The Interlinear Hebrew-Greek-English Bible

Volume 1 of 4 Volumes of the
Paperback Edition of the
Interlinear Hebrew Greek English Bible
Revised Fourth Edition

With Strong's Concordance Numbers
Above Each Word

The Interlinear Hebrew-Greek-English Bible

Volume 1 of 4 Volumes of the
Paperback Edition of the
Interlinear Hebrew Greek English Bible
Revised Fourth Edition

With Strong's Concordance Numbers
Above Each Word

Jay P. Green, Sr.
General Editor and Translator

Authors For Christ, Inc.
P.O. Box 4998
Lafayette, In 47905
Http://www.authorsforchrist.com

The Interlinear Hebrew Greek English Bible, Volume 1 of 4 Vols.
Four Volume Paperback Edition

ISBN: 1-58960-356-7

First Printing of Paperback Fourth Edition — 2009
Printed in the United States of America

A NOTE FROM THE PUBLISHER

With much thanksgiving, our Lord has enabled us to reissue the highly popular four-volume edition of *The Interlinear Hebrew-Greek-English Bible*.

It has been our plan to newly typeset all four volumes in order to give the reader a much clearer, easier-to-read text. By now the typesetting of the New Testament has been completed and appears in this issue of the set. The typesetting of the three Old Testament volumes is far more laborious, time-consuming, and expensive. Therefore, it is not possible for us to issue the newly typeset Hebrew-English until late 2001.

In the meantime, there has been such a demand for the set that we have been urged to go ahead and issue the Old Testament volumes in the 1985 edition. At last, we have bowed to this insistence for immediate access to these study volumes.

In the past issues, the Strong's Concordance numbers were added so that the reader who knew no Greek or Hebrew could use these numbers to go into the Hebrew and Greek lexicons to learn more of the meanings of the original words. This very helpful and popular addition was not part of the original design. The only way to add them was to take each page and by use of a typewriter to put the numbers over the original words. The adding of hundreds of thousands of numbers in this fashion was a gigantic task. In the doing of it, it was inevitable that some few numbers would prove to be wrongly assigned. As it turned out, however, this proved to be less than 1% of the numbers.

The English translations, however, did not suffer to that extent. Everyone has been so delighted with the usefulness of this set, that few sets (of the over 125,000 copies in circulation) ever show up in the used book marketplace, though by now those sets in distribution are quite worn from heavy use. In addition, so many have seen or heard of the set that new buyers are eagerly seeking to buy a set for themselves.

It is for this reason that we have decided not to wait until the entire set can be typeset. It is apparent that serious Bible students want to immediately acquire this unique Bible, not being in the least deterred by the relatively few errors left in the 1985 edition.

The newly typeset New Testament volume is a welcome bonus to all the ones who have been clamoring for an immediate reissue. An additional blessing has been added, too. The *Authorized/King James Version* appears in the right margin of the New Testament pages and will eventually appear in the Old Testament as it is typeset. These newly typeset pages are also so much clearer and easier to read.

May God be with you as you use these volumes to accelerate your growth in grace and in the knowledge of our Lord and Savior, Jesus Christ.

JAY P. GREEN, SR., Publisher

PREFACE

After nearly forty centuries of desperate failure, has Satan, aided and cheerfully abetted by deceitful and desperately wicked men (Jer. 17:9), finally succeeded in destroying the written word of God, the Bible, as a single-voiced witness to his great arch-enemy, our God and Savior Jesus Christ? Has the old Devil, like a sleight-of-hand shell-game artist, finally brought us to the point where we are searching desperately for the true word of God? Are we to believe that it cannot now be intact after all this time, having been run through the shredder of unholy hands and heads? Let it not be said! For not only has God warned us that, "*Man shall not live by bread alone, but by every word that proceeds out of the mouth of God,*" (Deut. 8:3; Matt. 4:4), but God has provided us with the very words that we are to live by, and He has most certainly also preserved for us the very words by which we are to live. Else, how could He plainly say, "*And if anyone hears My words and does not believe, I do not judge him . . . the word which I spoke is that which will judge him in the last day,*" (John 12:47,48)?

God has given us His life-giving words in words which all men may receive and believe. From the least intelligent to the most brilliant, men from all backgrounds and in all lands and languages must be able to hear, understand, believe and obey; else the Divine purpose cannot be fulfilled. In order to leave every person without excuse, God the Holy Spirit breathed out through the divinely chosen penmen words in common use among the Hebrew people, and, later, words commonly in use by the Greek-speaking world. However, since few today read Hebrew and Greek, and since the Scriptdures are intended for every nation and tongue, a translation into the common language of each person is needed. This Tyndale wrote in his preface, "which thing moved me to translate the New Testament. Because I had perceived by experience that it was impossible to establish the lay people in any truth except the Scripture were plainly laid before their eyes in their mother tongue, that they might see the process, order and meaning of the text." Tyndale labored to translate so that "every plowboy might understand," and such a great spiritual revolution followed that J. R. Green, the noted English historian, felt compelled to write, "No greater moral change ever passed over a nation than passed over England in the latter part of the reign of Queen Elizabeth. England became the people of a Book, and that Book was the Bible. Itwas read by every class of people. And the effect was amazing. The whole moral tone of the nation was changed."

With these considerations in mind, and also with much fear and trembling before our majestic and awesome God, we have sought to provide in *The Interlinear Hebrew-Greek-English Bible* both the original God-breathed Hebrew, Aramaic and Greek words (as incorporated in the texts received by the vast majority of Bible-believing peoples), and two literal English translations of these words. Our purpose in doing so is that the reader and student of this work might be led to "*receive in meekness the implanted word, which is able to save your souls*" (James 1:21). It now is submitted to you in the hope that the Almighty God who enabled us to conceive and to execute this monumental task will also enable you to grow in grace and in the knowledge of our Lord Jesus Christ by the use of it.

THE INTERLINEAR BIBLE

This work, we believe, contains all the Hebrew and Aramaic words which have been preserved for us by the Masoretes, and which in total has come to be known as the Masoretic Text. This work also contains the Greek words as printed in the Stephens Edition of 1550, which has become known as the Textus Receptus, or, Received Text, for the past four centuries. We have not followed the order of the Hebrew Bible (The Law, The Prophets, The Writings), but the order of the English Bible.

Why did we use these particular texts? It is simply because these are the only texts which can justly be designated as 'received' texts. In worldwide acceptance they tower so far above any other original Hebrew or Greek texts that there is no doubt but what they must be used in a work such as this is, a work that is intended to become a standard work for all the English-speaking peoples in the world. They are the 'Received Texts' because no other text has been able to win the adherence of any group powerful enough to displace either the Masoretic or the Received Text from their place as the standard by which all others are measured.

Since there will be separate prefaces supplied with each volume of this work, we will confine our remarks here to matters concerning the Hebrew and English printed in this volume. The Hebrew text in the Old Testament volumes of this work was first typeset in 1866 by the British and Foreign Bible Society, and it is from the Masoretic text. It was chosen over other beautiful Hebrew texts simply because it provided, for the most part, adequate room for the interlineary addition of the English equivalents under the original words.

The English, both that under the Hebrew words and that in the translation on the side, constitutes the original translation work of Jay P. Green, Sr., improved by scholars on a Board of Review, and from a volunteer Editorial Board. For purposes of fixing responsibility, the English translations are both those of Jay P. Green, Sr., since he was the sole judge of what changes would, or would not, be allowed in either the English equivalents placed under the Hebrew words, or the translation in the column at the side of the page.

THE INTERLINEAR BIBLE: WHAT IT IS; WHAT IT IS NOT.

This being the only complete interlineary Bible in existence, we give our concept of what this work is, and what it is not:

1. This *Interlinear Bible* is a Bible in every sense of the word, having both the original words, and two English translations for English-speaking people. Some may use this Bible in order to read the Bible in the original languages; others may read only the English translation, referring to the original words only in order to further investigate the meaning in lexicons or other reference works. It is our firm belief that all the benefits promised within the Bible itself may fairly be expected from the reading studying of this Bible.

2. It is the most literal English translation every produced, certainly the only one with literal meanings placed under the original words. Still, it is not in a true sense an absolutely literal representation of the Hebrew or Greek words. To begin with, no foreign language could adequately capture all the fullness of expression of either the Hebrew or Greek languages. In the Hebrew particularly, it being a pictorially-based language, it is impossible for the English translator to bring out in English the many shades of thought which are found in the Hebrew Bible (*e.g.* when the translation reads *"meek"*, this will hardly convey to you that the word is derived from a root signifying to "afflict"; and when you read *"delight"*, you will not realize that the original word pictures out a bending down toward the object being delighted in).

3. It not only gives the English reader insight into the literal meanings of the original languages, but opens to the understanding many idiomatic expressions. However, at this point, it must be admitted that the final product is somewhat of a hybrid production. On the one hand, it is not possible to express all the Hebrew idiom in English. On the other hand, if all idioms were attempted in English, many English readers would not always receive the sense, being unfamiliar with the background of the idiomatic expression. It is for this reason that two English translations are sometimes provided, one under each word of the original, it being more literal and more idiomatic at times; and the other on the side, giving a more standard treatment of translation so that the reader might more easily collect the sense of the entire context. There is another reason for the lack of expression of some of the idiom of the Hebrew language, and that is the limitation in space with which the translator was faced in this format. The cost of resetting the Hebrew to fit a fully literal translation into English would have been so great that the average serious Bible student would have found the final cost to be prohibitive. Also this work being intended for general use among all English-understanding peoples, it was necessary to avoid expressions which could only be comprehended by the more advanced Hebrew scholars. It is hoped that this work as you now see it will be useful to all classes of Bible readers, whatever may be their educational

level, and that it will be the most useful Bible ever produced in the matter of conveying spiritual truths and insights to the reader.

4. This Bible should prove to be a word book of considerable value for the study of Biblical vocabulary, both Hebrew and English.

5. It is intended to be a reader, both for those who are reading the English only, and for those who desire to read the original and at the same time to have help in understanding the meaning of each word. It will provide a much more rapid-reading Hebrew Bible than any that has been in existence until now. It will give the English reader a feel for Hebrew expressions which may not have been experienced before.

6. Although it gives some immediate lexiconal help, it is not intended to serve as a lexicon (dictionary).

7. It is most certainly not a grammar. Students must not use it in learning Hebrew or Greek grammar.

8. It is not intended to be a substitute for the person, in-depth study of the original. Students of the word should continue to make their own studies, using every reference work available to them. Each one should attempt to make his own independent translation. It would be neither seemly nor wise for anyone to take these words and present them as his own translation.

9. This work should be of considerable use to pastors and teachers. To those who have been trained in the original Biblical languages this work will be a refresher. It should help the trained student to remain sharp and fresh in his recognition of the meanings of all the words in any context. To the untrained pastor or teacher, it should be realized that without some knowledge of the literal meanings of the Hebrew, Aramaic and Greek words, one cannot be certain in a single instance that the sermon or lesson based on a text of Scripture is the accurate teaching of that text. This work is intended to give you encouragement and help in attaining such a knowledge of the meanings of the original Hebrew, Aramaic and Greek words.

10. Because all the nearly nineteen hundred Hebrew root words and the seven hundred and fifty or so Greek root words are here, along with English equivalents, this work is ideal for the use of those who must prepare written manuscripts or articles for publication. To find the original word with which you are concerned, one needs only to know the Biblical reference in order to quickly refer to them in this work.

11. *The Interlinear Bible* is the fulfillment of a long-recognized need. Martin Luther is reported as saying that he would not part with his knowledge of Hebrew for untold gold. Yet the vast majority of English-speaking people have been shut out of this precious knowledge, not having the time, or the money, to attend schools that teach Hebrew. One of the most often-voiced desires, especially since the hundreds of thou-

sands of interlineary New Testaments have been distributed in the past century, is the desire for a complete interlineary Bible. And this obviously is because it is the next best thing to a formal opportunity to study the Hebrew and Greek languages in depth. Until now, however, the formidable task of producing such an immeasureably useful Bible had never been completed.

There has been some progress for several centuries. First, for the purpose of creating study tools of the magnitude that the Bible necessitates, there must have been provided a standard translation in English. This came to us in the form of the King James Version of the Bible, the first edition issued in 1611, and the final form of it being established by 1730 a.d. Then it was possible to make a concordance which could be used by one and all, whether learned or unlearned — only the ability to read being necessary for its use. After another century or so, lexicon-dictionaries and grammars found fertile soil, and these added their input to the growing knowledge of the Bible. These at first were for the learned, or those formally trained. Then came the two big concordances, one by James Strong, the other by Robert Young. These gave abundant help to those who had only been trained in the English language. By the use of these one could laboriously make a study of the original individual words of the Bible. In the past century useful Bible dictioaries have helped in word studies, and wordbooks such as W. E. Vine's *Expository Dictionary of New Testament Words*, other studies by Trench and Girdlestone, etc. have advanced Biblical knowledge. Now in this present age there are more Biblical helps than ever before, a time when *The Interlinear Bible* can now be used as a means to shorten the time and effort to make Biblical studies in the lexicons, dictionaries, concordances, etc. Anyone who will learn the Hebrew alphabet and the Greek alphabet (the work of only one or two days) will be blessed with even more help from this *Interlinear Bible*.

12. *The Interlinear Bible* is up-to-date, having used the latest lexicons and study helps in the fixing of meanings, and a trustworthy guide to an accurate understanding of the Biblical words.

SPECIFIC DIFFICULTIES ENCOUNTERED.

It should be kept in mind in the use of this word that there is a wide difference in time and culture and language, not only between Hebrew and Greek, but also between those languages, times and cultures, and those of our day. In rendering the Biblical languages into English we particularly found it difficult to deal with the following:

A. Figures of Speech. The Hebrew speaks of the 'lip' of the river, rather than the 'bank'; sometimes the 'mouth' of Jehovah, rather than the 'word' or 'command' of Jehovah; 'lifting the heads' rather than counting, etc. If the figure of speech were considered intelligible to the English reader, the literal meaning is often given in this work.

B. Parts of Speech. It is not always possible to render the parts of speech in literal form, and at the same time convey the meaning to the English reader.

C. Interpretation. There is always interpretation in rendering one language into another, and it is necessary to consider the entire context before making a translation. There may be differences of opinion as to what the context teaches, but the purpose of this work has been to give the sense of the original language as we interpreted it after lengthy study.

D. Untranslated Words. There are some Hebrew words which are not translated in this work. For instance, אֶת־ an untranslated sign defining the direct object of a verb, and at places, אֲשֶׁר , the relative particle, which is sometimes redundant.

E. Implied Words. There are many instances in which the verb, or other words, are implied within the Hebrew word, either by the sentence structure, the syntax, or the context. In such cases the translator has supplied the word, even though it is not represented by Hebrew characters. In these instances the word supplied has been put in parentheses so that the reader will know that they were supplied by the translator. In the marginal translation these supplied words may be in italic type.

F. Punctuation and Capitalization. It should be realized that in the original Biblical languages, both Hebrew and Greek, all letters were capital letters, as we think of them. Therefore in the use of capitals and small letters, as we do in modern-day English, any capital letter can be counted as supplied. Capital letters have been used in this work for the following: for the beginning of all sentences; for the beginning word in all speeches; for specific events or places, such as, The Passover, The Feast of Tabernacles, The Negeb, The River (either Nile, or Euphrates), etc.; and we have also capitalized all pronouns which we deem to refer to the Deity, whether God the Father, God the Son, or God the Holy Spirit.

It should also be noted that there was no punctuation in the original manuscripts, either in the Hebrew or Greek. In the Hebrew text which we are using for this volume, the Masoretes (*c.* 700 a.d.) have placed certain punctuation marks for the benefit of the Hebrew reader. In this work we have generally followed the Masoretic punctuation, keeping in mind that punctuation is an aid to the reader. For this reason the punctuation may seen strange to the English reader at first, but since the reader is reading the English in Hebrew order (from right to left), and is oftentimes reading very literally, the reader will be aided by the punctuation as it appears under the Hebrew words. In the English translation in the margin we have followed modern English punctuation rules, our authority being *The Chicago Manual of Style.*

In regard to the use of question marks and the indication of interrogation, it should be noted that a question is often indicated in the Hebrew at the beginning of a sentence, sometimes by interrogative words, or at times only by the context.

G. The name of Jehovah, יְהוָה. The Old Testament contained this name in some fifty-five hundred places, and in this *Interlinear Bible* we have always rendered it Jehovah, or in its shortened form, Jah. The Jews, of course, considered this name to be incommunicable, never pronouncing it. The root bears the meaning of continuing being, a personal, absolute, self-determining Existence. It is very likely best translated as in Exodus 3:14, where the Lord said to Moses, "*I AM THAT I AM*" — "*Thus you shall say to the sons of Israel, I AM has sent me to you . . . .*" Because of the vagueness of the Hebrew tense (which is the same in both parts of the sentence) other renderings are possible, but in our opinion none better than "*I AM THAT I AM*". The name Jehovah is, of course, an English word which is based on the Masorete's choice of writing. They so revered this holy name that they wrote the vowels of the word signifying Lord (*adonai*) with the consonants of the name which God gave to Himself, JHWH, resulting in יְהוָה Jehovah — or as some prefer to render it, Yahweh, the consonants being in the Hebrew properly transliterated YHWH. In the history of the English language, however, the letter *J* has a written counterpart in the German *J*, although the letter *J* in German is pronounced like an English *Y*. The bulk of theological studies having come from German sources, there has been an intermixed usage in English of the *J* and the *Y*. Our English translations of the Bible reflect this, so we have chosen to use *J*, thus Jehovah, rather than Yahweh, because this is established English usage for Biblical names beginning with this Hebrew letter. No one suggests that we ought to change Jacob, Joseph, Jehoshaphat, Joshua, etc. to begin with a *Y*, and neither should we at this late date change Jehovah to Yahweh.

H. Non-literal Translation. Various forms of the Hebrew verb, idioms, and repetitions are sometimes rendered here by their intention, rather than by their exact expression. Examples of such are: (1) The Hebrew superlative (literally קֹדֶשׁ קָדָשִׁים is herein as "*most holy*. In Genesis 10:L9 it is said, "*Nimrod was a mighty hunter before the Lord*", or, *a hunter of God*, indicating that he was the greatest of hunters. (2) The Hebrew infinitive absolute, (literally מוֹת יָמוּת is "*dying, he shall die*", but it is usually translated by such words as surely, or certainly. (3) Hebrew idioms (literally *the mouth of the sword* may be translated herein as *the edge of the sword*. In successive editions the more literal idioms have been inserted. (4) Figures of Speech. (Literally אֵין לוֹ is *non-existence to him*, or, *not to him is*, but herein it is often rendered as, "he does not have," or, "not to him

Also, *seven years and twenty years and one hundred years* will appear herein as "*twenty-seven and one hundred years*", the word years being printed only once in English).

I. Non-concordant Translation. As in all languages, parts of speech may be fluid enough to have many meanings for one word or particle, usually depending on its contextual circumstance. For example, in Hebrew, we have וְ — *and, but, then, or*, and many others. Also דָּבָר for *word, thing, matter*. Although an attempt is made in *The Interlinear Bible* to translate certain Hebrew words with the same English word throughout a book, especially translating those words which have distinct doctrinal meaning, it is not always possible to fulfill the sense of the context by using the same English word. Many times reference to the English translation in the margin will help to explain difficult expressions.

J. Non-agreement of Number. Singular pronouns are often translated by the plural (normally a Hebrew collective) — for example, literally *to him* may appear as *to them*. Numbered objects are often singular in Hebrew. For example, literally it is written *four hundred man* but herein it will be rendered in the plural, *four hundred men*.

K. Space Limitations. Apart from the linguistic considerations, the interlineary format posed many mechancial problems as well. A moment's reflection on the difficult task of putting English meanings under Hebrew words will show that many short words require long English translations, or even more than one English word at places. In order to serve the reader best, a two-line format has been chosen in order to allow in nearly all instances a full expression of the meaning of the Hebrew words. At times the English, especially on the second line, is allowed to extend beyond the space under the Hebrew word, if no confusion results. Nevertheless, in certain places, and particularly in translating certain words, it has been necessary for us to adopt either a different word for translation, or a shortened form of construction. For example, in dealing with the Hebrew verb construct state, the possessive form was used to meet space requirements, such as *the sons of Israel* being rendered as *Israel's sons*. And whereas כְּ is normally *according to*, because of space limitations it is sometimes rendered as *by, as to*, etc. Also normally וַיְהִי would be rendered *and it came to be*, herein it is rendered *and it was*, because of the shortness of the Hebrew word. You will find in causative verb tenses that a shortening is often unavoidable, but happily in English the sense still comes through. Literally it may be, *he shall cause to put to death*, but herein, *he will execute*, especially where judicial execution is intended.

Jay P. Green, Sr., General Editor and Translator

HOW TO USE THE NUMBERING SYSTEM IN THIS WORK

The number over each Hebrew word is designed to be the key to a fuller understanding of that word, and of the context. The student will obtain more information on the word by referring to any or all of the reference works which are also keyed to Strong's numbering system. To find every single place where the word is used in the Bible, look up that number in *The New Englishman's Hebrew Concordance*, at which place will be listed in Biblical order all the places the holy penmen have used that word. This will help fix the meaning by Biblical usage. To discover more information on the root, the origin, the usage in other languages, and particularly the variations in the conjugations of verbs, look up the number in *The New BrownDriver-Briggs Hebrew-Aramaic Lexicon with Index* (or for quicker reference use *A Concise Lexicon to the Biblical Languages*). Also there is a Hebrew lexicon in the back of *Strong's Exhaustive Concordance*.

By this quick means of searching the individual usages of the words in a phrase, a sentence, or a paragraph, a far more accurate knowledge of the spiritual meaning of that passage will develop in the mind of the student. Thus spiritual heights will be climbed; ever higher will the spirit of the searcher rise, and the soul will soar with blessing on top of blessing, nevermore to return to its former state.

The editor wishes to express his deep appreciation to Dr. Allan A. MacRae for his encouragement through the years, and to the staff of Biblical School of Theology for their help in this work, particularly in improving the translation of the New Testament. We also want to express our appreciation for the space provided for the work of the Board of Review by Faith Theological Seminary and Westminster Theological Seminary. We owe particular appreciation to Rev. Maurice Robinson and Rev. Frank Coho, who have spent more time in improving this work than any other. We also owe a deep debt of gratitude to the many others who have contributed to this work, whether in the original edition, or by sending in their suggestions for the present improved edition.

Despite a widespread scepticism that such a work could ever be completed, now by God's grace, it is our pleasure to commend this work to you for your spiritual benefit. May Jehovah be praised!

Jay P. Green, Sr., General Editor

HOW TO READ THE ENGLISH LINES UNDER THE HEBREW, OR GREEK

1. Read the English in Hebrew order, that is from right to left.
2. Read the top line first, the line directly under the Hebrew.
3. Read from right to left on the first line, then on the second line.
4. Proceed to the next Hebrew word, reading the top English line first.

In reading the Greek New Testament section, however:

1. You will read in English order, that is from left to right.
2. Since Greek sentence structure is different, words will not be in order.
3. Refer to the English translation on the side to pick up word order.

INVITATION TO PARTICIPATE IN THE NEXT EDITION OF *THE INTERLINEAR BIBLE*

God's people want, and desperately need, the word of God in its most accurate form, not in a paraphrase, much less in a commentary disguised as a Bible. ***The Interlinear Bible*** demonstrates that word-for-word translation is the only way to achieve such an accurate Bible. In translating into English the original languages, we have attempted within the limitations noted before to give the true sense and the meaning of each of God's words to the reader of ***The Interlinear Bible***. We recognize, however, that God gives gifts of time, talent, and specialized knowledge to many different individuals. Some of you may very well be able to suggest to us improved renderings of certain portions of the Bible. You may be sure your suggestions will be very welcome.

However, because we do not want to invite a state of confusion in the submission of such suggestions for improvement, we must establish the following rules under which such suggestions are submitted:

A. A clear communication from the word of God is a matter of interest and the responsibility of the whole body of Christ. To sharpen such a communication is the duty of each of you, provided you have abilities in that area.

B. Your suggestions must be for constructive purposes only, and must be submitted within the framework and format which is now in use in this Bible.

C. Please observe the following instructions: (1) Suggestions must be brief. There is no staff to read long dissertations on the reasoning behind your suggestions. (2) Give relative evidence. Particularly cite Biblical usage, because we consider that to be more important than etymology alone; also cite authorities, periodicals, or significant monographs. (3) Your suggestion must be on the basis of a word-on-word translation, rather than "conceptual idea"-on-word. It is not our purpose to re-express the word of God according to our concepts, but render each word according to its Biblical meaning. (4) All suggestions must be based on the received texts, either the Masoretic text or the Received Text of Stephens, 1550. No emendations, variant readings, repointing, or editorial interpolations will be used. (5) Place all your suggestions on a separate page. Do not include suggestions in the body of a letter regarding other matters. (6) You must realize that you will receive no correspondence in regard to your suggestions. Be assured, however, that our editors will carefully consider every suggestion. Your contribution to this work, which will undoubtedly become a standard work worldwide, will be of great value to the people of God from now on, and that should be reason enough to do all you can do to make this Bible an accurate rendering of the written word of God. By improving ***The Interlinear Bible***, you can do this.

Hebrew Alphabet

1. The Hebrew is read *from right to left.* The Alphabet consists of 22 letters (and their variations), which are all regarded as *consonants*, being enunciated by the aid of certain "points" or marks, mostly beneath the letters, and which serve as *vowels*. There is no distinction of *capitals*, *italics*, etc.

2. The letters are as follows:

No.	Form.	Name.		Transliteration and Power.
1.	א	'Aleph	(*aw'-lef*)	' unappreciable
2.	בּ	Bêyth	(*bayth*)	**b**
3.	גּ	Gîymel	(*ghee'-mel*)	**g** hard = γ
4.	דּ	Dâleth	(*daw'-leth*)	**d** [cent
5.	ה	Hê'	(*hay*)	**h**, often quies-
6.	ו	Vâv	(*vawv*)	**v**, or **w** quies-
7.	ז	Zayin	(*zah'-yin*)	**z**, as in zeal [cent
8.	ח	Chêyth	(*khayth*)	German **ch** = χ [(nearly *kh*)
9.	ט	Têyth	(*tayth*)	**ṭ** = ת [cent
10.	י	Yôwd	(*yode*)	**y** often quies-
11.	כּ, final ך	Kaph	(*caf*)	**k** = ק
12.	ל	Lâmed	(*law'-med*)	**l**
13.	מ, final ם	Mêm	(*mame*)	**m**
14.	נ, final ן	Nûwn	(*noon*)	**n**
15.	ס	Çâmek	(*saw'-mek*)	**ç** = *s* sharp = שׂ
16.	ע	'Ayin	(*ah'-yin*)	' peculiar *
17.	פ, final ף	Phê'	(*fay*)	**ph** = *f* = φ
	פּ	Pê'	(*pay*)	**p**
18.	צ, final ץ	Tsâdêy	(*tsaw-day'*)	**ts**
19.	ק	Qôwph	(*cofe*)	**q** = *k* = כּ
20.	ר	Rêysh	(*raysh*)	**r**
21.	שׂ	Sîyn	(*seen*)	**s** sharp = ס = σ
	שׁ	Shîyn	(*sheen*)	**sh**
22.	ת	Thâv	(*thawv*)	**th**, as in THin
	תּ	Tâv	(*tawv*)	**t** = ט = τ [= ϑ

* The letter *'Ayin*, owing to the difficulty experienced by Occidentals in pronouncing it accurately (it is a deep guttural sound, like that made in *gargling*), is generally neglected (i.e. passed over silently) in reading. We have represented it to the eye (but not exactly to the ear) by the Greek *rough breathing* (for distinctness and typographical convenience, a *reversed apostrophe*) in order to distinguish it from *'Âleph*, which is likewise treated as silent, being similarly represented by the Greek *smooth breathing* (the apostrophe).

3. The *vowel-points* are the following:

Form.*	Name.		Representation and Power.
(ָ)	Qâmêts	(*caw-mates'*)	**â**, as in ALL
(ַ)	Pattach	(*pat'-takh*)	**a**, as in mAn, (*fâr*)
(ֲ)	Shevâ'-Pattach	(*she-vaw' pat'-takh*)	**ă**, as in hAt
(ֵ)	Tsêrêy	(*tsay-ray'*)	**ê**, as in thEy = η
(ֶ)	Çegôwl	(*seg-ole'*)	**e**, as in thEir; **e**, as in mEn = ε
(ֱ)	Shevâ'-Çegôwl	(*she-vaw' seg-ole'*)	**ĕ**, as in mEt
(ְ)	Shevâ' †	(*she-vaw'*)	e obscure, as in [avErage; silent, as *e* in madE
(ִ)	Chîyriq	(*khee'-rik*)	**î**, as in machIne ‡; **i**, as in suppliant, [(mîsery, hIt)
(ֹ)	Chôwlem §	(*kho'-lem*)	**ô**, as in no = ω
(ָ)	Short Qâmêts ‖		**o**, as in nor = ο
(ֳ)	Shevâ'-Qâmêts	(*she-vaw' caw-mates'*)	**ŏ**, as in not
(וּ)	Shûwrêq *	(*shoo-ruke'*)	**û**, as in cruel
(ֻ)	Qibbûts *	(*kib'-boots*)	**u**, as in fUll, rûde

4. A point in the bosom of a letter is called *Dâgêsh'*, and is of two kinds, which must be carefully distinguished.

a. Dâgêsh *lenè* occurs only in the letters בּ, גּ, דּ, כּ, פּ, תּ, (technically vocalized *Begad'-Kephath'*,) when they *begin* a clause or sentence, or are preceded by a consonant *sound;* and simply has the effect of removing their aspiration.†

b. Dâgêsh *fortè* may occur in any letter except א, ה, ח, ע or ר; it is equivalent to *doubling* the letter, and at the same time it removes the aspiration of a Begad-Kephath letter.‡

5. The *Maqqêph'* (־), like a *hyphen*, unites words only for purposes of pronunciation (by removing the primary accent from all except the last of them), but does not affect their meaning or their grammatical construction.

* The parenthesis-marks ( ) are given here in order to show the place of the vowel-points, whether below, above, or in the middle of the letter.

† *Silent Shevâ'* is not represented by any mark in our method of transliteration, as it is understood whenever there is no other vowel-point.

‡ *Chîyriq* is thus long only when it is followed by a quiescent *yôwd* (either expressed or implied).

§ *Chôwlem* is written *fully* only over *Vâv*, which is then quiescent (*w*): but when used "defectively" (without the *Vâv*) it may be written either over the left-hand corner of the letter to which it belongs, or over the right-hand corner of the following one.

‖ Short *Qâmêts* is found only in *unaccented syllables ending with a consonant sound.*

* *Shûwrêq* is written only in the bosom of *Vâv*. Sometimes it is said to be "defectively" written (without the *Vâv*), and then takes the form of *Qibbûts*, which in such cases is called *vicarious*.

† In our system of transliteration Dâgêsh *lenè* is represented only in the letters פּ and תּ, because elsewhere it does not affect the pronunciation (with most Hebraists).

‡ A point in the bosom of הּ is called *Mappîyq* (*map-peek'*). It occurs only in the final vowelless letter of a few words, and we have represented it by *hh*. A Dâgêsh *fortè* in the bosom of וּ may easily be distinguished from the vowel *Shûwrêq* by noticing that in the former case the letter has a proper vowel-point accompanying it.

It should be noted that both kinds of Dâgêsh are often omitted in writing (being then said to be *implied*), but (in the case at least of Dâgêsh *fortè*) the word is (by most Hebraists) pronounced the same as if it were present.

בראשית
(THE BOOK OF)
GENESIS

A LITERAL TRANSLATION OF THE BIBLE

THE BOOK OF GENESIS

CHAPTER 1

[1]In the beginning God created the heavens and the earth; [2]and the earth being without form and empty, and darkness on the face of the deep, and the Spirit of God moving gently on the face of the waters, [3]then God said, Let light be—and there was light. [4]And God saw the light, that *it was* good, and God separated between the light and the darkness. [5]And God called the light, Day. And He called the darkness, Night. And there was evening, and there was morning the first day.

[6]And God said, Let an expanse be in the midst of the waters, and let it divide between the waters *and* the waters. [7]And God made the expanse, and He separated between the waters which *were* under the expanse and the waters which *were* above the expanse. And it was so. [8]And God called the expanse, Heavens. And there was evening, and there was morning the second day.

[9]And God said, Let the waters under the heavens be collected to one place, and let the dry land appear. And it was so. [10]And God called the dry land, Earth. And He called the collection of the waters, Seas.

CAPUT. I א

CHAPTER 1

776 776 8064 430 1254 7225
1 2 בְּרֵאשִׁית בָּרָא אֱלֹהִים אֵת הַשָּׁמַיִם וְאֵת הָאָרֶץ׃ וְהָאָרֶץ
the and earth | the earth | and | the heavens | God | created | the In beginning

430 7307 8415 6440 5921 2822 922 8414 1961
הָיְתָה תֹהוּ וָבֹהוּ וְחֹשֶׁךְ עַל־פְּנֵי תְהוֹם וְרוּחַ אֱלֹהִים
God | the and of Spirit | ;deep the | the of face | on | and darkness | and ,empty | without form | was

1961 216 1961 430 559 4325 6440 7363
3 מְרַחֶפֶת עַל־פְּנֵי הַמָּיִם׃ וַיֹּאמֶר אֱלֹהִים יְהִי אוֹר וַיְהִי
and was | light | Let be | ,God | said Then | the .waters | the of face | on | moving gently

996 430 914 2896 216 430 7200 216
4 אוֹר׃ וַיַּרְא אֱלֹהִים אֶת־הָאוֹר כִּי־טוֹב וַיַּבְדֵּל אֱלֹהִים בֵּין
be- tween | God | and separated | good that (was it) | light the | God | saw And | .light

2822 3117 216 430 7121 2822 996 216
5 הָאוֹר וּבֵין הַחֹשֶׁךְ׃ וַיִּקְרָא אֱלֹהִים ׀ לָאוֹר יוֹם וְלַחֹשֶׁךְ
the and darkness | ,Day | light the | God | called And | the .darkness | and | the light

259 3117 1242 1961 6153 1961 7121
קָרָא לָיְלָה וַיְהִי־עֶרֶב וַיְהִי־בֹקֶר יוֹם אֶחָד׃ פ
.one | day | mor- ning | and was | eve- ,ning | and was | ;Night | He called

996 914 1961 4325 8432 7549 1961 430 559
6 וַיֹּאמֶר אֱלֹהִים יְהִי רָקִיעַ בְּתוֹךְ הַמָּיִם וִיהִי מַבְדִּיל בֵּין
be- tween | (be) dividing | and it let | the ,waters | the in of midst | an expanse | be Let | ,God | said And

4325 996 914 7549 430 6213 4325 4325
7 מַיִם לָמָיִם׃ וַיַּעַשׂ אֱלֹהִים אֶת־הָרָקִיעַ וַיַּבְדֵּל בֵּין הַמַּיִם
the waters | between | He and separated | the ,expanse | God | And made | the (and) .waters | waters

1961 7549 5921 834 4325 996 7549 8478 834
אֲשֶׁר מִתַּחַת לָרָקִיעַ וּבֵין הַמַּיִם אֲשֶׁר מֵעַל לָרָקִיעַ וַיְהִי־
it and was | the ,expanse | above | which (were) | the waters | and | the expanse | under | which (were)

1242 1961 6153 1961 8064 7549 430 7121 3651
8 כֵן׃ וַיִּקְרָא אֱלֹהִים לָרָקִיעַ שָׁמָיִם וַיְהִי־עֶרֶב וַיְהִי־בֹקֶר
mor- ning | and was | eve- ,ning | and was | ;heavens | the expanse | God | And called | .so

8145 3117
יוֹם שֵׁנִי׃ פ
.second day

259 4725 413 8064 8478 4325 6960 430 559
9 וַיֹּאמֶר אֱלֹהִים יִקָּווּ הַמַּיִם מִתַּחַת הַשָּׁמַיִם אֶל־מָקוֹם אֶחָד
,one | place | to | the heavens | under | the waters | be Let collected | ,God | said And

776 3004 430 7121 3651/1961 3004 7200
10 וְתֵרָאֶה הַיַּבָּשָׁה וַיְהִי־כֵן׃ וַיִּקְרָא אֱלֹהִים ׀ לַיַּבָּשָׁה אֶרֶץ
,Earth | dry the land | God | And called | so it and was | dry the ;land | let and appear

559 2896 430 7200 3220 7121 4325 4723
11 וּלְמִקְוֵה הַמַּיִם קָרָא יַמִּים וַיַּרְא אֱלֹהִים כִּי־טוֹב׃ וַיֹּאמֶר
said And | good .(was it) | God | and saw | ,Seas | He called | the waters | the and of collection

the earth sprout tender
sprouts, *the* plant seeding
seed, the fruit tree pro-
ducing fruit according to its
kind, whichever seed *is* in it
on the earth. And it was
so. 12And the earth bore
tender sprouts, *the* plant
seeding seed according to
its *kind, and the fruit tree*
producing fruit according to
its kind, whichever seed *is*
in it. And God saw that *it*
was good. 13And there
was evening, and there was
morning the third day.

14And God said, Let
luminaries be in the
expanse of the heavens, to
divide between the day and
the night. And let them be
for signs and for seasons,
and for days and years.
15And let them be for
luminaries in the expanse of
the heavens, to give light
on the earth. And it was so.
16And God made the two
great luminaries: the great

luminary to rule the day,
and the small luminary and
the stars to rule the night.
17And God set them in the
expanse of the heavens, to
give light on the earth,
18and to rule over the day
and over the night; and to
divide between the light
and the darkness. And God
saw that *it was* good. 19And
there was evening, and
there was morning the
fourth day.

20And God said, Let the
waters swarm *with* the
swarmers *having* a soul of
life; and let the birds fly over
the earth, on the face of the
expanse of the heavens.
21And God created the great
sea animals, and all that
creeps, *having* a living soul,
which swarmed the waters,

אלהים תדשא הארץ דשא עשב מזריע זרע עץ פרי
עשה פרי למינו אשר זרעו בו על הארץ ויהי כן
12 ותוצא הארץ דשא עשב מזריע זרע למינהו ועץ עשה
13 פרי אשר זרעו בו למינהו וירא אלהים כי טוב ויהי
ערב ויהי בקר יום שלישי פ
14 ויאמר אלהים יהי מארת ברקיע השמים להבדיל בין
היום ובין הלילה והיו לאתת ולמועדים ולימים ושנים
15 והיו למאורת ברקיע השמים להאיר על הארץ ויהי
16 כן ויעש אלהים את שני המארת הגדלים את המאור
הגדל לממשלת היום ואת המאור הקטן לממשלת
17 הלילה ואת הכוכבים ויתן אתם אלהים ברקיע
18 השמים להאיר על הארץ ולמשל ביום ובלילה
ולהבדיל בין האור ובין החשך וירא אלהים כי טוב
19 ויהי ערב ויהי בקר יום רביעי פ
20 ויאמר אלהים ישרצו המים שרץ נפש חיה ועוף יעופף
21 על הארץ על פני רקיע השמים ויברא אלהים את
התנינם הגדלים ואת כל נפש החיה הרמשת אשר

according to its kind; and every bird *with* wing according to its kind. And God saw that *it was* good.

[22]And God blessed them, saying, Be fruitful and multiply, and fill the waters in the seas; and let the birds multiply in the earth. [23]And there was evening, and there was morning the fifth day.

[24]And God said, Let the earth bring forth the soul of life according to its kind: cattle, and creepers, and its beasts of the earth, according to its kind. And it was so. [25]And God made the animals of the earth according to its kind, and cattle according to its kind, and every creeping thing of the ground according to its kind. And God saw that *it was* good. [26]And God said, Let Us make man in Our image, according to Our likeness; and let them rule over the fish of the sea, and over the birds of the heavens, and over the cattle, and over all the earth, and over all the creepers creeping on the earth.

[27]And God created the man in His own image; in the image of God He created him. He created them male and female. [28]And God blessed them; and God said to them, Be fruitful and multiply, and fill the earth, and subdue it, and rule over the fish of the sea, and over birds of the heavens, and over all living things creeping on the earth. [29]And God said, Behold, I have given you every plant seeding seed which *is* on the face of all the earth, and every tree in which *is* the fruit of a tree seeding seed—it shall be food for you. [30]And to every living thing of the earth, and

7200 4327 3671 5775 3605 4327 4325 8317
שָׁרְצוּ הַמַּיִם לְמִינֵהֶם וְאֵת כָּל־עוֹף כָּנָף לְמִינֵהוּ וַיַּרְא
and after (with) bird every and after the swarmed
saw ;kind its wing ,kind their waters

7235 6509 559 430 1288 2896 430
22 אֱלֹהִים כִּי־טוֹב׃ וַיְבָרֶךְ אֹתָם אֱלֹהִים לֵאמֹר פְּרוּ וּרְבוּ
be and Be ,saying God them And good that God
,many fruitful blessed .(was it)

6153 1961 776 5775 3220 4325 4390
23 וּמִלְאוּ אֶת־הַמַּיִם בַּיַּמִּים וְהָעוֹף יִרֶב בָּאָרֶץ׃ וַיְהִי־עֶרֶב
eve- And the on let the and the in waters the fill and
ning was .earth multiply birds ;seas

2549 3117 1242 1961
וַיְהִי־בֹקֶר יוֹם חֲמִישִׁי׃ פ
fifth day mor- and
ning was

929 4327 2416 5315 776 3318 430 559
24 וַיֹּאמֶר אֱלֹהִים תּוֹצֵא הָאָרֶץ נֶפֶשׁ חַיָּה לְמִינָהּ בְּהֵמָה
cattle after living soul the bring Let ,God said And
kind its earth forth

430 6213 1961 4327 776 2416 7431
25 וָרֶמֶשׂ וְחַיְתוֹ־אֶרֶץ לְמִינָהּ וַיְהִי־כֵן׃ וַיַּעַשׂ אֱלֹהִים אֶת־
— God And ,so and after the of its and and
made was it ;kind its earth beasts ,creepers

7431 3605 4327 929 4327 776 2416
חַיַּת הָאָרֶץ לְמִינָהּ וְאֶת־הַבְּהֵמָה לְמִינָהּ וְאֵת כָּל־רֶמֶשׂ
creepers all and after cattle the and after the the
of ,kind its kind its earth of beasts

430 559 2090 430 7200 4327 127
26 הָאֲדָמָה לְמִינֵהוּ וַיַּרְא אֱלֹהִים כִּי־טוֹב׃ וַיֹּאמֶר אֱלֹהִים
,God said And good that God saw and after the of
(was it) ;kind their ground

5775 3220 1710 7287 1823 6754 120 6213
נַעֲשֶׂה אָדָם בְּצַלְמֵנוּ כִּדְמוּתֵנוּ וְיִרְדּוּ בִדְגַת הַיָּם וּבְעוֹף
over and the over let and to according Our in man Us Let
of birds sea of fish rule them likeness Our ,image make

5921 7430 7431 3605 776 3605 929 8064
הַשָּׁמַיִם וּבַבְּהֵמָה וּבְכָל־הָאָרֶץ וּבְכָל־הָרֶמֶשׂ הָרֹמֵשׂ עַל־
on creeping the over and the over and over and the
creepers all earth all ,cattle the ,heavens

430 6754 120 430 1254 776
27 הָאָרֶץ׃ וַיִּבְרָא אֱלֹהִים ׀ אֶת־הָאָדָם בְּצַלְמוֹ בְּצֶלֶם אֱלֹהִים
God the In His in man the God And .earth the
of image ,image created

430 1288 1254 5347 2145 1254
28 בָּרָא אֹתוֹ זָכָר וּנְקֵבָה בָּרָא אֹתָם׃ וַיְבָרֶךְ אֹתָם אֱלֹהִים
,God them And .them He and male ;him He
blessed created female created

3533 776 4390 6509 430 559
וַיֹּאמֶר לָהֶם אֱלֹהִים פְּרוּ וּרְבוּ וּמִלְאוּ אֶת־הָאָרֶץ וְכִבְשֻׁהָ
it and ,earth the fill and and Be ,God to said and
;subdue ,multiply fruitful them

5921 7430 2416 3605 8064 5775 3220 1710 7287
וּרְדוּ בִּדְגַת הַיָּם וּבְעוֹף הַשָּׁמַיִם וּבְכָל־חַיָּה הָרֹמֶשֶׂת עַל־
on creeping beasts and the over and the the over and
all over ,heavens of birds ,sea of fish rule

6212 3605 5414 2009 430 559 776
29 הָאָרֶץ׃ וַיֹּאמֶר אֱלֹהִים הִנֵּה נָתַתִּי לָכֶם אֶת־כָּל־עֵשֶׂב ׀
herb every you to have I ,Behold ,God said And the
given .earth

834 6086 3665 776 3605 6440 834 2233 2232
זֹרֵעַ זֶרַע אֲשֶׁר עַל־פְּנֵי כָל־הָאָרֶץ וְאֶת־כָּל־הָעֵץ אֲשֶׁר־
which tree every and the all the on which seed seed-
earth of face (is) ing

2416 402 1961 2233 2232 6086 6629
30 בּוֹ פְרִי־עֵץ זֹרֵעַ זָרַע לָכֶם יִהְיֶה לְאָכְלָה׃ וּלְכָל־חַיַּת
beast to and ,food for it shall to ;seed seeding (the) fruit it in
of every be you tree of (is)

to every bird of the heavens, and to every creeper on the earth, in which *is* a living soul, every green plant *is* for food. And it was so. [31]And God saw everything that He had made; and, behold, *it was* very good. And there was evening, and there was morning the sixth day.

834 776 7430 8064 5775 772
הָאָרֶץ וּֽלְכָל־עוֹף הַשָּׁמַיִם וּלְכֹל ׀ רוֹמֵשׂ עַל־הָאָרֶץ אֲשֶׁר
which earth the on creeper to and the of bird to and the
every ,heavens every ,earth

7200 3651 1961 402 6212 3418 2416 5315
31 בּוֹ נֶפֶשׁ חַיָּה אֶת־כָּל־יֶרֶק עֵשֶׂב לְאָכְלָה וַֽיְהִי־כֵֽן׃ וַיַּרְא
saw And .so it ;food for herb of green every living soul a it in
was (is)

6153 1961 3966 2896 2009 6213 834 3605 430
אֱלֹהִים אֶת־כָּל־אֲשֶׁר עָשָׂה וְהִנֵּה־טוֹב מְאֹד וַֽיְהִי־עֶרֶב
,evening And !very (was it) and had He which all God
was good behold made

8345 3117 1242 1961
וַֽיְהִי־בֹקֶר יוֹם הַשִּׁשִּֽׁי׃
.sixth day mor- and
ning was

CAP. II ב

CHAPTER 2

CHAPTER 2

[1]And the heavens and the earth were finished, and all their host. [2]And on the seventh day God completed His work which He had made. And He rested on the seventh day from all His work which He had made. [3]And God blessed the seventh day and sanctified it, because He rested from all His work on it, which God had created to make.

3117 430 3615 6635 3605 776 8064 3615
1
2 וַיְכֻלּוּ הַשָּׁמַיִם וְהָאָרֶץ וְכָל־צְבָאָֽם׃ וַיְכַל אֱלֹהִים בַּיּוֹם
on God And their and the and the were And
day finished .host all earth heavens finished

7637 3117 7673 6213 834 4399 7637
הַשְּׁבִיעִי מְלַאכְתּוֹ אֲשֶׁר עָשָׂה וַיִּשְׁבֹּת בַּיּוֹם הַשְּׁבִיעִי
the day on He And had He which work His the
seventh rested .made seventh

3117 430 1288 6213 834 4399 3605
3 מִכָּל־מְלַאכְתּוֹ אֲשֶׁר עָשָֽׂה׃ וַיְבָרֶךְ אֱלֹהִים אֶת־יוֹם
day God And had He which work His all from
blessed .made

834 4399 3605 7673 3588 6942 7637
הַשְּׁבִיעִי וַיְקַדֵּשׁ אֹתוֹ כִּי בוֹ שָׁבַת מִכָּל־מְלַאכְתּוֹ אֲשֶׁר
which work His all from He it on be- ;it and the
rested cause sanctified seventh

6213 430 1254
בָּרָא אֱלֹהִים לַעֲשֽׂוֹת׃
.make to God had
created

[4]These are the births of the heavens and of the earth when they *were* created in the day *that* Jehovah *was* making earth and heavens—[5]and every shrub of the field was not yet on the earth, and every plant of the field had not yet sprung up; for Jehovah God had not sent rain on the earth, and there was no man to till the ground. [6]And mist went up from the earth and watered the whole face of the ground. [7]And Jehovah God formed the man *out of* dust from the ground, and blew into his nostrils *the* breath of life; and man became a living soul.

3068 6213 3117 1254 776 8064 8435 428
4 אֵלֶּה תוֹלְדוֹת הַשָּׁמַיִם וְהָאָרֶץ בְּהִבָּֽרְאָם בְּיוֹם עֲשׂוֹת יְהוָה
Jehovah the the in they when the and the genera- the These
of making of day created (were) earth heavens of tions (are)

1961 2962 7704 7880 3605 8064 776 430
5 אֱלֹהִים אֶרֶץ וְשָׁמָֽיִם׃ וְכֹל ׀ שִׂיחַ הַשָּׂדֶה טֶרֶם יִֽהְיֶה
was it yet not the shrub And and earth God's
—field of every .heavens

3808 3068 4305 6779 7704 6212 3605 776
בָאָרֶץ וְכָל־עֵשֶׂב הַשָּׂדֶה טֶרֶם יִצְמָח כִּי לֹא הִמְטִיר יְהוָה
Jehovah rain had not for had it not —field the of herb and the on
sent ,up sprung yet every ,earth

108 125 5647 369 120 772 430
6 אֱלֹהִים עַל־הָאָרֶץ וְאָדָם אַיִן לַֽעֲבֹד אֶת־הָֽאֲדָמָֽה׃ וְאֵד
a and ;ground the till to was a and the on God
mist not man ,earth

3335 125 6440 3605 8248 776 5927
7 יַעֲלֶה מִן־הָאָרֶץ וְהִשְׁקָה אֶֽת־כָּל־פְּנֵֽי־הָאֲדָמָֽה׃ וַיִּיצֶר
And .ground the the all and the from went
formed of face watered earth up

639 5301 125 6083 120 430 3068
יְהוָה אֱלֹהִים אֶת־הָֽאָדָם עָפָר מִן־הָאֲדָמָה וַיִּפַּח בְּאַפָּיו
his into and the from (of) dust man the God Jehovah
nostrils blew ,ground

[8]And Jehovah God planted a garden in Eden, to

430 3068 5193 2416 5315 120 1961 2416 5397
8 נִשְׁמַת חַיִּים וַֽיְהִי הָֽאָדָם לְנֶפֶשׁ חַיָּֽה׃ וַיִּטַּע יְהוָה אֱלֹהִים
God Jehovah And living soul a man the and ;life breath
planted became of

the east; and He put the man whom He had formed there. 9 And out of the ground Jehovah God made to spring up every tree that is pleasant to the sight, and good for food. The Tree of Life *was* also in the middle of the garden; also the Tree of Knowledge of Good and Evil. 10 And a river went out of Eden to water the garden, and from there it was divided and became four heads. 11 The name of the first *was* Pishon—it *is* the *one* surrounding all the land of Havilah, where gold *is*; 12 and the gold of that land *is* good; there *is* bdellium gum resin, *and* the onyx stone. 13 And the name of the second river *is* Gihon—it is the one surrounding all the land of Cush. 14 And the name of the third river *is* Hiddakel—it *is* the one going east of Assyria. And the fourth river *is* Euphrates.

15 And Jehovah God took the man and put him into the garden of Eden, to work it and to keep it. 16 And Jehovah God commanded the man, saying, You may freely eat of every tree in the garden; 17 but of the Tree of Knowledge of Good and Evil you may not eat, for in the day that you eat of it, you shall surely die.

18 And Jehovah God said, It is not *good*, the man being alone. I will make a helper suited to him. 19 And Jehovah God formed every animal of the field, and every bird of the heavens out of the ground. And *He* brought *them* to the man, to see what he would call it. And all which the man might call it, *each* living soul, that *was* its name.

1588 5731 6924 7760 8033 120 834 3335 6779
9 גַּן־בְּעֵדֶן מִקֶּדֶם וַיָּשֶׂם שָׁם אֶת־הָאָדָם אֲשֶׁר יָצָר׃ וַיַּצְמַח
made And had He whom the there and the to in a
spring .formed man put east ,Eden garden

3068 430 4480 127 3605 6086 2530 4758 2895
יְהוָה אֱלֹהִים מִן־הָאֲדָמָה כָּל־עֵץ נֶחְמָד לְמַרְאֶה וְטוֹב
and the to pleasant tree every the from God Jehovah
good sight ground

3978 6086 2416 8432 1588 1847 2896 7451
לְמַאֲכָל וְעֵץ הַחַיִּים בְּתוֹךְ הַגָּן וְעֵץ הַדַּעַת טוֹב וָרָע׃
and good knowl- the the and the the in life the and ;food for
.evil of edge of tree .garden of midst (was) of tree

5104 5927 5731 4325 1588 8033 6504 1961
10 וְנָהָר יֹצֵא מֵעֵדֶן לְהַשְׁקוֹת אֶת־הַגָּן וּמִשָּׁם יִפָּרֵד וְהָיָה
and was it from and the water to from went a And
became divided there ,garden Eden out river

702 7218 8034 259 6376 1931 5437
11 לְאַרְבָּעָה רָאשִׁים׃ שֵׁם הָאֶחָד פִּישׁוֹן הוּא הַסֹּבֵב אֵת
(one) the (is it) ;Pishon one the The .heads four into
surrounding (is) of name

776 2341 834 8033 2091 2091 776 1931
12 כָּל־אֶרֶץ הַחֲוִילָה אֲשֶׁר־שָׁם הַזָּהָב׃ וּזֲהַב הָאָרֶץ הַהִוא
that land the And .(is) gold where ,Havilah the all
of gold of land

2896 8033 916 68 7718 8034 5104 8145 1521
13 טוֹב שָׁם הַבְּדֹלַח וְאֶבֶן הַשֹּׁהַם׃ וְשֵׁם־הַנָּהָר הַשֵּׁנִי גִּיחוֹן
Gihon second the the And .onyx the and bdellium there ;good
(is) river of name of stone resin gum (is) (is)

5437 776 3570 8034 5104 7992
14 הוּא הַסּוֹבֵב אֵת כָּל־אֶרֶץ כּוּשׁ׃ וְשֵׁם־הַנָּהָר הַשְּׁלִישִׁי
(is) third the the And .Cush the all – one the (is) it
river of name of land surrounding

2313 1931 1980 6926 804 5104 7243
חִדֶּקֶל הוּא הַהֹלֵךְ קִדְמַת אַשּׁוּר וְהַנָּהָר הָרְבִיעִי הוּא
(is) fourth the and ;Assyria of east one the (is) it .Tigris
river going

6576 3947 3068 430 120 3240 1588 5731
15 פְרָת׃ וַיִּקַּח יְהוָה אֱלֹהִים אֶת־הָאָדָם וַיַּנִּחֵהוּ בְגַן־עֵדֶן
Eden the in put and man the God Jehovah And .Euphrates
of garden him took

5647 8104 6680 3068 430 120 559
16 לְעָבְדָהּ וּלְשָׁמְרָהּ׃ וַיְצַו יְהוָה אֱלֹהִים עַל־הָאָדָם לֵאמֹר
,saying ,man the to God Jehovah And to and it till to
commanded .it keep

3605 6086 1588 398 398 6086 1847 2896 7451
17 מִכֹּל עֵץ־הַגָּן אָכֹל תֹּאכֵל׃ וּמֵעֵץ הַדַּעַת טוֹב וָרָע לֹא
not and good knowl- the of but may you surely the tree Of
evil of edge of tree the ;eat garden of every

398 3117 398 4191 4191 559
18 תֹאכַל מִמֶּנּוּ כִּי בְּיוֹם אֲכָלְךָ מִמֶּנּוּ מוֹת תָּמוּת׃ וַיֹּאמֶר
said And shall you surely from your the in for from shall you
.die it eating of day ;it eat

3068 430 2896 1961 120 905 6213 5828
יְהוָה אֱלֹהִים לֹא־טוֹב הֱיוֹת הָאָדָם לְבַדּוֹ אֶעֱשֶׂה־לּוֹ עֵזֶר
a for will I ;alone man the being is it not ,God Jehovah
helper him make of good

5048 3335 3068 430 127 3605 2416 7704
19 כְּנֶגְדּוֹ׃ וַיִּצֶר יְהוָה אֱלֹהִים מִן־הָאֲדָמָה כָּל־חַיַּת הַשָּׂדֶה
field the beast every the from God Jehovah And correspond
of ground formed .him to ing

3605 5775 8064 935 120 7200 7121
וְאֵת כָּל־עוֹף הַשָּׁמַיִם וַיָּבֵא אֶל־הָאָדָם לִרְאוֹת מַה־יִּקְרָא־
would he what see to man the to and the bird every and
call brought ,heavens of

3605 834 7121 120 5315 2416 1931 8034
לוֹ וְכֹל אֲשֶׁר יִקְרָא־לוֹ הָאָדָם נֶפֶשׁ חַיָּה הוּא שְׁמוֹ׃
its that ,living (each) man the it call might which and
.name (was) soul all

[20]And the man called names to all the cattle, and to the bird of the heavens, and to every animal of the field. But no helper suited to him was found for a man. [21]And Jehovah God caused a deep sleep to fall on the man, and he slept. And He took one of his ribs, and closed up the flesh underneath. [22]And Jehovah God formed the rib which He had taken from the man into a woman, and brought her to the man. [23]And the man said, This now at last *is* bone of my bones, and flesh from my flesh. For this shall be called Woman, because this has been taken out of man. [24]Therefore, a man shall leave his father and his mother, and shall cleave to his wife; and they shall become one flesh. [25]And they were both naked, the man and his wife, and they were not ashamed.

3605 8064 5775 929 3605 8034 120 7121
20 וַיִּקְרָא הָאָדָם שֵׁמוֹת לְכָל־הַבְּהֵמָה וּלְעוֹף הַשָּׁמַיִם וּלְכֹל
and ,heavens the to and the all to names man the And
every to of bird and cattle called

3068 5307 5048 5828 4672 120 7704 2416
21 חַיַּת הַשָּׂדֶה וּלְאָדָם לֹא־מָצָא עֵזֶר כְּנֶגְדּוֹ׃ וַיַּפֵּל יְהוָה
Jehovah made And suited a was not for but ;field the beast
fall to .him to helper found man a of

6763 259 39 47 3462 120 8415/8439 430
אֱלֹהִים ׀ תַּרְדֵּמָה עַל־הָאָדָם וַיִּישָׁן וַיִּקַּח אַחַת מִצַּלְעֹתָיו
ribs his from one He And he and ,man the on deep a God
took .slept sleep

834 6763 430 3068 1127 8478 1320 5462
22 וַיִּסְגֹּר בָּשָׂר תַּחְתֶּנָּה׃ וַיִּבֶן יְהוָה אֱלֹהִים ׀ אֶת־הַצֵּלָע אֲשֶׁר־
which rib the God Jehovah And underneath flesh the and
formed up closed

120 559 120 935 802 120 3947
23 לָקַח מִן־הָאָדָם לְאִשָּׁה וַיְבִאֶהָ אֶל־הָאָדָם׃ וַיֹּאמֶר הָאָדָם
,man the said And .man the to brought and a into man the from had He
in her ,woman taken

802 7121 2063 1320 1320 6106 6106 6470 2063
זֹאת הַפַּעַם עֶצֶם מֵעֲצָמַי וּבָשָׂר מִבְּשָׂרִי לְזֹאת יִקָּרֵא אִשָּׁה
,Woman shall this For my from and my from bone at now This
called be .flesh flesh ,bones last (is)

376 5800 3947 376 3588
24 כִּי מֵאִישׁ לֻקֳחָה־זֹּאת׃ עַל־כֵּן יַעֲזָב־אִישׁ אֶת־אָבִיו וְאֶת־
and his man a shall Therefore .this been has of out be-
father leave taken man cause

8147 1961 259 1320 1961 802 1692 517
25 אִמּוֹ וְדָבַק בְּאִשְׁתּוֹ וְהָיוּ לְבָשָׂר אֶחָד׃ וַיִּהְיוּ שְׁנֵיהֶם
both And .one flesh into they and his to shall and his
were they become shall ,wife cling mother

954 3808 802 120 6174
עֲרוּמִּים הָאָדָם וְאִשְׁתּוֹ וְלֹא יִתְבֹּשָׁשׁוּ׃
were they and his and man the ,naked
.ashamed not ,wife

CHAPTER 3

[1]And the serpent was cunning above every animal of the field which Jehovah God had made. And he said to the woman, *Is it* true that God has said, You shall not eat from any tree of the garden? [2]And the woman said to the serpent, We may eat of the fruit of the trees of the garden, [3]but of the fruit of the tree which *is* in the middle of the garden, God has said, You shall not eat of it, nor shall you touch it, lest you die. [4]And the serpent said to the woman, You shall not surely die, [5]for God knows that in the day you eat of it, your eyes shall be opened, and you shall be as God, knowing

CAP. III ג

CHAPTER 3

3068 6213 834 7704 2416 3605 6175 1961 5175
1 וְהַנָּחָשׁ הָיָה עָרוּם מִכֹּל חַיַּת הַשָּׂדֶה אֲשֶׁר עָשָׂה יְהוָה
Jehovah had which field the beast above cunning was the And
made of every serpent

398 430 559 641 802 559 430
אֱלֹהִים וַיֹּאמֶר אֶל־הָאִשָּׁה אַף כִּי־אָמַר אֱלֹהִים לֹא תֹאכְלוּ
shall You not ,God said has (it Is) ,woman the to he And .God
eat that so said

1588/6086 6529 5175 802 559 1588 6086 3605
2 מִכֹּל עֵץ הַגָּן׃ וַתֹּאמֶר הָאִשָּׁה אֶל־הַנָּחָשׁ מִפְּרִי עֵץ־הַגָּן
gar-the the the Of the to the said And the tree from
den of trees of fruit ,serpent woman ?garden of any

3808 430 559 1588/8432 834 6086 6529 398
3 נֹאכֵל׃ וּמִפְּרִי הָעֵץ אֲשֶׁר בְּתוֹךְ־הַגָּן אָמַר אֱלֹהִים לֹא
not ,God said had the the in which the of but may We
garden of middle (is) tree of fruit the ,eat

5175 559 4191 6435 5060 398
4 תֹאכְלוּ מִמֶּנּוּ וְלֹא תִגְּעוּ בּוֹ פֶּן־תְּמֻתוּן׃ וַיֹּאמֶר הַנָּחָשׁ
the said And .die you lest ,it you shall nor ,it of shall You
serpent touch eat

3117 430 3045 4191 4191 803
5 אֶל־הָאִשָּׁה לֹא־מוֹת תְּמֻתוּן׃ כִּי יֹדֵעַ אֱלֹהִים כִּי בְּיוֹם
the in that God knows for shall you surely Not woman the to
day .die

2596 3045 430 1961 5869 6491 398
אֲכָלְכֶם מִמֶּנּוּ וְנִפְקְחוּ עֵינֵיכֶם וִהְיִיתֶם כֵּאלֹהִים יֹדְעֵי טוֹב
good knowing ,God as you and eyes your shall then ,it of eat you
be shall opened be

good and evil. 6And the woman saw that the tree was good for food, and that it was pleasant to the eyes, and the tree desirable to make *one* wise. And she took of its fruit and ate. And she also gave to her husband with her, and he ate. 7And the eyes of both of them were opened and they knew that they *were* naked. And they sewed leaves of the fig-tree and made girdles for themselves.

8And they heard the sound of Jehovah God walking up and down in the garden at the breeze of the day. And the man and his wife hid themselves from the face of Jehovah God in the middle of the trees of the garden. 9And Jehovah God called to the man and said to him, Where are you? 10And he said, I have heard Your sound in the garden, and I was afraid, for I *am* naked, and I hid myself. 11And He said, Who told you that you *were* naked? Have you eaten of the tree *of* which I commanded you not to eat? 12And the man said, The woman whom You gave *to be* with me, she has given to me of the tree, and I ate. 13And Jehovah God said to the woman, What *is* this you have done? And the woman said, The serpent deceived me, and I ate.

14And Jehovah God said to the serpent, Because you have done this, you are cursed above all beasts, and above every animal of the field. You shall go on your belly, and you shall eat dust all the days of your life. 15And I will put enmity between you and the woman, and between your seed and her seed—He will bruise your head, and you shall bruise His heel. 16He said to the woman, I will greatly increase your

6 וָרָע׃ וַתֵּרֶא הָאִשָּׁה כִּי טוֹב הָעֵץ לְמַאֲכָל וְכִי תַאֲוָה־הוּא
לָעֵינַיִם וְנֶחְמָד הָעֵץ לְהַשְׂכִּיל וַתִּקַּח מִפִּרְיוֹ וַתֹּאכַל וַתִּתֵּן
7 גַּם־לְאִישָׁהּ עִמָּהּ וַיֹּאכַל׃ וַתִּפָּקַחְנָה עֵינֵי שְׁנֵיהֶם וַיֵּדְעוּ כִּי
עֵירֻמִּם הֵם וַיִּתְפְּרוּ עֲלֵה תְאֵנָה וַיַּעֲשׂוּ לָהֶם חֲגֹרֹת׃
8 וַיִּשְׁמְעוּ אֶת־קוֹל יְהוָה אֱלֹהִים מִתְהַלֵּךְ בַּגָּן לְרוּחַ הַיּוֹם
וַיִּתְחַבֵּא הָאָדָם וְאִשְׁתּוֹ מִפְּנֵי יְהוָה אֱלֹהִים בְּתוֹךְ עֵץ הַגָּן׃
9 10 וַיִּקְרָא יְהוָה אֱלֹהִים אֶל־הָאָדָם וַיֹּאמֶר לוֹ אַיֶּכָּה׃ וַיֹּאמֶר
אֶת־קֹלְךָ שָׁמַעְתִּי בַּגָּן וָאִירָא כִּי־עֵירֹם אָנֹכִי וָאֵחָבֵא׃
11 וַיֹּאמֶר מִי הִגִּיד לְךָ כִּי עֵירֹם אָתָּה הֲמִן־הָעֵץ אֲשֶׁר צִוִּיתִיךָ
12 לְבִלְתִּי אֲכָל־מִמֶּנּוּ אָכָלְתָּ׃ וַיֹּאמֶר הָאָדָם הָאִשָּׁה אֲשֶׁר
13 נָתַתָּה עִמָּדִי הִוא נָתְנָה־לִּי מִן־הָעֵץ וָאֹכֵל׃ וַיֹּאמֶר יְהוָה
אֱלֹהִים לָאִשָּׁה מַה־זֹּאת עָשִׂית וַתֹּאמֶר הָאִשָּׁה הַנָּחָשׁ
14 הִשִּׁיאַנִי וָאֹכֵל׃ וַיֹּאמֶר יְהוָה אֱלֹהִים ׀ אֶל־הַנָּחָשׁ כִּי עָשִׂיתָ
זֹּאת אָרוּר אַתָּה מִכָּל־הַבְּהֵמָה וּמִכֹּל חַיַּת הַשָּׂדֶה עַל־
15 גְּחֹנְךָ תֵלֵךְ וְעָפָר תֹּאכַל כָּל־יְמֵי חַיֶּיךָ׃ וְאֵיבָה ׀ אָשִׁית
בֵּינְךָ וּבֵין הָאִשָּׁה וּבֵין זַרְעֲךָ וּבֵין זַרְעָהּ הוּא יְשׁוּפְךָ רֹאשׁ
16 וְאַתָּה תְּשׁוּפֶנּוּ עָקֵב׃ ס אֶל־הָאִשָּׁה אָמַר הַרְבָּה אַרְבֶּה

sorrow and your con-
ception; you shall bear
sons in sorrow, and your
desire shall be toward
your husband; and he
shall rule over you.
[17]And He said to the man,
Because you have lis-
tened to the voice of your
wife, and have eaten of
the tree about which I
commanded you, saying,
You shall not eat from it,
the ground shall be
cursed because of you;
you shall eat of it in
sorrow all the days of
your life. [18]And it shall
bring forth thorns and
thistles for you, and you
shall eat the plant of the
field. [19]By the sweat of
your face you shall eat
bread until your return to
the ground. For you have
been taken out of it; for
you are dust, and to dust
you shall return. [20]And
the man called the name
of his wife, Eve, because
she became the mother
of all living. [21]And
Jehovah made coats of
skin for the man and his
wife, and clothed them.

[22]And Jehovah God said,
Behold! *The man has be-*
come as one of Us, to know
good and evil. And now,
lest he put forth his hand
and also take from the Tree
of Life, and eat, and live
forever. [23]And Jehovah
God sent him out of the
garden of Eden to till the
ground out of which he was
taken. [24]And He drove the
man out. And He caused to
dwell the cherubs at the
east of the Garden of Eden,
and the flaming sword
whirling around, to guard
the way of the Tree of Life.

8669 376 1121 80,85 6089 2032 6093
עִצְּבוֹנֵךְ וְהֵרֹנֵךְ בְּעֶצֶב תֵּלְדִי בָנִים וְאֶל־אִישֵׁךְ תְּשׁוּקָתֵךְ
desire your be shall | your husband | and | ;sons | you bear shall | sorrow in | your and conception | your sorrow

6963 8085 559 120 4910
17 וְהוּא יִמְשָׁל־בָּךְ׃ ס וּלְאָדָם אָמַר כִּי שָׁמַעְתָּ לְקוֹל
the to of voice | have you listened | Because | He ,said | to And man the | over ,you | rule shall | he and

398 559 6680 834 6086 398 802
אִשְׁתֶּךָ וַתֹּאכַל מִן־הָעֵץ אֲשֶׁר צִוִּיתִיךָ לֵאמֹר לֹא תֹאכַל
shall you eat | not | ,saying | com- I ,you manded | about which | the tree | of | have you eaten | your wife

3117 3605 398 6093 127 779
מִמֶּנּוּ אֲרוּרָה הָאֲדָמָה בַּעֲבוּרֶךָ בְּעִצָּבוֹן תֹּאכֲלֶנָּה כֹּל יְמֵי
the of days | all | shall you it of eat | sorrow in | because ;you of | ground the | cursed be shall | from ,it

7704 6212 398 6779 1863 6975 2416
18 חַיֶּיךָ׃ וְקוֹץ וְדַרְדַּר תַּצְמִיחַ לָךְ וְאָכַלְתָּ אֶת־עֵשֶׂב הַשָּׂדֶה׃
field the | plant the of | you eat shall | and ;you | for | shall it forth bring | and thistles | And thorns | your .life

127 7725 5704 3899 398 639 2188
19 בְּזֵעַת אַפֶּיךָ תֹּאכַל לֶחֶם עַד שׁוּבְךָ אֶל־הָאֲדָמָה
;ground the | to | return your | until | bread | shall you eat | face your | the By of sweat

7725 6083 857 6083 3947
כִּי מִמֶּנָּה לֻקָּחְתָּ כִּי־עָפָר אַתָּה וְאֶל־עָפָר תָּשׁוּב׃
shall you .return | dust | to and | ,are you | dust - | for | have you ;taken been | it of out | for

3605 517 1961 3588 2332 802 8034 120 7121
20 וַיִּקְרָא הָאָדָם שֵׁם אִשְׁתּוֹ חַוָּה כִּי הִוא הָיְתָה אֵם כָּל־
all | the of mother | became | she because | ;Eve | his wife's | name | man the | And called

5785 3801 802 120 430 3068 6213 2416
21 חָי׃ וַיַּעַשׂ יְהוָה אֱלֹהִים לְאָדָם וּלְאִשְׁתּוֹ כָּתְנוֹת עוֹר
skin | of coats | wife his | and | man the for | God | Jehovah | And made | .living

3843
וַיַּלְבִּשֵׁם׃
clothed and .them

3045 259 1961 120 2005 430 3068 559
22 וַיֹּאמֶר ׀ יְהוָה אֱלֹהִים הֵן הָאָדָם הָיָה כְּאַחַד מִמֶּנּוּ לָדַעַת
know to | ,Us of | one as | has become | The man | !Behold | ,God | Jehovah | said And

2416 6086 3947 7971 6435 6258 7451 2896
טוֹב וָרָע וְעַתָּה ׀ פֶּן־יִשְׁלַח יָדוֹ וְלָקַח גַּם מֵעֵץ הַחַיִּים
.life | from also of tree the | and take | his hand | put he forth | lest | ,now And | and evil | good

5647 1588 430 3068 7971 5769 2425 398
23 וְאָכַל וָחַי לְעֹלָם׃ וַיְשַׁלְּחֵהוּ יְהוָה אֱלֹהִים מִגַּן־עֵדֶן לַעֲבֹד
till to | the of out Eden of garden | God | Jehovah | therefore him sent | ,forever | and live | and eat

7931 120 1644 3947 834 127
24 אֶת־הָאֲדָמָה אֲשֶׁר לֻקַּח מִשָּׁם׃ וַיְגָרֶשׁ אֶת־הָאָדָם וַיַּשְׁכֵּן
He and lodged | ;man the | He And out drove | .from | was he taken | which | ground the

2015 2719 3858 3742 5731 1588 6924
מִקֶּדֶם לְגַן־עֵדֶן אֶת־הַכְּרֻבִים וְאֵת לַהַט הַחֶרֶב הַמִּתְהַפֶּכֶת
around whirling | the sword | flaming | and | .cherubim the | of the Eden | of the garden | at east

2416 6086 1870 8104
לִשְׁמֹר אֶת־דֶּרֶךְ עֵץ הַחַיִּים׃
.life | the of tree | of way the | guard to

CAP. IV ד

CHAPTER 4

[1]And the man knew his wife Eve. And she conceived and bore Cain, and said, I have gotten a man *with the help* of Jehovah. [2]And she continued to bear his brother, Abel. And Abel became a shepherd of flocks. And Cain became a tiller of the ground. [3]And in the end of days, it happened that Cain brought an offering to Jehovah from the fruit of the ground. [4]And Abel brought, he also, from the firstlings of his flocks, even from their fat. And Jehovah looked to Abel and to his offering. [5]And He did not look to Cain and to his offering. And Cain glowed greatly *with anger*, and his face fell. [6]And Jehovah said to Cain, Why have you angrily glowed, and why has your face fallen? [7]If you do well, is there not exaltation? And if you do not do well, sin is crouching at the door; and its desire *is* toward you; but you should rule over it.

[8]And Cain talked with his brother Abel. And as they were in the field, Cain rose up against His brother Abel, and killed him. [9]And Jehovah said to Cain, Where *is* your brother Abel? And he said, I do not know. Am I my brother's keeper? [10]And He said, What have you done? The voice of the blood of your brother cries to Me from the ground. [11]And now you *are* cursed more than the ground which opened its mouth to receive your brother's blood from your hand. [12]When you till the ground, it will not again give its strength to you. You shall be a vagabond and a fugitive on the earth. [13]And Cain said to Jehovah, My punishment is greater than I can bear.

CHAPTER 4

559 7014 853 3205 2029 802 853 3045 120
1 וְהָאָדָם יָדַע אֶת־חַוָּה אִשְׁתּוֹ וַתַּהַר וַתֵּלֶד אֶת־קַיִן וַתֹּאמֶר
,said and ,Cain and she And .wife his Eve knew the And
bore conceived man

1893 251 3205 3254 3068 854 376 7069
2 קָנִיתִי אִישׁ אֶת־יְהוָה׃ וַתֹּסֶף לָלֶדֶת אֶת־אָחִיו אֶת־הָבֶל
.Abel brother his to she And (help the with) man a have I
bear continued .Jehovah of gotten

7093 1961 127 5647 1961 7014 6629 2462 1961
3 וַיְהִי־הֶבֶל רֹעֵה צֹאן וְקַיִן הָיָה עֹבֵד אֲדָמָה׃ וַיְהִי מִקֵּץ
the in And .ground the a became and ,flocks a Abel And
of end was it of tiller Cain of shepherd became

935 1893 3068 4503 127 6529 7014 935 3117
4 יָמִים וַיָּבֵא קַיִן מִפְּרִי הָאֲדָמָה מִנְחָה לַיהוָה׃ וְהֶבֶל הֵבִיא
brought And .Jehovah to an the the from Cain that days
Abel offering ground of fruit brought

1893 3068 8159 2459 6629 1062 1931
גַם־הוּא מִבְּכֹרוֹת צֹאנוֹ וּמֵחֶלְבֵהֶן וַיִּשַׁע יְהוָה אֶל־הֶבֶל
Abel to Jehovah And from even his the from ,he also
looked .fat their ,flocks of firstlings

7014 2734 8159 4503 7014 4503
5 וְאֶל־מִנְחָתוֹ׃ וְאֶל־קַיִן וְאֶל־מִנְחָתוֹ לֹא שָׁעָה וַיִּחַר לְקַיִן
Cain And did He not his to and Cain to and his to and
glowed .look offering ;offering

2734 4100 7014 3068 559 6440 5307 3966
6 מְאֹד וַיִּפְּלוּ פָּנָיו׃ וַיֹּאמֶר יְהוָה אֶל־קָיִן לָמָּה חָרָה לָךְ
you have Why ,Cain to Jehovah said And .face his and ,greatly
glowed angrily fell

7613 3190 518 6440 5307 4100
7 וְלָמָּה נָפְלוּ פָנֶיךָ׃ הֲלוֹא אִם־תֵּיטִיב שְׂאֵת וְאִם לֹא
not if And exalta- do you If there is ?face your has why and
?tion ,well not fallen

8669 7257 2403 6607 3190
תֵיטִיב לַפֶּתַח חַטָּאת רֹבֵץ וְאֵלֶיךָ תְּשׁוּקָתוֹ וְאַתָּה תִּמְשָׁל־
rule should but its toward and is sin the at do you
you .(is) desire you ;crouching door ,well

6965 7704 1961 251 1893 413 7014 557
8 בּוֹ׃ וַיֹּאמֶר קַיִן אֶל־הֶבֶל אָחִיו וַיְהִי בִּהְיוֹתָם בַּשָּׂדֶה וַיָּקָם
rose the in they as and his Abel with Cain And over
up ,field were ;brother talked .it

335 7014 3068 559 2026 251 1893 413 7014
9 קַיִן אֶל־הֶבֶל אָחִיו וַיַּהַרְגֵהוּ׃ וַיֹּאמֶר יְהוָה אֶל־קַיִן אֵי
Where ,Cain to Jehovah said And killed and his Abel against Cain
(is) .him brother

559 251 8104 3045 559 251 1893
10 הֶבֶל אָחִיךָ וַיֹּאמֶר לֹא יָדַעְתִּי הֲשֹׁמֵר אָחִי אָנֹכִי׃ וַיֹּאמֶר
He And ?I (am) my keeper do I not he And your Abel
said brother's ;know said ?brother

6248 127 6817 251 1818 6963 6213 4100
11 מֶה עָשִׂיתָ קוֹל דְּמֵי אָחִיךָ צֹעֲקִים אֵלַי מִן־הָאֲדָמָה׃ וְעַתָּה
And ,ground the from to cries your blood The have you What
now Me brother's of voice ?done

3947 6310 6425 834 127 779
אָרוּר אָתָּה מִן־הָאֲדָמָה אֲשֶׁר פָּצְתָה אֶת־פִּיהָ לָקַחַת אֶת־
to mouths its opened which the more (are) cursed
receive ground than you

3581 5414 3254 127 5647 3588 3027 251 1818
12 דְּמֵי אָחִיךָ מִיָּדֶךָ׃ כִּי תַעֲבֹד אֶת־הָאֲדָמָה לֹא־תֹסֵף תֵּת־כֹּחָהּ
its give again not ,ground the you When your from your blood
strength it will till hand brother's

5771 1419 3068 7014 559 776 1961 5110 5128
13 לָךְ נָע וָנָד תִּהְיֶה בָאָרֶץ׃ וַיֹּאמֶר קַיִן אֶל־יְהוָה גָּדוֹל עֲוֺנִי
pun- My is ,Jehovah to Cain said And the on shall you a and a ;you to
ishment greater .earth be fugitive vagabond

14Lo, You have driven me
out from the face of the
earth today. And I shall be
hidden from Your face. And
I shall be a vagabond and a
fugitive on the earth. And it
will be *that* anyone who
finds me shall kill me.
15And Jehovah said to him,
If anyone kills Cain, he shall
be avenged sevenfold. And
Jehovah set a mark on Cain,
so that anyone who found
him should not kill him.
16And Cain went out from
the presence of Jehovah.
And *he* lived in the land of
Nod, east of Eden. 17And
Cain knew his wife, and she
conceived and bore Enoch.
And he built a city, and he
called the name of the city
according to the name of
his son, Enoch.
18And Irad was born to
Enoch; and Irad fathered
Mehujael. And Mehujael
fathered Methusael; and
Methusael fathered La-
mech. 19And Lamech took
two wives to himself: the
name of the first was Adah;
and the name of the second
was Zillah. 20And Adah
bore Jabal; he was the
father of those living in
tents, and with cattle.
21And the name of his
brother *was* Jubal; he was
the father of all those
playing the harp and the
organ. 22And Zillah also
bore Tubalcain, the ham-
merer of every engraving
tool of bronze and iron. And
the sister of Tubalcain *was*
Naamah. 23And Lamech
said to his wives, Adah and
Zillah, Hear my voice, you
wives of Lamech; listen to
my words—for I have killed
a man because of my
wound, and a young man
because of my hurt; 24for
Cain is avenged sevenfold,
and Lamech seventy-seven.
25And Adam knew his
wife again, and she bore a
son. And she called his
name, Seth, for God has
appointed to me another
seed in place of Abel,
because Cain killed him.

5640 6440 127 6440 5921 3117 1644 5375
14 מִנְּשֹׂא׃ הֵן גֵּרַשְׁתָּ אֹתִי הַיּוֹם מֵעַל פְּנֵי הָאֲדָמָה וּמִפָּנֶיךָ אֶסָּתֵר
be shall I from and earth the the from ,today me have You ,Lo I than
;hidden face Your of face out driven bear can

3068 559 2026 4672 3605 1961 776 5110/5128 1961
15 וְהָיִיתִי נָע וָנָד בָּאָרֶץ וְהָיָה כָל־מֹצְאִי יַהַרְגֵנִי׃ וַיֹּאמֶר לוֹ יְהוָה
Jehovah to And kill shall who anyone it And the on a and vage- a I and
him said me me finds be will .earth fugitive bond be shall

3605 1115 226 7760 5358 7659 7014 5206 3651
לָכֵן כָּל־הֹרֵג קַיִן שִׁבְעָתַיִם יֻקָּם וַיָּשֶׂם יְהוָה לְקַיִן אוֹת לְבִלְתִּי
that so a on Jehovah And shall he sevenfold ,Cain kills any- If
not mark Cain set avenged be one

776 2416 3068 6440 7014 5927 4672 3605 2026
16 הַכּוֹת־אֹתוֹ כָּל־מֹצְאוֹ׃ וַיֵּצֵא קַיִן מִלִּפְנֵי יְהוָה וַיֵּשֶׁב בְּאֶרֶץ
the in and Jehovah the from Cain And who anyone him should
of land lived of presence out went him found kill

3205 2029 802 7014 3045 5731 6926 5112
17 נוֹד קִדְמַת־עֵדֶן׃ וַיֵּדַע קַיִן אֶת־אִשְׁתּוֹ וַתַּהַר וַתֵּלֶד אֶת־
and she and ,wife his Cain And .Eden of east ,Nod
bore conceived knew

2585 3205 2027 5892 8034 7121 5892 1529 2585
חֲנוֹךְ וַיְהִי בֹּנֶה עִיר וַיִּקְרָא שֵׁם הָעִיר כְּשֵׁם בְּנוֹ חֲנוֹךְ׃
.Enoch his according the the he and ,city a he And .Enoch
son's ,name to city of name called built

4232 4232 3205 5897 5897 2585 3205
18 וַיִּוָּלֵד לַחֲנוֹךְ אֶת־עִירָד וְעִירָד יָלַד אֶת־מְחוּיָאֵל וּמְחִיָּיאֵל
and ;Mehujael fathered And .Irad to And
Mehujael Irad Enoch born was

3929 3947 3929 3205 4967 4967 3205
19 יָלַד אֶת־מְתוּשָׁאֵל וּמְתוּשָׁאֵל יָלַד אֶת־לָמֶךְ׃ וַיִּקַּח־לוֹ לֶמֶךְ
Lamech to And .Lamech fathered And .Methusael fathered
himself took Methusael

5711 3205 6741 8145 8034 5711 259 8034 802 8147
20 שְׁתֵּי נָשִׁים שֵׁם הָאַחַת עָדָה וְשֵׁם הַשֵּׁנִית צִלָּה׃ וַתֵּלֶד עָדָה
Adah And .Zillah other the the and ,Adah first the the ;wives two
bore was of name was of name

251 8034 4735 168 2416 1 1961 2489
21 אֶת־יָבָל הוּא הָיָה אֲבִי יֹשֵׁב אֹהֶל וּמִקְנֶה׃ וְשֵׁם אָחִיו יוּבָל הוּא
he (was) his And (raising) and tents those the was he ;Jabal
;Jubal brother's name ;livestock in living of father

3205 1571 6741 5748 3658 8610 1 1961
22 הָיָה אֲבִי כָּל־תֹּפֵשׂ כִּנּוֹר וְעוּגָב׃ וְצִלָּה גַם־הִוא יָלְדָה אֶת־
bore she also And the and the those all the was
Zillah .organ harp playing of father

8423 269 1170 5178 2714 3113 8423
תּוּבַל קַיִן לֹטֵשׁ כָּל־חֹרֵשׁ נְחֹשֶׁת וּבַרְזֶל וַאֲחוֹת תּוּבַל־קַיִן
Tubalcain the And and bronze engraving every the ,Tubalcain
of sister .iron of tool of hammerer

802 6963 8085 6741 5711 802 3929 559 5279
23 נַעֲמָה׃ וַיֹּאמֶר לֶמֶךְ לְנָשָׁיו עָדָה וְצִלָּה שְׁמַעַן קוֹלִי נְשֵׁי
you my Hear and Adah his to Lamech said And (was)
of wives ,voice ,Zillah wives .Naamah

3206 6482 2026 376 3588 565 238 3929
לֶמֶךְ הַאְזֵנָּה אִמְרָתִי כִּי אִישׁ הָרַגְתִּי לְפִצְעִי וְיֶלֶד
a and of because have I man a for —words my to listen ,Lamech
man young ,wound my killed

7651 7657 3929 7014 5358 7659 3588 2250
24 לְחַבֻּרָתִי׃ כִּי שִׁבְעָתַיִם יֻקַּם־קָיִן וְלֶמֶךְ שִׁבְעִים וְשִׁבְעָה׃
.seven seventy- and is Cain sevenfold for ;hurt my for
Lamech avenged

8034 7121 1121 3205 802 5750 120 3045
25 וַיֵּדַע אָדָם עוֹד אֶת־אִשְׁתּוֹ וַתֵּלֶד בֵּן וַתִּקְרָא אֶת־שְׁמוֹ
name his she and son a she and ,wife his again Adam And
called bore knew

2026 3588 1893 312 2233 430 7896 3588 8352
שֵׁת כִּי שָׁת־לִי אֱלֹהִים זֶרַע אַחֵר תַּחַת הֶבֶל כִּי הֲרָגוֹ
killed be- ,Abel place in another seed God me has for ,Seth
him cause of appointed

[26]And a son was also born to Seth, and he called his name, Enos. Then it was begun to call on the name of Jehovah.

583 80 34 7121 1121 3205 1931 1571 8352 7014
26 קָיִן׃ וּלְשֵׁת גַּם־הוּא יֻלַּד־בֵּן וַיִּקְרָא אֶת־שְׁמוֹ אֱנוֹשׁ אָז
Then .Enos name his he and ,son a called was born he also to And Seth .Cain

3068 8034 7121 2490
הוּחַל לִקְרֹא בְּשֵׁם יְהוָה׃ ס
.Jehovah the on of name call to was it begun

CAP. V ה

CHAPTER 5

[1]This is the book of the generations of Adam: In the day that God created man, He made him in the likeness of God. [2]He created them male and female, and blessed them, and called their name Adam in the day when they were created. [3]And Adam lived one hundred and thirty years and fathered a son in his own likeness, according to his image, and called his name Seth. [4]And the days of Adam after he fathered Seth were eight hundred years. And he fathered sons and daughters. [5]And all the days that Adam lived were nine hundred and thirty years. And he died.

1823 120 430 1254 3117 120 8435 5612 2088
1 זֶה סֵפֶר תּוֹלְדֹת אָדָם בְּיוֹם בְּרֹא אֱלֹהִים אָדָם בִּדְמוּת
the in of likeness ,man God that created the in day :Adam genera- tions of the book of the (is) This

1288 1254 5347 2145 6213 430
2 אֱלֹהִים עָשָׂה אֹתוֹ׃ זָכָר וּנְקֵבָה בְּרָאָם וַיְבָרֶךְ אֹתָם
,them He and blessed created He ;them and female male .him made He God

430 120 2421 1254 3117 120 8034 7121
3 וַיִּקְרָא אֶת־שְׁמָם אָדָם בְּיוֹם הִבָּרְאָם׃ וַיְחִי אָדָם שְׁלֹשִׁים
thirty Adam And lived they when created were the in day man name their and called

8352 8034 7121 6754 1823 3205 8141 3967
וּמְאַת שָׁנָה וַיּוֹלֶד בִּדְמוּתוֹ כְּצַלְמוֹ וַיִּקְרָא אֶת־שְׁמוֹ שֵׁת׃
.Seth name his and called to according ,image his own his in likeness fath- ered and a son years one and hundred

8141 3967 8083 8352 3205 310 120 3117 1961
4 וַיִּהְיוּ יְמֵי־אָדָם אַחֲרֵי הוֹלִידוֹ אֶת־שֵׁת שְׁמֹנֶה מֵאֹת שָׁנָה
.years hundred eight Seth fathered he after Adam the of days And were

8672 2425 120 3117 1961 1323 1121 3205
5 וַיּוֹלֶד בָּנִים וּבָנוֹת׃ וַיִּהְיוּ כָּל־יְמֵי אָדָם אֲשֶׁר־חַי תְּשַׁע
nine he lived that Adam the days all And were and daughters sons he And fathered

[6]And Seth lived one hundred and five years, and fathered Enos. [7]And after he fathered Enos, Seth lived eight hundred and seven years. And he fathered sons and daughters. [8]And all the days of Seth were nine hundred and twelve years. And he died.

2568 8352 2416 4191 8141 7970 8141 3967
6 מֵאוֹת שָׁנָה וּשְׁלֹשִׁים שָׁנָה וַיָּמֹת׃ ס וַיְחִי־שֵׁת חָמֵשׁ
five Seth And lived he and .died ;years thirty and years hundred

3205 310 8352 2421 583 3205 8141 3967 8141
7 שָׁנִים וּמְאַת שָׁנָה וַיּוֹלֶד אֶת־אֱנוֹשׁ׃ וַיְחִי־שֵׁת אַחֲרֵי הוֹלִידוֹ
after Seth And lived .Enosh and fathered ;years one and hundred years

1121 3205 8141 3967 8083 8141 7651 583
אֶת־אֱנוֹשׁ שֶׁבַע שָׁנִים וּשְׁמֹנֶה מֵאוֹת שָׁנָה וַיּוֹלֶד בָּנִים
sons he and fathered ;years hundred eight and years seven ,Enosh

3967 8672 8141 6240 8147 8352 3117 3605 1961 1323
8 וּבָנוֹת׃ וַיִּהְיוּ כָּל־יְמֵי־שֵׁת שְׁתֵּים עֶשְׂרֵה שָׁנָה וּתְשַׁע מֵאוֹת
hundred and nine years twelve Seth the of days all And were and .daughters

[9]And Enos lived ninety years and fathered Cainan. [10]After he fathered Cainan, Enos lived eight hundred and fifteen years, and he fathered sons and daughters. [11]And all the days of Enos were nine hundred and five years. And he died.

7018 3205 8141 8673 583 2421 4191 8141
9 שָׁנָה וַיָּמֹת׃ ס וַיְחִי אֱנוֹשׁ תִּשְׁעִים שָׁנָה וַיּוֹלֶד אֶת־קֵינָן׃
.Cainan and fathered years ninety Enosh And lived he And .died .years

8141 6240 2568 7018 3205 310 583 2416
10 וַיְחִי אֱנוֹשׁ אַחֲרֵי הוֹלִידוֹ אֶת־קֵינָן חֲמֵשׁ עֶשְׂרֵה שָׁנָה
years fifteen ,Cainan he fathered after Enosh And lived

3117 3605 1961 1323 1121 3205 8141 3967 8083
11 וּשְׁמֹנֶה מֵאוֹת שָׁנָה וַיּוֹלֶד בָּנִים וּבָנוֹת׃ וַיִּהְיוּ כָּל־יְמֵי
the of days all And were and .daughters sons he and fathered ;years hundred eight and

[12]And Cainan lived seven-

2421 8141 3967 8672 8141 2568 583
12 אֱנוֹשׁ חָמֵשׁ שָׁנִים וּתְשַׁע מֵאוֹת שָׁנָה וַיָּמֹת׃ ס וַיְחִי קֵינָן
Cainan And lived he and .died ;years hundred and nine years five Enosh

ty years and fathered Mahalaleel. [13]And after he fathered Mahalaleel, Cainan lived eight hundred and forty years. And he fathered sons and daughters. [14]And all the days of Cainan were nine hundred and ten years. And he died. [15]And Mahalaleel lived sixty-five years and fathered Jared. [16]And after he fathered Jared, Mahalaleel lived eight hundred and thirty years. And he fathered sons and daughters. [17]And all the days of Mahalaleel were eight hundred and ninety five years. And he died.

[18]And Jared lived one hundred and sixty two years and fathered Enoch. [19]And after he fathered Enoch, Jared lived eight hundred years. And he fathered sons and daughters. [20]And all the days of Jared were nine hundred and sixty-two years. And he died.

[21]And Enoch lived sixty-five years and fathered Methuselah. [22]And Enoch walked with God three hundred years after he fathered Methuselah. And he fathered sons and daughters. [23]And all the days of Enoch were three hundred and sixty-five years. [24]And Enoch walked with God; then he was not —for God took him.

[25]And Methuselah lived one hundred and eighty-seven years and fathered Lamech. [26]And after he

3205 310 7018 2421 4111 3205 8141 7657
13 שִׁבְעִים שָׁנָה וַיּוֹלֶד אֶת־מַהֲלַלְאֵל׃ וַיְחִי קֵינָן אַחֲרֵי הוֹלִידוֹ
he fathered after Cainan And lived .Mahalaleel and fathered years seventy

3205 8141 3967 8083 8141 705 4111
אֶת־מַהֲלַלְאֵל אַרְבָּעִים שָׁנָה וּשְׁמֹנֶה מֵאוֹת שָׁנָה וַיּוֹלֶד
he and fathered ,years hundred eight and years forty ,Mahalaleel

3967 8672 8141 6235 7018/3117/3605 1961 1323 1121
14 בָּנִים וּבָנוֹת׃ וַיִּהְיוּ כָּל־יְמֵי קֵינָן עֶשֶׂר שָׁנִים וּתְשַׁע מֵאוֹת
hundred and nine years ten Cainan the all of days And were and .daughters sons

8141 8346 8141 2568 4111 2421 4191 8141
15 שָׁנָה וַיָּמֹת׃ ס וַיְחִי מַהֲלַלְאֵל חָמֵשׁ שָׁנִים וְשִׁשִּׁים שָׁנָה
;years sixty- years five Mahalaleel And lived he and .died ;years

3382 3205 310 4111 2421 3382 3205
16 וַיּוֹלֶד אֶת־יָרֶד׃ וַיְחִי מַהֲלַלְאֵל אַחֲרֵי הוֹלִידוֹ אֶת־יֶרֶד
Jared fathered he after Mahalaleel And lived .Jared he and fathered

1323 1121 3205 8141 3967 8083 8141 7970
שְׁלֹשִׁים שָׁנָה וּשְׁמֹנֶה מֵאוֹת שָׁנָה וַיּוֹלֶד בָּנִים וּבָנוֹת׃
and .daughters sons he and fathered ;years hundred eight and years thirty

3967 8083 8141 8673 2568 4111 3117/3605 1961
17 וַיִּהְיוּ כָּל־יְמֵי מַהֲלַלְאֵל חָמֵשׁ וְתִשְׁעִים שָׁנָה וּשְׁמֹנֶה מֵאוֹת
hundred and eight years ninety- five Mahalaleel the all of days And were

3967 8141 8346 8147 3382/2421 4191 8141
18 שָׁנָה וַיָּמֹת׃ ס וַיְחִי־יֶרֶד שְׁתַּיִם וְשִׁשִּׁים שָׁנָה וּמְאַת
one and hundred years sixty- two Jared And lived he and .died ;years

2585 3205 310 3382/2421 2585 3205 8141
19 שָׁנָה וַיּוֹלֶד אֶת־חֲנוֹךְ׃ וַיְחִי־יֶרֶד אַחֲרֵי הוֹלִידוֹ אֶת־חֲנוֹךְ
,Enoch fathered he after Jared And lived .Enoch and fathered ;years

3382/3117/3605 1961 1323 1121 3205 8141 3967 8083
20 שְׁמֹנֶה מֵאוֹת שָׁנָה וַיּוֹלֶד בָּנִים וּבָנוֹת׃ וַיִּהְיוּ כָּל־יְמֵי־יֶרֶד
Jared the all of days And were and .daughters sons and fathered years hundred eight

2421 4191 8141 3967 8672 8141 8346 8147
21 שְׁתַּיִם וְשִׁשִּׁים שָׁנָה וּתְשַׁע מֵאוֹת שָׁנָה וַיָּמֹת׃ ס וַיְחִי
And lived he and .died ;years hundred and nine years sixty- two

1980 4968 3205 8141 8346 2568 2585
22 חֲנוֹךְ חָמֵשׁ וְשִׁשִּׁים שָׁנָה וַיּוֹלֶד אֶת־מְתוּשָׁלַח׃ וַיִּתְהַלֵּךְ
And walked .Methuselah and fathered years sixty- five Enoch

7969 4968 3205 310 430 854 2585
חֲנוֹךְ אֶת־הָאֱלֹהִים אַחֲרֵי הוֹלִידוֹ אֶת־מְתוּשֶׁלַח שְׁלֹשׁ
three Methuselah fathered he after God with Enoch

2568 2585 3117/3605 1961 1323 1121 3205 8141 3967
23 מֵאוֹת שָׁנָה וַיּוֹלֶד בָּנִים וּבָנוֹת׃ וַיְהִי כָּל־יְמֵי חֲנוֹךְ חָמֵשׁ
five Enoch the all of days And were and .daughters sons he and fathered ,years hundred

2585 1980 8141 3967 7969 8141 8346
24 וְשִׁשִּׁים שָׁנָה וּשְׁלֹשׁ מֵאוֹת שָׁנָה׃ וַיִּתְהַלֵּךְ חֲנוֹךְ אֶת־
with Enoch And walked .years hundred three and years sixty-

4968 2421 430 3947 369 430
25 הָאֱלֹהִים וְאֵינֶנּוּ כִּי־לָקַח אֹתוֹ אֱלֹהִים׃ ס וַיְחִי מְתוּשֶׁלַח
Methuselah And lived .God him took for he then —not was ,God

2421 3927 3205 8141 3967 8141 8084 7651
26 שֶׁבַע וּשְׁמֹנִים שָׁנָה וּמְאַת שָׁנָה וַיּוֹלֶד אֶת־לָמֶךְ׃ וַיְחִי
And lived .Lamech he and fathered years one and hundred years eighty- seven

fathered Lamech, Methuse-
lah lived seven hundred and
eighty-two years. And he
fathered sons and daugh-
ters. [27]And all the days of
Methuselah were nine hun-
dred and sixty nine years;
and he died.

[28]And Lamech lived one
hundred and eighty-two
years and fathered a son.
[29]And he called his name
Noah, saying, This one shall
comfort us concerning our
work and the toil of our
hands, because of the
ground which the Lord has
cursed. [30]And after he
fathered Noah, Lamech
lived five hundred and
ninety-five years. And he
fathered sons and daugh-
ters. [31]And all the days of
Lamech were seven hun-
dred and seventy-seven
years. And he died. [32]And
Noah was five hundred
years old. And Noah
fathered Shem, Ham, and
Japheth.

8141 8084 8147 3929 3205 310 4968
מְתוּשֶׁלַח אַחֲרֵי הוֹלִידוֹ אֶת־לֶמֶךְ שְׁתַּיִם וּשְׁמוֹנִים שָׁנָה
years eighty- two Lamech fathered he after Methuselah

3117 1961 1323 1121 3205 8141 3967 7651
27 וְשֶׁבַע מֵאוֹת שָׁנָה וַיּוֹלֶד בָּנִים וּבָנוֹת׃ וַיִּהְיוּ כָּל־יְמֵי
the all And and sons he and ;years hundred and
of days were .daughters fathered seven

4191 8141 3967 8672 8141 8346 8672 4968
מְתוּשֶׁלַח תֵּשַׁע וְשִׁשִּׁים שָׁנָה וּתְשַׁע מֵאוֹת שָׁנָה וַיָּמֹת׃
he and ;years hundred nine and years sixty- nine Methuselah
died

1121 3205 8141 3967 8141 8084 8147 3929 2421
28 וַיְחִי־לֶמֶךְ שְׁתַּיִם וּשְׁמֹנִים שָׁנָה וּמְאַת שָׁנָה וַיּוֹלֶד בֵּן׃
.son a he and ;years one and years eighty- two Lamech And
fathered hundred lived

6093 4639 5162 2088 559 5146 8034 7121
29 וַיִּקְרָא אֶת־שְׁמוֹ נֹחַ לֵאמֹר זֶה יְנַחֲמֵנוּ מִמַּעֲשֵׂנוּ וּמֵעִצְּבוֹן
the and from shall This ,saying ,Noah name his he And
of toil work our us comfort one called

310 2929 2421 3068 779 834 127 4480 3027
30 יָדֵינוּ מִן־הָאֲדָמָה אֲשֶׁר אֵרְרָהּ יְהוָה׃ וַיְחִי־לֶמֶךְ אַחֲרֵי
after Lamech And .Jehovah has which the from our
lived cursed ground hands

3967 2568 8141 8673 2568 5146 3205
הוֹלִידוֹ אֶת־נֹחַ חָמֵשׁ וְתִשְׁעִים שָׁנָה וַחֲמֵשׁ מֵאֹת
hundred five and years ninety- five ,Noah he
fathered

7651 3929 3605 1961 1323 1121 3205 8141
31 שָׁנָה וַיּוֹלֶד בָּנִים וּבָנוֹת׃ וַיְהִי כָּל־יְמֵי־לֶמֶךְ שֶׁבַע
seven Lamech the all And and sons he and ;years
of days were .daughters fathered

1961 4191 8141 3967 7651 8141 7657
32 וְשִׁבְעִים שָׁנָה וּשְׁבַע מֵאוֹת שָׁנָה וַיָּמֹת׃ ס וַיְהִי־
And he and ;years hundred and years seventy-
was .died seven

2526 8055 5146 3205 8141 3967 2568 1121 5146
נֹחַ בֶּן־חֲמֵשׁ מֵאוֹת שָׁנָה וַיּוֹלֶד נֹחַ אֶת־שֵׁם אֶת־חָם
,Ham ,Shem Noah And .years hundred five a Noah
fathered of man

3315
וְאֶת־יָפֶת׃
.Japheth and

CAP. VI ו

CHAPTER 6

CHAPTER 6

[1]And it came about that
men began to multiply on
the face of the earth, and
daughters were born to
them. [2]The sons of God
saw the daughters of men,
that they *were* good. And
they took wives for them-
selves from all those whom
they chose. [3]And Jehovah
said, My Spirit shall not
always strive with man; in
their erring he *is* flesh. And
his days shall be a hundred
and twenty years.

[4]The giants were in the
earth in those days, and
even afterwards when the

3205 1323 127 6440 5921/7235 120 2490 1961
1 וַיְהִי כִּי־הֵחֵל הָאָדָם לָרֹב עַל־פְּנֵי הָאֲדָמָה וּבָנוֹת יֻלְּדוּ
were and ,earth the the on to men began that it And
born daughters of face multiply was

2007 2896 120 1323 430 1121 7200
2 לָהֶם׃ וַיִּרְאוּ בְנֵי־הָאֱלֹהִים אֶת־בְּנוֹת הָאָדָם כִּי טֹבֹת הֵנָּה
they (were) that ,men daughters the God the (that) to
good

3808 3068 559 977 834 3605 802 3947
3 וַיִּקְחוּ לָהֶם נָשִׁים מִכֹּל אֲשֶׁר בָּחָרוּ׃ וַיֹּאמֶר יְהוָה לֹא־
not ,Jehovah said And they whom all from wives for they and
.chose those themselves took

3967 3117 1961 1320 7683 5769 120 7307 1777
יָדוֹן רוּחִי בָאָדָם לְעֹלָם בְּשַׁגַּם הוּא בָשָׂר וְהָיוּ יָמָיו מֵאָה
a his and ;flesh (is) he their in always with My shall
hundred days be shall ;erring man Spirit strive

310 1571 1992 3117 776 1961 5303 8141 6242
4 וְעֶשְׂרִים שָׁנָה׃ הַנְּפִלִים הָיוּ בָאָרֶץ בַּיָּמִים הָהֵם וְגַם אַחֲרֵי־
after- and ,those days in the on were giants The .years twenty and
wards even earth

sons of God came in to the
daughters of men, and they
bore to them—they were
heroes which *existed* from
ancient time, the men of
name.

5 And Jehovah saw that
the evil of man *was* great on
the earth, and every imagination of the thought of his
heart *was* only evil all the
day *long*. 6 And Jehovah
repented that He had made
man on the earth, and He
was grieved to His heart.
7 And Jehovah said, I will
wipe off man whom I have
created from the face of the
earth, from man to beast, to
the creeping thing and to
the bird of the heavens; for I
repent that I made them.
8 And Noah found grace in
the eyes of Jehovah.

9 These are the genera-
tions of Noah. Noah, a
righteous man, had been
perfected among his family
— Noah walked with God.
10 And Noah fathered three
sons, Shem, Ham, and
Japheth. 11 And the earth
was corrupt before God,
and the earth was filled with
violence. 12 And God
looked on the earth, and
behold, it was corrupted.
For all flesh had corrupted
its way on the earth. 13 And
God said to Noah, The end
of all flesh has come before
Me, for the earth is filled
with violence through them.
And behold, I will destroy
them *along with* the earth.
14 Make an ark of cyprus
timbers for yourself. You
shall make rooms in the ark;
and you shall cover it with
asphalt inside and out.
15 And you shall make it this
way: The length of the ark

3205 120 1323 430 1121 935 834 3651
כן אשר יבאו בני האלהים אל־בנות האדם וילדו להם
to them; they and bore men the of daughters to God the of sons came in when
8034 582 5769 834 1368 1992
המה הגברים אשר מעולם אנשי השם׃
.name the of men ancient time from who (existed) heroes they were

3336 3605 776 120 7451 7227 3068 7200
5 וירא יהוה כי רבה רעת האדם בארץ וכל־יצר
imagina- tion of every and the earth on man the of evil great (was) that Jehovah And saw
6213 3068 5162 3117 7451 7535 3820 4284
6 מחשבת לבו רק רע כל־היום׃ וינחם יהוה כי־עשה
had made He that Jehovah And repented day the (long) all evil only (was) heart his the of thoughts
4229 3068 559 3820 413 6087 776 120
7 את־האדם בארץ ויתעצב אל־לבו׃ ויאמר יהוה אמחה
will I wipe off ,Jehovah And said His heart to He and angered was the earth on man
5704 120 127 6440 1254 834 120
את־האדם אשר־בראתי מעל פני האדמה מאדם עד־
to man from ,earth the of face the from have I created whom man
6213 5162 8064 5775 7431 929
בהמה עד־רמש ועד־עוף השמים כי נחמתי כי עשיתם׃
made I .them that regret I for ;heavens the of fowl the to and the thing creeping to ,beast
3068/5869 2580 4672 5146
8 ונח מצא חן בעיני יהוה׃
.Jehovah of eyes the in grace found But Noah

8435 1961 8549 6662 376 5146 5146 8435
9 אלה תולדת נח נח איש צדיק תמים היה בדרתיו
his among ;peers had been perfected ,righteous a man ,Noah .Noah the of generations These are
1121 7969 5146 3205 1980 5146 430
10 את־האלהים התהלך־נח׃ ויולד נח שלשה בנים את־
;sons three Noah And fathered .walked Noah God with
430 6440 776 7843 3315 2526 8035
11 שם את־חם ואת־יפת׃ ותשחת הארץ לפני האלהים
,God before earth the And corrupt was .Japheth and ,Ham ,Shem
2009 776 430 7200 2555 776 4390
12 ותמלא הארץ חמס׃ וירא אלהים את־הארץ והנה
and ,behold ,earth the God saw And .violence earth the was and with filled
776 1870 1320 7843 7843
נשחתה כי־השחית כל־בשר את־דרכו על־הארץ׃ ס
.earth the on way its flesh all had corrupted for ;corrupted was it
4390 6440 935 1320 7093 5146 430 559
13 ויאמר אלהים לנח קץ כל־בשר בא לפני כי־מלאה
filled with is for before ,me has come flesh all The of end ,Noah to God said And
6213 776 7843 2005 6440 2555 776
14 הארץ חמס מפניהם והנני משחיתם את־הארץ׃ עשה
Make the .earth (along) (with) destroy will them and I ,behold of because ;them violence the earth
3722 8392 854 6213 7064 7613/6086 8392
לך תבת עצי־גפר קנים תעשה את־התבה וכפרת אתה
it you and cover shall ;ark the in shall you make rooms cypress ,timbers ark an for of yourself
3967 7969 6213 3724 2351 1004
15 מבית ומחוץ בכפר׃ וזה אשר תעשה אתה שלש מאות
hundred three :it shall you make And thus with ,asphalt out and inside

shall be three hundred cubits, its breadth fifty cubits, and its height thirty cubits. [16]You shall make a window in the ark, and you shall finish it above to a cubit. And you shall set the door of the ark in its side. You shall make it with lower, second, and third stories. [17]And behold, I, even I, am bringing a flood of waters on the earth in order to destroy all flesh in which *is* the breath of life from under the heavens. Everything which is on the earth shall die. [18]And I will establish My covenant with you. And you shall come into the ark, you and your sons and your wife, and your sons' wives with you. [19]And you shall bring into the ark two of every kind, of every living thing of all flesh, to keep alive with you; they shall be male and female; [20]from the fowl after its kind, and from the cattle after its kind, from every creeping thing of the ground after its kind—two from each shall come in to you to keep alive. [21]And take for yourself all food that is eaten, and gather to yourself. And let it be for you and for them for food. [22]And Noah did so, according to all that God commanded him, so he did.

אַמָּה אֹרֶךְ הַתֵּבָה חֲמִשִּׁים אַמָּה רָחְבָּהּ וּשְׁלֹשִׁים אַמָּה

cubits thirty and (be shall) its ;breadth cubits (be shall) fifty ;ark the the of length cubits (be shall)

16 קוֹמָתָהּ׃ צֹהַר ׀ תַּעֲשֶׂה לַתֵּבָה וְאֶל־אַמָּה תְּכַלֶּנָּה מִלְמַעְלָה

.above shall you finish it cubit a to and the in ark shall You make a window .height its

וּפֶתַח הַתֵּבָה בְּצִדָּהּ תָּשִׂים תַּחְתִּיִּם שְׁנִיִּם וּשְׁלִשִׁים

third and stories second with lower shall you ;set .side its in ark the the and of door

17 תַּעֲשֶׂהָ׃ וַאֲנִי הִנְנִי מֵבִיא אֶת־הַמַּבּוּל מַיִם עַל־הָאָרֶץ

earth the on waters of flood the am bringing ,behold I And I even shall You .it make

לְשַׁחֵת כָּל־בָּשָׂר אֲשֶׁר־בּוֹ רוּחַ חַיִּים מִתַּחַת הַשָּׁמַיִם כֹּל

every thing ;sky the from under life the of breath (is) in which it flesh all order in destroy to

18 אֲשֶׁר־בָּאָרֶץ יִגְוָע׃ וַהֲקִמֹתִי אֶת־בְּרִיתִי אִתָּךְ וּבָאתָ אֶל־

into you and come shall with ;you covenant My I And establish will shall .die the on earth is which

19 הַתֵּבָה אַתָּה וּבָנֶיךָ וְאִשְׁתְּךָ וּנְשֵׁי־בָנֶיךָ אִתָּךְ׃ וּמִכָּל־הָחַי

living thing And every of with .you your sons' wives and your wife and your sons and you ,ark the

מִכָּל־בָּשָׂר שְׁנַיִם מִכֹּל תָּבִיא אֶל־הַתֵּבָה לְהַחֲיֹת אִתָּךְ

with ;you keep to alive ark the into shall you bring every of ,kind two ,flesh all of

20 זָכָר וּנְקֵבָה יִהְיוּ׃ מֵהָעוֹף לְמִינֵהוּ וּמִן־הַבְּהֵמָה לְמִינָהּ

its after ,kind cattle the and from its after kind the From fowl they .be shall and female male

מִכֹּל רֶמֶשׂ הָאֲדָמָה לְמִינֵהוּ שְׁנַיִם מִכֹּל יָבֹאוּ אֵלֶיךָ

you to shall in come from each two its after ,kind ground the creeping of thing from every

21 לְהַחֲיוֹת׃ וְאַתָּה קַח־לְךָ מִכָּל־מַאֲכָל אֲשֶׁר יֵאָכֵל וְאָסַפְתָּ

and gather ,eaten is that food all of for yourself take And ,you to keep .alive

22 אֵלֶיךָ וְהָיָה לְךָ וְלָהֶם לְאָכְלָה׃ וַיַּעַשׂ נֹחַ כְּכֹל אֲשֶׁר צִוָּה

told that as all to Noah And did .food for for and them for you let and be it to ;yourself

אֹתוֹ אֱלֹהִים כֵּן עָשָׂה׃

.did he so ,God him

CAP. VII ז

CHAPTER 7

CHAPTER 7

[1]And Jehovah said to Noah, You and all your house come into the ark, for I have seen you righteous before Me in this generation. [2]You shall take to yourself from every clean animal by sevens, male and female; and from the animal

1 וַיֹּאמֶר יְהוָה לְנֹחַ בֹּא־אַתָּה וְכָל־בֵּיתְךָ אֶל־הַתֵּבָה כִּי־

for ,ark the into your house and all You come to ,Noah Jehovah And said

2 אֹתְךָ רָאִיתִי צַדִּיק לְפָנַי בַּדּוֹר הַזֶּה׃ מִכֹּל ׀ הַבְּהֵמָה

animal From every .this in generation before Me righteous have I seen you

הַטְּהוֹרָה תִּקַּח־לְךָ שִׁבְעָה שִׁבְעָה אִישׁ וְאִשְׁתּוֹ וּמִן

and of and ;female male ,sevens by to yourself shall you take clean

that *is* not clean by two, male and female. [3]And *take* of the fowl of the heavens by sevens, male and female, to keep alive seed on the face of the earth. [4]For after seven more days I will cause it to rain on the earth forty days and forty nights, and will wipe away every living substance that I have made from off the face of the earth. [5]And Noah did according to all that Jehovah commanded him.

[6]Noah was six hundred years old, and the flood of waters was on the earth. [7]And Noah went in, and his sons, and his wife, and his sons' wives with him into the ark, because of the waters of the flood. [8]And they went in to Noah into the ark, male and female of clean animals, and of animals that are not clean, and of fowl, and of every thing that creeps on the earth, [9]two by two, as God had commanded Noah.

[10]And in time, after the seven days, the waters of the flood came into being on the earth. [11]In the six hundredth year of Noah's life, in the second month, in the seventeenth day of the month, in this day all the fountains of the great deep were risen, and the windows of the heavens were opened up. [12]And the rain was on the earth forty days and forty nights. [13]In this same day Noah and Shem and Ham and Japheth, the sons of Noah, and Noah's wife and the three wives of his sons with them, went into the ark; [14]they, and every animal after its kind,

802 376 8147 1931 2889 3808 834 929
3 הַבְּהֵמָה אֲשֶׁר לֹא טְהֹרָה הִוא שְׁנַיִם אִישׁ וְאִשְׁתּוֹ׃ גַּם־
And and male ,two by it clean not that animal the
female (is)

5921 2233 2421 5347 2145 7651 8064 5775
מֵעוֹף הַשָּׁמַיִם שִׁבְעָה שִׁבְעָה זָכָר וּנְקֵבָה לְחַיּוֹת זֶרַע עַל־
upon seed keep to and male ,sevens by the the of
alive ;female heavens of fowl

5921 4305 7651 5750 3117 776
4 פְּנֵי כָל־הָאָרֶץ׃ כִּי לְיָמִים עוֹד שִׁבְעָה אָנֹכִי מַמְטִיר עַל־
on cause will I seven after the to For .earth the all the
rain to more days of face

3605 4229 3915 202 3117 705 776
הָאָרֶץ אַרְבָּעִים יוֹם וְאַרְבָּעִים לָיְלָה וּמָחִיתִי אֶת־כָּל־
every will and ,nights forty and days forty earth the
away wipe

3605 5146 6213 127 6440 5921 6213 834 3351
5 הַיְקוּם אֲשֶׁר עָשִׂיתִי מֵעַל פְּנֵי הָאֲדָמָה׃ וַיַּעַשׂ נֹחַ כְּכֹל
as Noah And .earth the the from have I that living
all to did of face off made substance

1961 3999 8141 3967 8337 3068 6680 834
6 אֲשֶׁר־צִוָּהוּ יְהוָה׃ וְנֹחַ בֶּן־שֵׁשׁ מֵאוֹת שָׁנָה וְהַמַּבּוּל הָיָה
was the and ;years hundred six a Noah .Jehovah ordered that
flood of son was him

1121 802 802 1121 935 776 4325
7 מַיִם עַל־הָאָרֶץ׃ וַיָּבֹא נֹחַ וּבָנָיו וְאִשְׁתּוֹ וּנְשֵׁי־בָנָיו אִתּוֹ אֶל־
into with his and his and his and Noah And .earth the on waters
him sons' wives wife sons in went

2889 929 3999 4325 8392
8 הַתֵּבָה מִפְּנֵי מֵי הַמַּבּוּל׃ מִן־הַבְּהֵמָה הַטְּהוֹרָה וּמִן־
of and clean animals the Of .flood the the because ark the
of waters of

7430 834 3605 5775 2889 929
הַבְּהֵמָה אֲשֶׁר אֵינֶנָּה טְהֹרָה וּמִן־הָעוֹף וְכֹל אֲשֶׁר־רֹמֵשׂ
creeps that of and the and ,clean not were that animals
thing every ,fowl of

2145 8392 5146 935 8147 8147 127
9 עַל־הָאֲדָמָה׃ שְׁנַיִם שְׁנַיִם בָּאוּ אֶל־נֹחַ אֶל־הַתֵּבָה זָכָר
male ,ark the into Noah to they by Two .earth the on
in went two

3117 7651 5146 430 6680 5347
10 וּנְקֵבָה כַּאֲשֶׁר צִוָּה אֱלֹהִים אֶת־נֹחַ׃ וַיְהִי לְשִׁבְעַת הַיָּמִים
.days the after in And .Noah God had as and
seven ,time commanded female

2416 8141 3967 8337 8141 776 1961 3999 4325
11 וּמֵי הַמַּבּוּל הָיוּ עַל־הָאָרֶץ׃ בִּשְׁנַת שֵׁשׁ־מֵאוֹת שָׁנָה לְחַיֵּי־
life of year hundredth the in the upon came flood the the
six ;earth being into of waters

2088 3117 2320 3117 6240 7651 8145 2320
נֹחַ בַּחֹדֶשׁ הַשֵּׁנִי בְּשִׁבְעָה־עָשָׂר יוֹם לַחֹדֶשׁ בַּיּוֹם הַזֶּה
this day in the of day seventeenth the in ,second the in Noah's
month month

6605 8064 699 227 4599 1234
נִבְקְעוּ כָּל־מַעְיְנוֹת תְּהוֹם רַבָּה וַאֲרֻבֹּת הַשָּׁמַיִם נִפְתָּחוּ׃
were heavens the the and great the fountains the all were
up opened of windows deep of risen

3915 702 3117 702 776 1653
12 וַיְהִי הַגֶּשֶׁם עַל־הָאָרֶץ אַרְבָּעִים יוֹם וְאַרְבָּעִים לָיְלָה׃
.nights forty and days forty earth the on rain the And
was

802 1121 3315 2526 8035 5146 935 3117 6106
13 בְּעֶצֶם הַיּוֹם הַזֶּה בָּא נֹחַ וְשֵׁם־וְחָם וָיֶפֶת בְּנֵי־נֹחַ וְאֵשֶׁת
wife and sons the and and and Noah entered this day In
Noah of Japheth Ham Shem same

2416 3605 1992 8392 1121 802 7969
14 נֹחַ וּשְׁלֹשֶׁת נְשֵׁי־בָנָיו אִתָּם אֶל־הַתֵּבָה׃ הֵמָּה וְכָל־הַחַיָּה
animal and They .ark the into with his wives the and Noah's
every them sons of three

and every beast after its kind, and every creeping thing that creeps on the earth after its kind; and every fowl after its kind, every bird of every wing. [15]And they went in to Noah and to the ark, two and two of all flesh, in which *is* the breath of life. [16]And those going in went in male and female of all flesh, as God had commanded him. And Jehovah shut behind him.

[17]And the flood was on the earth forty days. And the waters increased, and bore up the ark, and it was lifted up above the earth. [18]And the waters prevailed, and were greatly increased on the earth. And the ark floated on the face of the waters. [19]And the waters were strong, exceedingly violent on the earth, and all the high mountains under the heavens were covered. [20]The waters grew strong, fifteen cubits upward, and the mountains were covered. [21]And all flesh that moved on the earth died: the fowl, and cattle, and beast, and every swarming thing that swarms on the earth, and all mankind; [22]all died in whose nostrils *was* the breath of life, of all that *was* in the dry land. [23]And every living thing which was on the face of the earth was wiped away, from man to cattle, and to the creeping things, and the fowl of the heavens. And they were wiped off from the earth, and only Noah was left, and those who were with him in the ark. [24]And the waters were strong on the earth a hundred and fifty days.

5921 7430 7431 3605 4327 929 3605 4327
לְמִינָהּ וְכָל־הַבְּהֵמָה לְמִינָהּ וְכָל־הָרֶמֶשׂ הָרֹמֵשׂ עַל־
on that creeping and its after beast and its after
creeps thing every ,kind every ,kind

3671/3 605 6833 3605 432 7 5775/36 05 4327 776
הָאָרֶץ לְמִינֵהוּ וְכָל־הָעוֹף לְמִינֵהוּ כֹּל צִפּוֹר כָּל־כָּנָף׃
.sort every of bird every its after fowl and its after earth the
,kind every ,kind

834 1320 3605 8147 8147 8392 5146 935
15 וַיָּבֹאוּ אֶל־נֹחַ אֶל־הַתֵּבָה שְׁנַיִם שְׁנַיִם מִכָּל־הַבָּשָׂר אֲשֶׁר
which ,flesh all of two by two ,ark the into Noah to they And
in went

935 1320 3605 5347 2145 935 2416 7307
16 בּוֹ רוּחַ חַיִּים׃ וְהַבָּאִים זָכָר וּנְקֵבָה מִכָּל־בָּשָׂר בָּאוּ
went ,flesh all of and male those And .life the is in
in female in going of breath it

3999 1961 5462 3068 5462 430 3117 702
17 כַּאֲשֶׁר צִוָּה אֹתוֹ אֱלֹהִים וַיִּסְגֹּר יְהוָה בַּעֲדוֹ׃ וַיְהִי הַמַּבּוּל
flood the And behind Jehovah And .God him had as
was ,him shut commanded

8392 5375 4325 7235 776 3117 702
אַרְבָּעִים יוֹם עַל־הָאָרֶץ וַיִּרְבּוּ הַמַּיִם וַיִּשְׂאוּ אֶת־הַתֵּבָה
,ark the and the and ;earth the on days forty
up bore waters increased

776 5921/3 966 7235 4325 1396 776 7311
18 וַתָּרָם מֵעַל הָאָרֶץ׃ וַיִּגְבְּרוּ הַמַּיִם וַיִּרְבּוּ מְאֹד עַל־הָאָרֶץ
the upon greatly were and the And .earth the above it and
,earth increased waters prevailed lifted was

3966 3966 1396 4325 4325 6440 8392 5375
19 וַתֵּלֶךְ הַתֵּבָה עַל־פְּנֵי הַמָּיִם׃ וְהַמַּיִם גָּבְרוּ מְאֹד מְאֹד
exceedingly pre- the And the the on ark the and
vailed waters ,waters of face floated

3605 8478 1364 2022 3605 3680 776 5921
עַל־הָאָרֶץ וַיְכֻסּוּ כָּל־הֶהָרִים הַגְּבֹהִים אֲשֶׁר־תַּחַת כָּל־
all under which high the all were and ;earth the on
are mountains covered

3680 4325 1396 4605 520 6240 2568 8064
20 הַשָּׁמָיִם׃ חֲמֵשׁ עֶשְׂרֵה אַמָּה מִלְמַעְלָה גָּבְרוּ הַמָּיִם וַיְכֻסּוּ
and the pre- upwards cubits Fifteen the
hid were ;waters vailed .heavens

929 5775 776 7430 1320 1478 2022
21 הֶהָרִים׃ וַיִּגְוַע כָּל־בָּשָׂר ׀ הָרֹמֵשׂ עַל־הָאָרֶץ בָּעוֹף וּבַבְּהֵמָה
and the the on that flesh all And the
cattle ,fowl earth moved died .mountains

120 3605 776 5921 8317 8318 3605 2416
22 וּבַחַיָּה וּבְכָל־הַשֶּׁרֶץ הַשֹּׁרֵץ עַל־הָאָרֶץ וְכֹל הָאָדָם׃ כֹּל
All ,mankind and the upon that creeping and and
all ,earth creeps thing every ,beast (the)

4191 2724 3605 639 2416 7307 5397 834
אֲשֶׁר נִשְׁמַת־רוּחַ חַיִּים בְּאַפָּיו מִכֹּל אֲשֶׁר בֶּחָרָבָה מֵתוּ׃
.died the in (was) that all of whose in ,life the breathed which
,land dry nostrils of breath

120 127 6440 834 3351 3605 4229
23 וַיִּמַח אֶת־כָּל־הַיְקוּם ׀ אֲשֶׁר ׀ עַל־פְּנֵי הָאֲדָמָה מֵאָדָם
man from ;earth the the on which living every was And
of face was thing destroyed

776 4229 8064 5775 7431 929
עַד־בְּהֵמָה עַד־רֶמֶשׂ וְעַד־עוֹף הַשָּׁמַיִם וַיִּמָּחוּ מִן־הָאָרֶץ
the from they and the the and the to ,cattle to
;earth off wiped were ,heavens of fowl ,things creeping

5921 4325 1396 8392 834 5146/389 7604
24 וַיִּשָּׁאֶר אַךְ־נֹחַ וַאֲשֶׁר אִתּוֹ בַּתֵּבָה׃ וַיִּגְבְּרוּ הַמַּיִם עַל־
on the And .ark the in (were) the and Noah only and
waters mighty were him with who ones left was

3117 3967 2572 776
הָאָרֶץ חֲמִשִּׁים וּמְאַת יוֹם׃
.days hundred a fifty earth the
and

CHAPTER 8

1 And God remembered Noah and every living thing, and all the cattle, which were with him in the ark. And God made a wind to pass over the earth, and the waters subsided. 2 And the fountains of the deep and the windows of the heavens were stopped, and the rain from the heavens was restrained. 3 And the waters retreated from the earth, going and retreating. And the waters diminished at the end of a hundred and fifty days.

4 And in the seventh month, on the seventeenth day of the month, the ark rested on the mountains of Ararat. 5 And the waters were going and falling until the tenth month. In the tenth *month*, on the first of the month, the tops of the mountains were seen. 6 And it happened, at the end of forty days, and Noah opened the window of the ark which he had made. 7 And he sent out a raven, and it went out, going out and returning until the waters were dried up from off the earth. 8 He also sent out from him the dove, to see if the waters had gone down from off the face of the earth. 9 But the dove found no rest for the sole of her foot, and she returned to him into the ark, for the waters were on the face of all the earth. And he put out his hand and took her, and pulled her in to him into the ark.

10 And he waited yet another seven days, and again he sent forth the dove out of the ark. 11 And the dove came in to him in the evening. And, behold! In her mouth *was* a newly plucked olive leaf. So Noah

CAP. VIII ח

CHAPTER 8

929 3605 2416 3605 5146 430 2142
1 וַיִּזְכֹּר אֱלֹהִים אֶת־נֹחַ וְאֵת כָּל־הַחַיָּה וְאֶת־כָּל־הַבְּהֵמָה
cattle the all and living thing every and Noah God And remembered

7918 776 5921 7307 430 5674 8392 834
אֲשֶׁר אִתּוֹ בַּתֵּבָה וַיַּעֲבֵר אֱלֹהִים רוּחַ עַל־הָאָרֶץ וַיָּשֹׁכּוּ
and subsided earth the over a wind God made And pass to the in ark with him which were

3607 8064 699 8415 4599 5534 4325
2 הַמָּיִם׃ וַיִּסָּכְרוּ מַעְיְנֹת תְּהוֹם וַאֲרֻבֹּת הַשָּׁמָיִם וַיִּכָּלֵא
was and restrained the ;heavens the and of windows the ,deep fountains the of And stopped .waters the

7725 776 4325 7725 8064 1053
3 הַגֶּשֶׁם מִן־הַשָּׁמָיִם׃ וַיָּשֻׁבוּ הַמַּיִם מֵעַל הָאָרֶץ הָלוֹךְ וָשׁוֹב
and ;retreating going the ,earth from the waters And retreated the .heavens from rain the

8392 5117 3117 3967 2572 7097 4325 2637
4 וַיַּחְסְרוּ הַמַּיִם מִקְצֵה חֲמִשִּׁים וּמְאַת יוֹם׃ וַתָּנַח הַתֵּבָה
ark the And rested .days and hundred fifty the at of end the waters and diminished

2022 2320 3117 6240 7651 7637 2320
בַּחֹדֶשׁ הַשְּׁבִיעִי בְּשִׁבְעָה־עָשָׂר יוֹם לַחֹדֶשׁ עַל הָרֵי אֲרָרָט׃
.Ararat the of heights on the of ,month day seventeenth the on seventh the in .month

6224 6224 2320 5704 2637 1980 4325
5 וְהַמַּיִם הָיוּ הָלוֹךְ וְחָסוֹר עַד הַחֹדֶשׁ הָעֲשִׂירִי בָּעֲשִׂירִי
tenth the in (month) ;tenth the month until and falling going were the And waters

702 7093 1961 2022 7218 7200 2320 259
6 בְּאֶחָד לַחֹדֶשׁ נִרְאוּ רָאשֵׁי הֶהָרִים׃ וַיְהִי מִקֵּץ אַרְבָּעִים
forty the at of end it And was the .mountains tops the of were seen the of month the on first

7971 6213 834 8392 2474 5146 6605 3117
7 יוֹם וַיִּפְתַּח נֹחַ אֶת־חַלּוֹן הַתֵּבָה אֲשֶׁר עָשָׂה׃ וַיְשַׁלַּח אֶת־
he And out sent had he .made which ark the the of window Noah and opened ;days

776 4325 3001 7725 3318 3318 6158
הָעֹרֵב וַיֵּצֵא יָצוֹא וָשׁוֹב עַד־יְבֹשֶׁת הַמַּיִם מֵעַל הָאָרֶץ׃
.earth the off from the waters were up dried until and returning going out it and ,out went the ;raven

6440 4325 7043 7200 3128 7971
8 וַיְשַׁלַּח אֶת־הַיּוֹנָה מֵאִתּוֹ לִרְאוֹת הֲקַלּוּ הַמַּיִם מֵעַל פְּנֵי
face from off the waters had if receded see to from ,him dove the also He out sent

7725 7272 3709 4494 3128 4672 127
9 הָאֲדָמָה׃ וְלֹא־מָצְאָה הַיּוֹנָה מָנוֹחַ לְכַף־רַגְלָהּ וַתָּשָׁב
she and returned ,foot her the for of sole rest the dove found But no .earth's the

3027 7971 776 3605 6440 4325 8392
אֵלָיו אֶל־הַתֵּבָה כִּי מַיִם עַל־פְּנֵי כָל־הָאָרֶץ וַיִּשְׁלַח יָדוֹ
his hand he And out put the .earth all the on of face the were waters for ,ark the into to him

7651 5750 2342 8392 935 3947
10 וַיִּקָּחֶהָ וַיָּבֵא אֹתָהּ אֵלָיו אֶל־הַתֵּבָה׃ וַיָּחֶל עוֹד שִׁבְעַת
seven yet he And waited .ark the into him to her and in pulled took and her

935 8392 3128 7971 3254 312 3117
11 יָמִים אֲחֵרִים וַיֹּסֶף שַׁלַּח אֶת־הַיּוֹנָה מִן־הַתֵּבָה׃ וַתָּבֹא
And in came .ark the of out dove the sent he forth and again ,another days

3045 6310 2965 2132 5929 2009 6153 6256 3128
אֵלָיו הַיּוֹנָה לְעֵת עֶרֶב וְהִנֵּה עֲלֵה־זַיִת טָרָף בְּפִיהָ וַיֵּדַע
So knew her in !mouth newly plucked leaf olive an ,And ,behold the .evening of time the dove the to him

knew that the waters had
gone down from off the
earth. [12]And he waited
another seven days and
sent forth the dove. And she
did not return again to him
any more.
[13]And in the six hundred
and first year, at the beginning, on the first of the
month, the waters were
dried up from off the earth.
And Noah removed the
covering of the ark and
looked. And, behold! The
face of the earth was dried.
[14]And in the second month,
on the twenty-seventh day
of the month, the earth was
dry. [15]And God spoke to
Noah, saying, [16]Go out of
the ark, you and your wife,
and your sons and your
sons' wives with you.

[17]Bring out from you every
living thing that *is* with you,
of all flesh, of fowl, of cattle,
and of every creeping thing
that creeps on the earth;
and let them swarm on the
earth, and bear, and
multiply on the earth. [18]And
Noah went out, and his
sons, and his wife, and his
sons' wives with him;
[19]every animal, every creeping thing, and every fowl; all
which creeps on the earth.
They went forth out of the
ark according to their
families.
[20]Then Noah built an altar
to Jehovah, and took of
every clean animal, and of
every clean bird, and
offered burnt offerings on
the altar. [21]And Jehovah
smelled the delightful odor,
and Jehovah said in His
heart, I will never again
curse the ground for the
sake of man, because the
imagination of the heart of
man is evil from his youth.
Yea, I will not again smite
every living thing as I have
done; [22]while the earth
remains, seedtime and

3117 7651 5750 3176 776 4325 7043 5146
12 נח כי־קלו המים מעל הארץ׃ וייחל עוד שבעת ימים
days seven yet he And .earth the from the had that Noah
waited off waters receded

1961 5750 7725 3254 3808 3128 7971 312
13 אחרים וישלח את־היונה ולא־יספה שוב־אליו עוד׃ ויהי
And any to return did she and ,dove the sent and ;another
was it .more him again not forth

2717 2320 259 7223 8141 8337 259
באחת ושש־מאות שנה בראשון באחד לחדש חרבו
were the of the on the at ,year hundred and the in
up dried month one ,beginning six one

7200 8392 4372 5146 776 4325
המים מעל הארץ ויסר נח את־מכסה התבה וירא והנה
,lo and and ark the the Noah And the from the
looked of covering removed .earth off waters

3117 6242 7651 8145 2320 127 2717
14 חרבו פני האדמה׃ ובחדש השני בשבעה ועשרים יום
day twenty- the on ,second in And .earth the the was
seventh month the of face dried

559 430 1696 776 3001 2320
15 לחדש יבשה הארץ׃ ס וידבר אלהים אל־נח לאמר׃
,saying ,Noah to God spoke And .earth the dry was the of
,month

1121 802 1121 802 8392
16 צא מן־התבה אתה ואשתך ובניך ונשי־בניך אתך׃
with your and your and your and you ,ark the of Go
,you sons' wives sons ,wife out

3605 929 5775 1320 3605 2416 3605
17 כל־החיה אשר־אתך מכל־בשר בעוף ובבהמה ובכל־
of and ,cattle of ,fowl of ,flesh all of with (is) that living Every
every ,you thing

6509 776 8317 3318 776 7430 7431
הרמש הרמש על־הארץ הוצא אתך ושרצו בארץ ופרו
and the on them let and with bring ,earth the upon that creeping
bear ,earth swarm ;you out creeps thing

1121 802 802 1121 5927 776 7235
18 ורבו על־הארץ׃ ויצא־נח ובניו ואשתו ונשי־בניו אתו׃
with his and his and his and ;Noah And .earth the on and
,him sons' wives wife sons out went multiply

776 7430 5775 7431 2416
19 כל־החיה כל־הרמש וכל־העוף כל רומש על־הארץ
;earth the upon which all ,fowl and creeping every animal Every
creeps every thing

3068 4196 1129 8392 4940
20 למשפחתיהם יצאו מן־התבה׃ ויבן נח מזבח ליהוה
to altar an Noah Then .ark the of out they ,families their after
,Jehovah built forth went

5927 2889 5775 2889 929 3605 3947
ויקח מכל ׀ הבהמה הטהרה ומכל העוף הטהר ויעל
and clean bird of and clean animal of and
offered every every took

3068 559 5207 7381 3068 7306 4196 5930
21 עלת במזבח׃ וירח יהוה את־ריח הניחח ויאמר יהוה
Jehovah and soothing frag- the Jehovah And the on burnt
said rance smelled .altar offerings

5668 127 7043 3254 3820 413
אל־לבו לא־אסף לקלל עוד את־האדמה בעבור
the for ground the again curse will I Not His in
of sake ,heart

5750 3254 3808 5271 7451 120 3820 3336 3588 120
האדם כי יצר לב האדם רע מנעריו ולא־אסף עוד
again will I and from evil is man's heart the because ,man
not ;youth his of thought

776 3117 6213 2416 3605 5221
22 להכות את־כל־חי כאשר עשיתי׃ עד כל־ימי הארץ
,earth the remains While have I as living every strike
.done thing

harvest, cold and heat, summer and winter, and day and night shall not cease.

3808 3915 3117 2779 7019 2527 7120 7102 2233
זרע וקציר וקר וחם וקיץ וחרף ויום ולילה לא
not | and night | day | and ,winter | summer | and ,heat | cold | and ,harvest | seed-time

7673
ישבתו:
shall .cease

CAP. IX ט

CHAPTER 9

CHAPTER 9

[1]And God blessed Noah
and his sons. And He said
to them, Be fruitful and
multiply, and fill the earth.
[2]And your fear and your
dread shall be on all the
animals of the earth, and on
every bird of the heavens,
on all that moves on the
earth, and on all the fish of
the sea. They are given into
your hands. [3]Every creeping thing which is alive shall
be food for you. I have given
you all things, even as the
green plant. [4]But you shall
not eat flesh in its life, its
blood. [5]And surely the
blood of your lives I will
demand. At the hand of
every animal I will demand
it, and at the hand of man. I
will demand the life of man
at the hand of every man's
brother. [6]Whoever sheds
man's blood, his blood shall
be shed by man. For He
made man in the image of
God. [7]And you, be fruitful
and multiply. Swarm over
the earth and multiply in it.
[8]And God spoke to Noah,
and to his sons with him,
saying, [9]Behold, I, even I,
am establishing My cov-
enant with you, and with
your seed after you, [10]and
with every living creature
which is with you, among
fowl, among cattle, and
among every animal of the
earth with you, from all that
go out from the ark, to every
animal of the earth. [11]And
I have made stand My
covenant with you, and all

1 6509 559 1121 5146 430 1288
ויברך אלהים את־נח ואת־בניו ויאמר להם פרו ורבו
and multiply | Be fruitful | ,them to | And said He | .sons his and | Noah | God | And blessed

2 2416 2844 4172 776
ומלאו את־הארץ: ומוראכם וחתכם יהיה על כל־חית
the all of animals | on | be shall | the and you of dread | the And you of fear | .earth the | fill and

127 7430 8064 5775 776
הארץ ועל כל־עוף השמים בכל אשר תרמש האדמה
,earth the | on moves | that | all on | the ;heavens | of bird every | and earth the on

3 2416 7431 3220 1709 3605
ובכל־דגי הים בידכם נתנו: כל־רמש אשר הוא־חי לכם
for you | alive is | which | creeping thing | Every | are they .given | into hands your | ;sea the | the fish of | on and all

4 1320 389 6212 3418 402
יהיה לאכלה כירק עשב נתתי לכם את־כל: אך־בשר
flesh | But | .things all | you | have I given | the green | as even plant | ;food | shall be

5 1818 389 398 1818
בנפשו דמו לא תאכלו: ואך את־דמכם לנפשתיכם
lives your | of | blood the | And surely | shall you .eat | not | its ,blood | its in ,life

251 376 120 1875 2416 1875
אדרש מיד כל־חיה אדרשנו ומיד האדם מיד איש אחיו
brother | every the at man's of hand | ,man | the at and of hand | will I ;it demand | animal every the at of hand | will I ,demand

6 1818 120 120 1818 8210 120 1875
אדרש את־נפש האדם: שפך דם האדם באדם דמו
his blood | man by | ,man's | blood | Whoever sheds | .man | of life the | will I demand

7 6509 120 430 6754 8210
ישפך כי בצלם אלהים עשה את־האדם: ואתם פרו
be fruitful | ,you And | .man | made He | God | the in of image | for | be shall ;shed

8 430 559 7235 776 8317 7235
ורבו שרצו בארץ ורבו־בה: ס ויאמר אלהים אל־
to | God | And spoke | .it on | and multiply | the over earth | swarm | and ;multiply

9 1285 6965 559 1121 5146
נח ואל־בניו אתו לאמר: ואני הנני מקים את־בריתי
covenant My | am establishing | ,Behold ,I | even ,I | ,saying | with ,him | his sons | and ,Noah to

10 2416 310 2233
אתכם ואת־זרעכם אחריכם: ואת כל־נפש החיה אשר
which is | living creature every | and with | after ,you | seed your | and with | with ,you

776 2416 929 5775
אתכם בעוף בבהמה ובכל־חית הארץ אתכם מכל יצאי
go that from out | from all | ;you with | the earth | animal and of every | among ,cattle | among ,fowl | with ,you

11 1285 6965 776 2416 8392
התבה לכל חית הארץ: והקמתי את־בריתי אתכם
,you with | covenant My | have I And established | .earth the | animal of | to every | ,ark the

ולא־יכרת כל־בשר עוד ממי המבול ולא־יהיה עוד
12 מבול לשחת הארץ׃ ויאמר אלהים זאת אות־הברית
אשר־אני נתן ביני וביניכם ובין כל־נפש חיה אשר אתכם
13 לדרת עולם׃ את־קשתי נתתי בענן והיתה לאות ברית
14 ביני ובין הארץ׃ והיה בעננו ענן על־הארץ ונראתה
15 הקשת בענן׃ וזכרתי את־בריתי אשר ביני וביניכם ובין
כל־נפש חיה בכל־בשר ולא־יהיה עוד המים למבול
16 לשחת כל־בשר׃ והיתה הקשת בענן וראיתיה לזכר
ברית עולם בין אלהים ובין כל־נפש חיה בכל־בשר
17 אשר על־הארץ׃ ויאמר אלהים אל־נח זאת אות־הברית
אשר הקמתי ביני ובין כל־בשר אשר על־הארץ׃

18 ויהיו בני־נח היצאים מן־התבה שם וחם ויפת וחם הוא
19 אבי כנען׃ שלשה אלה בני־נח ומאלה נפצה כל־הארץ׃
20 ויחל נח איש האדמה ויטע כרם׃ וישת מן־היין וישכר
21
22 ויתגל בתוך אהלה׃ וירא חם אבי כנען את ערות אביו
23 ויגד לשני־אחיו בחוץ׃ ויקח שם ויפת את־השמלה
וישימו על־שכם שניהם וילכו אחרנית ויכסו את ערות

flesh shall not be cut off again by the waters of a flood; nor shall there ever again be a flood to destroy the earth. [12]And God said, This is the sign of the covenant which I am about to make between Me and you, and every living soul which is with you, for everlasting generations: [13]I have set My bow in the cloud, and it shall be a sign of a covenant between Me and the earth. [14]And when I gather the clouds on the earth, then the bow shall be seen in the clouds. [15]And I will remember My covenant which is between Me and you, and every living soul in all flesh. And the waters shall not again become a flood to destroy all flesh. [16]And the bow shall be in the clouds, and I shall see it, to remember the everlasting covenant between God and every living soul, in all flesh which is on the earth.

[17]And God said to Noah, This is the sign of the covenant which I have made stand between Me and all flesh that is on the earth.

[18]And the sons of Noah that went out of the ark were Shem, Ham, and Japheth. And Ham is the father of Canaan. [19]These *are* the three sons of Noah, and the whole earth was overspread from them.

[20]And Noah, a man of the ground, began and planted a vineyard. [21]And he drank from the wine, and was drunk. And he uncovered himself inside his tent. [22]And Ham, the father of Canaan, saw the nakedness of his father. And he told his two brothers outside. [23]And Shem and Japheth took a garment and put it on both their shoulders. And they went backwards and covered the nakedness of

their father, their faces backward. And they did not see the nakedness of their father. 24 And Noah awoke from his wine. And he came to know what his younger son had done to him. 25 And he said, Cursed be Canaan. He shall be a slave of slaves to his brothers. 26 And he said, Blessed be Jehovah, the God of Shem; and may Canaan be his slave. 27 God shall enlarge Japheth, and he shall live in the tents of Shem, and Canaan shall be their slave.

28 And Noah lived three hundred and fifty years after the flood. 29 And all the days of Noah were nine hundred and fifty years. And he died.

CHAPTER 10

1 And these are the generations of the sons of Noah, Shem, Ham, and Japheth. And sons were born to them after the flood.

2 The sons of Japheth: Gomer, and Magog, and Madai, and Javan, and Tubal, and Meshech, and Tiras. 3 And Gomer's sons *were* Ashkenaz, and Riphath, and Togarmah. 4 And Javan's sons *were* Elishah, and Tarshish, Kittim, and Dodanim. 5 The coasts of the nations were divided by these in their lands, each by his tongue, by their families, in their nations.

6 And Ham's sons *were* Cush, and Mizraim, and Put, and Canaan. 7 And the sons of Cush *were* Seba, and Havilah, and Sabtah, and Raamah, and Sabtecha. And Raamah's sons *were* Sheba and Dedan. 8 And Cush fathered Nimrod; he began to be a mighty one in the land. 9 He was a mighty hunter before Jehovah; so it is said, Even as Nimrod the mighty hunter before Jehovah.

3364 7200 3808 1 6172 322 6440 1
24 אֲבִיהֶם וּפְנֵיהֶם אֲחֹרַנִּית וְעֶרְוַת אֲבִיהֶם לֹא רָאוּ׃ וַיִּיקֶץ
And they not their and ,backward faces their their
awoke .see did father's nakedness ,father

559 6996 1121 6213 3045 3196 5146
25 נֹחַ מִיֵּינוֹ וַיֵּדַע אֵת אֲשֶׁר־עָשָׂה לוֹ בְּנוֹ הַקָּטָן׃ וַיֹּאמֶר
he And .younger his to had what he and from Noah
said son him done knew ,wine his

3068 1288 559 251 1961 5650 5650 3667 779
26 אָרוּר כְּנָעַן עֶבֶד עֲבָדִים יִהְיֶה לְאֶחָיו׃ וַיֹּאמֶר בָּרוּךְ יְהוָה
,Jehovah Blessed he And his to shall slaves a ;Canaan Cursed
be said .brothers be he of slave be

7931 3315 430 6607 5650 3667 8035 430
27 אֱלֹהֵי שֵׁם וִיהִי כְנַעַן עֶבֶד לָמוֹ׃ יַפְתְּ אֱלֹהִים לְיֶפֶת וְיִשְׁכֹּן
he and ,Japheth God shall .his slave Canaan and ,Shem the
live shall enlarge be may of God

3999 310 5146 2421 5650 3667 1961 8035 168
28 בְּאָהֳלֵי־שֵׁם וִיהִי כְנַעַן עֶבֶד לָמוֹ׃ וַיְחִי־נֹחַ אַחַר הַמַּבּוּל
.flood the after Noah And to a Canaan and ,Shem the in
lived .them slave be shall of tents

8672 5146 3605 1961 8141 2572 8141 3967 7969
29 שְׁלֹשׁ מֵאוֹת שָׁנָה וַחֲמִשִּׁים שָׁנָה׃ וַיְהִי כָּל־יְמֵי־נֹחַ תְּשַׁע
nine Noah the all And .years fifty and years hundred three
of days were

4191 8141 2572 8141 3967
מֵאוֹת שָׁנָה וַחֲמִשִּׁים שָׁנָה וַיָּמֹת׃
he And ;years fifty and years hundred
.died

CAP. X

CHAPTER 10

1121 3205 2526 8035 5146 1121 8435
1 וְאֵלֶּה תּוֹלְדֹת בְּנֵי־נֹחַ שֵׁם חָם וָיָפֶת וַיִּוָּלְדוּ לָהֶם בָּנִים
sons to were and and Ham ,Shem ,Noah the genera- the And
them born ;Japheth of sons of tions are these

4902 8422 3120 4074 4031 1586 3315 1121 3999 310
2 אַחַר הַמַּבּוּל׃ בְּנֵי יֶפֶת גֹּמֶר וּמָגוֹג וּמָדַי וְיָוָן וְתֻבָל וּמֶשֶׁךְ
and and and and and ,Gomer Ja- The .flood the after
,Meshech ,Tubal ,Javan ,Madai ,Magog :pheth of sons

3120 1121 8425 7384 813 1586 1121 8494
3 4 וְתִירָס׃ וּבְנֵי גֹּמֶר אַשְׁכְּנַז וְרִיפַת וְתֹגַרְמָה׃ וּבְנֵי יָוָן
Ja- And and and .Ashkenaz :Gomer's And .Tiras and
:van's sons .Togarmah ,Riphath sons

1471 336 6504 1721 3794 8659 473
5 אֱלִישָׁה וְתַרְשִׁישׁ כִּתִּים וְדֹדָנִים׃ מֵאֵלֶּה נִפְרְדוּ אִיֵּי הַגּוֹיִם
the coasts the were these By and ,Kittim and ,Elishah
nations of divided .Dodanim ,Tarshish

2526 1121 1471 4940 3956 376 776
6 בְּאַרְצֹתָם אִישׁ לִלְשֹׁנוֹ לְמִשְׁפְּחֹתָם בְּגוֹיֵהֶם׃ וּבְנֵי חָם
:Ham's And their in ,families their by his by each their in
sons .nations ,tongue ,lands

5454 2341 5434 3568 1121 3667 6316 4714 3568
7 כּוּשׁ וּמִצְרַיִם וּפוּט וּכְנָעַן׃ וּבְנֵי כוּשׁ סְבָא וַחֲוִילָה וְסַבְתָּה
and and ,Seba :Cush And and and and ,Cush
,Sabtah ,Havilah of sons the .Canaan ,Put ,Mizraim

3205 3568 1719 2614 7484 1121 5455 7484
8 וְרַעְמָה וְסַבְתְּכָא וּבְנֵי רַעְמָה שְׁבָא וּדְדָן׃ וְכוּשׁ יָלַד אֶת־
fathered And and Sheba :Raamah's and and and
Cush .Dedan sons ;Sabtecha ,Raamah

6718 1368 1961 776 1368 1961 2490 5248
9 נִמְרֹד הוּא הֵחֵל לִהְיוֹת גִּבֹּר בָּאָרֶץ׃ הוּא־הָיָה גִבֹּר־צַיִד
hunter a was He the in hero a be to began he ;Nimrod
great .land

3068 6440 6718 1368 5248 559 3651 3068 6440
לִפְנֵי יְהוָה עַל־כֵּן יֵאָמַר כְּנִמְרֹד גִּבּוֹר צַיִד לִפְנֵי יְהוָה׃
.Jehovah before hunter the as Even is it so ;Jehovah be-
great Nimrod ,said fore

[10]And the beginning of his
kingdom was Babel, and
Erech, and Accad, and
Calneh, in the land of
Shinar. [11]From that land he
went forth to Assyria and
built Nineveh, and Reho-
both the city, and Calah,
[12]and Resen between Nineveh and Calah, which is a
great city. [13]And Mizraim
fathered Ludim, and Ana-
mim, and Lehabim, and
Naphtuhim, [14]and Pathru-
sim, and Casluhim, who
came from the Philistines
and Caphtorim.

[15]And Canaan fathered
his firstborn Sidon, and
Heth, [16]and the Jebusite,
and the Amorite, and the
Girgashite, [17]and the Hivite,
and the Arkite, and the
Sinite, [18]and the Arvadite,
and the Zemarite, and the
Hamathite. And afterward
the families of the Canaanites were routed.

[19]And the border of the
Canaanites was from Sidon,
as you come to Gerar, as far
as Gaza, as you go in
towards Sodom and Go-
morrah, and Admah, and
Zeboim, even to Lasha.
[20]These *were* the sons of
Ham, according to their
families, according to their
tongues, in their countries,
in their nations.

[21]And to Shem was born,
even *to* him, the father of all
the sons of Eber, the
brother of Japheth the
elder. [22]The sons of Shem
were Elam, and Asshur, and
Arpachshad, and Lud, and
Aram. [23]And Aram's sons
were Uz, and Hul, and
Gether, and Mash. [24]And
Arpachsnad fathered Sha-
lach; and Shalach fathered
Eber. [25]And two sons were
born to Eber; the name of
the one *was* Peleg, for in his
days the earth was divided;
and his brother's name *was*
Joktan. [26]And Joktan

776 3641 390 751 894 4467 7225 1961
10 וַתְּהִי רֵאשִׁית מַמְלַכְתּוֹ בָּבֶל וְאֶרֶךְ וְאַכַּד וְכַלְנֵה בְּאֶרֶץ
the in and and and ,Babel kingdom his the And
of land ,Calneh ,Accad ,Erech of beginning was

5210 1129 804 5927 776 8152
11 שִׁנְעָר׃ מִן־הָאָרֶץ הַהִוא יָצָא אַשּׁוּר וַיִּבֶן אֶת־נִינְוֵה וְאֶת־
and ,Nineveh and to went he that of Out .Shinar
built Assyria forth land

3625 5210 996 7449 3625 5892 7344
12 רְחֹבֹת עִיר וְאֶת־כָּלַח׃ וְאֶת־רֶסֶן בֵּין נִינְוֵה וּבֵין כָּלַח
,Calah and Nineveh be- Resen and ,Calah and the ,Rehoboth
tween 3205 city

6047 3866 4714 1419 5892
13 הִוא הָעִיר הַגְּדֹלָה׃ וּמִצְרַיִם יָלַד אֶת־לוּדִים וְאֶת־עֲנָמִים
,Anamim and ,Ludim fathered And .great the which
Mizraim city is

3695 6625 5320 3853
14 וְאֶת־לְהָבִים וְאֶת־נַפְתֻּחִים׃ וְאֶת־פַּתְרֻסִים וְאֶת־כַּסְלֻחִים
,Casluhim and ,Pathrusim and ,Naphtuhim and ,Lehabim and

3667 3732 6430 8033 3318
15 אֲשֶׁר יָצְאוּ מִשָּׁם פְּלִשְׁתִּים וְאֶת־כַּפְתֹּרִים׃ ס וּכְנַעַן
And .Caphtorim and the from came who
Canaan Philistim

567 2983 2845 1060 6721 3205
16 יָלַד אֶת־צִידֹן בְּכֹרוֹ וְאֶת־חֵת׃ וְאֶת־הַיְבוּסִי וְאֶת־הָאֱמֹרִי
the and the and ,Heth and his ,Sidon fathered
,Amorite ,Jebusite ,firstborn

5513 6208 2340 1622
17 18 וְאֵת הַגִּרְגָּשִׁי׃ וְאֶת־הַחִוִּי וְאֶת־הַעַרְקִי וְאֶת־הַסִּינִי׃ וְאֶת־
and ,Sinite the and the and the and the and
Arkite ,Hivite ,Girgashite

4940 6327 310 2577 6786 721
הָאַרְוָדִי וְאֶת־הַצְּמָרִי וְאֶת־הַחֲמָתִי וְאַחַר נָפֹצוּ מִשְׁפְּחוֹת
the were and the and the and the
of families routed afterward ;Hamathite ,Zemarite ,Arvadite

5804 1642 935 6721 3669 1366 1961 3664
19 הַכְּנַעֲנִי׃ וַיְהִי גְּבוּל הַכְּנַעֲנִי מִצִּידֹן בֹּאֲכָה גְרָרָה עַד־עַזָּה
as far as ,Gerar to you as from Canaan-the the And the
,Gaza come ,Sidon ites of border was .Canaanites

396 2 6636 126 6012 5467 935
20 בֹּאֲכָה סְדֹמָה וַעֲמֹרָה וְאַדְמָה וּצְבֹיִם עַד־לָשַׁע׃ אֵלֶּה
These as far as and and and towards you as
(were) .Lasha ,Zeboim Admah ,Gomorrah Sodom go

1471 776 3956 4940 2526
בְנֵי־חָם לְמִשְׁפְּחֹתָם לִלְשֹׁנֹתָם בְּאַרְצֹתָם בְּגוֹיֵהֶם׃
their in their in to according to according ,Ham the
.nations ,countries ,tongues their ,families their of sons

1419 3315 251 5677/1121/3605 1571 3208 8035
21 וּלְשֵׁם יֻלַּד גַּם־הוּא אֲבִי כָּל־בְּנֵי־עֵבֶר אֲחִי יֶפֶת הַגָּדוֹל׃
.elder the Japheth the ,Eber the all the (to) also was to And
of brother of sons of father ,him born Shem

758 1121 758 3815 775 804 5867 8035 1121
22 23 בְּנֵי שֵׁם עֵילָם וְאַשּׁוּר וְאַרְפַּכְשַׁד וְלוּד וַאֲרָם׃ וּבְנֵי אֲרָם
:Aram's And and and and and ,Elam :Shem The
sons ,Aram ,Lud ,Arpachshad ,Asshur of sons

7874 7874 3205 775 48•51 1666 2343 5780
24 עוּץ וְחוּל וְגֶתֶר וָמַשׁ׃ וְאַרְפַּכְשַׁד יָלַד אֶת־שָׁלַח וְשֶׁלַח
and ;Shalach fathered And and and and ,Uz
Shalach Arpachshad .Mash ,Gether ,Hul

6389 259 8034 1121 8147 3205 5677 5677 3205
25 יָלַד אֶת־עֵבֶר׃ וּלְעֵבֶר יֻלַּד שְׁנֵי בָנִים שֵׁם הָאֶחָד פֶּלֶג
,Peleg one the the ;sons two were to And .Eber fathered
(was) of name born Eber

3205 3355 3355 251 8034 776 914 3117 3588
26 כִּי בְיָמָיו נִפְלְגָה הָאָרֶץ וְשֵׁם אָחִיו יָקְטָן׃ וְיָקְטָן יָלַד אֶת־
fathered And (was) his and ,earth the was his in for
Joktan .Joktan brother's name divided days

fathered Almodad, and Sheleph, and Hazarmaveth, and Jerah, 27 and Hadoram, and Uzal, and Diklah, 28 and Obal, and Abimael, and Sheba, 29 and Ophir, and Havilah, and Jobab. These all *were* the sons of Joktan. 30 And their dwelling was from Mesha, as you go to Sephar, an eastern mountain. 31 These *were* the sons of Shem, according to their families, according to their tongues, in their lands, according to their nations.

32 These *were* the families of the sons of Noah, by their generations, in their nations. And from these the nations were divided in the earth after the flood.

27 אלמודד ואת־שלף ואת־חצרמות ואת־ירח׃ ואת־הדורם
1913 3392 2700 8026 486
.Hadoram and ,Jerah and ,Hazarmaveth and ,Sheleph and ,Almodad

28 ואת־אוזל ואת־דקלה׃ ואת־עובל ואת־אבימאל ואת־
39 5745 1853 186
and ,Abimael and ,Obal and ,Diklah and ,Uzal and

29 שבא׃ ואת־אופר ואת־חוילה ואת־יובב כל־אלה בני
1121 3103 2341 211 7614
the these all ;Jobab and ,Havilah and ,Ophir and ,Sheba
of sons (were)

30 יקטן׃ ויהי מושבם ממשא באכה ספרה הר הקדם׃
6924 2022/5611 935 4852 4186 1961 3355
,east the a ,Sephar to as from their And Joktan
of hill go you Mesha dwelling was

31 אלה בני־שם למשפחתם ללשנתם בארצתם לגויהם׃
1471 776 3956 4940 8035 1121
to according their in to according to according ,Shem the These
nations their ,lands ,tongues their ,families their of sons (are)

32 אלה משפחת בני־נח לתולדתם בגויהם ומאלה נפרדו
6504 1471 8435 5146/1121 4940
were from and their in their by ,Noah the families the These
divided these ;nations ,generations of sons of (were)

הגוים בארץ אחר המבול׃
3999 310 776 1471
.flood the after the on the
earth nations

CAP. XI יא

CHAPTER 11

CHAPTER 11

1 And the whole earth was of one lip and of one speech 2 And it happened, as they traveled from the east, they found a level valley in the land of Shinar. And they lived there. 3 And each one said to his neighbor, Come, let us make brick, and thoroughly burn *them.* And they had brick for stone, and they had asphalt for mortar. 4 And they said, Come, let us build a city and a tower with its top in the heavens, and make a name for ourselves, that we not be scattered on the face of all the earth. 5 And Jehovah came down to see the city and the tower which the sons of Adam had built. 6 And Jehovah said, Behold, the people *is* one, and the lip one to all of them, and this they are beginning to do, and now all which they have imagined to do will not be restrained from

1 ויהי כל־הארץ שפה אחת ודברים אחדים׃ ויהי בנסעם
2 5265 1961 259 1697 376 8193 776 1961
they as And .one of and ;one lip of earth all And
traveled was it speech the was

3 מקדם וימצאו בקעה בארץ שנער וישבו שם׃ ויאמרו
559 8033 2416 8152 776 1234 4672 6924
said And .there they and ,Shinar the in level a they the from
lived of land valley found ,east

איש אל־רעהו הבה נלבנה לבנים ונשרפה לשרפה
8316 8313 3843 3835 3053 7453 376
.thoroughly burn and bricks us let ,Come his to each
(them) make ,neighbor one

ותהי להם הלבנה לאבן והחמר היה להם לחמר׃
2563 1961 2564 68 3843 1961
.mortar for to it the and ,stone for brick the to And
them was asphalt them was

4 ויאמרו הבה נבנה־לנו עיר ומגדל וראשו בשמים
8064 7214 4026 5892 1129 3653 559
the in its with a and city a our- for us let ,Come they And
heavens top tower selves build ,said

5 ונעשה־לנו שם פן־נפוץ על־פני כל־הארץ׃ וירד יהוה
3068 3381 776 3605 6440 6327 8034 6213
Jehovah And the all the on be we lest a for and
down came ,earth of face scattered ,name ourselves make

לראת את־העיר ואת־המגדל אשר בנו בני האדם׃
120 1121 1129 834 4026 5892 7200
.Adam the had which tower the and city the see to
of sons built

6 ויאמר יהוה הן עם אחד ושפה אחת לכלם וזה החלם
2490 3605 376 8193 259 5941 3068 559
are they and all to (is) the and (is) the ,See ,Jehovah And
beginning this them one lip one people said

לעשות ועתה לא־יבצר מהם כל אשר יזמו לעשות׃
6213 2161 834 3605 1219 3808 6258 6213
do to have they which all from be will not now and ;do to
imagined them restrained

them. [7]Come, let Us go down and confuse their lip so that they cannot understand one another's speech. [8]And Jehovah scattered them from there, over the face of all the earth. And they stopped building the city. [9]On account of this its name is called Babel, because Jehovah confused the lip of all the earth there. And Jehovah scattered them abroad from there on the face of all the earth.

[10]These are the generations of Shem: Shem was a hundred years old and fathered Arpachshad two years after the flood. [11]And after he fathered Arpachshad, Shem lived five hundred years. And he fathered sons and daughters. [12]And Arpachshad lived thirty-five years and fathered Shalach. [13]And after he fathered Shalach, Arpachshad lived four hundred and three years. And he fathered sons and daughters. [14]And Shalach lived thirty years and fathered Eber. [15]And after he fathered Eber, Shalach lived four hundred and three years. And he fathered sons and daughters. [16]And Eber lived thirty-four years and fathered Peleg. [17]And after he fathered Peleg, Eber lived four hundred and thirty years. And he fathered sons and daughters.

[18]And Peleg lived thirty years and fathered Reu. [19]And after he fathered Reu, Peleg lived two hundred and nine years. And he

376 8085 3808 834 8193 8033 1101 3212 3053
7 הבה נרדה ונבלה שם שפתם אשר לא ישמעו איש
one can they understand not that so their language there and mix up go Us let ,Come

776 3605 6440 8033 3068 6327 7451 8193
8 שפת רעהו׃ ויפץ יהוה אתם משם על־פני כל־הארץ
;earth the all the face of over from , there them Jehovah And scattered their neighbor's language

8033 3588 894 8034 7121 5892 1129 2308
9 ויחדלו לבנת העיר׃ על־כן קרא שמה בבל כי־שם
there be- cause ,Babel its name was called Therefore the .city from building they and ceased

6440 30 68 6327 8033 776 3605 8193 30 68 1101
בלל יהוה שפת כל־הארץ ומשם הפיצם יהוה על־פני
the of face on Jehovah scattered abroad them from and there the earth all the of speech Jehovah mixed up

776 3605
כל־הארץ׃
פ
.earth the all

775 3205 8141 3967 1121 8035 8035 8435 428
10 אלה תולדת שם שם בן־מאת שנה ויולד את־ארפכשד
Arpachshad and fathered years a hundred was Shem old :Shem the of generations These (are)

775 3205 310 2421 3999 310 8147
11 שנתים אחר המבול׃ ויחי־שם אחרי הולידו את־ארפכשד
,Arpachshad he fathered after Shem And lived .flood the after two years

775 1323 1121 3205 8141 3967 2568
12 חמש מאות שנה ויולד בנים ובנות׃ ס וארפכשד
And Arpachshad and .daughters sons and fathered ,years hundred five

775 2425 2421 3205 8141 7970 2568 2421
13 חי חמש ושלשים שנה ויולד את־שלח׃ ויחי ארפכשד
Arpachshad And lived .Shalach and fathered years thirty- five lived

8141 3967 702 8141 7969 2421 3208 310
אחרי הולידו את־שלח שלש שנים וארבע מאות שנה
;years hundred and four years three Shalach he fathered after

3205 8141 7970 2425 2421 1323 1121 3205
14 ויולד בנים ובנות׃ ס ושלח חי שלשים שנה ויולד
and fathered years thirty lived And Shalach and .daughters sons and fathered

8141 7969 5677 3205 310 2421 5677
15 את־עבר׃ ויחי־שלח אחרי הולידו את־עבר שלש שנים
years three ,Eber he fathered after Shalach And lived .Eber

2425 1323 1121 3205 8141 3967 702
16 וארבע מאות שנה ויולד בנים ובנות׃ ס ויחי־
And lived and .daughters sons and fathered years hundred and four

5677 2425 6389 3205 8141 7970 702 5677
17 עבר ארבע ושלשים שנה ויולד את־פלג׃ ויחי־עבר
Eber And lived .Peleg and fathered years thirty- four Eber

8141 3967 702 8141 7970 6389 3205 310
אחרי הולידו את־פלג שלשים שנה וארבע מאות שנה
years hundred and four years thirty ,Peleg he fathered after

3205 8141 7970 6389 2425 1323 1121 3205
18 ויולד בנים ובנות׃ ס ויחי־פלג שלשים שנה ויולד
and fathered years thirty Peleg And lived and .daughters sons and fathered

8141 8672 7466 3205 310 6389 2421 7466
19 את־רעו׃ ויחי־פלג אחרי הולידו את־רעו תשע שנים
years .nine ,Reu he fathered after Peleg And lived .Reu

fathered sons and daughters. [20]And Reu lived thirty-two years and fathered Serug. [21]And after he fathered Serug, Reu lived two hundred and seven years. And he fathered sons and daughters. [22]And Serug lived thirty years and fathered Nahor. [23]And after he fathered Nahor, Serug lived two hundred years. And he fathered sons and daughters. [24]And Nahor lived twenty-nine years and fathered Terah. [25]And after he fathered Terah, Nahor lived a hundred and nineteen years. And he fathered sons and daughters. [26]And Terah lived seventy years and fathered Abram, Nahor, and Haran.

[27]And these are the generations of Terah: Terah fathered Abram, Nahor, and Haran. And Haran fathered Lot. [28]And Haran died before his father Terah in the land of his birth, in Ur of the Chaldeans. [29]And Abram and Nahor took wives for themselves. The name of Abram's wife *was* Sarai. And the name of Nahor's wife *was* Milcah, the daughter of Haran, the father of Milcah, and the father of Iscah.

[30]And Sarai was barren; she had no child. [31]And Terah took his son Abram, and Lot, Haran's son, his son's son, and his daughter-in-law Sarai, his son Abram's wife. And *he* went forth with them from Ur of the Chaldeans, to go into the land of Canaan. And they came to Haran and lived there. [32]And the days of Terah were two hundred

8147 7466 2421 1323 1121 3205 8141 3967
20 ומאתים שנה ויולד בנים ובנות׃ ויחי רעו שתים
two Reu And lived and .daughters sons and fathered years two and hundred

3205 310 7466 2421 8286 3205 8141 7970
21 ושלשים שנה ויולד את־שרוג׃ ויחי רעו אחרי הולידו
he fathered after Reu And lived .Serug and fathered years thirty-

1323 1121 3205 8141 3967 8141 7651 8286
את־שרוג שבע שנים ומאתים שנה ויולד בנים ובנות׃
and daughters sons and fathered ;years two and hundred years seven ,Serug

8286 2416 5752 3205 8141 7970 8286 2421
22 ס ויחי שרוג שלשים שנה ויולד את־נחור׃ ויחי שרוג
23 Serug And lived .Nahor and fathered years thirty Serug And lived

1323 1121 3205 8141 3967 5152 3205 310
אחרי הולידו את־נחור מאתים שנה ויולד בנים ובנות׃
and .daughters sons and fathered ,years two hundred ,Nahor he fathered after

2421 8646 3205 8141 6242 8672 5152 2421
24 ס ויחי נחור תשע ועשרים שנה ויולד את־תרח׃ ויחי
25 And lived .Terah and fathered years twenty- nine Nahor And lived

3967 8141 6240 8672 8646 3205 310 5652
נחור אחרי הולידו את־תרח תשע־עשרה שנה ומאת
a and hundred years ten (and) nine ,Terah he fathered after Nahor

8141 7657 8646 2421 1323 1121 3205 8141
26 שנה ויולד בנים ובנות׃ ס ויחי־תרח שבעים שנה
years seventy Terah And lived and .daughters sons and fathered years

8646 8435 2039 5752 87 3205
27 ויולד את־אברם את־נחור ואת־הרן׃ ואלה תולדת תרח
:Terah genera- of tions the these And .Haran and Nahor ,Abram and fathered

3205 2039 2039 5152 87 3205 8646
תרח הוליד את־אברם את־נחור ואת־הרן והרן הוליד
fathered and Haran ;Haran and ,Nahor Abram fathered Terah

4138 776 1 8646 6440 2039 4191 3876
28 את־לוט׃ וימת הרן על־פני תרח אביו בארץ מולדתו
,birth his the in of land his father Terah before of face the Haran died And .Lot

802 8034 802 87 3947 3778 219
29 באור כשדים׃ ויקח אברם ונחור להם נשים שם אשת־
the of wife the of name ;wives for themselves and Abram Nahor And took the .Chaldeans in of Ur

4435 2039 1323 4435 802 803 8247 87
אברם שרי ושם אשת־נחור מלכה בת־הרן אבי־מלכה
Milcah the of father ,Haran the of daughter ,Milcah Nahor the of wife the and of name (was) Sarai Abram

8646 3947 2056 6135 8299 1961 3252
30 ואבי יסכה׃ ותהי שרי עקרה אין לה ולד׃ ויקח תרח
31 Terah And took .Child to her was ;barren no Sarai And was .Iscah the and of father

3618 8297 1121 1121 2039/1121 3876 1121/87
את־אברם בנו ואת־לוט בן־הרן בן־בנו ואת שרי כלתו
his daughter-in-law Sarai and of son the .son his ,Haran the of son ,Lot and his son ,Abram

776 1980 3778 219 3318 1121 87 802
אשת אברם בנו ויצאו אתם מאור כשדים ללכת ארצה
the of land go to the Chaldeans Ur from with them left and his son Abram the of wife

2568 8646 3117 1961 8033 2421 2771 935
32 כנען ויבאו עד־חרן וישבו שם׃ ויהיו ימי־תרח חמש
five Terah the of days And were .there lived and Haran to And came they .Canaan

2771 8646 4191 8141 3967 8141

שְׁנִים וּמָאתַיִם שָׁנָה וַיָּמָת תֶּרַח בְּחָרָן׃

.Haran in Terah and died years two and hundred years

and five years; and Terah died in Haran.

CAP. XII יב

CHAPTER 12

1004 4138 776 3212 87 3068 559

1 וַיֹּאמֶר יְהוָה אֶל־אַבְרָם לֶךְ־לְךָ מֵאַרְצְךָ וּמִמּוֹלַדְתְּךָ וּמִבֵּית

from and your from and your from for Go ,Abram to Jehovah And / house ,kindred ,land yourself said had

1288 1419 1471 6213 7200 834 776

2 אָבִיךָ אֶל־הָאָרֶץ אֲשֶׁר אַרְאֶךָּ׃ וְאֶעֶשְׂךָ לְגוֹי גָּדוֹל וַאֲבָרֶכְךָ

will I and ,great a for will I And will I which land the to your / you bless nation you make .you show ,father's

7043 1288 1288 1293 1961 8034 1430

3 וַאֲגַדְּלָה שְׁמֶךָ וֶהְיֵה בְּרָכָה׃ וַאֲבָרְכָה מְבָרְכֶיךָ וּמְקַלֶּלְךָ

one the and who those will I And .blessing a you and your make and / you despising you bless bless be will ;name great

87 3212 127 4940 3605 1288 779

4 אָאֹר וְנִבְרְכוּ בְךָ כֹּל מִשְׁפְּחֹת הָאֲדָמָה׃ וַיֵּלֶךְ אַבְרָם כַּאֲשֶׁר

as even Abram And .earth the the all in shall and I will / went of families you blessed be ;curse

8141 2568 1121 87 3876 3212 3068 1696

דִּבֶּר אֵלָיו יְהוָה וַיֵּלֶךְ אִתּוֹ לוֹט וְאַבְרָם בֶּן־חָמֵשׁ שָׁנִים

five a And ;Lot with and ,Jehovah to had / of son Abram him went him spoken

802 8297 87 3947 2771 3318 8141 7657

5 וְשִׁבְעִים שָׁנָה בְּצֵאתוֹ מֵחָרָן׃ וַיִּקַּח אַבְרָם אֶת־שָׂרַי אִשְׁתּוֹ

his Sarai Abram And from he when years seventy- / ,wife took ,Haran departed

7408 7339 3605 251 1121 3876

וְאֶת־לוֹט בֶּן־אָחִיו וְאֶת־כָּל־רְכוּשָׁם אֲשֶׁר רָכָשׁוּ וְאֶת־

and had they that their all and his son Lot and / gained substance ,brother's

935 3667 776 3212 3318 2771 6213 2272

הַנֶּפֶשׁ אֲשֶׁר־עָשׂוּ בְחָרָן וַיֵּצְאוּ לָלֶכֶת אַרְצָה כְּנַעַן וַיָּבֹאוּ

they and Canaan into go to they And in had they whom the / in came of land the departed .Haran gotten persons

5704 7927 4725 5704 776 87 5674 3667 776

6 אַרְצָה כְּנָעַן׃ וַיַּעֲבֹר אַבְרָם בָּאָרֶץ עַד מְקוֹם שְׁכֶם עַד

to ,Shechem the far as land the Abram And .Caanan the to / of place as over passed of land

87 3068 7200 776 227 3669 4176 437

7 אֵלוֹן מוֹרֶה וְהַכְּנַעֲנִי אָז בָּאָרֶץ׃ וַיֵּרָא יְהוָה אֶל־אַבְרָם

Abram to Jehovah And the in was the and ;Moreh the / appeared .land then Canaanite of oak

3068 4196 8033 1129 2063 776 5414 2233 559

וַיֹּאמֶר לְזַרְעֲךָ אֶתֵּן אֶת־הָאָרֶץ הַזֹּאת וַיִּבֶן שָׁם מִזְבֵּחַ לַיהוָה

to an there and ;this land I your to and / Jehovah altar built he give will seed ,said

5186 1008 6924 2022 8033 6275 7200

8 הַנִּרְאֶה אֵלָיו׃ וַיַּעְתֵּק מִשָּׁם הָהָרָה מִקֶּדֶם לְבֵית־אֵל וַיֵּט

and ,Bethel the on a to from he And .him to who / stretched of east mountain there moved appeared

3068 4196 1129 6924 5857 5320 1008 168

אָהֳלֹה בֵּית־אֵל מִיָּם וְהָעַי מִקֶּדֶם וַיִּבֶן־שָׁם מִזְבֵּחַ לַיהוָה

to an there and the on Ai and toward Bethel ;tent his / Jehovah altar built he ,east ,sea the

5045 5265 3212 87 5265 3068 8034 7121

9 וַיִּקְרָא בְּשֵׁם יְהוָה׃ וַיִּסַּע אַבְרָם הָלוֹךְ וְנָסוֹעַ הַנֶּגְבָּה׃ פ

toward setting and on going Abram And .Jehovah the on and / Negeb the forth forth set of name called

3515 8033 1481 4714 87 3381 776 7458 1961

10 וַיְהִי רָעָב בָּאָרֶץ וַיֵּרֶד אַבְרָם מִצְרַיְמָה לָגוּר שָׁם כִּי־כָבֵד

(was) for ,there to Egypt into Abram and the in a And / severe stay down went ;land famine was

CHAPTER 12

1 And Jehovah had said to Abram, Go out from your land, and from your kindred, and from your father's house, to the land which I will show you. 2 And I will make of you a great nation. And I will bless you and make your name great; and you will be a blessing. 3 And I will bless those who bless you, and curse the one despising you. And in you all families of the earth shall be blessed.

4 And Abram went out, even as Jehovah had spoken to him. And Lot went with him. And Abram *was* seventy-five years old when he departed from Haran. 5 And Abram took his wife Sarai, and his brother's son, Lot, and all their substance that they had gathered, and the persons they had gained in Haran. And they went out to go into the land of Canaan. And they came into the land of Canaan. 6 And Abram passed through the land as far as the place of Shechem, to the oak of Moreh. And the Canaanite was then in the land. 7 And Jehovah appeared to Abram and said I will give this land to your seed. And he built an altar there to Jehovah, who appeared to him. 8 And he moved from there to a mountain on the east of Bethel, and stretched his tent *with* Bethel toward the sea, and Ai on the east. And he built an altar there to Jehovah, and called on the name of Jehovah. 9 And Abram traveled, going on and traveling toward the south.

10 And a famine was in the land, so Abram went down into Egypt to stay there. For the famine *was* severe in

the land. [11]And it was
when he had drawn near
to come to Egypt, he said
to his wife Sarai, Behold!
Please, I know that you
are a beautiful woman to
look upon. [12]And it will
be when the Egyptians
see you, then they will
say, This is his wife; and
they will kill me, and they
will save you alive.
[13]Please say that you are my
sister, so that it may be well
with me for your sake, and
my soul shall live because of
you. [14]And it happened,
when Abram had come into
Egypt, the Egyptians saw
the woman, that she *was*
very beautiful. [15]And
Pharoah's princes saw her,
and *they* praised her before
Pharaoh. And the woman
was taken into Pharaoh's
house. [16]And he treated
Abram well for her sake.
And he had sheep, and
oxen, and he-asses, and
men-slaves, and slave-girls,
and she-asses, and camels.
[17]And Jehovah touched
Pharaoh and his house with
great plagues because of
Sarai, Abram's wife. [18]And
Pharaoh called for Abram
and said, What *is* this you
have done to me? Why did
you not tell me she *is* your
wife? [19]Why did you say,
She *is* my sister? And so I
was taking her for my wife.
Now, then, see your wife.
Take *her* and go. [20]And as
Pharaoh ordered *his* men as
to him, even they sent him
and his wife and all that he
had away.

559 4714 935 7126 2961 776 7458
11 הָרָעָב בָּאָרֶץ׃ וַיְהִי כַּאֲשֶׁר הִקְרִיב לָבוֹא מִצְרָיְמָה וַיֹּאמֶר
he even ,Egypt to come to had he when And the in the
near drawn ,was it .land famine

4758 3303 802 3045 2009 802 8297
אֶל־שָׂרַי אִשְׁתּוֹ הִנֵּה־נָא יָדַעְתִּי כִּי אִשָּׁה יְפַת־מַרְאֶה אָתְּ׃
you look to beautiful a that I ,Behold ,wife his Sarai to
(are) upon woman know ,please

2026 802 1696 4714 7200 1961
12 וְהָיָה כִּי־יִרְאוּ אֹתָךְ הַמִּצְרִים וְאָמְרוּ אִשְׁתּוֹ זֹאת וְהָרְגוּ
they and This wife his they and the you see when it and
kill will ;is ,say will ,Egyptians be will

4616 3190 269 4994 559 2421
13 אֹתִי וְאֹתָךְ יְחַיּוּ׃ אִמְרִי־נָא אֲחֹתִי אָתְּ לְמַעַן יִיטַב־לִי
with may it that so ;are you sister my Please say will they you and ,me
me well be that .alive save

4714 87 935 7558 2212 2421 5668
14 בַּעֲבוּרֵךְ וְחָיְתָה נַפְשִׁי בִּגְלָלֵךְ׃ וַיְהִי כְּבוֹא אַבְרָם מִצְרָיְמָה
,Egypt into Abram when And because soul my and of because
come had ,was it .you of live shall ,you

7200 3303 802 4714 7200
15 וַיִּרְאוּ הַמִּצְרִים אֶת־הָאִשָּׁה כִּי־יָפָה הִוא מְאֹד׃ וַיִּרְאוּ
And ,very she beautiful that ,woman the Egyptians the then
saw (was) saw

802 3947 6547 413 1984 6547 8269
אֹתָהּ שָׂרֵי פַרְעֹה וַיְהַלְלוּ אֹתָהּ אֶל־פַּרְעֹה וַתֻּקַּח הָאִשָּׁה
the was and ;Pharaoh before her and Pharaoh the her
woman into taken praised of princes

1241 6629 1961 5668 3190 87 6547 1004
16 בֵּית פַּרְעֹה׃ וּלְאַבְרָם הֵיטִיב בַּעֲבוּרָהּ וַיְהִי־לוֹ צֹאן־וּבָקָר
and ,sheep he and her for did he to And ,Pharaoh's house
,oxen had ,sake good Abram

3068 5060 1581 860 8198 5650 2543
17 וַחֲמֹרִים וַעֲבָדִים וּשְׁפָחֹת וַאֲתֹנֹת וּגְמַלִּים׃ וַיְנַגַּע יְהוָה
Jehovah And ,camels and and and male and and
touched ,she-asses slave-girls slaves ,he-asses

802 8297 1697 1004 1419 5061 6547
אֶת־פַּרְעֹה נְגָעִים גְּדֹלִים וְאֶת־בֵּיתוֹ עַל־דְּבַר שָׂרַי אֵשֶׁת
the ,Sarai of because house his and great with Pharaoh
of wife plagues

6213 559 87 6547 7121 87
18 אַבְרָם׃ וַיִּקְרָא פַרְעֹה לְאַבְרָם וַיֹּאמֶר מַה־זֹּאת עָשִׂיתָ לִּי
to have you (is) What ,said and for Pharaoh And .Abram
?me done this Abram called

269 559 4100 802 3947
19 לָמָּה לֹא־הִגַּדְתָּ לִּי כִּי אִשְׁתְּךָ הִוא׃ לָמָה אָמַרְתָּ אֲחֹתִי
my you did Why ?(is) she wife your that me you did not Why
sister ,say tell

3212 3947 802 2009 6258 802 3947
הִוא וָאֶקַּח אֹתָהּ לִי לְאִשָּׁה וְעַתָּה הִנֵּה אִשְׁתְּךָ קַח וָלֵךְ׃
and take your behold and ;wife for to her I so And She
.go (her) ,wife now me took ?(is)

802 7971 582 6547 6680
20 וַיְצַו עָלָיו פַּרְעֹה אֲנָשִׁים וַיְשַׁלְּחוּ אֹתוֹ וְאֶת־אִשְׁתּוֹ וְאֶת־
and wife his and him they and ;men (his) Pharaoh to as And
away sent him ordered

1961/834 3605
כָּל־אֲשֶׁר־לוֹ׃
.had he that all

CAP. XIII יג

CHAPTER 13

CHAPTER 13
[1]And Abram went up out
of Egypt into the Negeb, he
and his wife and all that he
had, and Lot *being* with
him. [2]And Abram was very

3876 3605 802 4714 87 5927
1 וַיַּעַל אַבְרָם מִמִּצְרַיִם הוּא וְאִשְׁתּוֹ וְכָל־אֲשֶׁר־לוֹ וְלוֹט עִמּוֹ
with and to that and his and ,he of out Abram And
him Lot ,him (was) all ,wife ,Egypt up went

rich in livestock, in silver 2
and in gold. [3]And he went 3
on his journeys from the
south, even to Bethel, to the
place where his tent had
been there at the begin-
ning, between Bethel and
Ai, [4]to the place of the altar 4
which he had made there at
the first. And Abram called
on the name of Jehovah
there. [5]And Lot, who went 5
with Abram, also had flocks
and herds and tents. [6]And 6
the land was not able to
bear them, for dwelling
together, for their wealth
was great, so that they
could not dwell together.
[7]And there was strife be- 7
tween the herdsmen of
Abram's livestock and the
herdsmen of Lot's livestock.
And the Canaanite and the
Perizzite lived then in the
land.

[8]And Abram said to Lot, 8
Please let there be no strife
between me and you, and
between my herdsmen and
your herdsmen, for we *are* 9
men, brothers. [9]Is not all
the land before you? Please
separate from me. If *you go*
to the left, then I will go to
the right. Or if *you go* to the
right, then I will go to the
left. [10]And Lot lifted up his 10
eyes and saw all the circuit
of Jordan, that it was well-
watered — before Jehovah
destroyed Sodom and Go-
morrah — even like the
garden of Jehovah, like the
land of Egypt as you come
to Zoar. [11]Then Lot chose 11
all the circuit of Jordan for
himself. And Lot journeyed
east. And they were
separated, each one from
his brother. [12]And Abram 12
lived in the land of Canaan,
and Lot lived in the cities of
the circuit, and pitched *his*
tent as far as Sodom. [13]And 13
the men of Sodom were
wicked and sinners before
Jehovah—exceedingly so.
[14]And after Lot had 14

3212 2091 3701 4735 3966 3513 87 5045
הנגבה: ואברם כבד מאד במקנה בכסף ובזהב: וילך
And went he | in and gold | silver in | in ,livestock | very | was rich | And Abram | the into .Negeb

8033 1961 4725 1008 5045 4550
למסעיו מנגב ועד-בית-אל עד-המקום אשר-היה שם
there | had been | where | place the | to | ,Bethel | to even | from south the | his on journeys

419 :6 4725 5857 1008 996 8462 168
אהלה בתחלה בין בית-אל ובין העי: אל-מקום המזבח
altar the | the of place | to | ,Ai | and | Bethel | between | at beginning the | tent his

3068 8034 8033 7121 7223 8033 6213 834
אשר-עשה שם בראשנה ויקרא שם אברם בשם יהוה:
.Jehovah | the on of name | Abram | there | And called | .first the at | there | had he made | which

168 1241 6629 1961 87 854 3212 3876 1571
וגם-ללוט ההלך את-אברם היה צאן-ובקר ואהלים:
.tents and | and oxen | sheep | there was | ,Abram | with | went who | to Lot | And also

7227 7339 1961 3162 2416 776 5375
ולא-נשא אתם הארץ לשבת יחדו כי-היה רכושם רב
,great | their substance | was for | ,together | for living | land the | them | able was And bear to not

4735 7473 996 7379 3162 2421 3201
ולא-יכלו לשבת יחדו: ויהי-ריב בין רעי מקנה-אברם
Abram's livestock | those tending | be- tween | strife | And was | .together | live | they that so could not

776 3427 6522 3669 3876 4735 7462
ובין רעי מקנה-לוט והכנעני והפרזי אז ישב בארץ:
the in .land | lived | then | the and Perizzite | the And Canaanite | .Lot's live- stock | those tending | and

996 996 4808 1961 408 3876 87 559
ויאמר אברם אל-לוט אל-נא תהי מריבה ביני ובינך ובין
be- tween | and ,you | and me | between | strife | be let | Please no | ,Lot to | Abram | And said

776 3605 3808 251 582 7462 996 7462
רעי ובין רעיך כי-אנשים אחים אנחנו: הלא כל-הארץ
the land | all | not Is | we .(are) | brothers | men (are) for | your ;tenders | and | my tenders

3231 3225 8040 4994 6504 6440
לפניך הפרד נא מעלי אם-השמאל ואימנה ואם-הימין
the to right | if or | go will I so ;right the to | ,left the to | if | from ;me | Please | be separated | before ?you

3383 3603 3605 7200 5869 3876 5375 8041
ואשמאילה: וישא-לוט את-עיניו וירא את-כל-ככר הירדן
the ,Jordan | the of circuit | all | saw and | his eyes | Lot | And up lifted | go will I then .left the to

6017 5467 3068 7843 6440 4945 3605
כי כלה משקה לפני | שחת יהוה את-סדם ואת-עמרה
,Gomorrah and | Sodom | Jehovah | de- stroyed | before | watered ;well | was it that all

3876 977 6820 935 4714 776 3068 1588
כגן-יהוה כארץ מצרים באכה צער: ויבחר-לו לוט את
Lot | for himself | And chose | .Zoar | you as to come | Egypt | the like of land | Jehovah's as ,garden

251 376 6504 6924 5265 3603 3605
כל-ככר הירדן ויסע לוט מקדם ויפרדו איש מעל אחיו:
his .brother | from | each one | they And ,separated | east- .ward | Lot set forth | and the Jordan | the of circuit | all

167 3603 5892 3427 3876 3667 776 3427 87
אברם ישב בארץ-כנען ולוט ישב בערי הככר ויאהל
and tented | the ,circuit | the in of cities | lived | Lot and | ;Canaan | the in of land | lived | Abram

3068 3966 3068 2401 7451 5467 376 5467 5704
עד-סדם: ואנשי סדם רעים וחטאים ליהוה מאד: ויהוה
And Jehovah | greatly .so | before Jehovah | and sinners | were evil | Sodom | the And of men | .Sodom as as far

separated from him, Jehovah said to Abram, Now lift up your eyes and look northward and southward and eastward and westward from the place where you are. [15]For all the land which you see I will give to you, and to your seed forever. [16]And I will make your seed as the dust of the earth, so that if a man can count the dust of the earth, then your seed also will be counted. [17]Rise up! Walk through the land, in its length and in its breadth, for I will give it to you. [18]Then Abram moved *his* tent and came and lived among the oaks of Mamre, which *were* in Hebron; and he built an altar to Jehovah there.

5869 5375 3876 6504 310 87 559
אָמַר אֶל־אַבְרָם אַחֲרֵי הִפָּרֶד־לוֹט מֵעִמּוֹ שָׂא נָא עֵינֶיךָ
your eyes · Now up lift · ,him from · Lot · had separated · after · ,Abram to · said

6924 5045 6828 8033 4725 7200
וּרְאֵה מִן־הַמָּקוֹם אֲשֶׁר־אַתָּה שָׁם צָפֹנָה וָנֶגְבָּה וָקֵדְמָה
and eastward · and southward · and northward · ;there are you · where · place the from · look and

5414 720 0 834 776 3605 3220
15 וָיָמָּה׃ כִּי אֶת־כָּל־הָאָרֶץ אֲשֶׁר־אַתָּה רֹאֶה לְךָ אֶתְּנֶנָּה
will I ;it give · you to · see · you · which · land the all · for · and westward

834 776 6083 2233 7760 5769/5704/2233
16 וּלְזַרְעֲךָ עַד־עוֹלָם׃ וְשַׂמְתִּי אֶת־זַרְעֲךָ כַּעֲפַר הָאָרֶץ אֲשֶׁר ׀
which · ,earth the · the as of dust · seed your · I And make will · .forever until · to and seed your

4487 2233 776 6083 4487 376 3201
אִם־יוּכַל אִישׁ לִמְנוֹת אֶת־עֲפַר הָאָרֶץ גַּם זַרְעֲךָ יִמָּנֶה׃
be will counted · your seed · also · the ,earth · of dust the · count to · man a · able is if

5414 7341 753 776 1980 6965
17 קוּם הִתְהַלֵּךְ בָּאָרֶץ לְאָרְכָּהּ וּלְרָחְבָּהּ כִּי לְךָ אֶתְּנֶנָּה׃
will I .it give · you to for · in and ;breadth its · its in length · through land the · Walk · Rise !up

2275 834 4471 437 3427 935 87 167
18 וַיֶּאֱהַל אַבְרָם וַיָּבֹא וַיֵּשֶׁב בְּאֵלֹנֵי מַמְרֵא אֲשֶׁר בְּחֶבְרוֹן
in ;Hebron · which (were) · ,Mamre · the by of oaks · and lived · and came · Abram · moved And tent (his)

3068 4196 1129
וַיִּבֶן־שָׁם מִזְבֵּחַ לַיהוָה׃
to Jehovah · altar an · there · and built he

CAP. XIV יד

CHAPTER 14

CHAPTER 14

1 [1]And in the days of
Amraphel king of Shinar,
Arioch king of Ellasar,
Chedor-laomer king of
2 Elam and Tidal king of the
nations, [2]they warred
with Bera king of Sodom,
and with Birsha king of
Gomorrah, Shinab king of
Admah, and Shemebar
3 king of Zeboiim, and the
king of Bela—it *is* Zoar.
[3]All these *were* joined
together to the valley of
Siddim, which *is* the Salt
4 Sea. [4]They served
Chedor-laomer *for* twelve
years, and the thirteenth
year they rebelled. [5]And
in the fourteenth year
Chedor-laomer and the
kings that were with
him came and struck
5 the giants in Ashteroth
Kamaim, and the Zuzim
in Ham, and the

495 4428 746 815 4428 569 3117 1961
וַיְהִי בִּימֵי אַמְרָפֶל מֶלֶךְ־שִׁנְעָר אַרְיוֹךְ מֶלֶךְ אֶלָּסָר
,Ellasar · of king · Arioch · ,Shinar · of king · Amraphel · the in of days · And ,was it

4421 6213 1471 4428 8413 5867 4428 3540
כְּדָרְלָעֹמֶר מֶלֶךְ עֵילָם וְתִדְעָל מֶלֶךְ גּוֹיִם׃ עָשׂוּ מִלְחָמָה
battle · they made · the ,nations · of king · Tidal and · ,Elam · of king · Chedorlaomer

4428 8134 6017 4428 1306 854 5467 4428 1298
אֶת־בֶּרַע מֶלֶךְ סְדֹם וְאֶת־בִּרְשַׁע מֶלֶךְ עֲמֹרָה שִׁנְאָב ׀ מֶלֶךְ
king of · Shinab · ,Gomorrah · king of · with Birsha · and · ,Sodom · king of · Bera with

6820 1931 1106 4428 6636 4428 8038 126
אַדְמָה וְשֶׁמְאֵבֶר מֶלֶךְ צְבוֹיִים וּמֶלֶךְ בֶּלַע הִיא־צֹעַר׃ כָּל־
All · Zoar (is) it · ,Bela · the and of king · ,Zeboiim · of king · and Shemebar · ,Admah

8147 4417 3220 7708 6010 2266
אֵלֶּה חָבְרוּ אֶל־עֵמֶק הַשִּׂדִּים הוּא יָם הַמֶּלַח׃ שְׁתֵּים
(and) two · .Salt the · Sea · which (is) · ,Siddim · the to of valley · joined together · these (were)

8141 6240 7969 3540 5647 8141 6240
עֶשְׂרֵה שָׁנָה עָבְדוּ אֶת־כְּדָרְלָעֹמֶר וּשְׁלֹשׁ־עֶשְׂרֵה שָׁנָה
year · ten (and) three · and · ,Chedor-laomer · They served · years · ten

4428 3540 935 8141 6240 702 4775
מָרָדוּ׃ וּבְאַרְבַּע עֶשְׂרֵה שָׁנָה בָּא כְדָרְלָעֹמֶר וְהַמְּלָכִים
kings the and · Chedor-laomer · came · year · ten (and) · in And four · they .rebelled

2504 6255 6255 7497 5221 834
אֲשֶׁר אִתּוֹ וַיַּכּוּ אֶת־רְפָאִים בְּעַשְׁתְּרֹת קַרְנַיִם וְאֶת־הַזּוּזִים
Zuzim the and · ,Karnaim · Ashteroth in · Giants the · and struck · with him · that were

Emim in Shaveh Kiriathaim, [6]and the Horites in their Mount Seir, as far as Elparan, which is by the wilderness. [7]And they turned back and came to Enmishpat which *is* Kadesh, and struck all the country of the Amalekites,and also the Amorites who lived in Hazazon Thamar. [8]And the king of Sodom went out, and the king of Gomorrah, and the king of Admah, and the king of Zeboiim, and the king of Bela, which *is* Zoar. And they set the battle with them in the valley of Siddim, [9]with Chedor-laomer the king of Elam, and with Tidal the king of the nations, and Amraphel the king of Shinar, and Arioch the king of Ellasar —four kings with the five. [10]And the valley of Siddim *was* full of asphalt pits and the kings of Sodom and Gomorrah fled, and fell there. And they that remained fled to the mountain. [11]And they took all the goods of Sodom and Gomorrah, and all their food, and went away. [12]And they took Lot, the son of Abram's brother, and his goods, and left; and he was living in Sodom.

[13]And one who had escaped came and told Abraham the Hebrew; for he was living among the oaks of Mamre the Amorite, *the* brother of Escol and Aner. And these had a covenant with Abram. [14]And when Abram heard that his brother was captured, even then he led out his trained men, born of his household, three hundred and eighteen. And *they* pursued as far as Dan. [15] And he divided against them by night, he and his slaves, and *he* struck them, and chased them as far as Hobah, which *is* on the left of Damascus.

2042 2753 7741 368 1990
6 בְּהָם וְאֵת הָאֵימִים בְּשָׁוֵה קִרְיָתָיִם׃ וְאֶת־הַחֹרִי בְּהַרְרָם
their the and ,Kiriathaim in Emim the and in
Mount Horite Shaveh ;Ham

935 7725 4057 834 6290 424 5704 8165
7 שֵׂעִיר עַד אֵיל פָּארָן אֲשֶׁר עַל־הַמִּדְבָּר׃ וַיָּשֻׁבוּ וַיָּבֹאוּ
and they And .wilderness the by is which Paran the far as ,Seir
came back turned of oak as

1571 6003 7704 5221 6946 5880 413
אֶל־עֵין מִשְׁפָּט הִוא קָדֵשׁ וַיַּכּוּ אֶת־כָּל־שְׂדֵה הָעֲמָלֵקִי וְגַם
and the country the all and ,Kadesh (is) it ,Enmishpat to
also ;Amalekite of struck

4428 5467 4428 5927 2688 2688 2416 567
8 אֶת־הָאֱמֹרִי הַיֹּשֵׁב בְּחַצְצֹן תָּמָר׃ וַיֵּצֵא מֶלֶךְ־סְדֹם וּמֶלֶךְ
the and Sodom the went And .Thamar in were Amorite the
of king of king out Hazezon living

6820 1931 1106 4428 6636 4428 126 4428 6017
עֲמֹרָה וּמֶלֶךְ אַדְמָה וּמֶלֶךְ צְבֹיִים וּמֶלֶךְ בֶּלַע הִוא־צֹעַר
.Zoar (is) it ,Bela the and ,Zeboim the and ,Admah the and Gomor-
of king of king of king ,rah

3540 7708 6010 4421 6186
9 וַיַּעַרְכוּ אִתָּם מִלְחָמָה בְּעֵמֶק הַשִּׂדִּים׃ אֵת כְּדָרְלָעֹמֶר
Chedor-laomer with ,Siddim the in battle the with they And
of valley them set

746 8152 4428 5691 1471 4428 8413 5869 4428
מֶלֶךְ עֵילָם וְתִדְעָל מֶלֶךְ גּוֹיִם וְאַמְרָפֶל מֶלֶךְ שִׁנְעָר וְאַרְיוֹךְ
and ,Shinar the and ,Goiim the with and ,Elam the
Arioch of king Amraphel of king Tidal of king

7708 6010 2568 4428 702 495 4428
10 מֶלֶךְ אֶלָּסָר אַרְבָּעָה מְלָכִים אֶת־הַחֲמִשָּׁה׃ וְעֵמֶק הַשִּׂדִּים
Siddim the And .five the with kings four —Ellasar the
of valley of king

8033 5307 6017 5467 4428 5127 2564 875 875
בֶּאֱרֹת בֶּאֱרֹת חֵמָר וַיָּנֻסוּ מֶלֶךְ־סְדֹם וַעֲמֹרָה וַיִּפְּלוּ־שָׁמָּה
;there fell and and Sodom the and ,asphalt (was) pits
Gomorrah of kings fled of full

6017 5467 7339 3605 3947 5127 2022 7604
11 וְהַנִּשְׁאָרִים הֶרָה נָּסוּ׃ וַיִּקְחוּ אֶת־כָּל־רְכֻשׁ סְדֹם וַעֲמֹרָה
and Sodom the all they And .fled the to those And
,Gomorrah of goods took mountain left

251 1121 7339 3876 3947 3212 400 3605
12 וְאֶת־כָּל־אָכְלָם וַיֵּלֵכוּ׃ וַיִּקְחוּ אֶת־לוֹט וְאֶת־רְכֻשׁוֹ בֶּן־אֲחִי
brother the his and ,Lot And went and their all and
of son ,goods took they ,away ,food

5046 6412 935 5467 7931 3212 87
13 אַבְרָם וַיֵּלֵכוּ וְהוּא יֹשֵׁב בִּסְדֹם׃ וַיָּבֹא הַפָּלִיט וַיַּגֵּד
and who one And .Sodom in was and went and Abram's
told escaped had came living he ;away

251 567 4471 457 7931 5680 87
לְאַבְרָם הָעִבְרִי וְהוּא שֹׁכֵן בְּאֵלֹנֵי מַמְרֵא הָאֱמֹרִי אֲחִי
brother the Mamre by was he and the Abram
,Amorite of oaks the living ;Hebrew

87 8085 87 1285 1167 60:63 251 812
14 אֶשְׁכֹּל וַאֲחִי עָנֵר וְהֵם בַּעֲלֵי בְרִית־אַבְרָם׃ וַיִּשְׁמַע אַבְרָם
Abram And with a had and ,Aner's and Eshcol's
heard ,Abram covenant they brother

6240 8083 1004 3205 2593 7324 251 7617
כִּי נִשְׁבָּה אָחִיו וַיָּרֶק אֶת־חֲנִיכָיו יְלִידֵי בֵיתוֹ שְׁמֹנָה עָשָׂר
eighteen his borne trained his he then and his was that
household of men out led ;brother captured

3915 2505 1835 7291 3967 7969
15 וּשְׁלֹשׁ מֵאוֹת וַיִּרְדֹּף עַד־דָּן׃ וַיֵּחָלֵק עֲלֵיהֶם לַיְלָה הוּא
he ,night by against he And .Dan as far as and hundred and
them divided pursued three

1834 8040 834 2327 7291 5221 5650
וַעֲבָדָיו וַיַּכֵּם וַיִּרְדְּפֵם עַד־חוֹבָה אֲשֶׁר מִשְּׂמֹאל לְדַמָּשֶׂק׃
.Damascus of left the on (is) which ,Hobah until chased and and his and
them ,them struck slaves

[16]And he brought back all the goods, and also brought back his brother, and also the women and the people.
[17]And the king of Sodom went out to meet him, after he returned from smiting Chedor-laomer and the kings which *were* with him, to the valley of Shaveh, it *being* the valley of the king
[18]And Melchizedek, king of Salem, brought out bread and wine; and he was the priest of the most high God.
[19]And he blessed him and said, Blessed be Abram of the most high God, possessor of Heaven and earth; [20]and blessed *be* the most high God, who has delivered your enemies into your hand. And he gave him a tithe of all.
[21]And the king of Sodom said to Abram, Give me the persons and take the goods for yourself. [22]And Abram said to the king of Sodom, I have lifted up my hand to Jehovah, the most high God, the possessor of Heaven and earth, [23]that I will not take from all that is yours, from a thread to a shoe-latchet, and *that* you *may* not say, I have made Abram rich. [24]Nothing for me; only what the young men have eaten, and the portion of the men who went with me: Aner, Eshcol, and Mamre; let them take their portion.

7725 7339 251 3876 1571 7339 7725
16 וַיָּשֶׁב אֵת כָּל־הָרְכֻשׁ וְגַם אֶת־לוֹט אָחִיו וּרְכֻשׁוֹ הֵשִׁיב
brought back his goods and his ,brother Lot and also ,goods all he And also retrieved

7125 5467 4428 5927 5971 802 1571
17 וְגַם אֶת־הַנָּשִׁים וְאֶת־הָעָם׃ וַיֵּצֵא מֶלֶךְ־סְדֹם לִקְרָאתוֹ
meet ,him to Sodom the of king And went the .people and women the and also

834 4428 3540 5221 7725 310
אַחֲרֵי שׁוּבוֹ מֵהַכּוֹת אֶת־כְּדָרְלָעֹמֶר וְאֶת־הַמְּלָכִים אֲשֶׁר
which (were) kings the and Chedor-laomer from striking his return after

4428 4442 4428 6010 1931 7740 6010
18 אִתּוֹ אֶל־עֵמֶק שָׁוֵה הוּא עֵמֶק הַמֶּלֶךְ׃ וּמַלְכִּי־צֶדֶק מֶלֶךְ
king of Melchizedek And .king the the of valley it (being) ,Shaveh the to of valley with ,him

1288 5945 410 3549 1961 3196 3899 3318 8004
19 שָׁלֵם הוֹצִיא לֶחֶם וָיָיִן וְהוּא כֹהֵן לְאֵל עֶלְיוֹן׃ וַיְבָרְכֵהוּ
he And him blessed most ,high the to God a priest he and was and ;wine bread brought out Salem

1288 776 8064 7069 5945 410 87 1288 559
20 וַיֹּאמַר בָּרוּךְ אַבְרָם לְאֵל עֶלְיוֹן קֹנֵה שָׁמַיִם וָאָרֶץ׃ וּבָרוּךְ
And (be) blessed and .earth Heaven possessor of most high the by ,God Abram Blessed be ,said and

3605 4643 5414 3027 6862 4042 5945 410
אֵל עֶלְיוֹן אֲשֶׁר־מִגֵּן צָרֶיךָ בְּיָדֶךָ וַיִּתֶּן־לוֹ מַעֲשֵׂר מִכֹּל׃
.all of a tithe to him he and gave your into ;hand your enemies has delivered who most high the ,God

3947 7339 5315 5414 87 5467 4428 559
21 וַיֹּאמֶר מֶלֶךְ־סְדֹם אֶל־אַבְרָם תֶּן־לִי הַנֶּפֶשׁ וְהָרְכֻשׁ קַח־לָךְ׃
for yourself take the goods and the persons to me Give ,Abram to Sodom the of king And said

430 3068 410 3027 7311 5467 4428 410 87 559
22 וַיֹּאמֶר אַבְרָם אֶל־מֶלֶךְ סְדֹם הֲרִמֹתִי יָדִי אֶל־יְהוָה אֵל
the ,God ,Jehovah to my hand have I lifted up ,Sodom of king the to Abram said And

518 5275 8288 5704 2339 518 776 8064 7069 5945
23 עֶלְיוֹן קֹנֵה שָׁמַיִם וָאָרֶץ׃ אִם־מִחוּט וְעַד שְׂרוֹךְ־נַעַל וְאִם־
that and shoe a ,latchet even to a from thread that and Heaven ,earth possess- of sor most high

87 6238 559 3808 834 3605 3947
אֶקַּח מִכָּל־אֲשֶׁר־לָךְ וְלֹא תֹאמַר אֲנִי הֶעֱשַׁרְתִּי אֶת־אַבְרָם׃
.Abram made rich have I 2506 ,say you not and ,yours that is all from will I take

3212 582 5288 398 7535 1107
24 בִּלְעָדַי רַק אֲשֶׁר אָכְלוּ הַנְּעָרִים וְחֵלֶק הָאֲנָשִׁים אֲשֶׁר הָלְכוּ
went who men the the and of portion young the ,men have eaten what only Nothing ;me for

2506 3947 4471 812 6063 853
אִתִּי עָנֵר אֶשְׁכֹּל וּמַמְרֵא הֵם יִקְחוּ חֶלְקָם׃ ס
their .portion let take them and :Mamre ,Eshcol ,Aner with ;me

CAP. XV טו

CHAPTER 15

CHAPTER 15

[1]After these things the word of Jehovah came to Abram in a vision, saying, Do not fear, Abram; I am your shield, your reward will increase greatly. [2]And Abram said, Lord Jehovah, what will You give to me, *since* I *am going* childless,

4236 87 3068 1697 1961 1697 310
1 אַחַר הַדְּבָרִים הָאֵלֶּה הָיָה דְבַר־יְהוָה אֶל־אַבְרָם בַּמַּחֲזֶה
a ,vision in Abram to Jehovah the of word was these things After

7235 7939 4043 87 3372 559
לֵאמֹר אַל־תִּירָא אַבְרָם אָנֹכִי מָגֵן לָךְ שְׂכָרְךָ הַרְבֵּה
will increase your reward to ,you a shield am I ;Abram Do not ,fear ,saying

5414 3068 136 87 559 3966
2 מְאֹד׃ וַיֹּאמֶר אַבְרָם אֲדֹנָי יְהוִה מַה־תִּתֶּן־לִי וְאָנֹכִי
I And to ?me You will give what ,Jehovah Lord ,Abram said And .greatly

and the son of the inheritance of my house *is* Eleazar of Damascus? 3And Abram said, Behold! You have given no seed to me; and lo, the son of my house is inheriting of me! 4And behold! The word of Jehovah *came* to him saying, This one shall not be your heir. But he that shall come forth out of your own bowels shall be your heir. 5And he brought him outside and said, Look now at the heavens and count the stars, if you are able to count them. And he said to him, So shall your seed be. 6And he believed in Jehovah. And He counted it to him for righteousness.

7And He said to him, I *am* Jehovah who caused you to come out of Ur of the Chaldeans, to give you this land to inherit it. 8And he said, My Lord Jehovah, by what shall I know that I shall inherit it? 9And He said to him, Take for Me a heifer three years old, and a she-goat three years old, and a ram three years old, and a turtledove, even a nestling. 10And he took all these for Him, and he divided them in the middle; and he laid each piece against one another, but he did not divide the bird. 11And the birds of prey came down on the carcases, and Abram drove them away. 12And it hap-them away.

12And it happened *as* the sun was setting, and a deep sleep fell on Abram; and behold, a terror of great darkness falling on him! 13And He said to Abram, You must surely know that your seed shall be an alien in a land not theirs; and they shall serve them. And they shall afflict them four hundred years; 14and I also will judge that nation whom they shall serve; and afterward they shall come out with great substance.

559 467 1834 1931 1004 4943 1121 6185 3212
3 הולך ערירי ובן־משק ביתי הוא דמשק אליעזר׃ ויאמר
said And .Eliezer Damascus of (is) he my the and ;childless (am)
house of heir going

3423 1004 1121 2009 2233 5414 3808 2009 87
אברם הן לי לא נתתה זרע והנה בן־ביתי יורש אתי׃
!me of is my son the and ;seed You not to Be- ,Abram
inheriting house of ,lo given have me !hold

2088 3423 3808 559 3068 1697 2009
4 והנה דבר־יהוה אליו לאמר לא יירשך זה כי־אם אשר
who but this be shall not ,saying to Jehovah The ,And
,one heir Your him of word !behold

559 2351 3318 3423 4578 5927
5 יצא ממעיך הוא יירשך׃ ויוצא אתו החוצה ויאמר
,said and outside him he And be shall he your of out will
brought .heir your bowels own go

5608 3201 3556 5608 8064 5027
הבט־נא השמימה וספר הכוכבים אם־תוכל לספר
count to are you if ,stars the and the Now look
able count heavens at

2503 3068 539 2233 1961 3541 559
6 אתם ויאמר לו כה יהיה זרעך׃ והאמן ביהוה ויחשבה
He and in he And .seed your be shall So to he and ;them
it reckoned ;Jehovah believed ,him said

3318 3068 559 6666
7 לו צדקה׃ ויאמר אליו אני יהוה אשר הוצאתיך מאור
of out you caused who Jehovah I to He And right- for to
Ur come to (am) ,him said .eousness him

559 3423 2088 776 5414 3778
8 כשדים לתת לך את־הארץ הזאת לרשתה׃ ויאמר
he And .it inherit to this land you to give to the
.said Chaldeans

3947 559 3423 3045 4100 3068 136
9 אדני יהוה במה אדע כי אירשנה׃ ויאמר אליו קחה
Take ,him to he And shall I that I shall by ,Jehovah My
said ?it inherit know what Lord

1469 8449 8027 352 8027 5795 8027 5697
לי עגלה משלשת ועז משלשת ואיל משלש ותר וגוזל׃
a even a and three being a and three being a and three being a for
.nestling dove ,old years ram ,old years she-goat ,old years heifer Me

1335 376 5414/8432 1334 3605 3947
10 ויקח־לו את־כל־אלה ויבתר אתם בתוך ויתן איש־בתרו
piece each he and the in them he and these all for he And
laid ;middle divided him took

5921 5861 3381 1334 3808 6833 7451 7125
11 לקראת רעהו ואת־הצפר לא בתר׃ וירד העיט על־
on birds the And did he not bird the but its opposite
prey of down came .divide ;neighbor

8637 935 8121 1961 87 5380 6297
12 הפגרים וישב אתם אברם׃ ויהי השמש לבוא ותרדמה
a and was sun the And .Abram them and the
sleep deep setting .was it away drove ,carcases

5307 1419 2835 367 2009 87 5307
נפלה על־אברם והנה אימה חשכה גדלה נפלת עליו׃
on falling great darkness a and ;Abram on fell
!him of terror ,behold

3808 776 2233 1961 1616 3045 3045 87 559
13 ויאמר לאברם ידע תדע כי־גר יהיה זרעך בארץ לא
not a in your be shall an that You must ,Abram to He And
land seed alien know surely said

1571 8141 3967 702 6031 5647
14 להם ועבדום וענו אתם ארבע מאות שנה׃ וגם את־
and ;years hundred four them they And will and to
also afflict will .them serve them

1419 7339 3651 310 1777 5647 1471
הגוי אשר יעבדו דן אנכי ואחרי־כן יצאו ברכש גדול׃
.great with shall they that and ;I will shall they whom the
substance out come after judge serve nation

[15]And you shall come to your fathers in peace. You shall be buried in a good old age. [16]And in the fourth generation they shall come here again; for the iniquity of the Amorites is not yet full. [17]And it was, the sun had gone down, and it was dark, behold! A smoking furnace, and a torch of fire that passed between those pieces! [18]In that day Jehovah made a covenant with Abram, saying, I have given this land to your seed, from the river of Egypt to the great river, the river Euphrates, [19]the Kenite, and the Kenizzite, and the Kadmonite, [20]and the Hittite, and the Perizzite, and the Rephaim, [21]and the Amorite, and the Canaanite, and the Girgashite, and the Jebusite.

2896 7872 6912 7965 1 935
15 וְאַתָּה תָּבוֹא אֶל־אֲבֹתֶיךָ בְּשָׁלוֹם תִּקָּבֵר בְּשֵׂיבָה טוֹבָה׃
.good | an in age old | shall you buried be | ;peace in | your fathers | to | shall come | And you

567 5771 8003 2008 7725 7243 8435
16 וְדוֹר רְבִיעִי יָשׁוּבוּ הֵנָּה כִּי לֹא־שָׁלֵם עֲוֺן הָאֱמֹרִי עַד־
until | the Amorites | the of iniquity | full is | not | for | ;here | they will return | the fourth | in And generation

6227 8574 2009 1961 5939 935 8121 1961 2008
17 הֵנָּה׃ וַיְהִי הַשֶּׁמֶשׁ בָּאָה וַעֲלָטָה הָיָה וְהִנֵּה תַנּוּר עָשָׁן
smoking | a furnace | ,behold | ;was it | and dark | gone had ,down | sun the | And ,was it | .now

193.1 3117 1506 996 5674 784 3940
18 וְלַפִּיד אֵשׁ אֲשֶׁר עָבַר בֵּין הַגְּזָרִים הָאֵלֶּה׃ בַּיּוֹם הַהוּא
that | day In | !these of | the parts | between | passed | that | of fire | a and torch

5414 2233 559 1285 87 3068 3772
כָּרַת יְהוָה אֶת־אַבְרָם בְּרִית לֵאמֹר לְזַרְעֲךָ נָתַתִּי אֶת־
have I given | your to seed | ,saying | a covenant | Abram with | Jehovah | cut

6578 5104 1419 5104 5704 4714 5104 2088 776
הָאָרֶץ הַזֹּאת מִנְּהַר מִצְרַיִם עַד־הַנָּהָר הַגָּדֹל נְהַר־פְּרָת׃
;Euphrates the river | ,great | the river | to | Egypt | the from of river | this | land

2850 6935 7074 7017
19 אֶת־הַקֵּינִי וְאֶת־הַקְּנִזִּי וְאֵת הַקַּדְמֹנִי׃ וְאֶת־הַחִתִּי וְאֶת־
20
and | ,Hittite the and | the ,Kadmonite | and | the Kenizzite | and | ,Kenite the

3669 567 7497 6522
21 הַפְּרִזִּי וְאֶת־הָרְפָאִים׃ וְאֶת־הָאֱמֹרִי וְאֶת־הַכְּנַעֲנִי וְאֶת־
and | ,Canaanite the and | the ,Amorite | and | ,Rephaim the | and | the Perizzite

2983 1622
הַגִּרְגָּשִׁי וְאֶת־הַיְבוּסִי׃
the .Jebusite | and | the ,Girgashite

CAP. XVI טז

CHAPTER 16

CHAPTER 16

[1]And Sarai, Abram's wife, did not bear to him; and to her *belonged* a female slave, an Egyptian, and her name *was* Hagar. [2]And Sarai said to Abram, See, now, Jehovah has kept me from bearing; go in now to my slave-girl; perhaps I may be built up from her. And Abram listened to the voice of Sarai. [3]And Sarai, Abram's wife, took her slave-girl, Hagar, the Egyptian, and gave her to her husband Abram to be his wife, after Abram had lived ten years in the land of Canaan. [4]And he went in to Hagar and she conceived; and she saw that she had conceived, and her mistress was despised in her

4713 8198 3205 3808 87 802 8297
1 וְשָׂרַי אֵשֶׁת אַבְרָם לֹא יָלְדָה לוֹ וְלָהּ שִׁפְחָה מִצְרִית
an Egyptian | a (was) ,slave-girl | to and her | to ;him | did bear | not | Abram | the of wife | And Sarai

6113 2009 87 8297 559 1904 8034
2 וּשְׁמָהּ הָגָר׃ וַתֹּאמֶר שָׂרַי אֶל־אַבְרָם הִנֵּה־נָא עֲצָרַנִי
kept has me | Please ,see | Abram | to | Sarai | said And | .Hagar | and name her

1129 194 8198 935 3205 3068
יְהוָה מִלֶּדֶת בֹּא־נָא אֶל־שִׁפְחָתִי אוּלַי אִבָּנֶה מִמֶּנָּה
from ;her | be may I up built | perhaps | maid-servant | my ;servant | to | please | go in | from ;bearing | Jehovah

87 802 8297 3947 8297 6963 87 8085
3 וַיִּשְׁמַע אַבְרָם לְקוֹל שָׂרָי׃ וַתִּקַּח שָׂרַי אֵשֶׁת־אַבְרָם
,Abram | the of wife | ,Sarai | took And | .Sarai | the to of voice | Abram | and listened

3427 8141 6235 7093 8198 4713 1904
אֶת־הָגָר הַמִּצְרִית שִׁפְחָתָהּ מִקֵּץ עֶשֶׂר שָׁנִים לְשֶׁבֶת
the of of living | years | ten | after | her maid-servant | ,Egyptian the | ,Hagar

802 376 87 5414 776 87
אַבְרָם בְּאֶרֶץ כְּנָעַן וַתִּתֵּן אֹתָהּ לְאַבְרָם אִישָׁהּ לוֹ לְאִשָּׁה׃
a for .wife | to him | her ,husband | to Abram | her | she and gave | ;Canaan | the in of land | Abram

1404 7043 2209 7200 2029 1904 935
4 וַיָּבֹא אֶל־הָגָר וַתַּהַר וַתֵּרֶא כִּי הָרָתָה וַתֵּקַל גְּבִרְתָּהּ
her mistress | was and despised | had she ,conceived | that | she and saw | she and ;conceived | Hagar to | he And in went

eyes. [5]And Sarai said to
Abram, My injury be upon
you; I gave my slave-girl
into your bosom, and she
saw that she had conceived,
and I was despised in her
eyes. Let Jehovah judge
between me and you. [6]But
Abram said to Sarai, See,
your slave-girl is in your
hand. Do to her what is
good in your eyes. And
Sarai dealt harshly with her,
and she fled from before
her.

[7]And the Angel of
Jehovah found her by a
fountain of water in the
wilderness; by the fountain
in the way of Shur. [8]And He
said, Hagar, Sarai's slave-
girl, where did you come
from? And where do you go?
And she said, I am fleeing
from the face of my
mistress, Sarai. [9]And the
Angel of Jehovah said to
her, Return to your mistress
and submit yourself under
her hand. [10]And the Angel
of Jehovah said to her, I will
exceedingly multiply your
seed, so that it shall not be
numbered for multitude.
[11]And the Angel of Jehovah
said to her, See you are with
child and shall bear a son;
and you shall call his name
Ishmael, because Jehovah
has attended to your affliction. [12]And he shall be a
wild ass of a man; his hand
against all, and the hand of
everyone against him; and
he shall live before all his
brothers. [13]And she called
the name of Jehovah, the
One speaking to her, You, a
God of vision! For she said,
Even here have I looked
after the One seeing me?
[14]On account of this, the
well was called, The Well of
the Living One Seeing Me.
Behold, *it is* between Kadesh and Bered. [15]And
Hagar bore a son to Abram,
and Abram called the name
of his son whom Hagar

5 בעיניה׃ ותאמר שרי אל־אברם חמסי עליך אנכי נתתי
שפחתי בחיקך ותרא כי הרתה ואקל בעיניה ישפט
6 יהוה ביני וביניך׃ ויאמר אברם אל־שרי הנה שפחתך
בידך עשי־לה הטוב בעיניך ותענה שרי ותברח מפניה׃
7 וימצאה מלאך יהוה על־עין המים במדבר על־העין
8 בדרך שור׃ ויאמר הגר שפחת שרי אי־מזה באת ואנה
9 תלכי ותאמר מפני שרי גברתי אנכי ברחת׃ ויאמר
לה מלאך יהוה שובי אל־גברתך והתעני תחת ידיה׃
10 ויאמר לה מלאך יהוה הרבה ארבה את־זרעך ולא
11 יספר מרב׃ ויאמר לה מלאך יהוה הנך הרה וילדת
בן וקראת שמו ישמעאל כי־שמע יהוה אל־עניך׃
12 והוא יהיה פרא אדם ידו בכל ויד כל בו ועל־פני כל־
13 אחיו ישכן׃ ותקרא שם־יהוה הדבר אליה אתה אל
14 ראי כי אמרה הגם הלם ראיתי אחרי ראי׃ על־כן קרא
15 לבאר באר לחי ראי הנה בין־קדש ובין ברד׃ ותלד
הגר לאברם בן ויקרא אברם שם־בנו אשר־ילדה הגר

bore, Ishmael. [16]And Abram
was eighty-six years old
when Hagar bore Ishmael
to Abram.

CHAPTER 17

[1]And when Abram was
ninety-nine years old,
Jehovah appeared to
Abram and said to him, I am
the Almighty God! Walk
before me and be perfect;
[2]and I will make My covenant between Me and you,
and will multiply you
exceedingly. [3]And Abram
fell on his face. And God
spoke with him, saying, [4]As
for Me,shall be a father of
many nations. [5]And your
name shall be Abraham; for
I have made you a father of
many nations. [6]And I will
make you very fruitful,
greatly *so.* And I will give
you (for) nations. And kings
shall come out of you. [7]And
I will establish My covenant
between Me and you, and
your seed after you in their
generations, for an ever-
lasting covenant, to be a
God to you and to your seed
after you. [8]And I will give to
you and to your seed after
you the land of your
sojourning, all the land of
Canaan, for an everlasting
possession, and I will be
their God.
[9]And God said to Abra-
ham, You shall keep My
covenant, you and your
seed after you in their
generations. [10]This is My
covenant which you shall
keep, between Me and you
and your seed after you:
Every man-child among you
shall be circumcised.

3205 8141 8337 8141 8084 1121 87 3450
16 יִשְׁמָעֵאל׃ וְאַבְרָם בֶּן־שְׁמֹנִים שָׁנָה וְשֵׁשׁ שָׁנִים בְּלֶדֶת־
bore when years six years eighty- was old And Abram .Ishmael

87 3450 1904
הָגָר אֶת־יִשְׁמָעֵאל לְאַבְרָם׃
.Abram to Ishmael Hagar

CAP. XVII יז

CHAPTER 17

3068 7200 8141 8672 8141 8673 1121 87 1961
1 וַיְהִי אַבְרָם בֶּן־תִּשְׁעִים שָׁנָה וְתֵשַׁע שָׁנִים וַיֵּרָא יְהוָה
Jehovah that appeared years (old) and nine years ninety of son a Abram (being) And ,was it

1961 6440 1980 7706 430 559 87
אֶל־אַבְרָם וַיֹּאמֶר אֵלָיו אֲנִי־אֵל שַׁדַּי הִתְהַלֵּךְ לְפָנַי וֶהְיֵה
and be before me Walk the !Almighty God am I to ,him said and Abram to

3966 7235 996 1285 6213 8549
2 תָמִים׃ וְאֶתְּנָה בְרִיתִי בֵּינִי וּבֵינֶךָ וְאַרְבֶּה אוֹתְךָ בִּמְאֹד
very you will and increase and ,you between Me My covenant I and make will ;perfect

559 430 1696 6440 87 5307 3966
3 מְאֹד׃ וַיִּפֹּל אַבְרָם עַל־פָּנָיו וַיְדַבֵּר אִתּוֹ אֱלֹהִים לֵאמֹר׃
,saying ,God with him And spoke his .face on Abram And fell .greatly

3808 7121 1471 1995 1 1961 1285 2009 589
4 אֲנִי הִנֵּה בְרִיתִי אִתָּךְ וְהָיִיתָ לְאַב הֲמוֹן גּוֹיִם׃ וְלֹא־יִקָּרֵא
5
be shall And called not .nations many father a of be shall you and ;you with (is) My covenant !behold ,I

1995 1 85 8034 1961 87 8034 5750
עוֹד אֶת־שִׁמְךָ אַבְרָם וְהָיָה שִׁמְךָ אַבְרָהָם כִּי אַב־הֲמוֹן
of father a many for ,Abraham your name but be shall ;Abram name your longer

1471 5414 3966 6213 6213 1471
6 גּוֹיִם נְתַתִּיךָ׃ וְהִפְרֵתִי אֹתְךָ בִּמְאֹד מְאֹד וּנְתַתִּיךָ לְגוֹיִם
for ;nations will I and you give ,greatly very you will I and fruitful make have I .you made nations

996 1285 6965 5927 4428
7 וּמְלָכִים מִמְּךָ יֵצֵאוּ׃ וַהֲקִמֹתִי אֶת־בְּרִיתִי בֵּינִי וּבֵינֶךָ
and ,you between Me covenant My will I And establish shall .come of out you kings and

1961 5769 1285 8435 310 2233
וּבֵין זַרְעֲךָ אַחֲרֶיךָ לְדֹרֹתָם לִבְרִית עוֹלָם לִהְיוֹת לְךָ
to you be to ;perpetual a for covenant their in ,generations you after your seed and

310 2233 5414 310 2230 430
8 לֵאלֹהִים וּלְזַרְעֲךָ אַחֲרֶיךָ׃ וְנָתַתִּי לְךָ וּלְזַרְעֲךָ אַחֲרֶיךָ
you after to and seed your to you will I And give .you after to and seed your for God a

1961 5769 272 3667/776 4033 776
אֵת אֶרֶץ מְגֻרֶיךָ אֵת כָּל־אֶרֶץ כְּנַעַן לַאֲחֻזַּת עוֹלָם וְהָיִיתִי
I and be will never- ;ending a for possession ,Canaan the of land all your ,sojourning of land the

85 430 559 430
9 לָהֶם לֵאלֹהִים׃ וַיֹּאמֶר אֱלֹהִים אֶל־אַבְרָהָם וְאַתָּה אֶת־
And you ,Abraham to God said And a for .God to them

1285 2088 8435 310 2233 8104 1285
10 בְּרִיתִי תִשְׁמֹר אַתָּה וְזַרְעֲךָ אַחֲרֶיךָ לְדֹרֹתָם׃ זֹאת בְּרִיתִי
My ,covenant is This their in .generations you after your and seed you ,keep shall My covenant

4135 310 2233 996 996 996 8104
אֲשֶׁר תִּשְׁמְרוּ בֵּינִי וּבֵינֵיכֶם וּבֵין זַרְעֲךָ אַחֲרֶיךָ הִמּוֹל
be to circumcised ;you after your seed and between you and between Me you keep shall which

[11]And you shall circumcise the flesh of your foreskin. And it shall be a token of the covenant between Me and you. [12]And a son of eight days shall be circumcised among you, every male in your generation, he that is born in the h ouse, or bought with silver from any son of a foreigner who *is* not of your seed. [13]Surely the child of your house and the purchase of your money must be circumcised. My covenant shall be in your flesh for a perpetual covenant. And an uncircumcised male who is not circumcised *in* the flesh of his foreskin, his soul shall be cut off from his people—he has broken My covenant.

[15]And God said to Abraham, You shall not call your wife Sarai *by* her name Sarai, for Sarah *shall be* her name; [16]and I have blessed her and have also given to you a son from her. Yea, I have blessed her and she shall become nations; kings of people shall be from her. [17]And Abraham fell on his face and laughed. And he said in his heart, Shall *a child* be born to a son of a hundred years? And shall Sarah bear, a daughter of ninety years? [18]And Abraham said to God, O that Ishmael might live before You! [19]And God said, Your wife Sarah truly shall bear you a son, and you shall call his name Isaac. And I have established My covenant with him for a perpetual covenant with his seed after him. [20]And as to Ishmael, I have heard you. Behold, I have blessed him and will make him fruitful and will multiply him exceedingly. He shall father twelve princes, and I will make him a great nation. [21]And

226 1961 6190 1320 5243 2145
11 לָכֶם כָּל־זָכָר׃ וּנְמַלְתֶּם אֵת בְּשַׂר עָרְלַתְכֶם וְהָיָה לְאוֹת
token a it and your flesh the you And male every among
of be shall ;foreskin of circumcise shall child you

2645 4135 3117 8083 996 1285
12 בְּרִית בֵּינִי וּבֵינֵיכֶם׃ וּבֶן־שְׁמֹנַת יָמִים יִמּוֹל לָכֶם כָּל־זָכָר
male every among be shall days eight the And .you and between the
,you circumcised 3701 of son Me covenant

3808 5236 4736 1004 3211 8435
לְדֹרֹתֵיכֶם יְלִיד בָּיִת וּמִקְנַת־כֶּסֶף מִכֹּל בֶּן־נֵכָר אֲשֶׁר לֹא
is who ,stranger from with bought or the in that he your in
not any silver ,house born is ,generation

3701 4731 1004 3211 4135 4135 2233
13 מִזַּרְעֲךָ הוּא׃ הִמּוֹל ׀ יִמּוֹל יְלִיד בֵּיתְךָ וּמִקְנַת כַּסְפֶּךָ
your of the and your the be must Surely .(is) he your of
;silver purchase ,house of child ;circumcised .seed

834 2145 6189 5769 1285 1320 1285 1961
14 וְהָיְתָה בְרִיתִי בִּבְשַׂרְכֶם לִבְרִית עוֹלָם׃ וְעָרֵל ׀ זָכָר אֲשֶׁר
who male an And never- a for flesh your in My shall and
uncircumcised .ending covenant covenant be

5971 2212 3772 6190 1320 4135
לֹא־יִמּוֹל אֶת־בְּשַׂר עָרְלָתוֹ וְנִכְרְתָה הַנֶּפֶשׁ הַהִוא מֵעַמֶּיהָ
his from his soul be shall his the (in) is not
;people off cut foreskin of flesh circumcised

8297 85 430 559 6565 1285
15 אֶת־בְּרִיתִי הֵפַר׃ ס וַיֹּאמֶר אֱלֹהִים אֶל־אַבְרָהָם שָׂרַי
Sarai ,Abraham to God said And has he covenant My
.broken

1288 8034 8283 3588 8297 8034 7121 802
16 אִשְׁתְּךָ לֹא־תִקְרָא אֶת־שְׁמָהּ שָׂרָי כִּי שָׂרָה שְׁמָהּ׃ וּבֵרַכְתִּי
have I and (be shall) Sarah for ;Sarai her (by) shall you not Your
blessed .name her name call wife

1471 1961 1288 1121 5414 1571
אֹתָהּ וְגַם נָתַתִּי מִמֶּנָּה לְךָ בֵּן וּבֵרַכְתִּיהָ וְהָיְתָה לְגוֹיִם
;nations she and have I ,yea ;son a to her from have and ,her
become shall ,her blessed you given also

6711 6440 85 5307 1961 5971 4428
17 מַלְכֵי עַמִּים מִמֶּנָּה יִהְיוּ׃ וַיִּפֹּל אַבְרָהָם עַל־פָּנָיו וַיִּצְחָק
and face his on Abraham fell And .be shall from people kings
;laughed her of

1323 8283 3205 3967 1121 3820 559
וַיֹּאמֶר בְּלִבּוֹ הַלְּבֶן מֵאָה־שָׁנָה יִוָּלֵד וְאִם־שָׂרָה הֲבַת־
daugh- a Sarah And be shall hundred a a To his in he and
of ter ?born years of son ,heart said

3863 430 85 559 3205 8141 8673
18 תִּשְׁעִים שָׁנָה תֵּלֵד׃ וַיֹּאמֶר אַבְרָהָם אֶל־הָאֱלֹהִים לוּ
O ,God to Abraham said And ?bear shall years ninety
that (old)

802 8283 61 430 559 6440 2421 3458
19 יִשְׁמָעֵאל יִחְיֶה לְפָנֶיךָ׃ וַיֹּאמֶר אֱלֹהִים אֲבָל שָׂרָה אִשְׁתְּךָ
your Sarah Truly ,God said And before might Ishmael
wife !You live

1285 6965 3327 8034 7121 1121 3205
יֹלֶדֶת לְךָ בֵּן וְקָרָאתָ אֶת־שְׁמוֹ יִצְחָק וַהֲקִמֹתִי אֶת־בְּרִיתִי
covenant My have I and ;Isaac name his you and a you shall
established call shall son bear

8085 3450 310 2233 5769 1285
20 אִתּוֹ לִבְרִית עוֹלָם לְזַרְעוֹ אַחֲרָיו׃ וּלְיִשְׁמָעֵאל שְׁמַעְתִּיךָ
heard have I as And .him after his with never- a for with
;you ,Ishmael for seed ending covenant him

3966 7235 6509 1288 2009
הִנֵּה ׀ בֵּרַכְתִּי אֹתוֹ וְהִפְרֵיתִי אֹתוֹ וְהִרְבֵּיתִי אֹתוֹ בִּמְאֹד
very him will and ,him will and him have I ,behold
multiply fruitful make blessed

1419 1471 5414 3205 5387 6240 8147
21 מְאֹד שְׁנֵים־עָשָׂר נְשִׂיאִם יוֹלִיד וּנְתַתִּיו לְגוֹי גָּדוֹל׃ וְאֶת־
And .great a will I and shall he ,princes ten (and) two much
nation him make father

I will establish My covenant with Isaac, whom Sarah shall bear to you at this time next year. [22]And He finished talking with him. And God went up from Abraham.

[23]And Abreaham took his son Ishmael and all the children of his house, and all that were bought with his silver — every male among the men of the house of Abraham. And he circumcised the flesh of their foreskins in that same day, even as God spoke to him.

[24]And Abraham was a son of ninety-nine years *when* being circumcised in the flesh of his foreskin. [25]And His son Ishmael was a son of thirteen years *when* being circumcised in the flesh of his foreskin. [26]In the same day that Abraham *was* circumcised, *so was* Ishmael his son. [27]And all the men of his house, born in the house or bought with silver from a son of a foreigner, were circumcised with him.

2088 4150 8283 3205 3327 6965 1285
בְּרִיתִי אָקִים אֶת־יִצְחָק אֲשֶׁר תֵּלֵד לְךָ שָׂרָה לַמּוֹעֵד הַזֶּה
this at Sarah to shall whom ,Isaac with will I My
season you bear establish covenant

430 5927 1696 3615 312 8141
22 בַּשָּׁנָה הָאַחֶרֶת׃ וַיְכַל לְדַבֵּר אִתּוֹ וַיַּעַל אֱלֹהִים מֵעַל
from God and with talking He And .next year
ascended ;him finished

3211 3605 1121 3458 85 3947 85
23 אַבְרָהָם׃ וַיִּקַּח אַבְרָהָם אֶת־יִשְׁמָעֵאל בְּנוֹ וְאֵת כָּל־יְלִידֵי
the all and his Ishmael Abraham And .Abraham
of children ,son took

85 1004 582 2145 3605 3701 4736 1004
בֵיתוֹ וְאֵת כָּל־מִקְנַת כַּסְפּוֹ כָּל־זָכָר בְּאַנְשֵׁי בֵּית אַבְרָהָם
,Abraham's house among male every his purchased all and his
of men the —money with ,house

1696 3117 6106 6190 1320 4135
וַיָּמָל אֶת־בְּשַׂר עָרְלָתָם בְּעֶצֶם הַיּוֹם הַזֶּה כַּאֲשֶׁר דִּבֶּר
said as even ,the day same in their flesh the he and
foreskins of circumcised

4135 8141 8672 8673 1121 85 430
24 אִתּוֹ אֱלֹהִים׃ וְאַבְרָהָם בֶּן־תִּשְׁעִים וָתֵשַׁע שָׁנָה בְּהִמֹּלוֹ
being at years nine ninety- was Abraham And .God to
circumcised (old) him

4135 8141 6240 7969 1121 3458 6190 1320
25 בְּשַׂר עָרְלָתוֹ׃ וְיִשְׁמָעֵאל בְּנוֹ בֶּן־שְׁלֹשׁ עֶשְׂרֵה שָׁנָה בְּהִמֹּלוֹ
being at years thirteen was his And his the in
circumcised (old) son Ishmael .foreskin of flesh

85 4135 2088 3117 6106 6190 1320
26 אֵת בְּשַׂר עָרְלָתוֹ׃ בְּעֶצֶם הַיּוֹם הַזֶּה נִמּוֹל אַבְרָהָם
;Abraham was the day same In .foreskin his the in
circumcised of flesh

3701 4736 1004 3211 1004 582 3605 1121 5458
27 וְיִשְׁמָעֵאל בְּנוֹ׃ וְכָל־אַנְשֵׁי בֵיתוֹ יְלִיד בָּיִת וּמִקְנַת־כֶּסֶף
with bought or the in (whether) his the And .son his and
silver house born ,house of men all Ishmael

4135 5236 1121
מֵאֵת בֶּן־נֵכָר נִמֹּלוּ אִתּוֹ׃
with were a of son from
.him circumcised foreigner

CAP. XVIII ח

CHAPTER 18

CHAPTER 18

[1]And Jehovah appeared to him by the oaks of Mamre. And he *was* sitting at the door of the tent in the heat of the day. [2]And *he* lifted up his eyes and looked; and, behold, three men were standing by him. And he saw, and *he* ran to meet them from the entrance of the tent. And he bowed to the ground. [3]And *he* said, My Lord, if now I have found favor in Your sight, I beg You, do not leave from near Your servant. [4]Please allow a little water to be taken and You wash Your feet, and rest under the tree. [5]And I will bring a bite of bread and will sustain Your heart. Then You may pass on, for

168 6607 3427 4471 437 3068 7200
1 וַיֵּרָא אֵלָיו יְהוָה בְּאֵלֹנֵי מַמְרֵא וְהוּא יֹשֵׁב פֶּתַח־הָאֹהֶל
the the at (was) he and ;Mamre the by Jehovah to And
tent door sitting of oaks him came

5324 582 7969 2009 7200 5869 5375 3117 2527
2 כְּחֹם הַיּוֹם׃ וַיִּשָּׂא עֵינָיו וַיַּרְא וְהִנֵּה שְׁלֹשָׁה אֲנָשִׁים נִצָּבִים
were men three ,lo and and his he And the the in
standing ;looked eyes up lifted .day of heat

776 7812 168 6607 7125 7323 7200
עָלָיו וַיַּרְא וַיָּרָץ לִקְרָאתָם מִפֶּתַח הָאֹהֶל וַיִּשְׁתַּחוּ אָרְצָה׃
the to he and the of the from meet to and and by
.ground bowed ,tent door them ran saw he ;him

5674 4994/3808/ 5869 2580 4672 4994 136 559
3 וַיֹּאמַר אֲדֹנָי אִם־נָא מָצָאתִי חֵן בְּעֵינֶיךָ אַל־נָא תַעֲבֹר מֵעַל
from do beg I not Your in favor have I ,please if My (he) And
near leave ,you ,sight found Lord said

8478 8172 7272 7364 4325 4595 4994/3947 5650
4 עַבְדֶּךָ׃ יֻקַּח־נָא מְעַט־מַיִם וְרַחֲצוּ רַגְלֵיכֶם וְהִשָּׁעֲנוּ תַּחַת
under rest and ;feet Your and water a Please let Your
wash you little ,taken be .servant

5674 310 3822 5582 3899 3947 6086
5 הָעֵץ׃ וְאֶקְחָה פַת־לֶחֶם וְסַעֲדוּ לִבְּכֶם אַחַר תַּעֲבֹרוּ כִּי־
for may You then Your and ,bread a let And the
,on go ;heart sustain of bite bring me tree

this is why You have passed
over to Your servant. And
they said, Do so, as you
have said. [6]And Abraham
ran into the tent to Sarah
and said, Hurry, *prepare*
three measures of fine
meal, knead *it* and make
cakes. [7]And Abraham ran
to the herd and brought a
son of the herd, tender and
good, and gave *it* to a youth.
And he hurried to prepare it.
[8]And he took curds and milk
and the son of the herd
which he had prepared, and
he set them before them.
And he stood by them
under the tree. And they
ate.

[9]And they said to him,
Where is your wife Sarah?
And he said, See, in the
tent. [10]And He said, I will
certainly return to you at the
time of life; and, behold, a
son *shall he* to your wife
Sarah. And Sarah *was*
listening at the entrance to
the tent, and it *was* behind
Him. [11]And Abraham and
Sarah *were* aged, going on
in days. The custom as to
women had ceased to be
to Sarah. [12]And Sarah
laughed within herself, saying, After my being old,
shall there be pleasure to
me, my lord also being old?
[13]And Jehovah said to
Abraham, Why has Sarah
laughed at this, saying,
Indeed, truly shall I bear,
even I who am old? [14]Is
anything too difficult for
Jehovah? At the appointed
time I will return to you, at
the time of life, and *there
will be* a son to Sarah.
[15]And Sarah denied, saying,
I did not laugh—for she was
afraid. And He said, No, but
you did laugh.

[16]And the men rose up
from there and looked
on the face of Sodom. And
Abraham was going with
them, to send them away.

עַל־כֵּן עֲבַרְתֶּם עַל־עַבְדְּכֶם וַיֹּאמְרוּ כֵּן תַּעֲשֶׂה כַּאֲשֶׁר
as | Do | so | they said And | Your servant | to | have You passed over | this why is

6 דִּבַּרְתָּ׃ וַיְמַהֵר אַבְרָהָם הָאֹהֱלָה אֶל־שָׂרָה וַיֹּאמֶר מַהֲרִי
,Hurry | ,said and | Sarah | to | the into tent | Abraham | ran And | have you said

7 שְׁלֹשׁ סְאִים קֶמַח סֹלֶת לוּשִׁי וַעֲשִׂי עֻגוֹת׃ וְאֶל־הַבָּקָר
oxen the And | .cakes | and make | knead (it) | fine | meal | measures | three of

רָץ אַבְרָהָם וַיִּקַּח בֶּן־בָּקָר רַךְ וָטוֹב וַיִּתֵּן אֶל־הַנַּעַר וַיְמַהֵר
he and hurried | the ;youth | to | and gave | and ,good | tender | the of a ,herd son | and brought | Abraham | ran

8 לַעֲשׂוֹת אֹתוֹ׃ וַיִּקַּח חֶמְאָה וְחָלָב וּבֶן־הַבָּקָר אֲשֶׁר עָשָׂה
had he ,prepared | which | the son a and herd of | and ,milk | curds | he And took | .it | to prepare

וַיִּתֵּן לִפְנֵיהֶם וְהוּא־עֹמֵד עֲלֵיהֶם תַּחַת הָעֵץ וַיֹּאכֵלוּ׃
they and .ate | the ,tree | under | them by | was he And standing | before .them | set and

9 וַיֹּאמְרוּ אֵלָיו אַיֵּה שָׂרָה אִשְׁתֶּךָ וַיֹּאמֶר הִנֵּה בָאֹהֶל׃
the in .tent | ,See | he And said | ?wife your | Sarah | Where is | ,him to | And said they

10 וַיֹּאמֶר שׁוֹב אָשׁוּב אֵלֶיךָ כָּעֵת חַיָּה וְהִנֵּה־בֵן לְשָׂרָה
(be shall) Sarah to | behold and son a | ;life | the at of time | you to | will I return | certainly | He And ,said

11 אִשְׁתֶּךָ וְשָׂרָה שֹׁמַעַת פֶּתַח הָאֹהֶל וְהוּא אַחֲרָיו׃ וְאַבְרָהָם
Now Abraham | behind .him | it and (was) | the tent | the at of door | (was) listening | and Sarah | your ;wife

וְשָׂרָה זְקֵנִים בָּאִים בַּיָּמִים חָדַל לִהְיוֹת לְשָׂרָה אֹרַח
the custom | to Sarah | be to | had it ceased | ;days in | advancing | (were) old | and Sarah

12 כַּנָּשִׁים׃ וַתִּצְחַק שָׂרָה בְּקִרְבָּהּ לֵאמֹר אַחֲרֵי בְלֹתִי
my old being | After | ,saying | within ,herself | Sarah | And laughed | to as .women

13 הָיְתָה־לִּי עֶדְנָה וַאדֹנִי זָקֵן׃ וַיֹּאמֶר יְהוָה אֶל־אַבְרָהָם
,Abraham | to | Jehovah | said And | being ?old | lord my also | ,pleasure | there shall me to be

לָמָּה זֶּה צָחֲקָה שָׂרָה לֵאמֹר הַאַף אֻמְנָם אֵלֵד וַאֲנִי זָקַנְתִּי׃
am ?old | who even | shall ,bear I | truly | ,Indeed | ,saying | ,Sarah | has laughed | at this | Why

14 הֲיִפָּלֵא מֵיְהוָה דָּבָר לַמּוֹעֵד אָשׁוּב אֵלֶיךָ כָּעֵת חַיָּה
,life | the at of time | ,you to | will I return | the at time set | ?anything | for Jehovah | Is hard too

15 וּלְשָׂרָה בֵן׃ וַתְּכַחֵשׁ שָׂרָה לֵאמֹר לֹא צָחַקְתִּי כִּי
for | did I —laugh | not | ,saying | ;Sarah | Then denied | a son | to and Sarah

16 יָרֵאָה וַיֹּאמֶר לֹא כִּי צָחָקְתְּ׃ וַיָּקֻמוּ מִשָּׁם הָאֲנָשִׁים
men the | from there | And up rose | did you .laugh | but | ,No | He And ,said | was she afraid

וַיַּשְׁקִפוּ עַל־פְּנֵי סְדֹם וְאַבְרָהָם הֹלֵךְ עִמָּם לְשַׁלְּחָם׃
send to away them | with ,them | was going | and Abraham | ;Sodom | the on of face | and looked

[17]And Jehovah said, Shall I hide from Abraham that which I am doing? [18]And Abraham shall become a great and powerful nation, and all the nations of the earth shall be blessed in him? [19]For I have known him, so that whatever he may command his sons and his house after him, even they may keep the way of Jehovah, to do righteousness and justice; to the intent that Jehovah may bring on Abraham that which He has spoken of him. [20]And Jehovah said, The cry of Sodom and Gomorrah is great, and their sin is exceedingly heavy. [21]I will go down and see if they have at all done according to the cry coming to Me. And if not, I will know.

[22]And the men faced around from there and went toward Sodom. And Abraham was still standing before Jehovah. [23]And Abraham drew near and said, Is it so? Will You cut off the righteous with the wicked? [24]Perhaps there are fifty righteous within the city; is it so You will cut off and will not spare the place for the sake of the fifty righteous ones that are within it? [25]Far be it from You to act in this way, to put to death the righteous with the wicked, that the righteous should be as the wicked. Far be it from You. The Judge of all the earth, shall He not do right?

[26]And Jehovah said, If I find fifty righteous within the city, in Sodom, then I will spare all the place because of them. [27]And Abraham answered and said, Behold, I beg You, I have undertaken to speak to the Lord, and I am dust and ash. [28]Perhaps there will be lacking from the

6213 834 85 3680 559 3068
17 וַיהוָה אָמָר הַֽמְכַסֶּה אֲנִי מֵאַבְרָהָם אֲשֶׁר אֲנִי עֹשֶֽׂה׃
am I that from I be Shall ,said And
?doing which Abraham hiding Jehovah

1471 3605 1288 6099 1419 1471 1961 85
18 וְאַבְרָהָם הָיוֹ יִהְיֶה לְגוֹי גָּדוֹל וְעָצוּם וְנִבְרְכוּ־בוֹ כֹּל גּוֹיֵי
the all be shall and and great a shall surely And
of nations him in blessed ;powerful nation become Abraham

1004 1121 6680 3045 776
19 הָאָֽרֶץ׃ כִּי יְדַעְתִּיו לְמַעַן אֲשֶׁר יְצַוֶּה אֶת־בָּנָיו וְאֶת־בֵּיתוֹ
his and sons his may he what- order in have I For ,earth the
house command ever that ,him known

4941 6666 6213 3068 1870 8104 310
אַחֲרָיו וְשָֽׁמְרוּ דֶּרֶךְ יְהוָה לַעֲשׂוֹת צְדָקָה וּמִשְׁפָּט לְמַעַן
order in and righteous- do to ,Jehovah way the they and after
that ;justice ness of keep may ;him

559 1696 85 3068 935
20 הָבִיא יְהוָה עַל־אַבְרָהָם אֵת אֲשֶׁר־דִּבֶּר עָלָֽיו׃ וַיֹּאמֶר
said And .him of has He which that Abraham on Jehovah may
spoken bring

3513 3588 2403 7227 6017 5467 2201 3068
יְהוָה זַעֲקַת סְדֹם וַעֲמֹרָה כִּי־רָבָּה וְחַטָּאתָם כִּי כָבְדָה
is it because and it because and Sodom cry The Jeho-
heavy sin their great is Gomorrah of vah

3588 6213 935/6818 7200 3381 3966
21 מְאֹֽד׃ אֵֽרְדָה־נָּא וְאֶרְאֶה הַכְּצַעֲקָתָהּ הַבָּאָה אֵלַי עָשׂוּ ׀
they Me to is that according if see and now go will I ,very
done have coming cry its to down

5467 3212 582 8033 6437 3045 3615
22 כָּלָה וְאִם־לֹא אֵדָֽעָה׃ וַיִּפְנוּ מִשָּׁם הָאֲנָשִׁים וַיֵּלְכוּ סְדֹמָה
toward and men the from And will I ,not and ;all at
;Sodom went there turned know if

559 85 5066 3068 6440 5975 5750 85
23 וְאַבְרָהָם עוֹדֶנּוּ עֹמֵד לִפְנֵי יְהוָֽה׃ וַיִּגַּשׁ אַבְרָהָם וַיֹּאמַר
,said and Abraham And .Jehovah before was still And
near came standing Abraham

6662 2572 3426 194 7568 5973 4662 5595
24 הַאַף תִּסְפֶּה צַדִּיק עִם־רָשָֽׁע׃ אוּלַי יֵשׁ חֲמִשִּׁים צַדִּיקִם
righteous fifty there Perhaps the with the will You it Is
are ?wicked righteous off cut so

2472 4616 4725 5375 5595 5892 8432
בְּתוֹךְ הָעִיר הַאַף תִּסְפֶּה וְלֹא־תִשָּׂא לַמָּקוֹם לְמַעַן חֲמִשִּׁים
fifty the for place the sparing and will You it Is the with-
not ,off cut so ;city in

1697 6213 2486 7130 834 6662
25 הַצַּדִּיקִם אֲשֶׁר בְּקִרְבָּֽהּ׃ חָלִלָה לְּךָ מֵעֲשֹׂת ׀ כַּדָּבָר
way in act to from it be Far within are that righteous
You ?it

2486 7563 6662 1961 7563 6662 4191 2088
הַזֶּה לְהָמִית צַדִּיק עִם־רָשָׁע וְהָיָה כַצַּדִּיק כָּרָשָׁע חָלִלָה
it be Far the so the as and the with the to ,this
;wicked righteous be should ,wicked righteous execute

3068 559 4941 6213 776 8199
26 לָּךְ הֲשֹׁפֵט כָּל־הָאָרֶץ לֹא יַעֲשֶׂה מִשְׁפָּֽט׃ וַיֹּאמֶר יְהוָה
,Jehovah said And ?right shall not ,earth the all The from
do He of Judge .You

5375 5892 8432 6662 2472 5467 4672
אִם־אֶמְצָא בִסְדֹם חֲמִשִּׁים צַדִּיקִם בְּתוֹךְ הָעִיר וְנָשָׂאתִי
I then ,city the within righteous fifty Sodom in find I If
spare will

2009 559 85 6030 4725 3605
27 לְכָל־הַמָּקוֹם בַּעֲבוּרָֽם׃ וַיַּעַן אַבְרָהָם וַיֹּאמַר הִנֵּה־נָא
,now Be- ,said and Abraham And of because place the all
hold answered them

2637 194 665 6083 136 1696 2974
28 הוֹאַלְתִּי לְדַבֵּר אֶל־אֲדֹנָי וְאָנֹכִי עָפָר וָאֵֽפֶר׃ אוּלַי יַחְסְרוּן
be will Perhaps and dust I and ,Lord the to speak to have I
lacking .ash am undertaken

fifty righteous; will You destroy all the city for the five? And He said, If I find forty-five there I will not destroy. [29]And he continued still to speak to Him and said, Perhaps forty will be found there. And He said, I will not do *it* because of the forty. [30]And he said, Please do not let my Lord be angry, that I may speak; perhaps thirty will be found there. And He said, I will not do *it* if I find thirty there. [31]And he said, Behold, now I have undertaken to speak to the Lord; perhaps twenty will be found there. And He said, I will not destroy because of the twenty. [32]And he said, Let not my Lord be angry now that I may speak only this time; perhaps ten will be found there. And He said, I will not destroy because of the ten. [33]And when He had finished speaking to Abraham Jehovah left. And Abraham returned to his place.

חֲמִשִּׁים הַצַּדִּיקִם חֲמִשָּׁה הֲתַשְׁחִית בַּחֲמִשָּׁה אֶת־כָּל־
all five the for You will destroy ;five righteous the (from) fifty

הָעִיר וַיֹּאמֶר לֹא אַשְׁחִית אִם־אֶמְצָא שָׁם אַרְבָּעִים וַחֲמִשָּׁה׃
.five forty- there find I if will I destroy not He And ,said the ?city

29 וַיֹּסֶף עוֹד לְדַבֵּר אֵלָיו וַיֹּאמַר אוּלַי יִמָּצְאוּן שָׁם אַרְבָּעִים
.forty there be will found Perhaps ,said and Him to speak to still he And went on

30 וַיֹּאמֶר לֹא אֶעֱשֶׂה בַּעֲבוּר הָאַרְבָּעִים׃ וַיֹּאמֶר אַל־נָא יִחַר
Be angry now not ,said he And .forty the of because will I (it) do not He And ,said

לַאדֹנָי וַאֲדַבֵּרָה אוּלַי יִמָּצְאוּן שָׁם שְׁלֹשִׁים וַיֹּאמֶר לֹא
not He And ,said .thirty there will found be perhaps may I that ;speak my ,Lord

31 אֶעֱשֶׂה אִם־אֶמְצָא שָׁם שְׁלֹשִׁים׃ וַיֹּאמֶר הִנֵּה־נָא הוֹאַלְתִּי
have I undertaken ,Behold now he And ,said .thirty there find I if will I (it) do

לְדַבֵּר אֶל־אֲדֹנָי אוּלַי יִמָּצְאוּן שָׁם עֶשְׂרִים וַיֹּאמֶר לֹא
not He And ,said .twenty there be will found perhaps the ;Lord to to speak

32 אַשְׁחִית בַּעֲבוּר הָעֶשְׂרִים׃ וַיֹּאמֶר אַל־נָא יִחַר לַאדֹנָי
my ,Lord Be angry now not he And ,said .twenty the because of will I destroy

וַאֲדַבְּרָה אַךְ־הַפַּעַם אוּלַי יִמָּצְאוּן שָׁם עֲשָׂרָה וַיֹּאמֶר לֹא
not He And ,said .ten there be will found perhaps this ;time only may I that speak

33 אַשְׁחִית בַּעֲבוּר הָעֲשָׂרָה׃ וַיֵּלֶךְ יְהוָה כַּאֲשֶׁר כִּלָּה לְדַבֵּר
speaking had He finished when Jehovah And off left .then the of because will I destroy

אֶל־אַבְרָהָם וְאַבְרָהָם שָׁב לִמְקֹמוֹ׃
his to .place returned and Abraham ;Abraham to

CAP. XIX יט

CHAPTER 19

[1]And the two angels came into Sodom at evening. And Lot was sitting at the gate of Sodom. And Lot saw, and *he* rose up to meet them and bowed his face to the earth. [2]And he said, Behold, now, my lords, please turn into your servant's house and lodge, and wash your feet; and rise early and go to your way. And they said, No, for we will lodge in the street. [3]And he much urged them, and they turned in to him and came into his house.

1 וַיָּבֹאוּ שְׁנֵי הַמַּלְאָכִים סְדֹמָה בָּעֶרֶב וְלוֹט יֹשֵׁב בְּשַׁעַר־
the at of gate was sitting and Lot at ;evening Sodom into angels the two And came

סְדֹם וַיַּרְא־לוֹט וַיָּקָם לִקְרָאתָם וַיִּשְׁתַּחוּ אַפַּיִם אָרְצָה׃
the to .earth face his and bowed meet to ,them rose and up Lot And (them) saw .Sodom

2 וַיֹּאמֶר הִנֶּה־נָּא אֲדֹנַי סוּרוּ נָא אֶל־בֵּית עַבְדְּכֶם וְלִינוּ
and stay your servant's house into please turn, my ,lords ,now Behold he And ,said

וְרַחֲצוּ רַגְלֵיכֶם וְהִשְׁכַּמְתֶּם וַהֲלַכְתֶּם לְדַרְכְּכֶם וַיֹּאמְרוּ
they And ,said your to .way go and early rise and ;feet your and wash

3 לֹּא כִּי בָרְחוֹב נָלִין׃ וַיִּפְצַר־בָּם מְאֹד וַיָּסֻרוּ אֵלָיו וַיָּבֹאוּ
and came him to they and in turned ,much them he And urged will we ,stay the in street for ,No

And he made a feast for them. And he baked cakes, and they ate. 4Before they had laid down, even the men of the city, the men of Sodom, surrounded the house; from the young to the aged, all the people from the limits. 5And they called to Lot and said to him, Where are the men who came to you tonight? Bring them out to us that we may know them. 6And Lot went out to them, to the door, and he closed the door behind him. 7And he said, My brothers, please do not act evilly. 8Behold, now, I have two daughters who have not known a man; please let me bring them out to you and do to them as you see fit. Only do not do a thing to these men, because on this account they came under my roof.

9And they said, Stand back! And they said, This one came in to visit, and must he always judge? Now we will do evil to you rather than to them. And they pressed on the man, upon Lot violently, and drew near to break the door. 10But the men put out their hands and pulled Lot to them, into the house, and shut the door. 11And they struck the men at the door of the house with blindness, from the small to the great; and they struggled to find the door. 12And the men said to Lot, Who still *is* here to you? Bring out of this place your sons and your sons-in-laws and your daughters, and whoever *belongs* to you in the city. 13For we are about to destroy this place, for the cry of them *is* great before Jehovah, and Jehovah has sent us to destroy it.

4 אֶל־בֵּיתוֹ וַיַּעַשׂ לָהֶם מִשְׁתֶּה וּמַצּוֹת אָפָה וַיֹּאכֵלוּ׃ טֶרֶם
יִשְׁכָּבוּ וְאַנְשֵׁי הָעִיר אַנְשֵׁי סְדֹם נָסַבּוּ עַל־הַבַּיִת מִנַּעַר
5 וְעַד־זָקֵן כָּל־הָעָם מִקָּצֶה׃ וַיִּקְרְאוּ אֶל־לוֹט וַיֹּאמְרוּ לוֹ
אַיֵּה הָאֲנָשִׁים אֲשֶׁר־בָּאוּ אֵלֶיךָ הַלָּיְלָה הוֹצִיאֵם אֵלֵינוּ
6 וְנֵדְעָה אֹתָם׃ וַיֵּצֵא אֲלֵהֶם לוֹט הַפֶּתְחָה וְהַדֶּלֶת סָגַר
7 אַחֲרָיו׃ וַיֹּאמַר אַל־נָא אַחַי תָּרֵעוּ׃ הִנֵּה־נָא לִי שְׁתֵּי בָנוֹת
8 אֲשֶׁר לֹא־יָדְעוּ אִישׁ אוֹצִיאָה־נָּא אֶתְהֶן אֲלֵיכֶם וַעֲשׂוּ לָהֶן
כַּטּוֹב בְּעֵינֵיכֶם רַק לָאֲנָשִׁים הָאֵל אַל־תַּעֲשׂוּ דָבָר כִּי־עַל
9 כֵּן בָּאוּ בְּצֵל קֹרָתִי׃ וַיֹּאמְרוּ ׀ גֶּשׁ־הָלְאָה וַיֹּאמְרוּ הָאֶחָד
בָּא־לָגוּר וַיִּשְׁפֹּט שָׁפוֹט עַתָּה נָרַע לְךָ מֵהֶם וַיִּפְצְרוּ בָאִישׁ
10 בְּלוֹט מְאֹד וַיִּגְּשׁוּ לִשְׁבֹּר הַדָּלֶת׃ וַיִּשְׁלְחוּ הָאֲנָשִׁים אֶת־
יָדָם וַיָּבִיאוּ אֶת־לוֹט אֲלֵיהֶם הַבָּיְתָה וְאֶת־הַדֶּלֶת סָגָרוּ׃
11 וְאֶת־הָאֲנָשִׁים אֲשֶׁר־פֶּתַח הַבַּיִת הִכּוּ בַּסַּנְוֵרִים מִקָּטֹן
12 וְעַד־גָּדוֹל וַיִּלְאוּ לִמְצֹא הַפָּתַח׃ וַיֹּאמְרוּ הָאֲנָשִׁים אֶל־
לוֹט עֹד מִי־לְךָ פֹה חָתָן וּבָנֶיךָ וּבְנֹתֶיךָ וְכֹל אֲשֶׁר־לְךָ בָּעִיר
13 הוֹצֵא מִן־הַמָּקוֹם׃ כִּי־מַשְׁחִתִים אֲנַחְנוּ אֶת־הַמָּקוֹם הַזֶּה
כִּי־גָדְלָה צַעֲקָתָם אֶת־פְּנֵי יְהוָה וַיְשַׁלְּחֵנוּ יְהוָה לְשַׁחֲתָהּ׃

[14] And Lot went out to speak to his sons-in-laws, those taking his daughters. And *he* said, Rise up, go out from this place, for Jehovah is about to destroy the city. And he seemed as one joking to his sons-in-laws. [15] And when the dawn rose, then the angels urged Lot, saying, Rise up, take your wife and your two daughters who *are* found, lest you be cut off in the perversity of the city. [16] And he lingered. And the men lay hold of his hand and the hand of his wife, and on the hand of his two daughters., Jehovah having mercy on him. And they caused him to go out, and *they* put him down outside the city. [17] And it happened as they led them outside, he said, Escape for your life! Do not look behind you, and do not stay in all the plain. Escape to the mountain, lest you be consumed. [18] And Lot said to them, Oh no, Lord!

[19] Behold, now, Your servant has found grace in Your sight, and You have magnified Your mercy which You have shown to me in saving my life. And I am not able to escape to the mountain lest *some* evil overtake me and I die. [20] Behold, now, this city is near, to flee there, and it *is* a little one. Please let me escape there! Is it not a little thing, that my soul may live? [21] And He said to him, See, I have accepted your face also as to this thing, without overthrowing the city *for* which you have spoken. [22] Hurry, escape there, for I am not able to do anything until you have come there. So the name of the city was called Zoar.

14 וַיֵּצֵא לוֹט וַיְדַבֵּר אֶל־חֲתָנָיו לֹקְחֵי בְנֹתָיו וַיֹּאמֶר קוּמוּ
צְאוּ מִן־הַמָּקוֹם הַזֶּה כִּי־מַשְׁחִית יְהוָה אֶת־הָעִיר וַיְהִי
15 כִמְצַחֵק בְּעֵינֵי חֲתָנָיו׃ וּכְמוֹ הַשַּׁחַר עָלָה וַיָּאִיצוּ הַמַּלְאָכִים
בְּלוֹט לֵאמֹר קוּם קַח אֶת־אִשְׁתְּךָ וְאֶת־שְׁתֵּי בְנֹתֶיךָ
16 הַנִּמְצָאֹת פֶּן־תִּסָּפֶה בַּעֲוֺן הָעִיר׃ וַיִּתְמַהְמָהּ וַיַּחֲזִקוּ
הָאֲנָשִׁים בְּיָדוֹ וּבְיַד־אִשְׁתּוֹ וּבְיַד שְׁתֵּי בְנֹתָיו בְּחֶמְלַת
17 יְהוָה עָלָיו וַיֹּצִאֻהוּ וַיַּנִּחֻהוּ מִחוּץ לָעִיר׃ וַיְהִי כְהוֹצִיאָם
אֹתָם הַחוּצָה וַיֹּאמֶר הִמָּלֵט עַל־נַפְשֶׁךָ אַל־תַּבִּיט אַחֲרֶיךָ
18 וְאַל־תַּעֲמֹד בְּכָל־הַכִּכָּר הָהָרָה הִמָּלֵט פֶּן־תִּסָּפֶה׃ וַיֹּאמֶר
19 לוֹט אֲלֵהֶם אַל־נָא אֲדֹנָי׃ הִנֵּה־נָא מָצָא עַבְדְּךָ חֵן בְּעֵינֶיךָ
וַתַּגְדֵּל חַסְדְּךָ אֲשֶׁר עָשִׂיתָ עִמָּדִי לְהַחֲיוֹת אֶת־נַפְשִׁי
וְאָנֹכִי לֹא אוּכַל לְהִמָּלֵט הָהָרָה פֶּן־תִּדְבָּקַנִי הָרָעָה וָמַתִּי׃
20 הִנֵּה־נָא הָעִיר הַזֹּאת קְרֹבָה לָנוּס שָׁמָּה וְהִוא מִצְעָר
21 אִמָּלְטָה נָּא שָׁמָּה הֲלֹא מִצְעָר הִוא וּתְחִי נַפְשִׁי׃ וַיֹּאמֶר
אֵלָיו הִנֵּה נָשָׂאתִי פָנֶיךָ גַּם לַדָּבָר הַזֶּה לְבִלְתִּי הָפְכִּי אֶת־
22 הָעִיר אֲשֶׁר דִּבַּרְתָּ׃ מַהֵר הִמָּלֵט שָׁמָּה כִּי לֹא אוּכַל
לַעֲשׂוֹת דָּבָר עַד־בֹּאֲךָ שָׁמָּה עַל־כֵּן קָרָא שֵׁם־הָעִיר

[23]The sun had risen on the earth, and Lot came into Zoar.

[24]And Jehovah rained brimstone and fire on Sodom and Gomorrah, from Jehovah out of the heavens. [25]And He overthrew those cities, and all the plain, and all those living in the cities, and the produce of the ground. [26]And his wife looked back from behind him, and she became a pillar of salt.

[27]And Abraham started up early in the morning, *going* to the place where he had stood there before Jehovah. [28]And he gazed toward Sodom and Gomorrah, and toward all the land of the plain. And he saw. And, behold, the smoke of the country went up like the smoke of a furnace. [29]And when God destroyed the cities of the plain, God remembered Abraham; and he sent Lot out from the overthrow when overturning the cities in which Lot lived.

[30]And Lot went up out of Zoar and lived in the mount. And his two daughters *were* with him. For he feared to live in Zoar. And he lived in a cave, he and his two daughters. [31]And the firstborn said to the younger, Our father is old, and there is no man in the land to come in to us as *is* the way of all the earth. [32]Come, let us make our father drink wine, and let us lie with him, that we may keep seed of our father.

[33]And they caused their father to drink wine that night. And the firstborn went in and lay with her father. And he did not know when she lay down nor when we rose up. [34]And on the next day it happened, the firstborn said to the younger, Behold, I lay with

3068 6820 935 3876 776 5921 3318 8121 6820
23 24 צוער׃ השמש יצא על־הארץ ולוט בא צערה׃ ויהוה
And into entered and ,earth the on had sun The .Zoar
Jehovah .Zoar Lot risen

3068 784 4614 6017 5467 4305
המטיר על־סדם ועל־עמרה גפרית ואש מאת יהוה מן
out Jehovah from and brimstone ,Gomorrah and Sodom on rained
of fire on

3603 3605 411 5892 2015 8064
25 השמים׃ ויהפך את־הערים האל ואת כל־הככר ואת
and ,plain the all and ,those cities He And the
overthrew .heavens

310 802 5027 127 6780 5892 3427
26 כל־ישבי הערים וצמח האדמה׃ ותבט אשתו מאחריו
from wife his And .ground the the and ,cities the those all
,him behind back looked of increase in living

4725 1242 85 7925 4417 5333 1961
27 ותהי נציב מלח׃ וישכם אברהם בבקר אל־המקום
place the to the in Abraham And .salt pillar a she and
morning early arose of became

5467 6440 8259 3068 6440 8033 5975
28 אשר־עמד שם את־פני יהוה׃ וישקף על־פני סדם
Sodom toward he And .Jehovah before there had he where
looked stood

7008 5927 2009 7200 3603 776 3605 6017
ועמרה ועל כל־פני ארץ הככר וירא והנה עלה קיטר
the went ,and he and ;plain the the of all and and
of smoke up ,lo ,saw of land toward ,Gomorrah

5892 430 7843 8574 7008 776
29 הארץ כקיטר הכבשן׃ ויהי בשחת אלהים את־ערי
cities the God when And .furnace a the as the
of destroyed of smoke country

8432 3876 7971 85 430 2142 3603
הככר ויזכר אלהים את־אברהם וישלח את־לוט מתוך
out Lot he and ;Abraham God remembered the
from sent ,plain

5927 3876 2004 3427 834 5892 2015 2019
30 ההפכה בהפך את־הערים אשר־ישב בהן לוט׃ ויעל
And .Lot them in lived which cities the in over- the
up went overturning ,throw

3427 3372 1323 8147 2022 3427 6820 3876
לוט מצוער וישב בהר ושתי בנתיו עמו כי ירא לשבת
live to he For (lived) his two and the in and of out Lot
feared ,him with daughters ;height lived Zoar

1067 559 1323 8147 4631 3427 6820
31 בצוער וישב במערה הוא ושתי בנתיו׃ ותאמר הבכירה
the said And his two and he ,cave a in he and ;Zoar in
firstborn .daughters lived

935 776 376 2204 1 6810
אל־הצעירה אבינו זקן ואיש אין בארץ לבוא עלינו
us to come to the in there a and is Our ,younger the to
in land no is man ,old father

7901 3196 1 8248 3212 776 3605 1870
32 כדרך כל־הארץ׃ לכה נשקה את־אבינו יין ונשכבה
let and ,wine father our make us let ,Come .earth the all (is) as
lie us drink of way the

3915 3146 1 8248 2233 1 2421
33 עמו ונחיה מאבינו זרע׃ ותשקין את־אביהן יין בלילה
night wine father their they And .seed our of keep and with
drink made seed father alive ,him

7901 3045 1 7901 1067 935
הוא ותבא הבכירה ותשכב את־אביה ולא־ידע בשכבה
she when did he and her with lay and firstborn the and ;that
down lay know not ;father in went

6810 1067 559 4283 1961 6965
34 ובקומה׃ ויהי ממחרת ותאמר הבכירה אל־הצעירה
,younger the to firstborn the said and the it And when nor
day next was .arose she

my father last night. Let us cause him to drink wine tonight also. And you go in and lie with him, so that we may keep alive seed of our father. [35]And they caused their father to drink wine that night also. And the younger rose up and lay with him. And he did not know when she lay down, or nor when she rose up. [36]And both the daughters of Lot were with child by their father. [37]And the firstborn bore a son and called his name Moab; he *is* the father of Moab to this kday. [38]And the younger also bore a son and called his name Ben-ammi; he *is* the father of the Ammonites to this day.

935 3915 3196 8248 1 570 7901
הֵן־שָׁכַבְתִּי אֶמֶשׁ אֶת־אָבִי נַשְׁקֶנּוּ יַיִן גַּם־הַלַּיְלָה וּבֹאִי
you and ,tonight also wine make us let my with last lay I Be-
in go drink him ;father night ,hold

1931 3915 1571 8248 2233 1 2421 7901
35 שִׁכְבִי עִמּוֹ וּנְחַיֶּה מֵאָבִינוּ זָרַע׃ וַתַּשְׁקֶיןָ גַּם בַּלַּיְלָה הַהוּא
that night also they And .seed our of we that with lie and
drink to caused father alive keep ,him

3045 7901 6810 6965 3196 1
אֶת־אֲבִיהֶן יַיִן וַתָּקָם הַצְּעִירָה וַתִּשְׁכַּב עִמּוֹ וְלֹא־יָדַע
did he and with lay and younger the and ,wine father their
know not ;him up rose

3205 1 3876 1323 8147 2029 6965 7901
36 בְּשִׁכְבָהּ וּבְקוּמָהּ׃ וַתַּהֲרֶיןָ שְׁתֵּי בְנוֹת־לוֹט מֵאֲבִיהֶן׃ וַתֵּלֶד
37
And their by Lot the both were So when nor she when
bore ,father of daughters child with .arose she down lay

4124 1 1931 4124 8034 7121 1121 1067
הַבְּכִירָה בֵּן וַתִּקְרָא שְׁמוֹ מוֹאָב הוּא אֲבִי־מוֹאָב עַד־
to Moab the (is) he ;Moab name his and son a the
of father called firstborn

5971 1121 8034 7121 1121 3205 1571 6810 3117
38 הַיּוֹם׃ וְהַצְּעִירָה גַם־הִוא יָלְדָה בֵּן וַתִּקְרָא שְׁמוֹ בֶּן־עַמִּי
;ammi Ben- his and son a bore she also the And this
name called younger .day

3117 5704 5983 1
הוּא אֲבִי בְנֵי־עַמּוֹן עַד־הַיּוֹם׃
.day this to Ammonites the the he
of father (is)

CAP. XX כ

CHAPTER 20

CHAPTER 20

[1]And Abraham moved from there to the land of the south, and lived between Kadesh and Shur, and stayed in Gerar. [2]And Abraham said with regards to his wife Sarah, She *is* my sister. And Abimelech the king of Gerar sent and took Sarah. [3]But God came to Abimelech in a dream by night and said to him, Behold, you *are* about to die because of the woman you have taken, she *being* married to a husband. [4]And Abimelech had not come near her. And he said, O Lord, will You slay even a righteous nation? [5]Did he not say to me, She *is* my sister? And she, even she herself said, He *is* my brother. In the honor of my heart and the purity of my hands I have done this. [6]And God said to him in a dream, Yes, I know that you did this in the honor of your heart, and I

996 6946 3427 5045 776 85 5265
1 וַיִּסַּע מִשָּׁם אַבְרָהָם אַרְצָה הַנֶּגֶב וַיֵּשֶׁב בֵּין־קָדֵשׁ וּבֵין
and Kadesh be- and the the to Abraham from And
tween lived ,Negeb of land there moved

169 802 8283 413 85 559 1642 1481 7783
2 שׁוּר וַיָּגָר בִּגְרָר׃ וַיֹּאמֶר אַבְרָהָם אֶל־שָׂרָה אִשְׁתּוֹ אֲחֹתִי
My ,wife his Sarah to Abraham said And .Gerar in he and ;Shur
sister stayed

935 8283 3947 1642 4428 40 7971
3 הִוא וַיִּשְׁלַח אֲבִימֶלֶךְ מֶלֶךְ גְּרָר וַיִּקַּח אֶת־שָׂרָה׃ וַיָּבֹא
But .Sarah and Gerar the Abimelech sent And She
came took of king .(is)

4191 559 3915 2472 40 430
אֱלֹהִים אֶל־אֲבִימֶלֶךְ בַּחֲלוֹם הַלָּיְלָה וַיֹּאמֶר לוֹ הִנְּךָ מֵת
about you ,Lo to and night by dream a in Abimelech to God
,die to (are) ,him said

40 1167 3947 3947 802
4 עַל־הָאִשָּׁה אֲשֶׁר־לָקַחְתָּ וְהִוא בְּעֻלַת בָּעַל׃ וַאֲבִימֶלֶךְ
And a married she have you whom the because
Abimelech .husband to (being) ,taken woman of

2026 6662 1571 1471 136 559 7126
5 לֹא קָרַב אֵלֶיהָ וַיֹּאמַר אֲדֹנָי הֲגוֹי גַּם־צַדִּיק תַּהֲרֹג׃ הֲלֹא
Did You will a even nation O he and ;her come had not
not ?slay righteous ,Lord said near

251 559 1570 1931 269 559
הוּא אָמַר־לִי אֲחֹתִי הִוא וְהִיא־גַם־הִוא אָמְרָה אָחִי הוּא
;(is) he My ,said she even And She my ,me to say he
brother herself she ?(is) sister

430 559 6213 3709 5356 3824 8537
6 בְּתָם־לְבָבִי וּבְנִקְיֹן כַּפַּי עָשִׂיתִי זֹאת׃ וַיֹּאמֶר אֵלָיו הָאֱלֹהִים
God him to And .this have I my the in and my of the in
said done hands of purity heart honor

2820 2088 6213 3824 8537 3045 2472
בַּחֲלֹם גַּם אָנֹכִי יָדַעְתִּי כִּי בְתָם־לְבָבְךָ עָשִׂיתָ זֹּאת וָאֶחְשֹׂךְ
I and ;this did you your the in that know I ,Yes a in
withheld ,heart of honor ,dream

also withheld you from sinning against Me. On account of this I did not allow you to touch her. [7]And now return the wife of the man, for he *is* a prophet, and he will pray for you, and you shall live. And if you do not return *her,* know that you shall surely die, you and all that are yours.

[8]And Abimelech started up early in the morning and called for all his servants. And *he* spoke all these words in their ears. And the men were greatly afraid. [9]And Abimelech called Abraham and said to him, What have you done to us? And in what have I offended you that you have brought on me and on my kingdom a great sin? You have done things to me that ought not to be done. [10]And Abimelech said to Abraham, What did you see that you have done this thing? [11]And Abraham said, Because I thought, Surely the fear of God is not in this place, and they will kill me for my wife's sake. [12]And yet she really is my sister, daughter of my father; only not daughter of my mother. And she became my wife.

[13]And when God made me wander from my father's house I said to her, This *is* your kindness which you do to me: at every place where we come there, say of me, He *is* my brother. [14]Abimelech took sheep and oxen, and male slaves, and slave-girls, and gave to Abraham. And he returned his wife Sarah to him.

[15]Abimelech said, Behold, my land is before you. Live where it pleases you. [16]And he said to Sarah,

5060 2820 3808 3651/5921 7398 1571
גַּם־אָנֹכִי אוֹתְךָ מֵחֲטוֹ־לִי עַל־כֵּן לֹא־נְתַתִּיךָ לִנְגֹּעַ אֵלֶיהָ׃
.her touch to did I not that For against from you I also
6419 you allow 5030 reason .Me sinning

1157 376 802 7725 6258
7 וְעַתָּה הָשֵׁב אֵשֶׁת־הָאִישׁ כִּי־נָבִיא הוּא וְיִתְפַּלֵּל בַּעַדְךָ
,you for he and ,(is) he a for ,wife man's the return Now
pray shall prophet ,then

3605 4191 4191 3045 7725 2421
וֶחְיֵה וְאִם־אֵינְךָ מֵשִׁיב דַּע כִּי־מוֹת תָּמוּת אַתָּה וְכָל־אֲשֶׁר
are that all and you you dying that know restore you if and you and
,die shall (her) not do ;live shall

1696 5650 7121 1242 40 7925
8 לָךְ׃ וַיַּשְׁכֵּם אֲבִימֶלֶךְ בַּבֹּקֶר וַיִּקְרָא לְכָל־עֲבָדָיו וַיְדַבֵּר
and his all for called and the in Abimelech rose And to
spoke servants morning early ,you

3966 582 2372 241 1697 3605
אֶת־כָּל־הַדְּבָרִים הָאֵלֶּה בְּאָזְנֵיהֶם וַיִּירְאוּ הָאֲנָשִׁים מְאֹד׃
.greatly men the were and ;ears their in these words all
afraid

6213 559 85 40 7121
9 וַיִּקְרָא אֲבִימֶלֶךְ לְאַבְרָהָם וַיֹּאמֶר לוֹ מֶה־עָשִׂיתָ לָּנוּ וּמֶה־
and ?us to have What to said and Abraham to Abimelech Then
.what done you ,him called

1419 2401 4467 5921 935 2398
חָטָאתִי לָךְ כִּי־הֵבֵאתָ עָלַי וְעַל־מַמְלַכְתִּי חֲטָאָה גְדֹלָה
?great sin a kingdom my and on have you that to have I
on me brought you offended

40 559 6213 6213 4639
10 מַעֲשִׂים אֲשֶׁר לֹא־יֵעָשׂוּ עָשִׂיתָ עִמָּדִי׃ וַיֹּאמֶר אֲבִימֶלֶךְ
Abimelech said And .me to have You not ought that things
done .done be to

559 2008 1697 6213 7200 85
11 אֶל־אַבְרָהָם מָה רָאִיתָ כִּי עָשִׂיתָ אֶת־הַדָּבָר הַזֶּה׃ וַיֹּאמֶר
said And ?this thing have you that did What ,Abraham to
done see you

2088 4725 430 3373 7535 559 3588 85
אַבְרָהָם כִּי אָמַרְתִּי רַק אֵין־יִרְאַת אֱלֹהִים בַּמָּקוֹם הַזֶּה
;this place in God the not is surely I Be- ,Abraham
of fear ,thought cause

1 1323 269 546 1571 802 3947 2026
12 וַהֲרָגוּנִי עַל־דְּבַר אִשְׁתִּי׃ וְגַם־אָמְנָה אֲחֹתִי בַת־אָבִי הִוא
;is she my daughter my really And .wife's my sake for they and
father of ,sister yet me kill will

8582 802 1961 517
13 אַךְ לֹא בַת־אִמִּי וַתְּהִי־לִי לְאִשָּׁה׃ וַיְהִי כַּאֲשֶׁר הִתְעוּ
made had when And .wife my she and my daughter not only
wander became ,mother of

6213 834 7617 2088 559 1 1004 430
אֹתִי אֱלֹהִים מִבֵּית אָבִי וָאֹמַר לָהּ זֶה חַסְדֵּךְ אֲשֶׁר תַּעֲשִׂי
do you which your This to said I my from God me
kindness (is) ,her ,father's house

251 559 935 834 4725
עִמָּדִי אֶל כָּל־הַמָּקוֹם אֲשֶׁר נָבוֹא שָׁמָּה אִמְרִי־לִי אָחִי
my ,me of say ,there we which place every at :me to
brother come

5414 8198 5650 1241 6629 40 3947
14 הוּא׃ וַיִּקַּח אֲבִימֶלֶךְ צֹאן וּבָקָר וַעֲבָדִים וּשְׁפָחֹת וַיִּתֵּן
and female and male and and sheep Abimelech And .(is) He
gave ,slaves ,slaves ,oxen took

40 559 802 8283 7725 85
15 לְאַבְרָהָם וַיָּשֶׁב לוֹ אֵת שָׂרָה אִשְׁתּוֹ׃ וַיֹּאמֶר אֲבִימֶלֶךְ
,Abimelech said And .wife his Sarah to he and to
him returned ;Abraham

559 8283 3427 5869 2896 6440 776 2009
16 הִנֵּה אַרְצִי לְפָנֶיךָ בַּטּוֹב בְּעֵינֶיךָ שֵׁב׃ וּלְשָׂרָה אָמַר
,said he to And .live your in where before is land my Be-
Sarah eyes good ;you ,hold

I, behold, I have given a thousand of silver to your brother. Behold, it is for you a covering of the eyes to all who *are* with you. And with all *this* you are justified.
[17]And Abraham prayed to God, and God healed Abimelech and his wife and his concubines, and they gave birth. [18]For Jehovah had closed up every womb of the house of Abimelech because of Sarah, the wife of Abraham.

5869 3682 2009 251 3701 505 5414 2009
הִנֵּה נָתַתִּי אֶלֶף כֶּסֶף לְאָחִיךְ הִנֵּה הוּא־לָךְ כְּסוּת עֵינַיִם
eyes the a for is it ,see your to silver thou- a have I Be-
of covering you ;brother of sand given ,hold

85 6419 3198 3605 3605
17 לְכֹל אֲשֶׁר אִתָּךְ וְאֵת כֹּל וְנֹכָחַת׃ וַיִּתְפַּלֵּל אַבְרָהָם אֶל־
to Abraham prayed And are you all and with who to
.justified (this) with ;you (are) all

519 802 40 430 7495 430
הָאֱלֹהִים וַיִּרְפָּא אֱלֹהִים אֶת־אֲבִימֶלֶךְ וְאֶת־אִשְׁתּוֹ וְאַמְהֹתָיו
his and wife his and Abimelech God healed and ;God
,concubines

40 1004 7358 3605 3068 6113 6113 3205
18 וַיֵּלֵדוּ׃ כִּי־עָצֹר עָצַר יְהוָה בְּעַד כָּל־רֶחֶם לְבֵית אֲבִימֶלֶךְ
Abimelech the of womb every Jehovah closed For they and
of house up closing .birth gave

85 802 8283 1697
עַל־דְּבַר שָׂרָה אֵשֶׁת אַבְרָהָם׃ ס
.Abraham's wife ,Sarah of because

CAP. XXI כא

CHAPTER 21

CHAPTER 21

[1]And Jehovah visited Sarah as He had said. Yea, the Lord did to Sarah as He had spoken. [2]And Sarah conceived and bore a son to Abraham in his old age, at the time appointed, that which God had spoken with him. [3]And Abraham called the name of the son who was born to him, whom Sarah had borne to him, Isaac. [4]And Abraham circumcised his son Isaac, a son of eight days, as God had commanded him.
[5]And Abraham was a son of a hundred years when his son Isaac was born to him. [6]And Sarah said, God has made laughter for me; all who hear will laugh with me. [7]And she said to Abraham, Will Sarah suckle sons? For I have borne a son to his old age.
[8]And the child grew and was weaned. And Abraham made a great feast on the day Isaac was weaned. [9]And Sarah saw the son of Hagar the Egyptian, *he* whom she had borne to Abraham, mocking. [10]And she said to Abraham, Drive

8283 3068 6213 559 8283 6485 3068
1 וַיהוָה פָּקַד אֶת־שָׂרָה כַּאֲשֶׁר אָמָר וַיַּעַשׂ יְהוָה לְשָׂרָה
Sarah to Lord the and had He as Sarah visited And
did said Jehovah

2208 1121 85 8283 3205 2029 1696
2 כַּאֲשֶׁר דִּבֵּר׃ וַתַּהַר וַתֵּלֶד שָׂרָה לְאַבְרָהָם בֵּן לִזְקֻנָיו
his in son a Abraham to Sarah bore and For had He as
,age old conceived .promised

85 7121 430 1696 4150
3 לַמּוֹעֵד אֲשֶׁר־דִּבֶּר אֹתוֹ אֱלֹהִים׃ וַיִּקְרָא אַבְרָהָם אֶת־
Abraham called And .God with had that ap- the at
him spoken time pointed

4135 3327 8283 3205 3205 1121 8034
4 שֶׁם־בְּנוֹ הַנּוֹלַד־לוֹ אֲשֶׁר־יָלְדָה־לּוֹ שָׂרָה יִצְחָק׃ וַיָּמָל
And .Isaac ,Sarah him to had whom to was who the the
circumcised borne ,him born son of name

6680 3117 8083 1121 1121 3327 85
אַבְרָהָם אֶת־יִצְחָק בְּנוֹ בֶּן־שְׁמֹנַת יָמִים כַּאֲשֶׁר צִוָּה אֹתוֹ
him had as ,days eight son a his Isaac Abraham
commanded of ,son

3327 3205 8141 3967 85 430
5 אֱלֹהִים׃ וְאַבְרָהָם בֶּן־מְאַת שָׁנָה בְּהִוָּלֶד לוֹ אֵת יִצְחָק
Isaac to when years a son a (was) And .God
him born was hundred of Abraham

8085 430 6213 6712 8283 559 1121
6 בְּנוֹ׃ וַתֹּאמֶר שָׂרָה צְחֹק עָשָׂה לִי אֱלֹהִים כָּל־הַשֹּׁמֵעַ
hear who all ;God for has laughter ,Sarah said And his
me made son

8283 1121 3243 85 4448 559 6717
7 יִצְחַק־לִי׃ וַתֹּאמֶר מִי מִלֵּל לְאַבְרָהָם הֵינִיקָה בָנִים שָׂרָה
?Sarah children Will ,Abraham to could Who she And with will
suckle said have ,said .me laugh

85 6213 1580 3206 1430 2208 1121 3205
8 כִּי־יָלַדְתִּי בֵן לִזְקֻנָיו׃ וַיִּגְדַּל הַיֶּלֶד וַיִּגָּמַל וַיַּעַשׂ אַבְרָהָם
Abraham and was and child the And his to son a have I For
made ,weaned grew .age old borne

8283 7200 3327 1580 3117 1419 4960
9 מִשְׁתֶּה גָדוֹל בְּיוֹם הִגָּמֵל אֶת־יִצְחָק׃ וַתֵּרֶא שָׂרָה אֶת־
Sarah saw And .Isaac was the on great feast a
weaned day

559 6711 85 3205 4713 1904/1121
10 בֶּן־הָגָר הַמִּצְרִית אֲשֶׁר־יָלְדָה לְאַבְרָהָם מְצַחֵק׃ וַתֹּאמֶר
she And .mocking ,Abraham to had she whom the Hagar the
said borne ,Egyptian of son

away this slavegirl and her son, for the son of this slavegirl shall not inherit with my son, with Isaac. [11]And the thing was very crushing in the eyes of Abraham, on account of his son. [12]And God said to Abraham, Let it not be crushing in your eyes because of the boy, and on your slavegirl. All that Sarah says to you, listen to her voice; for in Isaac your seed shall be called. [13]And also I will make a nation of the son of the slavegirl, for he *is* your seed. [14]And Abraham rose early in the morning and took bread and a skin of water. And *he* gave *them* to Hagar, putting *them* on her shoulder, and the boy, and sent her away. And she left and wandered in the wilderness of Beer-sheba.

[15]And the water from the skin was finished. And she put the boy under one of the shrubs. [16]And she went and sat down across from him, about a bowshot away. And *she* raised her voice and wept. [17]And God heard the voice of the young boy. And the angel of God called to Hagar out of the heavens. And he said to her, What ails you, Hagar? Do not fear, for God has heard the voice of the boy, there where he is. [18]Get up; lift up the boy and hold up your hand on him; for I will make a great nation of him. [19]And God opened her eyes, and she saw a well of water. And she went and filled the skin *with* water, and gave drink to the young boy.

לְאַבְרָהָם גָּרֵשׁ הָאָמָה הַזֹּאת וְאֶת־בְּנָהּ כִּי לֹא יִירַשׁ בֶּן
the of son shall inherit not for ;son her and this slave-girl Drive away .Abraham to

11 הָאָמָה הַזֹּאת עִם־בְּנִי עִם־יִצְחָק׃ וַיֵּרַע הַדָּבָר מְאֹד בְּעֵינֵי
the in of eyes very the thing was And evil .Isaac with my ,son with this slave-girl

12 אַבְרָהָם עַל אוֹדֹת בְּנוֹ׃ וַיֹּאמֶר אֱלֹהִים אֶל־אַבְרָהָם אַל־
not ,Abraham to God said And his son account of on ,Abraham

יֵרַע בְּעֵינֶיךָ עַל־הַנַּעַר וְעַל־אֲמָתֶךָ כֹּל אֲשֶׁר תֹּאמַר אֵלֶיךָ
you to says that All slave-girl your and of the boy because of your eyes in it Let evil be

13 שָׂרָה שְׁמַע בְּקֹלָהּ כִּי בְיִצְחָק יִקָּרֵא לְךָ זָרַע׃ וְגַם אֶת־
And ,also .seed your be shall called Isaac in for her voice to listen ,Sarah

14 בֶּן־הָאָמָה לְגוֹי אֲשִׂימֶנּוּ כִּי זַרְעֲךָ הוּא׃ וַיַּשְׁכֵּם אַבְרָהָם ׀
Abraham rose early And (is) he your seed for will I make him of a nation slave-girl of the son the

בַּבֹּקֶר וַיִּקַּח־לֶחֶם וְחֵמַת מַיִם וַיִּתֵּן אֶל־הָגָר שָׂם עַל־
on putting (them) ,Hagar to gave and (them) ,water a skin of and bread and took the in ,morning

שִׁכְמָהּ וְאֶת־הַיֶּלֶד וַיְשַׁלְּחֶהָ וַתֵּלֶךְ וַתֵּתַע בְּמִדְבַּר בְּאֵר
Beer- wilder-ness of the in and wandered she And left sent and away her ,boy the and her ,shoulder

15 שָׁבַע׃ וַיִּכְלוּ הַמַּיִם מִן־הַחֵמֶת וַתַּשְׁלֵךְ אֶת־הַיֶּלֶד תַּחַת
under boy the she and put ;skin the from the water was And gone .sheba

16 אַחַד הַשִּׂיחִם׃ וַתֵּלֶךְ וַתֵּשֶׁב לָהּ מִנֶּגֶד הַרְחֵק כִּמְטַחֲוֵי
a about shot ,away opposite for herself sat and down she And went .shrubs the one of

קֶשֶׁת כִּי אָמְרָה אַל־אֶרְאֶה בְּמוֹת הַיָּלֶד וַתֵּשֶׁב מִנֶּגֶד
opposite she and sat the ;boy death of the me Let see not ,said she For .bow

17 וַתִּשָּׂא אֶת־קֹלָהּ וַתֵּבְךְּ׃ וַיִּשְׁמַע אֱלֹהִים אֶת־קוֹל הַנַּעַר
young the ;boy voice of the God And heard .wept and voice her and raised

וַיִּקְרָא מַלְאַךְ אֱלֹהִים ׀ אֶל־הָגָר מִן־הַשָּׁמַיִם וַיֹּאמֶר לָהּ
to her he and said the ,heavens out of Hagar to God angel of the and called

מַה־לָּךְ הָגָר אַל־תִּירְאִי כִּי־שָׁמַע אֱלֹהִים אֶל־קוֹל הַנַּעַר
the ,boy voice of the God has heard for ,fear Do not ?Hagar ails What ,you

18 בַּאֲשֶׁר הוּא־שָׁם׃ קוּמִי שְׂאִי אֶת־הַנַּעַר וְהַחֲזִיקִי אֶת־
hold and up boy the up lift ,up Get .there he is where

19 יָדֵךְ בּוֹ כִּי־לְגוֹי גָּדוֹל אֲשִׂימֶנּוּ׃ וַיִּפְקַח אֱלֹהִים אֶת־עֵינֶיהָ
,eyes her God And opened make will I .him of great a nation for on him your hand

וַתֵּרֶא בְּאֵר מָיִם וַתֵּלֶךְ וַתְּמַלֵּא אֶת־הַחֵמֶת מַיִם וַתַּשְׁקְ
gave and drink (with) ,water skin the filled and she and went ;water well of a she and saw

[20]And God was with the boy. And he grew up. And he lived in the wilderness and became an archer. [21]And he lived in the wilderness of Parah. And his mother took a wife for him out of the land of Egypt.

[22]And at that time Abimelech and Phicol, the general of his army, spoke to Abraham, saying, God is with you in all that you do. [23]And now swear to me here by God, that you will not lie to me, and to my son, and to my heir, according to the kindness which I have sworn to you. Do to me and to the land in which you have lived. [24]And Abraham said, I will swear. [25]And Abraham reproved Abimelect on account of a well of water which the slaves of Abimelech had seized.

[26]And Abimelech said, I do not know who has done this thing; and also you have not told me, even I have not heard, except today. [27]And Abraham took sheep and oxen and gave to Abimelech, and both of them cut a covenant. [28]And Abraham set seven ewe lambs of the flock by themselves. [29]And Abimelech said to Abraham, What are these seven ewe lambs which you have set by themselves? [30]And he said, You shall take the seven ewe lambs from my hand so that it may become a *for* me a witness that I dug this well. [31]On account of this that place *is* called

4057 3427 1431 5288 430 1961 5288
20 אֶת־הַנַּעַר׃ וַיְהִי אֱלֹהִים אֶת־הַנַּעַר וַיִּגְדָּל וַיֵּשֶׁב בַּמִּדְבָּר
the in wilderness | he and lived | he and grew up | ,boy the with | God | And was | young the .boy | to

802 517 3947 6290 4057 3427 7198 1961
21 וַיְהִי רֹבֶה קַשָּׁת׃ וַיֵּשֶׁב בְּמִדְבַּר פָּארָן וַתִּקַּח־לוֹ אִמּוֹ אִשָּׁה
wife a | his mother | for him | and took | ;Paran | the in of wilderness | he And lived | .archer great a | and became

4714 776
מֵאֶרֶץ מִצְרָיִם׃
.Egypt | the of out of land

6635 8269 40 559 6256
22 וַיְהִי בָּעֵת הַהִוא וַיֹּאמֶר אֲבִימֶלֶךְ וּפִיכֹל שַׂר־צְבָאוֹ אֶל־
to | general the army his of | and Phicol | Abimelech | spoke | ,that | at time | it And was

6213 3605 430 559 85
אַבְרָהָם לֵאמֹר אֱלֹהִים עִמְּךָ בְּכֹל אֲשֶׁר־אַתָּה עֹשֶׂה׃
.do | you | that | all in | with is you | God | ,saying | ,Abraham

5209 8266 2008 430 7650 3046
23 וְעַתָּה הִשָּׁבְעָה לִּי בֵאלֹהִים הֵנָּה אִם־תִּשְׁקֹר לִי וּלְנִינִי
to and ,son my | to ,me | will you lie | that not | ,here | God by | to me | swear | So now

6213 7650 834 2617 5220
וּלְנֶכְדִּי כַּחֶסֶד אֲשֶׁר עָשִׂיתִי עִמְּךָ תַּעֲשֶׂה עִמָּדִי וְעִם־
to and | me to | Do | .you to | have I sworn | which | to according kindness the | to and ;heir my

7650 85 559 1481 776
24 הָאָרֶץ אֲשֶׁר־גַּרְתָּה בָּהּ׃ וַיֹּאמֶר אַבְרָהָם אָנֹכִי אִשָּׁבֵעַ׃
.swear will | I | ,Abraham | said And | .it in | have you lived | which | land the

4325 875 182 40 85 3198
25 וְהוֹכִחַ אַבְרָהָם אֶת־אֲבִימֶלֶךְ עַל־אֹדוֹת בְּאֵר הַמַּיִם אֲשֶׁר
which | water | of well a | of because | Abimelech | Abraham | And reproved

4310 3045 3808 40 559 40 5650 1497
26 גָּזְלוּ עַבְדֵי אֲבִימֶלֶךְ׃ וַיֹּאמֶר אֲבִימֶלֶךְ לֹא יָדַעְתִּי מִי
who | do I know | not | Abimelech | said And | Abimelech | the of slaves | had seized

5869 5046 3808 1571 2088 1697 6213
עָשָׂה אֶת־הַדָּבָר הַזֶּה וְגַם־אַתָּה לֹא־הִגַּדְתָּ לִּי וְגַם אָנֹכִי
I | even | ,me told have not | you also and | ;this | thing | done has

5414 1241 6629 3947 3117 1115 8085 3808
27 לֹא שָׁמַעְתִּי בִּלְתִּי הַיּוֹם׃ וַיִּקַּח אַבְרָהָם צֹאן וּבָקָר וַיִּתֵּן
gave and (them) | and oxen | sheep | Abraham | And took | .today | except | have ,heard | not

85 5324 1285 8147 3772 40
28 לַאֲבִימֶלֶךְ וַיִּכְרְתוּ שְׁנֵיהֶם בְּרִית׃ וַיַּצֵּב אַבְרָהָם אֶת־
Abraham | set And | .covenant a | of both them | cut | and | ,Abimelech to

85 40 559 6629 3535 7657
29 שֶׁבַע כִּבְשֹׂת הַצֹּאן לְבַדְּהֶן׃ וַיֹּאמֶר אֲבִימֶלֶךְ אֶל־אַבְרָהָם
,Abraham | to | Abimelech | said And | by .themselves | flock the | ewe of lambs | seven

5324 834 3535 7651 2008
מָה הֵנָּה שֶׁבַע כְּבָשֹׂת הָאֵלֶּה אֲשֶׁר הִצַּבְתָּ לְבַדָּנָה׃
by ?themselves | have you set | which | these | lambs ewe | seven | are | What

1961 5668 3027 3535 7651 559
30 וַיֹּאמֶר כִּי אֶת־שֶׁבַע כְּבָשֹׂת תִּקַּח מִיָּדִי בַּעֲבוּר תִּהְיֶה־לִּי
(for) me | may it become | that so | from shall you ,hand my | take | ewe lambs | seven The | he And said

4725 7121 2088 875 2658 5713
31 לְעֵדָה כִּי חָפַרְתִּי אֶת־הַבְּאֵר הַזֹּאת׃ עַל־כֵּן קָרָא לַמָּקוֹם
place | (is) called | this For reason | .this | well | dug I | that | a witness

The Well of Sheba, because the two of them swore there. [32]And they cut a covenant in Beer-sheba. And Abimelech and Phicol, the general of his army, rose up; and they returned to the land of the Philistines. [32]And he planted a tamarisk tree in Beer-sheba, and there he called on the name of Jehovah the everlasting God.

[34]And Abraham lived in the land of the Philistines many days.

CHAPTER 22

[1]And after these things, testing Abraham, God said to him, Abraham! And he said, Behold me. [2]And He said, Now take your son, Isaac, your only one, whom you love, and go into the land of Moriah. And there offer him for a burnt offering on one of the mountains which I will say to you. [3]And Abraham rose early in the morning and saddled his ass. And *he* took two *of* his young men with him, and his son Isaac. And he split wood for a burnt offering. And *he* rose up and went to the place which God had said to him.

[4]And on the third day Abraham lifted up his eyes and saw the place from a distance. [5]And Abraham said to his young men, You stay here with the ass. I and the boy will go on to that *place*, that we may worship, and may return to you. [6]And Abraham took the wood of the burnt offering and laid *it* on his son Isaac; and he took the fire and the knife in his hand. And the two went together.

[7]And Isaac spoke to his

1285 3772 8147 7650 8033 884
32 הַהוּא בְּאֵר שָׁבַע כִּי שָׁם נִשְׁבְּעוּ שְׁנֵיהֶם׃ וַיִּכְרְתוּ בְרִית
a they And of two the swore there be- ,sheba Beer- that
covenant cut .them cause

7725 6635 8269 6369 40 6965 884
בִּבְאֵר שָׁבַע וַיָּקָם אֲבִימֶלֶךְ וּפִיכֹל שַׂר־צְבָאוֹ וַיָּשֻׁבוּ אֶל־
to they and of general the and Abimelech and ;sheba Beer- in
returned army his Phicol up rose

8034 8033 7121 884 815 5193 6430 776
33 אֶרֶץ פְּלִשְׁתִּים׃ וַיִּטַּע אֶשֶׁל בִּבְאֵר שָׁבַע וַיִּקְרָא־שָׁם בְּשֵׁם
the on there and ,sheba Beer- in Tama- a he And .Philistines the the
of name called risk planted 5769 of land

7227 3117 6430 776 85 1481 410 3068
34 יְהוָה אֵל עוֹלָם׃ וַיָּגָר אַבְרָהָם בְּאֶרֶץ פְּלִשְׁתִּים יָמִים רַבִּים׃
.many days the the in Abraham And ever- the Jehovah
Philistines of land lived .lasting God

CAP. XXII כב

CHAPTER 22

85 5254 430 1697 310
1 וַיְהִי אַחַר הַדְּבָרִים הָאֵלֶּה וְהָאֱלֹהִים נִסָּה אֶת־אַבְרָהָם
Abraham testing God these things after And

3947 559 559 85 559
2 וַיֹּאמֶר אֵלָיו אַבְרָהָם וַיֹּאמֶר הִנֵּנִי׃ וַיֹּאמֶר קַח־נָא אֶת־
Take He And am I he And !Abraham ,him to said
,now ,said ,here ,said

776 3212 3327 157 3173 1121
בִּנְךָ אֶת־יְחִידְךָ אֲשֶׁר־אָהַבְתָּ אֶת־יִצְחָק וְלֶךְ־לְךָ אֶל־אֶרֶץ
land the into and ,Isaac ,love you whom your your
of go ,one only son

559 259 5930 5927 4179
הַמֹּרִיָּה וְהַעֲלֵהוּ שָׁם לְעֹלָה עַל אַחַד הֶהָרִים אֲשֶׁר אֹמַר
will I which the of one on a for there offer and ;Moriah
say ,mountains offering burnt him

3947 2543 2280 1242 85 7925
3 אֵלֶיךָ׃ וַיַּשְׁכֵּם אַבְרָהָם בַּבֹּקֶר וַיַּחֲבֹשׁ אֶת־חֲמֹרוֹ וַיִּקַּח
and ,ass his saddled and the in Abraham rose And .you to
took morning early

6965 5930 6086 1234 1121 3327 5288 8147
אֶת־שְׁנֵי נְעָרָיו אִתּוֹ וְאֵת יִצְחָק בְּנוֹ וַיְבַקַּע עֲצֵי עֹלָה וַיָּקָם
and burnt a wood he And his Isaac and with his (of) two
up rose,offering for split .son ,him youths

7992 430 559 4725 3212
4 וַיֵּלֶךְ אֶל־הַמָּקוֹם אֲשֶׁר־אָמַר־לוֹ הָאֱלֹהִים׃ בַּיּוֹם הַשְּׁלִישִׁי
third the on .God to had which place the to and
,day him said went

559 7350 4725 7200 5869 85
5 וַיִּשָּׂא אַבְרָהָם אֶת־עֵינָיו וַיַּרְא אֶת־הַמָּקוֹם מֵרָחֹק׃ וַיֹּאמֶר
said And a from place the and eyes his Abraham And
.distance saw up lifted

5288 2543 6311 5288 85
אַבְרָהָם אֶל־נְעָרָיו שְׁבוּ־לָכֶם פֹּה עִם־הַחֲמוֹר וַאֲנִי וְהַנַּעַר
the and I and ;ass the with here You stay his to Abraham
boy ;youths

85 3947 7725 7812 3541 3212
6 נֵלְכָה עַד־כֹּה וְנִשְׁתַּחֲוֶה וְנָשׁוּבָה אֲלֵיכֶם׃ וַיִּקַּח אַבְרָהָם
Abraham And .you to may and we that ,thus to go will
took return ,worship may

784 3027 3947 1121 3327 7760 5930 6086
אֶת־עֲצֵי הָעֹלָה וַיָּשֶׂם עַל־יִצְחָק בְּנוֹ וַיִּקַּח בְּיָדוֹ אֶת־הָאֵשׁ
fire the his in he and his Isaac on laid and burnt the wood the
hand took ;son (it) offering of

3327 559 3162 8147 3212 3979
7 וְאֶת־הַמַּאֲכֶלֶת וַיֵּלְכוּ שְׁנֵיהֶם יַחְדָּו׃ וַיֹּאמֶר יִצְחָק אֶל־
to Isaac spoke And .together two the went and ;knife the and

father Abraham and said,
My father. And he said,
Behold me. And he said,
See, the fire and the
wood! But where *is* the
lamb for a burnt offering?
[8]And Abraham said, My
son, God will see the
lamb for Himself for a
burnt offering. And the
two of them went to-
gether. [9]And they came
to the place that God had
said to him. And Abra-
ham built there the altar
and arranged the wood.
And he bound his son
Isaac and laid him on the
altar, on the wood.
[10]And Abraham stretched
out his hand and took the
knife to slay his son.
[11]And the Angel of
Jehovah called to him
from the heavens and
said, Abraham! And he
said, Behold me. [12]And
He said, Do not lay your
hand on the boy nor do
anything to him. For now
I know that you are a
fearer of God, and you
have not withheld your
son, your only one, from
Me.

[13]And Abraham lifted up his
eyes and looked. And
behold! A ram behind him
was entangled in a thicket
by its horns. And Abraham
went and took the ram and
offered him a burnt offering
instead of his son. [14]And
Abraham called the name of
that place Jehovah Will
See; so that it is said until
this day, In the mount of
Jehovah it will be seen.

[15]And the Angel of
Jehovah called to Abraham
out of the heavens a second
time. [16]And He said, I have
sworn by Myself, declares
Jehovah, that on account of
this thing you have done,
and not have withheld your
son, your only son, [17]that

2009 559 1121 559 559 1 1 85
אַבְרָהָם אָבִיו וַיֹּאמֶר אָבִי וַיֹּאמֶר הִנֶּנִּי בְנִי וַיֹּאמֶר הִנֵּה
,See he And my am I he And My ,said and his Abraham
,said ,son ,here ,said .father father

430 85 559 5930 7716 6086 784
8 הָאֵשׁ וְהָעֵצִים וְאַיֵּה הַשֶּׂה לְעֹלָה׃ וַיֹּאמֶר אַבְרָהָם אֱלֹהִים
God ,Abraham said And burnt a for the But the and the
?offering lamb (is) where !wood fire

935 3162 8147 3212 1121 5930 7716 7200
9 יִרְאֶה־לּוֹ הַשֶּׂה לְעֹלָה בְּנִי וַיֵּלְכוּ שְׁנֵיהֶם יַחְדָּו׃ וַיָּבֹאוּ
they And .together two the And my burnt a for the Him- for will
came them of went .son ,offering lamb self see

85 8033 1129 430 559 4725
אֶל־הַמָּקוֹם אֲשֶׁר אָמַר־לוֹ הָאֱלֹהִים וַיִּבֶן שָׁם אַבְרָהָם
Abraham there and ,God to had which place the to
built him said

7760 1121 3327 6123 6086 6186 4196
אֶת־הַמִּזְבֵּחַ וַיַּעֲרֹךְ אֶת־הָעֵצִים וַיַּעֲקֹד אֶת־יִצְחָק בְּנוֹ וַיָּשֶׂם
laid and his Isaac he and the and altar the
son bound wood arranged

85 7971 6086 4605 1196
10 אֹתוֹ עַל־הַמִּזְבֵּחַ מִמַּעַל לָעֵצִים׃ וַיִּשְׁלַח אַבְרָהָם אֶת־
Abraham And .wood the on altar the on him
out stretched

7121 1121 7819 3979 3947 3027
11 יָדוֹ וַיִּקַּח אֶת־הַמַּאֲכֶלֶת לִשְׁחֹט אֶת־בְּנוֹ׃ וַיִּקְרָא אֵלָיו
him to And .son his slay to knife the and his
called took hand

559 85 85 559 8064 3068 4397
מַלְאַךְ יְהוָה מִן־הַשָּׁמַיִם וַיֹּאמֶר אַבְרָהָם ׀ אַבְרָהָם וַיֹּאמֶר
he And !Abraham !Abraham ,said and the from Jehovah the
,said heavens of Angel

6213 3808 5288 413 3027 7971 3808 559
12 הִנֵּנִי׃ וַיֹּאמֶר אַל־תִּשְׁלַח יָדְךָ אֶל־הַנַּעַר וְאַל־תַּעַשׂ לוֹ
to do and ,boy the on your lay Do not He And am I
him not hand ,said .here

2820 3808 430 3373 3045 6258 3972
מְאוּמָה כִּי ׀ עַתָּה יָדַעְתִּי כִּי־יְרֵא אֱלֹהִים אַתָּה וְלֹא חָשַׂכְתָּ
have you and you God-fearer a that know I now For .anything
withheld not ,(are)

7200 5869 85 5375 3173 1121
13 אֶת־בִּנְךָ אֶת־יְחִידְךָ מִמֶּנִּי׃ וַיִּשָּׂא אַבְרָהָם אֶת־עֵינָיו וַיַּרְא
and eyes his Abraham And from only your your
;looked up lifted .Me ,one son

3947 85 1980 7161 5442 270 310 352 2009
וְהִנֵּה־אַיִל אַחַר נֶאֱחַז בַּסְּבַךְ בְּקַרְנָיו וַיֵּלֶךְ אַבְרָהָם וַיִּקַּח
and Abraham And its by a in was behind a and
took went .horns thicket entangled him ram !behold

8034 85 7121 1121 8478 5930 5927 352
14 אֶת־הָאַיִל וַיַּעֲלֵהוּ לְעֹלָה תַּחַת בְּנוֹ׃ וַיִּקְרָא אַבְרָהָם שֵׁם־
the Abraham And his instead a for offered and ram the
of name called .son of offering burnt it

3068 2022 3117 559 834 7200 3068 4725
הַמָּקוֹם הַהוּא יְהוָה ׀ יִרְאֶה אֲשֶׁר יֵאָמֵר הַיּוֹם בְּהַר יְהוָה
Jehovah the In until is it that so ;jireh Jehovah that place
mount ,day this said

8064 8145 85 3068 4397 7121 7200
15 יֵרָאֶה׃ וַיִּקְרָא מַלְאַךְ יְהוָה אֶל־אַבְרָהָם שֵׁנִית מִן־הַשָּׁמָיִם׃
the of out second a Abraham to Jehovah the And be will it
.heavens time of Angel called seen

6213 3282 3068 5002 7650 559
16 וַיֹּאמֶר בִּי נִשְׁבַּעְתִּי נְאֻם־יְהוָה כִּי יַעַן אֲשֶׁר עָשִׂיתָ אֶת־
have you because that utters have I By He And
done ,Jehovah ,sworn Myself said

1288 3173 1121 2820 3808 1697
17 הַדָּבָר הַזֶּה וְלֹא חָשַׂכְתָּ אֶת־בִּנְךָ אֶת־יְחִידֶךָ׃ כִּי־בָרֵךְ
surely that only your your have and ,this thing
,son ,son withheld not

blessing I will bless you, and multiplying I will multiply your seed like the stars of the heavens and as the sand which *is* on the seashore. And your Seed shall possess the gate of His enemies. [18]And in your Seed shall all the nations of the earth be blessed *as* reward *in* that you have obeyed My voice. [19]And Abraham returned to his young men, and they rose up and went together to Beer-sheba. And Abraham lived at Beer-sheba.

[20]And after these things it was told to Abraham, saying, Behold, Milcah, she also, has borne sons to your brother Nahor: [21]Uz, his firstborn, Buz, and Kemuel, the father of Aram, [22]and Chesed, and Hazo, and Pildash, and Jidlaph, and Bethuel. [23]And Bethuel fathered Rebekah. Milcah bore these eight to Nahor, the brother of Abraham. [24]And his concubine, whose name *was* Reuman, she also bore Tebah, and Gaham, and Thahash, and Maachah.

2344 8064 3556 2233 7235 7235 1288
אברכך והרבה ארבה את־זרעך ככוכבי השמים וכחול
as and ,heavens the the as seed your will I and will I
sand the of stars multiply surely you bless

1288 341 8179 2233 2423 3220 8193
18 אשר על־שפת הים וירש זרעך את שער איביו: והתברכו
shall And His the your And .sea the of lip the on which
blessed be .enemies of gate Seed own shall (is)

7725 6963 8085 6118 776 2233
19 בזרעך כל גויי הארץ עקב אשר שמעת בקלי: וישב
And My have you because the the all your in
returned .voice heard earth of nations Seed

884 3162 6965 5288 85
אברהם אל־נעריו ויקמו וילכו יחדו אל־באר שבע
.sheba Beer- to together and they and young his to Abraham
went up rose ,men

884 85 342
וישב אברהם בבאר שבע:
.sheba Beer- at Abraham and lived

2009 559 85 5646 1697 310 1961
20 ויהי אחרי הדברים האלה ויגד לאברהם לאמר הנה
,Behold ,saying ,Abraham to was it these things after it And
told was

1060 5780 251 5152 1121 1571 4435 3205
21 ילדה מלכה גם־הוא בנים לנחור אחיך: את־עוץ בכרו
his ,Uz your Nahor to sons she also Milcah has
firstborn :brother borne

2375 3777 768 1 7055 251 938
22 ואת־בוז אחיו ואת־קמואל אבי ארם: ואת־כשד ואת־חזו
,Hazo and ,Chesed and ,Aram the Kemuel and his ,Buz and
of father ;brother

3205 1328 1328 3044 6394
23 ואת־פלדש ואת־ידלף ואת בתואל: ובתואל ילד את־
fathered And .Bethuel and ,Jidlaph and ,Pildash and
Bethuel

85 251 5152 4435 3205 8083 7259
רבקה שמנה אלה ילדה מלכה לנחור אחי אברהם:
.Abraham's brother to Milcah bore these eight ;Rebekah
,Nahor

2876 1571 3205 7208 8034 6370
24 ופילגשו ושמה ראומה ותלד גם־הוא את־טבח ואת־
and ,Tebah she also bore ,Reuman whose his And
(was) name ,concubine

4601 8477 1514
גחם ואת־תחש ואת־מעכה:
.Maachah and ,Thahash and
,Gaham

CAP. XXIII כג

CHAPTER 23

CHAPTER 23

[1]And the life of Sarah *was* a hundred and twenty-seven years, the years of Sarah's life. [2]And Sarah died in Kirjath-arba which *is* Hebron, in the land of Canaan. And Abraham went in to mourn for Sarah and to weep for her. [3]And Abraham rose up from before his dead and spoke to the sons of Heth, saying,

8141 7651 8141 6242 8141 3967 8283 2416
1 ויהיו חיי שרה מאה שנה ועשרים שנה ושבע שנים
,years seven and — twenty and a Sarah the And
hundred of life was

2275 7153 8283 4191 2416
2 שני חיי שרה: ותמת שרה בקרית ארבע הוא חברון
,Hebron which arba in Sarah died and ;Sarah life the the
(is) Kirjath- of of years

1058 8283 5594 85 935 3667 776
בארץ כנען ויבא אברהם לספד לשרה ולבכתה:
weep to and ,Sarah for mourn to Abraham and ;Canaan the in
.her for in went of land

559 2845 1121 1696 4191 6440 85 6966
3 ויקם אברהם מעל פני מתו וידבר אל־בני־חת לאמר:
,saying ,Heth the to spoke and his before from Abraham And
of sons ,dead up rose

[4]I am an alien and a visitor with you. Give to me a possession among you, so that I may bury my dead from before the eyes. [5]And the sons of Heth answered Abraham, saying to him, [6]Hear us, my lord. You *are* a prince among us. Bury your dead in the best of our burying-places. Not a man of us will withhold his burying-place from you, from burying your dead. [7]And Abraham rose up and bowed himself to the people of the land, to the sons of Heth. [8]And he spoke with them, saying, If it is your desire to bury my dead from before my eyes, hear me. Entreat for me Ephron the son of Zohar, [9]that he may give to me the cave of Machpelah, which he has, which is in the edge of his field; for full silver let him give it to me among you, for a possession of a burying-place.

[10]And Ephron was sitting among the sons of Heth. And Ephron the Hittite answered Abraham in the ears of the sons of Heth, to all those entering the gate of the city, saying, [11]No, my lord, hear me. I have given the field to you, and I have given the cave that *is* in it. Before the eyes of the sons of my people I have given it to you. Bury your dead.

[12]And Abraham bowed before the people of the land, [13]and spoke to Ephron in the ears of the people of the land, saying, Only if you would hear me. I have given the silver for the field; take from me that I may bury my dead there. [14]And Ephron answered Abraham, saying to him, [15]My lord, hear me; the land *is worth* four hundred shekels of silver; what is that between me and you?

6912 6913 272 5414 8453 1616
4 גר־ותושב אנכי עמכם תנו לי אחזת־קבר עמכם ואקברה
I that so bury may among ,you burial a possession to Give me with ,you am I a and visitor an alien

8085 559 85 2845 1121 6030 5869 4191
5 מתי מלפני׃ ויענו בני־חת את־אברהם לאמר לו׃ שמענו
6 ,us Hear to saying ,him Abraham Heth of sons the And answered of out .sight my dead

6912 6913 4005 8432 430 5387 113
אדני נשיא אלהים אתה בתוכנו במבחר קברינו קבר
bury burying places our of best the in ;us among you (are) God of prince a ;lord my

6912 3607 3808 6913 376 4191
את־מתך איש ממנו את־קברו לא־יכלה ממך מקבר
from burying from you will not withhold burying- place his us of a man your ;dead

2845 776 5971 7812 85 6965 4191
7 מתך׃ ויקם אברהם וישתחו לעם־הארץ לבני־חת׃
.Heth the of sons to ,land the the to of people bowed and himself Abraham And up rose your .dead

4191 6912 5315 3426 559 1696
8 וידבר אתם לאמר אם־יש את־נפשכם לקבר את־מתי
my dead bury to desire your is it If ,saying with ,then he And spoke

5414 6714/1121 6085 6293 8085 5869
9 מלפני שמעוני ופגעו־לי בעפרון בן־צחר׃ ויתן־לי את־
to me he that give may ,Zohar the of son Ephron of entreat and me for ,me hear of out ,sight my

3701 7704 7097 834 4375 4631
מערת המכפלה אשר־לו אשר בקצה שדהו בכסף
in silver ;field his the of edge in which is he which .has ,Machpelah of cave the

8432 3427 6085 6913 272 8432 5414 4392
10 מלא יתננה לי בתוככם לאחזת־קבר׃ ועפרון ישב בתוך
among was sitting And Ephron burying- place a a for of possession ,you among to me him let it give full

2845/1121 241 85 2850 6085 1121
בני־חת ויען עפרון החתי את־אברהם באזני בני־חת
,Heth the of sons the in of ears Abraham Hittite the Ephron and answered ,Heth the of sons

7704 8085 113 3808 559 5892 8179 935 3605
11 לכל באי שער־עירו לאמר׃ לא־אדני שמעני השדה
field the ;me hear ,lord, No ,saying his city gate of the those entering all to

5971 1121/5869 5414 4631 5414
נתתי לך והמערה אשר־בו לך נתתיה לעיני בני־עמי
my people sons the of before eyes the have I it given to you it in (is) that cave the and to ,you have I given

776 5971/6440 7812 4141 6912 5414
12 נתתיה לך קבר מתך׃ וישתחו אברהם לפני עם־הארץ׃
,land the the of people before Abraham bowed And your .dead Bury to .you have I it given

559 776 5971 241 6085 1696
13 וידבר אל־עפרון באזני עם־הארץ לאמר אך אם־אתה
you If only ,saying ,land the the of people the in of ears Ephron to and spoke

6912 3947 7704 3701 5414 8085
לו שמעני נתתי כסף השדה קח ממני ואקברה את־
I that bury may from ,me (it) take the ;field the for silver have I given would ;hear me

113 559 85 6085 6030 8033 4191
14 מתי שמה׃ ויען עפרון את־אברהם לאמר לו׃ אדני
15 My ,lord ,him to saying ,Abraham Ephron And answered .there my dead

996 3701 8255 3967 702 776 8085
שמעני ארץ ארבע מאת שקל־כסף ביני ובינך מה־
is what you and between me ;silver of shekels hundred four land the (worth is) hear :me

And bury your dead. [16]And Abraham listened to Ephron, and Abraham weighed to Ephron the silver of which he had spoken in the ears of the sons of Heth, four hundred silver shekels *which* passes with the trader.

[17]And was certified the field of Ephron, which *was* in Machpelah, before Mamre, the field and the cave which *was* in it, and all the trees which *were* in the field, in all its borders around it, [18]to Abraham for a purchase before the sons of Heth, with all entering the gate of his city.

[19]And after this Abraham buried his wife Sarah at the cave of the field of Machpelah before Mamre, which *is* Hebron, in the land of Canaan. [20]And the field *was* certified, and the cave which *was* in it, to Abraham for a burial possession from the sons of Heth.

8254 6085 85 8085 6912 4191
16 הִוא וְאֶת־מֵתְךָ קְבֹר׃ וַיִּשְׁמַע אַבְרָהָם אֶל־עֶפְרוֹן וַיִּשְׁקֹל
and ,Ephron to Abraham And .bury your And ?that
weighed listened dead

2845 1121 241 1696 834 3701 6085 85
אַבְרָהָם לְעֶפְרֹן אֶת־הַכֶּסֶף אֲשֶׁר דִּבֶּר בְּאָזְנֵי בְנֵי־חֵת
,Heth the the in had he of silver the Ephron to Abraham
of sons of ears spoken which

6085 7704 6965 5503 3701 8255 3967 702
17 אַרְבַּע מֵאוֹת שֶׁקֶל כֶּסֶף עֹבֵר לַסֹּחֵר׃ וַיָּקָם ׀ שְׂדֵה עֶפְרוֹן
Ephron the was And the with (which) silver shekels hundred four
of field certified .merchant passes

834 4631 7704 4471 6440 834 4375 834
אֲשֶׁר בַּמַּכְפֵּלָה אֲשֶׁר לִפְנֵי מַמְרֵא הַשָּׂדֶה וְהַמְּעָרָה אֲשֶׁר־
which the and field the–Mamre before which–Machpelah in which
(was) cave (was) (was)

85 5439 1366 3605 7704 6086
18 בּוֹ וְכָל־הָעֵץ אֲשֶׁר בַּשָּׂדֶה אֲשֶׁר בְּכָל־גְּבֻלוֹ סָבִיב׃ לְאַבְרָהָם
Abraham to around its all in which the in which the and in
.it borders (were) ,field (were) trees all ,it

3651 310 5892 8179 935 3605 2845 1121 4736
19 לְמִקְנָה לְעֵינֵי בְנֵי־חֵת בְּכֹל בָּאֵי שַׁעַר־עִירוֹ׃ וְאַחֲרֵי־כֵן
this And his the entering with ,Heth the before a for
after .city of gate all of sons purchase

4375 7704 4631 802 8283 85 6912
קָבַר אַבְרָהָם אֶת־שָׂרָה אִשְׁתּוֹ אֶל־מְעָרַת שְׂדֵה הַמַּכְפֵּלָה
Machpelah the cave the at wife his Sarah Abraham buried
of field of

7704 6965 3667 776 2275 4471 6440
20 עַל־פְּנֵי מַמְרֵא הִוא חֶבְרוֹן בְּאֶרֶץ כְּנָעַן׃ וַיָּקָם הַשָּׂדֶה
,field the was And .Canaan the in Hebron which ,Mamre before
certified of land (is)

2845 1121 6913 272 85 834 4631
וְהַמְּעָרָה אֲשֶׁר־בּוֹ לְאַבְרָהָם לַאֲחֻזַּת־קָבֶר מֵאֵת בְּנֵי־חֵת׃
.Heth the from burial a for Abraham to it in which the and
of sons possession (is) cave

CAP. XXIV כד

CHAPTER 24

CHAPTER 24

[1]And Abraham *was* old, going on in days, and Jehovah had blessed Abraham in all things. [2]And Abraham said to his slave, oldest *in* his house, the one who governed in all that *was* to him, Please put your hand under my thigh. [3]And I will cause you to swear by Jehovah, God of the heavens and God of the earth, that you will not take a wife for my son from the daughters of the Canaanite, among whom I dwell. [4]But you shall go to my country and to my kindred and take a wife for my son, for Isaac. [5]And the slave said to him, Perhaps the woman will not be willing to go after me to this land; shall I indeed

3605 85 1288 3068 3117 935 2204 85
1 וְאַבְרָהָם זָקֵן בָּא בַּיָּמִים וַיהוָה בֵּרַךְ אֶת־אַבְרָהָם בַּכֹּל׃
all in Abraham had and in (far) (was) And
.things blessed Jehovah days gone ,old Abraham

3605 4910 1004 2205 5650 85 559
2 וַיֹּאמֶר אַבְרָהָם אֶל־עַבְדּוֹ זְקַן בֵּיתוֹ הַמֹּשֵׁל בְּכָל־אֲשֶׁר־
that all in one the his oldest his to Abraham said And
(was) ruled who house (in) ,slave

430 7650 3409 8478 3027 7760
3 לוֹ שִׂים־נָא יָדְךָ תַּחַת יְרֵכִי׃ וְאַשְׁבִּיעֲךָ בַּיהוָה אֱלֹהֵי
of God by make will I And my under your Please put to
,Jehovah swear you .thigh hand him

1323 1121 802 3947 776 430 8064
הַשָּׁמַיִם וֵאלֹהֵי הָאָרֶץ אֲשֶׁר לֹא־תִקַּח אִשָּׁה לִבְנִי מִבְּנוֹת
the from for wife a you not that ,earth the God and the
of girls son my take shall of heavens

776 7130 3427 3669
4 הַכְּנַעֲנִי אֲשֶׁר אָנֹכִי יוֹשֵׁב בְּקִרְבּוֹ׃ כִּי אֶל־אַרְצִי וְאֶל־
to and my to But .among dwell I whom the
country ,Canaanite

559 3327 1121 802 3947 1980 4138
5 מוֹלַדְתִּי תֵּלֵךְ וְלָקַחְתָּ אִשָּׁה לִבְנִי לְיִצְחָק׃ וַיֹּאמֶר אֵלָיו
him to said And .Isaac for my for wife a take and you my
,son go shall kindred

776 310 3212 802 14 3808 194 5650
הָעֶבֶד אוּלַי לֹא־תֹאבֶה הָאִשָּׁה לָלֶכֶת אַחֲרַי אֶל־הָאָרֶץ
land to me follow to woman the be will not Perhaps the
willing ,slave

bring back your son into the land from where you came out? [6]And Abraham said to him, Take heed for yourself that you do not take my son back there. [7]Jehovah, God of Heaven, who took me from the house of my father and from the land of my birth, and who spoke to me, and who swore to me, saying, I will give this land to your Seed; He shall send His Angel before you, and you shall take a wife from there for my son. [8]And if the woman will not be willing to to go after you, then you shall be clear from this my oath; only do not take back there my son. [9]And the slave put his hand under the thigh of his master Abraham and swore to him concerning this thing.

[10]And the slave took ten camels of the camels of his master, and *he* left. And all the good of his master *were* in his hand. And he rose up and went to Mesopotamia, to the city of Nahor. [11]And he made the camels kneel outside the city, by a well of water at the time of the evening, the time that women go out to draw. [12]And he said, Jehovan, God of my master Abraham, I beg you, cause *her* to meet before me this day, and show kindness to my master Abraham. [13]Lo, I am standing by the well of water, and the daughters of men of the city are coming out to draw water. [14]And let the girl to whom I shall speak *this*: Please let down your pitcher that I may drink; and she will say, Drink, and also I will water your camels; *let it be her* You have designed for Your servant, for Isaac. And by this I shall know that

האת השב אשיב את־בנך אל־הארץ אשר־יצאת
you out came which land the into your son I shall back bring truly ;this

6 משם׃ ויאמר אליו אברהם השמר לך פן־תשיב את־
take you back lest for yourself heed Take ,Abraham to him said And ?from

7 בני שמה׃ יהוה ׀ אלהי השמים אשר לקחני מבית
the from of house me took who the heavens God the of Jehovah .there my son

אבי ומארץ מולדתי ואשר דבר־לי ואשר נשבע־לי
me to swore who and to spoke ,me who and ,birth my from and of land the my father

לאמר לזרעך אתן את־הארץ הזאת הוא ישלח מלאכו
Angel His send shall He ;this land will I give your To seed ,saying

8 לפניך ולקחת אשה לבני משם׃ ואם־לא תאבה האשה
the woman be will willing not And if from .there for son my wife a you and take shall before ,you

לכת אחריך ונקית משבעתי זאת רק את־בני לא תשב
take do back not son my only ;this my from oath you then clear be shall after ,you go to

9 שמה׃ וישם העבד את־ידו תחת ירך אברהם אדניו
his master ,Abraham the of thigh under his hand the slave put And .there

10 וישבע לו על־הדבר הזה׃ ויקח העבד עשרה גמלים
camels ten the servant And took .this concerning thing to him and swore

מגמלי אדניו וילך וכל־טוב אדניו בידו ויקם וילך אל־
to and went he And arose in were .hand his his master goods the of and all and ;left his master the of camels

11 ארם נהרים אל־עיר נחור׃ ויברך הגמלים מחוץ לעיר
the city outside camels the he And knelt .Nahor city the of to Mesopotamia

12 אל־באר המים לעת ערב לעת צאת השאבת׃ ויאמר ׀
he And ,said to .draw they out go time the that the ,evening the at of time water well a of by

יהוה אלהי אדני אברהם הקרה־נא לפני היום ועשה־
show and this ,day before me please cause meet to (her) ,Abraham my master of God Jehovah

13 חסד עם אדני אברהם׃ הנה אנכי נצב על־עין המים
of water the by well (am) standing I ,Lo .Abraham my master to kindness

14 ובנות אנשי העיר יצאת לשאב מים׃ והיה הנער אשר
whom the girl let And .water draw to coming are out the city of men the and of daughters

אמר אליה הטי־נא כדך ואשתה ואמרה שתה וגם־
and also ,Drink she and ,say will I that ;drink may your pitcher Please let down ,to shall I speak

גמליך אשקה אתה הכחת לעבדך ליצחק ובה אדע
shall I know by and this ;Isaac for Your for ,servant have You designed (be it let) her will I ;water your camels

You have shown kindness to my master. [15]And it happened before he had finished speaking. Behold! Rebekah came out, *she* who was born to Bethuel the son of Milcah, the wife of Nahor, the brother of Abraham, *with* her pitcher on her neck. [16]And the girl *was* very good of form, a virgin, a man not knowing her. And she went down to the well and filled her pitcher and came up. [17]And the slave ran to meet her and said, Please let me sip a little water from your pitcher. [18]And she said, Drink, my lord. And she hurried and let down her pitcher on her hand and gave drink to him. [19]And she finished giving drink to him. And she said, I also will draw for your camels until they have finished drinking. [20]And she hurried and emptied her pitcher into the trough. And she again ran to the well to draw, and drew for all his camels. [21]And watching her, the man kept silent in order to know if Jehovah had blessed his way, or not.

[22]And it happened when the camels had finished drinking the man took a golden ring, its weighing a half-shekel, and two bracelets for her hands, then of gold their weighing. [23]And he said, Whose daughter are you? Please tell me, is there room for us to stay in your father's house? [24]And she said to him, I *am* the daughter of Bethuel, the son of Milcah, whom she bore to Nahor. [25]And she said to him, Both straw and fodder *are* plentiful with us, also a room to stay. [26]And the man bowed and worshiped Jehovah. [27]And he said, Blessed be Jehovah, God of my master Abraham, who has not

1696 3615 1961 113 2617 6213
15 כִּי־עָשִׂיתָ חֶסֶד עִם־אֲדֹנִי׃ וַיְהִי־הוּא טֶרֶם כִּלָּה לְדַבֵּר
,speaking had he before it And my to kindness have You that
finished ,happened .master done

802 4435 1121 1328 3205 3318 7259 2009
וְהִנֵּה רִבְקָה יֹצֵאת אֲשֶׁר יֻלְּדָה לִבְתוּאֵל בֶּן־מִלְכָּה אֵשֶׁת
wife the ,Milcah the ,Bethuel to was who came Rebekah be-
of of son born ,out ,hold

4758 2896 5291 7926 3537 85 251 3752
16 נָחוֹר אֲחִי אַבְרָהָם וְכַדָּהּ עַל־שִׁכְמָהּ׃ וְהַנַּעֲרָ טֹבַת מַרְאֶה
form of (was) the And her on her (with) ,Abraham the ,Nahor
good girl .shoulder pitcher of brother

3537 4390 3381 3045 376 1330 3966
מְאֹד בְּתוּלָה וְאִישׁ לֹא יְדָעָהּ וַתֵּרֶד הָעַיְנָה וַתְּמַלֵּא כַדָּהּ
her filled and the to she And knowing not man a ,virgin a ,very
pitcher well down went .her

4592 1572 559 7125 5650 7323 5927
17 וַתָּעַל׃ וַיָּרָץ הָעֶבֶד לִקְרָאתָהּ וַיֹּאמֶר הַגְמִיאִינִי נָא מְעַט
little a Please sip me let ,said and her meet to the And came and
slave ran .up

3537 3381 4116 113 8354 559 3537 4325
18 מַיִם מִכַּדֵּךְ׃ וַתֹּאמֶר שְׁתֵה אֲדֹנִי וַתְּמַהֵר וַתֹּרֶד כַּדָּהּ עַל־
on her let and she and my ,Drink she And your from water
pitcher down hurried ;lord ,said .pitcher

7579 1681 559 8248 3615 8354 3027
19 יָדָהּ וַתַּשְׁקֵהוּ׃ וַתְּכַל לְהַשְׁקֹתוֹ וַתֹּאמֶר גַּם לִגְמַלֶּיךָ אֶשְׁאָב
will I your for also she and him giving she And gave and her
draw camels ,said ,drink finished .drink him ,hand

7323 8268 3537 6168 4116 8354 3615 5704
20 עַד אִם־כִּלּוּ לִשְׁתֹּת׃ וַתְּמַהֵר וַתְּעַר כַּדָּהּ אֶל־הַשֹּׁקֶת וַתָּרָץ
she and ;trough the into her and she And .drinking have they until
ran pitcher emptied hurried finished

376 1581 7579 7579 875 5750
21 עוֹד אֶל־הַבְּאֵר לִשְׁאֹב וַתִּשְׁאַב לְכָל־גְּמַלָּיו׃ וְהָאִישׁ
the And .camels his all for drew and ,draw to well the to again
man

518 1870 3068 6743 3045 2790 7583
מִשְׁתָּאֵה לָהּ מַחֲרִישׁ לָדַעַת הַהִצְלִיחַ יְהוָה דַּרְכּוֹ אִם־
or ,way his Jehovah had if order in silent kept ,her watching
prospered know to

5141 376 3447 8354 1581 3615 1961 3808
22 לֹא׃ וַיְהִי כַּאֲשֶׁר כִּלּוּ הַגְּמַלִּים לִשְׁתּוֹת וַיִּקַּח הָאִישׁ נֶזֶם
a man the that ,drinking camels the had when it And .not
ring took finished ,happened

2091 6235 3027 6781 8147 4948 1234 2091
זָהָב בֶּקַע מִשְׁקָלוֹ וּשְׁנֵי צְמִידִים עַל־יָדֶיהָ עֲשָׂרָה זָהָב
gold of ten her for bracelets two and its half- a golden
,hands ,weighing ,shekel

1004 3426 4994 5046 859 4310 1323 559 4948
23 מִשְׁקָלָם׃ וַיֹּאמֶר בַּת־מִי אַתְּ הַגִּידִי נָא לִי הֲיֵשׁ בֵּית־
in Is ,me Please tell are Whose he And their
house there ?you daughter ,said .weighing

1121 1328 1323 559 3885 4725
24 אָבִיךְ מָקוֹם לָנוּ לָלִין׃ וַתֹּאמֶר אֵלָיו בַּת־בְּתוּאֵל אָנֹכִי בֶּן־
the ,(am) I ,Bethuel the to she And to for room your
of son of daughter ,him said ?stay us father's

1571 8401 1571 559 5152 3205 4436
25 מִלְכָּה אֲשֶׁר יָלְדָה לְנָחוֹר׃ וַתֹּאמֶר אֵלָיו גַּם־תֶּבֶן גַּם־
and straw Both ,him to she And .Nahor to bore she whom ,Milcah
said

7812 376 6915 3885 4725 1571 7227 4554
26 מִסְפּוֹא רַב עִמָּנוּ גַּם־מָקוֹם לָלוּן׃ וַיִּקֹּד הָאִישׁ וַיִּשְׁתַּחוּ
and man the And pass to room a also with (are) fodder
worshiped bowed ,night the ,us plentiful

85 113 430 3068 1288 559 3068
27 לַיהוָה׃ וַיֹּאמֶר בָּרוּךְ יְהוָה אֱלֹהֵי אֲדֹנִי אַבְרָהָם אֲשֶׁר
who ,Abraham my of God ,Jehovah Blessed And ,Jehovah
master be ,said he

left off His kindness and His truth with my master, I *being* in the way, Jehovah guided me to the house of the brother of my master.
28 And the girl ran and told these things to the house of her mother. 29 And Rebekah *had* a brother, his name *being* Laban. And Laban ran out to the man, to the fountain. 30 And when he saw the ring, and the bracelets on the hands of his sister, and when he heard the words of his sister Rebekah, saying, So the man spoke to me, then he came to the man and saw him standing by the camels at the fountain.
31 And he said, Come in, blessed of Jehovah. Why are you standing outside? I have prepared the house and a place for the camels.
32 And the man came into the house. And he unloaded the camels and gave straw and fodder to the camels, and water to wash his feet and the feet of the men who were with him. 33 And *food* was set before him to eat, but he said, I will not eat until I have spoken my message. And he said, Speak. 34 And he said, I am the slave of Abraham. 35 And Jehovah has blessed my master much, and he is great. And *He* has given to him flocks and herds, and silver and gold, and male slaves and slavegirls, and camels and asses. 36 And my master's wife bore a son to my master when she was old, and he has given to him all that *is* his. 37 And my master caused me to swear, saying, You shall not take a wife for my son from the daughters of the Canaanite, in whose land I live. 38 But you shall go to my father's house and to my family.

3068 5148 1870 113 5973 571 2617 5800
לֹא־עָזַב חַסְדּוֹ וַאֲמִתּוֹ מֵעִם אֲדֹנִי אָנֹכִי בַּדֶּרֶךְ נָחַנִי יְהוָה
Jehovah led in (being) I my with His and His has not
me ,way the ;master truth kindness forsaken

1697 517 1004 5046 5291 7323 113 251 1004
28 בֵּית אֲחִי אֲדֹנִי׃ וַתָּרָץ הַנַּעֲרָ וַתַּגֵּד לְבֵית אִמָּהּ כַּדְּבָרִים
things her house and girl the ran And my brother's to
mother's told ,master's house

376 3837 7323 3837 8034 251 7259
29 הָאֵלֶּה׃ וּלְרִבְקָה אָח וּשְׁמוֹ לָבָן וַיָּרָץ לָבָן אֶל־הָאִישׁ
man the to Laban and ;Laban name his a Rebekah And ,these
ran (being) ,brother (had)

6781 5141 7200 1961 5869 2351
30 הַחוּצָה אֶל־הָעָיִן׃ וַיְהִי ׀ כִּרְאֹת אֶת־הַנֶּזֶם וְאֶת־הַצְּמִדִים
bracelets the and ring the when And the to out
saw he was it .fountain

559 269 7259 1647 8085 269 3027 5921
עַל־יְדֵי אֲחֹתוֹ וּכְשָׁמְעוֹ אֶת־דִּבְרֵי רִבְקָה אֲחֹתוֹ לֵאמֹר
,saying his ,Rebekah words the when and ,sister his the on
sister of heard he of hands

5975 2009 376 935 376 3541
כֹּה־דִבֶּר אֵלַי הָאִישׁ וַיָּבֹא אֶל־הָאִישׁ וְהִנֵּה עֹמֵד עַל־
by standing and man the to he then the me to spoke Thus
him beheld came man

5975 4100 3068 1288 935 559 5869 1581
31 הַגְּמַלִּים עַל־הָעָיִן׃ וַיֹּאמֶר בּוֹא בְּרוּךְ יְהוָה לָמָּה תַעֲמֹד
you are Why !Jehovah blessed Come he And the at camels the
standing of ,in ,said .fountain

376 935 1581 4725 1004 6437 2351
32 בַּחוּץ וְאָנֹכִי פִּנִּיתִי הַבַּיִת וּמָקוֹם לַגְּמַלִּים׃ וַיָּבֹא הָאִישׁ
man the And the for a and house the have I ?outside
came .camels place prepared

1581 4554 8401 5414 1581 6605 1004
הַבַּיְתָה וַיְפַתַּח הַגְּמַלִּים וַיִּתֵּן תֶּבֶן וּמִסְפּוֹא לַגְּמַלִּים
,camels the to fodder and straw and ,camels the he and the into
gave unloaded ,house

3455 582 7272 7272 7364 4325
33 וּמַיִם לִרְחֹץ רַגְלָיו וְרַגְלֵי הָאֲנָשִׁים אֲשֶׁר אִתּוֹ׃ וַיִּישֶׂם
(food) And with that men the the and feet his wash to and
set was .him were of feet water

559 1697 1696 5704 398 559 398 6440
לְפָנָיו לֶאֱכֹל וַיֹּאמֶר לֹא אֹכַל עַד אִם־דִּבַּרְתִּי דְּבָרָי וַיֹּאמֶר
he and my have I until will I not but ;eat to before
,said ;message spoken eat ,said he him

113 1288 3068 85 5650 559 1696
34 דַּבֵּר׃ וַיֹּאמַר עֶבֶד אַבְרָהָם אָנֹכִי׃ וַיהוָה בֵּרַךְ אֶת־אֲדֹנִי
35
master my has And .am I Abraham's servant he And .Speak
blessed Jehovah said

8198 5650 2091 3701 1241 6629 1430 3966
מְאֹד וַיִּגְדָּל וַיִּתֶּן־לוֹ צֹאן וּבָקָר וְכֶסֶף וְזָהָב וַעֲבָדִם וּשְׁפָחֹת
slave- and male and and and and flocks to has and he and ,much
girls ,slaves ,gold silver ,herds him given ,great is

113 1121 113 802 8283 2543 1581
36 וּגְמַלִּים וַחֲמֹרִים׃ וַתֵּלֶד שָׂרָה אֵשֶׁת אֲדֹנִי בֵן לַאדֹנִי
my to son a my wife Sarah bore And .asses and and
master master's camels

113 7650 3605 5414 2209 310
37 אַחֲרֵי זִקְנָתָהּ וַיִּתֶּן־לוֹ אֶת־כָּל־אֲשֶׁר־לוֹ׃ וַיַּשְׁבִּעֵנִי אֲדֹנִי
my caused And to that all to he and was she when
,master swear to me .him (is) him given has ;old

3669 1323 1121 802 3947 559
לֵאמֹר לֹא־תִקַּח אִשָּׁה לִבְנִי מִבְּנוֹת הַכְּנַעֲנִי אֲשֶׁר אָנֹכִי
I whose the the from for wife a shall You not ,saying
,Canaanite of girls son my take

4940 1980 1 1004 518 776 3427
38 יֹשֵׁב בְּאַרְצוֹ׃ אִם־לֹא אֶל־בֵּית־אָבִי תֵּלֵךְ וְאֶל־מִשְׁפַּחְתִּי
,family my and shall you my house the to But .land in live
to go father of

and you shall take a wife for
my son. [39]And I said to my
master, Perhaps the woman
will not go after me. [40]And
he said to me, Jehovah,
before whom I walk, will
send His Angel with you
and prosper you way. And
you shall take a wife for my
son from my family, from my
father's house. [41]Then you
shall be released from my
oath, when you have come
to my family, and if they do
not give *one* to you; then
you shall be released from
my oath. [42]And today I
came to the well. And I said,
Jehovah, God of my master
Abraham, if You will, I pray,
prosper the way in which I
am about to go. [43]Behold, I
stand at the well of water,
and when the virgin comes
out to draw water, and I say
to her, Please let me drink a
little water from your
pitcher, [44]and she says to
me, Both you drink and also
I will draw for your camels,
may she *be* the woman
whom Jehovah has designed
for my master's son.
[45]Before I had finished
speaking within my heart,
even behold, Rebekah was
going out, her pitcher on
her neck. And she went
down to the well and drew.
And I said to her, Please let
me drink. [46]And she
hurried and let down her
pitcher from her and said,
Drink, and I also will water
your camels. And I drank,
and also she watered the
camels. [47]And I asked
her; and I said, Whose
daughter are you? And
she said, Bethuel's, the
son of Nahor, whom Milcah
bore to him. And I put
the ring on her nose and
the bracelets on her
hands. [48]And I bowed and
worshiped Jehovah, and I

802 1980 3808 113 559 1121 802 3947
39 וְלָקַחְתָּ אִשָּׁה לִבְנִי׃ וָאֹמַר אֶל־אֲדֹנִי אֻלַי לֹא־תֵלֵךְ הָאִשָּׁה
the will not Perhaps my to And my for wife a you and
woman go ,master said I .son take shall

6440 1980 3068 559 310
40 אַחֲרָי׃ וַיֹּאמֶר אֵלָי יְהוָה אֲשֶׁר־הִתְהַלַּכְתִּי לְפָנָיו יִשְׁלַח
will ,before walk I whom ,Jehovah to he And after
send me said .me

4940 1121 802 3947 1870 6743 854 4397
מַלְאָכוֹ אִתָּךְ וְהִצְלִיחַ דַּרְכֶּךָ וְלָקַחְתָּ אִשָּׁה לִבְנִי מִמִּשְׁפַּחְתִּי
my from for wife a you And your and with His
family son my take shall .way prosper you Angel

4940 935 422 5352 1004
41 וּמִבֵּית אָבִי׃ אָז תִּנָּקֶה מֵאָלָתִי כִּי תָבוֹא אֶל־מִשְׁפַּחְתִּי
,family my to you when from shall you Then my from and
come have ,oath my released be .father's house

3117 935 422 5355 1961 5414 3808
42 וְאִם־לֹא יִתְּנוּ לָךְ וְהָיִיתָ נָקִי מֵאָלָתִי׃ וָאָבֹא הַיּוֹם אֶל־
to today And from freed you then to do they not if and
came I .oath my be shall ;you (one) give

4994 85 430 3068 559 5869
הָעָיִן וָאֹמַר יְהוָה אֱלֹהֵי אֲדֹנִי אַבְרָהָם אִם־יֶשְׁךָ־נָּא
pray I You if ,Abraham my of God ,Jehovah I and the
,will master ,said ;well

5324 2009 1980 834 1870 6743
43 מַצְלִיחַ דַּרְכִּי אֲשֶׁר אָנֹכִי הֹלֵךְ עָלֶיהָ׃ הִנֵּה אָנֹכִי נִצָּב
stand I and .in about am I which way the prosper
,behold go to

559 7579 3318 5959 2009 4325 5869
עַל־עֵין הַמָּיִם וְהָיָה הָעַלְמָה הַיֹּצֵאת לִשְׁאֹב וְאָמַרְתִּי
say I and draw to comes virgin the when and ;water the at
,water forth of well

1571 559 3537 4325 4592 8248
44 אֵלֶיהָ הַשְׁקִינִי־נָא מְעַט־מַיִם מִכַּדֵּךְ׃ וְאָמְרָה אֵלַי גַּם־
Both to she and your from water little a me let Please ,her to
,me says ,pitcher drink

3198 802 7579 1581 8354
אַתָּה שְׁתֵה וְגַם לִגְמַלֶּיךָ אֶשְׁאָב הִוא הָאִשָּׁה אֲשֶׁר־הֹכִיחַ
has whom the she may will I your for and drink you
chosen woman (be) ,draw camels also

2009 3820 1696 3615 2962 113 1121 3068
45 יְהוָה לְבֶן־אֲדֹנִי׃ אֲנִי טֶרֶם אֲכַלֶּה לְדַבֵּר אֶל־לִבִּי וְהִנֵּה
,and my within speaking had Before I my for Jehovah
lo ,heart finished .master's son

7579 5869 3381 7926 3537 3318 7259
רִבְקָה יֹצֵאת וְכַדָּהּ עַל־שִׁכְמָהּ וַתֵּרֶד הָעַיְנָה וַתִּשְׁאָב
;drew and the to she And her on her was Rebekah
well down went .shoulder pitcher ,out going

3537 3381 4116 4994 8248 559
46 וָאֹמַר אֵלֶיהָ הַשְׁקִינִי נָא׃ וַתְּמַהֵר וַתּוֹרֶד כַּדָּהּ מֵעָלֶיהָ
her from her let and she And .Please me let ,her to I and
,(shoulder) pitcher down hurried drink said

1581 1571 8354 8248 1581 8354 559
וַתֹּאמֶר שְׁתֵה וְגַם־גְּמַלֶּיךָ אַשְׁקֶה וָאֵשְׁתְּ וְגַם הַגְּמַלִּים
camels the and I and will I your and ,Drink ,said and
also ,drank ;water camels also

559 1323 559 7592 8248
47 הִשְׁקָתָה׃ וָאֶשְׁאַל אֹתָהּ וָאֹמַר בַּת־מִי אַתְּ וַתֹּאמֶר בַּת־
she And are Whose I and her I And .watered she
said ?you daughter ,said asked

5141 7760 3205 5152 1121 1328
בְּתוּאֵל בֶּן־נָחוֹר אֲשֶׁר יָלְדָה־לּוֹ מִלְכָּה וָאָשִׂם הַנֶּזֶם עַל־
on ring the I And .Milcah to bore whom Nahor the Bethuel's
put him of son ,(daughter)

3068 7812 6915 3027 6781 639
48 אַפָּהּ וְהַצְּמִידִים עַל־יָדֶיהָ׃ וָאֶקֹּד וָאֶשְׁתַּחֲוֶה לַיהוָה
,Jehovah worshiped and I and her on the and her
bowed ;hands bracelets ,nose

blessed Jehovah, God of
my master Abraham, who
had guided me in the true
way, to take for his son the
daughter of the brother of
my master. 49And now, if
you are going to do kind-
ness and truth with my
master, tell me. And if not,
tell me so that I may turn to
the right or to the left.
50And Laban and Bethuel
answered and said, The
thing has come from
Jehovah; we are not able to
speak to you good or evil.
51Behold! Rebekah *is* before you, take *her* and go.
And let her become the
wife of the son of your
master, as Jehovah has
spoken. 52And when the
slave of Abraham heard
their words, he bowed himself to the earth to Jehovah.
53And the slave brought out
vessels of silver and vessels
of gold and garments, and
he gave to Rebekah. And he
gave precious things to her
brother and to her mother.
54And they ate and drank,
he and the men who *were*
with him; and they stayed
the night. And they rose up
in the morning, and he said,
Send me away to my
master. 55And her brother
and her mother said, Let the
girl stay with us, perhaps
ten days. Afterwards she
may go. 56And he said to
them, Do not delay me, *for*
Jehovah has propsered my
way. Send me away that I
may go to my master.
57And they said, we will call
the girl and ask of her
mouth. 58And they called
Rebekah and said to her,
Will you go with this man?
And she said, I will go.
59And they sent away their
sister Rebekah, and her
nurse, and Abraham's slave
and his men. 60And they
blessed Rebekah, and said

1870 5148 85 113 430 3068
וָאֲבָרֵךְ אֶת־יְהוָה אֱלֹהֵי אֲדֹנִי אַבְרָהָם אֲשֶׁר הִנְחַנִי בְּדֶרֶךְ
the in had who ,Abraham my of God ,Jehovah I and
way me guided master blessed

6258 1121 113 251 1323 3947 571
49 אֱמֶת לָקַחַת אֶת־בַּת־אֲחִי אֲדֹנִי לִבְנוֹ׃ וְעַתָּה אִם־יֶשְׁכֶם
are you if now And his for my brother's daughter take to ,true
going 3808 .son master's

5046 5046 113 571 2617 6213
עֹשִׂים חֶסֶד וֶאֱמֶת אֶת־אֲדֹנִי הַגִּידוּ לִי וְאִם־לֹא הַגִּידוּ
tell ,not and ;me tell my with and kindness do to
if ,master truth

1328 2837 6030 8040 176 3225 6437
50 לִי וְאֶפְנֶה עַל־יָמִין אוֹ עַל־שְׂמֹאל׃ וַיַּעַן לָבָן וּבְתוּאֵל
and Laban And .left the to or the to I that so me
Bethuel answered right turn may

176 7451 1696 3201 1697 3318 3068 559
וַיֹּאמְרוּ מֵיְהוָה יָצָא הַדָּבָר לֹא נוּכַל דַּבֵּר אֵלֶיךָ רַע אוֹ־
or evil you to to we not The has from ,said and
speak able are ;thing come Jehovah

113 1121 802 1961 1980 3947 7259 2009 2896
51 טוֹב׃ הִנֵּה־רִבְקָה לְפָנֶיךָ קַח וָלֵךְ וּתְהִי אִשָּׁה לְבֶן־אֲדֹנֶיךָ
*6440
your the of the let and and take before Rebekah Behold .good
,master of son wife be her ;go (her) ,you (is)

85 5650 8085 3068 1696
52 כַּאֲשֶׁר דִּבֶּר יְהוָה׃ וַיְהִי כַּאֲשֶׁר שָׁמַע עֶבֶד אַבְרָהָם אֶת־
Abraham's slave heard when And .Jehovah has as
spoken

3701 3627 5650 3318 3068 776 7812 1697
53 דִּבְרֵיהֶם וַיִּשְׁתַּחוּ אַרְצָה לַיהוָה׃ וַיּוֹצֵא הָעֶבֶד כְּלֵי־כֶסֶף
silver vessels the And to the to bowed he ,words their
of slave forth brought .Jehovah earth himself

251 5414 4030 7259 5414 899 2091 3627
וּכְלֵי זָהָב וּבְגָדִים וַיִּתֵּן לְרִבְקָה וּמִגְדָּנֹת נָתַן לְאָחִיהָ
her to he jewels and ;Rebekah to and pieces and gold and
brother gave gave clothing of of vessels

3885 582 8354 1398 517
54 וּלְאִמָּהּ׃ וַיֹּאכְלוּ וַיִּשְׁתּוּ הוּא וְהָאֲנָשִׁים אֲשֶׁר־עִמּוֹ וַיָּלִינוּ
they and with who the and he and they And her to and
;lodged him (were) men ,drank ate .mother

517 251 559 113 7971 559 1242 6965
55 וַיָּקוּמוּ בַבֹּקֶר וַיֹּאמֶר שַׁלְּחֻנִי לַאדֹנִי׃ וַיֹּאמֶר אָחִיהָ וְאִמָּהּ
her and her said And my to me Send he and the in they and
,mother brother .master away ,said ,morning up rose

559 1980 310 6218 176 3117 5291 3427
56 תֵּשֵׁב הַנַּעֲרָ אִתָּנוּ יָמִים אוֹ עָשׂוֹר אַחַר תֵּלֵךְ׃ וַיֹּאמֶר
he And she after- ,ten perhaps days us with girl the Let
said .go may wards stay

7971 1870 6743 3068 309 3808
אֲלֵהֶם אַל־תְּאַחֲרוּ אֹתִי וַיהוָה הִצְלִיחַ דַּרְכִּי שַׁלְּחוּנִי
me send ;way my has (since) ,me delay Do not ,them to
away prospered Jehovah

6310 7592 5291 7121 559 113 1980
57 וְאֵלְכָה לַאדֹנִי׃ וַיֹּאמְרוּ נִקְרָא לַנַּעֲרָ וְנִשְׁאֲלָה אֶת־פִּיהָ׃
her and girl the will We they And my to I that
mouth of inquire call ,said .master go may

2088 376 1980 559 7259 7121
58 וַיִּקְרְאוּ לְרִבְקָה וַיֹּאמְרוּ אֵלֶיהָ הֲתֵלְכִי עִם־הָאִישׁ הַזֶּה
?this man with you Will ,her to said and Rebekah they And
go called

3243 269 7259 7971 1980 559
59 וַתֹּאמֶר אֵלֵךְ׃ וַיְשַׁלְּחוּ אֶת־רִבְקָה אֲחֹתָם וְאֶת־מֵנִקְתָּהּ
,nurse her and their Rebekah they And will I she And
sister away sent .go ,said

559 7259 1288 582 85 5650
60 וְאֶת־עֶבֶד אַבְרָהָם וְאֶת־אֲנָשָׁיו׃ וַיְבָרְכוּ אֶת־רִבְקָה וַיֹּאמְרוּ
said and Rebekah they And .men his and Abraham's slave and
blessed

to her, Our sister, may you become myriads of thousands, and may your seed possess the gate of their haters. [61]And Rebekah and her maidens rose up, and they rode on the camels and went after the man. And the slave took Rebekah and went.

[62]And Isaac had come from the gate of the Well of the Living One, My Beholder — and he was dwelling in the land of the Negeb. [63]And Isaac had gone out to meditate in the field as *it* turned *to* evening. And he lifted his eyes and looked. And, behold! Camels were coming. [64]And Rebekah lifted her eyes, and she saw Isaac. And she quickly dismounted from the camel. [65]And she said to the slave, Who is this man who is walking in the field to meet us? And the slave said, It is my master. And she took the veil and covered herself. [66]And the slave told Isaac all the things that he had done. [67]And Isaac brought her into the tent of his mother Sarah. And he took Rebekah, and she became his wife; and he loved her. And Isaac was comforted after his mother.

לָהּ אֲחֹתֵנוּ אַתְּ הֲיִי לְאַלְפֵי רְבָבָה וְיִירַשׁ זַרְעֵךְ אֵת שַׁעַר
61 שֹׂנְאָיו׃ וַתָּקָם רִבְקָה וְנַעֲרֹתֶיהָ וַתִּרְכַּבְנָה עַל־הַגְּמַלִּים
וַתֵּלַכְנָה אַחֲרֵי הָאִישׁ וַיִּקַּח הָעֶבֶד אֶת־רִבְקָה וַיֵּלַךְ׃
62 וְיִצְחָק בָּא מִבּוֹא בְּאֵר לַחַי רֹאִי וְהוּא יוֹשֵׁב בְּאֶרֶץ הַנֶּגֶב׃
63 וַיֵּצֵא יִצְחָק לָשׂוּחַ בַּשָּׂדֶה לִפְנוֹת עָרֶב וַיִּשָּׂא עֵינָיו וַיַּרְא
64 וְהִנֵּה גְמַלִּים בָּאִים׃ וַתִּשָּׂא רִבְקָה אֶת־עֵינֶיהָ וַתֵּרֶא אֶת־
65 יִצְחָק וַתִּפֹּל מֵעַל הַגָּמָל׃ וַתֹּאמֶר אֶל־הָעֶבֶד מִי־הָאִישׁ
הַלָּזֶה הַהֹלֵךְ בַּשָּׂדֶה לִקְרָאתֵנוּ וַיֹּאמֶר הָעֶבֶד הוּא אֲדֹנִי
66 וַתִּקַּח הַצָּעִיף וַתִּתְכָּס׃ וַיְסַפֵּר הָעֶבֶד לְיִצְחָק אֵת כָּל־
67 הַדְּבָרִים אֲשֶׁר עָשָׂה׃ וַיְבִאֶהָ יִצְחָק הָאֹהֱלָה שָׂרָה אִמּוֹ
וַיִּקַּח אֶת־רִבְקָה וַתְּהִי־לוֹ לְאִשָּׁה וַיֶּאֱהָבֶהָ וַיִּנָּחֵם יִצְחָק
אַחֲרֵי אִמּוֹ׃

CAP. XXV כה

CHAPTER 25

[1]And Abraham added and took a wife, and her name *was* Keturah. [2]And she bore to him Zimran and Jokshan and Medan and Midian and Ishbak and Shuah. [3]And Jokshan fathered Sheba and Dedan. And the sons of Dedan were Asshurim, and Letushim and Leummim. [4]And the sons of Midian: Ephah, and Epher, and Hanoch.

1 2 וַיֹּסֶף אַבְרָהָם וַיִּקַּח אִשָּׁה וּשְׁמָהּ קְטוּרָה׃ וַתֵּלֶד לוֹ אֶת־
זִמְרָן וְאֶת־יָקְשָׁן וְאֶת־מְדָן וְאֶת־מִדְיָן וְאֶת־יִשְׁבָּק וְאֶת־
3 שׁוּחַ׃ וְיָקְשָׁן יָלַד אֶת־שְׁבָא וְאֶת־דְּדָן וּבְנֵי דְדָן הָיוּ
4 אַשּׁוּרִם וּלְטוּשִׁם וּלְאֻמִּים׃ וּבְנֵי מִדְיָן עֵיפָה וָעֵפֶר וַחֲנֹךְ

and Abida, and Eldaah. All these *were* the sons of Keturah. [5]And Abraham gave all that was his to Isaac. [6]And to the sons of the concubines who *were* to Abraham, Abraham gave gifts, and sent them away eastward, from his son Isaac, while still alive, to an eastern land.

[7]And these are the days of the years of the life of Abraham, which he lived, one hundred seventy five years. [8]And Abraham expired and died in a good old age, aged and satisfied, and was gathered to his people. [9]And his sons Isaac and Ishmael buried him at the cave of Machpelah, at the field of Ephron the son of Zohar the Hittite, which *is* before Mamre, [10]the field which Abraham bought from the sons of Heth. Abraham and his wife Sarah were buried there. [11]And it happened after the death of Abraham, God blessed his son Isaac. And Isaac lived by The Well of the Living One, My Beholder.

[12]And these *are* the generations of Ishmael, the son of Abraham, whom Hagar the Egyptian, the slavegirl of Sarah, bore to Abraham. [13]And these *are* the names of the sons of Ishmael, by their names, according to their generations: the firstborn of Ishmael was Nebajoth; then Kedar, and Adbeel, and Mibsam, [14]and Mishma, and Duman, and Massa, [15]Hadad, and Tema, Jetur, Naphish, and Kedemah. [16]These were the sons of Ishmael, and these their names in their settlements and in their camps, twelve chiefs according to their nations. [17]And these

85 5414 6989 1121 3605 420 28
5 וַאֲבִידָע וְאֶלְדָּעָה כָּל־אֵלֶּה בְּנֵי קְטוּרָה׃ וַיִּתֵּן אַבְרָהָם
Abraham And .Keturah the these All and and
gave of sons (were) .Eldaah Abida

6390 1121 3327 3605
6 אֶת־כָּל־אֲשֶׁר־לוֹ לְיִצְחָק׃ וְלִבְנֵי הַפִּילַגְשִׁים אֲשֶׁר
who ,concubines the the to And .Isaac to to that all
(were) of sons him was

3327 7971 4979 85 5414 85
לְאַבְרָהָם נָתַן אַבְרָהָם מַתָּנֹת וַיְשַׁלְּחֵם מֵעַל יִצְחָק בְּנוֹ
his Isaac from sent and ;gifts Abraham gave ,Abraham to
son away them

2416 8141 3117 6924 6924/776 6924 2416
7 בְּעוֹדֶנּוּ חַי קֵדְמָה אֶל־אֶרֶץ קֶדֶם׃ וְאֵלֶּה יְמֵי שְׁנֵי־חַיֵּי
life the the these And .east the of land a to ,eastward .alive yet while
of years of days are

8141 2568 7657 3967 2425 834 87
אַבְרָהָם אֲשֶׁר־חָי מְאַת שָׁנָה וְשִׁבְעִים שָׁנָה וְחָמֵשׁ שָׁנִים׃
.years five years seventy years one he which ,Abraham
hundred ,lived

622 7649 2205 2896 7872 85 4191 1478
8 וַיִּגְוַע וַיָּמָת אַבְרָהָם בְּשֵׂיבָה טוֹבָה זָקֵן וְשָׂבֵעַ וַיֵּאָסֶף אֶל־
to was and and aged ,good old an in Abraham died and And
,gathered ,satisfied age expired

6912 4631 1121 3458 3327 6912 5971
9 עַמָּיו׃ וַיִּקְבְּרוּ אֹתוֹ יִצְחָק וְיִשְׁמָעֵאל בָּנָיו אֶל־מְעָרַת הַמַּכְפֵּלָה
Machpelah of cave the at his Ishmael and Isaac him And his
sons buried .people

4471 6440 834 2850 6714 1121 6083 7704
אֶל־שְׂדֵה עֶפְרֹן בֶּן־צֹחַר הַחִתִּי אֲשֶׁר עַל־פְּנֵי מַמְרֵא׃
,Mamre before which the Zohar the Ephron the at
is ,Hittite of son of field

6912 8033 2845/1121 85 7069 7704
10 הַשָּׂדֶה אֲשֶׁר־קָנָה אַבְרָהָם מֵאֵת בְּנֵי־חֵת שָׁמָּה קֻבַּר
were there ;Heth the from Abraham bought which field the
buried of sons

1288 85 4194 310 1961 802 8283 85
11 אַבְרָהָם וְשָׂרָה אִשְׁתּוֹ׃ וַיְהִי אַחֲרֵי מוֹת אַבְרָהָם וַיְבָרֶךְ
that ,Abraham the after it And .wife his and Abraham
blessed of death was Sarah

2416 7200 875 33:27 2416 1121 3327 430
אֱלֹהִים אֶת־יִצְחָק בְּנוֹ וַיֵּשֶׁב יִצְחָק עִם־בְּאֵר לַחַי רֹאִי׃ פ
My Living the the by Isaac And his Isaac God
,seer One of Well lived ,son

1904 3205 85 1121 3458 8435
12 וְאֵלֶּה תֹּלְדֹת יִשְׁמָעֵאל בֶּן־אַבְרָהָם אֲשֶׁר יָלְדָה הָגָר
Hagar bore whom Abraham the ,Ishmael genera- the And
of son of tions are these

1121 8034 85 8283 8198 4713
13 הַמִּצְרִית שִׁפְחַת שָׂרָה לְאַבְרָהָם׃ וְאֵלֶּה שְׁמוֹת בְּנֵי
the names the And ,Abraham to Sarah slave- the the
of sons of are these of girl Egyptian

6938 50:32 3458 1060 8435 8034 3458
יִשְׁמָעֵאל בִּשְׁמֹתָם לְתוֹלְדֹתָם בְּכֹר יִשְׁמָעֵאל נְבָיֹת וְקֵדָר
and ,Nebajoth I The to according their by ,Ishmael
Kedar (was) of firstborn .generations their names

8485/2316 4851 746 4927 4017 110
14
15 וְאַדְבְּאֵל וּמִבְשָׂם׃ וּמִשְׁמָע וְדוּמָה וּמַשָּׂא׃ חֲדַד וְתֵימָא
and ,Hadar and and and and and
,Tema ,Massa ,Dumah ,Mishma Mibsam Adbeel and

8034 3458 1121 6929 5905 3195
16 יְטוּר נָפִישׁ וָקֵדְמָה׃ אֵלֶּה הֵם בְּנֵי יִשְׁמָעֵאל וְאֵלֶּה שְׁמֹתָם
their and ,Ishmael the These and ,Naphish and
names these of sons (were) .Kedemah ,Jetur

523 8269 6240 8147 2918 2691
17 בְּחַצְרֵיהֶם וּבְטִירֹתָם שְׁנֵים־עָשָׂר נְשִׂיאִם לְאֻמֹּתָם׃ וְאֵלֶּה
And to according rulers ten (and) two their in and their in
(are) these .nations their ;camps settlements

are the years of the life of Ishmael, a hundred thirty-seven years. And he expired and died and was gathered to his people. 18 And they lived from Havilah to Shur, which is facing Egypt *as* you come toward Assyria; he settled facing all his brothers.

19 And these (are) the generations of Isaac the son of Abraham: Abraham fathered Isaac. 20 And Isaac was a son of forty years when he took Rebekah, the daughter of Bethuel the Aramean from Padan-aram, the sister of Laban the Aramean, to him for a wife. 21 And Isaac prayed to Jehovah for his wife, for she *was* barren. And Jehovah was entreated for him. And his wife Rebekah conceived. 22 And the sons struggled together within her. And she said, If *this is* right why am I this way? And she went to ask Jehovah. 23 And Jehovah said to her, Two nations *are* in your womb; yea, two peoples shall break from your body. And one people shall be stronger than the other people; and the elder shall serve the younger.

24 And her days were fulfilled to bear. And, behold! Twins *were* in her womb. 25 And the first came out, all of him red like a hairy robe; and they called his name Esau. 26 And afterward his brother came out, and his hand was holding to the heel of Esau; and his name *was* called Jacob. And Issac was a son of sixty years when she bore them.

27 And the boys grew up. And Esau became a man knowing hunting, a man of the field. And Jaco was a simple man, living in tents. 28 And Isaac loved Esau, for game *was* in his mouth.

8141 7651 7970 3967 3468 2416 8141
שְׁנֵי חַיֵּי יִשְׁמָעֵאל מְאַת שָׁנָה וּשְׁלֹשִׁים שָׁנָה וְשֶׁבַע שָׁנִים
.years seven — thirty — hundred a ,Ishmael life the the
of of years

7793 2341 7931 5971 622 4191 1478
18 וַיִּגְוַע וַיָּמָת וַיֵּאָסֶף אֶל־עַמָּיו׃ וַיִּשְׁכְּנוּ מֵחֲוִילָה עַד־שׁוּר
.Shur to from they And .people his to was and and he And
Havilah lived gathered died expired

5307 251 3605/6440 804 935 4714 6440 834
אֲשֶׁר עַל־פְּנֵי מִצְרַיִם בֹּאֲכָה אַשּׁוּרָה עַל־פְּנֵי כָל־אֶחָיו נָפָל׃
he his all before toward you (as) ,Egypt before which
.settled brothers ;Assyria come is

3205 85 85 1121 3327 8435
19 וְאֵלֶּה תּוֹלְדֹת יִצְחָק בֶּן־אַבְרָהָם אַבְרָהָם הוֹלִיד אֶת־
fathered Abraham :Abraham's son ,Isaac genera- the And
of tions (are) these

7259 3947 8141 703 1121 3327 1961 3327
20 יִצְחָק׃ וַיְהִי יִצְחָק בֶּן־אַרְבָּעִים שָׁנָה בְּקַחְתּוֹ אֶת־רִבְקָה
,Rebekah he when years forty of son a Isaac And .Isaac
took was

761 3837 269 6307 761 1328 1323
בַּת־בְּתוּאֵל הָאֲרַמִּי מִפַּדַּן אֲרָם אֲחוֹת לָבָן הָאֲרַמִּי לוֹ
to the Laban the ,aram from the Bethuel the
him ,Aramean of sister Padan- Aramean of daughter

6135 802 5227 3068 3327 6279 802
21 לְאִשָּׁה׃ וַיֶּעְתַּר יִצְחָק לַיהוָה לְנֹכַח אִשְׁתּוֹ כִּי עֲקָרָה
(was) for his behalf in to Isaac And for
barren ,wife of Jehovah prayed .wife a

7533 802 7259 2029 3068 6279
22 הִוא וַיֵּעָתֶר לוֹ יְהוָה וַתַּהַר רִבְקָה אִשְׁתּוֹ׃ וַיִּתְרֹצֲצוּ
fought And his Rebekah and Jehovah for was And .she
together .wife conceived him entreated

1875 3212 2088 4100 3651 559 7130 1121
הַבָּנִים בְּקִרְבָּהּ וַתֹּאמֶר אִם־כֵּן לָמָּה זֶּה אָנֹכִי וַתֵּלֶךְ לִדְרֹשׁ
ask to she And am this why (this) If she and ,her within the
went ?I way ,right (is) said sons

8147 990 1471 8147 3068 559 3068
23 אֶת־יְהוָה׃ וַיֹּאמֶר יְהוָה לָהּ שְׁנֵי גֹיִים בְּבִטְנֵךְ וּשְׁנֵי
and your in nations Two to Jehovah said And .Jehovah
two ,womb (are) her

5647 7227 553 3816 3816 6504 4578 3816
לְאֻמִּים מִמֵּעַיִךְ יִפָּרֵדוּ וּלְאֹם מִלְאֹם יֶאֱמָץ וְרַב יַעֲבֹד
shall and be shall the than one and shall your from peoples
serve elder the ,stronger people other people ;break body

3318 990 8380 2009 3205 3117 4390 6810
24 צָעִיר׃ וַיִּמְלְאוּ יָמֶיהָ לָלֶדֶת וְהִנֵּה תוֹמִם בְּבִטְנָהּ׃ וַיֵּצֵא
25
And her in twins ,behold be to her were And the
out came !womb (were) ;delivered days fulfilled .younger

6215 8034 7121 8181 155 3605 132 7223
הָרִאשׁוֹן אַדְמוֹנִי כֻּלּוֹ כְּאַדֶּרֶת שֵׂעָר וַיִּקְרְאוּ שְׁמוֹ עֵשָׂו׃
.Esau his they and ;hairy a like of all red ,first the
name called robe him

7121 6215 6119 270 3027 251 3318 310
26 וְאַחֲרֵי־כֵן יָצָא אָחִיו וְיָדוֹ אֹחֶזֶת בַּעֲקֵב עֵשָׂו וַיִּקְרָא
and ,Esau's to holding his and his came And
called heel hand ,brother out afterward

1430 3205 8141 8346 1121 3327 3290 8034
27 שְׁמוֹ יַעֲקֹב וְיִצְחָק בֶּן־שִׁשִּׁים שָׁנָה בְּלֶדֶת אֹתָם׃ וַיִּגְדְּלוּ
grew And .them she when years sixty a (was) and ;Jacob his
up bore of son Isaac name

376 3290 7704 376 6718 3045 376 6215 1961 5288
הַנְּעָרִים וַיְהִי עֵשָׂו אִישׁ יֹדֵעַ צַיִד אִישׁ שָׂדֶה וְיַעֲקֹב אִישׁ
a And .field the a knowing a Esau and the
man was Jacob of man ,hunting man became boys

6310 6718 6215 3327 157 168 2401 8535
28 תָּם יֹשֵׁב אֹהָלִים׃ וַיֶּאֱהַב יִצְחָק אֶת־עֵשָׂו כִּי־צַיִד בְּפִיו
his in game for ,Esau Isaac And .tents in living simple
;mouth loved

And Rebekah loved Jacob.
[29]And Jacob boiled soup.
And Esau came from the
field, and he *was* faint.
[30]And Esau said to Jacob,
Please let me eat of the red,
this red *soup*, for I *am* faint
—on account of this his
name is called Edom.
[31]And Jacob said, Sell me
your birthright today. [32]And
Esau said, Behold, I *am*
going to die, and what *good*
is this, a birthright to me?
[33]And Jacob said, Swear to
me today. And he swore to
him and sold his birthright
to Jacob. [34]And Jacob
gave bread and soup of
lentils to Esau. And he ate
and drank, and rose up and
left. And Esau despised the
birthright.

6215 935 5138 3290 2102 3290 157 7259
29 וְרִבְקָה אֹהֶבֶת אֶת־יַעֲקֹב׃ וַיָּזֶד יַעֲקֹב נָזִיד וַיָּבֹא עֵשָׂו
Esau And .soup Jacob And .Jacob loved and
came boiled Rebekah

3938 3290 62/15 559 5889 7704
30 מִן־הַשָּׂדֶה וְהוּא עָיֵף׃ וַיֹּאמֶר עֵשָׂו אֶל־יַעֲקֹב הַלְעִיטֵנִי
eat me Let Jacob to Esau said And .faint he and the from
(was) field

7121 3651/5921 5889 20 88 122 122 4480
נָא מִן־הָאָדֹם הָאָדֹם הַזֶּה כִּי עָיֵף אָנֹכִי עַל־כֵּן קָרָא
is account on ;(am) I faint for ,this (soup) red ,red the of now
called this of

1062 3117 4376 3290 559 123 8034
31 שְׁמוֹ אֱדוֹם׃ וַיֹּאמֶר יַעֲקֹב מִכְרָה כַיּוֹם אֶת־בְּכֹרָתְךָ לִי׃
to your today Sell ,Jacob said And .Edom his
.me birthright name

1062 2088 4191 3212 2009 6265 559
32 וַיֹּאמֶר עֵשָׂו הִנֵּה אָנֹכִי הוֹלֵךְ לָמוּת וְלָמָּה־זֶּה לִי בְּכֹרָה׃
birth- a to what and ;die to (am) I ,See ,Esau And
?right me this (good) going said

43 76 7650 3117 7650 3290 559
33 וַיֹּאמֶר יַעֲקֹב הִשָּׁבְעָה לִּי כַּיּוֹם וַיִּשָּׁבַע לוֹ וַיִּמְכֹּר אֶת־
his he and to he and today me to Swear ,Jacob And
sold ;him swore said

574.2 5138 3899 6215/5414 3290 3290 1062
34 בְּכֹרָתוֹ לְיַעֲקֹב׃ וְיַעֲקֹב נָתַן לְעֵשָׂו לֶחֶם וּנְזִיד עֲדָשִׁים
.lentils and bread Esau to gave And .Jacob to birth-
of soup Jacob right

1062 6215 959 3212 6965 8354 398
וַיֹּאכַל וַיֵּשְׁתְּ וַיָּקָם וַיֵּלַךְ וַיִּבֶז עֵשָׂו אֶת־הַבְּכֹרָה׃
.birthright the Esau and and and and he And
despised ;left up got ,drank ate

CAP. XXVI כו

CHAPTER 26

CHAPTER 26
[1]And a famine was in the
land besides the famine
which was in the days of
Abraham. And Isaac went
to Abimelech king of the
Philistines, to Gerar. [2]And
Jehovah appeared to him
and said, Do not go down
into Egypt; stay in the land
which I shall say to you.
[3]Stay in this land, and I will
be with you and bless you,
for to you and to your seed I
will give all these lands.
And I will cause to rise My
oath which I swore to
your father Abraham. [4]And
I will increase your seed like
the stars of the heavens,
and I will give to your seed
all these lands. And all the
nations of the earth shall
bless themselves in your
seed, [5]because Abraham

3117 1961 834 7223 7458 806 776 7458 1961
1 וַיְהִי רָעָב בָּאָרֶץ מִלְּבַד הָרָעָב הָרִאשׁוֹן אֲשֶׁר הָיָה בִּימֵי
the in was which former the besides the in a And
of days famine land famine was

1642 6430 44 28 40 3227 3212 85
אַבְרָהָם וַיֵּלֶךְ יִצְחָק אֶל־אֲבִימֶלֶךְ מֶלֶךְ־פְּלִשְׁתִּים גְּרָרָה׃
.Gerar to ,Philistines the king Abimelech to Isaac and ;Abraham
of went

776 7931 4714 3381 559 3068 7200
2 וַיֵּרָא אֵלָיו יְהוָה וַיֹּאמֶר אַל־תֵּרֵד מִצְרָיְמָה שְׁכֹן בָּאָרֶץ
the in stay ;Egypt into go Do not ,said and Jehovah to And
land down him appeared

1288 1961 2088 776 1481 559 834
3 אֲשֶׁר אֹמַר אֵלֶיךָ׃ גּוּר בָּאָרֶץ הַזֹּאת וְאֶהְיֶה עִמְּךָ וַאֲבָרְכֶךָּ
bless and with will I and ,this land in Stay .you to shall I which
;you you be say

6965 776 3605 5414 2233
כִּי־לְךָ וּלְזַרְעֲךָ אֶתֵּן אֶת־כָּל־הָאֲרָצֹת הָאֵל וַהֲקִמֹתִי אֶת־
will I and ;these lands all will I to and for
establish give seed your you

7235 85 7650 834 7621
4 הַשְּׁבֻעָה אֲשֶׁר נִשְׁבַּעְתִּי לְאַבְרָהָם אָבִיךָ׃ וְהִרְבֵּיתִי אֶת־
will I and your Abraham to swore I which oath My
rise make .father

776 3605 2233 5414 8064 3556 2233
זַרְעֲךָ כְּכוֹכְבֵי הַשָּׁמַיִם וְנָתַתִּי לְזַרְעֲךָ אֵת כָּל־הָאֲרָצֹת
lands all seed your to I and ,heavens the the like your
give will of stars seed

8085 6118 776 1471 2233 1288
5 הָאֵל וְהִתְבָּרְכוּ בְזַרְעֲךָ כֹּל גּוֹיֵי הָאָרֶץ׃ עֵקֶב אֲשֶׁר־שָׁמַע
listened because the the all your in shall and ;these
;earth of nations seed themselves bless

listened to My voice and heeded My charge, My commands, My statutes, and My laws.

[6]And Isaac lived in Gerar. [7]And the men of the place asked about his wife. And he said, She *is* my sister, for he was afraid to say, My wife, lest the men of the place kill me on account of Rebekah, for she *was* beautiful of form. [8]And it happened when *his* days were many to him there, Abimelech king of the Philistines looked through the window and saw; and, behold, Isaac was sporting with his wife Rebekah. [9]And Abimelech called Isaac and said, See, surely she *is* your wife, and how have you said, She *is* my sister? And Isaac said to him, Because I said, lest I die on account of her. [10]And Abimelech said, What is this you have done to us? One of the people had almost lain with your wife, and you would have caused to come on us guilt.

[11]And Abimeleh commanded all the people, saying, Anyone touching this man and his wife shall surely be put to death.

[12]And Isaac sowed in that land. And a hundredfold *was* found in that year, and Jehovah blessed him.

[13]And the man grew great, and he went on, going on *to* be great, until he became very great. [14]And to him *were* possessions of flocks and possessions of herds and many slaves. And the Philistines envied him. [15]And all the wells which his father's slaves dug in the days of his father Abraham, the Philistines stopped them and filled them *with* dirt. [16]And Abimelech said to Isaac, Go

8451 2708 4687 4931 8104 6963 85
6 אַבְרָהָם בְּקֹלִי וַיִּשְׁמֹר מִשְׁמַרְתִּי מִצְוֺתַי חֻקּוֹתַי וְתוֹרֹתָי׃
My and My My ,charge My and My to Abraham
laws ,statutes ,commands heeded voice

559 802 4725 582 7592 1642 3327 559
7 וַיֵּשֶׁב יִצְחָק בִּגְרָר׃ וַיִּשְׁאֲלוּ אַנְשֵׁי הַמָּקוֹם לְאִשְׁתּוֹ וַיֹּאמֶר
he and his about place the men the asked And in Isaac And
said ,wife of Gerar lived

4725 582 2026 802 559 3372 269
אֲחֹתִי הִוא כִּי יָרֵא לֵאמֹר אִשְׁתִּי פֶּן־יַהַרְגֻנִי אַנְשֵׁי הַמָּקוֹם
the the kill lest ;wife my say to he for she My
place of men me feared ;(is) sister

8033 748 1961 4758 2896 7259
8 עַל־רִבְקָה כִּי־טוֹבַת מַרְאֶה הִוא׃ וַיְהִי כִּי אָרְכוּ־לוֹ שָׁם
there to many that And she form of good for of account on
him were was it .(was) Rebekah

7200 2474 1157 6130 4428 40 8259 3117
הַיָּמִים וַיַּשְׁקֵף אֲבִימֶלֶךְ מֶלֶךְ פְּלִשְׁתִּים בְּעַד הַחַלּוֹן וַיַּרְא
and the through the king Abimelech that ,days
,saw window Philistines of looked

40 7121 802 8259 6711 3327 2009
9 וְהִנֵּה יִצְחָק מְצַחֵק אֵת רִבְקָה אִשְׁתּוֹ׃ וַיִּקְרָא אֲבִימֶלֶךְ
Abimelech And .wife his Rebekah with sporting Isaac and
called ,lo

269 559 802 2009 389 559 3327
לְיִצְחָק וַיֹּאמֶר אַךְ הִנֵּה אִשְׁתְּךָ הִוא וְאֵיךְ אָמַרְתָּ אֲחֹתִי
My you have and she your ,lo ,Surely and (to)
sister ,said how (is) wife ,said Isaac

4191 559 3327 559
הִוא וַיֹּאמֶר אֵלָיו יִצְחָק כִּי אָמַרְתִּי פֶּן־אָמוּת עָלֶיהָ׃
her on die I Lest ,said I Because ,Isaac him to said And she
.account ?(is)

259 7901 4592 6213 2088 40 559
10 וַיֹּאמֶר אֲבִימֶלֶךְ מַה־זֹּאת עָשִׂיתָ לָּנוּ כִּמְעַט שָׁכַב אַחַד
one lain had a in ?us to did you What ,Abimelech And
of little this is said

40 6680 817 935 802 5971
11 הָעָם אֶת־אִשְׁתֶּךָ וְהֵבֵאתָ עָלֵינוּ אָשָׁם׃ וַיְצַו אֲבִימֶלֶךְ אֶת־
(to) Abimelech And ,guilt us on you and wife your with the
spoke sent had people

4191 4191 802 2088 376 5060 559 5971
כָּל־הָעָם לֵאמֹר הַנֹּגֵעַ בָּאִישׁ הַזֶּה וּבְאִשְׁתּוֹ מוֹת יוּמָת׃
be shall surely his and this man Anyone ,saying the all
.killed wife touching people

3967 8141 4672 776 3327 2232
12 וַיִּזְרַע יִצְחָק בָּאָרֶץ הַהִוא וַיִּמְצָא בַּשָּׁנָה הַהִוא מֵאָה
a that year in and ,that land in Isaac And
hundred found sowed

1433 3212 3212 376 1430 3068 1288 8180
13 שְׁעָרִים וַיְבָרְכֵהוּ יְהוָה׃ וַיִּגְדַּל הָאִישׁ וַיֵּלֶךְ הָלוֹךְ וְגָדֵל
be (to) going he and the grew And .Jehovah blessed and ,fold
great on went man great him

5627 1241 4735 6629 4135 1961 346 1430
14 עַד כִּי־גָדַל מְאֹד׃ וַיְהִי־לוֹ מִקְנֵה־צֹאן וּמִקְנֵה בָקָר וַעֲבֻדָּה
slaves and herds pos- and flocks pos- to And .very became he till
of sessions of sessions him was great

2658 834 875 3605 6430 7065 7227
15 רַבָּה וַיְקַנְאוּ אֹתוֹ פְּלִשְׁתִּים׃ וְכָל־הַבְּאֵרֹת אֲשֶׁר חָפְרוּ
dug which wells the all And .Philistines the him envied and ;many

6430 5640 1 85 3117 1 5650
עַבְדֵי אָבִיו בִּימֵי אַבְרָהָם אָבִיו סִתְּמוּם פְלִשְׁתִּים
Philistines the stopped his Abraham's days in his the
them father father of slaves

3212 3327 40 559 6083 4390
16 וַיְמַלְאוּם עָפָר׃ וַיֹּאמֶר אֲבִימֶלֶךְ אֶל־יִצְחָק לֵךְ מֵעִמָּנוּ
from Go ,Isaac to Abimelech said And (with) filled and
,us .dirt them

from us, for you are
stronger than we.
17And Isaac went from
there and camped in
Gerar Valley, and *he* lived
there. 18And again Isaac
dug the wells of water
which they dug in the
days of his father Abra-
ham; and the Philistines
stopped them after Abra-
ham's death. And he
called names to them like
the names which his
father had called them.
19And Isaac's slaves dug
in the torrent-bed, and
they found there a well of
living water. 20And the
shepherds of Gerar con-
tended with Isaac's shep-
herds, saying, The water
is ours; and he called the
name of the well, Conten-
tion, for they contended
with him. 21And they dug
another well and also
fought over it; and he
called its name Oppo-
sition. 22And he moved
from there and dug an-
other well, and they did
not fight over it; and he
called its name, Broad
Places. And *he* said, For
now Jehovah has broad-
ened for us and we shall
be fruitful in the land.
23And he went from there
to Beer-sheba. 24And
Jehovah appeared to him in
the same night, and said, I
am the God of your father
Abraham; do not fear, for I
am with you; and I will bless
you and increase your seed,
because of My servant
Abraham. 25And he built an
altar there and called on the
name of Jehovah. And he
pitched his tent there. And
the slaves of Isaac dug a
well there.
26And Abimelech went to
him from Gerar, and his aide
Ahuzzath, and Phicol the
general of his army. 27And
Isaac said to them, Why
have you come to me, *since*
you hate me and sent me
away from you? 28And

1642 5158 2583 3327 8033 3212 3966 6105
17 כִּי־עָצַמְתָּ מִמֶּנּוּ מְאֹד׃ וַיֵּלֶךְ מִשָּׁם יִצְחָק וַיִּחַן בְּנַחַל־גְּרָר
Gerar in and ,Isaac from And .much than are you for
Valley camped there went we stronger

834 4325 875 2658 3327 8033 2416
18 וַיֵּשֶׁב שָׁם׃ וַיָּשָׁב יִצְחָק וַיַּחְפֹּר ׀ אֶת־בְּאֵרֹת הַמַּיִם אֲשֶׁר
which water of wells the dug Isaac And .there and
again lived

4194 310 6430 5640 1 85 3117 2658
חָפְרוּ בִּימֵי אַבְרָהָם אָבִיו וַיְסַתְּמוּם פְלִשְׁתִּים אַחֲרֵי מוֹת
the after Philis- the had and his Abraham the in they
of death tines up them stopped ;father of days dug

8034 7121 834 8034 8034 7121 85
אַבְרָהָם וַיִּקְרָא לָהֶן שֵׁמוֹת כַּשֵּׁמֹת אֲשֶׁר־קָרָא לָהֶן אָבִיו׃
his them had which the like names to he And .Abraham
.father called names them called

2416 4325 875 4672 5158 3327 5650 2658
19 וַיַּחְפְּרוּ עַבְדֵי־יִצְחָק בַּנָּחַל וַיִּמְצְאוּ־שָׁם בְּאֵר מַיִם חַיִּים׃
.living water a there they and the in Isaac the And
of well found torrent-bed of slaves dug

7121 4325 559 3327 7462 7462 7378
20 וַיָּרִיבוּ רֹעֵי גְרָר עִם־רֹעֵי יִצְחָק לֵאמֹר לָנוּ הַמָּיִם וַיִּקְרָא
and ;water the To ,saying ,Isaac the with Gerar the con- And
called he (belongs) us of shepherds of shepherds tended

312 875 2658 6229 6230 875 8034
21 שֵׁם־הַבְּאֵר עֵשֶׂק כִּי הִתְעַשְּׂקוּ עִמּוֹ׃ וַיַּחְפְּרוּ בְּאֵר אַחֶרֶת
another well they And with con- they for Conten- well the the
dug .him tended tion of name

8033 6275 7856 8034 7121 5921 7378
22 וַיָּרִיבוּ גַּם־עָלֶיהָ וַיִּקְרָא שְׁמָהּ שִׂטְנָה׃ וַיַּעְתֵּק מִשָּׁם
from he And .Opposition its he and over also con- and
there moved name called ;it tended

7344 8034 7121 5921 7378 312 875 2658
3808 וַיַּחְפֹּר בְּאֵר אַחֶרֶת וְלֹא רָבוּ עָלֶיהָ וַיִּקְרָא שְׁמָהּ רְחֹבוֹת
Broad its he and ;it over they and ,another well dug and
Places name called contended not

5927 776 6509 3068 7337 6258 559
23 וַיֹּאמֶר כִּי־עַתָּה הִרְחִיב יְהוָה לָנוּ וּפָרִינוּ בָאָרֶץ׃ וַיַּעַל
he And .land the in we and for Jehovah has now For he and
went fruitful be shall us broadened said

559 1931 3915 3068 7200 884 8033
24 מִשָּׁם בְּאֵר שָׁבַע׃ וַיֵּרָא אֵלָיו יְהוָה בַּלַּיְלָה הַהוּא וַיֹּאמֶר
and the in Jehovah to And .Sheba (to) from
,said same night him appeared Beer- there

853 3372 1 85 430
אָנֹכִי אֱלֹהֵי אַבְרָהָם אָבִיךָ אַל־תִּירָא כִּי־אִתְּךָ אָנֹכִי
I with for ,fear do not your Abraham God the I
;(am) you ;father of (am)

5650 85 5668 2233 7235 1288
וּבֵרַכְתִּיךָ וְהִרְבֵּיתִי אֶת־זַרְעֲךָ בַּעֲבוּר אַבְרָהָם עַבְדִּי׃
My Abraham because ,seed your increase and will I and
.servant of you bless

3738 168 5186 3068 8034 7121 4196 1129
25 וַיִּבֶן שָׁם מִזְבֵּחַ וַיִּקְרָא בְּשֵׁם יְהוָה וַיֶּט־שָׁם אָהֳלוֹ וַיִּכְרוּ
dug and his there and ,Jehovah the on and altar an there And
;tent pitched he of name called built he

276 1642 3212 40 875 3327 5650
26 שָׁם עַבְדֵי־יִצְחָק בְּאֵר׃ וַאֲבִימֶלֶךְ הָלַךְ אֵלָיו מִגְּרָר וַאֲחֻזַּת
and from to went And a Isaac the there
Ahuzzath Gerar him Abimelech .well of slaves

3327 559 6635 8269 6369 4828
27 מֵרֵעֵהוּ וּפִיכֹל שַׂר־צְבָאוֹ׃ וַיֹּאמֶר אֲלֵהֶם יִצְחָק מַדּוּעַ
Why ,Isaac them to said And .army his the Phicol and his
of commander ,aide

7971 8130 935
בָּאתֶם אֵלָי וְאַתֶּם שְׂנֵאתֶם אֹתִי וַתְּשַׁלְּחוּנִי מֵאִתְּכֶם׃
?you from sent and me hate (since) to you have
away me you ,me come

they said, We have plainly seen that Jehovah has been with you, and we have said, let there be an oath now between us, between us and you, and let us cut a covenant with you, [29]whether you will do with us evil, as we did not touch you, and as we did only good with you, and we sent you away in peace; you now *being* blessed of Jehovah. [30]And he made a feast for them, and they ate and drank. [31]And they started up early at dawn, and each swore to his brother. And Isaac sent them away, and they left him in peace. [32]And it happened on that day Isaac's slaves came and told him about the well which they had dug, and said to him, We found water. [33]And he called it Shibah; so the name of the city *is* Beer-sheba until this day.
[34]And Esau was a son of forty years. And he took a wife, Judith, the daughter of Beeri the Hittite; also Basemath the daughter of Elon the Hittite. And they were a grief of spirit to Isaac and to Rebekah.

4994 1961 559 3068 1961 7200 7200 559
28 וַיֹּאמְרוּ רָאוֹ רָאִינוּ כִּי־הָיָה יְהוָה ׀ עִמָּךְ וַנֹּאמֶר תְּהִי נָא
now Let we and with Jehovah has that We plainly they And
be there ,said ,you been seen have ,said

1285 3772 996 996 1422
29 אָלָה בֵּינוֹתֵינוּ בֵּינֵינוּ וּבֵינֶךָ וְנִכְרְתָה בְרִית עִמָּךְ׃ אִם־
(that so) with a let and and between between an
you covenant cut us ;you us ;us oath

6213 5060 3808 7451 6213
תַּעֲשֵׂה עִמָּנוּ רָעָה כַּאֲשֶׁר לֹא נְגַעֲנוּךָ וְכַאֲשֶׁר עָשִׂינוּ עִמְּךָ
with did we as and did we not as (no) with will you
you you touch evil us do

6213 3068 1288 6258 7965 7971 2896 7535
30 רַק־טוֹב וַנְּשַׁלֵּחֲךָ בְּשָׁלוֹם אַתָּה עַתָּה בְּרוּךְ יְהוָה׃ וַיַּעַשׂ
he And .Jehovah blessed now you ;peace in we and ,good only
made of (being) you sent

7650 1242 7925 8354 398 4960
31 לָהֶם מִשְׁתֶּה וַיֹּאכְלוּ וַיִּשְׁתּוּ׃ וַיַּשְׁכִּימוּ בַבֹּקֶר וַיִּשָּׁבְעוּ
and ,dawn at they And and and ,feast a for
swore early rose .drank ate they them

1961 7965 3212 3327 7971 251 376
32 אִישׁ לְאָחִיו וַיְשַׁלְּחֵם יִצְחָק וַיֵּלְכוּ מֵאִתּוֹ בְּשָׁלוֹם׃ וַיְהִי ׀
And .peace in him they and Isaac sent and his to each
was it left them ;brother

875 182 5046 5650 935 3117
בַּיּוֹם הַהוּא וַיָּבֹאוּ עַבְדֵי יִצְחָק וַיַּגִּדוּ לוֹ עַל־אֹדוֹת הַבְּאֵר
well the concerning him and Isaac's slaves that ,that on
told came day

7656 7121 4325 4672 559 2658 834
33 אֲשֶׁר חָפָרוּ וַיֹּאמְרוּ לוֹ מָצָאנוּ מָיִם׃ וַיִּקְרָא אֹתָהּ שִׁבְעָה
;Shibah it he And .water We to said and had they which
called found ,him ,dug

1961 2088 3117 7651 875 5892 8034 3651
34 עַל־כֵּן שֵׁם־הָעִיר בְּאֵר שֶׁבַע עַד הַיּוֹם הַזֶּה׃ ס וַיְהִי
And .this day till sheba Beer- city's the so
was (is) name

882 1323 3067 802 3947 8141 703 1121 6215
עֵשָׂו בֶּן־אַרְבָּעִים שָׁנָה וַיִּקַּח אִשָּׁה אֶת־יְהוּדִית בַּת־בְּאֵרִי
Beeri's ,Judith wife a he and ;years forty a Esau
,daughter took of son

7307 4786 1961 2850 356 1323 1315 2850
35 הַחִתִּי וְאֶת־בָּשְׂמַת בַּת־אֵילֹן הַחִתִּי׃ וַתִּהְיֶיןָ מֹרַת רוּחַ
spirit grief a they and the Elon's Basemath and the
of were ;Hittite daughter ;Hittite

7259 3327
לְיִצְחָק וּלְרִבְקָה׃
to and to
.Rebekah Isaac

CAP. XXVII כז

CHAPTER 27

CHAPTER 27

[1]And it happened when Isaac *was* old and his eyes were dim for seeing, he called his elder son Esau and said to him, My son! And he said to him, Behold me. [2]And he said, See, now, I am old; I do not know the day of my death. [3]And now please lift up your weapons, your quiver and your bow, and go to the field and hunt game for me. [4]And make for me delicious

6215 7121 7200 5869 3543 3327 2204 1961
1 וַיְהִי כִּי־זָקֵן יִצְחָק וַתִּכְהֶיןָ עֵינָיו מֵרְאֹת וַיִּקְרָא אֶת־עֵשָׂו ׀
Esau he that for his were and (was) when And
called ,seeing eyes dim Isaac old ,was it

559 559 1121 559 1419 1121
2 בְּנוֹ הַגָּדֹל וַיֹּאמֶר אֵלָיו בְּנִי וַיֹּאמֶר אֵלָיו הִנֵּנִי׃ וַיֹּאמֶר
he And (am) I ,him to he And My to said and elder his
,said .here said !son ,him son

3627 5375 6258 4194 3045 3808 2204 2009
3 הִנֵּה־נָא זָקַנְתִּי לֹא יָדַעְתִּי יוֹם מוֹתִי׃ וְעַתָּה שָׂא־נָא כֵלֶיךָ
your now up lift And my day the I not am I now
,weapons now .death of know ,old

6213 6718 6679 7704 7198 8522
4 תֶּלְיְךָ וְקַשְׁתֶּךָ וְצֵא הַשָּׂדֶה וְצוּדָה לִּי צָיִדה׃ וַעֲשֵׂה־לִי
for And .game for and the to go and your and your
me make me hunt field ;bow quiver

things, such as I love, and
bring to me, and I will eat;
so that my soul may bless
you before I die. [5]And
Rebekah heard when Isaac
spoke to his son Esau. And
Esau went to the field to
hunt game, to bring *it* in.
[6]And Rebekah spoke to her
son Jacob, saying, Behold, I
heard your father speaking
to your brother Esau saying,
[7]Bring game to me and
make delicious things that I
may eat, and may bless you
before Jehovah before I die.
[8]And now my son hear my
voice, that which I com-
mand you. [9]Go now to the
flock and bring me from
there two good kids of the
goats. And I will make them
into delicious things for
your father, such as he
loves; [10]and you shall bring
it to your father and let him
eat, so that he may bless
you before his death.
[11]And Jacob said to his
mother Rebekah, Behold,
my brother Esau *is* a hairy
man, and I a smooth man.
[12]Perhaps my father will feel
me, and I shall be like a
deceiver in his eyes, and I
shall bring a curse on me,
and not blessing. [13]And his
mother said to him, Your
curse *be* on me, my son;
only listen to my voice and
go, take for me. [14]And he
went and took and came to
his mother. And his mother
made delicious things, such
as his father loved. [15]And
Rebekah took the clothing
of her elder son Esau, the
costly ones which were
with her in the house. And
she dressed her younger
son Jacob; [16]and she put
the skins of the kids of the
goats on his hands, and on

398 935 157 4303
מטעמים כאשר אהבתי והביאה לי ואכלה בעבור
that | I that eat may | me to | bring and | ,love I | like | delicacies

3327 1696 8085 7259 4191 2962 5315 1288
5 תברכך נפשי בטרם אמות: ורבקה שמעת בדבר יצחק
Isaac's | speech | heard | And Rebekah | .die I | before | soul my | may you bless

7259 935 6718 6679 7704 6215 3212 1121 6215
6 אל-עשו בנו וילך עשו השדה לצוד ציד להביא: ורבקה
And Rebekah | bring to .in | game hunt to | the to field | Esau | and went | his ;son | Esau | to

8085 2009 559 1121 3290 559
אמרה אל-יעקב בנה לאמר הנה שמעתי את-אביך
your father | I heard | ,See | ,saying | her son | Jacob | to | spoke

6213 6718 935 559 251 6215 1696
7 מדבר אל-עשו אחיך לאמר: הביאה לי ציד ועשה-לי
make and me | game | to me | Bring | ,saying | your brother | Esau | to | talking

6258 4194 6440 3068 6440 1288 398 4303
8 מטעמים ואכלה ואברככה לפני יהוה לפני מותי: ועתה
And now | .die I | before Jehovah before | may and you bless | I that ,eat may | delicacies

6629 4994 3212 6680 834 6963 8085 1121
9 בני שמע בקלי לאשר אני מצוה אתך: לך-נא אל-הצאן
the flock | to | now Go | .you | tell | I | that which | my voice | hear | my son

4303 6213 2896 5795 1423 8147 8033 3947
וקח-לי משם שני גדיי עזים טבים ואעשה אתם מטעמים
(into) delicacies | them | I and make will | ;good | the goats | kids of | two | from there | bring and me

398 935 157
10 לאביך כאשר אהב: והבאת לאביך ואכל בעבר אשר
that | so | let and eat him | your to father | you And bring shall | .loves he | like | your for father

2009 517 7259 3290 559 4194 6440 1288
11 יברכך לפני מותו: ויאמר יעקב אל-רבקה אמו הן
,See | his ,mother | Rebekah | to | Jacob | said And | his .death | before | may he you bless

1 4959 194 376 8163 376 251 6215
12 עשו אחי איש שער ואנכי איש חלק: אולי ימשני אבי
my ,father | feel will me | may It be | .smooth | a (am) man | I and | hairy | a (is) man | my brother | Esau

1293 7045 935 8591 5869 1961
והייתי בעיניו כמתעתע והבאתי עלי קללה ולא ברכה:
and .blessing | and not | curse a | me on | I and bring shall | a like ;deceiver | his in eyes | I and be shall

3212 6963 8085 1121 7045 517 559
13 ותאמר לו אמו עלי קללתך בני אך שמע בקלי ולך
and ,go | my voice | hear | only | my ;son | your (be) ,curse | On me | his ,mother | to him | said And

4303 517 6213 517 935 3947 3212 3947
14 קח-לי: וילך ויקח ויבא לאמו ותעש אמו מטעמים
delicacies | his mother | and made | his to ;mother | and brought | and took | he And went | for take .me

1121 6215 899 7259 3947 1 157
15 כאשר אהב אביו: ותקח רבקה את-בגדי עשו בנה
her son | Esau | clothes the of | Rebekah | took And | his .father | loved | like

1121 3290 3847 1004 834 2532 1419
הגדל החמדת אשר אתה בבית ותלבש את-יעקב בנה
her son | Jacob | she And clothed | the in .house | with her | which were | costly the ones | ,elder

5921 3027 3847 5795 1423 5785 6996
16 הקטן: ואת ערת גדיי העזים הלבישה על-ידיו ועל
and on | his ,hands | on | put she | goats the | the of kids | skins the of | and | ;younger

the smoothness of his neck. 17And she put the delicious things and the bread which she had made in the hand of her son Jacob. 18And he went in to his father and said, My father. And he said, Here I *am*. Who *are* you, my son? 19And Jacob said to his father, I *am* your firstborn, Esau. I have done as you said to me. Rise up now, sit and eat of my game, so that your soul may bless me. 20And Isaac said to his son, How then have you quickly found it, my son? And he said, Because Jehovah your God made it come to me.

21And Isaac said to Jacob, Come near now and let me feel you, whether then you *are* my son Esau, or not. 22And Jacob came near to his father Isaac. And he felt him. And he said, The voice *is* Jacob's voice, and the hands *are* Esau's hands. 23And he did not know him, because his hands were like the hairy hands of his brother Esau. And he blessed him. 24And he said, *Are* you then my son Esau? And he said, I *am*. 25And he said, Bring to me and let me eat of my son's game, so that my soul may bless you. And he came near to him. And he took and he ate. And he took wine to him, and he drank. 26And his father Isaac said to him, Now come and kiss me, my son. 27And he came and kissed him. And he smelled the odor of his clothes. And *he* blessed him and said, See, the smell of my son is as the smell of a field which Jehovah blessed. 28And may God give you of the dew of the heavens, and of the fatness of the earth, and much grain and wine. 29May the nations serve you and peoples bow to you. Be a ruler to your brothers,

834 3899 4303 3318 6677 2513
17 חֶלְקַת צַוָּארָיו׃ וַתִּתֵּן אֶת־הַמַּטְעַמִּים וְאֶת־הַלֶּחֶם אֲשֶׁר
which bread the and delicacies the And .neck his the
put she of smooth

1 559 1 935 1121 3290 3027 6213
18 עָשָׂתָה בְּיַד יַעֲקֹב בְּנָהּ׃ וַיָּבֹא אֶל־אָבִיו וַיֹּאמֶר אָבִי
My ,said and father his to he And her Jacob's in had she
father went .son hand made

3290 559 1121 4310 559
19 וַיֹּאמֶר הִנֶּנִּי מִי אַתָּה בְּנִי׃ וַיֹּאמֶר יַעֲקֹב אֶל־אָבִיו אָנֹכִי
(am) I ,father his to Jacob said And my (are) Who I Here he and
?son ,you .(am) ,said

342·7 6965 559 6213 1060 6215
עֵשָׂו בְּכֹרֶךָ עָשִׂיתִי כַּאֲשֶׁר דִּבַּרְתָּ אֵלָי קוּם־נָא שְׁבָה
sit .Please rise ;me to said you as have I your Esau
done .firstborn

3327 559 5315 1288 6718 398
20 וְאָכְלָה מִצֵּידִי בַּעֲבוּר תְּבָרְכַנִּי נַפְשֶׁךָ׃ וַיֹּאמֶר יִצְחָק אֶל־
to Isaac said And .soul your bless may that so my of eat and
his me ,game

3068 7136 559 1121 4672 4116 1121
בְּנוֹ מַה־זֶּה מִהַרְתָּ לִמְצֹא בְּנִי וַיֹּאמֶר כִּי הִקְרָה יְהוָה
Jehovah it made Be- he And my ,it found you have ,then ,How ,son
come cause ,said ?son quickly

4184 4994 5066 3290 3327 559 430
21 אֱלֹהֶיךָ לְפָנָי׃ וַיֹּאמֶר יִצְחָק אֶל־יַעֲקֹב גְּשָׁה־נָּא וַאֲמֻשְׁךָ
me let and ,now Come ,Jacob to Isaac said And .me to your
,you feel near God

3327 3290 5066 3808 6215 1121 2088 1121
22 בְּנִי הַאַתָּה זֶה בְּנִי עֵשָׂו אִם־לֹא׃ וַיִּגַּשׁ יַעֲקֹב אֶל־יִצְחָק
to Jacob And .not or ,Esau my then whether my
came son (are) you ;son

6215 3027 3027 3290 6963 6963 559 4959
אָבִיו וַיְמֻשֵּׁהוּ וַיֹּאמֶר הַקֹּל קוֹל יַעֲקֹב וְהַיָּדַיִם יְדֵי עֵשָׂו׃
.Esau's hands the and Jacob's (is) The he And he and his
hands voice voice ,said .him felt ,father

1288 8163 251 6215 3027 3027 1961 5234
23 וְלֹא הִכִּירוֹ כִּי־הָיוּ יָדָיו כִּידֵי עֵשָׂו אָחִיו שְׂעִרֹת וַיְבָרְכֵהוּ׃
he and ;hairy his Esau's like his were for knew he And
.him blessed brother hands hands him not

5066 559 559 6215 1121 559
24 25 וַיֹּאמֶר אַתָּה זֶה בְּנִי עֵשָׂו וַיֹּאמֶר אָנִי׃ וַיֹּאמֶר הַגִּשָׁה לִּי
to Bring he And .(am) I he And ?Esau my then (Are) he And
me ,said said son you ,said

398 3947 5315 1288 1121
וְאֹכְלָה מִצֵּיד בְּנִי לְמַעַן תְּבָרֶכְךָ נַפְשִׁי וַיַּגֶּשׁ־לוֹ וַיֹּאכַל
he and to he And my bless may that my game of let and
,ate ;him took .soul you son's eat me

5066 1 3327 559 8354 3196 935
26 וַיָּבֵא לוֹ יַיִן וַיֵּשְׁתְּ׃ וַיֹּאמֶר אֵלָיו יִצְחָק אָבִיו גְּשָׁה־נָּא
Now come his Isaac him to said And he and wine to he and
,father drank him brought

1288 899 7381 7306 5401 5066 1121 5401
27 וּשְׁקָה־לִּי בְּנִי׃ וַיִּגַּשׁ וַיִּשַּׁק־לוֹ וַיָּרַח אֶת־רֵיחַ בְּגָדָיו וַיְבָרְכֵהוּ
blessed and his odor the he And ,him and he And my ,me and
,him clothes of smelled kissed came ,son kiss

7704 7381 5414 3068 1288 1121 7381 7200 559
28 וַיֹּאמֶר רְאֵה רֵיחַ בְּנִי כְּרֵיחַ שָׂדֶה אֲשֶׁר בֵּרְכוֹ יְהוָה׃ וְיִתֶּן־
And Jehovah has which a as is my the ,See ,said and
give may blessed field's smell son of smell

8492 1715 7230 776 4924 8064 2919 430
לְךָ הָאֱלֹהִים מִטַּל הַשָּׁמַיִם וּמִשְׁמַנֵּי הָאָרֶץ וְרֹב דָּגָן וְתִירֹשׁ׃
.wine and grain and the of and the the of God you
much earth's fatness ,heavens of dew

251 1376 1933 3816 7812 1471 564
29 יַעַבְדוּךָ עַמִּים וְיִשְׁתַּחֲוּוּ לְךָ לְאֻמִּים הֱוֵה גְבִיר לְאַחֶיךָ
your to ruler a be ;peoples you to bow and ,nations serve May
,brothers you

וישתחוו לך בני אמך ארריך ארור ומברכיך ברוך׃
30 ויהי כאשר כלה יצחק לברך את־יעקב ויהי אך יצא
יצא יעקב מאת פני יצחק אביו ועשו אחיו בא מצידו׃
31 ויעש גם־הוא מטעמים ויבא לאביו ויאמר לאביו יקם
32 אבי ויאכל מציד בנו בעבר תברכני נפשך׃ ויאמר לו
33 יצחק אביו מי־אתה ויאמר אני בנך בכרך עשו׃ ויחרד
יצחק חרדה גדלה עד־מאד ויאמר מי־אפוא הוא הצד־
ציד ויבא לי ואכל מכל בטרם תבוא ואברכהו גם־ברוך
34 יהיה׃ כשמע עשו את־דברי אביו ויצעק צעקה גדלה
35 ומרה עד־מאד ויאמר לאביו ברכני גם־אני אבי׃ ויאמר
36 בא אחיך במרמה ויקח ברכתך׃ ויאמר הכי קרא שמו
יעקב ויעקבני זה פעמים את־בכרתי לקח והנה עתה
37 לקח ברכתי ויאמר הלא־אצלת לי ברכה׃ ויען יצחק
ויאמר לעשו הן גביר שמתיו לך ואת־כל־אחיו נתתי
לו לעבדים ודגן ותירש סמכתיו ולכה אפוא מה אעשה
38 בני׃ ויאמר עשו אל־אביו הברכה אחת הוא־לך אבי
39 ברכני גם־אני אבי וישא עשו קלו ויבך׃ ויען יצחק אביו

and may the sons of your
mother bow to you, and
cursed *be* those who
curse you, and blessed *be*
those who bless you.
And it happened when
Isaac made an end bless-
ing Jacob, then it was,
hardly had Jacob left
from before his father
Isaac, even his brother
Esau came in from his
hunting. [31]And he also
made delicious things
and took to his father.
And he said to his father,
Let my father rise and eat
from the game of his son,
so that your soul may
bless me. [32]And his father
Isaac said to him, Who
are you? And he said, I *am*
your son, your firstborn,
Esau. [33]And Isaac *was*
terrified with a very great
terror. And he said, Who
then *was* the one who
hunted game and came
to me; and I ate from all
before you came; and I
blessed him? Yea, he
shall be blessed. [34]When
Esau heard his father's
words he cried out a great
and very bitter cry. And
he said to is father, Bless
me, me also, my father.
[35]And he said, Your
brother came with deceit
and took your blessing.
[36]And he said, *It is* because his name *is* called
Jacob, and this twice he
took me by the heel; he
took my birthright, and,
behold, now he has taken
my blessing. And he said,
Have you not reserved a
blessing for me? [37]And
Isaac answered and said
to Esau, Behold, I have
set him over you *as* a ruler
and I have given him all
his brothers for servants; I
have girded him *with*
grain and wine. And what
then can I do for you, my
son? [38]And Esau said to
his father, Is one blessing
left to you, my father?
Bless me, me also, my
father. And Esau lifted up
his voice and wept.

[39]And his father Isaac
answered and said to

him. Behold, your abode shall be from the fat of the earth and from the dew of the heavens above; [40]and you shall live by your sword, and you shall serve your brother; and when it shall be that you fight, you shall break his yoke from your neck.

[41]And Esau hated Jacob because of the blessing with which his father had blessed him. And Esau said in his heart, The days of mourning *for* my father are near; then I will kill my brother Jacob. [42]And the words of her older son Esau were told to Rebekah. And she sent and called her younger son Jacob. And she said to him, See, your brother Esau *is* going to ease himself on you, to kill you. [43]And now, my son, listen to my voice, and rise, flee for yourself to my brother Laban, to Haran. [44]And stay with him some days until your brother's fury turns away, until your brother's anger turns back from you, and he forgets what you have done to him. And I will send you and take you from there. Why should I also be bereaved of two of you *in* one day?

[46]And Rebekah said to Isaac, I am weary of my life before the daughters of Heth. If Jacob takes a wife from the daughters of Heth, like these from the daughters of the land, what *is my* life to me?

וַיֹּאמֶר אֵלָיו הִנֵּה מִשְׁמַנֵּי הָאָרֶץ יִהְיֶה מוֹשָׁבֶךָ וּמִטַּל
from and your be shall earth the the from ,Behold ,him to and
of dew the abode of fat said

40 הַשָּׁמַיִם מֵעָל׃ וְעַל־חַרְבְּךָ תִחְיֶה וְאֶת־אָחִיךָ תַּעֲבֹד וְהָיָה
it and shall you your and shall you your and ;above the
,be shall ;serve brother ;live ,sword by heavens

41 כַּאֲשֶׁר תָּרִיד וּפָרַקְתָּ עֻלּוֹ מֵעַל צַוָּארֶךָ׃ וַיִּשְׂטֹם עֵשָׂו אֶת־
Esau hated And your from his shall you you when
.neck yoke break ,fight

יַעֲקֹב עַל־הַבְּרָכָה אֲשֶׁר בֵּרֲכוֹ אָבִיו וַיֹּאמֶר עֵשָׂו בְּלִבּוֹ
his in Esau said And his blessed had which the because Jacob
heart .father him blessing of

42 יִקְרְבוּ יְמֵי אֵבֶל אָבִי וְאַהַרְגָה אֶת־יַעֲקֹב אָחִי׃ וַיֻּגַּד
were And my Jacob I and my mourning the Are
told .brother kill will father (for) of days ,near

לְרִבְקָה אֶת־דִּבְרֵי עֵשָׂו בְּנָהּ הַגָּדֹל וַתִּשְׁלַח וַתִּקְרָא
called and she And .elder her Esau of words the to
sent son Rebekah

לְיַעֲקֹב בְּנָהּ הַקָּטָן וַתֹּאמֶר אֵלָיו הִנֵּה עֵשָׂו אָחִיךָ מִתְנַחֵם
to going (is) your Esau ,See ,him to she and ;younger her Jacob
himself ease brother said son

43 לְךָ לְהָרְגֶךָ׃ וְעַתָּה בְנִי שְׁמַע בְּקֹלִי וְקוּם בְּרַח־לְךָ אֶל־
to for flee and my to listen my ,now And kill to on
yourself ,rise ;voice son .you you

44 לָבָן אָחִי חָרָנָה׃ וְיָשַׁבְתָּ עִמּוֹ יָמִים אֲחָדִים עַד אֲשֶׁר־
until some days with stay And .Haran to my ,Laban
him ,brother

45 תָּשׁוּב חֲמַת אָחִיךָ׃ עַד־שׁוּב אַף־אָחִיךָ מִמְּךָ וְשָׁכַח אֶת
he and from your anger turns until your fury turns
forgets ,you brother's away ,brother's away

אֲשֶׁר־עָשִׂיתָ לּוֹ וְשָׁלַחְתִּי וּלְקַחְתִּיךָ מִשָּׁם לָמָה אֶשְׁכַּל גַּם־
also I should Why from take and I And to have you what
bereaved be .there you send will .him done

46 שְׁנֵיכֶם יוֹם אֶחָד׃ וַתֹּאמֶר רִבְקָה אֶל־יִצְחָק קַצְתִּי בְחַיַּי
my of am I ,Isaac to Rebekah said And ?one (in) two of
life weary day you (of)

מִפְּנֵי בְּנוֹת חֵת אִם־לֹקֵחַ יַעֲקֹב אִשָּׁה מִבְּנוֹת־חֵת כָּאֵלֶּה
like ,Heth the from a Jacob takes If ;Heth the before
these of daughters wife of daughters

מִבְּנוֹת הָאָרֶץ לָמָּה לִּי חַיִּים׃
(my) to what the the from
?life me (is) ,land of daughters

CAP. XXVIII כח

CHAPTER 28

CHAPTER 28

[1]And Isaac called Jacob. And he blessed him and commanded him, and said to him, You shall not take a wife from the daughters of Canaan. [2]Rise up, go to Padan-aram, to the house

1 וַיִּקְרָא יִצְחָק אֶל־יַעֲקֹב וַיְבָרֶךְ אֹתוֹ וַיְצַוֵּהוּ וַיֹּאמֶר לוֹ לֹא־
not to said and and ;him he and Jacob Isaac And
,him him directed blessed called

2 תִקַּח אִשָּׁה מִבְּנוֹת כְּנָעַן׃ קוּם לֵךְ פַּדֶּנָה אֲרָם בֵּיתָה
the to aram Padan to go ,Arise .Canaan the of a shall You
of house of daughters wife take

of Bethuel, your mother's father. And take a wife for yourself from there, from the daughters of Laban the brother of your mother. [3]And may God Almighty bless you and make you fruitful, and add to you; and may you become an assembly of nations. [4]And may He give to you the blessing of Abraham, to you and to your seed with you, for you to possess the land of your travels, which God gave to Abraham. [5]And Isaac sent away Jacob. And he went to Padan-aram, to Laban, son of Bethuel the Aramean, brother of Rebekah, the mother of Jacob and Esau. [6]And Esau saw that Isaac had blessed Jacob, and had sent him away to Padan-aram to take a wife for himself from there. In his blessing he had commanded him, saying, You shall not take a wife from the daughters of Canaan; [7]and that Jacob obeyed his father and his mother, and went to Padan-aram. [8]And when Esau saw that the daughters of Canaan were evil in the eyes of his father Isaac, then Esau went to Ishmael and took Mahalath the daughter of Ishmael, the son of Abraham, Nebajoth's sister. To his wives he *added her* for his wife.

[10]And Jacob went out from Beer-sheba and went toward Haran. [11]And he came on a place and stayed the night there, for the sun had gone. And he took stones of the place and placed *them* at his head; and he lay down in that place. [12]And he dreamed. And, behold, a ladder was placed on the earth, its top reaching to the heavens. And, behold, the angels of God *were* going up and going down on it! [13]And, behold, Jehovah stood above it and said, I *am* Jehovah the God of

251 3837 1323 802 8033 3947 517 1 1328
בתואל אבי אמך וקח־לך משם אשה מבנות לבן אחי
brother Laban the from a from for and your father Bethuel
of daughters wife there yourself take ;mother's

6951 7235 6509 1288 7706 410 517
3 אמך׃ ואל שדי יברך אתך ויפרך וירבך והיית לקהל
army an may and add and pros- and ,you may Almighty And your
of be you ;you to you per bless God .mother's

2233 85 1293 5414 1471
4 עמים׃ ויתן־לך את־ברכת אברהם לך ולזרעך אתך
with to and to Abraham blessing the to may and ;nations
;you seed your you of you give He

85 430 5414 4033 776 3423
לרשתך את־ארץ מגריך אשר־נתן אלהים לאברהם׃
.Abraham to God gave which your of land the to you for
travels possess

1121 3837 6307 3212 3290 3327 7971
5 וישלח יצחק את־יעקב וילך פדנה ארם אל־לבן בן
son ,Laban to aram Padan- to he and ,Jacob Isaac And
of went sent

6215 7200 6215 3290 517 7259 251 761 1328
6 בתואל הארמי אחי רבקה אם יעקב ועשו׃ וירא עשו
Esau And and Jacob's ,Rebekah brother the Bethuel
saw Esau's mother of Syrian

3947 6307 7971 3290 3327 1288
כי־ברך יצחק את־יעקב ושלח אתו פדנה ארם לקחת־
take to aram Padan- to him had and ,Jacob Isaac had that
sent blessed

3947 559 6680 1288 802 8033
לו משם אשה בברכו אתו ויצו עליו לאמר לא־תקח
shall You not ,saying ,him had he him his in ;wife a from for
take directed blessing there him

517 3290 8085 3667 1323 802
7 אשה מבנות כנען׃ וישמע יעקב אל־אביו ואל־אמו
his and his Jacob And .Canaan the from wife a
,mother father to listened of girls

5869 3667 1323 7451 6215 7200 6307 3212
8 וילך פדנה ארם׃ וירא עשו כי רעות בנות כנען בעיני
the in Canaan the was that Esau when And .aram Padan- to and
of eyes of girls evil saw went

4258 3947 3458 6215 3212 1 3327
9 יצחק אביו׃ וילך עשו אל־ישמעאל ויקח את־מחלת בת־
Mahalath and Ishmael to Esau then his Isaac
took went ,father

802 802 5032 269 85 1121 3458
ישמעאל בן־אברהם אחות נביות על־נשיו לו לאשה׃
his for which the to ,Nebajoth's sister ,Abraham the Ishmael's
.wife had he wives of son ,daughter

3885 4725 6293 2771 3212 7656 875 3290 5927
10 ויצא יעקב מבאר שבע וילך חרנה׃ ויפגע במקום וילן
11
and a upon he And toward and sheba from Jacob And
stayed place came .Haran went Beer- left

4763 7760 4725 68 3947 8121 935 8033
שם כי־בא השמש ויקח מאבני המקום וישם מראשתיו
his at put and place the the from he And .sun the had for
head (them) of stones took set there

776 5324 5551 2492 4725 7901
12 וישכב במקום ההוא׃ ויחלם והנה סלם מצב ארצה
the on was a ,and he And .that place in he and
earth placed ladder lo ;dreamed down lay

3381 5927 430 4397 8064 5060 7218
וראשו מגיע השמימה והנה מלאכי אלהים עלים וירדים
and going God angels the ,and the to reaching top its
down up of ,lo ;heavens

85 430 3068 559 5324 3068 2004
13 בו׃ והנה יהוה נצב עליו ויאמר אני יהוה אלהי אברהם
,Abraham the Jehovah I ,said and above stood Jehovah ,And on
of God am it ,behold it

your father Abraham, and the god of Isaac; the land on which you are lying, I will give it to you and to your seed. [14]And your seed shall be as the dust of the earth, and you shall spread to the west and to the east and to the north and to the south; and all the families of the earth shall be blessed in you and in your seed. [15]And, behold, I *will be* with you and will guard you in every *place in* which you may go, and will bring you back to this land; for I will not forsake you until I have surely done that which I have spoken to you. [16]And Jacob awakened from his sleep, and said, Surely Jehovah is in this place, and I did not know. [17]And he was afraid, and said, How fearful is this place! This is nothing except the house of God, and this *is* the doo to Heaven.

[18]And Jacob started up early in the morning and took the stone which he had placed at his head, and *he* placed it *as* a memorial pillar; and he poured oil on the top of it. [19]And he called the name of that place, The House of God. And yet the name of the city *was* at first Luz. [20]And Jacob vowed a vow, saying, If God is with me and keeps me in this way which I *am* going, and gives to me bread to eat and clothing to wear, [21]and I return in peace to the house of my father, then Jehovah shall be my God, [22]and this stone which I have placed *as* a memorial pillar shall become the house of God; and all which You shall give to me, I will tithe the tenth to You.

CAP. XXIX כט

CHAPTER 29

1 2 וַיִּשָּׂא יַעֲקֹב רַגְלָיו וַיֵּלֶךְ אַרְצָה בְנֵי־קֶדֶם׃ וַיַּרְא וְהִנֵּה
בְאֵר בַּשָּׂדֶה וְהִנֵּה־שָׁם שְׁלֹשָׁה עֶדְרֵי־צֹאן רֹבְצִים עָלֶיהָ
כִּי מִן־הַבְּאֵר הַהִוא יַשְׁקוּ הָעֲדָרִים וְהָאֶבֶן גְּדֹלָה עַל־
3 פִּי הַבְּאֵר׃ וְנֶאֶסְפוּ־שָׁמָּה כָל־הָעֲדָרִים וְגָלְלוּ אֶת־הָאֶבֶן
מֵעַל פִּי הַבְּאֵר וְהִשְׁקוּ אֶת־הַצֹּאן וְהֵשִׁיבוּ אֶת־הָאֶבֶן עַל־
4 פִּי הַבְּאֵר לִמְקֹמָהּ׃ וַיֹּאמֶר לָהֶם יַעֲקֹב אַחַי מֵאַיִן אַתֶּם
5 וַיֹּאמְרוּ מֵחָרָן אֲנָחְנוּ׃ וַיֹּאמֶר לָהֶם הַיְדַעְתֶּם אֶת־לָבָן
6 בֶּן־נָחוֹר וַיֹּאמְרוּ יָדָעְנוּ׃ וַיֹּאמֶר לָהֶם הֲשָׁלוֹם לוֹ וַיֹּאמְרוּ
7 שָׁלוֹם וְהִנֵּה רָחֵל בִּתּוֹ בָּאָה עִם־הַצֹּאן׃ וַיֹּאמֶר הֵן עוֹד
הַיּוֹם גָּדוֹל לֹא־עֵת הֵאָסֵף הַמִּקְנֶה הַשְׁקוּ הַצֹּאן וּלְכוּ
8 רְעוּ׃ וַיֹּאמְרוּ לֹא נוּכַל עַד אֲשֶׁר יֵאָסְפוּ כָל־הָעֲדָרִים
9 וְגָלְלוּ אֶת־הָאֶבֶן מֵעַל פִּי הַבְּאֵר וְהִשְׁקִינוּ הַצֹּאן׃ עוֹדֶנּוּ
מְדַבֵּר עִמָּם וְרָחֵל בָּאָה עִם־הַצֹּאן אֲשֶׁר לְאָבִיהָ כִּי רֹעָה
10 הִוא׃ וַיְהִי כַּאֲשֶׁר רָאָה יַעֲקֹב אֶת־רָחֵל בַּת־לָבָן אֲחִי
אִמּוֹ וְאֶת־צֹאן לָבָן אֲחִי אִמּוֹ וַיִּגַּשׁ יַעֲקֹב וַיָּגֶל אֶת־הָאֶבֶן
11 מֵעַל פִּי הַבְּאֵר וַיַּשְׁקְ אֶת־צֹאן לָבָן אֲחִי אִמּוֹ׃ וַיִּשַּׁק יַעֲקֹב

CHAPTER 29

1 And Jacob lifted his feet and went to the land of the sons of the east. 2 And he looked, and, behold, a well in the field. And, behold, three flocks of sheep *were* lying by it; for from that well they watered the flocks, and the stone on the mouth of the well *was* great. 3 And all the flocks were usually gathered there, and they rolled the stone off the mouth of the well and watered the sheep, and replaced the stone on the mouth of the well, to its place.

4 And Jacob said to them, My brothers, from where *are* you? And they said, We *are* from Haran. 5 And he said to them, Do you know Laban the son of Nahor? And they said, We know *him*. 6 And he said to them, *Is* he well? And they said, Well. And, behold, his daughter Rachel is coming with the sheep. 7 And he said, See, the day is still high; *it is* not time to gather the livestock. Water the sheep and go feed *them*. 8 And they said, We are not able until all the flocks are gathered and they roll the stone from the mouth of the well; then we water the sheep. 9 He still *was* speaking with them, and Rachel came with the sheep which *were* her father's; for she was a shepherdess. 10 And it happened when Jacob saw Rachel the daughter of Laban, brother to his mother, and the sheep of Laban, his mother's brother, Jacob came near and rolled the stone from the mouth of the well and watered the sheep of Laban, the brother of his mother. 11 And Jacob kissed Rachel and

lifted up his voice and wept.
[12]And Jacob told Rachel
that he *was* her father's
brother, and that he *was* the
son of Rebekah. And she
ran and told her father.
[13]And when Laban heard
the report of Jacob, his
sister's son, he ran to meet
him and embraced him and
kissed him. And *he* took
him to his house. And he
told Laban all these things.
[14]And Laban said to him,
Truly you are my bone and
my flesh. And he lived with
him a month of days. [15]And
Laban said to Jacob, Are
you not my brother? And
should you serve me for
nothing? Tell me, what shall
be your wages? [16]And
Laban *had* two daughters,
the name of the older, Leah,
and the name of the
younger, Rachel. [17]And the
eyes of Leah *were* weak,
and Rachel was beautiful of
form and beautiful of
appearance. [18]And Jacob
loved Rachel, and said, I will
serve you seven years for
Rachel, your younger
daughter. [19]And Laban
said, *It is* better for me to
give her to you *than* to give
her to another man; live
with me. [20]And Jacob
served seven years for
Rachel; and they were in his
eyes like a few days, in that
he loved her. [21]And Jacob
said to Laban, Give my wife,
for my days are fulfilled; and
let me go in to her. [22]And
Laban gathered all the men
of the place and made a
feast.

[23]And it happened in the
evening, he took his
daughter Leah and brought
her to him; and he went in
to her. [24]And Laban gave to
her Zilpah, his slavegirl, to
his daughter Leah *as* a
slave.

251 7354 3290 5046 1058 6963 5375 7354
12 לְרָחֵל וַיִּשָּׂא אֶת־קֹלוֹ וַיֵּבְךְּ׃ וַיַּגֵּד יַעֲקֹב לְרָחֵל כִּי אֲחִי
brother that Rachel Jacob And and his and ,Rachel
told ,wept voice up lifted

1961 1 5046 7323 7259 1121 1
13 אֲבִיהָ הוּא וְכִי בֶן־רִבְקָה הוּא וַתָּרָץ וַתַּגֵּד לְאָבִיהָ׃ וַיְהִי
And .father her and she and he Rebekah the and he her
,was it told ran ·(was) of son that (was) father's

7125 7323 269/1121 3290 8088 3837 8085
כִּשְׁמֹעַ לָבָן אֶת־שֵׁמַע ׀ יַעֲקֹב בֶּן־אֲחֹתוֹ וַיָּרָץ לִקְרָאתוֹ
him meet to ran he his son Jacob of report the Laban when
,sister's heard

3837 5608 1004 935 5401 2263
וַיְחַבֶּק־לוֹ וַיְנַשֶּׁק־לוֹ וַיְבִיאֵהוּ אֶל־בֵּיתוֹ וַיְסַפֵּר לְלָבָן אֵת
Laban he and his to took and him and him and
told ;house him kissed embraced

1320 6606 389 3837 559 1697 3605
14 כָּל־הַדְּבָרִים הָאֵלֶּה׃ וַיֹּאמֶר לוֹ לָבָן אַךְ עַצְמִי וּבְשָׂרִי
my and my ,Truly ,Laban to said And .these things all
flesh bone him

3290 3837 559 3117 2320 2416
15 אָתָּה וַיֵּשֶׁב עִמּוֹ חֹדֶשׁ יָמִים׃ וַיֹּאמֶר לָבָן לְיַעֲקֹב הֲכִי
not Are ,Jacob to Laban said And .days month a with he and you
of 5647 him lived ;(are)

4909 5046 2600
אָחִי אַתָּה וַעֲבַדְתַּנִי חִנָּם הַגִּידָה לִּי מַה־מַּשְׂכֻּרְתֶּךָ׃
?wages your (be shall) what me Tell for should and You my
?nothing me serve you brother

7354 6996 8034 3812/1419 8034 1323 8147 3837
16 וּלְלָבָן שְׁתֵּי בָנוֹת שֵׁם הַגְּדֹלָה לֵאָה וְשֵׁם הַקְּטַנָּה רָחֵל׃
.Rachel the tje amd Leah older the the ,daughters (had) And
,younger of name (was) of name two Laban

4758 3303 8389 3303 1961 7354 7390 3812 5869
17 וְעֵינֵי לֵאָה רַכּוֹת וְרָחֵל הָיְתָה יְפַת־תֹּאַר וִיפַת מַרְאֶה׃
.appearance and form of fair was and (were) Leah's And
of fair Rachel ,weak eyes

7354 8141 7651 5647 559 7354 3290 157
18 וַיֶּאֱהַב יַעֲקֹב אֶת־רָחֵל וַיֹּאמֶר אֶעֱבָדְךָ שֶׁבַע שָׁנִים בְּרָחֵל
for years seven will I ,said and ,Rachel Jacob And
Rachel you serve loved

5414 5414 2896 3837 559 6996 1323
19 בִּתְּךָ הַקְּטַנָּה׃ וַיֹּאמֶר לָבָן טוֹב תִּתִּי אֹתָהּ לָךְ מִתִּתִּי
(than) to her me for (is It) ,Laban said And ,younger your
give to you give to better daughter

7651 7354 3290 5647 2416 312 376
20 אֹתָהּ לְאִישׁ אַחֵר שְׁבָה עִמָּדִי׃ וַיַּעֲבֹד יַעֲקֹב בְּרָחֵל שֶׁבַע
seven Rachel for Jacob served And ,me with live ;another man to her

559 160 259 3117 5869 1961 8141
21 שָׁנִים וַיִּהְיוּ בְעֵינָיו כְּיָמִים אֲחָדִים בְּאַהֲבָתוֹ אֹתָהּ׃ וַיֹּאמֶר
said And .her that in ,few days like eyes his and ;years
loved he were they

935 3117 4390 802 3051 3837 3290
יַעֲקֹב אֶל־לָבָן הָבָה אֶת־אִשְׁתִּי כִּי מָלְאוּ יָמָי וְאָבוֹאָה
me let and my are for ,wife my (me) Give ,Laban to Jacob
in go ;days fulfilled

4960 6213/4925 582 3605 3837 622
22 אֵלֶיהָ׃ וַיֶּאֱסֹף לָבָן אֶת־כָּל־אַנְשֵׁי הַמָּקוֹם וַיַּעַשׂ מִשְׁתֶּה׃
.feast a made and place the of men the all Laban And .her to
gathered

935 935 1323 3812 3947 6153 1961
23 וַיְהִי בָעֶרֶב וַיִּקַּח אֶת־לֵאָה בִתּוֹ וַיָּבֵא אֹתָהּ אֵלָיו וַיָּבֹא
he and to her and his Leah took he the in it And
in went ;him brought daughter ,evening was

8198 1323 3812 8198 2153 3837/5414
24 אֵלֶיהָ׃ וַיִּתֵּן לָבָן לָהּ אֶת־זִלְפָּה שִׁפְחָתוֹ לְלֵאָה בִתּוֹ שִׁפְחָה׃
.slave a (as) his to ,slave-girl his ,Zilpah to Laban And to
daughter Leah her gave .her

[25]And it happened in the morning; behold! She *was* Leah. And he said to Laban, What have you done to me? *Did* I not serve with you for Rachel? And why have you tricked me? [26]And Laban said, It is not done this way in our place, to give the younger before the firstborn. [27]Fulfill the week of this one and we will also give you this *other* one, for the service which you will serve with me, yet another seven years. [28]And Jacob did so, and he fulfilled the week of this one, and he gave to him his daughter Rachel, to him for a wife. [29]And Laban gave his slave-girl Bilhah to his daughter Rachel, to her for a slave-girl. [30]And he also went in to Rachel, and he also loved Rachel *more than* Leah. And he served with him yet another seven years.

[31]And Jehovah saw that Leah *was* hated. And He opened her womb, but Rachel *was* barren. [32]And Leah conceived and bore a son. And she called his name Reuben; for she said, Surely Jehovah has looked on my affliction, for now my husband will love me. [33]And she conceived again and bore a son, and said, Surely Jehovah has heard that I *am* hated and has given this one to me also. And she called his name Simeon. [34]And she conceived again and bore a son. And she said, Now, *this* time, my husband will be joined to me, because I have borne to him three sons. So his name was called Levi.

[35]And she conceived again and bore a son. And she said, *This* time I praise Jehovah. So she called his name Judah. And she ceased from bearing.

3837 559 3812 2009 1242 1961
25 ויהי בבקר והנה־הוא לאה ויאמר אל־לבן מה־זאת
this What ,Laban to he and said ;Leah she (was) !behold the in ,morning it And was
559 7411 5647 7354 6213
26 עשית לי הלא ברחל עבדתי עמך ולמה רמיתני: ויאמר
said And you have ?me tricked And why with ?you serve I for Rachel (Did) not ?me to you have done
1067 6440 6810 5414 4725 6213 3837
לבן לא־יעשה כן במקומנו לתת הצעירה לפני הבכירה:
the .eldest before the younger give to ,place our in this way is It not done ,Laban
834 5656 2063 1571 5414 7620 4390
27 מלא שבע זאת ונתנה לך גם־את־זאת בעבדה אשר
which the for service this ,one (other) also you we and give will this ,one the of week Fulfill
3651 3290 6213 312 8141 7651 5750 5647
28 תעבד עמדי עוד שבע־שנים אחרות: ויעש יעקב כן
,so Jacob did And .another years seven yet with ,me shall you serve
5414 802 1323 7354 5414 7620 4390
29 וימלא שבע זאת ויתן־לו את־רחל בתו לו לאשה: ויתן
And gave a for .wife to him his ,daughter Rachel to he and him gave this ,one the of week he and fulfilled
935 8198 8198 1090 1323 7354 3837
30 לבן לרחל בתו את־בלהה שפחתו לה לשפחה: ויבא
he And in went a for .slave-girl to her his ,slave-girl ,Bilhah his daughter to Rachel Laban
5750 5647 3812 7351 1571 157 7354 1571
גם אל־רחל ויאהב גם־את־רחל מלאה ויעבד עמו עוד
yet with him he and served than more ;Leah Rachel also he and loved ,Rachel to also
6605 8130 3068 7200 312 8141 7651
31 שבע־שנים אחרות: וירא יהוה כי־שנואה לאה ויפתח
He and opened ,Leah (was) hated that Jehovah And saw .another years seven
7121 1121 3205 3812 2029 6135 7354 7358
32 את־רחמה ורחל עקרה: ותהר לאה ותלד בן ותקרא
she and called a ,son and bore Leah And conceived (was) .barren but Rachel ,womb her
6258 3588 6040 3068 7200 559 3588 7205 8034
שמו ראובן כי אמרה כי־ראה יהוה בעניי כי עתה
now for my on ,affliction Jehovah has looked Surely she ,said for ;Reuben his name
8085 3588 559 1121 3205 2029 376 157
33 יאהבני אישי: ותהר עוד ותלד בן ותאמר כי־שמע
has heard Surely ,said and a son bore and again she And conceived my .husband love will me
8034 7121 1571 5414 8130 3068
יהוה כי־שנואה אנכי ויתן־לי גם־את־זה ותקרא שמו
his name she and called this ;one also to has and me given I (am) hated that Jehovah
3867 6471 6258 559 1121 3205 5750 2029 8095
34 שמעון: ותהר עוד ותלד בן ותאמר עתה הפעם ילוה
be will joined (this) time Now she and ,said a ;son and bore again she And conceived .Simeon
8034 7121 1121 7969 3205 376
אישי אלי כי־ילדתי לו שלשה בנים על־כן קרא־שמו
his name was called so sons three him to have I him borne because to ,me my husband
3034 6471 559 1126 3205 2029 3878
35 לוי: ותהר עוד ותלד בן ותאמר הפעם אודה את־
will I praise (This) time she and ,said a ;son and bore again she And conceived .Levi
3205 5975 3063 8034 7121 3068
יהוה על־כן קראה שמו יהודה ותעמד מלדת:
from .bearing she and ceased ;Judah his name she called so ;Jehovah

CHAPTER 30

[1]And Rachel saw that she did not bear to Jacob, and Rachel was jealous of her sister. And she said to Jacob, Give me sons; and if there is none, I shall die. [2]And Jacob's anger glowed against Rachel, and he said, *Am* I in God's place, who has kept back from you the fruit of the womb? [3]And she said, Behold, my servant Bilhah! Go in to her and let her bear on my knees; yea, let me be built up from her, me also. [4]And she gave her slavegirl Bilhah to him for a wife. And Jacob went in to her. [5]And Bilhah conceived and bore a son to Jacob. [6]And Rachel said, God has judged and has also heard my voice, and has given me a son. So she called his name Dan. [7]And Bilhah, Rachel's slavegirl, conceived again, and bore a second son to Jacob. [8]And Rachel said, with struggles of God I have struggled with my sister; yea, I have been able. And she called his name Naphtali.

[9]And Leah saw that she had ceased from bearing. And she took Zilpah, her slavegirl, and gave her to Jacob for a wife. [10]And Leah's slavegirl Zilpah bore a son to Jacob. [11]And Leah said, With fortune. And she called his name Gad. [12]And Zilpah, Leah's slavegirl, bore a second son to Jacob. [13]And Leah said, In my happiness; for the daughters shall call me happy. And she called his name Asher.

[14]And in the days of wheat harvest Reuben went out and found love-apples in the field. And he

CAP. XXX ל

CHAPTER 30

1 וַתֵּרֶא רָחֵל כִּי לֹא יָלְדָה לְיַעֲקֹב וַתְּקַנֵּא רָחֵל בַּאֲחֹתָהּ

her of sister; Rachel was and jealous to Jacob did she bear not that Rachel And saw

וַתֹּאמֶר אֶל־יַעֲקֹב הָבָה־לִּי בָנִים וְאִם־אַיִן מֵתָה אָנֹכִי׃

.I shall die there none is and if ,sons me Give to ,Jacob to she and said

2 וַיִּחַר־אַף יַעֲקֹב בְּרָחֵל וַיֹּאמֶר הֲתַחַת אֱלֹהִים אָנֹכִי אֲשֶׁר־

who Am I God's in place he and ,said against ,Rachel Jacob's anger And burned

3 מָנַע מִמֵּךְ פְּרִי־בָטֶן׃ וַתֹּאמֶר הִנֵּה אֲמָתִי בִלְהָה בֹּא אֵלֶיהָ

her to Go in !Bilhah my slave ,See she And ,said the ?womb the of fruit from you kept

4 וְתֵלֵד עַל־בִּרְכַּי וְאִבָּנֶה גַם־אָנֹכִי מִמֶּנָּה׃ וַתִּתֶּן־לוֹ אֶת־

to him she And gave from ,her ,me also me let and ,up built be my knees on let and bear her

5 בִּלְהָה שִׁפְחָתָהּ לְאִשָּׁה וַיָּבֹא אֵלֶיהָ יַעֲקֹב׃ וַתַּהַר בִּלְהָה

Bilhah And conceived ,Jacob .to her and in went a for ;wife her slave Bilhah

6 וַתֵּלֶד לְיַעֲקֹב בֵּן׃ וַתֹּאמֶר רָחֵל דָּנַנִּי אֱלֹהִים וְגַם שָׁמַע

has heard and also God has judged ,Rachel said And .son a to Jacob and bore

7 בְּקֹלִי וַיִּתֶּן־לִי בֵּן עַל־כֵּן קָרְאָה שְׁמוֹ דָּן׃ וַתַּהַר עוֹד

again And conceived .Dan his name she called so ;son a has and me given my voice

8 וַתֵּלֶד בִּלְהָה שִׁפְחַת רָחֵל בֵּן שֵׁנִי לְיַעֲקֹב׃ וַתֹּאמֶר רָחֵל

,Rachel And said .Jacob to second a son Rachel's slave Bilhah and bore

נַפְתּוּלֵי אֱלֹהִים ׀ נִפְתַּלְתִּי עִם־אֲחֹתִי גַּם־יָכֹלְתִּי וַתִּקְרָא

she and called have I ,yea ;prevailed my ;sister with have I struggled God With of struggles

9 שְׁמוֹ נַפְתָּלִי׃ וַתֵּרֶא לֵאָה כִּי עָמְדָה מִלֶּדֶת וַתִּקַּח אֶת־

and took she from ;bearing had she ceased that Leah And saw .Naphtali his name

10 זִלְפָּה שִׁפְחָתָהּ וַתִּתֵּן אֹתָהּ לְיַעֲקֹב לְאִשָּׁה׃ וַתֵּלֶד זִלְפָּה

Zilpah And bore a for .wife to Jacob her and gave her slave Zilpah

11 שִׁפְחַת לֵאָה לְיַעֲקֹב בֵּן׃ וַתֹּאמֶר לֵאָה בָּגָד וַתִּקְרָא אֶת־

she and called With fortune ,Leah said And .son a Jacob to Leah the of slave

12 שְׁמוֹ גָּד׃ וַתֵּלֶד זִלְפָּה שִׁפְחַת לֵאָה בֵּן שֵׁנִי לְיַעֲקֹב׃

.Jacob to second a son Leah's slave Zilpah And bore .Gad his name

13 וַתֹּאמֶר לֵאָה בְּאָשְׁרִי כִּי אִשְּׁרוּנִי בָּנוֹת וַתִּקְרָא אֶת־שְׁמוֹ

name his she and called the daughters call shall me happy for my In ;happiness ,Leah said And

14 אָשֵׁר׃ וַיֵּלֶךְ רְאוּבֵן בִּימֵי קְצִיר־חִטִּים וַיִּמְצָא דוּדָאִים

love-apples and found wheat the harvest the in of days Reuben And went .Asher brought them to his mother Leah. And Rachel said to Leah, Please give to me from the love-apples of your son. [15]And she said to her, Is your taking my husband a little thing? Will you also take my son's love-apples? And Rachel said, So he shall be with you tonight, for your son's love-apples. [16]And Jacob came in from the field at evening. And Leah went out to meet him. And she said, You must come in to me, for surely I have hired you with my son's love-apples. And he lay with her during that night. [17]And God listened to Leah, and she conceived and bore a fifth son to Jacob. [18]And Leah said, God has given my hire; I gave my slavegirl to my husband. And she called his name Issachar.

[19]And Leah conceived again and bore a sixth son to Jacob. [20]And Leah said, God has given me a good present. *This* time my husband will live with me, because I have borne six sons to him. And she called his name Zebulun. [21]And afterwards she bore a daughter and called her name Dinah. [22]And God remembered Rachel; and God listened to her and opened her womb. [23]And she conceived and bore a son. And she said, God has taken away my reproach. [24]And she called his name Joseph, saying, May Jehovah add to me another son.

[25]And when Rachel had borne Joseph, Jacob said to Laban, Send me away so I may go to my own place and to my land. [26]Give my wives and my children, *for* whom I have served you, and let me go. For you

3812 7354 559 517 3812 803 935 7704
בַּשָּׂדֶה וַיָּבֵא אֹתָם אֶל־לֵאָה אִמּוֹ וַתֹּאמֶר רָחֵל אֶל־לֵאָה
,Leah to Rachel said And his Leah to them he and the in
.mother brought ;field

3947 4592 559 1121 1736 4994/5414
15 תְּנִי־נָא לִי מִדּוּדָאֵי בְּנֵךְ׃ וַתֹּאמֶר לָהּ הַמְעַט קַחְתֵּךְ אֶת־
your a Is to she And your the from me to Please
taking ,thing little ,her said .son of love-apples give

7901 3654 559 1121 1736 3947 376
אִישִׁי וְלָקַחַת גַּם אֶת־דּוּדָאֵי בְּנִי וַתֹּאמֶר רָחֵל לָכֵן יִשְׁכַּב
shall he then ,Rachel And my love the also you will my
lie said ?son of apples take ,husband

7704 3290 935 1121 1736 8178 3915
16 עִמָּךְ הַלַּיְלָה תַּחַת דּוּדָאֵי בְנֵךְ׃ וַיָּבֹא יַעֲקֹב מִן־הַשָּׂדֶה
field the from Jacob And your love the for tonight with
in came .son of apples you

7936 935 559 7125 3812 5927 6153
בָּעֶרֶב וַתֵּצֵא לֵאָה לִקְרָאתוֹ וַתֹּאמֶר אֵלַי תָּבוֹא כִּי שָׂכֹר
surely for ,must You to she and meet to Leah went and at
,in come me ,said ;him out evening

8085 3915 7901 1121 1736 7936
17 שְׂכַרְתִּיךָ בְּדוּדָאֵי בְּנִי וַיִּשְׁכַּב עִמָּהּ בַּלַּיְלָה הוּא׃ וַיִּשְׁמַע
And .that during with he and my love with have I
listened night her lay ;son's apples you hired

559 2549 1121 3290 3205 2029 3812 430
18 אֱלֹהִים אֶל־לֵאָה וַתַּהַר וַתֵּלֶד לְיַעֲקֹב בֵּן חֲמִישִׁי׃ וַתֹּאמֶר
said And .fifth a Jacob to and she and ,Leah to God
son bore conceived

7121 376 8198 5414 7939 430 5414 3812
לֵאָה נָתַן אֱלֹהִים שְׂכָרִי אֲשֶׁר־נָתַתִּי שִׁפְחָתִי לְאִישִׁי וַתִּקְרָא
she and my to my gave I because my God has ,Leah
called ;husband slave .hire given

3290 8345/1121 3205 3812 5750 2029 3485 8034
19 שְׁמוֹ יִשָּׂשכָר׃ וַתַּהַר עוֹד לֵאָה וַתֵּלֶד בֵּן־שִׁשִּׁי לְיַעֲקֹב׃
Jacob to sixth a and Leah again And .Issachar his
son bore conceived name

2082 6471 2896 2065 430 2064/3812 559
20 וַתֹּאמֶר לֵאָה זְבָדַנִי אֱלֹהִים ׀ אֹתִי זֵבֶד טוֹב הַפַּעַם יִזְבְּלֵנִי
live will (this) ;good a God has ,Leah said And
me with time present me given

2074 8034 7121 1121 8337 3205 3588 376
אִישִׁי כִּי־יָלַדְתִּי לוֹ שִׁשָּׁה בָנִים וַתִּקְרָא אֶת־שְׁמוֹ זְבֻלוּן׃
.Zebulun name his she and ;sons six to have I because my
called him borne ,husband

430 2142 1783 8034 7121 1323 3205 310
21 22 וְאַחַר יָלְדָה בַּת וַתִּקְרָא אֶת־שְׁמָהּ דִּינָה׃ וַיִּזְכֹּר אֱלֹהִים
God And .Dinah name her called and a she And
remembered daughter bore later

7358 6605 430 8085 7354
אֶת־רָחֵל וַיִּשְׁמַע אֵלֶיהָ אֱלֹהִים וַיִּפְתַּח אֶת־רַחְמָהּ׃
.womb her opened and God her to and ,Rachel
listened

7121 2781 430 6225 559 1121 3205 2029
23 24 וַתַּהַר וַתֵּלֶד בֵּן וַתֹּאמֶר אָסַף אֱלֹהִים אֶת־חֶרְפָּתִי׃ וַתִּקְרָא
she and ;reproach my God taken has she and a and she And
called away ,said ;son bore conceived

1961 312 1121 3068 3254 559 3127 8034
25 אֶת־שְׁמוֹ יוֹסֵף לֵאמֹר יֹסֵף יְהוָה לִי בֵּן אַחֵר׃ וַיְהִי כַּאֲשֶׁר
when And .another son to Jehovah May ,saying ,Joseph name his
was it me add

8212 7971 3837 3290 559 3127 7354 3205
יָלְדָה רָחֵל אֶת־יוֹסֵף וַיֹּאמֶר יַעֲקֹב אֶל־לָבָן שַׁלְּחֵנִי וְאֵלְכָה
I and Send ,Laban to Jacob said that Joseph Rachel had
go may ,away me ,borne

5647 3206 802 5414 776 4725
26 אֶל־מְקוֹמִי וּלְאַרְצִי׃ תְּנָה אֶת־נָשַׁי וְאֶת־יְלָדַי אֲשֶׁר עָבַדְתִּי
have I (for) my and wives my Give my to and own my to
served whom ,children .country place

know my service *with*
which I have served you.
[27]And Laban said to him, If I
have found favor in your
eyes, *stay*. I have seen
omens, also Jehovah has
blessed me because of you.
[28]And he said, Set your
wages on me and I will give.
[29]And he said to him, You
know how I have served
you and what has come to
be, your livestock *being*
with me. [30]For little was
yours before my mouth, and
it has spread out into a host.
And Jehovah has blessed
you at my foot. And now
when shall I work for my
house, I also? [31]And he
said, What shall I give you?
And Jacob said, You shall
not give me anything. If you
will do this thing for me, I
will remain. I will feed your
flock and keep *it*.

[32]I will pass among all
your flock today, taking
from there every speckled
and spotted sheep, and
every black sheep among
the lambs, also the spotted
and speckled goats; *these*
shall be my wages. [33]And
my righteousness shall
testify for me in the day to
come. When you come in
about my wages, before
your face everyone that is
not speckled and spotted
among the goats, and black
among the lambs, it *is*
stolen with me. [34]And
Laban said, Yes, truly let it
be as you speak. [35]And he
turned out in that day all the
striped and spotted lambs,
and all the speckled and
spotted goats, every one
which *had* white, and every
black one among the
lambs. And he gave them
into the hands of his sons.
[36]And he put three days'
journey between himself
and Jacob. And Jacob was
feeding the remaining
flocks of Laban.
[37]And Jacob took for

5647 5650 3045 3212 2004
אֹתְךָ בָּהֵן וְאֵלֵכָה כִּי אַתָּה יָדַעְתָּ אֶת־עֲבֹדָתִי אֲשֶׁר עֲבַדְתִּיךָ׃
have I with service my know you for let and for you
.you served which 3837 go me them 559

5172 5869 2540 4672 4994
27 וַיֹּאמֶר אֵלָיו לָבָן אִם־נָא מָצָאתִי חֵן בְּעֵינֶיךָ נִחַשְׁתִּי
have I your in favor have I ,Please if ,Laban him to said And
omens seen ,eyes found 1558 3068 1288

5414 7939 5344 559
28 וַיְבָרְכֵנִי יְהוָה בִּגְלָלֶךָ׃ וַיֹּאמַר נָקְבָה שְׂכָרְךָ עָלַי וְאֶתֵּנָה׃
I and me on wages your Set he And account on Jehovah has and
.give will ,said .you of me blessed

5647 3045 559
29 וַיֹּאמֶר אֵלָיו אַתָּה יָדַעְתָּ אֵת אֲשֶׁר עֲבַדְתִּיךָ וְאֵת אֲשֶׁר־
what and have I how know You ,him to he And
you served said

6555 6440 1961/834 4592 4735 1961
30 הָיָה מִקְנְךָ אִתִּי׃ כִּי מְעַט אֲשֶׁר־הָיָה לְךָ לְפָנַי וַיִּפְרֹץ
it and before you to was which little a For .me with your be-has
spread has ,me me livestock come

1571 6213 4970 7272 3068 1288 7230
לָרֹב וַיְבָרֶךְ יְהוָה אֹתְךָ לְרַגְלִי וְעַתָּה מָתַי אֶעֱשֶׂה גַם־
also I shall when now and my at you Jehovah has and a into
.work ,foot blessed ,host

5414 3290 559 5414 559 1004
31 אָנֹכִי לְבֵיתִי׃ וַיֹּאמֶר מָה אֶתֶּן־לָךְ וַיֹּאמֶר יַעֲקֹב לֹא־תִתֶּן־
You not Jacob said And ?you shall What he And my for ,I
give shall give I ,said ?house own

7462 3427 2088 1697 6213 3972
לִי מְאוּמָה אִם־תַּעֲשֶׂה־לִּי הַדָּבָר הַזֶּה אָשׁוּבָה אֶרְעֶה
feed will I stay will I ,this thing for do will you If .anything to
me me

3605 8033 5493 3117 6629 3605 5674 8104 6129
32 צֹאנְךָ אֶשְׁמֹר׃ אֶעֱבֹר בְּכָל־צֹאנְךָ הַיּוֹם הָסֵר מִשָּׁם כָּל־
every from taking ,today your among will I will and your
.there flock all pass, 2921 (it) keep, flock

5348 2921 3775 2345 7716 5348 7716
שֶׂה נָקֹד וְטָלוּא וְכָל־שֶׂה־חוּם בַּכְּשָׂבִים וְטָלוּא וְנָקֹד
and the and among black sheep and and speckled sheep
speckled spotted ,lambs the every ,spotted

4279 3117 6666 6030 7939 1961 5795
33 בָּעִזִּים וְהָיָה שְׂכָרִי׃ וְעָנְתָה־בִּי צִדְקָתִי בְּיוֹם מָחָר כִּי־
when ,come to the in my for shall And my (these) ;goats
day righteousness me testify .wages be shall

5795 2921 5348 3605 7939 935
תָבוֹא עַל־שְׂכָרִי לְפָנֶיךָ כֹּל אֲשֶׁר־אֵינֶנּוּ נָקֹד וְטָלוּא בָּעִזִּים
among and speckled is that every before my about you
goats the spotted not one .you wages come

3837 559 1589 3775 2345
34 וְחוּם בַּכְּשָׂבִים גָּנוּב הוּא אִתִּי׃ וַיֹּאמֶר לָבָן הֵן לוּ יְהִי
it let truly ,Yes ,Laban And with it (is) the among and
be said .me stolen ,lambs black

2921 6124 8495 3117 5493 1696
35 כִדְבָרֶךָ׃ וַיָּסַר בַּיּוֹם הַהוּא אֶת־הַתְּיָשִׁים הָעֲקֻדִּים וְהַטְּלֻאִים
and striped lambs the that day in he And you as
spotted out turned say

3605 3836 3605 2921 5348 6795
וְאֵת כָּל־הָעִזִּים הַנְּקֻדּוֹת וְהַטְּלֻאֹת כֹּל אֲשֶׁר־לָבָן בּוֹ וְכָל־
and ,white which every and speckled the all and
every (had) one ,spotted goats

3117 7969 1870 7760 1121 3027 5414 3775 2345
36 חוּם בַּכְּשָׂבִים וַיִּתֵּן בְּיַד־בָּנָיו׃ וַיָּשֶׂם דֶּרֶךְ שְׁלֹשֶׁת יָמִים
days three journey he And his into he and the among black
put .sons' hands them gave ,lambs one

3947 3498 3837 6629 7462 3290 3290 996 996
37 בֵּינוֹ וּבֵין יַעֲקֹב וְיַעֲקֹב רֹעֶה אֶת־צֹאן לָבָן הַנּוֹתָרֹת׃ וַיִּקַּח־
And remaining Laban flocks the was and ,Jacob and between
took of feeding Jacob himself

himself white rods of a fresh *tree*, and the almond and plane tree. And he peeled white stripes in them, laying bare the white on the rods. [38]And he set the rods which he had peeled by the troughs, by the water troughs where the flocks came to drink, across from the flocks. And they were in heat when they came to drink. [39]And the flocks bore striped, speckled and spotted *offspring*. [40]And Jacob separated the lambs, and *he* set the faces of the flock toward the striped, and every black one in the flocks of Laban. And he put his own droves by themselves, and did not put them with the flock of Laban. [41]And it happened that whenever the strong flocks conceived, Jacob placed the rods before the eyes of the flocks, before the troughs, that they might conceive by the rods. [42]And he did not set *them before* the weak flocks. And it came to be, the weak for Laban, and the strong for Jacob. [43]And the man increased very much, and were many flocks to him, and slavegirls, and male slaves, and camels and asses.

6479 6478 6196 3869 3892 3839 4731 3290
לו יעקב מקל לבנה לח ולוז וערמון ויפצל בהן פצלות
stripes in he and the and the and fresh a rods Jacob for
them peeled ,tree plane almond (tree) white of himself

33.22 4731 5921 834 3:8:3 6 4286 3839
38 לבנות מחשף הלבן אשר על־המקלות: ויצג את־
he And .rods the on which the laying ,white
set (was) white bare

4325 8268 7298 6478 834 4731
המקלות אשר פצל ברהטים בשקתות המים אשר
where ,water the by the by had he which rods the
troughs ,troughs peeled

8354 935 3179 6629 5227 8354 6629 935
תבאן הצאן לשתות לנכח הצאן ויחמנה בבאן לשתות:
.drink to they when they and the across ,drink to the came
came heat in were ,flocks from flocks

5348 6124 6629 3205 4731 6629 3179
39 ויחמו הצאן אל־המקלות ותלדן הצאן עקדים נקדים
,speckled ,striped flocks the And .rods the before the were And
bore flocks heat in

6124 413 6629/6440/5414 3290 6504 3775 2921
40 וטלאים: והכשבים הפריד יעקב ויתן פני הצאן אל־עקד
the toward the the and Jacob separated the And and
striped flock of faces set lambs ,spotted

7896 3808 5739 7896 3837 6629 2345
וכל־חום בצאן לבן וישת לו עדרים לבדו ולא שתם
put did and by droves his And .Laban the in black and
them not themselves own put he of flocks one every

7760 7194 6629 3170 1961 3837 6629
41 על־צאן לבן: והיה בכל־יחם הצאן המקשרות ושם
usually ,strong the conceived that it And .Laban the with
placed flocks whenever happened of flock

3179 7298 6629 5869 4731 3290
יעקב את־המקלות לעיני הצאן ברהטים ליחמנה
they that the before the the before rods the Jacob
conceive might ,troughs flocks of eyes

5848 1961 7760 3808 6629 5848 4731
42 במקלות: ובהעטיף הצאן לא ישים והיה העטפים
the usually and usually he not the being And .rods the by
weak was it (them) set ,flocks feeble

3966 3966 376 6555 3290 7194 3837
43 ללבן והקשרים ליעקב: ויפרץ האיש מאד מאד ויהי־
and ,much very man the And .Jacob for strong the and for
had increased Laban

2543 1581 5650 8198 7227 6629
לו צאן רבות ושפחות ועבדים וגמלים וחמרים:
.asses and camels and and girl- and ,many flocks he
,slaves male slaves

CAP. XXXI לא

CHAPTER 31

CHAPTER 31

[1]And he heard the words of Laban's sons, saying, Jacob has taken away all that *was* to our father; and from that which was our father's he has gotten all this wealth. [2]And Jacob saw the face of Laban. And, behold, it was not toward him as the day before yesterday. [3]And Jehovah said to Jacob, Go back to the land of your fathers, and to your kindred.

3605 3290 3947 559 3837/1121 1697 8085
1 וישמע את־דברי בני־לבן לאמר לקח יעקב את כל־
all — Jacob has ,saying ,Laban's sons words the he And
away taken of heard

2088 3519 6213 1 834 1
אשר לאבינו ומאשר לאבינו עשה את כל־הכבד הזה:
.this wealth all — has he - our was from and our to that
gotten father's which that ;father (was)

8032 8543 2009 3837 6440 3290 7200
2 וירא יעקב את־פני לבן והנה איננו עמו כתמול שלשום:
before the as toward was it and ;Laban face the Jacob And
.yesterday day him not ,behold of saw

4138 1 776 7725 3290 3068 559
3 ויאמר יהוה אל־יעקב שוב אל־ארץ אבותיך ולמולדתך
your to and your the to Go ,Jacob to Jehovah And
,kindred fathers of land back said

And I will be with you.
[4]And Jacob sent and
called for Rachel and for
Leah, to the field, to his
flocks. [5]And he said to
them, I see your father's
face, that it is not toward
me as the day before
yesterday. But the God
of my father has been with
me. [6]And you know that
with all my power I have
served your father. [7]And
your father has cheated me
and has changed my wages
ten times. And God has not
let him do evil to me. [8]If he
said this: The speckled
shall be your wages, then
all the flocks bore speckled.
And if he said this: The
striped shall be your wages,
then all the flocks bore
striped. [9]And God has
taken away the livestock of
your father and has given to
me. [10]And at the time the
flock was in heat, I lifted up
my eyes and saw in a
dream: And behold! The
rams going up on the flock
were striped, speckled, and
spotted. [11]And the Angel of
God spoke to me in a
dream, Jacob! And I said,
Behold me. [12]And He said,
Lift up your eyes and see all
the rams going up on the
flock; *they are* striped,
speckled and spotted. For I
have seen all that Laban *is*
doing to you. [13]I am the
God of Bethel, there where
you anointed the pillar,
where you vowed a vow to
Me. Now rise up; go out of
this land and go back to the
land of your kindred. [14]And
Rachel and Leah answered
and said to him, *Is there* yet
to us a portion and an
inheritance in the house of
our father for us? [15]Are we

7704 3812 7354 7121 3290 7971 1961
4 וְאֶהְיֶה עִמָּךְ׃ וַיִּשְׁלַח יַעֲקֹב וַיִּקְרָא לְרָחֵל וּלְלֵאָה הַשָּׂדֶה
the to for and for and Jacob And with I and
.field .Leah Rachel called sent .you be will
1 6440 7200 559 6629
5 אֶל־צֹאנוֹ׃ וַיֹּאמֶר לָהֶן רֹאֶה אָנֹכִי אֶת־פְּנֵי אֲבִיכֶן כִּי־
that your face the I see to he And his to
.father of .them said .flocks
859 1961 1 430 8032 8543
6 אֵינֶנּוּ אֵלַי כִּתְמֹל שִׁלְשֹׁם וֵאלֹהֵי אָבִי הָיָה עִמָּדִי׃ וְאַתֵּנָה
you And with has my the but before the as toward is it
.me been father of God yesterday day me not
2048 1 1 5647 3581 3045
7 יְדַעְתֶּן כִּי בְּכָל־כֹּחִי עָבַדְתִּי אֶת־אֲבִיכֶן׃ וַאֲבִיכֶן הֵתֶל בִּי
me has your And your have I my with that know
cheated father ;father served power all
7489 430 4489 6235 4909 2498
וְהֶחֱלִף אֶת־מַשְׂכֻּרְתִּי עֲשֶׂרֶת מֹנִים וְלֹא־נְתָנוֹ אֱלֹהִים לְהָרַע
do to God has and ;times ten my has and
evil him let not wages changed
6629 3605 3205/7939 1961 5348 559 5978
8 עִמָּדִי׃ אִם־כֹּה יֹאמַר נְקֻדִּים יִהְיֶה שְׂכָרֶךָ וְיָלְדוּ כָל־הַצֹּאן
the all then your shall The he thus If .me to
flocks bore ,wages be speckled ,said
3605 3205 7939 1961 6124 559 5348
נְקֻדִּים וְאִם־כֹּה יֹאמַר עֲקֻדִּים יִהְיֶה שְׂכָרֶךָ וְיָלְדוּ כָל־
all then your be shall The ,said he thus And .speckled
bore ,wages striped if
5414 4735 430 5337 6124 6629
9 הַצֹּאן עֲקֻדִּים׃ וַיַּצֵּל אֱלֹהִים אֶת־מִקְנֵה אֲבִיכֶם וַיִּתֶּן־לִי׃
has and your livestock the God has And .striped the
.me to given father of away taken flocks
2009 2472 7200 5869 5375 6629 3179 6256 1961
10 וַיְהִי בְּעֵת יַחֵם הַצֹּאן וָאֶשָּׂא עֵינַי וָאֵרֶא בַּחֲלוֹם וְהִנֵּה
,and a in saw and my lifted I the in was the at And
,behold ;dream eyes up ,flock heat time
1261 5348 6124 6629 5927 6260
הָעַתֻּדִים הָעֹלִים עַל־הַצֹּאן עֲקֻדִּים נְקֻדִּים וּבְרֻדִּים׃
and ,speckled were the on up going rams the
.dappled ,striped flock
559 3290 2472 430 4397 559
11 וַיֹּאמֶר אֵלַי מַלְאַךְ הָאֱלֹהִים בַּחֲלוֹם יַעֲקֹב וָאֹמַר הִנֵּנִי׃
(am) I I And !Jacob a in God the me to And
.here ,said ,dream of Angel spoke
5921 5927 6260 3605 7200 5869 5375 559
12 וַיֹּאמֶר שָׂא־נָא עֵינֶיךָ וּרְאֵה כָּל־הָעַתֻּדִים הָעֹלִים עַל־
upon up going rams the all see and eyes your Lift He And
up ,said
3837 3605 7200 1261 5348 6124 6629
הַצֹּאן עֲקֻדִּים נְקֻדִּים וּבְרֻדִּים כִּי רָאִיתִי אֵת כָּל־אֲשֶׁר לָבָן
Laban that all have I For and ,speckled (are they) the
4676 8033 4886 seen 1008 ,spotted 410 ,striped ;flock 6213
13 עֹשֶׂה לָּךְ׃ אָנֹכִי הָאֵל בֵּית־אֵל אֲשֶׁר מָשַׁחְתָּ שָּׁם מַצֵּבָה
the there you where ,Bethel the am I .you to is
,pillar anointed of God doing
2088 776 3318 6965 6258 5087 5087
אֲשֶׁר נָדַרְתָּ לִּי שָׁם נֶדֶר עַתָּה קוּם צֵא מִן־הָאָרֶץ הַזֹּאת
this land of go rise ,Now .vow a to you where
out ,up Me vowed
559 3812 7354 6030 4138 776 7725
14 וְשׁוּב אֶל־אֶרֶץ מוֹלַדְתֶּךָ׃ וַתַּעַן רָחֵל וְלֵאָה וַתֹּאמַרְנָה לוֹ
to said and and Rachel And your land the to and
,him Leah answered .kindred of return
5237 3808 1 1004 5159 2506
15 הַעוֹד לָנוּ חֵלֶק וְנַחֲלָה בְּבֵית אָבִינוּ׃ הֲלוֹא נָכְרִיּוֹת
strangers not Are our the in an and a to (there is)
?father of house inheritance portion us

3701 398 398 4376 2803
16 נֶחְשַׁבְנוּ לוֹ כִּי מְכָרָנוּ וַיֹּאכַל גַּם־אָכוֹל אֶת־כַּסְפֵּנוּ׃ כִּי
For .silver our entirely also he and has he For by we
spent has us sold ?him counted

1121 1 430 3947 6239 3605
כָל־הָעֹשֶׁר אֲשֶׁר הִצִּיל אֱלֹהִים מֵאָבִינוּ לָנוּ הוּא וּלְבָנֵינוּ
for and is it for our from God has which riches the all
.sons our us ,father taken

3290 6965 6213 430 559 831 3605 6258
17 וְעַתָּה כֹּל אֲשֶׁר אָמַר אֱלֹהִים אֵלֶיךָ עֲשֵׂה׃ וַיָּקָם יַעֲקֹב
Jacob Then .do ,you to God has that all ,Now
up got said which ,then

3605 5090 1581 5921 802 1121 5375
18 וַיִּשָּׂא אֶת־בָּנָיו וְאֶת־נָשָׁיו עַל־הַגְּמַלִּים׃ וַיִּנְהַג אֶת־כָּל־
all he And .camels on wives his and sons his and
drove lifted

834 7075 4735 7408 834 7339 3605 4735
מִקְנֵהוּ וְאֶת־כָּל־רְכֻשׁוֹ אֲשֶׁר רָכָשׁ מִקְנֵה קִנְיָנוֹ אֲשֶׁר
which his livestock had he which goods his all and his
property of ,gotten ,livestock

3667 776 1 3327 935 758 6307 7408
רָכַשׁ בְּפַדַּן אֲרָם לָבוֹא אֶל־יִצְחָק אָבִיו אַרְצָה כְּנָעַן׃
.Canaan the to his Isaac unto come to ;aram Padan-in had he
of land ,father acquired

834 8655 7354 1589 6629 1494 3212 3837
19 וְלָבָן הָלַךְ לִגְזֹז אֶת־צֹאנוֹ וַתִּגְנֹב רָחֵל אֶת־הַתְּרָפִים אֲשֶׁר
which household the Rachel And .sheep his to went And
idols stole shear Laban

5046 1097 5921 3837 761 3820 3290 1589 1
20 לְאָבִיהָ׃ וַיִּגְנֹב יַעֲקֹב אֶת־לֵב לָבָן הָאֲרַמִּי עַל־בְּלִי הִגִּיד
did he not because the Laban the Jacob And father her
tell ,Syrian of heart deceived .had

5674 6965 3605 1272 1272
21 לוֹ כִּי בֹרֵחַ הוּא׃ וַיִּבְרַח הוּא וְכָל־אֲשֶׁר־לוֹ וַיָּקָם וַיַּעֲבֹר
and he and to that and he fled And he about that him
crossed arose ,him (was) all .(was) flee to

3117 3837 5046 1568 2022 6440 7760 5104
22 אֶת־הַנָּהָר וַיָּשֶׂם אֶת־פָּנָיו הַר הַגִּלְעָד׃ וַיֻּגַּד לְלָבָן בַּיּוֹם
the on Laban was .Gilead the to his set and ,River the
day told of hill face

7291 251 3947 3290 1272 7992
23 הַשְּׁלִישִׁי כִּי בָרַח יַעֲקֹב׃ וַיִּקַּח אֶת־אֶחָיו עִמּוֹ וַיִּרְדֹּף
and with his he And .Jacob had that third
pursued him brothers took fled

935 1568 2022 1692 3117 7651 1870 310
24 אַחֲרָיו דֶּרֶךְ שִׁבְעַת יָמִים וַיַּדְבֵּק אֹתוֹ בְּהַר הַגִּלְעָד׃ וַיָּבֹא
And .Gilead the in him he and ;days seven journey after
came of hill overtook him

8104 559 3915 2472 761 3837 430
אֱלֹהִים אֶל־לָבָן הָאֲרַמִּי בַּחֲלֹם הַלָּיְלָה וַיֹּאמֶר לוֹ הִשָּׁמֶר
Watch to and ,night the a in the Laban to God
out him said of dream Syrian

3837 5381 7451 5704 3290 1696
25 לְךָ פֶּן־תְּדַבֵּר עִם־יַעֲקֹב מִטּוֹב עַד־רָע׃ וַיַּשֵּׂג לָבָן אֶת־
Laban Then bad to from Jacob with you lest for
overtook good speak ,yourself

251 8628 3837 2022 168 8628 3290 3290
יַעֲקֹב וְיַעֲקֹב תָּקַע אֶת־אָהֳלוֹ בָּהָר וְלָבָן תָּקַע אֶת־אֶחָיו
his with had And the at tent his had and ,Jacob
brothers pitched Laban .mount pitched Jacob

1589 6213 3290 3837 559 1568 2022
26 בְּהַר הַגִּלְעָד׃ וַיֹּאמֶר לָבָן לְיַעֲקֹב מֶה עָשִׂיתָ וַתִּגְנֹב אֶת־
you that you have What to Laban said And .Gilead the at
deceived have done Jacob of hill

2244 4100 2719 7617 1323 5090 3824
27 לְבָבִי וַתְּנַהֵג אֶת־בְּנֹתַי כִּשְׁבֻיוֹת חָרֶב׃ לָמָּה נַחְבֵּאתָ
you did Why the captives like my led and my
hide ?sword of daughters heart

not counted strangers by him. For he has sold us, and he has also entirely spent our silver. [16]For all the wealth which God has taken from our father, it is for us and for our sons. And now all that which God has said to you, do.

[17]And Jacob arose and set his sons and his wives on camels. [18]And he drove all the livestock, and *took* all his goods which he had gotten, livestock of his property which he had acquired in Padan-aram; to come to his father Isaac, to the land of Canaan.

[19]And Laban went to shear his sheep. And Rachel stole the household idols which *were* her father's. [20]And Jacob deceived the heart of Laban the Syrian, for he did not tell him that he *was* about to flee. [21]And he and all that *was* his fled. And he rose up and crossed the River; and *he* set his face to Mount Gilead. [22]And on the third day Laban was told that Jacob had fled. [23]And he took his brothers with him, and *they* ran after him, seven days journey. And he overtook him in Mount Gilead. [24]And God came to Laban the Syrian in a dream of the night. And *He* said to him, Watch out for yourself, that you not speak with Jacob from good to evil.

[25]And Laban overtook Jacob. And Jacob had pitched his tent at the Mount. And Laban with his brothers had pitched at Mount Gilead. [26]And Laban said to Jacob, What have you done? And you have deceived my heart and drove my daughters like captives of the sword? [27]Why did you hide so as

לִבְרֹחַ וַתִּגְנֹב אֹתִי וְלֹא־הִגַּדְתָּ לִּי וָאֲשַׁלֵּחֲךָ בְּשִׂמְחָה

with would I and ?me told have and ,me have and as so
rejoicing you sent have not deceived flee to

28 וּבְשִׁרִים בְּתֹף וּבְכִנּוֹר׃ וְלֹא נְטַשְׁתַּנִי לְנַשֵּׁק לְבָנַי וְלִבְנֹתָי

my and my kiss have you And with and with with and
.daughters sons me let not ,lyre tabret ,music

29 עַתָּה הִסְכַּלְתָּ עֲשׂוֹ׃ יֶשׁ־לְאֵל יָדִי לַעֲשׂוֹת עִמָּכֶם רָע וֵאלֹהֵי

the but ;harm you do to my the in It do to have you Now
of God hand of power is (this) foolish been

אֲבִיכֶם אֶמֶשׁ ׀ אָמַר אֵלַי לֵאמֹר הִשָּׁמֶר לְךָ מִדַּבֵּר עִם־

with you lest for Watch ,saying me to spoke last your
speak yourself out night fathers

30 יַעֲקֹב מִטּוֹב עַד־רָע׃ וְעַתָּה הָלֹךְ הָלַכְתָּ כִּי־נִכְסֹף נִכְסַפְתָּה

longed have in because you surely And .evil to from Jacob
longing left have now good

31 לְבֵית אָבִיךָ לָמָּה גָנַבְתָּ אֶת־אֱלֹהָי׃ וַיַּעַן יַעֲקֹב וַיֹּאמֶר

said and Jacob And ?gods my you have why your after
spoke stolen ;father's house

לְלָבָן כִּי יָרֵאתִי כִּי אָמַרְתִּי פֶּן־תִּגְזֹל אֶת־בְּנוֹתֶיךָ מֵעִמִּי׃

away your should you lest said I for was I Be- to
.me from daughters force by take ;afraid cause ,Laban

32 עִם אֲשֶׁר תִּמְצָא אֶת־אֱלֹהֶיךָ לֹא יִחְיֶה נֶגֶד אַחֵינוּ הַכֶּר־

see our here shall he not ,gods your find you whom-With
:brothers before live ever

לְךָ מָה עִמָּדִי וְקַח־לָךְ וְלֹא־יָדַע יַעֲקֹב כִּי רָחֵל גְּנָבָתַם׃

stolen had Rachel that Jacob did For to take and (is) what for
.them know not you (it) ,me with yourself

33 וַיָּבֹא לָבָן בְּאֹהֶל־יַעֲקֹב ׀ וּבְאֹהֶל לֵאָה וּבְאֹהֶל שְׁתֵּי

the into and ,Leah's into and ,Jacob's into Laban And
two of tent the tent tent went

הָאֲמָהֹת וְלֹא מָצָא וַיֵּצֵא מֵאֹהֶל לֵאָה וַיָּבֹא בְּאֹהֶל רָחֵל׃

.Rachel's into and Leah's tent he and did and ,slave-girls
tent entered left ;find not

34 וְרָחֵל לָקְחָה אֶת־הַתְּרָפִים וַתְּשִׂמֵם בְּכַר הַגָּמָל וַתֵּשֶׁב

sat and the the into put and household the had And
,camel of saddle them idols taken Rachel

35 עֲלֵיהֶם וַיְמַשֵּׁשׁ לָבָן אֶת־כָּל־הָאֹהֶל וְלֹא מָצָא׃ וַתֹּאמֶר

she And .find did but tent the all Laban felt and ;them on
said not around

אֶל־אָבִיהָ אַל־יִחַר בְּעֵינֵי אֲדֹנִי כִּי לוֹא אוּכַל לָקוּם מִפָּנֶיךָ

before rise to am I not that my the in Let not her to
you able lord of eyes be anger ,father

36 כִּי־דֶרֶךְ נָשִׁים לִי וַיְחַפֵּשׂ וְלֹא מָצָא אֶת־הַתְּרָפִים׃ וַיִּחַר

was And household the did and he And (is) women the for
angry .idols find not looked .me to of way

לְיַעֲקֹב וַיָּרֶב בְּלָבָן וַיַּעַן יַעֲקֹב וַיֹּאמֶר לְלָבָן מַה־פִּשְׁעִי

my (is) What to said and Jacob And with he and ,Jacob
;transgression ,Laban answered .Laban argued

37 מַה חַטָּאתִי כִּי דָלַקְתָּ אַחֲרָי׃ כִּי־מִשַּׁשְׁתָּ אֶת־כָּל־כֵּלַי

my all have you For after have you that my (is) what
.vessels around felt ?me pursued hotly ,sin

to flee, and have deceived me? And I would have sent you away with rejoicing and with music, with tabret and with harp. [28]And you have not let me kiss my sons and my daughters. Now you have been foolish to do *this*. [29]It is in the power of my hand to do you harm. But the God of your fathers spoke to me last night, saying, Watch out for yourself, that you not speak with Jacob from good to evil. [30]And now surely you have gone because you have longed after your father's house. Why have you stolen my household gods? [31]And Jacob answered and said to Laban, Because I *was* afraid. For I said, Lest by force you take your daughters from me. [32]With whomever you find your household gods, he shall not live here before our brothers. Search for yourself what *is* with me, and take *it* to you. For Jacob did not know that Rachel had stolen them.

[33]And Laban went into Jacob's tent, and into Leah's tent, and into the tent of the two slavegirls; and he did not find. And he went out of Leah's tent and came into Rachel's tent. [34]And Rachel had taken the household idols and put them into the saddle of the camel; and *she* sat on them. And Laban felt around all the tent, but did not find. [35]And she said to her father, Let no anger be in the eyes of my lord, for I am not able to rise before your face, for the way of women *is* to me. And he sought and did not find the household idols.
[36]And Jacob was angry, and he argued with Laban. And Jacob answered and said to Laban, What *is* my transgression; what *is* my sin, that you have hotly pursued after me? [37]For you have felt around all my

articles; what have you found from all the articles of your house? Set it here before my brothers and your brothers, and let them decide between the two of us. [38]Now I *was* with you twenty years. Your ewes and your she-goats have not failed to bear, and the rams of your flock I have not eaten. [39]I did not bring to you the mangled; I replaced it. From my hand you exacted it, that stolen *by* day and that stolen *by* night. [40]I was *there*; by day the heat consumed me, and by night the cold. And my sleep fled from my eyes. [41]Now I *have been* twenty years in your house. I served you fourteen years for your two daughters, and six years for your flock; and you have changed my wages ten times. [42]Except the God of my father, the God of Abraham and the Fear of Isaac, had been for me, truly now you would have sent me away empty. God has seen my affliction and the toil of my palm; and *last* night He judged.

[43]And Laban answered and said to Jacob, The daughters *are* my daughters and the sons my sons; and the flocks *are* my flocks; and all which you see, it *is* mine and my daughters'. What can I do to these today, or to their sons whom they have borne? [44]And come now, let us cut a covenant, you and me; and let it be for witness between you and me. [45]And Jacob took a stone and set it up as a memorial. [46]And Jacob said to his brothers, Gather stones. And they took stones and they made a heap. And they ate there on the heap. [47]And Laban called it Heap of the Testimony. And Jacob called it Heap of Testimony. [48]And Laban said, This heap *is*

251 251 3541 7760 1004 3605 4672
מַה־מָּצָאתָ מִכֹּל כְּלֵי־בֵיתֶךָ שִׂים כֹּה נֶגֶד אַחַי וְאַחֶיךָ
your and my before here it Set your the from you have What
,brothers brothers ?house of vessels all found

7353 8141 6242 8147 996 3198
38 וְיוֹכִיחוּ בֵּין שְׁנֵינוּ׃ זֶה עֶשְׂרִים שָׁנָה אָנֹכִי עִמָּךְ רְחֵלֶיךָ
your with I years twenty Now two the between let and
ewes ;you (was) .us of decide them

3808 2966 398 3808 6629 352 7921 5795
39 וְעִזֶּיךָ לֹא שִׁכֵּלוּ וְאֵילֵי צֹאנְךָ לֹא אָכָלְתִּי׃ טְרֵפָה לֹא־
not The have I not your the and failed have not your and
mangled .eaten flock of rams bear to she-goats

1589 1245 3027 2398 935
הֵבֵאתִי אֵלֶיךָ אָנֹכִי אֲחַטֶּנָּה מִיָּדִי תְּבַקְשֶׁנָּה גְּנֻבְתִי יוֹם
(by) that exacted you from recon- made ;you to did I
day stolen ,it hand my ;ciliation bring

3915 7140 2721 398 1961 3915 1589
40 וּגְנֻבְתִי לָיְלָה׃ הָיִיתִי בַיּוֹם אֲכָלַנִי חֹרֶב וְקֶרַח בַּלָּיְלָה
;night by the and the consumed by I so (by) that and
cold ,heat me day ;was ,night stolen

5647 1004 8141 6242 5869 8142 5074
41 וַתִּדַּד שְׁנָתִי מֵעֵינָי׃ זֶה־לִּי עֶשְׂרִים שָׁנָה בְּבֵיתֶךָ עֲבַדְתִּיךָ
served I your in years twenty I Now from my and
you ;house (been have) .eyes my sleep fled

6629 8141 8337 1323 8147 8141 6240 702
אַרְבַּע־עֶשְׂרֵה שָׁנָה בִּשְׁתֵּי בְנֹתֶיךָ וְשֵׁשׁ שָׁנִים בְּצֹאנֶךָ
your for years six and your two for years fourteen
;flocks daughters

430 3884 4489 6235 4909 2498
42 וַתַּחֲלֵף אֶת־מַשְׂכֻּרְתִּי עֲשֶׂרֶת מֹנִים׃ לוּלֵי אֱלֹהֵי אָבִי
my God the Except .times ten wages my you and
,father of changed have

7971 7387 6258 1961 3327 6343 85 430
אֱלֹהֵי אַבְרָהָם וּפַחַד יִצְחָק הָיָה לִי כִּי עַתָּה רֵיקָם שִׁלַּחְתָּנִי
would you empty now ,truly for had ,Isaac the and Abraham God the
.me sent have ,me been of Fear of

6030 510 3198 430 7200 3709 3018 6040
43 אֶת־עָנְיִי וְאֶת־יְגִיעַ כַּפַּי רָאָה אֱלֹהִים וַיּוֹכַח אָמֶשׁ׃ וַיַּעַן
And (last) He and ,God has my toil the and My
spoke .night judged seen palm of affliction

6629 1121 421 1323 1323 3290 559 3837
לָבָן וַיֹּאמֶר אֶל־יַעֲקֹב הַבָּנוֹת בְּנֹתַי וְהַבָּנִים בָּנַי וְהַצֹּאן
the and my the and my (are) The ,Jacob to and Laban
flocks ,sons sons daughters daughters said

6213 1323 7200 834 3605 6629
צֹאנִי וְכֹל אֲשֶׁר־אַתָּה רֹאֶה לִי־הוּא וְלִבְנֹתַי מָה־אֶעֱשֶׂה
do can I what my And .(is) it to ,see you which and my
,daughters me all ;flocks

3772 3252 6258 3205 1121 176 3117
44 לָאֵלֶּה הַיּוֹם אוֹ לִבְנֵיהֶן אֲשֶׁר יָלָדוּ׃ וְעַתָּה לְכָה נִכְרְתָה
us let ,come now So have they whom their to or ,today to
cut ?borne sons these

68 3290 3947 996 5707 1961 1285
45 בְרִית אֲנִי וָאָתָּה וְהָיָה לְעֵד בֵּינִי וּבֵינֶךָ׃ וַיִּקַּח יַעֲקֹב אָבֶן
a Jacob And .you and between for let and and me a
stone took me witness be it ;you ,covenant

3947 68 3950 251 3290 559 4676 7311
46 וַיְרִימֶהָ מַצֵּבָה׃ וַיֹּאמֶר יַעֲקֹב לְאֶחָיו לִקְטוּ אֲבָנִים וַיִּקְחוּ
they And .stones Gather his to Jacob said And a as set and
took brothers .memorial up it

3837 7121 1530 8033 398 1530 6213 68
47 אֲבָנִים וַיַּעֲשׂוּ־גָל וַיֹּאכְלוּ שָׁם עַל־הַגָּל׃ וַיִּקְרָא־לוֹ לָבָן
Laban it And .heap the on there they and a they and stones
called ate ;heap made

1530 3837 559 1567 7121 3290 7717 3026
48 יְגַר שָׂהֲדוּתָא וְיַעֲקֹב קָרָא לוֹ גַּלְעֵד׃ וַיֹּאמֶר לָבָן הַגַּל
heap ,Laban said For .Galeed it called and ;sahadutha Jegar-
Jacob

a witness between you and me today; so he called its name Heap of Testimony; [49]also, Watchtower; for he said, May Jehovah watch between you and me, for we are hidden, each from his neighbor. [50]If you will *not* afflict my daughters, and if you will *not* take wives above my daughters, no man is with us. See, God is a witness between you and me.

[51]And Laban said to Jacob, Behold this heap, and behold the pillar which I have set between you and me. [52]This heap *is* a witness, and the pillar *is* a witness. As for me, I will not pass over this heap to you; and as for you, you will not pass over this heap and this pillar for evil to me. [53]The God of Abraham, the God of Nahor, the God of their father, let judge between us. And Jacob swore by the Fear of his father Isaac. [54]And Jacob sacrificed a sacrifice on the mountain, and called his brothers to eat bread. And they ate bread and stayed on the mountain.

1567 8034 7121 3117 996 5707 2088
הזה עד ביני ובינך היום על־כן קרא־שמו גלעד׃
,Galeed its he so ,today and between a This
name called you me witness (is)

376 5640 996 3068 6822 559 4709
49 והמצפה אשר אמר יצף יהוה ביני ובינך כי נסתר איש
each are we when and between Jehovah May he for and
concealed ,you me watch ,said ,Mizpah

1323 802 3947 1323 6031 7453
50 מרעהו׃ אם־תענה את־בנתי ואם־תקח נשים על־בנתי
my above wives will you and my will you If his from
;daughters take (not) if daughters afflict (not) .neighbor

3837 559 996 5707 430 7200 376
51 אין איש עמנו ראה אלהים עד ביני ובינך׃ ויאמר לבן
Laban And and between a is God see with (is) man no
said ,you me witness ;us

996 3384 834 4676 2009 2088 1530 2009 3290
ליעקב הנה הגל הזה והנה המצבה אשר יריתי ביני
between I which pillar the look and ,this heap Look to
me set have on ,Jacob

5674 4676 5713/2088 1530 5707
52 ובינך׃ עד הגל הזה ועדה המצבה אם־אני לא־אעבר
will I not for as ;pillar the (is) and This heap a (is) and
over pass ,me witness a witness ,you

5674 3808 2088 1530 1530
אליך את־הגל הזה ואם־אתה לא־תעבר אלי את־הגל
heap me to will you not you for and ;this heap you to
over pass as

430 85 430 7451 2088 4676 2088
53 הזה ואת־המצבה הזאת לרעה׃ אלהי אברהם ואלהי
the and ,Abraham God The .evil for this pillar and ,this
of God of

6343 7650 1 430 996 8199 3837
נחור ישפטו בינינו אלהי אביהם וישבע יעקב בפחד
the by Jacob swore and their God the between judge let ,Nahor
of Fear ;father of us

398 251 7121 2022 2077 3290 2076 3327 1
54 אביו יצחק׃ ויזבח יעקב זבח בהר ויקרא לאחיו לאכל־
eat to his and the on a Jacob And .Isaac his
brothers called mount sacrifice offered father

2022 3885 3899 398 3899
לחם ויאכלו לחם וילינו בהר׃
the on and bread they and ;bread
.mountain stayed ate

CAP. XXXII לב

CHAPTER 32

[55]And Laban rose up early in the morning and kissed his sons and his daughters and blessed them. And Laban went away and returned to his own place.

CHAPTER 32

[1]And Jacob went on his way, and the angels of God met him. [2]And when he saw them, Jacob said, This *is* the camp of God. And he called the name of that place, Refuge.

[3]And Jacob sent messengers before his face to his brother Esau, to the land of Seir, the field of Edom.

1288 1323 1121 5401 1242 3837 7925
1 וישכם לבן בבקר וינשק לבניו ולבנותיו ויברך אתהם
;them and his and his and the in Laban rose And
blessed daughters sons kissed morning early up

6293 1870 3212 3290 4725 3837 7725 3212
2 וילך וישב לבן למקמו׃ ויעקב הלך לדרכו ויפגעו־בו
him and his on went And his to Laban returned and
met ,way Jacob .place own left

430 4264 7200 3290 559 430 4397
3 מלאכי אלהים׃ ויאמר יעקב כאשר ראם מחנה אלהים
(is) God the saw he when Jacob said And .God the
of camp ,them of angels

4266 4725 8034 7121
זה ויקרא שם־המקום ההוא מחנים׃
.Mahanaim that place the he and ;This
of name called

8165 776 251 6215 6440 4397 3290 7971
4 וישלח יעקב מלאכים לפניו אל־עשו אחיו ארצה שעיר
.Seir the to his Esau to before messengers Jacob And
of land ,brother him sent

4 And he commanded them, saying, You shall say to my lord, to Esau: Your servant Jacob says this: I have sojourned with Laban and remained until now. And it is that oxen, and asses, flocks, and slaves and slave-girls *are* mine. And I have sent to tell my lord, to find favor in your eyes. 6 And the messengers came back to Jacob, saying, We came to your brother Esau, and also *he is* coming to meet you, and four hundred men *are* with him. 7 And Jacob was afraid, and he was very distressed. And he divided the people with him, and the flocks, and the herds, and the camels, into two camps. 8 And he said, If Esau comes to the one company and strikes it, then it will be, the company that is left shall escape.

9 And Jacob said, O God of my father Abraham and God of my father Isaac, Jehovah, who said to me, Go back to your land and to your kindred and I will deal well with you. 10 I am not worthy of all the mercies and all the truth which You have done for Your servant, for I passed over this Jordan with my staff, and now I have become two companies. 11 Deliver me, I pray, from the hand of my brother, from the hand of Esau; for I fear him, lest he come and strike me, mother to sons. 12 And You said, I will surely deal well with you, and I will make your seed like the sand of the sea, which cannot be numbered for multitude.

13 And he remained there that night. And he took a present from what came into his hand, for his brother

6215 113 559 559 6680 123 7704
5 שדה אדום: ויצו אתם לאמר כה תאמרון לאדני לעשו
to my to shall You this ,saying ,them he And .Edom the
:Esau ,lord say directed of field

6258 5704 309 1481 3837 3290 5650 559
כה אמר עבדך יעקב עם־לבן גרתי ואחר עד־עתה:
.now until and have I Laban with ,Jacob your says Thus
stayed sojourned servant

5046 7971 8198 5650 6629 2543 7794
6 ויהי־לי שור וחמור צאן ועבד ושפחה ואשלחה להגיד
tell to have I and and and flocks and oxen to And
sent ;slave-girls slaves ,asses me is it

3290 4397 7725 5869 2580 4672 113
7 לאדני למצא־חן בעיניך: וישבו המלאכים אל־יעקב
,Jacob to the came And your in favor to my
messengers back .eyes find ,lord

702 7125 3212 6265 251 935 559
לאמר באנו אל־אחיך אל־עשו וגם הלך לקראתך וארבע־
four and meet to (is he) and Esau your to We ,saying
,you coming also brother came

2673 3334 3966 3290 3372 376 3967
8 מאות איש עמו: ויירא יעקב מאד ויצר לו ויחץ את־
he and ,he was and very Jacob was And with men hundred
divided distressed afraid .him

8147 1581 1241 6629 834 5971
העם אשר־אתו ואת־הצאן ואת־הבקר והגמלים לשני
into the and the and the and with which the
two camels herds flocks him (were) people

5221 259 4264 6215 935 559 4264
9 מחנות: ויאמר אם־יבוא עשו אל־המחנה האחת והכהו
and ,one the to Esau comes If he And .camps
,it strikes company ,said

430 3290 559 6413 7604 4264 1961
10 והיה המחנה הנשאר לפליטה: ויאמר יעקב אלהי
God O ,Jacob said And .escape shall which the it then
of left is company ,be shall

7725 559 3068 3027 1 430 85 1
אבי אברהם ואלהי אבי יצחק יהוה האמר אלי שוב
Return to said who ,Jehovah ,Isaac my God and Abraham my
,me father of father

2617 3605 6994 3190 4138 776
11 לארצך ולמולדתך ואיטיבה עמך: קטנתי מכל החסדים
the all of not am I with will I and to and your to
mercies worthy ;you well deal ,kindred your country

5674 4731 5650 6213 831 571 3605
ומכל־האמת אשר עשית את־עבדך כי במקלי עברתי
passed I my with for Your for have You which the all and
over staff ,servant done truth

4994 5337 4264 8147 1961 6258 2088 3383
12 את־הירדן הזה ועתה הייתי לשני מחנות: הצילני נא
I Deliver .camps two have I and this Jordan
,pray ,me become now

517 5221/935 3373 6215 3027 251 3027
מיד אחי מיד עשו כי־ירא אנכי אתו פן־יבוא והכני אם
mother and he lest him I fear for ,Esau's from my from
,me strike come hand ,brother's hand

7760 3190 3190 559 1121
13 על־בנים: ואתה אמרת היטב איטיב עמך ושמתי את־
I and with will I surely ,said You And .sons to
make will ,you well deal

3915 8033 3885 7230 5608 834 3220 2344 2233
14 זרעך כחול הים אשר לא־יספר מרב: וילן שם בלילה
night there he And for be can not which the the like your
stayed .multitude counted ,sea of sand seed

5795 251 6215 4503 3027 935 3947
15 ההוא ויקח מן־הבא בידו מנחה לעשו אחיו: עזים
she-goats his for a his into what from and ;that
:brother Esau present hand came took he

Esau: [14]two hundred she-goats, twenty he-goats, two hundred ewes, and twenty rams, [15]thirty milk camels with their thirty colts, forty cows and ten bulls, twenty she-asses and ten young asses. [16]And he gave into the hand of his slaves every drove by itself. And *he* said to his slaves, Pass over before my face and put a space between drove and drove. [17]And he commanded the first ones, saying, When my brother Esau meets you and asks, saying, Whose *are* you, and where do you go, and whose *are* these before your face? [18]Then you will say, Your servant Jacob's. It *is* a present sent to my lord, to Esau; and, behold, also he *is* behind us. [19]And he also commanded the second, also the third, even all the ones going after the droves, saying, Your shall speak this word to Esau when you find him. [20]And you shall also say, Behold, your servant Jacob *is* behind us. For he said, I will cover his face by the present, the one going before my face, and afterward I will see his face; perhaps he will lift up my face. [21]And the present passed before his face, and he remained in the camp that night.

[22]And he rose up that night and took his two wives, and his two slave-girls, and his eleven children. And *he* crossed the ford Jabbok. [23]And he took them and sent them over the stream, and sent over that which *was* his. [24]And Jacob was left alone. And a Man wrestled with him until

6242 352 3967 7353 6242 8495 3967
מָאתַיִם וּתְיָשִׁים עֶשְׂרִים רְחֵלִים מָאתַיִם וְאֵילִים עֶשְׂרִים׃
,twenty rams and ,hundred two ewes ,twenty he-goats two ,hundred

6499 702 6510 7970 1121 3293 1581
16 גְּמַלִּים מֵינִיקוֹת וּבְנֵיהֶם שְׁלֹשִׁים פָּרוֹת אַרְבָּעִים וּפָרִים
bulls and forty cows ,thirty their with nursing camels colts

5650 3027 5414 6240 5895 6242 860 6235
17 עֲשָׂרָה אֲתֹנֹת עֶשְׂרִים וַעְיָרִם עֲשָׂרָה׃ וַיִּתֵּן בְּיַד־עֲבָדָיו
his into he And .ten and twenty she-asses ,ten slaves' hand gave asses young

7305 6440 5674 5650 559 5739 5739
עֵדֶר עֵדֶר לְבַדּוֹ וַיֹּאמֶר אֶל־עֲבָדָיו עִבְרוּ לְפָנַי וְרֶוַח
a and front in Pass ,slaves his to said and by drove drove (by) space me of over ,itself

559 7223 6680 5739 996 5739 996 7760
18 תָּשִׂימוּ בֵּין עֵדֶר וּבֵין עֵדֶר׃ וַיְצַו אֶת־הָרִאשׁוֹן לֵאמֹר כִּי
When ,saying first the he And .drove and drove between put commanded

3212 559 7592 251 6215 6298
יִפְגָּשְׁךָ עֵשָׂו אָחִי וּשְׁאֵלְךָ לֵאמֹר לְמִי־אַתָּה וְאָנָה תֵלֵךְ
you do and ,you Whose ,saying asks and my Esau meets ;go where (are) ,you brother

4503 3290 5650 559
19 וּלְמִי אֵלֶּה לְפָנֶיךָ׃ וְאָמַרְתָּ לְעַבְדְּךָ לְיַעֲקֹב מִנְחָה הִוא
it gift a ;Jacob's Your you Then before (are) and (is) servant ,say will ?you these whose

1571 6680 310 2009 6265 113 7971
20 שְׁלוּחָה לַאדֹנִי לְעֵשָׂו וְהִנֵּה גַם־הוּא אַחֲרֵינוּ׃ וַיְצַו גַּם
also he And behind (is) he also ,and to my to sent commanded .us ,lo ;Esau ,lord

310 3212 3605 1571 7992 1571 8145
אֶת־הַשֵּׁנִי גַּם אֶת־הַשְּׁלִישִׁי גַּם אֶת־כָּל־הַהֹלְכִים אַחֲרֵי
after going ones the all even ,third also the ,second

4672 6215 1696 2088 1697 559 5739
הָעֲדָרִים לֵאמֹר כַּדָּבָר הַזֶּה תְּדַבְּרוּן אֶל־עֵשָׂו בְּמֹצַאֲכֶם
you when Esau to shall you This same ,saying ,droves the find speak word

559 310 3290 5650 2009 1571 559
21 אֹתוֹ׃ וַאֲמַרְתֶּם גַּם הִנֵּה עַבְדְּךָ יַעֲקֹב אַחֲרֵינוּ כִּי־אָמַר
,said he ,For behind (is) Jacob your ,Lo also you And .him .us servant ,say shall

7200 310 6440 3212 4503 6440 3722
אֲכַפְּרָה פָנָיו בַּמִּנְחָה הַהֹלֶכֶת לְפָנָי וְאַחֲרֵי־כֵן אֶרְאֶה
will I afterward and before one the the by his will I see :me going ,present face cover

3885 6440 4503 5674 6440 5375 194 6440
22 פָנָיו אוּלַי יִשָּׂא פָנָי׃ וַתַּעֲבֹר הַמִּנְחָה עַל־פָּנָיו וְהוּא לָן
stayed and before present the passed And my will he perhaps his he ;him over .face accept ;face

3947 3915 6965 4264 3915
23 בַּלַּיְלָה־הַהוּא בַּמַּחֲנֶה׃ וַיָּקָם ׀ בַּלַּיְלָה הוּא וַיִּקַּח אֶת־
and that night he And the in that night took up rose .camp

3206 6240 259 8198 8147 802 8147
שְׁתֵּי נָשָׁיו וְאֶת־שְׁתֵּי שִׁפְחֹתָיו וְאֶת־אַחַד עָשָׂר יְלָדָיו
boys his ten (and) one and his two and his two ,slave-girls ,wives

5674 5158 5674 3947 2999 4569 5674
24 וַיַּעֲבֹר אֵת מַעֲבַר יַבֹּק׃ וַיִּקָּחֵם וַיַּעֲבִרֵם אֶת־הַנָּחַל וַיַּעֲבֵר
sent and stream the sent and he And .Jabbok ford the and over over them them took crossed

5704 5973 376 79 905 3290 3498
25 אֶת־אֲשֶׁר־לוֹ׃ וַיִּוָּתֵר יַעֲקֹב לְבַדּוֹ וַיֵּאָבֵק אִישׁ עִמּוֹ עַד
until with a and ;alone Jacob was And .him to what him Man wrestled left was

the ascending of the dawn. [25]And He saw that He did not prevail over him, and He struck his hip-socket, and Jacob's hip-socket was unhinged as he grappled with Him.

[26]And He said, Send Me away, for the dawn has risen. And he said, I will not let You go unless You bless me. [27]And He said to him, What *is* your name? And he said, Jacob. [28]And He said, Your name no longer shall be called Jacob, but Israel, because you have persevered with God and with men and have been able.

[29]And Jacob requested and said, Please reveal Your name. And He said, Why this *that* you inquire about My name? And He blessed him there. [30]And Jacob called the name of the place Peniel, *saying,* Because I saw God face to face and my life is preserved.

[31]And the sun rose upon him as he passed over Penuel; and he *was* limping on his hip-socket. [32]On account of this the sons of Israel do not eat the sinew of the thigh which *is* on the hip-socket, until this day, because He struck the hip-socket of Jacob, the sinew of the thigh.

3363 3409 3709 5060 3201 3808 7200 7837 5937
26 עלות השחר: וירא כי לא יכל לו ויגע בכף ירכו ותקע
was and hip- his on and over did He not that He And .dawn the the
unhinged ,socket touched He him prevail saw of rise

5927 7971 559 79 3290 3409/3709
27 כף ירך יעקב בהאבקו עמו: ויאמר שלחני כי עלה
has for me Send He and with he as Jacob's hip-socket
risen away ,said .him wrestled

559 1288 518 7971 559 7837
28 השחר ויאמר לא אשלחך כי אם ברכתני: ויאמר אליו
to He And bless You unless will I not he And the
.him said .me go You let said .dawn

5750 559 3290 3808 559 3290 559 8034
29 מה שמך ויאמר יעקב: ויאמר לא יעקב יאמר עוד
longer shall Jacob Not He And .Jacob he And your What
called be ,said ,said ?name (is)

582 430 8280 3478 8034
שמך כי אם ישראל כי שרית עם אלהים ועם אנשים
men and God with you because ;Israel but your
with contended have ,name

559 8034 4994 5046 559 3290 7592 3201
30 ותוכל: וישאל יעקב ויאמר הגידה נא שמך ויאמר
He And Your Please reveal ,said and Jacob asked And have and
said ,name .prevailed

3290 7121 8033 1288 8034 7592 2088
31 למה זה תשאל לשמי ויברך אתו שם: ויקרא יעקב
Jacob And .there him He And about you this Why
called blessed ?name My ask

6440 6440 430 7200 3588 6439 4725 8034
שם המקום פניאל כי ראיתי אלהים פנים אל פנים
face to face God saw I Because ,Peniel place the the
of name

6439 5674 8121 2224 5315 5337
32 ותנצל נפשי: ויזרח לו השמש כאשר עבר את פנואל
;Penuel he as sun the upon And my is and
crossed him rose .life delivered

3478 1121 398 3808 3409/3709 6760
33 והוא צלע על ירכו: על כן לא יאכלו בני ישראל את
Israel of sons the eat do not this For his on limping and
,reason .thigh (was) he

3409 5060 2088 314 5704 3409 834 5384 1517
גיד הנשה אשר על כף הירך עד היום הזה כי נגע בכף
hip- He for ,this day until the hip- the on which the the
struck of socket (is) thigh of sinew

5384 1517 3290 3709
ירך יעקב בגיד הנשה:
.thigh the the (on) Jacob's
of sinew socket

CAP. XXXIII לג

CHAPTER 33

CHAPTER 33

[1]And Jacob lifted up his eyes and looked. And, behold, Esau was coming, and four hundred men with him. And he divided the children to Leah, and to Rachel, and to the two slave-girls. [2]And he put the slave-girls and their children first; and Leah and her children behind; and Rachel and Joseph last.

3967 702 935 6265 2009 7200 5869 3290 5375
1 וישא יעקב עיניו וירא והנה עשו בא ועמו ארבע מאות
hundred four with and (was) Esau and and his Jacob And
him ,coming !behold ,looked eyes raised

8147 7354 3812 3206 2673 376
איש ויחץ את הילדים על לאה ועל רחל ועל שתי
the to and ,Rachel to and ,Leah to [illegible] he and ;men
two divided

7223 3206 8198 7760 8198
2 השפחות: וישם את השפחות ואת ילדיהן ראשנה ואת
and ;first boys their and slave-girls the he And .slave-girls
put

314 3127 7354 314 3206 3812
לאה וילדיה אחרנים ואת רחל ואת יוסף אחרנים:
.last Joseph and Rachel and ;behind her and Leah
children

3And he passed over in front of them and bowed himself to the ground seven times, until he came even to his brother.
4And Esau ran to meet him, and embraced him, and fell on his neck and kissed him. And they wept. 5And he lifted up his eyes and saw the women and the children. And he said, Who are these *with* you? And he said, The children *with* whom God has favored your servant. 6And the slave-girls came near, they and their children; and they bowed. 7And Leah and her children also came near and bowed. And after this Rachel and Joseph came near and bowed. 8And he said, Whose *is* all this camp which I met? And he said, To find favor in the eyes of my lord. 9And Esau said, I have much, my brother. Let what you have be to yourself. 10And Jacob said, No, please, if I now have found favor in your eyes, take my present from my hands. For I have seen your face, like seeing the face of God; and you are pleased with me. 11Please take my blessing which has been brought to you, because God has favored me, and because I have all *things*. And he urged him; and he accepted. 12And he said, Let us depart and go, and I will go with you. 13And he said to him, My lord knows that the children are tender, and the flocks and the herds with me *are* suckling. And *if* they overdrive them one day, all the flocks will die. 14Please let my lord go before his servant, and I will move on by stages at my ease, according to the pace of the stock which *are* before me, and according to the pace of the children, until I come in to my lord to Seir. 15And

5704 6471 7651 776 7812 6440 5674
3 וְהוּא עָבַר לִפְנֵיהֶם וַיִּשְׁתַּחוּ אַרְצָה שֶׁבַע פְּעָמִים עַד־
until ,times seven the to ground bowed and himself front in them of went he And over

5921 5307 2263 7125 6215 7323 251 5066
4 גִּשְׁתּוֹ עַד־אָחִיו׃ וַיָּרָץ עֵשָׂו לִקְרָאתוֹ וַיְחַבְּקֵהוּ וַיִּפֹּל עַל־
upon fell and embraced him and meet to him Esau And ran his to brother even he came

802 7200 5869 5375 1058 5401 6677
5 צַוָּארָו וַיִּשָּׁקֵהוּ וַיִּבְכּוּ׃ וַיִּשָּׂא אֶת־עֵינָיו וַיַּרְא אֶת־הַנָּשִׁים
women the and saw his eyes he And raised and .wept they kissed and ;him his ,neck

3206 559 428 559 3206
וְאֶת־הַיְלָדִים וַיֹּאמֶר מִי־אֵלֶּה לָּךְ וַיֹּאמַר הַיְלָדִים אֲשֶׁר־
(with) whom boys The he And said (with) ?you (are) these Who he and .said ;boys the and

3206 8198 5066 5650 430 2603
6 חָנַן אֱלֹהִים אֶת־עַבְדֶּךָ׃ וַתִּגַּשְׁןָ הַשְּׁפָחוֹת הֵנָּה וְיַלְדֵיהֶן
their and boys they the slave-girls came And near .servant your God has favored

5066 310 7812 3206 3812 5066 7812
7 וַתִּשְׁתַּחֲוֶיןָ׃ וַתִּגַּשׁ גַּם־לֵאָה וִילָדֶיהָ וַיִּשְׁתַּחֲווּ וְאַחַר נִגַּשׁ
came near and after ;bowed and her and children Leah also And near came they and .bowed

2088 4264 3605 559 7812 7354 3127
8 יוֹסֵף וְרָחֵל וַיִּשְׁתַּחֲווּ׃ וַיֹּאמֶר מִי לְךָ כָּל־הַמַּחֲנֶה הַזֶּה
this camp all (with) you Who (is) he And ,said .bowed and and Rachel Joseph

559 113 5869 2580 4672 559 6298 834
9 אֲשֶׁר פָּגָשְׁתִּי וַיֹּאמֶר לִמְצֹא־חֵן בְּעֵינֵי אֲדֹנִי׃ וַיֹּאמֶר עֵשָׂו
,Esau said And my .lord the in of eyes favor find To he And ,said have I ?met which

4994/3808 3290 559 3426 251 7227 3426
10 יֶשׁ־לִי רָב אָחִי יְהִי לְךָ אֲשֶׁר־לָךְ׃ וַיֹּאמֶר יַעֲקֹב אַל־נָא
,please ,No ,Jacob said And you have what to yourself be let ;brother my ,much I have

3027 4503 3947 5869 2580 4672
אִם־נָא מָצָאתִי חֵן בְּעֵינֶיךָ וְלָקַחְתָּ מִנְחָתִי מִיָּדִי כִּי עַל־
there for my ;hands from my present take your ,eyes in favor have I found now If

3947 7521 430 6440 7200 6440 7200
11 כֵּן רָאִיתִי פָנֶיךָ כִּרְאֹת פְּנֵי אֱלֹהִים וַתִּרְצֵנִי׃ קַח־נָא אֶת־
Please take are you pleased .me with and ,God of face the seeing like ,face your have I seen fore

3605 3426 430 2603 935 834 1293
בִּרְכָתִי אֲשֶׁר הֻבָאת לָךְ כִּי־חַנַּנִי אֱלֹהִים וְכִי יֶשׁ־לִי־כֹל
all (things) I have and because ,God me favored has for ,you to been has brought which my blessing

5048 3212 3212 5265 559 3947 6484
12 וַיִּפְצַר־בּוֹ וַיִּקָּח׃ וַיֹּאמֶר נִסְעָה וְנֵלֵכָה וְאֵלְכָה לְנֶגְדֶּךָ׃
before .you I and go will ,go and us Let depart he And ,said he and ,accepted ,him he and urged

1241 6629 7390 3206 3045 113 559
13 וַיֹּאמֶר אֵלָיו אֲדֹנִי יֹדֵעַ כִּי־הַיְלָדִים רַכִּים וְהַצֹּאן וְהַבָּקָר
the and herds the and flocks are ,tender the boys that knows My lord to ,him he And said

4994 6629 4191 259 3117 1849 5764/5763
14 עָלוֹת עָלָי וּדְפָקוּם יוֹם אֶחָד וָמֵתוּ כָּל־הַצֹּאן׃ יַעֲבָר־נָא
Please go let the ,flocks all will die ,one day they if and them force with ;me (are) suckling

4399 7272 328 5095 5650 6440 113
אֲדֹנִי לִפְנֵי עַבְדּוֹ וַאֲנִי אֶתְנַהֲלָה לְאִטִּי לְרֶגֶל הַמְּלָאכָה
the livestock's according pace to my at ;ease on move will stages by and I his servant before my lord

113 935 834 5704 3206 7272 6440 834
אֲשֶׁר־לְפָנַי וּלְרֶגֶל הַיְלָדִים עַד אֲשֶׁר־אָבֹא אֶל־אֲדֹנִי
,lord my to come I until ;boys the according of pace to and before me which (are)

Esau said, Please let me place with you *some* of the people who *are* with me. And he said, Why, then? Let me find favor in the eyes of my lord. [16]And Esau returned on his way toward Seir that day.

[17]And Jacob traveled to Succoth. And he built himself a house, and made booths for his livestock. For this reason he called the name of the place Succoth.

[18]And Jacob came in peace to the city of Shechem, which *is* in the land of Canaan, as he came from Padan-aram. And he camped in front of the city. [19]And he bought that part of the field where he had stretched his tent, from the hand of the sons of Hamor, the father of Shechem, for a hundred kesitah. [20]And he set up an altar there. And he called it, El, the God of Israel.

5971 4994/3322 6215 559 8165
15 שֵׂעִירָה: וַיֹּאמֶר עֵשָׂו אַצִּיגָה־נָּא עִמְּךָ מִן־הָעָם אֲשֶׁר אִתִּי
with who the (some) with Please me let ,Esau said And .Seir to
.me (are) people of you place

1931 3117 7725 113 5869 2580 4672 4100 559
16 וַיֹּאמֶר לָמָּה זֶּה אֶמְצָא־חֵן בְּעֵינֵי אֲדֹנִי: וַיָּשָׁב בַּיּוֹם הַהוּא
that day And my the in favor me Let ?this Why he And
returned .lord of eyes find ,said

1004 1129 5523 5265 3290 8165 1870 6215
17 עֵשָׂו לְדַרְכּוֹ שֵׂעִירָה: וְיַעֲקֹב נָסַע סֻכֹּתָה וַיִּבֶן לוֹ בָּיִת
a himself and to traveled And toward his on Esau
house built he Succoth Jacob .Seir way

5523 4725 8034 7121 3651 5521 6213 4735
וּלְמִקְנֵהוּ עָשָׂה סֻכֹּת עַל־כֵּן קָרָא שֵׁם־הַמָּקוֹם סֻכּוֹת: ס
.Succoth the the he this for ;booths he for and
place of name called reason made livestock his

935 3667 776 834 7927 5892 8004 3290 935
18 וַיָּבֹא יַעֲקֹב שָׁלֵם עִיר שְׁכֶם אֲשֶׁר בְּאֶרֶץ כְּנַעַן בְּבֹאוֹ
he as ,Canaan the in which ,Shechem the in Jacob And
came of land (is) of city peace to came

7704 2513 7069 5892 6440 2583 758 6307
19 מִפַּדַּן אֲרָם וַיִּחַן אֶת־פְּנֵי הָעִיר: וַיִּקֶן אֶת־חֶלְקַת הַשָּׂדֶה
field the part that he And .city the front in he and ;aram from
of bought of camped Padan-

3967 7928 1 2544 1121 3027 168 5186 834
אֲשֶׁר נָטָה־שָׁם אָהֳלוֹ מִיַּד בְּנֵי־חֲמוֹר אֲבִי שְׁכֶם בְּמֵאָה
a for ,Shechem the ,Hamor the from his had he where
hundred of father of sons tent pitched

3478 430 410 7121 4196 8033 5324 7192
20 קְשִׂיטָה: וַיַּצֶּב־שָׁם מִזְבֵּחַ וַיִּקְרָא־לוֹ אֵל אֱלֹהֵי יִשְׂרָאֵל: ס
Israel of ,El ,it he and altar an there he and of pieces
of God called up set .money

CAP. XXXIV לד

CHAPTER 34

CHAPTER 34

[1]And Dinah, the daughter of Leah, whom she bore to Jacob, went out to see the daughters of the land. [2]And Shechem the son of Hamor the Hivite, the prince of the land, saw her, and took her, and lay with her, and humiliated her. [3]And his soul clung to Dinah, the daughter of Jacob. And he loved the girl, and spoke to the heart of the girl. [4]And Shechem spoke to his father Hamor, saying, Take this girl for me for a wife. [5]And Jacob heard that he had defiled his daughter Dinah. And his sons were with his livestock in the field. And Jacob kept silent until they had come.

[6]And Hamor the father of Shechem went out to Jacob to speak with him. [7]And the sons of Jacob came out of

1323 7200 3290 3205 3812 1783 5927
1 וַתֵּצֵא דִינָה בַּת־לֵאָה אֲשֶׁר יָלְדָה לְיַעֲקֹב לִרְאוֹת בִּבְנוֹת
the see to ,Jacob to she whom Leah the ,Dinah And
of daughters bore of daughter went out

776 5387 2340 2544 1121 7928 7200 776
2 הָאָרֶץ: וַיַּרְא אֹתָהּ שְׁכֶם בֶּן־חֲמוֹר הַחִוִּי נְשִׂיא הָאָרֶץ
,land the the the Hamor the Shechem her saw And .land the
of prince ,Hivite of son

1783 5315 1692 6031 7901 3947
3 וַיִּקַּח אֹתָהּ וַיִּשְׁכַּב אֹתָהּ וַיְעַנֶּהָ: וַתִּדְבַּק נַפְשׁוֹ בְּדִינָה
Dinah to soul his And and with lay and her and
clung .her humbled ,her took

559 5291 3820 1696 5291 157 3290 1323
4 בַּת־יַעֲקֹב וַיֶּאֱהַב אֶת־הַנַּעֲרָ וַיְדַבֵּר עַל־לֵב הַנַּעֲרָ: וַיֹּאמֶר
And ,girl the the to and girl the he and ;Jacob's
spoke of heart spoke loved daughter

2088 3207 3947 559 1 2544 7928
שְׁכֶם אֶל־חֲמוֹר אָבִיו לֵאמֹר קַח־לִי אֶת־הַיַּלְדָּה הַזֹּאת
this girl for Take ,saying his Hamor to Shechem
me ,father

1961 1121 1323 1783 2930 8085 3290 802
5 לְאִשָּׁה: וְיַעֲקֹב שָׁמַע כִּי טִמֵּא אֶת־דִּינָה בִתּוֹ וּבָנָיו הָיוּ
were Now his Dinah had he that heard And a for
sons his .daughter defiled Jacob .wife

2544 5927 935 3290 2790 7704 4735
6 אֶת־מִקְנֵהוּ בַּשָּׂדֶה וְהֶחֱרִשׁ יַעֲקֹב עַד־בֹּאָם: וַיֵּצֵא חֲמוֹר
Hamor And they until Jacob kept so the in his with
went .come had silent ;field livestock

935 3290 1121 850 1696 3290 7928 1
7 אֲבִי־שְׁכֶם אֶל־יַעֲקֹב לְדַבֵּר אִתּוֹ: וּבְנֵי יַעֲקֹב בָּאוּ מִן
from came Jacob's And with speak to Jacob to Shechem the
sons ,him of father

the field when they heard,
and the men were furious,
and they were very angry,
because he had done fool-
ishness in Israel, to lie with
the daughter of Jacob, and it
should not be done in this
way. [8]And Hamor spoke
with them, saying, My son
Shechem's soul is bound to
your daughter. Please give
her to him for a wife. [9]And
you intermarry with us; give
your daughters to us, and
take our daughters for yourselves. [10]And live with us,
and the land is before you;
live and trade *in* it, and get
property in it. [11]And
Shechem said to her father,
and to her brothers, Let me
find favor in your eyes, and
what you say to me I will
give. [12]Heap on me ever so
much bride-price and gift,
and I will give as you say to
me; but give me the girl for a
wife. [13]And the sons of
Jacob answered Shechem
and his father Hamor,
speaking with deceit be-
cause he had defiled their
sister Dinah. [14]And they
said to them, We are not
able to do this thing, to give
our sister to a man who is
uncircumcised. For it is a
reproach to us. [15]Only on
this *condition* will we
consent to you; if you will
become like us, to have
every male of you circum-
cised. [16]Then we will give
our daughters to you, and
we will take your daughters
to us; and we will live with
you and will become one
people. [17]And if you do not
listen to us, to be circumcised, then we will take our
daughter, and we will go.
[18]And their words
pleased Hamor and the son
of Hamor, Shechem. [19]And
the young man did not
hesitate to do the thing, for

הַשָּׂדֶה כְּשָׁמְעָם וַיִּתְעַצְּבוּ הָאֲנָשִׁים וַיִּחַר לָהֶם מְאֹד כִּי
נְבָלָה עָשָׂה בְיִשְׂרָאֵל לִשְׁכַּב אֶת־בַּת־יַעֲקֹב וְכֵן לֹא יֵעָשֶׂה׃
8 וַיְדַבֵּר חֲמוֹר אִתָּם לֵאמֹר שְׁכֶם בְּנִי חָשְׁקָה נַפְשׁוֹ בְּבִתְּכֶם
9 תְּנוּ נָא אֹתָהּ לוֹ לְאִשָּׁה׃ וְהִתְחַתְּנוּ אֹתָנוּ בְּנֹתֵיכֶם תִּתְּנוּ
10 לָנוּ וְאֶת־בְּנֹתֵינוּ תִּקְחוּ לָכֶם׃ וְאִתָּנוּ תֵּשֵׁבוּ וְהָאָרֶץ תִּהְיֶה
11 לִפְנֵיכֶם שְׁבוּ וּסְחָרוּהָ וְהֵאָחֲזוּ בָּהּ׃ וַיֹּאמֶר שְׁכֶם אֶל־
אָבִיהָ וְאֶל־אַחֶיהָ אֶמְצָא־חֵן בְּעֵינֵיכֶם וַאֲשֶׁר תֹּאמְרוּ אֵלַי
12 אֶתֵּן׃ הַרְבּוּ עָלַי מְאֹד מֹהַר וּמַתָּן וְאֶתְּנָה כַּאֲשֶׁר תֹּאמְרוּ
13 אֵלָי וּתְנוּ־לִי אֶת־הַנַּעֲרָ לְאִשָּׁה׃ וַיַּעֲנוּ בְנֵי־יַעֲקֹב אֶת־שְׁכֶם
וְאֶת־חֲמוֹר אָבִיו בְּמִרְמָה וַיְדַבֵּרוּ אֲשֶׁר טִמֵּא אֵת דִּינָה
14 אֲחֹתָם׃ וַיֹּאמְרוּ אֲלֵיהֶם לֹא נוּכַל לַעֲשׂוֹת הַדָּבָר הַזֶּה
לָתֵת אֶת־אֲחֹתֵנוּ לְאִישׁ אֲשֶׁר־לוֹ עָרְלָה כִּי־חֶרְפָּה הִוא
15 לָנוּ׃ אַךְ־בְּזֹאת נֵאוֹת לָכֶם אִם תִּהְיוּ כָמֹנוּ לְהִמֹּל לָכֶם
16 כָּל־זָכָר׃ וְנָתַנּוּ אֶת־בְּנֹתֵינוּ לָכֶם וְאֶת־בְּנֹתֵיכֶם נִקַּח־לָנוּ
17 וְיָשַׁבְנוּ אִתְּכֶם וְהָיִינוּ לְעַם אֶחָד׃ וְאִם־לֹא תִשְׁמְעוּ אֵלֵינוּ
18 לְהִמּוֹל וְלָקַחְנוּ אֶת־בִּתֵּנוּ וְהָלָכְנוּ׃ וַיִּיטְבוּ דִבְרֵיהֶם בְּעֵינֵי
19 חֲמוֹר וּבְעֵינֵי שְׁכֶם בֶּן־חֲמוֹר׃ וְלֹא־אֵחַר הַנַּעַר לַעֲשׂוֹת

he delighted in Jacob's daughter, and he was more honorable than all the house of his father. [20]And Hamor and his son Shechem came to the gate of their city. And they spoke with the men of their city, saying, [21]These men *are* peaceable with us; and, Let them live in the land and trade in it; and, Lo, the land *is* wide *on* both hands before them. Let us take their daughters for ourselves for wives, and let us give our daughters to them. [22]Only in this *way* will the men consent to us to live with us, to become one people: that every male of us be circumcised as they *are* circumcised. [23]Shall not their livestock, and their property, and all their beasts of burden *be* ours? Only let us consent to them, and let them live with us. [24]And all those going out o the gate of the city listeneo to Hamor, and to his son Shechem. And every male was circumcised, all those going out of the gate of the city. [25]And it happened on the third day, they being pained, that the two sons of Jacob, Simeon and Levi, Dinah's brothers, each took his sword. And they came on the city in *its* security, and killed every male. [26]And they killed Hamor and his son Shechem with the sword. And they took Dinah from the house of Shechem, and left. [27]The sons of Jacob came on the slain and plundered the city, because they had defiled their sister.

[28]They took their flocks and their herds and their asses, and whatever *was* in the city, and whatever *was* in the field. [29]And they seized all their wealth, and all their little ones, and their wives, and looted all that

1 1004 3605 3513 3290 1323 2654 1697
הַדָּבָר כִּי־חָפֵץ בְּבַת־יַעֲקֹב וְהוּא נִכְבָּד מִכֹּל בֵּית אָבִיו׃
his house than more (was) and ,Jacob's in he for the
.father's all honorable he daughter delighted ,thing

582 1696 5892 8179 1121 7928 2544 935
20 וַיָּבֹא חֲמוֹר וּשְׁכֶם בְּנוֹ אֶל־שַׁעַר עִירָם וַיְדַבְּרוּ אֶל־אַנְשֵׁי
the to they and their the to his and Hamor And
of men 853 spoke ;city of gate son Shechem came

3427 8003 582 559 5892
21 עִירָם לֵאמֹר׃ הָאֲנָשִׁים הָאֵלֶּה שְׁלֵמִים הֵם אִתָּנוּ וְיֵשְׁבוּ
let and with (are) peaceable These men ,saying their
live them ;us city

6440 3027 7342 2009 776 5583 776
בָאָרֶץ וְיִסְחֲרוּ אֹתָהּ וְהָאָרֶץ הִנֵּה רַחֲבַת־יָדַיִם לִפְנֵיהֶם
before both (on) (is) ,lo the and ;it in trade and the in
;them hands wide land land

389 5414 1323 802 3947 1323
22 אֶת־בְּנֹתָם נִקַּח־לָנוּ לְנָשִׁים וְאֶת־בְּנֹתֵינוּ נִתֵּן לָהֶם׃ אַךְ
Only to us let our and ,wives for for us let their
them give daughters ourselves take daughters

259 5971 1961 3427 582 225 2063
בְּזֹאת יֵאֹתוּ לָנוּ הָאֲנָשִׁים לָשֶׁבֶת אִתָּנוּ לִהְיוֹת לְעַם אֶחָד
;one people to with live to men the us to will this in
become ,us consent (way)

7075 4725 41 35 2145 4135
23 בְּהִמּוֹל לָנוּ כָּל־זָכָר כַּאֲשֶׁר הֵם נִמֹּלִים׃ מִקְנֵהֶם וְקִנְיָנָם
their and Their (are) they as male every us of be that
,property cattle .circumcised circumcised

3427 225 389 3808 929 3605
וְכָל־בְּהֶמְתָּם הֲלוֹא לָנוּ הֵם אַךְ נֵאוֹתָה לָהֶם וְיֵשְׁבוּ
let and to us let ,Only ?they (be) will beasts their and
live them ,them consent ours not —burden of all

8179 5927 1121 7928 2544 8085
24 אִתָּנוּ׃ וַיִּשְׁמְעוּ אֶל־חֲמוֹר וְאֶל־שְׁכֶם בְּנוֹ כָּל־יֹצְאֵי שַׁעַר
the those all his Shechem and Hamor to And .us with
of gate out going son to listened

3117 1961 5892 8179 5927 2145 4135 5892
25 עִירוֹ וַיִּמֹּלוּ כָּל־זָכָר כָּל־יֹצְאֵי שַׁעַר עִירוֹ׃ וַיְהִי בַיּוֹם
the on it And his gate the those all ,male every was and his
day ,was .city of out going circumcised ;city

8095 3290 1121/8147 3947 3510 1961 7992
הַשְּׁלִישִׁי בִּהְיוֹתָם כֹּאֲבִים וַיִּקְחוּ שְׁנֵי־בְנֵי־יַעֲקֹב שִׁמְעוֹן
Simeon ,Jacob sons the took ,pained they while ,third
of two (still) were

2026 983 5892 935 2719 376 1783 217 3878
וְלֵוִי אֲחֵי דִינָה אִישׁ חַרְבּוֹ וַיָּבֹאוּ עַל־הָעִיר בֶּטַח וַיַּהַרְגוּ
and (its) in the on they and his each ,Dinah brothers and
killed security city came ,sword of ,Levi

3947 2719 2026 1121 7928 2544 2145
26 כָּל־זָכָר׃ וְאֶת־חֲמוֹר וְאֶת־שְׁכֶם בְּנוֹ הָרְגוּ לְפִי־חָרֶב וַיִּקְחוּ
they and the by they his Shechem and Hamor And .male every
took ;sword's edge killed son

2491 935 1121 5927 7928 1004 1783
27 אֶת־דִּינָה מִבֵּית שְׁכֶם וַיֵּצֵאוּ׃ בְּנֵי יַעֲקֹב בָּאוּ עַל־הַחֲלָלִים
slain the on came Jacob The and Shechem's from Dinah
of sons .left house

1241 6629 269 2930 834 5892 962
28 וַיָּבֹזּוּ הָעִיר אֲשֶׁר טִמְּאוּ אֲחוֹתָם׃ אֶת־צֹאנָם וְאֶת־בְּקָרָם
herds their and flocks Their .sister their had they because the and
defiled ;city looted

3947 7704 834 5892 834 2543
וְאֶת־חֲמֹרֵיהֶם וְאֵת אֲשֶׁר־בָּעִיר וְאֶת־אֲשֶׁר בַּשָּׂדֶה לָקָחוּ׃
they the in whatever and the in whatever and their and
.took field (was) city (was) ,asses

962 7617 802 2945 2428 3605
29 וְאֶת־כָּל־חֵילָם וְאֶת־כָּל־טַפָּם וְאֶת־נְשֵׁיהֶם שָׁבוּ וַיָּבֹזּוּ וְאֵת
even and they their and their all and their all And
,looted took ,wives ,ones little ,wealth

was in the house. [30]And Jacob said to Simeon and to Levi, You have troubled me, to make me stink among the inhabitants of the land, among the Canaanites, and among the Perizzites. And I *being* few in number, and they gathering against me, they will strike me, and I and my house shall be wasted. [31]And they said, Should he treat our sister like a harlot?

5916 3878 8095 3290 559 1004 834 3605

30 כל־אשר בבית: ויאמר יעקב אל־שמעון ואל־לוי עכרתם

have You troubled ,Levi and Simeon to Jacob said And the in house which (was) all

4962 6522 3669 776 3427 887

אתי להבאישני בישב הארץ בכנעני ובפרזי ואני מתי

(being and few I ;Perizzite, the and Canaanite the among land's the among inhabitants me make to stink ,me

559 1004 8045 5221 622 4557

31 מספר ונאספו עלי והכוני ונשמדתי אני וביתי: ויאמרו

they And ,said my and ,house I shall I wasted be and will they me strike against ,me they and gather in ,number

269 6213 2181

הכזונה יעשה את־אחותנו:

?sister our Should treat he a like harlot

CAP. XXXV לה

CHAPTER 35

CHAPTER 35

[1]And God said to Jacob, Rise up, go to Bethel and live there. And make an altar to God there, who appeared to you when you fled before your brother Esau. [2]And Jacob said to his house, and to all those with him, Put away the strange gods which *are* in your midst, and purify yourselves, and change your clothing. [3]And let us rise up and go up to Bethel. And I will make an altar there to God, *He* who answered me in the day of my distress. And He was with me in the way *in* which I went. [4]And they gave all the strange gods in their hand to Jacob, and the earrings which *were* in their ears. And Jacob hid them under the oak which *was* in Shechem.

[5]And they pulled up *and went*. And the terror of God was on the cities that were all around them. They did not pursue the sons of Jacob.

[6]And Jacob came to Luz, which *is* in the land of Canaan, it *being* Bethel; and he and all the people with him. [7]And he built an altar there and called the place

8033 3427 1008 5927 6965 3290 430 559

1 ויאמר אלהים אל־יעקב קום עלה בית־אל ושב־שם

;there live and Bethel go to up Rise up ,Jacob to God said And

6215 6440 1272 7200 410 4196 8033 6213

ועשה־שם מזבח לאל הנראה אליך בברחך מפני עשו

Esau from before you when fled to you who appeared to God an altar there and make

5493 3605 1004 3290 559 251

2 אחיך: ויאמר יעקב אל־ביתו ואל כל־אשר עמו הסרו

Put away with ,him who (were) all and to his house to Jacob And said your .brother

2498 2891 8432 834 5236 430

את־אלהי הנכר אשר בתככם והטהרו והחליפו

change and purify and yourselves your in midst which (are) the strange gods

4196 8033 6213 1008 5927 6965 8071

3 שמלתיכם: ונקומה ונעלה בית־אל ואעשה־שם מזבח

altar an there I and make will ;Bethel go and to up let And arise us .clothing your

834 1870 1961 6864 6030 410

לאל הענה אתי ביום צרתי ויהי עמדי בדרך אשר

(in) which the in way with me He and was my ;distress the in of day me who answered ,God to

3027 834 5236 430 3605 3290 5414 3212

4 הלכתי: ויתנו אל־יעקב את כל־אלהי הנכר אשר בידם

their in hand which (were) the strange gods all Jacob to they And gave .I went

8478 3290 2934 241 834 5141

ואת־הנזמים אשר באזניהם ויטמן אתם יעקב תחת

under Jacob them hid and their in ;ears which (were) the rings and

430 2847 5265 7927 834 424

5 האלה אשר עם־שכם: ויסעו ויהי חתת אלהים על־

on God the of terror and they was And ,up pulled Shechem near which oak the (was)

3290 1121 310 7291 5439 5892

הערים אשר סביבותיהם ולא רדפו אחרי בני יעקב:

.Jacob the of sons after they pursue did and not around all ;them that (were) the cities

1008 3667 776 834 3870 3290 935

6 ויבא יעקב לוזה אשר בארץ כנען הוא בית־אל הוא

he ;Bethel it (being) ,Canaan the in of land which (is) to ,Luz Jacob And came

4725 7121 4196 8033 1129 834 5971

7 כל־העם אשר־עמו: ויבן שם מזבח ויקרא למקום

place the called and altar an there he And built with .him which (were) the people and all

El-Bethel; because God revealed Himself to him there
when he fled from his
brother. [8]And Rebekah's
nurse Deborah died, and
was buried below Bethel
under the oak. And he
called its name Oak of
Weeping.
[9]And God appeared to
Jacob again when he came
out of Padan-aram; and
blessed him. [10]And God
said to him, Your name is
Jacob; your name shall not
be called Jacob any more,
but Israel shall be your
name. And He called his
name Israel. [11]And God
said to him, I *am* God
Almighty. Be fruitful and
multiply. A nation and a
company of nations shall be
from you. And kings shall
go forth from your loins.
[12]And the land which I gave
to Abraham and to Isaac, I
will give it to you. And I will
give the land to your seed
after you. [13]And God went
up from him in the place
where He had spoken with
him. [14]And Jacob set up a
memorial pillar in the place
where He had spoken with
him, a pillar of stone. And
he poured a drink offering
on it, and he poured oil on
it. [15]And Jacob called the
name of the place where
God had spoken with him,
Bethel.
[16]And they pulled up from
Bethel. And there was a
kibrah of land *before they*
came to Ephrath. And
Rachel bore, and she had
hard labor in her bearing.
[17]And it happened as she
had hard labor in her
bearing, the midwife said to
her, Do not fear, for this also
is a son for you. [18]And it
happened as her soul was
going forth — for she died
— she called his name
Benoni. But his father called

6440 1272 430 1540 8033 1008 416
אֵל בֵּית־אֵל כִּי שָׁם נִגְלוּ אֵלָיו הָאֱלֹהִים בְּבָרְחוֹ מִפְּנֵי
from he when God him to revealed there for ;Bethel El-
before fled Himself

1008 8470 6912 7259 3243 1683 4191 251
8 אָחִיו׃ וַתָּמָת דְּבֹרָה מֵינֶקֶת רִבְקָה וַתִּקָּבֵר מִתַּחַת לְבֵית־
Beth- below was and ,Rebekah nurse the ,Deborah And his
buried of died brother

=439= 8034 7121 437 8478 416
אֵל תַּחַת הָאַלּוֹן וַיִּקְרָא שְׁמוֹ אַלּוֹן בָּכוּת׃ פ
.Weeping of Oak it he and ;oak the under el
name called

1288 758 6307 935 5750 3290 430 7200
9 וַיֵּרָא אֱלֹהִים אֶל־יַעֲקֹב עוֹד בְּבֹאוֹ מִפַּדַּן אֲרָם וַיְבָרֶךְ
and aram of out he when again Jacob to God And
blessed Padan- came appeared

5750 8034 7121 3808 3290 8034 430 559
10 אֹתוֹ׃ וַיֹּאמֶר־לוֹ אֱלֹהִים שִׁמְךָ יַעֲקֹב לֹא־יִקָּרֵא שִׁמְךָ עוֹד
any your will not ;Jacob Your ,God to And .him
more name called be (is) name him said

3478 8034 7121 8034 1961 3478 3290
יַעֲקֹב כִּי אִם־יִשְׂרָאֵל יִהְיֶה שְׁמֶךָ וַיִּקְרָא אֶת־שְׁמוֹ יִשְׂרָאֵל׃
.Israel his He and your will Israel but ,Jacob
name called ;name be

1471 6951 7235 6509 7706 410 430 559
11 וַיֹּאמֶר לוֹ אֱלֹהִים אֲנִי אֵל שַׁדַּי פְּרֵה וּרְבֵה גּוֹי וּקְהַל גּוֹיִם
nations a and a mul- and be ,Almighty I God to said And
of company nation ;tiply fruitful God (am) him

834 776 5927 2504 4428 1961
12 יִהְיֶה מִמֶּךָּ וּמְלָכִים מֵחֲלָצֶיךָ יֵצֵאוּ׃ וְאֶת־הָאָרֶץ אֲשֶׁר
which land the And go shall your from kings and from shall
.forth loins ,you be

5414 310 2233 5414 3327 85 5410
נָתַתִּי לְאַבְרָהָם וּלְיִצְחָק לְךָ אֶתְּנֶנָּה וּלְזַרְעֲךָ אַחֲרֶיךָ אֶתֵּן
will I after to and will I to to and Abraham to gave I
give you seed your ;it give you ,Isaac

1696 4725 430 5927 776
13 אֶת־הָאָרֶץ׃ וַיַּעַל מֵעָלָיו אֱלֹהִים בַּמָּקוֹם אֲשֶׁר־דִּבֶּר אִתּוֹ׃
with had He where place the in ,God from And .land the
.him spoken him up went

68 4073 1696 4725 4676 3290 5324
14 וַיַּצֵּב יַעֲקֹב מַצֵּבָה בַּמָּקוֹם אֲשֶׁר־דִּבֶּר אִתּוֹ מַצֶּבֶת אָבֶן
of pillar a with had He where the in pillar a Jacob And
;stone him spoken place up set

8034 3290 7121 8081 5921 5258 5262 5258
15 וַיַּסֵּךְ עָלֶיהָ נֶסֶךְ וַיִּצֹק עָלֶיהָ שָׁמֶן׃ וַיִּקְרָא יַעֲקֹב אֶת־שֵׁם
the Jacob And .oil it on he and drink a it on he and
of name called poured ;offering out poured

5265 1008 430 8033 1696 4725
16 הַמָּקוֹם אֲשֶׁר דִּבֶּר אִתּוֹ שָׁם אֱלֹהִים בֵּית־אֵל׃ וַיִּסְעוּ
they And .Bethel ,God there with had where place the
up pulled him spoken

3205 672 935 776 3530 5750 416 1008
מִבֵּית אֵל וַיְהִי־עוֹד כִּבְרַת־הָאָרֶץ לָבוֹא אֶפְרָתָה וַתֵּלֶד
and ;Ephrath come to land (some) still and ,Bethel from
bore to of length was there

559 3205 7185 1961 3205 7185 7354
17 רָחֵל וַתְּקַשׁ בְּלִדְתָּהּ׃ וַיְהִי בְהַקְשֹׁתָהּ בְּלִדְתָּהּ וַתֹּאמֶר
said that her in had she as it And her in had she and
bearing labor hard ,was bearing labor hard ,Rachel

5927 1961 1121 1571 3372 3205
18 לָהּ הַמְיַלֶּדֶת אַל־תִּירְאִי כִּי־גַם־זֶה לָךְ בֵּן׃ וַיְהִי בְּצֵאת
going in it And a for this also for ,fear Do not ,midwife the to
forth ,was .son you (is) her

7121 1 205 1121 8034 7121 4191 5315
נַפְשָׁהּ כִּי מֵתָה וַתִּקְרָא שְׁמוֹ בֶּן־אוֹנִי וְאָבִיו קָרָא־לוֹ
him called his but ;oni Ben- his she and she for her
father name called ,died that ,soul's

him Benjamin. 19And Rachel died and was buried in the way of Ephrath, which *is* Bethlehem. 20And Jacob set up a pillar on her grave; that *is* the pillar of Rachel's grave to today. 21And Israel pulled up *stakes*. And *he* stretched his tent beyond the Tower of the Flocks. 22And it happened, while Israel lived in that land, Reuben went and lay with Bilhah, his father's concubine. And Israel heard.

And the sons of Jacob were twelve: 23The sons of Leah: Reuben, the firstborn of Jacob; and Simeon, and Levi, and Judah, and Issachar, and Zebulun. 24The sons of Rachel: Joseph and Benjamin. 25And the sons of Bilhah, Rachel's slave-girl: Dan and Naphtali. 26And the sons of Zilpah, Leah's slave-girl: Gad and Asher. These *were* the sons of Jacob which *were* born to him in Padan-aram.

27And Jacob came to his father Isaac, to Mamre, to the city of Arba, which *is* Hebron, where had lived Abraham and Isaac. 28And the days of Isaac were a hundred and eighty years. 29And Isaac expired and died, and was gathered to his people, old and satisfied of days. And his sons, Esau and Jacob, buried him.

1008 672 1870 6912 7354 4191 11441121
19 בִּנְיָמִין׃ וַתָּמָת רָחֵל וַתִּקָּבֵר בְּדֶרֶךְ אֶפְרָתָה הִוא בֵּית
Beth- that ,Ephrath the on was and Rachel And .Benjamin
(is) to way buried died

6900 4673 6900 4676 13290 5324 1035
20 לָחֶם׃ וַיַּצֵּב יַעֲקֹב מַצֵּבָה עַל־קְבֻרָתָהּ הִוא מַצֶּבֶת קְבֻרַת־
the the that ,grave her on pillar a Jacob And .lehem
grave of pillar (is) 168 up set

4026 1973 5186 3478 5265 3117 7354
21 רָחֵל עַד־הַיּוֹם׃ וַיִּסַּע יִשְׂרָאֵל וַיֵּט אָהֳלֹה מֵהָלְאָה לְמִגְדַּל־
the beyond his and ,Israel And today to Rachel's
of tower tent pitched up pulled

7901 7205 3212 776 3478 7931 1961 5740
22 עֵדֶר׃ וַיְהִי בִּשְׁכֹּן יִשְׂרָאֵל בָּאָרֶץ הַהִוא וַיֵּלֶךְ רְאוּבֵן וַיִּשְׁכַּב
lay and Reuben that ,that land in Israel's during it And the
with went living ,was .flocks

3478 8085 1 6370 1090
אֶת־בִּלְהָה פִּילֶגֶשׁ אָבִיו וַיִּשְׁמַע יִשְׂרָאֵל
.Israel and his concubine ,Bilhah
heard ;father's

3290 1060 3812 1121 6240 8147 3290 1121 1961
23 וַיִּהְיוּ בְנֵי־יַעֲקֹב שְׁנֵים עָשָׂר׃ בְּנֵי לֵאָה בְּכוֹר יַעֲקֹב
Jacob's firstborn ,Leah The twelve Jacob the And
of sons of sons were

7354 1121 2074 3485 3063 3878 8095 7205
24 רְאוּבֵן וְשִׁמְעוֹן וְלֵוִי וִיהוּדָה וְיִשָּׂשכָר וּזְבוּלֻן׃ בְּנֵי רָחֵל
,Rachel the and and ,Judah and and and ,Reuben
of sons ;Zebulun Issachar ,Levi ,Simeon

1121 53 1126 1835 7354 8198 1090 1121 1144 3127
25
26 יוֹסֵף וּבִנְיָמִן׃ וּבְנֵי בִלְהָה שִׁפְחַת רָחֵל דָּן וְנַפְתָּלִי׃ וּבְנֵי
and and Dan Rachel's slave- ,Bilhah's and and Joseph
sons ;Naphtali ,girl sons ;Benjamin

3205 3290 1121 836 1410/3812 8198 2153
זִלְפָּה שִׁפְחַת לֵאָה גָּד וְאָשֵׁר אֵלֶּה בְּנֵי יַעֲקֹב אֲשֶׁר יֻלַּד־
were who Jacob's sons These and Gad Leah's slave- Zilpah's
born (were) ,Asher ,girl

4471 1 3327 3290 935 758 6307
27 לוֹ בְּפַדַּן אֲרָם׃ וַיָּבֹא יַעֲקֹב אֶל־יִצְחָק אָבִיו מַמְרֵא
to his Isaac to Jacob And .Aram Padan- in to
,Mamre ,father came him

3327 85 1481 2275 7153 5892
קִרְיַת הָאַרְבַּע הִוא חֶבְרוֹן אֲשֶׁר־גָּר־שָׁם אַבְרָהָם וְיִצְחָק׃
and Abraham stayed where ,Hebron that ,Arba the to
.Isaac (is) of city

3327 1478 8141 8084 8141 3967 3327 3117 1961
28
29 וַיִּהְיוּ יְמֵי יִצְחָק מְאַת שָׁנָה וּשְׁמֹנִים שָׁנָה׃ וַיִּגְוַע יִצְחָק
Isaac And .years eighty and — a Isaac the And
expired hundred of days were

6215 6912 3117 7649 2205 5971 622 4191
וַיָּמָת וַיֵּאָסֶף אֶל־עַמָּיו זָקֵן וּשְׂבַע יָמִים וַיִּקְבְּרוּ אֹתוֹ עֵשָׂו
Esau him And .days and old his to was and and
buried of satisfied people gathered died

1121 3290
וְיַעֲקֹב בָּנָיו׃
his and
.sons Jacob

CAP. XXXVI לו

CHAPTER 36

CHAPTER 36

1And these are the generations of Esau, that *is*, Edom: 2Esau took his wives from the daughters of Canaan, Adah the daughter of Elon the Hittite; and Oholibamah the daughter of Anah, the daughter of

1323 802 3947 6215 123 1931 6215 8435
1
2 וְאֵלֶּה תֹּלְדוֹת עֵשָׂו הוּא אֱדוֹם׃ עֵשָׂו לָקַח אֶת־נָשָׁיו מִבְּנוֹת
from his took Esau .Edom that ;Esau the are And
daughters wives (is) of generations these

6034 7323 173 2850 356 1323 5711 3667
כְּנָעַן אֶת־עָדָה בַּת־אֵילוֹן הַחִתִּי וְאֶת־אָהֳלִיבָמָה בַּת־עֲנָה
Anah's Oholibamah and the Elon's Adah :Canaan's
daughter ;Hittite ,daughter

Zibeon the Hivite; [3]and Basemath the daughter of Ishmael, sister of Nebajoth. [4]And Adah bore Eliphaz to Esau. And Basemath bore Reuel. [5]And Oholibamah bore Jeush, and Jalam, and Korah. These *were* the sons of Esau who were born to him in the land of Canaan.

[6]And Esau took his wives and his sons and his daughters, and all the souls of his house, and his livestock, and all his beasts of burden, and all his property which he had acquired in the land of Canaan, and he went to a land away from his brother Jacob. [7]For their possessions had become great, *keeping them* from dwelling together; and the land of their travels was not able to bear them, because of their livestock.

[8]And Esau dwelt on Mount Seir—Esau is Edom. [9]And these *were* the generations of Esau, the father of Edom on Mount Seir. [10]The names of the sons of Esau: Eliphaz the son of Adah, a wife of Esau, Reuel the son of Basemath, a wife Esau. [11]And the sons of Eliphaz: Teman, Omar, Zepho, and Gatam, and Kenaz. [12]And Timna was a concubine to Eliphaz the son of Esau; and she bore Amalek to Eliphaz. These *were* the sons of Esau's wife Adah.

[13]And the sons of Reuel: Nahath, and Zerah, Shammah, and Mizzah. These *were* the sons of Basemath, Esau's wife.

[14]And these *were* the sons of Oholibamah the daughter of Anah, the daughter of Zibeon, Esau's wife: even she bore Jeush to Esau, and Jalam, and Korah.

5032 269 3458 1323 1365 2340 6649 1323
3 בַּת־צִבְעוֹן הַחִוִּי׃ וְאֶת־בָּשְׂמַת בַּת־יִשְׁמָעֵאל אֲחוֹת נְבָיוֹת׃
Nebajoth sister of daughter Ishmael's ,Basemath and the ;Hivite Zibeon's daughter
7467 3205 1315 464 6215 5211 3205
4 וַתֵּלֶד עָדָה לְעֵשָׂו אֶת־אֱלִיפָז וּבָשְׂמַת יָלְדָה אֶת־רְעוּאֵל׃
.Reuel bore And Basemath .Eliphaz Esau to Adah And bore
7141 3281 3266 3205 173
5 וְאָהֳלִיבָמָה יָלְדָה אֶת־יְעִישׁ וְאֶת־יַעְלָם וְאֶת־קֹרַח אֵלֶּה
These (were) .Korah and ,Jalam and ,Jeush bore And Oholibamah
802 6215 3947 3667 776 3205 6215 1121
6 בְּנֵי עֵשָׂו אֲשֶׁר יֻלְּדוּ־לוֹ בְּאֶרֶץ כְּנָעַן׃ וַיִּקַּח עֵשָׂו אֶת־נָשָׁיו
his wives Esau And took .Canaan of land the in to him were born who Esau's sons
4735 1004 5315 3605 1323 1121
וְאֶת־בָּנָיו וְאֶת־בְּנֹתָיו וְאֶת־כָּל־נַפְשׁוֹת בֵּיתוֹ וְאֶת־מִקְנֵהוּ
his ,livestock and ,house his of souls the all and ,daughters his and ,sons his and
3667 776 7408 834 7075 3605 929 3605
וְאֶת־כָּל־בְּהֶמְתּוֹ וְאֵת כָּל־קִנְיָנוֹ אֲשֶׁר רָכַשׁ בְּאֶרֶץ כְּנָעַן
;Canaan of land the in gained had he which property his all and ,burden of beasts his all and
7227 7399 7961 251 3290 6440 776 3212
7 וַיֵּלֶךְ אֶל־אֶרֶץ מִפְּנֵי יַעֲקֹב אָחִיו׃ כִּי־הָיָה רְכוּשָׁם רָב
(too) great their possessions had become For his .brother Jacob from away land a to went he and
5375 4033 776 3201 3162 3427
מִשֶּׁבֶת יַחְדָּו וְלֹא יָכְלָה אֶרֶץ מְגוּרֵיהֶם לָשֵׂאת אֹתָם
them bear to travels their of land the able was not and ,together live to
123 6215 8165 2022 6215 3427 4735 6440
8 מִפְּנֵי מִקְנֵיהֶם׃ וַיֵּשֶׁב עֵשָׂו בְּהַר שֵׂעִיר עֵשָׂו הוּא אֱדוֹם׃
.Edom is Esau ;Seir Mount on Esau lived And livestock their of because
8034 8165 2022 123 1 6215 8435
9 וְאֵלֶּה תֹּלְדוֹת עֵשָׂו אֲבִי אֱדוֹם בְּהַר שֵׂעִיר׃ אֵלֶּה שְׁמוֹת
10 of names the (are) these ;Seir Mount on Edom of father the ,Esau of generations the (are) these And
1315 7467 6215 802 5711 1121 464 6215 1121
בְּנֵי־עֵשָׂו אֱלִיפַז בֶּן־עָדָה אֵשֶׁת עֵשָׂו רְעוּאֵל בֶּן־בָּשְׂמַת
,Basemath of son the Reuel ;Esau's wife Adah's son ,Eliphaz :Esau of sons the
1609 6825 201 8487 464 1121 7961 6215 802
11 אֵשֶׁת עֵשָׂו׃ וַיִּהְיוּ בְּנֵי אֱלִיפָז תֵּימָן אוֹמָר צְפוֹ וְגַעְתָּם
,Gatam and ,Zepho ,Omar ,Teman Eliphaz of sons the were And .Esau's wife
3205 6215 1121 464 6370 1961 8555 7073
12 וּקְנַז׃ וְתִמְנַע ׀ הָיְתָה פִילֶגֶשׁ לֶאֱלִיפַז בֶּן־עֵשָׂו וַתֵּלֶד
bore she and ,Esau's son ,Eliphaz to concubine a was Timna And .Kenaz and
1121 6215 802 5711 1121 6002 464
13 לֶאֱלִיפַז אֶת־עֲמָלֵק אֵלֶּה בְּנֵי עָדָה אֵשֶׁת עֵשָׂו׃ וְאֵלֶּה בְּנֵי
sons (were) these And .Esau's wife Adah of sons the (were) These .Amalek Eliphaz to
802 1315 1121 4199 8040 2226 5184 7467
רְעוּאֵל נַחַת וָזֶרַח שַׁמָּה וּמִזָּה אֵלֶּה הָיוּ בְּנֵי בָשְׂמַת אֵשֶׁת
wife Basemath of sons the were these ;Mizzah and Shammah and ,Zerah and ,Nahath :Reuel's
802 6649 1323 6034 1323 173 1121 6215
14 עֵשָׂו׃ וְאֵלֶּה הָיוּ בְּנֵי אָהֳלִיבָמָה בַת־עֲנָה בַּת־צִבְעוֹן אֵשֶׁת
wife Zibeon of daughter the Anah of daughter the Oholibamah of sons the were these And .Esau's
7141 3281 3266 6215 3205 6215
15 עֵשָׂו וַתֵּלֶד לְעֵשָׂו אֶת־יְעִישׁ וְאֶת־יַעְלָם וְאֶת־קֹרַח׃ אֵלֶּה
These (were) .Korah and ,Jalam and ,Jeush Esau to bore she and ,Esau's

[15]These *were* the chiefs of the sons of Esau: the sons of Eliphaz, Esau's firstborn: Chief Teman, Chief Omar, Chief Zepho, Chief Kenaz, [16]Chief Korah, Chief Gatam, Chief Amalek. These *were* the chiefs of Eliphaz in the land of Edom; these the sons of Adah.

[17]And these *were* the sons of Reuel, Esau's son: Chief Nathath, Chief Zerah, Chief Shammah, Chief Mizzah. These *were* the chiefs of Reuel in the land of Edom. These *were* the sons of Basemath, Esau's wife.

[18]And the sons of Oholibamah, Esau's wife: Chief Jeush, Chief Jalam, Chief Korah. These *were* the chiefs of Oholibamah, the daughter of Anah, Esau's wife. [19]These *were* the sons of Esau, and these their chiefs—he *is* Edom.

[20]These *were* the sons of Seir the Horite living in the land: Lotan, and Shobal, and Zibeon, and Anah, [21]and Dishon, and Ezer, and Dishan. These *were* the chiefs of the Horites, the sons of Seir, in the land of Edom. [22]And the sons of Lotan: Hori and Heman; and Lotan's sister, Timna. [23]And these *were* the sons of Shobal: Alvan, and Manahath, and Ebal, Shepho, and Onam. [24]And these *were* the sons of Zibeon, even Aiah and Anah—he *is* Anah who found the hot springs in the desert as he fed the asses of his father Zibeon. [25]And these *were* the sons of Anah: Dishon; and Oholibamah *was* the daughter of Anah. [26]And these *were* the sons of Dishon: Hemdan, and Eshban, and Ithran, and Cheran.

[27]These *were* Ezer's sons: Bilhan, and Zaavan, and Akan. [28]These *were* Dishan's sons: Uz and

441 8487 441 6215 1060 464 1121 6215 1121 441
אַלּוּפֵי בְנֵי־עֵשָׂו בְּנֵי אֱלִיפַז בְּכוֹר עֵשָׂו אַלּוּף תֵּימָן אַלּוּף
Chief ,Teman Chief ,Esau's first-born Eliphaz the of sons :Esau's sons the of chiefs

1609 441 7141 441 7073 441 6825 441 201
16 אוֹמָר אַלּוּף צְפוֹ אַלּוּף קְנַז׃ אַלּוּף קֹרַח אַלּוּף גַּעְתָּם
,Gatham Chief ,Korah Chief ,Kenas Chief ,Zepho Chief ,Omar

1121 428 123 776 464 441 428 6002 441
אַלּוּף עֲמָלֵק אֵלֶּה אַלּוּפֵי אֱלִיפַז בְּאֶרֶץ אֱדוֹם אֵלֶּה בְּנֵי
the of sons these (were) ;Edom the in of land Eliphaz chiefs of These (were) .Amalek Chief

2226 441 984 441 6215 1121 7469 1121 428 5711
17 עָדָה׃ וְאֵלֶּה בְּנֵי רְעוּאֵל בֶּן־עֵשָׂו אַלּוּף נַחַת אַלּוּף זֶרַח
,Zerah Chief ,Nahath Chief :Esau's son ,Reuel the of sons And these .Adah

123 776 7467 441 428 4199 8048 441
אַלּוּף שַׁמָּה אַלּוּף מִזָּה אֵלֶּה אַלּוּפֵי רְעוּאֵל בְּאֶרֶץ אֱדוֹם
;Edom the in of land Reuel chiefs of the these (were) ;Mizzah Chief ,Shammah Chief

802 173 428 6215 802 1315 1121 428
18 אֵלֶּה בְּנֵי בָשְׂמַת אֵשֶׁת עֵשָׂו׃ וְאֵלֶּה בְּנֵי אָהֳלִיבָמָה אֵשֶׁת
wife Oholibamah the of sons And these .Esau's wife ,Basemath the of sons these (were)

441 428 7141 441 3281 441 3266 441 6215
עֵשָׂו אַלּוּף יְעוּשׁ אַלּוּף יַעְלָם אַלּוּף קֹרַח אֵלֶּה אַלּוּפֵי
the of chiefs (were) these ;Korah Chief ,Jalam Chief ,Jeush Chief :Esau's

428 6215 1121 428 6215 802 6034 1323 173
19 אָהֳלִיבָמָה בַּת־עֲנָה אֵשֶׁת עֵשָׂו׃ אֵלֶּה בְנֵי־עֵשָׂו וְאֵלֶּה
and these Esau's sons These (were) .Esau's wife ,Anah the of daughter ,Oholibamah

2753 8165 1121 428 6215 441
20 אַלּוּפֵיהֶם הוּא אֱדוֹם׃ ס אֵלֶּה בְנֵי־שֵׂעִיר הַחֹרִי
the Horite Seir the of sons These (were) .Edom (is) he their (were) ;chiefs

687 1787 6034 6649 7732 3877 776 3427
21 יֹשְׁבֵי הָאָרֶץ לוֹטָן וְשׁוֹבָל וְצִבְעוֹן וַעֲנָה׃ וְדִשׁוֹן וְאֵצֶר
and Ezer and ,Dishon and ,Anah and ,Zibeon and ,Shobal ,Lotan the :land living (in)

1961 123 776 8165 1121 2753 441 428 1787
22 וְדִישָׁן אֵלֶּה אַלּוּפֵי הַחֹרִי בְּנֵי שֵׂעִיר בְּאֶרֶץ אֱדוֹם׃ וַיִּהְיוּ
And were .Edom the in of land ,Seir the of sons the .Horites chiefs the of these (were) and ;Dishan

1121 428 8535 3897 269 1967 2753 3877 1121
23 בְנֵי־לוֹטָן חֹרִי וְהֵימָם וַאֲחוֹת לוֹטָן תִּמְנָע׃ וְאֵלֶּה בְּנֵי
sons And (were) these (was) .Timna Lotan's sister and ;Heman and Hori sons the :Lotan of

6640 1121 428 208 8195 5956 4506 5935 7732
24 שׁוֹבָל עַלְוָן וּמָנַחַת וְעֵיבָל שְׁפוֹ וְאוֹנָם׃ וְאֵלֶּה בְנֵי־צִבְעוֹן
Zibeon the of sons And these .Onam and Shepho and .Ebal and ,Manahath ,Alvan :Shobal's

7462 4057 3222 4672 6034 6034 345
וְאַיָּה וַעֲנָה הוּא עֲנָה אֲשֶׁר מָצָא אֶת־הַיֵּמִם בַּמִּדְבָּר בִּרְעֹתוֹ
he as fed the in desert hot the springs found who Anah he (is) and :Anah even ,Aiah

173 1787/6034 1121 428 1 6649 2543
25 אֶת־הַחֲמֹרִים לְצִבְעוֹן אָבִיו׃ וְאֵלֶּה בְנֵי־עֲנָה דִּשֹׁן וְאָהֳלִיבָמָה
(was) and Oholibamah ,Dishon :Anah the of sons And these his .father for Zibeon asses the

3763 3506 790 2573 1789 1121 428 6034 1323
26 בַּת־עֲנָה׃ וְאֵלֶּה בְּנֵי דִישָׁן חֶמְדָּן וְאֶשְׁבָּן וְיִתְרָן וּכְרָן׃
and .Cheran and ,Ithran and ,Eshban ,Hemdan :Dishan the of sons And these .Anah the of daughter

765 5780 1789 1121 428 6130 2190 1092 687 1121 428
27 28 אֵלֶּה בְּנֵי־אֵצֶר בִּלְהָן וְזַעֲוָן וַעֲקָן׃ אֵלֶּה בְנֵי־דִישָׁן עוּץ וַאֲרָן׃
and .Aran Uz :Dishan the of sons These (were) and .Akan and ,Zaavan ,Bilhan :Ezer the of sons These (were)

Aran. 29 These *were* the chiefs of the Horites: Chief Lotan, Chief Shobal, Chief Zibeon, Chief Anah, 30 Chief Dishon, Chief Ezer, Chief Dishan. These *were* the chiefs of the Horites, according to their chiefs in the land of Seir.

31 And these *were* the kings who reigned in the land of Edom before the reigning of a king over the sons of Israel. 32 And Bela the son of Beor reigned in Edom, and the name of his city, Dinhabah. 33 And Bela died, and Jobab the son of Zerah, from Bozrah, reigned in his place. 34 And Jobab died, and Husham from the land of the Temanites reigned in his place. 35 And Husham died, and Hadad the son of Bedah, who smote Midian in the field of Moab, reigned in his place; and the name of his city, Avith. 36 And Hadad died, and Samlah from Masrekah reigned in his place. 37 And Samlah died, and Shaul from Rehoboth by the River reigned in his place. 38 And Shaul died, and Baal-hanan the son of Achbor reigned in his place. 39 And Baal-hanan the son of Achbor died, and Hadar reigned in his place. And the name of his city *was* Pau; and his wife's name, Mehetabel, the daughter of Matred, the daughter of Mezahab.

40 And these *were* the names of the chiefs of Esau, according to their families, according to their places, by their names: Chief Timnah, Chief Alvah, Chief Jetheth, 41 Chief Oholibamah, Chief Elah, Chief Pinon, 42 Chief Kenaz, Chief Teman, Chief Mibzar, 43 Chief Magdiel, Chief Iram. These *were* the chiefs of

6649 441 7732 441 3877 441 2753 441
29 אֵלֶּה אַלּוּפֵי הַחֹרִי אַלּוּף לוֹטָן אַלּוּף שׁוֹבָל אַלּוּף צִבְעוֹן
,Zibeon Chief ,Shobal Chief ,Lotan Chief the chiefs the These :Horites of (were)

1789 441 687 441 1787 441 6034 441
30 אַלּוּף עֲנָה׃ אַלּוּף דִּשֹׁן אַלּוּף אֵצֶר אַלּוּף דִּישָׁן אֵלֶּה
these ;Dishan Chief ,Ezer Chief ,Dishon Chief ,Anah Chief (were)

8165 776 441 2753 441
אַלּוּפֵי הַחֹרִי לְאַלֻּפֵיהֶם בְּאֶרֶץ שֵׂעִיר׃
.Seir the in of land to according chiefs their Horite the chiefs

4428 4428 6440 123 776 4428 4428
31 וְאֵלֶּה הַמְּלָכִים אֲשֶׁר מָלְכוּ בְּאֶרֶץ אֱדוֹם לִפְנֵי מְלָךְ־מֶלֶךְ
king a the of ruling before Edom the in of land ruled who the (were) kings And these

5892 8034 1160/1121 1106/123 4427 3478 1121
32 לִבְנֵי יִשְׂרָאֵל׃ וַיִּמְלֹךְ בֶּאֱדוֹם בֶּלַע בֶּן־בְּעוֹר וְשֵׁם עִירוֹ
his city the of name ;Beor the of son Bela Edom in And reigned .Israel the of sons over

1224 2126/1121 3103 4725 4427 1106/4191 1838
33 דִּנְהָבָה׃ וַיָּמָת בֶּלַע וַיִּמְלֹךְ תַּחְתָּיו יוֹבָב בֶּן־זֶרַח מִבָּצְרָה׃
from .Bozrah Zerah the of son ,Jobab his in place and reigned ;Bela And .died (was) .Dinhabah

4191 8489 776 2367 4725 4427 3103 4191
34 35 וַיָּמָת יוֹבָב וַיִּמְלֹךְ תַּחְתָּיו חֻשָׁם מֵאֶרֶץ הַתֵּימָנִי׃ וַיָּמָת
died And the .Temanites the of land ,Husham his in place and reigned ;Jobab and died

4080 5221 911/1121 1908 4725 4427 2367
חֻשָׁם וַיִּמְלֹךְ תַּחְתָּיו הֲדַד בֶּן־בְּדַד הַמַּכֶּה אֶת־מִדְיָן
Midian who struck ,Bedad the of son ,Hadad his in place and reigned ;Husham

4725 4427 1908 4191 5762 5892 8034 4124 7704
36 בִּשְׂדֵה מוֹאָב וְשֵׁם עִירוֹ עֲוִית׃ וַיָּמָת הֲדַד וַיִּמְלֹךְ תַּחְתָּיו
his in place and reigned ;Hadad And died .Avith his (was) city of the name and ;Moab the in of field

7586 4725 4427 8072 4191 4957 8072
37 שַׂמְלָה מִמַּשְׂרֵקָה׃ וַיָּמָת שַׂמְלָה וַיִּמְלֹךְ תַּחְתָּיו שָׁאוּל
Shaul his in place and reigned ;Samlah died And from Masrekah Samlah

1177 4725 4427 7586 4191 5104 7344
38 מֵרְחֹבוֹת הַנָּהָר׃ וַיָּמָת שָׁאוּל וַיִּמְלֹךְ תַּחְתָּיו בַּעַל חָנָן
Baalhanan his in place and reigned ;Shaul died And the .river from by Rehoboth

4725 4427 5907 1121 1177 4191 5907
39 בֶּן־עַכְבּוֹר׃ וַיָּמָת בַּעַל חָנָן בֶּן־עַכְבּוֹר וַיִּמְלֹךְ תַּחְתָּיו
his in place and reigned Achbor the of son ,Baalhanan died And .Achbor's son

4038 4105 802 8034 6464 5892 8034 1924
הֲדַר וְשֵׁם עִירוֹ פָּעוּ וְשֵׁם אִשְׁתּוֹ מְהֵיטַבְאֵל בַּת־מַטְרֵד
Matred the of daughter was ,Mehetabel his wife's and name (was) ,Pau his city the of name ;Hadar

4940 6215 441 8034 4314 1323
40 בַּת מֵי זָהָב׃ וְאֵלֶּה שְׁמוֹת אַלּוּפֵי עֵשָׂו לְמִשְׁפְּחֹתָם
their by ,families ,Esau chiefs the of the of names these And (were) .Mezahab the of daughter

3509 441 5933 441 8555 441 8034 4725
לִמְקֹמֹתָם בִּשְׁמֹתָם אַלּוּף תִּמְנָע אַלּוּף עַלְוָה אַלּוּף יְתֵת׃
,Jetheth Chief ,Alvah Chief ,Timnah Chief their by :names their by ,places

7073 441 6373 441 425 441 173 441
41 42 אַלּוּף אָהֳלִיבָמָה אַלּוּף אֵלָה אַלּוּף פִּינֹן׃ אַלּוּף קְנַז
,Kenaz Chief ,Pinon Chief ,Elah Chief ,Oholibamah Chief

5902 441 4025 441 4014 441 8487 441
43 אַלּוּף תֵּימָן אַלּוּף מִבְצָר׃ אַלּוּף מַגְדִּיאֵל אַלּוּף עִירָם
.Iram Chief ,Magdiel Chief ,Mibzar Chief ,Teman Chief

Edom, according to their dwellings, in the land of their possession—he *is* Esau, the father of Edom.

CHAPTER 37

[1]And Jacob lived in the land of his father's travels, in the land of Canaan.

[2]These *are* the generations of Jacob: Joseph, a son of seventeen years, was tending the flock with his brothers, with Bilhah's sons and with Zilpah's sons, his father's wives. And he was a youth. And Joseph came with an evil report of them to their father. [3]And Israel loved Joseph more than all his sons, because he *was* a son of old age to him. And he made a robe *reaching to* the feet. [4]And his brothers saw that their father loved him more than all his brothers, and they hated him. And they were not able to speak peaceably to him.

[5]And Joseph dreamed a dream, and told *it* to his brothers. And they increased to hate him still more. [6]And he said to them, Now hear this dream which I have dreamed: [7]And, behold! We *were* binding sheaves in the middle of the field. And, behold, my sheaf rose up and also stood up. And, behold, your sheaves came around and bowed themselves to my sheaf. [8]And his brothers said to him, Shall you indeed reign over us, or shall you really rule over us? And they hated him still more because of his dreams, and because of his words. [9]And he dreamed still another dream, and told it to his brothers. And he said, Behold, I have dreamed another dream:

אֵלֶּה ׀ אַלּוּפֵי אֱדוֹם לְמֹשְׁבֹתָם בְּאֶרֶץ אֲחֻזָּתָם הוּא עֵשָׂו

,Esau he their the in their by ,Edom chiefs the These
(is) ;possession of land ,dwellings of (were)

אֲבִי אֱדוֹם׃

.Edom the
of father

CAP. XXXVII לז

CHAPTER 37

1
2 וַיֵּשֶׁב יַעֲקֹב בְּאֶרֶץ מְגוּרֵי אָבִיו בְּאֶרֶץ כְּנָעַן׃ אֵלֶּה ׀ תֹּלְדוֹת

the (are) These .Canaan the in his the the in Jacob And
of generations of land father of travels of land lived

יַעֲקֹב יוֹסֵף בֶּן־שְׁבַע־עֶשְׂרֵה שָׁנָה הָיָה רֹעֶה אֶת־אֶחָיו

his with tending was ,years seventeen a ,Joseph :Jacob
brothers of son

בַּצֹּאן וְהוּא נַעַר אֶת־בְּנֵי בִלְהָה וְאֶת־בְּנֵי זִלְפָּה נְשֵׁי אָבִיו

his wives,Zilpah the and Bilhah the with a he and the
;father's of sons with of sons youth (was) ,flock

3 וַיָּבֵא יוֹסֵף אֶת־דִּבָּתָם רָעָה אֶל־אֲבִיהֶם׃ וְיִשְׂרָאֵל אָהַב

loved Israel And .father their to an ,report their Joseph and
one evil brought

אֶת־יוֹסֵף מִכָּל־בָּנָיו כִּי־בֶן־זְקֻנִים הוּא לוֹ וְעָשָׂה לוֹ כְּתֹנֶת

long a for he and to he old a for his more Joseph
coat him made ;him (was) age of son ,sons all than

4 פַּסִּים׃ וַיִּרְאוּ אֶחָיו כִּי־אֹתוֹ אָהַב אֲבִיהֶם מִכָּל־אֶחָיו

his than more their loved him that his saw And (reaching)
,brothers all father brothers .feet the (to)

5 וַיִּשְׂנְאוּ אֹתוֹ וְלֹא יָכְלוּ דַּבְּרוֹ לְשָׁלֹם׃ וַיַּחֲלֹם יוֹסֵף חֲלוֹם

a Joseph And for speak to they and ;him they and
dream dreamed .peace him (to) able were not hated

6 וַיַּגֵּד לְאֶחָיו וַיּוֹסִפוּ עוֹד שְׂנֹא אֹתוֹ׃ וַיֹּאמֶר אֲלֵיהֶם שִׁמְעוּ

,Hear ,them to he And .him to still they and his to (it) and
said hate more increased ;brothers told

7 נָא הַחֲלוֹם הַזֶּה אֲשֶׁר חָלָמְתִּי׃ וְהִנֵּה אֲנַחְנוּ מְאַלְּמִים

(were) We And have I which this dream ,now
binding !behold .dreamed

אֲלֻמִּים בְּתוֹךְ הַשָּׂדֶה וְהִנֵּה קָמָה אֲלֻמָּתִי וְגַם־נִצָּבָה וְהִנֵּה

and stood and my arose and ,field the the in sheaves
behold ;up even sheaf ,lo of midst

8 תְסֻבֶּינָה אֲלֻמֹּתֵיכֶם וַתִּשְׁתַּחֲוֶיןָ לַאֲלֻמָּתִי׃ וַיֹּאמְרוּ לוֹ אֶחָיו

his to said And .sheaf my to bowed and sheaves your came
brothers him themselves round

הֲמָלֹךְ תִּמְלֹךְ עָלֵינוּ אִם־מָשׁוֹל תִּמְשֹׁל בָּנוּ וַיּוֹסִפוּ עוֹד

still they And over you shall really or us over shall ,Indeed
on went ?us rule reign you

9 שְׂנֹא אֹתוֹ עַל־חֲלֹמֹתָיו וְעַל־דְּבָרָיו׃ וַיַּחֲלֹם עוֹד חֲלוֹם

dream again he And because and his of because him to
dreamed .words his of dreams hate

אַחֵר וַיְסַפֵּר אֹתוֹ לְאֶחָיו וַיֹּאמֶר הִנֵּה חָלַמְתִּי חֲלוֹם עוֹד

,again a have I ,Behold and his to it told and
dream dreamed ,said ,brothers ,another

And, behold, the sun and
the moon and the eleven
stars *were* bowing them-
selves to me. 10 And he told
it to his father, and to his
brothers. And his father
rebuked him, and said to
him, What *is* this dream
which you have dreamed?
Shall we indeed come to
bow ourselves to the earth
to you, I, your mother, and
your brothers? 11 And his
brothers were jealous of
him. But his father paid
attention to the word.
12 And his brothers went
to feed the flock of their
their father in Shechem.
13 And Israel said to Joseph,
Are not your brothers
feeding *the flocks* in Shechem? Come, and I will
send you to them. And he
said to him, Here I *am*.
14 And he said to him, Now
go, see the welfare of your
brothers, and the welfare of
the flock, and bring word
back *to* me. And he sent
him out of the valley of
Hebron. And he came to
Shechem.
15 And a man found him.
And, behold, he was
wandering in the field. And
the man asked him, saying,
What do you seek? 16 And
he said, I *am* looking for my
brothers. Please tell me
where they *are* feeding.
17 And the man said, They
pulled up from here, for I
heard *them* say, Let us go
toward Dothan. And Jo-
seph went after his
brothers and found them
in Dothan. 18 And they
saw him from afar. And
before he came near to
them they plotted against
him, to put him to death.
19 And they said, each to
his brother, Behold, this
master of dreams is
coming. 20 And, Come
now and let us kill him
and throw him into one of
the pits. And let us say,
An evil beast has eaten
him. And let us see what
will become of his
dreams.
21 And Reuben heard
and saved him from their

7812 3556 6240 259 3394 8121 2009
וְהִנֵּה הַשֶּׁמֶשׁ וְהַיָּרֵחַ וְאַחַד עָשָׂר כּוֹכָבִים מִשְׁתַּחֲוִים לִי׃
to bowing (were) .me themselves | stars | eleven and | the and moon | sun the | and ,behold
559 1 1605 251 1 5608
10 וַיְסַפֵּר אֶל־אָבִיו וְאֶל־אֶחָיו וַיִּגְעַר־בּוֹ אָבִיו וַיֹּאמֶר לוֹ מָה
What | to ,him | said and | his father | him | And rebuked | his .brothers | and to | his to father | he And (it) told
251 517 935 2492 834 2088 2472
הַחֲלוֹם הַזֶּה אֲשֶׁר חָלָמְתָּ הֲבוֹא נָבוֹא אֲנִי וְאִמְּךָ וְאַחֶיךָ
your and ,brothers | your and mother | I | we shall come | ,Indeed | have you ?dreamed | which | this | (is) dream
8104 1 251 7065 776 7812
11 לְהִשְׁתַּחֲוֺת לְךָ אָרְצָה׃ וַיְקַנְאוּ־בוֹ אֶחָיו וְאָבִיו שָׁמַר אֶת־
observed | his but father | his ;brothers | envied And him | the to ?earth | to you | bow to ourselves
7927 1 66.29 7461 251 3212 1697
12 הַדָּבָר׃ וַיֵּלְכוּ אֶחָיו לִרְעוֹת אֶת־צֹאן אֲבִיהֶם בִּשְׁכֶם׃
.Shechem in | their father | of flock the | feed to | his brothers | And went | .word the
3212 7927 7462 251 3808 3127 3478 559
13 וַיֹּאמֶר יִשְׂרָאֵל אֶל־יוֹסֵף הֲלוֹא אַחֶיךָ רֹעִים בִּשְׁכֶם לְכָה
Come | in ?Shechem | feeding | your brothers | (Are) not | ,Joseph to | Israel | And said
7200 3212 559 559 7971
14 וְאֶשְׁלָחֲךָ אֲלֵיהֶם וַיֹּאמֶר לוֹ הִנֵּנִי׃ וַיֹּאמֶר לוֹ לֶךְ־נָא רְאֵה
see | ,now Go | to ,him | he And said | (am) I .here | to ,him | he And said | to .them | will I and you send
7971 1697 7725 6629 7965 251 7965
אֶת־שְׁלוֹם אַחֶיךָ וְאֶת־שְׁלוֹם הַצֹּאן וַהֲשִׁבֵנִי דָּבָר וַיִּשְׁלָחֵהוּ
sent he And him | .word | bring and me to | the ,flock | the and of welfare | your ,brothers | welfare the of
8582 2009 376 4672 7927 935 2275 6010
15 מֵעֵמֶק חֶבְרוֹן וַיָּבֹא שְׁכֶמָה׃ וַיִּמְצָאֵהוּ אִישׁ וְהִנֵּה תֹעֶה
straying | and ,lo | ,man a | found And him | to .Shechem | he and came | ,Hebron | the from of valley
559 1245 559 376 7592 7704
16 בַּשָּׂדֶה וַיִּשְׁאָלֵהוּ הָאִישׁ לֵאמֹר מַה־תְּבַקֵּשׁ׃ וַיֹּאמֶר אֶת־
my | he And ,said | you do ?seek | What | ,saying | the ,man | asked And him | the in .field
559 7462 375 5046 1245 251
17 אַחַי אָנֹכִי מְבַקֵּשׁ הַגִּידָה־נָּא לִי אֵיפֹה הֵם רֹעִים׃ וַיֹּאמֶר
said And | (are) feeding | they | where | me | tell please | (am) ;seeking | I | brothers
3212 1886 3212 559 8085 2088 5265 376
הָאִישׁ נָסְעוּ מִזֶּה כִּי שָׁמַעְתִּי אֹמְרִים נֵלְכָה דֹּתָיְנָה וַיֵּלֶךְ
And went | towards .Dothan | us Let go | (them) ,saying | heard I | for | from ,here | They up pulled | the ,man
7350 7200 1886 4672 251 310 3127
18 יוֹסֵף אַחַר אֶחָיו וַיִּמְצָאֵם בְּדֹתָן׃ וַיִּרְאוּ אֹתוֹ מֵרָחֹק
from ;afar | him | they And saw | in .Dothan | found and them | his brothers | after | Joseph
559 4191 5230 7126 2962
19 וּבְטֶרֶם יִקְרַב אֲלֵיהֶם וַיִּתְנַכְּלוּ אֹתוֹ לַהֲמִיתוֹ׃ וַיֹּאמְרוּ
they And said | .him kill to | him | plotted they against | to ,them | came he near | and before
6258 935 1976 2472 1167 251 376
20 אִישׁ אֶל־אָחִיו הִנֵּה בַּעַל הַחֲלֹמוֹת הַלָּזֶה בָּא׃ וְעַתָּה
And now | !coming | this | dreams | master Behold of | his to ,brother | each
7451 2416 559 953 259 7993 2026 3212
לְכוּ וְנַהַרְגֵהוּ וְנַשְׁלִכֵהוּ בְּאַחַד הַבֹּרוֹת וְאָמַרְנוּ חַיָּה רָעָה
evil | An beast | let and ,say us | ;pits the | into of one | throw and him | us let him Kill | ,come
5337 7205 8085 2472 1961 7200 398
21 אֲכָלָתְהוּ וְנִרְאֶה מַה־יִּהְיוּ חֲלֹמֹתָיו׃ וַיִּשְׁמַע רְאוּבֵן וַיַּצִּלֵהוּ
saved and him | Reuben | And heard | his dreams | will what of become | let and see us | eaten has ;him

hands, and said, Let us not
smite his soul. [22]And
Reuben said to them, Do
not shed blood. Throw him
into this pit *here* in the
desert, but do not lay a hand
on him—so that *he might*
deliver him from their
hands, to return him to his
father. [23]And when Joseph
came to his brothers, they
stripped his long coat *from*
Joseph, the long coat on
him, *reaching to* his feet.
[24]And they took him and
threw him into the pit, the
pit *being* empty, no water in
it. [25]And they sat down to
eat bread. And they lifted up
their eyes and looked. And,
behold, a caravan of
Ishmaelites coming from
Gilead! And their camels
were bearing spices, and
balsam gum, and sticky
gum, going down to take
them to Egypt. [26]And
Judah said to his brothers,
What gain *is it* that we kill
our brother and conceal his
blood? [27]Come, let us sell
him to the Ishmaelites, and
do not let our hand be on
him. For he is our brother,
our flesh. And his brothers
listened. [28]And men, Midianites, traders, came by.
And they drew up Joseph
and took *him* out of the pit,
and they sold Joseph to the
Ishmaelites for twenty
pieces of silver. And they
brought Joseph into Egypt.
[29]And Reuben came back
to the pit. And, behold,
Joseph was not in the pit;
and he tore his garment.
[30]And he returned to his
brothers and said, The
child, he is not. And I,
where shall I go? [31]And
they took Joseph's long
coat, and killed a ram of the
goats, and dipped the long
coat in the blood. [32]And
they sent the long coat

3808 7205 559 5315 5221 3808 559 3027
22 מִיָּדָם וַיֹּאמֶר לֹא נַכֶּנּוּ נָפֶשׁ׃ וַיֹּאמֶר אֲלֵהֶם ׀ רְאוּבֵן אַל־
not ,Reuben them to said And .soul us Let his strike not ,said and from hand their

4057 834 2088 953 7993 1818 8210
תִּשְׁפְּכוּ־דָם הַשְׁלִיכוּ אֹתוֹ אֶל־הַבּוֹר הַזֶּה אֲשֶׁר בַּמִּדְבָּר
the in ;desert which (is) ,this put into him throw ;blood shed Do

7725 3027 5337 7760 3808 3027
וְיָד אַל־תִּשְׁלְחוּ־בוֹ לְמַעַן הַצִּיל אֹתוֹ מִיָּדָם לַהֲשִׁיבוֹ
return to him from hands their him deliver order in to ,him on lay not but hand a

854 6584 251 3127 935
23 אֶל־אָבִיו׃ וַיְהִי כַּאֲשֶׁר־בָּא יוֹסֵף אֶל־אֶחָיו וַיַּפְשִׁיטוּ אֶת־
stripped they (from) his to ,brothers Joseph came when And his to .father

3947 834 6446 3801 3801 3127
24 יוֹסֵף אֶת־כֻּתָּנְתּוֹ אֶת־כְּתֹנֶת הַפַּסִּים אֲשֶׁר עָלָיו׃ וַיִּקָּחֻהוּ
they And him took .him on which k(was) reaching feet the to coat long the ,coat long his Joseph

3427 4325 7386 953 953 7993
25 וַיַּשְׁלִכוּ אֹתוֹ הַבֹּרָה וְהַבּוֹר רֵק אֵין בּוֹ מָיִם׃ וַיֵּשְׁבוּ
they And down sat .water it in no ,empty pit the (being) the into ,pit him and threw

3459 732 2009 7200 5869 5375 3899 398
לֶאֱכָל־לֶחֶם וַיִּשְׂאוּ עֵינֵיהֶם וַיִּרְאוּ וְהִנֵּה אֹרְחַת יִשְׁמְעֵאלִים
Ismaelites cara-a of van and ,behold and ,looked eyes their they and raised bread eat to

3212 3910 6875 5219 5375 1581 1568 935
בָּאָה מִגִּלְעָד וּגְמַלֵּיהֶם נֹשְׂאִים נְכֹאת וּצְרִי וָלֹט הוֹלְכִים
going and ladanum and ,balm spices bearing their and camels from ;Gilead coming

1215 251 3063 559 4714 3381
26 לְהוֹרִיד מִצְרָיְמָה׃ וַיֹּאמֶר יְהוּדָה אֶל־אֶחָיו מַה־בֶּצַע כִּי
that gain What his to ,brothers Judah said And .Egypt to take to down (them)

3459 4376 3212 1818 3680 251 2026
27 נַהֲרֹג אֶת־אָחִינוּ וְכִסִּינוּ אֶת־דָּמוֹ׃ לְכוּ וְנִמְכְּרֶנּוּ לַיִּשְׁמְעֵאלִים
the to ;Ishmaelites us let him sell .Come ?blood his and conceal our brother we kill

251 8085 1320 251 3808 3027
וְיָדֵנוּ אַל־תְּהִי־בוֹ כִּי־אָחִינוּ בְשָׂרֵנוּ הוּא וַיִּשְׁמְעוּ אֶחָיו׃
his .brothers and listened ;is he flesh our our brother he for is upon ,him let be not our and hand

3127 5927 4900 5503 4084 582 5674
28 וַיַּעַבְרוּ אֲנָשִׁים מִדְיָנִים סֹחֲרִים וַיִּמְשְׁכוּ וַיַּעֲלוּ אֶת־יוֹסֵף
Joseph and took they And up drew .traders ,Midianites ,men came And by

3701 6242 3459 3127 4376 953
מִן־הַבּוֹר וַיִּמְכְּרוּ אֶת־יוֹסֵף לַיִּשְׁמְעֵאלִים בְּעֶשְׂרִים כָּסֶף
;silver twenty for of the to Ishmaelites Joseph they and sold the ,pit out of

2009 953 7725 7205 4714 3127 935
29 וַיָּבִיאוּ אֶת־יוֹסֵף מִצְרָיְמָה׃ וַיָּשָׁב רְאוּבֵן אֶל־הַבּוֹר וְהִנֵּה
and ,behold ,pit the to Reuben And came .Egypt into Joseph they and took

559 251 935 899 7167 953 3127 369
30 אֵין־יוֹסֵף בַּבּוֹר וַיִּקְרַע אֶת־בְּגָדָיו׃ וַיָּשָׁב אֶל־אֶחָיו וַיֹּאמַר
,said and his brothers to he And came .clothes his he and tore the in ;pit Joseph was not

3127 3801 3947 935 575 3206
31 הַיֶּלֶד אֵינֶנּוּ וַאֲנִי אָנָה אֲנִי־בָא׃ וַיִּקְחוּ אֶת־כְּתֹנֶת יוֹסֵף
Joseph's coat long they And took ?go shall I where ,I and is he not The ,child

7971 1818 3801 2881 5795 8163 7919
32 וַיִּשְׁחֲטוּ שְׂעִיר עִזִּים וַיִּטְבְּלוּ אֶת־הַכֻּתֹּנֶת בַּדָּם׃ וַיְשַׁלְּחוּ
they And sent the in .blood coat long the and dipped the goats a of ram and killed

reaching to the feet, and
they took it to their father,
and said, We have found
this. Now look, is it your
son's long coat?[33]And he
knew it, and said, My son's
long coat! An evil beast has
eaten him. Surely Joseph is
torn in pieces. [34]And Jacob
tore his clothing and put
sackcloth on his loins. And
he mourned many days for
his son. [35]And all his sons
and all his daughters rose
up to comfort him. And he
refused to be comforted,
and said, I will go down to
Sheol mourning for my son.
And his father wept for him.
[36]And the Midianites
sold him into Egypt, to
Potiphar, a eunuch of
Pharaoh, the chief of the
executioners.

4672 559 1 935 6446 3801
אֶת־כְּתֹנֶת הַפַּסִּים וַיָּבִיאוּ אֶל־אֲבִיהֶם וַיֹּאמְרוּ זֹאת מָצָאנוּ
have we found; This ,said and ,father their to they and (it) took reaching ,feet the to coat long the

559 5234 3808 1121 3801 4994 5234
33 הַכֶּר־נָא הַכְּתֹנֶת בִּנְךָ הִוא אִם־לֹא׃ וַיַּכִּירָהּ וַיֹּאמֶר
,said and he And it knew ?not or ,it your son's long (is) coat now know

7167 3127 2963 2963 398 7451 2416 1121 3801
34 כְּתֹנֶת בְּנִי חַיָּה רָעָה אֲכָלַתְהוּ טָרֹף טֹרַף יוֹסֵף׃ וַיִּקְרַע
tore and ;Joseph surely torn is pieces to eaten has ;him evil An beast My !son's long coat

3117 1121 56 4975 8242 7760 8071 3290
יַעֲקֹב שִׂמְלֹתָיו וַיָּשֶׂם שַׂק בְּמָתְנָיו וַיִּתְאַבֵּל עַל־בְּנוֹ יָמִים
days his son for he and mourned his on ;loins sack- cloth and put his clothes Jacob

5162 3985 5162 1323 3605 1121 3605 6965 7227
35 רַבִּים׃ וַיָּקֻמוּ כָל־בָּנָיו וְכָל־בְּנֹתָיו לְנַחֲמוֹ וַיְמָאֵן לְהִתְנַחֵם
be to ,comforted he but refused com- to ,him fort his all and daughters sons his all And arose .many

1058 7585 57 1121 3381 559
וַיֹּאמֶר כִּי־אֵרֵד אֶל־בְּנִי אָבֵל שְׁאֹלָה וַיֵּבְךְּ אֹתוֹ אָבִיו׃
his .father for him and wept ;Sheol to ,mourning my son to will I down go ,said and

6547 5631 6319 4714 4376 4092
36 וְהַמְּדָנִים מָכְרוּ אֹתוֹ אֶל־מִצְרָיִם לְפוֹטִיפַר סְרִיס פַּרְעֹה
.Pharaoh a of eunuch ,Potiphar to .Egypt into him sold the And Midianites

2876 8269
שַׂר הַטַּבָּחִים׃ פ
the .executioners the of chief

CAP. XXXVIII לח

CHAPTER 38

CHAPTER 38

[1]And it happened at that
time that Judah went down,
away from his brothers, and
turned aside to a man of
Adullam named Hirah.
[2]And Judah saw there a
daughter of a Canaanite
man named Shuah. And he
took her, and went in to
her. [3]And she conceived
and bore a son. And he
called his name Er. [4]And
she conceived again and
bore a son and called his
name Onan. [5]And she
continued still and bore a
son. And she called his
name Shelah. And he was
at Chezib when she bore
him. [6]And Judah took a
wife for his firstborn, Er,
named Tamar. [7]And Er,
Judah's firstborn, was evil
in the eyes of Jehovah. And
Jehovah killed him. [8]And
Judah said to Onan, Go in
to your brother's wife and
marry her, and raise up seed

376 5186 251 3063 3387 6256 1961
1 וַיְהִי בָּעֵת הַהִוא וַיֵּרֶד יְהוּדָה מֵאֵת אֶחָיו וַיֵּט עַד־אִישׁ
.man a to and turned in his ,brothers from away ,Judah went down ,that time at And was it

3669 376 3063 8033 7200 2437 8034 5726
2 עֲדֻלָּמִי וּשְׁמוֹ חִירָה׃ וַיַּרְא־שָׁם יְהוּדָה בַּת־אִישׁ כְּנַעֲנִי
Canaanite man a of daughter a Judah there saw And .Hirah named of Adullam

7121 1121 3205 2029 935 3947 7770 8034
3 וּשְׁמוֹ שׁוּעַ וַיִּקָּחֶהָ וַיָּבֹא אֵלֶיהָ׃ וַתַּהַר וַתֵּלֶד בֵּן וַיִּקְרָא
he And called a .son and bore she And conceived .her to and in went he And her took .Shuah named

269 8034 7121 1121 3205 5750 2928 6147 8034
4 אֶת־שְׁמוֹ עֵר׃ וַתַּהַר עוֹד וַתֵּלֶד בֵּן וַתִּקְרָא אֶת־שְׁמוֹ אוֹנָן׃
.Onan name his she and called a ,son bore and again she And conceived .Er name his

3580 1961 7956 8034 7121 1121 3205 5750 3254
5 וַתֹּסֶף עוֹד וַתֵּלֶד בֵּן וַתִּקְרָא אֶת־שְׁמוֹ שֵׁלָה וְהָיָה בִכְזִיב
at Chezib and was he ,Shelah his name she and called a son bore and still she And on went

8034 1060 6147 802 3063 3947 3205
6 בְּלִדְתָּהּ אֹתוֹ׃ וַיִּקַּח יְהוּדָה אִשָּׁה לְעֵר בְּכוֹרוֹ וּשְׁמָהּ
whose name was his ,firstborn for Er wife a Judah And took .him she when bore

4191 3068 5869 7451 3063 1060 6147 1961 8559
7 תָּמָר׃ וַיְהִי עֵר בְּכוֹר יְהוּדָה רַע בְּעֵינֵי יְהוָה וַיְמִתֵהוּ
and him killed Jehovah the in of eyes evil Judah the of firstborn Er And was .Tamar

2992 251 802 935 209 3063 559 3068
8 יְהוָה׃ וַיֹּאמֶר יְהוּדָה לְאוֹנָן בֹּא אֶל־אֵשֶׁת אָחִיךָ וְיַבֵּם
and marry your brother a of wife to Go ,Onan to Judah said And .Jehovah

to your brother. 9And Onan
knew that the seed would
not be his. And it happened
when he went *into* his
brother's wife, he wasted
his semen to the ground,
not giving seed to his
brother. 10And what he did
was evil in the eyes of
Jehovah, and He also killed
him. 11And Judah said to
his daughter-in-law Tamar,
Live *as* a widow in your
father's house until my son
Shelah is grown. For he
said, Lest he also die like
his brothers. And Tamar
went and lived in her
father's house.

12And the days were
many, and the wife of
Judah, the daughter of
Shuah, died. And Judah
was comforted, and *he*
went up to the shearers of
his flocks, he and his friend
Hirah of Adullam, to Tim-
nah. 13And Tamar was told,
saying, Behold, your father-
in-law *is* going up to
Timnah to shear his flocks.
14And she took off her
widow's robes from her,
and veiled herself with a
veil, and disguised herself.
And *she* sat at the entrance
to Enaim, which *is* on the
way to Timnah. For she saw
that Shelah had grown up,
and she had not been given
to him for a wife. 15And
Judah saw her. And he
thought she *was* a harlot,
because she had veiled her
face. 16And he turned aside
to her by the roadway, and
said, Come now, let me
come in to you. For he did
not know that she *was* his
daughter-in-law. And she
said, What will you give me
that you may come in to
me? 17And he said, I will
send a kid of the goats from
the flock. And she said, Will
you give me a pledge until
you send *it*? 18And he said,
What *is* the pledge which I
shall give to you? And she
said, Your signet ring, and
your bracelet, and your staff
in your hand. And he gave

1961 3808 209 3045 251 2233 6965
9 אתה והקם זרע לאחיך׃ וידע אונן כי לא לו יהיה
would be to him not that Onan And knew your to .brother seed and up raise ;her

1115 776 7843 251 802 935 518 1961/2233
הזרע והיה אם־בא אל־אשת אחיו ושחת ארצה לבלתי
not the to .ground he (it) wasted his ,brother wife the to of he when in went and ,was it the ;seed

1571 4191 6213 3068 5869 3415 251 2233 5414
10 נתן־זרע לאחיו׃ וירע בעיני יהוה אשר עשה וימת גם־
also He and he killed that ,did Jehovah the in of eyes was And evil his to .brother seed giving

1004 490 3427 3618 8559 3063 559
11 אתו׃ ויאמר יהודה לתמר כלתו שבי אלמנה בית־
in house widow a Live his ,daughter-in-law Tamar to Judah said And .him

1571 4191 559 1121 7956 1430 1
אביך עד־יגדל שלה בני כי אמר פן־ימות גם־הוא
he also die Lest ,said he for ;son my Shelah is until grown your ,father's

4191 3117 7235 1 1004 3427 8559 3212 251
12 כאחיו ותלך תמר ותשב בית אביה׃ וירבו הימים ותמת
and died ,days the And many were her .father's house and in lived Tamar and went his like ;brothers

6629 1494 5927 3063 5162 3063 802 1340/1323
בת־שוע אשת־יהודה וינחם יהודה ויעל על־גוזי צאנו
his ,sheep to of shearers and went Judah was And comforted .Judah the of wife Shuah's ,daughter

559 8559 5046 8553 5726 7453 2437
13 הוא וחירה רעהו העדלמי תמנתה׃ ויגד לתמר לאמר
,saying ,Tamar And told was .Timnah to ,Adullam of his friend and Hirah he

491 899 5493 6629 1494 8553 5927 2524 2009
14 הנה חמיך עלה תמנתה לגז צאנו׃ ותסר בגדי אלמנותה
widow's her robes she And off took his .flocks to shear Timnah goes your to father-in-law ,See

834 5869 6607 5968 6809 3680
מעליה ותכס בצעיף ותתעלף ותשב בפתח עינים אשר
which (is) of ,Enaim en- trance the at sat and dis- guised and herself a with ,veil veiled and herself from her

5414 3808 7856 1430 7200 8553 1870
על־דרך תמנתה כי ראתה כי־גדל שלה והוא לא־נתנה
had not given been and she ,Shelah had that up grown saw she For .Timnah to way the on

3680 2181 2803 3063 7200 802
15 לו לאשה׃ ויראה יהודה ויחשבה לזונה כי כסתה
had she veiled for a for ,harlot thought he (be to) her and ,Judah saw And her .wife a for to him

935 4994/3053 559 1870 5186 6440
16 פניה׃ ויט אליה אל־הדרך ויאמר הבה־נא אבוא אליך
to ;you me let in come ,now Come ,said and way the by her to he And in turned her .face

935 5414 559 3618 3045 3808/3588
כי לא ידע כי כלתו הוא ותאמר מה־תתן־לי כי תבוא
may you in come that to me will What give you she And said she his was daughter-in-law that he not did know for

559 6629 5795 1423 7971 559
17 אלי׃ ויאמר אנכי אשלח גדי־עזים מן־הצאן ותאמר
she And said the from .flock of goats the kid a send will I he And ,said ?me to

834 6162 559 7971 5704 6162 5414
18 אם־תתן ערבון עד שלחך׃ ויאמר מה הערבון אשר
which pledge the you ?send until pledge a you Will me give

5414 3027 834 4294 6616 2368 559 5414
אתן־לך ותאמר חתמך ופתילך ומטך אשר בידך ויתן
he And gave your in .hand which (is) your and staff your and bracelet Your ring signet she And ,said give will I ?you to

to her, and came in to her. And she conceived by him. 19 And she rose up and left, and took off her veil from her face. And *she* put on her widow's robes.

20 And Judah sent the kid of the goats by the hand of his friend, the Adullamite, to receive the pledge from the woman's hand. And he did not find her. 21 And he asked the men of her place, saying, Where *is* the harlot that *was* at Enaim, by the roadway? And they said, There was no harlot here. 22 And he returned to Judah and said, I have not found her. And also the men of the place said, There *was* no harlot here. 23 And Judah said, Let her take *them* for herself, that we not become a laughing-stock. See, I sent this kid, and you did not find her.

24 And after three months, it happened. It was told to Judah, saying, Your daughter-in-law Tamar has committed adultery, and also, behold, *she* is pregnant by whoredom. And Judah said, Bring her out and let her be burned. 25 She *was* being brought out, and she sent to her father-in-law, saying I *am* pregnant by a man to whom these *belong*. And she said, Note now whose *are* these, the signet ring, the bracelet, and the staff? 26 And Judah looked intently, and said, She is more righteous than I, because I did not give her to my son Shelah. And he never knew her again.

27 And in the time of her bearing, behold, it happened! Twins *were* in her womb. 28 And in her bearing, it happened that one put forth a hand, and the midwife took it and tied crimson on his hand, saying, This one came out first. 29 And it happened as he withdrew his hand, behold, his brother came out. And

6809 5493 3212 6965 2029 935
19 לָהּ וַיָּבֹא אֵלֶיהָ וַתַּהַר לוֹ׃ וַתָּקָם וַתֵּלֶךְ וַתָּסַר צְעִיפָהּ
her and ,left and she And by she and her to and to
veil removed arose .him conceived in came ,her

1423 3063 7971 491 899 3847 6440
20 מֵעָלֶיהָ וַתִּלְבַּשׁ בִּגְדֵי אַלְמְנוּתָהּ׃ וַיִּשְׁלַח יְהוּדָה אֶת־גְּדִי
the Judah sent And .widow's her robes put and her from
of kid on ,face

802 3027 6162 3947 5726 7453 3027 5795
הָעִזִּים בְּיַד רֵעֵהוּ הָעֲדֻלָּמִי לָקַחַת הָעֵרָבוֹן מִיַּד הָאִשָּׁה
the from pledge the get to the his by the
,woman's hand back ,Adullamite ,friend's hand goats

6948 559 4725 582 7592 4672 3808
21 וְלֹא מְצָאָהּ׃ וַיִּשְׁאַל אֶת־אַנְשֵׁי מְקֹמָהּ לֵאמֹר אַיֵּה הַקְּדֵשָׁה
harlot the Where ,saying her of men the he And did he and
is ,place asked .her find not

6948 2088 1961 559 1870 5879
הִוא בָעֵינַיִם עַל־הַדָּרֶךְ וַיֹּאמְרוּ לֹא־הָיְתָה בָזֶה קְדֵשָׁה׃
.harlot a here was There not they And ?way the by Enaim at that
,said (was)

4725 582 1571 4672 3808 559 3063 7725
22 וַיָּשָׁב אֶל־יְהוּדָה וַיֹּאמֶר לֹא מְצָאתִיהָ וְגַם אַנְשֵׁי הַמָּקוֹם
place the men the and have I not ,said and Judah to he And
of also her found returned

3947 3063 559 6948 1961 3808 559
23 אָמְרוּ לֹא־הָיְתָה בָזֶה קְדֵשָׁה׃ וַיֹּאמֶר יְהוּדָה תִּקַּח־לָהּ
for her Let ,Judah said And .harlot a here was There not ,said
herself take

4672 3808 2088 1423 7971 2009 937 1961
פֶּן נִהְיֶה לָבוּז הִנֵּה שָׁלַחְתִּי הַגְּדִי הַזֶּה וְאַתָּה לֹא מְצָאתָהּ׃
find did not you and ,this kid sent I ,see a be we lest
her ;laughing-stock

8559 2181 559 3063 5046 2320 7969 1961
24 וַיְהִי ׀ כְּמִשְׁלֹשׁ חֳדָשִׁים וַיֻּגַּד לִיהוּדָה לֵאמֹר זָנְתָה תָּמָר
Tamar has ,saying Judah to was it ,months three after And
adultery committed told ,was it

3318 3063 559 2783 2030 2009 2524 3618
כַּלָּתֶךָ וְגַם הִנֵּה הָרָה לִזְנוּנִים וַיֹּאמֶר יְהוּדָה הוֹצִיאוּהָ
her Bring ,Judah said And by is ,see also and your
out .whoredom pregnant ;daughter-in-law

559 2524 7971 3318 8313
25 וְתִשָּׂרֵף׃ הִוא מוּצֵאת וְהִיא שָׁלְחָה אֶל־חָמִיהָ לֵאמֹר
,saying her to sent she and being (was) She her let and
,father-in-law brought .burned be

4994/5234 559 2030 376
לְאִישׁ אֲשֶׁר־אֵלֶּה לּוֹ אָנֹכִי הָרָה וַתֹּאמֶר הַכֶּר־נָא לְמִי
to now Notice she And (am) I to these which a By
whom ,said .pregnant him (belong) man

559 3063 5234 4294 6616 2858
26 הַחֹתֶמֶת וְהַפְּתִילִים וְהַמַּטֶּה הָאֵלֶּה׃ וַיַּכֵּר יְהוּדָה וַיֹּאמֶר
,said and Judah And these the and ,bracelet the signet the
knew .(are) staff ,ring

1121 7956 5414 3808 3588 6663
צָדְקָה מִמֶּנִּי כִּי־עַל־כֵּן לֹא־נְתַתִּיהָ לְשֵׁלָה בְנִי וְלֹא־יָסַף
never and my Shelah to did I not because more is She
son her give ,I than righteous

990 8380 2009 3205 6256 1961 3045 5750
27 עוֹד לְדַעְתָּהּ׃ וַיְהִי בְּעֵת לִדְתָּהּ וְהִנֵּה תְאוֹמִים בְּבִטְנָהּ׃
her in twins ,that her the in it And he did again
.womb (were) ,behold bearing of time was .her know

3027 7194 3205 3947 5414 3205 1961
28 וַיְהִי בְלִדְתָּהּ וַיִּתֶּן־יָד וַתִּקַּח הַמְיַלֶּדֶת וַתִּקְשֹׁר עַל־יָדוֹ
his on tied and the and a put one her in it And
hand midwife it took hand out bearing ,was

3118 2009 3027 7725 1961 7223 3318 559 8144
29 שָׁנִי לֵאמֹר זֶה יָצָא רִאשֹׁנָה׃ וַיְהִי ׀ כְּמֵשִׁיב יָדוֹ וְהִנֵּה יָצָא
came ,that his he as it And .first came This ,saying ,crim-
out ,lo ,hand withdrew ,was out one son

she said, How have you broken a break for yourself? And one called his name Pharez. [30]And then his brother came out, on whose hand *was* the crimson. And one called his name Zarah.

CHAPTER 39

[1]And Joseph was made to go in to Egypt. And Potiphar, a eunuch of Pharaoh, the chief of the executioners, an Egyptian man, bought him from the Ishmaelites who had made him go there. [2]And Jehovah was with Joseph, and he was a prosperous man. And he was in the Egyptian's house, his master. [3]And his master saw that Jehovah *was* with him and in everything which Joseph did *was* prospering in his hand.

[4]And Joseph found favor in his sight, and served him. And he appointed him over his house, and he gave all he owned into his hand. [5]And it came about that from the time he appointed him over his house and over all he owned, Jehovah blessed the Egyptian's house for Joseph's sake. And the blessing of Jehovah was on all that he had, in the house and in the field. [6]And he left all he owned in Joseph's hand. And he did not know anything that he had, except the bread which he *was* eating. And Joseph was beautiful in form and beautiful of appearance.

[7]And after these things, it happened that his master's wife lifted up her eyes to Joseph, and said, Lie with me. [8]And he refused, and said to his master's wife, Behold, my master does not know what is in the house with me, and all that he owns he has given into my

6557 8034 7121 6555 6556 559 251
אָחִיו וַתֹּאמֶר מַה־פָּרַצְתָּ עָלֶיךָ פָּרֶץ וַיִּקְרָא שְׁמוֹ פָּרֶץ׃
.Pharez his name And called one ?break a for yourself have How broken you she And said his brother

30 2220 8034 7121 8144 3027 251 3318 310
וְאַחַר יָצָא אָחִיו אֲשֶׁר עַל־יָדוֹ הַשָּׁנִי וַיִּקְרָא שְׁמוֹ זָרַח׃ ס
.Zarah his name one And called the ,crimson hand on (was) whose his ,brother came out And then

CAP. XXXIX לט

CHAPTER 39

1 8269 6547 5631 6318 7069 4714 3381 3127
וְיוֹסֵף הוּרַד מִצְרָיְמָה וַיִּקְנֵהוּ פּוֹטִיפַר סְרִיס פַּרְעֹה שַׂר
the of chief ,Pharaoh a of eunuch ,Potiphar bought And him .Egypt to was brought And Joseph

3381 3459 4713 376 2876
הַטַּבָּחִים אִישׁ מִצְרִי מִיַּד הַיִּשְׁמְעֵאלִים אֲשֶׁר הוֹרִדֻהוּ
brought had down him who Ishmaelites the from Egyptian an man ,executioners the

2 1004 1961 6743 376 1961 3127 3068 1961 8033
שָׁמָּה׃ וַיְהִי יְהוָה אֶת־יוֹסֵף וַיְהִי אִישׁ מַצְלִיחַ וַיְהִי בְּבֵית
the of house in he was and ;prosperous man and was he Joseph with Jehovah And was .there

3 834 3068 113 7200 4713 113
אֲדֹנָיו הַמִּצְרִי׃ וַיַּרְא אֲדֹנָיו כִּי יְהוָה אִתּוֹ וְכֹל אֲשֶׁר
which and everything with ;him (was) Jehovah that his master saw And the .Egyptian his master

4 5869 2580 3127 4672 3027 6743 3127 6213
הוּא עֹשֶׂה יְהוָה מַצְלִיחַ בְּיָדוֹ׃ וַיִּמְצָא יוֹסֵף חֵן בְּעֵינָיו
his sight in favor Joseph And found his in .hand (was) prospering Joseph did he

3027 5414 3426 3605 1004 5921 6485 8334
וַיְשָׁרֶת אֹתוֹ וַיַּפְקִדֵהוּ עַל־בֵּיתוֹ וְכָל־יֶשׁ־לוֹ נָתַן בְּיָדוֹ׃
his .hand into he gave to him that was and all his ,house over he and him appointed ;him and served

5 1288 3426 8605 1004 6485 227 1961
וַיְהִי מֵאָז הִפְקִיד אֹתוֹ בְּבֵיתוֹ וְעַל כָּל־אֲשֶׁר יֶשׁ־לוֹ וַיְבָרֶךְ
and blessed to ,him was that all and over his over house him ap- pointed he from time that And ,was it

3068 1293 1961 3127 1558 4713 1004 3068
יְהוָה אֶת־בֵּית הַמִּצְרִי בִּגְלַל יוֹסֵף וַיְהִי בִּרְכַּת יְהוָה
Jehovah blessing of the was and ;Joseph's sake for the Egyptian the of house Jehovah

6 3027 834 3605 5800 7704 1004 3426 3605
בְּכָל־אֲשֶׁר יֶשׁ־לוֹ בַּבַּיִת וּבַשָּׂדֶה׃ וַיַּעֲזֹב כָּל־אֲשֶׁר־לוֹ בְּיַד
in hand to him that was all he And left in and .field the the in house to him was that all on

834 3899 518 3972 3045 3808 3127
יוֹסֵף וְלֹא־יָדַע אִתּוֹ מְאוּמָה כִּי אִם־הַלֶּחֶם אֲשֶׁר־הוּא
he which bread the except ,anything that had he did he know and not ;Joseph's

7 310 1961 4758 3303 8389 3303 3127 1961 398
אוֹכֵל וַיְהִי יוֹסֵף יְפֵה־תֹאַר וִיפֵה מַרְאֶה׃ וַיְהִי אַחַר
after it And was of appearance fair and form in fair Joseph And was was ,eating

3127 5869 113 802 5375 1697
הַדְּבָרִים הָאֵלֶּה וַתִּשָּׂא אֵשֶׁת־אֲדֹנָיו אֶת־עֵינֶיהָ אֶל־יוֹסֵף
Joseph to eyes her his master wife of the lifted up that these things

8 2009 113 802 559 3985 7901 559
וַתֹּאמֶר שִׁכְבָה עִמִּי׃ וַיְמָאֵן וַיֹּאמֶר אֶל־אֵשֶׁת אֲדֹנָיו הֵן
See ,master his of wife the to said and he And refused with .me Lie said and

3027 5414 3426 834 3605 1004 3045 3808 113
אֲדֹנִי לֹא־יָדַע אִתִּי מַה־בַּבַּיִת וְכֹל אֲשֶׁר־יֶשׁ־לוֹ נָתַן בְּיָדִי׃
my hand into has given he to him is which and all the in ;house what is with me does not know my master

hand. [9]No one in this house is greater than I, and he has not withheld anything from me except you, because you *are* his wife. And how should I do this great evil and sin against God? [10]And it happened, as she spoke to Joseph day *after* day, he did not listen to her, to lie beside her, to be with her. [11]And it happened *on* this day, that he went into the house to do his work. And none of the men of the house *were* there in the house. [12]And she caught him by his robe, saying, Lie with me! And he left his robe in her hand and fled, and went outside. [13]And it happened, when she saw that he had left his robe in her hand, and had fled outside, [14]she called to the men of her house and spoke to them, saying, See, he has brought to us a Hebrew man to mock at us. He came in to me to lie with me, and I cried with a loud voice. [15]And when he heard that I raised my voice and cried, he left his robe by me and fled, and went outside. [16]And she kept his robe beside her until the coming of his master to his house. [17]And she spoke these same words to him, saying, The Hebrew slave whom you brought in to us came in to me, to mock at me. [18]And it happened at my raising my voice and crying out, he left his robe beside me and fled outside.

[19]And it happened, when his master heard his wife's words which she spoke to him, saying, According to these words your slave did to me, his anger glowed. [20]And Joseph's master took

3972 2820 3808 2088 1004 1419
9 אֵינֶנּוּ גָדוֹל בַּבַּיִת הַזֶּה מִמֶּנִּי וְלֹא־חָשַׂךְ מִמֶּנִּי מְאוּמָה
,anything from has he and than this in is one No
me withheld not ;I house greater
1419 7451 62 13 802 859
כִּי אִם־אוֹתָךְ בַּאֲשֶׁר אַתְּ־אִשְׁתּוֹ וְאֵיךְ אֶעֱשֶׂה הָרָעָה הַגְּדֹלָה
great evil should and his you because ,you except
do I how ;wife (are)
3117 3117 3127 1696 1961 430 2398 2088
10 הַזֹּאת וְחָטָאתִי לֵאלֹהִים׃ וַיְהִי כְּדַבְּרָהּ אֶל־יוֹסֵף יוֹם ׀ יוֹם
,day day Joseph to her as it And ?God against sin and this
(after) speaking ,was
3117 1961 1961 5689 7901 8085 3808
11 וְלֹא־שָׁמַע אֵלֶיהָ לִשְׁכַּב אֶצְלָהּ לִהְיוֹת עִמָּהּ׃ וַיְהִי כְּהַיּוֹם
about it and with be to beside lie to ,her to did he that
day ,was ;her ,her listen not
582 376 4399 6213 1004 935 2088
הַזֶּה וַיָּבֹא הַבַּיְתָה לַעֲשׂוֹת מְלַאכְתּוֹ וְאֵין אִישׁ מֵאַנְשֵׁי
the of man and ;work his do to the into and ,this
of men no house went he
7901 559 899 8610 1004 8033 1004
12 הַבַּיִת שָׁם בַּבָּיִת׃ וַתִּתְפְּשֵׂהוּ בְּבִגְדוֹ לֵאמֹר שִׁכְבָה עִמִּי
with Lie ,saying his by she And the in (were) the
!me ,robe him caught ,house there house
7200 1961 2351 5127 3027 899 5800
13 וַיַּעֲזֹב בִּגְדוֹ בְּיָדָהּ וַיָּנָס וַיֵּצֵא הַחוּצָה׃ וַיְהִי כִּרְאוֹתָהּ
she when it And .outside and and her in his he And
saw was went fled hand robe left
1004 582 7121 2351 5127 3027 899 5800
14 כִּי־עָזַב בִּגְדוֹ בְּיָדָהּ וַיָּנָס הַחוּצָה׃ וַתִּקְרָא לְאַנְשֵׁי בֵיתָהּ
her the to called and ,outside and her in his he that
house of men fled had hand robe left had
6711 5680 376 935 7200 559 559
וַתֹּאמֶר לָהֶם לֵאמֹר רְאוּ הֵבִיא לָנוּ אִישׁ עִבְרִי לְצַחֶק
to Hebrew man a to has he ,See ,saying to and
laugh us brought ,them spoke
8085 1419 6963 7121 7901 935
15 בָּנוּ בָּא אֵלַי לִשְׁכַּב עִמִּי וָאֶקְרָא בְּקוֹל גָּדוֹל׃ וַיְהִי כְשָׁמְעוֹ
he when And .loud with I and with lie to to he at
heard voice a cried ,me me came ;us
5927 5127 681 899 5800 7121 6963 7311
כִּי־הֲרִימֹתִי קוֹלִי וָאֶקְרָא וַיַּעֲזֹב בִּגְדוֹ אֶצְלִי וַיָּנָס וַיֵּצֵא
and and me by his left he ,cried and my raised I that
went ,fled robe voice
1004 113 935 5704 681 899 3240 2351
16 הַחוּצָה׃ וַתַּנַּח בִּגְדוֹ אֶצְלָהּ עַד־בּוֹא אֲדֹנָיו אֶל־בֵּיתוֹ׃
.house his to his the until beside his And .outside
master of coming her robe kept she
5650 935 559 1697 1696
17 וַתְּדַבֵּר אֵלָיו כַּדְּבָרִים הָאֵלֶּה לֵאמֹר בָּא אֵלַי הָעֶבֶד
The me to came ,saying these words him to she And
slave in ,same spoke
6963 7311 1961 6711 935 5680
18 הָעִבְרִי אֲשֶׁר־הֵבֵאתָ לָּנוּ לְצַחֶק בִּי׃ וַיְהִי כַּהֲרִימִי קוֹלִי
my my at it And at to ,us to have you whom ,Hebrew
voice raising ,was .me laugh brought
8085 1961 2351 5127 681 899 5800 7121
19 וָאֶקְרָא וַיַּעֲזֹב בִּגְדוֹ אֶצְלִי וַיָּנָס הַחוּצָה׃ וַיְהִי כִשְׁמֹעַ
when it And .outside and beside his left he and
heard ,was fled me robe ,crying
1697 559 1696 802 1697 113
אֲדֹנָיו אֶת־דִּבְרֵי אִשְׁתּוֹ אֲשֶׁר דִּבְּרָה אֵלָיו לֵאמֹר כַּדְּבָרִים
According to ,saying ,him to she which his of words the his
words spoke wife master
3127 113 3947 639 2734 5650 6213
20 הָאֵלֶּה עָשָׂה לִי עַבְדֶּךָ וַיִּחַר אַפּוֹ׃ וַיִּקַּח אֲדֹנֵי יוֹסֵף אֹתוֹ
him Joseph's master And his glowed your to did these
took ,anger ,slave me

him and put him into the prison-house, the place where the king's prisoners *were* imprisoned. [21]And Jehovah was with Joseph, and extended kindness to him. And He gave him favor in the eyes of the warden of the prison-house. [22]And the warden of the prison-house gave all the prisoners in the prison-house into Joseph's hand. And all which they did there, he was doing. [23]There was no looking of the warden of the prison-house to anything in his hand, in that Jehovah *was* with him, and Jehovah *was* prospering what he *was* doing.

631 4428 615 834 4725 5470 1004 5414
וַיִּתְּנֵהוּ אֶל־בֵּית הַסֹּהַר מְקוֹם אֲשֶׁר־אֲסוּרֵי הַמֶּלֶךְ אֲסוּרִים
(were) king the prisoners where place the the house in put and
.bound of ,prison- him

5186 3127 3068 1961 5470 1004 1961
21 וַיְהִי־שָׁם בְּבֵית הַסֹּהַר׃ וַיְהִי יְהוָה אֶת־יוֹסֵף וַיֵּט אֵלָיו
to and Joseph with Jehovah And ,prison- the in there And
him extended was house was he

1004 8269 5470 1004 8269 5869 2580 2617
22 חָסֶד וַיִּתֵּן חִנּוֹ בְּעֵינֵי שַׂר בֵּית־הַסֹּהַר׃ וַיִּתֵּן שַׂר בֵּית־
house the And .prison-house the the the in favor He and kind-
of warden gave of warden of eyes gave ,ness

5470 1004 615 3605 3027 5470
הַסֹּהַר בְּיַד־יוֹסֵף אֵת כָּל־הָאֲסִירִם אֲשֶׁר בְּבֵית הַסֹּהַר
the house in who prisoners the all Joseph's into the
;prison- (were) hand prison-

1004 8269 6213 1961 8033 6213 834 3605
23 וְאֵת כָּל־אֲשֶׁר עֹשִׂים שָׁם הוּא הָיָה עֹשֶׂה׃ אֵין שַׂר בֵּית־
house the (for) I here .doing was he there they which all and
of warden no was did

3068 3027 3972 3605 7200 5470
הַסֹּהַר רֹאֶה אֶת־כָּל־מְאוּמָה בְּיָדוֹ בַּאֲשֶׁר יְהוָה אִתּוֹ
with Jehovah that in his in thing any to looking the
,him (was) ,hand prison-

6743 3068 6213
וַאֲשֶׁר־הוּא עֹשֶׂה יְהוָה מַצְלִיחַ׃
(was) Jehovah (was) he what and
.prospering doing

CAP. XL מ

CHAPTER 40

CHAPTER 40

[1]And after these things, it happened, the cupbearer and the baker of the king of Egypt sinned against their lord, against the king of Egypt. [2]And Pharaoh was angry against his two officers, against the chief of the cupbearers and against the chief of the bakers. [3]And he gave them into custody, in the house of the chief of the executioners, into the prison-house, the place where Joseph *was* imprisoned. [4]And the chief of the executioners assigned Joseph *to be* with them, and he ministered to them. And they were in custody *many* days. [5]And they dreamed a dream, both of them, each his dream in one night, each according to the interpretation of his dream, the cupbearer and the baker who *belonged* to the king of Egypt, who *were* imprisoned in the prison-house. [6]And Joseph came in to them in the morning. And he looked at them, and, behold, they *were* sad.

4713 8248 2398 1697 310 1961
1 וַיְהִי אַחַר הַדְּבָרִים הָאֵלֶּה חָטְאוּ מַשְׁקֵה מֶלֶךְ־מִצְרַיִם
Egypt king the cup- the sinned ,these things after it And
of of bearer ,was

8147 5921 6547 7107 4714 4428 113 644
2 וְהָאֹפֶה לַאֲדֹנֵיהֶם לְמֶלֶךְ מִצְרָיִם׃ וַיִּקְצֹף פַּרְעֹה עַל שְׁנֵי
two against Pharaoh was And .Egypt the against their against the and
angry of king ,lord baker

5414 644 8269 8248 8269 5631
3 סָרִיסָיו עַל שַׂר הַמַּשְׁקִים וְעַל שַׂר הָאוֹפִים׃ וַיִּתֵּן אֹתָם
them he And the the and cup- the the against his
gave .bakers of chief against bearers of chief ,eunuchs

4725 5470 1004 2876 8269 1004 4929
בְּמִשְׁמַר בֵּית שַׂר הַטַּבָּחִים אֶל־בֵּית הַסֹּהַר מְקוֹם אֲשֶׁר
where the the house into exe- the the the in into
place ,prison- ,cutioners of chief of house ,custody

3127 2876 8269 6485 8033 631 3127
4 יוֹסֵף אָסוּר שָׁם׃ וַיִּפְקֹד שַׂר הַטַּבָּחִים אֶת־יוֹסֵף אִתָּם
with Joseph execu- the the And .there was Joseph
,them tioners of chief appointed ;bound

8147 2472 2492 4929 3117 1961 8334
5 וַיְשָׁרֶת אֹתָם וַיִּהְיוּ יָמִים בְּמִשְׁמָר׃ וַיַּחַלְמוּ חֲלוֹם שְׁנֵיהֶם
of both a they And .custody in (many) and ;them he and
,them ,dream dreamed days were they served

8248 2472 6623 376 259 3915 2472 376
אִישׁ חֲלֹמוֹ בְּלַיְלָה אֶחָד אִישׁ כְּפִתְרוֹן חֲלֹמוֹ הַמַּשְׁקֶה
cup- the his the after each ,one night in his each
bearer ;dream of meaning dream

5470 1004 631 4714 4428 644
וְהָאֹפֶה אֲשֶׁר לְמֶלֶךְ מִצְרַיִם אֲשֶׁר אֲסוּרִים בְּבֵית הַסֹּהַר׃
.prison- the in were who ,Egypt the to who the and
house bound of king (belonged) baker

2196 2009 7200 1242 3127 935
6 וַיָּבֹא אֲלֵיהֶם יוֹסֵף בַּבֹּקֶר וַיַּרְא אֹתָם וְהִנָּם זֹעֲפִים׃
(were) they ,and at he and the in Joseph them to And
.sad ,behold ,them looked ;morning in came

7And he asked the officers of Pharaoh who *were* with him in custody, in the house of his lord, saying, Why *are* your faces sad today? 8And they said to him, We have dreamed a dream, and there is no interpreter. And Joseph said to them, Do not interpretations *belong* to God? Now tell it to me. 9And the chief of the cupbearers told his dream to Joseph, and said to him, In my dream, behold, a vine *was* before me. 10And in the vine *were* three branches. And at its budding, it went up *into* blossom, its clusters ripened *into* grapes. 11And Pharaoh's cup *was* in my hand, and I took the grapes and pressed them into the cup of Pharaoh; and I gave the cup into the hand of Pharaoh. 12And Joseph said to him, This *is* the interpretation: the three branches, they *are* three days. 13Yet within three days Pharaoh will lift up your head and will return you to your place. And you will give the cup of Pharaoh into his hand according to the former custom when you were his cupbearer.

14But remember me along with yourself, when it is well with you; and please do kindness with me and mention me to Pharaoh, and bring me out of this house. 15For truly I was stolen from the land of the Hebrews; and here also I have not done anything that they should have put me into the dungeon.

16And the chief of the bakers saw that the interpretation *was* good. And he said to Joseph, I also in my dream saw three baskets of white bread on my head. 17And in the top basket *some* from all the food of

113 1004 4929 6547 5631 7592
7 וַיִּשְׁאַל אֶת־סְרִיסֵי פַרְעֹה אֲשֶׁר אִתּוֹ בְמִשְׁמַר בֵּית אֲדֹנָיו
his in ,custody in with who Pharaoh officers the he And
lord's house him (were) of asked

2472 559 3117 7451 6440 4100 559
8 לֵאמֹר מַדּוּעַ פְּנֵיכֶם רָעִים הַיּוֹם׃ וַיֹּאמְרוּ אֵלָיו חֲלוֹם
a ,him to they And ?today sad your Why ,saying
dream said faces (are)

430 3808 3127 559 6622 2492
חָלַמְנוּ וּפֹתֵר אֵין אֹתוֹ וַיֹּאמֶר אֲלֵהֶם יוֹסֵף הֲלוֹא לֵאלֹהִים
God to not Do ,Joseph them to said and ;it is one and have We
(belong) not open to dreamed

2472 8248 8269 5608 4994 5608 6623
9 פִּתְרֹנִים סַפְּרוּ־נָא לִי׃ וַיְסַפֵּר שַׂר־הַמַּשְׁקִים אֶת־חֲלֹמוֹ
dream his the chief the told And .me to Now tell interpre-
cupbearers of it ?tations

7969 1612 6440 1612 2472 559 3127
10 לְיוֹסֵף וַיֹּאמֶר לוֹ בַּחֲלוֹמִי וְהִנֵּה־גֶפֶן לְפָנָי׃ וּבַגֶּפֶן שְׁלֹשָׁה
(were) in And before vine a ,behold my In to said and to
three vine the .me dream ,him ,Joseph

811 1310 5322 5927 6524 8299
שָׂרִיגִם וְהִוא כְפֹרַחַת עָלְתָה נִצָּהּ הִבְשִׁילוּ אַשְׁכְּלֹתֶיהָ
clusters its ripened (into) up went its at it and ;branches
,blossom ,budding

7818 6025 3947 6547 3563 6025
11 עֲנָבִים׃ וְכוֹס פַּרְעֹה בְּיָדִי וָאֶקַּח אֶת־הָעֲנָבִים וָאֶשְׂחַט
pressed and grapes the I and my in Pharaoh's And (into)
took hand (was) cup .grapes

6547 3709 3563 5414 6547 3563
אֹתָם אֶל־כּוֹס פַּרְעֹה וָאֶתֵּן אֶת־הַכּוֹס עַל־כַּף פַּרְעֹה׃
.Pharaoh the into cup the I and ;Pharaoh the into them
of palm gave of cup

3117 7969 8299 7969 6623 2088 3127 559
12 וַיֹּאמֶר לוֹ יוֹסֵף זֶה פִּתְרֹנוֹ שְׁלֹשֶׁת הַשָּׂרִגִים שְׁלֹשֶׁת יָמִים
days three ,branches the three inter- its This ,Joseph to And
;pretation (is) him said

7725 7218 6547 5375 3117 7969 5750
13 הֵם׃ בְּעוֹד שְׁלֹשֶׁת יָמִים יִשָּׂא פַרְעֹה אֶת־רֹאשֶׁךָ וַהֲשִׁיבְךָ
will and your Pharaoh will days three Yet they
you return head up lift within .(are)

7223 4941 3027 6547/3563 5414 3643
עַל־כַּנֶּךָ וְנָתַתָּ כוֹס־פַּרְעֹה בְּיָדוֹ כַּמִּשְׁפָּט הָרִאשׁוֹן אֲשֶׁר
when ,former to according into Pharaoh the you and your to
custom the hands his of cup give will ;place

3190 2142 8248 1961
14 הָיִיתָ מַשְׁקֵהוּ׃ כִּי אִם־זְכַרְתַּנִי אִתְּךָ כַּאֲשֶׁר יִיטַב לָךְ
with is it when with remember But his you
;you well ,yourself me .cupbearer were

3318 6547 2142 2617 6213
וְעָשִׂיתָ־נָּא עִמָּדִי חָסֶד וְהִזְכַּרְתַּנִי אֶל־פַּרְעֹה וְהוֹצֵאתַנִי
bring and ,Pharaoh to and kindness with please do and
out me me mention me

1571 5680 776 1589 1589 2088 1004
15 מִן־הַבַּיִת הַזֶּה׃ כִּי־גֻנֹּב גֻּנַּבְתִּי מֵאֶרֶץ הָעִבְרִים וְגַם־פֹּה
here and ;Hebrews the the from was I truly For .this house from
also of land stolen

644 8269 7200 953 7760 3972 6213
16 לֹא־עָשִׂיתִי מְאוּמָה כִּי־שָׂמוּ אֹתִי בַּבּוֹר׃ וַיַּרְא שַׂר־הָאֹפִים
the the And the into me they that anything have I not
bakers of chief saw .dungeon put have should done

7200 2472 634 3127 559 6622 2896
כִּי טוֹב פָּתָר וַיֹּאמֶר אֶל־יוֹסֵף אַף־אֲנִי בַּחֲלוֹמִי וְהִנֵּה
saw my in I also ,Joseph to he and inter- the (was) that
dream said ,pretation good

3978 3605 5945 5536 7218 2751 5536/7969
17 שְׁלֹשָׁה סַלֵּי חֹרִי עַל־רֹאשִׁי׃ וּבַסַּל הָעֶלְיוֹן מִכֹּל מַאֲכַל
the (some) top in and my upon white baskets three
of food all from basket the ;head bread of

Pharaoh, the work of a baker. And the birds *were* eating them from the basket off my head. [18]And Joseph answered and said, This *is* its interpretation: the three baskets *are* three days. [19]Yet within three days Pharaoh will lift up your head from you and hang you on a tree, and the birds will eat your flesh off you.

[20]And it happened, on the third day, the day of Pharaoh's birth, he made a feast for all his servants. And he lifted up the head of the chief of the cupbearers, and the head of the chief of the bakers, in the midst of his servants. [21]And he restored the chief of the cupbearers to his cupbearer *office*; and he gave the cup into Pharaoh's hand. [22]And he hanged the chief of the bakers, as Joseph interpreted to them. [23]And the chief of the cupbearers did not remember Joseph, but forgot him.

5921 5536 398 5775 644 4639 6547
פַּרְעֹה מַעֲשֵׂה אֹפֶה וְהָעוֹף אֹכֵל אֹתָם מִן־הַסַּל מֵעַל
off the from them (were) the and a work the ,Pharaoh
basket eating birds ;baker of

5536 7969 6623 2088 559 3127 6030 7218
18 רֹאשִׁי׃ וַיַּעַן יוֹסֵף וַיֹּאמֶר זֶה פִּתְרֹנוֹ שְׁלֹשֶׁת הַסַּלִּים
,baskets the three inter- its This ,said and Joseph And .head my
:pretation (is) answered

6547 5375 3117 7969 5750 3117 7969
19 שְׁלֹשֶׁת יָמִים הֵם׃ בְּעוֹד ׀ שְׁלֹשֶׁת יָמִים יִשָּׂא פַרְעֹה אֶת־
Pharaoh will days three Yet they days three
up lift within .(are)

5775 398 6086 8518 7218
רֹאשְׁךָ מֵעָלֶיךָ וְתָלָה אוֹתְךָ עַל־עֵץ וְאָכַל הָעוֹף אֶת־
the will and a on you hang and you from your
birds eat ,tree head

3205 3117 7969 3117 1961 1320
20 בְּשָׂרְךָ מֵעָלֶיךָ׃ וַיְהִי ׀ בַּיּוֹם הַשְּׁלִישִׁי יוֹם הֻלֶּדֶת אֶת־
the the ,third the on it And off from your
of birth of day day happened .you flesh

8269 7218 5375 5650 3605 4960 6213 6547
פַּרְעֹה וַיַּעַשׂ מִשְׁתֶּה לְכָל־עֲבָדָיו וַיִּשָּׂא אֶת־רֹאשׁ ׀ שַׂר
the head the he and his for feast a he ,Pharaoh
of chief of lifted ;servants of all made

7725 5650 8432 644 8269 7218 8248
21 הַמַּשְׁקִים וְאֶת־רֹאשׁ שַׂר הָאֹפִים בְּתוֹךְ עֲבָדָיו׃ וַיָּשֶׁב
he And his the in ,bakers the head the and the
restored .servants of midst of chief of ,cupbearers

6547 3709 3563 5414 4945 8248 8269
אֶת־שַׂר הַמַּשְׁקִים עַל־מַשְׁקֵהוּ וַיִּתֵּן הַכּוֹס עַל־כַּף פַּרְעֹה׃
.Pharaoh the into the he and cupbearer his to the the
of palm cup gave ;office cupbearers of chief

2142 3127 6622 8518 644 8269
22-23 וְאֵת שַׂר הָאֹפִים תָּלָה כַּאֲשֶׁר פָּתַר לָהֶם יוֹסֵף׃ וְלֹא־זָכַר
remem- And .Joseph to had as he the the And
bered not them interpreted ,hanged bakers of chief

7911 3127 8248 8269
שַׂר־הַמַּשְׁקִים אֶת־יוֹסֵף וַיִּשְׁכָּחֵהוּ׃
forgot but ,Joseph cupbearers the
.him of chief

CAP. XLI מא

CHAPTER 41

CHAPTER 41

[1]And it happened at the end of two years of days, Pharaoh was dreaming. And, lo, *he was* standing by the River. [2]And, behold, seven cows were going up from the River, beautiful of appearance and fat of flesh; and they were eating in the reeds. [3]And, behold, seven other cows *were* going up after them from the River, evil of appearance and lean of flesh. And they were standing beside the cows on the bank of the River. [4]And the evil-appearing and lean-fleshed cows were eating the seven cows of

5975 2009 2492 6547 3117 8141 7093 1961
1 וַיְהִי מִקֵּץ שְׁנָתַיִם יָמִים וּפַרְעֹה חֹלֵם וְהִנֵּה עֹמֵד עַל־
by (he was) ,and was that days two the at it And
standing ,lo ,dreaming Pharaoh of years of end was

4758 3303 6510 7651 5927 2975 2009 2975
2 הַיְאֹר׃ וְהִנֵּה מִן־הַיְאֹר עֹלֹת שֶׁבַע פָּרוֹת יְפוֹת מַרְאֶה
form beautiful ,cows seven were the from And the
of up going River ,behold .River

312 6510 7651 2009 260 7462 1320 1277
3 וּבְרִיאֹת בָּשָׂר וַתִּרְעֶינָה בָּאָחוּ׃ וְהִנֵּה שֶׁבַע פָּרוֹת אֲחֵרוֹת
other cows seven And the in they and ;flesh and
,behold .reeds eating were of fat

1320 1851 4758 7451 2975 310 5927
עֹלוֹת אַחֲרֵיהֶן מִן־הַיְאֹר רָעוֹת מַרְאֶה וְדַקּוֹת בָּשָׂר
;flesh and form of evil the from after (were)
of lean ,River them up going

6510 398 2975 8193 6510 681 5975
4 וַתַּעֲמֹדְנָה אֵצֶל הַפָּרוֹת עַל־שְׂפַת הַיְאֹר׃ וַתֹּאכַלְנָה הַפָּרוֹת
,cows the were they and the the on ,cows the beside they and
eating .River of lip standing were

3303 6510 7651 1320 1851 4758 7451
רָעוֹת הַמַּרְאֶה וְדַקֹּת הַבָּשָׂר אֵת שֶׁבַע הַפָּרוֹת יְפֹת
beautiful of cows seven the fleshed lean- and appearing evil-

beautiful and fat appearance. And Pharaoh awoke.
[5]And he slept and dreamed a second time. And, behold, seven ears of grain were coming up on one stalk, fat and good. [6]And, behold, seven ears of grain, lean and blasted *by* the east *wind*, sprouting forth after them. [7]And the seven lean ears were swallowing the seven fat and full ears. And Pharaoh awoke; and, lo, *it was* a dream. [8]And it happened in the morning his spirit was troubled. And he sent and called for all the magicians of Egypt, and all its wise men. And Pharaoh told them his dream, and *there* was no interpreter of them to Pharaoh.

[9]And the chief of the cupbearers spoke with Pharaoh, saying, I mention my sin today. [10]Pharaoh was angry against his servants, and gave me into custody in the house of the chief of the executioners, me and the chief of the bakers. [11]And we dreamed a dream in one night, he and I; we each dreamed according to the interpretation of his dream. [12]And a Hebrew youth was with us, a slave to the chief of the executioners. And we told him, and he interpreted our dreams to us; he interpreted to each according to his dream. [13]And it came about; as he had interpreted to us, so it was; he returned me to my place, and he hanged him.
[14]And Pharaoh sent and called Joseph; and they made him hasten from the dungeon. And he shaved and changed his clothing and came in to Pharaoh.
[15]And Pharaoh said to Joseph, I have dreamed a dream, and there is no one to interpret it; and I have heard about you, saying

8145 2492 3462 6547 3364 1277 4758
5 הַמַּרְאֶה וְהַבְּרִיאֹת וַיִּיקַץ פַּרְעֹה׃ וַיִּישָׁן וַיַּחֲלֹם שֵׁנִית
second a ;time and dreamed he And slept .Pharaoh and awoke ;fat and form

2896 1277 259 7070 5927 7641 7651 2009
וְהִנֵּה ׀ שֶׁבַע שִׁבֳּלִים עֹלוֹת בְּקָנֶה אֶחָד בְּרִיאוֹת וְטֹבוֹת׃
.good and fat ,one on stalk were coming of ears grain seven ,and behold

310 6779 6921 7710 1851 7641 7651 2009
6 וְהִנֵּה שֶׁבַע שִׁבֳּלִים דַּקּוֹת וּשְׁדוּפֹת קָדִים צֹמְחוֹת אַחֲרֵיהֶן׃
after .them sprouting the (by) (wind) east and blasted lean of ears ,grain seven ,And behold

1277 7641 7651 1851 7641 1104
7 וַתִּבְלַעְנָה הַשִּׁבֳּלִים הַדַּקּוֹת אֵת שֶׁבַע הַשִּׁבֳּלִים הַבְּרִיאוֹת
fat ears the seven lean ears the were And swallowing

6470 1242 1961 2472 2009 6547 3364 4392
8 וְהַמְּלֵאוֹת וַיִּיקַץ פַּרְעֹה וְהִנֵּה חֲלוֹם׃ וַיְהִי בַבֹּקֶר וַתִּפָּעֶם
was troubled the in ,morning it And was (was it) .dream a ,and ,lo :Pharaoh and awoke ;full and

3605 4714 2748 3605 7121 7971 7307
רוּחוֹ וַיִּשְׁלַח וַיִּקְרָא אֶת־כָּל־חַרְטֻמֵּי מִצְרַיִם וְאֶת־כָּל־
all and ,Egypt the of magicians all and for called he And sent his .spirit

6622 2472 6547 5608 2450
חֲכָמֶיהָ וַיְסַפֵּר פַּרְעֹה לָהֶם אֶת־חֲלֹמוֹ וְאֵין־פּוֹתֵר אוֹתָם
them interpreter of and no was his dream them Pharaoh and told wise its ;men

559 6547 8248 8269 1696 6547
9 לְפַרְעֹה׃ וַיְדַבֵּר שַׂר הַמַּשְׁקִים אֶת־פַּרְעֹה לֵאמֹר אֶת־
,saying ,Pharaoh with the cupbearers the of chief And spoke to .Pharaoh

5414 5650 7107 6547 3117 2142 2399
10 חֲטָאַי אֲנִי מַזְכִּיר הַיּוֹם׃ פַּרְעֹה קָצַף עַל־עֲבָדָיו וַיִּתֵּן אֹתִי
me and gave his against ,servants was angry Pharaoh .today mention I my sin

644 8269 2876 8269 1004 4929
בְּמִשְׁמַר בֵּית שַׂר הַטַּבָּחִים אֹתִי וְאֵת שַׂר הָאֹפִים׃
the .bakers the of chief and me execu- the ,tioners the of chief the (in) of house into custody

6623 376 259 3915 2472 2492
11 וַנַּחַלְמָה חֲלוֹם בְּלַיְלָה אֶחָד אֲנִי וָהוּא אִישׁ כְּפִתְרוֹן
to according interpretation each ;he and I ,one night in dream a we And dreamed

2876 8269 5650 5680 5288 2492 2472
12 חֲלֹמוֹ חָלָמְנוּ׃ וְשָׁם אִתָּנוּ נַעַר עִבְרִי עֶבֶד לְשַׂר הַטַּבָּחִים
execu- the ,tioners the to of chief a slave ,Hebrew a youth with us And was we .dreamed his dream's

6622 2472 376 2472 6622 5608
וַנְּסַפֶּר־לוֹ וַיִּפְתָּר־לָנוּ אֶת־חֲלֹמֹתֵינוּ אִישׁ כַּחֲלֹמוֹ פָּתָר׃
he .opened to according dream his each our ,dreams to us he and interpreted ,him we and told

8653 7725 1961 6622 1961
13 וַיְהִי כַּאֲשֶׁר פָּתַר־לָנוּ כֵּן הָיָה אֹתִי הֵשִׁיב עַל־כַּנִּי וְאֹתוֹ
and him my to ,place he returned me it ;was so to had he ,us interpreted as And ,was it

953 7323 3127 7121 6547 7971 8518
14 תָלָה׃ וַיִּשְׁלַח פַּרְעֹה וַיִּקְרָא אֶת־יוֹסֵף וַיְרִיצֻהוּ מִן־הַבּוֹר
the ;dungeon from they and him hurried ,Joseph and called Pharaoh And sent he .hanged

6547 559 6547 935 8071 2498 1548
15 וַיְגַלַּח וַיְחַלֵּף שִׂמְלֹתָיו וַיָּבֹא אֶל־פַּרְעֹה׃ וַיֹּאמֶר פַּרְעֹה
Pharaoh said And .Pharaoh to and in came his clothing and changed he and shaved

8085 369 6622 2492 2492 3127
אֶל־יוֹסֵף חֲלוֹם חָלַמְתִּי וּפֹתֵר אֵין אֹתוֹ וַאֲנִי שָׁמַעְתִּי
have heard and I ;it is one no to and interpret have I ,dreamed a dream ,Joseph to

you hear a dream to interpret it. 16 And Joseph answered Pharaoh, saying, Not I! God will answer the welfare of Pharaoh. 17 And Pharaoh said to Joseph, In my dream, lo, I *was* standing on the lip of the River.

18 And, behold, seven cows *were* going up from the River, fat of flesh and beautiful of form, and were feeding in the reeds. 19 And, behold, seven other cows *were* going up after them, poor and very evil of form, and lean of flesh; I have not seen *any* like them in all the land of Egypt for badness. 20 And the cows, the lean and the evil, ate the first seven fat cows. 21 And they went into their stomachs, and it could not be seen that they had gone into their stomachs; and their appearance *was as* evil as at the beginning. And I awakened.

22 And I looked in my dream. And, behold, seven ears of grain *were* coming up on one stalk, full and good. 23 And, behold, seven ears, withered, lean, blasted *by* the east *wind*, sprouting forth after them. 24 And the lean ears were swallowing the seven good ears. And I spoke to the magicians, but not one is making known *the meaning* to me.

25 And Joseph said to Pharaoh, The dream of Pharaoh is one. God has shown Pharaoh what He is about to do. 26 The seven good cows, they *are* seven years; and the seven good ears, they *are* seven years; it *is* one dream. 27 And the

3127 6030 6622 2472 8085 559
16 עָלֶיךָ לֵאמֹר תִּשְׁמַע חֲלוֹם לִפְתֹּר אֹתוֹ׃ וַיַּעַן יוֹסֵף אֶת־
Joseph And .it to a You ,saying about
answered interpret dream hear ,you

6547 7965 6030 430 1107 559 6547
פַּרְעֹה לֵאמֹר בִּלְעָדָי אֱלֹהִים יַעֲנֶה אֶת־שְׁלוֹם פַּרְעֹה׃
.Pharaoh the will God Not ,saying ,Pharaoh
of welfare answer !I

2975 8193 5975 2472 3127 6547 559
17 וַיְדַבֵּר פַּרְעֹה אֶל־יוֹסֵף בַּחֲלֹמִי הִנְנִי עֹמֵד עַל־שְׂפַת הַיְאֹר׃
the the on (was) behold my In ,Joseph to Pharaoh And
.River of bank standing I ,dream said

3303 1320 1277 6510 7651 5927 2975 2009
18 וְהִנֵּה מִן־הַיְאֹר עֹלֹת שֶׁבַע פָּרוֹת בְּרִיאוֹת בָּשָׂר וִיפֹת
and flesh of fat ,cows seven (were) the from ,And
of beautiful up going River ,behold

5927 312 6510 7641 2009 260 7462 8389
19 תֹּאַר וַתִּרְעֶינָה בָּאָחוּ׃ וְהִנֵּה שֶׁבַע־פָּרוֹת אֲחֵרוֹת עֹלוֹת
(were) other cows seven ,And the in were and ,form
going ,behold .reeds feeding

7200 3808 1320 7534 3966 8389 7951 1803 310
אַחֲרֵיהֶן דַּלּוֹת וְרָעוֹת תֹּאַר מְאֹד וְרַקּוֹת בָּשָׂר לֹא־רָאִיתִי
have I not ;flesh and ,very form and poor after
seen of lean of evil ,them

7534 6510 398 7455 4714 776 3605 2007
20 כָהֵנָּה בְּכָל־אֶרֶץ מִצְרַיִם לָרֹעַ׃ וַתֹּאכַלְנָה הַפָּרוֹת הָרַקּוֹת
lean cows the ate And for Egypt the all in like the
.badness of land them of

935 1277 7223 6510 7641 7451
21 וְהָרָעוֹת אֵת שֶׁבַע הַפָּרוֹת הָרִאשֹׁנוֹת הַבְּרִיאֹת׃ וַתָּבֹאנָה
they And .fat first cows the seven ,evil and
in went

7451 4758 7130 935 7200 3808 7130
אֶל־קִרְבֶּנָה וְלֹא נוֹדַע כִּי־בָאוּ אֶל־קִרְבֶּנָה וּמַרְאֵיהֶן רַע
(was) their and their to they that could it and their to
evil appearance ;stomachs in gone had seen be not ,stomachs

7641 7651 2009 2472 7200 3364 8462
22 כַּאֲשֶׁר בַּתְּחִלָּה וָאִיקָץ׃ וָאֵרֶא בַּחֲלֹמִי וְהִנֵּה שֶׁבַע שִׁבֳּלִים
of ears seven ,and my in I And I and the at as
grain ,behold dream looked .awoke ;beginning

7641 7651 2009 2896 4392 259 7070 5927
23 עֹלֹת בְּקָנֶה אֶחָד מְלֵאֹת וְטֹבוֹת׃ וְהִנֵּה שֶׁבַע שִׁבֳּלִים
ears seven ,And .good and full ,one stalk on (were)
,behold coming

1104 310 6779 6921 7710 1851 6798
24 צְנֻמוֹת דַּקּוֹת שְׁדֻפוֹת קָדִים צֹמְחוֹת אַחֲרֵיהֶם׃ וַתִּבְלַעְןָ
were And .them after sprouting the (by) blasted ,lean ,withered
swallowing forth ,(wind) east

559 2896 7641 7651 1851 7641
הַשִּׁבֳּלִים הַדַּקֹּת אֵת שֶׁבַע הַשִּׁבֳּלִים הַטֹּבוֹת וָאֹמַר אֶל־
to I and ;good ears the seven lean ears the
spoke

2472 6547 3127 559 5046 369 2748
25 הַחַרְטֻמִּים וְאֵין מַגִּיד לִי׃ וַיֹּאמֶר יוֹסֵף אֶל־פַּרְעֹה חֲלוֹם
The ,Pharaoh to Joseph said And to is one but ,magicians the
of dream .me revealing not

6547 5046 6213 430 259 6547
פַּרְעֹה אֶחָד הוּא אֵת אֲשֶׁר הָאֱלֹהִים עֹשֶׂה הִגִּיד לְפַרְעֹה׃
.Pharaoh has He about is God what — (is) it one ,Pharaoh
shown do to

7641 7651 8141 7651 2896 6510 7651
26 שֶׁבַע פָּרֹת הַטֹּבֹת שֶׁבַע שָׁנִים הֵנָּה וְשֶׁבַע הַשִּׁבֳּלִים
ears the and they years seven ,good The cows seven
seven ;(are)

6510 7651 259 2472 8141 7651 2896
27 הַטֹּבֹת שֶׁבַע שָׁנִים הֵנָּה חֲלוֹם אֶחָד הוּא׃ וְשֶׁבַע הַפָּרוֹת
cows the And .(is) it one dream they years seven ,good
seven ;(are)

seven thin and evil-appearing cows going up after them, they *are* seven years. And the seven empty ears blasted by the east *wind*, they are seven years of famine. [28]This *is* the word which I spoke to Pharaoh: What God *is* about to do, He has shown Pharaoh.

[29]Behold! Seven years of great plenty *are* coming in all the land of Egypt. [30]And seven years of famine will arise after them, and all the plenty of the land of Egypt will be forgotten. And the famine will consume the land. [31]And the plenty in the land will not be remembered in the face of that following, for it *will be* very severe. [32]And as to the dream being repeated to Pharah twice, that *is* the thing established from God, and God *is* hastening to do it.

[33]And now let Pharaoh look for a man who is intelligent and wise, and set him over the land of Egypt. [34]Let Pharaoh act, and let him appoint overseers over the land, and take a fifth *part of* the land of Egypt in the seven years of plenty. [35]And let them gather all the food of these coming good years. And let them heap up grain under the hand of Pharaoh *as* food in the cities, and let them store *it*. [36]And let the food be a store for the land, for the seven years of famine which will be in the land of Egypt. And let not the land be cut off by famine.

[37]And the word was good in Pharaoh's eyes, and in the eyes of all his servants. [38]And Pharaoh said to his servants, Can we find any man like this, *in* whom *is*

7651 8141 7651 310 5927 7451 7534
הָרַקּוֹת וְהָרָעֹת הָעֹלֹת אַחֲרֵיהֶן שֶׁבַע שָׁנִים הֵנָּה וְשֶׁבַע
and seven they (are); years seven ,them after up going evil and appearing thin

7458 8141 7651 6921 7710 738:6 7641
הַשִּׁבֳּלִים הָרֵקוֹת שְׁדֻפוֹת הַקָּדִים יִהְיוּ שֶׁבַע שְׁנֵי רָעָב׃
of .famine years seven they are the (with) (wind) east blasted ,empty ears the

6213 430 6547 1696 834 1697 2088
28 הוּא הַדָּבָר אֲשֶׁר דִּבַּרְתִּי אֶל־פַּרְעֹה אֲשֶׁר הָאֱלֹהִים עֹשֶׂה
about (is) do to God what :Pharaoh to spoke I which the word This (is)

1419 7647 935 8141 7651 2009 6547 7200
29 הֶרְאָה אֶת־פַּרְעֹה׃ הִנֵּה שֶׁבַע שָׁנִים בָּאוֹת שָׂבָע גָּדוֹל
great of plenty (are) coming years seven !Behold .Pharaoh has He shown

7911 310 7458 8141 7651 6965 4714 776 3605
30 בְּכָל־אֶרֶץ מִצְרָיִם׃ וְקָמוּ שֶׁבַע שְׁנֵי רָעָב אַחֲרֵיהֶן וְנִשְׁכַּח
be will and forgotten after ,them famine years of seven And arise will .Egypt the of land all in

3808 776 7458 3615 4714 776 7647 3605
31 כָּל־הַשָּׂבָע בְּאֶרֶץ מִצְרָיִם וְכִלָּה הָרָעָב אֶת־הָאָרֶץ׃ וְלֹא־
And not .land the the famine will and consume ;Egypt the in of land the plenty all

3515 3651 310 7458/6440 776 7647 3045
יִוָּדַע הַשָּׂבָע בָּאָרֶץ מִפְּנֵי הָרָעָב הַהוּא אַחֲרֵי־כֵן כִּי־כָבֵד
(be will) for severe ,following that famine the in of face the in land the plenty be will recalled

6471 6547 2472 8138 3966
32 הוּא מְאֹד׃ וְעַל הִשָּׁנוֹת הַחֲלוֹם אֶל־פַּרְעֹה פַּעֲמָיִם כִּי־
that ,twice Pharaoh to dream the being repeated And as to .very it

6213 430 4116 430 5973 1697 3559
נָכוֹן הַדָּבָר מֵעִם הָאֱלֹהִים וּמְמַהֵר הָאֱלֹהִים לַעֲשֹׂתוֹ׃
.it do to God is and hastening ,God from the thing (is) settled

559 5921 7896 2450 995 376 6547 7200 6258
33 וְעַתָּה יֵרֶא פַרְעֹה אִישׁ נָבוֹן וְחָכָם וִישִׁיתֵהוּ עַל־אֶרֶץ
the of land over set and him and ,wise is who intelligent a man Pharaoh let for look And ,now

2567 776 5921 6496 6485 6547 6213 4714
34 מִצְרָיִם׃ יַעֲשֶׂה פַרְעֹה וְיַפְקֵד פְּקִדִים עַל־הָאָרֶץ וְחִמֵּשׁ
take and fifth a the ,land over over-seers let and appoint him ,Pharaoh act Let .Egypt

3605 6908 7647 8141 7651 4714 776
35 אֶת־אֶרֶץ מִצְרַיִם בְּשֶׁבַע שְׁנֵי הַשָּׂבָע׃ וְיִקְבְּצוּ אֶת־כָּל־
all let And gather them .plenty of years the in seven Egypt the (part) of land (of)

3027/8478 1250/6651 935 2896 8141 400
אֹכֶל הַשָּׁנִים הַטֹּבוֹת הַבָּאֹת הָאֵלֶּה וְיִצְבְּרוּ־בָר תַּחַת יַד־
the under of hand grain let and heap up them ;these coming good years the of food

776 6487 400 1961 810 5892 400 6547
36 פַּרְעֹה אֹכֶל בֶּעָרִים וְשָׁמָרוּ׃ וְהָיָה הָאֹכֶל לְפִקָּדוֹן לָאָרֶץ
the for ,land store a for food the let And be let and .(it) store them the in ,cities (as) food Pharaoh

3772 3808 4714 776 1961 834 7458 8141 7651
לְשֶׁבַע שְׁנֵי הָרָעָב אֲשֶׁר תִּהְיֶיןָ בְּאֶרֶץ מִצְרָיִם וְלֹא־תִכָּרֵת
be let do off cut and not ,Egypt the of land in be shall which famine of years the for .seven

3625 5869 6547 5869 1697 3190 7458 776
37 הָאָרֶץ בָּרָעָב׃ וַיִּיטַב הַדָּבָר בְּעֵינֵי פַרְעֹה וּבְעֵינֵי כָּל־
all in and of eyes the ,Pharaoh the in of eyes word the was And good the by .famine the land

834 376 2088 4672 5650 7651 559 5650
38 עֲבָדָיו׃ וַיֹּאמֶר פַּרְעֹה אֶל־עֲבָדָיו הֲנִמְצָא כָזֶה אִישׁ אֲשֶׁר
whom any ,man like this find we Can his ,servants to Pharaoh said And his .servants

the Spirit of God? 39And Pharaoh said to Joseph, Since God has taught you all this, there is no one wise and intelligent like you. 40You shall be over my house, and at your mouth all my people shall kiss *the hand*. Only in respect to the throne will I be greater than you. 41And Pharaoh said to Joseph, Behold, I have set you over all the land of Egypt. 42And Pharaoh took off his ring from his hand and put it on the hand of Joseph; and he clothed him *with* fine white garments, and put a golden chain on his neck. 43And he caused him to ride in a chariot which *was* the second to him. And they cried before him, Bow the knee! And he put him over all the land of Egypt. 44And Pharaoh said to Joseph, I *am* Pharaoh, and without *a word* from you not a man shall lift his hand or his foot in all the land of Egypt. 45And Pharaoh called Joseph by the name of Zaphenath-paaneah. And He gave him Asenath the daughter of Poti-phera, priest of On, for a wife. And Joseph went out over the land of Egypt.

46And Joseph was thirty years old as he stood before Pharaoh king of Egypt. And Joseph went out from the face of Pharaoh and passed over in all the land of Egypt. 47And the land produced by handfuls in the seven years of plenty. 48And he gathered all the food of the seven years which were in the land of Egypt, and he put food in the cities. The food of the field of the city which *was* around it, he put in the middle of it. 49And Joseph heaped up grain

3045 310 3127 6547 559 430 7307
39 רוּחַ אֱלֹהִים בּוֹ׃ וַיֹּאמֶר פַּרְעֹה אֶל־יוֹסֵף אַחֲרֵי הוֹדִיעַ
has taught Since ,Joseph to Pharaoh said And (is) ?in God the of Spirit

2450 995 2088 3605 430
40 אֱלֹהִים אוֹתְךָ אֶת־כָּל־זֹאת אֵין־נָבוֹן וְחָכָם כָּמוֹךָ׃ אַתָּה
You .you like wise and is none intelligent ,this all you God

1431 3678 7535 5971 3605 5401/6310 1004 5921 1961
תִּהְיֶה עַל־בֵּיתִי וְעַל־פִּיךָ יִשַּׁק כָּל־עַמִּי רַק הַכִּסֵּא אֶגְדַּל
be will I greater throne the (in) only my ;people all be shall ordered your and mouth at my ,house over be shall

3605 5921 5414 2009 3127 6547 559
41 מִמֶּךָּ׃ וַיֹּאמֶר פַּרְעֹה אֶל־יוֹסֵף רְאֵה נָתַתִּי אֹתְךָ עַל כָּל־
all over you have I set ,See ,Joseph to Pharaoh said And than .you

5414 3027 2885 6547 5493 4714 776
42 אֶרֶץ מִצְרָיִם׃ וַיָּסַר פַּרְעֹה אֶת־טַבַּעְתּוֹ מֵעַל יָדוֹ וַיִּתֵּן
and put his hand from ring his Pharaoh took And off .Egypt the of land

7242 7760 7336 899 3847 3127 3027
אֹתָהּ עַל־יַד יוֹסֵף וַיַּלְבֵּשׁ אֹתוֹ בִּגְדֵי־שֵׁשׁ וַיָּשֶׂם רְבִד
a of chain put and fine linen (with) robes him he and clothed ;Joseph the of hand on it

8145 4818 7392 6677 5921 2091
43 הַזָּהָב עַל־צַוָּארוֹ׃ וַיַּרְכֵּב אֹתוֹ בְּמִרְכֶּבֶת הַמִּשְׁנֶה אֲשֶׁר־
which (was) second the a chariot in him he And ride made .neck his on gold

4814 776 3605 5921 5414 86 6440 7121
לוֹ וַיִּקְרְאוּ לְפָנָיו אַבְרֵךְ וְנָתוֹן אֹתוֹ עַל כָּל־אֶרֶץ מִצְרָיִם׃
.Egypt the of land all over him he And put the Bow !knee before ,him they and cried to him

7311 3127 6547 559
44 וַיֹּאמֶר פַּרְעֹה אֶל־יוֹסֵף אֲנִי פַרְעֹה וּבִלְעָדֶיךָ לֹא־יָרִים
shall lift not a without and you from word ,Pharaoh I (am) ,Joseph to Pharaoh said And

6547 7121 4714 776 3605 7272 3027 376
45 אִישׁ אֶת־יָדוֹ וְאֶת־רַגְלוֹ בְּכָל־אֶרֶץ מִצְרָיִם׃ וַיִּקְרָא פַרְעֹה
Pharaoh And called .Egypt the of land all in foot his or his hand a man

6319 1323 621 5414 =6847= 3127 8034
שֵׁם־יוֹסֵף צָפְנַת פַּעְנֵחַ וַיִּתֶּן־לוֹ אֶת־אָסְנַת בַּת־פּוֹטִי פֶרַע
,phera Poti- the of daughter Asenath he and him gave ,paaneah Zaphenath- Joseph's name

1121 3127 4714 776 3127 5927 802 204 3548
46 כֹּהֵן אֹן לְאִשָּׁה וַיֵּצֵא יוֹסֵף עַל־אֶרֶץ מִצְרָיִם׃ וְיוֹסֵף בֶּן־
son a of And Joseph .Egypt the of land over Joseph and out went a for ;wife On priest of

5927 4714 4428 6547 6440 5975 8141 7970
שְׁלֹשִׁים שָׁנָה בְּעָמְדוֹ לִפְנֵי פַּרְעֹה מֶלֶךְ־מִצְרַיִם וַיֵּצֵא
went and out ;Egypt of king Pharaoh before he as stood years thirty

6213 4714 776 3605 5674 6547 6440 3127
47 יוֹסֵף מִלִּפְנֵי פַרְעֹה וַיַּעֲבֹר בְּכָל־אֶרֶץ מִצְרָיִם׃ וַתַּעַשׂ
And produced .Egypt the of land all in passed and over Pharaoh the from of face Joseph

400 6908 7062 7647 8141 7651 776
48 הָאָרֶץ בְּשֶׁבַע שְׁנֵי הַשָּׂבָע לִקְמָצִים׃ וַיִּקְבֹּץ אֶת־כָּל־אֹכֶל
the of food all he And gathered by .handfuls plenty years of the in seven the land

5892 400 4714 776 1961 834 8141 7651
שֶׁבַע שָׁנִים אֲשֶׁר הָיוּ בְּאֶרֶץ מִצְרַיִם וַיִּתֶּן־אֹכֶל בֶּעָרִים
the in ;cities the food he and put ,Egypt the in of land were which the years seven

6651 8432 5414 5439 834 5892 7704 400
49 אֹכֶל שְׂדֵה־הָעִיר אֲשֶׁר סְבִיבֹתֶיהָ נָתַן בְּתוֹכָהּ׃ וַיִּצְבֹּר
And heaped among in .it he put around ,it which (was) the city the of field the of food

like the sand of the sea, exceedingly much, until he ceased to count it, because it was without number.

[50]And two sons were born to Joseph before the year of the famine came in, whom Asenath the daughter of Poti-phera, priest of On, bore to him. [51]And Joseph called the name of the firstborn Manasseh; for *he said*, God has made me forget all my toil, and all the house of my father. [52]And the name of the second he called Ephraim; for *he said*, God has made me fruitful in the land of my affliction.

[53]And the seven years of plenty which were in the land of Egypt were ended. [54]And the seven years of famine began to come, according as Joseph had said. And the famine was in all lands, but in all the land of Egypt there was bread. [55]And all the land of Egypt hungered, and the people cried to Pharaoh for bread. And Pharaoh said to all Egypt, Go to Joseph; what he says to you, do. [56]And the famine was on the face of all the land. And Joseph opened all which *was* in them, and sold to the Egyptians. And the famine was strong in the land of Egypt. [57]And all the earth came to Egypt to buy, to Joseph. For the famine was severe in all the earth.

4557 2308 5704 3966 7235 3220 2344 1250 3127
יוסף בר כחול הים הרבה מאד עד כי־חדל לספר כי־
for to he until ex- much the the like grain Joseph
,it count ceased ceedingly ,sea of sand

8141 935 2962 1121 8141 3205 3127 4557 369
50 אין מספר׃ וליוסף ילד שני בנים בטרם תבוא שנת
the came before ,sons two were to And .number was it
of year in born Joseph without

204 3548 =6319= 1323 621 3205 834 7458
הרעב אשר ילדה־לו אסנת בת־פוטי פרע כהן און׃
.On the ,phera Poti- the Asenath to bore whom the
of priest of daughter him ;famine

430 5382 4519 1060 8034 3127 7121
51 ויקרא יוסף את־שם הבכור מנשה כי־נשני אלהים את־
God made has for ;Manasseh the the Joseph And
forget me firstborn of name called

669 7121 8145 8034 1 1004 3605 5999 3605
52 כל־עמלי ואת כל־בית אבי׃ ואת שם השני קרא אפרים
;Ephraim he the the And my the all and toil my all
called second of name .father of house

7647 8141 7651 3615 6040 776 430 6509
53 כי־הפרני אלהים בארץ עניי׃ ותכלינה שבע שני השבע
plenty years the were And my the in God made has for
of seven ended .affliction of land fruitful me

7458 8141 7651 2490 4714 776 1961 834
54 אשר היה בארץ מצרים׃ ותחלינה שבע שני הרעב
famine years the began And .Egypt the in were which
of seven of land

3605 776 3605 7452 1961 3127 559 935
לבוא כאשר אמר יוסף ויהי רעב בכל־הארצות ובכל־
in but ,lands the all in the And .Joseph had according to
all famine was said as ,come

6817 4714 776 3605 7456 3899 1961 4714 776
55 ארץ מצרים היה לחם׃ ותרעב כל־ארץ מצרים ויצעק
and ,Egypt the all And .bread there Egypt the
cried of land hungered was of land

3212 4714 3605 6547 559 3899 6547 5971
העם אל־פרעה ללחם ויאמר פרעה לכל־מצרים לכו
Go ,Egypt all to Pharaoh said and for Pharaoh to the
;bread people

3605 6921 1961 7450 6213 559 3127
56 אל־יוסף אשר־יאמר לכם תעשו׃ והרעב היה על כל־
all on was the And .do ,you to says he what ;Joseph to
famine

4713 7666 834 3605 3127 6605 776 6440
פני הארץ ויפתח יוסף את־כל־אשר בהם וישבר למצרים
the to sold and in which all Joseph and the the
;Egyptians ,them (was) opened ;land of face

4714 935 776 3605 4714 776 7458 2388
57 ויחזק הרעב בארץ מצרים׃ וכל־הארץ באו מצרימה
Egypt to came earth the all And .Egypt the in the was and
of land famine severe

776 3605 7458 2388 3127 7666
לשבר אל־יוסף כי־חזק הרעב בכל־הארץ׃
.earth the all in the was for ;Joseph to ,buy to
famine severe

CAP. XLII מב

CHAPTER 42

CHAPTER 42

[1]And Jacob saw that grain was in Egypt. And Jacob said to his sons, Why do you look at each other? [2]And he said, Behold! I have heard grain is in Egypt. Go

1121 3290 559 4714 7668 3290 7200
1 וירא יעקב כי יש־שבר במצרים ויאמר יעקב לבניו
his to Jacob said and ,Egypt in grain was that Jacob And
,sons saw

4714 7668 3426 8085 2009 559 7200 4100
2 למה תתראו׃ ויאמר הנה שמעתי כי יש־שבר במצרים
;Egypt in grain is that have I ,Behold he And look you do Why
heard ,said ?other each at

down there and buy for us from there, so that we may live and not die. [3]And Joseph's ten brothers went down to buy grain from Egypt. [4]And Jacob did not send Benjamin the brother of Joseph with his brothers, because he said, Lest harm happen to him.

[5]And the sons of Israel came to buy among those that came, for the famine was in the land of Cannan. [6]And Joseph *was* the potentate over the land; he *was* the one selling to all the people of the earth. And Joseph's brothers came in and bowed themselves to him, face down to the earth. [7]And Joseph saw his brothers, and recognized them, and acted as a stranger toward them, and spoke harsh things to them, and said to them, Where have you come from? And they said, From the land of Canaan to buy food. [8]And Joseph recognized his brothers, but they did not recognize him. [9]And Joseph remembered the dreams which he had dreamed concerning them. And he said to them, You *are* spies! You have come in to see the bareness of the land. [10]And they said to him, No, my lord, but your servants have come to buy food. [11]We are all of us sons of one man; we are honest; your servants are not spies. [12]And he said to them, No, but you have come in to see the bareness of the land. [13]And they said, Your servants *are* twelve; we *are* brothers, sons of *one* man in the land of Canaan. And, lo, the youngest *is* with our father today; and the one is not. [14]And Joseph said to them, This is that which I have spoken to

3381 4191 3808 2421 8033 7666 8033 3381
3 רְדוּ־שָׁמָּה וְשִׁבְרוּ־לָנוּ מִשָּׁם וְנִחְיֶה וְלֹא נָמוּת׃ וַיֵּרְדוּ
And .die and that so from for and there go
went not live may we ,there us buy down

251 1144 4714 1250 7666 6235 3127 251
4 אֲחֵי־יוֹסֵף עֲשָׂרָה לִשְׁבֹּר בָּר מִמִּצְרָיִם׃ וְאֶת־בִּנְיָמִין אֲחִי
the Benjamin And from grain buy to ten Joseph the
of brother Egypt of brothers

611 7125 6435 559 251 3290 7971 3127
יוֹסֵף לֹא־שָׁלַח יַעֲקֹב אֶת־אֶחָיו כִּי אָמַר פֶּן־יִקְרָאֶנּוּ אָסוֹן׃
.harm happen Lest he for his with Jacob did not Joseph
him to said ,brothers send

7458 1961 935 8432 7666 3478 1121 935
5 וַיָּבֹאוּ בְּנֵי יִשְׂרָאֵל לִשְׁבֹּר בְּתוֹךְ הַבָּאִים כִּי־הָיָה הָרָעָב
the was for that those among buy to Israel the And
famine came of sons came

7666 776 5921 7989 3127 3667 776
6 בְּאֶרֶץ כְּנָעַן׃ וְיוֹסֵף הוּא הַשַּׁלִּיט עַל־הָאָרֶץ הוּא הַמַּשְׁבִּיר
one the he the over the (was) And .Canaan the in
selling (was) ,land governor Joseph of land

639 7812 3127 251 935 776 5971
לְכָל־עַם הָאָרֶץ וַיָּבֹאוּ אֲחֵי יוֹסֵף וַיִּשְׁתַּחֲווּ־לוֹ אַפַּיִם
face to bowed and Joseph the and the the to
down ,him themselves of brothers in came ;earth of people all

5234 5234 227 3127 7200 776
7 אָרְצָה׃ וַיַּרְא יוֹסֵף אֶת־אֶחָיו וַיַּכִּרֵם וַיִּתְנַכֵּר אֲלֵיהֶם
toward remained but knew and his Joseph And the to
;them stranger a ,them brothers saw .earth

559 935 370 559 7186 1696
וַיְדַבֵּר אִתָּם קָשׁוֹת וַיֹּאמֶר אֲלֵהֶם מֵאַיִן בָּאתֶם וַיֹּאמְרוּ
they And you have From ,them to said and harsh them to and
,said ?come where things spoke

251 3127 5234 400 7666 3667 776
8 מֵאֶרֶץ כְּנַעַן לִשְׁבָּר־אֹכֶל׃ וַיַּכֵּר יוֹסֵף אֶת־אֶחָיו וְהֵם
but his Joseph And .food buy to Canaan From
they ,brothers knew of land the

2492 2472 3127 2142 5234
9 לֹא הִכִּרֻהוּ׃ וַיִּזְכֹּר יוֹסֵף אֵת הַחֲלֹמוֹת אֲשֶׁר חָלַם לָהֶם
about had he which the Joseph And know did not
,them dreamed dreams remembered .him

776 6172 7200 7270 559
וַיֹּאמֶר אֲלֵהֶם מְרַגְּלִים אַתֶּם לִרְאוֹת אֶת־עֶרְוַת הָאָרֶץ
the the see to You spies ,them to he and
land of barrenness !(are) said

400 7666 935 5650 113 3808 559 935
10 בָּאתֶם׃ וַיֹּאמְרוּ אֵלָיו לֹא אֲדֹנִי וַעֲבָדֶיךָ בָּאוּ לִשְׁבָּר־אֹכֶל׃
.food buy to have your but my ,No to they And have You
come servants lord ,him said ,in come

5650 1961 5168 3651 259 376 1121
11 כֻּלָּנוּ בְּנֵי אִישׁ־אֶחָד נָחְנוּ כֵּנִים אֲנַחְנוּ לֹא־הָיוּ עֲבָדֶיךָ
your are not we ;honest we ;one man sons are We
servants (are) of us of all

935 776 6172 3808 559 7270
12 מְרַגְּלִים׃ וַיֹּאמֶר אֲלֵהֶם לֹא כִּי־עֶרְוַת הָאָרֶץ בָּאתֶם
have you the the but ,No ,them to he And .spies
come land of barrenness said

1121 251 5650 6240 8147 559 7200
13 לִרְאוֹת׃ וַיֹּאמְרוּ שְׁנֵים עָשָׂר עֲבָדֶיךָ אַחִים ׀ אֲנַחְנוּ בְּנֵי
sons we ;brothers your twelve they And .see to
of (are) (are) servants said

3117 1 6996 2009 3667 776 259 376
אִישׁ־אֶחָד בְּאֶרֶץ כְּנָעַן וְהִנֵּה הַקָּטֹן אֶת־אָבִינוּ הַיּוֹם
,today our (is) the ,and ;Canaan the in one man
father with youngest ,lo of land

1696 834 3127 559 369 259
14 וְהָאֶחָד אֵינֶנּוּ׃ וַיֹּאמֶר אֲלֵהֶם יוֹסֵף הוּא אֲשֶׁר דִּבַּרְתִּי
have I which This ,Joseph them to said And .not is the and
spoken that is one

you, saying, You *are* spies!
[15]By this you shall be tested: *As* Pharaoh lives, you shall not leave here except your younger brother come in here. [16]Send one of you and let him bring your brother, and you be bound, and let your words be proven, whether truth *is* with you. And if not, as Pharaoh lives, surely you *are* spies. [17]And he gathered them into custody three days.

[18]And on the third day Joseph said to them, Do *this* and live; I fear God. [19]If you *are* honest, let one, your brother, be bound in the house of your prison; and you go bring grain *for* the famine of your houses. [20]And you bring your youngest brother to me, and let your words be confirmed, and you shall not die. And so they did.

[21]And they said each to his brother, We *are* truly guilty because of our brother, whom we saw *in* distress of his soul, when he begged us, and we did not hear. That is why this distress has come to us.

[22]And Reuben answered them, saying, Did I not speak to you saying, Do not sin against the youth, and you did not hear? And, behold, his blood is also required. [23]And they did not know that Joseph heard, because the interpreter *was* between them. [24]And he turned away from them and wept, and returned to them and spoke to them. And he took Simeon from them and bound him before their eyes. [25]And Joseph commanded, and they filled their vessels *with* grain, and returned their

15 אֲלֵכֶם לֵאמֹר מְרַגְּלִים אַתֶּם׃ בְּזֹאת תִּבָּחֵנוּ חֵי פַרְעֹה אִם־
not ,Pharaoh (as) lives shall you be tested: this By You (are)! spies ,saying you to

16 תֵּצְאוּ מִזֶּה כִּי אִם־בְּבוֹא אֲחִיכֶם הַקָּטֹן הֵנָּה׃ שִׁלְחוּ
Send .here younger your brother in come except from here shall you leave

מִכֶּם אֶחָד וְיִקַּח אֶת־אֲחִיכֶם וְאַתֶּם הֵאָסְרוּ וְיִבָּחֲנוּ דִּבְרֵיכֶם
,words your let and be proven be shall bound and you your brother let and him bring one of you

הַאֱמֶת אִתְּכֶם וְאִם־לֹא חֵי פַרְעֹה כִּי מְרַגְּלִים אַתֶּם׃
.are you spies surely ,Pharaoh (as) lives ,not if and ;you with whether (is) truth

17 וַיֶּאֱסֹף אֹתָם אֶל־מִשְׁמָר שְׁלֹשֶׁת יָמִים׃
18 וַיֹּאמֶר אֲלֵהֶם
them to said And .days three custody into them he And gathered

יוֹסֵף בַּיּוֹם הַשְּׁלִישִׁי זֹאת עֲשׂוּ וִחְיוּ אֶת־הָאֱלֹהִים אֲנִי
I God and live ,Do this ,third the on day Joseph

19 יָרֵא׃ אִם־כֵּנִים אַתֶּם אֲחִיכֶם אֶחָד יֵאָסֵר בְּבֵית מִשְׁמַרְכֶם
;prison your the in of house be let bound of one your brothers ,you (are) honest If .fear

20 וְאַתֶּם לְכוּ הָבִיאוּ שֶׁבֶר רַעֲבוֹן בָּתֵּיכֶם׃ וְאֶת־אֲחִיכֶם
your brother and ;houses your the (for) of famine grain bring go and you

הַקָּטֹן תָּבִיאוּ אֵלַי וְיֵאָמְנוּ דִבְרֵיכֶם וְלֹא תָמוּתוּ וַיַּעֲשׂוּ־כֵן׃
.so did they and ;die shall you not and ,words your let and be confirmed ,me to you bring youngest

21 וַיֹּאמְרוּ אִישׁ אֶל־אָחִיו אֲבָל אֲשֵׁמִים ׀ אֲנַחְנוּ עַל־אָחִינוּ
our brother because of (are) We guilty truly his brother to each they And said

אֲשֶׁר רָאִינוּ צָרַת נַפְשׁוֹ בְּהִתְחַנְנוֹ אֵלֵינוּ וְלֹא שָׁמָעְנוּ עַל־
there- ;listen did we not and us he when begged his soul's pain saw we in that

22 כֵּן בָּאָה אֵלֵינוּ הַצָּרָה הַזֹּאת׃ וַיַּעַן רְאוּבֵן אֹתָם לֵאמֹר
,saying ,them Reuben And answered .this pain us to has come fore

הֲלוֹא אָמַרְתִּי אֲלֵיכֶם ׀ לֵאמֹר אַל־תֶּחֶטְאוּ בַיֶּלֶד וְלֹא
and not against youth the sin Do not ,saying you to I Did speak not

23 שְׁמַעְתֶּם וְגַם־דָּמוֹ הִנֵּה נִדְרָשׁ׃ וְהֵם לֹא יָדְעוּ כִּי שֹׁמֵעַ
heard that did know not And they is required ,behold his blood And also did you ?listen

24 יוֹסֵף כִּי הַמֵּלִיץ בֵּינֹתָם׃ וַיִּסֹּב מֵעֲלֵיהֶם וַיֵּבְךְּ וַיָּשָׁב
and came he and ;wept them from he And turned between (was) them the interpreter for ,Joseph

אֲלֵהֶם וַיְדַבֵּר אֲלֵהֶם וַיִּקַּח מֵאִתָּם אֶת־שִׁמְעוֹן וַיֶּאֱסֹר אֹתוֹ
him and bound Simeon from them he and took ,them to and spoke them to

25 לְעֵינֵיהֶם׃ וַיְצַו יוֹסֵף וַיְמַלְאוּ אֶת־כְּלֵיהֶם בָּר וּלְהָשִׁיב
and returned (with) ,grain their vessels they and filled ,Joseph And directed their before .eyes

money, each into his sack, and gave them food for the way; and one did so to them.

[26]And they loaded their grain on their asses and departed from there. [27]And one opened his sack to give fodder to his ass in the lodging place. And he saw his money; and, behold it *was* in the mouth of his sack! [28]And he said to his brothers, My money has been restored, and also look on my sack. And their hearts sank, and they each were terrified, saying to his brother, What is this God has done to us?

[29]And they came to their father Jacob to the land of Canaan, and told him all that had happened to them, saying, [30]The man, the ruler of the land, spoke harsh things with us, and gave us *to be* as spies in the land. [31]And we said to him, We *are* honest; we are not spies. [32]We *are* twelve brothers, sons of our father; the one is not, and the youngest *is* today with our father in the land of Canaan. [33]And the man, the ruler of the land, said to us, By this I shall know that you *are* honest; leave one, your brother, with me and take and go for the famine of your houses. [34]And bring your youngest brother to me, that I may know that you *are* not spies, but you *are* honest. I will give your brother to you, and you may go through the land.

[35]And it happened, they were emptying their sacks, and, behold, each one's bundle of money was in his sack; and they saw the bundles of their money, they and their father; and they were afraid. [36]And

כספיהם איש אל־שקו ולתת להם צדה לדרך ויעש
he and did | for ;way the | food | to them | gave and | his ,sack | into | each | their silver

להם כן: וישאו את־שברם על־חמריהם וילכו משם: 26
from .there | and departed | their asses | on | grain their | they And up lifted | .so | to them

ויפתח האחד את־שקו לתת מספוא לחמרו במלון וירא 27
he and saw | the in ;camp | his to ass | fodder | to give | his sack | one | And opened

את־כספו והנה־הוא בפי אמתחתו: ויאמר אל־אחיו 28
his ,brothers | to | he And said | his !sack's | in mouth | it (was) | ,and ,behold | ,silver his

הושב כספי וגם הנה באמתחתי ויצא לבם ויחרדו איש
,each | they and terrified were | their hearts | went and out | my in ;sack | ,look | and also | My ,money | been has restored

אל־אחיו לאמר מה־זאת עשה אלהים לנו: ויבאו אל־ 29
to | they And came | ?us to | God | has done | is this | What | ,saying | his brother | to

יעקב אביהם ארצה כנען ויגידו לו את כל־הקרת אתם
to ,them | that happened | all | him | told and | ,Canaan | the to of land | their father | Jacob

לאמר: דבר האיש אדני הארץ אתנו קשות ויתן אתנו 30
us | and gave | harsh ,things | us to | the ,land | the of lord | ,man The | spoke | ,saying

כמרגלים את־הארץ: ונאמר אליו כנים אנחנו לא היינו 31
we are | not | We ,(are) | honest | to ,him | we And said | the in .land | spies | as

מרגלים: שנים־עשר אנחנו אחים בני אבינו האחד איננו 32
is not | the one | our ;father | sons of | ,brothers | We are | twelve | .spies

והקטן היום את־אבינו בארץ כנען: ויאמר אלינו האיש 33
the man | us to | said And | .Canaan | the in of land | our father | with | (is) today | the and youngest

אדני הארץ בזאת אדע כי כנים אתם אחיכם האחד
one | your brother | you ;(are) | honest | that | shall I know | By this | the ,land | the of ruler

הניחו אתי ואת־רעבון בתיכם קחו ולכו: והביאו את־ 34
And bring | and go | take | your houses | the for of famine | and | with me | leave

אחיכם הקטן אלי ואדעה כי לא מרגלים אתם כי כנים
honest | but | you (are) | spies | not | that | I that know may | to ,me | youngest | your brother

אתם את־אחיכם אתן לכם ואת־הארץ תסחרו: ויהי 35
it And happened | may you .trade | the in land | and | to .you | will I give | your brother | you ;(are)

הם מריקים שקיהם והנה־איש צרור־כספו בשקו
in (was) ;sack his | one's silver | bundle of | each | ,and ,behold | their ,sacks | were emptying | they

ויראו את־צררות כספיהם המה ואביהם וייראו: ויאמר 36
said And | they and .afraid were | their and ,father | they | ,silver their | the of bundles | they and saw

their father Jacob said to them, You have bereaved me; Joseph is not, and Simeon is not, and you will take Benjamin. All of these are against me. [37]And Reuben spoke to his father, saying, You may kill my two sons if I do not bring him to you. Give him into my hand, and I will return him to you. [38]And he said, My son shall not go down with you; for his brother is dead, and he alone is left; and *if* harm should happen to him in the way in which you go, you would bring down my gray hair in sorrow to the grave.

8095 369 3127 7921 1 3290
אֱלֹהֶם יַעֲקֹב אֲבִיהֶם אֹתִי שִׁכַּלְתֶּם יוֹסֵף אֵינֶנּוּ וְשִׁמְעוֹן
and ,not is Joseph have You me their Jacob them to
Simeon ;bereaved ,father

7205 559 3605 1961 3947 1144 369
37 אֵינֶנּוּ וְאֶת־בִּנְיָמִן תִּקָּחוּ עָלַי הָיוּ כֻלָּנָה׃ וַיֹּאמֶר רְאוּבֵן
Reuben And of all are against will you Benjamin and is
spoke .these me ;take not

935 3808 4191 1121 8147 559 1
אֶל־אָבִיו לֵאמֹר אֶת־שְׁנֵי בָנַי תָּמִית אִם־לֹא אֲבִיאֶנּוּ
do I not if may You my two ,saying his to
him bring kill sons father

559 7725 3027 5414
38 אֵלֶיךָ תְּנָה אֹתוֹ עַל־יָדִי וַאֲנִי אֲשִׁיבֶנּוּ אֵלֶיךָ׃ וַיֹּאמֶר לֹא־
not he And .you to return will and my into him give ;you to
,said him I hand

7135 7604 905 1931 4191 251 1121 3381
יֵרֵד בְּנִי עִמָּכֶם כִּי־אָחִיו מֵת וְהוּא לְבַדּוֹ נִשְׁאָר וּקְרָאָהוּ
(if) and ;left is alone and is his for with My shall
him to come he ,dead brother ;you son go

3015 7872 3381 3212 834 1870 611
אָסוֹן בַּדֶּרֶךְ אֲשֶׁר תֵּלְכוּ־בָהּ וְהוֹרַדְתֶּם אֶת־שֵׂיבָתִי בְּיָגוֹן
in gray my would you ,in go you which the in harm
sorrow hair down bring way

7585
שְׁאוֹלָה׃
the to
.grave

CAP. XLIII מג

CHAPTER 43

CHAPTER 43

[1]And the famine was severe in the land. [2]And it happened, when they had finished eating the grain which they had brought from Egypt, their father said to them, Go back; buy a little food for us. [3]And Judah spoke to him, saying, The man vehemently protested to us, saying, You shall not see my face unless your brother *is* with you. [4]If you are sending our brother with us, we will go down and buy food for you. [5]And if you are not sending, we will not go down. For the man said to us, You shall not see my face unless your brother *is* with you. [6]And Israel said, Why did you do evil to me to tell the man whether you still *had* a brother? [7]And they said, The man keenly asked about us and about our kindred, saying, *Is* your father still alive? Is there a

7668 398 3615 1961 776 3515 7455
1 2 וְהָרָעָב כָּבֵד בָּאָרֶץ׃ וַיְהִי כַּאֲשֶׁר כִּלּוּ לֶאֱכֹל אֶת־הַשֶּׁבֶר
grain the eating had they when it And the in was the And
finished .was .land severe famine

7666 7725 1 559 4714 935 834
אֲשֶׁר הֵבִיאוּ מִמִּצְרָיִם וַיֹּאמֶר אֲלֵיהֶם אֲבִיהֶם שֻׁבוּ שִׁבְרוּ־
buy Go their them to said that from had they which
;back ,father ,Egypt brought

5749 5749 559 3063 559 400 4592
3 לָנוּ מְעַט־אֹכֶל׃ וַיֹּאמֶר אֵלָיו יְהוּדָה לֵאמֹר הָעֵד הֵעִד
testified fiercely ,saying Judah him to And .food little a for
spoke us

251 1115 6440 7200 559 376
בָּנוּ הָאִישׁ לֵאמֹר לֹא־תִרְאוּ פָנַי בִּלְתִּי אֲחִיכֶם אִתְּכֶם׃
with (is) your unless my shall You not ,saying The us to
.you brother face see ,man

7666 3381 251 7971
4 אִם־יֶשְׁךָ מְשַׁלֵּחַ אֶת־אָחִינוּ אִתָּנוּ נֵרְדָה וְנִשְׁבְּרָה לְךָ
for buy and will we with brother our sending you If
you down go us are

559 376 3381 3808 7971 369 400
5 אֹכֶל׃ וְאִם־אֵינְךָ מְשַׁלֵּחַ לֹא נֵרֵד כִּי־הָאִישׁ אָמַר אֵלֵינוּ
,us to said man the for will we not ,sending you if And food
go not are

4100 3478 559 251 6440/7200
6 לֹא־תִרְאוּ פָנַי בִּלְתִּי אֲחִיכֶם אִתְּכֶם׃ וַיֹּאמֶר יִשְׂרָאֵל לָמָה
Why ,Israel said And with (is) your unless my shall You not
.you brother face see

7592 559 251 5750 376 5046 7489
7 הֲרֵעֹתֶם לִי לְהַגִּיד לָאִישׁ הַעוֹד לָכֶם אָח׃ וַיֹּאמְרוּ שָׁאוֹל
keenly they And a you whether the tell to to you did
,said ?brother (had) still man me evil do

3426 2416 1 5750 559 4138 376 7592
שָׁאַל־הָאִישׁ לָנוּ וּלְמוֹלַדְתֵּנוּ לֵאמֹר הַעוֹד אֲבִיכֶם חַי הֲיֵשׁ
Is ?alive your still (Is) ,saying about and about man The asked
there father ,kindred out us

brother to you? And we answered him according to these words. Could we know certainly that he would say, Bring down your brother? 8 And Judah said to his father Israel, Send the young one with me, and let us rise up and go so that we may live and not die, both we and you and our little ones. 9 I will be surety for him; you may require him from my hand. If I do not bring him to you and set him before you, I shall be a sinner against you all the days. 10 For if we have not delayed, truly now we would have returned here twice. 11 And their father Israel said to them, If *it be* so then do this; take from the produce of the land in your vessels, and bring a present down to the man, a little balm, and a little honey, spices, and myrrh, nuts and almonds.

12 And take double silver in your hand. And take back in your hand the silver they returned in the mouth of your sacks. Perhaps it was an oversight. 13 And take your brother, and rise up; return to the man. 14 And may God Almighty give mercy to you before the man. And may he send your other brother and Benjamin to you. And I, if I am bereaved, I am bereaved.

15 And the men took this present, and they took double silver in their hand, and Benjamin. And they arose and went to Egypt and stood before Joseph.

16 And Joseph saw Benjamin with them, and said to the one over his house, Bring the men into the

3045 3045 1697 6310/5921 5046 251
לָכֶם אָח וַנַּגֶּד־לוֹ עַל־פִּי הַדְּבָרִים הָאֵלֶּה הֲיָדוֹעַ נֵדַע כִּי
that we Could .these words according to we And a to know certainly to him said ?brother you
3478 3063 559 251 3381 559
8 יֹאמַר הוֹרִידוּ אֶת־אֲחִיכֶם׃ וַיֹּאמֶר יְהוּדָה אֶל־יִשְׂרָאֵל
Israel to Judah said And ?brother your Bring down would he ,say
4191 3808 2421 3212 6965 5288 7971 1
אָבִיו שִׁלְחָה הַנַּעַר אִתִּי וְנָקוּמָה וְנֵלֵכָה וְנִחְיֶה וְלֹא נָמוּת
,die and not live may we that so ,go and us let and up rise with ,me the youth Send his ,father
1245 6148 2945 1571
9 גַּם־אֲנַחְנוּ גַּם־אַתָּה גַּם־טַפֵּנוּ׃ אָנֹכִי אֶעֶרְבֶנּוּ מִיָּדִי תְּבַקְשֶׁנּוּ
may you ;him require from me surety be will ;him for I our .ones little and you and we both
2398 6440 3322 935 3808 518
אִם־לֹא הֲבִיאֹתִיו אֵלֶיךָ וְהִצַּגְתִּיו לְפָנֶיךָ וְחָטָאתִי לְךָ
against you be shall I sinner a before ,you set and him you to bring do I him not If
2088 7725 6258 4102 3884 3117 3605
10 כָּל־הַיָּמִים׃ כִּי לוּלֵא הִתְמַהְמָהְנוּ כִּי־עַתָּה שַׁבְנוּ זֶה
this would we returned have now truly had we ,delayed not if For .days the all
645 1 3478 559 6471
11 פַעֲמָיִם׃ וַיֹּאמֶר אֲלֵהֶם יִשְׂרָאֵל אֲבִיהֶם אִם־כֵּן ׀ אֵפוֹא
,then ,so If their father Israel them to said And .twice
376 3381 3627 776 2172 3947 6213 2088
זֹאת עֲשׂוּ קְחוּ מִזִּמְרַת הָאָרֶץ בִּכְלֵיכֶם וְהוֹרִידוּ לָאִישׁ
the to man bring and down your in ,vessels the land the from of produce take ;do this
8247 992 3910 5219 1706 4592 6875 4592 4503
מִנְחָה מְעַט צֳרִי וּמְעַט דְּבַשׁ נְכֹאת וָלֹט בָּטְנִים וּשְׁקֵדִים׃
and ,almonds nuts and ,myrrh ,spices ,honey a and little ,balm little a a :present
6310 7725 3701 3027 3947 4932 3701
12 וְכֶסֶף מִשְׁנֶה קְחוּ בְיֶדְכֶם וְאֶת־הַכֶּסֶף הַמּוּשָׁב בְּפִי
in mouth they returned the silver and your in hand take double And silver
4870 3027 7725 572
13 אַמְתְּחֹתֵיכֶם תָּשִׁיבוּ בְיֶדְכֶם אוּלַי מִשְׁגֶּה הוּא׃ וְאֶת־
And it (was) an oversight perhaps your in ;hand back take ,sacks' your
5414/7706 410 376 7725 6965 3947 251
14 אֲחִיכֶם קְחוּ וְקוּמוּ שׁוּבוּ אֶל־הָאִישׁ׃ וְאֵל שַׁדַּי יִתֵּן לָכֶם
to you may give Almighty And God .man the to return and ,take up rise your brother
312 251 7971 376 6440 7356
רַחֲמִים לִפְנֵי הָאִישׁ וְשִׁלַּח לָכֶם אֶת־אֲחִיכֶם אַחֵר וְאֶת־
and other your brother to you may and send he the ,man before mercy
582 3947 7921 7921 1144
15 בִּנְיָמִין וַאֲנִי כַּאֲשֶׁר שָׁכֹלְתִּי שָׁכָלְתִּי׃ וַיִּקְחוּ הָאֲנָשִׁים אֶת־
— men the And took am I .bereaved am I ,bereaved if I and ;Benjamin
1144 3027 3947 3701 4932 2063 4503
הַמִּנְחָה הַזֹּאת וּמִשְׁנֶה־כֶּסֶף לָקְחוּ בְיָדָם וְאֶת־בִּנְיָמִן
;Benjamin and their in ,hand took they silver and double this present
3127 7200 3127 6440 5975 4714 3381 6965
16 וַיָּקֻמוּ וַיֵּרְדוּ מִצְרַיִם וַיַּעַמְדוּ לִפְנֵי יוֹסֵף׃ וַיַּרְא יוֹסֵף
Joseph And saw .Joseph before and stood ,Egypt to and went they and arose
582 935 1004 5921 559 1144 853
אִתָּם אֶת־בִּנְיָמִין וַיֹּאמֶר לַאֲשֶׁר עַל־בֵּיתוֹ הָבֵא אֶת־הָאֲנָשִׁים
men the Bring his over ,house the to one said and ,Benjamin with them

house, and make a great slaughter, and prepare. For the men shall eat with me at noon. 17And the man did as Joseph said. And the man brought the men into Joseph's house. 18And they said, *It is* on account of the silver that *was* returned in our sacks before that we are being brought in, to throw himself on us and to fall on us, and to take us and our asses for slaves. 19And they came near to the man over Joseph's house and spoke to him at the door of the house. 20And they said, O my lord, surely we came before to buy food. 21And it happened, when we came to the lodging place and opened our sacks, behold, the silver of each one *was* in the mouth of his sack, our silver in its weight. And we have brought other silver in our hand to buy food. We do not know who put our silver in our sacks. 23And he said, Peace to you. Do not fear. Your God and the God of your father has given treasure to you in your sacks. Your silver came to me. And he brought Simeon to them.

24And the man brought the men to the house of Joseph. And he furnished water, and they washed their feet. And he gave fodder for their asses. 25And they prepared the present, for the coming of Joseph at noon. For they had heard that they would eat bread there.

26And Joseph came into the house. And they

582 398 6213 2874 2873 1004
הַבַּיְתָה וּטְבֹחַ טֶבַח וְהָכֵן כִּי אִתִּי יֹאכְלוּ הָאֲנָשִׁים
men the | shall eat | with me | for | ;prepare and | an animal | and slaughter | the into .house

376 935 3127 559 376 6213 6672
17 בַּצָּהֳרָיִם׃ וַיַּעַשׂ הָאִישׁ כַּאֲשֶׁר אָמַר יוֹסֵף וַיָּבֵא הָאִישׁ
man the | and brought | ;Joseph | said | as | man the did And | .noon at

935 582 3372 3127 1004 582
18 אֶת־הָאֲנָשִׁים בֵּיתָה יוֹסֵף׃ וַיִּירְאוּ הָאֲנָשִׁים כִּי הוּבְאוּ
were they for to taken | ,men the | were And afraid | .Joseph's | house to | men the

572 7725 3701 559 3127 1004
בֵּית יוֹסֵף וַיֹּאמְרוּ עַל־דְּבַר הַכֶּסֶף הַשָּׁב בְּאַמְתְּחֹתֵינוּ
sacks our | in | (was) that returned | silver the | of Because | they and ,said | Joseph's house

5307 1556 935 8462
בַּתְּחִלָּה אֲנַחְנוּ מוּבָאִים לְהִתְגֹּלֵל עָלֵינוּ וּלְהִתְנַפֵּל עָלֵינוּ
,us on | fall to and | us upon | throw to himself | being are ,in brought | we | ,before

376 5066 2543 5650 3947
19 וְלָקַחַת אֹתָנוּ לַעֲבָדִים וְאֶת־חֲמֹרֵינוּ׃ וַיִּגְּשׁוּ אֶל־הָאִישׁ
man the | to | they And came | .asses our | and | ,slaves for | us | to and take

559 1004 6607 1696 3127 1004 834
20 אֲשֶׁר עַל־בֵּית יוֹסֵף וַיְדַבְּרוּ אֵלָיו פֶּתַח הַבָּיִת׃ וַיֹּאמְרוּ
they And ,said | the .house | the at of door | him to | spoke and | Joseph's house | over | which (was)

935 1961 400 7666 8462 3381 3381 113 994
21 בִּי אֲדֹנִי יָרֹד יָרַדְנוּ בַּתְּחִלָּה לִשְׁבָּר־אֹכֶל׃ וַיְהִי כִּי־בָאנוּ
we when came | it And ,was | .food | buy to | before | we came | surely | my ,lord | O

6310 376 3701 2009 572 6605 4411
אֶל־הַמָּלוֹן וַנִּפְתְּחָה אֶת־אַמְתְּחֹתֵינוּ וְהִנֵּה כֶסֶף־אִישׁ בְּפִי
in mouth | each one | the of silver | ,behold | sacks our | opened and | camp the to

312 3701 3027 7725 4948 3701 572
22 אַמְתַּחְתּוֹ כַּסְפֵּנוּ בְּמִשְׁקָלוֹ וַנָּשֶׁב אֹתוֹ בְּיָדֵנוּ׃ וְכֶסֶף אַחֵר
other | And silver | our .hand | in | it | we and bring | its ;weight | in | our silver | sack's his

3701 7760 3045 3808 400 7666 3027 3381
הוֹרַדְנוּ בְיָדֵנוּ לִשְׁבָּר־אֹכֶל לֹא יָדַעְנוּ מִי־שָׂם כַּסְפֵּנוּ
our silver | put who | do we know | not | ;food | buy to | our in hand | have we brought

430 3372 7965 559 572
23 בְּאַמְתְּחֹתֵינוּ׃ וַיֹּאמֶר שָׁלוֹם לָכֶם אַל־תִּירָאוּ אֱלֹהֵיכֶם
God your | ;fear do not | ;you to | Peace | he And said | .sacks our | in

3701 572 4301 5414 1 430
וֵאלֹהֵי אֲבִיכֶם נָתַן לָכֶם מַטְמוֹן בְּאַמְתְּחֹתֵיכֶם כַּסְפְּכֶם
silver your | ;sacks your | in | treasure a | you to | has given | your father | the and of God

376 935 8095 3318 935
24 בָּא אֵלָי וַיּוֹצֵא אֲלֵהֶם אֶת־שִׁמְעוֹן׃ וַיָּבֵא הָאִישׁ אֶת־
— | man the | And brought | .Simeon | them to | he And brought | .me to came

5414 7272 7364 4325 3127 1004 376
הָאֲנָשִׁים בֵּיתָה יוֹסֵף וַיִּתֶּן־מַיִם וַיִּרְחֲצוּ רַגְלֵיהֶם וַיִּתֵּן
he and gave | ;feet their | they and washed | he and ,water gave | ;Joseph | the to of house | men the

3127 935 5704 4503 3559 2543 4554
25 מִסְפּוֹא לַחֲמֹרֵיהֶם׃ וַיָּכִינוּ אֶת־הַמִּנְחָה עַד־בּוֹא יוֹסֵף
Joseph | the of coming | for | ,present the | they And prepared | their for .asses | fodder

1004 3127 935 3899 398 8033 8085 6672
26 בַּצָּהֳרָיִם כִּי שָׁמְעוּ כִּי־שָׁם יֹאכְלוּ לָחֶם׃ וַיָּבֹא יוֹסֵף הַבַּיְתָה
the ,house | Joseph | And into came | .bread | they eat would | there that | they heard had | for | ;noon at

brought the present which *was* in their hand in to him, into the house. And they bowed themselves to him, to the earth. [27]And he asked them of their welfare, and said, *Is* there peace to your father, the old man of whom you spoke? *Is* he still alive? [28]And they said, *There is* peace to your servant, to our father; he *is* still alive. And they bowed themselves and fell before *him*. [29]And he raised his eyes and saw his brother Benjamin, the son of his mother. And he said, *Is* this your youngest brother of whom you spoke to me? And he said, May God be gracious to you, my son. [30]And Joseph hurried, for his emotions were deeply moved towards his brother. And he looked for *a place* to weep; and he came into the inner room and wept there. [31]And he washed his face and went out, and controlled himself, and said, Lay out bread. [32]And they laid out for him by himself, and for them by themselves, and for the Egyptians eating with him by themselves. For the Egyptians cannot eat bread with the Hebrews; for it is an abomination in Egypt. [33]And they sat before him, the firstborn according to his birthright, and the younger according to his youth. And the men were astonished, each to his neighbor. [34]And one carried portions from before him to them, and the portion of Benjamin was greater than the portions of all of them, five times. And they drank and were drunken with him.

וַיָּבִיאוּ לוֹ אֶת־הַמִּנְחָה אֲשֶׁר־בְּיָדָם הַבָּיְתָה וַיִּשְׁתַּחֲווּ־לוֹ
27 אַרְצָה׃ וַיִּשְׁאַל לָהֶם לְשָׁלוֹם וַיֹּאמֶר הֲשָׁלוֹם אֲבִיכֶם
28 הַזָּקֵן אֲשֶׁר אֲמַרְתֶּם הַעוֹדֶנּוּ חָי׃ וַיֹּאמְרוּ שָׁלוֹם לְעַבְדְּךָ
29 לְאָבִינוּ עוֹדֶנּוּ חָי וַיִּקְּדוּ וַיִּשְׁתַּחֲווּ׃ וַיִּשָּׂא עֵינָיו וַיַּרְא אֶת־
בִּנְיָמִין אָחִיו בֶּן־אִמּוֹ וַיֹּאמֶר הֲזֶה אֲחִיכֶם הַקָּטֹן אֲשֶׁר
30 אֲמַרְתֶּם אֵלָי וַיֹּאמַר אֱלֹהִים יָחְנְךָ בְּנִי׃ וַיְמַהֵר יוֹסֵף כִּי־
נִכְמְרוּ רַחֲמָיו אֶל־אָחִיו וַיְבַקֵּשׁ לִבְכּוֹת וַיָּבֹא הַחַדְרָה
31 וַיֵּבְךְּ שָׁמָּה׃ וַיִּרְחַץ פָּנָיו וַיֵּצֵא וַיִּתְאַפַּק וַיֹּאמֶר שִׂימוּ
32 לָחֶם׃ וַיָּשִׂימוּ לוֹ לְבַדּוֹ וְלָהֶם לְבַדָּם וְלַמִּצְרִים הָאֹכְלִים
אִתּוֹ לְבַדָּם כִּי לֹא יוּכְלוּן הַמִּצְרִים לֶאֱכֹל אֶת־הָעִבְרִים
33 לֶחֶם כִּי־תוֹעֵבָה הִוא לְמִצְרָיִם׃ וַיֵּשְׁבוּ לְפָנָיו הַבְּכֹר
כִּבְכֹרָתוֹ וְהַצָּעִיר כִּצְעִרָתוֹ וַיִּתְמְהוּ הָאֲנָשִׁים אִישׁ אֶל־
34 רֵעֵהוּ׃ וַיִּשָּׂא מַשְׂאֹת מֵאֵת פָּנָיו אֲלֵהֶם וַתֵּרֶב מַשְׂאַת בִּנְיָמִן
מִמַּשְׂאֹת כֻּלָּם חָמֵשׁ יָדוֹת וַיִּשְׁתּוּ וַיִּשְׁכְּרוּ עִמּוֹ׃

CAP. XLIV מד

CHAPTER 44

[1]And he commanded the one over his house, saying, Fill the sacks of the men *with* food, as much as they are able to carry; and put the money of each one in the mouth of his sack. [2]And put

1 וַיְצַו אֶת־אֲשֶׁר עַל־בֵּיתוֹ לֵאמֹר מַלֵּא אֶת־אַמְתְּחֹת הָאֲנָשִׁים
אֹכֶל כַּאֲשֶׁר יוּכְלוּן שְׂאֵת וְשִׂים כֶּסֶף־אִישׁ בְּפִי אַמְתַּחְתּוֹ׃

my cup, the cup of silver, in the mouth of the sack of the youngest, and the silver for his grain. And he did according to the word of Joseph which he spoke. 3At the morning light the men were sent away, they and their asses. 4They had gone out from the city, not having gone far, and Joseph said to the one over his house, Rise up, follow after the men and overtake them, and say to them, Why have you repaid evil for good? 5Is this not *that* in which my lord is accustomed to drink, and divining he divines by it? You have done evil in what you have done.

6And he overtook them and spoke these words to them. 7And they said to him, Why should my lord speak according to these words? Far be it from your servants to do according to this word. 8See, the silver which we found in the mouth of our sacks, we returned to you from the land of Canaan. And how should we steal silver or gold from the house of your lord? 9*With* whomever it may be found, with him of your servants, he shall die. And we also will become slaves to my lord. 10And he said, Now also let it be according to your words; *with* whomever it is found with him, he will become a slave to me, and you shall be innocent. 11And they hurried, and each one brought down his sack to the earth. And each one opened his sack. 12And he searched, with the oldest first, and with the youngest last, and the cup was found in the sack of Benjamin.

13And they tore their clothes; and they each one loaded his ass and returned to the city.

2 וְאֶת־גְּבִיעִי גְּבִיעַ הַכֶּסֶף תָּשִׂים בְּפִי אַמְתַּחַת הַקָּטֹן וְאֵת
3 כֶּסֶף שִׁבְרוֹ וַיַּעַשׂ כִּדְבַר יוֹסֵף אֲשֶׁר דִּבֵּר׃ הַבֹּקֶר אוֹר
4 וְהָאֲנָשִׁים שֻׁלְּחוּ הֵמָּה וַחֲמֹרֵיהֶם׃ הֵם יָצְאוּ אֶת־הָעִיר
לֹא הִרְחִיקוּ וְיוֹסֵף אָמַר לַאֲשֶׁר עַל־בֵּיתוֹ קוּם רְדֹף אַחֲרֵי
הָאֲנָשִׁים וְהִשַּׂגְתָּם וְאָמַרְתָּ אֲלֵהֶם לָמָּה שִׁלַּמְתֶּם רָעָה
תַּחַת טוֹבָה׃ הֲלוֹא זֶה אֲשֶׁר יִשְׁתֶּה אֲדֹנִי בּוֹ וְהוּא נַחֵשׁ
6 יְנַחֵשׁ בּוֹ הֲרֵעֹתֶם אֲשֶׁר עֲשִׂיתֶם׃ וַיַּשִּׂגֵם וַיְדַבֵּר אֲלֵהֶם
7 אֶת־הַדְּבָרִים הָאֵלֶּה׃ וַיֹּאמְרוּ אֵלָיו לָמָּה יְדַבֵּר אֲדֹנִי
8 כַּדְּבָרִים הָאֵלֶּה חָלִילָה לַעֲבָדֶיךָ מֵעֲשׂוֹת כַּדָּבָר הַזֶּה׃ הֵן
כֶּסֶף אֲשֶׁר מָצָאנוּ בְּפִי אַמְתְּחֹתֵינוּ הֱשִׁיבֹנוּ אֵלֶיךָ מֵאֶרֶץ
9 כְּנָעַן וְאֵיךְ נִגְנֹב מִבֵּית אֲדֹנֶיךָ כֶּסֶף אוֹ זָהָב׃ אֲשֶׁר יִמָּצֵא
אִתּוֹ מֵעֲבָדֶיךָ וָמֵת וְגַם־אֲנַחְנוּ נִהְיֶה לַאדֹנִי לַעֲבָדִים׃
10 וַיֹּאמֶר גַּם־עַתָּה כְדִבְרֵיכֶם כֶּן־הוּא אֲשֶׁר יִמָּצֵא אִתּוֹ יִהְיֶה־
11 לִּי עָבֶד וְאַתֶּם תִּהְיוּ נְקִיִּם׃ וַיְמַהֲרוּ וַיּוֹרִדוּ אִישׁ אֶת־
12 אַמְתַּחְתּוֹ אָרְצָה וַיִּפְתְּחוּ אִישׁ אַמְתַּחְתּוֹ׃ וַיְחַפֵּשׂ בַּגָּדוֹל
הֵחֵל וּבַקָּטֹן כִּלָּה וַיִּמָּצֵא הַגָּבִיעַ בְּאַמְתַּחַת בִּנְיָמִן׃
13 וַיִּקְרְעוּ שִׂמְלֹתָם וַיַּעֲמֹס אִישׁ עַל־חֲמֹרוֹ וַיָּשֻׁבוּ הָעִירָה׃

[14]And Judah and his brothers came in to the house of Joseph, and he *was* still there. And they fell before him to the earth. [15]And Joseph said to them, What *is* this deed which you have done? Did you not know that a man like me would practice divination? [16]And Judah said, What can we say to my lord? What can we speak, and in what can we justify ourselves? God has found out the iniquity of your servants; behold, we *are* slaves to my lord, both we and he in whose hand the cup was found. [17]And he said, Far be it from me to do this. The man in whose hand the cup was found, he shall become a slave to me; and you go up in peace to your father.

14 וַיָּבֹא יְהוּדָה וְאֶחָיו בֵּיתָה יוֹסֵף וְהוּא עוֹדֶנּוּ שָׁם וַיִּפְּלוּ
they and ;there (was) and ,Joseph the to his and Judah And
fell still he of house brothers in came

15 לְפָנָיו אָרְצָה׃ וַיֹּאמֶר לָהֶם יוֹסֵף מָה־הַמַּעֲשֶׂה הַזֶּה אֲשֶׁר
which this deed (is) What ,Joseph to said And the to before
them .earth him

עֲשִׂיתֶם הֲלוֹא יְדַעְתֶּם כִּי־נַחֵשׁ יְנַחֵשׁ אִישׁ אֲשֶׁר כָּמֹנִי׃
?me like (is) who man a would that you Did not have you
divine divining know done

16 וַיֹּאמֶר יְהוּדָה מַה־נֹּאמַר לַאדֹנִי מַה־נְּדַבֵּר וּמַה־נִּצְטַדָּק
we can How we can What my to we can What ,Judah said And
?ourselves justify ?speak ?lord say

הָאֱלֹהִים מָצָא אֶת־עֲוֺן עֲבָדֶיךָ הִנֶּנּוּ עֲבָדִים לַאדֹנִי גַּם־
both my to (are) ,behold your the has God
lord slaves we ;servants of iniquity found

17 אֲנַחְנוּ גַּם אֲשֶׁר־נִמְצָא הַגָּבִיעַ בְּיָדוֹ׃ וַיֹּאמֶר חָלִילָה לִּי
from Be far he And his in cup the was he and we
me it said ,hand whom

מֵעֲשׂוֹת זֹאת הָאִישׁ אֲשֶׁר נִמְצָא הַגָּבִיעַ בְּיָדוֹ הוּא יִהְיֶה־לִּי
to shall he his in cup the was whom man the ;this do to
me become ,hand found

עָבֶד וְאַתֶּם עֲלוּ לְשָׁלוֹם אֶל־אֲבִיכֶם׃
your to peace in up go and a
.father you ;slave

[18]And Judah came near to him and said, O my lord, please let your servant speak a word in the ears of my lord, and let not your anger glow *on* your servant, for you are like Pharaoh. [19]My lord asked his servants, saying, *Is there* a brother or a father to you? [20]And we said to my lord, An aged father is to us, and a young child of *his* old age; and his brother is dead; and he alone is left of his mother; and his father loves him. [21]And you said to your servants, Bring him down to me, and let me see him. [22]And we said to my lord, The youth is not able to leave his father; and *if* he should leave his father, he will die. [23]And you said to your servants, If your youngest brother does not come down with you, you shall not see my face again. [24]And it happened, when we had gone up to your servant, my father, we told

18 וַיִּגַּשׁ אֵלָיו יְהוּדָה וַיֹּאמֶר בִּי אֲדֹנִי יְדַבֶּר־נָא עַבְדְּךָ דָבָר
a your let my ,O ,said and Judah him to And
word servant speak ,lord came

בְּאָזְנֵי אֲדֹנִי וְאַל־יִחַר אַפְּךָ בְּעַבְדֶּךָ כִּי כָמוֹךָ כְּפַרְעֹה׃
.Pharaoh as are you for your (on) your let and my ears in
,servant anger glow not lord's

19 אֲדֹנִי שָׁאַל אֶת־עֲבָדָיו לֵאמֹר הֲיֵשׁ־לָכֶם אָב אוֹ־אָח׃
a or a you to there Is ,saying servants his asked My
?brother father lord

20 וַנֹּאמֶר אֶל־אֲדֹנִי יֶשׁ־לָנוּ אָב זָקֵן וְיֶלֶד זְקֻנִים קָטָן וְאָחִיו
his and young old (his) a and an father to There my to we And
brother ,age of boy ,aged us is ,lord said

21 מֵת וַיִּוָּתֵר הוּא לְבַדּוֹ לְאִמּוֹ וְאָבִיו אֲהֵבוֹ׃ וַתֹּאמֶר אֶל־
to you And loves his and his of alone he is and is
said .him father ,mother left ,dead

22 עֲבָדֶיךָ הוֹרִדֻהוּ אֵלָי וְאָשִׂימָה עֵינִי עָלָיו׃ וַנֹּאמֶר אֶל־
to we And .him on my let and ,me to him Bring your
said eyes set me ,servants

אֲדֹנִי לֹא־יוּכַל הַנַּעַר לַעֲזֹב אֶת־אָבִיו וְעָזַב אֶת־אָבִיו וָמֵת׃
will he his (if) and his leave to The able is not my
.die ,father leave should he ;father youth ,lord

23 וַתֹּאמֶר אֶל־עֲבָדֶיךָ אִם־לֹא יֵרֵד אֲחִיכֶם הַקָּטֹן אִתְּכֶם לֹא
not with youngest your comes not If your to you And
,you brother ,servants said

24 תֹסִפוּן לִרְאוֹת פָּנָי׃ וַיְהִי כִּי עָלִינוּ אֶל־עַבְדְּךָ אָבִי וַנַּגֶּד־
we and my your to we that it And my see shall you
told ,father ,servant came happened .face again

him the words of my lord. [25]And our father said, Go back, buy a little food for us. [26]And we said, We cannot go down. If our youngest brother is with us, we will go down. For we cannot see the face of the man *if* our youngest brother is not with us. [27]And your servant, my father, said to us, You know that my wife bore two to me. [28]And one went out from me. And I said, Indeed, he surely is torn in pieces; and I have not seen him until now. [29]And *if* you take this one also from my face, and harm happen to him, you will bring my gray hair to the grave in sorrow. [30]And now when I come to your servant, my father, and the youth is not with us, and his soul *being* bound to his soul, it will be when he sees that the youth is not, he will die. And your servants will bring down the gray hair of your servant our father to the grave in sorrow. [32]For your servant was surety for the youth *with* my father, saying, If I do not bring him to you, I shall be a sinner against my father all the days. [33]And now please let your servant remain *as* a slave to my lord instead of the youth; and let the youth go up with his brothers. [34]For how can I go to my father, and the youth not be with me? Lest I look on the evil which will find my father.

4592 7666 7725 1 559 113 1697
25 לוֹ אֶת דִּבְרֵי אֲדֹנִי׃ וַיֹּאמֶר אָבִינוּ שֻׁבוּ שִׁבְרוּ־לָנוּ מְעַט
little a | us for | buy | Go ,back | our ,father | said And | my .lord | the of words | him

6996 251 3426 3381 3201 3808 559 400
26 אֹכֶל׃ וַנֹּאמֶר לֹא נוּכַל לָרֶדֶת אִם־יֵשׁ אָחִינוּ הַקָּטֹן אִתָּנוּ
with ,us | youngest | our brother | is | if | ;down go | We can | not | we And ,said | .food

6996 251 376 6440 7200 3201 38.08/3588 3381
וְיָרַדְנוּ כִּי־לֹא נוּכַל לִרְאוֹת פְּנֵי הָאִישׁ וְאָחִינוּ הַקָּטֹן
youngest | our (if) brother | man the | the of face | see | to | are we able | not | for | will we ;down go

3045 5650 559 369
27 אֵינֶנּוּ אִתָּנוּ׃ וַיֹּאמֶר עַבְדְּךָ אָבִי אֵלֵינוּ אַתֶּם יְדַעְתֶּם כִּי
that | know | You | ,us to | my father | your servant | said And | with .us | not is

559 259 5927 802 3205 8147
28 שְׁנַיִם יָלְדָה־לִּי אִשְׁתִּי׃ וַיֵּצֵא הָאֶחָד מֵאִתִּי וָאֹמַר אַךְ
,Truly | and said I | from ;me | one | And out went | my .wife | to me | bore | two

259 3947 4994/5704 7200 3808 2963 2963
29 טָרֹף טֹרָף וְלֹא רְאִיתִיו עַד־הֵנָּה׃ וּלְקַחְתֶּם גַּם־אֶת־זֶה
one this | also | (if) And take you | ,now until | have I him seen | and not | is he ;torn | torn

7451 7872 3381 611 7136 6440 5973
מֵעִם פָּנַי וְקָרָהוּ אָסוֹן וְהוֹרַדְתֶּם אֶת־שֵׂיבָתִי בְּרָעָה
in sorrow | my hair gray | will you bring | ,harm happen and him on | my ,face | from

369 5288 5650 935 6258 7585
30 שְׁאֹלָה׃ וְעַתָּה כְּבֹאִי אֶל־עַבְדְּךָ אָבִי וְהַנַּעַר אֵינֶנּוּ אִתָּנוּ
with us | not is | the and youth | my ,father | your to servant | I when come | And now | the to .grave

4191 5288 369 7200 5315 7194 5315
31 וְנַפְשׁוֹ קְשׁוּרָה בְנַפְשׁוֹ׃ וְהָיָה כִּרְאוֹתוֹ כִּי־אֵין הַנַּעַר וָמֵת
will he ;die | the ,youth | is not | that | he when sees | will it happen | his to ;soul | bound | his and (being) soul

7585 3615 5650 7822 5650 3381
וְהוֹרִידוּ עֲבָדֶיךָ אֶת־שֵׂיבַת עַבְדְּךָ אָבִינוּ בְּיָגוֹן שְׁאֹלָה׃
the to .grave | in sorrow | our father | your servant | gray the of hair | your servants | will and bring

935 3808 559 1 5973 5288 6148 5650 3588
32 כִּי עַבְדְּךָ עָרַב אֶת־הַנַּעַר מֵעִם אָבִי לֵאמֹר אִם־לֹא אֲבִיאֶנּוּ
bring I him | not If | ,saying | my father | (with) | for youth the | was surety | your servant | For

5650 7725 6258 3117 3605 1 2398
33 אֵלֶיךָ וְחָטָאתִי לְאָבִי כָּל־הַיָּמִים׃ וְעַתָּה יֵשֶׁב־נָא עַבְדְּךָ
your servant | please let remain | And now | .days the | all | against father my | be shall I sinner a | to ,you

349 251 5927 5288 113 5650 5288
34 תַּחַת הַנַּעַר עֶבֶד לַאדֹנִי וְהַנַּעַר יַעַל עִם־אֶחָיו׃ כִּי־אֵיךְ
how For | his ,brothers | with | go let | and youth the | my to ;lord | a (as) slave | the ,youth | instead of

834 7451 7200 369 5288 1 5927
אֶעֱלֶה אֶל־אָבִי וְהַנַּעַר אֵינֶנּוּ אִתִּי פֶּן אֶרְאֶה בָרָע אֲשֶׁר
which | on evil the | look I | Lest | with ?me | not be | the and youth | my ,father | to | I can go

1 4672
יִמְצָא אֶת־אָבִי׃
my .father | will find

CAP. XLV מה

CHAPTER 45

CHAPTER 45

[1]And Joseph was not able to control himself in regard to those standing beside him. And he called

7121 5324 3605 662 3127 3201 3808
1 וְלֹא־יָכֹל יוֹסֵף לְהִתְאַפֵּק לְכֹל הַנִּצָּבִים עָלָיו וַיִּקְרָא
he and ,cried | by ;him | those standing | before all | control to himself | Joseph | was able | And not

out, Cause every man to go
out from me. And no man
stood before him *as* Joseph
was making himself known
to his brothers. [2]And he
wept aloud; and the Egyp-
tians heard, and the house
of Pharaoh heard. [3]And
Joseph said to his brothers,
I am Joseph. *Is* my father
still alive? And his brothers
were not able to answer
him, for they trembled
before him. [4]And Joseph
said to his brothers, Now
come near to me. And they
came near. And he said, I
am your brother Joseph,
whom you sold into Egypt.
[5]And now do not be
grieved, and let no anger be
in your eyes because you
sold me here; for God sent
me before you to save life.
[6]For the famine *has been* in
the midst of the land for two
years. And *there are* still five
years in which no plowing
and harvest will be. [7]And
God sent me before you to
put a remnant in the land for
you, and to keep alive for
you a great deliverance.

[8]And now you did not send
me here, but God. And He
has placed me for a father to
Pharaoh, and for a lord in all
his house, and a ruler in all
the land of Egypt. [9]Hurry
and go up to my father, and
say to him, So says your son
Joseph, God has placed me
as a lord to all Egypt. Come
down to me, do not delay.

[10]And you shall live in the
land of Goshen, and you
shall be near to me, you and
your sons, and the sons of
your sons, and your flocks,
and your herds, and all you
have. [11]And I will nourish
you there, for *there are* still
five years *of* famine; lest you
be made poor, you and your

3127 3045 376 5975 3808 376 5927
הוֹצִיאוּ כָל־אִישׁ מֵעָלָי וְלֹא־עָמַד אִישׁ אִתּוֹ בְּהִתְוַדַּע יוֹסֵף
Joseph made when with man a stood and from man every to Cause
known himself him not ;me out go

8085 47:13 8085 1065 6963 5414 251
2 אֶל־אֶחָיו׃ וַיִּתֵּן אֶת־קֹלוֹ בִּבְכִי וַיִּשְׁמְעוּ מִצְרַיִם וַיִּשְׁמַע
and the and in his he And his to
heard Egyptians heard ;weeping voice gave .brothers

1 5750 31:27 251 3127 559 6547 1004
3 בֵּית פַּרְעֹה׃ וַיֹּאמֶר יוֹסֵף אֶל־אֶחָיו אֲנִי יוֹסֵף הַעוֹד אָבִי
my (Is) .Joseph I his to Joseph said And .Pharaoh's house
father still (am) ,brothers of

559 6440 1926 6030 251 3201 2416
4 חָי וְלֹא־יָכְלוּ אֶחָיו לַעֲנוֹת אֹתוֹ כִּי נִבְהֲלוּ מִפָּנָיו׃ וַיֹּאמֶר
said And before they for ,him to his were And ?alive
.him trembled answer brothers able not

251 3127 559 5066 5066 251 3127
יוֹסֵף אֶל־אֶחָיו גְּשׁוּ־נָא אֵלַי וַיִּגָּשׁוּ וַיֹּאמֶר אֲנִי יוֹסֵף אֲחִיכֶם
your Joseph I he and they and to Now come his to Joseph
,brother (am) ,said ;came ;me ,brothers

3808 6087 6258 4714 4376
5 אֲשֶׁר־מְכַרְתֶּם אֹתִי מִצְרָיְמָה׃ וְעַתָּה | אַל־תֵּעָצְבוּ וְאַל־
and be do not now And .Egypt into me sold you whom
not ,grieved

7971 24:21 4376 58:69 2734
יִחַר בְּעֵינֵיכֶם כִּי־מְכַרְתֶּם אֹתִי הֵנָּה כִּי לְמִחְיָה שְׁלָחַנִי
sent save to for ;here me you because your in be do
me life sold eyes angry

776 7130 7458 8141 2088 6440 430
6 אֱלֹהִים לִפְנֵיכֶם׃ כִּי־זֶה שְׁנָתַיִם הָרָעָב בְּקֶרֶב הָאָרֶץ
the the in the two this For before God
;land of midst famine years .you

7971 7102 2758 369 834 8141 2568 5750
7 וְעוֹד חָמֵשׁ שָׁנִים אֲשֶׁר אֵין־חָרִישׁ וְקָצִיר׃ וַיִּשְׁלָחֵנִי
sent And and (be will) in years five and
me .harvest plowing no which still

2421 776 7611 7760 6440 430
אֱלֹהִים לִפְנֵיכֶם לָשׂוּם לָכֶם שְׁאֵרִית בָּאָרֶץ וּלְהַחֲיוֹת לָכֶם
for to and the in a for put to before God
you alive keep land remnant you you

7971 3808 6258 1419 6413
8 לִפְלֵיטָה גְּדֹלָה׃ וְעַתָּה לֹא־אַתֶּם שְׁלַחְתֶּם אֹתִי הֵנָּה כִּי
but ,here me send did you not now And .great a
deliverance

4910 1004 3605 113 6547 1 7760 430
הָאֱלֹהִים וַיְשִׂימֵנִי לְאָב לְפַרְעֹה וּלְאָדוֹן לְכָל־בֵּיתוֹ וּמֹשֵׁל
a and his to for and to a for He and ;God
ruler ,house all lord a ,Pharaoh father me set has

559 1 5927 4116 4714 776 3605
9 בְּכָל־אֶרֶץ מִצְרָיִם׃ מַהֲרוּ וַעֲלוּ אֶל־אָבִי וַאֲמַרְתֶּם אֵלָיו
to say and my to and Hurry .Egypt the all in
,him ,father up go up of land

4714 3605 113 430 7760 31:27 1121 559
כֹּה אָמַר בִּנְךָ יוֹסֵף שָׂמַנִי אֱלֹהִים לְאָדוֹן לְכָל־מִצְרָיִם
;Egypt all to a as God has ,Joseph your says Thus
lord me placed 5915 son

7138 1961 1657 776 3427 3381
10 רְדָה אֵלַי אַל־תַּעֲמֹד׃ וְיָשַׁבְתָּ בְאֶרֶץ־גֹּשֶׁן וְהָיִיתָ קָרוֹב
near and Goshen the in you And do not to come
be shall of land live shall delay ,me down

834 3605 1241 6629 1121 1121 1121
אֵלַי אַתָּה וּבָנֶיךָ וּבְנֵי בָנֶיךָ וְצֹאנְךָ וּבְקָרְךָ וְכָל־אֲשֶׁר־לָךְ׃
to which and and your and your and your and ,you to
.you (is) all ,herds your ,flocks ,sons of sons sons ;me

3423 7458 8141 2568 5750 8033 3557
11 וְכִלְכַּלְתִּי אֹתְךָ שָׁם כִּי־עוֹד חָמֵשׁ שָׁנִים רָעָב פֶּן־תִּוָּרֵשׁ
be you lest ;famine years five still for ,there you will I And
,poor made (of) (are there) nourish

house and all which
belongs to you.
[12]And behold, your eyes
and the eyes of my brother
Benjamin see that my
mouth *is* speaking to you.
[13]And you tell my father of
all my honor in Egypt, and
all that you have seen. And
hurry and bring down my
father here. [14]And he fell
on the neck of his brother
Benjamin and wept, and
Benjamin wept on his neck.
[15]And he kissed all his
brothers, and wept on
them. And afterwards his
brothers spoke with him.
[16]And the report was
heard in Pharaoh's house,
saying, The brothers of
Joseph have come. And it
was good in the eyes of
Pharaoh and in the eyes of
his servants. [17]And Pharaoh
said to Joseph, Say to
your brothers, Do this;
load your animals and de-
part; go to the land of
Canaan. [18]And take your
father and your houses
and come to me. And I
will give to you the good
of the land of Egypt;
and you shall eat the fat
of the land. [19]And you
are commanded; you do
this: Take for yourselves
wagons from the land of
Egypt, for your little ones,
and for your wives. And
take your father and
come. [20]And your eye,
let it have no regard for
your vessels, for the good
of all the land of Egypt *is*
yours.

[21]And the sons of Israel
did so. And by the mouth
of Pharaoh Joseph gave
wagons to them. And he
gave food to them for the
way. [22]He gave to all of
them, to each one,
changes of clothing. And
he gave to Benjamin
three hundred *pieces* of
silver, and five changes of
clothing. [23]And to his
father he sent this: ten

12 אַתָּה וּבֵיתְךָ וְכָל־אֲשֶׁר־לָךְ׃ וְהִנֵּה עֵינֵיכֶם רֹאוֹת וְעֵינֵי
13 אָחִי בִנְיָמִין כִּי־פִי הַמְדַבֵּר אֲלֵיכֶם׃ וְהִגַּדְתֶּם לְאָבִי
אֶת־כָּל־כְּבוֹדִי בְּמִצְרַיִם וְאֵת כָּל־אֲשֶׁר רְאִיתֶם וּמִהַרְתֶּם
14 וְהוֹרַדְתֶּם אֶת־אָבִי הֵנָּה׃ וַיִּפֹּל עַל־צַוְּארֵי בִנְיָמִן־אָחִיו וַיֵּבְךְּ
15 וּבִנְיָמִן בָּכָה עַל־צַוָּארָיו׃ וַיְנַשֵּׁק לְכָל־אֶחָיו וַיֵּבְךְּ עֲלֵהֶם
16 וְאַחֲרֵי כֵן דִּבְּרוּ אֶחָיו אִתּוֹ׃ וְהַקֹּל נִשְׁמַע בֵּית פַּרְעֹה
לֵאמֹר בָּאוּ אֲחֵי יוֹסֵף וַיִּיטַב בְּעֵינֵי פַרְעֹה וּבְעֵינֵי עֲבָדָיו׃
17 וַיֹּאמֶר פַּרְעֹה אֶל־יוֹסֵף אֱמֹר אֶל־אַחֶיךָ זֹאת עֲשׂוּ טַעֲנוּ
18 אֶת־בְּעִירְכֶם וּלְכוּ־בֹאוּ אַרְצָה כְּנָעַן׃ וּקְחוּ אֶת־אֲבִיכֶם
וְאֶת־בָּתֵּיכֶם וּבֹאוּ אֵלָי וְאֶתְּנָה לָכֶם אֶת־טוּב אֶרֶץ מִצְרַיִם
19 וְאִכְלוּ אֶת־חֵלֶב הָאָרֶץ׃ וְאַתָּה צֻוֵּיתָה זֹאת עֲשׂוּ קְחוּ־
לָכֶם מֵאֶרֶץ מִצְרַיִם עֲגָלוֹת לְטַפְּכֶם וְלִנְשֵׁיכֶם וּנְשָׂאתֶם
20 אֶת־אֲבִיכֶם וּבָאתֶם׃ וְעֵינְכֶם אַל־תָּחֹס עַל־כְּלֵיכֶם כִּי־
21 טוּב כָּל־אֶרֶץ מִצְרַיִם לָכֶם הוּא׃ וַיַּעֲשׂוּ־כֵן בְּנֵי יִשְׂרָאֵל
וַיִּתֵּן לָהֶם יוֹסֵף עֲגָלוֹת עַל־פִּי פַרְעֹה וַיִּתֵּן לָהֶם צֵדָה
22 לַדָּרֶךְ׃ לְכֻלָּם נָתַן לָאִישׁ חֲלִפוֹת שְׂמָלֹת וּלְבִנְיָמִן נָתַן
23 שְׁלֹשׁ מֵאוֹת כֶּסֶף וְחָמֵשׁ חֲלִפֹת שְׂמָלֹת׃ וּלְאָבִיו שָׁלַח

asses bearing the good
things of Egypt, and ten
she-asses bearing grain,
and bread, and food for his
father for the way. [24]And he
sent his brothers away; and
they went. And he said to
them, Do not quarrel along
the way. [25]And they went
up from Egypt and came
into the land of Canaan, to
their father Jacob. [26]And
they told him, saying,
Joseph *is* still alive, and he
is ruler in all the land of
Egypt. And his heart froze
up, for he did not believe
them. [27]And they spoke to
him all Joseph's words
which he had spoken to
them. And he saw the
wagons that Joseph had
sent to carry him; and the
spirit of their father Jacob
revived. [28]And Israel said, *It*
is enough! My son Joseph
is alive; I will go and see
him before I die.

860 6235 4714 2898 5375 2543 6235 2063
כזאת עשרה חמרים נשאים מטוב מצרים ועשר אתנת
she-asses ten and ,Egypt good the of things bearing asses ten :this

251 7971 1870 1 4202 3899 1250 5375
24 נשאת בר ולחם ומזון לאביו לדרך: וישלח את־אחיו
his brothers he And sent the for .way his for father and food and ,bread ,grain bearing

4714 5927 1870 7264 3808 559 3212
25 וילכו ויאמר אלהם אל־תרגזו בדרך: ויעלו ממצרים
from Egypt they And up went along .way the Do tremble not ,them to he and said and ,went they

5750 559 5046 1 3290 3667 776
26 ויבאו ארץ כנען אל־יעקב אביהם: ויגדו לו לאמר עוד
(is) still ,saying him And told they their .father Jacob to Canaan the of land came and (to)

3808 3820 6313 4714 776 3605 4910 2416 3127
יוסף חי וכי־הוא משל בכל־ארץ מצרים ויפג לבו כי לא־
not for his ,heart And froze .Egypt the all in of land ruler he and (is) ,alive Joseph

1696 834 3127 1697 3605 1696 539
27 האמין להם: וידברו אליו את כל־דברי יוסף אשר דבר
had he spoken which Joseph the of words all to him they And spoke .them did he believe

5375 3127 7971 834 5699 7200 2421
אלהם וירא את־העגלות אשר־שלח יוסף לשאת אתו
;him carry to Joseph sent had which wagons the he and saw to them

3127 5750 7227 3478 559 1 3290 7307 2421
28 ותחי רוח יעקב אביהם: ויאמר ישראל רב עוד־יוסף
Joseph (is) still (is It) !enough ,Israel said And their father's Jacob's spirit and revived

4191 2962 7200 3212 2416 1121
בני חי אלכה ואראנו בטרם אמות:
.die I before see and him will I go ;alive my son

CAP. XLVI מו

CHAPTER 46

CHAPTER 46

[1]And Israel and all be-
longing to him departed,
and he came to Beer-sheba.
And he sacrificed sacrifices
to the God of his father
Isaac. [2]And God said to
Israel in visions of the night,
and He spoke, Jacob!
Jacob! And he answered, I
am here. [3]And He said, I
am God, the God of your
fathers. Do not fear to go
down into Egypt, for I will
make of you a great nation
there. [4]I will go down with
you into Egypt, and I will
also surely return you. And
Joseph shall put his hand
on your eyes.
[5]And Jacob rose up from
Beer-sheba; and the sons of
Israel carried their father
Jacob, and their little ones,

2077 2076 =884= 935 834 3605 3475 5265
1 ויסע ישראל וכל־אשר־לו ויבא בארה שבע ויזבח זבחים
sacrifices he and offered ;sheba Beer- to he and came to belonging ,him and all Israel And departed

4759 3478 430 559 3327 1 430
2 לאלהי אביו יצחק: ויאמר אלהים ׀ לישראל במראת
in of visions Israel to God said And .Isaac , his father the to of God

559 6030 3290 3290 559 3915
3 הלילה ויאמר יעקב ׀ יעקב ויאמר הנני: ויאמר אנכי
I am He And said (am) I here he and ,answered !Jacob !Jacob He and ,spoke the ,night

1419 1471 4714 3381 3372 3808 1 430 410
האל אלהי אביך אל־תירא מרדה מצרימה כי־לגוי גדול
great a nation for ,Egypt into go to down do fear not your ;fathers God the of ,God

5927 4714 3381 8033 7760
4 אשימך שם: אנכי ארד עמך מצרימה ואנכי אעלך
will I you return ,I and ,Egypt into with you will down go I .there will I you of make

875 3290 6965 5869 7896 3127 5927
5 גם־עלה ויוסף ישית ידו על־עיניך: ויקם יעקב מבאר
from -Beer Jacob And arose your upon .eyes his hand will put and Joseph ;surely also

2945 3290 3478 1121 5375 7614
שבע וישאו בני־ישראל את־יעקב אביהם ואת־טפם
their ,ones little and their father Jacob Israel the of sons up lifted and sheba

and their wives in the
wagons which Pharaoh had
sent to carry him. 6And they
took their livestock and
their property which they
had acquired in the land of
Canaan. And they came into
Egypt, Jacob and all his
seed with him. 7His sons
and the sons of his sons
were with him, his
daughters and his sons'
daughters, and all his seed
he brought with him into
Egypt.
8And these *were* the
names of the sons of Israel,
those coming into Egypt,
Jacob and his sons: the
firstborn of Jacob *was*
Reuben. 9And the sons of
Reuben: Hanoch, and Phal-
lu, and Hezron, and Carmi.
10And the sons of Simeon:
Jemuel, and Jamin, and
Ohad, and Jachin, and
Zohar, and Shaul, the son of
a Canaanitess. 11And the
sons of Levi: Gershon,
Kohath, and Merari. 12And
the sons of Judah: Er, and
Onan, and Shelah, and
Pharez, and Zerah. And Er
and Onan died in the land of
Canaan. And the sons of
Pharez: Hezron, and Hamul.
13And the sons of Issachar:
Tola, and Phuvah, and Job,
and Shimron. 14And the
sons of Zebulun: Sered, and
Elon, and Jahleel. 15These
were the sons of Leah,
whom she bore to Jacob in
Padan-aram, and his
daughter Dinah. All the
souls of his sons and his
daughters *were* thirty-three.
16And the sons of Gad:
Ziphion, and Haggi, Shuni,
and Ezbon, Eri, and Arodi,
and Areli. 17And the sons of
Asher: Jimnah, and Ishuah,
and Isui, and Beriah, and
their sister Serah. And the
sons of Beriah: Heber and
Malchiel. 18These *were* the
sons of Zilpah, whom
Laban gave to his daughter
Leah; and she bore these to
Jacob, sixteen souls. 19The
sons of Rachel the wife of
Jacob: Joseph and Benja-
min. 20And Manasseh and
Ephraim were born to

5375 6547 7971 834 5699 802
ואת־נשיהם בעגלות אשר־שלח פרעה לשאת אתו׃
.him carry to Pharaoh sent had which the in their and
wagons wives
3667 776 7408 834 7339 46,35 3947
6 ויקחו את־מקניהם ואת־רכושם אשר רכשו בארץ כנען
;Canaan the in they which their and their they And
of land gained property ,livestock took
1121 1121 2233/3290 4714/935
7 ויבאו מצרימה יעקב וכל־זרעו אתו׃ בניו ובני בניו אתו
with his and His with his and Jacob ,Egypt they and
,him sons of sons sons .him seed all entered
4714 935 2133 3605 1121 1323 1323
בנתיו ובנות בניו וכל־זרעו הביא אתו מצרימה׃
.Egypt to with he his and his and his
him brought seed all ,son's daughters daughters
1121 3290 4714 935 3478 1121 8034
8 ואלה שמות בני־ישראל הבאים מצרימה יעקב ובניו
his and Jacob ,Egypt to those ,Israel the the these And
:sons coming of sons of names (were)
3756 2696 6396 2585 7205 1121 7205 3290 1060
9 בכר יעקב ראובן׃ ובני ראובן חנוך ופלוא וחצרון וכרמי׃
and and and ,Hanoch :Reuben And (was) Jacob the
.Carmi Hezron Phallu of sons the Reuben of firstborn
1121 7586 6774 3199 161 3226 3223 8095 1121
10 ובני שמעון ימואל וימין ואהד ויכין וצחר ושאול בן־
the and and and and and ,Jemuel :Simeon And
of sons Shaul ,Zohar ,Jachin ,Ohad ,Jamin of sons the
6147 3063 1121 4841 6955 1648 3878/1121 3669
11 הכנענית׃ ובני לוי גרשון קהת ומררי׃ ובני יהודה ער
12 ,Er :Judah the And .Merari and Kohath, Gershon :Levi And woman a
of sons of sons the .Canaan of
1121 1961 3667 776 204/6167/4191 2226 6557 204
ואונן ושלה ופרץ וזרח וימת ער ואונן בארץ כנען ויהיו בני־
the and ;Canaan the in and Er and and and and
of sons were of land Onan died ;Zarah Pharez Shelah ,Onan
8110 3102 6312 8439 3485 1121 2538 2696 6557
13 פרץ חצרן וחמול׃ ובני יששכר תולע ופוה ויוב ושמרן׃
and and and ,Tola :Issachar the And and Pharez
.Shimron ,Job ,Phuvah of sons .Hamul Hezron
3205 3812 1121 3177 440 5620 2074 1121
14 ובני זבלון סרד ואלון ויחלאל׃ אלה בני לאה אשר ילדה
15 she whom ,Leah the These and and ,Sered the And
bore of sons (were) Jahleel Elon :Zebulun of sons
1323 1121 5315 1323 1783 6307 3290
ליעקב בפדן ארם ואת דינה בתו כל־נפש בניו ובנתיו
his and his the all his Dinah and .aram Padan- in to
daughters sons of souls ;daughter Jacob
6179 675 7764 2291 6837 1410 1121 7969 7970
16 שלשים ושלש׃ ובני גד צפיון וחגי שוני ואצבן ערי
,Eri ,Ezbon and ,Shuni and ,Ziphion :Gad And three (were)
,Haggi of sons the thirty-
1283 3449 3438 3232 836 1121 692 722
17 וארודי ואראלי׃ ובני אשר ימנה וישוה וישוי ובריעה
and and and ,Jimnah :Asher And .Areli and and
,Beriah ,Isui ,Ishuah of sons the ,Arodi
2153 1121 4439 2268 1283 1121 269 8294
18 ושרח אחתם ובני בריעה חבר ומלכיאל׃ אלה בני זלפה
,Zilpah the These .Malchiel and Heber ,Beriah and their and
of sons (were) of sons the ;sister Serah
8337 3290 3205 1323 3812 3837 5414
אשר־נתן לבן ללאה בתו ותלד את־אלה ליעקב שש
six- ,Jacob to these and his Leah to Laban gave whom
bore she daughter
3205 1144 3127 3290 802 7354 1121 5315 6240
19 עשרה נפש׃ בני רחל אשת יעקב יוסף ובנימן׃ ויולד
20 And and Joseph ,Jacob the Rachel The .souls ten (and)
born were .Benjamin of wife of sons

Joseph in the land of Egypt, whom Asenath the daughter of Poti-phera, priest of On, bore to him. [21]And the sons of Benjamin: Belah, and Becher, and Ashbel, Gera, and Naaman, Ehi, and Rosh, and Muppim, and Huppim, and Ard. [22]These *were* the sons of Rachel which were born to Jacob; all the souls *were* fourteen.

[23]And the son of Dan *was* Hushim. [24]And the sons of Naphtali: Jahzeel, and Guni, and Jezer, and Shillem. [25]These *were* the sons of Bilhah, whom Laban gave to his daughter Rachel; and she bore these to Jacob, all the souls *were* seven. [26]All the souls belonging to Jacob coming into Egypt, those springing from his loins, besides the wives of the sons of Jacob, all the souls *were* sixty-six. [27]And the sons of Joseph which were born to him in Egypt, two souls. All the souls belonging to the house of Jacob coming into Egypt *were* seventy.

[28]And he sent Judah before him to Joseph, to give directions before him to Goshen; and they came into the land of Goshen. [29]And Joseph prepared his chariot and went up to meet his father Israel to Goshen. And he appeared to him, and fell on his neck and wept on his neck a long time. [30]And Israel said to Joseph, This time let me die after seeing your face, because you *are* still alive. [31]And Joseph said to his brothers, and to the house of his father, I will go up and tell Pharaoh. And I will say to him, My brothers and the house of my father, who *were* in the land of Canaan, have come in to me. [32]And the men *are* shepherds of flocks, for they have been

6319 1323 621 3205 4714 776 3127
לְיוֹסֵף בְּאֶרֶץ מִצְרַיִם אֲשֶׁר יָלְדָה־לּוֹ אָסְנַת בַּת־פּוֹטִי פֶרַע
Poti- the Asenath to bore whom Egypt the in to
.phera of daughter him of land Joseph
1071 1106 1144 1121 669 4519 204 3548
21 כֹּהֵן אֹן אֶת־מְנַשֶּׁה וְאֶת־אֶפְרָיִם׃ וּבְנֵי בִנְיָמִן בֶּלַע וָבֶכֶר
and ,Belah :Benjamin And .Ephraim and Manasseh ,On priest
,Becher of sons the of
714 2650 4649 7220 278 5283 1617 788
22 וְאַשְׁבֵּל גֵּרָא וְנַעֲמָן אֵחִי וָרֹאשׁ מֻפִּים וְחֻפִּים וָאָרְדְּ׃ אֵלֶּה
These and and ,Muppim and ,Ehi and ,Gera and
(were) ,Ard ,Huppim ,Rosh ,Naaman Ashbel
6240 702 5315 3605 3290 3205 834 7354 1121
בְּנֵי רָחֵל אֲשֶׁר יֻלַּד לְיַעֲקֹב כָּל־נֶפֶשׁ אַרְבָּעָה עָשָׂר׃
.teen (were) the all . to were which ,Rachel the
four- souls ;Jacob born of sons
8006 3337 1476 3183 5320 1121 2366 1835 1121
23 וּבְנֵי־דָן חֻשִׁים׃ וּבְנֵי נַפְתָּלִי יַחְצְאֵל וְגוּנִי וְיֵצֶר וְשִׁלֵּם׃
24
and and and ,Jahzeel :Naphtali the And .Hushim :Dan And
.Shillem ,Jezer ,Guni of sons 1090 of sons the
3205 7354 38 37 5414 1121
25 אֵלֶּה בְּנֵי בִלְהָה אֲשֶׁר־נָתַן לָבָן לְרָחֵל בִּתּוֹ וַתֵּלֶד אֶת־
she and his to Laban gave whom ,Bilhah the These
bore daughter Rachel 5315 3605 of sons (were)
3290 935 5315 3605 7651 3290
26 אֵלֶּה לְיַעֲקֹב כָּל־נֶפֶשׁ שִׁבְעָה׃ כָּל־הַנֶּפֶשׁ הַבָּאָה לְיַעֲקֹב
with coming the All (were) the all to these
Jacob in souls seven souls Jacob
8346 5315 3605 3290 1121 802 3409 5927 4714
מִצְרַיְמָה יֹצְאֵי יְרֵכוֹ מִלְּבַד נְשֵׁי בְנֵי־יַעֲקֹב כָּל־נֶפֶשׁ שִׁשִּׁים
(were) the all ,Jacob's sons the besides his those to
sixty- souls 5315 4714 of wives loins from going Egypt
3605 8147 3205 834 3127 1121 8337
27 וָשֵׁשׁ׃ וּבְנֵי יוֹסֵף אֲשֶׁר־יֻלַּד־לוֹ בְמִצְרַיִם נֶפֶשׁ שְׁנָיִם כָּל־
all ;two souls in to were which Joseph's And .six
Egypt him born sons
7657 4714 935 3290 1004 5315
28 הַנֶּפֶשׁ לְבֵית־יַעֲקֹב הַבָּאָה מִצְרַיְמָה שִׁבְעִים׃ ס וְאֶת־
And (were) ,Egypt going ,Jacob belonging the
seventy into of house the to souls
935 1657 6440 3384 3127 6440 7971 3063
יְהוּדָה שָׁלַח לְפָנָיו אֶל־יוֹסֵף לְהוֹרֹת לְפָנָיו גֹּשְׁנָה וַיָּבֹאוּ
they and to before give to ,Joseph to before he Judah
into came ;Goshen him directions him sent
3478 7125 5927 4818 3127 631 1657 776
29 אַרְצָה גֹּשֶׁן׃ וַיֶּאְסֹר יוֹסֵף מֶרְכַּבְתּוֹ וַיַּעַל לִקְרַאת־יִשְׂרָאֵל
Israel meet to and his Joseph And .Goshen the
went chariot prepared of land
6677 5921 1058 6677 5921 5307 7200 1657 1
אָבִיו גֹּשְׁנָה וַיֵּרָא אֵלָיו וַיִּפֹּל עַל־צַוָּארָיו וַיֵּבְךְּ עַל־צַוָּארָיו
his upon and his on and to he And to his
neck wept neck fell he him appeared ;Goshen ,father
7200 310 6471 4191 3127 3478 559 5750
30 עוֹד׃ וַיֹּאמֶר יִשְׂרָאֵל אֶל־יוֹסֵף אָמוּתָה הַפָּעַם אַחֲרֵי רְאוֹתִי
seeing after this me Let ,Joseph to Israel And long a
time die said .time
1004 251 3127 559 2416 5750 6440
31 אֶת־פָּנֶיךָ כִּי עוֹדְךָ חָי׃ וַיֹּאמֶר יוֹסֵף אֶל־אֶחָיו וְאֶל־בֵּית
house and his to Joseph said And .alive you for ,face your
to ,brothers yet (are)
1 1004 251 559 6547 5046 5927 1
אָבִיו אֶעֱלֶה וְאַגִּידָה לְפַרְעֹה וְאֹמְרָה אֵלָיו אַחַי וּבֵית־אָבִי
my and My ,him to I and to tell and will I his
,father's house brothers say will .Pharaoh go ,father's
502 6629 7462 582 935 776
32 אֲשֶׁר בְּאֶרֶץ־כְּנַעַן בָּאוּ אֵלָי׃ וְהָאֲנָשִׁים רֹעֵי צֹאן כִּי־אַנְשֵׁי
men for ,flocks shepherds And to have ,Canaan the in who
of of (are) men the .me come of land (were)

men of livestock. And their flocks and their herds, and all which belongs to them they have brought in. [33]And it shall be, when Pharaoh calls to you and says, What *is* your occupation? [34]You shall say, Your servants have been men of livestock from our youth even until now, both we and our fathers. *This is* so that you may live in the land of Goshen. For the abomination of Egypt *is* every shepherd of flocks.

1961 935 834 3605 1241 6629 1961 4135
33 מִקְנֶה הָיוּ וְצֹאנָם וּבְקָרָם וְכָל־אֲשֶׁר לָהֶם הֵבִיאוּ׃ וְהָיָה
it And have they to which and their and and they cattle
be shall brought them (is) all herds flocks their ;been have

559 4039 559 6547 7121
34 כִּֽי־יִקְרָא לָכֶם פַּרְעֹה וְאָמַר מַה־מַּעֲשֵׂיכֶם׃ וַאֲמַרְתֶּם
you and your What and Pharaoh to calls when
,say shall ?occupation (is) ,says you

1571 6258 5704 5271 5650 1801 4735 582
אַנְשֵׁי מִקְנֶה הָיוּ עֲבָדֶיךָ מִנְּעוּרֵינוּ וְעַד־עַתָּה גַּם־אֲנַחְנוּ גַּם־
and we both ,now and our from Your have cattle men
until youth servants been of

3605 4714 8441 1657 776 3427 1
אֲבֹתֵינוּ בַּעֲבוּר תֵּשְׁבוּ בְּאֶרֶץ גֹּשֶׁן כִּֽי־תוֹעֲבַת מִצְרַיִם כָּל־
(is) Egypt abomi- the for ;Goshen the in you that so our
every of nation of land live may ;fathers

6629 7462
רֹעֵה צֹאן׃
.flocks shep-
of herd

CAP. XLVII מז

CHAPTER 47

CHAPTER 47

[1]And Joseph came in and made known to Pharaoh, and said, My father and my brothers, and their flocks and their herds, and all which *is* theirs, have come in from the land of Canaan. [2]And, behold, they (are) in the land of Goshen. And he took five men from among his brothers and set them before Pharaoh. [3]And Pharaoh said to his brothers, What *is* your occupation? And they said to Pharaoh, Your servants *are* shepherds of flocks, both we and our fathers. [4]And they said to Pharaoh, We have come in to stay in the land, because *there* is no pasture for the flocks which belong to your servants, for the famine is heavy in the land of Canaan. And now please, let your servants live in the land of Goshen. [5]And Pharaoh spoke to Joseph, saying, Your father and your brothers have come in to you. [6]The land of Egypt is before you; cause your father and your brothers to live in the best of the land; let them live in the land of Goshen. And if you know men of ability are among them, make them chiefs of livestock over what *is* mine.

1241 6629 251 1 559 6547 5046 3127 935
1 וַיָּבֹא יוֹסֵף וַיַּגֵּד לְפַרְעֹה וַיֹּאמֶר אָבִי וְאַחַי וְצֹאנָם וּבְקָרָם
their and their my and My and ,Pharaoh and Joseph And
,herds ,flocks ,brothers father ,said told came

7097 1657 776 2009 3667 776 935 834 3605
2 וְכָל־אֲשֶׁר לָהֶם בָּאוּ מֵאֶרֶץ כְּנָעַן וְהִנָּם בְּאֶרֶץ גֹּשֶׁן׃ וּמִקְצֵה
And .Goshen the in ,lo ,And .Canaan from have to which and
from of land (are they) of land the come them (is) all

559 6547 6440 3381 582 2568 3947 251
3 אֶחָיו לָקַח חֲמִשָּׁה אֲנָשִׁים וַיַּצִּגֵם לִפְנֵי פַרְעֹה׃ וַיֹּאמֶר
said And .Pharaoh before set and men five he his
them took brothers

7462 6547 559 4639 251 6547
פַּרְעֹה אֶל־אֶחָיו מַה־מַּעֲשֵׂיכֶם וַיֹּאמְרוּ אֶל־פַּרְעֹה רֹעֵה
(are) ,Pharaoh to they and your What his to Pharaoh
of shepherds said ?occupation (is) ,brothers

6547 559 1 1571 1571 5650 6629
4 צֹאן עֲבָדֶיךָ גַּם־אֲנַחְנוּ גַּם־אֲבוֹתֵינוּ׃ וַיֹּאמְרוּ אֶל־פַּרְעֹה
.Pharaoh to they And our and we both Your flocks
said .fathers ,servants

5650 834 6629 4829 369 935 776 1481
לָגוּר בָּאָרֶץ בָּאנוּ כִּי־אֵין מִרְעֶה לַצֹּאן אֲשֶׁר לַעֲבָדֶיךָ כִּֽי־
for your to which the for pasture no for have we the in To
,servants (are) flocks (left is) come land stay

776 5650 4994 3427 6258 3067 776 7458 3515
כָבֵד הָרָעָב בְּאֶרֶץ כְּנָעַן וְעַתָּה יֵשְׁבוּ־נָא עֲבָדֶיךָ בְּאֶרֶץ
the in your please let and ;Canaan the in the is
of land servants live now of land famine heavy

935 251 1 559 3127 6547 559 1657
5 גֹּשֶׁן׃ וַיֹּאמֶר פַּרְעֹה אֶל־יוֹסֵף לֵאמֹר אָבִיךָ וְאַחֶיךָ בָּאוּ
have your and Your ,saying Joseph to Pharaoh And .Goshen
come brothers father spoke

3427 776 4315 6440 4714 776
6 אֵלֶיךָ׃ אֶרֶץ מִצְרַיִם לְפָנֶיךָ הִוא בְּמֵיטַב הָאָרֶץ הוֹשֵׁב
cause the the in (is) it before Egypt The .you to
live to land of best ;you of land

3045 1657 776 3427 251 1
אֶת־אָבִיךָ וְאֶת־אַחֶיךָ יֵשְׁבוּ בְּאֶרֶץ גֹּשֶׁן וְאִם־יָדַעְתָּ וְיֶשׁ־
there you and ,Goshen the in them let your and your
are know if of land live ;brothers father

935 834 5921 4735 8269 7760 2428/582
7 בָּם אַנְשֵׁי־חַיִל וְשַׂמְתָּם שָׂרֵי מִקְנֶה עַל־אֲשֶׁר־לִי׃ וַיָּבֵא
And to what over livestock chiefs make ,men able among
in brought .me belongs of them them

[7]And Joseph brought in his father Jacob and placed him before Pharaoh. And Jacob blessed Pharaoh. [8]And Pharaoh said to Jacob, How many are the days of the years of your life? [9]And Jacob said to Pharaoh, The days of the years of my camps *are* a hundred and thirty years. Few and evil have been the days of the years of my life, and they have not reached the days of the years of the life of my fathers, in the days of their camps. [10]And Jacob blessed Pharaoh, and went out from before Pharaoh. [11]And Joseph caused his father and his brothers to live, and gave them a place in the land of Egypt, in the best of the land, in the land of Rameses, as Pharaoh commanded. [12]And Joseph nourished his father and his brothers, and all his father's house *with* bread for the mouth of the little ones.

[13]And no bread was in the land, because the famine was exceedingly severe. And the land of Egypt and the land of Canaan were exhausted from the famine. [14]And Joseph gathered up all the money found in the land of Egypt and in the land of Canaan in return for the grain they *were* buying. And Joseph brought in the money to the house of Pharaoh. [15]And the money failed from the land of Egypt, and from the land of Canaan. And all Egypt came in to Joseph, saying, Give us bread; and, Why should we die before you? For the money has failed. [16]And Joseph said, Give your livestock, and I will give to you for your livestock, if money has failed. [17]And they brought in their livestock to Joseph. And Joseph gave bread to them for the horses, and for the livestock of the flocks, for

3290 1288 6547 6440 5975 1 3290 3127
יוסף את־יעקב אביו ויעמדהו לפני פרעה ויברך יעקב
Jacob and blessed ;Pharaoh before placed and him his ,father Jacob Joseph

2416 8141 3117 4100 3290 6547 559 6547
8 את־פרעה׃ ויאמר פרעה אל־יעקב כמה ימי שני חייך׃
your ?life at- tained of the days How many Jacob to Pharaoh said And .Pharaoh

3967 7910 1033 8141 3117 6547 3290 559
9 ויאמר יעקב אל־פרעה ימי שני מגורי שלשים ומאת
a and hundred (are) thirty my camps the days of years The ,Pharaoh to Jacob said And

8141/3117 5381 2416/8141 3117/1961/1451 4592 8141
שנה מעט ורעים היו ימי שני חיי ולא השיגו את־ימי שני
the days of years the have reached they not and my life the days of years the have been and evil few ,years

5927 6547 3290 1288 4033 3117 1 2416
10 חיי אבתי בימי מגוריהם׃ ויברך יעקב את־פרעה ויצא
and left ,Pharaoh Jacob And blessed their camps the in of days my fathers the of life

5414 251 1 3127 3427 6547 6440
11 מלפני פרעה׃ ויושב יוסף את־אביו ואת־אחיו ויתן להם
them and gave his brothers and his father Joseph caused And live to .Pharaoh from before

7486 776 776 4315 4714 776 272
אחזה בארץ מצרים במיטב הארץ בארץ רעמסס כאשר
as ,Ramses the in of land the ,land the in of best ,Egypt the in of land a place

3605 251 1 3127 3557 6547 6680
12 צוה פרעה׃ ויכלכל יוסף את־אביו ואת־אחיו ואת כל־
all and his brothers and his father Joseph And nourished .Pharaoh di- rected

776 3605 369 38 99 2945 6310 3899 1 1004
13 בית אביו לחם לפי הטף׃ ולחם אין בכל־הארץ כי־
for the ,land all in was not And bread .ones little the of mouth for (with) bread his father's house

3667 776 4714 776 3856 3966 7458 3515
כבד הרעב מאד ותלה ארץ מצרים וארץ כנען מפני
from Canaan the and of land Egypt the of land and languished much the famine was severe

4714 776 4672 3701 3127 3950 7458
14 הרעב׃ וילקט יוסף את־כל־הכסף הנמצא בארץ־מצרים
Egypt the in of land found silver the all Joseph And gathered the .famine

3127 935 7666 834 7668 3667 776
ובארץ כנען בשבר אשר־הם שברים ויבא יוסף את־
Joseph and brought ;buying they (were) which the for grain Canaan in and of land the

776 4714 776 3701 8552 6547 1004 3701
15 הכסף ביתה פרעה׃ ויתם הכסף מארץ מצרים ומארץ
from and of land the ,Egypt the from of land the silver And failed .Pharaoh the to of house the silver

3899 3053 559 3127 4714 935 3667
כנען ויבאו כל־מצרים אל־יוסף לאמר הבה־לנו לחם
.bread us Give ,saying Joseph to Egypt all and came in ;Canaan

4735 3053 3127 559 3701 656 4191 4100
16 ולמה נמות נגדך כי אפס כסף׃ ויאמר יוסף הבו מקניכם
your ,livestock Give ,Joseph And said the money has failed For before ?you should we die and why

4735 935 3701 656 4735 5414
17 ואתנה לכם במקניכם אם־אפס כסף׃ ויביאו את־מקניהם
their livestock they brought And the silver has failed if your ,livestock for you to give will I and

6629 4735 5488 3899 3127 5414 3127
אל־יוסף ויתן להם יוסף לחם בסוסים ובמקנה הצאן
the ,flocks of livestock the for ,horses the for bread Joseph to them and gave ;Joseph to

the livestock of the herds, and for the asses. And he satisfied them with bread in that year for all their livestock. 18And that year ended. And they came in to him in the second year and said to him, We cannot hide from my lord *that* the silver and the herds of the animals have failed, *going* to my lord. Nothing is left before my lord except our bodies and our lands. 19Why should we die before your eyes, both we and also our land? Buy us and our land for bread, and let us, we and our land, become slaves to Pharaoh. And give seed so that we may live and not die, and the land not be waste.

20And Joseph bought all the land of Egypt for Pharaoh, because each one in Egypt sold his field, because this famine was severe on them; and the lands became Pharaoh's. 21And *as for* the people, he caused them to pass over into the cities, and from the end of the border of Egypt to its *other* end. 22Only he did not buy the land of the priests; for Pharaoh had appointed a portion for the priests, and they usually ate their appointed portion which Pharaoh gave to them. For this reason they did not sell their land. 23And Joseph said to the people, Behold, I have bought you and your land today. See, *here is* seed for you; and you sow the land. 24And it shall be, as you gather you shall give a fifth part to Pharaoh; and four parts shall be yours, for the seed of the field and for your food, and for those in your houses, and for food for your little ones. 25And they said, You have saved

במקנה הבקר ובחמרים וינהלם בלחם בכל־מקנהם
their livestock | all for | with bread | he and them satisfied | for and ;asses the | the ,herds | the for of livestock

18 בשנה ההוא: ותתם השנה ההוא ויבאו אליו בשנה
the in year | to him | they and came | that | year | And ended | .that | year in

השנית ויאמרו לו לא־נכחד מאדני כי אם־תם הכסף
the silver | has failed | that | my from lord | We conceal | not to ,him | said and | ,second

ומקנה הבהמה אל־אדני לא נשאר לפני אדני בלתי אם־
except | my lord | before | left is nothing | my (going) ;lord | the to beasts | the and of herds

19 גויתנו ואדמתנו: למה נמות לעיניך גם־אנחנו גם־אדמתנו
our ?land | and also | we both | before ,eyes your | should die we | Why | our and .lands | our bodies

קנה־אתנו ואת־אדמתנו בלחם ונהיה אנחנו ואדמתנו
our and ,land | we | let and ,become us | for ;bread | our land | and | us | Buy

עבדים לפרעה ותן־זרע ונחיה ולא נמות והאדמה לא
not | the and land | ,die | and not | we that live may | seed and give | to ;Pharaoh | slaves

20 תשם: ויקן יוסף את־כל־אדמת מצרים לפרעה כי־מכרו
sold | because | for ,Pharaoh | Egypt | the of land | all | Joseph | And bought | be .waste

מצרים איש שדהו כי־חזק עלהם הרעב ותהי הארץ
the land | and became | (this) ;famine | upon them | was for severe | his ,field | each one | the Egyptians

21 לפרעה: ואת־העם העביר אתו לערים מקצה גבול־
the of border | the from of end | the into ,cities | them | made he go | the people | And | .Pharaoh's

22 מצרים ועד־קצהו: רק אדמת הכהנים לא קנה כי חק
a portion | for ;buy | he did | not | priests the | the of land | Only | its .end | to (other) | Egypt

לכהנים מאת פרעה ואכלו את־חקם אשר נתן להם
to them | gave | which | set their portion | they and ate | ,Pharaoh | from | the for priests

23 פרעה על־כן לא מכרו את־אדמתם: ויאמר יוסף אל־
to | Joseph | said And | land their | they did not sell therefore | ;Pharaoh

העם הן קניתי אתכם היום ואת־אדמתכם לפרעה הא־
,see | for ;Pharaoh | land your | and | today | you | have I bought | ,See | the ,people

24 לכם זרע וזרעתם את־האדמה: והיה בתבואת ונתתם
shall you give | every in harvest | it And ,be shall | the .land | you and sow | ;seed | for you

חמישית לפרעה וארבע הידת יהיה לכם לזרע השדה
the field | the for of seed | ,yours | shall be | parts | and four | to ;Pharaoh | fifth a (part)

25 ולאכלכם ולאשר בבתיכם ולאכל לטפכם: ויאמרו
they And ,said | your for .ones little | for and food | your in ,houses | for and those | for and ,food your

our lives; let us find favor in the eyes of my lord, and we will become slaves to Pharaoh. 26 And Joseph made it a law until this day on the land of Egypt, the fifth *part is* for Pharaoh; only the land of the priests *being* excepted; it did not become Pharaoh's.

27 And Israel lived in the land of Egypt, in the land of Goshen. And they owned in it, and were fruitful, and multiplied exceedingly.

6547 5650 1961 113 5869 2580/4672 2421
הֶחֱיִתָנוּ נִמְצָא־חֵן בְּעֵינֵי אֲדֹנִי וְהָיִינוּ עֲבָדִים לְפַרְעֹה׃
.Pharaoh to slaves we and be will my ,lord the in of eyes favor us let find have You lives our saved

4714 127 5921 2088 3167 2706 3127 7760
26 וַיָּשֶׂם אֹתָהּ יוֹסֵף לְחֹק עַד־הַיּוֹם הַזֶּה עַל־אַדְמַת מִצְרַיִם
,Egypt the of land over this day until law a Joseph it And made

1961 3808 905 3548 127 7535 2549 6547
לְפַרְעֹה לַחֹמֶשׁ רַק אַדְמַת הַכֹּהֲנִים לְבַדָּם לֹא הָיְתָה
did it become not ,excepted the priests land the of only fifth the ;(part) for (is) Pharaoh

270 1657 776 4714 776 3478 3427 6547
27 לְפַרְעֹה׃ וַיֵּשֶׁב יִשְׂרָאֵל בְּאֶרֶץ מִצְרַיִם בְּאֶרֶץ גֹּשֶׁן וַיֵּאָחֲזוּ
they and owned ;Goshen the in of land Egypt the in of land Israel And lived .Pharaoh's

3966 7235 6509
בָהּ וַיִּפְרוּ וַיִּרְבּוּ מְאֹד׃
exceedingly and multiplied were and fruitful in ,it

28 And Jacob lived in the land of Egypt seventeen years. And the days of Jacob, the years of his life *were* a hundred and forty-seven years. 29 And the days of Israel to die drew near. And he called to his son Joseph and said to him, Now if I have found favor in your eyes, please put your hand under my thigh; and do kindness and truth with me. Please do not bury me in Egypt; 30 but let me lie with my fathers, and carry me from Egypt, and bury me in their burying-place. And he said, I will do according to your words. 31 And he said, Swear to me. And he swore to him. And Israel bowed on the head of the bed.

3117 1961 8141 6240 7651 4714 776 3290 2421
28 וַיְחִי יַעֲקֹב בְּאֶרֶץ מִצְרַיִם שְׁבַע עֶשְׂרֵה שָׁנָה וַיְהִי יְמֵי־
the of days and were ;years seventeen Egypt the in of land Jacob And lived

7136 8141 3967 702 8141 7651 2416 8141 3290
29 יַעֲקֹב שְׁנֵי חַיָּיו שֶׁבַע שָׁנִים וְאַרְבָּעִים וּמְאַת שָׁנָה׃ וַיִּקְרְבוּ
drew And near .years a and hundred and forty ,years seven his life the ,Jacob of years

559 3027 1121 7121 4191 3478 3117
יְמֵי־יִשְׂרָאֵל לָמוּת וַיִּקְרָא ׀ לִבְנוֹ לְיוֹסֵף וַיֹּאמֶר לוֹ אִם־נָא
If to said and ,him ,Joseph his to son he and called ,die to Israel the of days

6213 3409 8478 3027 7760 5869 2580 4672
מָצָאתִי חֵן בְּעֵינֶיךָ שִׂים־נָא יָדְךָ תַּחַת יְרֵכִי וְעָשִׂיתָ עִמָּדִי
with me do and my thigh under your hand please put your in eyes favor have I found

1 7901 4714 6912 4994 571 2617
30 חֶסֶד וֶאֱמֶת אַל־נָא תִקְבְּרֵנִי בְּמִצְרָיִם׃ וְשָׁכַבְתִּי עִם־אֲבֹתַי
my fathers with let But lie me ,Egypt in do me bury Please not and ,truth mercy

6213 559/6900 6912 4714 5375
וּנְשָׂאתַנִי מִמִּצְרַיִם וּקְבַרְתַּנִי בִּקְבֻרָתָם וַיֹּאמַר אָנֹכִי אֶעֱשֶׂה
do will I he And ,said their in place-burying bury and me from ,Egypt carry and

3478 7812 7650 559 1697
31 כִדְבָרֶךָ׃ וַיֹּאמֶר הִשָּׁבְעָה לִי וַיִּשָּׁבַע לוֹ וַיִּשְׁתַּחוּ יִשְׂרָאֵל
Israel bowed and to ;him he and swore to ,me Swear he And ,said to according .words your

4296 7218
עַל־רֹאשׁ הַמִּטָּה׃
.bed the the of head on

CAP. XLVIII מח

CHAPTER 48

CHAPTER 48

1 And after these things it happened, one said to Joseph, Behold, your father *is* sick. And he took his two sons with him, Manasseh and Ephraim. 2 And one spoke to Jacob and said, Behold, your son Joseph has come to you. And Israel took strength and sat on the bed.

1 2009 3127 559 1697 310 1961
1 וַיְהִי אַחֲרֵי הַדְּבָרִים הָאֵלֶּה וַיֹּאמֶר לְיוֹסֵף הִנֵּה אָבִיךָ
your father ,See to ,Joseph one that said these things after it And ,was

669 4519 1121 8147 3947 2470
חֹלֶה וַיִּקַּח אֶת־שְׁנֵי בָנָיו עִמּוֹ אֶת־מְנַשֶּׁה וְאֶת־אֶפְרָיִם׃
.Ephraim and Manasseh with ,him his sons two he And took (is) .sick

2388 935 3127 1121 2009 559 3290 5046
2 וַיַּגֵּד לְיַעֲקֹב וַיֹּאמֶר הִנֵּה בִּנְךָ יוֹסֵף בָּא אֵלֶיךָ וַיִּתְחַזֵּק
took and strength ;you to has come Joseph your son ,See ,said and Jacob to And spoke one

[3]And Jacob said to Joseph, God Almighty appeared to me in Luz in the land of Canaan and blessed me, [4]and said to me, Behold, I will make you fruitful and will multiply you, and will make you a multitude of peoples. And I will give this land to your seed after you *as* a continual possession. [5]And now your two sons, those born to you in the land of Egypt before my coming to you in Egypt, *are* mine, Ephraim and Manasseh, like Reuben and Simeon, even they shall be mine. [6]And your offspring which you father after them, they shall be yours. According to the name of their brothers they shall be called in their inheritance. [7]And I, when I came from Padan, Rachel died on me in the land of Canaan in the way, with only a little way to come to Ephrath. And I buried her there in the way to Ephrath, it *being* Bethlehem.

[8]And Israel saw the sons of Joseph, and he said, Who are these? [9]And Joseph said to his father, They *are* my sons, whom God has given to me here. And he said, Now bring them to me and I will bless them. [10]And the eyes of Israel were heavy from age, he not being able to see. And he brought them near to him. And he kissed them and embraced them. [11]And Israel said to Joseph, I did not think to see your face, and, behold, God also causes me to see your seed. [12]And Joseph brought them out from his knees; and he bowed his face to the earth. [13]And Joseph took both of them, Ephraim in his right hand, to the left of Israel;

7706 410 3127 3290 559 4296 3427 3478
3 יִשְׂרָאֵל וַיֵּשֶׁב עַל־הַמִּטָּה׃ וַיֹּאמֶר יַעֲקֹב אֶל־יוֹסֵף אֵל שַׁדַּי
Al- God ,Joseph to Jacob said And .bed the upon sat and Israel
mighty

559 1288 3667 776 3870 7200
4 נִרְאָה־אֵלַי בְּלוּז בְּאֶרֶץ כְּנָעַן וַיְבָרֶךְ אֹתִי׃ וַיֹּאמֶר אֵלַי
to said and ;me and Canaan the in in to appeared
,me blessed of land Luz me

5414 5971 6951 5414 7235 6509 2009
הִנְנִי מַפְרְךָ וְהִרְבִּיתִךָ וּנְתַתִּיךָ לִקְהַל עַמִּים וְנָתַתִּי אֶת־
I and ;peoples multi- a will and will and make will ,See
give will of tude you give ,you multiply fruitful you I

8147 6258 5769 272 310 2233 2088 776
5 הָאָרֶץ הַזֹּאת לְזַרְעֲךָ אַחֲרֶיךָ אֲחֻזַּת עוֹלָם׃ וְעַתָּה שְׁנֵי־
two And .perpetual a (as) after your to this land
now possession you seed

4714 935 5704 4714 776 3205 1121
בָנֶיךָ הַנּוֹלָדִים לְךָ בְּאֶרֶץ מִצְרַיִם עַד־בֹּאִי אֵלֶיךָ מִצְרַיְמָה
.Egypt into you to my before Egypt the in to were who your
coming of land you born ,sons

4138 1961 8095 7205 4519 669
6 לִי־הֵם אֶפְרַיִם וּמְנַשֶּׁה כִּרְאוּבֵן וְשִׁמְעוֹן יִהְיוּ־לִי׃ וּמוֹלַדְתְּךָ
your And to they and like and Ephraim they to
offspring .me be shall ,Simeon Reuben ,Manasseh (are) me

7121 251 8034 5921/1961 310 3205 834
אֲשֶׁר־הוֹלַדְתָּ אַחֲרֵיהֶם לְךָ יִהְיוּ עַל שֵׁם אֲחֵיהֶם יִקָּרְאוּ
shall they their the according they to after you which
called be brothers of name to ;be shall you ,them fathered

3667 776 7354 4191 6307 935 5159
7 בְּנַחֲלָתָם׃ וַאֲנִי בְּבֹאִי מִפַּדָּן מֵתָה עָלַי רָחֵל בְּאֶרֶץ כְּנַעַן
Canaan the in Rachel on died from when And their in
of land me ,Padan came I ,I .inheritance

8033 6912 672 935 776 3530 5750 1870
בַּדֶּרֶךְ בְּעוֹד כִּבְרַת־אֶרֶץ לָבֹא אֶפְרָתָה וָאֶקְבְּרֶהָ שָּׁם
there I and to to the length a when the in
her buried ;Ephrath come land of still ,way

1121 3478 7200 3899 1004 672 1870
8 בְּדֶרֶךְ אֶפְרָת הִוא בֵּית לָחֶם׃ וַיַּרְא יִשְׂרָאֵל אֶת־בְּנֵי
the Israel And .Bethlehem it ,Ephrath the in
of sons saw (being) of way

1121 3127 559 559 3127
9 יוֹסֵף וַיֹּאמֶר מִי־אֵלֶּה׃ וַיֹּאמֶר יוֹסֵף אֶל־אָבִיו בָּנַי הֵם
They my his to Joseph said And are Who he and ,Joseph
.(are) sons ,father ?these ,said

1288 3947 559 430 5414
אֲשֶׁר־נָתַן־לִי אֱלֹהִים בָּזֶה וַיֹּאמַר קָחֶם־נָא אֵלַי וַאֲבָרְכֵם׃
will I and me to Now bring he And .here God to has whom
.them bless them ,said me given

5066 7200 3201 3808 2207 3513 3478 5869
10 וְעֵינֵי יִשְׂרָאֵל כָּבְדוּ מִזֹּקֶן לֹא יוּכַל לִרְאוֹת וַיַּגֵּשׁ אֹתָם
them he and ;see to he not from were Israel's And
brought able was ,age heavy eyes

3127 3478 559 2263 5401
11 אֵלָיו וַיִּשַּׁק לָהֶם וַיְחַבֵּק לָהֶם׃ וַיֹּאמֶר יִשְׂרָאֵל אֶל־יוֹסֵף
,Joseph to Israel said And .them and them he and to
embraced kissed ,him

1571 430 7200 2009 6419 3808 6440 7200
רְאֹה פָנֶיךָ לֹא פִלָּלְתִּי וְהִנֵּה הֶרְאָה אֹתִי אֱלֹהִים גַּם
also God me causes ,and did I not your to
see to ,behold ;expect face see

639 7812 1290 5973 3127 5927 2233
12 אֶת־זַרְעֶךָ׃ וַיּוֹצֵא יוֹסֵף אֹתָם מֵעִם בִּרְכָּיו וַיִּשְׁתַּחוּ לְאַפָּיו
his he and his from them Joseph And .seed your
face bowed ;knees brought

8040 3225 669 8147 3127 3947 776
13 אָרְצָה׃ וַיִּקַּח יוֹסֵף אֶת־שְׁנֵיהֶם אֶת־אֶפְרַיִם בִּימִינוֹ מִשְּׂמֹאל
the to his in Ephraim of both Joseph And the to
of left hand right ,them took .earth

and Manasseh in his left hand, to the right of Israel. And he brought *them* to him. 14And Israel sent forth his right hand and put it on the head of Ephraim; and he *was* the younger. And *he put* his left hand on the head of Manasseh, crossing his hands; for Manasseh *was* the firstborn. 15And he blessed Joseph and said, The God *before* whom my fathers Abraham and Isaac walked, the God who has fed me since I was born until today; 16the Angel that redeemed me from every evil, may He bless the youths; and may my name be called on them, and the name of my fathers, Abraham and Isaac; and may they like the fishes increase into a multitude in the midst of the earth.

17And Joseph saw that his father was putting his right hand on the head of Ephraim; and it was evil in his eyes. And he took hold of his father's hand to turn it from Ephraim's head to the head of Manasseh. 18And Joseph said to his father, Not so, my father! For this one *is* the firstborn; put your right hand on his head. 19And his father refused, and said, I know, my son, I know. He also shall be a people, and he shall become great. But his younger brother shall become greater than he, and his seed shall become the fullness of the nations. 20And he blessed them in that day, saying, In you shall Israel bless, saying, May God make you like Ephraim and like Manasseh. 21And Israel said to Joseph, See, I am dying; and God will be with you, and will return you to

ישראל ואת־מנשה בשמאלו מימין ישראל ויגש אליו׃
14 וישלח ישראל את־ימינו וישת על־ראש אפרים והוא
הצעיר ואת־שמאלו על־ראש מנשה שכל את־ידיו כי
15 מנשה הבכור׃ ויברך את־יוסף ויאמר האלהים אשר
התהלכו אבתי לפניו אברהם ויצחק האלהים הרעה
16 אתי מעודי עד־היום הזה׃ המלאך הגאל אתי מכל־
רע יברך את־הנערים ויקרא בהם שמי ושם אבתי
17 אברהם ויצחק וידגו לרב בקרב הארץ׃ וירא יוסף כי־
ישית אביו יד־ימינו על־ראש אפרים וירע בעיניו ויתמך
יד־אביו להסיר אתה מעל ראש־אפרים על־ראש מנשה׃
18 ויאמר יוסף אל־אביו לא־כן אבי כי־זה הבכר שים ימינך
19 על־ראשו׃ וימאן אביו ויאמר ידעתי בני ידעתי גם־הוא
יהיה־לעם וגם־הוא יגדל ואולם אחיו הקטן יגדל ממנו
20 וזרעו יהיה מלא־הגוים׃ ויברכם ביום ההוא לאמור בך
יברך ישראל לאמר ישמך אלהים כאפרים וכמנשה
21 וישם את־אפרים לפני מנשה׃ ויאמר ישראל אל־יוסף
הנה אנכי מת והיה אלהים עמכם והשיב אתכם אל־

the land of your fathers. [22]And I will give to you one spur of land beyond your brothers, which I took from the hand of the Amorite with my sword and with my bow.

CHAPTER 49

[1]And Jacob called his sons and said, Gather yourselves and I will tell you what will happen to you in the days to come. [2]Gather yourselves and hear, sons of Jacob; yea, listen to your father Israel.

[3]Reuben you *are* my firstborn, my vigor, the beginning of my power, the highest in dignity and highest *in* might. [4]Like boiling water you shall not excel; for you went up to the bed of your father; then you defiled *it* — he went up to my couch.

[5]Simeon and Levi, brothers; their weapons *are* instruments of violence. [6]Let not my soul come into their counsel; let not my spirit be joined to their company. For in their anger they killed a man; and in self-will they hamstrung a bull. [7]Cursed *be* their anger, for it *was* fierce; and their wrath, for *it was* cruel. I will divide them in Jacob, and I will scatter them in Israel.

[8]Judah, may your brothers praise you, your hand *be* on the neck of your enemies. May the sons of your father bow themselves to you. [9]Judah *is* a lion's whelp. My son, you have risen up from the prey; he stoops, he crouches like a lion; and like a lioness, who can rouse him? [10]The scepter shall not depart from Judah, nor the lawmaker from between his feet, until Shiloh come, and the obedience of the peoples to him. [11]Binding his foal to the vine, and his ass's colt to the choice vine, he washes his clothing in wine, and his covering in

22 ארץ אבתיכם: ואני נתתי לך שכם אחד על־אחיך אשר

which your beyond one spur to will I And your the
,brothers land of you give .fathers of land

לקחתי מיד האמרי בחרבי ובקשתי:

with and my with the the from took I
.bow my sword Amorite of hand

CAP. XLIX מט

CHAPTER 49

1 ויקרא יעקב אל־בניו ויאמר האספו ואגידה לכם את

you I and Gather he and his to Jacob And
tell will yourselves ,said sons called

2 אשר־יקרא אתכם באחרית הימים: הקבצו ושמעו בני

sons and Gather .days the to in you to will what
of ,hear yourselves come happen

3 יעקב ושמעו אל־ישראל אביכם: ראובן בכרי אתה כחי

my you my ,Reuben your Israel to and ;Jacob
vigor ,(are) firstborn .father listen

4 וראשית אוני יתר שאת ויתר עז: פחז כמים אל־תותר

you not ,water Like .might and dignity the my begin- the
;excel shall boiling (in) highest highest ;power of ning

כי עלית משכבי אביך אז חללת יצועי עלה:

went he my to you then your the to you for
.up couch ;(it) defiled ;father of bed up went

5 שמעון ולוי אחים כלי חמס מכרתיהם: בסדם אל־תבא
6

let not their Into their violence (are) ;brothers and Simeon
enter counsel .weapons of tools ,Levi

נפשי בקהלם אל־תחד כבדי כי באפם הרגו איש וברצנם

in and a they their in for my be let not their to my
self-will ;man killed anger ;spirit joined company ;soul

7 עקרו־שור: ארור אפם כי עז ועברתם כי קשתה אחלקם

will I ;cruel for their and it for their Cursed .ox an they
them divide (was it) wrath ;fierce (was) ,anger (be) lamed

ביעקב ואפיצם בישראל:

.Israel in will I and in
them scatter Jacob

8 יהודה אתה יודוך אחיך ידך בערף איביך ישתחוו לך

to bow will your on (be) your your shall you ,Judah
you ;enemies of neck hand ;brothers praise

9 בני אביך: גור אריה יהודה מטרף בני עלית כרע רבץ

lies he he have you my from Judah a whelp your the
down stoops ;arisen son prey the ;(is) lion's .father of sons

10 כאריה וכלביא מי יקימנו: לא־יסור שבט מיהודה ומחקק

the nor from The shall not rouse can who like and a like
lawmaker ,Judah scepter depart ?him lioness a ;lion

11 מבין רגליו עד כי־יבא שילה ולו יקהת עמים: אסרי

Binding the obedi- the and ,Shiloh comes until his from
peoples of ence him to ,feet between

לגפן עירה ולשרקה בני אתנו כבס ביין לבשו ובדם־

the in and his in he his ,colt the to and foal his the to
of bloods ,clothing wine washes ,ass's vine choice vine

the bloods of grapes. 12 His eyes shall be dark from wine, and *his* teeth white from milk.

13 Zebulun shall live at the seashore, and he shall be a haven of ships, even his border beside Sidon.

14 Issachar *is* a strong ass, crouching between the sheepfolds. 15 And he saw a resting place, that *it was good*, and that the land *was* pleasant; and he bowed his shoulder to bear, and became a tribute-slave.

16 Dan shall judge his people, as one of the tribes of Israel. 17 Let Dan be a serpent on the way, a horned snake on the path that bites the horses' heels, and its rider falls backward. 18 I have waited for your salvation, O Jehovah.

19 Gad, a marauding band shall press upon him, and he shall press on *their* heel.

20 Out of Asher his bread shall be fat, and he shall give a king's delicacies.

21 Naphtali is a deer let loose, giving one beautiful sayings.

22 Joseph *is* a fruitful son, a fruitful son by a spring; *his* branches run over a wall. 23 And the masters of arrows harass him, and shoot, and lie in ambush for him. 24 His bow abides in strength, and the hands of his arms are made agile by the hands of the Mighty One of Jacob, from the Shepherd, the Rock of Israel. 25 From the God of your father, may He help you. And may the Almighty bless you with blessings of Heaven from above, blessings of the deep that lies beneath, blessings of the breasts and womb. 26 The blessings of your father are above the blessings of my offspring, to the limit of everlasting hills; may they be for the head of Joseph, and for the crown of the leader of his brothers.

27 Benjamin is a wolf that tears. In the morning he devours the prey, and at evening he divides the spoil.

2469 8127 3836 3196 5869 2447 5497 6025
12 ענבים סותה: חכלילי עינים מיין ולבן־שנים מחלב: פ
from (his) and with his Sparkling his grapes
.milk teeth white wine eyes of .raiment

6721 3411 5912/2348 7931 3220 2348 2074
13 זבולן לחוף ימים ישכן והוא לחוף אניות וירכתו על־צידן: פ
.Sidon beside his and ,ships a for and shall sea- the at Zebulun
border of shore he live shore

4496 7200 4942 996 7257 1634 2543 3485
14 יששכר חמר גרם רבץ בין המשפתים:
15 וירא מנחה
resting a he And sheepfolds the be- lying ,strong ass an Issachar
,place saw tween down (is)

4522 1961 5445 7926 5186 5276 776 2896
כי טוב ואת־הארץ כי נעמה ויט שכמו לסבל ויהי למס
a and bear to his he and (was) that land the and ,good that
tribute- became neck bowed ;pleasant (was)

1961 3478 7626 259 5971 1777 1835 5647
16 עבד: ס דן ידין עמו כאחד שבטי ישראל:
17 יהי
shall .Israel the of one as his shall Dan .slave
be of tribes .people judge

5483 6119 5391 734/5921 8207 1870 5921 5175 1835
דן נחש עלי־דרך שפיפן עלי־ארח הנשך עקבי־סוס
the heels that path the on horned a ,way the on a Dan
horse's bites snake serpent

1464 1418 3068 6960 3444 268 7392 5307
18 ויפל רכבו אחור: לישועתך קויתי יהוה: ס
19 גד גדוד
raiders ,Gad O have I Your For .backward its and
Jehovah ,waited salvation rider falls

3899 8082 836 6119 1464 1464
20 יגודנו והוא יגד עקב: ס מאשר שמנה לחמו והוא
and his (be shall) Of (their) shall and shall
he ,food fat Asher .heel on press he ,him raid

561 5414 7971 355 5320 4428 4574 5414
21 יתן מעדני־מלך: ס נפתלי אילה שלחה הנתן אמרי־
words giving let deer a Naphtali a dainties shall
one ,loose (is) .king's give

6805 1323 5869 6509 1121 3127 6509 1121 8233
22 שפר: ס בן פרת יוסף בן פרת עלי־עין בנות צעדה
run (his) a by fruitful a Joseph fruitful a .beautiful
daughters ,spring son ,(is) son

7232 3427 2671 1167 7852 4843 7791 5921
23 עלי־שור: וימררהו ורבו וישטמהו בעלי חצים:
24 ותשב
but ;arrows man a lurk and and vex And .wall a over
abides of him for ,shoot ,him

8033 3290 47 3027 3027 2220 6339 7198 386
באיתן קשתו ויפזו זרעי ידיו מידי אביר יעקב משם
from ,Jacob Mighty the from his the and his firmly
there of One of hands hands of arms (are) agile ,bow

1288 7706 5826 1 410 3478 68 7462
25 רעה אבן ישראל: מאל אביך ויעזרך ואת שדי ויברכך
He may the and He may your the From .Israel the Shep- the
you bless Almighty ;you help ,father of God of Rock ,herd

1293 8478 7257 8415 1293 5920 8064 1293
ברכת שמים מעל ברכת תהום רבצת תחת ברכת
blessings ,beneath that deep the blessings from Heaven with
of lies of ,above of blessings

2029 1293 1396 1 1293 7356 7699
26 שדים ורחם: ברכת אביך גברו על־ברכת הורי עד־
to my blessings the are your The and the
the offspring of above father of blessings .womb breasts

251 5139 6936 3127 7218 1961 5769 1389 8379
תאות גבעת עולם תהיין לראש יוסף ולקדקד נזיר אחיו: פ
his leader the for and ,Joseph for they may ever- hills limit
.brother's of prince of pole head be lasting of

7998 2505 6053 5706 398 1242 2963 2061 1144
27 בנימין זאב יטרף בבקר יאכל עד ולערב יחלק שלל:
the he at and the he the in that a Benjamin
.spoil divides evening .prey devours morning ;tears wolf (is)

[28]All these *were* the tribes of Israel, two *and* ten. And this *is* what their father spoke to them. And he blessed them, each one *with* what *was* according to his blessing, he blessed them. [29]And he commanded them and said to them, I am about to be gathered to my people. Bury me beside my fathers, at the cave which *is* in the field of Ephron the Hittite, [30]in the cave which *is* in the field of Machpelah, which *is* before Mamre, in the land of Canaan, the field which Abraham bought from Ephron the Hittite for a burying place. [31]They buried Abraham and his wife Sarah there, and they buried Isaac and his wife Rebekah; and I buried Leah there; [32]the purchase of the field and the cave in it, from the sons of Heth. [33]And Jacob finished commanding his sons, and he gathered his feet into the bed. And he expired, and was gathered to his people.

1696 834 2088 6240 8147 3478 7626 3605
28 כל־אלה שבטי ישראל שנים עשר וזאת אשר־דבר
spoke what this and twelve ,Israel tribes the these All
(is) of 1 (were)

1288 1293 376 1288
להם אביהם ויברך אותם איש אשר כברכתו ברך
he his after whom each ,them he and their to
blessed blessing one blessed ;father them

6912 5971 622 559 6680
29 אתם: ויצו אותם ויאמר אלהם אני נאסף אל־עמי קברו
bury my to to about am I ,them to said and them he And .them
;people gathered be commanded

2850 6085 7704 834 4631 1
אתי אל־אבתי אל־המערה אשר בשדה עפרון החתי:
the Ephron the in which cave the at my beside me
;Hittite of field (is) fathers

4471 6440 834 4375 7704 4631
30 במערה אשר בשדה המכפלה אשר־על־פני ממרא
,Mamre before which ,Machpelah the in which the in
(is) of land (is) cave

6085 7704 85 7069 3667 776
בארץ כנען אשר קנה אברהם את־השדה מאת עפרן
Ephron from the Abraham bought which ;Canaan the in
,field of field

8283 85 6912 8033 6913 272 2850
31 החתי לאחזת־קבר: שמה קברו את־אברהם ואת שרה
Sarah and Abraham They there .burying a for the
buried place ,Hittite

8033 802 7259 3327 6912 8033 802
אשתו שמה קברו את־יצחק ואת רבקה אשתו ושמה
and his Rebekah and Isaac they there his
there ;wife buried ;wife

834 4631 7704 4736 3812 6912
32 קברתי את־לאה: מקנה השדה והמערה אשר־בו מאת
from it in which the and ,field the the ;Leah I
(is) cave of purchase buried

7272 622 1121 6680 3290 3615 2845/1121
33 בני־חת: ויכל יעקב לצות את־בניו ויאסף רגליו אל־
into feet his he and his com- Jacob And .Heth the
gathered sons manding finished of sons

5971 622 1478 4296
המטה ויגוע ויאסף אל־עמיו:
his to was and he and the
.people gathered ,died ;bed

CAP. L נ

CHAPTER 50

CHAPTER 50

[1]And Joseph fell on the face of his father and wept on him, and kissed him. [2]And Joseph commanded his servants the physicians to embalm his father; and the physicians embalmed Israel. [3]And forty days went by, for so are fulfilled the days of those embalmed. And Egypt wept for him seventy days. [4]And the days of his weeping passed by, and Joseph spoke to the house of Pharaoh, saying, Now if I have found favor in

3127 6680 5401 5921 1058 1 6440 3127 5307
1
2 ויפל יוסף על־פני אביו ויבך עליו וישק־לו: ויצו יוסף
Joseph And .him and upon and his the on Joseph And
commanded kissed ,him wept father of face fell

7495 2590 1 2590 7495 5650
את־עבדיו את־הרפאים לחנט את־אביו ויחנטו הרפאים
the And his to the his
physicians embalmed .father embalm physicians servants

3117 4390 3651 3117 702 4390 3478
3 את־ישראל: וימלאו־לו ארבעים יום כי כן ימלאו ימי
the ful- are so for ,days forty for And ,Israel
of days filled him fulfilled

3117 5674 3117 7651 4714 1058 2590
4 החנטים ויבכו אתו מצרים שבעים יום: ויעברו ימי
days passed And .days seventy Egypt for and those
by him wept ;embalmed

4672 4994 559 6547 1004 3127 1696 1068
בכיתו וידבר יוסף אל־בית פרעה לאמר אם־נא מצאתי
have I Now if ,saying ,Pharaoh the to Joseph and his
found of house spoke ;weeping

your eyes, please speak in the ears of Pharaoh, saying, 5My father made me swear, saying, Lo, I am dying; you shall bury me there in the grave which I have dug for myself in the land of Canaan. And now please let me go up and bury my father, and return. 6And Pharaoh said, Go up and bury your father, as he made you swear. 7And Joseph went up to bury his father; and all the servants of Pharaoh went up with him, the elders of his house, even all the elders of the land of Egypt, 8and all the house of Joseph and his brothers, and the house of his father. Only, they left their little ones and their flocks and their herds in the land of Goshen. 9And both horsemen and chariots went up with him; and the company was very great. 10And they came as far as the threshing-floor of thorns, which *is* on the other side of the Jordan. And they mourned there with a great and very heavy mourning. And he made a lamentation for his father seven days. 11And the inhabitants of the land, the Canaanites, saw the lamentation in the threshing-floor of thorns. And they said, This is a very great lamentation to Egypt; for this reason its name was called Abel-mizraim, which *is* on the other side of Jordan. 12And his sons did to him as he had commanded them. 13And his sons carried him to the land of Canaan, and buried him in the cave of the field of Machpelah; which Abraham bought, the field for burying-place, from Ephron the Hittite, before Mamre.

14And after he buried his father, Joseph returned to Egypt, he and his brothers, and all those going up with him to bury his father.

7650 1 559 6547 241/4994/1696 5869 2580
5 חֵן בְּעֵינֵיכֶם דַּבְּרוּ־נָא בְּאָזְנֵי פַרְעֹה לֵאמֹר׃ אָבִי הִשְׁבִּיעַנִי
me made My ,saying Pharaoh the in please speak your in favor
,swear father of ears ,eyes

3667 776 3738 834 6913 4191 2009 559
לֵאמֹר הִנֵּה אָנֹכִי מֵת בְּקִבְרִי אֲשֶׁר כָּרִיתִי לִי בְּאֶרֶץ כְּנַעַן
Canaan the in for have I which the in am I ,Lo ,saying
of land me dug grave ;dying

7725 1 6912 4994/5927 6258 6912 8033
שָׁמָּה תִּקְבְּרֵנִי וְעַתָּה אֶעֱלֶה־נָּא וְאֶקְבְּרָה אֶת־אָבִי וְאָשׁוּבָה׃
and my bury and please me let and shall you there
.return ,father up go now ;me bury

7650 1 6912 5927 6547 559
6 וַיֹּאמֶר פַּרְעֹה עֲלֵה וּקְבֹר אֶת־אָבִיךָ כַּאֲשֶׁר הִשְׁבִּיעֶךָ׃
made he as your and up Go ,Pharaoh And
.swear you ,father bury said

6547 5650 3605 5927 6912 3127 5927
7 וַיַּעַל יוֹסֵף לִקְבֹּר אֶת־אָבִיו וַיַּעֲלוּ אִתּוֹ כָּל־עַבְדֵי פַרְעֹה
,Pharaoh the all with and ;father his to Joseph And
of servants him went bury up went

251 3127 1004 3605 4714 776 2205 3605 1004 2205
8 זִקְנֵי בֵיתוֹ וְכֹל זִקְנֵי אֶרֶץ־מִצְרָיִם׃ וְכֹל בֵּית יוֹסֵף וְאֶחָיו
his and Joseph the all and ,Egypt land the the and his the
brothers of house of of elders all ,house of elders

1657 776 5800 1241 6629 2945 7535 1 1004
וּבֵית אָבִיו רַק טַפָּם וְצֹאנָם וּבְקָרָם עָזְבוּ בְּאֶרֶץ גֹּשֶׁן׃
.Goshen the in they their and their and their only his the and
of land left herds flocks ones little ;father of house

3966 3515 4264 1961 6571 7393 1571 5927
9 וַיַּעַל עִמּוֹ גַּם־רֶכֶב גַּם־פָּרָשִׁים וַיְהִי הַמַּחֲנֶה כָּבֵד מְאֹד׃
.very great the and ;horsemen and chariots both with And
company was him went

8033 5594 3383 5676 834 329 1637 935
10 וַיָּבֹאוּ עַד־גֹּרֶן הָאָטָד אֲשֶׁר בְּעֵבֶר הַיַּרְדֵּן וַיִּסְפְּדוּ־שָׁם
there they and ;Jordan the on which thorns the to they And
mourned of side other (is) of floor grain came

3117 7651 1 60 6213 3966 3515 1419 4553
מִסְפֵּד גָּדוֹל וְכָבֵד מְאֹד וַיַּעַשׂ לְאָבִיו אֵבֶל שִׁבְעַת יָמִים׃
.days seven a his for he and ;very and great a
wailing father made heavy mourning

559 329 1637 60 3669 776 3427 7200
11 וַיַּרְא יוֹשֵׁב הָאָרֶץ הַכְּנַעֲנִי אֶת־הָאֵבֶל בְּגֹרֶן הָאָטָד וַיֹּאמְרוּ
they and ;thorns the at the the ,land the the And
said of floor grain wailing Canaanites of dwellers saw

4714 67 8034 7121 4713 2088 60 3515
אֵבֶל־כָּבֵד זֶה לְמִצְרָיִם עַל־כֵּן קָרָא שְׁמָהּ אָבֵל מִצְרַיִם
,mizraim- Abel name its they therefore the for This wailing a
called ;Egyptians heavy

6680 3651 1121 6213 3383 5676 834
12 אֲשֶׁר בְּעֵבֶר הַיַּרְדֵּן׃ וַיַּעֲשׂוּ בָנָיו לוֹ כֵּן כַּאֲשֶׁר צִוָּם׃
had he as thus to his did And .Jordan the on which
them told him sons of side other (is)

7704 4631 6912 3667 776 1121 5375
13 וַיִּשְׂאוּ אֹתוֹ בָנָיו אַרְצָה כְּנַעַן וַיִּקְבְּרוּ אֹתוֹ בִּמְעָרַת שְׂדֵה
the the in him and ,Canaan the to his him And
of field of cave buried of land sons carried

6913 272 7704 85 7069 834 4375
הַמַּכְפֵּלָה אֲשֶׁר קָנָה אַבְרָהָם אֶת־הַשָּׂדֶה לַאֲחֻזַּת־קֶבֶר
,burial a for field the Abraham bought which ,Machpelah
of place

4714 3127 7725 4471 6440 2850 6085
14 מֵאֵת עֶפְרֹן הַחִתִּי עַל־פְּנֵי מַמְרֵא׃ וַיָּשָׁב יוֹסֵף מִצְרַיְמָה
,Egypt to Joseph And .Mamre before the Ephron from
returned Hittite

6912 310 1 6912 3927 3605 251
הוּא וְאֶחָיו וְכָל־הָעֹלִים אִתּוֹ לִקְבֹּר אֶת־אָבִיו אַחֲרֵי קָבְרוֹ
he after ,father his bury to with those and his and he
buried him going all brothers

[15]And Joseph's brothers saw that their father was dead. And they said, What if Joseph should bear a grudge against us and should surely repay us all the evil which we did to him? [16]And they sent a message to Joseph, saying, [17]Your father commanded before his death, saying, So you shall say to Joseph, Please pardon now the revolt of your brothers, and their sin; for they did evil to you. And now please pardon the revolt of the servants of the God of your father. And Joseph wept when they spoke to him. [18]And his brothers also went and fell down before his face. And they said, Behold, we are your servants. [19]And Joseph said to them, Do not fear. For am I in the place of God? [20]And you, you intended evil against me, *but* God meant it for good, in order to make *it* as *it is* this day, to keep a great many people alive. [21]And now do not fear; I will nourish you and your little ones. And he comforted them, and spoke to their hearts.

[22]And Joseph lived in Egypt, he and the house of his father. And Joseph lived a hundred and ten years. [23]And Joseph saw the sons of Ephraim to the third generation. Also the sons of Machir the son of Manasseh were on Joseph's knees. [24]And Joseph said to his brothers, I am dying, and God will surely visit you and bring you up from this land to the land which He swore to Abraham, to Isaac, and to Jacob. [25]And Joseph made the sons of Israel swear, saying, God will surely visit you, and you

3863 559 1 4191 3127 251 7200 1
15 אֶת־אָבִיו׃ וַיִּרְאוּ אֲחֵי־יוֹסֵף כִּי־מֵת אֲבִיהֶם וַיֹּאמְרוּ לוּ
What they and their was that Joseph's brothers And his
if ,said ,father dead saw .father

1580 834 7451 3605 7725 7725 3127 7852
יִשְׂטְמֵנוּ יוֹסֵף וְהָשֵׁב יָשִׁיב לָנוּ אֵת כָּל־הָרָעָה אֲשֶׁר גָּמַלְנוּ
we which the all us should and Joseph against bear
did evil repay fully grudge a us

559 4194 6440 6680 1 559 3427 6680
16 אֹתוֹ׃ וַיְצַוּוּ אֶל־יוֹסֵף לֵאמֹר אָבִיךָ צִוָּה לִפְנֵי מוֹתוֹ לֵאמֹר׃
,saying his before com- Your ,saying ,Joseph they And to
,death manded father directed ?him

2403 251 6588 5375 577 3127 559
17 כֹּה־תֹאמְרוּ לְיוֹסֵף אָנָּא שָׂא נָא פֶּשַׁע אַחֶיךָ וְחַטָּאתָם
their and your the now Pardon we to shall you So
sin ,brothers of revolt pray ,Joseph say

430 5650 6588 5375 6250 1580 7451
כִּי־רָעָה גְמָלוּךָ וְעַתָּה שָׂא נָא לְפֶשַׁע עַבְדֵי אֱלֹהֵי אָבִיךָ
your God the the revolt the pray lift and did they the for
.father of of servants of up now ;you to evil

6440 5307 251 1571 3212 1696 3127 1058
18 וַיֵּבְךְּ יוֹסֵף בְּדַבְּרָם אֵלָיו׃ וַיֵּלְכוּ גַּם־אֶחָיו וַיִּפְּלוּ לְפָנָיו
before fell and his also And .him to they when Joseph And
;face his brothers went spoke wept

3127 559 5650 2009 559
19 וַיֹּאמְרוּ הִנֶּנּוּ לְךָ לַעֲבָדִים׃ וַיֹּאמֶר אֲלֵהֶם יוֹסֵף אַל־
not ,Joseph them to said And for to ,Behold they and
.servants you (are) we ,said

7451 5921 2803 430 8478 3372
20 תִּירָאוּ כִּי הֲתַחַת אֱלֹהִים אָנִי׃ וְאַתֶּם חֲשַׁבְתֶּם עָלַי רָעָה
,evil against you And ?I God's in (am) for Do
me intended ,you place ,fear

2421 2088 3117 6213 4616 2896 2803 430
אֱלֹהִים חֲשָׁבָהּ לְטֹבָה לְמַעַן עֲשֹׂה כַּיּוֹם הַזֶּה לְהַחֲיֹת
keep to ,this as make to in for meant (but)
alive day (is it) (it) order ,good it God

3557 3372 6258 7227 5971
21 עַם־רָב׃ וְעַתָּה אַל־תִּירָאוּ אָנֹכִי אֲכַלְכֵּל אֶתְכֶם וְאֶת־
and you will I ,fear do not And great a people
nourish now ,many

4714 3127 3427 3820 1696 5162 2945
22 טַפְּכֶם וַיְנַחֵם אוֹתָם וַיְדַבֵּר עַל־לִבָּם׃ וַיֵּשֶׁב יוֹסֵף בְּמִצְרַיִם
,Egypt in Joseph And their to and ,them he and your
lived .hearts spoke comforted ;ones little

7200 8141 6235 3967 3127 2421 1 1004
23 הוּא וּבֵית אָבִיו וַיְחִי יוֹסֵף מֵאָה וָעֶשֶׂר שָׁנִים׃ וַיַּרְא
And .years ten and a Joseph and his the and he
saw hundred lived father of house

3205 4519 1121 4353 1121 8029 1121 669 3127
יוֹסֵף לְאֶפְרַיִם בְּנֵי שִׁלֵּשִׁים גַּם בְּנֵי מָכִיר בֶּן־מְנַשֶּׁה יֻלְּדוּ
were Manasseh the Machir the also third the to sons Ephraim's Joseph
born of son of sons generation

430 4191 251 3127 559 3127 1290
24 עַל־בִּרְכֵּי יוֹסֵף׃ וַיֹּאמֶר יוֹסֵף אֶל־אֶחָיו אָנֹכִי מֵת וֵאלֹהִים
and am I his to Joseph said And .Joseph's knees on
God dying ,brothers

2088 776 5927 6485 6485
פָּקֹד יִפְקֹד אֶתְכֶם וְהֶעֱלָה אֶתְכֶם מִן־הָאָרֶץ הַזֹּאת אֶל־
to this land from you and you will surely
up bring visit

7650 3290 3327 85 7650 834 776
25 הָאָרֶץ אֲשֶׁר נִשְׁבַּע לְאַבְרָהָם לְיִצְחָק וּלְיַעֲקֹב׃ וַיַּשְׁבַּע
made And to and ,Isaac to to swore He which the
swear to ,Jacob Abraham land

430 6485 6485 559 3478 1121 3127
יוֹסֵף אֶת־בְּנֵי יִשְׂרָאֵל לֵאמֹר פָּקֹד יִפְקֹד אֱלֹהִים אֶתְכֶם
,you God will Surely ,saying ,Israel the Joseph
visit of sons

shall bring up my bones from here.
26And Joseph died, a son of a hundred and ten years. And they embalmed him and put *him* in a coffin in Egypt.

6236 3967/1121 3127 4191 2088 6106 5927

26 וְהַעֲלִתֶם אֶת־עַצְמֹתַי מִזֶּה׃ וַיָּמָת יוֹסֵף בֶּן־מֵאָה וָעֶשֶׂר

ten and / a hundred / a of son / Joseph / died And / from .here / bones my / you and up bring shall

4714 727 3455 2590 8141

שָׁנִים וַיַּחַנְטוּ אֹתוֹ וַיִּישֶׂם בָּאָרוֹן בְּמִצְרָיִם׃

.Egypt in / a in coffin / put and (him) / ,him they and embalmed / years

˙ואלה שמות

EXODUS

A LITERAL TRANSLATION
OF THE BIBLE
THE BOOK OF EXODUS

CAPUT. I א

CHAPTER 1

CHAPTER 1
[1]And these *were* the
names of the sons of Israel
who came into Egypt with
Jacob; they each one came
in with his house: [2]Reuben,
Simeon, Levi, and Judah,
[3]Issachar, Zebulun, and
Benjamin, [4]Dan, and Naphtali, Gad, and Asher. [5]And
all the souls that came out
of the loins of Jacob *were*
seventy souls, Joseph be-
ing in Egypt. [6]And Joseph
died, and all his brothers
and all that generation.
[7]And the sons of Israel were
fruitful and increased very
much, and multiplied, and
became very strong; and
the land was filled *with*
them.

[8]And a new king arose
over Egypt, who had not
known Joseph. [9]And he
said to his people, Behold,
the people of the sons of
Israel *are more* numerous
and strong than we.
[10]Come, let us deal craftily
towards them, lest they
multiply and it shall be that
when war occurs they will
also add to our enemies,
and will fight against us,
and go up from the land.
[11]And they put over them
slavemasters in order to
afflict them with their
burdens. And he built store-
cities for Pharaoh: Pithon
and Raamses. [12]And as
much as they afflicted
them, so much they multi-
plied and so much they
spread. And they were
afraid before the sons of
Israel. [13]And Egypt made
the sons of Israel to serve
with harshness. [14]And they
made their lives bitter by

376 3290 4714 935 3478 1121 8034
1 וְאֵלֶּה שְׁמוֹת בְּנֵי יִשְׂרָאֵל הַבָּאִים מִצְרָיְמָה אֵת יַעֲקֹב אִישׁ
each ;Jacob with Egypt into who Israel the the (were) And
one came of sons of names these

2074 3475 3063 3878 8095 7205 935 1004
2 וּבֵיתוֹ בָּאוּ׃ רְאוּבֵן שִׁמְעוֹן לֵוִי וִיהוּדָה׃ יִשָּׂשכָר זְבוּלֻן
3 Zebulun ,Issachar ,Judah and ,Levi ,Simeon ,Reuben they his with
:in came house

3409 3318 5315 3605 1961 836 1410 5320 1835 1144
4 וּבִנְיָמִן׃ דָּן וְנַפְתָּלִי גָּד וְאָשֵׁר׃ וַיְהִי כָּל־נֶפֶשׁ יֹצְאֵי יֶרֶךְ
5 the came that the all And and ,Gad and ,Dan and
of loins of out souls were .Asher Naphtali ,Benjamin

3605 3127 4191 4714 1961 3127 5315 7657 3290
6 יַעֲקֹב שִׁבְעִים נָפֶשׁ וְיוֹסֵף הָיָה בְמִצְרָיִם׃ וַיָּמָת יוֹסֵף וְכָל־
and ,Joseph And .Egypt in being Joseph ,souls seventy Jacob
all died

7235 8318 6509 3478 1121 1755 251
7 אֶחָיו וְכֹל הַדּוֹר הַהוּא׃ וּבְנֵי יִשְׂרָאֵל פָּרוּ וַיִּשְׁרְצוּ וַיִּרְבּוּ
mul- and and were Israel the And .that generation and his
tiplied teeming fruitful of sons all brothers

776 4390 3966 3966 6105
וַיַּעַצְמוּ בִּמְאֹד מְאֹד וַתִּמָּלֵא הָאָרֶץ אֹתָם׃
with land the was and ,very ,very became and
.them filled strong

3127 3045 4714 2319 4428 6965
8 וַיָּקָם מֶלֶךְ־חָדָשׁ עַל־מִצְרָיִם אֲשֶׁר לֹא־יָדַע אֶת־יוֹסֵף׃
Joseph had not who Egypt over new king a And
known arose

6099 7227 3478 1121 5971 2009 5971 559
9 וַיֹּאמֶר אֶל־עַמּוֹ הִנֵּה עַם בְּנֵי יִשְׂרָאֵל רַב וְעָצוּם מִמֶּנּוּ׃
than and (are) Israel the the ,Behold his to he And
we stronger many of sons of people ,people said

4421 7125 7235 2449 3053
10 הָבָה נִתְחַכְּמָה לוֹ פֶּן־יִרְבֶּה וְהָיָה כִּי־תִקְרֶאנָה מִלְחָמָה
,war occurs that it and he lest toward us let ,Come
when be shall ;multiply ,him slyly deal

776 5927 3898 8130 1931 3254
וְנוֹסַף גַּם־הוּא עַל־שֹׂנְאֵינוּ וְנִלְחַם־בָּנוּ וְעָלָה מִן־הָאָרֶץ׃
the from go and against will and our with he also will
.land up us fight enemies add

5892 1129 5450 6031 4522 8269 7760
11 וַיָּשִׂימוּ עָלָיו שָׂרֵי מִסִּים לְמַעַן עַנֹּתוֹ בְּסִבְלֹתָם וַיִּבֶן עָרֵי
cities And their with afflict as so ,slavemasters over they And
of built he .burdens them to them put

6031 7486 6619 6547 4543
12 מִסְכְּנוֹת לְפַרְעֹה אֶת־פִּתֹם וְאֶת־רַעַמְסֵס׃ וְכַאֲשֶׁר יְעַנּוּ
they as And .Raamses and Pithon for storage
afflicted as much ,Pharaoh

5647 3478 1121 6440 6973 6555 7235 3651
13 אֹתוֹ כֵּן יִרְבֶּה וְכֵן יִפְרֹץ וַיָּקֻצוּ מִפְּנֵי בְּנֵי יִשְׂרָאֵל׃ וַיַּעֲבִדוּ
made and ,Israel the before they and he and he so ,him
serve to of sons afraid were ;spread so multiplied

2416 4843 6531 3478 1121 4714
14 מִצְרַיִם אֶת־בְּנֵי יִשְׂרָאֵל בְּפָרֶךְ׃ וַיְמָרְרוּ אֶת־חַיֵּיהֶם
lives their they And with Israel of sons the Egypt
bitter made .harshness

hard work, in clay, and in bricks, and in all work in the field; all their work which they made them do with harshness.

[15]And the king of Egypt said to the midwives of the Hebrews, of whom the name of one *was* Shiphrah, and the name of the second, Puah; [16]and he said, When you midwife the Hebrew women, and look on the birth-stools, if it *is* a son, you will kill him; and if it *is* a daughter, it shall live. [17]And the midwives feared God, and they did not do as the king of Egypt said to them. And they kept the male children alive. [18]And the king of Egypt called to the midwives and said to them, Why do you do this thing and keep alive the male children? [19]And the midwives said to Pharaoh, Because the Hebrew women *are* not like the Egyptian women, for they *are* vigorous. Before the midwives come to them they bear. [20]And God dealt well with the midwives; and the people multiplied and became exceedingly strong. [21]And because the midwives feared God, He made houses for them.

[22]And Pharaoh commanded all his people, saying, Every son that is born, you shall cast him into the river. And you shall keep alive every daughter.

7704 5647 3605 3843 2563 7186 5656
בַּעֲבֹדָה קָשָׁה בְּחֹמֶר וּבִלְבֵנִים וּבְכָל־עֲבֹדָה בַּשָּׂדֶה אֵת
the in work in and in and clay in hard through
,field (of kind) all bricks work

4428 559 6531 6213 834 5647 3605
15 כָּל־עֲבֹדָתָם אֲשֶׁר־עָבְדוּ בָהֶם בְּפָרֶךְ׃ וַיֹּאמֶר מֶלֶךְ
the said And with them made they which work their all
of king ,harshness do

8034 823:6 259 8034 5680 3205 4714
מִצְרַיִם לַמְיַלְּדֹת הָעִבְרִיֹּת אֲשֶׁר שֵׁם הָאַחַת שִׁפְרָה וְשֵׁם
the and Shiphrah (was) one the of Hebrew the to Egypt
of name of name whom midwives

5921 7200 56:80 3205 559 6326 8145
16 הַשֵּׁנִית פּוּעָה׃ וַיֹּאמֶר בְּיַלֶּדְכֶן אֶת־הָעִבְרִיּוֹת וּרְאִיתֶן עַל־
on you and the you when he and ;Puah the
look women Hebrew midwife ,said ,second

2425 1323 4191 1121 70
הָאָבְנָיִם אִם־בֵּן הוּא וַהֲמִתֶּן אֹתוֹ וְאִם־בַּת הִיא וָחָיָה׃
shall it ,(is) it a and ,him will you (is) it son a if the
.live daughter if kill ,birth-stools

1696 621:3 3808 430 3205 3372
17 וַתִּירֶאןָ הַמְיַלְּדֹת אֶת־הָאֱלֹהִים וְלֹא עָשׂוּ כַּאֲשֶׁר דִּבֶּר אֲלֵיהֶן
them to said as did they and God midwives the And
do not feared

4714 4428 7121 3206 2421 4714 4428
18 מֶלֶךְ מִצְרָיִם וַתְּחַיֶּיןָ אֶת־הַיְלָדִים׃ וַיִּקְרָא מֶלֶךְ־מִצְרַיִם
Egypt the called And .children male the they And .Egypt the
of king alive kept of king

2421 2088 1697 6213 4069 559 3205
לַמְיַלְּדֹת וַיֹּאמֶר לָהֶן מַדּוּעַ עֲשִׂיתֶן הַדָּבָר הַזֶּה וַתְּחַיֶּיןָ
keep and this thing do you do Why to said and the to
alive ,them midwives

802 3808/3588/6547 3205 559 3206
19 אֶת־הַיְלָדִים׃ וַתֹּאמַרְןָ הַמְיַלְּדֹת אֶל־פַּרְעֹה כִּי לֹא כַנָּשִׁים
like not Be- ,Pharaoh to midwives the said And male the
women cause ?children

935 2962 2422 5680 4713
הַמִּצְרִיֹּת הָעִבְרִיֹּת כִּי־חָיוֹת הֵנָּה בְּטֶרֶם תָּבוֹא אֲלֵהֶן
to comes before they vigorous for the (are) the
them ;(are) ,women Hebrew ,Egyptian

6105 5971 7235 3205 430 3190 3205 3205
20 הַמְיַלֶּדֶת וְיָלָדוּ׃ וַיֵּיטֶב אֱלֹהִים לַמְיַלְּדֹת וַיִּרֶב הָעָם וַיַּעַצְמוּ
be- and the and the with God And they the
strong came people teemed ;midwives well dealt .bear ,midwife

6213 430 3205 3372 3966
21 מְאֹד׃ וַיְהִי כִּי־יָרְאוּ הַמְיַלְּדֹת אֶת־הָאֱלֹהִים וַיַּעַשׂ לָהֶם
for He ,God the because And .very
them made midwives feared

2975 320 1121/3605 559 5971 3605 6547 6680 1004
22 בָּתִּים׃ וַיְצַו פַּרְעֹה לְכָל־עַמּוֹ לֵאמֹר כָּל־הַבֵּן הַיִּלּוֹד הַיְאֹרָה
the into is that son Every ,saying his all Pharaoh And .houses
Nile ,born people commanded

2421 1323 3605 7993
תַּשְׁלִיכֻהוּ וְכָל־הַבַּת תְּחַיּוּן׃
will you daughter and will you
.alive keep every ,him cast

CAP. II ב

CHAPTER 2

CHAPTER 2

[1]And a man went from the house of Levi and took a daughter of Levi. [2]And the woman conceived and bore a son; and she saw him, that he *was* beautiful. And she concealed him three

802 2029 3878 1323 3947 1004 376 1980
1
2 וַיֵּלֶךְ אִישׁ מִבֵּית לֵוִי וַיִּקַּח אֶת־בַּת־לֵוִי׃ וַתַּהַר הָאִשָּׁה
the And .Levi a and Levi the from a And
woman conceived of daughter took of house man went

3391 7969 6845 2896 7200/1121 3205
וַתֵּלֶד בֵּן וַתֵּרֶא אֹתוֹ כִּי־טוֹב הוּא וַתִּצְפְּנֵהוּ שְׁלֹשָׁה יְרָחִים׃
.months three she and he that ,him she and a and
him hid (was) good saw ;son bore

months. [3]And she was not
able to hide him any longer,
and she took a basket *for*
him *made of* papyrus, and
she daubed it with bitumen
and with pitch. And she put
the child in it, and placed *it*
in the reeds by the lip of the
Nile. [4]And his sister took
her stand from a distance,
to know what would be
done to him.

[5]And the daughter of
Pharaoh went down to
bathe on the Nile. And her
maidens were walking on
the side of the Nile. And she
saw the basket in the midst
of the reeds, and sent her
slavegirl and took it. [6]And
she opened *it* and saw the
child, and, behold, a boy
crying! And she had pity on
him and said, This *one is* of
the children of the
Hebrews. [7]And his sister
said to Pharaoh's daughter,
Shall I go and call a woman
for you, a nurse of the
Hebrew women, that she
may nurse the child for you?
[8]And Pharaah's daughter
said to her, Go. And the girl
went and called *the* child's
mother. [9]And Pharaoh's
daughter said to her, Take
this child away and nurse
him for me, and I will give
your wages. And the
woman took the child and
nursed him.

[10]And the child grew, and
she brought him to the
daughter of Pharaoh. And
he became a son to her, and
she called his name Moses,
and said, Because I drew
him out of the water.

[11]And it happened in
those days, even Moses
was grown, and he went
out to his brothers and
looked upon their burdens.
And he saw an Egyptian
man striking a Hebrew man,
of his brothers. [12]And he
turned here and there and
saw that no man was *there*.
And he struck the Egyptian
and hid him in the sand.
[13]And he went out on the
second day, and, behold,

2560 1573 8392 3947 6845 5750 3201 3808
3 ולא־יכלה עוד הצפינו ותקח־לו תבת גמא ותחמרה
daubed and papy- ark an him she so hide to any was she And
it rus took ,him longer able not

5488 7760 3206 7760 2203 2564
בחמר ובזפת ותשם בה את־הילד ותשם בסוף על־
by the in and ,child the it in she and with and with
reeds (it) placed put ,pitch bitumen

6213 3045 7350 269 3320 2975 8193
4 שפת היאר ותתצב אחתו מרחק לדעה מה־יעשה
would what know to a from his took And .Nile the the
done be ,distance sister stand her of bank

1980 5291 2975 7364 6547 1323 3381
5 לו ותרד בת־פרעה לרחץ על־היאר ונערתיה הלכת
(were) her and ,Nile the at to Pharaoh the And to
walking maidens bathe of daughter went .him

5488 8432 8392 7200 2975 3027
על־יד היאר ותרא את־התבה בתוך הסוף ותשלח את־
sent and the the in ark the she and the the by
,reeds of midst saw ;Nile of hand

5288 2009 3206 7200 6605 3947 519
6 אמתה ותקחה ותפתח ותראהו את־הילד והנה־נער
boy a and ,child the saw and she And .it took and her
,behold him (it) opened girl-slave

559 5680 3206 559 2550 1058
7 בכה ותחמל עליו ותאמר מילדי העברים זה ותאמר
said And This Hebrews the the of ,said and on she And !crying
.(one is) of children him pity had

3243 802 7121 1980 6547 1323 269
אחתו אל־בת־פרעה האלך וקראתי לך אשה מינקת
nurse a a for call and I Shall ,Pharaoh the to his
woman you go of daughter sister

6547 1323 559 3206 3243 5680
8 מן העברית ותינק לך את־הילד ותאמר־לה בת־פרעה
,Pharaoh the to said And ?child the for she that Hebrew the of
of daughter her you nurse may ,women

559 3206 517 7121 5959 3318 1980
9 לכי ותלך העלמה ותקרא את־אם הילד ותאמר לה
to said And (the) mother called and girl the And .Go
her .child's went

5414 3243 3206 6547 1323
בת־פרעה היליכי את־הילד הזה והינקהו לי ואני אתן
will and for and this child Take ,Pharaoh the
give I me him nurse away of daughter

3206 1430 5134 3206 802 3947 7939
10 את־שכרך ותקח האשה הילד ותניקהו ויגדל הילד
the And nursed and child the the and ;wages your
child grew .him woman took

4872 8034 1121 1961 6547 1323 935
ותבאהו לבת־פרעה ויהי־לה לבן ותקרא שמו משה
,Moses his she and a for to And ,Pharaoh the to she and
name called ;son her was he of daughter him took

1430 3117 1961 4871 4325 559
11 ותאמר כי מן־המים משיתהו ויהי בימים ההם ויגדל
was those days in it And .him drew I the from For ,said and
grown was water

4713 376 7200 5450 7200 251 3318 4872
משה ויצא אל־אחיו וירא בסבלתם וירא איש מצרי
an man he And their saw and his to he And .Moses
Egyptian saw .burdens brothers went

376 7200 3541 6437 251 5680 376 5221
12 מכה איש־עברי מאחיו ויפן כה וכה וירא כי־אין איש
.man there that and and here he And his of a man striking
no was saw there turned .brothers ,Hebrew

2009 8145 3117 3318 2344 2934 4713 5221
13 ויך את־המצרי ויטמנהו בחול ויצא ביום השני והנה
and ,second the on he And the in hid and the he And
,behold day went .sand him Egyptian struck

two men, Hebrews, *were* fighting. And he said to the guilty one, Why should you strike your neighbor? 14 And he said, Who appointed you as a man, a prince and a judge over us? *Are* you saying to kill me, as you killed the Egyptian? And Moses feared, and said, Surely the thing is known. 15 And Pharaoh heard this word, and he sought to kill Moses. And Moses fled from before Pharaoh, and lived in the land of Midian. And *he* sat down by the well.

16 And seven daughters *were born to* the priest of Midian, and they came and drew and filled the troughs to water their father's flocks. 17 And the shepherds came and drove them away; and Moses rose up and saved them, and watered their flocks. 18 And they came to their father Reuel; and he said, Why have you hurried to come today? 19 And they said, An Egyptian man rescued us from the hand of the shepherds and he also drew for us and watered the flock. 20 And he said to his daughters, And where *is* he? Why then have you left the man? Call him, and let him eat bread. 21 And Moses consented to live with the man; and he gave his daughter Zipporah to Moses. 22 And she bore a son, and he called his name Gershom; for he said, I have become an alien in a foreign land.

23 And it happened during these many days, that the king of Egypt died, and the sons of Israel groaned from the slavery. And they cried, and their cry went up

7451 5221 7563 559 5327 5680 582 8147
שְׁנֵי־אֲנָשִׁים עִבְרִים נִצִּים וַיֹּאמֶר לָרָשָׁע לָמָּה תַכֶּה רֵעֶךָ׃
your you do Why the to he and were Hebrews ,men two
?neighbor strike ,one guilty said ;quarreling

2026 8199 8269 376 7760 559
14 וַיֹּאמֶר מִי שָׂמְךָ לְאִישׁ שַׂר וְשֹׁפֵט עָלֵינוּ הַלְהָרְגֵנִי אַתָּה
you me kill To ?us over a and a a as appointed Who he And
judge prince ,man you ,said

403 559 4872 3372 4713 2026 559
אֹמֵר כַּאֲשֶׁר הָרַגְתָּ אֶת־הַמִּצְרִי וַיִּירָא מֹשֶׁה וַיֹּאמַר אָכֵן
Surely, said and, Moses And /Egyptian the killed you as (are)
feared ,saying

2026 1245 2088 1697 6547 8085 1697 3045
15 נוֹדַע הַדָּבָר׃ וַיִּשְׁמַע פַּרְעֹה אֶת־הַדָּבָר הַזֶּה וַיְבַקֵּשׁ לַהֲרֹג
kill to he and this thing Pharaoh And .thing the is
sought heard known

4080 776 2416 6547 6440 4872 1272 4872
אֶת־מֹשֶׁה וַיִּבְרַח מֹשֶׁה מִפְּנֵי פַרְעֹה וַיֵּשֶׁב בְּאֶרֶץ־מִדְיָן
;Midian the in and ,Pharaoh from Moses fled And .Moses
of land lived before

935 1323 7651 4080 3548 875 3427
16 וַיֵּשֶׁב עַל־הַבְּאֵר׃ וּלְכֹהֵן מִדְיָן שֶׁבַע בָּנוֹת וַתָּבֹאנָה
they And .daughters seven Midian the And .well the by (he) and
came (had) of priest sat

1 6629 8248 7298 4390 1802
וַתִּדְלֶנָה וַתְּמַלֶּאנָה אֶת־הָרְהָטִים לְהַשְׁקוֹת צֹאן אֲבִיהֶן׃
their the water to troughs the filled and drew and
.father of flocks

8248 3462 4872 6965 1644 7462 935
17 וַיָּבֹאוּ הָרֹעִים וַיְגָרְשׁוּם וַיָּקָם מֹשֶׁה וַיּוֹשִׁעָן וַיַּשְׁקְ אֶת־
and freed and Moses and drove and the And
watered ,them arose ,away them shepherds came

4116 4069 559 1 7467 935 6629
18 צֹאנָם׃ וַתָּבֹאנָה אֶל־רְעוּאֵל אֲבִיהֶן וַיֹּאמֶר מַדּוּעַ מִהַרְתֶּן
you have Why he and their Reuel to they And their
hurried ,said ,father came .flocks

1571 7462 3022 5337 4713 376 559 935
19 בֹּא הַיּוֹם׃ וַתֹּאמַרְןָ אִישׁ מִצְרִי הִצִּילָנוּ מִיַּד הָרֹעִים וְגַם־
and the the from rescued An man they And ?today to
also shepherds of hand us Egyptian ,said come

1323 559 6629 8248 1802 1802
20 דָּלֹה דָלָה לָנוּ וַיַּשְׁקְ אֶת־הַצֹּאן׃ וַיֹּאמֶר אֶל־בְּנֹתָיו וְאַיּוֹ
And ,daughters his to And .flock the and for he even
?he (is) where said he watered us drew

2974 3899 398 7121 376 5800 4100
21 לָמָּה זֶּה עֲזַבְתֶּן אֶת־הָאִישׁ קִרְאֶן לוֹ וְיֹאכַל לָחֶם׃ וַיּוֹאֶל
And .bread let and him Call ?man the have then Why
agreed eat him left you

4872 1323 6855 5414 376 3427 4872
מֹשֶׁה לָשֶׁבֶת אֶת־הָאִישׁ וַיִּתֵּן אֶת־צִפֹּרָה בִתּוֹ לְמֹשֶׁה׃
.Moses to his Zipporah he and the with live to Moses
daughter gave ;man

1961 1616 559 1647 8037 7121 1121 3205
22 וַתֵּלֶד בֵּן וַיִּקְרָא אֶת־שְׁמוֹ גֵּרְשֹׁם כִּי אָמַר גֵּר הָיִיתִי
have I an ,said he for ;Gershom his name called and a she And
become alien ,son bore

5237 776
בְּאֶרֶץ נָכְרִיָּה׃
.foreign a in
land

1121 584 4714 4428 4191 1992 7227 1961
23 וַיְהִי בַיָּמִים הָרַבִּים הָהֵם וַיָּמָת מֶלֶךְ מִצְרַיִם וַיֵּאָנְחוּ בְנֵי־
the and Egypt king the even ,those many after it And
of sons groaned of died days was

430 7775 5927 2199 5656 4480 3478
יִשְׂרָאֵל מִן־הָעֲבֹדָה וַיִּזְעָקוּ וַתַּעַל שַׁוְעָתָם אֶל־הָאֱלֹהִים מִן־
from God to cry their and they and the from Israel
went ,cried ;slavery

to God from the slavery. 24And God heard their groaning, and God remembered His covenant with Abraham, with Isaac, and with Jacob. 25And God saw the sons of Israel, and God knew *them*.

CHAPTER 3

1And Moses was feeding the flock of his father-in-law Jethro, the priest of Midian. And he led the flock behind the wilderness and came to the mountain of God, to Horeb. 2And the Angel of Jehovah appeared to him in a flame of fire from the middle of a thorn bush. And he looked, and behold, the thorn bush *was* burning with fire, and the thorn bush was not burned up! 3And Moses said, I will turn aside now and see this great sight, why the thorn bush is not burned up. 4And Jehovah saw that he turned aside to see, and God called to him from the midst of the thorn bush, and said, Moses! Moses! And he said, I *am* here. 5And He said, Do not come near here, pull off your sandals from your feet, for the place on which you *are* standing *is* holy ground. 6And He said, I *am* the God of your fathers, the God of Abraham, the God of Isaac, and the God of Jacob. And Moses hid his face, for he feared to look upon God.

7And Jehovah said, I have certainly seen the affliction of My people who *are* in Egypt, and I have heard their cry from before their slavedrivers; for I know

24 430 2142 5009 430 8085 5656
העבדה׃ וישמע אלהים את־נאקתם ויזכר אלהים את־
God and their God And the
remembered ,groaning heard .slavery

430 7200 3290 3327 85 1285
בריתו את־אברהם את־יצחק ואת־יעקב׃ וירא אלהים
God And .Jacob and ,Isaac with ,Abraham with His
saw with covenant

430 3045 3478 1121
את־בני ישראל וידע אלהים׃
.God and ,Israel the
(them) knew of sons

CAP. III ג

CHAPTER 3

1 5090 4080 3548 2859 3503 6629 7462 1961 4872
ומשה היה רעה את־צאן יתרו חתנו כהן מדין וינהג
he and ;Midian the his Jethro the tending was And
led of priest ,father-in-law of flock Moses

2722 430 2022 935 4057 310 6629
את־הצאן אחר המדבר ויבא אל־הר האלהים חרבה׃
.Horeb to ,God the to and the behind flock the
of mountain came wilderness

2 7200 5572 8432 784 3827 3068 4397 7200
וירא מלאך יהוה אליו בלבת־אש מתוך הסנה וירא
he and thorn a of out fire a in him to Jehovah Angel the And
saw ;bush of flame of appeared

3 4872 559 398 5572 784 1197 5572 2009
והנה הסנה בער באש והסנה איננו אכל׃ ויאמר משה
Moses said And burned was the and with was thorn the and
,up not bush thorn fire burning bush ,behold

3808 4069 2088 1419 4758 7200 5493
אסרה־נא ואראה את־המראה הגדל הזה מדוע לא־
not why ,this great sight see and Now will I
aside turn

4 7121 7200 5493 3068 5572 1197
יבער הסנה׃ וירא יהוה כי סר לראות ויקרא אליו
to called and ,see to he that Jehovah And thorn the is
him turned saw .bush up burned

559 4872 4872 559 5572 8432 430
אלהים מתוך הסנה ויאמר משה משה ויאמר הנני׃
(am) I he And !Moses !Moses ,said and the the from God
.here ,said ,bush thorn of midst

5 4725 7272 5275 5394 1988 7126 559
ויאמר אל־תקרב הלם של־נעליך מעל רגליך כי המקום
place the for your from your pull ;here come Do not He And
,feet sandals off near ,said

6 559 6944 127 5921 5975 834
אשר אתה עומד עליו אדמת־קדש הוא׃ ויאמר אנכי
(am) I He And .(is) it holy ground it on standing you which
said (are)

3290 430 3327 430 85 430 1 430
אלהי אביך אלהי אברהם אלהי יצחק ואלהי יעקב
.Jacob the and ,Isaac the ,Abraham the your God the
of God of God of God ,fathers of

7 559 430 5027 3372 6440 4872 5641
ויסתר משה פניו כי ירא מהביט אל־האלהים׃ ויאמר
said And .God upon look to he for his Moses hid And
feared ,face

4714 5971 6040 7200 7200 3068
יהוה ראה ראיתי את־עני עמי אשר במצרים ואת־
and ,Egypt in who my the have I surely ,Jehovah
(are) people of affliction seen

4341 3045 5065 6440 8085 6818
צעקתם שמעתי מפני נגשיו כי ידעתי את־מכאביו׃
.sorrows his know I for his from have I cry their
;slavedrivers before heard

his sorrows. 8 And I have come down to deliver them from the hand of Egypt; yea, to deliver them from that land to a good and broad land, to a land flowing *with* milk and honey, to the place of the Canaanite, and the Hitite, and the Amorite, and the Perizzite, and the Hivite, and the Jebusite. 9 And now, behold, the cry of the sons of Israel has come to Me, and also I have seen the oppression *with* which the Egyptians oppress them. 10 And now, go, and I will send you to Pharaoh, and you bring out My people, the sons of Israel, from Egypt.

11 And Moses said to God, Who *am* I that I should go to Pharaoh, and that I should bring out the sons of Israel from Egypt? 12 And He said, I will be with you, and this *shall be* the sign for you that I have sent you, when you bring out the people from Egypt: You shall serve God on this mountain.

13 And Moses said to God, Behold, I *shall* come to the sons of Israel and say to them, The God of your fathers has sent me to you; and they will say to me, What *is* His name? What shall I say to them? 14 And God said to Moses, I AM THAT I AM; and He said, You shall say this to the sons of Israel, I AM has sent me to you. 15 And God said to Moses again, You shall say this to the sons of Israel, Jehovah the God of your fathers, the God of Abraham, the God of Isaac, and the God of Jacob, has sent me to you. This *is* My name forever, and this *is*

776 5337 3027 5337 3381
8 וארד להצילו ׀ מיד מצרים ולהעלתו מן־הארץ ההוא
.that land from to and Egypt the from deliver to I And
him deliver of hand him come have

1706 2461 776 7342 2896 776
אל־ארץ טובה ורחבה אל־ארץ זבת חלב ודבש אל־
to and milk flowing a to and good land a to
honey (with) land ,broad

2983 2340 6522 567 2850 3669 4725
מקום הכנעני והחתי והאמרי והפרזי והחוי והיבוסי׃
the and the and the and the and the and the place the
.Jebusite ,Hivite ,Perizzite ,Amorite ,Hittite ,Canaanite of

7200 1571 935 3478 1121 6818 2009 6258
9 ועתה הנה צעקת בני־ישראל באה אלי וגם־ראיתי את־
have I and to has Israel the cry the ,behold And
seen also ,Me come of sons of ,now

7971 3212 6258 3905 4713 3906
10 הלחץ אשר מצרים לחצים אתם׃ ועתה לכה ואשלחך
will I and ,go And .them are the (with) oppres the
you send ,now oppressing Egyptians which sion

559 4714 3478 1121 5971 3318 6547
11 אל־פרעה והוצא את־עמי בני־ישראל ממצרים׃ ויאמר
said And .Egypt of out Israel the My you and Pharaoh to
of sons people bring

6547 3212 430 4872
משה אל־האלהים מי אנכי כי אלך אל־פרעה וכי
and Pharaoh to should I that (am) Who ,God to Moses
that go I

1961 559 4714 3478 1121 3318
12 אוציא את־בני ישראל ממצרים׃ ויאמר כי־אהיה
be will I for he And ?Egypt from Israel sons the should I
,said of bring

3318 7971 3588 226 2088
עמך וזה־לך האות כי אנכי שלחתיך בהוציאך את־
you when sent have I that (be will) for and with
out bring ,you sign the you this ,you

2088 2022 430 5647 4714 5971
העם ממצרים תעבדון את־האלהים על ההר הזה׃
.this mountain on God shall you :Egypt from the
serve people

3478 1121 935 2009 430 4872 559
13 ויאמר משה אל־האלהים הנה אנכי בא אל־בני ישראל
Israel the to (shall) I ,Behold ,God to Moses said And
of sons come

559 7971 1 430 559
ואמרתי להם אלהי אבותיכם שלחני אליכם ואמרו־לי
to they and ;you to sent has your the to say and
me say will me fathers of God ,them

1961 4872 430 559 559 8034
14 מה־שמו מה אמר אלהם׃ ויאמר אלהים אל־משה אהיה
AM I ,Moses to God said And ?them to shall What his What
say I ?name (is)

7971 1961 3478 1121 559 559 1961
אשר אהיה ויאמר כה תאמר לבני ישראל אהיה שלחני
has AM I ,Israel the to will you Thus He And !AM I who
me sent of sons say ,said

559 4872 430 5750 559
15 אליכם׃ ויאמר עוד אלהים אל־משה כה תאמר אל־
to You thus ,Moses to God again said And .you to
say shall

430 85 430 1 430 3068 3478 1121
בני ישראל יהוה אלהי אבתיכם אלהי אברהם אלהי
the ,Abraham the your the ,Jehovah ,Israel the
of God of God ,fathers of God of sons

5769 8034 7971 3290 430 3327
יצחק ואלהי יעקב שלחני אליכם זה־שמי לעלם וזה
and ,forever My this ;you to has Jacob the and ,Isaac
(is) this name (is) me sent of God

My title from generation to generation. 16 Go, and gather the elders of Israel, and say to them, Jehovah the God of your fathers has appeared to me, the God of Abraham, Isaac, and Jacob, saying, I have surely visited you and *have seen what* is done to you in Egypt. 17 And I have said, I will bring you up from the affliction of Egypt to the land of the Canaanite, the Hittite, and the Amorite, and the Perizzite, and the Hivite, and the Jebusite; to a land flowing *with* milk and honey. 18 And they shall listen to your voice; and you shall come in, you and the elders of Israel to the king of Egypt. And you shall say to him, Jehovah the God of the Hebrews has met us; and now, please let us go for a journey of three days into the wilderness, and let us sacrifice to Jehovah our God. 19 And I know that the king of Egypt will not permit you to go, not even by a strong hand. 20 And I will stretch out My hand and strike Egypt with all My wonders, which I will do in its midst, and afterward he will send you away. 21 And I will give this people favor in the eyes of Egypt; and it will come to pass, when you go, you will not go empty. 22 And each woman shall ask of her neighbor, and from the stranger in her house, articles of silver, and articles of gold, and garments; and you shall put *these* on your sons and on your daughters. And you shall plunder Egypt.

16 זכרי לדר דר: לך ואספת את־זקני ישראל ואמרת
say and ,Israel the elders of and gather Go generation of to generation My title

אלהם יהוה אלהי אבתיכם נראה אלי אלהי אברהם
,Abraham the God of ,me to has appeared your fathers the God of ,Jehovah to them

יצחק ויעקב לאמר פקד פקדתי אתכם ואת־העשוי
(what) and done is you have I visited surely ,saying and Jacob ,Isaac

17 לכם במצרים: ואמר אעלה אתכם מעני מצרים אל־
to Egypt the from of affliction you will I up bring I And said have .Egypt in you to

ארץ הכנעני והחתי והאמרי והפרזי והחוי והיבוסי אל־
to the and Jebusite the and Hivite the and Perizzite the and ,Amorite the ,Hittite the ,Canaanite land the of

18 ארץ זבת חלב ודבש: ושמעו לקלך ובאת אתה וזקני
the and of elders you you and enter will your voice they And hear will and .honey milk flowing (with) a land

ישראל אל־מלך מצרים ואמרתם אליו יהוה אלהי
the of God ,Jehovah to him you and say will :Egypt the of king to ,Israel

*4994 העבריים נקרה עלינו ועתה נלכה־נא דרך שלשת ימים
days three a (for) of trip please us let go and ,now with ;us has met ,Hebrews the

19 במדבר ונזבחה ליהוה אלהינו: ואני ידעתי כי לא־יתן
will not permit that know And I .God our to Jehovah us let and sacrifice the into ,wilderness

20 אתכם מלך מצרים להלך ולא ביד חזקה: ושלחתי
will I And out stretch strong a by .hand not even ,go to Egypt the of king you

את־ידי והכיתי את־מצרים בכל נפלאתי אשר אעשה
do will I which My ,wonders with all Egypt and strike hand my

21 בקרבו ואחרי־כן ישלח אתכם: ונתתי את־חן העם־
people favor I And give will .you will he send and afterward its in ,midst

הזה בעיני מצרים והיה כי תלכון לא תלכו ריקם:
.empty will you go not ,go you when it and be shall ;Egypt the in of eyes this

22 ושאלה אשה משכנתה ומגרת ביתה כלי־כסף וכלי
and of things silver things of her in house from and stranger the her from ,neighbor each woman shall And ask

זהב ושמלת ושמתם על־בניכם ועל־בנתיכם ונצלתם
you and strip shall your ;daughters and on your sons on you and put shall and ;garments ,gold

את־מצרים:
.Egypt

CAP. IV ד

CHAPTER 4

CHAPTER 4

[1]And Moses answered and said, And, behold, they will not believe me and will not listen to my voice. For they will say, Jehovah has not appeared to you. [2]And Jehovah said to him, What *is* this in your hand? And he said, A staff. [3]And He said, Throw it to the ground. And he threw it to the ground, and it became a snake. And Moses fled before it. [4]And Jehovah said to Moses, Send out your hand and take it by the tail. And he sent out his hand and caught it, and it became a staff in his hand—[5]so that they may believe that Jehovah the God of their fathers has appeared to you, the God of Abraham, the God of Isaac, and the God of Jacob. [6]And Jehovah said to him again, Now put your hand into your bosom. And he put his hand into his bosom, and he brought it out, and, behold, his hand *was* leprous like snow. [7]And He said, Put your hand back into your bosom. And he put his hand back into his bosom, and he brought it out from his bosom; and, behold, it had turned like his flesh! [8]And it shall be, if they will not believe you and will not listen to the voice of the first sign, that they will believe the latter sign. [9]And it shall be, if they will not believe these two signs also, and will not listen to your voice, you shall take of the water of the Nile and pour *it on* the dry land. And the water which you take from the Nile shall become blood on the dry land. [10]And Moses said to Jehovah, O Lord, I *am* not a man of words, either from yesterday or the third day,

6963 8085 3808 539 3808 2009 559 4874 6030
1 וַיַּעַן מֹשֶׁה וַיֹּאמֶר וְהֵן לֹא־יַאֲמִינוּ לִי וְלֹא יִשְׁמְעוּ בְּקֹלִי
my to will and me they not And ,said and Moses And
;voice listen not believe will ,behold answered

3068 559 3068 7200 559
2 כִּי יֹאמְרוּ לֹא־נִרְאָה אֵלֶיךָ יְהוָה׃ וַיֹּאמֶר אֵלָיו יְהוָה מַזֶּה
What Jehovah to said And Jehovah you to has not will they for
this (is) him appeared ,say

7993 776 7993 559 4294 559 3027
3 בְיָדֶךָ וַיֹּאמֶר מַטֶּה׃ וַיֹּאמֶר הַשְׁלִיכֵהוּ אַרְצָה וַיַּשְׁלִכֵהוּ
he And the to it Throw He And .staff A he And your in
it threw ,ground ,said ,said hand

3068 559 6440 4872 5127 5175 1961 776
4 אַרְצָה וַיְהִי לְנָחָשׁ וַיָּנָס מֹשֶׁה מִפָּנָיו׃ וַיֹּאמֶר יְהוָה אֶל־
to Jehovah And its from Moses and a it and the to
said .face fled ,snake became ,ground

1961 2388 3027 7971 2180 270 3027 7971 4872
מֹשֶׁה שְׁלַח יָדְךָ וֶאֱחֹז בִּזְנָבוֹ וַיִּשְׁלַח יָדוֹ וַיַּחֲזֶק בּוֹ וַיְהִי
it and ,it and his he and its by and your Reach ,Moses
became caught hand out put ;tail it catch hand out

430 3068 7200 539 3709 4294
5 לְמַטֶּה בְּכַפּוֹ׃ לְמַעַן יַאֲמִינוּ כִּי־נִרְאָה אֵלֶיךָ יְהוָה אֱלֹהֵי
the Jehovah to has that may they so his in staff a
of God you appeared believe .palm

559 3290 430 3327 430 85 430 1
6 אֲבֹתָם אֱלֹהֵי אַבְרָהָם אֱלֹהֵי יִצְחָק וֵאלֹהֵי יַעֲקֹב׃ וַיֹּאמֶר
said And ,Jacob the and ,Isaac the ,Abraham the their
of God of God of God ,fathers

2436 935 2436 3027 935 5750 3068
יְהוָה לוֹ עוֹד הָבֵא־נָא יָדְךָ בְּחֵיקֶךָ וַיָּבֵא יָדוֹ בְּחֵיקוֹ
his into his he and your into your now Put ,again to Jehovah
.bosom hand put ,bosom hand him

3029 7725 559 7950 6879 3027 2009 3947
7 וַיּוֹצִאָהּ וְהִנֵּה יָדוֹ מְצֹרַעַת כַּשָּׁלֶג׃ וַיֹּאמֶר הָשֵׁב יָדְךָ אֶל־
into your Put He And like (was) his ,lo ,and he And
hand back ,said .snow leprous hand out it took

7725 2436 3947 2436 3027 7725 2436
חֵיקֶךָ וַיָּשֶׁב יָדוֹ אֶל־חֵיקוֹ וַיּוֹצִאָהּ מֵחֵיקוֹ וְהִנֵּה־שָׁבָה
had it ,lo, and his of he and his into his he and your
turned ;bosom out it took bosom hand back put ,bosom

226 6963 8085 3808 539 3808 1961 1320
8 כִּבְשָׂרוֹ׃ וְהָיָה אִם־לֹא יַאֲמִינוּ לָךְ וְלֹא יִשְׁמְעוּ לְקֹל הָאֹת
the the to will and you will they not if it And his like
sign of voice listen not believe ,be shall .flesh

3808 1961 314 226 6963 539 7223
9 הָרִאשׁוֹן וְהֶאֱמִינוּ לְקֹל הָאֹת הָאַחֲרוֹן׃ וְהָיָה אִם־לֹא
not if it And .latter the the they that ,first
,be shall sign of voice believe will

6963 8085 3808 226 8147 1571 539
יַאֲמִינוּ גַּם לִשְׁנֵי הָאֹתוֹת הָאֵלֶּה וְלֹא יִשְׁמְעוּן לְקֹלֶךָ
your to will not and ,these signs two also will they
,voice listen believe

834 4325 1961 3006 8210 2975 4325 3947
וְלָקַחְתָּ מִמֵּימֵי הַיְאֹר וְשָׁפַכְתָּ הַיַּבָּשָׁה וְהָיוּ הַמַּיִם אֲשֶׁר
which the it and the (on) pout and the water of will you
water ,be will ,land dry (it) out Nile's take

4874 559 1818 1961 2975 3947
10 תִּקַּח מִן־הַיְאֹר וְהָיוּ לְדָם בַּיַּבָּשֶׁת׃ וַיֹּאמֶר מֹשֶׁה אֶל־
to Moses said And dry the on blood will the from you
.land become Nile take

8543 518 1697 376 3068
יְהוָה בִּי אֲדֹנָי לֹא אִישׁ דְּבָרִים אָנֹכִי גַּם מִתְּמוֹל גַּם
or from either I words man a not Lord Please
yesterday ,(am) of ,Jehovah

nor since You have been speaking to Your slave. For I *am* heavy of mouth and heavy of tongue. [11]And Jehovah said to him, Who has made the mouth of man? Or who makes *one* dumb, or deaf, or seeing, or blind? Is it not I, Jehovah? [12]And now go, and I will be with your mouth and will teach you what you shall speak.

[13]And he said, O Lord, please send by the hand *of him whom* You will send. [14]And the anger of Jehovah glowed against Moses. And He said, Do I not know your brother, Aaron the Levite, that he can speak well? And, behold, he also *is* coming out to meet you, and he will see you and be glad in his heart. [15]And you shall speak to him, and you shall put the words in his mouth. And I will be with your mouth, and with his mouth, and I will teach you what you shall do. [16]And he shall speak for you to the people. And it shall be, he shall be a mouth for you, and you shall be a god for him. [17]And you shall take this staff in your hand *by* which you do the signs.

[18]And Moses went and returned to his father-in-law Jethro, and said to him, Please let me go and return to my brothers who are in Egypt, and see whether they *are* still alive. And Jethro said to Moses, Go in peace.

[19]And Jehovah said to Moses in Midian, Go! Return to Egypt. For all the men are dead, those seeking your life. [20]And Moses took his wife and his sons and set them on an ass.

3515 6310 3515 5650 1696 227 8032
מִשִּׁלְשֹׁם גַּם מֵאָז דַּבֶּרְךָ אֶל־עַבְדֶּךָ כִּי כְבַד־פֶּה וּכְבַד
and mouth heavy for Your to You since nor the from
of heavy of ;servant spoke ,day third

120 6310 7760 3068 559 3956
11 לְשׁוֹן אָנֹכִי׃ וַיֹּאמֶר יְהוָה אֵלָיו מִי שָׂם פֶּה לָאָדָם אוֹ
Or ?man's mouth has Who to Jehovah said And I tongue
3808 made ,him .(am)

3068 5787 6493 2795 483 7760
מִי־יָשׂוּם אִלֵּם אוֹ חֵרֵשׁ אוֹ פִקֵּחַ אוֹ עִוֵּר הֲלֹא אָנֹכִי יְהוָה׃
?Jehovah I it Is (the) or (the) or (the) or (the) makes who
not ?blind seeing deaf dumb

1696 3384 6310 1961 32,12 1258
12 וְעַתָּה לֵךְ וְאָנֹכִי אֶהְיֶה עִם־פִּיךָ וְהוֹרֵיתִיךָ אֲשֶׁר תְּדַבֵּר׃
will you what will and your with be will I and ,go And
.speak you teach ,mouth ,now

3068 639 2734 7971 3027 4994 7971 136 990 559
13 וַיֹּאמֶר בִּי אֲדֹנָי שְׁלַח־נָא בְּיַד־תִּשְׁלָח׃
14 וַיִּחַר־אַף יְהוָה
Jehovah the And will You the by now Send ,Lord Please he And
of anger glowed .send hand ,said

3045 3881 251 175 3808 559 4872
בְּמֹשֶׁה וַיֹּאמֶר הֲלֹא אַהֲרֹן אָחִיךָ הַלֵּוִי יָדַעְתִּי כִּי־דַבֵּר
well that ,know I the your ,Aaron not Do He And against
,Levite brother ,said .Moses

8056 7200 7125 3318 2009 1571 1696
יְדַבֵּר הוּא וְגַם הִנֵּה־הוּא יֹצֵא לִקְרָאתֶךָ וְרָאֲךָ וְשָׂמַח
be and he and meet to (is) he ,behold And ?he can
glad you see will ,you coming also speak

6310 1697 7760 1696 3820
15 בְּלִבּוֹ׃ וְדִבַּרְתָּ אֵלָיו וְשַׂמְתָּ אֶת־הַדְּבָרִים בְּפִיו וְאָנֹכִי
I and his in words the you and to you And his in
;mouth put shall ,him speak will .heart

6213 3384 6310 6310 1961
אֶהְיֶה עִם־פִּיךָ וְעִם־פִּיהוּ וְהוֹרֵיתִי אֶתְכֶם אֵת אֲשֶׁר תַּעֲשׂוּן׃
shall you what you will I and his and your with will
.do teach ,mouth with ,mouth be

6310 1961 1961 5971 1696
16 וְדִבֶּר־הוּא לְךָ אֶל־הָעָם וְהָיָה הוּא יִהְיֶה־לְּךָ לְפֶה וְאַתָּה
you and a for for shall he it And the to for he And
,mouth you be ,be shall .people you speak shall

834 3027 3947 4294 430 1961
17 תִּהְיֶה־לּוֹ לֵאלֹהִים׃ וְאֶת־הַמַּטֶּה הַזֶּה תִּקַּח בְּיָדֶךָ אֲשֶׁר
which your in you this staff And .god a for for shall
hand take shall him be

226 6213
תַּעֲשֶׂה־בּוֹ אֶת־הָאֹתֹת׃ פ ששי
.signs the by do you
it

3212 559 2859 3503 7725 4872 3212
18 וַיֵּלֶךְ מֹשֶׁה וַיָּשָׁב ׀ אֶל־יֶתֶר חֹתְנוֹ וַיֹּאמֶר לוֹ אֵלְכָה נָּא
now me Let to said and his Jethro to and Moses And
go ,him ,father-in-law returned went

2416 5750 7200 4714 251 7725
וְאָשׁוּבָה אֶל־אַחַי אֲשֶׁר־בְּמִצְרַיִם וְאֶרְאֶה הַעוֹדָם חַיִּים
.alive they whether and ,Egypt in who my to and
still (are) see (are) brothers return

4872 3068 559 7965 3212 4872 3503 559
19 וַיֹּאמֶר יִתְרוֹ לְמֹשֶׁה לֵךְ לְשָׁלוֹם׃ וַיֹּאמֶר יְהוָה אֶל־מֹשֶׁה
Moses to Jehovah said And .peace in Go ,Moses to Jethro said And

1245 582 3605 4191 4714 7725 3212 4080
בְּמִדְיָן לֵךְ שֻׁב מִצְרָיִם כִּי־מֵתוּ כָּל־הָאֲנָשִׁים הַמְבַקְשִׁים
seeking those men the all are for ,Egypt to return ,Go in
dead ,Midian

7392 1121 802 4872 3947 5315
20 אֶת־נַפְשֶׁךָ׃ וַיִּקַּח מֹשֶׁה אֶת־אִשְׁתּוֹ וְאֶת־בָּנָיו וַיַּרְכִּבֵם
made and sons his and wife his Moses took And .life your
ride them

And he returned to the land of Egypt. And Moses took the staff of God in his hand.
[21]And Jehovah said to Moses, As you go to return to Egypt, see all the wonders which I have put in your hand, and do them before Pharaoh. And I will harden his heart, and he will not send the people away.
[22]And you shall speak to Pharaoh, So says Jehovah, My son, My firstborn *is* Israel.
[23]And I said to you, Send My son away, and let him serve Me; and you refused to send him. Behold, I *am* about to kill your son, your firstborn!
[24]And it happened on the way, in the lodging place, Jehovah met him and sought to kill him.
[25]And Zipporah took a stone and cut off her son's foreskin, and caused *it* to touch his feet. And she said, You *are* a bridegroom of blood to me.
[26]And He pulled back from him. Then she said, A bridegroom of blood, for the circumcision.
[27]And Jehovah said to Aaron, Go to the wilderness to meet Moses. And he went and met him in the mountain of God; and he kissed him.
[28]And Moses told Aaron all the words of Jehovah *with* which He had sent him, and all the signs which He had commanded him.
[29]And Moses and Aaron went on and gathered all the elders of the sons of Israel.
[30]And Aaron spoke all the words which Jehovah had spoken to Moses. And he did the signs before the people.
[31]And the people believed. And they heard that

עַל־הַחֲמֹר וַיָּשָׁב אַרְצָה מִצְרָיִם וַיִּקַּח מֹשֶׁה אֶת־מַטֵּה
of staff the Moses And took .Egypt the to of land he and returned the ;ass on

21 הָאֱלֹהִים בְּיָדוֹ׃ וַיֹּאמֶר יְהוָה אֶל־מֹשֶׁה בְּלֶכְתְּךָ לָשׁוּב
to return go you As ,Moses to Jehovah said And his in .hand God

מִצְרַיְמָה רְאֵה כָּל־הַמֹּפְתִים אֲשֶׁר־שַׂמְתִּי בְיָדֶךָ וַעֲשִׂיתָם
them do and your in ,hand have I put which wonders the all see ,Egypt to

לִפְנֵי פַרְעֹה וַאֲנִי אֲחַזֵּק אֶת־לִבּוֹ וְלֹא יְשַׁלַּח אֶת־הָעָם׃
the .people will he away send not and his heart will I harden and ,Pharaoh before

22 וְאָמַרְתָּ אֶל־פַּרְעֹה כֹּה אָמַר יְהוָה בְּנִי בְכֹרִי יִשְׂרָאֵל׃
.Israel (is) My firstborn My ,son ,Jehovah says Thus ,Pharaoh to you And say shall

23 וָאֹמַר אֵלֶיךָ שַׁלַּח אֶת־בְּנִי וְיַעַבְדֵנִי וַתְּמָאֵן לְשַׁלְּחוֹ הִנֵּה אָנֹכִי
I ,lo send to ;him you and refused let and Me serve him son My Send away to you I And said

24 הֹרֵג אֶת־בִּנְךָ בְּכֹרֶךָ׃ וַיְהִי בַדֶּרֶךְ בַּמָּלוֹן וַיִּפְגְּשֵׁהוּ יְהוָה
Jehovah him met the in place lodging way the on it And happened your .firstborn your ,son about am kill to

25 וַיְבַקֵּשׁ הֲמִיתוֹ׃ וַתִּקַּח צִפֹּרָה צֹר וַתִּכְרֹת אֶת־עָרְלַת בְּנָהּ
her ,son foreskin of the off cut and a flint Zipporah And took slay to .him and sought

26 וַתַּגַּע לְרַגְלָיו וַתֹּאמֶר כִּי חֲתַן־דָּמִים אַתָּה לִי׃ וַיִּרֶף מִמֶּנּוּ
from .him He And desisted to .me you (are) bloods bride- a groom of For she and ,said his feet made And (it) touch

אָז אָמְרָה חֲתַן דָּמִים לַמּוּלֹת׃
the for circumcision bloods bride- A groom of she ,said Then

27 וַיֹּאמֶר יְהוָה אֶל־אַהֲרֹן לֵךְ לִקְרַאת מֹשֶׁה הַמִּדְבָּרָה וַיֵּלֶךְ
he And went the to .wilderness Moses meet to Go ,Aaron to Jehovah And said

28 וַיִּפְגְּשֵׁהוּ בְּהַר הָאֱלֹהִים וַיִּשַּׁק־לוֹ׃ וַיַּגֵּד מֹשֶׁה לְאַהֲרֹן
Aaron to Moses And told .him he and kissed ;God of mountain the in met and him

אֵת כָּל־דִּבְרֵי יְהוָה אֲשֶׁר שְׁלָחוֹ וְאֵת כָּל־הָאֹתֹת אֲשֶׁר
which signs the all and had He sent him (with) which Jehovah the of words all

29 צִוָּהוּ׃ וַיֵּלֶךְ מֹשֶׁה וְאַהֲרֹן וַיַּאַסְפוּ אֶת־כָּל־זִקְנֵי בְּנֵי יִשְׂרָאֵל׃
.Israel the of sons the of elders all and gathered and Aaron Moses And went him He ordered

30 וַיְדַבֵּר אַהֲרֹן אֵת כָּל־הַדְּבָרִים אֲשֶׁר־דִּבֶּר יְהוָה אֶל־
to Jehovah had spoken which words the all Aaron And spoke

31 מֹשֶׁה וַיַּעַשׂ הָאֹתֹת לְעֵינֵי הָעָם׃ וַיַּאֲמֵן הָעָם וַיִּשְׁמְעוּ כִּי־
that they and heard the ;people And believed the .people before the signs and did he ;Moses

Jehovah had visited the sons of Israel, and that He had seen their affliction. And they bowed and worshiped.

6915 6040 7200 3478 1121 3068 6485
פקד יהוה את־בני ישראל וכי ראה את־ענים ויקדו
they and their had He and ,Israel sons the Jehovah had
bowed ,affliction seen that of .visited
7812
וישתחוו:
and
.worshiped

CAP. V ה

CHAPTER 5

CHAPTER 5

[1]And afterward Moses and Aaron came in and said to Pharaoh, So says Jehovah the God of Israel, Send away My people, and they shall feast to Me in the wilderness. [2]And Pharaoh said, Who *is* Jehovah that I should listen to His voice to send away Israel? I do not know Jehovah, and I also will not send Israel away. [3]And they said, The God of the Hebrews has met with us. Now let us go a journey of three days into the wilderness and sacrifice to Jehovah our God, that He not strike us with plague or with sword. [4]And the king of Egypt said to them, Moses and Aaron, why do you loose the people from their work? You go to your burdens.

[5]And Pharaoh said, Behold, the people of the land *are* many now, and you make them cease from their burdens. [6]And Pharaoh commanded the slave-drivers of the people, and their overseers, that day, saying, [7]You shall not go on giving straw to the people to make bricks, as yesterday and the third day. They shall go and pick up straw for themselves. [8]And the fixed number of bricks which they *were* making yesterday *and* the third day you shall put on them. You shall not diminish from it. For they *are* idle: so they

559 6547 559 175 4872 935 310
1 ואחר באו משה ואהרן ויאמרו אל־פרעה כה־אמר
says Thus .Pharaoh to said and and Moses came And
Aaron in afterward
4057 2287 5971 7971 3478 430
יהוה אלהי ישראל שלח את־עמי ויחגו לי במדבר:
the in to they and My Send ,Israel the Jehovah
.wilderness Me feast shall people away of God
7971 6963 8085 3068 4310 6547 559
2 ויאמר פרעה מי יהוה אשר אשמע בקלו לשלח את־
send to His to should I that Jehovah Who ,Pharaoh And
away voice listen (is) said
7971 3808 3478 1571 3068 3045 3808 3478
ישראל לא ידעתי את־יהוה וגם את־ישראל לא אשלח:
I will not Israel and ,Jehovah do I not ?Israel
.send also know
1870 4994 3212 7125 5680 430 559
3 ויאמרו אלהי העברים נקרא עלינו נלכה נא דרך
trip a ,now go us let with met has Hebrews the the they And
of ;us of God said
6293 430 3068 2076 4057 3117 7969
שלשת ימים במדבר ונזבחה ליהוה אלהינו פן־יפגענו
fall He lest ;God our to us let and the into days three
us on Jehovah sacrifice wilderness
4872 4100 4714 4428 559 2719 1698
4 בדבר או בחרב: ויאמר אלהם מלך מצרים למה משה
Moses ,Why ,Egypt the them to said And with or with
of king .sword plague
5450 3212 4639 5971 6544 175
ואהרן תפריעו את־העם ממעשיו לכו לסבלתיכם:
.burdens your to You their from the you do and
go ?work people loose Aaron
7673 776 5971 6258 7227 6547 559
5 ויאמר פרעה הן־רבים עתה עם הארץ והשבתם אתם
them make you and the the now many ,See ,Pharaoh And
cease land of people (are) said
5971 5065 1931 3117 6547 6680 5450
6 מסבלתם: ויצו פרעה ביום ההוא את־הנגשים בעם
the slavedrivers the that day Pharaoh And their from
people of commanded .burdens
3835 8401 3254 559 7860
7 ואת־שטריו לאמר: לא תאספון לתת תבן לעם ללבן
to the to straw giving shall You not ,saying their and
make people continue ,overseers
8401 7197 3212 8032 8543 3843
הלבנים כתמול שלשם הם ילכו וקששו להם תבן:
.straw for pick and shall they the and as ,bricks
themselves up go ;before day ,yesterday
8032 8543 7760 834 3843 4971
8 ואת־מתכנת הלבנים אשר הם עשים תמול שלשם
day the yesterday were they which bricks fixed the And
before (and) making of number
3651 7503 1639 3808 7971
תשימו עליהם לא תגרעו ממנו כי־נרפים הם על־כן
So .they idle are for ;it from shall you not ;them upon shall you
diminish put

are crying, saying, Let us go, let us sacrifice to our God. [9]Let the bondage be heavy on the men, that they may work in it, and may not trust to the lying words.

[10]And the slavedrivers of the people, and their overseers, went out and spoke to the people, saying, Pharaoh has said this, I will not give you straw. [11]You go take straw for yourselves from wherever you may find *it*. For not a thing will be reduced from your work. [12]And the people scattered in all the land of Egypt to pick up stubble for straw. [13]And the slavedrivers *were* demanding, saying, Finish your work, the matter of a day in its day, as when there was straw. [14]And the overseers of the sons of Israel were beaten, those whom the slavedrivers of Pharaoh had put over them, saying, Why have you not finished your appointed task, to make bricks as a day ago *and* the day before, both yesterday and today?

[15]And the overseers of the sons of Israel came in and cried to Pharaoh, saying, Why do you do this way to your bondslaves? [16]No straw is given to your bondslaves, and they are saying to us, Make bricks. And, behold, your bondslaves are stricken, but your people are at fault. [17]And he said, Idle. You *are* idle. On this account you *are* saying, Let us go; let us sacrifice to Jehovah. [18]So now go serve. And straw will not be given to you, and you will give a quota of bricks.

[19]And the overseers of the sons of Israel saw themselves in evil, saying, You shall not diminish from your bricks, the matter of a day in its day. [20]And they met Moses and Aaron standing to

5656 3513 430 2076 3212 559 6817
9 הם צעקים לאמר נלכה נזבחה לאלהינו׃ תכבד העבדה
bondage the be Let .God our to us let us Let ,saying are they
heavy sacrifice ,go ,crying

5927 8267 1697 8159 5656 582
10 על־האנשים ויעשו־בה ואל־ישעו בדברי־שקר׃ ויצאו
And .lying in may and in they that the on
went words trust not ,it work may ,men

559 559 5971 559 7860 5971 5065
נגשי העם ושטריו ויאמרו אל־העם לאמר כה אמר
has Thus ,saying the to spoke and their and the slave- the
said ,people ,overseers ,people of drivers

8401 3947 3212 8401 5414 6547
11 פרעה אינני נתן לכם תבן׃ אתם לכו קחו לכם תבן
straw for take go You .straw you to will I ,Pharaoh
yourselves give not

5971 6327 1697 4639 1639 3588 4672
12 מאשר תמצאו כי אין נגרע מעבדתכם דבר׃ ויפץ העם
the And .thing a your from be will not for can you from
people scattered work reduced ;(it) find wherever

243 5065 8401 7179 7197 4714 776 3605
13 בכל־ארץ מצרים לקשש קש לתבן׃ והנגשים אצים
(were) the And for stubble to ,Egypt the all in
,urging slavedrivers .straw gather of land

1961 4639 3615 559
לאמר כלו מעשיכם דבר־יום ביומו כאשר בהיות
there when as a thing the work your Finish ,saying
was ,day of

5065 7760 3478 1121 7860 5221 8401
14 התבן׃ ויכו שטרי בני ישראל אשר־שמו עלהם נגשי
the over had those ,Israel the the were and ,straw
of drivers them put whom of sons of chiefs beaten

8543 3835 2706 3615 3808 4100 559 6547
פרעה לאמר מדוע לא כליתם חקכם ללבן כתמול
day a as make to task your you have not Why ,saying ,Pharaoh
ago bricks finished

3478 1121 7860 935 8032 865 8032
15 שלשם גם־תמול גם־היום׃ ויבאו שטרי בני ישראל
Israel the the came And ?today and yesterday both the (and)
of sons of chiefs ,before day

8401 5650 6213 4100 559 6547 6817
16 ויצעקו אל־פרעה לאמר למה תעשה כה לעבדיך׃ תבן
Straw your to thus you do Why ,saying ,Pharaoh to and
?servants do cried

5650 2009 6213 559 3843 5650 5414
אין נתן לעבדיך ולבנים אמרים לנו עשו והנה עבדיך
your ,and ,make us to are they bricks and your to is not
servants ,see saying ,servants given

8651 7503 7503 559 5971 2398 5221
17 מכים וחטאת עמך׃ ויאמר נרפים אתם נרפים על־כן
this on ;idle You .Idle he and your are But are
(are) ,said .people fault at .stricken

5647 3212 6258 3068 2076 559
18 אתם אמרים נלכה נזבחה ליהוה׃ ועתה לכו עבדו
(and) go now So to us let us Let are you
;work .Jehovah sacrifice ,go ,saying

1121 7860 7200 5414 3843 8506 5414 8401
19 ותבן לא־ינתן לכם ותכן לבנים תתנו׃ ויראו שטרי בני־
the the saw And will you bricks a and to will not and
of sons of chiefs .give of quota you given be straw

3117 1697 3843 1639 559 7451 3478
ישראל אתם ברע לאמר לא־תגרעו מלבניכם דבר־יום
a the your from shall You not ,saying in them- Israel
day of thing ,bricks diminish ,evil selves

7125 5324 175 4872 6293 3117
20 ביומו׃ ויפגעו את־משה ואת־אהרן נצבים לקראתם
them meet to standing Aaron and Moses they And its in
met .day

meet them when they
came from Pharaoh.
21 And they said to them,
May Jehovah look on you
and judge; who have
made our odor to stink in
Pharaoh's eyes and in the
eyes of his servants, to
give a sword in their
hands to kill us.
22 And Moses returned to
Jehovah and said, Lord,
why have You done evil to
this people? Why then have
You sent me? 23 And since I
came in to Pharaoh to
speak in Your name, he has
done evil to this people.
And You did not certainly
deliver your people.

3068 7200 559 6547 3318
21 בְּצֵאתָם מֵאֵת פַּרְעֹה׃ וַיֹּאמְרוּ אֲלֵהֶם יֵרֶא יְהוָה עֲלֵיכֶם
you on Jehovah May ,them to they And .Pharaoh from they when
look said came

5869 6547 5869 7381 887 8199
וְיִשְׁפֹּט אֲשֶׁר הִבְאַשְׁתֶּם אֶת־רֵיחֵנוּ בְּעֵינֵי פַרְעֹה וּבְעֵינֵי
in and Pharaoh's eyes in odor our made have who and
of eyes stink to judge

3068 4872 7725 2026 2719 5414 5650
22 עֲבָדָיו לָתֶת־חֶרֶב בְּיָדָם לְהָרְגֵנוּ׃ וַיָּשָׁב מֹשֶׁה אֶל־יְהוָה
Jehovah unto Moses And .us kill to into a give to his
returned hand their sword ,servants

7971 4100 2088 5971 7489 4100 136 559
וַיֹּאמַר אֲדֹנָי לָמָה הֲרֵעֹתָה לָעָם הַזֶּה לָמָּה זֶּה שְׁלַחְתָּנִי׃
you have ,this Why ?this to you have ,why ,Lord and
?me sent (that) people evil done ,said

5337 2088 5971 7489 8034 1696 6547 935
23 וּמֵאָז בָּאתִי אֶל־פַּרְעֹה לְדַבֵּר בִּשְׁמֶךָ הֵרַע לָעָם הַזֶּה וְהַצֵּל
and ;this to has he Your in to Pharaoh to came I And
surely people evil done ;name speak in since

5971 5337
לֹא־הִצַּלְתָּ אֶת־עַמֶּךָ׃
Your have you not
.people delivered

CAP. VI ו

CHAPTER 6

CHAPTER 6
1 And Jehovah said to
Moses, Now you will see
what I will do to Pharaoh.
For he will send them away
with a strong hand; yea, he
will drive them out from his
land with a strong hand.
2 And God spoke to
Moses and said to him, I *am*
Jehovah. 3 And I appeared
to Abraham, to Isaac and to
Jacob as God Almighty,
and *by* My name JEHOVAH
I never made Myself known
to them. 4 And I also
established My covenant
with them, to give to them
the land of Canaan, the land
of their travels, *in* which
they traveled. 5 And I also
have heard the groaning of
the sons of Israel, whom the
Egyptians are enslaving.
And I have remembered My
covenant. 6 Therefore, say
to the sons of Israel, I *am*
Jehovah, and I will bring
you out from under the
burdens of Egypt, and will
deliver you from their
slavery. And I will redeem
you with an outstretched
arm, and with great
judgments.

6547 6213 7200 6258 4872 3068 559
1 וַיֹּאמֶר יְהוָה אֶל־מֹשֶׁה עַתָּה תִרְאֶה אֲשֶׁר אֶעֱשֶׂה לְפַרְעֹה
to do will I what will you Now ,Moses to Jehovah And
;Pharaoh see said

776 1644 2389 3027 7971 2389 3027
כִּי בְיָד חֲזָקָה יְשַׁלְּחֵם וּבְיָד חֲזָקָה יְגָרְשֵׁם מֵאַרְצוֹ׃
his from will he strong with and will he strong with for
.land them drive hand a ,them send hand a

7200 3068 559 4872 430 1696
2 3 וַיְדַבֵּר אֱלֹהִים אֶל־מֹשֶׁה וַיֹּאמֶר אֵלָיו אֲנִי יְהוָה׃ וָאֵרָא
I and ;Jehovah I him to said and Moses to God And
appeared (am) spoke

3068 8034 7706 410 3290 3327 85
אֶל־אַבְרָהָם אֶל־יִצְחָק וְאֶל־יַעֲקֹב בְּאֵל שַׁדָּי וּשְׁמִי יְהוָה
Jehovah and ,Almighty as Jacob and ,Isaac to ,Abraham to
name My (by) God to

5414 1285 6965 1571 3045 3808
4 לֹא נוֹדַעְתִּי לָהֶם׃ וְגַם הֲקִמֹתִי אֶת־בְּרִיתִי אִתָּם לָתֵת
to with covenant My I And them to did I not
give ,them established also Myself reveal

1481 4033 776 3667 776
לָהֶם אֶת־אֶרֶץ כְּנָעַן אֵת אֶרֶץ מְגֻרֵיהֶם אֲשֶׁר־גָּרוּ בָהּ׃
in they which their the ;Canaan the to
.it traveled travels of land of land them

4714 3478 1121 5009 8085 1571
5 וְגַם ׀ אֲנִי שָׁמַעְתִּי אֶת־נַאֲקַת בְּנֵי יִשְׂרָאֵל אֲשֶׁר מִצְרַיִם
Egypt whom ,Israel the the heard have I And
of sons of groaning also

3478 1121 559 3651 1285 2142 5647
6 מַעֲבִדִים אֹתָם וָאֶזְכֹּר אֶת־בְּרִיתִי׃ לָכֵן אֱמֹר לִבְנֵי־יִשְׂרָאֵל
,Israel the to say There- My I And .them is
of sons fore .covenant remembered enslaving

5337 4714 5450 8478 3318 3068
אֲנִי יְהוָה וְהוֹצֵאתִי אֶתְכֶם מִתַּחַת סִבְלֹת מִצְרַיִם וְהִצַּלְתִּי
will and ,Egypt the from you I and ,Jehovah I
deliver of burdens under bring will (am)

8201 5186 2220 1350 5656
אֶתְכֶם מֵעֲבֹדָתָם וְגָאַלְתִּי אֶתְכֶם בִּזְרוֹעַ נְטוּיָה וּבִשְׁפָטִים
with and out- an with you will I and their from you
judgments stretched arm redeem ;slavery

[7]And I will take you for Myself for a people, and I will be a God for you. And you shall know that I *am* Jehovah your God, the One bringing you out from under the burdens of Egypt. [8]And I will bring you into the land which I raised My hand to give to Abraham, to Isaac, and to Jacob. And I will give it to you for a possession. I *am* Jehovah! [9]And Moses spoke to the sons of Israel. And they did not listen to Moses, from shortness of spirit and from hard bondage.

[10]And Jehovah spoke to Moses, saying, [11]Go, speak to Pharaoh king of Egypt, that he may send away the sons of Israel from his land. [12]And Moses spoke before Jehovah, saying, Behold the sons of Israel have not listened to me. And how should Pharaoh hear me, I *being* of uncircumcised lips? [13]And Jehovah spoke to Moses and to Aaron, and He commanded them as to the sons of Israel, and as to Pharaoh king of Egypt, to bring out the sons of Israel from the land of Egypt.

[14]These *were* the heads of the houses of their fathers: The sons of Reuben the firstborn of Israel *were* Hanoch, and Pallu, and Hezron, and Carmi; these *were* the families of Reuben. [15]And the sons of Simeon: Jemuel, and Jamin, and Ohad, and Jachin, and Zohar, and Shaul, the son of a Canaanitess; these *were* the families of Simeon. [16]And these *were* the names of the sons of Levi by their generations: Gershon, and Kohath, and Merari. And the years of the life of Levi *were* a hundred and

7 גְּדֹלִים׃ וְלָקַחְתִּי אֶתְכֶם לִי לְעָם וְהָיִיתִי לָכֶם לֵאלֹהִים
וִידַעְתֶּם כִּי אֲנִי יְהוָה אֱלֹהֵיכֶם הַמּוֹצִיא אֶתְכֶם מִתַּחַת
8 סִבְלוֹת מִצְרָיִם׃ וְהֵבֵאתִי אֶתְכֶם אֶל־הָאָרֶץ אֲשֶׁר נָשָׂאתִי
אֶת־יָדִי לָתֵת אֹתָהּ לְאַבְרָהָם לְיִצְחָק וּלְיַעֲקֹב וְנָתַתִּי אֹתָהּ
9 לָכֶם מוֹרָשָׁה אֲנִי יְהוָה׃ וַיְדַבֵּר מֹשֶׁה כֵּן אֶל־בְּנֵי יִשְׂרָאֵל
וְלֹא שָׁמְעוּ אֶל־מֹשֶׁה מִקֹּצֶר רוּחַ וּמֵעֲבֹדָה קָשָׁה׃ פ
10 11 וַיְדַבֵּר יְהוָה אֶל־מֹשֶׁה לֵּאמֹר׃ בֹּא דַבֵּר אֶל־פַּרְעֹה מֶלֶךְ
12 מִצְרָיִם וִישַׁלַּח אֶת־בְּנֵי־יִשְׂרָאֵל מֵאַרְצוֹ׃ וַיְדַבֵּר מֹשֶׁה
לִפְנֵי יְהוָה לֵאמֹר הֵן בְּנֵי־יִשְׂרָאֵל לֹא־שָׁמְעוּ אֵלַי וְאֵיךְ
יִשְׁמָעֵנִי פַרְעֹה וַאֲנִי עֲרַל שְׂפָתָיִם׃
13 וַיְדַבֵּר יְהוָה אֶל־מֹשֶׁה וְאֶל־אַהֲרֹן וַיְצַוֵּם אֶל־בְּנֵי יִשְׂרָאֵל
וְאֶל־פַּרְעֹה מֶלֶךְ מִצְרָיִם לְהוֹצִיא אֶת־בְּנֵי־יִשְׂרָאֵל מֵאֶרֶץ
14 מִצְרָיִם׃ ס אֵלֶּה רָאשֵׁי בֵית־אֲבֹתָם בְּנֵי רְאוּבֵן
בְּכֹר יִשְׂרָאֵל חֲנוֹךְ וּפַלּוּא חֶצְרֹן וְכַרְמִי אֵלֶּה מִשְׁפְּחֹת
15 רְאוּבֵן׃ וּבְנֵי שִׁמְעוֹן יְמוּאֵל וְיָמִין וְאֹהַד וְיָכִין וְצֹחַר
16 וְשָׁאוּל בֶּן־הַכְּנַעֲנִית אֵלֶּה מִשְׁפְּחֹת שִׁמְעוֹן׃ וְאֵלֶּה שְׁמוֹת
בְּנֵי־לֵוִי לְתֹלְדֹתָם גֵּרְשׁוֹן וּקְהָת וּמְרָרִי וּשְׁנֵי חַיֵּי לֵוִי שֶׁבַע •3878

thirty-seven years. [17]The sons of Gershon: Libni, and Shimei, by their families. [18]And the sons of Kohath: Amram, and Izhar, and Hebron, and Uzziel. And the years of the life of Kohath *were* a hundred and thirty-three years. [19]And the sons of Merari: Mahli, and Mushi. These are the families of Levi according to their generations.

[20]And Amram took his aunt Jochebed to him for a wife. And she bore to him Aaron and Moses. And the years of the life of Amram *were* a hundred and thirty-seven years. [21]And the sons of Izhar: Korah, and Nepheg, and Zichri. [22]And the sons of Uzziel: Mishael, and Elzaphan, and Zithri. [23]And Aaron took Elisheba the daughter of Amminadab, the sister of Nahshon, to him for a wife. And she bore to him Nadab, and Abihu, Eleazar, and Ithamar. [24]And the sons of Korah: Assir, and Elkanah, and Abiasaph. These *were* the families of the Korahites. [25]And Aaron's son Eleazar took of the daughters of Putiel for his wife. And she bore to him Phinehas. These *were* the heads of the fathers of the Levites by their families.

[26]That *is the* Aaron and Moses *to* whom Jehovah said, Bring out the sons of Israel from the land of Egypt, according to their armies. [27]Those *were* the ones speaking to Pharaoh king of Egypt to bring out the sons of Israel from Egypt—it *was* Moses and Aaron.

[28]And it happened on the day Jehovah spoke to Moses in the land of Egypt: [29]Jehovah spoke to Moses, saying, I *am* Jehovah!

4940 8096 3845 1648 1121 8141 3967 7970
17 ושלשים ומאת שנה: בני גרשון לבני ושמעי למשפחתם:
.families their by and ,Libni :Gershon The .years a and and
,Shimei of sons hundred thirty

6955 2416 8141 5816 2275 3324 6019 6099 1121
18 ובני קהת עמרם ויצהר וחברון ועזיאל ושני חיי קהת
Kohath the the and and ,Hebron and and ,Amram the And
of life of years ;Uzziel ,Izhar :Kohath sons of

4187 4249 4847 1121 8141 3967 7970 7969
19 שלש ושלשים ומאת שנה: ובני מררי מחלי ומושי אלה
these and ,Mahli :Merari the And .years a and and (were)
(are) ;Mushi of sons hundred thirty three

1733 3115 6019 3947 8435 3878 4940
20 משפחת הלוי לתלדתם: ויקח עמרם את־יוכבד דדתו
his Jochebed Amram And to according Levi the
aunt took .generations their of families

6019 2416 8141 4872 175 3205 802
לו לאשה ותלד לו את־אהרן ואת־משה ושני חיי עמרם
Amram the the and ;Moses and Aaron to she and a for to
of life of years him bore ;wife him

2147 5298 7141 3324 1121 8141 3967 7970 7651
21 שבע ושלשים ומאת שנה: ובני יצהר קרח ונפג וזכרי:
and and ,Korah :Izhar the And .years a and and (were)
.Zichri ,Nepheg of sons hundred thirty seven

175 3947 5644 469 4332 5816 1121
22 ובני עזיאל מישאל ואלצפן וסתרי: ויקח אהרן את־
23 Aaron And and and ,Mishael :Uzziel And
took .Zithri ,Elzaphan of sons the

3205 802 5177 269 5992 1323 472
אלישבע בת־עמינדב אחות נחשון לו לאשה ותלד לו
to she and a for to ,Nahshon the ,Amminadab the Elisheba
him bore ;wife him of sister of daughter

7141 1121 385 499 30 5070
24 את־נדב ואת־אביהוא את־אלעזר ואת־איתמר: ובני קרח
Korah the And .Ithamar and ,Eleazar ,Abihu and ,Nadab
of sons

499 7145 4940 23 511 617
25 אסיר ואלקנה ואביאסף אלה משפחת הקרחי: ואלעזר
And the families the these and and (were)
Eleazar Korahites of (were) ;Abiasaph Elkanah Assir

3205 802 6317 1323 3947 175 1121
בן־אהרן לקח־לו מבנות פוטיאל לו לאשה ותלד לו
to she and a for to Putiel the of to took Aaron the
him bore ,wife him of daughters him of son

1931 4940 3881 1 7218 6372
26 את־פינחס אלה ראשי אבות הלוים למשפחתם: הוא
It ,families their by the fathers the the these ;Phinehas
(was) Levites of of heads (were)

1121 3318 3068 559 4872 175
אהרן ומשה אשר אמר יהוה להם הוציאו את־בני
the out Bring to Jehovah said whom (to) Moses and
of sons ,them Aaron

1696 1992 6635 4714 776 3478
27 ישראל מארץ מצרים על־צבאתם: הם המדברים אל־
to ones the These their according Egypt the from Israel
speaking (were) armies to of land

4714 3478 1121 3318 4714 4428 6547
פרעה מלך־מצרים להוציא את־בני־ישראל ממצרים
;Egypt from Israel of sons the bring to ,Egypt of king Pharaoh
out

776 4872 3068 1696 1961 175 4872
28 הוא משה ואהרן: ויהי ביום דבר יהוה אל־משה בארץ
the in Moses to Jehovah spoke the on it And and Moses it
of land day was Aaron (was)

3068 559 4872 3068 1696
29 מצרים: ס וידבר יהוה אל־משה לאמר אני יהוה
;Jehovah I ,saying ,Moses to Jehovah spoke And ;Egypt
(am)

Speak to Pharaoh king of
Egypt all which I *am* about
to speak to you. 30 And
Moses said before Jehovah,
Behold, I *am* of uncircum-
cised lips. How could
Pharaoh listen to me?

1696 834 3605 4714 4428 6547 1696
דַּבֵּר אֶל־פַּרְעֹה מֶלֶךְ מִצְרַיִם אֵת כָּל־אֲשֶׁר אֲנִי דֹּבֵר אֵלֶיךָ׃
.you to | am I speaking | which | all | Egypt | king of | Pharaoh | to | speak

8085 8193 6189 2009 3068 6440 4872 559
30 וַיֹּאמֶר מֹשֶׁה לִפְנֵי יְהוָה הֵן אֲנִי עֲרַל שְׂפָתַיִם וְאֵיךְ יִשְׁמַע
could listen | how | ;lips | un-circumcised (am) I | See | Jeho-vah, | before | Moses | said And

6547
אֵלַי פַּרְעֹה׃ פ
?Pharaoh | to me

CAP. VII ז

CHAPTER 7

CHAPTER 7

1 And Jehovah said to
Moses, Come, see, I have
made you a god to Pharaoh;
and your brother Aaron
shall be your prophet. 2 You
shall speak all that I
command you, and your
brother Aaron shall speak to
Pharaoh. And he will send
away the sons of Israel from
his land. 3 And I will harden
the heart of Pharaoh. And I
will multiply My signs and
My wonders in the land of
Egypt. 4 And Pharaoh will
not listen to you. And I will
lay My hand on Egypt, and
will bring My armies, My
people, the sons of Israel,
from the land of Egypt with
great judgments. 5 And the
Egyptians shall know that I
am Jehovah when I send
forth My hand on Egypt and
bring out the sons of Israel
from their midst. 6 And
Moses and Aaron did as
Jehovah commanded them,
so they did. 7 And Moses
Moses *was* a son of eighty
years, and Aaron *was* a son
of eighty-three years when
they spoke to Pharaoh.

175 6547 430 6213 2009 4872 3068 559
1 וַיֹּאמֶר יְהוָה אֶל־מֹשֶׁה רְאֵה נְתַתִּיךָ אֱלֹהִים לְפַרְעֹה וְאַהֲרֹן
and Aaron | ;Pharaoh to | god a | have I you made | ,See | ,Moses to | Jehovah | And said

6680 3605 1696 5030 1961 251
2 אָחִיךָ יִהְיֶה נְבִיאֶךָ׃ אַתָּה תְדַבֵּר אֵת כָּל־אֲשֶׁר אֲצַוֶּךָּ
order I you | which | all | — | speak shall | You | your .prophet | be shall | your brother

3478 1121 7971 6547 1696 251 175
וְאַהֲרֹן אָחִיךָ יְדַבֵּר אֶל־פַּרְעֹה וְשִׁלַּח אֶת־בְּנֵי־יִשְׂרָאֵל
Israel | sons the of | he and send will | ,Pharaoh to | shall speak | your brother | and Aaron

226 7235 6547 3820 7185 776
3 מֵאַרְצוֹ׃ וַאֲנִי אַקְשֶׁה אֶת־לֵב פַּרְעֹה וְהִרְבֵּיתִי אֶת־אֹתֹתַי
signs My | will I and multiply | ;Pharaoh | the of heart | will harden | I And | his from .land

6547 8085 3808 4714 776 4159
4 וְאֶת־מוֹפְתַי בְּאֶרֶץ מִצְרָיִם׃ וְלֹא־יִשְׁמַע אֲלֵכֶם פַּרְעֹה
;Pharaoh | you to | listen will And not | .Egypt | the in of land | My wonders | and

5971 6635 3318 4714 3027 7760
וְנָתַתִּי אֶת־יָדִי בְּמִצְרָיִם וְהוֹצֵאתִי אֶת־צִבְאֹתַי אֶת־עַמִּי
My ,people | ,armies My | will and out bring | ,Egypt on | hand My | I and lay will

4713 3045 1419 8201 4714 776 3478 1121
5 בְּנֵי־יִשְׂרָאֵל מֵאֶרֶץ מִצְרַיִם בִּשְׁפָטִים גְּדֹלִים׃ וְיָדְעוּ מִצְרַיִם
the Egyptians | shall And know | .great | with judgments | Egypt | the from of land | ,Israel | the of sons

3318 4714 3027 5181 3068
כִּי־אֲנִי יְהוָה בִּנְטֹתִי אֶת־יָדִי עַל־מִצְרָיִם וְהוֹצֵאתִי אֶת־
— | bring and out | ,Egypt | on | hand My | I when out stretch | ,Jehovah | I (am) | that

3068 6680 175 4872 6213 8432 3478 1121
6 בְּנֵי־יִשְׂרָאֵל מִתּוֹכָם׃ וַיַּעַשׂ מֹשֶׁה וְאַהֲרֹן כַּאֲשֶׁר צִוָּה יְהוָה
Jehovah | com-manded | as | and Aaron | Moses | did And | their from .midst | Israel | the of sons

7969 1121 175 8141 8084 1121 4872 6213
7 אֹתָם כֵּן עָשׂוּ׃ וּמֹשֶׁה בֶּן־שְׁמֹנִים שָׁנָה וְאַהֲרֹן בֶּן־שָׁלֹשׁ
three | a of son | and (was) Aaron | ,years | eighty | a of son | And (was) Moses | they did | so ,them

6547 1696 8141 8084
וּשְׁמֹנִים שָׁנָה בְּדַבְּרָם אֶל־פַּרְעֹה׃ פ
.Pharaoh | to | they when spoke | ,years | and eighty

8 And Jehovah spoke to
Moses and to Aaron, say-
ing, 9 When Pharaoh speaks
to you, saying, Give a
miracle for yourselves, you
shall say to Aaron, Take

1696 559 175 4872 3068 559
8 וַיֹּאמֶר יְהוָה אֶל־מֹשֶׁה וְאֶל־אַהֲרֹן לֵאמֹר׃
9 כִּי יְדַבֵּר
speaks When | ,saying | Aaron to and | Moses to | Jehovah | And spoke

175 559 4159 5414 559 6547
אֲלֵכֶם פַּרְעֹה לֵאמֹר תְּנוּ לָכֶם מוֹפֵת וְאָמַרְתָּ אֶל־אַהֲרֹן
Aaron to | shall you say | a ,miracle | your-selves for | Give | ,saying | ,Pharaoh | you to

your staff and throw *it* before Pharaoh; and let it become a snake. [10]And Moses and Aaron came to Pharaoh, and they did so, as Jehovah had commanded. And Aaron threw his staff before Pharaoh and before his servants. And it became a snake. [11]And Pharaoh also called wise men and the sorcerers. And they, the priests of Egypt, also performed by their secret arts. [12]And they each one threw down his staff, and they became snakes. But Aaron's staff swallowed their staffs. [13]And the heart of Pharaoh was hardened, and he did not listen to them, as Jehovah had said.

[14]And Jehovah said to Moses, The heart of Pharaoh *is* heavy; he refuses to send away the people. [15]Go to Pharaoh in the morning. Behold, *he is* about to go out to the water. And you stand to meet him on the bank of the river. And you shall take in your hand the staff that was turned into a snake. [16]And you shall say to him, Jehovah the God of the Hebrews has sent me to you, saying, Send away My people, so that they may serve Me in the wilderness. And, behold, you have not listened until now. [17]So says Jehovah, By this you shall know that I *am* Jehovah: Behold, I *am* about to smite on the water in the river with the staff which is in My hand, and it shall be turned to blood. [18]And the fish in the river will die, and the river will stink, and the Egyptians will become weary *of* drinking water from the river.

[19]And Jehovah said to Moses, Say to Aaron, Take your staff, and stretch out your hand over the waters of Egypt, over the rivers,

4872 935 8577 6547 6440 7993 4294 3947
10 קַח אֶת־מַטְּךָ וְהַשְׁלֵךְ לִפְנֵי־פַרְעֹה יְהִי לְתַנִּין׃ וַיָּבֹא מֹשֶׁה
Moses And a become it let ;Pharaoh before throw and your Take
came .snake (it) staff

7993 3068 6680 3651 6213 6547 175
וְאַהֲרֹן אֶל־פַּרְעֹה וַיַּעֲשׂוּ כֵן כַּאֲשֶׁר צִוָּה יְהוָה וַיַּשְׁלֵךְ
and ;Jehovah had as ,so they and Pharaoh to and
threw commanded did Aaron

8577 1961 5650 6440 6547 6440 4294 175
אַהֲרֹן אֶת־מַטֵּהוּ לִפְנֵי פַרְעֹה וְלִפְנֵי עֲבָדָיו וַיְהִי לְתַנִּין׃
.snake a it and his and Pharaoh before staff his Aaron
became ;servants before

1571 6213 3784 2450 6547 7121
11 וַיִּקְרָא גַּם־פַּרְעֹה לַחֲכָמִים וְלַמְכַשְּׁפִים וַיַּעֲשׂוּ גַם־הֵם
,they also and the and men wise Pharaoh also and
performed ;sorcerers called

4294 376 7993 3651 3858 4714 2748
12 חַרְטֻמֵּי מִצְרַיִם בְּלַהֲטֵיהֶם כֵּן׃ וַיַּשְׁלִיכוּ אִישׁ מַטֵּהוּ
,staff his each ,they And .thus their by ,Egypt the
one threw arts secret of priests

3820 2388 4294 175 4294 1104 8577 1961
13 וַיִּהְיוּ לְתַנִּינִם וַיִּבְלַע מַטֵּה־אַהֲרֹן אֶת־מַטֹּתָם׃ וַיֶּחֱזַק לֵב
heart was And .staff their Aaron's staff but ;snakes they and
hardened swallowed became

559 3068 1696 8085 3808 6547
14 פַּרְעֹה וְלֹא שָׁמַע אֲלֵהֶם כַּאֲשֶׁר דִּבֶּר יְהוָה׃ וַיֹּאמֶר
said And Jehovah said had as ,them to did he and Pharaoh's
listen not

1980 5971 7971 3985 6547 3820 3515 4872 3068
15 יְהוָה אֶל־מֹשֶׁה כָּבֵד לֵב פַּרְעֹה מֵאֵן לְשַׁלַּח הָעָם׃ לֵךְ
Go the send to he ;Pharaoh the (is) ,Moses to Jehovah
.people away refuses of heart heavy

5921 7125 5324 4325 5927 2009 1242 6547
אֶל־פַּרְעֹה בַּבֹּקֶר הִנֵּה יֹצֵא הַמַּיְמָה וְנִצַּבְתָּ לִקְרָאתוֹ עַל־
on him meet to you and the to (is he) ,See the in Pharaoh to
stand ;water out going ;morning

3027 3947 5175 2015 4294 2975 8193
שְׂפַת הַיְאֹר וְהַמַּטֶּה אֲשֶׁר־נֶהְפַּךְ לְנָחָשׁ תִּקַּח בְּיָדֶךָ׃
your in shall you a into was that the and the the
.hand take snake turned staff ;Nile of bank

559 7971 5680 430 3068 559
16 וְאָמַרְתָּ אֵלָיו יְהוָה אֱלֹהֵי הָעִבְרִים שְׁלָחַנִי אֵלֶיךָ לֵאמֹר
.saying ,you to me sent has Hebrews the the Jehovah to you And
of God ,him say shall

3541 8085 3808 2009 4057 5647 5971 7971
שַׁלַּח אֶת־עַמִּי וְיַעַבְדֻנִי בַּמִּדְבָּר וְהִנֵּה לֹא־שָׁמַעְתָּ עַד־כֹּה׃
.now until have you not and the in they and My Send
listened ,behold ;wilderness Me serve may ,people away

5221 2009 3068 3045 2088 3068 559
17 כֹּה אָמַר יְהוָה בְּזֹאת תֵּדַע כִּי אֲנִי יְהוָה הִנֵּה אָנֹכִי מַכֶּה ׀
will I ,behold ;Jehovah I that you this By ,Jehovah says So
strike (am) (am) know shall

1818 2015 2975 834 4325 3027 4294
בַּמַּטֶּה אֲשֶׁר־בְּיָדִי עַל־הַמַּיִם אֲשֶׁר בַּיְאֹר וְנֶהֶפְכוּ לְדָם׃
to shall it and the in which water the on My in which the with
.blood turned be ;Nile (is) hand (is) staff

4713 3811 2975 887 4191 2975 834 1710
18 וְהַדָּגָה אֲשֶׁר־בַּיְאֹר תָּמוּת וּבָאַשׁ הַיְאֹר וְנִלְאוּ מִצְרַיִם
the will and the will and ,die will in (are) which the And
Egyptians weary be ;Nile stink Nile the fish

559 2975 4325 8354
19 לִשְׁתּוֹת מַיִם מִן־הַיְאֹר׃ וַיֹּאמֶר יְהוָה אֶל־מֹשֶׁה
,Moses to Jehovah said And the from water (of)
Nile drinking

4714 4325 3027 5186 4294 3947 175 559
אֱמֹר אֶל־אַהֲרֹן קַח מַטְּךָ וּנְטֵה־יָדְךָ עַל־מֵימֵי מִצְרַיִם
,Egypt the over your and ,staff your Take ,Aaron to Say
of waters hand out stretch

over their canals, and over their pools, and over every body of their waters, so that they may become blood. And blood shall be in all the land of Egypt, both in wooden and in stone *vessels.* [20]And Moses and Aaron did so, as Jehovah had commanded. And he lifted up the staff and smote the water which *was* in the river before Pharaoh's eyes, and before his servants' eyes. And all the water in the river turned to blood. [21]And the fish in the river died, and the river stunk. And the Egyptians were not able to drink water from the Nile. And the blood was in all the land of Egypt. [22]And the magicians of Egypt did so by their secret arts. And Pharaoh's heart was hardened, and he did not listen to them, as Jehovah had said. [23]And Pharaoh turned and went into his house. And he did not set his heart to this also.
[24]And all the Egyptians dug around the river to drink water, for they were not able to drink from the water of the river. [25]And seven days went by after Jehovah smote the river.

4723 3605 5921 98 5921 2975 5921 5104 5921
עַל־נַהֲרֹתָם ׀ עַל־יְאֹרֵיהֶם וְעַל־אַגְמֵיהֶם וְעַל כָּל־מִקְוֵה
reser- every and their over and their over their over
of voir over ,pools ,canals ,rivers
6086 4714 776 3605 1818 1961 1818 1961 4325
מֵימֵיהֶם וְיִהְיוּ־דָם וְהָיָה דָם בְּכָל־אֶרֶץ מִצְרַיִם וּבָעֵצִים
in both ,Egypt the all in blood and ;blood they that their
wooden of land be shall become may ,waters
3068 6680 175 4872 6213 68
20 וּבָאֲבָנִים׃ וַיַּעֲשׂוּ־כֵן מֹשֶׁה וְאַהֲרֹן כַּאֲשֶׁר ׀ צִוָּה יְהוָה
;Jehovah had as ,Aaron and Moses so And stone in and
commanded did .(vessels)
5869 6547 5869 2975 4325 5221 4294
וַיָּרֶם בַּמַּטֶּה וַיַּךְ אֶת־הַמַּיִם אֲשֶׁר בַּיְאֹר לְעֵינֵי פַרְעֹה וּלְעֵינֵי
in and ,Pharoah's before the in which the he and the he and
eyes eyes Nile (was) water smote staff up lifted
834 1710 1818 2975 4325 3605 2015 5650
21 עֲבָדָיו וַיֵּהָפְכוּ כָּל־הַמַּיִם אֲשֶׁר־בַּיְאֹר לְדָם׃ וְהַדָּגָה אֲשֶׁר־
which the And to the in which the all was and his
(were) fish .blood Nile (was) water turned ;servants'
4325 8354 4713 3201 2975 887 4191 2975
בַּיְאֹר מֵתָה וַיִּבְאַשׁ הַיְאֹר וְלֹא־יָכְלוּ מִצְרַיִם לִשְׁתּוֹת מַיִם
water drink to the were and the and ,died the in
Egyptians able not ;Nile stank Nile
2748 6213 4714 776 1818 1961 2975
22 מִן־הַיְאֹר וַיְהִי הַדָּם בְּכָל־אֶרֶץ מִצְרָיִם׃ וַיַּעֲשׂוּ־כֵן חַרְטֻמֵּי
priests so And .Egypt the in the and the from
did of land all blood was ;Nile
8085 3808 6547 3820 2388 3909 4714
מִצְרַיִם בְּלָטֵיהֶם וַיֶּחֱזַק לֵב־פַּרְעֹה וְלֹא־שָׁמַע אֲלֵהֶם כַּאֲשֶׁר
as to did he and ,Pharaoh the was and their by Egypt's
,them listen not of heart hardened ;arts secret
3820 7896 1004 935 6547 6437 3068 1696
23 דִּבֶּר יְהוָה׃ וַיִּפֶן פַּרְעֹה וַיָּבֹא אֶל־בֵּיתוֹ וְלֹא־שָׁת לִבּוֹ
his did he and his into and Pharaoh And .Jehovah had
heart set not ;house went turned said
8354 4325 2975 5439 4713 3605 2658 2088 1571
24 גַּם־לָזֹאת׃ וַיַּחְפְּרוּ כָל־מִצְרַיִם סְבִיבֹת הַיְאֹר מַיִם לִשְׁתּוֹת
;drink to water the around the all dug And to also
Nile about Egyptians .this
3117 7651 4390 2975 4325 8354 3201 3808
25 כִּי לֹא יָכְלוּ לִשְׁתֹּת מִמֵּימֵי הַיְאֹר׃ וַיִּמָּלֵא שִׁבְעַת יָמִים
days seven were And the the from to they not for
fulfilled .Nile of water drink able were
2975 3068 5221 310
אַחֲרֵי הַכּוֹת־יְהוָה אֶת־הַיְאֹר׃
.Nile the Jehovah struck after

CHAPTER 8

[1]And Jehovah said to Moses, Go to Pharaoh, and say to him, So says Jehovah, Send away My people that they may serve Me. [2]And if you refuse to send *them* away, behold, I *am* about to smite all your territory with frogs. [3]And the river will swarm *with* frogs. And they shall go up and enter into your house, and into your bedroom, and on your couch, and into

559 6547 935 4872 3068 559
26 וַיֹּאמֶר יְהוָה אֶל־מֹשֶׁה בֹּא אֶל־פַּרְעֹה וְאָמַרְתָּ אֵלָיו כֹּה
Thus to say and ,Pharaoh to Go ,Moses to Jehovah And
him said
7971 3986 5647 5971 7971 3068 559
27 אָמַר יְהוָה שַׁלַּח אֶת־עַמִּי וְיַעַבְדֻנִי׃ וְאִם־מָאֵן אַתָּה לְשַׁלֵּחַ
send to you refuse And they and My Send ,Jehovah says
(them) if .Me serve may people away
2975 8317 6854 1366 5062 2009
28 הִנֵּה אָנֹכִי נֹגֵף אֶת־כָּל־גְּבוּלְךָ בַּצְפַרְדְּעִים׃ וְשָׁרַץ הַיְאֹר
Nile the will And .frogs with your all to about I ,See
swarm territory smite (am)
4296 4904 2315 1004 935 5927 6854
צְפַרְדְּעִים וְעָלוּ וּבָאוּ בְּבֵיתֶךָ וּבַחֲדַר מִשְׁכָּבְךָ וְעַל־מִטָּתֶךָ
,bed your and your into and your into and they and (with)
on ,sleeping of room the ,house in go up go shall ;frogs

your servants' house, and on your people, and into your ovens, and into your kneading troughs. [4]And the frogs will come up on you, and on your people, and on all your servants.

[5]And Jehovah said to Moses, Say to Aaron, Stretch out your hand with your staff over the rivers, over the canals, and over the pools. And bring up frogs on the land of Egypt. [6]And Aaron stretched out his hand over the waters of Egypt, and the frogs came up and covered the land of Egypt. [7]And the priests did so with their secret arts. And they brought up the frogs on the land of Egypt.

[8]And Pharaoh called Moses and Aaron, and said, Pray to Jehovah that He may remove the frogs from me and from my people. And I will send away the people that they may sacrifice to Jehovah. [9]And Moses said to Pharaoh, Glory over me. For when shall I pray for you and for your servants and for your people, to cut off the frogs from you, and from your house, *that* they may be left only in the river? [10]And he said, For tomorrow. And he said, According to your word, so that you may know that there is none like Jehovah our God. [11]And the frogs will depart from you, and from your house, and from your servants, and from your people. They will only be in the river. [12]And Moses and Aaron went out from Pharaoh. And Moses cried to Jehovah concerning the frogs which He had set on Pharaoh.

4863 8574 5971 5650 1004
29 וּבְבֵית עֲבָדֶיךָ וּבְעַמֶּךָ וּבְתַנּוּרֶיךָ וּבְמִשְׁאֲרוֹתֶיךָ׃ וּבְכָה
on and you | your troughs kneading | into and ovens your | into and people your | on and servants' your | into and house

6854 5927 5650 3605 5971
וּבְעַמְּךָ וּבְכָל־עֲבָדֶיךָ יַעֲלוּ הַצְפַרְדְּעִים׃
frogs the | shall come | your servants | and all on | on and people your

CAP. VIII ח

CHAPTER 8

3027 5186 175 559 4872 3068 559
1 וַיֹּאמֶר יְהוָה אֶל־מֹשֶׁה אֱמֹר אֶל־אַהֲרֹן נְטֵה אֶת־יָדְךָ
hand your | Stretch out | Aaron to | Say | Moses | to Jehovah | And said

5927 98 5921 2975 5921 5104 5921 4294
בְּמַטֶּךָ עַל־הַנְּהָרֹת עַל־הַיְאֹרִים וְעַל־הָאֲגַמִּים וְהַעַל אֶת־
and up bring | the pools | and over | the canals | over | the rivers | over | your with staff

5921 3027 175 5186 4714 776 6854
2 הַצְפַרְדְּעִים עַל־אֶרֶץ מִצְרָיִם׃ וַיֵּט אַהֲרֹן אֶת־יָדוֹ עַל
over | hand his | Aaron | And out stretched | Egypt | the of land | on | frogs

4714 776 3680 6854 5927 4714 4325
מֵימֵי מִצְרַיִם וַתַּעַל הַצְּפַרְדֵּעַ וַתְּכַס אֶת־אֶרֶץ מִצְרָיִם׃
Egypt | the of land | and covered | frogs the | and came | Egypt's | waters

6854 5927 3000 2748 1571 6213
3 וַיַּעֲשׂוּ־כֵן הַחַרְטֻמִּים בְּלָטֵיהֶם וַיַּעֲלוּ אֶת־הַצְפַרְדְּעִים
frogs the | they and up brought | their with arts secret | priests | the | so did And

559 175 4872 6547 7121 4714 776
4 עַל־אֶרֶץ מִצְרָיִם׃ וַיִּקְרָא פַרְעֹה לְמֹשֶׁה וּלְאַהֲרֹן וַיֹּאמֶר
and said | to and Aaron | Moses to | Pharaoh | And called | Egypt | the of land | on

7971 5971 6854 5493 3068 6279
הַעְתִּירוּ אֶל־יְהוָה וְיָסֵר הַצְפַרְדְּעִים מִמֶּנִּי וּמֵעַמִּי וַאֲשַׁלְּחָה
will I send | and from people my | and from me | frogs the | He that remove may | Jehovah to | Pray

6286 6547 4872 559 3068 2076 5971
5 אֶת־הָעָם וְיִזְבְּחוּ לַיהוָה׃ וַיֹּאמֶר מֹשֶׁה לְפַרְעֹה הִתְפָּאֵר
Glory | to Pharaoh | Moses | said And | to Jehovah | they that sacrifice may | the people

3772 5971 5650 6279 4970 5921
עָלַי לְמָתַי ׀ אַעְתִּיר לְךָ וְלַעֲבָדֶיךָ וּלְעַמְּךָ לְהַכְרִית
off cut to | for and people your | your for and servants | for pray shall I you | For when | over me

559 7604 2975 7535 1004 6854
6 הַצְפַרְדְּעִים מִמְּךָ וּמִבָּתֶּיךָ רַק בַּיְאֹר תִּשָּׁאַרְנָה׃ וַיֹּאמֶר
he And said | may they left be | the in Nile | (that) only | from and house your | from you | the frogs

430 3068 3045 1697 559 4279
לְמָחָר וַיֹּאמֶר כִּדְבָרְךָ לְמַעַן תֵּדַע כִּי־אֵין כַּיהוָה אֱלֹהֵינוּ׃
our God | like Jehovah | none that is | you know | so may that | according word your to | he And said | to- For morrow

7535 5971 5650 1004 6854 5493
7 וְסָרוּ הַצְפַרְדְּעִים מִמְּךָ וּמִבָּתֶּיךָ וּמֵעֲבָדֶיךָ וּמֵעַמֶּךָ רַק
only | from and people your | your from and servants | from and house your | from you | the frogs | shall And depart

6817 6547 175 4872 5927 7604 2975
8 בַּיְאֹר תִּשָּׁאַרְנָה׃ וַיֵּצֵא מֹשֶׁה וְאַהֲרֹן מֵעִם פַּרְעֹה וַיִּצְעַק
and cried | Pharaoh | from | and Aaron | Moses | And out went | shall they left be | the in Nile

6547 7760 6854 1697 5921 3068 4872
מֹשֶׁה אֶל־יְהוָה עַל־דְּבַר הַצְפַרְדְּעִים אֲשֶׁר־שָׂם לְפַרְעֹה׃
on Pharaoh | He set had | which | the frogs | the of matter | over | Jehovah to | Moses

[13]And Jehovah did according to the word of Moses. And the frogs died from the houses, from the courts, and from the fields. [14]And they gathered them *in* heaps *and* heaps; and the land stunk. [15]And Pharaoh saw that *there* was relief. And he made his heart heavy, and he did not listen to them, as Jehovah had said.

[16]And Jehovah said to Moses, Say to Aaron, Stretch out your staff and smite the dust of the earth, and let it become lice in all the land of Egypt. [17]And they did so, and Aaron stretched out his hand with his staff and smote the dust of the earth. And the lice were on man and on beast. All the dust of the earth became lice in the land of Egypt. [18]And the priests performed with their secret arts to bring forth lice, and they could not. And the lice were on man and on beast. [19]And the priests said to Pharaoh, It is the finger of God. And Pharaoh's heart was hardened, and he did not listen to them, as Jehovah had said.

[20]And Jehovah said to Moses, Get up early in the morning, and stand before Pharao. Behold, he *is* about to go out to the water. And say to him, So says Jehovah, Send away My people that they may serve Me. [21]And if you do not send away My people, behold, I *am* about to send flies on you, and on your servants, and on your people, and on your house. And the houses of the Egyptians will be full *of* swarms of *flies*, and also the ground on which they *are*. [22]And in that day I will separate the land of

1004 6854 4191 4872 1697 3068 6213
9 וַיַּעַשׂ יְהוָה כִּדְבַר מֹשֶׁה וַיָּמֻתוּ הַצְפַרְדְּעִים מִן־הַבָּתִּים
the from the and ;Moses according Jehovah And
,houses frogs died of word the to did

2563 2563 6657 7704 2691
10 מִן־הַחֲצֵרֹת וּמִן־הַשָּׂדֹת׃ וַיִּצְבְּרוּ אֹתָם חֳמָרִם חֳמָרִם
(and) (in) them they And the and the from
;heaps heaps gathered .fields from courts

3513 7309 1961 6547 7200 776 887
11 וַתִּבְאַשׁ הָאָרֶץ׃ וַיַּרְא פַּרְעֹה כִּי הָיְתָה הָרְוָחָה וְהַכְבֵּד
he and ;relief there that Pharaoh And the and
heavy made was saw .land stank

559 3068 1696 8085 3808 3820
12 אֶת־לִבּוֹ וְלֹא שָׁמַע אֲלֵהֶם כַּאֲשֶׁר דִּבֶּר יְהוָה׃ וַיֹּאמֶר
said And .Jehovah had as to did he and his
said ,them listen not heart

5221 4294 5186 175 559 4872 3068
יְהוָה אֶל־מֹשֶׁה אֱמֹר אֶל־אַהֲרֹן נְטֵה אֶת־מַטְּךָ וְהַךְ
and staff your Stretch .Aaron to Say ,Moses to Jehovah
smite out

6213 4714 776 3654 1961 776 6083
13 אֶת־עֲפַר הָאָרֶץ וְהָיָה לְכִנִּם בְּכָל־אֶרֶץ מִצְרָיִם׃ וַיַּעֲשׂוּ
they And .Egypt the in lice it let and the the
did of land all become ,earth of dust

1961 776 6083 5221 4294 3027 175 5186
כֵן וַיֵּט אַהֲרֹן אֶת־יָדוֹ בְמַטֵּהוּ וַיַּךְ אֶת־עֲפַר הָאָרֶץ וַתְּהִי
and the the and his with his Aaron and so
were ,earth of dust smote staff hand out stretched

3605 3654 1961 776 6083 929 120 3654
הַכִּנָּם בָּאָדָם וּבַבְּהֵמָה כָּל־עֲפַר הָאָרֶץ הָיָה כִנִּים בְּכָל־
all in lice became the the all on and man on lice the
land of dust ;beast

3318 3909 2748 3651 6213 4714 776
14 אֶרֶץ מִצְרָיִם׃ וַיַּעֲשׂוּ־כֵן הַחַרְטֻמִּים בְּלָטֵיהֶם לְהוֹצִיא אֶת־
bring to their with the so And .Egypt the
forth arts secret priests did of land

559 929 120 3654 1961 3201 3808 3654
15 הַכִּנִּים וְלֹא יָכֹלוּ וַתְּהִי הַכִּנָּם בָּאָדָם וּבַבְּהֵמָה׃ וַיֹּאמְרוּ
said And .beast and man on lice the and they and ,lice
were ;could not

6547 3820 2388 430 676 6547 2748
הַחַרְטֻמִּם אֶל־פַּרְעֹה אֶצְבַּע אֱלֹהִים הִוא וַיֶּחֱזַק לֵב־פַּרְעֹה
,Pharaoh the was and It God the ,Pharaoh to the
of heart hardened ;(is) of finger priests

3068 559 3068 1696 8085
16 וְלֹא־שָׁמַע אֲלֵהֶם כַּאֲשֶׁר דִּבֶּר יְהוָה׃ וַיֹּאמֶר יְהוָה
Jehovah And .Jehovah had as ,them to did he and
said said listen not

5927 2009 6547 6440 3320 1242 7925 4872
אֶל־מֹשֶׁה הַשְׁכֵּם בַּבֹּקֶר וְהִתְיַצֵּב לִפְנֵי פַרְעֹה הִנֵּה יוֹצֵא
(is) he ,See ;Pharaoh before stand and the in Rise ,Moses to
going ,morning early

5647 5971 7971 3068 559 3651 559 4325
הַמָּיְמָה וְאָמַרְתָּ אֵלָיו כֹּה אָמַר יְהוָה שַׁלַּח עַמִּי וְיַעַבְדֻנִי׃
may they that My Send ,Jehovah says Thus to you and the to
.Me serve people ,him say ;water

5650 7971 2009 5971 7971
17 כִּי אִם־אֵינְךָ מְשַׁלֵּחַ אֶת־עַמִּי הִנְנִי מַשְׁלִיחַ בְּךָ וּבַעֲבָדֶיךָ
on and on am ,See My send you if For
servants your you sending I ,people away not do

4713 1004 4390 6157 1004 5971
וּבְעַמְּךָ וּבְבָתֶּיךָ אֶת־הֶעָרֹב וּמָלְאוּ בָּתֵּי מִצְרַיִם אֶת־
the the will and ;flies on and your on and
Egyptians of houses full be house your ,people

3117 6395 834 127 1571 6157
18 הֶעָרֹב וְגַם הָאֲדָמָה אֲשֶׁר־הֵם עָלֶיהָ׃ וְהִפְלֵיתִי בַיּוֹם
day in will I And .it on (are) they which the and swarms
separate ground also (flies of)

Goshen *with* My people resting on it, that there be no swarms of *flies*, so that you may know that I *am* Jehovah in the midst of the earth. [23]And I will put a distinction between My people and your people. This miracle shall be for tomorrow. [24]And Jehovah did so. And teeming swarms of *flies* came into Pharaoh's house, and the house of his servants, and into all the land of Egypt. And the land was destroyed before the swarms of *flies*.

[25]And Pharaoh called for Moses and for Aaron, and said, Go! Sacrifice to your God in the land. [26]And Moses said, It is not right to do so, for we sacrifice the abomination of the Egyptians to Jehovah our God. Behold, *if* we sacrifice the abomination of the Egyptians before their eyes, will they not stone us? [27]We will go into the wilderness, a journey of three days, and sacrifice to Jehovah our God, as He may say to us. [28]And Pharaoh said, I will send you away, and you may sacrifice to Jehovah your God in the wilderness; only do not go very far off. Pray for me.

[29]And Moses said, Behold, I *am* about to go out from you and to pray *to* Jehovah. And the swarms of *flies* will depart from Pharaoh, from his servants, and from his people tomorrow. But do not let Pharaoh continue to deceive, not to send the people to sacrifice to Jehovah. [30]And Moses went out from Pharaoh. And he prayed *to* Jehovah. [31]And Jehovah did according to the word of Moses, and the swarms of *flies* departed from Pharaoh.

1961 1115 5975 5971 1657 776
ההוא את־ארץ גשן אשר עמי עמד עליה לבלתי היות־
there be | that no | ;it on | resting My people | (with) Goshen | the of land | that

7760 776 7130 3068 3045 4616 6151
19 שם ערב למען תדע כי אני יהוה בקרב הארץ׃ ושמתי
I And put will | the .earth | the in of midst | Jehovah | I (am) | that know | may you | so that | of swarms (flies) | there

6213 2088 226 1961 4279 5971 996 5971 996 6304
20 פדת בין עמי ובין עמך למחר יהיה האת הזה׃ ויעש
And did | .this | miracle | shall be | for tomorrow | your ;people | and | My people | between | a difference

3605 5650 604 6547 1004 3515 6157 935 3068
יהוה כן ויבא ערב כבד ביתה פרעה ובית עבדיו ובכל־
into and all | his ,servants | the and of house | Pharaoh | the to of house | teeming | swarms (flies) of | and into came | ,so | Jehovah

6547 7121 6157 6440 776 7843 4714 776
21 ארץ מצרים תשחת הארץ מפני הערב׃ ויקרא פרעה
Pharaoh | And called | swarms the .(flies) of | before | the land | was destroyed | :Egypt | the of land

776 430 2076 3212 559 175 4872 413
אל־משה ולאהרן ויאמר לכו זבחו לאלהיכם בארץ׃
the in .land | God your to | Sacrifice !Go | and said | for and ,Aaron | Moses | for

4713 8441 6213 3559 3808 4872 559
22 ויאמר משה לא נכון לעשות כן כי תועבת מצרים
the Egyptians | abomi- of nation | the for | ,so | do to | right | is It not | ,Moses | said And

5869 4713 8441 2076 2005 430 3068 2076
נזבח ליהוה אלהינו הן נזבח את־תועבת מצרים לעיניהם
their eyes | before | the Egyptians | abomi- of nation | the | we (if) offer | ,See | ;God our | Jehovah to | we offer

2076 4057 3212 3117 7969 1870 5619
23 ולא יסקלנו׃ דרך שלשת ימים נלך במדבר וזבחנו
and sacrifice | the into ,wilderness | will We go | days | three | a of journey | they will ?us stone | not

6547 559 559 430 3068
24 ליהוה אלהינו כאשר יאמר אלינו׃ ויאמר פרעה אנכי
I | ,Pharaoh | said And | .us to | may He say | as | ,God our | to Jehovah

7535 4057 430 3068 2076 7971
אשלח אתכם וזבחתם ליהוה אלהיכם במדבר רק
only | the in ;wilderness | God your | to Jehovah | you and sacrifice may | ,you | send will away

4878 559 1157 6275 3212 7368 3966
25 הרחק לא־תרחיקו ללכת העתירו בעדי׃ ויאמר משה
,Moses | said And | .me for | pray | ;go Do | of far | not | very

6157 5414 3068 6279 5927 2009
הנה אנכי יוצא מעמך והעתרתי אל־יהוה וסר הערב
swarms the (flies) of | that depart | Jehovah to | pray will I and | from you | (am) going | I | ,Behold

2048 6547 3254 7535 4279 5971 5650 6547
מפרעה מעבדיו ומעמו מחר רק אל־יסף פרעה התל
to .deceive | Pharaoh | let do continue | not | but ;tomorrow | from and people his | his from servants | from ,Pharaoh

4872 5927 3068 2076 5971 7971 1115
26 לבלתי שלח את־העם לזבח ליהוה׃ ויצא משה מעם
from | Moses | went And out | to .Jehovah | to sacrifice | the people | to send | not

5493 4872 1697 3068 6213 3068 6279 6547
27 פרעה ויעתר אל־יהוה׃ ויעש יהוה כדבר משה ויסר
and departed | ,Moses | according of word the to | Jehovah | And did | .Jehovah to | he and prayed | ;Pharaoh

from his servants, and from his people; and not one was left. [32]And Pharaoh hardened his heart this time also, and he did not send away the people.

3513 259 7604 5971 5650 6547 6157

28 הֶעָרֹב מִפַּרְעֹה מֵעֲבָדָיו וּמֵעַמּוֹ לֹא נִשְׁאַר אֶחָד׃ וַיַּכְבֵּד

And .one left was not from and his from from of swarms
hardened ;people his servants ,Pharaoh *flies)*

5971 7971 3808 6471 3820 6547

פַּרְעֹה אֶת־לִבּוֹ גַּם בַּפַּעַם הַזֹּאת וְלֹא שִׁלַּח אֶת־הָעָם׃

the did he and ,this time also his Pharaoh
.people away send not heart

CAP. IX ט

CHAPTER 9

CHAPTER 9

[1]And Jehovah said to Moses, Go in to Pharaoh and say to him, So says Jehovah the God of the Hebrews, Send away My people that they may serve Me. [2]And if you refuse to send away, and you still hold onto them, [3]behold, the hand of Jehovah *is* going to be on your livestock in the field, on the horses, on the asses, on the camels, on the herds, and on the flocks, a very heavy pestilence. [4]And Jehovah will make a distinction between Israel's livestock and Egypt's livestock. Also of all *that belongs* to the sons of Israel, not a thing will die. [5]And Jehovah set a time, saying, Tomorrow Jehovah will do this thing in the land. [6]And Jehovah did this thing on the next day, and all the livestock of Egypt died. And from the livestock of the sons of Israel, not one died. [7]And Pharaoh sent, and behold, not even one was dead from Israel's livestock! And Pharaoh's heart was hardened, and he did not send away the people.

[8]And Jehovah said to Moses and to Aaron, Take for yourselves the fullness of your hands of soot from the furnace, and let Moses sprinkle it toward the heavens before Pharaoh's eyes. [9]And let it become dust on all the land of Egypt, and let it become an inflammation breaking out into a boil on man and on livestock in all the land of

3651 1696 6547 935 4872 3068 559

1 וַיֹּאמֶר יְהוָה אֶל־מֹשֶׁה בֹּא אֶל־פַּרְעֹה וְדִבַּרְתָּ אֵלָיו כֹּה־

Thus ,him to and ,Pharaoh to Go ,Moses to Jehovah And
speak in said

3588 5647 5971 7971 5680 430 3068 559

2 אָמַר יְהוָה אֱלֹהֵי הָעִבְרִים שַׁלַּח אֶת־עַמִּי וְיַעַבְדֻנִי׃ כִּי

For may they that My Send the the Jehovah says
.Me serve people away ,Hebrews of God

3068 3027 2388 5750 7971 3986

3 אִם־מָאֵן אַתָּה לְשַׁלֵּחַ וְעוֹדְךָ מַחֲזִיק בָּם׃ הִנֵּה יַד־יְהוָה

Jehovah the be- onto hold you and send to you refuse if
of hand ,hold ;them still ,away

1581 2543 5483 7704 834 4735 1961

הוֹיָה בְּמִקְנְךָ אֲשֶׁר בַּשָּׂדֶה בַּסּוּסִים בַּחֲמֹרִים בַּגְּמַלִּים

the on the on the on the in which your on going (is)
camels ,asses ,horses ,field (is) livestock be to

4735 996 3068 6395 3966 3515 1698 6629 1241

4 בַּבָּקָר וּבַצֹּאן דֶּבֶר כָּבֵד מְאֹד׃ וְהִפְלָה יְהוָה בֵּין מִקְנֵה

cattle be- Jehovah will And .very heavy pes- a on and the on
tween distinguish tilence ,flocks the ,herds

3478 1121 3605 4191 4714 4735 996 3478

יִשְׂרָאֵל וּבֵין מִקְנֵה מִצְרָיִם וְלֹא יָמוּת מִכָּל־לִבְנֵי יִשְׂרָאֵל

,Israel (given) all of will and ;Egypt's cattle and Israel's
of sons the to die not between

1697 3068 6213 4279 559 4150 3068 7760 1697

5 דָּבָר׃ וַיָּשֶׂם יְהוָה מוֹעֵד לֵאמֹר מָחָר יַעֲשֶׂה יְהוָה הַדָּבָר

thing Jehovah will Tomorrow ,saying a Jehovah And a
do time set .thing

4191 4283 2088 1697 3068 6213 996 2088

6 הַזֶּה בָּאָרֶץ׃ וַיַּעַשׂ יְהוָה אֶת־הַדָּבָר הַזֶּה מִמָּחֳרָת וַיָּמָת

and the on this thing Jehovah And the in this
died ;morrow did .land

259 4191 3478 1121 4735 4714 4735 3605

כֹּל מִקְנֵה מִצְרָיִם וּמִמִּקְנֵה בְנֵי־יִשְׂרָאֵל לֹא־מֵת אֶחָד׃

.one died not ,Israel the from and ;Egypt's of all
of sons of cattle the cattle

259 3478 4735 4191 3808 2009 6547 7971

7 וַיִּשְׁלַח פַּרְעֹה וְהִנֵּה לֹא־מֵת מִמִּקְנֵה יִשְׂרָאֵל עַד־אֶחָד

!one even Israel the from was not and ,Pharaoh And
of cattle dead ,behold sent

5971 7971 3808 6547 3820 3513

וַיִּכְבַּד לֵב פַּרְעֹה וְלֹא שִׁלַּח אֶת־הָעָם׃

the did he and Pharaoh's heart was And
.people away send not hardened

7651 4393 3947 175 4872 3068 559

8 וַיֹּאמֶר יְהוָה אֶל־מֹשֶׁה וְאֶל־אַהֲרֹן קְחוּ לָכֶם מְלֹא חָפְנֵיכֶם

your full for Take ,Aaron and Moses to Jehovah And
of hands yourselves to said

1961 6547 5869 8064 4872 2236 3536 6368

9 פִּיחַ כִּבְשָׁן וּזְרָקוֹ מֹשֶׁה הַשָּׁמַיְמָה לְעֵינֵי פַרְעֹה׃ וְהָיָה

let And .Pharaoh's before the towards Moses let and the from soot
be it eyes heavens it sprinkle ,furnace

929 5921 120 1961 4714 776 3605 80

לְאָבָק עַל כָּל־אֶרֶץ מִצְרָיִם וְהָיָה עַל־הָאָדָם וְעַל־הַבְּהֵמָה

livestock on and man on let and ,Egypt the all on dust
be it of land

Egypt. [10]And they took soot of the furnace and stood before Pharaoh. And Moses sprinkled it toward the heavens, and it became an inflammation breaking out into boils on man and on livestock. [11]And the priests were not able to stand before Moses, before the inflammation. For the inflammation was on the priests and on all the Egyptians. [12]And Jehovah hardened Pharaoh's heart, and he did not listen to them, as Jehovah had said to Moses.

[13]And Jehovah said to Moses, Get up early in the morning and stand before Pharaoh, and say to him, So says Jehovah the God of the Hebrews, Send away My people that they may serve Me. [14]For at this time I *am* going to send all My plagues to your heart, and on your servants, and on your people, so that you may know that *there* is none like Me in all the land. [15]For now I have sent forth My hand and have smitten you and your people with pestilence, and you have been destroyed from the earth. [16]And for this reason I have made you stand, in order to cause you to see My power, and in order to declare My name in all the land. [17]You are still exalting yourself against My people, not to send them away. [18]Behold, I will rain very heavy hail about this time tomorrow, *such as* has never been in Egypt from the day it was founded until now. [19]And now send out. Shelter your cattle and all belonging to

3947 4714 776 3605 76 6524 7822
10 לִשְׁחִין פֹּרֵחַ אֲבַעְבֻּעֹת בְּכָל־אֶרֶץ מִצְרָיִם׃ וַיִּקְחוּ אֶת־
– they And took .Egypt the of land all in (into) sores breaking out for boils

4872 2236 6547 6440 5975 3536 6368
פִּיחַ הַכִּבְשָׁן וַיַּעַמְדוּ לִפְנֵי פַרְעֹה וַיִּזְרֹק אֹתוֹ מֹשֶׁה
Moses it and sprinkled ;Pharaoh before stood and the furnace soot of

929 120 6524 76 7822 1961 8064
הַשָּׁמָיְמָה וַיְהִי שְׁחִין אֲבַעְבֻּעֹת פֹּרֵחַ בָּאָדָם וּבַבְּהֵמָה׃
on and .livestock man on breaking out sores (with) a boil it and became the toward ,heavens

7822 6440 4872 6440 5975 2748 3201
11 וְלֹא־יָכְלוּ הַחַרְטֻמִּים לַעֲמֹד לִפְנֵי מֹשֶׁה מִפְּנֵי הַשְּׁחִין כִּי־
for ;boil the before Moses before stand to priests the were able And not

3068 2388 4713 3605 2748 7822 1961
12 הָיָה הַשְּׁחִין בַּחֲרְטֻמִּם וּבְכָל־מִצְרָיִם׃ וַיְחַזֵּק יְהוָה אֶת־
Jehovah And hardened .Egyptians on and the all the on priests boil the was

3068 1696 8085 3808 6547 3820
לֵב פַּרְעֹה וְלֹא שָׁמַע אֲלֵהֶם כַּאֲשֶׁר דִּבֶּר יְהוָה אֶל־
to Jehovah had said as ;them to did he listen and not Pharaoh's heart

1242 7925 4872 3068 559 4872
13 מֹשֶׁה׃ וַיֹּאמֶר יְהוָה אֶל־מֹשֶׁה הַשְׁכֵּם בַּבֹּקֶר
the in morning up Get early ,Moses to Jehovah said And .Moses

430 3068 559 3551 559 6547 6440 3320
וְהִתְיַצֵּב לִפְנֵי פַרְעֹה וְאָמַרְתָּ אֵלָיו כֹּה־אָמַר יְהוָה אֱלֹהֵי
the of God Jehovah says Thus ,him to say and ,Pharaoh before and stand

6471 3588 5647 5971 7971 5680
14 הָעִבְרִים שַׁלַּח אֶת־עַמִּי וְיַעַבְדֻנִי׃ כִּי ׀ בַּפַּעַם הַזֹּאת אֲנִי
I (am) this time at For they that Me serve may people My Send away the ,Hebrews

5971 5650 3820 4046 3605 7971
שֹׁלֵחַ אֶת־כָּל־מַגֵּפֹתַי אֶל־לִבְּךָ וּבַעֲבָדֶיךָ וּבְעַמֶּךָ בַּעֲבוּר
that so on and ,people your on and ,servants your heart your to plagues my all going send to

7971 6258 776 3605 3045
15 תֵּדַע כִּי אֵין כָּמֹנִי בְּכָל־הָאָרֶץ׃ כִּי עַתָּה שָׁלַחְתִּי אֶת־
have I out stretched now For .land the all in Me like is none that you know may

776 3577 1698 5971 5221 3027
יָדִי וָאַךְ אוֹתְךָ וְאֶת־עַמְּךָ בַּדָּבֶר וַתִּכָּחֵד מִן־הָאָרֶץ׃
the .earth from have you and been destroyed with ,pestilence your people and you have and smitten My hand

581 7200 5668 5975 2088 5668 199
16 וְאוּלָם בַּעֲבוּר זֹאת הֶעֱמַדְתִּיךָ בַּעֲבוּר הַרְאֹתְךָ אֶת־כֹּחִי
My power you cause see to order in to made have I stand you this reason And for

5971 5549 5750 776 3605 8034 5608
17 וּלְמַעַן סַפֵּר שְׁמִי בְּכָל־הָאָרֶץ׃ עוֹדְךָ מִסְתּוֹלֵל בְּעַמִּי
against ,people My exalting are yourself You still the .land all in My name declare in and to order

3966 3515 1259 4279 4305 2009 7971
18 לְבִלְתִּי שַׁלְּחָם׃ הִנְנִי מַמְטִיר כָּעֵת מָחָר בָּרָד כָּבֵד מְאֹד
,very heavy hail tomorrow about time this will rain Behold I send to away them (as so) not

5704 3245 3117 4480 4714 3644 7961 3808
אֲשֶׁר לֹא־הָיָה כָמֹהוּ בְּמִצְרַיִם לְמִן־הַיּוֹם הִוָּסְדָה וְעַד־
until was it founded day the from of Egypt in it like has never been which

3426 834 3605 4735 5756 7971 6258
19 עָתָּה׃ וְעַתָּה שְׁלַח הָעֵז אֶת־מִקְנְךָ וְאֵת כָּל־אֲשֶׁר לְךָ
you have which all and your livestock shelter send ,out And now .now

you in the field. All men and livestock found in the field, and not brought to the house, the hail will come on them, and they will die.

[20]Of the servants of Pharaoh, the one who feared the word of Jehovah made his slaves and his livestock flee to the houses. [21]And the one who did not set his heart on the word of Jehovah left his slaves and his livestock in the field. [22]And Jehovah said to Moses, Stretch out your hand to the heavens, so that hail may be in all the land of Egypt, on man, and on livestock, and on every plant of the field in the land of Egypt. [23]And Moses stretched out his staff to the heavens. And Jehovah gave thunder and hail. And fire came down to the earth, and Jehovah rained hail on the land of Egypt. [24]And *there* was hail, and fire flashing in the midst of the hail, very heavy, which never had been in all the land of Egypt since it became a nation. [25]And the hail smote in all the land of Egypt, all that *was* in the field, from men and to livestock. And the hail struck every plant of the field, and it broke in pieces every tree of the field. [26]Only in the land of Goshen, where the sons of Israel *lived*, there was no hail.

[27]And Pharaoh sent and called Moses and Aaron, and said to them, I have sinned *this* time. Jehovah *is* the righteous One, and I and my people the wicked ones. [28]Pray to Jehovah and *let it be* enough of the

622 3808 7704 4672 834 929 120 3605 7704
בשדה כל-האדם והבהמה אשר-ימצא בשדה ולא יאסף
brought and not the in field are found which and livestock man all the in ;field

3068 1696 3372 4191 1259 5921 3381 1004
20 הביתה וירד עלהם הברד ומתו: הירא את-דבר יהוה
,Jehovah the of word one The feared who they and .die will the hail them on will come the to house

1004 4735 5650 5127 6547 5650
מעבדי פרעה הניס את-עבדיו ואת-מקנהו אל-הבתים:
.houses the to his livestock and servants his made flee ,Pharaoh the of servants

5650 5927/3068 1696 3820 834
21 ואשר לא-שם לבו אל-דבר יהוה ויעזב את-עבדיו ואת-
and slaves his left Jehovah the of word on his heart did not set he And who

7704 4735
מקנהו בשדה:
the in .field his livestock

1961 806:4 3027 5186 4872 3068 559
22 ויאמר יהוה אל-משה נטה את-ידך על-השמים ויהי
that be may the to heavens hand your Stretch out ,Moses to Jehovah And said

3605 5921 929 5921 120 4714 776 3605 1259
ברד בכל-ארץ מצרים על-האדם ועל-הבהמה ועל כל-
every and on ,livestock on and man on ;Egypt the of land all in hail

4294 4872 5186 4714 776 7704 6212
23 עשב השדה בארץ מצרים: ויט משה את-מטהו על-
to staff his Moses And stretched .Egypt the in of land field the plant of

4305 776 784 3212 1259 6963 5414 3068 8064
השמים ויהוה נתן קלת וברד ותהלך-אש ארצה וימטר
and rained the to ;earth fire and down came and ;hail sounds gave and Jehovah the ,heavens

3947 784 1259 1961 4714 776 1259 3068
24 יהוה ברד על-ארץ מצרים: ויהי ברד ואש מתלקחת
flashing and fire hail And was .Egypt the of land on hail Jehovah

776/3605 3644 1961 3808 3966 834 3515 1259
בתוך הברד כבד מאד אשר לא-היה כמהו בכל-ארץ
the of land all in like it had been never which ,very heavy ,hail the amidst

4714 776/3605 1259 5221 1471 1961 4714
25 מצרים מאז היתה לגוי: ויך הברד בכל-ארץ מצרים
Egypt the of land all in the hail And smote a .nation it became since Egypt

6212/3605 929 120 7704 834/3605
את כל-אשר בשדה מאדם ועד-בהמה ואת כל-עשב
plant every of and ;livestock and to from man the in ,field which (was) all —

776 7535 7665 7704 6086/3605 1259 5221 7704
26 השדה הכה הברד ואת-כל-עץ השדה שבר: רק בארץ
the in of land Only it .shattered the field tree every of and ,hail the smote field the

6547 7971 1259 1961 3808 3478 1121 8033/834 1657
27 גשן אשר-שם בני ישראל לא היה ברד: וישלח פרעה
Pharaoh sent And .hail there was no ,Israel the of sons where (lived) ,Goshen

3068 6471 2398 559 175 4872 7121
ויקרא למשה ולאהרן ויאמר אלהם חטאתי הפעם יהוה
Jehovah (this) ;time have I sinned ,them to said and ,Aaron and Moses and called

1961 7227 3068 6279 7563 5971 6662
28 הצדיק ואני ועמי הרשעים: העתירו אל-יהוה ורב מהית
being enough and Jehovah to Pray .wicked the my people and I and the (is) ,righteous

thunder and hail of God. And I will send you away, and you shall not stay any longer. [29]And Moses said to him, As I go out of the city I will spread out my palms to Jehovah. The thunder will cease, and the hail will not still be, so that you may know that the earth *belongs* to Jehovah. [30]And *as for* you and your servants, I know that you do not yet fear before Jehovah God.

[31]And the flax and the barley were smitten. For the barley *was in* the ear, and the flax *in* blossom. [32]And the wheat and the spelt were not smitten, for they *were* late. [33]And Moses went out from Pharaoh, *from* the city, and *he* spread out his hands to Jehovah. And the thunder and the hail ceased. And rain was not poured out toward the earth. [34]And Pharaoh saw that the rain and the hail and the thunder had ceased, and he continued to sin. And he hardened his heart, he and his servants. [35]And Pharaoh's heart was hardened, and he did not send away the sons of Israel, as Jehovah had said by the hand of Moses.

5975 3254 7971 1259 430 6963
קֹלֹת אֱלֹהִים וּבָרָד וַאֲשַׁלְּחָה אֶתְכֶם וְלֹא תֹסִפוּן לַעֲמֹד׃
any you shall and ,you will I and ;hail and God (that)
.longer continue not away send of sounds

3709 6566 5892 5927 4872 559
29 וַיֹּאמֶר אֵלָיו מֹשֶׁה כְּצֵאתִי אֶת־הָעִיר אֶפְרֹשׂ אֶת־כַּפַּי אֶל־
to palms my will I the of I So ,Moses to And
out spread city out go him said

3045 57:50 1259 2308 696 3068
יְהוָה הַקֹּלוֹת יֶחְדָּלוּן וְהַבָּרָד לֹא יִהְיֶה־עוֹד לְמַעַן תֵּדַע
you that so ,further shall not hail the and cease will the ;Jehovah
know may be sound

3372 2962 3045 5650 776 3068
30 כִּי לַיהוָה הָאָרֶץ׃ וְאַתָּה וַעֲבָדֶיךָ יָדַעְתִּי כִּי טֶרֶם תִּירְאוּן
do you not that I your and as) And the to (is) that
fear yet know ,servants you (for .earth Jehovah

8184 5221 8184 6593 430 3068
31 מִפְּנֵי יְהוָה אֱלֹהִים׃ וְהַפִּשְׁתָּה וְהַשְּׂעֹרָה נֻכָּתָה כִּי הַשְּׂעֹרָה
the for were the and the And .God Jehovah before
barley ;smitten barley flax

5221 3808 3698 2406 1392 6593 24
32 אָבִיב וְהַפִּשְׁתָּה גִּבְעֹל׃ וְהַחִטָּה וְהַכֻּסֶּמֶת לֹא נֻכּוּ כִּי
for were not the and the And (in) the and (in was)
;smitten spelt wheat ,blossom flax ,ear

6566 5892 6547 4672 5973 2007 648
33 אֲפִילֹת הֵנָּה׃ וַיֵּצֵא מֹשֶׁה מֵעִם פַּרְעֹה אֶת־הָעִיר וַיִּפְרֹשׂ
and from ,Pharaoh from Moses And .they (were)
spread ,city the out went late

5413 4306 1259 6963 2308 3068 3709
כַּפָּיו אֶל־יְהוָה וַיַּחְדְּלוּ הַקֹּלוֹת וְהַבָּרָד וּמָטָר לֹא־נִתַּךְ
was not rain and ,hail and thunder the and ;Jehovah to his
out poured ceased palms

6963 1259 4306 2308 6547 7200 776
34 אָרְצָה׃ וַיַּרְא פַּרְעֹה כִּי־חָדַל הַמָּטָר וְהַבָּרָד וְהַקֹּלֹת
the and hail the and rain the had that Pharaoh And toward
thunder ceased saw .earth the

6547 3820 2388 5650 3820 3513 2398 3254
35 וַיֹּסֶף לַחֲטֹא וַיַּכְבֵּד לִבּוֹ הוּא וַעֲבָדָיו׃ וַיֶּחֱזַק לֵב פַּרְעֹה
the was And his and he his he and ;sin to he and
,Pharaoh heart hardened .servants heart hardened increased

4872 3027 3068 1696 3478 1121 7971
וְלֹא שִׁלַּח אֶת־בְּנֵי יִשְׂרָאֵל כַּאֲשֶׁר דִּבֶּר יְהוָה בְּיַד־מֹשֶׁה׃
Moses the by Jehovah said had as ,Israel of sons the did he and
of hand send not

CAP. X

CHAPTER 10

CHAPTER 10

[1]And Jehovah said to Moses, Go in to Pharaoh, for I have hardened his heart and the heart of his servants, so that I may set these signs of Mine in their midst; [2]and so that you may relate in the ears of your son and the son of your son what I exerted Myself to do against Egypt, and My signs which I have done among them, and you may know that I *am* Jehovah. [3]And Moses and Aaron went in to Pharaoh and said to him, So says Jehovah the

3513 6547 935 4872 3068 559
1 וַיֹּאמֶר יְהוָה אֶל־מֹשֶׁה בֹּא אֶל־פַּרְעֹה כִּי־אֲנִי הִכְבַּדְתִּי
have I For ,Pharaoh to Go ,Moses to Jehovah And
hardened in said

7130 226 7896 5650 3820 3820
אֶת־לִבּוֹ וְאֶת־לֵב עֲבָדָיו לְמַעַן שִׁתִי אֹתֹתַי אֵלֶּה בְּקִרְבּוֹ׃
his in these My may I so his the and his
;midst signs set that ,servants of heart heart

5953 1121 1121 1121 241 5668
2 וּלְמַעַן תְּסַפֵּר בְּאָזְנֵי בִנְךָ וּבֶן־בִּנְךָ אֵת אֲשֶׁר הִתְעַלַּלְתִּי
exerted I what your the and your in may you so and
Myself son of son son's ear recount that

3045 3045 7760 834 226 4714
בְּמִצְרַיִם וְאֶת־אֹתֹתַי אֲשֶׁר־שַׂמְתִּי בָם וִידַעְתֶּם כִּי־אֲנִי
I that you and among have I which My and against
(am) know may ,them performed signs ,Egypt

3541 559 6547 175 4872 935 3068
3 יְהוָה׃ וַיָּבֹא מֹשֶׁה וְאַהֲרֹן אֶל־פַּרְעֹה וַיֹּאמְרוּ אֵלָיו כֹּה־
Thus to said and Pharaoh to and Moses And .Jehovah
,him Aaron in went

God of the Hebrews, How long will you refuse to humble yourself before Me? Send away My people so that they may serve Me. [4]For if you refuse to send away My people, behold, I *am* going to bring locusts into your territory tomorrow. [5]And they will cover the eye of the land, and no one will be able to see the land. And they will eat the rest of that which escaped, that which is left to you from the hail. And they will eat every tree that sprouts to you from the field. [6]And your houses will be full, and the houses of all your servants, and the houses of the Egyptians, which neither your fathers nor the fathers of your fathers have seen; from the day of their being on the earth until this day. And he turned and went out from Pharaoh.

[7]And Pharaoh's servants said to him, How long shall this one be a snare to us? Send away the men that they may serve Jehovah their God. Do you not yet know that Egypt is perishing? [8]And Moses and Aaron were brought back to Pharaoh. And he said to them, Go, serve Jehovah your God. Who and who *are* the ones going? [9]And Moses said, We will go with our young and with our old, with our sons and with our daughters. We will go with our flocks and with our herds. For *it is* a feast of Jehovah to us. [10]And he said to them, May Jehovah *be* so with you, as I send you away, and your little ones. Watch! For evil *is* before your face! [11]Not so! You and the men go now and serve Jehovah. For you *were* seeking it. And he drove them out from the face of Pharaoh.

אָמַר יְהוָה אֱלֹהֵי הָעִבְרִים עַד־מָתַי מֵאַנְתָּ לֵעָנֹת מִפָּנָי
4 שַׁלַּח עַמִּי וְיַעַבְדֻנִי׃ כִּי אִם־מָאֵן אַתָּה לְשַׁלֵּחַ אֶת־עַמִּי
5 הִנְנִי מֵבִיא מָחָר אַרְבֶּה בִּגְבֻלֶךָ׃ וְכִסָּה אֶת־עֵין הָאָרֶץ
וְלֹא יוּכַל לִרְאֹת אֶת־הָאָרֶץ וְאָכַל ׀ אֶת־יֶתֶר הַפְּלֵטָה
הַנִּשְׁאֶרֶת לָכֶם מִן־הַבָּרָד וְאָכַל אֶת־כָּל־הָעֵץ הַצֹּמֵחַ לָכֶם
6 מִן־הַשָּׂדֶה׃ וּמָלְאוּ בָתֶּיךָ וּבָתֵּי כָל־עֲבָדֶיךָ וּבָתֵּי כָל־
מִצְרַיִם אֲשֶׁר לֹא־רָאוּ אֲבֹתֶיךָ וַאֲבוֹת אֲבֹתֶיךָ מִיּוֹם
הֱיוֹתָם עַל־הָאֲדָמָה עַד הַיּוֹם הַזֶּה וַיִּפֶן וַיֵּצֵא מֵעִם פַּרְעֹה׃
7 וַיֹּאמְרוּ עַבְדֵי פַרְעֹה אֵלָיו עַד־מָתַי יִהְיֶה זֶה לָנוּ לְמוֹקֵשׁ
שַׁלַּח אֶת־הָאֲנָשִׁים וְיַעַבְדוּ אֶת־יְהוָה אֱלֹהֵיהֶם הֲטֶרֶם תֵּדַע
8 כִּי אָבְדָה מִצְרָיִם׃ וַיּוּשַׁב אֶת־מֹשֶׁה וְאֶת־אַהֲרֹן אֶל־
פַּרְעֹה וַיֹּאמֶר אֲלֵהֶם לְכוּ עִבְדוּ אֶת־יְהוָה אֱלֹהֵיכֶם מִי וָמִי
9 הַהֹלְכִים׃ וַיֹּאמֶר מֹשֶׁה בִּנְעָרֵינוּ וּבִזְקֵנֵינוּ נֵלֵךְ בְּבָנֵינוּ
10 וּבִבְנוֹתֵנוּ בְּצֹאנֵנוּ וּבִבְקָרֵנוּ נֵלֵךְ כִּי חַג־יְהוָה לָנוּ׃ וַיֹּאמֶר
אֲלֵהֶם יְהִי כֵן יְהוָה עִמָּכֶם כַּאֲשֶׁר אֲשַׁלַּח אֶתְכֶם וְאֶת־
11 טַפְּכֶם רְאוּ כִּי רָעָה נֶגֶד פְּנֵיכֶם׃ לֹא כֵן לְכוּ־נָא הַגְּבָרִים
וְעִבְדוּ אֶת־יְהוָה כִּי אֹתָהּ אַתֶּם מְבַקְשִׁים וַיְגָרֶשׁ אֹתָם מֵאֵת

[12]And Jehovah said to Moses, Stretch out your hand for the locusts over the land of Egypt, so that they may go up on the land of Egypt and may eat every plant of the land, all that the hail left. [13]And Moses stretched out his staff over the land of Egypt. And Jehovah brought an east wind on the land all that day and all that night. *And at* morning the east wind brought the locusts. [14]And the locusts went up over all the land of Egypt, and rested on all the territory of Egypt, exceedingly many. Never were there locusts like them before, and afterward none will be like them. [15]And they covered the eye of the earth, and the land became dark. And they ate every plant of the land, and all the fruit of the trees that the hail had left. And no greenness was left in the trees and in the plants of the field in all the land of Egypt. [16]And Pharaoh hurried to call Moses and Aaron. And he said, I have sinned against Jehovah your God and against you. [17]And now pray forgive my sins only *this* time, and pray *to* Jehovah your God that He may take away from me this death only. [18]And he went out from Pharaoh, and he prayed *to* Jehovah.

[19]And Jehovah changed *to* a west wind, very strong. And it carried the locusts and threw them into the Red Sea. Not one locust was left in all the territory of Egypt. [20]And Jehovah hardened the heart of Pharaoh, and he did not send away the sons of Israel.

776/5921 3027 5186 4872 3068 559 6547 6440
12 פְּנֵי פַרְעֹה׃ וַיֹּאמֶר יְהוָה אֶל־מֹשֶׁה נְטֵה יָדְךָ עַל־אֶרֶץ
the over your Stretch ,Moses to Jehovah said And .Pharaoh the
of land hand out of face

3605 398 4714 776 5927 697 4714
מִצְרַיִם בָּאַרְבֶּה וְיַעַל עַל־אֶרֶץ מִצְרָיִם וְיֹאכַל אֶת־כָּל־
every may and Egypt the on they that the for Egypt
eat of land go may ;locusts

5186 4872 1259 7604 834 776 6212
13 עֵשֶׂב הָאָרֶץ אֵת כָּל־אֲשֶׁר הִשְׁאִיר הַבָּרָד׃ וַיֵּט מֹשֶׁה אֶת־
Moses And .hail the left which all — ,land the plant
out stretched of

3605 776 6921 7307 5090 3061 4714 776 4294
מַטֵּהוּ עַל־אֶרֶץ מִצְרַיִם וַיהוָה נִהַג רוּחַ־קָדִים בָּאָרֶץ כָּל־
all the on east wind an brought and ,Egypt the over his
land Jehovah of land staff

5395 6921 7307 1961 1242 3415 3117
הַיּוֹם הַהוּא וְכָל־הַלַּיְלָה הַבֹּקֶר הָיָה וְרוּחַ הַקָּדִים נָשָׂא
brought east the and it (when and) the all and that day
wind ,was morning ;night

3605 5117 4714 776 597 5927 697
14 אֶת־הָאַרְבֶּה׃ וַיַּעַל הָאַרְבֶּה עַל כָּל־אֶרֶץ מִצְרַיִם וַיָּנַח בְּכֹל
on and ,Egypt the all over the And .locusts the
every rested of land locusts up went

697 3651 1961 6440 3966/3505 4714 1366
גְּבוּל מִצְרָיִם כָּבֵד מְאֹד לְפָנָיו לֹא־הָיָה כֵן אַרְבֶּה כָּמֹהוּ
like locusts such there never before ex- many ,Egypt border
them were it ;ceedingly of

2821 776 3605 5869 3680 1961 3808 310
15 וְאַחֲרָיו לֹא יִהְיֶה־כֵּן׃ וַיְכַס אֶת־עֵין כָּל־הָאָרֶץ וַתֶּחְשַׁךְ
became and the all surface the they And .so be will none and
dark ,earth of covered afterwards

834 6086 3605 776 6212 3605 398 776
הָאָרֶץ וַיֹּאכַל אֶת־כָּל־עֵשֶׂב הָאָרֶץ וְאֵת כָּל־פְּרִי הָעֵץ אֲשֶׁר
which the the all and the plant every they and the
,trees of fruit ,land of ate ;land

7704 6212 6086 3418 5414 3808 1259 3498
הוֹתִיר הַבָּרָד וְלֹא־נוֹתַר כָּל־יֶרֶק בָּעֵץ וּבְעֵשֶׂב הַשָּׂדֶה
.field the the in and the in green any was and ;hail the left had
of plants trees left not

175 4872 7121 6547 4116 4714 776 3605
16 בְּכָל־אֶרֶץ מִצְרָיִם׃ וַיְמַהֵר פַּרְעֹה לִקְרֹא לְמֹשֶׁה וּלְאַהֲרֹן
and Moses call to Pharaoh And .Egypt the all in
:Aaron hurried of land

2403 4994/5375 6258 430 3068 2398
17 וַיֹּאמֶר חָטָאתִי לַיהוָה אֱלֹהֵיכֶם וְלָכֶם׃ וְעַתָּה שָׂא נָא חַטָּאתִי
sin my pray forgive And and your against have I he and
now .you against God Jehovah sinned ,said

7535 5413 430 3068 6279 6471 389
אַךְ הַפַּעַם וְהַעְתִּירוּ לַיהוָה אֱלֹהֵיכֶם וְיָסֵר מֵעָלַי רַק אֶת־
only from He that your to pray and (this) only
me take may ,God Jehovah ,time

2015 3068 6279 6547 5927 2088 4194
18 19 הַמָּוֶת הַזֶּה׃ וַיֵּצֵא מֵעִם פַּרְעֹה וַיֶּעְתַּר אֶל־יְהוָה׃ וַיַּהֲפֹךְ
And .Jehovah to he and ,Pharaoh from he And .this death
changed prayed out went

3220 8628 697 5375 3966 2389 7307/3220 3068
יְהוָה רוּחַ־יָם חָזָק מְאֹד וַיִּשָּׂא אֶת־הָאַרְבֶּה וַיִּתְקָעֵהוּ יָמָּה
the threw and locusts the it and ,very strong a (to) Jehovah
of Sea into them carried wind west

3068 2380 4714 1366 3605/259 697 7604 5488
20 סּוּף לֹא נִשְׁאַר אַרְבֶּה אֶחָד בְּכֹל גְּבוּל מִצְרָיִם׃ וַיְחַזֵּק יְהוָה
Jehovah And .Egypt the all in one locust was Not .Reeds
hardened of territory left

3478 1121 7971 3808 6547 3820
אֶת־לֵב פַּרְעֹה וְלֹא שִׁלַּח אֶת־בְּנֵי יִשְׂרָאֵל׃
.Israel the did he and Pharaoh the
of sons away send not of heart

[21]And Jehovah said to Moses, Stretch out your hand to the heavens so that darkness may be on the land of Egypt, and one may feel darkness. [22]And Moses stretched out his hand to the heavens, and darkness of gloom was in all the land of Egypt three days. [23]They did not see each one his brother, and they did not rise up, each one from his place *for* three days. Yet to all the sons of Israel there was light in their dwellings. [24]And Pharaoh called to Moses and said, Go, serve Jehovah. Only leave your flocks and your herds behind. Your little ones may go with you. [25]And Moses said, You must also give into our hands sacrifices and burnt offerings so that we may prepare for Jehovah our God. [26]And also our livestock shall go with us. Not a hoof shall be left. For we shall take from them to serve Jehovah our God. And we do not know *with* what we shall serve Jehovah until we come there. [27]And Jehovah hardened the heart of Pharaoh, and he was not willing to send them away. [28]And Pharaoh said to him, Go away from me. Be careful for yourself. Do not see my face again, for in the day you see my face you shall die. [29]And Moses said, You have spoken rightly. I will not see your face again.

5921 2822 1961 8064 3027 5146 4872 3068 559
21 וַיֹּאמֶר יְהוָה אֶל־מֹשֶׁה נְטֵה יָדְךָ עַל־הַשָּׁמַיִם וִיהִי חֹשֶׁךְ עַל־
on darkness that be may the heavens to your hand Stretch out ,Moses to Jehovah And said

8064 3027 4872 5186 2822 4959 4714 776
22 אֶרֶץ מִצְרָיִם וְיָמֵשׁ חֹשֶׁךְ׃ וַיֵּט מֹשֶׁה אֶת־יָדוֹ עַל־הַשָּׁמָיִם
the ,heavens to his hand Moses And out stretched .darkness one and feel may ,Egypt the of land

7969 7200 3117 4714 776 3605 653 2822 1961
23 וַיְהִי חֹשֶׁךְ־אֲפֵלָה בְּכָל־אֶרֶץ מִצְרַיִם שְׁלֹשֶׁת יָמִים׃ לֹא־רָאוּ
they see not did ;days three Egypt the of land all in gloom darkness of and was

3117 1969 4714 776 6965 251 376
אִישׁ אֶת־אָחִיו וְלֹא־קָמוּ אִישׁ מִתַּחְתָּיו שְׁלֹשֶׁת יָמִים וּלְכָל־
to and all ;days three his from ,place each man they and ,arise did not his ,brother each man

4872 6547 7121 4186 216 1961 3478 1121
24 בְּנֵי יִשְׂרָאֵל הָיָה אוֹר בְּמוֹשְׁבֹתָם׃ וַיִּקְרָא פַרְעֹה אֶל־מֹשֶׁה
Moses to Pharaoh And called their in .dwellings light there was Israel the of sons

1571 3322 1241 6629 7535 3068 5647 3212 559
וַיֹּאמֶר לְכוּ עִבְדוּ אֶת־יְהוָה רַק צֹאנְכֶם וּבְקַרְכֶם יֻצָּג גַּם־
also leave ;behind your and herds your flocks only ;Jehovah serve Go and ;said

2077 3027 5414 1571 4872 559 3212 2945
25 טַפְּכֶם יֵלֵךְ עִמָּכֶם׃ וַיֹּאמֶר מֹשֶׁה גַּם־אַתָּה תִּתֵּן בְּיָדֵנוּ זְבָחִים
sacrifices into hand our must give you also ,Moses said And with .you may go your ones little

3808 3212 4735 430 3068 6213 5930
26 וְעֹלֹת וְעָשִׂינוּ לַיהוָה אֱלֹהֵינוּ׃ וְגַם־מִקְנֵנוּ יֵלֵךְ עִמָּנוּ לֹא
not with ;us shall go our livestock And also .God our for Jehovah may we that prepare burnt and ,offerings

430 3068 5647 3947 6541 7604
תִשָּׁאֵר פַּרְסָה כִּי מִמֶּנּוּ נִקַּח לַעֲבֹד אֶת־יְהוָה אֱלֹהֵינוּ
;God our Jehovah serve to shall we take from them for ;hoof a be shall left

2388 8033 935 5704 3068 5647 3045
27 וַאֲנַחְנוּ לֹא־נֵדַע מַה־נַּעֲבֹד אֶת־יְהוָה עַד־בֹּאֵנוּ שָׁמָּה׃ וַיְחַזֵּק
And hardened .there we come until Jehovah shall we serve (with) what do not know we and

6547 559 7971 14 3808 6547 3820 3068
28 יְהוָה אֶת־לֵב פַּרְעֹה וְלֹא אָבָה לְשַׁלְּחָם׃ וַיֹּאמֶר־לוֹ פַרְעֹה
,Pharaoh to him And said them let to .go was he willing and not ,Pharaoh the of heart Jehovah

3117 6440 7200 3254 8164 3212
לֵךְ מֵעָלָי הִשָּׁמֶר לְךָ אַל־תֹּסֶף רְאוֹת פָּנַי כִּי בְּיוֹם
the in day for my ,face see to again not ,yourself watch away ;me from Go

5750 3254 3808 1696 3651 4872 559 4191 6440 7200
29 רְאֹתְךָ פָנַי תָּמוּת׃ וַיֹּאמֶר מֹשֶׁה כֵּן דִּבַּרְתָּ לֹא־אֹסִף עוֹד
again yet will I not you ;spoken have as ,Moses said And shall you .die my face see you

6440 7200
רְאוֹת פָּנֶיךָ׃
your .face see

CAP. XI יא

CHAPTER 11

CHAPTER 11

[1]And Jehovah said to Moses, I will bring still one more plague on Pharaoh and on Egypt. Afterward he will send you from here. When he sends you away completely, he will surely

6547 5921 935 259 5061 5750 4872 3068 559
1 וַיֹּאמֶר יְהוָה אֶל־מֹשֶׁה עוֹד נֶגַע אֶחָד אָבִיא עַל־פַּרְעֹה
Pharaoh on will I bring one plague yet ,Moses to Jehovah And said

3617 7971 7971 310 4714
וְעַל־מִצְרַיִם אַחֲרֵי־כֵן יְשַׁלַּח אֶתְכֶם מִזֶּה כְּשַׁלְּחוֹ כָּלָה
com- pletely he when you sends from ;here you shall he send afterward ;Egypt on and

drive you out from here. [2]Now speak in the ears of the people, and let them ask, each man from his neighbor, articles of silver and articles of gold. [3]And Jehovah gave favor in the eyes of the Egyptians *toward* the people. And the man Moses *was* very great in the land of Egypt, in the eyes of the servants of Pharaoh, and in the eyes of the people.

[4]And Moses said, So says Jehovah, About the middle of the night I will go out in the midst of Egypt. [5]And every firstborn in the land of Egypt shall die, from the firstborn of Pharaoh, the one sitting on his throne, to the firstborn of the slave-girl who *is* behind the mill; and every firstborn of animals. [6]And a great cry shall be in all the land of Egypt, such as never has been, and nothing like it shall be again. [7]And a dog shall not sharpen his tongue against all the sons of Israel, toward man and toward livestock, so that you may know that Jehovah distinguishes *between* Egypt and Israel. [8]And all these servants of yours will come down to me, and bow to me, saying, Go out, you and all the people at your feet. And afterward I will go out. And he went out from Pharaoh in the heat of anger.

[9]And Jehovah said to Moses, Pharaoh will not listen to you, so that My miracles may multiply in the land of Egypt. [10]And Moses and Aaron did all these miracles before Pharaoh.

7592 5971 249 1696 1644 1644
2 גָּרֵשׁ יְגָרֵשׁ אֶתְכֶם מִזֶּה׃ דַּבֶּר־נָא בְּאָזְנֵי הָעָם וְיִשְׁאֲלוּ
let and ask them · the people · the in of ears · Now speak · from here · you · will he surely out drive
3627 3701 3627 7468 802 7451 376
אִישׁ ׀ מֵאֵת רֵעֵהוּ וְאִשָּׁה מֵאֵת רְעוּתָהּ כְּלֵי־כֶסֶף וּכְלֵי
and of articles · silver articles of · her ,neighbor · from every and woman · his ,neighbor · from · each man
376 1571 4714 5869 5971 2582 3068 5414 2091
3 זָהָב׃ וַיִּתֵּן יְהוָה אֶת־חֵן הָעָם בְּעֵינֵי מִצְרָיִם גַּם ׀ הָאִישׁ
the man · also · ;Egypt · the in of eyes · the people · favor (toward) · Jehovah · And gave · .gold
5869 6547 5650 5869 4714 776 3966 1419 4872
מֹשֶׁה גָּדוֹל מְאֹד בְּאֶרֶץ מִצְרַיִם בְּעֵינֵי עַבְדֵי־פַרְעֹה וּבְעֵינֵי
in and of eyes the · ,Pharaoh of servants · the in of eyes · Egypt · the in of land · very · (was) great · Moses
3915 2676 3068 559 3541 4872 559 5971
4 הָעָם׃ ס וַיֹּאמֶר מֹשֶׁה כֹּה אָמַר יְהוָה כַּחֲצֹת הַלַּיְלָה אֲנִי
I · night the · the About of middle · ,Jehovah · says · Thus · ,Moses · said And · the .people
4714 776 1060 3605 4191 4714 8432 5927
5 יוֹצֵא בְּתוֹךְ מִצְרָיִם׃ וּמֵת כָּל־בְּכוֹר בְּאֶרֶץ מִצְרַיִם
;Egypt · the in of land · first- born · every · shall and die · ;Egypt · the in of midst · go will out
8198 1060 3678 3427 6547 1060
מִבְּכוֹר פַּרְעֹה הַיֹּשֵׁב עַל־כִּסְאוֹ עַד בְּכוֹר הַשִּׁפְחָה אֲשֶׁר
who · the slave-girl · first- of born · the to · his ,throne · on · sitting · Pharaoh's · from first-born
1419 6818 1961 929 1060 3605 7347 310
6 אַחַר הָרֵחָיִם וְכֹל בְּכוֹר בְּהֵמָה׃ וְהָיְתָה צְעָקָה גְדֹלָה
great · cry a · shall And be · .animals · firstborn of · and every · of pair the millstones · (is) behind
3808 1961 3808 4714 776
בְּכָל־אֶרֶץ מִצְרַיִם אֲשֶׁר כָּמֹהוּ לֹא נִהְיָתָה וְכָמֹהוּ לֹא
none · and it like · has ;been · never · as such · — · ;Egypt · the of land · all in
376 3956 3611 2782 3478 1121 3254
7 תֹסִף׃ וּלְכֹל ׀ בְּנֵי יִשְׂרָאֵל לֹא יֶחֱרַץ־כֶּלֶב לְשֹׁנוֹ לְמֵאִישׁ
toward man · his ,tongue · dog a · shall sharpen · not · Israel · the of sons · And again all against · shall .be
4714 996 3068 6395 834 3045 929
וְעַד־בְּהֵמָה לְמַעַן תֵּדְעוּן אֲשֶׁר יַפְלֶה יְהוָה בֵּין מִצְרַיִם
Egypt · be- tween · Jehovah · dis- tinguishes · that · , may you know · order in that · ,livestock · and toward
7812 5650 3605 3381 3478 996
8 וּבֵין יִשְׂרָאֵל׃ וְיָרְדוּ כָל־עֲבָדֶיךָ אֵלֶּה אֵלַי וְהִשְׁתַּחֲווּ־לִי
,me to · bow and themselves · ,me to · these · your servants · all · will And down come · .Israel · and between
5927 310 7272 5971 3605 5927 559
לֵאמֹר צֵא אַתָּה וְכָל־הָעָם אֲשֶׁר־בְּרַגְלֶיךָ וְאַחֲרֵי־כֵן אֵצֵא
will I .out go · afterward and · your at ;feet · who (are) · the all and people · you · Go ,out · ,saying
4872 3068 559 639/2750 6547 5927
9 וַיֵּצֵא מֵעִם־פַּרְעֹה בָּחֳרִי־אָף׃ ס וַיֹּאמֶר יְהוָה אֶל־מֹשֶׁה
,Moses · to Jehovah · said And · .anger · the in of heat · Pharaoh · from · he And out went
776 4159 7235 6547 8085 3808
לֹא־יִשְׁמַע אֲלֵיכֶם פַּרְעֹה לְמַעַן רְבוֹת מוֹפְתַי בְּאֶרֶץ
the in of land · My miracles · to multiply · order in · ,Pharaoh · you to · will listen · not
4159 3605 6213 175 4872 4714
10 מִצְרָיִם׃ וּמֹשֶׁה וְאַהֲרֹן עָשׂוּ אֶת־כָּל־הַמֹּפְתִים הָאֵלֶּה
these · miracles · all · did · Aaron and · Moses And · .Egypt

And Jehovah hardened the heart of Pharaoh, and he did not send away the sons of Israel from his land.

7971 3808 3547 3820 3068 2388 6547 6440
לפני פרעה ויחזק יהוה את-לב פרעה ולא-שלח את-
did he send | and not | ,Pharaoh | heart the of | Jehovah | and hardened | ;Pharaoh | before

776 3478 1121
בני-ישראל מארצו׃
his from .land | Israel | the of sons

CAP. XII יב

CHAPTER 12

CHAPTER 12

[1]And Jehovah said to Moses and to Aaron in the land of Egypt, saying, [2]This month *shall be* the chief of months for you. It *shall be* the first of the months of the year for you. [3]Speak to all the congregation of Israel, saying, On the tenth of this month, they shall each take for themselves an animal of the flock for a father's house, a flock animal for a house. [4]And if the house is *too* small for a flock animal, he and his neighbor next to his house shall take. By the number of souls, each one according to the mouth of his eating, you shall count concerning the flock animal. [5]A flock animal, a perfect one, a male, a yearling, shall be to you. You shall take from the sheep or from the goats. [6]And it shall be for you to keep until the fourteenth day of this month. And all the assembly of the congregation of Israel shall kill it between the evenings. [7]And they shall take from the blood, and put *it* on the two side doorposts and on the upper doorpost, on the houses *in* which they eat it. [8]And they shall eat the flesh in this night, roasted with fire, and they shall eat it with unleavened bread and bitter herbs. [9]Do not eat it raw, or at all boiled in water, but roasted with fire; its head with its legs and with its inward parts. [10]And you shall not leave *any* of

559 4714 776 175 4872 3068 559
1 ויאמר יהוה אל-משה ואל-אהרן בארץ מצרים לאמר׃
,saying | ,Egypt | the in of land | Aaron to and | Moses | to | Jehovah | And spoke

2320 7223 2320 7218 2088 2320
2 החדש הזה לכם ראש חדשים ראשון הוא לכם לחדשי
the of of months | (be shall) you for | it | first the | ;months | the of chief | (be shall) you for | This | month

2320 6218 559 3478 5712 3605 413 1696 8141
3 השנה׃ דברו אל-כל-עדת ישראל לאמר בעשר לחדש
month of | the On tenth | ,saying | ,Israel | the of congregation | all | to | Speak | .year the

1004 7716 1 1004 7716 376 3947
4 הזה ויקחו להם איש שה לבית-אבת שה לבית׃ ואם-
if And | a for .house | flock a animal | ,father's | a for house | flock a animal | each one | for themselves | shall they take | ,this

7138 7934 3947 7716 1961 1004 4591
ימעט הבית מהית משה ולקח הוא ושכנו הקרב אל-
to | next | his and neighbor | he | take shall | a for animal flock | – | the house | (too) is small

7716 3699 408 6310 376 5315 4373 1004
ביתו במכסת נפשת איש לפי אכלו תכסו על-השה׃
flock the animal | to as | you count shall | his ,eating | the by of mouth | one each | ,souls | to according of number the | his ,house

3532 1961 8141 1121 2145 8549 7716
5 שה תמים זכר בן-שנה יהיה לכם מן-הכבשים ומן-
or from | sheep the | from | ;you to | shall be | a son ,year | of | ,male a | perfect a ,one | flock a animal

6240 702 5704 4931 1961 3947 5795
6 העזים תקחו׃ והיה לכם למשמרת עד ארבעה עשר
ten (and) four | until | keep to | you for | it And be shall | shall you .take | goats the

996 3478 5712 6944 3605 7919 2088 2320 3117
יום לחדש הזה ושחטו אתו כל קהל עדת-ישראל בין
twixt | Israel | con- the of gregation | the of assembly | all | it | shall and kill | ;this | month of | day

4201 8147 1818 3947 6153
7 הערבים׃ ולקחו מן-הדם ונתנו על-שתי המזוזת ועל-
and on | the doorposts | two on | and (it) put | the blood | from | they And take shall | the .evenings

398 398 1004 5921 4947
8 המשקוף על הבתים אשר-יאכלו אתו בהם׃ ואכלו
they And eat shall | in .them | it | eat they | which | houses the | on | the lintel

4844 4682 784 6748 2088 3915 1320
את-הבשר בלילה הזה צלי-אש ומצות על-מררים
bitter (herbs) | with | and bread unleavened | ,fire roasted with | ,this | night in | flesh the

4325 1310 1311 4995 398 3808 398
9 יאכלהו׃ אל-תאכלו ממנו נא ובשל מבשל במים כי
but | in ;water | boiled | or all at | raw | it | eat Do | not | shall they .it eat

3498 3808 7130 3167 7218 784 6748
10 אם-צלי-אש ראשו על-כרעיו ועל-קרבו׃ ולא-תותירו
shall you leave | And not | its with and parts inward | legs its | with | head its | ,fire | roasted with

it until morning. And you shall burn with fire that left from it until morning. [11]And you shall eat it this way: *with* your loins girded, your sandals on your feet, and your staff in your hand. And you shall eat it in haste. It *is the* Passover to Jehovah. [12]And I will pass through in the land of Egypt in this night. And I will smite every firstborn in the land of Egypt, from man and to livestock. And I will execute judgments on all the gods of Egypt. I *am* Jehovah! [13]And the blood shall be a sign to you, on the houses where you *are*. And I will see the blood, and I will pass over you. And the plague shall not be on you to destroy, when I smite in the land of Egypt.

[14]And the day shall be a memorial for you. And you shall celebrate it *as* a feast to Jehovah, for your generations. You shall celebrate it *as* a law forever.

[15]You shall eat unleavened bread seven days. Indeed, on the first day you shall cause leaven to cease from your houses. For anyone eating anything leavened, that soul shall be cut off from Israel, from the first day until the seventh day. [16]And on the first day *shall be* a holy convocation, and in the seventh day a holy convocation shall be to you. Not any work may be done on them. Only what must be eaten by your soul, that alone may be done by you. [17]And you shall observe the unleavened bread, for on this very day I brought out your armies from the land of Egypt. And you shall observe this day for your

3602 8313 784 1242 5704 3498 1242 5704
11 ממנו עד־בקר והנתר ממנו עד־בקר באש תשרפו׃ וככה
this And way | shall you .burn | with fire | morn- ing | until | from it | that and left | ;morning | until | (any) it of

47 31 7272 5275 2296 4975 398
תאכלו אתו מתניכם חגרים נעליכם ברגליכם ומקלכם
your and staff | your on feet | your sandals | ,girded | your (with) loins | ;it | shall you eat

5674 3068 6453 2649 398 3027
12 בידכם ואכלתם אתו בחפזון פסח הוא ליהוה׃ ועברתי
will I And through pass | to .Jehovah | (is) it | (the) ,Passover | haste in | it | you and eat shall | your in ;hand

776 1060 3605 5221 2088 3915 4714 776
בארץ־מצרים בלילה הזה והכיתי כל־בכור בארץ
the in of land | first- born | every | will I and smite | ,this | night in | Egypt | the in of land

6213 4714 430 3605 929 120 4714
מצרים מאדם ועד־בהמה ובכל־אלהי מצרים אעשה
will I execute | Egypt | gods the of | and all on | ;livestock to and | from man | ,Egypt

1004 5921 226 1818 1961 3068 8201
13 שפטים אני יהוה׃ והיה הדם לכם לאת על הבתים
houses the | on | for sign a | for you | the blood | And be shall | .Jehovah | I (am) | ;judgments

3808 6452 1818 7200 8033 834
אשר אתם שם וראיתי את־הדם ופסחתי עלכם ולא־
and not | ;you over | will I and pass | ,blood the | I and see will | ;there | you (are) | in which

1961 4714 776 5221 4889 5063 1961
14 יהיה בכם נגף למשחית בהכתי בארץ מצרים׃ והיה
And be shall | .Egypt | the in of land | I when smite | ,destroy to | the plague | on you | shall be

1755 3068 2282 2287 2146 2088/3117
היום הזה לכם לזכרון וחגתם אתו חג ליהוה לדרתיכם
your for ;generations | to ,Jehovah | a (as) feast | it | you and celebrate shall | ,memorial a | for you | this | day

3117 389 398 4682 3117 7651 2287 5769 2708
15 חקת עולם תחגהו׃ שבעת ימים מצות תאכלו אך ביום
on day | indeed | shall you ;eat | un- bread leavened | days | Seven | shall you .it celebrate | forever | a (as) law

2557 398 3605 1004 7603 7673 7223
הראשון תשביתו שאר מבתיכם כי כל־אכל חמץ
anything leavened | eating | any- one | for | your from houses | leaven | shall you cease to cause | first the

3117 7223 3117 3478 5315 3772
ונכרתה הנפש ההוא מישראל מיום הראשן עד־יום
day | until | first the | from day | ,Israel from | that | soul | be shall off cut

7637 3117 6944 4744 7223 3117 7637
16 השבעי׃ וביום הראשון מקרא־קדש וביום השביעי
the seventh | in and day | holy | (be shall) convocation a | first the | on And day | the .seventh

6213 3808 4399 3605 1961 6944 4744
מקרא־קדש יהיה לכם כל־מלאכה לא־יעשה בהם
on ;them | be shall done | not | work | any | ;you to | be shall | holy | a convocation

6213 5315 3605 398 389
אך אשר יאכל לכל־נפש הוא לבדו יעשה לכם׃
.you by | be may done | alone | that | ,soul | by each | be must eaten | what | only

3318 2088 3117 6106 4682 8104
17 ושמרתם את־המצות כי בעצם היום הזה הוצאתי את־
brought I out | this | day | very on | for | unleavened the ,bread | shall you And observe

2088 3117 8104 4714 776 6635
צבאותיכם מארץ מצרים ושמרתם את־היום הזה
this | day | you and observe shall | ;Egypt | the from of land | armies your

generations, a statute forever. [18]In the first *month,* on the fourteenth day of the month, at evening you shall eat unleavened bread, until the twenty-first day of the month, at evening. [19]*For* seven days no leaven shall be found in your houses. For anyone eating anything leavened, that soul shall be cut off from the congregation of Israel, among the aliens, and among the natives of the land. [20]You shall not eat anything leavened. You shall eat unleavened bread in all your dwellings.

[21]And Moses called to all the elders of Israel and said to them, Go out and take of the flock for you *and* for your families. And kill the passover. [22]And take a bunch of hyssop and dip in the blood which *is* in the basin. And apply some of the blood in the basin to the upper doorpost and to the two *side* doorposts. And you shall not go out, anyone from the door of his house until morning. [23]And Jehovah will pass through to smite Egypt. And He will see the blood on the upper doorpost and on the two *side* doorposts, and Jehovah will pass over the door. And He will not allow the destroyer to come into your house to strike *you.*

[24]And you shall observe this word for an ordinance for you, and for your sons forever. [25]And it shall be, when you come into the land which Jehovah shall give to you, as He has spoken, you shall observe this service. [26]And it shall be, when your sons say to you, What *is* this service to you? [27]Then you shall say, A sacrifice of a passover of

2320 3117 6240 702 7223 5769 2708 1755
18 לדרתיכם חקת עולם׃ בראשן בארבעה עשר יום לחדש
the of day the on the In .forever a your for
,month fourteenth ,(month) first statute ,generations

2320 6242 259 3117 4682 398 6153
בערב תאכלו מצת עד יום האחד ועשרים לחדש
the of twenty- first the day until un- shall you at
month bread leavened eat ,evening

3605 1004 4672 3808/7603 3117 7651 6153
19 בערב׃ שבעת ימים שאר לא ימצא בבתיכם כי כל־
anyone for your in be shall no leaven days (for) at
;houses found seven ;evening

1616 3478 5712 5315 3772 2556 398
אכל מחמצת ונכרתה הנפש ההוא מעדת ישראל בגר
among ,Israel the from that soul be shall anything eating
aliens the of congregation off cut ,leavened

4186 3605 398 3808 2556 776 249
20 ובאזרח הארץ׃ כל־מחמצת לא תאכלו בכל מושבתיכם
dwellings your all in shall You not leavened any- the among and
.eat thing .land of natives the

4682 398
תאכלו מצות׃
unleavened shall you
.bread eat

3947 4900 559 3478 2205 4872 7121
21 ויקרא משה לכל־זקני ישראל ויאמר אלהם משכו וקחו
and Draw ,them to said and ,Israel the all to Moses And
take out of elders called

92 3947 6453 7919 4940 6621
22 לכם צאן למשפחתיכם ושחטו הפסח׃ ולקחתם אגדת
a take And the kill and ,families your for the of for
of bunch passover flock you

4947 5060 1592 834 1818 2881 231
אזוב וטבלתם בדם אשר־בסף והגעתם אל־המשקוף
the to apply and the in which the in dip and hyssop
lintel ;basin (is) blood

5927 3808 5592 1818 4201 8147
ואל־שתי המזוזת מן־הדם אשר בסף ואתם לא תצאו
shall not you and the in which the some the two to and
out go ;basin (is) blood of doorposts

4714 5061 3068 5674 1242 5704 1004 6607 376
23 איש מפתח־ביתו עד־בקר׃ ועבר יהוה לנגף את־מצרים
;Egypt to Jehovah will And morn- until his the from any-
smite on pass .ing ,house of door one

6452 4201 8147 4947 1818 7200
וראה את־הדם על־המשקוף ועל שתי המזוזת ופסח
will and the two and lintel the on blood the He and
pass ;doorposts on see will

5061 1004 935 7843 5414 6607 5921 3068
יהוה על־הפתח ולא יתן המשחית לבא אל־בתיכם לנגף׃
to houses your into to destroyer the He not and the over Jehovah
.(you) strike come allow will

5769 1121 2706 2088 1697 8104
24 ושמרתם את־הדבר הזה לחק־לך ולבניך עד־עולם׃
.forever for and for an for this word you and
sons your you ordinance observe shall

3068 5414 776 935 1961
25 והיה כי־תבאו אל־הארץ אשר יתן יהוה לכם כאשר
as you to Jehovah will which land the into you when it And
give come be shall

559 1961 2088 5656 8104 1696
26 דבר ושמרתם את־העבדה הזאת׃ והיה כי־יאמרו
say when it And .this service shall you has he
be shall observe ,spoken

2077 559 5656 1121
27 אליכם בניכם מה העבדה הזאת לכם׃ ואמרתם זבח־
the you And to this service What your you to
of sacrifice say shall ?you (is) ,sons

Jehovah, who passed over the houses of the sons of Israel in Egypt when He struck Egypt. And he delivered our houses. And the people bowed and worshiped.
28And the sons of Israel went out and did as Jehovah commanded Moses and Aaron. So they did.
29And it happened at midnight. Jehovah struck every firstborn in the land of Egypt, from the firstborn of Pharaoh, the one sitting on the throne, to the firstborn of the captive who *was* in the prison-house, and every firstborn of animals.
30And Pharaoh arose by night, he and all his servants, and all the Egyptians. And *there* was a great cry in Egypt, for there was not a house where *there* was not a dead one.
31And he called Moses and Aaron by night, and said, Arise, go out from the midst of my people, both you and the sons of Israel. And go serve Jehovah according to your word.
32Take both your flocks and your herds, as you said, and go. And bless me also.
33And the Egyptians pressed on the people, to hasten to send them away from the land. For they said, All of us *are* about to die.
34And the people took up their dough before it was leavened, their kneading-troughs being bound up in their clothing on their shoulders.
35And the sons of Israel did according to the word of Moses. And they asked from the Egyptians articles of silver and articles of gold, and clothing.
36And Jehovah gave favor *to* the people in the eyes of the Egyptians. And they granted their requests. And they plundered Egypt.

פֶּסַח הוּא לַיהוָה אֲשֶׁר פָּסַח עַל־בָּתֵּי בְנֵי־יִשְׂרָאֵל בְּמִצְרַיִם
,Egypt in Israel the the over passed who to (is) It the
of sons of houses ,Jehovah Passover

בְּנָגְפּוֹ אֶת־מִצְרַיִם וְאֶת־בָּתֵּינוּ הִצִּיל וַיִּקֹּד הָעָם וַיִּשְׁתַּחֲווּ׃

28 וַיֵּלְכוּ וַיַּעֲשׂוּ בְּנֵי יִשְׂרָאֵל כַּאֲשֶׁר צִוָּה יְהוָה אֶת־מֹשֶׁה

29 וְאַהֲרֹן כֵּן עָשׂוּ׃ ס וַיְהִי ׀ בַּחֲצִי הַלַּיְלָה וַיהוָה הִכָּה כָל־בְּכוֹר

בְּאֶרֶץ מִצְרַיִם מִבְּכֹר פַּרְעֹה הַיֹּשֵׁב עַל־כִּסְאוֹ עַד בְּכוֹר

30 הַשְּׁבִי אֲשֶׁר בְּבֵית הַבּוֹר וְכֹל בְּכוֹר בְּהֵמָה׃ וַיָּקָם פַּרְעֹה

לַיְלָה הוּא וְכָל־עֲבָדָיו וְכָל־מִצְרַיִם וַתְּהִי צְעָקָה גְדֹלָה

31 בְּמִצְרָיִם כִּי־אֵין בַּיִת אֲשֶׁר אֵין־שָׁם מֵת׃ וַיִּקְרָא לְמֹשֶׁה

וּלְאַהֲרֹן לַיְלָה וַיֹּאמֶר קוּמוּ צְּאוּ מִתּוֹךְ עַמִּי גַּם־אַתֶּם גַּם־

32 בְּנֵי יִשְׂרָאֵל וּלְכוּ עִבְדוּ אֶת־יְהוָה כְּדַבֶּרְכֶם׃ גַּם־צֹאנְכֶם

גַּם־בְּקַרְכֶם קְחוּ כַּאֲשֶׁר דִּבַּרְתֶּם וָלֵכוּ וּבֵרַכְתֶּם גַּם־אֹתִי׃

33 וַתֶּחֱזַק מִצְרַיִם עַל־הָעָם לְמַהֵר לְשַׁלְּחָם מִן־הָאָרֶץ כִּי

34 אָמְרוּ כֻּלָּנוּ מֵתִים׃ וַיִּשָּׂא הָעָם אֶת־בְּצֵקוֹ טֶרֶם יֶחְמָץ

35 מִשְׁאֲרֹתָם צְרֻרֹת בְּשִׂמְלֹתָם עַל־שִׁכְמָם׃ וּבְנֵי־יִשְׂרָאֵל

עָשׂוּ כִּדְבַר מֹשֶׁה וַיִּשְׁאֲלוּ מִמִּצְרַיִם כְּלֵי־כֶסֶף וּכְלֵי זָהָב

36 וּשְׂמָלֹת׃ וַיהוָה נָתַן אֶת־חֵן הָעָם בְּעֵינֵי מִצְרַיִם וַיַּשְׁאִלוּם

וַיְנַצְּלוּ אֶת־מִצְרָיִם׃

37And the sons of Israel
pulled up from Rameses
to Succoth, the men *be-
ing* about six hundred
thousand on foot, apart
from little ones. 38And
also a mixed multitude
went up with them, and
flocks and herds, very
many livestock. 39And
they baked the dough
which they brought out
from Egypt *into* unleav-
ened cakes. For it was
not leavened, because
they were driven out from
Egypt, and they were not
able to delay. And also
they had not prepared
for themselves food for a
journey.
40And the time of the
dwelling of the sons of
Israel, which they dwelt
in Egypt, *was* four hun-
dred and thirty years.
41And it happened, from
the end of four hundred
and thirty years, on this
very day all the armies of
Jehovah went out from
the land of Egypt. 42It *is* a
night of celebration to
Jehovah, for bringing
them out of the land of
Egypt. This night *is* it, a
celebration for all the
sons of Israel to their
generations.
43And Jehovah said to
Moses and Aaron This *is*
the ordinance of the Passover. No alien may eat of
it. 44And every man's
slave, a purchase of silver,
you shall circumcise him,
then he may eat of it.
45An alien and a hired servant may not eat of it.
46It shall be eaten in one
house. You shall not
carry *any* of the flesh outside from the house. And
you shall not break a
bone in it. 47All the congregation of Israel shall
prepare it. 48And when
a foreigner shall stay with
you, and will do the Passover to Jehovah, let every
male of his be circum-
cised, and then he may
come to prepare it, and
he shall be like a native of
the land. But any uncir-
cumcised one may not
eat of it. 49One law shall

505 3967 8337 5523 7486 3478 1121 5265
37 ויסעו בני־ישראל מרעמסס סכתה כשש־מאות אלף
thousand hundred about to from Israel sons the and
six ,Succoth Rameses of up pulled

6629 5927 7227 6154 2945 905 1397 7273
38 רגלי הגברים לבד מטף: וגם־ערב רב עלה אתם וצאן
and with .vent a mixed And from apart ,men the on
,flocks ,them up multitude also .ones little foot

3318 1217 644 3966 3515 4735 1241
39 ובקר מקנה כבד מאד: ויאפו את־הבצק אשר הוציאו
they which dough the they And .very many and and
out brought baked livestock ,herds

4714 1644 2556 4682 5692 4714
ממצרים עגת מצות כי לא חמץ כי־גרשו ממצרים ולא
and from they because was it not for un- (into) from
not ;Egypt out driven were ;leavened ,leavened cakes Egypt

1121 4186 6213 6720 1571 4102 3201
40 יכלו להתמהמה וגם־צדה לא־עשו להם: ומושב בני
sons the And them- for had they food also and to they
living-time .selves made not journey a for ;delay able were

3967 702 8141 7970 4714 3427 834 3478
ישראל אשר ישבו במצרים שלשים שנה וארבע מאות
hundred and years (was) .Egypt in lived which Israel's
four thirty

1961 8141 3967 702 8141 7970 7093 1961 8141
41 שנה: ויהי מקץ שלשים שנה וארבע מאות שנה ויהי
.years hundred and years thirty the from it And .years
was four of end ,was

4714 776 3068 6635 3605 5927 3117 6106
בעצם היום הזה יצאו כל־צבאות יהוה מארץ מצרים:
.Egypt the from Jehovah the all went ,this day on
of land of armies out very

4714 776 3318 3068 8107 3915
42 ליל שמרים הוא ליהוה להוציאם מארץ מצרים הוא־
(is) it ;Egypt the of out bringing for to (is) It celebration a
of land them Jehovah of night

1755 3478 1121 3605 8107 3068 2088 3915
הלילה הזה ליהוה שמרים לכל־בני ישראל לדרתם:
their for Israel the all for a to this night
.generations of sons celebration Jehovah

1121 6453 2708 175 4872 3068 559
43 ויאמר יהוה אל־משה ואהרן זאת חקת הפסח כל־בן־
son every the the (is) This and Moses to Jehovah And
of ;Passover of ordinance .Aaron said

4135 3701 4736 376 5650 3605 398 5236
44 נכר לא־יאכל בו: וכל־עבד איש מקנת־כסף ומלתה
shall you ,silver a man's slave But .it of eat shall not an
circumcise of purchase every alien

259 1004 398 7916 8453 398
45 46 אתו אז יאכל בו: תושב ושכיר לא־יאכל בו: בבית אחד
one house In .it of may not a and alien An .it of he then ,him
eat servant hired eat may

3808 6106 2351 1320 1004 3318 398
יאכל לא־תוציא מן־הבית מן־הבשר חוצה ועצם לא־
not a and ,outside the (any) the from shall you not shall it
bone flesh of house carry ;eaten be

1481 6213 3478 5712 3605 7665
47 48 תשברו־בו: כל־עדת ישראל יעשו אתו: וכי־יגור אתך
with shall And .it shall Israel the All .it shall you
you stay when prepare of congregation break

7126 227 3605 2145 4135 3068 6453 6213 1616
גר ועשה פסח ליהוה המול לו כל־זכר ואז יקרב
may he then ,male every to be let ,Jehovah to the will and for-a
come him circumcised Passover do eigner

8451 398 3808 6189 3605 776 249 1961 6213
49 לעשתו והיה כאזרח הארץ וכל־ערל לא־יאכל בו: תורה
law .it of shall not not but land the a like he and pre- to
eat circumcised anyone of native be shall ,it pare

be to the native, and to the stranger, the one staying in your midst.

[50]And all the sons of Israel did as Jehovah commanded Moses and Aaron. So they did. [51]And it happened on this day, Jehovah brought out the sons of Israel from the land of Egypt by their armies.

1121 6213 8432 1481 1616 249 1961 259
50 אַחַת יִהְיֶה לָאֶזְרָח וְלַגֵּר הַגָּר בְּתוֹכְכֶם׃ וַיַּעֲשׂוּ כָּל־בְּנֵי
the all did And your in one the to and the to be shall One
of sons .midst staying visitor the native

6213 3651 175 4872 3068 6680 3478
יִשְׂרָאֵל כַּאֲשֶׁר צִוָּה יְהוָה אֶת־מֹשֶׁה וְאֶת־אַהֲרֹן כֵּן עָשׂוּ׃
they so ;Aaron and Moses Jehovah com- as Israel
.did manded

3478 1121 3068 3318 2088 3117 6106 1961
51 וַיְהִי בְּעֶצֶם הַיּוֹם הַזֶּה הוֹצִיא יְהוָה אֶת־בְּנֵי יִשְׂרָאֵל ס
Israel the Jehovah brought this day on it And
of sons out very was

6635 4714 776
מֵאֶרֶץ מִצְרַיִם עַל־צִבְאֹתָם׃
their by Egypt the from
.armies of land

CAP. XIII יג

CHAPTER 13

[1]And Jehovah spoke to Moses, saying, [2]Set apart every firstborn to Me, the one opening every womb among the sons of Israel, among men and among livestock— it *shall* belong to Me.

[3]And Moses said to the people, Remember this day *in* which you went out from Egypt, from the house of the slaves. For by the might of *His* hand Jehovah brought you out from here. And no leavened bread shall be eaten. [4]Today you are going out in the month of Abib. [5]And it shall be when Jehovah brings you into the land of the Canaanites, and the Hittites, and the Amorites, and the Hivites, and the Jebusites, which He swore to your fathers, to give to you, a land flowing *with* milk and honey, you shall do this service in this month. [6]Seven days you shall eat unleavened bread, and on the seventh day *keep* a feast to Jehovah. [7]Unleavened bread shall be eaten the seven days. And leavened bread shall not be seen for you, and leaven shall not be seen for you in all your boundaries. [8]And you shall tell your son on that day, saying, *It is* because of what Jehovah did to me, in my going out from Egypt. [9]And it shall be

6363 1060 3605 6942 559 4872 3068 1696
1 וַיְדַבֵּר יְהוָה אֶל־מֹשֶׁה לֵּאמֹר׃ קַדֶּשׁ־לִי כָל־בְּכוֹר פֶּטֶר
2
one the first- every to Set ,saying ,Moses to Jehovah And
opening born Me apart spoke

559 929 120 3478 1121 7358 3605
3 כָּל־רֶחֶם בִּבְנֵי יִשְׂרָאֵל בָּאָדָם וּבַבְּהֵמָה לִי הוּא׃ וַיֹּאמֶר
said And it belong among and among ,Israel among womb every
.(shall) Me to ;livestock men of sons the

4714 3318 834 2088/3117 2142 5971 4872
מֹשֶׁה אֶל־הָעָם זָכוֹר אֶת־הַיּוֹם הַזֶּה אֲשֶׁר יְצָאתֶם מִמִּצְרַיִם
from went you (in) this day Remember the to Moses
Egypt out which people

3808 3088 3068 3318 3027 2392 5650 1004
מִבֵּית עֲבָדִים כִּי בְּחֹזֶק יָד הוֹצִיא יְהוָה אֶתְכֶם מִזֶּה וְלֹא
and from you Jehovah brought (His) the by For .slaves the from
no ;here out hand of might of house

1961 24 2320 3318 3117 2557 398
4 יֵאָכֵל חָמֵץ׃ הַיּוֹם אַתֶּם יֹצְאִים בְּחֹדֶשׁ הָאָבִיב׃ וְהָיָה
5
it And .Abib the in going are you Today leavened be shall
be will of month ,out .bread eaten

2340 567 2850 3669 776 3068 935
כִּי־יְבִיאֲךָ יְהוָה אֶל־אֶרֶץ הַכְּנַעֲנִי וְהַחִתִּי וְהָאֱמֹרִי וְהַחִוִּי
the and the and the and the the into Jehovah brings when
,Hivites ,Amorites ,Hittites ,Canaanites of land you

2461 2100 776 5414 1 7650 834 2983
וְהַיְבוּסִי אֲשֶׁר נִשְׁבַּע לַאֲבֹתֶיךָ לָתֶת לָךְ אֶרֶץ זָבַת חָלָב
milk flowing a ,you give to your to He which the and
(with) land fathers swore ,Jebusites

7651 2088 2320 5656 5647 1706
6 וּדְבָשׁ וְעָבַדְתָּ אֶת־הָעֲבֹדָה הַזֹּאת בַּחֹדֶשׁ הַזֶּה׃ שִׁבְעַת
Seven .this month in this service shall you and
do ;honey

4682 3068 2282 7637 3117 4682 398 3117
7 יָמִים תֹּאכַל מַצֹּת וּבַיּוֹם הַשְּׁבִיעִי חַג לַיהוָה׃ מַצּוֹת
Unleavened to (keep) seventh on and unleavened you days
bread .Jehovah feast a day the .bread eat shall

7200 3808 2557 7200 3117 7651 398
יֵאָכֵל אֵת שִׁבְעַת הַיָּמִים וְלֹא־יֵרָאֶה לְךָ חָמֵץ וְלֹא־יֵרָאֶה
shall and leavened for be shall and ;days the seven be shall
seen be not ,bread you seen not eaten

559 3117 1121 5046 1366 7603
8 לְךָ שְׂאֹר בְּכָל־גְּבֻלֶךָ׃ וְהִגַּדְתָּ לְבִנְךָ בַּיּוֹם הַהוּא לֵאמֹר
,saying ,that day in your you And your all in leaven among
son tell shall .boundaries you

1961 4714 5927 3068 6213 2088 5668
9 בַּעֲבוּר זֶה עָשָׂה יְהוָה לִי בְּצֵאתִי מִמִּצְרָיִם׃ וְהָיָה לְךָ
to it And .Egypt from I when ,me for Jehovah did what (is It)
you be shall out came of because

a sign to you on your hand, and a memorial between your eyes, so that a law of Jehovah may be in your mouth. For with a strong hand Jehovah brought you out from Egypt. [10]And you shall keep this ordinance at its appointed time from days to days.

[11]And it shall be, when Jehovah breings you into the land of the Canaanites, as He swore to you and to your fathers, and gives it to you, [12]you shall set apart to Jehovah every one opening the womb, and every firstling, the young of the animals belonging to you, the males *are* to Jehovah. [13]And every firstling of an ass you shall redeem with a flock animal. And if you do not redeem *it*, you shall break its neck. And every firstborn of men among your sons you shall redeem. [14]And it shall be, when your son asks you in the future, saying, What *is* this? You shall say to him, Jehovah brought us out from Egypt by the might of *His* hand, from the house of slaves. [15]And it happened when Pharaoh hardened *himself* against sending us away, Jehovah killed every firstborn in the land of Egypt, from the firstborn of men and to the firstborn of animals. For this reason I sacrifice to Jehovah every one opening the womb, the males; and I redeem every firstborn of my sons. [16]And it shall be a sign on your hand, and frontlets between your eyes. For Jehovah brought us out from Egypt by the might of *His* hand.

[17]And it happened, in Pharaoh's sending away the people, God did not lead them *by* the way of the land of the Philistines, though it *was* near. For God said, Lest the people repent when they see war, and return to Egypt. [18]But God made the people turn

3068 8451 1961 5869 996 2146 3027/5921 226
לְאוֹת עַל־יָדְךָ וּלְזִכָּרוֹן בֵּין עֵינֶיךָ לְמַעַן תִּהְיֶה תּוֹרַת יְהוָה
Jehovah a be may that so your be- a for and your on for
8104 of law 4714 3068 ;eyes tween memorial ,hand sign a
3368 2389 3027 6313
10 בְּפִיךָ כִּי בְּיָד חֲזָקָה הוֹצִאֲךָ יְהוָה מִמִּצְרָיִם׃ וְשָׁמַרְתָּ
you And .Egypt from Jehovah brought strong with for your in
keep shall out you hand a mouth
3117 3117 4150 2088 2708
אֶת־הַחֻקָּה הַזֹּאת לְמוֹעֲדָהּ מִיָּמִים יָמִימָה׃
.days to from its at this ordinance
days ,time appointed
7650 3669 776 3068 935 1961
11 וְהָיָה כִּי־יְבִאֲךָ יְהוָה אֶל־אֶרֶץ הַכְּנַעֲנִי כַּאֲשֶׁר נִשְׁבַּע לְךָ
to swore He as the the into Jehovah brings when it And
you ,Canaanites of land you be shall
3068 7350 6363 5674 5414
12 וְלַאֲבֹתֶיךָ וּנְתָנָהּ לָךְ׃ וְהַעֲבַרְתָּ כָל־פֶּטֶר־רֶחֶם לַיהוָה
to the open- every shall you ,you to and to and
,Jehovah womb ing one apart set it gives ,fathers your
3068 2145 1961 834 929 7698 6363/3605
וְכָל־פֶּטֶר | שֶׁגֶר בְּהֵמָה אֲשֶׁר יִהְיֶה לְךָ הַזְּכָרִים לַיהוָה׃
to (are) males the to are which the off- first- and
.Jehovah ,you animals of spring born every
6202 6299 3808 7716 6299 2543 6363/3605
13 וְכָל־פֶּטֶר חֲמֹר תִּפְדֶּה בְשֶׂה וְאִם־לֹא תִפְדֶּה וַעֲרַפְתּוֹ וְכֹל
and shall you re- do you not if and a with shall you ass an first And
every ;neck its break ;(it) deem ,animal flock redeem of born every
4299 1121 7592 1961 6299 1121 120 1060
14 בְּכוֹר אָדָם בְּבָנֶיךָ תִּפְדֶּה׃ וְהָיָה כִּי־יִשְׁאָלְךָ בִנְךָ מָחָר
the in your you asks when it And shall you among men firstborn
future son be shall .redeem sons your of
3068 3318 3027 2392 559 2088 559
לֵאמֹר מַה־זֹּאת וְאָמַרְתָּ אֵלָיו בְּחֹזֶק יָד הוֹצִיאָנוּ יְהוָה
Jehovah brought (His) the by ,him to shall you ?this what ,saying
7971 out us hand of might 1961 say (is)
6547 7185 5650 1004 4714
15 מִמִּצְרַיִם מִבֵּית עֲבָדִים׃ וַיְהִי כִּי־הִקְשָׁה פַרְעֹה לְשַׁלְּחֵנוּ
against Pharaoh hardened when it And .slaves the from from
,us sending (himself) was of house ,Egypt
5704 120 1060 4714 776 1060/3605 3068 2026
וַיַּהֲרֹג יְהוָה כָּל־בְּכוֹר בְּאֶרֶץ מִצְרַיִם מִבְּכֹר אָדָם וְעַד
even men the from ,Egypt the in first- every Jehovah and
to of firstborn of land born killed
7358 6363/3605 3068 2076 929 1060
בְּכוֹר בְּהֵמָה עַל־כֵּן אֲנִי זֹבֵחַ לַיהוָה כָּל־פֶּטֶר רֶחֶם
the opening every to sacrifice I therefore ;animals the
,womb one Jehovah of firstborn
3027 5921 226 1961 6299 1121 1060 3605 2145
16 הַזְּכָרִים וְכָל־בְּכוֹר בָּנַי אֶפְדֶּה׃ וְהָיָה לְאוֹת עַל־יָדְכָה
your on a for it And I my first- and ,males the
,hand sign be shall .redeem sons of born every
4714 3068 3318 3067 2392 5869 996 2903
וּלְטוֹטָפֹת בֵּין עֵינֶיךָ כִּי בְּחֹזֶק יָד הוֹצִיאָנוּ יְהוָה מִמִּצְרָיִם׃
.Egypt from Jehovah brought (His) the by for your between and
out us hand of might ;eyes 7971 frontlets
776 1870 430 5148 5971 6547 1961
17 וַיְהִי בְּשַׁלַּח פַּרְעֹה אֶת־הָעָם וְלֹא־נָחָם אֱלֹהִים דֶּרֶךְ אֶרֶץ
the the God lead did not ,people the Pharaoh's when And
of land of way them sent was it
5971 5162 430 559 7138 3588 6430
פְּלִשְׁתִּים כִּי קָרוֹב הוּא כִּי | אָמַר אֱלֹהִים פֶּן־יִנָּחֵם הָעָם
the repent Lest ,God said for it near al- the
people (was) though Philistines
5971 430 5437 4714 7725 4421 7200
18 בִּרְאֹתָם מִלְחָמָה וְשָׁבוּ מִצְרָיְמָה׃ וַיַּסֵּב אֱלֹהִים | אֶת־הָעָם
people the God But .Egypt to and war they when
turn to made return see

toward the way of the
wilderness, *to* the Red Sea.
And the sons of Israel went
up armed from the land of
Egypt.
[19]And Moses took the
bones of Joseph with him.
For he had made the sons of
Israel certainly swear, saying, God will surely visit
you, and you shall cause my
bones to go from here with
you.
[20]And they traveled from
Succoth, and they camped
at Etham, in the edge of the
wilderness. [21]And Jehovah
was going before them by
day in a pillar of cloud, to
lead them *in* the way; and
by night in a pillar of fire, to
give light to them, to go by
day and by night. [22]The
pillar of cloud did not cease
by day, and the pillar of fire
by night, before the people.

דרך המדבר ים־סוף וחמשים עלו בני־ישראל מארץ
19 מצרים׃ ויקח משה את־עצמות יוסף עמו כי השבע
השביע את־בני ישראל לאמר פקד יפקד אלהים אתכם
20 והעליתם את־עצמתי מזה אתכם׃ ויסעו מסכת ויחנו
21 באתם בקצה המדבר׃ ויהוה הלך לפניהם יומם בעמוד
ענן לנחתם הדרך ולילה בעמוד אש להאיר להם
22 ללכת יומם ולילה׃ לא־ימיש עמוד הענן יומם ועמוד
האש לילה לפני העם׃

CAP. XIV יד

CHAPTER 14

CHAPTER 14
[1]And Jehovah spoke to
Moses, saying, [2]Speak to
the sons of Israel, and let
them return and camp
before Pihahiroth, between
Migdol and the sea, before
Baal-Zephon. You shall
camp opposite *it*, by the
sea. [3]And Pharaoh will say
as to the sons of Israel,
They *are* entangled in the
land, the wilderness has
shut them in. [4]And I will
harden Pharaoh's heart,
and he will pursue you. And
I will be honored through
Pharaoh, and through all his
armies. And the Egyptians
shall know that I *am*
Jehovah. And they did so.
[5]And it was told to the
king of Egypt that the
people had fled; and the
heart of Pharaoh and his
servants was turned as to
the people. And they said,
What *is* this we have done?
For we have sent away
Israel from serving us.

1 2 וידבר יהוה אל־משה לאמר׃ דבר אל־בני ישראל וישבו
ויחנו לפני פי החירת בין מגדל ובין הים לפני בעל
3 צפן נכחו תחנו על־הים׃ ואמר פרעה לבני ישראל
4 נבכים הם בארץ סגר עליהם המדבר׃ וחזקתי את־לב־
פרעה ורדף אחריהם ואכבדה בפרעה ובכל־חילו וידעו
5 מצרים כי־אני יהוה ויעשו־כן׃ ויגד למלך מצרים כי
ברח העם ויהפך לבב פרעה ועבדיו אל־העם ויאמרו
6 מה־זאת עשינו כי־שלחנו את־ישראל מעבדנו׃ ויאסר

[6]And he prepared his chariots. And he took his people with him. [7]And he took six hundred chosen chariots, and all the chariots of Egypt, and officers over all of them. [8]And Jehovah hardened Pharaoh king of Egypt's heart. And he pursued after the sons of Israel. And the sons of Israel *were* going out with a high hand. [9]And the Egyptians pursued them. And they overtook them camping by the sea, all the horses and the chariots of Pharaoh, and his horsemen, and his army, by Pihahiroth, before Baal-Zephon.

[10]And Pharaoh came near, and the sons of Israel raised their eyes, and, behold! The Egyptians *were* marching after them! And they were greatly afraid. And the sons of Israel cried to Jehovah. [11]And they said to Moses, Were there no graves in Egypt, that you have taken us away to die in the wilderness? What *is* this you have done to us, to bring us out from Egypt? [12]*Is* this not the word which we spoke to you in Egypt, saying, Go away from us, and let us serve the Egyptians. For *it is* better for us to serve the Egyptians, than to die in the wilderness. [13]And Moses said to the people, Do not be afraid. Take your stand and see the salvation of Jehovah, which He will prepare for you today. For as you see the Egyptians today, you shall not continue to see them again forever. [14]Jehovah will fight for you, and you be silent.

[15]And Jehovah said to Moses, Why do you cry to Me? Speak to the sons of

7393 3967 8337 3947 3947 5971 7393
7 את־רכבו ואת־עמו לקח עמו׃ ויקח שש־מאות רכב
chariots hundred six he And with took he his and his
took .him people ,chariots 977

3068 2388 3605 5921 7991 4714 7393 3605
8 בחור וכל רכב מצרים ושלשם על־כלו׃ ויחזק יהוה
Jehovah And of all over and ,Egypt the all and ,chosen
hardened .them officers of chariots

1121 3478 1121 310 7291 4714 4428 6547 3820
את־לב פרעה מלך מצרים וירדף אחרי בני ישראל ובני
the And .Israel the after he and ,Egypt king Pharaoh the
of sons of sons pursued of of heart

5381 310 4713 7291 7311 3027 5927 3478
9 ישראל יצאים ביד רמה׃ וירדפו מצרים אחריהם וישיגו
and after the And .high with were Israel
overtook them Egyptians pursued hand a out going

2428 6571 6547 7393 5483 3220 2583
אותם חנים על־הים כל־סוס רכב פרעה ופרשיו וחילו
his and his and ,Pharaoh's and horses all ,sea the by camping them
army ,horsemen chariots

5375 7126 6547 =1189= 6440 6367
10 על־פי החירת לפני בעל צפן׃ ופרעה הקריב וישאו
And .near came And .Baalzephon before ,Pihahiroth by
lifted Pharoah

310 5265 4713 2009 5869 3478 1121
בני־ישראל את־עיניהם והנה מצרים נסע אחריהם
after were the and ,eyes their Israel the
!them marching Egyptians ,behold of sons

559 3068 3478 1121 6817 3966 3372
11 וייראו מאד ויצעקו בני־ישראל אל־יהוה׃ ויאמרו אל־
to they And .Jehovah to Israel the and ;greatly they And
said of sons cried feared

4057 4191 3947 4714 6913 4872
משה המבלי אין־קברים במצרים לקחתנו למות במדבר
the in die to you that ,Egypt in graves no is It ,Moses
?wilderness us taken have (were) because

1697 3808 4714 3318 6213 2043
12 מה־זאת עשית לנו להוציאנו ממצרים׃ הלא־זה הדבר
the this not Is ?Egypt from bring to to have you this What
word out us ,us done (is)

5647 2308 559 4714 1696 834
אשר דברנו אליך במצרים לאמר חדל ממנו ונעבדה
let and us Let ,saying ,Egypt in you to we which
serve us alone spoke

4057 4191 4713 5647 2896 4713
את־מצרים כי טוב לנו עבד את־מצרים ממתנו במדבר׃
the in than the to us for (is it) For the
.wilderness die to Egyptians serve better ?Egyptians

7200 3320 3372 5971 4872 559
13 ויאמר משה אל־העם אל־תיראו התיצבו וראו את־
see and your take be Do not the to Moses And
stand ;afraid people said

7200 3117 6213 834 3068 3444
ישועת יהוה אשר־יעשה לכם היום כי אשר ראיתם את־
you as for ;today for will He which Jehovah the
see you perform of salvation

3068 5769 6287 200 3254 3808 3117 4713
14 מצרים היום לא תספו לראתם עוד עד־עולם׃ יהוה
Jehovah .forever again see to shall you not ,today the
them continue Egyptians

2790 3898
ילחם לכם ואתם תחרישון׃
.silent be you and for will
,you fight

1121 1696 6817 4872 3068 559
15 ויאמר יהוה אל־משה מה־תצעק אלי דבר אל־בני־
the to Speak to you do Why ,Moses to Jehovah And
of sons ?me cry said

Israel, and let them move forward. [16]And you raise your staff, and stretch out your hand over the sea, and divide it so that the sons of Israel may go in the midst of the sea on dry ground. [17]And I, behold, I *am* about to harden the heart of the Egyptians. And they will go after them. And I will be honored through Pharaoh, and through his armies, through his chariots, and through his horsemen. [18]And the Egyptians shall know that I *am* Jehovah, in my being honored through Pharaoh, through his chariots, and through his horsemen.

[19]And the Angel of God withdrew, the One going before the camp of Israel. And He went behind them. And the pillar of cloud withdrew from before them, and it stood behind them. [20]And it came between the camp of Egypt and the camp of Israel. And it was cloudy and dark. And it gave light to the night; and this one did not come near to that one all night.

[21]And Moses stretched out his hand over the sea, and Jehovah caused the sea to go back by a strong east wind all night. And He made the sea dry land, and the waters divided. [22]And the sons of Israel came into the middle of the sea on dry ground, the waters *being* a wall to them from their right and from their left. [23]And the Egyptians pursued, and all the horses of Pharaoh came after them, his chariots and his horsemen, into the middle of the sea. [24]And it happened in the morning watch: Jehovah looked on the camp of the Egyptians in the pillar of fire and cloud. And He confused the camp of the Egyptians. [25]And He took off the wheels of their chariots, and made them

5971 3027 5186 4294 7311 5265 3478
16 ישראל ויסעו: ואתה הרם את־מטך ונטה את־ידך על־
over hand your and staff your raise And and ,Israel
out stretch ,you .up pull

3006 3220 8432 3478 1121 935 1234 3220
הים ובקעהו ויבאו בני־ישראל בתוך הים ביבשה:
dry on sea the the in Israel the may that and the
ground of midst of sons go it divide ,sea

3513 310 935 4713 3820 2388 2009
17 ואני הנני מחזק את־לב מצרים ויבאו אחריהם ואכבדה
will I and after they and the heart the ,behold And
honored be ;them go will ,Egyptians of hardening (am) I I

4713 3045 6571 7393 2428 6547
18 בפרעה ובכל־חילו ברכבו ובפרשיו: וידעו מצרים
the shall And through and through his through and through
Egyptians know .horsemen his ,chariots his ,armies all Pharaoh

5265 6571 7393 6547 3513 3068
19 כי־אני יהוה בהכבדי בפרעה ברכבו ובפרשיו: ויסע
And through and his through through being my in ,Jehovah I that
moved .horsemen his ,chariots ,Pharaoh honored (am)

310 3212 3470 4264 6440 1980 430 4397
מלאך האלהים ההלך לפני מחנה ישראל וילך מאחריהם
behind He and ,Israel the before One the ,God the
,them went of camp going of Angel

996 935 310 5975 6440 6051 5982 5265
20 ויסע עמוד הענן מפניהם ויעמד מאחריהם: ויבא בין
be- it And behind it and before from the pillar and
tween came .them stood ;them cloud of moved

215 2822 6051 1961 3478 4264 996 4714 4264
מחנה מצרים ובין מחנה ישראל ויהי הענן והחשך ויאר
it and the and the it and ;Israel the and Egypt camp the
up lit ,darkness cloud was of camp of

4872 5186 3915 3605/2088 2088 7126 3808 3915
21 את־הלילה ולא־קרב זה אל־זה כל־הלילה: ויט משה
Moses And .night all that to this did and ;night the
out stretched near come not

5794/6921 7307 3220 3068 3212 3220 3027
את־ידו על־הים ויולך יהוה את־הים ברוח קדים עזה
strong east an by sea the Jehovah and ,sea the over his
wind recede made hand

935 4325 1234 2724 3220 7760 3915 3605
22 כל־הלילה וישם את־הים לחרבה ויבקעו המים: ויבאו
And the were and dry sea the He and .night all
came .waters divided ,land made

3225 2346 4325 3006 3220 8432 3478 1121
בני־ישראל בתוך הים ביבשה והמים להם חומה מימינם
their from a to the and ,dry the on the the into Israel the
(hand) right wall them (were) waters ,ground sea of middle of sons

5483 3605 310 935 4713 7291 8040
23 ומשמאלם: וירדפו מצרים ויבאו אחריהם כל סוס
the all after and the And from and
of horses them came Egyptians pursued .(hand) left their

1242 821 1961 3220 8432 6571 7393 6547
24 פרעה רכבו ופרשיו אל־תוך הים: ויהי באשמרת הבקר
the in it And the the into his and his ,Pharaoh
,morning watch happened .sea of middle ,horsemen ,chariots

2000 6051 784 5982 4713 4264 3068/8250
וישקף יהוה אל־מחנה מצרים בעמוד אש וענן ויהם את
He and and fire the in the camp the on Jehovah looked
confused ,cloud of pillar Egyptians of down

3517 5090 4818 212 5493 4713 4264
25 מחנה מצרים: ויסר את אפן מרכבתיו וינהגהו בכבדת
with made and their the He And the camp the
;difficulty drive them ,chariots of wheels off took .Egyptians of

drive with difficulty. And the Egyptians said, I will flee from the face of Israel, for Jehovah *is* fighting for them against the Egyptians.

[26]And Jehovah said to Moses, Stretch out your hand over the sea, and let the waters return on the Egyptians, on their chariots, and on their horsemen. [27]And Moses stretched out his hand over the sea, and the sea returned to its usual flow, at the turning of the morning, and the Egyptians *were* fleeing to meet it. And Jehovah shook off the Egyptians into the middle of the sea. [28]And the waters returned and covered the chariots and the horsemen, together with all the army of Pharaoh, those going after them into the sea. And not even one was left among them. [29]And the sons of Israel walked on dry ground in the middle of the sea, the waters *being* a wall for them, from their right and from their left.

[30]And Jehovah saved Israel in that day from the hand of Egypt. And Israel saw the Egyptians dead on the seashore. [31]And Israel saw the great hand with which Jehovah worked against Egypt, and the people feared Jehovah; and they believed in Jehovah and in His servant Moses.

3898 3068 3478 6440 5127 4713 559
ויאמר מצרים אנוסה מפני ישראל כי יהוה נלחם להם
for is Jehovah for ,Israel from will I the said and
them fighting of face the flee ,Egyptians
4713
במצרים:
the against Egyptians

4325 7725 3220 5921 3027 5186 4872 3068 559
26 ויאמר יהוה אל-משה נטה את-ידך על-הים וישבו המים
the let and the over your Stretch ,Moses to Jehovah And
waters return ,sea hand out said
3027 4872 5186 6571 7393 4713
27 על-מצרים על-רכבו ועל-פרשיו: ויט משה את-ידו
his Moses And their and their on the on
hand out stretched .horsemen on chariots ,Egyptians
5127 4713 386 1242 6437 3220 7725 3220
על-הים וישב הים לפנות בקר לאיתנו ומצרים נסים
(were) the And its to ,morning the at the and ,sea the over
fleeing Egyptians .flow usual of dawn sea returned
7725 3220 8432 4713 3068 5287 7125
28 לקראתו וינער יהוה את-מצרים בתוך הים: וישבו
And .sea the the into the Jehovah and ;it meet to
returned of middle Egyptians off shook
6547 2428 3605 6571 7393 3680 4325
המים ויכסו את-הרכב ואת-הפרשים לכל חיל פרעה
,Pharaoh the together the and the and the
of army all with ,horsemen chariots covered waters
1121 259 5704 7604 3220 310 935
29 הבאים אחריהם בים לא-נשאר בהם עד-אחד: ובני
the And .one even among was and into after those
of sons them left not ;sea the them going
3225 2346 4325 3220 8432 3006 1980 3478
ישראל הלכו ביבשה בתוך הים והמים להם חמה מימינם
their from a to the and the the in dry on walked Israel
(hand) right wall them waters ,sea of middle ground
3027 3478 3117 3068 3462 8040
30 ומשמאלם: ויושע יהוה ביום ההוא את-ישראל מיד
from Israel that day in Jehovah And their from and
of hand the saved .(hand) left
7200 3220 8193 4191 4713 3478 7200 4713
31 מצרים וירא ישראל את-מצרים מת על-שפת הים: וירא
And the the upon dead the Israel and the
saw .sea of shore Egyptians saw ;Egyptians
3372 4714 3068 5647 1419 3027 3478
ישראל את-היד הגדלה אשר עשה יהוה במצרים וייראו
and against Jehovah worked with great hand the Israel
feared ,Egypt which
5650 4872 3068 539 3068 5971
העם את-יהוה ויאמינו ביהוה ובמשה עבדו:
His in and in they and ;Jehovah the
.servant Moses Jehovah believed people

CAP. XV טו
CHAPTER 15

CHAPTER 15

[1]Then Moses and the sons of Israel sang this song to Jehovah, and spoke, saying, I will sing to Jehovah, for He is highly exalted. He has thrown *the* horse and its rider into the sea. [2]My strength and song is Jehovah, and He

559 3068 7892 3478 1121 4872 7891
1 אז ישיר-משה ובני ישראל את-השירה הזאת ליהוה ויאמרו
and to this song Israel the and Moses Then
spoke Jehovah of sons sang
5483 1342 1342 3068 7891 559
לאמר אשירה ליהוה כי-גאה גאה סוס
Horse is He highly for to will I ,saying
exalted ,Jehovah sing
1961 3050 2176 5797 3220 7411 7392
2 ורכבו רמה בים: עזי וזמרת יה ויהי-לי
He And is and my into has He its and
me to was ;Jah praise strength .sea the thrown rider

has become salvation to
me. This *is* my God and I
will glorify Him; the God
of my father, and I will exalt Him. 3Jehovah *is* a
man of war; Jehovah *is*
His name. 4He has thrown
Pharaoh's chariots and
his army into the sea; yea,
the choice ones of his
officers are drowned in
the Sea of Reeds. 5The
deep covers them; they
went down into the
depths like a stone.
6Your right *hand*, O
Jehovah *is* glorious in
power; Your right *hand*, O
Jehovah, dashes the
enemy to pieces. 7And in
the greatness of Your
majesty You pull down
those rising against You;
You send forth Your
wrath; it consumes them
like stubble. 8And by the
spirit of Your anger were
heaped up waters; the
running *waters* stood like
a wall; the depths con-
gealed in the heart of the
sea. 9The enemy said, I
will pursue, I will over-
take; I will divide the
spoil; my soul shall be
filled *with* them; I will
draw my sword; my hand
shall destroy them.

10You blew with Your
wind; the sea covered
them; they sank like lead
in mighty waters. 11Who
is like You among the
gods, O Jehovah? Who *is*
like You, glorified in holiness, fearful in praises, O
Worker of wonders.
12You stretched out Your
right *hand*; the earth
swallowed them. 13In
Your mercy You led the
people whom You had
redeemed; in Your
strength You guided to
Your holy dwelling.
14Peoples heard; they
tremble, trembling seized

430 5115 410 2088 3444
אֱלֹהֵי זֶה אֵלִי וְאַנְוֵהוּ לִישׁוּעָה
God the of — will I and Him glorify, my God, this (is) — for ;salvation

3 3068 4421 376 3068 7311 1
יְהוָה מִלְחָמָה אִישׁ יְהוָה אָבִי וַאֲרֹמְמֶנְהוּ׃
Jehovah (is) ;war — Man a of — Jehovah (is) — will I and Him exalt ,father my

4 4005 3220 3384 2428 6547 4818 8034
וּמִבְחַר בַיָּם יָרָה וְחֵילוֹ פַּרְעֹה מַרְכְּבֹת שְׁמוֹ׃
the and of ones choice — the sea; in — has He cast — his and army — Pharaoh — chariots The of — His .name

5 3644 3966 3381 3680 8415 5488 2883 7991
כְּמוֹ בִמְצוֹלֹת יָרְדוּ יְכַסְיֻמוּ תְּהֹמֹת בְיַם־סוּף׃ טֻבְּעוּ שָׁלִשָׁיו
like — the into depths — they down went — ;them cover — deep the — Reeds of Sea — in sank — are — his officers

6 3225 3581 142 3068 3225 68
יְמִינְךָ בַּכֹּחַ נֶאְדָּרִי יְהוָה יְמִינְךָ אָבֶן׃
right Your (hand), — in ;power — (is) glorious — O ,Jehovah — right Your (hand) — .stone a

7 2040 1347 7230 341 7492 3068
תַּהֲרֹס גְּאוֹנְךָ וּבְרֹב אוֹיֵב׃ תִּרְעַץ יְהוָה
pull You down — Your majesty — in And of greatness — the .enemy — to dashes pieces — O ,Jehovah

8 7307 7179 398 2740 7971 6965
וּבְרוּחַ כַּקַּשׁ׃ יֹאכְלֵמוֹ חֲרֹנְךָ תְּשַׁלַּח קָמֶיךָ
the by And of spirit — like .stubble — con- it them sumes — Your ;wrath — send You forth — who those ;You oppose

5067 5324 4325 6192 639
כְמוֹ־נֵד נִצְּבוּ מַיִם נֶעֶרְמוּ אַפֶּיךָ
a like wall — stood — ;waters the — were up heaped — Your anger

9 559 3220 3820 8415 7087 5140
אָמַר בְּלֶב־יָם׃ תְהֹמֹת קָפְאוּ נֹזְלִים
said — ,sea the of heart — the in — the depths — congealed — running the ;(waters)

4390 7998 2505 5381 7291 341
תִּמְלָאֵמוֹ שָׁלָל אֲחַלֵּק אַשִּׂיג אֶרְדֹּף אוֹיֵב
filled be shall them (with) — the ;spoil — will I divide — will I ,overtake — will I ,pursue — the ,enemy

10 5397 7218 3027 2719 7324 5315
נָשַׁפְתָּ יָדִי׃ תּוֹרִישֵׁמוֹ חַרְבִּי אָרִיק נַפְשִׁי
blew You — my .hand — destroy shall them — my ,sword — will I draw — ;soul my

4325 5777 6749 3220 3680 7307
בְּמַיִם כַּעוֹפֶרֶת צָלְלוּ יָם כִּסָּמוֹ בְרוּחֲךָ
in waters — lead like — they sank — the ;sea — covered them — Your with ;wind

11 3068 410 117
מִי יְהוָה בָּאֵלִם מִי־כָמֹכָה אַדִּירִים׃
Who (is) — O ?Jehovah — among ,gods the — like You — Who (is) — .mighty

6213 6382 8416 3372 6944 142
עֹשֵׂה תְהִלֹּת נוֹרָא בַּקֹּדֶשׁ נֶאְדָּר כָּמֹכָה
Worker O of — (in) ,praises — fearful — in holiness — glorified — like ,You

12 13 5148 776 1104 3225 5186 6382
נָחִיתָ אָרֶץ׃ תִּבְלָעֵמוֹ יְמִינְךָ נָטִיתָ פֶלֶא׃
led You — the .earth — swallowed them — Your ,(hand) right — stretched You — ?wonders

5116 5797 5095 1350 2098 5971 2617
אֶל־נְוֵה בְעָזְּךָ נֵהַלְתָּ גָּאָלְתָּ עַם־זוּ בְחַסְדְּךָ
to dwelling — Your in strength — You guided — had You ;redeemed — whom the people — Your in mercy

14 2427 7264 5971 8085 6944
חִיל יִרְגָּזוּן עַמִּים שָׁמְעוּ קָדְשֶׁךָ׃
trembling — they ;tremble — ,peoples — Have heard — .holy Your

the inhabitants of Philistia.
15 Then the leaders of Edom
were confounded; the
leaders of Moab *were*
seized by trembling; all the
inhabitants of Canaan were
melted. 16 Terror and dread
fell on them; by the greatness of Your arm they are
silent as a stone; until Your
people pass through, O
Jehovah, until pass through
the people whom You have
bought. 17 You shall bring
them in and plant them in
the mountain of Your
inheritance, the place You
have made for Your
dwelling-place, O Jehovah;
the sanctuary which Your
hands have prepared, O
Lord. 18 Jehovah reigns forever and ever!

19 For the horses of
Pharaoh went in with his
chariots and his horsemen
into the sea, and Jehovah
brought back the waters of
the sea on them; and the
sons of Israel went on dry
land in the midst of the sea.

20 And the sister of Aaron,
Miriam the prophetess,
took the timbrel in her
hand, and all the women
went out after her with
timbrels and with dances.
21 And Miriam answered to
them, Sing to Jehovah, for
surely He has triumphed
gloriously; He has thrown
the horse and its rider into
the sea.

22 And Moses made Israel
to pull out from the Red
Sea. And they went out into
the wilderness of Shur. And
they went into the wilderness three days, and did not
find water. 23 And they came
to Marah. And they were
not able to drink water from
Marah, for it *was* bitter.
Therefore, one called its
name Marah. 24 And the
people murmured against
Moses, saying, What shall

אָחַז יֹשְׁבֵי פְּלָשֶׁת׃ 15 אָז נִבְהֲלוּ אַלּוּפֵי
אֱדוֹם אֵילֵי מוֹאָב יֹאחֲזֵמוֹ רָעַד נָמֹגוּ
כֹּל יֹשְׁבֵי כְנָעַן׃ 16 תִּפֹּל עֲלֵיהֶם אֵימָתָה
וָפַחַד בִּגְדֹל זְרוֹעֲךָ יִדְּמוּ כָּאָבֶן עַד
יַעֲבֹר עַמְּךָ יְהוָה עַד־יַעֲבֹר עַם־זוּ
קָנִיתָ׃ 17 תְּבִאֵמוֹ וְתִטָּעֵמוֹ בְּהַר נַחֲלָתְךָ מָכוֹן
לְשִׁבְתְּךָ פָּעַלְתָּ יְהוָה מִקְּדָשׁ אֲדֹנָי כּוֹנְנוּ
יָדֶיךָ׃ 18 יְהוָה ׀ יִמְלֹךְ לְעֹלָם וָעֶד׃ 19 כִּי
בָא סוּס פַּרְעֹה בְּרִכְבּוֹ וּבְפָרָשָׁיו בַּיָּם וַיָּשֶׁב יְהוָה עֲלֵהֶם
אֶת־מֵי הַיָּם וּבְנֵי יִשְׂרָאֵל הָלְכוּ בַיַּבָּשָׁה בְּתוֹךְ הַיָּם׃ פ
20 וַתִּקַּח מִרְיָם הַנְּבִיאָה אֲחוֹת אַהֲרֹן אֶת־הַתֹּף בְּיָדָהּ וַתֵּצֶאןָ
21 כָל־הַנָּשִׁים אַחֲרֶיהָ בְּתֻפִּים וּבִמְחֹלֹת׃ וַתַּעַן לָהֶם מִרְיָם
שִׁירוּ לַיהוָה כִּי־גָאֹה גָּאָה סוּס וְרֹכְבוֹ רָמָה בַיָּם׃ ס
22 וַיַּסַּע מֹשֶׁה אֶת־יִשְׂרָאֵל מִיַּם־סוּף וַיֵּצְאוּ אֶל־מִדְבַּר־שׁוּר
23 וַיֵּלְכוּ שְׁלֹשֶׁת־יָמִים בַּמִּדְבָּר וְלֹא־מָצְאוּ מָיִם׃ וַיָּבֹאוּ
מָרָתָה וְלֹא יָכְלוּ לִשְׁתֹּת מַיִם מִמָּרָה כִּי מָרִים הֵם עַל־
24 כֵּן קָרָא־שְׁמָהּ מָרָה׃ וַיִּלֹּנוּ הָעָם עַל־מֹשֶׁה לֵּאמֹר מַה־

we drink? [25]And he cried to Jehovah, and Jehovah showed him a tree. And he threw *it* into the water, and the water became sweet.

He made a statute and an ordinance for them there, and He tested them there. [26]And he said, If you carefully listen to the voice of Jehovah your God, and you do what is right in His eyes, and you give ear to His commandments, and keep all His statutes, I will not put on you all the diseases which I have put on Egypt; for I *am* Jehovah your healer.

[27]And they came to Elim. And there *were* twelve springs of water and seventy palm trees. And they camped by the waters.

7993 6086 3068 5384 3068 6817 8354

25 נִשְׁתֶּה׃ וַיִּצְעַק אֶל־יְהוָה וַיּוֹרֵהוּ יְהוָה עֵץ וַיַּשְׁלֵךְ אֶל־

into (it) threw he and tree, a Jehovah him showed and Jehovah to cried he And ?drink we shall

5254 8033 4941 2706 7760 4325 4985 4325

הַמַּיִם וַיִּמְתְּקוּ הַמָּיִם שָׁם שָׂם לוֹ חֹק וּמִשְׁפָּט וְשָׁם נִסָּהוּ׃

.them tried He there and ,ordinance an and statute a them for made He There .water the sweet be came and ,water the

5869 3477 430 3068 6963 8085 8085 559

26 וַיֹּאמֶר אִם־שָׁמוֹעַ תִּשְׁמַע לְקוֹל ׀ יְהוָה אֱלֹהֶיךָ וְהַיָּשָׁר בְּעֵינָיו

His eyes in right the and ,God your Jehovah of voice the to listen you carefully If said he And

4245 3605 2706 8104 4687 238 6213

תַּעֲשֶׂה וְהַאֲזַנְתָּ לְמִצְוֺתָיו וְשָׁמַרְתָּ כָּל־חֻקָּיו כָּל־הַמַּחֲלָה

diseases the all ,statutes His all keep and ,commands His to listen you and ,do

3068 7760 4714 7760 834

אֲשֶׁר־שַׂמְתִּי בְמִצְרַיִם לֹא־אָשִׂים עָלֶיךָ כִּי אֲנִי יְהוָה

Jehovah (am) I for ;you on put will I not Egypt on put have I which

4325 5869 6240 8147 8033 362 935 7495

27 רֹפְאֶךָ׃ ס וַיָּבֹאוּ אֵילִמָה וְשָׁם שְׁתֵּים עֶשְׂרֵה עֵינֹת מַיִם

water of springs twelve (were) there and ;Elim to came they And .healer your

4325 8033 2583 8558 7657

וְשִׁבְעִים תְּמָרִים וַיַּחֲנוּ־שָׁם עַל־הַמָּיִם׃

.waters the by there camped they and ;trees palm seventy and

CAP. XVI טז

CHAPTER 16

CHAPTER 16

[1]And they pulled out from Elim. And all the congregation of the sons of Israel came into the Wilderness of Sin, which *is* between Elim and Sinai, on the fifteenth day of the second month *after* their going out from the land of Egypt. [2]And all the congregation of the sons of Israel murmured against Moses and against Aaron in the wilderness. [3]And the sons of Israel said to them, Would that we had died by the hand of Jehovah in the land of Egypt, in our sitting by the flesh-pots, in our eating bread to satisfaction. For you have brought us out into this wilderness to kill all this assembly with hunger.

5512 4057 3478 1121 5712 935 362 5265

1 וַיִּסְעוּ מֵאֵילִם וַיָּבֹאוּ כָּל־עֲדַת בְּנֵי־יִשְׂרָאֵל אֶל־מִדְבַּר־סִין

,Sin of wilderness the into Israel of sons the of congregation the all came and ,Elim from up pulled they And

2320 3117/6240 2568 5514 996 362 996 834

אֲשֶׁר בֵּין־אֵילִם וּבֵין סִינָי בַּחֲמִשָּׁה עָשָׂר יוֹם לַחֹדֶשׁ

month the of day fifteenth the on ,Sinai and between Elim between (is) which

3478 1121 5712 3885 4714 776 3318 8145

2 הַשֵּׁנִי לְצֵאתָם מֵאֶרֶץ מִצְרָיִם׃ וַיִּלּוֹנוּ כָּל־עֲדַת בְּנֵי־יִשְׂרָאֵל

Israel of sons the of congregation the all murmured And .Egypt of land the from their leaving (after) second

3478 1121 559 4057 175 4872

3 עַל־מֹשֶׁה וְעַל־אַהֲרֹן בַּמִּדְבָּר׃ וַיֹּאמְרוּ אֲלֵהֶם בְּנֵי יִשְׂרָאֵל

.Israel of sons the them to said And .wilderness the in Aaron against and Moses against

5518 3427 4714 776 3068 4191 4310

מִי־יִתֵּן מוּתֵנוּ בְיַד־יְהוָה בְּאֶרֶץ מִצְרַיִם בְּשִׁבְתֵּנוּ עַל־סִיר

pots the by sitting our in ,Egypt of land the in Jehovah of hand the by died had we that Would

3318 7648 3899 398 1320

הַבָּשָׂר בְּאָכְלֵנוּ לֶחֶם לָשֹׂבַע כִּי־הוֹצֵאתֶם אֹתָנוּ אֶל־

into us out brought have you for ;satisfaction to bread eating our in ,flesh

7458 2088 6951 3605 4191 4057

הַמִּדְבָּר הַזֶּה לְהָמִית אֶת־כָּל־הַקָּהָל הַזֶּה בָּרָעָב׃ ס

.hunger with this assembly all kill to this wilderness

[4]And Jehovah said to Moses, Behold, *I AM*! Bread will rain from the heavens for you. And the people shall go out and gather the matter of a day in its day, so that I may test them, whether they will walk in

8064 3899 4305 2009 4872 3068 559

4 וַיֹּאמֶר יְהוָה אֶל־מֹשֶׁה הִנְנִי מַמְטִיר לָכֶם לֶחֶם מִן־הַשָּׁמָיִם

;heavens the from bread you for rain will (am) I ,behold ,Moses to Jehovah said And

3212 5254 3117 3117 1697 3950 5971 5927

וְיָצָא הָעָם וְלָקְטוּ דְּבַר־יוֹם בְּיוֹמוֹ לְמַעַן אֲנַסֶּנּוּ הֲיֵלֵךְ

walk they will if ,them test may I that so ,day its in day a of matter the gather and people the out go shall and

My law or not. 5 And it shall
be on the sixth day they
shall prepare what they
bring in. And it shall be
double what they gather
day by day.
6 And Moses and Aaron
said to all the sons of Israel,
At evening, you shall know
that Jehovah has brought
you from the land of Egypt;
7 and in the morning you
shall see the glory of
Jehovah, in His hearing
your murmurings against
Jehovah. And we, what *are*
we that you murmur against
us? 8 And Moses said,
When Jehovah gives you
flesh to eat in *the* evening,
and bread in the morning,
to satisfaction; when
Jehovah hears your mur-
murings which you are
murmuring against Him,
you will see. And what *are*
we? Your murmurings *are*
not against us, but against
Jehovah.

9 And Moses spoke to
Aaron, Say to all the
congregation of the sons of
Israel, Come near before
Jehovah; for He has heard
your murmurings. 10 And it
happened, as Aaron was
speaking to all the congregation of the sons of Israel,
they turned toward the
wilderness. And, behold!
The glory of Jehovah
appeared in the cloud!
11 And Jehovah spoke to
Moses, saying, 12 I have
heard the murmurings of
the sons of Israel. Speak to
them, saying, Between the
evenings you shall eat
flesh; and in the morning
you shall be satisfied *with*
bread; and you shall know
that I *am* Jehovah your
God.

13 And it happened in the
evening: the quail came up
and covered the camp. And
in the morning a layer of
dew was around the camp.
14 And the layer of dew went
up, and, behold, *something*

small *was* on the face of the wilderness, scale-like, small like the hoar-frost on the earth. 15 And the sons of Israel looked. And they said, each one to his brother, *Is* that a whatness? For they did not know what it *was*. And Moses said to them, That *is* the bread which Jehovah has given to you for food. 16 This *is* the thing which Jehovah commanded. Gather from it, each one according to the mouth of his eating; an omer for a head, *by* the number of your souls you shall take for each man who *is* in your tent. 17 And so the sons of Israel did. And they gathered—the one gathering much and the one gathering little. 18 And they measured with an omer. And the one gathering much did not have too much. And the one gathering little did not have any need. Each one gathered according to the mouth of his eating. 19 And Moses said to them, Do not let anyone leave from it until morning. 20 And they did not listen to Moses. And some left from it until morning; and it became rotten *with* maggots, and stunk. And Moses was angry against them. 21 And they gathered it in the morning, each one in the morning according to the mouth of his eating. And it melted *in* the heat of the sun. 22 And it came about on the sixth day, they gathered double bread, two omers for one. And all the leaders of the congregation came and reported to Moses. 23 And he said to them, That *is* what Jehovah said, Tomorrow is a rest, a holy sabbath to Jehovah. What you will bake, bake. And boil what you will boil. And lay up for yourselves all that is left over, to keep it until the morning. 24 And they laid it up until the morning, as Moses

776 3713 1851 2636 1851 4057 6440
עַל־פְּנֵי הַמִּדְבָּר דַּק מְחֻסְפָּס דַּק כַּכְּפֹר עַל־הָאָרֶץ׃
.earth the on the like small ,scale-like (something) the the on
hoar-frost small wilderness of face

3808 4478 251 376 559 3478 1121 7200
15 וַיִּרְאוּ בְנֵי־יִשְׂרָאֵל וַיֹּאמְרוּ אִישׁ אֶל־אָחִיו מָן הוּא כִּי לֹא
not For ?that What his to each ,said and ,Israel the And
(is) ,brother one of sons looked

5414 3899 4872 559 3045
יָדְעוּ מַה־הוּא וַיֹּאמֶר מֹשֶׁה אֲלֵהֶם הוּא הַלֶּחֶם אֲשֶׁר נָתַן
has which the This ,them to Moses said And it what did they
given bread (is) .(was) know

3947 3068 6680 834 1697 2088 402 3068
16 יְהוָה לָכֶם לְאָכְלָה׃ זֶה הַדָּבָר אֲשֶׁר צִוָּה יְהוָה לִקְטוּ
gather ;Jehovah has which the This .food for to Jehovah
commanded thing (is) you

5315 4557 1538 6016 400 6310 376
מִמֶּנּוּ אִישׁ לְפִי אָכְלוֹ עֹמֶר לַגֻּלְגֹּלֶת מִסְפַּר נַפְשֹׁתֵיכֶם
,souls your the (by) a for an his to according each from
of number ,head omer ;eating of mouth the one ,it

3950 3478 1121 6213 3947 168 376
17 אִישׁ לַאֲשֶׁר בְּאָהֳלוֹ תִּקָּחוּ׃ וַיַּעֲשׂוּ־כֵן בְּנֵי יִשְׂרָאֵל וַיִּלְקְטוּ
they and ;Israel the so did And you in who each
,gathered of sons .take shall tent his (is) man

4591 5736 6076 4058 4591 7235/4591
18 הַמַּרְבֶּה וְהַמַּמְעִיט׃ וַיָּמֹדּוּ בָעֹמֶר וְלֹא הֶעְדִּיף הַמַּרְבֶּה
gath- one the have did and an with they And one the and gath one the
,much ering surplus a not ,omer measured .little gathering much ering

559 3950 400 6310 376 2637 3808 4591
19 וְהַמַּמְעִיט לֹא הֶחְסִיר אִישׁ לְפִי־אָכְלוֹ לָקָטוּ׃ וַיֹּאמֶר
said And .gathered his to according each have did not one the and
eating of mouth the one ;need any little gathering

8085 3808 1242 5704 3498 376 4872
20 מֹשֶׁה אֲלֵהֶם אִישׁ אַל־יוֹתֵר מִמֶּנּוּ עַד־בֹּקֶר׃ וְלֹא־שָׁמְעוּ
did they And .morning until from let do not Anyone to Moses
listen not it leave ,them

8438 7311 1242 5704 582 3498 4872
אֶל־מֹשֶׁה וַיּוֹתִרוּ אֲנָשִׁים מִמֶּנּוּ עַד־בֹּקֶר וַיָּרֻם תּוֹלָעִים
(with) it and ;morning until from men left and ,Moses to
maggots rotten became it

376 1242 1242 3950 4872 7107 887
21 וַיִּבְאַשׁ וַיִּקְצֹף עֲלֵהֶם מֹשֶׁה׃ וַיִּלְקְטוּ אֹתוֹ בַּבֹּקֶר בַּבֹּקֶר אִישׁ
each the in the in it they And .Moses against was and and
one morning ;morning gathered them angry ;stank

3950 8315 3117 1961 4549 8121 2552 400 6310
22 כְּפִי אָכְלוֹ וְחַם הַשֶּׁמֶשׁ וְנָמָס׃ וַיְהִי בַּיּוֹם הַשִּׁשִּׁי לָקְטוּ
they the day on it And it and sun the the and his the by
gathered ,sixth was .melted of heat eating of mouth

5712 8269 3605 935 259 6016 8147 4932 3899
לֶחֶם מִשְׁנֶה שְׁנֵי הָעֹמֶר לָאֶחָד וַיָּבֹאוּ כָּל־נְשִׂיאֵי הָעֵדָה
the leaders the all and ;one for omers two ,double bread
congregation of came

3068 1696 559 4872 5046
23 וַיַּגִּידוּ לְמֹשֶׁה׃ וַיֹּאמֶר אֲלֵהֶם הוּא אֲשֶׁר דִּבֶּר יְהוָה
,Jehovah said what That ,them to he And .Moses to and
(is) said reported

644 644 4279 3068 6944/7676 7677
שַׁבָּתוֹן שַׁבַּת־קֹדֶשׁ לַיהוָה מָחָר אֵת אֲשֶׁר־תֹּאפוּ אֵפוּ
,bake will you what ,tomorrow to holy a a (is)
,bake Jehovah sabbath ,rest

3240 5736 3605 1310 1310
וְאֵת אֲשֶׁר־תְּבַשְּׁלוּ בַּשֵּׁלוּ וְאֵת כָּל־הָעֹדֵף הַנִּיחוּ לָכֶם
for up lay is that all and ,boil will you what and
yourselves over left ,boil

6680 1242 5704 3240 1242 5704 4931
24 לְמִשְׁמֶרֶת עַד־הַבֹּקֶר׃ וַיַּנִּיחוּ אֹתוֹ עַד־הַבֹּקֶר כַּאֲשֶׁר צִוָּה
directed as the until it they And the until keep to
morning up laid .morning

commanded. And it did not
stink and no maggot was in
it. 25 And Moses said, Eat it
today, for today *is* a sabbath
to Jehovah. Today you will
not find it in the field. 26 You
shall gather it six days, and
on the seventh *is* a sabbath;
in it none shall be found.
27 And it happened on the
seventh day, *some* of the
people went out to gather,
and did not find *any*. 28 And
Jehovah said to Moses,
Until when do you refuse to
keep My commandments
and My laws? 29 See, be-
cause Jehovah has given
the sabbath to you, therefore He *is* giving to you two
days of bread on the sixth
day. Each one of you remain
in his place. Do not let
anyone go out from his
place on the seventh day.
30 And the people rested on
the seventh day.

31 And the house of Israel
called its name, Manna.
And it *was* like the seed of
coriander, white; and its
taste like cakes with honey.
32 And Moses said, This *is*
the thing which Je' ovah
has commanded, . ill an
omer from it, to keep for
your generations, so that
they may see the bread
which I caused you to eat in
the wilderness, as I brought
you out from the land of
Egypt. 33 And Moses said to
Aaron, Take a pitcher and
put manna there, the fullness of an omer, and lay it
up before Jehovah, to keep
for your generations. 34 Even
as Jehovah commanded
Moses, Aaron laid it up before the Testimony, to keep
it.

35 And the sons of Israel
ate the manna forty years,
until their coming into an
inhabited land. They ate the

4872 559 1961 3808 7415 887 3808 4872
25 משה ולא הבאיש ורמה לא היתה בו׃ ויאמר משה
.Moses said And .it in was no and did it and ;Moses
maggot ,stink not

4672 3808 3117 3068 3117 7676 3117 398
אכלהו היום כי־שבת היום ליהוה היום לא תמצאהו
will you not today to today a for ,today it Eat
it find ;Jehovah (is) sabbath

7676 7637 3117 3950 3117 8337 7704
26 בשדה׃ ששת ימים תלקטהו וביום השביעי שבת לא
none (is it) seventh on and shall you days Six the in
;sabbath day the ,it gather .field

3808 3950 5971 5927 7637 3117 1961 1961
27 יהיה־בו׃ ויהי ביום השביעי יצאו מן־העם ללקט ולא
and to the (some) went ,seventh the on it And in be shall
not ,gather people of out day was .it (found)

3985 5704 4872 3068 559 4672
28 מצאו׃ ס ויאמר יהוה אל־משה עד־אנה מאנתם
you do long How ,Moses to Jehovah said And find did
refuse .(any)

7676 5414 3068 3588 8451 4687 8104
29 לשמר מצותי ותורתי׃ ראו כי־יהוה נתן לכם השבת
the you to has Jehovah be- ,See My and My keep to
,Sabbath given cause ?laws commands

376 3427 3117 3899 8345 3117 5414
על־כן הוא נתן לכם ביום הששי לחם יומים שבו איש
each remain two bread sixth the on to is He therefore
one ;days of day you giving

5971 7673 7637 3117 4725 376 5927 8478
30 תחתיו אל־יצא איש ממקמו ביום השביעי׃ וישבתו העם
the rested And .seventh the on his from any do not his in
people day place one out go ;place

4478 8034 3478 1004 7121 7637 3117
31 ביום השבעי׃ ויקראו בית־ישראל את־שמו מן והוא
and
an it ,Manna its Israel the called And .seventh the on
(was) name of house day

2088 4872 559 1706 6838 2940 3836 1407 2233
32 כזרע גד לבן וטעמו כצפיחת בדבש׃ ויאמר משה זה
This Moses said And with like its and ,white cor- the like
(is) .honey cakes taste iander of seed

4931 6016 4393 3068 6680 834 1697
הדבר אשר צוה יהוה מלא העמר ממנו למשמרת
keep to from omer an Fill ,Jehovah has which the
,it commanded thing

398 834 3899 7200 1755
לדרתיכם למען יראו את־הלחם אשר האכלתי אתכם
you caused I which bread the they so your for
eat to see may ;generations

4872 559 4714 776 3318 4057
33 במדבר בהוציאי אתכם מארץ מצרים׃ ויאמר משה אל־
to Moses said And .Egypt the from you I when the in
of land out brought, wilderness

3240 4478 6016 4393 8033 5414 259 6803 3947 175
אהרן קח צנצנת אחת ותן־שמה מלא־העמר מן והנח
and ,manna an the there and one pitcher Take ,Aaron
deposit of omer of fullness put

3068 6680 1755 4931 3068 6440
34 אתו לפני יהוה למשמרת לדרתיכם׃ כאשר צוה יהוה
Jehovah com- As your for keep to ,Jehovah before it
manded .generations

3478 1121 4931 5715 6440 175 3240 4872
35 אל־משה ויניחהו אהרן לפני העדת למשמרת׃ ובני ישראל
Israel the And be to the before Aaron deposited ,Moses to
of sons kept Testimony it

3427 776 935 8141 703 4478 398
אכלו את־המן ארבעים שנה עד־באם אל־ארץ נושבת
an .land into their until ,years forty the ate
.inhabited coming manna

36 אֶת־הַמָּן אָכְלוּ עַד־בֹּאָם אֶל־קְצֵה אֶרֶץ כְּנָעַן׃ וְהָעֹמֶר
עֲשִׂרִית הָאֵיפָה הוּא׃

manna until their coming to the border of the land of Canaan. [36]And the omer, it *was* the tenth of an ephah.

CAP. XVII ז

CHAPTER 17

1 וַיִּסְעוּ כָּל־עֲדַת בְּנֵי־יִשְׂרָאֵל מִמִּדְבַּר־סִין לְמַסְעֵיהֶם עַל־
2 פִּי יְהוָה וַיַּחֲנוּ בִּרְפִידִים וְאֵין מַיִם לִשְׁתֹּת הָעָם׃ וַיָּרֶב
הָעָם עִם־מֹשֶׁה וַיֹּאמְרוּ תְּנוּ־לָנוּ מַיִם וְנִשְׁתֶּה וַיֹּאמֶר לָהֶם
3 מֹשֶׁה מַה־תְּרִיבוּן עִמָּדִי מַה־תְּנַסּוּן אֶת־יְהוָה׃ וַיִּצְמָא שָׁם
הָעָם לַמַּיִם וַיָּלֶן הָעָם עַל־מֹשֶׁה וַיֹּאמֶר לָמָּה זֶּה הֶעֱלִיתָנוּ
4 מִמִּצְרַיִם לְהָמִית אֹתִי וְאֶת־בָּנַי וְאֶת־מִקְנַי בַּצָּמָא׃ וַיִּצְעַק
מֹשֶׁה אֶל־יְהוָה לֵאמֹר מָה אֶעֱשֶׂה לָעָם הַזֶּה עוֹד מְעַט
5 וּסְקָלֻנִי׃ וַיֹּאמֶר יְהוָה אֶל־מֹשֶׁה עֲבֹר לִפְנֵי הָעָם וְקַח
אִתְּךָ מִזִּקְנֵי יִשְׂרָאֵל וּמַטְּךָ אֲשֶׁר הִכִּיתָ בּוֹ אֶת־הַיְאֹר קַח
6 בְּיָדְךָ וְהָלָכְתָּ׃ הִנְנִי עֹמֵד לְפָנֶיךָ שָּׁם ׀ עַל־הַצּוּר בְּחֹרֵב
וְהִכִּיתָ בַצּוּר וְיָצְאוּ מִמֶּנּוּ מַיִם וְשָׁתָה הָעָם וַיַּעַשׂ כֵּן מֹשֶׁה
7 לְעֵינֵי זִקְנֵי יִשְׂרָאֵל׃ וַיִּקְרָא שֵׁם הַמָּקוֹם מַסָּה וּמְרִיבָה
עַל־רִיב ׀ בְּנֵי יִשְׂרָאֵל וְעַל נַסֹּתָם אֶת־יְהוָה לֵאמֹר הֲיֵשׁ
יְהוָה בְּקִרְבֵּנוּ אִם־אָיִן׃

CHAPTER 17

[1]And all the congregation of the sons of Israel traveled from the Wilderness of Sin, according to their journeys, by the mouth of Jehovah. And they camped in Rephidim. And there was no water for the drinking of the people. [2]And the people wrangled with Moses, and said, Give us water that we may drink. And Moses said to them, Why do you wrangle with me? Why do you tempt Jehovah? [3]And the people thirsted there for water, and the people murmured against Moses, and said, Why, then, have you caused us to go up from Egypt, to kill me and my sons and my livestock with thirst? [4]And Moses cried to Jehovah, saying, What shall I do to this people? Yet a little and they will stone me. [5]And Jehovah said to Moses, Pass on in front of the people, and take with you *some* of the elders of Israel. And take in your hand your staff with which you smote the River, and go. [6]Behold, I will stand before you there on the rock in Horeb. And you shall smite the rock, and water will come out of it; and the people will drink. And Moses did so before the eyes of the elders of Israel. [7]And one called the name of the place, Massah, and, Meribah, because of the wrangling of the sons of Israel, and because of their testing of Jehovah, saying, Is Jehovah in our midst, or not?

[8]And Amalek came and fought against Israel in Rephidim. [9]And Moses said to Joshua, Choose men for us, and go fight against Amalek. Tomorrow I will stand on the top of the hill, and the staff of God in my hand. [10]And Joshua did as Moses had said to him, to fight against Amalek. And Moses, Aaron and Hur went up to the top of the hill. [11]And so it was that when Moses lifted his hand, Israel prevailed. And when he rested his hand, Amalek prevailed. [12]And the hands of Moses *became* heavy. And they took a stone and put *it* under him. And he sat on it. And Aaron and Hur held up his hands, from this one and from that one. And his hands were steady until the going of the sun. [13]And Joshua defeated Amalek and his people by the mouth of the sword.

4872 559 7508 3478 3898 6002 935
8 9 ויבא עמלק וילחם עם־ישראל ברפידם: ויאמר משה
Moses said And .Rephidim in Israel against and fought Amalek And came

4279 6002 3898 5927 582 977 3091
אל־יהושע בחר־לנו אנשים וצא הלחם בעמלק מחר
Tomorrow against Amalek fight go and men us for Choose ,Joshua to

6213 3027 430 4294 1389 7218 5324
10 אנכי נצב על־ראש הגבעה ומטה האלהים בידי: ויעש
did And my in .hand God the and of staff ,hill the the on of head will stand I

4872 6002 3898 559 4872 3091
יהושע כאשר אמר־לו משה להלחם בעמלק ומשה
and Moses against ;Amalek fight to Moses him to had said as Joshua

4872 7311 1961 1389 7218 5927/2354 175
11 אהרן וחור עלו ראש הגבעה: והיה כאשר ירים משה
Moses lifted when so And ,was it .hill the the of head went to up and Hur ,Aaron

3027 6002 1396 3027 5117 3478 1396 3027
12 ידו וגבר ישראל וכאשר יניח ידו וגבר עמלק: וידי
And hands .Amalek prevailed his ,hand rested he when and ;Israel prevailed his ,hand

175 5921 3427 8478 7760 68 3947 3515 4872
משה כבדים ויקחו־אבן וישימו תחתיו וישב עליה ואהרן
and Aaron ;it on he and sat under ;him put and (it) a ,stone they and took (became) ;heavy Moses'

530 3027 259 259 2088 3027 8551 2354
וחור תמכו בידיו מזה אחד ומזה אחד ויהי ידיו אמונה
steady his hands And were .one and that from one from this his ,hands up held and Hur

5971 6002 3091 2522 8121 935 5704
13 עד־בא השמש: ויחלש יהושע את־עמלק ואת־עמו
his people and Amalek Joshua And defeated .the sun the of going until

2719/6310
לפי־חרב:
the sword the of mouth by

[14]And Jehovah said to Moses, Write this, a memorial in a book, and set *it* in the ears of Joshua, that I will utterly wipe away the remembrance of Amalek under the heavens. [15]And Moses built an altar. And he called its name, Jehovah My Banner. [16]And He said, A hand *is* on the throne of Jehovah; war *is* to Jehovah with Amalek from generation to generation.

241 7760 5612 2146 3789 4872 3068 559
14 ויאמר יהוה אל־משה כתב זאת זכרון בספר ושים באזני
in ears and (it) set a in ,book a memorial ,this Write ,Moses to Jehovah And said

8064 8478 6002 2143 4229 4229 3091
יהושע כי־מחה אמחה את־זכר עמלק מתחת השמים:
the .heavens from under Amalek the of remembrance will I away wipe utterly that ,Joshua's

5921 3027 559 5251 3068 8034 7121 4196 4872 1129
15 16 ויבן משה מזבח ויקרא שמו יהוה נסי: ויאמר כי־יד על
(is) on A hand he and ,said my ;Banner Jehovah its name he and called an ,altar Moses And built

1755 1755 6002 3068 4421 3050 3676
כס יה מלחמה ליהוה בעמלק מדר דר:
generation from .generation to with Amalek to (is) Jehovah war Jah the of throne

CAP. XVIII יח

CHAPTER 18

[1]And Jethro the priest of Midian, father-in-law of Moses, heard all which God had done for Moses, and for His people Israel, that Jehovah had caused Israel to go out of Egypt.

6213 834 3605 4872 2859 4080 3548 3503 8085
1 וישמע יתרו כהן מדין חתן משה את כל־אשר עשה
had done which all ,Moses' father-in-law ,Midian the of priest Jethro And heard

3478 3068 3318 5971 3478 3503 430
אלהים למשה ולישראל עמו כי־הוציא יהוה את־ישראל
Israel Jehovah had that brought out His ,people for and Israel for ,Moses God

2 And Jethro, Moses' father-in-law, took Zipporah, Moses' wife, after sending her away, 3 and her two sons, *of* whom the name of one *was* Gershom—for he said, I have become an alien in a foreign land; 4 and the name of one *was* Eliezer—for the God of my father *was* my Help, and delivered me from the sword of Pharaoh. 5 And Jethro, Moses' father-in-law, and his sons and his wife came to Moses, to the wilderness where he camped, *at* the mount of God. 6 And he said to Moses, I, your father-in-law Jethro, have come to you, and your wife, and your two sons with her. 7 And Moses went out to meet his father-in-law, and bowed, and kissed him. And they asked, each to his neighbor, as to *their* welfare. And they came into the tent. 8 And Moses told his father-in-law all that Jehovah had done to Pharaoh and to Egypt on account of Israel, all the trouble which they had found in the way, and Jehovah had delivered them. 9 And Jethro rejoiced regarding all the good which Jehovah had done to Israel, whom He had delivered from the hand of Egypt. 10 And Jethro said, Blessed *be* Jehovah who has delivered you from the hand of Egypt, and from the hand of Pharaoh; who has delivered the people from under the hand of Egypt. 11 Now I know that Jehovah *is* greater than all the gods; truly, in the way in which they were proved against them.

12 And Jethro, the father-in-law of Moses, took a burnt offering and sacrifices to God. And Aaron and all the elders of Israel came to

4872 802 6855 4872 2859 3503 3947 4714
2 מִמִּצְרָיִם׃ וַיִּקַּח יִתְרוֹ חֹתֵן מֹשֶׁה אֶת־צִפֹּרָה אֵשֶׁת מֹשֶׁה
,Moses the Zipporah Moses the Jethro took And from
of wife of father-in-law .Egypt

1647 259 8034 1121 8147 7964 310
3 אַחַר שִׁלּוּחֶיהָ׃ וְאֵת שְׁנֵי בָנֶיהָ אֲשֶׁר שֵׁם הָאֶחָד גֵּרְשֹׁם
(was) one the (of) her two and her sending after
Gershom of name whom ,sons ,away

461 259 8034 5237 776 1961 1616 559
4 כִּי אָמַר גֵּר הָיִיתִי בְּאֶרֶץ נָכְרִיָּה׃ וְשֵׁם הָאֶחָד אֱלִיעֶזֶר
(was) one and foreign a in have I An ,said he for
,Eliezer of name the land become alien

3503 935 6547 2719 5337 5828 1 430
5 כִּי־אֱלֹהֵי אָבִי בְּעֶזְרִי וַיַּצִּלֵנִי מֵחֶרֶב פַּרְעֹה׃ וַיָּבֹא יִתְרוֹ
Jethro And .Pharaoh's from and (was) my the for
came sword me saved ,Help my father of God

4057 4872 802 1121 4872 2859
חֹתֵן מֹשֶׁה וּבָנָיו וְאִשְׁתּוֹ אֶל־מֹשֶׁה אֶל־הַמִּדְבָּר אֲשֶׁר־הוּא
he where the to ,Moses to his and and Moses' father-
wilderness wife sons his in-law

2859 4872 559 430 2022 8033 2583
6 חֹנֶה שָׁם הַר הָאֱלֹהִים׃ וַיֹּאמֶר אֶל־מֹשֶׁה אֲנִי חֹתֶנְךָ
your ,I ,Moses to he And .God the (at) ,camped
father-in-law said of mount

4872 5927 1121 8147 802 935 4503
7 יִתְרוֹ בָּא אֵלֶיךָ וְאִשְׁתְּךָ וּשְׁנֵי בָנֶיהָ עִמָּהּ׃ וַיֵּצֵא מֹשֶׁה
Moses And with her and your and to have ,Jethro
out went .her sons two ,wife ,you come

7453 376 7592 5401 7812 2859 7125
לִקְרַאת חֹתְנוֹ וַיִּשְׁתַּחוּ וַיִּשַּׁק־לוֹ וַיִּשְׁאֲלוּ אִישׁ־לְרֵעֵהוּ
his to each they and ;him and bowed and his meet to
,neighbor ,asked kissed father-in-law

3605 2859 4872 5608 168 935 7965
8 לְשָׁלוֹם וַיָּבֹאוּ הָאֹהֱלָה׃ וַיְסַפֵּר מֹשֶׁה לְחֹתְנוֹ אֵת כָּל־
all his to Moses told And .tent the they and (their) to as
father-in-law entered ;welfare

3478 182 4714 6547 3068 6213 834
אֲשֶׁר עָשָׂה יְהוָה לְפַרְעֹה וּלְמִצְרַיִם עַל אוֹדֹת יִשְׂרָאֵל
,Israel of account on to and to Jehovah had which
Egypt Pharoah done

2302 3068 5337 1870 4672 834 8513 3605
9 אֵת כָּל־הַתְּלָאָה אֲשֶׁר מְצָאָתַם בַּדֶּרֶךְ וַיַּצִּלֵם יְהוָה׃ וַיִּחַדְּ
And .Jehovah had and the in had they which the all
rejoiced them delivered ,way found trouble

3478 3068 6213 834 2896 3605 3503
יִתְרוֹ עַל כָּל־הַטּוֹבָה אֲשֶׁר־עָשָׂה יְהוָה לְיִשְׂרָאֵל אֲשֶׁר
whom ,Israel to Jehovah had which the all to as Jethro
done good

5337 3068 1288 3503 559 4714 3027 5337
10 הִצִּילוֹ מִיַּד מִצְרָיִם׃ וַיֹּאמֶר יִתְרוֹ בָּרוּךְ יְהוָה אֲשֶׁר הִצִּיל
has who Jehovah Blessed ,Jethro said And .Egypt the from had He
saved (be) of hand delivered

5971 5337 6547 3027 4714 3027
אֶתְכֶם מִיַּד מִצְרַיִם וּמִיַּד פַּרְעֹה אֲשֶׁר הִצִּיל אֶת־הָעָם
the has who ;Pharaoh from and Egypt from you
people delivered of hand the of hand the

3605 3068 1419 3045 6258 4714 3027 8478
11 מִתַּחַת יַד־מִצְרָיִם׃ עַתָּה יָדַעְתִּי כִּי־גָדוֹל יְהוָה מִכָּל־
than Jehovah (is) that know I Now .Egypt the from
all greater of hand under

2859 3503 3947 2102 834 1870 430
12 הָאֱלֹהִים כִּי בַדָּבָר אֲשֶׁר זָדוּ עֲלֵיהֶם׃ וַיִּקַּח יִתְרוֹ חֹתֵן
father- Jethro And against were they in the in ,truly the
in-law took .them proved which manner ;gods

3478 2205 3605 175 935 430 2077 5930 4872
מֹשֶׁה עֹלָה וּזְבָחִים לֵאלֹהִים וַיָּבֹא אַהֲרֹן וְכֹל זִקְנֵי יִשְׂרָאֵל
Israel the all and Aaron and ;God to and burnt a Moses'
of elders came sacrifices offering

eat bread before God with
Moses' father-in-law.
[13]And it happened on the
next day that Moses sat to
judge the people. And the
people stood beside Moses
from the morning until the
evening. [14]And Moses'
father-in-law saw all he *was*
doing to the people. And he
said, What *is* this thing
which yoiu are doing to the
people? Why *are* you sitting
by yourself, and all the
people standing beside you
from morning until even
ing? [15]And Moses said to
his father-in-law, Because
the people come to me to
seek God. [16]When they
have a matter, they come to
me, and I judge between a
man and his neighbor. And I
reveal the statutes of God,
and His laws. [17]And the
father-in-law of Moses said
to him, The thing which you
do *is* not good. [18]Surely
you will wear out, both you
and this people which *is*
with you. For the thing *is*
heavy for you. You are not
able to do it by yourself.
[19]Now listen to my voice. I
will counsel you, and may
God be with you. You be for
this people before God, and
you bring the matters to
God. [20]And you warn them
as to the statutes and the
laws, and make known to
them the way in which they
should walk, and the work
which they should do.

[21]And you, you shall look
out men of ability out of all
the people, who fear God,
men of truth, haters of
unjust gain. And you place
these over them *as* rulers of
thousands, rulers of hun-
dreds, rulers of fifties, and

4283 1961 430 6440 4872 2859 3899 398
13 לֶאֱכָל־לֶחֶם עִם־חֹתֵן מֹשֶׁה לִפְנֵי הָאֱלֹהִים׃ וַיְהִי מִמָּחֳרָת
the on next day, it was And .God before ,Moses' father-in-law with bread eat to
4872 5971 5975 5971 8199 4872 3427
וַיֵּשֶׁב מֹשֶׁה לִשְׁפֹּט אֶת־הָעָם וַיַּעֲמֹד הָעָם עַל־מֹשֶׁה מִן
from Moses beside the people and stood the ;people judge to Moses sat
3605 4872 2859 7200 6153 5704 1242
14 הַבֹּקֶר עַד־הָעָרֶב׃ וַיַּרְא חֹתֵן מֹשֶׁה אֵת כָּל־אֲשֶׁר־הוּא
he all Moses father-in-law And saw the .evening until the morning
5971 6213 834 2088 1697 559 5971 6213
עֹשֶׂה לָעָם וַיֹּאמֶר מָה־הַדָּבָר הַזֶּה אֲשֶׁר אַתָּה עֹשֶׂה לָעָם
the to ?people are doing you which this thing What (is) he and ,said the to ;people was doing
1242 5324 5971 3605 3427 4100
מַדּוּעַ אַתָּה יוֹשֵׁב לְבַדֶּךָ וְכָל־הָעָם נִצָּב עָלֶיךָ מִן־בֹּקֶר
morning from beside you standing the people and all by ,yourself sitting (are) you Why
1875 5971 935 2859 4872 559 6153 5704
15 עַד־עָרֶב׃ וַיֹּאמֶר מֹשֶׁה לְחֹתְנוֹ כִּי־יָבֹא אֵלַי הָעָם לִדְרֹשׁ
to seek the people to me For come his to ,father-in-law Moses said And ?evening until
376 996 8199 935 1697 430
16 אֱלֹהִים׃ כִּי־יִהְיֶה לָהֶם דָּבָר בָּא אֵלַי וְשָׁפַטְתִּי בֵּין אִישׁ
a man between I and judge to ,me they come a ,matter to them there is When .God
8451 430 2706 3045 7453 996
וּבֵין רֵעֵהוּ וְהוֹדַעְתִּי אֶת־חֻקֵּי הָאֱלֹהִים וְאֶת־תּוֹרֹתָיו׃
.laws His and God the of statutes I and reveal his ;neighbor and
6213 834 1697 2896 4872 2859 559
17 וַיֹּאמֶר חֹתֵן מֹשֶׁה אֵלָיו לֹא־טוֹב הַדָּבָר אֲשֶׁר אַתָּה עֹשֶׂה׃
.do you which thing The (is) not good ,him to Moses father-in-law And said
3555 834 2088 5971 1571 5034 5034
18 נָבֹל תִּבֹּל גַּם־אַתָּה גַּם־הָעָם הַזֶּה אֲשֶׁר עִמָּךְ כִּי־כָבֵד
(too) heavy is for with ;you (is) which this people and you both will you outwear Surely
6963 8085 6258 6213 3201 1697
19 מִמְּךָ הַדָּבָר לֹא־תוּכַל עֲשֹׂהוּ לְבַדֶּךָ׃ עַתָּה שְׁמַע בְּקֹלִי
my to .voice listen Now by .yourself it do to you able are not the ;thing for you
430 4136 5971 1961 430 1961 3289
אִיעָצְךָ וִיהִי אֱלֹהִים עִמָּךְ הֱיֵה אַתָּה לָעָם מוּל הָאֱלֹהִים
,God before for the people you be with ,you God may and be will I advise you
2094 430 1697 935
20 וְהֵבֵאתָ אַתָּה אֶת־הַדְּבָרִים אֶל־הָאֱלֹהִים׃ וְהִזְהַרְתָּה
you And warn .God to matters the you and bring
1870 3045 8451 2706 853
אֶתְהֶם אֶת־הַחֻקִּים וְאֶת־הַתּוֹרֹת וְהוֹדַעְתָּ לָהֶם אֶת־הַדֶּרֶךְ
way the to them make and known ,laws the and the (to as) statutes them
3605 2372 6213 834 4639 32:12
21 יֵלְכוּ בָהּ וְאֶת־הַמַּעֲשֶׂה אֲשֶׁר יַעֲשׂוּן׃ וְאַתָּה תֶחֱזֶה מִכָּל־
of out all shall you out look And ,you they .do should which work the and it in they walk should
1215 8130 571 582 430 3373 2428/582 5971
הָעָם אַנְשֵׁי־חַיִל יִרְאֵי אֱלֹהִים אַנְשֵׁי אֱמֶת שֹׂנְאֵי בָצַע
unjust ;gain haters of ,truth of men ,God who fear ,ability of men the ,people
8269 2572 8269 396:7 8269 505 8269 7760
וְשַׂמְתָּ עֲלֵהֶם שָׂרֵי אֲלָפִים שָׂרֵי מֵאוֹת שָׂרֵי חֲמִשִּׁים וְשָׂרֵי
and of rulers ,fifties rulers of ,hundreds rulers of ,thousands (as) of rulers over ,them you and (these) set

rulers of tens. [22]And let
them judge the people at all
times. And it shall be that
every great matter they
shall bring to you, and every
small matter they shall
judge. And you make *it* easy
on yourself, and let them
bear with you. [23]If you do
this thing, and God com-
mand you, you will be able
to stand; and also this
people will go in peace to
their place.

[24]And Moses listened to
the voice of his father-in-
law, and he did all that he
had said. [25]And Moses
chose men of ability from all
Israel and made them
heads over the people;
rulers of thousands, rulers
of hundreds, rulers of fifties,
and rulers of tens. [26]And
they judged the people at
all times; the hard matters
they brought to Moses, and
every small matter they
judged themselves. [27]And
Moses sent his father-in-
law away, and he went to
his own land.

22 עֲשָׂרֹת׃ וְשָׁפְטוּ אֶת־הָעָם בְּכָל־עֵת וְהָיָה כָּל־הַדָּבָר הַגָּדֹל
יָבִיאוּ אֵלֶיךָ וְכָל־הַדָּבָר הַקָּטֹן יִשְׁפְּטוּ־הֵם וְהָקֵל מֵעָלֶיךָ
23 וְנָשְׂאוּ אִתָּךְ׃ אִם אֶת־הַדָּבָר הַזֶּה תַּעֲשֶׂה וְצִוְּךָ אֱלֹהִים
וְיָכָלְתָּ עֲמֹד וְגַם כָּל־הָעָם הַזֶּה עַל־מְקֹמוֹ יָבֹא בְשָׁלוֹם׃
24 וַיִּשְׁמַע מֹשֶׁה לְקוֹל חֹתְנוֹ וַיַּעַשׂ כֹּל אֲשֶׁר אָמָר׃ וַיִּבְחַר
25 מֹשֶׁה אַנְשֵׁי־חַיִל מִכָּל־יִשְׂרָאֵל וַיִּתֵּן אֹתָם רָאשִׁים עַל־
הָעָם שָׂרֵי אֲלָפִים שָׂרֵי מֵאוֹת שָׂרֵי חֲמִשִּׁים וְשָׂרֵי עֲשָׂרֹת׃
26 וְשָׁפְטוּ אֶת־הָעָם בְּכָל־עֵת אֶת־הַדָּבָר הַקָּשֶׁה יְבִיאוּן אֶל־
27 מֹשֶׁה וְכָל־הַדָּבָר הַקָּטֹן יִשְׁפּוּטוּ הֵם׃ וַיְשַׁלַּח מֹשֶׁה אֶת־
חֹתְנוֹ וַיֵּלֶךְ לוֹ אֶל־אַרְצוֹ׃

CAP. XIX יט

CHAPTER 19

CHAPTER 19

[1]In the third month of
the going out of the sons
of Israel from the land of
Egypt, on this day they
came to the wilderness of
Sinai. [2]And they pulled
up *stakes* from Rephidim
and came to the wilder-
ness of Sinai. And they
camped in the wilderness.
And Israel camped there
before the mountain.
[3]And Moses went up to
God. And Jehovah called
to him from the mountain,
saying, You shall say this
to the house of Jacob, and
tell *it* to the sons of
Israel. [4]You have seen
what I did to Egypt; and I
bore you on wings of
eagles and brought you to

1 בַּחֹדֶשׁ הַשְּׁלִישִׁי לְצֵאת בְּנֵי־יִשְׂרָאֵל מֵאֶרֶץ מִצְרָיִם בַּיּוֹם
2 הַזֶּה בָּאוּ מִדְבַּר סִינָי׃ וַיִּסְעוּ מֵרְפִידִים וַיָּבֹאוּ מִדְבַּר
3 סִינַי וַיַּחֲנוּ בַּמִּדְבָּר וַיִּחַן־שָׁם יִשְׂרָאֵל נֶגֶד הָהָר׃ וּמֹשֶׁה
עָלָה אֶל־הָאֱלֹהִים וַיִּקְרָא אֵלָיו יְהוָה מִן־הָהָר לֵאמֹר כֹּה
4 תֹאמַר לְבֵית יַעֲקֹב וְתַגֵּיד לִבְנֵי יִשְׂרָאֵל׃ אַתֶּם רְאִיתֶם
אֲשֶׁר עָשִׂיתִי לְמִצְרָיִם וָאֶשָּׂא אֶתְכֶם עַל־כַּנְפֵי נְשָׁרִים

Me. [5]And now if you will surely listen to My voice, and will keep My covenant, you shall become a special treasure to Me above all the nations, for all the earth *is* Mine. [6]And you shall become a kingdom of priests for Me, a holy nation. These *are* the words which you shall speak to the sons of Israel.

[7]And Moses came and called the elders of the people. And he put all these words before them which Jehovah commanded him. [8]And all the people answered together and said, All which Jehovah has spoken we will do. And Moses brought back the words of the people to Jehovah. [9]And Jehovah said to Moses, Behold, I come to you in a darkness of clouds, so that the people may hear My speaking with you, and in you they may believe forever. And Moses told the words of the people to Jehovah.

[10]And Jehovah said to Moses, Go to the people and sanctify them today and tomorrow. And let them wash their clothes. [11]And be ready for the third day. For on the third day Jehovah will go down before the eyes of all the people on the mountain of Sinai. [12]And you shall set limits to the people all around, saying, Be careful for yourselves, *not* going up into the mountain and touching its border—everyone touching the mountain shall surely be killed. [13]Not a hand shall touch him, but surely he shall be stoned, or surely he shall be shot through. He shall not live, whether animal or man. At the sounding of the ram's horn, they shall go up into the mountain. [14]And Moses went from the mountain to the people. And he sanctified the people, and they

8104 6963 8085 8085 6258 935
5 ואבא אתכם אלי׃ ועתה אם־שמוע תשמעו בקלי ושמרתם
will and My to will you surely if And to you and
keep ,voice listen now .Me brought

3605 1471 5459 1961 1285
את־בריתי והייתם לי סגלה מכל־העמים כי־לי כל־
all to for the all above special a to shall you My
(is) Me ;nations treasure Me become .covenant

6918 1471 3548 4467 1961 776
6 הארץ׃ ואתם תהיו־לי ממלכת כהנים וגוי קדוש אלה
these ;holy a and priests kingdom a for shall you And .earth the
(are) nation of Me become

7121 4872 935 3478 1121 1696 834 1697
7 הדברים אשר תדבר אל־בני ישראל׃ ויבא משה ויקרא
and Moses And .Israel the to you which words the
called came of sons speak shall

1697 3605 6440 7760 5971 2205
לזקני העם וישם לפניהם את כל־הדברים האלה אשר
which these words all before and the elders the
them put he ,people of

1696 834 3605 559 3162 5971 6030 3068 6680
8 צוהו יהוה׃ ויענו כל־העם יחדו ויאמרו כל אשר־דבר
has which All ,said and together the all And .Jehovah had
spoken people answered him told

559 3068 5971 1697 4872 3318 6213 3068
9 יהוה נעשה וישב משה את־דברי העם אל־יהוה׃ ויאמר
said And .Jehovah to the words the Moses and will we Jehovah
people of brought ;do

6051 5645 935 2009 4872 3068
יהוה אל־משה הנה אנכי בא אליך בעב הענן בעבור
that so ,clouds a in you to come I ,Behold ,Moses to Jehovah
of darkness

5046 5769 539 1696 5971 8085
ישמע העם בדברי עמך וגם־בך יאמינו לעולם ויגד
And .forever may they in and with My the may
told believe you ,you speaking people hear

4872 3068 559 3068 5971 1697 4872
10 משה את־דברי העם אל־יהוה׃ ויאמר יהוה אל־משה
,Moses to Jehovah said And .Jehovah to the words the Moses
people of

1961 8071 3526 4279 3117 6942 5971 3212
11 לך אל־העם וקדשתם היום ומחר וכבסו שמלתם׃ והיו
be and their let and and today sanctify and the to Go
;clothes wash them ,tomorrow them people

3068 3381 7992 3117 7992 3117 3559
נכנים ליום השלישי כי ביום השלישי ירד יהוה לעיני
before Jehovah go will third the on for ;third the for ready
down day day

559 5439 5971 1379 5511 2022 5971 3605
12 כל־העם על־הר סיני׃ והגבלת את־העם סביב לאמר
,saying all the you And .Sinai the on the all
,around people to limits set shall of mountain people

2022 5060 7097 5060 2022 5927 8104
השמרו לכם עלות בהר ונגע בקצהו כל־הנגע בהר
the touching every its and the into (not) for Watch
mountain one ;edge touching mountain up going ,yourselves

3384 3384 5619 5619 3027 5060 4191 4191
13 מות יומת׃ לא־תגע בו יד כי־סקול יסקל או־ירה יירה
shall he surely or shall he surely but a him shall not be will surely
pierced be stoned be ,hand touch killed

5927 3104 4900 2421 3808 376 518 929
אם־בהמה אם־איש לא יחיה במשך היבל המה יעלו
shall they ram's the the At shall he not ,man or animal whether
up go ,horn of sounding .live

5971 6942 5971 2022 4872 3381 2022
14 בהר׃ וירד משה מן־ההר אל־העם ויקדש את־העם
the he and the to the from Moses And the into
,people sanctified ;people mountain went .mountain

washed their clothes.
[15]And he said to the people,
Be ready for the third day.
Do not approach a woman.
[16]And on the third day, it
being morning, it happened:
There *were* thunders and
lightnings, and a heavy
cloud on the mountain, and
the sound of a ram's horn,
very strong! And all the
people in the camp
trembled. [17]And Moses
caused the people to go up
from the camp to meet God.
And they took their stand at
the lower part of the
mountain. [18]And the mountain of Sinai was smoking,
all of it, because Jehovah
came down on it in fire. And
its smoke went up like the
smoke of a furnace; and the
mountain quaked exceed-
ingly. [19]And it happened,
while the sound of the ram's
horn *was* sounding, and
becoming very strong,
Moses spoke. And God
answered him by a voice.
[20]And Jehovah came down
on the mountain of Sinai, to
the top of the mountain;
and Jehovah called Moses
to the top of the mountain,
and Moses went up. [21]And
Jehovah said to Moses, Go
down, warn the people lest
they break through to gaze
at Jehovah, and many of
them fall. [22]And also the
priests, those approaching
Jehovah, let them sanctify
themselves that Jehovah
not burst forth among them.
[23]And Moses said to
Jehovah, The people are
not able to come up to the
mountain of Sinai. For You
warned us, saying, Set
limits to the mountain and
sanctify it. [24]And Jehovah
said to him, Come, go
down. And you come up,
and Aaron with you. And let
not the priests and the
people break through to
come up to Jehovah, lest

7969 3559 1961 5971 559 8071 3526
15 יְכַבְּסוּ שִׂמְלֹתָם׃ וַיֹּאמֶר אֶל־הָעָם הֱיוּ נְכֹנִים לִשְׁלֹשֶׁת
third for ready Be the to he And their they and
people said .clothes washed

1961 7992 3117 1961 802 5066 3117
16 יָמִים אַל־תִּגְּשׁוּ אֶל־אִשָּׁה׃ וַיְהִי בַיּוֹם הַשְּׁלִישִׁי בִּהְיֹת
being it ,third the on And .woman a to do not the
day was it approach ;day

7782 6913 2022 3515 6051 7300 6963 1961 1242
הַבֹּקֶר וַיְהִי קֹלֹת וּבְרָקִים וְעָנָן כָּבֵד עַל־הָהָר וְקֹל שֹׁפָר
ram's a a and the on heavy a and and sounds it ,morning
horn of voice ,mountain cloud ,lightnings was

4872 3318 4264 5971 3605 2729 3966 2389
17 חָזָק מְאֹד וַיֶּחֱרַד כָּל־הָעָם אֲשֶׁר בַּמַּחֲנֶה׃ וַיּוֹצֵא מֹשֶׁה
Moses And the in who the all and ;very strong
brought .camp (were) people trembled

8482 3320 4264 430 7125 5971
אֶת־הָעָם לִקְרַאת הָאֱלֹהִים מִן־הַמַּחֲנֶה וַיִּתְיַצְּבוּ בְּתַחְתִּית
the at they and the from God meet to the
of bottom stood ;camp people

3068 3381 3588 3605 6226 5514 2022 2022
18 הָהָר׃ וְהַר סִינַי עָשַׁן כֻּלּוֹ מִפְּנֵי אֲשֶׁר יָרַד עָלָיו יְהוָה
Jehovah it on came because of all was Sinai And the
down ,it ,smoking Mount .mount

3966 2022 3605 2729 3536 6225 6227 5927 784
בָּאֵשׁ וַיַּעַל עֲשָׁנוֹ כְּעֶשֶׁן הַכִּבְשָׁן וַיֶּחֱרַד כָּל־הָהָר מְאֹד׃
exceed- whole the and ,furnace a the like its and ;fire in
.ingly mountain trembled of smoke smoke up went

430 1696 4872 3966 2390 1980 7782 6963 1961
19 וַיְהִי קוֹל הַשֹּׁפָר הוֹלֵךְ וְחָזֵק מְאֹד מֹשֶׁה יְדַבֵּר וְהָאֱלֹהִים
God and ,spoke Moses ,very be- and sound- ram's a the it And
strong coming ing horn of sound was

2022 7218 5514 2022 3068 3381 6963 6030
20 יַעֲנֶנּוּ בְקוֹל׃ וַיֵּרֶד יְהוָה עַל־הַר סִינַי אֶל־רֹאשׁ הָהָר
the the to Sinai Mount on Jehovah And a by answered
;mount of head down came .voice him

559 4872 5927 2022 7218 413 4872 3068 7121
21 וַיִּקְרָא יְהוָה לְמֹשֶׁה אֶל־רֹאשׁ הָהָר וַיַּעַל מֹשֶׁה׃ וַיֹּאמֶר
said And .Moses and the head the to Moses Jehovah and
up went ,mount of called

3068 2040 5971 5749 3381 4872 3068
יְהוָה אֶל־מֹשֶׁה רֵד הָעֵד בָּעָם פֶּן־יֶהֶרְסוּ אֶל־יְהוָה לִרְאוֹת
to Jehovah to they lest the warn Go ,Moses to Jehovah
,see through break ,people ,down

6942 3068 5066 3548 1571 7227 5307
22 וְנָפַל מִמֶּנּוּ רָב׃ וְגַם הַכֹּהֲנִים הַנִּגָּשִׁים אֶל־יְהוָה יִתְקַדָּשׁוּ
sanctify shall ,Jehovah to those the And .many of and
,themselves approaching ,priests also them fall

3201 3808 3068 4872 559 3068 6555
23 פֶּן־יִפְרֹץ בָּהֶם יְהוָה׃ וַיֹּאמֶר מֹשֶׁה אֶל־יְהוָה לֹא־יוּכַל
are Not ,Jehovah to Moses said And .Jehovah among burst lest
able them forth

559 5749 5514 2022 5927 5971
הָעָם לַעֲלֹת אֶל־הַר סִינָי כִּי־אַתָּה הַעֵדֹתָה בָּנוּ לֵאמֹר
,saying ,us warned You for ,Sinai Mount to come to the
up people

3381 3068 559 6942 2022 1379
24 הַגְבֵּל אֶת־הָהָר וְקִדַּשְׁתּוֹ׃ וַיֹּאמֶר אֵלָיו יְהוָה לֶךְ־רֵד
go ,Come ,Jehovah to said And and the limits set
;down him ,it sanctify mountain to

2040 3808 5971 3548 175 5927
וְעָלִיתָ אַתָּה וְאַהֲרֹן עִמָּךְ וְהַכֹּהֲנִים וְהָעָם אַל־יֶהֶרְסוּ
shall not the and the and with and you and
through break ,people priests ;you Aaron ,up come

He burst forth among them.
25 [25]And Moses went down to
the people and spoke to
them.

5927 3068 6555 3381 4872 5971
לעלת אל־יהוה פן־יפרץ־בם׃ 25 וירד משה אל־העם
the people | to | Moses | And down went | .them among | forth burst He | lest | ,Jehovah to | come to up

559
ויאמר אלהם׃
.them to | and spoke

CAP. XX כ

CHAPTER 20

CHAPTER 20
1 [1]And God spoke all these
2 words, saying:
[2]I *am* Jehovah your God,
who has brought you out
from the land of Egypt, from
the house of bondage.
[3]You shall not have any
other gods beside Me.
3 [4]You shall not make a
4 graven image for yourself,
of any likeness which *is* in
the heavens above, or
which *is* in the earth
beneath, or which *is* in the
waters under the earth;
5 [5]you shall not bow to them,
and you shall not serve
them; for I *am* Jehovah your
God, a jealous God, visiting
the iniquity of fathers on
children, on the third and
on the fourth *generation*, to
those that hate Me; [6]and
6 doing kindness to thou-
sands, to those loving Me,
and to those keeping My
commandments.
7 [7]You shall not take the
name of Jehovah your God
in vain; for Jehovah will not
leave unpunished *the one*
who takes His name in vain.

1696 430 3605 1697 559
1 וידבר אלהים את כל־הדברים האלה לאמר׃ ס 2 אנכי
I (am) | ,saying | ,these | words | all | God | And spoke

3068 430 3318 772 4714 1004 5650
יהוה אלהיך אשר הוצאתיך מארץ מצרים מבית עבדים׃
:bondage | the from of house | ,Egypt | the from of land | brought has out you | who | your God | Jehovah

1961 430 312 6213
3 לא־יהיה לך אלהים אחרים על־פני׃ 4 לא־תעשה לך
for yourself | shall You make | not | .Me besides | any other | gods | to you | shall be there | not

6459 8544 834 8064 4605 834 776
פסל וכל־תמונה אשר בשמים ממעל ואשר בארץ
the in earth | or (is) which | ,above | the in heavens | which (is) | likeness | or any | graven a ,image

8478 834 4325 8478 776 7812
מתחת ואשר במים מתחת לארץ׃ 5 לא־תשתחוה להם
to ,them | shall you down bow | not | ;earth | the | under | the in waters | or (is) which | beneath

3808 5647 3068 430 410 7067 6485 5771
ולא תעבדם כי אנכי יהוה אלהיך אל קנא פקד עון
the of iniquity | visiting | jealous | a God | ,God your | Jehovah | I (am) | for | shall you ;them serve | and not

1 1121 8029 7243 8130 6213
אבת על־בנים על־שלשים ועל־רבעים לשנאי׃ 6 ועשה
and doing | those to ;Me hate that | fourth the and .(generation) on | third the on (generation) | ,children on | fathers

2617 505 157 8104 4687 3808 5375
חסד לאלפים לאהבי ולשמרי מצותי׃ ס 7 לא תשא
shall You take | not | com- .mandments | My | to and keeping those | those to Me loving | ,thousands to | kind- ness

8034 3068 430 7723 5352 3068
את־שם־יהוה אלהיך לשוא כי לא ינקה יהוה את אשר־
(him) who | Jehovah | will unpunished leave | not for | ;vain in | your God | Jehovah | the of name

5375 8034 7723
ישא את־שמו לשוא׃
.vain in | name His | takes

8 [8]Remember the sabbath
9 day, to keep it holy; [9]six
days you shall labor and do
all your work; [10]and the
10 seventh day *is* a sabbath to
Jehovah your God; you
shall not do any work, you,
and your son, and your
daughter, your male slave
and your slave-girl, and your
livestock, and your stranger
who *is* in your gates. [11]For
11 *in* six days Jehovah made

2142 3117 7676 6942 8337 5647 6213
8 זכור את־יום השבת לקדשו׃ 9 ששת ימים תעבד ועשית
do and | shall you labor | days | Six | it keep to .holy | the Sabbath | day | Remem- ber

3605 4399 3117 7637 7676 3068 430
כל־מלאכתך׃ 10 ויום השביעי שבת ליהוה אלהיך לא־
not | your ;God | to Jehovah | a is Sabbath | the seventh | And day | .work your | all

6213 3605 4399 1121 1323 5650 519
תעשה כל־מלאכה אתה ובנך־ובתך עבדך ואמתך
your and ,slave-girl | your ,slave male | your and ,daughter | and son your | ,you | ,work | any | shall You do

929 1616 8179 3117 8337 6213
ובהמתך וגרך אשר בשעריך׃ 11 כי ששת־ימים עשה
made | days six | (in) | for | your in ,gates | (is) | who | and stranger your | your and ,cattle

the heavens and the earth, the sea, and all which *is* in them, and He rested on the seventh day; on account of this Jehovah blessed the sabbath day and sanctified it.

12 [12]Honor your father and your mother, so that your days may be long on the land which Jehovah your God is giving to you.

13 [13]You shall not murder.

14 [14]You shall not commit adultery.

15 [15]You shall not steal.

16 [16]You shall not testify a witness of falsehood against your neighbor.

17 [17]You shall not covet your neighbor's house; you shall not covet your neighbor's wife, or his male slave, or his slave-girl, or his ox, or his ass, or anything which *belongs* to your neighbor.

18 [18]And all the people saw the thunders, and the lightnings, and the sound of the ram's horn, and the smoking mountain. And the people looked, and they trembled, and they stood from a distance.

19 [19]And they said to Moses, You speak with us, and we will hear. And let us not speak with God, that we not die.

20 [20]And Moses said to the people, Do not be afraid, for God has come in order to test you, and so that His fear may be on your faces, that you may not sin.

21 [21]And the people stood from a distance, and Moses went near the thick darkness where God *was*.

22 [22]And Jehovah said to Moses, You shall say this to the sons of Israel: You have seen that I have spoken with you from the heavens.

23 [23]You shall not make gods

834 3605 3220 776 8064 3068
יְהוָה אֶת־הַשָּׁמַיִם וְאֶת־הָאָרֶץ אֶת־הַיָּם וְאֶת־כָּל־אֲשֶׁר־בָּם
in (is) which all and ,sea the ,earth the and the Jehovah
them heavens

7676 3117 3068 1288 3651/5921 7637 3117 5117
וַיָּנַח בַּיּוֹם הַשְּׁבִיעִי עַל־כֵּן בֵּרַךְ יְהוָה אֶת־יוֹם הַשַּׁבָּת
the day Jehovah blessed therefore ;seventh the on He and
Sabbath day rested

748 517 1 3513 6942
12 וַיְקַדְּשֵׁהוּ׃ ס כַּבֵּד אֶת־אָבִיךָ וְאֶת־אִמֶּךָ לְמַעַן יַאֲרִכוּן
be may so your and your Honor sanctified and
long that mother father .it

3808 5414 430 3068 127 5921/3117
13 יָמֶיךָ עַל הָאֲדָמָה אֲשֶׁר־יְהוָה אֱלֹהֶיךָ נֹתֵן לָךְ׃ ס לֹא
14
not to is your Jehovah which the on your
you giving God land days

3808 1589 5003 3808 7523
15 תִּרְצָח׃ ס לֹא תִּנְאָף׃ ס לֹא תִּגְנֹב׃ ס לֹא־
16
not shall You not shall You not shall You
.steal .adultery commit .murder

7453 1004 2530 8267 5707 7453 6030
17 תַעֲנֶה בְרֵעֲךָ עֵד שָׁקֶר׃ ס לֹא תַחְמֹד בֵּית רֵעֶךָ
your house shall You not .false a your against shall You
;neighbor's covet witness neighbor testify

2543 7794 519 5650 7453 802 2530
ס לֹא־תַחְמֹד אֵשֶׁת רֵעֶךָ וְעַבְדּוֹ וַאֲמָתוֹ וְשׁוֹרוֹ וַחֲמֹרוֹ
his or his or his or male his or your wife shall you not
,ass ,ox ,slave-girl ,slave ,neighbor's covet

7453 834 3605
וְכֹל אֲשֶׁר לְרֵעֶךָ׃
to (belongs) which or
.neighbor your anything

6963 3940 6963 7200 5971 3605
18 וְכָל־הָעָם רֹאִים אֶת־הַקּוֹלֹת וְאֶת־הַלַּפִּידִם וְאֵת קוֹל
the and the and the saw the And
of sound ,lightnings ,sounds people all

7350 5975 5128 5971 7200 6225 2022 7782
הַשֹּׁפָר וְאֶת־הָהָר עָשֵׁן וַיַּרְא הָעָם וַיָּנֻעוּ וַיַּעַמְדוּ מֵרָחֹק׃
a from they and they and the and ;smoking the and ram's the
.distance stood ,trembled people looked mountain horn

1696 3808 8085 1696 4872 559
19 וַיֹּאמְרוּ אֶל־מֹשֶׁה דַּבֵּר־אַתָּה עִמָּנוּ וְנִשְׁמָעָה וְאַל־יְדַבֵּר
let and we and with You speak ,Moses to they And
speak not ;hear will ,us said

3372 5971 4872 559 4191 430
20 עִמָּנוּ אֱלֹהִים פֶּן־נָמוּת׃ וַיֹּאמֶר מֹשֶׁה אֶל־הָעָם אַל־תִּירָאוּ
be Do not the to Moses said And .die we lest ,God with
,afraid ,people us

1961 430 935 5254 5668
כִּי לְבַעֲבוּר נַסּוֹת אֶתְכֶם בָּא הָאֱלֹהִים וּבַעֲבוּר תִּהְיֶה
be may that so .God has you test to order in for
come

7350 5971 5975 2398 6440 3373
21 יִרְאָתוֹ עַל־פְּנֵיכֶם לְבִלְתִּי תֶחֱטָאוּ׃ וַיַּעֲמֹד הָעָם מֵרָחֹק
a from the And you may that your upon His
,distance people stood .sin not ,faces fear

430 8033 6205 5066 4872
וּמֹשֶׁה נִגַּשׁ אֶל־הָעֲרָפֶל אֲשֶׁר־שָׁם הָאֱלֹהִים׃
.God there where thick the approached and
(was) darkness Moses

3478 1121 559 3651 4878 3068 559
22 וַיֹּאמֶר יְהוָה אֶל־מֹשֶׁה כֹּה תֹאמַר אֶל־בְּנֵי יִשְׂרָאֵל אַתֶּם
You ,Israel the to you Thus ,Moses to Jehovah said And
of sons say shall

6213 3808 1696 8064 7200
23 רְאִיתֶם כִּי מִן־הַשָּׁמַיִם דִּבַּרְתִּי עִמָּכֶם׃ לֹא תַעֲשׂוּן אִתִּי
with shall You not .you with have I the from that have
Me make spoken heavens seen

of silver along with Me, and you shall not make gods of gold for yourselves.

24You shall make an altar of earth for Me, and you shall sacrifice your burnt offerings and your peace offerings on it, your sheep and your cattle. In every place *in* which I cause My name to be remembered, I will come to you and will bless you. 25And if you make an altar of stone for Me, you shall not build them of cut stones. When you swing your tool on it, you defile it. 26And you shall not go up by steps to My altar, that your nakedness may not be uncovered on it.

CHAPTER 21

1And these *are* the judgments which you shall put before them:

2When you buy a Hebrew slave, he shall serve six years. And in the seventh he shall go out free for nothing. 3If he comes in with his body, he shall go out with his body. If he *was* the husband of a wife, his wife shall go out with him. 4If his master gives him a wife, and she bears sons or daughters to him, the wife and her children shall belong to her master; and he shall go out with his body. 5And if the slave truly says, I love my master, my wife and my children; I do not desire to go out free,

6his master shall bring him to God, and one shall bring him to the door, or to the doorpost; and his master shall pierce his ear with an awl, and he shall serve him forever.

7And when a man sells his daughter for a slave-girl, she shall not go out as the

127 4196 6213 3808 2091 430 3701 430
24 אֱלֹהֵי כֶסֶף וֵאלֹהֵי זָהָב לֹא תַעֲשׂוּ לָכֶם׃ מִזְבַּח אֲדָמָה
earth altar An for shall you not ;gold and ,silver of gods
of .yourselves make of gods

8002 5930 5921 2076 6213
תַּעֲשֶׂה־לִּי וְזָבַחְתָּ עָלָיו אֶת־עֹלֹתֶיךָ וְאֶת־שְׁלָמֶיךָ אֶת־
peace your and burnt your it on you and ,Me for you
,offerings offerings sacrifice shall make shall

8034 2142 4725 3605 1241 6629
צֹאנְךָ וְאֶת־בְּקָרֶךָ בְּכָל־הַמָּקוֹם אֲשֶׁר אַזְכִּיר אֶת־שְׁמִי
My bring I (in) place every in your and your
,name memory to which ;cattle sheep

6213 68 4196 1288 935
25 אָבוֹא אֵלֶיךָ וּבֵרַכְתִּיךָ׃ וְאִם־מִזְבַּח אֲבָנִים תַּעֲשֶׂה־לִּי
for you stone an if And will and you to will I
,Me make of altar .you bless come

2490 5921 5130 2719 1496 1129
לֹא־תִבְנֶה אֶתְהֶן גָּזִית כִּי חַרְבְּךָ הֵנַפְתָּ עָלֶיהָ וַתְּחַלְלֶהָ׃
you it on you your when of them shall you not
.it profane wield tool ;stones cut build

1540 3808 4196 4609 5927 3808
26 וְלֹא־תַעֲלֶה בְמַעֲלֹת עַל־מִזְבְּחִי אֲשֶׁר לֹא־תִגָּלֶה
be may not that My to steps by shall you And
uncovered ,altar up go not

6172
עֶרְוָתְךָ עָלָיו׃
.it on your
nakedness

CAP. XXI כא

CHAPTER 21

5650 7069 6440 7760 834 4941
1
2 וְאֵלֶּה הַמִּשְׁפָּטִים אֲשֶׁר תָּשִׂים לִפְנֵיהֶם׃ כִּי תִקְנֶה עֶבֶד
a buy you When before shall you which the these And
slave .them put judgments (are)

2600 2670 7637 5647 8141 8337 5680
3 עִבְרִי שֵׁשׁ שָׁנִים יַעֲבֹד וּבַשְּׁבִעִת יֵצֵא לַחָפְשִׁי חִנָּם׃ אִם־
If for ,free shall he the in and he years six ,Hebrew
.nothing out go seventh serve shall

802 5927 802 1167 5927 1610 935 1610
בְּגַפּוֹ יָבֹא בְּגַפּוֹ יֵצֵא אִם־בַּעַל אִשָּׁה הוּא וְיָצְאָה אִשְׁתּוֹ
wife his go shall he wife a the If shall he with he his with
out ,(was) of husband .out go body his ,in comes body

1323 1121 3205 802 5414 113
4 עִמּוֹ׃ אִם־אֲדֹנָיו יִתֶּן־לוֹ אִשָּׁה וְיָלְדָה־לוֹ בָנִים אוֹ בָנוֹת
,daughters or sons to she and a to gives his If with
him bears wife him master .him

1610 5927 113 1961 3206 802
5 הָאִשָּׁה וִילָדֶיהָ תִּהְיֶה לַאדֹנֶיהָ וְהוּא יֵצֵא בְגַפּוֹ׃ וְאִם־
if and with shall he and her to shall her and wife the
.body his out go ,master belong children

1121 802 113 157 5650 559 559
אָמֹר יֹאמַר הָעֶבֶד אָהַבְתִּי אֶת־אֲדֹנִי אֶת־אִשְׁתִּי וְאֶת־בָּנָי
my and my my love I the says truly
;sons ,wife ,master ,slave

5066 430 113 5066 2670 5927 3808
6 לֹא אֵצֵא חָפְשִׁי׃ וְהִגִּישׁוֹ אֲדֹנָיו אֶל־הָאֱלֹהִים וְהִגִּישׁוֹ אֶל־
to he and ,God to his shall Then .free will I not
him bring shall master him bring out go

4836 241 113 7527 4201 1817
הַדֶּלֶת אוֹ אֶל־הַמְּזוּזָה וְרָצַע אֲדֹנָיו אֶת־אָזְנוֹ בַּמַּרְצֵעַ
an with ear his his shall and the to or door the
awl master pierce ;doorpost

519 1323 376 4376 5769 5647
7 וַעֲבָדוֹ לְעֹלָם׃ ס וְכִי־יִמְכֹּר אִישׁ אֶת־בִּתּוֹ לְאָמָה
a for his man a sells And .forever he and
,slave-girl daughter when him serve shall

male slaves go out. 8 If she is bad in the eyes of her master who has chosen her for himself, he shall allow her redemption. He shall not have power to sell her to a strange people, in his deceiving her. 9 And if he chooses her for his son, he shall do to her as is the custom of daughters. 10 If he takes another for himself, her flesh, her clothing, and her conjugal right shall not be diminished. 11 And if he does not do these three for her, she shall go out for nothing, without money.

12 He that strikes a man so that he dies, surely he shall be put to death. 13 And he who does not lie in wait, and God lets fall into his hand, I will appoint a place for you where he may flee.

14 And when a man seethes insolently against his neighbor, to kill him by deceit, you shall take him from My altar to die.

15 And he who strikes his father or his mother shall surely be put to death.

16 And he that steals a man and sells him, or if he is found in his hand, he shall surely be put to death.

17 And he who curses his father or his mother, he shall surely be put to death.

18 And when men strive, and one strikes his neighbor with a stone, or with a fist, and he does not die, but falls on his bed, 19 if he rises and walks about in the street on his staff, the one who struck *him* shall be innocent—only he shall pay his sitting; surely he shall pay for *his* healing.

20 And if a man strikes his male slave or his slave-girl with a rod, and he dies under his hand, he shall surely be avenged. 21 But if he continues a day or two, he shall not be avenged, for he *is* his silver.

22 And when men fight, and they strike a pregnant woman, and her child goes

113 5869 7451 5650 5927 5927 3808
8 לֹא תֵצֵא כְּצֵאת הָעֲבָדִים׃ אִם־רָעָה בְּעֵינֵי אֲדֹנֶיהָ אֲשֶׁר־
who her the in is she If male the go as she not
,master of eyes bad .slaves out out go shall

898 4376 4910 5237 5971 6299 3259
לֹא יְעָדָהּ וְהֶפְדָּהּ לְעַם נָכְרִי לֹא־יִמְשֹׁל לְמָכְרָהּ בְּבִגְדוֹ־
his in sell to shall He not strange a to her let shall he has for
deceiving ,her power have people redeemed be chosen him

6213 1323 4941 3259 1121
9 בָהּ׃ וְאִם־לִבְנוֹ יִיעָדֶנָּה כְּמִשְׁפַּט הַבָּנוֹת יַעֲשֶׂה־לָּהּ׃ אִם־
10 If to will he ,daughters the is as chooses he his for And .her
.her do of custom her son if

1639 3808 5772 3682 7607 3947 312
11 אַחֶרֶת יִקַּח־לוֹ שְׁאֵרָהּ כְּסוּתָהּ וְעֹנָתָהּ לֹא יִגְרָע׃ וְאִם־
if And be shall not her and cloth- her ,flesh her for he another
.diminished rights conjugal ,ing ,himself takes

3701 5927 6213 7969
שְׁלָשׁ־אֵלֶּה לֹא יַעֲשֶׂה לָהּ וְיָצְאָה חִנָּם אֵין כָּסֶף׃ ס
.silver with- for shall she for does he not these three
out ,nothing out go ,her do

430 6658 3808 4191 4191 4191 376 5221
12 מַכֵּה אִישׁ וָמֵת מוֹת יוּמָת׃ וַאֲשֶׁר לֹא צָדָה וְהָאֱלֹהִים
13 God and lie does not he And shall he surely he that so a that He
,wait in who .executed be dies he man strikes

8033 5127 834 4725 7760 579
14 אִנָּה לְיָדוֹ וְשַׂמְתִּי לְךָ מָקוֹם אֲשֶׁר יָנוּס שָׁמָּה׃ ס וְכִי־
And .there may he where place a for will I his into lets
when flee you appoint ,hand fall

3947 4196 6195 2026 7453 376 2102
יָזִד אִישׁ עַל־רֵעֵהוּ לְהָרְגוֹ בְעָרְמָה מֵעִם מִזְבְּחִי תִּקָּחֶנּוּ
shall you My from by kill to his against a burns
him take altar ,deceit him ;neighbor ,man

1589 4191 4191 517 1 5221 4191
15 לָמוּת׃ ס וּמַכֵּה אָבִיו וְאִמּוֹ מוֹת יוּמָת׃ ס וְגֹנֵב
16 he And be shall surely his or his he And .die to
steals that .executed mother father strikes who

1 7043 4191 4191 3027 4672 4376 376
17 אִישׁ וּמְכָרוֹ וְנִמְצָא בְיָדוֹ מוֹת יוּמָת׃ ס וּמְקַלֵּל אָבִיו
his who he And be shall surely his in is he if or and man a
father curses .executed ,hand found ,him sells

376 5221 582 7378 4191 4191 517
18 וְאִמּוֹ מוֹת יוּמָת׃ ס וְכִי־יְרִיבֻן אֲנָשִׁים וְהִכָּה־אִישׁ
a and ,men strive And be shall surely his or
man smites when .executed mother

4904 5307 4191 3808 106 176 68 7453
אֶת־רֵעֵהוּ בְּאֶבֶן אוֹ בְאֶגְרֹף וְלֹא יָמוּת וְנָפַל לְמִשְׁכָּב׃
his on but does and a with or a with his
;bed falls ,die not ,fist stone neighbor

7535 5221 5352 4938 2351 1980 6965
19 אִם־יָקוּם וְהִתְהַלֵּךְ בַּחוּץ עַל־מִשְׁעַנְתּוֹ וְנִקָּה הַמַּכֶּה רַק
only one the be shall his on the in walks and he if
;smote who innocent ,staff street about rises

5650 376 5221 7495 7495 5414 7674
20 שִׁבְתּוֹ יִתֵּן וְרַפֹּא יְרַפֵּא׃ וְכִי־יַכֶּה אִישׁ אֶת־עַבְדּוֹ
male his man a strikes And pay shall he surely shall he his for
slave if .healing for ,pay sitting

389 5358 5358 3027 8478 4191 7626 519
21 אוֹ אֶת־אֲמָתוֹ בַּשֵּׁבֶט וּמֵת תַּחַת יָדוֹ נָקֹם יִנָּקֵם׃ אַךְ אִם־
if but shall he surely his under he and a with female his or
;avenged be hand dies rod slave

3701 5358 5975 8147 3117
22 יוֹם אוֹ יוֹמַיִם יַעֲמֹד לֹא יֻקַּם כִּי כַסְפּוֹ הוּא׃ ס וְכִי־
And .(is) he his for shall he not he two or day a
when money ,avenged be ,continued

611 1961 3808 3206 5927 2550 802 5061 582 5327
יִנָּצוּ אֲנָשִׁים וְנָגְפוּ אִשָּׁה הָרָה וְיָצְאוּ יְלָדֶיהָ וְלֹא יִהְיֶה אָסוֹן
;injury there and her and ,pregnant a they and ,men fight
is no ,children forth goes woman strike

forth, and there is no injury, surely he shall be fined. As *much as* the husband of the woman shall put on him, even he shall give through the judges. [23]But if injury occurs, you shall give life for life, [24]eye for eye, tooth for tooth, hand for hand, foot for foot, [25]branding for branding, wound for wound, stripe for stripe.

[26]And when a man strikes the eye of his male slave, or the eye of his slave-girl, and destroys it, he shall send him away free for his eye. [27]And if he causes the tooth of his male slave, or the tooth of his slave-girl, to fall out, he shall send him away free for his tooth.

[28]And when an ox gores a man or a woman, so that he dies, the ox shall surely be stoned, and its flesh shall not be eaten, and the owner of the ox *is* innocent. [29]And if he *was* an ox apt to gore from yesterday and the third day, and its owner is given warning, and he does not watch him, and he kills a man or a woman, the ox shall be stoned, and its owner also shall be put to death.

[30]If a ransom is put on him, he shall give the redemption of his life, according to all which is put on him. [31]Whether he gores a son, or he gores a daughter, according to this judgment it shall be done to him. [32]If the ox gores a male slave or a slave-girl, he shall give thirty silver shekels to his master, and the ox shall be stoned.

[33]And when a man opens a pit, or when a man digs a pit, and does not cover it, and an ox or an ass falls into it, [34]the owner of the pit shall pay; he shall give silver to its owner, and the dead shall be his. [35]And

6414 5414 802 1167 7896 6064 6064
ענוש יענש כאשר ישית עליו בעל האשה ונתן בפללים׃
the through he and the the upon may as shall he surely
judges , give shall woman's husband him put fined be

23 24 8127 5869 5869 5315 5315 5414 1961 611
ואם־אסון יהיה ונתתה נפש תחת נפש׃ עין תחת עין שן
tooth ,eye for eye ,life for life shall you ,occurs injury But
give if

25 3555 3555 7272 7272 3027 3027 8127
תחת שן יד תחת יד רגל תחת רגל׃ כויה תחת כויה
,branding for branding ,foot for foot ,hand for hand ,tooth for

26 376 5221 2250 2250 6482 6482
פצע תחת פצע חבורה תחת חבורה׃ ס וכי־יכה איש
a strikes And .stripe for stripe ,wound for wound
man when

7971 2670 7843 519 5869 5650 5869
את־עין עבדו או־את־עין אמתו ושחתה לחפשי ישלחנו
shall he free and is of eye the or his of eye the
him send ,it destroys ,slave-girl slave male

27 7971 2670 5307 519 8127 5650 8127 5869 8478
תחת עינו׃ ואם־שן עבדו או־שן אמתו יפיל לחפשי ישלחנו
shall he free makes he his the or his the And his for
him send out fall slave- tooth male tooth if .eye
girl of slave of

8127
תחת שנו׃
his for
.tooth

28 5619 5619 4191 802 376 7794 5055
וכי־יגח שור את־איש או את־אשה ומת סקול יסקל
be shall surely that so ,woman a or man a ox an gores And
.stoned dies he when

29 7794 5355 7794 1167 1320 398 7794
השור ולא יאכל את־בשרו ובעל השור נקי׃ ואם שור
ox an And (is) ox the the and ,flesh his be shall and ,ox the
if .innocent of owner eaten not

8104 3808 1167 5749 8032 8543 5056
נגח הוא מתמל שלשם והועד בבעליו ולא ישמרנו
does he and owner his is and day and from he to apt
him watch not ,warning given ,third the yesterday (was) gore

4191 1167 1571 5619 7794 802 376 4191
והמית איש או אשה השור יסקל וגם־בעליו יומת׃
be shall its and be shall the a or man a he and
.killed owner also stoned ox ,woman kills

30 7896 834 3605 5315 6306 5414 1 7896 3724
אם־כפר יושת עליו ונתן פדין נפשו ככל אשר־יושת
put is which according his re- the shall he upon put is a If
all to ,life of demption give ,him ransom

31 6213 2088 4941 5055 1323 5055 1121 5921
עליו׃ או־בן יגח או־בת יגח כמשפט הזה יעשה לו׃
to shall it ,this to according gores a or he a Whether upon
.him done be judgment ;daughter gores son .him

32 5414 8255 7970 3701 519 7794 5055 5650
אם־עבד יגח השור או אמה כסף ׀ שלשים שקלים יתן
he shekels thirty of a or ox the gores a If
give shall silver ,slave-girl slave male

33 376 6605 5619 7794 113
לאדניו והשור יסקל׃ ס וכי־יפתח איש בור או כי־
when or ,pit a man a opens And be shall the and his to
when .stoned ox ,master

2543 7794 5307 368 953 376 3738
יכרה איש בר ולא יכסנו ונפל־שמה שור או חמור׃
;ass an or ox an it into and does and a man a digs
falls ,it cover not ,pit

34 1961 4191 1167 7725 3701 7999 953 1167
בעל הבור ישלם כסף ישיב לבעליו והמת יהיה־לו׃
.his shall the and its to shall he silver ;pay shall pit the the
be dead ,owner give of owner

when a man's ox hurts the ox of a man, the ox of his neighbor, and it dies, they shall sell the living ox; they shall divide its silver. And they shall also divide the dead. [36]Or if it was known that he *was* an ox apt to gore from yesterday *and* the third day, and his owner does not watch him, surely he shall repay ox for ox, and the dead shall be his.

[37]When a man steals an ox or a sheep, and slaughters it or sells it, he shall repay five cattle for an ox, and four of a flock animal for a sheep.

35 וכי־יגף שור־איש את־שור רעהו ומת ומכרו את־
36 השור החי וחצו את־כספו וגם את־המת יחצון׃ או נודע
כי שור נגח הוא מתמול שלשם ולא ישמרנו בעליו
37 שלם ישלם שור תחת השור והמת יהיה־לו׃ ס כי
יגנב־איש שור או־שה וטבחו או מכרו חמשה בקר ישלם
תחת השור וארבע־צאן תחת השה׃

CAP. XXII כב

CHAPTER 22

[1]If the thief is found breaking in and is smitten and dies, no blood shall be *shed* for him. [2]If the sun has risen on him, blood *is* due for him; surely he shall repay. If he has nothing, then he should be sold for his theft. [3]If the stolen thing is surely found in his hand alive, from ox to ass to flock animal, he shall pay double.

[4]When a man burns a field or a vineyard, and he lets loose his beast and it feeds in another's field, he shall repay the best of his field and the best of his vineyard.

[5]When fire breaks out and finds thorns, and shocked grain, or standing grain, or the field is burned up, surely the one kindling the fire shall repay.

[6]When a man gives silver or vessels to his neighbor to keep, and it is stolen from the man's house, if the thief is found he shall repay double. [7]If the thief is not found, the master of the house shall be brought to

1 אם־במחתרת ימצא הגנב והכה ומת אין לו דמים׃
2 אם־זרחה השמש עליו דמים לו שלם ישלם אם־אין
3 לו ונמכר בגנבתו׃ אם־המצא תמצא בידו הגנבה
4 משור עד־חמור עד־שה חיים שנים ישלם׃ ס כי
יבער־איש שדה או־כרם ושלח את־בעירה ובער בשדה
5 אחר מיטב שדהו ומיטב כרמו ישלם׃ ס כי־תצא
אש ומצאה קצים ונאכל גדיש או הקמה או השדה
6 שלם ישלם המבער את־הבערה׃ ס כי־יתן איש
אל־רעהו כסף או־כלים לשמר וגנב מבית האיש אם־
7 ימצא הגנב ישלם שנים׃ אם־לא ימצא הגנב ונקרב

God, whether or not he put out his hand to his neighbor's goods.
[9]In every case of trespass, for ox, for ass, for sheep, for clothing, for anything lost of which it is said that it is his, the case of both of them shall come to God. Whom God declares guilty, he shall repay double to his neighbor. [10]When a man gives an ass or an ox to his neighbor, or a sheep, or any animal to keep, and it dies, or is injured, or is captured, no one seeing it, [11]an oath of Jehovah shall be between them both, that he has not put his hand to his neighbor's goods. And its owner shall take it, and he shall not repay. [12]And if it is indeed stolen from him, he shall repay to its owner. [13]If it is completely torn in pieces, he shall bring it *as* a witness; he shall not repay that which was torn.

[14]And when a man borrows from his neighbor, and it is hurt, or dies, its owner not being with it, surely he shall repay. [15]If its owner *is* with it, he shall not repay. If it *is* hired, it comes for its hire.
[16]And when a man lures a virgin who is not betrothed, and lies with her, he shall surely pay her dowry for a wife to himself. [17]If her father absolutely refuses to give her to him, he shall weigh silver according to the dowry of virgins.
[18]You shall not allow a sorceress to live.
[19]Anyone lying with an animal, he surely shall be put to death.
[20]One sacrificing to a god shall be destroyed, unless *it is* only to Jehovah.

4399 3027 7971 3808 430 1004 1167
בַּעַל־הַבַּיִת אֶל־הָאֱלֹהִים אִם־לֹא שָׁלַח יָדוֹ בִּמְלֶאכֶת
the on his has he or whether ,God to the master the
of goods hand out put not house of

7716 2543 7794 6588 1697 3605 7453
8 רֵעֵהוּ׃ עַל־כָּל־דְּבַר־פֶּשַׁע עַל־שׁוֹר עַל־חֲמוֹר עַל־שֶׂה
,sheep for ass for ,ox for trespass case every For his
of neighbor

2088 559 834 9 3605 8008
עַל־שַׂלְמָה עַל־כָּל־אֲבֵדָה אֲשֶׁר יֹאמַר כִּי־הוּא זֶה עַד
to this his that said is it of ,thing lost any for ,clothing for
.(is) which

7999 430 7561 8147 1697 935 430
הָאֱלֹהִים יָבֹא דְּבַר־שְׁנֵיהֶם אֲשֶׁר יַרְשִׁיעֻן אֱלֹהִים יְשַׁלֵּם
shall he ,God declares whom of both the shall God
repay guilty ;them of case come

7794 2543 7453 376 5414 7453 8147
9 שְׁנַיִם לְרֵעֵהוּ׃ ס כִּי־יִתֵּן אִישׁ אֶל־רֵעֵהוּ חֲמוֹר אוֹ־שׁוֹר
ox an or ,ass an his to man a gives When his to double
.neighbor .neighbor

369 7617 7665 4191 8104 929 3605 7716
אוֹ־שֶׂה וְכָל־בְּהֵמָה לִשְׁמֹר וּמֵת אוֹ־נִשְׁבַּר אוֹ־נִשְׁבָּה אֵין
no is or ,injured is or it and ,keep to animal or a or
,captured ,dies any ,sheep

3027 7971 3808 8147 996 1961 3068 7650 7200
10 רֹאֶה׃ שְׁבֻעַת יְהוָה תִּהְיֶה בֵּין שְׁנֵיהֶם אִם־לֹא שָׁלַח יָדוֹ
his has he not that them be- be shall Jehovah oath an seeing
hand put ,both tween of ,it

1589 7999 3808 1167 3947 7453 4399
11 בִּמְלֶאכֶת רֵעֵהוּ וְלָקַח בְּעָלָיו וְלֹא יְשַׁלֵּם׃ וְאִם־גָּנֹב
And shall he and its shall And his goods to
indeed if ,repay not ,owner take ;neighbor's

5707 935 2960 2960 1167 7999 1589
12 יִגָּנֵב מֵעִמּוֹ יְשַׁלֵּם לִבְעָלָיו׃ אִם־טָרֹף יִטָּרֵף יְבִאֵהוּ עֵד
a (as) shall he is it completely If its to shall he from is it
;witness it bring torn pieces in .master repay ,him stolen

7999 3808 2963
הַטְּרֵפָה לֹא יְשַׁלֵּם׃ פ
shall he not which that
.repay torn was

369 1167 4191 7665 7453 376 7592
13 וְכִי־יִשְׁאַל אִישׁ מֵעִם רֵעֵהוּ וְנִשְׁבַּר אוֹ־מֵת בְּעָלָיו אֵין
not its ,dies or is it and his from a borrows And
being owner ,hurt ,neighbor man when

7939 7999 3808 1167 7999 7999 5973
14 עִמּוֹ שַׁלֵּם יְשַׁלֵּם׃ אִם־בְּעָלָיו עִמּוֹ לֹא יְשַׁלֵּם אִם־שָׂכִיר
is it If shall he not (is) its If shall he paying with
,hired .repay ,it with master .repay ,it

1330 376 6601 7939 935
15 הוּא בָּא בִּשְׂכָרוֹ׃ ס וְכִי־יְפַתֶּה אִישׁ בְּתוּלָה אֲשֶׁר
who virgin a man a seduces When his with came it
.hire

802 4117 4117 7901 781 3808
16 לֹא־אֹרָשָׂה וְשָׁכַב עִמָּהּ מָהֹר יִמְהָרֶנָּה לּוֹ לְאִשָּׁה׃ אִם־
If a for to pay he shall paying with and is not
.wife him dowry her ,her lies ,betrothed

1330 4117 8254 3701 5414 3985 3985
מָאֵן יְמָאֵן אָבִיהָ לְתִתָּהּ לוֹ כֶּסֶף יִשְׁקֹל כְּמֹהַר הַבְּתוּלֹת׃
.virgins according shall he silver to give to her refuses re-
of dowry the to weight ,him her father fusing

4191 929 7901 3605 2421 3808 3984
17 18 ס מְכַשֵּׁפָה לֹא תְחַיֶּה׃ כָּל־שֹׁכֵב עִם־בְּהֵמָה מוֹת
dying ,animal an with lying Any shall you not A
.live to allow sorceress

3068 1115 2763 430 2076 4191
19 יוּמָת׃ ס זֹבֵחַ לָאֱלֹהִים יָחֳרָם בִּלְתִּי לַיהוָה לְבַדּוֹ׃
.only to unless be shall a to One shall he
Jehovah (is it) ,destroyed god sacrificing .executed be

[21]You shall not be violent toward an alien. You shall not oppress *him*, for you were aliens in the land of Egypt. [22]You shall not afflict an orphan or a widow. [23]If you afflict him, if he at all cries to Me, I will surely hear his cry, [24]and My anger shall glow, and I will kill you with the sword; and your wives shall become widows, and your sons orphans.

[25]If you lend silver to My people, the poor with you, you shall not be as a money-lender to him; you shall not put interest on him. [26]If you indeed take the clothing of your neighbor as a pledge, you shall return it to him by the going of the sun, [27]for that is his only covering, that *is* his covering for his skin. In what shall he lie down? And it shall be, when he cries to Me, I will hear, for I *am* compassionate.

[28]You shall not revile God, and you shall not curse a ruler among your people.

[29]You shall not delay *giving* your harvest and your vintage. You shall give to Me the firstborn of your sons. [30]So you shall do to your oxen, to your sheep: it shall be seven days with its mother; on the eighth day you shall give it to Me. And you shall be holy men to Me. [31]And you shall not eat flesh torn in pieces in the field; you shall throw it to the dogs.

20 וְגֵר לֹא־תוֹנֶה וְלֹא תִלְחָצֶנּוּ כִּי־גֵרִים הֱיִיתֶם בְּאֶרֶץ מִצְרָיִם׃
21 כָּל־אַלְמָנָה וְיָתוֹם לֹא תְעַנּוּן׃ 22 אִם־עַנֵּה תְעַנֶּה אֹתוֹ כִּי
23 אִם־צָעֹק יִצְעַק אֵלַי שָׁמֹעַ אֶשְׁמַע צַעֲקָתוֹ׃ וְחָרָה אַפִּי
וְהָרַגְתִּי אֶתְכֶם בֶּחָרֶב וְהָיוּ נְשֵׁיכֶם אַלְמָנוֹת וּבְנֵיכֶם יְתֹמִים׃ פ
24 אִם־כֶּסֶף ׀ תַּלְוֶה אֶת־עַמִּי אֶת־הֶעָנִי עִמָּךְ לֹא־תִהְיֶה לוֹ
25 כְּנֹשֶׁה לֹא־תְשִׂימוּן עָלָיו נֶשֶׁךְ׃ אִם־חָבֹל תַּחְבֹּל שַׂלְמַת
26 רֵעֶךָ עַד־בֹּא הַשֶּׁמֶשׁ תְּשִׁיבֶנּוּ לוֹ׃ כִּי הִוא כְסוּתֹה לְבַדָּהּ
הִוא שִׂמְלָתוֹ לְעֹרוֹ בַּמֶּה יִשְׁכָּב וְהָיָה כִּי־יִצְעַק אֵלַי וְשָׁמַעְתִּי
27 כִּי־חַנּוּן אָנִי׃ ס אֱלֹהִים לֹא תְקַלֵּל וְנָשִׂיא בְעַמְּךָ לֹא
28 תָאֹר׃ מְלֵאָתְךָ וְדִמְעֲךָ לֹא תְאַחֵר בְּכוֹר בָּנֶיךָ תִּתֶּן־לִּי׃
29 כֵּן־תַּעֲשֶׂה לְשֹׁרְךָ לְצֹאנֶךָ שִׁבְעַת יָמִים יִהְיֶה עִם־אִמּוֹ בַּיּוֹם
30 הַשְּׁמִינִי תִּתְּנוֹ־לִי׃ וְאַנְשֵׁי־קֹדֶשׁ תִּהְיוּן לִי וּבָשָׂר בַּשָּׂדֶה
טְרֵפָה לֹא תֹאכֵלוּ לַכֶּלֶב תַּשְׁלִכוּן אֹתוֹ׃

CAP. XXIII כג

CHAPTER 23

[1]You shall not utter a false report; You shall not put your hand with the wicked, to become a violent witness. [2]You shall not *run* after many to *gain* evil things. And you shall not testify as to a lawsuit, to turn aside after many in order to pervert *justice*. [3]And you shall not favor the lowly in his lawsuit.

1 לֹא תִשָּׂא שֵׁמַע שָׁוְא אַל־תָּשֶׁת יָדְךָ עִם־רָשָׁע לִהְיֹת עֵד
2 חָמָס׃ לֹא־תִהְיֶה אַחֲרֵי־רַבִּים לְרָעֹת וְלֹא־תַעֲנֶה עַל־רִב
3 לִנְטֹת אַחֲרֵי רַבִּים לְהַטֹּת׃ וְדָל לֹא תֶהְדַּר בְּרִיבוֹ׃ ס

[4]When you happen on the ox of your enemy, or his wandering ass, you shall surely return it to him. [5]When you see the ass of one who hates you crouching under its burden, you shall refrain from leaving *it* to him; you shall surely loose *it* from him.

[6]You shall not pervert the judgment of your needy one in his lawsuit. [7]You shall keep far away from a false matter. And do not kill the innocent and the righteous; for I will not justify the wicked. [8]And you shall not take a bribe, for the bribe blinds the seeing one, and *it* perverts the words of the righteous.

[9]And you shall not oppress an alien; and you know the life of an alien, since you were aliens in the land of Egypt.

[10]And you shall sow your land six years, and you shall gather its produce. [11]And the seventh *year* you shall let it rest and lie fallow, and the needy of your people shall eat. And what they leave, the animals of the field shall eat. So you shall do to your vineyard, to your oliveyard.

[12]You shall do your work six days, and on the seventh day you shall rest, so that your ox and your ass may rest, and the son of your slave-girl and your alien may be refreshed. [13]And be watchful in all that I have said to you. And you shall not mention another god by name; it shall not be heard from your mouth.

[14]Three times in the year you shall make a feast to Me. [15]You shall keep the Feast of Unleavened Bread. Seven days you shall eat unleavened bread, as I have commanded you, at the set time of the month of Abib. For in it you came out from Egypt, and they shall not appear before Me empty.

[16]Also the Feast of Harvest, the firstfruits of your labor, *of* what you sow in the

8582 2543 341 6293
4 כִּי תִפְגַּע שׁוֹר אֹיִבְךָ אוֹ חֲמֹרוֹ תֹּעֶה הָשֵׁב תְּשִׁיבֶנּוּ לוֹ׃
to shall you surely wander- ass his or your ox the you When
.him it return ,ing ,enemy of on happen
2308 4853 7257 8130 2543 7200
5 ס כִּי־תִרְאֶה חֲמוֹר שֹׂנַאֲךָ רֹבֵץ תַּחַת מַשָּׂאוֹ וְחָדַלְתָּ
shall you its under crouching who one the see you When
refrain ,burden you hates of ass
34 4941 5186 5800 5800 5800
6 מֵעֲזֹב לוֹ עָזֹב תַּעֲזֹב עִמּוֹ׃ ס לֹא תַטֶּה מִשְׁפַּט אֶבְיֹנְךָ
your the shall You not from shall you surely ;him to from
poor of judgment pervert .him (it) loose (it) leaving
2026 5662 5355 7368 8267 1697 7379
7 בְּרִיבוֹ׃ מִדְּבַר־שֶׁקֶר תִּרְחָק וְנָקִי וְצַדִּיק אַל־תַּהֲרֹג
;kill do not the and the and shall you false a From his in
righteous innocent ;away keep matter .law-suit
5786 7810 3588 3947 3808 7810 7563 6663 3588
8 כִּי לֹא־אַצְדִּיק רָשָׁע׃ וְשֹׁחַד לֹא תִקָּח כִּי הַשֹּׁחַד יְעַוֵּר
blinds the for you not a And the will I not for
bribe ,take shall bribe .wicked justify
3905 1616 6662 1697 5559 6493
9 פִּקְחִים וִיסַלֵּף דִּבְרֵי צַדִּיקִים׃ וְגֵר לֹא תִלְחָץ וְאַתֶּם
and shall you not an And the words the and seeing the
you ;oppress alien .righteous of perverts ,one
4714 776 1961 1616 3588 1616 5315 3045
יְדַעְתֶּם אֶת־נֶפֶשׁ הַגֵּר כִּי־גֵרִים הֱיִיתֶם בְּאֶרֶץ מִצְרָיִם׃
.Egypt the in were you aliens since an life the know
of land ,alien of
8393 622 776 2232 8141 8337
10 וְשֵׁשׁ שָׁנִים תִּזְרַע אֶת־אַרְצֶךָ וְאָסַפְתָּ אֶת־תְּבוּאָתָהּ׃
.produce its you and ,land your shall you years And
gather shall sow six
3499 7971 34 398 5203 8058 7651
11 וְהַשְּׁבִיעִת תִּשְׁמְטֶנָּה וּנְטַשְׁתָּהּ וְאָכְלוּ אֶבְיֹנֵי עַמֶּךָ וְיִתְרָם
what and your the shall And lie and let shall you the And
leave they ;people of needy eat .fallow rest it seventh
8117 8337 2132 3754 6213 7704 2416 398
12 תֹּאכַל חַיַּת הַשָּׂדֶה כֵּן־תַּעֲשֶׂה לְכַרְמְךָ לְזֵיתֶךָ׃ שֵׁשֶׁת יָמִים
days six your to your to shall you so the the eat shall
.olive-yard ,vineyard do ;field of animals
7794 5117 7673 7637 3117 4639 6213
תַּעֲשֶׂה מַעֲשֶׂיךָ וּבַיּוֹם הַשְּׁבִיעִי תִּשְׁבֹּת לְמַעַן יָנוּחַ שׁוֹרְךָ
your may that so shall you seventh on and your shall you
ox rest ,rest day the ,work do
559 834 3605 1616 519 1121 5314 2543
13 וַחֲמֹרֶךָ וְיִנָּפֵשׁ בֶּן־אֲמָתְךָ וְהַגֵּר׃ וּבְכֹל אֲשֶׁר־אָמַרְתִּי
have I that in And the and your son the be may and and
said all .alien slave-girl of refreshed ,ass your
2142 3808 312 430 8104
אֲלֵיכֶם תִּשָּׁמֵרוּ וְשֵׁם אֱלֹהִים אֲחֵרִים לֹא תַזְכִּירוּ לֹא
not shall you not another god and be you to
;mention name by ;watchful
2282 8141 2287 7272 7969 6310 5921 8085
14 15 יִשָּׁמַע עַל־פִּיךָ׃ שָׁלֹשׁ רְגָלִים תָּחֹג לִי בַּשָּׁנָה׃ אֶת־חַג
the the in Me to you times Three your from shall it
of feast .year feast shall .mouth heard be
6680 4682 398 3117 7651 8104 4682
הַמַּצּוֹת תִּשְׁמֹר שִׁבְעַת יָמִים תֹּאכַל מַצּוֹת כַּאֲשֶׁר צִוִּיתִךָ
have I as unleavened shall you days seven shall you unleavened
you commanded ,bread eat ;keep bread
7200 4714 5927 3588 24 2320 4150
לְמוֹעֵד חֹדֶשׁ הָאָבִיב כִּי־בוֹ יָצָאתָ מִמִּצְרָיִם וְלֹא־יֵרָאוּ
they not and from you it in for ;Abib the set the at
appear shall ,Egypt out came of month of time
7704 2232 834 4639 1061 7102 2282 7387
16 פָנַי רֵיקָם׃ וְחַג הַקָּצִיר בִּכּוּרֵי מַעֲשֶׂיךָ אֲשֶׁר תִּזְרַע בַּשָּׂדֶה
the in you (of) your first- the ,harvest And .empty before
.field sow what ,labor of fruit's of feast Me

field. Also the Feast of Ingathering, at the end of the year, at your gathering your work from the field. 17 Three times in the year every one of your males shall appear before the Lord Jehovah.

18 You shall not offer the blood of My sacrifice with leavened bread. And the fat of My feast shall not pass the night until morning. 19 The first, the firstfruits of your ground you shall bring *to* the house of Jehovah your God. You shall not boil a kid in its mother's milk.

20 Behold, I *am* about to send an Angel before you, to guard you in the way, and to bring you to the place which I have prepared. 21 Be observant before Him, and listen to His voice. Do not be rebellious against Him, for He will not forgive your transgressions; for My name *is* in Him. 22 For if you fully listen to his voice and do all which I speak, I will be a hater to all your haters, and will be a foe to your foes. 23 For My Angel shall go before you and bring you in to the Amorites, and the Hittites, and the Perizzites, and the Canaanites, and the Hivites, and the Jebusites; and I will destroy them.

24 You shall not bow down to their gods, and you shall not serve them. And you shall not do according to their works. But you shall surely pull down, and surely you shall smash their idols. 25 And you shall serve Jehovah your God, and He will bless your bread and your water. And I will remove sickness from your midst. 26 There shall not be one aborting, nor one barren in your land. I will fulfill the number of your days. 27 I will send My terror before you, and I will confound all the people among whom you come. And I will

7704 4639 622 8141 5927 614 2282
וְחַג הָאָסִף בְּצֵאת הַשָּׁנָה בְּאָסְפְּךָ אֶת־מַעֲשֶׂיךָ מִן־הַשָּׂדֶה׃
.field the from work your your at the when ingather- and
gathering ,year out goes ,ing of feast the

113 6440 2138 7200 8141 6471 7969
17 שָׁלֹשׁ פְּעָמִים בַּשָּׁנָה יֵרָאֶה כָּל־זְכוּרְךָ אֶל־פְּנֵי הָאָדֹן
the before your every shall the in times Three
Lord males of one appear year

2282 2459 3885 2077 1818 2557 2076 3068
18 יְהוִה׃ לֹא־תִזְבַּח עַל־חָמֵץ דַּם־זִבְחִי וְלֹא־יָלִין חֵלֶב־חַגִּי
My fat the pass shall and My of the leavened with You not .Jehovah
feast of night the not ;sacrifice blood bread offer shall

3068 1004 935 127 1061 7225 1242 5704
19 עַד־בֹּקֶר׃ רֵאשִׁית בִּכּוּרֵי אַדְמָתְךָ תָּבִיא בֵּית יְהוָה
Jehovah the shall you your first The ,first the .morning until
of house (to) bring ground of fruits

517 2461 1423 1310 3808 430
אֱלֹהֶיךָ לֹא־תְבַשֵּׁל גְּדִי בַּחֲלֵב אִמּוֹ׃
its the in kid a shall You not your
.mother of milk boil .God

935 1870 8104 6440 4397 7971 2009
20 הִנֵּה אָנֹכִי שֹׁלֵחַ מַלְאָךְ לְפָנֶיךָ לִשְׁמָרְךָ בַּדָּרֶךְ וְלַהֲבִיאֲךָ
to and the in guard to before an sending I ,Behold
you bring ,way you ,you Angel (am)

6963 8085 6440 8104 3559 834 4725
21 אֶל־הַמָּקוֹם אֲשֶׁר הֲכִנֹתִי׃ הִשָּׁמֶר מִפָּנָיו וּשְׁמַע בְּקֹלוֹ
His to and before on Be have I which place the to
;voice listen ,Him guard .prepared

3588 7130 8034 6588 5375 3808 3588 4843
22 אַל־תַּמֵּר בּוֹ כִּי לֹא יִשָּׂא לְפִשְׁעֲכֶם כִּי שְׁמִי בְּקִרְבּוֹ׃ כִּי
For in is My for your will He not for against be do not
.Him name ,transgressions up lift ,Him rebellious

341 1696 834 3605 6213 6963 8085 8085
אִם־שָׁמוֹעַ תִּשְׁמַע בְּקֹלוֹ וְעָשִׂיתָ כֹּל אֲשֶׁר אֲדַבֵּר וְאָיַבְתִּי
an be will I speak I which all do and His to listen you fully If
to enemy ,voice

6440 4397 3212 6887 6696 341
23 אֶת־אֹיְבֶיךָ וְצַרְתִּי אֶת־צֹרְרֶיךָ׃ כִּי־יֵלֵךְ מַלְאָכִי לְפָנֶיךָ
before My shall For .foes your be will and your
you Angel go to foe a ,enemies

2983 2340 3669 6522 2850 567 935
וֶהֱבִיאֲךָ אֶל־הָאֱמֹרִי וְהַחִתִּי וְהַפְּרִזִּי וְהַכְּנַעֲנִי הַחִוִּי וְהַיְבוּסִי
the and the and the and the and the and the to bring and
;Jebusites ,Hivites ,Canaanites ,Perizzites ,Hittites ,Amorites in you

5647 430 7812 3808 3582
24 וְהִכְחַדְתִּיו׃ לֹא־תִשְׁתַּחֲוֶה לֵאלֹהֵיהֶם וְלֹא תָעָבְדֵם וְלֹא
and shall you and their to shall You not will I and
not ,them serve not ,gods down bow .them off cut

7665 7665 2040 2040 4639 6213
תַעֲשֶׂה כְּמַעֲשֵׂיהֶם כִּי הָרֵס תְּהָרְסֵם וְשַׁבֵּר תְּשַׁבֵּר
shall you and shall you surely but to according shall you
smash surely ,down pull ;works their do

1288 430 3068 5647 4676
25 מַצֵּבֹתֵיהֶם׃ וַעֲבַדְתֶּם אֵת יְהוָה אֱלֹהֵיכֶם וּבֵרַךְ אֶת־
He and ,God your Jehovah you And ,pillars idol their
bless will serve shall

3808 7130 4245 5493 4325 3899
26 לַחְמְךָ וְאֶת־מֵימֶיךָ וַהֲסִרֹתִי מַחֲלָה מִקִּרְבֶּךָ׃ ס לֹא
not your from sickness I and your and your
.midst remove will ;water bread

4390 3117 4557 776 6135 7921 1961
תִהְיֶה מְשַׁכֵּלָה וַעֲקָרָה בְּאַרְצֶךָ אֶת־מִסְפַּר יָמֶיךָ אֲמַלֵּא׃
will I your number the your in one nor one shall There
.fulfill days of ;land barren ,aborting be

834 5971 3605 2000 6440 7971 367
27 אֶת־אֵימָתִי אֲשַׁלַּח לְפָנֶיךָ וְהַמֹּתִי אֶת־כָּל־הָעָם אֲשֶׁר
whom the all I and before will I terror My
people confound will ,you send

give the neck of your enemies to you. 28And I will send hornets before you which shall drive out the Hivites, the Canaanites, and the Hittites before you. 29I will not drive them out from before you in one year, that the land not become a waste, and the beast of the field multiply on you. 30I will drive them out before you little by little, until you are fruitful and possess the land. 31And I will set your border from the Red Sea as far as the Sea of the Philistines, and from the wilderness as far as the River. For I will give the people of the land into your hand. And you shall drive them out before you. 32You shall not cut a covenant for them and for their gods. 33They shall not dwell in your land, lest they cause you to sin towards Me. Surely when you serve their gods, it will be a snare to you.

28 תָּבֹא בָּהֶם וְנָתַתִּי אֶת־כָּל־אֹיְבֶיךָ אֵלֶיךָ עֹרֶף׃ וְשָׁלַחְתִּי
אֶת־הַצִּרְעָה לְפָנֶיךָ וְגֵרְשָׁה אֶת־הַחִוִּי אֶת־הַכְּנַעֲנִי וְאֶת־
29 הַחִתִּי מִלְּפָנֶיךָ׃ לֹא אֲגָרְשֶׁנּוּ מִפָּנֶיךָ בְּשָׁנָה אֶחָת פֶּן
30 תִּהְיֶה הָאָרֶץ שְׁמָמָה וְרַבָּה עָלֶיךָ חַיַּת הַשָּׂדֶה׃ מְעַט
מְעַט אֲגָרְשֶׁנּוּ מִפָּנֶיךָ עַד אֲשֶׁר תִּפְרֶה וְנָחַלְתָּ אֶת־הָאָרֶץ׃
31 וְשַׁתִּי אֶת־גְּבֻלְךָ מִיַּם־סוּף וְעַד־יָם פְּלִשְׁתִּים וּמִמִּדְבָּר
עַד־הַנָּהָר כִּי ׀ אֶתֵּן בְּיֶדְכֶם אֵת יֹשְׁבֵי הָאָרֶץ וְגֵרַשְׁתָּמוֹ
32 מִפָּנֶיךָ׃ לֹא־תִכְרֹת לָהֶם וְלֵאלֹהֵיהֶם בְּרִית׃ לֹא יֵשְׁבוּ
33 בְּאַרְצְךָ פֶּן־יַחֲטִיאוּ אֹתְךָ לִי כִּי תַעֲבֹד אֶת־אֱלֹהֵיהֶם כִּי־
יִהְיֶה לְךָ לְמוֹקֵשׁ׃

CAP. XXIV כד

CHAPTER 24

CHAPTER 24

1And He said to Moses, Come up to Jehovah, you and Aaron, Nadab, and Abihu, and seventy from the elders of Israel. And bow yourselves from a distance. 2And let Moses approach by himself to Jehovah, and they shall not approach. And the people shall not go up with him. 3And Moses came and told all the words of Jehovah to the people, and all the judgments. And all the people answered with one voice and said, We will do all the words which Jehovah has spoken. 4And Moses wrote all the words of Jehovah. And he rose early in the morning

1 וְאֶל־מֹשֶׁה אָמַר עֲלֵה אֶל־יְהוָה אַתָּה וְאַהֲרֹן נָדָב וַאֲבִיהוּא
2 וְשִׁבְעִים מִזִּקְנֵי יִשְׂרָאֵל וְהִשְׁתַּחֲוִיתֶם מֵרָחֹק׃ וְנִגַּשׁ מֹשֶׁה
3 לְבַדּוֹ אֶל־יְהוָה וְהֵם לֹא יִגָּשׁוּ וְהָעָם לֹא יַעֲלוּ עִמּוֹ׃ וַיָּבֹא
מֹשֶׁה וַיְסַפֵּר לָעָם אֵת כָּל־דִּבְרֵי יְהוָה וְאֵת כָּל־הַמִּשְׁפָּטִים
וַיַּעַן כָּל־הָעָם קוֹל אֶחָד וַיֹּאמְרוּ כָּל־הַדְּבָרִים אֲשֶׁר־דִּבֶּר
4 יְהוָה נַעֲשֶׂה׃ וַיִּכְתֹּב מֹשֶׁה אֵת כָּל־דִּבְרֵי יְהוָה וַיַּשְׁכֵּם

and built an altar below the
mountain, and twelve
memorial pillars for the
twelve tribes of Israel.
[5]And he sent young men of
the sons of Israel. And they
offered up burnt offerings,
and offered sacrifices of
bullocks, peace offerings to
Jehovah. [6]And Moses took
half of the blood, and he put
it in basins. And he
sprinkled half of the blood
on the altar. [7]And he took
the book of the covenant,
and read in the ears of the
people. And they said, We
will do all that Jehovah has
spoken, and we will hear.
[8]And Moses took the blood
and sprinkled on the
people, and said, Behold,
the blood of the covenant
which Jehovah has cut with
you concerning these
words.

[9]And Moses and Aaron
went up *with* Nadab and
Abihu, and seventy from the
elders of Israel. [10]And they
saw the God of Israel. And
under His feet *was* as the
work of a pavement of
sapphire, and as the
heavens for clearness.
[11]And He did not stretch out
His hand to the nobles of
the sons of Israel. And they
saw God, and they ate and
drank.

[12]And Jehovah said to
Moses, Come up to Me to
the mountain, and be there.
And I will give to you the
tablets of stone, and the
law, and the command-
ments which I have writ-
ten, to teach them. [13]And
Moses rose up, and Joshua
his attendant. And Moses
went up to the mountain of
God. [14]And he said to the
elders, Wait here for us,
until we return to you. And,
behold, Aaron, who *is* a
master of matters, and Hur
are with you—let him
approach to them.

בַּבֹּקֶר וַיִּבֶן מִזְבֵּחַ תַּחַת הָהָר וּשְׁתֵּים עֶשְׂרֵה מַצֵּבָה
5 לִשְׁנֵים עָשָׂר שִׁבְטֵי יִשְׂרָאֵל׃ וַיִּשְׁלַח אֶת־נַעֲרֵי בְּנֵי יִשְׂרָאֵל
6 וַיַּעֲלוּ עֹלֹת וַיִּזְבְּחוּ זְבָחִים שְׁלָמִים לַיהוָה פָּרִים׃ וַיִּקַּח
מֹשֶׁה חֲצִי הַדָּם וַיָּשֶׂם בָּאַגָּנֹת וַחֲצִי הַדָּם זָרַק עַל־
7 הַמִּזְבֵּחַ׃ וַיִּקַּח סֵפֶר הַבְּרִית וַיִּקְרָא בְּאָזְנֵי הָעָם וַיֹּאמְרוּ
8 כֹּל אֲשֶׁר־דִּבֶּר יְהוָה נַעֲשֶׂה וְנִשְׁמָע׃ וַיִּקַּח מֹשֶׁה אֶת־הַדָּם
וַיִּזְרֹק עַל־הָעָם וַיֹּאמֶר הִנֵּה דַם־הַבְּרִית אֲשֶׁר כָּרַת יְהוָה
9 עִמָּכֶם עַל כָּל־הַדְּבָרִים הָאֵלֶּה׃ וַיַּעַל מֹשֶׁה וְאַהֲרֹן נָדָב
10 וַאֲבִיהוּא וְשִׁבְעִים מִזִּקְנֵי יִשְׂרָאֵל׃ וַיִּרְאוּ אֵת אֱלֹהֵי יִשְׂרָאֵל
וְתַחַת רַגְלָיו כְּמַעֲשֵׂה לִבְנַת הַסַּפִּיר וּכְעֶצֶם הַשָּׁמַיִם
11 לָטֹהַר׃ וְאֶל־אֲצִילֵי בְּנֵי יִשְׂרָאֵל לֹא שָׁלַח יָדוֹ וַיֶּחֱזוּ אֶת־
12 הָאֱלֹהִים וַיֹּאכְלוּ וַיִּשְׁתּוּ׃ ס וַיֹּאמֶר יְהוָה אֶל־מֹשֶׁה
עֲלֵה אֵלַי הָהָרָה וֶהְיֵה־שָׁם וְאֶתְּנָה לְךָ אֶת־לֻחֹת הָאֶבֶן
13 וְהַתּוֹרָה וְהַמִּצְוָה אֲשֶׁר כָּתַבְתִּי לְהוֹרֹתָם׃ וַיָּקָם מֹשֶׁה
14 וִיהוֹשֻׁעַ מְשָׁרְתוֹ וַיַּעַל מֹשֶׁה אֶל־הַר הָאֱלֹהִים׃ וְאֶל־
הַזְּקֵנִים אָמַר שְׁבוּ־לָנוּ בָזֶה עַד אֲשֶׁר־נָשׁוּב אֲלֵיכֶם וְהִנֵּה
15 אַהֲרֹן וְחוּר עִמָּכֶם מִי־בַעַל דְּבָרִים יִגַּשׁ אֲלֵהֶם׃ וַיַּעַל

15And Moses went up into the mountain. And a cloud covered the mountain. 16And the glory of Jehovah dwelt on the mountain of Sinai. And the cloud covered it six days. And He called to Moses on the seventh day from the midst of the cloud. 17And the appearance of the glory of Jehovah *was* like fire burning on the top of the mountain before the eyes of the sons of Israel. 18And Moses came into the midst of the cloud, and he went up into the mountain. And Moses was in the mountain forty days and forty nights.

3068 3519 7931 2022 6051 3680 2022 4872
16 משה אל־ההר ויכס הענן את־ההר׃ וישכן כבוד־יהוה
Jehovah the And .mountain the a and the into Moses
of glory dwelt cloud covered ;mountain

4872 7121 3117 8337 6051 3680 5514 2022
על־הר סיני ויכסהו הענן ששת ימים ויקרא אל־משה
Moses to He and ;days six the and ,Sinai on
called cloud it covered Mount

784 3068 3519 4758 6051 8432 7637 3117
17 ביום השביעי מתוך הענן׃ ומראה כבוד יהוה כאש
like (was) Jehovah the the And .cloud the from seventh the on
fire of glory of appearance of midst the day

4872 935 3478 1121 2022 7218 398
18 אכלת בראש ההר לעיני בני ישראל׃ ויבא משה
Moses And .Israel the before the head on burning
came of sons mount of

3117 703 2022 4872 1961 2022 5927 6051 8432
בתוך הענן ויעל אל־ההר ויהי משה בהר ארבעים יום
days forty the in Moses and the into he and the into
mount was ;mount up went ,cloud of midst

3915 705
וארבעים לילה׃
.nights forty and

CAP. XXV כה

CHAPTER 25

CHAPTER 25

1And Jehovah spoke to Moses, saying, 2Speak to the sons of Israel, and let them take an offering for Me from every man whose heart impels him—let them take My offering. 3And this *is* the offering which you shall take from them: gold, and silver, and bronze; 4and blue, and purple, and crimson, and fine linen, and goats' hair; 5and rams' skin dyed red, and dugong skins, and acacia-wood; 6oil for the light, spices for the oil of anointing, and for the incense of perfumes; 7onyx stones, and stones *for* setting, for the ephod, and for the pouch. 8And let them make a sanctuary for Me, that I may dwell in their midst. 9According to all which I *am* going to reveal to you, the plan of the tabernacle, and the plan of all its vessels. And so you shall do.

10And they shall make an ark of acacia-wood, two and a half cubits long, and a cubit and a half wide, and a

3478 1121 1696 559 4872 3068 1696
1 וידבר יהוה אל־משה לאמר׃ דבר אל־בני ישראל
2 ,Israel the to Speak ,saying Moses to Jehovah And
of sons spoke

3947 3820 5068 376 3605 8641 3947
ויקחו־לי תרומה מאת כל־איש אשר ידבנו לבו תקחו
them let ;heart impels whose man every from heave a for let and
take him ;offering Me take them

2091 3947 8641 8641
3 את־תרומתי׃ וזאת התרומה אשר תקחו מאתם זהב
,gold from shall you which heave the And heave My
:them take offering (is) this .offering

5795 8336 8144 8438 713 8504 5178 3701
4 כסף ונחשת׃ ותכלת וארגמן ותולעת שני ושש ועזים׃
goat's and and and and .blue and ,bronze and and
,(hair) linen fine crimson ,purple ,silver

8081 7848 6086 8476 5785 119 352 5785
5
6 וערת אילם מאדמים וערת תחשים ועצי שטים׃ שמן
oil ,acacia- and ,dugong's and dyed ram's and
wood skins ,red skins

68 5561 7004 4888 8081 1314 3974
7 למאור בשמים לשמן המשחה ולקטרת הסמים׃ אבני
stones ;perfumes for and ,anointing the for spices the for
of incense the of oil ,lamp

4720 6213 2833 646 4294 68 7718
8 שהם ואבני מלאים לאפד ולחשן׃ ועשו לי מקדש
a Me for let And the for And the for (for) and ,onyx
,sanctuary make them pocket ,ephod ,setting stones

8403 7200 834 3605 8432 7931
9 ושכנתי בתוכם׃ ככל אשר אני מראה אותך את תבנית
the ,you to to going I which According their in I that
of plan reveal (am) all to ,midst dwell may

6213 6213 3651 3627 3605 8403 4908
10 המשכן ואת תבנית כל־כליו וכן תעשו׃ ס ועשו
they And shall you and its all plan the and the
make shall .do so ;vessels of tabernacle

7341 3677 520 753 2677 520 7848 6086 727
ארון עצי שטים אמתים וחצי ארכו ואמה וחצי רחבו
its a and a and its a and two ,acacia- wood an
,width half cubit ,length half cubits of ark

cubit and a half high. 11And you shall overlay it *with* pure gold; you shall overlay it inside and outside. And you shall make a wreath of gold all around on it. 12And you shall cast four rings of gold for it, and shall put it on its four feet; two rings on the one side, and two rings on the second side. 13And you shall make poles of acacia-wood, and you shall overlay them *with* gold. 14And you shall put the poles into the rings on the sides of the ark, to carry the ark by them. 15The poles shall be in the rings of the ark; they shall not depart from it. 16And you shall put the testimony into the ark, which I shall give to you.

17And you shall make a mercy-seat of pure gold, its length two and a half cubits, and its width a cubit and a half. 18And you shall make two cherubs of gold; you shall make them of beaten work from the two ends of the mercy-seat. 19And make one cherub from the end here, and one cherub from the end there. You shall make the cherubs from the mercy-seat, on its two ends. 20And the cherubs shall be spreading out wings above, covering the mercy-seat with their wings, and their faces each toward its brother; the faces of the cherubs shall be toward the mercy-seat.

21And you shall put the mercy-seat on the ark from above. And you shall put the testimony into the ark, which I shall give to you. 22And I will meet you there, and will speak with you, above the mercy-seat, from between the two cherubs which *are* on the ark of

2351 1004 2889 2091 6823 6967 2677 520
11 וְאַמָּה וָחֵצִי קֹמָתוֹ׃ וְצִפִּיתָ אֹתוֹ זָהָב טָהוֹר מִבַּיִת וּמִחוּץ
and outside | inside | ,pure | (with) gold | it | you And overlay shall | its .height | a and half | a and cubit

702 3332 5439 2091 2221 5921 6213 6823
12 תְּצַפֶּנּוּ וְעָשִׂיתָ עָלָיו זֵר זָהָב סָבִיב׃ וְיָצַקְתָּ לּוֹ אַרְבַּע
four | it for | you and cast shall | all ,around | gold of | a wreath | it on | you and make shall | shall you ;it overlay

5921 2885 8147 6471 702 5921 5414 2091 2885
טַבְּעֹת זָהָב וְנָתַתָּה עַל אַרְבַּע פַּעֲמֹתָיו וּשְׁתֵּי טַבָּעֹת עַל־
on | rings | two | ;feet its | four | on | shall and it put | ,gold | of rings

905 6213 8145 6684 /5921 2885 8147 259 6763
13 צַלְעוֹ הָאֶחָת וּשְׁתֵּי טַבָּעֹת עַל־צַלְעוֹ הַשֵּׁנִית׃ וְעָשִׂיתָ בַדֵּי
poles of | you And make shall | .second | side its | on | rings | two and | ,one | side its

2885 905 935 2091 6823 7840 6086
14 עֲצֵי שִׁטִּים וְצִפִּיתָ אֹתָם זָהָב׃ וְהֵבֵאתָ אֶת־הַבַּדִּים בַּטַּבָּעֹת
the into ,rings | poles the | you And put shall | (with) .gold | them | and overlay | ,acacia-wood

727 2885 727 5375 727 6763 5921
15 עַל צַלְעֹת הָאָרֹן לָשֵׂאת אֶת־הָאָרֹן בָּהֶם׃ בְּטַבְּעֹת הָאָרֹן
ark the | the In of rings | .them by | ark the | carry to | ,ark the | the of sides | on

5715 727 5414 5493 3808 905 1961
16 יִהְיוּ הַבַּדִּים לֹא יָסֻרוּ מִמֶּנּוּ׃ וְנָתַתָּ אֶל־הָאָרֹן אֵת הָעֵדֻת
the testimony | ark the | into | you And put shall | .it from | they depart shall | not | ;poles the | shall be

2677 520 2889 2091 3727 6213 5414 834
17 אֲשֶׁר אֶתֵּן אֵלֶיךָ׃ וְעָשִׂיתָ כַפֹּרֶת זָהָב טָהוֹר אַמָּתַיִם וָחֵצִי
a and half | two cubits | ,pure | gold | a of mercy-seat | shall you And make | .you | shall I give | which

2091 3742 8147 6213 7341 2677 520 753
18 אָרְכָּהּ וְאַמָּה וָחֵצִי רָחְבָּהּ׃ וְעָשִׂיתָ שְׁנַיִם כְּרֻבִים זָהָב
;gold | cherubs of | two | you And make shall | .width its | a and half | a and cubit | its length

3742 6213 3707 7098 8147 6213 4749
19 מִקְשָׁה תַּעֲשֶׂה אֹתָם מִשְּׁנֵי קְצוֹת הַכַּפֹּרֶת׃ וַעֲשֵׂה כְּרוּב
cherub | And make | the .mercy-seat | of ends | from two the | ,them shall you make | beaten of work

3727 2088 7098 3742 2088 7098 259
אֶחָד מִקָּצָה מִזֶּה וּכְרוּב־אֶחָד מִקָּצָה מִזֶּה מִן־הַכַּפֹּרֶת
the mercy-seat | from ;there | the from end | one | and cherub | ,here | the from end | one

3742 1961 7098 8147 5921 3742 6213
20 תַּעֲשׂוּ אֶת־הַכְּרֻבִים עַל־שְׁנֵי קְצוֹתָיו׃ וְהָיוּ הַכְּרֻבִים
cherubs the | shall And be | of ends .it | two the on | ,cherubs the | shall you make

3727 3671 5526 4605 3671 6566
פֹּרְשֵׂי כְנָפַיִם לְמַעְלָה סֹכְכִים בְּכַנְפֵיהֶם עַל־הַכַּפֹּרֶת
the ,mercy-seat | their with wings | covering | ,above | wings | spreading out

3742 6440 1961 3727 251 376 6440
וּפְנֵיהֶם אִישׁ אֶל־אָחִיו אֶל־הַכַּפֹּרֶת יִהְיוּ פְּנֵי הַכְּרֻבִים׃
.cherubs the | the of faces | be shall | the mercy-seat | toward | his brother | to | each | their and faces

5414 727 4605 727 3727 5414
21 וְנָתַתָּ אֶת־הַכַּפֹּרֶת עַל־הָאָרֹן מִלְמָעְלָה וְאֶל־הָאָרֹן תִּתֵּן
you put shall | ark the | and into | ;above from | ark the | on | the mercy-seat | you And put shall

1696 8033 3259 5414 834 5715
22 אֶת־הָעֵדֻת אֲשֶׁר אֶתֵּן אֵלֶיךָ׃ וְנוֹעַדְתִּי לְךָ שָׁם וְדִבַּרְתִּי
will and speak | there | you | will I And meet | .you to | shall I give | which | the ,testimony

727 5921 834 3742 8147 996 3727 5921
אִתְּךָ מֵעַל הַכַּפֹּרֶת מִבֵּין שְׁנֵי הַכְּרֻבִים אֲשֶׁר עַל־אֲרוֹן
ark the of | on | which (are) | ,cherubs the | two | from between | the ,mercy-seat | above | ,you to

testimony, all which I shall command you concerning the sons of Israel.

23 And you shall make a table of acacia-wood, its length two cubits, and its width a cubit, and its height a cubit and a half. 24 And you shall overlay it *with* pure gold, and you shall make it a wreath of gold all around. 25 And you shall make a border of a hand's breadth for it all around. And you shall make a wreath of gold all around on its border. 26 And you shall make four rings of gold for it, and you shall put the rings on the four corners which *are* to its four feet. 27 The rings shall be near the border for housings for the poles, to carry the table. 28 And you shall make the poles of acacia-wood, and you shall overlay them *with* gold. And the table shall be carried by them. 29 And you shall make its platters, and its bowls, and its pitchers, and its sacrificial cups *with* which a drink offering is made. You shall make them of pure gold. 30 And you shall put the Bread of the Presence on the table before Me continually.

31 And you shall make a lampstand of pure gold. The lampstand shall be made of beaten work; its base and its shaft, its cups, its knobs, and its blossoms shall be from it. 32 And six branches shall go out from its sides, three branches of the lamp from its one side, and three branches of the lamp from its second side; 33 three almond-like cups on the one branch *with* knob and blossom; and three almond-like cups on the one branchd *with* knob and blossom — so for the six branches, those

3478 1121 6680 834 5715
הָעֵדֻת אֵת כָּל־אֲשֶׁר אֲצַוֶּה אוֹתְךָ אֶל־בְּנֵי יִשְׂרָאֵל׃
.Israel of sons the to as you command shall I which all the ,testimony

23 520 7341 520 753 520 7848 6086 7979 6213
וְעָשִׂיתָ שֻׁלְחָן עֲצֵי שִׁטִּים אַמָּתַיִם אָרְכּוֹ וְאַמָּה רָחְבּוֹ וְאַמָּה
a cubit and its ,width a cubit and its ,length two cubits ,acacia-wood of table a you And make shall

24 2091 2213 6213 2889 2091 6823 6967 2677
וָחֵצִי קֹמָתוֹ׃ וְצִפִּיתָ אֹתוֹ זָהָב טָהוֹר וְעָשִׂיתָ לּוֹ זֵר זָהָב
gold of wreath a it for you and make shall ,pure (with) gold it you And overlay shall ,height its a half and

25 2091 2213 6213 5439 2948 4526 3947 5439
סָבִיב׃ וְעָשִׂיתָ לּוֹ מִסְגֶּרֶת טֹפַח סָבִיב וְעָשִׂיתָ זֵר־זָהָב
gold of wreath a you and make shall ;around all breadth hand's a of border a it for you And make shall all around

26 5414 2096 2885 702 6213 5439 4526
לְמִסְגַּרְתּוֹ סָבִיב׃ וְעָשִׂיתָ לּוֹ אַרְבַּע טַבְּעֹת זָהָב וְנָתַתָּ
you and put shall ,gold of rings four it for you And make shall all .around its on border

5980 7272 702 834 6285 702 2885
אֶת־הַטַּבָּעֹת עַל אַרְבַּע הַפֵּאֹת אֲשֶׁר לְאַרְבַּע רַגְלָיו׃ לְעֻמַּת
Near .feet its four for which (are) the ,corners four as rings the

27 5375 905 1004 2885 1961 4526
הַמִּסְגֶּרֶת תִּהְיֶיןָ הַטַּבָּעֹת לְבָתִּים לְבַדִּים לָשֵׂאת אֶת־
carry to the for ,poles housings for ,rings the be shall borders the

28 6823 7848 6086 905 6213 7979
הַשֻּׁלְחָן׃ וְעָשִׂיתָ אֶת־הַבַּדִּים עֲצֵי שִׁטִּים וְצִפִּיתָ אֹתָם
them you and overlay shall ,acacia- wood of poles the you And make shall .table the

29 3709 7086 6213 7979 5375 2091
זָהָב וְנִשָּׂא־בָם אֶת־הַשֻּׁלְחָן׃ וְעָשִׂיתָ קְּעָרֹתָיו וְכַפֹּתָיו
its and ,bowls platters its you And make shall .table the by shall and them carried be (with) ;gold

6213 2889 2091 2004 5258 834 4518 7175
וּקְשׂוֹתָיו וּמְנַקִּיֹּתָיו אֲשֶׁר יֻסַּךְ בָּהֵן זָהָב טָהוֹר תַּעֲשֶׂה אֹתָם׃
.them shall you make pure of gold ;with made is libation a which its and cups sacrificial its and ,pitchers

30 8548 6440 6440 3899 7979 5414
וְנָתַתָּ עַל־הַשֻּׁלְחָן לֶחֶם פָּנִים לְפָנַי תָּמִיד׃
.continually before Me the showbread table the of on you And put shall

31 3409 4501 6213 4744 2889 2091 4501 6213
וְעָשִׂיתָ מְנֹרַת זָהָב טָהוֹר מִקְשָׁה תֵּעָשֶׂה הַמְּנוֹרָה יְרֵכָהּ
base its the ,lampstand be shall made beaten of work ;pure gold of lamp-a stand you And make shall

32 8337 1961 6525 3730 1375 7070
וְקָנָהּ גְּבִיעֶיהָ כַּפְתֹּרֶיהָ וּפְרָחֶיהָ מִמֶּנָּה יִהְיוּ׃ וְשִׁשָּׁה
six And shall .be it from its and blossoms ,knobs its ,cups is ,cups its and ,shaft

259 6654 4501 7070 7969 6654 5927 7070
קָנִים יֹצְאִים מִצִּדֶּיהָ שְׁלֹשָׁה ׀ קְנֵי מְנֹרָה מִצִּדָּהּ הָאֶחָד
,one its from side the lamp branches of three its from sides go shall out branches

33 8246 1375 7969 8145 6654 4501 7070 7969
וּשְׁלֹשָׁה קְנֵי מְנֹרָה מִצִּדָּהּ הַשֵּׁנִי׃ שְׁלֹשָׁה גְבִעִים מְשֻׁקָּדִים
almond-like cups three ;second its from side the lampstand of branches and three

8246 1375 7969 6525 3730 259 7070
בַּקָּנֶה הָאֶחָד כַּפְתֹּר וָפֶרַח וּשְׁלֹשָׁה גְבִעִים מְשֻׁקָּדִים
almond-like cups three and ;blossom and (with) knob ,one the on branch

5927 7070 8337 6525 3730 259 7070
בַּקָּנֶה הָאֶחָד כַּפְתֹּר וָפֶרַח כֵּן לְשֵׁשֶׁת הַקָּנִים הַיֹּצְאִים
going those out the ,branches six for so ;blossom and (with) knob ,one the on branch

going out from the lampstand. [34]And on the lampstand *shall be* four almond-like cups, each *with* its knobs and its blossoms, [35]and a knob under two branches of it; and a knob under two branches of it; and a knob under two branches of it, to the six branches, those going from the lampstand. [36]Their knobs and their branches shall be of it, all of it one beaten work *of* pure gold. [37]And you shall make its seven lamps. And one shall set up its lamps, and they shall give light on its face. [38]And its tongs, and its pans *shall be* of pure gold. [39]One shall make it of a talent of pure gold, with all these vessels. [40]And see *that they are* made by their patterns which you *were* made to see in the mountain.

3730 8246 1375 702 4501 4501
34 מִן־הַמְּנֹרָה׃ וּבַמְּנֹרָה אַרְבָּעָה גְבִעִים מְשֻׁקָּדִים כַּפְתֹּרֶיהָ
(with each) its ,almond-like cups four the on And the from
knobs lampstand .lampstand

8478 3730 7070 8147 8478 3730 6525
35 וּפְרָחֶיהָ׃ וְכַפְתֹּר תַּחַת שְׁנֵי הַקָּנִים מִמֶּנָּה וְכַפְתֹּר תַּחַת
under a and ;it of branches two under a and its and
knob knob ;blossoms

8337 7070 8147 8478 3730 7070 8147
שְׁנֵי הַקָּנִים מִמֶּנָּה וְכַפְתֹּר תַּחַת־שְׁנֵי הַקָּנִים מִמֶּנָּה לְשֵׁשֶׁת
six to ;it of branches two under a and ;it of branches two
knob

7070 3730 4501 5927 7070
36 הַקָּנִים הַיֹּצְאִים מִן־הַמְּנֹרָה׃ כַּפְתֹּרֵיהֶם וּקְנֹתָם מִמֶּנָּה
it of their and Their the from going those the
branches knobs .lampstand ,branches

5216 6213 2889 2091 259 4749 3605 1961
37 יִהְיוּ כֻּלָּהּ מִקְשָׁה אַחַת זָהָב טָהוֹר׃ וְעָשִׂיתָ אֶת־נֵרֹתֶיהָ
lamps its you And .pure gold (of) one beaten of all shall
make shall ,work ,it ,be

4457 5676 215 5927 7651
38 שִׁבְעָה וְהֶעֱלָה אֶת־נֵרֹתֶיהָ וְהֵאִיר עַל־עֵבֶר פָּנֶיהָ׃ וּמֶלְקָחֶיהָ
its And its opposite they and its one and ;seven
,tongs ,face light give shall .lamps up set shall

6213 2889 2091 3603 2889 2091 4289
39 וּמַחְתֹּתֶיהָ זָהָב טָהוֹר׃ כִּכָּר זָהָב טָהוֹר יַעֲשֶׂה אֹתָהּ אֵת
with ,it shall one pure gold a Of .pure gold its and
make of talent (of) pans

834 8403 6213 7200 3627 3605
40 כָּל־הַכֵּלִים הָאֵלֶּה׃ וּרְאֵה וַעֲשֵׂה בְּתַבְנִיתָם אֲשֶׁר־אַתָּה
you which their by (they that see And .these vessels all
patterns made (are)

7200
מָרְאֶה בָּהָר׃
the in been have
.mountain shown

CAP. XXVI כו

CHAPTER 26

CHAPTER 26

[1]And you shall make the tabernacle *with* ten curtains. You shall make them *with* cherubs, the work of a skilled workman, *of* twined linen, and blue and purple and crimson. [2]The length of one curtain *shall be* twenty-eight by the cubit; and the width four by the cubit, *for* the one curtain; one measure to all the curtains. [3]Five curtains shall be joined together, each to her sister. And five curtains joined each to her sister. [4]And you shall make loops of blue on the edge of one curtain, from the end at

8504 7806 8336 3407 6235 4908
1 וְאֶת־הַמִּשְׁכָּן תַּעֲשֶׂה עֶשֶׂר יְרִיעֹת שֵׁשׁ מָשְׁזָר וּתְכֵלֶת
,blue and ,twined linen ;curtains (with) shall you the And
ten make tabernacle

6213 2803 4639 3742 8144 8438 713
וְאַרְגָּמָן וְתֹלַעַת שָׁנִי כְּרֻבִים מַעֲשֵׂה חֹשֵׁב תַּעֲשֶׂה אֹתָם׃
.them shall you skilled a work the (with) and and
make workman of ,cherubs ,crimson ,purple

7341 520 6242 8083 259 3407 753
2 אֹרֶךְ הַיְרִיעָה הָאַחַת שְׁמֹנֶה וְעֶשְׂרִים בָּאַמָּה וְרֹחַב
the and the by twenty (be shall) one the curtain The
,width ;cubit -eight of length

3407 3605 259 4060 3407 520 702
אַרְבַּע בָּאַמָּה הַיְרִיעָה הָאַחַת מִדָּה אַחַת לְכָל־הַיְרִיעֹת׃
the to one measure the (for) curtain the by four
.curtains all ,one ,cubit

3407 2568 269 802 2266 1961 3407 2568
3 חֲמֵשׁ הַיְרִיעֹת תִּהְיֶיןָ חֹבְרֹת אִשָּׁה אֶל־אֲחֹתָהּ וְחָמֵשׁ יְרִיעֹת
curtains and its to each joined be shall curtains Five
five ;sister-piece ,together

8193 5921 8504 3924 6213 269 802 2266
4 חֹבְרֹת אִשָּׁה אֶל־אֲחֹתָהּ׃ וְעָשִׂיתָ לֻלְאֹת תְּכֵלֶת עַל שְׂפַת
the on blue of loops you And its to each ,joined
of edge make shall .sister-piece

3407 8193 6213 4225 7098 259 3407
הַיְרִיעָה הָאֶחָת מִקָּצָה בַּחֹבָרֶת וְכֵן תַּעֲשֶׂה בִּשְׂפַת הַיְרִיעָה
the the at shall you and the at the from ,one curtain
curtain of edge do so ;juncture end

the juncture; and so you shall do at the edge of the last curtain, at the second juncture. [5]You shall make fifty loops on the one curtain; and you shall make fifty loops in the end of the curtain which *is* at the second juncture; the corresponding loops each to her sister. [6]And you shall make fifty hooks of gold. And you shall join the curtains, each to her sister, by the hooks. And it shall become one tabernacle.

[7]And you shall make curtains of goats' *hair* for a tent over the tabernacle; you shall make eleven curtains. [8]The length of the one curtain *shall be* thirty by the cubit; and the width four by the cubit *for* the one curtain; one measure to the eleven curtains. [9]And you shall join the five curtains separately, and the six curtains separately. And you shall double the six curtains before the front of the tabernacle. [10]And you shall make fifty loops on the edge of the one curtain, the last at the juncture; and fifty loops on the edge of the second curtain that joins.

[11]And you shall make fifty hooks of bronze. And you shall put the hooks in the loops and join the tent together. And it shall become one. [12]And the overlapping part of the rest of the curtains of the tabernacle, the half curtain that remains, shall hang on the back of the tabernacle. [13]And the cubit from this *side*, and the cubit from that *side* that remains in the length of the curtains of the tent shall be hung over the sides of the tabernacle from

6213 3924 2572 8145 4225 7020
5 הַקִּיצֹנָה בַּמַּחְבֶּרֶת הַשֵּׁנִית׃ חֲמִשִּׁים לֻלָאֹת תַּעֲשֶׂה
shall you make | loops | Fifty | .second | the at juncture | ,last

3407 7097 6213 3924 2572 259 3407
בַּיְרִיעָה הָאֶחָת וַחֲמִשִּׁים לֻלָאֹת תַּעֲשֶׂה בִּקְצֵה הַיְרִיעָה
curtain the | the in of end | shall you make | loops | fifty and | ,one | the on curtain

802 3924 6901 8145 4225 834
אֲשֶׁר בַּמַּחְבֶּרֶת הַשֵּׁנִית מַקְבִּילֹת הַלֻּלָאֹת אִשָּׁה אֶל־
to | each | loops the | corresponding | ;second | the at (is) juncture | which

3407 2266 2091 7165 2572 6213 269
6 אֲחֹתָהּ׃ וְעָשִׂיתָ חֲמִשִּׁים קַרְסֵי זָהָב וְחִבַּרְתָּ אֶת־הַיְרִיעֹת
,curtains the | you and join shall | ;gold | hooks of | fifty | you And make shall | its sister-piece

6213 259 4908 1961 7165 269 802
7 אִשָּׁה אֶל־אֲחֹתָהּ בַּקְּרָסִים וְהָיָה הַמִּשְׁכָּן אֶחָד׃ וְעָשִׂיתָ
you And make shall | .one | tabernacle | it and be shall | the by ,hooks | its ,sister-piece | to | each

3407 6240 6249 4908 5921 168 5795 3407
יְרִיעֹת עִזִּים לְאֹהֶל עַל־הַמִּשְׁכָּן עַשְׁתֵּי־עֶשְׂרֵה יְרִיעֹת
curtains | eleven | the ;tabernacle | over | a for tent | goat's (hair) | curtains of

520 7970 259 3407 753 6213
8 תַּעֲשֶׂה אֹתָם׃ אֹרֶךְ ׀ הַיְרִיעָה הָאַחַת שְׁלֹשִׁים בָּאַמָּה
the by ;cubit | thirty | ,one | curtain the | the of length | ;them | shall you make

6249 259 4060 259 3407 520 702 7341
וְרֹחַב אַרְבַּע בָּאַמָּה הַיְרִיעָה הָאֶחָת מִדָּה אַחַת לְעַשְׁתֵּי
to the | one | measure | ;one | the (for) curtain | the by cubit | four | the and ,width

905 3407 2568 2266 3407 6240
9 עֶשְׂרֵה יְרִיעֹת׃ וְחִבַּרְתָּ אֶת־חֲמֵשׁ הַיְרִיעֹת לְבָד וְאֶת־
and | separately | the curtains | five | you And join shall | .curtains | eleven

4136 8337 3407 3717 905 3407 8345
שֵׁשׁ הַיְרִיעֹת לְבָד וְכָפַלְתָּ אֶת־הַיְרִיעָה הַשִּׁשִּׁית אֶל־מוּל
front the of | six | the curtains | you and double shall | ;separately | the curtains | six

3407 8193 3924 2572 6213 168 6440
10 פְּנֵי הָאֹהֶל׃ וְעָשִׂיתָ חֲמִשִּׁים לֻלָאֹת עַל שְׂפַת הַיְרִיעָה
the curtain | the of edge | on | loops | fifty | you And make shall | the .tabernacle | before

8193 3924 2572 2279 7020 259
הָאֶחָת הַקִּיצֹנָה בַּחֹבָרֶת וַחֲמִשִּׁים לֻלָאֹת עַל שְׂפַת
edge the of | on | loops | fifty and | the at ;juncture | last the | ,one

2572 5178 7165 6213 8145 2279 3407
11 הַיְרִיעָה הַחֹבֶרֶת הַשֵּׁנִית׃ וְעָשִׂיתָ קַרְסֵי נְחֹשֶׁת חֲמִשִּׁים
;fifty | bronze | hooks of | you And make shall | .second | joins that | the curtain

1961 168 2266 3924 7165 935
וְהֵבֵאתָ אֶת־הַקְּרָסִים בַּלֻּלָאֹת וְחִבַּרְתָּ אֶת־הָאֹהֶל וְהָיָה
it and be shall | ,tent the | join and together | the in loops | hooks the | out | And make go shall

5736 3407 2677 168 3407 5736 5629 259
12 אֶחָד׃ וְסֶרַח הָעֹדֵף בִּירִיעֹת הָאֹהֶל חֲצִי הַיְרִיעָה הָעֹדֶפֶת
that ,remains | the curtain | half | the tent | of curtains | rest the | the and of part overlapping | ,one

2088 520 2088 520 4908 268 5628
13 תִּסְרַח עַל אֲחֹרֵי הַמִּשְׁכָּן׃ וְהָאַמָּה מִזֶּה וְהָאַמָּה מִזֶּה
from (side) that | the and cubit | from (side) this | the And cubit | the .tabernacle | back the of | on | shall hang

4908 5785 5628 1961 168 3407 753 5736
בָּעֹדֵף בְּאֹרֶךְ יְרִיעֹת הָאֹהֶל יִהְיֶה סָרוּחַ עַל־צִדֵּי הַמִּשְׁכָּן
the tabernacle | of sides the | over | hung | shall be | tent the | the of curtains | the in of length | that remains

this and from that *side*, to
cover it. [14]And you shall
make a cover for the tent of
rams' skins dyed red, and a
covering of dugong skins
from above.

[15]And you shall make the
boards for the tabernacle *of*
acacia-wood standing up.
[16]Ten cubits shall be the
length of one board; and a
cubit and a half the width of
one board. [17]Two *pins*
shall be in one board, each
connected to her sister. So
you shall do to all the
boards of the tabernacle.
[18]And you shall make the
boards for the tabernacle;
twenty boards on the south
side, southward. [19]And you
shall make forty sockets of
silver *for* the twenty boards;
two sockets under the one
board, for its two *pins*, and
two sockets under the one
board for its two *pins*.
[20]And for the second side of
the tabernacle, on the north
side twenty boards; [21]and
their forty silver sockets;
two sockets under the one
board, and two sockets
under the one board. [22]And
you shall make six boards
for the sides of the
tabernacle westward. [23]And
you shall make two boards
for the corners of the
tabernacle, in the sides.
[24]And they shall be double
from beneath. And in like
manner they shall be
complete on the top, to the
one ring. So it shall be to
both of them; they shall be
for the two corners. [25]And
there shall be eight boards,
and their silver sockets,
sixteen sockets, two soc-
kets under the one board,

352 5985 168 4372 6213 3680 2088 2088
14 מִזֶּה וּמִזֶּה לְכַסֹּתוֹ׃ וְעָשִׂיתָ מִכְסֶה לָאֹהֶל עֹרֹת אֵלִם
rams' skins the for of tent cover a you And make shall cover to .it from and (side) that from (side) this

5921 8476 5785 4372 119
מְאָדָּמִים וּמִכְסֵה עֹרֹת תְּחָשִׁים מִלְמָעְלָה׃
.above from dugong skins a and of cover ;red dyed

6235 5975 7848 6086 4908 7175 6213
15
16 וְעָשִׂיתָ אֶת־הַקְּרָשִׁים לַמִּשְׁכָּן עֲצֵי שִׁטִּים עֹמְדִים׃ עֶשֶׂר
Ten standing up acacia- (of) wood the for tabernacle boards the you And make shall

7175 7341 520 2677 520 7175 753 520
אַמּוֹת אֹרֶךְ הַקָּרֶשׁ וְאַמָּה וַחֲצִי הָאַמָּה רֹחַב הַקָּרֶשׁ
the board the of width a of cubit a and half a and cubit one ;board the of length cubits (be shall)

802 7947 259 7175 3489 8147 259
17 הָאֶחָד׃ שְׁתֵּי יָדוֹת לַקֶּרֶשׁ הָאֶחָד מְשֻׁלָּבֹת אִשָּׁה אֶל־
to each connected ,one for board pins (be shall) two ,one

7175 6213 4908 7175 6213 269
18 אֲחֹתָהּ כֵּן תַּעֲשֶׂה לְכֹל קַרְשֵׁי הַמִּשְׁכָּן׃ וְעָשִׂיתָ אֶת־הַקְּרָשִׁים
boards the you And make shall the .tabernacle the of boards all to do shall you so its ;sister-piece

703 8486 5045 6285 7175 6242 4908
19 לַמִּשְׁכָּן עֶשְׂרִים קֶרֶשׁ לִפְאַת נֶגְבָּה תֵימָנָה׃ וְאַרְבָּעִים
forty And .southward ,south side the for boards twenty the for ;tabernacle

8478 134 8147 7175 6242 8478 6213 3701 209
אַדְנֵי־כֶסֶף תַּעֲשֶׂה תַּחַת עֶשְׂרִים הַקָּרֶשׁ שְׁנֵי אֲדָנִים תַּחַת
under sockets two ;boards the twenty under shall you make silver sockets of

7175 8478 134 8147 3489 8147 259 7175
הַקֶּרֶשׁ הָאֶחָד לִשְׁתֵּי יְדֹתָיו וּשְׁנֵי אֲדָנִים תַּחַת־הַקֶּרֶשׁ
the board under sockets and two its ,pins two for ,one the board

6828 6285 8145 4908 6763 3489 8147 259
20 הָאֶחָד לִשְׁתֵּי יְדֹתָיו׃ וּלְצֶלַע הַמִּשְׁכָּן הַשֵּׁנִית לִפְאַת צָפוֹן
north the on side ,second the tabernacle of side the for And .pins its two for one

8478 134 8147 3701 134 703 7175 6242
21 עֶשְׂרִים קָרֶשׁ׃ וְאַרְבָּעִים אַדְנֵיהֶם כָּסֶף שְׁנֵי אֲדָנִים תַּחַת
under sockets two ,silver their of sockets forty and ,boards twenty

3411 259 7175 8478 134 8147 259 7175
22 הַקֶּרֶשׁ הָאֶחָד וּשְׁנֵי אֲדָנִים תַּחַת הַקֶּרֶשׁ הָאֶחָד׃ וּלְיַרְכְּתֵי
the for And of sides .one the board under sockets and two ,one the board

6213 7175 8147 7175 8337 6213 3220 4908
23 הַמִּשְׁכָּן יָמָּה תַּעֲשֶׂה שִׁשָּׁה קְרָשִׁים׃ וּשְׁנֵי קְרָשִׁים תַּעֲשֶׂה
shall you make boards And two .boards six shall you make west- ward the tabernacle

3162 4295 8382 1961 3411 4908 4742
24 לִמְקֻצְעֹת הַמִּשְׁכָּן בַּיַּרְכָתָיִם׃ וְיִהְיוּ תֹאֲמִם מִלְּמַטָּה וְיַחְדָּו
and together from ;below double they And be shall the in .sides the tabernacle the for of corners

1961 259 2885 7175 5921 8382 1961
יִהְיוּ תַמִּים עַל־רֹאשׁוֹ אֶל־הַטַּבַּעַת הָאֶחָת כֵּן יִהְיֶה
shall it be so ;one ring the to its head on complete they be shall

7175 8083 1961 1961 4740 8147 8147
25 לִשְׁנֵיהֶם לִשְׁנֵי הַמִּקְצֹעֹת יִהְיוּ׃ וְהָיוּ שְׁמֹנָה קְרָשִׁים
,boards eight And be shall they be shall the corners two for both to ;them of

3478 7175 8147 134 6240 8337 3701 134
וְאַדְנֵיהֶם כֶּסֶף שִׁשָּׁה עָשָׂר אֲדָנִים שְׁנֵי אֲדָנִים תַּחַת
under sockets two ;sockets sixteen ,silver their and sockets

and two sockets under the
one board. 26 And you shall
make bars of acacia-wood;
five to the boards of the one
side of the tabernacle;
27 and five bars to the boards
of the second side of the
tabernacle; and five bars to
the boards of the side of the
tabernacle, for the rear,
westward. 28 And *there*
shall be a middle bar in the
midst of the boards, going
through from end to end.
29 And you shall overlay the
boards *with* gold, and you
shall make their rings gold,
housings for the bars. And
you shall overlay the bars
with gold. 30 And you shall
set up the tabernacle ac-
cording to the decree which
you were shown in the
mountain. 31 And you shall
make a veil *of* blue and
purple and crimson, and
twined linen. One shall
make it by the work of the
skilled workman, *with*
cherubs. 32 And you shall
put it on four pillars of
acacia-wood overlaid *with*
gold, their nails gold, on
four sockets of silver.

33 And you shall hang the
veil under the hooks. And
you shall bring the ark of the
testimony there inside to
the veil. And the veil shall
divide for you between the
holy place and the Holy of
Holies. 34 And you shall put
the mercy-seat on the ark of
the testimony, in the Holy of
Holies. 35 And you shall set
the table outside the veil,
and the lamp across from
the table on the side of the
tabernacle southward. And
you shall put the table on
the north side.
36 And you shall make a
screen for the door of the
tent of blue, and of purple

6213 259 7175 3478 134 8147 259 7175
26 הַקֶּרֶשׁ הָאֶחָד וּשְׁנֵי אֲדָנִים תַּחַת הַקֶּרֶשׁ הָאֶחָד׃ וְעָשִׂיתָ
you And .one the under sockets two and ,one the
make shall board board

259 4908 6763 7175 2568 7848 6086 1280
בְרִיחִם עֲצֵי שִׁטִּים חֲמִשָּׁה לְקַרְשֵׁי צֶלַע־הַמִּשְׁכָּן הָאֶחָד׃
;one the the of side the to five ;acacia· wood of bars
tabernacle of boards

2568 8145 4908 6763 7175 1280 2568
27 וַחֲמִשָּׁה בְרִיחִם לְקַרְשֵׁי צֶלַע־הַמִּשְׁכָּן הַשֵּׁנִית וַחֲמִשָּׁה
five and the the of side the for bars five and
;second tabernacle of boards

1280 3220 3411 4908 6763 7175 1280
28 בְרִיחִם לְקַרְשֵׁי צֶלַע הַמִּשְׁכָּן לַיַּרְכָתַיִם יָמָּה׃ וְהַבְּרִיחַ
a And west- the for the side the the to bars
bar .ward rear tabernacle of of boards

7097 7097 1272 7175 8432 1280
הַתִּיכֹן בְּתוֹךְ הַקְּרָשִׁים מַבְרִחַ מִן־הַקָּצֶה אֶל־הַקָּצֶה׃
.end to end from going ;boards the the in middle a
through of midst bar

2091 6213 2885 2091 6823 7175
29 וְאֶת־הַקְּרָשִׁים תְּצַפֶּה זָהָב וְאֶת־טַבְּעֹתֵיהֶם תַּעֲשֶׂה זָהָב
,gold shall you rings their and (with) shall you boards the And
make gold overlay

6965 2091 1280 6823 1280 1004
30 בָּתִּים לַבְּרִיחִם וְצִפִּיתָ אֶת־הַבְּרִיחִם זָהָב׃ וַהֲקֵמֹתָ אֶת־
you And (with) bars the you and the for housing
up set shall .gold overlay shall ;bars

6213 2022 7200 834 4941 4908
31 הַמִּשְׁכָּן כְּמִשְׁפָּטוֹ אֲשֶׁר הָרְאֵיתָ בָּהָר׃ חמישי וְעָשִׂיתָ
you And the in were you which to according the
make shall .mountain shown decree the tabernacle

4639 7806 8336 8144 8438 713 8504 6532
פָרֹכֶת תְּכֵלֶת וְאַרְגָּמָן וְתוֹלַעַת שָׁנִי וְשֵׁשׁ מָשְׁזָר מַעֲשֵׂה
the by ;twined and and and blue ,veil a
of work linen crimson purple

702 5921 5414 3742 6213 2803
32 חֹשֵׁב יַעֲשֶׂה אֹתָהּ כְּרֻבִים׃ וְנָתַתָּה אֹתָהּ עַל־אַרְבָּעָה
four on it you And (with) ,it shall one the
put shall .cherubs make artisan

134 702 2091 2053 2091 6823 7848 5982
עַמּוּדֵי שִׁטִּים מְצֻפִּים זָהָב וָוֵיהֶם זָהָב עַל־אַרְבָּעָה אַדְנֵי־
sockets four on ,gold their (with) overlaid acacia· pillars
of nails gold ,wood of

8033 935 7165 8478 6532 5414 3701
33 כָסֶף׃ וְנָתַתָּה אֶת־הַפָּרֹכֶת תַּחַת הַקְּרָסִים וְהֵבֵאתָ שָׁמָּה
there you and ,hooks the under veil the you And .silver
bring shall hang shall

6532 914 5715 727 6532 1004
מִבֵּית לַפָּרֹכֶת אֵת אֲרוֹן הָעֵדוּת וְהִבְדִּילָה הַפָּרֹכֶת לָכֶם
for veil the shall and the ark the the to
you divide ;testimony of veil

5921 3726 5414 6944 6944 996 6944 996
34 בֵּין הַקֹּדֶשׁ וּבֵין קֹדֶשׁ הַקֳּדָשִׁים׃ וְנָתַתָּ אֶת־הַכַּפֹּרֶת עַל
on the you And .holies the and the between
mercy-seat set shall of holy place holy

2351 7999 7760 6944 6944 5715 727
35 אֲרוֹן הָעֵדֻת בְּקֹדֶשׁ הַקֳּדָשִׁים׃ וְשַׂמְתָּ אֶת־הַשֻּׁלְחָן מִחוּץ
outside table the you And .holies the in the the
set shall of holy ,testimony of ark

8486 4908 6763 7979 5227 5216 6532
לַפָּרֹכֶת וְאֶת־הַמְּנֹרָה נֹכַח הַשֻּׁלְחָן עַל צֶלַע הַמִּשְׁכָּן תֵּימָנָה
south- the side the on table the across the and ,veil the
;ward tabernacle of from lamp

168 6607 4539 6213 6828 6763 5414 7979
36 וְהַשֻּׁלְחָן תִּתֵּן עַל־צֶלַע צָפוֹן׃ וְעָשִׂיתָ מָסָךְ לְפֶתַח הָאֹהֶל
,tent the the for a you And .north the on shall you the and
of door screen make shall side put table

and crimson, and twined linen, the work of an embroiderer. [37]And you shall make five pillars of acacia-wood for the screen. And you shall overlay them *with* gold, their nails gold. And you shall cast for them five sockets of bronze.

תְּכֵלֶת וְאַרְגָּמָן וְתוֹלַעַת שָׁנִי וְשֵׁשׁ מָשְׁזָר מַעֲשֵׂה רֹקֵם׃

an embroiderer's work ,twined linen and crimson and of and purple ,blue of

37 וְעָשִׂיתָ לַמָּסָךְ חֲמִשָּׁה עַמּוּדֵי שִׁטִּים וְצִפִּיתָ אֹתָם זָהָב וָוֵיהֶם

and (with) nails their ,gold them you and overlay shall acacia- wood pillars of five the for screen you And make shall

זָהָב וְיָצַקְתָּ לָהֶם חֲמִשָּׁה אַדְנֵי נְחֹשֶׁת׃ ס

.bronze sockets of five for them you and cast shall ,gold

CAP. XXVII כז

CHAPTER 27

[1]And you shall make the altar of acacia timbers; five cubits long and five cubits wide. The altar shall be square, and its height three cubits. [2]And you shall make its horns on its four corners. It's horns shall be *a part* of itself. And you shall overlay it *with* bronze. [3]And you shall make its pots to remove its ashes, and its shovels, and its sacrificial bowls, and its flesh-forks, and its pans. You shall make all its vessels to be bronze. [4]And you shall make a grating for it, a network of bronze. And you shall make four rings of bronze on the four ends of the net. [5]And you shall put it under the ledge of the altar from beneath. And the net shall be as far as half of the altar. [6]And you shall make poles for the altar, poles of acacia timbers. And you shall overlay them *with* bronze. [7]And its poles shall be brought into the rings. And the poles shall be on the two sides of the altar, for carrying it. [8]You shall make it hollow *with* boards; as *He* showed you in the mountain, so they shall make it.

[9]And you shall make the court of the tabernacle; for the south side southward, hangings for the court *of* twined linen, a hundred by

1 וְעָשִׂיתָ אֶת־הַמִּזְבֵּחַ עֲצֵי שִׁטִּים חָמֵשׁ אַמּוֹת אֹרֶךְ וְחָמֵשׁ

and five ,long cubits five ;acacia- timbers of altar the you And make shall

אַמּוֹת רֹחַב רָבוּעַ יִהְיֶה הַמִּזְבֵּחַ וְשָׁלֹשׁ אַמּוֹת קֹמָתוֹ׃

its height cubits three and ;altar the be shall square ;wide cubits

2 וְעָשִׂיתָ קַרְנֹתָיו עַל אַרְבַּע פִּנֹּתָיו מִמֶּנּוּ תִּהְיֶיןָ קַרְנֹתָיו

its ;horns shall it be (part a) itself of its ,corners four on horns it you And make shall

3 וְצִפִּיתָ אֹתוֹ נְחֹשֶׁת׃ וְעָשִׂיתָ סִּירֹתָיו לְדַשְּׁנוֹ וְיָעָיו וּמִזְרְקֹתָיו

sacri- ficial ,bowls its and ,shovels its and remove to ,ashes its pots its you And make shall (with) .bronze it you and overlay shall

4 וּמִזְלְגֹתָיו וּמַחְתֹּתָיו לְכָל־כֵּלָיו תַּעֲשֶׂה נְחֹשֶׁת׃ וְעָשִׂיתָ

you And make shall (of) .bronze shall you make its vessels all its and ;pans its and ,flesh-forks

לּוֹ מִכְבָּר מַעֲשֵׂה רֶשֶׁת נְחֹשֶׁת וְעָשִׂיתָ עַל־הָרֶשֶׁת אַרְבַּע

four net the on you and make shall ;bronze a net- work of a grating for it

5 טַבְּעֹת נְחֹשֶׁת עַל אַרְבַּע קְצוֹתָיו׃ וְנָתַתָּה אֹתָהּ תַּחַת

under it you And put shall its .corners four on ,bronze of rings

כַּרְכֹּב הַמִּזְבֵּחַ מִלְּמָטָּה וְהָיְתָה הָרֶשֶׁת עַד חֲצִי הַמִּזְבֵּחַ׃

.altar the half of far as as net the shall and be from ;beneath altar the the of ledge

6 וְעָשִׂיתָ בַדִּים לַמִּזְבֵּחַ בַּדֵּי עֲצֵי שִׁטִּים וְצִפִּיתָ אֹתָם נְחֹשֶׁת׃

(with) .bronze them you and overlay shall ;acacia- timbers of poles the for ,altar poles you And make shall

7 וְהוּבָא אֶת־בַּדָּיו בַּטַּבָּעֹת וְהָיוּ הַבַּדִּים עַל־שְׁתֵּי צַלְעֹת

the of sides two on poles the and be shall the into ;rings poles its shall And brought be

8 הַמִּזְבֵּחַ בִּשְׂאֵת אֹתוֹ׃ נְבוּב לֻחֹת תַּעֲשֶׂה אֹתוֹ כַּאֲשֶׁר

as ;it shall you make polished hollow boards ,it for carrying altar the

9 הֶרְאָה אֹתְךָ בָּהָר כֵּן יַעֲשׂוּ׃ ס וְעָשִׂיתָ אֵת חֲצַר

the of court you And make shall shall they so .(it) make the in ,mountain you showed

הַמִּשְׁכָּן לִפְאַת נֶגֶב־תֵּימָנָה קְלָעִים לֶחָצֵר שֵׁשׁ מָשְׁזָר

,twined (of) linen the for court hangings south- ,ward ,south the for side the ;tabernacle the cubit *in* length, for the one side. [10]And its pillars *shall be* twenty, and their sockets twenty *in* bronze; the nails of the pillars and their bands *of* silver. [11]And so for the north side in length, hangings a hundred *in* length; and its pillars twenty, and their sockets twenty *in* bronze; the nails of the pillars and their bands *of* silver. [12]And the width of the west side of the court *shall have* fifty cubits *of* hangings; their pillars ten, and their sockets ten. [13]And the width of the court for the east side eastward, fifty cubits; [14]and the hangings to the side fifteen cubits; their pillars three, and their sockets three. [15]And to the hangings for the second side, fifteen; their pillars three, and their sockets three. [16]And for the gate of the court, a screen *of* twenty cubits, blue and purple and crimson, and twined linen, the work of an embroiderer; their pillars four, and their sockets four. [17]All the pillars of the court round about *shall be* banded *with* silver, their nails silver, and their sockets bronze. [18]The length of the court *shall be* a hundred by the cubit, and the width fifty by fifty, and the height five cubits, twined linen; and their sockets bronze. [19]As to all the vessels of the tabernacle, in all its service, and all its pins, and all the pins of the court, *they shall be* bronze.

[20]And you shall command the sons of Israel, and let them bring to you pure olive oil beaten for the light,

134 6242 5982 259 6285 753 520 3967
10 מֵאָה בָּאַמָּה אֹרֶךְ לַפֵּאָה הָאֶחָת׃ וְעַמֻּדָיו עֶשְׂרִים וְאַדְנֵיהֶם
their and sockets | (be shall) ,twenty | its And pillars | .one | the for side | (in) length | the by cubit | a hundred

6285 3651 3701 2838 5982 2053 5178 6242
11 עֶשְׂרִים נְחֹשֶׁת וָוֵי הָעַמֻּדִים וַחֲשֻׁקֵיהֶם כָּסֶף׃ וְכֵן לִפְאַת
the for side | so And | (of) ,silver | their and bands | pillars the | the of nails | (or) ;bronze | twenty

134 6242 5982 753 3967 7050 753 6828
צָפוֹן בָּאֹרֶךְ קְלָעִים מֵאָה אֹרֶךְ וְעַמֻּדָו עֶשְׂרִים וְאַדְנֵיהֶם
their and sockets | twenty | its and pillars | (in) ;length | a hundred | hangings | in length | north

2691 7341 3701 2838 5982 2053 5178 6242
12 עֶשְׂרִים נְחֹשֶׁת וָוֵי הָעַמֻּדִים וַחֲשֻׁקֵיהֶם כָּסֶף׃ וְרֹחַב הֶחָצֵר
the court | the and of width | (of) ,silver | their and bands | the pillars | the of nails | (of) ;bronze | twenty

134 6235 5982 520 2572 7050 3220 6285
לִפְאַת־יָם קְלָעִים חֲמִשִּׁים אַמָּה עַמֻּדֵיהֶם עֲשָׂרָה וְאַדְנֵיהֶם
their and sockets | ten | their pillars | ;cubits | fifty | (have shall) (of) hangings | the on west side

2572 4217 6924 6285 2691 7341 6235
13 עֲשָׂרָה׃ וְרֹחַב הֶחָצֵר לִפְאַת קֵדְמָה מִזְרָחָה חֲמִשִּׁים
fifty | ,eastward | east | the for side | court the | the And of width | .ten

598 3802 7050 520 6240 2568 520
14 אַמָּה׃ וַחֲמֵשׁ עֶשְׂרֵה אַמָּה קְלָעִים לַכָּתֵף עַמֻּדֵיהֶם
pillars their | the to ;side | the hangings | cubits | fifteen and | ;cubits

6240 2568 8145 3802 7969 134 7969
15 שְׁלֹשָׁה וְאַדְנֵיהֶם שְׁלֹשָׁה׃ וְלַכָּתֵף הַשֵּׁנִית חֲמֵשׁ עֶשְׂרֵה
fifteen | second | for And side the | .three | their and sockets | three

2691 8179 7969 134 7969 5982 7050
16 קְלָעִים עַמֻּדֵיהֶם שְׁלֹשָׁה וְאַדְנֵיהֶם שְׁלֹשָׁה׃ וּלְשַׁעַר הֶחָצֵר
,court the | for And of gate the | .three | their and sockets | ,three | their pillars | the (to) ;hangings

8336 8144 8438 713 8504 520 6242 4539
מָסָךְ עֶשְׂרִים אַמָּה תְּכֵלֶת וְאַרְגָּמָן וְתוֹלַעַת שָׁנִי וְשֵׁשׁ
and linen | crimson | and purple and | blue | ,cubits | twenty | a (of) screen

702 134 702 5982 7551 4639 7806
מָשְׁזָר מַעֲשֵׂה רֹקֵם עַמֻּדֵיהֶם אַרְבָּעָה וְאַדְנֵיהֶם אַרְבָּעָה׃
.four | their and sockets | four | their pillars | an ;embroiderer's | ,work | twined

3701 2053 3701 2836 5439 2691 5982
17 כָּל־עַמּוּדֵי הֶחָצֵר סָבִיב מְחֻשָּׁקִים כֶּסֶף וָוֵיהֶם כָּסֶף
,silver | their nails | (with) ,silver | (be shall) banded | round about | court the | the of pillars | All

2572 7341 520 3967 2691 753 5178 134
18 וְאַדְנֵיהֶם נְחֹשֶׁת׃ אֹרֶךְ הֶחָצֵר מֵאָה בָאַמָּה וְרֹחַב חֲמִשִּׁים בַּחֲמִשִּׁים
fifty | the and width | the by ,cubit | (be shall) hundred a | the court | The of length | .bronze | their and sockets

5178 134 7806 8336 520 2568 6967 2572
בַּחֲמִשִּׁים וְקֹמָה חָמֵשׁ אַמּוֹת שֵׁשׁ מָשְׁזָר וְאַדְנֵיהֶם נְחֹשֶׁת׃
.bronze | their and sockets | ;twined | linen | ,cubits | five | the and height | ,fifty by

3489 3605 5489 3605 5656 3605 4908 3627 3605
19 לְכֹל כְּלֵי הַמִּשְׁכָּן בְּכֹל עֲבֹדָתוֹ וְכָל־יְתֵדֹתָיו וְכָל־יִתְדֹת
pins the of | and all | ,pins its | all and | its ,service | all in | taber- ,nacle | the of vessels | the | to As all

5178 2691
הֶחָצֵר נְחֹשֶׁת׃
(be shall they) .bronze | the court

2134/2132 8081 3947 3478 1121 6680
20 וְאַתָּה תְּצַוֶּה אֶת־בְּנֵי יִשְׂרָאֵל וְיִקְחוּ אֵלֶיךָ שֶׁמֶן זַיִת זָךְ
pure olive | oil of | you to | let and bring them | ,Israel | the of sons | shall command | you And

to set up lamps perpetually. [21]In the tabernacle of the congregation from outside the veil which *is* by the testimony, Aaron and his sons shall arrange them from evening until morning before Jehovah; a never-ending statute for their generations, from the sons of Israel.

כָּתִית לַמָּאוֹר לְהַעֲלֹת נֵר תָּמִיד׃ בְּאֹהֶל מוֹעֵד מִחוּץ 21
לַפָּרֹכֶת אֲשֶׁר עַל־הָעֵדֻת יַעֲרֹךְ אֹתוֹ אַהֲרֹן וּבָנָיו מֵעֶרֶב עַד־
בֹּקֶר לִפְנֵי יְהוָה חֻקַּת עוֹלָם לְדֹרֹתָם מֵאֵת בְּנֵי יִשְׂרָאֵל׃ ס

CAP. XXVIII כח

CHAPTER 28

[1]And you shall take to yourself your brother Aaron, and his sons with him, from among the sons of Israel, for him to serve as priest to Me; Aaron, Nadab, and Abihu, Eleazar, and Ithamar, the sons of Aaron. [2]And you shall make holy garments for your brother Aaron, for glory and for beauty. [3]And you shall speak to all the wise-hearted whom I have filled with a spirit of wisdom; and they shall make the garments of Aaron to sanctify him for his serving as priest to Me.

[4]And these *are* the garments which they shall make: a *breast*pocket, and a tunic of woven stuff, a miter and a girdle. And they shall make holy garments for your brother Aaron and for his sons, even for him to serve as priest to Me.

[5]And they shall take the gold, and the blue, and the purple, and the crimson, and the bleached *linen*.

[6]And they shall make the ephod of gold, blue, and purple, crimson and bleached, twined *linen*, the work of a weaver. It shall have two shoulder-pieces at its two ends; and it shall be joined together. [8]And the band of the ephod which *is* on it, like its work, shall be of it, gold, blue, and purple, and crimson, and bleached, twined *linen*.

1 וְאַתָּה הַקְרֵב אֵלֶיךָ אֶת־אַהֲרֹן אָחִיךָ וְאֶת־בָּנָיו אִתּוֹ מִתּוֹךְ
בְּנֵי יִשְׂרָאֵל לְכַהֲנוֹ־לִי אַהֲרֹן נָדָב וַאֲבִיהוּא אֶלְעָזָר וְאִיתָמָר
2 בְּנֵי אַהֲרֹן׃ וְעָשִׂיתָ בִגְדֵי־קֹדֶשׁ לְאַהֲרֹן אָחִיךָ לְכָבוֹד
3 וּלְתִפְאָרֶת׃ וְאַתָּה תְּדַבֵּר אֶל־כָּל־חַכְמֵי־לֵב אֲשֶׁר מִלֵּאתִיו
רוּחַ חָכְמָה וְעָשׂוּ אֶת־בִּגְדֵי אַהֲרֹן לְקַדְּשׁוֹ לְכַהֲנוֹ־לִי׃
4 וְאֵלֶּה הַבְּגָדִים אֲשֶׁר יַעֲשׂוּ חֹשֶׁן וְאֵפוֹד וּמְעִיל וּכְתֹנֶת
תַּשְׁבֵּץ מִצְנֶפֶת וְאַבְנֵט וְעָשׂוּ בִגְדֵי־קֹדֶשׁ לְאַהֲרֹן אָחִיךָ
5 וּלְבָנָיו לְכַהֲנוֹ־לִי׃ וְהֵם יִקְחוּ אֶת־הַזָּהָב וְאֶת־הַתְּכֵלֶת
וְאֶת־הָאַרְגָּמָן וְאֶת־תּוֹלַעַת הַשָּׁנִי וְאֶת־הַשֵּׁשׁ׃
6 וְעָשׂוּ אֶת־הָאֵפֹד זָהָב תְּכֵלֶת וְאַרְגָּמָן תּוֹלַעַת שָׁנִי וְשֵׁשׁ
7 מָשְׁזָר מַעֲשֵׂה חֹשֵׁב׃ שְׁתֵּי כְתֵפֹת חֹבְרֹת יִהְיֶה־לּוֹ אֶל־
8 שְׁנֵי קְצוֹתָיו וְחֻבָּר׃ וְחֵשֶׁב אֲפֻדָּתוֹ אֲשֶׁר עָלָיו כְּמַעֲשֵׂהוּ
מִמֶּנּוּ יִהְיֶה זָהָב תְּכֵלֶת וְאַרְגָּמָן וְתוֹלַעַת שָׁנִי וְשֵׁשׁ

[9]And you shall take two
onyx stones; and you shall
engrave on them the names
of the sons of Israel.
[10]Six of their names *shall be*
on the one stone, and six of
the remaining names on the
second stone, according to
their birth. [11]You shall
engrave the two stones, the
work of an stone-engraver,
the engravings of a signet,
according to the names of
the sons of Israel; you shall
make them set *in* plaited
work of gold. [12]And you
shall put the two stones on
the shoulder-pieces of the
ephod, stones of remem-
brance for the sons of Israel.
And Aaron shall bear their
names before the face of
Jehovah, on his two
shoulders for a remem-
brance. [13]And you shall
make plaited work of gold:
[14]and two chains of pure
gold, you shall make them
woven work, a work of cord;
and you shall put chains of
the cords on the plaited
work.

[15]And you shall make a
*breast*pocket of judg-
ment, a work of a weaver,
like the work of the
ephod you shall make it:
gold, blue, and purple,
and crimson, and
bleached, twined *linen*
you shall make it. [16]It
shall be square, being
doubled; its length a span
and its width a span.
[17]And you shall fill in it
settings of stones, four
rows of stones: a row of
sardius, topaz and car-
buncle *shall be* the first
row. [18]And the second
row: emerald, sapphire
and jasper. [19]And the
third row: opal, agate and
amethyst. [20]And the
fourth row: chrysolyte,
onyx and beryl. They
shall be plaited with
gold in their settings.

21 והאבנים תהיין על־שמת בני־ישראל שתים עשרה על־
שמתם פתוחי חותם איש על־שמו תהיין לשני עשר
22 שבט׃ ועשית על־החשן שרשת גבלת מעשה עבת זהב
23 טהור׃ ועשית על־החשן שתי טבעות זהב ונתת את־
24 שתי הטבעות על־שני קצות החשן׃ ונתתה את־שתי
25 עבתת הזהב על־שתי הטבעת אל־קצות החשן׃ ואת
שתי קצות שתי העבתת תתן על־שתי המשבצות ונתתה
26 על־כתפות האפד אל־מול פניו׃ ועשית שתי טבעות זהב
ושמת אתם על־שני קצות החשן על־שפתו אשר אל־
27 עבר האפד ביתה׃ ועשית שתי טבעות זהב ונתתה
אתם על־שתי כתפות האפוד מלמטה ממול פניו לעמת
28 מחברתו ממעל לחשב האפוד׃ וירכסו את־החשן
מטבעתו אל־טבעת האפוד בפתיל תכלת להית על־
29 חשב האפוד ולא־יזח החשן מעל האפוד׃ ונשא אהרן
את־שמות בני־ישראל בחשן המשפט על־לבו בבאו אל־
30 הקדש לזכרן לפני־יהוה תמיד׃ ונתת אל־חשן המשפט
את־האורים ואת־התמים והיו על־לב אהרן בבאו לפני

21 And the stones shall be according to the names of the sons of Israel, twelve according to their names, the engraving of a signet; they shall be each according to his name for the twelve tribes. 22 And you shall make chains of woven work on the pocket, a work of cords, *in* pure gold. 23 And you shall make two rings of gold on the pocket. And you shall put the two rings on the two ends of the pocket. 24 And you shall put the two cords of gold on the two rings, at the end of the pocket. 25 And you shall put the two ends of the two cords on the two plaitings. And you shall put *them* on the shoulder-pieces of the ephod, to the front of it. 26 And you shall make two rings of gold, and you shall put them on the two ends of the pocket, on its edge, inward across from the ephod. 27 And you shall make two rings of gold, and you shall put them on the two shoulder-pieces of the ephod, from beneath, at its front, near its joining, above the band of the ephod.

28 And they shall fasten the pocket from its rings to the rings of the ephod; and the pocket may not move itself from the ephod. 29 And Aaron shall bear the names of the sons of Israel on the pocket of judgment on his heart, in his going into the holy place, for a memorial before the face of Jehovah continually. 30 And you shall put the Urim and the Thummim into the pocket of judgment. And they shall be on the heart of Aaron in his going

before the face of
Jehovah. And Aaron shall
bear the judgment of the
sons of Israel on his heart
before the face of
Jehovah continually.

[31]And you shall make
the robe of the ephod all
of blue. [32]And the mouth
in its top shall be in its
middle; a binding shall be
all around its mouth, of
woven work — it shall be
like the mouth of a
corselet; it may not be
torn. [33]And you shall make
pomegranates of blue and
purple and crimson on its
hem, all around on its hem;
also bells of gold *shall be*
among them all around: [34]a
bell of gold and a pome-
granate, a bell of gold and a
pomegrranate, on the hem
of the robe all around.
[35]And it shall be on Aaron
for ministering; and its
sound shall be heard in his
going into the holy place
before the face of Jehovah,
and in his coming out, that
he should not die.

[36]And you shall make a
plate of pure gold. And you
shall engrave on it the
engravings of a signet:
HOLINESS TO JEHOVAH.
[37]And you shall put a ribbon
of blue on it, and it shall be
on the miter, to the front of
the miter it shall be.
[38]And it shall be on Aaron's
forehead, and Aaron shall
bear the iniquity of the holy
things which will sanctify
the sons of Israel to all their
holy gifts. And it shall be on
his forehead continually, for
acceptance for them before
the face of Jehovah.

[39]And you shall weave
the tunic *of* bleached *linen*,
and you shall make a miter
of bleached *linen*, and you
shall make a girdle, the
work of an embroiderer.
[40]And you shall make tunics
for the sons of Aaron; and
you shall make girdles for
them; and you shall make
bonnets for them, for glory
and for beauty. [41]And you
shall clothe your brother
Aaron *with* them, and his
sons with him; and you

6213 3548/3547 6942 4390
42 וַעֲשֵׂה וְכִהֲנוּ לִי׃ אֹתָם וְקִדַּשְׁתָּ אֹתָם וּמִלֵּאתָ אֶת־יָדָם
And make .Me to priests as minister they and them you and sanctify shall ,them you and consecrate shall ,them

3409 5704 4975 6172 1320 3680 906/4370
לָהֶם מִכְנְסֵי־בָד לְכַסּוֹת בְּשַׂר עֶרְוָה מִמָּתְנַיִם וְעַד־יְרֵכַיִם
the thighs far as as the from loins naked- ,ness the of flesh cover to linen breeches for them

41-50 168 935 1121 175 1961 1961
43 יִהְיוּ׃ וְהָיוּ עַל־אַהֲרֹן וְעַל־בָּנָיו בְּבֹאָם ׀ אֶל־אֹהֶל מוֹעֵד אוֹ
or ,meeting the of tent into their in going his sons and on Aaron on they And be shall they .be shall

4191 5771 5375 6944 8334 4196 5066
בְגִשְׁתָּם אֶל־הַמִּזְבֵּחַ לְשָׁרֵת בַּקֹּדֶשׁ וְלֹא־יִשְׂאוּ עָוֺן וָמֵתוּ
and ;die iniquity they so and bear shall not the in ;sanctuary to minister altar the to their in approaching

310 2233 5769 2708
חֻקַּת עוֹלָם לוֹ וּלְזַרְעוֹ אַחֲרָיו׃ ס
after .him to and seed his to him never- ending a (is it) statute

CAP. XXIX כט

CHAPTER 29

3947 3547 6942 6213 834 1697 2088
1 וְזֶה הַדָּבָר אֲשֶׁר־תַּעֲשֶׂה לָהֶם לְקַדֵּשׁ אֹתָם לְכַהֵן לִי לְקַח
take :Me to priests as minister to them to sanctify to ,them shall you do which the thing And (is) this

4682 3899 8549 8147 352 1241/1121 259 6499
2 פַּר אֶחָד בֶּן־בָּקָר וְאֵילִם שְׁנַיִם תְּמִימִם׃ וְלֶחֶם מַצּוֹת
unlea- ,vened and bread ;perfect two and rams the herd the of son ,one bullock

8081 4886 4682 7550 8081 1101 4682 2471
וְחַלֹּת מַצֹּת בְּלוּלֹת בַּשֶּׁמֶן וּרְקִיקֵי מַצּוֹת מְשֻׁחִים בַּשָּׁמֶן
with ;oil anointed unlea- vened and wafers with ,oil poured over unlea- vened and cakes

259 5536 5414 6213 2406 5560
3 סֹלֶת חִטִּים תַּעֲשֶׂה אֹתָם׃ וְנָתַתָּ אוֹתָם עַל־סַל אֶחָד
one basket into them you And put shall .them shall you make wheat fine (of) of flour

352 8147 6499 5536 7126
4 וְהִקְרַבְתָּ אֹתָם בַּסָּל וְאֶת־הַפָּר וְאֵת שְׁנֵי הָאֵילִם׃ וְאֶת־
And .rams the two and the bullock and the in ,basket them shall and near bring

7364 4150 168 6607 3947 1121 175
אַהֲרֹן וְאֶת־בָּנָיו תַּקְרִיב אֶל־פֶּתַח אֹהֶל מוֹעֵד וְרָחַצְתָּ
you And wash shall the .meeting tent the of the of door to shall you near bring his sons and Aaron

175 3847 899 3947 4325
5 אֹתָם בַּמָּיִם׃ וְלָקַחְתָּ אֶת־הַבְּגָדִים וְהִלְבַּשְׁתָּ אֶת־אַהֲרֹן
Aaron you and clothe shall the ,garments you And take shall .water in them

2833 646 646 4598 3801
אֶת־הַכֻּתֹּנֶת וְאֵת מְעִיל הָאֵפֹד וְאֶת־הָאֵפֹד וְאֶת־הַחֹשֶׁן
the ;pocket and ,ephod the and the ,ephod robe the of and the ,tunic (with)

5414 7218 4701 7760 646 2805 640
6 וְאָפַדְתָּ לוֹ בְּחֵשֶׁב הָאֵפֹד׃ וְשַׂמְתָּ הַמִּצְנֶפֶת עַל־רֹאשׁוֹ וְנָתַתָּ
you and put shall his :head on miter the you And put shall the .ephod the with of band to him it bind will you and

4888 8081 3947 4701 5921 6944 5145
7 אֶת־נֵזֶר הַקֹּדֶשׁ עַל־הַמִּצְנָפֶת׃ וְלָקַחְתָּ אֶת־שֶׁמֶן הַמִּשְׁחָה
anointing oil the of you And take shall .miter the on the holy crown

3947 1121 4886 7218 5921 3332
8 וְיָצַקְתָּ עַל־רֹאשׁוֹ וּמָשַׁחְתָּ אֹתוֹ׃ וְאֶת־בָּנָיו תַּקְרִיב
shall you take his sons And .him shall and anoint his head on shall and pour

shall anoint them, and you shall consecrate them, and you shall sanctify them. And they shall minister as priests to Me. [42]And make breeches of linen for them, to cover the flesh of nakedness, from the loins as far as the thighs they shall be. [43]And they shall be on Aaron and on his sons in their going into the tabernacle of the congregation or in their drawing near to the altar to minister in the holy place, and so that they shall not raise up iniquity and die. It is a perpetual statute to him and to his seed after him.

CHAPTER 29

[1]And this *is* the thing which you shall do to them, to sanctify them to minister as priests to Me: Take one bull, the son of the herd, and two perfect rams, [2]and unleavened bread, and unleavened cakes poured over with oil, and unleavened wafers anointed with oil — you shall make them *of* fine wheat flour. [3]And you shall put them into one basket and shall bring them near in the basket, and the bull and the two rams. [4]And you shall take Aaron and his sons to the door of the tabernacle of the congregation. And you shall wash them in water. [5]And you shall take the garments and you shall clothe Aaron *with* the tunic, and the robe of the ephod, and the ephod, and the *breast*pocket. And you shall bind it to him with the band of the ephod. [6]And you shall put the miter on his head; and you shall put the holy crown on the miter. [7]And you shall take the oil of anointing and shall pour on his head, and shall anoint him. [8]And you shall take his sons and

clothe them *with* tunics.
[9]And you shall gird them
with girdles, Aaron and his
sons; and you shall bind on
bonnets for them; and *it*
shall be a never-ending
statute for them *in* the
priest's office. And you shall
consecrate Aaron and his
sons. [10]And you shall bring
near the bullock before the
tabernacle of the congregation. And Aaron and his
sons shall lay their hands
on the head of the bullock.
[11]And you shall slaughter
the bullock before the face
of Jehovah, *at* the door of
the tabernacle of the congregation. [12]And you shall
take of the blood of the
bullock and shall put *it* on
the horns of the altar with
your finger. And you shall
pour out all the blood at the
base of the altar. [13]And you
shall take all the fat that
covers the inward parts,
and the lobe on the liver,
and the two kidneys, and
the fat on them, and you
shall burn on the altar.
[14]And you shall burn the
flesh of the bullock, and its
skin,and its dung, with fire
outside the camp; it *is* a sin
offering.

[15]And you shall take one
ram,and Aaron and his sons
shall lay their hands on the
head of the ram. [16]And you
shall slaughter the ram, and
you shall take its blood and
shall sprinkle *it* on the altar
all around. [17]And you shall
cut the ram into pieces; and
you shall wash its inward
parts, and its legs, and shall
place *them* on its pieces
and on its head. [18]And you
shall burn all the ram on the
altar; it *is* a burnt offering to
Jehovah, a soothing fra-
grance; it *is* a fire offering to
Jehovah.

[19]And you shall take the
second ram and Aaron and
his sons shall lay their
hands on the head of the
ram. [20]And you shall

1121 175 73 2296 3801 3847
9 וְהִלְבַּשְׁתָּם כֻּתֳּנֹת׃ וְחָגַרְתָּ אֹתָם אַבְנֵט אַהֲרֹן וּבָנָיו
his and ,sons | Aaron | (with) ,girdles | them | you And gird shall | (with) .tunics | shall you and them clothe

5769 2708 3550 1961 4021 2280
וְחָבַשְׁתָּ לָהֶם מִגְבָּעֹת וְהָיְתָה לָהֶם כְּהֻנָּה לְחֻקַּת עוֹלָם
never- ,ending | a for statute | priest's the office | for them | shall and be | ,bonnets | for them | you and bind shall

168 6440 6499 7126 1121 175 4390
10 וּמִלֵּאתָ יַד־אַהֲרֹן וְיַד־בָּנָיו׃ וְהִקְרַבְתָּ אֶת־הַפָּר לִפְנֵי אֹהֶל
the of tent | before | the bullock | you And near bring shall | his .sons | and | Aaron | shall you and consecrate

6499 7218 3027 1121 175 5564 4150
מוֹעֵד וְסָמַךְ אַהֲרֹן וּבָנָיו אֶת־יְדֵיהֶם עַל־רֹאשׁ הַפָּר׃
the .bullock | the of head | on | hands their | his and sons | Aaron | shall And lay | meet- .ing

3947 4150 168 6607 3068 6440 6499 7819
11 12 וְשָׁחַטְתָּ אֶת־הַפָּר לִפְנֵי יְהוָה פֶּתַח אֹהֶל מוֹעֵד׃ וְלָקַחְתָּ
you And take shall | .meeting | the of tent | the at of door | ,Jehovah before | the bullock | you And kill shall

3605 676 4196 7161 5921 5414 6499 1818
מִדַּם הַפָּר וְנָתַתָּה עַל־קַרְנֹת הַמִּזְבֵּחַ בְּאֶצְבָּעֶךָ וְאֶת־כָּל־
all | and | your with ;finger | altar the | the of horns | on | shall and (it) put | the bullock's | of blood

2459 3605 3947 4196 3247 413 8210 1818
13 הַדָּם תִּשְׁפֹּךְ אֶל־יְסוֹד הַמִּזְבֵּחַ׃ וְלָקַחְתָּ אֶת־כָּל־הַחֵלֶב
fat the | all | you And take shall | .altar the | the of base | at | shall you out pour | the blood

8147 3516 5921 3508 7130 3680
הַמְכַסֶּה אֶת־הַקֶּרֶב וְאֵת הַיֹּתֶרֶת עַל־הַכָּבֵד וְאֵת שְׁתֵּי
two | and | ,liver the | on | lobe the | and | the ,inwards | that covers

4196 6999 5921 834 2459 3629
14 הַכְּלָיֹת וְאֶת־הַחֵלֶב אֲשֶׁר עֲלֵיהֶן וְהִקְטַרְתָּ הַמִּזְבֵּחָה׃ וְאֶת־
And | the on .altar | you and burn shall | ;them on | which (is) | fat the | and | the ,kidneys

4264 2351 784 8313 6569 5785 6499 1320
בְּשַׂר הַפָּר וְאֶת־עֹרוֹ וְאֶת־פִּרְשׁוֹ תִּשְׂרֹף בָּאֵשׁ מִחוּץ לַמַּחֲנֶה
the ;camp | outside | with ,fire | shall you burn | its dung | and | its skin | and | the bullock's | flesh

1121 175 5561 3937 259 352 2403
15 חַטָּאת הוּא׃ וְאֶת־הָאַיִל הָאֶחָד תִּקָּח וְסָמְכוּ אַהֲרֹן וּבָנָיו
and sons his | Aaron | and lay shall | shall you ,take | one | ram | And | .(is) it | sin a offering

3947 352 7819 352 7218 5921 3027
16 אֶת־יְדֵיהֶם עַל־רֹאשׁ הָאָיִל׃ וְשָׁחַטְתָּ אֶת־הָאַיִל וְלָקַחְתָּ
you and take shall | ;ram the | you And kill shall | .ram the | the of head | on | hands their

5408 352 5439 4196 2236 1818
17 אֶת־דָּמוֹ וְזָרַקְתָּ עַל־הַמִּזְבֵּחַ סָבִיב׃ וְאֶת־הָאַיִל תְּנַתֵּחַ
shall you cut | ram the | and | all ;around | altar the | on | you and sprinkle shall | ,blood its

5409 5408 3767 7130 7364 5409
לִנְתָחָיו וְרָחַצְתָּ קִרְבּוֹ וּכְרָעָיו וְנָתַתָּ עַל־נְתָחָיו וְעַל־
and on | its pieces | on | shall and (them) put | its and ,legs | its inwards | you and wash shall | its into ;pieces

3068 5930 4196 352 3605 6999 7218
18 רֹאשׁוֹ׃ וְהִקְטַרְתָּ אֶת־כָּל־הָאַיִל הַמִּזְבֵּחָה עֹלָה הוּא לַיהוָה
to ;Jehovah | it (is) | burnt a offering | the on ,altar | ram the | all | you And burn shall | .head its

8145 352 3947 3068 801 5207 7381
19 רֵיחַ נִיחוֹחַ אִשֶּׁה לַיהוָה הוּא׃ וְלָקַחְתָּ אֵת הָאַיִל הַשֵּׁנִי
;second ram the | you And take shall | .(is) it | to Jehovah | fire a offering | soothing | a fragrance

7919 352 7218 3027 1121 175 5564
20 וְסָמַךְ אַהֲרֹן וּבָנָיו אֶת־יְדֵיהֶם עַל־רֹאשׁ הָאָיִל׃ וְשָׁחַטְתָּ
you And kill shall | .ram the | the of head | on | hands their | his and sons | Aaron | and lay shall

slaughter the ram; and you shall take of its blood and shall put *it* on the tip of Aaron's ear, and on the tip of the right ear of Aaron and on the tip of the ear of his sons, and on the thumb of the right hand, and on the big toe of their right foot; and you shall sprinkle the blood on the altar all around. [21]And you shall take of the blood on the altar, and the oil of anointing, and you shall sprinkle on Aaron and on his garments, and on his sons, and on his sons' garments with him.

[22]And you shall take the fat from the ram, and the fat tail, and the fat that covers the inward parts, and the lobe of the liver, and the two kidneys, and the fat on them, and the right shoulder; for it *is* a ram of consecration; [23]and one loaf of bread, and one cake of oil bread, and one wafer, from the basket of unleavened bread which *is* before the face of Jehovah. [24]And you shall put all on the palms of Aaron and on the palms of his sons. And you shall wave them for a wave offering before the face of Jehovah. [25]And you shall take them from their hand, and you shall burn the burnt offering on the altar for a soothing fragrance before the face of Jehovah; it *is* a fire offering to Jehovah.

[26]And you shall take the breast from the ram of consecration which *is* on Aaron. And you shall wave it as a wave offering before Jehovah; it shall be your share. [27]And you shall sanctify the breast of the wave offering and the shoulder of the heave offering which *is* waved and which *is* lifted from the ram of consecration, from what *is* Aaron's, and

from what *is* to his sons.
[28]And it shall be for Aaron
and for his sons for a never-
ending statute from the
sons of Israel; it *is* for a
heave offering, and it shall
be a heave offering from the
sons of Israel, from the
sacrifices of their peace
offerings, their heave offering to Jehovah.
[29]And the holy garments
which *are* Aaron's shall be
his sons' after him, for
anointing in them and for
filling their hands in them.
[30]The priest shall put them
on seven days, *he* from his
sons taking his place; he
who comes into the taber-
nacle of the congregation
to minister in the sanctuary.
[31]And you shall take the
ram of consecration, and
you shall boil its flesh in a
holy place. [32]And Aaron
and his sons shall eat the
flesh of the ram and the
bread which *is* in the basket
at the door of the tabernacle
of the congregation. [33]And
they shall eat those *things*
by which atonement is
made, to consecrate them,
to sanctify them; and a
stranger shall not eat, for
they *are* holy. [34]And if *any*
is left of the flesh of consecration, and of the bread,
until the morning, you shall
burn what is left with fire; it
shall not be eaten, for it *is*
holy.
[35]And so you shall do to
Aaron and to his sons,
according to all which I
have commanded you; you
shall consecrate them
seven days. [36]And you
shall offer a bullock of a sin
offering daily for atonement,
and you shall purify the altar
in your making atonement
for it; and you shall anoint it
to sanctify it. [37]You shall
make atonement seven
days for the altar, and shall
sanctify it; and the altar
shall become most holy,
everything touching the
altar becomes holy.
[38]And this *is* what you
shall offer on the altar: two
lambs daily, sons of a year;

28 וּמֵאֲשֶׁר לְבָנָיו׃ וְהָיָה לְאַהֲרֹן וּלְבָנָיו לְחָק־עוֹלָם מֵאֵת
בְּנֵי יִשְׂרָאֵל כִּי תְרוּמָה הוּא וּתְרוּמָה יִהְיֶה מֵאֵת בְּנֵי
29 יִשְׂרָאֵל מִזִּבְחֵי שַׁלְמֵיהֶם תְּרוּמָתָם לַיהוָה׃ וּבִגְדֵי הַקֹּדֶשׁ
אֲשֶׁר לְאַהֲרֹן יִהְיוּ לְבָנָיו אַחֲרָיו לְמָשְׁחָה בָהֶם וּלְמַלֵּא־
30 בָם אֶת־יָדָם׃ שִׁבְעַת יָמִים יִלְבָּשָׁם הַכֹּהֵן תַּחְתָּיו מִבָּנָיו
31 אֲשֶׁר יָבֹא אֶל־אֹהֶל מוֹעֵד לְשָׁרֵת בַּקֹּדֶשׁ׃ וְאֵת אֵיל הַמִּלֻּאִים
32 תִּקָּח וּבִשַּׁלְתָּ אֶת־בְּשָׂרוֹ בְּמָקֹם קָדֹשׁ׃ וְאָכַל אַהֲרֹן וּבָנָיו
אֶת־בְּשַׂר הָאַיִל וְאֶת־הַלֶּחֶם אֲשֶׁר בַּסָּל פֶּתַח אֹהֶל מוֹעֵד׃
33 וְאָכְלוּ אֹתָם אֲשֶׁר כֻּפַּר בָּהֶם לְמַלֵּא אֶת־יָדָם לְקַדֵּשׁ אֹתָם
34 וְזָר לֹא־יֹאכַל כִּי־קֹדֶשׁ הֵם׃ וְאִם־יִוָּתֵר מִבְּשַׂר הַמִּלֻּאִים
וּמִן־הַלֶּחֶם עַד־הַבֹּקֶר וְשָׂרַפְתָּ אֶת־הַנּוֹתָר בָּאֵשׁ לֹא יֵאָכֵל
35 כִּי־קֹדֶשׁ הוּא׃ וְעָשִׂיתָ לְאַהֲרֹן וּלְבָנָיו כָּכָה כְּכֹל אֲשֶׁר
36 צִוִּיתִי אֹתָכָה שִׁבְעַת יָמִים תְּמַלֵּא יָדָם׃ וּפַר חַטָּאת תַּעֲשֶׂה
לַיּוֹם עַל־הַכִּפֻּרִים וְחִטֵּאתָ עַל־הַמִּזְבֵּחַ בְּכַפֶּרְךָ עָלָיו
37 וּמָשַׁחְתָּ אֹתוֹ לְקַדְּשׁוֹ׃ שִׁבְעַת יָמִים תְּכַפֵּר עַל־הַמִּזְבֵּחַ
וְקִדַּשְׁתָּ אֹתוֹ וְהָיָה הַמִּזְבֵּחַ קֹדֶשׁ קָדָשִׁים כָּל־הַנֹּגֵעַ בַּמִּזְבֵּחַ
38 יִקְדָּשׁ׃ ס וְזֶה אֲשֶׁר תַּעֲשֶׂה עַל־הַמִּזְבֵּחַ כְּבָשִׂים בְּנֵי

the one lamb you shall offer
in the morning, and the
second lamb you shall offer
between the evenings.
40And a tenth of fine flour
anointed with beaten oil, a
fourth of a hin, and a drink
offering, a fourth of a hin *of*
wine, for the one lamb.
41And you shall offer the
second lamb between the
evenings; you shall do to it
like the morning food
offering and its drink offering, for a soothing fra-
grance, a fire offering to
Jehovah. 42*This shall be* a
continual burnt offering to
your generations, *at* the
door of the tabernacle of
the congregation before the
face of Jehovah; there
where I meet you to speak
to you there. 43And I will
meet the sons of Israel
there, and it shall be
sanctified by My glory.
44And I will sanctify the
tabernacle of the congregation and the altar. And I will
sanctify Aaron and his sons
to minister as priests to Me.
45And I will dwell in the
midst of the sons of Israel;
and I will be God to them.

46And they shall know that I
am Jehovah their God, who
brought them out from the
land of Egypt, that I may
dwell in their midst. I *am*
Jehovah their God.

39
6213 259 3532 8548 3117 8147 8141
שָׁנָה שְׁנַיִם לַיּוֹם תָּמִיד׃ אֶת־הַכֶּבֶשׂ הָאֶחָד תַּעֲשֶׂה
shall you offer | one the | lamb | ;continually | ,daily | two | year a

40
6241 6153 996 6213 8145 3532 1242
בַּבֹּקֶר וְאֵת הַכֶּבֶשׂ הַשֵּׁנִי תַּעֲשֶׂה בֵּין הָעַרְבָּיִם׃ וְעִשָּׂרֹן
a And of tenth | the .evenings | between | shall you offer | second | lamb the | and | the in ,morning

1969 7253 5262 1969 7243 3795 8081 1101 5560
סֹלֶת בָּלוּל בְּשֶׁמֶן כָּתִית רֶבַע הַהִין וְנֵסֶךְ רְבִיעִת הַהִין
hin a | fourth a of | a and ,libation | ,hin a | fourth a of | ,beaten | with oil | anointed | fine flour

41
6153 996 6213 8145 3532 259 3532 3196
יַיִן לַכֶּבֶשׂ הָאֶחָד׃ וְאֵת הַכֶּבֶשׂ הַשֵּׁנִי תַּעֲשֶׂה בֵּין הָעַרְבָּיִם
the ;evenings | between | shall you offer | second | the lamb | And | .one | the for lamb | (of) ,wine

801 5207 7381 6213 5262 1242 4503
כְּמִנְחַת הַבֹּקֶר וּכְנִסְכָּהּ תַּעֲשֶׂה־לָּהּ לְרֵיחַ נִיחֹחַ אִשֶּׁה
fire a offering | soothing | a for fragrance | ,it to | shall you do | its and libation | the morning | food like offering

42
6440 4150 168 6607 1755 8548 5930 3068
לַיהוָה׃ עֹלַת תָּמִיד לְדֹרֹתֵיכֶם פֶּתַח אֹהֶל־מוֹעֵד לִפְנֵי
before | meeting of | the tent | the (at) of door | your to ,generations | contin-ual | burnt a offering | to ,Jehovah

43
3259 8033 1696 8033 3259 3068
יְהוָה אֲשֶׁר אִוָּעֵד לָכֶם שָׁמָּה לְדַבֵּר אֵלֶיךָ שָׁם׃ וְנֹעַדְתִּי
I And meet will | .there | you to | speak to | ,you | meet I | where | ;Jehovah

44
168 6942 3519 6942 3478 1121 8033
שָׁמָּה לִבְנֵי יִשְׂרָאֵל וְנִקְדַּשׁ בִּכְבֹדִי׃ וְקִדַּשְׁתִּי אֶת־אֹהֶל
of tent the | will I And sanctify | My by .glory | will it and sanctified be | ;Israel | the of sons | there

3547 6942 1121 175 4196 4150
מוֹעֵד וְאֶת־הַמִּזְבֵּחַ וְאֶת־אַהֲרֹן וְאֶת־בָּנָיו אֲקַדֵּשׁ לְכַהֵן
minister to priests as | will I sanctify | his sons | and | Aaron | and | ;altar the | and | the meeting

45
430 1961 3478 1122 8432 7931
לִי׃ וְשָׁכַנְתִּי בְּתוֹךְ בְּנֵי יִשְׂרָאֵל וְהָיִיתִי לָהֶם לֵאלֹהִים׃
.God a | to them | I and be will | ;Israel | the of sons | the in of midst | I And dwell will | to .Me

46
776 5927 430 3068 3045
וְיָדְעוּ כִּי אֲנִי יְהוָה אֱלֹהֵיהֶם אֲשֶׁר הוֹצֵאתִי אֹתָם מֵאֶרֶץ
from of land the | them | brought out | who | ,God their | Jehovah | I (am) | that | they And know shall

430 3068 8462 7931 4714
מִצְרַיִם לְשָׁכְנִי בְתוֹכָם אֲנִי יְהוָה אֱלֹהֵיהֶם׃ פ
.God their | Jehovah | I (am) | their in ,midst | I that dwell may | ,Egypt

CAP. XXX ל

CHAPTER 30

CHAPTER 30

1And you shall make an
altar, a place for burning
incense; you shall make it of
acacia-wood. 2It shall be
a cubit in length and a cubit
in width; it shall be square.
And its height *shall be* two
cubits, its horns from itself.
3And you shall overlay it
with pure gold, its top, and
its walls all around, and its
horns. And you shall make a
wreath of gold for it all
around. 4And you shall

1
6213 7848 6086 7004 4729 4196 6213
וְעָשִׂיתָ מִזְבֵּחַ מִקְטַר קְטֹרֶת עֲצֵי שִׁטִּים תַּעֲשֶׂה אֹתוֹ׃
;it | shall you make | acacia- wood | of ,incense | place a burn to | ,altar an | you And make shall

2
6967 520 1961 7251 7341 520 753 520
אַמָּה אָרְכּוֹ וְאַמָּה רָחְבּוֹ רָבוּעַ יִהְיֶה וְאַמָּתַיִם קֹמָתוֹ
its ;height | two and cubits | shall it be | square | in ;width | a and cubit | in ,length | cubit a

3
1406 2889 2091 6823 7161
מִמֶּנּוּ קַרְנֹתָיו׃ וְצִפִּיתָ אֹתוֹ זָהָב טָהוֹר אֶת־גַּגּוֹ וְאֶת־
and | ,top its | ,pure | (with) gold | it | you And overlay shall | .horns its | (part a) itself of

5439 2091 2213 6213 7161 5439 7023
קִירֹתָיו סָבִיב וְאֶת־קַרְנֹתָיו וְעָשִׂיתָ לּוֹ זֵר זָהָב סָבִיב׃
all ,around | gold | a wreath | for it | you and make shall | ;horns its | and | all ,around | walls its

4 make two rings of gold for
it, under its wreath; you
shall make its two corners
on its two sides; and they
shall be housings for poles,
to lift them up by it. [5]And
you shall make the poles of
acacia-wood; and you shall
overlay them *with* gold.
[6]And you shall put it in front
of the veil which *is* beside
the ark of the testimony; in
front of the mercy-seat
which *is* over the testimony, there where I meet
you. [7]And Aaron shall burn
incense of perfume on it
morning by morning, when
he dresses the lamps he
shall burn it. [8]And when
Aaron sets up the lamps
between the evenings he
shall burn it, a perpetual
incense before the face of
Jehovah for your genera-
tions. [9]You shall not offer
up strange incense on it,
and burnt offering and food
offering; and you shall not
pour out a drink offering, to
go up on it. [10]And Aaron
shall make atonement on
its horns once in a year,
from the blood of the sin
offering of the atonement
once in the years he shall
make atonement on it for
your generations; it is most
holy to Jehovah.

[11]And Jehovah spoke to
Moses, saying: [12]When
you lift up the head of the
sons of Israel, of those
numbered, each one shall
give the ransom of his soul
to Jehovah when number-
ing them; and there shall
not be a plague among
them when numbering
them. [13]They shall give
this, everyone passing over
to those numbered: half a
shekel, by the shekel of the
sanctuary, twenty gerahs
being a shekel; half a shekel
as an offering to Jehovah.
[14]Every one passing over to
those numbered, from a son
of twenty years and upward,
shall give the offering of
Jehovah. [15]The rich shall

8147 5921 2213 8478 6213 2091 2885 8147
4 וּשְׁתֵּי טַבְּעֹת זָהָב תַּעֲשֶׂה־לּוֹ ׀ מִתַּחַת לְזֵרוֹ עַל שְׁתֵּי
two on its under for shall you gold of rings and
;wreath .it make two

5375 905 1004 1961 6763 8147 6213 6763
צַלְעֹתָיו תַּעֲשֶׂה עַל־שְׁנֵי צִדָּיו וְהָיָה לְבָתִּים לְבַדִּים לָשֵׂאת
carry to the for housings they and its two shall you sides its
,poles be shall ;corners make

6823 7848 6086 905 6213 1992
5 אֹתוֹ בָּהֵמָּה׃ וְעָשִׂיתָ אֶת־הַבַּדִּים עֲצֵי שִׁטִּים וְצִפִּיתָ אֹתָם
them you and ;acacia- of poles the you And them by it
overlay shall wood make shall

6440 5715 727 6532 6440 5414 2091
6 זָהָב׃ וְנָתַתָּה אֹתוֹ לִפְנֵי הַפָּרֹכֶת אֲשֶׁר עַל־אֲרֹן הָעֵדֻת לִפְנֵי
before the the beside which ,veil the before it you And (with)
;testimony of ark (is) put shall .gold

6999 8033 3259 5715 834 3727
7 הַכַּפֹּרֶת אֲשֶׁר עַל־הָעֵדֻת אֲשֶׁר אִוָּעֵד לְךָ שָׁמָּה׃ וְהִקְטִיר
shall And .you I where the over which the
burn .there meet ,testimony (is) mercy seat

5216 3190 1242 1242 5561 7004 175 5921
עָלָיו אַהֲרֹן קְטֹרֶת סַמִּים בַּבֹּקֶר בַּבֹּקֶר בְּהֵיטִיבוֹ אֶת־הַנֵּרֹת
lamps the he when by morn- perfume incense Aaron it on
dresses ;morning ing of

6999 6153 996 5216 175 5927 6999
8 יַקְטִירֶנָּה׃ וּבְהַעֲלֹת אַהֲרֹן אֶת־הַנֵּרֹת בֵּין הָעַרְבַּיִם יַקְטִירֶנָּה
shall he the between lamps the Aaron when And shall he
.it burn ,evenings up sets .it burn

7004 5921 5927 3808 1755 3068 6440 8548 7004
9 קְטֹרֶת תָּמִיד לִפְנֵי יְהוָה לְדֹרֹתֵיכֶם׃ לֹא־תַעֲלוּ עָלָיו קְטֹרֶת
incense it on shall You not your for Jehovah before a incense
up offer .generations perpetual

5921 175 3722 5927 5258 5262 4503 5930 2114
10 זָרָה וְעֹלָה וּמִנְחָה וְנֵסֶךְ לֹא תִסְּכוּ עָלָיו׃ וְכִפֶּר אַהֲרֹן עַל־
on Aaron shall And go to shall you not a and food and and ,strange
atone .it on up out pour libation ;offering offering burnt

8141 259 57 22 2403 1818 8141 259 7161
קַרְנֹתָיו אַחַת בַּשָּׁנָה מִדַּם חַטַּאת הַכִּפֻּרִים אַחַת בַּשָּׁנָה
the in once the sin the the from a in once horns its
year atonement of offering of blood ;year

3068 6944 1756 5921 3722
יְכַפֵּר עָלָיו לְדֹרֹתֵיכֶם קֹדֶשׁ־קָדָשִׁים הוּא לַיהוָה׃
to (is) it most holy your for it upon shall he
Jehovah ;generations atonement make

1121 7218 5375 559 4872 3068 1696
11 וַיְדַבֵּר יְהוָה אֶל־מֹשֶׁה לֵּאמֹר׃ כִּי תִשָּׂא אֶת־רֹאשׁ בְּנֵי־
12
the head the you When ,saying .Moses to Jehovah And
of sons of up lift spoke

6485 3068 5315 3724 376 5414 6485 3478
יִשְׂרָאֵל לִפְקֻדֵיהֶם וְנָתְנוּ אִישׁ כֹּפֶר נַפְשׁוֹ לַיהוָה בִּפְקֹד
when to his the one each shall those of ,Israel
counting Jehovah soul of ransom give ,counted

3605 5414 2088 6485 5063 1961 3808
13 אֹתָם וְלֹא־יִהְיֶה בָהֶם נֶגֶף בִּפְקֹד אֹתָם׃ זֶה ׀ יִתְּנוּ כָּל־
every they This .them when a among shall and ;them
one ,give shall counting plague them be not

6242 6944 8255 8255 4276 6485 5921 5674
הָעֹבֵר עַל־הַפְּקֻדִים מַחֲצִית הַשֶּׁקֶל בְּשֶׁקֶל הַקֹּדֶשׁ עֶשְׂרִים
twenty the the by ,shekel a half those to over passing
,sanctuary of shekel ,counted

5674 3605 3068 8641 8255 4276 8255 1626
14 גֵּרָה הַשֶּׁקֶל מַחֲצִית הַשֶּׁקֶל תְּרוּמָה לַיהוָה׃ כֹּל הָעֹבֵר
passing Every to an as shekel a half a gerahs
one .Jehovah offering ;shekel (being)

3068 8641 5414 4605 8141 6242 1121 6485 5921
עַל־הַפְּקֻדִים מִבֶּן עֶשְׂרִים שָׁנָה וָמָעְלָה יִתֵּן תְּרוּמַת יְהוָה׃
.Jehovah the shall and years twenty from those to over
of offering give ,upward of son a ,counted

give more, and the poor shall not give less than half a shekel, to give the offering of Jehovah, to make atonement for your souls. [16]And you shall take the money of atonement from the sons of Israel, and you shall give it to the service of the tabernacle of the congregation; and it shall be for the sons of Israel for remembrance before the face of Jehovah, to make atonement for your souls.

[17]And Jehovah spoke to Moses, saying: [18]And you shall make a laver of bronze, and its base bronze, for washing. And you shall put it between the tabernacle of the congregation and the altar; and you shall put water there. [19]And Aaron and his sons shall wash from it, their hands and their feet, [20]as they go into the tabernacle of the congregation they shall wash *with* water, and shall not die; or as they draw near to the altar to minister, to burn a fire offering to Jehovah. [21]And they shall wash their hands and their feet, and shall not die. And it shall be a never-ending statute to them, to him and to his seed for their generations.

[22]And Jehovah spoke to Moses, saying: [23]And you take spices for yourself, the best, five hundred of pure myrrh, and its half of spicy cinnamon, two hundred and fifty *shekels*, and two hundred and fifty of aromatic calamus; [24]and five hundred of cassia, by the shekel of the sanctuary; and a hin of olive oil. [25]And you shall make it an oil of holy anointing, ointment compound, the work of a perfumer, an oil of

8255 4276 4591 3808 1800 7235 6223
15 העשיר לא־ירבה והדל לא ימעיט ממחצית השקל
a shekel, half than of, give shall less, not, the and poor, shall more give, not, rich the

3947 5315 3722 8641 5414
16 לתת את־תרומת יהוה לכפר על־נפשתיכם: ולקחת את־
you And take shall, .souls your, for, make to atonement, ,Jehovah offering the of, give to

5656 5414 3478 1121 3725 3701
כסף הכפרים מאת בני ישראל ונתת אתו על־עבדת
the of service, to, it, you and give shall, ,Israel, the of sons, from, the atonement, the of silver

3722 3068 6440 2146 3478 1121 1961 4150 168
אהל מועד והיה לבני ישראל לזכרון לפני יהוה לכפר
make to atonement, ,Jehovah before, for remembrance, Israel, the for of sons, it and be shall, meeting, the of tent

5315
על־נפשתיכם:
.souls your for

3653 5178 3595 6213 559 4872 3068 1696
17 וידבר יהוה אל־משה לאמר: ועשית כיור נחשת וכנו
18 and base its, ,bronze, laver a of, you And make shall, ,saying, ,Moses, to, Jehovah, And spoke

4196 4150 168 996 5414 7364 5178
נחשת לרחצה ונתת אתו בין־אהל מועד ובין המזבח
,altar the, and, meeting, the between of tent, it, you and put shall, for ;washing, ,bronze

3027 1121 175 7364 4325 8033 5414
19 ונתת שמה מים: ורחצו אהרן ובניו ממנו את־ידיהם
hands their, from it, his and sons, Aaron, shall And wash, .water, there, you and put shall

3808 4325 7364 4150 168 935 7272
20 ואת־רגליהם: בבאם אל־אהל מועד ירחצו־מים ולא
and not, ,water shall they (with) wash, meeting, the of tent, into, they as go, ;feet their, and

801 6999 8334 4196 5066 4191
ימתו או בגשתם אל־המזבח לשרת להקטיר אשה
fire a offering, burn to, minister to, altar the, to, they as approach, or, shall ;die

1961 4191 3808 7272 3027 7364 3068
21 ליהוה: ורחצו ידיהם ורגליהם ולא ימתו והיתה להם
to them, it and be shall, shall ;die, not and, their and ,feet, their hands, they and wash shall, to ;Jehovah

1755 2233 5769/2706
חק־עולם לו ולזרעו לדרתם:
their .generations, for, to and seed his, to him, never- ,ending, a statute

1314 3947 559 4872 3068 1696
22 וידבר יהוה אל־משה לאמר: ואתה קח־לך בשמים
23 ,spices, for yourself, take, you And, ,saying, ,Moses, to, Jehovah, And spoke

2572 4276 1314 7076 3967 2568 1865/4733 7218
ראש מר־דרור חמש מאות וקנמן־בשם מחציתו חמשים
fifty, half its, spicy cinnamon, of and, hundred, five, pure myrrh, the ,best

2568 6916 3967 2572 1314 7070 3967
24 ומאתים וקנה־בשם חמשים ומאתים: וקדה חמש
five, of and cassia, two and ;hundred, fifty, aromatic calamus, of and, two and ,hundred

8081 6213 1969 2132 8081 6944 8255 3967
25 מאות בשקל הקדש ושמן זית הין: ועשית אתו שמן
an of oil, it, you And make shall, .hin a, olive, of and oil, the ,sanctuary, the by of shekel, hundred

4888 8081 7543 4639 4842 7545 6944 4888
משחת־קדש רקח מרקחת מעשה רקח שמן משחת־
anointing of, oil an, a ,perfumer, the of work, **compound ointment**, ,holy, anointing

holy anointing it shall be. [26]And you shall anoint with it the tabernacle of the congregation and the ark of the testimony, [27]and the table and all its vessels, and the altar of incense, [28]and the altar of burnt offering, and all its vessels, and the laver and its base. [29]And you shall sanctify them, and they shall become most holy; everything touching them shall become holy. [30]And you shall anoint Aaron and his sons, and you shall consecrate them to minister as priests to Me. [31]And you shall speak to the sons of Israel, saying, This shall be a holy anointing oil for Me for your generations. [32]It shall not be poured on the flesh of man, and you shall not make *any* like it in its proportion; it *is* holy. It shall be holy to you. [33]A man prepares *any* like it, or who gives from it to a stranger, shall be cut off from his people.

[34]And Jehovah said to Moses, Take perfumes for yourself, spices, stacte, and onycha, and galbanum, spices, and pure frankincense, a part shall be for a part. [35]And you shall make it incense, an ointment, a work of a perfumer, salted, pure and holy. [36]And you shall grind *some* of it fine, and put *some* of it in front of the testimony in the tabernacle of the congregation, where I meet you. It shall be most holy to you. [37]And the incense which you make, in its proportion, you shall not make for yourselves; it shall be holy to you for Jehovah. [38]A man who makes *any* like it, to smell of it, he shall be cut off from his people.

26 קדש יהיה: ומשחת בו את־אהל מועד ואת ארון העדת:
27 ואת־השלחן ואת־כל־כליו ואת־המנרה ואת־כליה ואת
28 מזבח הקטרת: ואת־מזבח העלה ואת־כל־כליו ואת־
29 הכיר ואת־כנו: וקדשת אתם והיו קדש קדשים כל־
30 הנגע בהם יקדש: ואת־אהרן ואת־בניו תמשח וקדשת
31 אתם לכהן לי: ואל־בני ישראל תדבר לאמר שמן
32 משחת־קדש יהיה זה לי לדרתיכם: על־בשר אדם
לא ייסך ובמתכנתו לא תעשו כמהו קדש הוא קדש
33 יהיה לכם: איש אשר ירקח כמהו ואשר יתן ממנו על־
34 זר ונכרת מעמיו: ס ויאמר יהוה אל־משה קח־לך
סמים נטף ושחלת וחלבנה סמים ולבנה זכה בד בבד
35 יהיה: ועשית אתה קטרת רקח מעשה רוקח ממלח
36 טהור קדש: ושחקת ממנה הדק ונתתה ממנה לפני
העדת באהל מועד אשר אועד לך שמה קדש קדשים
37 תהיה לכם: והקטרת אשר תעשה במתכנתה לא
38 תעשו לכם קדש תהיה לך ליהוה: איש אשר־יעשה
כמוה להריח בה ונכרת מעמיו:

CHAPTER 31

[1]And Jehovah spoke to
Moses, saying: [2]Behold, I
have called by name Beza-
leel, the son of Uri, the son
of Hur, to the tribe of Judah.
[3]And I have filled him *with*
the spirit of God in wisdom,
and in intelligence, and in
knowledge, and in all work-
manship, [4]to devise de-
signs, to work in gold and in
silver and in bronze, [5]and
in cutting of stones for
settings, and in carving of
wood, to work in all work-
manship. [6]And behold, I
have given with him
Aholiab, the son of Ahisamach, of the tribe of Dan;
and in the heart of every
wise-hearted one I have
given wisdom; and they
shall make all which I have
commanded you: [7]the
tabernacle of the congregation, and the ark of the
testimony, and the mercy-
seat which *is* going up over
it, and all the vessels of the
tabernacle, [8]and the table
and its vessels, and the
pure lampstand and all its
vessels, and the altar of
incense; [9]and the altar of
burnt offering and all its
vessels, and the laver and
its base; [10]and the woven
garments, and the holy garments for Aaron the priest,
and the garments of his
sons, to minister as priests;
[11]and the oil of anointing,
and the incense of per-
fumes for the sanctuary;
according to all which I
have commanded you, they
shall do.

[12]And Jehovah spoke to
Moses, saying: [13]And you
speak to the sons of Israel,
saying, You shall surely
keep My sabbaths; for it *is* a
sign between Me and you

CAP. XXXI לא

CHAPTER 31

1212 8038 7129 2009 559 4872 3068 1696
1 2 וַיְדַבֵּר יְהוָה אֶל־מֹשֶׁה לֵּאמֹר׃ רְאֵה קָרָאתִי בְשֵׁם בְּצַלְאֵל
Bezaleel by have I ,See ,saying ,Moses to Jehovah And
name called spoke

430 7307 4390 3063 4294 2354/1121 221/1121
3 בֶּן־אוּרִי בֶן־חוּר לְמַטֵּה יְהוּדָה׃ וָאֲמַלֵּא אֹתוֹ רוּחַ אֱלֹהִים
God (with) him I And .Judah the of ,Hur the Uri the
of spirit the filled have of tribe of son of son

4284 2803 4399 3605 1847 8394 2451
4 בְּחָכְמָה וּבִתְבוּנָה וּבְדַעַת וּבְכָל־מְלָאכָה׃ לַחְשֹׁב מַחֲשָׁבֹת
,designs to workman- in and in and in and in
devise ;ship all ,knowledge ,intelligence ,wisdom

4390 68 2799 5178 3701 2091 6213
5 לַעֲשׂוֹת בַּזָּהָב וּבַכֶּסֶף וּבַנְּחֹשֶׁת׃ וּבַחֲרֹשֶׁת אֶבֶן לְמַלֹּאת
for stones in and in and in and in to
,finishings of cutting ;bronze ,silver ,gold work

5414 2009 4399 3605 6213 6086 2799
6 וּבַחֲרֹשֶׁת עֵץ לַעֲשׂוֹת בְּכָל־מְלָאכָה׃ וַאֲנִי הִנֵּה נָתַתִּי אִתּוֹ
with have behold ,And .workmanship all in work to ,wood in and
him given I of carving

3820 2450 3820 1835 4294 294 1121 171
אֵת אָהֳלִיאָב בֶּן־אֲחִיסָמָךְ לְמַטֵּה־דָן וּבְלֵב כָּל־חֲכַם־לֵב
wise-hearted every in and ;Dan the of ,Ahisamach the Aholiab
one of heart the of tribe of son

4150 168 6680 834 3605 6213 2451 5414
7 נָתַתִּי חָכְמָה וְעָשׂוּ אֵת כָּל־אֲשֶׁר צִוִּיתִךָ׃ אֵת ׀ אֹהֶל מוֹעֵד
meeting the have I which all they and ,wisdom have I
of tent :you commanded make shall given

3627/3605 5921 834 3727 5715 727
וְאֶת־הָאָרֹן לָעֵדֻת וְאֶת־הַכַּפֹּרֶת אֲשֶׁר עָלָיו וְאֵת כָּל־כְּלֵי
the all and ,it on which the and the ark the and
of vessels (is) mercy-seat ,testimony of

2889 4501 3627 7979 168
8 הָאֹהֶל׃ וְאֶת־הַשֻּׁלְחָן וְאֶת־כֵּלָיו וְאֶת־הַמְּנֹרָה הַטְּהֹרָה
pure the and its and the and the
lampstand ,vessels table ;tent

5930 4196 7004 4196 3627 3605
9 וְאֶת־כָּל־כֵּלֶיהָ וְאֵת מִזְבַּח הַקְּטֹרֶת׃ וְאֶת־מִזְבַּח הָעֹלָה
burnt altar the and ;incense altar the and its all and
,offering of of vessels

8278 899 3653 3595 3627 3605
10 וְאֶת־כָּל־כֵּלָיו וְאֶת־הַכִּיּוֹר וְאֶת־כַּנּוֹ׃ וְאֵת בִּגְדֵי הַשְּׂרָד וְאֶת־
and the garments and its and the ,and its all and
woven ;base laver ,vessels

3547 1121 899 3548 175 6944 899
11 בִּגְדֵי הַקֹּדֶשׁ לְאַהֲרֹן הַכֹּהֵן וְאֶת־בִּגְדֵי בָנָיו לְכַהֵן׃ וְאֵת
and minister to his the and the for holy the
;priests as sons of garments ,priest Aaron garments

834 3605 6944 5561 7004 4888 8081
שֶׁמֶן הַמִּשְׁחָה וְאֶת־קְטֹרֶת הַסַּמִּים לַקֹּדֶשׁ כְּכֹל אֲשֶׁר־
which according the for perfumes the and ,anointing the
all to ;sanctuary of incense of oil

6213 6680
צִוִּיתִךָ יַעֲשׂוּ׃ פ
.do shall they have I
,you commanded

3478 1121 1696 559 4872 3068 559
12 13 וַיֹּאמֶר יְהוָה אֶל־מֹשֶׁה לֵּאמֹר׃ וְאַתָּה דַּבֵּר אֶל־בְּנֵי יִשְׂרָאֵל
,Israel the to speak ,you And ,saying ,Moses to Jehovah And
of sons spoke

996 226 8104 7676 389 559
לֵאמֹר אַךְ אֶת־שַׁבְּתֹתַי תִּשְׁמֹרוּ כִּי אוֹת הִוא בֵּינִי וּבֵינֵיכֶם
you and between it a for shall you My Surely ,saying
Me (is) sign ;keep sabbaths

for your generations; to know that I *am* Jehovah your sanctifier. [14]And you shall keep the Sabbath, for it *is* holy for you; the profaners of it surely shall be put to death; for everyone doing work in it, that soul shall be cut off frm the midst of his people. [15]Work may be done six days, and on the seventh day *is* a sabbath of rest, holy to Jehovah; everyone doing work on the Sabbath day surely shall be put to death. [16]And the sons of Israel shall observe the Sabbath, to do the Sabbath for their generations; *it is* a never-ending covenant. [17]It is a sign forever between Me and the sons of Israel; for *in* six days Jehovah made the heavens and the earth, and on the seventh day He rested and was refreshed.

[18]And when He finished speaking with him on Mount Sinai, He gave to Moses the two tablets of the testimony, tablets of stone, written by the finger of God.

8104 6942 3068 3045 1755
14 לְדֹרֹתֵיכֶם לָדַעַת כִּי אֲנִי יְהוָה מְקַדִּשְׁכֶם׃ וּשְׁמַרְתֶּם אֶת־
you And keep shall | your .sanctifier | Jehovah I (am) | that know to | your for ;generations

3605 4191 4191 2490 6944 7676
הַשַּׁבָּת כִּי קֹדֶשׁ הִוא לָכֶם מְחַלְלֶיהָ מוֹת יוּמָת כִּי כָּל־
every one | for ;executed | be shall surely | one the it profaning | ;you for | (is) it | holy | for | the ,Sabbath

5971 7130 5315 3772 4399 6213
הָעֹשֶׂה בָהּ מְלָאכָה וְנִכְרְתָה הַנֶּפֶשׁ הַהִוא מִקֶּרֶב עַמֶּיהָ׃
his .people | the from of midst | that | soul | be shall off cut | ,work | it in | doing

7677 7676 7637 3117 4399 6213 3117 8337
15 שֵׁשֶׁת יָמִים יֵעָשֶׂה מְלָאכָה וּבַיּוֹם הַשְּׁבִיעִי שַׁבַּת שַׁבָּתוֹן
,rest | a (is) of sabbath | the seventh | on and day | ;work | be may done | days | Six

4191 4191 7676 3117 4399 6213 3605 3068 6944
קֹדֶשׁ לַיהוָה כָּל־הָעֹשֶׂה מְלָאכָה בְּיוֹם הַשַּׁבָּת מוֹת יוּמָת׃
be shall surely .executed | the Sabbath | day on | work | doing every one | to ,Jehovah | holy

7676 6213 7676 3478 1121 8104
16 וְשָׁמְרוּ בְנֵי־יִשְׂרָאֵל אֶת־הַשַּׁבָּת לַעֲשׂוֹת אֶת־הַשַּׁבָּת
the Sabbath | observe to | the Sabbath | Israel | sons the of | shall And keep

226 3478 1121 996 996 5769 1285 1755
17 לְדֹרֹתָם בְּרִית עוֹלָם׃ בֵּינִי וּבֵין בְּנֵי יִשְׂרָאֵל אוֹת הִוא
It (is) | sign a | .Israel | sons the of | and between | Me | never- ,ending | covenant a | their for ,generations

776 8064 3068 6213 3117 8337 5769
לְעֹלָם כִּי־שֵׁשֶׁת יָמִים עָשָׂה יְהוָה אֶת־הַשָּׁמַיִם וְאֶת־הָאָרֶץ
the earth | and | the heavens | Jehovah | made | days | (in) six | for | ,forever

3615 4872 5414 5314 7673 7637 3117
18 וּבַיּוֹם הַשְּׁבִיעִי שָׁבַת וַיִּנָּפַשׁ׃ ס וַיִּתֵּן אֶל־מֹשֶׁה כְּכַלֹּתוֹ
He when finished | Moses | to | He And gave | was and .refreshed | He rested | the seventh | on and day

3789 68 3871 5715 3871 8147 5514 2022 1696
לְדַבֵּר אִתּוֹ בְּהַר סִינַי שְׁנֵי לֻחֹת הָעֵדֻת לֻחֹת אֶבֶן כְּתֻבִים
written | ,stone | tablets of | the ,testimony | tablets of | the two | ,Sinai | on Mount | with him | speaking

430 676
בְּאֶצְבַּע אֱלֹהִים׃
.God | the by of finger

CAP. XXXII לב

CHAPTER 32

CHAPTER 32

[1]And the people saw that Moses delayed to come down form the mountain. And the people gathered to Aaron. And they said to him, Rise up, make for us gods who may go before our face. As for this Moses, the man who brought us up from the land of Egypt, we do not know what has become of him. [2]And Aaron said to them, Tear off the rings of gold which *are* in the ears of your wives, your sons and your daughters; and bring *them*

5971 6950 2022 3381 954 5971 7200
1 וַיַּרְא הָעָם כִּי־בֹשֵׁשׁ מֹשֶׁה לָרֶדֶת מִן־הָהָר וַיִּקָּהֵל הָעָם
the people | and gathered | the ,mountain | from | come to down | Moses | delayed | that | the people | And saw

430 6213 6965 559 175
עַל־אַהֲרֹן וַיֹּאמְרוּ אֵלָיו קוּם ׀ עֲשֵׂה־לָנוּ אֱלֹהִים אֲשֶׁר
who | gods | for us | make | ,Arise | ,him to | they and said | ,Aaron | to

776 5927 376 4872 2088 6440 3212
יֵלְכוּ לְפָנֵינוּ כִּי־זֶה ׀ מֹשֶׁה הָאִישׁ אֲשֶׁר הֶעֱלָנוּ מֵאֶרֶץ
the from of land | brought up us | who | man the | ,Moses | this | as for | before ;us | may go

175 559 1961 3045 3808 4714
2 מִצְרַיִם לֹא יָדַעְנוּ מֶה־הָיָה לוֹ׃ וַיֹּאמֶר אֲלֵהֶם אַהֲרֹן
,Aaron | them to | said And | of .him | has become | what | do we know | not | ,Egypt

1323 1121 802 241 834 2091 5141 6561
פָּרְקוּ נִזְמֵי הַזָּהָב אֲשֶׁר בְּאָזְנֵי נְשֵׁיכֶם בְּנֵיכֶם וּבְנֹתֵיכֶם
your and ;daughters | your ,sons | your ,wives | the in of ears | which (are) | gold | the of rings | Break off

to me. 3And all the people
tore off the rings of gold
which *were* in their ears,
and they brought to Aaron.
4And he took from their
hand and formed it with an
engraving tool. And he
made it a casted calf. And
they said, These *are* your
gods, O Israel, who made
you go up from the land of
Egypt. 5And Aaron saw,
and he built an altar before
it. And Aaron called and
said, A feast to Jehovah
tomorrow. 6And they rose
early on the morrow, and
they offered burnt offer-
ings brought near peace
offerings. And the people
sat down to eat and drink,
and rose up to make merry.
7And Jehovah spoke to
Moses, Come, go down,
for your people whom you
caused to go up from
Egypt are corrupted; 8they
have quickly turned off
from the way which I
commanded them; they
have made for themselves
a casted calf and have
bowed to it, and have
sacrificed to it. And *they*
have said, These *are* your
gods, O Israel, who made
you go up from the land of
Egypt. 9And Jehovah said
to Moses, I have seen this
people, and, behold, it *is* a
stiff-necked people.
10And now leave Me
alone that My anger
may glow against them,
that I may consume them.
And I will make you a great
nation. 11And Moses
prayed before the face of
Jehovah his God, and he
said, Why, O Jehovah,
does Your anger glow
against Your people whom
You caused to go up from
the land of Egypt with
great power, and with a
mighty hand? 12Why
should the Egyptians say,
saying, For evil He has
caused them to go up, to
kill them in the mountains,
and to consume them on
the face of the earth? Turn
from Your fierce anger and
change Your purpose as to
the evil to Your people.

834 2091 5141 5971 3605 6561 935
3 וְהָבִיאוּ אֵלָי׃ וַיִּתְפָּרְקוּ כָּל־הָעָם אֶת־נִזְמֵי הַזָּהָב אֲשֶׁר
which (were) gold rings of the the people all broke off And .me to bring and (them)

2747 6696 3947 175 935 241
4 בְּאָזְנֵיהֶם וַיָּבִיאוּ אֶל־אַהֲרֹן׃ וַיִּקַּח מִיָּדָם וַיָּצַר אֹתוֹ בַּחֶרֶט
an with .tool engraving it formed and their hand from And took he .Aaron to they and (them) brought their in ,ears

834 3478 430 559 4541 5695 6213
וַיַּעֲשֵׂהוּ עֵגֶל מַסֵּכָה וַיֹּאמְרוּ אֵלֶּה אֱלֹהֶיךָ יִשְׂרָאֵל אֲשֶׁר
who ,Israel O your ,gods these (are) they And ,said .casted calf a he And it made

7121 6440 4196 1129 175 7200 4714 776 5927
5 הֶעֱלוּךָ מֵאֶרֶץ מִצְרָיִם׃ וַיַּרְא אַהֲרֹן וַיִּבֶן מִזְבֵּחַ לְפָנָיו וַיִּקְרָא
And called before ;it altar an he and built ,Aaron And saw .Egypt the from of land brought up you

5930 5927 4283 7925 4279 3068 2282 559 175
6 אַהֲרֹן וַיֹּאמַר חַג לַיהוָה מָחָר׃ וַיַּשְׁכִּימוּ מִמָּחֳרָת וַיַּעֲלוּ עֹלֹת
burnt offerings they and offered the on ,morrow they And early rose Tomorrow .(is) to Jehovah a feast and ,said Aaron

6711 6965 8354 398 5971 3427 8002 5066
וַיַּגִּשׁוּ שְׁלָמִים וַיֵּשֶׁב הָעָם לֶאֱכֹל וְשָׁתוֹ וַיָּקֻמוּ לְצַחֵק׃ פ
make to .merry rose and up and ,drink eat to the people sat and down peace ;offerings and brought

5927 834 5971 7843 3588 3381 4872 3068 1696
7 וַיְדַבֵּר יְהוָה אֶל־מֹשֶׁה לֶךְ־רֵד כִּי שִׁחֵת עַמְּךָ אֲשֶׁר הֶעֱלֵיתָ
*3212 you brought whom your people are corrupted for go ,down ,Come ,Moses to Jehovah And spoke

6213 6680 834 1870 4118 5493 4714 776
8 מֵאֶרֶץ מִצְרָיִם׃ סָרוּ מַהֵר מִן־הַדֶּרֶךְ אֲשֶׁר צִוִּיתִם עָשׂוּ
they made com- ;them manded I which way the from quickly they swerved have ;Egypt the from of land

559 2076 7812 4541 5695
לָהֶם עֵגֶל מַסֵּכָה וַיִּשְׁתַּחֲווּ־לוֹ וַיִּזְבְּחוּ־לוֹ וַיֹּאמְרוּ אֵלֶּה
These (are) and ,said have ,it to have and sacrificed ,it to have and bowed ,casted calf a for themselves

3068 559 4714 776 5927 834 3478 430
9 אֱלֹהֶיךָ יִשְׂרָאֵל אֲשֶׁר הֶעֱלוּךָ מֵאֶרֶץ מִצְרָיִם׃ וַיֹּאמֶר יְהוָה
Jehovah And said .Egypt the from of land brought up you who O ,Israel ,gods your

6203 7186 5971 2009 5971 7200 4872
אֶל־מֹשֶׁה רָאִיתִי אֶת־הָעָם הַזֶּה וְהִנֵּה עַם־קְשֵׁה־עֹרֶף הוּא׃
.(is) it necked stiff- a people and ,behold ,this people have I seen ,Moses to

6213 3615 639 2734 3240 6258
10 וְעַתָּה הַנִּיחָה לִּי וְיִחַר־אַפִּי בָהֶם וַאֲכַלֵּם וְאֶעֱשֶׂה אוֹתְךָ
you will I and make may I that ;them consume against them My anger that ,Me glow may leave alone And ,now

4100 559 430 3068 6440 4872 2470 1419 1471
11 לְגוֹי גָּדוֹל׃ וַיְחַל מֹשֶׁה אֶת־פְּנֵי יְהוָה אֱלֹהָיו וַיֹּאמֶר לָמָה
,Why he and ,said ,God his Jehovah before Moses And prayed .great a nation

3587 4714 776 5927 834 5971 639 2734 3068
יְהוָה יֶחֱרֶה אַפְּךָ בְּעַמֶּךָ אֲשֶׁר הוֹצֵאתָ מֵאֶרֶץ מִצְרַיִם בְּכֹחַ
with power Egypt the from of land have You brought whom against people Your Your anger does glow O ,Jehovah

7451 559 4713 559 4100 2389 3027 1419
12 גָּדוֹל וּבְיָד חֲזָקָה׃ לָמָּה יֹאמְרוּ מִצְרַיִם לֵאמֹר בְּרָעָה
For evil ,saying the ,Egyptians should speak Why ?mighty a and hand great

127 6440 3615 2022 2026 5927
הוֹצִיאָם לַהֲרֹג אֹתָם בֶּהָרִים וּלְכַלֹּתָם מֵעַל פְּנֵי הָאֲדָמָה
?earth the the of face from on to and consume them the in ,mountains them kill to has He ,them brought

85 2142 5971 7451 5162 639 2740 7725
13 שׁוּב מֵחֲרוֹן אַפֶּךָ וְהִנָּחֵם עַל־הָרָעָה לְעַמֶּךָ׃ זְכֹר לְאַבְרָהָם
,Abraham Recall Your to .people the to evil as change and purpose Your Your ,anger from fierce Turn

[13]Recall Abraham, Isaac, and Israel, Your servants, to whom You swore by Yourself, and You spoke to them, I will multiply your seed like the stars of the heavens, and all this land which I have said, I will give to your seed. And they shall possess it forever. [14]And Jehovah changed His purpose concerning the evil which He had spoken to do to His people.

[15]And Moses turned and went down from the mountain, the two tablets of the testimony in his hand, tablets written on their two sides, on this and on that they *were* written. [16]And the tablets *were* the work of God, and the writing *was* the writing of God; it *was* engraved on the tablets. [17]And Joshua heard the voice of the people in their shouting. And he said to Moses, A sound of war in the camp! [18]And he said, It is not a sound of a cry of victory nor a sound of a cry of defeat; I *am* hearing the sound of singing. [19]And it happened, as he came near to the camp and saw the calf and dances, the anger of Moses glowed. And he threw the tablets from his hands, and he broke them below the mountain. [20]And he took the calf which they had made and burned *it* with fire, and *he* ground *it* until it *was* fine, then he scattered *it* on the face of the water. And he made the sons of Israel to drink *it*.

[21]And Moses said to Aaron, What has this people done to you that you have made to come on them a great sin? [22]And Aaron said, Let not the anger of my lord glow. You know the people, that it *is* in evil. [23]And they said to me, Make for us gods

1696 7650 834 5650 3478 3327
ליצחק ולישראל עבדיך אשר נשבעת להם בך ותדבר
You and by to swore You whom Your ,Israel and ,Isaac
spoke ,Yourself ,servants

776 3605 8064 3556 2233 7235
אלהם ארבה את־זרעכם ככוכבי השמים וכל־הארץ
land all and the the like seed your will I ,them to
;heavens of stars multiply

5162 5769 5157 2233 5414 559 834 2088
14 הזאת אשר אמרתי אתן לזרעכם ונחלו לעלם׃ וינחם
changed And for- they and your to will I have I which this
purpose His .ever it own shall ;seed give of spoken

5971 6213 1696 834 7451 3068
יהוה על־הרעה אשר דבר לעשות לעמו׃ פ
His to do to had He which the to as Jehovah
.people spoken evil

3871 3027 5715 3871 8147 2022 4872 3381 6437
15 ויפן וירד משה מן־ההר ושני לחת העדת בידו לחת
tablets his in the tablets the the from Moses went and And
,hand testimony of two ,mountain down turned

3871 3789 2088 2088 5676 8147 3789
16 כתבים משני עבריהם מזה ומזה הם כתבים׃ והלחת
the And .written they on and on ,sides their on written
tablets (were) that this two

2801 430 4385 4385 430 4639
מעשה אלהים המה והמכתב מכתב אלהים הוא חרות
engraved it ,God the the and they God work the
,(was) of writing writing ;(were) of

559 7452 5971 6963 3091 8085 3871
17 על־הלחת׃ וישמע יהושע את־קול העם ברעה ויאמר
he and their in the sound the Joshua And the on
said ,shouting people of heard .tablets

6030 6963 559 4264 4421 6963 4872
18 אל־משה קול מלחמה במחנה׃ ויאמר אין קול ענות
cry a a is It he And the in war A ,Moses to
of of sound not ,said .camp of sound

1961 8085 6031 2476 6030 6963 1369
19 גבורה ואין קול ענות חלושה קול ענות אנכי שמע׃ ויהי
it And .hearing I singing the ;defeat cry a a and ,victory
,was (am) of sound of of sound not

2734 4246 5695 7200 4264 7126
כאשר קרב אל־המחנה וירא את־העגל ומחלת ויחר
glowed ,dances and calf the and camp the to he as
saw near came

8478 7665 3871 3027 7993 4872 639
אף משה וישלך מידו את־הלחת וישבר אתם תחת
below them he and the his from he and ,Moses' anger
broke ,tablets hands threw

5704 2912 784 8313 6213 834 5695 3947 2022
20 ההר׃ ויקח את־העגל אשר עשו וישרף באש ויטחן עד
until and with and had they which calf the he And the
(it) ground ,fire (it) burned made took .mount

3478 1121 8248 4325 6440 2219 1852
אשר־דק ויזר על־פני המים וישק את־בני ישראל׃
.Israel the he and ,water the the on he and ,fine it
of sons drink to caused of face (it) scattered (was)

935 2088 5971 6213 175 4872 559
21 ויאמר משה אל־אהרן מה־עשה לך העם הזה כי־הבאת
have you that ,this people to has What ,Aaron to Moses said And
brought you done

113 639 2734 175 559 1419 2401
22 עליו חטאה גדלה׃ ויאמר אהרן אל־יחר אף אדני אתה
you my the glow Let not ,Aaron said And ?great sin a on
;lord of anger them

430 6213 559 7451 5971 3045
23 ידעת את־העם כי ברע הוא׃ ויאמרו לי עשה־לנו אלהים
gods for Make to they And .(is) it in that the know
us ,me said evil ,people

who may go before us; as
for Moses, the man who
caused us to go up from
the land of Egypt, we do
not know what has
become of him. 24And I
said to them, Whoever *has*
gold, let them tear off. And
they gave to me, and I cast
it into the fire, and this calf
came out.

25And Moses saw the
people, that it was un-
loosed, for Aaron had let *it*
loose for a derision among
their enemies. 26And
Moses stood in the gate of
the camp and said, Who *is*
for Jehovah? *Come* to me!
And all the sons of Levi
assembled to him. 27And
he said to them, So says
Jehovah, God of Israel,
each one put his sword on
his thigh; pass over to and
fro from gate to gate in the
camp, and each one kill his
brother, and each one his
neighbor, and each one
his kindred. 28And the
sons of Levi did according
to the word of Moses. And
about three thousand men
of the people fell on that
day. 29And Moses said,
Fill your hand today for
Jehovah, since each one
has been against his son
and against his brother,
and in order to give you a
blessing today.

30And it happened on
the morrow, Moses said to
the people, You have
sinned a great sin. And
now I will go up to
Jehovah; perhaps I can
make atonement for your
sin. 31And Moses went
back to Jehovah and said,
Oh, this people has sinned
a great sin, and they have
made for themselves gods
of gold. 32And now if You
will, lift up their sin. And if
not, I pray, blot me out
from Your book which You
have written. 33And
Jehovah said to Moses,

776 5927 376 4872 2088 6440 3212
אשר ילכו לפנינו כי־זה משה האיש אשר העלנו מארץ
the from brought who man the ,Moses this as before may who
of land up us for ;us go

2091 559 1961 3045 3808 4714
24 מצרים לא ידענו מה־היה לו׃ ואמר להם למי זהב
,gold Whoever to I And of has what do we not ,Egypt
has ,them said .him become know

2088 5695 5927 784 7993 5414 6561
התפרקו ויתנו־לי ואשלכהו באש ויצא העגל הזה׃
.this calf came and the into it cast I and to and them let
out ,fire ,me gave they ;off tear

175 6544 6544 5971 4872 7200
25 וירא משה את־העם כי פרע הוא כי־פרעה אהרן
,Aaron let had for ,it was that the Moses And
loose (it) unloosed people saw

559 4264 8179 4872 5975 6965 8103
26 לשמצה בקמיהם׃ ויעמד משה בשער המחנה ויאמר
and ,camp the the in Moses stood And their among a for
,said of gate .enemies derision

559 3878 1121 622 3068
27 מי ליהוה אלי ויאספו אליו כל־בני לוי׃ ויאמר להם
,them to he And .Levi the all to And (Come) for who
said of sons him gathered !me to Jehovah (is)

3409 2719 376 7760 3478 430 3068 559
כה־אמר יהוה אלהי ישראל שימו איש־חרבו על־ירכו
his on his each put ,Israel of God ,Jehovah says Thus
;thigh sword one

251 376 2026 4264 8179 8179 7725 5674
עברו ושובו משער לשער במחנה והרגו איש־את־אחיו
his each kill and the in gate to from and to pass
,brother one ;camp gate fro over

1697 3878 1121 6213 7138 376 7453 376
28 ואיש את־רעהו ואיש את־קרבו׃ ויעשו בני־לוי כדבר
according ,Levi the And his each and his each and
word to of sons did .relative one ,neighbor one

376 505 7969 1931 3117 5971 5307 4872
משה ויפל מן־העם ביום ההוא כשלשת אלפי איש׃
.men thousand about that day on the of and ;Moses'
three people fell

1121 376 3588 3068 3117 3027 4390 4872 559
29 ויאמר משה מלאו ידכם היום ליהוה כי איש בבנו
against each since for today your fill ,Moses said And
son his one ,Jehovah hand

559 4283 1961 1293 3117 5414 251
30 ובאחיו ולתת עליכם היום ברכה׃ ויהי ממחרת ויאמר
that the on it And .blessing a today you in and against and
said ,morrow was give to order ;brother his

5927 6258 1419 2401 2398 5971 4872
משה אל־העם אתם חטאתם חטאה גדלה ועתה אעלה
will I and ;great sin a sinned have You the to Moses
up go now ,people

4872 7725 2403 1157 3722 194 3068
31 אל־יהוה אולי אכפרה בעד חטאתכם׃ וישב משה אל־
to Moses And .sin your for make can I perhaps ;Jehovah to
returned atonement

6213 1419 2401 2088 5971 2398 577 559 3068
יהוה ויאמר אנא חטא העם הזה חטאה גדלה ויעשו
they and ,great sin a this people has Oh and Jehovah
made have sinned said

4229 369 2403 5375 6258 1091 430
32 להם אלהי זהב׃ ועתה אם־תשא חטאתם ואם־אין מחני
blot ,not if and —sin their will You if now And .gold gods for
,out me up lift of gods themselves

4872 3068 559 3789 834 5612 4994
33 נא מספרך אשר כתבת׃ ויאמר יהוה אל־משה מי אשר
whoever ,Moses to Jehovah said And You which from ,pray I
.written have book Your

Whoever has sinned against Me, I will blot him from My book. [34]And now go, lead the people to that *place* which I have spoken to you. Behold, My Angel shall go before your face. And in the day of My visitation I will visit their sin on them. [35]And Jehovah plagued the people because they made the calf, which Aaron made.

34 חטא־לי אמחנו מספרי׃ ועתה לך ׀ נחה את־העם אל
אשר־דברתי לך הנה מלאכי ילך לפניך וביום פקדי
35 ופקדתי עלהם חטאתם׃ ויגף יהוה את־העם על אשר
עשו את־העגל אשר עשה אהרן׃

CAP. XXXIII לג

CHAPTER 33

CHAPTER 33

[1]And Jehovah spoke to Moses, Come, go up from here, you and the people whom you have caused to go up out from the land of Egypt, to the land which I swore to Abraham, to Isaac, and to Jacob, saying, I will give it to your seed. [2]And I will send an angel before your face, and I will drive out the Canaanites, the Amorites, and the Hittites, and the Perizzites, the Hivites, and the Jebusites; [3]to a land flowing *with* milk and honey. For I will not go up among you, for you *are* a stiff-necked people, lest I consume you in the way. [4]And the people heard this evil word, and they mourned, and did not put any ornaments on himself. [5]And Jehovah said to Moses, Say to the sons of Israel, You are a stiff-necked people; in one instant I will go up among you and I will consume you. And now lay off from you your ornaments, that I may know what I shall do to you. [6]And the sons of Israel pulled off their ornaments, from Mount Horeb. [7]And Moses took the tent and pitched it outside the camp, far off from the camp. And he called it the

1 וידבר יהוה אל־משה לך עלה מזה אתה והעם אשר
העלית מארץ מצרים אל־הארץ אשר נשבעתי לאברהם
2 ליצחק וליעקב לאמר לזרעך אתננה׃ ושלחתי לפניך
מלאך וגרשתי את־הכנעני האמרי והחתי והפרזי החוי
3 והיבוסי׃ אל־ארץ זבת חלב ודבש כי לא אעלה בקרבך
4 כי עם־קשה־ערף אתה פן־אכלך בדרך׃ וישמע העם
את־הדבר הרע הזה ויתאבלו ולא־שתו איש עדיו עליו׃
5 ויאמר יהוה אל־משה אמר אל־בני־ישראל אתם עם־
קשה־ערף רגע אחד אעלה בקרבך וכליתיך ועתה הורד
6 עדיך מעליך ואדעה מה אעשה־לך׃ ויתנצלו בני־
7 ישראל את־עדים מהר חורב׃ ומשה יקח את־האהל
ונטה־לו ׀ מחוץ למחנה הרחק מן־המחנה וקרא לו

tabernacle of the congregation. And it happened that everyone seeking Jehovah went to the tabernacle of the congregation which *was* outside the camp. 8And it happened as Moses went to the tabernacle, the people all rose and stood, each one at the door of his tent. And *they* looked after Moses until he had gone into the tabernacle. 9And it happened as Moses' went into the tabernacle, the pillar of cloud would come down and stand *at* the door of the tabernacle. And He spoke with Moses. 10And all the people would see the pillar of the cloud standing *at* the door of the tabernacle. And all the people rose and bowed themselves, each one *at* the door of his tent. 11And Jehovah would speak to Moses face to face, as a man speaks to his friend. And he would return to the camp. And his attendant, Joshua the son of Nun, a young man, did not leave the middle of the tabernacle.

12And Moses said to Jehovah, Behold, You *are* saying to me, Cause this people to go up. And You, You have not told me whom You will send with me. And yet You have said, I know you by name, and also you have found favor in My eyes. 13And now, if I have found favor in Your eyes, please make me see Your ways, and let me know You, so that I may find favor in Your eyes; and consider that this nation is Your people. 14And He said, My presence will go *with you*, and I will give you rest. 15And he said to Him, If Your presence does not go, do not cause us to go up from here. 16And now by what can it be known that I and Your people have found favor in

אֹהֶל מוֹעֵד וְהָיָה כָּל־מְבַקֵּשׁ יְהוָה יֵצֵא אֶל־אֹהֶל מוֹעֵד
8 אֲשֶׁר מִחוּץ לַמַּחֲנֶה׃ וְהָיָה כְּצֵאת מֹשֶׁה אֶל־הָאֹהֶל
יָקוּמוּ כָּל־הָעָם וְנִצְּבוּ אִישׁ פֶּתַח אָהֳלוֹ וְהִבִּיטוּ אַחֲרֵי
9 מֹשֶׁה עַד־בֹּאוֹ הָאֹהֱלָה׃ וְהָיָה כְּבֹא מֹשֶׁה הָאֹהֱלָה יֵרֵד
10 עַמּוּד הֶעָנָן וְעָמַד פֶּתַח הָאֹהֶל וְדִבֶּר עִם־מֹשֶׁה׃ וְרָאָה
כָל־הָעָם אֶת־עַמּוּד הֶעָנָן עֹמֵד פֶּתַח הָאֹהֶל וְקָם כָּל־הָעָם
11 וְהִשְׁתַּחֲווּ אִישׁ פֶּתַח אָהֳלוֹ׃ וְדִבֶּר יְהוָה אֶל־מֹשֶׁה פָּנִים
אֶל־פָּנִים כַּאֲשֶׁר יְדַבֵּר אִישׁ אֶל־רֵעֵהוּ וְשָׁב אֶל־הַמַּחֲנֶה
וּמְשָׁרְתוֹ יְהוֹשֻׁעַ בִּן־נוּן נַעַר לֹא יָמִישׁ מִתּוֹךְ הָאֹהֶל׃ פ
12 וַיֹּאמֶר מֹשֶׁה אֶל־יְהוָה רְאֵה אַתָּה אֹמֵר אֵלַי הַעַל אֶת־
הָעָם הַזֶּה וְאַתָּה לֹא הוֹדַעְתַּנִי אֵת אֲשֶׁר־תִּשְׁלַח עִמִּי וְאַתָּה
13 אָמַרְתָּ יְדַעְתִּיךָ בְשֵׁם וְגַם־מָצָאתָ חֵן בְּעֵינָי׃ וְעַתָּה אִם־
נָא מָצָאתִי חֵן בְּעֵינֶיךָ הוֹדִעֵנִי נָא אֶת־דְּרָכֶךָ וְאֵדָעֲךָ לְמַעַן
14 אֶמְצָא־חֵן בְּעֵינֶיךָ וּרְאֵה כִּי עַמְּךָ הַגּוֹי הַזֶּה׃ וַיֹּאמַר פָּנַי
15 יֵלֵכוּ וַהֲנִחֹתִי לָךְ׃ וַיֹּאמֶר אֵלָיו אִם־אֵין פָּנֶיךָ הֹלְכִים אַל־
16 תַּעֲלֵנוּ מִזֶּה׃ וּבַמֶּה יִוָּדַע אֵפוֹא כִּי־מָצָאתִי חֵן בְּעֵינֶיךָ אֲנִי

Your eyes? *Is it* not in Your going with us? And we are distinguished, I and Your people, from all the nations which *are* on the face of the earth?

[17]And Jehovah said to Moses, This thing which you have spoken I will do. For you have found favor in My eyes, and I know you by name. [18]And he said, I pray, let me see Your glory. [19]And He said, I will cause all My goodness to pass before your face. And I will call out the name of Jehovah before your face. And I will favor whom I will favor, and I will have mercy on whom I will have mercy. [20]And he said, You are not able to see My face; for no man sees Me and lives. [21]And Jehovah said, Behold, a place by Me! And you shall stand on a rock. [22]And as My glory is passing it will be that I will put you in a cleft of the rock; and I will cover My palm over you during My passing. [23]And I will remove My palm, and you shall see My back; but My face cannot be seen.

1471 5971 6395 3212 5971
וְעַמֶּךָ הֲלוֹא בְּלֶכְתְּךָ עִמָּנוּ וְנִפְלֵינוּ אֲנִי וְעַמְּךָ מִכָּל־הָעָם
the nations from all Your people, and I distinguished are, we So ?us with Your going in (it Is) not ?people Your and
127 6440 834
אֲשֶׁר עַל־פְּנֵי הָאֲדָמָה׃
?earth the face of the on which (are)

1696 834 2088 1697 1571 4872 3068 559
17 וַיֹּאמֶר יְהוָה אֶל־מֹשֶׁה גַּם אֶת־הַדָּבָר הַזֶּה אֲשֶׁר דִּבַּרְתָּ
have you spoken which this thing Also ,Moses to Jehovah And said
7200 559 8034 3045 5869 2580 4672 6213
18 אֶעֱשֶׂה כִּי־מָצָאתָ חֵן בְּעֵינַי וָאֵדָעֲךָ בְּשֵׁם׃ וַיֹּאמַר הַרְאֵנִי
me Let see he And said .name by I and you know My in ,eyes favor have you found for will I ;do
6440 2898 3605 5674 559 3519 4994
19 נָא אֶת־כְּבֹדֶךָ׃ וַיֹּאמֶר אֲנִי אַעֲבִיר כָּל־טוּבִי עַל־פָּנֶיךָ
your before ,face My goodness all cause will pass to I He And ,said Your .glory I ,pray
7355 2603 6440 3068 8034 7121
וְקָרָאתִי בְשֵׁם יְהוָה לְפָנֶיךָ וְחַנֹּתִי אֶת־אֲשֶׁר אָחֹן וְרִחַמְתִּי
have will I on mercy will I ,favor whom will I and favor before ,you Jehovah the of name will I and proclaim
6440 7200 3201 559 7355
20 אֶת־אֲשֶׁר אֲרַחֵם׃ וַיֹּאמֶר לֹא תוּכַל לִרְאֹת אֶת־פָּנָי כִּי
for My ;face see to are You able not He And ,said have will I .mercy whom
5324 4725 2009 3068 559 2425 120 7200
21 לֹא־יִרְאַנִי הָאָדָם וָחָי׃ וַיֹּאמֶר יְהוָה הִנֵּה מָקוֹם אִתִּי וְנִצַּבְתָּ
you And stand shall by ;Me place a ,Behold ,Jehovah And said and .live man see can Me no
6697 5366 7760 3519 5674 1961 6697 5921
22 עַל־הַצּוּר׃ וְהָיָה בַּעֲבֹר כְּבֹדִי וְשַׂמְתִּיךָ בְּנִקְרַת הַצּוּר
the ;rock a in of cleft put will I you My ,glory is as passing it And be shall .rock a on
7200 3709 5493 5674/5704 5921 3709 5526
23 וְשַׂכֹּתִי כַפִּי עָלֶיךָ עַד־עָבְרִי׃ וַהֲסִרֹתִי אֶת־כַּפִּי וְרָאִיתָ
you and see shall ,palm My I And remove will My .passing during over you My palm will I and cover
7200 3808 6440 268
אֶת־אֲחֹרָי וּפָנַי לֹא יֵרָאוּ׃
be can .seen not My face but My ;back

CAP. XXXIV לד

CHAPTER 34

CHAPTER 34

[1]And Jehovah said to Moses, Cut out for yourself two tablets of stone, like the former. And I will write on the tablets the words which were on the former tablet, which you broke. [2]And be prepared in the morning, and go up in the morning to Mount Sinai. And place yourself there by Me, on the top of the mountain. [3]And a man shall not go up with you. And also let no man be seen on all the mountain. Also do not allow the flocks and the

7223 68 3871 8147 4872 3068 559
1 וַיֹּאמֶר יְהוָה אֶל־מֹשֶׁה פְּסָל־לְךָ שְׁנֵי־לֻחֹת אֲבָנִים כָּרִאשֹׁנִים
the like ;former ,stone tablets of two out Cut yourself for ,Moses to Jehovah And said
3871 1961 834 1697 3871 5921 3789
וְכָתַבְתִּי עַל־הַלֻּחֹת אֶת־הַדְּבָרִים אֲשֶׁר הָיוּ עַל־הַלֻּחֹת
the tablets on were which words the the tablets on I and write will
1242 5927 1242 3559 1961 7665 834 7223
2 הָרִאשֹׁנִים אֲשֶׁר שִׁבַּרְתָּ׃ וֶהְיֵה נָכוֹן לַבֹּקֶר וְעָלִיתָ בַבֹּקֶר
the in morning go and up the in morning prepared And be you .broke which ,former
3808 376 2022 7218 5921 8033 5324 5514 2022
3 אֶל־הַר סִינַי וְנִצַּבְתָּ לִי שָׁם עַל־רֹאשׁ הָהָר׃ וְאִישׁ לֹא־
not a And man the .mount top the of on there by Me place and yourself ,Sinai Mount to
1241 6629 1571 2022/3605 7200 408 376 1571 5927
יַעֲלֶה עִמָּךְ וְגַם־אִישׁ אַל־יֵרָא בְּכָל־הָהָר גַּם־הַצֹּאן וְהַבָּקָר
the and herds the flocks also the ;mountain all on be let seen no man And also with .you shall up go

herds to feed before that 4
mountain. [4]And he cut out
two tablets of stone like the
former. And Moses rose
early in the morning and
went up into Mount Sinai,
as Jehovah had com-
manded him. And he took 5
in his hand the two tablets
of stone. [5]And Jehovah
came down in the cloud.
And he placed himself there 6
with Him, and *he* called on
the name of Jehovah. [6]And
Jehovah passed by before
his face and called out:
Jehovah! Jehovah, God!
Merciful and gracious, slow
to anger, and great in goodness and truth, [7]keeping 7
mercy for thousands, for-
giving iniquity and transgression and sin, and not
leaving entirely unpun-
ished, visiting *the* iniquity of
fathers on sons, and on
sons of sons, to the third
and to the fourth *generation*. 8
[8]And Moses hurried and
bowed to the earth and
worshiped. [9]And he said, If 9
now I have found favor in
Your eyes, O Lord, please
let my Lord go in our midst,
for it *is* a stiff-necked
people; and You forgive our
iniquity and our sin, and
take us as a possession.
[10]And He said, Behold, I 10
am cutting a covenant; I will
do wonderful things before
all your people, which not
have been done in all the
earth and among all nations.
And all the people, in
whose midst you *are*, shall
see the work of Jehovah,
for that which I *am* about to
do *is* awesome.

[11]Take note for yourself 11
what I *am* commanding you
today. Behold, I *am* about to
drive out from before your
face the Amorites, and the
Canaanites, and the Hit-
tites, and the Perizzites,
and the Hivites, and the
Jebusites. [12]Take heed to 12
yourself, that you not cut a
covenant with the people of
the land *to* which you *are*

68 3871 8147 6458 1931 2022 4136 7462
אַל־יִרְעוּ אֶל־מוּל הָהָר הַהוּא׃ וַיִּפְסֹל שְׁנֵי־לֻחֹת אֲבָנִים
stone tablets two he And .that mountain before let do not
of out cut feed

5514 2022 5927 1242 4872 7925 7223
כָּרִאשֹׁנִים וַיַּשְׁכֵּם מֹשֶׁה בַבֹּקֶר וַיַּעַל אֶל־הַר סִינַי כַּאֲשֶׁר
as ,Sinai Mount into and the in Moses rose And the like
up went morning early .former

3068 3381 68 3871 8147 3027 3947 3068 6680
צִוָּה יְהוָה אֹתוֹ וַיִּקַּח בְּיָדוֹ שְׁנֵי לֻחֹת אֲבָנִים׃ וַיֵּרֶד יְהוָה
Jehovah And .stone tablets the his in he and ;him Jehovah had
down came of two hand took commanded

3068 5674 3068 8034 7121 8033 3320 6051
בֶּעָנָן וַיִּתְיַצֵּב עִמּוֹ שָׁם וַיִּקְרָא בְשֵׁם יְהוָה׃ וַיַּעֲבֹר יְהוָה ׀
Jehovah And .Jehovah the on and there Him with he and the in
by passed of name called himself placed ;cloud

639 750 2587 7349 410 3068 3068 7121 6440
עַל־פָּנָיו וַיִּקְרָא יְהוָה ׀ יְהוָה אֵל רַחוּם וְחַנּוּן אֶרֶךְ אַפַּיִם
,anger to slow and merciful !God ,Jehovah !Jehovah and his before
,gracious :proclaimed face

6588 5771 5375 505 2617 5341 571 2617 7227
וְרַב־חֶסֶד וֶאֱמֶת׃ נֹצֵר חֶסֶד לָאֲלָפִים נֹשֵׂא עָוֺן וָפֶשַׁע
and iniquity forgiving for mercy keeping and good- in and
transgression ,thousands ,truth ness great

5921 1121 1 5771 6485 5352 3808 5352 2403
וְחַטָּאָה וְנַקֵּה לֹא יְנַקֶּה פֹּקֵד ׀ עֲוֺן אָבוֹת עַל־בָּנִים וְעַל־
on and ,sons on fathers (the) visiting leaving not and ,sin and
of iniquity ,unpunished entirely

6915 4872 4116 7243 8029 1121 1121
בְּנֵי בָנִים עַל־שִׁלֵּשִׁים וְעַל־רִבֵּעִים׃ וַיְמַהֵר מֹשֶׁה וַיִּקֹּד
and Moses And fourth the and third the to sons sons
bowed hurried .(generation) to of

5869 136 2580 4672 4994 559 7812 776
אַרְצָה וַיִּשְׁתָּחוּ׃ וַיֹּאמֶר אִם־נָא מָצָאתִי חֵן בְּעֵינֶיךָ אֲדֹנָי
O Your in favor have I ,now If he And and the to
,Lord ,eyes found ,said .worshiped earth

5545 6203 7186 5971 7130 136 4994/3212
יֵלֶךְ־נָא אֲדֹנָי בְּקִרְבֵּנוּ כִּי עַם־קְשֵׁה־עֹרֶף הוּא וְסָלַחְתָּ
You and ,(is) it stiff-necked a for our in my I let
forgive people ;midst Lord ,pray go

3772 2009 559 5157 2403 5771
לַעֲוֺנֵנוּ וּלְחַטָּאתֵנוּ וּנְחַלְתָּנוּ׃ וַיֹּאמֶר הִנֵּה אָנֹכִי כֹּרֵת
cutting (am) I Behold He And us take and our and our
,said .possession a as sin ,iniquity

3605 1254 3808 834 6381 6213 5971/3605 1285
בְּרִית נֶגֶד כָּל־עַמְּךָ אֶעֱשֶׂה נִפְלָאֹת אֲשֶׁר לֹא־נִבְרְאוּ בְכָל־
all in been have not which wonderful will I your all before a
done ,things do people ;covenant

7130 5971 3605 1471 8605 776
הָאָרֶץ וּבְכָל־הַגּוֹיִם וְרָאָה כָל־הָעָם אֲשֶׁר־אַתָּה בְקִרְבּוֹ
midst in you whose the shall all and ;nations and the
(are) people see all among earth

6213 834 3372 3068 4639
אֶת־מַעֲשֵׂה יְהוָה כִּי־נוֹרָא הוּא אֲשֶׁר אֲנִי עֹשֶׂה עִמָּךְ׃
with about (am) I which that (is) for ,Jehovah work the
,you do to awesome of

6440 1644 3117 6680 8104
שְׁמָר־לְךָ אֵת אֲשֶׁר אָנֹכִי מְצַוְּךָ הַיּוֹם הִנְנִי גֹרֵשׁ מִפָּנֶיךָ
from to about behold ;today command- I what for Take
you before out drive (am) I you ing (am) yourself heed

2983 2340 6522 2850 3669 567
אֶת־הָאֱמֹרִי וְהַכְּנַעֲנִי וְהַחִתִּי וְהַפְּרִזִּי וְהַחִוִּי וְהַיְבוּסִי׃
the and the and the and the and the and the
.Jebusites ,Hivites ,Perizzites ,Hittites ,Canaanites ,Amorites

935 776 5971 1285 3772 8104
הִשָּׁמֶר לְךָ פֶּן־תִּכְרֹת בְּרִית לְיוֹשֵׁב הָאָרֶץ אֲשֶׁר אַתָּה בָּא
going you (to) land the the with a cut you lest for Be
(are) which of people covenant yourself careful

going in, that it not be a
snare in your midst. 13But
you shall cut down their
altars, and break their
images, and you shall cut
off their shrines. 14For
you shall not bow to an-
other god; for Jehovah's
name *is* Jealous; He *is* a
jealous God; 15that you
not cut a covenant with
the people of the land,
and *lest* they whore after
their gods, and they
sacrifice to their gods,
and one call to you, and
you eat from his sacrifice;
16and you take from their
daughters for your sons
and commit whoredom
after their daughters,
after their gods, and they
lead your sons to whore-
dom after their gods.
17You shall not make
for yourself casted gods.
18You shall keep the
Feast of Unleavened
Bread. Seven days you
shall eat unleavened
bread, which I com-
manded you, at the time
appointed, the month of
Abib. For in the month
of Abib you went out from
Egypt. 19Every one open-
ing the womb *is* Mine;
and of all your male livestock, a firstling of ox or
sheep, 20and a firstling of
an ass you shall redeem
with a lamb. And if you do
not redeem, you shall
break its neck. You shall
redeem every firstborn of
your sons, and they shall
not appear before My
face empty.
21You may work six
days, and on the seventh
day you shall rest. 22And
you shall observe a Feast
of Weeks for yourself, the
firstfruits of the harvest of
wheat; also the Feast of
Ingathering *at* the turn of
the year. 23Three times
in the year every male of
yours shall appear before
the Lord Jehovah, the
God of Israel. 24For I will
expel nations from before
your face, and you will
make broad your border;

5422 4196 7130 4170
13 עָלֶיהָ פֶּן־יִהְיֶה לְמוֹקֵשׁ בְּקִרְבֶּךָ׃ כִּי אֶת־מִזְבְּחֹתָם תִּתֹּצוּן
shall you down cut | their altars | But | your in .midst | snare a | be it lest | ;in

3808 3772 842 7605 4676
14 וְאֶת־מַצֵּבֹתָם תְּשַׁבֵּרוּן וְאֶת־אֲשֵׁרָיו תִּכְרֹתוּן׃ כִּי לֹא
not | For | shall you off cut | their and shrines | ,break | their and images

7067 410 8034 7067 3068 312 410 7812
תִשְׁתַּחֲוֶה לְאֵל אַחֵר כִּי יְהוָה קַנָּא שְׁמוֹ אֵל קַנָּא הוּא׃
He ;(is) | jealous | a God | whose ,name | (is) Jehovah Jealous | for | ;another god | to | shall you bow

430 310 2181 776 5971 1285 3772
15 פֶּן־תִּכְרֹת בְּרִית לְיוֹשֵׁב הָאָרֶץ וְזָנוּ ׀ אַחֲרֵי אֱלֹהֵיהֶם
,gods their | after | they and whore the play | land the | the with of people | a covenant | cut you | lest

3947 2077 398 7121 430 2076
16 וְזָבְחוּ לֵאלֹהֵיהֶם וְקָרָא לְךָ וְאָכַלְתָּ מִזִּבְחוֹ׃ וְלָקַחְתָּ
you and take | his from ;sacrifice | you and eat | to ,you | one and call | their to ,gods | they and sacrifice

2181 430 310 1323 2181 1121 1323
מִבְּנֹתָיו לְבָנֶיךָ וְזָנוּ בְנֹתָיו אַחֲרֵי אֱלֹהֵיהֶן וְהִזְנוּ אֶת־
lead they and whoredom to | ,gods their | after | their daughters | com- and mit whoredom | your for ,sons | their from daughters

6213 3808 4541 430 430 310 1121
17 בָּנֶיךָ אַחֲרֵי אֱלֹהֵיהֶן׃ אֱלֹהֵי מַסֵּכָה לֹא תַעֲשֶׂה־לָּךְ׃ אֶת־
18
for ,yourself | shall You make | not | casted | gods | .gods their | after | your sons

6680 834 4682 398 3117 7651 8104 4682 2282
חַג הַמַּצּוֹת תִּשְׁמֹר שִׁבְעַת יָמִים תֹּאכַל מַצּוֹת אֲשֶׁר צִוִּיתִךָ
com- I ;you manded | which | unlea- ,bread vened | shall you eat | days | seven | shall You ;keep | unleavened the bread of feast

4714 3318 24 2320 24 2320 4150
לְמוֹעֵד חֹדֶשׁ הָאָבִיב כִּי בְּחֹדֶשׁ הָאָבִיב יָצָאתָ מִמִּצְרָיִם׃
from .Egypt | went you out | Abib | the in of month | for | ;Abib | the of month | the at ,time fixed

7716 7794 6363 2142 4735 3605 7358 6363 3605
19 כָּל־פֶּטֶר רֶחֶם לִי וְכָל־מִקְנְךָ תִּזָּכָר פֶּטֶר שׁוֹר וָשֶׂה׃
or ;sheep | ox | a of firstling | ,male | your livestock | all and (is) ;Mine | the opening womb | Every of

3605 6202 6299 3808 7716 6299 2543 6363
20 וּפֶטֶר חֲמוֹר תִּפְדֶּה בְשֶׂה וְאִם־לֹא תִפְדֶּה וַעֲרַפְתּוֹ כֹּל
every | shall you ;neck its break | do you ,redeem | not if and | a with ;lamb | shall you redeem | ,ass an | a and of firstling

3117 8337 7387 6440 7200 6299 1121 1060
21 בְּכוֹר בָּנֶיךָ תִּפְדֶּה וְלֹא־יֵרָאוּ פָנַי רֵיקָם׃ שֵׁשֶׁת יָמִים
days | Six | .empty | before Me | shall they and appear not | shall you redeem | your sons | first- of born

7673 7102 2758 7673 7637 3117 5647
תַּעֲבֹד וּבַיּוֹם הַשְּׁבִיעִי תִּשְׁבֹּת בֶּחָרִישׁ וּבַקָּצִיר תִּשְׁבֹּת׃
shall you .rest | in and harvest | in plowing | shall you ;rest | seventh | on and day the | may you ,work

614 2282 2406 7105 1061 8104 7620 2282
22 וְחַג שָׁבֻעֹת תַּעֲשֶׂה לְךָ בִּכּוּרֵי קְצִיר חִטִּים וְחַג הָאָסִיף
gath- the in ering | and of feast | ;wheat | the of harvest | first- the of fruits | for ,yourself | shall you observe | weeks | a And of feast

2138 3605 7200 8141 6471 7969 8141 8622
23 תְּקוּפַת הַשָּׁנָה׃ שָׁלֹשׁ פְּעָמִים בַּשָּׁנָה יֵרָאֶה כָּל־זְכוּרְךָ
of male yours | every | shall appear | the in year | times | Three | .year the | the (at) of turn

1471 3423 3478 430 3068 113 6440
24 אֶת־פְּנֵי הָאָדֹן ׀ יְהוָה אֱלֹהֵי יִשְׂרָאֵל׃ כִּי־אוֹרִישׁ גּוֹיִם
nations | will I dispossess | For | .Israel | the of God | Jehovah | the Lord | before

776 376 2530 3808 1366 7337 6440
מִפָּנֶיךָ וְהִרְחַבְתִּי אֶת־גְּבוּלֶךָ וְלֹא־יַחְמֹד אִישׁ אֶת־אַרְצְךָ
your ,land | one | shall covet | no and | your ;territory | will you and broad make | be- from you fore

and no one shall covet your land, as you go up to appear before Jehovah your God three times in the year. 25 You shall not slaughter the blood of My sacrifice on leavened bread, nor shall the sacrifice of the feast of the Passover pass the night until morning. 26 You shall bring the first of the firstfruits of your ground *to* the house of Jehovah your God. You shall not boil a kid in the milk of its mother.

27 And Jehovah said to Moses, Write these words for **yourself**, for on the mouth of these words I will cut a covenant with you and with Israel. 28 And he was there with Jehovah forty days and forty nights; he did not eat bread and he did not drink water. And He wrote on the tablets the words of the covenant, the Ten Commandments.

29 And it happened as Moses was going down from the mountain of Sinai, the two tablets of the testimony being in Moses' hand as he went down from the mountain, Moses did not know that the skin of his face had become luminous through His speaking with him. 30 And Aaron and all the sons of Israel saw Moses, and, behold, the skin of his face had become luminous. And they were afraid to draw near to him. 31 And Moses called to them. And Aaron and all the leaders among the congregation turned back to him. And Moses spoke to them. 32 And afterwards all the sons of Israel drew near. And he commanded them *to do* all which Jehovah had spoken with him in the mountain of Sinai. 33 And Moses finished speaking with them, and he put a veil on his face. 34 And as Moses came in before Jehovah to speak with Him, he would remove the veil until he went out; and he would go

8141 6471 7969 430 3068 6440 7200 5927
בַּעֲלֹתְךָ לֵרָאוֹת אֶת־פְּנֵי יְהוָה אֱלֹהֶיךָ שָׁלֹשׁ פְּעָמִים בַּשָּׁנָה׃
the in times three your Jehovah before to you as
year God appear up go

2282/2077 1242 3885 2077 1818 2557 7919 3808
25 לֹא־תִשְׁחַט עַל־חָמֵץ דַּם־זִבְחִי וְלֹא־יָלִין לַבֹּקֶר זֶבַח חַג
the sacri- the the till shall not and sacri- My the leavened on shall you Not
of feast of fice morning remain ,fice of blood bread slaughter

430 3068 1004 935 127 1061 7225 6453
26 הַפָּסַח׃ רֵאשִׁית בִּכּוּרֵי אַדְמָתְךָ תָּבִיא בֵּית יְהוָה אֱלֹהֶיךָ
your Jehovah the (to) shall you your first- the the the
;God of house bring ground of fruits of first .Passover

517 2461 1423 1310 3808
לֹא־תְבַשֵּׁל גְּדִי בַּחֲלֵב אִמּוֹ׃
its the in kid a shall you not
.mother of milk boil

1697 3789 4872 3068 559
27 וַיֹּאמֶר יְהוָה אֶל־מֹשֶׁה כְּתָב־לְךָ אֶת־הַדְּבָרִים הָאֵלֶּה כִּי
for ;these words for Write ,Moses to Jehovah said And
yourself

3478 1285 3772 1697 6310
עַל־פִּי ׀ הַדְּבָרִים הָאֵלֶּה כָּרַתִּי אִתְּךָ בְּרִית וְאֶת־יִשְׂרָאֵל׃
.Israel and a with will I these words the on
with covenant you cut of mouth

3899 3915 703 3117 705 3068 8033/1961
28 וַיְהִי־שָׁם עִם־יְהוָה אַרְבָּעִים יוֹם וְאַרְבָּעִים לַיְלָה לֶחֶם
bread ;nights forty and days forty Jehovah with there And was he

1697 3871 5921 3789 8354 3808 4325 398
לֹא אָכַל וּמַיִם לֹא שָׁתָה וַיִּכְתֹּב עַל־הַלֻּחֹת אֵת דִּבְרֵי
the the on he and did he not and did he not
of words tablets wrote ;drink water ,eat

5514 2022 4872 3381 1961 6680 6235 1285
29 הַבְּרִית עֲשֶׂרֶת הַדְּבָרִים׃ וַיְהִי בְּרֶדֶת מֹשֶׁה מֵהַר סִינַי
,Sinai from Moses was as it And the ten the
Mount down going ,was commandments ,covenant

3808 4872 2022 3381 4872 3027 5715 3871 8147
וּשְׁנֵי לֻחֹת הָעֵדֻת בְּיַד־מֹשֶׁה בְּרִדְתּוֹ מִן־הָהָר וּמֹשֶׁה לֹא־
not that the from he as Moses' being the tablets the
Moses mountain down went hand in testimony of two

1121 3605 175 7200 1696 6440 5785 7160 3045
30 יָדַע כִּי קָרַן עוֹר פָּנָיו בְּדַבְּרוֹ אִתּוֹ׃ וַיַּרְא אַהֲרֹן וְכָל־בְּנֵי
the and Aaron saw with through his skin had that did
of sons all ;him speaking His face- shiny become know

5066 3372 6440 5785 7160 2009 4872 3478
יִשְׂרָאֵל אֶת־מֹשֶׁה וְהִנֵּה קָרַן עוֹר פָּנָיו וַיִּירְאוּ מִגֶּשֶׁת
to they and his skin had ,lo ,and ;Moses Israel
approach afraid were ;face- shiny become

3605 175 7725 4872 7121
31 אֵלָיו׃ וַיִּקְרָא אֲלֵהֶם מֹשֶׁה וַיָּשֻׁבוּ אֵלָיו אַהֲרֹן וְכָל־
all and Aaron him to and ,Moses them to And .him
back turned called

3605/5066 310 4872 1696 5712 8260
32 הַנְּשִׂאִים בָּעֵדָה וַיְדַבֵּר מֹשֶׁה אֲלֵהֶם׃ וְאַחֲרֵי־כֵן נִגְּשׁוּ כָּל־
all came And .them to Moses And the of chiefs the
near afterwards spoke .congregation

2022 3068 1696 834 3605 6680 3478 1121
בְּנֵי יִשְׂרָאֵל וַיְצַוֵּם אֵת כָּל־אֲשֶׁר דִּבֶּר יְהוָה אִתּוֹ בְּהַר
in with Jehovah had which all he And .Israel the
Mount him spoken them commanded of sons

935 4533 6440/5921 5414 1696 4872 3615 5514
33 34 סִינָי׃ וַיְכַל מֹשֶׁה מִדַּבֵּר אִתָּם וַיִּתֵּן עַל־פָּנָיו מַסְוֶה׃ וּבְבֹא
as And .veil a his on he and with speaking Moses And .Sinai
in came face put ,them finished

5927 5704 4533 5493 1696 3068 6440 4872
מֹשֶׁה לִפְנֵי יְהוָה לְדַבֵּר אִתּוֹ יָסִיר אֶת־הַמַּסְוֶה עַד־צֵאתוֹ
went he until veil the he with to Jehovah before Moses
;out off took Him speak

out and speak to the sons of Israel what he was commanded. [35]And the sons of Israel would see the face of Moses, that the skin of the face of Moses had become luminous. And Moses would put the veil back on his face until he went to speak with Him.

CHAPTER 35

[1]And Moses assembled all the congregation of the sons of Israel and said to them, These *are* the words which Jehovah has commanded, to do them: [2]Work may be done six days, and on the seventh day it shall be holy to you, a sabbath of rest to Jehovah; everyone doing work in it shall be put to death. [3]You shall not kindle a fire in all your dwellings on the day of the Sabbath.

[4]And Moses said to all the congregation of the sons of Israel, saying, This *is* the thing which Jehovah commanded, saying: [5]Take from among you an offering to Jehovah. Everyone willing of heart shall bring it, the offering of Jehovah: gold and silver and bronze, [6]and blue, and purple, and crimson, and bleached *linen*, and goats' *hair*, [7]and rams' skins dyed red, and dugong skins, and acacia-wood, [8]and oil for the light, and spices for the oil of anointing, and for the incense of perfumes; [9]and onyx stones, and stones of settings, for the ephod and for the pocket. [10]And every wise-hearted one of you, let them come and make all which Jehovah has commanded: [11]the tabernacle, its tent,

1121 7200 6680 3478 1121 1696 5927

35 יצא ודבר אל־בני ישראל את אשר יצוה׃ וראו בני

the And was he what Israel the to speak and he and
of sons see would .commanded of sons leave would

4872 7725 4872 6440 5785 7160 4872 6440 3478

ישראל את־פני משה כי קרן עור פני משה והשיב משה

Moses would and ;Moses the skin had that ,Moses the Israel
back put of face- shiny become of face

1696 935 5704 6440 4533

את־המסוה על־פניו עד־באו לדבר אתו׃

with speak to he until his on veil the
.Him went face

CAP. XXXV לה

CHAPTER 35

559 3478 1121 5712 3605 4872 6950

1 ויקהל משה את־כל־עדת בני ישראל ויאמר אלהם

,them to said and Israel the the all Moses And
of sons of congregation assembled

3177 8337 6213 3068 6680 834 1697

2 אלה הדברים אשר־צוה יהוה לעשת אתם׃ ששת ימים

days Six :them do to ,Jehovah has which the These
commanded words (are)

7676 6944 1961 7637 3117 4399 6213

תעשה מלאכה וביום השביעי יהיה לכם קדש שבת

a ,holy you to shall it ,seventh on and ,work be may
of sabbath be day the done

1197 3808 4191 4399 6213 3605 3068 7677

3 שבתון ליהוה כל־העשה בו מלאכה יומת׃ לא־תבערו

shall you Not be shall work it in doing every to rest
kindle .executed one ;Jehovah

7676 3117 4186 3605 784

אש בכל משבתיכם ביום השבת׃

the the on your all in fire a
Sabbath of day dwellings

1697 559 3478 1121 5712 3605 4872 559

4 ויאמר משה אל־כל־עדת בני־ישראל לאמר זה הדבר

the This ,saying ,Israel the con- the all to Moses And
thing (is) of sons of gregation spoke

3605/3068 8641 3947 559 3068 6680 834

5 אשר־צוה יהוה לאמר׃ קחו מאתכם תרומה ליהוה כל

Every to an among from Take ,saying ,Jehovah has which
one .Jehovah offering you commanded

5178 3701 2091 3068 8641 935/3820 5081

נדיב לבו יביאה את תרומת יהוה זהב וכסף ונחשת׃

and and ,gold ;Jehovah the shall heart willing
,bronze silver of offering ,it bring of

5785 352 5795 8336 8144 8438 713 8504

6 ותכלת וארגמן ותולעת שני ושש ועזים׃ וערת אילם
7

rams' skins and goats' and and crimson and and ,blue and
(hair) ,bleached ,purple

3974 8081 7848 6086 8476 5785 119

8 מאדמים וערת תחשים ועצי שטים׃ ושמן למאור

the for oil and ,acacia- and ,dugong and ,red died
light wood skins

7718 68 5561 7004 4888 8081 1314

9 ובשמים לשמן המשחה ולקטרת הסמים׃ ואבני־שהם

,onyx and the for and the oil for and
stones ,perfumes of incense ,anointing of spices

935 3820 2450 2833 646 4396 68

10 ואבני מלאים לאפוד ולחשן׃ וכל־חכם־לב בכם יבאו

let among hearted-wise And the for and the for ,settings and
come them ,you one every .pocket ephod of stones

168 4908 3068 6680 834 3605 6213

11 ויעשו את כל־אשר צוה יהוה׃ את־המשכן את־אהלו

its the ;Jehovah has which all and
,tent ,tabernacle commanded make

and its cover, its hooks, its boards, its bars, its pillars, and its sockets; 12 the ark, and its poles, the mercy-seat and the veil of the covering, 13 the table and its poles, and all its vessels, and the Bread of the Presence; 14 and the lampstand of the light, and its vessels, and its lamps, and the oil of the light; 15 and the incense altar and its poles, and the oil of anointing, and the incense of perfumes, and the hanging of the door, at the door of the tabernacle; 16 the altar of burnt offering, and its bronze grating, its poles, and all its vessels, the laver and its base; 17 the hangings of the court, its pillars, and its sockets, and the hanging for the gate of the court; 18 the pins of the tabernacle, and the pins of the court, and their cords; 19 the woven garments to minister in the holy place, the holy garments for Aaron the priest, and the garments for his sons, to minister as priests.

20 And all the congregation of the sons of Israel went out from Moses. 21 And they came, every one whose heart was lifted up, and every one whose spirit made him willing. They brought the offering of Jehovah for the work of the tabernacle of the congregation, and for all its service and for the holy garments. 22 And the men came in together with the women, every one willing of heart. They brought in bracelets, and nose-rings and rings, and jewels, every gold article, and everyone who waved a wave offering.

5982 1280 7175 7165 4372
ואת־מכסהו את־קרסיו ואת־קרשיו את־בריחו את־עמדיו
,pillars its ,bars its ,boards its and ,hooks its ,cover its and

6532 3727 905 727 134
12 ואת־אדניו׃ את־הארן ואת־בדיו את־הכפרת ואת פרכת
the and of veil | the mercy-seat | ,poles its and | ,ark the | its ;sockets | and

3899 3627 3605 905 7979 4539
13 המסך׃ את־השלחן ואת־בדיו ואת־כל־כליו ואת לחם
bread | and | its ,vessels | all | and | its and ,poles | the ,table | the ,covering

5216 3627 3974 4501 6440
14 הפנים׃ ואת־מנרת המאור ואת־כליה ואת־נרתיה ואת
and | its ,lamps | and | its ,vessels | and | the ,light | the of lampstand | and | the show-

8081 905 7004 4196 3974 8081
15 שמן המאור׃ ואת־מזבח הקטרת ואת־בדיו ואת שמן
of oil | and | its poles | and | the ,incense- | altar | and | ;light the | the of oil

6607 6607 4539 5561 7004 4888
המשחה ואת קטרת הסמים ואת־מסך הפתח לפתח
the at of door | the door | the of hanging | and | the ,perfumes | incense of | and | the ,anointing

5178 4345 5930 4196 4908
16 המשכן׃ את | מזבח העלה ואת־מכבר הנחשת אשר
bronze | and grating | burnt the ,offering | altar the of | the ;tabernacle

7050 3653 3595 3627/8605 905
17 לו את־בדיו ואת־כל־כליו את־הכיר ואת־כנו׃ את קלעי
the of hangings | its ;base | and | the ,laver | its ,vessels | all | and | its ,poles | ,its

2691 8179 4539 134 5982 2691
החצר את־עמדיו ואת־אדניה ואת מסך שער החצר׃
the ;court | the of gate | the for hanging | and | its ,sockets | and | its ,pillars | the ,court

1697 2691 3489 4908 3489
18 את־יתדת המשכן ואת־יתדת החצר ואת־מיתריהם׃
;cords their | and | ,court the of | pins the | and | the tabernacle | the of pins

1 6944 899 6944 8334 8278 899
19 את־בגדי השרד לשרת בקדש את־בגדי הקדש לאהרן
for Aaron | holy the | garments | the in ,sanctuary | to minister | the woven | garments

3478 1121 5712 5927 3547 1121 899 3548
20 הכהן ואת־בגדי בניו לכהן׃ ויצאו כל־עדת בני־ישראל
Israel | the of sons | con- the gregation | all | went And out | priest- of ,hood | his sons' | garments and | the ,priest

3605 38 20/5375 376 3605/935 4872
21 מלפני משה׃ ויבאו כל־איש אשר־נשאו לבו וכל אשר
whose | and one every | ,heart | was up lifted | whose | one every | they And ,came | .Moses | from

168 4399 3068 8641 935 7307 5068
נדבה רוחו אתו הביאו את־תרומת יהוה למלאכת אהל
the of tent | the for of work | Jehovah | the of offering | they brought | ;him spirit | made willing

582 935 6944 899 3605 4150
22 מועד ולכל־עבדתו ולבגדי הקדש׃ ויבאו האנשים
men the | came And in | .holy the | for and garments | its ,service | for and all | ,meeting

3558 2885 5141 2397 935 3820 5081 3605 802 5921
על־הנשים כל | נדיב לב הביאו חח ונזם וטבעת וכומז
and ,jewels | ,rings and | and nose-rings | brace- ,lets | they in brought | ;heart | willing of | every one | the ,women | together with

3068 2091 8573 5130 376 3605 2091 3627
כל־כלי זהב וכל־איש אשר הניף תנופת זהב ליהוה׃
to .Jehovah | gold | wave a of offering | waved | who | one every | and | ;gold article every

to Jehovah. [23]And everyone *with* whom blue was
found, and purple, and
crimson, and bleached
linen, and goats' *hair*, and
rams' skins dyed red, and
dugong skins, they brought.
[24]Everyone rising up *with* an
offering of silver and
bronze, they brought the
offering of Jehovah; and
everyone *with* whom was
found acacia-wood for any
work of the service, they
brought. [25]And every wise-
hearted woman spun with
her hands; and they brought
spun yarn, blue, and purple,
and crimson and bleached
linen. [26]And all the women
whose hearts were lifted up
in wisdom spun the goats'
hair. [27]And the leaders
brought the onyx stones,
and stones for the setting,
for the ephod and for the
breastplate, [28]and the
spice, and the oil for the
light, and for the anointing
oil, and for the incense of
the perfumes. [29]And every
man and woman whose
hearts impelled them to
bring for all the work
which Jehovah com-
manded to be done by
the hand of Moses; the
sons of Israel brought a
willing offering to
Jehovah.

[30]And Moses said to the
sons of Israel, See, Jehovah
has called by name Beza-
leel the son of Uri, the son
of Hur, of the tribe of Judah.
[31]And He has filled him *with*
the spirit of God, in wisdom,
in intelligence, and in
knowledge, and in all work-
manship, and to devise
designs, to work in gold,
and in silver, and in bronze,
and in cuttings of stones for
finishing, and in carving of
wood, to work in all work-
manship of design. [34]And

8144/8438 713 8504 4672 376
23 וְכָל־אִישׁ אֲשֶׁר־נִמְצָא אִתּוֹ תְּכֵלֶת וְאַרְגָּמָן וְתוֹלַעַת שָׁנִי
.crimson and | and | .blue | with | was found | whom | one Every

935 8476 .purple 5785 119 352 5785 5795 8336
וְשֵׁשׁ וְעִזִּים וְעֹרֹת אֵילִם מְאָדָּמִים וְעֹרֹת תְּחָשִׁים הֵבִיאוּ׃
they brought | ,dugongs | skins and of | ,red dyed | rams' | and skins | and (hair) goats' | and ,linen

3068 8641 935 5178 3701 8641 7311 3605
24 כָּל־מֵרִים תְּרוּמַת כֶּסֶף וּנְחֹשֶׁת הֵבִיאוּ אֵת תְּרוּמַת יְהוָה
;Jehovah | the offering of | they brought | and bronze | silver | an offering of | lifting up | Every one

5656 4399 3605 7848 6086 4672 3605
וְכֹל אֲשֶׁר נִמְצָא אִתּוֹ עֲצֵי שִׁטִּים לְכָל־מְלֶאכֶת הָעֲבֹדָה
the service, | work of | any for | acacia | wood | with | was found | whom | and every one

4299 935 2906 3820 2450 802 935
25 הֵבִיאוּ׃ וְכָל־אִשָּׁה חַכְמַת־לֵב בְּיָדֶיהָ טָווּ וַיָּבִיאוּ מַטְוֶה
spun yarn | they brought and | ;spun | her with hands | wise hearted | woman And every | they ,brought

8336 8144 8438 713 8504
אֶת־הַתְּכֵלֶת וְאֶת־הָאַרְגָּמָן אֶת־תּוֹלַעַת הַשָּׁנִי וְאֶת־הַשֵּׁשׁ׃
bleached and .(linen) | ,crimson | ,purple | and | ,blue

2901 2437 3820 5375 802 3605
26 וְכָל־הַנָּשִׁים אֲשֶׁר נָשָׂא לִבָּן אֹתָנָה בְּחָכְמָה טָווּ אֶת־
spun | wisdom in | them | hearts lifted up | whose | the women | all And

68 7718 68 935 8260 5795
27 הָעִזִּים׃ וְהַנְּשִׂאִם הֵבִיאוּ אֵת אַבְנֵי הַשֹּׁהַם וְאֵת אַבְנֵי
stones for | and | onyx the | stones | brought | the And leaders | goats' the .(hair)

3974 8081 1314 2833 646 4394
28 הַמִּלֻּאִים לָאֵפוֹד וְלַחֹשֶׁן׃ וְאֶת־הַבֹּשֶׂם וְאֶת־הַשֶּׁמֶן לְמָאוֹר
the for ,light | oil the | and ,spice the | and the for .breastplate | and the for ephod | the ,setting

802 376 5561 7004 4888 8081
29 וּלְשֶׁמֶן הַמִּשְׁחָה וְלִקְטֹרֶת הַסַּמִּים׃ כָּל־אִישׁ וְאִשָּׁה אֲשֶׁר
whose | and woman | man Every | the perfumes | for and incense | the ,anointing | for and of oil

3068 6680 834 4399 935 3820 5068
נָדַב לִבָּם אֹתָם לְהָבִיא לְכָל־הַמְּלָאכָה אֲשֶׁר צִוָּה יְהוָה
Jehovah has commanded | which | work the | all for | bring to | them | hearts | impelled

3068 5071 3478 1121 935 4872 3027 6213
לַעֲשׂוֹת בְּיַד־מֹשֶׁה הֵבִיאוּ בְנֵי־יִשְׂרָאֵל נְדָבָה לַיהוָה׃
to .Jehovah | voluntary a offering | Israel | the of sons | brought | ;Moses | the by of hand | be to done

8034 3068 7121 7200 3478 1121 4872 559
30 וַיֹּאמֶר מֹשֶׁה אֶל־בְּנֵי יִשְׂרָאֵל רְאוּ קָרָא יְהוָה בְשֵׁם
by name | Jehovah | has called | ,See | ,Israel | the of sons | to | Moses | said And

4390 3063 4294 2354/1121 221/1121 1212
31 בְּצַלְאֵל בֶּן־אוּרִי בֶן־חוּר לְמַטֵּה יְהוּדָה׃ וַיְמַלֵּא אֹתוֹ
him | He and filled has | ;Judah | the of tribe | Hur the of son | ,Uri the of son | Bezaleel

4399 3605 1847 8394 2451 430 7307
רוּחַ אֱלֹהִים בְּחָכְמָה בִּתְבוּנָה וּבְדַעַת וּבְכָל־מְלָאכָה׃
;workmanship in and all | in and knowledge | in intelligence | in ,wisdom | ,God | the (with) of spirit

2799 5178 3701 2091 6213 4284 2803
32 33 וְלַחְשֹׁב מַחֲשָׁבֹת לַעֲשֹׂת בַּזָּהָב וּבַכֶּסֶף וּבַנְּחֹשֶׁת׃ וּבַחֲרֹשֶׁת
in and of cuttings | in and bronze | in and silver | in ,gold | to work | ,designs | to and devise

4284 4399 3605 6213 6086 2799 4390 68
אֶבֶן לְמַלֹּאת וּבַחֲרֹשֶׁת עֵץ לַעֲשׂוֹת בְּכָל־מְלֶאכֶת מַחֲשָׁבֶת׃
.design | workmanship of | in all | work to | ,wood | in and of carving | for ,finishings | stones

He has put in his heart to teach, he and Aholiab the son of Ahisamach, of the tribe of Dan. [35]He has filled them *with* wisdom of heart, to do every work of a smith, and an artisan, and an embroiderer in blue, and in purple, and in crimson, and in bleached *linen*, and a weaver; doers of every work and devisers of designs.

1835/ 4294 294 1121 171 3820 5414 3384

34 וּלְהוֹרֹת נָתַן בְּלִבּוֹ הוּא וְאָהֳלִיאָב בֶּן־אֲחִיסָמָךְ לְמַטֵּה־דָן׃

.Dan the of tribe Ahisamach the of son and Aholiab he his in heart has He put to And teach

2803 2796 4399 3605 6213 38:20 2451 4390

35 מִלֵּא אֹתָם חָכְמַת־לֵב לַעֲשׂוֹת כָּל־מְלֶאכֶת חָרָשׁ וְחֹשֵׁב

an and artisan smith a of work every do to ,heart wisdom of them has He (with) filled

707 8336 8144 8438 713 8504 7551

וְרֹקֵם בַּתְּכֵלֶת וּבָאַרְגָּמָן בְּתוֹלַעַת הַשָּׁנִי וּבַשֵּׁשׁ וְאֹרֵג

a and ;weaver in and ,linen in and crimson in and ,purple ,blue in an and embroiderer

4284 2803 4399 3605 6213

עֹשֵׂי כָּל־מְלָאכָה וְחֹשְׁבֵי מַחֲשָׁבֹת׃

.designs and of devisers ,work every doers of

CAP. XXXVI לו

CHAPTER 36

CHAPTER 36

[1]And Bezaleel and Aholiab shall work *with* everyone wise of heart *to* whom Jehovah has given wisdom and intelligence, to know how to do every work of the service of the holy place, concerning all which Jehovah had commanded. [2]And Moses called to Bezaleel, and to Aholiab, and to everyone wise of heart, to whom Jehovah had given a heart of wisdom, everyone whose heart had lifted him up to come near the work, to do it. [3]And they took every offering before Moses which the sons of Israel had brought for the work of the service *in* the holy place, to do it. And they brought to him still more willing offerings morning by morning. [4]And all the wise men came, those doing every kind of work *for* the holy place, each one from his work they *were* doing.

[5]And they spoke to Moses, saying, The people *are* bringing more than enough *for* the service of the work that Jehovah commanded, to do it. [6]And Moses commanded, and they caused it to be voiced in the camp,

5414 3820 2450 376 171 1212 6213

1 וְעָשָׂה בְצַלְאֵל וְאָהֳלִיאָב וְכֹל אִישׁ חֲכַם־לֵב אֲשֶׁר נָתַן

has given (to) ,heart wise of everyone (with) and Aholiab Bezaleel shall And work

3605 6213 3045 1992 8394 2451 3068

יְהוָה חָכְמָה וּתְבוּנָה בָּהֵמָּה לָדַעַת לַעֲשֹׂת אֶת־כָּל־

every do to know to how ,whom and intelligence wisdom Jehovah

3068 7121 3068 6680 834 3605 6944 5656 4399

2 מְלֶאכֶת עֲבֹדַת הַקֹּדֶשׁ לְכֹל אֲשֶׁר־צִוָּה יְהוָה׃ וַיִּקְרָא מֹשֶׁה

Moses And called .Jehovah had commanded which to as all the ,sanctuary service of the work of

3820/2450 376 3605 171 1212

אֶל־בְּצַלְאֵל וְאֶל־אָהֳלִיאָב וְאֶל כָּל־אִישׁ חֲכַם־לֵב אֲשֶׁר

to whom heart wise of everyone and to ,Aholiab to and ,Bezaleel to

7126 38:20/5375 3605 3820 2451 3068 5414

נָתַן יְהוָה חָכְמָה בְּלִבּוֹ כֹּל אֲשֶׁר נְשָׂאוֹ לִבּוֹ לְקָרְבָה אֶל־

to come near to heart had up him lifted whose everyone a ,heart of wisdom Jehovah had given

3605 4872 6440 3947 6213 4399

3 הַמְּלָאכָה לַעֲשֹׂת אֹתָהּ׃ וַיִּקְחוּ מִלִּפְנֵי מֹשֶׁה אֵת כָּל־

every Moses before they And took .it do to ,work the

6944 5656 4399 3478 1121 935 834 8641

הַתְּרוּמָה אֲשֶׁר הֵבִיאוּ בְּנֵי יִשְׂרָאֵל לִמְלֶאכֶת עֲבֹדַת הַקֹּדֶשׁ

the ,sanctuary service (in) the for of work Israel the of sons had brought which ,offering

1242 1242 5071 5750 935 6213

לַעֲשֹׂת אֹתָהּ וְהֵם הֵבִיאוּ אֵלָיו עוֹד נְדָבָה בַּבֹּקֶר בַּבֹּקֶר׃

(by) morning ,morning voluntary offerings still more to him brought And they .it to build

376 6944 4399 6213 2450 3605 935

4 וַיָּבֹאוּ כָּל־הַחֲכָמִים הָעֹשִׂים אֵת כָּל־מְלֶאכֶת הַקֹּדֶשׁ אִישׁ־

each the for ,sanctuary work every of kind those doing the ,men wise all And came

4872 559 6213 4399 376

5 אִישׁ מִמְּלַאכְתּוֹ אֲשֶׁר־הֵמָּה עֹשִׂים׃ וַיֹּאמְרוּ אֶל־מֹשֶׁה

,Moses to they And spoke. were .doing they his from work one

834 4399 5656 1767 935 5971 7235 559

לֵאמֹר מַרְבִּים הָעָם לְהָבִיא מִדֵּי הָעֲבֹדָה לַמְּלָאכָה אֲשֶׁר־

which the of work the (for) service than enough (are) bringing The people much more ,saying

4264 6963 5674 4872 6680 6213 3068 6680

6 צִוָּה יְהוָה לַעֲשֹׂת אֹתָהּ׃ וַיְצַו מֹשֶׁה וַיַּעֲבִירוּ קוֹל בַּמַּחֲנֶה

the in ,camp caused they and voiced be to it ,Moses And commanded .it build to ,Jehovah commanded saying, Let neither man nor woman make any more offering for the holy place; and the people were held back from bringing. [7]And their property was sufficient for all the work, to do it, and *it was* too much.

[8]And every wise-hearted one among the doers of the work of the tabernacle made ten curtains, twined, bleached *linen*, and blue, and purple, and crimson — he made them *with* cherubs, the work of an artisan. [9]The length of one curtain *was* twenty-eight by the cubit; and the width *was* four by the cubit; the one curtain *was* the same measure for all the curtains. [10]And he joined five curtains, one to another; and he joined five curtains, one to another. [11]And he made loops of blue on the edge of the one curtain, from the end to the juncture; so he did at the edge of the last curtain at the second juncture. [12]He made fifty loops on one curtain; and he made fifty loops on the end of the curtain which *was* at the second juncture; the loops corresponded, one with another. [13]And he made fifty hooks of gold; and he joined the curtains by the hooks, one to another. And the tabernacle became one.

[14]And he made curtains of goats' *hair* for a tent over the tabernacle; he made them eleven curtains. [15]The length of the one curtain *was* thirty by the cubit, and four cubits the

לאמר איש ואשה אל־יעשו־עוד מלאכה לתרומת הקדש

for offering work any make Let nor man ,saying / sanctuary the more neither woman

7 ויכלא העם מהביא׃ והמלאכה היתה דים לכל־המלאכה

,work the all for sufficient was their And property from bringing the people were and kept

8 לעשות אתה והותר׃ ויעשו כל־חכם־לב בעשי

the among hearted-wise every And made one of doers (was) there and .remainder a do to

המלאכה את־המשכן עשר יריעת שש משזר ותכלת

,blue and twined bleached (linen) ,curtains ten the ,tabernacle of work the

וארגמן ותולעת שני כרבים מעשה חשב עשה אתם׃

.them he made an artisan work the of (with) ,cherubs ;crimson and ,purple and

9 ארך היריעה האחת שמנה ועשרים באמה ורחב ארבע

four the and ,width the by ;cubit twenty- eight one (was) curtain The of length

10 באמה היריעה האחת מדה אחת לכל־היריעת׃ ויחבר

he And joined the .curtains all for same the measure (was) one the curtain the by ;cubit

את־חמש היריעת אחת אל־אחת וחמש יריעת חבר אחת

one he ,joined curtains and five ;another to one ,curtains five

11 אל־אחת׃ ויעש ללאת תכלת על שפת היריעה האחת

,one curtain the of edge on blue of loops he And made .another to

מקצה במחברת כן עשה בשפת היריעה הקיצונה

last the curtain the at of edge did he so the at ;juncture the from end

12 במחברת השנית׃ חמשים ללאת עשה ביריעה האחת

;one on curtain He made loops fifty .second the at juncture

וחמשים ללאת עשה בקצה היריעה אשר במחברת

the at juncture which (was) the curtain the on of end he made loops fifty and

13 השנית מקבילת הללאת אחת אל־אחת׃ ויעש חמשים

fifty he And made .another with one ,loops the corresponded ;second

קרסי זהב ויחבר את־היריעת אחת אל־אחת בקרסים

the by ,hooks another to one curtains the he and joined ;gold hooks of

ויהי המשכן אחד׃

.one the tabernacle became and

14 ויעש יריעת עזים לאהל על־המשכן עשתי־עשרה יריעת

curtains eleven the ;tabernacle over a for tent goats' (hair) curtains of he And made

15 עשה אתם׃ ארך היריעה האחת שלשים באמה וארבע

four and the by ,cubit thirty ,one curtain The of length .them he made width of the one curtain; one measue to the eleven curtains. [16]And he joined the five curtains separately, and the six curtains separately. [17]And he made fifty loops on the edge of the last curtain at the juncture; and he made fifty loops on the edge of the curtain that joined the second. [18]And he made fifty hooks of bronze to join the tent, to unite it in one.

[19]And he made a cover for the tent of rams' skins dyed red; and a cover of dugong skins from above.

[20]And he made the boards for the tabernacle, standing planks of acacia-wood. [21]The length of the board *was* ten cubits, and a cubit and a half *was* the width of the one board. [22]The one board *was* connect *by* two pins, one to another; so he did to all the boards of the tabernacle.

[23]And he made the boards for the tabernacle: twenty boards for the south side southward. [24]And he made forty sockets of silver under the twenty boards; two sockets under the one board for its two *pins*. [25]And for the second side of the tabernacle, to the north side, he made twenty boards, [26]and their forty silver sockets; two sockets under the one board, and two sockets under the other board. [27]And he made six boards for the sides of the tabernacle westward.

6240 6249 259 4060 259 3407 7341 520
אמת רחב היריעה האחת מדה אחת לעשתי עשרה
eleven the to one measure ;one the curtain the of width cubits

16 3407 8337 905 3407 2568 2266 3407
יריעת׃ ויחבר את־חמש היריעת לבד ואת־שש היריעת
curtains the six and separately curtains five the he And joined .curtains

17 7020 3407 8193 2572 3924 6213 905
לבד׃ ויעש ללאת חמשים על שפת היריעה הקיצנה
last the curtain the of edge on fifty loops he And made separately

2266 3407 8193 6213 3924 2572 4225
במחברת וחמשים ללאת עשה על־שפת היריעה החברת
that joined the curtain the of edge on he made loops and fifty the at ;juncture

18 168 2266 2572 5178 7165 6213 8145
השנית׃ ויעש קרסי נחשת חמשים לחבר את־האהל
,tent the join to fifty bronze hooks of he And made the .second

19 119 352 5785 168 4372 6213 259 259
להיות אחד׃ ויעש מכסה לאהל ערת אילם מאדמים
;(red) dyed rams' skins the for of tent cover a he And made .one it untie to

20 7175 6213 4605 8471 5785 4372
ומכסה ערת תחשים מלמעלה׃ ויעש את־הקרשים
boards the he And made .above from dugong skins a and of cover

21 7175 753 520 6235 5975 7848 6086 4908
למשכן עצי שטים עמדים׃ עשר אמת ארך הקרש
the ;board The of length cubits ten (was) ,standing .up acaca- wood planks of the for ,tabernacle

22 7175 3489 8147 259 7175 7341 2676 520
ואמה וחצי האמה רחב הקרש האחד׃ שתי ידת לקרש
board pins (by) two .one the board the of width was a and half a and cubit

7175 3605 6213 3651 259 259 7947 259
האחד משלבת אחת אל־אחת כן עשה לכל קרשי
the of boards all to did he so ;another to one (was) ,connected one The

23 7175 6242 4908 7175 6213 4908
המשכן׃ ויעש את־הקרשים למשכן עשרים קרשים
boards twenty the for ;tabernacle the boards he And made the .tabernacle

24 8478 6213 3701 134 703 8486 5045 6285
לפאת נגב תימנה׃ וארבעים אדני־כסף עשה תחת
under he made silver sockets of forty And .southward the south for side

8147 259 7175 8478 134 8147 7175 6242
עשרים הקרשים שני אדנים תחת־הקרש האחד לשתי
for two one the board under sockets two ;boards the twenty

3489 8147 259 7175 8478 134 8147 3489
ידתיו ושני אדנים תחת־הקרש האחד לשתי ידתיו׃
.pins its two for one the board under sockets and two its pins

25 7175 6242 6213 6828 6285 8145 4908 6763
ולצלע המשכן השנית לפאת צפון עשה עשרים קרשים׃
,boards twenty he made ,north the to side ,second the tabernacle for And of side the

26 259 7175 8478 134 8147 3701 134 703
וארבעים אדניהם כסף שני אדנים תחת הקרש האחד
,one the board under sockets two ;silver their sockets forty and

27 3720 4908 3411 259 7175 8478 134 8147
ושני אדנים תחת הקרש האחד׃ ולירכתי המשכן ימה
west- ward the tabernacle for And of sides the .other the board under sockets and two

28And he made two boards for the corners of the tabernacle, in the sides. 29And they were double from from below, and in like manner they were complete to its top, to the first ring. So he did to both of them, for the two corners. 30And there were eight boards, and their silver sockets, sixteen sockets; two sockets *and* two sockets under the one board.

31And he made bars of acacia-wood; five to the boards of the second side of the tabernacle; and five bars to the boards of the sides of the tabernacle westward. 33And he made the middle bar to go through the middle of the boards, from end to end. 34And he overlaid the boards *with* gold. And he made the rings gold, housing for the poles; and he overlaid the bars *with* gold.

35And he made a veil *of* blue, and purple, and crimson, and twined, bleached *linen*. He made it the work of an artisan, *with* cherubs. 36And he made four pillars of acacia for it. And he overlaid them *with* gold, their nails gold; and he cast four sockets of silver for them.

37And he made a hanging for the door of the tabernacle, blue, and purple, and crimson, and twined, bleached *linen*, the work of an embroiderer; 38and its five pillars, and their nails; and he overlaid their tops and their bands *with* gold; and their five sockets *were* of bronze.

4908 4742 6213 7175 8147 7175 8337 6213
28 עָשָׂה שִׁשָּׁה קְרָשִׁים׃ וּשְׁנֵי קְרָשִׁים עָשָׂה לִמְקֻצְעֹת הַמִּשְׁכָּן
the tabernacle, the of corners for made he boards And two .boards six he made
8582 1961 3162 4295 8382 1961 3411
29 בַּיַּרְכָתָיִם׃ וְהָיוּ תוֹאֲמִם מִלְּמַטָּה וְיַחְדָּו יִהְיוּ תַמִּים אֶל־
to complete they were in and manner like from below double And were they .sides the in
8147 8147 6213 259 2885 7218
רֹאשׁוֹ אֶל־הַטַּבַּעַת הָאֶחָת כֵּן עָשָׂה לִשְׁנֵיהֶם לִשְׁנֵי
the for two both to them of did he so ;first ring the to top its
6240 8337 3701 134 7175 8083 1961 4740
30 הַמִּקְצֹעֹת׃ וְהָיוּ שְׁמֹנָה קְרָשִׁים וְאַדְנֵיהֶם כֶּסֶף שִׁשָּׁה עָשָׂר
sixteen ,silver their and sockets ,boards eight And were there .corners
6213 259 7175 8478 134 8147 134 8147 134
31 אֲדָנִים שְׁנֵי אֲדָנִים שְׁנֵי אֲדָנִים תַּחַת הַקֶּרֶשׁ הָאֶחָד׃ וַיַּעַשׂ
he And made .one board the under sockets (and) sockets two two ;sockets
259 4908 6763 7175 2568 7848 6086 1280
בְּרִיחֵי עֲצֵי שִׁטִּים חֲמִשָּׁה לְקַרְשֵׁי צֶלַע־הַמִּשְׁכָּן הָאֶחָת׃
;one the tabernacle the of side the to of boards five ;acacia-wood of bars
2568 8145 4908 6763 7175 1280 2568
32 וַחֲמִשָּׁה בְרִיחִם לְקַרְשֵׁי צֶלַע־הַמִּשְׁכָּן הַשֵּׁנִית וַחֲמִשָּׁה
five and ;second the tabernacle the of side the to of boards bars five and
1280 6213 3220 3411 4908 7175 1280
33 בְרִיחִם לְקַרְשֵׁי הַמִּשְׁכָּן לַיַּרְכָתַיִם יָמָּה׃ וַיַּעַשׂ אֶת־הַבְּרִיחַ
bar the he And made west- ward the of sides the tabernacle the to of boards bars
7097 7097 7175 8432 1272 8484
34 הַתִּיכֹן לִבְרֹחַ בְּתוֹךְ הַקְּרָשִׁים מִן־הַקָּצֶה אֶל־הַקָּצֶה׃ וְאֶת־
And .end to end from ,boards the the of middle go to through middle
905 1004 2091 6213 2885 2091 6823 7175
הַקְּרָשִׁים צִפָּה זָהָב וְאֶת־טַבְּעֹתָם עָשָׂה זָהָב בָּתִּים לַבְּרִיחִם
the for .poles housing ,gold he made rings the and (with) ,gold he overlaid the boards
713 8504 6532 6213 2091 1280 6823
35 וַיְצַף אֶת־הַבְּרִיחִם זָהָב׃ וַיַּעַשׂ אֶת־הַפָּרֹכֶת תְּכֵלֶת וְאַרְגָּמָן
and purple blue a (of) veil he And made (with) .gold bars the he And overlaid
3742 6213 2803 4639 7806 8336 8144 8438
וְתוֹלַעַת שָׁנִי וְשֵׁשׁ מָשְׁזָר מַעֲשֵׂה חֹשֵׁב עָשָׂה אֹתָהּ כְּרֻבִים׃
(with) .cherubs ,it he made skilled a workman the of work ;twined and linen crimson and
2091 2053 2091 6823 7848 5982 702 6213
36 וַיַּעַשׂ לָהּ אַרְבָּעָה עַמּוּדֵי שִׁטִּים וַיְצַפֵּם זָהָב וָוֵיהֶם זָהָב
;gold their nails (with) ,gold them he and overlaid ,acacia pillars of four for it he And made
168 6607 4539 6213 3701 134 702 3332
37 וַיִּצֹק לָהֶם אַרְבָּעָה אַדְנֵי־כָסֶף׃ וַיַּעַשׂ מָסָךְ לְפֶתַח הָאֹהֶל
the tabernacle the for of door a hanging he And made .silver sockets of four for them he and cast
7551 4639 7806 8336 8144 8438 713 8504
תְּכֵלֶת וְאַרְגָּמָן וְתוֹלַעַת שָׁנִי וְשֵׁשׁ מָשְׁזָר מַעֲשֵׂה רֹקֵם׃
and ;embroiderers work ,twined and linen ,crimson and and purple (of) blue
2838 7218 6823 2053 2568 5982
38 וְאֶת־עַמּוּדָיו חֲמִשָּׁה וְאֶת־וָוֵיהֶם וְצִפָּה רָאשֵׁיהֶם וַחֲשֻׁקֵיהֶם
their and bands their tops he and overlaid ;their nails and five its pillars and
5178 2568 134 2091
זָהָב וְאַדְנֵיהֶם חֲמִשָּׁה נְחֹשֶׁת׃
(of) .bronze five their and ,sockets (with) ;gold

CAP. XXXVII לז

CHAPTER 37

CHAPTER 37

[1]And Bezaleel made the ark *of* acacia-wood; two cubits and a half long, and a cubit and a half wide, and a cubit and a half high. [2]And he overlaid it *with* pure gold, inside and outside. And he made for it a wreath of gold all around. [3]And he cast four rings of gold for it, on its four feet; two rings on its one side, and two rings on its second side. [4]And he made poles of acacia-wood; and he overlaid them *with* gold. [5]And he put the poles into the rings, on the sides of the ark, to carry the ark. [6]And he made a mercy-seat of pure gold; two cubits and a half long, and a cubit and a half wide. [7]And he made two cherubs *of* gold; he made them of beaten work, from the two ends of the mercy-seat; [8]one cherub herer at one end, and one cherub there at the *other* end. He made the cherubs from the mercy-seat, from its two ends. [9]And the cherubs were spreading out *their* wings above, covering the mercy-seat with their wings, their faces *with* their faces each toward its brother, towards the mercy-seat were the faces of the cherubs.

[10]And he made the table of planks of acacia; two cubits long, and a cubit wide, and a cubit and a half high. [11]And he overlaid it *with* pure gold; and he made for it a wreath of gold all around. [12]And he made for it a border of a hand's breadth all around. And made a wreath of gold for

753 2677 520 7848 6086 727 2212 6213
1 וַיַּעַשׂ בְּצַלְאֵל אֶת־הָאָרֹן עֲצֵי שִׁטִּים אַמָּתַיִם וָחֵצִי אָרְכּוֹ
,long a and half two cubits ;acacia-wood (of) ark the Bezaleel And made

2889 2091 6823 6967 2677 520 7341 2677 520
2 וְאַמָּה וָחֵצִי רָחְבּוֹ וְאַמָּה וָחֵצִי קֹמָתוֹ׃ וַיְצַפֵּהוּ זָהָב טָהוֹר
,pure (with) gold he And it overlaid .high a and half a and cubit ,wide a and half a and cubit

702 3332 5439 2091 2213 6213 2351 1004
3 מִבַּיִת וּמִחוּץ וַיַּעַשׂ לוֹ זֵר זָהָב סָבִיב׃ וַיִּצֹק לוֹ אַרְבַּע
four for it he And cast all .around gold a of wreath it for he and made and ;outside inside

6763 2885 8147 6471 702 5921 2091 2885
טַבְּעֹת זָהָב עַל אַרְבַּע פַּעֲמֹתָיו וּשְׁתֵּי טַבָּעֹת עַל־צַלְעוֹ
its side on rings two ;feet its four on ,gold rings of

6086 905 6213 8145 6763 5921 2885 8147 259
4 הָאֶחָת וּשְׁתֵּי טַבָּעֹת עַל־צַלְעוֹ הַשֵּׁנִית׃ וַיַּעַשׂ בַּדֵּי עֲצֵי
wood of poles he And made .second its side on rings and two ,one

5921 2885 905 935 2091 6823 7848
5 שִׁטִּים וַיְצַף אֹתָם זָהָב׃ וַיָּבֵא אֶת־הַבַּדִּים בַּטַּבָּעֹת עַל
on the into rings poles the he And put (with) .gold them he and overlaid ;acacia-

2889 2091 3727 6213 727 5375 727 6763
6 צַלְעֹת הָאָרֹן לָשֵׂאת אֶת־הָאָרֹן׃ וַיַּעַשׂ כַּפֹּרֶת זָהָב טָהוֹר
,pure gold a of mercy-seat he And made .ark the carry to ,ark the the of sides

3742 8147 6213 7341 2677 520 753 2677 520
7 אַמָּתַיִם וָחֵצִי אָרְכָּהּ וְאַמָּה וָחֵצִי רָחְבָּהּ׃ וַיַּעַשׂ שְׁנֵי כְרֻבִים
cherubs two he And made .wide a and half a and cubit ,long a and half two cubits

259 3742 3727 7098 8147 6213 4749 2091
8 זָהָב מִקְשָׁה עָשָׂה אֹתָם מִשְּׁנֵי קְצוֹת הַכַּפֹּרֶת׃ כְּרוּב אֶחָד
one cherub the ;mercy-seat of ends the two from ,them he made beaten of work (of) ;gold

6213 3727 7098 259/3742 7098
מִקָּצָה מִזֶּה וּכְרוּב־אֶחָד מִקָּצָה מִזֶּה מִן־הַכַּפֹּרֶת עָשָׂה
he made the mercy-seat out of ;there the at end (other) one and cherub ,here one at end

3674 6566 3742 1961 7098 8147 3742
9 אֶת־הַכְּרֻבִים מִשְּׁנֵי קְצוֹותָו׃ וַיִּהְיוּ הַכְּרֻבִים פֹּרְשֵׂי כְנָפַיִם
their wings spreading out the cherubs And were .ends its from two ,cherubs the

376 6440 3727 3671 5526 4605
לְמַעְלָה סֹכְכִים בְּכַנְפֵיהֶם עַל־הַכַּפֹּרֶת וּפְנֵיהֶם אִישׁ אֶל־
toward each faces their the ,mercy-seat their with wings covering ,above

3742 6440 1961 3727 251
אָחִיו אֶל־הַכַּפֹּרֶת הָיוּ פְּנֵי הַכְּרֻבִים׃
the .cherubs the of faces were the mercy-seat towards the ;other

7341 520 753 520 7848 6086 7979 6213
10 וַיַּעַשׂ אֶת־הַשֻּׁלְחָן עֲצֵי שִׁטִּים אַמָּתַיִם אָרְכּוֹ וְאַמָּה רָחְבּוֹ
,wide a and cubit ,long two cubits ;acacia of planks table the And made he

2091/2213 6213 2889 2091 6823 6967 2677 520
11 וְאַמָּה וָחֵצִי קֹמָתוֹ׃ וַיְצַף אֹתוֹ זָהָב טָהוֹר וַיַּעַשׂ לוֹ זֵר זָהָב
gold a wreath it for he and made ;pure (with) gold it he And overlaid .high a and half a and cubit

2091/2213 6213 5439 2948 4526 6213 5439
12 סָבִיב׃ וַיַּעַשׂ לוֹ מִסְגֶּרֶת טֹפַח סָבִיב וַיַּעַשׂ זֵר־זָהָב
gold a wreath he and made all ;around hand's a breadth border a of for it he And made all .around

its border all around. [13]And he cast four rings of gold for it; and he put the rings on the four corners, which *were* to its four feet. [14]The rings were near the border, the housings for the poles, to carry the table. [15]And he made the poles of acacia-wood; and he overlaid them *with* gold, to lift up the table. [16]And he made the vessels which *were* on the table, its platters, and its bowls, and its sacrificial cups, and its pitchers *by* which *is* made a drink offering, with pure gold.

[17]And he made the lampstand *of* pure gold; he made the lampstand *of* beaten work, its side, and its branch, its cups, its knobs and its blossoms were from it. [18]And six branches went out from its sides; three branches of the lampstand from one side, and three branches of the lampstand from its second side. [19]Three almond-like cups *were* on the one branch, *with* knob and blossom; and three almond-like cups on the one branch, *with* knob and blossom; so for the six branches, those going out from it. [20]And on the lampstand *were* four almond-like cups, its knobs and its blossoms. [21]And a knob *was* under two branches of it; to the six branches, those going out from it. [22]The knobs and the branches of

13 לְמִסְגַּרְתּוֹ סָבִיב׃ וַיִּצֹק לוֹ אַרְבַּע טַבְּעֹת זָהָב וַיִּתֵּן אֶת־
14 הַטַּבָּעֹת עַל אַרְבַּע הַפֵּאֹת אֲשֶׁר לְאַרְבַּע רַגְלָיו׃ לְעֻמַּת
הַמִּסְגֶּרֶת הָיוּ הַטַּבָּעֹת בָּתִּים לַבַּדִּים לָשֵׂאת אֶת־הַשֻּׁלְחָן׃
15 וַיַּעַשׂ אֶת־הַבַּדִּים עֲצֵי שִׁטִּים וַיְצַף אֹתָם זָהָב לָשֵׂאת אֶת־
16 הַשֻּׁלְחָן׃ וַיַּעַשׂ אֶת־הַכֵּלִים אֲשֶׁר עַל־הַשֻּׁלְחָן אֶת־קְעָרֹתָיו
וְאֶת־כַּפֹּתָיו וְאֵת מְנַקִּיֹּתָיו וְאֶת־הַקְּשָׂוֹת אֲשֶׁר יֻסַּךְ בָּהֵן
זָהָב טָהוֹר׃

17 וַיַּעַשׂ אֶת־הַמְּנֹרָה זָהָב טָהוֹר מִקְשָׁה עָשָׂה אֶת־הַמְּנֹרָה
18 יְרֵכָהּ וְקָנָהּ גְּבִיעֶיהָ כַּפְתֹּרֶיהָ וּפְרָחֶיהָ מִמֶּנָּה הָיוּ׃ וְשִׁשָּׁה
קָנִים יֹצְאִים מִצִּדֶּיהָ שְׁלֹשָׁה קְנֵי מְנֹרָה מִצִּדָּהּ הָאֶחָד
19 וּשְׁלֹשָׁה קְנֵי מְנֹרָה מִצִּדָּהּ הַשֵּׁנִי׃ שְׁלֹשָׁה גְבִעִים מְשֻׁקָּדִים
בַּקָּנֶה הָאֶחָד כַּפְתֹּר וָפֶרַח וּשְׁלֹשָׁה גְבִעִים מְשֻׁקָּדִים
בְּקָנֶה אֶחָד כַּפְתֹּר וָפָרַח כֵּן לְשֵׁשֶׁת הַקָּנִים הַיֹּצְאִים מִן־
20 הַמְּנֹרָה׃ וּבַמְּנֹרָה אַרְבָּעָה גְבִעִים מְשֻׁקָּדִים כַּפְתֹּרֶיהָ
21 וּפְרָחֶיהָ׃ וְכַפְתֹּר תַּחַת שְׁנֵי הַקָּנִים מִמֶּנָּה וְכַפְתֹּר תַּחַת
שְׁנֵי הַקָּנִים מִמֶּנָּה וְכַפְתֹּר תַּחַת־שְׁנֵי הַקָּנִים מִמֶּנָּה
22 לְשֵׁשֶׁת הַקָּנִים הַיֹּצְאִים מִמֶּנָּה׃ כַּפְתֹּרֵיהֶם וּקְנֹתָם מִמֶּנָּה

it were one beaten work of
pure gold. 23 And he made
its seven lamps, and its
snuffers, and its pans *of*
pure gold. 24 He made it *of* a
talent of pure gold, and all
its vessels.

25 And he made the altar
of incense of acacia-wood;
its length a cubit, and its
width a cubit, square; and
its height *was* two cubits;
its horns were of it. 26 And
he overlaid it *with* pure
gold, its top and its sides all
around, and its horns. And
he made for it a wreath of
gold all around. 27 And he
made for it two rings of
gold, from beneath its
wreath, on its two corners,
on its two sides, for
housings for poles, to lift it.
28 And he made its poles of
acacia-wood; and he over-
laid them *with* gold. 29 And
he made the holy oil of
anointing, and the pure incense of soothing fra-
grance, the work of a
perfumer.

5216 6213 2889 2091 259 4749 3605 1961
23 הָיוּ כֻּלָּהּ מִקְשָׁה אַחַת זָהָב טָהוֹר׃ וַיַּעַשׂ אֶת־נֵרֹתֶיהָ
lamps its | he And made | .pure | gold | of one | beaten work | all | were

2889 2091 3683 2889 2091 4289 4451 7651
24 שִׁבְעָה וּמַלְקָחֶיהָ וּמַחְתֹּתֶיהָ זָהָב טָהוֹר׃ כִּכָּר זָהָב טָהוֹר
pure | gold | a (of) of talent | .pure | gold | of pan its and | its ,snuffers | and | .seven

3627 6213
עָשָׂה אֹתָהּ וְאֵת כָּל־כֵּלֶיהָ׃
its vessels | all | and | ,it | he made

520 753 520 7848 6086 7004 4196 6213
25 וַיַּעַשׂ אֶת־מִזְבַּח הַקְּטֹרֶת עֲצֵי שִׁטִּים אַמָּה אָרְכּוֹ וְאַמָּה
a and cubit | its ,length | cubit a | ,acacia- | wood | incense | the of altar | he And made

6823 7161 1961 6967 520 7251 7341
26 רָחְבּוֹ רָבוּעַ וְאַמָּתַיִם קֹמָתוֹ מִמֶּנּוּ הָיוּ קַרְנֹתָיו׃ וַיְצַף אֹתוֹ
it | he And overlaid | its .horns | were | from it | its ;height | two and cubits | ,square | its ,width

6213 7161 5439 7023 1406 2889 2091
זָהָב טָהוֹר אֶת־גַּגּוֹ וְאֶת־קִירֹתָיו סָבִיב וְאֶת־קַרְנֹתָיו וַיַּעַשׂ
he and made | its ;horns | and | all around | its sides | and | its tip | ,pure | (with) gold

8478 6213 2091 2885 8147 5439 2091 2213
27 לוֹ זֵר זָהָב סָבִיב׃ וּשְׁתֵּי טַבְּעֹת זָהָב עָשָׂה־לּוֹ מִתַּחַת
from beneath | for ,it | he made | gold | of rings | two And | all .around | gold | a | for of wreath it

5375 905 1004 6654 8147/6921/6763 8147 2213
לְזֵרוֹ עַל שְׁתֵּי צַלְעֹתָיו עַל שְׁנֵי צִדָּיו לְבָתִּים לְבַדִּים לָשֵׂאת
carry to | for ,poles | for housings | its ;sides | two | on | its ,corners | two | on | its ,wreath

6823 7848 6086 905 6213
28 אֹתוֹ בָּהֶם׃ וַיַּעַשׂ אֶת־הַבַּדִּים עֲצֵי שִׁטִּים וַיְצַף אֹתָם
them | he and overlaid | ;acacia- | wood | the of poles | he And made | by .them | it

5561 7004 6944 4888 8081 6213 2091
29 זָהָב׃ וַיַּעַשׂ אֶת־שֶׁמֶן הַמִּשְׁחָה קֹדֶשׁ וְאֶת־קְטֹרֶת הַסַּמִּים
fragrant spices | the of incense | and | ,holy | anointing | of oil the | he And made | (with) ,gold

7543 4639 2889
טָהוֹר מַעֲשֵׂה רֹקֵחַ׃
a .perfumer | work the of | pure

CAP. XXXVIII לה

CHAPTER 38

CHAPTER 38
1 And he made the altar of
burnt offering of acacia-
wood; its length five cubits,
and its width five cubits,
square; and its height *was*
three cubits. 2 And he made
its horns on its four corners,
its horns were of it. And he
overlaid it *with* bronze.
3 And he made all the
vessels of the altar, the pots,
and the shovels, and the
sacrificial bowls, the flesh-
hooks, and the firepans; he
made all its vessels *of*

753 520 2568 7848 6086 5930 4196 6213
1 וַיַּעַשׂ אֶת־מִזְבַּח הָעֹלָה עֲצֵי שִׁטִּים חָמֵשׁ אַמּוֹת אָרְכּוֹ
its ,length | cubits | five | ;acacia- | wood | burnt the of offering | the of altar | he And made

6213 6967 520 7969 7251 7341 520 2568
2 וְחָמֵשׁ־אַמּוֹת רָחְבּוֹ רָבוּעַ וְשָׁלֹשׁ אַמּוֹת קֹמָתוֹ׃ וַיַּעַשׂ
he And made | its .height | cubits | three and | ,square | its ,width | cubits | and five

6823 7161 1961 6438 702 5921 7161
קַרְנֹתָיו עַל אַרְבַּע פִּנֹּתָיו מִמֶּנּוּ הָיוּ קַרְנֹתָיו וַיְצַף אֹתוֹ
it | he and overlaid | its ;horns | were | from it | its ,corners | four | on | horns its

3276 5518 4196 3627 3605 6213 5178
3 נְחֹשֶׁת׃ וַיַּעַשׂ אֶת־כָּל־כְּלֵי הַמִּזְבֵּחַ אֶת־הַסִּירֹת וְאֶת־הַיָּעִים
the ,shovels | and | ,pots the | the ,altar | the of vessels | all | he And made | (with) .bronze

6213 3627 3605 4289 4207 4219
וְאֶת־הַמִּזְרָקֹת אֶת־הַמִּזְלָגֹת וְאֶת־הַמַּחְתֹּת כָּל־כֵּלָיו עָשָׂה
he made | its vessels | all | the pans fire | and | the fleshhooks | sacrificial the and ,bowls

bronze. [4]And he made a
network of bronze grating
for the altar, under its ledge
from below, as far as its
middle. [5]And he cast four
rings in the four ends to the
bronze grating, housings for
the poles. [6]And he made
the poles of acacia-wood;
and he overlaid them *with*
bronze. [7]And he put the
poles into the rings, on the
sides of the altar, to lift it
with them; he made it
hollow *with* planks.

[8]And he made the laver
bronze, and its base
bronze, from the mirrors
of the serving women
who served *at* the door of
the tabernacle of the
congregation. [9]And he
made the court: to the
side of the Negeb, to the
south, the hangings of
the court *with* bleached
twined *linen*, a hundred
by the cubit. [10]Their pillars
were twenty, and their
sockets twenty, of bronze.
The nails of the pillars and
their bands *were* silver.
[11]And for the north side, a
hundred by the cubit, their
pillars twenty and their
sockets twenty, *of* bronze.
The nails of the pillars and
their bands *were* silver.
[12]And for the west side,
hangings of fifty cubits; their
pillars *were* ten, and their
sockets ten; the nails of the
pillars and their bands *were*
silver. [13]And for the east
side eastward, fifty cubits.
[14]Hangings of fifteen cubits
to the side, their pillars
three, and their sockets
were three. [15]And for the
second side, on this side
and on that side to the gate
of the court, hangings of
fifteen cubits; their pillars
were three, and their

4 נחשת: ויעש למזבח מכבר מעשה רשת נחשת תחת
5 כרכבו מלמטה עד־חציו: ויצק ארבע טבעת בארבע
6 הקצות למכבר הנחשת בתים לבדים: ויעש את־הבדים
7 עצי שטים ויצף אתם נחשת: ויבא את־הבדים בטבעת
על צלעת המזבח לשאת אתו בהם נבוב לחת עשה
8 אתו: ס ויעש את הכיור נחשת ואת כנו נחשת
במראת הצבאת אשר צבאו פתח אהל מועד: ס
9 ויעש את־החצר לפאת נגב תימנה קלעי החצר שש
10 משזר מאה באמה: עמודיהם עשרים ואדניהם עשרים
11 נחשת ווי העמודים וחשקיהם כסף: ולפאת צפון מאה
באמה עמודיהם עשרים ואדניהם עשרים נחשת ווי
12 העמודים וחשקיהם כסף: ולפאת־ים קלעים חמשים
באמה עמודיהם עשרה ואדניהם עשרה ווי העמדים
13 וחשוקיהם כסף: ולפאת קדמה מזרחה חמשים אמה:
14 קלעים חמש־עשרה אמה אל־הכתף עמודיהם שלשה
15 ואדניהם שלשה: ולכתף השנית מזה ומזה לשער
החצר קלעים חמש עשרה אמה עמדיהם שלשה

sockets three. [16]All the hangings of the court all around *were* twined, bleached *linen*.

[17]And the sockets to the pillars *were* bronze, the nails of the pillars and their bands *were* silver. And the overlaying of their capitals *were* silver; they being bound together *with* silver, all the pillars of the court. [18]And the hanging of the gate of the court *was* a work of an embroiderer, blue, and purple, and crimson, and twined, bleached *linen*; and twenty cubits long, and the height and the width, five cubits, near the hangings of the court. [19]And their pillars *were* four, and their sockets four, *of* bronze; their nails *were* silver, and the overlaying of their capitals and their bands *were* silver. [20]And all the pins for the tabernacle and for the court all around *were* bronze.

[21]These *are* the numbered things of the tabernacle, the tabernacle of the testimony, which were numbered at the mouth of Moses; the service of the Levites in the hand of Ithamar, the son of Aaron the priest. [22]And Bezaleel the son of Uri, the son of Hur, of the tribe of Judah, made all that Jehovah commanded Moses. [23]And with him Aholiab the son of Ahisamach, of the tribe of Dan, and engraver, and an artisan, and an embroiderer in blue, and in purple, and crimson, and in bleached *linen*. [24]All the gold used for the work, in all the work of the holy place, was the gold of the wave offering: twenty-nine talents and seven hundred and thirty shekels, by the shekel of the sanctuary. [25]And the silver of those numbered of the congregation *was* a hundred talents, and a thousand and seven hundred and seventy-five shekels,

7806 8336 5439 2691 7050 7969 134
16 וְאַדְנֵיהֶם שְׁלֹשָׁה׃ כָּל־קַלְעֵי הֶחָצֵר סָבִיב שֵׁשׁ מָשְׁזָר׃
.twined bleached all the the All .three their and
(linen) around court of hangings sockets

3701 2838 5982 2053 5178 5982 134
17 וְהָאֲדָנִים לָעַמֻּדִים נְחֹשֶׁת וָוֵי הָעַמּוּדִים וַחֲשׁוּקֵיהֶם כֶּסֶף
;silver their and pillars the the (were) the for the And
bands of nails ,bronze pillars sockets

5982 3605 3701 2836 3701 7218 6826
וְצִפּוּי רָאשֵׁיהֶם כָּסֶף וְהֵם מְחֻשָּׁקִים כֶּסֶף כֹּל עַמֻּדֵי
the all ,silver bound and ;silver their the and
of pillars (with) they capitals of overlaying

713 8504 7551 4639 2691 8179 4509 2691
18 הֶחָצֵר׃ וּמָסַךְ שַׁעַר הֶחָצֵר מַעֲשֵׂה רֹקֵם תְּכֵלֶת וְאַרְגָּמָן
and ,blue an work the the the And the
,purple ,embroiderer's court of gate of hanging .court

7341 6967 753 520 6242 7806 8336 8144 8438
וְתוֹלַעַת שָׁנִי וְשֵׁשׁ מָשְׁזָר וְעֶשְׂרִים אַמָּה אֹרֶךְ וְקוֹמָה בְרֹחַב
in the and ,long cubits and ;twined and and
width height twenty bleached ,crimson

702 5982 2691 7050 5980 520 2568
19 חָמֵשׁ אַמּוֹת לְעֻמַּת קַלְעֵי הֶחָצֵר׃ וְעַמֻּדֵיהֶם אַרְבָּעָה
,four their And .court the the joining ,cubits five
pillars of hangings

7218 6826 3701 2053 5178 702 134
וְאַדְנֵיהֶם אַרְבָּעָה נְחֹשֶׁת וָוֵיהֶם כֶּסֶף וְצִפּוּי רָאשֵׁיהֶם
their the and ;silver their of ,four their and
capitals of overlaying nails ;bronze sockets

5178 5439 2691 4908 3480 3701 2838
20 וַחֲשֻׁקֵיהֶם כָּסֶף׃ וְכָל־הַיְתֵדֹת לַמִּשְׁכָּן וְלֶחָצֵר סָבִיב נְחֹשֶׁת׃
(were) all for and the for pins the And .silver their and
.bronze around court the tabernacle all bands

6310 6485 5715 4908 4908 6485 428
21 אֵלֶּה פְקוּדֵי הַמִּשְׁכָּן מִשְׁכַּן הָעֵדֻת אֲשֶׁר פֻּקַּד עַל־פִּי
the at were which the taber- the taber- the (those) These
of mouth counted ,testimony ,of nacle ,nacle of counted (are)

1212 3548 175/1121 385 3027 3878 5656 4872
22 מֹשֶׁה עֲבֹדַת הַלְוִיִּם בְּיַד אִיתָמָר בֶּן־אַהֲרֹן הַכֹּהֵן׃ וּבְצַלְאֵל
And the Aaron the ,Ithamar's in the the ;Moses
Bezaleel .priest of son hand Levites of service

6680 834 3605 6213 3063 4294 2354/1121 221/1121
בֶּן־אוּרִי בֶן־חוּר לְמַטֵּה יְהוּדָה עָשָׂה אֵת כָּל־אֲשֶׁר־צִוָּה
com- which all made ,Judah the of ,Hur the Uri the
manded of tribe of son of son

1835 4294 294 1121 171 4872 3068
23 יְהוָה אֶת־מֹשֶׁה׃ וְאִתּוֹ אָהֳלִיאָב בֶּן־אֲחִיסָמָךְ לְמַטֵּה־דָן
,Dan the of ,Ahisamach the Aholiab And .Moses Jehovah
of tribe of son him with

8104 8438 713 8504 7551 2803 2796
חָרָשׁ וְחֹשֵׁב וְרֹקֵם בַּתְּכֵלֶת וּבָאַרְגָּמָן וּבְתוֹלַעַת הַשָּׁנִי
and in and ,blue in an and an and en- an
crimson ,purple embroiderer ,artisan graver

4399 3605 4399 6213 2091 3605 8336
24 וּבַשֵּׁשׁ׃ ס כָּל־הַזָּהָב הֶעָשׂוּי לַמְּלָאכָה בְּכֹל מְלֶאכֶת
work the all in the for was the All in and
of ,work used gold linen

7651 3603 6242 8672 8573 2091 1961 6944
הַקֹּדֶשׁ וַיְהִי ׀ זְהַב הַתְּנוּפָה תֵּשַׁע וְעֶשְׂרִים כִּכָּר וּשְׁבַע
and talents twenty nine wave the the and the
seven ,offering of gold was sanctuary

5712 6485 3701 6944 8255 8255 7970 3967
25 מֵאוֹת וּשְׁלֹשִׁים שֶׁקֶל בְּשֶׁקֶל הַקֹּדֶשׁ׃ וְכֶסֶף פְּקוּדֵי הָעֵדָה
the these the And the the by ,shekels thirty and hundred
assembly of numbered of silver .sanctuary of shekel

8255 7657 2568 3967 7651 505 3603 3967
מְאַת כִּכָּר וְאֶלֶף וּשְׁבַע מֵאוֹת וַחֲמִשָּׁה וְשִׁבְעִים שָׁקֶל
,shekels seventy- five and hundred seven a and talents a (was)
thousand hundred

by the shekel of the
sanctuary; [26]a bekah for a
head, half a shekel, by the
shekel of the sanctuary, for
every one passing over to
those numbered, from a son
of twenty years and upward,
for six hundred thousand
and three thousand and five
hundred and fifty. [27]And the
hundred talents of silver
were for casting the sockets
of the holy place, and the
sockets of the veil; a hundred sockets for the hun-
dred talents, a talent for a
socket. [28]And the thou-
sand, seven hundred and
seventy-five *shekels* he
made into nails for the
pillars; and he overlaid their
capitals and joined them.

[29]And the bronze of the
wave offering *was* seventy
talents and two thousand
and four hundred shekels.
[30]And he made with it the
sockets of the door of the
tabernacle of the congre-
gation, and the altar of
bronze and its bronze
grating; and all the vessels
of the altar. [31]And the
sockets of the court all
around, and the sockets of
the gate of the court; and all
the pins of the tabernacle,
and all the pins of the court
all around.

8255 8255 4276 1538 1235 6944 8255
26 בְּשֶׁקֶל הַקֹּדֶשׁ׃ בֶּקַע לַגֻּלְגֹּלֶת מַחֲצִית הַשֶּׁקֶל בְּשֶׁקֶל
the by a half a for a the the by
of shekel ,shekel ,head ,bekah ;sanctuary of shekel
4665 8141 6242 1121 6485 5674 6944
הַקֹּדֶשׁ לְכֹל הָעֹבֵר עַל־הַפְּקֻדִים מִבֶּן עֶשְׂרִים שָׁנָה וָמַעְלָה
and years twenty a from those to passing for the
,upward of son ,numbered over one every ,sanctuary
2572 3907 2568 505 7969 505 3967 8337
לְשֵׁשׁ־מֵאוֹת אֶלֶף וּשְׁלֹשֶׁת אֲלָפִים וַחֲמֵשׁ מֵאוֹת וַחֲמִשִּׁים׃
.fifty and hundred and ,thousand three and thou- hundred for
five sand six
134 6944 134 3332 3701 3602 3967/1961
27 וַיְהִי מְאַת כִּכַּר הַכֶּסֶף לָצֶקֶת אֵת אַדְנֵי הַקֹּדֶשׁ וְאֵת אַדְנֵי
the and the the for silver the talents the And
of sockets ,sanctuary of sockets casting of hundred were
134 3603 3603 3967 134 3967 6532
28 הַפָּרֹכֶת מְאַת אֲדָנִים לִמְאַת הַכִּכָּר כִּכָּר לָאָדֶן׃ וְאֶת־
And a for a ,talents the for sockets a ;veil the
.socket talent hundred hundred
5982 3053 6213 7657 2568 3967 7651 505
הָאֶלֶף וּשְׁבַע הַמֵּאוֹת וַחֲמִשָּׁה וְשִׁבְעִים עָשָׂה וָוִים לָעַמּוּדִים
the for (into) he seventy- five and hundred seven the
;pillars nails made (shekels) ,thousand
7657 8573 5178 2836 7218 6823
29 וְצִפָּה רָאשֵׁיהֶם וְחִשַּׁק אֹתָם׃ וּנְחֹשֶׁת הַתְּנוּפָה שִׁבְעִים
(was) wave the the And .them and their he and
seventy offering of bronze joined ,capitals overlaid
134 6213 8255 3967 702 505 3603
30 כִּכָּר וְאַלְפַּיִם וְאַרְבַּע־מֵאוֹת שָׁקֶל׃ וַיַּעַשׂ בָּהּ אֶת־אַדְנֵי
sockets the with he And .shekels hundred four two and talents
of it made ,thousand
5178 4345 5178 4196 4150 168 6607
פֶּתַח אֹהֶל מוֹעֵד וְאֵת מִזְבַּח הַנְּחֹשֶׁת וְאֶת־מִכְבַּר הַנְּחֹשֶׁת
bronze grating and ,bronze the and ,meeting the the
of altar of tent of door
5439 2691 134 4196 3627 3605 834
31 אֲשֶׁר־לוֹ וְאֵת כָּל־כְּלֵי הַמִּזְבֵּחַ׃ וְאֶת־אַדְנֵי הֶחָצֵר סָבִיב
all the the and ;altar the the all and for which
,around court of sockets of vessels ;it (was)
3605 4908 3489/3605 2691 8179 134
וְאֶת־אַדְנֵי שַׁעַר הֶחָצֵר וְאֵת כָּל־יִתְדֹת הַמִּשְׁכָּן וְאֶת־כָּל־
all and the pins the all and the gate the the and
,tabernacle of ;court of of sockets
5439 2691 3489
יִתְדֹת הֶחָצֵר סָבִיב׃
all court the of pins the
around

CAP. XXXIX לט

CHAPTER 39

CHAPTER 39

[1]And from the blue, and
the purple, and the crimson,
they made woven garments
for ministering in the holy
place; and they made the
holy garments which *were*
to Aaron, as Jehovah com-
manded Moses. [2]And he
made the ephod of gold,
blue, and purple, and

8278 899 6213 8144 8438 713 8504
1 וּמִן־הַתְּכֵלֶת וְהָאַרְגָּמָן וְתוֹלַעַת הַשָּׁנִי עָשׂוּ בִגְדֵי־שְׂרָד
woven garments they the and the and ,blue the And
made crimson ,purple from
175 6944 899 6213 6944 8334
לְשָׁרֵת בַּקֹּדֶשׁ וַיַּעֲשׂוּ אֶת־בִּגְדֵי הַקֹּדֶשׁ אֲשֶׁר לְאַהֲרֹן כַּאֲשֶׁר
as ,Aaron's which holy the garments and the in for
(were) made they ;place holy serving
4872 3068 6680
צִוָּה יְהוָה אֶת־מֹשֶׁה׃
.Moses Jehovah com-
manded
8336 8144 8438 713 8504 2091 646 6213
2 וַיַּעַשׂ אֶת־הָאֵפֹד זָהָב תְּכֵלֶת וְאַרְגָּמָן וְתוֹלַעַת שָׁנִי וְשֵׁשׁ
and and and ,blue ,gold ephod the he And
linen ,crimson ,purple of made

crimson, and twined,
bleached *linen*. [3]And they
hammered out sheets of
gold, and cut threads to
work into the midst of the
blue, and into the midst of
the purple, and into the
midst of the crimson, and
into the midst of the
bleached *linen*, the work of
an artisan. [4]They made
shoulder-pieces for it,
joined together; by its two
ends it *was* joined.
[5]And the band of its
fastening which *was* on it,
it *was* of like work: gold,
blue, and purple, and crimson, and twined, bleached
linen, as Jehovah com-
manded Moses. [6]And they
made the onyx stones, set *in*
plaited work of gold,
engraved *with* the engravings of a signet, according
to the names of the sons of
Israel. [7]And he put them on
the shoulder-pieces of the
ephod, stones of memorial,
for the sons of Israel,
as Jehovah commanded
Moses.

[8]And he made the
pocket, a work of an artisan, like the work of the
ephod: gold, blue, purple
and crimson, and twined,
bleached *linen*; [9]it was
square. They made the
pocket double; its length
was a span, its width a
span, doubled. [10]And
they filled in it four rows
of stones: one row *was* a
ruby, a topaz, and a car-
buncle; the first row.
[11]And the second row: an
emerald, a sapphire, and
a diamond. [12]And the
third row: a jacinth, an
agate, and an amethyst.
[13]And the fourth row: a
chrysolite, an onyx, and a
jasper; set in plaited work
of gold in their settings.
[14]And the stones *were*
according to the names
of the sons of Israel; they
were twelve, accord-
ing to their names, the
engravings of a signet,

6213 6616 7112 2091 6341/854 7554 7806
3 מָשְׁזָר׃ וַיְרַקְּעוּ אֶת־פַּחֵי הַזָּהָב וְקִצֵּץ פְּתִילִם לַעֲשׂוֹת
work to ,threads and cut ,gold sheets of they And hammered out ,twined

8144 8438 8432 713 8432 8504 8432
בְּתוֹךְ הַתְּכֵלֶת וּבְתוֹךְ הָאַרְגָּמָן וּבְתוֹךְ תּוֹלַעַת הַשָּׁנִי
;crimson the into and of midst the the purple into and of midst the ,blue the the into of midst

8147 2266 6213 3802 2803 4639 8336 8432
4 וּבְתוֹךְ הַשֵּׁשׁ מַעֲשֵׂה חֹשֵׁב׃ כְּתֵפֹת עָשׂוּ־לוֹ חֹבְרֹת עַל־שְׁנֵי
two on joined ,together for ,it They made shoulder-pieces an .artisan work the of the ,linen into and of midst

59,21 834 642 2805 2266 7098
5 קְצוֹוֹתָו חֻבָּר׃ וְחֵשֶׁב אֲפֻדָּתוֹ אֲשֶׁר עָלָיו מִמֶּנּוּ הוּא
it (was) it of ,it on which (was) its fastening the And of band was it joined ends its

7806 8336 8141 8438 713 8504 2091 4639
כְּמַעֲשֵׂהוּ זָהָב תְּכֵלֶת וְאַרְגָּמָן וְתוֹלַעַת שָׁנִי וְשֵׁשׁ מָשְׁזָר
,twined (linen) bleached and ,crimson and and ,purple ,blue ,gold its like ,work

7718 68 6213 4872 3068 6680
6 כַּאֲשֶׁר צִוָּה יְהוָה אֶת־מֹשֶׁה׃ ס וַיַּעֲשׂוּ אֶת־אַבְנֵי הַשֹּׁהַם
,onyx stones of they And made .Moses Jehovah commanded as

8034 2368 6603 6605 2091 4865 4374
מֻסַבֹּת מִשְׁבְּצוֹת זָהָב מְפֻתָּחֹת פִּתּוּחֵי חוֹתָם עַל־שְׁמוֹת
the according of names to a ,signet en- the of gravings engraved (with) ,gold plaited of work (in) set

2146 68 646 3802 5921 7760 3478 1121
7 בְּנֵי יִשְׂרָאֵל׃ וַיָּשֶׂם אֹתָם עַל כִּתְפֹת הָאֵפֹד אַבְנֵי זִכָּרוֹן
memorial stones of the ,ephod shoulder- of pieces the on them he And put .Israel the of sons

4872 3068 6680 3478 1121
לִבְנֵי יִשְׂרָאֵל כַּאֲשֶׁר צִוָּה יְהוָה אֶת־מֹשֶׁה׃ פ
.Moses Jehovah com- manded as ,Israel the for of sons

8504 2091 646 4639 2803 6213 2833 6213
8 וַיַּעַשׂ אֶת־הַחֹשֶׁן מַעֲשֵׂה חֹשֵׁב כְּמַעֲשֵׂה אֵפֹד זָהָב תְּכֵלֶת
,blue gold the :ephod the like of work an ,artisan of work a (breast-) the ,pocket he And made

6213 3717 1961 7251 7806 8336 8144 8438 713
9 וְאַרְגָּמָן וְתוֹלַעַת שָׁנִי וְשֵׁשׁ מָשְׁזָר׃ רָבוּעַ הָיָה כָּפוּל עָשׂוּ
they made double it ;was square twined and (linen) bleached ,crimson and ,purple

4390 3717 7341 2239 753 2239 6833
10 אֶת־הַחֹשֶׁן זֶרֶת אָרְכּוֹ וְזֶרֶת רָחְבּוֹ כָּפוּל׃ וַיְמַלְאוּ־בוֹ
it in they And set .doubled ,width its a and span its ,length span a .pocket the

259 2905 1304 6357 127 2905 68 2905 702
אַרְבָּעָה טוּרֵי אָבֶן טוּר אֹדֶם פִּטְדָה וּבָרֶקֶת הַטּוּר הָאֶחָד׃
.first row the an and ;emerald a ,topaz a ruby one was row ;stones of rows four

3958 7992 2904 3095 5601 5306 8145 2905
11 12 וְהַטּוּר הַשֵּׁנִי נֹפֶךְ סַפִּיר וְיַהֲלֹם׃ וְהַטּוּר הַשְּׁלִישִׁי לֶשֶׁם
a ,jacinth third the And row a and .diamond a ,sapphire a ,turquoise second the And row

3471 7718 8658 7243 2905 306 7618
13 שְׁבוֹ וְאַחְלָמָה׃ וְהַטּוּר הָרְבִיעִי תַּרְשִׁישׁ שֹׁהַם וְיָשְׁפֵה
a and ;jasper onyx an a ,chrysolite ,fourth the And row an and ,amethyst an agate

8034 68 4396 2091 4865 4374
14 מוּסַבֹּת מִשְׁבְּצוֹת זָהָב בְּמִלֻּאֹתָם׃ וְהָאֲבָנִים עַל־שְׁמֹת
the according of names to the And stones their in .settings gold plaited of work in set

2368 6603 8034 6240 8147 3478 1121
בְּנֵי־יִשְׂרָאֵל הֵנָּה שְׁתֵּים עֶשְׂרֵה עַל־שְׁמֹתָם פִּתּוּחֵי חוֹתָם
a ,signet the of engravings their ;names according to twelve they (were) ,Israel the of sons

each according to his name, for the twelve tribes. 15 And they made cords of chains on the pocket, a work of cords, *of* pure gold. 16 And they made two plaitings of gold; and they put the two rings on the two ends of the pocket. 17 And they shall put the two cords of gold on the two rings on the ends of the pocket. 18 And the two ends of the two cords they put on the two settings. And they put them on the shoulder-pieces of the ephod, on its front. 19 And they made two rings of gold, and they put *them* on the two ends of the pocket, on its edge, which *was* on the inward side of the ephod. 20 And they made two rings of gold, and they put them on the two shoulder-pieces of the ephod from beneath, toward its front, near its joining; from above to the band of the ephod. 21 And they fastened the pocket from its rings to the rings of the ephod with a ribbon of blue, to be above the band of the ephod. And the pocket could not move itself from the ephod, as Jehovah commanded Moses.

2833 6213 7626 6240 8147 8034 376
15 איש על-שמו לשנים עשר שבט : ויעשו על-החשן
the pocket | on | they And made | .tribes | ten (and) two | his according each ,names to

8147 6213 2889 2091 5688 4639 1383 8333
16 שרשרת גבלת מעשה עבת זהב טהור : ויעשו שתי
two | they and made | ,pure | gold | cords | work of | ,chains | of cords

2885 8147 5414 2091 2885 8147 2091 4865
משבצת זהב ושתי טבעת זהב ויתנו את-שתי הטבעת
rings the | two | they and put | ;gold | rings of | two and | ,gold | plaitings of

5921 2091 5688 8147 5414 2833 7098 8147 5921
17 על-שני קצות החשן : ויתנו שתי העבתת הזהב על-
on | gold of cords the | two | they And put shall | the .pocket | of ends the | on two

8147 7098 8147 2833 7098 2885 8147
18 שתי הטבעת על-קצות החשן : ואת שתי קצות שתי
two | of ends | two the | and | the .pocket | the of ends | on | rings the | two

3802 5921 5414 4865 8147 5414 5688
העבתת נתנו על-שתי המשבצת ויתנם על-כתפת
the of shoulder-pieces | on | they and them put | ;settings the | two | on | they put | cords the

646 4136 6440 6213 8147 2885 2091 7760 5921
19 האפד אל-מול פניו : ויעשו שתי טבעת זהב וישימו על-
(them) on | they and put | ,gold | of rings | two | they And made | toward front its | the ,ephod

8147 7098 2833 8193 834 5676 646 1004
שני קצות החשן על-שפתו אשר אל-עבר האפד ביתה :
,inward | the ephod | the of side | on | which (was) | .edge its | on | the ,pocket | of ends | the two

6213 8147 2885 2091 5414 5921 8147 3802 646
20 ויעשו שתי טבעת זהב ויתנם על-שתי כתפת האפד
the ephod | shoulder-of pieces | the two | on | they and them put | ,gold | of rings | two | they And made

4295 4136 6440 5980 4225 4605 2805 646
מלמטה ממול פניו לעמת מחברתו ממעל לחשב האפד :
the .ephod | the to of band | from above | ;joining its | near | the toward ,it of front | from ,beneath

7405 2833 2885 646 6616
21 וירכסו את-החשן מטבעתיו אל-טבעת האפד בפתיל
a with of ribbon | the ephod | of rings the to | rings its from | the pocket | they And fastened

8504 1961 2805 2833 2118 3808 646
תכלת להיות על-חשב האפד ולא-יזח החשן מעל האפד
the ;ephod | from | the pocket | not that itself move | the ;ephod | band the | on | be to | ,blue of

4872 3068 6680
כאשר צוה יהוה את-משה :
.Moses | Jehovah com-manded | as

22 And he made the robe of the ephod, a work of a weaver, all of blue. 23 And the mouth of the robe in the middle *was* like the mouth of a woven garment, the edge of its mouth all around, that it might not be torn. 24 And they made bells of pure gold. And they put the

6310 8504 3632 707 4639 646 4598 6213
22 ויעש את-מעיל האפד מעשה ארג כליל תכלת : ופי-
23
the And of mouth | .blue | entirely | a ,weaver | of work a | the ,ephod | robe the of | he And made

7167 3808 5439 6310 8193 8473 6310 8432 4598
המעיל בתוכו כפי תחרא שפה לפיו סביב לא יקרע :
it that .torn be might | not | all ,around | its of mouth | the edge | coat a ,mail of | the like of mouth | its in midst | robe the

8438 713 8504 7416 4598 7757 6213
24 ויעשו על-שולי המעיל רמוני תכלת וארגמן ותולעת
and ,crimson | and ,purple | ,blue | pomegrantes of | the robe | the of hem | on they And made

6472 5414 2089 2091 6472 6213 7806 8138
25 שני משזר : ויעשו פעמני זהב טהור ויתנו את-הפעמנים
bells the | and they put | ;pure | gold | of bells | And they made | twined

bells in the midst of the pomegranates, on the hem of the robe all around, among the pomegranates, a bell and a pomegranate, a bell and a pomegranate on the hem of the robe all around, for ministering, as Jehovah commanded Moses.

[27]And they made the tunics of bleached *linen*, the work of a weaver, for Aaron and for his sons; [28]also the miter *of* bleached *linen*, and the headdress of the caps *of* bleached *linen*, and the breeches of twined linen bleached; and the girdle *of* bleached, twined *linen*, and blue, and purple, and crimson, the work of an embroiderer, as Jehovah commanded Moses.

[30]And they made the plate of the holy crown *of* pure gold. And they wrote on it the writing of the engravings of a signet, HOLINESS TO JEHOVAH. [31]And they put on it a ribbon of blue, to fasten *it* on the miter from above, as Jehovah commanded Moses.

[32]And all the work of the tent of the tabernacle was finished. And the sons of Israel did according to all which Jehovah had commanded Moses; so they did.

[33]And they brought the tabernacle to Moses, the tent and all its vessels, its hooks, it boards, its bars, and its pillars, and its sockets, [34]and the cover of rams' skins dyed red, and the cover of dugong skins, and the veil of the covering, [35]the ark of the testimony, and its poles, and the mercy-seat, [36]the table, and all its vessels, and the Bread of the Presence, [37]the pure lampstand, its lamps, the

7416 8432 5439 4598 7757 7416 8432
בְּתוֹךְ הָרִמֹּנִים עַל־שׁוּלֵי הַמְּעִיל סָבִיב בְּתוֹךְ הָרִמֹּנִים׃
the among all robe the the on pome- the the in
;pomegranates ,around of hem ;granates of midst

83 34 5439 4598 7757 7416 6472 7416 6472
26 פַּעֲמֹן וְרִמֹּן פַּעֲמֹן וְרִמֹּן עַל־שׁוּלֵי הַמְּעִיל סָבִיב לְשָׁרֵת
for all robe the the on a and bell a a and bell a
,ministering ,around of hem ,pomegranate ,pomegranate

3801 6213 4872 3068 6680
27 כַּאֲשֶׁר צִוָּה יְהוָה אֶת־מֹשֶׁה׃ ס וַיַּעֲשׂוּ אֶת־הַכָּתְנֹת
(of) tunics the they And made .Moses Jehovah com- manded as

8336 4701 1121 175 707 4639 8336
28 שֵׁשׁ מַעֲשֵׂה אֹרֵג לְאַהֲרֹן וּלְבָנָיו׃ וְאֵת הַמִּצְנֶפֶת שֵׁשׁ
(,linen) miter the and for and Aaron for a work the (,linen)
bleached (of) ;sons his ,weaver of bleached

7806 8336 906 4370 8336 4021 6287
וְאֶת־פַּאֲרֵי הַמִּגְבָּעֹת שֵׁשׁ וְאֶת־מִכְנְסֵי הַבָּד שֵׁשׁ מָשְׁזָר׃
;twined bleached ,linen the and bleached the the and
(linen) of breeches (linen) (of) caps of headdress

8144 8438 713 8504 7806 8336 73
29 וְאֶת־הָאַבְנֵט שֵׁשׁ מָשְׁזָר וּתְכֵלֶת וְאַרְגָּמָן וְתוֹלַעַת שָׁנִי
,crimson and and ,blue and ,twined bleached the and
,purple (linen) (of) girdle

4872 3068/6680 7551 4639 6213
30 מַעֲשֵׂה רֹקֵם כַּאֲשֶׁר צִוָּה יְהוָה אֶת־מֹשֶׁה׃ ס וַיַּעֲשׂוּ אֶת־
they And made .Moses Jehovah com- manded as an ,embroiderer's work

6603 4385 3789 2889 2091 6944 5145 6731
צִיץ נֵזֶר־הַקֹּדֶשׁ זָהָב טָהוֹר וַיִּכְתְּבוּ עָלָיו מִכְתַּב פִּתּוּחֵי
the writing the it on they and ;pure (of) the crown the
of engravings of wrote gold holy of plate

8504 6616 5414 3068 6944 2368
31 חוֹתָם קֹדֶשׁ לַיהוָה׃ וַיִּתְּנוּ עָלָיו פְּתִיל תְּכֵלֶת לָתֵת עַל־
on to ,blue a it on they And TO HOLINESS a
(it) fasten of ribbon put .JEHOVAH ,signet

3615 4872 3068 6680 4605 4701
32 הַמִּצְנֶפֶת מִלְמָעְלָה כַּאֲשֶׁר צִוָּה יְהוָה אֶת־מֹשֶׁה׃ ס וַתֵּכֶל
was And finished .Moses Jehovah com- manded as from ;above miter the

3605 3478 1121 6213 4150 168 4908 5656 3605
כָּל־עֲבֹדַת מִשְׁכַּן אֹהֶל מוֹעֵד וַיַּעֲשׂוּ בְּנֵי יִשְׂרָאֵל כְּכֹל
according all to Israel the of sons did And .meeting the of tent the of tabernacle work the of all

6213 3651 4872 3068 6680 834
אֲשֶׁר צִוָּה יְהוָה אֶת־מֹשֶׁה כֵּן עָשׂוּ׃
they .did so ,Moses Jehovah has commanded which

3627 3605 168 4872 4908 935
33 וַיָּבִיאוּ אֶת־הַמִּשְׁכָּן אֶל־מֹשֶׁה אֶת־הָאֹהֶל וְאֶת־כָּל־כֵּלָיו
its ,vessels all and tent the ,Moses to the tabernacle they And brought

5785 4372 134 5982 1280 7175 7165
34 קְרָסָיו קְרָשָׁיו בְּרִיחָו וְעַמֻּדָיו וַאֲדָנָיו׃ וְאֶת־מִכְסֵה עוֹרֹת
skins cover the of and its and ;sockets its and ,pillars ,bars its its ,boards its ,hooks

6532 8476 5785 4372 119 352
הָאֵילִם הַמְאָדָּמִים וְאֶת־מִכְסֵה עֹרֹת הַתְּחָשִׁים וְאֵת פָּרֹכֶת
the of veil and the dugong skins cover the of and of ,red dyed rams'

3727 905 5715 727 4539
35 הַמָּסָךְ׃ אֶת־אֲרוֹן הָעֵדֻת וְאֶת־בַּדָּיו וְאֵת הַכַּפֹּרֶת׃ אֶת־
36
mercy- ;seat the and its ,poles and the ,testimony of ark the the ;covering

4501 6440 3899 3627 3605 7979
37 הַשֻּׁלְחָן אֶת־כָּל־כֵּלָיו וְאֵת לֶחֶם הַפָּנִים׃ אֶת־הַמְּנֹרָה
the lampstand the ;presence the of bread and its ,vessels all and ,table the

הַטְּהֹרָה אֶת־נֵרֹתֶיהָ נֵרֹת הַמַּעֲרָכָה וְאֶת־כָּל־כֵּלֶיהָ וְאֵת
38 שֶׁמֶן הַמָּאוֹר׃ וְאֵת מִזְבַּח הַזָּהָב וְאֵת שֶׁמֶן הַמִּשְׁחָה וְאֵת
39 קְטֹרֶת הַסַּמִּים וְאֵת מָסַךְ פֶּתַח הָאֹהֶל׃ אֵת ׀ מִזְבַּח
הַנְּחֹשֶׁת וְאֶת־מִכְבַּר הַנְּחֹשֶׁת אֲשֶׁר־לוֹ אֶת־בַּדָּיו וְאֶת־כָּל־
40 כֵּלָיו אֶת־הַכִּיֹּר וְאֶת־כַּנּוֹ׃ אֵת קַלְעֵי הֶחָצֵר אֶת־עַמֻּדֶיהָ
וְאֶת־אֲדָנֶיהָ וְאֶת־הַמָּסָךְ לְשַׁעַר הֶחָצֵר אֶת־מֵיתָרָיו וִיתֵדֹתֶיהָ
41 וְאֵת כָּל־כְּלֵי עֲבֹדַת הַמִּשְׁכָּן לְאֹהֶל מוֹעֵד׃ אֶת־בִּגְדֵי
הַשְּׂרָד לְשָׁרֵת בַּקֹּדֶשׁ אֶת־בִּגְדֵי הַקֹּדֶשׁ לְאַהֲרֹן הַכֹּהֵן
42 וְאֶת־בִּגְדֵי בָנָיו לְכַהֵן׃ כְּכֹל אֲשֶׁר־צִוָּה יְהוָה אֶת־מֹשֶׁה
43 כֵּן עָשׂוּ בְּנֵי יִשְׂרָאֵל אֵת כָּל־הָעֲבֹדָה׃ וַיַּרְא מֹשֶׁה אֶת־
כָּל־הַמְּלָאכָה וְהִנֵּה עָשׂוּ אֹתָהּ כַּאֲשֶׁר צִוָּה יְהוָה כֵּן עָשׂוּ
וַיְבָרֶךְ אֹתָם מֹשֶׁה׃

lamps of arrangement and all its vessels, and the oil of the light, [38]and the altar of gold, and the oil of anointing, and the incense of perfumes, and the hanging of the door of the tabernacle, [39]the altar of bronze, and its bronze grating, its poles and all its vessels, the laver and its base, [40]the hangings of the court, its pillars, and its sockets, and the hanging for the gate of the court, its cords, and its pins, and all the vessels of the service of the tabernacle, for the tabernacle of the congregation, [41]the woven garments for ministering in the holy place, the holy garments for Aaron the priest, and the garments of his sons for ministering as priests.

[42]According to all which Jehovah had commanded Moses, so the sons of Israel did all the work. [43]And Moses saw all the work. And, behold, they had done it as Jehovah had commanded; so they had done. And Moses blessed them.

CAP. XL מ

CHAPTER 40

1 וַיְדַבֵּר יְהוָה אֶל־מֹשֶׁה לֵּאמֹר׃ בְּיוֹם־הַחֹדֶשׁ הָרִאשׁוֹן
2
3 בְּאֶחָד לַחֹדֶשׁ תָּקִים אֶת־מִשְׁכַּן אֹהֶל מוֹעֵד׃ וְשַׂמְתָּ שָׁם
4 אֵת אֲרוֹן הָעֵדוּת וְסַכֹּתָ עַל־הָאָרֹן אֶת־הַפָּרֹכֶת׃ וְהֵבֵאתָ
אֶת־הַשֻּׁלְחָן וְעָרַכְתָּ אֶת־עֶרְכּוֹ וְהֵבֵאתָ אֶת־הַמְּנֹרָה וְהַעֲלֵיתָ

CHAPTER 40

[1]And Jehovah spoke to Moses, saying, [2]On the first day of the month, on the first of the month, you shall raise up the tent of the tabernacle of the congregation. [3]And you shall put there the ark of testimony, and you shall cover the ark with the veil. [4]And you shall bring in the table and set in order its arrangement. And you shall bring in the lampstand and

set up its lamps. [5]And you shall put the altar of gold for incense before the ark of testimony. And you shall set up the hanging of the door of the tabernacle. [6]And you shall set up the altar of burnt offerings before the door of the tent of the tabernacle of the congregation. [7]And you shall put the laver between the tabernacle of the congregation and the altar. And you shall put water there. [8]And you shall set up the court all around. And you shall place the hanging of the gate of the court. [9]And you shall take the oil of anointing, and you shall anoint the tabernacle and all in it. And you shall sanctify it and all its vessels, and it shall become holy. [10]And you shall anoint the altar of burnt offering and all its vessels. And you shall sanctify the altar, and the altar shall become most holy.

[11]And you shall anoint the laver and its base, and you shall sanctify it. [12]And you shall bring Aaron and his sons near the door of the tabernacle of the congregation, and you shall wash them with water. [13]And you shall clothe Aaron *with* the holy garments. And you shall anoint him and sanctify him. And he shall minister as priest to Me. [14]And you shall bring near his sons. And you shall clothe them *with* tunics. [15]And you shall anoint them, as you anointed their father. And they shall minister as priests to Me. And their anointing shall be for a perpetual priesthood for their generations. [16]And Moses did so, according to all Jehovah had commanded him, so he did.

[17]And it happened in the first month, in the second year, on the first of the month, the tabernacle was raised up. [18]And Moses raised up the tabernacle,

5 את־נרתיה׃ ונתתה את־מזבח הזהב לקטרת לפני ארון
6 העדת ושמת את־מסך הפתח למשכן׃ ונתתה את
7 מזבח העלה לפני פתח משכן אהל־מועד׃ ונתת את־
8 הכיר בין־אהל מועד ובין המזבח ונתת שם מים׃ ושמת
9 את־החצר סביב ונתת את־מסך שער החצר׃ ולקחת
את־שמן המשחה ומשחת את־המשכן ואת־כל־אשר־בו
10 וקדשת אתו ואת־כל־כליו והיה קדש׃ ומשחת את־
מזבח העלה ואת־כל־כליו וקדשת את־המזבח והיה
11 המזבח קדש קדשים׃ ומשחת את־הכיר ואת־כנו וקדשת
12 אתו׃ והקרבת את־אהרן ואת־בניו אל־פתח אהל מועד
13 ורחצת אתם במים׃ והלבשת את־אהרן את בגדי הקדש
14 ומשחת אתו וקדשת אתו וכהן לי׃ ואת־בניו תקריב
15 והלבשת אתם כתנת׃ ומשחת אתם כאשר משחת את־
אביהם וכהנו לי והיתה להית להם משחתם לכהנת
16 עולם לדרתם׃ ויעש משה ככל אשר צוה יהוה אתו
17 כן עשה׃ ס ויהי בחדש הראשון בשנה השנית
18 באחד לחדש הוקם המשכן׃ ויקם משה את־המשכן

and he placed its sockets, and he set up its boards, and he placed its bars, and he raised up its pillars. [19]And he spread out the tent over the tabernacle. And he put the cover of the tent over it from above, as Jehovah had commanded Moses.

[20]And he took and placed the testimony into the ark. And he put the poles on the ark. And he placed the mercy-seat on the ark from above. [21]And he brought the ark into the tabernacle. And he placed the veil of the covering, and he covered the ark of testimony, as Jehovah had commanded Moses. [22]And he placed the table in the tabernacle of the congregation, on the north side of the tabernacle, outside the veil. [23]And he set the bread in order before the face of Jehovah, as Jehovah had commanded Moses.

[24]And he put the lampstand in the tabernacle of the congregation, opposite the table, on the south side of the tabernacle. [25]And he set up the lambs before the face of Jehovah, as Jehovah had commanded Moses. [26]And he put the altar of gold in the tabernacle of the congregation, in front of the veil. [27]And he burned incense of perfumes on it, as Jehovah had commanded Moses. [28]And he set up the hanging of the door to the tabernacle.

[29]And he put the altar of burnt offering *at* the door of the tent of the tabernacle of the congregation. And he offered up on it the burnt offering, and the food offering, as Jehovah had commanded Moses. [30]And he put the laver between the tabernacle of the congregation and the altar, and he

6965 1280 5414 7175 7760 134 5414
וַיִּתֵּן אֶת־אֲדָנָיו וַיָּשֶׂם אֶת־קְרָשָׁיו וַיִּתֵּן אֶת־בְּרִיחָיו וַיָּקֶם
he and up raised | ,bars its | he and placed | its ,boards | he and up set | its ,sockets | he and placed

7760 4908 168 6566 5982
19 אֶת־עַמּוּדָיו׃ וַיִּפְרֹשׂ אֶת־הָאֹהֶל עַל־הַמִּשְׁכָּן וַיָּשֶׂם אֶת־
he and put | the tabernacle | over | tent the | he And out spread | .pillars its

4872 3068 6680 4605 5921 168 4372
מִכְסֵה הָאֹהֶל עָלָיו מִלְמָעְלָה כַּאֲשֶׁר צִוָּה יְהוָה אֶת־מֹשֶׁה׃
.Moses | Jehovah | had commanded | as | from .above | over it | the tent | the of cover

5921/905 7760 727 5715 5414 3947
20 ס וַיִּקַּח וַיִּתֵּן אֶת־הָעֵדֻת אֶל־הָאָרֹן וַיָּשֶׂם אֶת־הַבַּדִּים עַל־
on | poles the | he and put | the ark | into | the testimony | and placed | he And took

935 4605 727 3727 5414 727
21 הָאָרֹן וַיִּתֵּן אֶת־הַכַּפֹּרֶת עַל־הָאָרֹן מִלְמָעְלָה׃ וַיָּבֵא אֶת־
he And brought | from .above | the ark | on | mercy- the seat | he and placed | the ;ark

727 5921 5526 4539 6532 7760 4908 727
הָאָרֹן אֶל־הַמִּשְׁכָּן וַיָּשֶׂם אֵת פָּרֹכֶת הַמָּסָךְ וַיָּסֶךְ עַל אֲרוֹן
the of ark | over | he and covered | the ,covering | veil the of | he and placed | the .tabernacle | into | the ark

5414 4872 3068 6680 5715
22 הָעֵדוּת כַּאֲשֶׁר צִוָּה יְהוָה אֶת־מֹשֶׁה׃ ס וַיִּתֵּן אֶת־
he And placed | .Moses | Jehovah | had commanded | as | ,testimony

6532 235 6828 4908 3409 4150 168 7979
הַשֻּׁלְחָן בְּאֹהֶל מוֹעֵד עַל יֶרֶךְ הַמִּשְׁכָּן צָפֹנָה מִחוּץ לַפָּרֹכֶת׃
.veil the | outside | north- ward | the ,tabernacle | side of | on | ,meeting | the in of tent | the table

2009 6680 3068 6440 3899 6187 6186
23 וַיַּעֲרֹךְ עָלָיו עֵרֶךְ לֶחֶם לִפְנֵי יְהוָה כַּאֲשֶׁר צִוָּה יְהוָה אֶת־
Jehovah had commanded | as | ,Jehovah before | the bread | in order | on it | he And set

7979 5227 4150 168 4501 7760 4872
24 מֹשֶׁה׃ ס וַיָּשֶׂם אֶת־הַמְּנֹרָה בְּאֹהֶל מוֹעֵד נֹכַח הַשֻּׁלְחָן
the ;table | opposite | ,meeting | the in of tent | the lampstand | he And put | .Moses

3068 6440 5216 5927 5045 4908 3409 5921
25 עַל יֶרֶךְ הַמִּשְׁכָּן נֶגְבָּה׃ וַיַּעַל הַנֵּרֹת לִפְנֵי יְהוָה כַּאֲשֶׁר
as | ,Jehovah before | the lamps | he And up set | south- .ward | the tabernacle | side of | on

168 2091 4196 7760 4872 3068 6680
26 צִוָּה יְהוָה אֶת־מֹשֶׁה׃ ס וַיָּשֶׂם אֶת־מִזְבַּח הַזָּהָב בְּאֹהֶל
the in of tent | gold | the of altar | he And put | .Moses | Jehovah had commanded

5561 7004 5921 6999 6532 6440 4150
27 מוֹעֵד לִפְנֵי הַפָּרֹכֶת׃ וַיַּקְטֵר עָלָיו קְטֹרֶת סַמִּים כַּאֲשֶׁר
as | fragrant ,perfumes | incense of | it on | he And burned | .veil the | before ,meeting

6607 4539 7760 4872 3068 6680
28 צִוָּה יְהוָה אֶת־מֹשֶׁה׃ ס וַיָּשֶׂם אֶת־מָסַךְ הַפֶּתַח
the door | the of hanging | he And up set | .Moses | Jehovah had commanded

4150 168 4908 6607 7760 5930 4196 4908
29 לַמִּשְׁכָּן׃ וְאֵת מִזְבַּח הָעֹלָה שָׂם פֶּתַח מִשְׁכַּן אֹהֶל־מוֹעֵד
;meeting | the of tent | the of tabernacle | the (at) of door | he put | burnt offering | the of altar | And | the to .tabernacle

3068 6680 4503 5930 5927
וַיַּעַל עָלָיו אֶת־הָעֹלָה וְאֶת־הַמִּנְחָה כַּאֲשֶׁר צִוָּה יְהוָה
Jehovah | had commanded | as | food the ,offering | and | the offering burnt | it on | he and up offered

996 4150 168 3595 7760 4872
30 אֶת־מֹשֶׁה׃ ס וַיָּשֶׂם אֶת־הַכִּיֹּר בֵּין־אֹהֶל מוֹעֵד וּבֵין
and | meeting | the between of tent | laver the | he And put | .Moses

placed water there for
washing. [31]And from it
Moses and Aaron and his
sons washed their hands
and their feet. [32]As they
came into the tabernacle of
the congregation, and as
they came near to the altar,
they would wash, as
Jehovah had commanded
Moses.

[33]And he raised up the
court all around the tabernacle, and the altar. And he
set up the hanging of the
gate of the court. And
Moses finished the work.

[34]And the cloud covered
the tabernacle of the
congregation; and the glory
of Jehovah filled the
tabernacle. [35]And Moses
was not able to come into
the tabernacle of congregation, because the cloud
dwelt on it. And the glory of
Jehovah filled the taber-
nacle. [36]And as the cloud
rose up from the tabernacle
the sons of Israel traveled in
all their journeys. [37]And
if the cloud did not rise
up, then they did not pull
up *stakes* until the day it
rose up. [38]For the cloud
of Jehovah *was* on the
tabernacle by day, and
fire was on it by night,
before the eyes of all the
house of Israel in all their
journeyings.

4872 7364 7364 4325 8033 5414 4196
31 הַמִּזְבֵּחַ וַיִּתֵּן שָׁמָּה מַיִם לְרָחְצָה׃ וְרָחֲצוּ מִמֶּנּוּ מֹשֶׁה
Moses from it And washed for .washing water there he and placed the ;altar

168 935 7272 3027 1121 175
32 וְאַהֲרֹן וּבָנָיו אֶת־יְדֵיהֶם וְאֶת־רַגְלֵיהֶם׃ בְּבֹאָם אֶל־אֹהֶל
the of tent into they As came .feet their and hands their his and sons and Aaron

3068 6680 7364 4196 7126 4150
מוֹעֵד וּבְקָרְבָתָם אֶל־הַמִּזְבֵּחַ יִרְחָצוּ כַּאֲשֶׁר צִוָּה יְהוָה
Jehovah had commanded as would they wash the altar to they as and near came meeting

4196 4908 5439 2691 6965 4872
33 אֶת־מֹשֶׁה׃ ס וַיָּקֶם אֶת־הֶחָצֵר סָבִיב לַמִּשְׁכָּן וְלַמִּזְבֵּחַ
the and ;altar the tabernacle all around court the he And up raised .Moses

4399 4872 3615 2691 8179 4539 5414
וַיִּתֵּן אֶת־מָסַךְ שַׁעַר הֶחָצֵר וַיְכַל מֹשֶׁה אֶת־הַמְּלָאכָה׃ פ
.work the Moses And finished the .court the of gate the of hanging he and up set

4390 3068 3519 4150 168 6051 3680
34 וַיְכַס הֶעָנָן אֶת־אֹהֶל מוֹעֵד וּכְבוֹד יְהוָה מָלֵא אֶת־
filled Jehovah the and of glory ;meeting the of tent the cloud And covered

3588 4150 168 935 4872 3201 4908
35 הַמִּשְׁכָּן׃ וְלֹא־יָכֹל מֹשֶׁה לָבוֹא אֶל־אֹהֶל מוֹעֵד כִּי־
because ,meeting the of tent into come to Moses was And able not the .tabernacle

5927 4908 4390 3068 3519 6051 5921 7931
36 שָׁכַן עָלָיו הֶעָנָן וּכְבוֹד יְהוָה מָלֵא אֶת־הַמִּשְׁכָּן׃ וּבְהֵעָלוֹת
as And arose the .tabernacle filled Jehovah the and of glory the cloud it on dwelt

4550 3605 3478 1121 5265 4908 5921 6051
הֶעָנָן מֵעַל הַמִּשְׁכָּן יִסְעוּ בְּנֵי יִשְׂרָאֵל בְּכֹל מַסְעֵיהֶם׃
their journeys all in ,Israel the of sons journeyed the tabernacle from the cloud

6051 3588 5927 3117/5704 5265 3808 6051 5927/3808
37 וְאִם־לֹא יֵעָלֶה הֶעָנָן וְלֹא יִסְעוּ עַד־יוֹם הֵעָלֹתוֹ׃ כִּי עֲנַן
38
the of cloud For its of rising the day until did they up pull and not the ,cloud did arise not And if

3605 5869 3915 1961 784 3119 4908 5921 3068
יְהוָה עַל־הַמִּשְׁכָּן יוֹמָם וְאֵשׁ תִּהְיֶה לַיְלָה בּוֹ לְעֵינֵי כָל־
all before ,it on of eyes the by night was and fire by ,day the tabernacle on Jehovah (was)

4550 3605 3478 1004
בֵּית־יִשְׂרָאֵל בְּכָל־מַסְעֵיהֶם׃
their .journeyings all in Israel the of house

ויקרא

LEVITICUS

(THE) BOOK OF LEVITICUS

CAPUT. I א

A LITERAL TRANSLATION
OF THE BIBLE

THE BOOK OF LEVITICUS

CHAPTER 1

1And Jehovah called to Moses and spoke to him out of the tabernacle of the congregation, saying:
2Speak to the sons of Israel and say to them, If any one of you brings an offering to Jehovah, from livestock of the herd, or from the flock, you shall bring near your offering.
3If his offering *is* out of the herd, a male, a perfect one, he shall bring it to the opening of the tabernacle of the congregation, at his pleasure, before the face of Jehovah. 4And he shall lay his hand on the head of the burnt offering, and it is accepted for him to make atonement for him. 5And he shall kill the son of the herd before the face of Jehovah. And the sons of Aaron, the priests, shall bring near the blood and sprinkle the blood on the altar all around, which *is* at the opening of the tabernacle of the congregation. 6And he shall skin the burnt offering, and shall cut it into pieces. 7And the sons of Aaron the priest shall put fire on the altar and arrange wood on the fire. 8And the sons of Aaron, the priests, shall arrange the pieces, with the head and the fat, on the wood which is on the fire, which *is* on the altar. 9And he shall wash its inward parts, and its legs, with water. And the priest shall burn as incense the whole *of it* on the altar for a burnt offering, a fire offering of soothing fragrance to Jehovah.

CHAPTER 1

559 4150 168 3068 1696 4872 7121
1 וַיִּקְרָא אֶל־מֹשֶׁה וַיְדַבֵּר יְהוָה אֵלָיו מֵאֹהֶל מוֹעֵד לֵאמֹר׃
,saying ,meeting the of out him to Jehovah and Moses to And
of tent spoke called

7126 120 559 3478 1121 1696
2 דַּבֵּר אֶל־בְּנֵי יִשְׂרָאֵל וְאָמַרְתָּ אֲלֵהֶם אָדָם כִּי־יַקְרִיב מִכֶּם
you of brings If one any ,them to say and ,Israel the to Speak
of sons

7126 6629 1241 929 3068 7133
קָרְבָּן לַיהוָה מִן־הַבְּהֵמָה מִן־הַבָּקָר וּמִן־הַצֹּאן תַּקְרִיבוּ
shall you the from or ,herd the of the from to an
bring ,flock cattle :Jehovah offering

8549 2145 1241 7133 5930 7133
3 אֶת־קָרְבַּנְכֶם׃ אִם־עֹלָה קָרְבָּנוֹ מִן־הַבָּקָר זָכָר תָּמִים
perfect a a ,herd the of out his burnt If .offering your
,one ,male (is) offering

6440 7522 7126 4150 168 6607 7126
יַקְרִיבֶנּוּ אֶל־פֶּתַח אֹהֶל מוֹעֵד יַקְרִיב אֹתוֹ לִרְצֹנוֹ לִפְנֵי
before his at ,it shall he ;meeting the the to shall he
,pleasure bring of tent of opening it bring

3722 7521 5930 7218 5921 3027 5564 3068
4 יְהוָה׃ וְסָמַךְ יָדוֹ עַל רֹאשׁ הָעֹלָה וְנִרְצָה לוֹ לְכַפֵּר עָלָיו׃
;him for make to for is it and burnt- the head the on his he And .Jehovah
atonement him accepted ,offering of hand lay shall

175 1121 7126 3068 6440 1241 1121 7819
5 וְשָׁחַט אֶת־בֶּן הַבָּקָר לִפְנֵי יְהוָה וְהִקְרִיבוּ בְּנֵי אַהֲרֹן
,Aaron the shall And .Jehovah before herd the the he and
of sons near bring of son kill shall

5439 4196 5921 1818 2236 1818 3548
הַכֹּהֲנִים אֶת־הַדָּם וְזָרְקוּ אֶת־הַדָּם עַל־הַמִּזְבֵּחַ סָבִיב
all altar the on blood the and blood the ,priests the
,around sprinkle

5408 5930 6584 4150 168 6607 834
6 אֲשֶׁר־פֶּתַח אֹהֶל מוֹעֵד׃ וְהִפְשִׁיט אֶת־הָעֹלָה וְנִתַּח אֹתָהּ
it shall and burnt the shall he And .meeting the the at which
cut ;offering skin of tent of door (is)

6186 4196 5921 784 3548 175 1121 5414 5409
7 לִנְתָחֶיהָ׃ וְנָתְנוּ בְּנֵי אַהֲרֹן הַכֹּהֵן אֵשׁ עַל־הַמִּזְבֵּחַ וְעָרְכוּ
and ,altar the on fire the Aaron the shall And .pieces into
arrange priest of sons put

5409 3548 175 1121 6186 784 5921 6086
8 עֵצִים עַל־הָאֵשׁ׃ וְעָרְכוּ בְּנֵי אַהֲרֹן הַכֹּהֲנִים אֵת הַנְּתָחִים
,pieces the ,priests the ,Aaron the shall And .fire the on wood
of sons arrange

834 784 834 6086 5921 6309 7218
אֶת־הָרֹאשׁ וְאֶת־הַפָּדֶר עַל־הָעֵצִים אֲשֶׁר עַל־הָאֵשׁ אֲשֶׁר
which ,fire the on is which ,wood the upon fat the and head the with

3548 6999 4325 7364 3767 7130 4196 5921
9 עַל־הַמִּזְבֵּחַ׃ וְקִרְבּוֹ וּכְרָעָיו יִרְחַץ בַּמָּיִם וְהִקְטִיר הַכֹּהֵן
priest the burn shall with shall he its and its And .altar the on (is)
incense as ;water wash legs parts inward

3068 5207 7381 801 5930 4196 3605
אֶת־הַכֹּל הַמִּזְבֵּחָה עֹלָה אִשֵּׁה רֵיחַ־נִיחוֹחַ לַיהוָה׃
to sooth- fragrance fire- a a for the on whole the
.Jehovah ing offering burnt altar
of ,offering

10 And if his offering *is*
out of the flock, out of the
sheep, or out of the goats,
for a burnt offering, a male,
a perfect one, he shall
bring it near. 11 And he
shall slaughter it by the
side of the altar northward,
before the face of Jehovah.
And the sons of Aaron, the
priests, shall sprinkle its
blood all around on the
altar. 12 And he shall wash
the inward parts, and the
legs, with water, and shall
legs, with water, and the
priest shall bring near the
whole *of it* and burn it as
incense on the altar; it *is* a
burnt offering, a fire offering
of soothing fragrance to
Jehovah.

14 And if the burnt offering
is a burnt offering out of the
fowls to Jehovah, then he
shall bring near his offering,
of turtle-doves or of the
offspring of the dove.
15 And the priest shall bring
it near to the altar and shall
nip off its head. And *he* shall
burn it as incense on the
altar; its blood shall be
drained by the side of the
altar. 16 And he shall
remove its crop with its
feathers, and shall throw it
near the altar eastward, to
the place of the ashes.
17 And he shall cleave it with
its wings, not dividing *it*,
and the priest shall burn it
as incense on the altar, on
the wood which *is* on the
fire; a burnt offering; it *is* a
fire offering of soothing
fragrance to Jehovah.

5930 5795 3775 7133 6629
10 וְאִם־מִן־הַצֹּאן קָרְבָּנוֹ מִן הַכְּשָׂבִים אוֹ מִן־הָעִזִּים לְעֹלָה
burnt a for the out or sheep the out his (is) the out if And
:offering goats of of ,offering flock of
6828 4196 3409 7819 7126 8549 2145
11 זָכָר תָּמִים יַקְרִיבֶנּוּ׃ וְשָׁחַט אֹתוֹ עַל יֶרֶךְ הַמִּזְבֵּחַ צָפֹנָה
north- altar the the by it he And shall he perfect a a
ward of side kill shall it bring ,one male
4196 1818 3548 175 1121 2236 3068 6440
לִפְנֵי יְהוָה וְזָרְקוּ בְּנֵי אַהֲרֹן הַכֹּהֲנִים אֶת־דָּמוֹ עַל־הַמִּזְבֵּחַ
altar the on blood its ,priests the ,Aaron the and ;Jehovah before
of sons sprinkle shall
6186 6309 7218 5409 5408 5439
12 סָבִיב׃ וְנִתַּח אֹתוֹ לִנְתָחָיו וְאֶת־רֹאשׁוֹ וְאֶת־פִּדְרוֹ וְעָרַךְ
and fat its and head its with pieces to it he And all
arrange shall both cut shall .around
4196 5921 834 784 5921 834 6086 3548
הַכֹּהֵן אֹתָם עַל־הָעֵצִים אֲשֶׁר עַל־הָאֵשׁ אֲשֶׁר עַל־הַמִּזְבֵּחַ׃
.altar the on which the on which wood the on them priest the
(is) fire (is)
3605 3548 7126 4325 7364 3767 7130
13 וְהַקֶּרֶב וְהַכְּרָעַיִם יִרְחַץ בַּמָּיִם וְהִקְרִיב הַכֹּהֵן אֶת־הַכֹּל
,whole the the shall and with shall he the and the And
priest near bring ,water wash legs innards
3068 5207 7381 801 5930 4196 6999
וְהִקְטִיר הַמִּזְבֵּחָה עֹלָה הוּא אִשֵּׁה רֵיחַ נִיחוֹחַ לַיהוָה׃ פ
.Jehovah to sooth- fragrance fire a (is) it a ,altar the on burn and
ing of offering ,offering burnt incense as it
8449 7126 3068 7133 5930 5775
14 וְאִם מִן־הָעוֹף עֹלָה קָרְבָּנוֹ לַיהוָה וְהִקְרִיב מִן־הַתֹּרִים
turtle-doves of he then to (his) burnt a the out And
bring shall ,Jehovah offering offering fowls of if
4196 3548 7126 7133 3123 1121
15 אוֹ מִן־בְּנֵי הַיּוֹנָה אֶת־קָרְבָּנוֹ׃ וְהִקְרִיבוֹ הַכֹּהֵן אֶל־הַמִּזְבֵּחַ
altar the to the shall And his dove the the of or
priest near it bring .offering of offspring
7023 1818 4680 4196 6999 7218 4454
וּמָלַק אֶת־רֹאשׁוֹ וְהִקְטִיר הַמִּזְבֵּחָה וְנִמְצָה דָמוֹ עַל קִיר
the by its be shall the upon shall and ,head its shall and
of side blood drained ;altar incense as it burn off nip
681 7993 5133 4760 5493 4196
16 הַמִּזְבֵּחַ׃ וְהֵסִיר אֶת־מֻרְאָתוֹ בְּנֹצָתָהּ וְהִשְׁלִיךְ אֹתָהּ אֵצֶל
near it shall and its with crop its he And .altar the
throw feathers remove shall
3808 3671 8156 1880 4725 6924 4196
17 הַמִּזְבֵּחַ קֵדְמָה אֶל־מְקוֹם הַדָּשֶׁן׃ וְשִׁסַּע אֹתוֹ בִכְנָפָיו לֹא
not its with it he And .ashes the to ,eastward altar the
wings cleave shall of place
834 6086 4196 3548 6999 914
יַבְדִּיל וְהִקְטִיר אֹתוֹ הַכֹּהֵן הַמִּזְבֵּחָה עַל־הָעֵצִים אֲשֶׁר
which wood the on the on the it shall and dividing
altar priest incense as burn ,two in (it)
3068 5207 7381 801 5930 784
עַל־הָאֵשׁ עֹלָה הוּא אִשֵּׁה רֵיחַ נִיחֹחַ לַיהוָה׃ ס
.Jehovah to sooth- fragrance fire a (is) it burnt a the (is)
ing of offering ,offering ;fire on

CAP. II ב

CHAPTER 2

1 And when a person
brings near an offering, an
offering, a food offering to
Jehovah, his offering shall
be of flour. And he shall
pour oil on it; and he shall
put on it frankincense.
2 And he shall bring to the
sons of Aaron the priest,

7133 1961 5560 3068 4503 7133 7126 5315
1 וְנֶפֶשׁ כִּי־תַקְרִיב קָרְבַּן מִנְחָה לַיהוָה סֹלֶת יִהְיֶה קָרְבָּנוֹ
his be shall of to food a an brings when a And
offering flour ,Jehovah ,offering ,offering near person
1121 935 3828 5921 5414 8081 3332
2 וְיָצַק עָלֶיהָ שֶׁמֶן וְנָתַן עָלֶיהָ לְבֹנָה׃ וֶהֱבִיאָהּ אֶל־בְּנֵי
the to shall he And .frankincense it on he and ;oil it on he and
of sons it bring put shall pour shall

And he shall take out of it his handful from its flour, and from its oil, with all its frankincense. And the priest shall burn it as incense on the altar, a memorial offering, a fire offering, a soothing fragrance to Jehovah. [3]And the rest of the food offering *is* for Aaron and for his sons, most holy, of the fire offerings of Jehovah.

[4]And when you bring near an offering, a food offering baked in an oven, fine flour, unleavened cakes mixed with oil, and unleavened thin cakes anointed with oil.

[5]And if your offering *is* a food offering on a griddle, your offering *shall be* fine flour mixed with oil; it shall be unleavened. [6]You shall divide ite into parts, and you shall pour oil on it; it *is* a food offering.

[7]And if the food offering *is* in a pan, your offering *shall be* of fine flour; it shall be made with oil. [8]And you shall bring the food offering made of these things to Jehovah. And the priest shall bring it near to the altar. [9]And the priest shall lift up the food offering, its memorial offering, and shall burn it as incense on the altar, a fire offering, a soothing fragrance to Jehovah. [10]And the rest of the food offering *is* for Aaron and his sons, most holy, of the fire offering of Jehovah. [11]Any food offering which you shall bring near to Jehovah, you shall not make *it* leavened; for all leaven and all honey you shall not burn it as incense, a fire offering to Jehovah.

[12]*As* an offering of first-fruits, you shall bring them to Jehovah, but they shall not go up on the altar for a soothing fragrance. [13]And every offering of your food offering you shall season

8081 6560 7062 4393 8033 7061 3548 175
אַהֲרֹן הַכֹּהֲנִים וְקָמַץ מִשָּׁם מְלֹא קֻמְצוֹ מִסָּלְתָּהּ וּמִשַּׁמְנָהּ
from and its from his fulness from he and the ,Aaron
,oil its flour fine handful of it grasp shall ;priests

4196 234 3548 6999 3828 3605
עַל כָּל־לְבֹנָתָהּ וְהִקְטִיר הַכֹּהֵן אֶת־אַזְכָּרָתָהּ הַמִּזְבֵּחָה
the on memorial its the burn shall and its all with
altar offering priest incense as it ;frankincense

3 175 4503 3498 3068 5207 7381 801
אִשֵּׁה רֵיחַ נִיחֹחַ לַיהוָה׃ וְהַנּוֹתֶרֶת מִן־הַמִּנְחָה לְאַהֲרֹן
for (is) food the of the And .Jehovah to soothing a fire a
Aaron offering rest fragrance ,offering

4 7126 3068 801 6944 6944 1121
וּלְבָנָיו קֹדֶשׁ קָדָשִׁים מֵאִשֵּׁי יְהוָה׃ וְכִי תַקְרִב
you And .Jehovah fire of most holy for and
bring when of offerings ,sons his

8081 1101 4682 2471 5560 8574 3989 4503 7133
קָרְבַּן מִנְחָה מַאֲפֵה תַנּוּר סֹלֶת חַלּוֹת מַצֹּת בְּלוּלֹת בַּשֶּׁמֶן
with mixed unleavened cakes fine an baked food a an
,oil flour ,oven in offering ,offering

5 4503 8081 4886 4682 7550
וּרְקִיקֵי מַצּוֹת מְשֻׁחִים בַּשָּׁמֶן׃ וְאִם־מִנְחָה עַל־
on food a And with spread unleavened and
offering if .oil over cakes thin

6 6626 1961 4682 8081 1101 5560 7133 4227
הַמַּחֲבַת קָרְבָּנֶךָ סֹלֶת בְּלוּלָה בַשֶּׁמֶן מַצָּה תִהְיֶה׃ פָּתוֹת
shall you shall it unlea- with mixed fine your griddle the
divide ;be vened oil flour ,(is) offering

7 4503 8081 5921 3332 6595
אֹתָהּ פִּתִּים וְיָצַקְתָּ עָלֶיהָ שָׁמֶן מִנְחָה הִוא׃ וְאִם־
And .(is) it food a ;oil it on you and into it
if offering pour shall ,bits

8 935 6213 8081 5560 7133 4802 4503
מִנְחַת מַרְחֶשֶׁת קָרְבָּנֶךָ סֹלֶת בַּשֶּׁמֶן תֵּעָשֶׂה׃ וְהֵבֵאתָ
you And shall it with fine of offering your a in food a
bring shall ,made be oil flour (made is) ,pan offering

7126 3068 6213 834 4503
אֶת־הַמִּנְחָה אֲשֶׁר יֵעָשֶׂה מֵאֵלֶּה לַיהוָה וְהִקְרִיבָהּ אֶל־
to shall and to these of made is which food the
it bring Jehovah (things) offering

9 4503 3548 7311 4196 5066 3548
הַכֹּהֵן וְהִגִּישָׁהּ אֶל־הַמִּזְבֵּחַ׃ וְהֵרִים הַכֹּהֵן מִן־הַמִּנְחָה
food the from the shall And .altar the to he and the
,offering priest remove it bring shall ,priest

3068 5207 7381 801 4196 6999 234
אֶת־אַזְכָּרָתָהּ וְהִקְטִיר הַמִּזְבֵּחָה אִשֵּׁה רֵיחַ נִיחֹחַ לַיהוָה׃
to soothing a fire a the on burn shall and memorial its
.Jehovah fragrance ,offering ,altar incense as it ,offering

10 801/6944 6944 1121 175 4503 3498
וְהַנּוֹתֶרֶת מִן־הַמִּנְחָה לְאַהֲרֹן וּלְבָנָיו קֹדֶשׁ קָדָשִׁים מֵאִשֵּׁי
the of most holy for and for food the of the And
of offering fire ,sons his Aaron (is) offering rest

11 6213 3808 3068 7126 834 4503 3068
יְהוָה׃ כָּל־הַמִּנְחָה אֲשֶׁר תַּקְרִיבוּ לַיהוָה לֹא תֵעָשֶׂה
shall you not to bring shall you which food Any .Jehovah
make Jehovah offering

801 6999 1706 3605 7603 7557
חָמֵץ כִּי כָל־שְׂאֹר וְכָל־דְּבַשׁ לֹא־תַקְטִירוּ מִמֶּנּוּ אִשֶּׁה
fire a it as shall you not honey and leaven all for lea-
offering incense as burn all ,vened

12 4196 3068 7126 7225 7133 3068
לַיהוָה׃ קָרְבַּן רֵאשִׁית תַּקְרִיבוּ אֹתָם לַיהוָה וְאֶל־הַמִּזְבֵּחַ
the but to them shall you first an (As) to
altar on ,Jehovah bring fruits of offering ,Jehovah

13 4414 4417 4503 7133/ 3605 5207 7381 5927
לֹא־יַעֲלוּ לְרֵיחַ נִיחֹחַ׃ וְכָל־קָרְבַּן מִנְחָתְךָ בַּמֶּלַח תִּמְלָח
shall you with food your offering And .soothing a for they not
season salt offering of every fragrance up go shall

with salt, and you shall not let the salt of the covenant of your God be lacking from your food offering; you shall offer salt with all your offerings.

[14]And if you bring near a food offering of first-fruits to Jehovah, fresh ears roasted with fire, kernels from a garden, you shall bring near your first-fruits for a food offering. [15]And you shall put oil on it, and lay on it frankincense; ite *is* a food offering. [16]And the priest shall burn it as incense, with its memorial offering from its kernels, and from its oil, besides all its frankincense, a fire offering to Jehovah.

3605 4503 430 1285 4417 7673
וְלֹא תַשְׁבִּית מֶלַח בְּרִית אֱלֹהֶיךָ מֵעַל מִנְחָתֶךָ עַל כָּל־
all with food your from your the salt the shall you and
;offering God of covenant of lacking be let not

1061 4503 7126 4417 7126 7133
14 קָרְבָּנְךָ תַּקְרִיב מֶלַח׃ וְאִם־תַּקְרִיב מִנְחַת בִּכּוּרִים
first- food a bring you if And .salt shall you your
fruits of offering near offer offerings

4503 7126 3759 1643 784 7033 24 3068
לַיהוָה אָבִיב קָלוּי בָּאֵשׁ גֶּרֶשׂ כַּרְמֶל תַּקְרִיב אֵת מִנְחַת
food a for shall you ;garden a of with roasted fresh to
of offering near bring kernels ,fire ,ears :Jehovah

4503 3828 7760 8081 5414 1061
15 בִּכּוּרֶיךָ׃ וְנָתַתָּ עָלֶיהָ שֶׁמֶן וְשַׂמְתָּ עָלֶיהָ לְבֹנָה מִנְחָה
food a frank- it on lay and ,oil it on you And your
offering ;incense put shall .first-fruits

8081 1643 234 3548 6999
16 הִוא׃ וְהִקְטִיר הַכֹּהֵן אֶת־אַזְכָּרָתָהּ מִגִּרְשָׂהּ וּמִשַּׁמְנָהּ
from and its from memorial its with the burn shall And .(is) it
,oil its kernels offering priest incense as (it)

3068 801 3828
עַל כָּל־לְבֹנָתָהּ אִשֶּׁה לַיהוָה׃
to fire a its all besides
.Jehovah offering ,frankincense

CAP. III ג

CHAPTER 3

CHAPTER 3

[1]And if his offering *is* a sacrifice of peace offering, if he *is* offering *it* from the herd, whether male or female, a perfect one, he shall bring it near before the face of Jehovah. [2]And he shall lay his hand on the head of his offering and slaughter it at the opening of the tabernacle of the congregation. And the sons of Aaron, the priests, shall sprinkle the blood on the altar all around.

[3]And he shall bring near from the sacrifice of the peace offering a fire offering to Jehovah, the fat which covers the inward parts, and all the fat which *is* on the loins, and the fatty fold by the liver beside the kidneys, which you shall remove. [5]And the sons of Aaron shall burn it as incense on the altar, on the burnt offering which *is* on the wood, which *is* on the fire, a fire offering of a soothing fragrance to Jehovah.

7126 1241 7133 8002 2077
1 וְאִם־זֶבַח שְׁלָמִים קָרְבָּנוֹ אִם מִן־הַבָּקָר הוּא מַקְרִיב אִם־
whether offering he herd the from if his peace a (is) if And
(it) (is) ,offering offering of sacrifice

3027 7971 3068 6440 7126 8849 5347 2145
2 זָכָר אִם־נְקֵבָה תָּמִים יַקְרִיבֶנּוּ לִפְנֵי יְהוָה׃ וְסָמַךְ יָדוֹ
his he And .Jehovah before shall he perfect a ,female or male
hand lay shall it near bring one

1121 2236 4150 168 6607 7819 7133 7218
עַל־רֹאשׁ קָרְבָּנוֹ וּשְׁחָטוֹ פֶּתַח אֹהֶל מוֹעֵד וְזָרְקוּ בְּנֵי
the shall and ,meeting the the at shall and his the on
of sons sprinkle of tent of door it kill offering of head

7126 5439 4196 1818 3548 175
3 אַהֲרֹן הַכֹּהֲנִים אֶת־הַדָּם עַל־הַמִּזְבֵּחַ סָבִיב׃ וְהִקְרִיב
he And all altar the on blood the ,priests the ,Aaron
near bring shall .around

3680 2459 3068 801 8002 2077
מִזֶּבַח הַשְּׁלָמִים אִשֶּׁה לַיהוָה אֶת־הַחֵלֶב הַמְכַסֶּה אֶת־
which fat the to fire a peace the the from
covers ,Jehovah offering ,offering of sacrifice

3629 8147 7130 834 2459 3605 7130
4 הַקֶּרֶב וְאֵת כָּל־הַחֵלֶב אֲשֶׁר עַל־הַקֶּרֶב׃ וְאֵת שְׁתֵּי הַכְּלָיֹת
the two and the (is) which fat the all in- the
,kidneys ,innards on parts ward

3506 3689 834 834 2459
וְאֶת־הַחֵלֶב אֲשֶׁר עֲלֵהֶן אֲשֶׁר עַל־הַכְּסָלִים וְאֶת־הַיֹּתֶרֶת
fatty the and ,loins the on which on which fat the and
fold (is) ,them (is)

1121 6999 5493 3629 3516
5 עַל־הַכָּבֵד עַל־הַכְּלָיוֹת יְסִירֶנָּה׃ וְהִקְטִירוּ אֹתוֹ בְנֵי־
sons it shall And you which ,kidneys the beside liver the by
incense as burn .remove shall

5921 834 6086 834 5930 4196 175
אַהֲרֹן הַמִּזְבֵּחָה עַל־הָעֹלָה אֲשֶׁר עַל־הָעֵצִים אֲשֶׁר עַל־
on which wood the on which burnt the on ,altar the on Aaron's
(is) (is) offering

3068 5207 7381 801 784
הָאֵשׁ אִשֵּׁה רֵיחַ נִיחֹחַ לַיהוָה׃
to soothing a fire a the
.Jehovah fragrance of offering ,fire

6 And if his offering for a sacrifice of peace offerings *is* from the flock, male or female, a perfect one, he shall bring it near. 7 If he is bringing near a sheep for his offering, then he shall bring it near before the face of Jehovah. 8 And *he* shall lay his hand on the head of his offering and shall slaughter it in front of the tabernacle of the congregation. And the sons of Aaron shall sprinkle its blood on the altar all around.

9 And he shall bring near from the sacrifice of the peace offerings a fire offering to Jehovah, its fat; he shall remove the entire fat tail close by the backbone, and all the fat that covers the inward parts, and all the fat that *is* on the inward parts, 10 and the two kidneys, and the fat that *is* on them, which *is* on the loins, and he shall remove the fold by the liver, beside the kidneys. 11 And the priest shall burn it as incense on the altar, bread of the fire offering to Jehovah.

12 And if his offering *is* a goat, then he shall bring it near before the face of Jehovah. 13 And *he* shall lay his hand on its head and shall slaughter it in front of the tabernacle of the congregation. And the sons of Aaron shall spring its blood all around on the altar. 14 And he shall bring near from it his offering, a fire offering to Jehovah, the fat covering the inward parts, and all the fat on the inward parts. 15 And the two kidneys and the fat on them, which *is* on the loins, and the fold on the liver, beside the kidneys, he shall remove. 16 And the priest shall burn them as incense on the altar, bread of the fire offering for soothing fragrance; all the fat *is* Jehovah's.

5347 2145 3068 8002 2077 7133 6629
6 ואם־מן־הצאן קרבנו לזבח שלמים ליהוה זכר או נקבה
,female or male to peace a for his the out (is) And
Jehovah offerings of sacrifice offering flock of if

7126 7133 7126 3775 7126 8549
7 תמים יקריבנו׃ אם־כשב הוא־מקריב את־קרבנו והקריב
shall he then his for is he sheep a If shall he perfect a
near bring ,offering bringing .it bring one

7819 7133 7218 3027 5564 3068 6440
8 אתו לפני יהוה׃ וסמך את־ידו על־ראש קרבנו ושחט
shall and his the on hand his shall And .Jehovah before it
kill offering of head lay

5921 1818 175 1121 2236 4150 168 6440
אתו לפני אהל מועד וזרקו בני אהרן את־דמו על־
on blood its Aaron the shall and ,meeting the before it
of sons sprinkle of tent

3068 801 8002 2077 7126 5439 4196
9 המזבח סביב׃ והקריב מזבח השלמים אשה ליהוה
to fire a peace the the from he And all altar the
:Jehovah offering offerings of sacrifice near bring shall .around

2459 5493 6096 5980 8549 451 2459
חלבו האליה תמימה לעמת העצה יסירנה ואת־החלב
fat the all shall he the by close whole fat the ,fat its
;remove backbone tail

7130 834 2459 3605 7130 3680
המכסה את־הקרב ואת כל־החלב אשר על־הקרב׃
the on that fat the all and the that
,parts inward (is) ,innards covers

5921 834 834 2459 3629 8147
10 ואת שתי הכלית ואת־החלב אשר עלהן אשר על־
on which on that fat the and the two and
(is) them (is) kidneys

5493 3629 3516 3508 3689
הכסלים ואת־היתרת על־הכבד על־הכלית יסירנה׃
shall he the beside liver the by fold the and ,loins the
.it remove ,kidneys

3068 801 3899 4196 3548 6999
11 והקטירו הכהן המזבחה לחם אשה ליהוה׃
to fire the bread the on the burn shall And
.Jehovah offering of ,altar priest incense as it

5921 3027 5564 3068 6440 7126 7133 5795
12 ואם־עז קרבנו והקריבו לפני יהוה׃
13 וסמך את־ידו על־
on hand his he And .Jehovah before shall he then his a (is) And
lay shall near it bring ,offering goat if

175 1121 2236 4150 168 6440 7819 7218
ראשו ושחט אתו לפני אהל מועד וזרקו בני אהרן את־
Aaron the shall And .meeting the before it shall and its
of sons sprinkle of tent kill head

3068 801 7133 7126 5439 4196 1818
14 דמו על־המזבח סביב׃ והקריב ממנו קרבנו אשה ליהוה
to fire a his from shall he And all altar the on its
,Jehovah offering ,offering it near bring .around blood

834 2459 3605 7130 3680 2459
את־החלב המכסה את־הקרב ואת כל־החלב אשר על־
on which fat the all and the (is) which fat the
(is) ,parts inward covering

834 834 2459 3629 8147 7130
15 הקרב׃ ואת שתי הכלית ואת־החלב אשר עלהן אשר
which on which fat the and the two and inward the
,them (is) ,kidneys parts

5493 3629 3516 3508 3689 5921
על־הכסלים ואת־היתרת על־הכבד על־הכלית יסירנה׃
shall he the beside liver the on fold the and ,loins the on (is)
.it remove ;kidneys

2459 5207 7381 801 3899 4196 3548 6999
16 והקטירם הכהן המזבחה לחם אשה לריח ניחח כל־חלב
fat the all sooth- for fire the bread the on the burn shall and
;ing fragrance offering of ,altar priest incense as them

[17]*It shall be* a never-ending statute for your generations. You shall not eat any fat or any blood.

CHAPTER 4

[1]And Jehovah spoke to Moses, saying: [2]Speak to the sons of Israel, saying, When a person sins against any of the commands of Jehovah through ignorance, which *is* not to be done, and shall do any one of them; [3]if the priest who is anointed sins, resulting in guilt to the people, then he shall bring near for his sin which he has sinned a bullock, a son of the herd, a perfect one, to Jehovah for a sin offering. [4]And he shall bring the bullock in to the opening of the tabernacle of the congregation, before the face of Jehovah. And *he* shall lay his hand on the head of the bullock and shall slaughter the bullock before the face of Jehovah. [5]And the priest who is anointed shall take of the blood of the bullock and shall bring it to the tabernacle of the congregation. [6]And the priest shall dip his finger in the blood and sprinkle of the blood seven times before Jehovah, at the front of the veil of the holy place. [7]And the priest shall put of the blood on the horns of the altar of sweet incense, which *is* at the opening of the tabernacle of the congregation, before the and he shall pour out all the bullock''s blood at the base of the altar of the burnt offering, which *is at* the door of the tabernacle of the congregation. [8]And he shall lift up from it all the fat of the bullock of the sin offering, the fat which *is* covering over the inward parts, and all the fat which

2459 3605 4186 3605 7755 5769 2708 3068
17 לַיהוָה: חֻקַּת עוֹלָם לְדֹרֹתֵיכֶם בְּכֹל מוֹשְׁבֹתֵיכֶם כָּל־חֵלֶב
Jehovah's (is) a statute never-ending your generations throughout in all your dwellings any fat
398 3808 1818 3605
וְכָל־דָּם לֹא תֹאכֵלוּ:
any nor blood not you shall eat.

CAP. IV ד

CHAPTER 4

3478 1121 1696 559 4872 3068 1696
1 וַיְדַבֵּר יְהוָה אֶל־מֹשֶׁה לֵּאמֹר: דַּבֵּר אֶל־בְּנֵי יִשְׂרָאֵל
2 And spoke Jehovah to Moses, saying Speak to the sons of Israel
834 3068 4687 7684 2398 5315 559
לֵאמֹר נֶפֶשׁ כִּי־תֶחֱטָא בִשְׁגָגָה מִכֹּל מִצְוֹת יְהוָה אֲשֶׁר
saying, a person When sins through ignorance against any of commands Jehovah's, which
4899 3548 2007 259 6213 6213 3808
3 לֹא תֵעָשֶׂינָה וְעָשָׂה מֵאַחַת מֵהֵנָּה: אִם הַכֹּהֵן הַמָּשִׁיחַ
not (ought) to be done, and shall do any one of them; if the priest who is anointed
2398 834 2403 7126 5971 819 2398
יֶחֱטָא לְאַשְׁמַת הָעָם וְהִקְרִיב עַל חַטָּאתוֹ אֲשֶׁר חָטָא
sins, resulting in guilt to the people, then he shall bring near for his sin which he has sinned
6499 935 2401 3068 8549 1241 1121 6499
4 פַּר בֶּן־בָּקָר תָּמִים לַיהוָה לְחַטָּאת: וְהֵבִיא אֶת־הַפָּר
a bullock, a son of the herd, a perfect one, to Jehovah for a sin offering. And he shall bring the bullock
7218 5921 3027 5564 3068 6440 4150 168 6607
אֶל־פֶּתַח אֹהֶל מוֹעֵד לִפְנֵי יְהוָה וְסָמַךְ אֶת־יָדוֹ עַל־רֹאשׁ
in to the door of the tent of meeting before Jehovah, and shall lay his hand on the head of
4899 3548 3947 3068 6440 6499 7819 6499
5 הַפָּר וְשָׁחַט אֶת־הַפָּר לִפְנֵי יְהוָה: וְלָקַח הַכֹּהֵן הַמָּשִׁיחַ
the bullock and shall kill the bullock before Jehovah. And shall take the priest who is anointed
3548 2881 4150 168 935 6499 1818
6 מִדַּם הַפָּר וְהֵבִיא אֹתוֹ אֶל־אֹהֶל מוֹעֵד: וְטָבַל הַכֹּהֵן אֶת־
of the blood of the bullock and shall bring it to the tent of meeting. And shall dip the priest
3068 6440 6471 7651 1818 5137 1818 676
אֶצְבָּעוֹ בַּדָּם וְהִזָּה מִן־הַדָּם שֶׁבַע פְּעָמִים לִפְנֵי יְהוָה
his finger in the blood and sprinkle of the blood seven times before Jehovah
7161 1818 3548 5414 6944 6532 6440
7 אֶת־פְּנֵי פָּרֹכֶת הַקֹּדֶשׁ: וְנָתַן הַכֹּהֵן מִן־הַדָּם עַל־קַרְנוֹת
at the front of the veil of the sanctuary. And shall put the priest of the blood on the horns of
4150 168 834 3068 6440 5561 7004 4196
מִזְבַּח קְטֹרֶת הַסַּמִּים לִפְנֵי יְהוָה אֲשֶׁר בְּאֹהֶל מוֹעֵד וְאֵת
the altar of incense sweet before Jehovah which (is) in the tent of meeting, and
6607 834 5930 4196 3247 8210 6499 1818
כָּל־דַּם הַפָּר יִשְׁפֹּךְ אֶל־יְסוֹד מִזְבַּח הָעֹלָה אֲשֶׁר־פֶּתַח
all the blood bullock's he shall pour out at the base of the altar of the burnt offering which (is) (at) the door of
7311 2403 6499 2459 3605 4150 168
8 אֹהֶל מוֹעֵד: וְאֶת־כָּל־חֵלֶב פַּר הַחַטָּאת יָרִים מִמֶּנּוּ אֶת־
the tent of meeting. And all the fat of the bullock of the sin offering, he shall lift up from it
5921 834 2459 3605 7130 5921 3680 2459
הַחֵלֶב הַמְכַסֶּה עַל־הַקֶּרֶב וְאֵת כָּל־הַחֵלֶב אֲשֶׁר עַל־
the fat which is covering over the inward parts, and all the fat which (is) on

is on the inward parts, and the two kidneys and the fat on them, which *is* beside the loins, and he shall remove the fold on the liver beside the kidneys. [10]As it is raised up from the sacrifice of the peace offerings of the bullock, the priest shall burn them as incense on the altar of burnt offering. [11]And the skin of the bullock, and all its flesh with its head, and with its legs, and the inward parts, and its dung, [12]he shall bring out all the bullock to the outside of the camp, to a clean place, to the place of the pouring of ashes; and he shall burn it on the wood with fire; it shall be at the place of pouring of ashes.

[13]And if the whole company f Israel shall err, and the thing has been hidden from the eyes of the congregation, and they do that which *is* to be done to any of all the commands of Jehovah, and are guilty; [14]when the sin shall be known, that which they have sinned against it, then the congregation shall bring near a bullock, a son of the herd, for a sin offering. And they shall bring it in front of the tabernacle of the congregation. [15]And the elders of the congregation shall lay their hands on the head of the bullock before the face of Jehovah. And *they* shall slaughter the bullock before the face of Jehovah. [16]And the priest who is anointed shall bring in of the blood of the bullock to the tabernacle of the congregation. [17]And the priest shall dip his finger in the blood and shall sprinkle seven times before the face of Jehovah, at the front of the veil. [18]And he shall put of the blood on the horns of the altar which *is* before the face of Jehovah, which *is* in the tabernacle of the congregation. And he shall pour out all the blood at the base of the altar of burnt offering which *is at*

9 הַקֶּרֶב׃ וְאֵת שְׁתֵּי הַכְּלָיֹת וְאֶת־הַחֵלֶב אֲשֶׁר עֲלֵיהֶן אֲשֶׁר
עַל־הַכְּסָלִים וְאֶת־הַיֹּתֶרֶת עַל־הַכָּבֵד עַל־הַכְּלָיוֹת יְסִירֶנָּה׃
10 כַּאֲשֶׁר יוּרַם מִשּׁוֹר זֶבַח הַשְּׁלָמִים וְהִקְטִירָם הַכֹּהֵן עַל
11 מִזְבַּח הָעֹלָה׃ וְאֶת־עוֹר הַפָּר וְאֶת־כָּל־בְּשָׂרוֹ עַל־רֹאשׁוֹ
12 וְעַל־כְּרָעָיו וְקִרְבּוֹ וּפִרְשׁוֹ׃ וְהוֹצִיא אֶת־כָּל־הַפָּר אֶל־
מִחוּץ לַמַּחֲנֶה אֶל־מָקוֹם טָהוֹר אֶל־שֶׁפֶךְ הַדֶּשֶׁן וְשָׂרַף
אֹתוֹ עַל־עֵצִים בָּאֵשׁ עַל־שֶׁפֶךְ הַדֶּשֶׁן יִשָּׂרֵף׃
13 וְאִם כָּל־עֲדַת יִשְׂרָאֵל יִשְׁגּוּ וְנֶעְלַם דָּבָר מֵעֵינֵי הַקָּהָל
וְעָשׂוּ אַחַת מִכָּל־מִצְוֺת יְהוָה אֲשֶׁר לֹא־תֵעָשֶׂינָה וְאָשֵׁמוּ׃
14 וְנוֹדְעָה הַחַטָּאת אֲשֶׁר חָטְאוּ עָלֶיהָ וְהִקְרִיבוּ הַקָּהָל פַּר
15 בֶּן־בָּקָר לְחַטָּאת וְהֵבִיאוּ אֹתוֹ לִפְנֵי אֹהֶל מוֹעֵד׃ וְסָמְכוּ
זִקְנֵי הָעֵדָה אֶת־יְדֵיהֶם עַל־רֹאשׁ הַפָּר לִפְנֵי יְהוָה וְשָׁחַט
16 אֶת־הַפָּר לִפְנֵי יְהוָה׃ וְהֵבִיא הַכֹּהֵן הַמָּשִׁיחַ מִדַּם הַפָּר
17 אֶל־אֹהֶל מוֹעֵד׃ וְטָבַל הַכֹּהֵן אֶצְבָּעוֹ מִן־הַדָּם וְהִזָּה
18 שֶׁבַע פְּעָמִים לִפְנֵי יְהוָה אֶת־פְּנֵי הַפָּרֹכֶת׃ וּמִן־הַדָּם
יִתֵּן עַל־קַרְנֹת הַמִּזְבֵּחַ אֲשֶׁר לִפְנֵי יְהוָה אֲשֶׁר בְּאֹהֶל
מוֹעֵד וְאֵת כָּל־הַדָּם יִשְׁפֹּךְ אֶל־יְסוֹד מִזְבַּח הָעֹלָה אֲשֶׁר־

פתח אהל מועד׃ ואת כל־חלבו ירים ממנו והקטיר 19
המזבחה׃ ועשה לפר כאשר עשה לפר החטאת כן 20
יעשה־לו וכפר עלהם הכהן ונסלח להם׃ והוציא את־ 21
הפר אל־מחוץ למחנה ושרף אתו כאשר שרף את הפר
הראשון חטאת הקהל הוא׃ פ
אשר נשיא יחטא ועשה אחת מכל־מצות יהוה אלהיו 22
אשר לא־תעשינה בשגגה ואשם׃ או־הודע אליו חטאתו 23
אשר חטא בה והביא את־קרבנו שעיר עזים זכר תמים׃
וסמך ידו על־ראש השעיר ושחט אתו במקום אשר־ 24
ישחט את־העלה לפני יהוה חטאת הוא׃ ולקח הכהן 25
מדם החטאת באצבעו ונתן על־קרנת מזבח העלה ואת־
דמו ישפך אל־יסוד מזבח העלה׃ ואת־כל־חלבו יקטיר 26
המזבחה כחלב זבח השלמים וכפר עליו הכהן מחטאתו
ונסלח לו׃ פ
ואם־נפש אחת תחטא בשגגה מעם הארץ בעשתה 27
אחת ממצות יהוה אשר לא־תעשינה ואשם׃ או הודע 28
אליו חטאתו אשר חטא והביא קרבנו שעירת עזים

the opening of the tabernacle of the congregation. [19]And he shall take off all its fat from it and shall burn it as incense on the altar. [20]And he shall do with the bullock as he has done to the bullock of the sin offering, so he shall do to is. And the priest shall atone for them; and it shall be forgiven them. [21]And he shall bring the bullock to the outside of the camp, and *he* shall burn it as he burned the first bullock; it is a sin offering of the congregation.

[22]When a ruler sins and has acted *against* one of all the commands of Jehovah his God, which not *is* to be done, through ignorance, and *is* guilty; [23]or his sin which he has sinned shall be made known to him then he shall bring his offering, a buck of the goats, a male, a perfect one; [24]and he shall lay his hand on the head of the goat and shall slaughter it in the place where he slaughters the burnt offering, before the face of Jehovah; it *is* a sin offering. [25]And the priest shall take of the blood of the sin offering, and with his finger he shall put it on the horns of the altar of burnt offering; and he shall pour out its blood at the base of the altar of burnt offering. [26]And he shall burn it as incense on the altar, with all its fat, as the fat of the sacrifice of the peace offerings. And the priest shall atone for him because of his sin; and it shall be forgiven him.

[27]And if any person of the people of the land sins through ignorance, by doing that which *is* not to be done, *against* one of the commands of Jehovah, and is guilty; [28]or his sin which he has sinned shall be made known to him, then he shall bring his offering, a ewe of the goats, a perfect

29 תמימה נקבה על־חטאתו אשר חטא׃ וסמך את־ידו
על ראש החטאת ושחט את־החטאת במקום העלה׃
30 ולקח הכהן מדמה באצבעו ונתן על־קרנת מזבח העלה
31 ואת־כל־דמה ישפך אל־יסוד המזבח׃ ואת־כל־חלבה
יסיר כאשר הוסר חלב מעל זבח השלמים והקטיר
הכהן המזבחה לריח ניחח ליהוה וכפר עליו הכהן
ונסלח לו׃

one, a female, for his sin which he has sinned; [29]then he shall lay his hand on the head of the sin offering and shall slaughter the sin offering in the place of the burnt offering. [30]And the priest shall take of its blood with his finger and shall put *it* on the horns of the altar of burnt offering. And he shall pour out all its blood at the base of the altar; [31]and he shall turn off all its fat, as has been turned off the sacrifice of peace offerings. And the priest shall burn it as incense on the altar for a soothing fragrance to Jehovah. And the priest shall atone for him, and it is forgiven him.

32 ואם־כבש יביא קרבנו לחטאת נקבה תמימה יביאנה׃
33 וסמך את־ידו על ראש החטאת ושחט אתה לחטאת
34 במקום אשר ישחט את־העלה׃ ולקח הכהן מדם
החטאת באצבעו ונתן על־קרנת מזבח העלה ואת־כל־
35 דמה ישפך אל־יסוד המזבח׃ ואת־כל־חלבה יסיר
כאשר יוסר חלב־הכשב מזבח השלמים והקטיר הכהן
אתם המזבחה על אשי יהוה וכפר עליו הכהן על־
חטאתו אשר־חטא ונסלח לו׃

[32]And if he brings as his offering for a sin offering a female, a perfect one, he shall bring it and he shall lay his hand on the head of the sin offering, and *he* shall slaughter it for a sin offering in the place where he slaughters the burnt offering. [34]And the priest shall take of the blood of the sin offering with his finger and put it on the horns of the altar of burnt offering. And he shall pour out its blood at the base of the altar. And he shall turn off all its fat, as is turned off the fat of the lamb from the sacrifice of peace offerings. And the priest shall burn them as incense on the altar, on the fire offerings of Jehovah. And the priest shall atone for him for his sin which he has sinned; and it is forgiven him.

CAP. V ה

CHAPTER 5

1 ונפש כי־תחטא ושמעה קול אלה והוא עד או ראה

CHAPTER 5

[1]And when a person sins, and hears the voice of swearing, and he *is* witness or has seen, or has known,

if he does not reveal *it*, then he shall bear his iniquity. [2]Or if a soul touches any unclean thing, or the unclean dead body of an animal, or the unclean dead body of livestock, or the dead body of unclean swarming things, it being hidden from him that he *is* unclean and is guilty, [3]or if he touches the uncleanness of man, any of his uncleanness by which he *is* unclean, and it is hidden from him, and he knows, then he is guilty. [4]Or if a person swears, speaking rashly with the lips, to do evil, or to do good, anything which the man speaks rashly with an oath, and it is hidden from him, and he knows, then he is guilty of one of these.

[5]And it shall be, when he is guilty of one of these, then he shall confess that in which he has sinned. [6]And he shall bring his guilt offering to Jehovah for his sin which he has sinned, a female out of the flock, a lamb, or a ewe of the goats, for a sin offering. And the priest shall atone for him regarding his sin.

[7]And if his hand does not reach to a lamb, then he shall bring his guilt offering, he who has sinned: two turtle doves, or two offspring of a dove, to Jehovah; one for a sin offering and one for a burnt offering. [8]And he shall bring them to the priest, *who* shall bring near that which *is* for a sin offering first. And *he* shall nip off his head from his neck, but shall not divide *it*. [9]And he shall sprinkle of the blood of the sin offering on the side of the altar, and that which remains of the blood shall be drained at the base of the altar; it *is* a sin offering. [10]And he shall *offer* the second *for* a burnt offering, as by ordinance. And the priest shall atone for

3605 5060 5315 176 5771 5375 5046 3045
2 אוֹ יָדָע אִם־לוֹא יַגִּיד וְנָשָׂא עֲוֹנוֹ׃ אוֹ נֶפֶשׁ אֲשֶׁר תִּגַּע בְּכָל־
any- touches if soul a or his iniquity he then bear shall he ,tells not if has ,known or

929 5038 2931 2416 5038 2931 1697
דָּבָר טָמֵא אוֹ בְנִבְלַת חַיָּה טְמֵאָה אוֹ בְּנִבְלַת בְּהֵמָה
,cattle dead the of body or ,unclean an animal dead the of body or ,unclean thing

2931 5956 2931 8318 5038 2931
טְמֵאָה אוֹ בְּנִבְלַת שֶׁרֶץ טָמֵא וְנֶעְלַם מִמֶּנּוּ וְהוּא טָמֵא
,unclean that (is) he from him being it hidden ,unclean swarming things dead the of body or ,unclean

2930 834 2932 120 2932 5060 816
3 וְאָשֵׁם׃ אוֹ כִי יִגַּע בְּטֻמְאַת אָדָם לְכֹל טֻמְאָתוֹ אֲשֶׁר יִטְמָא
is he unclean which his uncleanness any of ,man un- cleanness of the he touches if is and guilty

7650 5315 816 3045 5956
4 בָּהּ וְנֶעְלַם מִמֶּנּוּ וְהוּא יָדַע וְאָשֵׁם׃ אוֹ נֶפֶשׁ כִּי תִשָּׁבַע
,swears if a person Or .guilty is he then knows he when ,him hidden is from it and ,it by

981 834 3605 7489 8193 981
לְבַטֵּא בִשְׂפָתַיִם לְהָרַע ׀ אוֹ לְהֵיטִיב לְכֹל אֲשֶׁר יְבַטֵּא
speaks rashly which any- thing do to ,good or do to evil the with lips speaking rashly

259 816 3045 5956 7621 120
הָאָדָם בִּשְׁבֻעָה וְנֶעְלַם מִמֶּנּוּ וְהוּא־יָדַע וְאָשֵׁם לְאַחַת
one of he then guilty is has ,known when he from ,him it and hidden is an with ,oath the man

834 3034 259 816 1961
5 מֵאֵלֶּה׃ וְהָיָה כִי־יֶאְשַׁם לְאַחַת מֵאֵלֶּה וְהִתְוַדָּה אֲשֶׁר
which he then confess ,these of one of is he guilty when it And ,be shall .these of

834 2403 3068 816 935 2398
6 חָטָא עָלֶיהָ׃ וְהֵבִיא אֶת־אֲשָׁמוֹ לַיהוָה עַל חַטָּאתוֹ אֲשֶׁר
which sin his for to Jehovah guilt his offering he And bring shall .that in has he sinned

2403 5795 8166 3776 6629 5347 2398
חָטָא נְקֵבָה מִן־הַצֹּאן כִּשְׂבָּה אוֹ־שְׂעִירַת עִזִּים לְחַטָּאת
sin a for offering the ,goats ewe a of or ,lamb a the ,flock of out a female has he ,sinned

7716 1767 3027 5060 3808 2403 3548 3722
7 וְכִפֶּר עָלָיו הַכֹּהֵן מֵחַטָּאתוֹ׃ וְאִם־לֹא תַגִּיעַ יָדוֹ דֵּי שֶׂה
a ,lamb to his hand reaches not if And regarding .sin his the priest for him shall and atone

1121 8147 8449 8147 2398 834 816 854 935
וְהֵבִיא אֶת־אֲשָׁמוֹ אֲשֶׁר חָטָא שְׁתֵּי תֹרִים אוֹ־שְׁנֵי בְנֵי־
off- spring two or turtle- ,doves two has ,sinned who he guilt his ,offering he then bring shall

935 5930 259 2403 259 3068 3128
8 יוֹנָה לַיהוָה אֶחָד לְחַטָּאת וְאֶחָד לְעֹלָה׃ וְהֵבִיא אֹתָם
them he And bring shall burnt a for ,offering and one sin a for ,offering one to ,Jehovah a ,dove

4454 7223 2403 834 7126 3548
אֶל־הַכֹּהֵן וְהִקְרִיב אֶת־אֲשֶׁר לַחַטָּאת רִאשׁוֹנָה וּמָלַק אֶת־
shall and off nip ,first sin a for offering that (is) which shall and near bring the priest to

2403 1818 5137 914 6203 4136 7218
9 רֹאשׁוֹ מִמּוּל עָרְפּוֹ וְלֹא יַבְדִּיל׃ וְהִזָּה מִדַּם הַחַטָּאת עַל־
on sin the offering the of blood he And sprinkle shall shall .divide not but his ,neck from his head

2401 4196 3247 4680 1818 7604 4196 7023
קִיר הַמִּזְבֵּחַ וְהַנִּשְׁאָר בַּדָּם יִמָּצֵה אֶל־יְסוֹד הַמִּזְבֵּחַ חַטָּאת
sin a offering ;altar the the of base at be shall out drained the of blood that and left is which ,altar the the of side

3548 3722 4941 5930 8145
10 הוּא׃ וְאֶת־הַשֵּׁנִי יַעֲשֶׂה עֹלָה כַּמִּשְׁפָּט וְכִפֶּר עָלָיו הַכֹּהֵן
the priest for him shall and atone by ;ordinance as a (for) burnt offering shall he (offer) the second And .(is) it

him, because of his sin which he has sinned; and it shall be forgiven him.

11 And if his hand cannot reach to two turtle-doves, or two offspring of a dove, then *he* who sinned shall bring his offering, a tenth of an ephah of fine flour for a sin offering; he shall not put on it oil, nor put on it frankincense; for it is a sin offering. 12 And he shall bring it to the priest, and the priest shall take from it his full handful, the memorial offering, and shall burn it as incense on the altar, on the fire offering of Jehovah; it *is* a sin offering. 13 And the priest shall atone for him, for his sin which he sinned from one of these; and it shall be forgiven him. And it shall be for the priest as a food offering.

14 And Jehovah spoke to Moses, saying, 15 If a person acts unfaithfully and sins in ignorance against the holy things of Jehovah, then he shall bring his guilt offering to Jehovah, a ram, a perfect one, out of the flock, at your evaluation *in* silver, by the shekel of the sanctuary, for a guilt offering. 16 And he shall make good that *in* which he sinned, of the holy thing. And he shall add the fifth part to it and give it to the priest. And the priest shall atone for him with a ram of the guilt offering. And it shall be forgiven him. 17 And if a person sins, and he has done *any* one of all the commands of Jehovah, and which ought not to be done, and he is guilty, and bears his iniquity. 18 Then he shall bring a ram, a perfect one from the flock, at your evaluation, for a guilt offering to the priest. And the priest shall atone for him, for his sin of ignorance which he erred, and he did not know. And it shall be forgiven him. It *is* a guilt offering.

מֵחַטָּאתוֹ אֲשֶׁר־חָטָא וְנִסְלַח לוֹ׃ 11 וְאִם־לֹא תַשִּׂיג
can touch | not | And if | him. | shall it and forgiven be | he sinned; | which | regarding his sins

יָדוֹ לִשְׁתֵּי תֹרִים אוֹ לִשְׁנֵי בְנֵי־יוֹנָה וְהֵבִיא אֶת־קָרְבָּנוֹ
his offering, | he then bring shall | dove a, | off- of spring | two to | or | turtle-doves | two to | his hand

אֲשֶׁר חָטָא עֲשִׂירִת הָאֵפָה סֹלֶת לְחַטָּאת לֹא־יָשִׂים עָלֶיהָ
it on | shall he not put | sin a for ;offering | fine flour | ephah of | tenth a of | ,sinned | (he) who

שֶׁמֶן וְלֹא־יִתֵּן עָלֶיהָ לְבֹנָה כִּי חַטָּאת הִוא׃ 12 וֶהֱבִיאָהּ אֶל־
to | he And it bring shall | .(is) it | sin a offering | for | frank- ,incense | it on | put | and not | ,oil

הַכֹּהֵן וְקָמַץ הַכֹּהֵן ׀ מִמֶּנָּה מְלוֹא קֻמְצוֹ אֶת־אַזְכָּרָתָהּ
memorial the offering | his ,handful | fulness of | it from | the priest | shall and take | the priest

וְהִקְטִיר הַמִּזְבֵּחָה עַל אִשֵּׁי יְהוָה חַטָּאת הִוא׃ 13 וְכִפֶּר
shall And atone | .(is) it | sin a offering | ;Jehovah | fire the of offering | on | the ,altar | on | burn shall and incense as

עָלָיו הַכֹּהֵן עַל־חַטָּאתוֹ אֲשֶׁר־חָטָא מֵאַחַת מֵאֵלֶּה וְנִסְלַח
shall it and forgiven be | of ;these | from one | he sinned | which | sin his | for | the ,priest | for him

לוֹ וְהָיְתָה לַכֹּהֵן כַּמִּנְחָה׃ 14 וַיְדַבֵּר יְהוָה אֶל־מֹשֶׁה
,Moses | to | Jehovah | And spoke | food a as .offering | the for priest | it and be shall | ,him

לֵּאמֹר׃ 15 נֶפֶשׁ כִּי־תִמְעֹל מַעַל וְחָטְאָה בִּשְׁגָגָה מִקָּדְשֵׁי
against things holy | in ignorance | sins and | unfaith- fully | acts | If | a person | ,saying

יְהוָה וְהֵבִיא אֶת־אֲשָׁמוֹ לַיהוָה אַיִל תָּמִים מִן־הַצֹּאן בְּעֶרְכְּךָ
your at evaluation | the out ,flock of | perfect a ,one | a ,ram | to Jehovah | guilt his offering | then he bring shall | ,Jehovah's

כֶּסֶף־שְׁקָלִים בְּשֶׁקֶל־הַקֹּדֶשׁ לְאָשָׁם׃ 16 וְאֵת אֲשֶׁר חָטָא
he sinned | (in) which | And that | guilt a for .offering | the sanctuary | the by of shekel | ,shekels | (in) silver

מִן־הַקֹּדֶשׁ יְשַׁלֵּם וְאֶת־חֲמִישִׁתוֹ יוֹסֵף עָלָיו וְנָתַן אֹתוֹ לַכֹּהֵן
the to ;priest | it | and give | ,it to | shall he add | fifth its part | and | shall he ,good make | the thing holy | of

וְהַכֹּהֵן יְכַפֵּר עָלָיו בְּאֵיל הָאָשָׁם וְנִסְלַח לוֹ׃
.him | shall it and forgiven be | guilt the ;offering | the with of ram | for him | shall atone | the and priest

17 וְאִם־נֶפֶשׁ כִּי תֶחֱטָא וְעָשְׂתָה אַחַת מִכָּל־מִצְוֹת יְהוָה אֲשֶׁר
which | Jehovah | com- mand | the from of all | (any) one | has and done | ,sins he | if | a person | And if

לֹא תֵעָשֶׂינָה וְלֹא־יָדַע וְאָשֵׁם וְנָשָׂא עֲוֺנוֹ׃ 18 וְהֵבִיא אַיִל
a ,ram | he Then bring shall | his .iniquity | and bears | he and ,guilty is | knows (it) | and not | to ought done be | not

תָּמִים מִן־הַצֹּאן בְּעֶרְכְּךָ לְאָשָׁם אֶל־הַכֹּהֵן וְכִפֶּר עָלָיו הַכֹּהֵן
the ,priest | for him | shall and atone | the priest | to | guilt a for offering | your at ,evaluation | the flock | from | perfect a one

עַל שִׁגְגָתוֹ אֲשֶׁר־שָׁגָג וְהוּא לֹא־יָדַע וְנִסְלַח לוֹ׃ 19 אָשָׁם הוּא
it :(is) | guilt a offering | ;him | shall it and forgiven be | did not ;know | and he | he ,erred | which | sin his of ignorance | for

Truly he is guilty before Jehovah.

CHAPTER 6

[1]And Jehovah spoke to Moses, saying, [2]If any person sins and (is) slyly treacherous against Jehovah, and deals falsely with his neighbor concerning a deposit, or concerning security, or by robbery, or has extorted his neighbor; [3]or has found a lost thing and has lied about it, and has sworn to a falsehood—as regards to any one of all *these* which a man does, sinning in them—[4]then it shall be, when he sins and is guilty, he shall return what he got by robbery, *that which* he robbed, the extorted thing which he extorted, or the deposit which had been deposited with him, or the lost thing which he had found; [5]or all that about which he swore falsely; he shall even repay it in its principal, and the fifth part he shall add to it; to whomever it belongs. He shall give it on the day of his guilt offering. [6]And he shall bring his guilt offering to Jehovah: a ram, a perfect one out of the flock, at your evaluation for a guilt offering, to the priest. [7]And the priest shall make atonement for him before Jehovah, and as regards to one thing of all that he has done, it shall be forgiven him, by being guilty in it.

[8]And Jehovah spoke to Moses, saying, [9]Command Aaron and his sons, saying, This *is* the law of the burnt offering; it *is* the burnt offering because it is burned on the altar all the night until the morning, and the fire of the altar is kept burning on it. [10]The priest

אשם אשם ליהוה:

20 21 וידבר יהוה אל־משה לאמר: נפש כי תחטא ומעלה

מעל ביהוה וכחש בעמיתו בפקדון או־בתשומת יד או

22 בגזל או עשק את־עמיתו: או־מצא אבדה וכחש בה

ונשבע על־שקר על־אחת מכל אשר־יעשה האדם לחטא

23 בהנה: והיה כי־יחטא ואשם והשיב את־הגזלה אשר

גזל או את־העשק אשר עשק או את־הפקדון אשר הפקד

24 אתו או את־האבדה אשר מצא: או מכל אשר־ישבע

עליו לשקר ושלם אתו בראשו וחמשתיו יסף עליו לאשר

25 הוא לו יתננו ביום אשמתו: ואת־אשמו יביא ליהוה איל

26 תמים מן־הצאן בערכך לאשם אל־הכהן: וכפר עליו

הכהן לפני יהוה ונסלח לו על־אחת מכל אשר־יעשה

לאשמה בה:

CAP. VI ו

CHAPTER 6

1 2 וידבר יהוה אל־משה לאמר: צו את־אהרן ואת־בניו

לאמר זאת תורת העלה הוא העלה על מוקדה על־

המזבח כל־הלילה עד־הבקר ואש המזבח תוקד בו:

shall put on his long robe of fine linen, and he shall put his linen underpants on his flesh. And he shall lift up the ashes which the fire consumed with the burnt offering on the altar, and shall put them beside the altar. [11]And he shall strip off his garments, and shall put on other garments, and shall bring the ashes out to the outside of the camp, to a clean place. [12]And the fire on the altar shall be kept burning on it; it shall not be put out. And the priest shall burn wood on it morning by morning. And he shall lay the burnt offering in order on it. And he shall burn it as incense *with* the fat of the peace offering. [13]Fire shall be continually burning on the altar; it shall never go out.

[14]And this *is* the law of the food offering: the sons of Aaron shall bring it near before Jehovah, to the front of the altar. [15]And *he* shall lift from it his handful of the flour of the food offering, and of its oil, and all the frankincense which is on the food offering. And *he* shall burn it as incense on the altar, a sweet fragrance from its memorial to Jehovah. [16]And Aaron and his sons shall eat the rest. It shall be eaten *with* unleavened things in the holy place, in the court of the tabernacle of the congregation they shall eat it. [17]It shall not be baked *with* leaven. I have given it as their portion out of My fire offerings. It *is* most holy, like the *sin* offering, and like the guilt offering. [18]Every male among the sons of Aaron shall eat it, a never-ending statute throughout your generations from the fire offerings of Jehovah. All that touches them shall be holy.

[19]And Jehovah spoke to Moses, saying, [20]This *is* the offering of Aaron and his

3 ולבש הכהן מדו בד ומכנסי-בד ילבש על-בשרו
והרים את-הדשן אשר תאכל האש את-העלה על-
4 המזבח ושמו אצל המזבח: ופשט את-בגדיו ולבש
בגדים אחרים והוציא את-הדשן אל-מחוץ למחנה אל-
5 מקום טהור: והאש על-המזבח תוקד-בו לא תכבה
ובער עליה הכהן עצים בבקר בבקר וערך עליה העלה
6 והקטיר עליה חלבי השלמים: אש תמיד תוקד על-
7 המזבח לא תכבה: ס וזאת תורת המנחה הקרב
8 אתה בני-אהרן לפני יהוה אל-פני המזבח: והרים
ממנו בקמצו מסלת המנחה ומשמנה ואת כל-הלבנה
אשר על-המנחה והקטיר המזבח ריח ניחח אזכרתה
9 ליהוה: והנותרת ממנה יאכלו אהרן ובניו מצות תאכל
10 במקום קדש בחצר אהל-מועד יאכלוה: לא תאפה
חמץ חלקם נתתי אתה מאשי קדש קדשים הוא כחטאת
11 וכאשם: כל-זכר בבני אהרן יאכלנה חק-עולם לדרתיכם
מאשי יהוה כל אשר-יגע בהם יקדש: פ
12 13 וידבר יהוה אל-משה לאמר: זה קרבן אהרן ובניו

sons which they shall bring near to Jehovah on the day he is anointed: a tenth of an ephah of flour, a continual food offering; half of it in the morning, and half of it in the evening. [21]It shall be made on a griddle with oil. You shall bring it in mixed. You shall bring baked pieces of the food offering, a sweet fragrance to Jehovah. [22]And the priest who is anointed in his place, from among his sons, shall make it. *It is* a never-ending statute of Jehovah. It shall be completely burned; [23]and every food offering of a priest is a whole burnt offering. It shall not be eaten.

[24]And Jehovah spoke to Moses, saying, [25]Speak to Aaron and to his sons, saying, This *is* the law of the sin offering: In the place where the burnt offering is killed, the sin offering shall be killed before Jehovah. It *is* It *is* most holy. [26]The priest who offers it for sin shall eat it. It shall be eaten in the holy place, in the court of the tabernacle of the congregation. [27]All that touches its flesh shall be holy. And when *any* of its blood is sprinkled on the garment, that on which it is sprinkled shall be washed in the holy place. [28]And an earthen vessel in which it is boiled shall be broken. And if it is boiled in a bronze vessel, then it shall be scoured and rinsed with water. [29]Every male among the priests shall eat of it. It *is* most holy. [30]And any sin offering of whose blood is brought into the tabernacle of the congregation to make atonement in the sanctuary shall not be eaten. It shall be burned with fire.

374 6224 4886 3117 3068 7126 834
אֲשֶׁר־יַקְרִיבוּ לַיהוָה בְּיוֹם הִמָּשַׁח אֹתוֹ עֲשִׂירִת הָאֵפָה
ephah an tenth a .him be to the on to shall they which
of of anointed of day Jehovah near bring

6153 4276 1242 4276 8548 4503 5560
סֹלֶת מִנְחָה תָּמִיד מַחֲצִיתָהּ בַּבֹּקֶר וּמַחֲצִיתָהּ בָּעָרֶב׃
the in half and the in it of half continual food a flour
;evening it of morning ,offering

4503 6595 935 7246 6213 8081 4227 5921
14 עַל־מַחֲבַת בַּשֶּׁמֶן תֵּעָשֶׂה מֻרְבֶּכֶת תְּבִיאֶנָּה תֻּפִינֵי מִנְחַת
food the pieces shall you mixed shall it with griddle a on
offering of in it bring ;made be oil

8478 4899 3548 3068 5207 7381 7126 8601
15 פִּתִּים תַּקְרִיב רֵיחַ־נִיחֹחַ לַיהוָה׃ וְהַכֹּהֵן הַמָּשִׁיחַ תַּחְתָּיו
his in is who the And to sooth- a shall you ;baked
place anointed priest .Jehovah ing fragrance offer

3605 6999 3632 3068 5769 2706 6213 1121
16 מִבָּנָיו יַעֲשֶׂה אֹתָהּ חָק־עוֹלָם לַיהוָה כָּלִיל תָּקְטָר׃ וְכָל־
And shall it completely of never a (is it) ,it shall his of
every .burned be ,Jehovah -ending statute offer sons

398 3808 3632 3548 4503
מִנְחַת כֹּהֵן כָּלִיל תִּהְיֶה לֹא תֵאָכֵל׃
shall it not ;is whole a a food
.eaten be offering burnt priest of offering

175 1696 559 4872 3068 1696
17 18 וַיְדַבֵּר יְהוָה אֶל־מֹשֶׁה לֵּאמֹר׃ דַּבֵּר אֶל־אַהֲרֹן וְאֶל־
to and Aaron to Speak ,saying Moses to Jehovah And
spoke

7819 4725 2403 8451 2063 559 1121
בָּנָיו לֵאמֹר זֹאת תּוֹרַת הַחַטָּאת בִּמְקוֹם אֲשֶׁר תִּשָּׁחֵט
killed is where the in sin the law the This ,saying his
place :offering of (is) sons

6944 6944 3068 6440 2403 7819 5930
הָעֹלָה תִּשָּׁחֵט הַחַטָּאת לִפְנֵי יְהוָה קֹדֶשׁ קָדָשִׁים הִוא׃
.(is) it most holy ;Jehovah before sin the be shall burnt the
offering killed offering

398 6918 4725 398 2398 3548
19 הַכֹּהֵן הַמְחַטֵּא אֹתָהּ יֹאכְלֶנָּה בְּמָקוֹם קָדֹשׁ תֵּאָכֵל
shall it holy the in eat shall it offers who The
eaten be ,place ;it sin for priest

6918 1320 5060 834 3605 4150 168 2691
20 בַּחֲצַר אֹהֶל מוֹעֵד׃ כֹּל אֲשֶׁר־יִגַּע בִּבְשָׂרָהּ יִקְדָּשׁ
be shall flesh its touches that All .meeting the the in
;holy of tent of court

4725 3526 5921 5137 834 899 1818 5137
וַאֲשֶׁר יִזֶּה מִדָּמָהּ עַל־הַבֶּגֶד אֲשֶׁר יִזֶּה עָלֶיהָ תְּכַבֵּס בְּמָקוֹם
the in be shall on is it that the on its of is when and
place washed which sprinkled ,garment blood sprinkled (any)

3627 7665 1310 834 2789 3627 6942
21 קָדֹשׁ׃ וּכְלִי־חֶרֶשׂ אֲשֶׁר תְּבֻשַּׁל־בּוֹ יִשָּׁבֵר וְאִם־בִּכְלִי
a in if and be shall in is it which earthen an And .holy
vessel ;broken boiled vessel

3548 2145 3605 4325 7857 4838 1310 5178
22 נְחֹשֶׁת בֻּשָּׁלָה וּמֹרַק וְשֻׁטַּף בַּמָּיִם׃ כָּל־זָכָר בַּכֹּהֲנִים
the among male Every with and it then ,boiled is it copper
priests .water rinsed scoured be shall

834 2403 3605 6944 6944 398
23 יֹאכַל אֹתָהּ קֹדֶשׁ קָדָשִׁים הִוא׃ וְכָל־חַטָּאת אֲשֶׁר
which sin And .(is) it most holy its of eat shall
offering any blood

398 3808 6944 3722 4150 168 1818 935
יוּבָא מִדָּמָהּ אֶל־אֹהֶל מוֹעֵד לְכַפֵּר בַּקֹּדֶשׁ לֹא תֵאָכֵל
be shall not the in make to meeting the into of its is
;eaten sanctuary atonement of tent blood brought

8313 284
בָּאֵשׁ תִּשָּׂרֵף׃
be shall it with
.burned fire

CHAPTER 7

[1]And this *is* the law of the guilt offering; it *is* most holy. [2]In the place where they kill the burnt offering, they shall kill the guilt offering, and its blood shall be sprinkled on the altar all around. [3]And all its fat shall be brought near, he shall offer the fat tail of it, and the fat which covers the inward parts, [4]and the two kidneys, and the fat which *is* on them, which *is* on the flanks, and the fold above the liver, which you shall take away beside the kidneys. [5]And the priest shall burn them as incense on the altar, a fire offering to Jehovah; it *is* a guilt offering. [6]Every male among the priests shall eat it; it shall be eaten in the holy place. It is most holy. [7]As a sin offering *is*, so a guilt offering. One law *is* for them. The priest who makes atonement by it, it is his. [8]And the priest who brings near any man's burnt offering, the skin of the burnt offering which he has brought near, it is the priest's, his own. [9]And every food offering which was baked in an oven, and every one that is prepared in the stewing-pan, and on the griddle, shall be the priest's that offers it; it is his. [10]And every food offering, mixed with oil or dry, is for all the sons of Aaron *to* a man, as his brother.

[11]And this *is* the law of the sacrifice of the peace offerings which shall be brought to Jehovah: [12]If he brings it for a thanksgiving, then he shall bring with the sacrifice of thanksgiving unleavened cakes mixed with oil,

CAP. VII ז

CHAPTER 7

4725 6944 6944 816 8451 2088
1 וְזֹאת תּוֹרַת הָאָשָׁם קֹדֶשׁ קָדָשִׁים הוּא׃ בִּמְקוֹם אֲשֶׁר
2 where | the In place | .(is) it | most | holy | guilt the ;offering | the of law | And (is) this

2236 1818 816 7819 5930 7819
יִשְׁחֲטוּ אֶת־הָעֹלָה יִשְׁחֲטוּ אֶת־הָאָשָׁם וְאֶת־דָּמוֹ יִזְרֹק
be shall sprinkled | its blood | and | guilt the offering | shall they kill | burnt the offering | kill they

7126 2459 3605 5439 4196 5921
3 עַל־הַמִּזְבֵּחַ סָבִיב׃ וְאֵת כָּל־חֶלְבּוֹ יַקְרִיב מִמֶּנּוּ אֵת
shall he ,it of offer | be shall near brought | fat its | all | And | all .around | altar the | on

8147 7130 3680 2459 451
4 הָאַלְיָה וְאֶת־הַחֵלֶב הַמְכַסֶּה אֶת־הַקֶּרֶב׃ וְאֵת שְׁתֵּי
two | And | the .innards | which covers | fat the | and | the ,tail fat

3689 5921 834 5921 834 2459 3629
הַכְּלָיֹת וְאֶת־הַחֵלֶב אֲשֶׁר עֲלֵיהֶן אֲשֶׁר עַל־הַכְּסָלִים וְאֶת־
and | the ,loins | on (is) | which | on (is) ,them | which | fat the | and | the ,kidneys

6999 5493 3629 3516 3508
5 הַיֹּתֶרֶת עַל־הַכָּבֵד עַל־הַכְּלָיוֹת יְסִירֶנָּה׃ וְהִקְטִיר אֹתָם
them | shall And incense as burn | shall he it remove | the kidneys | by | the liver | on | fold the

2145 3605 816 3068 801 4196 3548
6 הַכֹּהֵן הַמִּזְבֵּחָה אִשֶּׁה לַיהוָה אָשָׁם הוּא׃ כָּל־זָכָר
male | Every | (is) it | guilt a ,offering | to ;Jehovah | fire a offering | the on ,altar | the priest

6944 6944 398 6918 4725 398 3548
בַּכֹּהֲנִים יֹאכְלֶנּוּ בְּמָקוֹם קָדוֹשׁ יֵאָכֵל קֹדֶשׁ קָדָשִׁים הוּא׃
(is) it | most | holy | shall it ;eaten be | holy | the in place | eat shall ,it | the among priests

3722 834 3548 259 8451 816 2403
7 כַּחַטָּאת כָּאָשָׁם תּוֹרָה אַחַת לָהֶם הַכֹּהֵן אֲשֶׁר יְכַפֶּר־בּוֹ
by ,it | makes atonement | who | the priest | for ;them | one | (is there) law | guilt a so ;offering | sin a As ,(is) offering

834 5930 5785 376 5930 7126 3548
8 לוֹ יִהְיֶה׃ וְהַכֹּהֵן הַמַּקְרִיב אֶת־עֹלַת אִישׁ עוֹר הָעֹלָה אֲשֶׁר
which | burnt the offering | the of skin, | any man's | burnt offering | brings who near | And priest the | is it | .his

8574 644 834 4503 3605 3548 7126
9 הִקְרִיב לַכֹּהֵן לוֹ יִהְיֶה׃ וְכָל־מִנְחָה אֲשֶׁר תֵּאָפֶה בַּתַּנּוּר
an in ,oven | was baked | which | food offering | And every | .is it | his own | the to ,priest | has he brought

7126 3548 4802 5921 4227 6213
וְכָל־נַעֲשָׂה בַמַּרְחֶשֶׁת וְעַל־מַחֲבַת לַכֹּהֵן הַמַּקְרִיב אֹתָהּ
;it | offering | the to priest | the griddle | on and | a in pan stewing | that all and made is

3605 1121 2720 8081 1101 4503 3605
10 לוֹ תִהְיֶה׃ וְכָל־מִנְחָה בְלוּלָה־בַשֶּׁמֶן וַחֲרֵבָה לְכָל־בְּנֵי
the of sons | all for | ,dry or | ,oil with | mixed | food offering | And every | .is it | his

251 376 175
אַהֲרֹן תִּהְיֶה אִישׁ כְּאָחִיו׃
his as ,brother | a (to) man | shall it ,be | Aaron

3068 7126 834 8002 2077 8451
11 וְזֹאת תּוֹרַת זֶבַח הַשְּׁלָמִים אֲשֶׁר יַקְרִיב לַיהוָה׃ אִם עַל־
12 for | if | to :Jehovah | be shall brought | which | peace the offerings | the of sacrifice | law the | And (is) this

4682 2471 8426 2077 7126 7126 8426
תּוֹדָה יַקְרִיבֶנּוּ וְהִקְרִיב עַל־זֶבַח הַתּוֹדָה חַלּוֹת מַצּוֹת
unleavened | cakes | thanksgiving | the with of sacrifice | he then bring shall | brings he ,it | a thanksgiving

and thin unleavened wafers anointed with oil, and of well-mixed flour, cakes mingled with oil. [13]He shall bring his offering with the cakes of unleavened bread with the sacrifice of thanksgiving, his peace offerings. [14]And he shall bring out of it one of every offering, a heave offering to Jehovah, to the priest who is sprinkling the blood of the peace offering; it is his. [15]As to the flesh of the sacrifice of the thanksgiving peace offerings, it shall be eaten in the day of his offering. He shall not leave of it until morning. [16]And if the sacrifice of his offering *is* a vow, or free-will offering, in the day he brings his sacrifice near, it shall be eaten. And on the morrow the rest of it shall also be eaten. [17]And the rest of the flesh of the sacrifice on the third day shall be burned with fire. [18]And if any of the flesh of the sacrifice of his peace offerings is at all eaten on the third day, it is not pleasing. It shall not be reckoned for him who has brought it. It shall be a hateful thing, and the person who eats of it shall bear his iniquity.

[19]And the flesh which touches any unclean thing shall not be eaten. It shall be burned with fire. As to the flesh, every clean one shall eat of the flesh. [20]And the person who eats of the flesh of the sacrifice of the peace offerings which *are* Jehovah's *when* his uncleanness *is* upon him, even that person shall be cut off from his people. [21]And when a person touches any unclean thing, of the uncleanness of man, or of the uncleanness of animals, or of any unclean swarming creature, and shall eat of the flesh of the sacrifice of the peace offerings which *are* Jehovah's, even that person shall be cut off from his people.

[22]And Jehovah spoke to

בלולת בשמן ורקיקי מצות משחים בשמן וסלת מרבכת
13 חלת בלולת בשמן׃ על־חלת לחם חמץ יקריב קרבנו
14 על־זבח תודת שלמיו׃ והקריב ממנו אחד מכל־קרבן
תרומה ליהוה לכהן הזרק את־דם השלמים לו יהיה׃
15 ובשר זבח תודת שלמיו ביום קרבנו יאכל לא־יניח
16 ממנו עד־בקר׃ ואם־נדר | או נדבה זבח קרבנו ביום
הקריבו את־זבחו יאכל וממחרת והנותר ממנו יאכל׃
17 18 והנותר מבשר הזבח ביום השלישי באש ישרף׃ ואם
האכל יאכל מבשר־זבח שלמיו ביום השלישי לא
ירצה המקריב אתו לא יחשב לו פגול יהיה והנפש
19 האכלת ממנו עונה תשא׃ והבשר אשר־יגע בכל־טמא
לא יאכל באש ישרף והבשר כל־טהור יאכל בשר׃
20 והנפש אשר־תאכל בשר מזבח השלמים אשר ליהוה
21 וטמאתו עליו ונכרתה הנפש ההוא מעמיה׃ ונפש כי־
תגע בכל־טמא בטמאת אדם או | בבהמה טמאה או
בכל־שקץ טמא ואכל מבשר־זבח השלמים אשר ליהוה
22 ונכרתה הנפש ההוא מעמיה׃ וידבר יהוה אל־משה

Moses, saying. [23]Speak to the sons of Israel, saying, You shall not eat any fat of ox, or of sheep, or of goat. [24]And the fat of a dead body, and the fat of a thing torn may be used for any work, but you certainly shall not eat it. [25]for whoever eats the fat of the animal, of which *one* brings near a fire offering to Jehovah, even the person who eats shall be cut off from his people. [26]And you shall not eat any blood in all your dwellings, of fowl, or of animal. [27]Any person who eats any blood, even that person shall be cut off from his people.

23 לֵאמֹר׃ דַּבֵּר אֶל־בְּנֵי יִשְׂרָאֵל לֵאמֹר כָּל־חֵלֶב שׁוֹר וְכֶשֶׂב
of or sheep ,ox of fat Any ,saying Israel the of sons to Speak ,saying
24 וָעֵז לֹא תֹאכֵלוּ׃ וְחֵלֶב נְבֵלָה וְחֵלֶב טְרֵפָה יֵעָשֶׂה לְכָל־
for any be may used thing a torn the and of fat dead a ,body the And of fat shall you .eat not of or goat
25 מְלָאכָה וְאָכֹל לֹא תֹאכְלֻהוּ׃ כִּי כָּל־אֹכֵל חֵלֶב מִן־
of fat the eats whoever For shall you .it eat not but certainly ,work
הַבְּהֵמָה אֲשֶׁר יַקְרִיב מִמֶּנָּה אִשֶּׁה לַיהוָה וְנִכְרְתָה הַנֶּפֶשׁ
the person shall even off cut be to Jehovah fire a offering ,if of near bring (one) which the animal
26 הָאֹכֶלֶת מֵעַמֶּיהָ׃ וְכָל־דָּם לֹא תֹאכְלוּ בְּכֹל מוֹשְׁבֹתֵיכֶם
,dwellings your all in shall You eat not blood any from .people his eats who
27 לָעוֹף וְלַבְּהֵמָה׃ כָּל־נֶפֶשׁ אֲשֶׁר־תֹּאכַל כָּל־דָּם וְנִכְרְתָה
shall even off cut be ,blood any eats who person Any of or .animal of ,fowl
הַנֶּפֶשׁ הַהִוא מֵעַמֶּיהָ׃
his from .people that person

[28]And Jehovah spoke to Moses, saying, [29]Speak to the sons of Israel, saying, He who brings near the sacrifice of his peace offerings to Jehovah shall bring his offering to Jehovah from the sacrifice of his peace offerings; [30]his own hands shall bring in the fire offerings of Jehovah; the fat beside the breast he shall bring in with the breast, to wave it *as* a wave offering before Jehovah. [31]And the priest shall burn the fat on the altar as incense; and the breast shall be Aaron's and his sons. [32]And you shall make a heave offering of the right leg to the priest of the sacrifices of your peace offerings; [33]one of the sons of Aaron who is bringing near the blood of the peace offerings, and the fat, the right leg is his for a portion. [34]For the breast of the wave offering, and the leg of the heave offering, I have taken from the sons of Israel, from the sacrifices of their peace offerings, and I have given them to Aaron the priest,

28 וַיְדַבֵּר יְהוָה אֶל־מֹשֶׁה לֵּאמֹר׃ דַּבֵּר אֶל־בְּנֵי יִשְׂרָאֵל
29 Israel the of sons to Speak ,saying Moses to Jehovah And spoke
לֵאמֹר הַמַּקְרִיב אֶת־זֶבַח שְׁלָמָיו לַיהוָה יָבִיא אֶת־קָרְבָּנוֹ
his (in) offering shall bring to Jehovah peace his offerings the of sacrifice who He near brings ,saying
30 לַיהוָה מִזֶּבַח שְׁלָמָיו׃ יָדָיו תְּבִיאֶינָה אֵת אִשֵּׁי יְהוָה אֶת־
.Jehovah fire the of offerings — bring shall His hands own peace his .offerings the from of sacrifice to Jehovah
הַחֵלֶב עַל־הֶחָזֶה יְבִיאֶנּוּ אֵת הֶחָזֶה לְהָנִיף אֹתוֹ תְּנוּפָה
wave a (as) offering it wave to the breast with shall he ;it bring the ,breast with fat the
31 לִפְנֵי יְהוָה׃ וְהִקְטִיר הַכֹּהֵן אֶת־הַחֵלֶב הַמִּזְבֵּחָה וְהָיָה
shall and be the on ;altar fat the the priest shall And incense as burn .Jehovah before
32 הֶחָזֶה לְאַהֲרֹן וּלְבָנָיו׃ וְאֵת שׁוֹק הַיָּמִין תִּתְּנוּ תְרוּמָה
heave a offering you give shall right the leg And his and .son's Aaron's the breast
33 לַכֹּהֵן מִזִּבְחֵי שַׁלְמֵיכֶם׃ הַמַּקְרִיב אֶת־דַּם הַשְּׁלָמִים וְאֶת־
and peace the ,offerings blood the of is who he near bringing peace your ;offerings the from of sacrifices the to priest
34 הַחֵלֶב מִבְּנֵי אַהֲרֹן לוֹ תִהְיֶה שׁוֹק הַיָּמִין לְמָנָה׃ כִּי
For a for .portion right the leg is his ,Aaron's of sons fat the
אֶת־חֲזֵה הַתְּנוּפָה וְאֵת ׀ שׁוֹק הַתְּרוּמָה לָקַחְתִּי מֵאֵת
from have I taken heave the offering the of leg and wave the offering breast the of
בְּנֵי־יִשְׂרָאֵל מִזִּבְחֵי שַׁלְמֵיהֶם וָאֶתֵּן אֹתָם לְאַהֲרֹן הַכֹּהֵן
the priest to Aaron them I and given have peace their offerings the from of sacrifices ;Israel the of sons

and to his sons, by a never-
ending statute, from the
sons of Israel. [35]This is *the*
portion of the anointing of
Aaron, and the anointing of
his sons out of the fire
offerings of Jehovah, in the
day he shall bring them
near to act as priests to
Jehovah, [36]which Jehovah
has commanded to give to
them the day of His
anointing them, from the
sons of Israel, a never-
ending statute throughout
their generations.
[37]This *is* the law for burnt
offering, for the food
offering, and for sin offering, and for guilt offering,
and for consecrations, and
for a sacrifice of the peace
offerings, [38]which Jehovah
had commanded Moses in
Mount Sinai, in the days of
His commanding the sons
of Israel to bring near their
offerings to Jehovah, in the
wilderness of Sinai.

175 4888 3478 1121 5769 2706 1121
35 ולבניו לחק־עולם מאת בני ישראל: זאת משחת אהרן
,Aaron anointing the This .Israel the from never- a by to and
of is of sons ending statute sons his
3547 7126 3117 3068 801 1121 4888
ומשחת בניו מאשי יהוה ביום הקריב אתם לכהן
act to them shall he the in ,Jehovah the of out his the and
priests as ,near bring day of offering fire ,sons of anointing
4886 3117 5414 3068 6680 834 3068
36 ליהוה: אשר צוה יהוה לתת להם ביום משחו אתם
,them his day the to give to Jehovah has which to
anointing of them commanded ;Jehovah
8451 2088 1755 5769 2708 3478 1121
37 מאת בני ישראל חקת עולם לדרתם: זאת התורה
law the This their for never- a ;Israel the from
(is) .generations ending statute of sons
2077 4394 816 2403 4503 5930
לעלה למנחה ולחטאת ולאשם ולמלואים ולזבח
a for and for and for and for and the for burnt the for
sacrifice ,consecrations ,offering guilt ,offering sin ,offering food ,offering
3117 5514 2022 4872 3068 6680 834 8002
38 השלמים: אשר צוה יהוה את־משה בהר סיני ביום
the in Sinai in Moses Jehovah had which the of
of days Mount commanded ,offerings peace
3068 7133 7126 3478 1121 6680
צותו את־בני ישראל להקריב את־קרבניהם ליהוה
to their bring to ,Israel the His
Jehovah offerings near of sons commanding
5414 4057
במדבר סיני:
.Sinai the in
of wilderness

CHAPTER 8

[1]And Jehovah spoke to
Moses, saying, [2]Take
Aaron, and his sons with
him, and the garments, and
the anointing oil, and the
bullock of the sin offering,
and the two rams, and the
basket of unleavened
things, [3]and gather all the
congregation together at
the door of the tabernacle
of the congregation. [4]And
Moses did as Jehovah had
commanded him, and the
congregation was gathered
to the door of the taber-
nacle of the congregation.
[5]And Moses said to the
congregation, This *is* the
thing which Jehovah has
commanded done. [6]And
Moses brought Aaron and
his sons, and bathed them
in water, [7]and put on him
the tunic, and girded him
with the girdle, and clothed

CAP. VIII ח
CHAPTER 8

1121 175 3947 559 4872 3068 1696
1
2 וידבר יהוה אל־משה לאמר: קח את־אהרן ואת־בניו
his and Aaron Take ,saying ,Moses to Jehovah And
sons spoke
2403 6499 4888 8081 899
אתו ואת הבגדים ואת שמן המשחה ואת | פר החטאת
sin the the and ,anointing of oil and the and with
offering of bullock garments ,him
5712 3605 4682 5536 352 8147
3 ואת שני האילים ואת סל המצות: ואת כל־העדה
the all and unleavened the and ,rams the two and
congregation things of basket
6680 4872 6213 4150 168 6607 6950
4 הקהל אל־פתח אהל מועד: ויעש משה כאשר צוה
had as Moses did And .meeting the the at gather
commanded of tent of door
559 4150 168 6607 5712 6950 3068
5 יהוה אתו ותקהל העדה אל־פתח אהל מועד: ויאמר
said And .meeting the the to the was and ;him Jehovah
of tent of door congregation gathered
6213 3068 6680 834 1697 2088 5712 4872
משה אל־העדה זה הדבר אשר־צוה יהוה לעשות:
to Jehovah has which the This the to Moses
.do commanded thing (is) ,congregation
4325 7364 1121 175 4872 7126
6 ויקרב משה את־אהרן ואת־בניו וירחץ אתם במים:
;water in them and his and Aaron Moses And
bathed ,sons brought
3847 73 2296 3801 5414
7 ויתן עליו את־הכתנת ויחגר אתו באבנט וילבש אתו
him and the with him and ,tunic the on and
clothed ,girdle girded him put

him with the upper robe, and put the ephod on him, and girded him with the the ephod on him, and girded him with the girdle of the ephod, and bound it to him with it; 8 and put the breastplate on him, and put the Urim and the Thummim into the breastplate, 9 and put the miter on his head, and on the miter, on its front, *he* put the golden plate, the holy crown; as Jehovah commanded Moses.

10 And Moses took the anointing oil, and anointed the tabernacle, and all in it, and sanctified them; 11 and he sprinkled of it on the altar seven times, and anointed the altar, and all its vessels, and the laver, and its base, to sanctify them. 12 And he poured of the anointing oil on the head of Aaron, and anointed him, to sanctify him. 13 And Moses brought the sons of Aaron near, and clothed them with tunics, and girded them with girdles, and bound bonnets on them, as Jehovah had commanded Moses.

14 And he brought the bullock of the sin offering, and Aaron and his sons laid their hands on the head of the bullock of the sin offering; 15 and *one* killed *it;* and Moses took the blood and put *it* on the horns of the altar round about with his finger, and cleansed the altar; and he poured out the blood at the foundation of the altar, and sanctified it, to make atonement on it. 16 And he took all the fat on the inward parts, and the fold above the liver, and the two kidneys, and their fat,

2805 2296 646 5921 5414 4598
אֶת־הַמְּעִיל וַיִּתֵּן עָלָיו אֶת־הָאֵפֹד וַיַּחְגֹּר אֹתוֹ בְּחֵשֶׁב
the with him and the on and upper the with
of girdle girded ,ephod him put robe

5414 2833 7760 640 646
8 הָאֵפֹד וַיֶּאְפֹּד לוֹ בּוֹ׃ וַיָּשֶׂם עָלָיו אֶת־הַחֹשֶׁן וַיִּתֵּן אֶל־
into and the on and with to and the
put ,pouch him put ;it him it bound ephod

5921 4701 7760 8537 224 2833
9 הַחֹשֶׁן אֶת־הָאוּרִים וְאֶת־הַתֻּמִּים׃ וַיָּשֶׂם אֶת־הַמִּצְנֶפֶת עַל־
on miter the put and the and the the
;Thummin Urim ,pouch

2091 6731 4136 4701 7760 7218
רֹאשׁוֹ וַיָּשֶׂם עַל־הַמִּצְנֶפֶת אֶל־מוּל פָּנָיו אֵת צִיץ הַזָּהָב
the ,plate its ,front on miter the in and his
golden put ,head

4872 3947 4872 3068 6680 6944 5145
10 נֵזֶר הַקֹּדֶשׁ כַּאֲשֶׁר צִוָּה יְהוָה אֶת־מֹשֶׁה׃ וַיִּקַּח מֹשֶׁה
Moses And ,Moses Jehovah com- as the crown
took manded holy

834 3605 4908 4886 4888 8081
אֶת־שֶׁמֶן הַמִּשְׁחָה וַיִּמְשַׁח אֶת־הַמִּשְׁכָּן וְאֶת־כָּל־אֲשֶׁר־בּוֹ
,it in which all and the and the oil
(was) tabernacle anointed anointing

4886 647 7651 4196 5921 5137 6942
11 וַיְקַדֵּשׁ אֹתָם׃ וַיַּז מִמֶּנּוּ עַל־הַמִּזְבֵּחַ שֶׁבַע פְּעָמִים וַיִּמְשַׁח
and ;times seven altar the on it of And them and
anointed sprinkled he sanctified

6942 3653 3595 3627 3605 4196
אֶת־הַמִּזְבֵּחַ וְאֶת־כָּל־כֵּלָיו וְאֶת־הַכִּיֹּר וְאֶת־כַּנּוֹ לְקַדְּשָׁם׃
sanctify to its and the and its all and altar the
,them ,base laver ,vessels

4886 175 7218 5921 4888 8081 3332
12 וַיִּצֹק מִשֶּׁמֶן הַמִּשְׁחָה עַל רֹאשׁ אַהֲרֹן וַיִּמְשַׁח אֹתוֹ
,him and ,Aaron head the on the oil of he And
anointed of anointing poured

3801 3847 175 1121 4872 7126 6942
13 לְקַדְּשׁוֹ׃ וַיַּקְרֵב מֹשֶׁה אֶת־בְּנֵי אַהֲרֹן וַיַּלְבִּשֵׁם כֻּתֳּנֹת
with and Aaron the Moses And sanctify to
,tunics them clothed of sons near brought ,him

6680 4021 2280 73 2296
וַיַּחְגֹּר אֹתָם אַבְנֵט וַיַּחֲבֹשׁ לָהֶם מִגְבָּעוֹת כַּאֲשֶׁר צִוָּה
had as ,bonnets on and with them and
commanded them bound ,girdles girded

175 5564 2403 6499 5066 4872 3068
14 יְהוָה אֶת־מֹשֶׁה׃ וַיַּגֵּשׁ אֵת פַּר הַחַטָּאת וַיִּסְמֹךְ אַהֲרֹן
Aaron laid and sin the the he And ,Moses Jehovah
:offering of bullock brought

3947 7819 2403 6499 7218/5921 3027 1121
15 וּבָנָיו אֶת־יְדֵיהֶם עַל־רֹאשׁ פַּר הַחַטָּאת׃ וַיִּשְׁחָט וַיִּקַּח
and (one) And sin the the head the on hands their and
took (it) killed ,offering of bullock of sons his

676 5439 4196 7161 5921 5414 1818 4872
מֹשֶׁה אֶת־הַדָּם וַיִּתֵּן עַל־קַרְנוֹת הַמִּזְבֵּחַ סָבִיב בְּאֶצְבָּעוֹ
his with round altar the the on and blood the Moses
,finger about of horns (it) put

4196 3247 3332 1818 4196 2398
וַיְחַטֵּא אֶת־הַמִּזְבֵּחַ וְאֶת־הַדָּם יָצַק אֶל־יְסוֹד הַמִּזְבֵּחַ
,altar the the at he blood the and ;altar the and
of base out poured cleansed

5921 834 2459 3605 3947 3722 6942
16 וַיְקַדְּשֵׁהוּ לְכַפֵּר עָלָיו׃ וַיִּקַּח אֶת־כָּל־הַחֵלֶב אֲשֶׁר עַל־
on which fat the all he And ,it on make to and
(was) took atonement ,it sanctified

2459 3629 8147 3516 3508 7130
הַקֶּרֶב וְאֵת יֹתֶרֶת הַכָּבֵד וְאֶת־שְׁתֵּי הַכְּלָיֹת וְאֶת־חֶלְבְּהֶן
;fat their and the two and ,liver the the and the
,kidneys of fold ,parts inward

and Moses burned it as incense on the altar. 17And the bullock, and its skin, and its flesh, and its dung, he burned with fire, at the outside of the camp, as Jehovah had commanded Moses.

18And he brought the ram of the burnt offering, and Aaron and his sons laid their hands on the head of the ram; 19and *one* killed *it*, and Moses sprinkled the blood on the altar all around; 20and he cut the ram into its pieces, and Moses burned it as incense with the head, and the pieces, and the fat. 21And he washed the inward parts and the legs with water, and Moses burned it as incense with the whole ram on the altar; it *is* a burnt offering, for a sweet fragrance; it *is* a fire offering to Jehovah, as Jehovah had commanded Moses.

22And he brought the second ram, a ram of the consecrations, and Aaron and his sons lay their hands on the head of the ram. 23And *one* killed *it*, and Moses took of its blood and put *it* on the tip of the right ear of Aaron, and on the thumb of his right hand, and on the big toe of his right foot. 24And he brought Aaron's sons, and Moses put of the blood on the tip of their right ear, and on the thumb of their right hand, and on the big toe of their right foot. And Moses sprinkled the blood on the altar all around, 25and took the fat, and the fat tail, and all the fat on the inward parts, and the fold above the liver, and the two kidneys, and their fat, and

1320 5785 6499 4196 4872 6999
17 וַיַּקְטֵר מֹשֶׁה הַמִּזְבֵּחָה׃ וְאֶת־הַפָּר וְאֶת־עֹרוֹ וְאֶת־בְּשָׂרוֹ
its flesh and its skin and the bullock And the on altar Moses and incense as it burned
3068 6680 4264 2351 784 8313 6569
וְאֶת־פִּרְשׁוֹ שָׂרַף בָּאֵשׁ מִחוּץ לַמַּחֲנֶה כַּאֲשֶׁר צִוָּה יְהוָה
Jehovah had commanded as the of camp the at outside with fire he burned its dung and
1121 175 5564 5930 352 7126 4872
18 אֶת־מֹשֶׁה׃ וַיַּקְרֵב אֵת אֵיל הָעֹלָה וַיִּסְמְכוּ אַהֲרֹן וּבָנָיו
and sons his Aaron laid and burnt the offering of ram the he And brought .Moses
4872 2236 7819 352 7218 3027
19 אֶת־יְדֵיהֶם עַל־רֹאשׁ הָאָיִל׃ וַיִּשְׁחָט וַיִּזְרֹק מֹשֶׁה אֶת־
Moses and sprinkled and (it) killed ,ram the the of head on hands their
6999 5409 5408 352 5439 4196 5921 1818
20 הַדָּם עַל־הַמִּזְבֵּחַ סָבִיב׃ וְאֶת־הָאַיִל נִתַּח לִנְתָחָיו וַיַּקְטֵר
burned and incense as its into pieces he cut the ram and all ,around altar the on the blood
7130 6309 5409 7218 4872
21 מֹשֶׁה אֶת־הָרֹאשׁ וְאֶת־הַנְּתָחִים וְאֶת־הַפָּדֶר׃ וְאֶת־הַקֶּרֶב
the parts inward And suet the and the pieces and the ,head with ,Moses
352 3605 4872 6999 4325 7364 3767
וְאֶת־הַכְּרָעַיִם רָחַץ בַּמַּיִם וַיַּקְטֵר מֹשֶׁה אֶת־כָּל־הָאַיִל
the ram whole with Moses burned and incense as it with ,water he washed legs the and
3068 801 5207 7381 5930 4196
הַמִּזְבֵּחָה עֹלָה הוּא לְרֵיחַ־נִיחֹחַ אִשֶּׁה הוּא לַיהוָה
to Jehovah (is) it fire a offering sooth :ing a for fragrance (is) it burnt a offering the on ;altar
8145 352 7126 4872 3068 6680
22 כַּאֲשֶׁר צִוָּה יְהוָה אֶת־מֹשֶׁה׃ וַיַּקְרֵב אֶת־הָאַיִל הַשֵּׁנִי
,second ram the he And brought .Moses Jehovah had commanded as
7218 5921 3027 1121 175 5564 4394 352
אֵיל הַמִּלֻּאִים וַיִּסְמְכוּ אַהֲרֹן וּבָנָיו אֶת־יְדֵיהֶם עַל־רֹאשׁ
the of head on their hands and sons his Aaron laid and the :consecrations ram a of
241 8571 5921 5414 1818 4872 3947 7819 352
23 הָאָיִל׃ וַיִּשְׁחָט ׀ וַיִּקַּח מֹשֶׁה מִדָּמוֹ וַיִּתֵּן עַל־תְּנוּךְ אֹזֶן
ear the of tip on and (it) put its of blood Moses and took and (it) killed the :ram
7272 931 5921 3233 3027 931 3233 175
אַהֲרֹן הַיְמָנִית וְעַל־בֹּהֶן יָדוֹ הַיְמָנִית וְעַל־בֹּהֶן רַגְלוֹ
his foot big the of toe and on ,right his hand the of thumb on and ,right Aaron's
5921 1818 4872 5414 175 1121 7126 3233
24 הַיְמָנִית׃ וַיַּקְרֵב אֶת־בְּנֵי אַהֲרֹן וַיִּתֵּן מֹשֶׁה מִן־הַדָּם עַל־
on the blood of Moses and put Aaron's ,sons he And brought .right
7272 931 3233 931 3233 244 8571
תְּנוּךְ אָזְנָם הַיְמָנִית וְעַל־בֹּהֶן יָדָם הַיְמָנִית וְעַל־בֹּהֶן רַגְלָם
their foot big the of toe and on ,right their hand the of thumb on and ,right their ear the of tip
3947 5439 4196 5921 1818 4872 2236 3233
25 הַיְמָנִית וַיִּזְרֹק מֹשֶׁה אֶת־הַדָּם עַל־הַמִּזְבֵּחַ סָבִיב׃ וַיִּקַּח
he And took all ,around altar the on blood the Moses And sprinkled right
7130 5921 834 2459 3605 451 2459
אֶת־הַחֵלֶב וְאֶת־הָאַלְיָה וְאֶת־כָּל־הַחֵלֶב אֲשֶׁר עַל־הַקֶּרֶב
the parts inward on which (is) fat the all and the tail fat and ,fat the
2459 3629 8147 3516 3508
וְאֵת יֹתֶרֶת הַכָּבֵד וְאֶת־שְׁתֵּי הַכְּלָיֹת וְאֶת־חֶלְבְּהֶן וְאֶת
and fat their and the ,kidneys two and the ,liver the of fold and

the right leg. 26And out of
the basket of unleavened
bread which *was* before
Jehovah, he took one
unleavened cake, and one
cake of oiled bread, and one
wafer, and put *them* on the
fat, and on the right leg;
27and placed the whole on
the hands of Aaron, and on
the hands of his sons, and
waved them, a wave
offering before Jehovah.
28And Moses took them off
their hands and burned
them with incense on the
altar, on the burnt offering;
they *are* consecrations for
sweet fragrance; it *is* a fire
offering to Jehovah. 29And
Moses took the breast and
waved it, a wave offering
before Jehovah, of the ram
of the consecrations. It was
Moses' portion, as Jehovah
had commanded Moses.
30And Moses took of the
anointing oil, and of the
blood on the altar, and
sprinkled on Aaron, on his
garments, and on his sons,
and on his sons' garments
with him. And he sanctified
Aaron, his garments, and
his sons, and the garments
of his sons with him.

31And Moses said to
Aaron and to his sons, Boil
the flesh at the door of the
tabernacle of the congre-
gation, and you shall eat it
there, and the bread which
is in the basket of the
consecrations, as I have
commanded, saying, Aaron
and his sons shall eat it.
32And the rest of the flesh
and of the bread you shall
burn with fire; 33and you
shall not go out of the door
of the tabernacle of the
congregation for seven
days, until the days of your
consecration are fulfilled.
For He shall consecrate you
seven days; 34as He has
done on this day, Jehovah
has commanded *you* to do,

2471 3947 3068 6440 834 4682 5536 3225 7785
26 שׁוֹק הַיָּמִין׃ וּמִסַּל הַמַּצּוֹת אֲשֶׁר לִפְנֵי יְהוָה לָקַח חַלַּת
cake he ,Jehovah before which unleavened out and the leg
took (was) bread of basket the of right

7760 259 7550 259 8081 3899 2471 259 4682
מַצָּה אַחַת וְחַלַּת לֶחֶם שֶׁמֶן אַחַת וְרָקִיק אֶחָד וַיָּשֶׂם
put and one and ,one oiled bread and ,one unlea-
(them) wafer of cake vened

3729/5921 3605 5414 3225 7785 5921 2459
27 עַל־הַחֲלָבִים וְעַל שׁוֹק הַיָּמִין׃ וַיִּתֵּן אֶת־הַכֹּל עַל כַּפֵּי
the on whole the and the leg and ,fat the on
of hands placed ;right on

3947 3068 6440 8573 5130 1121 3709 5921 175
28 אַהֲרֹן וְעַל כַּפֵּי בָנָיו וַיָּנֶף אֹתָם תְּנוּפָה לִפְנֵי יְהוָה׃ וַיִּקַּח
And .Jehovah before wave a them and his the and Aaron
took offering waved ,sons of palms on

5930 4196 6999 3709 4872
מֹשֶׁה אֹתָם מֵעַל כַּפֵּיהֶם וַיַּקְטֵר הַמִּזְבֵּחָה עַל־הָעֹלָה
burnt the with the on burned and their off them Moses
;offering altar incense with them hands

4872 3947 3068 801 5207 7381 4394
29 מִלֻּאִים הֵם לְרֵיחַ נִיחֹחַ אִשֶּׁה הוּא לַיהוָה׃ וַיִּקַּח מֹשֶׁה
Moses And to (is) it fire a ;soothing a for they conse-
took .Jehovah offering fragrance (are) crations

4394 352 3068 6440 8573 5130 2373
אֶת־הֶחָזֶה וַיְנִיפֵהוּ תְנוּפָה לִפְנֵי יְהוָה מֵאֵיל הַמִּלֻּאִים
the the of ,Jehovah before wave a and the
;consecrations of ram offering it waved breast

3947 4872 3068 6680 4940 1961 4872
30 לְמֹשֶׁה הָיָה לְמָנָה כַּאֲשֶׁר צִוָּה יְהוָה אֶת־מֹשֶׁה׃ וַיִּקַּח
And .Moses Jehovah had as a for it for
took commanded portion was Moses

5130 4196 5921 1898 4888 8081 4872
מֹשֶׁה מִשֶּׁמֶן הַמִּשְׁחָה וּמִן־הַדָּם אֲשֶׁר עַל־הַמִּזְבֵּחַ וַיַּז עַל־
on and altar the on which the and the oil of Moses
sprinkled (was) blood of anointing (of)

6942 1121 899 1121 899 5921 175
אַהֲרֹן עַל־בְּגָדָיו וְעַל־בָּנָיו וְעַל־בִּגְדֵי בָנָיו אִתּוֹ וַיְקַדֵּשׁ
he and with his the and his and his on ,Aaron
sanctified ;him sons garments on ,sons on ,garments

1121 899 1121 899 175
אֶת־אַהֲרֹן אֶת־בְּגָדָיו וְאֶת־בָּנָיו וְאֶת־בִּגְדֵי בָנָיו אִתּוֹ׃
with his the and his and his ,Aaron
.him sons of garments ,sons ,garments

6607 1320 1310 1121 175 4872 559
31 וַיֹּאמֶר מֹשֶׁה אֶל־אַהֲרֹן וְאֶל־בָּנָיו בַּשְּׁלוּ אֶת־הַבָּשָׂר פֶּתַח
the at the Boil his and Aaron to Moses And
of door flesh ,sons to said

5536 834 3899 398 8033 4150 168
אֹהֶל מוֹעֵד וְשָׁם תֹּאכְלוּ אֹתוֹ וְאֶת־הַלֶּחֶם אֲשֶׁר בְּסַל
the in which the and it shall you and ;meeting the
of basket (is) bread eat there of tent

3498 398 1121 175 559 6680 4394
32 הַמִּלֻּאִים כַּאֲשֶׁר צִוֵּיתִי לֵאמֹר אַהֲרֹן וּבָנָיו יֹאכְלֻהוּ׃ וְהַנּוֹתָר
the And shall and Aaron ,saying have I as the
of rest .it eat sons his ,commanded ,consecrations

4150 168 6607 8313 784 3899 1320
33 בַּבָּשָׂר וּבַלָּחֶם בָּאֵשׁ תִּשְׂרֹפוּ׃ וּמִפֶּתַח אֹהֶל מוֹעֵד לֹא
not ,meeting the of And shall you with of and the
of tent of door the burn fire bread the flesh

7651 4394 4390 3117/5704 3117 7651 5927
תֵצְאוּ שִׁבְעַת יָמִים עַד יוֹם מְלֹאת יְמֵי מִלֻּאֵיכֶם כִּי שִׁבְעַת
seven for conse- your the ful- of the until ,days for shall you
;crations of days filling day seven out go

3068 6680 2088 3117 6213 3027 4390 3117
34 יָמִים יְמַלֵּא אֶת־יֶדְכֶם׃ כַּאֲשֶׁר עָשָׂה בַּיּוֹם הַזֶּה צִוָּה יְהוָה
Jehovah has ,this on has He As your shall he days
commanded day done .hands fill

to make atonement for you. [35]And you shall remain at the door of the tabernacle of the congregation day and night for seven days, and you shall keep the charge of Jehovah and shall not die; for so I have been commanded. [36]And Aaron and his sons did all the things which Jehovah had commanded by the hand of Moses.

3117 7725 4150 168 6607 3722 6213
35 לַעֲשֹׂת לְכַפֵּר עֲלֵיכֶם׃ וּפֶתַח אֹהֶל מוֹעֵד תֵּשְׁבוּ יוֹמָם
day shall you meeting the the at And for make to to
remain of tent of door .you atonement do

3808 3068 4931 8104 3117 7651 3915
וָלַיְלָה שִׁבְעַת יָמִים וּשְׁמַרְתֶּם אֶת־מִשְׁמֶרֶת יְהוָה וְלֹא
and Jehovah charge the you and ;days for and
not of keep shall seven night

1697 3605 1121 175 6213 6680 4191
36 תָמוּתוּ כִּי־כֵן צֻוֵּיתִי׃ וַיַּעַשׂ אַהֲרֹן וּבָנָיו אֵת כָּל־הַדְּבָרִים
things the all his and Aaron And have I so for shall
sons did .commanded ;die

4872 3027 3068 6680 834
אֲשֶׁר־צִוָּה יְהוָה בְּיַד־מֹשֶׁה׃
.Moses the by Jehovah had which
of hand commanded

CAP. IX ט

CHAPTER 9

CHAPTER 9

[1]And it happened, on the eighth day, Moses called for Aaron and for his sons, and for the elders of Israel. [2]And he said to Aaron, Take a calf to yourself, a son of the herd, for a sin offering, and a ram for a burnt offering, perfect ones, and bring near before Jehovah. [3]And speak to the sons of Israel, saying, Take a kid of the goats for a sin offering, and a calf, and a lamb, sons of a year, perfect ones, for a burnt offering; [4]and a bullock and a ram for peace offerings, to sacrifice before Jehovah; and a food offering mixed with oil; for today Jehovah will appear to you. [5]And they took that which Moses had commanded to the front of the tabernacle of the congregation, and all the congregation drew near and stood before Jehovah. [6]And Moses said, This *is* the thing that Jehovah has commanded; do *it*, and the glory of Jehovah shall appear to you. [7]And Moses said to Aaron, Draw near to the altar and make your sin offering, and your burnt offering, and make atonement for yourself, and for the people, and make the offering of the people, and atone for them, as Jehovah has commanded. [8]And Aaron drew near to the altar

2205 1121 175 4872 7121 8066 3117 1961
1 וַיְהִי בַּיּוֹם הַשְּׁמִינִי קָרָא מֹשֶׁה לְאַהֲרֹן וּלְבָנָיו וּלְזִקְנֵי
the for and for and for Moses called eighth on it And
of elders ,sons his Aaron day the was

2403 1241/1121 5695 3947 175 559 3478
2 יִשְׂרָאֵל׃ וַיֹּאמֶר אֶל־אַהֲרֹן קַח־לְךָ עֵגֶל בֶּן־בָּקָר לְחַטָּאת
sin a for the a a to Take ,Aaron to he And .Israel
offering herd of son ,calf yourself said

3478 1121 3068 6440 7126 8549 5930 352
3 וְאַיִל לְעֹלָה תְּמִימִם וְהַקְרֵב לִפְנֵי יְהוָה׃ וְאֶל־בְּנֵי יִשְׂרָאֵל
Israel the And .Jehovah before bring and perfect burnt a for a and
of sons to near ones offering ram

1121 3532 5695 2403 5795 8163 3947 559 1696
תְּדַבֵּר לֵאמֹר קְחוּ שְׂעִיר־עִזִּים לְחַטָּאת וְעֵגֶל וָכֶבֶשׂ בְּנֵי־
sons a and a and sin a for the male a Take ,saying speak
of ,lamb ,calf ,offering goats of

6440 2076 8002 352 7794 5930 8549 8147
4 שָׁנָה תְּמִימִם לְעֹלָה׃ וְשׁוֹר וָאַיִל לִשְׁלָמִים לִזְבֹּחַ לִפְנֵי
before to peace for a and a and burnt a for perfect a
sacrifice ,offerings ram bullock ;offering ,ones ,year

7200 3068 3117 8081 1101 4503 3068
יְהוָה וּמִנְחָה בְּלוּלָה בַשָּׁמֶן כִּי הַיּוֹם יְהוָה נִרְאָה
will Jehovah today for ,oil with mixed a and ;Jehovah
appear offering food

4150 168 6440 4872 6680 834 3947
5 אֲלֵיכֶם׃ וַיִּקְחוּ אֵת אֲשֶׁר צִוָּה מֹשֶׁה אֶל־פְּנֵי אֹהֶל מוֹעֵד
;meeting the the to Moses had that they And .you to
of tent of front commanded which took

4872 559 3068 6440 5975 5712 3605 7126
6 וַיִּקְרְבוּ כָּל־הָעֵדָה וַיַּעַמְדוּ לִפְנֵי יְהוָה׃ וַיֹּאמֶר מֹשֶׁה
,Moses said And .Jehovah before stood and the all drew and
congregation near

3519 7200 6213 3068 6680 834 1697 2088
זֶה הַדָּבָר אֲשֶׁר־צִוָּה יְהוָה תַּעֲשׂוּ וְיֵרָא אֲלֵיכֶם כְּבוֹד
the you to shall and (it) do ;Jehovah has which the This
of glory appear commanded thing (is)

6213 4196 7126 175 4872 559 3068
7 יְהוָה׃ וַיֹּאמֶר מֹשֶׁה אֶל־אַהֲרֹן קְרַב אֶל־הַמִּזְבֵּחַ וַעֲשֵׂה
and altar the to Draw ,Aaron to Moses said And .Jehovah
make near

6213 5971 3722 5930 2403
אֶת־חַטָּאתְךָ וְאֶת־עֹלָתֶךָ וְכַפֵּר בַּעַדְךָ וּבְעַד הָעָם וַעֲשֵׂה
and the for and for and burnt your and sin your
make ;people ,yourself atone ,offering offering

7126 3069 6680 3722 5971 7133
8 אֶת־קָרְבַּן הָעָם וְכַפֵּר בַּעֲדָם כַּאֲשֶׁר צִוָּה יְהוָה׃ וַיִּקְרַב
drew And .Jehovah has as for and the offering the
near commanded them atone people of

and killed the calf of the sin
offering, which *is* for
himself; 9and Aaron's sons
brought the blood near to
him, and he dipped his
finger in the blood and put *it*
on the horns of the altar.
And he poured out the
blood at the foundation of
the altar; 10and the fat, and
the kidneys, and the fold of
the liver, of the sin offering,
he burned with incense on
the altar, as Jehovah had
commanded Moses. 11And
he burned the flesh and the
skin with fire, at the outside
of the camp.

12And he killed the burnt
offering. And Aaron's sons
presented the blood to him
and he sprinkled it on the
altar all around; 13and they
presented to him the burnt
offering, by its pieces, and
the head, and he burned
them with incense on the
altar. 14And he washed the
inward parts and the legs,
and burned them as
incense for the burnt
offering on the altar.
15And he brought the
offering of the people, and
took the goat of the sin
offering which *is* for the
people, and killed it, and
made it a sin offering like
the first. 16And he brought
the burnt offering, and
offered it, according to the
ordinance. 17And he
brought the food offering
and filled his palm from it,
and burned it as incense on
the altar, besides the burnt
offering of the morning.
18And he killed the
bullock and the ram, a
sacrifice of the peace
offerings, which *are* for the
people, and Aaron's sons
presented the blood to Him,
and he sprinkled it on the
altar all around; 19and the
fat of the bullock, and of the
ram, the fat tail, and the
covering, and the kidneys,
and the fold above the liver.

834 2403 5695 7919 4196 175
אהרן אל־המזבח וישחט את־עגל החטאת אשר־לו׃
for which (is) himself | sin the offering | calf the of | and killed | altar the | to | Aaron

18 18 676 2881 1818 175 1121 7126
9 ויקרבו בני אהרן את־הדם אליו ויטבל אצבעו בדם
the in blood | his finger | he and dipped | to him | the blood | Aaron's | sons | And brought

4196 3247 3332 1818 4196 7161 5921 5414
ויתן על־קרנות המזבח ואת־הדם יצק אל־יסוד המזבח׃
altar the | the of base | at | he poured out | blood the and | altar the | the of horns | on | and (it) put

3516 3508 3629 2459
10 ואת־החלב ואת־הכלית ואת־היתרת מן־הכבד מן
of | the liver | of | the fold | and | the kidneys | and | fat the | And

3068 6680 4196 6999 2403
החטאת הקטיר המזבחה כאשר צוה יהוה את־
Jehovah | had commanded | as | the on altar | burned he incense with | sin the offering

4264 2351 784 8313 5785 1320 4872
11 משה׃ ואת־הבשר ואת־העור שרף באש מחוץ למחנה׃
the of camp | the at outside | with fire | he burned | the skin | and | the flesh | And | Moses

1818 175 1121 4672 5930 7919
12 וישחט את־העלה וימצאו בני אהרן אליו את־הדם
blood the | him to | Aaron's | sons | and presented | burnt the offering | he And killed

5930 4672 5439 4196 5921 2236
13 ויזרקהו על־המזבח סביב׃ ואת־העלה המציאו אליו
to him | they presented | burnt the offering | And | all around | altar the | on | he and it sprinkled

7364 4196 6999 7218 5409
14 לנתחיה ואת־הראש ויקטר על־המזבח׃ וירחץ את־
he And washed | altar the | on burned he and incense with them | the head | and | its by pieces

7126 4196 5930 6999 3767 7130
15 הקרב ואת־הכרעים ויקטר על־העלה המזבחה׃ ויקרב
he And brought | the on altar | burnt the offering | with burned and incense as | legs the | and | the parts inward

5971 834 2403 8163 3947 5971 7133
את קרבן העם ויקח את־שעיר החטאת אשר לעם
the for people | which (is) | sin the offering | the of goat | and took | the people | the of offering

6213 5930 7126 7223 2398 7919
16 וישחטהו ויחטאהו כראשון׃ ויקרב את־העלה ויעשה
and it offered | burnt the offering | he And brought | the like first | it made and offering sin a | killed and it

6999 3709 4390 4503 7126 4941
17 כמשפט׃ ויקרב את־המנחה וימלא כפו ממנה ויקטר
burned and incense as | it of | his palm | and filled | food the offering | he And brought | to according ordinance the

7794 7919 1242 5930 905 4196
18 על־המזבח מלבד עלת הבקר׃ וישחט את־השור ואת־
and | the bullock | he And killed | the morning | burnt the offering of | besides | altar the | on

175 1121 4672 5971 834 8002 2077 352
האיל זבח השלמים אשר לעם וימצאו בני אהרן את־
Aaron's | sons | and presented | the for people | which (are) | peace the offerings | a sacrifice of | the ram

2459 5439 4196 5921 2236 1818
19 הדם אליו ויזרקהו על־המזבח סביב׃ ואת־החלבים
fat the | And | all around | altar the | on | he and it sprinkled | to him | the blood

3508 3629 4374 451 352 7794
מן־השור ומן־האיל האליה והמכסה והכלית ויתרת
the and of fold | the and kidneys | the and covering | fat the tail | the ram | and of | the bullock | of

20And they set the fat on the
breasts, and he burned as
incense the fat on the altar.
21And Aaron waved the
breasts, and the right leg *as*
a wave offering before
Jehovah, as He had com-
manded Moses.
22And Aaron lifted up his
hands toward the people
and blessed them, and
came down from offering
the sin offering, and the
burnt offering, and the
peace offerings. 23And
Moses and Aaron went into
the tabernacle of the
congregation. And they
came out and blessed the
people; and the glory of
Jehovah appeared to all the
people. 24And fire came
out from before Jehovah
and consumed the burnt
offering and the fat on the
altar. And all the people
saw, and cried aloud, and
fell on their faces.

2459 6999 2373 2459 7760 3516
20 הַכָּבֵד׃ וַיָּשִׂימוּ אֶת־הַחֲלָבִים עַל־הֶחָזוֹת וַיַּקְטֵר הַחֲלָבִים
the burned he and the on fat the they And .liver the
(portions) fat incense as ,breasts portions set

175 5130 3225 7785 2373 4196
21 הַמִּזְבֵּחָה׃ וְאֵת הֶחָזוֹת וְאֵת שׁוֹק הַיָּמִין הֵנִיף אַהֲרֹן
Aaron waved the leg and the And on
right breasts .altar the

175 5375 4872 6680 3068 6440 8573
22 תְּנוּפָה לִפְנֵי יְהוָה כַּאֲשֶׁר צִוָּה מֹשֶׁה׃ וַיִּשָּׂא אַהֲרֹן אֶת־
Aaron And .Moses had He as ,Jehovah before a (as)
up lifted commanded offering wave

5930 2403 6213 3381 1288 5971 3027
יָדָו אֶל־הָעָם וַיְבָרְכֵם וַיֵּרֶד מֵעֲשֹׂת הַחַטָּאת וְהָעֹלָה
the and sin the from came and and the toward his
,offering burnt ,offering offering down ,them blessed ,people hands

1288 5927 4150 168 175 4872 935 8002
23 וְהַשְּׁלָמִים׃ וַיָּבֹא מֹשֶׁה וְאַהֲרֹן אֶל־אֹהֶל מוֹעֵד וַיֵּצְאוּ וַיְבָרְכוּ
and they and ,meeting the into and Moses And peace the and
blessed out came of tent Aaron went .offerings

784 5927 5971 3605 3068 3519 7200 5971
24 אֶת־הָעָם וַיֵּרָא כְבוֹד־יְהוָה אֶל־כָּל־הָעָם׃ וַתֵּצֵא אֵשׁ
fire And the all to Jehovah the And the
out came .people of glory appeared .people

2459 5930 4196 398 3068 6440
מִלִּפְנֵי יְהוָה וַתֹּאכַל עַל־הַמִּזְבֵּחַ אֶת־הָעֹלָה וְאֶת־הַחֲלָבִים
;fat the and burnt the ,altar the on and Jehovah from
offering consumed before

6440 5921 5307 7442 5971 3605 7200
וַיַּרְא כָּל־הָעָם וַיָּרֹנּוּ וַיִּפְּלוּ עַל־פְּנֵיהֶם׃
their on and and the all and
.faces fell ,aloud cried ,people saw

CAP. X

CHAPTER 10

CHAPTER 10
1And Nadab and Abihu,
the sons of Aaron, each
took his censer and put fire
in them; and they put
incense on it and brought
strange fire before Jehovah,
which He had not com-
manded them. 2And fire
went out from before
Jehovah and consumed
them; and they died before
Jehovah. 3And Moses said
to Aaron, It *is* that which
Jehovah has spoken, say-
ing, I will be sanctified by
those drawing near to Me;
and I will be honored before
all the people. And Aaron
was silent.
4And Moses called
Mishael and Elzaphan, sons
of Uzziel, Aaron's uncle,
and said to them, Come
near, carry your brothers
from the front of the
sanctuary to the outside of
the camp. 5And they came
near and carried them in

2004 5414 4289 376 30 5070 175 1121 3947
1 וַיִּקְחוּ בְנֵי־אַהֲרֹן נָדָב וַאֲבִיהוּא אִישׁ מַחְתָּתוֹ וַיִּתְּנוּ בָהֵן
in put and his each and Nadab ,Aaron the And
them censer Abihu of sons took

2114 784 3068 6440 7126 7004 7760 784
אֵשׁ וַיָּשִׂימוּ עָלֶיהָ קְטֹרֶת וַיַּקְרִבוּ לִפְנֵי יְהוָה אֵשׁ זָרָה
strange fire ,Jehovah before and incense it on they and ;fire
brought put

398 3068 6440 784 5927 6680 834
2 אֲשֶׁר לֹא צִוָּה אֹתָם׃ וַתֵּצֵא אֵשׁ מִלִּפְנֵי יְהוָה וַתֹּאכַל
and Jehovah from fire And .them had He not which
consumed before out went commanded

175 4872 559 3068 6440 4191
3 אוֹתָם וַיָּמֻתוּ לִפְנֵי יְהוָה׃ וַיֹּאמֶר מֹשֶׁה אֶל־אַהֲרֹן הוּא
(is) It ,Aaron to Moses said And .Jehovah before they and ;them
died

5971 3605/6440 6942 7130 559 3068 1696/834
אֲשֶׁר־דִּבֶּר יְהוָה לֵאמֹר בִּקְרֹבַי אֶקָּדֵשׁ וְעַל־פְּנֵי כָל־הָעָם
the all before and be will I those by ,saying Jehovah has that
people holy treated Me approaching spoken which

469 4332 4872 7121 175 1826 3513
4 אֶכָּבֵד וַיִּדֹּם אַהֲרֹן׃ וַיִּקְרָא מֹשֶׁה אֶל־מִישָׁאֵל וְאֶל אֶלְצָפָן
,Elzaphan and Mishael to Moses And .Aaron was and will I
to called silent ;honored be

251 5375 7126 559 175 1730 5816 1121
בְּנֵי עֻזִּיאֵל דֹּד אַהֲרֹן וַיֹּאמֶר אֲלֵהֶם קִרְבוּ שְׂאוּ אֶת־אֲחֵיכֶם
your carry Come ,them to said and Aaron's uncle ,Uzziel sons
brothers ,near of

5375 7126 4264 2351 6944 6440
5 מֵאֵת פְּנֵי־הַקֹּדֶשׁ אֶל־מִחוּץ לַמַּחֲנֶה׃ וַיִּקְרְבוּ וַיִּשָּׂאֻם
carried and they And .camp the the to the front the from
them near came of outside sanctuary of

their coats to the outside of the camp, as Moses had commanded.

[6]And Moses said to Aaron, and to Eleazar, and to Ithamar, his sons, You shall not uncover your heads and you shall not tear your garments, that you may not die, and He be angry on all the congregation. As to your brothers, the whole house of Israel, they shall mourn the burning which Jehovah has kindled. [7]And you shall not go out of the door of the tabernacle of the congregation lest you die. For the anointing oil of Jehovah *is* on you. And they did according to the words of Moses.

[8]And Jehovah spoke to Aaron, saying, [9]You shall not drink wine and strong drink, you nor your sons with you, as you go into the the tabernacle of the congregation, and you shall not die; a never-ending statute throughout your generations; [10]and to make a distinction between the holy and profane, and between the unclean and the clean; [11]and to teach the sons of Israel all the statutes which Jehovah has spoken to them by the hand of Moses.

[12]And Moses spoke to Aaron, and to Eleazar, and to Ithamar, his sons who were left, Take the food offering that remains from the fire offerings of Jehovah, and eat it unleavened near the altar, for it *is* most holy. [13]And you shall eat it in the holy place, for it *is* your portion, and the portion of your sons, from the fire offerings of Jehovah; for so I have been commanded. [14]And the breast of the wave offering, and the leg of the heave offering, you shall eat in a clean place, you and your sons, and your daughters with you. For they have been given for your portion

559 4872 1696 4264 2351 3801
6 בְּכֻתֳּנֹתָם אֶל־מִחוּץ לַמַּחֲנֶה כַּאֲשֶׁר דִּבֶּר מֹשֶׁה׃ וַיֹּאמֶר
said And .Moses had as the the to their in
commanded camp of outside coats
7218 1121 385 599 175 4872
מֹשֶׁה אֶל־אַהֲרֹן וּלְאֶלְעָזָר וּלְאִיתָמָר ׀ בָּנָיו רָאשֵׁיכֶם אַל־
not your his to and to and ,Aaron to Moses
heads ,sons Ithamar Eleazar
5712 4191 3808 6533 899 6544
תִּפְרָעוּ ׀ וּבִגְדֵיכֶם לֹא־תִפְרֹמוּ וְלֹא תָמֻתוּ וְעַל כָּל־הָעֵדָה
the all and may you that you not your and shall you
congregation on ,die not ,tear shall garments ,uncover
834 8316 1058 3478 1004 3605 251 7107
יִקְצֹף וַאֲחֵיכֶם כָּל־בֵּית יִשְׂרָאֵל יִבְכּוּ אֶת־הַשְּׂרֵפָה אֲשֶׁר
which the shall they ,Israel house the your to As He
burning mourn of whole ,brothers .angry be
4191 5927 4150 168 6607 3068 8313
7 שָׂרַף יְהוָה׃ וּמִפֶּתַח אֹהֶל מוֹעֵד לֹא תֵצְאוּ פֶּן־תָּמֻתוּ כִּי־
For .die you lest shall you not ,meeting the the of And .Jehovah has
out go of tent of door burned
4872 1697 6213 5921 3068 4888 8081
שֶׁמֶן מִשְׁחַת יְהוָה עֲלֵיכֶם וַיַּעֲשׂוּ כִּדְבַר מֹשֶׁה׃
.Moses' according And upon (is) of the of oil
words to did they .you Jehovah anointing
8354 7941 3196 559 175 3068 1696
8
9 וַיְדַבֵּר יְהוָה אֶל־אַהֲרֹן לֵאמֹר׃ יַיִן וְשֵׁכָר אַל־תֵּשְׁתְּ
You not strong and wine ,saying ',Aaron to Jehovah And
,drink shall drink spoke
4191 3808 4150 168 935 1121
אַתָּה ׀ וּבָנֶיךָ אִתָּךְ בְּבֹאֲכֶם אֶל־אֹהֶל מוֹעֵד וְלֹא תָמֻתוּ
You and ,meeting the into you as with your nor you
;die shall not of tent go ,you sons
2455 996 6944 914 1755 5769/2708
10 חֻקַּת עוֹלָם לְדֹרֹתֵיכֶם׃ וּלְהַבְדִּיל בֵּין הַקֹּדֶשׁ וּבֵין הַחֹל
the and the between for And your for never- a
,profane holy distinction ,generations ending statute
3478 1121 3384 2889 996 2931 996
11 וּבֵין הַטָּמֵא וּבֵין הַטָּהוֹר׃ וּלְהוֹרֹת אֶת־בְּנֵי יִשְׂרָאֵל אֵת
Israel the to and ;clean the and the and
of sons teach unclean between
4872 3027 3068 1696 2706 3605
כָּל־הַחֻקִּים אֲשֶׁר דִּבֶּר יְהוָה אֲלֵיהֶם בְּיַד־מֹשֶׁה׃
.Moses by them to Jehovah has which the all
of hand the spoken statutes
1121 385 499 175 4872 1696
12 וַיְדַבֵּר מֹשֶׁה אֶל־אַהֲרֹן וְאֶל אֶלְעָזָר וְאֶל־אִיתָמָר ׀ בָּנָיו
his Ithamar and Eleazar and ,Aaron to Moses And
sons to to spoke
398 3068 801 3498 4503 3947 3498
הַנּוֹתָרִים קְחוּ אֶת־הַמִּנְחָה הַנּוֹתֶרֶת מֵאִשֵּׁי יְהוָה וְאִכְלוּהָ
and Jehovah the from remains that the Take were who
it eat of offerings offering food ,left
398 6944 6944 4196 681 4682
13 מַצּוֹת אֵצֶל הַמִּזְבֵּחַ כִּי קֹדֶשׁ קָדָשִׁים הִוא׃ וַאֲכַלְתֶּם
you And .(is) it most holy for ,altar the near unlea-
eat shall vened
3068 801 1121 2706 2706 6918 4725
אֹתָהּ בְּמָקוֹם קָדֹשׁ כִּי חָקְךָ וְחָק־בָּנֶיךָ הִוא מֵאִשֵּׁי יְהוָה
;Jehovah from (is) it your the and your for holy the in it
of offerings fire the ;sons of portion portion place
8641 7785 8573 2373 6680
14 כִּי־כֵן צֻוֵּיתִי׃ וְאֵת חֲזֵה הַתְּנוּפָה וְאֵת ׀ שׁוֹק הַתְּרוּמָה
heave the leg the and wave the breast the And have I thus for
offering of offering of ,commanded
2706 1323 1121 2889 4725 398
תֹּאכְלוּ בְּמָקוֹם טָהוֹר אַתָּה וּבָנֶיךָ וּבְנֹתֶיךָ אִתָּךְ כִּי־חָקְךָ
your for with your and and you ,clean a in shall you
portion ,you daughters sons your place eat

and the portion of your sons out of the sacrifices of peace offerings of the sons of Israel. [15]The leg of the heave offering, and the breast of the wave offering, besides fire offerings of the fat, they shall bring in to wave a wave offering before Jehovah; and it shall be to you, and to your sons with you, a never-ending statute, as Jehovah has commanded.

[16]And Moses sought carefully for the goat of the sin offering; and, behold, it had been burned! And he was angry against Eleazar and against Ithamar, Aaron's remaining sons, saying, [17]Why have you not eaten the sin offering in the holy place, for it *is* most holy, and He has given it to you to take away the iniquity of the congregation, to make atonement of them before Jehovah? [18]Behold, its blood has not been brought in to the holy place inside. You should certainly have eaten it in the holy place, as I have commanded. [19]And Aaron said to Moses, Behold, today they have brought their sin offering and their burnt offering before Jehovah; and such things have happened to me. And if I had eaten the sin offering today, would it have been accepted in the sight of Jehovah? [20]And when Moses heard, then it was good in his eyes.

15 וחק־בניך נתנו מזבחי שלמי בני ישראל׃ שוק התרומה
וחזה התנופה על אשי החלבים יביאו להניף תנופה
לפני יהוה והיה לך ולבניך אתך לחק־עולם כאשר
16 צוה יהוה׃ ואת שעיר החטאת דרש דרש משה והנה
שרף ויקצף על־אלעזר ועל־איתמר בני אהרן הנותרם
17 לאמר׃ מדוע לא־אכלתם את־החטאת במקום הקדש
כי קדש קדשים הוא ואתה נתן לכם לשאת את־עון
18 העדה לכפר עליהם לפני יהוה׃ הן לא־הובא את־
דמה אל־הקדש פנימה אכול תאכלו אתה בקדש כאשר
19 צויתי׃ וידבר אהרן אל־משה הן היום הקריבו את־
חטאתם ואת־עלתם לפני יהוה ותקראנה אתי כאלה
20 ואכלתי חטאת היום הייטב בעיני יהוה׃ וישמע משה
וייטב בעיניו׃

CAP. XI יא

CHAPTER 11

CHAPTER 11

[1]And Jehovah spoke to Moses and to Aaron, saying to them, [2]Speak to the sons of Israel, saying, These *are* the living things which you shall eat out of all the animals which *are* on the earth. [3]Any *that* divides the hoof and is wholly

1 וידבר יהוה אל־משה ואל־אהרן לאמר אלהם׃ דברו
2 אל־בני ישראל לאמר זאת החיה אשר תאכלו מכל־
3 הבהמה אשר על־הארץ׃ כל מפרסת פרסה ושסעת

cloven-footed, bringing up the cud, among the living things, you may eat it. [4]Only, you may not eat these, of those bringing up the cud, and of those dividing the hoof: the camel, though it brings up the cud, yet it does not divide *the* hoof; it *is* unclean to you; [5]and the rock badger, though it brings up the cud, yet it does not divide the hoof; it *is* unclean to you; [6]and the hare, though it brings up the cud, yet it does not divide *the* hoof; it *is* unclean to you; [7]and the swine, though it divides the hoof and *is* cloven-footed, yet it does not bring up the cud; it *is* unclean to you. [8]You shall not eat of their flesh, and you shall not touch their dead body; they *are* unclean to you.

[9]Of all *that are* in the waters, you shall eat these; any one that has fins and scales in the waters, in the seas, and in the brooks, you may eat them. [10]But any one that does not have fins and scales in the seas, and in the brooks, of any swarming creature of the waters, and of any creature which lives, which *is* in the waters; they *are* an abomination to you. [11]Yes, they are an abomination to you; you shall not eat of their flesh and you shall shun their dead bodies. [12]Any one that does not have fins and scales in the waters, it *shall be* a hateful thing to you.

[13]And these you shall count unclean among the fowls; they shall not be eaten; they are unclean: the eagle, and the black vulture and the bearded vulture, [14]and the kite, and the falcon, according to its kind; [15]every raven according to its kind; [16]and the

389 398 929 1625 5927 6541 8157
4 שֶׁסַע פְּרָסֹת מַעֲלַת גֵּרָה בַּבְּהֵמָה אֹתָהּ תֹּאכֵלוּ׃ אַךְ אֶת־
,Only may You eat it the among animals, the cud bringing up the cleft hooves the of

6541 6536 1625 5927 398
זֶה לֹא תֹאכְלוּ מִמַּעֲלֵי הַגֵּרָה וּמִמַּפְרִסֵי הַפַּרְסָה אֶת־
:hoof the of and dividing those cud the those of up bringing may you eat not these

2930 6536 369 6541 1625 5927 1581
הַגָּמָל כִּי־מַעֲלֵה גֵרָה הוּא וּפַרְסָה אֵינֶנּוּ מַפְרִיס טָמֵא הוּא
(is) it unclean is dividing it not (the) yet hoof ,it the cud brings up for the camel

6536 3808 6541 1625 5927 8227
5 לָכֶם׃ וְאֶת־הַשָּׁפָן כִּי־מַעֲלֵה גֵרָה הוּא וּפַרְסָה לֹא יַפְרִיס
divides not (the) yet hoof cud the brings up for the and ,rock badger ;you to

1625 5927 768 2931
6 טָמֵא הוּא לָכֶם׃ וְאֶת־הָאַרְנֶבֶת כִּי־מַעֲלַת גֵּרָה הִוא
,it the cud brings up for the ,hare and ;you to (is) it unclean

2386 2931 6536 3808 6541
7 וּפַרְסָה לֹא הִפְרִיסָה טְמֵאָה הִוא לָכֶם׃ וְאֶת־הַחֲזִיר כִּי־
though the swine and ;you to (is) it unclean ,divides not (the) yet hoof

3808 1625 6541 8157 8156 6541 6536
מַפְרִיס פַּרְסָה הוּא וְשֹׁסַע שֶׁסַע פַּרְסָה וְהוּא גֵּרָה לֹא־
does not the ,cud yet it the ,hoof wholly divided and it ,(is) hoof the divided

3808 5038 398 1320 2931 1641
8 יִגָּר טָמֵא הוּא לָכֶם׃ מִבְּשָׂרָם לֹא תֹאכֵלוּ וּבְנִבְלָתָם לֹא
not their dead body and ,You shall eat not their of flesh .you to it (is) unclean bring ;up

4325 398 2088 2931 5060
9 תִגָּעוּ טְמֵאִים הֵם לָכֶם׃ אֶת־זֶה תֹּאכְלוּ מִכֹּל אֲשֶׁר בַּמָּיִם
the in waters that (is) all of you shall eat This .you to they (are) unclean you ;touch shall

5158 3220 4325 7193 5579
כֹּל אֲשֶׁר־לוֹ סְנַפִּיר וְקַשְׂקֶשֶׂת בַּמַּיִם בַּיַּמִּים וּבַנְּחָלִים
in and ,brooks the the in ,seas the in ,waters and scales fins has that any

3220 7193 5579 369 3605 398
10 אֹתָם תֹּאכֵלוּ׃ וְכֹל אֲשֶׁר אֵין־לוֹ סְנַפִּיר וְקַשְׂקֶשֶׂת בַּיַּמִּים
the in ,seas scales and fins not does have that But any them may you .eat

4325 834 2416 5315 3605 4325 8318 3605 5158
וּבַנְּחָלִים מִכֹּל שֶׁרֶץ הַמַּיִם וּמִכֹּל נֶפֶשׁ הַחַיָּה אֲשֶׁר בַּמָּיִם
the in ,waters which (is) which lives creature of and any the ,waters swarmer of any in and ,brooks the

398 3808 1320 1961 8263 8263
11 שֶׁקֶץ הֵם לָכֶם׃ וְשֶׁקֶץ יִהְיוּ לָכֶם מִבְּשָׂרָם לֹא תֹאכֵלוּ
shall you ,eat not their of flesh ,you to they be shall an and abomination ;you to (are) they an abomination

7193 5579 369 3605 8262 5038
12 וְאֶת־נִבְלָתָם תְּשַׁקֵּצוּ׃ כֹּל אֲשֶׁר אֵין־לוֹ סְנַפִּיר וְקַשְׂקֶשֶׂת
scales and fins not does have that Any you and .detest shall their bodies dead

3808 5775/4480 8262 428 8263 4325
13 בַּמָּיִם שֶׁקֶץ הוּא לָכֶם׃ וְאֶת־אֵלֶּה תְּשַׁקְּצוּ מִן־הָעוֹף לֹא
not the among ,fowls shall you detest these And .you to (is) it an abomination the in waters

5822 6538 5404 8263 398
יֵאָכְלוּ שֶׁקֶץ הֵם אֶת־הַנֶּשֶׁר וְאֶת־הַפֶּרֶס וְאֵת הָעָזְנִיָּה׃
bearded the vulture and black the vulture and eagles the (are) they an abomination shall they ,eaten be

4327 6158 3605 4327 344 1676
14 15 וְאֶת־הַדָּאָה וְאֶת־הָאַיָּה לְמִינָהּ׃ אֵת כָּל־עֹרֵב לְמִינוֹ׃
according raven every to its ,kind according ,falcon the and ,kite the and to its ,kind

16 ostrich, and the great owl, and the gull, and small hawks, according to its kind;
17 [17]and the little owl, and the cormorant, and the
18 eared owl; [18]and the barn owl, and the pelican and the owl-vulture; [19]and the stork,
19 *and* the heron according to its kind, and the hoopoe, and the bat.

20 [20]Every flying swarming creature going on all four—it *is* an abomination to you.
21 [21]Only, this you may eat of any swarming thing which flies, which goes on all four, which *has* legs above its feet, to leap with them on the earth;
22 [22]these *are* those you may eat: the locusts according to its kind, and the bald locust according to its kind, and the long horned locust according to its kind, and the short horned grasshopper according to its kind.
23 [23]But every swarming thing which flies, which has four feet, it *is* unclean to you.

24 [24]And by these you shall be made unclean; any who touches their dead body is unclean until the evening.
25 [25]And anyone who lifts up their dead body shall wash his garments and shall be unclean until the evening;
26 [26]even every living thing which divides the hoof, and is not cloven-footed, and does not bring up the cud, they *are* unclean to you; anyone who touches them shall be unclean.
27 [27]And any one going on its paws among all the living things which go on all four; they *are* unclean to you; anyone who touches their dead body is unclean until the evening;
28 [28]and he who lifts up their dead body shall wash his garments and shall be unclean until the evening; they *are* unclean to you.

5322 7828 8464 3284
16 ואת בת היענה ואת התחמס ואת השחף ואת הנץ
small ,hawks and the gull and the ,owl great and the ,ostrich and

3244 7994 3559 4327
17 18 למינהו: ואת הכוס ואת השלך ואת הינשוף: ואת
and eared the ,owl and Egyptian the vulture and the ,owl little and according .kind its to

601 2624 7360 6893 8580
19 התנשמת ואת הקאת ואת הרחם: ואת החסידה האנפה
the (and) ,heron ,stork the and owl- ,vulture the and the ,pelican and the barn-owl

5775 8318 5847 1744 4327
20 למינה ואת הדוכיפת ואת העטלף: כל שרץ העוף
which ,flies swarming creature Every .bat the and the hoopoe and ,kind its to according

398 2088 389 8263 702 5921 3212
21 ההלך על ארבע שקץ הוא לכם: אך את זה תאכלו
may you ,eat this ,Only .you to (is) it an abomination four all on going

3767 834 702 5921 3212 5775 8318 3605
מכל שרץ העוף ההלך על ארבע אשר לא כרעים
lower legs which (has) ,four all on which goes which ,flies swarming thing of any

428 776 5921 2004 5425 7272 4605
22 ממעל לרגליו לנתר בהן על הארץ: את אלה מהם
from them (are) these ;earth the on with them leap to feet its above

4327 5556 4327 697 398
תאכלו את הארבה למינו ואת הסלעם למינהו ואת
and according ,kind its to bald the locust and according ,kind its to the locusts may you :eat

5775 8318 4327 2284 4327 2728
23 החרגל למינהו ואת החגב למינהו: וכל שרץ העוף
which ,flies swarming thing But every its by .kind horned short the and grasshopper its by ,kind horned long the grasshopper

2930 428 8263 7272 702 834
24 אשר לו ארבע רגלים שקץ הוא לכם: ולאלה תטמאו
shall you unclean be by And these .you to (is) it an abomination ,feet four to it which (is)

5038 5375 3605 6153 2930 5038 5060
25 כל הנגע בנבלתם יטמא עד הערב: וכל הנשא מנבלתם
dead their body lifts up who and anyone the ;evening until is unclean dead their body who touches any one

834 929 3605 6153 2430 899 3576
26 יכבס בגדיו וטמא עד הערב: לכל הבהמה אשר הוא
which living thing even every the ;evening until shall and unclean be his garments shall wash

6927 369 1625 8167 369 8156 1541 6536
מפרסת פרסה ושסע איננה שסעת וגרה איננה מעלה
bring up does not the and cud cloven ,footed not is and hoof the wholly divides

5921 3212 3605 2930 5060 3605 2930
27 טמאים הם לכם כל הנגע בהם יטמא: וכל הולך על
on going And anyone be shall .unclean them who any- touches one to ;you they (are) unclean

1992 2930 702 5921 3212 2416 3605 3709
כפיו בכל החיה ההלכת על ארבע טמאים הם לכם
to ;you they (are) unclean ,four all on go which the living things among all its paws

5038 5375 6153 2930 5038 5060 3605
28 כל הנגע בנבלתם יטמא עד הערב: והנשא את נבלתם
dead their body he And up lifts who the .evening until is unclean dead their body who touches any one

2930 6153 2930 899 3526
יכבס בגדיו וטמא עד הערב טמאים המה לכם:
.you to they (are) unclean the ,evening until shall and unclean be his garments shall wash

[29]And these *shall be* unclean to you among the swarming things which swarm on the earth: the weasel, and the mouse, and the great lizard according to its kind, [30]and the gecko, and the monitor, and the lizard, and the sand lizard, and the barn owl. [31]These *are* unclean to you among all which swarm; anyone who touches them in their death is unclean until the evening. [32]And anything on which any one of them falls, in their death, is unclean, of any vessel of wood, or garment, or skin, or sack; any vessel in which work is done shall be caused to go into water, and shall be unclean until the evening; then it shall be cleaned. [33]And any earthen vessel into the midst of which *any* one of them falls, whatever *is* in it shall be unclean, and you shall break it. [34]Of all the food which may be eaten, that on which *such* water falls shall be unclean, and all drink that may be drunk in any *such* vessel shall be unclean. [35]And anything on which *any part* of their dead body falls shall be unclean, oven and hearth, shall be broken down; they *are* unclean; yes, they are unclean to you. [36]But a fountain or a well, a collection of water, shall be clean; only that touching the dead body is unclean. [37]And when *any part* of their dead body falls on any sowing seed which is sown, it shall be clean; [38]but when water is put on the seed, and *any* of its dead body has fallen on it, it *shall be* unclean to you.

[39]And when any of the animals which *are* food for you dies, he who touches its dead body is unclean until the evening; [40]and he who eats of its dead body shall wash his garments and shall be unclean until the evening; and he who lifts up its dead body shall

29 וְזֶה לָכֶם הַטָּמֵא בַּשֶּׁרֶץ הַשֹּׁרֵץ עַל־הָאָרֶץ הַחֹלֶד וְהָעַכְבָּר

the and mouse, the weasel, the earth: on which swarm the among swarmers unclean you to (be shall) And this

30 וְהַצָּב לְמִינֵהוּ׃ וְהָאֲנָקָה וְהַכֹּחַ וְהַלְּטָאָה וְהַחֹמֶט וְהַתִּנְשָׁמֶת׃

the and owl barn, the and lizard sand, the and lizard, the and monitor, the and gecko, its by kind, the and lizard great

31 אֵלֶּה הַטְּמֵאִים לָכֶם בְּכָל־הַשָּׁרֶץ כָּל־הַנֹּגֵעַ בָּהֶם בְּמֹתָם

their in death them who touches any- one which swarm among all you to unclean These (are)

32 יִטְמָא עַד־הָעָרֶב׃ וְכֹל אֲשֶׁר־יִפֹּל עָלָיו מֵהֶם ׀ בְּמֹתָם

their in death of them on one falls which And anything the evening, until is unclean

יִטְמָא מִכָּל־כְּלִי־עֵץ אוֹ בֶגֶד אוֹ עוֹר אוֹ שָׂק כָּל־כְּלִי

vessel any sack, or skin, or garment, or wood, vessel of any of is unclean

אֲשֶׁר־יֵעָשֶׂה מְלָאכָה בָּהֶם בַּמַּיִם יוּבָא וְטָמֵא עַד־הָעָרֶב

the evening, until shall and unclean be shall be put into water in them, work done is which

33 וְטָהֵר׃ וְכָל־כְּלִי־חֶרֶשׂ אֲשֶׁר־יִפֹּל מֵהֶם אֶל־תּוֹכוֹ כֹּל

all its midst, into them of anyone falls of which earthen- ware vessel And any shall it then cleaned be

34 אֲשֶׁר בְּתוֹכוֹ יִטְמָא וְאֹתוֹ תִּשְׁבֹּרוּ׃ מִכָּל־הָאֹכֶל אֲשֶׁר

which the food all Of shall you break it and be shall unclean its in midst that (is)

יֵאָכֵל אֲשֶׁר יָבוֹא עָלָיו מַיִם יִטְמָא וְכָל־מַשְׁקֶה אֲשֶׁר יִשָּׁתֶה

be may drunk that drink all and be shall unclean, (and) water on it falls which be may eaten

35 בְּכָל־כְּלִי יִטְמָא׃ וְכֹל אֲשֶׁר־יִפֹּל מִנִּבְלָתָם ׀ עָלָיו יִטְמָא

be shall unclean; on dead their body falls which And anything be shall unclean. vessel any in (such)

36 תַּנּוּר וְכִירַיִם יֻתָּץ טְמֵאִים הֵם וּטְמֵאִים יִהְיוּ לָכֶם׃ אַךְ

But you to. yea, they are unclean they (are), unclean be shall smashed; or hearth an oven

מַעְיָן וּבוֹר מִקְוֵה־מַיִם יִהְיֶה טָהוֹר וְנֹגֵעַ בְּנִבְלָתָם יִטְמָא׃

is unclean. dead (their) body that only touches which ;clean be shall water, of collection a well, a or a spring

37 וְכִי יִפֹּל מִנִּבְלָתָם עַל־כָּל־זֶרַע זֵרוּעַ אֲשֶׁר יִזָּרֵעַ טָהוֹר

;clean is sown which sowing seed of any on their of body dead falls And when

38 הוּא׃ וְכִי יֻתַּן־מַיִם עַל־זֶרַע וְנָפַל מִנִּבְלָתָם עָלָיו טָמֵא

unclean on it, their of body dead has and fallen the seed on water is put but when it (be shall)

39 הוּא לָכֶם׃ וְכִי יָמוּת מִן־הַבְּהֵמָה אֲשֶׁר־הִיא לָכֶם

for you which (are) the animals of dies And when you to. it (be shall)

40 לְאָכְלָה הַנֹּגֵעַ בְּנִבְלָתָהּ יִטְמָא עַד־הָעָרֶב׃ וְהָאֹכֵל מִנִּבְלָתָהּ

its of body dead he and eats who the evening; until is unclean dead its body who he touches for food,

יְכַבֵּס בְּגָדָיו וְטָמֵא עַד־הָעָרֶב וְהַנֹּשֵׂא אֶת־נִבְלָתָהּ יְכַבֵּס

shall wash dead its body who he and lifts up the evening; until shall and be unclean his garments shall wash

776 5921 8317 8318 3605 6153 5704 2930 899
41 בְּגָדָיו וְטָמֵא עַד־הָעָרֶב׃ וְכָל־הַשֶּׁרֶץ הַשֹּׁרֵץ עַל־הָאָרֶץ
the on which swarming And the until shall and his
earth swarms thing every .evening unclean be garments

3212 3605 1512 3212 3605 398 3808 8263
42 שֶׁקֶץ הוּא לֹא יֵאָכֵל׃ כֹּל הוֹלֵךְ עַל־גָּחוֹן וְכֹל ׀ הוֹלֵךְ
going and its on going anything be shall not it an (is)
any belly .eaten ;abomination

5921 8317 8318 3605 7272 7235 3605 702
עַל־אַרְבַּע עַד כָּל־מַרְבֵּה רַגְלַיִם לְכָל־הַשֶּׁרֶץ הַשֹּׁרֵץ עַל־
on that swarming even feet having all even (all) on
swarms thing every many ,four

8262 8263 398 776
43 הָאָרֶץ לֹא תֹאכְלוּם כִּי־שֶׁקֶץ הֵם׃ אַל־תְּשַׁקְּצוּ אֶת־
shall You not they an for shall you not the
pollute (are) abomination ,them eat ,earth

2930 2933 8317 8318 3605 5315
נַפְשֹׁתֵיכֶם בְּכָל־הַשֶּׁרֶץ הַשֹּׁרֵץ וְלֹא תִטַּמְּאוּ בָּהֶם וְנִטְמֵתֶם
you that so with shall you nor which swarming with yourselves
unclean are them yourselves defile ,swarms thing any

6918 1961 6942 430 3068
44 בָּם׃ כִּי אֲנִי יְהוָה אֱלֹהֵיכֶם וְהִתְקַדִּשְׁתֶּם וִהְיִיתֶם קְדֹשִׁים
,holy you and have you and ,God your Jehovah I For by
become have ,yourselves sanctified 3808 (am) .them

8318 3605 5315 2930 6944
כִּי קָדוֹשׁ אָנִי וְלֹא תְטַמְּאוּ אֶת־נַפְשֹׁתֵיכֶם בְּכָל־הַשֶּׁרֶץ
swarming with persons your shall you and I (am) for
thing any defile not ;holy

776 5927 3068 776 430
45 הָרֹמֵשׂ עַל־הָאָרֶץ׃ כִּי ׀ אֲנִי יְהוָה הַמַּעֲלֶה אֶתְכֶם מֵאֶרֶץ
the of out you brought who ,Jehovah I For the on which
of land up (am) .earth creeps

6918 6918 1961 430 1961 4714
מִצְרַיִם לִהְיֹת לָכֶם לֵאלֹהִים וִהְיִיתֶם קְדֹשִׁים כִּי קָדוֹשׁ
holy for ,holy you and for to to ,Egypt
be shall ,God you become

7430 2416 5315 3605 5775 929 8451 2088
46 אָנִי׃ זֹאת תּוֹרַת הַבְּהֵמָה וְהָעוֹף וְכֹל נֶפֶשׁ הַחַיָּה הָרֹמֶשֶׂת
which living creature and of and ,animals the the This I
moves every of ,fowl the of law (is) .(am)

996 914 776 5921 8317 5315 3605 4325
47 בַּמָּיִם וּלְכָל־נֶפֶשׁ הַשֹּׁרֶצֶת עַל־הָאָרֶץ׃ לְהַבְדִּיל בֵּין
between make to ;earth the on which creature and the in
distinction a swarms every ,waters

834 2416 996 398 2416 996 2889 996 2930
הַטָּמֵא וּבֵין הַטָּהֹר וּבֵין הַחַיָּה הַנֶּאֱכֶלֶת וּבֵין הַחַיָּה אֲשֶׁר
that the and may that the and ,clean the and the
thing living ,eaten be thing living between unclean

398 3808
לֹא תֵאָכֵל׃
be may not
.eaten

wash his garments and shall be unclean until the evening.
[41]And every swarming thing which swarms on the earth is unclean; it shall not be eaten; [42]anything going on its belly, and any going on *all* four, and all having many feet, even every swarming thing that swarms on the earth, you shall not eat them, for they *are* unclean; [43]you shall not pollute yourselves with any swarming thing which swarms, nor shall you make yourselves unclean with them, so that you should be defiled by them. [44]For I *am* Jehovah your God, and you have sanctified yourselves, and you have become holy, for I *am* holy. And you shall not defile your persons with any swarming thing which creeps on the earth; [45]for I *am* Jehovah who brought you up out of the land of Egypt to become your God; and you shall be holy, for I *am* holy.
[46]This *is* the law of the animals, and of the fowl, and of every living creature which moves in the waters, and every creature which swarms on the earth, [47]to make a distinction between the unclean and the clean, and between the living thing that may be eaten, and the living thing that may not be eaten.

CAP. XII יב

CHAPTER 12

3478 1121 1696 559 4872 3068 1696
1 2 וַיְדַבֵּר יְהוָה אֶל־מֹשֶׁה לֵּאמֹר׃ דַּבֵּר אֶל־בְּנֵי יִשְׂרָאֵל
,Israel the to Speak ,saying ,Moses to Jehovah And
of sons spoke

3117 7651 2930 7145 3205 2232 802 559
לֵאמֹר אִשָּׁה כִּי תַזְרִיעַ וְיָלְדָה זָכָר וְטָמְאָה שִׁבְעַת יָמִים
;days seven she shall ,male a has and con- has if a ,saying
unclean be shall borne seed ceived woman

1320 4135 8066 3117 2930 1738 3117
3 כִּימֵי נִדַּת דְּוֺתָהּ תִּטְמָא׃ וּבַיּוֹם הַשְּׁמִינִי יִמּוֹל בְּשַׂר
the be shall eighth on And shall she her impurity the as
of flesh circumcised day the .unclean be menstrual of days

CHAPTER 12
[1]And Jehovah spoke to Moses, saying, [2]Speak to the sons of Israel, saying, If a woman has conceived seed, and has borne a male, then she shall be unclean seven days; as on the days of her menstrual impurity she shall be unclean. [3]And on the eighth day the flesh of his foreskin shall be

circumcised. [4]And she shall remain in the blood of her cleansing thirty-three days; she shall not touch any holy thing, and she shall not go into the sanctuary, until the days of her cleansing are fulfilled. [5]And if she bears a female, then she shall be unclean two weeks, as in her menstruation; and she shall continue in the blood of her cleansing sixty-six days.

[6]And when the days of her cleansing are fulfilled for son or for daughter, she shall bring in a lamb, a son of a year, for a burnt offering, and a young pigeon or a turtle-dove for a sin offering, to the door of the tabernacle of the congregation, to the priest. [7]And he shall bring it near before Jehovah, and shall make atonement for her; and she shall be cleansed from the fountain of her blood; this *is* the law of her who bears, whether a male or a female. [8]And if her hand is not able to find a lamb, then she shall take two turtle-doves, or two young pigeons, one for a burnt offering, and one for a sin offering, and the priest shall make atonement for her; and she shall be cleansed.

4 עָרְלָתוֹ׃ וּשְׁלֹשִׁים יוֹם וּשְׁלֹשֶׁת יָמִים תֵּשֵׁב בִּדְמֵי טָהֳרָה

her cleansing; the in blood of shall she remain days (and) three days thirty his foreskin.

בְּכָל־קֹדֶשׁ לֹא־תִגָּע וְאֶל־הַמִּקְדָּשׁ לֹא תָבֹא עַד־מְלֹאת

are fulfilled until she go shall not the sanctuary and into shall she not touch holy any thing

5 יְמֵי טָהֳרָהּ׃ וְאִם־נְקֵבָה תֵלֵד וְטָמְאָה שְׁבֻעַיִם כְּנִדָּתָהּ

her menstruation; as two weeks she then unclean be shall she a female bears, if And her cleansing. days the of

6 וְשִׁשִּׁים יוֹם וְשֵׁשֶׁת יָמִים תֵּשֵׁב עַל־דְּמֵי טָהֳרָה׃ וּבִמְלֹאת ׀

when And fulfilled are her cleansing. the in of blood shall she remain days (and) six days and sixty

יְמֵי טָהֳרָהּ לְבֵן אוֹ לְבַת תָּבִיא כֶּבֶשׂ בֶּן־שְׁנָתוֹ לְעֹלָה וּבֶן־

a and young a for offering burnt year a of son a lamb a shall she bring for or daughter, for son, the days the cleansing of

יוֹנָה אוֹ־תֹר לְחַטָּאת אֶל־פֶּתַח אֹהֶל־מוֹעֵד אֶל־הַכֹּהֵן׃

the priest. to meeting, the of tent door the of to sin a for offering, a turtle-dove or dove

7 וְהִקְרִיבוֹ לִפְנֵי יְהוָה וְכִפֶּר עָלֶיהָ וְטָהֲרָה מִמְּקֹר דָּמֶיהָ

her blood. the from of fountain shall she and cleansed be for her, shall and atone Jehovah before shall he And it bring

8 זֹאת תּוֹרַת הַיֹּלֶדֶת לַזָּכָר אוֹ לַנְּקֵבָה׃ וְאִם־לֹא תִמְצָא

able is find to not if And female. a or whether male, a who her bears law the of This (is)

יָדָהּ דֵּי שֶׂה וְלָקְחָה שְׁתֵּי־תֹרִים אוֹ שְׁנֵי בְּנֵי יוֹנָה אֶחָד

one doves, young two or turtle-doves two she then take shall lamb a so much as her hand

לְעֹלָה וְאֶחָד לְחַטָּאת וְכִפֶּר עָלֶיהָ הַכֹּהֵן וְטָהֵרָה׃ פ

shall she and be cleansed. the priest her for shall and atone sin a for offering one and a for offering burnt

CAP. XIII יג

CHAPTER 13

1 [1]And Jehovah spoke to Moses and to Aaron, saying, [2]When a man has a rising in the skin of his flesh, or a scab, or a bright spot, and it shall become in the skin of his flesh the plague of leprosy, then he shall be brought in to Aaron the priest, or to one of his sons the priests. [3]And the priest shall look upon the plague in the skin of the flesh; and if the hair in the plague has turned white, and the appearance of the plague is deeper than the skin of his flesh, it *is* a plague of leprosy, and the priest shall look upon him and shall pronounce him unclean. [4]And if the bright

1
2 וַיְדַבֵּר יְהוָה אֶל־מֹשֶׁה וְאֶל־אַהֲרֹן לֵאמֹר׃ אָדָם כִּי־יִהְיֶה

has When man a saying, Aaron to and Moses to Jehovah And spoke

בְעוֹר־בְּשָׂרוֹ שְׂאֵת אוֹ־סַפַּחַת אוֹ בַהֶרֶת וְהָיָה בְעוֹר־בְּשָׂרוֹ

flesh his the in of skin it and becomes bright a spot or scab, a or a swelling, flesh his the in of skin

לְנֶגַע צָרָעַת וְהוּבָא אֶל־אַהֲרֹן הַכֹּהֵן אוֹ אֶל־אַחַד מִבָּנָיו

his of sons one to or priest, the Aaron to shall he then brought be leprosy, the of plague

3 הַכֹּהֲנִים׃ וְרָאָה הַכֹּהֵן אֶת־הַנֶּגַע בְּעוֹר־הַבָּשָׂר וְשֵׂעָר

if and hair the flesh, the the in of skin plague the priest the shall And look on priests. the

בַּנֶּגַע הָפַךְ לָבָן וּמַרְאֵה הַנֶּגַע עָמֹק מֵעוֹר בְּשָׂרוֹ נֶגַע צָרַעַת

leprosy. (is) it of plague a flesh, his the than of skin is deeper the plague the and look of white has turned the in plague

4 הוּא וְרָאָהוּ הַכֹּהֵן וְטִמֵּא אֹתוֹ׃ וְאִם־בַּהֶרֶת לְבָנָה הִוא

it (is) white bright the spot And if he shall and unclean be. priest the And look shall it (is).

spot *is* white in the skin of his flesh, and its appearance is not deeper than the skin, and its hair has not turned white, then the priest shall shut up the plague seven days. [5]And the priest shall look upon him on the seventh day, and, behold, if the plague stays in its appearance, and the plague has not spread in the skin, then the priest shall shut him up seven more days. [6]And the priest shall look upon him again the seventh day; and, behold, if the plague has become dim, and the plague has not spread in the skin, then the priest shall pronounce him clean; it *is* a scab, and he shall wash his garments and shall be clean. [7]But if the scab spreads greatly in the skin, after he has been seen by the priest for his cleansing, then he shall be seen a second time by the priest. [8]And the priest shall look, and, behold, if the scab has spread in the skin, the priest shall pronounce him unclean; it *is* leprosy.

[9]When the plague of leprosy is in a man, then he shall be brought in to the priest. [10]And the priest shall look, and, behold, if a white rising *is* in the skin, and it has turned the hair white, and a living flesh *is* in the swelling, [11]it *is* an old leprosy in the skin of his flesh, and the priest shall pronounce him unclean; he shall not shut him up, for he *is* unclean. [12]And if the leprosy breaks out greatly on the skin, and the leprosy covers all the skin of *the one who has* the plague, from his head even to his feet, to all that appears to the priest's eyes, [13]then the priest shall look, and behold, if the leprosy has covered all his flesh, he shall pronounce *the one who has* the plague clean; it has all turned white; he *is* clean. [14]And in the day living flesh is seen in him, he is unclean. [15]And the the priest shall look on the

3808
2015 8181 5785 4758 6013 1320 5785
בְּעוֹר בְּשָׂרוֹ וְעָמֹק אֵין־מַרְאֶהָ מִן־הָעוֹר וּשְׂעָרָה לֹא־הָפַךְ
has not turned | its and hair | the than skin | appearance is no | and deeper | ,flesh his | the in of skin

3548 7200 3117 7651 5061 3548 5462 3836
5 לָבָן וְהִסְגִּיר הַכֹּהֵן אֶת־הַנֶּגַע שִׁבְעַת יָמִים׃ וְרָאָהוּ הַכֹּהֵן
the priest | shall And him on look | .days | seven | plague the | the priest | shall then up shut | ,white

5061 6581 3808 5869 5975 5061 2009 7637 3117
בַּיּוֹם הַשְּׁבִיעִי וְהִנֵּה הַנֶּגַע עָמַד בְּעֵינָיו לֹא־פָשָׂה הַנֶּגַע
the plague | has spread | (and) not | his in eyes | has stood | the plague | if ,behold | and seventh the | on ,day

3548 7200 3117 8145 7651 3548 5462 5785
6 בָּעוֹר וְהִסְגִּירוֹ הַכֹּהֵן שִׁבְעַת יָמִים שֵׁנִית׃ וְרָאָה הַכֹּהֵן
the priest | shall And look | .more | days | seven | priest the | shall then up him shut | the in ,skin

6581 5061 3544 2009 8145 7637 3117
אֹתוֹ בַּיּוֹם הַשְּׁבִיעִי שֵׁנִית וְהִנֵּה כֵּהָה הַנֶּגַע וְלֹא־פָשָׂה
has spread | and not | the plague | has become dim | and if ,behold | second .time | the seventh | the in day | upon him

2891 899 3526 4556 3548 2891 5785 5061
הַנֶּגַע בָּעוֹר וְטִהֲרוֹ הַכֹּהֵן מִסְפַּחַת הִוא וְכִבֶּס בְּגָדָיו וְטָהֵר׃
shall and .clean be | his garments | he and wash shall | (is) it ,scab a | the priest | call shall him clean | the in ,skin | the plague

7200 310 5785 4556 6581 6581
7 וְאִם־פָּשֹׂה תִפְשֶׂה הַמִּסְפַּחַת בָּעוֹר אַחֲרֵי הֵרָאֹתוֹ אֶל־
to | has he appeared | after | the in skin | scab the | spreads | greatly if But

3548 7200 3548 8145 7200 2093 3548
8 הַכֹּהֵן לְטָהֳרָתוֹ וְנִרְאָה שֵׁנִית אֶל־הַכֹּהֵן׃ וְרָאָה הַכֹּהֵן
the priest | shall And look | .priest the | to | second a time | shall he then appear | his for ,cleansing | the priest

6883 2930 4556 6581
וְהִנֵּה פָּשְׂתָה הַמִּסְפַּחַת בָּעוֹר וְטִמְּאוֹ הַכֹּהֵן צָרַעַת הִוא׃
(is) it .leprosy | the priest | call shall him unclean | the in skin | scab the | has spread | and if ,behold

3548 7200 3548 935 120 6883 5061
9 נֶגַע צָרַעַת כִּי תִהְיֶה בְּאָדָם וְהוּבָא אֶל־הַכֹּהֵן׃ וְרָאָה הַכֹּהֵן
10
the priest | shall And look | the priest | to | he then brought be shall | ,man a in | is | when leprosy | the of plague

4241 3836 8181 2015 5785 3836 7613 2009
וְהִנֵּה שְׂאֵת־לְבָנָה בָּעוֹר וְהִיא הָפְכָה שֵׂעָר לָבָן וּמִחְיַת
emer- of gence | or ;white | the hair | has turned | it and | in (is) ,skin the | white | a swelling | and ,behold

2930 1320 5785 3462 6883 7613 2416 1320
11 בָּשָׂר חַי בַּשְׂאֵת׃ צָרַעַת נוֹשֶׁנֶת הִוא בְּעוֹר בְּשָׂרוֹ וְטִמְּאוֹ
shall and ;unclean him call | ,flesh his | the in of skin | (is) it | old an | leprosy | the in (is) swelling | raw flesh

6883 6524 6524 2931 5462 3808 3548
12 הַכֹּהֵן לֹא יַסְגִּרֶנּוּ כִּי טָמֵא הוּא׃ וְאִם־פָּרוֹחַ תִּפְרַח הַצָּרַעַת
the leprosy | breaks | greatly if And | .(is) he | unclean for | shall he not ,up him shut | the priest

5704 5785 3605 6883 3680 5785
בָּעוֹר וְכִסְּתָה הַצָּרַעַת אֵת כָּל־עוֹר הַנֶּגַע מֵרֹאשׁוֹ וְעַד־
even to | his from head | ,plagued | skin the all | leprosy the | covers and | the on ,skin

3680 2009 3548 7200 3548 5869 4758 3605 7272
13 רַגְלָיו לְכָל־מַרְאֵה עֵינֵי הַכֹּהֵן׃ וְרָאָה הַכֹּהֵן וְהִנֵּה כִסְּתָה
has if covered | and ,behold | the ,priest | shall then look | the ;priest | the of eyes | appears that | to all | his ,feet

3836 2015 3605 5061 2891 1320 3605 6883
הַצָּרַעַת אֶת־כָּל־בְּשָׂרוֹ וְטִהַר אֶת־הַנֶּגַע כֻּלּוֹ הָפַךְ לָבָן
;white | has turned | all it | the ;plagued | shall he clean call | flesh his | all | the leprosy

7200 2930 2416 1320 7200 3117 2891
14 טָהוֹר הוּא׃ וּבְיוֹם הֵרָאוֹת בּוֹ בָּשָׂר חַי יִטְמָא׃ וְרָאָה
15
shall And on look | is he .unclean | raw | flesh | in him | seen (is) | in And day the | .(is) he | clean

living flesh and shall pronounce him unclean; the
living flesh is unclean; it *is*
leprosy. 16 Or when the
living flesh turns back and
shall be turned to white,
then he shall come in to the
priest; 17 and the priest
shall look on him; and,
behold, the plague has
turned to white; the priest
shall pronounce *the one*
who has the plague clean;
he *is* clean.

18 And when the flesh has
the skin of a boil in it, and it
has been healed, 19 and a
white swelling has replaced
the boil, or a bright white
spot, very red, then it shall
be looked upon by the
priest. 20 And the priest shall
look; and, behold, if its
appearance *is* lower than
the skin, and its hair has
turned white, the priest
shall pronounce him
unclean; it *is* the plague of
leprosy; it has broken out in
a boil. 21 But if the priest
looks at it,; and, behold,
there is no white hair in it,
and it is not lower than the
skin, and has become dim,
then the priest shall shut
him up seven days. 22 And if
it spreads greatly in the
skin, then the priest shall
pronounce him unclean; it
is a plague. 23 And if in its
place the bright spot is
stayed, it has not spread; it
is an inflamed boil, and the
priest shall pronounce him
clean.

24 Or if there is flesh in
which the skin has a hot
burning, and the raw *flesh*
of the burning *becomes* a
bright white spot, being
very red or white; 25 and the
priest shall look on it; and,
behold, the hair has turned
white in the bright spot, and
its appearance is deeper
than the skin, it *is* leprosy. It
has broken out in the burning, and the priest shall
pronounce him unclean; it
is the plague of leprosy.
26 But if the priest looks on
it,, and, behold, there is no

הַכֹּהֵן אֶת־הַבָּשָׂר הַחַי וְטִמְּאוֹ הַבָּשָׂר הַחַי טָמֵא הוּא
16 צָרַעַת הוּא׃ אוֹ כִי יָשׁוּב הַבָּשָׂר הַחַי וְנֶהְפַּךְ לְלָבָן וּבָא
17 אֶל־הַכֹּהֵן׃ וְרָאָהוּ הַכֹּהֵן וְהִנֵּה נֶהְפַּךְ הַנֶּגַע לְלָבָן וְטִהַר
הַכֹּהֵן אֶת־הַנֶּגַע טָהוֹר הוּא׃
18 19 וּבָשָׂר כִּי־יִהְיֶה בוֹ־בְעֹרוֹ שְׁחִין וְנִרְפָּא׃ וְהָיָה בִּמְקוֹם
הַשְּׁחִין שְׂאֵת לְבָנָה אוֹ בַהֶרֶת לְבָנָה אֲדַמְדָּמֶת וְנִרְאָה
20 אֶל־הַכֹּהֵן׃ וְרָאָה הַכֹּהֵן וְהִנֵּה מַרְאֶהָ שָׁפָל מִן־הָעוֹר
וּשְׂעָרָהּ הָפַךְ לָבָן וְטִמְּאוֹ הַכֹּהֵן נֶגַע־צָרַעַת הִוא בַּשְּׁחִין
21 פָּרָחָה׃ וְאִם יִרְאֶנָּה הַכֹּהֵן וְהִנֵּה אֵין־בָּהּ שֵׂעָר לָבָן וּשְׁפָלָה
אֵינֶנָּה מִן־הָעוֹר וְהִיא כֵהָה וְהִסְגִּירוֹ הַכֹּהֵן שִׁבְעַת יָמִים׃
22 23 וְאִם־פָּשֹׂה תִפְשֶׂה בָּעוֹר וְטִמֵּא הַכֹּהֵן אֹתוֹ נֶגַע הִוא׃ וְאִם
תַּחְתֶּיהָ תַּעֲמֹד הַבַּהֶרֶת לֹא פָשָׂתָה צָרֶבֶת הַשְּׁחִין הִוא
24 וְטִהֲרוֹ הַכֹּהֵן׃ אוֹ בָשָׂר כִּי־יִהְיֶה בְעֹרוֹ מִכְוַת־אֵשׁ
וְהָיְתָה מִחְיַת הַמִּכְוָה בַּהֶרֶת לְבָנָה אֲדַמְדֶּמֶת אוֹ לְבָנָה׃
25 וְרָאָה אֹתָהּ הַכֹּהֵן וְהִנֵּה נֶהְפַּךְ שֵׂעָר לָבָן בַּבַּהֶרֶת וּמַרְאֶהָ
עָמֹק מִן־הָעוֹר צָרַעַת הִוא בַּמִּכְוָה פָּרָחָה וְטִמֵּא אֹתוֹ הַכֹּהֵן
26 נֶגַע צָרַעַת הִוא׃ וְאִם יִרְאֶנָּה הַכֹּהֵן וְהִנֵּה אֵין־בַּבַּהֶרֶת

white hair in the bright spot, and it is no lower than the *other* skin, but is somewhat dark, then the priest shall shut him up seven days. [27]And the priest shall look at him the seventh day. And if it is spread abroad very much in the skin, the priest shall pronounce him unclean. It is the plague of leprosy. [28]And if the bright spot stays in its place, and does not spread in the skin, but is somewhat dark, it is a swelling of the burning; and the priest shall pronounce him clean, for it *is* a scar of the burning.

[29]And if a man or a woman has in him a plague in the head or in the beard, [30]then the priest shall look on the plague. And, behold, if its appearance is deeper than the skin, and a thin shining hair in it, the priest shall pronounce him unclean; it *is* a scurf, a leprosy on the head or beard. [31]And when the priest looks on the plague of the scurf; and, behold, it is not in sight deeper than the skin, and there is no black hair in it, then the priest shall shut up *the one who has* the plague of the scurf seven days. [32]And in the seventh day the priest shall look on the plague. And, behold, if the scurf has not spread, and there is no shining hair in it, and the appearance of the scurf is not deeper than the skin, [33]then he shall shave himself, but he shall not shave the scurf. And the priest shall shut up *the one who has* the scurf a second seven days. [34]And the priest shall look on the scurf on the seventh day. And, behold, if the scurf has not spread in the skin, and its appearance is not deeper than the skin, then the priest shall pronounce him clean. And he shall wash his garments, and shall be clean. [35]And if the scurf has spread further in the skin after his cleansing, [36]and

שֵׂעָר לָבָן וּשְׁפָלָה אֵינֶנָּה מִן־הָעוֹר וְהִוא כֵהָה וְהִסְגִּירוֹ
shall then up him shut somewhat colorless it but (is),skin (other) the than no is it and lower ,white hair

27 הַכֹּהֵן שִׁבְעַת יָמִים׃ וְרָאָהוּ הַכֹּהֵן בַּיּוֹם הַשְּׁבִיעִי אִם־
And if .seventh day the the priest shall And him at look .days seven the priest

פָּשֹׂה תִפְשֶׂה בָּעוֹר וְטִמֵּא הַכֹּהֵן אֹתוֹ נֶגַע צָרַעַת הִוא׃
(is) it .leprosy the of plague him the priest call shall ;unclean the in ,skin it spreads farther

28 וְאִם־תַּחְתֶּיהָ תַעֲמֹד הַבַּהֶרֶת לֹא־פָשְׂתָה בָעוֹר וְהִוא כֵהָה
,faded but (is) it the in skin does spread and not bright the ,spot stays its in place if And

שְׂאֵת הַמִּכְוָה הִוא וְטִהֲרוֹ הַכֹּהֵן כִּי־צָרֶבֶת הַמִּכְוָה הִוא׃
.(is) it the burn scar a of for the ,priest shall and ,clean him call ;(is) it the burn the of swelling

29 וְאִישׁ אוֹ אִשָּׁה כִּי־יִהְיֶה בוֹ נֶגַע בְּרֹאשׁ אוֹ בְזָקָן׃ וְרָאָה
30
shall then on look the in ,beard or the in head a plague in him has that a woman or And man a

הַכֹּהֵן אֶת־הַנֶּגַע וְהִנֵּה מַרְאֵהוּ עָמֹק מִן־הָעוֹר וּבוֹ שֵׂעָר
hair a and it in the ,skin than is deeper its appearance if ,behold and the ,plague the priest

צָהֹב דַּק וְטִמֵּא אֹתוֹ הַכֹּהֵן נֶתֶק הוּא צָרַעַת הָרֹאשׁ אוֹ
or the head leprosy a on ,(is) it the scurf the priest him call shall ;unclean ,thin shining yellow

31 הַזָּקָן הוּא׃ וְכִי־יִרְאֶה הַכֹּהֵן אֶת־נֶגַע הַנֶּתֶק וְהִנֵּה אֵין
is no and ,behold the ,scurf the of plague the priest on looks And when it (is) beard

מַרְאֵהוּ עָמֹק מִן־הָעוֹר וְשֵׂעָר שָׁחֹר אֵין בּוֹ וְהִסְגִּיר הַכֹּהֵן
the priest shall then up shut in ,it there no is black and hair the ,skin than deeper appear- ance ,it of

32 אֶת־נֶגַע הַנֶּתֶק שִׁבְעַת יָמִים׃ וְרָאָה הַכֹּהֵן אֶת־הַנֶּגַע בַּיּוֹם
the on day the plague the priest shall And on look .days seven the (has who him) of plague the scurf

הַשְּׁבִיעִי וְהִנֵּה לֹא־פָשָׂה הַנֶּתֶק וְלֹא־הָיָה בוֹ שֵׂעָר צָהֹב
,shining yellow hair it in there is no and the scurf has spread if not and ,behold ;seventh

33 וּמַרְאֵה הַנֶּתֶק אֵין עָמֹק מִן־הָעוֹר׃ וְהִתְגַּלָּח וְאֶת־הַנֶּתֶק
the scurf but shall he then himself shave the ,skin than deeper is not the scurf the and of look

לֹא יְגַלֵּחַ וְהִסְגִּיר הַכֹּהֵן אֶת־הַנֶּתֶק שִׁבְעַת יָמִים שֵׁנִית׃
a second days seven (has who him) scurf the the priest shall and up shut shall he shave not

34 וְרָאָה הַכֹּהֵן אֶת־הַנֶּתֶק בַּיּוֹם הַשְּׁבִיעִי וְהִנֵּה לֹא־פָשָׂה
has spread not if and ,behold ,seventh the on day scurf the the priest shall And on look

הַנֶּתֶק בָּעוֹר וּמַרְאֵהוּ אֵינֶנּוּ עָמֹק מִן־הָעוֹר וְטִהַר אֹתוֹ
him call shall clean the ,skin than deeper not is its and appearance the in ,skin the scurf

35 הַכֹּהֵן וְכִבֶּס בְּגָדָיו וְטָהֵר׃ וְאִם־פָּשֹׂה יִפְשֶׂה הַנֶּתֶק בָּעוֹר
the in skin the scurf spread has further And if be and .clean his garments he and wash shall the ;priest

the priest has looked on him; and, lo, the scurf has spread on the skin, the priest shall not seek for the shining yellow hair; he is unclean. [37]But if in his eyes the scurf has stabilized, and black hair has sprung up in it, the scurf has been healed; he *is* clean. And the priest shall call him clean. [38]And when a man or a woman has bright spots, white bright spots, in the skin, [39]and the priest has seen it; and, behold, there are pale white bright spots in the skin of their flesh; it *is* a pale spot springing up in the skin; he *is* clean.

[40]And when a man's head grows bald; he *is* bald; he *is* clean. [41]And if his head grows bald from the edge of his face, his head grows bald; he *is* forehead bald; he *is* clean. [42]And if there is in the bald head or the bald forehead, a reddish-white plague, it *is* a leprosy breaking out in his bald head, or in his bald forehead. [43]And the priest shall look on him. And, behold, *if* the swelling of the plague is reddish-white in his bald head, or in his bald forehead, as the appearance of leprosy in the skin of the flesh, [44]he *is* a leprous man; he *is* unclean. The priest calling shall call him unclean; his plague *is* in his head.

[45]And the leper who *has* the plague in him, his garments shall be torn, and his head shall be uncovered, and he shall cover on the upper lip. And he shall call out Unclean! Unclean! [46]And the days that the plague *shall be* in him, he *is* unclean; he shall live alone; he is uclean; he shall live outside the camp.

[47]And if there is in any garment a plague of leprosy; in a wool garment, or in a linen garment, [48]or in the warp, or in the woof or of linen, or of wool, or in leather, or in a

5785 5424 6581 2009 3548 7200 2893 310
36 אחרי טהרתו: וראהו הכהן והנה פשה הנתק בעור
the in the has and the shall and his after
skin scurf spread ,behold priest him on look ! ;cleansing

5869 2931 6669 8181 3548 1239 3808
37 לא־יבקר הכהן לשער הצהב טמא הוא: ואם־בעיניו
his in And .(is) he unclean shining the for the shall not
eyes if ;yellow hair priest seek

2889 5424 7495 3779 7838 8181 5424 5975
עמד הנתק ושער שחר צמח־בו נרפא הנתק טהור הוא
he clean the been has ,it in has black and the has
;(is) ;scurf healed up sprung hair ,scurf stayed

1320 5785 1961 802 376 3548 2891
38 וטהרו הכהן: ס ואיש או־אשה כי־יהיה בעור־בשרם
their the in has when a or a And .priest the shall and
flesh of skin woman man .clean him call

1320 5785 2009 3548 7200 3836 934 934
39 בהרת בהרת לבנת: וראה הכהן והנה בעור־בשרם
their the in and the has and ,white bright bright
flesh of skin ,behold ,priest it on looked spots spots

2889 6524 933 3836 3544 934
בהרת כהות לבנת בהק הוא פרח בעור טהור הוא: ס
.(is) he clean the in springing it pale a ,white pale (are there)
;skin up (is) spot spots bright

6285 2889 7142 7218 4803 3588 376
40 ואיש כי ימרט ראשו קרח הוא טהור הוא: ואם מפאת
41
the from And .(is) he clean ,(is) he bald his grows when a And
of edge if head bald man

7742 1961 2889 1371 7218 4803 6440
42 פניו ימרט ראשו גבח הוא טהור הוא: וכי־יהיה בקרחת
the in there And .(is) he clean he forehead his grows
head bald is if ;(is) bald ,head bald ,face his

7142 6542 6883 125 3836 5061 1372
או בגבחת נגע לבן אדמדם צרעת פרחת הוא בקרחתו
his in (is) it breaking a ,reddish-white a bald the or
head bald out leprosy plague ,forehead

3836 5061 7613 2009 3548 7200 1372
43 או בגבחתו: וראה אתו הכהן והנה שאת־הנגע לבנה
(is) the the (if) and the him shall And his in or
white plague of swelling ,behold, priest see forehead bald

1320 6883 4758 1372 7142 125
אדמדמת בקרחתו או בגבחתו כמראה צרעת עור בשר:
the the in ,leprosy the as bald his in or bald his in reddish
flesh of skin of appearance ,forehead head

7218 3548 2930 2930 2931 6879 376
44 איש־צרוע הוא טמא הוא טמא יטמאנו הכהן בראשו
his in the him call shall utterly he unclean he leprous man a
head ;priest unclean ;(is) ;(is)

7218 6533 1961 899 5061 834 6879 5061
45 נגעו: והצרוע אשר־בו הנגע בגדיו יהיו פרמים וראשו
his and ,torn shall his the in who the And his (is)
head be garments ,plague him (has) leper .plague

31 3605 7121 2931 2931 5844 8222 6544 1961
46 יהיה פרוע ועל־שפם יעטה וטמא טמא יקרא: כל־ימי
the All shall he !Unclean and shall he the on and ;loose shall
days .out call !Unclean cover lip upper be

4264 2351 3427 910 2931 2930 5061
אשר הנגע בו יטמא טמא הוא בדד ישב מחוץ למחנה
the outside he ;alone .(is) he unclean is he in (is) the that
camp live shall ;unclean him plague

6785 899 6883 5061 1961 899 4186
47 מושבו: ס והבגד כי־יהיה בו נגע צרעת בבגד צמר
,wool a in ,leprosy a in there if any And his (be shall)
of garment of plague it is garment .dwelling

6785 6593 6154 8359 6593 899
48 או בבגד פשתים: או בשתי או בערב לפשתים ולצמר
of or of or the in or the in or ,linen a in or
,wool ,linen ,woof warp of garment

work of leather. [49]And if the plague is greenish or reddish in the garment, or in the leather, or in the warp, or in the woof, or in anything of leather, it *is* a plague of leprosy; and it shall be shown to the priest. [50]And the priest shall look on the plague, and shall shut up *that which has* the plague seven days. [51]And he shall look on the plague on the seventh day. And if the plague has spread in the garment, or in the warp, or in the woof, or in the leather, of all that is made of skin for use, the plague is a corroding leprosy; it *is* unclean. [52]And he shall burn the garment, or the warp, or the woof, in wool or in linen, or anything of leather, in which the plague is; for it *is* a corroding leprosy; it shall be burned with fire. [53]And if the priest shall look, and, behold, the plague has not spread in the garment, or in the warp, or in the woof, or in anything of leather, [54]then the priest shall command, and they shall wash that in which the plague *is*. And he shall shut it up a second seven days.

[55]And the priest shall look on *that which has* the plague after it has been washed. And, behold, if the plague has not changed its appearance, and if the plague has not spread, it *is* unclean; you shall burn it with fire; it *is* eaten away in its inside or in its outside. [56]And if the priest shall look, and, behold, the plague has become pale after it has been washed, then he shall tear it out of the garment, or out of the leather, or out of the warp, or out of the woof. [57]And if it is still seen in the garment, or in the warp, or in the woof, or in anything

176 3422 5061 5785 4399 3605 5785
49 אוֹ בְעוֹר אוֹ בְּכָל־מְלֶאכֶת עוֹר׃ וְהָיָה הַנֶּגַע יְרַקְרַק | אוֹ
or greenish the if and ,leather work in or ,in or
plague is of any leather

3627 3605 6154 8359 5785 899 125
אֲדַמְדָּם בַּבֶּגֶד אוֹ בָעוֹר אוֹ־בַשְּׁתִי אוֹ־בָעֵרֶב אוֹ בְכָל־כְּלִי־
thing in or the in or the in or the in or the in reddish
of any ,woof ,warp ,skin ,garment

3548 7200 3548 7200 6883 5061 5785
50 עוֹר נֶגַע צָרַעַת הוּא וְהָרְאָה אֶת־הַכֹּהֵן׃ וְרָאָה הַכֹּהֵן אֶת־
the shall And the shall it and ;(is) it leprosy a ,leather
priest on look .priest to shown be of plague

5061 7200 3117 7651 5061 5462 5061
51 הַנֶּגַע וְהִסְגִּיר אֶת־הַנֶּגַע שִׁבְעַת יָמִים׃ וְרָאָה אֶת־הַנֶּגַע
plague the he And .days seven (has which that) shut and the
on look shall plague the up ,plague

6154 8359 899 5061 6581 7637 3117
בַּיּוֹם הַשְּׁבִיעִי כִּי־פָשָׂה הַנֶּגַע בַּבֶּגֶד אוֹ־בַשְּׁתִי אוֹ־בָעֵרֶב
the in or the in or the in the has and ,seventh the on
woof warp ,garment plague spread if 3605 day

3992 6883 4399 5785 6213 5785
אוֹ בָעוֹר לְכֹל אֲשֶׁר־יֵעָשֶׂה הָעוֹר לִמְלָאכָה צָרַעַת מַמְאֶרֶת
an a (is) for leather made is that all of lea- or
of eruption leprosy ;use of ,ther

8359 899 8313 2931 5061
52 הַנֶּגַע טָמֵא הוּא׃ וְשָׂרַף אֶת־הַבֶּגֶד אוֹ אֶת־הַשְּׁתִי | אוֹ אֶת־
or ,warp the or the he And .(is) it unclean the
,garment burn shall (is) plague

834 5785 3627 3605 6593 6785 6154
הָעֵרֶב בַּצֶּמֶר אוֹ בַפִּשְׁתִּים אוֹ אֶת־כָּל־כְּלִי הָעוֹר אֲשֶׁר־
which leather thing any or ,linen in or ,wool in the
of ,woof

8313 784 3992 6883 5061
53 יִהְיֶה בוֹ הַנֶּגַע כִּי־צָרַעַת מַמְאֶרֶת הִוא בָּאֵשׁ תִּשָּׂרֵף׃ וְאִם
And be shall it with ;(is) it an a for the in is
if burned .fire eruption ,leprosy ;plague it

176 8359 899 5061 6581 3808 2009 3548 7200
יִרְאֶה הַכֹּהֵן וְהִנֵּה לֹא־פָשָׂה הַנֶּגַע בַּבֶּגֶד אוֹ בַשְּׁתִי אוֹ
or the in or the in the has not and the shall
,warp garment plague spread ,behold ,priest look

834 3526 3548 6680 5785 3627 3605 6154
54 בָעֵרֶב אוֹ בְּכָל־כְּלִי־עוֹר׃ וְצִוָּה הַכֹּהֵן וְכִבְּסוּ אֵת אֲשֶׁר־
that they and the shall then lea- thing in or the in
which wash shall ,priest command ,ther of any ,woof

310 3548 7200 8145 3117 7651 5462 5061
55 בּוֹ הַנֶּגַע וְהִסְגִּירוֹ שִׁבְעַת־יָמִים שֵׁנִית׃ וְרָאָה הַכֹּהֵן אַחֲרֵי
after the shall And a days seven shall he and the (is) it in
priest on look .second up it shut ,plague

3808 5061 5869 5061 2015 2009 5061 3526
הֻכַּבֵּס אֶת־הַנֶּגַע וְהִנֵּה לֹא־הָפַךְ הַנֶּגַע אֶת־עֵינוֹ וְהַנֶּגַע לֹא־
not if and its the has if ,lo and (having that) its
plague the ,appearance plague changed not ;plague the ,washing

7142 6356 8313 784 2931 6581
פָשָׂה טָמֵא הוּא בָּאֵשׁ תִּשְׂרְפֶנּוּ פְּחֶתֶת הִוא בְּקָרַחְתּוֹ אוֹ
or its on (is) it eaten shall you with ;(is) it unclean has
inside away it burn fire ,spread

3526 310 5061 1961 2009 3548 7200 518 1372
56 בְגַבַּחְתּוֹ׃ וְאִם רָאָה הַכֹּהֵן וְהִנֵּה כֵּהָה הַנֶּגַע אַחֲרֵי הֻכַּבֵּס
been has after the be- has and the shall if And its in
washed plague pale come ,behold ,priest look .outside

8359 4481 5785 4481 899 4481 7167
אֹתוֹ וְקָרַע אֹתוֹ מִן־הַבֶּגֶד אוֹ מִן־הָעוֹר אוֹ מִן־הַשְּׁתִי אוֹ
or the out or the out or the out it he then it
,warp of ,leather of ,of garment of ,tear shall

6154 8359 899 5750 7200 6154 4481
57 מִן־הָעֵרֶב׃ וְאִם־תֵּרָאֶה עוֹד בַּבֶּגֶד אוֹ־בַשְּׁתִי אוֹ־בָעֵרֶב
the in or the in or the in still is it if and the of out
,woof ,warp ,garment seen ;woof

of leather, it *is* a spreading *plague;* you shall burn it with fire, that in which the plague *is.* [58]And the garment, or the warp, or the woof, or anything of leather which you shall wash when the plague has been taken off them, then it shall be washed a second time, and shall be clean.

[59]This is the law of the plague of leprosy *in* a garment of wool or of linen, or of the warp, or of the woof, or of anything of leather, to pronounce it clean, or to pronounce it unclean.

834 8313 784 6524 5750 3627 3605
אוֹ בְכָל־כְּלִי־עוֹר פֹּרַחַת הִוא בָּאֵשׁ תִּשְׂרְפֶנּוּ אֵת אֲשֶׁר־
that which | shall you burn ;it | with fire | ;(is) it spreading a (plague) | leather | thing in of any | or

5785 3627 3605 6154 8359 899 5061
58 כּוֹ הַנָּגַע׃ וְהַבֶּגֶד אוֹ־הַשְּׁתִי אוֹ־הָעֵרֶב אוֹ־כָל־כְּלִי הָעוֹר
leather | thing of | any | or | the ,woof | or | the warp | or | the And garment | .(is) the plague | in it

2088 2891 8145 3526 5061 5493 3526 834
59 אֲשֶׁר תְּכַבֵּס וְסָר מֵהֶם הַנָּגַע וְכֻבַּס שֵׁנִית וְטָהֵר׃ זֹאת
This (is) | shall and .clean be | second a time | it then washed be shall | ,plague the | off them | has when taken been | shall you ,wash | which

8359 6593 6785 899 6883 8451
תּוֹרַת נֶגַע־צָרַעַת בֶּגֶד הַצֶּמֶר ׀ אוֹ הַפִּשְׁתִּים אוֹ הַשְּׁתִי אוֹ
or | the of ,warp | or | ,linen of | or | ,wool of garment | a (in) leprosy of plague | the law the of

2930 2889 5785 3627 3605 6154
הָעֵרֶב אוֹ כָּל־כְּלִי־עוֹר לְטַהֲרוֹ אוֹ לְטַמְּאוֹ׃
call to .unclean it | or | call to clean it | lea- ;ther | thing of any | or | the of ,woof

CAP. XIV יד

CHAPTER 14

[1]And Jehovah spoke to Moses, saying, [2]This shall be the law of the leper in the day of his cleansing, that he shall be brought to the priest. [3]And the priest shall go out to the outside of the camp. And the priest shall look; and, behold, if the plague of leprosy is healed in the leper, [4]then the priest shall command, and he shall take for him who is to be cleansed two clean living birds, and cedar wood, and scarlet, and hyssop. [5]And the priest shall command, and he shall kill the one bird on an earthen vessel, over running water; [6]he shall take the living bird, and the cedar wood, and the scarlet, and the hyssop, and shall dip them and the living bird in the blood of the slain bird, over the running water. [7]And he shall sprinkle on him who is to be cleansed from the leprosy seven times, and shall pronounce him clean. And he shall send out the living bird into the open field. [8]And he who is to be cleansed shall wash his garments, and shall shave all his hair, and shall bathe with water, and shall be

6879 8451 1961 2088 559 4872 3068 1696
1
2 וַיְדַבֵּר יְהוָה אֶל־מֹשֶׁה לֵּאמֹר׃ זֹאת תִּהְיֶה תּוֹרַת הַמְּצֹרָע
,leper the | the of law | be shall | This | ,saying | ,Moses | to Jehovah | And spoke

2351 3588 5927 3548 935 2893 3117
3 בְּיוֹם טָהֳרָתוֹ וְהוּבָא אֶל־הַכֹּהֵן׃ וְיָצָא הַכֹּהֵן אֶל־מִחוּץ
the outside | to | the priest | shall and out go | the ,priest | to | shall he that brought be | his cleansing | the in of day

6879 6883 5061 7495 2009 3548 7200 4264
לַמַּחֲנֶה וְרָאָה הַכֹּהֵן וְהִנֵּה נִרְפָּא נֶגַע־הַצָּרַעַת מִן־הַצָּרוּעַ׃
the ;leper | in | leprosy of plague | the healed | is if | and behold | the ,priest | shall and look | the of ,camp

2889 2416 6833 8147 2891 3947 3548 6680
4 וְצִוָּה הַכֹּהֵן וְלָקַח לַמִּטַּהֵר שְׁתֵּי־צִפֳּרִים חַיּוֹת טְהֹרוֹת
,clean | living | birds | two | who him for cleansed be to is | he and take shall | ,priest the | then direct shall

7919 3548 6680 231 8438 8144 730 6086
5 וְעֵץ אֶרֶז וּשְׁנִי תוֹלַעַת וְאֵזֹב׃ וְצִוָּה הַכֹּהֵן וְשָׁחַט אֶת־
he and kill shall | the priest | shall And command | and .hyssop | the (dye) | and scarlet | ,cedar | and wood

6833 2416 4325 2789 3627 259 6833
6 הַצִּפּוֹר הָאֶחָת אֶל־כְּלִי־חֶרֶשׂ עַל־מַיִם חַיִּים׃ אֶת־הַצִּפֹּר
bird the | ;running | water over | an earthen | vessel upon | one the | bird

8438 8144 730 6086 3947 2416
הַחַיָּה יִקַּח אֹתָהּ וְאֶת־עֵץ הָאֶרֶז וְאֶת־שְׁנִי הַתּוֹלַעַת וְאֶת
and | scarlet the (dye) | and | the cedar | wood and | ,(it) | shall he take | living

7919 1818 2416 6833 2881 231
הָאֵזֹב וְטָבַל אוֹתָם וְאֵת ׀ הַצִּפֹּר הַחַיָּה בְּדַם הַצִּפֹּר הַשְּׁחֻטָה
,slaughtered | the bird | the in of blood | living | bird the | and | them | shall and dip | the hyssop

7651 6879 2891 5137 2416 4325
7 עַל הַמַּיִם הַחַיִּים׃ וְהִזָּה עַל הַמִּטַּהֵר מִן־הַצָּרַעַת שֶׁבַע
seven | the leprosy | from | is who him cleansed be to | on | he And sprinkle shall | .running | the water | over

7704 6440 2416 6833 7971 2889 6471
פְּעָמִים וְטִהֲרוֹ וְשִׁלַּח אֶת־הַצִּפֹּר הַחַיָּה עַל־פְּנֵי הַשָּׂדֶה׃
.field the | open | into | living | bird the | he and out send shall | shall and ;clean him call | ,times

4325 7364 8181 3605 1548 899 2891 3526
8 וְכִבֶּס הַמִּטַּהֵר אֶת־בְּגָדָיו וְגִלַּח אֶת־כָּל־שְׂעָרוֹ וְרָחַץ בַּמַּיִם
with ,water | shall and bathe | ,hair his | all | and shave shall | his ,garment | to one the cleansed be | shall And wash

clean. And afterwards he shall come into the camp, and shall live on the outside of his tent seven days. [9]And it shall be on the seventh day, he shall shave all his hair, his head, and his beard, and his eyebrows; he shall even shave all his hair. And he shall wash his garments, and shall bathe his flesh with water, and shall be clean.

[10]And on the eighth day he shall take two male lambs, perfect ones, and one ewe lamb, daughter of a year, a perfect one, and three-tenth parts of flour *for* a food offering, mixed with oil, and one log of oil.

[11]And the priest who is cleansing the man who is to be cleansed shall stand with them before Jehovah, at the door of the tabernacle of the congregation. [12]And the priest shall take the one male lamb and shall bring it near for a guilt offering, and the log of oil, and shall wave them *as* a wave offering before Jehovah. [13]And he shall kill the lamb in the place where he killed the sin offering and the burnt offering, in the holy place. For like the sin offering, the guilt offering belongs to the priest; it *is* most holy. [14]And the priest shall take of the blood of the guilt offering; and the priest shall put on the tip of the right ear of him who is to be cleansed, and on the thumb of his right hand, and on the big toe of his right foot; [15]and the priest shall take of the log of oil and shall pour on the left palm of the priest. [16]And the priest shall dip his right finger in the oil that *is* on his left palm and shall sprinkle of the oil with his finger seven times before Jehovah. [17]And of the rest of the oil

וְטָהֵר וְאַחַר יָבוֹא אֶל־הַמַּחֲנֶה וְיָשַׁב מִחוּץ לְאָהֳלוֹ שִׁבְעַת
9 יָמִים׃ וְהָיָה בַיּוֹם הַשְּׁבִיעִי יְגַלַּח אֶת־כָּל־שְׂעָרוֹ אֶת־רֹאשׁוֹ
וְאֶת־זְקָנוֹ וְאֵת גַּבֹּת עֵינָיו וְאֶת־כָּל־שְׂעָרוֹ יְגַלֵּחַ וְכִבֶּס אֶת־
10 בְּגָדָיו וְרָחַץ אֶת־בְּשָׂרוֹ בַּמַּיִם וְטָהֵר׃ וּבַיּוֹם הַשְּׁמִינִי יִקַּח
שְׁנֵי־כְבָשִׂים תְּמִימִם וְכַבְשָׂה אַחַת בַּת־שְׁנָתָהּ תְּמִימָה
וּשְׁלֹשָׁה עֶשְׂרֹנִים סֹלֶת מִנְחָה בְּלוּלָה בַשֶּׁמֶן וְלֹג אֶחָד
11 שָׁמֶן׃ וְהֶעֱמִיד הַכֹּהֵן הַמְטַהֵר אֵת הָאִישׁ הַמִּטַּהֵר וְאֹתָם
12 לִפְנֵי יְהוָה פֶּתַח אֹהֶל מוֹעֵד׃ וְלָקַח הַכֹּהֵן אֶת־הַכֶּבֶשׂ
הָאֶחָד וְהִקְרִיב אֹתוֹ לְאָשָׁם וְאֶת־לֹג הַשָּׁמֶן וְהֵנִיף אֹתָם
13 תְּנוּפָה לִפְנֵי יְהוָה׃ וְשָׁחַט אֶת־הַכֶּבֶשׂ בִּמְקוֹם אֲשֶׁר
יִשְׁחַט אֶת־הַחַטָּאת וְאֶת־הָעֹלָה בִּמְקוֹם הַקֹּדֶשׁ כִּי כַּחַטָּאת
14 הָאָשָׁם הוּא לַכֹּהֵן קֹדֶשׁ קָדָשִׁים הוּא׃ וְלָקַח הַכֹּהֵן מִדַּם
הָאָשָׁם וְנָתַן הַכֹּהֵן עַל־תְּנוּךְ אֹזֶן הַמִּטַּהֵר הַיְמָנִית וְעַל־
15 בֹּהֶן יָדוֹ הַיְמָנִית וְעַל־בֹּהֶן רַגְלוֹ הַיְמָנִית׃ וְלָקַח הַכֹּהֵן
16 מִלֹּג הַשָּׁמֶן וְיָצַק עַל־כַּף הַכֹּהֵן הַשְּׂמָאלִית׃ וְטָבַל הַכֹּהֵן
אֶת־אֶצְבָּעוֹ הַיְמָנִית מִן־הַשֶּׁמֶן אֲשֶׁר עַל־כַּפּוֹ הַשְּׂמָאלִית
17 וְהִזָּה מִן־הַשֶּׁמֶן בְּאֶצְבָּעוֹ שֶׁבַע פְּעָמִים לִפְנֵי יְהוָה׃ וּמִיֶּתֶר

which *is* on his palm, the priest shall put on the tip of the right ear of him who is to be cleansed, and on the thumb of his right hand, and on the big toe of his right foot, on the blood of the guilt offering; [18]and the rest of the oil which *is* on the palm of the priest, he shall put on the head of him who is to be cleansed. And the priest shall make atonement for him before Jehovah. [19]And the priest shall make a sin offering, and shall make atonement for him who is to be cleansed from his uncleanness. And afterwards he shall slaughter the burnt offering; [20]and the priest shall offer the burnt offering, and the food offering, on the altar; and the priest shall make atonement for him; and he shall be clean.

[21]And if he *is* poor, and his hand is not able to reach *these things*, then he shall take one lamb *as* a guilt offering, for a wave offering, to make atonement for himself, and one-tenth part of flour mixed with oil for a food offering, and a log of oil, [22]and two turtle-doves, or two young doves, which he is able to afford; and one shall be a sin offering, and the other a burnt offering. [23]And he shall bring them in to the priest on the eighth day for his cleansing, to the door of the tabernacle of the congregation, before Jehovah. [24]And the priest shall take the lamb of the guilt offering, and the log of oil, and the priest shall wave them *as* a wave offering before Jehovah; [25]and he shall kill the lamb of the guilt offering; and the priest shall take of the blood of the guilt offering, and *he* shall put on the tip of the right ear of him who is to be cleansed, and on the thumb of his right hand, and on the big toe of his right foot. [26]And the priest shall pour the oil on the left palm of the priest; [27]and the priest shall sprinkle with his right finger of the oil which *is* on

2891 241 8571 3548 5414 3409 834 8081
השמן אשר על־כפו יתן הכהן על־תנוך אזן המטהר
is who him ear the on the shall his on which oil the
cleansed be to of of tip priest put ,palm (is)

5921 3233 7272 931 5921 3233 3027 931 3233
הימנית ועל־בהן ידו הימנית ועל־בהן רגלו הימנית על
on the his great on and the his thumb and the
,right foot of toe ,right hand of on ,right

5921 5414 3548 3709 834 8081 3498 816 1818
18 דם האשם: והנותר בשמן אשר על־כף הכהן יתן על־
on he the the on which the of the and guilt the the
put shall ,priest of palm (is) oil rest ;offering of blood

3548 6213 3068 6440 3548 3722 2891 7218
19 ראש המטהר וכפר עליו הכהן לפני יהוה: ועשה הכהן
the shall And .Jehovah before the for shall and is who him the
priest make priest him atone ;cleansed be to of head

7919 310 2932 2891 3722 2403
את־החטאת וכפר על־המטהר מטמאתו ואחר ישחט
shall he and his from is who him for shall and sin a
slaughter later ;uncleanness cleansed be to atone offering

4196 4503 5930 3548 5927 5930
20 את־העלה: והעלה הכהן את־העלה ואת־המנחה המזבחה
the on food the and burnt the the shall and burnt the
;altar ,offering ,offering priest offer ;offering

3027 369 1800 2891 3548 3722
21 וכפר עליו הכהן וטהר: ס ואם־דל הוא ואין ידו
his and he poor if And shall he and the for shall and
hand not ,(is) .clean be ;priest him atone

6241 3722 8573 816 259 3532 3947
משגת ולקח כבש אחד אשם לתנופה לכפר עליו ועשרון
tenth and for to wave a for a (as) one lamb he then can
of part himself atone offering ,offering guilt take shall ,reach

8449 8147 8081 3849 4503 8081 1101 259 5560
22 סלת אחד בלול בשמן למנחה ולג שמן: ושתי תרים
turtle- and ,oil a and food a for with mixed one flour
,doves two of log ,offering oil

259 2403 259 1961 834 3128 1121 8147 176
או שני בני יונה אשר תשיג ידו והיה אחד חטאת והאחד
the and sin a one and his can which a sons two or
other ,offering be shall ;hand reach ,dove of

3548 2893 8066 3117 935 5930
23 עלה: והביא אתם ביום השמיני לטהרתו אל־הכהן
the to his for eighth the on them shall he and burnt a
,priest cleansing day in bring ;offering

3532 3548 3947 3068 6440 4150 168 6607
24 אל־פתח אהל־מועד לפני יהוה: ולקח הכהן את־כבש
lamb the the shall And .Jehovah before meeting the the to
of priest take of tent of door

6440 8573 3548 5130 8081 3849 816
האשם ואת־לג השמן והניף אתם הכהן תנופה לפני
before a (as) the them shall and ,oil the of log and guilt the
offering wave priest wave ,offering

816 1818 3947 816 3532 7919 3068
25 יהוה: ושחט את־כבש האשם ולקח הכהן מדם האשם
guilt the the of the shall and guilt the lamb the he and ;Jehovah
offering of blood priest take ;offering of kill shall

3233 3027 931 3233 2891 241 8571 5414
ונתן על־תנוך און־המטהר הימנית ועל־בהן ידו הימנית
the his thumb and the is who him ear tip the on and
right hand of on ,right cleansed be to of of put shall

3709 3548 3332 8081 3233 7272 931 5921
26 ועל־בהן רגלו הימנית: ומן־השמן יצק הכהן על־כף
palm on the shall oil the and the his great and
of priest pour of ;right foot of toe on

8081 3233 676 3548 5137 8042 3548
27 הכהן השמאלית: והזה הכהן באצבעו הימנית מן־השמן
oil the of right his with the and ;left the the
finger priest sprinkle shall priest

his left palm, seven times before Jehovah. 28 And the priest shall put of the oil which *is* on his palm on the tip of the right ear of him who is to be cleansed, and on the thumb of the right hand, and on the big toe of his right foot, on the place of the blood of the guilt offering. 29 And the rest of the oil which is on the priest's palm he shall put on the head of him who is to be cleansed, to make atonement for him, before Jehovah. 30 And he shall offer one of the turtle-doves, or of the young doves, from that which he is able to reach; 31 that which his hand has reached out to, the one a sin offering, and the other a burnt offering, besides the food offering. And the priest shall make atonement for him who is to be cleansed before Jehovah. 32 This *is* the law of him in whom *is* a plague of leprosy whose hand could not reach to his cleansing.

33 And Jehovah spoke to Moses and to Aaron, saying, 34 When you come into the land of Canaan, which I am giving to you for a possession, and I have put a plague of leprosy in the house *in* the land of your possession; 35 then *if* he who owns the house shall come in and declare to the priest, saying, *I have* seen a plague in the house. 36 And the priest shall command, and they shall turn out the house before the priest comes in to see the plague, that all in the house may not be unclean; and afterwards the priest shall come in to see the house. 37 And he shall look upon the plague; and, behold, if the plague *is* in the walls of the house with depressions, greenish or reddish, and the appearance of it is lower than the wall; 38 then the priest shall

5414 3068 6440 6471 7651 8042 3208 5921 834
28 אֲשֶׁר עַל־כַּפּוֹ הַשְּׂמָאלִית שֶׁבַע פְּעָמִים לִפְנֵי יְהוָה׃ וְנָתַן
And .Jehovah before times seven ,left his on which
put shall palm (is)

2891 241 8571 3709 834 8081 3548
הַכֹּהֵן מִן־הַשֶּׁמֶן אֲשֶׁר עַל־כַּפּוֹ עַל־תְּנוּךְ אֹזֶן הַמִּטַּהֵר
to is who his ear tip the on his on which oil the of the
cleansed be of palm (is) priest

3233 7272 931 3233 931 5921 3233
הַיְמָנִית וְעַל־בֹּהֶן יָדוֹ הַיְמָנִית וְעַל־בֹּהֶן רַגְלוֹ הַיְמָנִית עַל־
on the his great and the his thumb and the
,right foot of toe on ,right hand of on ,right

3548 3709 5921 834 8081 3498 816 1818 4725
29 מְקוֹם דַּם הָאָשָׁם׃ וְהַנּוֹתָר מִן־הַשֶּׁמֶן אֲשֶׁר עַל־כַּף הַכֹּהֵן
the palm on which oil the of the and guilt the the place the
priest's (is) rest ;offering of blood of

6213 3068 6440 3722 2891 7218 5921 5414
30 יִתֵּן עַל־רֹאשׁ הַמִּטַּהֵר לְכַפֵּר עָלָיו לִפְנֵי יְהוָה׃ וְעָשָׂה
he And .Jehovah before for to is who him head the on he
offer shall ,him atone cleansed be to of put shall

3027 5381 834 3128 1121 176 8449 259
אֶת־הָאֶחָד מִן־הַתֹּרִים אוֹ מִן־בְּנֵי הַיּוֹנָה מֵאֲשֶׁר תַּשִּׂיג יָדוֹ׃
his can that from the the or the of one
;hand reach which ,doves of sons ,turtledoves

5930 259 2403 259 3027 5381 834
31 אֵת אֲשֶׁר־תַּשִּׂיג יָדוֹ אֶת־הָאֶחָד חַטָּאת וְאֶת־הָאֶחָד עֹלָה
burnt a the and sin a one the his has which that
,offering other ,offering ,hand to reached

8451 2088 3068 6440 2891 3548 3722 4503
32 עַל־הַמִּנְחָה וְכִפֶּר הַכֹּהֵן עַל הַמִּטַּהֵר לִפְנֵי יְהוָה׃ זֹאת תּוֹרַת
law the This .Jehovah before is who him for the shall and food the be-
of (is) cleansed be to priest atone ;offering sides

2893 3027 5381 3808 834 6883 5061
אֲשֶׁר־בּוֹ נֶגַע צָרָעַת אֲשֶׁר לֹא־תַשִּׂיג יָדוֹ בְּטָהֳרָתוֹ׃ פ
his in his could not which ,leprosy a in which
cleansing hand reach of plague him (is)

935 559 175 4872 3068 1696
33 וַיְדַבֵּר יְהוָה אֶל־מֹשֶׁה וְאֶל־אַהֲרֹן לֵאמֹר׃ כִּי תָבֹאוּ אֶל־
34
into you When ,saying ,Aaron to and Moses to Jehovah And
come spoke

6883 5061 5414 272 5414 834 3667 776
אֶרֶץ כְּנַעַן אֲשֶׁר אֲנִי נֹתֵן לָכֶם לַאֲחֻזָּה וְנָתַתִּי נֶגַע צָרַעַת
leprosy a I and a as you to am I which Canaan the
of plague put have ,possession giving of land

3548 5046 1004 834 935 272 776 1004
35 בְּבֵית אֶרֶץ אֲחֻזַּתְכֶם׃ וּבָא אֲשֶׁר־לוֹ הַבַּיִת וְהִגִּיד לַכֹּהֵן
the to and the owns who he then your the (in) the in
priest declare house come shall ;possession of land house

1004 6437 3548 6680 1004 7200 5061 559
36 לֵאמֹר כְּנֶגַע נִרְאָה לִי בַּבָּיִת׃ וְצִוָּה הַכֹּהֵן וּפִנּוּ אֶת־הַבַּיִת
the they and the shall And the in to is plague A ,saying
house turn shall priest charge .house me seen

834 3605 2930 3808 5061 7200 3548 935 2962
בְּטֶרֶם יָבֹא הַכֹּהֵן לִרְאוֹת אֶת־הַנֶּגַע וְלֹא יִטְמָא כָּל־אֲשֶׁר
which all be may that the see to the comes before
(is) unclean not ,plague priest

7200 1004 7200 3548 935 310 1004
37 בַּבָּיִת וְאַחַר כֵּן יָבֹא הַכֹּהֵן לִרְאוֹת אֶת־הַבָּיִת׃ וְרָאָה אֶת־
he and the see to the shall and the in
on look shall ;house priest come afterwards ;house

176 3422 8258 1004 7023 5061 2009 5061
הַנֶּגַע וְהִנֵּה הַנֶּגַע בְּקִירֹת הַבַּיִת שְׁקַעֲרוּרֹת יְרַקְרַקֹּת אוֹ
or greenish ith the the in (is) the if and the
depressions house of walls plague ,behold ;plague

1004 3548 5927 7023 4480 8217 4758 125
38 אֲדַמְדַּמֹּת וּמַרְאֵיהֶן שָׁפָל מִן־הַקִּיר׃ וְיָצָא הַכֹּהֵן מִן־הַבַּיִת
the of the shall then the than is its and ,reddish
house priest out go ;wall lower appearance

7725 3117 7651 1004 5462 1004 6607
39 אֶל־פֶּתַח הַבָּיִת וְהִסְגִּיר אֶת־הַבַּיִת שִׁבְעַת יָמִים׃ וְשָׁב
shall And .days seven the shut and the the to
return house up ,house of door

1004 7023 5061 6581 2009 7200 7637 3117 3548
הַכֹּהֵן בַּיּוֹם הַשְּׁבִיעִי וְרָאָה וְהִנֵּה פָּשָׂה הַנֶּגַע בְּקִירֹת הַבָּיִת׃
the the in the has if and shall and ,seventh the the
;house of walls plague spread ,behold look day priest

7993 5061 834 68 2502 3548 6680
40 וְצִוָּה הַכֹּהֵן וְחִלְּצוּ אֶת־הָאֲבָנִים אֲשֶׁר בָּהֵן הַנָּגַע וְהִשְׁלִיכוּ
throw and the in which the they that the shall then
plague them (is) stones out take priest order

7096 1004 2931 4725 5892 2351
41 אֶתְהֶן אֶל־מִחוּץ לָעִיר אֶל־מָקוֹם טָמֵא׃ וְאֶת־הַבַּיִת יַקְצִעַ
shall he the And an place into the of the to them
scrape house .unclean city outside

2351 7106 834 6083 8210 5439 1004
מִבַּיִת סָבִיב וְשָׁפְכוּ אֶת־הֶעָפָר אֲשֶׁר הִקְצוּ אֶל־מִחוּץ
the at have they which dust the they and all inside
outside off scraped out pour shall ,around

935 312 68 3947 2931 4725 5892
42 לָעִיר אֶל־מָקוֹם טָמֵא׃ וְלָקְחוּ אֲבָנִים אֲחֵרוֹת וְהֵבִיאוּ
bring and other stones they and an place at the of
them take shall ;unclean ,city

1004 2902 3947 312 6083 68 8478
43 אֶל־תַּחַת הָאֲבָנִים וְעָפָר אַחֵר יִקַּח וְטָח אֶת־הַבָּיִת׃ וְאִם־
And .house the and he other and the the to
if daub take shall clay ;stones of place

310 68 2502 310 1004 6524 5061 7725
יָשׁוּב הַנֶּגַע וּפָרַח בַּבַּיִת אַחַר חִלֵּץ אֶת־הָאֲבָנִים וְאַחֲרֵי
and the has he after the in and the comes
after stones removed house out breaks plague again

2009 7200 3548 935 2902 1004 7096
44 הִקְצוֹת אֶת־הַבַּיִת וְאַחֲרֵי הִטּוֹחַ׃ וּבָא הַכֹּהֵן וְרָאָה וְהִנֵּה
and and the shall then has it and ,house the has he
,behold ;look priest come daubed been after scraped

2931 1004 3992 6883 1004 5061 6581
פָּשָׂה הַנֶּגַע בַּבָּיִת צָרַעַת מַמְאֶרֶת הִוא בַּבַּיִת טָמֵא הוּא׃
(is) it unclean the in is it a leprosy the in the has if
;house malignant ,house plague spread

1004 6083 6086 68 1004 5422
45 וְנָתַץ אֶת־הַבַּיִת אֶת־אֲבָנָיו וְאֶת־עֵצָיו וְאֵת כָּל־עֲפַר הַבָּיִת
the the all and its and its ,house the he And
;house of clay ,wood ,stones raze shall

1004 935 2931 4725 5892 2351 3318
46 וְהוֹצִיא אֶל־מִחוּץ לָעִיר אֶל־מָקוֹם טָמֵא׃ וְהַבָּא אֶל־הַבַּיִת
the into he And an place to the of the to he and
house goes who .unclean ,city outside bear shall

1004 7901 6153 2930 5462 3117/3605
47 כָּל־יְמֵי הִסְגִּיר אֹתוֹ יִטְמָא עַד־הָעָרֶב׃ וְהַשֹּׁכֵב בַּבַּיִת
the in he and the until be shall it has he the all
house lies who ;evening unclean up shut days

935 899 3526 1004 398 899 3526
48 יְכַבֵּס אֶת־בְּגָדָיו וְהָאֹכֵל בַּבַּיִת יְכַבֵּס אֶת־בְּגָדָיו׃ וְאִם־בֹּא
surely And his shall the in he and his shall
if clothes wash house eats who ;clothes wash

2902 310 1004 5061 6581 2009 7200 3548 935
יָבֹא הַכֹּהֵן וְרָאָה וְהִנֵּה לֹא־פָשָׂה הַנֶּגַע בַּבַּיִת אַחֲרֵי הִטֹּחַ
been has after the in the has not and and the shall
daubed house plague spread ,behold ,look priest come

3947 5061 7495 1004 3548 2891 1004
49 אֶת־הַבָּיִת וְטִהַר הַכֹּהֵן אֶת־הַבַּיִת כִּי נִרְפָּא הַנָּגַע׃ וְלָקַח
he And the been has for ,house the the shall then ,house the
take shall .plague healed priest clean call

231 8438 8144 730 6086 6833 8144 1004 2398
לְחַטֵּא אֶת־הַבַּיִת שְׁתֵּי צִפֳּרִים וְעֵץ אֶרֶז וּשְׁנִי תוֹלַעַת וְאֵזֹב׃
and scarlet and ,cedar and ,birds two the the for
;hyssop (dye) wood house of cleansing

go out of the house to the door of the house, and shut up the house seven days. [39]And the priest shall come again the seventh day, and shall look: and, behold, if the plague has spread in the walls of the house; [40]then the priest shall command that they take out the stones in which the plague is, and throw them into an unclean place outside the city. [41]And he shall cause the house to be scraped inside all around, and they shall pour out the dust which they have scraped off at the outside of the city, at an unclean place. [42]And they shall take other stones and bring them in to the place of the stones; and he shall take other clay and shall daub the house.

[43]And if the plague returns and breaks out in the house after he has taken away the stones, and after he has scraped the house, and after it has been daubed, [44]then the priest shall come in and look; and, behold, if the plague has spread in the house, it is a corroding leprosy in the house; it *is* unclean. [45]And he shall break down the house; its stones, and its wood, and all the clay of the house; and he shall carry out to the outside of the city, to an unclean place. [46]And he who goes into the house all the days he has shut it up shall be unclean until the evening. [47]And he who lies in the house shall wash his clothes; and he who eats in the house shall wash his clothes.

[48]And if the priest shall come in and carefully look, and, behold, the plague has not spread in the house after the house has been daubed, then the priest shall pronounce the house clean; for the plague has been healed. [49]And he shall take two birds for the cleansing of the house, and cedar wood, and scarlet *dye*, and hyssop; [50]and he

shall kill the one bird on an earthen vessel, over running water; [51]and he shall take the cedar wood, and the hyssop, and the scarlet, and the living bird, and shall dip them in the blood of the slain bird, and in the running water, and shall sprinkle on the house seven times. [52]And he shall cleanse the house with the blood of the bird, and with the running water, and with the living bird, and with the cedar wood, and with the hyssop, and with the scarlet yarn; [53]and he shall send away the living bird to the outside of the city, to the open field, and shall atone for the house; and it shall be clean.

[54]This *is* the law for every plague of the leprosy and for scurf; [55]and for leprosy of a garment, and of a house, [56]and for a swelling, and for a scurf, and for a bright spot; [57]to teach when it is unclean and when it is clean; this *is* the law of leprosy.

2416 4325 2789 3627 259 6833 7919
50 וְשָׁחַט אֶת־הַצִּפֹּר הָאֶחָת אֶל־כְּלִי־חֶרֶשׂ עַל־מַיִם חַיִּים׃
;running water over an vessel on one bird the he and
earthen kill shall
8438 8144 231 730 6086 3947
51 וְלָקַח אֶת־עֵץ־הָאֶרֶז וְאֶת־הָאֵזֹב וְאֶת ׀ שְׁנִי הַתּוֹלַעַת וְאֵת
and grub scarlet the and the and the wood he and
(dye) hyssop cedar take shall
4325 79:19 6833 1818 2881 2416 6833
הַצִּפֹּר הַחַיָּה וְטָבַל אֹתָם בְּדַם הַצִּפֹּר הַשְּׁחוּטָה וּבַמַּיִם
in and ,slaughtered bird the the in them shall and ,living bird the
water the of blood dip
1004 2398 6471 7651 1004 5137 2416
52 הַחַיִּים וְהִזָּה אֶל־הַבַּיִת שֶׁבַע פְּעָמִים׃ וְחִטֵּא אֶת־הַבַּיִת
house the he And .times seven the on and ,running
cleanse shall house sprinkle shall
730 6086 2416 6833 2416 4325 6833 1818
בְּדַם הַצִּפּוֹר וּבַמַּיִם הַחַיִּים וּבַצִּפֹּר הַחַיָּה וּבְעֵץ הָאֶרֶז
the with and living with and ,running with and the the with
,cedar wood bird the water the ,bird of blood
2416 6833 1921 8438 8144
53 וּבָאֵזֹב וּבִשְׁנִי הַתּוֹלָעַת׃ וְשִׁלַּח אֶת־הַצִּפֹּר הַחַיָּה אֶל־
to living bird the shall he and grub with and with and
away send ;(dye) scarlet the ,hyssop the
2088 2891 1004 3722 7704 6440 5892 2351
54 מִחוּץ לָעִיר אֶל־פְּנֵי הַשָּׂדֶה וְכִפֶּר עַל־הַבַּיִת וְטָהֵר׃ זֹאת
This it and ;house the for and ;field the open to the of the
(is) .clean be shall atone shall ,city outside
1004 899 6683 5424 6883 5061 3605 8451
55 הַתּוֹרָה לְכָל־נֶגַע הַצָּרַעַת וְלַנָּתֶק׃ וּלְצָרַעַת הַבֶּגֶד וְלַבָּיִת׃
a of and a for and for and the plague for law the
,house ,garment of leprosy ,scurf ,leprosy of every
2931 3384 934 5597 7613
56
57 וְלַשְׂאֵת וְלַסַּפַּחַת וְלַבֶּהָרֶת׃ לְהוֹרֹת בְּיוֹם הַטָּמֵא וּבְיוֹם
and is it when teach to a for and a for and a for and
when unclean ;spot bright ,scab ,rising
6883 8451 2088 2889
הַטָּהֹר זֹאת תּוֹרַת הַצָּרָעַת׃ פ
.leprosy law the this is it
of (is) ;clean

CAP. XV טו

CHAPTER 15

CHAPTER 15

[1]And Jehovah spoke to Moses and to Aaron, saying, [2]Speak to the sons of Israel, and you shall say to them, When there is a discharge from his flesh; he *is* unclean because of his flow. [3] And this is his uncleanness in his discharge, *if* his flesh has run with his discharge, *or* his flesh has stopped from his discharge; it *is* his uncleanness. [4]Every bed on which he who discharges lies shall be unclean. And everything on which he sits shall be unclean. [5]And anyone who touches his bed shall wash his garments, and shall bathe with water, and shall be

1121 1696 559 175 4872 3068 1696
1
2 וַיְדַבֵּר יְהוָה אֶל־מֹשֶׁה וְאֶל־אַהֲרֹן לֵאמֹר׃ דַּבְּרוּ אֶל־בְּנֵי
the to Speak ,saying ,Aaron and Moses to Jehovah And
of sons to spoke
1320 2100 1961 376 376 559 3478
יִשְׂרָאֵל וַאֲמַרְתֶּם אֲלֵהֶם אִישׁ אִישׁ כִּי יִהְיֶה זָב מִבְּשָׂרוֹ
his from a there when man any to shall you and ,Israel
,flesh discharge is ,them say
1320 3381 2101 2932 1961 2088 2931 2101
3 זוֹבוֹ טָמֵא הוּא׃ וְזֹאת תִּהְיֶה טֻמְאָתוֹ בְּזוֹבוֹ רָר בְּשָׂרוֹ
his has his in his is this And .(is) it unclean for
flesh run ;flow uncleanness flow his
3605 2932 2101 1320 2856 2101
4 אֶת־זוֹבוֹ אוֹ־הֶחְתִּים בְּשָׂרוֹ מִזּוֹבוֹ טֻמְאָתוֹ הִוא׃ כָּל־
Every .(is) it his his from flesh his stopped has or his with
uncleanness ;flow ,flow
834 3627/3605 2930 2100 5921 7901 834 4904
הַמִּשְׁכָּב אֲשֶׁר יִשְׁכַּב עָלָיו הַזָּב יִטְמָא וְכָל־הַכְּלִי אֲשֶׁר־
which thing and be shall who he on lies which bed
every ;unclean flows it
899 3526 4904 5060 376 2930 5921 3427
5 יֵשֵׁב עָלָיו יִטְמָא׃ וְאִישׁ אֲשֶׁר יִגַּע בְּמִשְׁכָּבוֹ יְכַבֵּס בְּגָדָיו
his shall bed his touches who And be shall on he
.clothes wash anyone .unclean it sits

unclean until the evening.
[6]And he who sits on anything on which he that has
the issue sat shall wash his
clothes, and bathe himself
in water, and shall be
unclean until the evening.
[7]And he that touches the
flesh of him that has the
discharge shall wash his
clothes, and bathe himself
in water, and be unclean
until evening. [8]And if he
that has the issue spits on
him that is clean, then he
shall wash his clothes and
bathe himself in water, and
be unclean until the evening. [9]And whatever saddle
he that has the issue rides
on shall be unclean. [10]And
whoever touches anything
that was under him shall be
unclean until the evening.
And he that carries those
things shall wash his
clothes and bathe himself
in water, and be unclean
until the evening. [11]And
whomever he that has the
discharge touches, and has
not rinsed his hands in
water, he shall wash his
clothes and bathe himself
in water, and be unclean
until the evening. [12]And
the earthen vessel that he
who discharges shall be
broken; and every wooden
vessel shall be rinsed with
water.

[13]And when he that dis-
charges is cleansed of his
discharge, then he shall
number to himself seven
days for his cleansing, and
wash his clothes. And he
shall bathe his flesh in running water, and shall be
clean. [14]And on the eighth
day he shall take to himself
two turtle-doves, or two
young doves, and come
before Jehovah to the door
of the tabernacle of the
congregation and give
them to the priest. [15]And
the priest shall offer them,
the one for a sin offering,
and the other for a burnt
offering. And the priest
shall make atonement for
him before Jehovah for his
discharge.

[16]And if any man's semen
pass from him, then he shall
bathe all his flesh in water,
and be unclean until the

834 3627 5921 3427 6153 5704 2930 4325 7364
6 וְרָחַץ בַּמַּיִם וְטָמֵא עַד־הָעָרֶב׃ וְהַיֹּשֵׁב עַל־הַכְּלִי אֲשֶׁר־
which anything on he And the until shall and with shall and
sits who ,evening unclean be ,water bathe

6153 5704 2930 4325 7364 899 3526 2100 3427
יֵשֵׁב עָלָיו הַזָּב יְכַבֵּס בְּגָדָיו וְרָחַץ בַּמַּיִם וְטָמֵא עַד־הָעָרֶב׃
the until shall and in and his shall who he on has
evening unclean be water bathe clothes wash discharges it sat

5704 2930 4325 7364 899 3526 2100 1320 5060
7 וְהַנֹּגֵעַ בִּבְשַׂר הַזָּב יְכַבֵּס בְּגָדָיו וְרָחַץ בַּמַּיִם וְטָמֵא עַד־
until shall and in and his shall who him flesh the he And
unclean be ,water bathe ,clothes wash discharges of touches that

4325 7364 899 3526 2889 2100 7556 6153
8 הָעָרֶב׃ וְכִי־יָרֹק הַזָּב בַּטָּהוֹר וְכִבֶּס בְּגָדָיו וְרָחַץ בַּמַּיִם
in and his he then a on who he spits if And the
,water bathe clothes wash shall ,one clean discharges .evening

2100 7392 4817 3605 6153/5704 2930
9 וְטָמֵא עַד־הָעָרֶב׃ וְכָל־הַמֶּרְכָּב אֲשֶׁר יִרְכַּב עָלָיו הַזָּב
who he it on rides which saddle And the until be and
discharges every .evening unclean

5704 2930 8478 1961 3604 5060 3605 2930
10 יִטְמָא׃ וְכָל־הַנֹּגֵעַ בְּכֹל אֲשֶׁר יִהְיֶה תַחְתָּיו יִטְמָא עַד־
until be shall under was that any- touch And be shall
unclean him thing who any .unclean

5704 2930 4325 7364 899 3526 5375 6153
הָעָרֶב וְהַנֹּשֵׂא אוֹתָם יְכַבֵּס בְּגָדָיו וְרָחַץ בַּמַּיִם וְטָמֵא עַד־
until be and in and his shall them that he and the
unclean ,water bathe clothes wash carries ;evening

4325 7857 3027 2100 5060 3605 6153
11 הָעָרֶב׃ וְכֹל אֲשֶׁר יִגַּע־בּוֹ הַזָּב וְיָדָיו לֹא־שָׁטַף בַּמָּיִם
in has not his and who on touch who And the
,water rinsed hands ,flows him all .evening

2789 3605 6153 2930 4325 7364 899 3526
12 וְכִבֶּס בְּגָדָיו וְרָחַץ בַּמַּיִם וְטָמֵא עַד־הָעָרֶב׃ וּכְלִי־חֶרֶשׂ
earthen the And the until be and in and his shall he
vessel .evening unclean ,water bathe ,clothes wash

4325 7857 6086 3627 7665 2100 5060 834
13 אֲשֶׁר־יִגַּע־בּוֹ הַזָּב יִשָּׁבֵר וְכָל־כְּלִי־עֵץ יִשָּׁטֵף בַּמָּיִם׃ וְכִי־
And with be shall wood vessel and be shall he who touches
when .water rinsed of every ,broken discharges which

3526 2893 3117 7651 5608 2101 2100/2891
יִטְהַר הַזָּב מִזּוֹבוֹ וְסָפַר לוֹ שִׁבְעַת יָמִים לְטָהֳרָתוֹ וְכִבֶּס
and his for days seven to he then his of who he is
wash cleansing himself count shall flow flows cleansed

8066 3117 2891 2416 4325 1320 7364 899
14 בְּגָדָיו וְרָחַץ בְּשָׂרוֹ בְּמַיִם חַיִּים וְטָהֵר׃ וּבַיּוֹם הַשְּׁמִינִי
eighth on And shall and ,running in his he and his
day the .clean be water flesh bathe shall ;clothes

3068 6440 935 3123 1121 8147 8449 8147 3947
יִקַּח־לוֹ שְׁתֵּי תֹרִים אוֹ שְׁנֵי בְּנֵי יוֹנָה וּבָא לִפְנֵי יְהוָה אֶל־
to Jehovah before and a of sons two or turtle- two to shall he
come dove doves himself take

3548 6213 3548 5414 4150 168 6607
15 פֶּתַח אֹהֶל מוֹעֵד וּנְתָנָם אֶל־הַכֹּהֵן׃ וְעָשָׂה אֹתָם הַכֹּהֵן
the them shall And the to give and ,meeting the door the
priest offer .priest them of tent of

3068/6440 3548 5921 3722 5930 259 2403 259
אֶחָד חַטָּאת וְהָאֶחָד עֹלָה וְכִפֶּר עָלָיו הַכֹּהֵן לִפְנֵי יְהוָה
Jehovah before the for shall and burnt a the and sin a one
priest him atone ;offering for other ,offering for

7364 2235 7902 5927 376 2101
16 מִזּוֹבוֹ׃ ס וְאִישׁ כִּי־תֵצֵא מִמֶּנּוּ שִׁכְבַת־זֶרַע וְרָחַץ
he then semen from goes if a And his for
bathe shall him out man flow

3605 899 6053 5704 2930 1320 3605 4325
17 בַּמַּיִם אֶת־כָּל־בְּשָׂרוֹ וְטָמֵא עַד־הָעָרֶב׃ וְכָל־בֶּגֶד וְכָל־
and ,garment And the until be and his all in
every every .evening unclean ,flesh water

evening. [17]And every garment, and every skin on which the semen shall be, shall be washed with water, and be unclean until the evening. [18]And a woman with whom a man lies with an emission of semen shall bathe with water, and be unclean until the evening. [20]And if a woman's discharge in her flesh is a flow of blood, she shall be in her impurity seven days; and whoever touches her shall be unclean until the evening. [20]And anything that she lies on in her impurity shall be unclean; and anything that she sits on shall be unclean. [21]And whoever touches her bed shall wash his clothes and bathe in water, and be unclean until the evening. [22]And whoever touches anything that she sits on shall wash his clothes and bathe himself in water, and be unclean until the evening. [23]And if it is on the bed, or on anything on which she sits when he touches it, he shall be unclean until the evening. [24]And if any man lies with her, and her impurity is on him, he shall be unclean seven days, and every bed on which he lies shall be unclean.

[25]And if a woman has an issue of her blood many days outside the time of her impurity, or if she has an issue beyond the time of her impurity, all the days of the flow of her uncleanness, she shall be as in the days of her impurity; she *is* unclean. [26]Every bed on which she lies all the days of her discharge shall be as the bed of her impurity to her; and everything on which she sits shall be unclean as the uncleanness of her impurity. [27]And whoever touches those things shall be unclean, and shall wash

5704 2930 4325 3526 2233 7902 5921 1961 834 5785
עוֹר אֲשֶׁר־יִהְיֶה עָלָיו שִׁכְבַת־זָרַע וְכֻבַּס בַּמַּיִם וְטָמֵא עַד־
until shall and with be shall semen on shall which leather
unclean be ,water washed it be
7364 2233 7902 376 7901 802 6153
18 הָעָרֶב׃ וְאִשָּׁה אֲשֶׁר יִשְׁכַּב אִישׁ אֹתָהּ שִׁכְבַת־זָרַע וְרָחֲצוּ
bathe shall semen an with with man a lies who a And the
of emission her woman .evening
6153/5704 2930 4325
בַמַּיִם וְטָמְאוּ עַד־הָעָרֶב׃
the until be and with
.evening unclean ,water
3117 7651 1320 2100 1961 1818 2101 802
19 וְאִשָּׁה כִּי־תִהְיֶה זָבָה דָּם יִהְיֶה זֹבָהּ בִּבְשָׂרָהּ שִׁבְעַת יָמִים
days seven her in her is of a is if a And
flesh discharge blood flow woman
3604 6153 2930 5060 5079 1961
20 תִּהְיֶה בְנִדָּתָהּ וְכָל־הַנֹּגֵעַ בָּהּ יִטְמָא עַד־הָעָרֶב׃ וְכֹל אֲשֶׁר
that And the until be shall her touches and her in shall she
anything .evening unclean whoever ;impurity be
2930 3427 3605 2930 5079 5921 7901
תִּשְׁכַּב עָלָיו בְּנִדָּתָהּ יִטְמָא וְכֹל אֲשֶׁר־תֵּשֵׁב עָלָיו יִטְמָא׃
be shall on sits she that and be shall her in on lies she
.unclean it anything ;unclean impurity it
5704 2930 4325 7364 899 3526 4904 5060
21 וְכָל־הַנֹּגֵעַ בְּמִשְׁכָּבָהּ יְכַבֵּס בְּגָדָיו וְרָחַץ בַּמַּיִם וְטָמֵא עַד־
until be and in and his shall bed her touches And
unclean ,water bathe clothes wash whoever
899 3526 5414 3427 3627 3605 5060 6153
22 הָעָרֶב׃ וְכָל־הַנֹּגֵעַ בְּכָל־כְּלִי אֲשֶׁר־תֵּשֵׁב עָלָיו יְכַבֵּס בְּגָדָיו
his shall on sits she that thing any touches And the
clothes wash it whoever .evening
176 4904 5921 6153 5704 2930 4325 7364
23 וְרָחַץ בַּמַּיִם וְטָמֵא עַד־הָעָרֶב׃ וְאִם עַל־הַמִּשְׁכָּב הוּא אוֹ
or ,(is) it bed the on if And the until be and in and
.evening unclean ,water bathe
5704 2930 5060 5921 3427 834 3627
עַל־הַכְּלִי אֲשֶׁר־הִוא יֹשֶׁבֶת־עָלָיו בְּנָגְעוֹ־בוֹ יִטְמָא עַד־
until shall he it he when on sits she which anything on
unclean be touches ,it
5921 5079 1961 376 7901 7901 6153
24 הָעָרֶב׃ וְאִם שָׁכֹב יִשְׁכַּב אִישׁ אֹתָהּ וּתְהִי נִדָּתָהּ עָלָיו
on her and with any lies actually if And the
,him impurity is ,her man .evening
2930 5921 3427 834 4904 3605 3117 7651 2930
וְטָמֵא שִׁבְעַת יָמִים וְכָל־הַמִּשְׁכָּב אֲשֶׁר־יִשְׁכַּב עָלָיו יִטְמָא׃
be shall on lies he which bed and ;days seven shall he
.unclean every unclean be
5079 6250 3808 7227 3117 1818 2101 1961 802
25 ס וְאִשָּׁה כִּי־יָזוּב זוֹב דָּמָהּ יָמִים רַבִּים בְּלֹא עֶת־נִדָּתָהּ
her time the outside many days her dis- a has she if a And
,impurity of blood of charge ,woman
5079 3117 2932 2101 3117 5079 2101 176
אוֹ כִי־תָזוּב עַל־נִדָּתָהּ כָּל־יְמֵי זוֹב טֻמְאָתָהּ כִּימֵי נִדָּתָהּ
her in as unclean- her the days the all time the beyond she if or
impurity of days the ness of flow of impurity her of discharges
3605 5921 7901 834 4904 3605 2931 1961
26 תִּהְיֶה טְמֵאָה הִוא׃ כָּל־הַמִּשְׁכָּב אֲשֶׁר־תִּשְׁכַּב עָלָיו כָּל־
all on lies she which bed Every she unclean shall she
it (is) be;
3427 834 3627 3605 1961 5079 4904 2101 3117
יְמֵי זוֹבָהּ כְּמִשְׁכַּב נִדָּתָהּ יִהְיֶה־לָּהּ וְכָל־הַכְּלִי אֲשֶׁר תֵּשֵׁב
sits she which thing and to be shall her the as her the
every ;her impurity of bed discharge of days
2930 5060 5079 2932 1961 2931
27 עָלָיו טָמֵא יִהְיֶה כְּטֻמְאַת נִדָּתָהּ׃ וְכָל־הַנּוֹגֵעַ בָּם יִטְמָא
be shall those touches And her the as be shall unclean on
,unclean things whoever .impurity of uncleanness it

his clothes and bathe himself in water, and be unclean until the evening. [28]And if she is cleansed of her discharge, then she shall number to herself seven days, and after that she shall be clean. [29]And on the eighth day she shall take to herself two turtle-doves, or two young doves, and bring them to the priest, to the door of the tabernacle of the congregation. [30]And the priests shall offer the one for a sin offering, and the other for a burnt offering; and the priest shall make atonement for her before Jehovah for the discharge of her uncleanness.

[31]So you shall separate the sons of Israel from their uncleanness, and they shall not die in their uncleanness, when they defile My tabernacle that *is* in their midst.

[32]This *is* the law of him that discharges, and of him from whom semen flows out, for uncleanness by it; [33]and of her who is sick in her impurity, and of him from whom the discharge flows; of a male or of a female, and of a man who lies with an unclean woman.

2891 6153 5704 2930 4325 7364 899 3326
28 וְכִבֶּס בְּגָדָיו וְרָחַץ בַּמַּיִם וְטָמֵא עַד־הָעָרֶב׃ וְאִם־טָהֲרָה
is she if And the until be and in and his shall and
cleansed evening, unclean ,water bathe clothes wash

3117 2889 310 3117 7651 5608 2101
29 מִזּוֹבָהּ וְסָפְרָה לָּהּ שִׁבְעַת יָמִים וְאַחַר תִּטְהָר׃ וּבַיּוֹם
on And shall she after and days seven to she then her of
day the .clean be that herself count shall ;discharge

935 3128 1121 8147 176 8449 8147 3947 8066
הַשְּׁמִינִי תִּקַּח־לָהּ שְׁתֵּי תֹרִים אוֹ שְׁנֵי בְּנֵי יוֹנָה וְהֵבִיאָה
and a sons two or turtle- two to shall she eighth
bring ,dove of doves herself take

3548 6213 4150 168 6607 3548
30 אוֹתָם אֶל־הַכֹּהֵן אֶל־פֶּתַח אֹהֶל מוֹעֵד׃ וְעָשָׂה הַכֹּהֵן
the shall And .meeting the the to the to them
priest offer of tent of door priest

3548 3722 5930 259 2403 259
אֶת־הָאֶחָד חַטָּאת וְאֶת־הָאֶחָד עֹלָה וְכִפֶּר עָלֶיהָ הַכֹּהֵן
the her for shall and burnt a the and sin a one the
priest atone ,offering for other ,offering for

3478 1121 5144 2932 2101 3068 6440
31 לִפְנֵי יְהוָה מִזּוֹב טֻמְאָתָהּ׃ וְהִזַּרְתֶּם אֶת־בְּנֵי־יִשְׂרָאֵל
Israel sons the you So her the for Jehovah before
of separate shall .uncleanness of discharge

834 4908 2930 2932 4191 3808 2932
מִטֻּמְאָתָם וְלֹא יָמֻתוּ בְּטֻמְאָתָם בְּטַמְּאָם אֶת־מִשְׁכָּנִי אֲשֶׁר
which My they when their from they and their from
(is) tabernacle defile ,uncleanness die shall not ,uncleanness

2233 7902 5927 2100 8451 2088 8432
32 בְּתוֹכָם׃ זֹאת תּוֹרַת הַזָּב וַאֲשֶׁר תֵּצֵא מִמֶּנּוּ שִׁכְבַת־זֶרַע
,semen from flows of and him law the This their in
him out him ,flows that of (is) .midst

5347 2145 2100 3526 1739 2930
33 לְטָמְאָה־בָהּ׃ וְהַדָּוָה בְּנִדָּתָהּ וְהַזָּב אֶת־זוֹבוֹ לַזָּכָר וְלַנְּקֵבָה
a of or a of flow the of and her in her of and ,it by for
,female male ,flows who him ,impurity sick is who uncleanness

2931 7901 376
וּלְאִישׁ אֲשֶׁר יִשְׁכַּב עִם־טְמֵאָה׃
unclean an with lies who of and
.woman man a

CAP. XVI טז

CHAPTER 16

CHAPTER 16

[1]And Jehovah spoke to Moses after the death of the two sons of Aaron, as they drew near before Jehovah, and they died; [2]and Jehovah said to Moses, Speak to your brother Aaron, and he shall not come in at all times to the sanctuary within the veil, to the front of the mercy-seat. [3]With this Aaron shall come into the sanctuary: with a bullock, a son of the herd, for a sin offering, and a ram for a burnt offering. [4]He shall put on a holy linen coat, and linen underpants

7126 175 1121 8147 4194 310 4872 3068 1696
1 וַיְדַבֵּר יְהוָה אֶל־מֹשֶׁה אַחֲרֵי מוֹת שְׁנֵי בְּנֵי אַהֲרֹן בְּקָרְבָתָם
they when ,Aaron sons the the after Moses to Jehovah And
came of two of death spoke

175 1696 4872 3068 559 4191 3068 6440
2 לִפְנֵי־יְהוָה וַיָּמֻתוּ׃ וַיֹּאמֶר יְהוָה אֶל־מֹשֶׁה דַּבֵּר אֶל־אַהֲרֹן
Aaron to Speak ,Moses to Jehovah said And they and ,Jehovah
.died before

6532 1004 6944 6256 935 251
אָחִיךָ וְאַל־יָבֹא בְכָל־עֵת אֶל־הַקֹּדֶשׁ מִבֵּית לַפָּרֹכֶת אֶל־
,veil the within the to times at shall he and your
sanctuary all come not ,brother

7200 6051 4194 3808 727 5921 834 3727 6440
פְּנֵי הַכַּפֹּרֶת אֲשֶׁר עַל־הָאָרֹן וְלֹא יָמוּת כִּי בֶּעָנָן אֵרָאֶה
appear I the in For shall he and ,ark the on which the before
cloud .die not (is) mercy-seat

1121 6499 6944 175 935 2063 3727 5921
3 עַל־הַכַּפֹּרֶת׃ בְּזֹאת יָבֹא אַהֲרֹן אֶל־הַקֹּדֶשׁ בְּפַר בֶּן
a a with the into Aaron shall With the on
of son ,bullock :sanctuary come this .mercy-seat

4137 3844 6944 906 3801 5930 352 2403 1241
4 בָּקָר לְחַטָּאת וְאַיִל לְעֹלָה׃ כְּתֹנֶת־בַּד קֹדֶשׁ יִלְבָּשׁ וּמִכְנְסֵי־
under- and shall he holy linen coat a burnt a for a and sin a for the
pants ,on put ;offering ram ,offering ,herd

shall be on his flesh, and he shall gird himself with a linen girdle, and he shall wrap himself in a linen miter; they *are* holy garments. And he shall bathe his flesh with water and shall put them on. 5And he shall take from the congregation of the sons of Israel two kids of the goats for a sin offering, and one ram for a burnt offering. 6And Aaron shall bring near the bullock of the sin offering which *is* his own, and shall make atonement for himself, and for his house. 7And he shall take the two goats and shall cause them to stand before Jehovah, at the door of the tabernacle of the congregation. 8And Aaron shall give lots over the two goats, one lot for Jehovah, and one lot for complete removal. 9And Aaron shall bring the goat on which the lot fell for Jehovah, and shall make it a sin offering. 10And the goat on which the lot for complete removal fell shall be set alive before Jehovah, to atone by it, to send it away for complete removal to the wilderness.

11And Aaron shall bring the bull of the sin offering which *is* his own, and shall atone for himself and for his house, and shall kill the bull of the sin offering which *is* his own. 12And he shall take a censer full of coals of fire from off the altar before Jehovah, and his hands full of incense of fragrant perfumes beaten small, and bring *it* within the veil. 13And he shall put the incense on the fire before Jehovah. And the cloud of the incense shall cover the mercy-seat that *is* on the testimony; and he shall not die. 14And he shall take of the blood of the bull and shall sprinkle with his finger on the front of the mercy-seat eastward. And he shall sprinkle at the front of the mercy-seat seven

6801 906 4701 2296 906 73 1320 5921 1961 906
בד יהיו על־בשרו ובאבנט בד יחגר ובמצנפת בד יצנף
shall he linen a with and shall he linen a with and his on shall linen
;wrap miter gird girdle ,flesh be

5 3847 1320 4325 7364 1992 6944 899
בגדי־קדש הם ורחץ במים את־בשרו ולבשם׃ ומאת
And shall and his with he and they holy ;garments
from on them put flesh water bathe shall (are)

352 2403 5795 8163 8147 3947 3478 1121 5712
עדת בני ישראל יקח שני־שעירי עזים לחטאת ואיל
and · sin a for the bucks two shall he Israel sons the the
ram ,offering goats of take of company

6 834 2403 6499 175 7126 5930 259
אחד לעלה׃ והקריב אהרן את־פר החטאת אשר־לו
his which sin the bullock the Aaron shall and burnt a for one
,own (is) offering of bring ,offering

7 5975 8163 8147 3947 1004 1157 3722
וכפר בעדו ובעד ביתו׃ ולקח את־שני השעירם והעמיד
shall and goats the two he and his and for shall and
stand take shall ;house for ,himself atone

8 8147 175 5414 4150 168 6607 3068 6440
אתם לפני יהוה פתח אהל מועד׃ ונתן אהרן על־שני
two over Aaron shall And .meeting the the (at) ,Jehovah before them
cast of tent of door

5799 259 1486 3068 259 1486 1486 8163
השעירם גרלות גורל אחד ליהוה וגורל אחד לעזאזל׃
a for one and for one lot ,lots goats the
scapegoat lot Jehovah

9 3068 1486 5921 5927 834 8163 175 7126
והקריב אהרן את־השעיר אשר עלה עליו הגורל ליהוה
for lot the it on fell which goat the Aaron shall And
Jehovah bring

10 5799 1486 5921 5927 834 8163 2403 6213
ועשהו חטאת׃ והשעיר אשר עלה עליו הגורל לעזאזל
com- for lot the it on fell which the And sin a shall and
removal plete goat .offering it make

5799 7971 3722 3068 6440 2416 5975
יעמד־חי לפני יהוה לכפר עליו לשלח אתו לעזאזל
com- for it send to ,it by atone to Jehovah before alive be shall
removal plete away stand made

11 834 2403 6499 175 7126 4057
המדברה׃ והקריב אהרן את־פר החטאת אשר־לו
his which sin the the Aaron shall And the into
,own (is) offering of bullock bring .wilderness

834 2403 6499 7919 1004 3722
וכפר בעדו ובעד ביתו ושחט את־פר החטאת אשר־לו׃
his which sin the the shall and his for and for shall and
;own (is) offering of bullock kill ,house ,himself atone

12 3068 6440 4194 784 1513 4289 4393 3947
ולקח מלא־המחתה גחלי־אש מעל המזבח מלפני יהוה
Jehovah before the from fire coals censer a of full he and
altar off of take shall

6532 1004 935 1851 5561 7004 2651 4393
ומלא חפניו קטרת סמים דקה והביא מבית לפרכת׃
.veil the within and beaten fragrant incense his and
(it) bring small perfumes of hands of full

13 7004 6051 3680 3068 6440 784 7004 5414
ונתן את־הקטרת על־האש לפני יהוה וכסה ׀ ענן הקטרת
the the shall And .Jehovah be- fire the on incense the he And
incense of cloud cover fore put shall

14 1818 3947 4191 3808 5715 834 3727
את־הכפרת אשר על־העדות ולא ימות׃ ולקח מדם
the of he And shall he and the on which the
of blood take shall .die not ;testimony (is) mercy-seat

3727 6440 6924 3727 6440 676 5137 6499
הפר והזה באצבעו על־פני הכפרת קדמה ולפני הכפרת
the at and eastward the the on his with shall and the
mercy-seat of front the mercy-seat of front finger sprinkle bullock

times from the blood with his finger.

15And he shall kill the goat of the sin offering which *is* the people's, and shall bring in its blood to the inside of the veil, and shall do with its blood as he has done with the blood of the bullock, and shall sprinkle it on the mercy-seat, and at the front of the mercy-seat. 16And he shall make atonement for the sanctuary because of the pollutions of the sons of Israel, and because of their transgressions for all their sins. And so he shall do for the tabernacle of the congregation which is dwelling in the midst of their pollutions. 17And not any man shall be in the tabernacle of the congregation as he goes in to make atonement in the sanctuary, until he comes out. And he shall make atonement for himself, and for his house, and for all the congregation of Israel. 18And he shall go out to the altar which *is* before Jehovah, and shall make atonement for it. And he shall take of the blood of the bullock, and of the blood of the goat, and shall put *it* on the horns of the altar all around. 19And he shall sprinkle on it from the blood with his finger seven times, and shall cleanse it, and shall purify it from the uncleannesses of the sons of Israel.

20And when he having finished atoning *for* the sanctuary, and the tabernacle of the congregation, and the altar, and having brought near the living goat; 21then Aaron shall lay his two hands on the head of the living goat, and shall confess over it all the iniquities of the sons of Israel, and all their transgressions, and all their sins, and shall put them on the head of the goat, and shall send *it* by the hand of a chosen man into the wilderness. 22And the goat shall bear on him all their iniquities to a land cut off. And he shall send the goat away into the wilderness.

8163 7919 676 1818 6471 7651 5137
15 יזה שבע־פעמים מן־הדם באצבעו׃ ושחט את־שעיר
goat the of | he And kill shall | his with .finger | the blood | of | times | seven | shall he sprinkle

6532 1004 1818 935 5971 834 2403
החטאת אשר לעם והביא את־דמו אל־מבית לפרכת
the of veil | the inside | to | its blood | shall and in bring | the ,people's | which (is) | sin the offering

5921 5137 6499 1818 6213 1818 6213
ועשה את־דמו כאשר עשה לדם הפר והזה אתו על־
on | it | shall and sprinkle | the bullock | the with of blood | has he done | as | its blood | with | shall and do

1121 2932 6944 3722 3727 6440 3727
16 הכפרת ולפני הכפרת׃ וכפר על־הקדש מטמאת בני
the of sons | the for of pollutions | sanctuary the for | he and atone shall | the ;mercy-seat | and before | the ,mercy-seat

4150 168 6213 996/2403 3605 6588 3478
ישראל ומפשעיהם לכל־חטאתם וכן יעשה לאהל מועד
meeting | the for of tent | shall he do | and so | their ;sins | all for | of because and transgressions their | ,Israel

168 1961 120 3605 2932 854 7931
17 השכן אתם בתוך טמאתם׃ וכל־אדם לא־יהיה באהל
the in of tent | be shall | not | man | And any | their .pollutions | the in of midst | with them | is which dwelling

3722 5927 5704 6944 3722 935 4150
מועד בבאו לכפר בקדש עד־צאתו וכפר בעדו ובעד
and for | for himself | he and atone shall | comes he until ,out | the in ,sanctuary | make to atonement | he as in goes | meeting

834 4196 5927 3471 6951 1004
18 ביתו ובעד כל־קהל ישראל׃ ויצא אל־המזבח אשר
which (is) | the altar | to | he And out go shall | .Israel | the of assembly | all for and | his ,house

8163 1818 6499 1818 3947 3722 3068 6440
לפני־יהוה וכפר עליו ולקח מדם הפר ומדם השעיר
,goat the | of out of blood the | the ,bullock | the of blood | he and take shall | ;it for | shall and atone | ,Jehovah | be-fore

1818 5921 5137 5439 4196 7161 5414
19 ונתן על־קרנות המזבח סביב׃ והזה עליו מן־הדם
the blood | of | it on | he and sprinkle shall | all ;around | altar the | the of horns | on | shall and (it) put

3478 1121 2930 6942 2891 6471 7651 676
באצבעו שבע פעמים וטהרו וקדשו מטמאת בני ישראל׃
,Israel | the of sons | the from pollutions | shall and of it purify | shall and it cleanse | ,times | seven | his with finger

4196 4150 168 6944 3722 3615
20 וכלה מכפר את־הקדש ואת־אהל מועד ואת־המזבח
,altar the | and | ,meeting | the of tent | and | the (for) ,sanctuary | atoning | having And finished

3027 8147 175 5564 2416 8163 7126
21 והקריב את־השעיר החי׃ וסמך אהרן את־שתי ידו על־
on | his hands | two | Aaron | shall then lay | ,living | goat the | has and brought

3478 1121 5771/3605 3034 2416 8163 7218
ראש השעיר החי והתודה עליו את־כל־עונת בני ישראל
,Israel | the of sons | the of iniquities | all | over it | shall and confess | ,living | goat the | the of head

7218/5921 5414 2403 3605 6588 3605
ואת־כל־פשעיהם לכל־חטאתם ונתן אתם על־ראש
head the of | on | them | and put shall | ,sins their | all and | their ,transgressions | all | and

8163 5375 4057 6261 376 3027 7971 8163
22 השעיר ושלח ביד־איש עתי המדברה׃ ונשא השעיר
goat the | And bear shall | the into .wilderness | chosen | man a | the by of hand | shall and (it) send | ,goat the

8163 7971 1509 776 5771 3605 5921
עליו את־כל־עונתם אל־ארץ גזרה ושלח את־השעיר
goat the | he And send shall | soli- .tary | land a | to | their iniquities | all | upon itself

²³And Aaron shall come
into the tabernacle of the
congregation, and shall
strip off the linen garments
which he had put on as he
went into the sanctuary,
and shall leave them there.
²⁴And he shall bathe his
flesh with water in the holy
place, and shall put on his
garments, and shall come
out, and shall offer his burnt
offering, and the burnt
offering of the people, and
shall make atonement for
himself and for his people.
²⁵And he shall burn as
incense the fat of the sin
offering on the altar. ²⁶And
he who let the goat go for a
scapegoat shall wash his
garments, and shall bathe
his flesh with water; and
afterwards he shall come
into the camp. ²⁷And the
bullock of the sin offering,
and the goat of the sin
offering, whose blood has
been brought in to make
atonement in the sanctuary,
one shall carry out to the
outside of the camp; and
they shall burn their skins
with fire, and their flesh,
and their dung. ²⁸And he
who shall burn them shall
wash his garments, and
shall bathe his flesh with
water, and afterwards he
shall come into the camp.
²⁹And it shall be for a
never-ending statute, in the
seventh month, in the tenth
of the month, you shall
humble yourself and do no
work, the native, and the
alien who is staying in your
midst. ³⁰For on this day he
shall make atonement for
you, to cleanse you from all
your sins; you shall be clean
before Jehovah. ³¹It *is* a
sabbath of rest to you, and
you shall humble yourself. *It*
is a never-ending statute.
³²And the priest whom He
shall anoint, and whose
hand He shall consecrate to
act as priest instead of his
father, shall make atone-
ment, and shall put on the

23 במדבר: ובא אהרן אל־אהל מועד ופשט את־בגדי
garments shall and ,meeting the into Aaron shall And the into
off strip of tent come .wilderness

24 הבד אשר לבש בבאו אל־הקדש והניחם שם: ורחץ
he And .there shall and the into he as has he which the
bathe shall them leave ,sanctuary went on put linen

את־בשרו במים במקום קדוש ולבש את־בגדיו ויצא
shall and his he and ;holy the in with flesh his
,out come ,clothes on put shall place water

ועשה את־עלתו ואת־עלת העם וכפר בעדו ובעד העם:
the and for shall and the burnt the and burnt his shall and
;people for himself atone ,people of offering ,offering offer

25 ואת חלב החטאת יקטיר המזבחה: והמשלח את־
26
who he And the on shall he sin the fat the and
go let .altar incense as burn offering of

השעיר לעזאזל יכבס בגדיו ורחץ את־בשרו במים
with flesh his shall and his shall the for goat the
,water bathe ,garments wash scapegoat

27 ואחרי־כן יבוא אל־המחנה: ואת פר החטאת ואת
and sin the the And .camp the into shall he and
,offering of bullock come afterward

שעיר החטאת אשר הובא את־דמם לכפר בקדש יוציא
shall one the in atone to their been have which sin the goat the
carry ,sanctuary blood brought ,offering of

אל־מחוץ למחנה ושרפו באש את־ערתם ואת־בשרם
,flesh their and ,skins their with they and the of the to
fire burn shall ;camp outside

28 ואת־פרשם: והשרף אתם יכבס בגדיו ורחץ את־בשרו
flesh his shall and his shall them who he And their and
bathe clothes wash burn shall .dung

29 במים ואחרי־כן יבוא אל־המחנה: והיתה לכם לחקת
statute a you for it And .camp the into shall he and with
be shall come afterward ,water

עולם בחדש השביעי בעשור לחדש תענו את־נפשתיכם
yourselves shall you the of the in ,seventh the in never-
humble month tenth month ,ending

וכל־מלאכה לא תעשו האזרח והגר הגר בתוככם:
your in is who the and the ,do no work and
midst staying alien native

30 כי־ביום הזה יכפר עליכם לטהר אתכם מכל חטאתיכם
your from ;you to ,you for shall he this on For
sins all cleanse atone day

31 לפני יהוה תטהרו: שבת שבתון היא לכם ועניתם
you and ,you to (is) It rest sabbath a shall you Jehovah before
humble shall of .clean be

2 את־נפשתיכם חקת עולם: וכפר הכהן אשר־ימשח
shall he whom the shall And never- a (is it) ;yourselves
,anoint priest atone .ending statute

אתו ואשר ימלא את־ידו לכהן תחת אביו ולבש את־
shall and his instead act to his shall he and him
on put ,father of priest as hand consecrate whom

linen garments, the holy garments. 33 And he shall make atonement *for* the holy sanctuary, and *for* the tabernacle of the congregation, and *for* the altar he shall make atonement; yes, for the priests, and for all the people of the congregation he shall make atonement. 34 And this shall be to you a never-ending statute, to make atonement for the sons of Israel, because of all their sins, once a year.

And he did as Jehovah had commanded Moses.

6944 4720 3722 6944 899 906 899
33 בגדי הבד בגדי הקדש: וכפר את־מקדש הקדש ואת־
and ;holy the (for) he and ,holy the garments the garments
sanctuary atone shall linen

5971 3605 3548 3722 4196 4150 168
אהל מועד ואת־המזבח יכפר ועל הכהנים ועל־כל־עם
the all and the And shall he the (for) and ,meeting the
of people for priests for atone altar of tent

3722 5769/2288 2088 1961 3722 6951
34 הקהל יכפר: והיתה־זאת לכם לחקת עולם לכפר על־
for to never- statute a you to this shall And shall he the
atone ending be. .atone assembly

6680 6213 8141 259 2403 3605 3478 1121
בני ישראל מכל־חטאתם אחת בשנה ויעש כאשר צוה
ordered as he And a in once ,sins their because ,Israel the
did .year all of of sons

4872 3068
יהוה את־משה:
.Moses Jehovah

CAP. XVII יז

CHAPTER 17

1 And Jehovah spoke to Moses, saying, 2 Speak to Aaron, and to his sons, and to all the sons of Israel, and you shall say to them, This *is* the thing which Jehovah has commanded, saying, 3 Any man of the house of Israel who kills an ox, or lamb, or goat, in the camp, or who kills at the outside of the camp, 4 and has not brought it in to the door of the tabernacle of the congregation as an offering to Jehovah, before the tabernacle of Jehovah, blood shall be imputed to that man; he has shed blood. And that man shall be cut off from the midst of his people; 5 so that the sons of Israel shall bring in their sacrifices which they are sacrificing in the open field to the door of the tabernacle of the congregation, to the priest, and sacrifice them for sacrifices of peace offerings to Jehovah. 6 And the priest shall sprinkle the blood on the altar of Jehovah, at the door of the tabernacle of the congregation, and shall burn the fat as incense for a

1121 175 1696 559 4872 3068 1696
1
2 וידבר יהוה אל־משה לאמר: דבר אל־אהרן ואל־בניו
his to and ,Aaron to Speak ,saying ,Moses to Jehovah And
sons spoke

1697 2088 559 3478 1121/3605
ואל כל־בני ישראל ואמרת אליהם זה הדבר אשר־
which the This ,them to you and ;Israel the all and
word (is) say shall of sons to

7819 3478 1004 376 376 559 3068 6680
3 צוה יהוה לאמר: איש איש מבית ישראל אשר ישחט
kills who Israel the of man Any ,saying Jehovah has
of house commanded

2351 7819 4264 5795 3775 7794
שור או־כשב או־עז במחנה או אשר ישחט מחוץ
the at kills who or the in goat or ,lamb or an
outside ,camp ,ox

7126 935 3808 4150 168 6607 4264
4 למחנה: ואל־פתח אהל מועד לא הביאו להקריב
offer to has not meeting the door the and the of
it brought of tent of to ,camp

376 2803 1818/3068 4908 6440 3068 7133
קרבן ליהוה לפני משכן יהוה דם יחשב לאיש ההוא
;that man to be shall blood ,Jehovah the before to an as
imputed of tabernacle Jehovah offering

5971 7130 376 3772 8210 1818
5 דם שפך ונכרת האיש ההוא מקרב עמו: למען אשר
that so his the from that man shall and has he blood
;people of midst off cut be ;shed

5921 2076 834 2077 3478 1121 935
יביאו בני ישראל את־זבחיהם אשר הם זבחים על־
in are they which their Israel the shall
sacrificing sacrifices of sons in bring

4150 168 6607 3068 935 7704 6440
פני השדה והביאם ליהוה אל־פתח אהל מועד אל־
to meeting the the to to they that the open
of tent of door Jehovah them bring may ,field

3548 2236 3068 8002 2077 2076 3548
6 הכהן וזבחו זבחי שלמים ליהוה אותם: וזרק הכהן
the shall And .them to peace sacrifices and ;priest the
priest sprinkle Jehovah offerings of (for) sacrifice

2459 6999 4150 168 6607 3068 4196 1818
את־הדם על־מזבח יהוה פתח אהל מועד והקטיר החלב
fat the shall and meeting the the at ,Jehovah the on blood the
incense as burn of tent of door of altar

sweet fragrance to Jehovah.
7 [7]And they shall not sacrifice their sacrifices any to goats, after which they have gone whoring. This is a never-ending statute to them throughout their generations.
8 [8]And you shall say to them, Any man of the house of Israel, or of aliens who sojourn in your midst, who offers burnt offering or sacrifice, [9]and does not bring it in to the door of the tabernacle of the congregation to offer it to Jehovah, that man shall be cut off from his people. [10]And any man of the house of Israel, or of the aliens who is staying in your midst, who eats any blood, I will set My face against that person that eats blood and will cut him of from his people. [11]For the life of the flesh is in the blood, and I have given it to you on the altar, to make atonement for your souls; for it *is* the blood which makes atonement for the soul. [12]For this reason I have said to the sons of Israel, No person among you shall eat blood; and the alien who is staying in your midst shall not eat blood.
[13]And any man of the sons of Israel, or of the aliens who reside in your midst, who hunt game of beast or fowl which may be eaten, then *he* shall pour out its blood and cover it with dust. [14]For the life of all flesh *is* its blood. And I say to the sons of Israel, You shall not eat blood of any flesh, for the life of all flesh *is* its blood; anyone eating it shall be cut off.
[15]And any person who eats a dead body or a torn thing, be he a native or an alien, he shall wash his

8163 2077 5750 2076 3068 5207 7381
7 לְרֵיחַ נִיחֹחַ לַיהוָה׃ וְלֹא־יִזְבְּחוּ עוֹד אֶת־זִבְחֵיהֶם לַשְּׂעִירִם
goats to sacrifices their any shall they and to soothing a for
more sacrifice not Jehovah fragrance

2088 5769 2708 310 2181
אֲשֶׁר הֵם זֹנִים אַחֲרֵיהֶם חֻקַּת עוֹלָם תִּהְיֶה־זֹּאת לָהֶם
them to This is never- a after gone have they which
ending statute them whoring

3478 1004 376 376 559 1755
8 לְדֹרֹתָם׃ וַאֲלֵהֶם תֹּאמַר אִישׁ אִישׁ מִבֵּית יִשְׂרָאֵל וּמִן־
of or ,Israel the of Any shall you to And their for
of house man ,say them .generations

2077 5930 5927 8432 1481 1616
9 הַגֵּר אֲשֶׁר־יָגוּר בְּתוֹכָם אֲשֶׁר־יַעֲלֶה עֹלָה אוֹ־זָבַח׃ וְאֶל־
and ,sacrifice or burnt offers who your in stays who the
to offering ,midst alien

3772 3068 6213 935 4250 168 6607
פֶּתַח אֹהֶל מוֹעֵד לֹא יְבִיאֶנּוּ לַעֲשׂוֹת אֹתוֹ לַיהוָה וְנִכְרַת
be shall to it offer to does not meeting the the
off cut ,Jehovah it bring of tent of door

3478 1004 376 376 5971 376
10 הָאִישׁ הַהוּא מֵעַמָּיו׃ וְאִישׁ אִישׁ מִבֵּית יִשְׂרָאֵל וּמִן־
of or Israel the of any And his from that man
of house man .people

5315 6440 5414 1818 398 7130 1481 1616
הַגֵּר הַגָּר בְּתוֹכָם אֲשֶׁר יֹאכַל כָּל־דָּם וְנָתַתִּי פָנַי בַּנֶּפֶשׁ
against My will I ,blood any eats who your in is who the
person the face set ,midst staying alien

5971 7130 3772 1818 398
11 הָאֹכֶלֶת אֶת־הַדָּם וְהִכְרַתִּי אֹתָהּ מִקֶּרֶב עַמָּהּ׃ כִּי־
For his the from him will I and the eats that
.people of midst off cut blood

4196 5921 5414 1818 1320 5315
נֶפֶשׁ הַבָּשָׂר בַּדָּם הִוא וַאֲנִי נְתַתִּיו לָכֶם עַל־הַמִּזְבֵּחַ
,altar the on you to have I and it the in flesh the the
it given (is) blood of life

3651 3722 5315 1818 5315 3722
12 לְכַפֵּר עַל־נַפְשֹׁתֵיכֶם כִּי־הַדָּם הוּא בַּנֶּפֶשׁ יְכַפֵּר׃ עַל־כֵּן
this For which the for (is) it the for ;souls your for to
reason .atones soul blood atone

1616 1818 398 8432 5315 3478 1121 559
אָמַרְתִּי לִבְנֵי יִשְׂרָאֵל כָּל־נֶפֶשׁ מִכֶּם לֹא־תֹאכַל דָּם וְהַגֵּר
the and ,blood shall not among soul Any ,Israel the to have I
alien eat you of sons said

3478 1121 376 376 1818 398 3808 8432 1481
13 הַגָּר בְּתוֹכְכֶם לֹא־יֹאכַל דָּם׃ וְאִישׁ אִישׁ מִבְּנֵי יִשְׂרָאֵל
,Israel the of any And .blood shall not your in staying
of sons man eat midst

5775 2416 6718 6679 8432 1481 1616
וּמִן־הַגֵּר הַגָּר בְּתוֹכָם אֲשֶׁר יָצוּד צֵיד חַיָּה אוֹ־עוֹף אֲשֶׁר
which fowl or of game hunts who your in who the of or
beast ,midst stay aliens

1320 3605 5315 6083 3680 1818 8210 398
14 יֵאָכֵל וְשָׁפַךְ אֶת־דָּמוֹ וְכִסָּהוּ בֶּעָפָר׃ כִּי־נֶפֶשׁ כָּל־בָּשָׂר
flesh all the for with and its shall then be may
of life ;dust it cover blood out pour ;eaten

3808 1320 3605 1818 3478 1121 559 5315 1818
דָּמוֹ בְנַפְשׁוֹ הוּא וָאֹמַר לִבְנֵי יִשְׂרָאֵל דַּם כָּל־בָּשָׂר לֹא
not ;flesh any blood ,Israel the to I and it its with its (is)
of of sons say (one is) life ;blood

3772 398 3605 1818 1320 3605 5315 398
תֹאכֵלוּ כִּי נֶפֶשׁ כָּל־בָּשָׂר דָּמוֹ הִוא כָּל־אֹכְלָיו יִכָּרֵת׃
be shall eating any it flesh all the for shall You
off cut it one (is) blood of life eat

3526 1616 249 2966 5038 398 5315 3605
15 וְכָל־נֶפֶשׁ אֲשֶׁר תֹּאכַל נְבֵלָה וּטְרֵפָה בָּאֶזְרָח וּבַגֵּר וְכִבֶּס
shall he an or a he be torn a or dead a eats who person And
wash ,alien native ,thing body any

clothes, and bathe in water, and be unclean until the evening; then he shall be clean. [16]And if he does not wash them, nor bathe his flesh, then he shall bear his iniquity.

CHAPTER 18

[1]And Jehovah spoke to Moses, saying, [2]Speak to the sons of Israel and say to them, I am Jehovah your God. [3]You shall not do according to the doings of the land of Egypt in which you lived; and you shall not do according to the doings of the land of Canaan where I am bringing you; nor shall you walk in their statutes. [4]You shall do My judgments and you shall keep My statutes, to walk in them; I *am* Jehovah your God. [5]and you shall keep My statutes and My judgments, which if a man do, he shall live by them. I *am* Jehovah.

[6]None of you shall draw near to any relative of his flesh to uncover the*ir* nakedness; I *am* Jehovah. [7]You shall not uncover the nakedness of your father or the nakedness of your mother; she is your mother; you shall not uncover her nakedness. [8]You shall not uncover the nakedness of your father's wife; it *is* the nakedness of your father. [9]You shall not uncover the nakedness of your sister, the daughter of your father, or the daughter of your mother, born at home, or born away; you shall not uncover their nakedness. [10]You shall not uncover the nakedness of your son's daughter, or your daughter's daughter; you shall not uncover their nakedness, got theirs *is* your own nakedness. [11]The nakedness of the daughter of your father's wife, begotten by your father, she *is* your

16 בְּגָדָיו וְרָחַץ בַּמַּיִם וְטָמֵא עַד־הָעֶרֶב וְטָהֵר׃ וְאִם לֹא יְכַבֵּס

does he not And he then the until be and in and his / ,them wash if .clean be shall ;evening unclean ,water bathe clothes

וּבְשָׂרוֹ לֹא יִרְחָץ וְנָשָׂא עֲוֹנוֹ׃

his he then ,bathe not his and / .iniquity bear shall flesh

CAP. XVIII יח

CHAPTER 18

1 2 וַיְדַבֵּר יְהוָה אֶל־מֹשֶׁה לֵּאמֹר׃ דַּבֵּר אֶל־בְּנֵי יִשְׂרָאֵל

Israel the to Speak ,saying ,Moses to Jehovah And / of sons spoke

3 וְאָמַרְתָּ אֲלֵהֶם אֲנִי יְהוָה אֱלֹהֵיכֶם׃ כְּמַעֲשֵׂה אֶרֶץ־מִצְרַיִם

Egypt the the Like .God your Jehovah I ,them to say and / of land of deeds (am)

אֲשֶׁר יְשַׁבְתֶּם־בָּהּ לֹא תַעֲשׂוּ וּכְמַעֲשֵׂה אֶרֶץ־כְּנַעַן אֲשֶׁר

where Canaan the the like and shall you not in lived you which / of land of deeds ;do ,it

אֲנִי מֵבִיא אֶתְכֶם שָׁמָּה לֹא תַעֲשׂוּ וּבְחֻקֹּתֵיהֶם לֹא תֵלֵכוּ׃

you shall not their in and shall you not ,there you am I / .walk statutes ;do bringing

4 אֶת־מִשְׁפָּטַי תַּעֲשׂוּ וְאֶת־חֻקֹּתַי תִּשְׁמְרוּ לָלֶכֶת בָּהֶם אֲנִי

I ;them in walk to shall you My and shall You My / (am) ,keep statutes do judgments

5 יְהוָה אֱלֹהֵיכֶם׃ וּשְׁמַרְתֶּם אֶת־חֻקֹּתַי וְאֶת־מִשְׁפָּטַי אֲשֶׁר

which My and My you And .God your Jehovah / ,judgments statutes keep shall

6 יַעֲשֶׂה אֹתָם הָאָדָם וָחַי בָּהֶם אֲנִי יְהוָה׃ אִישׁ אִישׁ

Any .Jehovah I ;them by he and man a them do shall / man (am) live shall

אֶל־כָּל־שְׁאֵר בְּשָׂרוֹ לֹא תִקְרְבוּ לְגַלּוֹת עֶרְוָה אֲנִי יְהוָה׃

.Jehovah I naked- the to shall you not flesh his relative any to / (am) ;ness uncover near draw of

7 עֶרְוַת אָבִיךָ וְעֶרְוַת אִמְּךָ לֹא תְגַלֵּה אִמְּךָ הִוא לֹא

not she your shall you not your the and your The / ;(is) mother ;uncover ,mother of nakedness ,father of nakedness

8 תְגַלֶּה עֶרְוָתָהּ׃ עֶרְוַת אֵשֶׁת־אָבִיךָ לֹא תְגַלֵּה

shall you not your wife The her shall you / ;uncover father's of nakedness .nakedness uncover

9 עֶרְוַת אָבִיךָ הִוא׃ עֶרְוַת אֲחוֹתְךָ בַת־אָבִיךָ אוֹ

or your the ,sister your The .(is) it father your the / ,father of daughter of nakedness of nakedness

בַּת־אִמְּךָ מוֹלֶדֶת בַּיִת אוֹ מוֹלֶדֶת חוּץ לֹא תְגַלֶּה עֶרְוָתָן׃

their shall you not ,away born or at born ,mother your the / .nakedness uncover home of daughter

10 עֶרְוַת בַּת־בִּנְךָ אוֹ בַת־בִּתְּךָ לֹא תְגַלֶּה עֶרְוָתָן כִּי

for their shall you not your of or your daughter The / ;nakedness uncover daughter's daughter ,son's of nakedness

11 עֶרְוָתְךָ הֵנָּה׃ עֶרְוַת בַּת־אֵשֶׁת אָבִיךָ מוֹלֶדֶת

begotten your wife a naked- the theirs own your / by ,father's of daughter of ness .(is) nakedness

sister; you shall not uncover
her nakedness. 12You shall
not uncover the nakedness
of a sister of your father; she
is a relative of your father.
13You shall not uncover the
nakedness of your mother's
sister; for she is your
mother's relative. 14You
shall not uncover the
nakedness of your father's
brother; you shall not draw
near to his wife; she is your
aunt. 15You shall not un-
cover the nakedness of your
daughter-in-law; she is your
son's wife; you shall not
uncover her nakedness.
16You shall not uncover the
nakedness of your brother's
wife; it *is* your brother's
nakedness. 17You shall not
uncover the nakedness of a
woman and her daughter;
you shall not undertake to
uncover her son's daughter,
and her daughter's daugh-
ter; they *are* her relatives; it
is evil. 18And you shall
not take a wife with her
sister, to be a vexer to
her, to uncover her
nakedness, beside the
other in her lifetime.
19And you shall not
draw near to uncover the
nakedness of a woman in
the impurity of her un-
cleanness. 20And you
shall not give to your
neighbor's wife, lying
with semen, to be un-
clean with her. 21And you
shall not give your seed
to pour over them to
Molech; nor shall you
pollute the name of your
God; I *am* Jehovah.
22And you shall not lie
with a male as one lies
with a woman; it *is* de-
testable. 23And you shall
not give, lying down with
any animal, for unclean-
ness with it. And a
woman shall not stand
before an animal, to lie
with it; it *is* a shameful
mixing.
24Do not defile yourself
with all these, for with all
these the nations have
been defiled, which I am
expelling before you 25and
the land is defiled, and I
will visit its iniquity on

6172 6172 1540 3808 269 1
12 ערות אביך אחותך היא לא תגלה ערותה׃
The her shall you not ;(is) she your your
of nakedness .nakedness uncover sister ,father

6172 7607 1 1540 3808 269
13 ערות אחות־אביך לא תגלה שאר אביך הוא׃
The .(is) she your relative a shall you not your sister a
of nakedness father of ;uncover ,father of

6172 517 7607 1540 517 269
14 ערות אחות־אמך לא תגלה כי־שאר אמך הוא׃
The .(is) she your relative for shall you not your ,sister
of nakedness mother's ;uncover mother's

1733 7126 802 1540 251
אחי־אביך לא תגלה אל־אשתו לא תקרב דדתך הוא׃
.(is) she your shall you not wife his to shall you not your brother
aunt ;near draw ;uncover ,father's

1540 3808 1121 802 1540 3618 6172
15 ערות כלתך לא תגלה אשת בנך הוא לא תגלה
shall you not she your wife shall you not your The
uncover ;(is) son's ;uncover ,daughter-in-law of nakedness

6172 1540 3808 251 802 6172 6172
16 ערותה׃ ערות אשת־אחיך לא תגלה ערות
nakedness shall you not your wife The her
;uncover brother's of nakedness .nakedness

1540 251 802 6172 251
17 אחיך הוא׃ ערות אשה ובתה לא תגלה את־
shall you not her and a The .(is) it your
;uncover ,daughter woman of nakedness brother's

7608 6172 1540 3947 3808 1323 1323 1121/1323
בת־בנה ואת־בת־בתה לא תקח לגלות ערותה שארה
her naked- her to shall you not her daughter and her daugh-
relatives ;ness uncover undertake ,daughter's son's ter

1540 6887 3947 269 802 2154
18 הנה זמה הוא׃ ואשה אל־אחתה לא תקח לצרר לגלות
to a be to shall you not her with a And .(is) it .evil they
uncover vexer take ,sister wife :(are)

7126 3808 2932 5079 802 2416 6172
19 ערותה עליה בחייה׃ ואל־אשה בנדת טמאתה לא תקרב
shall you not her the in woman a And her in beside naked- her
near draw ,uncleanness of impurity to .lifetime other the ,ness

7903 5414 5997 802 6172 1540
20 לגלות ערותה׃ ואל־אשת עמיתך לא־תתן שכבתך
your shall you not your the to And her uncover to
lying give ,neighbor of wife .nakedness

3808 4432 5674 5414 2233 2930 2233
21 לזרע לטמאה־בה׃ ומזרעך לא־תתן להעביר למלך ולא
not ;Molech to pour to shall you not And with be to with
them over give seed your .her unclean semen

7901 3808 2145 3068 430 8034 2490
22 תחלל את־שם אלהיך אני יהוה׃ ואת־זכר לא תשכב
shall you not ,male a And .Jehovah I your name the shall you
lie with (am) ;God of pollute

7903 5414 929 3605 8397 802 4904
23 משכבי אשה תועבה הוא׃ ובכל־בהמה לא־תתן שכבתך
your shall you not ,animal And .(is) it detestable a one as
down lying give any with ;woman with lies

7250 929 6440 5975 3808 802 2930
לטמאה־בה ואשה לא־תעמד לפני בהמה לרבעה תבל
a down lie to an before shall not a and with for
mixing ;it with animal stand woman ;it uncleanness

1471 2930 428 3605 411 2930
24 הוא׃ אל־תטמאו בכל־אלה כי בכל־אלה נטמאו הגוים
the been have these with for ,these with defile Do not .(is) it
,nations defiled all all yourselves

5771 6485 776 2930 6440 7971 834
25 אשר־אני משלח מפניכם׃ ותטמא הארץ ואפקד עונה
its I and the is And before am I which
iniquity visit will ,land defiled .you out casting

it; and the land is vomiting out its inhabitants; [26]and you, you shall keep My statutes and My judgments, and shall not do *any* of all these disgusting acts; *neither* the native nor the alien who is staying in your midst. [27]For the men of the land who are before you have done all these disgusting things, and the land is defiled; [28]lest the land vomit you out for your defiling it, as it has vomited out the nation that *was* before you. [29]For anyone who does *any* of these disgusting things, even the persons who are doing *them*, shall be cut off from the midst of their people. [30]And you shall keep My charge, so as not to do *any* of the disgusting customs which were committed before you; and you shall not defile yourselves with them; I *am* Jehovah your God.

2708 8104 3427 776 6958 5921
26 עָלֶיהָ וַתָּקִא הָאָרֶץ אֶת־יֹשְׁבֶיהָ׃ וּשְׁמַרְתֶּם אַתֶּם אֶת־חֻקֹּתַי
My statutes ,you you And keep shall its ,inhabitants the land shall and out vomit it on

249 428 8441 6213/ 4941
וְאֶת־מִשְׁפָּטַי וְלֹא תַעֲשׂוּ מִכֹּל הַתּוֹעֵבֹת הָאֵלֶּה הָאֶזְרָח
the native ,these detestable acts of (any) all do shall not and My ,judgments and

582 6213 8441 3605 3588/8432 1481/1616
27 וְהַגֵּר הַגָּר בְּתוֹכְכֶם׃ כִּי אֶת־כָּל־הַתּוֹעֵבֹת הָאֵל עָשׂוּ אַנְשֵׁי־
men the of have done these detestable things all for your in ;midst who is staying the alien

776 6958 776 2930 776
28 הָאָרֶץ אֲשֶׁר לִפְנֵיכֶם וַתִּטְמָא הָאָרֶץ׃ וְלֹא־תָקִיא הָאָרֶץ
land the vomit out lest the ;land is and defiled before ,you who (were) the land

1471 6958 2930
אֶתְכֶם בְּטַמַּאֲכֶם אֹתָהּ כַּאֲשֶׁר קָאָה אֶת־הַגּוֹי אֲשֶׁר
that (was) nation the it out vomited as ,it your for defiling you

3772 428 8441 6213 3605 6440
29 לִפְנֵיכֶם׃ כִּי כָּל־אֲשֶׁר יַעֲשֶׂה מִכֹּל הַתּוֹעֵבֹת הָאֵלֶּה וְנִכְרְתוּ
be shall ,off cut these abomin- ations of (any) all does who anyone For before ,you

4931 8104 5971 7130 6213 5315
30 הַנְּפָשׁוֹת הָעֹשֹׂת מִקֶּרֶב עַמָּם׃ וּשְׁמַרְתֶּם אֶת־מִשְׁמַרְתִּי
,charge My you and keep shall their ;people from among are who ,(them) doing the even persons

3808 6440 6213 834 8441 2708 6213
לְבִלְתִּי עֲשׂוֹת מֵחֻקּוֹת הַתּוֹעֵבֹת אֲשֶׁר נַעֲשׂוּ לִפְנֵיכֶם וְלֹא
and not before ;you were done which detestable customs the of (any) do to as so not

430 3068 2930
תִטַּמְּאוּ בָּהֶם אֲנִי יְהוָה אֱלֹהֵיכֶם׃
.God your Jehovah I (am) ;them with shall you yourselves defile

CAP. XIX יט

CHAPTER 19

CHAPTER 19

[1]And Jehovah spoke to Moses, saying, [2]Speak to all the congregation of the sons of Israel, and you shall say to them, You are holy, for I *am* holy, Jehovah your God. [3]Each man of you shall fear his mother and his father, and keep My sabbaths; I *am* Jehovah your God. [4]Do not turn yourself to the idols; and you shall not make molten gods for yourselves; I *am* Jehovah your God.

[5]And if you sacrifice a sacrifice of peace offerings to Jehovah, you shall sacrifice it at your pleasure; [6]it shall be eaten in the day of your sacrificing it, and on the morrow, and that which is left on the third day shall be burned with fire. [7]And if it is at all eaten on the third

1121 5712/3605 1696 559 4872 3068 1696
1
2 וַיְדַבֵּר יְהוָה אֶל־מֹשֶׁה לֵּאמֹר׃ דַּבֵּר אֶל־כָּל־עֲדַת בְּנֵי־
the company the all to of sons of Speak ,saying ,Moses to Jehovah And spoke

3068 6918 6918 559 3478
יִשְׂרָאֵל וְאָמַרְתָּ אֲלֵהֶם קְדֹשִׁים תִּהְיוּ כִּי קָדוֹשׁ אֲנִי יְהוָה
Jehovah I (am) holy for ,are You holy ,them to you and say shall ,Israel

8104 7676 3372 1 517 376 430
3 אֱלֹהֵיכֶם׃ אִישׁ אִמּוֹ וְאָבִיו תִּירָאוּ וְאֶת־שַׁבְּתֹתַי תִּשְׁמֹרוּ
;keep My Sabbaths and shall fear his and ,father his mother Each man .God your

4547 430 457 6437 430 3068
4 אֲנִי יְהוָה אֱלֹהֵיכֶם׃ אַל־תִּפְנוּ אֶל־הָאֱלִילִם וֵאלֹהֵי מַסֵּכָה
casted and gods ;idols the to turn Do yourselves not .God your Jehovah I (am)

2077 2076 430 3068 6213
5 לֹא תַעֲשׂוּ לָכֶם אֲנִי יְהוָה אֱלֹהֵיכֶם׃ וְכִי תִזְבְּחוּ זֶבַח
a sacrifice of sacrifice you And when .God your Jehovah I (am) ;you for shall you make not

398 2077 3117 2076 7522 3068 8002
6 שְׁלָמִים לַיהוָה לִרְצֹנְכֶם תִּזְבָּחֻהוּ׃ בְּיוֹם זִבְחֲכֶם יֵאָכֵל
shall it ;eaten be your sacrificing the in of day shall you ;it sacrifice your of ;will free to .Jehovah peace offerings

8313 784 7992 3117 3498 4283
7 וּמִמָּחֳרָת וְהַנּוֹתָר עַד־יוֹם הַשְּׁלִישִׁי בָּאֵשׁ יִשָּׂרֵף׃ וְאִם
And if be shall .burned with fire the third day on that and left is which on and ,morrow the

day, it *is* unclean; it shall not
be accepted. [8]And he who
shall eat his shall bear his
iniquity; for he has polluted
the holy thing of Jehovah,
and that person shall be cut
off from his people.

[9]And as you reap the harvest of your land, you shall
not completely reap the
corner of your field; and you
shall not gather the gleaning of your harvest; [10]and
you shall not glean your
vineyard and you shall not
gather what has been left of
your vineyard; you shall
leave them to the poor and
to the alien; I *am* Jehovah
your God.

[11]You shall not steal, nor
lie, nor deceive to one
another. [12]And you shall
not swear by My name to a
falsehood; nor shall you
pollute the name of your
God; I *am* Jehovah.

[13]You shall not extort
your neighbor; nor rob; you
shall not allow the wages of
one hired to remain with
you until morning. [14]You
shall not revile the deaf, nor
put a stumbling-block be-
fore the blind; for you shall
be afraid of your God;I *am*
Jehovah.

[15]You shall do no un-
righteousness in judgment;
you shall not respect the
person of the poor, nor
favor the person of the
mighty; but in righteous-
ness you shall judge your
neighbor. [16]You shall not go
slandering among your
people; you shall not stand
up against the blood of your
neighbor; I *am* Jehovah.
[17]You shall not hate your
brother in your heart; you
shall certainly reprove your
neighbor, and not allow sin
on him. [18]You shall not
take vengeance, nor bear
any grudge against the sons
of your people; and you
shall love your neighbor as
yourself; I *am* Jehovah.

[19]You shall keep my
statutes; you shall not
cause your livestock to
breed with different kinds;
you shall not sow your field
with different kinds; and
you shall not allow a garment mingled of linen and
wool to come upon you.

8 הָאָכֹל יֵאָכֵל בַּיּוֹם הַשְּׁלִישִׁי פִּגּוּל הוּא לֹא יֵרָצֶה׃ וְאֹכְלָיו
עֲוֺנוֹ יִשָּׂא כִּי־אֶת־קֹדֶשׁ יְהוָה חִלֵּל וְנִכְרְתָה הַנֶּפֶשׁ הַהִוא
9 מֵעַמֶּיהָ׃ וּבְקֻצְרְכֶם אֶת־קְצִיר אַרְצְכֶם לֹא תְכַלֶּה פְּאַת
10 שָׂדְךָ לִקְצֹר וְלֶקֶט קְצִירְךָ לֹא תְלַקֵּט׃ וְכַרְמְךָ לֹא תְעוֹלֵל
וּפֶרֶט כַּרְמְךָ לֹא תְלַקֵּט לֶעָנִי וְלַגֵּר תַּעֲזֹב אֹתָם אֲנִי יְהוָה
11 אֱלֹהֵיכֶם׃ לֹא תִּגְנֹבוּ וְלֹא־תְכַחֲשׁוּ וְלֹא־תְשַׁקְּרוּ אִישׁ
12 בַּעֲמִיתוֹ׃ וְלֹא־תִשָּׁבְעוּ בִשְׁמִי לַשָּׁקֶר וְחִלַּלְתָּ אֶת־שֵׁם
13 אֱלֹהֶיךָ אֲנִי יְהוָה׃ לֹא־תַעֲשֹׁק אֶת־רֵעֲךָ וְלֹא תִגְזֹל לֹא־
14 תָלִין פְּעֻלַּת שָׂכִיר אִתְּךָ עַד־בֹּקֶר׃ לֹא־תְקַלֵּל חֵרֵשׁ וְלִפְנֵי
15 עִוֵּר לֹא תִתֵּן מִכְשֹׁל וְיָרֵאתָ מֵּאֱלֹהֶיךָ אֲנִי יְהוָה׃ לֹא־תַעֲשׂוּ
עָוֶל בַּמִּשְׁפָּט לֹא־תִשָּׂא פְנֵי־דָל וְלֹא תֶהְדַּר פְּנֵי גָדוֹל
16 בְּצֶדֶק תִּשְׁפֹּט עֲמִיתֶךָ׃ לֹא־תֵלֵךְ רָכִיל בְּעַמֶּיךָ לֹא תַעֲמֹד
17 עַל־דַּם רֵעֶךָ אֲנִי יְהוָה׃ לֹא־תִשְׂנָא אֶת־אָחִיךָ בִּלְבָבֶךָ
18 הוֹכֵחַ תּוֹכִיחַ אֶת־עֲמִיתֶךָ וְלֹא־תִשָּׂא עָלָיו חֵטְא׃ לֹא־
תִקֹּם וְלֹא־תִטֹּר אֶת־בְּנֵי עַמֶּךָ וְאָהַבְתָּ לְרֵעֲךָ כָּמוֹךָ אֲנִי
19 יְהוָה׃ אֶת־חֻקֹּתַי תִּשְׁמְרוּ בְּהֶמְתְּךָ לֹא־תַרְבִּיעַ כִּלְאַיִם
שָׂדְךָ לֹא־תִזְרַע כִּלְאָיִם וּבֶגֶד כִּלְאַיִם שַׁעַטְנֵז לֹא יַעֲלֶה

[20]And when a man lies with a woman with semen, and she *is* a slave-girl, betrothed to a man, and not truly redeemed, and freedom not having been given to her, there shall be an inquest; they shall not be put to death, because she was not free. [21]And he shall bring in his guilt offering to Jehovah, to the door of the tabernacle of the congregation, a ram *for* a guilt offering. [22]And the priest shall make atonement for him with the ram of the guilt offering before Jehovah, for his sin which he has sinned; and it shall be forgiven him because of his sin he has sinned.

[23]And when you come into the land and have planted all of the food trees, then you shall expose its foreskin, its fruit, it shall be uncircumcised for you three years; it shall not be eaten. [24]And in the fourth year all its fruit is holy; *it is for* praises for Jehovah. [25]And in the fifth year you shall eat its fruit, that it may yield to you its increase; I *am* Jehovah your God.

[26]You shall not eat with the blood; you shall not divine, nor conjure *spirits*. [27]You shall not round the corner of your head, nor mar the corner of your beard. [28]And you shall not make any cuttings in your flesh for the dead; and you shall not put on yourself any writing or mark; I *am* Jehovah.

[29]You shall not pollute your daughter, to cause her to go whoring, that the land may not go whoring, and the land become full of wickedness. [30]You shall keep My sabbaths; and you shall revere My sanctuary. I *am* Jehovah.

[31]You shall not turn to those having familiar spirits; and you shall not seek to spiritists to be defiled by them; I *am* Jehovah your God.

8198 2233 7902 802 7901 376 5921
20 עָלֶיךָ׃ וְאִישׁ כִּי־יִשְׁכַּב אֶת־אִשָּׁה שִׁכְבַת־זֶרַע וְהִוא שִׁפְחָה
slave- a and semen lying a with lies he if And upon
girl (is) she (with) woman down ,man a ,you

5414 2668 176 6299 3808 6299 376 2778
נֶחֱרֶפֶת לְאִישׁ וְהָפְדֵּה לֹא נִפְדָּתָה אוֹ חֻפְשָׁה לֹא נִתַּן־
given not freedom or ransomed not but a to betrothed
actually man

935 2666 3808 4191 1961 1244
21 לָהּ בִּקֹּרֶת תִּהְיֶה לֹא יוּמְתוּ כִּי־לֹא חֻפָּשָׁה׃ וְהֵבִיא אֶת־
he And was she not for shall they not ;be shall an to
bring shall .free executed be inquest her

3722 816 352 4150 168 6607 3068 816
22 אֲשָׁמוֹ לַיהוָה אֶל־פֶּתַח אֹהֶל מוֹעֵד אֵיל אָשָׁם׃ וְכִפֶּר
shall and guilt a ,ram a ,meeting the the to to guilt his
atone ;offering of tent of door Jehovah offering

834 2403 3068 6440 816 352 3548
עָלָיו הַכֹּהֵן בְּאֵיל הָאָשָׁם לִפְנֵי יְהוָה עַל־חַטָּאתוֹ אֲשֶׁר
which sin his for ,Jehovah before guilt the the with the for
offering of ram priest him

2403 834 2403 5545 2398
חָטָא וְנִסְלַח לוֹ מֵחַטָּאתוֹ אֲשֶׁר חָטָא׃
has he which because him shall and has he
.sinned sin his of forgiven be ;sinned

6188 3978 6086 5193 776 935
23 וְכִי־תָבֹאוּ אֶל־הָאָרֶץ וּנְטַעְתֶּם כָּל־עֵץ מַאֲכָל וַעֲרַלְתֶּם
shall you then (for) tree any and the into you And
expose food plant land come when

398 6189 1961 8141 7969 6529 6190
עָרְלָתוֹ אֶת־פִּרְיוֹ שָׁלֹשׁ שָׁנִים יִהְיֶה לָכֶם עֲרֵלִים לֹא יֵאָכֵל׃
shall it not uncircum- for shall it years three its its
;eaten be ;cised you be fruit foreskin

3068 1974 6944 6529 3605 1961 7243 8141
24 וּבַשָּׁנָה הָרְבִיעִת יִהְיֶה כָּל־פִּרְיוֹ קֹדֶשׁ הִלּוּלִים לַיהוָה׃
for (for is it) ;holy its all is fourth in and
.Jehovah praises fruit year the

8393 3254 6529 398 2549 8141
25 וּבַשָּׁנָה הַחֲמִישִׁת תֹּאכְלוּ אֶת־פִּרְיוֹ לְהוֹסִיף לָכֶם תְּבוּאָתוֹ
its for to its shall you fifth in And
;increase you yield ;fruit eat year the

5172 1818 398 430 3068
26 אֲנִי יְהוָה אֱלֹהֵיכֶם׃ לֹא תֹאכְלוּ עַל־הַדָּם לֹא תְנַחֲשׁוּ
shall you not the with shall You not .God your Jehovah I
divine ;blood eat (am)

7843 3808 7218 6255 5362 3808 5172
27 וְלֹא תְעוֹנֵנוּ׃ לֹא תַקִּפוּ פְּאַת רֹאשְׁכֶם וְלֹא תַשְׁחִית אֵת
mar nor ,head your the shall You not conjure nor
of side round .(spirits)

3793 1320 643 4191 8296 2206 6285
28 פְּאַת זְקָנֶךָ׃ וְשֶׂרֶט לָנֶפֶשׁ לֹא תִתְּנוּ בִּבְשַׂרְכֶם וּכְתֹבֶת
and your in shall you not the for And your the
mark ;flesh make dead cuttings .beard of edge

1323 2490 3068 5414 7085
29 קַעֲקַע לֹא תִתְּנוּ בָּכֶם אֲנִי יְהוָה׃ אַל־תְּחַלֵּל אֶת־בִּתְּךָ
your shall You not .Jehovah I on shall you not tattoo
,daughter profane (am) ;yourself put

2154 776 4390 776 2181 2181
30 לְהַזְנוֹתָהּ וְלֹא־תִזְנֶה הָאָרֶץ וּמָלְאָה הָאָרֶץ זִמָּה׃ אֶת־
.evil land the become and the go may that her make to
of full land whoring not ,harlot a

6437 3068 3372 4720 8104 7676
31 שַׁבְּתֹתַי תִּשְׁמֹרוּ וּמִקְדָּשִׁי תִּירָאוּ אֲנִי יְהוָה׃ אַל־תִּפְנוּ
shall You not .Jehovah I shall you My and shall you My
turn (am) ;revere sanctuary ;keep sabbaths

2930 1245 3049 178
אֶל־הָאֹבֹת וְאֶל־הַיִּדְּעֹנִים אַל־תְּבַקְשׁוּ לְטָמְאָה בָהֶם אֲנִי
I by be to shall you not spiritists to and mediums to
(am) ;them defiled seek

[32]You shall rise up in the face of gray hairs; and you shall honor the face of an old man; and be afraid of your God. I *am* Jehovah.

[33]And when an alien lives with you in your land, you shall not oppress him; [34]as the native among you, so shall be the alien who is staying with you; and you shall love him as yourself, for you were aliens in the land of Egypt; I *am* Jehovah your God.

[35]You shall do no unrighteousness in judgment, in measures and weights, or in quantity. [36]You shall have just balances, just weights, a just ephah, and a just hin. I *am* Jehovah your God, who brought you out from the land of Egypt; [37]and you shall observe all My statutes, and all My judgments and shall do them; I *am* Jehovah.

3372 2205/6440 1921 6965 7872 6440 430 3068
32 יְהוָה אֱלֹהֵיכֶם׃ מִפְּנֵי שֵׂיבָה תָּקוּם וְהָדַרְתָּ פְּנֵי זָקֵן וְיָרֵאתָ
fear and old an the you and shall you gray the In .God your Jehovah
;man of face honor shall ;rise hairs of face

3808 776 1616 1481 3068 430
33 מֵאֱלֹהֶיךָ אֲנִי יְהוָה׃ ס וְכִי־יָגוּר אִתְּךָ גֵּר בְּאַרְצְכֶם לֹא
not your in an with stays And .Jehovah I ;God your
,land alien you when (am)

1481/ 1616 1961 854 249 3238
34 תוֹנוּ אֹתוֹ׃ כְּאֶזְרָח מִכֶּם יִהְיֶה לָכֶם הַגֵּר הַגָּר אִתְּכֶם
with is who the you to shall (so) among the as ;him shall you
you staying alien be ,you native oppress

3068 4714 776 1961 1616 157
וְאָהַבְתָּ לוֹ כָּמוֹךָ כִּי־גֵרִים הֱיִיתֶם בְּאֶרֶץ מִצְרָיִם אֲנִי יְהוָה
Jehovah I ;Egypt the in you aliens for as him you and
(am) of land were ,yourself love shall

4948 4060 4941 5766 6213 430
35 אֱלֹהֵיכֶם׃ לֹא־תַעֲשׂוּ עָוֶל בַּמִּשְׁפָּט בַּמִּדָּה בַּמִּשְׁקָל
and in ,judgment in evil shall You no .God your
weights measures do

6664 1969 6664 374 6664 68 6664 3976 4884
36 וּבַמְּשׂוּרָה׃ מֹאזְנֵי צֶדֶק אַבְנֵי־צֶדֶק אֵיפַת צֶדֶק וְהִין צֶדֶק
just a and a ephah just weights ,just balances liquid in and
hin ,just ; ;capacity

776 3318 430 3068 1961
יִהְיֶה לָכֶם אֲנִי יְהוָה אֱלֹהֵיכֶם אֲשֶׁר־הוֹצֵאתִי אֶתְכֶם מֵאֶרֶץ
the from you brought who ,God your Jehovah I to shall
of land out (am) .you be

4941 3605 2708 3605 8104 4714
37 מִצְרָיִם׃ וּשְׁמַרְתֶּם אֶת־כָּל־חֻקֹּתַי וְאֶת־כָּל־מִשְׁפָּטַי
My all and My all shall you And .Egypt
judgments ,statutes observe

3068 6213
וַעֲשִׂיתֶם אֹתָם אֲנִי יְהוָה׃
.Jehovah I ;them shall and
(am) do

CAP. XX כ

CHAPTER 20

[1]And Jehovah spoke to Moses, saying, [2]And you shall say to the sons of Israel, Any man of the sons of Israel, and of the aliens who are living in Israel, who gives of his seed to Molech shall certainly be put to death; the people of the land shall stone him with stones! [3]And I, I shall set My face against that man, and shall cut him off from the midst of his people, for he has given of his seed to Molech, so as to defile My sanctuary, and to pollute My holy name. [4]And if the people of the land truly hide their eyes from that man, as he gives his seed to Molech, so as not to put him to death, [5]then I shall

559 3478 1121 559 4872 3068 1696
1
2 וַיְדַבֵּר יְהוָה אֶל־מֹשֶׁה לֵּאמֹר׃ וְאֶל־בְּנֵי יִשְׂרָאֵל תֹּאמַר
shall you Israel the to And ,saying ,Moses to Jehovah And
say of sons spoke

3478 1481 1616 3478 1121 376 376
אִישׁ אִישׁ מִבְּנֵי יִשְׂרָאֵל וּמִן־הַגֵּר ׀ הַגָּר בְּיִשְׂרָאֵל אֲשֶׁר
who ,Israel in are who the of or ,Israel the of Any
staying aliens of sons man

68 7275 776 5971 4191 4191 4432 2233
יִתֵּן מִזַּרְעוֹ לַמֹּלֶךְ מוֹת יוּמָת עַם הָאָרֶץ יִרְגְּמֻהוּ בָאָבֶן׃
with stone shall the the be shall surely to his of give
;stones him land of people ,executed ,Molech seed

5971 7130 3772 376 6440 5414
3 וַאֲנִי אֶתֵּן אֶת־פָּנַי בָּאִישׁ הַהוּא וְהִכְרַתִּי אֹתוֹ מִקֶּרֶב עַמּוֹ
his from him shall and ,that against My shall I and
;people among off cut man face set ,I

2490 4720 2930 4432 5414 2233
כִּי מִזַּרְעוֹ נָתַן לַמֹּלֶךְ לְמַעַן טַמֵּא אֶת־מִקְדָּשִׁי וּלְחַלֵּל אֶת־
to and My to as so to has he his of for
pollute sanctuary defile ,Molech given seed

5869 776 5971 5956 5956 6944 8034
4 שֵׁם קָדְשִׁי׃ וְאִם הַעְלֵם יַעְלִימוּ עַם הָאָרֶץ אֶת־עֵינֵיהֶם
eyes their land the the hide all at if And My .name
of people holy

4191 1115 4432 2233 5414 376
מִן־הָאִישׁ הַהוּא בְּתִתּוֹ מִזַּרְעוֹ לַמֹּלֶךְ לְבִלְתִּי הָמִית אֹתוֹ׃
,him to as so to seed his he as ,that man from
execute not ,Molech gives

set My face against that man, and against his family, and shall cut him off, and all who go whoring after him, even going whoring after Molech, from the midst of their people.

[6]And the person who turns to those having familiar spirits, and to the spiritists, to go whoring after them, I shall set my face against that person, and cut him off from the midst of his people. [7]And you shall sanctify yourselves, and you shall be holy, for I *am* Jehovah your God; [8]and you shall keep My statutes and shall do them; I *am* Jehovah who is sanctifying you. [9]And any man who curses his father and his mother shall certainly be put to death; he has cursed his father and his mother; his blood *shall be* on him.

[10]And a man who commits adultery with a man's wife, who commits adultery with the wife of his neighbor, the adulterer and the adulteress are surely to be put to death. [11]And a man who lies with his father's wife, who has uncovered the nakedness of his father, both of them shall surely be put to death; their blood *shall be* on them. [12]And a man who lies with his daughter-in-law, both of them shall surely be put to death; they have made a *shameful* mixture; their blood *shall be* on them. [13]And a man who lies with a male as one lies with a woman, both of them have done a disgusting thing; they shall certainly be put to death; their blood *shall be* on them. [14]And a man who takes a woman and her mother, it is wickedness; they shall burn him and them; and there shall be no wickedness in your midst. [15]And a man who lies with an animal shall certainly be put to death; and you shall kill the animal. [16]And if a woman draws near to any animal to

3772 4940 376 6440 7760
5 וְשַׂמְתִּי אֲנִי אֶת־פָּנַי בָּאִישׁ הַהוּא וּבְמִשְׁפַּחְתּוֹ וְהִכְרַתִּי
shall I and off cut | against and family his | that | against man | My face | I | shall then set

7130 4432 2181 310 2181
אֹתוֹ וְאֵת ׀ כָּל־הַזֹּנִים אַחֲרָיו לִזְנוֹת אַחֲרֵי הַמֹּלֶךְ מִקֶּרֶב
from among | ,Molech | after | go to whoring | after him | go who whoring | all | and | ,him

3049 413 178 6437 5315 5971
6 עַמָּם׃ וְהַנֶּפֶשׁ אֲשֶׁר תִּפְנֶה אֶל־הָאֹבֹת וְאֶל־הַיִּדְּעֹנִים
the' spiritists | to and | ,mediums to | turns | who | the And person | their .people

3772 5315 6440 5414 310 2181
לִזְנוֹת אַחֲרֵיהֶם וְנָתַתִּי אֶת־פָּנַי בַּנֶּפֶשׁ הַהוּא וְהִכְרַתִּי אֹתוֹ
him | cut and off | ,that | against person | My face | shall I set | after ,them | go to whoring

3068 6918 1961 6942 5971 7130
7 מִקֶּרֶב עַמּוֹ׃ וְהִתְקַדִּשְׁתֶּם וִהְיִיתֶם קְדֹשִׁים כִּי אֲנִי יְהוָה
Jehovah | I (am) | for | ;holy | you and be shall | shall you And yourselves sanctify | his .people | from among

3068 6213 2708 8104 430
8 אֱלֹהֵיכֶם׃ וּשְׁמַרְתֶּם אֶת־חֻקֹּתַי וַעֲשִׂיתֶם אֹתָם אֲנִי יְהוָה
Jehovah | I (am) | ;them | shall and do | My statutes | shall you And keep | .God your

517 1 7043 376 376 6942
9 מְקַדִּשְׁכֶם׃ כִּי־אִישׁ אִישׁ אֲשֶׁר יְקַלֵּל אֶת־אָבִיו וְאֶת־אִמּוֹ
his mother | and | his father | curses | who | man any | And | is who .you sanctifying

5003 376 1818 7043 517 1 4191
10 מוֹת יוּמָת אָבִיו וְאִמּוֹ קִלֵּל דָּמָיו בּוֹ׃ וְאִישׁ אֲשֶׁר יִנְאַף
commits adultery | who | a And man | (be shall) him on | his blood | has he ;cursed | his and mother | his father | be shall surely ;executed

4191 4191 7453 802 5003 376 802
אֶת־אֵשֶׁת אִישׁ אֲשֶׁר יִנְאַף אֶת־אֵשֶׁת רֵעֵהוּ מוֹת־יוּמַת
shall surely ,executed be | his ,neighbor | of the wife | with | commits adultery | who | a man's | wife | with

6172 1 802 7901 376 5003 5003
11 הַנֹּאֵף וְהַנֹּאָפֶת׃ וְאִישׁ אֲשֶׁר יִשְׁכַּב אֶת־אֵשֶׁת אָבִיו עֶרְוַת
naked-ness | his father's | wife | with | lies | who | a And man | the and .adulteress | the adulterer

376 1818 8147 4191 1540 1
12 אָבִיו גִּלָּה מוֹת־יוּמְתוּ שְׁנֵיהֶם דְּמֵיהֶם בָּם׃ וְאִישׁ אֲשֶׁר
who | a And man | (be shall) .them on | their blood | of both ,them | shall surely ,executed be | has who uncovered | his father's

1818 6213 8397 8147 4191 4191 3618 7901
יִשְׁכַּב אֶת־כַּלָּתוֹ מוֹת יוּמְתוּ שְׁנֵיהֶם תֶּבֶל עָשׂוּ דְּמֵיהֶם
their blood | ;made have they | mixing a | of both them | surely shall ,executed be | his | with daughter-in-law | lies

8441 802 4904 2145 7901 376
13 בָּם׃ וְאִישׁ אֲשֶׁר יִשְׁכַּב אֶת־זָכָר מִשְׁכְּבֵי אִשָּׁה תּוֹעֵבָה
abom-,ination | an | a woman | one as with lies | male a with | lies | who | a And man | (be shall) .them on

3947 376 1818 4191 4191 8147 6213
14 עָשׂוּ שְׁנֵיהֶם מוֹת יוּמָתוּ דְּמֵיהֶם בָּם׃ וְאִישׁ אֲשֶׁר יִקַּח
takes | who | a And man | (be shall) .them on | their blood | shall they surely ;executed be | of both ;them | have done

8313 784 2154 517 802
אֶת־אִשָּׁה וְאֶת־אִמָּהּ זִמָּה הִוא בָּאֵשׁ יִשְׂרְפוּ אֹתוֹ וְאֶתְהֶן
and ;them | him | shall they burn | with fire | (is) it | wicked-,ness | her ,mother | and | woman a

7903 5414 376 8436 2154 1961 3808
15 וְלֹא־תִהְיֶה זִמָּה בְּתוֹכְכֶם׃ וְאִישׁ אֲשֶׁר יִתֵּן שְׁכָבְתּוֹ
lies | gives | who | a And man | your in .midst | wicked-ness | there be shall | and no

802 2026 929 4191 4191 929
16 בִּבְהֵמָה מוֹת יוּמָת וְאֶת־הַבְּהֵמָה תַּהֲרֹגוּ׃ וְאִשָּׁה אֲשֶׁר
when | a And woman | shall you kill | the .animal | and | shall surely ,executed be | an with animal

lie with it, you shall even put
to death the woman and the
animal; they are surely to be
put to death; their blood
shall be on them.
17And if a man takes his
sister, the daughter of his
father or daughter of his
mother, and he has seen
her nakedness, and she
sees his nakedness, it is a
shame; and they shall be
cut off before the eyes of
the sons of their people; he
has uncovered his sister's
nakedness; he shall bear
his iniquity. 18And if a man
lies with a menstruous
woman, and has un-
covered her nakedness, he
has made her fountain bare;
and she has uncovered the
fountain of her blood; even
both of them shall be cut off
from the midst of their
people. 19And you shall not
uncover the nakedness of
your mother's sister, nor of
your father's sister, because
he has made naked his near
kin; they shall bear their
iniquity. 20If a man lies with
his aunt, he has uncovered
the nakedness of his uncle;
they shall bear their sin;
they shall die childless.
21And if a man takes his
brother's wife, it is an
unclean thing; he has
uncovered his brother's
nakedness; they shall be
childless.
21And if a man takes his
brother's wife, it is an
unclean thing; he has
uncovered his brother's
nakedness; they shall be
childless.
22And you shall keep all
My statutes, and all My
judgments, and shall do
them, and the land where I
am bringing you to live in it
shall not vomit you out.
23And you shall not walk in
the statutes of the nation
which I am casting out from
before you, for all these they
have done, and I am
disgusted with them. 24But
I have said to you, You shall
surely possess their land;
and, I, I am giving it to you
to possess it, a land flowing
with milk and honey; I *am*
Jehovah your God, who has
set you apart from the

802 2026 7250 929 3605 7126
תִּקְרַב אֶל־כָּל־בְּהֵמָה לְרִבְעָה אֹתָהּ וְהָרַגְתָּ אֶת־הָאִשָּׁה
the woman | then shall you execute | with it | lie to | animal | any | to | draws near

3927 376 1818 4191 4191 929
17 וְאֶת־הַבְּהֵמָה מוֹת יוּמָתוּ דְּמֵיהֶם בָּם׃ וְאִישׁ אֲשֶׁר־יִקַּח
takes | who | a And man | (be shall) .them on | their blood | surely are they ;executed be to | the animal | and

6172 7200 517 176 1 1323 269
אֶת־אֲחֹתוֹ בַּת־אָבִיו אוֹ בַת־אִמּוֹ וְרָאָה אֶת־עֶרְוָתָהּ וְהִיא
and she | her ,nakedness | he and seen has | his ,mother | the of daughter | or | his father | the of daughter | ,sister his

5971 1121 5869 3772 2617 6172 6172 7200
תִרְאֶה אֶת־עֶרְוָתוֹ חֶסֶד הוּא וְנִכְרְתוּ לְעֵינֵי בְּנֵי עַמָּם
their ;people | the of sons | the in .of eyes | shall they and off cut be | it ;(is) | a disgrace | his ,nakedness | sees

802 7901 834 376 5375 5771 1540 269 6172
18 עֶרְוַת אֲחֹתוֹ גִּלָּה עֲוֺנוֹ יִשָּׂא׃ וְאִישׁ אֲשֶׁר־יִשְׁכַּב אֶת־אִשָּׁה
a woman | with | lies down | who | a And man | shall he .bear | his iniquity | has he ,bared | his sister's | naked-ness

1540 1540 4726 6172 1540 1739
דָּוָה וְגִלָּה אֶת־עֶרְוָתָהּ אֶת־מְקֹרָהּ הֶעֱרָה וְהִוא גִּלְּתָה אֶת־
has bared | and she | has he ,bared | her fountain | her ,nakedness | hasand bared | men- ,Strous

269 6172 5971 7130 8147 3772 1818 4726
19 מְקוֹר דָּמֶיהָ וְנִכְרְתוּ שְׁנֵיהֶם מִקֶּרֶב עַמָּם׃ וְעֶרְוַת אֲחוֹת
sister | the And of nakedness | their .people | from among | of both them | shall even off cut be | her ;blood | foun- of tain | the

5771 7607 1540 3808 269 517
אִמְּךָ וַאֲחוֹת אָבִיךָ לֹא תְגַלֵּה כִּי אֶת־שְׁאֵרוֹ הֶעֱרָה עֲוֺנָם
their iniquity | has he ;bared | nearest his kin | for | shall you ,bare | not | your ,father's | and sister | your ,mother's

1540 1730 6172 1733 7901 376 5375
20 יִשָּׂאוּ׃ וְאִישׁ אֲשֶׁר יִשְׁכַּב אֶת־דֹּדָתוֹ עֶרְוַת דֹּדוֹ גִּלָּה
has he ;bared | his uncle | the of nakedness | ,aunt his | with | lies | who | man A | they .bear shall

802 3947 376 4191 6185 5375 2399
21 חֶטְאָם יִשָּׂאוּ עֲרִירִים יָמֻתוּ׃ וְאִישׁ אֲשֶׁר יִקַּח אֶת־אֵשֶׁת
wife | takes | who | a And man | they .die shall | .childless | they bear shall | their ;sin

8104 1961 6185 1540 251 6172 5079 251
22 אָחִיו נִדָּה הִוא עֶרְוַת אָחִיו גִּלָּה עֲרִירִים יִהְיוּ׃ וּשְׁמַרְתֶּם
you And keep shall | they .be shall | .childless | has he ;bared | his brother's | nakedness | it :(is) | ,impurity | his ,brother's

6958 6213 4941 3605 2708 3605
אֶת־כָּל־חֻקֹּתַי וְאֶת־כָּל־מִשְׁפָּטַי וַעֲשִׂיתֶם אֹתָם וְלֹא־תָקִיא
shall out spue | and not | ,them | do shall and | My ,judgments | all | and | My ,statutes | all

3427 8033 935 834 776
אֶתְכֶם הָאָרֶץ אֲשֶׁר אֲנִי מֵבִיא אֶתְכֶם שָׁמָּה לָשֶׁבֶת בָּהּ׃
.it in | live to | there | you | am bringing | I | (in) which | land the | you

3588 6440 7971 1471 2708 3212 3808
23 וְלֹא תֵלְכוּ בְּחֻקֹּת הַגּוֹי אֲשֶׁר־אֲנִי מְשַׁלֵּחַ מִפְּנֵיכֶם כִּי
for | before .you | from | casting out | am | I | which | the nation | the in of statutes | shall you walk | And not

3423 559 6973 6213 3605
24 אֶת־כָּל־אֵלֶּה עָשׂוּ וָאָקֻץ בָּם׃ וָאֹמַר לָכֶם אַתֶּם תִּירְשׁוּ
shall possess | You | ,you to said have | I But | with .them | am I and disgusted; | they done have | these | all

2100 776 3423 5414 127
אֶת־אַדְמָתָם וַאֲנִי אֶתְּנֶנָּה לָכֶם לָרֶשֶׁת אֹתָהּ אֶרֶץ זָבַת
flowing (with) | a land | ,it | possess to | you to | am I it giving | ,I and | .land their

914 430 3068 1706 2461
חָלָב וּדְבָשׁ אֲנִי יְהוָה אֱלֹהֵיכֶם אֲשֶׁר־הִבְדַּלְתִּי אֶתְכֶם
you | has separated | who | ,God your | Jehovah | I (am) | and ;honey | milk

nations. 25And you shall make a difference between the clean animals and the unclean, and between the unclean fowl and the clean. And you shall not defile your souls by beast or by fowl, or by anything which swarms the ground, which I have set apart to you as unclean —26and you shall be holy to Me, for I, Jehovah, *am* holy; and I have set you apart from the nations to become Mine.

27And a man or woman, when there is among them a medium or a fortune-teller, shall certainly be put to death; they shall stone them with stones; their blood *is* on them.

2931 2889 929 996 914 1471
25 מִן־הָעַמִּים׃ וְהִבְדַּלְתֶּם בֵּין־הַבְּהֵמָה הַטְּהֹרָה לַטְּמֵאָה
the and unclean clean the animals between shall you And separate the from nations.

5315 8262 3808 2889 2931 5775 996
וּבֵין־הָעוֹף הַטָּמֵא לַטָּהֹר וְלֹא־תְשַׁקְּצוּ אֶת־נַפְשֹׁתֵיכֶם
souls your shall you defile and not the and clean, unclean the fowl and between

914 834 127 7430 834 3605 5775 929
בַּבְּהֵמָה וּבָעוֹף וּבְכֹל אֲשֶׁר תִּרְמֹשׂ הָאֲדָמָה אֲשֶׁר־הִבְדַּלְתִּי
set have I apart which the ground, swarms which by or anything by or fowl, beast by

3068 6918 6918 1961 2930
26 לָכֶם לְטַמֵּא׃ וִהְיִיתֶם לִי קְדֹשִׁים כִּי קָדוֹשׁ אֲנִי יְהוָה
Jehovah, I (am) holy for holy, to Me you and be shall as unclean; you to

3588 802 376 1961 1471 914
27 וָאַבְדִּל אֶתְכֶם מִן־הָעַמִּים לִהְיוֹת לִי׃ וְאִישׁ אוֹ־אִשָּׁה כִּי
when a woman or a And man .Mine to become the nations from you have I and apart set

7275 68 4191 4191 3049 176 178 854 1961
יִהְיֶה בָהֶם אוֹב אוֹ יִדְּעֹנִי מוֹת יוּמָתוּ בָּאֶבֶן יִרְגְּמוּ אֹתָם
;them shall they stone with stones be shall surely ;executed a fortune-teller or a medium among them there is

1818
דְּמֵיהֶם בָּם׃
on (is) .them their blood

CAP. XXI כא

CHAPTER 21

CHAPTER 21

1And Jehovah said to Moses, Speak to the priests, Aaron's sons, and you shall say to them, None shall be defiled for the dead among his people. 2But for his relative who is near to him, for his mother, and for his father, and for his son, and for his daughter, and for his brother, 3and for his sister, the virgin, who is near to him, who has not been with a man, for her he may be defiled. 4A leader shall not defile himself among his people, to pollute himself; 5they shall not make their heads bald, and they shall not shave the edge of their beard; and they shall not make a cutting in their flesh; 6they are holy to their God, and they shall not pollute the name of their God. For they offer the fire offerings of Jehovah, bread of their God, and they are holy. 7They shall not take a woman *who is* a harlot, or polluted; nor shall they take a woman put away from her husband; for he *is* holy to

175 1121 3548 559 4872 3068 559
1 וַיֹּאמֶר יְהוָה אֶל־מֹשֶׁה אֱמֹר אֶל־הַכֹּהֲנִים בְּנֵי אַהֲרֹן
,Aaron's sons ,priests the to Speak ,Moses to Jehovah said And

7607 5971 2430 4191 559
2 וְאָמַרְתָּ אֲלֵהֶם לְנֶפֶשׁ לֹא־יִטַּמָּא בְּעַמָּיו׃ כִּי אִם־לִשְׁאֵרוֹ
his for relative but his among ,people be shall None defiled the for .dead ,them to you and say shall

269 251 1323 1121 1 517 7138
3 הַקָּרֹב אֵלָיו לְאִמּוֹ וּלְאָבִיו וְלִבְנוֹ וּלְבִתּוֹ וּלְאָחִיו׃ וְלַאֲחֹתוֹ
his for and ,sister for and his ,brother for and his ,daughter for and his ,son for and his ,father his for ,mother ,him to is who near

2930 376 1961 834 7138 1330
הַבְּתוּלָה הַקְּרוֹבָה אֵלָיו אֲשֶׁר לֹא־הָיְתָה לְאִישׁ לָהּ יִטַּמָּא׃
be may he .defiled for her a with ,man has been not who to ,him is who near ,virgin the

7218 7142 7139 3808 2490 5971 1167 2930
4 5 לֹא יִטַּמָּא בַּעַל בְּעַמָּיו לְהֵחַלּוֹ׃ לֹא־יִקְרְחוּ קָרְחָה בְּרֹאשָׁם
their ;head bald shall they make not pollute to himself among people his leader A be shall not ;defiled

8296 8295 3808 1320 1548 3808 2206 6285
וּפְאַת זְקָנָם לֹא יְגַלֵּחוּ וּבִבְשָׂרָם לֹא יִשְׂרְטוּ שָׂרָטֶת׃
;cutting a shall they make not in and flesh their shall they not ;shave their beard the and of edge

430 8034 2490 3808 430 1961 6944
6 קְדֹשִׁים יִהְיוּ לֵאלֹהֵיהֶם וְלֹא יְחַלְּלוּ שֵׁם אֱלֹהֵיהֶם כִּי
for ;God their the of name shall they pollute and not ,God their to they be shall holy

6918 1961 7126 430 3899 3068 801
אֶת־אִשֵּׁי יְהוָה לֶחֶם אֱלֹהֵיהֶם הֵם מַקְרִיבִם וְהָיוּ קֹדֶשׁ׃
.holy they and are ,offer they ,God their bread of ,Jehovah fire the of offerings

376 1644 802 3947 2491 2181 802
7 אִשָּׁה זֹנָה וַחֲלָלָה לֹא יִקָּחוּ וְאִשָּׁה גְּרוּשָׁה מֵאִישָׁהּ לֹא
not her from husband is who away put woman a ;take shall they not or ,polluted is who a harlot A woman

his God. [8]And you shall sanctify him, for he brings near the bread of your God; he is holy to you; for I, Jehovah, *am* holy, who is sanctifying you. [9]And when a daughter of any priest pollutes herself by going whoring, she is polluting her father; she shall be burned with fire.

[10]And the high priest of his brothers, on whose head the anointing oil is poured, and whose hand is consecrated to put on the garments, his head shall not be uncovered, nor his garments torn; [11]nor shall he come near any dead person; he shall not defile himself for his father or for his mother; [12]nor shall he go out from the sanctuary; nor shall he pollute the sanctuary of his God. For the separation of the anointing oil of his God is on him; I *am* Jehovah.

[13]And he shall take a wife in her virginity. [14]He shall not take a widow, or one put away, or a polluted one, a harlot, but he shall take a virgin of his own people *for* a wife; [15]and he shall not pollute his seed among his people; for I *am* Jehovah who sanctifies him.

[16]And Jehovah spoke to Moses, saying, [17]Speak to Aaron, saying, No man of your seed throughout their generations shall draw near to offer the bread of his God if there is a blemish in him. [18]For no man in whom *there is* a blemish shall draw near, a blind man, or one lame, or disfigured, or deformed; [19]or a broken-footed man, or a broken-handed man, [20]or one hump-backed, or a crushed one, or with a spot in his eye, or a scurvy or

8 יקחו כי־קדש הוא לאלהיו: וקדשתו כי את־לחם אלהיך
הוא מקריב קדש יהיה־לך כי קדוש אני יהוה מקדשכם:
9 ובת איש כהן כי תחל לזנות את־אביה היא מחללת
10 באש תשרף: ס והכהן הגדול מאחיו אשר־יוצק
על־ראשו שמן המשחה ומלא את־ידו ללבש את־
11 הבגדים את־ראשו לא יפרע ובגדיו לא יפרם: ועל
12 כל־נפשת מת לא יבא לאביו ולאמו לא יטמא: ומן
המקדש לא יצא ולא יחלל את מקדש אלהיו כי נזר
13 שמן משחת אלהיו עליו אני יהוה: והוא אשה בבתוליה
14 יקח: אלמנה וגרושה וחללה זנה את־אלה לא יקח
15 כי אם־בתולה מעמיו יקח אשה: ולא־יחלל זרעו בעמיו
16 כי אני יהוה מקדשו: ס וידבר יהוה אל־משה
17 לאמר: דבר אל־אהרן לאמר איש מזרעך לדרתם אשר
18 יהיה בו מום לא יקרב להקריב לחם אלהיו: כי כל־
איש אשר־בו מום לא יקרב איש עור או פסח או חרם
19 או שרוע: או איש אשר־יהיה בו שבר רגל או שבר
20 יד: או־גבן או־דק או תבלל בעינו או גרב או ילפת

scabbed person, or one with crushed testicles. [21]No man of the seed of Aaron the priest in whom there is a blemish shall come near to offer the fire offerings of Jehovah; a blemish is in him; he shall not come near to offer the bread of his God. [22]He shall eat of the bread of his God, of the most holy things, and of the holy things. [23]But he shall not enter into the veil, and he shall not draw near to the altar; for a blemish *is* in him; and he shall not pollute My sanctuary; for I *am* Jehovah who sanctifies them. [24]And Moses spoke to Aaron, and to his sons, and to all the sons of Israel.

175 2233 3971 834 376 3605 810 4790 176
21 אוֹ מְרוֹחַ אָשֶׁךְ׃ כָּל־אִישׁ אֲשֶׁר־בּוֹ מוּם מִזֶּרַע אַהֲרֹן
Aaron the of seed (is there) a blemish in whom man Any .testicles crushed or

3899 3971 801 7126 5066 3548
הַכֹּהֵן לֹא יִגַּשׁ לְהַקְרִיב אֶת־אִשֵּׁי יְהוָה מוּם בּוֹ אֵת לֶחֶם
the of bread in (is) a ;him blemish ;Jehovah fire the of offerings offer to shall not near come the priest

6944 6944 430 3899 7126 5927 430
22 אֱלֹהָיו לֹא יִגַּשׁ לְהַקְרִיב׃ לֶחֶם אֱלֹהָיו מִקָּדְשֵׁי הַקֳּדָשִׁים
the things holy of most ,God his The of bread .offer to shall he not near come God his

936 6532 398 6944
23 וּמִן־הַקֳּדָשִׁים יֹאכֵל׃ אַךְ אֶל־הַפָּרֹכֶת לֹא יָבֹא וְאֶל־
to and shall he not ,enter veil the into But shall he .eat holy the ,things and of

4720 2490 3808 3971 5066 4196
הַמִּזְבֵּחַ לֹא יִגַּשׁ כִּי־מוּם בּוֹ וְלֹא יְחַלֵּל אֶת־מִקְדָּשַׁי כִּי
for My ;sanctuary shall he pollute and not in (is) ,him a blemish for shall he not ;near draw altar the

1121 175 4872 1696 6942 3068
24 אֲנִי יְהוָה מְקַדְּשָׁם׃ וַיְדַבֵּר מֹשֶׁה אֶל־אַהֲרֹן וְאֶל־בָּנָיו
his sons and to Aaron to Moses And spoke who .them sanctifies Jehovah I (am)

3478 1121 3605
וְאֶל־כָּל־בְּנֵי יִשְׂרָאֵל׃
.Israel the of sons all and to

CAP. XXII כב

CHAPTER 22

CHAPTER 22

[1]And Jehovah spoke to Moses, saying, [2]Speak to Aaron, and to his sons, that they set themselves apart from the holy things of the sons of Israel, and that they do not profane My holy name in what they devote to Me; I *am* Jehovah. [3]Say to them, Out of all your seed throughout your generations, any man who draws near to the holy things which the sons of Israel set apart to Jehovah, and his uncleanness being upon him, that person shall be cut off from before me; I *am* Jehovah. [4]Any man of the seed of Aaron that is leprous, or has an issue, he shall not eat of the holy things until he is clean. And he who touches any uncleanness of a person, or a man whose semen has gone out of him; [5]or a man who touches any swarming thing which is unclean to him, or touches a man who is unclean to him, by any of

1121 175 1696 559 4872 3068 1696
1 וַיְדַבֵּר יְהוָה אֶל־מֹשֶׁה לֵּאמֹר׃ דַּבֵּר אֶל־אַהֲרֹן וְאֶל־בָּנָיו
2 his ,sons and to ,Aaron to Speak ,saying ,Moses to Jehovah And spoke

6944 8034 2490 3808 3478 1121 6944 5144
וְיִנָּזְרוּ מִקָּדְשֵׁי בְנֵי־יִשְׂרָאֵל וְלֹא יְחַלְּלוּ אֶת־שֵׁם קָדְשִׁי
My holy name profane and not ,Israel the of sons holy the of things from they apart keep that

1755 559 3068 6942 834
3 אֲשֶׁר הֵם מַקְדִּשִׁים לִי אֲנִי יְהוָה׃ אֱמֹר אֲלֵהֶם לְדֹרֹתֵיכֶם
your generations In ,them to Say .Jehovah I (am) ;Me to devote they in what

834 6944 2233 7126 834 376 3605
כָּל־אִישׁ ׀ אֲשֶׁר־יִקְרַב מִכָּל־זַרְעֲכֶם אֶל־הַקֳּדָשִׁים אֲשֶׁר
which holy the things to your seed of out all draws near who man any

5315 3772 2932 3068 3478 1121 6942
יַקְדִּישׁוּ בְנֵי־יִשְׂרָאֵל לַיהוָה וְטֻמְאָתוֹ עָלָיו וְנִכְרְתָה הַנֶּפֶשׁ
person be shall off cut on (be) ,him his and uncleanness to ,Jehovah Israel the of sons set apart

175 2233 376 376 3068 6440
4 הַהִוא מִלְּפָנַי אֲנִי יְהוָה׃ אִישׁ אִישׁ מִזֶּרַע אַהֲרֹן וְהוּא
he and (is) Aaron the of seed man any .Jehovah I (am) ;Me before from that

5060 5704 398 6944 2100 6879
צָרוּעַ אוֹ זָב בַּקֳּדָשִׁים לֹא יֹאכַל עַד אֲשֶׁר יִטְהָר וְהַנֹּגֵעַ
who he touches is he ;clean until shall he not eat the of things holy a has ,flow or ,leprous

2233 7902 5927 834 376 2931 3605
בְּכָל־טְמֵא־נֶפֶשׁ אוֹ אִישׁ אֲשֶׁר־תֵּצֵא מִמֶּנּוּ שִׁכְבַת־זָרַע׃
emission an ,semen of from him go has out who man a or a ,person unclean- of ness any

120 176 2930 834 8318 5060 834 376
5 אוֹ־אִישׁ אֲשֶׁר יִגַּע בְּכָל־שֶׁרֶץ אֲשֶׁר יִטְמָא־לוֹ אוֹ בְאָדָם
man a or to ,him is unclean which swarming thing any touches who man a or

his uncleanness, the person who touches it shall even be unclean until the evening, and shall not eat of the holy things, but shall bathe his flesh with water. 7And when the sun goes in, he shall be clean, and afterwards he shall eat of the holy things, for it *is* his food; 8he shall not eat a dead body or torn thing, for it is unclean; I *am* Jehovah. 9And they shall keep My charge, and shall bear no sin for it, that they may not die for it when they pollute it; I *am* Jehovah, who is sanctifying them.

10And no stranger shall eat of the holy things; a tenant of a priest, or a hired servant, shall not eat of the holy thing. 11And if a priest buys a person, the purchase of his silver, he shall eat of it; also one born in his house, they shall eat of his bread. 12And a priest's daughter, when she belongs to an alien man, she shall not eat of the heave offering of the holy things. 13But a priest's daughter, when she is a widow, or put away, and has no seed, and has turned back to her father's house, as *in* her youth, she shall eat of her father's bread. But no stranger shall eat of it. 14And if a man shall eat of a holy thing through ignorance, then he shall add the fifth part of it, and shall give it to the priest along with the holy thing. 15And they shall not pollute the holy things of the sons of Israel, that which they lift up to Jehovah; 16and so cause them to bear the iniquity of the guilt offering in their eating their holy things. For I *am* Jehovah who sanctifies them.

17And Jehovah spoke to Moses, saying, 18Speak to Aaron, and to his sons, and to all the sons of Israel, and

6 אֲשֶׁר יִטְמָא־לוֹ לְכֹל טֻמְאָתוֹ׃ נֶפֶשׁ אֲשֶׁר תִּגַּע־בּוֹ וְטָמְאָה
עַד־הָעָרֶב וְלֹא יֹאכַל מִן־הַקֳּדָשִׁים כִּי אִם־רָחַץ בְּשָׂרוֹ
7 בַּמָּיִם׃ וּבָא הַשֶּׁמֶשׁ וְטָהֵר וְאַחַר יֹאכַל מִן־הַקֳּדָשִׁים
8 כִּי לַחְמוֹ הוּא׃ נְבֵלָה וּטְרֵפָה לֹא יֹאכַל לְטָמְאָה־בָהּ
9 אֲנִי יְהוָה׃ וְשָׁמְרוּ אֶת־מִשְׁמַרְתִּי וְלֹא־יִשְׂאוּ עָלָיו חֵטְא
10 וּמֵתוּ בוֹ כִּי יְחַלְּלֻהוּ אֲנִי יְהוָה מְקַדְּשָׁם׃ וְכָל־זָר לֹא־
11 יֹאכַל קֹדֶשׁ תּוֹשַׁב כֹּהֵן וְשָׂכִיר לֹא־יֹאכַל קֹדֶשׁ׃ וְכֹהֵן
כִּי־יִקְנֶה נֶפֶשׁ קִנְיַן כַּסְפּוֹ הוּא יֹאכַל בּוֹ וִילִיד בֵּיתוֹ הֵם
12 יֹאכְלוּ בְלַחְמוֹ׃ וּבַת־כֹּהֵן כִּי תִהְיֶה לְאִישׁ זָר הִוא בִּתְרוּמַת
13 הַקֳּדָשִׁים לֹא תֹאכֵל׃ וּבַת־כֹּהֵן כִּי תִהְיֶה אַלְמָנָה וּגְרוּשָׁה
וְזֶרַע אֵין לָהּ וְשָׁבָה אֶל־בֵּית אָבִיהָ כִּנְעוּרֶיהָ מִלֶּחֶם
14 אָבִיהָ תֹּאכֵל וְכָל־זָר לֹא־יֹאכַל בּוֹ׃ וְאִישׁ כִּי־יֹאכַל קֹדֶשׁ
15 בִּשְׁגָגָה וְיָסַף חֲמִשִׁיתוֹ עָלָיו וְנָתַן לַכֹּהֵן אֶת־הַקֹּדֶשׁ׃ וְלֹא
יְחַלְּלוּ אֶת־קָדְשֵׁי בְּנֵי יִשְׂרָאֵל אֵת אֲשֶׁר־יָרִימוּ לַיהוָה׃
16 וְהִשִּׂיאוּ אוֹתָם עֲוֹן אַשְׁמָה בְּאָכְלָם אֶת־קָדְשֵׁיהֶם כִּי אֲנִי
יְהוָה מְקַדְּשָׁם׃
17 18 וַיְדַבֵּר יְהוָה אֶל־מֹשֶׁה לֵּאמֹר׃ דַּבֵּר אֶל־אַהֲרֹן וְאֶל־בָּנָיו

you shall say to them, Any man of the house of Israel, or of the aliens in Israel, who brings near his offering, of all his vows, or of all his free-will offerings which they bring near to Jehovah for a burnt offering; [19]at your own will a male, a perfect one, of the oxen, of the sheep, or of the goats *may be offered.* [20]You shall not offer that which has a blemish; for it shall not be acceptable for you. [21]And when a man brings near a sacrifice of peace offerings to Jehovah, to complete a vow, or for a free-will offering, of the herd or of the flock, it shall be perfect to be accepted; no blemish shall be in it; [22]blind, or broken, or maimed, or having a running sore, or scurvy, or scabbed, you shall not bring these near to Jehovah; and you shall not make of them a fire offering on the altar to Jehovah. [23]As to an ox or a sheep deformed or dwarfed, you shall make it a free-will offering; but it is not acceptable for a vow. [24]As to *anything* bruised, or beaten, or enlarged, or anything cut, you shall not bring it near to Jehovah; even you shall not do it in your land. [25]And you shall not bring near the bread of your God from the hand of a son of a stranger, or any of these, for their corruption *is* in them, they are blemished; they are not acceptable for you.

[26]And Jehovah spoke to Moses, saying, [27]When an ox, or lamb, or goat is born, and when it has been seven days under its dam, then from the eighth day and onward it is acceptable for an offering, a fire offering to Jehovah; [28]but an ox or sheep, it and its young one, you shall not slaughter in one day. [29]And when you sacrifice a sacrifice of

1004 376 376 559 3478 1121 3605
וְאֶל כָּל־בְּנֵי יִשְׂרָאֵל וְאָמַרְתָּ אֲלֵהֶם אִישׁ אִישׁ מִבֵּית
the of of house | Any man | ,them to | you and say shall | ,Israel | the of sons | all | and to

3605 7133 7126 834 3478 1616 3478
יִשְׂרָאֵל וּמִן־הַגֵּר בְּיִשְׂרָאֵל אֲשֶׁר יַקְרִיב קָרְבָּנוֹ לְכָל־
all of | his ,offering | brings near | who | ,Israel in | the of or aliens | ,Israel

5930 7126 834 5071 5088
נִדְרֵיהֶם וּלְכָל־נִדְבוֹתָם אֲשֶׁר־יַקְרִיבוּ לַיהוָה לְעֹלָה׃
burnt a for offering | to Jehovah | bring they near | which | free- their offering will | of or all | their ,vows

834 3605 5795 3775 1241 2145 8549 7522
19 לִרְצֹנְכֶם תָּמִים זָכָר בַּבָּקָר בַּכְּשָׂבִים וּבָעִזִּים׃ כֹּל אֲשֶׁר־
20 which | all | the of or ;goats | the of sheep | the of ,oxen | a ,male | perfect a ,one | your at ,will own

376 1961 7522 7126 3971
21 בּוֹ מוּם לֹא תַקְרִיבוּ כִּי־לֹא לְרָצוֹן יִהְיֶה לָכֶם׃ וְאִישׁ כִּי־
when a And man | .you for | shall it be | accept- able | not for | shall you offer | not a ;blemish | has

1241 5071 5088 6381 3068 8002 2077 7126
יַקְרִיב זֶבַח־שְׁלָמִים לַיהוָה לְפַלֵּא־נֶדֶר אוֹ לִנְדָבָה בַבָּקָר
the of herd | free- a of offering will | or | ,vow a to complete | to Jehovah | peace offerings | a of sacrifice | brings near

5788 1961 3808 3971 7522 1961 8549 6629
22 אוֹ בַצֹּאן תָּמִים יִהְיֶה לְרָצוֹן כָּל־מוּם לֹא יִהְיֶה־בּוֹ׃ עַוֶּרֶת
,blind | :it in | shall be | not blemish any | be to acceptable | shall it be | ,perfect | the of ,flock | or

3808 3217 176 1618 2990 2782 7665
אוֹ שָׁבוּר אוֹ־חָרוּץ אוֹ־יַבֶּלֶת אוֹ גָרָב אוֹ יַלֶּפֶת לֹא־
not | ,scabbed | or | ,scurvy | or | a having ,flow | or | ,maimed | or | ,broken | or

4196 5921 5414 801 3068 428 7126
תַקְרִיבוּ אֵלֶּה לַיהוָה וְאִשֶּׁה לֹא־תִתְּנוּ מֵהֶם עַל־הַמִּזְבֵּחַ
the altar | on them of | you make shall | not | a and offering fire | ;Jehovah to | these | shall you near bring

5088 6213 5071 7038 8311 7716 7794 3068
23 לַיהוָה׃ וְשׁוֹר וָשֶׂה שָׂרוּעַ וְקָלוּט נְדָבָה תַּעֲשֶׂה אֹתוֹ וּלְנֵדֶר
for but vow a | ;it | shall you make | free a offering will | or | ,deformed dwarfed | a or ,sheep | to As ,ox an | to .Jehovah

7126 3772 5423 3807 4600 7521
24 לֹא יֵרָצֶה׃ וּמָעוּךְ וְכָתוּת וְנָתוּק וְכָרוּת לֹא תַקְרִיבוּ לַיהוָה
to ;Jehovah | shall you near it bring | not | any- or ,cut thing | ,torn or | or ,beaten | to As ,bruised | is it .acceptable | not

3899 7126 5236 1121 3027 6213 3808 776
25 וּבְאַרְצְכֶם לֹא תַעֲשׂוּ׃ וּמִיַּד בֶּן־נֵכָר לֹא תַקְרִיבוּ אֶת־לֶחֶם
bread the of | shall you near bring | not | stranger's a son | And of hand | shall you .it do | not | your land | in even

7521 3971 4893 428 3605 430
אֱלֹהֵיכֶם מִכָּל־אֵלֶּה כִּי מָשְׁחָתָם בָּהֶם מוּם בָּם לֹא יֵרָצוּ
are they not acceptable | in them | blemish a (is) | their corruption | for | these | of any of | ,God your

3775 7794 559 4872 3068 1696
26 לָכֶם׃ ס וַיְדַבֵּר יְהוָה אֶל־מֹשֶׁה לֵּאמֹר׃ שׁוֹר אוֹ־כֶשֶׂב
27 ,lamb a | or | ,ox an | ,saying | ,Moses | to | Jehovah | And spoke | for .you

3117 517 8476 3117 7651 1961 3205 5795
אוֹ־עֵז כִּי יִוָּלֵד וְהָיָה שִׁבְעַת יָמִים תַּחַת אִמּוֹ וּמִיּוֹם
from the day | and its ,mother | under | days | seven | it and been has | is ,born | when | a or ,goat

7794 3068 801 7133 7521 1973 8066
28 הַשְּׁמִינִי וָהָלְאָה יֵרָצֶה לְקָרְבַּן אִשֶּׁה לַיהוָה׃ וְשׁוֹר אוֹ־
or ox an | And .Jehovah | to | fire a offering | an for ,offering | is it acceptable | and onward | eighth

2076 259 3117 7919 3808 1121 7716
29 שֶׂה אֹתוֹ וְאֶת־בְּנוֹ לֹא תִשְׁחֲטוּ בְּיוֹם אֶחָד׃ וְכִי־תִזְבְּחוּ
you sacrifice when | And | .one | day in | shall you slaughter | not | its young | and | it | a ,sheep

30 וְזָבַח־תּוֹדָה לַיהוָה לִרְצֹנְכֶם תִּזְבָּחוּ׃ בַּיּוֹם הַהוּא יֵאָכֵל
31 לֹא־תוֹתִירוּ מִמֶּנּוּ עַד־בֹּקֶר אֲנִי יְהוָה׃ וּשְׁמַרְתֶּם מִצְוֹתַי
32 וַעֲשִׂיתֶם אֹתָם אֲנִי יְהוָה׃ וְלֹא תְחַלְּלוּ אֶת־שֵׁם קָדְשִׁי
וְנִקְדַּשְׁתִּי בְּתוֹךְ בְּנֵי יִשְׂרָאֵל אֲנִי יְהוָה מְקַדִּשְׁכֶם׃
33 הַמּוֹצִיא אֶתְכֶם מֵאֶרֶץ מִצְרַיִם לִהְיוֹת לָכֶם לֵאלֹהִים
אֲנִי יְהוָה׃

thanksgiving to Jehovah, you shall sacrifice it of your free will; [30]it shall be eaten on that day; you shall not leave of it until morning; I *am* Jehovah.

[31]And you shall keep My commands and shall do them; I *am* Jehovah. [32]And you shall not profane My holy name, and I shall be counted holy among the sons of Israel; I *am* Jehovah, who is sanctifying you, [33]who is bringing you up out of the land of Egypt, to become your God; I *am* Jehovah.

CAP. XXIII כג

CHAPTER 23

1
2 וַיְדַבֵּר יְהוָה אֶל־מֹשֶׁה לֵּאמֹר׃ דַּבֵּר אֶל־בְּנֵי יִשְׂרָאֵל
וְאָמַרְתָּ אֲלֵהֶם מוֹעֲדֵי יְהוָה אֲשֶׁר־תִּקְרְאוּ אֹתָם מִקְרָאֵי
3 קֹדֶשׁ אֵלֶּה הֵם מוֹעֲדָי׃ שֵׁשֶׁת יָמִים תֵּעָשֶׂה מְלָאכָה וּבַיּוֹם
הַשְּׁבִיעִי שַׁבַּת שַׁבָּתוֹן מִקְרָא־קֹדֶשׁ כָּל־מְלָאכָה לֹא תַעֲשׂוּ
שַׁבָּת הִוא לַיהוָה בְּכֹל מוֹשְׁבֹתֵיכֶם׃
4 אֵלֶּה מוֹעֲדֵי יְהוָה מִקְרָאֵי קֹדֶשׁ אֲשֶׁר־תִּקְרְאוּ אֹתָם
5 בְּמוֹעֲדָם׃ בַּחֹדֶשׁ הָרִאשׁוֹן בְּאַרְבָּעָה עָשָׂר לַחֹדֶשׁ בֵּין
6 הָעַרְבָּיִם פֶּסַח לַיהוָה׃ וּבַחֲמִשָּׁה עָשָׂר יוֹם לַחֹדֶשׁ הַזֶּה
7 חַג הַמַּצּוֹת לַיהוָה שִׁבְעַת יָמִים מַצּוֹת תֹּאכֵלוּ׃ בַּיּוֹם
הָרִאשׁוֹן מִקְרָא־קֹדֶשׁ יִהְיֶה לָכֶם כָּל־מְלֶאכֶת עֲבֹדָה לֹא

CHAPTER 23

[1]And Jehovah spoke to Moses, saying, [2]Speak to the sons of Israel, and you shall say to them, The appointed seasons of Jehovah which you shall proclaim, holy gatherings, shall be these: These *are* My appointed seasons: [3]Work is to be done six days, and in the seventh day *shall be* a sabbath of rest, a holy gathering; you shall do no work; it *is* a sabbath to Jehovah in all your dwellings.

[4]These *are* appointed seasons of Jehovah, holy gatherings which you shall proclaim in their appointed seasons: [5]In the first month, on the fourteenth of the month, between the evenings, *is* the Passover to Jehovah. [6]And on the fifteenth of this month *is* the Feast of Unleavened *Bread* to Jehovah; you shall eat unleavened *things* seven days.

[7]On the first day you shall have a holy gathering; you shall do no work of service; [8]and you shall bring near a

fire offering to Jehovah seven days; and the seventh day *shall be* a holy gathering; you shall do no work of service.

[9]And Jehovah spoke to Moses, saying, [10]Speak to the sons of Israel, and you shall say to them, When you come in to the land which I am giving to you, and have reaped its harvest, and have brought in the sheaf, the beginning of your harvest, to the priest, [11]then he shall wave the sheaf before Jehovah for your acceptance; on the morrow of the sabbath the priest shall wave it. [12]And you shall prepare a lamb in the day you wave the sheaf, a perfect one, a son of a year, for a burnt offering to Jehovah. [13]And its food offering *shall be* two-tenth parts of flour mixed with oil, a fire offering to Jehovah, a sweet fragrance; and its drink offering, a fourth of a hin of wine. [14]And you shall not eat bread and roasted grain and fresh ears until this self-same day, until you have brought the offering of your God; *it is* a never-ending statute throughout your generations in all your dwellings.

[15]And you shall number to you from the next day after the sabbath, from the day you bring in the sheaf of the wave offering; they shall be seven perfect sabbaths; [16]to the next day after the seventh sabbath, you shall number fifty days; and you shall bring near a new food offering to Jehovah; [17]you shall bring in bread out of your dwellings for a wave offering, two *loaves*; they shall be of two-tenth parts of flour; they shall be baked with leaven; firstfruits to

3117 3117 7651 3068 801 7126 6213
8 תַעֲשׂוּ׃ וְהִקְרַבְתֶּם אִשֶּׁה לַיהוָה שִׁבְעַת יָמִים בַּיּוֹם
the and ;days seven to fire a shall you And shall you
day 3808 Jehovah offering near bring .do

6213 5656 4399 6944 4744 7637
הַשְּׁבִיעִי מִקְרָא־קֹדֶשׁ כָּל־מְלֶאכֶת עֲבֹדָה לֹא תַעֲשׂוּ׃
shall you not of work any holy a (be shall) seventh
.do service ;gathering

3478 1121 1696 559 4872 3068 1696
9 וַיְדַבֵּר יְהוָה אֶל־מֹשֶׁה לֵּאמֹר׃ דַּבֵּר אֶל־בְּנֵי יִשְׂרָאֵל
10
,Israel the to Speak ,saying ,Moses to Jehovah And
of sons spoke

5414 834 776 935 559
וְאָמַרְתָּ אֲלֵהֶם כִּי־תָבֹאוּ אֶל־הָאָרֶץ אֲשֶׁר אֲנִי נֹתֵן לָכֶם
to am I which the to you When to you and
,you giving land in come ,them say shall

7102 7225 6016 935 7102 7114
וּקְצַרְתֶּם אֶת־קְצִירָהּ וַהֲבֵאתֶם אֶת־עֹמֶר רֵאשִׁית קְצִירְכֶם
your the sheaf the have and its have and
harvest of beginning of in brought ,harvest reaped

7522 3068 6440 6016 5130 3548
11 אֶל־הַכֹּהֵן׃ וְהֵנִיף אֶת־הָעֹמֶר לִפְנֵי יְהוָה לִרְצֹנְכֶם
your for Jehovah before sheaf the he then the to
;acceptance wave shall ,priest

5130 3117 6213 3548 5130 7676 4283
12 מִמָּחֳרַת הַשַּׁבָּת יְנִיפֶנּוּ הַכֹּהֵן׃ וַעֲשִׂיתֶם בְּיוֹם הֲנִיפְכֶם
wave you the in you And .priest the shall the the on
day prepare shall it wave sabbath of morrow

4503 3068 5930 1121 8549 3532 6616
13 אֶת־הָעֹמֶר כֶּבֶשׂ תָּמִים בֶּן־שְׁנָתוֹ לְעֹלָה לַיהוָה׃ וּמִנְחָתוֹ
food its and to burnt a for its a perfect a a sheaf the
offering ;Jehovah offering ,year of son ,one ,ram

7381 3068 801 8081 1101 5560 6241
שְׁנֵי עֶשְׂרֹנִים סֹלֶת בְּלוּלָה בַשֶּׁמֶן אִשֶּׁה לַיהוָה רֵיחַ
a ,Jehovah to fire a ,oil with mixed flour tenths (be shall)
fragrance offering of (ephah) two

3759 7039 3899 1969 7243 3196 5262 5207
14 נִיחֹחַ וְנִסְכֹּה יַיִן רְבִיעִת הַהִין׃ וְלֶחֶם וְקָלִי וְכַרְמֶל לֹא
not new or roast or And .hin a fourth a of its and ,soothing
grain ,grain ,bread of ,wine offering drink

7133 935 5704 2088 3117 6106 398
תֹאכְלוּ עַד־עֶצֶם הַיּוֹם הַזֶּה עַד הֲבִיאֲכֶם אֶת־קָרְבַּן
offering the have you until this ;day self-same until shall you
of brought eat

4186 3605 1755 5769 2708 430
אֱלֹהֵיכֶם חֻקַּת עוֹלָם לְדֹרֹתֵיכֶם בְּכֹל מֹשְׁבֹתֵיכֶם׃
.dwellings your all in your for never- a (is it) ;God your
generations ending statute

6016 935 347 7676 4283 5608
15 וּסְפַרְתֶּם לָכֶם מִמָּחֳרַת הַשַּׁבָּת מִיּוֹם הֲבִיאֲכֶם אֶת־עֹמֶר
sheaf the bring you from the the from you to you And
of in day the ,sabbath after day number shall

4283 5704 1961 7676 7651 8573
16 הַתְּנוּפָה שֶׁבַע שַׁבָּתוֹת תְּמִימֹת תִּהְיֶינָה׃ עַד מִמָּחֳרַת
day the to shall they perfect sabbaths seven wave the
after ,be ,offering

4503 7126 3117 2572 5608 7637 7676
הַשַּׁבָּת הַשְּׁבִיעִת תִּסְפְּרוּ חֲמִשִּׁים יוֹם וְהִקְרַבְתֶּם מִנְחָה
food a shall you And .days fifty shall you ;seventh the
offering bring number sabbath

8573 3899 935 4186 3068 2319
17 חֲדָשָׁה לַיהוָה׃ מִמּוֹשְׁבֹתֵיכֶם תָּבִיאוּ ׀ לֶחֶם תְּנוּפָה
wave a bread shall you your of Out to new
,offering for in bring dwellings ,Jehovah

1061 644 1961 5560 6241 8147 8147
שְׁתַּיִם שְׁנֵי עֶשְׂרֹנִים סֹלֶת תִּהְיֶינָה חָמֵץ תֵּאָפֶינָה בִּכּוּרִים
first shall they with shall they flour tenths of two
fruits ;baked be yeast ;be of (ephah) two ,(loaves)

Jehovah. [18]And besides the bread, you shall offer seven lambs, perfect ones, sons of a year, and one bullock, a son of the herd, and two rams; they are a burnt offering to Jehovah, with their food offering and their drink offerings, a fire offering of sweet fragrance to Jehovah. [19]And you shall offer one he-goat for a sin offering, and two lambs, sons of a year, for a sacrifice of peace offerings. [20]And the priest shall wave them, besides the bread of the firstfruits, a wave offering before Jehovah, besides the two lambs; they are holy to Jehovah for the priest. [21]And you shall make a proclamation on this same day; *it* is a holy gathering to you. You shall do no work of service. *It is* a never-ending statute in all your dwellings throughout your generations.

[22]And when you reap the harvest of your land, you shall not completely reap the corner of your field, nor shall you gather the gleaning of your harvest; you shall leave them for the poor, and for the alien: I am Jehovah your God.

[23]And Jehovah spoke to Moses, saying, [24]Speak to the sons of Israel, saying, In the seventh month, on the first of the month, you shall have a sabbath, a memorable acclamation, a holy gathering. [25]You shall do no work of service, and you shall bring a fire offering to Jehovah.

[26]And Jehovah spoke to Moses, saying, [27]Also, on the tenth of this seventh month shall be a day of atonement; you shall have a holy gathering, and you shall humble yourselves, and shall bring a fire

8549 3532 7651 3899 7126 3068
18 לַיהוָה׃ וְהִקְרַבְתֶּם עַל־הַלֶּחֶם שִׁבְעַת כְּבָשִׂים תְּמִימִם
perfect ,lambs seven the besides shall you And to
,ones bread offer .Jehovah

1961 8147 352 259 1241 1121 6499 8141 1121
בְּנֵי שָׁנָה וּפַר בֶּן־בָּקָר אֶחָד וְאֵילִם שְׁנָיִם יִהְיוּ עֹלָה
burnt a they ;two and one the a and a sons
offering are rams ,herd of son ,bullock ,year of

3068 5207 7381 801 5262 4503 3068
לַיהוָה וּמִנְחָתָם וְנִסְכֵּיהֶם אִשֵּׁה רֵיחַ־נִיחֹחַ לַיהוָה׃
to soothing aroma fire a their and their with ,Jehovah to
.Jehovah of offering ,offerings drink ,offerings food

1121 3532 8147 2403 259 5795 8163 6213
19 וַעֲשִׂיתֶם שְׂעִיר־עִזִּים אֶחָד לְחַטָּאת וּשְׁנֵי כְבָשִׂים בְּנֵי
sons ,lambs and sin a for one he-goat you And
of two ,offering offer shall

3899 3548 5130 8002 2077 8141
20 שָׁנָה לְזֶבַח שְׁלָמִים׃ וְהֵנִיף הַכֹּהֵן ׀ אֹתָם עַל לֶחֶם
the besides ;them the shall and peace a for a
of bread priest wave ,offering of sacrifice ,year

1961 6944 3532 8147 3068 6440 8573 1061
הַבִּכֻּרִים תְּנוּפָה לִפְנֵי יְהוָה עַל־שְׁנֵי כְּבָשִׂים קֹדֶשׁ יִהְיוּ
they holy ;lambs the besides ;Jehovah before wave a first- the
are two offering ,fruits

6944 4744 2088 3117 6106 7121 3548 3068
21 לַיהוָה לַכֹּהֵן׃ וּקְרָאתֶם בְּעֶצֶם ׀ הַיּוֹם הַזֶּה מִקְרָא־קֹדֶשׁ
holy a ;this day same on shall you And the for to
gathering proclaim .priest Jehovah

5769 2708 6213 5656 4399 3605
יִהְיֶה לָכֶם כָּל־מְלֶאכֶת עֲבֹדָה לֹא תַעֲשׂוּ חֻקַּת עוֹלָם
never- a (is It) shall you not of work any to is it
ending statute .do ,service ;you

776 7102 7114 1755 4186 3605
22 בְּכָל־מוֹשְׁבֹתֵיכֶם לְדֹרֹתֵיכֶם׃ וּבְקֻצְרְכֶם אֶת־קְצִיר אַרְצְכֶם
your the when And your in dwellings your all in
,land of harvest reap you ,generations

3950 3808 7102 3951 7114 7704 6285
לֹא־תְכַלֶּה פְּאַת שָׂדְךָ בְּקֻצְרֶךָ וְלֶקֶט קְצִירְךָ לֹא תְלַקֵּט
shall you not your the you when your the shall you not
;gather harvest of gleaning reap ,field of corner finish

430 3068 5800 1616 6041
לֶעָנִי וְלַגֵּר תַּעֲזֹב אֹתָם אֲנִי יְהוָה אֱלֹהֵיכֶם׃ פ
.God your Jehovah I ;them shall you for and for
(am) leave alien the poor the

3478 1121 1696 559 4872 3068 1696
23 24 וַיְדַבֵּר יְהוָה אֶל־מֹשֶׁה לֵּאמֹר׃ דַּבֵּר אֶל־בְּנֵי יִשְׂרָאֵל
,Israel the to Speak ,saying ,Moses to Jehovah And
of sons spoke

7677 1961 2320 259 7637 2320 559
לֵאמֹר בַּחֹדֶשׁ הַשְּׁבִיעִי בְּאֶחָד לַחֹדֶשׁ יִהְיֶה לָכֶם שַׁבָּתוֹן
a to shall the of the on ,seventh the In ,saying
,sabbath you be ,month first month

6213 5656 4399 6944 4744 8643 2146
25 זִכְרוֹן תְּרוּעָה מִקְרָא־קֹדֶשׁ׃ כָּל־מְלֶאכֶת עֲבֹדָה לֹא תַעֲשׂוּ
shall you no of work any ;holy a ,signaled a
.do service ;gathering reminder

4872 3068 1696 3068 801 7126
26 וְהִקְרַבְתֶּם אִשֶּׁה לַיהוָה׃ ס וַיְדַבֵּר יְהוָה אֶל־מֹשֶׁה
,Moses to Jehovah And to fire a shall you And
spoke .Jehovah offering bring

3725 3117 2088 7637 2320 6218 389 559
27 לֵאמֹר׃ אַךְ בֶּעָשׂוֹר לַחֹדֶשׁ הַשְּׁבִיעִי הַזֶּה יוֹם הַכִּפֻּרִים
;atonement a (is) ,this seventh of the in ,saying
of day month tenth Only

5315 6031 1961 6944 4744 1961
הוּא מִקְרָא־קֹדֶשׁ יִהְיֶה לָכֶם וְעִנִּיתֶם אֶת־נַפְשֹׁתֵיכֶם
souls your you and to shall holy (be) shall
humble shall you be convocation a

28 וְהִקְרַבְתֶּם אִשֶּׁה לַיהוָה׃ וְכָל־מְלָאכָה לֹא תַעֲשׂוּ בְּעֶצֶם

in same / shall you do / not / work / And any / to .Jehovah / fire a offering / shall and bring

הַיּוֹם הַזֶּה כִּי יוֹם כִּפֻּרִים הוּא לְכַפֵּר עֲלֵיכֶם לִפְנֵי יְהוָה

Jehovah / before / you for / make to atonement / ,(is) it / atonement a / for / ,this / day of day

29 אֱלֹהֵיכֶם׃ כִּי כָל־הַנֶּפֶשׁ אֲשֶׁר לֹא־תְעֻנֶּה בְּעֶצֶם הַיּוֹם

day / same in / is humbled / not / who / person any / For / .God your

30 הַזֶּה וְנִכְרְתָה מֵעַמֶּיהָ׃ וְכָל־הַנֶּפֶשׁ אֲשֶׁר תַּעֲשֶׂה כָּל־

any / does / who / person any and / his from ;people / be shall off cut / this

מְלָאכָה בְּעֶצֶם הַיּוֹם הַזֶּה וְהַאֲבַדְתִּי אֶת־הַנֶּפֶשׁ הַהִוא

that / person / even shall I destroy / ,this / day / same in / work

31 מִקֶּרֶב עַמָּהּ׃ כָּל־מְלָאכָה לֹא תַעֲשׂוּ חֻקַּת עוֹלָם

never-ending / a (is it) statute / shall you do / not / work / Any / his .people / from among

32 לְדֹרֹתֵיכֶם בְּכֹל מֹשְׁבֹתֵיכֶם׃ שַׁבַּת שַׁבָּתוֹן הוּא לָכֶם

,you to / (is) it / rest / A of sabbath / .dwellings your / all in / your for ,generations

וְעִנִּיתֶם אֶת־נַפְשֹׁתֵיכֶם בְּתִשְׁעָה לַחֹדֶשׁ בָּעֶרֶב מֵעֶרֶב עַד־

to / from evening / at ,evening / the of month / the in ninth / yourselves / you and humble shall

עֶרֶב תִּשְׁבְּתוּ שַׁבַּתְּכֶם׃

your .sabbath / shall you keep / evening

33
34 וַיְדַבֵּר יְהוָה אֶל־מֹשֶׁה לֵּאמֹר׃ דַּבֵּר אֶל־בְּנֵי יִשְׂרָאֵל

,Israel / the of sons / to / Speak / ,saying / ,Moses / to / Jehovah / And spoke

לֵאמֹר בַּחֲמִשָּׁה עָשָׂר יוֹם לַחֹדֶשׁ הַשְּׁבִיעִי הַזֶּה חַג הַסֻּכּוֹת

booths of feast a / (is) / this / seventh / of month / day / the in fifteenth / ,saying

35 שִׁבְעַת יָמִים לַיהוָה׃ בַּיּוֹם הָרִאשׁוֹן מִקְרָא־קֹדֶשׁ כָּל־

any / ;holy / a gathering / first / the on day / to ;Jehovah / days / seven

36 מְלֶאכֶת עֲבֹדָה לֹא תַעֲשׂוּ׃ שִׁבְעַת יָמִים תַּקְרִיבוּ אִשֶּׁה

fire a offering / shall you bring / days / seven / shall you ;do / not / of service / work

לַיהוָה בַּיּוֹם הַשְּׁמִינִי מִקְרָא־קֹדֶשׁ יִהְיֶה לָכֶם וְהִקְרַבְתֶּם

shall you and near bring / to you / shall be / holy / a gathering / eighth / the on day / to ;Jehovah

אִשֶּׁה לַיהוָה עֲצֶרֶת הִוא כָּל־מְלֶאכֶת עֲבֹדָה לֹא תַעֲשׂוּ׃

shall you .do / not / of service / work / any / ;(is) it / festive assembly / to ;Jehovah / fire the offering

37 אֵלֶּה מוֹעֲדֵי יְהוָה אֲשֶׁר־תִּקְרְאוּ אֹתָם מִקְרָאֵי קֹדֶשׁ לְהַקְרִיב

bring to / holy / ,gatherings / ;them / shall you proclaim / which / Jehovah / set the of feasts / These (are)

אִשֶּׁה לַיהוָה עֹלָה וּמִנְחָה זֶבַח וּנְסָכִים דְּבַר־יוֹם בְּיוֹמוֹ׃

its own ;day / a day / the of thing / drink and ,offerings / a sacrifice / a and food ,offering / burnt a ,offering / to .Jehovah / fire a offering

offering to Jehovah. [28]And you shall do no work in this same day, for it is a day of atonement, to make atonement for you before Jehovah your God. [29]For any person who is not humbled in this same day shall be cut off from his people. [30]And any person who does any work in this same day, I shall even destroy that person from the midst of his people. [31]You shall do no work; *it is* a never-ending statute throughout your generations, in all your dwellings. [32]It *is* a sabbath of rest to you, and you shall humble yourselves in the ninth of the month at evening; from evening until evening you shall keep your sabbath.

[33]And Jehovah spoke to Moses, saying, [34]Speak to the sons of Israel, saying, In the fifteenth day of this seventh month *shall be* a Feast of Booths seven days to Jehovah. [35]On the first day *shall be* a holy gathering; you shall do no work of service. [36]even days you shall bring a fire offering to Jehovah; on the eighth day you shall have a holy gathering; and you shall burn the fire offering to Jehovah; it is a solemn assembly; you shall do no work of service.

[37]These *are* the set feasts of Jehovah which you shall proclaim holy gatherings, to bring a fire offering to Jehovah, a burnt offering, and a food offering, a sacrifice, and drink offer-*ings*, the thing of a day on

its own day; [38]besides the sabbaths of Jehovah, and besides your gifts, and besides all your free-will offerings, which you shall give to Jehovah.

[39]Also, in the fifteenth day of the seventh month, when you gather in the increase of the land, you shall keep the feast of Jehovah seven days; on the first day a sabbath, and on the eighth day a sabbath. [40]And you shall take to yourselves on the first day the fruit of majestic trees, palm branches, and boughs of oak trees, and willows of the brook, and shall rejoice before Jehovah your God seven days. [41]And you shall keep a feast to Jehovah, seven days in a year, a never-ending statute throughout your generations; in the seventh month you shall keep it a feast. [42]You shall live in booths seven days; all who are home-born in Israel shall live in booths, [43]so that your generations shall know that I caused the sons of Israel to live in booths, when I brought them out of the land of Egypt; I *am* Jehovah your God.

[44]And Moses announced the appointed season of Jehovah to the sons of Israel.

905
5088 3605 4979 905 3068 7676 905
38 מִלְּבַד שַׁבְּתֹת יְהוָה וּמִלְּבַד מַתְּנוֹתֵיכֶם וּמִלְּבַד כָּל־נִדְרֵיכֶם
,vows your all and ,gifts your and ,Jehovah the besides
besides besides of sabbaths

2568 389 3068 5414 834 5071 905
39 וּמִלְּבַד כָּל־נִדְבֹתֵיכֶם אֲשֶׁר תִּתְּנוּ לַיהוָה׃ אַךְ בַּחֲמִשָּׁה
five the on ,Only to shall you which free- your all and
.Jehovah give offerings will besides

776 4768 622 7637 2320 3117 6240
עָשָׂר יוֹם לַחֹדֶשׁ הַשְּׁבִיעִי בְּאָסְפְּכֶם אֶת־תְּבוּאַת הָאָרֶץ
,land the the you when ,seventh the of day (and)
. of increase gather month ten

7677 7223 3117 3117 7651 3068 2282 2287
תָּחֹגּוּ אֶת־חַג־יְהוָה שִׁבְעַת יָמִים בַּיּוֹם הָרִאשׁוֹן שַׁבָּתוֹן
a first the on ;days seven Jehovah the shall you
,sabbath day of feast keep

7223 3117 3947 7677 8066 3117
40 וּבַיּוֹם הַשְּׁמִינִי שַׁבָּתוֹן׃ וּלְקַחְתֶּם לָכֶם בַּיּוֹם הָרִאשׁוֹן
first the on to you and a eighth on and
day yourselves take shall ;sabbath day the

5158 6155 5687 6086 6057 3709 1926 6086 6529
פְּרִי עֵץ הָדָר כַּפֹּת תְּמָרִים וַעֲנַף עֵץ־עָבֹת וְעַרְבֵי־נָחַל
;brook the and ,oak trees and ,palm branches ma- trees the
of willows of boughs jestic of fruit

2282 3117 7651 430 3068 8056
41 וּשְׂמַחְתֶּם לִפְנֵי יְהוָה אֱלֹהֵיכֶם שִׁבְעַת יָמִים׃ וְחַגֹּתֶם אֹתוֹ
it you And .days seven God your Jehovah before you and
celebrate shall rejoice shall

1755 5769 2208 8141 3117 7637 3068 2282
חַג לַיהוָה שִׁבְעַת יָמִים בַּשָּׁנָה חֻקַּת עוֹלָם לְדֹרֹתֵיכֶם
your for never- a a in days seven to a
;generations ending statute ,year Jehovah feast

3117 7651 3427 5521 2287 7637 2320
42 בַּחֹדֶשׁ הַשְּׁבִיעִי תָּחֹגּוּ אֹתוֹ׃ בַּסֻּכֹּת תֵּשְׁבוּ שִׁבְעַת יָמִים
days seven shall You in it shall you seventh the in
live booths celebrate month

1755 3045 5521 3427 3478 249 3605
43 כָּל־הָאֶזְרָח בְּיִשְׂרָאֵל יֵשְׁבוּ בַּסֻּכֹּת׃ לְמַעַן יֵדְעוּ דֹרֹתֵיכֶם
your may that so in shall Israel in are who all
generations know ,booths live homeborn

3318 3478 1121 3427 5521
כִּי בַסֻּכּוֹת הוֹשַׁבְתִּי אֶת־בְּנֵי יִשְׂרָאֵל בְּהוֹצִיאִי אוֹתָם
them I when Israel the caused I in that
out brought of sons live to booths

4872 1696 430 3068 4714 776
44 מֵאֶרֶץ מִצְרַיִם אֲנִי יְהוָה אֱלֹהֵיכֶם׃ וַיְדַבֵּר מֹשֶׁה אֶת־
Moses And .God your Jehovah I ;Egypt the of
announced (am) of land

3478 1121 3068 4150
מֹעֲדֵי יְהוָה אֶל־בְּנֵי יִשְׂרָאֵל׃
.Israel the to Jehovah set the
of sons of feasts

CAP. XXIV כד

CHAPTER 24

CHAPTER 24

[1]And Jehovah spoke to Moses, saying, [2]Command the sons of Israel, and they shall bring to you pure olive oil, beaten, for the light, to cause a light to burn continually. [3]Outside the veil of the testimony in the tabernacle of the congregation Aaron shall arrange it

3947 3478 1121 6680 559 4872 3068 1696
1
2 וַיְדַבֵּר יְהוָה אֶל־מֹשֶׁה לֵּאמֹר׃ צַו אֶת־בְּנֵי יִשְׂרָאֵל וְיִקְחוּ
they and ,Israel the Command ,saying ,Moses to Jehovah And
bring shall of sons spoke

8548 5216 5927 3974 3795 2134 2132 8081
אֵלֶיךָ שֶׁמֶן זַיִת זָךְ כָּתִית לַמָּאוֹר לְהַעֲלֹת נֵר תָּמִיד׃
contin- a to cause the for beaten pure olive oil you
;ually lamp up go light

175 6186 4150 168 5715 6532 2351
3 מִחוּץ לְפָרֹכֶת הָעֵדֻת בְּאֹהֶל מוֹעֵד יַעֲרֹךְ אֹתוֹ אַהֲרֹן
Aaron it shall ,meeting the in the veil the outside
arrange of tent testimony of

from evening until morning before Jehovah continually, a never-ending statute throughout your generations. [4]He shall arrange the lamps on the pure lampstand before Jehovah continually.

[5]And you shall take flour, and shall bake twelve cakes with it; two tenths shall be in the one cake. [6]And you shall set them *in* two rows, six *on* a row on the pure table before Jehovah. [7]And you shall put pure frankincense on the row, and it shall be the bread of a memorial, a fire offering to Jehovah. [8]On each sabbath day he shall arrange it before Jehovah continually, from the sons of Israel, a never-ending covenant. [9]And it shall belong to Aaron and to his sons, and they shall eat it in the holy placea, for it *is* most holy to him, from the fire offerings of Jehovah, a never-ending statute.

[10]And the son of an Israelite woman, and he a son of an Egyptian man, went out among the sons of Israel. And the son of the woman of Israel and a man of Israel struggled together in the camp. [11]And the son of the woman of Israel blasphemed the Name, and cursed. And they brought him in to Moses—and his mother's name *was* Shelomith, the daughter of Dibri, of the tribe of Dan. [12]And they put him under guard, that it might be declared to them at the mouth of Jehovah.

[13]And Jehovah spoke to Moses, saying, [14]Bring out the reviler to the outside of the camp. And all those who heard shall lay their hands on his head, and all

1755 5769 2708 8548 3068 6440 1242 6153
מֵעֶרֶב עַד־בֹּקֶר לִפְנֵי יְהוָה תָּמִיד חֻקַּת עוֹלָם לְדֹרֹתֵיכֶם׃
your for never- a contin- Jehovah before morning until from
;generations ending statute ,ually evening

8548 3068 6440 5216 6186 2889 4501
4 עַל הַמְּנֹרָה הַטְּהֹרָה יַעֲרֹךְ אֶת־הַנֵּרוֹת לִפְנֵי יְהוָה תָּמִיד׃
.continually Jehovah before the shall he pure the on
lamps arrange (gold) lampstand

8147 2471 6240 8147 644 5560 3947
5 וְלָקַחְתָּ סֹלֶת וְאָפִיתָ אֹתָהּ שְׁתֵּים עֶשְׂרֵה חַלּוֹת שְׁנֵי
two ;cakes twelve with shall and ,flour you And
it bake take shall

8147 7760 259 2471 1961 6241
6 עֶשְׂרֹנִים יִהְיֶה הַחַלָּה הָאֶחָת׃ וְשַׂמְתָּ אוֹתָם שְׁתַּיִם
two (in) them you And .one the (in) be shall tenths
set shall cake (ephah)

3068 6440 2889 7979 4635 8337 4634
מַעֲרָכוֹת שֵׁשׁ הַמַּעֲרָכֶת עַל־הַשֻּׁלְחָן הַטָּהֹר לִפְנֵי יְהוָה׃
.Jehovah before pure table the on a (to) six ,rows
(gold) ,row

234 3899 1961 2134 4635 5921 5414
7 וְנָתַתָּ עַל־הַמַּעֲרֶכֶת לְבֹנָה זַכָּה וְהָיְתָה לַלֶּחֶם לְאַזְכָּרָה
a for the for it and ;pure frankin- row the on you And
memorial bread be shall cense put shall

6440 6186 7677 3117 7676 3117 3068 801
8 אִשֶּׁה לַיהוָה׃ בְּיוֹם הַשַּׁבָּת בְּיוֹם הַשַּׁבָּת יַעַרְכֶנּוּ לִפְנֵי
before shall he sabbath day every On to fire a
it arrange .Jehovah offering

175 1961 5769 1285 3478 1121 8548 3068
9 יְהוָה תָּמִיד מֵאֵת בְּנֵי־יִשְׂרָאֵל בְּרִית עוֹלָם׃ וְהָיְתָה לְאַהֲרֹן
Aaron to it And never- a ,Israel the from con- Jehovah
belong shall ending covenant of sons ,tinually

6944 6944 6918 4725 398 1121
וּלְבָנָיו וַאֲכָלֻהוּ בְּמָקוֹם קָדֹשׁ כִּי קֹדֶשׁ קָדָשִׁים הוּא לוֹ
to (is) it holy most for ,holy the in they and to and
,him place it eat shall ,sons his

3482 802 1121 3318 5769 3068 801
10 מֵאִשֵּׁי יְהוָה חָק־עוֹלָם׃ וַיֵּצֵא בֶּן־אִשָּׁה יִשְׂרְאֵלִית
,Israel woman a a went And never- a Jehovah the from
of of son out .ending statute of offerings fire

4264 5327 3478 1121 8432 4713 376 1121
וְהוּא בֶּן־אִישׁ מִצְרִי בְּתוֹךְ בְּנֵי יִשְׂרָאֵל וַיִּנָּצוּ בַּמַּחֲנֶה
the in fought and ;Israel the among an a of a he and
camp together of sons Egyptian ,man son (was)

802 1121 5344 3471 376 3482 1121
11 בֶּן הַיִּשְׂרְאֵלִית וְאִישׁ הַיִּשְׂרְאֵלִי׃ וַיִּקֹּב בֶּן־הָאִשָּׁה
the the And .Israelite an and of woman the the
of woman of son blasphemed man Israel of son

8034 4872 935 7043 8034 3478
הַיִּשְׂרְאֵלִית אֶת־הַשֵּׁם וַיְקַלֵּל וַיָּבִיאוּ אֹתוֹ אֶל־מֹשֶׁה וְשֵׁם
and ;Moses to him they And and ,Name the Israel
name brought ,cursed

4929 3240 1835 4294 1704 1323 8019 517
12 אִמּוֹ שְׁלֹמִית בַּת־דִּבְרִי לְמַטֵּה־דָן׃ וַיַּנִּיחֻהוּ בַּמִּשְׁמָר
under they And .Dan the of ,Dibri the (was) his
guard him put of tribe of daughter ;Shelomith mother's

3068 6310 6567
לִפְרֹשׁ לָהֶם עַל־פִּי יְהוָה׃
.Jehovah the at to be to
of mouth them declared

7043 3318 559 4872 3068 1696
13
14 וַיְדַבֵּר יְהוָה אֶל־מֹשֶׁה לֵּאמֹר׃ הוֹצֵא אֶת־הַמְקַלֵּל אֶל־
to reviler the Bring ,saying ,Moses to Jehovah And
out spoke

7218 5921 3027 8085 5564 4264 2351
מִחוּץ לַמַּחֲנֶה וְסָמְכוּ כָל־הַשֹּׁמְעִים אֶת־יְדֵיהֶם עַל־רֹאשׁוֹ
his on hands their who those all shall and the of the
head heard lay ;camp outside

the congregation shall stone him. [15]And you shall say to the sons of Israel, saying, When any man curses his God, then he shall bear his sin.[16]And he who blasphemes the name of Jehovah shall certainly be put to death. All the congregation shall certainly cast stones at him. As *to* the alien, so *to* a native, when he blasphemes the Name, he is put to death.

[17]And a man, when he strikes the life from any man, he shall surely be put to death. [18]And he who smites an animal to death shall make it good, body for body. [19]And when a man causes a blemish in his neighbor, as he has done, so it shall be done to him; [20]break for break, eye for eye, tooth for tooth. As he has caused a blemish in a man, so it shall be done to him. [21]And he who smites an animal to death shall repay it; and he who smites a man to death shall be put to death. [22]One judgment shall be for you, whether an alien or a native; for I *am* Jehovah your God. [23]And Moses spoke to the sons of Israel, and they brought the reviler to the outside of the camp and stoned him *with* stones. And the sons of Israel did as Jehovah had commanded Moses.

15 ורגמו אתו כל-העדה: ואל-בני ישראל תדבר לאמר
16 איש איש כי-יקלל אלהיו ונשא חטאו: ונקב שם-יהוה
מות יומת רגום ירגמו-בו כל-העדה כגר כאזרח בנקבו
17 18 שם יומת: ואיש כי יכה כל-נפש אדם מות יומת: ומכה
19 נפש-בהמה ישלמנה נפש תחת נפש: ואיש כי-יתן
20 מום בעמיתו כאשר עשה כן יעשה לו: שבר תחת
שבר עין תחת עין שן תחת שן כאשר יתן מום באדם
21 כן ינתן בו: ומכה בהמה ישלמנה ומכה אדם יומת:
22 משפט אחד יהיה לכם כגר כאזרח יהיה כי אני
23 יהוה אלהיכם: וידבר משה אל-בני ישראל ויוציאו
את-המקלל אל-מחוץ למחנה וירגמו אתו אבן ובני-
ישראל עשו כאשר צוה יהוה את-משה:

CAP. XXV כה

CHAPTER 25

CHAPTER 25

[1]And Jehovah spoke to Moses in Mount Sinai, saying. [2]Speak to the sons of Israel, and you shall say to them, When you come into the land which I am giving to you, then the land shall keep a sabbath to Jehovah. [3]You shall sow your field six years, and you shall prune your vineyard six years, and shall gather its produce.

1 2 וידבר יהוה אל-משה בהר סיני לאמר: דבר אל-בני
ישראל ואמרת אלהם כי תבאו אל-הארץ אשר אני
3 נתן לכם ושבתה הארץ שבת ליהוה: שש שנים תזרע
שדך ושש שנים תזמר כרמך ואספת את-תבואתה:

3068 7676 776 1961 7677 767 7637 8141
4 וּבַשָּׁנָה הַשְּׁבִיעִת שַׁבַּת שַׁבָּתוֹן יִהְיֶה לָאָרֶץ שַׁבָּת לַיהוָה
to a the for be shall rest a seventh the in and
;Jehovah .sabbath ,land of sabbath year

7102 5599 2168 3808 3954 2232 7704
5 שָׂדְךָ לֹא תִזְרָע וְכַרְמְךָ לֹא תִזְמֹר׃ אֵת סְפִיחַ קְצִירְךָ
your after- the shall you not your and shall you not your
,harvest of growth ;prune vineyard ,sow field

1961 7677 8141 1219 3808 5139 6025 7114
לֹא תִקְצוֹר וְאֶת־עִנְּבֵי נְזִירֶךָ לֹא תִבְצֹר שְׁנַת שַׁבָּתוֹן יִהְיֶה
shall it rest year a shall you not your grapes the and shall you not
be of ;gather ,vine unkept of ;reap

5650 402 776 7676 1961 776
6 לָאָרֶץ׃ וְהָיְתָה שַׁבַּת הָאָרֶץ לָכֶם לְאָכְלָה לְךָ וּלְעַבְדְּךָ
your to and to ,food for you to land the the shall And the for
,slave male ,you of sabbath be .land

929 1481 8453 7916 519
7 וְלַאֲמָתֶךָ וְלִשְׂכִירְךָ וּלְתוֹשָׁבְךָ הַגָּרִים עִמָּךְ׃ וְלִבְהֶמְתְּךָ
your to and among who those your to and your to and your to and
,cattle ;you living are tenant ,one hired ,slave-girl

398 8393 3605 1961 776 834 2416
וְלַחַיָּה אֲשֶׁר בְּאַרְצֶךָ תִּהְיֶה כָל־תְּבוּאָתָהּ לֶאֱכֹל׃ ס
.food for produce the all be shall your in which to and
it of ,land (is) beast the

6471 7651 8141 7651 8141 7676 7651 5608
8 וְסָפַרְתָּ לְךָ שֶׁבַע שַׁבְּתֹת שָׁנִים שֶׁבַע שָׁנִים שֶׁבַע פְּעָמִים
,times seven years seven ,years sabbaths seven you to you And
of count shall

8141 703 8672 8141 7676 7651 3117 1961
וְהָיוּ לְךָ יְמֵי שֶׁבַע שַׁבְּתֹת הַשָּׁנִים תֵּשַׁע וְאַרְבָּעִים שָׁנָה׃
.years forty- nine years sabbaths the the to and
of seven of days you be shall

7320 6218 7637 2320 8643 7782 5674
9 וְהַעֲבַרְתָּ שׁוֹפַר תְּרוּעָה בַּחֹדֶשׁ הַשְּׁבִעִי בֶּעָשׂוֹר לַחֹדֶשׁ
the of the in ,seventh the in a ram's a shall you And
;month tenth month signal ,horn resound let

6942 776 3605 7782 5674 3725 3117
10 בְּיוֹם הַכִּפֻּרִים תַּעֲבִירוּ שׁוֹפָר בְּכָל־אַרְצְכֶם׃ וְקִדַּשְׁתֶּם
shall you and your throughout ram's a let shall atonement the in
holy make ;land all horn pass of day

3605 776 1865 7121 8141 2572 8141
אֵת שְׁנַת הַחֲמִשִּׁים שָׁנָה וּקְרָאתֶם דְּרוֹר בָּאָרֶץ לְכָל־
all to the in liberty you and (one),fiftieth the year
land proclaim shall ;year

272 376 7725 1961 3104 3427
יֹשְׁבֶיהָ יוֹבֵל הִוא תִּהְיֶה לָכֶם וְשַׁבְתֶּם אִישׁ אֶל־אֲחֻזָּתוֹ
his to every you and to be shall it jubilee a its
;possession man return shall ;you ;dwellers

2572 8141 3104 7725 4940 376
11 וְאִישׁ אֶל־מִשְׁפַּחְתּוֹ תָּשֻׁבוּ׃ יוֹבֵל הִוא שְׁנַת הַחֲמִשִּׁים
the year ;(is) it a shall you family his to and
,fiftieth jubilee ;return each

5599 7114 3808 2232 3808 1961 8141
שָׁנָה תִּהְיֶה לָכֶם לֹא תִזְרָעוּ וְלֹא תִקְצְרוּ אֶת־סְפִיחֶיהָ
grows which that reap nor shall You not to is it a
,itself of ,sow .you year

6944 3104 3588 5139 1219 3808
12 וְלֹא תִבְצְרוּ אֶת־נְזִרֶיהָ׃ כִּי יוֹבֵל הִוא קֹדֶשׁ תִּהְיֶה לָכֶם
;you to is it holy (is) it a for unkept its gather nor
jubilee ,vines

2088 3104 8141 4768 398 7704
13 מִן־הַשָּׂדֶה תֹּאכְלוּ אֶת־תְּבוּאָתָהּ׃ בִּשְׁנַת הַיּוֹבֵל הַזֹּאת
this jubilee year the in ;increase its shall you the out
of eat field of

5997 4465 4376 272 376 7725
14 תָּשֻׁבוּ אִישׁ אֶל־אֲחֻזָּתוֹ׃ וְכִי־תִמְכְּרוּ מִמְכָּר לַעֲמִיתֶךָ
your to anything sell you if And his to each shall you
.neighbor .possession one return

[4]And in the seventh year shall be a sabbath of rest to the land, a sabbath to Jehovah. You shall not sow your field, and you shall not prune your vineyard. [5]You shall not reap that which grows of itself of your harvest; and you shall not gather the grapes of your unkept vine; it shall be a year of rest to the land. [6]And the sabbath of the land shall be to you for food, to you, and to your male slave, and to your female slave, and to your hired one, and to your tenant, *those* who are living with you; [7]and to your livestock, and to the beast which *is* in your land, all the produce of it shall be for food.

[8]And you shall number to yourself seven sabbaths of years, seven years times seven, and all the days of the seven sabbaths of years shall be to you forty-nine years. [9]And you shall cause an alarum, the ram's horn to pass over in the seventh month, in the tenth of the month; in the day of atonement shall pass over a ram's horn throughout all your land; and you shall make holy the fiftieth year. And you shall proclaim liberty in the land to all its inhabitants; it shall be a julilee to you. And you shall return every man to his possession; yea, you shall turn back each to his family. [11]It is a jubilee, the fiftieth year; it is a year to you. You shall not sow, nor reap that which grows of itself, nor gather from its unkept vines; [12]for it is a jubilee, it is holy to you; you shall eat its increase out of the field. [13]In the year of jubilee you shall return each one to his possession.

[14]And if you sell anything to your neighbor, or buy

from the hand of your
neighbor, you shall not
each man oppress his
brother. [15]By the number of
years after the jubilee you
shall buy from your
neighbor; by the number of
the years of increase he
shall sell to you; [16]accord-
ing to the many years you
shall multiply its price; and
by the fewness of the years
you shall diminish its price;
for he is selling to you the
number of crops. [17]And
you shall not oppress each
man his neighbor, and you
shall fear your God, for I *am*
Jehovah your God.

[18]And you shall do My
statutes, and you shall keep
my judgments and shall do
them; and you shall live on
the land securely. [19]And
the land shall give its fruit,
and you shall eat to satisfaction; and you shall dwell
securely on it. [20]And when
you say, What shall we eat
in the seventh year; for, lo,
we may not sow nor gather
our increase? [21]Then I have
commanded My blessing
on you in the sixth year, and
it shall produce the
increase for three years;
[22]and you shall sow the
eighth year, and shall eat of
the old crop until the ninth
year, until the coming in of
its crop; you shall eat of the
old. [23]And the land shall
not be sold in perpetuity; for
the land is Mine; for you are
aliens and tenants with Me.
[24]And you shall grant a
redemption for the land in
all the land of your
possession.

[25]If your brother has
become poor and has sold
his possessions, then his
kinsman-redeemer shall
come, and he shall redeem
the thing his brother sold.
[26]But when a man has no

4557 251 376 3238 5997 3027 7069
15 או קנה מיד עמיתך אל-תונו איש את-אחיו: במספר
the by his each shall you not your the from buy or
of number ;brother man oppress ,neighbor of hand

8141 4557 5997 7069 3104 310 8141
שנים אחר היובל תקנה מאת עמיתך במספר שני-
the the by your from shall you the after years
of years of number ;neighbor buy jubilee

6310 4736 7235 8141 7230 4376 4768
16 תבואת ימכר-לך: לפי רב השנים תרבה מקנתו ולפי
and ,price its shall you ,years the by to he shall increase
by multiply many ;you sell

8393 4557 4736 4591 8141 4591
מעט השנים תמעיט מקנתו כי מספר תבואת הוא
he crops the for ;price its shall you the the
of number diminish years of fewness

430 3372 5997 376 3238 4376
17 מכר לך: ולא תונו איש את-עמיתו ויראת מאלהיך כי
for ,God your you and his each shall you and to is
fear shall ;neighbor man oppress not ,you selling

4941 2708 6213 430 3068
18 אני יהוה אלהיכם: ועשיתם את-חקתי ואת-משפטי
My and My shall you And .God your Jehovah I
judgments statutes do (am)

5414 983 776 5921 3427 6213 8104
19 תשמרו ועשיתם אתם וישבתם על-הארץ לבטח: ונתנה
shall and ;securely the on you and ;them shall and shall you
give land live shall do keep

983 3427 7648 398 6529 776
הארץ פריה ואכלתם לשבע וישבתם לבטח עליה:
.it on securely you and satis- to you and its the
dwell shall ;faction eat shall ,fruit land

2232 380,8 7637 8141 398 559
20 וכי תאמרו מה-נאכל בשנה השביעת הן לא נזרע
may we not (for) ,seventh the in shall What you And
sow ,lo year eat we ,say when

5921 1293 6680 4768 622
21 ולא נאסף את-תבואתנו: וצויתי את-ברכתי לכם
you on blessing my have I Then ?increase our gather nor
commanded

8141 7965 4768 6213 8345 8141
בשנה הששית ועשת את-התבואה לשלש השנים:
;years three for increase the it and ,sixth the in
make will year

3465 8393 398 8066 8141 2232
22 וזרעתם את השנה השמינת ואכלתם מן-התבואה ישן
old ;crop the of shall and ,eighth year the you and
eat sow shall

3465 398 8393 935 5704 8671 5704
עד השנה התשיעת עד-בוא תבואתה תאכלו ישן:
the shall you ,crop its the until ,ninth year the until
.old of eat of coming

1616 776 6783 4376 3808 776
23 והארץ לא תמכר לצמתת כי-לי הארץ כי-גרים
aliens for the (is) for in be shall not the And
;land Mine perpetuity sold land

1353 272 776 3605 8453
24 ותושבים אתם עמדי: ובכל ארץ אחזתכם גאלה תתנו
you a your the in And with you tenants and
give redemption possession of land all .Me (are)

1350 935 272 4376 259 4134 776
25 לארץ: כי-ימוך אחיך ומכר מאחזתו ובא גאלו
his then his has and your has If the for
redeemer comes ,property sold brother poor become .land

1961 380,8 376 251 4465 1350 7138
26 הקרב אליו וגאל את ממכר אחיו: ואיש כי לא יהיה
there not when a But his thing the and to near a
is man ,brother (by) sold redeems ,him relative

redeemer, and his own hand has reached out, and he has enough *for* its redemption, 27then he shall count the years since its sale, and shall give back the surplus to the man to whom he sold; and he shall return to his possession. 28And if his hand has not found enough to give back to him, then the thing he sold shall be in the hand of him who buys it until the year of jubilee. And it shall go out in the jubilee, and he shall return to his possession.

29And when a man sells a dwelling-house *in* a walled city, then his right of redemption shall be the end of the year from its selling date; his right of redemption shall be *a year of* days. 30And if it is not redeemed until a full year is complete, then the house in the walled city shall be established to perpetuity to its buyer, throughout his generations; it shall not out in the jubilee. 31But the houses of the villages which have no walls all around shall be counted as the field of the country; it may be redeemed, and it shall go out in the jubilee. 32As to the cities of the Levites, houses of the cities of their possession, the Levites shall have never-ending redemption. 33And that which is redeemed from the Levites, both the sale of a house, and the city of his possession shall go out in the jubilee. For the houses of the cities of the Levites are their possession in the midst of the sons of Israel. 34And the field, the open land of their cities, shall not be sold; for it is a never-ending possession to them.

35And when your brother has become poor, and his hand has failed with you, then you shall uphold him. He shall live with you as an alien and a tenant. 36You shall take no interest from him, or increase; and you shall fear your God; and the life of your brother *is* with you. 37You shall not give

2803 1353 1767 4672 3027 5381 1350
27 לוֹ גֹּאֵל וְהִשִּׂיגָה יָדוֹ וּמָצָא כְּדֵי גְאֻלָּתוֹ׃ וְחִשַּׁב אֶת־
re- a to its (for) enough he and his has and redeemer to
deemer him redemption finds ,hand reached him

4376 376 5736 7725 4465 8141
שְׁנֵי מִמְכָּרוֹ וְהֵשִׁיב אֶת־הָעֹדֵף לָאִישׁ אֲשֶׁר מָכַר־לוֹ
to he whom the to the shall and its the
him sold man remainder back give sale of years

1961 7725 1767 3027 4672 3808 272 7725
28 וְשָׁב לַאֲחֻזָּתוֹ׃ וְאִם לֹא־מָצְאָה יָדוֹ דֵּי הָשִׁיב לוֹ וְהָיָה
then to give to enough his has not And his to he and
be shall ,him back hand found if ,property return shall

7725 3104 5927 8104 8141 5704 7069 3027 4465
מִמְכָּרוֹ בְּיַד הַקֹּנֶה אֹתוֹ עַד שְׁנַת הַיּוֹבֵל וְיָצָא בַּיֹּבֵל וְשָׁב
he and the in shall and ,jubilee the until it who him the in thing the
return shall jubilee out go of year buys of hand sold he

2346 5892 4186 1004 4376 376 272
29 לַאֲחֻזָּתוֹ׃ וְאִישׁ כִּי־יִמְכֹּר בֵּית־מוֹשַׁב עִיר חוֹמָה
,walled a (in) dwelling a sells when a And his to
city house man ,property

1353 1961 3117 4465 8141 8552/5704 1353 1961
וְהָיְתָה גְּאֻלָּתוֹ עַד־תֹּם שְׁנַת מִמְכָּרוֹ יָמִים תִּהְיֶה גְאֻלָּתוֹ׃
his shall (year a) its of the the until his shall then
;redemption be days (of) ;sale year of end redemption be

1004 6965 8546 8141 4390 5704 1350
30 וְאִם לֹא־יִגָּאֵל עַד־מְלֹאת לוֹ שָׁנָה תְמִימָה וְקָם הַבַּיִת
the shall then ,full a to is until is it not and
house remain year him complete redeemed if

1755 7069 6783 2346 5892 834
אֲשֶׁר־בָּעִיר אֲשֶׁר־לֹא חֹמָה לַצְּמִיתֻת לַקֹּנֶה אֹתוֹ לְדֹרֹתָיו
his for (of) the to to wall a to that the in which
:generations it buyer perpetuity it (has) city is

2316 369 2691 1004 3104 5927 3808
31 לֹא יֵצֵא בַּיֹּבֵל׃ וּבָתֵּי הַחֲצֵרִים אֲשֶׁר אֵין־לָהֶם חֹמָה
a to there which the But the in shall it not
wall them not is villages of houses .jubilee out go

3104 1961 1353 2803 776 7704 5439
סָבִיב עַל־שְׂדֵה הָאָרֶץ יֵחָשֵׁב גְּאֻלָּה תִּהְיֶה־לּוֹ וּבַיֹּבֵל
the in and to there redemption be shall the the as all
jubilee ;it is rights ,counted land of field ,around

1961 5769 1353 272 5892/1004 3881 5892 5927
32 יֵצֵא׃ וְעָרֵי הַלְוִיִּם בָּתֵּי עָרֵי אֲחֻזָּתָם גְּאֻלַּת עוֹלָם תִּהְיֶה
shall never-redemption their cities the the the the And shall it
be ending right ,possession of of houses ,Levites of cities .out go

5892 1004 4465 5927 3881 5892 1004 834 3881
33 לַלְוִיִּם׃ וַאֲשֶׁר יִגְאַל מִן־הַלְוִיִּם וְיָצָא מִמְכַּר־בַּיִת וְעִיר
the or a sale the shall then the from (one) that And the to
of city ,house of out go ,Levites redeems which ,Levites

8432 272 3881 5892 1004 3104 272
אֲחֻזָּתוֹ בַּיֹּבֵל כִּי בָתֵּי עָרֵי הַלְוִיִּם הִוא אֲחֻזָּתָם בְּתוֹךְ
among their (are) the the the for the in their
property Levites of cities of houses ;jubilee possession

272 4376 3808 5892 4054 7704 3478 1121
34 בְּנֵי יִשְׂרָאֵל׃ וּשְׂדֵה מִגְרַשׁ עָרֵיהֶם לֹא יִמָּכֵר כִּי־אֲחֻזַּת
a for shall not their pasture the the And .Israel the
possession ;sold be ,cities of land ,field of sons

3027 4131 251 4134 5769
35 עוֹלָם הוּא לָהֶם׃ וְכִי־יָמוּךְ אָחִיךָ וּמָטָה יָדוֹ עִמָּךְ
with his has and your becomes And .them to (is) it never-
,you hand failed ,brother poor when ending

5392 3947 2416 8453 1616 2388
36 וְהֶחֱזַקְתָּ בּוֹ גֵּר וְתוֹשָׁב וָחַי עִמָּךְ׃ אַל־תִּקַּח מֵאִתּוֹ נֶשֶׁךְ
interest from shall you not with shall he a and an him you then
him take ;you live tenant alien help shall

3701 251 2416 430 3372 4768
37 וְתַרְבִּית וְיָרֵאתָ מֵאֱלֹהֶיךָ וְחֵי אָחִיךָ עִמָּךְ׃ אֶת־כַּסְפְּךָ
Your with (is) your the and ;God your you and or
silver ;you brother of life fear shall ;increase

money to him with interest, and you shall not give your food for increase; [38]I *am* Jehovah your God, who has brought you out of the land of Egypt, to give to you the land of Canaan, to become your God.

[39]And when your brother becomes poor with you, and he has been sold to you, you shall not lay on him the service of a slave. [40]He shall be with you as a hireling, as a tenant; he shall serve with you until the year of jubilee; [41]then he shall go out from you, he and his sons with him, and shall return to his family; he shall even return to the possession of his father. [42]For they *are* My servants, whom I have brought out from the land of Egypt; they shall not be sold *with* the sale of a slave. [43]You shall not rule over him with severity, and you shall fear your God. [44]And your male slave and your female slave whom you have from the nations who are all around you, you shall buy them as male slave or female slave; [45]and also you may buy of the sons of the tenants who are sojourning with you, and of their families who *are* with you, which they have fathered in your land. And they shall be a possession to you. [46]And you shall take them for inheritance to your sons after you, to hold *for* a possession; you may lay service on them forever. But on your brothers, the sons of Israel, one over another, you shall not rule over him with severity.

[47]And if lifts up a hand of an alien or a tenant with you, and your brother grows poor with him, and he sells himself to an alien, a tenant with with you, or to the offshoot of the family of an alien; [48]after he has been sold, there is a redemption to him; one of his brothers

38 לא־תתן לו בנשך ובמרבית לא־תתן אכלך׃ אני יהוה
אלהיכם אשר־הוצאתי אתכם מארץ מצרים לתת לכם
39 את־ארץ כנען להיות לכם לאלהים׃ וכי־ימוך
אחיך עמך ונמכר־לך לא־תעבד בו עבדת עבד׃
40 כשכיר כתושב יהיה עמך עד־שנת היבל יעבד עמך׃
41 ויצא מעמך הוא ובניו עמו ושב אל־משפחתו ואל־
42 אחזת אבתיו ישוב׃ כי־עבדי הם אשר־הוצאתי אתם
43 מארץ מצרים לא ימכרו ממכרת עבד׃ לא־תרדה בו
44 בפרך ויראת מאלהיך׃ ועבדך ואמתך אשר יהיו־לך
מאת הגוים אשר סביבתיכם מהם תקנו עבד ואמה׃
45 וגם מבני התושבים הגרים עמכם מהם תקנו וממשפחתם
אשר עמכם אשר הולידו בארצכם והיו לכם לאחזה׃
46 והתנחלתם אתם לבניכם אחריכם לרשת אחזה לעלם
בהם תעבדו ובאחיכם בני־ישראל איש באחיו לא־
47 תרדה בו בפרך׃ וכי תשיג יד גר ותושב עמך
ומך אחיך עמו ונמכר לגר תושב עמך או לעקר
48 משפחת גר׃ אחרי נמכר גאלה תהיה־לו אחד מאחיו

may redeem him. [49]or his
uncle, or a son of his uncle,
may redeem him, or any of
his fleshly relations of his
family may redeem him. Or,
if his own hand has reached
out *to gain*, then he may be
redeemed. [50]And he shall
count with his buyer from
the year of his being sold to
him until the year of jubilee,
and the silver of his sale
shall be by the number of
years. As the days of a
hireling, it shall be with
him. [51]If *there are* yet many
years, according to them he
shall give back his
redemption, from the silver
of his purchase. [52]And if
few are left of the years till
the year of jubilee, then he
shall count with him;
according to his years he
shall give back his
redemption price. [53]As a
hireling, year by year, he
shall be with him, and he
shall not rule him with
severity before your eyes.
[54]And if he is not redeemed
in this way, then he shall go
out in the year of jubilee, he
and his sons with him.
[55]For the sons of Israel *are*
servants to Me; they are My
servants whom I brought
forth out of the land of
Egypt; I *am* Jehovah your
God.

1320 7607 1350 1730/1121 176 7607 1350
49 יִגְאָלֶנּוּ: אוֹ־דֹדוֹ אוֹ בֶן־דֹּדוֹ יִגְאָלֶנּוּ אוֹ־מִשְּׁאֵר בְּשָׂרוֹ
his the of any or may his son a or his or may
flesh of kin ,him redeem ,uncle of ,uncle ,him redeem

2803 1350 3027 5381 1350 4940
50 מִמִּשְׁפַּחְתּוֹ יִגְאָלֶנּוּ אוֹ־הִשִּׂיגָה יָדוֹ וְנִגְאָל: וְחִשַּׁב עִם־
with he And he then hand has if may his of
count shall redeem may ,reached him redeem ,family

4465 3701 1961 3104 8141 4376 8141 7069
קֹנֵהוּ מִשְּׁנַת הִמָּכְרוֹ לוֹ עַד שְׁנַת הַיֹּבֵל וְהָיָה כֶּסֶף מִמְכָּרוֹ
his silver and the year the until to being his the from his
sale be shall ,jubilee of him sold of year buyer

7227 5750 1961 7916 3117 8141 4557
51 בְּמִסְפַּר שָׁנִים כִּימֵי שָׂכִיר יִהְיֶה עִמּוֹ: אִם־עוֹד רַבּוֹת
many yet if with shall it a the as ;years the by
,him be ,hireling of days of number

4592 4736 3701 1353 7725 6310 8141
52 בַּשָּׁנִים לְפִיהֶן יָשִׁיב גְּאֻלָּתוֹ מִכֶּסֶף מִקְנָתוֹ: וְאִם־מְעַט
few if And pur- his the from his shall he according ,years
if price chase of silver ,redemption repay them to

7725 8141 6310 2803 3104 8141 8141 7604
נִשְׁאַר בַּשָּׁנִים עַד־שְׁנַת הַיֹּבֵל וְחִשַּׁב־לוֹ כְּפִי שָׁנָיו יָשִׁיב
shall he his as with he then of the till the of are
repay years ,him count shall ,jubilee year years left

7287 3808 1961 8141 8141 7916 1353
53 אֶת־גְּאֻלָּתוֹ: כִּשְׂכִיר שָׁנָה בְּשָׁנָה יִהְיֶה עִמּוֹ לֹא־יִרְדֶּנּוּ
shall he not with shall he by year a as redemp- his
him rule ;him be ,year ,hireling ;price tion

3104 8141 5927 428 1350 3808 5869 6531
54 בְּפֶרֶךְ לְעֵינֶיךָ: וְאִם־לֹא יִגָּאֵל בְּאֵלֶּה וְיָצָא בִּשְׁנַת הַיֹּבֵל
,jubilee the in he then this in is he not And before with
year of out go shall (way) redeemed if ,eyes your severity

5650 5650 3478 1121 1121
55 הוּא וּבָנָיו עִמּוֹ: כִּי־לִי בְנֵי־יִשְׂרָאֵל עֲבָדִים עֲבָדַי הֵם
they My (are) Israel the to For with and he
(are) servants ;servants of sons Me ,him sons his

430 3068 4714 776 3318
אֲשֶׁר־הוֹצֵאתִי אוֹתָם מֵאֶרֶץ מִצְרָיִם אֲנִי יְהוָה אֱלֹהֵיכֶם:
.God your Jehovah I ;Egypt of out brought I whom
(am) of land the forth

CAP. XXVI כו

CHAPTER 26

CHAPTER 26

[1]You shall not make idols
to yourselves; and you shall
not set up for yourselves
graven images, or a
memorial pillar. And you
shall not place any stone
image in your land, to bow
yourselves to it; for I *am*
Jehovah your God.
[2]You shall keep My
sabbaths and revere My
Holy Place; I *am* Jehovah!

6965 4676 6459 457 6213
1 לֹא־תַעֲשׂוּ לָכֶם אֱלִילִם וּפֶסֶל וּמַצֵּבָה לֹא־תָקִימוּ לָכֶם
for shall you not a or carved or ;idols to shall You not
;you up set ,pillar ,images yourselves make

7812 776 5414 4906 68
וְאֶבֶן מַשְׂכִּית לֹא תִתְּנוּ בְּאַרְצְכֶם לְהִשְׁתַּחֲוֹת עָלֶיהָ כִּי
for ,it to bow to your in you not image and
yourselves ,land place shall stone

3372 4720 8104 7676 430 3068
2 אֲנִי יְהוָה אֱלֹהֵיכֶם: אֶת־שַׁבְּתֹתַי תִּשְׁמֹרוּ וּמִקְדָּשִׁי תִּירָאוּ
;revere My and shall you My .God your Jehovah I
sanctuary ,keep sabbaths (am)

3068
אֲנִי יְהוָה:
.Jehovah I
(am)

[3]If you walk in My
statutes, and keep My commandments, and do them,
[4]then I will give your rains
in their season, and the land
shall yield her produce,
and the tree of the field

6213 8104 4687 3212 2708
3 אִם־בְּחֻקֹּתַי תֵּלֵכוּ וְאֶת־מִצְוֹתַי תִּשְׁמְרוּ וַעֲשִׂיתֶם אֹתָם:
,them do and ,keep My and you My in If
commandments ,walk statutes

7704 6086 2981 776 5414 6256 1653 5414
4 וְנָתַתִּי גִשְׁמֵיכֶם בְּעִתָּם וְנָתְנָה הָאָרֶץ יְבוּלָהּ וְעֵץ הַשָּׂדֶה
the the and its the shall and their in your I then
field of tree produce land yield ,season rains give will

field shall give its fruit; [5]and your threshing shall overtake the vintage, and the vintage shall overtake the sowing time; and you shall eat your bread until you have enough, and live in your land securely. [6]And I will give peace in the land, and you shall lie down, and none shall make you afraid. And I shall cause evil beasts to cease out of the land, and the sword shall not pass over into your land. [7]And you shall pursue your enemies, and they shall fall before you by the sword. [8]And five of you shall pursue a hundred, and a hundred of you shall pursue a myriad; and your enemies shall fall before you by the sword. [9]And I shall turn My face toward you and make you fruitful, and multiply you, and shall establish My covenant with you. [10]And you shall eat very old provision, and clear away the old because of the new. [11]And I will set My tabernacle in your midst, and My soul shall not loathe you; [12]and I shall walk always in your midst, and shall be God to you, and you, you shall be people to Me; [13]I *am* Jehovah your God, who has brought you out of the land of the Egyptians, from being their slaves; and I will break the bars of your yoke, and cause you to stand erect.

5381 1208 1210 1786 5381 6529 5414
5 יִתֵּן פִּרְיוֹ׃ וְהִשִּׂיג לָכֶם דַּיִשׁ אֶת־בָּצִיר וּבָצִיר יַשִּׂיג אֶת־
shall the and ,vintage the threshing your shall and its shall
to reach vintage to reach ;fruit give

776 983 3427 7648 3899 398 2233
זֶרַע וַאֲכַלְתֶּם לַחְמְכֶם לָשֹׂבַע וִישַׁבְתֶּם לָבֶטַח בְּאַרְצְכֶם׃
your in securely live and unto your you and sowing
.land ,satiation bread eat shall ;time

2416 7673 2729 369 7901 776 7965 5414
6 וְנָתַתִּי שָׁלוֹם בָּאָרֶץ וּשְׁכַבְתֶּם וְאֵין מַחֲרִיד וְהִשְׁבַּתִּי חַיָּה
beasts will I and shall and you and the in peace I And
eliminate ;terrify none rest shall ,land give will

7291 776 5674 2719 776 7451
7 רָעָה מִן־הָאָרֶץ וְחֶרֶב לֹא־תַעֲבֹר בְּאַרְצְכֶם׃ וּרְדַפְתֶּם
you And your into shall not the and the out evil
pursue shall .land over pass sword ,land of

2568 7291 2719 6440 5307 341
8 אֶת־אֹיְבֵיכֶם וְנָפְלוּ לִפְנֵיכֶם לֶחָרֶב׃ וְרָדְפוּ מִכֶּם חֲמִשָּׁה
five you of shall and the by before they and your
pursue ;sword you fall shall ,enemies

6440 341 5307 7291 7233 3967 3967
מֵאָה וּמֵאָה מִכֶּם רְבָבָה יִרְדֹּפוּ וְנָפְלוּ אֹיְבֵיכֶם לִפְנֵיכֶם
before your shall And shall ten you of a and a
you enemies fall pursue thousand hundred ,hundred

7235 6509 6437 2719
9 לֶחָרֶב׃ וּפָנִיתִי אֲלֵיכֶם וְהִפְרֵיתִי אֶתְכֶם וְהִרְבֵּיתִי אֶתְכֶם
,you and ,you make and toward I And the by
multiply fruitful you turn shall .sword

3462 3462 3465 398 1285 6965
10 וַהֲקִימֹתִי אֶת־בְּרִיתִי אִתְּכֶם׃ וַאֲכַלְתֶּם יָשָׁן נוֹשָׁן וְיָשָׁן
and store very you And with my shall and
old old eat shall .you covenant establish

1602 3808 8432 4908 5414 3318 2319
11 מִפְּנֵי חָדָשׁ תּוֹצִיאוּ׃ וְנָתַתִּי מִשְׁכָּנִי בְּתוֹכְכֶם וְלֹא־תִגְעַל
shall and your in My I And clear (the) because
loathe not ,midst tabernacle set will :away new of

430 1961 8432 3212 5315
12 נַפְשִׁי אֶתְכֶם׃ וְהִתְהַלַּכְתִּי בְּתוֹכְכֶם וְהָיִיתִי לָכֶם לֵאלֹהִים
.God for to shall and your in shall I And .you My
you be ,midst walk (always) soul

5927 430 3068 5971 1961
13 וְאַתֶּם תִּהְיוּ־לִי לְעָם׃ אֲנִי יְהוָה אֱלֹהֵיכֶם אֲשֶׁר הוֹצֵאתִי
brought has who God your Jehovah I a for to you and
out (am) ;people Me be shall ,you

4135 7661 5650 1961 4713 776
אֶתְכֶם מֵאֶרֶץ מִצְרַיִם מִהְיֹת לָהֶם עֲבָדִים וָאֶשְׁבֹּר מֹטֹת
bars the I and ;slaves to from the the of you
of break will them being ,Egyptians of land

6968 3212 5923
עֻלְּכֶם וָאוֹלֵךְ אֶתְכֶם קוֹמְמִיּוּת׃
.erect you cause and your
walk to ,yoke

[14]And if you will not listen to Me, and do not do all these commands; [15]and if you reject My statutes, and if your soul hates My judgments, so as not to do all My commands, to the breakng of My covenant, [16]I will do this to you also, and I shall appoint terror over you, the burning

4687 3605 6213 3808 8085 3808
14 וְאִם־לֹא תִשְׁמְעוּ לִי וְלֹא תַעֲשׂוּ אֵת כָּל־הַמִּצְוֹת הָאֵלֶּה׃
;these commands all do and to will you not if And
not ,Me listen

5315 1602 4941 3985 2708
15 וְאִם־בְּחֻקֹּתַי תִּמְאָסוּ וְאִם אֶת־מִשְׁפָּטַי תִּגְעַל נַפְשְׁכֶם
,soul your hates My if and ,reject you My if and
judgments statutes

1285 6565 4687 3605 6213
16 לְבִלְתִּי עֲשׂוֹת אֶת־כָּל־מִצְוֹתַי לְהַפְרְכֶם אֶת־בְּרִיתִי׃ אַף־
also My you that My all do to as so
,covenant break commands - not

928 6485 6213
אֲנִי אֶעֱשֶׂה־זֹּאת לָכֶם וְהִפְקַדְתִּי עֲלֵיכֶם בֶּהָלָה אֶת־
,terror you over shall I And .you to this do will I
appoint

fever, destroying the eyes
and consuming the soul;
and you shall sow your seed
in vain; and your enemies
will eat it. [17]And I shall set
My face against you, and
you shall be smitten before
your enemies; and those
hating you shall rule over
you, and you will flee, and
no one will be pursuing
you. [18]And if *after* these
things you will not listen to
Me, then I will chastise you
seven times more for your
sin; [19]and I will break the
pride of your strength, and
will make your heavens as
iron, and your earth as
bronze; [20]and your strength
shall be consumed in vain,
and your land shall not give
her produce, and the tree of
the land shall not give its
fruit.

[21]And if you walk contrary
to Me, and are not willing to
listen to Me, then I will
bring seven times more
plagues on you according
to your sins, [22]and send
against you the beast of the
field, and it shall bereave
you. And I shall cut off your
livestock and shall make
you few, and shall cause
your ways to become
desolate.
[23]And if you are not
instructed by Me by these
things, and shall walk
contrary to Me, [24]then I, I
also, shall walk contrary to
you, and shall smite you,
even I, seven *times more* for
your sins; [25]and I will bring
a sword on you, executing
the vengeance of the
covenant, and you shall be
gathered to your cities, and
I shall send pestilence
among you, and you will be
given into the hand of an
enemy. [26]When I break the
staff of bread to you, ten
women will bake your
bread in one oven, and will
give back your bread by
weight; and you shall eat
and not be satisfied.
[27]And if you will not

2232 5315 1727 5869 3615 6920 7829
השחפת ואת־הקדחת מכלות עינים ומדיבת נפש וזרעתם
you and sow shall | the ;soul | and consuming | the ,eyes | destroy-ing | burning the and ,fever | wasting a

5061 6440/5414 341 398 2233 7385
17 לריק זרעכם ואכלהו איביכם׃ ונתתי פני בכם ונגפתם
shall you and smitten be | against ,you | My face | I and set shall | your ;enemies | will and it eat | your ,seed | vain in

7291 5727 8130 7287 341 6440
לפני איביכם ורדו בכם שנאיכם ונסתם ואין־רדף
pursues one no | When flee shall | you And | who those .you hate | over you | shall and rule | your ;enemies | before

3256 3254 8085 3808 428
18 אתכם׃ ואם־עד־אלה לא תשמעו לי ויספתי ליסרה
chastise | more I will | then | to ,Me | will you listen | not | these to (things) | if And | .you

5797 1347 7665 2403 7651
19 אתכם שבע על־חטאתיכם׃ ושברתי את־גאון עזכם
your ;might | the of pride | will I and break | ;sins your | for | seven (times) | ,you

8552 5154 776 1270 8064 5414
20 ונתתי את־שמיכם כברזל ואת־ארצכם כנחשה׃ ותם
shall and spent be | as ,bronze | earth your | and | ,iron as | heavens your | will and make

776 6086 2981 776 5414 2581 7385
לריק כחכם ולא־תתן ארצכם את־יבולה ועץ הארץ לא
not | the land | the and of tree | its ,produce | your land | shall give | and not | your ;strength | vain in

8085 14 7147 3212 6529/5414
21 יתן פריו׃ ואם־תלכו עמי קרי ולא תאבו לשמע לי
to .Me | to listen | are you (if) willing | and not | ,contrary | to Me | you walk | if And | its ,fruit | shall give

7971 2403 7651 4347 3254
22 ויספתי עליכם מכה שבע כחטאתיכם׃ והשלחתי בכם
against you | I and send will | to according ,sins your | seven ,(times) | the plague | ,you on | will I then more bring

929 3772 7921 7704 2416
את־חית השדה ושכלה אתכם והכריתה את־בהמתכם
,livestock your | shall I and off cut | ;you | shall it and bereave | ,field the | beast the of

3256 3808 428 1870 8074 4591
23 והמעיטה אתכם ונשמו דרכיכם׃ ואם־באלה לא תוסרו
are you chastised | not | these by things | And if | .roads your | that so deserted are | ,you | shall and few make

7147 3212 7147 3212
24 לי והלכתם עמי קרי׃ והלכתי אף־אני עמכם בקרי
,contrary | you to | ,I | also | I then ,walk shall | ,contrary | Me to | shall and walk | to ,Me

935 2403 7651 1571 5221
25 והכיתי אתכם גם־אני שבע על־חטאתיכם׃ והבאתי
will I and bring | .sins your | for | seven (more times) | ,I even | ,you | shall and strike

5892 413 622 1285 5359 5358 2719
עליכם חרב נקמת נקם־ברית ונאספתם אל־עריכם
,cities your | to | shall you and gathered be | the ;covenant | the of vengeance | executing | a sword | you on

7665 341 3027 5414 8432 1698 7971
26 ושלחתי דבר בתוככם ונתתם ביד־אויב׃ בשברי לכם
you to | I When break | an .enemy | the into of hand | you and given be shall | among ,you | pestilence | I and send shall

7725 259 8574 3899 802 6235 644 3899 4294
מטה־לחם ואפו עשר נשים לחמכם בתנור אחד והשיבו
shall and back give | ;one | oven in | your bread | women | ten | shall bake | ,bread | the of staff

7646 3808 398 4948 3899
27 לחמכם במשקל ואכלתם ולא תשבעו׃ ואם־
if And | be shall .satisfied | and not | you and ,eat shall | ;weight by | your bread

Me for this, and shall walk contrary to Me, 28 then I also will walk contrary to you in fury. I also will chastise you, I also, seven *times* for your sins. 29 And you shall eat of the flesh of your sons, and you shall eat of the flesh of your daughters. 30 And I shall destroy your high places and cut down your altars, and shall put your dead bodies on the carcases of your idols. And My soul shall loathe you. 31 And I shall make your cities a waste, and shall make your sanctuaries desolate; and I shall not smell your sweet fragrances. 32 And I shall make the land desolate, and your enemies who are living in it shall be astonished at it. 33 And I will scatter you among nations, and shall draw out the sword after you, and your land shall become a waste, and your cities shall be a desolation.

34 Then the land shall enjoy its sabbaths, all the days of the desolation. And you shall be in the land of your enemies; then the land shall enjoy rest, and shall enjoy its sabbaths. 35 It shall rest all the days of the desolation, that which it has not rested in your sabbaths while you lived on it. 36 And those who are left of you, I shall also bring a faintness into their heart in the lands of their enemies; and the sound of a driven leaf shall chase them; and they shall flee, as one flees from the sword; and they shall fall when no one pursues. 37 And they shall stumble upon one another, as if it were before the sword, when no one pursues. And you shall have no power to stand before your enemies. 38 And you shall perish among the nations, and the land of your enemies shall devour you. 39 And of those who are left of you, they shall

3212 7147 3212 8085 2063
28 בזאת לא תשמעו לי והלכתם עמי בקרי׃ והלכתי
I then walk will ,contrary Me to shall and walk to ,Me will you listen not this for

7651 637 3256 7147 2534
עמכם בחמת־קרי ויסרתי אתכם אף־אני שבע על־
for seven (times) ,I also ,you I and chastise will ;contrary fury in you to

398 1320 1121 1320 398 2403
29 חטאתיכם׃ ואכלתם בשר בניכם ובשר בנתיכם תאכלו׃
shall you eat your daughters the and of flesh your ,sons the of flesh you And of eat shall .sins your

5414 2553 3772 1116 8045
30 והשמדתי את־במתיכם והכרתי את־חמניכם ונתתי את־
put shall and ;altars your cut and down high your places shall I And destroy

5414 5315 1602 1544 6297 6297
31 פגריכם על־פגרי גלוליכם וגעלה נפשי אתכם׃ ונתתי
I and make shall ;you soul My shall and loathe ;idols your the of carcasses on dead your bodies

7306 4720 8074 2723 5869
את־עריכם חרבה והשמותי את־מקדשיכם ולא אריח
shall I smell and not ;sanctuaries your shall and desolate make ,waste a cities your

8074 776 8074 5207 7381
32 בריח ניחחכם׃ והשמתי אני את־הארץ ושממו עליה
it at shall and astonished be ,land the I shall and desolate make your soothing fragrances

7324 1471 2219 3427 341
33 איביכם הישבים בה׃ ואתכם אזרה בגוים והריקתי
shall and out draw among nations will I scatter you And .it in are who living your enemies

2123 1961 5892 8077 776 1961 2719 310
אחריכם חרב והיתה ארצכם שממה ועריכם יהיו חרבה׃
a .desolation shall be your and cities ;waste a your land shall and become the ,sword after you

8074 3117 7676 776 7521
34 אז תרצה הארץ את־שבתתיה כל ימי השמה ואתם
you and (be will) the ,desolation of days the all ,sabbaths its land the shall enjoy Then

7676 7521 776 7673 341 776
בארץ איביכם אז תשבת הארץ והרצת את־שבתתיה׃
;sabbaths its shall and enjoy the ,land rest shall then your ;enemies the in of land

7676 7673 7673 874 3117/3605
35 כל־ימי השמה תשבת את אשר לא־שבתה בשבתתיכם
,sabbaths your in rested had it not that which shall it ,rest the desolation the of days all

3824 4816 935 7604 3427
36 בשבתכם עליה׃ והנשארים בכם והבאתי מרך בלבבם
their heart into a faintness also shall I bring ,you of those left are who And .it on you while lived

4449 5086 5929 6963 7291 341 776
בארצת איביהם ורדף אתם קול עלה נדף ונסו מנסת־
one (as) flees the flee shall and driven a ;leaf of sound the them shall and chase their ;enemies the in of lands

2719 251 376 3782 7291 5307 2719
37 חרב ונפלו ואין רדף׃ וכשלו איש־באחיו כמפני־חרב
the ,sword if as before his on ,brother each man they And stumble shall .pursues when one no they and fall shall the sword

6 341 6440 5797 1961 369 7291
38 ורדף אין ולא־תהיה לכם תקומה לפני איביכם׃ ואבדתם
you And perish shall your .enemies before power stand to to you shall be and is not one and pursuing not

7604 341 776 398 1471
39 בגוים ואכלה אתכם ארץ איביכם׃ והנשארים בכם
.you of those left of And your .enemies the of land you shall and consume among ,nations the

putrefy in their iniquity, in the lands of your enemies; and also in the iniquities of their fathers, they shall putrefy with them.

40 And if they shall confess their iniquity, and the iniquity of their fathers, in their trespass with which they have trespassed against Me; and, also, that they have walked contrary to Me— 41 I also walked contrary to them, and I brought them into the land of their enemies. If their uncircumcised heart is then humbled, and they then *have* paid for their iniquity; 42 then I will remember My covenant *with* Jacob; and also My covenant with Isaac; and I shall also remember My covenant *with* Abraham, and I shall remember the land. 43 For the land shall be forsaken by them, and shall enjoy its sabbaths, in the desolation without them. And they shall enjoy their iniquity, because, even because, they have kicked against My judgments, and their soul has loathed My statutes. 44 And yet for all that, when they are in the land of their enemies, I will not reject them, nor will I hate them, to consume them, to break My covenant with them; for I *am* Jehovah their God. 45 Then I shall remember for them the covenant of the first *fathers*, whom I brought forth out of the land of Egypt in the sight of the nations, that I might be their God; I *am* Jehovah.

46 These *are* the statutes and the judgments and the laws which Jehovah has given between Him and the sons of Israel, in Mount Sinai, by the hand of Moses.

1 5771 637 341 776 5771 4743
יִמַּקּוּ בַּעֲוֹנָם בְּאַרְצֹת אֹיְבֵיכֶם וְאַף בַּעֲוֹנֹת אֲבֹתָם אִתָּם
with their in and your the in their in shall they
them ,fathers' iniquities also ,enemies of lands ,iniquity putrefy

834 4604 1 5771 5771 3034 4743
40 יִמָּקּוּ׃ וְהִתְוַדּוּ אֶת־עֲוֹנָם וְאֶת־עֲוֹן אֲבֹתָם בְּמַעֲלָם אֲשֶׁר
which their in their iniquity and their they (if) And shall they
sin fathers' ,iniquity confess shall ,putrefy

3212 637 7147 3212 4604
41 מָעֲלוּ־בִי וְאַף אֲשֶׁר־הָלְכוּ עִמִּי בְּקֶרִי׃ אַף־אֲנִי אֵלֵךְ עִמָּם
to will I also ;contrary to have they that and against they
them walk Me walked also ,Me sinned have

3824 3665 341 776 935 7147
בְּקֶרִי וְהֵבֵאתִי אֹתָם בְּאֶרֶץ אֹיְבֵיהֶם אוֹ־אָז יִכָּנַע לְבָבָם
their is then If their the into them will and ,contrary
heart humbled ,enemies of land bring

3290 1285 2142 5771 7521 176 6189
42 הֶעָרֵל וְאָז יִרְצוּ אֶת־עֲוֹנָם׃ וְזָכַרְתִּי אֶת־בְּרִיתִי יַעֲקוֹב
,Jacob covenant My will I then their pay they and uncircum-
(with) remember ;iniquity for then ,cised

2142 85 1285 637 3327 1285 389
וְאַף אֶת־בְּרִיתִי יִצְחָק וְאַף אֶת־בְּרִיתִי אַבְרָהָם אֶזְכֹּר
will I Abraham covenant My and ;Isaac covenant My and
;remember (with) also (with) also

7676 7521 5800 776 2142 776
43 וְהָאָרֶץ אֶזְכֹּר׃ וְהָאָרֶץ תֵּעָזֵב מֵהֶם וְתִרֶץ אֶת־שַׁבְּתֹתֶיהָ
,sabbaths its shall and by be shall the For will I the and
enjoy ,them forsaken land .remember land

4941 3282 5771 7521 8074
בָּהְשַׁמָּה מֵהֶם וְהֵם יִרְצוּ אֶת־עֲוֹנָם יַעַן וּבְיַעַן בְּמִשְׁפָּטַי
My even ,because their shall and without the in
judgments ,because ,iniquity for pay they ;them desolation

2063 637 1602 2708 3973
44 מָאָסוּ וְאֶת־חֻקֹּתַי גָּעֲלָה נַפְשָׁם׃ וְאַף גַּם־זֹאת בִּהְיוֹתָם
they when this even And their has My and have they
are (after) yet .soul loathed statutes ,rejected

6565 3615 1602 3973 341 776
בְּאֶרֶץ אֹיְבֵיהֶם לֹא־מְאַסְתִּים וְלֹא־גְעַלְתִּים לְכַלֹּתָם לְהָפֵר
to consume to will I not and will I not their the in
break ,them ,them hate ,them reject ,enemies of land

1285 2142 430 3068 1285
45 בְּרִיתִי אִתָּם כִּי אֲנִי יְהוָה אֱלֹהֵיהֶם׃ וְזָכַרְתִּי לָהֶם בְּרִית
the them for I Then .God their Jehovah I for with My
of covenant remember will (am) ;them covenant

1471 5869 4714 776 3318 7223
רִאשֹׁנִים אֲשֶׁר הוֹצֵאתִי־אֹתָם מֵאֶרֶץ מִצְרַיִם לְעֵינֵי הַגּוֹיִם
the the before Egypt of out brought I whom first the
,nations of eyes of land the forth (fathers)

4941 2706 428 3068 430 1961
46 לִהְיוֹת לָהֶם לֵאלֹהִים אֲנִי יְהוָה׃ אֵלֶּה הַחֻקִּים וְהַמִּשְׁפָּטִים
the and the These .Jehovah I ;God for to to
judgments statutes (are) (am) them be

5514 2022 3478 1121 996 996 3068 5414 834 8451
וְהַתּוֹרֹת אֲשֶׁר נָתַן יְהוָה בֵּינוֹ וּבֵין בְּנֵי יִשְׂרָאֵל בְּהַר סִינַי
,Sinai in ,Israel the and between Jehovah has which the and
Mount of sons Him given laws

4872 3027
בְּיַד־מֹשֶׁה׃
.Moses the by
of hand

CAP. XXVII כז

CHAPTER 27

CHAPTER 27

1 And Jehovah spoke to Moses, saying, 2 Speak to the sons of Israel, and you

3478 1121 1696 559 4872 3068 1696
1 וַיְדַבֵּר יְהוָה אֶל־מֹשֶׁה לֵּאמֹר׃ דַּבֵּר אֶל־בְּנֵי יִשְׂרָאֵל
2
,Israel the to Speak ,saying ,Moses to Jehovah And
of sons spoke

shall say to them, When a man makes a difficult vow by your evaluation, the persons *shall be* Jehovah's. [3]And your evaluation shall be of the male from a son of twenty years even until a son of sixty years; then your evaluation shall be fifty shekels of silver by the shekel of the sanctuary. [4]And if it is a female, then your evaluation shall be thirty shekels. [5]And if from a son of five years to a son of twenty years, then your evaluation shall be twenty shekels for the male and ten shekels for the female. [6]And if a son of a month even to a son of five years, then your evaluation shall be five shekels of silver for the male and three shekels of silver for the female. [7]And if from a son of sixty years and above, if a male, then your evaluation shall be fifteen shekels, and for a female ten shekels. [8]But if he is too poor for your evaluation, then he shall be made to stand before the priest, and the priest shall value him; the priest shall value him according to the reach of him who vowed.

[9]And if *it is* an animal of which they bring an offering to Jehovah, all that *one* gives of it to Jehovah is holy. [10]He shall not replace it, or change it, a good for a bad, or a bad for a good. And if he shall at all change animal for animal, then both it and that for which it is changed shall be holy. [11]And if any unclean animal, of which they may not bring an offering to Jehovah, then he shall make stand the animal before the priest. [12]And the priest shall value

ואמרת אלהם איש כי יפלא נדר בערכך נפשת ליהוה:
3 והיה ערכך הזכר מבן עשרים שנה ועד בן־ששים שנה
4 והיה ערכך חמשים שקל כסף בשקל הקדש: ואם־
5 נקבה הוא והיה ערכך שלשים שקל: ואם מבן־חמש
שנים ועד בן־עשרים שנה והיה ערכך הזכר עשרים
6 שקלים ולנקבה עשרת שקלים: ואם מבן־חדש ועד
בן־חמש שנים והיה ערכך הזכר חמשה שקלים כסף
7 ולנקבה ערכך שלשת שקלים כסף: ואם מבן־ששים
שנה ומעלה אם־זכר והיה ערכך חמשה עשר שקל
8 ולנקבה עשרה שקלים: ואם־מך הוא מערכך והעמידו
לפני הכהן והעריך אתו הכהן על־פי אשר תשיג יד הנדר
9 יעריכנו הכהן: ואם־בהמה אשר יקריבו ממנה
10 קרבן ליהוה כל אשר יתן ממנו ליהוה יהיה־קדש: לא
יחליפנו ולא־ימיר אתו טוב ברע או־רע בטוב ואם־המר
ימיר בהמה בבהמה והיה־הוא ותמורתו יהיה־קדש:
11 ואם כל־בהמה טמאה אשר לא־יקריבו ממנה קרבן
12 ליהוה והעמיד את־הבהמה לפני הכהן: והעריך הכהן

it, whether it is good or bad; as you the priest value it, so it shall be. [13]But if he really redeems it, then he shall add its fifth to your evaluation.

[14]And when a man sanctifies his house as a holy thing to Jehovah, then the priest shall value it, whether good or bad. As the priest values it, so it shall stand. [15]And if he who is sanctifying shall redeem the house, then he shall add a fifth of the silver of its valuation, and it shall become his.

[16]And if a man sanctifies a field of his property to Jehovah, then your valuation shall be according to its seed; a homer of barley seed at fifty shekels of silver. [17]If he shall sanctify his field from the year of jubilee, it shall stand according to your evaluation. [18]And if he shall sanctify his field after the jubilee, then the priest shall count to him the silver according to the years which are left, to the year of the jubilee. And it shall be deducted from your estimation. [19]And if the one sanctifying the field really will redeem it, then he shall add a fifth of the silver of your evaluation to it, and it shall rise to become his. [20]And if he does not redeem the field, or if he has sold the field to another man, it is not to be redeemed any more. [21]And the field shall be holy to Jehovah when it goes out in the jubilee, as a field that is devoted. It shall be a possession to the priest. [22]And if he should devote a field of his purchase, which *is* not of the fields of his possession, [23]then the priest shall count to him the amount of your evaluation to the year of the jubilee. And he shall give your evaluation in that day, a holy thing to Jehovah. [24]In the year of the jubilee

1961 3548 6187 7451 996 2896 996
13 אתה בין טוב ובין רע כערכך הכהן כן יהיה׃ ואם־
if But shall it so the you as ;bad or good whether ,it
.be ,priest it value
6942 376 6187 2549 3254 1350
14 גאל יגאלנה ויסף חמישתו על־ערכך׃ ואיש כי־יקדש
sancti- when a And your to fifth its he then he all at
fies man .evaluation add shall ,it redeems
7451 996 2896 996 3548 6186 3068 6944 1004
את־ביתו קדש ליהוה והעריכו הכהן בין טוב ובין רע
;bad or good whether the shall then to (be to) house his
,priest it value Jehovah holy
1350 6942 6965 3651 3548 6186
15 כאשר יעריך אתו הכהן כן יקום׃ ואם־המקדיש יגאל
shall is who he if and it shall so the it values as
redeem sanctifying ,stand ,priest
5921 1961 6187 3701/2549 3259 1004
16 את־ביתו ויסף חמישית כסף־ערכך עליו והיה לו׃ ואם
And to it and to your the fifth a he then ,house his
if ,him be shall it valuation of silver add shall
2233 63 10 6187 1961 3068 376 6942 272 7704
משדה אחזתו יקדיש איש ליהוה והיה ערכך לפי זרעו
its per your then ,Jehovah to a shall his field a
:seed valuation be shall man sanctify property of
8141 3701 8255 2572 8184 2565 2233
17 זרע חמר שערים בחמשים שקל כסף׃ אם־משנת
the from If .silver shekels fifty at barley homer a seed
of year of of
3104 310 6965 6187 7704 6942 8104
18 היבל יקדיש שדהו כערכך יקום׃ ואם־אחר היבל
the after if and shall it your as his shall he the
jubilee ;stand valuation ,field sanctify jubilee
8141 6360 3701 3548 2803 7704 6942
יקדיש שדהו וחשב־לו הכהן את־הכסף על־פי השנים
years the according silver the the to shall then his shall he
to priest him count ,field sanctify
1350 518 6187 1639 3104 8141 3498
19 הנותרת עד שנת היבל ונגרע מערכך׃ ואם־גאל יגאל
shall ever And your from shall and the the to are which
redeem if ,valuation (it) deduct ,jubilee of year ,left
6187 3701 2549 3254 6942 7704
את־השדה המקדיש אתו ויסף חמשית כסף־ערכך עליו
,it to your silver the of fifth a he then ,it who he field the
evaluation of ley add shall sanctified
7704 4376 7704 1350 3808 6965
20 וקם לו׃ ואם־לא יגאל את־השדה ואם־מכר את־השדה
field the has he if or ,field the does he not if And (as) it and
sold redeem rises his
3104 5927 7704 1961 5750 1350/3808 312 376
21 לאיש אחר לא־יגאל עוד׃ והיה השדה בצאתו ביבל
the in it when field the and any to is it not ,another man to
jubilee out goes be shall ;more redeemed be
272 1961 3548 2761 7704 3068 6942
22 קדש ליהוה כשדה החרם לכהן תהיה אחזתו׃ ואם
if And his shall it the to is which like to holy
,possession be priest ;devoted field a Jehovah
3068 2761 272 7704 3808 4736 7704
את־שדה מקנתו אשר לא משדה אחזתו יקדיש ליהוה׃
to should he his the of not which his of field a
,Jehovah devote ,estate of fields (is) ,purchase
5414 3104 8141 5704 6187 4373 3548 2803
23 וחשב־לו הכהן את מכסת הערכך עד שנת היבל ונתן
he and year the to your the the to shall then
give shall ,jubilee of valuation of amount priest him count
7725 3104 8141 3068 6944 3117 6187
24 את־הערכך ביום ההוא קדש ליהוה׃ בשנת היובל ישוב
shall the year in to holy a ,that day in your
return jubilee ;Jehovah thing valuation

the field shall return to him from whom he bought it, to him who owns *it in* the land. 25And all your evaluation shall be by the shekel of the sanctuary: twenty gerahs shall be the shekel.

26However, no man shall dedicate a firstling, which is firstborn to Jehovah among animals, whether ox or sheep; it *is* Jehovah's.

27And if among the unclean animals, then he shall ransom *it* at your evaluation, and he shall add its fifty to it. And if it is not redeemed, then it shall be sold at your evaluation. 28But any devoted thing which a man devotes to Jehovah from all which *belongs* to him, of man or of animal, or of the field of his possession, it shall not be sold nor redeemed. Every one devoted to Jehovah *is* most holy. 29No devoted thing which is dedicated by man shall be ransomed; it shall surely be put to death. 30And all the tithe of the land, of the seed of the land, of the fruit of the tree, shall be Jehovah's — *it is* holy to Jehovah.

31If a man at all redeems *any* of his tithes, he shall add its fifth to it. 32And all the tithe of the herd and of the flock, all that passes under the rod, a tenth shall be holy to Jehovah. 33He shall not search between good or bad, nor shall he change it. And if he at all changes it, then it shall be, and its substitute shall be holy; it shall not be redeemed.

34These *are* the commands which Jehovah commanded Moses for the sons of Israel on Mount Sinai.

3605 776 272 7069 7704
25 הַשָּׂדֶה לַאֲשֶׁר קָנָהוּ מֵאִתּוֹ לַאֲשֶׁר־לוֹ אֲחֻזַּת הָאָרֶץ׃ וְכָל־
all And the posses- a to to from bought he to field the
.land of sion him whom ,him it whom
8255 1961 1626 6242 6944 8255 1961 6187
עֶרְכְּךָ יִהְיֶה בְּשֶׁקֶל הַקֹּדֶשׁ עֶשְׂרִים גֵּרָה יִהְיֶה הַשָּׁקֶל׃
the shall gerahs twenty the the by be shall your
.shekel be ;sanctuary of shekel valuation
376 6942 38,08 929 3068 1069 1060
26 אַךְ־בְּכוֹר אֲשֶׁר־יְבֻכַּר לַיהוָה בִּבְהֵמָה לֹא־יַקְדִּישׁ אִישׁ
a shall not among to is which a However
,man dedicate ,animals Jehovah firstborn firstling
2731 929 3068 7716 7794
27 אֹתוֹ אִם־שׁוֹר אִם־שֶׂה לַיהוָה הוּא׃ וְאִם בַּבְּהֵמָה הַטְּמֵאָה
,unclean the among And (is) it .Jehovah's a an it
animals if ;sheep or ox whether
4376 1350 2549 3254 6181 6299
וּפָדָה בְעֶרְכֶּךָ וְיָסַף חֲמִשִׁתוֹ עָלָיו וְאִם־לֹא יִגָּאֵל וְנִמְכַּר
shall it is it re- not if and ;it to fifth its he and your at shall then
sold be ,deemed add shall ,valuation ransom he
3605 3068 376 2763 2761 3605 6187
28 בְּעֶרְכֶּךָ׃ אַךְ כָּל־חֵרֶם אֲשֶׁר יַחֲרִם אִישׁ לַיהוָה מִכָּל־
all of to man a devotes which devoted any But your at
Jehovah thing .valuation
38,08 4376 272 7704 929 120 834
אֲשֶׁר־לוֹ מֵאָדָם וּבְהֵמָה וּמִשְּׂדֵה אֲחֻזָּתוֹ לֹא יִמָּכֵר וְלֹא
nor shall it not posses- his the of or of or ,man of to which
sold be sion of field ,animal ,him (is)
834 2761 3068 6944 6944 2761 1350
29 יִגָּאֵל כָּל־חֵרֶם קֹדֶשׁ־קָדָשִׁים הוּא לַיהוָה׃ כָּל־חֵרֶם אֲשֶׁר
which devoted Any to it holy most every ,redeemed
thing one .Jehovah (is) (one) devoted
776 4643 3605 4191 1961 6299 120 2763
30 יָחֳרַם מִן־הָאָדָם לֹא יִפָּדֶה מוֹת יוּמָת׃ וְכָל־מַעְשַׂר הָאָרֶץ
the tithe the all And to put dying be shall not man by is
,land of .death to ;ransomed devoted
3068 6944 3068 6086 6529 776 2233
31 מִזֶּרַע הָאָרֶץ מִפְּרִי הָעֵץ לַיהוָה הוּא קֹדֶשׁ לַיהוָה׃ וְאִם־
if And to (is it) it for the the of the the of
.Jehovah holy ;(is) Jehovah ,tree of fruit .land of seed
4643 3605 3254 2549 4643 376 1350 1350
32 גָּאֹל יִגְאַל אִישׁ מִמַּעַשְׂרוֹ חֲמִשִׁיתוֹ יֹסֵף עָלָיו׃ וְכָל־מַעְשַׂר
the all And .it to he fifth its of (any) man a redeems at
of tithe add shall ,tithes his all
1961 6224 4626 8478 5674 3605 6629 1241
בָּקָר וָצֹאן כֹּל אֲשֶׁר־יַעֲבֹר תַּחַת הַשָּׁבֶט הָעֲשִׂירִי יִהְיֶה־
be shall tenth a ,rod the under passes that all of and the
,flock the herd
4171 7451 2896 1239 3808 3068 6944
33 קֹדֶשׁ לַיהוָה׃ לֹא יְבַקֵּר בֵּין־טוֹב לָרַע וְלֹא יְמִירֶנּוּ וְאִם־
if and he shall nor or good between shall He not to holy
;it change ,bad search .Jehovah
1350 6944 1961 8545 1961 8545
הָמֵר יְמִירֶנּוּ וְהָיָה־הוּא וּתְמוּרָתוֹ יִהְיֶה־קֹּדֶשׁ לֹא יִגָּאֵל׃
shall it not ;holy shall its and it then he at
.redeemed be be substitute be shall ,it changes all
3478 1121 4872 3068 6680 4687 428
34 אֵלֶּה הַמִּצְוֹת אֲשֶׁר צִוָּה יְהוָה אֶת־מֹשֶׁה אֶל־בְּנֵי יִשְׂרָאֵל
Israel the for Moses Jehovah has which the These
of sons commanded commands (are)
5514 2022
בְּהַר סִינָי׃
.Sinai on
Mount

A LITERAL TRANSLATION
OF THE BIBLE
THE BOOK OF NUMBERS

CHAPTER 1

1And Jehovah spoke to
Moses in the wilderness of
Sinai, in the tabernacle of
the congregation on the
first day of the second
month, in the second year
after they had come out of
the land of Egypt, saying,
2Lift the heads of all the
congregation of the sons of
Israel, by their families, by
their fathers' houses, according to the number of
names, every male, by their
heads; 3from twenty years
old and upward, all that are
able to go forth to war in
Israel. You shall number
them by their armies, even
you and Aaron. 4And there
shall be a man of every tribe
with you, every one head of
his father's house. 5And
these are the names of the
men that shall stand with
you: Of Reuben, Elizur the
son of Shedeur; 6Of
Simeon, Shelumiel the son
of Zurishaddai; 7of Judah,
Nahshon the son of
Amminadab; 8of Issachar,
Nethaneel the son of Zuar;
9of Zebulun, Eliab the son of
Helon; 10of the sons of
Joseph; of Ephraim, Eli-
shama the son of Ammihud;
of Manasseh, Gamaliel the
son of Pedahzur; 11of
Benjamin, Abidan the son
of Gideoni; 12of Dan,
Ahiezer the son of Ammi-
shaddai; 13of Asher, Pagiel
the son of Ocran; 14of Gad,
Eliasaph the son of Deuel;
15of Naphtali, Ahira the son
of Enan. 16These *were*
those called from the

ב מ ד ב ר

(THE BOOK OF)

NUMERI

NUMBERS

CAPUT. I א

CHAPTER 1

259 4150 168 5514 4057 4872 3068 1696
1 וַיְדַבֵּר יְהוָה אֶל־מֹשֶׁה בְּמִדְבַּר סִינַי בְּאֹהֶל מוֹעֵד בְּאֶחָד
the on ,meeting the in ,Sinai the in Moses to Jehovah And
day first of tent of wilderness spoke

4714 776 3318 8145 8141 8145 2320
לַחֹדֶשׁ הַשֵּׁנִי בַּשָּׁנָה הַשֵּׁנִית לְצֵאתָם מֵאֶרֶץ מִצְרַיִם
,Egypt the of they after ,second the in ,second the of
of land left had year month

4940 3478 1121 5712 3605 7218 5375 559
2 לֵאמֹר׃ שְׂאוּ אֶת־רֹאשׁ כָּל־עֲדַת בְּנֵי־יִשְׂרָאֵל לְמִשְׁפְּחֹתָם
their by ,Israel the the all of heads the Lift ,saying
,families of sons of company

1121 1538 2145 8034 4551 1 1004
3 לְבֵית אֲבֹתָם בְּמִסְפַּר שֵׁמוֹת כָּל־זָכָר לְגֻלְגְּלֹתָם׃ מִבֶּן
from their by ,male every ,names to according their by
old heads of number the ,fathers' house

6485 3478 6635 5927 4605 8141 6242
עֶשְׂרִים שָׁנָה וָמַעְלָה כָּל־יֹצֵא צָבָא בְּיִשְׂרָאֵל תִּפְקְדוּ אֹתָם
them shall you ;Israel in war to are that all and years twenty
number go to able ,upward

4294 376 376 1961 175 6635
4 לְצִבְאֹתָם אַתָּה וְאַהֲרֹן׃ וְאִתְּכֶם יִהְיוּ אִישׁ אִישׁ לַמַּטֶּה
,tribe of man a there with And and even their by
every be shall you .Aaron you armies

582 8034 1 1004 7218 376
5 אִישׁ רֹאשׁ לְבֵית־אֲבֹתָיו הוּא׃ וְאֵלֶּה שְׁמוֹת הָאֲנָשִׁים
men the the And who his house head every
of names are these .(is) father's of one

8095 7707 1121 468 7205 5975
6 אֲשֶׁר יַעַמְדוּ אִתְּכֶם לִרְאוּבֵן אֱלִיצוּר בֶּן־שְׁדֵיאוּר׃ לְשִׁמְעוֹן
of ;Shedeur the Elizur of with shall that
,Simeon of son ,Reuben :you stand

2497 5992 5179 30 63 6701 1121 8017
7 שְׁלֻמִיאֵל בֶּן־צוּרִישַׁדָּי׃ לִיהוּדָה נַחְשׁוֹן בֶּן־עַמִּינָדָב׃
:Amminadab the ,Nahshon of ;Zurishaddai the Shelumiel
of son Judah of son

2497 446 2074 6686 1121 5417 3485
8
9 לְיִשָּׂשכָר נְתַנְאֵל בֶּן־צוּעָר׃ לִזְבוּלֻן אֱלִיאָב בֶּן־חֵלֹן׃
;Helon the Eliab of ;Zuar the Nethaneel of
of son Zebulun of son Issachar

1583 4519 5989 1121 476 669 3127 1121
10 לִבְנֵי יוֹסֵף לְאֶפְרַיִם אֱלִישָׁמָע בֶּן־עַמִּיהוּד לִמְנַשֶּׁה גַּמְלִיאֵל
Gamaliel of ;Ammihud the Elishama of :Joseph the of
Manasseh of son Ephraim of sons

1121 295 1835/1441 1121 27 1144 6301 1121
11
12 בֶּן־פְּדָהצוּר׃ לְבִנְיָמִן אֲבִידָן בֶּן־גִּדְעֹנִי׃ לְדָן אֲחִיעֶזֶר בֶּן־
the Ahiezer of ;Gideoni the Abidan of ;Pedahzur the
of son ,Dan of son ,Benjamin of son

1121/460 1410 5918 1121 6295 836 5996
13
14 עַמִּישַׁדָּי׃ לְאָשֵׁר פַּגְעִיאֵל בֶּן־עָכְרָן׃ לְגָד אֶלְיָסָף בֶּן־
the Eliasaph of ;Ocran the Pagiel of ;Ammishaddai
of son ,Gad of son ,Asher

5712 7148 428 5881 1121 299 5320 1845
15
16 דְּעוּאֵל׃ לְנַפְתָּלִי אֲחִירַע בֶּן־עֵינָן׃ אֵלֶּה קְרִיאֵי הָעֵדָה
con- the those These .Enan the Ahira of ;Deuel
,gregation called (were) of son ,Naphtali
from

congregation, rulers of the tribes of their fathers. They *were* heads of the thousands of Israel.

[17]And Moses and Aaron took these men who were marked out by name. [18]And they assembled all the congregation on the first of the second month. And they declared their pedigrees according to their families, by their fathers' house, according to the number of names, from twenty years old and upward, by their heads. [19]As Jehovah commanded Moses, so he numbered them in the wilderness of Sinai.

[20]And the sons of Reuben, Israel's firstborn, their generations, by their families, by their fathers' house, in the number of names, by their heads, every male from twenty years old and upward, everyone able to go out to war: [21]those that were numbered of them for the tribe of Reuben *were* forty-six thousand and five hundred.

[22]Of the sons of Simeon, their generations, by their families, by their fathers' house, his numbered ones in the number of names, by their heads, every male from twenty years old and upward, everyone able to go out to war: [23]those that were numbered of them for the tribe of Simeon *were* fifty-nine thousand and three hundred.

[24]Of the sons of Gad, their generations, by their families, by their fathers' house, in the number of names, every male from twenty years old and upward, everyone able to go out to war: [25]those that were numbered of them for the tribe of Gad *were* forty-five thousand and six hundred and fifty.

17 נשיאי מטות אבותם ראשי אלפי ישראל הם׃ ויקח
משה ואהרן את האנשים האלה אשר נקבו בשמות׃
18 ואת כל־העדה הקהילו באחד לחדש השני ויתילדו
על־משפחתם לבית אבתם במספר שמות מבן עשרים
19 שנה ומעלה לגלגלתם׃ כאשר צוה יהוה את־משה
20 ויפקדם במדבר סיני׃ ס ויהיו בני־ראובן בכר
ישראל תולדתם למשפחתם לבית אבתם במספר
שמות לגלגלתם כל־זכר מבן עשרים שנה ומעלה כל
21 יצא צבא׃ פקדיהם למטה ראובן ששה וארבעים אלף
וחמש מאות׃
22 לבני שמעון תולדתם למשפחתם לבית אבתם פקדיו
במספר שמות לגלגלתם כל־זכר מבן עשרים שנה
23 ומעלה כל יצא צבא׃ פקדיהם למטה שמעון תשעה
וחמשים אלף ושלש מאות׃
24 לבני גד תולדתם למשפחתם לבית אבתם במספר שמות
25 מבן עשרים שנה ומעלה כל יצא צבא׃ פקדיהם למטה
גד חמשה וארבעים אלף ושש מאות וחמשים׃ פ

26 Of the sons of Judah, their generations, by their families, by their fathers' house, in the number of names, every male from twenty years old and upward, everyone able to go out to war: 27 those that were numbered of them for the tribe of Judah *were* seventy-four thousand and six hundred.

28 Of the sons of Issachar, their generations, by their families, by their fathers' house, in the number of names, every male from twenty years old and upward, everyone able to go out to war: 29 those that were numbered of them for the tribe of Issachar *were* fifty-four thousand and four hundred.

30 Of the sons of Zebulun, their generations, by their families, by their fathers' house, in the number of names, every male from twenty years old and upward, everyone able to go out to war: 31 those that were numbered of them for the tribe of Zebulun *were* fifty-seven thousand and four hundred.

32 Of the sons of Joseph, of the sons of Ephraim, their generations, by their families, by their fathers' house, in the number of names, every male from twenty years old and upward, everyone able to go out to war: 33 those that were numbered of them for the tribe of Ephraim *were* forty thousand and five hundred.

34 Of the sons of Manasseh, their generations, by their families, by their fathers' house, in the number of names, every male from twenty years old and upward, everyone able to go out to war: 35 those that were numbered of them for the tribe of Manasseh *were* thirty-two thousand and two hundred.

36 [O]f the sons of Benjamin, their generations, by their families, by their fathers' house, in the number of

4557 1 1004 4940 8435 3063 1121
26 לִבְנֵי יְהוּדָה תּוֹלְדֹתָם לְמִשְׁפְּחֹתָם לְבֵית אֲבֹתָם בְּמִסְפַּר
the in | their | by | their by | their | ,Judah | the Of
of number | ,fathers' | house | ,families | ,generations | | of sons

6485 6635 5927 3605 4605 8141 6242 1121 80·34
27 שֵׁמוֹת מִבֶּן עֶשְׂרִים שָׁנָה וָמַעְלָה כֹּל יֹצֵא צָבָא׃ פְּקֻדֵיהֶם
numbered those | to | able | every- | and | years | twenty | from | ,names
them of | :war | go to | one | ,upward | | | of son a

3967 8337 505 7657 702 3063 4294
לְמַטֵּה יְהוּדָה אַרְבָּעָה וְשִׁבְעִים אֶלֶף וְשֵׁשׁ מֵאוֹת׃ פ
.hundred | and | thousand | seventy- | (were) | Judah | the of
| six | | four | | | of sons

4557 1 1004 4940 8435 3485 1121
28 לִבְנֵי יִשָּׂשכָר תּוֹלְדֹתָם לְמִשְׁפְּחֹתָם לְבֵית אֲבֹתָם בְּמִסְפַּר
the in | their | by | their by | their | ,Issachar | the Of
of number | ,fathers' | house | ,families | ,generations | | of sons

6485 6635 5927 3605 1608 8141 6242 1121 80·34
29 שֵׁמוֹת מִבֶּן עֶשְׂרִים שָׁנָה וָמַעְלָה כֹּל יֹצֵא צָבָא׃ פְּקֻדֵיהֶם
numbered those | to | able | every- | and | years | twenty | from | ,names
them of | :war | go to | one | ,upward | | | of son a

3967 702 505 2572 702 3485 4294
לְמַטֵּה יִשָּׂשכָר אַרְבָּעָה וַחֲמִשִּׁים אֶלֶף וְאַרְבַּע מֵאוֹת׃ פ
.hundred | and | thousand | fifty- | (were) | Issachar | the of
| four | | | four | | of tribe

4557 1 1004 4940 8435 2074 1121
30 לִבְנֵי זְבוּלֻן תּוֹלְדֹתָם לְמִשְׁפְּחֹתָם לְבֵית אֲבֹתָם בְּמִסְפַּר
the in | their | by | their by | their | Zebulun | the Of
of number | ,fathers' | house | ,families | ,generations | | of sons

6485 6635 5927 3605 4605 8141 6242 1121 80·34
31 שֵׁמוֹת מִבֶּן עֶשְׂרִים שָׁנָה וָמַעְלָה כֹּל יֹצֵא צָבָא׃ פְּקֻדֵיהֶם
numbered those | to | able | every- | and | years | twenty | from | names
them of | :war | go to | one | ,upward | | | of son a

3967 702 505 2572 7651 2074 4294
לְמַטֵּה זְבוּלֻן שִׁבְעָה וַחֲמִשִּׁים אֶלֶף וְאַרְבַּע מֵאוֹת׃ פ
.hundred | and | thousand | fifty | (were) | Zebulun | the of
| four | | | seven | | of tribe

1004 4940 8435 669 1121 3127 1121
32 לִבְנֵי יוֹסֵף לִבְנֵי אֶפְרַיִם תּוֹלְדֹתָם לְמִשְׁפְּחֹתָם לְבֵית
by | their by | their | ,Ephraim | the of | :Joseph | the Of
house | ,families | generation | | of sons | | of sons

3605 4605 8141 6242 1121 80·34 4557 1
אֲבֹתָם בְּמִסְפַּר שֵׁמוֹת מִבֶּן עֶשְׂרִים שָׁנָה וָמַעְלָה כֹּל
every- | and | years | twenty | from | ,names | the in | their
one | ,upward | | | of son a | | of number | ,fathers'

505 703 669 4294 6485 6635 5927
33 יֹצֵא צָבָא׃ פְּקֻדֵיהֶם לְמַטֵּה אֶפְרָיִם אַרְבָּעִים אֶלֶף
thousand | (were) | Ephraim | the of | numbered those | to | able
| forty | | of tribe | them of | :war | go to

3967 2568
וַחֲמֵשׁ מֵאוֹת׃
.hundred | and
| five

4557 1 1004 4940 8435 4519 1121
34 לִבְנֵי מְנַשֶּׁה תּוֹלְדֹתָם לְמִשְׁפְּחֹתָם לְבֵית אֲבֹתָם בְּמִסְפַּר
the in | their | by | their by | their | ,Manasseh | the Of
of number | ,fathers' | house | ,families | ,generations | | of sons

6685 6635 5927 3605 4605 8141 6242 1121 80·34
35 שֵׁמוֹת מִבֶּן עֶשְׂרִים שָׁנָה וָמַעְלָה כֹּל יֹצֵא צָבָא׃ פְּקֻדֵיהֶם
numbered those | to | able | every- | and | years | twenty | from | ,names
them of | :war | go to | one | ,upward | | | of son a

3967 505 7970 8147 4519 4294
לְמַטֵּה מְנַשֶּׁה שְׁנַיִם וּשְׁלֹשִׁים אֶלֶף וּמָאתָיִם׃
two and | thousand | thirty- | (were) | Manasseh | the of
.hundred | | | two | | of tribe

4557 1 1004 4940 8435 1144 1121
36 לִבְנֵי בִנְיָמִן תּוֹלְדֹתָם לְמִשְׁפְּחֹתָם לְבֵית אֲבֹתָם בְּמִסְפַּר
the in | their | by | their by | their | ,Benjamin | the Of
of number | ,fathers' | house | ,families | ,generations | | of sons

names, every male from twenty years old and upward, everyone able to go out to war: [37]those that were numbered of them for the tribe of Benjamin *were* thirty-five thousand and four hundred.

[38]Of the sons of Dan, their generations, by their families, by their fathers' house, in the number of names, every male from twenty years old and upward, everyone able to go out to war: [39]those that were numbered of them for the tribe of Dan *were* sixty-two thousand and seven hundred.

[40]Of the sons of Asher, their generations, by their families, by their fathers' house, in the number of names, every male from twenty years old and upward, everyone able to go out to war: [41]those that were numbered of them for the tribe of Asher *were* forty-one thousand and five hundred.

[42]Of the sons of Naphtali, their generations, by their families, by their fathers' house, in the number of names, from twenty years old and upward, everyone able to go out to war: [43]those that were numbered of them for the tribe of Naphtali *were* fifty-three thousand and four hundred.

[44]These *were* numbered, whom Moses and Aaron numbered, and the rulers of Israel being twelve men; they were each one of his fathers' house. [45]And all those that were numbered of the sons of Israel by their fathers' house, from twenty years old and upward, all that were able to go out to war in Israel; [46]even all those that were numbered *were* six hundred and three thousand, and five hundred and fifty. [47]But the Levites, according to the tribe of their fathers, were not numbered among them.

6485 6635 5927 3605 4605 8141 6242 1121 8034
37 שְׁמֹת מִבֶּן עֶשְׂרִים שָׁנָה וָמַעְלָה כֹּל יֹצֵא צָבָא׃ פְּקֻדֵיהֶם
numbered those to able every- and years twenty from ,names
them of :war go to one ,upward of son a

3967 702 505 7970 2568 1144 4294
לְמַטֵּה בִנְיָמִן חֲמִשָּׁה וּשְׁלֹשִׁים אֶלֶף וְאַרְבַּע מֵאוֹת׃
.hundred and thousand thirty- (were) Benjamin the of
four five of tribe

4557 1 1004 4940 8435 1835 1121
38 לִבְנֵי דָן תּוֹלְדֹתָם לְמִשְׁפְּחֹתָם לְבֵית אֲבֹתָם בְּמִסְפַּר
the in their by their by their ,Dan the Of
of number ,fathers' house ,families generations of sons

6485 6635 5927 3605 4605 8141 6242 1121 8034
39 שְׁמֹת מִבֶּן עֶשְׂרִים שָׁנָה וָמַעְלָה כֹּל יֹצֵא צָבָא׃ פְּקֻדֵיהֶם
numbered those to able every- and years twenty from ,names
them of :war go to one ,upward of son a

3967 7651 505 8346 8147 1835 4294
לְמַטֵּה דָן שְׁנַיִם וְשִׁשִּׁים אֶלֶף וּשְׁבַע מֵאוֹת׃
.hundred and thousand sixty- (were) Dan the of
seven two of tribe

4557 1 1004 4940 8435 836 1121
40 לִבְנֵי אָשֵׁר תּוֹלְדֹתָם לְמִשְׁפְּחֹתָם לְבֵית אֲבֹתָם בְּמִסְפַּר
the in their by their by their ,Asher the Of
of number ,fathers' house ,families generations of sons

6485 6635 5927 3605 4605 8141 6242 1121 8034
41 שְׁמֹת מִבֶּן עֶשְׂרִים שָׁנָה וָמַעְלָה כֹּל יֹצֵא צָבָא׃ פְּקֻדֵיהֶם
numbered those to able every and years twenty from ,names
them of :war go to one ,upward of son a

3967 2568 505 703 259 836 4294
לְמַטֵּה אָשֵׁר אֶחָד וְאַרְבָּעִים אֶלֶף וַחֲמֵשׁ מֵאוֹת׃
.hundred and thousand forty- (were) Asher the of
five one of tribe

4557 1 1004 4940 8435 5320 1121
42 בְּנֵי נַפְתָּלִי תּוֹלְדֹתָם לְמִשְׁפְּחֹתָם לְבֵית אֲבֹתָם בְּמִסְפַּר
the in their by their by their ,Naphtali the Of
of number ,fathers' house ,families generations of sons

6485 6635 5927 3605 4605 8141 6242 1121 8034
43 שְׁמֹת מִבֶּן עֶשְׂרִים שָׁנָה וָמַעְלָה כֹּל יֹצֵא צָבָא׃ פְּקֻדֵיהֶם
numbered those to able every- and years twenty from ,names
them of :war go to one ,upward of son a

3967 702 505 2572 7969 5320 4294
לְמַטֵּה נַפְתָּלִי שְׁלֹשָׁה וַחֲמִשִּׁים אֶלֶף וְאַרְבַּע מֵאוֹת׃
.hundred and thousand fifty- (were) Naphtali the of
four three of tribe

3478 8269 175 4872 6485 6485 428
44 אֵלֶּה הַפְּקֻדִים אֲשֶׁר פָּקַד מֹשֶׁה וְאַהֲרֹן וּנְשִׂיאֵי יִשְׂרָאֵל
,Israel the and and Moses numbered whom those These
of rulers ;Aaron ,numbered (were)

3605 1961 1 1004 259 376 376 6240 8147
45 שְׁנֵים עָשָׂר אִישׁ אִישׁ־אֶחָד לְבֵית־אֲבֹתָיו הָיוּ׃ וַיִּהְיוּ כָּל־
all And they his for one each ;men twelve
were fathers' house

4605 8141 6242 1121 1 1004 3478 1121 6485
פְּקוּדֵי בְנֵי־יִשְׂרָאֵל לְבֵית אֲבֹתָם מִבֶּן עֶשְׂרִים שָׁנָה וָמַעְלָה
and years twenty from their by Israel sons the those
,upward of son a fathers' house of of numbered

3967 8337 6485 3605 1961 3478 6635 5927/3605
46 כָּל־יֹצֵא צָבָא בְּיִשְׂרָאֵל׃ וַיִּהְיוּ כָּל־הַפְּקֻדִים שֵׁשׁ־מֵאוֹת
hundred six numbered those all even ;Israel in war to able every-
were go to one

3881 2572 3967 2568 505 7969 505
47 אֶלֶף וּשְׁלֹשֶׁת אֲלָפִים וַחֲמֵשׁ מֵאוֹת וַחֲמִשִּׁים׃ וְהַלְוִיִּם
the But and hundred five ,thousand and thousand
,Levites ,fifty three

8432 6485 3808 1 4294
לְמַטֵּה אֲבֹתָם לֹא הִתְפָּקְדוּ בְּתוֹכָם׃
among were not their according
.them numbered ,fathers' tribe to

48 [48]And Jehovah spoke to Moses, saying, [49]However, you shall not number the tribe of Levi, nor shall you *count* their heads among the sons of Israel. [50]But you shall appoint the Levites over the tabernacle of the testimony, and over all its furniture, and over all that belongs to it. They shall bear the tabernacle, and all its furniture. And they shall serve it, and shall encamp around the tabernacle. [51]And when the tabernacle goes forward, the Levites shall take it down. And when the tabernacle is to be pitched, the Levites shall set it up. And the stranger that draws near shall be put to death. [52]And the sons of Israel shall pitch their tents, each man with his own camp, and each man with his own standard, according to their armies. [53]But the Levites shall pitch around the tabernacle of the testimony, that there be no wrath on the congregation of the sons of Israel. And the Levites shall keep the charge of the tabernacle of the testimony. [54]And the sons of Israel did according to all that Jehovah commanded Moses — so they did.

6485 3808/3881/4294 559 4872 3068 1696
48 וַיְדַבֵּר יְהוָה אֶל־מֹשֶׁה לֵּאמֹר׃ אַךְ אֶת־מַטֵּה לֵוִי לֹא תִפְקֹד
49
shall you not Levi tribe the ,Only ,saying Moses to Jehovah And
,number of spoke

6485 3478 1121 8432 5375 3808 7218
50 וְאֶת־רֹאשָׁם לֹא תִשָּׂא בְּתוֹךְ בְּנֵי יִשְׂרָאֵל׃ וְאַתָּה הַפְקֵד
shall you but ;Israel the among shall you not their and
appoint of sons lift heads

3605 5921 3627 3605 5921 5715 4908 3881
אֶת־הַלְוִיִּם עַל־מִשְׁכַּן הָעֵדֻת וְעַל כָּל־כֵּלָיו וְעַל כָּל־אֲשֶׁר
that all and its all and the the over Levites the
belongs over furniture over, testimony of tabernacle

8334 3627 3605 4908 5375
לוֹ הֵמָּה יִשְׂאוּ אֶת־הַמִּשְׁכָּן וְאֶת־כָּל־כֵּלָיו וְהֵם יְשָׁרְתֻהוּ
shall and its all and tabernacle the shall they to
it serve they ;furniture bear ;it

3881 3381 4908 5265 2583 4908 5439
51 וְסָבִיב לַמִּשְׁכָּן יַחֲנוּ׃ וּבִנְסֹעַ הַמִּשְׁכָּן יוֹרִידוּ אֹתוֹ הַלְוִיִּם
the it take shall the when And shall the and
;Levites down ,tabernacle forward goes ,encamp tabernacle around

4191 7131 2114 3881 6965 4908 2583
וּבַחֲנֹת הַמִּשְׁכָּן יָקִימוּ אֹתוֹ הַלְוִיִּם וְהַזָּר הַקָּרֵב יוּמָת׃
be shall draws that the and the it shall the is when and
.killed near stranger ;Levites up set tabernacle pitched be to

6635 1714 376 4264 376 3478 1121 2583
52 וְחָנוּ בְּנֵי יִשְׂרָאֵל אִישׁ עַל־מַחֲנֵהוּ וְאִישׁ עַל־דִּגְלוֹ לְצִבְאֹתָם׃
to according own his with and own his with each ,Israel sons the And
.armies their ,standard man each ,tent man of pitch shall

7110 1961 5715 4908 5439 2520 3881
53 וְהַלְוִיִּם יַחֲנוּ סָבִיב לְמִשְׁכַּן הָעֵדֻת וְלֹא־יִהְיֶה קֶצֶף עַל־
on wrath there that the the around shall the But
be not ,testimony of tabernacle pitch Levites

4908 4931 3881 8104 3478 1121 5712
עֲדַת בְּנֵי יִשְׂרָאֵל וְשָׁמְרוּ הַלְוִיִּם אֶת־מִשְׁמֶרֶת מִשְׁכַּן
the charge the the shall and ;Israel sons the the
of tabernacle of Levites keep of of company

3068 6680 3605 3478 1121 6213 5715
54 הָעֵדוּת׃ וַיַּעֲשׂוּ בְּנֵי יִשְׂרָאֵל כְּכֹל אֲשֶׁר צִוָּה יְהוָה אֶת־
Jehovah com- that according Israel the And the
manded all to of sons did .testimony

6213 4872
מֹשֶׁה כֵּן עָשׂוּ׃
they so ,Moses
.did

CHAPTER 2

[1]And Jehovah spoke to Moses and Aaron, saying, [2]The sons of Israel shall pitch by their fathers' house, every man with his own standard, according to the ensigns. They shall pitch around the tabernacle of the congregation, afar off. [3]And those who pitch on the east side, toward the sunrising, are *of* the standard of Judah's camp, according to their armies, the ruler of the sons of Judah *being* Nahshon the son of Amminadab. [4]And his army and those numbered of them *were* seventy-four thousand and six hundred. [5]And those

CAP. II ב

CHAPTER 2

1714 376 559 175 4872 3068 1696
1 וַיְדַבֵּר יְהוָה אֶל־מֹשֶׁה וְאֶל־אַהֲרֹן לֵאמֹר׃ אִישׁ עַל־דִּגְלוֹ
2
own his by Every ,saying Aaron to and Moses to Jehovah And
,standard man spoke

168 5439 5048 3478 1121 2583 1 1004 226
בְּאֹתֹת לְבֵית אֲבֹתָם יַחֲנוּ בְּנֵי יִשְׂרָאֵל מִנֶּגֶד סָבִיב לְאֹהֶל־
tent the around off afar ;Israel the shall their of with
of of sons pitch ,fathers' house ensigns the

3063 4264 1714 4217 6924 2583 2583 4150
3 מוֹעֵד יַחֲנוּ׃ וְהַחֹנִים קֵדְמָה מִזְרָחָה דֶּגֶל מַחֲנֵה יְהוּדָה
Judah's camp (of) are the toward the on those And shall they
of standard the ,sunrising side east pitch who .pitch meeting

6635 5992 1121 5177 3063 1121 5387 6635
4 לְצִבְאֹתָם וְנָשִׂיא לִבְנֵי יְהוּדָה נַחְשׁוֹן בֶּן־עַמִּינָדָב׃ וּצְבָאוֹ
his and ;Amminadab the Nahshon Judah the ruler the to according
,army of son (being) of son of ;armies their

2583 3967 8337 505 7657 702 6485
5 וּפְקֻדֵיהֶם אַרְבָּעָה וְשִׁבְעִים אֶלֶף וְשֵׁשׁ מֵאוֹת׃ וְהַחֹנִים
those And .hundred and thousand seventy- (were) those and
pitch that six four them of numbered

pitching next to him *shall*
be the tribe of Issachar; the
ruler of the sons of Issachar
being Nethaneel the son of
Zuar; [6]and his army, and
those that were numbered
of them *were* fifty-four thousand and four hundred.
[7]And the tribe of Zebulun;
the ruler of the sons of
Zebulun *being* Eliab the son
of Helon. [8]And his army,
and those that were num-
bered of them *were* fifty-
seven thousand and four
hundred. [9]All that were
numbered of the camp of
Judah *were* a hundred and
eighty-six thousand and
four hundred, by their
armies. They shall set forth
first.
[10]On the south side
shall be the standard of the
camp of Reuben, according
to their armies; the ruler of
the sons of Reuben *being*
Elizur the son of Shedeur.
[11]And his army, and those
numbered of it *were* forty-
six thousand and five
hundred. [12]And those that
pitch next to him shall be
the tribe of Simeon; the
ruler of the sons of Simeon
being Shelumiel the son of
Zurishaddi. [13]And his army,
and those numbered of
them *were* fifty-nine thousand and three hundred.
[14]And the tribe of Gad: the
ruler of the sons of Gad
being Eliasaph the son of
Reuel. [15]And his army, and
those numbered of them
were forty-five thousand,
six hundred and fifty. [16]All
that were numbered of the
camp of Reuben *were* a
hundred and fifty-one thousand four hundred and fifty,
according to their armies.
And they shall pull out
second.
[17]And the camp of the
Levites, *with* the tabernacle
of the congregation shall
pull out in the middle of the
camps. As they encamp, so
they shall pull out, each
man in his place, by their
standards.
[18]On the west side shall
be the standard of the camp
of Ephraim, according to
their armies; the ruler of the
sons of Ephraim *being*

6686 5417 3485 1121 5387 3485 4294
עליו מטה יששכר ונשיא לבני יששכר נתנאל בן־צוער׃
of son Nethaneel Issachar the ruler the ,Issachar (be shall) next
;Zuar (being) of sons of of tribe the him to

6 3967 702 505 2572 702 6485 6635
6 וצבאו ופקדיו ארבעה וחמשים אלף וארבע מאות׃
.hundred four and thousand fifty- four (were) those and his and
it of numbered ,army

7 6635 2497/1121 446 2074 1121 5387 2074 4294
7 8 מטה זבולן ונשיא לבני זבולן אליאב בן־חלן׃ וצבאו
his and ;Helon the (being) Zebulun the of the ;Zebulun the And
,army of son Eliab of sons ruler of tribe

9 3605 3967 702 505 2572 7651 6485
9 ופקדיו שבעה וחמשים אלף וארבע מאות׃ כל־
All .hundred four and thousand fifty- seven those and
,it of numbered

8337 505 8084 505 3967 3063 4264 6485
הפקדים למחנה יהודה מאת אלף ושמנים אלף וששת־
six and (were) Judah the of were that
eighty- hundred a of camp numbered

10 1714 5265 7223 6635 3967 702 505
10 אלפים וארבע־מאות לצבאתם ראשנה יסעו׃ דגל
The shall They first their by ,hundred and thousand
of standard up pull .armies four

468 7205 1121 5387 6635 8486 7205 4264
מחנה ראובן תימנה לצבאתם ונשיא לבני ראובן אליצור
(being) Reuben the of the to according be shall Reuben the
Elizur of sons ruler ;armies their ,side south the on of camp

11 2568 505 703 8337 6485 6635 7707 1121
11 בן־שדיאור׃ וצבאו ופקדיו ששה וארבעים אלף וחמש
five and thousand forty- (were) those and his and ;Shedeur the
six it of numbered army of son

12 8095 1121 5387 8095 4294 2583 3967
12 מאות׃ והחונם עליו מטה שמעון ונשיא לבני שמעון
Simeon the of the ;Simeon be shall to next those And .hundred
of sons ruler of tribe the him pitch that

13 2572 8672 6455 6635 6701 1121 8017
13 שלמיאל בן־צורישדי׃ וצבאו ופקדיהם תשעה וחמשים
fifty- nine those and his and ;Zurishaddai the (being)
them of numbered army of son Shelumiel

14 460 1410 1121 5387 1410 4294 3967 7969 505
14 אלף ושלש מאות׃ ומטה גד ונשיא לבני גד אליסף
(being) Gad the of ruler the ,Gad the And .hundred and thousand
Eliasaph of sons of tribe three

15 505 703 2568 6485 6635 7467 1121
15 בן־רעואל׃ וצבאו ופקדיהם חמשה וארבעים אלף
thousand forty- five those and his and ;Reuel the
,them of numbered ,army of son

16 3967 7205 4264 6485 3605 2572 3967 8337
16 ושש מאות וחמשים׃ כל־הפקדים למחנה ראובן מאת
(were) Reuben the of were that All .fifty and hundred six
hundred a of camp numbered

6635 2572 3967 702 505 2572 259 505
אלף ואחד וחמשים אלף וארבע־מאות וחמשים לצבאתם
to according and hundred four ,thousand fifty and one
.armies their ,fifty

17 8432 3881 4264 4150 168 5265 5265 8145
17 ושנים יסעו׃ ונסע אהל־מועד מחנה הלוים בתוך
the in the camp the ,meeting the shall And shall they And
of middle ,Levites of of tent up pull up pull second

1714 3027 376 52·65 2583 4264
המחנת כאשר יחנו כן יסעו איש על־ידו לדגליהם׃
their by his at each set shall so they as ;camp the
.standards hand man forth they ,encamp

18 669 1121 5387 3220 6635 669 4264 1714
18 דגל מחנה אפרים לצבאתם ימה ונשיא לבני אפרים
Ephraim the of ruler the (be shall) to according ,Ephraim camp the The
of sons side west the on armies their of of standard

Elishama the son of
Ammihud. [19]And his army,
and those numbered of
them *were* forty thousand
and five hundred. [20]And
next to him shall be the
tribe of Manasseh; the ruler
of the sons of Manasseh
being Gamaliel the son of
Pedahzur. [21]And his army,
and those numbered of
them *were* thirty-two thousand and two hundred.
[22]And the tribe of Benjamin; the ruler of the sons of
Benjamin *being* Abidan the
son of Gideoni. [23]And his
army, and those that were
numbered of them were
thirty-five thousand and
four hundred. [24]All that
were numbered of the
camp of Ephraim *were* a
hundred *and* eight thou-
sand and one hundred,
according to their armies.
And they shall pull out third.

[25]*On the north side shall*
be the standard of the camp
of Dan, according to their
armies; the ruler of the sons
of Dan *being* Ahiezer the
son of Ammishaddai. [26]And
his army, and those num-
bered of them *were* sixty-
two thousand and seven
hundred. [27]And those that
pitch next to him shall be
the tribe of Asher; the ruler
of the sons of Asher *being*
Pagiel the son of Ocran.
[28]And his army, and those
that were numbered of
them *were* forty-one thousand and five hundred.
[29]And the tribe of Naphtali;
the ruler of the sons of
Naphtali *being* Ahira the
son of Enan. [30]And his
army, and those numbered
of them *were* fifty-three
thousand and four hundred.
[31]All that were numbered of
the camp of Dan *were* a
hundred and fifty-seven
thousand and six hundred.
They shall pull out last by
their standards.

[32]These are those num-
bered of the sons of Israel
by their fathers' houses; all
that were numbered of the
camps according to their
armies *were* six hundred
and three thousand, five

505 703 6485 6635 5989 1121 476
19 אֱלִישָׁמָע בֶּן־עַמִּיהוּד׃ וּצְבָאוֹ וּפְקֻדֵיהֶם אַרְבָּעִים אֶלֶף
thousand (were) those and his and ;Ammihud the (being)
forty it of numbered ,army of son Elishama

4519 1121 5387 4519 4294 3967 2568
20 וַחֲמֵשׁ מֵאוֹת׃ וְעָלָיו מַטֵּה מְנַשֶּׁה וְנָשִׂיא לִבְנֵי מְנַשֶּׁה
Manasseh the of the ;Manasseh tribe the next And .hundred five and
of sons ruler of him to

7970 8147 6385 6635 6301 1121 1583
21 גַּמְלִיאֵל בֶּן־פְּדָהצוּר׃ וּצְבָאוֹ וּפְקֻדֵיהֶם שְׁנַיִם וּשְׁלֹשִׁים
thirty- two those and his and ;Pedahzur the (being)
them of numbered army of son Gamaliel

27 1144 1121 5387 1144 4294 3967 505
22 אֶלֶף וּמָאתָיִם׃ וּמַטֵּה בִּנְיָמִן וְנָשִׂיא לִבְנֵי בִנְיָמִן אֲבִידָן
(being) Benjamin the of the ,Benjamin the And two and thousand
Abidan of son ruler of tribe .hundred

702 505 7970 2568 6485 6635 1441/1121
23 בֶּן־גִּדְעֹנִי׃ וּצְבָאוֹ וּפְקֻדֵיהֶם חֲמִשָּׁה וּשְׁלֹשִׁים אֶלֶף וְאַרְבַּע
and thousand thirty- five those and his and ,Gideoni the
four ,them of numbered ;army of son

8083 505 3907 669 4264 6485 3605 3967
24 מֵאוֹת׃ כָּל־הַפְּקֻדִים לְמַחֲנֵה אֶפְרַיִם מְאַת אֶלֶף וּשְׁמֹנַת־
eight and a (were) Ephraim the of were that All .hundred
hundred of camp numbered

1714 5265 7992 6635 3967 505
25 אֲלָפִים וּמֵאָה לְצִבְאֹתָם וּשְׁלִשִׁים יִסָּעוּ׃ דֶּגֶל
The shall they third And to according one and thousand
of standard .up pull .armies their ,hundred

1121 295 1835/1121 5387 6635 6828 1835 4264
מַחֲנֵה דָן צָפֹנָה לְצִבְאֹתָם וְנָשִׂיא לִבְנֵי דָן אֲחִיעֶזֶר בֶּן
the (being) Dan the ruler the to according be shall Dan camp the
of son Ahiezer of sons of ;armies their side north the on of

7651 505 8346 8147 6385 6635 5996
26 עַמִּישַׁדָּי׃ וּצְבָאוֹ וּפְקֻדֵיהֶם שְׁנַיִם וְשִׁשִּׁים אֶלֶף וּשְׁבַע
and thousand sixty- two those and his and ;Ammishaddai
seven ,them of numbered army

836 1121 5387 836 4294 2583 3967
27 מֵאוֹת׃ וְהַחֹנִם עָלָיו מַטֵּה אָשֵׁר וְנָשִׂיא לִבְנֵי אָשֵׁר
Asher the of ruler the ;Asher the to next those And .hundred
of sons of tribe him pitch that

505 703 259 6385 6635 5918 1121 6295
28 פַּגְעִיאֵל בֶּן־עָכְרָן׃ וּצְבָאוֹ וּפְקֻדֵיהֶם אֶחָד וְאַרְבָּעִים אֶלֶף
thousand forty- one those and his and ;Ocran the (being)
,them of numbered ;army of son Pagiel

299 5320 1121 5387 5320 4294 3967 2568
29 וַחֲמֵשׁ מֵאוֹת׃ וּמַטֵּה נַפְתָּלִי וְנָשִׂיא לִבְנֵי נַפְתָּלִי אֲחִירַע
(being) Naphtali the of ruler the ,Naphtali the and ;hundred five and
Ahira of sons of tribe

702 505 2572 7969 6485 6635 5881/1121
30 בֶּן־עֵינָן׃ וּצְבָאוֹ וּפְקֻדֵיהֶם שְׁלֹשָׁה וַחֲמִשִּׁים אֶלֶף וְאַרְבַּע
and thousand fifty- three those and his and ;Enan the
four them of numbered army of son

7651 505 3967 1835 4264 6485 3605 3967
31 מֵאוֹת׃ כָּל־הַפְּקֻדִים לְמַחֲנֵה דָן מְאַת אֶלֶף וְשִׁבְעָה
seven and thousand a (were) Dan the of were that All .hundred
hundred of camp numbered

1714 5265 314 3967 8337 505 2572
וַחֲמִשִּׁים אֶלֶף וְשֵׁשׁ מֵאוֹת לָאַחֲרֹנָה יִסְעוּ לְדִגְלֵיהֶם׃
their by shall They last ;hundred and thousand fifty-
.standards up pull six

4264 6485 1 1004 3478 1121 6485 428
32 אֵלֶּה פְּקוּדֵי בְנֵי־יִשְׂרָאֵל לְבֵית אֲבֹתָם כָּל־פְּקוּדֵי הַמַּחֲנֹת
camps the were that all their by Israel sons the the those These
of numbered ;fathers' houses of of numbered are

3967 2568 505 7969 505 3967 8337 6635
לְצִבְאֹתָם שֵׁשׁ־מֵאוֹת אֶלֶף וּשְׁלֹשֶׁת אֲלָפִים וַחֲמֵשׁ מֵאוֹת
hundred five ,thousand three and hundred (were) to according
six armies their

hundred and fifty. [33]But the Levites were not numbered among the sons of Israel, as Jehovah commanded Moses.

[34]And the sons of Israel did according to all that Jehovah had commanded Moses, so they pitched by their standards, and so they pulled out, each one according to his family, and according to the house of his father.

33 חֲמִשִּׁים׃ וְהַלְוִיִּם לֹא הָתְפָּקְדוּ בְּתוֹךְ בְּנֵי יִשְׂרָאֵל כַּאֲשֶׁר

as ,Israel the among were not the But .fifty and
of sons numbered Levites

34 צִוָּה יְהוָה אֶת־מֹשֶׁה׃ וַיַּעֲשׂוּ בְּנֵי יִשְׂרָאֵל כְּכֹל אֲשֶׁר־צִוָּה

had that according Israel the did And .Moses Jehovah commanded
commanded all to of sons

יְהוָה אֶת־מֹשֶׁה כֵּן־חָנוּ לְדִגְלֵיהֶם וְכֵן נָסָעוּ אִישׁ לְמִשְׁפְּחֹתָיו

to according each they and their by they so ;Moses Jehovah
family his one ,forth set so .standards pitched

עַל־בֵּית אֲבֹתָיו׃ פ

.father his house the and
of to according

CAP. III ג

CHAPTER 3

CHAPTER 3

[1]And these are the generations of Aaron and Moses, in the day of the speaking of Jehovah with Moses in Mount Sinai. [2]And these *are* the names of Aaron's sons: Nadab, the firstborn; and Abihu, Eleazar, and Ithamar. [3]These are the names of Aaron's sons, the anointed priests whose hands he consecrated to act as priests. [4]And Nadab and Abihu died before Jehovah in the wilderness of Sinai, for bringing strange fire before Jehovah. And they had no sons. And Eleazar and Ithamar acted as priests in the presence of their father Aaron.

1 וְאֵלֶּה תּוֹלְדֹת אַהֲרֹן וּמֹשֶׁה בְּיוֹם דִּבֶּר יְהוָה אֶת־מֹשֶׁה

Moses with Jehovah's speaking the in and Aaron the these And
of day Moses of generations are

2 בְּהַר סִינָי׃ וְאֵלֶּה שְׁמוֹת בְּנֵי־אַהֲרֹן הַבְּכֹר ׀ נָדָב וַאֲבִיהוּא

and ,Nadab the :Aaron the the these And .Sinai on
,Abihu firstborn of sons of names (are) Mount

3 אֶלְעָזָר וְאִיתָמָר׃ אֵלֶּה שְׁמוֹת בְּנֵי אַהֲרֹן הַכֹּהֲנִים

priests the ,Aaron's sons names the these are and ,Eleazar ;Ithamar

4 הַמְּשֻׁחִים אֲשֶׁר־מִלֵּא יָדָם לְכַהֵן׃ וַיָּמָת נָדָב וַאֲבִיהוּא

Abihu and Nadab And as act to hands He whose ,anointed
died .priests filled

לִפְנֵי יְהוָה בְּהַקְרִבָם אֵשׁ זָרָה לִפְנֵי יְהוָה בְּמִדְבַּר סִינַי

;Sinai the in ,Jehovah before strange fire bringing for ,Jehovah before
of wilderness

וּבָנִים לֹא־הָיוּ לָהֶם וַיְכַהֵן אֶלְעָזָר וְאִיתָמָר עַל־פְּנֵי אַהֲרֹן

Aaron the in and Eleazar acted and they no and
of presence Ithamar priests as ;had sons

אֲבִיהֶם׃

their .father

[5]And Jehovah spoke to Moses, saying, [6]Bring the tribe of Levi near, and you shall cause it to stand before Aaron the priest. And they shall serve him, [7]and keep his charge, and the charge of all the congregation before the tabernacle of the congregation, to do the work of the tabernacle. [8]And they shall keep all the vessels of the tabernacle of the congregation, and the charge of the sons of Israel, to do the work of the tabernacle.

5 וַיְדַבֵּר יְהוָה אֶל־מֹשֶׁה לֵּאמֹר׃ הַקְרֵב אֶת־מַטֵּה לֵוִי
6

,Levi tribe the Bring ,saying ,Moses to Jehovah And
of near spoke

7 וְהַעֲמַדְתָּ אֹתוֹ לִפְנֵי אַהֲרֹן הַכֹּהֵן וְשֵׁרְתוּ אֹתוֹ׃ וְשָׁמְרוּ

keep and ,him they and the Aaron before it cause and
serve shall ,priest stand to

אֶת־מִשְׁמַרְתּוֹ וְאֶת־מִשְׁמֶרֶת כָּל־הָעֵדָה לִפְנֵי אֹהֶל מוֹעֵד

,meeting the before the all charge the and ,charge his
of tent congregation of

8 לַעֲבֹד אֶת־עֲבֹדַת הַמִּשְׁכָּן׃ וְשָׁמְרוּ אֶת־כָּל־כְּלֵי אֹהֶל

the the all they And the work the do to
of tent of vessels keep shall .tabernacle of

מוֹעֵד וְאֶת־מִשְׁמֶרֶת בְּנֵי יִשְׂרָאֵל לַעֲבֹד אֶת־עֲבֹדַת הַמִּשְׁכָּן׃

the work the do to ,Israel the charge the and ,meeting
.tabernacle of of sons of

[9]And you shall give the
Levites to Aaron and to his
son. They shall surely be
given to him out of the sons
of Israel. [10]And you shall
appoint Aaron and his sons,
and they shall keep their
priesthood. And the foreign
one who comes near shall
be put to death.
[11]And Jehovah spoke to
Moses, saying, [12]And I,
behold, I have taken the
Levites from the midst of
the sons of Israel in the
place of every firstborn
opening a womb among
the sons of Israel; and the
Levites have become Mine.
[13]for every firstborn is Mine,
from the day I struck every
firstborn in the land of
Egypt, I have set apart to
Myself every firstborn in
Israel, from men to animal.
They are Mine. I *am*
Jehovah.

[14]And Jehovah spoke to
Moses in the wilderness of
Sinai, saying, [15]Visit the
sons of Levi by their
families, by their fathers'
house. You shall number
every male from a month
old and upward. [16]And
Moses numbered them according
to the command of
Jehovah, as he had been
commanded.
[17]And these are the sons
of Levi by their names:
Gershon, and Kohath, and
Merari. [18]And these are the
names of the sons of
Gershon by their families:
Libni and Shimei. [19]And the
sons of Kohath, by their
families *were* Amram, and
Izehar, Hebron, and Uzziel.
[20]And the sons of Merari by
their families: Mahli and
Mushi. These are the
families of the Levites by
their fathers' houses.
[21]Of Gershon *is* the family
of the Libnites, and the
family of the Shimites.
These are the families of the
Gershonites. [22]Those that
were numbered of them,

8418 5414 1121 175 3881 5414
9 וְנָתַתָּה אֶת־הַלְוִיִּם לְאַהֲרֹן וּלְבָנָיו נְתוּנִם נְתוּנִם הֵמָּה
they surely shall to and Aaron to the you And
given be ;son his Levites give shall

8104 6485 1121 175 3478 1121
10 לוֹ מֵאֵת בְּנֵי יִשְׂרָאֵל׃ וְאֶת־אַהֲרֹן וְאֶת־בָּנָיו תִּפְקֹד וְשָׁמְרוּ
they and shall you his and Aaron And .Israel the of out to
keep shall ,appoint sons of sons ,him

4191 7131 2114 3550
אֶת־כְּהֻנָּתָם וְהַזָּר הַקָּרֵב יוּמָת׃
put be shall who the and priest- their
.death to near comes stranger hood

3947 2009 559 4872 3068 1696
11 12 וַיְדַבֵּר יְהוָה אֶל־מֹשֶׁה לֵּאמֹר׃ וַאֲנִי הִנֵּה לָקַחְתִּי אֶת־
have I ,behold ,I And ,saying ,Moses to Jehovah And
taken spoke

1121 7358 6363 1060 8478 3478 1121 8432 3881
הַלְוִיִּם מִתּוֹךְ בְּנֵי יִשְׂרָאֵל תַּחַת כָּל־בְּכוֹר פֶּטֶר רֶחֶם מִבְּנֵי
among the opening first- every the in Israel sons the from the
of sons the womb born of place of among Levites

3605 5221 3117 1060 8605 3881 1961 3478
13 יִשְׂרָאֵל וְהָיוּ לִי הַלְוִיִּם׃ כִּי לִי כָּל־בְּכוֹר בְּיוֹם הַכֹּתִי כָל־
every smote I from first- every Mine For the Mine and ;Israel
day the .born is .Levites become have

3478 1060 3605 6942 4714 776 1060
בְכוֹר בְּאֶרֶץ מִצְרַיִם הִקְדַּשְׁתִּי לִי כָל־בְּכוֹר בְּיִשְׂרָאֵל
,Israel in first- every to have I ,Egypt the in firstborn Myself sanctified of land born

3068 929 120
מֵאָדָם עַד־בְּהֵמָה לִי יִהְיוּ אֲנִי יְהוָה׃
.Jehovah I they Mine ,animal to from
(am) ;are men

6485 559 5514 4057 4872 3068 1696
14 15 וַיְדַבֵּר יְהוָה אֶל־מֹשֶׁה בְּמִדְבַּר סִינַי לֵאמֹר׃ פְּקֹד אֶת־
Count ,saying ,Sinai the in Moses to Jehovah And
of wilderness spoke

2320 2145 4940 1 1004 3881
בְּנֵי לֵוִי לְבֵית אֲבֹתָם לְמִשְׁפְּחֹתָם כָּל־זָכָר מִבֶּן־חֹדֶשׁ
a a from male every their by their the by Levi the
month of son ,families ,fathers of house of sons

3068 6310 4872 6485 6485 4605
16 וָמַעְלָה תִּפְקְדֵם׃ וַיִּפְקֹד אֹתָם מֹשֶׁה עַל־פִּי יְהוָה
,Jehovah the according Moses them And shall you and
of mouth to numbered .number upward

6955 1648 8034 1121 8034 6680
17 כַּאֲשֶׁר צֻוָּה׃ וַיִּהְיוּ־אֵלֶּה בְנֵי־לֵוִי בִּשְׁמֹתָם גֵּרְשׁוֹן וּקְהָת
and ,Gershon their by Levi the these And had he as
,Kohath ;names of sons are .commanded been

3845 4940 1648 1121 8034 428 4847
18 וּמְרָרִי׃ וְאֵלֶּה שְׁמוֹת בְּנֵי־גֵרְשׁוֹן לְמִשְׁפְּחֹתָם לִבְנִי
Libni their by Gershon the names the And and
:families of sons of are these .Merari

2275 3324 6019 4940 6955 1121 8096
19 וְשִׁמְעִי׃ וּבְנֵי קְהָת לְמִשְׁפְּחֹתָם עַמְרָם וְיִצְהָר חֶבְרוֹן
,Hebron and ,Amram their by Kohath the And and
,Izehar (are) families of sons .Shimei

428 4187 4249 4940 4847 1121 5826
20 וְעֻזִּיאֵל׃ וּבְנֵי מְרָרִי לְמִשְׁפְּחֹתָם מַחְלִי וּמוּשִׁי אֵלֶּה הֵם
(are) These .Mushi and Mahli their by Merari the And and
(are) families of sons .Uzziel

3846 4940 1648 1 1004 3881 4940
21 מִשְׁפְּחֹת הַלֵּוִי לְבֵית אֲבֹתָם׃ לְגֵרְשׁוֹן מִשְׁפַּחַת הַלִּבְנִי
the the (is) Of their by the families the
,Libnites of family Gershon .fathers' houses Levites of

6485 1649 4940 1992 8047 4940
22 וּמִשְׁפַּחַת הַשִּׁמְעִי אֵלֶּה הֵם מִשְׁפְּחֹת הַגֵּרְשֻׁנִּי׃ פְּקֻדֵיהֶם
numbered Those the families the (are) these the the and
them of Gershonites of ;Shimites of family

according to the number of all the males, from a month old and upward, even those that were numbered of them *were* seven thousand and five hundred. [23]The families of the Gershonites were to pitch behind the tabernacle westward. [24]The ruler of the fathers' house of the Gershonites *was* Eliasaph the son of Lael. [25]And the duty of the sons of Gershon in the tabernacle of the congregation *is* the tabernacle, and the tent, and its coverings, and the veil at the door of the tabernacle of the congregation; [26]and the hangings of the court, and the veil at the door of the court, which *is* by the tabernacle and by the altar all around, and its cords, to all its service.

[27]And of Kohath *is* the family of the Amramites, and the family of the Izeharites, and the family of the Hebronites, and the family of the Uzzielites. These are the families of the Kohathites. [28]In number, all the males, from a month old and upward *were* eight thousand and six hundred, keepers of the charge of the sanctuary. [29]The families of the sons of Kohath were to pitch on the side of the tabernacle southward; [30]the ruler of the fathers' house of the families of the Kohathites *being* Elizaphan the son of Uzziel. [31]And their charge *was* the ark, and the table, and the lampstand, and the altars, and the vessels of the sanctuary with which they minister, and the veil, and all the service of it. [32]Eleazar the son of Aaron the priest was ruler over the rulers of the Levites, and had the oversight of those that keep the charge of the sanctuary.

[33]Of Merari was the family of the Mahlites and the family of the Mushites. These are the families of Merari. [34]And those that were numbered of them, according to the number of all the males, from a month

7651 6485 4615 2320/1121 2145 4557
במספר כל-זכר מבן-חדש ומעלה פקדיהם שבעת
(were) those even ,upward and a a from the all to according
seven them of numbered month of son ,males of number the

4908 310 1649 4940 3967 2568 505
23 אלפים וחמש מאות: משפחת הגרשני אחרי המשכן
the behind families The .hundred five and thousand
tabernacle Gershonites of

3815 1121 460 1649 1004 5387 3220 2583
24 יחנו ימה: ונשיא בית-אב לגרשני אליסף בן-לאל:
;Lael the (being) the of father's the ruler the ;westward were
of son Eliasaph Gershonite house of camp to

4372 168 4918 4150 168 1648 1121 4931
25 ומשמרת בני-גרשון באהל מועד המשכן והאהל מכסהו
its and the and the is meeting the in Gershon the the and
,coverings ,tent ,tabernacle of tent of sons of duty

6607 4539 2691 7050 4150 168 6607 4539
26 ומסך פתח אהל מועד: וקלעי החצר ואת-מסך פתח
the at veil the and ,court the the and ,meeting the the at the and
of door of hangings of tent of door veil

4340 5439 4196 4908 834 2691
החצר אשר על-המשכן ועל-המזבח סביב ואת מיתריו
,cords its and all altar the by and the by which the
,around tabernacle (is) ,court

4940 6020 4940 6955 5656 3605
27 לכל עבדתו: ס ולקהת משפחת העמרמי ומשפחת
the and the the (is) of And its all for
of family ,Amramite of family Kohath .service

428 5877 4940 2276 4940 3325
היצהרי ומשפחת החברני ומשפחת העזיאלי אלה הם
are These the the and the the and the
.Uzzielite of family ,Hebronite of family ,Izeharite

4605 2320 1121 2145 3605 4557 6956 4940
28 משפחת הקהתי: במספר כל-זכר מבן-חדש ומעלה
and a a from the all In the families the
,upward month of son ,males number 8337 :Kohathite of

6944 4931 8104 3967 8337 505 8083
שמנת אלפים ושש מאות שמרי משמרת הקדש:
the charge the of keepers ,hundred six and thousand were
.sanctuary of eight

5387 8486 4908 3409 5921 2583 6955/1121 4940
29
30 משפחת בני-קהת יחנו על ירך המשכן תימנה: ונשיא
the And .southward the the on were Kohath the The
of ruler tabernacle of side pitch to of sons of families

4931 5816 469 6956 4940 1004
31 בית-אב למשפחת הקהתי אליצפן בן-עזיאל: ומשמרתם
their and ;Uzziel the (being) the the of father's the
(was) charge of son Elizaphan Kohathites of families house

834 6944 3627 4196 4501 7979 727
הארן והשלחן והמנרה והמזבחת וכלי הקדש אשר
which the the and the and the and the and ,ark the
sanctuary of vessels .altars lampstand ,table

3881 5387 5387 5656 3605 4539 8334
32 ישרתו בהם והמסך וכל עבדתו: ונשיא נשיאי הלוי
the rulers the the And service the and the and ,with minister
Levites of over ruler .it of all veil they

6944 4931 8104 6486 3548 175/1121 499
אלעזר בן-אהרן הכהן פקדת שמרי משמרת הקדש:
the charge the who those the (having) the Aaron the (is)
.sanctuary of keep of oversight ,priest of son Eleazar

428 4188 4940 4250 4940 4847
33 למררי משפחת המחלי ומשפחת המושי אלה הם
are these the the and the the was Of
;Mushites of family ,Mahlites of family Merari

2320 1121 2145 3605 4557 6485 4847 4940
34 משפחת מררי: ופקדיהם במספר כל-זכר מבן-חדש
a a from the all to according those And .Merari the
month of son ,males of number the ,them of numbered of families

old and upward *were* six
thousand and two hundred.
35 The ruler of the fathers'
house of the families of
Merari *was* Zuriel the son of
Abihail. They were to pitch
on the side of the taber-
nacle northward. 36 The appointed duty of the sons of
Merari *being* the boards of
the tabernacle, and its bars,
and its pillars, and its
sockets, and all its vessels,
and all its service; 37 and
the pillars of the court all
around, and their sockets,
and their pins, and their
cords.
38 And those that were to
pitch before the tabernacle
eastward, before the tabernacle of the congregation,
toward the sunrising, *were*
Moses, and Aaron, and his
sons, keeping the charge of
the sanctuary, and the
charge of the sons of Israel.
And the foreigner who goes
near shall be put to death.
39 All that were numbered of
the Levites, whom Moses
and Aaron numbered at the
mouth of Jehovah, by their
families, all the males from
a month old and upward
were twenty-two thousand.
40 And Jehovah said to
Moses, Count every first-
born male of the sons of
Israel from a month old and
upward, and take the
number of their names.
41 And you shall take the
Levites for Me, I *am*
Jehovah, instead of every
firstborn among the sons of
Israel; and the cattle of the
Levites instead of every
firstling among the cattle of
the sons of Israel.
42 And Moses numbered as
Jehovah commanded him,
all the firstborn among the
sons of Israel. 43 And all
the firstborn males ac-
cording to the number of
their names, from a son of a
month and upward of
those that were numbered
of them, were twenty-two
thousand, two hundred
and seventy-three. 44 And

4940 1 5387 3967 505 8336 4605
35 ומעלה ששת אלפים ומאתים: ונשיא בית־אב למשפחת
families the of father's the the and and thousand were and
of house of ruler ;two hundred six ,upward

6828 2583 4808 3409 32 1121 6700 4847
מררי צוריאל בן־אביחיל על ירך המשכן יחנו צפנה:
.northward they the the on ;Abihail the (was) Merari
camped tabernacle of side of son Zuriel

1280 4908 7175 4847 1121 4931 6486
36 ופקדת משמרת בני מררי קרשי המשכן ובריחיו
its and the (were) ,Merari the charge the the And
bars tabernacle boards of sons of ,oversight

2691 5982 5656 3605 3627 134 5982
37 ועמדיו ואדניו וכל־כליו וכל עבדתו: ועמדי החצר
the the and its all and its and its and its and
court of pillars ,service ,vessels all sockets ,pillars

4908 6440 2583 4340 3489 134 5439
38 סביב ואדניהם ויתדתם ומיתריהם: והחנים לפני המשכן
the before those And their and their and their and all
tabernacle pitched that .cords pins sockets ,around

1121 175 4872 4217 4150 168 6440 6924
קדמה לפני אהל־מועד ׀ מזרחה משה ׀ ואהרן ובניו
his and and were the toward ,meeting the before ,eastward
sons ,Aaron ,Moses ,sun-rising of tent

2114 3478 1121 4931 4720 4931 8104
שמרים משמרת המקדש למשמרת בני ישראל והזר
the and ;Israel the the and the charge the keeping
stranger of sons for charge sanctuary of

175 4872 6485 3881 6485 4191 7131
39 הקרב יומת: כל־פקודי הלוים אשר פקד משה ואהרן
and Moses numbered whom the the All he shall goes who
Aaron Levites of numbered .executed near

4605 2320 1121 2145 3605 4940 3068 6310
על־פי יהוה למשפחתם כל־זכר מבן־חדש ומעלה
and a a from the all their by ,Jehovah
upward month of son males ,families

6485 4872 3068 559 505 6242 8147
40 שנים ועשרים אלף: ס ויאמר יהוה אל־משה פקד
Number ,Moses to Jehovah said And .thousand twenty- (were)
two

7 5375 4605 2320 3478 1121 2145 1060 3605
כל־בכר זכר לבני ישראל מבן־חדש ומעלה ושא את
and and a from ,Israel the of male first- every
up take ,upward month of son a of sons born

3605 8478 3068 3881 3947 8034 4557
41 מספר שמתם: ולקחת את־הלוים לי אני יהוה תחת כל־
every instead ,Jehovah I for the you And their the
of (am) ,Me Levites take shall .names of number

1060 3605 8478 3881 929 3478 1121 1060
בכר בבני ישראל ואת בהמת הלוים תחת כל־בכור
firstling every instead the the and ;Israel the among first-
of Levites of cattle of sons born

3068 6680 4872 6485 3478 1121 929
42 בבהמת בני ישראל: ויפקד משה כאשר צוה יהוה
Jehovah had as Moses And .Israel the the among
commanded numbered of sons of cattle

2145 1060 3478 1121 1060 3605
43 אתו את־כל־בכור בבני ישראל: ויהי כל־בכור זכר
males the all And .Israel among the all ,him
firstborn of sons the firstborn

6242 8147 6485 4605 2320 1121 8034 4557
במספר שמת מבן־חדש ומעלה לפקדיהם שנים ועשרים
twenty- were their of and a a from their the by
two ,numbered upward month of son names of number

3967 7657 7969 505
אלף שלשה ושבעים ומאתים:
two and three ,thousand
.hundred seventy-

Jehovah spoke to Moses, saying, [45]Take the Levites instead of all the firstborn among the sons of Israel, and the cattle of the Levites instead of their cattle. And the Levites shall be Mine; I *am* Jehovah. [46]And *from* those redeemed of the two hundred and seventy-three who are more than the Levites, of the firstborn of the sons of Israel, [47]you shall even take five shekels a piece, by the head—you shall take by the shekel of the sanctuary; twenty gerahs *to* the shekel. [48]And you shall give the silver to Aaron,and to his sons, by which these over and above are redeemed. [49]And Moses shall take the redemption silver from those that are over and above those that were redeemed by the Levites, [50]from the firstborn of the sons of Israel he shall take the silver, a thousand, three hundred and sixty-five by the sanctuary shekel. [51]And Moses shall give the silver of those redeemed to Aaron and to his sons, according to Jehovah's command, as Jehovah has commanded Moses.

3605 8478 3881 3947 559 4872 3068 1696
44 וַיְדַבֵּר יְהוָה אֶל־מֹשֶׁה לֵּאמֹר׃ קַח אֶת־הַלְוִיִּם תַּחַת כָּל־
45 all Instead of Levites the Take ,saying ,Moses to Jehovah And spoke

929 8478 3881 929 3478 1121 1060
בְּכוֹר בִּבְנֵי יִשְׂרָאֵל וְאֶת־בֶּהֱמַת הַלְוִיִּם תַּחַת בְּהֶמְתָּם
;cattle their instead of the Levites of cattle the and ,Israel the among of sons the firstborn

7657 7969 6302 3068 3881 1961
46 וְהָיוּ־לִי הַלְוִיִּם אֲנִי יְהוָה׃ וְאֵת פְּדוּיֵי הַשְּׁלֹשָׁה וְהַשִּׁבְעִים
seventy- three the the of ;redeemed And Jehovah I (am) the ;Levites Mine and be shall

3947 3478 1121 1060 3881 5921 5736 3967
47 וְהַמָּאתַיִם הָעֹדְפִים עַל־הַלְוִיִּם מִבְּכוֹר בְּנֵי יִשְׂרָאֵל׃ וְלָקַחְתָּ
even you take shall Israel the of sons the of firstborn the than ,Levites were who more two and ,hundred

3947 6944 8255 1538 8255 2568 2568
חֲמֵשֶׁת חֲמֵשֶׁת שְׁקָלִים לַגֻּלְגֹּלֶת בְּשֶׁקֶל הַקֹּדֶשׁ תִּקָּח
shall you ;take the sanctuary the by of shekel ;head the by shekels five apiece

6302 1121 175 3701 5414 8255 1626 6242
48 עֶשְׂרִים גֵּרָה הַשָּׁקֶל׃ וְנָתַתָּה הַכֶּסֶף לְאַהֲרֹן וּלְבָנָיו פְּדוּיֵי
the of redeemed to and ,sons his Aaron to silver the your And give shall the to ,shekel gerahs twenty

6306 3701 4872 3947 5736
49 הָעֹדְפִים בָּהֶם׃ וַיִּקַּח מֹשֶׁה אֵת כֶּסֶף הַפִּדְיוֹם מֵאֵת
from redemption silver the Moses And take shall among .them were who more

3947 3478 1121 1060 3881 6302 5921 5736
50 הָעֹדְפִים עַל פְּדוּיֵי הַלְוִיִּם׃ מֵאֵת בְּכוֹר בְּנֵי יִשְׂרָאֵל לָקַח
he took Israel the of sons (the) of firstborn from the by ;Levites the redeemed above over those and

8255 505 3967 7969 8346 2568 3701
אֶת־הַכָּסֶף חֲמִשָּׁה וְשִׁשִּׁים וּשְׁלֹשׁ מֵאוֹת וָאֶלֶף בְּשֶׁקֶל
the by of shekel a ,thousand and hundred three and sixty- and five ,silver the

1121 175 6302 3701 4872 5414 6944
51 הַקֹּדֶשׁ׃ וַיִּתֵּן מֹשֶׁה אֶת־כֶּסֶף הַפְּדֻיִם לְאַהֲרֹן וּלְבָנָיו עַל־
by ,sons his to and ,Aaron to those redeemed silver the of Moses And gave the ,sanctuary

4872 3068 6680 3068 6310
פִּי יְהוָה כַּאֲשֶׁר צִוָּה יְהוָה אֶת־מֹשֶׁה׃
.Moses Jehovah com- manded as ,Jehovah the of mouth

CAP. IV ד

CHAPTER 4

CHAPTER 4

[1]And Jehovah spoke to Moses and to Aaron, saying, [2]Lift the heads of the sons of Kohath from among the sons of Levi, by their families, by their fathers' houses, [3]from thirty years old and upward, even until fifty years old, all that enter upon the service, to do work in the tabernacle of the congregation. [4]This *shall be* the service of the sons of Kohath in the tabernacle of the congregation, the Holy of Holies. [5]Aaron and his sons shall come in, when the camp

7218 5375 559 175 4872 3068 1696
1 וַיְדַבֵּר יְהוָה אֶל־מֹשֶׁה וְאֶל־אַהֲרֹן לֵאמֹר׃ נָשֹׂא אֶת־רֹאשׁ
2 of heads the Lift ,saying Aaron to and Moses to Jehovah And spoke

1121 1 1004 4940 3881 1121 8432 6955 1121
3 בְּנֵי קְהָת מִתּוֹךְ בְּנֵי לֵוִי לְמִשְׁפְּחֹתָם לְבֵית אֲבֹתָם׃ מִבֶּן
from of son a their ,fathers' by houses their by ,families ,Levi the of sons from among Kohath the of sons

6635 935 3605 8141 2572 1121 5704 4605 8141 7970
שְׁלֹשִׁים שָׁנָה וָמַעְלָה וְעַד בֶּן־חֲמִשִּׁים שָׁנָה כָּל־בָּא לַצָּבָא
the ,service that that all ,years fifty of son a even until and upward years thirty

6955 1121 5656 2088 4150 168 4399 6213
4 לַעֲשׂוֹת מְלָאכָה בְּאֹהֶל מוֹעֵד׃ זֹאת עֲבֹדַת בְּנֵי־קְהָת
Kohath the of sons the of service (is) This .meeting the of tent in work do to

5265 1121 175 935 6944 6944 4150 168
5 בְּאֹהֶל מוֹעֵד קֹדֶשׁ הַקֳּדָשִׁים׃ וּבָא אַהֲרֹן וּבָנָיו בִּנְסֹעַ
when travels his and sons Aaron shall And go in .(place) most the holy ,meeting the of tent in

pulls out, and shall take down the veil of the hanging, and shall cover the ark of the testimony with it. [6]And *he* shall put a covering of dugong skins on it, and shall spread a garment entirely of blue on top, and shall put in its staves. [7]And they shall spread a blue cloth on the table of the showbread, and shall put its dishes, and the spoons, and the bowls, and the cups of the drink offering, and the continual bread on it. [8]And they shall spread a cloth of scarlet over them, and shall cover it with a covering of dugong skin, and shall put in its staves. [9]And *he* shall take a blue cloth and shall cover the lampstand of the lamp, and its lights, and its tongs, and its firepans, and all its oil vessels with which they minister to it. [10]And they shall put it and all its vessels into a covering of dugong skin, and shall put *it* on the bar

[11]And they shall spread a blue cloth on the golden altar, and shall cover it with a covering of dugong skin, and shall put in its staves. [12]And they shall take all the vessels of ministry with which they minister in the sanctuary, and shall put *them* into a blue cloth, and shall cover them with a covering of dugong skin, and shall put *them* on the bar. [13]And *they* shall remove the ashes of the altar, and shall spread over it a purple cloth; [14]and shall put on it all its vessels with which they minister around it, the firepans, the hooks, and the shovels, and the bowls, all the vessels of the altar. And *they* shall spread

727 3680 4539 6532 33,81 4264
הַֽמַּחֲנֶה וְהוֹרִדוּ אֵת פָּרֹכֶת הַמָּסָךְ וְכִסּוּ־בָהּ אֵת אֲרֹן
the with shall and the veil the shall and the / of ark it cover hanging of down take ,camp

36 32 899 6566 8476 5785 3681 5921 5414 5715
6 הָעֵדֻת׃ וְנָתְנוּ עָלָיו כְּסוּי עוֹר תַּחַשׁ וּפָרְשׂוּ בֶגֶד־כְּלִיל
entirely a shall and ,dugong skins a it on shall and the / of cloth spread of covering put ;testimony

6566 6440 7979 905 7760 8504
7 תְּכֵלֶת מִלְמָעְלָה וְשָׂמוּ בַּדָּיו׃ וְעַל ׀ שֻׁלְחַן הַפָּנִים יִפְרְשׂוּ
shall they the the And its shall and ,top on blue / spread showbread of table on .staves in put

3709 7086 5414 8504 899
בֶּגֶד תְּכֵלֶת וְנָתְנוּ עָלָיו אֶת־הַקְּעָרֹת וְאֶת־הַכַּפֹּת וְאֶת־
and the and dishes its it on and ,blue a / ,spoons put shall of cloth

1961 5921 8548 3899 5262 7184 4518
הַמְּנַקִּיֹּת וְאֵת קְשׂוֹת הַנָּסֶךְ וְלֶחֶם הַתָּמִיד עָלָיו יִהְיֶה׃
;be shall it on the and drink the the and the / continual bread ,offering of cups ,bowls

5785 4372 3680 8144 8438 899 6566
8 וּפָרְשׂוּ עֲלֵיהֶם בֶּגֶד תּוֹלַעַת שָׁנִי וְכִסּוּ אֹתוֹ בְּמִכְסֵה עוֹר
skin a with it shall and ,scarlet a over they and / of covering cover of cloth them spread shall

3680 8504 899 3947 905 7760 8476
9 תָּחַשׁ וְשָׂמוּ אֶת־בַּדָּיו׃ וְלָקְחוּ ׀ בֶּגֶד תְּכֵלֶת וְכִסּוּ אֶת־
shall and blue a shall and its on shall and ,dugong / cover of cloth take ;staves it put

4289 4457 3974 5216 4501
מְנֹרַת הַמָּאוֹר וְאֶת־נֵרֹתֶיהָ וְאֶת־מַלְקָחֶיהָ וְאֶת־מַחְתֹּתֶיהָ
,firepans and ,tongs its and ,lights its and lamp the the / of lampstand

5414 8334 834 8081 3627
10 וְאֵת כָּל־כְּלֵי שַׁמְנָהּ אֲשֶׁר יְשָׁרְתוּ־לָהּ בָּהֶם׃ וְנָתְנוּ אֹתָהּ
it they and ;with it to they which oil its vessels all and / put shall minister

4132 5921 5414 8476 5785 4372 3627 3605
וְאֶת־כָּל־כֵּלֶיהָ אֶל־מִכְסֵה עוֹר תָּחַשׁ וְנָתְנוּ עַל־הַמּוֹט׃
.bar the on shall and ,dugong skin a into its all and / (it) put of covering vessels

4372 3680 8504 6566 2091 4196 5921
11 וְעַל ׀ מִזְבַּח הַזָּהָב יִפְרְשׂוּ בֶּגֶד תְּכֵלֶת וְכִסּוּ אֹתוֹ בְּמִכְסֵה
a with it shall and ,blue a shall they golden altar the And / of covering cover of cloth spread on

8335 3627 3947 905 7760 8476 5785
12 עוֹר תָּחַשׁ וְשָׂמוּ אֶת־בַּדָּיו׃ וְלָקְחוּ אֶת־כָּל־כְּלֵי הַשָּׁרֵת
ministry the all they And its shall and ,dugong skin / of vessels take shall .staves in put

3680 8504 899 5414 6944 8334 834
אֲשֶׁר יְשָׁרְתוּ־בָם בַּקֹּדֶשׁ וְנָתְנוּ אֶל־בֶּגֶד תְּכֵלֶת וְכִסּוּ
shall and ,blue a in they and the in with they which / cover of cloth (them) put shall ,sanctuary minister

1878 4132 5921 5414 8476 5785 4372
13 אוֹתָם בְּמִכְסֵה עוֹר תָּחַשׁ וְנָתְנוּ עַל־הַמּוֹט׃ וְדִשְּׁנוּ אֶת־
remove shall and ;bar the on shall and ,dugong skin a with them / of ashes the (them) put of covering

3615 5921 5414 713 899 6566 4196
14 הַמִּזְבֵּחַ וּפָרְשׂוּ עָלָיו בֶּגֶד אַרְגָּמָן׃ וְנָתְנוּ עָלָיו אֶת־כָּל־
all it on shall and ,purple a over shall and ,altar the / put of cloth it spread

4207 4289 5921 8334 834 3627
כֵּלָיו אֲשֶׁר יְשָׁרְתוּ עָלָיו בָּהֶם אֶת־הַמַּחְתֹּת אֶת־הַמִּזְלָגֹת
,hooks the ,firepans the ,with around they which its / it minister vessels

5921 6566 4196 3627/3605 4219 3276
וְאֶת־הַיָּעִים וְאֶת־הַמִּזְרָקֹת כֹּל כְּלֵי הַמִּזְבֵּחַ וּפָרְשׂוּ עָלָיו
it on shall and ,altar the the all ,bowls the and the and / spread of vessels ,shovels

a covering of dugong skin
on it, and shall put in its
staves. 15 And when Aaron
and his sons have finished
covering the sanctuary, and
all the sanctuary vessels, as
the camp sets forward, then
afterwards the sons of
Kohath shall come in to
carry. And they shall not
touch the holy thing, that
they may not die. These are
the burden of the sons of
Kohath in the tabernacle of
the congregation.
16 And the oversight of
Eleazar the son of Aaron the
priest *shall be* the oil of the
lamp, and the sweet
incense, and the continual
food offering, and the
anointing oil. He shall have
the charge of all the
tabernacle, of all that is in it,
whether it is the sanctuary,
or its furniture.
17 And Jehovah spoke to
Moses and to Aaron, say-
ing, 18 Do not cut off the
tribe of the families of the
Kohathites from among the
Levites. 19 but do this to
them, and they shall live
and not die as they draw
near the Holy of Holies.
Aaron and his sons shall go
in, and shall appoint them
each man to his service,
and to his burden. 20 And
they shall not go in to see
when the holy thing is
covered, that they may not
die.

21 And Jehovah spoke to
Moses, saying, 22 Lift the
heads of the sons of
Gershon also, by their
fathers' house, by their
families, 23 from thirty years
old and upward, you shall
number them, until fifty
years old; all that enter to
wait on the service, to serve
in the tabernacle of the
congregation. 24 This is the
duty of the families of the
Gershonites in serving and
in bearing burdens. 25 They
shall bear the curtains of the

3680 1121 175 3615 905 7760 8476 5785 3681
15 כְּסוּי עוֹר תַּחַשׁ וְשָׂמוּ בַדָּיו׃ וְכִלָּה אַהֲרֹן וּבָנָיו לְכַסֹּת
covering his and Aaron when And its shall and ,dugong skin a
sons finished have .staves in put of covering

310 4264 5265 6944 3627 6944
אֶת־הַקֹּדֶשׁ וְאֶת־כָּל־כְּלֵי הַקֹּדֶשׁ בִּנְסֹעַ הַמַּחֲנֶה וְאַחֲרֵי־כֵן
then the sets as the the all and ,sanctuary the
afterward ,camp forward ,sanctuary of vessels

428 4191 6944 5060 5375 6955 1121 935
יָבֹאוּ בְנֵי־קְהָת לָשֵׂאת וְלֹא־יִגְּעוּ אֶל־הַקֹּדֶשׁ וָמֵתוּ אֵלֶּה
these they lest the shall they but to Kohath the shall
(are) ;die ,thing holy touch not ;carry of sons in come

1121 499 6486 4150 168 6955 1121 4853
16 מַשָּׂא בְנֵי־קְהָת בְּאֹהֶל מוֹעֵד׃ וּפְקֻדַּת אֶלְעָזָר ׀ בֶּן
son ,Eleazar the And .meeting the in Kohath sons the the
of of oversight of tent of of burden

8548 4503 5561 7004 3974 8081 3548 175
אַהֲרֹן הַכֹּהֵן שֶׁמֶן הַמָּאוֹר וּקְטֹרֶת הַסַּמִּים וּמִנְחַת הַתָּמִיד
,continual the and ,sweet the and ,lamp the (be shall) the Aaron
offering food incense of oil the ,priest

6944 3605 4908 6486 4888 8081
וְשֶׁמֶן הַמִּשְׁחָה פְּקֻדַּת כָּל־הַמִּשְׁכָּן וְכָל־אֲשֶׁר־בּוֹ בְּקֹדֶשׁ
the in in that all and the all shall he ;anointing the and
,sanctuary it is ,tabernacle oversee oil

3427
וּבְכֵלָיו׃
its and
furnishings

3772 3808 559 175 4872 3068 1696
17 וַיְדַבֵּר יְהוָה אֶל־מֹשֶׁה וְאֶל־אַהֲרֹן לֵאמֹר׃ אַל־תַּכְרִיתוּ
18
off cut Do not ,saying ,Aaron to and Moses to Jehovah And
spoke

6213 2088 3881 8432 6956 4940 7626
19 אֶת־שֵׁבֶט מִשְׁפְּחֹת הַקְּהָתִי מִתּוֹךְ הַלְוִיִּם׃ וְזֹאת ׀ עֲשׂוּ
do this but ;Levites the from the families the of tribe the
among Kohathites of

175 6944 6944 5066 4191 3808 2421
לָהֶם וְחָיוּ וְלֹא יָמֻתוּ בְּגִשְׁתָּם אֶת־קֹדֶשׁ הַקֳּדָשִׁים אַהֲרֹן
Aaron :holies of holy the they as ,die and they and to
near draw not live shall ,them

4853 5656 376 376 7760 935 1121
וּבָנָיו יָבֹאוּ וְשָׂמוּ אוֹתָם אִישׁ אִישׁ עַל־עֲבֹדָתוֹ וְאֶל־מַשָּׂאוֹ׃
his to and his to man each them shall and shall his and
;burden ,service appoint ,in go sons

4191 6944 1104 7200 935
20 וְלֹא־יָבֹאוּ לִרְאוֹת כְּבַלַּע אֶת־הַקֹּדֶשׁ וָמֵתוּ׃
they lest the is when see to they and
.die ,thing holy covered in go shall not

1648 1121 7218 5375 559 4872 3068/1696
21 וַיְדַבֵּר יְהוָה אֶל־מֹשֶׁה לֵּאמֹר׃ נָשֹׂא אֶת־רֹאשׁ בְּנֵי גֵרְשׁוֹן
22
Gershon the of heads the Lift ,saying ,Moses to Jehovah And
of sons spoke

8141 7970 1121 4940 1 1004 1571
23 גַּם־הֵם לְבֵית אֲבֹתָם לְמִשְׁפְּחֹתָם׃ מִבֶּן שְׁלֹשִׁים שָׁנָה
years thirty from ,families their by their the by ,also
old ,fathers of house

5921 935 3605 6485 2572 1121 5704 4605
וָמַעְלָה עַד בֶּן־חֲמִשִּׁים שָׁנָה תִּפְקֹד אוֹתָם כָּל־הַבָּא לִצְבֹא
wait to that all ;them shall you years fifty son a until and
on enter number of ,upward

4940 5656 2088 4150 168 5656 5647 6635
24 צָבָא לַעֲבֹד עֲבֹדָה בְּאֹהֶל מוֹעֵד׃ זֹאת עֲבֹדַת מִשְׁפְּחֹת
families the the This meeting the in service do to the
of of duty is of tent ,service

4908 3407 5375 4853 5647 1649
25 הַגֵּרְשֻׁנִּי לַעֲבֹד וּלְמַשָּׂא׃ וְנָשְׂאוּ אֶת־יְרִיעֹת הַמִּשְׁכָּן וְאֶת־
and the of curtains the shall They bear to and to the
,tabernacle bear .burdens serve ,Gershonite

tabernacle, and the tabernacle of the congregation,
its covering, and the covering of dugong skins that is
on its top, and the hanging
for the door of the tabernacle of the congregation;
26and the hangings of thea
court, and the hanging for
the door of the gate of the
court which is by the tabernacle and by the altar all
around, and their cords, and
all the vessels of their
service, and whatever there
may be to do with them; in
this they shall serve. 27At
the mouth of Aaron, and of
his sons, shall be all the
service of the sons of the
Gershonites, and all their
burden, and all their service.
And you shall lay a charge
on them concerning the
duty of all their burden
28This is the service of the
families of the sons of the
Gershonites in the taber-
nacle of the congregation;
and their charge *is* under
the hand of Ithamar, son of
Aaron the priest.
29You shall number the
sons of Merari by their
families, by their fathers'
house, 30from thirty years
old and upward, even to
fifty years old you shall
number them, everyone
who is going into the
service, to do the work of
the tabernacle of the congregation. 31And this is the
charge of their burden,
according to all their
service in the tabernacle of
the congregation: the
boards of the tabernacle,
and its bars, and its pillars,
and its sockets, 32and the
pillars of the court all
around, and their sockets,
and their pins, and their
cords, of all their vessels,
and of all their service. And
you shall number the
vessels of the charge of
their burden by name.
33This is the service of the
families of the sons of
Merari, for all their service,
in the tabernacle of the congregation, by the hand of
Ithamar, son of Aaron the
priest.
34And Moses and Aaron
numbered; also the ruler of
the congregation, the sons

5921 834 8476 4372 4372 4150 168
אֹהֶל מוֹעֵד מִכְסֵהוּ וּמִכְסֵה הַתַּחַשׁ אֲשֶׁר־עָלָיו מִלְמָעְלָה
,it of | top on | is that | dugong skins | the and of covering | its ,covering | ,meeting | the of tent

4539 2691 7050 4150 168 6607 4539
26 וְאֶת־מָסַךְ פֶּתַח אֹהֶל מוֹעֵד׃ וְאֵת קַלְעֵי הֶחָצֵר וְאֶת־מָסַךְ
the hanging | and | the ,court | the of hangings | and | ;meeting | the of tent | the of door | hanging the for | and

5439 4196 4908 2691 8179 6607
פֶּתַח ׀ שַׁעַר הֶחָצֵר אֲשֶׁר עַל־הַמִּשְׁכָּן וְעַל־הַמִּזְבֵּחַ סָבִיב
all ,around | altar the | by and | the tabernacle | .by | which is | ,court the | the of gate | the for of door

6213 5656 3627 4340
וְאֵת מֵיתְרֵיהֶם וְאֶת־כָּל־כְּלֵי עֲבֹדָתָם וְאֵת כָּל־אֲשֶׁר יֵעָשֶׂה
do to | whatever be may there | and | their service | the of vessels | all | and | ,cords their | and

1121 5656 3605 1961 1121 175 6310 5647
27 לָהֶם וְעָבָדוּ׃ עַל־פִּי אַהֲרֹן וּבָנָיו תִּהְיֶה כָּל־עֲבֹדַת בְּנֵי
the of sons | service the of | all | be shall | his and sons | Aaron | the At of mouth | they this in .serve will | with ;them

5921 6485 5656 3605 4853 1649
הַגֵּרְשֻׁנִּי לְכָל־מַשָּׂאָם וּלְכֹל עֲבֹדָתָם וּפְקַדְתֶּם עֲלֵהֶם
them on | shall you charge a lay | and | their ;service | all and | their ,burden | all and | the ,Gershonites

1121 4940 5656 2088 4853 3605 4931
28 בְּמִשְׁמֶרֶת אֵת כָּל־מַשָּׂאָם׃ זֹאת עֲבֹדַת מִשְׁפְּחֹת בְּנֵי
the of sons | families of | the of service | is This | their .burden | all | concerning of duty the

175 1121 385 3027 4931 4150 168 1649
הַגֵּרְשֻׁנִּי בְּאֹהֶל מוֹעֵד וּמִשְׁמַרְתָּם בְּיַד אִיתָמָר בֶּן־אַהֲרֹן
Aaron | son of | Ithamar's | under hand | their And (is) charge | .meeting | the in of tent | the Gershonites

6485 1 1004 4940 4847 1121 3548
29 הַכֹּהֵן׃ ס בְּנֵי מְרָרִי לְמִשְׁפְּחֹתָם לְבֵית־אֲבֹתָם תִּפְקֹד
shall you number | their ,fathers | the by of house | their by ,families | ,Merari | The of sons | the .priest

8141 2572 1121 4605 8141 7970 1121
30 אֹתָם׃ מִבֶּן שְׁלֹשִׁים שָׁנָה וָמַעְלָה וְעַד בֶּן־חֲמִשִּׁים שָׁנָה
years | fifty | old to even | and ,upward | years | thirty | from old | ;them

4150 168 5656 5647 6635 935 3605 6485
תִּפְקְדֵם כָּל־הַבָּא לַצָּבָא לַעֲבֹד אֶת־עֲבֹדַת אֹהֶל מוֹעֵד׃
.meeting | the of tent | work the of | do to | the into ,service | who every- going is one | shall you ,them number

7175 4150 168 5656 3605 4853 4931
31 וְזֹאת מִשְׁמֶרֶת מַשָּׂאָם לְכָל־עֲבֹדָתָם בְּאֹהֶל מוֹעֵד קַרְשֵׁי
the of boards | :meeting | the in of tent | their service | according all to | their ,burden | charge the of | And is this

5439 4691 5982 134 5982 1280 4908
32 הַמִּשְׁכָּן וּבְרִיחָיו וְעַמּוּדָיו וַאֲדָנָיו׃ וְעַמּוּדֵי הֶחָצֵר סָבִיב
all ,around | court the | the and of pillars | its and ,sockets | its and ,pillars | its and ,bars | the ,tabernacle

5656 3605 3627 3605 4340 3489 134
וְאַדְנֵיהֶם וִיתֵדֹתָם וּמֵיתְרֵיהֶם לְכָל־כְּלֵיהֶם וּלְכֹל עֲבֹדָתָם
their ;service | of and all | their ,vessels | all of | their and ,cords | their and ,pins | their and ,sockets

5656 2088 4853 4931 3627 6485 8034
33 וּבְשֵׁמֹת תִּפְקְדוּ אֶת־כְּלֵי מִשְׁמֶרֶת מַשָּׂאָם׃ זֹאת עֲבֹדַת
the of service | is This | their .burden | charge the of | vessels the of | shall you number | by and name

385 3027 4150 168 5656 3605 4847 1121 4940
מִשְׁפְּחֹת בְּנֵי מְרָרִי לְכָל־עֲבֹדָתָם בְּאֹהֶל מוֹעֵד בְּיַד אִיתָמָר
Ithamar's | by hand | ,meeting | the in of tent | their service | all for | ,Merari | the of sons | the of families

5712 5387 175 4872 6485 3548 175 1121
34 בֶּן־אַהֲרֹן הַכֹּהֵן׃ וַיִּפְקֹד מֹשֶׁה וְאַהֲרֹן וּנְשִׂיאֵי הָעֵדָה אֶת־
the ,congregation | the and of ruler | and ,Aaron | Moses | And numbered | .priest the | Aaron | son of

of the Kohathites by their
families, and by their
fathers' house, 35from thirty
years old and upward, even
to fifty years old, everyone
who is going into the
service, for work in the
tabernacle of the congre-
gation. 36their numbered
ones, by their families, were
two thousand, seven hun-
dred and fifty. 37These are
those numbered of the
families of the Kohathites,
everyone who is serving in
the tabernacle of the congregation, whom Moses
and Aaron numbered by the
mouth of Jehovah, by the
hand of Moses.
38And those numbered of
the sons of Gershon, by
their families, and by their
fathers' house, 39from thirty
years old and upward, even
to fifty years old, and everyone who is going into the
service, for work in the
tabernacle of the congre-
gation, 40even those num-
bered of them, by their
families, by their father's
house *were* two thousand,
six hundred and thirty.
41These *were* those num-
bered of the families of
Gershon, everyone who is
serving in the tabernacle of
the congregation, whom
Moses and Aaron num-
bered at the mouth of
Jehovah.
42And those numbered of
the families of the sons of
Merari, by their families, by
their fathers' house, 43from
thirty years old and upward,
even to fifty years old,
everyone who is going into
the service, for work in the
tabernacle of the congre-
gation, 44even their num-
bered ones by their families
were three thousand and
two hundred. 45These
were those numbered of
the families of the sons of
Merari, whom Moses and
Aaron numbered by the
mouth of Jehovah, by
Moses' hand.
46All those numbered,
whom Moses and Aaron
and the rulers of Israel

35 בְּנֵי הַקְּהָתִי לְמִשְׁפְּחֹתָם וּלְבֵית אֲבֹתָם׃ מִבֶּן שְׁלֹשִׁים
שָׁנָה וָמַעְלָה וְעַד בֶּן־חֲמִשִּׁים שָׁנָה כָּל־הַבָּא לַצָּבָא
36 לַעֲבֹדָה בְּאֹהֶל מוֹעֵד׃ וַיִּהְיוּ פְקֻדֵיהֶם לְמִשְׁפְּחֹתָם אַלְפַּיִם
37 שְׁבַע מֵאוֹת וַחֲמִשִּׁים׃ אֵלֶּה פְקוּדֵי מִשְׁפְּחֹת הַקְּהָתִי כָּל־
הָעֹבֵד בְּאֹהֶל מוֹעֵד אֲשֶׁר פָּקַד מֹשֶׁה וְאַהֲרֹן עַל־פִּי יְהוָה
38 בְּיַד־מֹשֶׁה׃ ס וּפְקוּדֵי בְּנֵי גֵרְשׁוֹן לְמִשְׁפְּחוֹתָם וּלְבֵית
39 אֲבֹתָם׃ מִבֶּן שְׁלֹשִׁים שָׁנָה וָמַעְלָה וְעַד בֶּן־חֲמִשִּׁים
40 שָׁנָה כָּל־הַבָּא לַצָּבָא לַעֲבֹדָה בְּאֹהֶל מוֹעֵד׃ וַיִּהְיוּ
פְּקֻדֵיהֶם לְמִשְׁפְּחֹתָם לְבֵית אֲבֹתָם אַלְפַּיִם וְשֵׁשׁ מֵאוֹת
41 וּשְׁלֹשִׁים׃ אֵלֶּה פְקוּדֵי מִשְׁפְּחֹת בְּנֵי גֵרְשׁוֹן כָּל־הָעֹבֵד
בְּאֹהֶל מוֹעֵד אֲשֶׁר פָּקַד מֹשֶׁה וְאַהֲרֹן עַל־פִּי יְהוָה׃
42 וּפְקוּדֵי מִשְׁפְּחֹת בְּנֵי מְרָרִי לְמִשְׁפְּחֹתָם לְבֵית אֲבֹתָם׃
43 מִבֶּן שְׁלֹשִׁים שָׁנָה וָמַעְלָה וְעַד בֶּן־חֲמִשִּׁים שָׁנָה כָּל־הַבָּא
44 לַצָּבָא לַעֲבֹדָה בְּאֹהֶל מוֹעֵד׃ וַיִּהְיוּ פְקֻדֵיהֶם לְמִשְׁפְּחֹתָם
45 שְׁלֹשֶׁת אֲלָפִים וּמָאתָיִם׃ אֵלֶּה פְקוּדֵי מִשְׁפְּחֹת בְּנֵי
46 מְרָרִי אֲשֶׁר פָּקַד מֹשֶׁה וְאַהֲרֹן עַל־פִּי יְהוָה בְּיַד־מֹשֶׁה׃ כָּל־
הַפְּקֻדִים אֲשֶׁר פָּקַד מֹשֶׁה וְאַהֲרֹן וּנְשִׂיאֵי יִשְׂרָאֵל אֶת־

numbered, of the Levites, by their families, and by their fathers' house, [47]from thirty years old and upward, even to fifty years old, everyone who is going in to do the work of the service, even the service of burden in the tabernacle of the congregation, [48]even their numbered ones were eight thousand, five hundred and eighty; [49]*one* numbered them by the mouth of Jehovah, by the hand of Moses, each man according to his service, and according to his burden,; even they were numbered by him, as Jehovah commanded Moses.

CHAPTER 5

[1]And Jehovah spoke to Moses, saying, [2]Command the sons of Israel, and they shall send every leper out of the camp, and everyone with an issue, and everyone defiled by a dead body. [3]You shall send out from male and female. You shall send them to the outside of the camp. And they shall not defile their camps in the midst of which I dwell. [4]And the sons of Israel did so, and put them outside the camp. As Jehovah spoke to Moses, so the sons of Israel did.

[5]And Jehovah spoke to Moses, saying, [6]Speak to the sons of Israel, man or woman, when they commit any of the sins of man, by committing a trespass against Jehovah, and that person is guilty: [7]Then they shall confess their sin which they have done. And he shall restore his guilt in its principal, and add its fifth to it, *and shall give it* to him against whom he has been guilty. [8]And if a man has no kinsman to whom the guilt may be restored, the guilt which is restored *shall*

4605 8141 7970 1121 1 1004 4940 3881
47 הַלְוִיִּם לְמִשְׁפְּחֹתָם וּלְבֵית אֲבֹתָם׃ מִבֶּן שְׁלֹשִׁים שָׁנָה וָמַעְלָה
and upward years thirty from old their fathers' by and house their by families the of Levites

5656 5656 5656 5647 935 3605 8141 2572 1121 5704
וְעַד בֶּן־חֲמִשִּׁים שָׁנָה כָּל־הַבָּא לַעֲבֹד עֲבֹדַת עֲבֹדָה וַעֲבֹדַת
the even of service the service of work do to who every-in going is one years fifty old even to

2568 505 8083 6485 1961 4150 168 4853
48 מַשָּׂא בְּאֹהֶל מוֹעֵד׃ וַיִּהְיוּ פְּקֻדֵיהֶם שְׁמֹנַת אֲלָפִים וַחֲמֵשׁ
five thousand eight their ones numbered even were meeting the in of tent burden

376 376 4872 3027 6485 3068 6310 8084 3967
49 מֵאוֹת וּשְׁמֹנִים׃ עַל־פִּי יְהוָה פָּקַד אוֹתָם בְּיַד־מֹשֶׁה אִישׁ אִישׁ
man each Moses' hand by numbered (one) them Jehovah the By of mouth and hundred eighty

4872 3068 6680 6485 4853 5656
עַל־עֲבֹדָתוֹ וְעַל־מַשָּׂאוֹ וּפְקֻדָיו אֲשֶׁר־צִוָּה יְהוָה אֶת־מֹשֶׁה׃
Moses. Jehovah had commanded as were they him by numbered and his by burden his service by

CAP. V ה

CHAPTER 5

3478 1121 6680 559 4872 3068 1696
1 וַיְדַבֵּר יְהוָה אֶל־מֹשֶׁה לֵּאמֹר׃ צַו אֶת־בְּנֵי יִשְׂרָאֵל
2
Israel. sons the of Charge saying, Moses to Jehovah And spoke

5315 2931 3605 2100 6879 4264 7971
וִישַׁלְּחוּ מִן־הַמַּחֲנֶה כָּל־צָרוּעַ וְכָל־זָב וְכֹל טָמֵא לָנָפֶשׁ׃
a by body; defiled and everyone every and flowing one every leper the camp of out they and send shall

3808 7971 4264 2351 7971 5347 2145
3 מִזָּכָר עַד־נְקֵבָה תְּשַׁלֵּחוּ אֶל־מִחוּץ לַמַּחֲנֶה תְּשַׁלְּחוּם וְלֹא
and not shall you them send; camp the of outside the to shall you out send; female to from male

1121 6213 8432 7931 834 4264 2930
4 יְטַמְּאוּ אֶת־מַחֲנֵיהֶם אֲשֶׁר אֲנִי שֹׁכֵן בְּתוֹכָם׃ וַיַּעֲשׂוּ־כֵן בְּנֵי
the of sons so did And the in of midst dwell I which camps their shall they defile

1696 4264 2351 7971 3478
יִשְׂרָאֵל וַיְשַׁלְּחוּ אוֹתָם אֶל־מִחוּץ לַמַּחֲנֶה כַּאֲשֶׁר דִּבֶּר
spoke as camp the; outside them put and Israel,

3478 1121 6213 4872 3068
יְהוָה אֶל־מֹשֶׁה כֵּן עָשׂוּ בְּנֵי יִשְׂרָאֵל׃
Israel. the of sons did so Moses to Jehovah

376 3478 1121 1696 559 4872 3068 1696
5 וַיְדַבֵּר יְהוָה אֶל־מֹשֶׁה לֵּאמֹר׃ דַּבֵּר אֶל־בְּנֵי יִשְׂרָאֵל אִישׁ
6
man Israel, the of sons to Speak saying, Moses to Jehovah And spoke

3068 4604 4603 120 2403 6213 802
אוֹ־אִשָּׁה כִּי יַעֲשׂוּ מִכָּל־חַטֹּאת הָאָדָם לִמְעֹל מַעַל בַּיהוָה
against Jehovah a trespass, com- mitting by man, sins the of any of they commit When woman, or

6213 834 2403 3034 5315 816
7 וְאָשְׁמָה הַנֶּפֶשׁ הַהִוא׃ וְהִתְוַדּוּ אֶת־חַטָּאתָם אֲשֶׁר עָשׂוּ
they done have; which sin their they then confess shall that; person is and guilty

5414 3254 2549 7218 816 7725
וְהֵשִׁיב אֶת־אֲשָׁמוֹ בְּרֹאשׁוֹ וַחֲמִישִׁתוֹ יֹסֵף עָלָיו וְנָתַן לַאֲשֶׁר
him to and (it) give it to; add its and fifth its in principal guilt his he and restore shall

816 816 7725 1350 376 369 816
8 אָשַׁם לוֹ׃ וְאִם־אֵין לָאִישׁ גֹּאֵל לְהָשִׁיב הָאָשָׁם אֵלָיו הָאָשָׁם
guilt the whom, to guilt be may restored redeemer a man no has And if against has he whom. guilty been

be Jehovah's, a priest's, besides the ram of the atonement by which he makes atonement for him. [9]And every heave offering of all the holy things of the sons of Israel which they bring to the priest shall be his. [10]And any man's dedicated things shall become his, that which any man gives to the priest becomes his.

[11]And Jehovah spoke to Moses, saying, [12]Speak to the sons of Israel, and you shall say to them, When any man's wife goes astray, and has committed a trespass against him, [13]and a man lies with her *with* semen, and it has been hidden from her husband's eyes, and is kept hidden, and she has been defiled, and there is no witness against her, and she has not been caught; [14]and a spirit of jealousy has passed over him, and he has become jealous of his wife, and she has been defiled. Or, a spirit of jealousy has passed over him, and he has become jealous of his wife, and she has not become defiled: [15]then the man shall bring his wife in to the priest, and he shall bring in her offering for her, a tenth of an ephah of barley meal. He shall not pour oil on it, nor shall he put frankincense on it, for it *is* a food offering of jealousy, a food offering of memorial, bringing iniquity to remembrance. [16]And the priest shall bring her near, and shall cause her to stand before Jehovah. [17]And the priest shall take holy water in an earthen vessel. And the priest shall take of the dust which is on the tabernacle floor, and shall put *it* into the water. [18]And the priest shall cause the woman to stand before Jehovah, and shall uncover the woman's head, and shall give into her hand

3722 3725 352 3548 3068 7725
הַמּוּשָׁב לַיהוָה לַכֹּהֵן מִלְּבַד אֵיל הַכִּפֻּרִים אֲשֶׁר יְכַפֶּר
he the ram the besides a (is) is which
atones ,atonement of ,priest's ,Jehovah's restored

834 3478 1121 6944 3605 8641
9 בּוֹ עָלָיו׃ וְכָל־תְּרוּמָה לְכָל־קָדְשֵׁי בְנֵי־יִשְׂרָאֵל אֲשֶׁר
which ,Israel the holy the all of heave And by for
of sons of things offering every ,which him

376 1961 6944 376 1961 3548 7126
10 יַקְרִיבוּ לַכֹּהֵן לוֹ יִהְיֶה׃ וְאִישׁ אֶת־קֳדָשָׁיו לוֹ יִהְיוּ אִישׁ
any shall his dedicated any and ;becomes his the to they
man ;become things man's priest bring

1961 3548 5414 834
אֲשֶׁר־יִתֵּן לַכֹּהֵן לוֹ יִהְיֶה׃
.becomes his the to gives that
priest which

3478 1121 1696 559 4872 3068 1696
11 וַיְדַבֵּר יְהוָה אֶל־מֹשֶׁה לֵּאמֹר׃ דַּבֵּר אֶל־בְּנֵי יִשְׂרָאֵל
12
,Israel the to Speak ,saying ,Moses to Jehovah And
of sons spoke

4603 802 7847 376 376 559
וְאָמַרְתָּ אֲלֵהֶם אִישׁ אִישׁ כִּי־תִשְׂטֶה אִשְׁתּוֹ וּמָעֲלָה בוֹ
against has and ,wife goes When man's any ,them to you and
,him committed astray say shall

376 5869 5956 2233 7902 376 7901 4603
13 מָעַל׃ וְשָׁכַב אִישׁ אֹתָהּ שִׁכְבַת־זֶרַע וְנֶעְלַם מֵעֵינֵי אִישָׁהּ
her from has it and ,semen lying with man a lie and a
husband's eyes hidden been (with) her ,trespass

8610 3808 5707 2930 5640
וְנִסְתְּרָה וְהִיא נִטְמָאָה וְעֵד אֵין בָּהּ וְהִוא לֹא נִתְפָּשָׂה׃
been has not and against no and been has and kept is and
;caught she ;her witness ,defiled she ,hidden

2930 802 7065 7068 7307 5674
14 וְעָבַר עָלָיו רוּחַ־קִנְאָה וְקִנֵּא אֶת־אִשְׁתּוֹ וְהִוא נִטְמָאָה אוֹ־
or been has and ,wife his is he and ,jealousy a over has and
;defiled she of jealous of spirit him passed

2930 3808 802 7065 7068 7307 5674
עָבַר עָלָיו רוּחַ־קִנְאָה וְקִנֵּא אֶת־אִשְׁתּוֹ וְהִיא לֹא נִטְמָאָה׃
become has not and ,wife his is he and jealousy a over has
;defiled she of jealous of spirit him passed

7133 935 3548 802 376 935
15 וְהֵבִיא הָאִישׁ אֶת־אִשְׁתּוֹ אֶל־הַכֹּהֵן וְהֵבִיא אֶת־קָרְבָּנָהּ
offering her he and the to wife his the shall then
bring shall ,priest man in bring

8081 5921 3332 8184 7058 374 6224
עָלֶיהָ עֲשִׂירִת הָאֵיפָה קֶמַח שְׂעֹרִים לֹא־יִצֹק עָלָיו שֶׁמֶן
,oil it on shall he not ;barley meal an tenth a ,her for
pour of ephah of

2146 4503 7068 4503 3828 5921 5414
וְלֹא־יִתֵּן עָלָיו לְבֹנָה כִּי־מִנְחַת קְנָאֹת הוּא מִנְחַת זִכָּרוֹן
,memorial food a ,(is) it jealousy food a for ,frankincense on shall nor
of offering of offering it put

3068 6440 5975 3548 7126 5771 2142
16 מַזְכֶּרֶת עָוֹן׃ וְהִקְרִיב אֹתָהּ הַכֹּהֵן וְהֶעֱמִדָהּ לִפְנֵי יְהוָה׃
;Jehovah before shall and the her shall And .sin bring to
her stand priest near bring mind to

834 6083 2789 3627 6944 4325 3548 3947
17 וְלָקַח הַכֹּהֵן מַיִם קְדֹשִׁים בִּכְלִי־חָרֶשׂ וּמִן־הֶעָפָר אֲשֶׁר
which the and ,earthen an in holy water the shall and
dust from vessel priest take

5975 4325 5414 3548 3947 4908 7172 1961
18 יִהְיֶה בְּקַרְקַע הַמִּשְׁכָּן יִקַּח הַכֹּהֵן וְנָתַן אֶל־הַמָּיִם׃ וְהֶעֱמִיד
shall and the into shall and the shall the the on is
stand ;water (it) put ,priest take tabernacle of floor

5414 802 7218 6544 3068 6440 802 3548
הַכֹּהֵן אֶת־הָאִשָּׁה לִפְנֵי יְהוָה וּפָרַע אֶת־רֹאשׁ הָאִשָּׁה וְנָתַן
shall and the head the and ,Jehovah before woman the the
give ,woman of bare priest

the food offering of memorial; it is a food offering of jealousy; and in the priest's hand shall be the bitter waters which cause the curse. [19]And the priest shall cause her to swear and shall say to the woman, If no man has lain with you, and if you have not turned aside *to* impurity under your husband, be free from these bitter waters which cause the curse. [20]And you, if you have turned aside under your husband, and if you have been defiled, and any man besides your husband has given his semen to you, [21]then the priest shall cause the woman to swear with an oath of cursing, and the priest shall say to the woman: Jehovah shall make you a curse and an oath among your people, when Jehovah makes your thigh to fall away, and your belly to swell, [22]and these waters which cause the curse shall go into your bowels to cause the belly to swell, and the thigh to fall. And the woman shall say, Amen, amen.

[23]And the priest shall write these curses in a book, and shall blot *them* with the bitter waters. [24]And *he* shall cause the woman to drink the bitter waters which cause the curse. And the waters which cause the curse shall enter into her for bitter things. [25]And the priest shall take the food offering of jealousy out of the woman's hand, and shall wave the food offering before Jehovah, and shall bring it near to the altar. [26]And the priest shall take a handful of the food offering, its memorial, and shall burn it as incense on the altar. And afterward *he* shall cause the woman to drink the water. [27]And when he shall cause her to drink the water, then it shall be, if she has been defiled and has committed a trespass against her husband, the waters which

3548 3027 4068 4503 2146 4503 3709
עַל־כַּפֶּיהָ אֵת מִנְחַת הַזִּכָּרוֹן מִנְחַת קְנָאֹת הִוא וּבְיַד הַכֹּהֵן
the in and ;is it of food a ;memorial food the her into
priest's hand jealousy offering of offering palm
1961 4325 4751 779 7650 3548 559
19 יִהְיוּ מֵי הַמָּרִים הַמְאָרְרִים׃ וְהִשְׁבִּיעַ אֹתָהּ הַכֹּהֵן וְאָמַר
shall and the her shall And cause which bitter the shall
say priest swear to cause ,curse the waters be
802 7901 376 784
אֶל־הָאִשָּׁה אִם־לֹא שָׁכַב אִישׁ אֹתָךְ וְאִם־לֹא שָׂטִית
have you not if and with man has no If the to
strayed ,you lain ,woman
2932 8478 376 5352 4335 4751 779 428
טֻמְאָה תַּחַת אִישֵׁךְ הִנָּקִי מִמֵּי הַמָּרִים הַמְאָרְרִים הָאֵלֶּה׃
.these cause which bitter from be your under (to)
curse the waters free ,husband impurity
7847 8478 376 5414/2930 376
20 וְאַתְּ כִּי שָׂטִית תַּחַת אִישֵׁךְ וְכִי נִטְמֵאת וַיִּתֵּן אִישׁ בָּךְ אֶת־
to any has and have you and your under have you if But
man given ,defiled been if ,husband strayed ,you
7903 1107 376 7650 3548 802
21 שְׁכָבְתּוֹ מִבַּלְעֲדֵי אִישֵׁךְ׃ וְהִשְׁבִּיעַ הַכֹּהֵן אֶת־הָאִשָּׁה
woman the priest the shall then your besides his
swear to cause —husband ,semen
7621 422 559 3548 5414/802 3068 422
בִּשְׁבֻעַת הָאָלָה וְאָמַר הַכֹּהֵן לָאִשָּׁה יִתֵּן יְהוָה אוֹתָךְ לְאָלָה
curse a you Jehovah shall the to the shall and ;cursing an with
make ,woman priest say of oath
7621 8432 5971 5414 3068 3409 5307
וְלִשְׁבֻעָה בְּתוֹךְ עַמֵּךְ בְּתֵת יְהוָה אֶת־יְרֵכֵךְ נֹפֶלֶת וְאֶת־
and fall thigh your Jehovah when your among an and
,away makes ,people oath
990 6639 935 4325 428 779 4578 6638
22 בִּטְנֵךְ צָבָה׃ וּבָאוּ הַמַּיִם הַמְאָרְרִים הָאֵלֶּה בְּמֵעַיִךְ לַצְבּוֹת
cause to your into these cause which waters and to your
swell to bowels curse the go shall ,swell belly
990 5307 3409 559 802 543 543 3789
23 בֶּטֶן וְלַנְפִּל יָרֵךְ וְאָמְרָה הָאִשָּׁה אָמֵן ׀ אָמֵן׃ וְכָתַב אֶת־
shall And !Amen ,Amen the shall And the to and the
write ,woman say ,thigh fall ,belly
422 428 3548 5612 4229 4325 4751 8248
24 הָאָלֹת הָאֵלֶּה הַכֹּהֵן בַּסֵּפֶר וּמָחָה אֶל־מֵי הַמָּרִים׃ וְהִשְׁקָה
shall and the with shall and a in the these curses
drink make ,bitter waters blot book priest
802 4325 4751 779 935 4325
אֶת־הָאִשָּׁה אֶת־מֵי הַמָּרִים הַמְאָרְרִים וּבָאוּ בָהּ הַמַּיִם
the into shall and cause which bitter waters the woman the
waters her enter ;curse the
779 4751 3947 3548 3027 802 4503
25 הַמְאָרְרִים לְמָרִים׃ וְלָקַח הַכֹּהֵן מִיַּד הָאִשָּׁה אֵת מִנְחַת
food the the of out the shall And bitter for cause which
of offering woman's hand priest take .things curse the
7068 5130 4503 6440 3068 7126
הַקְּנָאֹת וְהֵנִיף אֶת־הַמִּנְחָה לִפְנֵי יְהוָה וְהִקְרִיב אֹתָהּ אֶל־
to it shall and ,Jehovah before food the shall and ,jealousy
near bring offering wave
4196 7061 3548 4503 234 6999
26 הַמִּזְבֵּחַ׃ וְקָמַץ הַכֹּהֵן מִן־הַמִּנְחָה אֶת־אַזְכָּרָתָהּ וְהִקְטִיר
shall and its food the of the shall and ;altar the
it burn ,memorial ,offering priest hand the fill
4196 310 8248 802 4325 8248
27 הַמִּזְבֵּחָה וְאַחַר יַשְׁקֶה אֶת־הָאִשָּׁה אֶת־הַמָּיִם׃ וְהִשְׁקָהּ
he when And .water the woman the make shall and the on
drink her makes drink then ;altar
4325 1961 2930 4603 4604 376 935
אֶת־הַמַּיִם וְהָיְתָה אִם־נִטְמְאָה וַתִּמְעֹל מַעַל בְּאִישָׁהּ וּבָאוּ
shall that against a has and has she if it then ,water the
go ,husband her trespass committed defiled been ,be shall

cause the curse shall go
into her for bitter things;
and her belly shall swell,
and her thigh shall fall
away, and the woman shall
become a curse in the midst
of her people. [28]And if the
woman has not been
defiled, and is pure, then
she shall be clean and shall
conceive seed.
[29]This is the law of
jealousies when a wife
turns aside under her
husband, and has been
defiled; [30]or when a spirit
of jealousy passes over a
man, and he has become
jealous of his wife, then he
shall cause the woman to
stand before Jehovah, and
the priest shall do to her all
this law; [31]and the man
shall be clean from sin, and
the woman shall bear her
iniquity.

3409 5307 990 6638 4151 779 4325
בָּהּ הַמַּיִם הַמְאָרְרִים לְמָרִים וְצָבְתָה בִטְנָהּ וְנָפְלָה יְרֵכָהּ
her shall and her shall and bitter for cause which the into
,thigh away fall ,belly swell ,things curse the waters her

28 2930 3808 5971 7130 422 802 1961
וְהָיְתָה הָאִשָּׁה לְאָלָה בְּקֶרֶב עַמָּהּ׃ וְאִם־לֹא נִטְמְאָה
been has not if And her the in curse a the shall and
defiled .people of midst woman become

29 8451 2233 2232 5352 2889 802
הָאִשָּׁה וּטְהֹרָה הִוא וְנִקְּתָה וְנִזְרְעָה זָרַע׃ זֹאת תּוֹרַת
law the This .seed shall and shall then she is and the
of is conceive clean be shall ,pure woman

30 2930 376 8478 802 7847 7068
הַקְּנָאֹת אֲשֶׁר תִּשְׂטֶה אִשָּׁה תַּחַת אִישָׁהּ וְנִטְמָאָה׃ אוֹ
or been has and her under wife a goes when ,jealousies
;defiled ,husband astray

802 7065 7068 7307 5921 5674 376
אִישׁ אֲשֶׁר תַּעֲבֹר עָלָיו רוּחַ קִנְאָה וְקִנֵּא אֶת־אִשְׁתּוֹ
,wife his is he and ,jealousy a over passes whom man a
of jealous of spirit

3605 3548 6213 3068 6440 802 5975
וְהֶעֱמִיד אֶת־הָאִשָּׁה לִפְנֵי יְהוָה וְעָשָׂה לָהּ הַכֹּהֵן אֵת כָּל־
all the to shall and ,Jehovah before the he then
priest her do woman stand shall

31 5375 1931 802 5771 376 5352 2088 8451
הַתּוֹרָה הַזֹּאת׃ וְנִקָּה הָאִישׁ מֵעָוֺן וְהָאִשָּׁה הַהִוא תִּשָּׂא
shall the and from the shall and ;this law
bear woman ,sin man clear be

5771
אֶת־עֲוֹנָהּ׃
her
.inquity

CAP. VI ו

CHAPTER 6

CHAPTER 6
[1]And Jehovah spoke to
Moses, saying, [2]Speak to
the sons of Israel and you
shall say to them, When a
man or woman shall vow
the special vow of a
Nazarite, to be separated to
Jehovah: [3]He shall sep-
arate from wine and fer-
mented drink; he shall not
drink vinegar of wine, or
vinegar of fermented drink;
he shall not drink any juice
of the grapes; and he shall
not eat dry or moist grapes.
[4]All the days of his
separation he shall not eat
from all that is made of the
vine, from pressed grapes,
even to the grapestone. [5]All
the days of the vow of his
separation, a razor shall not
pass over his head; he shall
be holy until all the days are
fulfilled which he has
separated to Jehovah. He
shall allow the locks of the
hair of his head to grow
long. [6]All the days of his
separation to Jehovah he

1 2 3478 1121 1696 559 4872 3068 1696
וַיְדַבֵּר יְהוָה אֶל־מֹשֶׁה לֵּאמֹר׃ דַּבֵּר אֶל־בְּנֵי יִשְׂרָאֵל
,Israel the to Speak ,saying ,Moses to Jehovah And
of sons spoke

5139/5087 5088 5087 802 376 559
וְאָמַרְתָּ אֲלֵהֶם אִישׁ אוֹ־אִשָּׁה כִּי יַפְלִא לִנְדֹּר נֶדֶר נָזִיר
a of special the shall When a or man a ,them to you and
,Nazarite vow vow woman say shall

3 3808 7941 2858 3196 2558 5144 7941 3196 3068 5144
לְהַזִּיר לַיהוָה׃ מִיַּיִן וְשֵׁכָר יַזִּיר חֹמֶץ יַיִן וְחֹמֶץ שֵׁכָר לֹא
not strong vinegar or vinegar shall he and from to be to
drink of wine of ;separate drink strong wine ;Jehovah separated

3892 3892 6025 8354 3808 6025 4952 3605 8354
יִשְׁתֶּה וְכָל־מִשְׁרַת עֲנָבִים לֹא יִשְׁתֶּה וַעֲנָבִים לַחִים וִיבֵשִׁים
,moist or dry and shall he not the of juice any he
grapes drink grapes ;drink shall

4 3196 1612 6213 3605 5145 3117 3605 398
לֹא יֹאכֵל׃ כֹּל יְמֵי נִזְרוֹ מִכֹּל אֲשֶׁר יֵעָשֶׂה מִגֶּפֶן הַיַּיִן
the the of made is which any- from his days all he shall not
wine,grapevine thing ,separation of ;eat

5 8593 5145 5088 3117 3605 398 3808 3085 2785
מֵחַרְצַנִּים וְעַד־זָג לֹא יֹאכֵל׃ כָּל־יְמֵי נֶדֶר נִזְרוֹ תַּעַר לֹא־
not razor a his vow the All shall he not to even pressed from
,separation of days .eat grapestone the grapes

6918 3068 5144 3117 4390 5704 7218 5674
יַעֲבֹר עַל־רֹאשׁוֹ עַד־מְלֹאת הַיָּמִם אֲשֶׁר־יַזִּיר לַיהוָה קָדֹשׁ
holy to has he which the all are until his over shall
;Jehovah separated days fulfilled ,head pass

6 5921 3068 5144 3117/3605 7218 8181 6545 1430 1961
יִהְיֶה גַּדֵּל פֶּרַע שְׂעַר רֹאשׁוֹ׃ כָּל־יְמֵי הַזִּירוֹ לַיהוָה עַל־
to his days All his the long shall he shall he
,Jehovah ,separation of .head of hair of locks grow ;be

shall not go near a dead
person. 7He shall not make
himself unclean for his
father, or for his mother, or
for his brother, or for his
sister, at their death; because his separation to his
God is on his head. 8All
the days of his separation
he shall be holy to Jehovah.
9And if any man dies very
suddenly beside him, and
he defiles his consecrated
head, then he shall shave
his head on the day of his
cleansing, on the seventh
day he shall shave it. 10And
on the eighth day he shall
bring two turtle-doves or
two young pigeons to the
priest, to the door of the
tabernacle of the congre-
gation. 11And the priest
shall prepare one for a sin
offering, and one for a burnt
offering, and shall make
atonement for him, be-
cause he sinned by reason
of the dead body. And he
shall dedicate his head on
that day. 12And he shall
consecrate to Jehovah the
days of his Nazariteship,
and shall bring a he-lamb of
the first year for a guilt
offering. But the former
days shall be void, for his
separation was defiled.
13And this is the law of
the Nazarite: when the *one*
shall bring him in to the
door of the tabernacle of
the congregation, 14and he
shall offer his offering to
Jehovah, one he-lamb of
the first year, a perfect one,
for a burnt offering; and one
she-lamb, a yearling, a
perfect one, for a sin-
offering; and one ram, a
perfect one, for a peace
offering; 15and a basket of
unleavened cakes of flour,
cakes mixed with oil, and
unleavened wafers an-
ointed with oil, and their
food offering, and their
drink offerings. 16And the
priest shall bring them
before Jehovah, and shall
offer his sin offering and his
burnt offering. 17And he
shall offer the ram *for* a
sacrifice of peace offering
to Jehovah, with the basket
of unleavened cakes. And
the priest shall offer its food
offering and its drink

3808 269 251 517 1 935 3808 4191 5315
7 נֶפֶשׁ מֵת לֹא יָבֹא: לְאָבִיו וּלְאִמּוֹ לְאָחִיו וּלְאַחֹתוֹ לֹא־
not shall | his for or sister | his for brother, | his for or mother, | his for father, | shall he not ;near go | dead | a person

3117 3605 7218 430 5145 4194 2930
8 יִטַּמָּא לָהֶם בְּמֹתָם כִּי נֵזֶר אֱלֹהָיו עַל־רֹאשׁוֹ: כֹּל יְמֵי
the of days | All | his .head | (is) upon | God his | separ-ation to | for | their at ;death | for them | defile he himself

6597 6621 4191 4191 3068 6918 5145
9 נִזְרוֹ קָדֹשׁ הוּא לַיהוָה: וְכִי־יָמוּת מֵת עָלָיו בְּפֶתַע פִּתְאֹם
,very | suddenly | beside him | one dies | And if | to .Jehovah | he (be shall) | holy | his separation

7637 3117 2893 3117 7218 1548 5145 2930
וְטִמֵּא רֹאשׁ נִזְרוֹ וְגִלַּח רֹאשׁוֹ בְּיוֹם טָהֳרָתוֹ בַּיּוֹם הַשְּׁבִיעִי
seventh | the in day | his ,cleansing | the in of day | his head | he then shave shall | his head ,separation | the he and of defiles

3128 1121 8147 176 8441 8147 935 8066 3117 1548
10 יְגַלְּחֶנּוּ: וּבַיּוֹם הַשְּׁמִינִי יָבִא שְׁתֵּי תֹרִים אוֹ שְׁנֵי בְּנֵי יוֹנָה
doves | young | two | or | turtle-doves | two | he bring shall | eighth | in And day the | shall he .it shave

259 3548 6213 4150 168 6607 3548
11 אֶל־הַכֹּהֵן אֶל־פֶּתַח אֹהֶל מוֹעֵד: וְעָשָׂה הַכֹּהֵן אֶחָד
one | the priest | shall and prepare | ,meeting | the of tent | the of door | to | the ,priest | to

5375 2398 3722 5930 259 2403
לְחַטָּאת וְאֶחָד לְעֹלָה וְכִפֶּר עָלָיו מֵאֲשֶׁר חָטָא עַל־הַנָּפֶשׁ
(dead) ;body | the con-cerning | he sinned | because | for ,him | shall and atone | a for ,offering burnt | one and | sin a for ,offering

5145 3117 3068 5144 3117 7218 6942
12 וְקִדַּשׁ אֶת־רֹאשׁוֹ בַּיּוֹם הַהוּא: וְהִזִּיר לַיהוָה אֶת־יְמֵי נִזְרוֹ
his separation | days | to Jehovah | shall he and separate | ;that | on day | his head | he and dedicate shall

1313 5307 7223 3117 816 8141 1121 3532 935
וְהֵבִיא כֶּבֶשׂ בֶּן־שְׁנָתוֹ לְאָשָׁם וְהַיָּמִים הָרִאשֹׁנִים יִפְּלוּ כִּי
for | shall ,fall | former | the but days | guilt a for ;offering | yearling a | he-lamb male | a | shall and bring

935 5145 3117 4390 3117 5139 8451 5139 2930
13 טָמֵא נִזְרוֹ: וְזֹאת תּוֹרַת הַנָּזִיר בְּיוֹם מְלֹאת יְמֵי נִזְרוֹ יָבִיא
shall bring | sepa-ration his | days (which) fulfilled are | the in day | the :Nazirite | the of law | this And (is) | his .separation | de-filed was

3068 7133 7126 4150 168 6607
14 אֹתוֹ אֶל־פֶּתַח אֹהֶל מוֹעֵד: וְהִקְרִיב אֶת־קָרְבָּנוֹ לַיהוָה
to Jehovah | his offering | he and bring shall | ;meeting | the of tent | door the of | to | him

1323 259 3535 5930 259 8549 8141 1121 3532
כֶּבֶשׂ בֶּן־שְׁנָתוֹ תָמִים אֶחָד לְעֹלָה וְכַבְשָׂה אַחַת בַּת־
a female | ,one | she-lamb | and burnt a for ,offering | ,one | perfect | ,yearling a | he-lamb male

5536 8002 8549 259 352 2403 8549 8141
15 שְׁנָתָהּ תְּמִימָה לְחַטָּאת וְאַיִל־אֶחָד תָּמִים לִשְׁלָמִים: וְסַל
a and of basket | peace a for ,offering | ,perfect | one | and ram | sin a for ,offering | ,perfect | ,yearling

4886 4682 7550 8081 1101 2471 5560 4682
מַצּוֹת סֹלֶת חַלֹּת בְּלוּלֹת בַּשֶּׁמֶן וּרְקִיקֵי מַצּוֹת מְשֻׁחִים
anointed | unleavened | and wafers | with oil | mixed | cakes | ,flour | unlea-vened of cakes

6213 3068 6440 3548 7126 5262 4503 8081
16 בַּשָּׁמֶן וּמִנְחָתָם וְנִסְכֵּיהֶם: וְהִקְרִיב הַכֹּהֵן לִפְנֵי יְהוָה וְעָשָׂה
shall and perform | Jeho-vah | be fore | the priest | shall And bring (them) | the .offerings drink | food their and ,offering | with ,oil

8002 2077 352 5930 2403
17 אֶת־חַטָּאתוֹ וְאֶת־עֹלָתוֹ: וְאֶת־הָאַיִל יַעֲשֶׂה זֶבַח שְׁלָמִים
peace a offering | a (for) ,sacrifice | shall he perform | the ram | and | burnt his and ;offering | sin his offering

5262 4503 3548 6213 4682 5536 3068
לַיהוָה עַל סַל הַמַּצּוֹת וְעָשָׂה הַכֹּהֵן אֶת־מִנְחָתוֹ וְאֶת־נִסְכּוֹ:
drink his and .offering | food his offering | the priest | shall and perform | unleavened the ;cakes of basket | with | to ,Jehovah

offering. [18]And the Nazarite shall shave the head of his separation at the door of the tabernacle of the congregation, and shall take the hair of the head of his separation and shall put *it* on the fire which is under the sacrifice of the peace offering. [19]And the priest shall take the boiled shoulder from the ram, and one unleavened cake out of the basket, and one unleavened wafer, and shall put *them* on the palms of the Nazarite after he has shaved his separation. [20]And the priest shall wave them, a wave offering before Jehovah. It *is* holy to the priest, besides the breast of the wave offering, and besides the leg of the heave offering. And afterward the Nazarite shall drink wine. [21]This is the law of the Nazarite who vows his offering to Jehovah for his separation, besides that which his hand may get. According to his vow which he vows, so he shall do by the law of his separation.

[22]And Jehovah spoke to Moses, saying, [23]Speak to Aaron and to his sons, saying, In this way you shall bless the sons of Israel, saying to them: [24]Jehovah bless you and keep you; [25]Jehovah cause His face to shine on you, and be gracious to you; [26]Jehovah lift up His face to you, and give you peace. [27]So they shall put My name on the sons of Israel, and I Myself will bless them.

18 וגלח הנזיר פתח אהל מועד את־ראש נזרו ולקח את־
שער ראש נזרו ונתן על־האש אשר־תחת זבח השלמים׃
19 ולקח הכהן את־הזרע בשלה מן־האיל וחלת מצה אחת
מן־הסל ורקיק מצה אחד ונתן על־כפי הנזיר אחר
20 התגלחו את־נזרו׃ והניף אותם הכהן תנופה לפני יהוה
קדש הוא לכהן על חזה התנופה ועל שוק התרומה
21 ואחר ישתה הנזיר יין׃ זאת תורת הנזיר אשר ידר קרבנו
ליהוה על־נזרו מלבד אשר־תשיג ידו כפי נדרו אשר
ידר כן יעשה על תורת נזרו׃ פ
22 וידבר יהוה אל־משה לאמר׃ דבר אל־אהרן ואל־בניו
23
לאמר כה תברכו את־בני ישראל אמור להם׃ ס
24 יברכך יהוה וישמרך׃ ס יאר יהוה פניו אליך
25
26 ויחנך׃ ס ישא יהוה פניו אליך וישם לך שלום׃
27 ושמו את־שמי על־בני ישראל ואני אברכם׃

CAP. VII ז

CHAPTER 7

CHAPTER 7

[1]And it happened on the day that Moses finished setting up the tabernacle, he anointed it, and sanctified it, and all its vessels, and the altar and all its vessels. And he anointed

1 ויהי ביום כלות משה להקים את־המשכן וימשח אתו
ויקדש אתו ואת־כל־כליו ואת־המזבח ואת־כל־כליו

them and sanctified them.
[2]And the rulers of Israel, the
chiefs of their fathers'
houses offered. These *were*
the rulers of the tribes;
these they that stood over
the ones that were num-
bered. [3]And they brought
their offering before
Jehovah, six covered
wagons and twelve oxen; a
wagon for every two of the
rulers, for each one an ox.
And they presented them
before the tabernacle. [4]And
Jehovah spoke to Moses,
saying, [5]Take it from them,
that they may be used to do
the service of the taber-
nacle of the congregation.
And you shall give them to
the Levites, to each man
according to his service.
[6]And Moses took the
wagons and the oxen and
gave them to the Levites.
[7]He gave two wagons and
four oxen to the sons of
Gershon, according to their
service. [8]And he gave four
wagons and eight oxen to
the sons of Merari, according to their service under
Ithamar, the son of Aaron
the priest. [9]But he did not
give any to the sons of
Kohath, because the ser-
vice of the holy things belonged to them. They bore
them on *their* shoulders.
[10]And the rulers brought the
dedication offering of the
altar in the day it was
anointed. And the rulers
brought near their offering
before the altar. [11]And
Jehovah said to Moses,
They shall present their
offering, one to the day, one
ruler to the day, for the dedication of the altar.

[12]And he who brought his
offering the first day *was*
Nahshon the son of
Amminadab, of the tribe of
Judah; [13]his offering *was*:

376 3478 5387 7126 6942 4886
2 וימשחם ויקדש אתם ויקריבו נשיאי ישראל ראשי
the ,Israel the And .them and he and
of chiefs of rulers offered sanctified them anointed

6485 5976 4294 5387 1 1004
בית אבתם הם נשיאי המטת הם העמדים על־הפקדים
who ones the over who they these the the these their houses
.numbered were stood (were) ,tribes of rulers (were) ;fathers'

6240 8147 6632 5699 8337 3068 6440 7133 935
3 ויביאו את־קרבנם לפני יהוה שש־עגלת צב ושני עשר
and covered wagons six ,Jehovah before their they And
twelve offering brought

7126 259 7794 5387 8147 5699 1241
בקר עגלה על־שני הנשאים ושור לאחד ויקריבו אותם
them they and for an the (every) for a :oxen
brought ;each ox ,rulers of two wagon

3947 559 4872 3068 559 4908 6440
4
5 לפני המשכן ויאמר יהוה אל־משה לאמר קח מאתם
from Take ,saying ,Moses to Jehovah And the before
,them (it) spoke .tabernacle

5414 4150 168 5656 5647
והיו לעבד את־עבדת אהל מועד ונתתה אותם אל־
to them you and ;meeting the the (at) to they that
give shall of tent of service serve be may

5699 4872 3947 5650 6310 376 3881
6 הלוים איש כפי עבדתו ויקח משה את־העגלת ואת־
and the Moses And his according each the
wagons took .service to ,Levites

5699 8147 3881 5414 1241
7 הבקר ויתן אותם אל־הלוים את | שתי העגלות ואת
and wagons two the to them and the
.Levites gave oxen

5656 6310 1648 1121 5414 1241 702
8 ארבעת הבקר נתן לבני גרשון כפי עבדתם ואת |
And their according ,Gershon the to He oxen four
.service to of sons gave

6310 4847 1121 5414 1241 8083 5699 702
ארבע העגלת ואת שמנת הבקר נתן לבני מררי כפי
for ,Merari the to he oxen eight and wagons four
of sons gave

3808 6955 1121 3548 1121 385 3027 5656
9 עבדתם ביד איתמר בן־אהרן הכהן ולבני קהת לא
not Kohath to But the Aaron the ,Ithamar the in their
(any) of sons the .priest of son of hand ,service

7126 5375 3802 6944 5656 5414
10 נתן כי־עבדת הקדש עליהם בכתף ישאו ויקריבו
And bore they (their) on belonged holy the the because he
brought .(them) shoulders ;them to things of service ,gave

7126 4886 3117 4196 2598 5387
הנשאים את חנכת המזבח ביום המשח אתו ויקריבו
brought and ;it was the in the dedication the the
near anointed day altar of offering rulers

3068 559 4196 6440 7133 5387
11 הנשיאם את־קרבנם לפני המזבח ויאמר יהוה אל־
to Jehovah said And the before their the
.altar offering rulers

7126 3117 5387 3117 259 5387 4872
משה נשיא אחד ליום נשיא אחד ליום יקריבו את־
shall they to one ruler the to One ruler ,Moses
bring ,day the ,day

7223 3117 7126 1961 4196 2598 7133
12 קרבנם לחנכת המזבח ויהי המקריב ביום הראשון
first the who he And the the for their
day brought was .altar of dedication ,offering

7133 3063 4284 5992 1121 5177 7133
13 את־קרבנו נחשון בן־עמינדב למטה יהודה וקרבנו
his and ;Judah the of Ammina- the Nahshon his
offering of tribe ,dab of son offering

one silver dish, its weight a hundred and thirty, one silver basin *of* seventy shekels after the sanctuary shekel, both of them full of flour mixed with oil for a food offering; [14]one golden pan *of* ten shekels full of incense; [15]one young bullock, one ram, one he-lamb of the first year, for a burnt offering; [16]one male of the goats for a sin offering; [17]and for the sacrifice of the peace offering, two oxen, five rams, five he-goats, five yearling he-lambs. This *was* the offering of Nahshon the son of Amminadab.

[18]On the second day Nethaneel the son of Zuar, ruler of Issachar, offered; [19]he brought for his offering: one silver dish, its weight a hundred and thirty, one silver basin *of* seventy shekels after the sanctuary shekel, both of them full of flour mixed with oil for a food offering; [20]one golden pan *of* ten shekels full of incense; [21]one young bullock, one ram, one he-lamb of the first year, for a burnt offering; [22]one male of the goats for a sin offering; [23]and for the sacrifice of the peace offering, two oxen, five rams, five he-goats, five yearling he-lambs. This *was* the offering of Nethaneel the son of Zuar.

[24]On the third day Eliab the son of Helon, ruler of the sons of Zebulun: [25]his offering *was*: one silver dish, its weight a hundred and thirty, one silver basin

259 4219 4948 3967 7970 259 3701 7086
קַעֲרַת־כֶּסֶף אַחַת שְׁלֹשִׁים וּמֵאָה מִשְׁקָלָהּ מִזְרָק אֶחָד
one basin its a and thirty ,one silver (was)
weight hundred dish

55,60 4392 8147 6944 8255 8255 7657 3701:
כֶּסֶף שִׁבְעִים שֶׁקֶל בְּשֶׁקֶל הַקֹּדֶשׁ שְׁנֵיהֶם ׀ מְלֵאִים סֹלֶת
of full of both the the by ,shekels (of) silver
flour them ;sanctuary of shekel seventy

4392 2091 6235 259 3709 4503 8081 1101
14 בְּלוּלָה בַשֶּׁמֶן לְמִנְחָה׃ כַּף אַחַת עֲשָׂרָה זָהָב מְלֵאָה
.full ,golden ten (of) one pan food a for with mixed
of shekels ;offering ,oil

8141/1121 259 3532 259 352 1241/1121 6499 2004
15 קְטֹרֶת׃ פַּר אֶחָד בֶּן־בָּקָר אַיִל אֶחָד כֶּבֶשׂ־אֶחָד בֶּן־שְׁנָתוֹ
a one he- one ram the a ,one bullock of
,yearling lamb ,herd of son ;incense

8002 1241 2077 2403 259 5795 8163 5930
16 17 לְעֹלָה׃ שְׂעִיר־עִזִּים אֶחָד לְחַטָּאת׃ וּלְזֶבַח הַשְּׁלָמִים בָּקָר
oxen peace the the for and sin a for one the buck burnt a for
offering of sacrifice ;offering goats of ;offering

8141 1121 3532 2568 6260 2568 352 8147
שְׁנַיִם אֵילִם חֲמִשָּׁה עַתֻּדִים חֲמִשָּׁה כְּבָשִׂים בְּנֵי־שָׁנָה
,yearlings ,he-lambs ,five he-goats ,five rams ,two

5992 1121 5177 7133 2568
חֲמִשָּׁה זֶה קָרְבַּן נַחְשׁוֹן בֶּן־עַמִּינָדָב׃
.Amminadab the Nahshon the This .five
of son of offering (was)

7126 3485 5387 6686 1121 5416 7126 8145 3117
18 19 בַּיּוֹם הַשֵּׁנִי הִקְרִיב נְתַנְאֵל בֶּן־צוּעָר נְשִׂיא יִשָּׂשכָר׃ הִקְרִב
he ;Issachar rulers ,Zuar the Nethaneel brought second On
brought of of son day the

4941 3967 7970 259 3701 7086 7133
אֶת־קָרְבָּנוֹ קַעֲרַת־כֶּסֶף אַחַת שְׁלֹשִׁים וּמֵאָה מִשְׁקָלָהּ
its a and thirty ,one silver dish his
;weight hundred :offering

8147 6944 8255 8255 7659 3701 259 4219
מִזְרָק אֶחָד כֶּסֶף שִׁבְעִים שֶׁקֶל בְּשֶׁקֶל הַקֹּדֶשׁ שְׁנֵיהֶם ׀
of both the the by ,shekels (of) silver one basin
them ;sanctuary of shekel seventy

6235 259 3709 4503 8081 1101 55,60 4392
20 מְלֵאִים סֹלֶת בְּלוּלָה בַשֶּׁמֶן לְמִנְחָה׃ כַּף אַחַת עֲשָׂרָה
ten (of) one pan food a for with mixed of full
(shekels) ;offering oil flour

3532 259 352 1241/1121 6499 7004 4392 2091
21 זָהָב מְלֵאָה קְטֹרֶת׃ פַּר אֶחָד בֶּן־בָּקָר אַיִל אֶחָד כֶּבֶשׂ־
he-lamb ,one ram the a ,one bullock of full ,golden
herd of son ;incense

2077 2403 259 5795 8163 5930 8141/1121 259
22 23 אֶחָד בֶּן־שְׁנָתוֹ לְעֹלָה׃ שְׂעִיר־עִזִּים אֶחָד לְחַטָּאת׃ וּלְזֶבַח
a for and sin a for one the buck burnt a for a ,one
of sacrifice ;offering goats of ;offering ,yearling

3532 2568 6260 2568 352 8147 1241 8002
הַשְּׁלָמִים בָּקָר שְׁנַיִם אֵילִם חֲמִשָּׁה עַתֻּדִים חֲמִשָּׁה כְּבָשִׂים
,he-lambs ,five he-goats ,five rams ,two oxen peace the
offering

6686 5417 7133 2088 2568 8141/1121
בְּנֵי־שָׁנָה חֲמִשָּׁה זֶה קָרְבַּן נְתַנְאֵל בֶּן־צוּעָר׃
.Zuar the Nethaneel the This .five ,yearlings
of son of offering (was)

7133 2497/1121 446 2074 1121 5387 7992 3117
24 25 בַּיּוֹם הַשְּׁלִישִׁי נָשִׂיא לִבְנֵי זְבוּלֻן אֱלִיאָב בֶּן־חֵלֹן׃ קָרְבָּנוֹ
his —Helon the Eliab ,Zebulun the of the third On
:offering of son of sons ruler (offered) day the

259 4519 4918 3967 7970 259 3701 7086
קַעֲרַת־כֶּסֶף אַחַת שְׁלֹשִׁים וּמֵאָה מִשְׁקָלָהּ מִזְרָק אֶחָד
one basin its a and thirty ,one silver dish
;weight hundred

of seventy shekels after the sanctuary shekel, both of them full of flour mixed with oil for a food offering; [26]one golden pan *of* ten shekels full of incense; [27]one young bullock, one ram, one he-lamb of the first year, for a burnt offering; [28]one male of the goats for a sin offering. [29]and for the sacrifice of the peace offering, two oxen, five rams, five he-goats, five yearling he-lambs. This *was* the offering of Eliab the son of Helon.

[30]On the fourth day Elizur the son of Shedeur, the ruler of the sons of Reuben: [31]his offering *was*: one silver dish, its weight a hundred and thirty, one silver basin *of* seventy shekels after the sanctuary shekel, both of them full of flour mixed with oil for a food offering; [32]one golden pan *of* ten shekels full of incense; [33]one young bullock, one ram, one he-lamb of the first year, for a burnt offering; [34]one male of the goats for a sin offering; [35]and for the sacrifice of the peace offering, two oxen, five rams, five he-goats, five yearling he-lambs. This *was* the offering of Elizur the son of Shedeur.

[36]On the fifth day Shelumiel the son of Zurishaddai, ruler of the sons of Simeon: [37]his offering *was*: one silver dish, its weight a hundred and thirty, one silver basin *of* seventy shekels after the sanctuary shekel, both of them full of

5560 4392 8147 6944 8255 8255 7657 3701
כֶּסֶף שִׁבְעִים שֶׁקֶל בְּשֶׁקֶל הַקֹּדֶשׁ שְׁנֵיהֶם ׀ מְלֵאִים סֹלֶת
of full of both the the by shekels (of) silver
flour them ;sanctuary of shekel seventy

4392 2091 6235 259 3709 4503 8081 1101
26 בְּלוּלָה בַשֶּׁמֶן לְמִנְחָה׃ כַּף אַחַת עֲשָׂרָה זָהָב מְלֵאָה
full ,golden ten (of) one pan food a for with mixed
shekels ;offering ,oil

1121 259 352 259 352 1241/1121 259 6499 7004
27 קְטֹרֶת׃ פַּר אֶחָד בֶּן־בָּקָר אַיִל אֶחָד כֶּבֶשׂ־אֶחָד בֶּן
a ,one he-lamb ,one ram the a ,one bullock of
,herd of son ;incense

8002 2077 2403 259 5795 8163 5930 8141
28 29 שְׁנָתוֹ לְעֹלָה׃ שְׂעִיר־עִזִּים אֶחָד לְחַטָּאת׃ וּלְזֶבַח הַשְּׁלָמִים
peace the the for and sin a for one the buck burnt a for year-
,offering of sacrifice ;offering goats of ;offering ,ling

8141/1121 3532 2568 6260 2568 352 8147 1241
בָּקָר שְׁנַיִם אֵילִם חֲמִשָּׁה עַתֻּדִים חֲמִשָּׁה כְּבָשִׂים בְּנֵי־שָׁנָה
,yearlings ,he-lambs ,five he-goats ,five rams ,two oxen

2497/1121 446 7133 2088 2568
חֲמִשָּׁה זֶה קָרְבַּן אֱלִיאָב בֶּן־חֵלֹן׃
.Helon the Eliab the This .five
of son of offering (was)

7707 1121 468 7205 1121 5387 7243 3117
30 בַּיּוֹם הָרְבִיעִי נָשִׂיא לִבְנֵי רְאוּבֵן אֱלִיצוּר בֶּן־שְׁדֵיאוּר׃
—Shedeur the Elizur ,Reuben the of the fourth the On
of son of sons ruler (offered) day

4219 4948 3967 7970 259 3701 7086 7133
31 קָרְבָּנוֹ קַעֲרַת־כֶּסֶף אַחַת שְׁלֹשִׁים וּמֵאָה מִשְׁקָלָהּ מִזְרָק
basin its a and thirty ,one silver dish his
;weight hundred ;offering

4392 8147 6944 8255 8255 7657 3701 259
אֶחָד כֶּסֶף שִׁבְעִים שֶׁקֶל בְּשֶׁקֶל הַקֹּדֶשׁ שְׁנֵיהֶם ׀ מְלֵאִים
full of both the the by ,shekels (of) silver one
them ,sanctuary of shekel seventy

4392 2091 6235 259 3709 4503 8081 1101 5560
32 סֹלֶת בְּלוּלָה בַשֶּׁמֶן לְמִנְחָה׃ כַּף אַחַת עֲשָׂרָה זָהָב מְלֵאָה
full ,golden ten (of) one pan food a for with mixed of
shekels ;offering ,oil flour

8141/1121 259 3532 259 352 1241/1121 259 6499 7004
33 קְטֹרֶת׃ פַּר אֶחָד בֶּן־בָּקָר אַיִל אֶחָד כֶּבֶשׂ־אֶחָד בֶּן־שְׁנָתוֹ
a ,one he- ,one ram the a ,one bullock of
,yearling lamb ,herd of son ;incense

1241 8002 2077 2403 259 5795 8163 5930
34 35 לְעֹלָה׃ שְׂעִיר־עִזִּים אֶחָד לְחַטָּאת׃ וּלְזֶבַח הַשְּׁלָמִים בָּקָר
oxen peace the the for and sin a for one the buck burnt a for
,offering of sacrifice ;offering goats of ;offering

8141/1121 3532 2568 6260 2568 352 8147
שְׁנַיִם אֵילִם חֲמִשָּׁה עַתֻּדִים חֲמִשָּׁה כְּבָשִׂים בְּנֵי־שָׁנָה
,yearlings ,he-lambs ,five he-goats ,five rams ,two

7707 1121 468 7133 2088 2568
חֲמִשָּׁה זֶה קָרְבַּן אֱלִיצוּר בֶּן־שְׁדֵיאוּר׃
.Shedeur the Elizur the This .five
of son of offering (was)

6701 1121 8017 8095 1121 5387 2549 3117
36 בַּיּוֹם הַחֲמִישִׁי נָשִׂיא לִבְנֵי שִׁמְעוֹן שְׁלֻמִיאֵל בֶּן־צוּרִישַׁדָּי׃
—Zurishaddai the Shelumiel ,Simeon the of the fifth the On
of son of sons ruler (offered) day

4219 4948 3967 7970 259 3701 7086 7133
37 קָרְבָּנוֹ קַעֲרַת־כֶּסֶף אַחַת שְׁלֹשִׁים וּמֵאָה מִשְׁקָלָהּ מִזְרָק
basin its a and thirty ,one silver dish his
;weight hundred ;offering

4392 8147 6944 4825 8255 7657 3701 259
אֶחָד כֶּסֶף שִׁבְעִים שֶׁקֶל בְּשֶׁקֶל הַקֹּדֶשׁ שְׁנֵיהֶם ׀ מְלֵאִים
full of both the the by ,shekels (of) silver one
them ,sanctuary of shekel seventy

flour mixed with oil for a food offering; 38one golden pan *of* ten shekels full of incense; 39one young bullock, one ram, one he-lamb of the first year, for a burnt offering; 40one male of the goats for a sin offering; 41and for the sacrifice of the peace offering, two oxen, five rams, five he-goats, five yearling he-lambs. This *was* the offering of Shelumiel the son of Zurishaddai.

42On the sixth day Eliasaph the son of Deuel, ruler of the sons of Gad: 43his offering *was* one silver dish, its weight a hundred and thirty, one silver basin *of* seventy shekels after the sanctuary shekel, both of them full of flour mixed with oil for a food offering; 44one golden pan *of* ten shekels full of incense; 45one young bullock, one ram, one he-lamb of the first year, for a burnt offering; 46one male of the goats for a sin offering; 47and for the sacrifice of the peace offering, two oxen, five rams, five he-goats, five yearling he-lambs. This *was* the offering of Eliasaph the son of Deuel.

48On the seventh day Elishama the son of Ammihud, ruler of the sons of Ephraim: 49his offering *was*: one silver dish, its weight a hundred and thirty, one silver basin *of* seventy shekels after the sanctuary shekel, both of them full of flour mixed with oil for a food offering; 50one golden pan *of* ten shekels full of

4392 2091 6235 259 3709 4503 8081 1107 5560
38 סלת בלולה בשמן למנחה׃ כף אחת עשרה זהב מלאה
full ,golden ten of (shekels) one pan food a for ;offering with ,oil mixed of flour

8141/1121 259 3532 259 352 1241/1121 259/6499 7004
39 קטרת׃ פר אחד בן־בקר איל אחד כבש־אחד בן־שנתו
a yearling ,one he-lamb ,one ram the a herd of son ,one bullock of ;incense

1241 8002 2077 2403 259 5795 8163 5930
40 41 לעלה׃ שעיר־עזים אחד לחטאת׃ ולזבח השלמים בקר
oxen peace the offering the for and sacrifice of sin a for ;offering one the goats buck of burnt a for ;offering

8141/1121 3532 2568 6260 2568 352 8147
שנים אילם חמשה עתדים חמשה כבשים בני־שנה
,yearlings ,he-lambs ,five he-goats ,five rams ,two

6701 1121 8017 7133 2088 2568
חמשה זה קרבן שלמיאל בן־צורישדי׃
.Zurishaddai the of son Shelumiel the of offering This (was) .five

7133 1845 1121 460 1410 1121 5387 8345 3117
42 43 ביום הששי נשיא לבני גד אליסף בן־דעואל׃ קרבנו
his ;offering —Deuel the of son Eliasaph ,Gad the of sons of ruler the (offered) sixth the on day

259 4219 4948 3967 7970 259 3701 7086
קערת־כסף אחת שלשים ומאה משקלה מזרק אחד
one basin its ;weight a and hundred thirty ,one silver dish

5560 4392 8147 6944 8255 8255 7657 3701
כסף שבעים שקל בשקל הקדש שניהם ׀ מלאים סלת
of flour full of both them the sanctuary the by of shekel ,shekels seventy of silver

7004 4392 2091 6235 259 3709 4503 8081 1101
44 בלולה בשמן למנחה׃ כף אחת עשרה זהב מלאה קטרת׃
of ;incense full ,golden ten of (shekels) one pan food a for ;offering with ,oil mixed

5930 8141/1121 259 3532 259 352 1241/1121 259 6499
45 פר אחד בן־בקר איל אחד כבש־אחד בן־שנתו לעלה׃
burnt a for ;offering a yearling ,one he-lamb ,one ram the a herd of son ,one bullock

8147 1241 8002 2077 2403 259 5795 8163
46 47 שעיר־עזים אחד לחטאת׃ ולזבח השלמים בקר שנים
,two oxen peace the offering of the for and sacrifice sin a for ;offering one the goats buck of

2568 8141/1121 3532 2568 6260 2568 352
אילם חמשה עתדים חמשה כבשים בני־שנה חמשה
.five ,yearling ,he-lambs ,five he-goats ,five rams

1845 1121 460 7133 2088
זה קרבן אליסף בן־דעואל׃
.Deuel the of son Eliasaph the of offering This (was)

5989 1121 476 669 1121 5387 7637 3117
48 ביום השביעי נשיא לבני אפרים אלישמע בן־עמיהוד׃
—Ammihud the of son Elishama ,Ephraim the of sons of ruler the (offered) seventh the On day

4219 4948 3967 7970 259 3701 7086 7133
49 קרבנו קערת־כסף אחת שלשים ומאה משקלה מזרק
basin by ;weight a and hundred thirty ,one silver dish his ;offering

4392 8147 6944 8255 8255 7657 3701 259
אחד כסף שבעים שקל בשקל הקדש שניהם ׀ מלאים
of full of both them the sanctuary the by of shekel shekels seventy silver one of (bowl)

4392 2091 6235 259 3709 4503 8081 1101 5560
50 סלת בלולה בשמן למנחה׃ כף אחת עשרה זהב מלאה
full ,golden ten of (shekels) one pan food a for ;offering ,oil with mixed flour of

incense; [51]one young bullock, one ram, one he-lamb of the first year, for a burnt offering; [52]one male of the goats for a sin offering; [53]and for the sacrifice of the peace offering, two oxen, five rams, five he-goats, five yearling he-lambs. This *was* the offering of Elishama, the son of Ammihud.

[54]On the eighth day Gamaliel the son of Pedahzur, ruler of the sons of Manasseh: [55]his offering *was* one silver dish, its weight a hundred and thirty, one silver basin *of* seventy shekels after the sanctuary shekel, both of them full of flour mixed with oil for a food offering; [56]one golden pan *of* ten shekels full of incense; [57]one young bullock, one ram, one he-lamb of the first year, for a burnt offering;

[58]one male of the goats for a sin offering; [59]and for the sacrifice of the peace offering, two oxen, five rams, five he-goats, five yearling he-lambs. This *was* the offering of Gamaliel the son of Pedahzur.

[60]On the ninth day Abidan the son of Gideoni, ruler of the sons of Benjamin: [61]his offering *was* one silver dish, its weight a hundred and thirty, one silver basin *of* seventy shekels after the sanctuary shekel, both of them full of flour mixed with oil for a food offering; [62]one golden pan *of* ten shekels full of incense; [63]one young bullock, one ram, one he-lamb of the first

8141/1121 269 3532 259 352 1241/1121 259 6499 7004
51 קְטֹֽרֶת׃ פַּר אֶחָד בֶּן־בָּקָר אַיִל אֶחָד כֶּבֶשׂ־אֶחָד בֶּן־שְׁנָתוֹ
a yearling ,one he-lamb ,one ram the herd of son a ,one bullock of ;incense

1241 8002 2077 2403 259 5795 8163 5930
52 53 לְעֹלָה׃ שְׂעִיר־עִזִּים אֶחָד לְחַטָּאת׃ וּלְזֶבַח הַשְּׁלָמִים בָּקָר
oxen peace the offering the for and sacrifice sin a for offering one the goats buck of burnt a for ;offering

8141/1121 3532 2568 6260 2568 352 8147
שְׁנַיִם אֵילִם חֲמִשָּׁה עַתֻּדִים חֲמִשָּׁה כְּבָשִׂים בְּנֵי־שָׁנָה
a year a of son ,he-lambs ,five he-goats ,five rams ,two

5989 1121 476 7133 2088 2568
חֲמִשָּׁה זֶה קָרְבַּן אֱלִישָׁמָע בֶּן־עַמִּיהוּד׃ פ
.Ammihud the of son Elishama the of offering This (was) .five

6301 1121 1583 4519 1121 5387 8066 3117
54 בַּיּוֹם הַשְּׁמִינִי נָשִׂיא לִבְנֵי מְנַשֶּׁה גַּמְלִיאֵל בֶּן־פְּדָהצוּר׃
—Pedahzur the of son Gamaliel ,Manasseh the of sons the ruler eighth (offered) the On day

4219 4948 3967 7970 259 3701 7086 7133
55 קָרְבָּנוֹ קַעֲרַת־כֶּסֶף אַחַת שְׁלֹשִׁים וּמֵאָה מִשְׁקָלָהּ מִזְרָק
basin its ;weight a and hundred thirty ,one silver dish his :offering

4392 8147 6944 8255 8255 7657 3701 259
אֶחָד כֶּסֶף שִׁבְעִים שֶׁקֶל בְּשֶׁקֶל הַקֹּדֶשׁ שְׁנֵיהֶם ׀ מְלֵאִים
full of both them the sanctuary the by of shekel ,shekels of seventy silver one

4392 2091 6235 259 3709 4503 8081 1101 5560
56 סֹלֶת בְּלוּלָה בַשֶּׁמֶן לְמִנְחָה׃ כַּף אַחַת עֲשָׂרָה זָהָב מְלֵאָה
full ,golden ten of (shekels) one pan food a for ;offering with ,oil mixed of flour

8141/1121 259 3532 259 352 1241/1121 259 6499 7004
57 קְטֹֽרֶת׃ פַּר אֶחָד בֶּן־בָּקָר אַיִל אֶחָד כֶּבֶשׂ־אֶחָד בֶּן־שְׁנָתוֹ
a ,yearling ,one he-lamb ,one ram the herd of son a ,one bullock of ;incense

1241 8002 2077 2403 259 5795 8163 5930
58 59 לְעֹלָה׃ שְׂעִיר־עִזִּים אֶחָד לְחַטָּאת׃ וּלְזֶבַח הַשְּׁלָמִים בָּקָר
oxen peace the offering the for and sacrifice sin a for offering one the goats buck of burnt a for ;offering

8141/1121 3532 2568 6260 2568 352 8147
שְׁנַיִם אֵילִם חֲמִשָּׁה עַתֻּדִים חֲמִשָּׁה כְּבָשִׂים בְּנֵי־שָׁנָה
,yearlings ,he-lambs ,five he-goats ,five rams ,two

6301 1121 1583 7133 2088 2568
חֲמִשָּׁה זֶה קָרְבַּן גַּמְלִיאֵל בֶּן־פְּדָהצוּר׃ פ
.Pedahzur the of son Gamaliel the of offering This (was) .five

7133 1441/1121 27 1144 1121 5387 8671 3117
60 61 בַּיּוֹם הַתְּשִׁיעִי נָשִׂיא לִבְנֵי בִנְיָמִן אֲבִידָן בֶּן־גִּדְעֹנִי׃ קָרְבָּנוֹ
his :offering —Gideoni the of son Abidan ,Benjamin the of sons the ruler ninth (offered) the On day

259 4219 4948 3967 7970 259 3701 7086
קַעֲרַת־כֶּסֶף אַחַת שְׁלֹשִׁים וּמֵאָה מִשְׁקָלָהּ מִזְרָק אֶחָד
one basin its ;weight a and hundred thirty ,one silver dish

5560 4392 8147 6944 8255 8255 7657 3701
כֶּסֶף שִׁבְעִים שֶׁקֶל בְּשֶׁקֶל הַקֹּדֶשׁ שְׁנֵיהֶם ׀ מְלֵאִים סֹלֶת
of flour full of both them the sanctuary the by of shekel ,shekels of seventy silver

4392 2091 6235 259 3709 4503 8081 1101
62 בְּלוּלָה בַשֶּׁמֶן לְמִנְחָה׃ כַּף אַחַת עֲשָׂרָה זָהָב מְלֵאָה
full ,golden ten of (shekels) one pan food a for ;offering with ,oil mixed

8141/1121 269 3532 259 352 1241/1121 259 6499 7004
63 קְטֹֽרֶת׃ פַּר אֶחָד בֶּן־בָּקָר אַיִל אֶחָד כֶּבֶשׂ־אֶחָד בֶּן־שְׁנָתוֹ
a ,year a of son ,one he-lamb ,one ram the herd of son a ,one bullock of ;incense

year, for a burnt offering; [64]one male of the goats for a sin offering; [65]and for the sacrifice of the peace offering, two oxen, five rams, five he-goats, five yearling he-lambs. This *was* the offering of Abidan the son of Gideoni.

[66]On the tenth day Ahiezer the son of Ammishaddai, ruler of the sons of Dan: [67]his offering *was* one silver dish, its weight a hundred and thirty, one silver basin *of* seventy shekels after the sanctuary shekel, both of them full of flour mixed with oil for a food offering; [68]one golden pan *of* ten shekels full of incense; [69]one young bullock, one ram, one he-lamb of the first year, for a burnt offering; [70]one male of the goats for a sin offering; [71]and for the sacrifice of the peace offering, two oxen, five rams, five he-goats, five yearling he-lambs. This *was* the offering of Ahiezer the son of Ammishaddai.

[72]On the eleventh day Pagiel the son of Ocran, ruler of the sons of Asher: [73]his offering *was* one silver dish, its weight a hundred and thirty, one silver basin *of* seventy shekels after the sanctuary shekel, both of them full of flour mixed with oil for a food offering; [74]one golden pan *of* ten shekels full of incense; [75]one young bullock, one ram, one he-lamb of the first year, for a burnt offering; [76]one male of the goats for a sin offering; [77]and for the sacrifice of the peace offering, two oxen, five

1241 8002 2077 2403 259 5795 8165 5930
64 65 לְעֹלָה: שְׂעִיר־עִזִּים אֶחָד לְחַטָּאת: וּלְזֶבַח הַשְּׁלָמִים בָּקָר
oxen peace the the for and sin a for one the buck burnt a for
offering of sacrifice ;offering goats of ;offering

8141/1121 3532 2568 6260 2568 352 8147
שְׁנַיִם אֵילִם חֲמִשָּׁה עַתֻּדִים חֲמִשָּׁה כְּבָשִׂים בְּנֵי־שָׁנָה
,yearlings ,he-lambs ,five he-goats ,five rams ,two

1441 1121 27 7133 2088 2568
חֲמִשָּׁה זֶה קָרְבַּן אֲבִידָן בֶּן־גִּדְעֹנִי:
.Gideoni the Abidan the This .five
of son of offering (was)

7133 5996 1121 295 1835/1121 5387 6221 3117
66 בַּיּוֹם הָעֲשִׂירִי נָשִׂיא לִבְנֵי דָן אֲחִיעֶזֶר בֶּן־עַמִּישַׁדָּי: קָרְבָּנוֹ
his Ammishad- the Ahiezer ,Dan the of the tenth the On
offering -dai of son of sons ruler (offered) day

259 4219 4948 3967 7970 259 3701 7086
67 קַעֲרַת־כֶּסֶף אַחַת שְׁלֹשִׁים וּמֵאָה מִשְׁקָלָהּ מִזְרָק אֶחָד
one basin its a and thirty ,one silver dish
;weight hundred

5560/4392 8147 6944 8255 8255 7657 3701
כֶּסֶף שִׁבְעִים שֶׁקֶל בְּשֶׁקֶל הַקֹּדֶשׁ שְׁנֵיהֶם ׀ מְלֵאִים סֹלֶת
of full of both the the by ,shekels of silver
flour them ,sanctuary of shekel seventy

4392 2091 6235 259 3709 4503 8081 1101
68 בְּלוּלָה בַשֶּׁמֶן לְמִנְחָה: כַּף אַחַת עֲשָׂרָה זָהָב מְלֵאָה
full ,golden ten of one pan food a for with mixed
(shekels) ;offering ,oil

8141/1121 259 3532 259 352 1241/1121 259 6499 7004
69 קְטֹרֶת: פַּר אֶחָד בֶּן־בָּקָר אַיִל אֶחָד כֶּבֶשׂ־אֶחָד בֶּן־שְׁנָתוֹ
a ,one he-lamb ,one ram the a ,one bullock of
yearling ,herd of son ;incense

1241 8002 2077 2403 259 5795 8163 5930
70 71 לְעֹלָה: שְׂעִיר־עִזִּים אֶחָד לְחַטָּאת: וּלְזֶבַח הַשְּׁלָמִים בָּקָר
oxen peace the the for and sin a for one the buck burnt a for
offering of sacrifice ;offering goats of ;offering

8141/1121 3532 2568 6260 2568 352 8147
שְׁנַיִם אֵילִם חֲמִשָּׁה עַתֻּדִים חֲמִשָּׁה כְּבָשִׂים בְּנֵי־שָׁנָה
,yearlings ,he-lambs ,five he-goats ,five rams ,two

5996/1121 295 7133 2088 2568
חֲמִשָּׁה זֶה קָרְבַּן אֲחִיעֶזֶר בֶּן־עַמִּישַׁדָּי:
.Amminshaddai the Ahiezer the This .five
of son of offering (was)

5918 1121 6295 836 1121 5387 3117 6240 6249 3117
72 בְּיוֹם עַשְׁתֵּי עָשָׂר יוֹם נָשִׂיא לִבְנֵי אָשֵׁר פַּגְעִיאֵל בֶּן־עָכְרָן:
—Ocran the Pagiel ,Asher the as the day the the On
of son of sons ruler eleventh ,day

4219 4948 3967 7970 259 3701 7086 7133
73 קָרְבָּנוֹ קַעֲרַת־כֶּסֶף אַחַת שְׁלֹשִׁים וּמֵאָה מִשְׁקָלָהּ מִזְרָק
basin its a and thirty ,one silver dish his
;weight hundred :offering

4392 8147 6944 8255 8255 7657 3701 259
אֶחָד כֶּסֶף שִׁבְעִים שֶׁקֶל בְּשֶׁקֶל הַקֹּדֶשׁ שְׁנֵיהֶם ׀ מְלֵאִים
full of both the the by ,shekels of silver one
them ,sanctuary of shekel seventy

4392 2091 6235 259 3709 4503 8081 1101 5560
74 סֹלֶת בְּלוּלָה בַשֶּׁמֶן לְמִנְחָה: כַּף אַחַת עֲשָׂרָה זָהָב מְלֵאָה
full ,golden ten of one pan food a for with mixed of
(shekels) ;offering ,oil flour

8141/1121 3532 259 352 1241/1121 259 /6499 7004
75 קְטֹרֶת: פַּר אֶחָד בֶּן־בָּקָר אַיִל אֶחָד כֶּבֶשׂ־אֶחָד בֶּן־שְׁנָתוֹ
a ,one he-lamb ,one ram the a ,one bullock of
,yearling ,herd of son ;incense

1241 8002 2077 2403 259 5795 8163 5930
76 77 לְעֹלָה: שְׂעִיר־עִזִּים אֶחָד לְחַטָּאת: וּלְזֶבַח הַשְּׁלָמִים בָּקָר
oxen peace the the for and sin a for one the buck burnt a for
,offering of sacrifice ;offering goats of ;offering

rams, five he-goats, five yearling he-lambs. This *was* the offering of Pagiel the son of Ocran.

[78]On the twelfth day Ahira the son of Enan, ruler of the sons of Naphtali: [79]his offering *was* one silver dish, its weight a hundred and thirty, one silver basin *of* seventy shekels after the sanctuary shekel, both of them full of flour mixed with oil for a food offering; [80]one golden pan *of* ten shekels full of incense; [81]one young bullock, one ram, one he-lamb of the first year, for a burnt offering; [82]one male of the goats for a sin offering; [83]and for the sacrifice of the peace offering, two oxen, five rams, five he-goats, five yearling he-lambs. This *was* the offering of Ahira the son of Enan.

[84]This *was* the dedication of the altar, in the day when it was anointed, at the hand of the rulers of Israel: twelve silver dishes, twelve silver basins, twelve golden pans; [85]each silver dish a hundred and thirty in weight, and each basin seventy—all the silver of the vessels *was* two thousand and four hundred *shekels* by the sanctuary shekel—[86]twelve golden pans full of incense, ten *to this* and ten *to that* pan, according to the sanctuary shekel —all the gold of the pans *was* a hundred and twenty— [87]all the animals for the burnt offering, twelve bullocks, twelve

8141/1121 3532 2568 6260 2568 352 8147
שְׁנַיִם אֵילִם חֲמִשָּׁה עַתֻּדִים חֲמִשָּׁה כְּבָשִׂים בְּנֵי־שָׁנָה
,yearlings ,he-lambs ,five he-goats ,five rams ,two

5918 6295 7133 2088 2568
חֲמִשָּׁה זֶה קָרְבַּן פַּגְעִיאֵל בֶּן־עָכְרָן׃
.Ocran the of son Pagiel the of offering This (was) .five

5881/1121 299 5320 1121 5387 3117 6240 8147 3117
78 בַּיּוֹם שְׁנֵים עָשָׂר יוֹם נָשִׂיא לִבְנֵי נַפְתָּלִי אֲחִירַע בֶּן־עֵינָן׃
—Enan the of son Ahira ,Naphtali the of sons of the ruler ,day the twelfth the On day

4219 4948 3967 7970 259 3701 7086 7133
79 קָרְבָּנוֹ קַעֲרַת־כֶּסֶף אַחַת שְׁלֹשִׁים וּמֵאָה מִשְׁקָלָהּ מִזְרָק
basin its weight a and hundred thirty ,one silver dish his :offering

4392 8147 6944 8255 8255 7657 3701 259
אֶחָד כֶּסֶף שִׁבְעִים שֶׁקֶל בְּשֶׁקֶל הַקֹּדֶשׁ שְׁנֵיהֶם ׀ מְלֵאִים
full of both them the sanctuary the by shekel ,shekels of seventy silver one

4392 2091 6235 259 3709 4503 8081 1101 5560
80 סֹלֶת בְּלוּלָה בַשֶּׁמֶן לְמִנְחָה׃ כַּף אַחַת עֲשָׂרָה זָהָב מְלֵאָה
full ,golden ten of (shekels) one pan food a for ;offering with ,oil mixed of flour

8141/1121 259 3532 259 352 1241/1121 259/6499 7004
81 קְטֹרֶת׃ פַּר אֶחָד בֶּן־בָּקָר אַיִל אֶחָד כֶּבֶשׂ־אֶחָד בֶּן־שְׁנָתוֹ
a ,yearling ,one he-lamb ,one ram the a herd of son ,one bullock of ;incense

1241 8002 2077 2403 259 5795 8163 5930
82 לְעֹלָה׃ שְׂעִיר־עִזִּים אֶחָד לְחַטָּאת׃ וּלְזֶבַח הַשְּׁלָמִים בָּקָר
83
oxen peace the offering the of sacrifice for and sin a for ;offering ,one the goats buck of burnt a for ;offering

8141/1121 3532 2568 6260 2568 352 8147
שְׁנַיִם אֵילִם חֲמִשָּׁה עַתֻּדִים חֲמִשָּׁה כְּבָשִׂים בְּנֵי־שָׁנָה
,yearlings ,he-lambs ,five he-goats ,five rams two

5881/1121/ 299 7133 2088 2568
חֲמִשָּׁה זֶה קָרְבַּן אֲחִירַע בֶּן־עֵינָן׃
.Enan the of son Ahira the of offering This (was) .five

3478 5387 4886 3117 4196 2598 2088
84 זֹאת ׀ חֲנֻכַּת הַמִּזְבֵּחַ בְּיוֹם הִמָּשַׁח אֹתוֹ מֵאֵת נְשִׂיאֵי יִשְׂרָאֵל
:Israel the of rulers by was it ,anointed the in day the ,altar dedi- of cation the This (was)

3709 6240 8147 3701 4219 6240 8147 3701 7086
קַעֲרֹת כֶּסֶף שְׁתֵּים עֶשְׂרֵה מִזְרְקֵי־כֶסֶף שְׁנֵים עָשָׂר כַּפּוֹת
pans twelve silver basins ,twelve silver dishes

3701 259 7086 3967/7970 6240 8147 2091
85 זָהָב שְׁתֵּים עֶשְׂרֵה׃ שְׁלֹשִׁים וּמֵאָה הַקְּעָרָה הָאַחַת כֶּסֶף
,silver each dish (was) a and hundred thirty (shekels) ;twelve golden

702 505 3627 3701 3605 259 4219 7657
וְשִׁבְעִים הַמִּזְרָק הָאֶחָד כֹּל כֶּסֶף הַכֵּלִים אַלְפַּיִם וְאַרְבַּע־
and four two (was) thousand the vessels the of silver all ;each basin and seventy

4392 6240 8147 2091 3709 6944 8255 3967
86 מֵאוֹת בְּשֶׁקֶל הַקֹּדֶשׁ׃ כַּפּוֹת זָהָב שְׁתֵּים־עֶשְׂרֵה מְלֵאֹת
full ,twelve golden pans the sanctuary the by of shekel hundred (shekels)

3709 2091 3605 6944 4825 3709 6235 6235 7004
קְטֹרֶת עֲשָׂרָה עֲשָׂרָה הַכַּף בְּשֶׁקֶל הַקֹּדֶשׁ כָּל־זְהַב הַכַּפּוֹת
,pans the of gold the all the ;sanctuary the by of shekel ,pan ten (and) (that to) ten (this to) of ;incense

352 6499 6240 8147 5930 1241 3605 3967 6242
87 עֶשְׂרִים וּמֵאָה׃ כָּל־הַבָּקָר לָעֹלָה שְׁנֵים עָשָׂר פָּרִים אֵילִם
rams ,bullocks twelve burnt the for ,offering the animals all a and ;hundred twenty (shekels)

rams, twelve yearling he-lambs, and their food offering; and the twelve males of the goats for a sin offering; [88]and all the animals for the sacrifice of the peace offering, twenty-four bullocks, sixty rams, sixty he-goats, sixty yearling he-lambs. This *was* the dedication of the altar, after it was anointed.

[89]And when Moses went into the tent of the congregation to speak with Him, he heard the voice speaking to him from the mercy-seat which *is* on the ark of the testimony, from between the two cherubs; and He spoke to him.

8163 4503 6240 8147 8141/1121 3532 6240 8147
שְׁנֵים־עָשָׂר כְּבָשִׂים בְּנֵי־שָׁנָה שְׁנֵים עָשָׂר וּמִנְחָתָם וּשְׂעִירֵי
the and food their and ;twelve ,yearlings ,he-lambs ,twelve
of bucks ;offering
6242 8002 2077 1241 3605 2403 6240 8147 5795
88 עִזִּים שְׁנֵים עָשָׂר לְחַטָּאת׃ וְכֹל בְּקַר זֶבַח הַשְּׁלָמִים עֶשְׂרִים
twenty- peace the sac- the the all and sin a for ,twelve the
,offering of rifice for animals ;offering ,goats
1121 3532 7970 6260 8346 352 6499 702
וְאַרְבָּעָה פָּרִים אֵילִם שִׁשִּׁים עַתֻּדִים שִׁשִּׁים כְּבָשִׂים בְּנֵי־
year- ,he-lambs ,sixty he-goats ,sixty rams ,bullocks four
935 4886 310 4196 2598 2088 8346 8141
89 שָׁנָה שִׁשִּׁים זֹאת חֲנֻכַּת הַמִּזְבֵּחַ אַחֲרֵי הִמָּשַׁח אֹתוֹ׃ וּבְבֹא
when And — was it after the dedi- the This .sixty ,lings
went .anointed ,altar of cation (was)
1696 6963 8085/ 1696 4150 168 4872
מֹשֶׁה אֶל־אֹהֶל מוֹעֵד לְדַבֵּר אִתּוֹ וַיִּשְׁמַע אֶת־הַקּוֹל מִדַּבֵּר
speaking voice the he with to meeting the into Moses
heard ,Him speak of tent
3742 8147/996 5715 727/5921 834 3727
אֵלָיו מֵעַל הַכַּפֹּרֶת אֲשֶׁר עַל־אֲרֹן הָעֵדֻת מִבֵּין שְׁנֵי הַכְּרֻבִים
the two from the the on which the from to
;cherubs between ,testimony of ark (is) ,mercy-seat him
1696
וַיְדַבֵּר אֵלָיו׃
.him to He and
spoke

CAP. VIII ח

CHAPTER 8

CHAPTER 8

[1]And Jehovah spoke to Moses, saying, [2]Speak to Aaron and say to him, When you light the lamps, the seven lamps shall give light in the front of the lampstand. [3]And Aaron did so. He lit its lamps *so as to give light* in front of the lampstand, as Jehovah commanded Moses. [4]And this was the work of the lampstand: beaten work of gold to its base, and to its flowers; it *was* beaten work, according to the pattern which Jehovah caused Moses to see, so he made the lampstand.

559 175 1696 559 4872 3068 1696
1 וַיְדַבֵּר יְהוָה אֶל־מֹשֶׁה לֵּאמֹר׃ דַּבֵּר אֶל־אַהֲרֹן וְאָמַרְתָּ
2 say and Aaron to Speak ,saying ,Moses to Jehovah And
spoke
7651 215 4501 6440 5922 5216 5927
אֵלָיו בְּהַעֲלֹתְךָ אֶת־הַנֵּרֹת אֶל־מוּל פְּנֵי הַמְּנוֹרָה יָאִירוּ שִׁבְעַת
seven give shall the of front in the go you When to
light lampstand ,lamps (with) up ,him
5216 5927 4501 6440 5922 175 6213 5216
3 הַנֵּרוֹת׃ וַיַּעַשׂ כֵּן אַהֲרֹן אֶל־מוּל פְּנֵי הַמְּנוֹרָה הֶעֱלָה נֵרֹתֶיהָ
its went he the of front in ;Aaron so And the
,lamps (with) up lampstand did .lamps
4749 4501 4639 2088 4872 3068 6680
4 כַּאֲשֶׁר צִוָּה יְהוָה אֶת־מֹשֶׁה׃ וְזֶה מַעֲשֵׂה הַמְּנֹרָה מִקְשָׁה
hammered the the this And .Moses Jehovah com- as
;lampstand of work (was) manded
7200 834 4758 4749 6525 3409 2091
זָהָב עַד־יְרֵכָהּ עַד־פִּרְחָהּ מִקְשָׁה הִוא כַּמַּרְאֶה אֲשֶׁר הֶרְאָה
showed which to according it hammered its to its to gold
pattern the ;(was) work flowers ,base
1501 6213 3651 4872 3068
יְהוָה אֶת־מֹשֶׁה כֵּן עָשָׂה אֶת־הַמְּנֹרָה׃
the he so (to) Jehovah
.lampstand made ,Moses

[5]And Jehovah spoke to Moses, saying, [6]Take the Levites from among the sons of Israel, and you shall cleanse them: sprinkle on them water of sin offering. And they shall cause a razor to pass over all their flesh, and shall wash their

1121 8432 3881 3947 559 4872 3068 1696
5 וַיְדַבֵּר יְהוָה אֶל־מֹשֶׁה לֵּאמֹר׃ קַח אֶת־הַלְוִיִּם מִתּוֹךְ בְּנֵי
6 the the from the Take ,saying ,Moses to Jehovah And
of sons of midst Levites spoke
5137 2891 6213 3651 2891 3478
7 יִשְׂרָאֵל וְטִהַרְתָּ אֹתָם׃ וְכֹה־תַעֲשֶׂה לָהֶם לְטַהֲרָם הַזֵּה
sprinkle cleanse to to will you And .them and ,Israel
:them them do thus cleanse
3526 1320 3605 5921 8593 5674 240 4325
עֲלֵיהֶם מֵי חַטָּאת וְהֶעֱבִירוּ תַעַר עַל־כָּל־בְּשָׂרָם וְכִבְּסוּ
shall and their all over a shall they and sin- water on
wash ,flesh razor pass to cause ,offering of them

garments and cleanse themselves. [8]And *they* shall take a bullock of the first year, and its food offering, flour mixed with oil. And you shall take for a sin offering a second bullock, a son of the herd. [9]And you shall bring the Levites near before the tabernacle of the congregation. And you shall assemble the whole congregation of the sons of Israel. [10]And you shall bring the Levites before Jehovah, and the sons of Israel shall lay their hands on the Levites. [11]And Aaron shall wave the Levites *as* a wave offering before Jehovah, from the sons of Israel, that they may serve *at* the service of Jehovah.

[12]And the Levites shall lay their hands on the head of the bullocks. And you shall offer the one *for* a sin offering, and one a burnt offering to Jehovah, to atone for the Levites. [13]And you shall cause the Levites to stand before Aaron, and before his sons, and shall wave them *as* a wave offering to Jehovah. [14]And you shall separate the Levites from the midst of the sons of Israel, and the Levites shall become Mine. [15]And afterward the Levites shall come in to serve the tabernacle of the congregation; and you shall cleanse them, and shall wave them, a wave offering. [16]For they *are* wholly given to Me from among the sons of Israel; instead of the one who opens any womb, the firstborn of all, from the sons of Israel. I have taken them to Myself. [17]For every firstborn among the sons of Israel among man and among animal is Mine; I set them apart for Myself in the day I smote every firstborn in the land of Egypt. [18]And I take the Levites instead of every firstborn among the sons of Israel. [19]And I have given the Levites *as gifts* to

1101 5560 4503 1241/1121 6499 3947 2889 899
8 בִּגְדֵיהֶם וְהִטֶּהָרוּ׃ וְלָקְחוּ פַּר בֶּן־בָּקָר וּמִנְחָתוֹ סֹלֶת בְּלוּלָה
mixed flour food its and the son a a shall and cleanse and their
,offering ,herd of ,bullock take ,themselves garments

7126 2403 3947 1241/1121 8145 6499 8081
9 בַּשֶּׁמֶן וּפַר־שֵׁנִי בֶן־בָּקָר תִּקַּח לְחַטָּאת׃ וְהִקְרַבְתָּ אֶת־
shall you and sin a for shall you the a ,second a and with
near bring ;offering take ,herd of son bullock ;oil

1121/5712 7126 4150 168 6440 3881
הַלְוִיִּם לִפְנֵי אֹהֶל מוֹעֵד וְהִקְהַלְתָּ אֶת־כָּל־עֲדַת בְּנֵי
the company the all shall you and ;meeting the before the
of sons of assemble of tent Levites

1121 5564 3068 6440 3881 7126 3478
10 יִשְׂרָאֵל׃ וְהִקְרַבְתָּ אֶת־הַלְוִיִּם לִפְנֵי יְהוָה וְסָמְכוּ בְנֵי
the and ,Jehovah before the shall you and ;Israel
of sons lay shall Levites near bring

3881 175 5130 3881 5921 3027 3478
11 יִשְׂרָאֵל אֶת־יְדֵיהֶם עַל־הַלְוִיִּם׃ וְהֵנִיף אַהֲרֹן אֶת־הַלְוִיִּם
the Aaron shall and the on their Israel
Levites wave ;Levites hands

5647 1961 3478 1121 3068 6440 8573
תְּנוּפָה לִפְנֵי יְהוָה מֵאֵת בְּנֵי יִשְׂרָאֵל וְהָיוּ לַעֲבֹד אֶת־
serve that ;Israel the from ,Jehovah before wave a
might they of sons offering

6499 7218 3027 5564 3881 3068 5656
12 עֲבֹדַת יְהוָה׃ וְהַלְוִיִּם יִסְמְכוּ אֶת־יְדֵיהֶם עַל רֹאשׁ הַפָּרִים
the the on their shall the And .Jehovah the (at)
;bullocks of head hands lay Levites of service

3722 3068 5930 259 2403 259 6213
וַעֲשֵׂה אֶת־הָאֶחָד חַטָּאת וְאֶת־הָאֶחָד עֹלָה לַיהוָה לְכַפֵּר
to to burnt a the and sin a the and
atone ,Jehovah offering one ,offering one make

1121 6440 175 6440 3881 5975 3881
13 עַל־הַלְוִיִּם׃ וְהַעֲמַדְתָּ אֶת־הַלְוִיִּם לִפְנֵי אַהֲרֹן וְלִפְנֵי בָנָיו
his and ,Aaron before the shall you and the for
sons before Levites stand to cause ;Levites

8432 3881 914 3068 8573 5130
14 וְהֵנַפְתָּ אֹתָם תְּנוּפָה לַיהוָה׃ וְהִבְדַּלְתָּ אֶת־הַלְוִיִּם מִתּוֹךְ
the from the shall you and to wave a them shall and
of midst Levites separate ;Jehovah offering present

3881 935 310 3881 1961 3478 1121
15 בְּנֵי יִשְׂרָאֵל וְהָיוּ לִי הַלְוִיִּם׃ וְאַחֲרֵי־כֵן יָבֹאוּ הַלְוִיִּם
the shall and the Me to shall and ,Israel the
Levites in come afterward ;Levites be of sons

8573 5130 2891 4150 168 5647
לַעֲבֹד אֶת־אֹהֶל מוֹעֵד וְטִהַרְתָּ אֹתָם וְהֵנַפְתָּ אֹתָם תְּנוּפָה׃
wave a them and ,them you and ;meeting the to
.offering present cleanse shall of tent serve

6363 8478 3478 1121 8432 5414 5414
16 כִּי נְתֻנִים נְתֻנִים הֵמָּה לִי מִתּוֹךְ בְּנֵי יִשְׂרָאֵל תַּחַת פִּטְרַת
one the instead ;Israel the from to they given wholly ,For
opens who of of sons among Me (are)

3947 3478 1121 3605 1060 7358 3605
17 כָּל־רֶחֶם בְּכוֹר כֹּל מִבְּנֵי יִשְׂרָאֵל לָקַחְתִּי אֹתָם לִי׃ כִּי
For to them have I ,Israel the from ,all the ,womb every
.Myself taken of sons of firstborn

5221 3117/929 120 3478 1121 1060 3605
לִי כָל־בְּכוֹר בִּבְנֵי יִשְׂרָאֵל בָּאָדָם וּבַבְּהֵמָה בְּיוֹם הַכֹּתִי
I the in among and among ,Israel among first- every (is)
struck day ;animal man of sons the born Mine

3947 6942 4714 776 1060 3605
18 כָל־בְּכוֹר בְּאֶרֶץ מִצְרַיִם הִקְדַּשְׁתִּי אֹתָם לִי׃ וָאֶקַּח אֶת־
I and to them I ;Egypt the in first- every
take ;Myself sanctified of land born

5414 3478 1121 1060 8478 3881
19 הַלְוִיִּם תַּחַת כָּל־בְּכוֹר בִּבְנֵי יִשְׂרָאֵל׃ וָאֶתְּנָה אֶת־
I And .Israel among first- every instead the
given have of sons the born of Levites

Aaron and to his sons from among the sons of Israel, to do the service of the sons of Israel in the tabernacle of the congregation, and to make atonement for the sons of Israel through the sons of Israel's drawing near to the sanctuary.
[20]And Moses and Aaron, and all the congregation of the sons of Israel did to the Levites according to all that Jehovah had commanded Moses concerning the Levites; so the sons of Israel did to them. [21]And the Levites cleansed themselves, and washed their garments. And Aaron waved them *as* a wave offering before Jehovah; and Aaron atoned for them, to cleanse them. [22]And afterward the Levites went in to do their service in the tabernacle of the congregation, before Aaron and before his sons; as Jehovah commanded Moses concerning the Levites, so they did to them.
[23] [1]And Jehovah spoke to Moses, saying [24]This *is* that which *pertains* to the Levites: from twenty-five years old and upward he shall go in to do the service and the works of the tabernacle of the congregation. [25]And from the age of fifty years they shall return from the service of the work, and shall not serve any more. [26]But he shall serve with his brothers in the tabernacle of the congregation, to keep the charge; only *he* shall not serve *at* a service. So you shall do to the Levites concerning their charge.

5647 3478 1121 8432 1121 175 5414 3881
הַלְוִיִּם נְתֻנִים ׀ לְאַהֲרֹן וּלְבָנָיו מִתּוֹךְ בְּנֵי יִשְׂרָאֵל לַעֲבֹד
to ,Israel the the from to and to (as) the
serve of sons of midst ,sons his Aaron gifts Levites

1121 3722 4150 168 3478 1121 5656
אֶת־עֲבֹדַת בְּנֵי־יִשְׂרָאֵל בְּאֹהֶל מוֹעֵד וּלְכַפֵּר עַל־בְּנֵי
the for to and ,meeting the in Israel the the (at)
of sons atone of tent of sons of service

3478 1121 5066 5061 3478 1121 1961 3478
יִשְׂרָאֵל וְלֹא יִהְיֶה בִּבְנֵי יִשְׂרָאֵל נֶגֶף בְּגֶשֶׁת בְּנֵי־יִשְׂרָאֵל
Israel the coming by a Israel among shall and ;Israel
of sons near plague of sons the be not

3478 1121 5712/3605 175 4872 6213 6944
20 אֶל־הַקֹּדֶשׁ׃ וַיַּעַשׂ מֹשֶׁה וְאַהֲרֹן וְכָל־עֲדַת בְּנֵי־יִשְׂרָאֵל
Israel the the all and and Moses And the to
of sons of company Aaron did .sanctuary

6213 3651 3881 4872 3068 6680 3605 3881
לַלְוִיִּם כְּכֹל אֲשֶׁר־צִוָּה יְהוָה אֶת־מֹשֶׁה לַלְוִיִּם כֵּן־עָשׂוּ
did so concerning Moses Jehovah had that according the to
;Levites the commanded all to ,Levites

899 3526 3881 2398 3478 1121
21 לָהֶם בְּנֵי יִשְׂרָאֵל׃ וַיִּתְחַטְּאוּ הַלְוִיִּם וַיְכַבְּסוּ בִּגְדֵיהֶם
their and the purified And .Israel the to
,garments washed ,Levites themselves of sons them

175 3722 3068 6440 8573 175/5130
וַיָּנֶף אַהֲרֹן אֹתָם תְּנוּפָה לִפְנֵי יְהוָה וַיְכַפֵּר עֲלֵיהֶם אַהֲרֹן
Aaron for and ,Jehovah before wave a them Aaron and
them atoned offering waved

168 5657 5647 3881 935 310 2891
22 לְטַהֲרָם׃ וְאַחֲרֵי־כֵן בָּאוּ הַלְוִיִּם לַעֲבֹד אֶת־עֲבֹדָתָם בְּאֹהֶל
the in their (at) to the went And cleanse to
of tent service serve Levites in afterward .them

4872 3068 6680 1121 6440 175 6440 4150
מוֹעֵד לִפְנֵי אַהֲרֹן וְלִפְנֵי בָנָיו כַּאֲשֶׁר צִוָּה יְהוָה אֶת־מֹשֶׁה
Moses Jehovah had as his and Aaron before ,meet-
commanded ;sons before ing

4872 3068 1696 6213 3651 3881
23 עַל־הַלְוִיִּם כֵּן עָשׂוּ לָהֶם׃ וַיְדַבֵּר יְהוָה אֶל־מֹשֶׁה
,Moses to Jehovah And to they so the con-
spoke .them did Levites cerning

4605 8141 6240 2568 1121/3881 834 2088 559
24 לֵאמֹר׃ זֹאת אֲשֶׁר לַלְוִיִּם מִבֶּן חָמֵשׁ וְעֶשְׂרִים שָׁנָה וָמַעְלָה
and years twenty- five the from the to that This ,saying
upward of son ;Levites (is) which (is)

2572 1121 4150 168 5656 6635 6633 935
25 יָבוֹא לִצְבֹא צָבָא בַּעֲבֹדַת אֹהֶל מוֹעֵד׃ וּמִבֶּן חֲמִשִּׁים
fifty from and ;meeting the the in duty do to shall he
of son a of tent of service in go

8334 5750 5647 3808 5656 6635 7725 8141
26 שָׁנָה יָשׁוּב מִצְּבָא הָעֲבֹדָה וְלֹא יַעֲבֹד עוֹד׃ וְשֵׁרֵת אֶת־
with shall he but any shall and the the from shall he years
minister ;more serve not ,service of duty return

5647 5656 4931 8104 4150 168 251
אֶחָיו בְּאֹהֶל מוֹעֵד לִשְׁמֹר מִשְׁמֶרֶת וַעֲבֹדָה לֹא יַעֲבֹד כָּכָה
so they not a (at) but the to ,meeting the in his
;serve shall service ,charge keep of tent brothers

4931 3881 6213
תַּעֲשֶׂה לַלְוִיִּם בְּמִשְׁמְרֹתָם׃
concerning the to shall you
.charge their Levites do

CAP. IX ט

CHAPTER 9

CHAPTER 9

[1]And Jehovah spoke to Moses in the wilderness of Sinai, in the first month of the second year after they

8145 8141 5514 4057 4872 3068 1696
1 וַיְדַבֵּר יְהוָה אֶל־מֹשֶׁה בְמִדְבַּר־סִינַי בַּשָּׁנָה הַשֵּׁנִית
second the in Sinai the in Moses to Jehovah And
year of wilderness spoke

had come out of the land of Egypt, saying, 2Also the sons of Israel shall prepare the Passover in its appointed season. 3In the fourteenth day of this month, between the evenings, you shall prepare it according to all its statutes, and according to all its ordinances. 4And Moses spoke to the sons of Israel to prepare the Passover. 5And they prepared the Passover in the first *month* on the fourteenth day of the month, between the evenings, in the wilderness of Sinai, according to all that Jehovah had commanded Moses—so the sons of Israel did.

6And *there were* men who had been defiled by the body of a man, and they had not been able to prepare the Passover on that day. And they came near before Moses, and before Aaron on that day. 7And those men said to him, We *are* defiled by the body of a man. Why are we restrained so as not to be able to offer the offering of Jehovah in its appointed season, in the midst of the sons of Israel? 8And Moses said to them, You wait, so that I may hear what Jehovah will command concerning you. 9And Jehovah spoke to Moses, saying, 10Speak to the sons of Israel, saying, If any man of you or of your generations shall be unclean by reason of a body, or be in a distant journey, yet he shall keep the Passover to Jehovah. 11In the second month, on the fourteenth day at dusk, they shall keep it, they shall eat it with unleavened bread and

6213 559 7223 2320 4714 776 5927
2 לְצֵאתָם מֵאֶרֶץ מִצְרַיִם בַּחֹדֶשׁ הָרִאשׁוֹן לֵאמֹר׃ וְיַעֲשׂוּ
shall Also prepare ,saying ,first the in month ,Egypt the from of land their after coming

3117 6240 702 4150 6453 3478 1121
3 בְנֵי־יִשְׂרָאֵל אֶת־הַפָּסַח בְּמוֹעֲדוֹ׃ בְּאַרְבָּעָה עָשָׂר־יוֹם
day fourteenth the in set its in ;season the Passover Israel the of sons

2708 3605 4150 6213 6153 996 2088 2320
בַּחֹדֶשׁ הַזֶּה בֵּין הָעַרְבַּיִם תַּעֲשׂוּ אֹתוֹ בְּמוֹעֲדוֹ כְּכָל־חֻקֹּתָיו
its statutes according all to set its in ;season it shall you prepare the evenings between ,this in month

3478 1121 4872 1696 6213 4941 3605
4 וּכְכָל־מִשְׁפָּטָיו תַּעֲשׂוּ אֹתוֹ׃ וַיְדַבֵּר מֹשֶׁה אֶל־בְּנֵי יִשְׂרָאֵל
Israel the of sons to Moses And spoke .it shall you prepare its ordinances according and all to

6240 702 7223 6453 6213 6453 6213
5 לַעֲשׂוֹת הַפָּסַח׃ וַיַּעֲשׂוּ אֶת־הַפֶּסַח בָּרִאשׁוֹן בְּאַרְבָּעָה עָשָׂר
the on fourteenth first the in (month) the Passover they and prepared the Passover to prepare

3068 6680 3605 5514 4057 6153 996 2320 3117
יוֹם לַחֹדֶשׁ בֵּין הָעַרְבַּיִם בְּמִדְבַּר סִינָי כְּכֹל אֲשֶׁר צִוָּה יְהוָה
Jehovah had commanded that all by ;Sinai wild- of erness the in the evenings between the of ,month day

1961 582 3478 1121 6213 3651 4872
6 אֶת־מֹשֶׁה כֵּן עָשׂוּ בְּנֵי יִשְׂרָאֵל׃ וַיְהִי אֲנָשִׁים אֲשֶׁר הָיוּ
were who (were there) men And .Israel the of sons did so ,Moses

3117 6453 6213 3201 3808 120 5315 2931
טְמֵאִים לְנֶפֶשׁ אָדָם וְלֹא־יָכְלוּ לַעֲשֹׂת־הַפֶּסַח בַּיּוֹם הַהוּא
;that day on the Passover to prepare had they able been and not a ,man the by of body defiled

559 3117 175 6440 4872 6440 7126
7 וַיִּקְרְבוּ לִפְנֵי מֹשֶׁה וְלִפְנֵי אַהֲרֹן בַּיּוֹם הַהוּא׃ וַיֹּאמְרוּ
said and ;that day on Aaron and before ,Moses before they and near came

4100 120 5315 2931 1992 582
הָאֲנָשִׁים הָהֵמָּה אֵלָיו אֲנַחְנוּ טְמֵאִים לְנֶפֶשׁ אָדָם לָמָּה
why a ;man the by of body defiled We (are) to ,him those men

1121 8432 4150 3068 7133 7126 1639
נִגָּרַע לְבִלְתִּי הַקְרִיב אֶת־קָרְבַּן יְהוָה בְּמֹעֲדוֹ בְּתוֹךְ בְּנֵי
the of sons the in of midst set its in season Jehovah the of offering to bring not we are ,restrained

6680 8085 5975 4872 559 3478
8 יִשְׂרָאֵל׃ וַיֹּאמֶר אֲלֵהֶם מֹשֶׁה עִמְדוּ וְאֶשְׁמְעָה מַה־יְצַוֶּה
will command what may I that hear You ,wait ,Moses to them said And ?Israel

3068
יְהוָה לָכֶם׃
concerning .you Jehovah

3478 1121 1697 559 4872 3068 1696
9
10 וַיְדַבֵּר יְהוָה אֶל־מֹשֶׁה לֵּאמֹר׃ דַּבֵּר אֶל־בְּנֵי יִשְׂרָאֵל
,Israel the of sons to Speak ,saying ,Moses to Jehovah And spoke

7350 1870 176/5315 2931 1961 376 376 559
לֵאמֹר אִישׁ אִישׁ כִּי־יִהְיֶה טָמֵא׀ לָנֶפֶשׁ אוֹ בְדֶרֶךְ רְחֹקָה
,distant a on journey or a by ,body (dead) unclean shall be if man Any ,saying

8145 2320 3068 6453 6213 1755 176
11 לָכֶם אוֹ לְדֹרֹתֵיכֶם וְעָשָׂה פֶסַח לַיהוָה׃ בַּחֹדֶשׁ הַשֵּׁנִי
,second the in month to ;Jehovah the Passover shall he yet prepare your of generations or of you

4682 6213 6153 996 3117 6240 702
בְּאַרְבָּעָה עָשָׂר יוֹם בֵּין הָעַרְבַּיִם יַעֲשׂוּ אֹתוֹ עַל־מַצּוֹת
cakes with unleavened ;it shall they prepare the ,evenings between day ten (and) four the on

bitter herbs; [12]they shall
leave none of it until
morning, nor break a bone
of it. According to all the
statutes of the Passover,
they shall keep it. [13]But
the man that is clean, and is
not on a journey, and has
failed to prepare the
Passover, even that person
shall be cut off from his
people; because he did not
bring the offering of
Jehovah in its appointed
season—that man shall
bear his sin. [14]And if a
stranger shall reside with
you, and desires to keep the
Passover to Jehovah; he
shall do according to the
statute of the Passover, and
according to its ordinance.
You shall have one statute,
both for the alien and for the
native of the land.
[15]And on the day that the
tabernacle was reared up,
the cloud covered the
tabernacle, even the tabernacle of the testimony. And
at evening there was on the
tabernacle the appearance
of fire, until morning. [16]So it
was always; the cloud
covered it, and the appearance of fire by night. [17]And
whenever the cloud was
taken up from over the
tabernacle, then after that
the sons of Israel pulled up
stakes; and in the place
where the cloud abode,
there the sons of Israel encamped. [18]By the mouth of
Jehovah the sons of Israel
pulled up; and by the mouth
of Jehovah they encamped.
All the days that the cloud
remained over the taber-
nacle, they remained in
camp. [19]And when the
cloud tarried on the tabernacle many days, then the
sons of Israel kept the
charge of Jehovah, and did
not pull up. [20]And so when
the cloud was a number of
days over the tabernacle, by
the mouth of Jehovah they
camped; and by the mouth
of Jehovah they pulled up
stakes.
[21]And so when the cloud

3808 6106 1242/5704 7604 3808 398 4844
12 וּמְרֹרִים יֹאכְלֻהוּ׃ לֹא־יַשְׁאִירוּ מִמֶּנּוּ עַד־בֹּקֶר וְעֶצֶם לֹא
not a and ,morn- until any shall they not shall they bitter and
bone ing it of leave ;it eat herbs

376 6213 6453 2708 7665
13 יִשְׁבְּרוּ־בוֹ כְּכָל־חֻקַּת הַפֶּסַח יַעֲשׂוּ אֹתוֹ׃ וְהָאִישׁ אֲשֶׁר־
who the But .it shall they the the according of shall they
man prepare ,Passover of statutes all to ;it break

3772 6453 6213 2308 1961 3808 1879 2889
הוּא טָהוֹר וּבְדֶרֶךְ לֹא־הָיָה וְחָדַל לַעֲשׂוֹת הַפֶּסַח וְנִכְרְתָה
be shall even the to has and ,is not a on and ,clean (is)
off cut ,Passover prepare failed journey

4150 7126 3068 7133 5971 5315
הַנֶּפֶשׁ הַהִוא מֵעַמֶּיהָ כִּי קָרְבַּן יְהוָה לֹא הִקְרִיב בְּמֹעֲדוֹ
set its in did he not Jehovah the for his from that person
;season bring of offering ;people

6213 1616 1481 376 5375 2399
14 חֶטְאוֹ יִשָּׂא הָאִישׁ הַהוּא׃ וְכִי־יָגוּר אִתְּכֶם גֵּר וְעָשָׂה
and an with sojourns And .that man shall his
prepares ,alien you if bear sin

2708 6213 3651 4941 6453 2708 3068 6453
פֶסַח לַיהוָה כְּחֻקַּת הַפֶּסַח וּכְמִשְׁפָּטוֹ כֵּן יַעֲשֶׂה חֻקָּה
statute he so by and the the by to Pass- the
;do shall ,ordinance its ,Passover of statute ;Jehovah over

3117 776 249 1616 1961 259
15 אַחַת יִהְיֶה לָכֶם וְלַגֵּר וּלְאֶזְרַח הָאָרֶץ׃ ס וּבְיוֹם
on And the the for and for both for there one
day the .land of native alien the ,you be will

5715 168 4908 6051 3680 4908 6965
הָקִים אֶת־הַמִּשְׁכָּן כִּסָּה הֶעָנָן אֶת־הַמִּשְׁכָּן לְאֹהֶל הָעֵדֻת
the the even the the covered the was
;testimony of tent ,tabernacle cloud ,tabernacle up raised

1961 3651 1242 5704/784 4758 4908 1961 6153
16 וּבָעֶרֶב יִהְיֶה עַל־הַמִּשְׁכָּן כְּמַרְאֵה־אֵשׁ עַד־בֹּקֶר׃ כֵּן יִהְיֶה
it So morn- until ,fire the as the on there at and
was ing of appearance tabernacle was evening

5927/6310 3915 984 4758 3680 6051 8548
17 תָמִיד הֶעָנָן יְכַסֶּנּוּ וּמַרְאֵה־אֵשׁ לָיְלָה׃ וּלְפִי הֵעָלֹת
went And by fire the and covered the ;always
up whenever .night of appearance ,it cloud

4725 3478 1121 5265 310 168 5921 6051
הֶעָנָן מֵעַל הָאֹהֶל וְאַחֲרֵי כֵן יִסְעוּ בְּנֵי יִשְׂרָאֵל וּבִמְקוֹם
the in and ;Israel the set that then the from the
place of sons forth after ,tent over cloud

6310 3478 1121 2583 8033 6051 7931 8033
18 אֲשֶׁר יִשְׁכָּן־שָׁם הֶעָנָן שָׁם יַחֲנוּ בְּנֵי יִשְׂרָאֵל׃ עַל־פִּי
the by ;Israel the camped there the abode where
of mouth of sons ,cloud

3117 3605 2583 3068 6310 3478 1121 5265 3068
יְהוָה יִסְעוּ בְּנֵי יִשְׂרָאֵל וְעַל־פִּי יְהוָה יַחֲנוּ כָּל־יְמֵי אֲשֶׁר
that the all they Jehovah the by and ,Israel the set Jehovah
days ;camped of mouth of sons forth

4908 6051 748 2583 4908 6051 7931
19 יִשְׁכֹּן הֶעָנָן עַל־הַמִּשְׁכָּן יַחֲנוּ׃ וּבְהַאֲרִיךְ הֶעָנָן עַל־הַמִּשְׁכָּן
the on the when And they the over the abode
tabernacle cloud tarried .camped ,tabernacle cloud

3808 3068 4931 3478 1121 8104 7227 3117
יָמִים רַבִּים וְשָׁמְרוּ בְנֵי־יִשְׂרָאֵל אֶת־מִשְׁמֶרֶת יְהוָה וְלֹא
and ,Jehovah charge the Israel the then ,many days
not of of sons kept

4908 4557 3117 6051 1961 5265
20 יִסָּעוּ׃ וְיֵשׁ אֲשֶׁר יִהְיֶה הֶעָנָן יָמִים מִסְפָּר עַל־הַמִּשְׁכָּן עַל־
by the over numerous days the was when And did
,tabernacle cloud .forth set

6057 1961 5265 3068 6310 2583 3063 6310
21 פִּי יְהוָה יַחֲנוּ וְעַל־פִּי יְהוָה יִסָּעוּ׃ וְיֵשׁ אֲשֶׁר יִהְיֶה הֶעָנָן
the was when And they Jehovah the by and they Jehovah the
cloud (there) .forth set of mouth ;camped of mouth

was there from evening until morning, when the cloud was taken up in the morning, then they pulled up. Whether by day or by night, when the cloud was taken up, then they pulled up. [22]Whether two days, or a month, or days, when the cloud tarried over the tabernacle, to remain over it, the sons of Israel remained in camp, and did not pull up. And when it was lifted up, they pulled up. [23]By the mouth of Jehovah they encamped, and by the mouth of Jehovah they pulled up *stakes*. They kept the charge of Jehovah, by the mouth of Jehovah, by the hand of Moses.

CHAPTER 10

[1]And Jehovah spoke to Moses, saying, [2]Make two trumpets of silver for yourself. You shall make them of beaten work, and they shall be to you for the calling of the congregation, and for causing the camps to pull up. [3]And when they shall blow with them, all the congregation shall gather themselves to you at the door of the tabernacle of the congregation. [4]And if they blow with one, then the rulers, the heads of the thousands of Israel, shall assemble to you. [5]And when you blow an alarm, the camps that lie on the east side shall then pull up. [6]And when you blow an alarm the second time, the camps that lie on the south side shall pull up; they shall blow an alarm for their journeys. [7]But when the assembly is gathered, you shall blow, but you shall not sound an alarm. [8]And the sons of Aaron, the priests, shall blow with the trumpets. And they shall be to you for a never-ending statute throughout your generations. [9]And when you go into battle in your land against the foe distressing you, then you shall blow with the trumpets, and you shall be remembered before Jehovah your God.

3915 3119 5265 1242 6051 3947 1242 6153

מֵעֶרֶב עַד־בֹּקֶר וְנַעֲלָה הֶעָנָן בַּבֹּקֶר וְנָסָעוּ אוֹ יוֹמָם וָלַיְלָה

by or night by day if they then set forth. the in morning the cloud was taken up and morning till from evening

748 3117 2320 3117 5265 6051 3947

22 וְנַעֲלָה הֶעָנָן וְנָסָעוּ׃ אוֹ־יֹמַיִם אוֹ־חֹדֶשׁ אוֹ־יָמִים בְּהַאֲרִיךְ

when tarried ,days or a ,month or two ,days Whether they then set forth. the cloud, was when taken up

5265 3808 3478 1121 2583 5921 7931 4908 5921 6051

הֶעָנָן עַל־הַמִּשְׁכָּן לִשְׁכֹּן עָלָיו יַחֲנוּ בְנֵי־יִשְׂרָאֵל וְלֹא יִסָּעוּ

set forth; did not and ,Israel the of sons camped over ,it to dwell the ,tabernacle over the cloud

5265 3068 6310 2583 3068 6310 5265 3947

23 וּבְהֵעָלֹתוֹ יִסָּעוּ׃ עַל־פִּי יְהוָה יַחֲנוּ וְעַל־פִּי יְהוָה יִסָּעוּ אֶת־

they forth; Jehovah the by of mouth and they ,camped Jehovah by the of mouth ,camped they forth; set was it taken up when and

4872 3027 3068 6310 8104 3068 4931

מִשְׁמֶרֶת יְהוָה שָׁמָרוּ עַל־פִּי יְהוָה בְּיַד־מֹשֶׁה׃

.Moses the by of hand ,Jehovah the by of mouth they ,kept Jehovah charge the of

CAP. X

CHAPTER 10

2689 8147 6213 551 4872 3068/1696

1 וַיְדַבֵּר יְהוָה אֶל־מֹשֶׁה לֵּאמֹר׃ עֲשֵׂה לְךָ שְׁתֵּי חֲצוֹצְרֹת

2 trumpets of two for yourself Make ,saying ,Moses to Jehovah And spoke

4550 5712 4744 1961 6213 4749 3701

כֶּסֶף מִקְשָׁה תַּעֲשֶׂה אֹתָם וְהָיוּ לְךָ לְמִקְרָא הָעֵדָה וּלְמַסַּע

for and moving the congregation for calling the to you they and shall be them you make shall hammered work ;silver

5712 3259 2004 8628 4264

3 אֶת־הַמַּחֲנוֹת׃ וְתָקְעוּ בָּהֵן וְנוֹעֲדוּ אֵלֶיךָ כָּל־הָעֵדָה אֶל־

at the congregation all to you gather shall themselves with ,them when And blow they .camps the

3259 8628 259 4150 168 6607

4 פֶּתַח אֹהֶל מוֹעֵד׃ וְאִם־בְּאַחַת יִתְקָעוּ וְנוֹעֲדוּ אֵלֶיךָ

to you gather shall themselves then they ,blow with one And if .meeting the of tent the of door

5265 8643 8628 3478 505 7218 5387

5 הַנְּשִׂיאִים רָאשֵׁי אַלְפֵי יִשְׂרָאֵל׃ וּתְקַעְתֶּם תְּרוּעָה וְנָסְעוּ

shall and up pull a ,signal when And blow you .Israel the of thousands the of heads the ,rulers

5265 8145 8643 8628 6924 4264 2583

6 הַמַּחֲנוֹת הַחֹנִים קֵדְמָה׃ וּתְקַעְתֶּם תְּרוּעָה שֵׁנִית וְנָסְעוּ

shall up pull second the ,time the signal when And blow you the on .east which camp the camps

4550 8628 8643 8486 4264 2583

הַמַּחֲנוֹת הַחֹנִים תֵּימָנָה תְּרוּעָה יִתְקְעוּ לְמַסְעֵיהֶם׃

their for .journeys shall they blow the signal the on ;south which camp the camps

175 1121 7321 3808 8628 6951 6950

7 וּבְהַקְהִיל אֶת־הַקָּהָל תִּתְקְעוּ וְלֹא תָרִיעוּ׃ וּבְנֵי אַהֲרֹן

8 .Aaron the of sons And the sound .signal but not shall you ,blow the ,assembly is when But assembled

5769 2708 1961 2689 8628 3548

הַכֹּהֲנִים יִתְקְעוּ בַּחֲצֹצְרוֹת וְהָיוּ לָכֶם לְחֻקַּת עוֹלָם

perpetual a for statute to you they and be shall the with ;trumpets shall blow the priests

6887 6862 776 4421 935 1755

9 לְדֹרֹתֵיכֶם׃ וְכִי־תָבֹאוּ מִלְחָמָה בְּאַרְצְכֶם עַל־הַצַּר הַצֹּרֵר

vexing the against adversary your in land battle you into go And when your to .generations

430 3068 6440 2142 2689 7321

אֶתְכֶם וַהֲרֵעֹתֶם בַּחֲצֹצְרֹת וְנִזְכַּרְתֶּם לִפְנֵי יְהוָה אֱלֹהֵיכֶם

your ;God Jehovah before will you and remembered be the with ,trumpets shall you then signal ,you

And you shall be saved from your enemies. [10]And in the day of your gladness, and in your appointed times, and in your new moons, you shall blow the trumpets over your burnt offerings, and over the sacrifices of your peace offerings. And they shall be to you for a memorial before your God. I *am* Jehovah your God.

[11]And it happened in the second year, in the second month, in the twentieth of the month, the cloud went up from off the tabernacle of the testimony. [12]And the sons of Israel went forward in their journeyings from the wilderness of Sinai. And the cloud stayed *on it* in the wilderness of Paran. [13]And they set forth first at the mouth of Jehovah, by the hand of Moses. [14]And in the front, the standard of the camp of the sons of Judah pulled up *stakes*, by their armies. And over its army *was* Nahshon the son of Amminadab. [15]And over the army of the tribe of the sons of Issachar *was* Nethaneel the son of Zuar. [16]And over the army of the tribe of the sons of Zebulun *was* Eliab the son of Helon. [17]And the tabernacle was taken down, and the sons of Gershon and the sons of Merari pulled up, bearing the tabernacle. [18]And the standard of the camp of Reuben pulled up, by their armies. And over its army *was* Elizur the son of Shedeur. [19]And over the army of the tribe of the sons of Simeon, Shelumiel son of Zurishaddai. [20]And over the army of the tribe of Gad *was* Eliasaph son of Deuel. [21]And the Kohathites pulled up, bearing the sanctuary. And *others* set up the tabernacle while they came. [22]And the standard of the camp of the sons of Ephraim pulled up, by their armies. And over its army *was* Elishama the son of Ammihud. [23]And over the

4150 8057 3117 341 3467
10 וְנוֹשַׁעְתֶּם מֵאֹיְבֵיכֶם׃ וּבְיוֹם שִׂמְחַתְכֶם וּבְמוֹעֲדֵיכֶם
your in and | your | the in And | your from | shall you and
,times appointed | ,gladness | of day | .enemies | delivered be
5921/5930 2681 8628 2320 7218
וּבְרָאשֵׁי חָדְשֵׁכֶם וּתְקַעְתֶּם בַּחֲצֹצְרֹת עַל עֹלֹתֵיכֶם וְעַל
and burnt your | over | the with | shall you | your | the in and
over ,offerings | trumpets | blow | ,months | of beginnings
430 6440 2146 1961 8002 2077
זִבְחֵי שַׁלְמֵיכֶם וְהָיוּ לָכֶם לְזִכָּרוֹן לִפְנֵי אֱלֹהֵיכֶם אֲנִי
I | your | before | a for | to | they and | peace your | sac- the
(am) | ;God | memorial | you | be shall | ;offerings | of fices
430 3068
יְהוָה אֱלֹהֵיכֶם׃
.God your Jehovah

3947 2320 6242 8145 2320 8145 8141 1961
11 וַיְהִי בַּשָּׁנָה הַשֵּׁנִית בַּחֹדֶשׁ הַשֵּׁנִי בְּעֶשְׂרִים בַּחֹדֶשׁ נַעֲלָה
was | the of | the in | ,second | the in | ,second | the in | And
up taken | ,month | twentieth | | month | | year |
4550 3478 1121 5265 5715 4908 6051
12 הֶעָנָן מֵעַל מִשְׁכַּן הָעֵדֻת׃ וַיִּסְעוּ בְנֵי־יִשְׂרָאֵל לְמַסְעֵיהֶם
their in | Israel | the | And | the | the | from the
journeyings | | of sons | up pulled | .testimony | of tabernacle | cloud
7223 5265 6290 4057 6051 7931 5514 4057
13 מִמִּדְבַּר סִינָי וַיִּשְׁכֹּן הֶעָנָן בְּמִדְבַּר פָּארָן׃ וַיִּסְעוּ בָּרִאשֹׁנָה
first | they and | ;Paran | the in | the | and | ;Sinai | the from
| forth set | | of wilderness | cloud | stayed | | of wilderness
3063 4264 1121 1714 5265 4872 3027 3068 6310
14 עַל־פִּי יְהוָה בְּיַד־מֹשֶׁה׃ וַיִּסַּע דֶּגֶל מַחֲנֵה בְנֵי־יְהוּדָה
Judah | the camp the | the | pulled and | .Moses | the by | Jehovah | the at
| of sons | of of standard | up | | of hand | | of mouth
5992 1121 5177 6635 6635 7223
15 בָּרִאשֹׁנָה לְצִבְאֹתָם וְעַל־צְבָאוֹ נַחְשׁוֹן בֶּן־עַמִּינָדָב׃ וְעַל־
And | Ammina- | son | (was) | its | and | their by | the at
over | .dab | of | Nahshon | army | over | ;armies | front
4294 6635 6686/1121 5417 3485/ 1121 4294 6635
16 צְבָא מַטֵּה בְּנֵי יִשָּׂשכָר נְתַנְאֵל בֶּן־צוּעָר׃ וְעַל־צְבָא מַטֵּה
the | the | And | .Zuar | son | (was) | Issachar | the | tribe the | the
of tribe | of army | over | | of | Nethaneel | | of sons | of | of army
1121 5265 4908 3381 2497/1121 446 2079 1121
17 בְּנֵי זְבוּלֻן אֱלִיאָב בֶּן־חֵלֹן׃ וְהוּרַד הַמִּשְׁכָּן וְנָסְעוּ בְנֵי־
the | pulled and | the | was And | .Helon | son | (was) | Zebulun | the
of sons | up | ,tabernacle | down taken | | of | Eliab | | of sons
7228 4264 1714 5265 4968 5375 4847 1121 1648
18 גֵרְשׁוֹן וּבְנֵי מְרָרִי נֹשְׂאֵי הַמִּשְׁכָּן׃ וְנָסַע דֶּגֶל מַחֲנֵה רְאוּבֵן
Reuben | camp the | the | pulled and | the | bearing | ,Merari | and | Gershon
| of | of standard | up | .tabernacle | | | of sons the |
4294 6635 7707 1121 468 6635/5921 6635
19 לְצִבְאֹתָם וְעַל־צְבָאוֹ אֱלִיצוּר בֶּן־שְׁדֵיאוּר׃ וְעַל־צְבָא מַטֵּה
the | army the | And | .Shedeur | son | (was) | its | and | their by
of tribe | of | over | | of | Elizur | army | over | ,armies
1121 4291 6635 6701 1121 8017 8095 1121
20 בְּנֵי שִׁמְעוֹן שְׁלֻמִיאֵל בֶּן־צוּרִישַׁדָּי׃ וְעַל־צְבָא מַטֵּה בְנֵי־
the | tribe the | the | And | Zuri- | son | (was) | Simeon | the
of sons | of | of army | over | .shaddai | of | Shelumiel | | of sons
4720 5375 6956 5265 1845 460 1410
21 גָד אֶלְיָסָף בֶּן־דְּעוּאֵל׃ וְנָסְעוּ הַקְּהָתִים נֹשְׂאֵי הַמִּקְדָּשׁ
the | bearing | the | pulled and | .Deuel | son | (was) | Gad
sanctuary | | Kohathites | up | | of | Eliasaph |
1121 4264 1714 5265 935 4908 6965
22 וְהֵקִימוּ אֶת־הַמִּשְׁכָּן עַד־בֹּאָם׃ וְנָסַע דֶּגֶל מַחֲנֵה בְנֵי־
the | camp the | the | pulled and | they | until | the | (others) and
of sons | of | of standard | up | .came | | tabernacle | up set
5989 476 6635/5921 6635 669
23 אֶפְרַיִם לְצִבְאֹתָם וְעַל־צְבָאוֹ אֱלִישָׁמָע בֶּן־עַמִּיהוּד׃ וְעַל־
And | Ammihud | of son | Elishama | (was) | army its | and | their by | ,Ephraim
over | | | | | | over | ;armies |

army of the tribe of the sons of Manasseh *was* Gamaliel the son of Pedahzur. 24And over the army of the tribe of the sons of Benjamin *was* Abidan the son of Gideoni.

25And the standard of the camp of the sons of Dan pulled up, to the rear of all the camps, by their armies. And over its army *was* Ahiezer the son of Ammishaddai. 26And over the army of the tribe of the sons of Asher *was* Pagiel the son of Ocran. 27And over the army of the tribe of the sons of Naphtali *was* Ahira the son of Enan. 28These *were* the travels of the sons of Israel according to their armies. And they pulled up *stakes.*

29And Moses said to Hobab the son of Reuel the Midianite, Moses' father-in-law, We are traveling to the place of which Jehovah has said, I will give it to you. Go with us, and we will do good to you; for Jehovah has spoken good concerning Israel. 30And he said to him, I shall not go, but I shall go to my land and to my kindred. 31And he said, Please do not forsake us, because you know *as to how* we encamp in the wilderness, and you shall be to us for eyes. 32And it shall come to pass when you go with us; yea, it shall be that what good Jehovah shall do to us, we shall do good to you.

33And they pulled up from the mount of Jehovah three days' journey. And the ark of the covenant of Jehovah pulled out before them, three days' journey, to seek out a resting place for them. 34And the cloud of Jehovah *was* on them by day as they pulled out from the camp. 35And it happened when the ark pulled out, Moses said, Rise, O Jehovah, and Your enemies shall be scattered, and those hating You shall flee from Your

24 צְבָא מַטֵּה בְּנֵי מְנַשֶּׁה גַּמְלִיאֵל בֶּן־פְּדָהצוּר׃ וְעַל־צְבָא
25 מַטֵּה בְּנֵי בִנְיָמִן אֲבִידָן בֶּן־גִּדְעוֹנִי׃ וְנָסַע דֶּגֶל מַחֲנֵה בְנֵי־
דָן מְאַסֵּף לְכָל־הַמַּחֲנֹת לְצִבְאֹתָם וְעַל־צְבָאוֹ אֲחִיעֶזֶר
26 בֶּן־עַמִּישַׁדָּי׃ וְעַל־צְבָא מַטֵּה בְּנֵי אָשֵׁר פַּגְעִיאֵל בֶּן־
27 28 עָכְרָן׃ וְעַל־צְבָא מַטֵּה בְּנֵי נַפְתָּלִי אֲחִירַע בֶּן־עֵינָן׃ אֵלֶּה
29 מַסְעֵי בְנֵי־יִשְׂרָאֵל לְצִבְאֹתָם וַיִּסָּעוּ׃ וַיֹּאמֶר
מֹשֶׁה לְחֹבָב בֶּן־רְעוּאֵל הַמִּדְיָנִי חֹתֵן מֹשֶׁה נֹסְעִים ׀
אֲנַחְנוּ אֶל־הַמָּקוֹם אֲשֶׁר אָמַר יְהוָה אֹתוֹ אֶתֵּן לָכֶם לְכָה
30 אִתָּנוּ וְהֵטַבְנוּ לָךְ כִּי־יְהוָה דִּבֶּר־טוֹב עַל־יִשְׂרָאֵל׃ וַיֹּאמֶר
אֵלָיו לֹא אֵלֵךְ כִּי אִם־אֶל־אַרְצִי וְאֶל־מוֹלַדְתִּי אֵלֵךְ׃
31 וַיֹּאמֶר אַל־נָא תַּעֲזֹב אֹתָנוּ כִּי ׀ עַל־כֵּן יָדַעְתָּ חֲנֹתֵנוּ בַּמִּדְבָּר
32 וְהָיִיתָ לָּנוּ לְעֵינָיִם׃ וְהָיָה כִּי־תֵלֵךְ עִמָּנוּ וְהָיָה ׀ הַטּוֹב
33 הַהוּא אֲשֶׁר יֵיטִיב יְהוָה עִמָּנוּ וְהֵטַבְנוּ לָךְ׃ וַיִּסְעוּ מֵהַר
יְהוָה דֶּרֶךְ שְׁלֹשֶׁת יָמִים וַאֲרוֹן בְּרִית־יְהוָה נֹסֵעַ לִפְנֵיהֶם
34 דֶּרֶךְ שְׁלֹשֶׁת יָמִים לָתוּר לָהֶם מְנוּחָה׃ וַעֲנַן יְהוָה
35 עֲלֵיהֶם יוֹמָם בְּנָסְעָם מִן־הַמַּחֲנֶה׃ וַיְהִי בִּנְסֹעַ
הָאָרֹן וַיֹּאמֶר מֹשֶׁה קוּמָה ׀ יְהוָה וְיָפֻצוּ אֹיְבֶיךָ וְיָנֻסוּ

presence. 36And when it rested, he said, Return, O Jehovah, *to* the myriads, the thousands of Israel.

7233 3068 7725 559 5117 6440 8130

36 מְשַׂנְאֶיךָ מִפָּנֶיךָ׃ וּבְנֻחֹה יֹאמַר שׁוּבָה יְהוָה רִבְבוֹת

the (to) O ,Return he when And Your from hating those
,myriads ;Jehovah ,said ,rested it .face You

3478 505

אַלְפֵי יִשְׂרָאֵל׃

.Israel the
of thousands

CAP. XI יא

CHAPTER 11

1And the people *were* evil, as those complaining in the ears of Jehovah. And Jehovah heard, and His anger glowed, and the fire of Jehovah burned among them, and devoured in the *extreme* edge of the camp. 2And the people cried to Moses, and Moses prayed to Jehovah, and the fire was quenched. 3And he called the name of that place Taberah, because the fire of Jehovah burned among them

4And the mixed multitude that *was* among them lusted *with a great* lust; and the sons of Israel also turned back and wept, and said, Who shall cause us to eat meat? 5We remember the fish that we ate in Egypt for nothing; the cucumbers, and the melons, and the leeks, and the onions, and the garlic; 6and now our soul withers. There is nothing except this manna *before* our eyes. 7And the manna *was* like coriander seed, and its look like the look of bdellium resin gum. 8And the people went around and gathered *it* and ground *it* in mills, or beat *it* in mortars, and boiled *it* in a pan, and made it into cakes. And its taste was like the taste of fresh oil. 9And when the dew came down on the camp by night, the manna came down on it.

10And Moses heard the people weeping by its families, each at the door of his tent; and the anger of Jehovah glowed exceedingly, and in the eyes of

2734 3068 8085 3068 241 7451 596 5971 1961

1 וַיְהִי הָעָם כְּמִתְאֹנְנִים רַע בְּאָזְנֵי יְהוָה וַיִּשְׁמַע יְהוָה וַיִּחַר

and ,Jehovah and ;Jehovah the in (were) those as the And
glowed heard of ears evil complaining people

4264 7097 398 3068 784 1197 639

אַפּוֹ וַתִּבְעַר־בָּם אֵשׁ יְהוָה וַתֹּאכַל בִּקְצֵה הַמַּחֲנֶה׃

the the at and ,Jehovah the among and His
.camp of edge devoured of fire them burned ;anger

8257 3068 4872 6419 4872 5971 6817

2 וַיִּצְעַק הָעָם אֶל־מֹשֶׁה וַיִּתְפַּלֵּל מֹשֶׁה אֶל־יְהוָה וַתִּשְׁקַע

was and ,Jehovah to Moses and ,Moses to the And
quenched prayed people cried

1197/3588 8404 1931 4725 8034 7121 784

3 הָאֵשׁ׃ וַיִּקְרָא שֵׁם־הַמָּקוֹם הַהוּא תַּבְעֵרָה כִּי־בָעֲרָה בָם

among because ,Taberah that place the he and the
them burned of name called ;fire

7725 8378 183 7130 628 3068 784

4 אֵשׁ יְהוָה׃ וְהָאסַפְסֻף אֲשֶׁר בְּקִרְבּוֹ הִתְאַוּוּ תַּאֲוָה וַיָּשֻׁבוּ

and (great with) lusted their in that mixed the And .Jehovah the
turned ;lust midst (was) multitude of fire

2142 1320 398 559 3478 1121 1571 1058

5 וַיִּבְכּוּ גַּם בְּנֵי יִשְׂרָאֵל וַיֹּאמְרוּ מִי יַאֲכִלֵנוּ בָּשָׂר׃ זָכַרְנוּ

We ?meat cause will Who ,said and ,Israel the also and
remember eat to us of sons wept

7180 2600 4714 398 834 1710

אֶת־הַדָּגָה אֲשֶׁר־נֹאכַל בְּמִצְרַיִם חִנָּם אֵת הַקִּשֻּׁאִים וְאֵת

and the for in we which fish the
,cucumbers ;nothing Egypt ate

7762 1211 2682 20

הָאֲבַטִּחִים וְאֶת־הֶחָצִיר וְאֶת־הַבְּצָלִים וְאֶת־הַשּׁוּמִים׃

the and the and the and the
;garlic ,onions leeks ,melons

4478 5869 4478 1115 3605/369 3001 5315 6258

6
7 וְעַתָּה נַפְשֵׁנוּ יְבֵשָׁה אֵין כֹּל בִּלְתִּי אֶל־הַמָּן עֵינֵינוּ׃ וְהַמָּן

the And (before) the except any there :withers our and
manna .eyes our manna thing no is soul now

3950 5971 7751 911 5869 5869 1407/2233

8 כִּזְרַע־גַּד הוּא וְעֵינוֹ כְּעֵין הַבְּדֹלַח׃ שָׁטוּ הָעָם וְלָקְטוּ

gath- and the went And bdellium the as its and ,(was) coriander like
,(it) ered people about .(resin gum) of look look seed

6213 6517 1310 4085 1793 7347 2912

וְטָחֲנוּ בָרֵחַיִם אוֹ דָכוּ בַּמְּדֹכָה וּבִשְּׁלוּ בַּפָּרוּר וְעָשׂוּ אֹתוֹ

it and the in boiled and in beat or in and
made ,pan (it) mortars (it) ,mills (it) ground

2919 3381 8081 3956 2940 2940 1961 5692

9 עֻגוֹת וְהָיָה טַעְמוֹ כְּטַעַם לְשַׁד הַשָּׁמֶן׃ וּבְרֶדֶת הַטַּל

the when And the the the as its and (into)
dew down came .oil of delicacy of taste taste was ;cakes

4872 8085 4478 3381 3915 4264 5921

10 עַל־הַמַּחֲנֶה לָיְלָה יֵרֵד הַמָּן עָלָיו׃ וַיִּשְׁמַע מֹשֶׁה אֶת־

Moses And .it on the came by the on
heard manna down ,night camp

3068 6392 734 168 6607 376 4940 1058 5971

הָעָם בֹּכֶה לְמִשְׁפְּחֹתָיו אִישׁ לְפֶתַח אָהֳלוֹ וַיִּחַר־אַף יְהוָה

Jeho- anger and his the at each its by weeping the
vah's glowed ;tent of door ,families people

Moses *it was* evil. 11 And Moses said to Jehovah, Why have You done evil to Your servant; and why have I not found grace in Your eyes, to put the burden of all this people on me? 12 I, have I conceived all this people? I, have I begotten it, that You say to me, Carry it in your bosom as the foster father bears the suckling, to the land which You have sworn to its fathers? 13 *Where* shall I get flesh to give to all this people? For they weep to me, saying, Give to us flesh that we may eat. 14 I am not able, I alone, to bear all this people, for *it is* too heavy for me; 15 and if You deal thus with me, please quickly kill me, if I have found grace in Your eyes, and let me not look on my affliction.

16 And Jehovah said to Moses, Gather to Me seventy men of the elders of Israel, whom you have known that they *are* elders of the people, and its officers. And you shall take them to the tabernacle of the congregation; and they shall station themselves there with you. 17 And I shall come down and speak with you there; and I will take of the spirit which *is* upon you, and will put *it* on them; and they will bear the burden of the people with you, that you may not bear it yourself alone. 18 And you shall say to the people, Sanctify yourselves for tomorrow, and you shall eat flesh. For you have wept in the ears of Jehovah, saying, Who shall give us flesh, for we *had* good in Egypt? And

4100 3068 4872 559 7451 4872 5869 3966
11 מְאֹד וּבְעֵינֵי מֹשֶׁה רָע׃ וַיֹּאמֶר מֹשֶׁה אֶל־יְהוָה לָמָה
Why .Jehovah to Moses said And (was it) Moses' in and exceed-
.evil eyes .ingly

7760 5869 2580 46 72 4100 5650 7489
הֲרֵעֹתָ לְעַבְדֶּךָ וְלָמָּה לֹא־מָצָתִי חֵן בְּעֵינֶיךָ לָשׂוּם אֶת־
to Your in grace I have not And Your to You have
put ,eyes found why ?servant evil done

5971 2029 2088 5971/ 8605 4853
12 מַשָּׂא כָּל־הָעָם הַזֶּה עָלָי׃ הֶאָנֹכִי הָרִיתִי אֵת כָּל־הָעָם
people all I have ,I on this people all the
conceived ?me of burden

2436 5375 559 3205 2088
הַזֶּה אִם־אָנֹכִי יְלִדְתִּיהוּ כִּי־תֹאמַר אֵלַי שָׂאֵהוּ בְחֵיקֶךָ
your in Carry to You that I have ,I ?this
bosom it ,me say ,it begotten

7650 127 3243 539 53
כַּאֲשֶׁר יִשָּׂא הָאֹמֵן אֶת־הַיֹּנֵק עַל הָאֲדָמָה אֲשֶׁר נִשְׁבַּעְתָּ
have You which the to the foster the bears as
sworn land ,suckling father

658 2088 5971 5414 1320 370 1
13 לַאֲבֹתָיו׃ מֵאַיִן לִי בָּשָׂר לָתֵת לְכָל־הָעָם הַזֶּה כִּי־יִבְכּוּ
they For ?this people to to meat to (Where) its to
weep all give me is ?fathers

3201 3808 398 1320 5414 559
14 עָלַי לֵאמֹר תְּנָה־לָּנוּ בָשָׂר וְנֹאכֵלָה׃ לֹא־אוּכַל אָנֹכִי
I am I not we that meat to Give ,saying on
,able .eat may us ,me

3515 2088 5971 3605 5375 905
15 לְבַדִּי לָשֵׂאת אֶת־כָּל־הָעָם הַזֶּה כִּי כָבֵד מִמֶּנִּי׃ וְאִם־
and for (is it) for ,this people all bear to ,alone
if ;me heavy too

5869 2580 4672 2026 176 2026 6213.
כָּכָה ׀ אַתְּ־עֹשֶׂה לִּי הָרְגֵנִי נָא הָרֹג אִם־מָצָאתִי חֵן בְּעֵינֶיךָ
Your in grace have I if ,quickly I kill to do You thus
,eyes found ;You beg ,me ,me

7451 7200 3808
וְאַל־אֶרְאֶה בְּרָעָתִי׃
.evil my on me let and
look not

2205 376 7657 622 4872 3068 559
16 וַיֹּאמֶר יְהוָה אֶל־מֹשֶׁה אֶסְפָה־לִּי שִׁבְעִים אִישׁ מִזִּקְנֵי
the of men seventy to Gather ,Moses to Jehovah And
of elders Me said

3947 7860 5971 2205 3045 3478
יִשְׂרָאֵל אֲשֶׁר יָדַעְתָּ כִּי־הֵם זִקְנֵי הָעָם וְשֹׁטְרָיו וְלָקַחְתָּ
you and its and the elders they that have you whom ,Israel
take shall ;officers ,people of (are) ,known

1696 3381 8033 3320 4150 168
17 אֹתָם אֶל־אֹהֶל מוֹעֵד וְהִתְיַצְּבוּ שָׁם עִמָּךְ׃ וְיָרַדְתִּי וְדִבַּרְתִּי
and will I and with there they and ;meeting the to them
speak down come ,you up line will of tent

7760 59 21 834 7307 680 8033
עִמְּךָ שָׁם וְאָצַלְתִּי מִן־הָרוּחַ אֲשֶׁר עָלֶיךָ וְשַׂמְתִּי עֲלֵיהֶם
on will and upon which the of will I and ;there with
;them (it) put ,you (is) spirit take you

905 5375 5971 4853 5375
18 וְנָשְׂאוּ אִתְּךָ בְּמַשָּׂא הָעָם וְלֹא־תִשָּׂא אַתָּה לְבַדֶּךָ׃ וְאֶל־
And .alone yourself will you and the the with they and
to (it) bear not people of burden you bear will

1058 1320 398 4279 6972 559 59 71
הָעָם תֹּאמַר הִתְקַדְּשׁוּ לְמָחָר וַאֲכַלְתֶּם בָּשָׂר כִּי בְּכִיתֶם
have you For .meat you and for Sanctify shall you the
wept eat shall ,tomorrow yourselves say people

4714 2895 1320 398 559 3068 241
בְּאָזְנֵי יְהוָה לֵאמֹר מִי יַאֲכִלֵנוּ בָּשָׂר כִּי־טוֹב לָנוּ בְּמִצְרָיִם
in we good for ,meat cause shall Who ,saying ,Jehovah the in
?Egypt (had) eat to us of ears

Jehovah shall give meat to you, and you shall eat. [19]You shall not eat one day, nor two days, nor five days, nor ten days, nor twenty days; [20]*but* to a month of days, until it comes out of your nostrils, and it shall become to you a loathsome thing; because you have loathed Jehovah, who *is* in your midst, and weep before Him, saying, Why *is it* that we have come out of Egypt?

[21]And Moses said, The people in whose midst I *am* are six hundred thousand footmen; and You, You have said, I shall give meat to them, and they shall eat a month of days. [22]Shall flock and herd be slaughtered for them, so *one* may find for them? Are all the fish of the sea to be gathered for them, that *one* may find for them? [23]And Jehovah said to Moses, Is the hand of Jehovah shortened? Now you shall see whether My word shall come to pass to you or not.

[24]And Moses went out and spoke to the people the words of Jehovah, and gathered seventy men of the elders of the people, and caused them to stand around the tabernacle. [25]And Jehovah came down in the cloud and spoke to him, and took of the spirit which *was* on him, and put *it* on the seventy men of the elders. And it happened, as the spirit rested on them, that they prophesied, but they did not continue. [26]And two of the men were left in the camp, the name of the one *being* Eldad, and the name of the second Medad; and the spirit rested on them, and they *were* among those written, but did not go out to the

398 259 3117 3808 398 1320 3068 5414
19 ונתן יהוה לכם בשר ואכלתם׃ לא יום אחד תאכלון
shall you one day Not you and ;meat to Jehovah And
.eat .eat shall you give shall

3117 6235 3808 3117 2568 3117
ולא יומים ולא חמשה ימים ולא עשרה ימים ולא
nor ,days ten nor ,days five nor two nor
,days

1961 639 5927 5704 3117 2320 3117 6242
20 עשרים יום׃ עד חדש ימים עד אשר־יצא מאפכם והיה
it and your of comes it until ,days a (but) ,days twenty
be will ,nostrils out of month to

7130 3068 3973 3282 2214
לכם לזרא יען כי־מאסתם את־יהוה אשר בקרבכם
your in who ,Jehovah have you because loath- a to
,midst (is) loathed ;thing some you

559 4714 5927 4100 559 6440 1058
21 ותבכו לפניו לאמר למה זה יצאנו ממצרים׃ ויאמר
said And of have we (is) Why ,saying before and
?Egypt out come (it) ,Him weep

7130 595 5971 7273 505 5967 8337 4872
משה שש־מאות אלף רגלי העם אשר אנכי בקרבו
whose in I (are) footmen thousand hundred six ,Moses
;midst (am) people the

6629 3117 2320 398 5414 1320 559
22 ואתה אמרת בשר אתן להם ואכלו חדש ימים׃ הצאן
Shall .days a they and to shall I meat have You and
flock of month eat shall ,them give ,said ,You

622 3220/1709 4672 7919 4241
ובקר ישחט להם ומצא להם אם את־כל־דגי הים יאסף
be to Are the the all for (one) that for be and
gathered sea of fish ?them find may them killed herd

4672
להם ומצא להם׃
for (one) that for
?them find may ,them

7200 6258 7114 3068 3027 4872 3068 559
23 ויאמר יהוה אל־משה היד יהוה תקצר עתה תראה
shall you Now Is Jehovah the ,Moses to Jehovah And
see ?shortened of hand said

5971 1696 4872 5927 3808 1697 7136
24 היקרך דברי אם־לא׃ ויצא משה וידבר אל־העם את
the to and Moses And .not or My shall whether
people spoke out went word you befall

8033 5975 5971 2205 376 7657 622 3068 1697
דברי יהוה ויאסף שבעים איש מזקני העם ויעמד אתם
them and the the of men seventy and ,Jehovah the
stood ,people of elders gathered of words

680 1696 6051 3068 3381 168 5439
25 סביבת האהל׃ וירד יהוה בענן וידבר אליו ויאצל
set and to and the in Jehovah came And the around
apart ,him spoke cloud down .tent

1961 2205 376 7657 5414 7307
מן־הרוח אשר עליו ויתן על־שבעים איש הזקנים ויהי
and the ,men the on and on which the from
was it ,elders seventy (it) put ,him (was) spirit

8147 7604 3254 5612 7307 5117
26 כנוח עליהם הרוח ויתנבאו ולא יספו׃ וישארו שני־
two were And did they but they the on as
left ,continue not prophesied spirit them rested

4312 8145 8034 419 259 8033 4264 582
אנשים במחנה שם האחד אלדד ושם השני מידד
;Medad the the and (being) the the the in men
second of name ,Eldad one of name ,camp

168 5927 3808 3789 7307 5117
ותנח עלהם הרוח והמה בכתבים ולא יצאו האהלה
the to go did but those among they and the on and
.tent out not ,written (were) ,spirit them rested

tabernacle. And they
prophesied in the camp.
27And a young man ran and
told Moses, and said, Eldad
and Medad are prophesy-
ing in the camp. 28And
Joshua the son of Nun,
minister *to* Moses, of his
young men, answered and
said, My lord Moses, stop
them. 29And Moses said to
him, Are you jealous for my
sake? Oh that all Jehovah's
people *were* prophets, that
Jehovah would put His
spirit on them! 30And
Moses withdrew into the
camp, he and the elders of
Israel.
31And a wind went forth
from Jehovah and cut off
quails from the sea, and let
them fall by the camp, as a
day's journey here, and as a
day's journey there, all
around the camp, and about
two cubits deep on the face
of the land. 32And the
people rose up all that day,
and all that night, and the
day after, and gathered the
quails; he who had least
had gathered ten homers.
And they spread them out
for themselves around the
camp. 33The meat *was* yet
between their teeth, it was
not yet cut off, and the
anger of Jehovah glowed
among the people. And
Jehovah struck among the
people *with* a very great
plague. 34And one called
the name of that place The
Graves of Lust; for there
they buried the people who
lusted.

35From the Graves of Lust
the people pulled up to *go*
to Hazeroth, and they
remained in Hazeroth.

419 559 4872 5046 5288 7323 4264 5012
27 ויתנבאו במחנה: וירץ הנער ויגד למשה ויאמר אלדד
Eldad ,said and ,Moses and young a and the in they And
8334 5126 3091 told 6030 man 4264 ran 5012 camp prophesied 43:12
28 ומידד מתנבאים במחנה: ויען יהושע בן־נון משרת
minister ,Nun the Joshua And the in are and
of son answered .camp prophesying Medad
4872 559 3607 4872 113 559 979 4872
29 משה מבחריו ויאמר אדני משה כלאם: ויאמר לו משה
,Moses to And stop ,Moses my and young his of (to)
him said .them lord said men ,Moses
3068 5414 5030 3068/ 5971 3605/ 5414/ 7065
המקנא אתה לי ומי־יתן כל־עם יהוה נביאים כי־יתן יהוה
Jehovah would that (were) Jeho- people all that Oh for you Are
put prophets vah's ?me jealous
2205 4264 4872 622 7307
30 את־רוחו עליהם: ויאסף משה אל־המחנה הוא וזקני
the and he the into Moses And on His
of elders ,camp gathered was !them spirit
5903 3220 7958/1468/ 3068 5265 7307 3478
31 ישראל: ורוח נסע מאת יהוה ויגז שלוים מן־הים ויטש
let and the from quails and Jehovah from set a And .Israel
fall (them) ,sea off cut forth wind
4264 5439 3541 3117 1879 3541/3117 1879 4264
על־המחנה כדרך יום כה וכדרך יום כה סביבות המחנה
the all ,there day's a as and here day's a as the by
,camp around journey journey ,camp
3605 3117/3605 5971 6865 776 6440 5921 520
32 וכאמתים על־פני הארץ: ויקם העם כל־היום ההוא וכל־
and ,that day all the And the the above about even
all people rose .land of face cubits two
622 4591 7958 622 4283 3117 3605 3915
הלילה וכל יום המחרת ויאספו את־השלו הממעיט אסף
took who he the and ,after the and the
up least had ;quails gathered day all ,night
4264 5439 78 49 7849 2563 6235
עשרה חמרים וישטחו להם שטוח סביבות המחנה:
the around out for they and ;homers ten
.camp themselves spread
5971 2734 3068 639 3772 2962 8127 996 5750 1320
33 הבשר עודנו בין שניהם טרם יכרת ואף יהוה חרה בעם
the at glowed Jeho- when was it not their between (was) The
;people vah's anger ,off cut yet ,teeth still meat
4725 8034 7121 3966 7227 4317 5971 3068/5221
34 ויך יהוה בעם מכה רבה מאד: ויקרא את־שם־המקום
place the one and ;very great a (with) among Jeho- and
of name called plague people the vah struck
183 5971 6912 8033 8378 6913
ההוא קברות התאוה כי־שם קברו את־העם המתאוים:
who the they there for ,Lust of the that
.lusted people buried Graves
2698 1961 2698 5971 5265 8378 6913
35 מקברות התאוה נסעו העם חצרות ויהיו בחצרות:
in they and (for) the set Lust From
.Hazeroth were ,Hazeroth people forth of Graves the

CAP. XII יב

CHAPTER 12

CHAPTER 12
1And Miriam and Aaron
spoke against Moses, be-
cause of the Cushite
woman whom he had
taken. For he had taken a
Cushite woman. 2And they
said, Has Jehovah spoken
only by Moses? Has He not

3569 802 182 4872 175 4813 1696
1 ותדבר מרים ואהרן במשה על־אדות האשה הכשית
Cushite the because against and Miriam And
woman of ,Moses Aaron spoke
4872 389 559 3947 3569 802 3947
2 אשר לקח כי־אשה כשית לקח: ויאמרו הרק אך־במשה
by Only they and had he Cushite a for had he whom
Moses ,said taken woman ;taken

also spoken by us? And Jehovah heard. [3]And the man Moses *was* very meek, more than any man who *was* on the face of the earth. [4]And Jehovah said suddenly to Moses, and to Aaron, and to Miriam, You three come out to the tabernacle of the congregation. And the three of them came out. [5]And Jehovah came down in the pillar of the cloud and stood at the tabernacle door, and called Aaron and Miriam. And both of them came out. [6]And He said, Now hear My words. If your prophet is of Jehovah, I shall make Myself known to him in an appearance; I will speak to him in a dream. [7]*It is* not so *with* My servant Moses! He *is* faithful in all My house. [8]I speak to him mouth to mouth, and *by* an appearance, and not in riddles; and he carefully looks upon the form of Jehovah. So why have you not been afraid to speak against My servant, against Moses? [9]And the anger of Jehovah glowed against them, and He left. [10]And the cloud turned away from the tent. And, behold, Miriam *was* leprous as snow! And Aaron turned toward Miriam, and, behold, *she was* leprous! [11]And Aaron said to Moses, Oh my lord, I beg you, do not lay sin upon us, by which we have done foolishly, and by which we have sinned. [12]I beg you, do not let her be as *one* dead, of whom the flesh is half-consumed when he comes out of his mother's womb. [13]And Moses cried to Jehovah, saying, O God, I beg You, give healing to her, I beseech You.

[14]And Jehovah said to Moses, If her father had but spat in her face, should she not be ashamed seven

376 3068 8085 1696 1571 3808 3068 1696
3 דבר יהוה הלא גם־בנו דבר וישמע יהוה׃ והאיש
the And man | .Jehovah | And heard | He ?spoken | by us | also | Has ?Jehovah not | has spoken

127 6440 120 3605 3966 6041 4872
משה ענו מאד מכל האדם אשר על־פני האדמה׃
the .earth | the of face | on | who (was) | man | more any than | ,very meek | Moses (was)

4813 175 4872 6597 3068 559
4 ויאמר יהוה פתאם אל־משה ואל־אהרן ואל־מרים
Miriam and to | ,Aaron and to | ,Moses to | suddenly | Jehovah | said And

3381 7969 5927 4150 168 7969 5927
5 צאו שלשתכם אל־אהל מועד ויצאו שלשתם׃ וירד
And came | they .three | and out came | ;meeting | the tent | to | you ,three | Come ,out

4813 175 7121 168 6607 5975 6051 5982 3068
יהוה בעמוד ענן ויעמד פתח האהל ויקרא אהרן ומרים
and ;Miriam | Aaron | and called | the ,tent | the at of door | and stood | the cloud | the in of pillar | Jehovah

5030 1697 4994 8085 559 8147 5927
6 ויצאו שניהם׃ ויאמר שמעו־נא דברי אם־יהיה נביאכם
your prophet | is | If | My .words | Now | hear | He And ,said | of both .them | and came

3651/5821 1696 2472 7200 4759 3068
7 יהוה במראה אליו אתודע בחלום אדבר־בו׃ לא־כן
so Not | with ;him | will I speak | a in dream | will I ;myself reveal | to ,him | an by appearance | of Jehovah

1696 6310 6310 539 1004 3605 4872 5650
8 עבדי משה בכל־ביתי נאמן הוא׃ פה אל־פה אדבר־
speak I | mouth to Mouth | he .(is) | faithful | My house | In all | !Moses | (with) servant My

3808 4100 5027 3068 8544 2420 3808 4758
בו ומראה ולא בחידת ותמנת יהוה יביט ומדוע לא
not | so why | he ;regards | Jehovah | the and of form | in ;riddles | and not | an (by) ,appearance | and with ,him

3068 639 2734 4872 5650 1696 3372
9 יראתם לדבר בעבדי במשה׃ ויחר־אף יהוה בם
against ,them | Jehovah | the of anger | And glowed | against ?Moses | My against ,servant | to speak | you have feared

7950 6879 4813 2009 168 6051 3212
10 וילך׃ והענן סר מעל האהל והנה מרים מצרעת כשלג
as !snow | (was) ;leprous | Miriam | ,and behold | the ;tent | from turned away | the and cloud | He and ;left

175 559 6879 2009 4813 175 6437
11 ויפן אהרן אל־מרים והנה מצרעת׃ ויאמר אהרן אל־
to | Aaron | said And | (was she) !leprous | ,and behold | ,Miriam | toward | Aaron | And turned

2973 834 2403 5921 7896 4994/3808 113 4872
משה בי אדני אל־נא תשת עלינו חטאת אשר נואלנו
have we .foolishly done | which by | sin | upon us | do lay | beg I ,you ,not | my ,lord Oh | ,Moses

7358 5927 4191 4994/3808 2398 834
12 ואשר חטאנו׃ אל־נא תהי כמת אשר בצאתו מרחם
of womb | he when out comes | (one) as ,dead | let do be her | beg I ,you not | have we ,sinned | by and which

410 559 3068 4872 6817 1320 2677 398 517
13 אמו ויאכל חצי בשרו׃ ויצעק משה אל־יהוה לאמר אל
O ,God | ,saying | ,Jehovah | to | Moses | And cried | whose .flesh | half | of con-sumed | is | his ,mother's

7495 4994
נא רפא נא לה׃
.her | I ,You beg | ,heal | I ,You beg

3808 6440 3417 3417 1 4872 3068 559
14 ויאמר יהוה אל־משה ואביה ירק ירק בפניה הלא
should not | her in ,face | had spit | surely | her If father | ,Moses | to | Jehovah | said And

days? She shall be shut out
seven days at the outside of
the camp, and afterward
she shall be brought in.
15And Miriam was shut out
at the outside of the camp
seven days, and the people
did not pull up *stakes* until
Miriam was brought in.
16And afterward the people
pulled up from Hazeroth,
and they encamped in the
wilderness of Paran.

4264 2351 3117 7651 5462 3117 7651 3637
תִּכָּלֵם שִׁבְעַת יָמִים תִּסָּגֵר שִׁבְעַת יָמִים מִחוּץ לַמַּחֲנֶה
the of camp, outside days seven be her Let out shut ?days seven be she humiliated

3117 7651 4264 2351 4813 5462 622 310
15 וְאַחַר תֵּאָסֵף׃ וַתִּסָּגֵר מִרְיָם מִחוּץ לַמַּחֲנֶה שִׁבְעַת יָמִים
,days seven the of camp outside Miriam was And out shut be shall she in brought and afterward

2698 5971 5265 310 4813 622 5704 5265 5971
16 וְהָעָם לֹא נָסַע עַד־הֵאָסֵף מִרְיָם׃ וְאַחַר נָסְעוּ הָעָם מֵחֲצֵרוֹת
from ,Hazeroth the people pulled up and then ;Miriam was in brought until did up pull not the and people

6290 4056 2583
וַיַּחֲנוּ בְּמִדְבַּר פָּארָן׃
.Paran the in of wilderness they and camped

CAP. XIII יג

CHAPTER 13

CHAPTER 13
1And Jehovah spoke to
Moses, saying, 2Send men
for you, and they shall spy
out the land of Canaan
which I am giving to the
sons of Israel; you shall send
one man for the tribe of his
fathers, one man, every one
a leader among them. 3And
by the mouth of Jehovah
Moses sent them from the
wilderness of Paran; they
were all of them men, heads
of the sons of Israel. 4And
these *were* their names: of
the tribe of Reuben, Sham-
mua the son of Zaccur; 5of
the tribe of Simeon, Sha-
phat the son of Hori; 6of the
tribe of Judah, Caleb the son
of Jephunneh; 7of the tribe
of Issachar, Igal the son of
Joseph; 8of the tribe of
Ephraim, Joshua the son of
Nun; 9of the tribe of
Benjamin, Palti the son of
Raphu; 10of the tribe of
Zebulun, Gaddiel the son of
Sodi; 11of the tribe of
Joseph, of the tribe of
Manasseh, Gaddi the son of
Susi; 12of the tribe of Dan,
Ammiel the son of Gemalli;
13of the tribe of Asher,
Sethur the son of Michael;
14of the tribe of Naphtali,
Nahbi the son of Vophsi;
15of the tribe of Gad, Geuel
the son of Machi. 16These
were the names of the men

8446 562 7971 559 4872 3068 1696
1 2 וַיְדַבֵּר יְהוָה אֶל־מֹשֶׁה לֵּאמֹר׃ שְׁלַח־לְךָ אֲנָשִׁים וְיָתֻרוּ
they and search shall ,men for you Send ,saying ,Moses to Jehovah And spoke

259 376 3478 1121 5414 834 3667 776
אֶת־אֶרֶץ כְּנַעַן אֲשֶׁר־אֲנִי נֹתֵן לִבְנֵי יִשְׂרָאֵל אִישׁ אֶחָד
one man ;Israel the to of sons am giving I which ,Canaan the of land

7971 854 5387 3605 7971 1 4294 259 376
3 אִישׁ אֶחָד לְמַטֵּה אֲבֹתָיו תִּשְׁלָחוּ כֹּל נָשִׂיא בָהֶם׃ וַיִּשְׁלַח
sent And among .them a leader every one shall you ,send his fathers the for of tribe one (by) man

582 3605 3068 6310 6290 4057 4872
אֹתָם מֹשֶׁה מִמִּדְבַּר פָּארָן עַל־פִּי יְהוָה כֻּלָּם אֲנָשִׁים
(were) ;men they all ;Jehovah the at of mouth Paran the from of wilderness Moses them

7205 4294 8034 7992 3478 1121 7218
4 רָאשֵׁי בְנֵי־יִשְׂרָאֵל הֵמָּה׃ וְאֵלֶּה שְׁמוֹתָם לְמַטֵּה רְאוּבֵן
,Reuben the of of tribe their :names these And (were) they .(were) Israel the of sons heads of

4294 2753/1121 8202 8095 4294 2139/1121 8851
5 6 שַׁמּוּעַ בֶּן־זַכּוּר׃ לְמַטֵּה שִׁמְעוֹן שָׁפָט בֶּן־חוֹרִי׃ לְמַטֵּה
the of of tribe ;Hori the of son Shaphat ,Simeon the of of tribe ;Zaccur the of son Sham- mua

3127 1121 3008 3485 4294 3312 1121 3612 3063
7 יְהוּדָה כָּלֵב בֶּן־יְפֻנֶּה׃ לְמַטֵּה יִשָּׂשכָר יִגְאָל בֶּן־יוֹסֵף׃
;Joseph the of son Igal ,Issachar the of of tribe Jephun- ;neh the of son Caleb ,Judah

1121 6406 1144 4294 5126 1954 669 4294
8 9 לְמַטֵּה אֶפְרָיִם הוֹשֵׁעַ בִּן־נוּן׃ לְמַטֵּה בִנְיָמִן פַּלְטִי בֶּן
the of son Palti ,Benjamin the of of tribe ;Nun the of son Oshea ,Ephraim the of tribe

3127 4294 5476/1121 1426 2074 4294 7505
10 11 רָפוּא׃ לְמַטֵּה זְבוּלֻן גַּדִּיאֵל בֶּן־סוֹדִי׃ לְמַטֵּה יוֹסֵף
,Joseph the of of tribe ;Sodi the of son Gaddiel ,Zebulun the of of tribe ;Raphu

1582 1121 5988 1835 4294 5485 1121/1427 4519 4294
12 לְמַטֵּה מְנַשֶּׁה גַּדִּי בֶּן־סוּסִי׃ לְמַטֵּה דָן עַמִּיאֵל בֶּן־גְּמַלִּי׃
;Gemalli the of son Ammiel ,Dan the of of tribe ;Susi the of son Gaddi ,Manasseh the of of tribe

5147 5320 4294 4317/1121 5639 836 4294
13 14 לְמַטֵּה אָשֵׁר סְתוּר בֶּן־מִיכָאֵל׃ לְמַטֵּה נַפְתָּלִי נַחְבִּי
Nahbi ,Naphtali the of of tribe ;Michael the of son Sethur ,Asher the of of tribe

8034 428 4352/1121 1345 1410 4294 2058/1121
15 16 בֶּן־וָפְסִי׃ לְמַטֵּה גָד גְּאוּאֵל בֶּן־מָכִי׃ אֵלֶּה שְׁמוֹת
the of names These (were) .Machi the of son Geuel ,Gad the of of tribe ;Vophsi the of son

whom Moses sent to spy out the land. And Moses called Oshea the son of Nun, Joshua.

[17]And Moses sent them to spy out the land of Canaan, and said to them, You go up this *way* into the Negeb, and go up *into* the hills; [18]and you shall see the land, what it *is*, and the people who are living on it, whether it *is* strong or feeble; whether it *is* few or many; [19]and what the land *is* in which they live, whether good or bad; and what *are* the cities in which they live, whether in camps or in fortresses; [20]and what the land *is*, whether it is fat or lean; whether wood is in it or not. And you shall make yourselves strong and shall take of the fruit of the land. And *it was* the days of the first-ripe grapes.

[21]And they went up and spied out the land, from the wilderness of Zin to Rehob, at the entrance to Hamath. [22]And they went up into the Negeb, and came to Hebron. And Ahiman, Sheshai, and Talmai, the sons of Anak, *were* there. And Hebron had been built seven years before Zoan *in* Egypt. [23]And they came in to the valley of Eshcol, and cut down from there a branch and one cluster of grapes. And they carried it on a staff by two; also of the pomegranates, and of the figs. [24]That place was called the Torrent of Eshcol, because of the cluster which the sons of Israel cut from there.

[25]And they returned from spying out the land at the end of forty days. [26]And they traveled and came in to

7121 776 8446 4872 7921 582
הָאֲנָשִׁים אֲשֶׁר־שָׁלַח מֹשֶׁה לָתוּר אֶת־הָאָרֶץ וַיִּקְרָא
and the spy to Moses sent whom the
called ;land out men

8446 4872 7971 3091 5126/1121/1954 4872
17 מֹשֶׁה לְהוֹשֵׁעַ בִּן־נוּן יְהוֹשֻׁעַ׃ וַיִּשְׁלַח אֹתָם מֹשֶׁה לָתוּר
to Moses them And .Joshua ,Nun the ,Oshea Moses
search sent of son

5927 5045 2088 5927 559 3667 776
אֶת־אֶרֶץ כְּנָעַן וַיֹּאמֶר אֲלֵהֶם עֲלוּ זֶה בַּנֶּגֶב וַעֲלִיתֶם
go and the into this Go to said and ,Canaan the
up Negeb (way) up ,them of land

3427 5971 1961 776 7200 2022
18 אֶת־הָהָר׃ וּרְאִיתֶם אֶת־הָאָרֶץ מַה־הִוא וְאֶת־הָעָם הַיֹּשֵׁב
are who the and it what the see and the (into)
dwelling people ,(is) land ;hills

776 7227 4592 7504 2389
19 עָלֶיהָ הֶחָזָק הוּא הֲרָפֶה הַמְעַט הוּא אִם־רָב׃ וּמָה הָאָרֶץ
the and ;many or it whether whether it whether ,it on
land what (has) few ;weak ,(is) strong

5892 7451 2896 3427 834
אֲשֶׁר־הוּא יֹשֵׁב בָּהּ הֲטוֹבָה הִוא אִם־רָעָה וּמָה הֶעָרִים
the what and ;bad (is) it whether ,in are (they) (is)
cities (are) or good dwelling which

4013 4264 2009 3427 834
20 אֲשֶׁר־הוּא יוֹשֵׁב בָּהֵנָּה הַבְּמַחֲנִים אִם בְּמִבְצָרִים׃ וּמָה
and in or whether ,in are (they) which
what ;fortresses camps in dwelling

6086 3426 7330 8082 776
הָאָרֶץ הַשְּׁמֵנָה הִוא אִם־רָזָה הֲיֵשׁ־בָּהּ עֵץ אִם־אַיִן
;not or wood it in whether ,lean or (is) it whether land the
is there fat (is)

1061 3117 776 6529 3947 2388
וְהִתְחַזַּקְתֶּם וּלְקַחְתֶּם מִפְּרִי הָאָרֶץ וְהַיָּמִים יְמֵי בִּכּוּרֵי
first the the Now .land the of and strengthen and
ripe of days (were) days of fruit take yourselves

935 7690 5704 6798 4057 776 8446 5927 6025
21 עֲנָבִים׃ וַיַּעֲלוּ וַיָּתֻרוּ אֶת־הָאָרֶץ מִמִּדְבַּר־צִן עַד־רְחֹב לְבֹא
the to ,Rehob to Zin the from the and they And .grapes
of gate of wilderness ,land searched up went

8344 289 8033 2275 935 5045 5927 2574
22 חֲמָת׃ וַיַּעֲלוּ בַנֶּגֶב וַיָּבֹא עַד־חֶבְרוֹן וְשָׁם אֲחִימַן שֵׁשַׁי
,Sheshai ,Ahiman and ;Hebron to and the into they And Ha-
there (were) came ,Negeb up went .math

6814/6440 1129 8141 7651 2275 6061 3211 8526
וְתַלְמַי יְלִידֵי הָעֲנָק וְחֶבְרוֹן שֶׁבַע שָׁנִים נִבְנְתָה לִפְנֵי צֹעַן
Zoan before been had years seven And .Anak chil- the and
built Hebron of dren ,Talmai

2156 8033 3772 811 5158 935 4714
23 מִצְרָיִם׃ וַיָּבֹאוּ עַד־נַחַל אֶשְׁכֹּל וַיִּכְרְתוּ מִשָּׁם זְמוֹרָה
a from cut and ,Eshcol the to they And (in)
branch there down of valley came .Egypt

7416 1571 8147 4132 5375 259 6025 811
וְאֶשְׁכּוֹל עֲנָבִים אֶחָד וַיִּשָּׂאֻהוּ בַמּוֹט בִּשְׁנָיִם וּמִן־הָרִמֹּנִים
the of also ,two by a on they and ;one grapes and
,pomegranates staff it bore of cluster

182 812 3759 7121 4725 8384
24 וּמִן־הַתְּאֵנִים׃ לַמָּקוֹם הַהוּא קָרָא נַחַל אֶשְׁכּוֹל עַל אֹדוֹת
because ,Eshcol the (one) That place the and
of of valley called .figs of

8446 7725 3478 1121 8033 3772 811
25 הָאֶשְׁכּוֹל אֲשֶׁר־כָּרְתוּ מִשָּׁם בְּנֵי יִשְׂרָאֵל׃ וַיָּשֻׁבוּ מִתּוּר
from they And .Israel the from cut which the
searching returned of sons there off cluster

4872 935 3212 3117 703 7093 776
26 הָאָרֶץ מִקֵּץ אַרְבָּעִים יוֹם׃ וַיֵּלְכוּ וַיָּבֹאוּ אֶל־מֹשֶׁה וְאֶל
and Moses to and they And .days forty the at the
to came traveled of end land

Moses and to Aaron, and to
all the tabernacle of the
congregation of the sons of
Israel, to the wilderness of
Paran, to Kadesh. And they
brought them and all the
congregation word, and
showed them the fruit of
the land. 27 And they re-
ported to him and said, We
came to the land where you
sent us, and it surely does
flow with milk and honey;
and this is its fruit. 28 But the
people that live in the land
are fierce, and the cities are
fortified, very great. And
also we have seen the
children of Anak there.
29 Amalek lives in the
land of the Negeb, and the
Hittite, and the Jebusite,
and the Amorites live in the
hills. And the Canaanite is
living by the sea, and
beside the Jordan. 30 And
Caleb stilled the people
before Moses, and said, We
will certainly go up, and we
will seize it, for we are well
able *to do* it. 31 And the men
who had gone up with him
said, We are not able to go
up against the people, for it
is stronger than we. 32 And
they sent out an evil report
of the land which they had
spied out to the sons of
Israel, saying, The land into
which we traveled, to spy it
out, *is* a land eating up its
inhabitants. And all the
people we saw in its midst
were men of stature. 33 And
we saw the giants there, the
sons of Anak, of the giants.
And we were in our own
eyes as grasshoppers, and
so we were in their eyes.

אַהֲרֹן וְאֶל־כָּל־עֲדַת בְּנֵי־יִשְׂרָאֵל אֶל־מִדְבַּר פָּארָן קָדֵשָׁה
וַיָּשִׁבוּ אֹתָם דָּבָר וְאֶת־כָּל־הָעֵדָה וַיַּרְאוּם אֶת־פְּרִי הָאָרֶץ׃
27 וַיְסַפְּרוּ־לוֹ וַיֹּאמְרוּ בָּאנוּ אֶל־הָאָרֶץ אֲשֶׁר שְׁלַחְתָּנוּ וְגַם
28 זָבַת חָלָב וּדְבַשׁ הִוא וְזֶה־פִּרְיָהּ׃ אֶפֶס כִּי־עַז הָעָם הַיֹּשֵׁב
בָּאָרֶץ וְהֶעָרִים בְּצֻרוֹת גְּדֹלֹת מְאֹד וְגַם־יְלִדֵי הָעֲנָק רָאִינוּ
29 שָׁם׃ עֲמָלֵק יוֹשֵׁב בְּאֶרֶץ הַנֶּגֶב וְהַחִתִּי וְהַיְבוּסִי וְהָאֱמֹרִי
30 יוֹשֵׁב בָּהָר וְהַכְּנַעֲנִי יֹשֵׁב עַל־הַיָּם וְעַל יַד הַיַּרְדֵּן׃ וַיַּהַס
כָּלֵב אֶת־הָעָם אֶל־מֹשֶׁה וַיֹּאמֶר עָלֹה נַעֲלֶה וְיָרַשְׁנוּ אֹתָהּ
31 כִּי־יָכוֹל נוּכַל לָהּ׃ וְהָאֲנָשִׁים אֲשֶׁר־עָלוּ עִמּוֹ אָמְרוּ לֹא
32 נוּכַל לַעֲלוֹת אֶל־הָעָם כִּי־חָזָק הוּא מִמֶּנּוּ׃ וַיֹּצִיאוּ דִּבַּת
הָאָרֶץ אֲשֶׁר תָּרוּ אֹתָהּ אֶל־בְּנֵי יִשְׂרָאֵל לֵאמֹר הָאָרֶץ
אֲשֶׁר עָבַרְנוּ בָהּ לָתוּר אֹתָהּ אֶרֶץ אֹכֶלֶת יוֹשְׁבֶיהָ הִוא
33 וְכָל־הָעָם אֲשֶׁר־רָאִינוּ בְתוֹכָהּ אַנְשֵׁי מִדּוֹת׃ וְשָׁם רָאִינוּ
אֶת־הַנְּפִילִים בְּנֵי עֲנָק מִן־הַנְּפִלִים וַנְּהִי בְעֵינֵינוּ כַּחֲגָבִים
וְכֵן הָיִינוּ בְּעֵינֵיהֶם׃

CAP. XIV יד

CHAPTER 14

CHAPTER 14
1 And all the congregation
lifted up their voice and
cried; and the people wept
during that night. 2 And all
the sons of Israel

1 וַתִּשָּׂא כָּל־הָעֵדָה וַיִּתְּנוּ אֶת־קוֹלָם וַיִּבְכּוּ הָעָם בַּלַּיְלָה

murmured against Moses
and against Aaron. And
all the congregation said
to them, Oh that we had
died in the land of Egypt,
or in this wilderness; oh
that we had died! [3]And
why is Jehovah bringing
us into this land to fall by
the sword? Our wives and
our infants will be a prey.
Is it not good for us to
return to Egypt? [4]And they
said each to his brother,
Let us appoint a leader
and return to Egypt.
[5]And Moses and Aaron
fell on their faces before all
the assembly of the con-
gregation of the sons of
Israel. [6]And Joshua the
son of Nun, and Caleb the
son of Jephunneh, of those
who spied out the land, tore
their garments. [7]And they
spoke to all the congregation of the sons of Israel,
saying, The land into which
we traveled, to spy it out, *is*
an exceedingly good land.

[8]If Jehovah has delighted in
us, then He will bring us
into this land and will give it
to us, a land which is
flowing with milk and
honey. [9]Only, do not rebel
against Jehovah. And you,
do not fear the people of the
land, for they *are* our bread;
their defense has turned
away from them; and
Jehovah *is* with us; do not
be afraid of them. [10]And all
the congregation said to
stone them with stones.
And the glory of Jehovah
appeared in the tabernacle
of the congregation, to all
the sons of Israel.
[11]And Jehovah said to
Moses, How long will this
people despise Me? And
How long will they continue
not to believe in Me, for all
the signs which I have done
in its midst? [12]I shall strike

559 3478 1121 3605 175 4872 3885
2 ההוא׃ וילנו על־משה ועל־אהרן כל בני ישראל ויאמרו
said and ;Israel the all Aaron and Moses against and ;that
of sons against murmured

4057 176 4714 776 4191 3863 5712 3605
אלהם כל־העדה לו־מתנו בארץ מצרים או במדבר
in or ,Egypt the in had we Oh the all to
wilderness of land died that ,congregation them

2088 776 935 3068 4100 4191 3863
3 הזה לו־מתנו׃ ולמה יהוה מביא אתנו אל־הארץ הזאת
this land into us is Jehovah And had we Oh !this
bringing why !died that

7725 2896 3808 957 1961 2945 802 2719 5307
לנפל בחרב נשינו וטפנו יהיו לבז הלוא טוב לנו שוב
to for good it Is a will our and our the by to
return us not !prey become infants wives ?sword fall

7725 7218 5414 251 376 559 4714
4 מצרימה׃ ויאמרו איש אל־אחיו נתנה ראש ונשובה
and a us Let his to each they And ?Egypt to
return head appoint ,brother ,said

6951 3605/6440 6440 5921 175 4872 5307 4714
5 מצרימה׃ ויפל משה ואהרן על־פניהם לפני כל־קהל
the all before their on and Moses And .Egypt to
of assembly faces Aaron fell

3312/1121 3612 5126/1121/3091 3478 1121 5712
6 עדת בני ישראל׃ ויהושע בן־נון וכלב בן־יפנה מן־
of Jephun- the and Nun the And .Israel of sons the the
,neh of son Caleb of son Joshua of company

5712 3605 559 899 7167 776 8466
7 התרים את־הארץ קרעו בגדיהם׃ ויאמרו אל־כל־עדת
the all to they and their tore the who those
of company spoke ,garments land searched

8446 5674 834 776 559 3478 1121
בני־ישראל לאמר הארץ אשר עברנו בה לתור אתה
,it spy to ,in passed we which The ,saying ,Israel the
out through land of sons

935 3068 2654 3966 3966 776 2896
8 טובה הארץ מאד מאד׃ אם־חפץ בנו יהוה והביא
He then ,Jehovah us in has if exceed- very land a (is)
bring will delighted ;ingly good

2461/2100 834 776 5414 2088 776
אתנו אל־הארץ הזאת ונתנה לנו ארץ אשר־הוא זבת חלב
milk is which a to will and this land into us
with flowing land ,us it give

5971 3372 3808 4775 3808 3068 1706
9 ודבש׃ אך ביהוה אל־תמרדו ואתם אל־תיראו את־עם
the do not And do not against Only and
of people fear ,you !rebel Jehovah .honey

3068 6738/5493 3899 776
הארץ כי לחמנו הם סר צלם מעליהם ויהוה אתנו אל־
not with (is) and from their has they our for the
;us Jehovah ;them defense turned ;(are) bread ,land

3519 68 7275 5712 3605 559 3372
10 תיראם׃ ויאמרו כל־העדה לרגום אתם באבנים וכבוד
the and with them stone to the all said And fear do
of glory ;stones congregation .them

3478 1121 3605 4150 168 7200 3068
יהוה נראה באהל מועד אל־כל־בני ישראל׃
.Israel the all to meeting the in appeared Jeho-
of sons of tent vah

5704 2088 5971 5006 5704 4872 3068 559
11 ויאמר יהוה אל־משה עד־אנה ינאצני העם הזה ועד־
And ?this people will when Until ,Moses to Jehovah said And
until Me despise

7130 6213 834 226 3605 539 3808
אנה לא־יאמינו בי בכל האתות אשר עשיתי בקרבו׃
its in have I which the for in will they not when
?midst done signs all ,Me believe

it with pestilence and dispossess it. And I will make you a nation greater and mightier than it. 13And Moses said to Jehovah, And the Egyptians will hear. For You have brought up this people out of their midst with Your power. 14And they will say to the inhabitant of this land, They have heard that You, Jehovah, *are* in the midst of this people, who is seen eye with eye. You *are* Jehovah, and Your cloud stands over them; in a pillar of cloud You go before them by day, and in a pillar of fire by night. 15And will you execute this people as one man? Then the nations who have heard Your fame will speak, saying, 16Because Jehovah is not able to bring this people into the land which He swore to them, therefore He has slain them in the wilderness. 17And now, I beseech You, let the power of my Lord be great, as You have spoken, saying, 18Jehovah is slow to anger, and of great mercy, bearing away iniquity and transgression; and by no means will clear *the guilty*, visiting the iniquity of the fathers on the sons, on the third and on the fourth *generation*. 19I beseech You, forgive the iniquity of this people, according to the greatness of Your mercy, and as You have borne with this people from Egypt, even until now.

20And Jehovah said, I have forgiven according to your words; 21but as I live, all the earth shall be filled *with* the glory of Jehovah; 22for all the men who are seeing My glory, and My signs which I have done in Egypt and in the wilderness, and have tried Me these ten times, and have not listened to My voice,

12 אַכֶּנּוּ בַדֶּבֶר וְאוֹרִשֶׁנּוּ וְאֶעֱשֶׂה אֹתְךָ לְגוֹי־גָּדוֹל וְעָצוּם
13 מִמֶּנּוּ׃ וַיֹּאמֶר מֹשֶׁה אֶל־יְהוָה וְשָׁמְעוּ מִצְרַיִם כִּי־הֶעֱלִיתָ
14 בְכֹחֲךָ אֶת־הָעָם הַזֶּה מִקִּרְבּוֹ׃ וְאָמְרוּ אֶל־יוֹשֵׁב הָאָרֶץ
הַזֹּאת שָׁמְעוּ כִּי־אַתָּה יְהוָה בְּקֶרֶב הָעָם הַזֶּה אֲשֶׁר־עַיִן
בְּעַיִן נִרְאָה ׀ אַתָּה יְהוָה וַעֲנָנְךָ עֹמֵד עֲלֵהֶם וּבְעַמֻּד עָנָן
15 אַתָּה הֹלֵךְ לִפְנֵיהֶם יוֹמָם וּבְעַמּוּד אֵשׁ לָיְלָה׃ וְהֵמַתָּה
אֶת־הָעָם הַזֶּה כְּאִישׁ אֶחָד וְאָמְרוּ הַגּוֹיִם אֲשֶׁר־שָׁמְעוּ אֶת־
16 שִׁמְעֲךָ לֵאמֹר׃ מִבִּלְתִּי יְכֹלֶת יְהוָה לְהָבִיא אֶת־הָעָם
17 הַזֶּה אֶל־הָאָרֶץ אֲשֶׁר־נִשְׁבַּע לָהֶם וַיִּשְׁחָטֵם בַּמִּדְבָּר׃ וְעַתָּה
18 יִגְדַּל־נָא כֹּחַ אֲדֹנָי כַּאֲשֶׁר דִּבַּרְתָּ לֵאמֹר׃ יְהוָה אֶרֶךְ
אַפַּיִם וְרַב־חֶסֶד נֹשֵׂא עָוֹן וָפָשַׁע וְנַקֵּה לֹא יְנַקֶּה פֹּקֵד עֲוֹן
19 אָבוֹת עַל־בָּנִים עַל־שִׁלֵּשִׁים וְעַל־רִבֵּעִים׃ סְלַח־נָא לַעֲוֹן
הָעָם הַזֶּה כְּגֹדֶל חַסְדֶּךָ וְכַאֲשֶׁר נָשָׂאתָה לָעָם הַזֶּה מִמִּצְרַיִם
20
21 וְעַד־הֵנָּה׃ וַיֹּאמֶר יְהוָה סָלַחְתִּי כִּדְבָרֶךָ׃ וְאוּלָם חַי־אָנִי
22 וְיִמָּלֵא כְבוֹד־יְהוָה אֶת־כָּל־הָאָרֶץ׃ כִּי כָל־הָאֲנָשִׁים
הָרֹאִים אֶת־כְּבֹדִי וְאֶת־אֹתֹתַי אֲשֶׁר־עָשִׂיתִי בְמִצְרַיִם
וּבַמִּדְבָּר וַיְנַסּוּ אֹתִי זֶה עֶשֶׂר פְּעָמִים וְלֹא שָׁמְעוּ בְּקוֹלִי׃

23 they shall not see the land which I have sworn to their fathers. Yea, not one of those scorning Me shall see it. 24 And My servant Caleb, because there is another spirit in him, and he is fully following Me, I shall bring him into the land into which he has gone, and his seed shall possess it— 25 and the Amalekite and the Canaanite were living in the valley. Tomorrow turn and pull up *stakes* for yourselves; *going* into the wilderness, the way of the Red Sea.

26 And Jehovah spoke to Moses and to Aaron, saying, 27 How long shall I bear *with* this evil company who *are* murmuring against Me? I have heard the murmurings of the sons of Israel which they are murmuring against Me. 28 Say to them, *As* I live, says Jehovah, as surely as you have spoken in My ears, so I will do to you. 29 Your dead bodies shall fall in this wilderness, even all your numbered ones, as to your whole number, from twenty years old and upward, in that you have murmured against Me.

30 You shall certainly not come into the land which I lifted up My hand to cause you to live in it, except Caleb the son of Jephunneh and Joshua the son of Nun. 31 As for your infants, of whom you have said, They shall be a prey, I shall bring them in, and they shall know the land which you have rejected. 32 As for you, your carcases shall fall in this wilderness. 33 And your sons shall be shepherds in the wilderness forty years, and shall bear your fornications until your carcases are wasted in the wilderness; 34 by the number of the days in which you

5006 3605 1 7650 834 776 7200 518
23 אם־יראו את־הארץ אשר נשבעתי לאבתם וכל־מנאצי
those all and their to sworn have I which land the they not
Me despising ;fathers see shall

312 7351 1961 6118 3612 5650 7200 3808
24 לא יראוה׃ ועבדי כלב עקב היתה רוח אחרת עמו
with another spirit has there since ,Caleb My But .it see shall not
,him been servant

2233 935 834 776 935 310 4390
וימלא אחרי והביאתיו אל־הארץ אשר־בא שמה וזרעו
his and has he which land the into shall I following he and
seed ;entered him bring ,Me fully is

5265 6437 4279 6010 3427 3669 6003 3423
25 ירשנה׃ והעמלקי והכנעני יושב בעמק מחר פנו וסעו
and turn Tomorrow the in were the and the And shall
up pull .valley living Canaanite Amalekite .it possess

5488 3220 1870 4057
לכם המדברה דרך ים־סוף׃
.Reeds the way the the into you
of Sea of ,wilderness

5712 5704 559 175 4872 3068 1696
26 27 וידבר יהוה אל־משה ואל־אהרן לאמר׃ עד־מתי לעדה
company long How ,saying ,Aaron to and ,Moses to Jehovah And
bear I shall spoke

1121 3885 3885 2088 7451
הרעה הזאת אשר המה מלינים עלי את־תלנות בני
the murmurings The against murmuring (are) who this evil
of sons of ?Me

2416 559 8085 3885 834 3478
28 ישראל אשר המה מלינים עלי שמעתי׃ אמר אלהם חי־
As ,them to Say have I against murmuring they which ,Israel
live heard ,Me (are)

6213 241 1696 3808 / 518 3068 /5002
אני נאם־יהוה אם־לא כאשר דברתם באזני כן אעשה
do will I so My in have you as If ,Jehovah says ,I
ears spoken surely

3605 1121 6485 3605 6297 5307 4057
29 לכם׃ במדבר הזה יפלו פגריכם וכל־פקדיכם לכל־
to as counted your even dead your shall this in ;you to
whole ,ones all ,bodies fall wilderness

3885 4605 8141 6242 1121 4557
מספרכם מבן עשרים שנה ומעלה אשר הלינתם עלי׃
against have you that and years twenty from your
;Me murmured ,upward old ,number

7931 3027 5375 834 776 935 518
30 אם־אתם תבאו אל־הארץ אשר נשאתי את־ידי לשכן
cause to My lifted which land the into shall you certainly
live to hand up come not

2945 5126/1121/3091 3312/1121 3612 518 3588
31 אתכם בה כי אם־כלב בן־יפנה ויהושע בן־נון׃ וטפכם
for As .Nun the and Jephunneh the Caleb except ,it in you
infants your of son Joshua of son

776 3045 935 3068 957 559
אשר אמרתם לבז יהיה והביאתי אתם וידעו את־הארץ
land the they and ,them shall I They a ,said you of
know shall in bring be shall pray whom

2088 4057 5307 6297 3973 834
32 אשר מאסתם בה׃ ופגריכם אתם יפלו במדבר הזה׃
.this in shall for As your have you which
wilderness fall ,you carcases .rejected

5375 8141 703 4057 7467 1961 1121
33 ובניכם יהיו רעים במדבר ארבעים שנה ונשאו את־
shall and ,years forty the in shepherds shall your and
bear wilderness be sons

834 3117 4557 4057 6299 8552/5704 2184
34 זנותיכם עד־תם פגריכם במדבר׃ במספר הימים אשר־
in days the the by the in your are until your
which of number ;wilderness carcases wasted fornications

spied out the land, forty
days, a day for a year, a day
for a year; you shall bear
your iniquities forty years;
you shall know My alien-
ation *from you.* [35]I *am*
Jehovah; I have spoken. I
shall do this to all this evil
company who are gathered
together against Me; they
shall be brought to an end
in this wilderness, and
there they shall die.

[36]And the men whom
Moses had sent to spy out
the land, and who, when
they returned, made all the
congregation to murmur
against him, by bringing up
an evil report against the
land, [37]even those men
bringing up an evil report of
the land died by the plague
before Jehovah. [38]But
Joshua the son of Nun, and
Caleb the son of Jephun-
neh, remained alive of
those men that went to spy
out the land. [39]And Moses
told these words to all the
sons of Israel; and the
people mourned deeply.
[40]And they rose up early in
the morning and went up to
the top of the mountain,
saying, Behold, we are
here, and *we* will go up to
the place which Jehovah
has said, for we have
sinned. [41]And Moses said,
Why do you now trans-
gress the mouth of
Jehovah, since it will not
prosper? [42]Do not go up,
for Jehovah *is* not in your
midst. And shall you not
be defeated before your
enemies? [43]For the Amalekite and the Canaanite
are there before your face,
and you shall fall by the
sword, because you have
turned back from follow-
ing Jehovah, and Jehovah
is not with you. [44]And
they presumed to go up
to the top of the moun-
tain, but the ark of the
covenant of Jehovah
and Moses did not
leave the middle of the

8141 3117 8141 3117 3117 703 776 8446
תרתם את־הארץ ארבעים יום יום לשנה יום לשנה
;year a for day a a for day a ,year ,days forty ,land the spied you out

8569 3045 8141 703 5771 5375
תשאו את־עונתיכם ארבעים שנה וידעתם את־תנואתי:
alienation My ;(you from) shall you know ;years forty ,iniquities your shall you bear

35 7451 5712 3605 6213 2063 3808/518 1696 3068
אני יהוה דברתי אם־לא ׀ זאת אעשה לכל־העדה הרעה
evil company all to shall I do this ,surely have I spoken ;Jehovah I (am)

4191 8033 8552 4057 3259 2088
הזאת הנועדים עלי במדבר הזה יתמו ושם ימתו:
shall they .die and there shall they be ended this in wilderness against ;Me are who gathered this

36 7725 776 8446 4872 7971 582
והאנשים אשר־שלח משה לתור את־הארץ וישבו
they and returned —land the spy to out Moses sent had whom the And men

776 1681 3318 5712/3605 3885
וילונו עליו את־כל־העדה להוציא דבה על־הארץ:
the —land against evil an report by up bringing congre- gation the all against him made and murmur to

37 6440 5061 7451 776 1681 3318 582 4191
וימתו האנשים מוצאי דבת־הארץ רעה במגפה לפני
before the by plague evil an land the of report (who) brought men those died and

38 1992 582 2416 3312/1121 3612 5126/1121 3091 3068
יהוה: ויהושע בן־נון וכלב בן־יפנה חיו מן־האנשים ההם
those men out of lived of son the Jephunneh ,Caleb and ,Nun the of son Joshua But .Jehovah

39 1697 4872 1696 776 8446 3212
ההלכים לתור את־הארץ: וידבר משה את־הדברים
words Moses told And .land the to out spy went that

40 7925 3966 5971 56 3478 1121 3605 428
האלה אל־כל־בני ישראל ויתאבלו העם מאד: וישכמו
they And early rose ,deeply the people and mourned ;Israel of sons the all to these

4725 3212/2009 559 2022 7218 5927 1242
בבקר ויעלו אל־ראש־ההר לאמר הננו ועלינו אל־המקום
place the to will and go ,See here are we ,saying the top the mountain of to and went the in morning

41 4994/4100 4872 559 2398 3068 559 834
אשר־אמר יהוה כי חטאנו: ויאמר משה למה זה אתם
you now why ,Moses said And have we .sinned for ;Jehovah has said which

42 369/3588 5927/3808 6743 3808 3068 6310 5674
עברים את־פי יהוה והוא לא תצלח: אל־תעלו כי אין
is not for up Go not shall ?prosper not it since ,Jehovah the of mouth you do trangress

43 6003 341 6440 5061 7130 3068
יהוה בקרבכם ולא תנגפו לפני איביכם: כי העמלקי
the Amalekite For your .enemies before shall you be defeated and not your ;midst in Jehovah

7725 2719 5307 6440 8033 3669
והכנעני שם לפניכם ונפלתם בחרב כי־על־כן שבתם
have you back turned because the by ,sword you and fall shall before face your (are) there the and Canaanite

44 5927 6075 3068 3808 3068 310
מאחרי יהוה ולא־יהיה יהוה עמכם: ויעפלו לעלות אל־
to up go to they And presumed with .you Jehovah is not and ;Jehovah from following

7130 4185 3808 4872 3068 1285 127 2022 7218
ראש ההר וארון ברית־יהוה ומשה לא־משו מקרב
the from of midst did leave not and Moses Jehovah the of covenant the but of ark the ,mount the of top

camp. [45]And the Amalekite and the Canaanite who were living in that mountain came down and struck them, and beat them down, to Hormah.

5221 2022 3427 3669 6003 3381 4264
45 המחנה׃ וירד העמלקי והכנעני הישב בהר ההוא ויכום
and smote them, that mount in living were who the Canaanite and the Amalekite the came down And the camp.
2767 3807
ויכתום עד־החרמה׃
.Hormah to beat and down them

CAP. XV טו

CHAPTER 15

CHAPTER 15

[1]And Jehovah spoke to Moses, saying, [2]Speak to the sons of Israel and say to them, When you have come to the land of your dwellings, which I am giving to you, [3]then you shall prepare a fire offering to Jehovah, a burnt offering, or a sacrifice, in fulfillment of a vow, or as a free-will offering, or in your appointed seasons, to make a sweet fragrance to Jehovah, out of the herd, or out of the flock.

[4]And he who is bringing his offering to Jehovah shall bring near a food offering of flour, a tenth part, mixed with a fourth of a hin of oil; [5]and wine for a drink offering, a fourth of a hin you shall prepare for the burnt offering, or for a sacrifice, for the one lamb. [6]Or you shall prepare a food offering of flour for a ram, two tenth parts mixed with oil, a third of a hin; [7]and wine for a drink offering, a third part of a hin. You shall bring *it* near, a sweet fragrance to Jehovah. [8]And when you prepare a bullock for a burnt offering, or for a sacrifice, in fulfillment of a vow, or peace offerings to Jehovah, [9]then he shall bring near for the son of the herd a food offering of flour, three tenth parts, mixed with oil, a half of a hin; [10]and you shall bring wine near for a drink offering, a half of a hin, *as* a fire offering of soothing fragrance to Jehovah. [11]So it shall be done for one ox, or for the one ram, or for a lamb of the sheep, or of the

3478 1121 1696 559 4872 3068 1696
1 וידבר יהוה אל־משה לאמר׃ דבר אל־בני ישראל
2 .Israel of sons the to Speak ,saying ,Moses to Jehovah And spoke
834 4186 776 935 559
ואמרת אלהם כי תבאו אל־ארץ מושבתיכם אשר אני
I which your dwellings the of land to have you come When to them say and
6381 2077 5930 3068 801 6213 5414
3 נתן לכם׃ ועשיתם אשה ליהוה עלה או־זבח לפלא־
special for a sacrifice or a offering to Jehovah fire offering a you and prepare shall ;you to giving am
3068 5207 7381 6213 4150 176 5071 176 5088
נדר או בנדבה או במעדיכם לעשות ריח ניחח ליהוה
to Jehovah soothing fragrance a make to your feasts set in or free- will offering a as or a vow
3068 7133 7126 7121 6620 176 1241
4 מן־הבקר או מן־הצאן׃ והקריב המקריב קרבנו ליהוה
to Jehovah his offering is who bringing he shall near bring And the flock out of or the herd of out
3196 8081 1969 7243 1101 6241 5560 4503
5 מנחה סלת עשרון בלול ברבעית ההין שמן׃ ויין
and wine ;oil hin a of a fourth with mixed tenth a part ,flour food a of offering
3512 2077 176 5930 6213 1969 7243 5262
לנסך רביעית ההין תעשה על־העלה או לזבח לכבש
the for lamb a for ,sacrifice or burnt the for offering shall you prepare hin a fourth a of a for offering drink
1001 6241 8147 5560 4503 6213 352 176 259
6 האחד׃ או לאיל תעשה מנחה סלת שני עשרנים בלולה
mixed tenth parts two ,flour food a of offering shall you prepare for ram a Or .one
7126 1969 7992 5262 3196 1969 7992 8081
7 בשמן שלשית ההין׃ ויין לנסך שלשית ההין תקריב
shall you ,(it) bring hin a third a of part drink a for offering and wine ;hin a third a of with ,oil
2077 5930 1241/1121 6213 3068 5207 7381
8 ריח־ניחח ליהוה׃ וכי־תעשה בן־בקר עלה או־זבח
a for ,sacrifice or burnt a offering the of son a herd you prepare And when to Jehovah soothing a fragrance
1241/1121 7126 3068 8002 5088 6381
9 לפלא־נדר או־שלמים ליהוה׃ והקריב על־בן־הבקר
the herd the of son for he and bring shall ,Jehovah to peace offerings or a ,vow for special
1969 2677 8081 1101 6241 7969 5560 4503
מנחה סלת שלשה עשרנים בלול בשמן חצי ההין׃
;hin a half a of with ,oil mixed tenth parts three ,flour food a of offering
3068 5207/7381 801 1969 2677 5262 7126 3196
10 ויין תקריב לנסך חצי ההין אשה ריח־ניחח ליהוה׃
to Jehovah sooth- ing frag- rance a fire a of offering ,hin a half a of a for ,offering drink shall you bring and wine
7716 259 352 176 259 7794 6213
11 ככה יעשה לשור האחד או לאיל האחד או־לשה
the for animal flock or ,one the for ram or one the for ox shall it be done Thus

goats. [12]You shall prepare
according to the number.
So you shall do for everyone
according to their number.
[13]All that are home-born
shall do these things in this
way, in presenting an
offering made by fire, of a
soothung fragrance to
Jehovah. [14]And if an alien
lives with you, or whoever
may be among you,
throughout your genera-
tions, and desires to offer a
fire offering of a soothing
fragrance to Jehovah; as
you do, so he shall do. [15]*As
for* the congregation, there
shall be one statute both for
you and for the alien that
lives with you, a never-
ending statute throughout
your generations; as you
are, so shall the alien be
before Jehovah. [16]There
shall be one law and one
ordinance both for you and
for the alien that lives with
you.
[17]And Jehovah spoke to
Moses, saying, [18]Speak to
the sons of Israel and say to
them, When you come into
the land to which I bring
you, [19]then it shall be that
when you eat of the bread of
the land, you shall lift up a
heave offering to Jehovah.
[20]You shall lift up a cake of
the first of your dough *as* a
heave offering; as the of the
threshing-floor, so you shall
heave it. [21]You shall give of
the first of your dough to
Jehovah, a heave offering
for your generations.
[22]And when you shall err,
and not observe all these
commands which Jehovah
has spoken to Moses,
[23]even all that Jehovah has
commanded you by the
hand of Moses from the day
that Jehovah commanded,
and onward for your gene-
rations; [24]then it shall be,
if it be done in error by the
congregation, by ignorance,
even all the congregation
shall offer a son of the herd
for a burnt offering, for
soothing fragrance to

6213 3602 6213 4557 5795 176 3532
12 כַּכְּבָשִׂים אוֹ בָעִזִּים׃ כַּמִּסְפָּר אֲשֶׁר תַּעֲשׂוּ כָּכָה תַּעֲשׂוּ
shall you so shall you that the the of or ,sheep the of
do prepare number ;goats

428 3602 6213 249 4557 259
13 לָאֶחָד כְּמִסְפָּרָם׃ כָּל־הָאֶזְרָח יַעֲשֶׂה־כָּכָה אֶת־אֵלֶּה
these this in shall are that All to according every for
things way do homeborn number their one

176 1616 1481 3068 5207/7381 801 7126
14 לְהַקְרִיב אִשֵּׁה רֵיחַ־נִיחֹחַ לַיהוָה׃ וְכִי־יָגוּר אִתְּכֶם גֵּר אוֹ
or an with lives if And to soothing a fire a bringing in
alien you Jehovah fragrance of offering near

3068 5207/7381 801 6213 1755 854
אֲשֶׁר־בְּתוֹכְכֶם לְדֹרֹתֵיכֶם וְעָשָׂה אִשֵּׁה רֵיחַ־נִיחֹחַ לַיהוָה
to soothing a of fire a and your for be may whoever
Jehovah fragrance ,offering makes generations ,you among

2416 1616 259 2708 6951 6213 6213
15 כַּאֲשֶׁר תַּעֲשׂוּ כֵּן יַעֲשֶׂה׃ הַקָּהָל חֻקָּה אַחַת לָכֶם וְלַגֵּר הַגָּר
who for and for one statute the (for as) shall so ,do you as
lives alien the you ,assembly .do he

8451 3068 6440 1961 1616 1755 5769 2708
16 חֻקַּת עוֹלָם לְדֹרֹתֵיכֶם כָּכֶם כַּגֵּר יִהְיֶה לִפְנֵי יְהוָה׃ תּוֹרָה
law .Jehovah before shall the so you as your for never- a
be alien ,are ;generations ending statute

1481 16 16 1961 259 4941 259
אַחַת וּמִשְׁפָּט אֶחָד יִהְיֶה לָכֶם וְלַגֵּר הַגָּר אִתְּכֶם׃
with who for and for there one and One
.you lives alien the you be shall ordinance

3478 1121 1696 559 4872 3068 1696
17 וַיְדַבֵּר יְהוָה אֶל־מֹשֶׁה לֵּאמֹר׃ דַּבֵּר אֶל־בְּנֵי יִשְׂרָאֵל
18
Israel the to Speak ,saying ,Moses to Jehovah And
of sons spoke

935 834 776 935 559
וְאָמַרְתָּ אֲלֵהֶם בְּבֹאֲכֶם אֶל־הָאָרֶץ אֲשֶׁר אֲנִי מֵבִיא אֶתְכֶם
;you bring I to the into you When to say and
which land come ,them

8641 7311 776 3899 398 1961 8033
19 שָׁמָּה׃ וְהָיָה בַּאֲכָלְכֶם מִלֶּחֶם הָאָרֶץ תָּרִימוּ תְרוּמָה
heave a shall you the the of you when it then
offering up lift ,land of bread eat that be shall

8641 8641 7311 2471 6182 7225 3068
20 לַיהוָה׃ רֵאשִׁית עֲרִסֹתֵכֶם חַלָּה תָּרִימוּ תְרוּמָה כִּתְרוּמַת
heave the as heave- a shall you a your the Of to
of offering ;offering up lift cake ,dough of first .Jehovah

3068 5414 6182 7225 7311 3651 1637
21 גֹּרֶן כֵּן תָּרִימוּ אֹתָהּ׃ מֵרֵאשִׁית עֲרִסֹתֵיכֶם תִּתְּנוּ לַיהוָה
to shall you dough your first the Of .it shall you so the
Jehovah give of up lift floor

6213 3808 7686 1755 8641
22 תְּרוּמָה לְדֹרֹתֵיכֶם׃ וְכִי תִשְׁגּוּ וְלֹא תַעֲשׂוּ אֵת
shall and shall you And your for heave- a
observe not err when .generations offering

4872 3068 1696 834 428 4687 3605
23 כָּל־הַמִּצְוֹת הָאֵלֶּה אֲשֶׁר־דִּבֶּר יְהוָה אֶל־מֹשֶׁה׃ אֵת כָּל־
even ,Moses to Jehovah has which these commands all
all spoken

6680 3117 4872 3027 3068 6680
אֲשֶׁר צִוָּה יְהוָה אֲלֵיכֶם בְּיַד־מֹשֶׁה מִן־הַיּוֹם אֲשֶׁר צִוָּה
com- that the from Moses the by you Jehovah has that
manded day of hand commanded

6213 5712 7684 1961 1755 1973 3068
24 יְהוָה וָהָלְאָה לְדֹרֹתֵיכֶם׃ וְהָיָה אִם מֵעֵינֵי הָעֵדָה נֶעֶשְׂתָה
be it con- the of by if it then your for and ,Jehovah
done gregation ignorance be shall ;generations onward

7381 5930 259 1241/1121 6499 5712/3605 6213 7686
לִשְׁגָגָה וְעָשׂוּ כָל־הָעֵדָה פַּר בֶּן־בָּקָר אֶחָד לְעֹלָה לְרֵיחַ
a for a for one young bullock the all that ,error in
fragrance, offering burnt congregation offer shall

Jehovah, and its food
offering, and its drink offering, according to the
ordinance, and one kid of
the goats for a sin offering.
25 And the priest shall make
atonement for all the congregation of the sons of
Israel, and it shall be
forgiven them. For it *was* in
error, and they have
brought their offering, a fire
offering to Jehovah, and
their sin offering before
Jehovah, for their error.
26 And all the congregation
of the sons of Israel shall be
forgiven, and the alien that
lives among them; for as to
all the people, *it was* in
ignorance.
27 And if one person sins
through error, then he shall
offer a she-goat of the first
year for a sin offering.
28 And the priest shall make
atonement for the soul that
errs, when he sins through
error, before Jehovah, to
make atonement for him;
and he shall be forgiven,
29 both he that is home-born
among the sons of Israel,
and the alien that lives
among them; you shall have
one law for him that acts in
error. 30 And the soul that
does anything with a high
hand, whether home-born
or of the alien, the same
blasphemes Jehovah. And
that person shall be cut off
from the midst of his
people. 31 Because he has
despised the word of
Jehovah, and has broken
His commandment, that
soul shall utterly be cut off,
his iniquity shall be on him.

32 And while the sons of
Israel were in the wilderness, they found a man
gathering sticks on the
sabbath day. 33 And those
who found him gathering
sticks brought him to
Moses and Aaron, and to all
the congregation. 34 And
they put him under guard,
because it had not been
declared what should be
done to him. 35 And Jehovah
said to Moses, The man

shall surely be put to death; all the congregation shall stone him with stones outside the camp. [36]And all the congregation brought him outside the camp and stoned him with stones, and he died, as Jehovah commanded Moses.

[37]And Jehovah spoke to Moses, saying, [38]Speak to the sons of Israel and you shall tell them that they shall make themselves fringes on the corners of their garments for their generations, and they shall put with the fringe of each corner a thread of blue. [39]And it shall be to you for a fringe, that you may look upon it, and remember all the commandments of Jehovah, and do them; and that you do not go about after your own heart and your own eyes, after which you usually go astray; [40]that you may remember and do all My commandments, and be holy to your God. [41]I *am* Jehovah your God, who brought you out of the land of Egypt, to be your God; I *am* Jehovah your God.

2351 5712 3605 68 7275 376 4191 1961
מוֹת יוּמַת הָאִישׁ רָגוֹם אֹתוֹ בָאֲבָנִים כָּל־הָעֵדָה מִחוּץ
outside con- the all with him shall the Surely shall
gregation stones stone ;man executed be

7275 4264 2351 5712 3605 3318 4264
36 לַמַּחֲנֶה׃ וַיֹּצִיאוּ אֹתוֹ כָּל־הָעֵדָה אֶל־מִחוּץ לַמַּחֲנֶה וַיִּרְגְּמוּ
and the outside con- the all him And .camp the
stoned camp gregation brought

4872 3068 6680 4191 68
אֹתוֹ בָּאֲבָנִים וַיָּמֹת כַּאֲשֶׁר צִוָּה יְהוָה אֶת־מֹשֶׁה׃
.Moses Jehovah com- as he and with him
manded ,died stones

3478 1121 1696 559 4872 3068 559
37 וַיֹּאמֶר יְהוָה אֶל־מֹשֶׁה לֵּאמֹר׃ דַּבֵּר אֶל־בְּנֵי יִשְׂרָאֵל
38
,Israel the to Speak ,saying ,Moses to Jehovah And
of sons spoke

1755 899 3671 6734 6213 559
וְאָמַרְתָּ אֲלֵהֶם וְעָשׂוּ לָהֶם צִיצִת עַל־כַּנְפֵי בִגְדֵיהֶם לְדֹרֹתָם
their for their the on fringes them- they that them you and
;generations garments of corners selves make shall tell shall

6734 1961 8541 6616 3671 6734 5414
39 וְנָתְנוּ עַל־צִיצִת הַכָּנָף פְּתִיל תְּכֵלֶת׃ וְהָיָה לָכֶם לְצִיצִת
a for to it And .blue thread a each the on they and
;fringe you be shall of corner of fringe put shall

6213 3068 4687 3605 2142 7200
וּרְאִיתֶם אֹתוֹ וּזְכַרְתֶּם אֶת־כָּל־מִצְוֹת יְהוָה וַעֲשִׂיתֶם אֹתָם
;them do and ,Jehovah the all and upon you that
of commands remember it look may

834 5869 3824 310 8446 3808
וְלֹא־תָתוּרוּ אַחֲרֵי לְבַבְכֶם וְאַחֲרֵי עֵינֵיכֶם אֲשֶׁר־אַתֶּם
you which own your and own your after shall you and
,eyes heart follow not

4687 3605 6213 2142 2181
40 זֹנִים אַחֲרֵיהֶם׃ לְמַעַן תִּזְכְּרוּ וַעֲשִׂיתֶם אֶת־כָּל־מִצְוֹתָי
My all do and may you that ;after go
,commands remember astray

430 3068 430 6918 1961
41 וִהְיִיתֶם קְדֹשִׁים לֵאלֹהֵיכֶם׃ אֲנִי יְהוָה אֱלֹהֵיכֶם אֲשֶׁר
who ,God your Jehovah I your to holy be and
(am) ;God

430 1961 4714 776 3318
הוֹצֵאתִי אֶתְכֶם מֵאֶרֶץ מִצְרַיִם לִהְיוֹת לָכֶם לֵאלֹהִים אֲנִי
I ;God your be to ,Egypt of out you brought
(am) of land the

430 3068
יְהוָה אֱלֹהֵיכֶם׃
.God your Jehovah

CAP. XVI טז

CHAPTER 16

CHAPTER 16

[1]And Korah, the son of Izhar, the son of Kohath, the son of Levi, took both Dathan and Abiram, the sons of Eliab, and On, the son of Peleth, the sons of Reuben; [2]and they rose up before Moses, with certain of the sons of Israel, two hundred and fifty rulers of the congregation, elect men of the assembly, men of name. [3]And they were assembled against Moses and against Aaron, and said

1121 48 1885 3881/1121 6955/1121 3324/1121 7141 3947
1 וַיִּקַּח קֹרַח בֶּן־יִצְהָר בֶּן־קְהָת בֶּן־לֵוִי וְדָתָן וַאֲבִירָם בְּנֵי
the and both ,Levi the ,Kohath the ,Izhar the ,Korah And
of sons ,Abiram Dathan of son of son of son took

4872 6440 6965 7205 1121 6451/1121 203 446
2 אֱלִיאָב וְאוֹן בֶּן־פֶּלֶת בְּנֵי רְאוּבֵן׃ וַיָּקֻמוּ לִפְנֵי מֹשֶׁה
,Moses before they and ;Reuben the ,Peleth the and ,Eliab
arose of sons of sons ;On

5712 5387 3967 2572 3478 1121 582
וַאֲנָשִׁים מִבְּנֵי־יִשְׂרָאֵל חֲמִשִּׁים וּמָאתָיִם נְשִׂיאֵי עֵדָה
the leaders two and fifty ,Israel the of with
,company of hundred of sons certain

175 4872 6950 8034/582 4150 7148
3 קְרִאֵי מוֹעֵד אַנְשֵׁי־שֵׁם׃ וַיִּקָּהֲלוּ עַל־מֹשֶׁה וְעַל־אַהֲרֹן
,Aaron and Moses against they And .name of men the elect
against assembled ,company of men

to them, You *take* too much! For all the congregation, all of them *are* holy, and Jehovah is among them. Why then do you lift up yourselves above the assembly of Jehovah?

[4]And Moses heard and fell on his face. [5]And he spoke to Korah, and to all his company, saying, In the morning Jehovah will show who are His, and him who is holy, and shall cause him to come near Him; even him whom He may choose He will cause to come near to Him. [6]Do this: take censers for yourselves, Korah, and all his company, [7]and put fire in them, and put incense on them before Jehovah tomorrow; and it shall be, the men whom Jehovah chooses, he shall be the holy one. You *take* too much, sons of Levi! [8]And Moses said to Korah, Hear now, you sons of Levi, [9]is it but a small thing to you that the God of Israel has separated you from the congregation of Israel to bring you near to Himself, to do the service of the tabernacle of Jehovah, and to stand before the congregation to minister to them? [10]Yea, He has brought you near, and all your brothers, the sons of Levi, with you. And will you seek the priesthood also? [11]Therefore, you and all your company that have gathered together against Jehovah: What is Aaron that you murmur against him?

[12]And Moses sent to call for Dathan and for Abiram, the sons of Eliab; and they said, We will not come up. [13]Is it a small thing that you have brought us up out of a land flowing with milk and honey, to kill us in the wilderness, but must you also certainly seize dominion over us? [14]Yea, you have not brought us into a land flowing with milk and honey, nor given

ויאמרו אלהם רב־לכם כי כל־העדה כלם קדשים
(are) holy of all them the congregation all for You (take)! too much to ,them said and

4 ובתוכם יהוה ומדוע תתנשאו על־קהל יהוה׃ וישמע
And heard ?Jehovah the of assembly above lift you do yourselves Why then ;Jehovah is and them among

5 משה ויפל על־פניו׃ וידבר אל־קרח ואל־כל־עדתו
his ,company all to and Korah to he and spoke his ,face on and fell Moses

לאמר בקר וידע יהוה את־אשר־לו ואת־הקדוש והקריב
shall and near him draw who him ,holy is and ,His are who Jehovah will show the In morning ,saying

6 אליו ואת אשר יבחר־בו יקריב אליו׃ זאת עשו קחו־
take ;Do this .Him to he will draw him may He choose whom even ;Him

7 לכם מחתות קרח וכל־עדתו׃ ותנו בהן ׀ אש ושימו
put and ,fire in them put and his ;company and all Korah ,censers for you

עליהן ׀ קטרת לפני יהוה מחר והיה האיש אשר־יבחר
chooses whom the man it and be shall ;tomorrow Jehovah be- fore incense on them

8 יהוה הוא הקדוש רב־לכם בני לוי׃ ויאמר משה אל־
to Moses And said !Levi sons of You (take) much too the be shall one holy he ,Jehovah

9 קרח שמעו־נא בני לוי׃ המעט מכם כי־הבדיל אלהי
the of God has separated that you to it is little too ,Levi you of sons ,now ,Hear ,Korah

ישראל אתכם מעדת ישראל להקריב אתכם אליו לעבד
do to to Himself you bring to near ,Israel the from of company you Israel

את־עבדת משכן יהוה ולעמד לפני העדה לשרתם׃
minister to ?them the congregation to before to and stand ,Jehovah the of tabernacle service the of

10 ויקרב אתך ואת־כל־אחיך בני־לוי אתך ובקשתם גם־
also you will seek And with ,you Levi the of sons your brothers all and ,you has He drawn ,Yea

11 כהנה׃ לכן אתה וכל־עדתך הנעדים על־יהוה ואהרן
and Aaron ;Jehovah against have that gathered your company and all you ,So priest- the ?hood

12 מה־הוא כי תלונו עליו׃ וישלח משה לקרא לדתן
for Dathan call to Moses sent And against ?him you murmur that ,he what (is)

13 ולאבירם בני אליאב ויאמרו לא נעלה׃ המעט כי
that it is little too will We ;come not they and said ;Eliab the of sons for and ,Abiram

העליתנו מארץ זבת חלב ודבש להמיתנו במדבר כי־
but the in ,wilderness us kill to and ,honey milk flowing with of out and a have you us brought

14 תשתרר עלינו גם־השתרר׃ אף לא אל־ארץ זבת חלב
milk flowing with land a into not ,Yea ?certainly also us over seize you dominion

us inheritance in fields and vineyards; will you put out the eyes of these men? We will not come up! [15]And Moses was very angry, and said to Jehovah, Do not respect their offering; I have not taken one ass from them, nor have I hurt one of them. [16]And Moses said to Korah, You and all your company, you be there before Jehovah, you and they, and Aaron, tomorrow.

[17]And each one take his censer, and you shall put incense on them, and shall offer before Jehovah, each his censer, two hundred and fifty censers; even you and Aaron, each his censer. [18]And they each took his censer, and put fire on them, and lay incense on them, and they stood at the door of the tabernacle of the congregation, with Moses and Aaron. [19]And Korah assembled all the congregation against them, to the door of the tabernacle of the congregation, and the glory of Jehovah was seen by all the congregation.

[20]And Jehovah spoke to Moses and to Aaron, saying, [21]Separate yourselves from the midst of this company, and I will consume them in a moment. [22]And they fell on their faces, and said, O God, God of the spirits of all flesh; shall one man sin, and will You be angry with all the congregation?

[23]And Jehovah spoke to Moses, saying, [24]Speak to the congregation, saying, You get away from around the tent of Korah, Dathan, and Abiram. [25]And Moses rose up and went to Dathan

ודבש הביאתנו ותתן-לנו נחלת שדה וכרם העיני
the Will of eyes · and vineyards · fields · inheritance of · us · nor given · have you us brought · and honey

15 האנשים ההם תנקר לא נעלה: ויחר למשה מאד
very · Moses · was angry And · will We up come · not · put you out? · these · men

ויאמר אל-יהוה אל-תפן אל-מנחתם לא חמור אחד
one · ass · not · their offering; · Do respect · not · Jehovah · to · said and

16 מהם נשאתי ולא הרעתי את-אחד מהם: ויאמר משה
Moses · said And · them of · one · I have treated badly · nor · have I taken · from them

אל-קרח אתה וכל-עדתך היו לפני יהוה אתה והם
and they · you · Jehovah · before · be you there · your all company · and · You · Korah · to

17 ואהרן מחר: וקחו איש מחתתו ונתתם עליהם קטרת
incense · them on · you and put shall · his censer · each one · and take · tomorrow; · and Aaron

והקרבתם לפני יהוה איש מחתתו חמשים ומאתים
two and hundred · fifty · his censer · each · Jehovah · before · shall and offer

18 מחתת ואתה ואהרן איש מחתתו: ויקחו איש מחתתו
his censer · each · they And took · his censer · each · and Aaron · and you · censers;

ויתנו עליהם אש וישימו עליהם קטרת ויעמדו פתח
the at of door · they and stood · incense; · them on · lay and · fire · them on · and put

19 אהל מועד ומשה ואהרן: ויקהל עליהם קרח את-כל
all · Korah · against them · And assembled · Aaron · and · Moses with · meeting · of tent the

העדה אל-פתח אהל מועד וירא כבוד-יהוה אל-כל
all · by · Jehovah · the of glory · was and seen · meeting · the of tent · the of door · to · the congregation

20 העדה: ס וידבר יהוה אל-משה ואל-אהרן לאמר:
saying · Aaron · and to · Moses · to · Jehovah · And spoke · the congregation

21 22 הבדלו מתוך העדה הזאת ואכלה אתם כרגע: ויפלו
they And fell · a in moment · them · I and consume will · this · congregation · from among · Separate yourselves

על-פניהם ויאמרו אל אלהי הרוחת לכל-בשר האיש
shall man · flesh; · all of · the spirits · of God · O God · said and · their faces · on

23 אחד יחטא ועל כל-העדה תקצף: ס וידבר יהוה
Jehovah · And spoke · You will be angry? · the congregation · all · and with · sin · one

24 אל-משה לאמר: דבר אל-העדה לאמר העלו מסביב
from around · Get you away · saying · the congregation · to · Speak · saying · Moses · to

25 למשכן-קרח דתן ואבירם: ויקם משה וילך אל-
to · and went · Moses · rose And · and Abiram · Dathan · Korah · the of tent

and Abiram, and the elders of Israel went after him. 26 And he spoke to the congregation, saying, Please turn away from the tents of these wicked men and do not touch anything that they have, lest you be consumed in all their sins. 27 And they went away from around the tent of Korah, Dathan and Abiram. And Dathan and Abiram came out, standing at the door of their tents, and their wives, their sons, and their infants. 28 And Moses said, by this you shall know that Jehovah has sent me to do all these works, *and* that not from my own heart. 29 If these die according to the death of all men, and the visitionat of all men is visited upon them, Jehovah has not sent me.

30 And if Jehovah makes a new thing, and the ground opens her mouth and swallows them, and all that they have, and they go down alive to Sheol, then you shall know that these men have despised Jehovah. 31 And it happened, as he made an end of speaking all these words, that the ground which was under them split apart, 32 and the earth opened her mouth and swallowed them, and their houses, and all the men who *were* for Korah, and all their possessions. 33 And they went down, they and all that they had, alive to Sheol, and the earth closed over them; and they perished from the midst of the assembly. 34 And all Israel who *were* around them fled at their cry; for they said, Lest the earth swallow us up.

1696 3478 2205 310 5927 48 1885
26 דָּתָן וַאֲבִירָם וַיֵּלְכוּ אַחֲרָיו זִקְנֵי יִשְׂרָאֵל׃ וַיְדַבֵּר אֶל־
to he And .Israel the after and and Dathan
spoke of elders him went ;Abiram

7563 582 168 4994 5493 559 5712
הָעֵדָה לֵאמֹר סוּרוּ נָא מֵעַל אָהֳלֵי הָאֲנָשִׁים הָרְשָׁעִים
wicked men the from Please turn ,saying con- the
of tents away ,gregation

3605 5595 6435/1992 834 3605 5060
הָאֵלֶּה וְאַל־תִּגְּעוּ בְּכָל־אֲשֶׁר לָהֶם פֶּן־תִּסָּפוּ בְּכָל־
all in be you lest they that anything do not and ,these
consumed have touch

5439 48 1885 7141 4908 5927 2403
27 חַטֹּאתָם׃ וַיֵּעָלוּ מֵעַל מִשְׁכַּן־קֹרַח דָּתָן וַאֲבִירָם מִסָּבִיב
;around and ,Dathan ,Korah the from they And .sins their
Abiram of tent away went

802 168 6607 5324 5927 48 1885
וְדָתָן וַאֲבִירָם יָצְאוּ נִצָּבִים פֶּתַח אָהֳלֵיהֶם וּנְשֵׁיהֶם
their and ,tents their the at standing came and and
,wives of door out Abiram Dathan

7971 3068 3045 4872 559 2995 1121
28 וּבְנֵיהֶם וְטַפָּם׃ וַיֹּאמֶר מֹשֶׁה בְּזֹאת תֵּדְעוּן כִּי־יְהוָה שְׁלָחַנִי
sent has Jehovah that shall you by ,Moses said And their and their and
me know this ,infants ,sons

4194 3820 3808 4639 3605 6213
29 לַעֲשׂוֹת אֵת כָּל־הַמַּעֲשִׂים הָאֵלֶּה כִּי־לֹא מִלִּבִּי׃ אִם־כְּמוֹת
the like If my from not (and) ,these works all do to
of death heart own that

5921 6485 120 3605 6486 428 4191 120 3605
כָּל־הָאָדָם יְמֻתוּן אֵלֶּה וּפְקֻדַּת כָּל־הָאָדָם יִפָּקֵד עֲלֵיהֶם
upon is men all the and these die men all
,them visited of visitation

6475 3068 1254 1278 7971 3068 3808
30 לֹא יְהוָה שְׁלָחָנִי׃ וְאִם־בְּרִיאָה יִבְרָא יְהוָה וּפָצְתָה
opens and ,Jehovah creates new a if But sent has Jehovah
thing .me not

3381 1992 3605 1104 6310 127
הָאֲדָמָה אֶת־פִּיהָ וּבָלְעָה אֹתָם וְאֶת־כָּל־אֲשֶׁר לָהֶם וְיָרְדוּ
and they that all and ,them and mouth her ground the
go they ,have swallows

428 582 5006 3045 7585 2416
חַיִּים שְׁאֹלָה וִידַעְתֶּם כִּי נִאֲצוּ הָאֲנָשִׁים הָאֵלֶּה אֶת־
these men have that you then ;Sheol to alive
despised know shall

1234 428 1697 3605 1696 3615 1961 3068
31 יְהוָה׃ וַיְהִי כְּכַלֹּתוֹ לְדַבֵּר אֵת כָּל־הַדְּבָרִים הָאֵלֶּה וַתִּבָּקַע
that ,these words all speaking he as it And .Jehovah
apart split finished ,was

1104 6310 776 6605 8478 834 127
32 הָאֲדָמָה אֲשֶׁר תַּחְתֵּיהֶם׃ וַתִּפְתַּח הָאָרֶץ אֶת־פִּיהָ וַתִּבְלַע
and ,mouth its the and ,them under which the
swallowed earth opened (was) ground

3605 7141 834 120 3605 1004
אֹתָם וְאֶת־בָּתֵּיהֶם וְאֵת כָּל־הָאָדָם אֲשֶׁר לְקֹרַח וְאֵת כָּל־
all and for who men the all and their and ;them
.Korah (were) ,houses

3680 7585 2416 1992 834/3605 3381 7339
33 הָרְכוּשׁ׃ וַיֵּרְדוּ הֵם וְכָל־אֲשֶׁר לָהֶם חַיִּים שְׁאֹלָה וַתְּכַס
and ;Sheol to alive they all and they they And their
covered ,had ,sank property

3478 3605 6951 8432 6 776
34 עֲלֵיהֶם הָאָרֶץ וַיֹּאבְדוּ מִתּוֹךְ הַקָּהָל׃ וְכָל־יִשְׂרָאֵל אֲשֶׁר
who Israel all And the from they and the over
(were) .assembly among perished ;earth them

776 1104 559 6963 5127 5439
סְבִיבֹתֵיהֶם נָסוּ לְקֹלָם כִּי אָמְרוּ פֶּן־תִּבְלָעֵנוּ הָאָרֶץ׃
the swallow lest they for their at fled around
.earth up us ,said ;cry them

[35]And fire came forth from Jehovah and consumed the two hundred and fifty men that offered the incense.

376 3967 2572 398 3068 5927 784
35 ואש יצאה מאת יהוה ותאכל את החמשים ומאתים איש
men | two and hundred | fifty the | and consumed | ,Jehovah | from | came forth | And fire
7004 7126
מקריבי הקטרת׃
the .incense | that offered

CAP. XVII ז׳

CHAPTER 17

[36]And Jehovah spoke to Moses, saying, [37]Speak to Eleazar, the son of Aaron, the priest, and he shall lift up the censers from the midst of the burning, and shall scatter the fire yonder, for they have become holy, [38]the firepans of these sinners against their own souls. And they shall make of them spread-out plates, a covering for the altar, for they have brought them before Jehovah, and they are holy. And they shall become a sign to the sons of Israel. [39]And Eleazar the priest took the bronze firepans which the those burning had brought near, and they spread them out, a covering for the altar; [40]a memorial to the sons of Israel, so that an alien who *is* not of the seed of Aaron shall not draw near to offer incense before Jehovah,a And shall not be as Korah and as his company, as Jehovah spoken to him by the hand of Moses.

[41]And all the congregation of the sons of Israel murmured on the next day against Moses and against Aaron, saying, You have killed the people of Jehovah. [42]And it happened, as the company was assembled against Moses and against Aaron, that they turned toward the tabernacle of the congregation. And, behold, the cloud had covered it, and the glory of Jehovah appeared! [43]And Moses and Aaron came to the front of the tabernacle of the congregation. [44]And

175/1121 499 559 559 4872 3068 1696
1 וידבר יהוה אל־משה לאמר׃ אמר אל־אלעזר בן־אהרן
,Aaron the of son | ,Eleazar | to | Speak | ,saying | ,Moses | to | Jehovah | And spoke
2219 784 8316 946 4289 7311 3548
2 הכהן וירם את־המחתת מבין השרפה ואת־האש זרה־
scatter | fire the | and | ,burning the | of out | censers the | he that lift | the ,priest
5315 2400 4289 6942 1973
3 הלאה כי קדשו׃ את מחתות החטאים האלה בנפשתם
their against souls own | these | sinners | firepans the of | are they ;holy | for | ;yonder
6440 7126 4196 6826 6341 7555 6213
ועשו אתם רקעי פחים צפוי למזבח כי־הקריבם לפני־
before | they them brought | for | the for ,altar | a covering | ,plates | beaten | of them | they And make shall
499 3947 3478 1121 226 1961 6942 3068
4 יהוה ויקדשו ויהיו לאות לבני ישראל׃ ויקח אלעזר
Eleazar | took And | .Israel | the to of sons | sign a | they and be shall | they and ;holy are | ;Jehovah
8313 7126 834 5178 4289 3548
הכהן את מחתות הנחשת אשר הקריבו השרפים
were who they ,burned | had brought | which | ,bronze | firepans the | the priest
4616 3478 1121 2146 4196 6826 7554
5 וירקעום צפוי למזבח׃ זכרון לבני ישראל למען אשר
that so | ;Israel | the to of sons | a as memorial | the for ,altar | a (into) cover | they and them beat
6999 175 2233 3808 2114 376 7126
לא־יקרב איש זר אשר לא מזרע אהרן הוא להקטיר
offer to | ,(is) | Aaron | the of of seed | not | who | an alien | man | shall near draw | not
1696 5712 7141 1961 3808 3068 6440 7004
קטרת לפני יהוה ולא־יהיה כקרח וכעדתו כאשר דבר
had spoken | as | as and ,company his | as ,Korah | shall be | and not | ;Jehovah | before | incense
4872 3027 3068
יהוה ביד־משה לו׃
to .him | Moses | the by of hand | Jehovah
175 4872 4283 3478 1121 5712 3605 3885
6 וילנו כל־עדת בני־ישראל ממחרת על־משה ועל־אהרן
,Aaron | and against | Moses against | the on ,day next | Israel | sons the of | the of company | all | And murmured
5712 6950 1961 3068 5971 4191 559
7 לאמר אתם המתם את־עם יהוה׃ ויהי בהקהל העדה
the company | was as assembled | it And ,was | .Jehovah | the of people | have killed | You | ,saying
3680 2009 4150 168 6437 175 4872
על־משה ועל־אהרן ויפנו אל־אהל מועד והנה כסהו
had it covered | ,and ,behold | ;meeting | the toward of tent | that turned they | ,Aaron | and against | Moses against
168 6440 175 4872 935 3068 3519 7200 6051
8 הענן וירא כבוד יהוה׃ ויבא משה ואהרן אל־פני אהל
the of tent | the of front | to | and Aaron | Moses | And came | !Jehovah | the of glory | and appeared | the ,cloud

Jehovah spoke to Moses, saying, [45]Get away from the midst of this company, and I shall consume them in a moment; and they fell on their faces. [46]And Moses said to Aaron, Take the censer, and put fire on it from the altar, and lay on incense, and go, hurry to the congregation, and make atonement for them, for the wrath has gone out from the presence of Jehovah; the plague has begun. [47]And Aaron did as Moses had spoken, and ran into the midst of the assembly. And, behold, the plague had begun among the people! And he laid on the incense and made atonement for the people, [48]and stood between the dead and the living, and the plague was stayed. [49]And those who died by the plague were fourteen thousand and seven hundred, besides those who died for the matter of Korah. [50]And Aaron turned back to Moses, to the door of the tabernacle of the congregation; and the plague was stayed.

8432 7426 559 4872 3068 1696 4150
9 מוֹעֵד׃ ס וַיְדַבֵּר יְהוָה אֶל־מֹשֶׁה לֵּאמֹר׃ הֵרֹמּוּ מִתּוֹךְ
10 the from up Rise ,saying ,Moses to Jehovah And .meeting
of midst spoke

559 6440 5921 5307 7281 3615 5712
11 הָעֵדָה הַזֹּאת וַאֲכַלֶּה אֹתָם כְּרָגַע וַיִּפְּלוּ עַל־פְּנֵיהֶם׃ וַיֹּאמֶר
said And their on they and a in them shall I and ,this congre-
.faces fell ;moment consume gation

5921 784 5414 4289 3947 175 4872
מֹשֶׁה אֶל־אַהֲרֹן קַח אֶת־הַמַּחְתָּה וְתֶן־עָלֶיהָ אֵשׁ מֵעַל
from fire it on and the Take ,Aaron to Moses
put ,censer

3722 5712 4120 3212 7004 7760 4196
הַמִּזְבֵּחַ וְשִׂים קְטֹרֶת וְהוֹלֵךְ מְהֵרָה אֶל־הָעֵדָה וְכַפֵּר
and the to hurry ,go and ,incense and ,altar the
atone ,congregation on lay

3947 5063 2490 3068 6440 7110 5927/3588
12 עֲלֵיהֶם כִּי־יָצָא הַקֶּצֶף מִלִּפְנֵי יְהוָה הֵחֵל הַנָּגֶף׃ וַיִּקַּח
did And the has ;Jehovah from the has for for
.plague begun wrath out gone ;them

2490 2009 6951 8432 7323/4872 1696 175
אַהֲרֹן כַּאֲשֶׁר דִּבֶּר מֹשֶׁה וַיָּרָץ אֶל־תּוֹךְ הַקָּהָל וְהִנֵּה הֵחֵל
had and the midst the into and ,Moses had as Aaron
begun ,behold ;assembly of ran 7004 spoken

5975 5971 3722 5414 5971 5063
13 הַנֶּגֶף בָּעָם וַיִּתֵּן אֶת־הַקְּטֹרֶת וַיְכַפֵּר עַל־הָעָם׃ וַיַּעֲמֹד
he And the for and incense the he And the in the
stood .people atoned on laid !people plague

4191 1061 4046 6113 2416 4191 996
14 בֵּין־הַמֵּתִים וּבֵין הַחַיִּים וַתֵּעָצַר הַמַּגֵּפָה׃ וַיִּהְיוּ הַמֵּתִים
who those And .plague the was and the and the between
died were stayed ,living dead

4191 3967 7651 505 6240 704 4046
בַּמַּגֵּפָה אַרְבָּעָה עָשָׂר אֶלֶף וּשְׁבַע מֵאוֹת מִלְּבַד הַמֵּתִים
who those besides ,hundred and thousand fourteen the by
died seven plague

168 6607 4872 175 7725 7141 1697
15 עַל־דְּבַר־קֹרַח׃ וַיָּשָׁב אַהֲרֹן אֶל־מֹשֶׁה אֶל־פֶּתַח אֹהֶל
the the to ,Moses to Aaron And .Korah the for
of tent of door back turned of matter

4046 6113 4150
מוֹעֵד וְהַמַּגֵּפָה נֶעֱצָרָה׃
was the and ;meeting
.stayed plague

CHAPTER 17

[1]And Jehovah spoke to Moses, saying, [2]Speak to the sons of Israel, and take from each of them a rod, for a father's house, from all their rulers, for the house of their fathers, twelve rods. You shall write the name of each on his rod. [3]And you shall write Aaron's name on the tribe of Levi; for one rod shall be for the head of their fathers' house. [4]And you shall place them in the tabernacle of the congregation, before the testimony, where I shall meet with you. [5]And it shall be that the man's rod which I

3478 1121 1696 559 4872 3068 1696
16 וַיְדַבֵּר יְהוָה אֶל־מֹשֶׁה לֵּאמֹר׃ דַּבֵּר ׀ אֶל־בְּנֵי יִשְׂרָאֵל
17 ,Israel the to Speak ,saying ,Moses to Jehovah And
of sons spoke

5387 3605 1 1004 4294 4294 259 3947
וְקַח מֵאִתָּם מַטֶּה מַטֶּה לְבֵית אָב מֵאֵת כָּל־נְשִׂיאֵהֶם
their all from the for rod a ,rod a each from and
,rulers ,fathers' house them of take

5921 5189 8034 376 4294 6240 8147 1 1004
לְבֵית אֲבֹתָם שְׁנֵים עָשָׂר מַטּוֹת אִישׁ אֶת־שְׁמוֹ תִּכְתֹּב עַל־
on shall you the each ;rods twelve their the for
write of name fathers of house

259 4294 3881 4294 3789 175 8034 4294
18 מַטֵּהוּ׃ וְאֵת שֵׁם אַהֲרֹן תִּכְתֹּב עַל־מַטֵּה לֵוִי כִּי מַטֶּה אֶחָד
one rod for ;Levi the on you Aaron's name And his
of rod write shall rod

5715 6440 4150 168 3240 1 1004 7218
19 לְרֹאשׁ בֵּית אֲבוֹתָם׃ וְהִנַּחְתָּם בְּאֹהֶל מוֹעֵד לִפְנֵי הָעֵדוּת
the before meeting the in you And their house for is
,testimony of tent them place shall .father's of head the

977 834 376 1961 8033 3259
20 אֲשֶׁר אִוָּעֵד לָכֶם שָׁמָּה׃ וְהָיָה הָאִישׁ אֲשֶׁר אֶבְחַר־בּוֹ
which which the it And .there ,you shall I where
choose I man's be shall meet

choose shall blossom. And I shall cause the murmurings of the sons of Israel, which they are murmuring against you, to cease from Me. [6]And Moses spoke to the sons of Israel, and all their rulers gave to him one rod for each ruler, one rod for a ruler, for their fathers' house, twelve rods, and the rod of Aaron *was* among the rods.

[7]And Moses placed the rods before Jehovah, in the the tabernacle of the testimony. [8]And it happened on the next day, Moses went into the tabernacle of the testimony, and, behold! The rod of Aaron for the house of Levi had budded, and put forth buds, and bloomed blossoms, and bore ripe almonds. [9]And Moses brought out all the rods from before Jehovah to all the sons of Israel. And they looked, and each one took his rod.

[10]And Jehovah said to Moses, Put back the rod of Aaron, before the testimony, to be kept as a token to the sons of rebellion. And you shall take their murmurings off Me; and they shall not die. [11]And Moses did as Jehovah had commanded him; so he did.
[12]And the sons of Israel spoke to Moses, saying, Behold, we die, we perish, we all perish. [13]Anyone who draws near to the tabernacle of Jehovah shall die; shall we be consumed to die?

834 3478 1121 8519 7918 6524 4294
מטהו יפרח והשכתי מעלי את־תלנות בני ישראל אשר
which ,Israel the murmurings the from shall I and shall rod
of sons of Me stop ;bloom

5414 3478 1121 4872 1696 3885
21 הם מלינם עליכם׃ וידבר משה אל־בני ישראל ויתנו
and ,Israel the to Moses And against are they
gave of sons spoke .you murmuring

259 5387 4294 259 5387 4294 5387 3605
אליו כל־נשיאיהם מטה לנשיא אחד מטה לנשיא אחד
,one a for rod ,one each for rod rulers their all to
ruler ruler him

4294 8432 175 4294 4294 6240 8147 1 1004
לבית אבתם שנים עשר מטות ומטה אהרן בתוך מטותם׃
.rods the among Aaron the and ;rods twelve their for
(was) of rod ;father's house

1961 5715 168 3068 6440 4294 4872 3240
22 וינח משה את־המטת לפני יהוה באהל העדת׃
23 ויהי
it and the the in Jehovah before rods the Moses And
.was ;testimony of tent placed

4294 6524 2009 5715 168 4872 935 4283
ממחרת ויבא משה אל־אהל העדות והנה פרח מטה
rod had ,and the the into Moses that next the on
budded ,behold ;testimony of tent went ,day

3318 8247 1580 6731 6692 6525 3318 3881 1004 175
24 אהרן לבית לוי ויצא פרח ויצץ ציץ ויגמל שקדים׃ ויצא
And ripe and a and buds it and ,Levi the for Aaron's
bore .almonds bore flower bloomed out put of house

3478 1121 3605 3068 6440 4294 3605 4872
משה את־כל־המטת מלפני יהוה אל־כל־בני ישראל
;Israel the all to Jehovah from the all Moses
of sons before rods

4294 376 3947 7200
ויראו ויקחו איש מטהו׃
.rod his each and they and
one took ,looked

5715 6440 175 4294 7725 4872 3068 559
25 ויאמר יהוה אל־משה השב את־מטה אהרן לפני העדות
the before ,Aaron of rod the Put ,Moses to Jehovah And
,testimony back said

3808 8519 3615 4805 1121 226 4931
למשמרת לאות לבני־מרי ותכל תלונתם מעלי ולא
and from their you and rebel- the to a as kept be to
not ,Me murmurings end shall ;ion of sons token

6213 3651 3068 6680 4872 6213 4191
26 ימתו׃ ויעש משה כאשר צוה יהוה אתו כן עשה׃
.did he so ;him Jehovah charged as Moses And shall they
did .die

3605 6 1478 559 4872 3478 1121 559
27 ויאמרו בני ישראל אל־משה לאמר הן גוענו אבדנו כלנו
all we we ,See ,saying ,Moses to Israel the And
,perish die of sons spoke

4191 3068 4908 7131 3605 6
28 אבדנו׃ כל הקרב הקרב אל־משכן יהוה ימות האם
Shall shall Jehovah the to draws who any we
.die of tabernacle near one ;perish

1478 8552
תמנו לגוע׃
?die to be we
consumed

CAP. XVIII. יח

CHAPTER 18

CHAPTER 18
[1]And Jehovah said to Aaron, You, and your sons, and your father's house with you shall bear the

5375 1 1004 1121 175 3068 559
1 ויאמר יהוה אל־אהרן אתה ובניך ובית־אביך אתך תשאו
shall with your and and You ,Aaron to Jehovah And
bear ,you father's house ,sons your said

iniquity of the sanctuary. And you, and your sons with you, shall bear the iniquity of your priesthood; [2]and also your brothers, the tribe of Levi, the tribe of your father, you shall bring near with you, that they may be joined to you and may minister to you, you and your sons in your being before the tabernacle of the testimony. [3]And they shall keep your charge and the charge of all the tabernacle; only, they shall not go near to the vessels of the sanctuary and to the altar. And they shall not die, either they or you. [4]And they shall be joined to you, and shall keep the charge of the tabernacle of the congregation, for all the service of the tabernacle, and a stranger shall not go near to you. [5]And you shall keep the charge of the sanctuary, and the charge of the altar, and there shall be no more wrath against the sons of Israel. [6]And I, behold, I have taken your brothers the Levites from the midst of the sons of Israel; as a gift they are given to you by Jehovah, to do the service of the tabernacle of the congregation. [7]And you, and your sons with you, shall keep your priesthood, in everything that pertains to the altar, and to that inside the veil. And you shall serve; I have given you the priesthood as a service of gift; and the stranger who comes near shall be put to death.

[8]And Jehovah spoke to Aaron, *saying,* And I, behold, I have given to you the charge of My heave offerings, of all the dedicated things of the sons of Israel. I have given them to you for the anointing, and to your sons, by a never-ending statute. [9]This shall be yours of the most holy things, from the fire: every offering of theirs, even every food offering of theirs, and every sin offering of theirs, and every guilt

3550 5771 5375 1121 4720 5771
אֶת־עֲוֹן הַמִּקְדָּשׁ וְאַתָּה וּבָנֶיךָ אִתָּךְ תִּשְׂאוּ אֶת־עֲוֹן כְּהֻנַּתְכֶם׃
your iniquity the shall with and And the the
.priesthood of bear you sons your you .sanctuary of iniquity

3867 7126 1 7626 3881 4294 251 1571
2 וְגַם אֶת־אַחֶיךָ מַטֵּה לֵוִי שֵׁבֶט אָבִיךָ הַקְרֵב אִתָּךְ וְיִלָּווּ
they and with shall you your the ,Levi the your And
join shall ,you bring ,father of tribe of tribe brothers also

5715 168 6440 1121 8334
עָלֶיךָ וִישָׁרְתוּךָ וְאַתָּה וּבָנֶיךָ אִתָּךְ לִפְנֵי אֹהֶל הָעֵדֻת׃
the the before with your and you and you
.testimony of tent ,you sons ,you to minister

6944 3627 168 3605 4931 4931 8104
3 וְשָׁמְרוּ מִשְׁמַרְתְּךָ וּמִשְׁמֶרֶת כָּל־הָאֹהֶל אַךְ אֶל־כְּלֵי הַקֹּדֶשׁ
the the to ,only the all the and your they And
sanctuary of vessels ;tent of charge charge keep shall

3867 4191 7126 3808 4196
4 וְאֶל־הַמִּזְבֵּחַ לֹא יִקְרָבוּ וְלֹא־יָמֻתוּ גַּם־הֵם גַּם־אַתֶּם׃ וְנִלְווּ
they And .you or they either they that shall they not ,altar the and
join shall ,die not near go to

168 5656 3605 4150 168 4931 8104
עָלֶיךָ וְשָׁמְרוּ אֶת־מִשְׁמֶרֶת אֹהֶל מוֹעֵד לְכֹל עֲבֹדַת הָאֹהֶל
the the all for meeting the charge the shall and ,you
;tent of service of tent of keep

6944 4931 8104 7126 2114
5 וְזָר לֹא־יִקְרַב אֲלֵיכֶם׃ וּשְׁמַרְתֶּם אֵת מִשְׁמֶרֶת הַקֹּדֶשׁ
the charge the you And .you to go shall not a and
,sanctuary of keep shall near stranger

3478 1121 7110/5750/1961 3808 4196 4931
וְאֵת מִשְׁמֶרֶת הַמִּזְבֵּחַ וְלֹא־יִהְיֶה עוֹד קֶצֶף עַל־בְּנֵי יִשְׂרָאֵל׃
.Israel the against wrath more there and ,altar the charge the and
of sons be shall no of

3478 1121 8436 3881 251 3947 2009
6 וַאֲנִי הִנֵּה לָקַחְתִּי אֶת־אֲחֵיכֶם הַלְוִיִּם מִתּוֹךְ בְּנֵי יִשְׂרָאֵל
;Israel the from the your have I ,behold And
of sons among Levites brothers taken ,I

4150 168 5656 5647 3068 5414 4979
לָכֶם מַתָּנָה נְתֻנִים לַיהוָה לַעֲבֹד אֶת־עֲבֹדַת אֹהֶל מוֹעֵד׃
.meeting the service the do to by are they a as to
of tent of ,Jehovah given gift you

4196 1697 3605 3550 8104 1121
7 וְאַתָּה וּבָנֶיךָ אִתְּךָ תִּשְׁמְרוּ אֶת־כְּהֻנַּתְכֶם לְכָל־דְּבַר הַמִּזְבֵּחַ
the of thing in your shall with and you And
,altar every ,priesthood keep ,you sons your

3550 5414 4979 5647 5656 6530 1004
וּלְמִבֵּית לַפָּרֹכֶת וַעֲבַדְתֶּם עֲבֹדַת מַתָּנָה אֶתֵּן אֶת־כְּהֻנַּתְכֶם
your have I gift a as you and ;veil the that to and
;priesthood given of service ;serve shall inside

4191 7131 2114
וְהַזָּר הַקָּרֵב יוּמָת׃
be shall coming the and
.executed near stranger

4931 5414 2009 175 3068 1696
8 וַיְדַבֵּר יְהוָה אֶל־אַהֲרֹן וַאֲנִי הִנֵּה נָתַתִּי לְךָ אֶת־מִשְׁמֶרֶת
charge the you have I ,behold ,And ,Aaron to Jehovah And
of given I spoke

4888 5414 3478 1121 6944 3605 8641
תְּרוּמֹתָי לְכָל־קָדְשֵׁי בְנֵי־יִשְׂרָאֵל לְךָ נְתַתִּים לְמָשְׁחָה
the for have I you to ;Israel the the all of heave My
,anointing them given of sons of things devoted ,offerings

6944 6944 1961 2088 5769 2706 1121
9 וּלְבָנֶיךָ לְחָק־עוֹלָם׃ זֶה יִהְיֶה לְךָ מִקֹּדֶשׁ הַקֳּדָשִׁים מִן
from most the of yours shall This never- a by to and
,things holy be .ending statute sons your

3605 2403 3605 4503 3605 7133 3605 784
הָאֵשׁ כָּל־קָרְבָּנָם לְכָל־מִנְחָתָם וּלְכָל־חַטָּאתָם וּלְכָל־
all and their all and their all even offering every the
,offering sin ,food-offering ;theirs of ,fire

offering of theirs which they may give back to Me; it *shall be* most holy to you and to your sons.
[10]You shall eat it in the holy of holies; every male shall eat it; it shall be holy to you. [11]And this is yours, the heave offering of their gift, with all the waver offerings of the sons of Israel. I have given them to you, and to your sons, and to your daughters with you, by a never-ending statute; every clean one in your house shall eat it. [12]All the best of the oil, and all the best of the new wine, and wheat, the firstfruits of them which they give to Jehovah, I have given to you. [13]The firstfruits of all that *is* in their land, which they bring in to Jehovah shall be yours; every clean one in your house shall eat it; [14]every devoted thing in Israel shall be yours; [15]every one opening a womb of all flesh which they offer to Jehovah, among man and among animal, shall be yours. Only, you shall certainly redeem the firstborn of man, and you shall redeem the firstling of the unclean beasts. [16]And their redeemed ones, from a month old, you shall redeem with your valuation, of silver, five shekels, by the shekel of the sanctuary; it *is* twenty gerahs. [17]But the firstling of a cow, or the firstling of a sheep, or the firstling of a goat, you shall not redeem; they *are* holy. You shall sprinkle their blood on the altar, and you shall burn their fat as incense, a fire offering of soothing fragrance to Jehovah. [18]And their flesh shall be yours, as the breast of the wave offering, and as the right leg; it shall be yours. [19]All the heave offerings of the holy things which the sons of Israel shall lift up to Jehovah, I have given to you and to

1121 6944 6944 7725 834 816
אֲשָׁמָם אֲשֶׁר יָשִׁיבוּ לִי קֹדֶשׁ קָדָשִׁים לְךָ הוּא וּלְבָנֶיךָ׃
to and (shall) it to most holy ;Me to may they which guilt their
.sons your (be) you back give ,offering

1961 6944 398 2145 3605 398 6944
10 בְּקֹדֶשׁ הַקֳּדָשִׁים תֹּאכְלֶנּוּ כָּל־זָכָר יֹאכַל אֹתוֹ קֹדֶשׁ יִהְיֶה־
shall it holy ;it shall male every shall you most the In
be eat ;it eat holy

3478 1121 8641 3605 4976 8641 2088
11 לָּךְ׃ וְזֶה־לְּךָ תְּרוּמַת מַתָּנָם לְכָל־תְּנוּפֹת בְּנֵי יִשְׂרָאֵל לְךָ
to ;Israel the wave the with their heave the is And to
you of sons of offerings all ,gift of offering ;yours this .you

2889 3605 5769 2756 1323 1121 5414
נְתַתִּים וּלְבָנֶיךָ וְלִבְנֹתֶיךָ אִתְּךָ לְחָק־עוֹלָם כָּל־טָהוֹר
clean every never- a by with to and to and given have I
one ;ending statute ,you daughters your ,sons your ,them

8492 2459 3605 3323 2459 3605 398 1004
12 בְּבֵיתְךָ יֹאכַל אֹתוֹ׃ כֹּל חֵלֶב יִצְהָר וְכָל־חֵלֶב תִּירוֹשׁ
the the all and ,oil the the All .it shall your in
,wine of best of best eat house

3605 1061 5414 3068 5414 834 7225 1715
13 וְדָגָן רֵאשִׁיתָם אֲשֶׁר־יִתְּנוּ לַיהוָה לְךָ נְתַתִּים׃ בִּכּוּרֵי כָּל־
All first-the have I to to they which their and
of fruits .given you ,Jehovah give firstfruits ,wheat

2889 3605 1961 3068 935 834 776
אֲשֶׁר בְּאַרְצָם אֲשֶׁר־יָבִיאוּ לַיהוָה לְךָ יִהְיֶה כָּל־טָהוֹר
clean every shall yours to they which their in that
one ;be ,Jehovah bring ,land (is)

6363 3605 1961 3478 2764 3605 398 1004
14 בְּבֵיתְךָ יֹאכְלֶנּוּ׃ כָּל־חֵרֶם בְּיִשְׂרָאֵל לְךָ יִהְיֶה׃ כָּל־פֶּטֶר
15
opening Every shall yours Israel in devoted Every shall your in
one be thing it eat house

929 120 3068 7126 834 1320 3605 7358
רֶחֶם לְכָל־בָּשָׂר אֲשֶׁר־יַקְרִיבוּ לַיהוָה בָּאָדָם וּבַבְּהֵמָה
among and among to offer they which flesh all of the
,animal ,men ,Jehovah womb

1060 120 1060 6299 2931 389 1961
יִהְיֶה־לָּךְ אַךְ ׀ פָּדֹה תִפְדֶּה אֵת בְּכוֹר הָאָדָם וְאֵת בְּכוֹר־
the and ,man the surely shall you ,only ;yours shall
of firstling of firstborn redeem be

6299 2320 1121 6299 6299 2931 929
16 הַבְּהֵמָה הַטְּמֵאָה תִּפְדֶּה׃ וּפְדוּיָו מִבֶּן־חֹדֶשׁ תִּפְדֶּה
shall you a of son a their And shall you unclean beasts the
redeem month redeemed .redeem

6242 6944 8255 8255 2568 3701 6187
בְּעֶרְכְּךָ כֶּסֶף חֲמֵשֶׁת שְׁקָלִים בְּשֶׁקֶל הַקֹּדֶשׁ עֶשְׂרִים
twenty the the by ,shekels five of your with
sanctuary of shekel ,silver ,valuation

5795/1060 3775 1060 176 7794 1060 389 1626
17 גֵּרָה הוּא׃ אַךְ בְּכוֹר־שׁוֹר אוֹ בְכוֹר כֶּשֶׂב אוֹ־בְכוֹר עֵז
a the or ,sheep a the or ,cow a the But .(is) it gerahs
,goat of firstling of firstling of firstling

4196 2236 1818 6944 6299 3808
לֹא תִפְדֶּה קֹדֶשׁ הֵם אֶת־דָּמָם תִּזְרֹק עַל־הַמִּזְבֵּחַ וְאֶת־
and ,altar the on shall you blood their ;they holy shall you not
sprinkle (are) ;redeem

1961 1320 3068 5207 7381 801 6999 2459
18 חֶלְבָּם תַּקְטִיר אִשֶּׁה לְרֵיחַ נִיחֹחַ לַיהוָה׃ וּבְשָׂרָם יִהְיֶה־
shall their And to soothing a fire a as burn fat their
be flesh ,Jehovah fragrance, offering ,incense

8641 3605 1961 3225 7785 8573 2373
19 לָּךְ כַּחֲזֵה הַתְּנוּפָה וּכְשׁוֹק הַיָּמִין לְךָ יִהְיֶה׃ כֹּל תְּרוּמֹת
heave the All shall it yours the as and wave the the as ,yours
of offerings .be ;right leg ,offering of breast

1121 5414 3068 3478 1121 7311 834 6944
הַקֳּדָשִׁים אֲשֶׁר יָרִימוּ בְנֵי־יִשְׂרָאֵל לַיהוָה נָתַתִּי לְךָ וּלְבָנֶיךָ
to and to have I to Israel the lift shall which holy the
,sons your you given ,Jehovah of sons up things

your sons, and to your
daughters with you, by a
never-ending statute, a
covenant of salt, it *shall be*
forever before Jehovah to
you and to your seed with
you.
20 And Jehovah said to
Aaron, You shall have no
inheritance in their land,
nor shall you have any
portion among them; I am
your portion and your
inheritance among the sons
of Israel. 21 And, behold, I
have given all the tithe in
Israel to the sons of Levi for
an inheritance, in return for
their service which they are
serving, the service of the
tabernacle of the congre-
gation. 22 And the sons of
Israel shall not come near to
the tabernacle of the
congregation any more, lest
they bear sin, and die. 23 But
the Levites shall do the
service of the tabernacle of
the congregation, and they
shall bear their iniquity; it
shall be a never-ending
statute throughout your
generations, that in the
midst of the sons of Israel
they shall have no inheritance; 24 but the tithes of
the sons of Israel which
they shall lift up to Jehovah,
a heave offering, I have
given to the Levites for
inheritance; therefore I
have said to them, They
shall have no inheritance
among the sons of Israel.

ולבנתיך אתך לחק־עולם ברית מלח עולם הוא לפני
20 יהוה לך ולזרעך אתך׃ ויאמר יהוה אל־אהרן בארצם
לא תנחל וחלק לא־יהיה לך בתוכם אני חלקך
21 ונחלתך בתוך בני ישראל׃ ס ולבני לוי הנה נתתי
כל־מעשר בישראל לנחלה חלף עבדתם אשר־הם
22 עבדים את־עבדת אהל מועד׃ ולא־יקרבו עוד בני
23 ישראל אל־אהל מועד לשאת חטא למות׃ ועבד הלוי
הוא את־עבדת אהל מועד והם ישאו עונם חקת עולם
24 לדרתיכם ובתוך בני ישראל לא ינחלו נחלה׃ כי את־
מעשר בני־ישראל אשר ירימו ליהוה תרומה נתתי
ללוים לנחלה על־כן אמרתי להם בתוך בני ישראל
לא ינחלו נחלה׃

25 And Jehovah spoke to
Moses, saying, 26 And you
shall say to the Levites; and
you shall speak to them,
When you take the tithe
from the sons of Israel,
which I have given to you
from them, for your inheritance, then you shall offer
from it a heave offering of
Jehovah, a tithe of the
tithe. 27 And your heave
offering shall be counted to
you as grain from the
threshing-floor, and as fullness from the wine-press.
28 So you also shall lift up the
heave offering of Jehovah

25 וידבר יהוה אל־משה לאמר׃ ואל־הלוים תדבר ואמרת
26 אלהם כי־תקחו מאת בני־ישראל את־המעשר אשר
נתתי לכם מאתם בנחלתכם והרמתם ממנו תרומת
27 יהוה מעשר מן־המעשר׃ ונחשב לכם תרומתכם כדגן
28 מן־הגרן וכמלאה מן־היקב׃ כן תרימו גם־אתם תרומת

from all your tithes which
you receive from the sons of
Israel. And you shall give
from it the heave offering of
Jehovah to Aaron the
priest. [29]You shall lift up
the whole heave offering of
Jehovah out of all your gifts,
out of all its fat, its hallowed
part, out of it. [30]And you
shall say to them, When
you lift up its fat out of it,
then it shall be counted to
the Levites as increase of a
threshing-floor, and as
increase of a wine-press.
[31]And you shall eat it in
every place, you and your
households, for it *is* your
reward in return for your
service in the tabernacle of
the congregation. [32]And
you shall bear no sin
because of it, since you
have set apart from it the
best of it. And you shall not
profane the holy things of
the sons of Israel, so that
you may not die.

יְהוָה מִכֹּל מַעְשְׂרֹתֵיכֶם אֲשֶׁר תִּקְחוּ מֵאֵת בְּנֵי יִשְׂרָאֵל
29 וּנְתַתֶּם מִמֶּנּוּ אֶת־תְּרוּמַת יְהוָה לְאַהֲרֹן הַכֹּהֵן׃ מִכֹּל
מַתְּנֹתֵיכֶם תָּרִימוּ אֵת כָּל־תְּרוּמַת יְהוָה מִכָּל־חֶלְבּוֹ אֶת־
30 מִקְדְּשׁוֹ מִמֶּנּוּ׃ וְאָמַרְתָּ אֲלֵהֶם בַּהֲרִימְכֶם אֶת־חֶלְבּוֹ
מִמֶּנּוּ וְנֶחְשַׁב לַלְוִיִּם כִּתְבוּאַת גֹּרֶן וְכִתְבוּאַת יָקֶב׃
31 וַאֲכַלְתֶּם אֹתוֹ בְּכָל־מָקוֹם אַתֶּם וּבֵיתְכֶם כִּי־שָׂכָר הוּא
32 לָכֶם חֵלֶף עֲבֹדַתְכֶם בְּאֹהֶל מוֹעֵד׃ וְלֹא־תִשְׂאוּ עָלָיו
חֵטְא בַּהֲרִימְכֶם אֶת־חֶלְבּוֹ מִמֶּנּוּ וְאֶת־קָדְשֵׁי בְנֵי־יִשְׂרָאֵל
לֹא תְחַלְּלוּ וְלֹא תָמוּתוּ׃

CAP. XIX ט

CHAPTER 19

CHAPTER 19
[1]And Jehovah spoke to
Moses and to Aaron, say-
ing, [2]This *is* the statute of
the law which Jehovah has
commanded, saying, Speak
to the sons of Israel, that
they bring you a red heifer, a
perfect one, in which there
is no blemish, on which no
yoke ever came. [3]And you
shall give her to Eleazar the
priest, and she shall be
brought forth outside the
camp; and she shall be
slaughtered before his face.
[4]And Eleazar the priest shall
take of her blood with his
finger, and shall sprinkle of
her blood toward the front of
the tabernacle of the congregation seven times. [5]And
the heifer shall be burned
before his eyes; her skin,

1 וַיְדַבֵּר יְהוָה אֶל־מֹשֶׁה וְאֶל־אַהֲרֹן לֵאמֹר׃ זֹאת חֻקַּת
2 הַתּוֹרָה אֲשֶׁר־צִוָּה יְהוָה לֵאמֹר דַּבֵּר ׀ אֶל־בְּנֵי יִשְׂרָאֵל
וְיִקְחוּ אֵלֶיךָ פָרָה אֲדֻמָּה תְּמִימָה אֲשֶׁר אֵין־בָּהּ מוּם
3 אֲשֶׁר לֹא־עָלָה עָלֶיהָ עֹל׃ וּנְתַתֶּם אֹתָהּ אֶל־אֶלְעָזָר הַכֹּהֵן
4 וְהוֹצִיא אֹתָהּ אֶל־מִחוּץ לַמַּחֲנֶה וְשָׁחַט אֹתָהּ לְפָנָיו׃ וְלָקַח
אֶלְעָזָר הַכֹּהֵן מִדָּמָהּ בְּאֶצְבָּעוֹ וְהִזָּה אֶל־נֹכַח פְּנֵי אֹהֶל־
5 מוֹעֵד מִדָּמָהּ שֶׁבַע פְּעָמִים׃ וְשָׂרַף אֶת־הַפָּרָה לְעֵינָיו

and her flesh, and her blood with her dung, shall be burned. 6 And the priest shall take cedar wood, and hyssop and scarlet, and shall cast it into the midst of the burning of the heifer. 7 Then the priest shall wash his clothes, and he shall bathe his flesh in water, and afterward he may come into the camp; and the priest shall be unclean until the evening. 8 And he that burned her shall wash his clothes in water, and shall bathe his flesh in water, and shall be unclean until the evening. 9 And a man that is clean shall gather up the ashes of the heifer, and shall lay them up outside the camp in a clean place. And it shall be kept for the congregation of the sons of Israel for a water of impurity; it is a purging offering.

10 And he that gathers the ashes of the heifer shall wash his clothes, and shall be unclean until the evening; and it shall be to the sons of Israel, and to the stranger that lives among them, for a never-ending statute.

11 He that touches the dead body of any man shall be unclean seven days. 12 He shall cleanse himself for it on the third day, and on the seventh day he shall be clean. And if he does not cleanse himself on the third day, then on the seventh day he shall not be clean. 13 Anyone who touches the dead body, the body of a man who dies, and does not cleanse himself, he shall have defiled the tabernacle of Jehovah; and that person shall be cut off from Israel, for the water of impurity shall not be sprinkled upon him. He shall be unclean; his uncleanness *shall be* still on him.

14 This *is* the law when a man dies in a tent: Everyone who comes into the tent, and all that *is* in the tent, shall be

6 אֶת־עֹרָהּ וְאֶת־בְּשָׂרָהּ וְאֶת־דָּמָהּ עַל־פִּרְשָׁהּ יִשְׂרֹף׃ וְלָקַח
הַכֹּהֵן עֵץ אֶרֶז וְאֵזוֹב וּשְׁנִי תוֹלָעַת וְהִשְׁלִיךְ אֶל־תּוֹךְ
7 שְׂרֵפַת הַפָּרָה׃ וְכִבֶּס בְּגָדָיו הַכֹּהֵן וְרָחַץ בְּשָׂרוֹ בַּמַּיִם
8 וְאַחַר יָבֹא אֶל־הַמַּחֲנֶה וְטָמֵא הַכֹּהֵן עַד־הָעָרֶב׃ וְהַשֹּׂרֵף
אֹתָהּ יְכַבֵּס בְּגָדָיו בַּמַּיִם וְרָחַץ בְּשָׂרוֹ בַּמָּיִם וְטָמֵא עַד־
9 הָעָרֶב׃ וְאָסַף ׀ אִישׁ טָהוֹר אֵת אֵפֶר הַפָּרָה וְהִנִּיחַ
מִחוּץ לַמַּחֲנֶה בְּמָקוֹם טָהוֹר וְהָיְתָה לַעֲדַת בְּנֵי־יִשְׂרָאֵל
10 לְמִשְׁמֶרֶת לְמֵי נִדָּה חַטָּאת הִוא׃ וְכִבֶּס הָאֹסֵף אֶת־אֵפֶר
הַפָּרָה אֶת־בְּגָדָיו וְטָמֵא עַד־הָעָרֶב וְהָיְתָה לִבְנֵי יִשְׂרָאֵל
11 וְלַגֵּר הַגָּר בְּתוֹכָם לְחֻקַּת עוֹלָם׃ הַנֹּגֵעַ בְּמֵת לְכָל־נֶפֶשׁ
12 אָדָם וְטָמֵא שִׁבְעַת יָמִים׃ הוּא יִתְחַטָּא־בוֹ בַּיּוֹם הַשְּׁלִישִׁי
וּבַיּוֹם הַשְּׁבִיעִי יִטְהָר וְאִם־לֹא יִתְחַטָּא בַּיּוֹם הַשְּׁלִישִׁי
13 וּבַיּוֹם הַשְּׁבִיעִי לֹא יִטְהָר׃ כָּל־הַנֹּגֵעַ בְּמֵת בְּנֶפֶשׁ הָאָדָם
אֲשֶׁר־יָמוּת וְלֹא יִתְחַטָּא אֶת־מִשְׁכַּן יְהוָה טִמֵּא וְנִכְרְתָה
הַנֶּפֶשׁ הַהִוא מִיִּשְׂרָאֵל כִּי מֵי נִדָּה לֹא־זֹרַק עָלָיו טָמֵא
14 יִהְיֶה עוֹד טֻמְאָתוֹ בוֹ׃ זֹאת הַתּוֹרָה אָדָם כִּי־יָמוּת בְּאֹהֶל
כָּל־הַבָּא אֶל־הָאֹהֶל וְכָל־אֲשֶׁר בָּאֹהֶל יִטְמָא שִׁבְעַת

unclean seven days. 15 And
every open vessel which
has no covering of thread on
it shall be unclean. 16 And
whoever in the open field
touches one that has been
pierced with a sword, or one
that has died of himself, or
the bone of a man, or a
grave, shall be unclean
seven days. 17 And for the
unclean they shall take the
ashes of the burning of the
purging offering, and running water in a vessel shall
be put on it. 18 And a clean
person shall take hyssop,
and shall dip it in the water,
and shall sprinkle it upon
the tent, and upon all the
vessels, and upon the
persons that were there,
and upon him that touched
the bone, or the slain, or the
dead, or the grave. 19 And the
clean person shall sprinkle
on the unclean on the third
day, and on the seventh day;
and on the seventh day he
shall purify himself; and he
shall wash his clothes, and
bathe himself in water, and
shall be clean at evening.
20 But the man that shall be
unclean, and shall not purify
himself, that soul shall be
cut off from the midst of the
congregation, because he
has defiled the sanctuary of
Jehovah; the water for
impurity has not been
sprinkled on him; he *shall*
be unclean. 21 And it shall
be a never-ending statute to
them; and he that sprinkles
the water of sprinkling shall
wash his clothes; and he
touches the water of
sprinkling shall be unclean
until evening. 22 And whatever the unclean person
touches shall be unclean;
and the soul that touches *it*
shall be unlean until
evening.

2931 6616 6781 369 834 6605 3627 3605 3117
15 יָמִים׃ וְכֹל כְּלִי פָתוּחַ אֲשֶׁר אֵין־צָמִיד פָּתִיל עָלָיו טָמֵא
unclean; it on thread covering has which open vessel and ;days
of no every

4191 176 2719/2491 7704 6440 5060 3605
16 הוּא׃ וְכֹל אֲשֶׁר־יִגַּע עַל־פְּנֵי הַשָּׂדֶה בַּחֲלַל־חֶרֶב אוֹ בְמֵת
one or pierced one field the open in touches who- And .(is) it
.dead ,sword a by ever

3947 3117 7651 2930 6913 176 120 6106
17 אוֹ־בְעֶצֶם אָדָם אוֹ בְקָבֶר יִטְמָא שִׁבְעַת יָמִים׃ וְלָקְחוּ
they And .days seven be shall ,grave a or ,man a bone the or
take shall unclean of

2416 4325 5921 5414 2403 8316 6083 2931
לַטָּמֵא מֵעֲפַר שְׂרֵפַת הַחַטָּאת וְנָתַן עָלָיו מַיִם חַיִּים אֶל־
in running water on and purging the burning the the of the for
it put ,offering of of ashes unclean

168 5921 5137 2889 376 4325 2881 231 3947 3627
18 כֶּלִי׃ וְלָקַח אֵזוֹב וְטָבַל בַּמַּיִם אִישׁ טָהוֹר וְהִזָּה עַל־הָאֹהֶל
,tent the on shall and ,clean a the in shall and hyssop shall and a
sprinkle person water it dip take ,vessel

5060 5921 8033 5315 3627 3605 5921
וְעַל־כָּל־הַכֵּלִים וְעַל־הַנְּפָשׁוֹת אֲשֶׁר הָיוּ־שָׁם וְעַל־הַנֹּגֵעַ
that him and ,there were that the and ,vessels the all and
touched on persons on upon

2889 5137 6913 4191 176 2491 6106
19 בַּעֶצֶם אוֹ בֶחָלָל אוֹ בַמֵּת אוֹ בַקָּבֶר׃ וְהִזָּה הַטָּהֹר עַל־
on clean the shall And the or the or the or the
person sprinkle .grave ,dead ,slain ,bone

7637 3117 2398 7637 3117 7992 3117 2931
הַטָּמֵא בַּיּוֹם הַשְּׁלִישִׁי וּבַיּוֹם הַשְּׁבִיעִי וְחִטְּאוֹ בַּיּוֹם הַשְּׁבִיעִי
;seventh the on he and ;seventh on and ,third the on the
day him purify shall day the day unclean

2930 376 6153 2891 4325 7364 899 3526
20 וְכִבֶּס בְּגָדָיו וְרָחַץ בַּמַּיִם וְטָהֵר בָּעָרֶב׃ וְאִישׁ אֲשֶׁר־יִטְמָא
unclean is that the But at shall and in shall and his shall and
man .evening clean be ,water bathe clothes wash

6951 8432 5315 3772 2398 3808
וְלֹא יִתְחַטָּא וְנִכְרְתָה הַנֶּפֶשׁ הַהִוא מִתּוֹךְ הַקָּהָל כִּי אֶת־
the from that soul be shall does not and
for ,assembly among off cut ,himself purify

1961 2931 /5921 2236 5079 4325/2930 3068 4720
21 מִקְדַּשׁ יְהוָה טִמֵּא מֵי נִדָּה לֹא־זֹרַק עָלָיו טָמֵא הוּא׃ וְהָיְתָה
it And .(is) he un- on has not impurity the has he Jeho- sanc- the
be shall clean him sprinkled been of water defiled ;vah of tuary

4325 5060 899 3526 5079 4325 5137 5769 2708
לָהֶם לְחֻקַּת עוֹלָם וּמַזֵּה מֵי־הַנִּדָּה יְכַבֵּס בְּגָדָיו וְהַנֹּגֵעַ בְּמֵי
the that he and his shall im- for the that he and never- a to
of water touches ;clothes wash purity water sprinkles ;ending statute them

2930 2931 5060 834 3605 6153 2930 5079
22 הַנִּדָּה יִטְמָא עַד־הָעָרֶב׃ וְכֹל אֲשֶׁר־יִגַּע־בּוֹ הַטָּמֵא יִטְמָא
be shall the touches what- And .evening until be shall im-
;unclean person unclean ever unclean purity

6153 2930 5060 5315
וְהַנֶּפֶשׁ הַנֹּגַעַת תִּטְמָא עַד־הָעָרֶב׃
.evening until be shall that the and
unclean (it) touches soul

CAP. XX כ

CHAPTER 20

1 And the sons of Israel,
even the whole congrega-
tion, came into the wilderness of Zin in the first
month; and the people re-
mained in Kadesh. And
Miriam died there, and was
buried there. 2 And there

7223 2320 6790/ 4052 5712 3478 1121 935
1 וַיָּבֹאוּ בְנֵי־יִשְׂרָאֵל כָּל־הָעֵדָה מִדְבַּר־צִן בַּחֹדֶשׁ הָרִאשׁוֹן
.first the in Zin the in whole the ,Israel the And
month of wilderness congregation of sons came

3808 8033 6912 4813 8033 4191 6946 5971 7725
2 וַיֵּשֶׁב הָעָם בְּקָדֵשׁ וַתָּמָת שָׁם מִרְיָם וַתִּקָּבֵר שָׁם׃ וְלֹא־
And .there was and ,Miriam there and in the And
not buried died ;Kadesh people remained

was no water for the congregation, and they were gathered against Moses, and against Aaron. 3 And the people contended with Moses, and spoke, saying, Oh that we had died when our brothers died before Jehovah! 4 And, why have you brought the assembly of Jehovah to this wilderness to die there, we and our animals? 5 And, why have you brought us up out of Egypt to bring us to this evil place, not a place of seed, nor fig, nor vine, nor pomegranate; and there is no water to drink? 6 And Moses and Aaron went in from the eyes of the assembly, to the door of the tabernacle of the congregation; and fell on their faces. And the glory of Jehovah appeared to them.

7 And Jehovah spoke to Moses, saying, 8 Take the rod, and assemble the congregation, you and your brother Aaron. And speak to the rock before their eyes. And it shall give forth its water; and you shall bring water out of the rock to them; so you shall water the congregation and their animals. 9 And Moses took the rod from before Jehovah, as He commanded him. 10 And Moses and Aaron assembled the congregation before the rock. And he said to them, Hear now, you rebels, shall we bring forth water to you out of this rock? 11 And Moses lifted up his hand and smote the rock with his rod twice; and much water came out; and the congregation and their animals drank. 12 And Jehovah said to Moses and Aaron, Because you did not believe

7378 175 4872 6950 5712 4325 1961
3 היה מים לעדה ויקהלו על־משה ועל־אהרן׃ וירב
And .Aaron and Moses against they and the for water there
contended against gathered ;congregation was
6440 251 1478 1478 3863 559 4872 5971
העם עם־משה ויאמרו לאמר ולו גוענו בגוע אחינו לפני
before our when had we O ,saying and .Moses with the
brothers died died that spoke people
4057 3068 6951 935 4100 3068
4 יהוה׃ ולמה הבאתם את־קהל יהוה אל־המדבר הזה
this wilderness to Jehovah the you have And !Jehovah
of assembly brought why
4714 5927 4100 1165 4191
5 למות שם אנחנו ובעירנו׃ ולמה העליתנו ממצרים
of out you have why And our and we ,there die to
Egypt us brought ?animals
8384 22,33/4725 2088 7451 4725 935
להביא אתנו אל־המקום הרע הזה לא מקום זרע ותאנה
,fig nor ,seed place a not ,this evil place to us bring to
of
5869 175 4872/ 935 8354 369 4325 7416 16,12
6 וגפן ורמון ומים אין לשתות׃ ויבא משה ואהרן מפני
from and Moses And ?drink to there and nor ,vine nor
eyes Aaron in went no is water ;pomegranate
3519 7200 6440 5921 5307 4150 168 6607 6951
הקהל אל־פתח אהל מועד ויפלו על־פניהם וירא כבוד־
the and their on and ,meeting the the to the
of glory appeared ;faces fell of tent of door ,assembly's
3068
יהוה אליהם׃ פ
to Jehovah
them

6950 4294 3947 559 4872 3068 1696
7 וידבר יהוה אל־משה לאמר׃ קח את־המטה והקהל
8
and rod the Take ,saying ,Moses to Jehovah And
assemble spoke
5553 1696 251 175 5712
את־העדה אתה ואהרן אחיך ודברתם אל־הסלע
rock the to speak and your and you the
,brother Aaron ,congregation
8248 5553 4325 3318 4325 5414 5869
לעיניהם ונתן מימיו והוצאת להם מים מן־הסלע והשקית
will you so the out water for you and its it And before
to drink give rock of them bring will water give will .eyes their
6440 4294 4872 3947 1165 5712
9 את־העדה ואת־בעירם׃ ויקח משה את־המטה מלפני
from rod the Moses And their and the
before took ,animals congregation
6951 175 4872 6450 6680 3068
10 יהוה כאשר צוהו׃ ויקהלו משה ואהרן את־הקהל
the and Moses And said He as ,Jehovah
assembly Aaron assembled .him to
5553 4984 4994 8085 559 5553/6440
אל־פני הסלע ויאמר להם שמעו־נא המרים המן־הסלע
rock Shall you ,now Hear to he and the before
from !rebels them said :rock
5553 5221 4872 7311 4325 3318
11 הזה נוציא לכם מים׃ וירם משה את־ידו ויך את־הסלע
rock the and hand his Moses And ?water to bring we this
struck lifted you forth
1165 5712 8354 7221 4325 3318 6471 4294
במטהו פעמים ויצאו מים רבים ותשת העדה ובעירם׃ ס
their and the and ;much water and ;twice his with
.animals congregation drank out came rod
559 3808 175 4872 3068 559
12 ויאמר יהוה אל־משה ואל־אהרן יען לא־האמנתם בי
in did you not Because ,Aaron and Moses to Jehovah And
Me believe to said

in Me, to sanctify Me before the eyes of the sons of Israel, so that you shall not bring in this congregation to the land which I have given to them. [13]These *are* the Waters of Strife, because the sons of Israel contended with Jehovah, and He was sanctified upon them.

[14]And Moses sent messengers from Kadesh to the king of Edom: So says your brother Israel, You surely have known all the travail which has befallen us; [15]that our fathers went down to Egypt, and we lived in Egypt many days, and the Egyptians did evil to us and to our fathers. [16]And we cried to Jehovah, and He heard our voice, and sent a messenger, and is bringing us out of Egypt; and, behold, we *are* in Kadesh, a city *on* the edge of your border. [17]Please let us pass over, through your land; we shall not pass over through a field, nor through a vineyard, nor shall we drink water of a well; we shall go along the king's highway. We will not turn aside to the right hand or to the left, until we have passed your border. [18]And Edom said to him, You shall not pass through me, lest I come out with the sword against you. [19]And the sons of Israel said to him, We shall go in the highway; and if we drink of your waters, our cattle and us, then I shall give their price. Only let me pass through on my feet; there shall be no harm. [20]And he said, You shall not pass through. And Edom came out against him with many people, and with a strong hand. [21]And Edom refused to allow Israel to pass over through his border. And Israel turned away from him.

[22]And the sons of Israel, the whole congregation, pulled up *stakes* from Kadesh and came in to

6951 935 3478 1121 5869 6942
לְהַקְדִּישֵׁנִי לְעֵינֵי בְּנֵי יִשְׂרָאֵל לָכֵן לֹא תָבִיאוּ אֶת־הַקָּהָל
assembly you not there- ,Israel the the in sanctify to
bring shall fore of sons of eyes Me
2088 4808 4325 1992 5414 834 776
13 הַזֶּה אֶל־הָאָרֶץ אֲשֶׁר־נָתַתִּי לָהֶם׃ הֵמָּה מֵי מְרִיבָה אֲשֶׁר־
because ,Meribah the These to have I which the to this
of waters (are) .them given land
5971 854 6942 3068 3478/1121/7378
14 רָבוּ בְנֵי־יִשְׂרָאֵל אֶת־יְהוָה וַיִּקָּדֵשׁ בָּם׃ ס וַיִּשְׁלַח
sent And among was He and ;Jehovah with Israel the con-
.them sanctified of sons tended
251 559 123 4428 6946 4397 4872
מֹשֶׁה מַלְאָכִים מִקָּדֵשׁ אֶל־מֶלֶךְ אֱדוֹם כֹּה אָמַר אָחִיךָ
your says Thus :Edom the to from messengers Moses
brother of king Kadesh
4671 834 8573 3605 3045 3478
יִשְׂרָאֵל אַתָּה יָדַעְתָּ אֵת כָּל־הַתְּלָאָה אֲשֶׁר מְצָאָתְנוּ׃
;us found has which the all have You ,Israel
travail known
7227 3117 4714 3427 4714 1 3381
15 וַיֵּרְדוּ אֲבֹתֵינוּ מִצְרַיְמָה וַנֵּשֶׁב בְּמִצְרַיִם יָמִים רַבִּים
.many days Egypt in we and ;Egypt to our that
lived fathers went
6963 8085 3068 3427 4714 7489
16 וַיָּרֵעוּ לָנוּ מִצְרַיִם וְלַאֲבֹתֵינוּ׃ וַנִּצְעַק אֶל־יְהוָה וַיִּשְׁמַע קֹלֵנוּ
our He and ,Jehovah to we and to and the to did And
,voice heard cried ;fathers our Egyptians us evil
7097 5892 6946 2009 4714 3318 4397 7971
וַיִּשְׁלַח מַלְאָךְ וַיֹּצִאֵנוּ מִמִּצְרָיִם וְהִנֵּה אֲנַחְנוּ בְקָדֵשׁ עִיר קְצֵה
at city a in we And of out is and a sent and
edge ,Kadesh (are) ,behold .Egypt us bringing ,messenger
3808 3754 7704 5674 3808 776 4994 5674 1366
17 גְבוּלֶךָ׃ נַעְבְּרָה־נָּא בְאַרְצֶךָ לֹא נַעֲבֹר בְּשָׂדֶה וּבְכֶרֶם וְלֹא
nor through nor through will we not through Please us let your
,vineyard a ,field a pass ;land your pass .border's
8040 3225 5186 3808 3212 4428 1870 875 4325 8354
נִשְׁתֶּה מֵי בְאֵר דֶּרֶךְ הַמֶּלֶךְ נֵלֵךְ לֹא נִטֶּה יָמִין וּשְׂמֹאול
to or the to will we not will we the road ;well a water we shall
,left the right turn ;(by) go king's of drink
5634 3808 123 559 1366 5674 5704
18 עַד אֲשֶׁר־נַעֲבֹר גְּבֻלֶךָ׃ וַיֹּאמֶר אֵלָיו אֱדוֹם לֹא תַעֲבֹר
shall You not ,Edom him to said And your have we until
pass .border passed
3478 1121 559 7125 3318 2719
19 בִּי פֶּן־בַּחֶרֶב אֵצֵא לִקְרָאתֶךָ׃ וַיֹּאמְרוּ אֵלָיו בְּנֵי־יִשְׂרָאֵל
,Israel the him to said And against come I with lest through
of sons .you out sword the me
4377 5414 4735 8354 4325 3212 4546
בַּמְסִלָּה נַעֲלֶה וְאִם־מֵימֶיךָ נִשְׁתֶּה אֲנִי וּמִקְנַי וְנָתַתִּי מִכְרָם
their I then my and I we your of if and will We the on
;price give will ,cattle ,drink waters ;go highway
3318 5674 3808 559 5674 7272 1697 369 7535
20 רַק אֵין־דָּבָר בְּרַגְלַי אֶעֱבֹרָה׃ וַיֹּאמֶר לֹא תַעֲבֹר וַיֵּצֵא
And shall You not he And me let my on ;hurt there ,only
out came .pass ,said .pass feet no be shall
5414/125 3985 2389 3027 3515 5971 7125 123
21 אֱדוֹם לִקְרָאתוֹ בְּעַם כָּבֵד וּבְיָד חֲזָקָה׃ וַיְמָאֵן ׀ אֱדוֹם נְתֹן
to Edom And .strong with and ,many with against Edom
allow refused hand a people him
3478 5186 1366 5674 3478
אֶת־יִשְׂרָאֵל עֲבֹר בִּגְבֻלוֹ וַיֵּט יִשְׂרָאֵל מֵעָלָיו׃ פ
from Israel and through pass to Israel
.him turned ,border his
2022 2023 712 3605 3478 1121 935 6946 5265
22 וַיִּסְעוּ מִקָּדֵשׁ וַיָּבֹאוּ בְנֵי־יִשְׂרָאֵל כָּל־הָעֵדָה הֹר הָהָר׃
.Mount Hor the whole ,Israel the came and from And
,congregation of sons to ;Kadesh up pulled

Mount Hor. 23 And Jehovah
spoke to Moses and Aaron
in Mount Hor, on the edge
of the land of Edom, say-
ing, 24 Aaron shall be
gathered to his people, for
he shall not go into the land
which I have given to the
sons of Israel, because you
rebelled againt My word at
the waters of Meribah.
25 Take Aaron and his son
Eleazar, and cause them to
go up to Mount Hor; 26 and
strip Aaron of his gar-
ments, and you shall put
them on his son Eleazar.
And Aaron shall be
gathered and shall die
there. 27 And Moses did as
Jehovah had commanded;
and they went up to Mount
Hor before the eyes of all
the congregation. 28 And
Moses stripped Aaron of his
garments, and clothed his
son Eleazar with them. And
Aaron died there on the top
of the mountain. And
Moses and Eleazar came
down from the mountain.
29 And all the congregation
saw that Aaron had died,
and they mourned Aaron
thirty days, all the house of
Israel.

1366 2022 2023 175 4872 3068 559
23 וַיֹּאמֶר יְהֹוָה אֶל־מֹשֶׁה וְאֶל־אַהֲרֹן בְּהֹר הָהָר עַל־גְּבוּל
the at ,Mount Hor on Aaron to and Moses to Jehovah And
of edge spoke

935 3808 5971 175 622 559 123 776
24 אֶרֶץ־אֱדוֹם לֵאמֹר׃ יֵאָסֵף אַהֲרֹן אֶל־עַמָּיו כִּי לֹא יָבֹא אֶל־
into he not for his to Aaron be shall ,saying ,Edom the
go shall ,people gathered of land

6310 4784 3478 1121 5414 834 776
הָאָרֶץ אֲשֶׁר נָתַתִּי לִבְנֵי יִשְׂרָאֵל עַל אֲשֶׁר־מְרִיתֶם אֶת־פִּי
My rebelled you because ,Israel the to have I which land the
mouth against of sons given

5927 1121 499 175 3947 4808 4325
25 לְמֵי מְרִיבָה׃ קַח אֶת־אַהֲרֹן וְאֶת־אֶלְעָזָר בְּנוֹ וְהַעַל אֹתָם
them and his Eleazar and Aaron Take .Meribah the at
send ,son of waters

3847 899 175 6584 2022 2023
26 הֹר הָהָר׃ וְהַפְשֵׁט אֶת־אַהֲרֹן אֶת־בְּגָדָיו וְהִלְבַּשְׁתָּם אֶת־
them put and his of Aaron strip and ;Mount to
on garments Hor

4872 6213 8033 4191 622 175 1121 499
27 אֶלְעָזָר בְּנוֹ וְאַהֲרֹן יֵאָסֵף וּמֵת שָׁם׃ וַיַּעַשׂ מֹשֶׁה כַּאֲשֶׁר
as Moses did And .there shall and be shall and his Eleazar
die gathered Aaron son

6584 5712 3605 2022 2023 5927 3068 6680
28 צִוָּה יְהֹוָה וַיַּעֲלוּ אֶל־הֹר הָהָר לְעֵינֵי כָּל־הָעֵדָה׃ וַיַּפְשֵׁט
And the all before Mount Hor to they and ,Jehovah had
stripped .congregation up went ordered

1121 499 3847 899 175 4872
מֹשֶׁה אֶת־אַהֲרֹן אֶת־בְּגָדָיו וַיַּלְבֵּשׁ אֹתָם אֶת־אֶלְעָזָר בְּנוֹ
his Eleazar with and his of Aaron Moses
son them clothed garments

2022 499 4872/3381 2022 7218 8033 175 4191
וַיָּמָת אַהֲרֹן שָׁם בְּרֹאשׁ הָהָר וַיֵּרֶד מֹשֶׁה וְאֶלְעָזָר מִן־הָהָר׃
the from and Moses and the the on there Aaron and
.mountain Eleazar down came ;mount of top died

7970 175 1058 175 1478 5712/8605 7200
29 וַיִּרְאוּ כָּל־הָעֵדָה כִּי גָוַע אַהֲרֹן וַיִּבְכּוּ אֶת־אַהֲרֹן שְׁלֹשִׁים
thirty Aaron they and ,Aaron had that the all And
mourned ,died congregation saw

3478 1004 3605/3117
יוֹם כֹּל בֵּית יִשְׂרָאֵל׃
.Israel the all ,days
of house

CAP. XXI כא

CHAPTER 21

CHAPTER 21
1 And king Arad the
Canaanite, who lived
in the south, heard that
Israel had come the way of
Atharim; and he fought
against Israel, and took
some of them captive. 2 And
Israel vowed a vow to
Jehovah, and said, If you
will indeed deliver this
people into my hand, then I
will utterly destroy their
cities. 3 And Jehovah
listened to the voice of
Israel, and delivered up the
Canaanites; and they utterly
destroyed them and their
cities; and the name of the
place was called Hormah.

3478 935 5045 3427 6166/4428 3669 8085
1 וַיִּשְׁמַע הַכְּנַעֲנִי מֶלֶךְ־עֲרָד יֹשֵׁב הַנֶּגֶב כִּי בָּא יִשְׂרָאֵל
Israel had that the who ,Arad king the And
come south in lived Canaanite heard

5087 7628 7617 3478 389 871 1870
2 דֶּרֶךְ הָאֲתָרִים וַיִּלָּחֶם בְּיִשְׂרָאֵל וַיִּשְׁבְּ ׀ מִמֶּנּוּ שֶׁבִי׃ וַיִּדַּר
And .captive some took and against he and ;Atharim the
vowed them of Israel fought of way

2088 5971 5414 5414 559 3068 5088 3478
יִשְׂרָאֵל נֶדֶר לַיהֹוָה וַיֹּאמַר אִם־נָתֹן תִּתֵּן אֶת־הָעָם הַזֶּה
this people You will If ,said and to vow a Israel
truly deliver ,Jehovah

3478 6963 3068 8085 5892 2763 3027
3 בְּיָדִי וְהַחֲרַמְתִּי אֶת־עָרֵיהֶם׃ וַיִּשְׁמַע יְהֹוָה בְּקוֹל יִשְׂרָאֵל
,Israel the to Jehovah And .cities their will I then my into
of voice listened exterminate ,hand

8034 7121 5892 2763 3669 5414
וַיִּתֵּן אֶת־הַכְּנַעֲנִי וַיַּחֲרֵם אֶתְהֶם וְאֶת־עָרֵיהֶם וַיִּקְרָא שֵׁם
the was and their and them they and the and
of name called ;cities exterminated ;Canaanites up gave

המקום הרמה׃
.Hormah the place

4 ויסעו מהר ההר דרך ים־סוף לסבב את־ארץ אדום
.Edom land of the go around to ,Reeds Sea of the way the ,Mount Hor from they And moved

5 ותקצר נפש־העם בדרך׃ וידבר העם באלהים ובמשה
against Moses and against God the people And spoke .way the because of the people of soul the was impatient And

למה העליתנו ממצרים למות במדבר כי אין לחם
bread no for ?wilderness the in die to Egypt of out you have brought us Why

6 ואין מים ונפשנו קצה בלחם הקלקל׃ וישלח יהוה
Jehovah sent And .light bread this hates our soul and ;(here is) water no and

בעם את הנחשים השרפים וינשכו את־העם וימת עם־
people died and ;people the bit they and ;fiery serpents among people the

7 רב מישראל׃ ויבא העם אל־משה ויאמרו חטאנו כי־
for ,sinned have We ,said and Moses to people the And came in .Israel of many

דברנו ביהוה ובך התפלל אל־יהוה ויסר מעלינו את־
from us He will turn and ,Jehovah to Pray .you against and Jehovah against have we spoken

8 הנחש ויתפלל משה בעד העם׃ ויאמר יהוה אל־
to Jehovah And spoke .people the for Moses And prayed .serpent the

משה עשה לך שרף ושים אתו על־נס והיה כל־הנשוך
,bitten is one any when it shall be and ;pole a on it set and (serpent) fiery a yourself Make ,Moses

9 וראה אתו וחי׃ ויעש משה נחש נחשת וישמהו על־
on it put and ,bronze of serpent a Moses made And .live shall he ,it sees he when

הנס והיה אם־נשך הנחש את־איש והביט אל־נחש
serpent of the to looked he when ,man any serpent a bitten had if ,was it and pole a

10 11 הנחשת וחי׃ ויסעו בני ישראל ויחנו באבת׃ ויסעו
And pulled up .Oboth in camped and Israel of sons the And pulled up .lived he ,bronze

מאבת ויחנו בעיי העברים במדבר אשר על־פני מואב
,Moab before (is) that wilderness the in Ijeabarim in camped and ,Oboth from

12 13 ממזרח השמש׃ משם נסעו ויחנו בנחל זרד׃ משם
From there .Zered of valley the in camped and pulled up they From there .sun the of rising the toward

נסעו ויחנו מעבר ארנון אשר במדבר היצא מגבל
of border the of out comes that wilderness the in (is) which ,Arnon beyond pitched and pulled they

האמרי כי ארנון גבול מואב בין מואב ובין האמרי׃
;Amorite the and Moab between ,Moab's border (is) Arnon for ;Amorite the

4 And they moved from Mount Hor by the way to the Red Sea, to go around the land of Edom. And the soul of the people became impatient because of the way. 5 And the people spoke against God, and against Moses, Why have you brought us out of Egypt to die in the wilderness? For *there is* no bread, and there is no water, and our soul hates the light bread. 6 And Jehovah sent fiery serpents among the people; and they bit the people, and many people of Israel died. 7 And the people came in to Moses and said, We have sinned, for we have spoken against Jehovah, and against you. Pray to Jehovah, and He shall turn the serpent away from us. And Moses prayed on behalf of the people. 8 And Jehovah spoke to Moses, Make yourself a fiery serpent, and set it on a pole; and it shall be that when anyone is bitten, when he sees it, he shall live. 9 And Moses made a serpent of copper and put it on a pole; and it happened, if a serpent had bitten any man, when he looked to the copper serpent, he lived.

10 And the sons of Israel journeyed, and encamped in Oboth. 11 And they moved from Oboth, and camped in Ije-abarim, in the wilderness that is before Moab, toward the rising of the sun. 12 From there they pulled up and camped in the valley of Zered. 13 From there they pulled up and camped beyond Arnon, which is in the wilderness that comes out of the border of the Amorite; for Arnon *is* the border of Moab, between Moab and the Amorite;

14 On account of this it is said in the Book of the Wars of Jehovah: Vaheb in Suphah, and the torrents of Arnon, 15 and the slope of the torrent-beds that goes down to the site of Ar and leans on the border of Moab.

16 And from there *they went* to Beer; that *is* the well of which Jehovah spoke to Moses, *saying*, Gather the people and I will give water to them.

17 Then Israel sang this song: Spring up, O well, sing to it; 18 the well which the princes dug, which the nobles of the people dug with their staves, at *the word of* the Lawgiver. And *they departed* from the desert to Mattanah. 19 And from Mattanah *they went* to Nahaliel; and from Nahaliel to Bemoth; 20 and from Bemoth in the valley which *is* in the field of Moab *to* the top of Pisgah, and looking toward the wilderness.

21 And Israel sent messengers to Sihon king of the Amorites, saying, 22 Let me pass through your land; we will not turn into a field or into a vineyard; we will not drink waters of a well; we will go in the king's highway until we have passed over your border. 23 And Sihon would not allow Israel to pass through his border. And Sihon gathered all his people and went out to meet Israel in the wilderness, and *they* came to Jahaz and fought against Israel. 24 And Israel struck him by the mouth of the sword and seized his land, from Arnon to Jabbok, to the sons of Ammon. For the border of the sons of Ammon *was* strong. 25 And Israel took all these cities. And Israel dwelt in all the cities of the

5497 2052 3068 4421 5612 559 3651/5921
14 עַל־כֵּן יֵאָמַר בְּסֵפֶר מִלְחֲמֹת יְהוָה אֶת־וָהֵב בְּסוּפָה וְאֶת־
and in Vaheb :Jehovah the the in is it ,Therefore
Suphah of wars of book said

6144 3427 5186 834 5158 793 769 5158
15 הַנְּחָלִים אַרְנוֹן׃ וְאֶשֶׁד הַנְּחָלִים אֲשֶׁר נָטָה לְשֶׁבֶת עָר
;Ar the to turns that torrent-the the and ,Arnon the
of site down beds of slope of torrents

834 875 876 8033 4124 1366 8172
16 וְנִשְׁעַן לִגְבוּל מוֹאָב׃ וּמִשָּׁם בְּאֵרָה הִוא הַבְּאֵר אֲשֶׁר
of well the that (went they) And .Moab the on and
which (is) ;Beer to there from of border leans

4325 5414 5971 622 4872 3068 559
אָמַר יְהוָה לְמֹשֶׁה אֱסֹף אֶת־הָעָם וְאֶתְּנָה לָהֶם מָיִם׃
.water to I and the Gather to Jehovah spoke
them give will people Moses

7891 875 5921 2088 7892 3478 7891
17 אָז יָשִׁיר יִשְׂרָאֵל אֶת־הַשִּׁירָה הַזֹּאת עֲלִי בְאֵר עֱנוּ־לָהּ׃
;it to sing O Spring :this song Israel sang Then
,well ,up

4938 2710 5971 5081 3738 8269 2658 875
18 בְּאֵר חֲפָרוּהָ שָׂרִים כָּרוּהָ נְדִיבֵי הָעָם בִּמְחֹקֵק בְּמִשְׁעֲנֹתָם
their with the by the the which the which the
staffs lawgiver ,people of nobles dug ,leaders dug well

1120 5160 5160 4980 4980 4057
19 וּמִמִּדְבָּר מַתָּנָה׃ וּמִמַּתָּנָה נַחֲלִיאֵל וּמִנַּחֲלִיאֵל בָּמוֹת׃
to from and to from and to from And
,Bamoth Nahaliel ;Nahaliel Mattanah ;Mattanah desert the

8259 6449 7218 4124 7704 834 1516 1120
20 וּמִבָּמוֹת הַגַּיְא אֲשֶׁר בִּשְׂדֵה מוֹאָב רֹאשׁ הַפִּסְגָּה וְנִשְׁקָפָה
which ,Pisgah the (to) ,Moab the in which the in from and
looks of top of field (is) valley Bamoth

3452 6440
עַל־פְּנֵי הַיְשִׁימֹן׃
the toward
.wilderness

559 567 4428 5511 4397 3478 7971
21 וַיִּשְׁלַח יִשְׂרָאֵל מַלְאָכִים אֶל־סִיחֹן מֶלֶךְ־הָאֱמֹרִי לֵאמֹר׃
,saying the of king Sihon to messengers Israel sent And
Amorites

4325 8354 3808 3754 7704 5186 3808 776 5674
22 אֶעְבְּרָה בְאַרְצֶךָ לֹא נִטֶּה בְּשָׂדֶה וּבְכֶרֶם לֹא נִשְׁתֶּה מֵי
waters will we not into or a into will we not through me Let
of drink ;vineyard a field turn ;land your pass

5414 1366 5674 5704/3212 4428 1870 875
23 בְּאֵר בְּדֶרֶךְ הַמֶּלֶךְ נֵלֵךְ עַד אֲשֶׁר־נַעֲבֹר גְּבֻלֶךָ׃ וְלֹא־נָתַן
would But your have we will we king's the on ;well a
allow not .border crossed until go highway

5971 3605 5511 622 1366 5674 3478 5511
סִיחֹן אֶת־יִשְׂרָאֵל עֲבֹר בִּגְבֻלוֹ וַיֶּאֱסֹף סִיחֹן אֶת־כָּל־עַמּוֹ
his all Sihon and through to Israel Sihon
people gathered ;border his pass

3898 3086 935 4057 3478 7125 3318
וַיֵּצֵא לִקְרַאת יִשְׂרָאֵל הַמִּדְבָּרָה וַיָּבֹא יָהְצָה וַיִּלָּחֶם
and to and the in Israel meet to and
fought Jahaz came ,wilderness out went

776 3423 2719/6310 3478 5221 3478
24 בְּיִשְׂרָאֵל׃ וַיַּכֵּהוּ יִשְׂרָאֵל לְפִי־חָרֶב וַיִּירַשׁ אֶת־אַרְצוֹ
his and the the by Israel And against
land seized sword of edge him struck .Israel

3947 5983 1121 1366 5794 5983 1121 2999 769
25 מֵאַרְנֹן עַד־יַבֹּק עַד־בְּנֵי עַמּוֹן כִּי עַז גְּבוּל בְּנֵי עַמּוֹן׃ וַיִּקַּח
And .Ammon the the (was) for ;Ammon the to ,Jabbok to from
took of sons of border strong of sons Arnon

5892 3605 3478 3427 428 5892 3605 3478
יִשְׂרָאֵל אֵת כָּל־הֶעָרִים הָאֵלֶּה וַיֵּשֶׁב יִשְׂרָאֵל בְּכָל־עָרֵי
the all in Israel and ;these cities all Israel
of cities lived

Amorite, in Heshbon and
in all its daughter villages.
26 For Heshbon *was* the[B]
city of Sihon king of the
Amorites. And he had
fought against the former
king of Moab and had
taken his land out of his
hand, to Arnon. 27 On
account of this the
parable-speakers say,
Come to Heshbon! Let the
city of Sihon be built and
established! 28 For a fire
has gone out of Heshbon,
a flame from the city of
Sihon; it has consumed Ar
of Moab, the lords of the
high places of Arnon.
29 Woe to you, Moab!
You are undone, O people
of Chemosh! He has given
his sons as fugitives and
his daughters into cap-
tivity, to Sihon king of the
Amorites. 30 We have cast
them down; Heshbon has
perished, even to Dibon;
and we have ravaged even
to Nophah, which *is* to
Medeba.
31 And Israel dwelt in the
land of the Amorites.
32 And Moses sent to spy
out Jaazer, and they took
its villages and drove out
the Amorite who was
there. 33 And they turned
and went the way of
Bashan. And Og king of
Bashan came out to meet
them, he and all his
people, to battle *at* Edrei.
34 And Jehovah said to
Moses, Do not fear him,
for I have given him into
your hand, and all his
people and his land. And
you shall do to him as you
have done to Sihon king of
the Amorites, who dwelt
at Heshbon. 35 And they
struck him and his sons
and all his people until he
did not have a remnant
left. And they seized his
land.

5511 5892 2809 3588 1323 3605 2809 567
26 הָאֱמֹרִי בְּחֶשְׁבּוֹן וּבְכָל־בְּנֹתֶיהָ׃ כִּי חֶשְׁבּוֹן עִיר סִיחֹן
Sihon the Heshbon for its in and in the
of city (was) villages all Heshbon ,Amorite

7223 4124 4428 3898 567 4428
מֶלֶךְ הָאֱמֹרִי וְהוּא נִלְחַם בְּמֶלֶךְ מוֹאָב הָרִאשׁוֹן
,former the Moab against had he And the king
of king fought ,Amorites of

491 1 559 769 3027 776 3605 3947
27 וַיִּקַּח אֶת־כָּל־אַרְצוֹ מִיָּדוֹ עַד־אַרְנֹן׃ עַל־כֵּן יֹאמְרוּ הַמֹּשְׁלִים
:poets the say therefore ;Arnon to of out his all had and
hand his land taken

3318 784 5511 5892 3559 1129 2809 935
28 בֹּאוּ חֶשְׁבּוֹן תִּבָּנֶה וְתִכּוֹנֵן עִיר סִיחוֹן׃ כִּי־אֵשׁ יָצְאָה
gone has a For !Sihon the and be let !Heshbon Come
out fire of city settled built to

1167 4124 6144 398 5511 7151 3852 2809
מֵחֶשְׁבּוֹן לֶהָבָה מִקִּרְיַת סִיחֹן אָכְלָה עָר מוֹאָב בַּעֲלֵי
the ,Moab of Ar has it ;Sihon the from ,flame a of
of lords consumed of city ,Heshbon

1121 5414 3645 6 4124 188 769 1116
29 בָּמוֹת אַרְנֹן׃ אוֹי־לְךָ מוֹאָב אָבַדְתָּ עַם־כְּמוֹשׁ נָתַן בָּנָיו
his He !Chemosh O are you !Moab to Woe .Arnon high the
sons given has of people ,undone ,you of places

6 3384 5511 661 4428 7628 1323 6412
30 פְּלֵיטִם וּבְנֹתָיו בַּשְּׁבִית לְמֶלֶךְ אֱמֹרִי סִיחוֹן׃ וַנִּירָם אָבַד
has cast we And .Sihon the king to into his and as
perished ;down them Amorites of ,captivity daughters fugitives

3427 4311 5704 834 5307 8074 1769 2809
31 חֶשְׁבּוֹן עַד־דִּיבֹן וַנַּשִּׁים עַד־נֹפַח אֲשֶׁר עַד־מֵידְבָא׃ וַיֵּשֶׁב
So .Medeba (reaches) which ,Nophah to we and ;Dibon even ,Hesh-
lived to ravaged to bon

3270 7270 4872 7971 567 776 3478
32 יִשְׂרָאֵל בְּאֶרֶץ הָאֱמֹרִי׃ וַיִּשְׁלַח מֹשֶׁה לְרַגֵּל אֶת־יַעְזֵר
,Jaazer spy to Moses sent And the the in Israel
out .Amorites of land

5927 6437 8033 567 3423 1323 3920
33 וַיִּלְכְּדוּ בְּנֹתֶיהָ וַיּוֹרֶשׁ אֶת־הָאֱמֹרִי אֲשֶׁר־שָׁם׃ וַיִּפְנוּ וַיַּעֲלוּ
and they and was who the drove and its they and
went turned ;there Amorite out ,villages took

3605 7125 1316 5747/5927 1316 1870
דֶּרֶךְ הַבָּשָׁן וַיֵּצֵא עוֹג מֶלֶךְ־הַבָּשָׁן לִקְרָאתָם הוּא וְכָל־
all and he meet to Bashan of king Og And .Bashan the
them came of way

3372 4872 3068 559 159 4421 5971
34 עַמּוֹ לַמִּלְחָמָה אֶדְרֶעִי׃ וַיֹּאמֶר יְהוָה אֶל־מֹשֶׁה אַל־תִּירָא
fear Do not ,Moses to Jehovah said And .Edrei (at) battle to

6213 776 5971 3605 5414 3027
אֹתוֹ כִּי בְיָדְךָ נָתַתִּי אֹתוֹ וְאֶת־כָּל־עַמּוֹ וְאֶת־אַרְצוֹ וְעָשִׂיתָ
you and his and his all and ,him have I into for ,him
do shall ;land people given hand your

2809 3427 567 4428 5511 6213
לּוֹ כַּאֲשֶׁר עָשִׂיתָ לְסִיחֹן מֶלֶךְ הָאֱמֹרִי אֲשֶׁר יוֹשֵׁב בְּחֶשְׁבּוֹן׃
at lived who the king to have you as to
.Heshbon Amorite of Sihon done him

7604 1115 5971 3605 1121 5221
35 וַיַּכּוּ אֹתוֹ וְאֶת־בָּנָיו וְאֶת־כָּל־עַמּוֹ עַד־בִּלְתִּי הִשְׁאִיר־לוֹ
did he left not until his all and ,sons his and him And
have ,people struck they

776 3423 8300
שָׂרִיד וַיִּירְשׁוּ אֶת־אַרְצוֹ׃
.land his they and a
seized ;remnant

CAP. XXII כב

CHAPTER 22

[1]And the sons of Israel
1 pulled up *stakes* and
camped on the plains of
Moab, beyond the Jordan,
by Jericho.
[2]And Balak the son of
2 Zippor saw all that Israel
had done to the Amorites.
[3]And Moab greatly feared
because of the people, for
3 it *was* many. And Moab
was vexed by the
presence of the sons of
Israel. [4]And Moab said to
4 the elders of Midian, Now
this assembly is licking up
all that is around us, as the
ox licks up the grass of the
field. And Balak the son of
Zippor *was* king of Moab
at that time. [5]And he sent
5 messengers to Balaam the
son of Beor, to Pethor
which *is* beside the River
of the land of the sons of
his people, to call for him,
saying, Behold! A people
has come out of Egypt.
Behold! it has covered the
face of the earth, and it is
setting next to me. [6]And
6 now please come, curse
this people for me, for it *is*
stronger than I. Perhaps I
will prevail, that we may
strike them, that I may
drive them out from the
land. For I know that
whoever you bless *is*
blessed, and whoever you
curse is cursed.
[7]And the elders of Moab
7 and the elders of Midian
left with the rewards of the
seer in their hand. And
they came to Balaam and
8 spoke the words of Balak
to him. [8]And he said to
them, Stay here tonight,
and I will bring back word
to you, even as Jehovah
may speak to me. And the
leaders of Moab stayed
9 with Balaam. [9]And God

3383 5676 4124 6160 2583 3478 1121 5265
1 וַיִּסְעוּ בְּנֵי יִשְׂרָאֵל וַיַּחֲנוּ בְּעַרְבוֹת מוֹאָב מֵעֵבֶר לְיַרְדֵּן
the Jordan | beyond | ,Moab | the on of plains | and camped | Israel | the of sons | And moved
3405
יְרֵחוֹ׃
(by) Jericho.

567 3478 6213 3605 6834/1121 1111 7200
2 וַיַּרְא בָּלָק בֶּן־צִפּוֹר אֵת כָּל־אֲשֶׁר־עָשָׂה יִשְׂרָאֵל לָאֱמֹרִי׃
the to ;Amorites | Israel | had done | that | all | Zippor the of son | Balak | And saw

6440 4124/6973 1961/7227 3966 5971 6640 4124 1481
3 וַיָּגָר מוֹאָב מִפְּנֵי הָעָם מְאֹד כִּי רַב־הוּא וַיָּקָץ מוֹאָב מִפְּנֵי
to due | Moab was vexed | and | it (was) | many | for | ,greatly | the people | Moab | and feared

3897 6258 4080 2205 4124 559 3478 1121
4 בְּנֵי יִשְׂרָאֵל׃ וַיֹּאמֶר מוֹאָב אֶל־זִקְנֵי מִדְיָן עַתָּה יְלַחֲכוּ
licking up | is Now | ;Midian | the of elders | to | Moab | said And | .Israel | the of sons

7704 3418 7794 3897 5439 3605 6951
הַקָּהָל אֶת־כָּל־סְבִיבֹתֵינוּ כִּלְחֹךְ הַשּׁוֹר אֵת יֶרֶק הַשָּׂדֶה
.field the | the of grass | ox the | licks up | as | that is ,us around | all | this assembly

4397 7971 6256 4124 4428 6839/1121 1111
5 וּבָלָק בֶּן־צִפּוֹר מֶלֶךְ לְמוֹאָב בָּעֵת הַהִוא׃ וַיִּשְׁלַח מַלְאָכִים
messengers | he And sent | .that | at time | Moab of | (was) king | Zippor the of son | And Balak

1121 776 5104 834 6604 1160 1121 1109
אֶל־בִּלְעָם בֶּן־בְּעוֹר פְּתוֹרָה אֲשֶׁר עַל־הַנָּהָר אֶרֶץ בְּנֵי־
the of sons | land the of | the River | beside | which (is) | to ,Pethor | ,Beor | the of son | Balaam | to

3680 2009 4714 3318 5971 2009 559 7121 5971
עַמּוֹ לִקְרֹא־לוֹ לֵאמֹר הִנֵּה עַם יָצָא מִמִּצְרַיִם הִנֵּה כִסָּה
has it covered | ,behold | of out ;Egypt | has come | a people | ,Behold | ,saying | for him | to call | his ,people

779 4994/3212 6258 4136 3427 776 5869
6 אֶת־עֵין הָאָרֶץ וְהוּא יֹשֵׁב מִמֻּלִי׃ וְעַתָּה לְכָה־נָּא אָרָה־
curse | ;please come | And ,now | to next .me | is setting | it and | the ;earth | face the of

5221 3201 194 6099 2088 5971
לִּי אֶת־הָעָם הַזֶּה כִּי־עָצוּם הוּא מִמֶּנִּי אוּלַי אוּכַל נַכֶּה־
we that strike may | shall I ,prevail | perhaps | than ;I | (is) it | stronger | ,this | people | for me

1288 1288 3045 776 1644
בּוֹ וַאֲגָרְשֶׁנּוּ מִן־הָאָרֶץ כִּי יָדַעְתִּי אֵת אֲשֶׁר־תְּבָרֵךְ מְבֹרָךְ
is ,blessed | you bless | he whom | know I that | for | the ;land | from | may I expel them | that ;them

3027 7081 4080/2205 4124 2205/3212 779 779 834
7 וַאֲשֶׁר תָּאֹר יוּאָר׃ וַיֵּלְכוּ זִקְנֵי מוֹאָב וְזִקְנֵי מִדְיָן וּקְסָמִים בְּיָדָם
their in .hand | the with fee seer's | Midian | and of elders the | Moab | the of elders | left And | is .cursed | you curse | he and whom

559 1111 1697 1696 1109 935
8 וַיָּבֹאוּ אֶל־בִּלְעָם וַיְדַבְּרוּ אֵלָיו דִּבְרֵי בָלָק׃ וַיֹּאמֶר אֲלֵיהֶם
,them to | he And said | .Balak | the of words | him to | and spoke | Balaam to | they And came

3068/1696 1697 7725 3915 3885
לִינוּ פֹה הַלַּיְלָה וַהֲשִׁבֹתִי אֶתְכֶם דָּבָר כַּאֲשֶׁר יְדַבֵּר יְהוָה
Jehovah | may speak | as | ,word | you | will I and back bring | ,tonight | here | Stay

430 935 1109 4124 8269 3427
9 אֵלָי וַיֵּשְׁבוּ שָׂרֵי־מוֹאָב עִם־בִּלְעָם׃ וַיָּבֹא אֱלֹהִים אֶל־
to | God | And came | .Balaam | with | Moab | the of leaders | And stayed | to ,me

came to Balaam and said, Who *are* these men with you? [10]And Balaam said to God, Balak the son of Zippor, king of Moab, has sent to me, *saying*, [11]Behold! A people has come out of Egypt and covers the eye of the earth. Come now, curse them for me; perhaps I will be able to overcome it and expel it. [12]And God said to Balaam, You shall not go with them; you shall not curse the people, for it *is* blessed.

[13]And Balaam rose in the morning and said to the leaders of Balak, Go to your land, for Jehovah has refused to allow me to go with you.

[14]And the leaders of Moab arose and came to Balak and said, Balaam refuses to come with us.

[15]And yet again Balak sent more leaders, even more honorable than they. [16]And they came to Balaam and said to him, So says Balak the son of Zippor, Please do not be kept back from coming to me, [17]for I will honor you with very much honor. And all that you say to me, I will do; and, Please come, curse this people for me. [18]And Balaam replied and said to the servants of Balak, If Balak would give to me his house full of silver and gold, I would not be able to go beyond the mouth of Jehovah my God, to do anything, small or great. [19]But now please remain here tonight, you also, and I shall know what more Jehovah may speak to me. [20]And God came to Balaam at night and said to him, If the men have come to call you, rise up,

10 בלעם ויאמר מי האנשים האלה עמך׃ ויאמר בלעם
Balaam said And with (are) these you? men Who said and ,Balaam

11 אל־האלהים בלק בן־צפר מלך מואב שלח אלי׃ הנה
(saying) to me sent has ,Moab of king ,Zippor of son the Balak ,God to See

העם היצא ממצרים ויכס את־עין הארץ עתה לכה קבה־
curse ;come ,now the earth of eye the covers which Egypt of out come has A people

12 לי אתו אולי אוכל להלחם בו וגרשתיו׃ ויאמר אלהים
God said And expel and .it it overcome to able be shall I perhaps ;them for me

אל־בלעם לא תלך עמהם לא תאר את־העם כי ברוך
blessed for ;people the curse shall you not ;them with shall You not go ,Balaam to

13 הוא׃ ויקם בלעם בבקר ויאמר אל־שרי בלק לכו אל־
to Go ,Balak of chiefs the to said and morning the in Balaam rose And .(is) it

14 ארצכם כי מאן יהוה לתתי להלך עמכם׃ ויקומו שרי
of chiefs the arose And you with to go me allow to Jehovah refused has for ,land your

מואב ויבאו אל־בלק ויאמרו מאן בלעם הלך עמנו׃
.us with come to Balaam refuses ,said and ,Balak to came and Moab

15 ויסף עוד בלק שלח שרים רבים ונכבדים מאלה׃
.they than honorable more and more chiefs sent Balak again yet And

16 ויבאו אל־בלעם ויאמרו לו כה אמר בלק בן־צפור אל־
not ,Zippor of son the Balak says Thus him to said and Balaam to came they And

17 נא תמנע מהלך אלי׃ כי־כבד אכבדך מאד וכל אשר־
that all and much very honor you will I honor for me to coming from hindered be do Please

18 תאמר אלי אעשה ולכה־נא קבה־לי את העם הזה׃ ויען
replied And .this people for me curse ,please come and do will I me to say you

בלעם ויאמר אל־עבדי בלק אם־יתן־לי בלק מלא ביתו
house his of full Balak me to give would If ,Balak of servants the to said and Balaam

כסף וזהב לא אוכל לעבר את־פי יהוה אלהי לעשות
anything do to God my Jehovah of mouth the beyond go could I not ,gold and silver

19 קטנה או גדולה׃ ועתה שבו נא בזה גם־אתם הלילה
;tonight ,you also ,here please stay now And .great or small

20 ואדעה מה־יסף יהוה דבר עמי׃ ויבא אלהים אל־
to God came And .me to speak may Jehovah more what know shall I and

בלעם לילה ויאמר לו אם־לקרא לך באו האנשים קום
arise ,men the come have you call to If ,him to said and ,night at Balaam

with them and say only the
thing that I speak to you
— it you shall do. [21]And
Balaam rose up in the
morning and saddled his
ass and went with the
leaders of Moab.

[22]And the anger of God
glowed because he went.
And the Angel of Jehovah
stationed Himself in the
road, as an enemy against
him. And he was riding on
his ass, and two of his
servants with him. [23]And
the ass saw the Angel of
Jehovah standing in the
road, and His sword *was*
drawn in His hand. And the
ass turned out of the road
and went into a field.
And Balaam struck the ass,
to turn it back into the
road. [24]And the Angel of
Jehovah stood in a narrow
path of the vineyards, a
wall *being* on this
side and a wall on that.

[25]And the ass saw the
Angel of Jehovah, and
she pushed herself to the
wall and crushed the foot
of Balaam against the
wall. And again he struck
her. [26]And the Angel of
Jehovah passed on and
stood in a narrow place,
where there *was* no way
to turn, either to the right
or to the left. [27]And the
ass saw the Angel of
Jehovah, and she lay
down under Balaam. And
Balaam's anger glowed,
and he struck the ass
with his staff. [28]And
Jehovah opened the
mouth of the ass. And
she said to Balaam, What
have I done to you
that you have struck
me these three times?
[29]And Balaam said to the
ass, because you have
insulted me. If only there
were a sword in my hand
now I would kill you.
[30]And the ass said to
Balaam, Am I not your
ass on which you have
ridden all your life long
to this day? Was I ever

לך אתם ואך את־הדבר אשר־אדבר אליך אתו תעשה׃
21 ויקם בלעם בבקר ויחבש את־אתנו וילך עם־שרי מואב׃
22 ויחר־אף אלהים כי־הולך הוא ויתיצב מלאך יהוה בדרך
23 לשטן לו והוא רכב על־אתנו ושני נעריו עמו׃ ותרא
האתון את־מלאך יהוה נצב בדרך וחרבו שלופה בידו
ותט האתון מן־הדרך ותלך בשדה ויך בלעם את־האתון
24 להטתה הדרך׃ ויעמד מלאך יהוה במשעול הכרמים
25 גדר מזה וגדר מזה׃ ותרא האתון את־מלאך יהוה
ותלחץ אל־הקיר ותלחץ את־רגל בלעם אל־הקיר ויסף
26 להכתה׃ ויוסף מלאך־יהוה עבור ויעמד במקום צר
27 אשר אין־דרך לנטות ימין ושמאול׃ ותרא האתון את־
מלאך יהוה ותרבץ תחת בלעם ויחר־אף בלעם ויך
28 את־האתון במקל׃ ויפתח יהוה את־פי האתון ותאמר
לבלעם מה־עשיתי לך כי הכיתני זה שלש רגלים׃
29 ויאמר בלעם לאתון כי התעללת בי לו יש־חרב בידי
30 כי עתה הרגתיך׃ ותאמר האתון אל־בלעם הלוא אנכי
אתנך אשר־רכבת עלי מעודך עד־היום הזה ההסכן

known to do so to you? And
he said, No. [31]And Jehovah
opened the eyes of Balaam,
and he saw the Angel of
Jehovah standing in the
road with His sword drawn
in His hand. And he bowed
and fell on his face.
[32]And the Angel of Jehovah
said to him, Why have you
struck your ass these three
times? Behold, I have come
out as an enemy because
your way *is* contrary to Me.
[33]And the ass saw Me and
turned aside before Me
these three times. If she
had not turned aside surely
now I would have killed you
and saved her alive.
[34]And Balaam said to the
Angel of Jehovah, I have
sinned, for I did not know
that You stood against me
in the way. Now if evil *is* in
Your eyes, I will turn back
by myself. [35]And the Angel
of Jehovah said to Balaam,
Go with the men. But only
the word that I speak to you,
it you shall speak. And
Balaam went with the
leaders of Balak.

[36]And when Balak heard
that Balaam had come, and
had gone out to meet him,
to a city of Moab which *is*
on the border of Arnon,
which *is* in the outermost
border, [37]then Balak said
to Balaam, Sending did I
not send to you, to call for
you? Why did you not come
to me? Am I not truly able
to honor you? [38]And
Balaam said to Balak, Behold,
I have come to you.
Now am I able to speak anything
at all? The word that
God puts in my mouth,
that I will speak. [39]And
Balaam went with Balak;

3869 3068 1540 3808 559 6213 5532
31 הִסְכַּנְתִּי לַעֲשׂוֹת לְךָ כֹּה וַיֹּאמֶר לֹא׃ וַיְגַל יְהוָה אֶת־עֵינֵי
eyes the of Jehovah Then opened .No he And said ?so to you do to known I

8025 2719 1870 5324 3068 4397 7200 1109
בִלְעָם וַיַּרְא אֶת־מַלְאַךְ יְהוָה נִצָּב בַּדֶּרֶךְ וְחַרְבּוֹ שְׁלֻפָה
drawn His sword with the road in standing Jehovah the of Angel he and saw ,Balaam

3068 4397 559 639 7812 6911 3027
32 בְּיָדוֹ וַיִּקֹּד וַיִּשְׁתַּחוּ לְאַפָּיו׃ וַיֹּאמֶר אֵלָיו מַלְאַךְ יְהוָה עַל־
Why ,Jehovah the of Angel him to said And his on .face fell and he and bowed His in ;hand

3318 2009 7272 7969 860 5221
מָה הִכִּיתָ אֶת־אֲתֹנְךָ זֶה שָׁלוֹשׁ רְגָלִים הִנֵּה אָנֹכִי יָצָאתִי
have come I Behold ?times three these ass your you have struck

6440 5186 860 7200 1870 3399 7854
33 לְשָׂטָן כִּי־יָרַט הַדֶּרֶךְ לְנֶגְדִּי׃ וַתִּרְאַנִי הָאָתוֹן וַתֵּט לְפָנַי
before Me and turned off ass the saw And .Me to your way is because contrary an as enemy

6258 5186 194 7272 7969
זֶה שָׁלֹשׁ רְגָלִים אוּלַי נָטְתָה מִפָּנַי כִּי עַתָּה גַּם־אֹתְכָה
you now surely from Me had she turned off not if ;times three these

3068 4397 1109 559 2421 2026
34 הָרַגְתִּי וְאוֹתָהּ הֶחֱיֵיתִי׃ וַיֹּאמֶר בִּלְעָם אֶל־מַלְאַךְ יְהוָה
Jehovah the of Angel to Balaam said And saved .alive her and would I have killed

6258/1870 7125 5324 3045 3808 2398
חָטָאתִי כִּי לֹא יָדַעְתִּי כִּי אַתָּה נִצָּב לִקְרָאתִי בַּדָּרֶךְ וְעַתָּה
,now the in ;way against me stood You that did I know not for have I sinned

3068 4397 559 7725 5869 7451 518
35 אִם־רַע בְּעֵינֶיךָ אָשׁוּבָה לִּי׃ וַיֹּאמֶר מַלְאַךְ יְהוָה אֶל־
to Jehovah the of Angel said And by .myself turn shall I back Your in ,eyes evil (is) If

1696 834 1697 657 582 3212 1109
בִּלְעָם לֵךְ עִם־הָאֲנָשִׁים וְאֶפֶס אֶת־הַדָּבָר אֲשֶׁר־אֲדַבֵּר
speak I which word the and only ,men the with Go ,Balaam

8085 1111 8269 1109 3212 1696
36 אֵלֶיךָ אֹתוֹ תְדַבֵּר וַיֵּלֶךְ בִּלְעָם עִם־שָׂרֵי בָלָק׃ וַיִּשְׁמַע
And heard when .Balak of chiefs the with Balaam And went shall you .speak it ,you to

834 4124 5892 7125 3318 1109 935 1111
בָלָק כִּי־בָא בִלְעָם וַיֵּצֵא לִקְרָאתוֹ אֶל־עִיר מוֹאָב אֲשֶׁר
which (is) ,Moab of city a to meet to ,him had and gone ,Balaam had come that Balak

1111 559 1366 7097 834 769 1366
37 עַל־גְּבוּל אַרְנֹן אֲשֶׁר בִּקְצֵה הַגְּבוּל׃ וַיֹּאמֶר בָּלָק אֶל־
to Balak said Then the .border outermost in which (is) ,Arnon the of border on

3808 4100 7121 7971 1109
בִּלְעָם הֲלֹא שָׁלֹחַ שָׁלַחְתִּי אֵלֶיךָ לִקְרֹא־לָךְ לָמָּה לֹא
not Why ?you for call to you to earnestly I send Did not ,Balaam

1109 559 3513 3201 3808 552 3212
38 הָלַכְתָּ אֵלָי הַאֻמְנָם לֹא אוּכַל כַּבְּדֶךָ׃ וַיֹּאמֶר בִּלְעָם אֶל־
to Balaam said And honor to ?you able I not truly Am ?me to you did come

3972 1696 3201 3605 6258 935 2009 1111
בָּלָק הִנֵּה־בָאתִי אֵלֶיךָ עַתָּה הֲיָכֹל אוּכַל דַּבֵּר מְאוּמָה
?anything speak to able I am all at ,now ,you to have I come ,See ,Balak

1109 3212 1696 6310 430 7760 834 1697
39 הַדָּבָר אֲשֶׁר יָשִׂים אֱלֹהִים בְּפִי אֹתוֹ אֲדַבֵּר׃ וַיֵּלֶךְ בִּלְעָם
Balaam And went I will .speak that my in ,mouth God puts which The word

and they came to the City of
Huzoth. [40]And Balak sacrificed oxen and sheep and
sent to Balaam and to the
leaders who *were* with him.
[41]And it happened in the
morning, Balak took Balaam
and caused him to go up to
the high places of Baal. And
from there he saw the
farthest edge of the people.

CHAPTER 23
[1]And Balaam said to
Balak, Build seven altars
for me here, and prepare
seven bullocks and seven
rams for me here. [2]And
Balak did as Balaam had
spoken. And Balak and
Balaam offered a bullock
and a ram on the altar. [3]And
Balaam said to Balak,
Station yourself by your
burnt offering, and I will go
on; it may be that Jehovah
will come to meet me, and I
will declare to you the
things which He reveals to
me. And he went to a high
place. [4]And God came to
Balaam, and he said to Him,
I have set up seven altars.
And I have offered a bul-
lock and a ram on the altar.
[5]And Jehovah put a word in
Balaam's mouth, and said,
Return to Balak, and you
shall say this. [6]And he returned to him. And, lo, he
was standing by his burnt
offering, he and all the
leaders of Moab. [7]And he
took up his parable and
said, He has led me from
Aram, Balak king of Moab;
from the mountains of the
east, *saying*, Come, curse
Jacob for me; and, Come,
denounce Israel. [8]How
shall I curse *him* whom God
has not cursed? And how
shall I denounce *him* whom
Jehovah has not de-
nounced? [9]For from the top
of the rocks I see him, and I
behold him from the
heights. Behold, it is a
people that shall dwell
alone, and shall not be
reckoned among the

7971 6629 1241 1111 2076 2351 7155 935 1111
40 עִם־בָּלָק וַיָּבֹאוּ קִרְיַת חֻצוֹת׃ וַיִּזְבַּח בָּלָק בָּקָר וָצֹאן וַיְשַׁלַּח
sent and and cattle Balak And ,huzoth Kirjath- and Balak with
sheep sacrificed to came they

1111 3947 1242 1961 8269 1109
41 לְבִלְעָם וְלַשָּׂרִים אֲשֶׁר אִתּוֹ׃ וַיְהִי בַבֹּקֶר וַיִּקַּח בָּלָק אֶת־
Balak that the in it And with who to and to
took ,morning was .him (were) leaders the ,Balaam

5971 7097 8033 7200 1120 1116 5927 1109
בִּלְעָם וַיַּעֲלֵהוּ בָּמוֹת בָּעַל וַיַּרְא מִשָּׁם קְצֵה הָעָם׃
the the from he and ;Baal high the sent and Balaam
.people of edge there saw of places to up him

CAP. XXIII כג

CHAPTER 23

3559 4196 7651 1129 1111 1109 559
1 וַיֹּאמֶר בִּלְעָם אֶל־בָּלָק בְּנֵה־לִי בָזֶה שִׁבְעָה מִזְבְּחֹת וְהָכֵן
and ,altars seven here for Build ,Balak to Balaam said And
prepare me

1111 6213 352 7651 6499 7651 2088
2 לִי בָּזֶה שִׁבְעָה פָרִים וְשִׁבְעָה אֵילִים׃ וַיַּעַשׂ בָּלָק כַּאֲשֶׁר
as Balak did And .rams and bullocks seven here for
seven me

559 4196 352 6499 1109 1111 5927 1109 1696
3 דִּבֶּר בִּלְעָם וַיַּעַל בָּלָק וּבִלְעָם פַּר וָאַיִל בַּמִּזְבֵּחַ׃ וַיֹּאמֶר
said And the on a and a and Balak and ,Balaam had
.altar ram bullock Balaam offered spoken

7136 194 1980 5930 3320 1111 1109
בִּלְעָם לְבָלָק הִתְיַצֵּב עַל־עֹלָתֶךָ וְאֵלְכָה אוּלַי יִקָּרֵה
will may it I and burnt your by Station to Balaam
come that be ;on go will ,offering yourself ,Balak

8205 1980 5046 7200 1697 7125 3068
יְהוָה לִקְרָאתִי וּדְבַר מַה־יַּרְאֵנִי וְהִגַּדְתִּי לָךְ וַיֵּלֶךְ שֶׁפִי׃
high a to And to will I that He which the and meet to Jehovah
;place went he .you declare ,me to reveals things ;me

4196 7651 559 1109 430 7136
4 וַיִּקָּר אֱלֹהִים אֶל־בִּלְעָם וַיֹּאמֶר אֵלָיו אֶת־שִׁבְעַת הַמִּזְבְּחֹת
altars seven to he and ,Balaam to God and
.Him said came

6310 1697 3068 7760 4196 352 6499 5927 6186
5 עָרַכְתִּי וָאַעַל פַּר וָאַיִל בַּמִּזְבֵּחַ׃ וַיָּשֶׂם יְהוָה דָּבָר בְּפִי
in a Jehovah put And the on a and a have I and have I
mouth word .altar ram bullock offered ;up set

7725 1696 1111 7725 559 1109
6 בִלְעָם וַיֹּאמֶר שׁוּב אֶל־בָּלָק וְכֹה תְדַבֵּר׃ וַיָּשָׁב אֵלָיו
,him to he And shall you and ,Balak to Go ,said and ,Balaam's
returned .say this back

4912 5375 4124 8269 5930 5324 2009
7 וְהִנֵּה נִצָּב עַל־עֹלָתוֹ הוּא וְכָל־שָׂרֵי מוֹאָב׃ וַיִּשָּׂא מְשָׁלוֹ
his he And .Moab the and he burnt his by was he and
parable up took of chiefs all ,offering standing ,behold

6924 2042 4124 4428 1111 5148 758 559
וַיֹּאמַר מִן־אֲרָם יַנְחֵנִי בָלָק מֶלֶךְ־מוֹאָב מֵהַרְרֵי־קֶדֶם
the the from ;Moab of king Balak has he Aram From ,said and
east of mountains me led

3808 5344 4100 3478 2194 3212 3290 779 3212
8 לְכָה אָרָה־לִּי יַעֲקֹב וּלְכָה זֹעֲמָה יִשְׂרָאֵל׃ מָה אֶקֹּב לֹא
not I shall How Israel denounce and ;Jacob for curse ,Come
curse come me

6697 7218 3068 2194 2194 410 6895
9 קַבֹּה אֵל וּמָה אֶזְעֹם לֹא זָעַם יְהוָה׃ כִּי־מֵרֹאשׁ צֻרִים
the the from For ?Jehovah has not I shall And ?God whom
rocks of top at raged at rage how cursed has

3808 1471 7931 910 5971 7200 1389 7200
אֶרְאֶנּוּ וּמִגְּבָעוֹת אֲשׁוּרֶנּוּ הֶן־עָם לְבָדָד יִשְׁכֹּן וּבַגּוֹיִם לֹא
not among and shall alone the ,See behold I from and see I
nations the dwell people to :him heights the ,him

nations. [10]Who can count
the dust of Jacob, and the
number of the fourth part
of Israel? Let me die the
death of the righteous;
yea, let my last end be
like his! [11]And Balak said
to Balaam, What have
you done to me? I took
you to curse my enemies,
and, behold, blessing you
have blessed. [12]And he
answered and said, Must
not I take heed to speak
that which Jehovah has
put in my mouth? [13]And
Balak said to him, Please
come with me to another
place, from where you
shall see it; only you shall
see its edge, and you
shall not see all of it; and
curse it for me there.
[14]And he took him to the
field of Zophim, to the top
of Pisgah, and *he* built
seven altars and offered a
bull and a ram on the
altar. [15]And he said to
Balak, Stand here by the
burnt offering while I go
to meet *Him* over there.
[16]And Jehovah met Ba-
laam and put a word in
his mouth, and said, Go
back to Balak, and
you shall say this.

[17]And he came to him, and
behold, he stood by his
burnt offering, and the
leaders of Moab with him.
And he said to him, What
has Jehovah spoken? [18]And
he took up his parable and
said, Rise up, Balak, and
hear; give ear to me, son of
Zippor. [19]God is not a man
that He should lie; nor a son
of man that He should
repent. Has He said, and
shall He not do it? And *has*
He spoken, and shall He not
make it good? [20]Behold, I
have received *word* to
bless; yes, He has blessed; I
cannot reverse it. [21]He has
seen no iniquity in Jacob,
nor has He seen mischief in
Israel. Jehovah his God *is*
with him, and the shout of a
king *is* in him. [22]God who

10 יתחשב׃ מי מנה עפר יעקב ומספר את־רבע ישראל
11 תמת נפשי מות ישרים ותהי אחריתי כמהו׃ ויאמר
בלק אל־בלעם מה עשית לי לקב איבי לקחתיך והנה
12 ברכת ברך׃ ויען ויאמר הלא את אשר ישים יהוה
13 בפי אתו אשמר לדבר׃ ויאמר אליו בלק לך־נא אתי
אל־מקום אחר אשר תראנו משם אפס קצהו תראה
14 וכלו לא תראה וקבנו־לי משם׃ ויקחהו שדה צפים
אל־ראש הפסגה ויבן שבעה מזבחת ויעל פר ואיל
15 במזבח׃ ויאמר אל־בלק התיצב כה על־עלתך ואנכי
16 אקרה כה׃ ויקר יהוה אל־בלעם וישם דבר בפיו
17 ויאמר שוב אל־בלק וכה תדבר׃ ויבא אליו והנו נצב
על־עלתו ושרי מואב אתו ויאמר לו בלק מה־דבר
18 יהוה׃ וישא משלו ויאמר קום בלק ושמע האזינה
19 עדי בנו צפר׃ לא איש אל ויכזב ובן־אדם ויתנחם
20 ההוא אמר ולא יעשה ודבר ולא יקימנה׃ הנה ברך
21 לקחתי וברך ולא אשיבנה׃ לא־הביט און ביעקב ולא־
ראה עמל בישראל יהוה אלהיו עמו ותרועת מלך בו׃

5173 3808 3588 7214 8443 4714 3318 410

22 אֵל מוֹצִיאָם מִמִּצְרָיִם כְּתוֹעֲפֹת רְאֵם לוֹ׃ כִּי לֹא־נַחַשׁ
23

(is) spell a not For for the the like (is) of out brought who God
.him ox wild of horns lofty Egypt them

3478 3290 559 6256 3478 7081 3290

בְיַעֲקֹב וְלֹא־קֶסֶם בְּיִשְׂרָאֵל כָּעֵת יֵאָמֵר לְיַעֲקֹב וּלְיִשְׂרָאֵל

Israel and Jacob of is it Now against fortune- and against
said ;Israel telling not Jacob

3808 5375 738 6965 3833 5971 410 6466

24 מַה־פָּעַל אֵל׃ הֶן־עָם כְּלָבִיא יָקוּם וְכַאֲרִי יִתְנַשָּׂא לֹא

not lift shall he like and shall a like the Behold God! has What
;up himself lion a .rise lioness people done

1111 559 8354 2491 1818 2964 398 5704 3427

25 יִשְׁכַּב עַד־יֹאכַל טֶרֶף וְדַם־חֲלָלִים יִשְׁתֶּה׃ וַיֹּאמֶר בָּלָק

Balak said And .drinks slain the and .prey eats he until shall he
of blood down lie

6030 1288 3808 5344 3808

26 אֶל־בִּלְעָם גַּם־קֹב לֹא תִקֳּבֶנּוּ גַּם־בָּרֵךְ לֹא תְבָרֲכֶנּוּ׃ וַיַּעַן

And .it bless nor all at curse Do not all at .Balaam to
replied .it

3605 559 1696 1111 559 1109

בִּלְעָם וַיֹּאמֶר אֶל־בָּלָק הֲלֹא דִּבַּרְתִּי אֵלֶיךָ לֵאמֹר כֹּל

All ,saying you to speak I not Did ,Balak to said and Balaam

1109 1111 559 6213 3068 1696

27 אֲשֶׁר־יְדַבֵּר יְהוָה אֹתוֹ אֶעֱשֶׂה׃ וַיֹּאמֶר בָּלָק אֶל־בִּלְעָם

,Balaam to Balak said And ?do I will that ,Jehovah speaks that

430 5869 8477 312 4725 3947 4994 3212

לְכָה־נָּא אֶקָּחֲךָ אֶל־מָקוֹם אַחֵר אוּלַי יִישַׁר בְּעֵינֵי הָאֱלֹהִים

God the in be it may ;another place to will I ,come
of eyes right you take Please

6465 7218 1109 1111 3947 8033 6895

28 וְקַבֹּתוֹ לִי מִשָּׁם׃ וַיִּקַּח בָּלָק אֶת־בִּלְעָם רֹאשׁ הַפְּעוֹר

.Peor the to Balaam Balak And from for curse to
of top took .there me it

1129 1111 1109 559 4057 6440 8259

29 הַנִּשְׁקָף עַל־פְּנֵי הַיְשִׁימֹן׃ וַיֹּאמֶר בִּלְעָם אֶל־בָּלָק בְּנֵה־

Build ,Balak to Balaam said And the toward which
.wilderness looks

6499 7651 3559 4196 7651

לִי בָזֶה שִׁבְעָה מִזְבְּחֹת וְהָכֵן לִי בָּזֶה שִׁבְעָה פָרִים

bullocks seven here for and ,altars seven here for
me prepare me

6499 5927 1109 559 1111 6213 352 7651

30 וְשִׁבְעָה אֵילִים׃ וַיַּעַשׂ בָּלָק כַּאֲשֶׁר אָמַר בִּלְעָם וַיַּעַל פַּר

a he and ,Balaam said as Balak did And .rams seven and
bullock offered

4196 352

וָאַיִל בַּמִּזְבֵּחַ׃

the on a and
.altar ram

brought them out of Egypt *is* for him like the lofty horns of the wild ox. [23]For there *is* not a spell against Jacob, nor any fortune-telling against Israel. Now it is said of Jacob and Israel, *See* what God has done! [24]Behold, the people shall rise like a lioness, and as a lion he shall lift himself up; he shall not lie down until he eats the prey and drinks the blood of the slain. [25]And Balak said to Balaam, Do not curse it at all, nor bless it at all. [26]And Balaam answered and said to Balak, Did I not speak to you, saying, All that Jehovah speaks, that I will do? [27]And Balak said to Balaam, Come, please, I will take you to another place. It may be that it will be right in the eyes of God to curse it for me from there. [28]And Balak took Balaam to the top of Peor, which looks toward the wilderness. [29]And Balaam said to Balak, Build seven altars for me here, and prepare seven bullocks and seven rams for me here. [30]And Balak did as Balaam said; and he offered a bullock and a ram on the altar.

CAP. XXIV

CHAPTER 24

3808 3478 1288 3068 5869 2895 1109 7200

1 וַיַּרְא בִּלְעָם כִּי טוֹב בְּעֵינֵי יְהוָה לְבָרֵךְ אֶת־יִשְׂרָאֵל וְלֹא

not and ,Israel bless to Jehovah the in was it that Balaam And
of eyes good saw

4057 7896 5173 7125 6471 6471 3212

הָלַךְ כְּפַעַם־בְּפַעַם לִקְרַאת נְחָשִׁים וַיָּשֶׁת אֶל־הַמִּדְבָּר

the toward he but ;spells seek to ,times other at as did he
wilderness set .go

7931 3478 7200 5869 1109 5375 6440

2 פָּנָיו׃ וַיִּשָּׂא בִלְעָם אֶת־עֵינָיו וַיַּרְא אֶת־יִשְׂרָאֵל שֹׁכֵן

,camping Israel saw and ,eyes his Balaam And his
up lifted .face

CHAPTER 24

[1]And Balaam saw that it pleased Jehovah to bless Israel, and he did not go, as at other times, to seek spells. And he set his face toward the wilderness. [2]And Balaam lifted up his eyes and saw Israel camping by its tribes. And

the Spirit of God was on him. [3]And he took up his parable and said, The saying of Balaam the son of Beor, and the saying of the man whose eyes have been opened; [4]the saying of him who hears the words of God, who sees the vision of the Almighty, fallen down, yet with open eyes: [5]How good are your tents, O Jacob, your dwellings, O Israel! [6]They are spread out like valleys, like gardens by a river; and Jehovah has planted aloes, as cedars beside the water. [7]He makes water flow from his buckets, and his seed *shall be* in mighty waters; and his king shall be higher than Agag, and his kingdom exalted. [8]God who has brought him out of Egypt *is* for him like the lofty horns of the wild ox; he shall eat up the nations that are his foes, and shall break their bones in pieces, and shall pierce them through *with* his arrows. [9]He has crouched; he has lain down like a lion, and like a lioness; who shall rouse him up? Blessed is everyone that blesses you, and cursed is everyone that curses you.

[10]And Balak's anger glowed against Balaam, and he struck his palms together. And Balak said to Balaam, I called you to curse my enemies; and, behold, you have altogether blessed them these three times. [11]And now, flee to your place. I thought to honor you with great honor, but, behold, Jehovah has kept you back from honor. [12]And Balaam said to Balak, Did I not speak to your messengers that you sent to me, saying, [13]If Balak would give me his house full of silver and gold, I cannot go beyond the mouth of Jehovah, to do good or bad of my own heart what Jehovah speaks, that I will speak? [14]And

559 4912 5375 430 7307 1901 7626
3 לשבטיו ותהי עליו רוח אלהים׃ וישא משלו ויאמר
,said and his he And .God the him on was and its by
parable up took of Spirit ;tribes

5002 5869 8365 1397 5002 1160 1121 1109 5002
4 נאם בלעם בנו בער ונאם הגבר שתם העין׃ נאם
the his having man the the and ,Beor the ,Balaam The
of saying :eyes opened of saying of son of saying

1540 5307 7706 4236 834 410 561 8085
שמע אמרי־אל אשר מחזה שדי יחזה נפל וגלוי
un- and fallen ,sees the the who ,God the one
of covered down Almighty of vision of words hearing

3478 4908 3290 168 2895 5869
5 עינים׃ מה־טבו אהליך יעקב משכנתיך ישראל׃
!Israel O your ,Jacob O ,tents your good How :eyes
dwellings are

730 3068 5193 174 5104 1593 5186 5158
6 כנחלים נטיו כגנת עלי נהר כאהלים נטע יהוה כארזים
cedars as ,Jehovah has aloes like a by like they valleys Like
planted ;river gardens out spread

7311 7227 4325 2233 1805 4325 4325
7 עלי־מים׃ יזל־מים מדליו וזרעו במים רבים וירם
and ;mighty (be shall) his and His from waters He the beside
higher waters in seed ,buckets flow makes ,waters

4714 5927 410 4428 5375 4428 90
8 מאגג מלכו ותנשא מלכתו׃ אל מוציאו ממצרים
of out has Who God his and his (is) than
Egypt him brought .kingdom exalted ,king Agag

1633 6106 6862 398 7214 8443
כתועפת ראם לו יאכל גוים צריו ועצמתיהם יגרם
gnaw shall their and are that the shall he for wild the the like (is)
bones ,foes his nations up eat ;him ox of horns lofty

6965 3833 738 7901 3766 4272 2671
9 וחציו ימחץ׃ כרע שכב כארי וכלביא מי יקימנו
stir shall who like and a like has he has He shall he (with) and
?up him :lioness a ,lion down lain ,crouched .dash arrows his

1109 1111 639 2734 779 779 1288 1288
10 מברכיך ברוך וארריך ארור׃ ויחר־אף בלק אל־בלעם
,Balaam against Balak's anger And .cursed he and Blessed who he
glowed. is curses who you ,is you blesses

7121 341 6895 1109 1111 559 3709 5606
ויספק את־כפיו ויאמר בלק אל־בלעם לקב איבי קראתיך
called I my to ,Balaam to Balak and ,palms his he and
;you enemies curse said struck

1272 6471 7969 1288 2009
11 והנה ברכת ברך זה שלש פעמים׃ ועתה ברח־לך
flee And .times three these, altogether have you and
,now blessed ,behold

3068 4513 2009 3513 3513 559 4725
אל־מקומך אמרתי כבד אכבדך והנה מנעך יהוה
Jehovah kept has but honor to great thought I your to
back you ,behold ;you honor ;place

4397 1571 1111 1109 559 3519
12 מכבוד׃ ויאמר בלעם אל־בלק הלא גם אל־מלאכיך
your to also Did ,Balak to Balaam said And from
messengers not .honor

4393 1111 5414 559 1696 7971
13 אשר־שלחת אלי דברתי לאמר׃ אם־יתן־לי בלק מלא
full Balak me would If ,saying ,speak I me to sent you that
of give

6213 3068 6310 5674 3201 2091 3701 1004
ביתו כסף וזהב לא אוכל לעבר את־פי יהוה לעשות
do to ,Jehovah the go can I not and silver his
of mouth beyond ,gold house

1696 3068 1696 834 3820 7451 2896
טובה או רעה מלבי אשר־ידבר יהוה אתו אדבר׃
I will that ,Jehovah speaks what my of bad or (either)
?speak ;heart own good

now, behold, I go to my
people. Come, and I will tell
you what this people shall
do to your people in the
latter days. [15]And he took
up his parable and said, The
saying of Balaam the son of
Beor, and the saying of the
man whose eyes *are*
opened; [16]the saying of
him who hears the words of
God, and knows the
knowledge of the Most
High, who sees the vision of
the Almighty, falling down,
yet with open eyes: [17]I shall
see him, but not now; I shall
behold him, but not near. A
star shall come forth out of
Jacob, and a scepter shall
rise out of Israel and shall
dash the corners of Moab,
and break down all the sons
of tumult. [18]And Edom
shall be a possession; and
Seir shall be a possession,
for *his* foes; but Israel shall
do mightily. [19]And *one* out
of Jacob shall rule, and will
destroy the survivors from
Ar.
[20]And he looked upon
Amalek, and took up his
parable and said, Amalek
was the first of the nations,
but his latter end *is* to
destruction. [21]And he
looked upon the Kenites,
and took up his parable, and
said, Your dwelling-place
may be enduring, and your
nest may be set in a rock,
[22]but the Kenites shall be
consumed, until Assyria
shall carry you away.
[23]And he took up his
parable and said, Alas! Who
shall live when God puts
out? [24]And ships *shall*
come from the coast of Chit-
tim, and they shall humble
Assyria, and they shall
humble Eber, and he also
shall come to destruction.
[25]And Balaam rose up and
left, and returned to his
place; and Balak also went
on his way.

14 ועתה הנני הולך לעמי לכה איעצך אשר יעשה העם
15 הזה לעמך באחרית הימים: וישא משלו ויאמר נאם
16 בלעם בנו בער ונאם הגבר שתם העין: נאם שמע
אמרי־אל וידע דעת עליון מחזה שדי יחזה נפל וגלוי
17 עינים: אראנו ולא עתה אשורנו ולא קרוב דרך כוכב
מיעקב וקם שבט מישראל ומחץ פאתי מואב וקרקר
18 כל־בני־שת: והיה אדום ירשה והיה ירשה שעיר איביו
19 וישראל עשה חיל: וירד מיעקב והאביד שריד מעיר:
20 וירא את־עמלק וישא משלו ויאמר ראשית גוים עמלק
21 ואחריתו עדי אבד: וירא את־הקיני וישא משלו ויאמר
22 איתן מושבך ושים בסלע קנך: כי אם־יהיה לבער קין
23 עד־מה אשור תשבך: וישא משלו ויאמר אוי מי יחיה
24 משמו אל: וצים מיד כתים וענו אשור וענו־עבר וגם־
25 הוא עדי אבד: ויקם בלעם וילך וישב למקמו וגם־
בלק הלך לדרכו:

CAP. XXV כה

CHAPTER 25

[1]And Israel lived in Shittim. And the people began
to fornicate with the
daughters of Moab. [2]And

1 וישב ישראל בשטים ויחל העם לזנות אל־בנות מואב:

they called the people to the sacrifices of their gods. And the people ate and bowed themselves to their gods. [3]And Israel was joined to Baal-peor, and the anger of Jehovah burned against Israel. [4]And Jehovah said to Moses, Take all the leaders of the people and hang them up to Jehovah before the sun, that the fierce anger of Jehovah may be turned away from Israel. [5]And Moses said to the judges of Israel, Each one of you kill his men, *those* who joined to Baal-peor. [6]And, behold, a man of the sons of Israel came and brought in to his brothers a woman of Midian, before the eyes of Moses and before the eyes of all the congregation of the sons of Israel, who were weeping at the door of the tabernacle of the congregation. [7]And Phinehas, the son of Eleazar, the son of Aaron, the priest saw. And *he* rose from amidst the congregation and took a javelin in his hand, [8]and went in after the man of Israel, into the tent room. And *he* pierced both of them through, the man of Israel and the woman, through her belly. So the plague was stayed from the sons of Israel. [9]And those that died by the plague *were* twenty-four thousand.

[10]And Jehovah spoke to Moses, saying, [11]Phinehas the son of Eleazar, the son of Aaron the priest, has turned My wrath away from the sons of Israel while he was zealous for My sake among them, so that I did not consume the sons of Israel in My jealousy. [12]Therefore say, Behold, I give to him My covenant of peace; [13]and it shall be to

2 ותקראן לעם לזבחי אלהיהן ויאכל העם וישתחוו
bowed and the and ;gods their the to the they And
people ate of sacrifices people called

3 לאלהיהן׃ ויצמד ישראל לבעל פעור ויחר־אף יהוה
Jehovah the and ,peor-Baal to Israel was And their to
of anger burned joined .gods

4 בישראל׃ ויאמר יהוה אל־משה קח את־כל־ראשי העם
the the all Take ,Moses to Jehovah said And against
,people of chiefs .Israel

והוקע אותם ליהוה נגד השמש וישב חרון אף־יהוה
Jehovah anger the may that sun the before before them and
of fierce turned be ,Jehovah hang

5 מישראל׃ ויאמר משה אל־שפטי ישראל הרגו איש
Each you ,Israel the to Moses said And from
of kill of judges .Israel

6 אנשיו הנצמדים לבעל פעור׃ והנה איש מבני ישראל
Israel the of a And .Baal-Peor to who his
of sons man ,behold joined ,men

בא ויקרב אל־אחיו את־המדינית לעיני משה ולעיני כל־
all and Moses' before woman a his to and came
before ,eyes ,Midian of brothers brought

7 עדת בני־ישראל והמה בכים פתח אהל מועד׃ וירא
And .meeting the the at were who ;Israel the the
looked of tent of door weeping of sons of company

פינחס בן־אלעזר בן־אהרן הכהן ויקם מתוך העדה ויקח
and congre- the from and the Aaron the ,Eleazar the ,Phinehas
took ,gation amid rose ,priest of son of son

8 רמח בידו׃ ויבא אחר איש־ישראל אל־הקבה וידקר
and tent- the into Israel the after and his in a
pierced ,chamber of man in went ,hand javelin

את־שניהם את איש ישראל ואת־האשה אל־קבתה
her through the and Israel man the of both
.belly ,woman of ,them

9 ותעצר המגפה מעל בני ישראל׃ ויהיו המתים במגפה
the by that those And .Israel the from plague the was So
plague died were of sons stayed

ארבעה ועשרים אלף׃
.thousand and four
twenty

10 וידבר יהוה אל־משה לאמר׃
11 פינחס בן־אלעזר בן
the ,Eleazar the Phinehas ,saying ,Moses to Jehovah And
of son of son spoke

אהרן הכהן השיב את־חמתי מעל בני־ישראל בקנאו
he while Israel the from wrath My has the Aaron
zealous was of sons away turned ,priest

את־קנאתי בתוכם ולא־כליתי את־בני־ישראל בקנאתי׃
My in Israel the did I that so among My with
.jealousy of sons consume not ,them zeal

12 לכן אמר הנני נתן לו את־בריתי שלום׃
13 והיתה לו
to it and ;peace covenant My to I ,Behold ,say ,So
,him be shall of him give

him, and to his seed after
him, the covenant of an
everlasting priesthood; because he was zealous for
his God, and made atone-
ment for the sons of Israel.
[14]And the name of the man
of Israel who was smitten,
who was smitten with the
woman of Midian, *was*
Zimri, the son of Salu, ruler
of a father's house of the
Simeonites. [15]And the
name of the woman who
was smitten, the woman of
Midian, *was* Cozbi, the
daughter of Zur; he was
head of the people of a
father's house in Midian.

[16]And Jehovah spoke to
Moses, saying, [17]Vex the
Midianites; and you shall
strike them; [18]for they are
vexers to you, because of
the wiles with which they
have beguiled you in the
matter of Peor, and in the
matter of Cozbi, the
daughter of a ruler of
Midian, their sister, who
was smitten in the day of
the plague because of the
matter of Peor.

430 7065 8478 5769 3554 1285 2233
ולזרעו אחריו ברית כהנת עולם תחת אשר קנא לאלהיו
his for God | was he zealous | because | a perpetual | priest-hood of | the covenant | after him | to and seed his

14 5221 3478 370 8034 3478 1121 3722
ויכפר על-בני ישראל׃ ושם איש ישראל המכה אשר
who | was who struck | ,Israel | the of man | the And of name | .Israel | the for of sons | and atoned

8099 1 1004 5387 5543 1121 2174 4084 5221
הכה את-המדינית זמרי בן-סלוא נשיא בית-אב לשמעני׃
the of Simeonites | father's a house | ruler of | ,Salu | the of son | (was) ,Zimri | woman the ,Midian of | with | was struck

15 523 7218 6698 3579 4080 5221 802 8034
ושם האשה המכה המדינית כזבי בת-צור ראש אמות
the of people of | head | ;Zur of daughter | the | (was) ,Cozbi | woman the ,Midian of | was who ,struck | the | the And woman of name

4080 1004
בית-אב במדין הוא׃
.was he | in Midian | father's a house

16
17 5221 4084 6887 559 4872 3068 1696
וידבר יהוה אל-משה לאמר׃ צרור את-המדינים והכיתם
you and strike shall | the ;Midianites | Trouble | ,saying | ,Moses | to Jehovah | And spoke

18 5230 5231 6887
אתם׃ כי צררים הם לכם בנכליהם אשר-נכלו לכם על-
in | you | have they beguiled | with which | of because wiles the | to you | they are | vexers | for | ,them

5221 209 4000 5307 1570 1697 6465 1697
דבר פעור ועל-דבר כזבי בת-נשיא מדין אחתם המכה
was who struck | their ,sister | ,Midian ruler a | the of daughter | ,Cozbi | the in and of matter | ,Peor | the of matter

19 4046 310 1961 6465 1697 4046 3117
ביום-המגפה על-דבר-פעור׃ ויהי אחרי המגפה׃
,plague the | after | it And was | .Peor | the because of matter of | the ,plague | the in of day

CAP. XXVI כו

CHAPTER 26

CHAPTER 26

[1]And it happened, after
the plague, Jehovah spoke
to Moses, and to Eleazar
the son of Aaron the priest,
saying, [2]Lift the heads of all
the congregation of the
sons of Israel, from twenty
years old and upward,
throughout their fathers'
house, all that are able to go
to war in Israel. [3]And Moses
and Eleazar the priest
spoke with them in the
plains of Moab beside
Jordan, *at* Jericho, saying,
[4]*Count* a son of twenty
years and upward, as
Jehovah commanded
Moses and the sons of
Israel, who went out of
the land of Egypt.

[5]Reuben, the firstborn of
Israel, the sons of Reuben:
of Hanoch *came* the family
of the Hanochites; of Pallu
the family of the Palluites;

1 559 3548 175 1121 499 4872 3068 559
ויאמר יהוה אל-משה ואל אלעזר בן-אהרן הכהן לאמר׃
,saying | the priest | Aaron of son | the Eleazar | and to | ,Moses | to Jehovah | that spoke

2 8141 6242 1121 3478 1121 5712 3605 7218 5375
שאו את-ראש כל-עדת בני-ישראל מבן עשרים שנה
years | twenty | from old | ,Israel | the of sons | the of company | all | heads the of | Lift

3 1696 3478 6635 3605 1 1004 4605
ולמעלה לבית אבתם כל-יצא צבא בישראל׃ וידבר
And spoke | .Israel in | war to | that all go can | their ,fathers' | by house | and ,upward

3405 3383 4124 6160 3548 499 4872
משה ואלעזר הכהן אתם בערבת מואב על-ירדן ירחו
(at) ,Jericho | ,Jordan beside | Moab | the on of plains | with them | the priest | and Eleazar | Moses

4 3068 6680 4105 8141 6242 559
לאמר׃ מבן עשרים שנה ומעלה כאשר צוה יהוה את-
Jehovah | com-manded | as | and ,upward | years | twenty (Count) of son a | ,saying

5 1060 7205 4714 776 5927 3478 1121 4872
משה ובני ישראל היצאים מארץ מצרים׃ ראובן בכור
first-born | Reuben | :Egypt | the of out of land | who came | ,Israel | the and of sons | Moses

4940 6396 2599 4940 2585 7205 1121 3478
ישראל בני ראובן חנוך משפחת החנכי לפלוא משפחת
family the of | .Pallu of | the ;Hanochites | the of family (came) | (of) Hanoch | :Reuben | the of sons | ;Israel's

6 from Hezron the family of
the Hezronites; of Carmi,
the family of the Carmites.
7 These are the families of
the Reubenites; and those
who were numbered with
them were forty-three thousand, seven hundred and
thirty. 8 And the son of Pallu
was Eliab. 9 And the sons
of Eliab *were* Nemuel, and
Dathan, and Abiram. This *is*
that Dathan and Abiram
who were called ones *in* the
congregation, who fought
against Moses and against
Aaron in the company of
Korah, when they fought
against Jehovah. 10 And the
earth opened its mouth and
swallowed them up to-
gether with Korah, when
that company died, when
the fire ate up two
hundred and fifty men. And
they became a sign; 11 but
the sons of Korah did not
die.

12 The sons of Simeon
according to their fami-
lies: of Nemuel, the fam-
ily of the Nemuelites;
of Jamin, the family of
the Jaminites; of Jachin,
the family of the Jachin-
ites; 13 of Zerah, the
family of the Zerahites;
of Shaul, the family of
the Sahulites. These *are*
the families of the
Simeonites, twenty-two
thousand, two hundred.

15 The sons of Gad ac-
cording to their families: of
Zephon, the family of the
Zephonites; of Haggi, the
family of the Haggites; of
Shuni, the family of the
Shunites; 16 of Ozni, the
family of the Oznites; of Eri,
the family of the Erites; 17 of
Arod, the family of the
Arodites; of Areli, the family
of the Arelites. 18 These are
the families of the sons of
Gad according to those
numbered of them, forty
thousand, five hundred.
19 The sons of Judah: Er
and Onan; and Er and Onan
died in the land of Canaan.

4940 3766 2697b 4940 2696 6384
6 הַפַּלֻּאִי׃ לְחֶצְרֹן מִשְׁפַּחַת הַחֶצְרוֹנִי לְכַרְמִי מִשְׁפַּחַת
family the ,Carmi of the family the of the
of ;Hezronites of Hezron ;Palluites

7969 6485 1961 7206 • 4940 428 3757
7 הַכַּרְמִי׃ אֵלֶּה מִשְׁפְּחֹת הָראוּבֵנִי וַיִּהְיוּ פְקֻדֵיהֶם שְׁלֹשָׁה
three their and the families the These the
numbered were ;Reubenites of are .Carmites

446 6396 1121 7970 3969 7651 505 703
8 וְאַרְבָּעִים אֶלֶף וּשְׁבַע מֵאוֹת וּשְׁלֹשִׁים׃ וּבְנֵי פַלּוּא אֱלִיאָב׃
(was) Pallu the And .thirty and hundred and thousand forty and
.Eliab of son seven

7148 48 1885 48 1885 5241 446 1121
9 וּבְנֵי אֱלִיאָב נְמוּאֵל וְדָתָן וַאֲבִירָם הוּא־דָתָן וַאֲבִירָם קְרוּאֵי
called and (is) This and and ,Nemuel Eliab the And
ones ,Abiram Dathan that .Abiram ,Dathan (were) of sons

7141 5712 175 4872 5327 834 5712
הָעֵדָה אֲשֶׁר הִצּוּ עַל־מֹשֶׁה וְעַל־אַהֲרֹן בַּעֲדַת־קֹרַח
,Korah the in Aaron and Moses against fought who the of
of company against congregation

1104 6310 776 6605 3068 5327
10 בְּהַצֹּתָם עַל־יְהוָה׃ וַתִּפְתַּח הָאָרֶץ אֶת־פִּיהָ וַתִּבְלַע אֹתָם
them and mouth its the And .Jehovah against when
swallowed earth opened fought they

3967 2572 784 398 5712 4194 7141
וְאֶת־קֹרַח בְּמוֹת הָעֵדָה בַּאֲכֹל הָאֵשׁ אֵת חֲמִשִּׁים וּמָאתַיִם
two and fifty the when that the at ,Korah to-
hundred fire up ate ,group of death with gether

8095 1121 4191 7141 1121 5257 376
11 12 אִישׁ וַיִּהְיוּ לְנֵס׃ וּבְנֵי־קֹרַח לֹא־מֵתוּ׃ ס בְּנֵי שִׁמְעוֹן
Simeon The .die did not Korah the but a they and ;men
of sons of sons sign became

4940 3226 5242 4940 5241 4940
לְמִשְׁפְּחֹתָם לִנְמוּאֵל מִשְׁפַּחַת הַנְּמוּאֵלִי לְיָמִין מִשְׁפַּחַת
family the of the family the ,Nemuel of their by
of ,Jamin ;Nemuelites of :families

2227 4940 2226 3200 4940 3199 3228
13 הַיָּמִינִי לְיָכִין מִשְׁפַּחַת הַיָּכִינִי׃ לְזֶרַח מִשְׁפַּחַת הַזַּרְחִי
the family the of the family the of the
;Zerahites of Zerah ;Jachinites of ,Jachin ;Jaminites

8147 8099 4940 428 7587 4940 7586
14 לְשָׁאוּל מִשְׁפַּחַת הַשָּׁאוּלִי׃ אֵלֶּה מִשְׁפְּחֹת הַשִּׁמְעֹנִי שְׁנַיִם
two the families the These the family the of
,Simeonites of are .Shaulities of ,Shaul

6827 4940 1410 1121 3967 505 6242
15 וְעֶשְׂרִים אֶלֶף וּמָאתָיִם׃ ס בְּנֵי גָד לְמִשְׁפְּחֹתָם לִצְפוֹן
of their by Gad The two and thousand twenty-
,Zephon :families of sons .hundred

4940 7764 2291 4940 2291 6830 4940
מִשְׁפַּחַת הַצְּפוֹנִי לְחַגִּי מִשְׁפַּחַת הַחַגִּי לְשׁוּנִי מִשְׁפַּחַת
family the of the family the of the family the
of ,Shuni ;Haggites of ,Haggi ;Zephonites of

6180 4940 6179 244 4940 244 7765
16 הַשּׁוּנִי׃ לְאָזְנִי מִשְׁפַּחַת הָאָזְנִי לְעֵרִי מִשְׁפַּחַת הָעֵרִי׃
the family the ,Eri of the family the of the
;Erites of ;Oznites of ,Ozni ;Shunites

692 4940 692 722 4940 720
17 לַאֲרוֹד מִשְׁפַּחַת הָאֲרוֹדִי לְאַרְאֵלִי מִשְׁפַּחַת הָאַרְאֵלִי׃
the family the ,Areli of the family the ,Arod of
.Arelites of ;Arodites of

2869 505 703 4940 1410 1121 4940 428
18 אֵלֶּה מִשְׁפְּחֹת בְּנֵי־גָד לִפְקֻדֵיהֶם אַרְבָּעִים אֶלֶף וַחֲמֵשׁ
five and thousand forty their by sons the families the These
,ones numbered Gad of of are

776 209 6117 4191 209 6147 3063 1121 3967
19 מֵאוֹת׃ ס בְּנֵי יְהוּדָה עֵר וְאוֹנָן וַיָּמָת עֵר וְאוֹנָן בְּאֶרֶץ
the in and Er and and Er :Judah The .hundred
of land Onan died ;Onan of sons

[20]And the sons of Judah by their families: of Shelah, the family of the Shelanites; of Pharez, the family of the Pharzites; of Zerah, the family of the Zarhites. [21]And the sons of Pharez: of Hezron, the family of the Hezronites; of Hamul, the family of the Hamulites. [22]These are the families of Judah, according to those numbered of them, seventy-six thousand, five hundred.

[23]Of the sons of Issachar, according to their families: of Tola, the family of the Tolaites; of Pua, the family of the Punites; [24]of Jashub, the family of the Jashubites; of Shimron, the family of the Shimronites. [25]These are the families of Issachar according to those numbered to them, sixty-four thousand, three hundred.

[26]Of the sons of Zebulun, according to their families: of Sered, the family of the Seredites; of Elong, the family of the Elonites; of Jahleel, the family of the Jahleelites. [27]These are the families of the Zebulunites according to those numbered to them, sixty thousand, five hundred.

[28]And the sons of Joseph according to their families: Manasseh and Ephraim. [29]The sons of Manasseh: of Machir, the family of the Machirites; and Machir fathered Gilead; of Gilead, the family of the Gileadites. [30]These are the sons of Gilead: of Jeezer, the family of the Jeezerites; of Helek, the family of the Helekites. [31]And of Asriel, the family of the Asrielites; and of Shechem, the family of the Shechemites; [32]and of Shemida, the family of the Shemidaites; and of Hepher, the family of the Hepherites. [33]And Zelophehad the son of Hepher had no sons, but

20 כְּנָעַן׃ וַיִּהְיוּ בְנֵי־יְהוּדָה לְמִשְׁפְּחֹתָם לְשֵׁלָה מִשְׁפַּחַת
הַשֵּׁלָנִי לְפֶרֶץ מִשְׁפַּחַת הַפַּרְצִי לְזֶרַח מִשְׁפַּחַת הַזַּרְחִי׃
21 וַיִּהְיוּ בְנֵי־פֶרֶץ לְחֶצְרֹן מִשְׁפַּחַת הַחֶצְרֹנִי לְחָמוּל מִשְׁפַּחַת
22 הֶחָמוּלִי׃ אֵלֶּה מִשְׁפְּחֹת יְהוּדָה לִפְקֻדֵיהֶם שִׁשָּׁה וְשִׁבְעִים
23 אֶלֶף וַחֲמֵשׁ מֵאוֹת׃ בְּנֵי יִשָּׂשכָר לְמִשְׁפְּחֹתָם תּוֹלָע
24 מִשְׁפַּחַת הַתּוֹלָעִי לְפֻוָּה מִשְׁפַּחַת הַפּוּנִי׃ לְיָשׁוּב מִשְׁפַּחַת
25 הַיָּשֻׁבִי לְשִׁמְרֹן מִשְׁפַּחַת הַשִּׁמְרֹנִי׃ אֵלֶּה מִשְׁפְּחֹת יִשָּׂשכָר
26 לִפְקֻדֵיהֶם אַרְבָּעָה וְשִׁשִּׁים אֶלֶף וּשְׁלֹשׁ מֵאוֹת׃ בְּנֵי
זְבוּלֻן לְמִשְׁפְּחֹתָם לְסֶרֶד מִשְׁפַּחַת הַסַּרְדִּי לְאֵלוֹן מִשְׁפַּחַת
27 הָאֵלֹנִי לְיַחְלְאֵל מִשְׁפַּחַת הַיַּחְלְאֵלִי׃ אֵלֶּה מִשְׁפְּחֹת
28 הַזְּבוּלֹנִי לִפְקֻדֵיהֶם שִׁשִּׁים אֶלֶף וַחֲמֵשׁ מֵאוֹת׃ בְּנֵי
29 יוֹסֵף לְמִשְׁפְּחֹתָם מְנַשֶּׁה וְאֶפְרָיִם׃ בְּנֵי מְנַשֶּׁה לְמָכִיר
מִשְׁפַּחַת הַמָּכִירִי וּמָכִיר הוֹלִיד אֶת־גִּלְעָד לְגִלְעָד מִשְׁפַּחַת
30 הַגִּלְעָדִי׃ אֵלֶּה בְּנֵי גִלְעָד אִיעֶזֶר מִשְׁפַּחַת הָאִיעֶזְרִי לְחֵלֶק
31 מִשְׁפַּחַת הַחֶלְקִי׃ וְאַשְׂרִיאֵל מִשְׁפַּחַת הָאַשְׂרְאֵלִי וְשֶׁכֶם
32 מִשְׁפַּחַת הַשִּׁכְמִי׃ וּשְׁמִידָע מִשְׁפַּחַת הַשְּׁמִידָעִי וְחֵפֶר
33 מִשְׁפַּחַת הַחֶפְרִי׃ וּצְלָפְחָד בֶּן־חֵפֶר לֹא־הָיוּ לוֹ בָּנִים כִּי

daughters; and the names of the daughters of Zelophehad *were* Mahlah, Noah, Hoglah, Milcah and Tirzah. [34]These are the families of Manasseh, and those numbered of them, fifty-two thousand, seven hundred.

[35]These are the sons of Ephraim, according to their families: of Shuthelah, the family of the Shuthelahites; of Becher, the family of the Becherites; of Tahan, the family of the Tahanites. [36]And these are the sons of Shuthelah: of Eran, the family of the Eranites. [37]These are the families of the sons of Ephraim according to those numbered of them, thirty-two thousand, five hundred. These are the sons of Joseph according to their families.

[38]The sons of Benjamin according to their families: of Bela, the family of the Belaites; of Ashbel, the family of the Ashbelites; of Ahiram, the family of the Ahiramites; [39]of Shupham, the family of the Shuphamites; of Hupham, the family of the Huphamites. [40]And Bela's sons *were* Ard and Naaman. *Of Ard,* the family of the Ardites; of Naaman the family of the Naamites. [41]These are the sons of Benjamin according to their families, and their numbered ones, forty-five thousand, six hundred.

[42]These are the sons of Dan according to their families: of Shuham, the family of the Shuhamites. These are the families of Dan according to their families. [43]All the families of the Shuhamites according to those numbered of them, sixty-four thousand, four hundred.

[44]Of the sons of Asher according to their families: of Jimna, the family of the Jimnites; of Jesui, the family of the Jesuites; of Beriah, the family of the

אִם־בָּנוֹת וְשֵׁם בְּנוֹת צְלָפְחָד מַחְלָה וְנֹעָה חָגְלָה מִלְכָּה

34 וְתִרְצָה׃ אֵלֶּה מִשְׁפְּחֹת מְנַשֶּׁה וּפְקֻדֵיהֶם שְׁנַיִם וַחֲמִשִּׁים

35 אֶלֶף וּשְׁבַע מֵאוֹת׃ אֵלֶּה בְנֵי־אֶפְרַיִם לְמִשְׁפְּחֹתָם

לְשׁוּתֶלַח מִשְׁפַּחַת הַשֻּׁתַלְחִי לְבֶכֶר מִשְׁפַּחַת הַבַּכְרִי

36 לְתַחַן מִשְׁפַּחַת הַתַּחֲנִי׃ וְאֵלֶּה בְּנֵי שׁוּתָלַח לְעֵרָן מִשְׁפַּחַת

37 הָעֵרָנִי׃ אֵלֶּה מִשְׁפְּחֹת בְּנֵי־אֶפְרַיִם לִפְקֻדֵיהֶם שְׁנַיִם

וּשְׁלֹשִׁים אֶלֶף וַחֲמֵשׁ מֵאוֹת אֵלֶּה בְנֵי־יוֹסֵף לְמִשְׁפְּחֹתָם׃

38 בְּנֵי בִנְיָמִן לְמִשְׁפְּחֹתָם לְבֶלַע מִשְׁפַּחַת הַבַּלְעִי לְאַשְׁבֵּל

39 מִשְׁפַּחַת הָאַשְׁבֵּלִי לַאֲחִירָם מִשְׁפַּחַת הָאֲחִירָמִי׃ לִשְׁפוּפָם

40 מִשְׁפַּחַת הַשּׁוּפָמִי לְחוּפָם מִשְׁפַּחַת הַחוּפָמִי׃ וַיִּהְיוּ בְנֵי־

בֶלַע אַרְדְּ וְנַעֲמָן מִשְׁפַּחַת הָאַרְדִּי לְנַעֲמָן מִשְׁפַּחַת הַנַּעֲמִי׃

41 אֵלֶּה בְנֵי־בִנְיָמִן לְמִשְׁפְּחֹתָם וּפְקֻדֵיהֶם חֲמִשָּׁה וְאַרְבָּעִים

42 אֶלֶף וְשֵׁשׁ מֵאוֹת׃ אֵלֶּה בְנֵי־דָן לְמִשְׁפְּחֹתָם לְשׁוּחָם

43 מִשְׁפַּחַת הַשּׁוּחָמִי אֵלֶּה מִשְׁפְּחֹת דָּן לְמִשְׁפְּחֹתָם׃ כָּל־

מִשְׁפְּחֹת הַשּׁוּחָמִי לִפְקֻדֵיהֶם אַרְבָּעָה וְשִׁשִּׁים אֶלֶף וְאַרְבַּע

44 מֵאוֹת׃ בְּנֵי אָשֵׁר לְמִשְׁפְּחֹתָם לְיִמְנָה מִשְׁפַּחַת

הַיִּמְנָה לְיִשְׁוִי מִשְׁפַּחַת הַיִּשְׁוִי לִבְרִיעָה מִשְׁפַּחַת הַבְּרִיעִי׃

Berites. [45]Of the sons of
45 Beriah: of Heber, the family
of the Heberites; of Mal-
chiel, the family of the
Malchielites. [46]And Asher's
46 daughter's name was Sarah.
47 [47]These are the families of
the sons of Asher according
to those numbered of them,
fifty-three thousand, four
hundred.
48 [48]The sons of Naphtali
according to their families:
of Jahzeel, the family of the
Jahzeelites; of Guni, the
family of the Gunites; [49]of
49 Jezer, the family of the
Jezerites; of Shillem, the
family of the Shillemites.
50 [50]These are the families of
Naphtali by their families,
and their numbered ones
were forty-five thousand,
four hundred.
51 [51]These were the numbered ones of the sons of
Israel, six hundred and one
thousand, seven hundred
and thirty.

52 [52]And Jehovah spoke to
53 Moses, saying, [53]The land
shall be divided to those for
an inheritance, according to
the number of names. [54]To
54 the many you shall increase
their inheritance; and to the
few you shall diminish their
inheritance; each according
to the mouth of his num-
bered ones shall be given
55 his inheritance. [55]But the
land shall be divided by lot.
They shall inherit according
to the names of the tribes of
their fathers. [56]According to
56 the lot, possession of it shall
be divided between the
many and few.
57 [57]And these are the
numbered ones of the
Levites by their families: of
Gershon, the family of the
Gershonites; of Kohath, the
family of the Kohathites; of
Merari, the family of the
58 Merarites. [58]These are the
families of the Levites: the
family of the Libnites; the
family of the Hebronites; the
family of the Mahlites; the
family of the Mushites; the
family of the Korathites.
And Kohath fathered

4940 4439 2277 4940 2268 1283 1121
45 לִבְנֵי בְרִיעָה לְחֶבֶר מִשְׁפַּחַת הַחֶבְרִי לְמַלְכִּיאֵל מִשְׁפַּחַת
of family the Malchiel of the family the Heber of :Beriah the Of
;Heberites of . of sons

1121 4940 428 8294 836 1323 8034 4440
46 47 הַמַּלְכִּיאֵלִי׃ וְשֵׁם בַּת־אָשֵׁר שָׂרַח׃ אֵלֶּה מִשְׁפְּחֹת בְּנֵי־
the families the These was Asher's daugh- And the
of sons of are Sarah ter's name .Malchielites

3967 702 515 2572 7969 6485 836
אָשֵׁר לִפְקֻדֵיהֶם שְׁלֹשָׁה וַחֲמִשִּׁים אֶלֶף וְאַרְבַּע מֵאוֹת׃
.hundred and thousand fifty three their by ,Asher
four ones numbered

1476 3184 4440 3183 4940 5320 1121
48 בְּנֵי נַפְתָּלִי לְמִשְׁפְּחֹתָם לְיַחְצְאֵל מִשְׁפַּחַת הַיַּחְצְאֵלִי לְגוּנִי
,Guni of the family the ,Jahzeel of their by Naphtali The
;Jahzeelites of families of sons

4940 8006 3339 4940 3337 1477 4940
49 מִשְׁפַּחַת הַגּוּנִי׃ לְיֵצֶר מִשְׁפַּחַת הַיִּצְרִי לְשִׁלֵּם מִשְׁפַּחַת
family the of the family the of the family the
of ,Shillem ;Jezerites of Jezer ;Gunites of

6485 4940 5320 4940 428 8016
50 הַשִּׁלֵּמִי׃ אֵלֶּה מִשְׁפְּחֹת נַפְתָּלִי לְמִשְׁפְּחֹתָם וּפְקֻדֵיהֶם
their and their by Naphtali families the These the
ones numbered ,families of are . Shillemites

1121 6485 428 3967 702 505 703 2568
51 חֲמִשָּׁה וְאַרְבָּעִים אֶלֶף וְאַרְבַּע מֵאוֹת׃ אֵלֶּה פְּקוּדֵי בְּנֵי
the num- the These .hundred four and thousand forty five
of sons of bered were

7970 3967 7651 505 505 3967 8337 3478
יִשְׂרָאֵל שֵׁשׁ־מֵאוֹת אֶלֶף וָאָלֶף שְׁבַע מֵאוֹת וּשְׁלֹשִׁים׃
.thirty and hundred seven one and thousand hundred six ,Israel
,thousand

776 2505 428 559 4872 3068 1696
52 53 וַיְדַבֵּר יְהוָה אֶל־מֹשֶׁה לֵּאמֹר׃ לָאֵלֶּה תֵּחָלֵק הָאָרֶץ
the be shall To ,saying ,Moses to Jehovah And
land divided these spoke

4592 5159 7235 7227 8034 4557 5159
54 בְּנַחֲלָה בְּמִסְפַּר שֵׁמוֹת׃ לָרַב תַּרְבֶּה נַחֲלָתוֹ וְלַמְעַט
to and their shall you the To .names the by an for
few the ,inheritance increase many of number ,inheritance

1486 5159 5414 6485 6310 376 5159 4591
55 תַּמְעִיט נַחֲלָתוֹ אִישׁ לְפִי פְקֻדָיו יֻתַּן נַחֲלָתוֹ׃ אַךְ־בְּגוֹרָל
lot by Only his be shall num- his the by each their shall you
.inheritance given ones bered mouth ;inheritance ,diminish

6310 5157 1 4294 8034 776 2505
56 יֵחָלֵק אֶת־הָאָרֶץ לִשְׁמוֹת מַטּוֹת־אֲבֹתָם יִנְחָלוּ׃ עַל־פִּי
By shall they their the the by ;land the be shall
mouth .inherit fathers of tribes of names divided

6485 428 4592 7227 5159 2505 1486
57 הַגּוֹרָל תֵּחָלֵק נַחֲלָתוֹ בֵּין רַב לִמְעָט׃ וְאֵלֶּה פְקוּדֵי
the these And .few and many be- his be shall lot the
of numbered are tween inheritance divided

6956 1649 4940 1648 4940 3881
הַלֵּוִי לְמִשְׁפְּחֹתָם לְגֵרְשׁוֹן מִשְׁפַּחַת הַגֵּרְשֻׁנִּי לִקְהָת
of the family the of their by the
Kohath ;Gershonites of ,Gershon :families ,Levites

4940 428 4848 4940 4847 6956 4940
58 מִשְׁפַּחַת הַקְּהָתִי לִמְרָרִי מִשְׁפַּחַת הַמְּרָרִי׃ אֵלֶּה מִשְׁפְּחֹת
families the These the family the of the family the
of are .Merarites of ,Merari ;Kohathites ,of

4250 4940 2276 4940 3846 4940 3881
לֵוִי מִשְׁפַּחַת הַלִּבְנִי מִשְׁפַּחַת הַחֶבְרֹנִי מִשְׁפַּחַת הַמַּחְלִי
the family the the family the the family the the
,Mahlites. of ,Hebronites of ,Libnites of :Levites

6019 3205 6955 7145 4940 4188 4940
מִשְׁפַּחַת הַמּוּשִׁי מִשְׁפַּחַת הַקָּרְחִי וּקְהָת הוֹלִד אֶת־עַמְרָם׃
.Amram fathered And the the family of the family the
Kohath .Korathites of ,Mushites of

Amram; 59And the name
of Amram's wife *was*
Jochebed, the daughter
of Levi, whom *one* bore
her to Levi in Egypt. And
she bore Aaron and
Moses and their sister
Miriam to Amram. 60And
Nadab and Abihu, Elea-
zar and Ithamar *were*
born to Aaron. 61And Na-
dab and Abi died for
bringing strange fire be-
fore Jehovah. 62And their
numbered ones were
three thousand twenty-
three, all males from a
son of a month and up-
ward. For they were not
counted among the sons
of Israel, for no inheri-
tance *was* given to them
among the sons of Israel.
63These *are* those num-
bered by Moses and Ele-
azar the priest, who num-
bered the sons of Israel in
the plains of Moab be-
side Jordan, *near* Jeri-
cho. 64And among these
there was not a man of
those numbered by
Moses and Aaron the
priest, who numbered
the sons of Israel in the
wilderness of Sinai.

65For Jehovah had said to
them, They shall surely die
in the wilderness; and not a
man of them should be left
except Caleb the son of
Jephunneh, and Joshua the
son of Nun.

59 וְשֵׁם אֵשֶׁת עַמְרָם יוֹכֶבֶד בַּת־לֵוִי אֲשֶׁר יָלְדָה אֹתָהּ
her (one) bore whom Levi the of daughter ,Jochebed Amram's (was) wife the And of name
לְלֵוִי בְּמִצְרָיִם וַתֵּלֶד לְעַמְרָם אֶת־אַהֲרֹן וְאֶת־מֹשֶׁה וְאֵת
and ,Moses and Aaron Amram to she and bore in ;Egypt to Levi
60 מִרְיָם אֲחֹתָם׃ וַיִּוָּלֵד לְאַהֲרֹן אֶת־נָדָב וְאֶת־אֲבִיהוּא אֶת־
,Abihu and Nadab :Aaron to And born their .sister Miriam
61 אֶלְעָזָר וְאֶת־אִיתָמָר׃ וַיָּמָת נָדָב וַאֲבִיהוּא בְּהַקְרִיבָם
bringing for Abihu and Nadab And died .Ithamar and Eleazar
62 אֵשׁ־זָרָה לִפְנֵי יְהוָה׃ וַיִּהְיוּ פְקֻדֵיהֶם שְׁלֹשָׁה וְעֶשְׂרִים אֶלֶף
,thousand twenty- three their ,ones numbered And were .Jehovah before strange fire
כָּל־זָכָר מִבֶּן־חֹדֶשׁ וָמָעְלָה כִּי לֹא הָתְפָּקְדוּ בְּתוֹךְ בְּנֵי
the of sons among were they counted not for and ;upward a month from old males all
63 יִשְׂרָאֵל כִּי לֹא־נִתַּן לָהֶם נַחֲלָה בְּתוֹךְ בְּנֵי יִשְׂרָאֵל׃ אֵלֶּה
These are .Israel the of sons among inheritance to them was given not for ,Israel
פְּקוּדֵי מֹשֶׁה וְאֶלְעָזָר הַכֹּהֵן אֲשֶׁר פָּקְדוּ אֶת־בְּנֵי יִשְׂרָאֵל
Israel the of sons numbered who the ,priest and Eleazar by Moses those counted
64 בְּעַרְבֹת מוֹאָב עַל יַרְדֵּן יְרֵחוֹ׃ וּבְאֵלֶּה לֹא־הָיָה אִישׁ
a of man there was not among and these (near) ;Jericho ,Jordan beside ,Moab the on of plains
מִפְּקוּדֵי מֹשֶׁה וְאַהֲרֹן הַכֹּהֵן אֲשֶׁר פָּקְדוּ אֶת־בְּנֵי יִשְׂרָאֵל
Israel the of sons numbered who the ,priest and Aaron by Moses those numbered
65 בְּמִדְבַּר סִינָי׃ כִּי־אָמַר יְהוָה לָהֶם מוֹת יָמֻתוּ בַּמִּדְבָּר וְלֹא־
and not the in ;wilderness shall they die Surely to ,them Jehovah had said For .Sinai the in of wilderness
נוֹתַר מֵהֶם אִישׁ כִּי אִם־כָּלֵב בֶּן־יְפֻנֶּה וִיהוֹשֻׁעַ בִּן־נוּן׃
.Nun the of son and ,Joshua ,Jephunnah the of son Caleb except a man of ,them should left be

CAP. XXVII כז

CHAPTER 27

1And came the daughters
of Zelophehad the son of
Hepher, the son of Gilead,
the son of Machir, the son
of Manasseh, of the family
of Manasseh, the son of
Joseph. And these are his
daughters' names: Mahlah,
Noah, Hoglah, Milcah, and
Tirzah. 2And they stood
before Moses and Eleazar
the priest, and before the
rulers and all the congregation at the door of the
tabernacle of the congre-
gation, saying, 3Our father

1 וַתִּקְרַבְנָה בְּנוֹת צְלָפְחָד בֶּן־חֵפֶר בֶּן־גִּלְעָד בֶּן־מָכִיר בֶּן־
the of son ,Machir the of son ,Gilead the of son ,Hepher the of son ,Zelophehad the of daughters came And
מְנַשֶּׁה לְמִשְׁפְּחֹת מְנַשֶּׁה בֶן־יוֹסֵף וְאֵלֶּה שְׁמוֹת בְּנֹתָיו מַחְלָה
,Mahlah :daughters the (are) of names And these ,Joseph the of son Manasseh the of of family ,Manasseh
2 נֹעָה וְחָגְלָה וּמִלְכָּה וְתִרְצָה׃ וַתַּעֲמֹדְנָה לִפְנֵי מֹשֶׁה וְלִפְנֵי
and before Moses before they stood And and .Tirzah ,Milcah ,Hoglah ,Noah
אֶלְעָזָר הַכֹּהֵן וְלִפְנֵי הַנְּשִׂיאִם וְכָל־הָעֵדָה פֶּתַח אֹהֶל־מוֹעֵד
,meeting the of tent the at of door the ,congregation all and rulers the and before the ,priest Eleazar

died in the wilderness, and he was not among the company who met together against Jehovah in the company of Korah, but he died for his own sins, and had no sons. 4 Why is the name of our father taken away from the midst of his family because there *is* no son to him? Give a possession to us among the brothers of our father. 5 And Moses brought their cause before Jehovah.

6 And Jehovah spoke to Moses saying, 7 The daughters of Zelophehad speak rightly. You shall surely give them a possession of an inheritance among the brothers of their father. And you shall cause the inheritance of their father to pass to them. 8 And you shall speak to the sons of Israel, saying, When a man dies, and has no son, then you shall cause his inheritance to pass to his daughter. 9 And if he has no daughter, then you shall give his inheritance to his brothers. 10 And if he has no brothers, then you shall give his inheritance to his nearest relation, of his family. And he shall possess it, and it shall be a statute of judgment to the sons of Israel as Jehovah has commanded Moses.

12 And Jehovah said to Moses, Get up into this mountain of Abarim, and see the land which I have given to the sons of Israel. 13 And when you have seen it, you also shall be gathered to your people as your brother Aaron was

5712 8432 1961 4357 4191 559
3 לֵאמֹר׃ אָבִינוּ מֵת בַּמִּדְבָּר וְהוּא לֹא־הָיָה בְּתוֹךְ הָעֵדָה
con- the among was not he and the in died Our ,saying
gregation ,wilderness father

1121 2399 7141 5712 3068 3259
הַנּוֹעָדִים עַל־יְהוָה בַּעֲדַת־קֹרַח כִּי־בְחֶטְאוֹ מֵת וּבָנִים לֹא־
not and he his for but ,Korah the in Jehovah against met who
sons ,died sins own of company together

369 3588 4940 8432 8034 1639 4100 1961
4 הָיוּ לוֹ׃ לָמָּה יִגָּרַע שֵׁם־אָבִינוּ מִתּוֹךְ מִשְׁפַּחְתּוֹ כִּי אֵין
(is) because his the from our the taken is Why to
no family of midst father of name away him were

4872 7126 251 8432 272 5414 1121
5 לוֹ בֵּן תְּנָה־לָּנוּ אֲחֻזָּה בְּתוֹךְ אֲחֵי אָבִינוּ׃ וַיַּקְרֵב מֹשֶׁה אֶת־
Moses And our the among an us to Give !son to
brought .father of brothers inheritance him

3068 6440 4941
מִשְׁפָּטָן לִפְנֵי יְהוָה׃
.Jehovah before their
cause

1696 6765 1323 3651 559 4872 3068 559
6
7 וַיֹּאמֶר יְהוָה אֶל־מֹשֶׁה לֵּאמֹר׃ כֵּן בְּנוֹת צְלָפְחָד דֹּבְרֹת
;speak Zelophehad The rightly ,saying Moses to Jehovah And
of daughters spoke

5674 251 8432 5159 272 5414 5414
נָתֹן תִּתֵּן לָהֶם אֲחֻזַּת נַחֲלָה בְּתוֹךְ אֲחֵי אֲבִיהֶם וְהַעֲבַרְתָּ
cause and their brothers among an pos- a them you surely
on pass to ,father's inheritance ,session give shall

560 1090 3478 1121 1 5159
8 אֶת־נַחֲלַת אֲבִיהֶן לָהֶן׃ וְאֶל־בְּנֵי יִשְׂרָאֵל תְּדַבֵּר לֵאמֹר
,saying shall you Israel the to And to their the
,speak of sons .them father of inheritance

1323 5159 5674 369 1121 4191 376
אִישׁ כִּי־יָמוּת וּבֵן אֵין לוֹ וְהַעֲבַרְתֶּם אֶת־נַחֲלָתוֹ לְבִתּוֹ׃
his to his shall you and to is and ,dies When a
.daughter inheritance on pass ,him no son man

369 251 5159 5414 1323 369
9
10 וְאִם־אֵין לוֹ בַּת וּנְתַתֶּם אֶת־נַחֲלָתוֹ לְאֶחָיו׃ וְאִם־אֵין לוֹ
to are and his to his you then daugh- to is And
him not if ;brothers inheritance give shall ,ter him no if

251 369 1 251 5159 5414 251
11 אַחִים וּנְתַתֶּם אֶת־נַחֲלָתוֹ לַאֲחֵי אָבִיו׃ וְאִם־אֵין אַחִים
brothers has and his to his you then ,brothers
no if ;father's brothers inheritance give shall

4940 7607 5159 5414 1
לְאָבִיו וּנְתַתֶּם אֶת־נַחֲלָתוֹ לִשְׁאֵרוֹ הַקָּרֹב אֵלָיו מִמִּשְׁפַּחְתּוֹ
his of to nearest his to his you then his to
;family him relative inheritance give shall ,father

4941 2708 3478 1121 1961 3423
וְיָרַשׁ אֹתָהּ וְהָיְתָה לִבְנֵי יִשְׂרָאֵל לְחֻקַּת מִשְׁפָּט כַּאֲשֶׁר
as judgment a Israel the to it and ;it he and
of statute of sons be shall own shall

4872 3068 6680
צִוָּה יְהוָה אֶת־מֹשֶׁה׃
.Moses Jehovah has
commanded

7218 2088 5682 2022 5927 4872 3068 559
12 וַיֹּאמֶר יְהוָה אֶל־מֹשֶׁה עֲלֵה אֶל־הַר הָעֲבָרִים הַזֶּה וּרְאֵה
see and ,this Arabim Mount to Get ,Moses to Jehovah And
up said

7200 3478 1121 5414 834 776
13 אֶת־הָאָרֶץ אֲשֶׁר נָתַתִּי לִבְנֵי יִשְׂרָאֵל׃ וְרָאִיתָה אֹתָהּ
,it when And .Israel the to have I which land the
seen have you of sons given

251 175 622 1571 5971 622
וְנֶאֱסַפְתָּ אֶל־עַמֶּיךָ גַּם־אָתָּה כַּאֲשֶׁר נֶאֱסַף אַהֲרֹן אָחִיךָ׃
your Aaron was as ,you also your to you then
.brother gathered ,people gathered be shall

gathered. 14 For you re-
belled against My mouth in
the desert of Zin, in the
strife of the congregation,
to sanctify Me at the waters
before their eyes — they
were the waters of Meribah
in Kadesh, in the desert of
Zin.
15 And Moses spoke to
Jehovah, saying, 16 Let
Jehovah, the God of the
spirits of all flesh, appoint a
man over the congregation
17 who may go out before
them, and who may go in
before them, and who may
lead them out, and who
may bring them in, so that
the assembly of Jehovah
may not be as sheep to
whom there is no shepherd.
18 And Jehovah said to
Moses, Take Joshua the
son of Nun, a man in whom
is the Spirit, and lay your
hand on him. 19 And cause
him to stand before Eleazar
the priest, and before all the
congregation, and give him
a charge in their sight.
20 And you shall put
some of your dignity on
him, so that all the con-
gregation of the sons of
Israel will listen. 21 And
he shall stand before Eleazar the priest, who shall
ask for him according to
the judgment of the Urim
before Jehovah. At his
word they shall go out,
and at his word they shall
enter, and all the sons of
Israel with him, even all
the congregation. 22 And
Moses did as Jehovah
commanded him. And he
took Joshua and made
him stand before Eleazar
the priest, and before all
the congregation. 23 And
he laid his hands on him
and gave him a charge,
even as Jehovah com-
manded by the hand of
Moses.

CHAPTER 28
1 And Jehovah spoke to
Moses, saying 2 Command
the sons of Israel, and you
shall say to them, My

6942 5712 4808 6790 4057 6310 4784
14 כַּאֲשֶׁר מְרִיתֶם פִּי בְּמִדְבַּר־צִן בִּמְרִיבַת הָעֵדָה לְהַקְדִּישֵׁנִי
sanc- to congre- the the in ,Zin the in against you For
Me tify ,gation of strife of desert mouth My rebelled
6790 4057 6946 4808 4325 5869 4325
בַמַּיִם לְעֵינֵיהֶם הֵם מֵי־מְרִיבַת קָדֵשׁ מִדְבַּר־צִן׃ ס
.Zin the in in Meribah the (were) they before the at
of desert ,Kadesh of waters ;eyes their waters
7307 430 3068 6485 559 3068 4872 1696
15 16 וַיְדַבֵּר מֹשֶׁה אֶל־יְהוָה לֵאמֹר׃ יִפְקֹד יְהוָה אֱלֹהֵי הָרוּחֹת
the God the ,Jehovah Let ,saying ,Jehovah to Moses And
of spirits of appoint spoke
834 6440 5927 834 5712 376 1320 3605
17 לְכָל־בָּשָׂר אִישׁ עַל־הָעֵדָה׃ אֲשֶׁר־יֵצֵא לִפְנֵיהֶם וַאֲשֶׁר
who and before may who the over a ,flesh all
.them out go ,congregation man
5712 1961 935 834 3318 834 6440 935
יָבֹא לִפְנֵיהֶם וַאֲשֶׁר יוֹצִיאֵם וַאֲשֶׁר יְבִיאֵם וְלֹא תִהְיֶה עֲדַת
the be may so bring may and lead may and before may
of company not that .in them who .out them who .them in go
4872 3068 559 7462 369 834 6629 3068
18 יְהוָה כַּצֹּאן אֲשֶׁר אֵין־לָהֶם רֹעֶה׃ וַיֹּאמֶר יְהוָה אֶל־מֹשֶׁה
,Moses to Jehovah And .shepherd to is whom as Jehova
said them no sheep
5564 7307 376 5126 1121 3091 3947
קַח־לְךָ אֶת־יְהוֹשֻׁעַ בִּן־נוּן אִישׁ אֲשֶׁר־רוּחַ בּוֹ וְסָמַכְתָּ אֶת־
lay and ,in the is whom a ,Nun the Joshua for Take
Spirit man of son you
3605 6440 3548 499 6440 5975 3027
19 יָדְךָ עָלָיו׃ וְהַעֲמַדְתָּ אֹתוֹ לִפְנֵי אֶלְעָזָר הַכֹּהֵן וְלִפְנֵי כָּל־
all and the Eleazar before him cause And on your
before .priest stand to .him hand
1935 5414 5869 6680 5712
20 הָעֵדָה וְצִוִּיתָה אֹתוֹ לְעֵינֵיהֶם׃ וְנָתַתָּה מֵהוֹדְךָ עָלָיו לְמַעַן
that so on of (some) you And .eyes before him give and con-
.him dignity your put shall charge a ;gregation
5975 3548 499 6440 3478 1121 5712 3605 8085
21 יִשְׁמְעוּ כָּל־עֲדַת בְּנֵי יִשְׂרָאֵל׃ וְלִפְנֵי אֶלְעָזָר הַכֹּהֵן יַעֲמֹד
will he the Eleazar And .Israel the the all will
;stand priest before of sons of company listen
5927 6310 3068 6440 224 4941 7592
וְשָׁאַל לוֹ בְּמִשְׁפַּט הָאוּרִים לִפְנֵי יְהוָה עַל־פִּיו יֵצְאוּ וְעַל־
and shall they his At .Jehovah before the the by for he and
at ,out go word Urim of judgment him ask will
4872 6213 5712 3605 3478 1121 3605 935 6316
22 פִּיו יָבֹאוּ הוּא וְכָל־בְּנֵי־יִשְׂרָאֵל אִתּוֹ וְכָל־הָעֵדָה׃ וַיַּעַשׂ מֹשֶׁה
Moses And the even with Israel the and .he shall they his
did .congregation all ,him of sons all enter mouth
6440 5975 3091 3947 3068 6680
כַּאֲשֶׁר צִוָּה יְהוָה אֹתוֹ וַיִּקַּח אֶת־יְהוֹשֻׁעַ וַיַּעֲמִדֵהוּ לִפְנֵי
before made and Joshua he And .him Jehovah com- as
stand him took manded
6680 3027 5564 5712 3605 3548 499
23 אֶלְעָזָר הַכֹּהֵן וְלִפְנֵי כָּל־הָעֵדָה׃ וַיִּסְמֹךְ אֶת־יָדָיו עָלָיו וַיְצַוֵּהוּ
charged and on his he And the all and the Eleazar
,him him hands laid .congregation before ,priest
4872 3027 3068 1696
כַּאֲשֶׁר דִּבֶּר יְהוָה בְּיַד־מֹשֶׁה׃ פ
.Moses the by Jehovah com- even
of hand manded as

CAP. XXVIII. כח

CHAPTER 28

559 3478 1121 6680 559 4872 3068 1696
1 2 וַיְדַבֵּר יְהוָה אֶל־מֹשֶׁה לֵּאמֹר׃ צַו אֶת־בְּנֵי יִשְׂרָאֵל וְאָמַרְתָּ
you and ,Israel the Order ,saying Moses to Jehovah And
say shall of sons spoke

offering, My bread for My fire offerings, My sweet fragrance, you shall be careful to offer to Me in its appointed season. [3]And you shall say to them, This *is* the fire offering which you shall offer to Jehovah, two yearling lambs without blemish, day by day, as a continual burnt offering. [4]You shall offer the one lamb in the morning, and you shall offer the other lamb between the two evenings; [5]and a tenth of an ephah of flour for a food offering, mixed with beaten oil, a fourth of a hin; [6]a continual burnt offering which was offered in Mount Sinai for a sweet fragrance, a fire offering to Jehovah; [7]and its drink offering, a fourth of a hin for the one lamb; pour a drink offering *of* strong drink to Jehovah in the sanctuary. [8]And you shall offer the other lamb between the evenings, even as the food offering of the morning, and as its drink offering, you shall offer *as* a sacrifice made by fire, a sweet fragrance to Jehovah. [9]And on the sabbath day, two yearling lambs, perfect ones, and two tenth parts of flour, a food offering mixed with oil, and its drink offering; [10]the burnt offering of the sabbath on its sabbath, besides the continual burnt offering and its drink offering.

[11]And in the beginning of your months you shall present a burnt offering to Jehovah: two bullocks, sons of the herd, and one ram, seven yearling lambs, perfect ones.; [12]and three tenth parts of flour, a food offering mixed with oil for the one bullock; and two tenths parts of flour *as* a food offering mixed with oil

אלהם את־קרבני לחמי לאשי ריח ניחחי תשמרו להקריב
3 לי במועדו׃ ואמרת להם זה האשה אשר תקריבו ליהוה
4 כבשים בני־שנה תמימם שנים ליום עלה תמיד׃ את־
הכבש אחד תעשה בבקר ואת הכבש השני תעשה
5 בין הערבים׃ ועשירית האיפה סלת למנחה בלולה
6 בשמן כתית רביעת ההין׃ עלת תמיד העשיה בהר סיני
7 לריח ניחח אשה ליהוה׃ ונסכו רביעת ההין לכבש
8 האחד בקדש הסך נסך שכר ליהוה׃ ואת הכבש השני
תעשה בין הערבים כמנחת הבקר וכנסכו תעשה אשה
ריח ניחח ליהוה׃
9 וביום השבת שני־כבשים בני־שנה תמימם ושני עשרנים
10 סלת מנחה בלולה בשמן ונסכו׃ עלת שבת בשבתו
על־עלת התמיד ונסכה׃
11 ובראשי חדשיכם תקריבו עלה ליהוה פרים בני־בקר
שנים ואיל אחד כבשים בני־שנה שבעה תמימם׃
12 ושלשה עשרנים סלת מנחה בלולה בשמן לפר האחד
ושני עשרנים סלת מנחה בלולה בשמן לאיל האחד׃

for the one ram; [13]and a
tenth part of flour mixed
with oil as a food offering
for the one lamb; a burnt
offering, a sweet fragrance,
a fire offering to Jehovah;
[14]and their drink offerings
shall be a half of a hin to a
bullock, and a third of a hin
to a ram, and a fourth of a hin
to a lamb, of wine. This *shall*
be the burnt offering of
every month for the months
of the year. [15]And one kid of
the goats for a sin offering to
Jehovah; it shall be pre-
pared besides the continual
burnt offering, and its drink
offering.

[16]And in the fourteenth
day of the first month *is* the
Passover of Jehovah.
[17]And in the fifteenth day of
this month a feast: unleavened bread shall be eaten
seven days. [18]In the first
day *shall be* a holy
convocation; you shall do
no work of service. [19]And
you shall offer a fire
offering, a burnt offering to
Jehovah — two young
bullocks, and one ram, and
seven yearling lambs; they
shall be perfect ones for
you; [20]and their food offering, flour mixed with oil.
You shall prepare three
tenths parts for a bullock,
and two tenths parts for a
ram. [21]You shall prepare
one tenth part for the one
lamb, and for the seven
lambs; [22]and one goat, a
sin offering to atone for
you, [23]besides the burnt
offering of the morning, the
continual burnt offering,
you shall prepare these.

[24]In this way you shall
prepare daily, seven days,
bread for a fire offering, a
sweet fragrance to Jehovah.
It shall be prepared besides
the continual burnt offering
and its drink offering.
[25]And on the seventh day
you shall have a holy
convocation; you shall do
no work of service. [26]And

259 3532 8081 1101 4503 5560 6241 6241
13 וְעִשָּׂרֹן עִשָּׂרוֹן סֹלֶת מִנְחָה בְּלוּלָה בַשֶּׁמֶן לַכֶּבֶשׂ הָאֶחָד
;one the | for lamb | oil with | mixed | food a as ,flour offering | of part | a and tenth

1961 1969 2677 5262 3068 801 5207 7381 5930
14 עֹלָה רֵיחַ נִיחֹחַ אִשֶּׁה לַיהוָה׃ וְנִסְכֵּיהֶם חֲצִי הַהִין יִהְיֶה
shall be | ,hin a | half a of | their and ,offerings drink | to ;Jehovah | fire a offering | ,soothing a fragrance | burnt a ,offering

2088 3532 1969 7243 352 1969 7992 6499
לַפָּר וּשְׁלִישִׁת הַהִין לָאַיִל וּרְבִיעִת הַהִין לַכֶּבֶשׂ יָיִן זֹאת
this (is) | of ;wine | a ,lamb | to | hin a | a and of fourth | a to ,ram | hin a | a and of third | a to ,bullock

259 5795 8163 8141 2320 2320 2320 5930
15 עֹלַת חֹדֶשׁ בְּחָדְשׁוֹ לְחָדְשֵׁי הַשָּׁנָה׃ וּשְׂעִיר עִזִּים אֶחָד
one | the goats | and of kid | ;year the | the for of months | every | month burnt the of offering

5262 6213 8548 5930 3068 2403
לְחַטָּאת לַיהוָה עַל־עֹלַת הַתָּמִיד יֵעָשֶׂה וְנִסְכּוֹ׃ ס
its and .offering drink | be shall ,prepared | the continual | burnt besides offering | to ,Jehovah | sin a for offering

3068 6453 2320 3117 6240 702 7223 2320
16 וּבַחֹדֶשׁ הָרִאשׁוֹן בְּאַרְבָּעָה עָשָׂר יוֹם לַחֹדֶשׁ פֶּסַח לַיהוָה׃
;Jehovah | the (is) of Passover | the month | day of | the fourteenth | in | first | the in And month

4682 3117 7651 2282 2088 2320 3117 6240 2568
17 וּבַחֲמִשָּׁה עָשָׂר יוֹם לַחֹדֶשׁ הַזֶּה חָג שִׁבְעַת יָמִים מַצּוֹת
unleavened bread | days | seven | a ;feast | this | of month | day | the in and fifteenth

3808 5656 4399 6944 4744 7223 3117 398
18 יֵאָכֵל׃ בַּיּוֹם הָרִאשׁוֹן מִקְרָא־קֹדֶשׁ כָּל־מְלֶאכֶת עֲבֹדָה לֹא
not | of service | work | any | ;holy a | (be shall) convocation | first | the In day | be shall eaten

1241 1121 6499 3068 5930 801 7126 6213
19 תַעֲשׂוּ׃ וְהִקְרַבְתֶּם אִשֶּׁה עֹלָה לַיהוָה פָּרִים בְּנֵי־בָקָר
young | bullocks | to :Jehovah | burnt a offering | fire a ,offering | you and offer shall | shall you do

1961 8549 8141 1121 3532 7651 259 352 8147
שְׁנַיִם וְאַיִל אֶחָד וְשִׁבְעָה כְבָשִׂים בְּנֵי שָׁנָה תְּמִימִם יִהְיוּ
they be shall | perfect ones | ;yearling | lambs | and seven | ,one | and ram | ,two

6241 7969 8081 1101 5560 4503
20 לָכֶם׃ וּמִנְחָתָם סֹלֶת בְּלוּלָה בַשָּׁמֶן שְׁלֹשָׁה עֶשְׂרֹנִים
tenth parts | three | with ;oil | mixed | flour | their and offering food | for ;you

6213 6224 6241 6213 352 6224 8147 6499
21 לַפָּר וּשְׁנֵי עֶשְׂרֹנִים לָאַיִל תַּעֲשׂוּ׃ עִשָּׂרוֹן עִשָּׂרוֹן תַּעֲשֶׂה
shall you prepare | part | tenth one | shall you ;prepare | a for ram | tenth parts | and two ,bullock | a for

259 2403 8163 3532 7651 259 3532
22 לַכֶּבֶשׂ הָאֶחָד לְשִׁבְעַת הַכְּבָשִׂים׃ וּשְׂעִיר חַטָּאת אֶחָד
,one | sin a offering | and goat | ,lambs | for and seven the | ,one | the for lamb

8548 5930 834 1242 5930 3722
23 לְכַפֵּר עֲלֵיכֶם׃ מִלְּבַד עֹלַת הַבֹּקֶר אֲשֶׁר לְעֹלַת הַתָּמִיד
,continual | the for offering burnt | which (is) | the ,morning | burnt the of offering | Besides | .you for | to atone

3899 3117 7651 3117 6213 428 428 6213
24 תַּעֲשׂוּ אֶת־אֵלֶּה׃ כָּאֵלֶּה תַּעֲשׂוּ לַיּוֹם שִׁבְעַת יָמִים לֶחֶם
bread | ,days | seven | ,daily | shall you prepare | this in way | ;these | shall you prepare

5262 6213 8548 5930 3068 5207 7381 801
אִשֵּׁה רֵיחַ־נִיחֹחַ לַיהוָה עַל־עוֹלַת הַתָּמִיד יֵעָשֶׂה וְנִסְכּוֹ׃
its and ;offering drink | be shall it prepared | continual | the burnt offering | besides | to ;Jehovah | soothing a fragrance | fire a for ,offering

5656 4399 3605 1961 6944 4744 7637 3117
25 וּבַיּוֹם הַשְּׁבִיעִי מִקְרָא־קֹדֶשׁ יִהְיֶה לָכֶם כָּל־מְלֶאכֶת עֲבֹדָה
work | of labor | any to ;you | shall be | a holy | convo-cation | the seventh | on and day

in the day of the firstfruits,
as you offer a new food
offering to Jehovah in your
Feast of Weeks, you shall
have a holy convocation;
you shall do no work of
service; 27 and you shall
offer a burnt offering for a
sweet fragrance to Jehovah:
two bullocks, sons of the
herd, one ram, seven
yearling lambs, 28 and their
food offering, flour mixed
with oil, three tenth parts to
the one bullock, two tenth
parts to the one ram, 29 one
tenth part to the one lamb,
for the seven lambs; 30 one
kid of the goats to make
atonement for you. 31 You
shall offer them besides the
continual burnt offering and
its food offering and drink
offerings; they shall be
perfect ones for you.

4503 7126 1061 3117 6213
26 לֹא תַעֲשׂוּ׃ וּבְיוֹם הַבִּכּוּרִים בְּהַקְרִיבְכֶם מִנְחָה
food a offering | you as offer | the ,firstfruits | the in And of day | shall you not .do

3605 1961 6944 4744 7620 3068 2319
חֲדָשָׁה לַיהוָה בְּשָׁבֻעֹתֵיכֶם מִקְרָא־קֹדֶשׁ יִהְיֶה לָכֶם כָּל־
any | to :you | shall be | a holy | convocation | feast your in ,weeks of | to ,Jehovah | new

5207 7381 5930 7126 6213 3808 5656 4399
27 מְלֶאכֶת עֲבֹדָה לֹא תַעֲשׂוּ׃ וְהִקְרַבְתֶּם עֹלָה לְרֵיחַ נִיחֹחַ
sooth ing | a fragrance | for | burnt a offering | you and offer shall | shall you :do | not | work | of labor

1121 3532 7651 259 352 8147 1241 1121 6499 3068
לַיהוָה פָּרִים בְּנֵי־בָקָר שְׁנַיִם אַיִל אֶחָד שִׁבְעָה כְבָשִׂים בְּנֵי
lambs | seven | ,one | ram | two | the of herd | a of son | bullocks | to ;Jehovah

6499 6224 7969 8081 1101 5560 4503 8141
28 שָׁנָה׃ וּמִנְחָתָם סֹלֶת בְּלוּלָה בַשֶּׁמֶן שְׁלֹשָׁה עֶשְׂרֹנִים לַפָּר
to bullock | tenth parts | three | ,oil with | mixed | flour | their and ,offering food | ,yearling

3532 6224 6224 259 352 6224 8147 259
29 הָאֶחָד שְׁנֵי עֶשְׂרֹנִים לָאַיִל הָאֶחָד׃ עִשָּׂרוֹן עִשָּׂרוֹן לַכֶּבֶשׂ
lamb to | part tenth one | ,one | the to ram | tenth parts | two | ,one the

3722 259 5795 8163 3532 7651 259
30 הָאֶחָד לְשִׁבְעַת הַכְּבָשִׂים׃ שְׂעִיר עִזִּים אֶחָד לְכַפֵּר עֲלֵיכֶם׃
;you for | to atone | ,one | the goats | of kid | ;lambs | the for seven | ,one the

1961 8549 6213 4503 8548 5930
31 מִלְּבַד עֹלַת הַתָּמִיד וּמִנְחָתוֹ תַּעֲשׂוּ תְּמִימִם יִהְיוּ־לָכֶם
for you | they be shall | perfect ones | shall you ;them offer | its and offering food | continual | the offering burnt | besides

5262
וְנִסְכֵּיהֶם׃
drink their and .offerings

CAP. XXIX כט

CHAPTER 29

CHAPTER 29
1 And in the seventh
month, on the first of the
month you shall have a holy
gathering; you shall do no
work of service. It shall be a
day of blowing the trumpets
to you. 2 And you shall
prepare a burnt offering for
a sweet fragrance to
Jehovah: one young bul-
lock, one ram, seven yearling lambs, perfect ones;
3 and their food offering,
flour mixed with oil, three
tenths parts for the bullock,
two tenths parts for the ram,
4 and one tenth part for each
of the seven lambs; 5 and
one kid of the goats, a sin
offering to make atonement
for you; 6 besides the
burnt offering of the month,

1961 6944 4744 2320 259 7637 2320
1 וּבַחֹדֶשׁ הַשְּׁבִיעִי בְּאֶחָד לַחֹדֶשׁ מִקְרָא־קֹדֶשׁ יִהְיֶה לָכֶם
to ;you | shall be | holy | convo- a cation | the ,month | the on of first | ,seventh the | in And month

1961 8643 3117 6213 3808 5656 4399 3605
כָּל־מְלֶאכֶת עֲבֹדָה לֹא תַעֲשׂוּ יוֹם תְּרוּעָה יִהְיֶה לָכֶם׃
;you to | shall it be | blowing the trumpets | day a of | shall you :do | not | service | of work | any

352 259 1241 1121 6499 3068 5207 7381 5930 6213
2 וַעֲשִׂיתֶם עֹלָה לְרֵיחַ נִיחֹחַ לַיהוָה פַּר בֶּן־בָּקָר אֶחָד אַיִל
ram | ,one | young | bullock | to :Jehovah | soothing | a fragrance | for | burnt a offering | shall you and prepare

5560 4503 8549 7651 8141 1121 3532 259
3 אֶחָד כְּבָשִׂים בְּנֵי־שָׁנָה שִׁבְעָה תְּמִימִם׃ וּמִנְחָתָם סֹלֶת
flour | their and ,offering food | perfect :ones | ,seven | yearling | lambs | ,one

352 6241 8147 6499 6241 7969 8081 1101
בְּלוּלָה בַשֶּׁמֶן שְׁלֹשָׁה עֶשְׂרֹנִים לַפָּר שְׁנֵי עֶשְׂרֹנִים לָאָיִל׃
the for ,ram | tenth parts | two | the for ,bullock | tenth parts | three | with ,oil | mixed

8163 3532 7651 259 3532 259 6241
4 5 וְעִשָּׂרוֹן אֶחָד לַכֶּבֶשׂ הָאֶחָד לְשִׁבְעַת הַכְּבָשִׂים׃ וּשְׂעִיר
kid and of | ;lambs | the for seven | ,one | the for lamb | one | and part tenth

2320 5930 3722 2403 259 5795
6 עִזִּים אֶחָד חַטָּאת לְכַפֵּר עֲלֵיכֶם׃ מִלְּבַד עֹלַת הַחֹדֶשׁ
the ,month | burnt the of offering | besides | ;you for | to atone | sin a ,offering | ,one | the goats

and its food offering, and the continual burnt offering, and its food offering, and their drink offerings, according to their ordinance for sweet fragrance, a fire offering to Jehovah.
[7]And on the tenth of this seventh month you shall have a holy gathering; you shall do no work of service, you shall humble your souls. [8]And you shall offer a burnt offering to Jehovah, a sweet fragrance: one bullock, a son of the herd, one ram, seven yearling lambs; they shall be perfect ones for you; [9]and their food offering, flour mixed with oil, three tenths parts for the bullock, two tenths parts for the one ram; [10]one tenth part for the one lamb, for the seven lambs; [11]one kid of the goats, a sin offering, besides the sin offering of the atonement, and the continual burnt offering, and its food offering, and their drink offerings.

[12]And on the fifteenth day of the seventh month, you shall have a holy gathering; you shall do no work of service; and you shall celebrate a feast to Jehovah seven days. [13]And *you* shall offer a burnt offering, a fire offering, a sweet fragrance to Jehovah: thirteen bullocks, sons of the herd, two rams, fourteen yearling lambs; they shall be perfect ones; [14]and their food offerings, flour mixed with oil, three tenths parts to the one bullock, for the thirteen bullocks; two tenths parts to each of the two rams; [15]and one tenth part to each of the fourteen lambs; [16]and one kid of the goats, a sin offering,

7381 4941 5262 4503 8548 5930 4503
וּמִנְחָתָהּ וְעֹלַת הַתָּמִיד וּמִנְחָתָהּ וְנִסְכֵּיהֶם כְּמִשְׁפָּטָם לְרֵיחַ
a for odor | to according ,ordinance | their and offerings drink | its and ,offering food | ,continual offering burnt | the and food its and ,offering

2088 7637 2320 6218 3068 801 5207
7 נִיחֹחַ אִשֶּׁה לַיהוָה׃ וּבֶעָשׂוֹר לַחֹדֶשׁ הַשְּׁבִיעִי הַזֶּה
,this | seventh | month of | the on And tenth | to Jehovah | fire a offering | ,soothing

3605 5315 6031 1961 6944 4744
מִקְרָא־קֹדֶשׁ יִהְיֶה לָכֶם וְעִנִּיתֶם אֶת־נַפְשֹׁתֵיכֶם כָּל־
any | ;souls your | you and humble shall | you to | shall be | holy | a convocation

5207 7381 3068 5930 7126 6213 3808 4399
8 מְלָאכָה לֹא תַעֲשׂוּ׃ וְהִקְרַבְתֶּם עֹלָה לַיהוָה רֵיחַ נִיחֹחַ
;soothing | a ;fragrance | Jehovah to | burnt a offering | shall you and offer | shall you ;do | not | laboring (work)

7651 8141 1121 3532 259 352 259 1241 1121 6499
פַּר בֶּן־בָּקָר אֶחָד אַיִל אֶחָד כְּבָשִׂים בְּנֵי־שָׁנָה שִׁבְעָה
;seven | the of herd | a of son | lambs | ,one | ram | ,one | the herd | a of son | bull

7969 8081 1101 5560 4503 1961 8549
9 תְּמִימִם יִהְיוּ לָכֶם׃ וּמִנְחָתָם סֹלֶת בְּלוּלָה בַשֶּׁמֶן שְׁלֹשָׁה
three | ,oil with | mixed | flour | their and .offering food | for ;you | they be shall | perfect ones

6241 6241 259 352 8241 8147 6499 6241
10 עֶשְׂרֹנִים לַפָּר שְׁנֵי עֶשְׂרֹנִים לָאַיִל הָאֶחָד׃ עִשָּׂרוֹן עִשָּׂרוֹן
one | tenth part | ,one | the for ram | tenth parts | two | the for bullock | tenth parts

2403 259 5795 8163 3532 7651 259 3532
11 לַכֶּבֶשׂ הָאֶחָד לְשִׁבְעַת הַכְּבָשִׂים׃ שְׂעִיר־עִזִּים אֶחָד חַטָּאת
sin- a ;offering | ,one | the goats | of kid | ;lambs the | seven for | ,one | the for lamb

5262 4503 8548 5930 3725 2403
מִלְּבַד חַטַּאת הַכִּפֻּרִים וְעֹלַת הַתָּמִיד וּמִנְחָתָהּ וְנִסְכֵּיהֶם׃
their and .offerings drink | food its and offering | the ,continual | burnt and offering | the ,atonement | sin the of offering | besides

6944 4744 7637 2320 3117 6240 2568
12 וּבַחֲמִשָּׁה עָשָׂר יוֹם לַחֹדֶשׁ הַשְּׁבִיעִי מִקְרָא־קֹדֶשׁ ס
convocation a holy | ,seventh | the on month | day | fifteenth | the on And

3068 2282 2287 6213 3808 5656 4399 3605 1961
יִהְיֶה לָכֶם כָּל־מְלֶאכֶת עֲבֹדָה לֹא תַעֲשׂוּ וְחַגֹּתֶם חַג לַיהוָה
to Jehovah | a feast | shall You celebrate | you .do shall | no | service | of work | any | to ;you | shall be

6491 3068 5207 7381 801 5930 7126 3117 7651
13 שִׁבְעַת יָמִים׃ וְהִקְרַבְתֶּם עֹלָה אִשֵּׁה רֵיחַ נִיחֹחַ לַיהוָה פָּרִים
bullocks | to ;Jehovah | soothing a fragrance | fire a offering | burnt a ,offering | shall and offer | ,days | seven

8141 1121 3532 8147 352 6248 7969 8141 1121
בְּנֵי־בָקָר שְׁלֹשָׁה עָשָׂר אֵילִם שְׁנַיִם כְּבָשִׂים בְּנֵי־שָׁנָה
year a of son | lambs | ,two | rams | ten (and) three | young
1101

8081 5560 4503 1961 8549 6240 702
14 אַרְבָּעָה עָשָׂר תְּמִימִם יִהְיוּ׃ וּמִנְחָתָם סֹלֶת בְּלוּלָה בַשֶּׁמֶן
with .oil | mixed | flour | their and ,offering food | they ;be shall | perfect ones | ;fourteen

8147 6499 6240 702 259 6499 6241 7969
שְׁלֹשָׁה עֶשְׂרֹנִים לַפָּר הָאֶחָד לִשְׁלֹשָׁה עָשָׂר פָּרִים שְׁנֵי
two ;bullocks | thirteen the for | ,one | the to bullock | tenth parts | three

3532 6241 6241 352 8147 259 352 6241
15 עֶשְׂרֹנִים לָאַיִל הָאֶחָד לִשְׁנֵי הָאֵילִם׃ וְעִשָּׂרוֹן עִשָּׂרוֹן לַכֶּבֶשׂ
the to lamb | part tenth one and | ;rams the | for two | ,one | the for ram | tenth parts

2403 259 5795 8163 3532 6242 702 259
16 הָאֶחָד לְאַרְבָּעָה עָשָׂר כְּבָשִׂים׃ וּשְׂעִיר־עִזִּים אֶחָד חַטָּאת
sin a ;offering | ,one | the goats | and of kid | ;lambs | fourteen the for | ,one the

besides the continual burnt offering, its food offering and its drink offering. [17]And on the second day twelve bullocks, sons of the herd, two rams, fourteen yearling lambs, perfect ones; [18]and their food offerings, and their drink offerings for the bullocks, for the rams, and for the lambs, in their number, according to the ordinance; [19]and one kid of the goats, a sin offering; besides the continual burnt offering, and its food offering, and their drink offerings. [20]And in the third day eleven bullocks, two rams, fourteen yearling lambs, perfect ones; [21]and their food offerings, and their drink offerings for the bullocks, for the rams, and for the lambs, in their number, according to the ordinance; [22]and one goat as a sin offering; besides the continual burnt offering, and its food offering, and its drink offering. [23]And on the fourth day ten bullocks, two rams, fourteen yearling lambs, perfect ones; [24]their food offering, and their drink offerings for the bullocks, for the rams, and for the lambs, in their number, according to the ordinance;

[25]and one kid of the goats, a sin offering, besides the continual burnt offering, and its food offering, and its drink offering. [26]And on the fifth day nine bullocks two rams, fourteen yearling lambs, perfect ones; [27]their food offering, and their drink offerings for the bullocks, for the rams, and for the lambs, in their number, according to the ordinance; [28]and one goat, a sin offering; besides the continual burnt offering, and its food offering, and its drink offering. [29]And on the sixth day eight bullocks, two

8145 3117 5262 4503 8548 5930
17 מִלְּבַד עֹלַת הַתָּמִיד מִנְחָתָהּ וְנִסְכָּהּ׃ וּבַיּוֹם הַשֵּׁנִי
second on And its and food its the burnt besides
day the .offering drink ,offering ,continual offering

1121 3532 8147 352 6240 8147 1241 1121 6499
פָּרִים בְּנֵי־בָקָר שְׁנֵים עָשָׂר אֵילִם שְׁנָיִם כְּבָשִׂים בְּנֵי
lambs ,two rams ,twelve the of a bullocks
herd of son

6499 5262 4503 8549 6240 702 8141
18 שָׁנָה אַרְבָּעָה עָשָׂר תְּמִימִם׃ וּמִנְחָתָם וְנִסְכֵּיהֶם לַפָּרִים
the for their and their and perfect ,fourteen yearling
,bullocks ,offerings drink ,offering food ;ones

259 5795 8163 4941 4557 3532 352
19 לָאֵילִם וְלַכְּבָשִׂים בְּמִסְפָּרָם כַּמִּשְׁפָּט׃ וּשְׂעִיר־עִזִּים אֶחָד
,one the and the by their in the for and the for
goats of kid ;ordinance ,number lambs ,rams

3117 5262 4503 85 : 28 59;30 2403
20 חַטָּאת מִלְּבַד עֹלַת הַתָּמִיד וּמִנְחָתָהּ וְנִסְכֵּיהֶם׃ וּבַיּוֹם
on And their and food its and the burnt besides sin a
day the .offerings drink ,offering ,continual offering offering

8141 1121 3532 8147 352 6240 6249 6499 7992
הַשְּׁלִישִׁי פָּרִים עַשְׁתֵּי־עָשָׂר אֵילִם שְׁנָיִם כְּבָשִׂים בְּנֵי־שָׁנָה
yearling lambs ,two rams ,eleven bullocks third

352 6499 5262 4503 8549 6240 702
21 אַרְבָּעָה עָשָׂר תְּמִימִם׃ וּמִנְחָתָם וְנִסְכֵּיהֶם לַפָּרִים לָאֵילִם
the for the for their and food their and perfect ,fourteen
,rams ,bullocks ,offerings drink ,offering ;ones

259 2403 8163 4941 4557 3532
22 וְלַכְּבָשִׂים בְּמִסְפָּרָם כַּמִּשְׁפָּט׃ וּשְׂעִיר חַטָּאת אֶחָד
;one sin a goat and the by their in the for and
,offering ;ordinance ,number ,lambs

3117 5262 4503 8548 59:30
23 מִלְּבַד עֹלַת הַתָּמִיד וּמִנְחָתָהּ וְנִסְכָּהּ׃ וּבַיּוֹם
on And its and food its and the burnt besides
day the .offering drink ,offering ,continual offering

8141 1121 3532 8147 352 6235 6499 7243
הָרְבִיעִי פָּרִים עֲשָׂרָה אֵילִם שְׁנָיִם כְּבָשִׂים בְּנֵי־שָׁנָה
yearling lambs ,two rams ,ten bullocks fourth

352 6499 5262 4503 8549 6240 702
24 אַרְבָּעָה עָשָׂר תְּמִימִם׃ מִנְחָתָם וְנִסְכֵּיהֶם לַפָּרִים לָאֵילִם
the for the for their and food their perfect ,fourteen
,rams ,bullocks ,offerings drink ,offering ;ones

2403 259 5795 4941 4557 3532
25 וְלַכְּבָשִׂים בְּמִסְפָּרָם כַּמִּשְׁפָּט׃ וּשְׂעִיר־עִזִּים אֶחָד חַטָּאת
sin a ,one the and the by their in for and
,offering goats of kid ;ordinance ,number lambs the

2549 3117 5262 4503 8548 5930
26 מִלְּבַד עֹלַת הַתָּמִיד מִנְחָתָהּ וְנִסְכָּהּ׃ וּבַיּוֹם הַחֲמִישִׁי
fifth on And its food its the burnt besides
day the .offering drink ,offering ,continual offering

702 8141/1121 3532 8147 352 8672 6499
פָּרִים תִּשְׁעָה אֵילִם שְׁנָיִם כְּבָשִׂים בְּנֵי־שָׁנָה אַרְבָּעָה
four- yearling lambs ,two rams ,nine bullocks

3532 352 6499 5262 4503 8549 6240
27 עָשָׂר תְּמִימִם׃ וּמִנְחָתָם וְנִסְכֵּיהֶם לַפָּרִים לָאֵילִם וְלַכְּבָשִׂים
for and the for the for their and their and perfect ;teen
.lambs the ,rams ,bullocks offering drink offering food ;ones

5930 259 2403 8163 4941 4557
28 בְּמִסְפָּרָם כַּמִּשְׁפָּט׃ וּשְׂעִיר חַטָּאת אֶחָד מִלְּבַד עֹלַת
burnt besides ,one sin a goat and the by their in
offering ,offering ;ordinance ,number

8083 6499 8345 3117 5262 4503 8548
29 הַתָּמִיד וּמִנְחָתָהּ וְנִסְכָּהּ׃ וּבַיּוֹם הַשִּׁשִּׁי פָּרִים שְׁמֹנָה
,eight bullocks sixth on And its and its and the
day the .offering drink offering food ,continual

rams, fourteen yearling
lambs, perfect ones; [30]their
food offerings, and their
drink offerings for the
bullocks, for the rams, and
for the lambs, in their
number, according to the
ordinance; [31]and one
goat, a sin offering; besides
the continual burnt offering,
and its food offering, and its
drink offering. [32]And on the
seventh day seven bullocks,
two rams, fourteen yearling
lambs, perfect ones; [33]their
food offerings, and their
drink offerings for the bullocks, for the rams, and for
the lambs, in their number,
according to the ordinance;

[34]and one goat, a sin
offering; besides the continual burnt offering, and its
food offering, and its drink
offering.
[35]And you shall have a
solemn assembly on the
eighth day; you shall do no
work of service. [36]And you
shall offer a burnt offering, a
fire offering, a sweet
fragrance to Jehovah: one
bullock, one ram, seven
yearling lambs, perfect
ones; [37]their food offerings,
and their drink offerings for
the bullock, for the ram, and
for the lambs, in their
number, according to the
ordinance; [38]and one goat,
a sin offering, besides the
continual burnt offering, and
its food offering, and its
drink offering. [39]You shall
prepare these in your
appointed seasons, apart
from your vows and your
free-will offerings, for your
burnt offerings and for your
food offerings, and for your
drink offerings, and for your
peace offerings.

8549 6240 702 8141 1121 3532 8147 352
אֵילִם שְׁנָיִם כְּבָשִׂים בְּנֵי־שָׁנָה אַרְבָּעָה עָשָׂר תְּמִימִם׃
perfect ;ones ;fourteen yearling lambs ,two rams

4557 3532 352 6499 5262 4503
30 וּמִנְחָתָם וְנִסְכֵּיהֶם לַפָּרִים לָאֵילִם וְלַכְּבָשִׂים בְּמִסְפָּרָם
their in number for and ,lambs the for and ,rams the the for ,bullocks their and drink offerings their and food ,offering

8548 5930 259 2403 8163 4941
31 כַּמִּשְׁפָּט׃ וּשְׂעִיר חַטָּאת אֶחָד מִלְּבַד עֹלַת הַתָּמִיד
the ,continual burnt offering besides ,one sin a ,offering ,goat and the by ;ordinance

7651 6499 7637 3117 5262 4503
32 מִנְחָתָהּ וְנִסְכֶּהָ׃ וּבַיּוֹם הַשְּׁבִיעִי פָּרִים שִׁבְעָה
seven bullocks ,seventh on And day the its and .offering drink food its ,offering

8549 6240 702 8141 1121 3532 8147 352
אֵילִם שְׁנָיִם כְּבָשִׂים בְּנֵי־שָׁנָה אַרְבָּעָה עָשָׂר תְּמִימִם׃
perfect ;ones ;fourteen yearling lambs ,two rams

4557 3532 352 6499 5262 4503
33 וּמִנְחָתָם וְנִסְכֵּהֶם לַפָּרִים לָאֵילִם וְלַכְּבָשִׂים בְּמִסְפָּרָם
their in ,number for and ,lambs the the for ,rams the for ,bulls their and drink offerings their and food ,offering

8548 5930 259 2403 8163 4941
34 כְּמִשְׁפָּטָם׃ וּשְׂעִיר חַטָּאת אֶחָד מִלְּבַד עֹלַת הַתָּמִיד
the ,continual burnt offering besides ,one sin a ,offering goat and their by ;ordinance

1961 6116 8066 3117 5262 4503
35 מִנְחָתָהּ וְנִסְכָּהּ׃ בַּיּוֹם הַשְּׁמִינִי עֲצֶרֶת תִּהְיֶה לָכֶם
to ;you shall be solemn a assembly eighth on And day the its and .offering drink food its offering

801 5930 7126 6213 3808 5656 4399 3605
36 כָּל־מְלֶאכֶת עֲבֹדָה לֹא תַעֲשׂוּ׃ וְהִקְרַבְתֶּם עֹלָה אִשֵּׁה
fire a ,offering burnt a ,offering you And bring shall shall you .do not service of work any

8141 1121 3532 259 352 259 6499 3068 5207 7381
רֵיחַ נִיחֹחַ לַיהוָה פַּר אֶחָד אַיִל אֶחָד כְּבָשִׂים בְּנֵי־שָׁנָה
year a of son lambs ,one ram ,one bullock to Jehovah soothing a fragrance

3532 352 6499 5262 4503 8549 7651
37 שִׁבְעָה תְּמִימִם׃ מִנְחָתָם וְנִסְכֵּיהֶם לַפָּר לָאַיִל וְלַכְּבָשִׂים
for and ,lambs the the for ram the for ,bullock their and ,offerings drink food their ,offering perfect ;ones ,seven

5930 259 2403 8163 4941 4557
38 בְּמִסְפָּרָם כַּמִּשְׁפָּט׃ וּשְׂעִיר חַטָּאת אֶחָד מִלְּבַד עֹלַת
burnt offering besides ,one sin a ,offering goat and the by ;ordinance their in ,number

4150 3068 6213 428 5262 4503 8548
39 הַתָּמִיד וּמִנְחָתָהּ וְנִסְכָּהּ׃ אֵלֶּה תַּעֲשׂוּ לַיהוָה בְּמוֹעֲדֵיכֶם
your feast in set for Jehovah shall You prepare these its and .offering drink food its and ,offering the ,continual

4503 5930 5071 5088 905
לְבַד מִנִּדְרֵיכֶם וְנִדְבֹתֵיכֶם לְעֹלֹתֵיכֶם וּלְמִנְחֹתֵיכֶם
your for and ,offerings food burnt your for ,offerings burnt free- your and ,offerings will vows your apart from

8002 5262
וּלְנִסְכֵּיכֶם וּלְשַׁלְמֵיכֶם׃
your for and .offerings peace your for and ,offerings drink

CAP. XXX. ל
CHAPTER 30

[40]And Moses spoke to the sons of Israel according to all that Jehovah had commanded Moses.

CHAPTER 30

[1]And Moses spoke to the heads of the tribes of the sons of Israel, saying, This is the thing which Jehovah has commanded: [2]When a man vows a vow to Jehovah, or has sworn an oath to bind his soul with a bond, he shall not break his word; he shall do all that has gone out of his mouth. [3]And when a woman vows a vow to Jehovah, and has bound a bond in the house of her father in her youth, [4]and her father has heard her vow, and her bond with which she has bound her soul, and her father has remained silent as to her, then all her vows shall stand; and every bond with which she has bound her soul shall stand. [5]But if her father has prohibited her in the day he heard, none of her vows and her bond with which she has bound her soul shall stand. And Jehovah will forgive her because her father prohibited her. [6]And if she belongs to a husband, and her vows *are* on her, or a rash utterance *on* her lips with which she has bound her soul, [7]and her husband has heard, and in the day he heard he has remained silent as to her, then her vows shall stand, and her bond with which she has bound her soul shall stand. [8]And if in the day her husband hears, he prohibits her, then he has broken her vow which *is* on her, and the rash utterance of her lips with which she has bound her soul. And

3068 6680 3605 3478 1121 4872 1696
1 וַיֹּאמֶר מֹשֶׁה אֶל־בְּנֵי יִשְׂרָאֵל כְּכֹל אֲשֶׁר־צִוָּה יְהוָה אֶת־
Jehovah had that according Israel the to Moses And
commanded all to of sons spoke
4872
מֹשֶׁה׃
.Moses

2088 559 3478 1121 4294 7218 4872 1696
2 וַיְדַבֵּר מֹשֶׁה אֶל־רָאשֵׁי הַמַּטּוֹת לִבְנֵי יִשְׂרָאֵל לֵאמֹר זֶה
This ,saying ,Israel the of tribes the the to Moses And
(is) of sons of heads spoke
3068 5088 5087 376 3068 6680 834 1697
3 הַדָּבָר אֲשֶׁר צִוָּה יְהוָה׃ אִישׁ כִּי־יִדֹּר נֶדֶר לַיהוָה אוֹ
or to vow a vows When a :Jehovah has which the
Jehovah man commanded thing
3605 1697 2490 3808 5921 632 631 7621 7650
הִשָּׁבַע שְׁבֻעָה לֶאְסֹר אִסָּר עַל־נַפְשׁוֹ לֹא יַחֵל דְּבָרוֹ כְּכָל־
all his he not him- on with bind to oath an has
;word break shall ,self bond a sworn
631 3068 5088 5087 802 6213 6310 3318
4 הַיֹּצֵא מִפִּיו יַעֲשֶׂה׃ וְאִשָּׁה כִּי־תִדֹּר נֶדֶר לַיהוָה וְאָסְרָה
has and to vow a vows when a And shall he his of has that
bound ,Jehovah woman .do mouth out gone
5088 1 8085 5271 1 1004 631
5 אִסָּר בְּבֵית אָבִיהָ בִּנְעֻרֶיהָ׃ וְשָׁמַע אָבִיהָ אֶת־נִדְרָהּ
,vow her her has and her in her the in a
father heard ,youth father of house bond
6965 1 2790 5921 631 834 631
וֶאֱסָרָהּ אֲשֶׁר אָסְרָה עַל־נַפְשָׁהּ וְהֶחֱרִישׁ לָהּ אָבִיהָ וְקָמוּ
shall then her to as has and her- on has she her and
stand ,father her silent kept ,self bound which bond
6965 5315 631 834 631 3605 5088
6 כָּל־נְדָרֶיהָ וְכָל־אִסָּר אֲשֶׁר־אָסְרָה עַל־נַפְשָׁהּ יָקוּם׃ וְאִם־
But shall her- on has she which bond and ,vows her all
if stand self bound every
834 631 5088 3605 8085 3117 1 5106
הֵנִיא אָבִיהָ אֹתָהּ בְּיוֹם שָׁמְעוֹ כָּל־נְדָרֶיהָ וֶאֱסָרֶיהָ אֲשֶׁר־
which her and her any he the in her her has
bonds vows of heard day father denied
1 5106 5545 3068 6965 3808 5315 631
אָסְרָה עַל־נַפְשָׁהּ לֹא יָקוּם וַיהוָה יִסְלַח־לָהּ כִּי־הֵנִיא אָבִיהָ
her because her will and shall none her- on has she
father denied forgive Jehovah ;stand ,self bound
4008 176 5088 376 1961 518
7 אֹתָהּ׃ וְאִם־הָיוֹ תִהְיֶה לְאִישׁ וּנְדָרֶיהָ עָלֶיהָ אוֹ מִבְטָא
rash a or on (are) her and a to she all at And .her
utterance ,her vows ,husband is if
8085 3117 376 8085 5315 631 834 8193
8 שְׂפָתֶיהָ אֲשֶׁר אָסְרָה עַל־נַפְשָׁהּ׃ וְשָׁמַע אִישָׁהּ בְּיוֹם שָׁמְעוֹ
he in and her has and her- on has she which her (on)
heard day the ,husband heard self bound ,lips
5921 631 834 632 5088 6965 2790
וְהֶחֱרִישׁ לָהּ וְקָמוּ נְדָרֶיהָ וֶאֱסָרֶהָ אֲשֶׁר־אָסְרָה עַל־נַפְשָׁהּ
her- on has she which her and her then to as has he
self bound bond ,vows stand shall ,her silent kept
5088 6565 5106 376 8085 3117 518 6965
9 יָקֻמוּ׃ וְאִם בְּיוֹם שְׁמֹעַ אִישָׁהּ יָנִיא אוֹתָהּ וְהֵפֵר אֶת־נִדְרָהּ
vow her he then ,her he her hears the in And shall
broken has denied husband day if ,stand
5315 631 834 8193 4008 5921 834
אֲשֶׁר עָלֶיהָ וְאֵת מִבְטָא שְׂפָתֶיהָ אֲשֶׁר אָסְרָה עַל־נַפְשָׁהּ
;herself on has she which lips her rash the and ,her on which
bound of utterance (is)

Jehovah will forgive her.
[9]And *as* to the vow of a widow, or her that is divorced, all that she has bound on her soul shall be established on her. [10]And if she has vowed *in* the house of her husband, or bound a bond on her soul with an oath, [11]and her husband has heard, and has remained silent as to her, *and* he has not prohibited her, then all her vows shall be established, and every bond with which she has bound her soul shall stand. [12]And if her husband has certainly broken them in the day he heard, none of the utterance of her lips concerning her vows, or concerning the bond of her soul, shall stand; her husband has broken them. And Jehovah will forgive her.
[13]Every vow and every oath, any bond to humble a soul, her husband shall establish it, or her husband shall break it. [14]And if her husband is altogether silent at her from day to day, then he has established all her vows, or all her bonds which *are* on her; he has established them; for he remained silent as to her in the day he heard. [15]And if he at all breaks them after he hears, then he has borne her iniquity.
[16]These are the statutes which Jehovah has commanded Moses between a man and his wife, between a father and his daughter in her youth *in* the house of her father.

631 834 3605 1644 490 5088 5545 3068
10 וַיהוָה יִסְלַח־לָהּ׃ וְנֵדֶר אַלְמָנָה וּגְרוּשָׁה כֹּל אֲשֶׁר־אָסְרָה
has she that all a and ,widow a to And .her will and
bound ,one divorced of vow the forgive Jehovah

631 5087 376 1004 5921 5315
11 עַל־נַפְשָׁהּ יָקוּם עָלֶיהָ׃ וְאִם־בֵּית אִישָׁהּ נָדָרָה אוֹ־אָסְרָה
bound or has she her the (in) And upon be shall her on
,vowed husband of house if .her settled soul

3808 2790 376 8085 7621 5315 5921 6321
12 אִסָּר עַל־נַפְשָׁהּ בִּשְׁבֻעָה׃ וְשָׁמַע אִישָׁהּ וְהֶחֱרִשׁ לָהּ לֹא
(and) to as has and her has and an with her on a
not ,her silent kept husband heard ,oath soul bond

5921 631 834 632 3605 5088 6965 5106
הֵנִיא אֹתָהּ וְקָמוּ כָּל־נְדָרֶיהָ וְכָל־אִסָּר אֲשֶׁר־אָסְרָה עַל־
has she with bond and her all then ,her has
bound which every ,vows settled be shall denied

8085 3117 376 6565 6565 6965 5315
13 נַפְשָׁהּ יָקוּם׃ וְאִם־הָפֵר יָפֵר אֹתָם ׀ אִישָׁהּ בְּיוֹם שָׁמְעוֹ
he the in her them has certainly And shall her
,heard day husband broken if .stand soul

376 6965 3808 5315 632 5088 8193 4161
כָּל־מוֹצָא שְׂפָתֶיהָ לִנְדָרֶיהָ וּלְאִסַּר נַפְשָׁהּ לֹא יָקוּם אִישָׁהּ
her shall none her to as or to as lips her the of
husband ;stand ,soul bond of the ,vows her of utterance

6031 631 7621 3605 5088 3605 5545 3068 6565
14 הֲפֵרָם וַיהוָה יִסְלַח־לָהּ׃ כָּל־נֵדֶר וְכָל־שְׁבֻעַת אִסָּר לְעַנֹּת
to any ,oath and vow Every .her will and broken has
humble bond every forgive Jehovah ;them

2790 2790 6565 376 6965 376 5315
15 נֶפֶשׁ אִישָׁהּ יְקִימֶנּוּ וְאִישָׁהּ יְפֵרֶנּוּ׃ וְאִם־הַחֲרֵשׁ יַחֲרִישׁ לָהּ
at altogether is and shall her or shall her a
.her silent if ;it break husband .it settle husband ,soul

3605 5088 3605 6965 3117 3117 376
אִישָׁהּ מִיּוֹם אֶל־יוֹם וְהֵקִים אֶת־כָּל־נְדָרֶיהָ אוֹ אֶת־כָּל־
all or her all he then ,day to from her
,vows settled has day husband

8085 3117 2790 6965 5921 834 631
אֱסָרֶיהָ אֲשֶׁר עָלֶיהָ הֵקִים אֹתָם כִּי־הֶחֱרִשׁ לָהּ בְּיוֹם שָׁמְעוֹ׃
he the in to as has he for ;them has he on which her
;heard day her silent kept settled ;her (are) bonds

428 5771 8085 310 6565 6565
16 וְאִם־הָפֵר יָפֵר אֹתָם אַחֲרֵי שָׁמְעוֹ וְנָשָׂא אֶת־עֲוֺנָהּ׃ אֵלֶּה
17
These her he then he after them he all at and
(are) ,iniquity borne has ,hears breaks if

996 802 376 996 4872 3068 6680 834 2706
הַחֻקִּים אֲשֶׁר צִוָּה יְהוָה אֶת־מֹשֶׁה בֵּין אִישׁ לְאִשְׁתּוֹ בֵּין
between and a between Moses Jehovah com- which the
,wife his man manded statutes

1 1004 5271 1323 1
אָב לְבִתּוֹ בִּנְעֻרֶיהָ בֵּית אָבִיהָ׃
her the (in) her in his and a
.father of house ,youth ,daughter father

CAP. XXXI. לא

CHAPTER 31

CHAPTER 31
[1]And Jehovah spoke to Moses, saying, [2]Execute the vengeance of the sons of Israel against the Midianites. Afterward you shall be gathered to your people.
[3]And Moses spoke to the people, saying, Some men of you be armed for the army, and they shall be against Midian, to execute

3478 1121 5360 5358 559 4872 3068 1696
1 וַיְדַבֵּר יְהוָה אֶל־מֹשֶׁה לֵּאמֹר׃ נְקֹם נִקְמַת בְּנֵי יִשְׂרָאֵל
2
Israel the the Execute ,saying ,Moses to Jehovah And
of sons of vengeance spoke

4872 1696 5971 622 310 4080
3 מֵאֵת הַמִּדְיָנִים אַחַר תֵּאָסֵף אֶל־עַמֶּיךָ׃ וַיְדַבֵּר מֹשֶׁה אֶל־
to Moses And your to shall you after- the against
spoke ,people gathered be ward ;Midianites

1961 6635 582 582 2502 559 5971
הָעָם לֵאמֹר הֵחָלְצוּ מֵאִתְּכֶם אֲנָשִׁים לַצָּבָא וְיִהְיוּ עַל־
against and the for men of men (Some) armed be ,saying the
be shall they ,army ,you of ,people

the vengeance of Jehovah on Midian; [4]you shall send to the army a thousand for a tribe as to all the tribes of Israel. [5]And a thousand for a tribe were given out of the thousands of Israel, twelve thousand armed ones of the army. [6]And Moses sent them to the army, a thousand for a tribe, them and Phinehas the son of Eleazar the priest to the army; also the holy vessels, and the trumpets to sound in his hand. [7]And they warred against Midian, as Jehovah had commanded Moses, and killed every male. [8]And they killed the kings of Midian, besides the rest of their slain: Evi, and Rekem, and Zur, and Hur, and Reba, five kings of Midian. They also killed Balaam the son of Beor with the sword. [9]And the sons of Israel took the women of Midian captive, and their infants, and all their livestock, and all their purchased things. And they plundered all their wealth. [10]And they burned all their cities with fire, their homes, and all their towers. [11]And they took all the spoil, and all the prey, among man and among animal. [12]And they brought it to Moses, and to Eleazar the priest, and to the congregation of the sons of Israel; the captives, and the prey, and the spoil—to the camp, to the plains of Moab which *are* by Jordan, *near* Jericho.

[13]And Moses and Eleazar the priest, and all the rulers of the congregation went out to meet them outside the camp. [14]And Moses was angry

4 מדין לתת נקמת־יהוה במדין׃ אלף למטה אלף למטה
a of a a of a on Jehovah the to Midian
,tribe thousand ,tribe thousand ;Midian of vengeance give

5 לכל מטות ישראל תשלחו לצבא׃ וימסרו מאלפי
the of out there And the to shall you ,Israel the of
of thousands given were .army send of tribes all

6 ישראל אלף למטה שנים־עשר אלף חלוצי צבא׃ וישלח
sent And the armed thousand twelve a of a ,Israel
.army of ones ,tribe thousand

אתם משה אלף למטה לצבא אתם ואת־פינחס בן
the Phinehas and them the to a of a ,Moses them
of son army tribe thousand

אלעזר הכהן לצבא וכלי הקדש וחצצרות התרועה
sound to the and ,holy the and the to the Eleazar
trumpets vessels ;army .priest

7 בידו׃ ויצבאו על־מדין כאשר צוה יהוה את־משה
,Moses Jehovah com- as ,Midian against they And his in
manded warred .hand

8 ויהרגו כל־זכר׃ ואת־מלכי מדין הרגו על־חלליהם את־
:slain their besides they Midian the and ;male every and
.killed of kings killed

אוי ואת־רקם ואת־צור ואת־חור ואת־רבע חמשת מלכי
kings five ,Rebah and ,Hur and ,Zur and ,Rekem and Evi
of

9 מדין ואת בלעם בן־בעור הרגו בחרב׃ וישבו בני־
the took And the with they Beor the Balaam also ;Midian
of sons captive .sword killed of son

ישראל את־נשי מדין ואת־טפם ואת כל־בהמתם ואת־
and their all and their and ,Midian the Israel
livestock ;infants of women

10 כל־מקנהם ואת־כל־חילם בזזו׃ ואת כל־עריהם
their all and they their all and their all
,cities ;plundered wealth ;possessions

11 במושבתם ואת כל־טירתם שרפו באש׃ ויקחו את־כל־
all they And with they their all and their
took .fire burned towers ,habitations

12 השלל ואת כל־המלקוח באדם ובבהמה׃ ויבאו אל־
to they And among and among ,prey the all and the
it brought .animal man ,spoil

משה ואל־אלעזר הכהן ואל־עדת בני־ישראל את־השבי
the :Israel sons the the to and the Eleazar to and Moses
,captives of of company ,priest

ואת־המלקוח ואת־השלל אל־המחנה אל־ערבת מואב
,Moab the to ,camp the to ;spoil the and ,prey the and
of plains

13 אשר על־ירדן ירחו׃ ס ויצאו משה ואלעזר הכהן
the and Moses And (near) the by which
priest Eleazar out went Jericho Jordan (are)

14 וכל־נשיאי העדה לקראתם אל־מחוץ למחנה׃ ויקצף
was And .camp the outside meet to con- the the all and
angry them gregation of rulers

with the officers of the army, the captains of thousands and the captains of hundreds who came from the service of the war.
[15]And Moses said to them, Have you saved all the women alive? [16]Behold, these through the counsel of Balaam caused the sons of Israel a deliverance of treachery against Jehovah in the matter of Peor; and the plague was on the company of Jehovah. [17]And now kill every male among the infants; yea, you shall kill every woman having known a man by lying with a male. [18]And you shall keep alive for yourselves all the female children who have not known *a man* by lying with a male. [19]And pitch outside the camp seven days. Whoever has killed any person, and whoever touched a polluted one, purify yourselves on the third day and on the seventh day, you and your captives. [20]And as to every garment, and all that is made of skin, and all work of goats' hair, and all things made of wood, you shall purify *them*.

[21]And Eleazar the priest said to the men of war who went to battle, This *is* the statute of the law which Jehovah has commanded Moses: [22]only the gold, the silver, the copper, the iron, the tin, and the lead, [23]everything that passes through the fire, you shall make it go through the fire; and it shall be clean. Only it shall be purified with the water for impurity. And every thing that cannot go through the fire, you shall make go through the water. [24]And you shall wash your clothes on the seventh day, and you shall be clean. And afterwards you shall come into the camp.

[25]And Jehovah spoke to Moses, saying, [26]Lift the heads of the prey of the

935 3967 8269 505 8269 2428 6485 4872
משה על פקדי החיל שרי האלפים ושרי המאות הבאים
who came ,hundreds the and thousands of captains the of captains ,army the of officers the with Moses

15 3605 2421 4872 559 4421 6635
מצבא המלחמה: ויאמר אלהם משה החייתם כל-
all you Have alive saved ,Moses them to said And the battle the from of service

16 4560 1109 1697 3478 1121 1961 2007 5347
נקבה: הן הנה היו לבני ישראל בדבר בלעם למסר-
deliv- a erance Balaam of counsel the through Israel of sons the to become these ,Behold the ?females

3068 5712 5061 1961 6965 1697 3068 4604
מעל ביהוה על-דבר-פעור ותהי המגפה בעדת יהוה:
.Jehovah the on of company the plague was and ,Peor of matter the in against Jehovah of treachery

17 4904 376 3045 802 3605 2945 2145 3605 2026 6258
ועתה הרגו כל-זכר בטף וכל-אשה ידעת איש למשכב
lying with by man a has known who woman and every among male every ;infants the kill And ,now

18 2145 4904 3045 834 802 2945 3605 2026 2145
זכר הרגו: וכל הטף בנשים אשר לא-ידעו משכב זכר
a male lying with have known not who female the children but all shall you ;kill a male

19 3605 3117 7651 4264 2351 2583 2421
החיו לכם: ואתם חנו מחוץ למחנה שבעת ימים כל
any who ;days seven camp the outside pitch And for shall you .yourselves alive keep

3117 7992 3117 2398 2491 5060 3605 5315 2026
הרג נפש וכל נגע בחלל תתחטאו ביום השלישי וביום
on and day the ,third day the on purify yourselves pierced a , one has any and touched any who person has killed

20 3605 5785 3627 899 3605 7628 7637
השביעי אתם ושביכם: וכל-בגד וכל-כלי-עור וכל-
and all ,skin of made things and all ,garment And every your and .captives you ,seventh

21 499 559 2398 6086 3627 3605 5795 4639
מעשה עזים וכל-כלי-עץ תתחטאו: ס ויאמר אלעזר
Eleazar said And shall you .purify ,wood of made things and all goat's (hair) work of

8451 2708 2088 4421 935 6635 582 3548
הכהן אל-אנשי הצבא הבאים למלחמה זאת חקת התורה
law the of statute the This (is) the to ,battle went who the army men of to the priest

22 3701 389 4872 3068 6680 834
אשר-צוה יהוה את-משה: אך את-הזהב ואת-הכסף
the ,silver and ,gold the Only :Moses Jehovah has commanded which

23 3605 5777 913 1270 5178
את-הנחשת את-הברזל את-הבדיל ואת-העפרת: כל-
every- ,lead the and ,tin the ,iron the ,copper the

5079 6325 389 2891 784 5674 784 935 834 1697
דבר אשר-יבא באש תעבירו באש וטהר אך במי נדה
for the impurity with water only is it clean and through fire the shall you pass make through fire the goes that thing

24 3526 4325 5674 784 935 3808 834 3605 2398
יתחטא וכל אשר לא-יבא באש תעבירו במים: וכבסתם
you And wash shall through .water the shall you pass through fire the can not go that and thing every be shall it ;purified

4264 935 310 2891 7637 3117 899
בגדיכם ביום השביעי וטהרתם ואחר תבאו אל-המחנה:
.camp the to shall you come in and afterwards shall you and clean be ,seventh the day on your clothes

25 26 4455 7218 5375 559 4872 3068 559
ויאמר יהוה אל-משה לאמר: שא את ראש מלקוח
prey the of heads (of) the Lift ,saying ,Moses to Jehovah And spoke

captives among man and
among beast, you and
Eleazar the priest, and the
heads of the fathers of the
congregation. 27And you
shall divide the prey
between those skilled in
war, that went out to battle,
and all the congregation.
28And you shall levy a
tribute to Jehovah from the
men of war who went out to
the battle: one body out of
five hundred, of men, and of
the herd, and of the asses,
and of the flock, 29you shall
take from their half, and you
shall give to Eleazar the
priest *as* the heave offering
of Jehovah. 30And from the
sons of Israel's half, you
shall take one portion out of
fifty, of man, and of the
herd, and of the asses, and
of the flock, of all the
livestock, and you shall give
them to the Levites keeping
the charge of the tabernacle
of Jehovah.

31And Moses and Eleazar
the priest did as Jehovah
had commanded Moses.
32And the prey, the rest of
the spoil which the people
of the army plundered, was
six hundred and seventy-
five thousand sheep, 33and
seventy-two thousand oxen,
34sixty-one thousand of the
asses; 35and of human
beings, of the women who
had not known *a man* by
lying *with* a male, the
persons *were* thirty-two
thousand. 36And the half,
the portion of those who
went out to the war, the
number of the flock *was*
three hundred and thirty-
seven thousand, five hun-
dred. 37And the tribute to
Jehovah of the sheep was
six hundred and seventy-
five, 38and the oxen,

7218 3548 499 929 120 7628
השבי באדם ובבהמה אתה ואלעזר הכהן וראשי אבות
the the and the and you among and among the
of fathers of heads ,priest Eleazar ;beast man ,captives

4421 8610 996 4455 2673 5712
27 העדה: וחצית את־המלקוח בין תפשי המלחמה
.battle the those between prey the you and con- the
in skilled divide shall ;gregation

3068 4371 7311 5712 3605 6635 5927
28 היצאים לצבא ובין כל־העדה: והרמת מכס ליהוה
to a you and the all and the to went who
Jehovah tribute levy shall ;congregation ,war out

2568 259 6635 5927 4421 582
מאת אנשי המלחמה היצאים לצבא אחד נפש מחמש
of out body one the to went who ,battle the men from
five ;war out of

6629 2543 1241 120 3967
המאות מן־האדם ומן־הבקר ומן־החמרים ומן־הצאן:
the and ,asses the of the of ,man of ,hundred
;flock of ,herd

3068 8641 3548 499 5414 3947 4276
29 ממחציתם תקחו ונתתה לאלעזר הכהן תרומת יהוה:
.Jehovah heave the the to you and shall you from and
of offering priest Eleazar give shall ;take half their

2572 270 259 3947 3478 1121 4276
30 וממחצת בני־ישראל תקח אחד | אחז מן־החמשים
,fifty of out portion one shall you ,Israel's the from And
take of sons half

929 6620 2543 1241 120
מן־האדם מן־הבקר מן־החמרים ומן־הצאן מכל־הבהמה
the all of the and ,asses the of the of ,man of
livestock flock of herd

6213 3068 4908 4931 8104 3881 5414
31 ונתתה אתם ללוים שמרי משמרת משכן יהוה: ויעש
And .Jehovah the charge the keeping the to them you and
did of tabernacle of Levites give shall

1961 4872 3068 6680 834 3548 499 4872
32 משה ואלעזר הכהן כאשר צוה יהוה את־משה: ויהי
And .Moses Jehovah com- as the and Moses
was manded priest Eleazar

3967 8337 6629 6635 5971 962 834 957 3499 4455
המלקוח יתר הבז אשר בזזו עם הצבא צאן שש־מאות
hundred six sheep the the had which the the ,prey the
army of people seized spoil of rest

7657 8147 1241 505 2568 505 7657 505
33 אלף ושבעים אלף וחמשת אלפים: ובקר שנים ושבעים
seventy- two and ;thousand five and
oxen seventy

802 120 5315 505 8346 259 2543 505
34
35 אלף: וחמרים אחד וששים אלף: ונפש אדם מן־הנשים
the of :human of and -thousand sixty- one the of ;thousand
women beings asses

505 7970 8147 3605 2145 4905 3045 3808 834
אשר לא־ידעו משכב זכר כל־נפש שנים ושלשים אלף:
.thousand thirty- (were) the all a lying had not who
two persons ,male (with) known

7969 6629 4557 6635 5927 2506 4275 1961
36 ותהי המחצה חלק היצאים בצבא מספר הצאן שלש־
three the the the to who those half the And
flock of number war out went of portion was

3967 2568 505 7651 505 7970 505 3967
מאות אלף ושלשים אלף ושבעת אלפים וחמש מאות:
.hundred and thousand seven thirty- hundred
five

7657 2568 3967 8337 6629 3068 4371 1961
37 ויהי המכס ליהוה מן־הצאן שש מאות חמש ושבעים:
and five hundred six the of to the And
,seventy- sheep Jehovah tribute was

thirty-six thousand; and
their tribute to Jehovah,
seventy-two; [39]and the
asses thirty thousand, five
hundred; and their tribute to
Jehovah, sixty-one; [40]and
the human beings sixteen
thousand; and their tribute
to Jehovah *was* thirty-two
persons. [41]And Moses
gave the tribute, the heave
offering of Jehovah, to
Eleazar the priest, as
Jehovah had commanded
Moses.

[42]And of the sons of
Israel's half, which Moses
divided from the men who
warred: [43]even the congregation's half was three hundred and thirty-seven thousand, five hundred of the
flock; [44]and of the oxen,
thirty-six thousand; [45]and
thirty thousand, five hundred asses; [46]and sixteen
thousand human beings.

[47]Moses took from the sons
of Israel's half the one
portion from the fifty of man
and of animal. And *he* gave
them to the Levites keeping
the charge of the tabernacle
of Jehovah, as Jehovah had
commanded Moses.

[48]And the officers who
were over the thousands of
the army, heads of the
thousands and heads of the
hundreds, drew near to
Moses. [49]And they said to
Moses, You servants have
lifted the heads of the men
of war who *were* with us,
and not a man of us is
missing. [50]And we bring
near Jehovah's offering,
each what he has found,
vessels of gold, chains, and
bracelets, rings, earrings,
and jewels, to make
atonement for ourselves

7657 8147 3068 4371 505 7970 8337 1241
38 וְהַבָּקָר שִׁשָּׁה וּשְׁלֹשִׁים אָלֶף וּמִכְסָם לַיהוָה שְׁנַיִם וְשִׁבְעִים׃
;seventy- (was) to their and ,thousand thirty- six the and
two Jehovah tribute oxen

259 3068 4371 3967 2568 505 7970 2543
39 וַחֲמֹרִים שְׁלֹשִׁים אֶלֶף וַחֲמֵשׁ מֵאוֹת וּמִכְסָם לַיהוָה אֶחָד
(was) to their and ,hundred and ,thousand thirty the and
one Jehovah tribute five asses

3068 505 6240 8337 120 5315 8346
40 שִׁשִּׁים׃ וְנֶפֶשׁ אָדָם שִׁשָּׁה עָשָׂר אָלֶף וּמִכְסָם לַיהוָה
to their and ,thousand sixteen human the and and
Jehovah tribute beings ;sixty-

3068 8641 4371 4872 5414 5315 7970 8147
41 שְׁנַיִם וּשְׁלֹשִׁים נָפֶשׁ׃ וַיִּתֵּן מֹשֶׁה אֶת־מֶכֶס תְּרוּמַת יְהוָה
,Jehovah's heave the Moses And .persons thirty- (was)
offering ,tribute gave two

4276 4872 3068 6680 834 3546 499
42 לְאֶלְעָזָר הַכֹּהֵן כַּאֲשֶׁר צִוָּה יְהוָה אֶת־מֹשֶׁה׃ וּמִמַּחֲצִית
the of And .Moses Jehovah had as the to
of half commanded ,priest Eleazar

6633 582 4872 2673 834 3478 1121
בְּנֵי יִשְׂרָאֵל אֲשֶׁר חָצָה מֹשֶׁה מִן־הָאֲנָשִׁים הַצֹּבְאִים׃
who the from Moses divided which ,Israel the
;warred men of sons

7970 505 3967 7969 6629 4480 5712 4275 1961
43 וַתְּהִי מֶחֱצַת הָעֵדָה מִן־הַצֹּאן שְׁלֹשׁ־מֵאוֹת אֶלֶף וּשְׁלֹשִׁים
thirty- hundred three the of the half and
flock ;congregation's was

7970 8337 1249 3967 2568 505 7651 505
44 אֶלֶף שִׁבְעַת אֲלָפִים וַחֲמֵשׁ מֵאוֹת׃ וּבָקָר שִׁשָּׁה וּשְׁלֹשִׁים
thirty- six of and ;hundred and thousand seven
oxen the five

120 5315 3967 2568 505 7970 2543 505
45
46 אָלֶף׃ וַחֲמֹרִים שְׁלֹשִׁים אֶלֶף וַחֲמֵשׁ מֵאוֹת׃ וְנֶפֶשׁ אָדָם
human of and ;hundred and thousand thirty and ;thousand
beings five asses

3478/1121 4276 4872 3947 505 6240 8337
47 שִׁשָּׁה עָשָׂר אָלֶף׃ וַיִּקַּח מֹשֶׁה מִמַּחֲצִת בְּנֵי־יִשְׂרָאֵל אֶת־
Israel's sons the from Moses And .thousand sixteen
of half took

5414 929 120 2572 259 270
הָאָחֻז אֶחָד מִן־הַחֲמִשִּׁים מִן־הָאָדָם וּמִן־הַבְּהֵמָה וַיִּתֵּן
and ,animal of and man of ,fifty the from one the
gave portion

6680 3068 4908 4931 8104 3881
אֹתָם לַלְוִיִּם שֹׁמְרֵי מִשְׁמֶרֶת מִשְׁכַּן יְהוָה כַּאֲשֶׁר צִוָּה
had as ,Jehovah the the keeping the to them
commanded of tabernacle of charge Levites

505 834 6485 4872 7126 4872 3068
48 יְהוָה אֶת־מֹשֶׁה׃ וַיִּקְרְבוּ אֶל־מֹשֶׁה הַפְּקֻדִים אֲשֶׁר לְאַלְפֵי
the the Moses to drew And .Moses Jehovah
of thousands (of) officers near

4872 559 3967 8269 505 8269 6635
49 הַצָּבָא שָׂרֵי הָאֲלָפִים וְשָׂרֵי הַמֵּאוֹת׃ וַיֹּאמְרוּ אֶל־מֹשֶׁה
,Moses to they And the and the heads the
said .hundreds of heads of thousands of army

3808 3027 4421 582 7218 5375 5650
עֲבָדֶיךָ נָשְׂאוּ אֶת־רֹאשׁ אַנְשֵׁי הַמִּלְחָמָה אֲשֶׁר בְּיָדֵנוּ וְלֹא־
and our at who battle the the heads the have Your
not ;hand (were) of men of lifted servants

4672 376 3068 7133 7126 376 6485
50 נִפְקַד מִמֶּנּוּ אִישׁ׃ וַנַּקְרֵב אֶת־קָרְבַּן יְהוָה אִישׁ אֲשֶׁר מָצָא
has he what each ,Jehovah's offering we and ;man a us of is
,found bring missed

3722 3558 5694 2885 6781 685 2091/3627
כְלִי־זָהָב אֶצְעָדָה וְצָמִיד טַבַּעַת עָגִיל וְכוּמָז לְכַפֵּר עַל־
for to and ear ,rings and ,chains ,gold vessels
atone ,jewels ,rings ,bracelets of

before Jehovah. 51 And Moses and Eleazar the priest took the gold from them, all crafted things. 52 And all the gold of the heave offering which they lifted up to Jehovah *was* sixteen thousand, seven hundred and fifty shekels, from the head sof thousands and from the heads of hundreds, 53 men of the army *who* had each taken spoil for himself. 54 And Moses and Eleazar the priest took the gold from the heads of the thousands and of the hundreds. And they brought it into the tabernacle of the congregation, a memorial for the sons of Israel before Jehovah.

2091 3548 499 4872 3947 3068 6440 5315
51 נַפְשֹׁתֵינוּ לִפְנֵי יְהוָה׃ וַיִּקַּח מֹשֶׁה וְאֶלְעָזָר הַכֹּהֵן אֶת־הַזָּהָב
gold the | the priest | and Eleazar | Moses | And took | .Jehovah before ourselves

834 8641 2091 1961 4639 3627 3605
52 מֵאִתָּם כֹּל כְּלִי מַעֲשֶׂה׃ וַיְהִי ׀ כָּל־זְהַב הַתְּרוּמָה אֲשֶׁר
which | heave the offering | the of gold | all | and was | crafted things all | from them

8255 2572 3967 7651 505 6240 8337 3068 7311
הֵרִימוּ לַיהוָה שִׁשָּׁה עָשָׂר אֶלֶף שְׁבַע־מֵאוֹת וַחֲמִשִּׁים שָׁקֶל
,shekels | and fifty | hundred seven ,thousand sixteen | to Jehovah | they up lifted

6635 582 3967 8269 505 8269
53 מֵאֵת שָׂרֵי הָאֲלָפִים וּמֵאֵת שָׂרֵי הַמֵּאוֹת׃ אַנְשֵׁי הַצָּבָא
army the of men | the ;hundreds of rulers | the from | and | the ,thousands | the of rulers | from

2091 3548 499 4872 3947 376 962
54 בָּזְזוּ אִישׁ לוֹ׃ וַיִּקַּח מֹשֶׁה וְאֶלְעָזָר הַכֹּהֵן אֶת־הַזָּהָב מֵאֵת
from | the gold | the priest | and Eleazar | Moses | And took | for man each .himself | had ,spoil taken

2146 4150 168 935 3967 505 8267
שָׂרֵי הָאֲלָפִים וְהַמֵּאוֹת וַיָּבִאוּ אֹתוֹ אֶל־אֹהֶל מוֹעֵד זִכָּרוֹן
a memorial | for meeting | the into of tent | it | they and brought | of and ,hundreds | the the thousands | the of heads

3068 6440 3478 1121
לִבְנֵי־יִשְׂרָאֵל לִפְנֵי יְהוָה׃
.Jehovah before | Israel | the for of sons

CAP. XXXII לב

CHAPTER 32

CHAPTER 32

1 And the sons of Reuben and the sons of Gad had many livestock, a very great multitude. And they saw the land of Jazer, and the land of Gilead. And, behold, the place *was* a place *for* livestock. 2 And the sons of Gad and the sons of Reuben came in and spoke to Moses, and to Eleazar the priest, and to the rulers of the congregation, saying, 3 Ataroth, and Dibon, and Jazer, and Nimrah, and Heshbon, and Elealeh, and Shebam, and Nebo, and Beon, 4 the land which Jehovah has struck before the congregation of Israel *is* a land for livestock, and your servants *own* livestock. 5 And they said, If we have found favor in your eyes, let this land be given to your servants for a possession. Do not make us pass over the Jordan. 6 And Moses said to the sons of Gad and to the sons of Reuben, Do your brothers go into the battle, and you, do you sit

7200 3966 7227 1410 1121 7205 1121 1961 7227 4735
1 וּמִקְנֶה ׀ רַב הָיָה לִבְנֵי רְאוּבֵן וְלִבְנֵי־גָד עָצוּם מְאֹד וַיִּרְאוּ
And saw they | .very | great a multitude | Gad to and of sons the | Reuben | the to of sons | were | many | And cattle

4735 4725 4725 2009 1568 776 3270 776
אֶת־אֶרֶץ יַעְזֵר וְאֶת־אֶרֶץ גִּלְעָד וְהִנֵּה הַמָּקוֹם מְקוֹם מִקְנֶה׃
,livestock | a (was) place | the (for) place | and ,behold | ;Gilead land the | and | Jazer of | the of land

499 4872 559 7205 1121 1410 1121 935
2 וַיָּבֹאוּ בְנֵי־גָד וּבְנֵי רְאוּבֵן וַיֹּאמְרוּ אֶל־מֹשֶׁה וְאֶל־אֶלְעָזָר
Eleazar | and to | Moses to | and spoke | Reuben the of sons | and Gad the of sons | in came And

3270 1769 5852 559 5712 5387 3548
3 הַכֹּהֵן וְאֶל־נְשִׂיאֵי הָעֵדָה לֵאמֹר׃ עֲטָרוֹת וְדִיבֹן וְיַעְזֵר
and Jazer | and ,Dibon | ,Ataroth | ,saying | the ,congregation | the of rulers to | and | the priest

834 776 1194 5015 7643 500 2809 5247
4 וְנִמְרָה וְחֶשְׁבּוֹן וְאֶלְעָלֵה וּשְׂבָם וּנְבוֹ וּבְעֹן׃ הָאָרֶץ אֲשֶׁר
which | the land | and ,Beon | and ,Nebo | and ,Sebam | and ,Elealeh | and ,Heshbon | and ,Nimrah

5650 4735 776 3478 5712 6440 3068 5221
הִכָּה יְהוָה לִפְנֵי עֲדַת יִשְׂרָאֵל אֶרֶץ מִקְנֶה הִוא וְלַעֲבָדֶיךָ
your to and servants | (is) it | livestock | land a for | ,Israel of | the company | before | Jehovah | has struck

5414 5869 2580 4672 559 4735
5 וַיֹּאמְרוּ אִם־מָצָאנוּ חֵן בְּעֵינֶיךָ יֻתַּן אֶת־ מִקְנֶה׃
be let given | your ,eyes | in favor | have we If found | they And said | livestock (is)

3383 5674 272 5650 2088 776
הָאָרֶץ הַזֹּאת לַעֲבָדֶיךָ לַאֲחֻזָּה אַל־תַּעֲבִרֵנוּ אֶת־הַיַּרְדֵּן׃
.Jordan the | make Do not over cross us | a for possession | your to servants | this | land

4421 935 251 7205 1121 1410 1121 4872 559
6 וַיֹּאמֶר מֹשֶׁה לִבְנֵי־גָד וְלִבְנֵי רְאוּבֵן הַאַחֵיכֶם יָבֹאוּ לַמִּלְחָמָה
the into ,battle | shall go | Your brothers | ,Reuben of sons the to | and Gad the to of sons | Moses | And said

here? 7And why do you discourage the heart of the sons of Israel from passing over to the land which Jehovah has given to them? 8So your fathers did when I sent them from Kadesh-barnea to see the land. 9And they went up to the valley of Eshcol and saw the land, and discouraged the hearts of the sons of Israel, so as *for them* not to go into the land which Jehovah had given to them. 10And the anger of Jehovah burned in that day, and He sword, saying, 11Surely none of the men that came up out of Egypt, from twenty years old and upward, shall see the land which I swore to Abraham, to Isaac, and to Jacob; because they have not wholly followed Me; 12except Caleb the son of Jephunneh, the Kenezite, and Joshua the son of Nun, for they have fully followed Jehovah. 13And Jehovah's anger was kindled against Israel. And He made them wander in the wilderness forty years, until all the generation that had done evil in the sight of Jehovah was destroyed. 14And, behold, you have risen up in your fathers' stead, an increase of sinful men, to add still more to the fierce anger of Jehovah toward Israel! 15For if you turn away from following Him, He will yet again leave them in the wilderness; and so you will destroy all this people.

16And they came near to him and said, We will build sheepfolds here for our livestock, and cities for our little ones. 17And we ourselves shall go armed, ready before the sons of Israel, until we have brought them to their place. And our little ones shall live

3478 1121 3820 5106 4100 6311 3427
7 ואתם תשבו פה: ולמה תנואון את־לב בני ישראל
Israel the heart the you do And ?here you will and
of sons of discourage why sit ,you

1 6213 3068 5414/834 776 5674
8 מעבר אל־הארץ אשר־נתן להם יהוה: כה עשו אבתיכם
your did So ?Jehovah to has which the to from
fathers them given land crossing

5927 776 7200 6947 7971
9 בשלחי אתם מקדש ברנע לראות את־הארץ: ויעלו
they and ;land the see to barnea from them I when
up went Kadesh- sent

1121 3820 5106 776 7200 811 5158
עד־נחל אשכול ויראו את־הארץ ויניאו את־לב בני
the hearts the and ,land the and Eshcol the to
of sons of discouraged saw of valley

3068 5414/834 776 935 3478
ישראל לבלתי־בא אל־הארץ אשר־נתן להם יהוה:
.Jehovah to had which the into to as so Israel
them given land go not

7200 518 559 7650 3117 3068 639 2734
10 11 ויחר־אף יהוה ביום ההוא וישבע לאמר: אם־יראו
shall Surely ,saying He and ,that day in Jehovah the and
see not ,swore of anger glowed

4605 8141 6242 1121 4714 5927 582
האנשים העלים ממצרים מבן עשרים שנה ומעלה את
and years twenty from of out came who men the
,upward of son a ,Egypt up

3808 3290 3327 85 7650 834 127
האדמה אשר נשבעתי לאברהם ליצחק וליעקב כי לא־
not for to and ,Isaac to to swore I which land the
;Jacob Abraham

5126/1121/3091 7074 3312/1121 3612 310 4390
12 מלאו אחרי: בלתי כלב בן־יפנה הקנזי ויהושע בן־נון
,Nun the and the Jephunneh the Caleb except followed they
of son Joshua ,Kenezite of son ;Me wholly have

5128 3478 3068 639 2734 3068 310 4390 3588
13 כי מלאו אחרי יהוה: ויחר־אף יהוה בישראל וינעם
set He so against Jehovah's anger And .Jehovah followed they for
astray them ,Israel glowed wholly

7451 6213 1755 3605 8552 8141 703 4057
במדבר ארבעים שנה עד־תם כל־הדור העשה הרע
evil which the all was until ,years forty the in
done had generation destroyed wilderness

582 8635 1 8478 6965 2009 3068 5869
14 בעיני יהוה: והנה קמתם תחת אבתיכם תרבות אנשים
men increase an your in have you And Jehovah the in
of ,fathers' stead up risen ,behold of eyes

3588 3478 3068 639 2740 5921 5750 5595 2400
15 חטאים לספות עוד על חרון אף־יהוה אל־ישראל: כי
For .Israel toward anger the the to still add to ,sinful
Jehovah of of heat more

3605 7843 4057 3240 3254 310 7725
תשובן מאחריו ויסף עוד להניחו במדבר ושחתם לכל־
all you and the in leave yet will He following from if
hurt will wilderness them again ,Him turn you

1129 6629 1448 559 5066 2088 5971
16 העם הזה: ויגשו אליו ויאמרו גדרת צאן נבנה
will We sheep folds ,said and him to they And this .people
build came

6440 2363 2502 587 2945 5892 6311 / 4735
17 למקננו פה וערים לטפנו: ואנחנו נחלץ חשים לפני
before hastened shall we we but our for and ,here our for
armed go ourselves ;ones little cities livestock

3427 4725 935 5704 3478 1121
בני ישראל עד אשר אם־הביאנם אל־מקומם וישב
shall and their to have we until ,Israel the
live ;place them brought of sons

in the fortified cities because of the inhabitants of the land. [18]We will not return to our houses until each man of the sons of Israel has inherited his inheritance. [19]For we will not inherit with them on the other side of the Jordan, and beyond; for our inheritance has fallen to us eastward on this side of Jordan. [20]And Moses said to them, If you will do this thing; if you will arm for battle before Jehovah, [21]and all of you will go over Jordan armed before Jehovah, until He has driven His enemies out before Him, [22]and the land is subdued before Jehovah, then afterwards you shall return and be guiltless before Jehovah, and before Israel. And this land shall be your possession before Jehovah. [23]But if you will not do so, behold, you have sinned against Jehovah, and know that your sin will find you out. [24]Build cities for your little ones, and folds for your sheep, and do that which has come out of your mouth.

[25]And the sons of Gad and the sons of Reuben spoke to Moses, saying, Your servants will do as my lord commands. [26]Our little ones, our wives, our flocks, and all our livestock shall be there in the cities of Gilead. [27]But your servants will go over, every man armed for war, before Jehovah to battle, as my lord says. [28]And Moses commanded Eleazar the priest concerning them, and Joshua the son of Nun, and the heads of the fathers of the tribes of the sons of Israel; [29]even

3808 7725 776 3427 6440 4013 5892 2945
18 טַפֵּנוּ בְּעָרֵי הַמִּבְצָר מִפְּנֵי יֹשְׁבֵי הָאָרֶץ׃ לֹא נָשׁוּב אֶל־
to will We not the the because the cities in our
return .land of inhabitants of fortified children

6157 3808 5159 376 3478 1121 5157 5704 1004
19 בָּתֵּינוּ עַד הִתְנַחֵל בְּנֵי יִשְׂרָאֵל אִישׁ נַחֲלָתוֹ׃ כִּי לֹא נִנְחַל
will we not For his each Israel the has until our
inherit .inheritance man of sons inherited houses

5676 5159 935 1973 3383 5676
אִתָּם מֵעֵבֶר לַיַּרְדֵּן וָהָלְאָה כִּי בָאָה נַחֲלָתֵנוּ אֵלֵינוּ מֵעֵבֶר
this on us to our has for and the of the on with
of side inheritance come ,beyond ,Jordan side other them

4217 3383
הַיַּרְדֵּן מִזְרָחָה׃
.eastward ,Jordan

518 2088 1697 6213 4872 559
20 וַיֹּאמֶר אֲלֵיהֶם מֹשֶׁה אִם־תַּעֲשׂוּן אֶת־הַדָּבָר הַזֶּה אִם־
if ;this thing will you If ,Moses them to And
do said

2502 3605 5674 4421 3068 6440 2502
21 תֵּחָלְצוּ לִפְנֵי יְהוָה לַמִּלְחָמָה׃ וְעָבַר לָכֶם כָּל־חָלוּץ אֶת־
armed all you of will and ,battle for Jehovah before will you
over go arm

3533 6440 341 3423 5704 3068 6440 3383
22 הַיַּרְדֵּן לִפְנֵי יְהוָה עַד הוֹרִישׁוֹ אֶת־אֹיְבָיו מִפָּנָיו׃ וְנִכְבְּשָׁה
is and before His has He until ,Jehovah before Jordan
subdued Him enemies out driven

3068 5355 1961 7725 310 3068 6440 776
הָאָרֶץ לִפְנֵי יְהוָה וְאַחַר תָּשֻׁבוּ וִהְיִיתֶם נְקִיִּם מֵיְהוָה
before guiltless you and shall you then ;Jehovah before the
Jehovah be shall return later land

3068 6440 272 2088 776 1961 3478
וּמִיִּשְׂרָאֵל וְהָיְתָה הָאָרֶץ הַזֹּאת לָכֶם לַאֲחֻזָּה לִפְנֵי יְהוָה׃
.Jehovah before possession to this land and before and
you be shall Israel

2403 3045 3068 2398 2009 6213 518
23 וְאִם־לֹא תַעֲשׂוּן כֵּן הִנֵּה חֲטָאתֶם לַיהוָה וּדְעוּ חַטַּאתְכֶם
*3808
sin your know and against have you ,behold ,so do you not But
Jehovah sinned if

1448 2945 5892 1129 4672 834
24 אֲשֶׁר תִּמְצָא אֶתְכֶם׃ בְּנוּ־לָכֶם עָרִים לְטַפְּכֶם וּגְדֵרֹת
folds and your for cities for build ;you find will which
ones little you out

1121 1410 1121 559 6213 6310 5927 6792
25 לְצֹנַאֲכֶם וְהַיֹּצֵא מִפִּיכֶם תַּעֲשׂוּ׃ וַיֹּאמֶר בְּנֵי־גָד וּבְנֵי
the and Gad the And .do your of the and your for
of sons of sons spoke mouth issuing flock

6680 113 6213 5650 559 4872 7205
רְאוּבֵן אֶל־מֹשֶׁה לֵאמֹר עֲבָדֶיךָ יַעֲשׂוּ כַּאֲשֶׁר אֲדֹנִי מְצַוֶּה׃
com- my as do will Your ,saying ,Moses to Reuben
.mands lord servants

1568 5892 8033 1961 929 3605 4735 802 2945
26 טַפֵּנוּ נָשֵׁינוּ מִקְנֵנוּ וְכָל־בְּהֶמְתֵּנוּ יִהְיוּ־שָׁם בְּעָרֵי הַגִּלְעָד׃
.Gilead the in there shall our all and our our Our
of cities be cattle ,livestock ,wives ,babes

4421 3068 6440 6635 2502 3605 5674 5650
27 וַעֲבָדֶיךָ יַעַבְרוּ כָּל־חֲלוּץ צָבָא לִפְנֵי יְהוָה לַמִּלְחָמָה
battle to Jehovah before ,war armed every go will your But
for man ,over servants

3548 499 4872 6680 1696 113
28 כַּאֲשֶׁר אֲדֹנִי דֹּבֵר׃ וַיְצַו לָהֶם מֹשֶׁה אֵת אֶלְעָזָר הַכֹּהֵן
the Eleazar Moses to as And .says lord my as
priest them directed

3478 1121 4294 1 7218 5126 1121 3091
וְאֵת יְהוֹשֻׁעַ בִּן־נוּן וְאֶת־רָאשֵׁי אֲבוֹת הַמַּטּוֹת לִבְנֵי יִשְׂרָאֵל׃
;Israel the of tribes the the the and ,Nun the Joshua and
of sons of fathers of heads of son

Moses said to them, If the sons of Gad and the sons of Reuben pass over the Jordan with you, each armed for battle before Jehovah, and the land shall be subdued before you, then you shall give to them the land of Gilead for a possession. 30But if they will not go over armed with you, they shall have possessions among you in the land of Canaan. 31And the sons of Gad and the sons of Reuben replied, saying, As Jehovah has said to your servants, so we will do. 32We ourselves will go over armed before Jehovah *into* the land of Canaan, so that the land of our inheritance on that side of Jordan may be ours.

33And Moses gave to them, even to the sons of Gad and to the sons of Reuben, and to the half tribe of Manasseh the son of Joseph, the kingdom of Sihon king of the Amorites, and the kingdom of Og king of of Bashan, the land, by its cities, with *their* borders, even the cities of the land all around.

34And the sons of Gad built Dibon, and Ataroth, and Aroer, 35and Atroth-shophan, and Jaazer, and Jogbehah, 36and Beth-nimrah, and Beth-haran, fortified cities, and folds for sheep.

37And the sons of Reuben built Heshbon, and Elealeh, and Kirjath-aim, 38and Nebo, and Baal-meon, their names being changed, and Shibmah. And they called by name the names of the cities which they had built. 39And the sons of Machir the son of Manasseh went to Gilead and captured it, and expelled the Amorite who *was* in it. 40And Moses gave Gilead to Machir the son of

7205/1121 1410/1121/ 5674 518 4872 559

29 וַיֹּאמֶר מֹשֶׁה אֲלֵהֶם אִם־יַעַבְרוּ בְנֵי־גָד וּבְנֵי־רְאוּבֵן ׀ אִתְּכֶם

you with Reuben and Gad the pass If to Moses And
of sons the of sons over ,them said

776 3544 3068 6440 2421 2502 3605 3383

אֶת־הַיַּרְדֵּן כָּל־חָלוּץ לַמִּלְחָמָה לִפְנֵי יְהוָה וְנִכְבְּשָׁה הָאָרֶץ

the be shall and ,Jehovah before for armed each ,Jordan the
land subdued battle (man)

3808 272 1568 776 5414 6440

30 לִפְנֵיכֶם וּנְתַתֶּם לָהֶם אֶת־אֶרֶץ הַגִּלְעָד לַאֲחֻזָּה׃ וְאִם־לֹא

not but a for the of land to you then before
if ;possession Gilead them give shall ,you

6030 3667 776 8432 270 2502 5674

31 יַעַבְרוּ חֲלוּצִים אִתְּכֶם וְנֹאחֲזוּ בְתֹכְכֶם בְּאֶרֶץ כְּנָעַן׃ וַיַּעֲנוּ

And ,Canaan the in among shall they with armed will they
replied of land you inherit ,you over go

3068 1696 559 1205 1121 1410

בְנֵי־גָד וּבְנֵי רְאוּבֵן לֵאמֹר אֵת אֲשֶׁר דִּבֶּר יְהוָה אֶל־

to Jehovah has As ,saying ,Reuben the and Gad the
said of sons of sons

776 3068 6440 2502 5674/ 5168 6213 3651 5650

32 עֲבָדֶיךָ כֵּן נַעֲשֶׂה׃ נַחְנוּ נַעֲבֹר חֲלוּצִים לִפְנֵי יְהוָה אֶרֶץ

the (into) Jehovah be- armed pass will We will we so your
of land fore over ourselves .do ,servants

4872 5414 3383 5676 5159 272 3667

33 כְּנָעַן וְאִתָּנוּ אֲחֻזַּת נַחֲלָתֵנוּ מֵעֵבֶר לַיַּרְדֵּן׃ וַיִּתֵּן לָהֶם ׀ מֹשֶׁה

,Moses to And Jordan of that on our land the that ,Canaan
them gave side inheritance of ours be may

3127/1121 4519 7626 2677 7205 1121 1410/1121

לִבְנֵי־גָד וְלִבְנֵי רְאוּבֵן וְלַחֲצִי ׀ שֵׁבֶט ׀ מְנַשֶּׁה בֶן־יוֹסֵף אֶת־

,Joseph the Manasseh tribe to and ,Reuben to and ,Gad the to
of son of half the of sons the of sons

1316 4428/5147/4467 567 4428 5511 4467

מַמְלֶכֶת סִיחֹן מֶלֶךְ הָאֱמֹרִי וְאֶת־מַמְלֶכֶת עוֹג מֶלֶךְ הַבָּשָׁן

,Bashan king Og the of and the king Sihon the of
of of kingdom ,Amorites of of kingdom

1410/1121/ 1129 5439 776 5892 1367 5892 776

34 הָאָרֶץ לְעָרֶיהָ בִּגְבֻלֹת עָרֵי הָאָרֶץ סָבִיב׃ וַיִּבְנוּ בְנֵי־גָד

Gad the And all the the even (their) with its by the
of sons built around land of cities ,borders cities ,land

5855 5852 6177 5852 1769

35 אֶת־דִּיבֹן וְאֶת־עֲטָרֹת וְאֵת עֲרֹעֵר׃ וְאֶת־עַטְרֹת שׁוֹפָן וְאֶת־

and ,Shophan Ataroth and ,Aroer and ,Ataroth and ,Dibon

4013 6872 = 1028 = = 1039 = 3011 3270

36 יַעְזֵר וְיָגְבְּהָה׃ וְאֶת־בֵּית נִמְרָה וְאֶת־בֵּית הָרָן עָרֵי מִבְצָר

forti- cities ,haran-Beth and ,nimrah-Beth and and ,Jaazer
.fied ,Jogbehah

1500 2809 1129 7205 1121 6629 1448

37 וְגִדְרֹת צֹאן׃ וּבְנֵי רְאוּבֵן בָּנוּ אֶת־חֶשְׁבּוֹן וְאֶת־אֶלְעָלֵא

,Elealeh and ,Heshbon built Reuben And ,sheep folds and
of sons the for

8034 5437 = 1186 = 5015 7156

38 וְאֶת קִרְיָתָיִם׃ וְאֶת־נְבוֹ וְאֶת־בַּעַל מְעוֹן מוּסַבֹּת שֵׁם וְאֶת־

and ,names being ,Meon-Baal and ,Nebo and ,Kirjathaim and
changed

1129 834 5892 8034 8034 7121 7643

שִׂבְמָה וַיִּקְרְאוּ בְשֵׁמֹת אֶת־שְׁמוֹת הֶעָרִים אֲשֶׁר בָּנוּ׃

they which the of names the name by they and ;Sibmah
built had cities called

3423 3920 1568 4519 1121 4353 1121 3212

39 וַיֵּלְכוּ בְּנֵי מָכִיר בֶּן־מְנַשֶּׁה גִּלְעָדָה וַיִּלְכְּדֻהָ וַיּוֹרֶשׁ אֶת־

and seized and Gilead to Manasseh the Machir the And
expelled it of son of sons went

1121 4353 1568 4872 5414 834 567

40 הָאֱמֹרִי אֲשֶׁר־בָּהּ׃ וַיִּתֵּן מֹשֶׁה אֶת־הַגִּלְעָד לְמָכִיר בֶּן

the to Gilead Moses And .it in who the
of son Machir gave (was) Amorite

Manasseh, and he lived in it. 41 And Jair the son of Manasseh went out and captured their towns, and called them Towns of Jair. 42 And Nobah went and took Kenath and its villages; and he called it Nobah after his own name.

2333 3920 3212 4519 1121 2971 3427 4519
41 מְנַשֶּׁה וַיֵּשֶׁב בָּהּ׃ וְיָאִיר בֶּן־מְנַשֶּׁה הָלַךְ וַיִּלְכֹּד אֶת־חַוֹּתֵיהֶם
,towns their | and seized | went out | Manasseh the of son | And Jair | .it in | he and lived | Manas- ,seh

7079 3920 1980 5025 2971 2333 7121
42 וַיִּקְרָא אֶתְהֶן חַוֹּת יָאִיר׃ וְנֹבַח הָלַךְ וַיִּלְכֹּד אֶת־קְנָת וְאֶת־
and | Kenath | took and | went | And Nobah | .Jair | towns of | them | and called

8034 5025 7121 1323
בְּנֹתֶיהָ וַיִּקְרָא לָה נֹבַח בִּשְׁמוֹ׃
his after .name own | ,Nobah | it | he and called | its ;villages

CAP. XXXIII לג

CHAPTER 33

1 Thes *are* the journeys of the sons of Israel who went out from the land of Egypt according to their armies under the hand of Moses and Aaron. 2 And Moses wrote their departures according to their journeys by the mouth of Jehovah. And these are their journeys, according to their departures:

3 And they pulled up *stakes* from Rameses in the first month on the fifteenth day of the first month. On the next day after the Passover the sons of Israel went out with a high hand, before the eyes of all the Egyptians. 4 And the Egyptians were burying those whom Jehovah had smitten among them, every first-born, and Jehovah had executed judgments on their gods. 5 And the sons of Israel pulled up from Rameses and camped in Succoth. 6 And they pulled up from Succoth and camped at Etham, which is in the edge of the wilderness. 7 And they pulled up from Etham and turned back to Pihahiroth, which is before Baal-zephon; and they camped before Migdol. 8 And they pulled up from Pihahiroth and passed over through the midst of the Sea, into the wilderness, and went a journey of three days inthe wilderness of Etham, and camped at Marah. 9 And they pulled up from Marah and came to Elim. And in Elim *were* twelve springs of water and seventy palm trees. And

6635 4714 776 5927 834 3478 1121 4550 428
1 אֵלֶּה מַסְעֵי בְנֵי־יִשְׂרָאֵל אֲשֶׁר יָצְאוּ מֵאֶרֶץ מִצְרַיִם לְצִבְאֹתָם
their by armies | ,Egypt | the from of land | went out | who | ,Israel | sons the of | jour- the of neys | These (are)

4550 4161 4872 3789 175 4872 3027
2 בְּיַד־מֹשֶׁה וְאַהֲרֹן׃ וַיִּכְתֹּב מֹשֶׁה אֶת־מוֹצָאֵיהֶם לְמַסְעֵיהֶם
to according .journeys their | their departures | Moses | And wrote | .Aaron and | Moses | the by of mouth

7486 5265 4161 4550 428 3068 6310
3 עַל־פִּי יְהוָה וְאֵלֶּה מַסְעֵיהֶם לְמוֹצָאֵיהֶם׃ וַיִּסְעוּ מֵרַעְמְסֵס
from Rameses | the And up pulled | their by :departures | their ,journeys | and these of | ;Jehovah | the by command

7223 2320 3117 6240 2568 7223 2320
בַּחֹדֶשׁ הָרִאשׁוֹן בַּחֲמִשָּׁה עָשָׂר יוֹם לַחֹדֶשׁ הָרִאשׁוֹן
;first | the of month | day | fifteenth | the on | first | the in month

3605 5869 7311 3027 3478 1121 5927 6453 4283
מִמָּחֳרַת הַפֶּסַח יָצְאוּ בְנֵי־יִשְׂרָאֵל בְּיָד רָמָה לְעֵינֵי כָּל־
all | before of eyes the | ,high | a with hand | Israel | the of sons | went out | the Passover | the on after day

854 3068 5221 834 6912 4713 4713
4 מִצְרָיִם׃ וּמִצְרַיִם מְקַבְּרִים אֵת אֲשֶׁר הִכָּה יְהוָה בָּהֶם
among them | ,Jehovah | had struck | whom | were burying | the and Egyptians | the ;Egyptians

1121 5265 8201 3068 6213 430 1060 3605
5 כָּל־בְּכוֹר וּבֵאלֹהֵיהֶם עָשָׂה יְהוָה שְׁפָטִים׃ וַיִּסְעוּ בְנֵי־
the of sons | And traveled | judgments | Jehovah | had executed | on and gods their | first- ,born | every

864 2583 5523 5265 5523 2583 7486 3478
6 יִשְׂרָאֵל מֵרַעְמְסֵס וַיַּחֲנוּ בְּסֻכֹּת׃ וַיִּסְעוּ מִסֻּכֹּת וַיַּחֲנוּ בְאֵתָם
at ,Etham | and camped | from Succoth | they And traveled | at Succoth | and camped | from Rameses | Israel

6367 7725 864 5265 4057 7097 834
7 אֲשֶׁר בִּקְצֵה הַמִּדְבָּר׃ וַיִּסְעוּ מֵאֵתָם וַיָּשָׁב עַל־פִּי הַחִירֹת
,Pihahiroth | to | and returned | from ,Etham | they And traveled | the .wilderness | the on of edge | which (is)

5265 4024 6440 2583 1189 6440 834
8 אֲשֶׁר עַל־פְּנֵי בַּעַל צְפוֹן וַיַּחֲנוּ לִפְנֵי מִגְדֹּל׃ וַיִּסְעוּ מִפְּנֵי
from Pi | they and traveled | .Migdol | before | they and pitched | ;zephon-Baal | before | which (is)

7969 1870 3212 4057 3221 8432 5674 6367
הַחִירֹת וַיַּעַבְרוּ בְתוֹךְ־הַיָּם הַמִּדְבָּרָה וַיֵּלְכוּ דֶּרֶךְ שְׁלֹשֶׁת
three | a of journey | and went | the into ,wilderness | the Sea of | through midst | and the crossed | Hahiroth

935 4785 5265 4785 2583 864 4057 3117
9 יָמִים בְּמִדְבַּר אֵתָם וַיַּחֲנוּ בְּמָרָה׃ וַיִּסְעוּ מִמָּרָה וַיָּבֹאוּ
and came | from Marah | they And traveled | .Marah at | and pitched | ,Etham | the in of wilderness | days

8558 7657 4325 5869 6240 8147 362 362
אֵילִמָה וּבְאֵילִם שְׁתֵּים עֶשְׂרֵה עֵינֹת מַיִם וְשִׁבְעִים תְּמָרִים
palm ;trees | and seventy | ,water | springs of | (were) twelve | at and Elim | ;Elim to

they camped there. [10]And
they pulled up from Elim
and camped by the Red
Sea. [11]And they pulled up
from the Red Sea and
camped in the wilderness
of Sin. [12]And they pulled up
from the wilderness of Sin
and camped in Dophkah.
[13]And they pulled up from
Dophkah and camped in
Alush. [14]And they pulled up
from Alush and camped in
Rephidim; and no water
was there for the people to
drink. [15]And they pulled up
from Rephidim and camped
in the wilderness of Sinai.
[16]And they pulled up from
the wilderness of Sinai and
camped in The Graves of
Lust. [17]And they pulled up
from The Graves of Lust and
camped in Hazeroth. [18]And
they pulled up from
Hazeroth and camped in
Rithmath. [19]And they pulled
up from Rithmah and
camped in The Pomegran-
ate Breach. [20]And they
pulled up from The
Pomegranate Breach and
camped in Libnah. [21]And
they pulled up from Libnah
and camped in Rissah.
[22]And they pulled up from
Rissah and camped in the
Meeting Place. [23]And they
pulled up from the Meeting
Place and camped in Mount
Shaphar. [24]And they pulled
up from Mount Shaphar and
camped in Haradah. [25]And
they pulled up from
Haradah and pitched in
Makheloth. [26]And they
pulled up eled from Mak-
heloth and camped in
Tahath. [27]And they pulled
up from Tahath and camped
in Tarah. [28]And they pulled
up from Tarah and camped
in Mithcah. [29]And they
pulled up from Mithcah and
camped in Hashmonah.
[30]And they pulled up from
Hashmonah and camped in
Moseroth. [31]And they pulled
up from Moseroth and
camped in Benejaakan.
[32]And they pulled up from
Benejaakan and camped in
the Hole of the Cleft. [33]And
they pulled up from the
Hole in the Cleft camped in
Jotbathah. [34]And they
pulled up from Jotbathah
and camped in Abronah.

8033
3220 5265 5488 3220 2583 362 5265 2583
10 וַיַּחֲנוּ־שָׁם׃ וַיִּסְעוּ מֵאֵילִם וַיַּחֲנוּ עַל־יַם־סוּף׃ וַיִּסְעוּ מִיַּם־
11
the from they And the by and from they And .there and
of Sea traveled Reeds of Sea pitched ,Elim up pulled pitched they

1850 2583 5512 4057 5265 5512 4057 2583 5488
12 סוּף וַיַּחֲנוּ בְּמִדְבַּר־סִין׃ וַיִּסְעוּ מִמִּדְבַּר־סִין וַיַּחֲנוּ בְּדָפְקָה׃
in and ,Sin the from they And .Sin the in and ,Reeds
.Dophkah pitched of wilderness traveled of wilderness pitched

2583 442 5265 442 2583 1850 5265
13 וַיִּסְעוּ מִדָּפְקָה וַיַּחֲנוּ בְּאָלוּשׁ׃ וַיִּסְעוּ מֵאָלוּשׁ וַיַּחֲנוּ
14
and from they And in and from they And
pitched ,Alush up pulled .Alush pitched ,Dophkah traveled

7508 5265 8354 5971 4325 8033 1961 7508
15 בִּרְפִידִם וְלֹא־הָיָה שָׁם מַיִם לָעָם לִשְׁתּוֹת׃ וַיִּסְעוּ מֵרְפִידִם
*3808
from they And .drink to the for water there no and in
,Rephidim up pulled people was ;Rephidim

6913 2583 5514 4057 5265 5514 4057 2583
16 וַיַּחֲנוּ בְּמִדְבַּר סִינָי׃ וַיִּסְעוּ מִמִּדְבַּר סִינָי וַיַּחֲנוּ בְּקִבְרֹת
in and Sinai the from they And .Sinai the in and
Graves the pitched of wilderness up pulled of wilderness pitched

5265 2698 2583 8378 6913 5265 8378
17 הַתַּאֲוָה׃ וַיִּסְעוּ מִקִּבְרֹת הַתַּאֲוָה וַיַּחֲנוּ בַּחֲצֵרֹת׃ וַיִּסְעוּ
18
they And in and ,Lust the from they And .Lust of
up pulled ,Hazeroth pitched of Graves up pulled

7428 2583 7575 5265 7575 2583 2698
19 מֵחֲצֵרֹת וַיַּחֲנוּ בְּרִתְמָה׃ וַיִּסְעוּ מֵרִתְמָה וַיַּחֲנוּ בְּרִמֹּן פָּרֶץ׃
Breach the in and from they And .Rithmah in and from
Pomegranate pitched Rithmah up pulled .Rithmah pitched Hazeroth

2583 3841 5268 3841 2583 7428 5265
20 וַיִּסְעוּ מֵרִמֹּן פָּרֶץ וַיַּחֲנוּ בְּלִבְנָה׃ וַיִּסְעוּ מִלִּבְנָה וַיַּחֲנוּ
21
and from they And .Libnah in and Breach the from they And
pitched ,Libnah up pulled pitched Pomegranate up pulled

6954 5265 6954 2583 7446 5265 7446
22 בְּרִסָּה׃ וַיִּסְעוּ מֵרִסָּה וַיַּחֲנוּ בִּקְהֵלָתָה׃ וַיִּסְעוּ מִקְּהֵלָתָה
23
the from they And the in and from they And in
.Place Meeting up pulled .Place Meeting pitched Rissah up pulled .Rissah

2732 2583 8234 2022 5265 8234 2022 2583
24 וַיַּחֲנוּ בְּהַר־שָׁפֶר׃ וַיִּסְעוּ מֵהַר־שָׁפֶר וַיַּחֲנוּ בַּחֲרָדָה׃
in and ,Shapher from they And .Shapher in and
.Haradah pitched Mount up pulled Mount pitched

2583 4722 5265 4722 2583 2732 5265
25 וַיִּסְעוּ מֵחֲרָדָה וַיַּחֲנוּ בְּמַקְהֵלֹת׃ וַיִּסְעוּ מִמַּקְהֵלֹת וַיַּחֲנוּ
26
and from they And in and from they And
pitched ,Makheloth up pulled .Makheloth pitched Haradah up pulled

2583 8646 5265 8646 2583 8480 5265 8480
27 בְּתָחַת׃ וַיִּסְעוּ מִתָּחַת וַיַּחֲנוּ בְּתָרַח׃ וַיִּסְעוּ מִתָּרַח וַיַּחֲנוּ
28
and from they And in and from they And in
pitched ,Tarah up pulled .Tarah pitched ,Tahath up pulled .Tahath

2832 5265 2832 2583 4989 5265 4989
29 בְּמִתְקָה׃ וַיִּסְעוּ מִמִּתְקָה וַיַּחֲנוּ בְּחַשְׁמֹנָה׃ וַיִּסְעוּ מֵחַשְׁמֹנָה
30
from they And in and from they And in
Hashmonah up pulled .Hashmonah pitched ,Mithcah up pulled .Mithcah

1142 1121 2583 4149 5265 4149 2583
31 וַיַּחֲנוּ בְּמֹסֵרוֹת׃ וַיִּסְעוּ מִמֹּסֵרוֹת וַיַּחֲנוּ בִּבְנֵי יַעֲקָן׃
in Bene- and from they And in and
jaakan pitched .Moseroth up pulled .Moseroth pitched

2735 5265 2735 2583 1142 1121 5265
32 וַיִּסְעוּ מִבְּנֵי יַעֲקָן וַיַּחֲנוּ בְּחֹר הַגִּדְגָּד׃ וַיִּסְעוּ מֵחֹר הַגִּדְגָּד
33
the in the from they And . the in the at and ;jaakan from they And
Cleft Hole up pulled Cleft Hole pitched Bene- up pulled

5684 2583 3193 5265 3193 2583
34 וַיַּחֲנוּ בְּיָטְבָתָה׃ וַיִּסְעוּ מִיָּטְבָתָה וַיַּחֲנוּ בְּעַבְרֹנָה׃
at and from they And in and
.Abronah pitched Jotbathah up pulled .Jotbathah pitched

6100 5265 6100 2583 5684 5265
35 וַיִּסְעוּ מֵעַבְרֹנָה וַיַּחֲנוּ בְּעֶצְיֹן גָּבֶר׃ וַיִּסְעוּ מֵעֶצְיֹן גָּבֶר
36
from they And .geber Ezion- at and from they And
,geber Ezion up pulled pitched Abronah up pulled

35 And they pulled up from
Abronah and camped in
Ezion-geber. 36 And they
pulled up from Ezion-geber
and camped in the wilder-
ness of Zin; it *is* Kadesh.
37 And they pulled up from
Kadesh and camped in
Mount Hor, in the edge of
the land of Edom.
38 And Aaron the priest
went up into Mount Hor at
the mouth of Jehovah; and
he died there in the fortieth
year after the sons of Israel
had come out of the land of
Egypt, in the fifth month, on
the first of the month. 39 And
Aaron *was* a hundred and
twenty-three years old
at his death in Mount Hor.
40 And king Arad the
Canaanite, who lived in the
Negeb, in the land of
Canaan, heard of the
coming of the sons of Israel.
41 And they traveled from
Mount Hor and camped in
Zalmonah. 42 And they
pulled up from Zalmonah
and camped in Punon.
43 And they pulled up from
Punon and camped in
Oboth. 44 And they pulled
up from Oboth and camped
in Ije-abarim, in the border
of Moab. 45 And they pulled
up from Ijim and camped in
Dibongad. 46 And they
pulled up from Dibon-gad
and camped in Almon-
diblathaim. 47 And they
pulled up from Almon-
diblathaim and camped in
the Abarim mountains, by
Nebo. 48 And they pulled up
from the Abarim mountains
and camped in the plains of
Moab beside Jordan, *near*
Jericho. 49 And they
camped by the Jordan, from
the House of Deserts even
to the Meadow of Acacias in
the plains of Moab.
50 And Jehovah spoke to
Moses in the plains of
Moab, beside Jordan, *near*
Jericho, saying, 51 Speak to
the sons of Israel and say to
them, When you have
crossed the Jordan into the
land of Canaan, 52 then you
shall drive out all the
inhabitants of the land from

37 ויחנו במדבר־צן הוא קדש: ויסעו מקדש ויחנו בהר
2023 2583 6946 5265 6946 6790 4057 2583
Hor in and pitched from Kadesh they And pulled up .Kadesh (is) it ,Zin of the wilderness in and pitched

38 ההר בקצה ארץ אדום: ויעל אהרן הכהן אל־הר
2023 3548 175 5927 123 776 7097 2022
Hor into the priest Aaron And went up .Edom the of land the at of border ,Mount

ההר על־פי יהוה וימת שם בשנת הארבעים לצאת
5927 705 8141 8033 4191 3068 6310 2022
after came the fortieth year in ,there and died ,Jehovah the of mouth at Mount

בני־ישראל מארץ מצרים בחדש החמישי באחד לחדש:
2320 259 2549 2320 4714 776 3478 1121
.month the the on of first fifth month the in ,Egypt of land the of out Israel the of sons

39 ואהרן בן־שלש ועשרים ומאת שנה במתו בהר ההר:
2022 2023 4194 8141 3967 6242 7969 1121 175
.Mount Hor in the at of death years hundred a twenty- three (was) of son a And Aaron

40 וישמע הכנעני מלך ערד והוא־ישב בנגב בארץ
776 5045 3427 6166 4428 3669 8085
the in of land the in Negeb lived who ,Arad king the Canaanite heard And

41 כנען בבא בני ישראל: ויסעו מהר ההר ויחנו בצלמנה:
6758 2583 2022 2023 5265 3478 1121 935 3667
.Zalmonah in and pitched Mount Hor from they And up pulled .Israel the of sons the of coming ,Canaan

42 43 ויסעו מצלמנה ויחנו בפונן: ויסעו מפונן ויחנו באבת:
88 2583 6325 5265 6325 2583 6758 5265
.Oboth in and pitched ,Punon from they And up pulled .Punon in and pitched Zalmonah from they And up pulled

44 45 ויסעו מאבת ויחנו בעיי העברים בגבול מואב: ויסעו
5265 4124 1366 5682 5856 2583 88 5265
they And up pulled .Moab the of border in abarim Ije- at and pitched ,Oboth from they And up pulled

46 מעיים ויחנו בדיבן גד: ויסעו מדיבן גד ויחנו בעלמן
5963 2583 1408 1769 5265 1408 1769 2583 5856
Almon- in and pitched ,gad Dibon- from they And up pulled .gad Dibon- at and camped from Ijim

47 דבלתימה: ויסעו מעלמן דבלתימה ויחנו בהרי העברים
5682 2022 2583 5963 5963 5265 5963
the Abarim mountains in and pitched ,diblathaim Almon- from they And up pulled diblathaim

48 לפני נבו: ויסעו מהרי העברים ויחנו בערבת מואב על
4124 6160 2583 5682 2022 5265 5015 6440
beside ,Moab the of plains in and pitched the ,Abarim mountains from they And up pulled .Nebo be- fore

49 ירדן ירחו: ויחנו על־הירדן מבית הישמת עד אבל
59 5704 3451 1004 3383 2583 3405 3383
the Meadow to even of Deserts the of House from the ,Jordan by they And pitched (near) ,Jericho the Jordan

50 השטים בערבת מואב: וידבר יהוה אל־משה
4872 3068 1696 4124 6160 7848
Moses to Jehovah And spoke .Moab the of plains in of ,Acacias

51 בערבת מואב על־ירדן ירחו לאמר: דבר אל־בני
1121 1696 559 3405 3383 4872 6160
the of sons to Speak ,saying (near) ,Jericho ,Jordan beside ,Moab the of plains in

ישראל ואמרת אלהם כי אתם עברים את־הירדן אל־
3383 5674 559 3478
into the Jordan have crossed you When ,them to say and ,Israel

52 ארץ כנען: והורשתם את־כל־ישבי הארץ מפניכם
6440 776 3427 3605 3423 3667 776
before from ,face your land the the of inhabitants all shall you and out drive ,Canaan the of land

וְאִבַּדְתֶּם אֵת כָּל־מַשְׂכִּיֹּתָם וְאֵת כָּל־צַלְמֵי מַסֵּכֹתָם תְּאַבֵּדוּ
53 וְאֵת כָּל־בָּמוֹתָם תַּשְׁמִידוּ׃ וְהוֹרַשְׁתֶּם אֶת־הָאָרֶץ וִישַׁבְתֶּם־
54 בָּהּ כִּי לָכֶם נָתַתִּי אֶת־הָאָרֶץ לָרֶשֶׁת אֹתָהּ׃ וְהִתְנַחַלְתֶּם
אֶת־הָאָרֶץ בְּגוֹרָל לְמִשְׁפְּחֹתֵיכֶם לָרַב תַּרְבּוּ אֶת־נַחֲלָתוֹ
וְלַמְעַט תַּמְעִיט אֶת־נַחֲלָתוֹ אֶל אֲשֶׁר־יֵצֵא לוֹ שָׁמָּה הַגּוֹרָל
55 לוֹ יִהְיֶה לְמַטּוֹת אֲבֹתֵיכֶם תִּתְנֶחָלוּ׃ וְאִם־לֹא תוֹרִישׁוּ
אֶת־יֹשְׁבֵי הָאָרֶץ מִפְּנֵיכֶם וְהָיָה אֲשֶׁר תּוֹתִירוּ מֵהֶם לְשִׂכִּים
בְּעֵינֵיכֶם וְלִצְנִינִם בְּצִדֵּיכֶם וְצָרְרוּ אֶתְכֶם עַל־הָאָרֶץ אֲשֶׁר
56 אַתֶּם יֹשְׁבִים בָּהּ׃ וְהָיָה כַּאֲשֶׁר דִּמִּיתִי לַעֲשׂוֹת לָהֶם
אֶעֱשֶׂה לָכֶם׃

before you, and destroy all their engraved images; yea, you shall destroy all their casted images, and demolish all their high places. 53 And you shall possess the land, and live in it, for I have given you the land, to possess it. 54 And you shall inherit the land by lot, by your families. You shall increase the inheritance to the many, and you shall diminish the inheritance to the few; wherever the lot falls out to him, it is his. You shall inherit by the tribes of your fathers. 55 And if you will not drive out the inhabitants of the land from before you, then it shall be, those whom you let remain of them *shall be* thorns in your eyes, and as goads in your sides. And they will vex you on the land in which you are living. 56 And it shall be, as I thought to do to them, *so* I shall do to you.

CAP. XXXIV לד

CHAPTER 34

1 וַיְדַבֵּר יְהוָה אֶל־מֹשֶׁה לֵּאמֹר׃
2 צַו אֶת־בְּנֵי יִשְׂרָאֵל
וְאָמַרְתָּ אֲלֵהֶם כִּי־אַתֶּם בָּאִים אֶל־הָאָרֶץ כְּנָעַן זֹאת הָאָרֶץ
3 אֲשֶׁר תִּפֹּל לָכֶם בְּנַחֲלָה אֶרֶץ כְּנַעַן לִגְבֻלֹתֶיהָ׃ וְהָיָה
לָכֶם פְאַת־נֶגֶב מִמִּדְבַּר־צִן עַל־יְדֵי אֱדוֹם וְהָיָה לָכֶם
4 גְּבוּל נֶגֶב מִקְצֵה יָם־הַמֶּלַח קֵדְמָה׃ וְנָסַב לָכֶם הַגְּבוּל
מִנֶּגֶב לְמַעֲלֵה עַקְרַבִּים וְעָבַר צִנָה וְהָיוּ תּוֹצְאֹתָיו מִנֶּגֶב

CHAPTER 34

1 And Jehovah spoke to Moses, saying, 2 Command the sons of Israel, and you shall say to them, When you have come into the land of Canaan, this *is* the land which falls to you by inheritance, the land of Canaan, by its borders: 3 And your south quarter shall be from the wilderness of Zin, along by the hand of Edom, and it shall be to you a south border from the end of the Salt Sea, eastward. 4 And the border shall turn around to you from the south to the ascent of Akrabbim, and shall pass on to Zin, and its end shall be from the south to Kadesh-barnea; and it

shall go out at Hazar-addar, and it shall pass on to Azmon. [5]And the border shall turn from Azmon to the brook of Egypt, and its border shall be at the sea. [6]As to the western border, even the Great Sea shall be a border to you; this is your western border. [7]And this is your northern border: from the Great Sea you shall mark out for yourselves Mount Hor; [8]from Mount Hor you shall mark out a line to the entrance to Hamath; and the edge of the border shall be at Zedad. [9]And the border shall go forth to Ziphron, and the edge of it shall be at Hazar-enan; this shall be your northern border. [10]And you shall mark out your line for the eastern border from Hazar-enan to Shepham; [11]and the border shall go down from Shepham to Riblah, on the east side of Ain; and the border shall go down, and shall reach upon the slopes of the sea of Chinnereth eastward. [12]And the border shall go down to the Jordan, and the edge of it shall be at the Salt Sea; this shall be your land according to the borders of it all around.

[13]And Moses commanded the sons of Israel, saying, This *is* the land which you shall receive *as an* inheritance by lot, which Jehovah has commanded to give to the nine tribes, and to the half tribe; [14]for the tribe of the sons of Reuben according to their fathers' houses have received by their fathers' houses; and the tribe of the sons of Gad by their fathers' houses, and the half tribe of Manasseh have received their inheritance; [15]the two tribes and half the tribe shall have received their inheritance beyond the Jordan *at* Jericho eastward, toward the sunrising.

5 לקדש ברנע ויצא חצר־אדר ועבר עצמנה׃ ונסב
הגבול מעצמון נחלה מצרים והיו תוצאתיו הימה׃
6 וגבול ים והיה לכם הים הגדול וגבול זה־יהיה לכם
7 גבול ים׃ וזה־יהיה לכם גבול צפון מן־הים הגדל
8 תתאו לכם הר ההר׃ מהר ההר תתאו לבא חמת והיו
9 תוצאת הגבל צדדה׃ ויצא הגבל זפרנה והיו תוצאתיו
10 חצר עינן זה־יהיה לכם גבול צפון׃ והתאויתם לכם
11 לגבול קדמה מחצר עינן שפמה׃ וירד הגבל משפם
הרבלה מקדם לעין וירד הגבל ומחה על־כתף ים־
12 כנרת קדמה׃ וירד הגבול הירדנה והיו תוצאתיו ים
13 המלח זאת תהיה לכם הארץ לגבלתיה סביב׃ ויצו
משה את־בני ישראל לאמר זאת הארץ אשר תתנחלו
אתה בגורל אשר צוה יהוה לתת לתשעת המטות
14 וחצי המטה׃ כי לקחו מטה בני הראובני לבית אבתם
ומטה בני־הגדי לבית אבתם וחצי מטה מנשה לקחו
15 נחלתם׃ שני המטות וחצי המטה לקחו נחלתם מעבר
לירדן ירחו קדמה מזרחה׃ פ

[16]And Jehovah spoke to
Moses, saying, [17]Theese
are the names of the men
that shall take possession
of the land for you: Eleazar
the priest and Joshua the
son of Nun. [18]And you
shall take one ruler, one
ruler of every tribe, to take
possession of the land.
[19]And these *are* the names
of the men: Of the tribe of
Judah, Caleb the son of
Jephunneh. [20]And of the
tribe of the sons of Simeon,
Shemuel the son of Ammi-
hud. [21]Of the tribe of Benjamin, Elidad the son of
Chislon. [22]And of the tribe
of Dan, Bukki the ruler, son
of Jogli. [23]Of the sons of
Joseph, of the tribe of
the sons of Manasseh,
Hanniel the ruler, the son
of Ephod. [24]And of the
tribe of the sons of
Ephraim, Kemuel the ruler,
the son of Shiphtan.
[25]And of the tribe of the
sons of Zebulun, Eliza-
phan the ruler, the son of
Parnach. [26]And of the tribe
of the sons of Issachar,
Paltiel the ruler, the son
of Azzan. [27]And of the
tribe of the sons of Asher,
Ahihud the ruler, the son
of Shelomi. [28]And of the
tribe of the sons of Naphtali, Pedahel the ruler, the
son of Ammihud. [29]These
are they whom Jehovah
commanded to divide the
inheritance to the sons of
Israel in the land of
Canaan.

582 8034 428 559 4872 3068 1696
16 וַיְדַבֵּר יְהוָה אֶל־מֹשֶׁה לֵּאמֹר׃ אֵלֶּה שְׁמוֹת הָאֲנָשִׁים
17
men the | the | These | ,saying | ,Moses | to Jehovah | And
of names (are) | spoke

5126 3091 3548 499 776 5157
אֲשֶׁר־יִנְחֲלוּ לָכֶם אֶת־הָאָרֶץ אֶלְעָזָר הַכֹּהֵן וִיהוֹשֻׁעַ בִּן־נוּן׃
.Nun the | and | the | Eleazar | the of | for | take shall | who
of son | Joshua | priest | land | you | possession

776 5157 3947 4294 259 5387 259 5387
18 וְנָשִׂיא אֶחָד נָשִׂיא אֶחָד מִמַּטֶּה תִּקְחוּ לִנְחֹל אֶת־הָאָרֶץ׃
.land the | take to shall you | every of | one | ruler | ,one | And
of possession | take | tribe | ruler

3312/1121 3615 3063 4294 582 8034 428
19 וְאֵלֶּה שְׁמוֹת הָאֲנָשִׁים לְמַטֵּה יְהוּדָה כָּלֵב בֶּן־יְפֻנֶּה׃
Jephun- the | Caleb | ,Judah | the Of | :men the | the | these And
;neh of son | of tribe | of names (are)

1144 4294 5989/1121 8050 8095 1121 4294
20 וּלְמַטֵּה בְּנֵי שִׁמְעוֹן שְׁמוּאֵל בֶּן־עַמִּיהוּד׃ לְמַטֵּה בִנְיָמִן
21
,Benjamin the of | ;Ammihud the | Shemuel | ,Simeon | the the of And
of tribe | of son | of sons of tribe

3020 1231 5387 1835/1121/4294 3692 1121 449
22 אֱלִידָד בֶּן־כִּסְלוֹן׃ וּלְמַטֵּה בְנֵי־דָן נָשִׂיא בֻּקִּי בֶּן־יָגְלִי׃
;Jogli son | ,Bukki | the | ,Dan the | the of and | ;Chislon the | Elidad
of | ruler | of sons of tribe | of son

647/1121 2592 5387 4519 1121 4294 3127/1121
23 לִבְנֵי יוֹסֵף לְמַטֵּה בְנֵי־מְנַשֶּׁה נָשִׂיא חַנִּיאֵל בֶּן־אֵפֹד׃
.Ephod the | ,Hanniel | the | ,Manasseh the | the of | ,Joseph | the of
of son | ruler | of sons of tribe | of sons

4294 8204 1121 7055 5387 669 1121 4294
24 וּלְמַטֵּה בְנֵי־אֶפְרַיִם נָשִׂיא קְמוּאֵל בֶּן־שִׁפְטָן׃ וּלְמַטֵּה
25
the of and | ;Shiphtan the | ,Kemuel | the | ,Ephraim the | the of And
of tribe | of son | ruler | of sons of tribe

3485 1121 4294 6535 1121 469 5387 2074/1121
26 בְנֵי־זְבוּלֻן נָשִׂיא אֱלִיצָפָן בֶּן־פַּרְנָךְ׃ וּלְמַטֵּה בְנֵי־יִשָּׂשכָר
,Issachar | the | the of and | ;Parnach the | ,Elizaphan | the | ,Zebulon the
of sons of tribe | of son | ruler | of sons

282 5387 836 1121 4294 5821 1121 6409 5387
27 נָשִׂיא פַּלְטִיאֵל בֶּן־עַזָּן׃ וּלְמַטֵּה בְנֵי־אָשֵׁר נָשִׂיא אֲחִיהוּד
,Ahihud | the | ,Asher the | of and | ;Azzan the | ,Paltiel | the
ruler | of sons of tribe the | of son | ,ruler

5989 1121 6300 5387 5320 1121 4294 8015 1121
28 בֶּן־שְׁלֹמִי׃ וּלְמַטֵּה בְנֵי־נַפְתָּלִי נָשִׂיא פְּדַהְאֵל בֶּן־עַמִּיהוּד׃
.Ammihud the | ,Pedahel | the | ,Naphtali the | of and | ;Shelomi the
of son | ruler | of sons of tribe the | of son

3667 776 3478 1121 5157 3068 6680 834 428
29 אֵלֶּה אֲשֶׁר צִוָּה יְהוָה לְנַחֵל אֶת־בְּנֵי־יִשְׂרָאֵל בְּאֶרֶץ כְּנָעַן׃
.Canaan | the in | Israel | sons the | divide to | Jehovah | com- | whom | These
of land | of | to land the | manded | (are)

CAP. XXXV לה

CHAPTER 35

CHAPTER 35
[1]And Jehovah spoke to
Moses in the plains of
Moab, beside Jordan, *near*
Jericho, saying, [2]Command
the sons of Israel that they
give to the Levites cities to
live in, from the inheritance
of their possessions. And
you shall give to the Levites
open land around the cities.
[3]And they shall have the
cities to live in, and their
open lands shall be for their

3405 3383 4124 6160 4872 3068 1696
1 וַיְדַבֵּר יְהוָה אֶל־מֹשֶׁה בְּעַרְבֹת מוֹאָב עַל־יַרְדֵּן יְרֵחוֹ
(near) ,Jordan beside | ,Moab | the on | Moses | to Jehovah | And
Jericho | of plains | spoke

272 5159 3881 5414 3478 1121 6680 559
2 לֵאמֹר׃ צַו אֶת־בְּנֵי יִשְׂרָאֵל וְנָתְנוּ לַלְוִיִּם מִנַּחֲלַת אֲחֻזָּתָם
their | the from | the to | they that | ,Israel | the | Order | ,saying
possessions | of land | ,Levites | give | of sons

3881 5414 5439 5892 4054 3427 5892
עָרִים לָשָׁבֶת וּמִגְרָשׁ לֶעָרִים סְבִיבֹתֵיהֶם תִּתְּנוּ לַלְוִיִּם׃
the to | shall you | around | the of | open and | live to | cities
.Levites | give | cities | land | ;in

929 1961 4054 3427 5892 1961
3 וְהָיוּ הֶעָרִים לָהֶם לָשָׁבֶת וּמִגְרְשֵׁיהֶם יִהְיוּ לִבְהֶמְתָּם
their for | shall | their and | to | they | the | And
,cattle | be | lands open | ,in live | have | cities | shall

livestock, and for their substance, and for all their animals. [4]And the open land around the cities, which you shall give to the Levites, shall be from the wall of the city and outward a thousand cubits all around. [5]And you shall measure outside the city for the east side two thousand cubits, and for the south side two thousand cubits, and for the west side two thousand cubits, and for the north side two thousand cubits; the city being in the middle. This shall be to them the open land around the cities. [6]And the cities which you shall give to the Levites *shall be* the six cities of refuge, which you shall give for the manslayer that *he* may flee there. And besides them you shall give forty-two cities. [7]All the cities which you shall give to the Levites *shall be* forty-eight cities, them and the open land around them. [8]And you shall give the cities from the possession of the sons of Israel. From the many you shall multiply; and take away from the few; each tribe by the mouth of its inheritance which it inherits shall give of its cities to the Levites.

[9]And Jehovah spoke to Moses, saying, [10]Speak to the sons of Israel, and say to them, When you pass over the Jordan into the land of Canaan, [11]then you shall choose cities to be cities of refuge for you, so that the manslayer may flee there, he that kills any person through error. [12]And the cities shall be to you for refuge from the kinsman-avenger, that the manslayer may not die until he stands before the congregation for judgment. [13]As

5414 834 5892 4054 2416 3605 7339
4 ולרכשם ולכל חיתם: ומגרשי הערים אשר תתנו
shall you give which the cities, the and open land around their animals, for and all their for and substance

4058 5439 520 505 2351 5892 7023 3881
5 ללוים מקיר העיר וחוצה אלף אמה סביב: ומדתם
shall you And measure all around. cubits a thousand and outward city the the from wall of the to Levites:

5045/6285 520 505 6924 6285 5892 2351
מחוץ לעיר את־פאת־קדמה אלפים באמה ואת־פאת־נגב
south the for side and ,cubits two thousand eastward the for side the city outside

6285 520 505 3220/6285 520 505
אלפים באמה ואת־פאת־ים | אלפים באמה ואת פאת
the for side and ,cubits two thousand west the for side and ,cubits two thousand

4054 1961 2088 8432 5892 520 505 6828
צפון אלפים באמה והעיר בתוך זה יהיה להם מגרשי
open the land around to them shall be this the in middle; the and city ;cubits two thousand north

5892/8337 5414 5892 5892
6 הערים: ואת הערים אשר תתנו ללוים את שש־ערי
cities of six (be shall) the to Levites you give which cities the And .cities the

5414 7523 8033 5127 5414 834 4733
המקלט אשר תתנו לנס שמה הרצח ועליהם תתנו
you give besides and them the manslayer; there may flee that shall you give which the refuge,

3881 5414 834 5892 3605 5892 8147 703
7 ארבעים ושתים עיר: כל־הערים אשר תתנו ללוים
the to Levites shall you give which cities the All .cities two forty-

5892 4054 5892 8083 703
8 ארבעים ושמנה עיר אתהן ואת־מגרשיהן: והערים
the And cities open the land around .them and them ,cities eight (be shall) forty-

7235 7227 3478/1121 272 5414
אשר תתנו מאחזת בני־ישראל מאת הרב תרבו ומאת
and from shall you multiply, the many from ,Israel the sons of the possession of the from you which give shall

5414 5157 834 5159 6310 376 4591 4592
המעט תמעיטו איש כפי נחלתו אשר ינחלו יתן
shall give it inherits which its inheritance by mouth each tribe take away; few the

3881 5892
מעריו ללוים:
the to .Levites its of cities

3478 1121 1696 559 4872 3068 1696
9 וידבר יהוה אל־משה לאמר: דבר אל־בני ישראל
10 ,Israel the sons of to Speak ,saying ,Moses to Jehovah And spoke

3667 776 3383 5674 559
ואמרת אלהם כי אתם עברים את־הירדן ארצה כנען:
,Canaan the into land of Jordan the cross you When ,them to say and

8033 5127 1961 4733 5892 5892 7136
11 והקריתם לכם ערים ערי מקלט תהיינה לכם ונס שמה
there that so flee may for you, be to refuge of cities ,cities you for shall you then choose

4733 5892 1961 7684 5315/5221 7523
12 רצח מכה־נפש בשגגה: והיו לכם הערים למקלט
refuge for cities the you to And be shall through .error a person that he kills the ,manslayer

4941 5712 6440 5975/5704 7523 4191 3808 1350
מגאל ולא ימות הרצח עד־עמדו לפני העדה למשפט:
for .judgment con-the gregation before he stands until the manslayer may die not that the from ,avenger

to the cities which you shall
give, six *shall be* cities of
refuge to you; 14you shall
give three of the cities
beyond the Jordan, and you
shall give three of the cities
in the land of Canaan; they
shall be cities of refuge.
15These six cities shall be for
a refuge to the sons of
Israel, and to an alien, and
to a tenant in their midst; so
that anyone who strikes a
person unawares may flee
there. 16And if he strikes
him with an instrument of
iron, and he dies, he *is* a
murderer; the murderer
shall certainly be put to
death. 17And if he has
struck him with a stone *in*
the hand, by which he dies,
and he dies, he *is* a
murderer; the murderer
shall certainly be put to
death. 18And if he has
stricken him with a wooden
instrument *in* the hand, by
which he dies, and he dies,
he *is* a murderer; the
murderer shall certainly be
put to death. 19The avenger
of blood shall himself put
the murderer to death.
When he meets him, he
shall put him to death.
20And if he thrusts him
through in hatred, or has
thrown at him by lying in
wait, and he dies; 21or if he
has struck him with his
hand in enmity, and he dies,
he that struck him shall
surely be put to death; *he* is
a murderer. The avenger of
blood shall put the
murderer to death when he
meets him. 22And if, in an
instant, without enmity, he
has thrust him through, or
has thrown any instrument
at him, without lying in wait;
23or with any stone by
which he dies, without
seeing, and has caused *it* to
fall upon him, and he dies,
and he *is* not his enemy, or
seeking his evil; 24then the
congregation shall judge
between the one who
struck and the avenger of
blood, by these judg-
ments. 25And the congre-
gation shall deliver the
manslayer out of the hand
of the avenger of blood.

13 1961 4733 5892 8337 5414 834 5892
וְהֶעָרִים אֲשֶׁר תִּתֵּנוּ שֵׁשׁ־עָרֵי מִקְלָט תִּהְיֶינָה לָכֶם׃
;you to | be shall | refuge of | cities | six | shall you ,give | which | the And cities

14 5892 7969 3383 5676 5414 5892 7969
אֵת ׀ שְׁלֹשׁ הֶעָרִים תִּתְּנוּ מֵעֵבֶר לַיַּרְדֵּן וְאֵת שְׁלֹשׁ הֶעָרִים
cities the | three | and | the Jordan | beyond | shall you give | cities the | three

15 3478 1121 1961 4733 5892 3667 776 5414
תִּתְּנוּ בְּאֶרֶץ כְּנָעַן עָרֵי מִקְלָט תִּהְיֶינָה׃ לִבְנֵי יִשְׂרָאֵל
Israel | the To of sons | shall they .be | refuge | cities ;Canaan of | the in of land | shall you give

4733 428 5892 8337 1961 8432 8453 1616
וְלַגֵּר וְלַתּוֹשָׁב בְּתוֹכָם תִּהְיֶינָה שֵׁשׁ־הֶעָרִים הָאֵלֶּה לְמִקְלָט
a for ;refuge | these | cities | six | be shall | their in midst | a to and tenant | to and ,alien an

16 1270 3627 518 7684 5315 5221 8033 5127
לָנוּס שָׁמָּה כָּל־מַכֵּה־נֶפֶשׁ בִּשְׁגָגָה׃ וְאִם־בִּכְלִי בַרְזֶל ׀
iron | an with if And of instrument | .unawares | a person | who kills | any one | there | that flee may

17 3027 68 7523 4191 7523 4191 5221
הִכָּהוּ וַיָּמֹת רֹצֵחַ הוּא מוֹת יוּמַת הָרֹצֵחַ׃ וְאִם בְּאֶבֶן יָד
the (in) with And ,hand stone a if | the .murderer | shall surely executed be | ;(is) he | a murderer | he and ,dies | hits he ,him

4191 4191 7523 4191 5221 4191 834
אֲשֶׁר־יָמוּת בָּהּ הִכָּהוּ וַיָּמֹת רֹצֵחַ הוּא מוֹת יוּמַת הָרֹצֵחַ׃
the .murderer | shall surely executed be | he ;(is) | a murderer | he and ,dies | hit he ,him | ,by | dies he which

18 7523 4191 5221 4191 834 3027 6086 3627
אוֹ בִּכְלִי עֵץ־יָד אֲשֶׁר־יָמוּת בּוֹ הִכָּהוּ וַיָּמֹת רֹצֵחַ הוּא
;(is) he | mur-derer | a | he and ,dies | has he hit ,him | by | dies he which | (in) a hand the wood | with And instrument if

19 7523 4191 1818 1350 7523 4191 4191
מוֹת יוּמַת הָרֹצֵחַ׃ גֹּאֵל הַדָּם הוּא יָמִית אֶת־הָרֹצֵחַ
the ;murderer | shall execute | himself | The avenger blood | of | the .murderer | shall surely executed be

20 7993 1920 8130 4191 1931 6293
בְּפִגְעוֹ־בוֹ הוּא יְמִתֶנּוּ׃ וְאִם־בְּשִׂנְאָה יֶהְדֳּפֶנּוּ אוֹ־הִשְׁלִיךְ
thrown has or | he ,him pushes | in ,hatred | if And | shall .him execute | he | with him | when meets he

21 4191 4191 3027 5221 342 4191 6660
עָלָיו בִּצְדִיָּה וַיָּמֹת׃ אוֹ בְאֵיבָה הִכָּהוּ בְיָדוֹ וַיָּמֹת מוֹת־
surely | and dies | with ,hand his | has he him struck | in enmity | if or | he and ,dies | lying by ,wait in | at ,him

6293 7523 4191 1818 1350 7523 5221 4191
יוּמַת הַמַּכֶּה רֹצֵחַ הוּא גֹּאֵל הַדָּם יָמִית אֶת־הָרֹצֵחַ בְּפִגְעוֹ־
he when meets | the murderer | shall execute | the avenger blood | of | ;(is) he | a murderer | the ;smiter | be shall executed

22 3605 7993 1920 342 3808 6621
בוֹ׃ וְאִם־בְּפֶתַע בְּלֹא־אֵיבָה הֲדָפוֹ אוֹ־הִשְׁלִיךְ עָלָיו כָּל־
any | at him | has thrown | or | he ,him pushed | enmity without | an in ,instant | ,if And | with .him

23 7200 3808 4191 834 68 3605 6660 3627
כְּלִי בְּלֹא צְדִיָּה׃ אוֹ בְכָל־אֶבֶן אֲשֶׁר־יָמוּת בָּהּ בְּלֹא רְאוֹת
,seeing without (it) | ,by | dies he which | stone | with any | or | lying without ;wait in | ,thing

7451 1245 3808 341 3808 4191 5307
וַיַּפֵּל עָלָיו וַיָּמֹת וְהוּא לֹא־אוֹיֵב לוֹ וְלֹא מְבַקֵּשׁ רָעָתוֹ׃
;evil his | seeking | nor | ,to him | an enemy | not | then (is) he | he and ,dies | on ,him | made and fall (it)

24 4941 1818 1350 5221 5712 8199
וְשָׁפְטוּ הָעֵדָה בֵּין הַמַּכֶּה וּבֵין גֹּאֵל הַדָּם עַל הַמִּשְׁפָּטִים
judgments | by | the blood | avenger of | and | the striker | between | the congregation | shall then judge

25 7725 1818 1350 3027 7523 5712 5337 428
הָאֵלֶּה׃ וְהִצִּילוּ הָעֵדָה אֶת־הָרֹצֵחַ מִיַּד גֹּאֵל הַדָּם וְהֵשִׁיבוּ
shall and return | the ;blood | aven-ger of | the from of hand | the manslayer | the assembly | shall And deliver | .these

And the congregation shall return him to the city of refuge, to which he had fled, and he shall live in it until the high priest dies, he who was anointed with the holy oil.
26 But if the manslayer at all goes out from the border of the city of his refuge where he has fled, 27 and the avenger of blood finds him outside the border of the city of his refuge, and the avenger of blood kills the manslayer, there shall be no blood guiltinesss for him; 28 because he should have lived in the city of his refuge until the death of the high priest: and after the death of the high priest the manslayer shall return to the city of his possession. 29 And these things shall be to you for a statute of judgment throughout your generations, in all your dwellings.
30 Whoever kills any person, the murderer shall be put to death by the mouth of witnesses; and one witness shall not testify against a person, to die. 31 And you shall take no ransom for the life of a murderer who *is* condemned to die, for he shall certainly be put to death. 32 And you shall take no ransom *for him* to flee to the city of his refuge, to return to dwell in the land, until the death of the priest. 33 And you shall not pollute the land which you *are* in, for blood pollutes the land. And no ransom *is* to be taken for the land for blood which is shed in it, except for the blood of him who sheds it. 34 And you shall not defile the land in which you live, in the midst of which I dwell, for I, Jehovah, dwell in the midst of the sons of Israel.

5704 3427 5127 834 4733 5892 5712
אֹתוֹ הָעֵדָה אֶל־עִיר מִקְלָטוֹ אֲשֶׁר־נָס שָׁמָּה וְיָשַׁב בָּהּ עַד־
until ,it in he and ,to had he which refuge city the to the him
live shall fled of congregation

6944 8081 4886 834 1419 3548 4194
26 מוֹת הַכֹּהֵן הַגָּדֹל אֲשֶׁר־מָשַׁח אֹתוֹ בְּשֶׁמֶן הַקֹּדֶשׁ׃ וְאִם־
But .holy the oil with him has one whom ,high the the
if anointed priest of death

8033 5127 834 4733 5892 1366 7523
יָצֹא יֵצֵא הָרֹצֵחַ אֶת־גְּבוּל עִיר מִקְלָטוֹ אֲשֶׁר יָנוּס שָׁמָּה׃
,there has he which his the the man the indeed
fled refuge of city of border slayer leaves

7523 4733 5892 1366 2351 1818 1350 4672
27 וּמָצָא אֹתוֹ גֹּאֵל הַדָּם מִחוּץ לִגְבוּל עִיר מִקְלָטוֹ וְרָצַח
and his the border the outside the avenger him and
kills ,refuge of city of blood of finds

3427 4733 5892 1818 369 7523 1818 1350
28 גֹּאֵל הַדָּם אֶת־הָרֹצֵחַ אֵין לוֹ דָּם׃ כִּי בְעִיר מִקְלָטוֹ יֵשֵׁב
should he his the in for blood to (is) the the avenger
lived have refuge of city him no ,manslayer blood of

7523 7725 1419 3548 4194 310 1419 3548 4194 5704
עַד־מוֹת הַכֹּהֵן הַגָּדֹל וְאַחֲרֵי מוֹת הַכֹּהֵן הַגָּדֹל יָשׁוּב הָרֹצֵחַ
the shall high the the and ;high the the until
manslayer return priest of death after priest of death

1755 4941 2708 428 1961 272 776
29 אֶל־אֶרֶץ אֲחֻזָּתוֹ׃ וְהָיוּ אֵלֶּה לָכֶם לְחֻקַּת מִשְׁפָּט לְדֹרֹתֵיכֶם
your For .judgment a for you to these And his land the to
,generations of statute ,things be shall .possession

7523 5707 6310 5221 3605 4186 3605
30 בְּכֹל מוֹשְׁבֹתֵיכֶם׃ כָּל־מַכֵּה־נֶפֶשׁ לְפִי עֵדִים יִרְצַח אֶת־
be shall witness- the by any kills Who- your all in
executed es of mouth ,person ever .dwellings

3724 3947 4191 6630 3808 259 5707 7523
31 הָרֹצֵחַ וְעֵד אֶחָד לֹא־יַעֲנֶה בְנֶפֶשׁ לָמוּת׃ וְלֹא־תִקְחוּ כֹפֶר
ransom shall you And .die to against shall not one and the
take no ,person a testify witness ;murderer

3808 4191 4191 4191 7563 834 7523 53.15
32 לְנֶפֶשׁ רֹצֵחַ אֲשֶׁר־הוּא רָשָׁע לָמוּת כִּי־מוֹת יוּמָת׃ וְלֹא־
And surely shall he for for punish- he who mur- a the for
no .executed be ,death able (is) derer of life

776 3427 7725 4733 5892 5127 3724 3947
תִקְחוּ כֹפֶר לָנוּס אֶל־עִיר מִקְלָטוֹ לָשׁוּב לָשֶׁבֶת בָּאָרֶץ
the in dwell to to his the to flee to ransom you
,land return ,refuge of city (him for) take shall

834 776 2610 3808 3548 4194 5704
33 עַד־מוֹת הַכֹּהֵן׃ וְלֹא־תַחֲנִיפוּ אֶת־הָאָרֶץ אֲשֶׁר אַתֶּם בָּהּ
,in you which land the shall you And the the until
(are) pollute not .priest of death

1818 3722 776 776 2610 1818
כִּי הַדָּם הוּא יַחֲנִיף אֶת־הָאָרֶץ וְלָאָרֶץ לֹא־יְכֻפַּר לַדָּם
for ransom no for And ;land the pollutes it ,blood for
blood land the

2930 3808 8210 1818 8210 834
34 אֲשֶׁר שֻׁפַּךְ־בָּהּ כִּי־אִם בְּדַם שֹׁפְכוֹ׃ וְלֹא תְטַמֵּא אֶת־
shall you and who him the for except ,it in is which
defile not ;it sheds of blood shed

8432 7931 834 3427 834 776
הָאָרֶץ אֲשֶׁר אַתֶּם יֹשְׁבִים בָּהּ אֲשֶׁר אֲנִי שֹׁכֵן בְּתוֹכָהּ כִּי
for the in dwell I which ,in are you which the
;midst living land

3478 1121 8432 7931 3068
אֲנִי יְהוָה שֹׁכֵן בְּתוֹךְ בְּנֵי יִשְׂרָאֵל׃
.Israel the the in am ,Jehovah ,I
of sons of midst dwelling

CAP. XXXVI לו

CHAPTER 36

CHAPTER 36

[1]And the heads of the
1 fathers' *houses* of the
families of the sons of
Gilead, the son of Machir,
the son of Manasseh, of the
families of the sons of
Joseph, came near, and
spoke before Moses, and
before the rulers, the heads
2 of the fathers' *houses* of the
sons of Israel. [2]And they
said, Jehovah commanded
my lord to give the land for
inheritance by lot to the
sons of Israel. And my lord
was commanded by
Jehovah to give the inheritance of our brother
Zelophehad to his daugh-
ters. [3]And *if they* shall be
3 for wives to one of the sons
of the *other* tribes of the
sons of Israel; then their
inheritance will be taken
away from the inheritance
of our fathers, and will be
added to the inheritance of
the tribe to which they shall
4 belong. So it shall be taken
away from the lot of our
inheritance. [4]And when
the Jubilee of the sons of
Israel shall come, then their
inheritance shall be added
to the inheritance of the
tribe to which they shall
5 belong. So their inheritance
will be taken away from the
inheritance of the tribe of
our fathers. [5]And Moses
commanded the sons of
Israel according to the
mouth of Jehovah, saying,
The tribe of the sons of
6 Joseph speak right. [6]This
is the thing which Jehovah
has commanded concern-
ing the daughters of
Zelophehad, saying, Let
them be for wives to *those*
good in their eyes, only let
7 them be for wives to the
family of the tribe of their
father; [7]so no inheritance
of the sons of Israel shall
turn from tribe to tribe; for
the sons of Israel shall each
one cling to the inheritance
of the tribe of his fathers.
8 [8]And every daughter that
possesses an inheritance in
any tribe of the sons of

1121 4353 1121 1568 1121 4940 1 7218 7126
1 וַיִּקְרְבוּ רָאשֵׁי הָאָבוֹת לְמִשְׁפַּחַת בְּנֵי־גִלְעָד בֶּן־מָכִיר בֶּן
the ,Machir the ,Gilead the the of the the came And
of son of son of sons of families fathers of heads near
6440 4872 6440 1696 3127 1121 4940 4519
מְנַשֶּׁה מִמִּשְׁפְּחֹת בְּנֵי יוֹסֵף וַיְדַבְּרוּ לִפְנֵי מֹשֶׁה וְלִפְנֵי
and ,Moses before spoke and ,Joseph the the of ,Manasseh
before of sons of families
113 559 3478 1121 1 7218 5387
2 הַנְּשִׂאִים רָאשֵׁי אָבוֹת לִבְנֵי יִשְׂרָאֵל׃ וַיֹּאמְרוּ אֶת־אֲדֹנִי
lord my they and ;Israel the of the the ,rulers the
said of sons fathers of heads
3478 1121 1486 5159 776 5414 3068 6680
צִוָּה יְהוָה לָתֵת אֶת־הָאָרֶץ בְּנַחֲלָה בְּגוֹרָל לִבְנֵי יִשְׂרָאֵל
;Israel the to lot by for land the give to Jehovah com-
of sons inheritance manded
1323 251 6765 5159 5414 3068 6680 113
וַאדֹנִי צֻוָּה בַיהוָה לָתֵת אֶת־נַחֲלַת צְלָפְחָד אָחִינוּ לִבְנֹתָיו׃
his to our Zelophehad the give to by was my and
.daughters brother of inheritance Jehovah commanded lord
1639 802 3478 1121 7626 1121 259
3 וְהָיוּ לְאֶחָד מִבְּנֵי שִׁבְטֵי בְנֵי־יִשְׂרָאֵל לְנָשִׁים וְנִגְרְעָה
will then for Israel the (other) the the of one to (if) And
taken be wives of sons of tribes of sons be shall they
834 4294 5159 3254 1 5159 5159
נַחֲלָתָן מִנַּחֲלַת אֲבֹתֵינוּ וְנוֹסַף עַל נַחֲלַת הַמַּטֶּה אֲשֶׁר
which tribe the the to will and our the from inheri their
of inheritance added be ,fathers of inheritance tance
3104 1961 1639 5159 1486 1961
4 תִּהְיֶינָה לָהֶם וּמִגֹּרַל נַחֲלָתֵנוּ יִגָּרֵעַ׃ וְאִם־יִהְיֶה הַיֹּבֵל
the shall And be shall it our from so to shall they
Jubilee come when ,taken inheritance of lot the them be
834 4294 5159 5159 3254 3478 1121
לִבְנֵי יִשְׂרָאֵל וְנוֹסְפָה נַחֲלָתָן עַל נַחֲלַת הַמַּטֶּה אֲשֶׁר
which tribe the the to their shall then ,Israel the of
of inheritance inheritance added be of sons
6680 5159 1639 1 4294 5159 1961
5 תִּהְיֶינָה לָהֶם וּמִנַּחֲלַת מַטֵּה אֲבֹתֵינוּ יִגָּרַע נַחֲלָתָן׃ וַיְצַו
And their be shall our the from so to shall they
directed .inheritance taken fathers of tribe of inheritance ;them be
1121 4294 559 3068 6310 3478 1121 4872
מֹשֶׁה אֶת־בְּנֵי יִשְׂרָאֵל עַל־פִּי יְהוָה לֵאמֹר כֵּן מַטֵּה בְנֵי־
the The rightly ,saying ,Jehovah the by Israel the Moses
of sons of tribe of mouth of sons
6765 1323 3068 6680 834 1697 2088 1696 3127
6 יוֹסֵף דֹּבְרִים׃ זֶה הַדָּבָר אֲשֶׁר־צִוָּה יְהוָה לִבְנוֹת צְלָפְחָד
,Zelophehad to as Jehovah has which the This .speaks Joseph
of daughters the commanded thing (is)
4940 802 1961 5869 2896 559
לֵאמֹר לַטּוֹב בְּעֵינֵיהֶם תִּהְיֶינָה לְנָשִׁים אַךְ לְמִשְׁפַּחַת
the to only for them let their in the To ,saying
of family wives be eyes ,good
1121 5159 5437 802 1961 1 4294
7 מַטֵּה אֲבִיהֶם תִּהְיֶינָה לְנָשִׁים׃ וְלֹא־תִסֹּב נַחֲלָה לִבְנֵי
the of inner- the shall So .wives them let their tribe the
of sons itance turn not be ,father of
4294 5159 376 4294 4294 3478
יִשְׂרָאֵל מִמַּטֶּה אֶל־מַטֶּה כִּי אִישׁ בְּנַחֲלַת מַטֵּה אֲבֹתָיו
his the the to each for ;tribe to from Israel
fathers of tribe of inheritance one tribe
1121 4294 5159 3423 1323 3605 3478 1121 1692
8 יִדְבְּקוּ בְּנֵי יִשְׂרָאֵל׃ וְכָל־בַּת יֹרֶשֶׁת נַחֲלָה מִמַּטּוֹת בְּנֵי
the any from an own- daughter And .Israel the shall
of sons of tribe inheritance ing any of sons cling

Israel is to become a wife of
the family of the tribe of her
father, so that the sons of
Israel may each possess the
inheritance of his father;
[9]and the inheritance shall
not move from *one* tribe to
another tribe. For the tribes
of the sons of Israel shall
each one cling to its own
inheritance. [10]as Jehovah
commanded Moses, so the
daughters of Zelophehad
did. [11]For Mahlah, Tirzah,
and Hoglah, and Milcah,
and Noah, Zelophehad's
daughters, were for wives
to their father's brothers'
sons. [12]They were married
into the families of the sons
of Manasseh the son of
Joseph, and their inheritance
remained in the tribe
of the family of their father.
[13]These are the commandments
and the judgments which Jehovah
commanded by the hand of
Moses to the sons of Israel
in the plains of Moab,
beside the Jordan, *near*
Jericho.

802 1961 1 4294 4940 259 3478
ישראל לאחד ממשפחת מטה אביה תהיה לאשה למען
that so wife a to her the the of to Israel
become father of tribe of family one

5159 5437 3808 1 5159 376 3478 1121 3423
9 ירשו בני ישראל איש נחלת אבתיו׃ ולא־תסב נחלה
the shall And his the each Israel the may
inheritance turn not ;father of inheritance of sons possess

1121 4294 1692 5159 376 312 4294 4294
ממטה למטה אחר כי־איש בנחלתו ידבקו מטות בני
the tribes the shall own his to each for ;another to (one) from
of sons of cling inheritance one tribe tribe

6765 1323 6213 4872 3068 6680 3478
10 ישראל׃ כאשר צוה יהוה את־משה כן עשו בנות צלפחד׃
.Zelophehad's daugh- did so ,Moses Jehovah com- Even .Israel
ters manded as

6765 1323 5270 4435 2295 8656 4244
11 ותהיינה מחלה תרצה וחגלה ומלכה ונעה בנות צלפחד
Zelophe- daughters and and and ,Tirzah ,Mahlah were for
had of Noah Milcah Hoglah

1961 3127 4519 1121 4940 802 1730 1121
12 לבני דדיהן לנשים׃ ממשפחת בני־מנשה בן־יוסף היו
they Joseph the Manasseh the the Into for their sons to
were of son of sons of families .wives brothers father's

428 4940 4294 5159 1961 802
13 לנשים ותהי נחלתן על־מטה משפחת אביהן׃ אלה
These their family the the with their and for
(are) .father of of tribe inheritance was wives

1121 4872 3127 3068 6680 834 4941 4687
המצות והמשפטים אשר צוה יהוה ביד־משה אל־בני
the to Moses by Jehovah com- which the and com- the
of sons of hand the manded judgments mandments

3405 3383 4124 6160 3478
ישראל בערבת מואב על ירדן ירחו׃
(near) the beside ,Moab the on ,Israel
Jericho ,Jordan of plains

A LITERAL TRANSLATION
OF THE BIBLE

THE BOOK OF
DEUTERONOMY

CHAPTER 1

[1]These *are* the words
which Moses spoke to all
Israel beyond the Jordan; in
the wilderness, in the
Arabah, opposite to Suph,
between Paran and Tophel,
and Laban and Hazeroth,
and Dizahab; [2]eleven days
from Horeb by way of
Mount Seir to Kadesh-
barnea. [3]And it happened,
in the fortieth year, in the
eleventh month, on the first
of the month, Moses spoke
to the sons of Israel ac-
cording to all that Jehovah
had commanded him con-
cerning them; [4]after he had
smitten Sihon the king of
the Amorites, who lived in
Heshbon, and Og the king
of Bashan, who lived in
Ashtaroth in Edrei, [5]beyond
the Jordan, in the land of
Moab, Moses began to
explain this law, saying,
[6]Jehovah our God spoke to
us in Horeb, saying, You
have had enough of dwell-
ing in this mountain; [7]turn
and take your journey, and
enter the hill-country of the
Amorites, and to all its
neighboring places, in the
Arabah in the hill-country,
and in the low country, and
in the Negeb, and in the
shore of the sea, the land of
the Canaanites, and of
Lebanon, to the great river,
the river Euphrates. [8]Be-
hold, I have set before you
the land; go in and possess
the land which Jehovah has
sworn to your fathers, to

אלה הדברים
(THE BOOK OF)
DEUTERONOMIUM
DEUTERONOMY
CAPUT. I א
CHAPTER 1

5676 3478 3605 4872 1696 834 1697 428
1 אֵלֶּה הַדְּבָרִים אֲשֶׁר דִּבֶּר מֹשֶׁה אֶל־כָּל־יִשְׂרָאֵל בְּעֵבֶר
beyond Israel all to Moses spoke which words the These (are)

8603 6290 5488 4136 6160 4057 3383
הַיַּרְדֵּן בַּמִּדְבָּר בָּעֲרָבָה מוֹל סוּף בֵּין־פָּארָן וּבֵין־תֹּפֶל
Tophel and between Paran Reeds opposite to the on plain the in wilderness the Jordan

2022 1870 2722 3117 6240 259 1774 2698 3837
2 וְלָבָן וַחֲצֵרֹת וְדִי זָהָב׃ אַחַד עָשָׂר יוֹם מֵחֹרֵב דֶּרֶךְ הַר־
Mount the by of way from Horeb days eleven ;Dizahab and and Hazeroth and Laban

6240 6249 8141 703 1961 6947 5704 8165
3 שֵׂעִיר עַד קָדֵשׁ בַּרְנֵעַ׃ וַיְהִי בְּאַרְבָּעִים שָׁנָה בְּעַשְׁתֵּי־עָשָׂר
eleventh the in year the in fortieth it And came to pass .barnea Kadesh- to Seir

3605 3478 1121 4872 1696 2320 259 2320
חֹדֶשׁ בְּאֶחָד לַחֹדֶשׁ דִּבֶּר מֹשֶׁה אֶל־בְּנֵי יִשְׂרָאֵל כְּכֹל
according all to Israel the of sons to Moses spoke the of ,month the on first month

4428 6511 5221 310 3068 6680 834
4 אֲשֶׁר צִוָּה יְהוָה אֹתוֹ אֲלֵהֶם׃ אַחֲרֵי הַכֹּתוֹ אֵת סִיחֹן מֶלֶךְ
the of king Sihon — had he struck After concerning .them him Jehovah had commanded that

834 1316 4428 5747 2809 3427 834 567
הָאֱמֹרִי אֲשֶׁר יוֹשֵׁב בְּחֶשְׁבּוֹן וְאֵת עוֹג מֶלֶךְ הַבָּשָׁן אֲשֶׁר־
who ,Basham the of king Og and ,Heshbon in (was) living who the ,Amorites

4124 776 3383 5676 154 6252 3427
5 יוֹשֵׁב בְּעַשְׁתָּרֹת בְּאֶדְרֶעִי׃ בְּעֵבֶר הַיַּרְדֵּן בְּאֶרֶץ מוֹאָב
Moab the in of land the ,Jordan beyond ,Edrei in Ashtaroth in (was) living

3068 559 2088 8451 874 4872 2974
6 הוֹאִיל מֹשֶׁה בֵּאֵר אֶת־הַתּוֹרָה הַזֹּאת לֵאמֹר׃ יְהוָה
Jehovah ,saying ,this law to explain Moses began

2022 3427 7227 559 2722 1696 430
אֱלֹהֵינוּ דִּבֶּר אֵלֵינוּ בְּחֹרֵב לֵאמֹר רַב־לָכֶם שֶׁבֶת בָּהָר
in mountain (of) dwelling for much you ,saying ,Horeb in us to spoke God our

7934 3605 567 2022 935 5265 6437 2088
7 הַזֶּה׃ פְּנוּ וּסְעוּ לָכֶם וּבֹאוּ הַר הָאֱמֹרִי וְאֶל־כָּל־שְׁכֵנָיו
neigh- boring its ,places all to and the Amorites hill- of country the enter and your up pull and turn ;this

3667 776 3220 2348 5045 8219 2022 6160
בָּעֲרָבָה בָהָר וּבַשְּׁפֵלָה וּבַנֶּגֶב וּבְחוֹף הַיָּם אֶרֶץ הַכְּנַעֲנִי
the Canaanites the of land the ,sea the in of shore and in and Negeb the the in and foothills the in ,hills the in Arabah

6440 5414 2009 6578 5104 1419 5104 3844
8 וְהַלְּבָנוֹן עַד־הַנָּהָר הַגָּדֹל נְהַר־פְּרָת׃ רְאֵה נָתַתִּי לִפְנֵיכֶם
before you have I set ,See .Euphrates the ,Great River the River to and Lebanon

3068 7650 834 776 3423 935 776
אֶת־הָאָרֶץ בֹּאוּ וּרְשׁוּ אֶת־הָאָרֶץ אֲשֶׁר נִשְׁבַּע יְהוָה
Jehovah has sworn which the land and possess in go the ;land

Abraham, to Isaac, and to
Jacob, to give to them, and
to their seed after them.
9And I spoke to you at that
time, saying, I am not able to
bear you by myself.
10Jehovah your God has
multiplied you, and, behold,
today you *are* as the stars of
heaven for multitude. 11May
Jehovah the God of your
fathers make you a thou-
sand times more than you
are, and bless you as He has
said to you! 12How can I by
myself bear your pressure
and your burden, and your
strife? 13Give wise and
understanding men, and
those known to your tribes,
and I will appoint them
rulers over you. 14And you
answered me and said, The
thing which you have
spoken *is* good to do. 15And
I took the chiefs of your
tribes, wise and noted men,
and I appointed them rulers
over you, captains over
thousands, and captains
over hundreds, and captains
over fifties, and captains
over tens, and officers, for
your tribes. 16And I com-
manded your judges at that
time, saying, Hear between
your brothers; and judge
with righteousness be-
tween a man and his
brother, and his alien.
17You shall not discern
persons in judgment; you
shall hear the small as well
as the great; you shall not be
afraid because of the face of
a man, for the judgment is
God's; and the thing which
is too hard for you, you shall
bring near to me, and I shall
hear it. 18And at that time I
commanded you all the
things which you were to
do.
19And we pulled up
stakes from Horeb and went
through all that great and

2233 5414 3290 3327 85 1
לַאֲבֹתֵיכֶם לְאַבְרָהָם לְיִצְחָק וּלְיַעֲקֹב לָתֵת לָהֶם וּלְזַרְעָם
to and seed their | to them | to give | to and ,Jacob | Isaac to | Abraham to | your to ,fathers

9 3201 3808 559 6256 559 310
אַחֲרֵיהֶם׃ וָאֹמַר אֲלֵכֶם בָּעֵת הַהִוא לֵאמֹר לֹא־אוּכַל
am able | I | not | ,saying | that | time at | you to | I And spoke | .them after

10 2009 7235 430 3068 5375 905
לְבַדִּי שְׂאֵת אֶתְכֶם׃ יְהוָה אֱלֹהֵיכֶם הִרְבָּה אֶתְכֶם וְהִנְּכֶם
see and you | ,you | has multiplied | God your | Jehovah | ;you | bear to | by myself

11 3254 1 430 3068 7230 8064 3556 3117
הַיּוֹם כְּכוֹכְבֵי הַשָּׁמַיִם לָרֹב׃ יְהוָה אֱלֹהֵי אֲבוֹתֵכֶם יֹסֵף
May to add | your father's | the of God | Jehovah | for .multitude | the heavens | as (are) of stars the | today

1696 1288 6471 505
עֲלֵיכֶם כָּכֶם אֶלֶף פְּעָמִים וִיבָרֵךְ אֶתְכֶם כַּאֲשֶׁר דִּבֶּר
said He | as | ,you | bless and | times | a thousand | than more (are) you | you

12 7379 4853 2960 5375 349
לָכֶם׃ אֵיכָה אֶשָּׂא לְבַדִּי טָרְחֲכֶם וּמַשַּׂאֲכֶם וְרִיבְכֶם׃
your and ?strife | your and burden | load the you of | by myself | I can bear | How | .you to

13 7626 3045 995 2450 582 3053
הָבוּ לָכֶם אֲנָשִׁים חֲכָמִים וּנְבֹנִים וִידֻעִים לְשִׁבְטֵיכֶם
your ,tribes | to | and known | and understanding | wise | men | you for | Take

14 1697 2896 559 6030 7218 7760
וַאֲשִׂימֵם בְּרָאשֵׁיכֶם׃ וַתַּעֲנוּ אֹתִי וַתֹּאמְרוּ טוֹב־הַדָּבָר
the thing | (is) good | ,said and | me | you And answered | your as .heads | will I and them appoint

15 502 7626 7218 3947 6213 1696 834
אֲשֶׁר־דִּבַּרְתָּ לַעֲשׂוֹת׃ וָאֶקַּח אֶת־רָאשֵׁי שִׁבְטֵיכֶם אֲנָשִׁים
men | your ,tribes | heads the of | I And took | .do to | have you spoken | which

505 8269 5921 7218 5414 3045 2450
חֲכָמִים וִידֻעִים וָאֶתֵּן אוֹתָם רָאשִׁים עֲלֵיכֶם שָׂרֵי אֲלָפִים
,thousands captains | over | over ,you | heads | them | I and appointed | and ,known | wise

7626 7860 6235 8269 2572 8269 3967 8269
וְשָׂרֵי מֵאוֹת וְשָׂרֵי חֲמִשִּׁים וְשָׂרֵי עֲשָׂרֹת וְשֹׁטְרִים לְשִׁבְטֵיכֶם׃
your for .tribes | and officers | ,tens | cap- and over tains | ,fifties over captains | and hundreds over captains | and

16 251 996 8085 559 6256 8199 6680
וָאֲצַוֶּה אֶת־שֹׁפְטֵיכֶם בָּעֵת הַהִוא לֵאמֹר שָׁמֹעַ בֵּין־אֲחֵיכֶם
your between brothers | Hear | ,saying | that | time at | judges your | I And commanded

17 5234 1616 251 996 376 6664 8199
וּשְׁפַטְתֶּם צֶדֶק בֵּין־אִישׁ וּבֵין־אָחִיו וּבֵין גֵּרוֹ׃ לֹא־תַכִּירוּ
shall You not know | his .alien | and | his brother | and | a man | between (with) righteousness | judge and

376 1481/8808/8085 1419 6996 4941 5315
פָנִים בַּמִּשְׁפָּט כַּקָּטֹן כַּגָּדֹל תִּשְׁמָעוּן לֹא תָגוּרוּ מִפְּנֵי־אִישׁ
a ;man | because of | shall you not afraid be | shall you ,hear | the as great | the small | in ;judgment | persons

7185 834 1697 430 4941 3588
כִּי הַמִּשְׁפָּט לֵאלֹהִים הוּא וְהַדָּבָר אֲשֶׁר יִקְשֶׁה מִכֶּם
for ,you | too hard | which (is) | the and thing | ;(is) | God's | the judgment | for

18 6256 6680 8085 7126
תַּקְרִבוּן אֵלַי וּשְׁמַעְתִּיו׃ וָאֲצַוֶּה אֶתְכֶם בָּעֵת הַהִוא אֵת
that | time at | you | I And commanded | shall I and .it hear | me to | shall you near bring

19 3605 3212 2722 5265 6213 834 1697 3605
כָּל־הַדְּבָרִים אֲשֶׁר תַּעֲשׂוּן׃ וַנִּסַּע מֵחֹרֵב וַנֵּלֶךְ אֵת כָּל־
all | went and (through) | from Horeb | we And up pulled | were you .do to | which | things the | all

fearful wilderness which you have seen, the way of the hill-country of the Amorites, as Jehovah our God commanded us. And we came into Kadesh-barnea. [20]And I said to you, You have come into the hill-country of the Amorites, which Jehovah our God is giving to us. [21]See, Jehovah your God has set the land before you; go up, possess it, as Jehovah the God of your fathers has spoken to you; do not fear or be afraid. [22]And you came near to me, every one of you, and said, Let us send men before us, and they shall search out the land for us, and they shall bring us back word *as to* the way in which we shall go up, and the cities to which we shall come. [23]And the thing was good in my eyes, and I took twelve men of you, one man for each tribe. [24]And they turned and went up to the hill-country and came into the valley of Eshcol, and searched it. [25]And they took of the fruit of the land with their hands and brought it down *to* us, and brought us back word, and said, The land which Jehovah our God has given us *is* good. [26]And you were not willing to go up; yea, you rebelled against the mouth of Jehovah your God, [27]and murmured in your tents, and said, Because of Jehovah's hatred *for* us, He has brought us out of the land of Egypt, to give us into the land of the Amorite to destroy us. [28]Where *shall* we go up? Our brothers have melted our hearts, saying, We have seen there a people greater and taller than we, cities great and walled up to the heavens, and also the sons of the Anakim.

הַמִּדְבָּר הַגָּדוֹל וְהַנּוֹרָא הַהוּא אֲשֶׁר רְאִיתֶם דֶּרֶךְ הַר
הָאֱמֹרִי כַּאֲשֶׁר צִוָּה יְהוָה אֱלֹהֵינוּ אֹתָנוּ וַנָּבֹא עַד קָדֵשׁ
20 בַּרְנֵעַ׃ וָאֹמַר אֲלֵכֶם בָּאתֶם עַד־הַר הָאֱמֹרִי אֲשֶׁר־יְהוָה
21 אֱלֹהֵינוּ נֹתֵן לָנוּ׃ רְאֵה נָתַן יְהוָה אֱלֹהֶיךָ לְפָנֶיךָ אֶת־
הָאָרֶץ עֲלֵה רֵשׁ כַּאֲשֶׁר דִּבֶּר יְהוָה אֱלֹהֵי אֲבֹתֶיךָ לָךְ
22 אַל־תִּירָא וְאַל־תֵּחָת׃ וַתִּקְרְבוּן אֵלַי כֻּלְּכֶם וַתֹּאמְרוּ נִשְׁלְחָה
אֲנָשִׁים לְפָנֵינוּ וְיַחְפְּרוּ־לָנוּ אֶת־הָאָרֶץ וְיָשִׁבוּ אֹתָנוּ דָּבָר
אֶת־הַדֶּרֶךְ אֲשֶׁר נַעֲלֶה־בָּהּ וְאֵת הֶעָרִים אֲשֶׁר נָבֹא אֲלֵיהֶן׃
23 וַיִּיטַב בְּעֵינַי הַדָּבָר וָאֶקַּח מִכֶּם שְׁנֵים עָשָׂר אֲנָשִׁים אִישׁ
24 אֶחָד לַשָּׁבֶט׃ וַיִּפְנוּ וַיַּעֲלוּ הָהָרָה וַיָּבֹאוּ עַד־נַחַל אֶשְׁכֹּל
25 וַיְרַגְּלוּ אֹתָהּ׃ וַיִּקְחוּ בְיָדָם מִפְּרִי הָאָרֶץ וַיּוֹרִדוּ אֵלֵינוּ
וַיָּשִׁבוּ אֹתָנוּ דָבָר וַיֹּאמְרוּ טוֹבָה הָאָרֶץ אֲשֶׁר־יְהוָה אֱלֹהֵינוּ
26 נֹתֵן לָנוּ׃ וְלֹא אֲבִיתֶם לַעֲלֹת וַתַּמְרוּ אֶת־פִּי יְהוָה אֱלֹהֵיכֶם׃
27 וַתֵּרָגְנוּ בְאָהֳלֵיכֶם וַתֹּאמְרוּ בְּשִׂנְאַת יְהוָה אֹתָנוּ הוֹצִיאָנוּ
28 מֵאֶרֶץ מִצְרָיִם לָתֵת אֹתָנוּ בְּיַד הָאֱמֹרִי לְהַשְׁמִידֵנוּ׃ אָנָה
אֲנַחְנוּ עֹלִים אַחֵינוּ הֵמַסּוּ אֶת־לְבָבֵנוּ לֵאמֹר עַם גָּדוֹל וָרָם
מִמֶּנּוּ עָרִים גְּדֹלֹת וּבְצוּרֹת בַּשָּׁמָיִם וְגַם־בְּנֵי עֲנָקִים רָאִינוּ

29 And I said to you, Do
not be terrified, nor be
afraid of them. 30 Jehovah
your God, the One going
before you, He shall fight for
you according to all that He
did for you before your eyes
in Egypt; 31 and in the
wilderness, where you have
seen how Jehovah your
God has borne you, even as
a man bears his son, in all
the way which you have
gone until you have come
to this place. 32 Yet in this[t]
thing you *are* not believing
in Jehovah your God, 33 who
went before you in the way
to seek out for you a place
for your camping, with fire
by night to show you the
way in which you should
go, and with a cloud by
day.

34 And Jehovah heard the
sound of your words and
was angry, and swore, saying, 35 Not one of these men
of this evil generation shall
see the good land which I
have sworn to give to your
fathers, 36 except Caleb the
son of Jephunneh, he shall
see it, and I shall give the
land on which he has
walked to him, and to his
sons, because he has fully
followed Jehovah. 37 And
Jehovah was angry with me
for your sake, saying, Also
you shall not go in there.
38 Joshua the son of Nun,
who stands before you, he
shall go in there; you shall
strengthen him; for he shall
cause Israel to inherit.
39 And your infants, *of* whom
you said, They are a prey,
and your sons who today
have no knowledge of good
or evil, they shall go in there,
and I will give it to them, and
they shall possess it.

3372/3808 6206 3808 559 8033
29 שם: ואמר אלכם לא־תערצון ולא־תיראון מהם:
.them of | be afraid | and not | be Do terrified | not | ,you to | I And said | .there

834 3605 3898 6440 3212 430 3068
30 יהוה אלהיכם ההלך לפניכם הוא ילחם לכם ככל אשר
which | according all to | for you | shall fight | He | before ,you | One the going | God your | Jeho-vah

7200 4057 5869 4714 6213
31 עשה אתכם במצרים לעיניכם: ובמדבר אשר ראית
have you seen | where | in and wilderness the | before ;eyes your | Egypt in | you for | did He

3605 1121 376 5375 430 3068 5375
אשר נשאך יהוה אלהיך כאשר ישא־איש את־בנו בכל־
all in | his ,son | a man | bears | as | ,God your Jehovah | has you borne | how

1697 2088 4725 935 5704 3212 834 1870
32 הדרך אשר הלכתם עד־באכם עד־המקום הזה: ובדבר
in Yet thing | .this | place | to | have you until come | have you gone | which | way the

6440 3212 430 3068 539 369 2088
33 הזה אינכם מאמינם ביהוה אלהיכם: ההלך לפניכם
you before | went who | ,God your | Jehovah in | (are) believing | you not | this

7200 3915 784 2583 4725 8446 1870
בדרך לתור לכם מקום לחנתכם באש ׀ לילה לראתכם
you show to | by night | with fire | your for camping | place a | for you | seek to out | the in way

3068 8085 3119 6051 3212 834 1870
34 בדרך אשר תלכו־בה ובענן יומם: וישמע יהוה את־
Jehovah | And heard | by .day | with and cloud a | in | you should go | which | way the

376 7200 559 7650 7107 1697 6963
35 קול דבריכם ויקצף וישבע לאמר: אם־יראה איש
a of man | shall see | not | ,saying | ,swore and | was and angry | your words of | the sound

834 2876 776 2088 7451 1755 428 582
באנשים האלה הדור הרע הזה את הארץ הטובה אשר
which | good | the land | this | evil | genera-tion | ,these | men

3312/1121 3616 2108 1 5414 7650
36 נשבעתי לתת לאבתיכם: זולתי כלב בן־יפנה הוא
he | Jephun-,neh | the of son Caleb | except | ;fathers your to | give to | swore I

1121 1869 834 776 5414 7200
יראנה ולו־אתן את־הארץ אשר דרך־בה ולבניו יען אשר
because | to and sons his | ,on | he walked has | which | the land | I give shall | to and him | shall ;it see

559 1558 3068 599 3068 310 4390
37 מלא אחרי יהוה: גם־בי התאנף יהוה בגללכם לאמר
,saying | your for ,sake | Jehovah | angry was | with Also me | .Jehovah | after | has he filled

6440 5975 5121/1121/3091 8033 935
38 גם־אתה לא־תבא שם: יהושע בן־נון העמד לפניך הוא
he | before ,you | one the standing | ,Nun the of son | Joshua | .there | shall in go | not you Also

2945 3478 5157 2388 8033 935
39 יבא שמה אתו חזק כי־הוא ינחלנה את־ישראל: וטפכם
your And children | .Israel | (it) inherit to | cause shall | he for | shall strengthen | You him | .there | shall in go

3117 3045 3808 1121 1961 957 559
אשר אמרתם לבז יהיה ובניכם אשר לא־ידעו היום
today | have of knowledge | not | who | your and sons | They ;become shall | prey a | ,said you | (of) whom

3423 5414 8033 935 7 7451 2896
טוב ורע המה יבאו שמה ולהם אתננה והם יירשוה:
.it possess shall | and they | will I ,it give | to and them | ,there | shall in go | they | or ,evil | good

40And you, turn yourselves and travel toward the wilderness, the way of the Red Sea.

41And you answered and said to me, We have sinned against Jehovah; we shall go up, and we shall fight, according to all that which Jehovah our God has commanded us. And you each one girded on his weapons of war, and you thought it easy to go up to the hill country. 42And Jehovah said to me, Say to them, You shall not go up, nor fight, for I am not in your midst; lest you be struck before your enemies. 43And I spoke to you, and you did not listen, and rebelled against the mouth of Jehovah, and acted proudly, and went up into the hill-country. 44And the Amorites who lived in that hill-country came out to meet you, and they chased you, as the bees do, and struck you in Seir, to Hormah. 45And you returned and wept before Jehovah, but Jehovah did not listen to your voice, nor did He give ear to you. 46And you lived many days in Kadesh, according to the days that you remained there.

6030 5488/3220 1870 4057 5265 6437
40 41 וְאַתֶּם פְּנוּ לָכֶם וּסְעוּ הַמִּדְבָּרָה דֶּרֶךְ יַם־סוּף׃ וַתַּעֲנוּ
you And .Reeds the the (by) the toward and your- turn (as) And
answered of Sea of way ,wilderness journey selves ,you (for)
3605 3898 5927 3068 2398 559
וַתֹּאמְרוּ אֵלַי חָטָאנוּ לַיהוָה אֲנַחְנוּ נַעֲלֶה וְנִלְחַמְנוּ כְּכֹל
according we and shall We against have We ,me to said and
all to ,fight shall ,up go .Jehovah sinned
4121 3628 376 2296 430 3068 6680
אֲשֶׁר־צִוָּנוּ יְהוָה אֱלֹהֵינוּ וַתַּחְגְּרוּ אִישׁ אֶת־כְּלֵי מִלְחַמְתּוֹ
,his war weapons each you And .God our Jehovah com- which
of one on girded us manded
3808 559 3068 559 2022 5927 1951
42 וַתָּהִינוּ לַעֲלֹת הָהָרָה׃ וַיֹּאמֶר יְהוָה אֵלַי אֱמֹר לָהֶם לֹא
not to Say ,me to Jehovah But the to up go to re- and
,them said .hill-country easy as garded
6440 5061 3808 7130 369 3588 3898 3808 5927
תַעֲלוּ וְלֹא־תִלָּחֲמוּ כִּי אֵינֶנִּי בְּקִרְבְּכֶם וְלֹא תִּנָּגְפוּ לִפְנֵי
before be You lest ,midst your in am I for ;fight and shall you
struck not not ,up go
3068 6310 4784 8085 3808 1696 341
43 אֹיְבֵיכֶם׃ וָאֲדַבֵּר אֲלֵיכֶם וְלֹא שְׁמַעְתֶּם וַתַּמְרוּ אֶת־פִּי יְהוָה
Jeho- mouth re- and did you but ,you to I And your
,vah's against belled listen not spoke .enemies
2022 3427 567 5927 2022 5927 2102
44 וַתָּזִדוּ וַתַּעֲלוּ הָהָרָה׃ וַיֵּצֵא הָאֱמֹרִי הַיֹּשֵׁב בָּהָר הַהוּא
that in living the came And the into and acted and
hill-country Amorites out .hill-country up went proudly
3807 1682 6213 7291 7125
לִקְרַאתְכֶם וַיִּרְדְּפוּ אֶתְכֶם כַּאֲשֶׁר תַּעֲשֶׂינָה הַדְּבֹרִים וַיַּכְּתוּ
and ,bees the do as ,you they and ,you meet to
struck chased
3068 6440 1058 7725 2767 5704 8165
45 אֶתְכֶם בְּשֵׂעִיר עַד־חָרְמָה׃ וַתָּשֻׁבוּ וַתִּבְכּוּ לִפְנֵי יְהוָה
,Jehovah before and you And .Hormah as ,Seir in you
wept returned as far
6946 3427 238 3808 6963 3068 8085 3808
46 וְלֹא־שָׁמַע יְהוָה בְּקֹלְכֶם וְלֹא הֶאֱזִין אֲלֵיכֶם׃ וַתֵּשְׁבוּ בְקָדֵשׁ
Kadesh in you And ,you to He did and your to Jehovah did but
lived ,ear give not voice listen not
3427 834 3117 7227 3117
יָמִים רַבִּים כַּיָּמִים אֲשֶׁר יְשַׁבְתֶּם׃
lived you which according ,many days
.there days the to

CAP. II ב

CHAPTER 2

CHAPTER 2

1And we turned and traveled into the wilderness, the way of the Red Sea, as Jehovah had spoken to me; and we went around the mountain of Seir many days. 2And Jehovah spoke to me, saying, 3You have gone around this mountain long enough; turn yourselves northward. 4And command the people, saying, You shall pass over into the border of your brothers, the sons of Esau, who live in Seir, and they shall be afraid of you. And you shall be very careful;

3068 1696 5488/3220 1870 4057 5265 6437
1 וַנֵּפֶן וַנִּסַּע הַמִּדְבָּרָה דֶּרֶךְ יַם־סוּף כַּאֲשֶׁר דִּבֶּר יְהוָה
Jehovah had as ,Reeds the the the into and we And
spoken of Sea of way wilderness journeyed turned
559 7227 3117 8165 2022 5437
2 אֵלָי וַנָּסָב אֶת־הַר־שֵׂעִיר יָמִים רַבִּים׃ ס וַיֹּאמֶר
And .many days Seir Mount we and ,me to
spoke around went
6437 2088 2022 5439 7227 559 3068
3 יְהוָה אֵלַי לֵאמֹר׃ רַב־לָכֶם סֹב אֶת־הָהָר הַזֶּה פְּנוּ לָכֶם
your- turn ;this mountain going to Much ,saying to Jehovah
selves around you me
251 1366 5674 859 6680 5971 6828
4 צָפֹנָה׃ וְאֶת־הָעָם צַו לֵאמֹר אַתֶּם עֹבְרִים בִּגְבוּל אֲחֵיכֶם
your the (are) You ,saying com- the And north-
brothers of border over passing ,mand people .ward
3966 8104 3372 8165 3427 6215/1121
בְּנֵי־עֵשָׂו הַיֹּשְׁבִים בְּשֵׂעִיר וְיִירְאוּ מִכֶּם וְנִשְׁמַרְתֶּם מְאֹד׃
.very shall you and ;you they and ,Seir in ones the Esau the
careful be fear shall living of sons

[5]you shall not fight against
them, for I will not give their
land to you, *even* to a step of
a sole of a foot, for I have
given Mount Seir to Esau as
a possession. [6]You shall
buy food from them with
silver, and you shall eat; and
you shall buy water from
them with silver, and you
shall drink. [7]For Jehovah
your God has blessed you
with all the work of your
hands; He has known your
walking *through* this great
wilderness. Jehovah your
God *has been* with you
these forty years; you have
lacked nothing. [8]And when
we passed on from our
brothers, the sons of Esau,
those living in Seir, by the
way of the Arabah, by Elath,
and by Ezion-geber, we
turned and passed on by the
way of the wilderness of
Moab. [9]And Jehovah said
to me, Do not trouble Moab,
nor stir yourself up against
them in battle, for I will not
give their land to you *for* a
possession. For I have given
Ar *as* a possession to the
sons of Lot. [10]The Emim
lived there in days gone by,
a great and pletiful
people, and tall as the
Anakim; [11]they are reckoned
to be giants, they too, like
the Anakim; but the
Moabites call them Emim.
[12]And the Horites lived in
Seir before; and the sons of
Esau dispossessed them
and destroyed them from
before them, and lived in
their place, as Israel has
done to the land of his
possession, which Jehovah
has given to them. [13]Now,
rise up and pass yourselves
over the torrent Zered; and
we crossed over the torrent
Zered. [14]And the days in
which we came from
Kadesh-barnea, until we
had crossed over the torrent

3709 4096 776 5414 3808 3588 1624
5 אַל־תִּתְגָּרוּ בָם כִּי לֹא־אֶתֵּן לָכֶם מֵאַרְצָם עַד מִדְרַךְ כַּף־
a step a (even) ,land their to will I not for against be Do not
of sole of to you give them up stirred

7666 400 8165 2022 5414 6215 3425 7272
6 רָגֶל כִּי־יְרֻשָּׁה לְעֵשָׂו נָתַתִּי אֶת־הַר שֵׂעִיר׃ אֹכֶל תִּשְׁבְּרוּ
shall You food .Seir Mount have I to a as for a
buy given Esau possession ;foot

3701 3739 4325 398 3701
מֵאִתָּם בַּכֶּסֶף וַאֲכַלְתֶּם וְגַם־מַיִם תִּכְרוּ מֵאִתָּם בַּכֶּסֶף
with from shall you water and shall you and with from
,silver them bargain ;eat ,silver them

3045 3027 4639 3605 1288 430 3068 8354
7 וּשְׁתִיתֶם׃ כִּי יְהוָה אֱלֹהֶיךָ בֵּרַכְךָ בְּכֹל מַעֲשֵׂה יָדֶךָ יָדַע
has He your work the in has God your Jehovah For you and
known ;hand of all you blessed .drink shall

3068 8141 703 2088 2088 1419 4057 3212
לֶכְתְּךָ אֶת־הַמִּדְבָּר הַגָּדֹל הַזֶּה זֶה ׀ אַרְבָּעִים שָׁנָה יְהוָה
Jehovah years forty these ;this great wilderness your
(through) walking

1121 25 5674 1697 2637 3808 430
8 אֱלֹהֶיךָ עִמָּךְ לֹא חָסַרְתָּ דָּבָר׃ וַנַּעֲבֹר מֵאֵת אַחֵינוּ בְנֵי־
the our from when and a have you not (been has) your
of sons brothers with passed we ,thing lacked ;you with God

6100 359 6160 1870 6165 3427 6215
עֵשָׂו הַיֹּשְׁבִים בְּשֵׂעִיר מִדֶּרֶךְ הָעֲרָבָה מֵאֵילַת וּמֵעֶצְיֹן
from and from the the from ,Seir in ones the Esau
Ezion- Elath ,Arabah of way living

559 4124 4057 1870 5674 6437
9 גָּבֶר ס וַנֵּפֶן וַנַּעֲבֹר דֶּרֶךְ מִדְבַּר מוֹאָב׃ וַיֹּאמֶר
said And .Moab the the by and we ,geber
of wilderness of way passed turned

4421 1624/3808 4124 6696/3808 3068
יְהוָה אֵלַי אַל־תָּצַר אֶת־מוֹאָב וְאַל־תִּתְגָּר בָּם מִלְחָמָה
(in) against stir and Moab Do not ,me to Jeho-
,battle them up yourself not besiege vah

6144 5414 3876/1121 3425 776 5414 3808
כִּי לֹא־אֶתֵּן לְךָ מֵאַרְצוֹ יְרֻשָּׁה כִּי לִבְנֵי־לוֹט נָתַתִּי אֶת־עָר
Ar have I Lot the to for a (for) their to will I not for
given of sons ;possession land you give

7311 7227 1419 5971 3427 6440 368 3425
10 יְרֻשָּׁה׃ הָאֵמִים לְפָנִים יָשְׁבוּ בָהּ עַם גָּדוֹל וְרַב וָרָם
and and great a ,it in lived formerly Emim The a (as)
tall many people .possession

4125 6062 2803 7497 6062
11 כָּעֲנָקִים׃ רְפָאִים יֵחָשְׁבוּ אַף־הֵם כָּעֲנָקִים וְהַמֹּאָבִים
the but the like They also reck- are giants the as
Moabites ;Anakim be to oned .Anakim

1121 6440 2753 3427 8165 368 7121
12 יִקְרְאוּ לָהֶם אֵמִים׃ וּבְשֵׂעִיר יָשְׁבוּ הַחֹרִים לְפָנִים וּבְנֵי
the and ,formerly the lived in And .Emim them call
of sons Horites Seir

8478 3427 6440 8045 3423 6215
עֵשָׂו יִירָשׁוּם וַיַּשְׁמִידוּם מִפְּנֵיהֶם וַיֵּשְׁבוּ תַּחְתָּם כַּאֲשֶׁר
as their in and from destroyed and dispos- Esau
stead lived ,them before them them sessed

6258 3068 5414 834 3425 776 3478 6213
13 עָשָׂה יִשְׂרָאֵל לְאֶרֶץ יְרֻשָּׁתוֹ אֲשֶׁר־נָתַן יְהוָה לָהֶם׃ עַתָּה
Now to Jehovah has which his of the to Israel has
.them given possession land done

2218 5158 5674 2218 5158 5674 6965
קֻמוּ וְעִבְרוּ לָכֶם אֶת־נַחַל זָרֶד וַנַּעֲבֹר אֶת־נַחַל זָרֶד׃
.Zered the we And .Zered the your- cross and rise
torrent over crossed torrent selves over up

5674 5704 6947 3212 834 3117
14 וְהַיָּמִים אֲשֶׁר־הָלַכְנוּ ׀ מִקָּדֵשׁ בַּרְנֵעַ עַד אֲשֶׁר־עָבַרְנוּ אֶת־
had we until ,barnea from came we which the And
over passed Kadesh- days

Zered, *were* thirty-eight years, until the end of all the generation, *even* the men of war *were* destroyed from the midst of the camp, as Jehovah swore to them. [15]And the hand of Jehovah was also against them, to destroy them from the midst of the camp, until they were consumed.

[16]And it happened, when all the men of war had finished dying from among people, [17]Jehovah spoke to me, saying, [18]You *are* going over the border of Moab today, *to* Ar, [19]and you shall draw near, across from the sons of Ammon; you shall not vex them, nor stir yourself up against them, for I have not given of the land of the sons of Ammon to you *for* a possession, For I have given it *for* a possession to the sons of Lot. [20]It is reckoned a land of giants, even it; giants formerly lived in it, and the Ammonites call them Zamzummim; [21]a great and plentiful people, and tall as the Anakim. And Jehovah destroyed them before them, and they expelled them, and lived in their place; [22]as He had done for the sons of Esau, who live *in* Seir, when He destroyed the Horites from before them, and they expelled them, and lived in their place until today. [23]And the Avvim who lived in villages as far as Azzah, *the* Caphtorim coming out of Caphtor destroyed them, *and lived* in their place. [24]Rise up, set out and cross over the river Arnon; behold, I have given Sihon the king of Heshbon, the Amorite, and his land into your hands. Begin to possess, and stir yourselves up against him *in* battle. [25]Today I will begin to put your dread and your fear on the face of the people under all the heavens, who will

נחל זרד שלשים ושמנה שנה עד־תם כל־הדור אנשי

15 המלחמה מקרב המחנה כאשר נשבע יהוה להם׃ וגם

יד־יהוה היתה בם להמם מקרב המחנה עד תמם׃

16 ויהי כאשר־תמו כל־אנשי המלחמה למות מקרב העם׃

17 ס וידבר יהוה אלי לאמר׃
18 אתה עבר היום את־גבול

19 מואב את־ער׃ וקרבת מול בני עמון אל־תצרם ואל־

תתגר בם כי לא־אתן מארץ בני־עמון לך ירשה כי לבני־

20 לוט נתתיה ירשה׃ ארץ־רפאים תחשב אף־הוא רפאים

21 ישבו־בה לפנים והעמנים יקראו להם זמזמים׃ עם גדול

ורב ורם כענקים וישמידם יהוה מפניהם ויירשם וישבו

22 תחתם׃ כאשר עשה לבני עשו הישבים בשעיר אשר

השמיד את־החרי מפניהם ויירשם וישבו תחתם עד היום

23 הזה׃ והעוים הישבים בחצרים עד־עזה כפתרים היצאים

24 מכפתור השמידם וישבו תחתם׃ קומו סעו ועברו את־

נחל ארנן ראה נתתי בידך את־סיחן מלך־חשבון האמרי

25 ואת־ארצו החל רש והתגר בו מלחמה׃ היום הזה אחל

תת פחדך ויראתך על־פני העמים תחת כל־השמים

hear your fame, and will tremble and writhe because of you.

[26]And I sent messengers from the wilderness of Kedemoth to Sihon the king of Heshbon *with* words of peace, saying, [27]Let me pass on the highway through your land; I will go on the highway; I will not turn aside *to* the right or the left; [28]you shall sell me food for silver, and I shall eat; and you shall give me water for money, and I will drink. Only, let me pass through on my feet, [29]as the sons of Esau who live in Seir, and the Moabites who live in Ar, have done to me, until I have crossed over the Jordan, to the land which Jehovah our God *is* giving to us. [30]And Sihon the king of Heshbon was not willing to let us pass by him, for Jehovah your God had hardened his spirit, and had emboldened his heart, so as to give him into your hand, as it is this day.

[31]And Jehovah said to me, Behold, I have begun to give Sihon and his land before you; begin to possess, in order to possess his land. [32]And Sihon came out to meet us, he and all his people, to battle at Jahaz. [33]And Jehovah our God delivered him before us, and we struck him and his sons, and all his people. [34]And we captured all his cities at that time, and utterly destroyed every city; men and women and little ones. We did not leave a remnant. [35]Only, we plundered the cattle for ourselves, and we took the plunder of the cities. [36]From Aroer, which is by the lip of the river Arnon, and the city beside the river, even to Gilead, there was not a city which *was* too

4397 7971 2342 7264 8088 8085
26 אֲשֶׁר יִשְׁמְעוּן שִׁמְעֲךָ וְרָגְזוּ וְחָלוּ מִפָּנֶיךָ׃ וָאֶשְׁלַח מַלְאָכִים
messengers I And because and and your will who
sent you of writhe tremble name hear

7965 1697 2809 4428 5511 69:82 4057
מִמִּדְבַּר קְדֵמוֹת אֶל־סִיחוֹן מֶלֶךְ חֶשְׁבּוֹן דִּבְרֵי שָׁלוֹם
,peace (with) ,Heshbon the Sihon to Kedemoth the from
of words of king of wilderness

5493 32:12 1870 1870 776 5674 559
27 לֵאמֹר׃ אֶעְבְּרָה בְאַרְצֶךָ בַּדֶּרֶךְ בַּדֶּרֶךְ אֵלֵךְ לֹא אָסוּר
will I not will I the on the on through pass me Let ,saying
aside turn ;go way way ;land your

3701 4325 398 7666 3701 400 8040 3225
28 יָמִין וּשְׂמֹאול׃ אֹכֶל בַּכֶּסֶף תַּשְׁבִּרֵנִי וְאָכַלְתִּי וּמַיִם בַּכֶּסֶף
for and I and shall you for food ;left the or the (to)
silver ,water ;eat shall me sell silver right

1121 6213 7272 5674 7535 8354 5414
29 תִּתֶּן־לִי וְשָׁתִיתִי רַק אֶעְבְּרָה בְרַגְלָי׃ כַּאֲשֶׁר עָשׂוּ־לִי בְּנֵי
the to have as my on me let only shall I and ,me to you
of sons me done ;feet through pass ;drink give shall

5704 6144 3427 4125 8165 3427 6215
עֵשָׂו הַיֹּשְׁבִים בְּשֵׂעִיר וְהַמּוֹאָבִים הַיֹּשְׁבִים בְּעָר עַד אֲשֶׁר־
until ,Ar in living the and ,Seir in living Esau
Moabites

5414 430 3068 834 776 3383 5674
אֶעֱבֹר אֶת־הַיַּרְדֵּן אֶל־הָאָרֶץ אֲשֶׁר־יְהוָה אֱלֹהֵינוּ נֹתֵן לָנוּ׃
.us to (is) our Jehovah which the to the have I
giving God land Jordan over crossed

3068 / 7185 5674 2809 4428 5511 14 3808
30 וְלֹא אָבָה סִיחֹן מֶלֶךְ חֶשְׁבּוֹן הַעֲבִרֵנוּ בּוֹ כִּי־הִקְשָׁה יְהוָה
Jehovah had for through let to Heshbon the Sihon was And
hardened him pass of king willing not

3117 3027 5414 3824 553 7307 430
אֱלֹהֶיךָ אֶת־רוּחוֹ וְאִמֵּץ אֶת־לְבָבוֹ לְמַעַן תִּתּוֹ בְיָדְךָ כַּיּוֹם
(is it) as into give to as so his had and his your
day ,hand your him ,heart emboldened ,spirit God

6440 5414 2490 7200 3068 559 2088
31 הַזֶּה׃ ס וַיֹּאמֶר יְהוָה אֵלַי רְאֵה הַחִלֹּתִי תֵּת לְפָנֶיךָ
before to have I ,See ,me to Jehovah And .this
you give begun said

5927 776 3423 3423 2490 776 5511
32 אֶת־סִיחֹן וְאֶת־אַרְצוֹ הָחֵל רָשׁ לָרֶשֶׁת אֶת־אַרְצוֹ׃ וַיֵּצֵא
And his to order in to begin his and Sihon
out came .land possess ,possess ;land

5414 3096 4421 5971 3605 7125 5511
33 סִיחֹן לִקְרָאתֵנוּ הוּא וְכָל־עַמּוֹ לַמִּלְחָמָה יָהְצָה׃ וַיִּתְּנֵהוּ
gave And at battle to his and he ,us meet to Sihon
him Jahaz people all

5971 3605 1121 5221 6440 430 3068
יְהוָה אֱלֹהֵינוּ לְפָנֵינוּ וַנַּךְ אֹתוֹ וְאֶת־בָּנָיו וְאֶת־כָּל־עַמּוֹ׃
his all and his and him we and before God our Jehovah
,people sons struck ,us

4962 5892 3605 2763 6256 5892 3605 3920
34 וַנִּלְכֹּד אֶת־כָּל־עָרָיו בָּעֵת הַהִוא וַנַּחֲרֵם אֶת־כָּל־עִיר מְתִם
,men ,city every com- and that at his all we And
destroyed pletely time cities captured

962 929 7535 8300 7604 3808 2945 832
35 וְהַנָּשִׁים וְהַטָּף לֹא הִשְׁאַרְנוּ שָׂרִיד׃ רַק הַבְּהֵמָה בָּזַזְנוּ
we cattle the ,only a did we not and and
plundered ;survivor leave ;ones little women

8193 834 6177 3920 834 5892 7998
36 לָנוּ וּשְׁלַל הֶעָרִים אֲשֶׁר לָכָדְנוּ׃ מֵעֲרֹעֵר אֲשֶׁר עַל־שְׂפַת־
of edge the by which Aroer From .took we which cities the the and for
(is) of spoil ,ourselves

7151 1961 1568 5158 834 5892 769 5158
נַחַל אַרְנֹן וְהָעִיר אֲשֶׁר בַּנַּחַל וְעַד־הַגִּלְעָד לֹא הָיְתָה קִרְיָה
city a there not ,Gilead even beside which the and Arnon the
was to ,river the (is) city river

high for us. Jehovah our
God delivered all before us.
[37]Only, you did not come
near to the land of the sons
of Ammon, any part of the
river Jabbok, and the cities
of the hill-country, and all
which Jehovah our God had
forbidden us.

CHAPTER 3

[1]And we turned and went
up by the way of Bashan,
and Og the king of Bashan
came out to met us, he and
all his people, to battle *at*
Edrei. [2]And Jehovah said to
me, Do not fear him, for I
have given him into your
hand, and all his people, and
his land. And you shall do to
him as you have done to
Sihon the king of the
Amorites who lived in
Heshbon. [3]And Jehovah
your God also gave Og the
king of Bashan into our
hands, and all his people.
And we struck him until not
one survivor *was* left to
him. [4]And we captured all
his cities at that time, there
not being a city which we
did not take from them, sixty
cities, all the region of
Argob, the kingdom of Og in
Bashan. [5]All these cities
were fortified with high
walls, gates and double-
leaved doors, besides a
great many *of* the unwalled
towns. [6]And we utterly
destroyed them, as we had
done to Sihon the king of
Heshbon, destroying every
city, the men, the women
and the little ones. [7]And we
plundered for ourselves all
the livestock, and the
plunder of the cities.
[8]And we took the land
that was beyond the Jordan
from the valley of Arnon to
Mount Hermon, out of the
hand of the two kings of the
Amorites. [9]*The* Sidonians

6440 430 3068 5414 3605 7682
אֲשֶׁר שָׂגְבָה מִמֶּנּוּ אֶת־הַכֹּל נָתַן יְהוָה אֱלֹהֵינוּ לְפָנֵינוּ׃
before us God our Jehovah gave all ;us for too was high that

5892 2999 5158 3027 7126 3808 5983/1121 776 7535
37 רַק אֶל־אֶרֶץ בְּנֵי־עַמּוֹן לֹא קָרָבְתָּ כָּל־יַד נַחַל יַבֹּק וְעָרֵי
and of cities the ,Jabbok river the hand of any did you not ,near come Ammon the of sons the of land to ,Only

430 3068 6680 834 3605 2022
הָהָר וְכֹל אֲשֶׁר־צִוָּה יְהוָה אֱלֹהֵינוּ׃
.God our Jehovah had (us) commanded which and all hill- the ,country

CAP. III ג

CHAPTER 3

7125 1316 5747 5927 1316 1870 5927 6437
1 וַנֵּפֶן וַנַּעַל דֶּרֶךְ הַבָּשָׁן וַיֵּצֵא עוֹג מֶלֶךְ־הַבָּשָׁן לִקְרָאתֵנוּ
,us meet to Bashan the of king Og out came and ,Bashan the (by) way up went and we And turned

3808 3068 559 154 4421 5971 3605
2 הוּא וְכָל־עַמּוֹ לַמִּלְחָמָה אֶדְרֶעִי׃ וַיֹּאמֶר יְהוָה אֵלַי אַל־
not ,me to Jehovah said And (at) .Edrei to battle his people and all he

776 5971 3605 5414 3027/3588 3372
תִּירָא אֹתוֹ כִּי בְיָדְךָ נָתַתִּי אֹתוֹ וְאֶת־כָּל־עַמּוֹ וְאֶת־אַרְצוֹ
his ;land and his people all and ,him have I given into hand your for ,him Do fear

3427 834 567 4428 5511 6213 6213
וְעָשִׂיתָ לּוֹ כַּאֲשֶׁר עָשִׂיתָ לְסִיחֹן מֶלֶךְ הָאֱמֹרִי אֲשֶׁר יוֹשֵׁב
(was) living who the Amorite the of king ,Sihon to have you done as him to you and do shall

4428 5747 1571 3027 430 3068 5414 2809
3 בְּחֶשְׁבּוֹן׃ וַיִּתֵּן יְהוָה אֱלֹהֵינוּ בְּיָדֵנוּ גַּם אֶת־עוֹג מֶלֶךְ־
the of king Og also our into hands our God Jehovah And gave in .Heshbon

8300 7604 3808 5704 5221 5971 3605 1316
הַבָּשָׁן וְאֶת־כָּל־עַמּוֹ וַנַּכֵּהוּ עַד־בִּלְתִּי הִשְׁאִיר־לוֹ שָׂרִיד׃
a .survivor to him (one) left not until we and him struck his ;people all and ,Bashan

834 7151 1961 3808 6256 5892 3605 3920
4 וַנִּלְכֹּד אֶת־כָּל־עָרָיו בָּעֵת הַהִוא לֹא הָיְתָה קִרְיָה אֲשֶׁר
which a city there was not ;that at time his cities all we And captured

4467 709 2256 3605 5892 8346 3947
לֹא־לָקַחְנוּ מֵאִתָּם שִׁשִּׁים עִיר כָּל־חֶבֶל אַרְגֹּב מַמְלֶכֶת
the of kingdom ,Argob the of region all ,cities sixty from ,them did we take not

1817 1364 2346 1219 5892 428 3605 1316 5747
5 עוֹג בַּבָּשָׁן׃ כָּל־אֵלֶּה עָרִים בְּצֻרֹת חוֹמָה גְבֹהָה דְּלָתַיִם
double- (doors) leaved ,high walls fortified with cities (were) those All in .Bashan Og

2763 3966 7235 6521 5892 1280
6 וּבְרִיחַ לְבַד מֵעָרֵי הַפְּרָזִי הַרְבֵּה מְאֹד׃ וַנַּחֲרֵם אוֹתָם
,them we And destroyed completely .very many ,unwalled the towns besides and ,bars

4962 5892 3605 2763 2809 4428 5511 6213
כַּאֲשֶׁר עָשִׂינוּ לְסִיחֹן מֶלֶךְ חֶשְׁבּוֹן הַחֲרֵם כָּל־עִיר מְתִם
the ,men ,city every com- destroy pletely to ,Heshbon the of king to ,Sihon had we done as

962 5892 7998 929 3605 2945 802
7 הַנָּשִׁים וְהַטָּף׃ וְכָל־הַבְּהֵמָה וּשְׁלַל הֶעָרִים בַּזּוֹנוּ לָנוּ׃
for ourselves plun- dered we cities the the of spoil and the cattle and all the and ;ones little the ,women

567 4428 8147 3027 776 6256 3947
8 וַנִּקַּח בָּעֵת הַהִוא אֶת־הָאָרֶץ מִיַּד שְׁנֵי מַלְכֵי הָאֱמֹרִי
the Amorites the of kings two from the of hand land the that at time we And took

call Hermon Sirion, and the Amorites call it Senir—[10]all the cities of the tableland, and all Gilead, and all Bashan, to Salcah and Edrei, cities of the kingdom of Og in Bashan. [11]For only Og the king of Bashan remained of the rest of the giants. Behold, his bedstead *was* a bedstead of iron; is it not in Rabbah of the sons of Ammon, nine cubits long and four cubits broad, by the cubit of a man? [12]And this *is the* land we possessed at that time: from Aroer by the valley of Arnon, and half the hill-country of Gilead, and its cities I gave to the Reubenites and to the Gadites. [13]And the rest of Gilead, and all Bashan, the kingdom of Og, I gave to the half tribe of Manasseh; all the region of Argob, to all Bashan that is called the land of the giants. [14]Jair the son of Manasseh took all the region of Argob, to the border of the Geshurites and the Maachathites, and called them, even Bashan, after his own name, Towns of Jair, until today. [15]And I gave Gilead to Machir. [16]And to the Reubenites and to the Gadites I gave from Gilead even to the valley of Arnon, the middle of the valley and *its* border; even to the river Jabbok *which is* the border of the sons of Ammon; [17]and the Arabah, the Jordan and *its* border, from Chinnereth even to the sea of the Arabah, the Salt Sea, under the slopes of Pisgah eastward.

[18]And I commanded you at that time, saying,

6722 2768 2022 769 5158 3383 5676
9 אֲשֶׁר בְּעֵבֶר הַיַּרְדֵּן מִנַּחַל אַרְנֹן עַד־הַר חֶרְמוֹן׃ צִידֹנִים
(The) .Hermon Mount to Arnon the from the beyond that
Sidonians of valley torrent Jordan (was)

5892 3605 8148 7121 567 8503 2768 7121
10 יִקְרְאוּ לְחֶרְמוֹן שִׂרְיֹן וְהָאֱמֹרִי יִקְרְאוּ־לוֹ שְׂנִיר׃ כֹּל ׀ עָרֵי
the All .Senir it call the and ;Sirion Hermon call
of cities Amorites

5892 184 5548 5704 1316 3605 1568 3605 4334
הַמִּישֹׁר וְכָל־הַגִּלְעָד וְכָל־הַבָּשָׁן עַד־סַלְכָה וְאֶדְרֶעִי עָרֵי
cities and Salcah to ,Bashan and ,Gilead and the
of ,Edrei all all ,plain

3499 7604 1316 4428 5747 1316 5747 4467
11 מַמְלֶכֶת עוֹג בַּבָּשָׁן׃ כִּי רַק־עוֹג מֶלֶךְ הַבָּשָׁן נִשְׁאַר מִיֶּתֶר
the of remained Bashan the Og only For in Og the
of rest of king .Bashan of kingdom

1121 7237 3808 1270 6210 6210/2009 7497
הָרְפָאִים הִנֵּה עַרְשׂוֹ עֶרֶשׂ בַּרְזֶל הֲלֹה הִוא בְּרַבַּת בְּנֵי
the Rabbah in it is ;iron bed- a bed- his ,behold the
of sons of not of stead (was) stead ;giants

520 7341 520 702 753 520 8677 5983
עַמּוֹן תֵּשַׁע אַמּוֹת אָרְכָּהּ וְאַרְבַּע אַמּוֹת רָחְבָּהּ בְּאַמַּת־
the by its cubits and its cubits Nine ?Ammon
of cubit breadth (was) four length (was)

6171 6216 3423 2088 776 376
12 אִישׁ׃ וְאֶת־הָאָרֶץ הַזֹּאת יָרַשְׁנוּ בָּעֵת הַהִוא מֵעֲרֹעֵר
from :that time at we this land And a
,Aroer possessed .man

7206 5414 5892 1568 2022 2677 769 5158
אֲשֶׁר־עַל־נַחַל אַרְנֹן וַחֲצִי הַר־הַגִּלְעָד וְעָרָיו נָתַתִּי לָרְאוּבֵנִי
the to gave I its and Gilead the and ,Arnon the by which
Reubenites cities of hill-country half of valley torrent (is)

2677 5414 5747 4467 1316 3605 1568 3499 1425
13 וְלַגָּדִי׃ וְיֶתֶר הַגִּלְעָד וְכָל־הַבָּשָׁן מַמְלֶכֶת עוֹג נָתַתִּי לַחֲצִי
the to gave I ,Og the ,Bashan and Gilead the and to and
half of kingdom all of rest ;Gadites the

7121 1931 1316 3605 709 2256 3605 4519 7626
שֵׁבֶט הַמְנַשֶּׁה כֹּל חֶבֶל הָאַרְגֹּב לְכָל־הַבָּשָׁן הַהוּא יִקָּרֵא
is that ,Bashan concern- ;Argob the all ,Manasseh tribe
called all ing of region of

709 2256 3605 3947 1121 2971 7497 776
14 אֶרֶץ רְפָאִים׃ יָאִיר בֶּן־מְנַשֶּׁה לָקַח אֶת־כָּל־חֶבֶל אַרְגֹּב
,Argob the all took Manasseh the Jair the land the
region of son .giants of

8034 7121 4602 1651 1366
עַד־גְּבוּל הַגְּשׁוּרִי וְהַמַּעֲכָתִי וַיִּקְרָא אֹתָם עַל־שְׁמוֹ אֶת־
his after ,them and the and the border as
,name own called ,Maachatites Geshurites as far

1568 5414 4353 2088 3117/5704/2971 2333 1316
15 הַבָּשָׁן חַוֺּת יָאִיר עַד הַיּוֹם הַזֶּה׃ וּלְמָכִיר נָתַתִּי אֶת־הַגִּלְעָד׃
.Gilead gave I to And .this day until ,Jair towns ,Bashan
Machir of

8437 769 5158 1568 5414 1425 7206
16 וְלָרְאוּבֵנִי וְלַגָּדִי נָתַתִּי מִן־הַגִּלְעָד וְעַד־נַחַל אַרְנֹן תּוֹךְ
the ,Arnon the to and Gilead from gave I to and the to And
of middle of valley torrent Gadites the Reubenites

6160 5983 1121 1366 5104 2999 5704 1366 5104
17 הַנַּחַל וּגְבֻל וְעַד יַבֹּק הַנַּחַל גְּבוּל בְּנֵי עַמּוֹן׃ וְהָעֲרָבָה
the and ;Ammon the the the Jabbok even (its) and the
,Arabah of sons of border ,river to ,border valley

8478 4417 3220 6160 3220 5704 3672 1366 3383
וְהַיַּרְדֵּן וּגְבֻל מִכִּנֶּרֶת וְעַד יָם הָעֲרָבָה יָם הַמֶּלַח תַּחַת
under salt the the the even from (its) and the and
of sea ,Arabah of sea to Chinnereth ,border Jordan

559 6256 6680 4217 6449 798
18 אַשְׁדֹּת הַפִּסְגָּה מִזְרָחָה׃ וָאֲצַו אֶתְכֶם בָּעֵת הַהִוא לֵאמֹר
,saying ,that at you I And .eastward Pisgah the
time commanded of slopes

Jehovah your God has
given you this land to
possess it. And you shall
pass over armed before
your brothers, the sons of
Israel, all the warriors.
[19]Only, your wives and your
little ones, and your livestock, shall dwell in your
cities which I have given to
you—I know that you have
much livestock—[20]until
Jehovah shall give rest to
your brothers like your-
selves, and they, too, have
possessed the land which
Jehovah your God *is* giving
to them beyond the Jordan.
Then you shall *each* man
return to his possession
which I have given to you.
[21]And I at that time commanded Joshua, saying,
Your eyes have seen all that
Jehovah your God has done
to these two kings; so
Jehovah shall do to all the
kingdoms to which you *are*
passing over. [22]Do not fear
them; for Jehovah your
God, He shall fight for you.

2502 3423 2088 776 5414 430 3068
יְהוָה אֱלֹהֵיכֶם נָתַן לָכֶם אֶת־הָאָרֶץ הַזֹּאת לְרִשְׁתָּהּ חֲלוּצִים
armed to this land to has your Jehovah
;it possess you given God

7535 2428/1121 3605 3478 1121 251 6440 5674
19 תַּעַבְרוּ לִפְנֵי אֲחֵיכֶם בְּנֵי־יִשְׂרָאֵל כָּל־בְּנֵי־חָיִל׃ רַק
,Only .might the all .Israel the your before shall you
of sons of sons brothers over pass

7725 7227 4735 3045 4735 2945 802
נְשֵׁיכֶם וְטַפְּכֶם וּמִקְנֵכֶם יָדַעְתִּי כִּי־מִקְנֶה רַב לָכֶם יֵשְׁבוּ
shall you much cattle that I your and your and your
stay —have know —livestock ,ones little wives

251 3068 5117 5704 5414 834 5892
20 בְּעָרֵיכֶם אֲשֶׁר נָתַתִּי לָכֶם׃ עַד אֲשֶׁר־יָנִיחַ יְהוָה לַאֲחֵיכֶם
your to Jehovah shall until to have I which your in
,brothers rest give ;you given cities

5414 430 3068 776 1571 3423
כָּכֶם וְיָרְשׁוּ גַם־הֵם אֶת־הָאָרֶץ אֲשֶׁר יְהוָה אֱלֹהֵיכֶם נֹתֵן
(is) your Jehovah which the they too have and like
giving God land possessed ,yourselves

5414 834 3425 376 7725 3383 5676
לָהֶם בְּעֵבֶר הַיַּרְדֵּן וְשַׁבְתֶּם אִישׁ לִירֻשָּׁתוֹ אֲשֶׁר נָתַתִּי
have I which his to (each) you then the beyond to
given possession man return shall ;Jordan them

5869 559 6256 6680 3091
21 לָכֶם׃ וְאֶת־יְהוֹשׁוּעַ צִוֵּיתִי בָּעֵת הַהִוא לֵאמֹר עֵינֶיךָ
Your ,saying ,that at com- I Joshua And to
eyes time manded .you

4428 8147 430 3068 6213 3605 7200
הָרֹאֹת אֵת כָּל־אֲשֶׁר עָשָׂה יְהוָה אֱלֹהֵיכֶם לִשְׁנֵי הַמְּלָכִים
kings two to God your Jehovah has which all have
done seen

834 4467 3605 3068 6213 428
הָאֵלֶּה כֵּן־יַעֲשֶׂה יְהוָה לְכָל־הַמַּמְלָכוֹת אֲשֶׁר אַתָּה
you which the all to Jehovah shall so ;these
kingdoms do

430 3068 3372 3808 8033 5674
22 עֹבֵר שָׁמָּה׃ לֹא תִּירָאוּם כִּי יְהוָה אֱלֹהֵיכֶם הוּא
He ,God your Jehovah for fear do not ;there to (are)
,them over passing

3898
הַנִּלְחָם לָכֶם׃
for shall
you fight

[23]And I prayed to
Jehovah for favor at that
time, saying, [24]Lord
Jehovah, You have begun
to show Your servant Your
greatness and Your mighty
hand—for who *is* a God in
the heavens or in the earth
who can do according to
Your works and according
to Your might?—[25]I pray to
You, let me pass over and
see the good land which *is*
beyond the Jordan, this
good hill-country, and
Lebanon. [26]But Jehovah
was angry with me on your
account, and would not
listen to me. And Jehovah
said to me, Let it be much

3068 136 559 6256 3068 2603
23
24 וָאֶתְחַנַּן אֶל־יְהוָה בָּעֵת הַהִוא לֵאמֹר׃ אֲדֹנָי יְהוִה אַתָּה
You ,Jehovah Lord ,saying ,that at Jehovah to I And
time favor for prayed

2389 3027 1430 5650 7200 2490
הַחִלּוֹתָ לְהַרְאוֹת אֶת־עַבְדְּךָ אֶת־גָּדְלְךָ וְאֶת־יָדְךָ הַחֲזָקָה
;strong Your and Your Your show to have
hand ,greatness servant begun

4639 6213 834 776 8065 410
אֲשֶׁר מִי־אֵל בַּשָּׁמַיִם וּבָאָרֶץ אֲשֶׁר־יַעֲשֶׂה כְמַעֲשֶׂיךָ
to according can who the in or the in a Who
works Your do earth heavens God (is)

834 2896 776 7200 4994 5674 1368
25 וְכִגְבוּרֹתֶךָ׃ אֶעְבְּרָה־נָּא וְאֶרְאֶה אֶת־הָאָרֶץ הַטּוֹבָה אֲשֶׁר
which good the and Please me let to according and
(is) land see over pass ?might Your

3068 5674 3844 2088 2896 2022 3383 5676
26 בְּעֵבֶר הַיַּרְדֵּן הָהָר הַטּוֹב הַזֶּה וְהַלְּבָנֹן׃ וַיִּתְעַבֵּר יְהוָה בִּי
with Jehovah was But and ,this good hill- the beyond
me furious .Lebanon country ,Jordan

3808 7227 3068 559 8085 3808 6616
לְמַעַנְכֶם וְלֹא שָׁמַע אֵלָי וַיֹּאמֶר יְהוָה אֵלַי רַב־לָךְ אַל־
not for much ,me to Jehovah said and to would and your on
;you ,me listen not ,account

for you do not speak any more to Me about this thing. [27]Go up *to* the top of Pisgah and lift up your eyes westward and northward and southward and eastward, and see with your eyes; for you shall not cross over this Jordan. [28]And command Joshua and make him strong, and make him brave, for he shall cross over before this people, and he shall cause them to inherit the land which you shall see. [29]So we stayed in the valley across from Beth-peor.

CHAPTER 4

[1]And now, Israel, listen to the statutes and to the judgments which I *am* teaching you to do, so that you may live and go in, and possess the land which Jehovah the God of your fathers *is* giving to you. [2]You shall not add to the word which I command you, nor take from it, to keep the commandments of Jehovah your God which I command you.

[3]Your eyes have seen that which Jehovah has done in Baal-peor. For Jehovah your God has destroyed them from among you, the men that followed Baal-peor. [4]And you who held fast to Jehovah your God *are* alive today, all of you. [5]Behold, I have taught you statutes and ordinances, as Jehovah my God has commanded me, to do *them* in the midst of the land where you *are* going in, to possess it; [6]and you shall keep and do *them*, for it shall be your wisdom

5375 6449 7218 5927 2088 1697 1696 3254
27 תּוֹסֶף דַּבֵּר אֵלַי עוֹד בַּדָּבָר הַזֶּה׃ עֲלֵה ׀ רֹאשׁ הַפִּסְגָּה וְשָׂא
and ,Pisgah the up Go .this about ever to do again
up lift of head (to) thing Me speak

3808 5869 7200 4217 8486 6828 3220 5869
עֵינֶיךָ יָמָּה וְצָפֹנָה וְתֵימָנָה וּמִזְרָחָה וּרְאֵה בְעֵינֶיךָ כִּי־לֹא
not for your with and and and and west- your
;eyes see eastward southward ,northward ,ward eyes

553 2388 3091 6680 3383 5674
28 תַעֲבֹר אֶת־הַיַּרְדֵּן הַזֶּה׃ וְצַו אֶת־יְהוֹשֻׁעַ וְחַזְּקֵהוּ וְאַמְּצֵהוּ
make and and ,Joshua And Jordan this will you
,brave him ,him strengthen command over cross

776 5157 2088 5971 6440 5674
כִּי־הוּא יַעֲבֹר לִפְנֵי הָעָם הַזֶּה וְהוּא יַנְחִיל אוֹתָם אֶת־הָאָרֶץ
the them shall he and ,this people before shall he for
land inherit to cause over pass

1047 1516 3427 7200 834
29 אֲשֶׁר תִּרְאֶה׃ וַנֵּשֶׁב בַּגָּיְא מוּל בֵּית פְּעוֹר׃
.peor Beth- across the in we So shall you which
from valley stayed .see

CAP. IV ד

CHAPTER 4

834 4941 2706 8085 3478 6258
1 וְעַתָּה יִשְׂרָאֵל שְׁמַע אֶל־הַחֻקִּים וְאֶל־הַמִּשְׁפָּטִים אֲשֶׁר
which the and the to listen ,Israel O And
3423 judgments to statutes ,now

935 2421 6213 3925
אָנֹכִי מְלַמֵּד אֶתְכֶם לַעֲשׂוֹת לְמַעַן תִּחְיוּ וּבָאתֶם וִירִשְׁתֶּם
and go and may you so ,do to you (am) I
possess ,in ,live that teaching

3808 5414 1 430 3068 834 776
2 אֶת־הָאָרֶץ אֲשֶׁר יְהוָה אֱלֹהֵי אֲבֹתֵיכֶם נֹתֵן לָכֶם׃ לֹא
Not to (is) your the Jehovah which the
.you giving fathers of God land

1639 3808 6680 834 1697 3254
תֹסִפוּ עַל־הַדָּבָר אֲשֶׁר אָנֹכִי מְצַוֶּה אֶתְכֶם וְלֹא תִגְרְעוּ
take and ,you (am) I which the shall you
away not commanding word add

6680 834 430 3068 4687 8104
מִמֶּנּוּ לִשְׁמֹר אֶת־מִצְוֹת יְהוָה אֱלֹהֵיכֶם אֲשֶׁר אָנֹכִי מְצַוֶּה
(am) I which your Jehovah the to from
commanding God of commands keep ,it

1187 3068 6213 7200 5869
3 אֶתְכֶם׃ עֵינֵיכֶם הָרֹאֹת אֵת אֲשֶׁר־עָשָׂה יְהוָה בְּבַעַל
in Jehovah has what seeing Your .you
Baal- done eyes

8045 1187 310 5927 834 376 3605
פְעוֹר כִּי כָל־הָאִישׁ אֲשֶׁר הָלַךְ אַחֲרֵי בַעַל־פְּעוֹר הִשְׁמִידוֹ
de- has peor Baal- after went who man every for ;peor
him stroyed

430 3068 1695 7130 430 3068
4 יְהוָה אֱלֹהֶיךָ מִקִּרְבֶּךָ׃ וְאַתֶּם הַדְּבֵקִים בַּיהוָה אֱלֹהֵיכֶם
God your to clinging And among from your Jehovah
Jehovah you .you God

4941 2706 3925 7200 3117 2416
5 חַיִּים כֻּלְּכֶם הַיּוֹם׃ רְאֵה ׀ לִמַּדְתִּי אֶתְכֶם חֻקִּים וּמִשְׁפָּטִים
and statutes you have I ,See .today of all (are)
,judgments taught ,you ,alive

776 7130 3651 6213 430 3068 6680
כַּאֲשֶׁר צִוַּנִי יְהוָה אֱלֹהָי לַעֲשׂוֹת כֵּן בְּקֶרֶב הָאָרֶץ אֲשֶׁר
where the the in ,so do to my Jehovah com- as
land of midst ,God me manded

6213 8104 3423 995
6 אַתֶּם בָּאִים שָׁמָּה לְרִשְׁתָּהּ׃ וּשְׁמַרְתֶּם וַעֲשִׂיתֶם כִּי הִוא
that for do and you And possess to (are) you
(be will) ,(them) keep shall .it in going

חָכְמַתְכֶם וּבִינַתְכֶם לְעֵינֵי הָעַמִּים אֲשֶׁר יִשְׁמְעוּן אֵת
כָּל־הַחֻקִּים הָאֵלֶּה וְאָמְרוּ רַק עַם־חָכָם וְנָבוֹן הַגּוֹי
7 הַגָּדוֹל הַזֶּה׃ כִּי מִי־גוֹי גָּדוֹל אֲשֶׁר־לוֹ אֱלֹהִים קְרֹבִים
8 אֵלָיו כַּיהוָה אֱלֹהֵינוּ בְּכָל־קָרְאֵנוּ אֵלָיו׃ וּמִי גּוֹי גָּדוֹל
אֲשֶׁר־לוֹ חֻקִּים וּמִשְׁפָּטִים צַדִּיקִם כְּכֹל הַתּוֹרָה הַזֹּאת
9 אֲשֶׁר אָנֹכִי נֹתֵן לִפְנֵיכֶם הַיּוֹם׃ רַק הִשָּׁמֶר לְךָ וּשְׁמֹר
נַפְשְׁךָ מְאֹד פֶּן־תִּשְׁכַּח אֶת־הַדְּבָרִים אֲשֶׁר־רָאוּ עֵינֶיךָ
וּפֶן־יָסוּרוּ מִלְּבָבְךָ כֹּל יְמֵי חַיֶּיךָ וְהוֹדַעְתָּם לְבָנֶיךָ וְלִבְנֵי
10 בָנֶיךָ׃ יוֹם אֲשֶׁר עָמַדְתָּ לִפְנֵי יְהוָה אֱלֹהֶיךָ בְּחֹרֵב בֶּאֱמֹר
יְהוָה אֵלַי הַקְהֶל־לִי אֶת־הָעָם וְאַשְׁמִעֵם אֶת־דְּבָרָי אֲשֶׁר
יִלְמְדוּן לְיִרְאָה אֹתִי כָּל־הַיָּמִים אֲשֶׁר הֵם חַיִּים עַל־
11 הָאֲדָמָה וְאֶת־בְּנֵיהֶם יְלַמֵּדוּן׃ וַתִּקְרְבוּן וַתַּעַמְדוּן תַּחַת
הָהָר וְהָהָר בֹּעֵר בָּאֵשׁ עַד־לֵב הַשָּׁמַיִם חֹשֶׁךְ עָנָן וַעֲרָפֶל׃
12 וַיְדַבֵּר יְהוָה אֲלֵיכֶם מִתּוֹךְ הָאֵשׁ קוֹל דְּבָרִים אַתֶּם
13 שֹׁמְעִים וּתְמוּנָה אֵינְכֶם רֹאִים זוּלָתִי קוֹל׃ וַיַּגֵּד לָכֶם
אֶת־בְּרִיתוֹ אֲשֶׁר צִוָּה אֶתְכֶם לַעֲשׂוֹת עֲשֶׂרֶת הַדְּבָרִים
14 וַיִּכְתְּבֵם עַל־שְׁנֵי לֻחוֹת אֲבָנִים׃ וַיְצַו יְהוָה אֹתִי בָּעֵת

and your understanding before the eyes of the peoples who hear all these statutes. And they shall say, This great nation *is* a people wise and understanding. [7]For who *is* a great nation whose God is coming near to them, as Jehovah your God *is*, in all our calling on Him? [8]And who *is* a great nation whose statutes and judgments *are as* righteous as all this law which I set before you today?

[9]Only, take heed to yourself and keep your soul carefully, that you do not forget the things which your eyes have seen; and that they not depart from your heart all the days of your life. And you shall make them known to your sons, and to your sons' sons: [10]*The* day that you stood before Jehovah your God in Horeb, when Jehovah said to me, Gather the people to Me, and I will make them hear My words, that they may learn to fear Me all the days that they live on the earth; and that they may teach their sons. [11]And you drew near and stood below the mountain, and the mountain burned with fire to the heart of the heavens, darkness, cloud and thick gloom.

[12]And Jehovah spoke to you out of the midst of the fire; you heard the sound of words, but you did not see a form, only a voice.

[13]And He declared His covenant to you which He has commmanded you to do, the Ten Commandments; and He wrote them on two tablets of stone. [14]And Jehovah commanded me at that time to

teach you statutes and ordinances, for you to do them in the land which you shall pass over to possess it.
15 Therefore you shall carefully watch over your souls, for you have not seen any likeness in the day Jehovah spoke to you in Horeb out of the midst of the fire, 16 that you not deal corruptly, and make for yourselves a graven image, a likeness of any figure, the form of a male or female, 17 the form of any animal which *is* in the earth; the form of any winged bird that flies in the heavens; 18 the form of any creeping thing on the ground; the form of any fish in the waters under the earth; 19 and that you not lift up your eyes towards the heavens and shall see the sun, and the moon, and the stars, all the host of the heavens, and you be drawn away and worship them, and serve them; which Jehovah your God has allotted to all the peoples under all the heavens. 20 And Jehovah has taken you, and has brought you forth out of the iron furnace, out of Egypt, to be a people to Him, an inheritance, as *it is* this day. 21 And Jehovah was angry with me because of your words, and swore I would not pass over the Jordan, and that I might not go into the good land which Jehovah your God is giving to you *as* an inheritance. 22 For I *will* die in this land; I *shall* not pass over the Jordan. But you *shall* pass over, and shall possess this good land. 23 Take heed to yourselves, that you not forget the covenant of

6213 4941 2706 3925
הַהִוא לְלַמֵּד אֶתְכֶם חֻקִּים וּמִשְׁפָּטִים לַעֲשֹׂתְכֶם אֹתָם
them to you for do and judgments statutes you teach to that

8104 3423 8033 5674 834 776
15 בָּאָרֶץ אֲשֶׁר אַתֶּם עֹבְרִים שָׁמָּה לְרִשְׁתָּהּ׃ וְנִשְׁמַרְתֶּם
shall you guard Therefore your possess to on be there .it pass- over (are) ing you which the in land

1696 3117 2843 3605 7200 3808 5315 3966
מְאֹד לְנַפְשֹׁתֵיכֶם כִּי לֹא רְאִיתֶם כָּל־תְּמוּנָה בְּיוֹם דִּבֶּר
spoke the on day form any saw you not for your for ;souls very much

6213 7843 784 8432 2722 3068
16 יְהוָה אֲלֵיכֶם בְּחֹרֵב מִתּוֹךְ הָאֵשׁ׃ פֶּן־תַּשְׁחִתוּן וַעֲשִׂיתֶם
make and act you corruptly lest the ;fire the from of midst on Horeb to you Jehovah

8403 5347 2145 8403 5566 3605 8544 6459
17 לָכֶם פֶּסֶל תְּמוּנַת כָּל־סָמֶל תַּבְנִית זָכָר אוֹ נְקֵבָה׃ תַּבְנִית
shape the of a ;female or a male the of shape ,idol any form the of carved image for you

5774 3671 6833 3605 8403 776 834 929 3605
כָּל־בְּהֵמָה אֲשֶׁר בָּאָרֶץ תַּבְנִית כָּל־צִפּוֹר כָּנָף אֲשֶׁר תָּעוּף
flies that winged bird any shape the of the in ;earth which (is) animal any

834 1710 3605 8403 127 7430 3605 8403 8064
18 בַּשָּׁמָיִם׃ תַּבְנִית כָּל־רֹמֵשׂ בָּאֲדָמָה תַּבְנִית כָּל־דָּגָה אֲשֶׁר
which (is) fish any shape the of the on ;ground creeper any shape the of the in ;heavens

7200 8064 5869 5375 776 8478 4325
19 בַּמַּיִם מִתַּחַת לָאָרֶץ׃ וּפֶן־תִּשָּׂא עֵינֶיךָ הַשָּׁמַיְמָה וְרָאִיתָ
and see towards heavens the your eyes lift up you and lest the ;earth under the in waters

8064 6635 3605 3556 3394 8121
אֶת־הַשֶּׁמֶשׁ וְאֶת־הַיָּרֵחַ וְאֶת־הַכּוֹכָבִים כֹּל צְבָא הַשָּׁמָיִם
the ,heavens host the of all the stars and the ,moon and the ,sun

430 3068 2505 5647 7812 5080
וְנִדַּחְתָּ וְהִשְׁתַּחֲוִיתָ לָהֶם וַעֲבַדְתָּם אֲשֶׁר חָלַק יְהוָה אֱלֹהֶיךָ
your God Jehovah has allotted which serve and ,them to them bow and down be you and away drawn

3068 3947 8064 3605 8478 5971 3605
20 אֹתָם לְכֹל הָעַמִּים תַּחַת כָּל־הַשָּׁמָיִם׃ וְאֶתְכֶם לָקַח יְהוָה
Jehovah has taken And you the .heavens all under the peoples to all

5159 5971 1961 4714 1270 3564 3318
וַיּוֹצִא אֶתְכֶם מִכּוּר הַבַּרְזֶל מִמִּצְרַיִם לִהְיוֹת לוֹ לְעַם נַחֲלָה
inher- ,tance- peo- of a ple to Him to become of out ,Egypt ,iron the from of furnace you and out brought

7650 1697 599 3068 3117
21 כַּיּוֹם הַזֶּה׃ וַיהוָה הִתְאַנֶּף־בִּי עַל־דִּבְרֵיכֶם וַיִּשָּׁבַע לְבִלְתִּי
not (be would) and swore your ,words be- cause of with me was angry And Jehovah .this it) as day (is

834 2896 776 935 3383 5674
עָבְרִי אֶת־הַיַּרְדֵּן וּלְבִלְתִּי־בֹא אֶל־הָאָרֶץ הַטּוֹבָה אֲשֶׁר
which good the land into (my) going and not the Jordan pass- my over ing

2088 776 5159 5414 430 3068
22 יְהוָה אֱלֹהֶיךָ נֹתֵן לְךָ נַחֲלָה׃ כִּי אָנֹכִי מֵת בָּאָרֶץ הַזֹּאת
;this in land (will) be I For an (as) .inheritance to you is giving your God Jehovah

776 3423 5674 3383 5674
אֵינֶנִּי עֹבֵר אֶת־הַיַּרְדֵּן וְאַתֶּם עֹבְרִים וִירִשְׁתֶּם אֶת־הָאָרֶץ
land shall and possess pass- over (are) ing but you the ,Jordan (am) over passing .not I

3068 1285 7911 8104 2088 2896
23 הַטּוֹבָה הַזֹּאת׃ הִשָּׁמְרוּ לָכֶם פֶּן־תִּשְׁכְּחוּ אֶת־בְּרִית יְהוָה
Jehovah cov- of enant the you forget lest for ,yourselves on Be guard .this good

אֱלֹהֵיכֶם אֲשֶׁר כָּרַת עִמָּכֶם וַעֲשִׂיתֶם לָכֶם פֶּסֶל תְּמוּנַת
24 כֹּל אֲשֶׁר צִוְּךָ יְהוָה אֱלֹהֶיךָ׃ כִּי יְהוָה אֱלֹהֶיךָ אֵשׁ אֹכְלָה
הוּא אֵל קַנָּא׃
25 כִּי־תוֹלִיד בָּנִים וּבְנֵי בָנִים וְנוֹשַׁנְתֶּם בָּאָרֶץ וְהִשְׁחַתֶּם
וַעֲשִׂיתֶם פֶּסֶל תְּמוּנַת כֹּל וַעֲשִׂיתֶם הָרַע בְּעֵינֵי יְהוָה־
26 אֱלֹהֶיךָ לְהַכְעִיסוֹ׃ הַעִידֹתִי בָכֶם הַיּוֹם אֶת־הַשָּׁמַיִם וְאֶת־
הָאָרֶץ כִּי־אָבֹד תֹּאבֵדוּן מַהֵר מֵעַל הָאָרֶץ אֲשֶׁר אַתֶּם
עֹבְרִים אֶת־הַיַּרְדֵּן שָׁמָּה לְרִשְׁתָּהּ לֹא־תַאֲרִיכֻן יָמִים
27 עָלֶיהָ כִּי הִשָּׁמֵד תִּשָּׁמֵדוּן׃ וְהֵפִיץ יְהוָה אֶתְכֶם בָּעַמִּים
וְנִשְׁאַרְתֶּם מְתֵי מִסְפָּר בַּגּוֹיִם אֲשֶׁר יְנַהֶגְ יְהוָה אֶתְכֶם
28 שָׁמָּה׃ וַעֲבַדְתֶּם־שָׁם אֱלֹהִים מַעֲשֵׂה יְדֵי אָדָם עֵץ וָאֶבֶן
אֲשֶׁר לֹא־יִרְאוּן וְלֹא יִשְׁמְעוּן וְלֹא יֹאכְלוּן וְלֹא יְרִיחֻן׃
29 וּבִקַּשְׁתֶּם מִשָּׁם אֶת־יְהוָה אֱלֹהֶיךָ וּמָצָאתָ כִּי תִדְרְשֶׁנּוּ
30 בְּכָל־לְבָבְךָ וּבְכָל־נַפְשֶׁךָ׃ בַּצַּר לְךָ וּמְצָאוּךָ כֹּל הַדְּבָרִים
הָאֵלֶּה בְּאַחֲרִית הַיָּמִים וְשַׁבְתָּ עַד־יְהוָה אֱלֹהֶיךָ וְשָׁמַעְתָּ
31 בְּקֹלוֹ׃ כִּי אֵל רַחוּם יְהוָה אֱלֹהֶיךָ לֹא יַרְפְּךָ וְלֹא יַשְׁחִיתֶךָ
32 וְלֹא יִשְׁכַּח אֶת־בְּרִית אֲבֹתֶיךָ אֲשֶׁר נִשְׁבַּע לָהֶם׃ כִּי

Jehovah your God, which He has made with you, and make to yourselves a graven image, a likeness of anything which Jehovah your God has forbidden you. [24]For Jehovah your God *is* a consuming fire; He *is* a jealous God.

[25]When you father sons and son's sons, and you have been long in the land, and have dealt corruptly, and have made a graven image, a likeness of anything, and have done that which is evil in the sight of Jehovah your God, to provoke Him to anger; [26]I call heaven and earth to witness against you today, that you shall soon utterly perish from off the land to which you go over the Jordan to possess it; you shall not prolong *your* days on it, but shall utterly be destroyed. [27]And Jehovah shall scatter you among the peoples, and you shall be left few in number among the nations to which Jehovah shall lead you away. [28]And there you shall serve other gods, the work of man's hands, wood and stone, which cannot see, nor hear, nor eat, nor smell. [29]And if you shall seek Jehovah your God from there, then *you* shall find *Him*, if you seek Him with your whole heart, and with all your soul, [30]in your distress, when all these things have found you, in the latter days, then you shall return to Jehovah your God, and shall listen to His voice. [31]For Jehovah your God *is* a merciful God. He will not forsake you, nor destroy you, nor forget the covenant of your fathers which He swore to them.

[32]For ask now of the days

past, which were before
you, since the day that God
created man on the earth,
and from the one end of the
heavens to the other end of
the heavens, whether there
has been a thing as great *as*
this, or has *anything* like it
been heard. [33]Has a people
heard the voice of God
speaking from the midst of
the fire, as you have heard,
and lived? [34]Or has God
gone forth to take to
Himself a nation from the
midst of a nation, by trials,
by signs, and by wonders,
and by war, and by a mighty
hand, and by a stretched-
out arm, and by great
terrors, according to all that
Jehovah your God did for
you in Egypt before your
eyes? [35]*To* you it was
revealed, so that you might
know that Jehovah *is* God,
and no one else besides
Him. [36]He made you hear
His voice out of the
heavens, that He might
discipline you; and He
made you to see His great
fire on earth; and you heard
His word from the midst of
the fire. [37]And because He
loved your fathers, and
chose their seed after them,
and brought you out with
His presence, with His
great power, out of Egypt.

[38]in order to drive out
nations greater and
mightier than you from
before you, to bring you in,
to give their land for an
inheritance, as *it is* this day;
[39]know today, and lay *it* to
your heart, that Jehovah,
He *is* God in the heavens
above and on the earth
beneath; there is no other.
[40]And you shall keep His
statutes and His command-
ments which I am com-
manding you today, so that
it may be will with you, and
with your sons after you,

834 3117 6440 1961 834 7223 3117 4994/7592
שְׁאַל־נָא לְיָמִים רִאשֹׁנִים אֲשֶׁר־הָיוּ לְפָנֶיךָ לְמִן־הַיּוֹם אֲשֶׁר
when the since before were which ,former the of ,please ,ask
day ,you days

7097 5704 8064 7097 776 5921 120 430 1254
בָּרָא אֱלֹהִים ׀ אָדָם עַל־הָאָרֶץ וּלְמִקְצֵה הַשָּׁמַיִם וְעַד־קְצֵה
other the to the from and the on man God created
of end heavens of end one the ;earth

3644 8085 176 1419 1697 1961 8064
הַשָּׁמַיִם הֲנִהְיָה כַּדָּבָר הַגָּדוֹל הַזֶּה אוֹ הֲנִשְׁמַע כָּמֹהוּ׃
?it like been has or ;this great a like there whether the
heard thing been has .heavens

8085 784 8432 1696 430 6963 5971 8085
33 הֲשָׁמַע עָם קוֹל אֱלֹהִים מְדַבֵּר מִתּוֹךְ־הָאֵשׁ כַּאֲשֶׁר־שָׁמַעְתָּ
have as the the from speaking God the a heard Has
heard fire of midst of voice people

7130 1471 3947 3212 430 5254 176 2421
34 אַתָּה וַיֶּחִי׃ אוֹ ׀ הֲנִסָּה אֱלֹהִים לָבוֹא לָקַחַת לוֹ גוֹי מִקֶּרֶב
the from a to take to go to God set has Or and ,you
of midst nation Himself forth ?lived

2389 3027 4421 4159 226 4531 1471
גּוֹי בְּמַסֹּת בְּאֹתֹת וּבְמוֹפְתִים וּבְמִלְחָמָה וּבְיָד חֲזָקָה
,mighty by and by and by and ,signs by ,trials by a
hand a ,war ,wonders ,nation

6213 8605 1419 4172 5186 2220
וּבִזְרוֹעַ נְטוּיָה וּבְמוֹרָאִים גְּדֹלִים כְּכֹל אֲשֶׁר־עָשָׂה לָכֶם
for did that according ,great by and stretched-a by and
you all to terrors out arm

3045 7200 5869 4714 430 3068
35 יְהוָה אֱלֹהֵיכֶם בְּמִצְרַיִם לְעֵינֶיךָ׃ אַתָּה הָרְאֵתָ לָדַעַת כִּי
that that so was it you (To) your before in your Jehovah
know might you ,revealed ?eyes Egypt God

6213 8064 905 5750 369/430 3068
36 יְהוָה הוּא הָאֱלֹהִים אֵין עוֹד מִלְּבַדּוֹ׃ מִן־הַשָּׁמַיִם הִשְׁמִיעֲךָ
made He heavens the Out beside else (and) ,God (is) Jehovah
hear you of ,Him one no

1419 784 7200 776 5921 3256 6963
אֶת־קֹלוֹ לְיַסְּרֶךָּ וְעַל־הָאָרֶץ הֶרְאֲךָ אֶת־אִשּׁוֹ הַגְּדוֹלָה
,great His made He earth on and might He that His
fire see to you ,you correct ,voice

1 157 8478 784 8432 8085 1697
37 וּדְבָרָיו שָׁמַעְתָּ מִתּוֹךְ הָאֵשׁ׃ וְתַחַת כִּי אָהַב אֶת־אֲבֹתֶיךָ
your He And the the of out did you His and
,fathers loved because .fire of midst hear word

4714 1419 3581 6440 3318 310 2233 977
וַיִּבְחַר בְּזַרְעוֹ אַחֲרָיו וַיּוֹצִאֲךָ בְּפָנָיו בְּכֹחוֹ הַגָּדֹל מִמִּצְרָיִם׃
of out ,great with His with brought and after their He then
:Egypt power His ,presence out you ,them seed chose

5414 935 6440 6099 1419 1471 3423
38 לְהוֹרִישׁ גּוֹיִם גְּדֹלִים וַעֲצֻמִים מִמְּךָ מִפָּנֶיךָ לַהֲבִיאֲךָ לָתֶת־
give to bring to from than and greater nations to order in
,in you you before ,you mightier out drive

3427 3117 3045 2088 3117 5159 776
39 לְךָ אֶת־אַרְצָם נַחֲלָה כַּיּוֹם הַזֶּה׃ וְיָדַעְתָּ הַיּוֹם וַהֲשֵׁבֹתָ
lay and ,today Know .this (it) as an for their to
(it) day (is) inheritance land you

5921 4605 8064 430 3068 3824
אֶל־לְבָבֶךָ כִּי יְהוָה הוּא הָאֱלֹהִים בַּשָּׁמַיִם מִמַּעַל וְעַל־
on and above the in God He Jehovah that your to
heavens (is) ,heart

4687 2706 8104 5750 369 8478 776
40 הָאָרֶץ מִתָּחַת אֵין עוֹד׃ וְשָׁמַרְתָּ אֶת־חֻקָּיו וְאֶת־מִצְוֹתָיו
His and His you And .other there ;beneath the
commandments statutes keep shall no is earth

310 1121 3190 3117 6680 834
אֲשֶׁר אָנֹכִי מְצַוְּךָ הַיּוֹם אֲשֶׁר יִיטַב לְךָ וּלְבָנֶיךָ אַחֲרֶיךָ
after with and with may it so ,today com- am I which
,you sons your ,you well be that you manding

and so that you may prolong *your* days on the earth, which Jehovah our God is giving to you all the days.

[41]Then Moses separated three cities beyond the Jordan, toward the sunrising, [42]that the manslayer might flee there, he who killed his neighbor unawares, and did not hate him *in* times before, and he fleeing to one of these cities might live: [43]Bezer in the wilderness, in the tableland, for the Reubenites; and Ramoth in Gilead, for the Gadites; and Golan in Bashan, for the Manassites.

[44]And this *is* the law which Moses set before the sons of Israel; [45]these are the testimonies and the statutes and the ordinances which Moses spoke to the sons of Israel when they came out of Egypt;

[46]beyond the Jordan, in the valley opposite Beth-peor, in the land of Sihon the king of the Amorites, who lived at Heshbon, whom Moses and the sons of Israel struck when they came out of Egypt. [47]And they took possession of his land, and the land of Og the king of Bashan, the two kings of the Amorites who *were* beyond the Jordan, toward the sunrising; [48]from Aroer, which *is* on the lip of the river of Arnon, even to Mount Sion, which *is* Hermon; [49]and all the Arabah beyond the Jordan eastward, even to the sea of the Arabah, under the slopes of Pisgah.

5414 430 3068 834 127 5921 3117 748
ולמען תאריך ימים על־האדמה אשר יהוה אלהיך נתן
is giving God your Jehovah which the ,earth on (your) days may you prolong so and that

3117 3605
לך כל־הימים׃
the .days all to you

8121 4217 3383 5676 5892 7969 4872 914
41 אז יבדיל משה שלש ערים בעבר הירדן מזרחה שמש׃
,sun rising toward the Jordan beyond cities three Moses separated Then

1847 1097 7453 7523 7523 8033 5127
42 לנס שמה רוצח אשר ירצח את־רעהו בבלי־דעת
,knowing without his neighbor killed who the man-slayer there for fleeing

5892 259 5127 8032 8543 8130 1961
והוא לא־שנא לו מתמל שלשם ונס אל־אחת מן־הערים
cities of one to and fled he ;before times to him hating not and was

7206 4334 776 4057 1221 2425 411
43 האל וחי׃ את־בצר במדבר בארץ המישר לראובני
the of ;Reubenites level land the in the in ,wilderness Bezer he and :lived these

2088 4520 1316 1474 1425 1568 2216
44 ואת־ראמת בגלעד לגדי ואת־גולן בבשן למנשי׃ וזאת
And (is) this the of .Manassites in ,Bashan Golan and the of ;Gadites in ,Gilead Ramoth and

5713 428 3478 1121 6440 4872 7760 834 8451
45 התורה אשר־שם משה לפני בני ישראל׃ אלה העדת
the testimonies These are :Israel the of sons before Moses set which law the

3478 1121 4872 1696 834 4941 3478
והחקים והמשפטים אשר דבר משה אל־בני ישראל
,Israel the of sons to Moses spoke which the and judgments the and statutes

1047 4136 1516 3383 5676 4714 5927
46 בצאתם ממצרים׃ בעבר הירדן בגיא מול בית פעור
,peor Beth- opposite the in valley the ,Jordan beyond from ,Egypt they when out came

2809 3427 834 567 4428 5511 776
בארץ סיחן מלך האמרי אשר יושב בחשבון אשר
whom in ,Heshbon was living who the ,Amorites the of king Sihon the in of land

3423 4714 5927 3478 1121 4872 5221
47 הכה משה ובני ישראל בצאתם ממצרים׃ ויירשו
took they of possession And from .Egypt they when out came ,Israel the and of sons Moses struck

567 4428 8147 1316 4428 5747 776 776
את־ארצו ואת־ארץ עוג מלך־הבשן שני מלכי האמרי
the ,Amorites kings of the two ,Bashan the of king Og the of land and his ,land

5921 6177 8121 4217 3383 5676
48 אשר בעבר הירדן מזרח שמש׃ מערער אשר על־
on which (is) from ,Aroer ;sun- toward rising the Jordan the beyond what (were)

3605 2768 7865 2022 5704 769 5158 8193
49 שפת־נחל ארנן ועד־הר שיאן הוא חרמון׃ וכל־
and all :Hermon which (is) ,Sion Mount even to ,Arnon tor- of rent the the of edge

8478 6160 3220 5704 4217 3383 5676 6160
הערבה עבר הירדן מזרחה ועד ים הערבה תחת
under the ,Arabah the of sea even ,eastward the Jordan beyond the Arabah

6449 798
אשדת הפסגה׃
.Pisgah slopes the of

CAP. V ה

CHAPTER 5

CHAPTER 5

1And Moses called to all Israel and said to them, Hear, Israel, the statutes and the ordinances which I speak in your ears today. And you shall learn them, and shall take heed to do them. 2Jehovah your God cut a covenant with us in Horeb. 3Jehovah did not cut this covenant with our fathers, but with us, *even* us who are all of us here, alive today. 4Jehovah talked with you face to face in the mountain out of the midst of the fire. 5I stood between Jehovah and you at that time, to declare to you the word of Jehovah; for you were afraid from the face of the fire, and you did not go up into the mountain, *when He spoke,* saying:

6I *am* Jehovah your God who brought you out of the land of Egypt, from the house of bondage.

7You shall have no other gods before Me.

8You shall not make a graven image for you, any likeness which *is* in the heavens above, or which *is* in the earth beneath, and which *is* in the waters *from* under the earth. 9You shall not bow yourself to them nor serve them, for I, Jehovah your God, *am* a jealous God, visiting the iniquity of fathers on children, and on the third, and on the fourth *generation* of those that hate Me, 10and doing kindness to thousands of those who love Me and keep My commandments.

11You shall not take the name of Jehovah your God

3478 8085 559 3478 3605 4872 7121
1 וַיִּקְרָא מֹשֶׁה אֶל־כָּל־יִשְׂרָאֵל וַיֹּאמֶר אֲלֵהֶם שְׁמַע יִשְׂרָאֵל
,Israel ,Hear them to said and ,Israel all to Moses And called

241 1696 834 4941 2706
אֶת־הַחֻקִּים וְאֶת־הַמִּשְׁפָּטִים אֲשֶׁר אָנֹכִי דֹּבֵר בְּאָזְנֵיכֶם
ears your in speak I which judgments the and the statutes

430 3068 6213 8104 3925 3117
2 הַיּוֹם וּלְמַדְתֶּם אֹתָם וּשְׁמַרְתֶּם לַעֲשֹׂתָם׃ יְהוָה אֱלֹהֵינוּ
God our Jehovah .them do to guard on be and ,them learn and ;today

3068 3772 1 3808 2772 1285 3772
3 כָּרַת עִמָּנוּ בְּרִית בְּחֹרֵב׃ לֹא אֶת־אֲבֹתֵינוּ כָּרַת יְהוָה
Jehovah did cut our fathers with Not in .Horeb a covenant with us cut

3605 3117 428 587 2088 1285
אֶת־הַבְּרִית הַזֹּאת כִּי אִתָּנוּ אֲנַחְנוּ אֵלֶּה פֹה הַיּוֹם כֻּלָּנוּ
.us of all ,today here these ones (even) us ,us with but ,this covenant

8432 2022 3068 1696 6440 6440 2416
4 חַיִּים׃ פָּנִים ׀ בְּפָנִים דִּבֶּר יְהוָה עִמָּכֶם בָּהָר מִתּוֹךְ
of out of midst the in the mount you with Jehovah spoke face at Face .alive

5046 6256 3068 996 5975 784
5 הָאֵשׁ׃ אָנֹכִי עֹמֵד בֵּין־יְהוָה וּבֵינֵיכֶם בָּעֵת הַהִוא לְהַגִּיד
to declare ,that at time you and Jehovah be- tween stood I the ;fire

5927 3808 784 6440 3372 3068 1697
לָכֶם אֶת־דְּבַר יְהוָה כִּי יְרֵאתֶם מִפְּנֵי הָאֵשׁ וְלֹא־עֲלִיתֶם
go up did not and ,fire the the from of face were you afraid for Jehovah the of word to you

3318 430 3068 559 2022
6 בָּהָר לֵאמֹר׃ אָנֹכִי יְהוָה אֱלֹהֶיךָ אֲשֶׁר הוֹצֵאתִיךָ
brought you out who ,God your Jehovah (am) I ,saying the into mountain

430 1961 3808 5650 1004 4714 776
7 מֵאֶרֶץ מִצְרַיִם מִבֵּית עֲבָדִים׃ לֹא־יִהְיֶה לְךָ אֱלֹהִים
gods you to There be will not .slavery the from of house ,Egypt the of land

834 8544 3605 6459 6213 3808 6440 312
8 אֲחֵרִים עַל־פָּנָי׃ לֹא־תַעֲשֶׂה־לְךָ פֶסֶל ׀ כָּל־תְּמוּנָה אֲשֶׁר
which (is) likeness any carve a ,image for you You make shall not .Me above other

4325 834 8478 776 834 4605 8064
בַּשָּׁמַיִם ׀ מִמַּעַל וַאֲשֶׁר בָּאָרֶץ מִתַּחַת וַאֲשֶׁר בַּמַּיִם ׀
the in waters and (is) which ,beneath the in earth (is) which or ,above the in heavens

3588 5647 3808 7812 3808 776 8478
9 מִתַּחַת לָאָרֶץ׃ לֹא־תִשְׁתַּחֲוֶה לָהֶם וְלֹא תָעָבְדֵם כִּי אָנֹכִי
I (am) for serve ,them nor to them shall You yourself bow not the .earth under

5921 1121 5921 1 5771 6485 7067 410 430 3068
יְהוָה אֱלֹהֶיךָ אֵל קַנָּא פֹּקֵד עֲוֹן אָבוֹת עַל־בָּנִים וְעַל־
on and children on fathers the of iniquity visiting ,jealous a God your ,God Jehovah

505 2617 6213 8130 1755 8029
10 שִׁלֵּשִׁים וְעַל־רִבֵּעִים לְשֹׂנְאָי׃ וְעֹשֶׂה חֶסֶד לַאֲלָפִים
to thousands faith- fulness and doing those of .Me hating fourth the (generation) and on third the

3068 8034 5375 3808 4687 8104 157
11 לְאֹהֲבַי וּלְשֹׁמְרֵי מִצְוֹתָו׃ לֹא תִשָּׂא אֶת־שֵׁם־יְהוָה
Jehovah the of name You take shall not My .commandments and keeping those of Me loving

in vain; for Jehovah will not hold him guiltless who takes His name in vain.

[12]Observe the sabbath day, to keep it holy, as Jehovah your God has commanded you. [13]Six days you shall labor, and shall do all your work, [14]and the seventh day *shall be* a sabbath to Jehovah your God. You shall not do any work, you, nor your son, nor your daughter, nor your male slave, nor your female slave, nor your ox, nor your ass, nor any of your livestock, nor your stranger that *is* within your gates; so that your male slave and your female slave may rest like yourself. [15]And remember that you were a slave in the land of Egypt, and Jehovah your God brought you out from there by a mighty hand and by a stretched-out arm. On account of this Jehovah your God has commanded you to keep the sabbath day.

[16]Honor your father and your mother, as Jehovah your God has commanded you, so that your days may be prolonged, and so that it may be well with you in the land which Jehovah your God *is* giving to you.

[17]You shall not commit murder.

[18]You shall not commit adultery.

[19]You shall not steal.

[20]You shall not bear false witness against your neighbor.

[21]You shall not lust after your neighbor's wife; nor shall you covet your neighbor's house, his field, nor his male slave, nor his female slave, his ox, nor his ass, nor anything which *is* your neighbor's.

[22]Jehovah spoke these words to all your assembly, on the Mount, out of the midst of the fire of the cloud, and out of the thick darkness, with a great voice. And he added no more; and He wrote them

8034 5375/834 3068 5352 3808 7723 430
אֱלֹהֶיךָ לַשָּׁוְא כִּי לֹא יְנַקֶּה יְהוָה אֵת אֲשֶׁר־יִשָּׂא אֶת־שְׁמוֹ
His takes him Jehovah hold will not for in your
name who guiltless ;vain God

6680 6942 7676 3117 8104 7723
12 לַשָּׁוְא׃ שָׁמוֹר אֶת־יוֹם הַשַּׁבָּת לְקַדְּשׁוֹ כַּאֲשֶׁר צִוְּךָ
com- as it keep to the day Observe .vain in
you manded holy Sabbath

4399 3605 6213 5647 3117 8337 430 3068
13 יְהוָה אֱלֹהֶיךָ׃ שֵׁשֶׁת יָמִים תַּעֲבֹד וְעָשִׂיתָ כָּל־מְלַאכְתֶּךָ׃
your all do and shall you days Six your Jehovah
work labor God

3605 6213 3808 430 3068 7676 7637 3117
14 וְיוֹם הַשְּׁבִיעִי שַׁבָּת ׀ לַיהוָה אֱלֹהֶיךָ לֹא תַעֲשֶׂה כָל־
any shall you not your to a (be shall) the and
do ;God Jehovah sabbath seventh day

2543 7794 519 5650 1323 1121 4399
מְלָאכָה אַתָּה וּבִנְךָ וּבִתֶּךָ וְעַבְדְּךָ וַאֲמָתֶךָ וְשׁוֹרְךָ וַחֲמֹרְךָ
your nor your nor your nor your nor your nor nor you ,work
ass ,ox ,slave female ,slave male ,daughter son your

5650 5117 8179 1616 929 3605
וְכָל־בְּהֶמְתֶּךָ וְגֵרְךָ אֲשֶׁר בִּשְׁעָרֶיךָ לְמַעַן יָנוּחַ עַבְדְּךָ
male your may so your inside that your nor your nor
slave rest that ;gates (is) alien ,cattle of any

4714 776 1961 5650 2142 519
15 וַאֲמָתְךָ כָּמוֹךָ׃ וְזָכַרְתָּ כִּי־עֶבֶד הָיִיתָ ׀ בְּאֶרֶץ מִצְרַיִם
,Egypt the in you a that and ;you as your and
of land were slave remember slave female

5186/2220 2389 3027 8033 430 3068 3318
וַיֹּצִאֲךָ יְהוָה אֱלֹהֶיךָ מִשָּׁם בְּיָד חֲזָקָה וּבִזְרֹעַ נְטוּיָה עַל־
there- out- by and ,mighty a by from your Jehovah and
;stretched arm an hand there God you brought

3513 7676 3117 8104 430 3068 6680
16 כֵּן צִוְּךָ יְהוָה אֱלֹהֶיךָ לַעֲשׂוֹת אֶת־יוֹם הַשַּׁבָּת׃ כַּבֵּד אֶת־
Honor the day keep to your Jehovah com- fore
.Sabbath God you manded

748 430 3068 6680 517
אָבִיךָ וְאֶת־אִמֶּךָ כַּאֲשֶׁר צִוְּךָ יְהוָה אֱלֹהֶיךָ לְמַעַן ׀ יַאֲרִיכֻן
be may that so your Jehovah com- as your and your
prolonged ,God you manded ,mother ,father

430 3068 834 127 5921 3190 3117
יָמֶיךָ וּלְמַעַן יִיטַב לָךְ עַל הָאֲדָמָה אֲשֶׁר־יְהוָה אֱלֹהֶיךָ
your Jehovah which the on for may it so and your
God land you well be that ,days

3808 5003 3808 7523 5414
17 נֹתֵן לָךְ׃ לֹא תִּרְצָח׃ וְלֹא תִּנְאָף׃ וְלֹא
And shall you And shall You not to has
not .adultery commit not .murder .you given

3808 7723 5707 7453 6030 3808 1589
18 תִּגְנֹב׃ וְלֹא־תַעֲנֶה בְרֵעֲךָ עֵד שָׁוְא׃ וְלֹא
And .false a your against shall you And shall you
not witness neighbor testify not steal

7704 7453 1004 183 3808 7453 802 2530
תַחְמֹד אֵשֶׁת רֵעֶךָ וְלֹא תִתְאַוֶּה בֵּית רֵעֶךָ שָׂדֵהוּ
his your house you shall and your wife the shall you
,field ,neighbor's covet not ;neighbor's of desire

7453 834 3605 2543 7794 519 5650
19 וְעַבְדּוֹ וַאֲמָתוֹ שׁוֹרוֹ וַחֲמֹרוֹ וְכֹל אֲשֶׁר לְרֵעֶךָ׃ אֶת־
your to which any- or his or his female his or his or
.neighbor (is) thing ,ass ,ox ,slave ,slave male

8432 2022 6951 3605 3068 1696 1697
הַדְּבָרִים הָאֵלֶּה דִּבֶּר יְהוָה אֶל־כָּל־קְהַלְכֶם בָּהָר מִתּוֹךְ
the from the on your all to Jehovah spoke these words
of midst ,mount ,assembly

5921 3789 3254 3808 1419 6963 6205 6051 784
הָאֵשׁ הֶעָנָן וְהָעֲרָפֶל קוֹל גָּדוֹל וְלֹא יָסָף וַיִּכְתְּבֵם עַל־
on He and he no and ;great (with) of and the of the
them wrote ;added more voice a gloom the ,cloud ,fire

on two tablets of stone, and gave them to me. [23]And it happened, when you heard the voice out of the midst of the darkness, while the mountain burned with fire, you came near to me, all the rulers of your tribes, and your elders, [24]and you said, Behold, Jehovah your God has revealed His glory and His greatness to us, and we have heard His voice out of the midst of the fire; we have seen today that God speaks with man, and he lives. [25]Now then why should we die? For this great fire will consume us. If we hear the voice of Jehovah your God any more, then we shall die. [26]For who of all flesh that has heard the voice of the living God speaking out of the midst of the fire, as we *have,* and *has* lived? [27]You go near and hear all that Jehovah our God may say, and you shall speak to us all that Jehovah our God may speak to you. And we will hear it and do *it.* [28]And Jehovah heard the voice of your words when you spoke to me. And Jehovah said to me, I have heard the voice of the words of this people, which they have spoken to you; they have well *said* all that they have spoken. [29]Oh that this heart of theirs *would be* like this always, to fear Me, and to keep all My commandments, that it might be well with them, and with their sons forever.

[30]Go say to them, Return to your tents. [31]But as for you, you stand here by Me, and I will speak to you all the commandments and the

20 שְׁנֵי לֻחֹת אֲבָנִים וַיִּתְּנֵם אֵלָי׃ וַיְהִי כְּשָׁמְעֲכֶם אֶת־הַקּוֹל
the you when it And .me to gave and stone tablets two
voice heard ,was them of

מִתּוֹךְ הַחֹשֶׁךְ וְהָהָר בֹּעֵר בָּאֵשׁ וַתִּקְרְבוּן אֵלַי כָּל־רָאשֵׁי
the (even) me to you that with burned while dark- the the from
of heads all near came ,fire mountain the ,ness of midst

21 שִׁבְטֵיכֶם וְזִקְנֵיכֶם׃ וַתֹּאמְרוּ הֵן הֶרְאָנוּ יְהוָה אֱלֹהֵינוּ
God our Jehovah re- has ,Behold you and your and ,tribes your
us to vealed said ;elders

אֶת־כְּבֹדוֹ וְאֶת־גָּדְלוֹ וְאֶת־קֹלוֹ שָׁמַעְנוּ מִתּוֹךְ הָאֵשׁ הַיּוֹם
day the the from have we His and His and His
;fire of midst heard voice ,greatness glory

22 הַזֶּה רָאִינוּ כִּי־יְדַבֵּר אֱלֹהִים אֶת־הָאָדָם וָחָי׃ וְעַתָּה לָמָּה
why Now he and ,man with God speaks that have we this
,then .lives seen

נָמוּת כִּי תֹאכְלֵנוּ הָאֵשׁ הַגְּדֹלָה הַזֹּאת אִם־יֹסְפִים ׀ אֲנַחְנוּ
we again if ;this great fire will For should
us consume ?die we

23 לִשְׁמֹעַ אֶת־קוֹל יְהוָה אֱלֹהֵינוּ עוֹד וָמָתְנוּ׃ כִּי מִי כָל־
of all who For we then ,more our Jehovah the hear
(is there) .die shall God of voice

בָּשָׂר אֲשֶׁר שָׁמַע קוֹל אֱלֹהִים חַיִּים מְדַבֵּר מִתּוֹךְ־הָאֵשׁ
the the from speaking living the the has who flesh
fire of midst God of voice heard

24 כָּמֹנוּ וַיֶּחִי׃ קְרַב אַתָּה וּשְׁמָע אֵת כָּל־אֲשֶׁר יֹאמַר יְהוָה
Jehovah may that all and You come (has) and ,we as
say hear near ?lived

אֱלֹהֵינוּ וְאַתְּ ׀ תְּדַבֵּר אֵלֵינוּ אֵת כָּל־אֲשֶׁר יְדַבֵּר יְהוָה
Jehovah may that all us to shall and ;God our
speak speak you

25 אֱלֹהֵינוּ אֵלֶיךָ וְשָׁמַעְנוּ וְעָשִׂינוּ׃ וַיִּשְׁמַע יְהוָה אֶת־קוֹל
the Jehovah And and we and to God our
of voice heard .(it) do hear will ,you

דִּבְרֵיכֶם בְּדַבֶּרְכֶם אֵלַי וַיֹּאמֶר יְהוָה אֵלַי שָׁמַעְתִּי אֶת־
have I ,me to Jehovah said and ;me to you when your
heard spoke ,words

קוֹל דִּבְרֵי הָעָם הַזֶּה אֲשֶׁר דִּבְּרוּ אֵלֶיךָ הֵיטִיבוּ כָּל־אֲשֶׁר
that all have they to they which ,this people the the
well said ;you spoke of words of voice

26 דִּבֵּרוּ׃ מִי־יִתֵּן וְהָיָה לְבָבָם זֶה לָהֶם לְיִרְאָה אֹתִי וְלִשְׁמֹר
and ,Me fear to to as a such there that O have they
keep ,them this heart was .spoken

אֶת־כָּל־מִצְוֹתַי כָּל־הַיָּמִים לְמַעַן יִיטַב לָהֶם וְלִבְנֵיהֶם
with and with might it that the all My all
sons their ,them well be ,days commands

27 28 לְעֹלָם׃ לֵךְ אֱמֹר לָהֶם שׁוּבוּ לָכֶם לְאָהֳלֵיכֶם׃ וְאַתָּה פֹּה
,here But your to of Return to say Go .forever
you .tents yourselves ,them

עֲמֹד עִמָּדִי וַאֲדַבְּרָה אֵלֶיךָ אֵת כָּל־הַמִּצְוָה וְהַחֻקִּים
the and the all you to will I and ,Me by stand
statutes commands speak

statutes and the ordinances which you shall teach them, that they may do them in the land which I am giving to them, to possess it. 32And you shall be careful to do as Jehovah your God has commanded you; you shall not turn aside to the right or left. 33You shall walk in all the ways which Jehovah your God has commanded you, so that you may live, and *that* good *may be* to you, and you may prolong *your* days in the land which you will possess.

5414 834 776 6213 3925 834 4941
וְהַמִּשְׁפָּטִים אֲשֶׁר תְּלַמְּדֵם וְעָשׂוּ בָאָרֶץ אֲשֶׁר אָנֹכִי נֹתֵן
am I which the in they that shall you which the and
giving land (them) do may ,them teach judgments

3068 6680 6213 8104 3423
29 לָהֶם לְרִשְׁתָּהּ׃ וּשְׁמַרְתֶּם לַעֲשׂוֹת כַּאֲשֶׁר צִוָּה יְהוָֹה
Jehovah has as do to shall you And to to
commanded careful be .it possess ,them

1870 3605 8040 3225 5493 430
30 אֱלֹהֵיכֶם אֶתְכֶם לֹא תָסֻרוּ יָמִין וּשְׂמֹאל׃ בְּכָל־הַדֶּרֶךְ
the in or the to shall you not ;you God your
ways all ;left right aside turn

2896 2421 3212 430 3068 6680 834
אֲשֶׁר צִוָּה יְהוָֹה אֱלֹהֵיכֶם אֶתְכֶם תֵּלֵכוּ לְמַעַן תִּחְיוּן וְטוֹב
and may you so shall you you God your Jehovah has which
good live that ,walk commanded

3423 834 776 3117 748
לָכֶם וְהַאֲרַכְתֶּם יָמִים בָּאָרֶץ אֲשֶׁר תִּירָשׁוּן׃
will you which the in (your) you and (be may)
.possess land days prolong may ,you to

CAP. VI ו

CHAPTER 6

CHAPTER 6

1And this *is* the commandment, the statute and the judgments which Jehovah your God commanded to teach you, to do *them* in the land to which you are crossing over, to possess it, 2that you might fear Jehovah your God, to keep all His statutes and His commandments which I command you; you, and your son, and your sons' son, all the days of your life; and that your days may be prolonged. 3Hear, then, O Israel, and take heed to do *it*, that it may be well with you, that you may increase mightily, as Jehovah the God of your fathers has promised you, *in* the land flowing with milk and honey.

3068 6680 834 4941 2706 4687
1 וְזֹאת הַמִּצְוָה הַחֻקִּים וְהַמִּשְׁפָּטִים אֲשֶׁר צִוָּה יְהוָֹה
Jehovah com- which the and the com- the Now
manded judgments ,statutes ,mandment (is) this

5674 834 776 6213 3925 430
אֱלֹהֵיכֶם לְלַמֵּד אֶתְכֶם לַעֲשׂוֹת בָּאָרֶץ אֲשֶׁר אַתֶּם עֹבְרִים
are you which the in do to ,you teach to God your
over crossing land (them)

8104 430 3068 3372 3423
2 שָׁמָּה לְרִשְׁתָּהּ׃ לְמַעַן תִּירָא אֶת־יְהוָֹה אֱלֹהֶיךָ לִשְׁמֹר
keep to ,God your Jehovah you that possess to ,to
fear might ,it

1121 6680 834 4687 2708 3605
אֶת־כָּל־חֻקֹּתָיו וּמִצְוֹתָיו אֲשֶׁר אָנֹכִי מְצַוֶּךָ אַתָּה וּבִנְךָ
and ,you command I which His and His all
,son your commands statutes

8085 3117 748 2416 3117 3605 1121/1121
3 וּבֶן־בִּנְךָ כֹּל יְמֵי חַיֶּיךָ וּלְמַעַן יַאֲרִכֻן יָמֶיךָ׃ וְשָׁמַעְתָּ
Hear your be may and your the all your and
then .days prolonged that ;life of days son's son

7231 3190 6213 8104 3478
יִשְׂרָאֵל וְשָׁמַרְתָּ לַעֲשׂוֹת אֲשֶׁר יִיטַב לְךָ וַאֲשֶׁר תִּרְבּוּן
may you and with may it that do to take And O
increase that ,you well be ;(it) heed Israel

2100 776 1 430 3068 1696 3966
מְאֹד כַּאֲשֶׁר דִּבֶּר יְהוָֹה אֱלֹהֵי אֲבֹתֶיךָ לָךְ אֶרֶץ זָבַת
flowing (in) to your the Jehovah has as ,greatly
with land the ;you fathers of God spoken

1706 2461
חָלָב וּדְבָשׁ׃
and milk
.honey

4Hear, O Israel, Jehovah our God *is* one Jehovah. 5And you shall love Jehovah your God with all your heart, and with all your soul, and with all your might. 6And these words that I am commanding you today shall be on your heart. 7And you shall point out them to your sons.

157 259 3068 430 3068 3478 8085
4
5 שְׁמַע יִשְׂרָאֵל יְהוָֹה אֱלֹהֵינוּ יְהוָֹה ׀ אֶחָד׃ וְאָהַבְתָּ אֵת
you and ;one (is) our Jehovah O ,Hear
love shall Jehovah God ,Israel

3966 3605 5315 3605 3824 3605 430 3068
יְהוָֹה אֱלֹהֶיךָ בְּכָל־לְבָבְךָ וּבְכָל־נַפְשְׁךָ וּבְכָל־מְאֹדֶךָ׃
your and your and your with your Jehovah
;might all with ,soul all with ,heart all God

3824 5921 3117 6680 834 428 1697 1961
6 וְהָיוּ הַדְּבָרִים הָאֵלֶּה אֲשֶׁר אָנֹכִי מְצַוְּךָ הַיּוֹם עַל־לְבָבֶךָ׃
your on today com- I which these words and
,heart you manded be shall

and shall speak of them as
you sit in your house, and as
you walk in the way, and as
you are lying down, and as
your are rising up. [8]And *you*
shall bind them for a sign on
your hand; and they shall be
for frontlets between your
eyes. [9]And you shall write
them on the doorposts of
your house, and on your
gates.
[10]And it shall be, when
Jehovah your God shall
bring you into the land
which He has sworn to your
fathers, to Abraham, to
Isaac, and to Jacob, to give
to you great and good
cities, which you have not
built, [11]and houses full of
good things which you
have not filled, and wells
dug which you did not dig,
vineyards and oliveyards
which you did not plant —
and you shall eat and be
satisfied— [12]you shall be on
guard that you not forget
Jehovah who brought you
out of the land of Egypt, out
of the house of slaves.
[13]You shall fear Jehovah
your God, and you shall
serve Him, and you shall
swear by His name. [14]You
shall not go after other
gods, of the gods of the
peoples who *are* around
you— [15]for Jehovah your
God *is* a jealous God in your
midst—lest the anger of
Jehovah your God burn
against you, and He destroy
you from off the face of the
earth.
[16]You shall not test
Jehovah your God as you
tested *Him* in Massah.
[17]You shall diligently keep
the commands of Jehovah
your God, and His testi-
monies, and His statutes
which He has commanded
you. [18]And you shall do the
right thing and the good
thing in the eyes of
Jehovah, so that it may be
well with you, and that you
may go in and possess the
good land which Jehovah

3212 1004 3427 1696 1121 8150
7 וְשִׁנַּנְתָּם לְבָנֶיךָ וְדִבַּרְתָּ בָּם בְּשִׁבְתְּךָ בְּבֵיתֶךָ וּבְלֶכְתְּךָ
when and your in you when of shall and your to shall you and
walk you ,house sit them speak ,sons them sharpen
1961 3027 226 7194 6965 7901 1870
8 בַדֶּרֶךְ וּבְשָׁכְבְּךָ וּבְקוּמֶךָ׃ וּקְשַׁרְתָּם לְאוֹת עַל־יָדֶךָ וְהָיוּ
they and your on a for shall and you when and when and the in
be shall ;hand sign them bind ;up rise ,down lie you ,way
8179 1004 4201 3789 5869 996 2903
9 לְטֹטָפֹת בֵּין עֵינֶיךָ׃ וּכְתַבְתָּם עַל־מְזֻזוֹת בֵּיתֶךָ וּבִשְׁעָרֶיךָ׃
on and your door- the on shall you And your be- for
.gates your ;house of posts them write .eyes tween frontlets
7650 776 430 3068 935 1961
10 וְהָיָה כִּי־יְבִיאֲךָ יְהוָה אֱלֹהֶיךָ אֶל־הָאָרֶץ אֲשֶׁר נִשְׁבַּע
He which the into your Jehovah shall when it And
swore land God you bring ,be shall
5892 5414 3290 3327 85
לַאֲבֹתֶיךָ לְאַבְרָהָם לְיִצְחָק וּלְיַעֲקֹב לָתֶת לָךְ עָרִים
cities to give to to and ,Isaac to ,Abraham to your to
you Jacob ,fathers
2898 3605 4392 1004 1129 2896 1419
11 גְּדֹלֹת וְטֹבֹת אֲשֶׁר לֹא־בָנִיתָ׃ וּבָתִּים מְלֵאִים כָּל־טוּב
good every of full and you not which and great
thing houses built have good
3754 2672 2672 953 4390 3808 834
אֲשֶׁר לֹא־מִלֵּאתָ וּבֹרֹת חֲצוּבִים אֲשֶׁר לֹא־חָצַבְתָּ כְּרָמִים
vineyards did you not which dug and have you not which
dig wells ,filled
6435 8104 7646 398 5193 2132
12 וְזֵיתִים אֲשֶׁר לֹא־נָטָעְתָּ וְאָכַלְתָּ וְשָׂבָעְתָּ׃ הִשָּׁמֶר לְךָ פֶּן
lest (then) be and you and did you not which olive and
beware ;satisfied eat shall plant yards
1004 4714 776 3318 834 3068 7911
תִּשְׁכַּח אֶת־יְהוָה אֲשֶׁר הוֹצִיאֲךָ מֵאֶרֶץ מִצְרַיִם מִבֵּית
of out ,Egypt the of brought who Jehovah you
of house the of land out you forget
8034 5647 3372 430 3068 5650
13 עֲבָדִים׃ אֶת־יְהוָה אֱלֹהֶיךָ תִּירָא וְאֹתוֹ תַעֲבֹד וּבִשְׁמוֹ
by and shall you and shall you your Jehovah .slaves
name His ,serve Him ,fear God
5971 430 312 430 310 3212 3808 7650
14 תִּשָּׁבֵעַ׃ לֹא תֵלְכוּן אַחֲרֵי אֱלֹהִים אֲחֵרִים מֵאֱלֹהֵי הָעַמִּים
the the of ,other gods, after shall you not you shall
peoples of gods go ;swear
7130 430 3068 7067 410 5439
15 אֲשֶׁר סְבִיבוֹתֵיכֶם׃ כִּי אֵל קַנָּא יְהוָה אֱלֹהֶיךָ בְּקִרְבֶּךָ
your in your (is) jealous a for ;you around who
,midst God Jehovah God (are)
6440 8045 430 3068 639 2734
פֶּן־יֶחֱרֶה אַף־יְהוָה אֱלֹהֶיךָ בָּךְ וְהִשְׁמִידְךָ מֵעַל פְּנֵי
the from He and against your Jehovah the glow lest
of face off you destroy ,you God of anger
430 3068 5254 3808 127
16 הָאֲדָמָה׃ לֹא תְנַסּוּ אֶת־יְהוָה אֱלֹהֵיכֶם כַּאֲשֶׁר
as God your Jehovah You not the
test shall .earth
430 3068 4687 8104 8104 4531 5254
17 נִסִּיתֶם בַּמַּסָּה׃ שָׁמוֹר תִּשְׁמְרוּן אֶת־מִצְוֹת יְהוָה אֱלֹהֵיכֶם
your Jehovah the shall You diligently in you
God of commands keep ;Massah tested
5869 2896 3477 6213 6680 834 2706 5713
18 וְעֵדֹתָיו וְחֻקָּיו אֲשֶׁר צִוָּךְ׃ וְעָשִׂיתָ הַיָּשָׁר וְהַטּוֹב בְּעֵינֵי
the in the and right the you and com- He which His and His and
of eyes thing good thing do shall ;you manded statutes, testimonies
2896 776 3423 935 3190 3068
יְהוָה לְמַעַן יִיטַב לָךְ וּבָאתָ וְיָרַשְׁתָּ אֶת־הָאָרֶץ הַטֹּבָה
good land the and you and with may it so Jehovah
possess in go may ,you well be

has sworn to your fathers,
19to cast out all your
enemies from before you,
as Jehovah has spoken.
20When your son asks
you hereafter, saying, What
are the testimonies and the
statutes and the ordinances
which Jehovah your God
has commanded you?
21Then you shall say to your
son, We were Pharaoh's
slaves in Egypt, and
Jehovah brought us out of
Egypt with a mighty hand.
22And Jehovah gave signs
and great and grievous
wonders on Egypt, on
Pharaoh, and on all his
household, before our eyes.
23And He has brought us
out from there in order to
bring us in, to give us the
land which He had sworn to
our fathers. 24And Jehovah
commanded us to do all
these statutes, to fear
Jehovah our God for our
good forever, to keep us
alive, as today. 25And it
shall be righteousness for
us when we are careful to
do all this commandment
before Jehovah our God, as
He has commanded us.

6440 341 3605 3423 1 3068 7650 834
19 אֲשֶׁר־נִשְׁבַּע יְהוָה לַאֲבֹתֶיךָ: לַהֲדֹף אֶת־כָּל־אֹיְבֶיךָ מִפָּנֶיךָ
be-from your all drive to your to Jehovah has which
,you fore enemies out ,fathers sworn

559 4279 1121 7592 3068 1696
20 כַּאֲשֶׁר דִּבֶּר יְהוָה: כִּי־יִשְׁאָלְךָ בִנְךָ מָחָר לֵאמֹר
,saying here- your asks When .Jehovah has as
,after son you spoken

430 3068 6680 834 4941 2706 4713
מָה הָעֵדֹת וְהַחֻקִּים וְהַמִּשְׁפָּטִים אֲשֶׁר צִוָּה יְהוָה אֱלֹהֵינוּ
our Jehovah has which the and the and test- the What
God commanded judgments statutes imonies (are)

4714 6547 1961 5650 1121 559
21 אֶתְכֶם: וְאָמַרְתָּ לְבִנְךָ עֲבָדִים הָיִינוּ לְפַרְעֹה בְּמִצְרָיִם
,Egypt in to were We slaves your to you Then ?you
Pharaoh ,son say shall

226 3068 5414 2389 3027 4714 3068 3318
22 וַיֹּצִיאֵנוּ יְהוָה מִמִּצְרַיִם בְּיָד חֲזָקָה: וַיִּתֵּן יְהוָה אוֹתֹת
,signs Jehovah And .strong a with of out Jehovah and
gave hand Egypt us brought

1004 3605 6547 4714 7451 1419 4159
וּמֹפְתִים גְּדֹלִים וְרָעִים בְּמִצְרַיִם בְּפַרְעֹה וּבְכָל־בֵּיתוֹ
his against and against against and great and
,house all ,Pharaoh ,Egypt ,grievous wonders

5414 935 8033 3318 5869
23 לְעֵינֵינוּ: וְאוֹתָנוּ הוֹצִיא מִשָּׁם לְמַעַן הָבִיא אֹתָנוּ לָתֶת
to (and) us bring order in from He us and before
give in to ,there out brought ;eyes our

6213 3068 6680 7650 834 776
24 לָנוּ אֶת־הָאָרֶץ אֲשֶׁר נִשְׁבַּע לַאֲבֹתֵינוּ: וַיְצַוֵּנוּ יְהוָה לַעֲשׂוֹת
do to Jehovah And our to had He which the us to
us commanded .fathers sworn land

2896 430 3068 3372 428 2706 3605
אֶת־כָּל־הַחֻקִּים הָאֵלֶּה לְיִרְאָה אֶת־יְהוָה אֱלֹהֵינוּ לְטוֹב
for our Jehovah fear to ,these statutes all
good ,God

1961 6666 2088 3117 2421 3117 3605
25 לָנוּ כָּל־הַיָּמִים לְחַיֹּתֵנוּ כְּהַיּוֹם הַזֶּה: וּצְדָקָה תִּהְיֶה־לָּנוּ כִּי־
when for shall it And .this day as keep to the all our
us be righteousness ,alive us ,days

430 3068 6440 2063 4687 3605 6213 8104
נִשְׁמֹר לַעֲשׂוֹת אֶת־כָּל־הַמִּצְוָה הַזֹּאת לִפְנֵי יְהוָה אֱלֹהֵינוּ
,God our Jehovah before this command- all do to are we
ment careful

6680
כַּאֲשֶׁר צִוָּנוּ:
has He as
.us commanded

CHAPTER 7

1When Jehovah your
God shall bring you into
the land to which you are
going, to possess it, and
He casts out many
nations from before you,
the Hittite, and the Girgashite, and the Amorite
and the Caananite, and
the Perizzite, and the
Hivite, and the Jebusite
—seven nations larger
and mightier than you.
2And Jehovah your God
gives them up before you,
and you strike them,
then you shall utterly

CAP. VII ז

CHAPTER 7

935 834 776 430 3068 935
1 כִּי יְבִיאֲךָ יְהוָה אֱלֹהֶיךָ אֶל־הָאָרֶץ אֲשֶׁר־אַתָּה בָא־שָׁמָּה
,to are you which the into your Jehovah shall When
going land God you bring

567 1622 2850 6440 7227 1471 5394 3423
לְרִשְׁתָּהּ וְנָשַׁל גּוֹיִם־רַבִּים מִפָּנֶיךָ הַחִתִּי וְהַגִּרְגָּשִׁי וְהָאֱמֹרִי
the and the and the before from many nations He and possess to
Amorite ,Girgashite ,Hittite ,you out casts ,it

6099 7227 1471 7651 2983 2340 6522 3669
וְהַכְּנַעֲנִי וְהַפְּרִזִּי וְהַחִוִּי וְהַיְבוּסִי שִׁבְעָה גוֹיִם רַבִּים וַעֲצוּמִים
and larger nations seven the and the and the and the and
mightier Jebusite, ,Hivite ,Perizzite ,Canaanite

2763 5221 6440 430 3068 5414
2 מִמֶּךָּ: וּנְתָנָם יְהוָה אֱלֹהֶיךָ לְפָנֶיךָ וְהִכִּיתָם הַחֲרֵם
(then) you and before God your Jehovah gives and than
utterly ;them strike ,you up them ;you

destroy them; you shall not cut a covenant with them, nor show mercy to them; [3]nor shall you intermarry with them; you shall not give your daughter to his son, nor shall you take his daughter to your son. [4]For he will turn your son away from following Me, that they may serve other gods; and the anger of Jehovah will glow against you, and He will destroy you quickly. [5]But you shall deal with them in this way: you shall break down their altars, and dash in pieces the cult-stones; and you shall cut down their pillars; and you will burn their carved images with fire.

[6]For you *are* a holy people to Jehovah your God. Jehovah your God has chosen you to be His own treasure, out of all the people on the face of the earth. [7]Jehovah did not set His love on you or choose you because you were more in number than any people, for you *were* the fewest of all peoples. [8]But because Jehovah loved you, and because He kept the oath which He swore to your fathers, Jehovah has caused you to go out with a strong hand, and redeemed you from the house of slaves, from the hand of Pharaoh king of Egypt. [9]Because of this, know that Jehovah your God, He *is* God, the faithful God, keeping the covenant, and mercy to those who love Him, and to those who keep His commands, to a thousand generations; [10]and repaying to his face those that hate Him, to destroy him; He will not delay, He will repay him who hates Him to his face. [11]And you shall keep the commandments, and the statutes, and the ordinances which I am commanding you today, to do them.

3 תַּחֲרִים אֹתָם לֹא־תִכְרֹת לָהֶם בְּרִית וְלֹא תְחָנֵּם׃ וְלֹא
תִתְחַתֵּן בָּם בִּתְּךָ לֹא־תִתֵּן לִבְנוֹ וּבִתּוֹ לֹא־תִקַּח לִבְנֶךָ׃
4 כִּי־יָסִיר אֶת־בִּנְךָ מֵאַחֲרַי וְעָבְדוּ אֱלֹהִים אֲחֵרִים וְחָרָה
5 אַף־יְהוָה בָּכֶם וְהִשְׁמִידְךָ מַהֵר׃ כִּי־אִם־כֹּה תַעֲשׂוּ לָהֶם
מִזְבְּחֹתֵיהֶם תִּתֹּצוּ וּמַצֵּבֹתָם תְּשַׁבֵּרוּ וַאֲשִׁירֵהֶם תְּגַדֵּעוּן
6 וּפְסִילֵיהֶם תִּשְׂרְפוּן בָּאֵשׁ׃ כִּי עַם קָדוֹשׁ אַתָּה לַיהוָה
אֱלֹהֶיךָ בְּךָ בָּחַר ׀ יְהוָה אֱלֹהֶיךָ לִהְיוֹת לוֹ לְעַם סְגֻלָּה
7 מִכֹּל הָעַמִּים אֲשֶׁר עַל־פְּנֵי הָאֲדָמָה׃ לֹא מֵרֻבְּכֶם מִכָּל־
הָעַמִּים חָשַׁק יְהוָה בָּכֶם וַיִּבְחַר בָּכֶם כִּי־אַתֶּם הַמְעַט
8 מִכָּל־הָעַמִּים׃ כִּי מֵאַהֲבַת יְהוָה אֶתְכֶם וּמִשָּׁמְרוֹ אֶת־
הַשְּׁבֻעָה אֲשֶׁר נִשְׁבַּע לַאֲבֹתֵיכֶם הוֹצִיא יְהוָה אֶתְכֶם בְּיָד
חֲזָקָה וַיִּפְדְּךָ מִבֵּית עֲבָדִים מִיַּד פַּרְעֹה מֶלֶךְ־מִצְרָיִם׃
9 וְיָדַעְתָּ כִּי־יְהוָה אֱלֹהֶיךָ הוּא הָאֱלֹהִים הָאֵל הַנֶּאֱמָן שֹׁמֵר
הַבְּרִית וְהַחֶסֶד לְאֹהֲבָיו וּלְשֹׁמְרֵי מִצְוֹתָו לְאֶלֶף דּוֹר׃
10 וּמְשַׁלֵּם לְשֹׂנְאָיו אֶל־פָּנָיו לְהַאֲבִידוֹ לֹא יְאַחֵר לְשֹׂנְאוֹ אֶל־
11 פָּנָיו יְשַׁלֶּם־לוֹ׃ וְשָׁמַרְתָּ אֶת־הַמִּצְוָה וְאֶת־הַחֻקִּים וְאֶת־
הַמִּשְׁפָּטִים אֲשֶׁר אָנֹכִי מְצַוְּךָ הַיּוֹם לַעֲשׂוֹתָם׃

[12]And it shall be, because you hear judgments, and keep and do them, even Jehovah your God will keep with you the covenant and the mercy which He swore to your fathers. [13]And He will love you, and bless you, and multiply you. He will also bless the fruit of your body, and the fruit of your land, your grain and your wine and your oil, the increase of your oxen and the wealth of your flock, in the land which He has sworn to your fathers, to give *it* to you. [14]You shall be blessed above all people; there shall not be a barren man or a barren woman among you, nor among your livestock. [15]And Jehovah shall turn aside every sickness from you; and He will not put on you any of the evil diseases of Egypt, which you have known; but He will put them on all who hate you. [16]And you shall destroy all the peoples whom Jehovah your God is giving to you. And your eye shall have no pity on them; and you shall not serve their gods; for it *shall be* a snare to you.

[17]If you shall say in your heart, These nations *are* more plentiful than I; how can I throw them out?— [18]you shall not be afraid of them; you shall surely remember that which Jehovah your God has done to Pharaoh, and to all Egypt, [19]the great trials which your eyes have seen, and the miracles, and the wonders, and the mighty hand, and the stretched-out arm with which Jehovah your God has brought you out. So Jehovah your God shall do to all the peoples of whose face you are afraid. [20]And Jehovah your God shall send the hornets among

8104 428 4941 8085 6118 1961

12 וְהָיָה ׀ עֵקֶב תִּשְׁמְעוּן אֵת הַמִּשְׁפָּטִים הָאֵלֶּה וּשְׁמַרְתֶּם

keep and ,these judgments hear you because it And ,be shall

1285 430 3068 8104 6213

וַעֲשִׂיתֶם אֹתָם וְשָׁמַר יְהוָה אֱלֹהֶיךָ לְךָ אֶת־הַבְּרִית וְאֶת־

and the covenant with you God your Jehovah that keep will ,them do and

7235 1288 157 1 7650 834 2617

13 הַחֶסֶד אֲשֶׁר נִשְׁבַּע לַאֲבֹתֶיךָ׃ וַאֲהֵבְךָ וּבֵרַכְךָ וְהִרְבֶּךָ

multi- and ;you ply bless and ,you He and ,you love will your ;fathers to He swore which the mercy

808 8492 1715 127 6529 996 6527 1288

וּבֵרַךְ פְּרִי־בִטְנְךָ וּפְרִי־אַדְמָתֶךָ דְּגָנְךָ וְתִירֹשְׁךָ וְיִצְהָרֶךָ

your and oil fresh your and ,wine new your ,grain your ,land the and of fruit your ,body of fruit will He bless also

7650 834 127 6629 6251 504 7698

שְׁגַר־אֲלָפֶיךָ וְעַשְׁתְּרֹת צֹאנֶךָ עַל הָאֲדָמָה אֲשֶׁר־נִשְׁבַּע

has He sworn which the land in your ,flock young the and of ones your ,oxen off- the of spring

1961 3808 5971 3605 1961 1288 5414 1

14 לַאֲבֹתֶיךָ לָתֶת לָךְ׃ בָּרוּךְ תִּהְיֶה מִכָּל־הָעַמִּים לֹא־יִהְיֶה

there be shall not ;people above all shall You be blessed to .you give to your to fathers

3605 3068 5493 929 6135 6135

15 בְךָ עָקָר וַעֲקָרָה וּבִבְהֶמְתֶּךָ׃ וְהֵסִיר יְהוָה מִמְּךָ כָּל־חֹלִי

sick- every ;ness from you Jehovah shall and aside turn among ;cattle your nor barren a woman or man barren a among you

7760 3808 3045 834 7451 4714 4064 2483

וְכָל־מַדְוֵי מִצְרַיִם הָרָעִים אֲשֶׁר יָדַעְתָּ לֹא יְשִׂימָם בָּךְ

on you shall He them put not have you ;known have which ,evil Egypt dis- the of eases and all

3068 834 5971 3605 398 8130 3605 5414

16 וּנְתָנָם בְּכָל־שֹׂנְאֶיךָ׃ וְאָכַלְתָּ אֶת־כָּל־הָעַמִּים אֲשֶׁר יְהוָה

Jehovah whom the peoples all you And consume shall hate who ,you all on He but them put shall

5647 3808 5869 2347 3808 5414 430

אֱלֹהֶיךָ נֹתֵן לָךְ לֹא־תָחוֹס עֵינְךָ עֲלֵיהֶם וְלֹא תַעֲבֹד אֶת־

shall you serve and not on ,them your eye have shall pity not to ;you is giving your God

3824 559 4170 430

17 אֱלֹהֵיהֶם כִּי־מוֹקֵשׁ הוּא לָךְ׃ כִּי תֹאמַר בִּלְבָבְךָ

your in ,heart shall you say If to .you it (be shall) snare a for their ,gods

3808 3423 3201 349 428 1471 7227

18 רַבִּים הַגּוֹיִם הָאֵלֶּה מִמֶּנִּי אֵיכָה אוּכַל לְהוֹרִישָׁם׃ לֹא

not dispossess to ?them I shall able be how than ;I These nations (are) too many

430 3068 6213 834 2142 2142 3372

תִירָא מֵהֶם זָכֹר תִּזְכֹּר אֵת אֲשֶׁר־עָשָׂה יְהוָה אֱלֹהֶיךָ

your God Jehovah has done that which shall you remember surely of ;them shall You afraid be

5869 7200 834 1419 4531 4714 3605 6547

19 לְפַרְעֹה וּלְכָל־מִצְרָיִם׃ הַמַּסֹּת הַגְּדֹלֹת אֲשֶׁר־רָאוּ עֵינֶיךָ

your eyes have seen which great the trials ,Egypt to and all to ,Pharaoh

834 5186 2220 2389 3027 4154 226

וְהָאֹתֹת וְהַמֹּפְתִים וְהַיָּד הַחֲזָקָה וְהַזְּרֹעַ הַנְּטוּיָה אֲשֶׁר

with which stretched- out the and arm ,strong the and hand the and ,wonders the and ,signs

5971 3605 430 3068 6213 430 3068 3318

הוֹצִאֲךָ יְהוָה אֱלֹהֶיךָ כֵּן־יַעֲשֶׂה יְהוָה אֱלֹהֶיךָ לְכָל־הָעַמִּים

the peoples to all your God Jehovah shall do so your ;God Jeho- vah brought has out you

3068 7971 6880 1571 6440 3373 834

20 אֲשֶׁר־אַתָּה יָרֵא מִפְּנֵיהֶם׃ וְגַם אֶת־הַצִּרְעָה יְשַׁלַּח יְהוָה

Jehovah shall send hornets the And also their from .face are afraid you of whom

them, until the ones who are left perish, even *those* who hide themselves from your face.
[21]You shall not be afraid of them, for Jehovah your God *is* among you, a mighty and fearful God. [22]And Jehovah your God will clear out those nations before you by little and little. You may not destroy them at once, lest the beasts of the field increase upon you. [23]And Jehovah your God shall deliver them up before you, and destroy them with a great destruction until they are exterminated. [24]And He shall give their kings into your hand; and you shall destroy their name from under the heavens. No man shall be able to stand before you until you have destroyed them. [25]You shall burn the carved images of their gods with fire; and you shall not lust after the silver and gold on them, nor shall you take *it* to yourself, that you not be snared by it; for it *is* an abomination to Jehovah. [26]And you shall not bring an abomination into your house, that you not be a cursed thing like it. You shall utterly detest it, and you shall utterly hate it; for it *is* a cursed thing.

אֱלֹהֶיךָ בָּם עַד־אֲבֹד הַנִּשְׁאָרִים וְהַנִּסְתָּרִים מִפָּנֶיךָ׃ לֹא 21
not from hide who and who ones the perish until among your
.face your themselves left are ,them God

תַעֲרֹץ מִפְּנֵיהֶם כִּי־יְהוָה אֱלֹהֶיךָ בְּקִרְבֶּךָ אֵל גָּדוֹל
great a among (is) your Jehovah for before shall You
God you God ,them tremble

וְנוֹרָא׃ וְנָשַׁל יְהוָה אֱלֹהֶיךָ אֶת־הַגּוֹיִם הָאֵל מִפָּנֶיךָ מְעַט 22
little before those nations your Jehovah will And and
,you God out clear .fearful

מְעָט לֹא תוּכַל כַּלֹּתָם מַהֵר פֶּן־תִּרְבֶּה עָלֶיךָ חַיַּת הַשָּׂדֶה׃
.field the the upon multiply lest at finish may you not by
of beasts you once them ;little

וּנְתָנָם יְהוָה אֱלֹהֶיךָ לְפָנֶיךָ וְהָמָם מְהוּמָה גְדֹלָה עַד 23
until great a with destroy and before your Jehovah will And
destruction them you God up them give

הִשָּׁמְדָם׃ וְנָתַן מַלְכֵיהֶם בְּיָדֶךָ וְהַאֲבַדְתָּ אֶת־שְׁמָם מִתַּחַת 24
from their you and into their He And ex- are they
under name destroy shall ;hand your kings give shall .terminated

הַשָּׁמָיִם לֹא־יִתְיַצֵּב אִישׁ בְּפָנֶיךָ עַד הִשְׁמִדְךָ אֹתָם׃ פְּסִילֵי 25
carved the .them have you until before A shall not the
of images destroyed you man up stand ;heavens

אֱלֹהֵיהֶם תִּשְׂרְפוּן בָּאֵשׁ לֹא־תַחְמֹד כֶּסֶף וְזָהָב עֲלֵיהֶם
,them on and the shall you not with shall You their
gold silver desire ;fire burn gods

וְלָקַחְתָּ לָךְ פֶּן תִּוָּקֵשׁ בּוֹ כִּי תוֹעֲבַת יְהוָה אֱלֹהֶיךָ הוּא׃
;(is) it your to abomi- an for by be you lest to take nor
God Jehovah nation ;it snared ,yourself (it)

וְלֹא־תָבִיא תוֹעֵבָה אֶל־בֵּיתֶךָ וְהָיִיתָ חֵרֶם כָּמֹהוּ שַׁקֵּץ ׀ 26
utterly like cursed a you lest your into an shall you and
;it thing be ,house abomination bring not

תְּשַׁקְּצֶנּוּ וְתַעֵב ׀ תְּתַעֲבֶנּוּ כִּי־חֵרֶם הוּא׃ פ
it cursed a for shall you and shall you
.(is) thing ;it abhor utterly it detest

CAP. VIII

CHAPTER 8

[1]You shall take heed to do every commmandment which I am commanding you today, so that you may live and may multiply and may go in and possess the land which Jehovah has sworn to your fathers. [2]And you shall remember all the way which Jehovah your God has caused you to go these forty years in the wilderness, in order to humble you, to try you, to know that which *is* in your heart, whether you will keep His commandments or not. [3]And He has

כָּל־הַמִּצְוָה אֲשֶׁר אָנֹכִי מְצַוְּךָ הַיּוֹם תִּשְׁמְרוּן לַעֲשׂוֹת 1
,do to be shall you this com- I which com- Every
watchful day you mand mandment

לְמַעַן תִּחְיוּן וּרְבִיתֶם וּבָאתֶם וִירִשְׁתֶּם אֶת־הָאָרֶץ אֲשֶׁר־
which the and may and may and may you so
land possess in go mutliply live that

נִשְׁבַּע יְהוָה לַאֲבֹתֵיכֶם׃ וְזָכַרְתָּ אֶת־כָּל־הַדֶּרֶךְ אֲשֶׁר 2
which the all shall you and your to Jehovah has
way remember ;fathers sworn

הוֹלִיכְךָ יְהוָה אֱלֹהֶיךָ זֶה אַרְבָּעִים שָׁנָה בַּמִּדְבָּר לְמַעַן
order in the in years forty this your Jehovah has
to ,wilderness God you brought

עַנֹּתְךָ לְנַסֹּתְךָ לָדַעַת אֶת־אֲשֶׁר בִּלְבָבְךָ הֲתִשְׁמֹר מִצְוֹתָו
His you whether your in what know to try to humble
commands keep will ,heart (is) ,you ,you

humbled you, and caused you to hunger, and caused you to eat the manna, which you had not known, even your fathers had not known, in order to cause you to know that man shall not live by bread alone, but man shall live by every word that proceeds from the mouth of Jehovah. [4]Your clothing did not wear out on you, and your foot did not swell, these forty years. [5]And you have known with your heart that as a man disciplines his son, Jehovah your God disciplines you. [6]And you shall keep the commandments of Jehovah your God, to walk in His ways, and to fear Him. [7]For Jehovah your God brings you into a good land, a land of streams of water, of fountains and depths that spring out of valleys and hills, [8]a land of wheat and barley and vines and fig trees and pomegranates, a land of olive oil and honey, [9]a land in which you shall eat bread without want; you shall not lack anything in it; a land whose stones *are* iron; and you shall dig copper out of its mountains. [10]And you shall eat and be satisfied; and you shall bless Jehovah your God in the good land which He has given to you.

[11]Take heed to yourself, lest you forget Jehovah your God so as not to keep His commandments, and His ordinances, and His statutes, which I am commanding you today; [12]that *when* you have eaten and are satisfied, and have built goodly houses, and have lived *in them*; [13]and when your herds and your flocks multiply, and your silver and your gold have multiplied, and all that you have is multiplied; [14]then it rises up into your heart, and you forget Jehovah your

3 אִם־לֹא׃ וַיְעַנְּךָ וַיַּרְעִבֶךָ וַיַּאֲכִלְךָ אֶת־הַמָּן אֲשֶׁר לֹא־
not which the caused and gave and He And .not or
,manna eat to you ,hunger you ,you humbled

יָדַעְתָּ וְלֹא יָדְעוּן אֲבֹתֶיךָ לְמַעַן הוֹדִיעֲךָ כִּי לֹא עַל־הַלֶּחֶם
bread by not that you cause in your had even had you
know to to order ,fathers known not known

לְבַדּוֹ יִחְיֶה הָאָדָם כִּי עַל־כָּל־מוֹצָא פִי־יְהוָה יִחְיֶה הָאָדָם׃
.man shall Jehovah the coming every by but ,man shall alone
live of mouth of out word live

4 שִׂמְלָתְךָ לֹא בָלְתָה מֵעָלֶיךָ וְרַגְלְךָ לֹא בָצֵקָה זֶה אַרְבָּעִים
forty this did not your and on did not Your
swell foot ,you out wear mantle

5 שָׁנָה׃ וְיָדַעְתָּ עִם־לְבָבֶךָ כִּי כַּאֲשֶׁר יְיַסֵּר אִישׁ אֶת־בְּנוֹ
his a corrects as that your with you and ;years
son man heart known have

6 יְהוָה אֱלֹהֶיךָ מְיַסְּרֶךָּ׃ וְשָׁמַרְתָּ אֶת־מִצְוֹת יְהוָה אֱלֹהֶיךָ
your Jehovah the you and corrects your Jehovah
,God of commands kept have ;you God

7 לָלֶכֶת בִּדְרָכָיו וּלְיִרְאָה אֹתוֹ׃ כִּי יְהוָה אֱלֹהֶיךָ מְבִיאֲךָ
brings your Jehovah For .Him to and His in walk to
you God fear ,ways

אֶל־אֶרֶץ טוֹבָה אֶרֶץ נַחֲלֵי מָיִם עֲיָנֹת וּתְהֹמֹת יֹצְאִים
going and of ,water brooks a ,good a into
forth depths fountains of of land land

8 בַּבִּקְעָה וּבָהָר׃ אֶרֶץ חִטָּה וּשְׂעֹרָה וְגֶפֶן וּתְאֵנָה וְרִמּוֹן
and trees fig and and and wheat land a in and the in
pomegranates vines barley of ,hills the valleys

9 אֶרֶץ־זֵית שֶׁמֶן וּדְבָשׁ׃ אֶרֶץ אֲשֶׁר לֹא בְמִסְכֵּנֻת תֹּאכַל־
shall you with not which land a and oil olive a
eat poverty honey of land

בָּהּ לֶחֶם לֹא־תֶחְסַר כֹּל בָּהּ אֶרֶץ אֲשֶׁר אֲבָנֶיהָ בַרְזֶל
;iron stones whose a in any- shall you not ;bread in
(are) land ;it thing lack

10 וּמֵהֲרָרֶיהָ תַּחְצֹב נְחֹשֶׁת׃ וְאָכַלְתָּ וְשָׂבָעְתָּ וּבֵרַכְתָּ אֶת־
you and be and you and ;copper shall you from and
bless shall satisfied eat shall dig hills its

11 יְהוָה אֱלֹהֶיךָ עַל־הָאָרֶץ הַטֹּבָה אֲשֶׁר נָתַן־לָךְ׃ הִשָּׁמֶר
Take to has He which good the in your Jehovah
heed ,you given land God

לְךָ פֶּן־תִּשְׁכַּח אֶת־יְהוָה אֱלֹהֶיךָ לְבִלְתִּי שְׁמֹר מִצְוֹתָיו
His keep as so God your Jehovah you lest to
commands not to forget yourself

12 וּמִשְׁפָּטָיו וְחֻקֹּתָיו אֲשֶׁר אָנֹכִי מְצַוְּךָ הַיּוֹם׃ פֶּן־תֹּאכַל וְשָׂבָעְתָּ
are and (when) lest ;today com- I which His and His and
satisfied you eat you mand statutes judgments

13 וּבָתִּים טֹבִים תִּבְנֶה וְיָשָׁבְתָּ׃ וּבְקָרְךָ וְצֹאנְךָ יִרְבְּיֻן וְכֶסֶף
and ,multiply your and and live and ,build good and
silver flocks herds your (therein) houses

14 וְזָהָב יִרְבֶּה־לָּךְ וְכֹל אֲשֶׁר־לְךָ יִרְבֶּה׃ וְרָם לְבָבֶךָ וְשָׁכַחְתָּ
you and your to it then is to that and to has and
forget ,heart arises ;multiplied you (is) all ,you multiplied gold

brought you out of the land of Egypt, out of the house of slaves; [15]who led you through the great and dreadful wilderness, *with* burning serpent, and scorpion, and thirst, where there is no water; who brought you water out of the flinty rock; [16]who fed you with manna in the wilderness, which your fathers did not know; that He might humble you and that He might prove you, to do you good at your latter end; [17]that you not say in your heart, My power and the might of my hand have gotten me this wealth. [18]But you shall remember Jehovah your God, for *it is* He who gives to you power to get wealth; that He may establish His covenant which He swore to your fathers, as this day.

[19]And it shall be, if you shall forget Jehovah your God, and walk after other gods, and serve them, and worship them, I testify against you today that you shall utterly perish; [20]as the nations that Jehovah makes to perish before you, so you shall perish; because you did not listen to the voice of Jehovah your God.

5650 1004 4714 776 3318 430 3068
אֶת־יְהוָה אֱלֹהֶיךָ הַמּוֹצִיאֲךָ מֵאֶרֶץ מִצְרַיִם מִבֵּית עֲבָדִים׃
;slaves the from of house ,Egypt the of land brought who out you your God Jehovah

6137 8314 5175 3372 1419 4057 3212
15 הַמּוֹלִיכְךָ בַּמִּדְבָּר ׀ הַגָּדֹל וְהַנּוֹרָא נָחָשׁ ׀ שָׂרָף וְעַקְרָב
and scorpion ,burning (with) serpent and ,dreadful great the through wilderness led who you

2496 6697 4325 3318 4325 369 834 6774
וְצִמָּאוֹן אֲשֶׁר אֵין־מָיִם הַמּוֹצִיא לְךָ מַיִם מִצּוּר הַחַלָּמִישׁ׃
;flinty the rock of out water for you brought who ;water there no was where and ,thirst

6031 4478 4057 834 3045 3808 1 4478 398
16 הַמַּאֲכִלְךָ מָן בַּמִּדְבָּר אֲשֶׁר לֹא־יָדְעוּן אֲבֹתֶיךָ לְמַעַן עַנֹּתְךָ
humble you in to order your ;fathers did know not which the in manna wilderness fed who you

3581 3824 559 319 3190 5254
17 וּלְמַעַן נַסֹּתֶךָ לְהֵיטִבְךָ בְּאַחֲרִיתֶךָ׃ וְאָמַרְתָּ בִּלְבָבֶךָ כֹּחִי
My power your in ,heart you and say your at ;end latter do to good you prove ,you and to

3068 2142 2088 2428 6213 3027 6108
18 וְעֹצֶם יָדִי עָשָׂה לִי אֶת־הַחַיִל הַזֶּה׃ וְזָכַרְתָּ אֶת־יְהוָה
Jehovah you But remember shall .this wealth for me have made my hand the and of might

6965 2428 6213 3581 5414 430
אֱלֹהֶיךָ כִּי הוּא הַנֹּתֵן לְךָ כֹּחַ לַעֲשׂוֹת חָיִל לְמַעַן הָקִים
establish in to order wealth to make power to you who gives (is it) He for your ,God

2088 3117 7650 834 1285
אֶת־בְּרִיתוֹ אֲשֶׁר־נִשְׁבַּע לַאֲבֹתֶיךָ כַּיּוֹם הַזֶּה׃
.this day as your to fathers He swore which His covenant

310 3212 430 3068 7911 518 1961
19 וְהָיָה אִם־שָׁכֹחַ תִּשְׁכַּח אֶת־יְהוָה אֱלֹהֶיךָ וְהָלַכְתָּ אַחֲרֵי
after walk and your ,God Jehovah shall you forget indeed if it And ,be shall

5749 7812 5647 312 430
אֱלֹהִים אֲחֵרִים וַעֲבַדְתָּם וְהִשְׁתַּחֲוִיתָ לָהֶם הַעִדֹתִי בָכֶם
against you I testify to ,them down bow and serve and ,them ,other gods

6 3068 834 1471 6 6 3117
20 הַיּוֹם כִּי אָבֹד תֹּאבֵדוּן׃ כַּגּוֹיִם אֲשֶׁר יְהוָה מַאֲבִיד
to makes perish Jehovah that the as nations shall you ;perish utterly that today

3068 6963 8085 3808 6118 6 3651 6440
מִפְּנֵיכֶם כֵּן תֹּאבֵדוּן עֵקֶב לֹא תִשְׁמְעוּן בְּקוֹל יְהוָה
Jehovah the to of voice did you listen not because you shall ;perish so before ,you

430
אֱלֹהֵיכֶם׃
.God your

CAP. IX ט

CHAPTER 9

CHAPTER 9

[1]Hear, O Israel, you shall cross over the Jordan today, to go in to expel nations greater and mightier than yourself, cities great and walled up to the heavens; [2]a people great and tall, the sons of the Anakim, whom you know, and of whom you

3423 935 3383 3117 5674 3478 8085
1 שְׁמַע יִשְׂרָאֵל אַתָּה עֹבֵר הַיּוֹם אֶת־הַיַּרְדֵּן לָבֹא לָרֶשֶׁת
to dispossess go to in the ,Jordan today shall over cross you .Israel O ,Hear

8064 1219 1419 5892 6099 1419 1571
גּוֹיִם גְּדֹלִים וַעֲצֻמִים מִמֶּךָּ עָרִים גְּדֹלֹת וּבְצֻרֹת בַּשָּׁמָיִם׃
the to up ;heavens and walled great cities than ,yourself and mightier greater nations

3046 834 6062 1121 7311 1419 5971
2 עַם־גָּדוֹל וָרָם בְּנֵי עֲנָקִים אֲשֶׁר אַתָּה יָדַעְתָּ וְאַתָּה
,you and ,know you whom of Anakim the of sons and ,tall great a people

have heard it said, Who can
stand before the sons of
Anak? [3]And know today
that Jehovah your God *is*
He who passes over before
you *as* a consuming fire; He
will destroy them, and he
will bring them down
before you; so you shall
drive them out and make
them to perish quickly, as
Jehovah has spoken to you.
[4]Do not say in your heart,
when Jehovah your God
has cast them out from
before you, saying, Jehovah
has brought me in to
possess this land for my
righteousness. But *say,*
Jehovah drives them out
from before you because of
the wickedness of those
nations. [5]It is not for your
righteousness or for the
uprightness of your heart
that you go to possess their
land. But Jehovah your God
is dispossessing them from
before you because of the
wickedness of these
nations; and in order to
establish the word which
Jehovah has sworn to your
fathers, to Abraham, to
Isaac, and to Jacob. [6]And
you shall know that
Jehovah your God is not
giving you this good land,
to possess it, for your righteousness; for you *are* a
stiff-necked people.

[7]Remember; do not for-
get how you made Jehovah
your God angry in the
wilderness; even from the
day that you came out of the
land of Egypt until you came
into this place, you have
been rebellious against
Jehovah. [8]Even in Horeb
you made Jehovah angry;
and Jehovah showed Him-
self angry against you, to
destroy you. [9]When I went
up into the mountain to
receive the tablets of Stone,
tablets of the covenant
which Jehovah cut with
you, and I remained in the
mountain forty days and

3068 9 3117 3045 6061 1121 6440 3320 8085
3 שָׁמַעְתָּ מִי יִתְיַצֵּב לִפְנֵי בְּנֵי עֲנָק׃ וְיָדַעְתָּ הַיּוֹם כִּי יְהוָה
Jehovah that today ,Therefore ?Anak the before can Who have you
know of sons up stand ,said it heard
8045 1398 784 6440 5674 430
אֱלֹהֶיךָ הוּא הָעֹבֵר לְפָנֶיךָ אֵשׁ אֹכְלָה הוּא יַשְׁמִידֵם
destroy will He ;consuming (as) before who (is) God your
,them fire a you over passes He
4118 6 3423 6440 3665
וְהוּא יַכְנִיעֵם לְפָנֶיךָ וְהוֹרַשְׁתָּם וְהַאֲבַדְתָּם מַהֵר כַּאֲשֶׁר
as ,quickly them make and shall you so before will and
perish them dispossess ;you them humble He
430 9 3068 1920 3824 559 3068 1696
4 דִּבֶּר יְהוָה לָךְ׃ אַל־תֹּאמַר בִּלְבָבְךָ בַּהֲדֹף יְהוָה אֱלֹהֶיךָ
your Jehovah when your in ,say Do not to Jehovah has
God out casts ,heart ,you spoken
3423 3068 935 6666 559 6440
אֹתָם ׀ מִלְּפָנֶיךָ לֵאמֹר בְּצִדְקָתִי הֱבִיאַנִי יְהוָה לָרֶשֶׁת
possess to Jehovah brought has my For ,saying before from them
in me righteousness ,you
7564 3068 428 1471 3423 2088 776
אֶת־הָאָרֶץ הַזֹּאת וּבְרִשְׁעַת הַגּוֹיִם הָאֵלֶּה יְהוָה מוֹרִישָׁם
of because Jehovah these nations drives but ,this land
wickedness their out
3808 3423 935 3824 3476 6666 6440
5 מִפָּנֶיךָ׃ לֹא בְצִדְקָתְךָ וּבְיֹשֶׁר לְבָבְךָ אַתָּה בָא לָרֶשֶׁת אֶת־
possess to that you your the for or your for (is It) not from
go heart of uprightness righteousness .you before
7564 430 3068 428 1471 3423 776
אַרְצָם כִּי בְּרִשְׁעַת ׀ הַגּוֹיִם הָאֵלֶּה יְהוָה אֱלֹהֶיךָ מוֹרִישָׁם
of because God your Jehovah these nations is but their
wickedness their dispossessing land
3068 7650 834 1697 6440
מִפָּנֶיךָ וּלְמַעַן הָקִים אֶת־הַדָּבָר אֲשֶׁר נִשְׁבַּע יְהוָה לַאֲבֹתֶיךָ
your to Jehovah has which the to in and be- from
,fathers sworn word establish order ,you fore
3068 6666 3808 3045 3290 3327 85
6 לְאַבְרָהָם לְיִצְחָק וּלְיַעֲקֹב׃ וְיָדַעְתָּ כִּי לֹא בְצִדְקָתְךָ יְהוָה
Jehovah your for not that you and to and ,Isaac to ,Abraham to
righteousness know shall ;Jacob
3588 3423 2088 2896 776 5414 430 9
אֱלֹהֶיךָ נֹתֵן לְךָ אֶת־הָאָרֶץ הַטּוֹבָה הַזֹּאת לְרִשְׁתָּהּ כִּי
for to ,this good land you is God your
;it possess giving
7107 834 7911 2142 6203 7186 5971
7 עַם־קְשֵׁה־עֹרֶף אָתָּה׃ זְכֹר אַל־תִּשְׁכַּח אֵת אֲשֶׁר־הִקְצַפְתָּ
made you how do not ,Remem- you necked stiff- a
angry ,forget e ber .(are) people
776 5927 834 3117 4480 4057 430 3068
אֶת־יְהוָה אֱלֹהֶיךָ בַּמִּדְבָּר לְמִן־הַיּוֹם אֲשֶׁר־יָצָאתָ ׀ מֵאֶרֶץ
the from came you that the even the in your Jehovah
of land out day from ;wilderness God
5973 1961 4784 2088 4725 935 5704 4714
מִצְרַיִם עַד־בֹּאֲכֶם עַד־הַמָּקוֹם הַזֶּה מַמְרִים הֱיִיתֶם עִם־
against have you rebellious ,this place into you until Egypt
been come
3068 559 3068 7108 2722 3068
8 יְהוָה׃ וּבְחֹרֵב הִקְצַפְתֶּם אֶת־יְהוָה וַיִּתְאַנַּף יְהוָה בָּכֶם
against Jehovah showed and ;Jehovah made you in even ;Jehovah
,you angry Himself angry Horeb
68 3871 3947 2022 5927 8045
9 לְהַשְׁמִיד אֶתְכֶם׃ בַּעֲלֹתִי הָהָרָה לָקַחַת לוּחֹת הָאֲבָנִים
;stone the to the into I When .you destroy to
of tablets receive mountain up went
703 2022 3427 3068 3772 834 1285 3871
לוּחֹת הַבְּרִית אֲשֶׁר־כָּרַת יְהוָה עִמָּכֶם וָאֵשֵׁב בָּהָר אַרְבָּעִים
forty the in I and with Jehovah cut which the tablets
mountain remained ;you covenant of

forty nights—I did not eat bread nor did I drink water —[10]and Jehovah gave to me the two tablets of stone written with the finger of God, and on them was written according to all the words which Jehovah spoke with you in the mountain, out of the midst of the fire, in the day of the assembly; [11]then it happened, at the end of forty days and forty nights Jehovah gave the two tablets of stone to me, tablets of the covenant, [12]and Jehovah said to me, Rise up, go down quickly from here; for your people whom you have brought out of Egypt have acted corruptly; they have quickly turned aside out of the way which I commanded them; they have made themselves a molten image.

[13]And Jehovah spoke to me, saying, I have seen this people, and, behold, it *is* a stiff-necked people. [14]Let Me alone that I may destroy them and blot out their name from under the heavens; and I will make of you a nation mightier and greater than they. [15]And I turned and came down from the mountain, and the mountain was burning with fire, and the two tablets of the covenant *were* in my two hands; [16]and I looked; and, behold! You had sinned against Jehovah your God; you had made a molten calf for yourselves; you had quickly turned out of the way which Jehovah had commanded you. [17]And I took hold of the two tablets and threw them out of my two hands, and broke them before your eyes. [18]And I fell down before Jehovah, as at the first, forty days and forty nights; I ate no bread and drank no water; because of all your

יוֹם וְאַרְבָּעִים לַיְלָה לֶחֶם לֹא אָכַלְתִּי וּמַיִם לֹא שָׁתִיתִי׃
did I not and did I not bread ;nights and days
.drink water eat forty

10 וַיִּתֵּן יְהוָה אֵלַי אֶת־שְׁנֵי לוּחֹת הָאֲבָנִים כְּתֻבִים בְּאֶצְבַּע
the with written stone tablets two the me to Jehovah And
of finger of gave

אֱלֹהִים וַעֲלֵיהֶם כְּכָל־הַדְּבָרִים אֲשֶׁר דִּבֶּר יְהוָה עִמָּכֶם
you with Jehovah spoke which the according on and ,God
words all to them

11 בָּהָר מִתּוֹךְ הָאֵשׁ בְּיוֹם הַקָּהָל׃ וַיְהִי מִקֵּץ אַרְבָּעִים יוֹם
days forty the at it And the the in the the of out the in
of end was .assembly of day ,fire of midst ,mountain

וְאַרְבָּעִים לַיְלָה נָתַן יְהוָה אֵלַי אֶת־שְׁנֵי לֻחֹת הָאֲבָנִים
,stone tablets two the me to Jehovah gave ,nights forty and
of

12 לֻחוֹת הַבְּרִית׃ וַיֹּאמֶר יְהוָה אֵלַי קוּם רֵד מַהֵר מִזֶּה
from quickly go Rise ,me to Jehovah said and the tablets
;here down up ,covenant of

כִּי שִׁחֵת עַמְּךָ אֲשֶׁר הוֹצֵאתָ מִמִּצְרָיִם סָרוּ מַהֵר מִן־הַדֶּרֶךְ
the ot out quickly they ;Egypt of have you whom your acted have for
way aside turned have out brought ,people corruptly

13 אֲשֶׁר צִוִּיתִם עָשׂוּ לָהֶם מַסֵּכָה׃ וַיֹּאמֶר יְהוָה אֵלַי לֵאמֹר
,saying ,me to Jehovah And casted a them- have they have I which
spoke .image selves made ;them commanded

14 רָאִיתִי אֶת־הָעָם הַזֶּה וְהִנֵּה עַם־קְשֵׁה־עֹרֶף הוּא׃ הֶרֶף
let ;(is) it necked stiff- a and ;this people have I
alone people ,behold seen

מִמֶּנִּי וְאַשְׁמִידֵם וְאֶמְחֶה אֶת־שְׁמָם מִתַּחַת הַשָּׁמָיִם
the from their blot and may I that Me
;heavens under name out them destroy

15 וְאֶעֱשֶׂה אוֹתְךָ לְגוֹי־עָצוּם וָרָב מִמֶּנּוּ׃ וָאֵפֶן וָאֵרֵד מִן־
from came and I And than and mightier a you of I and
down turned .they greater nation make will

הָהָר וְהָהָר בֹּעֵר בָּאֵשׁ וּשְׁנֵי לוּחֹת הַבְּרִית עַל שְׁתֵּי יָדָי׃
my two (were) the tablets the and with was the and the
;hands in covenant of two ;fire burning mount, mount

16 וָאֵרֶא וְהִנֵּה חֲטָאתֶם לַיהוָה אֱלֹהֵיכֶם עֲשִׂיתֶם לָכֶם עֵגֶל
a for had you ;God your against had you and I and
calf yourselves made Jehovah sinned ,behold ,looked

מַסֵּכָה סַרְתֶּם מַהֵר מִן־הַדֶּרֶךְ אֲשֶׁר־צִוָּה יְהוָה אֶתְכֶם׃
.you Jehovah had which the out quickly had you casted
commanded way of turned

17 וָאֶתְפֹּשׂ בִּשְׁנֵי הַלֻּחֹת וָאַשְׁלִכֵם מֵעַל שְׁתֵּי יָדָי וָאֲשַׁבְּרֵם
broke and my two out cast and tablets the of I And
them ,hands of them two hold took

18 לְעֵינֵיכֶם׃ וָאֶתְנַפַּל לִפְנֵי יְהוָה כָּרִאשֹׁנָה אַרְבָּעִים יוֹם
days forty at as ,Jehovah before fell I And before
,first the down .eyes your

וְאַרְבָּעִים לַיְלָה לֶחֶם לֹא אָכַלְתִּי וּמַיִם לֹא שָׁתִיתִי עַל
because ;drank no and ate I no bread ;nights forty and
of water

sins which you had sinned, in doing that which was evil in the sight of Jehovah, to make Him angry. [19]For I was afraid because of the anger and the fury with which Jehovah had been angry against you, to destroy you. And Jehovah listened to me at this time also. [20]And Jehovah showed Himself very angry with Aaron, to destroy him, and I also prayed for Aaron at that time. [21]And I took your sin, the calf which you made, and I burned it with fire, and beat it, grinding it very small until it was as fine as dust; and I threw its dust into the brook that came down out of the mountain.

[22]And at Taberah, and at Massah, and at The Graves of Lust you provoked Jehovah to anger. [23]And when Jehovah sent you from Kadesh-barnea, saying, Go up and possess the land which I have given to you, then you rebelled against the mouth of Jehovah your God, and did not believe Him, nor listen to His voice. [24]You have been rebels against Jehovah from the day that I knew you.

[25]And I fell down before Jehovah the forty days and the forty nights that I had thrown myself down, for Jehovah had said to destroy you. [26]And I prayed to Jehovah, and said, O Lord Jehovah, do not destroy Your people, and Your inheritance whom You have redeemed in Your greatness; whom You have brought out of Egypt with a mighty hand. [27]Remember Your servants, Abraham, Isaac and Jacob; do not

3068 5869 7451 6213 2398 834 2403 3605
כָּל־חַטַּאתְכֶם אֲשֶׁר חֲטָאתֶם לַעֲשׂוֹת הָרַע בְּעֵינֵי יְהוָה
,Jehovah the in which that in had you which sins your all
of sight evil was doing ,sinned

3068 7107 834 2534 639 3025 3707
19 לְהַכְעִיסוֹ׃ כִּי יָגֹרְתִּי מִפְּנֵי הָאַף וְהַחֵמָה אֲשֶׁר קָצַף יְהוָה
Jehovah had with the and the because was I For make to
angry been which fury anger of afraid .angry Him

6421 1571 3068 8085 8045
עֲלֵיכֶם לְהַשְׁמִיד אֶתְכֶם וַיִּשְׁמַע יְהוָה אֵלַי גַּם בַּפַּעַם
time at also me to Jehovah and ;you destroy to against
listened ,you

6419 8045 3961 3068 599 175
20 הַהִוא׃ וּבְאַהֲרֹן הִתְאַנַּף יְהוָה מְאֹד לְהַשְׁמִידוֹ וָאֶתְפַּלֵּל
I and destroy to ,very Jehovah showed with And .that
prayed ,him angry Himself Aaron

6213 834 2403 6256 175 1571
21 גַּם־בְּעַד אַהֲרֹן בָּעֵת הַהִוא׃ וְאֶת־חַטַּאתְכֶם אֲשֶׁר־עֲשִׂיתֶם
made you which ,sin your And .that time at Aaron for also

2912 3807 784 8313 3947 5695
אֶת־הָעֵגֶל לָקַחְתִּי וָאֶשְׂרֹף אֹתוֹ ׀ בָּאֵשׁ וָאֶכֹּת אֹתוֹ טָחוֹן
grinding ,it I and with it I and ,took I calf the
it struck ,fire burned

5158 6083 7993 6083 1852 5704 3190
הֵיטֵב עַד אֲשֶׁר־דַּק לְעָפָר וָאַשְׁלִךְ אֶת־עֲפָרוֹ אֶל־הַנַּחַל
the into dust the I and ;dust as as it until very
brook if of threw fine was small

8378 6913 4531 8404 2022 3381
22 הַיֹּרֵד מִן־הָהָר׃ וּבְתַבְעֵרָה וּבְמַסָּה וּבְקִבְרֹת הַתַּאֲוָה
,"Lust of at and at and at And the out came that
Graves The" Massah ,Taberah of mountain of down

6947 3068 7971 3068 7107
23 מַקְצִפִים הֱיִיתֶם אֶת־יְהוָה׃ וּבִשְׁלֹחַ יְהוָה אֶתְכֶם מִקָּדֵשׁ
from you Jehovah when And .Jehovah you provoked
Kadesh- sent anger to

5414 834 776 3423 5927 559 6947
בַּרְנֵעַ לֵאמֹר עֲלוּ וּרְשׁוּ אֶת־הָאָרֶץ אֲשֶׁר נָתַתִּי לָכֶם
,you to have I which the and up Go ,saying ,barnea
given land possess

3808 539 3808 430 3068 6310 4784
וַתַּמְרוּ אֶת־פִּי יְהוָה אֱלֹהֵיכֶם וְלֹא הֶאֱמַנְתֶּם לוֹ וְלֹא
nor to did you and ,God your Jehovah the against you then
,Him trust not of mouth rebelled

3045 3117 3068 1961 4784 6963 8085
24 שְׁמַעְתֶּם בְּקֹלוֹ׃ מַמְרִים הֱיִיתֶם עִם־יְהוָה מִיּוֹם דַּעְתִּי
that the from Jehovah again you rebels His to listen
knew I day been have ;voice

3117 703 3068 6440 5307
25 אֶתְכֶם׃ וָאֶתְנַפַּל לִפְנֵי יְהוָה אֵת אַרְבָּעִים הַיּוֹם וְאֶת־
and days forty the Jehovah before I And .you
down fell

8045 3068 559 5307 3915 705
אַרְבָּעִים הַלַּיְלָה אֲשֶׁר הִתְנַפָּלְתִּי כִּי־אָמַר יְהוָה לְהַשְׁמִיד
destroy to Jehovah had for had I that nights forty the
said down myself thrown

7843 3068 136 559 3068 6419
26 אֶתְכֶם׃ וָאֶתְפַּלֵּל אֶל־יְהוָה וָאֹמַר אֲדֹנָי יְהוִה אַל־תַּשְׁחֵת
do not Jehovah O ,said and Jehovah to I and .you
destroy Lord prayed

4714 3318 834 1433 6299 834 5159 5971
עַמְּךָ וְנַחֲלָתְךָ אֲשֶׁר פָּדִיתָ בְּגָדְלֶךָ אֲשֶׁר־הוֹצֵאתָ מִמִּצְרַיִם
Egypt of have You whom Your in have You whom Your and Your
out brought ;greatness redeemed inheritance ,people

3808 3290 3327 85 5650 2142 2389 3027
27 בְּיָד חֲזָקָה׃ זְכֹר לַעֲבָדֶיךָ לְאַבְרָהָם לְיִצְחָק וּלְיַעֲקֹב אַל־
not ;Jacob and Isaac Abraham your Remember ,mighty with
,servants hand a

look to the stubbornness of this people, nor to their wickedness, nor to their sin, [28]lest the land from which You brought us say, Because Jehovah was not able to bring them into the land which He promised them; and, because He hated them, He has brought them out to kill them in the wilderness. [29]And they *are* Your people, and Your inheritance, whom You have brought out by Your great power, and by Your stretched-out arm.

559 6435 2403 7562 3808 2088 7971 7196 6437
28 תֵּפֶן אֶל־קְשִׁי הָעָם הַזֶּה וְאֶל־רִשְׁעוֹ וְאֶל־חַטָּאתוֹ׃ פֶּן־יֹאמְרוּ
say lest ,sin their nor their to nor ,this people the to do
to ,wickedness of stubbornness look

935 3068 3201 3808 3318 834 776
הָאָרֶץ אֲשֶׁר הוֹצֵאתָנוּ מִשָּׁם מִבְּלִי יְכֹלֶת יְהוָה לַהֲבִיאָם
bring to Jehovah able was because ,from You which the
them not us brought land

3318 8130 1697 834 776
אֶל־הָאָרֶץ אֲשֶׁר־דִּבֶּר לָהֶם וּמִשִּׂנְאָתוֹ אוֹתָם הוֹצִיאָם
brought He ,them because and ,them He which the into
out them hated He promised land

3581 3318 834 5159 5971 4057 4191
29 לַהֲמִתָם בַּמִּדְבָּר׃ וְהֵם עַמְּךָ וְנַחֲלָתֶךָ אֲשֶׁר הוֹצֵאתָ בְּכֹחֲךָ
Your by have You whom Your and Your they And the in kill to
power out brought ;inheritance ,people (are) .wilderness them

5186 2220 1419
הַגָּדֹל וּבִזְרֹעֲךָ הַנְּטוּיָה׃
stretched- by and ,great
.out arm Your

CAP. X

CHAPTER 10

CHAPTER 10

[1]At that time Jehovah said to me, Cut out for yourself two tablets of stone like the first, and come up to Me, into the mountain, and you shall make for yourself an ark of wood; [2]and I shall write on the tablets the words which were on the first tablets, which you have broken, and you shall place them in the ark. [3]And I made an ark of acacia-wood, and cut out two tablets of stone like the first, and went up into the mountain; and the two tablets *were* in my hand. [4]And He wrote on the tablets according to the writing, the Ten Words which Jehovah had spoken to you in the mountain, out of the midst of the fire, in the day of the assembly. And Jehovah gave them to me, [5]and I turned and came down from the mountain and put the tablets in the ark which I had made. And they are there, as Jehovah commanded me.

[6]And the sons of Israel traveled from Beeroth of the sons of Jaakan to Mosera; Aaron died there, and he was buried there; and his son Eleazar was acting as priest in his place. [7]From

68 3871 8147 6458 3068 559 6256
1 בָּעֵת הַהִוא אָמַר יְהוָה אֵלַי פְּסָל־לְךָ שְׁנֵי־לוּחֹת אֲבָנִים
stone tablets two for Carve ,me to Jehovah said that At
of yourself out time

3789 6086 727 6213 2022 5027 7223
2 כָּרִאשֹׁנִים וַעֲלֵה אֵלַי הָהָרָה וְעָשִׂיתָ לְּךָ אֲרוֹן עֵץ׃ וְאֶכְתֹּב
I And .wood an for you and the into Me to and the like
write shall of ark yourself make shall ;mountain up come ,first

7223 3871 5921 1961 834 1697 3871 5921
עַל־הַלֻּחֹת אֶת־הַדְּבָרִים אֲשֶׁר הָיוּ עַל־הַלֻּחֹת הָרִאשֹׁנִים
first the on were which the the on
tablets words tablets

7848 6086 727 6213 727 7760 7665 834
3 אֲשֶׁר שִׁבַּרְתָּ וְשַׂמְתָּם בָּאָרוֹן׃ וָאַעַשׂ אֲרוֹן עֲצֵי שִׁטִּים
acacia wood an And the in shall you and you which
of ark made I .ark them place ;broken have

8147 2022 5927 7223 68 3871 8147 6458
וָאֶפְסֹל שְׁנֵי־לֻחֹת אֲבָנִים כָּרִאשֹׁנִים וָאַעַל הָהָרָה וּשְׁנֵי
and the to I And the like stone tablets two cut and
two the mountain up went .first of out

7223 3789 3871 3789 3027 3871
4 הַלֻּחֹת בְּיָדִי׃ וַיִּכְתֹּב עַל־הַלֻּחֹת כַּמִּכְתָּב הָרִאשׁוֹן אֵת
the according the on And my in tablets
former writing the to tablets wrote He .hand (were)

784 8432 2022 3068 1696 834 1697 6235
עֲשֶׂרֶת הַדְּבָרִים אֲשֶׁר דִּבֶּר יְהוָה אֲלֵיכֶם בָּהָר מִתּוֹךְ הָאֵשׁ
fire the of out the in you to Jehovah had which Words the Ten
of midst the mountain spoken

7760 2022 3381 6437 3068 5414 6951 3117
5 בְּיוֹם הַקָּהָל וַיִּתְּנֵם יְהוָה אֵלָי׃ וָאֵפֶן וָאֵרֵד מִן־הָהָר וָאָשִׂם
put and the from came and And .me to And gave the the in
mountain down turned I Jehovah them .assembly of day

6680 8033 1961 6213 834 727 3871
אֶת־הַלֻּחֹת בָּאָרוֹן אֲשֶׁר עָשִׂיתִי וַיִּהְיוּ שָׁם כַּאֲשֶׁר צִוַּנִי
com- as ,there and had I which the in the
me manded are they ;made ark tablets

8033 4149 885 1121 881 5265 3478 1121 3068
6 יְהוָה׃ וּבְנֵי יִשְׂרָאֵל נָסְעוּ מִבְּאֵרֹת בְּנֵי־יַעֲקָן מוֹסֵרָה שָׁם
there to Jaakan the from set Israel the And .Jehovah
;Mosera of sons of Beeroth forth of sons

8033 8478 1121 499 3547 8033 6912 175 4191
7 מֵת אַהֲרֹן וַיִּקָּבֵר שָׁם וַיְכַהֵן אֶלְעָזָר בְּנוֹ תַּחְתָּיו׃ מִשָּׁם
From his in his Eleazar was and ;there he and ,Aaron died
there .place son priest as acting buried was

there they traveled to Gudgodah; and from Gudgodah to Jotbath, a land of water brooks. [8]At that time Jehovah separated the tribe of Levi, to bear the ark of the covenant before Jehovah, to stand before Jehovah and to minister to Him, and to bless in His name, until today. [9]Therefore, Levi has no portion nor inheritance according as Jehovah your God spoke to him.

[10]And I stayed in the mountain forty days and forty nights, as at the first. And Jehovah listened to me that time also; Jehovah would not destroy you. [11]And Jehovah said to me, Rise up! Go before the people, causing them to set forward, that they may go in and possess the land which I swore to their fathers, to give *it* to them.

[12]And now, Israel, what has Jehovah your God asked of you, except to fear Jehovah your God, to walk in all His ways, and to love Him, and to serve Jehovah your God with all your heart, and with all your soul; [13]to keep the commandments of Jehovah, and His statutes which I am commanding you today, for your good. [14]Behold, the heavens and the heavens of the heavens, the earth and all that *is* in it, *belong* to Jehovah your God. [15]Only, Jehovah has delighted in your fathers, to love them; and He chose their seed after them, on you out of all the peoples, as today.

6251 4325 5158 776 3193 1412 1412 5265
8 נָסְעוּ הַגֻּדְגֹּדָה וּמִן־הַגֻּדְגֹּדָה יָטְבָתָה אֶרֶץ נַחֲלֵי־מָיִם׃ בָּעֵת
At time | water brooks a of land | to Jotbath | Gudgodah and from | to Gudgodah | set they forth

729 5375 3881 7626 3068 914
הַהִוא הִבְדִּיל יְהוָה אֶת־שֵׁבֶט הַלֵּוִי לָשֵׂאת אֶת־אֲרוֹן
the of ark | bear to | Levi | the of tribe | Jehovah | separated | that

5714 8034 1288 8334 3068 6440 5975 3068 1285
בְּרִית־יְהוָה לַעֲמֹד לִפְנֵי יְהוָה לְשָׁרְתוֹ וּלְבָרֵךְ בִּשְׁמוֹ עַד
until | His name | to and bless | minister to Him | Jehovah before | to stand | Jehovah | the of covenant

251 5159 2506 3881 1961/3808 3117
9 הַיּוֹם הַזֶּה׃ עַל־כֵּן לֹא־הָיָה לְלֵוִי חֵלֶק וְנַחֲלָה עִם־אֶחָיו
his brothers; | with | nor inheritance | portion | Levi | has no | Therefore | .today

430 3068 1696 5159 3068
10 יְהוָה הוּא נַחֲלָתוֹ כַּאֲשֶׁר דִּבֶּר יְהוָה אֱלֹהֶיךָ לוֹ׃ וְאָנֹכִי
I And | to .him | God your | Jehovah | spoke | according as | his ,inheritance | Jehovah (is)

705 3117 703 7223 6471 2022 5975
עָמַדְתִּי בָהָר כַּיָּמִים הָרִאשֹׁנִים אַרְבָּעִים יוֹם וְאַרְבָּעִים
forty and | days | forty | first | at as time the | the in mountain | stayed

3068 14 3808 6471 1571 3068 8085 3915
לַיְלָה וַיִּשְׁמַע יְהוָה אֵלַי גַּם בַּפַּעַם הַהִוא לֹא־אָבָה יְהוָה
Jehovah | would not | that | time | also; | me to | Jehovah | and listened | ;nights

6440 4550 3212 6965 3068 559 7843
11 הַשְׁחִיתֶךָ׃ וַיֹּאמֶר יְהוָה אֵלַי קוּם לֵךְ לְמַסַּע לִפְנֵי
before them | causing forward set to | ,Go | ,Rise | me to | Jehovah | said And | .you destroy

1 7650 834 776 3423 935 5971
הָעָם וְיָבֹאוּ וְיִירְשׁוּ אֶת־הָאָרֶץ אֲשֶׁר־נִשְׁבַּעְתִּי לַאֲבֹתָם
their to ,fathers | swore I | which | the land | and possess | they that in go may | the people

5414
לָתֵת לָהֶם׃
to .them | give to (it)

7592 430 3068 3478 6258
12 וְעַתָּה יִשְׂרָאֵל מָה יְהוָה אֱלֹהֶיךָ שֹׁאֵל מֵעִמָּךְ כִּי אִם־
except | you of | has asked | God your | Jehovah | What | ,Israel | And ,now

157 1870 3605 3212 430 3068 3372
לְיִרְאָה אֶת־יְהוָה אֱלֹהֶיךָ לָלֶכֶת בְּכָל־דְּרָכָיו וּלְאַהֲבָה
to and love | His ,ways | all in | walk to | ,God your | Jehovah | fear to

5315 3824 3605 430 3068 5647
אֹתוֹ וְלַעֲבֹד אֶת־יְהוָה אֱלֹהֶיךָ בְּכָל־לְבָבְךָ וּבְכָל־נַפְשֶׁךָ׃
,soul your | and all with | your heart | with all | God your | Jehovah | to and serve | ,Him

3117 6680 834 2708 3068 4687 8104
13 לִשְׁמֹר אֶת־מִצְוֹת יְהוָה וְאֶת־חֻקֹּתָיו אֲשֶׁר אָנֹכִי מְצַוְּךָ הַיּוֹם
today | com- you manding | am I | which | His statutes | and | Jehovah | com- the of mandments | keep to

8064 8064 8064 430 3068 2009 2896
14 לְטוֹב לָךְ׃ הֵן לַיהוָה אֱלֹהֶיךָ הַשָּׁמַיִם וּשְׁמֵי הַשָּׁמָיִם
,heavens the | of heavens the and | the ,heavens | God your (belong) | to ,Jehovah | ,Behold | .your good | for

157 3068 2836 1 7535 3605 776
15 הָאָרֶץ וְכָל־אֲשֶׁר־בָּהּ׃ רַק בַּאֲבֹתֶיךָ חָשַׁק יְהוָה לְאַהֲבָה
love to | ,Jehovah | has delighted | your in fathers | Only | .it in | that (is) | with all | the ,earth

3117 5971 3605 310 2233 977
אוֹתָם וַיִּבְחַר בְּזַרְעָם אַחֲרֵיהֶם בָּכֶם מִכָּל־הָעַמִּים כַּיּוֹם
as .today | the ,peoples | of out all | on you | after ,them | seed their | He and chose | ;them

[16]And you shall circumcise the foreskin of your heart, and you shall not harden your neck any more. [17]For Jehovah your God, He is the God of gods, and the Lord of lords; the great, the mighty, the fearful God who does not lift up faces, nor take a bribe.

[18]He executes justice for the fatherless and the widow, and loves the alien, to give food and clothing for him. [19]And you shall love the alien, for you were aliens in the land of Egypt. [20]You shall fear Jehovah your God; you shall serve Him; and you shall cleave to Him; and you shall swear by His name. [21]He *shall be* your praise, and He your God, who has done for you these great and fearful *things* which your eyes have seen. [22]Your fathers went down to Egypt with seventy persons; and now Jehovah your God has made you as the stars of the heavens for multitude.

7185 3808 6203 3824 6190 4135 2088
16 הַזֶּה׃ וּמַלְתֶּם אֵת עָרְלַת לְבַבְכֶם וְעָרְפְּכֶם לֹא תַקְשׁוּ
shall you not harden | your neck | your ;heart | fore- of skin the | you And circumcise shall

113 113 430 430 430 3068 5715
17 עוֹד׃ כִּי יְהוָה אֱלֹהֵיכֶם הוּא אֱלֹהֵי הָאֱלֹהִים וַאֲדֹנֵי הָאֲדֹנִים
,lords | The and Lord of | ,gods | God The of | He (is) | ,God your | Jehovah for | any ;more

3947 3808 6440 5375 3808 834 3372 1368 1419 410
הָאֵל הַגָּדֹל הַגִּבֹּר וְהַנּוֹרָא אֲשֶׁר לֹא־יִשָּׂא פָנִים וְלֹא יִקַּח
take | nor | faces | does up lift | not | who | the ,fearful | the ,mighty | the ,great | ,God

5414 1616 157 490 3490 4941 6213 7810
18 שֹׁחַד׃ עֹשֶׂה מִשְׁפַּט יָתוֹם וְאַלְמָנָה וְאֹהֵב גֵּר לָתֶת לוֹ
for him | give to | the alien | and loving | the and widow | the for fatherless | justice | He executes | .bribe

776 1961 1616 1616 157 8071 3899
19 לֶחֶם וְשִׂמְלָה׃ וַאֲהַבְתֶּם אֶת־הַגֵּר כִּי־גֵרִים הֱיִיתֶם בְּאֶרֶץ
the in of land | you were | aliens for | ,alien the | you And love shall | and .clothing | food

1692 5647 3372 430 3068 4714
20 מִצְרָיִם׃ אֶת־יְהוָה אֱלֹהֶיךָ תִּירָא אֹתוֹ תַעֲבֹד וּבוֹ תִדְבָּק
shall you cling | and Him to | shall you ,serve | Him | shall You ;fear | God your | Jehovah | .Egypt

6213 834 430 8416 7650 8034
21 וּבִשְׁמוֹ תִּשָּׁבֵעַ׃ הוּא תְהִלָּתְךָ וְהוּא אֱלֹהֶיךָ אֲשֶׁר־עָשָׂה
has done | who | ,God your | He and (be shall) | ,praise your | He (be shall) | shall you .swear | by and name His

5869 7200 834 428 3372 1419
אִתְּךָ אֶת־הַגְּדֹלֹת וְאֶת־הַנּוֹרָאֹת הָאֵלֶּה אֲשֶׁר רָאוּ עֵינֶיךָ׃
your .eyes | have seen | which | these | fearful ,(things) | and | great | for you

3068 7760 6258 4714 1 3381 5315 7657
22 בְּשִׁבְעִים נֶפֶשׁ יָרְדוּ אֲבֹתֶיךָ מִצְרָיְמָה וְעַתָּה שָׂמְךָ יְהוָה
Jehovah | has you made | and now | ;Egypt to | your fathers | went down | persons | With seventy

7230 8064 3556 430
אֱלֹהֶיךָ כְּכוֹכְבֵי הַשָּׁמַיִם לָרֹב׃
for .multitude | the heavens | the as of stars | God your

CAP. XI יא

CHAPTER 11

CHAPTER 11

[1]And you shall love Jehovah your God, and keep His charge, and His statutes, and His judgments, and His commandments all the days. [2]And you know today, for *I do* not *speak* with your sons who have not known, and who have not seen the chastisement of Jehovah your God, His greatness, His mighty hand, and His stretched-out arm, [3]and His signs, and His works which He did in the midst of Egypt to Pharaoh the king of Egypt, and to all his land; [4]and that which He has done to the army of Egypt, to its horses, and to its chariots,

2708 4931 8104 430 3068 157
1 וְאָהַבְתָּ אֵת יְהוָה אֱלֹהֶיךָ וְשָׁמַרְתָּ מִשְׁמַרְתּוֹ וְחֻקֹּתָיו
His and statutes | charge His | keep and | ,God your | Jehovah | you And love shall

3808 3117 3045 3117 3605 4687 4941
2 וּמִשְׁפָּטָיו וּמִצְוֹתָיו כָּל־הַיָּמִים׃ וִידַעְתֶּם הַיּוֹם כִּי לֹא
not (speak I do) | for | ,today | you And know | .days the | all | His and commandments | His and judgments

3068 4148 7200 3808 834 3045 3808 834 1121
אֶת־בְּנֵיכֶם אֲשֶׁר לֹא־יָדְעוּ וַאֲשֶׁר לֹא־רָאוּ אֶת־מוּסַר יְהוָה
Jehovah | chas- the of tisement | have not seen | who and | have not known | who | your ,sons | with

5186 2220 2389 3027 1433 430
3 אֱלֹהֵיכֶם אֶת־גָּדְלוֹ אֶת־יָדוֹ הַחֲזָקָה וּזְרֹעוֹ הַנְּטוּיָה׃ וְאֶת־
and | stretched- ,out | His and arm | mighty | ,hand His | His greatness | ,God your

6547 4714 8432 6213 834 4639 226
אֹתֹתָיו וְאֶת־מַעֲשָׂיו אֲשֶׁר עָשָׂה בְּתוֹךְ מִצְרָיִם לְפַרְעֹה
Pharaoh to | ,Egypt | the in of midst | did he | which | His works | and | His signs

4714 2428 6213 834 776 3605 4714 4428
4 מֶלֶךְ־מִצְרַיִם וּלְכָל־אַרְצוֹ׃ וַאֲשֶׁר עָשָׂה לְחֵיל מִצְרַיִם
,Egypt | the to of army | has he done | that and which | his ,land | to and all | ,Egypt | the of king

when He caused the waters of the Red Sea to flow over them as they pursued you. And Jehovah destroyed them to this day. [5]Also *you know* that which He has done to you in the wilderness, until you came to this place; [6]and that which He has done to Dathan, and to Abiram, sons of Eliab, the son of Reuben, when the earth opened her mouth and swallowed them, and their houses, and their tents, and all the living substance which was at their feet, in the midst of all Israel. [7]But your eyes see all the great work of Jehovah which He has done. [8]And you shall keep all the commandments which I am commanding you today, so that you shall be strong, and shall go in and possess the land to which you are crossing over, to possess it; [9]and so that you may prolong *your* days in the land which Jehovah has sworn to your fathers, to give to them and to their seed, a land flowing with milk and honey.

[10]For the land to which you are going, to possess it, *is* not as the land of Egypt, from where you came, where you sowed your seed and watered *it* with your foot, as a garden of herbs. [11]But the land which you are entering, to possess it, *is* a land of hills and valleys, drinking water from the rain of the heavens; [12]a land which Jehovah your God cares for; the eyes of Jehovah your God *are* constantly on it from the beginning of the year to the end of the year.

לְסוּסָיו וּלְרִכְבּוֹ אֲשֶׁר הֵצִיף אֶת־מֵי יַם־סוּף עַל־פְּנֵיהֶם
them over Reeds the waters the made He when its to and its to
of Sea of flow ,chariots ,horses

5 בְּרָדְפָם אַחֲרֵיכֶם וַיְאַבְּדֵם יְהוָה עַד הַיּוֹם הַזֶּה׃ וַאֲשֶׁר
that and ,this place to came you until the in to has He
which wilderness you done

6 עָשָׂה לָכֶם בַּמִּדְבָּר עַד־בֹּאֲכֶם עַד־הַמָּקוֹם הַזֶּה׃ וַאֲשֶׁר
that and ,this place to you until the in to has He
which came wilderness you done

עָשָׂה לְדָתָן וְלַאֲבִירָם בְּנֵי אֱלִיאָב בֶּן־רְאוּבֵן אֲשֶׁר פָּצְתָה
opened when ,Reuben the ,Eliab of sons to and to has He
of son Abiram Dathan done

הָאָרֶץ אֶת־פִּיהָ וַתִּבְלָעֵם וְאֶת־בָּתֵּיהֶם וְאֶת־אָהֳלֵיהֶם
tents their and their and swallowed and her the
houses them mouth earth

7 וְאֵת כָּל־הַיְקוּם אֲשֶׁר בְּרַגְלֵיהֶם בְּקֶרֶב כָּל־יִשְׂרָאֵל׃ כִּי
But .Israel all the in their at (was) which the all and
of midst feet substance living

עֵינֵיכֶם הָרֹאֹת אֶת כָּל־מַעֲשֵׂה יְהוָה הַגָּדֹל אֲשֶׁר עָשָׂה׃
has He which great Jehovah of work the all see eyes your
.done

8 וּשְׁמַרְתֶּם אֶת־כָּל־הַמִּצְוָה אֲשֶׁר אָנֹכִי מְצַוְּךָ הַיּוֹם לְמַעַן
that so ,today com- am I which com- the all you And
you manding mandments keep shall

תֶּחֶזְקוּ וּבָאתֶם וִירִשְׁתֶּם אֶת־הָאָרֶץ אֲשֶׁר אַתֶּם עֹבְרִים
are you which the possess and shall and shall you
,over crossing land in go strong be

9 שָׁמָּה לְרִשְׁתָּהּ׃ וּלְמַעַן תַּאֲרִיכוּ יָמִים עַל־הָאֲדָמָה אֲשֶׁר
which a in (your) may you and possess to to
land days prolong that so ,it

נִשְׁבַּע יְהוָה לַאֲבֹתֵיכֶם לָתֵת לָהֶם וּלְזַרְעָם אֶרֶץ זָבַת
flowing a to and them to give to your to Jehovah has
land seed their ,fathers sworn

10 חָלָב וּדְבָשׁ׃ כִּי הָאָרֶץ אֲשֶׁר אַתָּה בָא־שָׁמָּה
to are you which the For and with
going land .honey milk

לְרִשְׁתָּהּ לֹא כְאֶרֶץ מִצְרַיִם הִוא אֲשֶׁר יְצָאתֶם מִשָּׁם
from came you ,Egypt the as (is) possess to
,where of land not it

11 אֲשֶׁר תִּזְרַע אֶת־זַרְעֲךָ וְהִשְׁקִיתָ בְרַגְלְךָ כְּגַן הַיָּרָק׃ וְהָאָרֶץ
the But .herbs a as your with watered and your you where
land of garden ,foot (it) seed sowed

אֲשֶׁר אַתֶּם עֹבְרִים שָׁמָּה לְרִשְׁתָּהּ אֶרֶץ הָרִים וּבְקָעֹת
and hills a (is) possess to ,to are you which
valleys of land ,it crossing

12 לִמְטַר הַשָּׁמַיִם תִּשְׁתֶּה־מָּיִם׃ אֶרֶץ אֲשֶׁר־יְהוָה אֱלֹהֶיךָ
God your Jehovah which a ,water drinking the the from
land heavens of rain

דֹּרֵשׁ אֹתָהּ תָּמִיד עֵינֵי יְהוָה אֱלֹהֶיךָ בָּהּ מֵרֵשִׁית הַשָּׁנָה
the the from upon (are) your Jehovah the constantly cares
year of beginning ,it God of eyes ;for

[13]And it shall be, if you carefully listen to My commands which I command you today, to love Jehovah your God, and to serve Him with all your heart, and with all your soul, [14]that I will give the rain of your land in its season, the former rain and the latter rain, that you may gather in your grain, and your wine, and your oil. [15]And I will give grass in your fields for your livestock; and you shall eat and be satisfied. [16]Take heed to yourselves, that your heart not be deceived, and you turn aside and worship other gods, and serve them; [17]and the anger of Jehovah glow against you, and He shut up the heavens, and there be no rain, and the ground not give her increase, and you perish quickly from off the good land which Jehovah is giving to you.

[18]And you shall lay these words up in your heart, and in your soul, and shall bind them for a sign on your hand. And they shall be for frontlets between your eyes. [19]And you shall teach them to your sons by speaking of them as you sit in your house, and as you go in the way, and as you lie down, and as you rise up. [20]And *you* shall write them on the sideposts of your house, and on your gates, [21]that your days may be multiplied, and the days of your sons, in the land which Jehovah has sworn to your fathers, to give to them, as the days of the heavens over the earth. [22]For if you will carefully keep this command which I am commanding you, to do

8085 8085 518 1961 8141 319 5704
13 ועד אחרית שנה: והיה אם־שמע תשמעו אל־
to you carefully if shall it And the end the to
listen ,pass to come .year of

3068 157 3117 4687 834 4687
מצותי אשר אנכי מצוה אתכם היום לאהבה את־יהוה
Jehovah love to ,today you command I which com- My
mandments

5414 5315 3605 3824 3605 5647 430
14 אלהיכם ולעבדו בכל־לבבכם ובכל־נפשכם: ונתתי
I that ,soul your and your with to and God your
give will all with heart all Him serve

8492 1715 622 4456 3138 6256 776 4306
מטר־ארצכם בעתו יורה ומלקוש ואספת דגנך ותירשך
your and your may you that the and the its in your the
wine grain in gather ,rain latter rain former ,season land of rain

7646 398 929 7704 6212 5414 3323
15 ויצהרך: ונתתי עשב בשדך לבהמתך ואכלת ושבעת:
be and you and your for your in grass I And and
.satisfied eat shall ,cattle fields give will .oil your

430 5647 3824 6601 8104
16 השמרו לכם פן־יפתה לבבכם וסרתם ועבדתם אלהים
gods serve and you and your in be lest your- to heed Take
aside turn heart deceived ,selves

6113 3068 639 2734 7812 312
17 אחרים והשתחויתם להם: וחרה אף־יהוה בכם ועצר
He and against Jehovah the and to bow and other
up shut ,you of anger glows them 3808 down

2981 5414 3808 127 4306 1961 8064
את־השמים ולא־יהיה מטר והאדמה לא תתן את־יבולה
her give not the and ,rain there and the
increase ground be no ,heavens

5414 3068 834 2896 776 4120 6
ואבדתם מהרה מעל הארץ הטבה אשר יהוה נתן
is Jehovah which good the from quickly you and
giving land off perish

5315 3824 428 1697 7760
18 לכם: ושמתם את־דברי אלה על־לבבכם ועל־נפשכם
,soul your and your in these words you And .you to
in heart up lay shall

5869 996 2903 1961 3027 226 7194
וקשרתם אתם לאות על־ידכם והיו לטוטפת בין עיניכם:
your between for they and your on a for them shall and
;eyes frontlets be shall ,hand sign bind

1004 3427 1696 1121 3925
19 ולמדתם אתם את־בניכם לדבר בם בשבתך בביתך
your in you as of by your to them you and
,house sit them speaking sons teach shall

4201 3789 6965 7901 1870 3212
20 ובלכתך בדרך ובשכבך ובקומך: וכתבתם על־מזוזות
the on shall and you as and you as and the in as and
of sideposts them write ;up rise down lie ,way go you

1121 3117 3117 7235 8179 1004
21 ביתך ובשעריך: למען ירבו ימיכם וימי בניכם על
in your the and your be may that so on and your
sons of days days multiplied ,gates your house

3117 5414 3068 7650 834 124
האדמה אשר נשבע יהוה לאבתיכם לתת להם כימי
the as to give to your to Jehovah has which the
of days ,them ,fathers sworn land

8104 8104 776 5921 8064
22 השמים על־הארץ: כי אם־שמר תשמרון את־
will you carefully if For the on the
keep .earth heavens

6213 6680 834 2088 4687 3605
כל־המצוה הזאת אשר אנכי מצוה אתכם לעשתה
,it do to ,you am I which this command- all
commanding ment

it, to love Jehovah your God, to walk in all His ways, and to cleave to Him, [23]then Jehovah shall expel all these nations from before you, and you shall possess nations greater and mightier than you. [24]Every place where the sole of your foot treads shall be yours, from the wilderness and Lebanon, from the river, the river Euphrates, even to the furthest sea shall be your border. [25]No man shall stand before you. Jehovah your God shall put your dread and your fear on the face of all the land on which you tread, as He has spoken to you.

[26]Behold, I set before you today a blessing and a curse: [27]A blessing if you obey the commandments of Jehovah your God which I command you today; [28]and a curse if you will not obey the commandments of Jehovah your God, but will turn aside out of the way which I command you today, to go after other gods which you have not known.
[29]And it shall be, when Jehovah your God shall bring you into the land to which you go to possess it, that you shall set the blessing on Mount Gerizim, and the curse on Mount Ebal. [30]Are they not beyond the Jordan, behind the way of the sunset, in the land of the Canaanites that live in the Arabah, opposite to Gilgal, beside the oaks of Moreh? [31]For you are to

1692 1870 3605 3212 430 3068 157
לְאַהֲבָה אֶת־יְהוָה אֱלֹהֵיכֶם לָלֶכֶת בְּכָל־דְּרָכָיו וּלְדָבְקָה־
to and cling | His ways | all in | walk to | ,God your | Jehovah | love to

3423 6440 428 1471 3605 3068 3423
23 בוֹ׃ וְהוֹרִישׁ יְהוָה אֶת־כָּל־הַגּוֹיִם הָאֵלֶּה מִלִּפְנֵיכֶם וִירִשְׁתֶּם
you and possess shall | from you before | these | nations all | Jehovah shall then dispossess | to ,Him

3709 1869 4725 3605 6099 1419 1471
24 גּוֹיִם גְּדֹלִים וַעֲצֻמִים מִכֶּם׃ כָּל־הַמָּקוֹם אֲשֶׁר תִּדְרֹךְ כַּף־
the of sole | treads | which | place | Every | than .you | and mightier | greater nations

5104 5104 3844 4057 1961 7272
רַגְלְכֶם בּוֹ לָכֶם יִהְיֶה מִן־הַמִּדְבָּר וְהַלְּבָנוֹן מִן־הַנָּהָר נְהַר־
the river | the ,river | from | and Lebanon | the wilderness | from | shall be | yours | on | foot your

376 3320 3808 1366 1961 314 3220 5704 6578
25 פְּרָת וְעַד הַיָּם הָאַחֲרוֹן יִהְיֶה גְּבֻלְכֶם׃ לֹא־יִתְיַצֵּב אִישׁ
man | shall stand | No | your .border | be shall | the farthest | sea the | even to | Eu- phrates

6440 430 3068 5414 4172 6343 6440
בִּפְנֵיכֶם פַּחְדְּכֶם וּמוֹרַאֲכֶם יִתֵּן ׀ יְהוָה אֱלֹהֵיכֶם עַל־פְּנֵי
the of face | on | God your | Jehovah | shall put | your and fear | dread your | before ;you

1696 1869 834 776 3605
כָל־הָאָרֶץ אֲשֶׁר תִּדְרְכוּ־בָהּ כַּאֲשֶׁר דִּבֶּר לָכֶם׃
.you to | has He spoken | as | ,on | you tread | which | the land | all

1293 7045 1293 3117 6440 5414 2009
26 רְאֵה אָנֹכִי נֹתֵן לִפְנֵיכֶם הַיּוֹם בְּרָכָה וּקְלָלָה׃ אֶת־הַבְּרָכָה
27
a blessing | a and ;curse | blessing a | today | before you | set | I | ,Behold

6680 834 430 3068 4687 8085
אֲשֶׁר תִּשְׁמְעוּ אֶל־מִצְוֺת יְהוָה אֱלֹהֵיכֶם אֲשֶׁר אָנֹכִי מְצַוֶּה
command | I | which | God your | Jehovah | com- the of mandments | hear you | if

4687 8085 3808 518 7045 3117
28 אֶתְכֶם הַיּוֹם׃ וְהַקְּלָלָה אִם־לֹא תִשְׁמְעוּ אֶל־מִצְוֺת
com- the of mandments | to | will you listen | not | if | a and curse | ,today | you

6680 834 1870 5493 430 3068
יְהוָה אֱלֹהֵיכֶם וְסַרְתֶּם מִן־הַדֶּרֶךְ אֲשֶׁר אָנֹכִי מְצַוֶּה
command | I | which | the way | out of | will but aside turn | ,God your | Jeho- vah

3808 834 312 430 310 3212 3117
אֶתְכֶם הַיּוֹם לָלֶכֶת אַחֲרֵי אֱלֹהִים אֲחֵרִים אֲשֶׁר לֹא־
not | which | ,other | gods | after | go to | ,today | you

776 430 3068 935 1961 3045
29 יְדַעְתֶּם׃ וְהָיָה כִּי יְבִיאֲךָ יְהוָה אֱלֹהֶיךָ אֶל־הָאָרֶץ
the land | into | God your | Jehovah | shall you bring | when | it And be shall | have you .known

1293 5414 3423 8033 935 834
אֲשֶׁר־אַתָּה בָא־שָׁמָּה לְרִשְׁתָּהּ וְנָתַתָּה אֶת־הַבְּרָכָה
the blessing | you that set shall | possess to ,it | there to | go | you | which

3808 5858 2022 7045 1630 2022
30 עַל־הַר גְּרִזִים וְאֶת־הַקְּלָלָה עַל־הַר עֵיבָל׃ הֲלֹא־הֵמָּה
they | Are not | .Ebal | Mount on | the curse | and | Gerizim | Mount on

3669 776 8121 3996 1870 310 3383 5676
בְּעֵבֶר הַיַּרְדֵּן אַחֲרֵי דֶּרֶךְ מְבוֹא הַשֶּׁמֶשׁ בְּאֶרֶץ הַכְּנַעֲנִי
the Canaanites | of land the in | ,sun the | going the of down | the of way | behind | the Jordan | beyond

4126 437 681 1537 4136 6160 3427
31 הַיֹּשֵׁב בָּעֲרָבָה מוּל הַגִּלְגָּל אֵצֶל אֵלוֹנֵי מֹרֶה׃ כִּי אַתֶּם
you | For | ?Moreh | the of oaks | beside | ,Gilgal | opposite to | the in .Arabah | that live

cross over the Jordan to go
in to possess the land
which Jehovah your God is
giving to you; and you shall
possess it and live in it.
[32]And take heed to do all
the statutes and the ordinances which I am setting
before you today.

3068 834 776 3423 935 3383 5674
עברים את־הירדן לבא לרשת את־הארץ אשר־יהוה
Jehovah which the land possess to to in go the Jordan to are over cross

8104 3427 3423 3414 430
32 אלהיכם נתן לכם וירשתם אתה וישבתם־בה: ושמרתם
take heed And .it in and live it you and possess shall ,you to is giving your God

5414 834 4941 2706 3605 6213
לעשות את כל־החקים ואת־המשפטים אשר אנכי נתן
am I setting which the judgments and the statutes all do to

3117 6440
לפניכם היום:
.today before you

CAP. XII יב

CHAPTER 12

CHAPTER 12
[1]These *are* the statutes
and the ordinances which
which you shall take heed
to do in the land which
Jehovah the God of your
fathers has given to you, to
possess it, all the days that
you live on the earth: [2]You
shall completely destroy all
the places where the
nations which you are
dispossessing served their
gods, on the high moun-
tains, and on the hills, and
under every leafy tree.
[3]And you shall break down
their altars, and shatter their
standing pillars. And you
shall burn their pillars with
fire. And you shall cut down
the carved images of their
gods, and shall destroy
their names out of that
place. [4]You shall not do so
to Jehovah your God. [5]But
you shall seek to the place
which Jehovah your God
shall choose out of all your
tribes; for you shall seek His
dwelling, to put His name
there. And you shall go
there. [6]And you shall bring
your burnt offerings there,
and your sacrifices, and
your tithes, and the offering
of your hand, and your
vows, and your free-will
offering, and the firstlings of
your herd and of your

776 6213 8104 834 4941 2706 428
1 אלה החקים והמשפטים אשר תשמרון לעשות בארץ
the in land do to shall you watchful be which the and judgments the statutes These (are)

3117 3605 3423 430 3068 5414 834
אשר נתן יהוה אלהי אבתיך לך לרשתה כל־הימים
the days all possess it to ,you your fathers the of God Jehovah has given which

3605 6 6 127 2416 834
2 אשר־אתם חיים על־האדמה: אבד תאבדון את־כל־
all shall You destroy completely the ,earth on live you that

3423 834 1471 8033 5647 4725
המקמות אשר עבדו־שם הגוים אשר אתם ירשים אתם
are ,dispossessing you which the ,nations served where the places

3605 8478 1389 7311 2022 5921 430
את־אלהיהם על־ההרים הרמים ועל־הגבעות ותחת כל־
every and under the hills and on high the mountains on their gods

4676 7665 4196 5422 7488 6086
3 עץ רענן: ונתצתם את־מזבחתם ושברתם את־מצבתם
standing their ,pillars and shatter their ,altars you And down break shall .leafy tree

6 2404 430 6456 784 8313 842
ואשריהם תשרפון באש ופסילי אלהיהם תגדעון ואבדתם
shall and destroy shall you ,down cut their gods of images carved the and ,fire with shall you burn their and pillars

3068 6213 3808 4725 8034
4 את־שמם מן־המקום ההוא: לא־תעשון כן ליהוה
to Jehovah so shall You do not .that place out of their names

430 3068 977 834 4725 430
5 אלהיכם: כי אם־אל־המקום אשר־יבחר יהוה אלהיכם
God your Jehovah shall choose which the place to But .God your

1875 7933 8033 8034 7760 7626 3605
מכל־שבטיכם לשום את־שמו שם לשכנו תדרשו
shall you ,seek His for dwelling there His name put to your ,tribes of out all

2077 5930 8033 935 8033 935
6 ובאת שמה: והבאתם שמה עלתיכם וזבחיכם ואת
and your and ,sacrifices burnt your ,offerings there you And bring shall .there you and go shall

5071 5088 3027 8641 4643
מעשרתיכם ואת תרומת ידכם ונדריכם ונדבתיכם
free- your and offering will your and ,offerings votive your hand heave the of offering and ,tithes your

flock. [7]And you shall eat
there before Jehovah your
God, and shall rejoice in all
that you put your hand to,
you and your households,
with which Jehovah your
God has blessed you. [8]You
shall not do according to all
that we *are* doing here
today, each *doing* all that *is*
right in his own eyes. [9]For
you have not come to the
rest and to the inheritance
which Jehovah your God is
giving to you. [10]And you
shall cross over the Jordan,
and shall live in the land
which Jehovah your God is
causing you to inherit. And
He shall give you rest from
all your enemies all around;
and you shall live securely.
[11]And it shall be, the place
which Jehovah your God
shall choose to cause His
name to dwell there, there
you shall bring all that I *am*
commanding you, your
burnt offerings, and your
sacrifices, your tithes, and
the heave offering of your
hand, and all your choice
free-will offerings which
you vow to Jehovah. [12]And
you shall rejoice before
Jehovah your God, you and
your sons, and your
daughters, and your male
slaves, and your slave-girls,
and the Levite who *is* within
your gates because he has
no portion or inheritance
with you. [13]Take heed to
yourself that you not offer
your burnt offerings in every
place that you see; [14]but
in the place which Jehovah
shall choose in one of your
tribes, there you shall offer
your burnt offerings, and
there you shall do all that I
command.
[15]Only with all the desire
of your soul you shall
sacrifice and shall eat flesh
within all your gates
according to the blessing of

3068 6440 8033 398 6629 1241 1060
7 וּבְכֹרֹת בְּקַרְכֶם וְצֹאנְכֶם׃ וַאֲכַלְתֶּם־שָׁם לִפְנֵי יְהוָה
Jehovah before there you And of and your the and
eat shall .flock your herd of firstlings

834 1004 3027 4916 3605 8056 430
אֱלֹהֵיכֶם וּשְׂמַחְתֶּם בְּכֹל מִשְׁלַח יֶדְכֶם אַתֶּם וּבָתֵּיכֶם אֲשֶׁר
with your and you your you that all in shall and your
which households hand to put rejoice God

6213 6213 430 3068 1288
8 בֵּרַכְךָ יְהוָה אֱלֹהֶיךָ׃ לֹא תַעֲשׂוּן כְּכֹל אֲשֶׁר אֲנַחְנוּ עֹשִׂים
(are) we that according You not your Jehovah has
doing all to do shall .God you blessed

5704 935 3808/3588 5869 3477 3605/376 3117
9 פֹּה הַיּוֹם אִישׁ כָּל־הַיָּשָׁר בְּעֵינָיו׃ כִּי לֹא־בָאתֶם עַד
till have you not for his in (is) that all each ,today here
come ;eyes own right (doing)

5414 430 3068 834 5159 4496 6258
עַתָּה אֶל־הַמְּנוּחָה וְאֶל־הַנַּחֲלָה אֲשֶׁר־יְהוָה אֱלֹהֶיךָ נֹתֵן
is God your Jehovah which the and rest the to now
giving inheritance to

3068 834 776 3427 3383 5674
10 לָךְ׃ וַעֲבַרְתֶּם אֶת־הַיַּרְדֵּן וִישַׁבְתֶּם בָּאָרֶץ אֲשֶׁר־יְהוָה
Jehovah which the in shall and the You And .you to
land live Jordan over cross shall

5439 341 3605 5117 5157 430
אֱלֹהֵיכֶם מַנְחִיל אֶתְכֶם וְהֵנִיחַ לָכֶם מִכָּל־אֹיְבֵיכֶם מִסָּבִיב
all your from you to He and ,you causing is God your
around enemies all rest give shall inherit to

430 3068 977 834 4725 1961 983 3427
11 וִישַׁבְתֶּם־בֶּטַח׃ וְהָיָה הַמָּקוֹם אֲשֶׁר־יִבְחַר יְהוָה אֱלֹהֵיכֶם
God your Jehovah shall which place the it And .securely you and
choose ,be shall live shall

3605 935 8033 8033 8034 7931
בּוֹ לְשַׁכֵּן שְׁמוֹ שָׁם שָׁמָּה תָבִיאוּ אֵת כָּל־אֲשֶׁר אָנֹכִי
I that all you (that) there ,there His cause to
bring shall name dwell to

8641 4643 2077 5930 6680
מְצַוֶּה אֶתְכֶם עוֹלֹתֵיכֶם וְזִבְחֵיכֶם מַעְשְׂרֹתֵיכֶם וּתְרֻמַת
the and tithes your your and burnt your :you (am)
of offering heave ,sacrifices offerings commanding

8056 3068 5087 834 5088 4005 3605 3027
12 יֶדְכֶם וְכֹל מִבְחַר נִדְרֵיכֶם אֲשֶׁר תִּדְּרוּ לַיהוָה׃ וּשְׂמַחְתֶּם
you and to you which votive your choice and your
rejoice shall .Jehovah vow offerings all hand

5650 1323 1121 430 3068 6440
לִפְנֵי יְהוָה אֱלֹהֵיכֶם אַתֶּם וּבְנֵיכֶם וּבְנֹתֵיכֶם וְעַבְדֵיכֶם
your and your and and sons .God your Jenovah before
slaves male daughters sons your

5159 2506 369/3588 8179 834 3881 519
וְאַמְהֹתֵיכֶם וְהַלֵּוִי אֲשֶׁר בְּשַׁעֲרֵיכֶם כִּי אֵין לוֹ חֵלֶק וְנַחֲלָה
of portion he not for within your who the and your and
inheritance has ,gates (is) Levite ,slaves female

4725 3605 5930 5927 8104
13 אִתְּכֶם׃ הִשָּׁמֶר לְךָ פֶּן־תַּעֲלֶה עֹלֹתֶיךָ בְּכָל־מָקוֹם אֲשֶׁר
that place in burnt your you lest to heed Take with
every offerings offer yourself ,you

7626 259 3068 977 834 4725 7200
14 תִּרְאֶה׃ כִּי אִם־בַּמָּקוֹם אֲשֶׁר־יִבְחַר יְהוָה בְּאַחַד שְׁבָטֶיךָ
your one in Jehovah shall which the in but you
:tribes of choose place only see

6680 3605 6213 8033 5930 5927 8033
שָׁם תַּעֲלֶה עֹלֹתֶיךָ וְשָׁם תַּעֲשֶׂה כֹּל אֲשֶׁר אָנֹכִי מְצַוֶּךָּ׃
command- I that all shall you and burnt your you there
.you ing (am) do there ,offering offer shall

3068 1293 1320 398 2076 185 3605 7535
15 רַק בְּכָל־אַוַּת נַפְשְׁךָ תִּזְבַּח וְאָכַלְתָּ בָשָׂר כְּבִרְכַּת יְהוָה
Jehovah according meat shall and shall you your the with Only
of blessing the to eat sacrifice soul of desire all

Jehovah your God which He has given you, the unclean and the clean one may eat of it, as of the gazelle and as of the hart. [16]Only, you shall not eat the blood; you shall pour it as water on the earth. [17]You may not eat the tithe of your grain within your gates, and of your new wine, and your oil, and the firstlings of your herd and of your flock, and any of your vows which you vow, and your free-will offering, and the heave offering of your hand. [18]But you shall eat it before Jehovah your God in the place which Jehovah your God shall choose, you and your son, and your daughter, and your male slave, and your slave-girl, and the Levite who *is* within your gates. And you shall rejoice before Jehovah your God in all that you put your hand to. [19]Take heed to yourself that you do not forsake the Levite as long as you live on the land.

[20]When Jehovah your God shall enlarge your border, as He has promised you, and you shall say, I will eat meat, because your soul longs to eat meat, you may eat meat according to all the desire of your soul. [21]If the place which Jehovah your God shall choose to put His name there is too far from you, then you shall sacrifice of your herd and of your flock which Jehovah has given you, as I have commanded you; and you shall eat within your gates according to all the desire of your soul. [22]Only, as the gazelle and the hart are eaten, so you shall eat of it; the unclean and the clean may eat of it alike. [23]Only, be sure not to eat the blood, for the blood *is* the life, and you shall not eat the life with the flesh; you shall not

24 25 לֹא תֹּאכְלֶנּוּ עַל־הָאָרֶץ תִּשְׁפְּכֶנּוּ כַּמָּיִם׃ לֹא תֹּאכְלֶנּוּ לְמַעַן
יִיטַב לְךָ וּלְבָנֶיךָ אַחֲרֶיךָ כִּי־תַעֲשֶׂה הַיָּשָׁר בְּעֵינֵי יְהוָה׃
26 רַק קָדָשֶׁיךָ אֲשֶׁר־יִהְיוּ לְךָ וּנְדָרֶיךָ תִּשָּׂא וּבָאתָ אֶל־
27 הַמָּקוֹם אֲשֶׁר־יִבְחַר יְהוָה׃ וְעָשִׂיתָ עֹלֹתֶיךָ הַבָּשָׂר וְהַדָּם
עַל־מִזְבַּח יְהוָה אֱלֹהֶיךָ וְדַם־זְבָחֶיךָ יִשָּׁפֵךְ עַל־מִזְבַּח
28 יְהוָה אֱלֹהֶיךָ וְהַבָּשָׂר תֹּאכֵל׃ שְׁמֹר וְשָׁמַעְתָּ אֵת כָּל־
הַדְּבָרִים הָאֵלֶּה אֲשֶׁר אָנֹכִי מְצַוֶּךָּ לְמַעַן יִיטַב לְךָ וּלְבָנֶיךָ
אַחֲרֶיךָ עַד־עוֹלָם כִּי תַעֲשֶׂה הַטּוֹב וְהַיָּשָׁר בְּעֵינֵי יְהוָה
29 אֱלֹהֶיךָ׃ כִּי־יַכְרִית יְהוָה אֱלֹהֶיךָ אֶת־הַגּוֹיִם אֲשֶׁר
אַתָּה בָא־שָׁמָּה לָרֶשֶׁת אוֹתָם מִפָּנֶיךָ וְיָרַשְׁתָּ אֹתָם וְיָשַׁבְתָּ
30 בְּאַרְצָם׃ הִשָּׁמֶר לְךָ פֶּן־תִּנָּקֵשׁ אַחֲרֵיהֶם אַחֲרֵי הִשָּׁמְדָם
מִפָּנֶיךָ וּפֶן־תִּדְרֹשׁ לֵאלֹהֵיהֶם לֵאמֹר אֵיכָה יַעַבְדוּ הַגּוֹיִם
31 הָאֵלֶּה אֶת־אֱלֹהֵיהֶם וְאֶעֱשֶׂה־כֵּן גַּם־אָנִי׃ לֹא־תַעֲשֶׂה
כֵן לַיהוָה אֱלֹהֶיךָ כִּי כָל־תּוֹעֲבַת יְהוָה אֲשֶׁר שָׂנֵא עָשׂוּ
לֵאלֹהֵיהֶם כִּי גַם אֶת־בְּנֵיהֶם וְאֶת־בְּנֹתֵיהֶם יִשְׂרְפוּ בָאֵשׁ
לֵאלֹהֵיהֶם׃

eat it; you shall pour it on the earth as water. [25]You shall not eat it in order that it may be well with you, and with your sons after you, when you do that which *is* right in the eyes of Jehovah. [26]Only, your holy things which you have, and your vows, you shall take up and shall go to the place which Jehovah shall choose. [27]And you shall offer your burnt offerings, the flesh and the blood, on the altar of Jehovah your God; and the blood of your sacrifices shall be poured out by the altar of Jehovah your God; and you shall eat the flesh. [28]And you take heed to obey all these words which I am commanding you, in order that it may be well with you and with your sons after you forever, when you do that which *is* good and right in the eyes of Jehovah your God.

[29]When Jehovah your God shall cut off the nations from before you, where you are going in to possess them, and you shall possess them, and shall live in their land, [30]take heed to yourself that you not be snared to follow them after they have been destroyed before you; and that you not inquire after their gods, saying, How did these nations serve their gods? And I shall do so, even I. [31]You shall not do so to Jehovah your God; for everything hateful to Jehovah, which He detests, they have done to their gods. For they have even burned their sons and their daughters in the fire to their gods.

CAP. XIII יג

CHAPTER 13

8104 6680 834 1697 3605

1 אֵת כָּל־הַדָּבָר אֲשֶׁר אָנֹכִי מְצַוֶּה אֶתְכֶם אֹתוֹ תִשְׁמְרוּ

take heed | them | ,you | (am) commanding | I | that | the things | All

1639 3808 3254 6213

לַעֲשׂוֹת לֹא־תֹסֵף עָלָיו וְלֹא תִגְרַע מִמֶּנּוּ׃

from it | take away | and not | it to | you not add shall | do to

226 5414 2472 2492 176 5030 7130 6965

2 כִּי־יָקוּם בְּקִרְבְּךָ נָבִיא אוֹ חֹלֵם חֲלוֹם וְנָתַן אֵלֶיךָ אוֹת

sign a | you gives | and | dreams of dreamer | a | or | a prophet | among you | rises | If

559 1696 834 4159 226 935 4159 176

3 אוֹ מוֹפֵת׃ וּבָא הָאוֹת וְהַמּוֹפֵת אֲשֶׁר־דִּבֶּר אֵלֶיךָ לֵּאמֹר

,saying | ,you to | he foretold | which | the or wonder | the sign | comes and pass to | a ,wonder | or

5647 3045 3808 834 312 430 310 3212

נֵלְכָה אַחֲרֵי אֱלֹהִים אֲחֵרִים אֲשֶׁר לֹא־יְדַעְתָּם וְנָעָבְדֵם׃

us let and ;them serve | have you known | not | which | other | gods | after | us Let go

2472 2492 176 5030 1697 8085

4 לֹא תִשְׁמַע אֶל־דִּבְרֵי הַנָּבִיא הַהוּא אוֹ אֶל־חוֹלֵם הַחֲלוֹם

dreams of | dreamer | to | or | that | prophet | the of words | to | shall You listen | not

3045 430 3068 5254

הַהוּא כִּי מְנַסֶּה יְהוָה אֱלֹהֵיכֶם אֶתְכֶם לָדַעַת הֲיִשְׁכֶם

whether are you | know to | ,you | God your | Jehovah | (is) testing | for | ,that

5315 3605 3824 3605 430 3068 157

אֹהֲבִים אֶת־יְהוָה אֱלֹהֵיכֶם בְּכָל־לְבַבְכֶם וּבְכָל־נַפְשְׁכֶם׃

:soul your | and all with | heart your | with all | God your | Jehovah | who ones love

4687 3372 3212 430 3068 310

5 אַחֲרֵי יְהוָה אֱלֹהֵיכֶם תֵּלֵכוּ וְאֹתוֹ תִירָאוּ וְאֶת־מִצְוֹתָיו

His commands | and | shall you ,fear | and Him | shall You ,walk | God your | Jehovah | after

5030 1692 5647 8085 6963 8104

6 תִּשְׁמֹרוּ וּבְקֹלוֹ תִשְׁמָעוּ וְאֹתוֹ תַעֲבֹדוּ וּבוֹ תִדְבָּקוּן׃ וְהַנָּבִיא

And prophet | shall you . to cling | and Him | shall you ,serve | and Him | shall you ,hear | His and voice | shall you ,keep

5627 4191 2492 2472 176

הַהוּא אוֹ חֹלֵם הַחֲלוֹם הַהוּא יוּמָת כִּי דִבֶּר־סָרָה עַל־

against apostasy | he spoken has | because be shall ,executed | that | dreams dreamer of | or | that

6299 4714 776 3318 430 3068

יְהוָה אֱלֹהֵיכֶם הַמּוֹצִיא אֶתְכֶם מֵאֶרֶץ מִצְרַיִם וְהַפֹּדְךָ

has and you redeemed | Egypt | the from of land | you | who out brought | ,God your | Jehovah

430 3068 6680 834 1870 5080 5650 1004

מִבֵּית עֲבָדִים לְהַדִּיחֲךָ מִן־הַדֶּרֶךְ אֲשֶׁר צִוְּךָ יְהוָה אֱלֹהֶיךָ

God your | Jehovah | has | which you commanded | the way | of | drive to out you | ,slavery | of out of house the

251 5496 7130 7451 1197 3212

7 לָלֶכֶת בָּהּ וּבִעַרְתָּ הָרָע מִקִּרְבֶּךָ׃ כִּי יְסִיתְךָ אָחִיךָ

your brother | entice shall When you | your from .midst | evil | you and away put shall | ;in | walk to

7453 176 2436 802 1323 1121 517 1121

בֶן־אִמֶּךָ אוֹ־בִנְךָ אוֹ־בִתְּךָ אוֹ ׀ אֵשֶׁת חֵיקֶךָ אוֹ רֵעֲךָ אֲשֶׁר

who (is) | your friend | or | your bosom | the of wife | or | your or daughter | your or son | your the mother of son

312 430 5647 3212 559 5643 5315

כְּנַפְשְׁךָ בַּסֵּתֶר לֵאמֹר נֵלְכָה וְנַעַבְדָה אֱלֹהִים אֲחֵרִים

other | gods | serve and | us Let go | ,saying | secretly | your as soul own

---

[32]All the things that I command you, take heed to do them, and you shall not add to it, nor take away from it.

CHAPTER 13

[1]If a prophet or a dreamer of dreams rises among you, and gives you a sign or a wonder, [2]and the sign or the wonder which he foretold to you occurs, saying, Let us go after other gods which you have not known, and let us serve them, [3]you shall not listen to the words of that prophet, or that dreamer of dreams. For Jehovah your God *is* testing you, to know if you love Jehovah your God with all your heart and with all your soul. [4]You shall walk after Jehovah your God, and you shall fear Him. And you shall keep His commandments, and you shall hear His voice, and you shall serve Him, and you shall cleave to Him. [5]And that prophet or that dreamer of dreams shall be put to death, because he has spoken apostasy against Jehovah your God, who is bringing you out of the land of Egypt, and has redeemed you out of the house of slavery, to drive you out of the way in which Jehovah your God has commanded you to walk. And you shall put away evil from among you.

[6]If your brother, your mother's son, or your son, or your daughter, or the wife of your bosom, or your friend who *is* as your own soul, shall entice you secretly, saying, Let us go and serve other gods,

which you have not known, you and your fathers, [7]of the gods of the people who are around you, who are near you, or who are far off from you, from one end of the earth even to the other end of the earth, [8]you shall not consent to him, nor listen to him, nor shall your eye have pity on him, nor shall you spare nor hide him. [9]But you shall surely kill him; your hand shall be first upon him to put him to death, and the hand of all the people last. [10]And you shall stone him with stones, and he shall die, for he has sought to drive you away from Jehovah your God, who brought you out of the land of Egypt, out of the house of slaves. [11]And all Israel shall hear and fear, and shall not again do any such wicked thing as this among you.

[12]If, in one of your cities which Jehovah your God is giving you to live in, you hear *one* saying, [13]*Certain* men, sons of Belial, have gone out from among you and have drawn away those who live in their city, saying, Let us go and serve other gods, which you have not known; [14]then you shall inquire and make search, and ask carefully; and, behold *if* the thing is truly established, *that* this abominable thing has been done among you, [15]you shall surely strike those who live in that city by the mouth of the sword, destroying it completely, and all that *is* in it, and its livestock, with the mouth of the sword. [16]And you shall gather all its spoil into the middle of its open place, and shall burn the city with fire, and all its spoil, completely, before

834 5971 430 1 3045 3808 834
8 אֲשֶׁר לֹא יָדַעְתָּ אַתָּה וַאֲבֹתֶיךָ׃ מֵאֱלֹהֵי הָעַמִּים אֲשֶׁר
who the the of your and you have you not which
are people of gods ,fathers ,known

7097 7350 176 7138 5439
סְבִיבֹתֵיכֶם הַקְּרֹבִים אֵלֶיךָ אוֹ הָרְחֹקִים מִמֶּךָּ מִקְצֵה
(one) from from are who or you to are who around
of end you off far near ,you

8085 3808 14 3808 776 7097 5704 776
9 הָאָרֶץ וְעַד־קְצֵה הָאָרֶץ׃ לֹא־תֹאבֶה לוֹ וְלֹא תִשְׁמַע אֵלָיו
to listen and to shall you not the (other) the even the
,him not him consent earth of end to earth

3680 2550 3808 5869 2347 3808
10 וְלֹא־תָחוֹס עֵינְךָ עָלָיו וְלֹא־תַחְמֹל וְלֹא־תְכַסֶּה עָלָיו׃ כִּי
But .him shall you and shall you and on your shall and
hide not spare not him eye pity have not

3605 3027 4191 7223 1961 3027 2026 2026
הָרֹג תַּהַרְגֶנּוּ יָדְךָ תִּהְיֶה־בּוֹ בָרִאשׁוֹנָה לַהֲמִיתוֹ וְיַד כָּל־
all the and him put to first upon shall your shall you surely
of hand ,death to him be hand ;him kill

5080 1245 4191 68 5619 314 5971
11 הָעָם בָּאַחֲרֹנָה׃ וּסְקַלְתּוֹ בָאֲבָנִים וָמֵת כִּי בִקֵּשׁ לְהַדִּיחֲךָ
drive to has he for he and with you And .afterwards the
away you sought ,die shall stones him stone shall people

5650 1004 4714 776 3318 430 3068
מֵעַל יְהוָה אֱלֹהֶיךָ הַמּוֹצִיאֲךָ מֵאֶרֶץ מִצְרַיִם מִבֵּית עֲבָדִים׃
.slavery of out ,Egypt the of out who God your Jehovah from
of house the of land you brought

1697 6213 3254 3808 3372 8085 3478
12 וְכָל־יִשְׂרָאֵל יִשְׁמְעוּ וְיִרָאוּן וְלֹא־יוֹסִפוּ לַעֲשׂוֹת כַּדָּבָר
thing as do shall and fear and shall Israel And
again not hear all

834 5892 259 8085 7130 2088 7451
13 הָרָע הַזֶּה בְּקִרְבֶּךָ׃ כִּי־תִשְׁמַע בְּאַחַת עָרֶיךָ אֲשֶׁר
which your one in you When among this evil
cities of hear ,you

582 5927 559 8033 3427 5414 430 3068
14 יְהוָה אֱלֹהֶיךָ נֹתֵן לְךָ לָשֶׁבֶת שָׁם לֵאמֹר׃ יָצְאוּ אֲנָשִׁים
(Certain) have (one) in live to to is your Jehovah
,men out gone ,saying you giving God

3212 559 5892 3427 5080 7130 1100/1121
בְנֵי־בְלִיַּעַל מִקִּרְבֶּךָ וַיַּדִּיחוּ אֶת־יֹשְׁבֵי עִירָם לֵאמֹר נֵלְכָה
us Let ,saying their who those have and from ,Belial sons
go ,city in live away drawn you among of

1875 3045 3808 834 312 430 5647
15 וְנַעַבְדָה אֱלֹהִים אֲחֵרִים אֲשֶׁר לֹא־יְדַעְתֶּם׃ וְדָרַשְׁתָּ
you then have you not which other gods serve and
inquire shall ;known

6213 1697 3559 571 2009 3190 7592 2713
וְחָקַרְתָּ וְשָׁאַלְתָּ הֵיטֵב וְהִנֵּה אֱמֶת נָכוֹן הַדָּבָר נֶעֶשְׂתָה
been has ,matter the (is) truly (if) and ;carefully and make and
done (that) established ,behold ask search

5892 3427 5221 5221 7130 2063 8441
16 הַתּוֹעֵבָה הַזֹּאת בְּקִרְבֶּךָ׃ הַכֵּה תַכֶּה אֶת־יֹשְׁבֵי הָעִיר
city who those shall you surely your in this hateful
in live strike midst thing

834 3605 2763 2719/6310
הַהִוא לְפִי־חָרֶב הַחֲרֵם אֹתָהּ וְאֶת־כָּל־אֲשֶׁר־בָּהּ וְאֶת־
an it in that all and it destroying the by that
(is) completely sword's edge

8432 6908 7998 3605 2719/6310 929
17 בְּהֶמְתָּהּ לְפִי־חָרֶב׃ וְאֶת־כָּל־שְׁלָלָהּ תִּקְבֹּץ אֶל־תּוֹךְ
the into shall you its all And the with cattle its
of middle gather spoil ,sword's mouth

3632 7998 3605 5892 784 8313 7339
רְחֹבָהּ וְשָׂרַפְתָּ בָאֵשׁ אֶת־הָעִיר וְאֶת־כָּל־שְׁלָלָהּ כָּלִיל
com- the all and city the with shall and open its
pletely it of spoil fire burn place

Jehovah your God. And it shall be a heap forever; it shall not be built any more. 17 And not any of the cursed thing shall cleave to your hand, so that Jehovah shall turn from the fierceness of His anger, and shall give mercies to you, and shall love you, and shall multiply you, as He has sworn to your fathers, 18 when you listen to the voice of Jehovah your God, to keep all His commandments which I *am* commanding you today, to do that which *is* right in the eyes of Jehovah your God.

18 לַיהוָה אֱלֹהֶיךָ וְהָיְתָה תֵּל עוֹלָם לֹא תִבָּנֶה עוֹד׃ וְלֹא־
יִדְבַּק בְּיָדְךָ מְאוּמָה מִן־הַחֵרֶם לְמַעַן יָשׁוּב יְהוָה מֵחֲרוֹן
אַפּוֹ וְנָתַן־לְךָ רַחֲמִים וְרִחַמְךָ וְהִרְבֶּךָ כַּאֲשֶׁר נִשְׁבַּע
19 לַאֲבֹתֶיךָ׃ כִּי תִשְׁמַע בְּקוֹל יְהוָה אֱלֹהֶיךָ לִשְׁמֹר אֶת־
כָּל־מִצְוֹתָיו אֲשֶׁר אָנֹכִי מְצַוְּךָ הַיּוֹם לַעֲשׂוֹת הַיָּשָׁר בְּעֵינֵי
יְהוָה אֱלֹהֶיךָ׃

CAP. XIV יד

CHAPTER 14

1 You *are* sons to Jehovah your God; you shall not cut yourselves, nor make *any* baldness between your eyes for the dead. 2 For you are holy people to Jehovah your God; and Jehovah has chosen you to be a people to Him, a special treasure out of all the peoples who are on the face of the earth.

3 You shall not eat any abominable thing. 4 These *are* the animals which you shall eat: the ox, the flocked sheep, and the flocked goats, 5 the hart and gazelle, and roebuck, and wild goat, and antelope, and oryx, and mouflon. 6 And you may eat every animal that divides the hoof, and divides two hoofs wholly, and causes the cud to come up among the animals. 7 But you shall not eat of those that *only* cause the cud to come up, or those *only* dividing the cloven hoof: the camel, and the hare, and the rock-badger — for they cause the cud to come up, but do not divide the hoof. They

1 בָּנִים אַתֶּם לַיהוָה אֱלֹהֵיכֶם לֹא תִתְגֹּדְדוּ וְלֹא־תָשִׂימוּ
2 קָרְחָה בֵּין עֵינֵיכֶם לָמֵת׃ כִּי עַם קָדוֹשׁ אַתָּה לַיהוָה
אֱלֹהֶיךָ וּבְךָ בָּחַר יְהוָה לִהְיוֹת לוֹ לְעַם סְגֻלָּה מִכֹּל
3 הָעַמִּים אֲשֶׁר עַל־פְּנֵי הָאֲדָמָה׃ לֹא תֹאכַל כָּל־
4 תּוֹעֵבָה׃ זֹאת הַבְּהֵמָה אֲשֶׁר תֹּאכֵלוּ שׁוֹר שֵׂה כְשָׂבִים
5 6 וְשֵׂה עִזִּים׃ אַיָּל וּצְבִי וְיַחְמוּר וְאַקּוֹ וְדִישֹׁן וּתְאוֹ וָזָמֶר׃ וְכָל־
בְּהֵמָה מַפְרֶסֶת פַּרְסָה וְשֹׁסַעַת שֶׁסַע שְׁתֵּי פְרָסוֹת מַעֲלַת
7 גֵּרָה בַּבְּהֵמָה אֹתָהּ תֹּאכֵלוּ׃ אַךְ אֶת־זֶה לֹא תֹאכְלוּ
מִמַּעֲלֵי הַגֵּרָה וּמִמַּפְרִיסֵי הַפַּרְסָה הַשְּׁסוּעָה אֶת־הַגָּמָל
וְאֶת־הָאַרְנֶבֶת וְאֶת־הַשָּׁפָן כִּי־מַעֲלֵה גֵרָה הֵמָּה וּפַרְסָה

shall be unclean to you. [8]And the swine, because it divides the hoof, but *does* not *bring up* the cud; it is unclean to you—you shall not eat of their flesh, nor touch their dead body.

[9]These you shall eat of all that are in the waters: you shall eat all that have fins and scales. [10]And whatever does not have fins and scales, you shall not eat. It *shall be* unclean to you.

[11]You shall eat of all clean birds. [12]But you shall not eat of these: the eagle, the black vulture and the bearded vulture, [13]and the hawk, and falcons, and the kite by its kinds, [14]and all ravens by their kinds; [15]and the ostrich, and the great owl, and the sea gull, and small hawks by their kinds, [16]the little owl and the eared owl, and the barn owl, [17]the pelican, and the owl, and the cormorant, [18]and the stork, and the heron by its kind, and the hoopoe, and the bat. [19]And every teeming thing that flies *shall be* unclean to you; they shall not be eaten. [20]You may eat of all clean birds.

[21]You shall not eat of anything that died of itself. You may give it to the alien who *is* within your gates, that he may eat it. Or you may sell *it* to a foreigner. For you *are* a holy people to Jehovah your God. You shall not simmer a kid in its mother's milk.

[22]You shall surely tithe all the produce of your seed that the field yields yearly. [23]And you shall eat before Jehovah your God in the place that He shall

8 לֹא הִפְרִיסוּ טְמֵאִים הֵם לָכֶם׃ וְאֶת־הַחֲזִיר כִּֽי־מַפְרִיס
divided because the swine and to you (be shall) they unclean they :divide not
פַּרְסָה הוּא וְלֹא גֵרָה טָמֵא הוּא לָכֶם מִבְּשָׂרָם לֹא תֹאכֵלוּ
shall you .eat not their of flesh to you (is) it unclean the cud but not (is) it hoof the
וּבְנִבְלָתָם לֹא תִגָּעוּ׃ 9 אֶת־זֶה תֹּאכְלוּ מִכֹּל אֲשֶׁר
that (are) all of shall you eat These you .touch shall not their and carcass
10 בַּמָּיִם כֹּל אֲשֶׁר־לוֹ סְנַפִּיר וְקַשְׂקֶשֶׂת תֹּאכֵלוּ׃ וְכֹל אֲשֶׁר
that And all shall you .eat and scales fins have that all the in :waters
אֵין־לוֹ סְנַפִּיר וְקַשְׂקֶשֶׂת לֹא תֹאכֵלוּ טָמֵא הוּא לָכֶם׃
.you to it (be shall) unclean shall you :eat not and scales fins not do have
11 כָּל־צִפּוֹר טְהֹרָה תֹּאכֵלוּ׃ 12 וְזֶה אֲשֶׁר לֹא־תֹאכְלוּ מֵהֶם
:of shall you eat not any But these shall you eat clean birds All
13 הַנֶּשֶׁר וְהַפֶּרֶס וְהָעָזְנִיָּה׃ וְהָרָאָה וְאֶת־הָאַיָּה וְהַדַּיָּה לְמִינָהּ׃
O,kinds its by the and kite falcons and the and hawk bearded and vulture black vulture eagle the
14 וְאֵת כָּל־עֹרֵב לְמִינוֹ׃ 15 וְאֵת בַּת הַיַּעֲנָה וְאֶת־הַתַּחְמָס וְאֶת־
and great the owl and the ostrich and by ,kinds their ravens all and
16 הַשָּׁחַף וְאֶת־הַנֵּץ לְמִינֵהוּ׃ אֶת־הַכּוֹס וְאֶת־הַיַּנְשׁוּף
eared the owl and little the owl their by ,kinds small hawks and gull the
17 וְהַתִּנְשָׁמֶת׃ וְהַקָּאָת וְאֶת־הָרָחָמָה וְאֶת־הַשָּׁלָךְ׃ 18 וְהַחֲסִידָה
the and stork Egyptian the and vulture owl the and pelican and the owl barn and
19 וְהָאֲנָפָה לְמִינָהּ וְהַדּוּכִיפַת וְהָעֲטַלֵּף׃ וְכֹל שֶׁרֶץ הָעוֹף טָמֵא
unclean that flies teeming thing And every the and bat the and hoopoe after ,kind its the and heron
20 הוּא לָכֶם לֹא יֵאָכֵלוּ׃ כָּל־עוֹף טָהוֹר תֹּאכֵלוּ׃ 21 לֹא תֹאכְלוּ
shall You eat not may you .eat clean birds All shall they .eaten be not to you (shall) (be)
כָל־נְבֵלָה לַגֵּר אֲשֶׁר־בִּשְׁעָרֶיךָ תִּתְּנֶנָּה וַאֲכָלָהּ אוֹ מָכֹר
may you or (it) sell he that ,it eat may may you it give within gates your who (is) the to alien died that any- ;(itself of) thing
לְנָכְרִי כִּי עַם קָדוֹשׁ אַתָּה לַיהוָה אֱלֹהֶיךָ לֹא־תְבַשֵּׁל גְּדִי
a kid shall You simmer not .God your to Jehovah you (are) holy a people For a to .foreigner
בַּחֲלֵב אִמּוֹ׃
its .mother the in of milk
22 עַשֵּׂר תְּעַשֵּׂר אֵת כָּל־תְּבוּאַת זַרְעֶךָ הַיֹּצֵא הַשָּׂדֶה שָׁנָה
year the field that yields your seed the of produce all shall you tithe Surely
23 שָׁנָה׃ וְאָכַלְתָּ לִפְנֵי יְהוָה אֱלֹהֶיךָ בַּמָּקוֹם אֲשֶׁר־יִבְחַר
shall He choose which the in place your ,God Jehovah before you And eat shall by .year

choose to cause to dwell
His name there, the tithe of
your grain, of your wine, and
of your oil, and the firstlings
of your herd and of your
flock; that you may learn to
fear Jehovah your God all
your days. [24]And if the
way is too long for you, so
that you cannot carry it,
because the place is too far
from you which Jehovah
your God shall choose to
set His name there, when
Jehovah your God shall
bless you; [25]then you shall
give *it* for silver, and bind up
the silver in your hand. And
you shall go to the place
which Jehovah your God
shall choose. [26]And you
shall pay the silver for
whatever your soul desires,
for oxen, or for sheep, or for
wine, or for fermented
drink, or for whatever your
soul desires. And you shall
eat there before Jehovah
your God, and you shall
rejoice, you and your
household. [27]And you shall
not forsake the Levite who
is within your gates, for he
has no portion nor inheritance with you.

[28]At the end of three
years, even the same year,
you shall bring forth all the
tithe of your increase, and
shall lay it up within your
gates. [29]And the Levite,
because he has no portion
nor inheritance with you,
and the alien, and the
fatherless, and the widow
who *are* within your gates
shall come and shall eat
and be satisfied; so that
Jehovah your God may
bless you in all the work of
your hand which you do.

לשכן שמו שם מעשר דגנך תירשך ויצהרך ובכרת
בקרך וצאנך למען תלמד ליראה את־יהוה אלהיך כל
24 הימים׃ וכי־ירבה ממך הדרך כי לא תוכל שאתו
כי־ירחק ממך המקום אשר יבחר יהוה אלהיך לשום
25 שמו שם כי יברכך יהוה אלהיך׃ ונתתה בכסף וצרת
הכסף בידך והלכת אל־המקום אשר יבחר יהוה
26 אלהיך בו׃ ונתתה הכסף בכל אשר־תאוה נפשך בבקר
ובצאן וביין ובשכר ובכל אשר תשאלך נפשך ואכלת
27 שם לפני יהוה אלהיך ושמחת אתה וביתך׃ והלוי
אשר־בשעריך לא תעזבנו כי אין לו חלק ונחלה עמך׃
28 מקצה שלש שנים תוציא את־כל־מעשר תבואתך
29 בשנה ההוא והנחת בשעריך׃ ובא הלוי כי אין־לו חלק
ונחלה עמך והגר והיתום והאלמנה אשר בשעריך ואכלו
ושבעו למען יברכך יהוה אלהיך בכל־מעשה ידך אשר
תעשה׃

CAP. XV טו

CHAPTER 15

[1]At the end of *every*
seven years you shall make
a release. [2]And this *is* the
manner of the release:

1 מקץ שבע־שנים תעשה שמטה׃
2 וזה דבר השמטה

Everyone who has a loan to his neighbor shall release it; he shall not exact *it* of his neighbor and his brother, because a release has been proclaimed for Jehovah. 3You may exact *it* from a foreigner, but your hand shall release whatever is yours with your brother, 4except when there shall be no one in need among you. For Jehovah will greatly bless you in the land that Jehovah your God is giving you for an inheritance, to possess it, 5only if you carefully listen to the voice of Jehovah your God, to take heed to do all this command which I *am* commanding you today. 6For Jehovah your God will bless you as He promised you. And you shall lend to many nations, but you shall not borrow. And you shall rule over many nations, but they shall not rule over you.

7If there is a poor man among you, one of your brothers inside any of your gates in your land which Jehovah your God is giving to you, you shall not harden your heart, nor shut your hand from your needy brother. 8But you shall surely open your hand to him, and shall surely lend him enough for his need in that which he lacks. 9Beware that there is no evil thought in your heart, saying, The seventh year, the year of release draws near; and your eye *be* evil against your needy brother, and you give him nothing, and he cry to Jehovah against you, and it be sin to you. 10You shall surely give to him, and your heart shall not be grieved when you give to him, because Jehovah your God will bless you for this thing, in

5065 7453 4874 834 3027 4874 1167 8058
שָׁמוֹט כָּל־בַּעַל מַשֵּׁה יָדוֹ אֲשֶׁר יַשֶּׁה בְּרֵעֵהוּ לֹא־יִגֹּשׂ
not he exact shall | his to neighbor | he lent | what | his hand | loan a of | holder every of | shall release

5237 3068 8059 7121 251 7453
3 אֶת־רֵעֵהוּ וְאֶת־אָחִיו כִּי־קָרָא שְׁמִטָּה לַיהוָה׃ אֶת־הַנָּכְרִי
a From foreigner | for :Jehovah | release a | been has proclaimed | for | his ,brother | and | his of neighbor | (it)

657 3027 8059 251 5065
4 תִּגֹּשׂ וַאֲשֶׁר יִהְיֶה לְךָ אֶת־אָחִיךָ תַּשְׁמֵט יָדֶךָ׃ אֶפֶס כִּי
that only | your ,hand | shall release | your brother | with | to you | is | but whatever | may you (it) exact

834 776 3068 1288 3966 34 854 1961 3808
לֹא יִהְיֶה־בְּךָ אֶבְיוֹן כִּי־בָרֵךְ יְבָרֶכְךָ יְהוָה בָּאָרֶץ אֲשֶׁר
that | in land the | Jehovah | will you bless | greatly | for | in one ,need | among you | there be shall | not

8104 7535 3423 5159 5414 430 3068
5 יְהוָה אֱלֹהֶיךָ נֹתֵן־לְךָ נַחֲלָה לְרִשְׁתָּהּ׃ רַק אִם־שָׁמוֹעַ
carefully | if | only | possess to it | an for inheritance | to you | is giving | your God | Jehovah

4687 3605 6213 8104 430 3068 6963 8085
תִּשְׁמַע בְּקוֹל יְהוָה אֱלֹהֶיךָ לִשְׁמֹר לַעֲשׂוֹת אֶת־כָּל־הַמִּצְוָה
command | all | do to | be to careful | your God | Jehovah | the to of voice | will you listen

1288 430 3068 3117 6680 834 2088
6 הַזֹּאת אֲשֶׁר אָנֹכִי מְצַוְּךָ הַיּוֹם׃ כִּי־יְהוָה אֱלֹהֶיךָ בֵּרַכְךָ
bless will you | God your | Jehovah | For | .today | . com- manding you | (am) I | which | this

5670 3808 7227 1471 5670 1696
כַּאֲשֶׁר דִּבֶּר־לָךְ וְהַעֲבַטְתָּ גּוֹיִם רַבִּים וְאַתָּה לֹא תַעֲבֹט
shall ;borrow | not | but you | ,many | to nations | you and lend shall | ;you | he promised | as

4191 3808 7227 1471 4910
7 וּמָשַׁלְתָּ בְּגוֹיִם רַבִּים וּבְךָ לֹא יִמְשֹׁלוּ׃ כִּי־יִהְיֶה
is there If | shall they rule | not | but you over | ,many | over nations | you and rule shall

834 776 8179 259 251 259 34 854
בְךָ אֶבְיוֹן מֵאַחַד אַחֶיךָ בְּאַחַד שְׁעָרֶיךָ בְּאַרְצְךָ אֲשֶׁר־
which | your in land | your gates | inside of any | your brothers | of one ,need | in one among you

7092 3808 3824 553 3808 5414 430 3068
יְהוָה אֱלֹהֶיךָ נֹתֵן לָךְ לֹא תְאַמֵּץ אֶת־לְבָבְךָ וְלֹא תִקְפֹּץ
shall you shut | and not | your heart | shall you harden | not | to ,you | is giving | your God | Jehovah

3027 6605 6605 34 251 3027
8 אֶת־יָדְךָ מֵאָחִיךָ הָאֶבְיוֹן׃ כִּי־פָתֹחַ תִּפְתַּח אֶת־יָדְךָ לוֹ
to him | your hand | shall you open | surely but | ,needy | your from brother | hand your

8104 2637 834 4270 1767 5670 5670
9 וְהַעֲבֵט תַּעֲבִיטֶנּוּ דֵּי מַחְסֹרוֹ אֲשֶׁר יֶחְסַר לוֹ׃ הִשָּׁמֶר לְךָ
to yourself | heed Take | to .him | is lacking | which | his need | enough for | lend shall him | and surely

8141 7126 559 1100 3824 1697 1961
פֶּן־יִהְיֶה דָבָר עִם־לְבָבְךָ בְלִיַּעַל לֵאמֹר קָרְבָה שְׁנַת־
year | draws near | ,saying | evil | your heart | in | a matter | there lest be

3808 34 251 5969 1100 8059 8141 7651
הַשֶּׁבַע שְׁנַת הַשְּׁמִטָּה וְרָעָה עֵינְךָ בְּאָחִיךָ הָאֶבְיוֹן וְלֹא
and nothing | needy | against brother your | your eye | (be) and evil | the ,release | year of | The seventh

5414 5414 2399 1961 3068 7121 5414
10 תִתֵּן לוֹ וְקָרָא עָלֶיךָ אֶל־יְהוָה וְהָיָה בְךָ חֵטְא׃ נָתוֹן תִּתֵּן
you give shall | Surely | .sin | with you | it and be | ,Jehovah to | against you | he and cry | to ,him | you give

2088 1697 1558 5414 3824 7489 3808
לוֹ וְלֹא־יֵרַע לְבָבְךָ בְּתִתְּךָ לוֹ כִּי בִּגְלַל ׀ הַדָּבָר הַזֶּה
this | thing | because of | for | to ,him | you when give | your heart | shall grieved be | and not | to ,him

all your work, and in all that you put your hand to. [11]For the poor will never cease from the midst of the land. On account of this I command you, saying, You shall surely open your hand to your poor and needy brother in your land.

[12]If your brother, a Hebrew man, or a Hebrew woman, is sold to you and serves you six years, then in the seventh year you shall let him go free from you. [13]And when you send him out free from you, you shall not let him go away empty. [14]You shall richly bestow on him from your flock, and from your threshing-floor, and from your winepress, with that which Jehovah your God has blessed you, you shall give to him. [15]And you shall remember that your were a slave in the land of Egypt, and Jehovah your God redeemed you—on account of this I command you this thing today. [16]And it shall be, if he says to you, I will not go out from you, because he loves you and your house, because *it was* good for him with you; [17]then you shall take an awl, and shall put it through his ear, and through the door, and he shall be your slave forever. And you shall do so to your slave-girl also. [18]It shall not seem hard in your eyes when you send him away free from you. For to the double of the hire of a hireling he has served you six years. And Jehovah your God will bless you in all that you do.

[19]All the firstling males that are born of your herd and of your flock, you shall sanctify to Jehovah your God. You shall do no work with the firstling of your ox,

יְבָרֶכְךָ יְהוָה אֱלֹהֶיךָ בְּכָל־מַעֲשֶׂךָ וּבְכֹל מִשְׁלַח יָדֶךָ׃ כִּי 11
לֹא־יֶחְדַּל אֶבְיוֹן מִקֶּרֶב הָאָרֶץ עַל־כֵּן אָנֹכִי מְצַוְּךָ לֵאמֹר
פָּתֹחַ תִּפְתַּח אֶת־יָדְךָ לְאָחִיךָ לַעֲנִיֶּךָ וּלְאֶבְיֹנְךָ בְּאַרְצֶךָ׃
כִּי־יִמָּכֵר לְךָ אָחִיךָ הָעִבְרִי אוֹ הָעִבְרִיָּה וַעֲבָדְךָ שֵׁשׁ שָׁנִים 12
וּבַשָּׁנָה הַשְּׁבִיעִת תְּשַׁלְּחֶנּוּ חָפְשִׁי מֵעִמָּךְ׃ וְכִי־תְשַׁלְּחֶנּוּ 13
חָפְשִׁי מֵעִמָּךְ לֹא תְשַׁלְּחֶנּוּ רֵיקָם׃ הַעֲנֵיק תַּעֲנִיק לוֹ 14
מִצֹּאנְךָ וּמִגָּרְנְךָ וּמִיִּקְבֶךָ אֲשֶׁר בֵּרַכְךָ יְהוָה אֱלֹהֶיךָ תִּתֶּן־
לוֹ׃ וְזָכַרְתָּ כִּי עֶבֶד הָיִיתָ בְּאֶרֶץ מִצְרַיִם וַיִּפְדְּךָ יְהוָה 15
אֱלֹהֶיךָ עַל־כֵּן אָנֹכִי מְצַוְּךָ אֶת־הַדָּבָר הַזֶּה הַיּוֹם׃ וְהָיָה 16
כִּי־יֹאמַר אֵלֶיךָ לֹא אֵצֵא מֵעִמָּךְ כִּי אֲהֵבְךָ וְאֶת־בֵּיתֶךָ
כִּי־טוֹב לוֹ עִמָּךְ׃ וְלָקַחְתָּ אֶת־הַמַּרְצֵעַ וְנָתַתָּה בְאָזְנוֹ 17
וּבַדֶּלֶת וְהָיָה לְךָ עֶבֶד עוֹלָם וְאַף לַאֲמָתְךָ תַּעֲשֶׂה־כֵּן׃
לֹא־יִקְשֶׁה בְעֵינֶךָ בְּשַׁלֵּחֲךָ אֹתוֹ חָפְשִׁי מֵעִמָּךְ כִּי מִשְׁנֶה 18
שְׂכַר שָׂכִיר עֲבָדְךָ שֵׁשׁ שָׁנִים וּבֵרַכְךָ יְהוָה אֱלֹהֶיךָ בְּכֹל
אֲשֶׁר תַּעֲשֶׂה׃

כָּל־הַבְּכוֹר אֲשֶׁר יִוָּלֵד בִּבְקָרְךָ וּבְצֹאנְךָ הַזָּכָר תַּקְדִּישׁ 19
לַיהוָה אֱלֹהֶיךָ לֹא תַעֲבֹד בִּבְכֹר שׁוֹרֶךָ וְלֹא תָגֹז בְּכוֹר

nor shear the firstling of your flock. [20]You shall eat it before Jehovah your God year by year in the place which Jehovah shall choose, you and your household. [21]And if there is *any* blemish in it, lameness, or blindness, or any evil blemish whatever, you shall not sacrifice it to Jehovah your God. [22]You shall eat it inside your gates; the unclean and the clean alike, as the gazelle and as the hart. [23]Only you shall not eat its blood; you shall pour it on the ground like water.

CHAPTER 16

[1]Observe the month Abib, and keep the Passover to Jehovah your God. For in the month of Abib Jehovah your God brought you out of Egypt by night. [2]And you shall sacrifice a Passover to Jehovah your God of the flock, and of the herd, in the place which He shall choose to cause His name to dwell there. [3]You shall eat no leavened bread with it. You shall eat unleavened bread with it seven days, even the bread of affliction. For you came out of the land of Egypt in haste, so that you may remember the day that you came out of the land of Egypt all the days of your life. [4]And there shall be no leaven seen with you in your borders seven days; nor shall *any* of the flesh which you sacrificed the first day at evening remain all night until the morning. [5]You may not sacrifice the Passover offering inside any of your gates, which Jehovah your God gives you. [6]But at the place which He shall choose to cause His name to dwell there, you shall sacrifice the Passover offering at evening, at the going of the sun

4725 8141 8141 398 430 3068 6440 6629

20 צֹאנֶךָ׃ לִפְנֵי יְהוָה אֱלֹהֶיךָ תֹּאכְלֶנּוּ שָׁנָה בְשָׁנָה בַּמָּקוֹם

the in place | by year | year | shall you it eat | your God | Jehovah | Before | your .flock

6455 3971 1961 1004 3068 977 834

21 אֲשֶׁר־יִבְחַר יְהוָה אַתָּה וּבֵיתֶךָ׃ וְכִי־יִהְיֶה בוֹ מוּם פִּסֵּחַ

lame- ness | (any) ,blemish | it in | there is | And if | your and .household | you | ,Jehovah | shall choose | which

8179 430 3068 2076 7451 3971 5787/176

22 אוֹ עִוֵּר כֹּל מוּם רָע לֹא תִזְבָּחֶנּוּ לַיהוָה אֱלֹהֶיךָ׃ בִּשְׁעָרֶיךָ

Inside gates your | .God your | to Jehovah | shall you it sacrifice | not | ,evil | blemish | any | blind- ,ness | or

1818 7535 354 6643 3162 2889 2931 398

23 תֹּאכְלֶנּוּ הַטָּמֵא וְהַטָּהוֹר יַחְדָּו כַּצְּבִי וְכָאַיָּל׃ רַק אֶת־דָּמוֹ

blood its | Only | as and .hart the | the as gazelle | ,alike | the and clean | the unclean | shall you ;it eat

4325 8210 776 5921 398 3808

לֹא תֹאכֵל עַל־הָאָרֶץ תִּשְׁפְּכֶנּוּ כַּמָּיִם׃

like .water | shall you it pour | the ground | on | shall you not ;eat

CAP. XVI טז

CHAPTER 16

430 3068 6453 6213 24 2320 8104

1 שָׁמוֹר אֶת־חֹדֶשׁ הָאָבִיב וְעָשִׂיתָ פֶּסַח לַיהוָה אֱלֹהֶיךָ כִּי

for ,God your | to Jehovah | the Passover | keep and | Abib | the month | Observe

3915 4714 430 3068 3318 24 2320

בְּחֹדֶשׁ הָאָבִיב הוֹצִיאֲךָ יְהוָה אֱלֹהֶיךָ מִמִּצְרַיִם לָיְלָה׃

.night by | Egypt of | God your | Jehovah | brought out you | Abib | the in of month

977 4725 1241 6629 430 3068 6453 2076

2 וְזָבַחְתָּ פֶּסַח לַיהוָה אֱלֹהֶיךָ צֹאן וּבָקָר בַּמָּקוֹם אֲשֶׁר יִבְחַר

shall choose | which | the in place | of and the herd | of the flock | your God | to Jehovah | pass- over | a sacrifice | you And shall

3117 7651 2557 398 3808 8033 8034 7931 3068

3 יְהוָה לְשַׁכֵּן שְׁמוֹ שָׁם׃ לֹא־תֹאכַל עָלָיו חָמֵץ שִׁבְעַת יָמִים

days | seven | leavened ;bread | with it | shall You eat | not | .there | his name | cause to dwell to | Jeho- vah

776 3318 2649 3588 6040 3899 4682 398

תֹּאכַל־עָלָיו מַצּוֹת לֶחֶם עֹנִי כִּי בְחִפָּזוֹן יָצָאתָ מֵאֶרֶץ

the from of land | you out came | haste in | for | afflic- tion | bread of | unleavened ,bread | with it | shall you eat

3605 4714 776 3318 3117 2142 4714

מִצְרַיִם לְמַעַן תִּזְכֹּר אֶת־יוֹם צֵאתְךָ מֵאֶרֶץ מִצְרַיִם כֹּל

all | Egypt | the of of land | you that out came | the day | may you remember | so that | —Egypt

3117 7651 1366 7603 7200/3808 2416 3117

4 יְמֵי חַיֶּיךָ׃ וְלֹא־יֵרָאֶה לְךָ שְׂאֹר בְּכָל־גְּבֻלְךָ שִׁבְעַת יָמִים

;days | seven | your borders | all in | leaven | with you | shall seen be | And not | your .life | the of days

7223 3117 6153 2076 834 1320 3885

וְלֹא־יָלִין מִן־הַבָּשָׂר אֲשֶׁר תִּזְבַּח בָּעֶרֶב בַּיּוֹם הָרִאשׁוֹן

first the | day on | at evening | you sacrificed | which | flesh the of | (any) | shall remain | and not

834 8179 259 6453 2076 3201 1242

5 לַבֹּקֶר׃ לֹא תוּכַל לִזְבֹּחַ אֶת־הַפָּסַח בְּאַחַד שְׁעָרֶיךָ אֲשֶׁר־

which | your gates | inside of any | the Passover | sacrifice | You may | not | the until .morning

977 4725 5414 430 3068

6 יְהוָה אֱלֹהֶיךָ נֹתֵן לָךְ׃ כִּי אִם־אֶל־הַמָּקוֹם אֲשֶׁר־יִבְחַר

shall choose | which | the place | at | but | ;you | (is) giving | your God | Jehovah

6153 6453 2076 8033 8034 7931 430 3068

יְהוָה אֱלֹהֶיךָ לְשַׁכֵּן שְׁמוֹ שָׁם תִּזְבַּח אֶת־הַפֶּסַח בָּעֶרֶב

at evening | the Passover | shall you sacrifice | ,there | his name | cause to dwell to | your God | Jehovah

at the time when you came
out of Egypt. 7And you
shall cook and eat in the
place which Jehovah your
God shall choose. And in
the morning you shall turn
and go into your tents.
8You shall eat unleavened
bread six days, and on the
seventh day *shall be* a
solemn assembly to Jeho-
vah your God. You shall do
no work.
9You shall number to
yourself seven weeks.
When the sickle begins *to
reap* in the standing grain,
you shall begin to number
seven weeks. 10And you
shall keep the Feast of
Weeks to Jehovah your
God according to the
measure of the free-will
offering of your hand, which
you shall give according as
Jehovah your God blesses
you. 11And you shall rejoice
before Jehovah your God,
you and your son, and your
daughter, and your male
slave, and your slave-girl,
and the Levite that *is* inside
your gates, and the alien,
and the fatherless, and the
widow that *are* among you,
in the place which Jehovah
your God shall choose to
cause His name to dwell
there. 12And you shall
remember that you were a
slave in Egypt; and you shall
take heed to do these
statutes.
13You shall keep the
Feast of Tabernacles seven
days, after you have
gathered in from your
threshing-floor and from
your winepress. 14And you
shall rejoice in your feast,
you and your son, and your
daughter, and your male
slave, and your slave-girl,
and the Levite, and the
alien, and the fatherless,
and the widow that *are*
inside your gates. 15You
shall keep a solemn feast
seven days to Jehovah your
God in the place which
Jehovah shall choose; for
Jehovah your God shall
bless you in all your
produce, and in every work
of your hands, and you shall

398 1310 4714 3318 4150 8121 935
7 כְּבוֹא הַשֶּׁמֶשׁ מוֹעֵד צֵאתְךָ מִמִּצְרָיִם׃ וּבִשַּׁלְתָּ וְאָכַלְתָּ
eat and (it) you And cook shall from .Egypt coming your out the at of season sun the when (down) goes

3212 1242 6437 430 3068 977 834 4725
בַּמָּקוֹם אֲשֶׁר יִבְחַר יְהוָה אֱלֹהֶיךָ בּוֹ וּפָנִיתָ בַבֹּקֶר וְהָלַכְתָּ
go and the in morning you and turn shall ;God your Jehovah shall which choose the in place

6116 7637 3117 4682 398 3117 8337 168
8 לְאֹהָלֶיךָ׃ שֵׁשֶׁת יָמִים תֹּאכַל מַצּוֹת וּבַיּוֹם הַשְּׁבִיעִי עֲצֶרֶת
solemn a assembly seventh the (be shall) on and day unleavened ,bread you eat shall days Six your into .tents

7620 7651 4399 6213 3808 430 3068
9 לַיהוָה אֱלֹהֶיךָ לֹא תַעֲשֶׂה מְלָאכָה׃ שִׁבְעָה שָׁבֻעֹת
weeks Seven (any) work you do shall not ;God your to Jehovah

7651 5608 2490 7054 2770 2490 5608
תִּסְפָּר־לָךְ מֵהָחֵל חֶרְמֵשׁ בַּקָּמָה תָּחֵל לִסְפֹּר שִׁבְעָה
seven to number shall you begin standing the ;grain the sickle (when) from begins for shall you ,yourself number

5071 4530 430 3068 7620 2282 6213 7620
10 שָׁבֻעוֹת׃ וְעָשִׂיתָ חַג שָׁבֻעוֹת לַיהוָה אֱלֹהֶיךָ מִסַּת נִדְבַת
votive a of offering enough of God your to Jehovah Weeks the of Feast you And perform shall .weeks

8056 430 3068 1288 5414 834 3027
11 יָדְךָ אֲשֶׁר תִּתֵּן כַּאֲשֶׁר יְבָרֶכְךָ יְהוָה אֱלֹהֶיךָ׃ וְשָׂמַחְתָּ
you and rejoice shall your .God Jehovah blesses you according as you give shall which your hand

519 5650 1323 1121 430 3068 6440
לִפְנֵי יְהוָה אֱלֹהֶיךָ אַתָּה וּבִנְךָ וּבִתֶּךָ וְעַבְדְּךָ וַאֲמָתֶךָ
your and slave female your and slave male your and daughter and son your you ,God your Jehovah before

490 3490 1616 8179 834 3881
וְהַלֵּוִי אֲשֶׁר בִּשְׁעָרֶיךָ וְהַגֵּר וְהַיָּתוֹם וְהָאַלְמָנָה אֲשֶׁר
who (are) the and widow the and orphan the and alien inside gates your who (is) the and Levite

8034 7931 430 3068 977 834 4725 7130
בְּקִרְבֶּךָ בַּמָּקוֹם אֲשֶׁר יִבְחַר יְהוָה אֱלֹהֶיךָ לְשַׁכֵּן שְׁמוֹ
His name cause to dwell to God your Jehovah shall choose which the in place your in ,midst

6213 8104 4714 1961 5650 2142 8033
12 שָׁם׃ וְזָכַרְתָּ כִּי־עֶבֶד הָיִיתָ בְּמִצְרָיִם וְשָׁמַרְתָּ וְעָשִׂיתָ אֶת־
do to you and heed take shall ,Egypt in you were a slave that you And remember shall .there

428 2706
הַחֻקִּים הָאֵלֶּה׃
.these statutes

1637 622 3117 7651 6213 5521 2282
13 חַג הַסֻּכֹּת תַּעֲשֶׂה לְךָ שִׁבְעַת יָמִים בְּאָסְפְּךָ מִגָּרְנְךָ
your from grain-floor you after in gathered have days seven for yourself shall you perform Tabernacles The of Feast

519 5650 1323/1121 2282 8056 3342
14 וּמִיִּקְבֶךָ׃ וְשָׂמַחְתָּ בְּחַגֶּךָ אַתָּה וּבִנְךָ וּבִתֶּךָ וְעַבְדְּךָ וַאֲמָתֶךָ
your and slave female your and slave male your and daughter and son your you your in ,feast you And rejoice shall your and press wine

7651 8179 834 490 3490 1616 3881
15 וְהַלֵּוִי וְהַגֵּר וְהַיָּתוֹם וְהָאַלְמָנָה אֲשֶׁר בִּשְׁעָרֶיךָ׃ שִׁבְעַת
Seven inside gates your who (are) the and widow the and fatherless the and alien the and Levite

3068 977 834 4725 430 3068 2287 3117
יָמִים תָּחֹג לַיהוָה אֱלֹהֶיךָ בַּמָּקוֹם אֲשֶׁר־יִבְחַר יְהוָה כִּי
for ;Jehovah shall choose which the in place God your to Jehovah shall you keep a feast days

3027 4639 3605 8393 3605 430 3068 1288
יְבָרֶכְךָ יְהוָה אֱלֹהֶיךָ בְּכֹל תְּבוּאָתְךָ וּבְכֹל מַעֲשֵׂה יָדֶיךָ
your ,hands work of in and every your produce all in God your Jehovah shall you bless

be altogether joyful.
[16]Three times in a year shall all your males appear before Jehovah your God in the place which He shall choose: In the Feast of Unleavened *Bread*, and in the Feast of Weeks, and in the Feast of Tabernacles. And they shall not appear before Jehovah empty, [17]*but* each with his gift of his hand, according to the blessing of Jehovah your God, which He has given you.
[18]You shall appoint judges and officers for yourself in all your gates which Jehovah your God gives you, tribe by tribe. And they shall judge the people with righteous judgment. [19]You shall not pervert judgment. You shall not regard faces, nor shall you take a bribe; for a bribe blinds the eyes of the wise, and perverts the words of the righteous. [20]You shall follow perfect justice, that you may live and possess the land which Jehovah your God is giving you.
[21]You shall not set up for yourself pillars of any trees which you make for yourself near the altar of Jehovah your God. [22]And you shall not raise up for yourself *any* standing image, which Jehovah your God detests.

2138 3605 7200 8141 6471 7969 8056 1961
16 וְהָיִיתָ אַךְ שָׂמֵחַ׃ שָׁלוֹשׁ פְּעָמִים ׀ בַּשָּׁנָה יֵרָאֶה כָל־זְכוּרְךָ
your all shall the in times Three .joyful only you and
males appear year be shall

4682 2282 977 834 4725 430 3068 6440
אֶת־פְּנֵי ׀ יְהוָה אֱלֹהֶיךָ בַּמָּקוֹם אֲשֶׁר יִבְחָר בְּחַג הַמַּצּוֹת
Unleavened the in He which the in God your Jehovah before
Bread of Feast choose shall place

3068 6440 7200 3808 5521 2282 7620 2282
וּבְחַג הַשָּׁבֻעוֹת וּבְחַג הַסֻּכּוֹת וְלֹא יֵרָאֶה אֶת־פְּנֵי יְהוָה
Jehovah before shall they and ;Tabernacles in and Weeks in and
appear not of Feast the of Feast The

5414 834 430 3068 1293 4979 376 7387
17 רֵיקָם׃ אִישׁ כְּמַתְּנַת יָדוֹ כְּבִרְכַּת יְהוָה אֱלֹהֶיךָ אֲשֶׁר נָתַן־לָךְ׃
.you has He which your Jehovah to according his the with (but) ,empty
given God of blessing the hand of gift each

430 3068 834 8179 5414 7860 8199
18 שֹׁפְטִים וְשֹׁטְרִים תִּתֶּן־לְךָ בְּכָל־שְׁעָרֶיךָ אֲשֶׁר יְהוָה אֱלֹהֶיךָ
your Jehovah which your all in for shall You and judges
God gates yourself appoint officers

3808 6664 4941 5971 8199 7626 5414
19 נֹתֵן לְךָ לִשְׁבָטֶיךָ וְשָׁפְטוּ אֶת־הָעָם מִשְׁפַּט־צֶדֶק׃ לֹא־
not righteous with the they and by tribe ,you is
judgment people judge shall ,tribe giving

7810 7810 3947 3808 6440 5234 3808 4941 5186
תַטֶּה מִשְׁפָּט לֹא תַכִּיר פָּנִים וְלֹא־תִקַּח שֹׁחַד כִּי הַשֹּׁחַד
bribe a for a shall you and ;faces shall you not ;judgment you
,bribe take not regard pervert shall

6664 6664 6662 1697 5557 2450 5869 5786
20 יְעַוֵּר עֵינֵי חֲכָמִים וִיסַלֵּף דִּבְרֵי צַדִּיקִם׃ צֶדֶק צֶדֶק
justice perfect the words the and wise the the blinds
.righteous of perverts of eyes

430 3068 834 776 3423 2421 7291
תִּרְדֹּף לְמַעַן תִּחְיֶה וְיָרַשְׁתָּ אֶת־הָאָרֶץ אֲשֶׁר־יְהוָה אֱלֹהֶיךָ
God your Jehovah which the and may you that shall You
land possess live ,follow

4196 681 6086 842 5193 5414
21 נֹתֵן לָךְ׃ לֹא־תִטַּע לְךָ אֲשֵׁרָה כָּל־עֵץ אֵצֶל מִזְבַּח
the near trees any of pillars for shall You not .you is
of altar you up set giving

4676 6965 3808 6213 834 430 3068
22 יְהוָה אֱלֹהֶיךָ אֲשֶׁר תַּעֲשֶׂה־לָּךְ׃ וְלֹא־תָקִים לְךָ מַצֵּבָה
(any) for shall you And for make you which God your Jehovah
standing your- up raise not .yourself
image self

430 3068 8130 834
אֲשֶׁר שָׂנֵא יְהוָה אֱלֹהֶיךָ׃
.God your Jehovah detests which

CAP. XVII יז

CHAPTER 17

[1]You shall not sacrifice to Jehovah your God an ox or sheep in which there is a blemish, any evil thing—for it *is* a hateful thing to Jehovah your God.
[2]When there is found among you, in one of your gates which Jehovah your God is giving to you, a man or woman who does that which is evil in the sight of Jehovah your God, in transgressing His covenant,

3971 1961 834 7716 7794 430 3068 2076 3808
1 לֹא־תִזְבַּח לַיהוָה אֱלֹהֶיךָ שׁוֹר וָשֶׂה אֲשֶׁר יִהְיֶה בוֹ מוּם
a it in there which or ox an God your to shall You not
,blemish is sheep Jehovah sacrifice

4672 430 3068 8441 7651 1697 3605
2 כֹּל דָּבָר רָע כִּי תוֹעֲבַת יְהוָה אֱלֹהֶיךָ הוּא׃ כִּי־יִמָּצֵא
is When .(is) it God your Jehovah hateful a for ,evil thing any
found to thing

376 5414 430 3068 834 8179 259 7130
בְקִרְבְּךָ בְּאַחַד שְׁעָרֶיךָ אֲשֶׁר־יְהוָה אֱלֹהֶיךָ נֹתֵן לָךְ אִישׁ
a to is ,God your Jehovah which gates your one in your in
man you giving of ,midst

5674 430 3068 5869 7451 6213 802
אוֹ־אִשָּׁה אֲשֶׁר יַעֲשֶׂה אֶת־הָרַע בְּעֵינֵי יְהוָה־אֱלֹהֶיךָ לַעֲבֹר
trans- in ,God your Jehovah the in what does who woman or
gressing of sight evil is

3 and has gone and served other gods, and worshiped them; or the sun, or the moon, or *of* the host of the heavens; which I hae not commanded; 4 and it has been revealed to you, and you have heard, and have searched carefully; and, behold, it is tdrue; and the thing is confirmed, *that* this hateful thing has been done in Israel— 5 then you shall bring out to your gates that man or that woman who has done this evil thing, the man or the woman; and you shall stone them with stones, and they shall die.

6 At the mouth of two witnesses or three witnesses shall he that is to die be put to death. He shall not be put to death at the mouth of one witness. 7 The hand of the witnesses shall be first on him, to put him to death; and the hand of all the people last. And you shall put away the evil from among you.

8 If a matter *is* too hard for you in judgment, between blood and blood, between cause and cause, or between stroke and stroke, matters of strife within your gates, then you shall rise and go up to the place which Jehovah your God shall choose. 9 And *you* shall come in to the priest, of the Levites, and to the judge who is in those days, and shall inquire. And they shall declare the sentence of judgment to you. 10 And you shall do according to the word which they declare to you from that place which Jehovah shall choose. And you shall be careful to do according to all that they direct you 11 You shall do according t the mouth of the law which they direct you, and according to the judgment which they deliver to you. You shall not turn aside

8121 7812 312 430 5647 3212 1285
3 בְּרִיתוֹ׃ וַיֵּלֶךְ וַיַּעֲבֹד אֱלֹהִים אֲחֵרִים וַיִּשְׁתַּחוּ לָהֶם וְלַשֶּׁמֶשׁ ׀
the or them and other gods and has and His
sun worshiped served gone ,covenant
5046 6680 3808 834 8064 6635 3605 176 3394
4 אוֹ לַיָּרֵחַ אוֹ לְכָל־צְבָא הַשָּׁמַיִם אֲשֶׁר לֹא־צִוִּיתִי׃ וְהֻגַּד־
it and have I not which the host the (any) or the or
told is ;commanded heavens of all (of) moon
6213 1697 3559 571 2009 3190 1875 8085
לְךָ וְשָׁמָעְתָּ וְדָרַשְׁתָּ הֵיטֵב וְהִנֵּה אֱמֶת נָכוֹן הַדָּבָר נֶעֶשְׂתָה
has (that) the is and is it ,and ,carefully have and you and to
done been ,thing confirmed true ,behold searched heard have you
176 376 3318 3478 2088 8441
5 הַתּוֹעֵבָה הַזֹּאת בְּיִשְׂרָאֵל׃ וְהוֹצֵאתָ אֶת־הָאִישׁ הַהוּא אוֹ
or that man you then ;Israel in this abomina-
out bring shall tion
7451 1697 6213 834 802
אֶת־הָאִשָּׁה הַהִוא אֲשֶׁר עָשׂוּ אֶת־הַדָּבָר הָרָע הַזֶּה אֶל־
to ,this evil thing has who that woman
done
4191 68 5619 802 176 376 8179
שְׁעָרֶיךָ אֶת־הָאִישׁ אוֹ אֶת־הָאִשָּׁה וּסְקַלְתָּם בָּאֲבָנִים וָמֵתוּ׃
they and with you and the or man the ,gates your
die shall ,stones them stone shall ,woman
4191 4191 4191 5707 7969 176/5707 8147 6310
6 עַל־פִּי ׀ שְׁנַיִם עֵדִים אוֹ שְׁלֹשָׁה עֵדִים יוּמַת הַמֵּת לֹא יוּמַת
shall he not the be shall witnesses three or witnesses two the At
executed be ; dying of mouth
4191 7223 1961 5707 3027 259 5707 6310
7 עַל־פִּי עֵד אֶחָד׃ יַד הָעֵדִים תִּהְיֶה־בּוֹ בָרִאשֹׁנָה לַהֲמִיתוֹ
him put to first him on shall the the ;one witness the at
,death to be witnesses of hand of mouth
7130 7451 1197 314 5971 3605 3027
וְיַד כָּל־הָעָם בָּאַחֲרֹנָה וּבִעַרְתָּ הָרָע מִקִּרְבֶּךָ׃
among from the you and ;afterward the all and
you evil off cut shall people of hand the
1779 1779 1818 1818/996 4941 1697 6381
8 כִּי יִפָּלֵא מִמְּךָ דָבָר לַמִּשְׁפָּט בֵּין־דָּם ׀ לְדָם בֵּין־דִּין לְדִין
and cause be- and blood be- in a you for too When
.cause tween ,blood tween judgment matter hard (is)
3212 6963 8179 7379 1697 5061 5061/996
וּבֵין נֶגַע לָנֶגַע דִּבְרֵי רִיבֹת בִּשְׁעָרֶיךָ וְקַמְתָּ וְעָלִיתָ אֶל־
to go and you then within legal matters and blow and
up rise shall ,gates your strife of blow between
3548 935 430 3068 977 834 4725
9 הַמָּקוֹם אֲשֶׁר יִבְחַר יְהוָה אֱלֹהֶיךָ בּוֹ׃ וּבָאתָ אֶל־הַכֹּהֲנִים
priests the to you and ,God your Jehovah shall which the
come shall choose place
1875 3117 8199 3881
הַלְוִיִּם וְאֶל־הַשֹּׁפֵט אֲשֶׁר יִהְיֶה בַּיָּמִים הָהֵם וְדָרַשְׁתָּ
shall and ,those days in is who the to and Levitical
inquire judge
1697 6310 6213 4941 1697 5046
10 וְהִגִּידוּ לְךָ אֵת דְּבַר הַמִּשְׁפָּט׃ וְעָשִׂיתָ עַל־פִּי הַדָּבָר
word the the by you And the the to they and
of mouth do shall .judgment of sentence you declare shall
8104 3068 977 834 1725 5046 834
אֲשֶׁר יַגִּידוּ לְךָ מִן־הַמָּקוֹם הַהוּא אֲשֶׁר יִבְחַר יְהוָה וְשָׁמַרְתָּ
you and ,Jehovah shall which that place from to they which
watch shall choose you declare
3384 834 8451 6310 3381 3605 6213
11 לַעֲשׂוֹת כְּכֹל אֲשֶׁר יוֹרוּךָ׃ עַל־פִּי הַתּוֹרָה אֲשֶׁר יוֹרוּךָ
they which law the the by they that according do to
,you direct of mouth you direct all to
1697 5493 3808 6213 559 834 4941
וְעַל־הַמִּשְׁפָּט אֲשֶׁר־יֹאמְרוּ לְךָ תַּעֲשֶׂה לֹא תָסוּר מִן־הַדָּבָר
the from you not shall you to they which the and
word turn shall ;do you deliver judgment by

from the word which they declare to you, right or left. [12]And the man who acts with pride so as not to listen to the priest who is standing to serve Jehovah your God there, or to the judge, even that man shall die; and you shall put away evil from Israel. [13]And all the people shall hear, and fear, and shall not presume any more.

[14]When you come into the land which Jehovah your God is giving to you, and have possessed it, and settled in it; and you shall say, Let me set a king over me like all the nations around me., [15]*then* you shall certainly set a king over you. You may not set an alien over you, one who is not your brother. [16]Only, he shall not multiply horses to himself, nor cause the people to turn back to Egypt so as to multiply horses, since Jehovah has said to you, You shall not again return in this way any more.

[17]And he shall not multiply wives to himself, and his heart shall not turn aside. And he shall not greatly multiply to himself silver and gold. [18]And it shall be, when he sits on the throne of his kingdom, he shall write for himself a copy of this law in a book, from before the priests, the Levites. [19]And it shall be with him, and he shall read in it all the days of his life, that he may learn to fear Jehovah your God, to keep all the words of this law and these statutes, to do them; [20]so that his heart may not be lifted up above his brothers, and that he may not turn aside from the

2087 6213 834 376 8040 3225 5046 834
12 אֲשֶׁר־יַגִּידוּ לְךָ יָמִין וּשְׂמֹאל׃ וְהָאִישׁ אֲשֶׁר־יַעֲשֶׂה בְזָדוֹן
with acts who the And .left or right to they which
pride man you declare

3068 8033 8334 5975 3548 8085
לְבִלְתִּי שְׁמֹעַ אֶל־הַכֹּהֵן הָעֹמֵד לְשָׁרֶת שָׁם אֶת־יְהוָה
Jehovah there serve to is who the to to as so
standing priest listen not

7451 1197 376 4191 8199 176 430
אֱלֹהֶיךָ אוֹ אֶל־הַשֹּׁפֵט וּמֵת הָאִישׁ הַהוּא וּבִעַרְתָּ הָרָע
the you and that man even ,judge the to or your
evil off cut shall die shall God

5750 2102 3808 3372 8085 5971 3605 3478
13 מִיִּשְׂרָאֵל׃ וְכָל־הָעָם יִשְׁמְעוּ וְיִרָאוּ וְלֹא יְזִידוּן עוֹד׃ כִּי־
14
When any shall and and shall the And from
.more presume not fear hear people all .Israel

3423 5414 430 3068 834 776 935
תָבֹא אֶל־הָאָרֶץ אֲשֶׁר יְהוָה אֱלֹהֶיךָ נֹתֵן לָךְ וִירִשְׁתָּהּ
have and to is your Jehovah which land the into you
it reseized you giving God come

834 1471 3605 4428 5921 7760 559 3427
וְיָשַׁבְתָּה בָּהּ וְאָמַרְתָּ אָשִׂימָה עָלַי מֶלֶךְ כְּכָל־הַגּוֹיִם אֲשֶׁר
which the all like king a over me Let you and ;it in have and
(are) nations me set ,say shall settled

430 3068 977 4428 7760 7760 5439
15 סְבִיבֹתָי׃ שׂוֹם תָּשִׂים עָלֶיךָ מֶלֶךְ אֲשֶׁר יִבְחַר יְהוָה אֱלֹהֶיךָ
your Jehovah shall whom king a over you (then)
;God choose you set shall surely ;me around

5414 3201 3808 4428 7760 251 7130
בּוֹ מִקֶּרֶב אַחֶיךָ תָּשִׂים עָלֶיךָ מֶלֶךְ לֹא תוּכַל לָתֵת עָלֶיךָ
over appoint may you not king a over shall you your from
you you set brothers among

5483 7235 7535 251 834 5237 376
16 אִישׁ נָכְרִי אֲשֶׁר לֹא־אָחִיךָ הוּא׃ רַק לֹא־יַרְבֶּה־לּוֹ סוּסִים
,horses himself he not Only .(is) your not who ,stranger a
to heap shall brother

3068 5483 7235 4714 5971 7725
וְלֹא־יָשִׁיב אֶת־הָעָם מִצְרַיְמָה לְמַעַן הַרְבּוֹת סוּס וַיהוָה
since ,horses up heap in Egypt to people the cause and
Jehovah to order return to not

7235 3808 5750 2088 1870 7725 3254 3808 559
17 אָמַר לָכֶם לֹא תֹסִפוּן לָשׁוּב בַּדֶּרֶךְ הַזֶּה עוֹד׃ וְלֹא יַרְבֶּה־
shall he And any this way in return shall You not ,you to has
multiply not .more again said

3966 7235 3808 2091 3701 3824 5493 3808 802
לּוֹ נָשִׁים וְלֹא יָסוּר לְבָבוֹ וְכֶסֶף וְזָהָב לֹא יַרְבֶּה־לּוֹ מְאֹד׃
.greatly shall he not and and his turn shall and ,wives to
himself to heap gold silver heart aside not himself

4932 3789 4467 3678 5921 3427 1961
18 וְהָיָה כְשִׁבְתּוֹ עַל כִּסֵּא מַמְלַכְתּוֹ וְכָתַב לוֹ אֶת־מִשְׁנֵה
of copy a for shall he that his the on he when it And
himself write ,kingdom of throne sits be shall

1961 3881 3548 6440 5612 2088 8451
19 הַתּוֹרָה הַזֹּאת עַל־סֵפֶר מִלִּפְנֵי הַכֹּהֲנִים הַלְוִיִּם׃ וְהָיְתָה
it And .Levitical priests the (what) from book a in this law
be shall before (is)

3068 3372 3925 2416 3117 3605 7200
עִמּוֹ וְקָרָא בוֹ כָּל־יְמֵי חַיָּיו לְמַעַן יִלְמַד לְיִרְאָה אֶת־יְהוָה
Jehovah fear to may he that ,life his the all it in he and with
learn of days read shall ,him

2706 2088 8451 1697 3605 8104 430
אֱלֹהָיו לִשְׁמֹר אֶת־כָּל־דִּבְרֵי הַתּוֹרָה הַזֹּאת וְאֶת־הַחֻקִּים
statutes and this law the all keep to God his
words

5993 3808 251 3824/7311 6213 428
20 הָאֵלֶּה לַעֲשֹׂתָם׃ לְבִלְתִּי רוּם־לְבָבוֹ מֵאֶחָיו וּלְבִלְתִּי סוּר
he not and above his be may that so do to these
turn may ,brothers his heart lifted not ;them

commandment, to the right or to the left; so that he may prolong *his* days over his kingdom, he and his sons in the midst of Israel.

4467 5921 3117 748 8040 3225 4687
מִן־הַמִּצְוָה יָמִין וּשְׂמֹאול לְמַעַן יַאֲרִיךְ יָמִים עַל־מַמְלַכְתּוֹ
his over (his) may he that so the to or the to the from
,kingdom days prolong ;left right command
3478 7130 1121
הוּא וּבָנָיו בְּקֶרֶב יִשְׂרָאֵל׃
.Israel the in and he
of midst ,sons his

CAP. XVIII יח

CHAPTER 18

CHAPTER 18

[1]the Priests, the Levites, all the tribe of Levi *shall have* no portion or inheritance with Israel. They shall eat fire offerings of Jehovah, even His inheritance. [2]And he shall have no inheritance among his brothers—Jehovah Himself is his inheritance, as He has spoken to him. [3]And this shall be the priest's due from the people, from those that offer a sacrifice, whether it is an ox or sheep, that they shall give to the priest the leg, and the two cheeks, and the stomach, [4]the first of your grain, of your new wine, and of your oil, and the first of the fleece of your flock, you shall give to him. [5]For Jehovah your God has chosen him out of all your tribes to stand to serve in the name of Jehovah, he and his sons continually.

[6]And if a Levite comes from one of your cities out of all Israel, where he has been living, and comes with all the desire of his soul to the place which Jehovah shall choose, [7]then he shall serve in the name of Jehovah his God, as all his brothers the Levites who stand before Jehovah do. [8]They shall eat portion like portion, except of the sales of *what belonged* to his father.

[9]When you come to the land which Jehovah your God is giving to you, you shall not learn to do according to the hateful acts of those nations. [10]There shall not be found in you one who passes his son or his daughter through

5159 2506 3881 7626 3605 3881 3548 1961 3808
1 לֹא־יִהְיֶה לַכֹּהֲנִים הַלְוִיִּם כָּל־שֵׁבֶט לֵוִי חֵלֶק וְנַחֲלָה עִם־
with or a ,Levi the all ,Levitical the for There not
inheritance portion of tribe priests be shall
1961 3808 5159 398 5159 801 3068 3478
2 יִשְׂרָאֵל אִשֵּׁי יְהוָה וְנַחֲלָתוֹ יֹאכֵלוּן׃ וְנַחֲלָה לֹא־יִהְיֶה־לּוֹ
he shall not an and shall they His even ,Jehovah fire ;Israel
have inheritance ;eat ,inheritance of offering
1696 5159 3068 251 7130
3 בְּקֶרֶב אֶחָיו יְהוָה הוּא נַחֲלָתוֹ כַּאֲשֶׁר דִּבֶּר־לוֹ׃ וְזֶה
And to has He as his (is) Himself Jehovah his among
this .him spoken ,inheritance ;brothers
518 2077 2076 5971 3548 4941 1961
יִהְיֶה מִשְׁפַּט הַכֹּהֲנִים מֵאֵת הָעָם מֵאֵת זֹבְחֵי הַזֶּבַח אִם־
whether a those from the from priests the due the shall
,sacrifice offering ,people of be
7716 6896 3895 2220 3548 5414 7716 7794
4 שׁוֹר אִם־שֶׂה וְנָתַן לַכֹּהֵן הַזְּרֹעַ וְהַלְּחָיַיִם וְהַקֵּבָה׃ רֵאשִׁית
first the the and the and the the to shall they a or ox an
of ;stomach ,cheeks two ,shoulder priest give ;sheep
5414 6629 1488 7218 3323 8492 1715
5 דְּגָנְךָ תִּירֹשְׁךָ וְיִצְהָרֶךָ וְרֵאשִׁית גֵּז צֹאנְךָ תִּתֶּן־לּוֹ׃ כִּי בוֹ
him For to you your the the and of and your of your
.him give shall ,flock of fleece of first ,oil your ,wine new ,grain
8034 8334 5975 7626 3605 430 3068 977
בָּחַר יְהוָה אֱלֹהֶיךָ מִכָּל־שְׁבָטֶיךָ לַעֲמֹד לְשָׁרֵת בְּשֵׁם־
the serve to stand to your of out your Jehovah has
of name ,tribes all God chosen
259 3881 935 3117 3605 1121 3068
6 יְהוָה הוּא וּבָנָיו כָּל־הַיָּמִים׃ וְכִי־יָבֹא הַלֵּוִי מֵאַחַד
one from a comes And .days the all his and he ,Jehovah
of Levite if sons
185 3605 935 8033 1481 3478 3605 8179
שְׁעָרֶיךָ מִכָּל־יִשְׂרָאֵל אֲשֶׁר־הוּא גָּר שָׁם וּבָא בְּכָל־אַוַּת
the with and ;there has he where ,Israel all of your
of desire all comes living been gates
3068 8034 8334 3068 977 4725 5315
7 נַפְשׁוֹ אֶל־הַמָּקוֹם אֲשֶׁר־יִבְחַר יְהוָה׃ וְשֵׁרֵת בְּשֵׁם יְהוָה
,Jehovah's in he then ,Jehovah shall which place the to his
name serve shall choose soul
2506 3068 6440 8033 5975 3881 251 3605 430
8 אֱלֹהָיו כְּכָל־אֶחָיו הַלְוִיִּם הָעֹמְדִים שָׁם לִפְנֵי יְהוָה׃ חֵלֶק
Portion .Jehovah before there who the his (do) as his
stand Levites brothers all ,God
935 1 4465 398 2506
9 כְּחֵלֶק יֹאכֵלוּ לְבַד מִמְכָּרָיו עַל־הָאָבוֹת׃ כִּי אַתָּה בָּא
come you When his (what) the of except they like
.fathers of (was) of sales eat shall portion
6213 3925 5414 430 3068 834 776
אֶל־הָאָרֶץ אֲשֶׁר־יְהוָה אֱלֹהֶיךָ נֹתֵן לָךְ לֹא־תִלְמַד לַעֲשׂוֹת
do to shall you not to (is) your Jehovah which land the to
(things) learn ,you giving God
784 1323 1121 5674 4672 1471 8441
10 כְּתוֹעֲבֹת הַגּוֹיִם הָהֵם׃ לֹא־יִמָּצֵא בְךָ מַעֲבִיר בְּנוֹ־וּבִתּוֹ בָּאֵשׁ
through or his (who) one in be shall not ;those nations the like
,fire daughter son passes you found of acts hateful

the fire, one that uses
divination, an observer of
clouds, or a fortune-teller,
or a whisperer of spells,
11or a magic-charmer, or
one asking of familiar
spirits, or a wizard, or one
inquiring of the dead. 12For
all doing these things *are*
an abomination to Jehovah.
And because of these filthy
acts Jehovah your God *is*
expelling *these nations*
before you. 13You shall be
perfect with Jehovah your
God. 14For these nations
whom you shall expel listen
to observers of clouds, and
to diviners. But *as to* you,
Jehovah your God has not
allowed you to do so.
15Jehovah your God shall
raise up to you a Prophet
from among you, of your
brothers, *One* like me—you
shall listen to Him, 16ac-
cording to all that you
desired of Jehovah your
God in Horeb in the day of
the assembly, saying, Let
me not hear again the voice
of Jehovah my God, nor let
me see this great fire any
more, lest I die. 17And
Jehovah said to me, They
have spoken well what they
have said. 18I shall raise up a
Prophet to them from
among their brothers, like
you; and I will put My words
in His mouth; and He shall
speak to them all that I shall
command Him. 19And it
shall be, whoever will not
listen to My words which
he shall speak in My name, I
will require *it* at his hand.
20But the prophet who
presumes to speak a word
in My name, that which I
have not commanded him
to speak, and who speaks
in the name of other gods,
even that prophet shall die.
21And if you say in your
heart, How shall we know
the word which Jehovah
has not spoken? 22When a

11 קֹסֵם קְסָמִים מְעוֹנֵן וּמְנַחֵשׁ וּמְכַשֵּׁף׃ וְחֹבֵר חָבֶר וְשֹׁאֵל
one or (of) a or a or fortune-a cloud-a practicing one
consulting magic charmer spell-caster teller ,reader ,divination

12 אוֹב וְיִדְּעֹנִי וְדֹרֵשׁ אֶל־הַמֵּתִים׃ כִּי־תוֹעֲבַת יְהוָה כָּל־עֹשֵׂה
doing all (are) Jeho abom- an For .dead the of one or a or ,spirits
(those) vah to ination inquiring wizard

אֵלֶּה וּבִגְלַל הַתּוֹעֵבֹת הָאֵלֶּה יְהוָה אֱלֹהֶיךָ מוֹרִישׁ אוֹתָם
them (is) God your Jehovah these acts filthy and these
expelling of because ;things

13 מִפָּנֶיךָ׃ תָּמִים תִּהְיֶה עִם יְהוָה אֱלֹהֶיךָ׃ כִּי הַגּוֹיִם הָאֵלֶּה
14
these nations for your Jehovah with shall You perfect before
;God be .you

אֲשֶׁר אַתָּה יוֹרֵשׁ אוֹתָם אֶל־מְעֹנְנִים וְאֶל־קֹסְמִים יִשְׁמָעוּ
;listen diviners to and cloud-readers to shall you which
them expel

15 וְאַתָּה לֹא כֵן נָתַן לְךָ יְהוָה אֱלֹהֶיךָ׃ נָבִיא מִקִּרְבְּךָ מֵאַחֶיךָ
your of from A your Jehovah you has so not but
,brothers ,you among prophet .God allowed ,you (to as)

16 כָּמֹנִי יָקִים לְךָ יְהוָה אֱלֹהֶיךָ אֵלָיו תִּשְׁמָעוּן׃ כְּכֹל אֲשֶׁר
that according shall you him to your Jehovah to shall (One)
all to ,listen ;God you up raise me like

שָׁאַלְתָּ מֵעִם יְהוָה אֱלֹהֶיךָ בְּחֹרֵב בְּיוֹם הַקָּהָל לֵאמֹר
,saying the the on Horeb at your Jehovah of you
assembly of day God asked

לֹא אֹסֵף לִשְׁמֹעַ אֶת־קוֹל יְהוָה אֱלֹהָי וְאֶת־הָאֵשׁ הַגְּדֹלָה
great fire and ,God my Jehovah the hear me Let not
of voice again

17 הַזֹּאת לֹא־אֶרְאֶה עוֹד וְלֹא אָמוּת׃ וַיֹּאמֶר יְהוָה אֵלָי
,me to Jehovah And .die I lest ,again me let not this
said see

18 הֵיטִיבוּ אֲשֶׁר דִּבֵּרוּ׃ נָבִיא אָקִים לָהֶם מִקֶּרֶב אֲחֵיהֶם
their from for shall I a have they (in) have They
brothers among them up raise prophet .said what well done

כָּמוֹךָ וְנָתַתִּי דְבָרַי בְּפִיו וְדִבֶּר אֲלֵיהֶם אֵת כָּל־אֲשֶׁר
that all them to he and his in my I and like
speak shall ;mouth words put will ;you

19 אֲצַוֶּנּוּ׃ וְהָיָה הָאִישׁ אֲשֶׁר לֹא־יִשְׁמַע אֶל־דְּבָרַי אֲשֶׁר
which My to will not what- man it And shall I
words listen (ever) ,be shall .him order

20 יְדַבֵּר בִּשְׁמִי אָנֹכִי אֶדְרֹשׁ מֵעִמּוֹ׃ אַךְ הַנָּבִיא אֲשֶׁר יָזִיד
pre- who the But .him of will I My in shall he
sumes prophet (it) require ,name speak

לְדַבֵּר דָּבָר בִּשְׁמִי אֵת אֲשֶׁר לֹא־צִוִּיתִיו לְדַבֵּר וַאֲשֶׁר
who and to have I not which My in word a speak to
,speak him ordered ,name

21 יְדַבֵּר בְּשֵׁם אֱלֹהִים אֲחֵרִים וּמֵת הַנָּבִיא הַהוּא׃ וְכִי
And .that prophet even ,other gods the in speaks
if die shall of name

תֹאמַר בִּלְבָבֶךָ אֵיכָה נֵדַע אֶת־הַדָּבָר אֲשֶׁר לֹא־דִבְּרוֹ
has not which word the shall How your in say you
spoken know we ,heart

prophet speaks in the name of Jehovah, if the thing does not happen or come about, that *is* the thing which Jehovah has not spoken—the prophet has spoken it proudly; you shall not be afraid of him.

1697 1961 3068 8034 5030 1696 3068
22 יְהוָה: אֲשֶׁר יְדַבֵּר הַנָּבִיא בְּשֵׁם יְהוָה וְלֹא־יִהְיֶה הַדָּבָר
thing the does if ,Jehovah the in a speaks When ?Jehovah
happen not of name prophet

1696 2087 3068 1696 3808 834 1697 935 3808
וְלֹא יָבֹא הוּא הַדָּבָר אֲשֶׁר לֹא־דִבְּרוֹ יְהוָה בְּזָדוֹן דִּבְּרוֹ
has proudly ;Jehovah has not which thing the this did and
spoken spoken (is) come not

1481 3808 5030
הַנָּבִיא לֹא תָגוּר מִמֶּנּוּ:
.him of shall you not the
afraid be ;prophet

CAP. XIX יט

CHAPTER 19

[1]When Jehovah your God shall cut off the nations whose land Jehovah your God is giving to you, and when you take their place, and live in their cities, and in their houses, [2]you shall separate three cities for you in the midst of your land, which Jehovah your God is giving you to possess it. [3]You shall prepare the way for yourself, and shall divide into three parts the border of your land which Jehovah your God shall cause you to inherit, so that every manslayer may flee there.

[4]And this is the case of the manslayer who shall flee there, that he may live: whoever strikes his neighbor unawares, and has not hated him yesterday *and* the day before; [5]even he who goes into the forest with his neighbor to cut wood, and his hand brings a stroke with the axe to cut down the tree, and the iron *head* slips from the wood and finds his neighbor so that he dies —he shall flee to one of these cities, and shall live; [6]that the avenger of blood not pursue the manslayer when his heart is hot, and shall overtake him because the way is long, and shall strike the life from him, and he had no sentence of death, for he did not hate him yesterday *or* the day before. [7]On account of this I *am* commanding you, saying,

430 3068 1471 430 3068 3772
1 כִּי־יַכְרִית יְהוָה אֱלֹהֶיךָ אֶת־הַגּוֹיִם אֲשֶׁר יְהוָה אֱלֹהֶיךָ
your Jehovah whose ,nations the your Jehovah shall When
God God off cut

1004 5892 3427 3423 776 5414
נֹתֵן לְךָ אֶת־אַרְצָם וִירִשְׁתָּם וְיָשַׁבְתָּ בְעָרֵיהֶם וּבְבָתֵּיהֶם:
their in and their in live and you and , land you to is
,houses cities them replace giving

430 3068 834 776 8432 914 5892 7969
2 שָׁלוֹשׁ עָרִים תַּבְדִּיל לָךְ בְּתוֹךְ אַרְצְךָ אֲשֶׁר יְהוָה אֱלֹהֶיךָ
your Jehovah which your the in for shall you cities three
God ,land of midst you separate

1366 8027 1870 3559 3423 5414
3 נֹתֵן לְךָ לְרִשְׁתָּהּ: תָּכִין לְךָ הַדֶּרֶךְ וְשִׁלַּשְׁתָּ אֶת־גְּבוּל
border the shall and way the for shall You possess to you (is)
of three into divide yourself prepare .it giving

3605 8033 5127 1961 430 3068 5157 834 776
אַרְצְךָ אֲשֶׁר יַנְחִילְךָ יְהוָה אֱלֹהֶיךָ וְהָיָה לָנוּס שָׁמָּה כָּל־
every there to it and your Jehovah make shall which your
flee be shall ,God inherit you land

5221 2425 8033 8127 7523 1697 7523
4 רֹצֵחַ: וְזֶה דְּבַר הָרֹצֵחַ אֲשֶׁר־יָנוּס שָׁמָּה וָחָי אֲשֶׁר יַכֶּה
strikes who- he that ,there shall who the case the And .manslayer
ever ;live may ,flee manslayer of (is) this

8032 865 8130 1847 1097 7453
אֶת־רֵעֵהוּ בִּבְלִי־דַעַת וְהוּא לֹא־שֹׂנֵא לוֹ מִתְּמֹל שִׁלְשֹׁם:
;times before him (was) not and know- without his
hating he ing neighbor

3027 5080 6086 2404 3293 7453 935 834
5 וַאֲשֶׁר יָבֹא אֶת־רֵעֵהוּ בַיַּעַר לַחְטֹב עֵצִים וְנִדְּחָה יָדוֹ
his and ,wood cut to the into his with goes he even
hand strikes forest neighbor who

4672 6086 1270 5394 6086 3772 1631
בַגַּרְזֶן לִכְרֹת הָעֵץ וְנָשַׁל הַבַּרְזֶל מִן־הָעֵץ וּמָצָא אֶת־
and the from (head) the and ,tree the cut to the with
finds wood iron slips down axe

2425 428 5892 259 5127 4191 7453
6 רֵעֵהוּ וָמֵת הוּא יָנוּס אֶל־אַחַת הֶעָרִים־הָאֵלֶּה וָחָי: פֶּן
lest and these cities of one to shall he that so his
;live flee ;dies he neighbor

5381 3824 3179 7523 310 1818 1350 7291
יִרְדֹּף גֹּאֵל הַדָּם אַחֲרֵי הָרֹצֵחַ כִּי יֵחַם לְבָבוֹ וְהִשִּׂיגוֹ
shall and his hot is when the after blood the pursue
,him catch ,heart manslayer of avenger

4194 4941 369 4191 5221 1870 7235
כִּי־יִרְבֶּה הַדֶּרֶךְ וְהִכָּהוּ נֶפֶשׁ וְלוֹ אֵין מִשְׁפַּט־מָוֶת כִּי
for ,death sentence had and ,life the strike and ,way the is because
of no he him (from) long

6680 8032 865 8130 3808
7 לֹא שֹׂנֵא הוּא לוֹ מִתְּמוֹל שִׁלְשׁוֹם: עַל־כֵּן אָנֹכִי מְצַוְּךָ
ordering I this on the (and) yesterday him he (was) not
,you (am) account before day hating

You shall separate to
yourself three cities. [8]And
if Jehovah your God shall
enlarge your border, as He
has sworn to your fathers,
and shall give to you all the
land which He has spoken
to give to your fathers, [9]if
you will keep these
commandments which I
am commanding you today,
to love Jehovah your God,
and to walk in His ways
forever, then you shall add
to yourself another three
cities to these three. [10]And
innocent blood shall not be
shed in the midst of your
land, which Jehovah your
God is giving to you *as* an
inheritance, and there be
blood on you.

[11]And if a man hates his
neighbor, and lies in wait
for him, and rises up against
him, and strikes his life from
him, so that he dies, and
flees to one of these cities,
[12]then the elders of his city
shall send and bring him
there, and deliver him into
the hand of the avenger of
blood, that he may die.
Your eye shall not pity him,
but you shall put away the
innocent blood from Israel,
and it shall be well with you.
[14]You may not remove
your neighbor's landmark,
which those formerly have
set in your inheritance,
which you shall inherit in
the land which Jehovah
your God is giving you, to
possess it.
[15]One witness shall not
rise against a man for any
iniquity, or for any sin, in
any sin which he sins. At
the mouth of two
witnesses, or at the mouth
of three witnesses, a thing
shall be established. [16]If a
vicious witness rises up
against any man to charge

3068 7337 914 5892 7969 559
8 לֵאמֹר שָׁלֹשׁ עָרִים תַּבְדִּיל לָךְ׃ וְאִם־יַרְחִיב יְהוָה
Jehovah shall if And to shall you cities three ,saying
enlarge .yourself separate

5414 7650 1366 430
אֱלֹהֶיךָ אֶת־גְּבֻלְךָ כַּאֲשֶׁר נִשְׁבַּע לַאֲבֹתֶיךָ וְנָתַן לְךָ אֶת־
to and your to has He as your your
you give shall ,fathers sworn ,border God

8104 5414 1696 776
9 כָּל־הָאָרֶץ אֲשֶׁר דִּבֶּר לָתֵת לַאֲבֹתֶיךָ׃ כִּי־תִשְׁמֹר אֶת־
will you if your to give to has He which land the all
keep ,fathers spoken

157 3117 6680 6213 4687 3605
כָּל־הַמִּצְוָה הַזֹּאת לַעֲשֹׂתָהּ אֲשֶׁר אָנֹכִי מְצַוְּךָ הַיּוֹם לְאַהֲבָה
love to ,today command- (am) I which do to these com- all
you ing mandments

3254 3117 3605 1870 3212 430 3068
אֶת־יְהוָה אֱלֹהֶיךָ וְלָלֶכֶת בִּדְרָכָיו כָּל־הַיָּמִים וְיָסַפְתָּ לְךָ
to you then (the) all His in to and your Jehovah
yourself add shall ,days ways walk God

5355 1818 8210 428 7969 5892 7969 5750
10 עוֹד שָׁלֹשׁ עָרִים עַל הַשָּׁלֹשׁ הָאֵלֶּה׃ וְלֹא יִשָּׁפֵךְ דָּם נָקִי
inno- blood shall and ;these three to cities three another
cent shed be not

1961 5159 5414 430 3068 834 776 7130
בְּקֶרֶב אַרְצְךָ אֲשֶׁר יְהוָה אֱלֹהֶיךָ נֹתֵן לְךָ נַחֲלָה וְהָיָה
be and an you to is God your Jehovah which your the in
inheritance giving ,land of midst

1818 5921
עָלֶיךָ דָּמִים׃
.blood upon
you

5221 6963 693 745:3 8130 376 1961
11 וְכִי־יִהְיֶה אִישׁ שֹׂנֵא לְרֵעֵהוּ וְאָרַב לוֹ וְקָם עָלָיו וְהִכָּהוּ
and against and for lies and his hating man a there And
his strikes him up rises ,him wait in ,neighbor be if

5892 2205 7971 411 5892 259 5127 4191 5315
12 נֶפֶשׁ וָמֵת וְנָס אֶל־אַחַת הֶעָרִים הָאֵל׃ וְשָׁלְחוּ זִקְנֵי עִירוֹ
his the shall then ,these cities of one to and that so life
city of elders send flees ,dies he

3808 4191 1818 1350 3027 5414 8033 3947
13 וְלָקְחוּ אֹתוֹ מִשָּׁם וְנָתְנוּ אֹתוֹ בְּיַד גֹּאֵל הַדָּם וָמֵת׃ לֹא־
not he that ,blood the into him and from him and
die may of avenger hand deliver ,there bring

2995 3478 5355 1818 1197 5869 2347
תָחוֹס עֵינְךָ עָלָיו וּבִעַרְתָּ דַם־הַנָּקִי מִיִּשְׂרָאֵל וְטוֹב לָךְ׃
with it and from the blood the shall but ,him Your shall
.you well be will ,Israel innocent of out cut eye pity

5159 7223 1379 7453 1366 5253 3808
14 לֹא תַסִּיג גְּבוּל רֵעֲךָ אֲשֶׁר גָּבְלוּ רִאשֹׁנִים בְּנַחֲלָתְךָ
your in first set have which your land- shall You not
,inheritance ,neighbor's mark remove

3423 5414 430 3068 834 776 5157
אֲשֶׁר תִּנְחַל בָּאָרֶץ אֲשֶׁר יְהוָה אֱלֹהֶיךָ נֹתֵן לְךָ לְרִשְׁתָּהּ׃
possess to you is God your Jehovah which the in shall you which
.it giving land inherit

2399 3605 5771 3605 376 259 5707 6965
15 לֹא־יָקוּם עֵד אֶחָד בְּאִישׁ לְכָל־עָוֺן וּלְכָל־חַטָּאת
,sin for or ,iniquity for against One witness shall not
any any man a rise

6310 176 5707 8147 6310 2398 2403
בְּכָל־חֵטְא אֲשֶׁר יֶחֱטָא עַל־פִּי ׀ שְׁנֵי עֵדִים אוֹ עַל־פִּי
at or witnesses two the at he which sin any in
of mouth of mouth ;sins

6030 376 2555 6965 1697 6965 5707 7969
16 שְׁלֹשָׁה־עֵדִים יָקוּם דָּבָר׃ כִּי־יָקוּם עֵד־חָמָס בְּאִישׁ לַעֲנוֹת
to against vicious a rises If .thing a shall witnesses three
charge man a witness up settled be

apostasy against him, [17]then both the men who have the dispute shall stand before Jehovah, before the priests and the judges who shall be in those days. [18]And the judges shall carefully investigate. And, behold, if the witness is a false witness, *and* he has testified falsely against his brother, [19]then you shall do to him as he plotted to do to his brother. And you shall put away the evil from among you. [20]And those who remain shall hear and fear, and thereafter not shall add to commit any such evil among you. [21]And your eye shall not pity; life shall go for life, eye for eye, tooth for tooth, hand for hand, foot for foot.

17 בּוֹ סָרָה׃ וְעָמְדוּ שְׁנֵי־הָאֲנָשִׁים אֲשֶׁר־לָהֶם הָרִיב לִפְנֵי

before the have who men the both shall then ,apostasy to
dispute stand him

יְהוָה לִפְנֵי הַכֹּהֲנִים וְהַשֹּׁפְטִים אֲשֶׁר יִהְיוּ בַּיָּמִים הָהֵם׃

;those days in shall who the and priests the before
(office in) be judges ,Jehovah

18 וְדָרְשׁוּ הַשֹּׁפְטִים הֵיטֵב וְהִנֵּה עֵד־שֶׁקֶר הָעֵד שֶׁקֶר עָנָה

has (and) the (is) false- a (if) and ,carefully judges the shall and
testified falsely witness hood of witness ,behold inquire

19 בְאָחִיו׃ וַעֲשִׂיתֶם לוֹ כַּאֲשֶׁר זָמַם לַעֲשׂוֹת לְאָחִיו וּבִעַרְתָּ

you and his to do to he as to shall you then against
off cut shall ;brother plotted him do brother his

20 הָרָע מִקִּרְבֶּךָ׃ וְהַנִּשְׁאָרִים יִשְׁמְעוּ וְיִרָאוּ וְלֹא־יֹסִפוּ לַעֲשׂוֹת

commit shall and and shall who those And from the
to add not ,fear hear remain .you among evil

21 עוֹד כַּדָּבָר הָרָע הַזֶּה בְּקִרְבֶּךָ׃ וְלֹא תָחוֹס עֵינֶךָ נֶפֶשׁ

life your shall And among this as evil such any there-
;eye pity not .you after

בְּנֶפֶשׁ עַיִן בְּעַיִן שֵׁן בְּשֵׁן יָד בְּיָד רֶגֶל בְּרָגֶל׃

for foot for hand for tooth for eye (go shall)
.foot ,hand ,tooth ,eye .life for

CAP. XX כ

CHAPTER 20

CHAPTER 20

[1]When you go out to battle against your enemies, and see horses and chariots, a people more than you, you shall not be afraid of them. For Jehovah your God is with you, who brought you up out of the land of Egypt. [2]And it shall be, when you draw near to battle, the priest shall come and speak to the people, [3]and say to them, Hear, Israel, you are drawing near today to battle against your enemies. Do not let your heart be faint; do not fear nor tremble, nor be terrified at their presence. [4]For Jehovah your God *is* He who is going before you, to fight for you with your enemies, to save you. [5]And the officers shall speak to the people, saying, who is the man that has built a new house, and has not dedicated it? Let him go and return to his house, that he

1 כִּי־תֵצֵא לַמִּלְחָמָה עַל־אֹיְבֶךָ וְרָאִיתָ סוּס וָרֶכֶב עַם רַב

more and horses see and your against to you When
people ,chariots ,enemies battle out go

מִמְּךָ לֹא תִירָא מֵהֶם כִּי־יְהוָה אֱלֹהֶיךָ עִמָּךְ הַמַּעַלְךָ

brought Who (is) your Jehovah for ;them shall you not than
up you ,you with God fear ,you

2 מֵאֶרֶץ מִצְרָיִם׃ וְהָיָה כְּקָרָבְכֶם אֶל־הַמִּלְחָמָה וְנִגַּשׁ

that ,battle the to you when it And .Egypt the of out
come shall near draw ,be shall of land

3 הַכֹּהֵן וְדִבֶּר אֶל־הָעָם׃ וְאָמַר אֲלֵהֶם שְׁמַע יִשְׂרָאֵל אַתֶּם

you ,Israel O ,Hear ,them to say and the to and the
people speak priest

קְרֵבִים הַיּוֹם לַמִּלְחָמָה עַל־אֹיְבֵיכֶם אַל־יֵרַךְ לְבַבְכֶם

your let not your against battle to today are
;heart faint be ;enemies near drawing

4 אַל־תִּירְאוּ וְאַל־תַּחְפְּזוּ וְאַל־תַּעַרְצוּ מִפְּנֵיהֶם׃ כִּי יְהוָה

Jehovah for their at be and ,tremble nor fear do not
;presence terrified not

אֱלֹהֵיכֶם הַהֹלֵךְ עִמָּכֶם לְהִלָּחֵם לָכֶם עִם־אֹיְבֵיכֶם לְהוֹשִׁיעַ

save to your with for fight to with (is) who He your
,enemies you you going God

5 אֶתְכֶם׃ וְדִבְּרוּ הַשֹּׁטְרִים אֶל־הָעָם לֵאמֹר מִי־הָאִישׁ אֲשֶׁר

who the (is) Who ,saying the to the shall And ,you
man people officers speak

בָּנָה בַיִת־חָדָשׁ וְלֹא חֲנָכוֹ יֵלֵךְ וְיָשֹׁב לְבֵיתוֹ פֶּן־יָמוּת

die he lest his to and Let dedicated and new house a has
,house return go him ?it not built

not die in battle and another
man dedicate it. 6And who
is the man that has planted
a vineyard, and has not
used its fruit? Let him go
and return to his house, that
he not die in the battle, and
another man use its fruit.
7And who *is* the man who
has betrothed a woman,
and has not taken her? Let
him go and return to his
house, that he not die in the
battle, and another man
take her. 8And the officers
shall speak further to the
people, and say, Who *is* the
man who is afraid, and faint
of heart? Let him go and
return to his house; then the
heart of his brothers will not
melt like his heart. 9And it
shall be, when the officers
have finished speaking to
the people, commanders of
the armies shall be
appointed at the head of the
people.
10When you come near a
city to fight against it, then
call to it for peace. 11And it
shall be, if it answers peace
to you, and shall open to
you, then it shall be that all
the people found in it shall
be a laborer for you, and
shall serve you. 12And if it
shall not make peace with
you, and shall make war
with you, then you shall lay
siege against it. 13And
Jehovah your God shall
give it into your hand; and
you shall strike every male
of it by the mouth of the
sword. 14Only, the women,
and the little ones, and the
livestock, and all that is in
the city, all its plunder, you
shall seize for yourself. And
you shall eat the plunder of
your enemies which
Jehovah your God has
given to you. 15So you shall
do to all the cities which are
very far away from you,
which are not of the cities of
these nations. 16But of the
cities of these peoples
which Jehovah your God is

6 בַּמִּלְחָמָה וְאִישׁ אַחֵר יַחְנְכֶנּוּ׃ וּמִי־הָאִישׁ אֲשֶׁר נָטַע
כֶּרֶם וְלֹא חִלְּלוֹ יֵלֵךְ וְיָשֹׁב לְבֵיתוֹ פֶּן־יָמוּת בַּמִּלְחָמָה
7 וְאִישׁ אַחֵר יְחַלְּלֶנּוּ׃ וּמִי־הָאִישׁ אֲשֶׁר אֵרַשׂ אִשָּׁה וְלֹא
לְקָחָהּ יֵלֵךְ וְיָשֹׁב לְבֵיתוֹ פֶּן־יָמוּת בַּמִּלְחָמָה וְאִישׁ אַחֵר
8 יִקָּחֶנָּה׃ וְיָסְפוּ הַשֹּׁטְרִים לְדַבֵּר אֶל־הָעָם וְאָמְרוּ מִי־
הָאִישׁ הַיָּרֵא וְרַךְ הַלֵּבָב יֵלֵךְ וְיָשֹׁב לְבֵיתוֹ וְלֹא יִמַּס אֶת־
9 לְבַב אֶחָיו כִּלְבָבוֹ׃ וְהָיָה כְּכַלֹּת הַשֹּׁטְרִים לְדַבֵּר אֶל־
10 הָעָם וּפָקְדוּ שָׂרֵי צְבָאוֹת בְּרֹאשׁ הָעָם׃ כִּי־תִקְרַב
11 אֶל־עִיר לְהִלָּחֵם עָלֶיהָ וְקָרָאתָ אֵלֶיהָ לְשָׁלוֹם׃ וְהָיָה
אִם־שָׁלוֹם תַּעַנְךָ וּפָתְחָה לָךְ וְהָיָה כָּל־הָעָם הַנִּמְצָא־בָהּ
12 יִהְיוּ לְךָ לָמַס וַעֲבָדוּךָ׃ וְאִם־לֹא תַשְׁלִים עִמָּךְ וְעָשְׂתָה
13 עִמְּךָ מִלְחָמָה וְצַרְתָּ עָלֶיהָ׃ וּנְתָנָהּ יְהוָה אֱלֹהֶיךָ בְּיָדֶךָ
14 וְהִכִּיתָ אֶת־כָּל־זְכוּרָהּ לְפִי־חָרֶב׃ רַק הַנָּשִׁים וְהַטַּף
וְהַבְּהֵמָה וְכֹל אֲשֶׁר יִהְיֶה בָעִיר כָּל־שְׁלָלָהּ תָּבֹז לָךְ
15 וְאָכַלְתָּ אֶת־שְׁלַל אֹיְבֶיךָ אֲשֶׁר נָתַן יְהוָה אֱלֹהֶיךָ לָךְ׃ כֵּן
תַּעֲשֶׂה לְכָל־הֶעָרִים הָרְחֹקֹת מִמְּךָ מְאֹד אֲשֶׁר לֹא־מֵעָרֵי
16 הַגּוֹיִם־הָאֵלֶּה הֵנָּה׃ רַק מֵעָרֵי הָעַמִּים הָאֵלֶּה אֲשֶׁר יְהוָה

giving to you *as* an inheritance, you shall not keep alive any that breathes. [17]But you shall utterly destroy them, the Hittites, and the Amorites, the Canaanites, and the Perizzites, the Hivites, and the Jebusites, as Jehovah your God has commanded you; [18]so that they may not teach you to do according to all their filthy deeds which they have done for their gods; and you would sin against Jehovah your God.

[19]When you shall lay siege to a city many days, to fight against it, to capture it, you shall not destroy its trees in order to force an axe against them. For you shall eat of them, and you shall not cut them down—for is the tree of the field *a* man that it should be used by you to lay siege? [20]Only the tree which you know not to be a fruit tree, you may destroy it, and may cut it down, and may build a bulwark against the city which is making war with you, until you have subdued it.

CAP. XXI כא

CHAPTER 21

[1]If one is found slain in the land which Jehovah your God is giving to you, to possess it, lying in the field, and it is not known who has struck him; [2]then your elders and your judges shall come out. And they shall measure to the cities which are around the one slain. [3]And it shall be, that the city which is nearest to the one slain, even the elders of that city shall take a heifer of the herd, which has not been worked with, and which has not drawn in the yoke. [4]And the elders of that city shall bring the heifer down to an ever-flowing stream, which is not plowed nor

sown. And *they* shall break the heifer's neck there by the stream. 5And the priests, the sons of Levi, shall come near — for Jehovah your God has chosen them to minister to Him, and to bless in the name of Jehovah—and by their mouth shall every controversy and every stroke be *tried*. 6And all the elders of that city which is nearest to the one slain shall wash their hands over the heifer whose neck was broken by the stream. 7And they shall answer and say, Our hands have not shed this blood, nor have our eyes seen it. 8O Jehovah, be merciful to Your people Israel, whom You have redeemed, and do not allow innocent blood in the midst of Your people Israel. And the blood shall be forgiven them. 9And you shall put away the innocent blood from among you, for you shall do that which is right in the eyes of Jehovah.

10When you go out to battle against your enemies, and Jehovah your God has given them into your hands, and you have taken them captive; 11and you have seen in the captivity a woman of beautiful face, and you desire her, even to take *her* to you for a wife, 12then you shall bring her into the midst of your household. And she shall shave her head, and prepare her nails, 13and shall remove the clothing of her captivity from her, and shall live in your house, and shall bewail her father and her mother a month of days. Then afterwards you shall go in to her, and shall marry her; and she shall be a wife to you. 14And it shall be, if you do not delight in her, you shall send her away at her desire; and you shall not at all sell her for silver; you shall not treat her as a slave, because you have humbled her.

5066 5158 5697 6202 2232 3808 5647
5 עבד בו ולא יזרע וערפו־שם את־העגלה בנחל׃ ונגשו
shall And near come | the by .brook | heifer's the | there shall and neck break | ,sown | nor | is plowed

1288 8334 430 3068 977 3881 1121 3548
הכהנים בני לוי כי בם בחר יהוה אלהיך לשרתו ולברך
to and bless | minister to Him to | your God | Jehovah | has chosen | them for | ,Levi | the of sons | the ,priests

2205 3605 5061 7379 3605 1961 6310 3068 8034
6 בשם יהוה ועל־פיהם יהיה כל־ריב וכל־נגע׃ וכל זקני
the of elders | And all | .stroke | and every | dispute every | shall (tried) be | their mouth | and by | ;Jehovah | the in of name

5921 3027 7364 2491 7138 5892
העיר ההוא הקרבים אל־החלל ירחצו את־ידיהם על־
over | hands their | shall wash | slain the man | to | is which nearest | that | city

8210 3808 3027 559 6030 5158 6202 5697
7 העגלה הערופה בנחל׃ וענו ואמרו ידינו לא שפכה
shed have | not | Our hands | ,say and | they And answer shall | the by .brook | neck whose broken was | heifer the

3478 5971 3722 7200 3808 5869 2088 1818
8 את־הדם הזה ועינינו לא ראו׃ כפר לעמך ישראל
,Israel | Your people | Forgive | have .(it) seen | not | our and eyes | ,this | blood

3478 5971 7130 5355 1818 5414 3068 6299
אשר־פדית יהוה ואל־תתן דם נקי בקרב עמך ישראל
;Israel | your people | the in of midst | inno- cent | blood | do not and put | O ;Jehovah | have You whom ,redeemed

7130 5355 1818 1197 1818 3722
9 ונכפר להם הדם׃ ואתה תבער הדם הנקי מקרבך
from ,you among | innocent | the blood | put shall you And away | the .blood | them shall and forgiven be

3068 5869 3477 6213
כי־תעשה הישר בעיני יהוה׃
.Jehovah | the in of eyes | which that right is | shall you for do

3027 430 3068 5414 341 4421 3318
10 כי־תצא למלחמה על־איביך ונתנו יהוה אלהיך בידך
your into ,hands | your God | Jehovah | has and them given | your against ,enemies | battle to | you When out go

2836 8389/ 3033 802 76 28 7200 7617 7617
11 ושבית שביו׃ וראית בשביה אשת יפת־תאר וחשקת
you and desire | beautiful form of | a woman | the in captivity | have and seen | them ;captive | you and taken have

1548 1004 8432 935 802 3947
12 בה ולקחת לך לאשה׃ והבאתה אל־תוך ביתך וגלחה
she and shave shall | your ,household | midst the of | into | you then her bring shall | a for ,wife | to you | take and (her) | ,her

8071 5493 6856 6213 7218
13 את־ראשה ועשתה את־צפרניה׃ והסירה את־שמלת
clothing the of | shall and off take | ,nails her | and dress | ,head her

1 1058 1004 3427 7628
שביה מעליה וישבה בביתך ובכתה את־אביה ואת־
and | father her | shall and bewail | your in ,house | shall and live | from her | her captivity

1961 1166 935 310 3117 3391 517
אמה ירח ימים ואחר כן תבוא אליה ובעלתה והיתה
she and be shall | shall and ,her marry | her to | shall you in go | after- wards | and of ;days | a month | her mother

5315 5414 2654 3808 518 1961 802
14 לך לאשה׃ והיה אם־לא חפצת בה ושלחתה לנפשה
her at :desire | shall you out her send | in ,her | you delight | not | if | it And ,be shall | .wife a | to you

8478 6014 3808 3701 4376 3808
ומכר לא־תמכרנה בכסף לא־תתעמר בה תחת אשר
because | ,her | shall you slave a as treat | not | for ,silver | shall you her sell | not | and at all

[15]If a man has two wives, the one loved, and the other hated; and they have borne him sons, both the loved one and the hated one; and if the firstborn son was of her who was hated, [16]then it shall be, in the day that he causes his son to inherit that which he has, he may not make the son of the loved one the firstborn before the son of the hated one, *he* who is *truly* the firstborn. [17]But he shall acknowledge the firstborn, the son of the hated one, by giving him a double portion of all that he has; for he is the firstfruit of his strength — the right of the firstborn is his.

[18]If a man has a stubborn and rebellious son who will not listen to his father's voice, or his mother's voice; even though they discipline him, *he* will not listen to them; [19]then his father and his mother shall lay hold on him and bring him out to the elders of his city, and to the gate of his place; [20]and they shall say to the elders of his city, This son of ours is stubborn and rebellious; he will not listen to our voice; he is a glutton, and a drunkard. [21]And all the men of his city shall stone him with stones, and he shall die. So you shall put away the evil from among you, that all Israel shall hear, and fear.

[22]And if a man has committed a sin worthy of death, and he is put to death, and you hang him on a tree, [23]his body shall not remain all night on the tree; but you shall surely bury him the same day. For he that is hanged is a reproach to God. And you shall not defile your land which Jehovah your God is giving to you *as* an inheritance.

15 עִנִּיתָהּ׃ ס כִּי־תִהְיֶיןָ לְאִישׁ שְׁתֵּי נָשִׁים הָאַחַת
אֲהוּבָה וְהָאַחַת שְׂנוּאָה וְיָלְדוּ־לוֹ בָנִים הָאֲהוּבָה וְהַשְּׂנוּאָה
16 וְהָיָה הַבֵּן הַבְּכֹר לַשְּׂנִיאָה׃ וְהָיָה בְּיוֹם הַנְחִילוֹ אֶת־בָּנָיו
אֵת אֲשֶׁר־יִהְיֶה לוֹ לֹא יוּכַל לְבַכֵּר אֶת־בֶּן־הָאֲהוּבָה עַל־
17 פְּנֵי בֶן־הַשְּׂנוּאָה הַבְּכֹר׃ כִּי אֶת־הַבְּכֹר בֶּן־הַשְּׂנוּאָה יַכִּיר
לָתֶת לוֹ פִּי שְׁנַיִם בְּכֹל אֲשֶׁר־יִמָּצֵא לוֹ כִּי־הוּא רֵאשִׁית
18 אֹנוֹ לוֹ מִשְׁפַּט הַבְּכֹרָה׃ ס כִּי־יִהְיֶה לְאִישׁ בֵּן סוֹרֵר
וּמוֹרֶה אֵינֶנּוּ שֹׁמֵעַ בְּקוֹל אָבִיו וּבְקוֹל אִמּוֹ וְיִסְּרוּ אֹתוֹ וְלֹא
19 יִשְׁמַע אֲלֵיהֶם׃ וְתָפְשׂוּ בוֹ אָבִיו וְאִמּוֹ וְהוֹצִיאוּ אֹתוֹ אֶל־
20 זִקְנֵי עִירוֹ וְאֶל־שַׁעַר מְקֹמוֹ׃ וְאָמְרוּ אֶל־זִקְנֵי עִירוֹ בְּנֵנוּ
21 זֶה סוֹרֵר וּמֹרֶה אֵינֶנּוּ שֹׁמֵעַ בְּקֹלֵנוּ זוֹלֵל וְסֹבֵא׃ וּרְגָמֻהוּ
כָּל־אַנְשֵׁי עִירוֹ בָאֲבָנִים וָמֵת וּבִעַרְתָּ הָרָע מִקִּרְבֶּךָ וְכָל־
22 יִשְׂרָאֵל יִשְׁמְעוּ וְיִרָאוּ׃ ס וְכִי־יִהְיֶה בְאִישׁ חֵטְא
23 מִשְׁפַּט־מָוֶת וְהוּמָת וְתָלִיתָ אֹתוֹ עַל־עֵץ׃ לֹא־תָלִין
נִבְלָתוֹ עַל־הָעֵץ כִּי־קָבוֹר תִּקְבְּרֶנּוּ בַּיּוֹם הַהוּא כִּי־קִלְלַת
אֱלֹהִים תָּלוּי וְלֹא תְטַמֵּא אֶת־אַדְמָתְךָ אֲשֶׁר יְהוָה אֱלֹהֶיךָ
נֹתֵן לְךָ נַחֲלָה׃

CAP. XXII כב

CHAPTER 22

CHAPTER 22
1 You shall not see your brother's ox or his sheep driven away, and hide yourself from them. You shall surely turn them back to your brother.
2 And if your brother is not near you, and you do not know him, then you shall surely bring it home to your house; and it shall be with you until your brother inquires of it; and you shall restore it to him.
3 And so you shall do with his ass; and so you shall do with his clothing; and so you shall do with everything lost of your brother's, which he has lost and you have found; you may not hide yourself.
4 You shall not see your brother's ass or his ox fallen down in the highway, and hide yourself from them. You shall surely *help* him lift *them* up.
5 There shall not be the thing of a man on a woman, nor shall a man put on a woman's garment. For whoever does these things is an abomination to Jehovah your God.

6 If a bird's nest happens to be before you in the way, in any tree, or on the ground, with young ones, or eggs; and the mother is sitting on the young, or on the eggs, you shall not take the mother with the young.
7 But in every case you shall let the mother go, and take the young for yourself, so that it may be well with you, and you may prolong *your* days.
8 When you build a new house, then you shall make a guard rail for your roof, so that you do not put blood on your house if someone falls from it.

1 לֹא־תִרְאֶה אֶת־שׁוֹר אָחִיךָ אוֹ אֶת־שֵׂיוֹ נִדָּחִים וְהִתְעַלַּמְתָּ
hide yourself and | driven away | sheep his | or | your brother's | ox | shall you see | Not

2 מֵהֶם הָשֵׁב תְּשִׁיבֵם לְאָחִיךָ׃ וְאִם־לֹא קָרוֹב אָחִיךָ אֵלֶיךָ
you, | your brother | near is | not | And if | your to brother. | shall you them return | surely | from them;

וְלֹא יְדַעְתּוֹ וַאֲסַפְתּוֹ אֶל־תּוֹךְ בֵּיתֶךָ וְהָיָה עִמְּךָ עַד דְּרֹשׁ
seeks | until | with you | it and be shall | your house, | | to home (it) | shall you and bring | you him know | and not

3 אָחִיךָ אֹתוֹ וַהֲשֵׁבֹתוֹ לוֹ׃ וְכֵן תַּעֲשֶׂה לַחֲמֹרוֹ וְכֵן תַּעֲשֶׂה
shall you do | and so | his with ass; | shall you do | And so | to him. | you and it restore shall | ;it | your brother

לְשִׂמְלָתוֹ וְכֵן תַּעֲשֶׂה לְכָל־אֲבֵדַת אָחִיךָ אֲשֶׁר־תֹּאבַד
loses | which | your brother's, | of lost | with everything | shall you do | and so | his with clothing;

4 מִמֶּנּוּ וּמְצָאתָהּ לֹא תוּכַל לְהִתְעַלֵּם׃ לֹא־תִרְאֶה
shall you see | Not | .(it) hide | you may | not | you and found have; | he

אֶת־חֲמוֹר אָחִיךָ אוֹ שׁוֹרוֹ נֹפְלִים בַּדֶּרֶךְ וְהִתְעַלַּמְתָּ מֵהֶם
.them | hide (from) | and | the in highway, | fallen down | his ox | or | your brother's | ass

5 הָקֵם תָּקִים עִמּוֹ׃ לֹא־יִהְיֶה כְלִי־גֶבֶר עַל־אִשָּׁה
a woman, | on | a man | the of thing | shall be | not | .it | shall you lift up | Surely

וְלֹא־יִלְבַּשׁ גֶּבֶר שִׂמְלַת אִשָּׁה כִּי תוֹעֲבַת יְהוָה אֱלֹהֶיךָ
your God | Jehovah to | an (is) abomination | for | a woman's; | garment | a man | take shall nor on

כָּל־עֹשֵׂה אֵלֶּה׃
these things. | does | whoever

6 כִּי יִקָּרֵא קַן־צִפּוֹר ׀ לְפָנֶיךָ בַּדֶּרֶךְ בְּכָל־עֵץ ׀ אוֹ עַל־
on | or | tree, any | in | the in way, | before you | a bird's | nest | happens be to | If

הָאָרֶץ אֶפְרֹחִים אוֹ בֵיצִים וְהָאֵם רֹבֶצֶת עַל־הָאֶפְרֹחִים
the nestlings, | on | is sitting | the and mother | eggs, | or | (with) nestlings | the ground,

7 אוֹ עַל־הַבֵּיצִים לֹא־תִקַּח הָאֵם עַל־הַבָּנִים׃ שַׁלֵּחַ תְּשַׁלַּח
shall you go let | (but) always | the young, | with | the mother | you take shall | not | eggs, the | on | or

אֶת־הָאֵם וְאֶת־הַבָּנִים תִּקַּח־לָךְ לְמַעַן יִיטַב לָךְ וְהַאֲרַכְתָּ
you and prolong may | with you, | may it be well | so that | for yourself | take | the young | but | the mother,

8 יָמִים׃ כִּי תִבְנֶה בַּיִת חָדָשׁ וְעָשִׂיתָ מַעֲקֶה לְגַגֶּךָ
your for roof, | guard a rail | you then make shall | new, | a house | you build | When | (your) days.

9 וְלֹא־תָשִׂים דָּמִים בְּבֵיתֶךָ כִּי־יִפֹּל הַנֹּפֵל מִמֶּנּוּ׃ לֹא־
not | .it from | someone falling | falls | If | your on house, | blood | do you put | that so not

9You shall not sow your vineyard with various kinds of seeds, that the fruit of your seed which you have sown and the fruit of your vineyard not be defiled. 10You shall not plow with an ox and an ass together. 11You shall not wear a garment of different kinds, of wool and linen together. 12You shall make tassels for yourself on the four corners of your cloak with which you cover.

13If any man takes a wife, and goes in to her, and hates her; 14then makes shameful charges against her, and brings up an evil name on her, and says, I took this woman, and when I came near her, I did not find in her the tokens of virginity. 15Then the girl's father and her mother shall take and bring the girl's tokens of virginity to the elders of the city in the gate. 16And the girl's father shall say to the elders, I have given my daughter to this man for a wife, and he hates her. 17And, behold, he has laid shameful charges, saying, I have not found in your daughter the tokens of virginity. And yet these are the tokens of my daughter's virginity. And they shall spread the garment before the elders of the city. 18And the elders of that city shall take that man and punish him. 19And they shall fine him a hundred pieces of silver, and give them to the girl's father, because he has caused an evil name to be spread abroad on a virgin of Israel. And she shall be his wife; he may not put her away all his days. 20But if this thing is true, *that* tokens of virginity have not been found for the girl, 21then they shall bring out the girl to the door of her father's house. And the men

2232 834 2233 4395 6942 3610 3754 2232
תִזְרַע כַּרְמְךָ כִּלְאָיִם פֶּן־תִּקְדַּשׁ הַמְלֵאָה הַזֶּרַע אֲשֶׁר תִּזְרָע
have you which the fruit the be lest with your shall You
sown seed (of) defiled ,seeds various vineyard sow

3162 2543 7794 2790 3754 8393
10 לֹא־תַחֲרֹשׁ בְּשׁוֹר־וּבַחֲמֹר יַחְדָּו׃ וּתְבוּאַת הַכָּרֶם׃
.together an and with shall You not (your) the and
ass ox an plow .vineyard of fruit

1434 3162 6593 6785 8162 3847
11
12 גְּדִלִים לֹא תִלְבַּשׁ שַׁעַטְנֵז צֶמֶר וּפִשְׁתִּים יַחְדָּו׃
tassels .together linen and wool of garment a shall You not
mixed wear

3680 834 3682 3671 702 6213
תַּעֲשֶׂה־לָּךְ עַל־אַרְבַּע כַּנְפוֹת כְּסוּתְךָ אֲשֶׁר תְּכַסֶּה־בָּהּ׃
.with you which your corners four the on for shall You
cover cloak of yourself make

7760 8130 935 802 376 3947
13
14 כִּי־יִקַּח אִישׁ אִשָּׁה וּבָא אֵלֶיהָ וּשְׂנֵאָהּ׃ וְשָׂם לָהּ
against and and ,her to and ,wife a man a takes If
her makes ,her hates in goes

802 7451 8034 5921 3318 1697 5949
עֲלִילֹת דְּבָרִים וְהוֹצִא עָלֶיהָ שֵׁם רָע וְאָמַר אֶת־הָאִשָּׁה
woman and an name her on and ,charges shameful
says evil brings

1331 4672 3808 7126 3947 2088
הַזֹּאת לָקַחְתִּי וָאֶקְרַב אֵלֶיהָ וְלֹא־מָצָאתִי לָהּ בְּתוּלִים׃
tokens the in did I not ,her to I when and took I This
;virginity of her find near came

5291 1331 3318 517 5291 1 3947
15 וְלָקַח אֲבִי הַנַּעַר וְאִמָּהּ וְהוֹצִיאוּ אֶת־בְּתוּלֵי הַנַּעַר אֶל־
to the tokens bring and her and the father then
girl's of virginity mother girl's take shall

2205 5291 1 559 8179 5892 2205
16 זִקְנֵי הָעִיר הַשָּׁעְרָה׃ וְאָמַר אֲבִי הַנַּעַר אֶל־הַזְּקֵנִים אֶת־
the to the father shall And the in the the
,elders girl's say .gate city of elders

2009 8130 802 2088 376 5414 1323
17 בִּתִּי נָתַתִּי לָאִישׁ הַזֶּה לְאִשָּׁה וַיִּשְׂנָאֶהָ׃ וְהִנֵּה־הוּא
he And he and a for this man to have I my
,behold .her hates ,wife given daughter

1331 1323 4672 3808 559 1697 5949 7760
שָׂם עֲלִילֹת דְּבָרִים לֵאמֹר לֹא־מָצָאתִי לְבִתְּךָ בְּתוּלִים
tokens the your in have I not ,saying ,charges shameful has
,virginity of daughter found laid

5892 2205 6440 8057 6566 1323 1331 428
וְאֵלֶּה בְּתוּלֵי בִתִּי וּפָרְשׂוּ הַשִּׂמְלָה לִפְנֵי זִקְנֵי הָעִיר׃
.city the the before garment the they And my of tokens yet and
of elders spread shall .daughter's virginity these (see)

6064 3256 376 5892 2205 3947
18
19 וְלָקְחוּ זִקְנֵי הָעִיר־הַהִוא אֶת־הָאִישׁ וְיִסְּרוּ אֹתוֹ׃ וְעָנְשׁוּ
they And .him and (that) that city the shall And
fine shall punish man of elders take

7451 8034 3318 5291 1 5414 3701 3967
אֹתוֹ מֵאָה כֶסֶף וְנָתְנוּ לַאֲבִי הַנַּעֲרָה כִּי הוֹצִיא שֵׁם רָע
an name has he because the the to and ,silver of a him
evil published girl of father give hundred

7971 3201 3808 802 1961 3478 1330 5921
עַל בְּתוּלַת יִשְׂרָאֵל וְלוֹ־תִהְיֶה לְאִשָּׁה לֹא־יוּכַל לְשַׁלְּחָהּ
her put he not ;wife shall she And .Israel virgin a upon
away may be his of

4672 1697 1961 571 3117 3605
20 כָּל־יָמָיו׃ וְאִם־אֱמֶת הָיָה הַדָּבָר הַזֶּה לֹא־נִמְצְאוּ
have (that and) ,this thing is true if But .days his all
found been not

1 1004 6607 5291 3318 5291 1331
21 בְּתוּלִים לַנַּעֲרָ׃ וְהוֹצִיאוּ אֶת־הַנַּעֲרָ אֶל־פֶּתַח בֵּית־אָבִיהָ
her house the to girl the they then the for of tokens
,father's of door out bring shall .girl virginity

of her city shall stone her with stones, and she shall die; for she has done folly in Israel, to commit fornication in her father's house. And you shall put away the evil from among you.

[22]If a man is found lying with a woman married to a husband, then they shall both of them die, the man that lay with the woman, and the woman. And you shall put away the evil from Israel. [23]If there is a girl that is a virgin, betrothed to a man, and a man finds her in the city, and lies with her; [24]then you shall bring them both out to the gate of that city. And you shall stone them with stones so that they die; the girl, because she did not cry out, being in the city; and the man, because he has humbled his neighbor's wife. And you shall put away the evil from among you. [25]But if a man finds a betrothed girl in the field, and the man seizes her and lies with her; then only the man that lay with her shall die. [26]And you shall do nothing to the girl; the girl has no sin worthy of death; for as when a man rises against his neighbor and murders him, even so is this matter.

[27]For he found her in the field, *and* the betrothed girl cried out, but no one saved her. [28]If a man finds a virgin girl, not being betrothed, and seizes her and lies with her, and they be found; [29]then the man lying with

5039 6213 4191 5619 5892 582 5619
וסקלוה אנשי עירה באבנים ומתה כי־עשתה נבלה
folly has she done for she and die shall with stones her city men the of shall and her stone

7130 7451 1197 1 1004 2181 3478
ס בישראל לזנות בית אביה ובערת הרע מקרבך׃
from you among evil the off cut shall you and her father's house in fornication commit to ,Israel in

4191 1167 1166 802 7901 376 4672
22 כי־ימצא איש שכב עם־אשה בעלת־בעל ומתו גם־
even they then die shall a husband, to married a woman with lying down man a is found If

7451 1197 802 802 7901 376 8147
שניהם האיש השכב עם־האשה והאשה ובערת הרע
evil the you so off cut shall the and woman; the woman, with that down lay man the of both them,

376 781 1330 5291 1961 3478
23 מישראל׃ כי יהיה נער בתולה מארשה לאיש
a to man, betrothed (is that) virgin a a girl there is If from Israel.

8147 3318 7901 5892 376 4672
24 ומצאה איש בעיר ושכב עמה׃ והוצאתם את־שניהם
both them you then out bring shall with her, lies and down the in city man a finds and her

4191 68 5619 5892 8179
אל־שער העיר ההוא וסקלתם אתם באבנים ומתו את־
that so die they; with stones them you and stone shall that, city the to of gate

376 5892 6817 5291
הנער על־דבר אשר לא־צעקה בעיר ואת־האיש על־
man the and (being) the in city; did she not out cry, because the girl

7130 7451 1197 7453 802 6030
ס דבר אשר־ענה את־אשת רעהו ובערת הרע מקרבך׃
from you among evil the ou so cut shall his neighbor's wife has he abased because

781 5291 376 4672 7704 518
25 ואם־בשדה ימצא האיש את־הנער המארשה
is that betrothed, girl a man the finds the in field if But

7901 376 4191 7901 376 2388
והחזיק־בה האיש ושכב עמה ומת האיש אשר־שכב
lies down who man the then die shall with her; lies and down man the her and seizes

4194 2399 5291 369 1697 6213 3808 5291
26 עמה לבדו׃ ולנער לא־תעשה דבר אין לנער חטא מות
death; of sin (worthy) girl the (done has) no thing; shall you do no to And girl the only. with her

1697 3651 7523 7453 376 6965
כי כאשר יקום איש על־רעהו ורצחו נפש כן הדבר
matter even so and him murders his against neighbor man a rises when as for

369 781 5291 6817 4672 7704 3588 2088
27 הזה׃ כי בשדה מצאה צעקה הנער המארשה ואין
and one no betrothed, girl the cried (and) out found he her, the in field For (is) this.

3808 1330 5291/376 4672 3467
28 מושיע לה׃ כי־ימצא איש נער בתולה אשר לא־
not who virgin a, girl a man a finds If her. saved

7901 376 5414 4672 7901 8610 781
29 ארשה ותפשה ושכב עמה ונמצאו׃ ונתן האיש השכב
lying down man the then give shall they and found be, with her, lies and down her seized, and betrothed (is)

8478 802 1961 3701 2572 5291 1
עִמָּהּ לַאֲבִי הַנַּעֲרָ חֲמִשִּׁים כָּסֶף וְלוֹ־תִהְיֶה לְאִשָּׁה תַּחַת
because , wife she his and of fifty the to with
be shall ,silver pieces girl's father her

*3808 3117 3605 7971 3201 6031
אֲשֶׁר עִנָּהּ לֹא־יוּכַל שַׁלְּחָהּ כָּל־יָמָיו׃
his all her put he not has he
.days away may ;her abased

CAP. XXIII כג

CHAPTER 23

3808 3671 1540 3808 1 802 376 3947 3808
1 לֹא־יִקַּח אִישׁ אֶת־אֵשֶׁת אָבִיו וְלֹא יְגַלֶּה כְּנַף אָבִיו׃
his skirt shall and his wife man A shall not
.father's uncover not ,father's take

3068 6951 8212 3772 1795 6481 935 3808
2 לֹא־יָבֹא פְצוּעַ־דַּכָּה וּכְרוּת שָׁפְכָה בִּקְהַל יְהוָה׃
.Jehovah the into male (his) cut or ,crushed being shall He not
of assembly ,member in wounded enter

3808 935 3808 6224 1755 1571 3068 6951 4464 935
3 לֹא־יָבֹא מַמְזֵר בִּקְהַל יְהוָה גַּם דּוֹר עֲשִׂירִי לֹא־יָבֹא לוֹ
of shall none ,tenth the even ;Jehovah the into A shall not
his enter generation (to) of assembly bastard enter

6951 4125 5984 935 3808 3068 6951
4 בִּקְהַל יְהוָה׃ לֹא־יָבֹא עַמּוֹנִי וּמוֹאָבִי בִּקְהַל
the into a or An shall not .Jehovah the into
of assembly Moabite Ammonite enter of assembly

5704 3068 6951 935 3808 6224 1755 1571 3068
יְהוָה גַּם דּוֹר עֲשִׂירִי לֹא־יָבֹא לָהֶם בִּקְהַל יְהוָה עַד־
Jehovah the into of shall none ,tenth the even ;Jehovah
of assembly them enter generation (to)

4325 3899 6923 3808 5769
5 עוֹלָם׃ עַל־דְּבַר אֲשֶׁר לֹא־קִדְּמוּ אֶתְכֶם בַּלֶּחֶם וּבַמַּיִם
with and with you did they not because ;perpetually
water bread meet

1109 7936 4714 3318 1870
בַּדֶּרֶךְ בְּצֵאתְכֶם מִמִּצְרָיִם וַאֲשֶׁר שָׂכַר עָלֶיךָ אֶת־בִּלְעָם
Balaam against they and ;Egypt of you when the in
you hired because out came way

3068 14 3808 7043 763 6604 1160 1121
6 בֶּן־בְּעוֹר מִפְּתוֹר אֲרַם נַהֲרַיִם לְקַלְלֶךָּ׃ וְלֹא־אָבָה יְהוָה
Jehovah would But curse to ,Mesopotamia from ,Beor the
not .you of Pethor of son

430 3068 2015 1109 8085 430
אֱלֹהֶיךָ לִשְׁמֹעַ אֶל־בִּלְעָם וַיַּהֲפֹךְ יְהוָה אֱלֹהֶיךָ לְּךָ אֶת־
for your Jehovah and ,Balaam to listen your
you God turned God

1875 3808 430 3068 157 1293 7045
7 הַקְּלָלָה לִבְרָכָה כִּי אֲהֵבְךָ יְהוָה אֱלֹהֶיךָ׃ לֹא־תִדְרֹשׁ
shall you not your Jehovah loved because a into curse the
seek ;God you ,blessing

8581 3808 5769 3117 3605 2896 7965
8 שְׁלֹמָם וְטֹבָתָם כָּל־יָמֶיךָ לְעוֹלָם׃ לֹא־תְתַעֵב
shall You not .perpetually your all their or their
despise days good peace

1961 1616 4713 8581 3808 251
אֲדֹמִי כִּי אָחִיךָ הוּא לֹא־תְתַעֵב מִצְרִי כִּי־גֵר הָיִיתָ
you an for an shall you not ;(is) he your for an
were alien ,Egyptian depise brother ,Edomite

935 7992 1755 3205 834 1121 776
9 בְאַרְצוֹ׃ בָּנִים אֲשֶׁר־יִוָּלְדוּ לָהֶם דּוֹר שְׁלִישִׁי יָבֹא לָהֶם
may third the of to born are who sons his in
enter ,generation them ;land

8104 341 4264 3318 3068 6951
10 בִּקְהַל יְהוָה׃ כִּי־תֵצֵא מַחֲנֶה עַל־אֹיְבֶיךָ וְנִשְׁמַרְתָּ
keep then your against (into) you When .Jehovah the-into
yourselves ,enemies camp forth go of assembly

her shall give to the girl's father fifty pieces of silver, and she shall be his wife, because he has humbled her. He may not put her away all his days.

[30]A man shall not take his father's wife, and shall not uncover his father's skirt.

CHAPTER 23

[1]He being wounded, crushed, or cut in his male member shall not enter into the assembly of Jehovah. [2]An illegitimate child shall not enter into the assembly of Jehovah, even to the tenth generation shall none of his enter into the assembly of Jehovah.

[3]An Ammonite or a Moabite shall not enter into the assembly of Jehovah; even to the tenth generation shall none of them enter into the assembly of Jehovah, perepetually; [4]because they did not meet you with bread and with water in the way when you came out of Egypt; and because they hired against you Balaam the son of Beor, from Pethor of Mesopotamia, to curse you. [5]But Jehovah your God would not listen to Balaam, and Jehovah your God turned the curse into a blessing to you, because Jehovah your God loved you. [6]You shall not seek their peace nor their prosperity all your days, perpetually.

[7]You shall not despise an Edomite, for he is your brother. You shall not despise an Egyptian, for you were an alien in his land; [8]sons of the third generation that are born to them may enter into the assembly of Jehovah.

[9]When you go forth *into* camp against your enemies, then keep yourselves from every evil thing.

[10]If there is among you *any* man who is not clean because of an accident at night, then he shall go to the outside of the camp; he shall not come in to the middle of the camp. [11]And it shall be, as evening *is* turning, he shall bathe with water, and as the sun is sinking, he shall come into the middle of the camp.

[12]Also you shall have a place outside the camp, and you shall go out there. [13]And you shall have an instrument on your staff. And it shall be, as you sit outside, you shall dig with it, and shall turn back, and shall cover that which comes from you. [14]For Jehovah your God walks in the middle of your camp, to deliver you and to give up your enemies before you; therefore your camp shall be holy, so that He may see no unclean thing in you, and turn away from you.

[15]You shall not hand over to his master a slave that has escaped from his master to you. [16]He shall live with you, among you, in the place which he chooses inside one of your gates, wherever it is pleasing to him. You shall not oppress him.

[17]There shall be no harlot among the daughters of Israel, nor shall there be a homosexual among the sons of Israel. [18]You shall not bring the hire of a harlot, or the price of a dog, into the house of Jehovah your God for any vow; for even both of these are an abomination to Jehovah your God.

[19]You shall not lend at interest to your brother; interest of silver, interest of food, interest on anything which is loaned at interest. [20]You may lend to a stranger, but you shall not lend at interest to your brother, so that Jehovah your God may bless you in all that you put your hand to.

11 מִכֹּל דָּבָר רָע׃ כִּי־יִהְיֶה בְךָ אִישׁ אֲשֶׁר לֹא־יִהְיֶה
is not who (any) among there If .evil thing from / man you is every-
טָהוֹר מִקְּרֵה־לָיְלָה וְיָצָא אֶל־מִחוּץ לַמַּחֲנֶה לֹא יָבֹא
shall he not the of the to he then at of because clean / in come ;camp outside go shall ,night accident an
12 אֶל־תּוֹךְ הַמַּחֲנֶה׃ וְהָיָה לִפְנוֹת־עֶרֶב יִרְחַץ בַּמָּיִם
with shall he ,evening turns as it and ;camp the the to / ,water bathe be shall of middle
13 וּכְבֹא הַשֶּׁמֶשׁ יָבֹא אֶל־תּוֹךְ הַמַּחֲנֶה׃ וְיָד תִּהְיֶה לְךָ
for will a Also .camp the the to shall he ,sun the as and / you be place of middle in come sinking is
14 מִחוּץ לַמַּחֲנֶה וְיָצָאתָ שָּׁמָּה חוּץ׃ וְיָתֵד תִּהְיֶה לְךָ עַל־
on you shall tool A .outside ,there you and the of the on / have out go shall ,camp outside
אֲזֵנֶךָ וְהָיָה בְּשִׁבְתְּךָ חוּץ וְחָפַרְתָּה בָהּ וְשַׁבְתָּ וְכִסִּיתָ
shall and shall and with you that ,outside you as it and your / cover ,back turn ,it dig shall sit ,be shall ;tool
15 אֶת־צֵאָתֶךָ׃ כִּי יְהוָה אֱלֹהֶיךָ מִתְהַלֵּךְ ׀ בְּקֶרֶב מַחֲנֶךָ
your the in walks your Jehovah For which that / ,camp of middle about God .you from comes
לְהַצִּילְךָ וְלָתֵת אֹיְבֶיךָ לְפָנֶיךָ וְהָיָה מַחֲנֶיךָ קָדוֹשׁ וְלֹא־
that so ,holy your Therefore before your to and deliver to / no camp be shall ,you enemies up give ,you
16 יִרְאֶה בְךָ עֶרְוַת דָּבָר וְשָׁב מֵאַחֲרֶיךָ׃ לֹא־
Not .you from and ,thing unclean in may He / away turn you see
תַסְגִּיר עֶבֶד אֶל־אֲדֹנָיו אֲשֶׁר־יִנָּצֵל אֵלֶיךָ מֵעִם אֲדֹנָיו׃
his from you to has who his to slave a shall you / ;master escaped master over hand
17 עִמְּךָ יֵשֵׁב בְּקִרְבְּךָ בַּמָּקוֹם אֲשֶׁר־יִבְחַר בְּאַחַד שְׁעָרֶיךָ
your inside he which the in among he with / ,gates of one ,chooses place ,you live shall you
18 בַּטּוֹב לוֹ לֹא תּוֹנֶנּוּ׃ לֹא־תִהְיֶה קְדֵשָׁה מִבְּנוֹת
among harlot There no shall you not to it where / daughters be shall .him oppress ;him pleasing is
19 יִשְׂרָאֵל וְלֹא־יִהְיֶה קָדֵשׁ מִבְּנֵי יִשְׂרָאֵל׃ לֹא־תָבִיא אֶתְנַן
hire the shall You not .Israel among homo- a shall nor ,Israel's / of bring of sons the sexual be there
זוֹנָה וּמְחִיר כֶּלֶב בֵּית יְהוָה אֱלֹהֶיךָ לְכָל־נֶדֶר כִּי תוֹעֲבַת
an for ;vow for your Jehovah (into) ,dog a the of a / to abomination any God of house the of price ,harlot
20 יְהוָה אֱלֹהֶיךָ גַּם־שְׁנֵיהֶם׃ לֹא־תַשִּׁיךְ לְאָחִיךָ
your to shall You not of both even your Jehovah / ;brother interest at lend .(are) these God
21 נֶשֶׁךְ כֶּסֶף נֶשֶׁךְ אֹכֶל נֶשֶׁךְ כָּל־דָּבָר אֲשֶׁר יִשָּׁךְ׃ לַנָּכְרִי
a to loaned is which thing any interest ,food interest ,money in- / stranger .interest at on on on terest
תַשִּׁיךְ וּלְאָחִיךָ לֹא תַשִּׁיךְ לְמַעַן יְבָרֶכְךָ יְהוָה אֱלֹהֶיךָ בְּכֹל
all in your Jehovah may that so you not your to but may You / God you bless lend shall brother ,lend

in the land where you go to possess it.

[21]When you shall vow a vow to Jehovah your God, you shall not delay to perform it; for Jehovah your God will certainly require it of you, and it shall be sin to you. [22]But if you shall forebear to vow, it shall be no sin to you. [23]That which has gone out of your lips, you shall keep, and shall do *it*. According as you have vowed as a free-will offering to Jehovah your God, *do* even that which you have promised with your mouth.

[24]When you come into your neighbor's vineyard, then you may eat grapes to your fill, at your pleasure. But you shall not put any in your vessel. [25]When you come into your neighbor's standing grain, then you may pluck heads with your hand; but you shall not move a sickle into your neighbor's standing grain.

3423 8033 935 834 776 3027 4916
מִשְׁלַח יָדֶךָ עַל־הָאָרֶץ אֲשֶׁר־אַתָּה בָא־שָׁמָּה לְרִשְׁתָּהּ׃
possess to it ,go you where land the in your (to) hand you that put

7999 309 3808 430 3068 5088 5087
22 כִּי־תִדֹּר נֶדֶר לַיהוָה אֱלֹהֶיךָ לֹא תְאַחֵר לְשַׁלְּמוֹ כִּי
for perform to ;it shall you delay not your ,God to Jehovah vow a vow you When

2599 1961 430 3068 1875 1875
23 דָרֹשׁ יִדְרְשֶׁנּוּ יְהוָה אֱלֹהֶיךָ מֵעִמָּךְ וְהָיָה בְךָ חֵטְא׃ וְכִי
But if .sin with you it and be shall ;you of your God Jehovah will it require surely

8104 8193 4161 2399 1961 5087 2308 3808
24 תֶחְדַּל לִנְדֹּר לֹא־יִהְיֶה בְךָ חֵטְא׃ מוֹצָא שְׂפָתֶיךָ תִּשְׁמֹר
shall you ,keep your lips What from gone has .sin for you shall it be no ,vow to shall you forbear

1696 834 5071 430 3068 5087 6213
וְעָשִׂיתָ כַּאֲשֶׁר נָדַרְתָּ לַיהוָה אֱלֹהֶיךָ נְדָבָה אֲשֶׁר דִּבַּרְתָּ
have you promised that which free- a will offering ,God your to Jehovah have you vowed according as shall and ;perform

6025 398 7453 3754 935 6310
25 כִּי תָבֹא בְּכֶרֶם רֵעֶךָ וְאָכַלְתָּ עֲנָבִים בְּפִיךָ׃
grapes you then eat may your ,neighbor's into vineyard you come When your with .mouth

935 5414 3627 7648 5315
26 כְּנַפְשְׁךָ שָׂבְעֶךָ וְאֶל־כֶּלְיְךָ לֹא תִתֵּן׃ כִּי תָבֹא
you When come you not .put shall (any) your vessel but into your to ;fill your at will

5130 3808 2770 3027 4425 6998 7453 7054
בְּקָמַת רֵעֶךָ וְקָטַפְתָּ מְלִילֹת בְּיָדֶךָ וְחֶרְמֵשׁ לֹא תָנִיף
you move shall not a but sickle with ;hand your heads you then pluck may your ,neighbor's into grain

7453 7054
עַל קָמַת רֵעֶךָ׃
your standing into .neighbor's grain

CAP. XXIV כד

CHAPTER 24

[1]When a man has taken a wife and married her, and it happens that she finds no favor in his eyes because he has found a thing of uncleanness in her, and he writes her a bill of divorce, and puts *it* in her hand, and sends her out of his house; [2]and if she leaves his house and goes and becomes another man's *wife*, [3]and the latter husband hates her, and writes her a bill of divorce, and puts *it* in her hand, and sends her out of his house; or if the latter husband who took her to be his wife dies; [4]her former husband who sent her away is not to take her again to be his wife, after she is defiled.

2580 4672 3808 1961 1166 802 376 3947
1 כִּי־יִקַּח אִישׁ אִשָּׁה וּבְעָלָהּ וְהָיָה אִם־לֹא תִמְצָא־חֵן
favor she finds not that it and happens ,her married and wife a man a has When taken

3748 5612 3789 1697 6172 4672 5869
בְּעֵינָיו כִּי־מָצָא בָהּ עֶרְוַת דָּבָר וְכָתַב לָהּ סֵפֶר כְּרִיתֻת
,divorce bill a of her he and writes a thing of disgrace in her he found has because in ,eyes his

1961 3212 1004 3318 1004 7971 3027 5414
2 וְנָתַן בְּיָדָהּ וְשִׁלְּחָהּ מִבֵּיתוֹ׃ וְיָצְאָה מִבֵּיתוֹ וְהָלְכָה וְהָיְתָה
and becomes and goes his house if and leaves she of out ,house his sends and her in her hand and (it) put

3748 5612 3789 314 376 8130 312 376
3 לְאִישׁ־אַחֵר׃ וּשְׂנֵאָהּ הָאִישׁ הָאַחֲרוֹן וְכָתַב לָהּ סֵפֶר כְּרִיתֻת
,divorce bill a her and writes ,latter the husband hates and her ,another man's (wife)

834 314 376 4191 1004 7971 3027 5414
וְנָתַן בְּיָדָהּ וְשִׁלְּחָהּ מִבֵּיתוֹ אוֹ כִי יָמוּת הָאִישׁ הָאַחֲרוֹן אֲשֶׁר
who ,latter the husband dies if or his of :house sends and out her her in ,hand and (it) puts

7971 834 7223 1167 3201 3808 802 3947
4 לְקָחָהּ לוֹ לְאִשָּׁה׃ לֹא־יוּכַל בַּעְלָהּ הָרִאשׁוֹן אֲשֶׁר־שִׁלְּחָהּ
her sent away who former her husband may (then) not be to ;wife his to him took her

2930 834 370 802 1961 3947 8147
לָשׁוּב לְקַחְתָּהּ לִהְיוֹת לוֹ לְאִשָּׁה אַחֲרֵי אֲשֶׁר הֻטַּמָּאָה
is she ;defiled that after ,wife his be to her take again

For it *is* a hateful thing before Jehovah, and you shall not cause the land to sin which Jehovah your God is giving to you *as* an inheritance.

[5]When a man has taken a new wife, he shall not go out to war, and he shall not be given any duty. He shall be free at his own house for one year, and shall gladden his wife whom he has taken. [6]No one shall take in pledge the lower and upper millstone, for he is taking a man's life to pledge. [7]If a man is found stealing a person of his brothers, of the sons of Israel, and has dealt with him as a slave, and sold him, then that thief shall die. And you shall put away the evil from among you.

[8]Be on guard in the plague of leprosy, that you watch closely and do according to all that the Levitical priests shall teach you. As I commanded them, so you shall be careful to do. [9]Remember that which Jehovah your God did to Miriam in the way, as you came out of Egypt.

[10]When you lend your neighbor any kind of loan, you shall not go to his house to get his pledge. [11]You shall stand outside, and the man to whom you loan shall bring the security outside to you. [12]And if the man is poor, you shall not sleep with his pledge. [13]You shall certainly give back to him the pledge at sundown; and he shall lie down in his own clothing, and shall bless you. And it shall be righteousness to you before Jehovah your God.

[14]You shall not oppress a poor and needy hired servant, of your brothers, or of your aliens who *are* in your land, within your gates. [15]In the same day you shall give him his hire; do not let the sun go down on it. For he is poor, and has lifted up his heart on it; that he not cry against you to Jehovah, and it be sin against you.

כי־תועבה הוא לפני יהוה ולא תחטיא את־הארץ אשר
5 יהוה אלהיך נתן לך נחלה׃ כי־יקח איש אשה
חדשה לא יצא בצבא ולא־יעבר עליו לכל־דבר נקי
יהיה לביתו שנה אחת ושמח את־אשתו אשר־לקח׃
6 7 לא־יחבל רחים ורכב כי־נפש הוא חבל׃ כי
ימצא איש גנב נפש מאחיו מבני ישראל והתעמר־בו
8 ומכרו ומת הגנב ההוא ובערת הרע מקרבך׃ השמר
בנגע־הצרעת לשמר מאד ולעשות ככל אשר־יורו אתכם
9 הכהנים הלוים כאשר צויתם תשמרו לעשות׃ זכור את
אשר־עשה יהוה אלהיך למרים בדרך בצאתכם
10 ממצרים׃ כי־תשה ברעך משאת מאומה לא־תבא
11 אל־ביתו לעבט עבטו׃ בחוץ תעמד והאיש אשר אתה
12 נשה בו יוציא אליך את־העבוט החוצה׃ ואם־איש עני
13 הוא לא תשכב בעבטו׃ השב תשיב לו את־העבוט
כבוא השמש ושכב בשלמתו וברכך ולך תהיה צדקה
14 לפני יהוה אלהיך׃ לא־תעשק שכיר עני ואביון
15 מאחיך או מגרך אשר בארצך בשעריך׃ ביומו תתן

[16]The fathers shall not be put to death for sons; and sons are not to be put to death for fathers; they each shall be put to death for his own sin.

[17]You shall not pervert judgment of an alien, *or* of an orphan; and you shall not take a widow's garment as pledge. [18]But you shall remember that you were a slave in Egypt, and Jehovah your God redeemed you from there. For that reason I command you to do this thing.

[19]When you cut down your harvest in your field, and have forgotten a sheaf in the field, you shall not turn back to take it. It shall be for the alien, for the orphan, and for the widow; so that Jehovah your God shall bless you in all the work of your hand. [20]When you beat your olive tree, you shall not search the branch behind you. It shall be for the alien, for the orphan, and for the widow. [21]When you gather the grapes of your vineyard, you shall not glean it afterward. It shall be for the alien, for the orphan, and for the widow. [22]And you shall remember that you were a slave in the land of Egypt. On account of this I am commanding you to do this thing.

5375 6921 6041 8121 6921 935 3808 7939
שְׂכָרוֹ וְלֹא־תָבוֹא עָלָיו הַשֶּׁמֶשׁ כִּי עָנִי הוּא וְאֵלָיו הוּא נֹשֵׂא
lifted he it on and ,(is) he poor for ;sun the it on let do not his
up down go ;hire

2398 1961 3068 7121 3808 3820
אֶת־נַפְשׁוֹ וְלֹא־יִקְרָא עָלֶיךָ אֶל־יְהוָה וְהָיָה בְךָ חֵטְא׃
.sin against and ,Jehovah to against cry he not and ;heart his
you be it you

376 1 4191 3808 1121 1121 4191 3808
16 לֹא־יוּמְתוּ אָבוֹת עַל־בָּנִים וּבָנִים לֹא־יוּמְתוּ עַל־אָבוֹת אִישׁ
each ;fathers for be shall not and ,sons for The be shall not
executed sons fathers executed

2254 3808 3490 1016 4941 5186 3808 4191 2399
17 בְּחֶטְאוֹ יוּמָתוּ׃ לֹא תַטֶּה מִשְׁפַּט גֵּר יָתוֹם וְלֹא תַחֲבֹל
as take and an an of judg- shall you Not shall they his for
pledge not ;orphan ;alien ment pervert execute sin own

3068 6299 4714 1961 5650 2142 490 899
18 בֶּגֶד אַלְמָנָה׃ וְזָכַרְתָּ כִּי עֶבֶד הָיִיתָ בְּמִצְרַיִם וַיִּפְדְּךָ יְהוָה
Jehovah and ,Egypt in you a that you But .widow's a
you redeemed were slave remember shall garment

2088 1697 6213 6680 8033 430
אֱלֹהֶיךָ מִשָּׁם עַל־כֵּן אָנֹכִי מְצַוְּךָ לַעֲשׂוֹת אֶת־הַדָּבָר הַזֶּה׃
.this thing do to command I that For from your
you reason ,there God

3808 7704 6016 7911 7704 7102 7114
19 כִּי תִקְצֹר קְצִירְךָ בְשָׂדֶךָ וְשָׁכַחְתָּ עֹמֶר בַּשָּׂדֶה לֹא־
not the in sheaf a have and your in your you When
,field forgotten ,field harvest down cut

1288 1961 490 3490 1616 3947 7725
תָשׁוּב לְקַחְתּוֹ לַגֵּר לַיָּתוֹם וְלָאַלְמָנָה יִהְיֶה לְמַעַן יְבָרֶכְךָ
may that so shall it the for and the for the for take to shall you
you bless ;be widow ,orphan ,alien ;it back turn

3808 2132 2251 3027 4639 3605 430 3068
20 יְהוָה אֱלֹהֶיךָ בְּכֹל מַעֲשֵׂה יָדֶיךָ׃ כִּי תַחְבֹּט זֵיתְךָ לֹא
not your beat you When your the all in your Jehovah
,tree olive .hand of work God

1219 1961 490 3490 1616 310 6286
21 תְפָאֵר אַחֲרֶיךָ לַגֵּר לַיָּתוֹם וְלָאַלְמָנָה יִהְיֶה׃ כִּי תִבְצֹר
gather you When it the for and the for the for behind shake do
of grapes the .be shall widow ,orphan ,alien ,you branch the

1961 490 3490 1616 310 5953 3808 3754
כַּרְמְךָ לֹא תְעוֹלֵל אַחֲרֶיךָ לַגֵּר לַיָּתוֹם וְלָאַלְמָנָה יִהְיֶה׃
shall it the for and the and the for ;afterward shall you not your
.be widow ,orphan ,alien (it) glean ,vineyard

6680 4714 776 1961 5650 2142
22 וְזָכַרְתָּ כִּי־עֶבֶד הָיִיתָ בְּאֶרֶץ מִצְרַיִם עַל־כֵּן אָנֹכִי מְצַוְּךָ
com- am I ,Therefore .Egypt the in you a that re- And
you manding of land were slave member

2088 1697 6213
לַעֲשׂוֹת אֶת־הַדָּבָר הַזֶּה׃
.this thing do to

CAP. XXV כה

CHAPTER 25

[1]If there is a contention between men, and they come to judgment; and they have been judged; and the righteous one *is* declared righteous, and the wrongdoer declared guilty; [2]then it shall be, if the wrongdoer *is* a son of stripes, the judge shall cause him to fall down. And *one* shall strike him in his presence, enough for his wickedness,

8199 4941 5066 582 996 7379 1961
1 כִּי־יִהְיֶה רִיב בֵּין אֲנָשִׁים וְנִגְּשׁוּ אֶל־הַמִּשְׁפָּט וּשְׁפָטוּם
they and ,judgment to they and ,men between a there If
,them judge come contention is

518 1961 7563 7561 6662 6663
2 וְהִצְדִּיקוּ אֶת־הַצַּדִּיק וְהִרְשִׁיעוּ אֶת־הָרָשָׁע׃ וְהָיָה אִם־
if it then the declare and the declare and
,be shall wrongdoer guilty ,one righteous righteous

7564 1767 6440 5221 8199 5307 7563 5221 1121
בִּן הַכּוֹת הָרָשָׁע וְהִפִּילוֹ הַשֹּׁפֵט וְהִכָּהוּ לְפָנָיו כְּדֵי רִשְׁעָתוֹ
his enough in (one) And the shall that wrong- the of a
wrong for his strike shall .judge him cause ,doer stripes son
,presence him down fall to

by number. [3]He may give him forty *stripes*; he shall not add more, lest, if he should exceed and beat him above *with* many stripes, then your brother would be dishonored before your eyes.

[4]You shall not muzzle an ox when he is treading out *grain*. [5]If brothers live together, and one of them dies, and has no son, the wife of the dead shall not go outside to a strange man; her brother-in-law shall go in to her, and take her to himself for a wife, and shall perform the duty of the levirate; [6]and it shall be, the firstborn which she bears shall rise up for his dead brother's name, and his name shall not be wiped out of Israel. [7]And if the man does not desire to take his brother's wife, then his brother's wife shall go up to the gate, to the elders, and say, My husband's brother is refusing to raise up a name to his brother in Israel; he has not been willing to perform the duty of my levirate. [8]And the elders of his city shall call for him and shall speak to him. And he shall stand and say, I have no desire to take her. [9]Then his brother's wife shall draw near to him before the elders, and shall take his shoe from his foot, and spit in his face, and shall answer and say, So it shall be done to the man who will not build up the house of his brother. [10]And his name shall be called in Israel, The house of him whose shoe was taken off.

[11]When men fight with one another, and the wife of the one shall come near to deliver her husband from his assailant's hand, and shall put out her hand and lay hold on his genitals, [12]then you shall cut off her hand; your eye shall not pity.

[13]You shall not have in your bag a weight and a weight, a great and a small. [14]You shall not have in your house an ephah and an

5221 6435 3254 3808 5221 703 4557
3 במספר׃ ארבעים יכנו לא יסיף פן־יסיף להכתו על־
above beat and he lest shall he not may He forty (a) with
him exceed (more) add ;him strike (times) .number

7794 2629 3808 5869 251 7034 7227 4347 428
4 אלה מכה רבה ונקלה אחיך לעיניך׃ לא־תחסם שור
ox an shall You not before your would then ;many (with) these
muzzle eyes your brother dishonored be stripes

1121 259 4191 3162 251 3427 1778
5 בדישו׃ ס כי־ישבו אחים יחדו ומת אחד מהם ובן
and of one and ,together brothers live If is he when
son ,them dies .(grain) out treading

935 2993 2114 376 2351 4191 802 1961 3808
אין־לו לא־תהיה אשת־המת החוצה לאיש זר יבמה יבא
shall brother- her an to outside the wife the shall not ,he has
in law-in alien man dead of go not

3605 834 1060 1961 2992 802 3947
6 עליה ולקחה לו לאשה ויבמה׃ והיה הבכור אשר תלד
she which the it And her do and a for to take and her to
bears firstborn be shall .levirate wife himself her

518 3478 8034 4229 3808 4191 251 8034 6965
7 יקום על־שם אחיו המת ולא־ימחה שמו מישראל׃ ואם־
if And from his be shall and ,dead his the for shall
.Israel name out wiped not brother of name up rise

8179 2994 5927 2994 3947 376 2654 3808
לא יחפץ האיש לקחת את־יבמתו ועלתה יבמתו השערה
,gate the to his shall then brother's his take to the does not
wife brother's up go ,wife man desire

3478 8034 251 6965 2993 3985 559 2205
אל־הזקנים ואמרה מאן יבמי להקים לאחיו שם בישראל
;Israel in a his to raise to My refuses say and the to
name brother up brother husband's ,elders

5975 1696 5892 2205 7121 2992 14 3808
8 לא אבה יבמי׃ וקראו־לו זקני־עירו ודברו אליו ועמד
he and to shall and his the him shall And my do is he not
stand shall ;him speak city of elders summon .levirate to willing

2994 5066 3947 2654 3808 559
9 ואמר לא חפצתי לקחתה׃ ונגשה יבמתו אליו לעיני
before to brother's his shall then take to do I not and
,him wife near draw ;her desire say

6030 6440 3417 7272 5275 2502 2205
הזקנים וחלצה נעלו מעל רגלו וירקה בפניו וענתה
shall and his in spit and his from his shall and the
answer face ,foot on shoe take ,elders

251 1004 1129 3808 834 376 6213 559
ואמרה ככה יעשה לאיש אשר לא־יבנה את־בית אחיו׃
his house will not who the to it shall thus ,say and
.brother's up build man done be

5327 5275 2502 1004 3478 8034 7121
10 11 ונקרא שמו בישראל בית חלוץ הנעל׃ ס כי־ינצו
fight When the removal the ,Israel in his shall And
.shoe's of house name called be

5337 259 802 7126 251 376 3162 582
אנשים יחדו איש ואחיו וקרבה אשת האחד להציל את־
to one the the shall and and man a together men
deliver of wife near come brother

7112 4016 2388 3027 7971 5221 3027 376
12 אישה מיד מכהו ושלחה ידה והחזיקה במבשיו׃ וקצתה
you then his on lay and her shall and his from her
off cut shall ,genitals hold hand out put ,assailant's hand husband

68 3599 1961 3808 5869 2347 3808 3709
13 את־כפה לא תחוס עינך׃ ס לא־יהיה לך בכיסך אבן
stone your in You shall not your shall not ;palm her
(weight) bag have .eye pity

374 374 1004 1961 3808 6996 1419 68
14 ואבן גדולה וקטנה׃ לא־יהיה לך בביתך איפה ואיפה
on and an your in You shall not a and great a a and
,ephah ephah house have .small ,stone

ephah, a great and a small. 15You shall have a perfect and just weight; you shall have a perfect and just ephah; so that they prolong your days in the land which Jehovah your God is giving to you. 16For anyone doing these things is hateful to Jehovah your God, everyone acting evilly.

17Remember what Amalek did to you by the way as you came forth out of Egypt; 18how he happened to meet you on the way and attacked your back, all the feeble *ones in* the rear, when you were faint and weary; and he did not fear God. 19And it shall be, when Jehovah your God gives you rest from all your enemies round about in the land which Jehovah your God is giving to you *as* an inheritance to possess it, you shall blot out the remembrance of Amalek from under the heavens; you shall not forget.

8003 374 1961 6664 8003 68 6996 1419
15 גְּדוֹלָה וּקְטַנָּה׃ אֶבֶן שְׁלֵמָה וָצֶדֶק יִהְיֶה־לָּךְ אֵיפָה שְׁלֵמָה
a ephah ;you shall and A stone a and great a
perfect have just perfect (weight) small

127 3117 798 1961 6664
וָצֶדֶק יִהְיֶה־לָּךְ לְמַעַן יַאֲרִיכוּ יָמֶיךָ עַל הָאֲדָמָה אֲשֶׁר־
which land the in your may they so ,you shall and
days prolong that have just

6213 3605 430 3068 8441 5414 430 3068
16 יְהוָה אֱלֹהֶיךָ נֹתֵן לָךְ׃ כִּי תוֹעֲבַת יְהוָה אֱלֹהֶיךָ כָּל־עֹשֵׂה
doing every- your Jehovah an for to (is) your Jehovah
one God to abomination ;you giving God

5761 6213 3605 428
אֵלֶּה כֹּל עֹשֵׂה עָוֶל׃
.evilly acting every- these
one ,things

4714 3318 1870 6002 6213 2142
17 זָכוֹר אֵת אֲשֶׁר־עָשָׂה לְךָ עֲמָלֵק בַּדֶּרֶךְ בְּצֵאתְכֶם מִמִּצְרָיִם׃
of out you as the by Amalek to did what Remember
;Egypt forth came way you

310 2826 3605 2179 1870 7136 834
18 אֲשֶׁר קָרְךָ בַּדֶּרֶךְ וַיְזַנֵּב בְּךָ כָּל־הַנֶּחֱשָׁלִים אַחֲרֶיךָ וְאַתָּה
when your (in) feeble the all your and the on met he how
you ,rear ,back attacked way you

430 3068 5117 1961 430 3373 3023 5889
19 עָיֵף וְיָגֵעַ וְלֹא יָרֵא אֱלֹהִים׃ וְהָיָה בְּהָנִיחַ יְהוָה אֱלֹהֶיךָ ׀
God your Jehovah when it And .God did he and and were
rest gives ,be shall fear not ;weary faint

5414 430 3068 834 776 5439 341
לְךָ מִכָּל־אֹיְבֶיךָ מִסָּבִיב בָּאָרֶץ אֲשֶׁר יְהוָה־אֱלֹהֶיךָ נֹתֵן
(is) God your Jehovah which the in round your from to
giving land ,about enemies all you

8064 8478 6002 2143 4229 3423 5159
לְךָ נַחֲלָה לְרִשְׁתָּהּ תִּמְחֶה אֶת־זֵכֶר עֲמָלֵק מִתַּחַת הַשָּׁמָיִם
the from Amalek the shall you possess to an (as) to
;heavens under of remembrance out blot ;it inheritance you

7911 3808
לֹא תִּשְׁכָּח׃
shall you not
.forget

CAP. XXVI כו

CHAPTER 26

CHAPTER 26

1And when you have come into the land which Jehovah your God is giving to you *as* an inheritance, and you have possessed it, and live in it; 2then you shall take of the first of all the fruits of the ground which you shall bring in from your land which Jehovah your God is giving to you, and shall put it in a basket, and shall go to the place which Jehovah your God shall choose to cause His name to dwell there. 3And you shall come to the priest who is in those days, and shall say to him, I declare today to Jehovah your God that I have come

5414 430 3068 834 776 935 1961
1 וְהָיָה כִּי־תָבוֹא אֶל־הָאָרֶץ אֲשֶׁר יְהוָה אֱלֹהֶיךָ נֹתֵן לְךָ
to (is) God your Jehovah which the to you when And
you giving land in come

6529 7225 3947 3427 3423 5159
2 נַחֲלָה וִירִשְׁתָּהּ וְיָשַׁבְתָּ בָּהּ׃ וְלָקַחְתָּ מֵרֵאשִׁית ׀ כָּל־פְּרִי
the all the of you then ;it in live and possess and an (as)
of fruits of first take shall it ,inheritance

5414 430 3068 776 935 834 127
הָאֲדָמָה אֲשֶׁר תָּבִיא מֵאַרְצְךָ אֲשֶׁר יְהוָה אֱלֹהֶיךָ נֹתֵן לָךְ
to (is) your Jehovah which from shall you which the
,you giving God land your in bring ground

430 3068 977 834 4725 3212 2935 7760
וְשַׂמְתָּ בַטֶּנֶא וְהָלַכְתָּ אֶל־הַמָּקוֹם אֲשֶׁר יִבְחַר יְהוָה אֱלֹהֶיךָ
your Jehovah shall which the to shall and a in shall and
God choose place go basket (it) put

3117 834 3548 935 8033 8034 7931
3 לְשַׁכֵּן שְׁמוֹ שָׁם׃ וּבָאתָ אֶל־הַכֹּהֵן אֲשֶׁר יִהְיֶה בַּיָּמִים הָהֵם
,those days in is who the to you And .there his cause to
(office in) priest come shall name dwell to

935 430 3068 3117 5046 559
וְאָמַרְתָּ אֵלָיו הִגַּדְתִּי הַיּוֹם לַיהוָה אֱלֹהֶיךָ כִּי־בָאתִי אֶל־
into have I that your to today declare I to shall and
come God Jehovah ,him say

into the land which
Jehovah has sworn to our
fathers to give to us. [4]And
the priest shall take the
basket out of your hand and
place it before the altar of
Jehovah your God. [5]And
you shall speak and say
before Jehovah your God,
My father *was* a perishing
Aramean! And he went
down to Egypt with few
men, and lived there, and
became a nation there,
great, mighty and many.
[6]And the Egyptians dealt ill
with us, and afflicted us,
and put hard bondage on
us. [7]And we cried to
Jehovah, the God of our
fathers, and Jehovah heard
our voice, and saw our
affliction, and our labor, and
our oppression. [8]And
Jehovah brought us out
from Egypt by a mighty
hand, and by a stretched-
out arm, and by great
terribleness, and with
signs, and with wonders.
[9]And He has brought us to
this place, and has given to
us this land, a land flowing
with milk and honey. [10]And
now, behold, I have brought
in the first of the fruits of the
ground which You have
given me, O Jehovah. And
you shall place it before
Jehovah your God, and bow
yourself before Jehovah
your God, [11]and rejoice in
all the good which Jehovah
your God has given to you,
and to your house, you, and
the Levite, and the alien
who *is* in your midst.

[12]When you have made
an end of tithing all the
tithes of your increase the
third year, the year of
tithing, and have given it to
the Levite, the alien, the
orphan, and the widow, that
they may eat inside your
gates, and be filled, [13]then
you shall say before
Jehovah your God I have
consumed the devoted

3947 5414 1 3068 7650 834 776
4 הארץ אשר נשבע יהוה לאבתינו לתת לנו׃ ולקח
and take shall | ;us to | give to | our to fathers | Jehovah | swore | which | land the

430 3068 4196 6440 3240 3117 2935 3548
הכהן הטנא מידך והניחו לפני מזבח יהוה אלהיך׃
.God your | Jehovah | the of altar | before | place and it | from hand your | the basket | the priest

3381 1 6 761 430 3068 6440 559 6030
5 וענית ואמרת לפני יהוה אלהיך ארמי אבד אבי וירד
went he down | my ;father | perish-ing | An Aramean | ,God your | Jehovah | before | say and | you And answer shall

6099 1419 1471 8033 1961 4592 4962 8033 1481 4714
מצרימה ויגר שם במתי מעט ויהי־שם לגוי גדול עצום
mighty | ,great | a nation | there | and became | few a | with men | there | and stayed | ,Egypt to

5656 5414 6031 4713 7489 7227
6 ורב׃ וירעו אתנו המצרים ויענונו ויתנו עלינו עבדה
bondage | us on | put and | and ,us afflicted | ,Egyptians the | with us | dealt and ill | and ;many

3068 8085 1 430 3068 6817 7186
7 קשה׃ ונצעק אל־יהוה אלהי אבתינו וישמע יהוה את־
Jehovah | and heard | our ,fathers | the of God | Jehovah | to | we and cried | ;hard

3318 3906 5999 6040 7200 6963
8 קלנו וירא את־ענינו ואת־עמלנו ואת־לחצנו׃ ויוצאנו
brought and out us | our ;oppression | and | our labor | and | our ,affliction | and saw | our ,voice

1419 4172 5186 2220 2389 3027 4714 3068
יהוה ממצרים ביד חזקה ובזרע נטויה ובמרא גדל
,great | by and terribleness | stretched out | by and arm an | ,mighty | a by hand | Egypt from | Jehovah

5414 4725 935 4159 226
9 ובאתות ובמפתים׃ ויבאנו אל־המקום הזה ויתן־לנו
to has and us given | ,this | place | to | He And us brought has | with and .wonders | with and signs

2009 6258 1706 2461 2100 776 2088 776
10 את־הארץ הזאת ארץ זבת חלב ודבש׃ ועתה הנה
,behold | And ,now | and .honey | milk | flowing | a (with) land | ,this | land

3068 3240 127 6529 7225 935
הבאתי את־ראשית פרי האדמה אשר־נתתה לי יהוה
Jeho-vah | O to .me | have you given | which | the ground | the of fruit | first the of | have I in brought

430 3068 6440 7812 430 3068 6440 5414
והנחתו לפני יהוה אלהיך והשתחוית לפני יהוה אלהיך׃
your ,God | Jehovah | before | bow and yourself | your ,God | Jehovah | before | you And it place shall

1004 430 3068 5414 834 2896 8056
11 ושמחת בכל־הטוב אשר נתן־לך יהוה אלהיך ולביתך
to and ,house your | your ,God | Jehovah | to you | has given | which | good the (things) | in all | and rejoice

6237 3615 7130 834 1616 3881
12 אתה והלוי והגר אשר בקרבך׃ כי תכלה לעשר
tithing | have you finished | When | your in .midst | who (is) | the and alien | the and ,Levite | you

4643 8141 7992 8141 8393 4643 3605
את־כל־מעשר תבואתך בשנה השלישת שנת המעשר
the .tithing | year of | ,third | the in year | your produce | the of tithes | all

8179 398 490 3490 1616 3881 5414
ונתתה ללוי לגר ליתום ולאלמנה ואכלו בשעריך
your inside gates | they that eat may | the and ,widow | the orphan | the ,aliens | the to ,Levite | have and (it) given

6944 1197 430 3068 6440 559 7646
13 ושבעו׃ ואמרת לפני יהוה אלהיך בערתי הקדש מן
from | sacred the (things) | have I consumed | ,God your | Jehovah | before | you then say shall | be and ,filled

things from the house, and also have given them to the Levite, and to the alien, to the orphan, and to the widow, according to all Your command which You have commanded me. I have not transgressed Your commands, and I have not forgotten. 14I have not eaten of it in my mourning; nor have I put *any* of it away for uncleanness; nor have I given of it for the dead. I have listened to the voice of Jehovah my God. I have done according to all that You have commanded me. 15Look down from Your holy habitation, from Heaven, and bless Your people Israel, and the land which You have given to us, as You swore to our fathers, a land flowing with milk and honey.

16Today Jehovah your God commands you to do these statutes and ordinances. You shall take heed to do them with all your heart, and with all your soul. 17You have today declared Jehovah to be your God, and to walk in His ways, and to keep His statutes and His commands, and His judgments, and to pay attention to His voice. 18And Jehovah has declared you today to be His people, a special treasure, as He has spoken to you, and to keep all His commandments. 19And *He will* make you high above all nations that He has made, in praise, and in name, and in glory; and that you may be a holy people to Jehovah your God, as He has spoken.

3605 490 3490 1616 3881 5414 1571 1004
הַבַּיִת וְגַם נְתַתִּיו לַלֵּוִי וְלַגֵּר לַיָּתוֹם וְלָאַלְמָנָה כְּכָל־
according the to and the to to and the to have and the
all to ,widow ,orphan ,alien the Levite them given also ,house
7941 3808 4687 5674 6680 834 4687
מִצְוָתְךָ אֲשֶׁר צִוִּיתָנִי לֹא־עָבַרְתִּי מִמִּצְוֹתֶיךָ וְלֹא שָׁכָחְתִּי׃
have I and Your have I not have You which Your
.forgotten not commands transgressed ;me commanded command
3808 2931 1197 205 398 3808
14 לֹא־אָכַלְתִּי בְאֹנִי מִמֶּנּוּ וְלֹא־בִעַרְתִּי מִמֶּנּוּ בְּטָמֵא וְלֹא־
not and for (any) removed not and ,it of my in have I not
uncleanness it of mourning eaten
3605 6213 430 3068 6963 8085 4191 5414
נָתַתִּי מִמֶּנּוּ לְמֵת שָׁמַעְתִּי בְּקוֹל יְהוָה אֱלֹהָי עָשִׂיתִי כְּכֹל
according have I my Jehovah the to have I the to it of have I
all to done ;God of voice listened ;dead given
1288 8064 6944 4583 8259 6680
15 אֲשֶׁר צִוִּיתָנִי׃ הַשְׁקִיפָה מִמְּעוֹן קָדְשְׁךָ מִן־הַשָּׁמַיִם וּבָרֵךְ
and the from ,holy Your from down Look have You that
bless ,heavens habitation .me commanded
5414 834 127 3478 5971
אֶת־עַמְּךָ אֶת־יִשְׂרָאֵל וְאֵת הָאֲדָמָה אֲשֶׁר נָתַתָּה לָנוּ כַּאֲשֶׁר
as to have you which land the and ,Israel Your
;us given people
3117 1706 2461 2100 176 1 7650
16 נִשְׁבַּעְתָּ לַאֲבֹתֵינוּ אֶרֶץ זָבַת חָלָב וּדְבָשׁ׃ הַיּוֹם הַזֶּה
Today and milk flowing a our to You
honey (with) land ,fathers swore
428 2706 6213 6680 430 3068
יְהוָה אֱלֹהֶיךָ מְצַוְּךָ לַעֲשׂוֹת אֶת־הַחֻקִּים הָאֵלֶּה וְאֶת־
and these statutes do to commands your Jehovah
you God
3605 3824 3605 6213 8104 4941
הַמִּשְׁפָּטִים וְשָׁמַרְתָּ וְעָשִׂיתָ אוֹתָם בְּכָל־לְבָבְךָ וּבְכָל־
with and your with them do to shall you ;judgments
all ,heart all careful be
430 1961 3117 559 3068 5315
17 נַפְשֶׁךָ׃ אֶת־יְהוָה הֶאֱמַרְתָּ הַיּוֹם לִהְיוֹת לְךָ לֵאלֹהִים
,God your to today have You Jehovah your
become declared .soul
8104 4941 4687 2706 8104 1870 3212
וְלָלֶכֶת בִּדְרָכָיו וְלִשְׁמֹר חֻקָּיו וּמִצְוֹתָיו וּמִשְׁפָּטָיו וְלִשְׁמֹעַ
to and His and His and His to and His in to and
listen ,judgments ,commands ,statutes heed ,ways walk
5459 5971 1961 3117 559 3068 6963
18 בְּקֹלוֹ׃ וַיהוָה הֶאֱמִירְךָ הַיּוֹם לִהְיוֹת לוֹ לְעַם סְגֻלָּה כַּאֲשֶׁר
as special a people His to today has And His to
treasure become you declared Jehovah .voice
1471 3605 5945 5414 4687 8104 1696
19 דִּבֶּר־לָךְ וְלִשְׁמֹר כָּל־מִצְוֹתָיו׃ וּלְתִתְּךָ עֶלְיוֹן עַל כָּל־הַגּוֹיִם
nations all above high to and His all to and to has He
you make ;commandments keep ,you spoken
6918 5971 1961 8597 8034 8416 6213
אֲשֶׁר עָשָׂה לִתְהִלָּה וּלְשֵׁם וּלְתִפְאָרֶת וְלִהְיֹתְךָ עַם־קָדֹשׁ
holy a that and in and in and ,praise in has He that
people be may you ;glory name ,made
1696 430 3068
לַיהוָה אֱלֹהֶיךָ כַּאֲשֶׁר דִּבֵּר׃
has He as ,God your to
.spoken Jehovah

CAP. XXVII כז

CHAPTER 27

1And Moses and the elders of Israel commanded the people, saying, Keep all the commands

3605 8104 559 5971 3478 2205 4872 6680
1 וַיְצַו מֹשֶׁה וְזִקְנֵי יִשְׂרָאֵל אֶת־הָעָם לֵאמֹר שָׁמֹר אֶת־כָּל־
all Keep ,saying the Israel the and Moses And
.people of elders commanded

which I *am* commanding
you today, [2]and it shall be in
the day you cross over the
Jordan to the land which
Jehovah your God is giving
to you, that you shall raise
up for yourself great stones,
and plaster them with
plaster. [3]And you shall write
on them all the words of
this law when you have
crossed over, so that you
may go into the land which
Jehovah your God *is* giving
you, a land flowing *with*
milk and honey, as Jehovah
the God of your fathers has
promised you. [4]And it shall
be when you have crossed
over the Jordan, that you
shall set up these stones *as*
to which I am commanding
you today, in Mount Ebal,
and you shall plaster them
with plaster. [5]And you shall
build an altar there to
Jehovah your God, an altar
of stones; you shall not
wield any iron tool on
them; [6]you shall build the
altar of Jehovah your God *of*
uncut stones. And you shall
offer burnt offerings on it to
Jehovah your God. [7]And
you shall offer peace
offerings, and shall eat
there. And you shall rejoice
before Jehovah your God.
[8]And you shall write on the
stones all the words of the
law very plainly.

[9]And Moses and the
priests, the Levites, spoke
to all Israel, saying, Keep
silence, and hear, O Israel:
Today you have become the
people of Jehovah your
God. [10]Therefore you shall
obey the voice of Jehovah
your God and do His
commandments and His
statutes which I command
you today.
[11]And Moses charged
the people the same day,

834 3117 1961 3117 6680 834 4687
2 הַמִּצְוָה אֲשֶׁר אָנֹכִי מְצַוֶּה אֶתְכֶם הַיּוֹם׃ וְהָיָה בַּיּוֹם אֲשֶׁר
(on) which | the in day | it and be shall | ;today | you | (am) | I | which commanding | com- mandments the

5414 430 3068 776 3383 5674
תַּעַבְרוּ אֶת־הַיַּרְדֵּן אֶל־הָאָרֶץ אֲשֶׁר־יְהוָה אֱלֹהֶיךָ נֹתֵן לָךְ
to ,you | is giving | your God | Jehovah | which | the land | to | the Jordan | cross you over

3789 7874 7874 1419 68 6965
3 וַהֲקֵמֹתָ לְךָ אֲבָנִים גְּדֹלוֹת וְשַׂדְתָּ אֹתָם בַּשִּׂיד׃ וְכָתַבְתָּ
you And write shall | with .plaster | them | and plaster | ,great | stones | for yourself | shall you erect

5674 2088 8451 1697 3605
עֲלֵיהֶן אֶת־כָּל־דִּבְרֵי הַתּוֹרָה הַזֹּאת בְּעָבְרֶךָ לְמַעַן אֲשֶׁר
that | order in | you when over cross | this | law | the of words | all | on them

2100 176 5414 430 3068 834 776 935
תָּבֹא אֶל־הָאָרֶץ אֲשֶׁר־יְהוָה אֱלֹהֶיךָ ׀ נֹתֵן לְךָ אֶרֶץ זָבַת
flowing (with) | a land | to ,you | (is) giving | your God | Jehovah | which | the land | into | you go may

1961 430 3068 1696 2461
4 חָלָב וּדְבַשׁ כַּאֲשֶׁר דִּבֶּר יְהוָה אֱלֹהֵי־אֲבֹתֶיךָ לָךְ׃ וְהָיָה
it And be shall | to .you | your fathers | the of God | Jehovah | has spoken | as | and ,honey | milk

834 68 6965 3383 5674
בְּעָבְרְכֶם אֶת־הַיַּרְדֵּן תָּקִימוּ אֶת־הָאֲבָנִים הָאֵלֶּה אֲשֶׁר
(to as) which | ,these | stones | you that up set shall | the ,Jordan | have you when over crossed

7874 7874 5858 2022 3117 6680
אָנֹכִי מְצַוֶּה אֶתְכֶם הַיּוֹם בְּהַר עֵיבָל וְשַׂדְתָּ אוֹתָם בַּשִּׂיד׃
with .plaster | them | you and plaster shall | ,Ebal | in Mount | today | you | am commanding | I

5130 68 4196 430 3068 4196 1129
5 וּבָנִיתָ שָּׁם מִזְבֵּחַ לַיהוָה אֱלֹהֶיךָ מִזְבַּח אֲבָנִים לֹא־תָנִיף
you wield shall | not | ;stones | altar an of | ,God your | to Jehovah | altar an | there | you And build shall

3068 4196 1129 8003 68 1270
6 עֲלֵיהֶם בַּרְזֶל׃ אֲבָנִים שְׁלֵמוֹת תִּבְנֶה אֶת־מִזְבַּח יְהוָה
Jehovah | altar the of | shall you build | uncut | (of) stones | iron any :tool | them on

8002 2076 430 3068 5930 5927 430
7 אֱלֹהֶיךָ וְהַעֲלִיתָ עָלָיו עוֹלֹת לַיהוָה אֱלֹהֶיךָ׃ וְזָבַחְתָּ שְׁלָמִים
peace ,offerings | you And sacrifice shall | your .God | to Jehovah | burnt offerings | it on | you and offer shall | your ;God

5921 3789 430 3068 6440 8056 8033 398
8 וְאָכַלְתָּ שָּׁם וְשָׂמַחְתָּ לִפְנֵי יְהוָה אֱלֹהֶיךָ׃ וְכָתַבְתָּ עַל־
on | you And write shall | .God your | Jehovah | before | , you and rejoice shall | ,there | shall and eat

3190 874 2088 8451 1697 3605 68
הָאֲבָנִים אֶת־כָּל־דִּבְרֵי הַתּוֹרָה הַזֹּאת בַּאֵר הֵיטֵב׃
.very | plainly | this | law | the of words | all | the stones

559 3478 3605 3881 3548 4872 1696
9 וַיְדַבֵּר מֹשֶׁה וְהַכֹּהֲנִים הַלְוִיִּם אֶל־כָּל־יִשְׂרָאֵל לֵאמֹר
,saying | Israel | all | to | the Levitical | the and priests | Moses | And spoke

430 3068 5971 1961 2088 3117 3478 8085 5535
הַסְכֵּת ׀ וּשְׁמַע יִשְׂרָאֵל הַיּוֹם הַזֶּה נִהְיֵיתָ לְעָם לַיהוָה אֱלֹהֶיךָ׃
.God your | to Jehovah | a people | have you become | this | day | O ,Israel | ,hear and | Keep silence

2706 4687 6213 430 3068 6963 8085
10 וְשָׁמַעְתָּ בְּקוֹל יְהוָה אֱלֹהֶיךָ וְעָשִׂיתָ אֶת־מִצְוֹתָו וְאֶת־חֻקָּיו
His statutes | and | His commandments | do and | ,God's your | Jehovah | voice | Therefore heed shall you

3117 5971 4872 6680 3117 6680 834
11 אֲשֶׁר אָנֹכִי מְצַוְּךָ הַיּוֹם׃ וַיְצַו מֹשֶׁה אֶת־הָעָם בַּיּוֹם
on day | the people | Moses | And charged | .today | (am) you commanding | I | which

saying, [12]These shall stand on Mount Gerizim to bless the people when you have crossed over the Jordan: Simeon, and Levi, and Judah, and Issachar, and Joseph, and Benjamin. [13]And these shall stand on Mount Ebal to curse: Reuben, Gad, and Asher, and Zebulun, Dan, and Naphtali. [14]And the Levites shall amswer, and shall say to all the men of Israel with a loud voice:

[15]Cursed *is* the man who makes a carved and molten image, an abomination to Jehovah, the work of a craftsman's hands; and *who* sets *it* up in a secret place! And all the people shall answer and say, Amen!

[16]Cursed *is* he who dishonors his father or his mother! And all the people shall say, Amen!

[17]Cursed *is* he who removes his neighbor's landmark! And all the people shall say, Amen!

[18]Cursed *is* he who makes the blind to wander out of the way! And all the people shall say, Amen!

[19]Cursed *is* he who perverts the judgment of the alien, the fatherless, and widow! And all the people shall say, Amen!

[20]Cursed is he who lies with his father's wife, because he uncovers his father's skirt! And all the people shall say, Amen!

[21]Cursed *is* he who lies with any kind of animal! And all the people shall say, Amen!

[22]Cursed *is* he who lies with his sister, his father's daughter, or his mother's daughter! And all the people shall say, Amen!

[23]Cursed *is* he who lies with his mother-in-law! And all the people shall say, Amen!

[24]Cursed *is* he who strikes his neighbor secretly! And all the people shall say, Amen!

[25]Cursed *is* he who takes a bribe to strike a life, to *shed* innocent blood! And all the people shall say, Amen!

12 ההוא לאמר: אלה יעמדו לברך את־העם על־הר גרזים
Gerizim Mount on the people bless to shall stand These ,saying that same
בעברכם את־הירדן שמעון ולוי ויהודה ויששכר ויוסף
and Joseph and Issachar and Judah and ,Levi ,Simeon ;Jordan the have you when over crossed
13 ובנימן: ואלה יעמדו על־הקללה בהר עיבל ראובן גד
,Gad ,Reuben ;Ebal on Mount curse the for shall stand And these and .Benjamin
14 ואשר וזבולן דן ונפתלי: וענו הלוים ואמרו אל־כל־איש
men of the all to say and the Levites shall answer And .Naphtali and ,Dan Zebulun and ,Asher and
15 ישראל קול רם: ארור האיש אשר יעשה פסל
a carved makes who man the Cursed (is) :loud a voice with Israel
ומסכה תועבת יהוה מעשה ידי חרש ושם בסתר וענו
And answer shall secret a !place in (it) sets and a craftsman's hands the of work —Jehovah to abomination an casted or —image
16 כל־העם ואמרו אמן: ארור מקלה אביו ואמו
his !mother or his father who he dishonors Cursed (is) !Amen ,say and the people all
17 ואמר כל־העם אמן: ארור מסיג גבול רעהו ואמר
shall say And his !neighbor's landmark who he removes Cursed (is) !Amen the ,people all shall say and
18 כל־העם אמן: ארור משגה עור בדרך ואמר
shall say And of out !way the the blind who he makes wander to Cursed (is) !Amen the ,people all
19 כל־העם אמן: ארור מטה משפט גר־יתום
father- ,less the ,alien the of judgment who he perverts Cursed (is) !Amen the ,people all
20 ואלמנה ואמר כל־העם אמן: ארור שכב עם־אשת אביו
his ,father's wife with who he lies Cursed (is) !Amen the ,people all shall say And and !widow
21 כי גלה כנף אביו ואמר כל־העם אמן: ארור שכב
who he lies Cursed (is) !Amen the ,people all shall say And his !father's skirt he uncovers be- cause
22 עם־כל־בהמה ואמר כל־העם אמן: ארור שכב
who he lies Cursed (is) !Amen the ,people all shall say And !animal any with
עם־אחתו בת־אביו או בת־אמו ואמר כל־העם אמן:
!Amen the ,people all shall say And his !mother's daughter or his ,father's daughter his sister with
23 ארור שכב עם־חתנתו ואמר כל־העם אמן:
24 ארור
Cursed (is) !Amen the ,people all shall say And his .mother-in-law with who he lies Cursed (is)
25 מכה רעהו בסתר ואמר כל־העם אמן: ארור
Cursed (is) !Amen the ,people all shall say And !secretly his neighbor who he strikes
לקח שחד להכות נפש דם נקי ואמר כל־העם אמן:
!Amen the ,people all shall say And inno- !cent blood (shed) (to) life a strike to a bribe who he takes

[26]Cursed *is* he who does not confirm all the words of this law, to do them! And all the people shall say, Amen!

CHAPTER 28

[1]And if you shall listen carefully to the voice of Jehovah your God, taking heed to do all His commandments which I command you this day, Jehovah your God shall set you on high above all nations of the earth. [2]And all these blessings shall come on you and overtake you, if you will listen to the voice of Jehovah your God. [3]You shall be blessed in the city, and you shall be blessed in the field. [4]The fruit of your body shall be blessed, and the fruit of your ground, and the fruit of your livestock, the offspring of your oxen, and the young ones of your flock. [5]Your basket and your kneading-trough shall be blessed. [6]You shall be blessed when you come in, and you shall be blessed when you go out.

[7]Jehovah shall cause your enemies that rise up against you to be stricken before your face. They shall come out against you one way, and flee before you seven ways. [8]Jehovah shall command the blessing on you in your storehouses and all that you set your hand *to*. And He shall bless you in the land which Jehovah your God is giving to you. [9]Jehovah shall establish you a holy people to Himself, as He has sworn to you, if you shall keep the commands of Jehovah your God and welcome His ways. [10]And all the people shall see that you are called by the name of Jehovah, and they shall be afraid of you. [11]And Jehovah shall prosper you in goods, in

6213 2088 8451 1697 6965 834 779
26 ארור אשר לא־יקים את דברי התורה־הזאת לעשות
do to ,this law the does not he Cursed
of words out carry who (is)
543 5971/36 05 559
אתם ואמר כל־העם אמן:
!Amen the all And !them
,people say shall

CAP. XXVIII כח

CHAPTER 28

8104 430 3068 6963 8085 8085 518 1961
1 היה אם־שמוע תשמע בקול יהוה אלהיך לשמר
taking ,God your Jehovah the to shall you carefully if it And
heed of voice listen shall be
5414 3117 6680 834 4687 3605 6213
לעשות את־כל־מצותיו אשר אנכי מצוך היום ונתנך
set will this command I which His all do to
you ,day you commandments
3605 5921 935 776 1471 3605 5945 430 3068
2 יהוה אלהיך עליון על כל־גויי הארץ: ובאו עליך כל־
all on And .earth the the all above on God your Jehovah
you come shall of nations ,high
430 3068 6963 8085 5381 428 1293
הברכות האלה והשיגך כי תשמע בקול יהוה אלהיך:
.God your Jehovah the to will you if and these blessings
of voice listen ,you overtake
990 6529 1288 7704 1288 5892 1288
3 ברוך אתה בעיר וברוך אתה בשדה: ברוך פרי־בטנך
4
your fruit The be (shall) the in you be and the in You be
body of blessed .field (shall) blessed city (shall) blessed
6629 6251 504 7698 929 6529 127 6529
ופרי אדמתך ופרי בהמתך שגר אלפיך ועשתרות צאנך:
your the and your the your the and your the and
.flock of ones young ,oxen of offspring ,cattle of fruit ,ground of fruit
1288 935 1288 4860 2935 1288
5 ברוך טנאך ומשארתך: ברוך אתה בבאך וברוך אתה
6
you (shall) and when You be (shall) your and Your be (shall)
blessed be in come you blessed .kneading-trough basket blessed
5061 6965 341 3068 5414 3318
7 בצאתך: יתן יהוה את־איביך הקמים עליך נגפים
be to against rise who your Jehovah shall you when
stricken ,you up enemies up give .out go
5127 1870 7651 3318 259 1870 6440
לפניך בדרך אחד יצאו אליך ובשבעה דרכים ינוסו
will they ways and against they one way by before
flee by seven ,you out come shall ;face your
4916 3605 618 1293 3068 6680/6440
8 לפניך: יצו יהוה אתך את־הברכה באסמיך ובכל משלח
you that all and your in the on Jehovah shall before
set storehouses blessing you command .you
6965 5414 430 3068 834 776 1288 3027
9 ידך וברכך בארץ אשר־יהוה אלהיך נתן לך: יקימך
shall .you to is God your Jehovah which the in shall He your
you establish giving land you bless ;(to) hand
8104 7650 6918 5971 3068
יהוה לו לעם קדוש כאשר נשבע־לך כי תשמר את־
shall you if to has He as ,holy a to Jehovah
keep ,you sworn people ,Himself
776 5971 7200 1870 3212 430 3068 4687
10 מצות יהוה אלהיך והלכת בדרכיו: וראו כל־עמי הארץ
earth the the all And His in walk and your Jehovah the
of peoples see shall .ways God of commands
3068 3498 3372 7121 3068 8034
11 כי שם יהוה נקרא עליך ויראו ממך: והותרך יהוה
Jehovah shall And .you of they and ;you on is Jehovah the that
you prosper afraid be shall named of name

the fruit of your livestock, and in the fruit of your ground in the land which Jehovah swore to your fathers to give you. [12]Jehovah shall open to you His good treasure, the heavens to give the rain to your land in its season, and to bless all the work of your hand. And you shall lend to many nations, but you shall not borrow. [13]And Jehovah shall make you the head, and not the tail. And you shall be only above, and you shall not be beneath; if you heed the commandments of Jehovah your God, which I am commanding you today, to be careful to do *them*. [14]And you shall not turn away from all the words which I am commanding you today, right or left, to go after other gods, to serve them.

[15]And it shall be, if you will not listen to the voice of your God, to take heed to do all His commandments and His statutes which I am commanding you today, that all these curses shall come on you and overtake you:

[16]You shall be cursed in the city, and you shall be cursed in the field.

[17]Your basket and your kneading-trough shall be cursed.

[18]The fruit of your body shall be cursed, and the fruit of your land, the offspring of your oxen, and the young ones of your sheep.

[19]You shall be cursed when you come in, and you shall be cursed when you go out.

[20]Jehovah shall send cursing on you, trouble and rebuke, in all that you set your hand *to*, *all* which you will do, until you are destroyed, or until you quickly perish, because of the badness of your doings *by* which you have forsaken

127 6529 929 6529 990 6529 2896
לְטֹבָה בִּפְרִי בִטְנְךָ וּבִפְרִי בְהֶמְתְּךָ וּבִפְרִי אַדְמָתְךָ עַל
in your in and your the in and your the in ,goods in
,ground of fruit the ,cattle of fruit ,body of fruit

12 6605 5414 1 3068 7650 834 776
הָאֲדָמָה אֲשֶׁר נִשְׁבַּע יְהוָה לַאֲבֹתֶיךָ לָתֶת לָךְ׃ יִפְתַּח
shall ,you give to your to Jehovah swore which land the
open fathers

776/4306 5414 8064 2896 214 3068
יְהוָה לְךָ אֶת־אוֹצָרוֹ הַטּוֹב אֶת־הַשָּׁמַיִם לָתֵת מְטַר־אַרְצְךָ
your the give to the ,good His to Jehovah
land to rain ,heavens treasure you

7227 1471 3867 3027 4639 3605 1288 6256
בְּעִתּוֹ וּלְבָרֵךְ אֵת כָּל־מַעֲשֵׂה יָדֶךָ וְהִלְוִיתָ גּוֹיִם רַבִּים
,many nations you and your the all to and its in
to lend shall ,hand of work bless ,season

13 7535/1961 2180 7218 3068 5414 3867
וְאַתָּה לֹא תִלְוֶה׃ וּנְתָנְךָ יְהוָה לְרֹאשׁ וְלֹא לְזָנָב וְהָיִיתָ רַק
only you and the and head the Jehovah shall And shall not but
be shall ;tail not you make .borrow you

3068 4687 8085 4295 1961 3808 4605
לְמַעְלָה וְלֹא תִהְיֶה לְמָטָּה כִּי־תִשְׁמַע אֶל־מִצְוֹת יְהוָה
Jehovah the to listen you if ;beneath shall you and ,above
of commands be not

14 5493 3808 6213 8104 3117 6680 430
אֱלֹהֶיךָ אֲשֶׁר אָנֹכִי מְצַוְּךָ הַיּוֹם לִשְׁמֹר וְלַעֲשׂוֹת׃ וְלֹא תָסוּר
turn do and do and be to ,today am I which your
away not ,(them) watchful you commanding ,God

8040 3225 3117 6680 834 1697 3605
מִכָּל־הַדְּבָרִים אֲשֶׁר אָנֹכִי מְצַוֶּה אֶתְכֶם הַיּוֹם יָמִין וּשְׂמֹאול
the or the to ,today you am I which words the from
,left right commanding all

5647 312 430 310 3212
לָלֶכֶת אַחֲרֵי אֱלֹהִים אֲחֵרִים לְעָבְדָם׃
serve to ,other gods after go to
,them

15 6213 8104 430 3068 6963 8104 3808 518 1961
וְהָיָה אִם־לֹא תִשְׁמַע בְּקוֹל יְהוָה אֱלֹהֶיךָ לִשְׁמֹר לַעֲשׂוֹת
do to be to your Jehovah the do you not if it And
careful ,God of voice heed ,be shall

935 3117 6680 834 2708 4687 3605
אֶת־כָּל־מִצְוֹתָיו וְחֻקֹּתָיו אֲשֶׁר אָנֹכִי מְצַוְּךָ הַיּוֹם וּבָאוּ
shall that ,today am I which His and His all
come you commanding statutes commands

16 5892 779 5381 428 7045 3605 5921
עָלֶיךָ כָּל־הַקְּלָלוֹת הָאֵלֶּה וְהִשִּׂיגוּךָ׃ אָרוּר אַתָּה בָּעִיר
the in You be (shall) overtake and these curses all upon
,city cursed .you you

17 18 6529 779 4863 2935 779 7704 779
וְאָרוּר אַתָּה בַּשָּׂדֶה׃ אָרוּר טַנְאֲךָ וּמִשְׁאַרְתֶּךָ׃ אָרוּר פְּרִי
The be (shall) your and Your be (shall) the in you (shall) and
of fruit ,cursed .kneading-trough ,basket cursed .field cursed be

19 779 6629 6251 504 7698 127 6529 990
בִטְנְךָ וּפְרִי אַדְמָתֶךָ שְׁגַר אֲלָפֶיךָ וְעַשְׁתְּרֹת צֹאנֶךָ׃ אָרוּר
be (shall) your the and your the ,land your the and your
cursed .sheep of ones young oxen of offering of fruit ,body

20 3068 7971 3318 779 935
אַתָּה בְּבֹאֶךָ וְאָרוּר אַתָּה בְּצֵאתֶךָ׃ יְשַׁלַּח יְהוָה בְּךָ אֶת־
on Jehovah shall you when you (shall) and you when You
you send .out go cursed be ,in come

3027 4916/3605 4045 4163 3994
הַמְּאֵרָה אֶת־הַמְּהוּמָה וְאֶת־הַמִּגְעֶרֶת בְּכָל־מִשְׁלַח יָדְךָ
your you that all in ,rebuke and ,trouble ,cursing
(to) hand set

7455 4118 6 5704 8045 5704 6213 834
אֲשֶׁר תַּעֲשֶׂה עַד הִשָּׁמֶדְךָ וְעַד־אֲבָדְךָ מַהֵר מִפְּנֵי רֹעַ
the because ,quickly you or are you until you will which
bad- of perish until ,destroyed ,do
ness

Me. 21 Jehovah shall make the plague cling to you until He has consumed you from off the land where you are going, to possess it. 22 Jehovah shall strike you with lung disease and with a fever, and with an inflammation, and with extreme burning, and with the sword, and with blasting and mildew. And they shall pursue you until you perish. 23 And your heavens which *are* over your head shall become bronze, and the earth under you iron. 24 Jehovah shall make the rain of your land *be* dust and ashes; it shall come down on you from the heavens until you are destroyed.

25 Jehovah shall cause you to be stricken before your enemies. You shall go out one way against them, and shall flee seven ways before them. And you shall be a trembling to all the kingdoms of the earth. 26 And your body shall be food to all the birds of the heavens, and to the beasts of the earth; and there shall be none to cause them to tremble. 27 Jehovah shall strike you with the ulcer of Egypt, and with hemorrhoids, and with the scab, and with itch, of which you cannot be healed. 28 Jehovah shall strike you with madness, and with blindness, and with astonishment of heart. 29 And you shall grope at noonday as the blind grope in darkness. And you shall not prosper in your ways. And you shall be always oppressed and plundered all the days; and there will be no one to save. 30 You shall betroth a wife, and another shall lie with her. You shall build a house, and you shall not live in it. You shall plant a vineyard, and shall not use its fruit. 31 Your ox *shall be* slaughtered before your eyes, and you shall not eat of it. Your ass *shall be* violently taken away from before you, and it shall not be given back to you. Your sheep *shall be* given to your enemies, and

5704 1698 3068 1692 5800 834 4611
21 מעלליך אשר עזבתני׃ ידבק יהוה בך את־הדבר עד
until the to Jehovah make shall have you (by) your
,plague you cling .Me forsaken which ,doings

3423 8033 935 127 3615
כלתו אתך מעל האדמה אשר־אתה בא־שמה לרשתה׃
to are you where ,land the from you has He
.it possess going off consumed

2719 2746 1816 6920 7829 3068 5221
22 יככה יהוה בשחפת ובקדחת ובדלקת ובחרחר ובחרב
with and with and with and with and with Jehovah shall
sword the ,burning extreme ,inflammation ,fever consumption you strike

5921 834 8064 1961 6 5704 7291 3420 7711
23 ובשדפון ובירקון ורדפוך עד אבדך׃ והיו שמיך אשר על
over which your be- And shall you until they and with and with and
(are) heavens come .perish you chase shall ;mildew ,blasting

3068 5414 1270 8478 834 776 5178 7218
24 ראשך נחשת והארץ אשר־תחתיך ברזל׃ יתן יהוה את־
Jehovah shall ;iron under which the and ,bronze your
give you (is) earth head

8045 5704 3381 8064 6083 80 776 4306
מטר ארצך אבק ועפר מן־השמים ירד עליך עד השמדך׃
are you until on shall it the from and (be) your the
.destroyed you down come heavens ;ashes dust land of rain

3318 259 1870 341 6440 5062 3068 5414
25 יתנך יהוה נגף לפני איביך בדרך אחד תצא אליו
against shall you one way by your before be to Jehovah shall
,them out go ;enemies stricken up you give

4467 8605 2189 1961 6440 5127 1870 7651
ובשבעה דרכים תנוס לפניו והיית לזעוה לכל ממלכות
the all to a you and before you ways and
of kingdoms trembling be shall ;them flee shall seven by

929 8064 5775 3605 3978 5038 1961 776
26 הארץ׃ והיתה נבלתך למאכל לכל־עוף השמים ולבהמת
to and the the all to food your shall and the
of beasts the ;heavens of birds body be ;earth

6076 4714 7822 3068 5221 2729 369 776
27 הארץ ואין מחריד׃ יככה יהוה בשחין מצרים ובעפלים
with and ,Egypt the with Jehovah shall terrifying and ;earth the
,hemorrhoids of ulcer you strike .(them) none be shall there

3068 5221 7495 3201 3808 834 2775 1618
28 ובגרב ובחרס אשר לא־תוכל להרפא׃ יככה יהוה
Jehovah shall .healed be can you not of with and with and
you strike which itch ,scab the

6672 4959 1961 3824 8541 5787 7697
29 בשגעון ובעורון ובתמהון לבב׃ והיית ממשש בצהרים
at grope you And .heart with and with and with
,noonday shall of astonishment ,blindness ,madness

1870 6743 3808 653 5787 4959
כאשר ימשש העור באפלה ולא תצליח את־דרכיך
;ways your shall you and in the gropes as
prosperous make not ;darkness blind

781 802 3462 369 3117 3605 1497 6231 1961
30 והיית אך עשוק וגזול כל־הימים ואין מושיע׃ אשה תארש
shall You a .save to there and ;days the all and op- always you but
,betroth wife one no be will plundered ,pressed be shall

5193 3754 3427 3808 1129 1004 7693 312 376
ואיש אחר ישגלנה בית תבנה ולא־תשב בו כרם תטע
shall you a ;it in you and shall you a lie shall another and
,plant vineyard live shall not ,build house ;her with

2543 398 3808 2873 7794 2490
31 ולא תחללנו׃ שורך טבוח לעיניך ולא תאכל ממנו חמרך
your ;it of shall you and before be (shall) Your use shall and
ass eat not ,eyes your slaughtered ox fruit its not

369 341 5414 6629 7725 3808 6440 1497
גזול מלפניך ולא ישוב לך צאנך נתנות לאיביך ואין לך
you and your to be (shall) your to shall it and before from (shall)
(shall) no ;enemies given sheep ;you be not ,you (be)
(have) returned robbed

there shall be no one to
save you. [32]Your sons and
your daughters *shall be*
given to another people;
and your eyes shall look and
fail for them all the day. And
no power *shall be* in your
hand.

[33]The fruit of your ground,
and all your labor, shall be
eaten up by a nation which
you do not know. And you
shall always be oppressed
and crushed. [34]And you
shall be maddened because
of that which you shall see
with the sight of your eyes.
[35]Jehovah shall strike you
with an evil ulcer on the
knees, and on the legs, of
which you cannot be
healed, from the sole of
your foot even to your
crown.

[36]Jehovah shall cause
you and your king whom
you shall raise up over you,
to go to a nation which you
have not known, you and
your fathers. And you shall
serve other gods there,
wood and stone. [37]And you
shall be an astonishment, a
proverb and a byword
among all the peoples
where Jehovah shall lead
you. [38]You shall carry much
seed out to the field, and
you shall gather in little; for
the locusts will devour it.
[39]You shall plant vineyards,
and shall labor, and you
shall not gather, nor drink
wine; for the worm will
devour it. [40]You shall have
olive trees in all your border,
and you shall not anoint
with oil; for your olive shall
fall off. [41]You shall father
sons and daughters, and
they shall not be with you;
for they shall go into
captivity. [42]The locust shall
possess all your trees and
fruits of your ground. [43]The
alien in your midst shall go
above you, higher *and*
higher; and you shall come
down, lower *and* lower.
[44]He shall lend to you, and
you shall not lend to him.
He shall be the head, and
you shall be the tail. [45]And
all these curses shall come

7200 5869 312 5971 5414 1323 1121 3462
32 מוֹשִׁיעַ׃ בָּנֶיךָ וּבְנֹתֶיךָ נְתֻנִים לְעַם אַחֵר וְעֵינֶיךָ רֹאוֹת
shall look | your eyes and | another people | to | (be shall) given | your daughters and | Your sons | deliverer.

3605 127 6529 3027 410 369 3117/3605 3616
33 וְכָלוֹת אֲלֵיהֶם כָּל־הַיּוֹם וְאֵין לְאֵל יָדֶךָ׃ פְּרִי אַדְמָתְךָ וְכָל־
all and | your ground, | The fruit of | your hand. | to power | and nothing | day the all | them for | fail and

7533 6231 7535 1961 3045 3808 834 5971 398 3018
יְגִיעֲךָ יֹאכַל עַם אֲשֶׁר לֹא־יָדָעְתָּ וְהָיִיתָ רַק עָשׁוּק וְרָצוּץ
and oppressed, crushed | always | you and be shall | do you know; | not | which | a people | be shall eaten | your labor,

7200 5869 4758 7696 1961 3117/3605
34 כָּל־הַיָּמִים׃ וְהָיִיתָ מְשֻׁגָּע מִמַּרְאֵה עֵינֶיךָ אֲשֶׁר תִּרְאֶה׃
shall you see. | what | your eyes, | of because of sight the | maddened | you And be shall | days the all

834 7785 5921 1290 5921 7451 7822 3068 5221
35 יַכְּכָה יְהוָה בִּשְׁחִין רָע עַל־הַבִּרְכַּיִם וְעַל־הַשֹּׁקַיִם אֲשֶׁר
(from) which | legs the, | and on | knees the, | on | evil, | an with boil | Jehovah | shall you strike

3068 3212 6936 5704 7272 3709 7495 3201
36 לֹא־תוּכַל לְהֵרָפֵא מִכַּף רַגְלְךָ וְעַד קָדְקֳדֶךָ׃ יוֹלֵךְ יְהוָה
Jehovah | shall go to cause | your crown. | even to | your foot | the from of sole | be healed; | you can | not

3808 834 1471 5921 6965 4428
אֹתְךָ וְאֶת־מַלְכְּךָ אֲשֶׁר תָּקִים עָלֶיךָ אֶל־גּוֹי אֲשֶׁר לֹא־
not | which | a nation | to | over you | shall you up raise | whom | your king | and | you

68 6086 312 430 8033 5647 1 3045
יָדַעְתָּ אַתָּה וַאֲבֹתֶיךָ וְעָבַדְתָּ שָּׁם אֱלֹהִים אֲחֵרִים עֵץ וָאָבֶן׃
and stone | wood | other, | gods | there | you and serve shall | your fathers or | you, | have you known

5090 5971 3605 8148 4912 8047 1961
37 וְהָיִיתָ לְשַׁמָּה לְמָשָׁל וְלִשְׁנִינָה בְּכֹל הָעַמִּים אֲשֶׁר־יְנַהֶגְךָ
shall you drive | where | the peoples | among all | a and taunt | a proverb, | horror a | you and become shall

2628 622 4592 7704 3318 7227/2233 8033 3068
38 יְהוָה שָׁמָּה׃ זֶרַע רַב תּוֹצִיא הַשָּׂדֶה וּמְעַט תֶּאֱסֹף כִּי יַחְסְלֶנּוּ
shall it devour | for | shall you in gather, | and little | the to field, | shall you out carry | Much seed | Jehovah

3808 8354 3808/3196 5647 5193 3754 697
39 הָאַרְבֶּה׃ כְּרָמִים תִּטַּע וְעָבָדְתָּ וְיַיִן לֹא־תִשְׁתֶּה וְלֹא
and not | shall you drink | not | and wine | and activate | shall you plant | vineyards | the locusts;

1366 3605 1961 2132 8438 398 103
40 תֶאֱגֹר כִּי תֹאכְלֶנּוּ הַתֹּלָעַת׃ זֵיתִים יִהְיוּ לְךָ בְּכָל־גְּבוּלֶךָ
your border, | all in | you shall have | olive trees | the worm; | shall it consume | for | gather,

3808 3205 1323 1121 2132 5394 5480 8081
41 וְשֶׁמֶן לֹא תָסוּךְ כִּי יִשַּׁל זֵיתֶךָ׃ בָּנִים וּבָנוֹת תּוֹלִיד וְלֹא־
and not | shall You beget; | and daughters | sons | your olive. | shall off fall | for | shall you anoint, | not | and oil (with)

3423 127 6529 6086 3605 7628 3212 1961
42 יִהְיוּ לָךְ כִּי יֵלְכוּ בַּשֶּׁבִי׃ כָּל־עֵצְךָ וּפְרִי אַדְמָתֶךָ יְיָרֵשׁ
shall possess | your ground | the and fruits of | your trees | all | into captivity; | they go shall | for | yours, | they be shall

4605 4605 5921 5927 7130 1616 6767
43 הַצְּלָצַל׃ הַגֵּר אֲשֶׁר בְּקִרְבְּךָ יַעֲלֶה עָלֶיךָ מַעְלָה מָּעְלָה
(and) higher, | higher | above you | shall up go | your in midst | who (is) | the alien | the locust;

3867 3808 3867 4295 4295 3381
44 וְאַתָּה תֵרֵד מַטָּה מָּטָּה׃ הוּא יַלְוְךָ וְאַתָּה לֹא תַלְוֶנּוּ
shall lend to him; | not | you and | lend shall to you, | he | (and) lower: | lower | shall come down | you and

3605 935 2180 1961 7218 1961
45 הוּא יִהְיֶה לְרֹאשׁ וְאַתָּה תִּהְיֶה לְזָנָב׃ וּבָאוּ עָלֶיךָ כָּל־
all | you on | And come shall | tail the. | shall become | you and | head the, | shall become | he

on you and shall pursue you
and overtake you, until you
are destroyed; for you did
not listen to the voice of
Jehovah your God, to keep
His commandments and
His statutes which He
commanded you. 46And
they shall be on you for a
sign and for a wonder, and
on your seed forever.
47Because you did not
serve Jehovah your God
with joyfulness and with
gladness of heart for the
abundance of all things,
48you shall serve your
enemies whom Jehovah
shall send on you, in
hunger, and in thirst, and in
nakedness, and in lack of all
things. And He shall put an
iron yoke on your neck until
He has destroyed you.
49Jehovah shall raise a
nation against you from
afar, from the end of the
earth, as the eagle flies; a
nation whose tongue you
will not understand; 50a
nation fierce of face, who
will not regard the person of
the aged, nor show favor *to*
the young. 51And he shall
eat the fruit of your
livestock, and the fruit of
your land, until you are destroyed. *He* shall not leave
to you grain, new wine,
and oil, offspring of your
oxen, or young ones of your
flock, until he has destroyed
you. 52And he shall lay
siege to you in all your
gates, until your high and
fenced walls in which you
are trusting come down, in
all your land; yea, he shall
lay siege to you in all your
gates, in all your land which
Jehovah your God has
given to you. 53And you
shall eat the fruit of your
body, the flesh of your sons
and your daughters whom
Jehovah your God has
given to you, in the siege,
and in the distress with
which your enemies shall
distress you. 54The man
who is tender among you,
and who *is* very delicate, his
eye shall be evil against his

הקללות האלה ורדפוך והשיגוך עד השמדך כי־לא
שמעת בקול יהוה אלהיך לשמר מצותיו וחקתיו אשר
46 47 צוך: והיו בך לאות ולמופת ובזרעך עד־עולם: תחת
אשר לא־עבדת את־יהוה אלהיך בשמחה ובטוב לבב
48 מרב כל: ועבדת את־איביך אשר ישלחנו יהוה בך
ברעב ובצמא ובעירם ובחסר כל ונתן על ברזל על־
49 צוארך עד השמידו אתך: ישא יהוה עליך גוי מרחק
מקצה הארץ כאשר ידאה הנשר גוי אשר לא־תשמע
50 לשנו: גוי עז פנים אשר לא־ישא פנים לזקן ונער לא
51 יחן: ואכל פרי בהמתך ופרי־אדמתך עד השמדך אשר
לא־ישאיר לך דגן תירוש ויצהר שגר אלפיך ועשתרת
52 צאנך עד האבידו אתך: והצר לך בכל־שעריך עד רדת
חמתיך הגבהת והבצרות אשר אתה בטח בהן בכל־
ארצך והצר לך בכל־שעריך בכל־ארצך אשר נתן יהוה
53 אלהיך לך: ואכלת פרי־בטנך בשר בניך ובנתיך אשר
נתן־לך יהוה אלהיך במצור ובמצוק אשר־יציק לך
54 איבך: האיש הרך בך והענג מאד תרע עינו באחיו

brother, and against the wife of his bosom, and against the remnant of his sons which he has left; 55so that he will not give to any of them of the flesh of his sons that he shall eat, because he has nothing left to him in the siege, and in the distress with which your enemies shall distress you in all your gates. 56The tender and delicate woman among you, who would not have ventured to set the sole of her foot on the ground for delicateness and tenderness, her eye shall be evil against the husband of her bosom, and against her son, and against her daughter; 57and against her fetus which comes out from between her feet, even against her sons whom she shall bear. For she shall eat them in secret, for the lack of everything in the siege and in the distress with which the enemy shall distress you within your gates.

58If you will not take heed to do all the words of this law which are written in this book, to fear this glorious and fearful Name, Jehovah your God, 59then Jehovah will make your plagues remarkable, and the plagues of your children *shall be* great and persistent plagues, with evil and long-lasting sicknesses. 60He shall also bring on you all the diseases of Egypt, of which you were afraid; and they shall cling to you. 61Also every sickness and every plague which is not written in the book of this law, Jehovah shall cause them to come on you until you are destroyed. 62And you shall be left few in number, whereas you were as the stars of the heavens for multitude, because you would not obey the voice of Jehovah your God. 63And it shall be, as Jehovah rejoiced over you to do you good, and to multiply you,

55 וּבְאֵשֶׁת חֵיקוֹ וּבְיֶתֶר בָּנָיו אֲשֶׁר יוֹתִיר׃ מִתֵּת ׀ לְאַחַד
מֵהֶם מִבְּשַׂר בָּנָיו אֲשֶׁר יֹאכֵל מִבְּלִי הִשְׁאִיר־לוֹ כֹּל
בְּמָצוֹר וּבְמָצוֹק אֲשֶׁר יָצִיק לְךָ אֹיִבְךָ בְּכָל־שְׁעָרֶיךָ׃
56 הָרַכָּה בְךָ וְהָעֲנֻגָּה אֲשֶׁר לֹא־נִסְּתָה כַף־רַגְלָהּ הַצֵּג עַל־
הָאָרֶץ מֵהִתְעַנֵּג וּמֵרֹךְ תֵּרַע עֵינָהּ בְּאִישׁ חֵיקָהּ וּבִבְנָהּ
57 וּבְבִתָּהּ׃ וּבְשִׁלְיָתָהּ הַיּוֹצֵת ׀ מִבֵּין רַגְלֶיהָ וּבְבָנֶיהָ אֲשֶׁר
תֵּלֵד כִּי־תֹאכְלֵם בְּחֹסֶר־כֹּל בַּסָּתֶר בְּמָצוֹר וּבְמָצוֹק אֲשֶׁר
58 יָצִיק לְךָ אֹיִבְךָ בִּשְׁעָרֶיךָ׃ אִם־לֹא תִשְׁמֹר לַעֲשׂוֹת אֶת־
כָּל־דִּבְרֵי הַתּוֹרָה הַזֹּאת הַכְּתֻבִים בַּסֵּפֶר הַזֶּה לְיִרְאָה
59 אֶת־הַשֵּׁם הַנִּכְבָּד וְהַנּוֹרָא הַזֶּה אֵת יְהוָה אֱלֹהֶיךָ׃ וְהִפְלָא
יְהוָה אֶת־מַכֹּתְךָ וְאֵת מַכּוֹת זַרְעֶךָ מַכּוֹת גְּדֹלֹת וְנֶאֱמָנוֹת
60 וָחֳלָיִם רָעִים וְנֶאֱמָנִים׃ וְהֵשִׁיב בְּךָ אֵת כָּל־מַדְוֵה מִצְרַיִם
61 אֲשֶׁר יָגֹרְתָּ מִפְּנֵיהֶם וְדָבְקוּ בָּךְ׃ גַּם כָּל־חֳלִי וְכָל־מַכָּה
אֲשֶׁר לֹא כָתוּב בְּסֵפֶר הַתּוֹרָה הַזֹּאת יַעְלֵם יְהוָה עָלֶיךָ
62 עַד הִשָּׁמְדָךְ׃ וְנִשְׁאַרְתֶּם בִּמְתֵי מְעָט תַּחַת אֲשֶׁר הֱיִיתֶם
כְּכוֹכְבֵי הַשָּׁמַיִם לָרֹב כִּי־לֹא שָׁמַעְתָּ בְּקוֹל יְהוָה אֱלֹהֶיךָ׃
63 וְהָיָה כַּאֲשֶׁר־שָׂשׂ יְהוָה עֲלֵיכֶם לְהֵיטִיב אֶתְכֶם וּלְהַרְבּוֹת

so Jehovah shall rejoice over you to destroy you, and to lay you waste. And you shall be plucked from the land you are going to possess.

64 And Jehovah shall scatter you among all people, from *one* end of the earth even to the *other*, and you shall serve other gods there—wood and stone—which you have not known, nor your fathers. 65 And among these nations you shall find no ease, nor shall the sole of your foot have rest. But Jehovah shall give you there a trembling heart and failing of eyes, and sorrow of mind. 66 And your life shall hang in doubt before you, and you shall fear day and night, and shall have no assurance of your life. 67 In the morning you shall say, O that it were evening! And in the evening you shall say, O that it were morning! For the fear of your heart with which you fear, and for the sight of your eyes which you shall see. 68 And Jehovah shall bring you into Egypt again with ships, by the way of which I said to you, You shall never see it again. And you shall be sold to your enemies there, for male slaves and slave-girls; and there shall be no buyer.

אֶתְכֶם כֵּן יָשִׂישׂ יְהוָה עֲלֵיכֶם לְהַאֲבִיד אֶתְכֶם וּלְהַשְׁמִיד
אֶתְכֶם וְנִסַּחְתֶּם מֵעַל הָאֲדָמָה אֲשֶׁר־אַתָּה בָא־שָׁמָּה
64 לְרִשְׁתָּהּ׃ וֶהֱפִיצְךָ יְהוָה בְּכָל־הָעַמִּים מִקְצֵה הָאָרֶץ וְעַד
קְצֵה הָאָרֶץ וְעָבַדְתָּ שָּׁם אֱלֹהִים אֲחֵרִים אֲשֶׁר לֹא־יָדַעְתָּ
65 אַתָּה וַאֲבֹתֶיךָ עֵץ וָאָבֶן׃ וּבַגּוֹיִם הָהֵם לֹא תַרְגִּיעַ וְלֹא־
יִהְיֶה מָנוֹחַ לְכַף־רַגְלֶךָ וְנָתַן יְהוָה לְךָ שָׁם לֵב רַגָּז וְכִלְיוֹן
66 עֵינַיִם וְדַאֲבוֹן נָפֶשׁ׃ וְהָיוּ חַיֶּיךָ תְּלֻאִים לְךָ מִנֶּגֶד וּפָחַדְתָּ
67 לַיְלָה וְיוֹמָם וְלֹא תַאֲמִין בְּחַיֶּיךָ׃ בַּבֹּקֶר תֹּאמַר מִי־יִתֵּן
עֶרֶב וּבָעֶרֶב תֹּאמַר מִי־יִתֵּן בֹּקֶר מִפַּחַד לְבָבְךָ אֲשֶׁר
68 תִּפְחָד וּמִמַּרְאֵה עֵינֶיךָ אֲשֶׁר תִּרְאֶה׃ וֶהֱשִׁיבְךָ יְהוָה מִצְרַיִם
בָּאֳנִיּוֹת בַּדֶּרֶךְ אֲשֶׁר אָמַרְתִּי לְךָ לֹא־תֹסִיף עוֹד לִרְאֹתָהּ
וְהִתְמַכַּרְתֶּם שָׁם לְאֹיְבֶיךָ לַעֲבָדִים וְלִשְׁפָחוֹת וְאֵין קֹנֶה׃

CHAPTER 29

1 These are the words of the covenant which Jehovah commanded Moses to make with the sons of Israel in the land of Moab, besides the covenant which He made with them in Horeb.

69 ס אֵלֶּה דִבְרֵי הַבְּרִית אֲשֶׁר־צִוָּה יְהוָה אֶת־מֹשֶׁה לִכְרֹת
אֶת־בְּנֵי יִשְׂרָאֵל בְּאֶרֶץ מוֹאָב מִלְּבַד הַבְּרִית אֲשֶׁר־כָּרַת
אִתָּם בְּחֹרֵב׃

CAP. XXIX כט

CHAPTER 29

2 And Moses called to all Israel, and said to them, You have seen all that

1 וַיִּקְרָא מֹשֶׁה אֶל־כָּל־יִשְׂרָאֵל וַיֹּאמֶר אֲלֵהֶם אַתֶּם רְאִיתֶם

Jehovah did before your eyes in the land of Egypt, to Pharaoh and to all his servants, and to all his land. [3]Your eyes have seen the great trials, the signs, and those great miracles

[4]Yet Jehovah has not given to you a heart to know, and eyes to see, and ears to hear, until this day. [5]And I have led you forty years in the wilderness; your garments have not worn out from off you, and your sandal has not worn away off your foot. [6]You have not eaten bread, and you have not drunk wine or strong drink, so that you might know that I *am* Jehovah your God. [7]And you came into this place, and Sihon the king of Heshbon, and Og the king of Bashan, came out to meet us, to battle. And we struck them, [8]and took their land, and gave it for an inheritance to the Reubenites, and to the Gadites, and for the half tribe of Manasseh. [9]Then pay attention to the words of this covenant, and do them, that you may act wisely *in* all that you do.

[10]You are standing today, all of you, before Jehovah your God; your rulers, your tribes, your elders, and your officers, every man of Israel; [11]your little ones, your wives, and your alien who *is* in the midst of your camps, from the woodchopper to the one drawing your water; [12]so that you should enter into the covenant of Jehovah your God, and into His oath, which Jehovah your God is making with you today; [13]so that He may establish you today for a

6547 4714 776 5869 3068 6213 834 3605
את כל־אשר עשה יהוה לעיניכם בארץ מצרים לפרעה
to Pharaoh ,Egypt the in of land before eyes your Jehovah did that all

2 7200 834 1419 4531 776 3605 5650 3605
ולכל־עבדיו ולכל־ארצו׃ המסות הגדלת אשר ראו
have seen which great trials the his ;land all to and his servants all to and

3 3068 5414 1419 4159 226 5869
עיניך האתת והמפתים הגדלים ההם׃ ולא־נתן יהוה
Jehovah has given ,yet not ;those great and miracles the signs your ,eyes

3117 5704 8085 241 7200 5869 3045 3820
לכם לב לדעת ועינים לראות ואזנים לשמע עד היום
day until ,hear to ears and ,see to eyes and to ,know a heart you

4 1086 4057 8141 703 3212 2088
הזה׃ ואולך אתכם ארבעים שנה במדבר לא־בלו
has out worn not the in ;wilderness years forty you have led ! .this

5 3899 7272 1086 5275 8008
שלמתיכם מעליכם ונעלך לא־בלתה מעל רגלך׃ לחם
bread your .foot off worn away has not and sandal your you off your clothing

3045 8354 3808 7941 3196 398 3808
לא אכלתם ויין ושכר לא שתיתם למען תדעו כי אני
I (am) that know might you that so have you ,drunk not and drink strong wine and have You ,eaten not

6 4428 5511 3318 2088 4725 935 430 3068
יהוה אלהיכם׃ ותבאו אל־המקום הזה ויצא סיחן מלך
king of Sihon and out came ,this place into you And came .God your Jehovah

7 3947 5221 4421 7125 1316 4428 5747 2809
חשבון ועוג מלך־הבשן לקראתנו למלחמה ונכם׃ ונקח
and took we and ,them struck ;battle for meet to us Bashan king of and Og Heshbon

7626 2677 1425 7206 5159 5414 776
את־ארצם ונתנה לנחלה לראובני ולגדי ולחצי שבט
tribe of for and half the to and ,Gadites the the to ,Reubenites an for inheritance and it gave ,land that

8 6213 2088 1285 1697 8104 4520
המנשי׃ ושמרתם את־דברי הברית הזאת ועשיתם אתם
,them do and ,this covenant the of words Therefore to heed take .Manasseh

6213 834 3605 7919
למען תשכילו את כל־אשר תעשון׃
.do you that (in) all may you wisely act that

9 8269 430 3068 6440 3605 3117 5324
אתם נצבים היום כלכם לפני יהוה אלהיכם ראשיכם
,rulers your ;God your Jehovah before of all ,you ,today are standing You

10 2945 3478 376 3605 7860 2205 7626
שבטיכם זקניכם ושטריכם כל איש ישראל׃ טפכם
little your ,ones ;Israel of man every your and officers your elders your tribes

7579 5704 6086 2404 4264 7130 834 1616 802
נשיכם וגרך אשר בקרב מחניך מחטב עציך עד שאב
one the drawing to your wood the from cutting one your ,camps the in of middle who (is) your and alien your ,wives

11 3068 834 423 430 3068 1285 5674 4325
מימיך׃ לעברך בברית יהוה אלהיך ובאלתו אשר יהוה
Jehovah which into and .oath His your ,God Jehovah the into of covenant that so enter you your ;water

12 3117 6965 3117 3772 430
אלהיך כרת עמך היום׃ למען הקים־אתך היום לו
to Himself today you may He establish that so ;today with you is cutting your God

people to Himself, and He Himself be your God, as He has spoken to you, and as He has sworn to your fathers, to Abraham, to Isaac, and to Jacob. [14]And I am not making this covenant and this oath with you alone, [15]but with him who stands here with us today before Jehovah your God; and also with him that is not here with us today. [16]For you know how we lived in the land of Egypt, and how we came through the nations through which you passed. [17]And you have seen their detestable things, and their idols *of* wood and stone, silver and gold, which were among them; [18]that there not be among you man, or woman, or family, or tribe, whose heart turns away today from Jehovah our God, to go and serve the gods of these nations; lest there should be among you today a root that bears gall and wormwood; [19]and it happens when he hears the words of this curse, that he should bless himself in his heart, saying, I shall have peace, even though I walk in the stubbornness of my heart, to snatch away the sated with the thirsty. [20]Jehovah will not be willing to forgive him, for then Jehovah's anger shall smoke, and His zeal *shall be* against that man, and all the curses written in this book shall lie upon him. And Jehovah shall blot out his name from under the heavens. [21]And Jehovah shall set him apart to evil, out of all the tribes of Israel, according to all the curses of the covenant that are written in this

1696 430 1961 5971
לְעָם וְהוּא יִהְיֶה־לְּךָ לֵאלֹהִים כַּאֲשֶׁר דִּבֶּר־לָךְ וְכַאֲשֶׁר
as and | to you has He spoken | as | ,God | your | He be may | and Himself | a for ,people

3808 3290 3327 85 1 7650
13 נִשְׁבַּע לַאֲבֹתֶיךָ לְאַבְרָהָם לְיִצְחָק וּלְיַעֲקֹב׃ וְלֹא אִתְּכֶם
with you | And not | to and Jacob | ,Isaac to | ,Abraham to | your to fathers | has He sworn

2088 422 2088 1285 3772 905
לְבַדְּכֶם אָנֹכִי כֹּרֵת אֶת־הַבְּרִית הַזֹּאת וְאֶת־הָאָלָה הַזֹּאת׃
,this | oath | and | this | covenant | am cutting | I | alone

430 3068 6440 3117 5975 3426
14 כִּי אֶת־אֲשֶׁר יֶשְׁנוֹ פֹּה עִמָּנוּ עֹמֵד הַיּוֹם לִפְנֵי יְהוָה אֱלֹהֵינוּ
,God our Jehovah before today stand-ing | with us | here | is | him who | with but

3045 3117 834
15 וְאֵת אֲשֶׁר אֵינֶנּוּ פֹּה עִמָּנוּ הַיּוֹם׃ כִּי־אַתֶּם יְדַעְתֶּם אֵת אֲשֶׁר־
how | know | you | for | ;today | with us | here | is not | him who | also and with

834 1471 7130 5674 4714 776 3427
יָשַׁבְנוּ בְּאֶרֶץ מִצְרָיִם וְאֵת אֲשֶׁר־עָבַרְנוּ בְּקֶרֶב הַגּוֹיִם אֲשֶׁר
which | the nations | through | we came | how | and | ,Egypt | the in of land | we lived

68 6086 1544 8251 7200 5674
16 עֲבַרְתֶּם׃ וַתִּרְאוּ אֶת־שִׁקּוּצֵיהֶם וְאֵת גִּלֻּלֵיהֶם עֵץ וָאֶבֶן
and ,stone | of wood | ,idols their | even | their things detestable | you and seen have | passed you ;through

802 376 3426 834 2091 3701
17 כֶּסֶף וְזָהָב אֲשֶׁר עִמָּהֶם׃ פֶּן־יֵשׁ בָּכֶם אִישׁ אוֹ־אִשָּׁה אוֹ
or | ,woman or | ,man | among you | there be should lest | among ;them | which (were) | and ,gold | silver

3068 3117 6437 3824 7626 4940
מִשְׁפָּחָה אוֹ־שֵׁבֶט אֲשֶׁר לְבָבוֹ פֹנֶה הַיּוֹם מֵעִם יְהוָה
Jehovah from | today | turns away | heart | whose | ,tribe or | ,family

3426 1471 430 5647 3212 430
אֱלֹהֵינוּ לָלֶכֶת לַעֲבֹד אֶת־אֱלֹהֵי הַגּוֹיִם הָהֵם פֶּן־יֵשׁ בָּכֶם
among you | there be should lest | ;those | nations | the of gods | (and) serve | go to | God our

422 1697 8085 1961 3939 7219 6509 8328
18 שֹׁרֶשׁ פֹּרֶה רֹאשׁ וְלַעֲנָה׃ וְהָיָה בְּשָׁמְעוֹ אֶת־דִּבְרֵי הָאָלָה
curse | the of words | when hears he | it and ,happens | and ;wormwood | gall | that bears | root a

3588 1961 7965 559 3824 1288 2088
הַזֹּאת וְהִתְבָּרֵךְ בִּלְבָבוֹ לֵאמֹר שָׁלוֹם יִהְיֶה־לִּי כִּי
though ,I | shall have | peace | ,saying | his in ,heart | he that himself bless should | ,this

6771 7302 5595 3212 3820 8307
בִּשְׁרִרוּת לִבִּי אֵלֵךְ לְמַעַן סְפוֹת הָרָוָה אֶת־הַצְּמֵאָה׃
;thirsty the with | the drunken | snatch away | to | ,walk I | my | the in heart of stubbornness

7068 3068 639 6225 5545 3068 14 3808
19 לֹא־יֹאבֶה יְהוָה סְלֹחַ לוֹ כִּי אָז יֶעְשַׁן אַף־יְהוָה וְקִנְאָתוֹ
His and zeal | ,Jehovah the of anger | shall smoke | then | for ,him | to forgive | Jehovah | be will willing | not

2088 5612 5789 422 3605 7257 376
בָּאִישׁ הַהוּא וְרָבְצָה בּוֹ כָּל־הָאָלָה הַכְּתוּבָה בַּסֵּפֶר הַזֶּה
;this | book in | are that written | the curses | all | upon him | shall and lie | ,that | against man

3068 914 8064 8478 8034 3068 4229
20 וּמָחָה יְהוָה אֶת־שְׁמוֹ מִתַּחַת הַשָּׁמָיִם׃ וְהִבְדִּילוֹ יְהוָה
Jehovah | shall And apart him set | .heavens the | from under | name his | Jehovah | shall and out blot

3789 1285 423 3605 3478 7626 3605 7451
לְרָעָה מִכֹּל שִׁבְטֵי יִשְׂרָאֵל כְּכֹל אָלוֹת הַבְּרִית הַכְּתוּבָה
is which written | the covenant | the of curses | according all to | ,Israel | the of tribes | of out all | unto evil

book of the law; [22]so that the generation to come, your sons who rise after you, and the foreigner who comes in from a distant land, shall say when they see the plagues of that land, and its sicknesses which Jehovah shall send into it— [23]the whole land shall be burned *with* brimstone and salt; it shall not be sown, nor shall it sprout; nor shall there be any herb in it. It *shall be like* the overthrow of Sodom and Gomorrah, Admah and Zeboim, which Jehovah overthrew in His anger and in His fury— [24]yes, all the nations shall say, Why has Jehovah done this to this land? *For* what *is* the heat of this great anger? [25]Then *men* shall say, Because they have forsaken the covenant of Jehovah, the God of their fathers, which He made with them when He brought them out of the land of Egypt. [26]For they went and served other gods, and worshiped them, gods which they did not know, and who had not given to them any portion.

[27]And the anger of Jehovah was kindled against this land, to bring on it all the curses that are written in this book. [28]And Jehovah rooted them out of their land in anger and wrath, and in great indignation, and cast them into another land, as it is today.

[29]The secret things *belong* to Jehovah our God; and the things revealed *belong* to us and to our sons forever, that we may do all the words of this law.

834 1121 314 1755 559 2088 8451 5612
21 ספר התורה הזה׃ ואמר הדור האחרון בניכם אשר
who sons your ,come to the generation that so say shall ,this Law the in of Book

7200 7350 776 935 5237 310 6965
יקומו מאחריכם והנכרי אשר יבא מארץ רחוקה וראו
when see they ,distant a from land comes in who the and foreigner ,you after rise

3068 7971 834 2471 8463 776 4347
את־מכות הארץ ההוא ואת־תחלאיה אשר־חלה יהוה
Jehovah shall send which its sicknesses and ,that land the of plagues

3808 2232 3808 776 3605 8316 4417 1614
22 בה׃ גפרית ומלח שרפה כל־ארצה לא תזרע ולא
nor shall it ,sown be not ,land whole the be shall burned and salt (with) brimstone into —it

6779 5927 3808 6212 3605 4114 5467 6017
תצמח ולא־יעלה בה כל־עשב כמהפכת סדם ועמרה
and ,Gomorrah Sodom of overthrow (be shall it) the like ;herb any it in shall up come nor ,sprout

126 6636 834 2015 3068 639 2534 559
23 אדמה וצביים אשר הפך יהוה באפו ובחמתו׃ ואמרו
shall yes say His in fury and His in anger Jehovah over- threw which and ,Zeboim Admah

3605 1471 5921 4100 6213 3068 3602 776 2063 4100 2750
כל־הגוים על־מה עשה יהוה ככה לארץ הזאת מה חרי
heat (for) of (is) what ?this land to this Jehovah has done Why the nations all

639 1419 2088 559 5921 834 5800 1285 3068
24 האף הגדול הזה׃ ואמרו על אשר עזבו את־ברית יהוה
Jehovah the of covenant have they forsaken Because shall Then say ?this great the anger

430 1 834 3772 5973 3318 853 776
אלהי אבתם אשר כרת עמם בהוציאו אתם מארץ
the from of land them He when out brought with them cut He which their ,fathers the of God

4714 3212 5647 430 312 7812
25 מצרים׃ וילכו ויעבדו אלהים אחרים וישתחוו להם
,them and worshiped other gods and served they For went .Egypt

430 834 3808 3045 3808 2505 2734 639 3068
26 אלהים אשר לא־ידעום ולא חלק להם׃ ויחר־אף יהוה
Jehovah the of anger And glowed to .them had who not given any portion did they not know whom gods

776 935 3605 7045 3789
בארץ ההוא להביא עליה את־כל־הקללה הכתובה
is that written curse every it on bring to ,that against land

5612 2088 5428 3068 127 631 2534
27 בספר הזה׃ ויתשם יהוה מעל אדמתם באף ובחמה
and ,wrath anger in land their of Jehovah And out them rooted .this book in

7110 1419 7993 776 312 3117 1961 5640
28 ובקצף גדול וישלכם אל־ארץ אחרת כיום הזה׃ הנסתרת
secret The things (is it) as .today ,another land into cast and them ,great in and indignation

3068 430 1540 1121 5769 6213
ליהוה אלהינו והנגלת לנו ולבנינו עד־עולם לעשות
(we) that do may ;forever to and sons our to us the and revealed things ;God our to (belong) Jehovah

3605 1697 8451 2088
את־כל־דברי התורה הזאת׃
.this law the of words all

CHAPTER 30

[1]And it shall be when all
these things have come on
you, the blessing and the
curse which I have set
before you; and among all
the nations where Jehovah
your God shall drive you,
you shall bring back to your
heart *these things*; [2]and
shall turn back to Jehovah
your God and listen to His
voice, according to all that I
am commanding you today,
you and your sons with all
your heart, and with all your
soul; [3]then Jehovah your
God will turn your captivity,
and He will have pity on
you, and will return and
gather you from all the
nations where Jehovah
your God has scattered you.
[4]If you are cast out to the
end of the heavens,
Jehovah your God shall
gather you from there, and
He shall take you from
there. [5]And Jehovah your
God shall bring you into the
land which your fathers
have possessed, and you
shall inherit it; and He shall
do you good and multiply
you above your fathers.
[6]And Jehovah your God will
circumcise your heart, and
the heart of your seed, to
love Jehovah your God with
all your heart, and with all
your soul, that you may live.
[7]And Jehovah your God will
put all these curses on your
enemies, and on those that
hate you, who have perse-
cuted you. [8]And you shall
return and obey the voice of
Jehovah, and do all His
commandments which I
am commanding you today.
[9]And Jehovah your God will
make you abundant in every
work of your hand, in the
fruit of your body, and in the
fruit of your livestock, and in
the fruit of your ground, for
good. For Jehovah will

CAP. XXX ל

CHAPTER 30

7045 1293 428 1697 3605 5921 935 1961
1 וְהָיָה כִי־יָבֹאוּ עָלֶיךָ כָּל־הַדְּבָרִים הָאֵלֶּה הַבְּרָכָה וְהַקְּלָלָה
the and the ,these things all upon have when it And
curse blessing you come ,be shall
834 1471 3605 3824 7725 6440 5414 834
אֲשֶׁר נָתַתִּי לְפָנֶיךָ וַהֲשֵׁבֹתָ אֶל־לְבָבֶךָ בְּכָל־הַגּוֹיִם אֲשֶׁר
which the among your to you and before have I which
nations all ,(them) heart back bring ,you set
430 3068 7725 8033 430 3068 5080
2 הִדִּיחֲךָ יְהוָה אֱלֹהֶיךָ שָׁמָּה׃ וְשַׁבְתָּ עַד־יְהוָה אֱלֹהֶיךָ
your Jehovah to shall And to your Jehovah shall
God back turn .there God you banish
1121 3117 6680 3605 6963 8085
וְשָׁמַעְתָּ בְקֹלוֹ כְּכֹל אֲשֶׁר־אָנֹכִי מְצַוְּךָ הַיּוֹם אַתָּה וּבָנֶיךָ
and you ,today com- I that according His to and
,sons your you manding (am) all to ,voice listen
7622 430 3068 7725 5315 3605 3824 3605
3 בְּכָל־לְבָבְךָ וּבְכָל־נַפְשֶׁךָ׃ וְשָׁב יְהוָה אֱלֹהֶיךָ אֶת־שְׁבוּתְךָ
your your Jehovah then your and your with
;captivity God turn will ;soul all with heart all
3068 6327 834 5971 3605 6908 7725 7355
וְרִחֲמֶךָ וְשָׁב וְקִבֶּצְךָ מִכָּל־הָעַמִּים אֲשֶׁר הֱפִיצְךָ יְהוָה
Jehovah has which the from and and will He and
you scattered nations all you gather return you pity
8033 8064 7097 5080 1961 8033 430
4 אֱלֹהֶיךָ שָׁמָּה׃ אִם־יִהְיֶה נִדַּחֲךָ בִּקְצֵה הַשָּׁמָיִם מִשָּׁם
from the the at out- your should If to your
there heavens of end casts be .there God
430 3068 935 3947 430 3068 6908
5 יְקַבֶּצְךָ יְהוָה אֱלֹהֶיךָ וּמִשָּׁם יִקָּחֶךָ׃ וֶהֱבִיאֲךָ יְהוָה אֱלֹהֶיךָ
your Jehovah shall and shall He from and your Jehovah gather shall
God you bring ,you take there God you
7235 3190 3423 1 3423 776
אֶל־הָאָרֶץ אֲשֶׁר־יָרְשׁוּ אֲבֹתֶיךָ וִירִשְׁתָּהּ וְהֵיטִבְךָ וְהִרְבְּךָ
mul- and will He and will you so your possessed which the into
you tiply good you do ,it possess ,fathers land
2233 3824 3824 430 3068 4135 1
6 מֵאֲבֹתֶיךָ׃ וּמָל יְהוָה אֱלֹהֶיךָ אֶת־לְבָבְךָ וְאֶת־לְבַב זַרְעֶךָ
your the and your your Jehovah will And than more
,seed of heart heart God circumcise .fathers your
5315 3605 3824 3605 430 3068 157
לְאַהֲבָה אֶת־יְהוָה אֱלֹהֶיךָ בְּכָל־לְבָבְךָ וּבְכָל־נַפְשְׁךָ לְמַעַן
so your and your with your Jehovah love to
that ,soul all with ,heart all God
5921 428 423 3605 430 3068 5414 2416
7 חַיֶּיךָ׃ וְנָתַן יְהוָה אֱלֹהֶיךָ אֵת כָּל־הָאָלוֹת הָאֵלֶּה עַל־
on these curses all your Jehovah And may you
God put will .live
8104 7725 7291 8130 5921 341
8 אֹיְבֶיךָ וְעַל־שֹׂנְאֶיךָ אֲשֶׁר רְדָפוּךָ׃ וְאַתָּה תָשׁוּב וְשָׁמַעְתָּ
and shall and have who those on and your
heed return you ;you persecuted ,you hating ,enemies
6680 834 4687 3605 6213 3068 6963
בְּקוֹל יְהוָה וְעָשִׂיתָ אֶת־כָּל־מִצְוֹתָיו אֲשֶׁר אָנֹכִי מְצַוְּךָ
command- I which com- His all do and ,Jehovah the
you ing (am) mandments of voice
6529 3027 4639 3605 430 3068 3498 3117
9 הַיּוֹם׃ וְהוֹתִירְךָ יְהוָה אֱלֹהֶיךָ בְּכֹל מַעֲשֵׂה יָדֶךָ בִּפְרִי
the your work in your Jehovah make will and ;today
of fruit ,hand of every God abundant you
7725 2896 127 6529 929 6529 990
בִטְנְךָ וּבִפְרִי בְהֶמְתְּךָ וּבִפְרִי אַדְמָתְךָ לְטֹבָה כִּי יָשׁוּב
will for for your the and your the and your
again ;good ,ground of fruit cattle of fruit womb

again rejoice over you for good, as He rejoiced over your fathers. 10For you shall listen to the voice of Jehovah your God, to keep His commandments and His statutes which are written in the book of this law. For you shall turn back toward Jehovah your God, with all your heart and with all your soul.

11For this command which I *am* command-ing you today *is* not too wonderful for you, nor *is* it too far off. 12It *is* not in the heavens *that you should* say, Who shall go up into the heavens for us, and bring it to us, and cause us to hear it, that we may do it? 13And it *is* not beyond the sea *that you should* say, Who shall cross over for us to the region beyond the sea and take it for us, and cause us to hear it, that we may do it? 14For the word *is* very near to you, in your mouth and in your heart, that you may do it.

15Behold, I have set before you today life and good, and death and evil,

16in that I *am* commanding you today to love Jehovah your God, to walk in His ways, and to keep His commands and His statutes, and His judgments, and you shall live and multiply, and Jehovah your God shall bless you in the land where you are going in, to possess it. 17But if you turn away your heart, and you do not listen, and are drawn on, even *you will* bow down to other gods, and serve them; 18I have declared to you today that you shall certainly perish. You shall not prolong *your* days in the land to which you are

1 7797 2896 5921 7797 3068
10 יְהוָה לָשׂוּשׂ עָלֶיךָ לְטוֹב כַּאֲשֶׁר־שָׂשׂ עַל־אֲבֹתֶיךָ׃ כִּי
for your over He as for over rejoice Jehovah
;fathers rejoiced good you

37 89 2708 4187 8104 430 3068 6963 8085
תִשְׁמַע בְּקוֹל יְהוָה אֱלֹהֶיךָ לִשְׁמֹר מִצְוֹתָיו וְחֻקֹּתָיו הַכְּתוּבָה
are which His and com- His to your Jehovah the to shall you
written statutes mandments keep ,God of voice listen

430 3068 7725 8451 5612
בְּסֵפֶר הַתּוֹרָה הַזֶּה כִּי תָשׁוּב אֶל־יְהוָה אֱלֹהֶיךָ בְּכָל־
all with your Jehovah to- shall you for ;this law the in
God return of book

834 4687 3588 5315 3605 3824
11 לְבָבְךָ וּבְכָל־נַפְשֶׁךָ׃ כִּי הַמִּצְוָה הַזֹּאת אֲשֶׁר
which this command- For your and your
ment .soul all with ,heart

7350 6381 3808 3117 6680
אָנֹכִי מְצַוְּךָ הַיּוֹם לֹא־נִפְלֵאת הִוא מִמְּךָ וְלֹא־רְחֹקָה הִוא׃
.it (is) far too and for it (is) too not today command- I
off not ,you wonderful you ing (am)

3947 8064 5927 559 8064
12 לֹא בַשָּׁמַיִם הִוא לֵאמֹר מִי יַעֲלֶה־לָּנוּ הַשָּׁמַיְמָה וְיִקָּחֶהָ
and the into us for shall Who (you that) ,(is) it the in Not
it get heavens up go say (should) heavens

559 3220 5676 3808 6213 8085
13 לָּנוּ וְיַשְׁמִעֵנוּ אֹתָהּ וְנַעֲשֶׂנָּה׃ וְלֹא־מֵעֵבֶר לַיָּם הִוא לֵאמֹר
(you that) it the beyond And we that ,it cause and for
,say (should) (is) sea not ?it do may hear to us ,us

8085 3947 3220 5676 5674
מִי יַעֲבָר־לָנוּ אֶל־עֵבֶר הַיָּם וְיִקָּחֶהָ לָּנוּ וְיַשְׁמִעֵנוּ אֹתָהּ
,it cause and for and the the to for shall Who
hear to us ,us it take ,sea beyond region us over cross

3824 6310 3966 1697 7138 6213
14 וְנַעֲשֶׂנָּה׃ כִּי־קָרוֹב אֵלֶיךָ הַדָּבָר מְאֹד בְּפִיךָ וּבִלְבָבְךָ
in and your in ,very the to (is) For we that
,heart your mouth word you near ?it do may

2416 3117 6440 5414 2009 2896
15 לַעֲשֹׂתוֹ׃ ס רְאֵה נָתַתִּי לְפָנֶיךָ הַיּוֹם אֶת־הַחַיִּים
life today before have I ,Behold you that
you set .it do may

6680 7451 4194 2896
16 וְאֶת־הַטּוֹב וְאֶת־הַמָּוֶת וְאֶת־הָרָע׃ אֲשֶׁר אָנֹכִי מְצַוְּךָ
command- I that in ,evil and death and ,good and
you ing (am)

8104 1870 3212 430 3068 157 3117
הַיּוֹם לְאַהֲבָה אֶת־יְהוָה אֱלֹהֶיךָ לָלֶכֶת בִּדְרָכָיו וְלִשְׁמֹר
to and His in walk to your Jehovah love to today
keep ,ways ,God

3068 1288 7235 2421 4941 2708 4687
מִצְוֹתָיו וְחֻקֹּתָיו וּמִשְׁפָּטָיו וְחָיִיתָ וְרָבִיתָ וּבֵרַכְךָ יְהוָה
Jehovah shall and and you and His and His and His
you bless ,multiply live shall ;judgments ,statutes ,commands

518 3423 935 776 430
17 אֱלֹהֶיךָ בָּאָרֶץ אֲשֶׁר־אַתָּה בָא־שָׁמָּה לְרִשְׁתָּהּ׃ וְאִם־
if But .it possess to are you where the in your
you going land God

430 7812 5080 8085 3808 3824 6437
יִפְנֶה לְבָבְךָ וְלֹא תִשְׁמָע וְנִדַּחְתָּ וְהִשְׁתַּחֲוִיתָ לֵאלֹהִים
gods down bow and you and do you and your turn
6 6 to 3117 impelled are ,listen not ,heart away

5046 5647 312
18 אֲחֵרִים וַעֲבַדְתָּם׃ הִגַּדְתִּי לָכֶם הַיּוֹם כִּי אָבֹד תֹּאבֵדוּן
shall you certainly that today to have I serve and ,other
;perish you declared ,them

5674 834 127 3117 748
לֹא־תַאֲרִיכֻן יָמִים עַל־הָאֲדָמָה אֲשֶׁר אַתָּה עֹבֵר אֶת־
are you which the on (your) shall you not
over crossing land day's prolong

crossing the Jordan, to go
in there to possess it. 19 I
call Heaven and earth to
witness against you today
that I have set before you
life and death, the blessing
and the curse. Therefore,
choose life, that you may
live, you and your seed, 20
to love Jehovah your God,
to listen to His voice, and to
cleave to Him—for He *is*
your life, and the length of
your days—to live in the
land which Jehovah has
sworn to your fathers, to
Abraham, to Isaac, and to
Jacob, to give *it* to them.

3117 5749 3423 8033 935 3383
19 הַיַּרְדֵּן לָבוֹא שָׁמָּה לְרִשְׁתָּהּ׃ הַעִדֹתִי בָכֶם הַיּוֹם אֶת־
– today against you to call I witness .it possess to there go to in the Jordan
1293 6440 5414 4194 2416 776 8064
הַשָּׁמַיִם וְאֶת־הָאָרֶץ הַחַיִּים וְהַמָּוֶת נָתַתִּי לְפָנֶיךָ הַבְּרָכָה
the blessing before you have I set and death that life the earth and the heavens
157 2233 2421 24:16 977 7045
20 וְהַקְּלָלָה וּבָחַרְתָּ בַּחַיִּים לְמַעַן תִּחְיֶה אַתָּה וְזַרְעֶךָ׃ לְאַהֲבָה
love to your and ,seed you may you ,live that ,life therefore choose the and ;curse
2416 1692 6963 8085 430 3068
אֶת־יְהוָה אֱלֹהֶיךָ לִשְׁמֹעַ בְּקֹלוֹ וּלְדָבְקָה־בוֹ כִּי הוּא חַיֶּיךָ
your ,life He (is) for to Him to and cling His to ,voice listen to your God Jehovah
1 3068 7650 834 127 5921 3427 3117 753
וְאֹרֶךְ יָמֶיךָ לָשֶׁבֶת עַל־הָאֲדָמָה אֲשֶׁר נִשְׁבַּע יְהוָה לַאֲבֹתֶיךָ
your to ,fathers Jehovah swore which the land on live to your days the and of length
5414 3290 3327 85
לְאַבְרָהָם לְיִצְחָק וּלְיַעֲקֹב לָתֵת לָהֶם׃
.them to to (it) give to and ,Jacob ,Isaac to to ,Abraham

CAP. XXXI לא

CHAPTER 31

1 And Moses went out and
spoke these words to all
Israel. 2 And he said to
them, I am a hundred and
twenty years old today. I am
not able any more to go out
and to come in. And
Jehovah has said to me,
You shall not cross over this
Jordan. 3 Jehovah your God
will cross over before you;
He shall destroy these
nations from before you,
and you shall possess
them. Joshua is the one
who shall cross over be-
fore you, as Jehovah has
spoken. 4 And Jehovah
shall do to them as He has
done to Sihon and to Og,
kings of the Amorites, and
to their land, which He
destroyed *before* them.

3478 3605 428 1697 1696 4872 3212
1 וַיֵּלֶךְ מֹשֶׁה וַיְדַבֵּר אֶת־הַדְּבָרִים הָאֵלֶּה אֶל־כָּל־יִשְׂרָאֵל׃
;Israel all to these words and spoke Moses And went
3808 3117 8141 6242 3967/1121 559
2 וַיֹּאמֶר אֲלֵהֶם בֶּן־מֵאָה וְעֶשְׂרִים שָׁנָה אָנֹכִי הַיּוֹם לֹא־
not ;today I (am) years and twenty hundred a of son ,them to He and said
5674 559 3068 935 3318 5750 3201
אוּכַל עוֹד לָצֵאת וְלָבוֹא וַיהוָה אָמַר אֵלַי לֹא תַעֲבֹר אֶת־
shall you over cross not ,me to has said and Jehovah to and ;in come go to out any more am I able
8045 6440 5674 430 3068 2088 3383
3 הַיַּרְדֵּן הַזֶּה׃ יְהוָה אֱלֹהֶיךָ הוּא עֹבֵר לְפָנֶיךָ הוּא־יַשְׁמִיד
shall destroy He before ;you crossing over (is) One the your God Jehovah .this Jordan
5674 3091 3423 6440 428 1471
אֶת־הַגּוֹיִם הָאֵלֶּה מִלְּפָנֶיךָ וִירִשְׁתָּם יְהוֹשֻׁעַ הוּא עֹבֵר
crossing over (is) one the Joshua will you and ;them dispossess before from these nations
6213 3068 6213 3068 1696 6440
4 לְפָנֶיךָ כַּאֲשֶׁר דִּבֶּר יְהוָה׃ וְעָשָׂה יְהוָה לָהֶם כַּאֲשֶׁר עָשָׂה
has He done as to them Jehovah And do shall .Jehovah has spoken as before ,you
8045 834 776 567 4428 5747 5511
לְסִיחוֹן וּלְעוֹג מַלְכֵי הָאֱמֹרִי וּלְאַרְצָם אֲשֶׁר הִשְׁמִיד אֹתָם׃
.them He destroyed which to and ,land their the ,Amorites kings of to and ,Og to Sihon

5 And Jehovah shall give
them up before your face,
and you shall do to them
according to all the
command which I have
commanded you. 6 Be strong
and brave. Do not fear
them, or be afraid of them.
For Jehovah your God *is* He
who is going with you; He
shall not fail you nor forsake
you.

834 4687 3605 6213 6440 3068/5414
5 וּנְתָנָם יְהוָה לִפְנֵיכֶם וַעֲשִׂיתֶם לָהֶם כְּכָל־הַמִּצְוָה אֲשֶׁר
which the command according all to to them you and do shall before ,you Jehovah shall And up them give
6206 3372 553 2388 6680
6 צִוִּיתִי אֶתְכֶם׃ חִזְקוּ וְאִמְצוּ אַל־תִּירְאוּ וְאַל־תַּעַרְצוּ מִפְּנֵיהֶם
because ;them of tremble and not fear do (them) not and ;courageous be strong ;you have I commanded
5800 3808 7503 3808 3212 430 3068
כִּי יְהוָה אֱלֹהֶיךָ הוּא הַהֹלֵךְ עִמָּךְ לֹא יַרְפְּךָ וְלֹא יַעַזְבֶךָּ׃
forsake .you and not shall He you fail not with ;you One the going (is) He your God Jehovah for

7 And Moses called for Joshua, and said to him before the eyes of all Israel, Be strong and brave, for you shall go in with this people to the land which Jehovah has sworn to their fathers, to give *it* to them, and you shall cause them to inherit it. 8 And Jehovah *is* He who is going before you; He Himself shall be with you; He shall not fail you nor forsake you. Do not fear nor be afraid.

9 And Moses wrote this law, and delivered it to the priests, the sons of Levi, those bearing the ark of the covenant of Jehovah, and to all the elders of Israel.

10 And Moses commanded them, saying, At the end of seven years, in the appointed time, the year of release, in the Feast of Tabernacles, 11 when all Israel comes in to see the face of Jehovah in the place which He chooses, you shall proclaim this law before all Israel, in their ears. 12 Assemble the people, men and women, and the little ones, and your alien who *is* within your gates, so that they may hear, and so that they may learn, and may fear Jehovah your God, and take heed to do all the words of this law; 13 and their sons, who have not known, shall hear, and shall learn to fear Jehovah your God all the days which you live on the land where you are crossing over the Jordan to possess it.

3478 3605 5869 559 3091 4872 7121
7 ויקרא משה ליהושע ויאמר אליו לעיני כל־ישראל
.Israel all before him to and Joshua Moses And
of eyes the said summoned

834 776 2088 5971 935 553 2388
חזק ואמץ כי אתה תבוא את־העם הזה אל־הארץ אשר
which the to this people with shall you for cou- and Be
land in go rageous strong

5157 5414 1 3068 7650
נשבע יהוה לאבתם לתת להם ואתה תנחילנה אותם:
;them cause shall and to give to their to Jehovah has
it inherit to you ,them ,fathers sworn

3808 7503 1961 6440 3212 3068
8 ויהוה הוא ההלך לפניך הוא יהיה עמך לא ירפך ולא
and shall He not with shall He Himself before One the (is) And
not you fail ;you be ;you going He Jehovah

8451 4872 3789 2865 3808 3372 5800
9 יעזבך לא תירא ולא תחת: ויכתב משה את־התורה
law Moses And be and do not forsake
wrote dismayed not fear ;you

727 5375 3881 1121 3548 5414
הזאת ויתנה אל־הכהנים בני לוי הנשאים את־ארון
ark the those ,Levi the priests the to and this
of bearing of sons it gave

4872 6680 3478 2205 3068 1285
10 ברית יהוה ואל־כל־זקני ישראל: ויצו משה אותם
them Moses And .Israel the all and ,Jehovah the
commanded of elders to of covenant

2282 8059 8141 4150 8141 7651 7093 559
לאמר מקץ שבע שנים במעד שנת השמטה בחג
the at ,release year the the in ,years seven the at ,saying
of feast of of time appointed of end

3068 6440 7200 3478 3605 935 5521
11 הסכות: בבוא כל־ישראל לראות את־פני יהוה
Jehovah the see to Israel all when ;tabernacles
of face in comes

2088 8451 7121 977 834 4725 430
אלהיך במקום אשר יבחר תקרא את־התורה הזאת
this law shall you He which the in your
proclaim ,chooses place God

582 5971 6950 241 3478 3605
12 נגד כל־ישראל באזניהם: הקהל את־העם האנשים
men the the Assemble their in ,Israel all before
people .ears

8085 8179 1616 2945 802
והנשים והטף וגרך אשר בשעריך למען ישמעו ולמען
so and may they that so within who and little and and
that hear ,gates your (is) alien your ones women

6213 8104 430 3068 3372 3925
ילמדו ויראו את־יהוה אלהיכם ושמרו לעשות את־
do to heed take and your Jehovah may and they
God fear ,learn may

8085 3045/3808 834 1121 2088 8451 1697 3605
13 כל־דברי התורה הזאת: ובניהם אשר לא־ידעו ישמעו
shall have not who their and ;this law the all
,hear ,known ,sons of words

834 3117 3605 430 3068 3372 3925
ולמדו ליראה את־יהוה אלהיכם כל־הימים אשר אתם
you which the all your Jehovah fear to shall and
(are) days God learn

8033 3383 5674 834 127 5921 2416
חיים על־האדמה אשר אתם עברים את־הירדן שמה
there Jordan the crossing you which the on living
over (are) land

3423
לרשתה:
possess to
,it

[14]And Jehovah said to Moses, Behold, your days are coming near, to die. Call Joshua, and present yourselves at the tabernacle of the congregation, and I shall charge him. And Moses and Joshua went, and they presented themselves at the tabernacle of the congregation. [15]And Jehovah appeared at the tabernacle in a pillar of cloud; and the pillar of cloud stood at the door of the tabernacle. [16]And Jehovah said to Moses, Behold, you shall sleep with your fathers, and this people shall rise up and go lusting after the gods of the strangers of the land into which they are going, and shall forsake Me, and shall break My covenant which I made with it. [17]And My anger shall burn against *this people* in that day, and I shall forsake them and hide My face from them. And it shall be consumed, and many evils and distresses shall find *this people*. And it shall say in that day, Is *it* not because my God is not in my midst, *that* these evils have found me? [18]And I will completely hide My face in that day, because of all the evil which *this people* has done, for it shall turn to other gods. [19]Now, then, write this song for you, and teach it to the sons of Israel. Put it in their mouths, so that this song shall be for a witness to Me against the sons of Israel. [20]And I shall bring them into the land flowing with milk and honey, which I have sworn to their fathers. And you shall eat and be satisfied, and become fat, and shall turn to other gods; and they shall serve them, and despise Me, and break My covenant. [21]And it shall be, when many evils

14 ויאמר יהוה אל-משה הן קרבו ימיך למות קרא את-
יהושע והתיצבו באהל מועד ואצונו וילך משה ויהושע
15 ויתיצבו באהל מועד: וירא יהוה באהל בעמוד ענן
16 ויעמד עמוד הענן על-פתח האהל: ויאמר יהוה אל-
משה הנך שכב עם-אבתיך וקם העם הזה וזנה | אחרי |
אלהי נכר-הארץ אשר הוא בא-שמה בקרבו ועזבני
17 והפר את-בריתי אשר כרתי אתו: וחרה אפי בו ביום-
ההוא ועזבתים והסתרתי פני מהם והיה לאכל ומצאהו
רעות רבות וצרות ואמר ביום ההוא הלא על כי-
18 אין אלהי בקרבי מצאוני הרעות האלה: ואנכי הסתר
אסתיר פני ביום ההוא על כל-הרעה אשר עשה
19 כי פנה אל-אלהים אחרים: ועתה כתבו לכם את-
השירה הזאת ולמדה את-בני-ישראל שימה בפיהם
20 למען תהיה-לי השירה הזאת לעד בבני ישראל: כי-
אביאנו אל-האדמה | אשר-נשבעתי לאבתיו זבת חלב
ודבש ואכל ושבע ודשן ופנה אל-אלהים אחרים
21 ועבדום ונאצוני והפר את-בריתי: והיה כי-תמצאן

and distresses have found them, this song shall testify against them as a witness. For it shall not be forgotten out of the mouths of their seed. For I know their imagination which they *are* making today, before I bring them into the land which I have sworn.

22 And Moses wrote this song on that day, and taught it to the sons of Israel. 23 And He commanded Joshua the son of Nun, and said, Be strong and brave. For you shall bring the sons of Israel into the land which I have sworn to them, and I shall be with you. 24 And it happened, when Moses completed writing the words of this law in a book, until their conclusion, 25 that Moses commanded the Levites who bore the ark of the covenant of Jehovah, saying, 26 Take this book of the law, and you shall put it in the side of the ark of the covenant of Jehovah your God, so that it may be there for a witness against you. 27 For I have known your rebellion and your stiff neck. Behold, while I am yet alive with you this day, you have been rebellious against Jehovah. And how much more after my death! 28 Assemble to me all the elders of your tribes, and your officers, and I shall speak in their ears these words, and cause the heavens and the earth to testify against them. 29 For I know that after my death you shall utterly corrupt yourselves, and will turn aside from the way which I have commanded you. And evil shall happen to you in the latter end of the days,

5707 6440 2088 7892 6030 6864 7227 7451
אֹתוֹ רָעוֹת רַבּוֹת וְצָרוֹת וְעָנְתָה הַשִּׁירָה הַזֹּאת לְפָנָיו לְעֵד
a for witness, before him, this, song, shall and testify, dis- and tresses, many, evils, him

3336 3045 2233 6310 7911 3808
כִּי לֹא תִשָּׁכַח מִפִּי זַרְעוֹ כִּי יָדַעְתִּי אֶת־יִצְרוֹ אֲשֶׁר
which, scheme their, know I, for, their seed's, from mouth, shall it be forgotten, not, for

7650 834 776 935 2962 3117 6213
הוּא עֹשֶׂה הַיּוֹם בְּטֶרֶם אֲבִיאֶנּוּ אֶל־הָאָרֶץ אֲשֶׁר נִשְׁבָּעְתִּי׃
have I sworn, which, the land, into, bring I them, before, ,today, (are) making, they

3925 3117 2088 7892 4872 3789
22 וַיִּכְתֹּב מֹשֶׁה אֶת־הַשִּׁירָה הַזֹּאת בַּיּוֹם הַהוּא וַיְלַמְּדָהּ
and it taught, ,that, day on, this, song, Moses, And wrote

2388 559 5126/1121/3091 6680 3478 1121
23 אֶת־בְּנֵי יִשְׂרָאֵל׃ וַיְצַו אֶת־יְהוֹשֻׁעַ בִּן־נוּן וַיֹּאמֶר חֲזַק
Be strong, and ,said, ,Nun the of son, Joshua, he and commanded, Israel, the to of sons

834 776 3478 1121 935 553
וֶאֱמָץ כִּי אַתָּה תָּבִיא אֶת־בְּנֵי יִשְׂרָאֵל אֶל־הָאָרֶץ אֲשֶׁר־
which, the land, into, Israel, the of sons, shall bring, you, for, and ,courageous

4872 3615 1961 1961 7650
24 נִשְׁבַּעְתִּי לָהֶם וְאָנֹכִי אֶהְיֶה עִמָּךְ׃ וַיְהִי ׀ כְּכַלּוֹת מֹשֶׁה
Moses, when finished, it And came to pass, with you, be shall, I and, ,them to, have I sworn

6680 8552 5704 5612 8451 1697 3789
25 לִכְתֹּב אֶת־דִּבְרֵי הַתּוֹרָה־הַזֹּאת עַל־סֵפֶר עַד תֻּמָּם׃ וַיְצַו
that ordered, their ,completion, until, ,book a in, this, law, the of words, writing

3947 559 3068 1285 727 5375 3881 4872
26 מֹשֶׁה אֶת־הַלְוִיִּם נֹשְׂאֵי אֲרוֹן בְּרִית־יְהוָה לֵאמֹר׃ לָקֹחַ
Take, ,saying, ,Jehovah the of covenant, ark the of, bearing, the Levites, Moses

1285 727 6654 7760 2088 8451 5612
אֵת סֵפֶר הַתּוֹרָה הַזֶּה וְשַׂמְתֶּם אֹתוֹ מִצַּד אֲרוֹן בְּרִית־
the of covenant, ark the of, the at of side, it, you and put shall, ,this, law, the of book

3045 5707 8033 1961 430 3068
27 יְהוָה אֱלֹהֵיכֶם וְהָיָה־שָׁם בְּךָ לְעֵד׃ כִּי אָנֹכִי יָדַעְתִּי אֶת־
know, I, for, a for ;witness, against you, there, that be may it, your ,God, Jehovah

2416 4784 3117 2009 7186 6203 4805
מֶרְיְךָ וְאֶת־עָרְפְּךָ הַקָּשֶׁה הֵן בְּעוֹדֶנִּי חַי עִמָּכֶם הַיּוֹם מַמְרִים
rebellious ,today, with you, alive, while yet am I, ,behold, ;stiff neck, your, and, your rebellion

6950 4194 310 3068 1961
28 הֱיִתֶם עִם־יְהוָה וְאַף כִּי־אַחֲרֵי מוֹתִי׃ הַקְהִילוּ אֵלַי אֶת־
to me, Gather, my !death, after, and ;Jehovah more much how, against, you been have

241 1696 7860 7626 2205
כָּל־זִקְנֵי שִׁבְטֵיכֶם וְשֹׁטְרֵיכֶם וַאֲדַבְּרָה בְּאָזְנֵיהֶם אֵת
their in ears, shall I and speak, your and ,officers, your ,tribes, the of elders, all

776 8064 5749 428 1697
הַדְּבָרִים הָאֵלֶּה וְאָעִידָה בָּם אֶת־הַשָּׁמַיִם וְאֶת־הָאָרֶץ׃
the ;earth, and, the heavens, against them, cause and testify to, ,these, words

5493 7843 7843 4194 310 3045
29 כִּי יָדַעְתִּי אַחֲרֵי מוֹתִי כִּי־הַשְׁחֵת תַּשְׁחִתוּן וְסַרְתֶּם מִן־
from, turn and away, shall you yourselves corrupt, utterly that, my death, after, know I, for

319 7451 7125 6680 834 1870
הַדֶּרֶךְ אֲשֶׁר צִוִּיתִי אֶתְכֶם וְקָרָאת אֶתְכֶם הָרָעָה בְּאַחֲרִית
latter the of end, in, evil, you, shall and to happen, ;you, have I commanded, which, way the

because you shall do evil in the eyes of Jehovah, to make Him angry with the work of your hands.
[30]And Moses spoke in the ears of all the assembly of Israel the words of this song, until their conclusion:

4639 3707 3068 5869 7451 6213 3117
הימים כי־תעשו את־הרע בעיני יהוה להכעיסו במעשה
the with of work | make and angry Him | Jehovah | the in of eyes | evil | you because do shall | the ;days

30 1697 3478 6951 241 4872 1696 3027
ידיכם: וידבר משה באזני כל־קהל ישראל את־דברי
words of | Israel | the of assembly | all | the in of ears | Moses | And spoke | your .hands

8552 5704 2088 7892
השירה הזאת עד תמם:
their .conclusion | until | ,this | song

CAP. XXXII לב

CHAPTER 32

CHAPTER 32

[1]Give ear, O heavens, and I will speak. And hear, O earth, the words of my mouth. [2]My doctrine shall drop as the rain; my speech shall drop down as the dew, as the small rain on the tender plant, and as the showers on the grass; [3]because I will proclaim the name of Jehovah *and* ascribe greatness to our God. [4]*He is* the Rock; His work *is* perfect. For all His ways *are* just, a God of faithfulness, and without evil; just and upright *is* He. [5]They have corrupted themselves; *they are* not His sons; *it is* their blemish; *they are* a crooked and perverse generation.

[6]Do you thus give back to Jehovah, O foolish and unwise people? Is He not your Father who bought you? *Has not* He made you and established you? [7]Remember the days of old, consider the years of many generations; ask your father, and he shall tell you; your elders, and they shall tell you; [8]when the Most High divided to the nations their inheritance; when He separated the sons of Adam, He set up the bounds of the peoples, according to the number of the sons of Israel.

1 6310/561 776 8085 1696 8064 238
האזינו השמים ואדברה ותשמע הארץ אמרי־פי:
my .mouth of words | the | ,earth O | ,hear and | will I and ;speak | O heavens | Give ,ear

2 565 2919 5140 3948 4306 6201
יערף כמטר לקחי תזל כטל אמרתי
my speech | the as dew | shall distil | My ;doctrine | the as rain | shall drip

6212 7241 1877 8164
כשעירם עלי־דשא וכרביבים עלי־עשב:
the ;herbs green | on | the as showers | fresh grass | as | the as rain light

3 430 1433 3053 7121 3068 8034 3588
כי שם יהוה אקרא הבו גדל לאלהינו:
our to !God | great- ness | Give | will I ;proclaim | Jehovah | the of name | be- cause

4 4941 1870 3605 6466 8549 6697
הצור תמים פעלו כי כל־דרכיו משפט
(are) ;judgment | His ways | all | for | His ;work | (is) perfect | (is He) ,Rock the

3477 6662 5766 369 530 410
אל אמונה ואין עול צדיק וישר הוא:
(is) .He | and upright | just | ;evil | and without | faithful- ,ness | God a of

5 6618 6141 1755 3971 1121 3808 7843
שחת לו לא בניו מומם דור עקש ופתלתל:
and !perverse | crooked | a generation | their ;blemish | (is it) | His sons | not | him | hath He self corrupted

6 2450 3808 5036 5971 2088 1580 3068
הליהוה תגמלו־זאת עם נבל ולא חכם
?wise | and not | foolish | O people | .thus | you Do repay | to Jehovah

3559 6213 7069 1 3808
הלוא־הוא אביך קנך הוא עשך ויכננך:
estab- ?you lished | and | made you | (not Has) He | bought ?you | Who | your ,father | He | not | Is

7 1755 8141 995 5769 3117 2142
זכר ימות עולם בינו שנות דר־ודר
(past) many ;generations | the of years | consider | ,old | days | Remem- ber

519 2205 5046 1 7592
שאל אביך ויגדך זקניך ויאמרו־לך:
;you | they and tell shall | your ,elders | he and ;you tell shall | your father | ask

8 120 1121 6504 1471 5945 5157
בהנחל עליון גוים בהפרידו בני אדם
;Adam | the of sons | He when separated | ,nations the (to) the divided When | High Most inheritance (their)

3478 1121 4557 5971 1367 5324
יצב גבלת עמים למספר בני ישראל:
.Israel | the of sons | to according of number the | the ,peoples | the of bounds | set He up

[9]For Jehovah's portion *is* His people; Jacob *is* the lot of His inheritance.

[10]He found him in a desert land, and in the waste, *a* howling wilderness. He encircled him *and* cared for him; He guarded him as the pupil of His eye. [11]As the eagle stirs up its nest; it hovers over its young; it spreads out its wings *and* takes it, and bears it on its wing. [12]Jehovah alone led him, and there was no strange god with him. [13]He made him ride on the high places of the earth, so that he might eat the increase of the fields. And He made him suck honey out of the rock, and oil out of the flinty rock; [14]butter from cows, and milk from sheep, with fat from lambs, and rams of the sons of Bashan, and he-goats, with the fat of the kidneys of wheat, and of the blood of the grape you shall drink wine.

[15]But Jeshurun grew fat, and kicked; you grew fat, thick *and* stubborn. And he abandoned God who made him, and dishonored the Rock of his salvation. [16]With strange gods they moved Him to jealousy; and with idols they provoked Him to anger. [17]They sacrificed to demons *who were* not God, *to* gods whom they did not know, new ones who came lately; your fathers had not dreaded them. [18]You forgot the Rock that brought you into being; and neglected God who formed you. [19]And Jehovah looked and de-

9 5971 3068 2506 כִּי חֵלֶק יְהוָה עַמּוֹ
His Jehovah's por- For
,people (is) tion
5159 2256 3290 יַעֲקֹב חֶבֶל נַחֲלָתוֹ׃
His lot the Jacob
.inheritance of

10 4057 776 4672 יִמְצָאֵהוּ בְּאֶרֶץ מִדְבָּר
,desert a in found He
land him
3452 3214/8414 וּבְתֹהוּ יְלֵל יְשִׁמֹן
;wilderness howling in and
waste the

995 5437 יְסֹבְבֶנְהוּ יְבוֹנְנֵהוּ
cared (and) encircled He
,him for him
5869 380 5341 יִצְּרֶנְהוּ כְּאִישׁוֹן עֵינוֹ׃
His the as guarded He
.eye of pupil him

11 7064 5782 5404 כְּנֶשֶׁר יָעִיר קִנּוֹ
its stirs the As
,nest up eagle
7363 1469 עַל־גּוֹזָלָיו יְרַחֵף
it its over
,hovers young

3947 3671 6566 יִפְרֹשׂ כְּנָפָיו יִקָּחֵהוּ
takes its spreads it
,it ,wings out
84 5375 יִשָּׂאֵהוּ עַל־אֶבְרָתוֹ׃
its on bears (and)
.wing it

12 5148 910 3068 יְהוָה בָּדָד יַנְחֶנּוּ
led alone Jehovah
,him
5236 369 וְאֵין עִמּוֹ אֵל נֵכָר׃
.strange god with there and
him no was

13 776 1116 7392 יַרְכִּבֵהוּ עַל־בָּמֳתֵי אָרֶץ
,earth the high the on made He
of places ride him
7704 8510 398 וַיֹּאכַל תְּנוּבֹת שָׂדָי
the the he and
;fields of produce ate

5553 1706 3243 וַיֵּנִקֵהוּ דְבַשׁ מִסֶּלַע
the from honey He and
rock suck him made
6697 2496 8081 וְשֶׁמֶן מֵחַלְמִישׁ צוּר׃
;rock the from and
flinty the oil

14 6629 2401 1241 2529 חֶמְאַת בָּקָר וַחֲלֵב צֹאן
the and ,cows curds
flocks of milk of
3733 2459 עִם־חֵלֶב כָּרִים
young fat with
,rams of

6260 1316 1121 352 וְאֵילִים בְּנֵי־בָשָׁן וְעַתּוּדִים
and ;Bashan the and
he-goats of sons of rams
2406 3629 2459 עִם־חֵלֶב כִּלְיוֹת חִטָּה
,wheat kidneys the the with
of of fat

15 2561 8354 6025/1818 וְדַם־עֵנָב תִּשְׁתֶּה־חָמֶר׃
!wine shall you the of and
drink ,grape of blood the
1163 3484 8080 וַיִּשְׁמַן יְשֻׁרוּן וַיִּבְעָט
and ,Jeshurun grew But
—kicked fat

3780 5666 8080 שָׁמַנְתָּ עָבִיתָ כָּשִׂיתָ
(and) ,thick you
stubborn fat grew
6213 433 5203 וַיִּטֹּשׁ אֱלוֹהַּ עָשָׂהוּ
who God he and
,him made abandoned

3444 6697 5034 וַיְנַבֵּל צוּר יְשֻׁעָתוֹ׃
salva- his the and
.vation of Rock scorned
16 2114 7065 יַקְנִאֻהוּ בְּזָרִים
with aroused They
,(gods) strange jealousy His

17 3707 8441 בְּתוֹעֵבֹת יַכְעִיסֻהוּ׃
provoked they with
,anger to Him abominations
433 3808 7700 2076 יִזְבְּחוּ לַשֵּׁדִים לֹא אֱלֹהַּ
(was) (who) to they
god not ,demons sacrificed

3045 3808 430 אֱלֹהִים לֹא יְדָעוּם
whom not gods
,knew they
435 7138 2319 חֲדָשִׁים מִקָּרֹב בָּאוּ
who lately ones new
,came

18 8175 3808 לֹא שְׂעָרוּם אֲבֹתֵיכֶם׃
your dreaded had not
.fathers them
7876 3205 6697 צוּר יְלָדְךָ תֶּשִׁי
you begat that the
;neglected you Rock

19 2342 410 7911 וַתִּשְׁכַּח אֵל מְחֹלְלֶךָ׃
formed who the and
.you God forgot
5001 3068 7200 וַיַּרְא יְהוָה וַיִּנְאָץ
and Jehovah And
,despised looked

spised because of the
provocation of His sons and
of His daughters. [20]And He
said, I will hide My face
from them; I will see what
their end *will be*; for they
are a perverse generation,
sons in whom *is* no faithfulness. [21]They made Me
jealous with a no-god; they
made Me angry by their
vanities; and I shall make
them jealous by a no-
people; by a foolish nation I
shall make them angry.
[22]For a fire has been kindled
in My anger, and it burns to
the lowest Sheol, and consumes the earth and its
produce; and sets on fire
the foundations of the
mountains.

[23]I will heap evils on
them; I will use up My
arrows on them. [24]I will
send on them exhaustion
by famine, and depletion by
burning heat, and bitter
destruction, and the teeth
of beasts, with the venom
of crawling things of the
dust. [25]The sword shall
bereave from without, and
terror from within, both the
young man and the virgin,
the suckling with the man
of gray hairs.

[26]I said, I will dash them
to pieces; I will make their
memory cease from among
men; [27]were it not the
provocation of an enemy I
feared, that their foes
should judge amiss, that
they might not say, Our
hand is high, and Jehovah
has not done all this. [28]For
they *are* a nation void of
counsel, and there is no
understanding in them. [29]If
they were wise, they would
understand this; they would
consider their latter end.

[30]How could one chase a

20 1323 1121 3708 מִכַּעַס בָּנָיו וּבְנֹתָיו׃ His of and His of the for .daughters sons provoking — 6440 5640 559 וַיֹּאמֶר אַסְתִּירָה פָנַי מֵהֶם from My will I He And ,them face hide ,said

319 7200 אֶרְאֶה מָה אַחֲרִיתָם end their what will I ,(be shall) see — 8419 1755 כִּי דוֹר תַּהְפֻּכֹת הֵמָּה they perverse a for ,(are) generation

21 529 1121 בָּנִים לֹא־אֵמֻן בָּם׃ in faith- (is) sons .whom fulness no — 410 3808 7065 הֵם קִנְאוּנִי בְלֹא־אֵל ;god with made have They no- a jealous Me

1892 3707 כִּעֲסוּנִי בְּהַבְלֵיהֶם their with aroused they ;vanities anger My — 5971 7065 וַאֲנִי אַקְנִיאֵם בְּלֹא־עָם ;people a by make shall I and no- jealous them

22 3707 5036 בְּגוֹי נָבָל אַכְעִיסֵם׃ make will I foolish a by .angry them nation — 639 6919 784 כִּי־אֵשׁ קָדְחָה בְאַפִּי My in breaking is a For anger out ,fire

8482 7585 3344 וַתִּיקַד עַד־שְׁאוֹל תַּחְתִּית ,lowest the to it and Sheol burn shall — 2981 776 398 וַתֹּאכַל אֶרֶץ וִיבֻלָהּ its and the shall it and ,produce earth devour

23 2022 4146 3857 וַתְּלַהֵט מוֹסְדֵי הָרִים׃ moun- the foun- the shall it and .tains of dations scorch — 7451 5921 5595 אַסְפֶּה עָלֵימוֹ רָעוֹת ;evils upon will I them increase

24 3615 2671 חִצַּי אֲכַלֶּה־בָּם׃ on use will I My .them up arrows — 7565 2898 7451 4198 מְזֵי רָעָב וּלְחֻמֵי רֶשֶׁף heat burning and ,famine Exhaustion by consumed by

4815 6986 וְקֶטֶב מְרִירִי ,bitter and destruction — 7971 929 8127 וְשֶׁן־בְּהֵמֹת אֲשַׁלַּח־בָּם upon will I ,beasts the and ,them send of teeth

25 6083 2119 2534 עִם־חֲמַת זֹחֲלֵי עָפָר׃ .dust the crawling the with of things of venom — 2719 7921 2351 מִחוּץ תְּשַׁכֶּל־חֶרֶב The shall from sword bereave without

367 2315 וּמֵחֲדָרִים אֵימָה ;terror from and within — 1330 1571 970 גַּם־בָּחוּר גַּם־בְּתוּלָה the and the both ,virgin man young

26 7872 376 3243 יוֹנֵק עִם־אִישׁ שֵׂיבָה׃ grey man the with the .hairs of suckling — 6284 559 אָמַרְתִּי אַפְאֵיהֶם them dash will I ,said I ; pieces to

27 2143 582 7673 אַשְׁבִּיתָה מֵאֱנוֹשׁ זִכְרָם׃ their among from will I .memory men cease make — 1481 341 3708 3884 לוּלֵי כַּעַס אוֹיֵב אָגוּר did I an pro- the not If fear enemy of vocation

6862 5234 פֶּן־יְנַכְּרוּ צָרֵימוֹ ad- their should lest ,versaries misconstrue — 7311 3027 559 פֶּן־יֹאמְרוּ יָדֵנוּ רָמָה is our should they lest ,high hand ,say

28 2088 3605 6466 3068 3808 וְלֹא יְהוָה פָּעַל כָּל־זֹאת׃ ;this all has Jehovah and done not — 6098 6 1471 כִּי־גוֹי אֹבַד עֵצוֹת הֵמָּה they counsel void a for ;(are) of nation

29 8394 369 וְאֵין בָּהֶם תְּבוּנָה׃ understand- in there and .ing them no is — 2088 7919 2449 לוּ חָכְמוּ יַשְׂכִּילוּ זֹאת ,this would they they If understand wise were

30 319 995 יָבִינוּ לְאַחֲרִיתָם׃ latter their would they .end comprehend — 505 259 7291 אֵיכָה יִרְדֹּף אֶחָד אֶלֶף a one shall How ,thousand chase

thousand and two put a
myriad to flight, if *it were*
not their Rock that sold
them, and Jehovah had
shut them up? [31]For their 31
rock *is* not our Rock, even
our enemies *being* judges.
[32]For their vine *is* of the vine
of Sodom, and their grapes 32
of the fields of Gomorrah,
grapes of gall; they *have*
bitter clusters.

[33]Their wine *is* the venom 33
of serpents, and the cruel
venom of asps. [34]Is it not
stored up with Me, sealed
in My treasuries? [35]Ven- 34
geance and retribution *be-*
long to Me; in due time their
foot will slip; for the day of
their calamity *is* near; and 35
the things prepared are
hurrying for them. [36]For
Jehovah will bring His
people justice; and He shall
have compassion on His
servants, for He sees that
their power is gone, and
only the imprisoned and 36
abandoned *remain*. [37]And
He will say, Where *are* their
gods, the rock in which
they sought refuge? [38]Who
ate the fat of their sacrifices, *and* drank the wine of
their drink offerings? Let
them rise up and help you; 37
let it be a hiding place for
you.
38

[39]See now that I, I *am* 39
He, and there is no other
God with Me. I kill, and I
keep alive. I wound and I
heal, and there is no
deliverer from My hand.

[40]For I lift up My hand to 40
the heavens and say, I live
forever!

8147 5127 7233
ושנים יניסו רבבה
ten to put and
,thousand flight two

4376 6697/3588 3808
אם־לא כי־צורם מכרם
sold who their for (were it) if
,them Rock not

3068 5462
ויהוה הסגירם:
shut had and
?up them Jehovah

31
6697 6697 3808
כי לא כצורנו צורם
their our as (is) For
,rock Rock not

341 6414
ואיבינו פלילים:
(being) our even
.judges enemies

32
1612 5467 1612
כי־מגפן סדם גפנם
their (is) Sodom the of For
,vine of vine

7709 6017
ומשדמת עמרה
;Gomorrah from and
of fields the

4846 6025 6025
ענבמו ענבי־רוש
;gall (are) their
of grapes grapes

811 4846
אשכלת מררת למו:
for bitter clusters
.them (are)

33
3196 8577 2534
חמת תנינם יינם
Their serpents the
,wine (is) of venom

7219 6620 393
וראש פתנים אכזר:
.cruel asps the and
of venom

34
3647 3808
הלא הוא כמס עמדי
with stored it not Is
,Me up

2856 214
חתום באוצרתי:
My in sealed
?treasuries up

35
8005 5359
לי נקם ושלם
and Ven- Me to
;retribution geance (belongs)

7272 4131 6256
לעת תמוט רגלם
their shall due in
;foot slip ,time

343 3117 7138
כי קרוב יום אידם
their day the (is) for
,calamity of near

6264 2363
וחש עתדת למו:
.them for things the are and
prepared hurrying

36
5971 3068 1777
כי־ידין יהוה עמו
His Jehovah will For
,people justice bring

5162 5650 5921
ועל־עבדיו יתנחם
have shall He His and
;compassion servants on

3027 235 7200
כי יראה כי־אזלת יד
(their) is that He for
,power gone sees

5800 6113 657
ואפס עצור ועזוב:
the and im- the only and
.abandoned ,prisoned (remain)

37
430 559
ואמר אי אלהימו
their Where He And
gods (are) ,say will

2620 6697
צור חסיו בו:
?it in they rock the
refuge sought

38
398 2077 2459 834
אשר חלב זבחימו יאכלו
,ate their fat the Who
sacrifices of

5257 3196 8354
ישתו יין נסיכם
drink their the (and)
?offering of wine drank

5826 6965
יקומו ויעזרכם
help and them Let
,you up rise

5643 1961
יהי עליכם סתרה:
hiding a for let
!place you be it

39
6258 7200
ראו עתה כי אני אני הוא
,He I ,I that now See
(am)

430 369
ואין אלהים עמדי
with god there And
;Me no is

2421 4191
אני אמית ואחיה
pre- I and ,kill I
;alive serve

7495 4272
מחצתי ואני ארפא
;heal I and
,wound

5337 369
ואין מידי מציל:
who from there and
.deliver hand My none is

40
3027 8064 5375
כי־אשא אל־שמים ידי
My the to up lift I For
hand heavens

5769 2416 559
ואמרתי חי אנכי לעלם:
!forever I live ,say and

[41]If I have sharpened My
glittering sword, and My
hand lays hold on judg-
ment, I will render ven-
geance to My foes, and I
will repay those who hate
Me. [42]I will make My arrows
drunk with blood, and My
sword shall devour flesh,
with the blood of the slain
and of the captives, from
the hairy head of the
enemy.

[43]Rejoice, O nations, of
His people; for He shall
avenge the blood of His
servants, and shall render
vengeance to His foes, and
shall have mercy on His
land *and* His people.
[44]And Moses came and
spoke all the words of this
song in the ears of the
people, he and Joshua the
son of Nun. [45]And Moses
finished speaking all these
words to all Israel, [46]and
said to them, Set your heart
on all the words which I
have testified against you
today, that you command
your sons to take heed to
do all the words of this law.

[47]For it is not a useless
word for you; for it *is* your
life; and by this you shall
prolong *your* days in the
land where you are cross-
ing over the Jordan, there
to possess it.

[48]And Jehovah spoke to
Moses in that same day,
saying, [49]Go up into this
Mount Abarim, *to* Mount
Nebo, which *is* in the land
of Moab, which *is* opposite
Jericho; and see the land of
Canaan which I am giving
to the sons of Israel for a
possession; [50]and die in

3027 4941 270 2719 1300 8150
41 אם־שנותי ברק חרבי ותאחז במשפט ידי
My ,hand | on judgment | lays and hold | My ,sword | lightning | I sharpen | When

7999 8130 6862 5359 7725
אשיב נקם לצרי ולמשנאי אשלם׃
will I ,repay | to and haters My | My to ,adversaries | venge- ance | will I render

1320 398 2719 1818 2671 7937
42 אשכיר חצי מדם וחרבי תאכל בשר
,flesh | shall devour | My and sword | with ,blood | My arrows | make will I drunk

341 6546 7218 7633 2491 1818
מדם חלל ושביה מראש פרעות אויב׃
the .enemy | hair the of | the from of head | the of and ,captives | the the with slain of blood

5358 5650 1818 5971 1471 7442
43 הרנינו גוים עמו כי דם־עבדיו יקום
shall He ,avenge | His servants | the of blood | for | His ;people | O of nations | ,Rejoice

5971 127 3722 6862 7725 5359
ונקם ישיב לצריו וכפר אדמתו עמו׃
His (and) .people | His land | will and for atone | His to ,adversaries | shall render | ven- and geance

5971 241 2088/7892 1697 3605 1696 4872 935
44 ויבא משה וידבר את־כל־דברי השירה־הזאת באזני העם
the ,people | the in of ears | this | song | the of words | all | and spoke | ,Moses | And came

1697 3605 1696 4872 3615 5126/1121 3091
45 הוא והושע בן־נון׃ ויכל משה לדבר את־כל־הדברים
words | all | speaking | Moses | and finished | ;Nun the of son | and Joshua | he

3824 7760 559 3478 3605 428
46 האלה אל־כל־ישראל׃ ויאמר אלהם שימו לבבכם
your hearts | set | ,them to | he and said | ,Israel | all | to | these

6680 3117 5749 834 1697 3605
לכל־הדברים אשר אנכי מעיד בכם היום אשר תצום
you command | that | ,today | against you | have testified | I | which | the words | on all

2088 8451 1697 3605 6213 8104 1121
את־בניכם לשמר לעשות את־כל־דברי התורה הזאת׃
.this | law | the of words | all | do to | take to heed | your sons

2088 1697 2416 7535 1697 3808 3588
47 כי לא־דבר רק הוא מכם כי־הוא חייכם ובדבר הזה
this | by and word | your ;life | (is) it for | for ,you | (is) it useless | a word | not | for

3383 5674 834 127 5921 3117 748
תאריכו ימים על־האדמה אשר אתם עברים את־הירדן
the Jordan | are over crossing | you | which | the land | on (your) days | you shall prolong

3423 8033
שמה לרשתה׃
possess to it | to there

5927 559 3117 6106 4872 3068 1696
48 וידבר יהוה אל־משה בעצם היום הזה לאמר׃ עלה
49
up Go | ,saying | ,that | day | same in | Moses | to Jehovah | And spoke

834 4124 776 834 5015/2022/2088 5682 2022
אל־הר העברים הזה הר־נבו אשר בארץ מואב אשר
which (is) | ,Moab | the in of land | which (is) | ,Nebo Mount | ,this Abarim | Mount into of

1121 5414 834 3667 776 7200 3405 6440
על־פני ירחו וראה את־ארץ כנען אשר אני נתן לבני
the to of sons | am giving | I | which | ,Canaan | the of land | see and | ;Jericho | opposite

the mountain where you are going, and be gathered to your people, even as your brother Aaron died on Mount Hor, and was gathered to his people; [51]in that you acted covertly toward Me among the sons of Israel at the waters of Meribah in Kadesh, in the wilderness of Zin; because you did not sanctify Me in the midst of the sons of Israel. [52]Yet you shall see the land across *from you*, but you shall not go in there to the land which I *am* giving to the sons of Israel.

50 יִשְׂרָאֵל לַאֲחֻזָּה׃ וּמֻת בָּהָר אֲשֶׁר אַתָּה עֹלֶה שָׁמָּה וְהֵאָסֵף
be gathered and there are going you where the mountain on and die a for possession ;Israel

אֶל־עַמֶּיךָ כַּאֲשֶׁר־מֵת אַהֲרֹן אָחִיךָ בְּהֹר הָהָר וַיֵּאָסֶף אֶל־
to was gathered and ,Mount Hor on your brother Aaron died as your ,people to

51 עַמָּיו׃ עַל אֲשֶׁר מְעַלְתֶּם בִּי בְּתוֹךְ בְּנֵי יִשְׂרָאֵל בְּמֵי־מְרִיבַת
Meribah the in of waters Israel the among of sons against Me you transgressed because His ;people

קָדֵשׁ מִדְבַּר־צִן עַל אֲשֶׁר לֹא־קִדַּשְׁתֶּם אוֹתִי בְּתוֹךְ בְּנֵי
the of sons the in of midst Me did you sanctify not because Zin the in ,Kadesh of wilderness

52 יִשְׂרָאֵל׃ כִּי מִנֶּגֶד תִּרְאֶה אֶת־הָאָרֶץ וְשָׁמָּה לֹא תָבוֹא אֶל־
to shall you not in go but there ,land the shall you see across (you from) Yet .Israel

הָאָרֶץ אֲשֶׁר־אֲנִי נֹתֵן לִבְנֵי יִשְׂרָאֵל׃
.Israel the to of sons (am) giving I which the land

CAP. XXXIII לג

CHAPTER 33

CHAPTER 33

[1]And this is the blessing *with* which Moses the man of God blessed the sons of Israel before his death. [2]And he said: Jehovah came from Sinai, and rose up from Seir for them; He shone forth from Mount Paran, and He came from the myriads of holy ones. At his right hand a law of fire *went forth* to them. [3]Yes, He loves the peoples; all His holy ones *are* in Your hand; and they sit down at Your feet—He lifts up *each* at Your words. [4]Moses has commanded a law to us, an inheritance *for* the congregation of Jacob. [5]And he was king in Jeshurun, when the heads of the people assembled, the tribes of Israel. [6]Let Reuben live, and not die, and let his men be numbered. [7]And this for Judah: And he said, Hear the voice of Judah, O Jehovah, and bring him in to his people; his hands *were* much for him, and You shall be a help against his foes.

[8]And of Levi he said, Your Thummim and Your Urim *are* for your devout men whom you did try at

1 וְזֹאת הַבְּרָכָה אֲשֶׁר בֵּרַךְ מֹשֶׁה אִישׁ הָאֱלֹהִים אֶת־בְּנֵי
the of sons God the of man Moses blessed (with) which the blessing this And (is)

2 יִשְׂרָאֵל לִפְנֵי מוֹתוֹ׃ וַיֹּאמֶר יְהוָה מִסִּינַי בָּא וְזָרַח מִשֵּׂעִיר
from Seir and up rose ,came from Sinai Jehovah he And ,said his .death before Israel

לָמוֹ הוֹפִיעַ מֵהַר פָּארָן וְאָתָה מֵרִבְבֹת קֹדֶשׁ מִימִינוֹ אֵשְׁדָּת
of law a (went) fire His from hand right holy ;ones the from of myriads He and came ,Paran from Mount shone He forth for ;them

3 לָמוֹ׃ אַף חֹבֵב עַמִּים כָּל־קְדֹשָׁיו בְּיָדֶךָ וְהֵם תֻּכּוּ לְרַגְלֶךָ
Your at ;feet sit down and they in (are) ;hand your His ones holy all the ,peoples He loves ,Yes to .them

4 יִשָּׂא מִדַּבְּרֹתֶיךָ׃ תּוֹרָה צִוָּה־לָנוּ מֹשֶׁה מוֹרָשָׁה קְהִלַּת
the of assembly poses- a (for) sion ,Moses to us has commanded law a Your at .words lifts He up (each)

5 יַעֲקֹב׃ וַיְהִי בִישֻׁרוּן מֶלֶךְ בְּהִתְאַסֵּף רָאשֵׁי עָם יַחַד שִׁבְטֵי
the of tribes together the ,people the of heads when gathered ,king in Jeshurun he And was .Jacob

6 יִשְׂרָאֵל׃ יְחִי רְאוּבֵן וְאַל־יָמֹת וִיהִי מְתָיו מִסְפָּר׃
7 וְזֹאת
And this num- .bered be his men and let ,die not and Reuben Let live .Israel

לִיהוּדָה וַיֹּאמַר שְׁמַע יְהוָה קוֹל יְהוּדָה וְאֶל־עַמּוֹ תְּבִיאֶנּוּ
him bring ;in his people and to ,Judah the of voice O ,Jehovah ,Hear he and ,said Judah for

יָדָיו רָב לוֹ וְעֵזֶר מִצָּרָיו תִּהְיֶה׃
shall You .be against foes his a and help (were) he ;him much his hands

8 וּלְלֵוִי אָמַר תֻּמֶּיךָ וְאוּרֶיךָ לְאִישׁ חֲסִידֶךָ אֲשֶׁר נִסִּיתוֹ
did you try whom your devout for (are) man your and Urim your Thummim ,said he of And Levi

Massah; You contended
with him at the waters of
Meribah; [9]who said of his
father and his mother, I
have not seen him. And he
has not acknowledge his
brothers, and did not know
his own son, for they have
kept Your word, and
observed Your covenant.
[10]They shall teach Your
ordinances to Jacob, and
Your law to Israel. They
shall put incense at Your
nostrils, and whole burnt
offering on Your altar.
[11]O Jehovah, bless his
strength, and accept the
work of his hands. Dash the
loins of those rising against
him, *those* who hate him,
that they may not rise!
[12]Of Benjamin he said,
The beloved of Jehovah
shall dwell securely beside
Him, covering him all the
day long; yea, he shall dwell
between His shoulders.
[13]And of Joseph he said,
Blessed of Jehovah *be* his
land, with the best of the
heavens, for the dew, for
the deep crouching be-
neath; [14]and with the best
of the produce of the sun,
and with the best yield of
the months; [15]and with the
first of the ancient mountains, and with the best of
the everlasting hills; [16]and
with the best of the earth,
and its fullness; and the
good will of Him who dwelt
in the Bush—let it come on
the head of Joseph, and on
the crown of the conse-
crated one *of* his brothers.
[17]His glory *is* as the firstborn
of his ox, and the horns of
the wild ox *are* his horns;
with them he shall butt the
peoples together *to* the
ends of the earth. And
they *are* the myriads of
Ephriam, and they *are* the
thousands of Manasseh.
[18]And of Zebulun he said,
Rejoice, O Zebulun, in your
going out, and O Issachar,
in your tents; [19]they call
the peoples *to* the mountains; they shall offer righteous sacrifices. For they
shall suck the seas' bounty
and treasures hidden in the
sand. [20]And of Gad he said,
Blessed *is* he who enlarges
Gad; he shall live like a lion-

517 1 559 4808 4325 7378 4531
9 בְּמַסָּה תְּרִיבֵהוּ עַל־מֵי מְרִיבָה׃ הָאֹמֵר לְאָבִיו וּלְאִמּוֹ
his and his of said who ;Meribah he at con-you ;Massah at
,mother father of waters him with tended

8104 3045 3808 1121 5234 3808 251 7200 3808
לֹא רְאִיתִיו וְאֶת־אֶחָיו לֹא הִכִּיר וְאֶת־בָּנָו לֹא יָדָע כִּי שָׁמְרוּ
have they for did not his and has he not his and have I not
kept ,know son own ,acknowledged brothers ;him seen

8451 3290 4941 3384 5341 1285 565
10 אִמְרָתֶךָ וּבְרִיתְךָ יִנְצֹרוּ׃ יוֹרוּ מִשְׁפָּטֶיךָ לְיַעֲקֹב וְתוֹרָתְךָ
Your and ,Jacob to Your shall They .observed Your and Your
law ordinances teach covenant word

1288 4196 3632 639 7004 7760 3478
11 לְיִשְׂרָאֵל יָשִׂימוּ קְטוֹרָה בְּאַפֶּךָ וְכָלִיל עַל־מִזְבְּחֶךָ׃ בָּרֵךְ
,Bless .altar your on whole and your at incense shall they ;Israel to
offering burnt nostrils put

8130 6965 4975 4272 7521 3027 6467 2428 3068
יְהוָה חֵילוֹ וּפֹעַל יָדָיו תִּרְצֶה מְחַץ מָתְנַיִם קָמָיו וּמְשַׂנְאָיו
hating those his loins the in dash ;accept his the and his Jeho- O
him adversaries of pieces hands of work strength ,vah

983 7931 3068 3039 559 1144 6965 4480
12 מִן־יְקוּמוּן׃ ס לְבִנְיָמִן אָמַר יְדִיד יְהוָה יִשְׁכֹּן לָבֶטַח
securely shall Jehovah the said he Benjamin Of may they that
dwell of beloved rise not

3127 7931 3862 996 3117 2653
13 עָלָיו חֹפֵף עָלָיו כָּל־הַיּוֹם וּבֵין כְּתֵפָיו שָׁכֵן׃ ס וּלְיוֹסֵף
of And shall he His ,yes day the all him covering beside
Joseph .dwell shoulders between :(long) ,Him

7257 8415 2919 8064 4022 776 3068 1288 559
אָמַר מְבֹרֶכֶת יְהוָה אַרְצוֹ מִמֶּגֶד שָׁמַיִם מִטָּל וּמִתְּהוֹם רֹבֶצֶת
crouching the for and the for the the with his (be) Jehovah Blessed he
deep ,dew heavens of best ,land of ,said

7218 3391 1645 4022 8121 1645 4022 8478
14 תָּחַת׃ וּמִמֶּגֶד תְּבוּאֹת שָׁמֶשׁ וּמִמֶּגֶד גֶּרֶשׁ יְרָחִים׃ וּמֵרֹאשׁ
15
with and (the) yield with and ;sun the the with and be-
of first the ;months of best the of produce of best the ;neath

4393 776 4022 5769 1389 4022 6924 2042
16 הַרְרֵי־קֶדֶם וּמִמֶּגֶד גִּבְעוֹת עוֹלָם׃ וּמִמֶּגֶד אֶרֶץ וּמְלֹאָהּ
its and the with and ever- hills the with and ;ancient the
;fullness ,earth of best the ,lasting hills of best the mountains

5139 6936 31:27 7218 935 5572 7931 7522
וּרְצוֹן שֹׁכְנִי סְנֶה תָּבוֹאתָה לְרֹאשׁ יוֹסֵף וּלְקָדְקֹד נְזִיר
conse- the on and Joseph the on come it let the who Him the and
one crated of crown of head ;bush in dwelt of goodwill

5971 7161 7214 7161 1926 7794 1060 251
17 אֶחָיו׃ בְּכוֹר שׁוֹרוֹ הָדָר לוֹ וְקַרְנֵי רְאֵם קַרְנָיו בָּהֶם עַמִּים
the with his (are) the the and His glory ,ox his the (as is) his (of) ;
peoples them ;horns ox wild of horns (is) of firstborn brothers

505 669 7233 776 657 3162 5055
יְנַגַּח יַחְדָּו אַפְסֵי־אָרֶץ וְהֵם רִבְבוֹת אֶפְרַיִם וְהֵם אַלְפֵי
thou- the and ,Ephraim myriads the and the the (to) together he
of sands they of (are) they earth of end ,butt shall

3485 3318 2074 8056 559 2074 4519
18 מְנַשֶּׁה׃ ס וְלִזְבוּלֻן אָמַר שְׂמַח זְבוּלֻן בְּצֵאתֶךָ וְיִשָּׂשכָר
,O and your in O ,Rejoice said he Zebulun of And .Manasseh
Issachar ,out going ,Zebulun

8228 6664 2077 2076 8033 7121 2022 5971 168
19 בְּאֹהָלֶיךָ׃ עַמִּים הַר־יִקְרָאוּ שָׁם יִזְבְּחוּ זִבְחֵי־צֶדֶק כִּי שֶׁפַע
the for ;righteous sacri- they there shall they (to) peoples your in
of bounty fices offer shall ;call mountain the ,tents

1288 559 1410 2344 2934 8226 3243 3220
20 יַמִּים יִינָקוּ וּשְׂפֻנֵי טְמוּנֵי חוֹל׃ ס וּלְגָד אָמַר בָּרוּךְ
Blessed he of And ,sand the hidden and shall they the
(is) said Gad in treasures suck seas

5869 6936 637 2220 2963 7931 3833 1410 7337
21 מַרְחִיב גָּד כְּלָבִיא שָׁכֵן וְטָרַף זְרוֹעַ אַף־קָדְקֹד׃ וַיַּרְא
he And top the and the shall and he a like ;Gad who he
eyes !head the of ,arm tear ,dwell shall lioness enlarges

ess and shall tear the arm and the top of the head. [21]And he eyes the first part for himself, for there was the portion of the lawgiver hidden; and he came *with* the rulers of the people; he executed the justice of Jehovah, and His judgments with Israel.

[22]And of Dan he said, Dan *is* a lion's whelp; he shall leap from Bashan.

[23]And of Naphtali he said, O Naphtali, satisfied with good will and full of the blessing of Jehovah; possess the west and the south.

[24]And of Asher he said, Asher *shall be* blessed with sons; let him be accepted by his brothers, and dip his foot in oil. [25]*May* your shoelatches *be* iron and bronze, and your days as your strength.

[26]There is none like the God of Jeshurun, riding the heavens for your help, and the clouds in His majesty. [27]The God of old *is* a refuge, and underneath *are* the everlasting arms. And He shall cast the enemy out from before you, and shall say, Destroy! [28]And Israel shall live alone in safety; the fountain of Jacob in a land of grain and wine; and his heavens *shall* drop down dew. [29]Blessed *are* you, O Israel! Who is like you? A people saved by Jehovah, the Shield of your help, and He who *is* the Sword of your excellency! And your enemies shall be found liars before you, and you shall tread on their high places.

5971 8269 857 5603 2710 2513 8033 7225
ראשית לו כי־שם חלקת מחקק ספון ויתא ראשי עם
the rulers he and was the por- the there for for first the
;people's (with) came ,hidden lawgiver of tion 6213 ,himself part

559 1835 3478 4944 3068 6666
22 צדקת יהוה עשה ומשפטיו עם־ישראל׃ ולדן אמר
he of And .Israel with His and he Jehovah the
said Dan judgments ,executed of justice

7649 5320 559 5320 1316 2182 138 1482 1835
23 דן גור אריה יזנק מן־הבשן׃ ולנפתלי אמר נפתלי שבע
satisfied O ,said he of And .Bashan from he ;lion's a whelp Dan
,Naphtali Naphtali leap shall (is)

836 3423 1864 3220 3068 1293 4392 7522
24 רצון ומלא ברכת יהוה ים ודרום ירשה׃ ולאשר
of And .possess the and the ,Jehovah the full and (with)
Asher south west of blessing of goodwill

7272 8081 2881 251 7521 1961 830 1121 1288 559
אמר ברוך מבנים אשר יהי רצוי אחיו וטבל בשמן רגלו׃
his oil in dip and his accepted (and) ;Asher with (be May) he
.foot ,brothers by be sons blessed ,said

3484 410 369 1679 3117 4515 5178 1270
25 ברזל ונחשת מנעליך וכימיך דבאך׃ אין כאל ישרון
26
Jeshu- the like None your as and (be may) and Iron
run of God is .strength days your ,latches your bronze

6924 430 4585 7834 1346 5828 8064 7392
27 רכב שמים בעזרך ובגאותו שחקים׃ מענה אלהי קדם
of The a (is) the His in and your for the riding
old God refuge .clouds majesty ,help heavens

8045 559 341 6440 1644 5769 2220 8478
ומתחת זרעת עולם ויגרש מפניך אויב ויאמר השמד׃
!Destroy ,said and the before from and ever- the (are) and
,enemy you out drove ;lasting arms underneath

8492 1715 776 3290 5869 910 983 3478 7931
28 וישכן ישראל בטח בדד עין יעקב אל־ארץ דגן ותירוש
new and grain a in Jacob's foun- ,alone in Israel So
wine of land tain safety dwells

3467 5971 3478 835 2919 6201 8064
29 אף־שמיו יערפו־טל׃ אשריך ישראל מי כמוך עם נושע
saved a like Who O (are) Blessed .dew shall His and
people ?you (is) !Israel ,you down drop heavens

341 3584 1346 2719 5828 4043 3068
ביהוה מגן עזרך ואשר־חרב גאותך ויכחשו איביך לך
before your be will And your the Who and your the Jeho- by
,you enemies liars .majesty of sword (is) ,help of shield ,vah

1869 1116 5921
ואתה על־במותימו תדרך׃
shall high their on and
.tread places you

CAP. XXXIV לד

CHAPTER 34

CHAPTER 34

[1]And Moses went up from the plains of Moab to Mount Nebo, the top of Pisgah, which *is* opposite Jericho. And Jehovah caused him to see all the land, Gilead to Dan; [2]and all Naphtali, and the land of Ephraim, and Manasseh, and all the land of Judah to the sea beyond; [3]and the south, and the plain of the

834 6449 7218 5015/2022 4124 6160 4872 5927
1 ויעל משה מערבת מואב אל־הר נבו ראש הפסגה אשר
which ,Pisgah the ,Nebo Mount to Moab the from Moses And
(is) of top of plains up went

1568 776 3605 3068 7200 3405 6440
על־פני ירחו ויראהו יהוה את־כל־הארץ את־הגלעד עד
to Gilead the all Jehovah and ;Jericho opposite
;land him showed

3605 459 669 776 5320 3605 1835
2 דן׃ ואת כל־נפתלי ואת־ארץ אפרים ומנשה ואת כל
all and and ,Ephraim the and Naphtali all and ,Dan
,Manasseh of land

3603 5045 314 3220 5704 3063 776
3 ארץ יהודה עד הים האחרון׃ ואת־הנגב ואת־הככר
of plain the and Negeb the and ;Hinder the to Judah the
Sea of land

valley of Jericho, the city of palm trees, to Zoar. [4]And Jehovah said to him, This *is* the land which I have sworn to Abraham, to Isaac, and to Jacob, saying, I will give it to your seed. I have caused you tosee with your eyes, but you shall not cross over there. [5]And Moses the servant of Jehovah died there in the land of Moab, according to the command of Jehovah. [6]And He buried him in a valley in the land of Moab, opposite Beth-peor. And no man knows his burying-place to this day.

[7]And Moses *was* a son of a hundred and twenty years when he died; his eye had not become dim, nor had his natural force abated. [8]And the sons of Israel mourned Moses in the plains of Moab thirty days. And the days of weeping *and* mourning for Moses were ended. [9]And Joshua the son of Nun was full of the spirit of wisdom, for Moses had laid his hands on him. And the sons of Israel listened to him and did as Jehovah commanded Moses. [10]And never since has a prophet like Moses arisen in Israel, whom Jehovah knew face to face,

[11]in regard to all the signs and wonders which Jehovah sent him to do in the land of Egypt, to Pharaoh, and to all his servants, and to all his land; [12]and in regard to all the mighty hand, and in all the great terror which Moses showed in the eyes of all Israel.

3068 559 6820 8558 5892 3405 1237
4 בִּקְעַת יְרֵחוֹ עִיר הַתְּמָרִים עַד־צֹעַר׃ וַיֹּאמֶר יְהוָה אֵלָיו
to Jehovah said And .Zoar to palm the ,Jericho valley the
,him trees of city of

3290 3327 85 7650 834 776 2088
זֹאת הָאָרֶץ אֲשֶׁר נִשְׁבַּעְתִּי לְאַבְרָהָם לְיִצְחָק וּלְיַעֲקֹב
to and ,Isaac to to have I which the This
Jacob ,Abraham sworn land (is)

5674 3808 8033 5869 7200 5414 2233 559
לֵאמֹר לְזַרְעֲךָ אֶתְּנֶנָּה הֶרְאִיתִיךָ בְעֵינֶיךָ וְשָׁמָּה לֹא תַעֲבֹר׃
will you not but your with caused have I will I your to ,saying
.over cross there ,eyes see to you ;it give seed

3068 6310 4124 776 3068 5650 4872 8033 4191
5 וַיָּמָת שָׁם מֹשֶׁה עֶבֶד־יְהוָה בְּאֶרֶץ מוֹאָב עַל־פִּי יְהוָה׃
.Jehovah the according ,Moab the in ,Jehovah the Moses there And
of mouth to of land of servant died

3045 =1042= 41:24 776 1516 6912
6 וַיִּקְבֹּר אֹתוֹ בַגַּי בְּאֶרֶץ מוֹאָב מוּל בֵּית פְּעוֹר וְלֹא־יָדַע
knows and ;peor Beth- opposite ,Moab the in the in him He And
not of land valley buried

6242 3967/1121 4872 3117 5704 6900 376
7 אִישׁ אֶת־קְבֻרָתוֹ עַד הַיּוֹם הַזֶּה׃ וּמֹשֶׁה בֶּן־מֵאָה וְעֶשְׂרִים
and a a (was) And .this day to his (any)
twenty hundred of son Moses place burial man

1121 1058 3893 3808 5869 3543 3808 4194 8141
8 שָׁנָה בְּמֹתוֹ לֹא־כָהֲתָה עֵינוֹ וְלֹא־נָס לֵחֹה׃ וַיִּבְכּוּ בְנֵי
the And (his) fled and his had not his at years
of sons bewailed .vigor (him) not ,eye dim become ;death

3117 8552 3117 7970 4124 6160 4872 3478
יִשְׂרָאֵל אֶת־מֹשֶׁה בְּעַרְבֹת מוֹאָב שְׁלֹשִׁים יוֹם וַיִּתְּמוּ יְמֵי
the and ;days thirty Moab the on Moses Israel
of days ended of plains

5564 2451 7307 4392 5126/1121/3091 4872 60 1065
9 בְכִי אֵבֶל מֹשֶׁה׃ וִיהוֹשֻׁעַ בִּן־נוּן מָלֵא רוּחַ חָכְמָה כִּי־סָמַךְ
had for ,wisdom the was Nun the And .Moses (and) weep-
laid of spirit of full of son Joshua for mourning ing

6213 3478 1121 8085 3027 4872
מֹשֶׁה אֶת־יָדָיו עָלָיו וַיִּשְׁמְעוּ אֵלָיו בְּנֵי־יִשְׂרָאֵל וַיַּעֲשׂוּ
and Israel the to listened and on his Moses
did of sons him ;him hands

3478 5750 5030 6965 4872 3068 6680
10 כַּאֲשֶׁר צִוָּה יְהוָה אֶת־מֹשֶׁה׃ וְלֹא־קָם נָבִיא עוֹד בְּיִשְׂרָאֵל
in again a has And .Moses Jehovah com- as
Israel prophet arisen not manded

226 3605 6440 6440 3068 3045 4872
11 כְּמֹשֶׁה אֲשֶׁר יְדָעוֹ יְהוָה פָּנִים אֶל־פָּנִים׃ לְכָל־הָאֹתֹת
the regard In .face to face ,Jehovah knew whom like
signs all to ,Moses

4714 776 6213 3068 7971 4159
וְהַמּוֹפְתִים אֲשֶׁר שְׁלָחוֹ יְהוָה לַעֲשׂוֹת בְּאֶרֶץ מִצְרָיִם
.Egypt the in do to Jehovah sent which and
of land him wonders

2389 3027 3605 776 3605 5650 3605 6547
12 לְפַרְעֹה וּלְכָל־עֲבָדָיו וּלְכָל־אַרְצוֹ׃ וּלְכֹל הַיָּד הַחֲזָקָה
the hand in and his and his for and to
,mighty all to regard ;land all to ,servants all ,Pharaoh

3478 3605 5869 4872 6213 834 1419 4172 3605
וּלְכֹל הַמּוֹרָא הַגָּדוֹל אֲשֶׁר עָשָׂה מֹשֶׁה לְעֵינֵי כָּל־יִשְׂרָאֵל׃
.Israel all the in Moses did which great the in and
of eyes terror all

יהושע

LIBER JEHOSUAH

(THE) BOOK OF JOSHUA

CAPUT. I א

CHAPTER 1

A LITERAL TRANSLATION
OF THE BIBLE

THE BOOK OF JOSHUA

CHAPTER 1

1 And after the death of Moses the servant of Jehovah, Jehovah spoke to Joshua the son of Nun, Moses' minister, saying, 2 My servant Moses is dead. And now rise up, cross over this Jordan, you and all this people, to the land which I am giving to them, to the sons of Israel. 3 Every place on which your foot shall tread, I have given it to you, as I spoke to Moses. 4 From the wilderness, and this Lebanon, even to the great river, the river Euphrates, all the land of the Hittites, and to the Great Sea toward the setting of the sun, shall be your border. 5 There shall not be any man able to stand before you all the days of your life. As I was with Moses, so I will be with you. I will not fail you nor will I forsake you. 6 Be strong and brave. For you shall cause this people to inherit the land which I swore to their fathers, to give to them. 7 Only be strong and very brave, so that you may take heed to do according to all the law which Moses My servant commanded you. Do not turn from it to the right or to the left, that you may act wisely wherever you go. 8 This book of the Law shall not depart out of your mouth, and you shall meditate on it by day and by night, so that you shall be on guard to do according to all

3091 3068 559 3068 5650 4872 4191 310 1961
1 ויהי אחרי מות משה עבד יהוה ויאמר יהוה אל־יהושע
Joshua to Jehovah that said ,Jehovah the servant of Moses the death of after And ,was it

6965 6258 4191 5650 4872 559 4872 8334 5126/1121
2 בן־נון משרת משה לאמר: משה עבדי מת ועתה קום
,arise and ,now is ;dead My servant Moses ,saying ,Moses' minister Nun the of son

834 776 20:88 5971 3605 859 2088 3383 5674
עבר את־הירדן הזה אתה וכל־העם הזה אל־הארץ אשר
which the land to ,this people and all ,you ;this Jordan cross over

1869 834 4725/3605 3478 1121 5414 595
3 אנכי נתן להם לבני ישראל: כל־מקום אשר תדרך
shall tread which place Every .Israel the to of sons ,them to am giving I

4872 1696 5414 7272 3709
כף־רגלכם בו לכם נתתיו כאשר דברתי אל־משה:
.Moses to spoke I as have I ,it given to you ,on it your foot sole the of

3605 6578 5104 1419 5104 5704 2088 3844 4057
4 מהמדבר והלבנון הזה ועד־הנהר הגדול נהר־פרת כל
all ,Euphrates river the ,Great the River even to ,this and Lebanon the From ,wilderness

1366 1961 8121 3996 1419 3220 2850 776
ארץ החתים ועד־הים הגדול מבוא השמש יהיה גבולכם:
your .border shall be sun the of setting the toward ,Great the Sea and to the ,Hittites of land the

1961 2416 3117 3605 6440 376 3320
5 לא־יתיצב איש לפניך כל ימי חייך כאשר הייתי עם־
with was I as your ;life the of days all before you A man be shall stand to able not

553 2388 5800 3808 7503 3808 1961 4872
6 משה אהיה עמך לא ארפך ולא אעזבך: חזק ואמץ
and ,brave Be strong will I .you forsake and not will I you fail not with ;you will I be ,Moses

7650 834 776 2088 5971 5157
כי אתה תנחיל את־העם הזה את־הארץ אשר־נשבעתי
swore I which land the this people cause shall inherit to you for

6213 8104 3966 553 2388 5414 1
7 לאבותם לתת להם: רק חזק ואמץ מאד לשמר לעשות
do to take to heed ,very and brave be strong Only .them give to their to ,fathers

3225 5493 5650 4872 6680 834 8451 3605
ככל־התורה אשר צוך משה עבדי אל־תסור ממנו ימין
the to right from it do not turn My ;servant Moses charged you which the Law according to all

5612 4185 3808 3212 3605 7919 8040
8 ושמאול למען תשכיל בכל אשר תלך: לא־ימוש ספר
Book of depart not shall you .go where every may you wisely act that the to or ,left

8104 3915 3119 1897 6310 2088 8451
התורה הזה מפיך והגית בו יומם ולילה למען תשמר
may you be watchful that by and ,night by day it on meditate shall, you and your mouth from This Law the

that is written in it. For then you shall prosper your way, and then you shall act wisely. 9Have I not commanded you? Be strong and brave. Do not be afraid or discouraged, for Jehovah your God *is* with you in all *places* where you go.

10Joshua commanded the officers of the people, saying, 11Pass through the camp and tell the people, saying, Prepare food for you. For within three days you *are* crossing over this Jordan to go in to possess it; the land which Jehovah your God is giving to you, to possess it.

12And Joshua spoke to the Reubenites, and to the Gadites, and to the half tribe of Manasseh, saying, 13Remember the word which Moses the servant of Jehovah commanded you, saying, Jehovah your God has given you rest, and He has given to you this land; 14your wives, your little ones, and your livestock shall remain in the land which Moses has given to you beyond the Jordan. But you shall cross over armed before your brothers, all the mighty warriors, and shall help them, 15until Jehovah has given rest to your brothers, as well as to you, and they, even they have possessed the land which Jehovah your God is giving to them. Then you may return to the land of your possession, and may possess it, which Moses the servant of Jehovah has given to you beyond the Jordan, toward the rising of the sun. 16And they answered Joshua, saying, We will do all that you command us; and we will go everywhere you shall send

1870 6743 3789 6213
לַעֲשׂוֹת כְּכָל־הַכָּתוּב בּוֹ כִּי־אָז תַּצְלִיחַ אֶת־דְּרָכֶךָ וְאָז
and ,way your shall then for in is that according do to
then prosper ;it written to all

2865 3808 6206 3808 553 / 2388 6680 3808 7919
9 תַּשְׂכִּיל׃ הֲלוֹא צִוִּיתִיךָ חֲזַק וֶאֱמָץ אַל־תַּעֲרֹץ וְאַל־תֵּחָת כִּי
for dis- nor be do not and Be charged I Have shall you
,couraged afraid ;brave strong ?you not wisely act

3091 6680 3212 3605 430 3068
10 עִמְּךָ יְהוָה אֱלֹהֶיךָ בְּכֹל אֲשֶׁר תֵּלֵךְ׃ וַיְצַו יְהוֹשֻׁעַ אֶת־
Joshua Then .go you where all in your Jehovah with
commanded (places) God (is) you

5971 6680 4264 7130 5674 559 5971 8269
11 שֹׁטְרֵי הָעָם לֵאמֹר׃ עִבְרוּ ׀ בְּקֶרֶב הַמַּחֲנֶה וְצַוּוּ אֶת־הָעָם
people the and camp the through Pass ,saying the the
tell ,people of officers

5674 3117 7969 6720 3559 559
לֵאמֹר הָכִינוּ לָכֶם צֵידָה כִּי בְּעוֹד ׀ שְׁלֹשֶׁת יָמִים אַתֶּם עֹבְרִים
crossing you days three within for ;food for Prepare ,saying
over (are) you

3068 834 776 3423 935 2088 3383
אֶת־הַיַּרְדֵּן הַזֶּה לָבוֹא לָרֶשֶׁת אֶת־הָאָרֶץ אֲשֶׁר יְהוָה
Jehovah which land the .it possess to in go to this Jordan

2677 1425 7206 3423 935 5414 430
12 אֱלֹהֵיכֶם נֹתֵן לָכֶם לְרִשְׁתָּהּ׃ וְלָרְאוּבֵנִי וְלַגָּדִי וְלַחֲצִי
to and the to and the to And .it possess to to is God your
half the ,Gadites ,Reubenites ,you giving

1697 2142 559 3091 559 4519 7626
13 שֵׁבֶט הַמְנַשֶּׁה אָמַר יְהוֹשֻׁעַ לֵאמֹר׃ זָכוֹר אֶת־הַדָּבָר אֲשֶׁר
which word the Recall ,saying ,Joshua spoke Manasseh tribe
of

5117 430 3068 559 3068 5650 4872 6680
צִוָּה אֶתְכֶם מֹשֶׁה עֶבֶד־יְהוָה לֵאמֹר יְהוָה אֱלֹהֵיכֶם מֵנִיחַ
gives God your Jehovah ,saying of the ,Moses you charged
rest ,Jehovah servant

4735 2945 802 2088 776 5414
14 לָכֶם וְנָתַן לָכֶם אֶת־הָאָרֶץ הַזֹּאת׃ נְשֵׁיכֶם טַפְּכֶם וּמִקְנֵיכֶם
your and your Your .this land you to and you
livestock ,infants wives give will

3383 5676 4872 5414 834 776 3427
יֵשְׁבוּ בָּאָרֶץ אֲשֶׁר נָתַן לָכֶם מֹשֶׁה בְּעֵבֶר הַיַּרְדֵּן וְאַתֶּם
But the beyond Moses you to has which the in shall
you .Jordan given land remain

5826 2428 1368 3605 251 6440 2571 5674
תַּעַבְרוּ חֲמֻשִׁים לִפְנֵי אֲחֵיכֶם כֹּל גִּבּוֹרֵי הַחַיִל וַעֲזַרְתֶּם
shall and ,warriors the all your before armed cross shall
help mighty ,brothers over

3423 251 3068 5117 5704
15 אוֹתָם׃ עַד אֲשֶׁר־יָנִיחַ יְהוָה ׀ לַאֲחֵיכֶם כָּכֶם וְיָרְשׁוּ גַם־
even they and to as your to Jehovah has until ,them
,possessed have you brothers rest given

7725 5414 430 3068 834 776
הֵמָּה אֶת־הָאָרֶץ אֲשֶׁר־יְהוָה אֱלֹהֵיכֶם נֹתֵן לָהֶם וְשַׁבְתֶּם
you then to is God your Jehovah which land the ,they
return may ;them giving

4872 5414 834 3423 3423 776
לְאֶרֶץ יְרֻשַּׁתְכֶם וִירִשְׁתֶּם אוֹתָהּ אֲשֶׁר ׀ נָתַן לָכֶם מֹשֶׁה
Moses you to has which ,it may and your of the to
given possess ,possession land

3091 6030 8121 4217 3383 5671 3068 5650
16 עֶבֶד יְהוָה בְּעֵבֶר הַיַּרְדֵּן מִזְרַח הַשָּׁמֶשׁ׃ וַיַּעֲנוּ אֶת־יְהוֹשֻׁעַ
,Joshua they And .sun the toward the beyond ,Jehovah the
answered of rising the Jordan of servant

7971 3605 6213 6680 3605 559
לֵאמֹר כֹּל אֲשֶׁר־צִוִּיתָנוּ נַעֲשֶׂה וְאֶל־כָּל־אֲשֶׁר תִּשְׁלָחֵנוּ
shall you where every and will we you that All ,saying
,us send (place) to ,do us command

us. 17 Acording to all we heard from Moses, so we will listen to you. Surely Jehovah your God is with you, as He has been with Moses. 18 Whoever rebels against your mouth, and will not listen to your commands in all that you say to him, he shall be put to death. Only, be strong and brave.

7535 8085 4872 8085 834 3605 3212
17 נֵלֵךְ׃ כְּכֹל אֲשֶׁר־שָׁמַעְנוּ אֶל־מֹשֶׁה כֵּן נִשְׁמַע אֵלֶיךָ רַק
surely to ;you will we so listen ,Moses to we listened which according all to will we ;go

376 8605 4872 1961 430 3068
18 יִהְיֶה יְהוָה אֱלֹהֶיךָ עִמָּךְ כַּאֲשֶׁר הָיָה עִם־מֹשֶׁה׃ כָּל־אִישׁ
man Every .Moses with has He been as with ,you your God Jehovah is

3605 1697 8085 6310 4784
אֲשֶׁר־יַמְרֶה אֶת־פִּיךָ וְלֹא־יִשְׁמַע אֶת־דְּבָרֶיךָ לְכֹל אֲשֶׁר־
that all in your words will hear and not your ,mouth resists who

553 2388 7535 4191 6680
תְּצַוֶּנּוּ יוּמָת רַק חֲזַק וֶאֱמָץ׃
and .brave be strong only be shall ;killed say you ,him to

CAP. II ב

CHAPTER 2

CHAPTER 2

1 And Joshua the son of Nun sent two men out of Shittim to spy secretly, saying, Go look over the land, and Jericho. And they went and came into the house of a woman, a harlot; and her name *was* Rahab. And they lay down there. 2 And it was reported to the king of Jericho, saying, Behold, men have come here tonight from the sons of Israel, to search the land. 3 And the king of Jericho sent to Rahab, saying, Bring out the men who have come in to you, who have come into your house. They have come in to search out all the land. 4 And the woman took the two men and hid them, and said, This way the men came in to me, but I did not know from where they were. 5 And it happened *as* the gate was to *be* shut at dark, even the men went out. I do not know where they have gone. You go after them, and hurry, for you may overtake them. 6 But she made them go up on the roof, and hid them with stalks of flax, which she arranged on the roof. 7 And the men went after them the way of the Jordan, by the

7270 502 8147 7851 5126/1121/3091 7971
1 וַיִּשְׁלַח יְהוֹשֻׁעַ בִּן־נוּן מִן־הַשִּׁטִּים שְׁנַיִם אֲנָשִׁים מְרַגְּלִים
spy to men two Shittim out of Nun the of son Joshua And sent

935 3212 3405 776 7200 3212 559 2791
חֶרֶשׁ לֵאמֹר לְכוּ רְאוּ אֶת־הָאָרֶץ וְאֶת־יְרִיחוֹ וַיֵּלְכוּ וַיָּבֹאוּ
and to came and ,went they ;Jericho and land the Look over ,Go ,saying ,secretly

4428 559 7001 7343 8034 2181 802 1004
2 בֵּית אִשָּׁה זוֹנָה וּשְׁמָהּ רָחָב וַיִּשְׁכְּבוּ־שָׁמָּה׃ וַיֵּאָמַר לְמֶלֶךְ
the to of king it And told was .there they and down lay ;Rahab her and ,name a ;harlot a ,woman house the of

3478 1121 3915 935 582 2009 559 3405
יְרִיחוֹ לֵאמֹר הִנֵּה אֲנָשִׁים בָּאוּ הֵנָּה הַלַּיְלָה מִבְּנֵי יִשְׂרָאֵל
,Israel the from of sons tonight here have come men See ,saying ,Jericho

559 7343 3405 4428 7971 776 2658
3 לַחְפֹּר אֶת־הָאָרֶץ׃ וַיִּשְׁלַח מֶלֶךְ יְרִיחוֹ אֶל־רָחָב לֵאמֹר
,saying ,Rahab to Jericho the of king sent And .land the to search

1004 935 935 582 3318
הוֹצִיאִי הָאֲנָשִׁים הַבָּאִים אֵלַיִךְ אֲשֶׁר־בָּאוּ לְבֵיתֵךְ כִּי
for your into ;house have come who ,you to have who in come men the Bring out

582 8147 802 3947 935 776 3605 2658
4 לַחְפֹּר אֶת־כָּל־הָאָרֶץ בָּאוּ׃ וַתִּקַּח הָאִשָּׁה אֶת־שְׁנֵי הָאֲנָשִׁים
,men the two the woman And took .came they land the all to out search

370 3045 3808 582 935 559 6845
וַתִּצְפְּנוֹ וַתֹּאמֶר כֵּן בָּאוּ אֵלַי הָאֲנָשִׁים וְלֹא יָדַעְתִּי מֵאַיִן
from where did I know but not ,men the me to came in Thus said and hid and ,them

3808 3318 582 2822 5462 8179 1961
5 הֵמָּה׃ וַיְהִי הַשַּׁעַר לִסְגּוֹר בַּחֹשֶׁךְ וְהָאֲנָשִׁים יָצָאוּ לֹא
not went ;out men the and ,dark at for shutting the gate and was they ;were

310 4118 7291 582 3212 3045
יָדַעְתִּי אָנָה הָלְכוּ הָאֲנָשִׁים רִדְפוּ מַהֵר אַחֲרֵיהֶם כִּי
for after ,them quickly run ;men the have gone where do I know

6086 6593 2934 1406 5927 5381
6 תַשִּׂיגוּם׃ וְהִיא הֶעֱלָתַם הַגָּגָה וַתִּטְמְנֵם בְּפִשְׁתֵּי הָעֵץ
with of stalks ,flax hid and them the on ,roof caused go to them But she may you .them catch

1870 310 7291 582 1406 6186
7 הָעֲרֻכוֹת לָהּ עַל־הַגָּג׃ וְהָאֲנָשִׁים רָדְפוּ אַחֲרֵיהֶם דֶּרֶךְ
the of way them after pursued men the And the .roof on by her were which arranged

fords. And they shut the gate afterwards, when the pursuers had gone after them.

8And before they had laid down, she came up to them on the roof. 9And she said to the men, I know that Jehovah has given the land to you, and that your terror has fallen on us, and that all the inhabitants of the land have melted before you. 10For we have heard how Jehovah dried up the water of the Red Sea before you, as you were going out of Egypt; also that which you have done to two kings of the Amorites who *were* beyond the Jordan; to Sihon, and to Og, whom you destroyed. 11And we have heard, and our heart has melted, and there not still rises spirit in *any* man, because of you. For Jehovah your God, He *is* God in the heavens above, and in the earth below.

12And now, please swear by me by Jehovah, since I have dealt with you in kindness, that you will also deal with my father's house in kindness, and shall give to me a true token; 13and shall keep alive my father, and my mother, and my brothers, and my sisters, and all that they *own*, and shall deliver our souls from death. 14And the men said to her, Our life is yours. If you do not tell this business of ours, then it shall be, when Jehovah gives this land to us, that we shall deal with you in kindness and truth.

15Then she let them down by a rope through the window, for her house *was* in the side of the wall, and

הַיַּרְדֵּן עַל הַמַּעְבְּרוֹת וְהַשַּׁעַר סָגָרוּ אַחֲרֵי כַּאֲשֶׁר יָצְאוּ
8 הָרֹדְפִים אַחֲרֵיהֶם׃ וְהֵמָּה טֶרֶם יִשְׁכָּבוּן וְהִיא עָלְתָה
9 עֲלֵיהֶם עַל־הַגָּג׃ וַתֹּאמֶר אֶל־הָאֲנָשִׁים יָדַעְתִּי כִּי־נָתַן
יְהוָה לָכֶם אֶת־הָאָרֶץ וְכִי־נָפְלָה אֵימַתְכֶם עָלֵינוּ וְכִי
10 נָמֹגוּ כָּל־יֹשְׁבֵי הָאָרֶץ מִפְּנֵיכֶם׃ כִּי שָׁמַעְנוּ אֵת אֲשֶׁר
הוֹבִישׁ יְהוָה אֶת־מֵי יַם־סוּף מִפְּנֵיכֶם בְּצֵאתְכֶם מִמִּצְרָיִם
וַאֲשֶׁר עֲשִׂיתֶם לִשְׁנֵי מַלְכֵי הָאֱמֹרִי אֲשֶׁר בְּעֵבֶר הַיַּרְדֵּן
11 לְסִיחֹן וּלְעוֹג אֲשֶׁר הֶחֱרַמְתֶּם אוֹתָם׃ וַנִּשְׁמַע וַיִּמַּס
לְבָבֵנוּ וְלֹא־קָמָה עוֹד רוּחַ בְּאִישׁ מִפְּנֵיכֶם כִּי יְהוָה
אֱלֹהֵיכֶם הוּא אֱלֹהִים בַּשָּׁמַיִם מִמַּעַל וְעַל־הָאָרֶץ מִתָּחַת׃
12 וְעַתָּה הִשָּׁבְעוּ־נָא לִי בַּיהוָה כִּי־עָשִׂיתִי עִמָּכֶם חָסֶד
וַעֲשִׂיתֶם גַּם־אַתֶּם עִם־בֵּית אָבִי חֶסֶד וּנְתַתֶּם לִי אוֹת
13 אֱמֶת׃ וְהַחֲיִתֶם אֶת־אָבִי וְאֶת־אִמִּי וְאֶת־אַחַי וְאֶת־אַחוֹתַי
14 וְאֵת כָּל־אֲשֶׁר לָהֶם וְהִצַּלְתֶּם אֶת־נַפְשֹׁתֵינוּ מִמָּוֶת׃ וַיֹּאמְרוּ
לָהּ הָאֲנָשִׁים נַפְשֵׁנוּ תַחְתֵּיכֶם לָמוּת אִם לֹא תַגִּידוּ אֶת־
דְּבָרֵנוּ זֶה וְהָיָה בְּתֵת יְהוָה לָנוּ אֶת־הָאָרֶץ וְעָשִׂינוּ עִמָּךְ
15 חֶסֶד וֶאֱמֶת׃ וַתּוֹרִדֵם בַּחֶבֶל בְּעַד הַחַלּוֹן כִּי בֵיתָהּ בְּקִיר

she lived in the wall. [16]And
she said to them, Go to the
mountain lest the pursuers
come upon you. And you
shall hide there three days
until the pursuers return;
and afterward you shall go
on your way. [17]And the men
said to her, We will be
guiltless from this oath of
yours which you made us
swear. [18]Behold, we are
coming into the land; you
shall bind this scarlet thread
of line in the window by
which you have let us down.
And you shall gather your
father, and your mother, and
your brothers, and all your
father's house to you, to the
house. [19]And it shall be,
anyone who goes outside
from the doors of your
house, his blood *shall be* on
his head, and we shall be
innocent. And anyone who
is with you in the house, his
blood *shall be* on our head,
if any hand is on him. [20]But
if you reveal this business of
ours, then we shall be
guiltless from you oath
which you make us swear.

[21]And she said, Let it *be*
according to your words.
And she sent them away.
And they went. And she
bound the line of scarlet
thread in the window.

[22]And they departed and
came to the mountain, and
stayed there three days,
until the pursuers had
returned. And the pursuers
searched in all the way, but
did not find *them*. [23]And
the two men returned and
came down from the
mountain, and crossed over,
and came to Joshua the son
of Nun, and reported to him
all that had happened to
them. [24]And they said to

3212 2022 559 3427 2346 2346
16 החומה ובחומה היא יושבת׃ ותאמר להם ההרה לכו
,Go the to to she And .lived she in and the
mountain ,them said wall the ,wall

3117 7969 8033 7247 7291 6293
פן־יפגעו בכם הרדפים ונחבתם שמה שלשת ימים
days three there shall you and the upon come lest
hide ;pursuers you

559 1870 3212 310 7291 7725 5704
17 עד שוב הרדפים ואחר תלכו לדרככם׃ ויאמרו אליה
her to said And .way your on you and the return until
go shall after ;pursuers

7650 834 2088 7621 5355 582
האנשים נקים אנחנו משבעתך הזה אשר השבעתנו׃
make you which this oath from We be will ,men the
.swear us yours of guiltless

8144 2339 8615 776 935 2009
18 הנה אנחנו באים בארץ את־תקות חוט השני הזה
this scarlet thread of line the into are we ,See
;land coming

517 1 3381 834 2474 7194
תקשרי בחלון אשר הורדתנו בו ואת־אביך ואת־אמך
your and your and ,it by have you which the to shall you
,mother father down us let window bind

1004 622 1 1004 3605 251
ואת־אחיך ואת כל־בית אביך תאספי אליך הביתה׃
the to ,you to shall you your the all and your and
house gather father of house ,brothers

7218 1818 2351 1004 1817 3318 1961
19 והיה כל אשר־יצא מדלתי ביתך החוצה דמו בראשו
his on his ,outside your the from goes who any- it And
,head (is) blood house of doors one ,be shall

7218 1818 1004 3605 5355
ואנחנו נקים וכל אשר יהיה אתך בבית דמו בראשנו
our on his the in with is who and be shall and
,head (is) blood ,house you anyone innocent we

5355 1961 2088 1697 5046 3027
20 אם־יד תהיה־בו׃ ואם־תגידי את־דברנו זה והיינו נקים
guiltless then ,this of business you if But .him on is a if
be shall we ours reveal hand

3651 1697 559 7650 834 7621
21 משבעתך אשר השבעתנו׃ ותאמר כדבריכם כן־הוא
it so to According And make you which your from
;(be will) ,words your ,said she .swear us oath

3212 2474 8144 8615 7194 3212 7971
22 ותשלחם וילכו ותקשר את־תקות השני בחלון׃ וילכו
they And the in scarlet line the she And and she and
left .window of bound .left they ,them sent

7291 7725 5704 3117 7969 8033 3427 2022 935
ויבאו ההרה וישבו שם שלשת ימים עד־שבו הרדפים
the had until ,days three there and the to and
;pursuers returned stayed ,mountain came

8147 7725 4672 1870 3605 7291 1245
23 ויבקשו הרדפים בכל־הדרך ולא מצאו׃ וישבו שני
two And found but ,way the in the and
returned .(them) not all pursuers searched

5126/1121/3091 935 5674 2022 3381 582
האנשים וירדו מההר ויעברו ויבאו אל־יהושע בן־נון
,Nun the Joshua to and and the from came and ,men the
of son came crossed ,mountain down

3091 559 4672 3605 5608
24 ויספרו־לו את כל־המצאות אותם׃ ויאמרו אל־יהושע
,Joshua to they And .them to had that all to and
said happened him reported

Joshua, Surely Jehovah has given all the land into our hands. And also, all the inhabitants of the land have melted before us.

כִּי־נָתַן יְהוָה בְּיָדֵנוּ אֶת־כָּל־הָאָרֶץ וְגַם־נָמֹגוּ כָּל־יֹשְׁבֵי

the of inhabitants all melted have ,also and ;land the all our into hands Jehovah has given truly

הָאָרֶץ מִפָּנֵינוּ׃

before .us land the

CAP. III ג

CHAPTER 3

CHAPTER 3

[1]And Joshua rose up early in the morning. And they moved from Shittim and came to the Jordan, he and all the sons of Israel. And they stayed there before they crossed over. [2]And it happened, at the end of three days, the officers passed into the midst of the camp. [3]And *they* commanded the people, saying, When you see the ark of the covenant of Jehovah your God, and the priests, and the Levites bearing it, then you shall move from your place and shall go after it. [4]Only, keep a distance between you and it, about two thousand cubits by measure. You shall not come near it, so that you may know the way in which you are to go. For you have not crossed over *this* way yesterday and the day before. [5]And Joshua said to the people, Sanctify yourselves, for tomorrow Jehovah will do wonders among you. [6]And Joshua spoke to the priests, saying, Take up the ark of the covenant and go before the people. And they took up the ark of the covenant and went before the people.

1 וַיַּשְׁכֵּם יְהוֹשֻׁעַ בַּבֹּקֶר וַיִּסְעוּ מֵהַשִּׁטִּים וַיָּבֹאוּ עַד־הַיַּרְדֵּן

the Jordan to and came from Shittim they and forth set the in ,morning Joshua rose And early

2 הוּא וְכָל־בְּנֵי יִשְׂרָאֵל וַיָּלִנוּ שָׁם טֶרֶם יַעֲבֹרוּ׃ וַיְהִי מִקְצֵה

the at of end it And ,was they .crossed before there they and stayed ;Israel the of sons and all he

3 שְׁלֹשֶׁת יָמִים וַיַּעַבְרוּ הַשֹּׁטְרִים בְּקֶרֶב הַמַּחֲנֶה׃ וַיְצַוּוּ

and charged ,camp the the in of midst officers the passed and over days three

אֶת־הָעָם לֵאמֹר כִּרְאֹתְכֶם אֵת אֲרוֹן בְּרִית־יְהוָה אֱלֹהֵיכֶם

,God your Jehovah the of covenant ark the of you When see ,saying ,people the

וְהַכֹּהֲנִים הַלְוִיִּם נֹשְׂאִים אֹתוֹ וְאַתֶּם תִּסְעוּ מִמְּקוֹמְכֶם

your from place set shall forth then you ,it bearing the ,Levites the and priests

4 וַהֲלַכְתֶּם אַחֲרָיו׃ אַךְ רָחוֹק יִהְיֶה בֵּינֵיכֶם וּבֵינָו כְּאַלְפַּיִם

two about thousand and ;it between you let be a distance Only after .it shall and go

אַמָּה בַּמִּדָּה אַל־תִּקְרְבוּ אֵלָיו לְמַעַן אֲשֶׁר־תֵּדְעוּ אֶת־הַדֶּרֶךְ

way the may you know that so ,it shall you near come not by ;measure cubits

אֲשֶׁר תֵּלְכוּ־בָהּ כִּי לֹא עֲבַרְתֶּם בַּדֶּרֶךְ מִתְּמוֹל שִׁלְשׁוֹם׃

past time in (this)on way have you crossed not for ;in are you go to which

5 וַיֹּאמֶר יְהוֹשֻׁעַ אֶל־הָעָם הִתְקַדָּשׁוּ כִּי מָחָר יַעֲשֶׂה

do will tomorrow for Sanctify ,yourselves the ,people to Joshua said And

6 יְהוָה בְּקִרְבְּכֶם נִפְלָאוֹת׃ וַיֹּאמֶר יְהוֹשֻׁעַ אֶל־הַכֹּהֲנִים

,priests the to Joshua And spoke among you Jehovah

לֵאמֹר שְׂאוּ אֶת־אֲרוֹן הַבְּרִית וְעִבְרוּ לִפְנֵי הָעָם וַיִּשְׂאוּ

they and up took the ;people before go and the covenant ark the of Take up ,saying

[7]And Jehovah said to Joshua, This day I will begin to make you great in the eyes of all Israel, so that they shall know that as I was with Moses, I am with you. [8]And

7 אֶת־אֲרוֹן הַבְּרִית וַיֵּלְכוּ לִפְנֵי הָעָם׃ וַיֹּאמֶר יְהוָה

Jehovah said And the .people before and went the covenant of ark the

אֶל־יְהוֹשֻׁעַ הַיּוֹם הַזֶּה אָחֵל גַּדֶּלְךָ בְּעֵינֵי כָּל־יִשְׂרָאֵל

,Israel all the in of eyes make to great you will I begin This day ,Joshua to

אֲשֶׁר יֵדְעוּן כִּי כַּאֲשֶׁר הָיִיתִי עִם־מֹשֶׁה אֶהְיֶה עִמָּךְ׃

with .you am I ,Moses with was I as that they shall know that so

8 you shall command the
priests bearing the ark of the
covenant, saying, When you
come to the edge of the
9 waters of the Jordan, you
shall stand *still* in the
Jordan. [9]And Joshua said
to the sons of Israel, Come
near here and hear the
words of Jehovah your
God. [10]And Joshua said, By
this you shall know that the
10 living God *is* among you.
And He shall certainly expel
from before you the
Canaanites, and the Hittites,
and the Hivites, and the
Perizzites, and the Girga-
shites, and the Amorites,
and the Jebusites. [11]Behold,
11 the ark of the covenant of
Jehovah of all the earth shall
pass over before you into
the Jordan. [12]And now,
12 take for yourselves twelve
men outof the tribes of
Israel, one man for each
tribe. [13]And it shall be,
when the soles of the feet
of the priests bearing the
ark of Jehovah, Lord of all
13 the earth, come to rest in
the waters of the Jordan,
the waters of the Jordan
shall be cut off, the waters
which come down from
above. And they shall stand
in one heap.
[14]And it happened, as the
14 people moved from their
tents to cross over the
Jordan, and as the priests
bore the ark of the covenant
before the people, [15]and as
those bearing the ark came
into the Jordan, and the
feet of the priests bearing
15 the ark were dipped in the
edge of the waters—and
the Jordan was full, over all
its banks all the days of
harvest—[16]that the waters
stood still, those coming
down from above rose up
into a heap, very far above
16 the city Adam, which *is*
beside Zaretan; and those
going down by the sea of
the Arabah, the Salt Sea,

8 ואתה תצוה את־הכהנים נשאי ארון־הברית לאמר
9 בבאכם עד־קצה מי הירדן בירדן תעמדו׃ ויאמר
יהושע אל־בני ישראל גשו הנה ושמעו את־דברי יהוה
10 אלהיכם׃ ויאמר יהושע בזאת תדעון כי אל חי בקרבכם
והורש יוריש מפניכם את־הכנעני ואת־החתי ואת־
11 החוי ואת־הפרזי ואת־הגרגשי והאמרי והיבוסי׃ הנה
12 ארון הברית אדון כל־הארץ עבר לפניכם בירדן׃ ועתה
קחו לכם שני־עשר איש משבטי ישראל איש־אחד
13 איש־אחד לשבט׃ והיה כנוח כפות רגלי הכהנים
נשאי ארון יהוה אדון כל־הארץ במי הירדן מי הירדן
14 יכרתון המים הירדים מלמעלה ויעמדו נד אחד׃ ויהי
בנסע העם מאהליהם לעבר את־הירדן והכהנים נשאי
15 הארון הברית לפני העם׃ וכבוא נשאי הארון עד־
הירדן ורגלי הכהנים נשאי הארון נטבלו בקצה המים
16 והירדן מלא על־כל־גדותיו כל ימי קציר׃ ויעמדו
המים הירדים מלמעלה קמו נד־אחד הרחק מאד
באדם העיר אשר מצד צרתן והירדים על ים הערבה

were completely cut off.
And the people passed over
opposite to Jericho. [17]And
the priests bearing the ark
of the covenant of Jehovah
stood firm on dry ground in
the middle of the Jordan.
And all Israel crossed over
on dry ground until all the
nation had completely
passed over the Jordan.

17 יַם־הַמֶּלַח תַּמּוּ נִכְרָתוּ וְהָעָם עָבְרוּ נֶגֶד יְרִיחוֹ׃ וַיַּעַמְדוּ
הַכֹּהֲנִים נֹשְׂאֵי הָאָרוֹן בְּרִית־יְהוָה בֶּחָרָבָה בְּתוֹךְ הַיַּרְדֵּן
הָכֵן וְכָל־יִשְׂרָאֵל עֹבְרִים בֶּחָרָבָה עַד אֲשֶׁר־תַּמּוּ כָּל־הַגּוֹי
לַעֲבֹר אֶת־הַיַּרְדֵּן׃

CAP. IV ד

CHAPTER 4

[1]And it happened, when
all the nation had
completely crossed over
the Jordan, Jehovah spoke
to Joshua, saying, [2]Take
twelve men for you out of
the people, one man of
each tribe. [3]And charge
them, saying, Take twelve
stones from this *place*, from
the middle of the Jordan,
from the place where the
feet of the priests *were*
fixed. And you shall carry
them over with you and lay
them down in the lodging
place which you stay the
night. [4]And Joshua called
to the twelve men whom he
had made ready out of the
sons of Israel, one man out
of each tribe. [5]And Joshua
said to them, Cross over
before the ark of Jehovah
your God to the middle of
the Jordan, and *each* man
of you lift up one stone on
his shoulder, according to
the number of the tribes of
the sons of Israel, [6]so that
this shall be a sign among
you, when you children ask
hereafter, saying, What *are*
these stones to you? [7]You
shall say to them, Because
the waters of the Jordan
were cut off before the ark

1 וַיְהִי כַּאֲשֶׁר־תַּמּוּ כָל־הַגּוֹי לַעֲבוֹר אֶת־הַיַּרְדֵּן וַיֹּאמֶר
2 יְהוָה אֶל־יְהוֹשֻׁעַ לֵאמֹר׃ קְחוּ לָכֶם מִן־הָעָם שְׁנֵים עָשָׂר
3 אֲנָשִׁים אִישׁ־אֶחָד אִישׁ־אֶחָד מִשָּׁבֶט׃ וְצַוּוּ אוֹתָם לֵאמֹר
שְׂאוּ־לָכֶם מִזֶּה מִתּוֹךְ הַיַּרְדֵּן מִמַּצַּב רַגְלֵי הַכֹּהֲנִים הָכִין
שְׁתֵּים־עֶשְׂרֵה אֲבָנִים וְהַעֲבַרְתֶּם אוֹתָם עִמָּכֶם וְהִנַּחְתֶּם
4 אוֹתָם בַּמָּלוֹן אֲשֶׁר־תָּלִינוּ בוֹ הַלָּיְלָה׃ וַיִּקְרָא יְהוֹשֻׁעַ
אֶל־שְׁנֵים הֶעָשָׂר אִישׁ אֲשֶׁר הֵכִין מִבְּנֵי יִשְׂרָאֵל אִישׁ־
5 אֶחָד אִישׁ־אֶחָד מִשָּׁבֶט׃ וַיֹּאמֶר לָהֶם יְהוֹשֻׁעַ עִבְרוּ לִפְנֵי
אֲרוֹן יְהוָה אֱלֹהֵיכֶם אֶל־תּוֹךְ הַיַּרְדֵּן וְהָרִימוּ לָכֶם אִישׁ
6 אֶבֶן אַחַת עַל־שִׁכְמוֹ לְמִסְפַּר שִׁבְטֵי בְנֵי־יִשְׂרָאֵל׃ לְמַעַן
תִּהְיֶה זֹאת אוֹת בְּקִרְבְּכֶם כִּי־יִשְׁאָלוּן בְּנֵיכֶם מָחָר לֵאמֹר
7 מָה הָאֲבָנִים הָאֵלֶּה לָכֶם׃ וַאֲמַרְתֶּם לָהֶם אֲשֶׁר נִכְרְתוּ

of the covenant of Jehovah, as it crossed over into the Jordan, the waters of the Jordan were cut off. And these stones are for a memorial to the sons of Israel all the days.

[8]And the sons of Israel did as Joshua commanded, and took up twelve stones out of the middle of the Jordan, as Jehovah had spoken to Joshua, according to the number of the tribes of the sons of Israel, and crossed over with them to the lodging place, and laid them down there; [9]even the twelve stones that Joshua lifted up in the middle of the Jordan, in the place *where* the feet of the priests bearing the ark of the covenant stood firm. And they are there until this day. [10]And the priests bearing the ark were standing in the middle of the Jordan until everything was finished that Jehovah had commanded Joshua to speak to the people, according to all that Moses commanded Joshua. And the people hastened and crossed over.

[11]And it happened, when the people had finished crossing over, the ark of Jehovah and the priests crossed over before the people. [12]And the sons of Reuben, and the sons of Gad, and the half tribe of Manasseh crossed over armed before the sons of Israel, as Moses had spoken to them; [13]about forty thousand armed men of the army crossed over before Jehovah for battle, to the plains of Jericho. [14]On that day Jehovah made Joshua great in the sight of all Israel. And they feared him all the days of his life, even as they feared Moses.

3772 3383 5674 3068 1285 727 6440 3383 4325
מימי הירדן מפני ארון ברית־יהוה בעברו בירדן נכרתו
were the into it as ;Jehovah the the before the the
off cut ,Jordan crossed of covenant of ark Jordan of waters

5704 3478 1121 2146 428 68 1961 3383 4325
מי הירדן והיו האבנים האלה לזכרון לבני ישראל עד־
unto Israel the to a for these stones are and the the
of sons memorial Jordan of waters

8 5375 3091 6680 834 3478 1121 6213 5769
עולם׃ ויעשו־כן בני־ישראל כאשר צוה יהושע וישאו
and ,Joshua ordered as Israel the so And .forever
up took of sons did

3068 1696 834 3383 8432 68 6240 8147
שתי־עשרה אבנים מתוך הירדן כאשר דבר יהוה אל־
to Jehovah had as the of out stones twelve
spoken Jordan of middle the

5674 3478 1121 7626 4557 3091
יהושע למספר שבטי בני־ישראל ויעברום עמם אל־
to with they and ;Israel the the the for Joshua
them over crossed of sons of tribes of number

9 3091 6965 68 6240 8147 8033 3240 4411
המלון וינחום שם׃ ושתים עשרה אבנים הקים יהושע
Joshua lifted stones twelve the And .there laid and the
up down them lodge

727 5375 3548 7272 4673 8478 3383 8432
בתוך הירדן תחת מצב רגלי הכהנים נשאי ארון
ark the bearing priests the the stood the in the the in
of of feet firm place Jordan of middle

10 727 5375 3548 2088 3117 5704 8033 1961 1285
הברית ויהיו שם עד היום הזה׃ והכהנים נשאי הארון
ark the bearing the And .this day to there they and the
priests are ;covenant

6680 834 1697 3605 8552 5704 3383 8432 5975
עמדים בתוך הירדן עד־תם כל־הדבר אשר־צוה
com- that thing every- was until the the in were
manded finished Jordan of middle standing

4872 6680 834 3605 5971 1696 3091 3068
יהוה את־יהושע לדבר אל־העם ככל אשר־צוה משה
Moses com- that according the to speak to ,Joshua to Jehovah
manded all to ,people

11 3605 8552 1961 5674 5971 4116 3091
את־יהושע וימהרו העם ויעברו׃ ויהי כאשר־תם כל־
all had when it And crossed and the and ;Joshua
finished was over people hurried

5971 6440 3548 3068 727 5674 5971
העם לעבור ויעבר ארון־יהוה והכהנים לפני העם׃
.people the before the and Jehovah the that crossing the
priests of ark ,over people

12 2571 4519 7626 2677 1410 1121 7205 1121 5674
ויעברו בני־ראובן ובני־גד וחצי שבט המנשה חמשים
battle in ,Manasseh of tribe the and ,Gad and ,Reuben the And
array half of sons the of sons crossed

13 703 4872 1696 3478 1121 6440
לפני בני ישראל כאשר דבר אליהם משה׃ כארבעים
forty About .Moses them to had as ,Israel the before
spoken of sons

6160 4421 3068 6440 5674 6635 2502 505
אלף חלוצי הצבא עברו לפני יהוה למלחמה אל ערבות
the to ,battle for Jehovah before they the armed thou-
of plains over crossed ,army of men sand

14 3605 5869 3091 3068 1430 3117 3405
יריחו׃ ביום ההוא גדל יהוה את־יהושע בעיני כל־
all the in Joshua Jehovah made that day On .Jericho
of eyes great

2416 3117 3605 4872 3372 3372 3478
ישראל וייראו אתו כאשר יראו את־משה כל־ימי חייו׃
his the all ,Moses they even him they and ;Israel
.life of days feared as feared

15 And Jehovah spoke to
Joshua, saying, 16 Command
the priests who carry the ark
of the testimony, and they
shall come up out of the
Jordan. 17 And Joshua
commanded the priests,
saying, Come up out of the
Jordan. 18 And when the
priests who bore the ark of
the covenant of Jehovah
had come up out of the
midst of the Jordan, and the
soles of the feet of the
priests had been lifted to the
dry land, the waters of the
Jordan returned to their
place, and flowed over all its
banks, as before. 19 And the
people came up out of the
Jordan on the tenth of the
first month, and camped in
Gilgal, in the east border of
Jericho. 20 And the twelve
stones which they took out
of the Jordan were raised up
in Gilgal by Joshua. 21 And
he spoke to the sons of
Israel, saying, when your
sons ask their fathers
hereafter, saying, What do
these stones *mean*? 22 Then
you shall make your sons
know, saying, Israel came
over this Jordan on dry land,
23 because Jehovah your
God dried up the waters of
the Jordan before you, until
you crossed over, as
Jehovah your God did to the
Red Sea, which He dried up
before you until we crossed
over; 24 so that all the people
of the land shall know that
the hand of Jehovah *is*
strong, so that you may fear
Jehovah your God all the
days.

3548 6680 559 3091 3068 559
15 וַיֹּאמֶר יְהוָה אֶל־יְהוֹשֻׁעַ לֵאמֹר׃ צַוֵּה אֶת־הַכֹּהֲנִים
16 priests the | Order | ,saying | ,Joshua | to Jehovah | And spoke

3091 6680 3383 5927 5715 727 5375
17 נֹשְׂאֵי אֲרוֹן הָעֵדוּת וְיַעֲלוּ מִן־הַיַּרְדֵּן׃ וַיְצַו יְהוֹשֻׁעַ אֶת־
Joshua | and ordered | the Jordan | of out | they that rise | the testimony | the of ark | who carry

3548 5927 3383 5927 559 3548
18 הַכֹּהֲנִים לֵאמֹר עֲלוּ מִן־הַיַּרְדֵּן׃ וַיְהִי בַּעֲלוֹת הַכֹּהֲנִים
priests the | had when up come | And | the Jordan | of out | Rise | ,saying | ,priests the

7272 3709 5423 3383 8432 3068 1285 727 5375
נֹשְׂאֵי אֲרוֹן בְּרִית־יְהוָה מִתּוֹךְ הַיַּרְדֵּן נִתְּקוּ כַּפּוֹת רַגְלֵי
the of feet | the of soles | were lifted | the Jordan | of out of midst the | Jehovah | the of covenant | the of ark | who carried

3212 4725 3383 4325 7725 2724 3548
הַכֹּהֲנִים אֶל הֶחָרָבָה וַיָּשֻׁבוּ מֵי־הַיַּרְדֵּן לִמְקוֹמָם וַיֵּלְכוּ
and flowed | their to place | the Jordan | the of waters | re- and turned | dry the ,land | to | the priests

3383 5927 5971 1415 3605 8032 8543
19 כִּתְמוֹל־שִׁלְשׁוֹם עַל־כָּל־גְּדוֹתָיו׃ וְהָעָם עָלוּ מִן־הַיַּרְדֵּן
the Jordan | of out | came up | the And people | .banks its | all over | before day the yesterday | as

3405 4217 7097 1537 2583 7223 2320 6218
בֶּעָשׂוֹר לַחֹדֶשׁ הָרִאשׁוֹן וַיַּחֲנוּ בַּגִּלְגָּל בִּקְצֵה מִזְרַח יְרִיחוֹ׃
;Jericho | east | the on of edge | in ,Gilgal | and camped | ,first | the of month | the on tenth

3947 834 428 68 6240 8147
20 וְאֵת שְׁתֵּים עֶשְׂרֵה הָאֲבָנִים הָאֵלֶּה אֲשֶׁר לָקְחוּ מִן־
out of | they took | which | these | stones | twelve | and

3478 1121 559 1537 3091 6965 3383
21 הַיַּרְדֵּן הֵקִים יְהוֹשֻׁעַ בַּגִּלְגָּל׃ וַיֹּאמֶר אֶל־בְּנֵי יִשְׂרָאֵל
,Israel | the of sons | to | he And spoke | in .Gilgal | by Joshua | were raised | the Jordan

559 4279 1121 7592 834 559
לֵאמֹר אֲשֶׁר יִשְׁאָלוּן בְּנֵיכֶם מָחָר אֶת־אֲבוֹתָם לֵאמֹר
,saying | ,fathers their | hereafter | your sons | ask shall | When | ,saying

559 1121 3045 428 68
22 מָה הָאֲבָנִים הָאֵלֶּה׃ וְהוֹדַעְתֶּם אֶת־בְּנֵיכֶם לֵאמֹר
,saying | ,sons your | shall you Then know to make | ?these | stones | What (mean)

3001 834 2088 3383 3478 5674 3006
23 בַּיַּבָּשָׁה עָבַר יִשְׂרָאֵל אֶת־הַיַּרְדֵּן הַזֶּה׃ אֲשֶׁר־הוֹבִישׁ
up dried | because | ;this | Jordan | Israel | crossed over | dry on land

5674 5704 6440 3383 4325 430 3068
יְהוָה אֱלֹהֵיכֶם אֶת־מֵי הַיַּרְדֵּן מִפְּנֵיכֶם עַד־עָבְרְכֶם
you ,over crossed | until | before you | the Jordan | the of waters | God your | Jehovah

3001 834 5488 3220 430 3068 6213
כַּאֲשֶׁר עָשָׂה יְהוָה אֱלֹהֵיכֶם לְיַם־סוּף אֲשֶׁר־הוֹבִישׁ
dried He up | which | ,Reeds the to of Sea | God your | Jehovah | did | as

3027 776 5971 3605 3047 5674 5704 6440
24 מִפָּנֵינוּ עַד־עָבְרֵנוּ׃ לְמַעַן דַּעַת כָּל־עַמֵּי הָאָרֶץ אֶת־יַד
the of hand | land the | the of people | all | shall know | Thus | had we ,over crossed | until | before us

430 3068 3372 2389 3068
יְהוָה כִּי חֲזָקָה הִיא לְמַעַן יְרָאתֶם אֶת־יְהוָה אֱלֹהֵיכֶם
God your | Jehovah | may you that so fear | ;(is) it | mighty | that ,Jehovah

3117 3605
כָּל־הַיָּמִים׃
the days. | all

CAP. V ה

CHAPTER 5

CHAPTER 5

1And it happened, when all the kings of the Amorites which *were* beyond the Jordan, toward the sea, and all the kings of the Canaanites which *were* by the sea, heard how Jehovah dried up the waters of the Jordan before the sons of Israel, until they crossed over, their heart was melted. And there was not any more spirit in them before the sons of Israel.

2At that time Jehovah said to Joshua, Make for yourself flint knives, and again circumcise the sons of Israel, the second time. 3And Joshua made flint knives for himself, and circumcised the sons of Israel at the hill of the foreskins. 4And this *is* the reason Joshua circumcised: All the people who had come out of Egypt, who were males, all the men of war, had died in the wilderness, in the way, as they came out of Egypt.

5For all the people who had come out were circumcised. And all the people who *were* born in the wilderness, in the way, as they came out from Egypt, had not been circumcised. 6For the sons of Israel had walked forty years in the wilderness, until all the nation, the men of war who had come out of Egypt, who did not listen to the voice of Jehovah, to whom Jehovah had sworn to them, not to show them the land which Jehovah swore to their fathers, to give to us, a land flowing with milk and honey—*these* were consumed. 7And He raised their sons up in their place. Joshua circumcised

3220 3383 5676 834 567 4428 3605 8085 1961
1 וַיְהִי כִשְׁמֹעַ כָּל־מַלְכֵי הָאֱמֹרִי אֲשֶׁר בְּעֵבֶר הַיַּרְדֵּן יָמָּה
toward the beyond who the the all when it And
Sea the Jordan (were) Amorites of kings heard ,was

3068 3001 3220 834 3669 4428 3605
וְכָל־מַלְכֵי הַכְּנַעֲנִי אֲשֶׁר עַל־הַיָּם אֵת אֲשֶׁר־הוֹבִישׁ יְהוָה
Jehovah dried how ,Sea the by who the the and
up (were) Canaanites of kings all

3824 4549 5674 5704 3478 1121 6440 3383 4325
אֶת־מֵי הַיַּרְדֵּן מִפְּנֵי בְנֵי־יִשְׂרָאֵל עַד־עָבְרָנוּ וַיִּמַּס לְבָבָם
their that they until ,Israel the before the the
,heart melted ,over crossed of sons Jordan of waters

6256 3478 1121 6440 7307 5750 1961 3808
2 וְלֹא־הָיָה בָם עוֹד רוּחַ מִפְּנֵי בְּנֵי־יִשְׂרָאֵל׃ בָּעֵת
time At .Israel the before spirit yet in was and
of sons them not

6697 2719 6213 3091 3068 559
הַהִיא אָמַר יְהוָה אֶל־יְהוֹשֻׁעַ עֲשֵׂה לְךָ חַרְבוֹת צֻרִים
,flint knives for Make ,Joshua to Jehovah said that
of you

2719 3091 6213 8145 3478 1121 4135 7725
3 וְשׁוּב מֹל אֶת־בְּנֵי־יִשְׂרָאֵל שֵׁנִית׃ וַיַּעַשׂ־לוֹ יְהוֹשֻׁעַ חַרְבוֹת
of knives Joshua for And the Israel the cir- and
himself made .time second of sons cumcise return

2088 6190 1389 3478 1121 4135 6697
4 צֻרִים וַיָּמָל אֶת־בְּנֵי יִשְׂרָאֵל אֶל־גִּבְעַת הָעֲרָלוֹת׃ וְזֶה
And the hill the at Israel sons the and ,flint
this .foreskins of of circumcised

4714 3318 5971 3605 3091 4135 834 1697
הַדָּבָר אֲשֶׁר־מָל יְהוֹשֻׁעַ כָּל־הָעָם הַיֹּצֵא מִמִּצְרַיִם
of out that the all Joshua circum- (for) the (is)
:Egypt came people cised which reason

3318 1870 4057 4191 4421 582 3605 2145
הַזְּכָרִים כֹּל ׀ אַנְשֵׁי הַמִּלְחָמָה מֵתוּ בַמִּדְבָּר בַּדֶּרֶךְ בְּצֵאתָם
they as the on the in had ,war the ,all males the
came way ,wilderness died of men

5971 3605 3318 5971 3605 1961 4135 4714
5 מִמִּצְרָיִם׃ כִּי־מֻלִים הָיוּ כָּל־הָעָם הַיֹּצְאִים וְכָל־הָעָם
the and that the all were circum- for of out
people all ;out came people cised ;Egypt

3588 4135 3808 4714 3318 1870 4057 3209
6 הַיִּלֹּדִים בַּמִּדְבָּר בַּדֶּרֶךְ בְּצֵאתָם מִמִּצְרַיִם לֹא־מָלוּ׃ כִּי ׀
For been had not of out they as the on the in were who
.circumcised ,Egypt came way ,wilderness born

3605 8558 5704 4057 3478 1121 8212 8141 203
אַרְבָּעִים שָׁנָה הָלְכוּ בְנֵי־יִשְׂרָאֵל בַּמִּדְבָּר עַד־תֹּם כָּל־
all was until the in Israel the had years forty
consumed ,wilderness of sons walked

8085 3808 834 4714 3318 4421 582 1471
הַגּוֹי אַנְשֵׁי הַמִּלְחָמָה הַיֹּצְאִים מִמִּצְרַיִם אֲשֶׁר לֹא־שָׁמְעוּ
did not who of out had who war the the
listen ,Egypt come of men ,nation

7200 3808 3068 765 834 3068 6963
בְּקוֹל יְהוָה אֲשֶׁר נִשְׁבַּע יְהוָה לָהֶם לְבִלְתִּי הַרְאוֹתָם
show to not to Jehovah had which ,Jehovah the to
them them sworn of voice

776 5414 3068 7650 834 776
אֶת־הָאָרֶץ אֲשֶׁר נִשְׁבַּע יְהוָה לַאֲבוֹתָם לָתֶת לָנוּ אֶרֶץ
a to to their to Jehovah swore which land the
land ,us give fathers

4135 8478 6965 1121 1706 2461 2100
7 זָבַת חָלָב וּדְבָשׁ׃ וְאֶת־בְּנֵיהֶם הֵקִים תַּחְתָּם אֹתָם מָל
cir- them their in He sons their And and milk flowing
cumcised ,place up raised .honey with

them, for they had been uncircumcised; for they had not been circumcised in the way.

[8]And it happened, when all the nation had finished being circumcised, they remained in their places in the camp until they revived. [9]And Jehovah said to Joshua, Today I have rolled the reproach of Egypt off of you. And he called the name of that place Gilgal to this day.

[10]And the sons of Israel camped in Gilgal, and prepared the Passover on the fourteenth day of the month, at evening, in the plains of Jericho. [11]And they ate the old grain of the land on the morrow of the Passover, unleavened bread and roasted *grain*, in this same day. [12]And the manna ceased on the next day after they ate of the old grain of the land. And there was no more manna to the sons of Israel, but they ate the produce of the land of Canaan in that year.

[13]And it happened, when Joshua was beside Jericho, that he lifted up his eyes and looked. And, behold! A Man stood opposite him, and His drawn sword *was* in His hand. And Joshua went to Him and said to Him, Are You for us, or for our foes? [14]And He said, No, for I now come *as* the Commander of the army of Jehovah. And Joshua fell on his face to the earth, and worshiped. And *he* said to Him, What does my Lord say to His bondslave? [15]And the Commander of the army of Jehovah said to Joshua, Take your shoe off your foot, for the place on which you are standing *is* holy. And Joshua did so.

8 יְהוֹשֻׁעַ כִּי־עֲרֵלִים הָיוּ כִּי לֹא־מָלוּ אוֹתָם בַּדָּרֶךְ׃ וַיְהִי
it And ,was the on .way them had they not for they uncircumcised for ;been had cumcised ;Joshua
כַּאֲשֶׁר־תַּמּוּ כָל־הַגּוֹי לְהִמּוֹל וַיֵּשְׁבוּ תַחְתָּם בַּמַּחֲנֶה עַד
until the in camp their in places they that remained being ,circumcised the nation all had finished when
9 חֲיוֹתָם׃ וַיֹּאמֶר יְהוָה אֶל־יְהוֹשֻׁעַ הַיּוֹם גַּלּוֹתִי אֶת־
have I rolled Today ,Joshua to Jehovah said And they lived
חֶרְפַּת מִצְרַיִם מֵעֲלֵיכֶם וַיִּקְרָא שֵׁם הַמָּקוֹם הַהוּא גִּלְגָּל
Gilgal that place the of name therefore called he of off ;you Egypt the of reproach
10 עַד הַיּוֹם הַזֶּה׃ וַיַּחֲנוּ בְנֵי־יִשְׂרָאֵל בַּגִּלְגָּל וַיַּעֲשׂוּ אֶת־הַפֶּסַח
Passover the and prepared at ,Gilgal Israel the of sons And camped .this day until
11 בְּאַרְבָּעָה עָשָׂר יוֹם לַחֹדֶשׁ בָּעֶרֶב בְּעַרְבוֹת יְרִיחוֹ׃ וַיֹּאכְלוּ
they and ate ;Jericho the on of plains at ,evening the of month day fourteenth the on
מֵעֲבוּר הָאָרֶץ מִמָּחֳרַת הַפֶּסַח מַצּוֹת וְקָלוּי בְּעֶצֶם הַיּוֹם
day · same in and (grain) roasted unleavened ,bread the Passover the on of morrow the land the of grain old
12 הַזֶּה׃ וַיִּשְׁבֹּת הַמָּן מִמָּחֳרָת בְּאָכְלָם מֵעֲבוּר הָאָרֶץ וְלֹא־
and not ;land the the of grain old they after ate the on day next the manna And ceased .this
הָיָה עוֹד לִבְנֵי יִשְׂרָאֵל מָן וַיֹּאכְלוּ מִתְּבוּאַת אֶרֶץ כְּנַעַן
Canaan the of land the of produce they but ate ,manna Israel the to of sons more (there) was
13 בַּשָּׁנָה הַהִיא׃ וַיְהִי בִּהְיוֹת יְהוֹשֻׁעַ בִּירִיחוֹ וַיִּשָּׂא עֵינָיו
his eyes he that lifted beside ,Jericho Joshua was when it And ,was .that year in
וַיַּרְא וְהִנֵּה־אִישׁ עֹמֵד לְנֶגְדּוֹ וְחַרְבּוֹ שְׁלוּפָה בְּיָדוֹ וַיֵּלֶךְ
and went His in ;hand (was) drawn His and sword opposite him stood a Man ,and ,behold and ;looked
14 יְהוֹשֻׁעַ אֵלָיו וַיֹּאמֶר לוֹ הֲלָנוּ אַתָּה אִם־לְצָרֵינוּ׃ וַיֹּאמֶר
He And said our for ?foes or You Are us for to ,Him said and to Him Joshua
לֹא כִּי אֲנִי שַׂר־צְבָא־יְהוָה עַתָּה בָאתִי וַיִּפֹּל יְהוֹשֻׁעַ
Joshua fell And have I come Now Jehovah the of army the of captain (am) I for ,No
אֶל־פָּנָיו אַרְצָה וַיִּשְׁתָּחוּ וַיֹּאמֶר לוֹ מָה אֲדֹנִי מְדַבֵּר אֶל־
to saying is my Lord What to ,Him said and and Him worshiped the to ,earth his face upon
15 עַבְדּוֹ׃ וַיֹּאמֶר שַׂר־צְבָא יְהוָה אֶל־יְהוֹשֻׁעַ שַׁל־נַעַלְךָ מֵעַל
off your shoe Take ,Joshua to Jehovah army the of the Captain of said And His ?servant
רַגְלֶךָ כִּי הַמָּקוֹם אֲשֶׁר אַתָּה עֹמֵד עָלָיו קֹדֶשׁ הוּא וַיַּעַשׂ
And did .(is) holy on are standing you place the for your foot
יְהוֹשֻׁעַ כֵּן׃
.so Joshua

CAP. VI

CHAPTER 6

CHAPTER 6

[1]And Jericho was shut in, even it was shut in from the face of the sons of Israel; no one going out, and no one coming in. [2]And Jehovah said to Joshua, See I have given Jericho and its king, mighty warriors, into your hand. [3]And you shall go around the city, all the men of battle, going around the city once; so you shall do six days. [4]And seven priests shall bear seven trumpets of ram's horns before the ark. And on the seventh day you shall go around the city seven times, and the priests shall blow with the trumpets. [5]And it shall be, when they make a long blast with the ram's horn, and when you hear the sound of the horn, all the people shall shout with a great shout. And the wall of the city shall fall down flat; and the people shall go up, each man in front of him. [6]And Joshua the son of Nun called the priests and said to them, Take up the ark of the covenant, and let seven priests bear seven trumpets of ram's horns before the ark of Jehovah. [7]And he said to the people, Pass on, go around the city, and he who is armed shall go on before the ark of Jehovah.

[8]And it happened, when Joshua spoke to the people, the seven priests bearing seven trumpets of the ram's horns before Jehovah passed on and blew with the trumpets. And the ark of the covenant of Jehovah went after them. [9]And he who was armed went before

369 3318 369 3478 1121 6440 5462 5462 3405
1 וִירִיחוֹ סֹגֶרֶת וּמְסֻגֶּרֶת מִפְּנֵי בְּנֵי יִשְׂרָאֵל אֵין יוֹצֵא וְאֵין
and going no ;Israel's sons of because was and was And
one no ,out one of face the in shut closed Jericho

3027 5414 7200 3091 3068 559 935
2 בָּא׃ וַיֹּאמֶר יְהוָה אֶל־יְהוֹשֻׁעַ רְאֵה נָתַתִּי בְיָדְךָ אֶת־
into have I ,See ,Joshua to Jehovah said And coming
hand your given .in

3605 5892 5437 2428 1368 4428 3405
3 יְרִיחוֹ וְאֶת־מַלְכָּהּ גִּבּוֹרֵי הֶחָיִל׃ וְסַבֹּתֶם אֶת־הָעִיר כֹּל
all ,city the you And .mighty warriors king its and Jericho
circle shall

6213 259 6471 5892 5362 4421 582
אַנְשֵׁי הַמִּלְחָמָה הַקֵּיף אֶת־הָעִיר פַּעַם אֶחָת כֹּה תַעֲשֶׂה
shall you so ;one time city the going ,war the
do around of men

7782 7651 5375 3548 7651 3117 8337
4 שֵׁשֶׁת יָמִים׃ וְשִׁבְעָה כֹהֲנִים יִשְׂאוּ שִׁבְעָה שׁוֹפְרוֹת
horns ram's seven bear shall priests seven and ;days six
of

5892 5437 7637 3117 727 6440 3104
הַיּוֹבְלִים לִפְנֵי הָאָרוֹן וּבַיּוֹם הַשְּׁבִיעִי תָּסֹבּוּ אֶת־הָעִיר
city the shall you seventh on and ;ark the in horn the
circle day the of front blast

4900 1961 7782 8628 3548 6471 7651
5 שֶׁבַע פְּעָמִים וְהַכֹּהֲנִים יִתְקְעוּ בַּשּׁוֹפָרוֹת׃ וְהָיָה בִּמְשֹׁךְ
they when it and the with shall the and ,times seven
long blow ,be shall ;horns ram's blow priests

5971 3605 7321 7782 6963 8085 3104 7161
בְּקֶרֶן הַיּוֹבֵל בְּשָׁמְעֲכֶם אֶת־קוֹל הַשּׁוֹפָר יָרִיעוּ כָל־הָעָם
the all shall ,horn the sound the you when the with
people shout of hear ,ram's horn

5971 5927 8478 5892 2346 5307 1419 8643
תְּרוּעָה גְדוֹלָה וְנָפְלָה חוֹמַת הָעִיר תַּחְתֶּיהָ וְעָלוּ הָעָם
the shall and down city the the shall and ,great a with
,people up go ;flat of wall fall shout

559 3548 5126 1121 3091 7121 5048 376
6 אִישׁ נֶגְדּוֹ׃ וַיִּקְרָא יְהוֹשֻׁעַ בִּן־נוּן אֶל־הַכֹּהֲנִים וַיֹּאמֶר
said and priests the Nun the Joshua And front in each
of son called .him of man

7651 5375 3548 7651 1285 727 5375
אֲלֵהֶם שְׂאוּ אֶת־אֲרוֹן הַבְּרִית וְשִׁבְעָה כֹהֲנִים יִשְׂאוּ שִׁבְעָה
seven let priests and the ark the Take ,them to
bear seven ,covenant of up

5971 559 3068 727 6440 3104 7782
7 שׁוֹפְרוֹת יוֹבְלִים לִפְנֵי אֲרוֹן יְהוָה׃ וַיֹּאמְרוּ אֶל־הָעָם
the to he and ;Jehovah the in blasting horns ram's
,people said of ark of front of

3068 727 6440 5674 2502 5892 5437 5674
עִבְרוּ וְסֹבּוּ אֶת־הָעִיר וְהֶחָלוּץ יַעֲבֹר לִפְנֵי אֲרוֹן יְהוָה׃
.Jehovah the before shall who he and ,city the and Pass
of ark on go armed is circle ,on

5375 3548 7651 5971 3091 559 1961
8 וַיְהִי כֶּאֱמֹר יְהוֹשֻׁעַ אֶל־הָעָם וְשִׁבְעָה הַכֹּהֲנִים נֹשְׂאִים
bearing priests the that the to Joshua when it And
seven ,people spoke ,was

8628 5674 3068 6440 3104 7782 7651
שִׁבְעָה שׁוֹפְרוֹת הַיּוֹבְלִים לִפְנֵי יְהוָה עָבְרוּ וְתָקְעוּ
and passed Jehovah in blasting horns ram's seven
blew on of front of

2502 310 3212 3068 1285 727 7782
9 בַּשּׁוֹפָרוֹת וַאֲרוֹן בְּרִית יְהוָה הֹלֵךְ אַחֲרֵיהֶם׃ וְהֶחָלוּץ
who he and ;them after went Jehovah the the and the with
armed was of covenant of ark horns ram's

the priests blowing the trumpets. And he who gathered up went after the ark, going on and blowing with the trumpets. 10And Joshua had commanded the people, saying, You shall not shout, nor cause your voice to be heard, nor shall there go from your mouth a word until the day I say to you, Shout! Then you shall shout. 11And the ark of Jehovah went around the city, going around one time. And they came into the camp, and remained in the camp.

12And Joshua rose early in the morning, and the priests bore the ark of Jehovah. 13And seven priests bearing seven trumpets of the ram's horns were walking before the ark of Jehovah, going on, and were blowing with the trumpets. And he who was armed went before them. And the rear guard went behind the ark of Jehovah, going on and blowing with the trumpets. 14And they circled the city on the second day one time, and returned to the camp. So they did six days.

15And it happened on the seventh day, they rose early, at the dawning of the day, and went around the city seven times. 16And it happened at the seventh time, the priests blew with the trumpets, and Joshua said to the people, Shout! For Jehovah has given you the city. 17And the city shall be devoted to Jehovah, it and all that are in it. Only Rahab the harlot shall live, she and

310 622 7782 8628 3548 6440 3212
הֹלֵךְ לִפְנֵי הַכֹּהֲנִים תָּקְעוּ הַשּׁוֹפָרוֹת וְהַמְאַסֵּף הֹלֵךְ אַחֲרֵי
after went the and ;horns ram's the blowing ,priests the before went
guard rear

10 3091 6680 5971 7782 8628 1980 727
הָאָרוֹן הָלוֹךְ וְתָקוֹעַ בַּשּׁוֹפָרוֹת׃ וְאֶת־הָעָם צִוָּה יְהוֹשֻׁעַ
,Joshua com- the And th with and going ,ark the
manded people .horns ram's blowing on

3318 3808 6963 8085 3808 7321 3808 559
לֵאמֹר לֹא תָרִיעוּ וְלֹא־תַשְׁמִיעוּ אֶת־קוֹלְכֶם וְלֹא־יֵצֵא
shall nor ,voice your to cause nor shall You not ,saying
go heard be ,shout

7321 7321 559 3117 5704 1697 6310
מִפִּיכֶם דָּבָר עַד יוֹם אָמְרִי אֲלֵיכֶם הָרִיעוּ וַהֲרֵיעֹתֶם׃
you Then !Shout ,you to say I the until ,word a from
.shout shall day mouth your

11 4264 935 259 6471 8362 5892 3068 727 5437
וַיַּסֵּב אֲרוֹן־יְהוָה אֶת־הָעִיר הַקֵּף פַּעַם אֶחָת וַיָּבֹאוּ הַמַּחֲנֶה
the to they and ;one time going ,city the Jehovah the And
,camp in came around of ark circled

12 3548 5375 1242 3091 7925 4264 3885
וַיָּלִינוּ בַּמַּחֲנֶה׃ וַיַּשְׁכֵּם יְהוֹשֻׁעַ בַּבֹּקֶר וַיִּשְׂאוּ הַכֹּהֲנִים
priests the and the in Joshua rose And the in and
bore ,morning early camp stayed

13 7782 7657 5375 3548 7651 3068 727
אֶת־אֲרוֹן יְהוָה׃ וְשִׁבְעָה הַכֹּהֲנִים נֹשְׂאִים שִׁבְעָה שׁוֹפְרוֹת
horns ram's seven bearing priests seven and ;Jehovah ark the
of of

7782 8628 3212 3212 3068 727 6440 3104
הַיֹּבְלִים לִפְנֵי אֲרוֹן יְהוָה הֹלְכִים הָלוֹךְ וְתָקְעוּ בַּשּׁוֹפָרוֹת
the with were and going were Jehovah the in blasting
;horns ram's blowing ;on ,walking of ark of front

3068 727 310 3212 622 6440 3212 2502
וְהֶחָלוּץ הֹלֵךְ לִפְנֵיהֶם וְהַמְאַסֵּף הֹלֵךְ אַחֲרֵי אֲרוֹן יְהוָה
Jehovah the behind went the and before went who he and
of ark guard rear ,them armed was

14 8145 3117 5892 5437 7782 8628 3212
הוֹלֵךְ וְתָקוֹעַ בַּשּׁוֹפָרוֹת׃ וַיָּסֹבּוּ אֶת־הָעִיר בַּיּוֹם הַשֵּׁנִי
second the on city the they And the with and going
day circled .horns ram's blowing ,on

3117 8337 6213 4264 7725 259 6471
פַּעַם אַחַת וַיָּשֻׁבוּ הַמַּחֲנֶה כֹּה עָשׂוּ שֵׁשֶׁת יָמִים׃
.days six did they so ;camp the to and ,one time
returned

15 5437 7837 7837 7925 7637 3117 1961
וַיְהִי | בַּיּוֹם הַשְּׁבִיעִי וַיַּשְׁכִּמוּ כַּעֲלוֹת הַשַּׁחַר וַיָּסֹבּוּ
and ,day the the at they that ,seventh the on it And
circled of dawning ,early rose day happened

2088 3117 7535 6471 7651 2088 4941 5892
אֶת־הָעִיר כַּמִּשְׁפָּט הַזֶּה שֶׁבַע פְּעָמִים רַק בַּיּוֹם הַהוּא
that day on only ;times seven ,this same in city the
way

16 7637 6471 1961 6471 7651 5892 5437
סָבְבוּ אֶת־הָעִיר שֶׁבַע פְּעָמִים׃ וַיְהִי בַּפַּעַם הַשְּׁבִיעִית
,seventh the time at it and ;times seven city the they
,was circled

5971 3091 559 7782 3548 8628
תָּקְעוּ הַכֹּהֲנִים בַּשּׁוֹפָרוֹת וַיֹּאמֶר יְהוֹשֻׁעַ אֶל־הָעָם
the to Joshua said and the with priests the blew
,people ,horns ram's

17 5892 1961 5892 3068 5414 7321
הָרִיעוּ כִּי־נָתַן יְהוָה לָכֶם אֶת־הָעִיר׃ וְהָיְתָה הָעִיר
the shall and ;city the you to Jehovah has For !Shout
city be given

2181 7343 7535 3068 834 3605 2764
חֵרֶם הִיא וְכָל־אֲשֶׁר־בָּהּ לַיהוָה רַק רָחָב הַזּוֹנָה
the Rahab only to it in that and it ;devoted
harlot ,Jehovah (are) all

all who are with her in the house, because she hid the messengers that we sent. [18]And you shall certainly keep clear of the cursed things, that you not become accursed by taking from the cursed things, and shall make the camp of Israel become accursed, and trouble it. [19]And all the silver and gold, and vessels of copper and iron, they *are* holy to Jehovah; they shall come into the treasury of Jehovah. [20]And the people shouted, and blew with the trumpets, and it happened, when the people heard the sound of the trumpet, the people shouted a great shout. And the wall fell under it; and the people went up into the city, each man in front of him; and they captured the city. [21]And they destroyed all that *was* in the city, from man even to woman, from young even to aged, and to ox, and sheep, and ass, by the mouth of the sword.

[22]And Joshua said to the two men who had spied out the land, Go into the house of the woman, the harlot, and bring the woman out from there, and all whom she has, as you have sworn to her. [23]And the young men, the spies, went in and brought out Rahab, and her father, and her mother, and her brothers, and all whom she had; yea, they brought all her family, and set them outside the camp of Israel.

[24]And they burned the city with fire, and all that *was* in it. Only they gave the silver and the gold, and the vessels of copper, and of iron, *to* the treasury of the house of Jehovah. [25]And Joshua kept alive Rahab the harlot, and the house of

thing *is* in your midst, O Israel; you are not able to stand before your enemies until you take away the

2244 1004 834 3605 2421
תִּחְיֶה הִיא וְכָל־אֲשֶׁר אִתָּהּ בַּבַּיִת כִּי הֶחְבְּאַתָה אֶת־
hid she because the in with that and she shall
,house her (are) all .live

2763 8104 7535 7971 834 4397
18 הַמַּלְאָכִים אֲשֶׁר שָׁלָחְנוּ׃ וְרַק־אַתֶּם שִׁמְרוּ מִן־הַחֵרֶם
the of keep you And .sent we that messengers the
.thing devoted clear certainly

4264 7760 2764 3947 2763
פֶּן־תַּחֲרִימוּ וּלְקַחְתֶּם מִן־הַחֵרֶם וְשַׂמְתֶּם אֶת־מַחֲנֵה
of camp the shall and the from taking by be you lest
make ;thing devoted accursed

3605 2091 3701 3605 5916 2764 3478
19 יִשְׂרָאֵל לְחֵרֶם וַעֲכַרְתֶּם אוֹתוֹ׃ וְכֹל ׀ כֶּסֶף וְזָהָב וּכְלֵי
and and the And .it trouble and become Israel
of vessels ,gold silver all accursed

7321 935 3068 214 3068 6944 1270 5178
20 נְחֹשֶׁת וּבַרְזֶל קֹדֶשׁ הוּא לַיהוָה אוֹצַר יְהוָה יָבוֹא׃ וַיָּרַע
And they Jehovah the (to) to they holy ,iron and copper
shouted .come shall of treasury ;Jehovah (are)

7782 6963 5971 8088 1961 7782 8628 5971
הָעָם וַיִּתְקְעוּ בַּשֹּׁפָרוֹת וַיְהִי כִשְׁמֹעַ הָעָם אֶת־קוֹל הַשּׁוֹפָר
ram's the the the when it and the with and the
,horn of sound people heard ,was horns ram's blew people

5927 8478 2346 5307 1419 7321 5971 7321
וַיָּרִיעוּ הָעָם תְּרוּעָה גְדוֹלָה וַתִּפֹּל הַחוֹמָה תַּחְתֶּיהָ וַיַּעַל
and under wall the fell and ,great shout a the that
up went ;it people shouted

2763 5892 3920 5048 376 5892 5971
21 הָעָם הָעִירָה אִישׁ נֶגְדּוֹ וַיִּלְכְּדוּ אֶת־הָעִיר׃ וַיַּחֲרִימוּ אֶת־
they And .city the they and front in each the to the
destroyed captured ,him of man ,city people

7794 5704 2205 5704 5288 802 5704 376 5892 834 3605
כָּל־אֲשֶׁר בָּעִיר מֵאִישׁ וְעַד־אִשָּׁה מִנַּעַר וְעַד־זָקֵן וְעַד שׁוֹר
,ox and ,aged even from ,woman even from the in that all
to to young to man ,city (was)

7270 582 8147 2719 6310 2543 7716
22 וָשֶׂה וַחֲמוֹר לְפִי־חָרֶב׃ וְלִשְׁנַיִם הָאֲנָשִׁים הַמְרַגְּלִים אֶת־
who they ,men the to And the the by and and
spied two .sword of edge ,ass ,sheep

3318 2181 802 1004 935 3091 559 776
הָאָרֶץ אָמַר יְהוֹשֻׁעַ בֹּאוּ בֵּית־הָאִשָּׁה הַזּוֹנָה וְהוֹצִיאוּ
bring and the the the Go ,Joshua said ,land the
out ,harlot ,woman of house into

7650 834 3605 802 8033
מִשָּׁם אֶת־הָאִשָּׁה וְאֶת־כָּל־אֲשֶׁר־לָהּ כַּאֲשֶׁר נִשְׁבַּעְתֶּם
have you as she whom all and woman the from
sworn ,has there

7343 3318 7270 5288 935
23 לָהּ׃ וַיָּבֹאוּ הַנְּעָרִים הַמְרַגְּלִים וַיֹּצִיאוּ אֶת־רָחָב וְאֶת־
and ,Rahab and ,spies the young the And to
out brought ,men in went .her

3605 834 3605 251 517 1
אָבִיהָ וְאֶת־אִמָּהּ וְאֶת־אַחֶיהָ וְאֶת־כָּל־אֲשֶׁר־לָהּ וְאֵת כָּל־
all and she whom all and her and her and her
.(yes) ;(had) ,brothers ,mother ,father

5892 3478 4264 2351 3240 3318 4940
24 מִשְׁפְּחוֹתֶיהָ הוֹצִיאוּ וַיַּנִּיחוּם מִחוּץ לְמַחֲנֵה יִשְׂרָאֵל׃ וְהָעִיר
And .Israel the outside set and they families her
city the of camp them ,brought

3605 2091 3701 7535 834 3605 784 8313
שָׂרְפוּ בָאֵשׁ וְכָל־אֲשֶׁר־בָּהּ רַק ׀ הַכֶּסֶף וְהַזָּהָב וּכְלֵי
the and the and the only ,it in that and with they
of vessels ,gold silver (was) all ,fire burned

2181 7343 3068 1004 214 5414 1270 5178
25 הַנְּחֹשֶׁת וְהַבַּרְזֶל נָתְנוּ אוֹצַר בֵּית־יְהוָה׃ וְאֶת־רָחָב הַזּוֹנָה
the Rahab and Jehovah the the (to) they iron of and copper
,harlot of house of treasury gave

her father, and all whom she had. And she lives in the midst of Israel to this day, for she hid the messengers whom Joshua sent to spy out Jericho.

[26]And at that time Joshua adjured, saying, Cursed *be* the man who rises up before the face of Jehovah and builds this city *of* Jericho. He shall lay its foundation in his firstborn, and he shall set up its doors in his youngest son. [27]And Jehovah was with Joshua, and his fame was in all the land.

וְאֶת־בֵּית אָבִיהָ וְאֶת־כָּל־אֲשֶׁר־לָהּ הֶחֱיָה יְהוֹשֻׁעַ וַתֵּשֶׁב

she and lives Joshua kept alive ,(had) she whom all and ,father's her house and

בְּקֶרֶב יִשְׂרָאֵל עַד הַיּוֹם הַזֶּה כִּי הֶחְבִּיאָה אֶת־הַמַּלְאָכִים

messengers the hid she for ,this day to Israel the in of midst

אֲשֶׁר־שָׁלַח יְהוֹשֻׁעַ לְרַגֵּל אֶת־יְרִיחוֹ׃ 26 וַיַּשְׁבַּע יְהוֹשֻׁעַ

Joshua And adjured .Jericho spy to out Joshua sent whom

בָּעֵת הַהִיא לֵאמֹר אָרוּר הָאִישׁ לִפְנֵי יְהוָה אֲשֶׁר יָקוּם

rises up who Jehovah before man the Cursed ,saying ,that at time

וּבָנָה אֶת־הָעִיר הַזֹּאת אֶת־יְרִיחוֹ בִּבְכֹרוֹ יְיַסְּדֶנָּה וּבִצְעִירוֹ

his of and son youngest ,it found he will of cast the at firstborn his ;Jericho this city and builds

יַצִּיב דְּלָתֶיהָ׃ 27 וַיְהִי יְהוָה אֶת־יְהוֹשֻׁעַ וַיְהִי שָׁמְעוֹ

fame his and was ,Joshua with Jehovah And was .doors its set up

בְּכָל־הָאָרֶץ׃

.land the all in

CAP. VII ז

CHAPTER 7

[1]And the sons of Israel committed a sin in the cursed thing. And Achan, the son of Carmi, the son of Zabdi, the son of Zerah, of the tribe of Judah took the cursed thing. And the anger of Jehovah glowed against the sons of Israel.

[2]And Joshua sent men from Jericho to Ai, which is near Beth-aven, on the east of Bethel, and spoke to them, saying, Go up and spy out the land. And the men went up and spied out Ai. [3]And they returned to Joshua, and said to him, Do not let all the people go up. Let about two thousand men, or about three thousand men, go up, and they shall strike Ai. Do not cause all the people to labor there, for they are few. [4]And about three thousand men of the people went up there. And they fled before the men of Ai. [5]And the

1 וַיִּמְעֲלוּ בְנֵי־יִשְׂרָאֵל מַעַל בַּחֵרֶם וַיִּקַּח עָכָן בֶּן־כַּרְמִי

,Carmi of son the ,Achan took and ;thing cursed the in sin a Israel of sons the And committed

בֶּן־זַבְדִּי בֶן־זֶרַח לְמַטֵּה יְהוּדָה מִן־הַחֵרֶם וַיִּחַר־אַף יְהוָה

Jehovah of anger the and glowed (some) of things cursed ;Judah of tribe the of ,Zerah of son the ,Zabdi of son the

2 בִּבְנֵי יִשְׂרָאֵל׃ וַיִּשְׁלַח יְהוֹשֻׁעַ אֲנָשִׁים מִירִיחוֹ הָעַי

to ,Ai from Jericho men Joshua sent And .Israel of sons the against

אֲשֶׁר עִם־בֵּית אָוֶן מִקֶּדֶם לְבֵית־אֵל וַיֹּאמֶר אֲלֵיהֶם

,them to and spoke ,Bethel of east ,aven Beth- near which (is)

לֵאמֹר עֲלוּ וְרַגְּלוּ אֶת־הָאָרֶץ וַיַּעֲלוּ הָאֲנָשִׁים וַיְרַגְּלוּ אֶת־

and out spied men the and went ;land the and out spy Go ,saying

3 הָעָי׃ וַיָּשֻׁבוּ אֶל־יְהוֹשֻׁעַ וַיֹּאמְרוּ אֵלָיו אַל־יַעַל כָּל־הָעָם

the ;people all Let go not ,him to said and Joshua to they And returned .Ai

כְּאַלְפַּיִם אִישׁ אוֹ כִּשְׁלֹשֶׁת אֲלָפִים אִישׁ יַעֲלוּ וְיַכּוּ אֶת־

and strike shall they ,go let men thousand about three or men two about thousand

4 הָעָי אַל־תְּיַגַּע שָׁמָּה אֶת־כָּל־הָעָם כִּי מְעַט הֵמָּה׃ וַיַּעֲלוּ

And up went they .(are) few for the ,people all there cause to labor not ;Ai

מִן־הָעָם שָׁמָּה כִּשְׁלֹשֶׁת אֲלָפִים אִישׁ וַיָּנֻסוּ לִפְנֵי אַנְשֵׁי

the of men before and fled they ,men thousand about three there the of people

5 men of Ai struck about
thirty-six men of them, and
pursued them before the
gate to Shebarim. And they
struck them in the descent.
And the heart of the people
was melted, and became as
water.
6 [6]And Joshua tore his
garments, and fell on his
face to the earth before the
ark of Jehovah until the
evening, he and the elders
of Israel. And they threw
dust on their heads. [7]And
7 Joshua said, O Lord
Jehovah, why have You at
all caused this people to
cross over the Jordan to
give us into the hands of the
Amorites, to destroy us?
And, O that we have been
willing, and that we had
dwelt beyond the Jordan!
8 [8]O Lord, what shall I say,
after Israel has turned its
back before its enemies?
9 [9]And the Canaanites, and
all the inhabitants of the
land shall hear, and shall
come around against us,
and shall cut off our name
out of the earth. And what
shall You do for Your great
name?
10 [10]And Jehovah said to
Joshua, Get up! Why do you
fall on your face this way?
[11]Israel has sinned, and
they also have transgressed
My covenant which I
commanded them, and
have also taken of the
11 cursed things, and have
also stolen, and also
deceived, and also put *it*
among their stuff. [12]And
the sons of Israel have not
been able to stand before
their enemies; they have
turned the back before their
12 enemies because they have
become cursed. I will not be
with you again if you do not
destroy the cursed things
from among you. [13]Rise
up, sanctify the people, and
you shall say, Sanctify
13 yourselves for tomorrow.
For so says Jehovah, the
God of Israel, A cursed

7291 376 8337 7970 5867 582 6321 5857
5 הָעַי׃ וַיַּכּוּ מֵהֶם אַנְשֵׁי הָעַי כִּשְׁלֹשִׁים וְשִׁשָּׁה אִישׁ וַיִּרְדְּפוּם
and ,men six about Ai the of and ;Ai
them chased thirty- of men them struck

5971 3824 4549 4174 6221 7671 5704 8179 6440
לִפְנֵי הַשַּׁעַר עַד־הַשְּׁבָרִים וַיַּכּוּם בַּמּוֹרָד וַיִּמַּס לְבַב־הָעָם
the the and ;Morad in and ;Shebarim to gate the before
people of heart melted them struck they

776 6440 5307 8071 3091 7167 4325 1961
6 וַיְהִי לְמָיִם׃ וַיִּקְרַע יְהוֹשֻׁעַ שִׂמְלֹתָיו וַיִּפֹּל עַל־פָּנָיו אַרְצָה
the to his on and clothing his Joshua And water as and
earth face fell tore became

6083 5927 3478 2205 6153 5704 3068 727 6440
לִפְנֵי אֲרוֹן יְהוָה עַד־הָעֶרֶב הוּא וְזִקְנֵי יִשְׂרָאֵל וַיַּעֲלוּ עָפָר
dust and ;Israel of the and he the until Jehovah the before
threw they elders ,evening of ark

5674 4100 3068 136 162 3091 559 7218 5921
7 עַל־רֹאשָׁם׃ וַיֹּאמֶר יְהוֹשֻׁעַ אֲהָהּ אֲדֹנָי יְהוִה לָמָה הֵעֲבַרְתָּ
you did why ,Jehovah Lord O Joshua said And their upon
cross make .heads

567 3027 5414 3383 2088 5971
הַעֲבִיר אֶת־הָעָם הַזֶּה אֶת־הַיַּרְדֵּן לָתֵת אֹתָנוּ בְּיַד הָאֱמֹרִי
the the into us give to ,Jordan the this people all at
,Amorites of hand

136 3383 5676 3427 2974 6
8 לְהַאֲבִידֵנוּ וְלוּ הוֹאַלְנוּ וַנֵּשֶׁב בְּעֵבֶר הַיַּרְדֵּן׃ בִּי אֲדֹנָי מָה
What ,Lord O !Jordan the beyond and had we And destroy to
dwelt had consented that O ?us

8085 341 6440 6203 3478 2015 834 310 559
9 אֹמַר אַחֲרֵי אֲשֶׁר הָפַךְ יִשְׂרָאֵל עֹרֶף לִפְנֵי אֹיְבָיו׃ וְיִשְׁמְעוּ
shall And its before (its) Israel has that after I shall
hear ?enemies back turned say

3772 5437 776 3427 3605 3669
הַכְּנַעֲנִי וְכֹל יֹשְׁבֵי הָאָרֶץ וְנָסַבּוּ עָלֵינוּ וְהִכְרִיתוּ אֶת־
shall and against come and ,land the the all and the
off cut ,us around of dwellers ,Canaanites

559 1419 8034 6213 776 8034
10 שְׁמֵנוּ מִן־הָאָרֶץ וּמַה־תַּעֲשֵׂה לְשִׁמְךָ הַגָּדוֹל׃ וַיֹּאמֶר
said And ?great Your for shall and the out our
name do You what ;earth of name

6440 5921 5307 2088 4100 6965 3091 3068
יְהוָה אֶל־יְהוֹשֻׁעַ קֻם לָךְ לָמָּה זֶּה אַתָּה נֹפֵל עַל־פָּנֶיךָ׃
your on (are) you this Why your- Get ,Joshua to Jehovah
?face falling (way) !self up

6680 834 1285 5674 1571 3478 2398
11 חָטָא יִשְׂרָאֵל וְגַם עָבְרוּ אֶת־בְּרִיתִי אֲשֶׁר צִוִּיתִי אוֹתָם
,them com- I which covenant My have they and Israel has
manded transgressed also sinned

7760 1571 3581 1571 1589 1571 2764 3947 1571
וְגַם לָקְחוּ מִן־הַחֵרֶם וְגַם גָּנְבוּ וְגַם כִּחֲשׁוּ וְגַם שָׂמוּ
put and ,deceived and ,stolen and the of have and
(it) also also also ,thing cursed taken also

341 6440 6965 3478 1121 3605 3808 3627
12 בִכְלֵיהֶם׃ וְלֹא יֻכְלוּ בְּנֵי יִשְׂרָאֵל לָקוּם לִפְנֵי אֹיְבֵיהֶם
their before to Israel the will And their among
;enemies stand of sons able be not .things

1961 3254 3808 2764 1961 341 6440 6437 6203
עֹרֶף יִפְנוּ לִפְנֵי אֹיְבֵיהֶם כִּי הָיוּ לְחֵרֶם לֹא אוֹסִיף לִהְיוֹת
will I not ;cursed they for their before they (their)
be again become have ,enemies turn will back

6942 6965 7130 2764 8045 3808
13 עִמָּכֶם אִם־לֹא תַשְׁמִידוּ הַחֵרֶם מִקִּרְבְּכֶם׃ קֻם קַדֵּשׁ אֶת־
sanctify Rise among from the do you not if with
,up .you thing cursed destroy you

430 3068 559 4279 6942 559 5971
הָעָם וְאָמַרְתָּ הִתְקַדְּשׁוּ לְמָחָר כִּי כֹה אָמַר יְהוָה אֱלֹהֵי
the ,Jehovah says thus for for Sanctify you and the
of God ;tomorrow yourselves ,say shall ,people

cursed thing from among you. [14]And you shall be brought near in the morning, by your tribes. And it shall be, the tribe which Jehovah takes shall draw near by families. And the family which Jehovah takes shall draw near by households. And the household which Jehovah takes shall draw near by men. [15]And it shall be, he who is taken with the accursed thing shall be burned with fire, he and all that he has, because he has transgressed the covenant of Jehovah, and because he has committed folly in Israel.

[16]And Joshua rose early in the morning, and brought Israel near by its tribes. And the tribe of Judah was taken. [17]And he brought the family of Judah near; and he took the family of the Zarchites. And he brought near the family of the Zarchites by men, and Zabdi was taken. [18]And he brought near his household by men, and Achan, the son of Carmi, the son of Zabdi, the son of Zerah, of the tribe of Judah, was taken. [19]And Joshua said to Achan, My son, I beg you, give glory to Jehovah, the God of Israel, and give thanks to Him, and please tell me what you have done. Do not hide it from me. [20]And Achan answered Joshua, and said, Truly I have sinned against Jehovah, the God of Israel, and this I have done: [21]When I saw among the spoil a goodly robe of Shinar, and two hundred shekels of silver, and a wedge of gold, one of fifty shekels in weight, then I lusted after them, and took

יִשְׂרָאֵל חֵרֶם בְּקִרְבְּךָ יִשְׂרָאֵל לֹא תוּכַל לָקוּם לִפְנֵי
14 אֹיְבֶיךָ עַד־הֲסִירְכֶם הַחֵרֶם מִקִּרְבְּכֶם׃ וְנִקְרַבְתֶּם בַּבֹּקֶר
לְשִׁבְטֵיכֶם וְהָיָה הַשֵּׁבֶט אֲשֶׁר־יִלְכְּדֶנּוּ יְהוָה יִקְרַב
לַמִּשְׁפָּחוֹת וְהַמִּשְׁפָּחָה אֲשֶׁר־יִלְכְּדֶנָּה יְהוָה תִּקְרַב לַבָּתִּים
15 וְהַבַּיִת אֲשֶׁר יִלְכְּדֶנּוּ יְהוָה יִקְרַב לַגְּבָרִים׃ וְהָיָה הַנִּלְכָּד
בַּחֵרֶם יִשָּׂרֵף בָּאֵשׁ אֹתוֹ וְאֶת־כָּל־אֲשֶׁר־לוֹ כִּי עָבַר אֶת־
16 בְּרִית יְהוָה וְכִי־עָשָׂה נְבָלָה בְּיִשְׂרָאֵל׃ וַיַּשְׁכֵּם יְהוֹשֻׁעַ
בַּבֹּקֶר וַיַּקְרֵב אֶת־יִשְׂרָאֵל לִשְׁבָטָיו וַיִּלָּכֵד שֵׁבֶט יְהוּדָה׃
17 וַיַּקְרֵב אֶת־מִשְׁפַּחַת יְהוּדָה וַיִּלְכֹּד אֵת מִשְׁפַּחַת הַזַּרְחִי
18 וַיַּקְרֵב אֶת־מִשְׁפַּחַת הַזַּרְחִי לַגְּבָרִים וַיִּלָּכֵד זַבְדִּי׃ וַיַּקְרֵב
אֶת־בֵּיתוֹ לַגְּבָרִים וַיִּלָּכֵד עָכָן בֶּן־כַּרְמִי בֶן־זַבְדִּי בֶן־זֶרַח
19 לְמַטֵּה יְהוּדָה׃ וַיֹּאמֶר יְהוֹשֻׁעַ אֶל־עָכָן בְּנִי שִׂים־נָא כָבוֹד
לַיהוָה אֱלֹהֵי יִשְׂרָאֵל וְתֶן־לוֹ תוֹדָה וְהַגֶּד־נָא לִי מֶה עָשִׂיתָ
20 אַל־תְּכַחֵד מִמֶּנִּי׃ וַיַּעַן עָכָן אֶת־יְהוֹשֻׁעַ וַיֹּאמַר אָמְנָה
אָנֹכִי חָטָאתִי לַיהוָה אֱלֹהֵי יִשְׂרָאֵל וְכָזֹאת וְכָזֹאת עָשִׂיתִי׃
21 וָאֵרֶא בַשָּׁלָל אַדֶּרֶת שִׁנְעָר אַחַת טוֹבָה וּמָאתַיִם שְׁקָלִים
כֶּסֶף וּלְשׁוֹן זָהָב אֶחָד חֲמִשִּׁים שְׁקָלִים מִשְׁקָלוֹ וָאֶחְמְדֵם

them. And behold, they *are*
hidden in the earth, in the
middle of my tent, and the
silver under it.
[22]And Joshua sent mes-
sengers, and they ran to the
tent; and behold, it was
hidden in his tent, and the
silver under it. [23]And they
took them out of the middle
of the tent, and brought
them to Joshua, and to all
the sons of Israel, and laid
them out before Jehovah.
[24]And Joshua, and all Israel
with him, took Achan the
son of Zerah, and the silver,
and the robe, and the
wedge of gold, and his
sons, and his daughters,
and his oxen, and his ass,
and his flock, and his tent,
and all that he had. And
they made them go up to
the valley of Achor. [25]And
Joshua said, How you have
troubled us! Jehovah shall
trouble you today! And all
Israel threw stones at him,
and they burned them with
fire, and they stoned them
with stones. [26]And they
raised over him a great heap
of stones to this day. And
Jehovah turned back from
the heat of His anger. On
this account the name of
that place *is* The Valley of
Grief until this day.

8478 3701 168 8432 776 779 2009 3947
וָאֶקָּחֵם וְהִנָּם טְמוּנִים בָּאָרֶץ בְּתוֹךְ הָאָהֳלִי וְהַכֶּסֶף תַּחְתֶּיהָ׃
.it under | the and (is) silver | ,tent my | the in of middle | the in ,ground | (are) they hidden | and ,behold | took and ;them

22
2934 2009 168 7323 4397 3091 7971
וַיִּשְׁלַח יְהוֹשֻׁעַ מַלְאָכִים וַיָּרֻצוּ הָאֹהֱלָה וְהִנֵּה טְמוּנָה
was it hidden | ,and ,behold | ;tent the | they and to ran | ,messengers | Joshua | sent And

23
935 168 8432 3447 8478 3701 168
בְּאָהֳלוֹ וְהַכֶּסֶף תַּחְתֶּיהָ׃ וַיִּקָּחוּם מִתּוֹךְ הָאֹהֶל וַיְבִאוּם
bore and them | the ,tent of | of out the middle | they and them took | ;it under | the and (was) silver | his in ,tent

3068 6440 3332 3478 1121 3605 3091
אֶל־יְהוֹשֻׁעַ וְאֶל כָּל־בְּנֵי יִשְׂרָאֵל וַיַּצִּקֻם לִפְנֵי יְהוָה׃
.Jehovah | before | poured and out them | Israel | the of sons | all | and to | ,Joshua | to

24
155 3701 2226 5912 3091 3947
וַיִּקַּח יְהוֹשֻׁעַ אֶת־עָכָן בֶּן־זֶרַח וְאֶת־הַכֶּסֶף וְאֶת־הָאַדֶּרֶת
,robe the | and | the ,silver | and | ,Zerah the of son | Achan | Joshua | And took

7794 1323 1121 2091 3956
וְאֶת־לְשׁוֹן הַזָּהָב וְאֶת־בָּנָיו וְאֶת־בְּנֹתָיו וְאֶת־שׁוֹרוֹ וְאֶת־
and | his ,oxen | and | his ,daughters | and | his ,sons | and | ,gold | the of bar | and

3605 834 3605 168 6629 2543
חֲמֹרוֹ וְאֶת־צֹאנוֹ וְאֶת־אָהֳלוֹ וְאֶת־כָּל־אֲשֶׁר־לוֹ וְכָל־
and all | (was) ,his | which | all | and | ,tent his | and | his ,flock | and | his ,asses

25
4100 3091 559 5911 6010 5921 3478
יִשְׂרָאֵל עִמּוֹ וַיַּעֲלוּ אֹתָם עֵמֶק עָכוֹר׃ וַיֹּאמֶר יְהוֹשֻׁעַ מֶה
How ,Joshua | said And | .Grief | the to of Valley | them | they and brought | with ,him | Israel

3478 3605 7275 2088 3117 3068 5916 5916
עֲכַרְתָּנוּ יַעְכָּרְךָ יְהוָה בַּיּוֹם הַזֶּה וַיִּרְגְּמוּ אֹתוֹ כָל־יִשְׂרָאֵל
Israel | all | him | And stoned | .this | on day | Jehovah | grieve will you | have you !us grieved

26
6965 68 5619 784 8313 68
אֶבֶן וַיִּשְׂרְפוּ אֹתָם בָּאֵשׁ וַיִּסְקְלוּ אֹתָם בָּאֲבָנִים׃ וַיָּקִימוּ
they And raised | with .stones | them | they and stoned | with ,fire | them | they and burned | with ,stones

2740 3068 7725 2088 3117 5704 1419 68 1530 5921
עָלָיו גַּל־אֲבָנִים גָּדוֹל עַד הַיּוֹם הַזֶּה וַיָּשָׁב יְהוָה מֵחֲרוֹן
the from of heat | Jehovah | And back turned | .this | day | to | great | stones | a of heap | over him

5704 5911 6010 4725 8034 7121 639
אַפּוֹ עַל־כֵּן קָרָא שֵׁם הַמָּקוֹם הַהוּא עֵמֶק עָכוֹר עַד
till | of Grief | the Valley | that | place of | the name | is called | there- fore | His ;anger

2088 3117
הַיּוֹם הַזֶּה׃
.this | day

CAP. VIII ח

CHAPTER 8

CHAPTER 8
[1]And Jehovah said to
Joshua, Do not fear, nor be
afraid. Take all the people of
war with you, and rise up,
go up to Ai. Behold, I have
given the king of Ai, and his
people, and his city, and his
land into your hand. [2]And
you shall do to Ai and to its

1
3947 2865 3372 3091 3068 559
וַיֹּאמֶר יְהוָה אֶל־יְהוֹשֻׁעַ אַל־תִּירָא וְאַל־תֵּחָת קַח עִמְּךָ
with you | take | be ;afraid | and not | Do ,fear | not | ,Joshua | to | Jehovah | And said

3027 5414 7200 5857 5921 6965 4421 5971 3605
אֵת כָּל־עַם הַמִּלְחָמָה וְקוּם עֲלֵה הָעָי רְאֵה נָתַתִּי בְיָדְךָ
into hand your | have I given | ,see | to ;Ai | to go | and ,arise | ,war | the of people | all | –

2
6213 776 5892 5971 5857 4428
אֶת־מֶלֶךְ הָעַי וְאֶת־עַמּוֹ וְאֶת־עִירוֹ וְאֶת־אַרְצוֹ׃ וְעָשִׂיתָ
you And do shall | his .land | and | his ,city | and | his ,people | and | ,Ai | the of king

לעי ולמלכה כאשר עשית ליריחו ולמלכה רק־שללה
3 ובהמתה תבזו לכם שים־לך ארב לעיר מאחריה׃ ויקם
יהושע וכל־עם המלחמה לעלות העי ויבחר יהושע
4 שלשים אלף איש גבורי החיל וישלחם לילה׃ ויצו
אתם לאמר ראו אתם ארבים לעיר מאחרי העיר אל־
5 תרחיקו מן־העיר מאד והייתם כלכם נכנים׃ ואני וכל־
העם אשר אתי נקרב אל־העיר והיה כי־יצאו לקראתנו
6 כאשר בראשנה ונסנו לפניהם׃ ויצאו אחרינו עד
התיקנו אותם מן־העיר כי יאמרו נסים לפנינו כאשר
7 בראשנה ונסנו לפניהם׃ ואתם תקמו מהאורב והורשתם
8 את־העיר ונתנה יהוה אלהיכם בידכם׃ והיה כתפשכם
את־העיר תציתו את־העיר באש כדבר יהוה תעשו ראו
9 צויתי אתכם׃ וישלחם יהושע וילכו אל־המארב וישבו
בין בית־אל ובין העי מים לעי וילן יהושע בלילה ההוא
10 בתוך העם׃ וישכם יהושע בבקר ויפקד את־העם
11 ויעל הוא וזקני ישראל לפני העם העי׃ וכל־העם
המלחמה אשר אתו עלו ויגשו ויבאו נגד העיר ויחנו

king as you have done to Jericho and its king. Only, its spoil and its cattle you shall take for yourselves. Set yourself an ambush for the city behind it. [3]And Joshua rose up, and all the people of war, to go up to Ai. And Joshua chose thirty thousand men, mighty warriors, and sent them away by night. [4]And *he* commanded them, saying, See, you *will be* an ambush against the city, at the rear of the city. You shall not go very far off from the city, and all of you shall be ready. [5]And I and all the people with me shall draw near to the city. And it shall be, when they come out to meet us as at the first, and we have fled before them, [6]and they have come out after us until we have drawn them out of the city—for they will say, They are fleeing before us, as at the first—and we are fleeing from them; [7]then you shall rise from the ambush and shall occupy the city. And Jehovah your God shall give it into your hand. [8]And it shall be, when you capture the city, you shall burn the city with fire. You shall do according to the word of Jehovah. See, I have commanded you. [9]And Joshua sent them away, and they went to the ambush, and stayed between Bethel and Ai, on the west of Ai. And Joshua remained that night in the midst of the people.

[10]And Joshua rose early in the morning, and inspected the people, and went up, he and the elders of Israel, in the sight of the people of Ai. [11]And all the people of war with him went up and drew near, and came before the city. And

they camped on the north of Ai, and the valley *was* between him and Ai. [12]And he took about five thousand men and set them as an ambush between Bethel and Ai, on the west of the city. [13]And they set the people, all the camp on the north of the city; and its rear on the west of the city. And Joshua went into the middle of the valley on that night. [14]And it happened, when the king of Ai saw, the men of the city rose early and hurried to go out to meet Israel in battle, he and all his people at the appointed time before the plain. He did not know that an ambush *was* against him behind the city. [15]And Joshua and all Israel *appeared* stricken before them, and fled the way of the wilderness. [16]And all the people in the city were called to chase them. And they pursued Joshua, and were drawn away out of the city. [17]And there was not a man left in Ai and Bethel who had not gone out after Israel. And they left the city open, and chased Israel.

[18]And Jehovah said to Joshua, Stretch out the javelin in your hand towar Ai. For I will give it into your hand. And Joshua stretched out the javelin in his hand toward the city. [19]And the ambush rose up quickly out of their place, and they ran as soon as he had stretched out his hand, and entered the city, and took it. And they hastened and burned the city with fire. [20]And the men of Ai looked behind them, and saw; and, behold! The smoke of the city had gone up into the sky. And there was no power in them to flee here or there.

12 מִצְּפוֹן לָעַי וְהַגַּי בֵּינוֹ וּבֵין הָעָי׃ וַיִּקַּח כַּחֲמֵשֶׁת אֲלָפִים
thousand about he And .Ai and between a and ;Ai north
five took him valley of

אִישׁ וַיָּשֶׂם אוֹתָם אֹרֵב בֵּין בֵּית־אֵל וּבֵין הָעַי מִיָּם לָעִיר׃
the west Ai and Bethel be- an as them and men
.city of tween ambush set

13 וַיָּשִׂימוּ הָעָם אֶת־כָּל־הַמַּחֲנֶה אֲשֶׁר מִצְּפוֹן לָעִיר וְאֶת־
and the north which the all the they And
,city of (was) camp people set

עֲקֵבוֹ מִיָּם לָעִיר וַיֵּלֶךְ יְהוֹשֻׁעַ בַּלַּיְלָה הַהוּא בְּתוֹךְ הָעֵמֶק׃
the the into that night Joshua and the west its
valley of middle went ;city of rear

14 וַיְהִי כִּרְאוֹת מֶלֶךְ־הָעַי וַיְמַהֲרוּ וַיַּשְׁכִּימוּ וַיֵּצְאוּ אַנְשֵׁי־הָעִיר
the the went and rose and that of the when it And
city of men out early hurried ,Ai king saw ,was

לִקְרַאת־יִשְׂרָאֵל לַמִּלְחָמָה הוּא וְכָל־עַמּוֹ לַמּוֹעֵד לִפְנֵי
before the at his and he ,battle in Israel meet to
time set ,people all

15 הָעֲרָבָה וְהוּא לֹא יָדַע כִּי־אֹרֵב לוֹ מֵאַחֲרֵי הָעִיר׃ וַיִּנָּגְעוּ
And .city the behind against am- an that knew not and ;plain the
touched him (was) bush he

16 יְהוֹשֻׁעַ וְכָל־יִשְׂרָאֵל לִפְנֵיהֶם וַיָּנֻסוּ דֶּרֶךְ הַמִּדְבָּר׃ וַיִּזָּעֲקוּ
were and the way the and before Israel and Joshua
called ;wilderness of fled ,them all

כָּל־הָעָם אֲשֶׁר בָּעִיר לִרְדֹּף אַחֲרֵיהֶם וַיִּרְדְּפוּ אַחֲרֵי יְהוֹשֻׁעַ
Joshua after they and after run to the in who the all
ran ;them city (were) people

17 וַיִּנָּתְקוּ מִן־הָעִיר׃ וְלֹא־נִשְׁאַר אִישׁ בָּעַי וּבֵית אֵל אֲשֶׁר
who or Ai in man a was And the from were and
Bethel left not .city drawn

לֹא־יָצְאוּ אַחֲרֵי יִשְׂרָאֵל וַיַּעַזְבוּ אֶת־הָעִיר פְּתוּחָה וַיִּרְדְּפוּ
ran and open city the they and ;Israel after had not
left out gone

18 אַחֲרֵי יִשְׂרָאֵל׃ וַיֹּאמֶר יְהוָה אֶל־יְהוֹשֻׁעַ נְטֵה בַּכִּידוֹן
the Stretch ,Joshua to Jehovah said And .Israel after
javelin forth

אֲשֶׁר־בְּיָדְךָ אֶל־הָעַי כִּי בְיָדְךָ אֶתְּנֶנָּה וַיֵּט יְהוֹשֻׁעַ בַּכִּידוֹן
the Joshua And will I your into for ;Ai toward your in that
javelin stretched ,it give hand hand (is)

19 אֲשֶׁר־בְּיָדוֹ אֶל־הָעִיר׃ וְהָאוֹרֵב קָם מְהֵרָה מִמְּקוֹמוֹ
its from quickly arose the And the toward his in that
place ambush ,city hand (was)

וַיָּרוּצוּ כִּנְטוֹת יָדוֹ וַיָּבֹאוּ הָעִיר וַיִּלְכְּדוּהָ וַיְמַהֲרוּ וַיַּצִּיתוּ
and they and seized and the and his as soon as ran and
burned hurried ;it city entered hand stretched he

20 אֶת־הָעִיר בָּאֵשׁ׃ וַיִּפְנוּ אַנְשֵׁי הָעַי אַחֲרֵיהֶם וַיִּרְאוּ וְהִנֵּה
,and and behind Ai the And with city the
,behold ;looked them of men turned .fire

עָלָה עֲשַׁן הָעִיר הַשָּׁמַיְמָה וְלֹא־הָיָה בָהֶם יָדַיִם לָנוּס הֵנָּה
here to power in there and the into city the the was
flee them was not ;sky of smoke rising

And the people who had
fled to the wilderness
turned back against the
pursuers. [21]And Joshua
and all Israel saw that the
ambush had captured the
city, and that the smoke of
the city had gone up. And
they turned back and struck
the men of Ai. [22]And the
others came out from the
city to meet them. and they
were in the midst of Israel,
some on this side, and
some on that. And they
struck them until he did not
leave them a survivor, not
one that escaped. [23]And
they caught the king of Ai
alive, and brought him to
Joshua.

[24]And it happened, when
Israel had made an end to
slaying all the inhabitants of
Ai in the field, even in the
wilderness where they
pursued them—and they all
of them fell by the mouth of
the sword until they were
consumed — all Israel
turned back to Ai, and
struck it with the mouth of
the sword. [25]And all who
fell during that day, of men
and of women, were twelve
thousand, all the men of
Ai. [26]And Joshua did not
draw back his hand with
which he stretched out the
javelin until he had
destroyed all the inhabi-
tants of Ai. [27]Only, Israel
seized for themselves the
livestock, and the plunder
of the city, according to the
word of Jehovah which He
commanded Joshua. [28]And
Joshua burned Ai, and
made it a heap forever, a
desolation to this day.

[29]And he hanged the king of
Ai on the tree until evening
time. And at sundown
Joshua commanded, and
they took his dead body
down from the tree, and
threw it into the opening of
the gate of the city; and
raised over it a great heap of

3091 7291 2015 4057 5127 5971 2008
21 וְהֵנָּה וְהָעָם הַנָּס הַמִּדְבָּר נֶהְפַּךְ אֶל־הָרוֹדֵף׃ וִיהוֹשֻׁעַ
and the against turned the to that the and or
Joshua ;pursuers back wilderness fled people ,there

5927 5892 693 3920 7200 3478 3605
וְכָל־יִשְׂרָאֵל רָאוּ כִּי־לָכַד הָאֹרֵב אֶת־הָעִיר וְכִי עָלָה
was and the the had that saw Israel and
rising that ,city ambush captured all

3318 428 5857 582 5221 7725 5892 6227
22 עֲשַׁן הָעִיר וַיָּשֻׁבוּ וַיַּכּוּ אֶת־אַנְשֵׁי הָעָי׃ וְאֵלֶּה יָצְאוּ מִן־
of came the And .Ai the and they and the the
out others of men struck turned city of smoke

428 2088 428 8432 3478 1961 7125 5892
הָעִיר לִקְרָאתָם וַיִּהְיוּ לְיִשְׂרָאֵל בַּתָּוֶךְ אֵלֶּה מִזֶּה וְאֵלֶּה
and on these the in Israel of they and meet to the
those this ;midst were them city

6412 8300 7604 1115 5704 5221 2088
מִזֶּה וַיַּכּוּ אוֹתָם עַד־בִּלְתִּי הִשְׁאִיר־לוֹ שָׂרִיד וּפָלִיט׃
an nor a them to was not until them they and on
.escape remnant left struck ;that

1961 3091 7126 2416 8610 5857 4428
23 וְאֶת־מֶלֶךְ הָעַי תָּפְשׂוּ חָי וַיַּקְרִבוּ אֹתוֹ אֶל־יְהוֹשֻׁעַ׃ וַיְהִי
24
it And .Joshua to him and alive they Ai of king And
was brought caught

4057 7704 5857 3427 3605 2026 3478 3615
כְּכַלּוֹת יִשְׂרָאֵל לַהֲרֹג אֶת־כָּל־יֹשְׁבֵי הָעַי בַּשָּׂדֶה בַּמִּדְבָּר
the in the in Ai natives all of Israel made when
desert field of the killing end an

8552 5704 2719 6440 3605 5307 7291 834
אֲשֶׁר רְדָפוּם בּוֹ וַיִּפְּלוּ כֻלָּם לְפִי־חֶרֶב עַד־תֻּמָּם
were they until the by all of had and —in pur- they where
,annihilated sword's edge them fallen them sued

3605 1961 2719 6310 5221 5857 3478 3605 7725
25 וַיָּשֻׁבוּ כָל־יִשְׂרָאֵל הָעַי וַיַּכּוּ אֹתָהּ לְפִי־חָרֶב׃ וַיְהִי כָל־
all And the with it and to Israel all turned
were .sword's mouth struck Ai back

505 6240 8147 802 5704 376 3117 5307
הַנֹּפְלִים בַּיּוֹם הַהוּא מֵאִישׁ וְעַד־אִשָּׁה שְׁנֵים עָשָׂר אֶלֶף
-thousand twelve to even from that day who
women men fell

3591 5186 834 3027 7725 3808 3091 5857 582 3605
26 כֹּל אַנְשֵׁי הָעָי׃ וִיהוֹשֻׁעַ לֹא־הֵשִׁיב יָדוֹ אֲשֶׁר נָטָה בַּכִּידוֹן
the had he (in) his did not And .Ai the all
javelin out put which hand back draw Joshua of men

7998 929 7535 5857 3427 3605 2763 834 5704
27 עַד אֲשֶׁר הֶחֱרִים אֵת כָּל־יֹשְׁבֵי הָעָי׃ רַק הַבְּהֵמָה וּשְׁלַל
the and cattle the ,only ;Ai the all had he until
of spoil of natives destroyed

6680 834 3068 1697 3478 962 5892
הָעִיר הַהִיא בָּזְזוּ לָהֶם יִשְׂרָאֵל כִּדְבַר יְהוָה אֲשֶׁר צִוָּה
com- He which Jehovah's according ,Israel for seized that city
manded word to themselves

5967 8510 7760 5857 3091 8313 3091
28 אֶת־יְהוֹשֻׁעַ׃ וַיִּשְׂרֹף יְהוֹשֻׁעַ אֶת־הָעָי וַיְשִׂימֶהָ תֵּל־עוֹלָם
,forever made and Ai Joshua And .Joshua
heap a it burned

5704 6086 8518 5857 4428 2088 3117 5704 8077
29 שְׁמָמָה עַד הַיּוֹם הַזֶּה׃ וְאֶת־מֶלֶךְ הָעַי תָּלָה עַל־הָעֵץ עַד־
until tree a on he Ai the And this day to ruin a
hanged of king

5038 3381 3091 6680 8121 935 6153 6256
עֵת הָעָרֶב וּכְבוֹא הַשֶּׁמֶשׁ צִוָּה יְהוֹשֻׁעַ וַיֹּרִידוּ אֶת־נִבְלָתוֹ
dead his they and Joshua ordered sun the the at and ;evening the
body down took of (down) going of time

5921 6965 5892 8179 6607 7993 6086
מִן־הָעֵץ וַיַּשְׁלִיכוּ אוֹתָהּ אֶל־פֶּתַח שַׁעַר הָעִיר וַיָּקִימוּ עָלָיו
over and the the the into it and the from
it raised ;city of gate of opening threw ,tree

stones until this day.
[30]Then Joshua built an
altar to Jehovah, the God of
Israel, in Mount Ebal, [31]as
Moses, the servant of
Jehovah, commanded the
sons of Israel, as it is written
in the book of the law of
Moses; an altar of whole
stones, on which had been
wielded no iron. And they
offered up on it burnt
offerings to Jehovah, and
offered peace offerings.
[32]And he wrote there on the
stones the copy of the law
of Moses, which he had
written in the presence of
the sons of Israel. [33]And
all Israel, and its elders, and
authorities, and its judges,
were standing on this side
and on that of the ark,
before the priests, the
Levites, who bore the ark of
the covenant of Jehovah—
the alien as well as the
home-born—half of them
in front of Mount Gerizim,
and half of them in front of
Mount Ebal, as Moses the
servant of Jehovah had
commanded at the first,
that they should bless the
people of Israel. [34]And
afterward he read all the
words of the law, the
blessing and the curse,
according to all that was
written in the book of the
law. [35]There was not a
word of all that Moses
commanded which Joshua
did not read before all the
assembly of Israel, and the
women, and the little ones,
and the aliens that walked
among them.

4196 3091 1129 2088 3117 5704 1419 68 1530

30 גַּל־אֲבָנִים גָּדוֹל עַד הַיּוֹם הַזֶּה׃ אָז יִבְנֶה יְהוֹשֻׁעַ מִזְבֵּחַ

an altar · Joshua · built · Then · this (stands it) · day · until · great · stones · a of heap

4872 6680 5858 2022 3478 430 3068

31 לַיהוָה אֱלֹהֵי יִשְׂרָאֵל בְּהַר עֵיבָל׃ כַּאֲשֶׁר צִוָּה מֹשֶׁה

Moses · com- manded · as · ,Ebal · in Mount · ,Israel of · the God · to Jehovah

4872 8451 5612 3789 3478 1121 3068 5650

עֶבֶד־יְהוָה אֶת־בְּנֵי יִשְׂרָאֵל כַּכָּתוּב בְּסֵפֶר תּוֹרַת מֹשֶׁה

:Moses · the of Law · the in of Book · is it as written · ;Israel · the of sons · Jehovah · the of servant

5927 1270 5921 5130 834 3808 8003 68 4196

מִזְבַּח אֲבָנִים שְׁלֵמוֹת אֲשֶׁר לֹא־הֵנִיף עֲלֵיהֶן בַּרְזֶל וַיַּעֲלוּ

they and offered · iron an ;(tool) · on · been had wielded · not · which · ,whole · stones · an of altar

68 5921 8033/3789 8002 2076 3068 5930 5921

32 עָלָיו עֹלוֹת לַיהוָה וַיִּזְבְּחוּ שְׁלָמִים׃ וַיִּכְתָּב־שָׁם עַל־הָאֲבָנִים

stones the · on · there he and wrote · peace ;offerings · and sacrificed · to ,Jehovah · burnt offerings · it on

3605 3478 1121 6440 3789/834 4872 8451 4932

33 אֵת מִשְׁנֵה תּוֹרַת מֹשֶׁה אֲשֶׁר כָּתַב לִפְנֵי בְּנֵי יִשְׂרָאֵל׃ וְכָל־

and all · ,Israel · the before of sons · had he written · which · Moses · the of Law · the of copy

2088 5975 8199 7860 2205 3478

יִשְׂרָאֵל וּזְקֵנָיו וְשֹׁטְרִים | וְשֹׁפְטָיו עֹמְדִים מִזֶּה | וּמִזֶּה |

on and (side) that · on this · (were) standing · and ,judges · and authorities · its and elders · Israel

1616 3068/1285 727 5375 3881 3548 5048 727

לָאָרוֹן נֶגֶד הַכֹּהֲנִים הַלְוִיִּם נֹשְׂאֵי | אֲרוֹן בְּרִית־יְהוָה כַּגֵּר

alike alien the · Jehovah's cove- nant · ark the of · (were who) bearing · the ,Levites · priests the of · before · of ark the

5858/2022 4136 2677 1630 2022 4136 2677 249

כָּאֶזְרָח חֶצְיוֹ אֶל־מוּל הַר־גְּרִזִים וְהַחֶצְיוֹ אֶל־מוּל הַר־עֵיבָל

,Ebal Mount · front in of · half and them of · ,Gerizim Mount · front in of · half them of · the and ,native

3478 5971 1288 3068 5650 4872 6680

כַּאֲשֶׁר צִוָּה מֹשֶׁה עֶבֶד־יְהוָה לְבָרֵךְ אֶת־הָעָם יִשְׂרָאֵל

Israel · the of people · bless to · ,Jehovah the of servant · Moses · com- manded · as

1293 8451 1697 3605 7121 310 7223

34 בָּרִאשֹׁנָה׃ וְאַחֲרֵי־כֵן קָרָא אֶת־כָּל־דִּבְרֵי הַתּוֹרָה הַבְּרָכָה

the blessing · the ,Law · the of words · all · he read · after- ward · And · .first the at

3605 1697/1961 8451 5612 3789 3605 7045

35 וְהַקְּלָלָה כְּכָל־הַכָּתוּב בְּסֵפֶר הַתּוֹרָה׃ לֹא־הָיָה דָבָר מִכֹּל

of all · a word · There was · not · .Law the · the in of Book · was that written · accord- ing all to · the and ,curse

6951 3605 3091 7121 3808 834 4872 6680

אֲשֶׁר־צִוָּה מֹשֶׁה אֲשֶׁר לֹא־קָרָא יְהוֹשֻׁעַ נֶגֶד כָּל־קְהַל

the of assembly · all · before · Joshua · did read · not · which · Moses · com- manded · that

7130 3212 1616 2945 802 3478

יִשְׂרָאֵל וְהַנָּשִׁים וְהַטַּף וְהַגֵּר הַהֹלֵךְ בְּקִרְבָּם׃

among .them · (were) who walking · and the aliens the · and the ,babes · the and ,women · ,Israel

CAP. IX ט

CHAPTER 9

CHAPTER 9
[1]And it happened, when
all the kings who *were*
beyond the Jordan in the
hills, and in the Lowland,
and in all the coast of the
Great Sea in front of

2022 3383 5676 834 4428 3605 8085 1961

1 וַיְהִי כִשְׁמֹעַ כָּל־הַמְּלָכִים אֲשֶׁר בְּעֵבֶר הַיַּרְדֵּן בָּהָר

the in ,hills · the Jordan · beyond · who (were) · kings the · all · when heard · it And ,was

2850 3844 4136 1419 3220 2348 3605 8219

וּבַשְּׁפֵלָה וּבְכֹל חוֹף הַיָּם הַגָּדוֹל אֶל־מוּל הַלְּבָנוֹן הַחִתִּי

the Hittite · ,Lebanon · toward · Great · the Sea · the of coast · in and all · the in and ,lowlands

Lebanon, heard of it, the Hittite, and the Amorite, the Canaanite, the Perizzite, the Hivite, and the Jebusite, [2]they with one mouth gathered themselves to fight with Joshua and with Israel.

[3]And the inhabitants of Gibeon heard what Joshua had done to Jericho and to Ai. [4]And they acted slyly, and they went and acted like envoys, and took old sacks for their asses, and old wineskins, even torn and bound up; [5]and old and patched sandals on their feet; and old garments on them. And all their provision of bread was dry; it was crumbs. [6]And they went to Joshua, to the camp at Gilgal. And *they* said to him and to the men of Israel, We have come from a distant land. And now cut a covenant with us. [7]And the men of Israel said to the Hivites, Perhaps you are living in our midst, and how shall we cut a covenant with you? [8]And they said to Joshua, We *are* your servants. And Joshua said to them, Who *are* you? And from where do you come? [9]And they said to him, Your servants have come from a very distant land, because of the name of Jehovah your God, for we have heard of His fame, and all that He has done in Egypt. [10]Also what He has done to the two kings of the Amorites beyond the Jordan, to Sihon the king of Heshbon, and to Og the king of Bashan who *was* in Ashtaroth. [11]And our elders and all the people of our land spoke to us,

3162 8179 2983 2340 6322 3669 567
2 וְהָאֱמֹרִי הַכְּנַעֲנִי הַפְּרִזִּי הַחִוִּי וְהַיְבוּסִי׃ וַיִּתְקַבְּצוּ יַחְדָּו
together gathered they themselves | the and Jebusite | the Hivite | the Perizzite | the Canaanite | the and Amorite

3427 259 6310 3478 3091 3898
3 לְהִלָּחֵם עִם־יְהוֹשֻׁעַ וְעִם־יִשְׂרָאֵל פֶּה אֶחָד׃ וְיֹשְׁבֵי
the And of natives | .one | (with) mouth | Israel | and with | Joshua | with | fight to

6213 5867 3405 3091 6213 8085 1391
4 גִבְעוֹן שָׁמְעוּ אֵת אֲשֶׁר עָשָׂה יְהוֹשֻׁעַ לִירִיחוֹ וְלָעָי׃ וַיַּעֲשׂוּ
and acted | to and ;Ai | to Jericho | Joshua | had done | what | heard | Gibeon

1087 8242 3947 6737 3212 6195 1571
גַּם־הֵמָּה בְּעָרְמָה וַיֵּלְכוּ וַיִּצְטַיָּרוּ וַיִּקְחוּ שַׂקִּים בָּלִים
old | sacks | and took | acted and envoys like | they and went | ,slyly | they also

8275 6887 1234 1087 3196/ 4997 2543
5 לַחֲמוֹרֵיהֶם וְנֹאדוֹת יַיִן בָּלִים וּמְבֻקָּעִים וּמְצֹרָרִים׃ וּנְעָלוֹת
and sandals | bound and ;up | and torn | worn out | wine-skins | and | their for ,asses

3605 1087 8008 7272 2921 1087
בָּלוֹת וּמְטֻלָּאוֹת בְּרַגְלֵיהֶם וּשְׂלָמוֹת בָּלוֹת עֲלֵיהֶם וְכֹל
and all | upon ;them | worn out | and garments | their on ,feet | patched and | worn out

3091 3212 5350 1961 3001 67:18 3899
6 לֶחֶם צֵידָם יָבֵשׁ הָיָה נִקֻּדִים׃ וַיֵּלְכוּ אֶל־יְהוֹשֻׁעַ אֶל־
to | Joshua | to they And went | .crumbs | was it | was ;dry | their of provision | the bread

776 3478 376 559 1537 4264
הַמַּחֲנֶה הַגִּלְגָּל וַיֹּאמְרוּ אֵלָיו וְאֶל־אִישׁ יִשְׂרָאֵל מֵאֶרֶץ
From land a | ,Israel | the of men | and to | ,him to | said and | (at) ,Gilgal | camp the

376 559 1285 3772 6258 935 7350
7 רְחוֹקָה בָּאנוּ וְעַתָּה כִּרְתוּ־לָנוּ בְרִית׃ וַיֹּאמְרוּ אִישׁ־
the of men | said And | a .covenant | with us | cut | and ,now | have we ,come | distant

3772 3427 7130 194 2340 3478
יִשְׂרָאֵל אֶל־הַחִוִּי אוּלַי בְּקִרְבִּי אַתָּה יוֹשֵׁב וְאֵיךְ אֶכְרָות־
we shall cut | and how | (are) ,living | you | our in midst | Perhaps | the ,Hivites | to | Israel

559 5650 3091 559 1285
8 לְךָ בְרִית׃ וַיֹּאמְרוּ אֶל־יְהוֹשֻׁעַ עֲבָדֶיךָ אֲנָחְנוּ וַיֹּאמֶר
said And | We .(are) | Your servants | ,Joshua to | they And said | a ?covenant | with you

559 935 370 3091
9 אֲלֵהֶם יְהוֹשֻׁעַ מִי אַתֶּם וּמֵאַיִן תָּבֹאוּ׃ וַיֹּאמְרוּ אֵלָיו
,him to | they And said | you do ?come | And where from | ?you | Who (are) | Joshua | to them

430 3068 8034 5650 935 3966 7350 776
מֵאֶרֶץ רְחוֹקָה מְאֹד בָּאוּ עֲבָדֶיךָ לְשֵׁם יְהוָה אֱלֹהֶיךָ כִּי־
for | your ,God | Jehovah | because of name the of | your ,servants | have come | very | distant | From land a

4714 6213 3605 8088 8085
10 שָׁמַעְנוּ שָׁמְעוֹ וְאֵת כָּל־אֲשֶׁר עָשָׂה בְּמִצְרָיִם׃ וְאֵת
and | ,Egypt in | has He done | that | all | and | His ,fame | have we heard of

3383 5676 567 4428 8147 6213 3605
כֹּל־אֲשֶׁר עָשָׂה לִשְׁנֵי מַלְכֵי הָאֱמֹרִי אֲשֶׁר בְּעֵבֶר הַיַּרְדֵּן
the Jordan | beyond | who (were) | the Amorites | kings of | the to two | has He done | that all

6252 1316 4428 5747 2809 4428 5511
לְסִיחוֹן מֶלֶךְ חֶשְׁבּוֹן וּלְעוֹג מֶלֶךְ־הַבָּשָׁן אֲשֶׁר בְּעַשְׁתָּרוֹת׃
.Ashtaroth in | who (was) | Bashan | the of king | to and Og | ,Heshbon | king of | to Sihon

3947 559 776 3427 3605 2205 559
11 וַיֹּאמְרוּ אֵלֵינוּ זְקֵינֵינוּ וְכָל־יֹשְׁבֵי אַרְצֵנוּ לֵאמֹר קְחוּ
Take | saying | our ,land | of dwellers the | all and | our elders | us to | And spoke

saying, Take provisions in your hand for the way, and go to meet them. And you shall say to them, We *are* your servants; and now, cut a covenant with us. [12]We provided ourselves with this hot bread out of our houses on the day we came out to go to you. And now, behold, *it is* dry and it is crumbs. [13]And these are the wineskins which we filled new; and, behold, they have torn. And these garments of ours, and our sandals, have become old because of the exceeding greatness of the way. [14]And the men took of their provision, and did not ask at the mouth of Jehovah. [15]And Joshua made peace with them, and cut a covenant with them, to keep them alive. And the leaders of the congregation swore to them.

[16]And at the end of three days they had cut a covenant with them, and it happened that they heard that they *were* their neighbors, and they *were* living in their midst. [17]And the sons of Israel journeyed and came to their cities on the third day. And their cities *were* Gibeon, and Chephirah, and Beeroth, and Kirjath-jearim. [18]And the sons of Israel did not strike them, for the leaders of the congregation swore to them by Jehovah the God of Israel. And all the congregation murmured against the leaders. [19]And all the leaders said to all the congregation, We have sworn to them by Jehovah the God of Israel; and now we cannot touch them. [20]We shall do this to them, and shall keep them alive and wrath shall not be on us because of the oath which we have sworn to them.

559 7125 3212 1870 6720 3027
בְּיֶדְכֶם צֵידָה לַדֶּרֶךְ וּלְכוּ לִקְרָאתָם וַאֲמַרְתֶּם אֲלֵיהֶם
.them to | you and say shall | meet to ;them | go and | the for ,way | provisions | your in hand

12 2525 3899 2088 1285 3772 6258 5650
עַבְדֵיכֶם אֲנַחְנוּ וְעַתָּה כִּרְתוּ־לָנוּ בְרִית׃ זֶה לַחְמֵנוּ חָם
hot | our bread | This | a covenant | with us | cut | and ,now | We (are) | your servants

6258 3212 3318 3117 1004 6679
הִצְטַיַּדְנוּ אֹתוֹ מִבָּתֵּינוּ בְּיוֹם צֵאתֵנוּ לָלֶכֶת אֲלֵיכֶם וְעַתָּה
and now | ;you to | go to | came we out | the on day | of out ,houses our | with it | took we ourselves for

13 4390 834 3196 4997 428 5350 3001 2009
הִנֵּה יָבֵשׁ וְהָיָה נִקֻּדִים׃ וְאֵלֶּה נֹאדוֹת הַיַּיִן אֲשֶׁר מִלֵּאנוּ
we filled | which | wineskins | And these | .crumbs | is it and | (is it) ,dry | ,see

1089/5225 8008 428 1234 2009 2319
חֲדָשִׁים וְהִנֵּה הִתְבַּקָּעוּ וְאֵלֶּה שַׂלְמוֹתֵינוּ וּנְעָלֵינוּ בָּלוּ
are out worn | our and sandals | our garments | and these | have they ;torn | ,and ,behold | (were) new

14 6310 6718 582 3947 3766 1870 7230
מֵרֹב הַדֶּרֶךְ מְאֹד׃ וַיִּקְחוּ הָאֲנָשִׁים מִצֵּידָם וְאֶת־פִּי
the and of mouth | their of provision | men the | And took | .exceeding | the way | from of length

15 3772 7965 3091 6213 7592 3068
יְהוָה לֹא שָׁאָלוּ׃ וַיַּעַשׂ לָהֶם יְהוֹשֻׁעַ שָׁלוֹם וַיִּכְרֹת לָהֶם
with them | and cut | ,peace | Joshua | with them | and made | ;ask did not | Jehovah

16 7097 1961 5712 5387 7650 2421 1285
בְּרִית לְחַיּוֹתָם וַיִּשָּׁבְעוּ לָהֶם נְשִׂיאֵי הָעֵדָה׃ וַיְהִי מִקְצֵה
the at of end | it And pass to came | con- the gregation | the of leaders | them to | and swore | keep to ;alive them | cove- a ,nant

8085 1285 3772 310 3117 7969
שְׁלֹשֶׁת יָמִים אַחֲרֵי אֲשֶׁר־כָּרְתוּ לָהֶם בְּרִית וַיִּשְׁמְעוּ כִּי־
that | they and heard | a ,covenant | with them | they cut had | after | days | three

17 1121 5265 3427 7130 7138
קְרֹבִים הֵם אֵלָיו וּבְקִרְבּוֹ הֵם יֹשְׁבִים׃ וַיִּסְעוּ בְנֵי־
the of sons | And journeyed | (were) .living | they | in and midst their | their | they (were) | neighbors

1391 5892 7992 3117 5892 935 3478
יִשְׂרָאֵל וַיָּבֹאוּ אֶל־עָרֵיהֶם בַּיּוֹם הַשְּׁלִישִׁי וְעָרֵיהֶם גִּבְעוֹן
,Gibeon | their :(were) cities | and ;third | the on day | their cities | to | and came | Israel

18 3478 1121 5221 3808 7157 881 3716
וְהַכְּפִירָה וּבְאֵרוֹת וְקִרְיַת יְעָרִים׃ וְלֹא הִכּוּם בְּנֵי יִשְׂרָאֵל
,Israel | the of sons | strike them | did And not | .jearim | and Kirjath- | and Beeroth | and ,Chephirah

3478 430 3068 5712 5387 7650
כִּי־נִשְׁבְּעוּ לָהֶם נְשִׂיאֵי הָעֵדָה בַּיהוָה אֱלֹהֵי יִשְׂרָאֵל
;Israel | the of God | by Jehovah | con- the gregation | the of chiefs | them to | swore for

19 5387 3605 559 5387 5712 3885
וַיִּלֹּנוּ כָל־הָעֵדָה עַל־הַנְּשִׂיאִים׃ וַיֹּאמְרוּ כָל־הַנְּשִׂיאִים
the chiefs | all | said And | .chiefs the | against | the congregation | all | and murmured

3478 430 3068 7650 5712 3605
אֶל־כָּל־הָעֵדָה אֲנַחְנוּ נִשְׁבַּעְנוּ לָהֶם בַּיהוָה אֱלֹהֵי יִשְׂרָאֵל
;Israel | the of God | by Jehovah | them to | have sworn | We | the ,congregation | all | to

20 2421 6213 2088 5060 3201 6258
וְעַתָּה לֹא נוּכַל לִנְגֹּעַ בָּהֶם׃ זֹאת נַעֲשֶׂה לָהֶם וְהַחֲיֵה
shall and alive keep | them to | we do shall | This | .them | touch | we can | not | and now

7650 834 7621 7110 5921 1961 3808
אוֹתָם וְלֹא־יִהְיֶה עָלֵינוּ קֶצֶף עַל־הַשְּׁבוּעָה אֲשֶׁר־נִשְׁבַּעְנוּ
have we sworn | which | oath the | because of | wrath | upon us | will be | and not | ,them

[21]And the leaders said to them, They shall live and be woodcutters, and drawers of water for all the congregation, as the leaders spoke to them.
[22]And Joshua called for them; and he spoke to them, saying, Why have you deceived us, saying, We are very far from you, yet you are living in our midst?

[23]And now, you *are* cursed, and none of you shall fail *to be* slaves, and woodcutters, and drawers of water for the house of my God. [24]And they answered Joshua and said, Because it was certainly told to your servants what Jehovah your God commanded His servant Moses, to give you all the land, and to destroy all the inhabitants of the land before you; and we were greatly afraid for ourselves, because of you. And we did this thing. [25]And now, behold, we *are* in your hand. Do whatever *is* good, and as *is* right in your eyes to do. [26]And he did so to them, and delivered them from the hand of the sons of Israel. And they did not kill them. [27]And on that day Joshua made them woodcutters, and drawers of water for the congregation, and for the altar of Jehovah at the place which He should choose, to this day.

21 לָהֶם׃ וַיֹּאמְרוּ אֲלֵיהֶם הַנְּשִׂיאִים יִחְיוּ וַיִּהְיוּ חֹטְבֵי עֵצִים
woodcutters they and they became ;live shall rulers the them to said And to them

וְשֹׁאֲבֵי־מַיִם לְכָל־הָעֵדָה כַּאֲשֶׁר דִּבְּרוּ לָהֶם הַנְּשִׂיאִים׃
.rulers the to them spoke as the congregation all for water and of drawers

22 וַיִּקְרָא לָהֶם יְהוֹשֻׁעַ וַיְדַבֵּר אֲלֵיהֶם לֵאמֹר לָמָּה רִמִּיתֶם
you have deceived Why ,saying ,them to he and spoke ,Joshua for them And called

אֹתָנוּ לֵאמֹר רְחוֹקִים אֲנַחְנוּ מִכֶּם מְאֹד וְאַתֶּם בְּקִרְבֵּנוּ
our in midst yet you ,very from you we (are) distant ,saying ,us

23 יֹשְׁבִים׃ וְעַתָּה אֲרוּרִים אַתֶּם וְלֹא־יִכָּרֵת מִכֶּם עֶבֶד
(being) slaves of (any) you will fail and not you ,(are) cursed And ,now are ?living

24 וְחֹטְבֵי עֵצִים וְשֹׁאֲבֵי־מַיִם לְבֵית אֱלֹהָי׃ וַיַּעֲנוּ אֶת־
answered And they my .God the for of house water and of drawers woodcutters and

יְהוֹשֻׁעַ וַיֹּאמְרוּ כִּי הֻגֵּד הֻגַּד לַעֲבָדֶיךָ אֵת אֲשֶׁר צִוָּה יְהוָה
Jehovah com- manded what your to ,servants was it surely told Since and ,said Joshua

אֱלֹהֶיךָ אֶת־מֹשֶׁה עַבְדּוֹ לָתֵת לָכֶם אֶת־כָּל־הָאָרֶץ
the ,land all you to give to His ,servant Moses your God

וּלְהַשְׁמִיד אֶת־כָּל־יֹשְׁבֵי הָאָרֶץ מִפְּנֵיכֶם וַנִּירָא מְאֹד
much we and feared before from ,you land the the of inhabitants all to and destroy

25 לְנַפְשֹׁתֵינוּ מִפְּנֵיכֶם וַנַּעֲשֵׂה אֶת־הַדָּבָר הַזֶּה׃ וְעַתָּה הִנְנוּ
behold (are) we and ,now ;this thing we and did because ,you of our for lives

26 בְיָדֶךָ כַּטּוֹב וְכַיָּשָׁר בְּעֵינֶיךָ לַעֲשׂוֹת לָנוּ עֲשֵׂה׃ וַיַּעַשׂ לָהֶם
to them he and did ;(it) do to ,us do to your in eyes as and right (is) (is) as good your in ;hand

27 כֵּן וַיַּצֵּל אוֹתָם מִיַּד בְּנֵי־יִשְׂרָאֵל וְלֹא הֲרָגוּם׃ וַיִּתְּנֵם יְהוֹשֻׁעַ
Joshua made and them did they ;them kill and not ;Israel's the of sons from hand them and saved he ,so

בַּיּוֹם הַהוּא חֹטְבֵי עֵצִים וְשֹׁאֲבֵי־מַיִם לָעֵדָה וּלְמִזְבַּח יְהוָה
Jehovah for and of altar the for ,congregation the water and of drawers wood cutters of that in day

עַד־הַיּוֹם הַזֶּה אֶל־הַמָּקוֹם אֲשֶׁר יִבְחָר׃
should He .choose which the place at ,this day to

CAP. X י

CHAPTER 10

CHAPTER 10

[1]And it happened, when Adonizedek king of Jerusalem heard that Joshua had captured Ai, and had destroyed it—as he had done to Jericho and to its king, so he had done to Ai

1 וַיְהִי כִשְׁמֹעַ אֲדֹנִי־צֶדֶק מֶלֶךְ יְרוּשָׁלַםִ כִּי־לָכַד יְהוֹשֻׁעַ
Joshua had captured that Jerusalem of king zedek Adoni- when heard it And ,was

אֶת־הָעַי וַיַּחֲרִימָהּ כַּאֲשֶׁר עָשָׂה לִירִיחוֹ וּלְמַלְכָּהּ כֵּן
so to and ,king her to Jericho had he done as and hand —it destroyed ,Ai

and to her king—and that
the inhabitants of Gibeon
had made peace with Israel,
and were in their midst,
[2]they were greatly afraid,
because Gibeon *was* a
great city, like one of the
royal cities, and because it
was greater than Ai, and all
its men *were* mighty.
[3]And Adonizedek king of
Jerusalem sent to Hoham
king of Hebron, and to
Piram king of Jarmuth, and
to Japhia king of Lachish,
and to Debir king of Eglon,
saying, [4]Come up to me
and help me. And we shall
strike Gibeon, for it has
made peace with Joshua,
and with the sons of Israel.
[5]And the five kings of the
Amorites assembled, the
king of Jerusalem, the king
of Hebron, the king of
Jarmuth, the king of
Lachish, the king of Eglon,
they and all their camps.
And *they* camped against
Gibeon, and fought against
it.

[6]And the men of Gibeon
sent to Joshua, and to the
camp at Gilgal, saying, Do
not withdraw your hand
from your servants. Come
up to us quickly, and save
us, and help us. for all the
kings of the Amorites living
in the hills have gathered
against us. [7]And Joshua
went up from Gilgal, he and
all the people of war with
him, even all the mighty
warriors. [8]And Jehovah
said to Joshua, Do not be
afraid of them, for I have
given them into your hands.
Not a man of them shall
stand before you. [9]And
Joshua came to them
suddenly—he had traveled
all night from Gilgal—[10]and

3478 1391 3427 7999 4824 5857 6213
עָשָׂה לָעַי וּלְמַלְכָּהּ וְכִי הִשְׁלִימוּ יֹשְׁבֵי גִבְעוֹן אֶת־יִשְׂרָאֵל
Israel with Gibeon the made had and to and to had he
of inhabitants peace that —king her Ai done

259 13:91 1419 5892 39:66 3372 7130 1961
2 וַיְהוּ בְקִרְבָּם׃ וַיִּירְאוּ מְאֹד כִּי עִיר גְּדוֹלָה גִּבְעוֹן כְּאַחַת
one like ,Gibeon great a for ,very they that their in and
of (was) city afraid were ,midst were

582 3605 5857 1419 3588 4467 5892
עָרֵי הַמַּמְלָכָה וְכִי הִיא גְדוֹלָה מִן־הָעַי וְכָל־אֲנָשֶׁיהָ
men its and ,Ai than greater it and ,royal the
(were) all (was) because cities

4428 1937 3389 4428 139 7971 1368
3 גִּבֹּרִים׃ וַיִּשְׁלַח אֲדֹנִי־צֶדֶק מֶלֶךְ יְרוּשָׁלַםִ אֶל־הוֹהָם מֶלֶךְ־
king Hoham to Jerusalem king zedek Adoni- And mighty
of of sent .men

3923 4824 3309 3412 4824 6502 2225
חֶבְרוֹן וְאֶל־פִּרְאָם מֶלֶךְ־יַרְמוּת וְאֶל־יָפִיעַ מֶלֶךְ־לָכִישׁ
,Lachish king Japhia and Jarmuth the Piram and ,Hebron
of to of king to

5221 58 26 59 27 559 5100/44 28 1688
4 וְאֶל־דְּבִיר מֶלֶךְ־עֶגְלוֹן לֵאמֹר׃ עֲלוּ־אֵלַי וְעִזְרֻנִי וְנַכֶּה
we and help and to Come ,saying ,Eglon king Debir and
strike shall ,me me up of to

3478 1121 3091 7999 1391
אֶת־גִּבְעוֹן כִּי־הִשְׁלִימָה אֶת־יְהוֹשֻׁעַ וְאֶת־בְּנֵי יִשְׂרָאֵל׃
.Israel the and ,Joshua with has it for ,Gibeon
of sons with peace made

44 28 3389 44 28 567 44 28 2568 5927 622
5 וַיֵּאָסְפוּ וַיַּעֲלוּ חֲמֵשֶׁת ׀ מַלְכֵי הָאֱמֹרִי מֶלֶךְ יְרוּשָׁלַםִ מֶלֶךְ־
the ,Jerusalem the the kings five the went and And
of king of king ,Amorites of up assembled

3605 5700/44 28 3923/ 4428 3412 44 28 2275
חֶבְרוֹן מֶלֶךְ־יַרְמוּת מֶלֶךְ־לָכִישׁ מֶלֶךְ־עֶגְלוֹן הֵם וְכָל־
and they ,Eglon the ,Lachish the ,Jarmuth the ,Hebron
all of king of king of king

582 7971 3898 1391 2583 4264
6 מַחֲנֵיהֶם וַיַּחֲנוּ עַל־גִּבְעוֹן וַיִּלָּחֲמוּ עָלֶיהָ׃ וַיִּשְׁלְחוּ אַנְשֵׁי
the sent And against and Gibeon against and their
of men .it fought camped ,camps

7503 3808 559 15 37 4264 3091 13 91
גִבְעוֹן אֶל־יְהוֹשֻׁעַ אֶל־הַמַּחֲנֶה הַגִּלְגָּלָה לֵאמֹר אַל־תֶּרֶף
Let not ,saying at camp the to ,Joshua to Gibeon
withdraw ,Gilgal

58:26 3462 4120 59 27 5650 3027
יָדֶיךָ מֵעֲבָדֶיךָ עֲלֵה אֵלֵינוּ מְהֵרָה וְהוֹשִׁיעָה לָּנוּ וְעָזְרֵנוּ
help and us save and ,quickly us to come your from your
;us up ;servants hand

5927 2022 3427 567 44 28 3605 6908
7 כִּי נִקְבְּצוּ אֵלֵינוּ כָּל־מַלְכֵי הָאֱמֹרִי יֹשְׁבֵי הָהָר׃ וַיַּעַל
and the in living the the all against have for
up went ;hill-country Amorites of kings us assembled

3605 4421 5971 3605 1537 3091
יְהוֹשֻׁעַ מִן־הַגִּלְגָּל הוּא וְכָל־עַם הַמִּלְחָמָה עִמּוֹ וְכֹל
even with war the and he ,Gilgal from Joshua
all ,him of people all

3372 38 08 3091 3068 559 2428 1368
8 גִּבּוֹרֵי הֶחָיִל׃ וַיֹּאמֶר יְהוָה אֶל־יְהוֹשֻׁעַ אַל־תִּירָא מֵהֶם
of Be not ,Joshua to Jehovah And the warriors
,them afraid said .mighty

935 6440 376 5975 38:08 5414 3027
9 כִּי בְיָדְךָ נְתַתִּים לֹא־יַעֲמֹד אִישׁ מֵהֶם בְּפָנֶיךָ׃ וַיָּבֹא
And before of man a shall not have I your into for
came .you them stand ;them given hands

1537 59 27 3915/ 3605 6597 3091
אֲלֵיהֶם יְהוֹשֻׁעַ פִּתְאֹם כָּל־הַלַּיְלָה עָלָה מִן־הַגִּלְגָּל׃
—Gilgal from had he the all —suddenly Joshua them to
up gone night

Jehovah troubled them before Israel, and struck them *with* a great slaughter at Gibeon, and *He* pursued by the way of the ascent of Beth-horon, and struck them to Azekah, and to Makkedah. [11]And it happened, as they fled from the face of Israel, they *were* in the descent of Beth-horon, even Jehovah cast great stones on them out of the heavens, to Azekah; and they died. *The* many who died by the hailstones *were* more than the sons of Israel had killed by the sword.

[12]Then Joshua spoke to Jehovah in the day when Jehovah gave the Amorites up before the sons of Israel; and he said, Sun, stand still before the eyes of Israel in Gibeon! And, Moon *stand still* in the valley of Aijalon! [13]And the sun *stood* still, and the moon *stood* still, until the nation *was* avenged *on* its foes. Is it not written in the Book of the Upright? Yea, the sun stood still in the middle of the heavens, and did not hasten to go down for a full day. [14]And there has not been a day such as that, before it or after it; for Jehovah listened to the voice of a man. For Jehovah fought for Israel.

[15]And Joshua returned, and all Israel with him, to the camp at Gilgal.

[16]And these five kings fled, and were hidden in a cave at Makkedah. [17]And it was told to Joshua, saying, the five kings have been found hidden in a cave at Makkedah. [18]And Joshua said, Roll great stones to the mouth of the cave, and set men over it to watch them. [19]And you, do not stand still. Pursue your enemies, and you shall strike the hindmost of

10 וַיְהֻמֵּם יְהוָה לִפְנֵי יִשְׂרָאֵל וַיַּכֵּם מַכָּה־גְדוֹלָה בְּגִבְעוֹן
וַיִּרְדְּפֵם דֶּרֶךְ מַעֲלֵה בֵית־חוֹרֹן וַיַּכֵּם עַד־עֲזֵקָה וְעַד־מַקֵּדָה׃
11 וַיְהִי בְּנֻסָם ׀ מִפְּנֵי יִשְׂרָאֵל הֵם בְּמוֹרַד בֵּית־חוֹרֹן וַיהוָה
הִשְׁלִיךְ עֲלֵיהֶם אֲבָנִים גְּדֹלוֹת מִן־הַשָּׁמַיִם עַד־עֲזֵקָה וַיָּמֻתוּ
רַבִּים אֲשֶׁר־מֵתוּ בְּאַבְנֵי הַבָּרָד מֵאֲשֶׁר הָרְגוּ בְּנֵי יִשְׂרָאֵל
12 בֶּחָרֶב׃ אָז יְדַבֵּר יְהוֹשֻׁעַ לַיהוָה בְּיוֹם תֵּת יְהוָה אֶת־
הָאֱמֹרִי לִפְנֵי בְּנֵי יִשְׂרָאֵל וַיֹּאמֶר ׀ לְעֵינֵי יִשְׂרָאֵל שֶׁמֶשׁ
13 בְּגִבְעוֹן דּוֹם וְיָרֵחַ בְּעֵמֶק אַיָּלוֹן׃ וַיִּדֹּם הַשֶּׁמֶשׁ וְיָרֵחַ עָמָד
עַד־יִקֹּם גּוֹי אֹיְבָיו הֲלֹא־הִיא כְתוּבָה עַל־סֵפֶר הַיָּשָׁר וַיַּעֲמֹד
14 הַשֶּׁמֶשׁ בַּחֲצִי הַשָּׁמַיִם וְלֹא־אָץ לָבוֹא כְּיוֹם תָּמִים׃ וְלֹא
הָיָה כַּיּוֹם הַהוּא לְפָנָיו וְאַחֲרָיו לִשְׁמֹעַ יְהוָה בְּקוֹל אִישׁ
15 כִּי יְהוָה נִלְחָם לְיִשְׂרָאֵל׃ וַיָּשָׁב יְהוֹשֻׁעַ וְכָל־יִשְׂרָאֵל
16 עִמּוֹ אֶל־הַמַּחֲנֶה הַגִּלְגָּלָה׃ וַיָּנֻסוּ חֲמֵשֶׁת הַמְּלָכִים הָאֵלֶּה
17 וַיֵּחָבְאוּ בַמְּעָרָה בְּמַקֵּדָה׃ וַיֻּגַּד לִיהוֹשֻׁעַ לֵאמֹר נִמְצְאוּ
18 חֲמֵשֶׁת הַמְּלָכִים נֶחְבָּאִים בַּמְּעָרָה בְּמַקֵּדָה׃ וַיֹּאמֶר יְהוֹשֻׁעַ
גֹּלּוּ אֲבָנִים גְּדֹלוֹת אֶל־פִּי הַמְּעָרָה וְהַפְקִידוּ עָלֶיהָ אֲנָשִׁים
19 לְשָׁמְרָם׃ וְאַתֶּם אַל־תַּעֲמֹדוּ רִדְפוּ אַחֲרֵי אֹיְבֵיכֶם וְזִנַּבְתֶּם

them. Do not allow them to
go into their cities, for
Jehovah your God has
given them into your hand.
20 And it happened, when
Joshua and the sons of
Israel had finished destroying them *with* a very great
blow, until they were
completely destroyed, and
the remnant of them *who*
escaped went into the
fortified cities, 21 that all
the people returned to the
camp in peace, to Joshua *at*
Makkedah. Not *one*
sharpened his tongue
against the sons of Israel,
against any man.

22 And Joshua said, Open
the mouth of the cave, and
bring out to me these five
kings from the cave. 23 And
they did so, and brought out
to him these five kings from
the cave, the king of
Jerusalem, the king of
Hebron, the king of
Jarmuth, the king of
Lachish, the king of Eglon.

24 And it happened, when
they brought out these
kings to Joshua, Joshua
called to every man of Israel
and said to the com-
manders of the men of war
who had gone with him,
Draw near, set your feet on
the necks of these kings.
And they drew near and set
their feet on their necks.

25 And Joshua said to them,
Do not fear nor be afraid. Be
strong and brave, for so
Jehovah shall do to all your
enemies with whom you
are fighting. 26 And afterward Joshua struck them,
and put them to death, and
hung them on five trees.
And they were hanging on

430 3068 5414 5892 935 5414 3808
אֹתָם אַל־תִּתְּנוּם לָבוֹא אֶל־עָרֵיהֶם כִּי נְתָנָם יְהוָה אֱלֹהֵיכֶם
your Jehovah has for their into go to grant do not ;them
God them given ,cities them

4347 5221 3478 1121 3091 3615 1961 3027
20 בְּיֶדְכֶם׃ וַיְהִי כְּכַלּוֹת יְהוֹשֻׁעַ וּבְנֵי יִשְׂרָאֵל לְהַכּוֹתָם מַכָּה
(with) striking Israel the and Joshua had when it And your into
defeat them of sons finished ,was .hand

935 8277 8300 8552 3966 1419
גְדוֹלָה־מְאֹד עַד־תֻּמָּם וְהַשְּׂרִידִים שָׂרְדוּ מֵהֶם וַיָּבֹאוּ אֶל־
into went of (who) survivors and were they until ,very a
them escaped the ;annihilated great

3091 4264 5971 3605 7725 4013 5892
21 עָרֵי הַמִּבְצָר׃ וַיָּשֻׁבוּ כָל־הָעָם אֶל־הַמַּחֲנֶה אֶל־יְהוֹשֻׁעַ
Joshua to camp the to the all that ,fortified its
people returned cities

3956 376 3478 1121 2782 7965 4779
מַקֵּדָה בְּשָׁלוֹם לֹא־חָרַץ לִבְנֵי יִשְׂרָאֵל לְאִישׁ אֶת־לְשֹׁנוֹ׃
.tongue his against Israel's against (one) Not .peace in at
man (any) sons sharpened Makkedah

3318 4631 631 6605 3091 559
22 וַיֹּאמֶר יְהוֹשֻׁעַ פִּתְחוּ אֶת־פִּי הַמְּעָרָה וְהוֹצִיאוּ אֵלַי אֶת־
me to bring and ,cave the the Open ,Joshua said And
out of mouth

3318 3651 6213 4631 428 4428 2568
23 חֲמֵשֶׁת הַמְּלָכִים הָאֵלֶּה מִן־הַמְּעָרָה׃ וַיַּעֲשׂוּ כֵן וַיֹּצִיאוּ
and so they and ;cave the from these kings five
out brought did

4428 4631 428 4428 2568
אֵלָיו אֶת־חֲמֵשֶׁת הַמְּלָכִים הָאֵלֶּה מִן־הַמְּעָרָה אֵת ׀ מֶלֶךְ
the ;cave the from these kings five to
of king him

3923 4428 3412 4428 2275 4428 3389
יְרוּשָׁלִַם אֶת־מֶלֶךְ חֶבְרוֹן אֶת־מֶלֶךְ יַרְמוּת אֶת־מֶלֶךְ לָכִישׁ
,Lachish the ,Jarmuth the ,Hebron the ,Jerusalem
of king of king of king

428 4428 3318 1961 5700 4428
24 אֶת־מֶלֶךְ עֶגְלוֹן׃ וַיְהִי כְּהוֹצִיאָם אֶת־הַמְּלָכִים הָאֵלֶּה
these kings they when it And .Eglon the
out brought was of king

559 3478 376 3605 3091 7121 3091
אֶל־יְהוֹשֻׁעַ וַיִּקְרָא יְהוֹשֻׁעַ אֶל־כָּל־אִישׁ יִשְׂרָאֵל וַיֹּאמֶר
said and ,Israel man every to Joshua that ,Joshua to
of called

7760 7126 3212 4421 582 7101
אֶל־קְצִינֵי אַנְשֵׁי הַמִּלְחָמָה הֶהָלְכוּא אִתּוֹ קִרְבוּ שִׂימוּ
set Draw with had who war the chiefs the to
,near ,him gone of men of

7760 7126 428 4428 6677 5921 7272
אֶת־רַגְלֵיכֶם עַל־צַוְּארֵי הַמְּלָכִים הָאֵלֶּה וַיִּקְרְבוּ וַיָּשִׂימוּ
set and they and ,these kings necks the on feet your
near drew of

3808 3091 559 6677 5921 7272
25 אֶת־רַגְלֵיהֶם עַל־צַוְּארֵיהֶם׃ וַיֹּאמֶר אֲלֵיהֶם יְהוֹשֻׁעַ אַל־
not ,Joshua them to said And .necks their on feet their

3068 6213 553 2388 2865 3372
תִּירְאוּ וְאַל־תֵּחָתּוּ חִזְקוּ וְאִמְצוּ כִּי כָכָה יַעֲשֶׂה יְהוָה
Jehovah shall so for and be be and fear do
do ;courageous strong ;afraid not

3091 5221 3898 834 341 3605
26 לְכָל־אֹיְבֵיכֶם אֲשֶׁר אַתֶּם נִלְחָמִים אוֹתָם׃ וַיַּכֵּם יְהוֹשֻׁעַ
Joshua And are you whom your all to
them struck ,fighting enemies

8518 1961 6086 2568 8518 4191 310
אַחֲרֵי־כֵן וַיְמִיתֵם וַיִּתְלֵם עַל חֲמִשָּׁה עֵצִים וַיִּהְיוּ תְּלוּיִם
hanging they and ;trees five on and and afterward
were them hanged executed
them

the trees until the evening.
27 And it happened at the
time of the going of the sun,
Joshua commanded, and
they took them down from
the trees, and threw them
into the cave where they
had been hidden, and put
great stones on the mouth
of the cave until this very
day.
28 And that day Joshua
captured Makkedah. And
he struck it by the mouth of
the sword, and he destroyed its king, them, and
every person in it. He did
not leave a survivor. And he
did to the king of Makkedah
as he did to the king of
Jericho.
29 And Joshua passed on,
and all Israel with him, from
Makkedah to Libnah. And
he fought with Libnah.
30 And Jehovah also gave it
into the hand of Israel, and
its king. And *they* struck it
by the mouth of the sword,
and every person in it; he
did not leave a survivor in it.
And he did to its king as he
did to the king of Jericho.
31 And Joshua passed on,
and all Israel with him, from
Libnah to Lachish. And *they*
camped against it, and
fought against it.
32 And Jehovah gave Lachish into
the hand of Israel, and he
captured it on the second
day, and struck it by the
mouth of the sword, and
every person in it, according to all that he did to
Libnah.
33 Then Horan the king of
Gezer came up to help
Lachish. And Joshua struck
him and his people until
there was not left to him a
survivor.
34 And Joshua
passed on, and all Israel
with him, from Lachish to
Eglon. And they camped
against it, and fought

27 עַל־הָעֵצִים עַד־הָעָרֶב׃ וַיְהִי לְעֵת בּוֹא הַשֶּׁמֶשׁ צִוָּה
יְהוֹשֻׁעַ וַיֹּרִידוּם מֵעַל הָעֵצִים וַיַּשְׁלִכֻם אֶל־הַמְּעָרָה אֲשֶׁר
נֶחְבְּאוּ־שָׁם וַיָּשִׂמוּ אֲבָנִים גְּדֹלוֹת עַל־פִּי הַמְּעָרָה עַד
28 עֶצֶם הַיּוֹם הַזֶּה׃ וְאֶת־מַקֵּדָה לָכַד יְהוֹשֻׁעַ בַּיּוֹם
הַהוּא וַיַּכֶּהָ לְפִי־חֶרֶב וְאֶת־מַלְכָּהּ הֶחֱרִם אוֹתָם וְאֶת־כָּל־
הַנֶּפֶשׁ אֲשֶׁר־בָּהּ לֹא הִשְׁאִיר שָׂרִיד וַיַּעַשׂ לְמֶלֶךְ מַקֵּדָה
29 כַּאֲשֶׁר עָשָׂה לְמֶלֶךְ יְרִיחוֹ׃ וַיַּעֲבֹר יְהוֹשֻׁעַ וְכָל־יִשְׂרָאֵל
30 עִמּוֹ מִמַּקֵּדָה לִבְנָה וַיִּלָּחֶם עִם־לִבְנָה׃ וַיִּתֵּן יְהוָה גַּם־
אוֹתָהּ בְּיַד יִשְׂרָאֵל וְאֶת־מַלְכָּהּ וַיַּכֶּהָ לְפִי־חֶרֶב וְאֶת־כָּל־
הַנֶּפֶשׁ אֲשֶׁר־בָּהּ לֹא־הִשְׁאִיר בָּהּ שָׂרִיד וַיַּעַשׂ לְמַלְכָּהּ
31 כַּאֲשֶׁר עָשָׂה לְמֶלֶךְ יְרִיחוֹ׃ וַיַּעֲבֹר יְהוֹשֻׁעַ וְכָל־
32 יִשְׂרָאֵל עִמּוֹ מִלִּבְנָה לָכִישָׁה וַיִּחַן עָלֶיהָ וַיִּלָּחֶם בָּהּ׃ וַיִּתֵּן
יְהוָה אֶת־לָכִישׁ בְּיַד יִשְׂרָאֵל וַיִּלְכְּדָהּ בַּיּוֹם הַשֵּׁנִי וַיַּכֶּהָ
לְפִי־חֶרֶב וְאֶת־כָּל־הַנֶּפֶשׁ אֲשֶׁר־בָּהּ כְּכֹל אֲשֶׁר־עָשָׂה
33 לְלִבְנָה׃ אָז עָלָה הֹרָם מֶלֶךְ גֶּזֶר לַעְזֹר אֶת־לָכִישׁ
וַיַּכֵּהוּ יְהוֹשֻׁעַ וְאֶת־עַמּוֹ עַד־בִּלְתִּי הִשְׁאִיר־לוֹ שָׂרִיד׃
34 וַיַּעֲבֹר יְהוֹשֻׁעַ וְכָל־יִשְׂרָאֵל עִמּוֹ מִלָּכִישׁ עֶגְלֹנָה וַיַּחֲנוּ עָלֶיהָ

against it, [35]and captured it
on that day, and struck it
with the mouth of the
sword. And he destroyed
every person in it on that
day, according to all that he
did to Lachish. [36]And
Joshua went on, and all
Israel with him, from Eglon
to Hebron. And they fought
against it, [37]and captured
it, and struck it by the mouth
of the sword, and its king,
and all its cities, and every
person in it; he did not leave
a survivor, according to all
that he did to Eglon, and
destroyed it and every
person in it.

[38]And Joshua returned
and all Israel with him, to
Debir, and fought against
it. [39]And *they* captured it
and its king, and all its
cities. And they struck them
by the mouth of the sword,
and destroyed every person
in it; he did not leave a
survivor. As he did to
Hebron, so he did to Debir,
and to its king; even as he
did to Libnah, and to its
king.

[40]And Joshua struck all
the land: the heights and
the Negeb, and the Low-
land, and the slopes, and all
their kings; he did not leave
a survivor, but he destroyed
all that breathed, as
Jehovah the God of Israel
had commanded. [41]And
Joshua struck them from
Kadesh-barnea, even to
Gaza, and all the land of
Goshen, even to Gibeon.

[42]And Joshua captured
all these kings in their land
at one time, for Jehovah the

2719/6310 5221 3117 3920 3898
35 וַיִּלָּחֲמוּ עָלֶיהָ׃ וַיִּלְכְּדוּהָ בַּיּוֹם הַהוּא וַיַּכּוּהָ לְפִי־חֶרֶב
the the by / sword of edge; and it struck; ,that; day on; and it captured; against ,it; and fought

834 3605 2763 3117 5315 3605
וְאֵת כָּל־הַנֶּפֶשׁ אֲשֶׁר־בָּהּ בַּיּוֹם הַהוּא הֶחֱרִים כְּכֹל אֲשֶׁר־
that; according all to; he ,destroyed; that; day on; it in; who (was); person every; and

5700 3478 3605 3091 5927 3923 6213
36 עָשָׂה לְלָכִישׁ׃ וַיַּעַל יְהוֹשֻׁעַ וְכָל־יִשְׂרָאֵל עִמּוֹ מֵעֶגְלוֹנָה
from Eglon; with ,him; Israel; and all; ,Joshua; And on went; to .Lachish; did he

2719/6310 5221 3920 3898 2275
37 חֶבְרוֹנָה וַיִּלָּחֲמוּ עָלֶיהָ׃ וַיִּלְכְּדוּהָ וַיַּכּוּהָ־לְפִי־חֶרֶב וְאֶת־
and; the the by ,sword of edge; and it struck; and it captured; against ,it; they and fought; to ;Hebron

3808 5315 3605 5892 3605 4428
מַלְכָּהּ וְאֶת־כָּל־עָרֶיהָ וְאֶת־כָּל־הַנֶּפֶשׁ אֲשֶׁר־בָּהּ לֹא־
not; ;it in; who (was); person; every and; its cities; all; and; its king

2763 5700 6213 3605 8300 7604
הִשְׁאִיר שָׂרִיד כְּכֹל אֲשֶׁר־עָשָׂה לְעֶגְלוֹן וַיַּחֲרֵם אוֹתָהּ וְאֶת־
and; it; he and destroyed; ;Eglon to; did he; that according all to; a ,survivor; did he leave

3478 3605 3091 7725 5315 3605
38 כָּל־הַנֶּפֶשׁ אֲשֶׁר־בָּהּ׃ וַיָּשָׁב יְהוֹשֻׁעַ וְכָל־יִשְׂרָאֵל עִמּוֹ
with him; Israel; and all; Joshua; And returned; .it in; who (was); person every

5892/3605 4428 3920 3898 1688
39 דְּבִרָה וַיִּלָּחֶם עָלֶיהָ׃ וַיִּלְכְּדָהּ וְאֶת־מַלְכָּהּ וְאֶת־כָּל־עָרֶיהָ
its ;cities; all; and; ,king its; and; and ,it captured; against ,it; he and fought; to ;Debir

3808 5315/3605 2763 2719/6310 5221
וַיַּכּוּם לְפִי־חֶרֶב וַיַּחֲרִימוּ אֶת־כָּל־נֶפֶשׁ אֲשֶׁר־בָּהּ לֹא
not; ;it in; who (was); person; every; and destroyed; ,sword of edge the the by; them struck they and

1688 6213 2275 6213 8300 7604
הִשְׁאִיר שָׂרִיד כַּאֲשֶׁר עָשָׂה לְחֶבְרוֹן כֵּן־עָשָׂה לִדְבִרָה
,Debir; to; did he; so; ,Hebron; to; did he; as just; a survivor; did he leave

3091 5221 4428 3841 6213 4428
40 וּלְמַלְכָּהּ וְכַאֲשֶׁר עָשָׂה לְלִבְנָה וּלְמַלְכָּהּ׃ וַיַּכֶּה יְהוֹשֻׁעַ
Joshua; And struck; to and .king its; to Libnah; did he; as and; to and ,king its

3605 798 8219 5045 2022 776 3605
אֶת־כָּל־הָאָרֶץ הָהָר וְהַנֶּגֶב וְהַשְּׁפֵלָה וְהָאֲשֵׁדוֹת וְאֵת כָּל־
all; and; the and ,slopes; the and ,lowland; the and ,Negeb; the ,heights; :land the; all

2763 5397 3605 8300 7604 3808 4428
מַלְכֵיהֶם לֹא הִשְׁאִיר שָׂרִיד וְאֵת כָּל־הַנְּשָׁמָה הֶחֱרִים
he ,destroyed; that breathed; all; and; a survivor; did he leave; not; their ;kings

6947 3091 5221 3478 430 3068 6680
41 כַּאֲשֶׁר צִוָּה יְהוָה אֱלֹהֵי יִשְׂרָאֵל׃ וַיַּכֵּם יְהוֹשֻׁעַ מִקָּדֵשׁ
from Kadesh; Joshua; And them struck; .Israel; the of God; Jehovah; had commanded; as

3605 1391 5704 1657 776 3605 5804 6947
42 בַּרְנֵעַ וְעַד־עַזָּה וְאֵת כָּל־אֶרֶץ גֹּשֶׁן וְעַד־גִּבְעוֹן׃ וְאֵת כָּל־
all; and; ;Gibeon; even until ,Goshen; the of land; all; and; ,Gaza; even until ,barnea

259 6471 3091 3920 776 428 4428
הַמְּלָכִים הָאֵלֶּה וְאֶת־אַרְצָם לָכַד יְהוֹשֻׁעַ פַּעַם אַחַת כִּי
for; ,one; time at; Joshua; captured; their land; and; these; kings

God of Israel fought for
Israel. [43]And Joshua returned, and all Israel with
him, to the camp at Gilgal.

CHAPTER 11
[1]And it happened, when
Jabin the king of Hazor
heard, he sent to Jobab the
king of Medon, and to the
king of Shimron, and to the
king of Achshaph, [2]and to
the kings that *were* on the
north of the heights, and in
the plains south of Chin-
neroth, and in the low
country, and in the hills of
Dor on the west; [3]to the
Canaanite on the east, and
on the west, and the
Amorite, and the Hittite,
and the Perizzite, and the
Jebusite in the heights, and
the Hivite below Hermon, in
the land of Mizpeh. [4]And
they went out, they and all
their camps with them, a
people plentiful as the sand
on the seashore in number,
and very many horses and
chariots. [5]And all these
kings met together. And
they came and camped to-
gether at the waters of
Merom, to fight with Israel.
[6]And Jehovah said to
Joshua, Do not fear before
them, for about this time
tomorrow I will give all of
them up wounded before
Israel. You shall hamstring
their horses, and burn their
chariots with fire. [7]And
Joshua came, and all the
people of war with him,
against them by the waters
of Merom. And they
suddenly fell on them.
[8]And Jehovah gave them
into Israel's hand, and they
struck them, and pursued
them to the great Sidon,
and to the burning waters,
and to the valley of Mizpeh

3605 3091 7725 3478 3898 3478 430 3068
43 יהוה אלהי ישראל נלחם לישראל׃ וישב יהושע וכל־
and ,Joshua And .Israel for fought Israel the Jehovah
all returned of God
1537 4264 3478
ישראל עמו אל־המחנה הגלגלה׃
.Gilgal at camp the to with Israel
,him

CAP. XI יא

CHAPTER 11

4068 4428 5103 7971 2674 4428 2985 8085 1961
1 ויהי כשמע יבין מלך־חצור וישלח אל־יובב מלך מדון
,Medon the Jobab to he that ,Hazor the Jabin when it And
of king sent of king heard happened
4428 407 4428 8110 4428
2 ואל־מלך שמרון ואל־מלך אכשף׃ ואל־המלכים אשר
that the to and ,Achshaph the and ,Shimron the to and
(were) kings of king to of king
1756 5299 8219 3672 5045 6160 2022 6828
מצפון בהר ובערבה נגב כנרות ובשפלה ובנפות דור
Dor in and the in and Chine- south on and the the on
of hills the country low ,roth of plains the ,heights of north
2983 6522 2850 567 3220 4217 3669 3220
3 מים׃ הכנעני ממזרח ומים והאמרי והחתי והפרזי והיבוסי
the and the and the and the and on and the on the and the on
Jebusite ,Perizzite ,Hittite ,Amorite ,west the east Canaanite ;west
3605 3318 4709 776 2768 8478 2340 2022
4 בהר והחוי תחת חרמון בארץ המצפה׃ ויצאו הם וכל־
and ,they they And .Mizpah in and ,Hermon below the and the in
all ,out went of land the Hivite ,heights
7230 3220 8193 834 2344 7227 4264
מחניהם עמם עם־רב כחול אשר על־שפת־הים לרב
in the of lip the on that the as many with their
;abundance sea (is) sand ,people ,them armies
935 428 4428 3605 3259 3966 7227 7393 5483
5 וסוס ורכב רב־מאד׃ ויועדו כל המלכים האלה ויבאו
and ;these kings all met And .very many and both
came they together chariots horses
3478 3898 4792 4325 3162 2583
ויחנו יחדו אל־מי מרום להלחם עם־ישראל׃
.Israel with fight to ,Merom the at together and
of waters camped
6256 4279 6440 3372 408 3091 3068 559
6 ויאמר יהוה אל־יהושע אל־תירא מפניהם כי מחר כעת
about tomor- for before be Do not ,Joshua to Jehovah said And
time row them afraid
3478 6440 2491 3605 5414 2088
הזאת אנכי נתן את־כלם חללים לפני ישראל את־
;Israel before slain of all will I this
them give
935 784 8313 4818 6131 5483
7 סוסיהם תעקר ואת־מרכבתיהם תשרף באש׃ ויבא
And with burn their and shall you their
came ,fire chariots ,hamstring horses
4792 4325 4421 5971 3605 3091
יהושע וכל־עם המלחמה עמו עליהם על־מי מרום
Merom the by against with war the and ,Joshua
of waters them him of people all
5221 3478 3027 3068 5414 5307 6597
8 פתאם ויפלו בהם׃ ויתנם יהוה ביד־ישראל ויכום
they and ,Israel the into Jehovah And upon they and ;suddenly
them struck of hand them gave .them fell
1237 4325 4955 5704 7227 6721 7291
וירדפום עד־צידון רבה ועד משרפות מים ועד־בקעת
the and ,waters the and the Sidon to pur- and
of valley to burning to ,great them sued

eastward. And they struck them until he did not have a survivor left to them. [9]And Joshua did to them as Jehovah said to him. He hamstrung their horses, and burned their chariots with fire.

[10]And Joshua returned and captured Hazor at that time. And he struck its king by the sword; for Hazor *was* formerly head of all these kingdoms. [11]And they struck every person in it by the mouth of the sword. He destroyed *them*, he did not leave anyone breathing; and he burned Hazor with fire. [12]And Joshua captured all the cities of these kings, and all their kings. And he struck them by the mouth of the sword. He destroyed them, as Moses the servant of Jehovah had commanded. [13]But *as for* all the cities which stood by their mounds, Israel did not burn them; but Joshua only burned Hazor. [14]And the sons of Israel seized for themselves all the plunder of these cities, and the livestock. But they struck every human being by the mouth of the sword, until they had destroyed them; they did not leave anyone breathing. [15]As Jehovah commanded His servant Moses, so Moses commanded Joshua, and so Joshua did. He did not turn aside from anything of all that Jehovah commanded Moses.

[16]And Joshua took all this land: the heights, and all the Negeb, and all the land of Goshen, and the Lowlands, and the Arabah, and the mountains of Israel, and its lowlands, [17]from

מצפה מזרחה ויכם עד־בלתי השאיר־להם שריד׃

9 ויעש להם יהושע כאשר אמר־לו יהוה את־סוסיהם עקר

10 ואת־מרכבתיהם שרף באש׃ וישב יהושע בעת

ההיא וילכד את־חצור ואת־מלכה הכה בחרב כי־חצור

11 לפנים היא ראש כל־הממלכות האלה׃ ויכו את־כל־

הנפש אשר־בה לפי־חרב החרם לא נותר כל־נשמה

12 ואת־חצור שרף באש׃ ואת־כל־ערי המלכים האלה

ואת־כל־מלכיהם לכד יהושע ויכם לפי־חרב החרים

13 אותם כאשר צוה משה עבד יהוה׃ רק כל־הערים

העמדות על־תלם לא שרפם ישראל זולתי את־חצור

14 לבדה שרף יהושע׃ וכל שלל הערים האלה והבהמה

בזזו להם בני ישראל רק את־כל־האדם הכו לפי־חרב

15 עד־השמדם אתם לא השאירו כל־נשמה׃ כאשר צוה

יהוה את־משה עבדו כן־צוה משה את־יהושע וכן עשה

יהושע לא־הסיר דבר מכל אשר־צוה יהוה את־משה׃

16 ויקח יהושע את־כל־הארץ הזאת ההר ואת־כל־הנגב

ואת כל־ארץ הגשן ואת־השפלה ואת־הערבה ואת־הר

17 Mount Halak, that goes up to Seir, even to Baal-gad in the Valley of Lebanon, below Mount Hermon. And he took all their kings, and and struck them, and killed them. 18 And Joshua made war many days with all those kings. 19 There was not a city that made peace with the sons of Israel except the Hivites, inhabitants of Gibeon. They took all in battle. 20 For it was of Jehovah to harden their hearts, so that they should come against Israel in battle, so that they might be destroyed, so that they might have no favor, but that He might destroy them, as Jehovah commanded Moses.

21 At that time Joshua came and cut off the Anakim from the mountains, from Hebron, from Debir, from Anab, and from all the mountains of Judah, and from all the mountains of Israel. Joshua completely destroyed them with their cities. 22 There were none of the Anakim left in the land of the sons of Israel; only some remained in Gaza, in Gath, and in Ashdod. 23 And Joshua took the whole of the land, according to all that Jehovah had spoken to Moses. And Joshua gave it for an inheritance to Israel according to their divisions, by their tribes. And the land had rest from war.

17 יִשְׂרָאֵל וּשְׁפֵלָתֹה׃ מִן־הָהָר הֶחָלָק הָעוֹלֶה שֵׂעִיר וְעַד־
5704 8165 5927 2569 2022 8219 3478
even to ,Seir to that up goes ,Halak Mount from its and lowlands Israel's

בַּעַל גָּד בְּבִקְעַת הַלְּבָנוֹן תַּחַת הַר־חֶרְמוֹן וְאֵת כָּל־
3605 2768 8478 3844 1237 1171
all and ;Hermon Mount below ,Lebanon the in of valley gad Baal-

18 מַלְכֵיהֶם לָכַד וַיַּכֵּם וַיְמִיתֵם׃ יָמִים רַבִּים עָשָׂה יְהוֹשֻׁעַ
3091 6213 7227 3117 4191 5221 3920 4428
Joshua did many days killed and .them and them struck ,took he their kings

19 אֶת־כָּל־הַמְּלָכִים הָאֵלֶּה מִלְחָמָה׃ לֹא־הָיְתָה עִיר אֲשֶׁר
5892 1961 3808 4421 428 4428 3605
that a city There was not .battle these kings all with

הִשְׁלִימָה אֶל־בְּנֵי יִשְׂרָאֵל בִּלְתִּי הַחִוִּי יֹשְׁבֵי גִבְעוֹן אֶת־
1391 3427 2340 3478 1121 7999
;Gibeon natives of the Hivites except ,Israel the of sons with made peace

20 הַכֹּל לָקְחוּ בַמִּלְחָמָה׃ כִּי־מֵאֵת יְהוָה הָיְתָה לְחַזֵּק אֶת־
2388 1961 3068 3588 4421 3947 3605
to harden was it Jehovah of For .battle in they took all (others)

לִבָּם לִקְרַאת הַמִּלְחָמָה אֶת־יִשְׂרָאֵל לְמַעַן הַחֲרִימָם
2763 3478 4421 7125 3820
might they ,destroyed be that so ,Israel battle the (in) come to against their hearts

לְבִלְתִּי הֱיוֹת־לָהֶם תְּחִנָּה כִּי לְמַעַן הַשְׁמִידָם כַּאֲשֶׁר צִוָּה
6680 8045 8467 1961 3808
com- manded as might he ,them destroy that but ,favor they might have that so no

21 יְהוָה אֶת־מֹשֶׁה׃ וַיָּבֹא יְהוֹשֻׁעַ בָּעֵת הַהִיא וַיַּכְרֵת
3772 6256 3091 935 4872 3068
cut and off that time at Joshua And came .Moses Jehovah

אֶת־הָעֲנָקִים מִן־הָהָר מִן־חֶבְרוֹן מִן־דְּבִר מִן־עֲנָב וּמִכֹּל
3605 6024 1688 2279 2022 6062
and all from Anab from ,Debir from ,Hebron from the from mountains the Anakim

הַר יְהוּדָה וּמִכֹּל הַר יִשְׂרָאֵל עִם־עָרֵיהֶם הֶחֱרִימָם יְהוֹשֻׁעַ׃
3091 2763 5892 3478 2022 3063 2022
.Joshua de- fully them stroyed their ;cities with ,Israel's mounts and all from Judah's hills

22 לֹא־נוֹתַר עֲנָקִים בְּאֶרֶץ בְּנֵי יִשְׂרָאֵל רַק בְּעַזָּה בְּגַת
1661 5804 7535 3478 1121 776 6062 3498
in ,Gath in ,Gaza only ;Israel the of sons the in of land the of Anakim There left was none

23 וּבְאַשְׁדּוֹד נִשְׁאָרוּ׃ וַיִּקַּח יְהוֹשֻׁעַ אֶת־כָּל־הָאָרֶץ כְּכֹל אֲשֶׁר
3605 776 3605 3091 3947 7604 795
that according all to the ,land the of whole Joshua And took some .remained in and Ashdod

דִּבֶּר יְהוָה אֶל־מֹשֶׁה וַיִּתְּנָהּ יְהוֹשֻׁעַ לְנַחֲלָה לְיִשְׂרָאֵל
3478 5159 3091 5414 4872 3068 1696
Israel to an for inheritance Joshua and it gave ;Moses to Jehovah had spoken

כְּמַחְלְקֹתָם לְשִׁבְטֵיהֶם וְהָאָרֶץ שָׁקְטָה מִמִּלְחָמָה׃
4421 8252 776 7626 4256
.war from rest had the and land their ;tribes by their ,divisions by

CAP. XII יב

CHAPTER 12

1 And these are the kings of the land whom the sons of Israel struck, and *they* seized their land beyond

1 וְאֵלֶּה מַלְכֵי הָאָרֶץ אֲשֶׁר הִכּוּ בְנֵי־יִשְׂרָאֵל וַיִּרְשׁוּ אֶת־
3423 3478 1121 5221 776 4428 428
— and seized ,Israel the of sons struck whom the land the of kings And these (are)

the Jordan, at the sunrising, from the river Arnon to Mount Hermon, and all the Arabah eastward: [2]Sihon
2 the king of the Amorites, who lived in Heshbon, and ruled from Aroer, which *is* on the lip of the river Arnon, and from its valley *floor*, and half Gilead, even to the river Jabbok, the border of the sons of Ammon; [3]and from the Arabah to the sea of Chinneroth on the east, and to the sea of the Arabah, even the Salt Sea,
3 eastward, the way to Beth-jeshimoth; and on the south under the slopes of Pisgah; [4]and the border of Og the king of Bashan, of the rest of the giants, who lived at Ashtaroth and at Edrei,
4 [5]and reigned in Mount Hermon, and in Salcah, and in all Bashan, to the border of the Geshurites
5 and the Maachathites, and half Gilead, the border of Sihon the king of Heshbon.

6 [6]Moses the servant of Jehovah and the sons of Israel struck them. And Moses the servant of Jehovah gave it for a possession to the Reubenites, and the Gadites, and the half tribe of Manasseh.
7 [7]And these are the kings of the land whom Joshua and the sons of Israel struck beyond the Jordan westward, from Baal-gad in the Valley of Lebanon even to Mount Halak that goes up to Seir, which Joshua gave to the tribes of Israel for a possession according to their divisions; [8]in the
8 mountains, and in the Lowlands, and in the Arabah, and in the slopes, and in the wilderness, and in the Negeb—the Hittites, the Amorites, and the Canaanites, the Perizzites,

5704 769 5158 8121 4217 3383 5676 776
ארצם בעבר הירדן מזרחה השמש מנחל ארנון עד־
to Arnon from sun the the at the beyond their
river the of rising Jordan ,land

567 4428 5511 4217 6160 3605 2268 2022
2 הר חרמון וכל־הערבה מזרחה׃ סיחון מלך האמרי
,Amorites king Sihon :eastward Arabah the and ,Hermon Mount
the of all

769 5158/8193 6177 4910 2809 3427
היושב בחשבון משל מערוער אשר על־שפת־נחל ארנון
,Arnon the the on which from ruled in who
River of bank (is) ,Aroer Heshbon lived

5908 1121 1366 5158 2999 5704 1568 2677 5104 8432
ותוך הנחל וחצי הגלעד ועד יבק הנחל גבול בני עמון׃
;Ammon the the the Jabbok even ,Gilead and its from and
of sons of border ,River to half valley (floor)

6160 3220 4217 3672 3220 5704 6160
3 והערבה עד־ים כנרות מזרחה ועד ים הערבה ים־
Sea the the and the on Chinneroth the until from and
,Arabah of sea to ,east of sea Arabah the

798 8478 8486 =1020= 1870 4217 4417
המלח מזרחה דרך בית הישמות ומתימן תחת אשדות
slopes the under on and ;Jeshimoth Beth- the ,eastward Salt
of ,south the to way

3427 7497 4217 1316 4428 5747 1366 6449
4 הפסגה׃ וגבול עוג מלך הבשן מיתר הרפאים היושב
who the of the of ,Bashan the Og the and ;Pisgah
lived giants rest of king of border

3605 5548 2768 2022 4910 164 6252
5 בעשתרות ובאדרעי׃ ומשל בהר חרמון ובסלכה ובכל־
in and in and Hermon in and in and ,Ashtaroth at
all Salcah Mount reigned ,Edrei

1366 1568 2677 4602 1651 1366 1316
הבשן עד־גבול הגשורי והמעכתי וחצי הגלעד גבול
the ,Gilead and the and the the to ,Bashan
of border half Maachathites ,Geshurites of border

5221 3478 1121 3068 5650 4872 2809 4428 5511
6 סיחון מלך חשבון׃ משה עבד־יהוה ובני ישראל הכום
struck Israel the and Jehovah the Moses .Heshbon king Sihon
;them of sons of servant of

7626 2677 1425 7206 3425 3068 5650 4872 5414
ויתנה משה עבד־יהוה ירשה לראובני ולגדי ולחצי שבט
tribe to and the to and the to pos- a Jehovah the Moses gave and
of half the Gadites ,Reubenites ,session of servant for it

1121 3091 5221 776 4428 428 4519
7 המנשה׃ ואלה מלכי הארץ אשר הכה יהושע ובני
and Joshua struck whom the the And .Manasseh
of sons the land of kings (are) these

3844 1237 =1171= 3220 3383 5676 3478
ישראל בעבר הירדן ימה מבעל גד בבקעת הלבנון
,Lebanon the in gad from west- the beyond Israel
of valley Baal- ,ward Jordan

7626 3091 5414 8165 5927 2509 2022 5704
ועד־ההר החלק העלה שעירה ויתנה יהושע לשבטי
the to Joshua which Seir to that Halak Mount even
of tribes for gave up goes to

6160 8219 2022 4256 3425 3478
8 ישראל ירשה כמחלקתם׃ בהר ובשפלה ובערבה
the in And the in and the in to according a Israel
Arabah ,lowland ,hills ;divisions their ,possession

6522 3669 567 2850 5045 4057 798
ובאשדות ובמדבר ובנגב החתי האמרי והכנעני הפרזי
the the the the the in and the in and the in and
,Perizzites ,Canaanites ,Amorites ,Hittites ,Negeb ,wilderness ,slopes

2903 2340
החוי והיבוסי׃
the and the
:Jebusites ,Hivites

9 מֶלֶךְ יְרִיחוֹ אֶחָד
4428 3405 259
the king of Jericho, one;

מֶלֶךְ הָעַי אֲשֶׁר־מִצַּד בֵּית־אֵל אֶחָד׃
4428 5857 6654 1008 259
the king of Ai, which is beside Bethel, one;

10 מֶלֶךְ יְרוּשָׁלִַם אֶחָד
4428 3389 259
the king of Jerusalem, one;

מֶלֶךְ חֶבְרוֹן אֶחָד׃
4428 2275 259
the king of Hebron, one;

11 מֶלֶךְ יַרְמוּת אֶחָד
4428 3412 259
the king of Jarmuth, one;

מֶלֶךְ לָכִישׁ אֶחָד׃
4428 3923 259
the king of Lachish, one;

12 מֶלֶךְ עֶגְלוֹן אֶחָד
4428 5700 259
the king of Eglon, one;

מֶלֶךְ גֶּזֶר אֶחָד׃
4428 1507 259
the king of Gezer, one;

13 מֶלֶךְ דְּבִר אֶחָד
4428 1688 259
the king of Debir, one;

מֶלֶךְ גֶּדֶר אֶחָד׃
4428 1445 259
the king of Geder, one;

14 מֶלֶךְ חָרְמָה אֶחָד
4428 2767 259
the king of Hormah, one;

מֶלֶךְ עֲרָד אֶחָד׃
4428 6166 259
the king of Arad, one;

15 מֶלֶךְ לִבְנָה אֶחָד
4428 3841 259
the king of Libnah, one;

מֶלֶךְ עֲדֻלָּם אֶחָד׃
4428 5725 259
the king of Adullam, one;

16 מֶלֶךְ מַקֵּדָה אֶחָד
4428 4719 259
the king of Makkedah, one;

מֶלֶךְ בֵּית־אֵל אֶחָד׃
4428 1008 259
the king of Bethel, one;

17 מֶלֶךְ תַּפּוּחַ אֶחָד
4428 8599 259
the king of Tappuah, one;

the Hivites, and the
Jebusites: [9]the king of
Jericho, one; the king of Ai,
which *is* beside Bethel,
one; [10]the king of Jeru-
salem, one; the king of
Hebron, one; [11]the king of
Jarmuth, one; the king of
Lachish, one; [12]the king of
Eglon, one; the king of
Gezer, one; [13]the king of
Debir, one; the king of
Geder, one; [14]the king of
Hormah, one; the king of
Arad, one; [15]the king of
Libnah, one; the king of
Adullam, one; [16]the king of
Makkedah, one; the king of
Bethel, one; [17]the king of
Tappuah, one; the king of
Hepher, one; [18]the king of

Aphek, one; the king of
Sharon, one; [19]the king of
Madon, one; the king of
Hazor, one; [20]the king of
Shimron-meron, one; the
king of Achshaph, one;
[21]the king of Taanach, one;
the king of Megiddo, one;
[22]the king of Kedesh, one;
the king of Jokneam in
Carmel, one; [23]the king of
Dor in the coast of Dor, one;
the king of the nations of
Gilgal, one; [24]the king of
Tirzah, one. All the kings
were thirty-one.

4428 2660 — 259
מֶלֶךְ חֵפֶר אֶחָד׃
the king of ,Hepher ;one

18 4428 663 — 259
מֶלֶךְ אֲפֵק אֶחָד
the king of ,Aphek ;one

4428 8289 — 259
מֶלֶךְ לַשָּׁרוֹן אֶחָד׃
the king of ,Sharon ;one

19 4428 4068 — 259
מֶלֶךְ מָדוֹן אֶחָד
the king of ,Madon ;one

4428 2674 — 259
מֶלֶךְ חָצוֹר אֶחָד׃
the king of ,Hazor ;one

20 4428 =8112= — 259
מֶלֶךְ שִׁמְרוֹן מְרֹאון אֶחָד
the king of Shimron- ,meron ;one

4428 407 — 259
מֶלֶךְ אַכְשָׁף אֶחָד׃
the king of Achshaph ;one

21 4428 8590 — 259
מֶלֶךְ תַּעְנַךְ אֶחָד
the king of ,Tannach ;one

4428 4023 — 259
מֶלֶךְ מְגִדּוֹ אֶחָד׃
the king of ,Megiddo ;one

22 4428 6943 — 259
מֶלֶךְ קֶדֶשׁ אֶחָד
the king of ,Kedesh ;one

4428 3362 3760 — 259
מֶלֶךְ־יָקְנְעָם לַכַּרְמֶל אֶחָד׃
the king of Jokneam in ,Carmel ;one

23 4428 1756 5299 1756 — 259
מֶלֶךְ דּוֹר לְנָפַת דּוֹר אֶחָד
the king of Dor in the height of ,Dor ;one

4428 1471 1537 — 259
מֶלֶךְ־גּוֹיִם לְגִלְגָּל אֶחָד׃
the king of Goiim in ,Gilgal ;one

24 4428 8656 — 259
מֶלֶךְ תִּרְצָה אֶחָד
the king of Tirzah .one

3605 4428 7970 259
כָּל־מְלָכִים שְׁלֹשִׁים וְאֶחָד׃
All the kings thirty and .one

CAP. XIII יג

CHAPTER 13

וִיהוֹשֻׁעַ זָקֵן בָּא בַּיָּמִים וַיֹּאמֶר יְהוָה אֵלָיו אַתָּה זָקַנְתָּה
2 בָּאתָ בַּיָּמִים וְהָאָרֶץ נִשְׁאֲרָה הַרְבֵּה־מְאֹד לְרִשְׁתָּהּ׃ זֹאת
3 הָאָרֶץ הַנִּשְׁאָרֶת כָּל־גְּלִילוֹת הַפְּלִשְׁתִּים וְכָל־הַגְּשׁוּרִי׃ מִן־
הַשִּׁיחוֹר אֲשֶׁר ׀ עַל־פְּנֵי מִצְרַיִם וְעַד גְּבוּל עֶקְרוֹן צָפוֹנָה
לַכְּנַעֲנִי תֵּחָשֵׁב חֲמֵשֶׁת ׀ סַרְנֵי פְלִשְׁתִּים הָעַזָּתִי וְהָאַשְׁדּוֹדִי
4 הָאֶשְׁקְלוֹנִי הַגִּתִּי וְהָעֶקְרוֹנִי וְהָעַוִּים׃ מִתֵּימָן כָּל־אֶרֶץ
הַכְּנַעֲנִי וּמְעָרָה אֲשֶׁר לַצִּידֹנִים עַד־אֲפֵקָה עַד גְּבוּל הָאֱמֹרִי׃
5 וְהָאָרֶץ הַגִּבְלִי וְכָל־הַלְּבָנוֹן מִזְרַח הַשֶּׁמֶשׁ מִבַּעַל גָּד תַּחַת
6 הַר־חֶרְמוֹן עַד לְבוֹא חֲמָת׃ כָּל־יֹשְׁבֵי הָהָר מִן־הַלְּבָנוֹן
עַד־מִשְׂרְפֹת מַיִם כָּל־צִידֹנִים אָנֹכִי אוֹרִישֵׁם מִפְּנֵי בְּנֵי
7 יִשְׂרָאֵל רַק הַפִּלֶהָ לְיִשְׂרָאֵל בְּנַחֲלָה כַּאֲשֶׁר צִוִּיתִךָ׃ וְעַתָּה
חַלֵּק אֶת־הָאָרֶץ הַזֹּאת בְּנַחֲלָה לְתִשְׁעַת הַשְּׁבָטִים וַחֲצִי
8 הַשֵּׁבֶט הַמְנַשֶּׁה׃ עִמּוֹ הָרֻאוּבֵנִי וְהַגָּדִי לָקְחוּ נַחֲלָתָם אֲשֶׁר
נָתַן לָהֶם מֹשֶׁה בְּעֵבֶר הַיַּרְדֵּן מִזְרָחָה כַּאֲשֶׁר נָתַן לָהֶם
9 מֹשֶׁה עֶבֶד יְהוָה׃ מֵעֲרוֹעֵר אֲשֶׁר עַל־שְׂפַת־נַחַל אַרְנוֹן
וְהָעִיר אֲשֶׁר בְּתוֹךְ־הַנַּחַל וְכָל־הַמִּישֹׁר מֵידְבָא עַד־דִּיבוֹן׃

CHAPTER 13

[1]And Joshua *was* old, going on *in* days. And Jehovah said to him, You have become aged, you are far along in days; yet very much land remains to be possessed. [2]This is the land that still remains: all the regions of the Philistines, and all Geshuri, [3]from Shihor which fronts on Egypt, and to the border of Ekron northward; it is counted to the Canaanites —five lords of the Philistines, of Gaza, of Ashdod, of Eshkalon, of Gath, and of Ekron; also the Avim. [4]From the south, all the land of the Canaanites, and Mearah which *belongs* to the Sidonians; to Aphek, to the border of the Amorites;

[5]and the land of the Giblites, and all Lebanon, toward the sunrising, from Baal-gad below Mount Hermon to the entering to Hamath; [6]all the inhabitants of the hills, from Lebanon to the burning waters; all the Sidonians—I will expel them before the sons of Israel. Only, cause it to fall to Israel for an inheritance, as I have commanded you. [7]Now, then, divide this land for an inheritance to the nine tribes, and the half tribe of Manasseh. [8]With him the Reubenites, and the Gadites received their inheritance, which Moses gave to them beyond the Jordan eastward, as Moses the servant of Jehovah has given to them; [9]from Aroer on the lip of the river Arnon, and the city which *is* in the middle of the valley, and all the plain of Medeba, to

Dibon; [10]and all the cities of Sihon the king of the Amorites, who reigned in Heshbon, to the border of the sons of Ammon; [11]and Gilead, and the border of the Geshurite, and of the Maachathite, and all Mount Hermon, and all Bashan to Salcah; [12]all the kingdom of Og in Bashan, who reigned in Ashtaroth and in Edrei; he remained of the remnant of the giants; and Moses struck them and expelled them. [13]But the sons of Israel did not expel the Geshurite and the Maachathite, but Geshur and Maachath live in the midst of Israel until today.

[14]Only, he has not given an inheritance to the tribe of Levi. The fire offerings of Jehovah the God of Israel are its inheritance, as He has spoken to it.

[15]And Moses gave to the tribe of the sons of Reuben, for their families; [16]and their border was from Aroer on the lip of the river Arnon, and the city which *is* in the middle of the valley, and all the plain by Medeba; [17]Heshbon, and all its cities in the tableland; Dibon, and Bamoth-baal, and Beth-baal-meon; [18]and Jahazah, and Kedemoth, and Mephaath; [19]and Kirjath-aim, and Sibmah, and Zareth-shahar in the mountain of the valley; [20]and Beth-peor, and the slopes of Pisgah, and Beth-jeshimoth; [21]and all the cities of the tableland, and all the kingdom of Sihon the king of the Amorite who reigned in Heshbon, whom Moses struck with the rulers of Midian, Evi, and Rekem, and Zur, and Hur, and Reba, chiefs of Sihon, the

2809 4427 834 567 4824 5511 5892 3605
10 וכל ערי סיחון מלך האמרי אשר מלך בחשבון עד
to in Heshbon reigned who the Amorites the of king Sihon the of cities and all

3605 4602 1651 1366 1568 5983/1121 1366
11 גבול בני־עמון׃ והגלעד וגבול הגשורי והמעכתי וכל
all and the Maachathite of and the Gehsurite the of border and Gilead and; Ammon the of sons of the border

1316 5747 4468 5548 1316 2768
12 הר חרמון וכל־הבשן עד־סלכה׃ כל־ממלכות עוג בבשן
in Bashan Og of kingdom the all ;Salcah to Bashan and all ,Hermon Mount

7497 3499 7604 1931 154 6252 4427
אשר־מלך בעשתרות ובאדרעי הוא נשאר מיתר הרפאים
,giants the the of remnant remained he ;Edrei in and Ashtaroth in reigned who

1651 3478/1121/3423 3808 3423 4872 5221
13 ויכם משה וירשם׃ ולא הורישו בני ישראל את־הגשורי
the Geshurite Israel the of sons expel did not and ex- pelled them; and Moses struck them and

3117 5704 3478 7130 4601 1650 3427 4601
ואת־המעכתי וישב גשור ומעכת בקרב ישראל עד היום
day until Israel the in of midst and Maachath Geshur but live the and ,Maachathite

430 3068 801 5159 5414 3808 3881 7626 7535 2088
14 הזה׃ רק לשבט הלוי לא נתן נחלה אשי יהוה אלהי
the of God ,Jehovah the fire of offerings an in- heritance He gave not ,Levi the of tribe to ,Only .this

4872 5414 1696 5159 3478
15 ישראל הוא נחלתו כאשר דבר־לו׃ ויתן משה
Moses And gave .it to He spoke as its inheritance are ,Israel

1366 1961 4940 7205/1121 4294
16 למטה בני־ראובן למשפחתם׃ ויהי להם הגבול
border their and was their by :families ,Reuben the of sons the of tribe to

8432 834 5892 769 5104/8193 834 6177
מערוער אשר על־שפת־נחל ארנון והעיר אשר בתוך
the in of middle which (is) the and city ,Arnon the river the of bank on which (is) from ,Aroer

834 3605 2809 4311 4334/3605 5104
17 הנחל וכל־המישר על־מידבא׃ חשבון וכל־עריה אשר
which (are) its cities and all ,Heshbon ;Medeba by the plain and all the ,valley

3096 =1010= =1120 1116 1769 4334
18 במישור דיבון ובמות בעל ובית בעל מעון׃ ויהצה
and ,Jahazah ;meon baal- and Beth- ,baal and Bamoth- ,Dibon the in ;tableland

2022 =6890= 7643 7136 4158 6932
19 וקדמת ומפעת׃ וקריתים ושבמה וצרת השחר בהר
the in of mountain shahar and Zareth- ,Sibmah and and Kirjath-aim and ;Mephaath and ,Kedemoth

=1020= 6449 798 =1047= 6040
20 העמק׃ ובית פעור ואשדות הפסגה ובית הישמות׃
;jeshimoth and Beth- ,Pisgah the and of slopes ,peor and Beth- the ;valley

834 567 4428 5511 4468 4334 5892 3605
21 וכל ערי המישר וכל־ממלכות סיחון מלך האמרי אשר
who the Amorite the of king Sihon king- the of dom and all table- the land the of cities and all

4080 5387 4872 5221 2809 4427
מלך בחשבון אשר הכה משה אתו ואת־נשיאי מדין
,Midian the of rulers and him Moses struck whom in ,Heshbon reigned

5257 7254 2354 6698 7552 189
את־אוי ואת־רקם ואת־צור ואת־חור ואת־רבע נסיכי
chiefs of ,Reba and ,Hur and ,Zur and ,Rekem and ,Evi

inhabitants of the land.
[22]And the sons of Israel
killed Balaam the son of
Beor, the diviner, with the
sword, among their slain.
[23]And the border of the
sons of Reuben was from
the Jordan, and *its* border.
This *was* the inheritance of
the sons of Reuben for their
families, the cities and their
villages.
[24]And Moses gave to the
tribe of Gad, to the sons of
Gad, for their families:
[25]And their border was to
Jazer, and all the cities of
Gilead, and half of the land
of the sons of Ammon, to
Aroer, which *is* before
Rabbah; [26]and from Heshbon to Ramath-mizpeh, and
Betonim, and from Maha-
naim to the border of Debir;
[27]and in the valley, Beth-
aram, and Beth-nimrah, and
Succoth, and Zaphon, the
rest of the kingdom of
Sihon the king of Heshbon;
the Jordan and *its* border,
to the edge of the Sea of
Chinnereth, beyond the
Jordan, eastward. [28]This is
the inheritance of the sons
of Gad, for their families, the
cities and their villages.
[29]And Moses gave to the
half of the tribe of
Manasseh. And it was to
the half of the tribe of the
sons of Manasseh, for their
families: [30]and their border
was from Mahanaim, all
Bashan, all the kingdom of
Og the king of Bashan, and
all the small towns of Jair in
Bashan, sixty cities; [31]and
the half of Gilead, and
Ashtaroth, and Edrei, cities
of the kingdom of Og in
Bashan, *belonged* to the
sons of Machir, the son of
Manasseh, to the half of the
sons of Machir for their
families.

[32]These *are* they whom
Moses caused to inherit in
the plains of Moab, beyond
the Jordan, *opposite* Jericho, eastward. [33]But

2026 7080 1160/1121 1109 776 3427 5511
22 סִיחוֹן יֹשְׁבֵי הָאָרֶץ׃ וְאֶת־בִּלְעָם בֶּן־בְּעוֹר הַקּוֹסֵם הָרְגוּ
killed the ,Beor the Balaam And the the Sihon
,diviner of son .land of dwellers

7205 1121 1366 1961 2491 413 2719 3478/1121
23 בְּנֵי־יִשְׂרָאֵל בַּחֶרֶב אֶל־חַלְלֵיהֶם׃ וַיְהִי גְּבוּל בְּנֵי רְאוּבֵן
Reuben the the And their among the with Israel the
of sons of border was slain sword of sons

5892 4940 7205 1121 5159 1366 3383
הַיַּרְדֵּן וּגְבוּל זֹאת נַחֲלַת בְּנֵי־רְאוּבֵן לְמִשְׁפְּחוֹתָם הֶעָרִים
the their for ,Reuben the inheri- the this (its) and the
cities ,families of sons tance (was) ;border ,Jordan

4940 1410/1121 1410/4294 48:72 5414 2691
24 וְחַצְרֵיהֶן׃ וַיִּתֵּן מֹשֶׁה לְמַטֵּה־גָד לִבְנֵי־גָד לְמִשְׁפְּחֹתָם׃
their by ,Gad the to ,Gad the to Moses And their and
;families of sons of tribe gave .villages

1121 776 2677 1568 5892 3605 3270 1366 1961
25 וַיְהִי לָהֶם הַגְּבוּל יַעְזֵר וְכָל־עָרֵי הַגִּלְעָד וַחֲצִי אֶרֶץ בְּנֵי
the land the and ,Gilead the and to border their and
of sons of of half of cities all ,Jazer was

2809 7237 6440 834 6177 5983
26 עַמּוֹן עַד־עֲרוֹעֵר אֲשֶׁר עַל־פְּנֵי רַבָּה׃ וּמֵחֶשְׁבּוֹן עַד־
to from and ;Rabbah before which ,Aroer to ;Ammon
Heshbon (is)

6010 1688 1366 5704 4266 993 = 7434 =
27 רָמַת הַמִּצְפֶּה וּבְטֹנִים וּמִמַּחֲנַיִם עַד־גְּבוּל לִדְבִר׃ וּבָעֵמֶק
in and ;Debir the to from and and ,mizpeh Ramoth-
,valley the of border Mahanaim ,Betonim

4468 3220 3499 6829 5523 = 1039 = 1027 =
בֵּית הָרָם וּבֵית נִמְרָה וְסֻכּוֹת וְצָפוֹן יֶתֶר מַמְלְכוּת
the rest the and and nimrah and ;aram Beth-
of kingdom of ,Zaphon ,Succoth Beth-

3672 3220 7097 1366 3383 2809 4428 5511
סִיחוֹן מֶלֶךְ חֶשְׁבּוֹן הַיַּרְדֵּן וּגְבֻל עַד־קְצֵה יָם־כִּנֶּרֶת
,Chinnereth the the to (its) and the ;Heshbon king the Sihon
of sea of edge ,border Jordan of

4940 1410/1121 5159 2088 4217 3383 5674
28 עֵבֶר הַיַּרְדֵּן מִזְרָחָה׃ זֹאת נַחֲלַת בְּנֵי־גָד לְמִשְׁפְּחֹתָם
their for ,Gad the inher- the This .eastward the beyond
,families of sons of itance is Jordan

4519 7626 2677 48:72 5414 2691 5892
29 הֶעָרִים וְחַצְרֵיהֶם׃ וַיִּתֵּן מֹשֶׁה לַחֲצִי שֵׁבֶט מְנַשֶּׁה
;Manasseh the the to Moses And their and the
of tribe of half gave .villages ,cities

1366 1961 4940 4519/1121 4294 2677 1961
30 וַיְהִי לַחֲצִי מַטֵּה בְנֵי־מְנַשֶּׁה לְמִשְׁפְּחוֹתָם׃ וַיְהִי גְבוּלָם
their and families their for ,Manasseh the the the to it and
border was of sons of tribe of half was

1316 4428 5747 4468 1316 3605 4266
מִמַּחֲנַיִם כָּל־הַבָּשָׁן כָּל־מַמְלְכוּת ׀ עוֹג מֶלֶךְ־הַבָּשָׁן
,Bashan the Og the all ,Bashan all from
of king of kingdom ,Mahanaim

1568 2677 4892 8346 1316 834 2971 2333
31 וְכָל־חַוֹּת יָאִיר אֲשֶׁר בַּבָּשָׁן שִׁשִּׁים עִיר׃ וַחֲצִי הַגִּלְעָד
,Gilead the and ;cities sixty in which ,Jair small the and
of half ,Bashan (are) of towns all

4653 1121 1316 5747 4468 5892 154 6252
וְעַשְׁתָּרוֹת וְאֶדְרֶעִי עָרֵי מַמְלְכוּת עוֹג בַּבָּשָׁן לִבְנֵי מָכִיר
,Machir the to in Og the cities and and
of sons ,Bashan of kingdom of ,Edrei ,Ashtaroth

428 4940 4353/1121 2677 4519/1121
32 בֶּן־מְנַשֶּׁה לַחֲצִי בְנֵי־מָכִיר לְמִשְׁפְּחוֹתָם׃ אֵלֶּה אֲשֶׁר־
they These their by Machir the the to ,Manasseh the
whom (are) .families of sons of half of son

4317 2405 3383 5676 4124 6160 4872 5157
נִחַל מֹשֶׁה בְּעַרְבוֹת מוֹאָב מֵעֵבֶר לְיַרְדֵּן יְרִיחוֹ מִזְרָחָה׃
east- (opposite) the beyond ,Moab the on Moses caused
.ward ,Jericho ,Jordan of plains inherit to

Moses did not give an
inheritance to the tribe of
Levi. Jehovah the God of
Israel Himself is their
inheritance, as He has
spoken to them.

CHAPTER 14

[1]And these *are* they *of*
the sons of Israel who
inherited in the land of
Canaan, whom Eleazar the
priest and Joshua the son
of Nun, and the heads of the
fathers of the tribes of the
sons of Israel caused to
inherit. [2]Their inheritance
was by lot, as Jehovah
commanded by the hand of
Moses, for the nine tribes,
and the half tribe—[3]for
Moses had given the inheritance of two of the tribes,
and the half tribe, beyond
the Jordan; and he did not
give any inheritance to the
Levites among them—[4]For
the sons of Joseph were
two tribes, Manasseh and
Ephraim. And they did not
give a portion to the Levites
in the land, except cities to
live in, with the open land
around them for their
livestock and for their
substance, [5]as Jehovah
commanded Moses, so the
sons of Israel did, and they
allotted the land.
[6]And the sons of Judah
came near to Joshua in
Gilgal, and Caleb the son of
Jephunneh the Kenezite
said to him, You know the
word that Jehovah spoke to
Moses the man of God as to
me and as to you in Kadesh-
barnea. [7]I was a son of
forty years when Moses the
servant of Jehovah sent me
from Kadesh-barnea to spy
out the land. And I brought

3478 430 3068 5159 4872 5414 3808 3881 7626
33 וּלְשֵׁבֶט הַלֵּוִי לֹא־נָתַן מֹשֶׁה נַחֲלָה יְהוָה אֱלֹהֵי יִשְׂרָאֵל
Israel the Jehovah an Moses did not ,Levi the to But
of God ;inheritance give of tribe

1696 5159
הוּא נַחֲלָתָם כַּאֲשֶׁר דִּבֶּר לָהֶם׃
to He as their Himself
.them spoke ,inheritance is

CAP. XIV יד

CHAPTER 14

5157 834 3667 776 3478 1121 5157 428
1 וְאֵלֶּה אֲשֶׁר־נָחֲלוּ בְנֵי־יִשְׂרָאֵל בְּאֶרֶץ כְּנָעַן אֲשֶׁר נִחֲלוּ
caused which ,Canaan the in Israel the inherited And
inherit to of land of sons these

4294 1 7218 5026/1121 3091 3548 1499
אוֹתָם אֶלְעָזָר הַכֹּהֵן וִיהוֹשֻׁעַ בִּן־נוּן וְרָאשֵׁי אֲבוֹת הַמַּטּוֹת
the fathers the the and ,Nun the and the Eleazar —
of tribes of of heads of son Joshua priest

3027 3068 6680 5159 1486 3478 1121
2 לִבְנֵי יִשְׂרָאֵל׃ בְּגוֹרַל נַחֲלָתָם כַּאֲשֶׁר צִוָּה יְהוָה בְּיַד־
by Jehovah com- as Their (was) .Israel the
hand manded inheritance ,lot by of sons

4872 5414 4294 2677 4294 8672 4872
3 מֹשֶׁה לְתִשְׁעַת הַמַּטּוֹת וַחֲצִי הַמַּטֶּה׃ כִּי־נָתַן מֹשֶׁה
Moses had for —tribe (the and) ,tribes the for ,Moses's
given half nine

3881 3383 5676 4294 2677 4294 8147 5159
נַחֲלַת שְׁנֵי הַמַּטּוֹת וַחֲצִי הַמַּטֶּה מֵעֵבֶר לַיַּרְדֵּן וְלַלְוִיִּם
to and the beyond ,tribe the and the two inher- the
Levites the ;Jordan half ,tribes of of itance

4294 8147 3127/1121 1961 8432 5159 5414
4 לֹא־נָתַן נַחֲלָה בְּתוֹכָם׃ כִּי־הָיוּ בְנֵי־יוֹסֵף שְׁנֵי מַטּוֹת
,tribes two Joseph the were for among any did he
of sons —them inheritance give not

776 3881 2506 5414 669 4519
מְנַשֶּׁה וְאֶפְרָיִם וְלֹא־נָתְנוּ חֵלֶק לַלְוִיִּם בָּאָרֶץ כִּי אִם־
except the in the to a did they and and Manasseh
.land Levites portion give not ;Ephraim

7075 4735 4054 3427 5892
5 עָרִים לָשֶׁבֶת וּמִגְרְשֵׁיהֶם לְמִקְנֵיהֶם וּלְקִנְיָנָם׃ כַּאֲשֶׁר
As their for and their for open the and live to cities
.substance livestock ,them of land ,in

2505 3478 1121 6213 3651/4872 3068/6680
צִוָּה יְהוָה אֶת־מֹשֶׁה כֵּן עָשׂוּ בְּנֵי יִשְׂרָאֵל וַיַּחְלְקוּ אֶת־
they and ,Israel the did so ,Moses Jehovah com-
allotted of sons manded

559 1537 3091 3063 1121 5066 776
6 הָאָרֶץ׃ וַיִּגְּשׁוּ בְנֵי־יְהוּדָה אֶל־יְהוֹשֻׁעַ בַּגִּלְגָּל וַיֹּאמֶר
said and in Joshua to Judah the came And the
,Gilgal of sons near .land

1697 3045 7074 3312/1121 3612
אֵלָיו כָּלֵב בֶּן־יְפֻנֶּה הַקְּנִזִּי אַתָּה יָדַעְתָּ אֶת־הַדָּבָר אֲשֶׁר־
that word the know You the Jephu- the Caleb to
,Kenezite neh of son ,him

182 430 376 4872 3068 1696
דִּבֶּר יְהוָה אֶל־מֹשֶׁה אִישׁ־הָאֱלֹהִים עַל אֹדוֹתַי וְעַל
and me to as God the Moses to Jehovah spoke
of man

7971 8141 703 1121 =6947=
7 אֹדוֹתֶיךָ בְּקָדֵשׁ בַּרְנֵעַ׃ בֶּן־אַרְבָּעִים שָׁנָה אָנֹכִי בִּשְׁלֹחַ
when (was) I years forty son a ;barnea in you to as
sent of Kadesh-

776 7270 =6947= 3068 5650 4872
מֹשֶׁה עֶבֶד־יְהוָה אֹתִי מִקָּדֵשׁ בַּרְנֵעַ לְרַגֵּל אֶת־הָאָרֶץ
;land the spy to barnea from me Jehovah the Moses
Kadesh- of servant

him back word as it was in
my heart. 8But my brothers
who went up with me
caused the heart of the
people to melt, yet I fully
followed after Jehovah my
God.

9And Moses swore in that
day, saying, Surely the land
on which your foot has
trodden shall be an
inheritance for you and for
your sons forever, because
you have fully followed after
Jehovah my God. 10And
now, behold, Jehovah has
kept me alive, as He said,
these forty-five years since
Jehovah spoke this word to
Moses, when Israel traveled
in the wilderness. And now,
behold, today I *am* eighty-
five years old; 11yet I *am* as
strong today as in the day
Moses sent me. As my
strength was then, so *is* my
strength now for war, both
to go out and to come in.
12And now, give to me this
mountain, of which
Jehovah spoke in that day,
for you heard in that day
how the Anakim *were*
there, and great walled
cities. If Jehovah shall be
with me, then I shall
expel them, as Jehovah
has spoken. 13And Joshua
blessed him, and *he* gave
Hebron to Caleb the son of
Jephunneh for an inheri-
tance. 14Therefore, Hebron
has belonged to Caleb the
son of Jephunneh, the
Kenezite, for an inheritance
to this day, because he fully
followed after Jehovah the
God of Israel. 15And the
name of Hebron before was

5927 834 251 3824 1697 7725
8 וָאָשֵׁב אֹתוֹ דָּבָר כַּאֲשֶׁר עִם־לְבָבִי׃ וְאַחַי אֲשֶׁר עָלוּ
went who my But my in as word him I and
up brothers .heart was it back brought

3068 310 4390 5971 3820 4529
עִמִּי הִמְסִיו אֶת־לֵב הָעָם וְאָנֹכִי מִלֵּאתִי אַחֲרֵי יְהוָה
Jehovah after fully I and the heart the caused with
followed ,people of melt to me

776 518 559 3117 4872 7650 430
9 אֱלֹהָי׃ וַיִּשָּׁבַע מֹשֶׁה בַּיּוֹם הַהוּא לֵאמֹר אִם־לֹא הָאָרֶץ
the Surely ,saying ,that day in Moses And my
land swore .God

5704 1121 5159 1961 7272 1869 834
אֲשֶׁר דָּרְכָה רַגְלְךָ בָּהּ לְךָ תִהְיֶה לְנַחֲלָה וּלְבָנֶיךָ עַד
to for and an shall for on your has which
sons your inheritance be you foot trodden

2421 2009 6258 430 3068 310 4390 5769
10 עוֹלָם כִּי מִלֵּאתָ אַחֲרֵי יְהוָה אֱלֹהָי׃ וְעַתָּה הִנֵּה הֶחֱיָה
kept has ,behold And .God my Jehovah after have you for ,forever
alive now followed

227 8141 2568 703 1696 3068
יְהוָה אוֹתִי כַּאֲשֶׁר דִּבֵּר זֶה אַרְבָּעִים וְחָמֵשׁ שָׁנָה מֵאָז
since years five forty- these He as ,me Jehovah
,said

3478 1980 4872 2088 1697 3068 1696
דִּבֶּר יְהוָה אֶת־הַדָּבָר הַזֶּה אֶל־מֹשֶׁה אֲשֶׁר־הָלַךְ יִשְׂרָאֵל
Israel traveled when ,Moses to this word Jehovah spoke

8141 8084 2568 1121 3117 2009 6258 4057
בַּמִּדְבָּר וְעַתָּה הִנֵּה אָנֹכִי הַיּוֹם בֶּן־חָמֵשׁ וּשְׁמוֹנִים שָׁנָה׃
;years eighty- five old today I ,behold And the in
(am) ,now .wilderness

3581 4872 7971 3117 2389 3117 5750
11 עוֹדֶנִּי הַיּוֹם חָזָק כַּאֲשֶׁר בְּיוֹם שְׁלֹחַ אוֹתִי מֹשֶׁה כְּכֹחִי
my as ;Moses me sent the in as as today I yet
strength day strong (am)

5414 6258 3212 3318 4421 6258 3581
12 אָז וּכְכֹחִי עָתָּה לַמִּלְחָמָה וְלָצֵאת וְלָבוֹא׃ וְעַתָּה תְּנָה־לִּי
to give And to and to both ,war for ,now my (is) so was
me ,now .in come out go strength ,then

8085 3117 3068 1696 834 2088 2022
אֶת־הָהָר הַזֶּה אֲשֶׁר־דִּבֶּר יְהוָה בַּיּוֹם הַהוּא כִּי־אַתָּה שָׁמַעְתָּ
heard you for ,that day in Jehovah spoke of ,this mountain
which

1219 1419 5892 8033 6062 3117
בַיּוֹם הַהוּא כִּי־עֲנָקִים שָׁם וְעָרִים גְּדֹלוֹת בְּצֻרוֹת אוּלַי
if ;walled great and (were) the (how) that day in
cities ,there Anakim

3091 1288 3068 1696 3423 3068
13 יְהוָה אוֹתִי וְהוֹרַשְׁתִּים כַּאֲשֶׁר דִּבֶּר יְהוָה׃ וַיְבָרְכֵהוּ יְהוֹשֻׁעַ
Joshua blessed And .Jehovah has as shall I then with Jehovah
him spoken ,them expel ,me be shall

1961 5159 3312 3612 2275 5414
14 וַיִּתֵּן אֶת־חֶבְרוֹן לְכָלֵב בֶּן־יְפֻנֶּה לְנַחֲלָה׃ עַל־כֵּן הָיְתָה־
has Therefore an for Jephun- the Caleb to Hebron and
belonged .inheritance neh of son gave

3117 5704 5159 7074 3312 3612 2275
חֶבְרוֹן לְכָלֵב בֶּן־יְפֻנֶּה הַקְּנִזִּי לְנַחֲלָה עַד הַיּוֹם הַזֶּה יַעַן
for ,this day to in- an for the of son the to Hebron
heritance ,Kenezite ,Jephunneh Caleb

6440 2275 8034 3478 430 3068 310 4390
15 אֲשֶׁר מִלֵּא אַחֲרֵי יְהוָה אֱלֹהֵי יִשְׂרָאֵל׃ וְשֵׁם חֶבְרוֹן לְפָנִים
before Hebron the And .Israel the Jehovah after fully he —
of name of God followed

City of Arba — that one *was* a great man among the Anakim.
And the land had rest from war.

קרית ארבע האדם הגדול בענקים הוא והארץ שקטה
ממלחמה:

CAP. XV טו

CHAPTER 15

[1]And the lot for the tribe of the sons of Judah for their families was to the border of Edom, the wilderness of Zin southward, in the extreme south. [2]And their south border was from the end of the Salt Sea, from the bay that looked southward. [3]And it went out southward to the ascent of Acrabbim, and passed on to Zin, and went up on the south of Kadesh-barnea, and passed to Hezron, and went up toward Adar, and turned toward Karkaa, [4]and passed on to Azmon, and went out by the torrent of Egypt; and the boundary line was at the sea. This shall be your south border. [5]And the east border *was* the Salt Sea to the end of the Jordan; and the border on the north side *was* from the bay of the sea at the end of the Jordan. [6]And the border went up to Beth-hoglah, and passed on the north of Beth-arabah; and the border went up to the stone of Bohan, the son of Reuben; [7]and the border went up toward Debir from the valley of Achor, and northward looking toward Gilgal, which is opposite to the ascent of Adummim, which *is* the south side of the torrent; and the border passed to the waters of En-shemesh, and its boundary line was at En-rogel. [8]And the border went up to the valley of the son of Hinnom, to the side of the Jebusite on the south—it *is* Jerusalem—and the border went up to the top of the

1 ויהי הגורל למטה בני יהודה למשפחתם אל־גבול
2 אדום מדבר־צן נגבה מקצה תימן: ויהי להם גבול נגב
3 מקצה ים המלח מן־הלשן הפנה נגבה: ויצא אל־
מנגב למעלה עקרבים ועבר צנה ועלה מנגב לקדש
4 ברנע ועבר חצרון ועלה אדרה ונסב הקרקעה: ועבר
עצמונה ויצא נחל מצרים והיה תצאות הגבול ימה
5 זה־יהיה לכם גבול נגב: וגבול קדמה ים המלח עד־
קצה הירדן וגבול לפאת צפונה מלשון הים מקצה
6 הירדן: ועלה הגבול בית חגלה ועבר מצפון לבית
7 הערבה ועלה הגבול אבן בהן בן־ראובן: ועלה הגבול
דברה מעמק עכור וצפונה פנה אל־הגלגל אשר־נכח
למעלה אדמים אשר מנגב לנחל ועבר הגבול אל־מי
8 עין־שמש והיו תצאתיו אל־עין רגל: ועלה הגבול גי
בן־הנם אל־כתף היבוסי מנגב היא ירושלם ועלה

mountain which *is* before
the valley of Hinnom westward, which is at the far end
of the Valley of the Giants
northward. 9And the border
was drawn from the top of
the mount to the fountain of
the waters of Nephtoah;
and *it* went up to the cities
of Mount Ephron; and the
border was drawn to
Baalah—it *is* Kirjath-jearim
—10and the border turned
around from Baalah west-
ward to Mount Seir, and
passed toward the side of
Mount Jearim on the north
—it *is* Chesalon—and went
down to Beth-shemesh,
and passed along by Tim-
nah; 11and the border went
out to the side of Ekron
northward; and the border
was drawn *to* Shikkeron,
and passed along to Mount
Baalah, and went out to
Jabneel. And the boundary
line was at the sea. 12And
the west border *was* to the
Great Sea, and *its* coast.
This is the border of the
sons of Judah all around, for
their families.

13And he gave a portion
to Caleb the son of
Jephunneh among the
sons of Judah, according to
the command of Jehovah to
Joshua: the City of Arba, the
father of Anak; it is Hebron.
14And Caleb dispossessed
the three sons of Anak from
there, Sheshai, Ahiman,
and Talmai, the sons of
Anak. 15And he went up
there to the inhabitants of
Debir; and the name of
Debir formerly was the city
of Sepher. 16And Caleb
said, He who strikes the city
of Sepher, and captures it, I
shall give my daughter
Achsah to him for a wife.
17And Othniel, the son of
Kenaz, the brother of Caleb,
captured it. And He gave his
daughter Achsah to him for
a wife. 18And it happened,
as she came, that she

834 3220 2011 1516 834 2022 7218 1366
הגבול אל־ראש ההר אשר על־פני גי־הנם ימה אשר
which west- Hinnom the before which the the to border the
is ,ward of valley (is) mount of top

2022 7218 1366 8388 6828 7497 6010 7097
9 בקצה עמק־רפאים צפנה׃ ותאר הגבול מראש ההר
the the from the was And north- Giants the the at
mount of top border drawn .ward of Valley of end far

1366 8388 6085 2022 5982 3318 425 4325 4599
אל־מעין מי נפתוח ויצא אל־ערי הר־עפרון ותאר הגבל
the was and ;Ephron Mount the to and ;Nephtoah the the to
border drawn of cities up went of waters of fountain

3220 1173 1366 5437 7157 1173
10 בעלה היא קרית יערים׃ ונסב הגבול מבעלה ימה
west- from the And .jearim Kirjath- (is) it to
ward Baalah border turned —Baalah

6828 3787 2022 3802 5674 8165 2022
אל־הר שעיר ועבר אל־כתף הר־יערים מצפונה היא
(is) it the on Jearim Mount the toward and ,Seir Mount to
,north of side passed

1366 3318 8553 5674 1050 3381 3693
11 כסלון וירד בית־שמש ועבר תמנה׃ ויצא הגבול אל־
to the went and by passed and shemesh to And .Chesalon
border out ;Timnah Beth- down went

2022 5674 7940 1366 8378 6828 6158 3802
כתף עקרון צפונה ותאר הגבול שכרונה ועבר הר־
to went and (to) the was and north- Ekron the
Mount on Shikkeron border drawn ,ward of side

1366 3220 1366 8444 1961 2995 3318 1173
12 הבעלה ויצא יבנאל והיו תצאות הגבול ימה׃ וגבול
the And the at the boundary the and to went and ,Baalah
border sea border of was ;Jabneel out

5439 3063 1121 1366 2088 1366 1419 3220
ים הימה הגדול וגבול זה גבול בני־יהודה סביב
all Judah the bor- the This (its) and ,Great the to west
,around of sons of der is .coast Sea (was)

1121 8432 2506 5414 3312/1121 3612 4940
13 למשפחתם׃ ולכלב בן־יפנה נתן חלק בתוך בני
the among a he of son the to And .families their for
of sons portion gave Jehphunneh Caleb

6061 1 704 7151 3092 3068 6310 413 3063
יהודה אל־פי יהוה ליהושע את־קרית ארבע אבי הענק
—Anak the Arba of city the ;Joshua to Jehovah the by Judah
of father of mouth

6061 1121 7969 3612 8033 3423 2275
14 היא חברון׃ וירש משם כלב את־שלושה בני הענק
;Anak of sons three the Caleb from And .Hebron (is) it
of there expelled

5927 6061 3211 8526 289 8344
15 את־ששי ואת־אחימן ואת־תלמי ילידי הענק׃ ויעל
he and ;Anak of sons the ,Talmai and ,Ahiman and ,Sheshai
up went

7158 7151 6440 1688 1688 3427 8033
משם אל־ישבי דבר ושם־דבר לפנים קרית־ספר׃
.Sepher the was before name the and ;Debir the to there
of city Debir of of inhabitants

5414 3920 7158 7151 5221 3612 559
16 ויאמר כלב אשר־יכה את־קרית־ספר ולכדה ונתתי לו
to shall I and ,Sepher of city the strikes Who- ,Caleb said And
him give ,it takes ever

251 7075/1121 6274 3920 802 1323 5915
17 את־עכסה בתי לאשה׃ וילכדה עתניאל בן־קנז אחי
brother ,Kenaz the ,Othniel captured And .wife a for my Achsah
of son it daughter

925 1961 852 1323 5915 5414 3612
18 כלב ויתן־לו את־עכסה בתו לאשה׃ ויהי בבואה
she as it And a for his Achsah to he and ;Caleb's
,came ,was .wife daughter him gave

persuaded him to ask from her father a field. And she alighted from the ass, and Caleb said to her, What do you *desire*? [19]And she said, Give a blessing to me. When you have given me the land of the south, then you shall give to me springs of water. And he gave to her the upper springs and the lower springs.

[20]This *is* the inheritance of the tribe of the sons of Judah, for their families: [21]And the cities at the furthest border of the tribe of the sons of Judah *were* to the border of Edom in the south: Kabzeel, and Eder, and Jagur, [22]and Kinah, and Dimonah, and Adadah, [23]and Kedesh, and Hazor, and Ithnan, [24]Ziph, and Telem, and Bealoth, [25]and Hazor, Hadattah, and Kerioth, and Hezron, which is Hazor, [26]Amam, and Shema, and Moladah, [27]and Hazar-gaddah, and Heshmon, and Beth-palet, [28]and Hazar-shual, and Beer-sheba, and Bizjothjah, [29]Baalah, and Iim, and Azem, [30]and Eltolad, and Chesil, and Hormah, [31]and Ziklag, and Madmannah, and Sansannah, [32]and Lebaoth, and Shilhim, and Ain, and Rimmon. All the cities are twenty-nine and their villages.

[33]In the Lowlands *were*: Eshtaol, and Zoreah, and Ashnah, [34]and Zanoah, and En-gannim, Tappuah, and Enam, [35]Jarmuth, and Adullam, Socoh, and Azekah, [36]and Sharaim, and Adithaim, and Gederah, and Gederothaim — fourteen cities and their villages— [37]Zenan, and Hadashah, and Migdal-gad, [38]and Dilan, and Mizpeh, and Joktheel, [39]Lachish, and Bozkath, and Eglon, [40]and Cabbon, and Lahmam, and Kithlish, [41]and Gederoth,

וַתְּסִיתֵהוּ לִשְׁאוֹל מֵאֵת־אָבִיהָ שָׂדֶה וַתִּצְנַח מֵעַל הַחֲמוֹר

19 וַיֹּאמֶר־לָהּ כָּלֵב מַה־לָּךְ׃ וַתֹּאמֶר תְּנָה־לִּי בְרָכָה כִּי

אֶרֶץ הַנֶּגֶב נְתַתָּנִי וְנָתַתָּה לִי גֻּלֹּת מָיִם וַיִּתֶּן־לָהּ אֵת גֻּלֹּת

20 עִלִּיּוֹת וְאֵת גֻּלֹּת תַּחְתִּיּוֹת׃ זֹאת נַחֲלַת מַטֵּה בְנֵי

21 יְהוּדָה לְמִשְׁפְּחֹתָם׃ וַיִּהְיוּ הֶעָרִים מִקְצֵה לְמַטֵּה בְנֵי

יְהוּדָה אֶל־גְּבוּל אֱדוֹם בַּנֶּגְבָּה קַבְצְאֵל וְעֵדֶר וְיָגוּר׃

22 23 וְקִינָה וְדִימוֹנָה וְעַדְעָדָה׃ וְקֶדֶשׁ וְחָצוֹר וְיִתְנָן׃ זִיף וָטֶלֶם

24 25 וּבְעָלוֹת׃ וְחָצוֹר ׀ חֲדַתָּה וּקְרִיּוֹת חֶצְרוֹן הִיא חָצוֹר׃

26 27 אֲמָם וּשְׁמַע וּמוֹלָדָה׃ וַחֲצַר גַּדָּה וְחֶשְׁמוֹן וּבֵית פָּלֶט׃

28 29 וַחֲצַר שׁוּעָל וּבְאֵר שֶׁבַע וּבִזְיוֹתְיָה׃ בַּעֲלָה וְעִיִּים וָעָצֶם׃

30 31 וְאֶלְתּוֹלַד וּכְסִיל וְחָרְמָה׃ וְצִקְלַג וּמַדְמַנָּה וְסַנְסַנָּה׃

32 וּלְבָאוֹת וְשִׁלְחִים וְעַיִן וְרִמּוֹן כָּל־עָרִים עֶשְׂרִים וָתֵשַׁע

33 34 וְחַצְרֵיהֶן׃ בַּשְּׁפֵלָה אֶשְׁתָּאוֹל וְצָרְעָה וְאַשְׁנָה׃ וְזָנוֹחַ

35 וְעֵין גַּנִּים תַּפּוּחַ וְהָעֵינָם׃ יַרְמוּת וַעֲדֻלָּם שׂוֹכֹה וַעֲזֵקָה׃

36 וְשַׁעֲרַיִם וַעֲדִיתַיִם וְהַגְּדֵרָה וּגְדֵרֹתָיִם עָרִים אַרְבַּע־עֶשְׂרֵה

37 38 וְחַצְרֵיהֶן׃ צְנָן וַחֲדָשָׁה וּמִגְדַּל־גָּד׃ וְדִלְעָן וְהַמִּצְפֶּה

39 40 וְיָקְתְאֵל׃ לָכִישׁ וּבָצְקַת וְעֶגְלוֹן׃ וְכַבּוֹן וְלַחְמָס וְכִתְלִישׁ׃

Beth-dagon, and Naamah,
and Makkedah — sixteen
cities and their villages—
42Libnah, and Ether, and
Ashan, 43and Jiphtah, and
Ashnah, and Nezib, 44and
Keilah, and Achzib, and
Mareshah—nine cities and
their villages—45Ekron with
its town and its villages;
46from Ekron even to the
sea, all that were at hand by
Ashdod, and their villages;
47Ashdod with its towns
and its villages; Gaza with
its towns and its villages, to
the river of Egypt, and the
Great Sea, and its coast.

48And in the hills: Shamir,
and Jattir, and Socoh,
49and Dannah, and Kirjath-
sannah, which is Debir;
50and Anab, and Estemoh,
and Anim, 51and Goshen,
and Holon, and Giloh—
eleven cities and their
villages—52Arab, and
Dumah, and Eshean, 53and
Janum, and Beth-tappuah,
and Aphekah, 54and Hum-
tah, and Kirjath-arba, which
is Hebron, and Zior—nine
cities and their villages—
55Maon, Carmel, and Ziph,
and Juttah, 56and Jezreel,
and Jokdeam, and Zanoah,
57Cain, Gibeah, and Tim-
nah—ten cities and their
villages—58Halhul, Beth-
zur, and Gedor, 59and
Maarath, and Beth-anoth,
and Eltekon —six cities and
their villages—60Kirjath-
baal, which is Kirjath-
jearim, and Rabbah—two
cities and their villages.
61In the wilderness, Beth-
arabah, Middin, and Se-
cacah, 62and Nibshan, and
the city of Salt, and En-
gedi—six cities and their
villages.
63As for the Jebusites,
the inhabitants of Jeru-
salem, the sons of Judah

6240 8337 5892 4719 5279 1016 1450
41 וּגְדֵרוֹת בֵּית־דָּגוֹן וְנַעֲמָה וּמַקֵּדָה עָרִים שֵׁשׁ־עֶשְׂרֵה
ten (and) six cities and and dagon Beth- and
—Makkedah Naamah Gederoth

5334 823 3316 6228 6281 3841 2691
42 וְחַצְרֵיהֶן׃ לִבְנָה וָעֶתֶר וְעָשָׁן׃
43 וְיִפְתָּח וְאַשְׁנָה וּנְצִיב׃
and and and and and ,Libnah their with
,Nezib ,Ashnah ,Jiphtah ,Ashan ,Ether —villages

2691 8672 5892 4762 392 7084
44 וּקְעִילָה וְאַכְזִיב וּמָרֵאשָׁה עָרִים תֵּשַׁע וְחַצְרֵיהֶן׃
their with nine cities and and and
—villages —Mareshah ,Achzib ,Keilah

3605 3220 6138 2691 1323 6138
45 עֶקְרוֹן וּבְנֹתֶיהָ וַחֲצֵרֶיהָ׃
46 מֵעֶקְרוֹן וָיָמָּה כֹּל אֲשֶׁר־עַל־
were that all to even from its and its with ;Ekron
sea the Ekron —villages towns

5804 2691 1323 795 2691 795 3027
47 יַד אַשְׁדּוֹד וְחַצְרֵיהֶן׃ אַשְׁדּוֹד בְּנוֹתֶיהָ וַחֲצֵרֶיהָ עַזָּה
Gaza its and its with Ashdod their with ,Ashdod the at
—villages towns —villages of hand

1366 1419 3220 4714 5158 2691 1323
בְּנוֹתֶיהָ וַחֲצֵרֶיהָ עַד־נַחַל מִצְרָיִם וְהַיָּם הַגָּדוֹל וּגְבוּל׃
its and ,Great the and ,Egypt the to its and its with
,coast Sea of torrent ,villages towns

1688 = 7158 = 1837 7755 3492 8069 2022
48 וּבָהָר שָׁמִיר וְיַתִּיר וְשׂוֹכֹה׃
49 וְדַנָּה וְקִרְיַת־סַנָּה הִיא דְבִר׃
,Debir which sannah and and and and ,Shamir in And
is Kirjath- ,Dannah ,Socoh ,Jattir :hill-country the

259 5892 1542 2473 1657 6044 851 6024
50 וַעֲנָב וְאֶשְׁתְּמֹה וְעָנִים׃
51 וְגֹשֶׁן וְחֹלֹן וְגִלֹה עָרִים אַחַת־
cities and and and and and and
—Giloh ,Holon ,Goshen ,Anim Eshtemoh ,Anab

1054 3241 824 1746 594 2691 6240
52 עֶשְׂרֵה וְחַצְרֵיהֶן׃ אֲרַב וְדוּמָה וְאֶשְׁעָן׃
53 וְיָנִים וּבֵית־
and and and and ,Arab their with eleven
Beth- ,Janum ,Eshean ,Dumah —villages

6730 2275 = 7153 = 2547 664 1054
54 תַּפּוּחַ וַאֲפֵקָה׃ וְחֻמְטָה וְקִרְיַת אַרְבַּע הִיא חֶבְרוֹן וְצִיעֹר
and ,Hebron which arba and and and ,tappuah
—Zior (is) Kirjath- ,Humtah ,Aphekah

3194 2128 6760 4584 2691 8672 5892
55 עָרִים תֵּשַׁע וְחַצְרֵיהֶן׃ מָעוֹן ׀ כַּרְמֶל וָזִיף וְיוּטָּה׃
and and ,Carmel ,Maon their with nine cities
,Juttah ,Ziph —villages

6235 5892 8553 1390 7014 2182 3347 3157
56 וְיִזְרְעֶאל וְיָקְדְעָם וְזָנוֹחַ׃
57 הַקַּיִן גִּבְעָה וְתִמְנָה עָרִים עֶשֶׂר
ten cities and ,Gibeah ,Cain and and and
—Timnah ,Zanoah ,Jokdeam ,Jezreel

1042 4638 1446 1049 2478 2691
58 וְחַצְרֵיהֶן׃ חַלְחוּל בֵּית־צוּר וּגְדוֹר׃
59 וּמַעֲרָת וּבֵית־
and and and zur Beth- ,Halhul their with
Beth- Maarath ,Gedor —villages

7154 2691 8337 5892 515 1042
60 עֲנוֹת וְאֶלְתְּקֹן עָרִים שֵׁשׁ וְחַצְרֵיהֶן׃ קִרְיַת־בַּעַל הִיא
which baal Kirjath- their with six cities and ,anoth
is —villages —Eltekon

4057 2691 8147 5892 7237 = 7157 =
61 קִרְיַת יְעָרִים וְהָרַבָּה עָרִים שְׁתַּיִם וְחַצְרֵיהֶן׃ בַּמִּדְבָּר
the In their with two cities and jearim Kirjath-
,wilderness ,villages —Rabbah

= 5872 = = 5898 = 5044 5527 4081 = 1026 =
62 בֵּית הָעֲרָבָה מִדִּין וּסְכָכָה׃ וְהַנִּבְשָׁן וְעִיר־הַמֶּלַח וְעֵין גֶּדִי
gedi En- Salt the and and and Middin arabah Beth-
of city ,Nibsham ,Secacah

3808 3389 3427 2983 2691 8337
63 עָרִים שֵׁשׁ וְחַצְרֵיהֶן׃ וְאֶת־הַיְבוּסִי יוֹשְׁבֵי יְרוּשָׁלַםִ לֹא־
not ,Jerusalem the the for As their with six cities
of natives ,Jebusites ,villages

could not drive them out. But the Jebusites dwell with the sons of Judah at Jerusalem to this day.

3363 1121 2983 3427 3423 3363 1121 3201

יָכְלוּ בְנֵי־יְהוּדָה לְהוֹרִישָׁם וַיֵּשֶׁב הַיְבוּסִי אֶת־בְּנֵי יְהוּדָה

Judah the with of sons the Jebusites But live them drive .out Judah the of sons could

2088 3117 5704 3389

בִּירוּשָׁלִַם עַד הַיּוֹם הַזֶּה׃

.this day to at Jerusalem

CAP. XVI טז

CHAPTER 16

CHAPTER 16

[1]And the lot of the sons of Joseph went out from the Jordan *at* Jericho, to the waters of Jericho eastward, to the wilderness which went from Jericho to the hills of Bethel. [2]And it went from Bethel to Luz, and passed on to the border of the Archites, to Ataroth; [3]and went down westward to the border of the Japhletites, to the border of Beth-horon the lower, and to Gezer, and its boundary line was at the sea. [4]And Manasseh and Ephraim, the sons of Joseph, inherited.

[5]And the border of the sons of Ephraim was by their families; the border of their inheritance on the east *was* Ataroth-addar to Beth-horon the upper. [6]And the border went out at the sea to Michmethah on the north; and the border went around eastward to Taanath-shiloh, and passed by it eastward to Janohah; [7]and went down from Janohah to Ataroth, and to Naarath, and touched on Jericho, and went out at the Jordan. [8]From Tappuah, the border went westward to the river Kanah, and its boundary line was at the sea. This is the inheritance of the tribe of the sons of Ephraim, for their families.

[9]And the separate cities of the sons of Ephraim *were* in the midst of the inheritance of the sons of Manasseh, all the cities and their villages. [10]And they did not expel the Canaanite

4217 3405 4325 3405 3383 3127 1121 1486 3318

1 וַיֵּצֵא הַגּוֹרָל לִבְנֵי יוֹסֵף מִיַּרְדֵּן יְרִיחוֹ לְמֵי יְרִיחוֹ מִזְרָחָה

,eastward Jericho the to of waters (beside) ,Jericho the from ,Jordan Joseph the of of sons the lot went And out

1008 3318 1008 2022 3405 5927 4057

2 הַמִּדְבָּר עֹלֶה מִירִיחוֹ בָּהָר בֵּית־אֵל׃ וְיָצָא מִבֵּית־אֵל

from Bethel it And went .Bethel the to of hills from Jericho which went the to wilderness

3220 3381 5852 757 1366 5674 3870

3 לוּזָה וְעָבַר אֶל־גְּבוּל הָאַרְכִּי עֲטָרוֹת׃ וְיָרַד יָמָּה אֶל־

to west- ward went and down to ;Ataroth the Archites the to of border passed and on to ,Luz

1961 1507 8481 1032 1366 3311 1366

גְּבוּל הַיַּפְלֵטִי עַד־גְּבוּל בֵּית־חוֹרֹן תַּחְתּוֹן וְעַד־גֶּזֶר וְהָיוּ

and was ,Gezer and to the ,lower horon Beth- the of border to Japh- ,letites the bor- the of der

1961 669 4519 3127/1121 5159 3220 8444

4 תֹּצְאֹתָו יָמָּה׃ וַיִּנְחֲלוּ בְנֵי־יוֹסֵף מְנַשֶּׁה וְאֶפְרָיִם׃ וַיְהִי

5 And was and .Ephraim Manasseh ,Joseph the of sons And inherited the at .sea its boundary

4217 5159 1366 1961 4940 669 1121 1366

גְּבוּל בְּנֵי־אֶפְרַיִם לְמִשְׁפְּחֹתָם וַיְהִי גְּבוּל נַחֲלָתָם מִזְרָחָה

the on east their inheritance bor- the of der :was their by families of sons the Ephraim bor- the of der

3220 1366 3318 5945 1032 5854

6 עַטְרוֹת אַדָּר עַד־בֵּית חוֹרֹן עֶלְיוֹן׃ וְיָצָא הַגְּבוּל הַיָּמָּה

the at sea the border went and out the ;upper horon Beth- to addar Araroth-

5674 8387 4217 1366 5437 6828 4366

הַמִּכְמְתָת מִצָּפוֹן וְנָסַב הַגְּבוּל מִזְרָחָה תַּאֲנַת שִׁלֹה וְעָבַר

and by went shiloh Taanath- eastward (to) the border went and around the on ;north to Michmethah

6293 5292 5852 3239 3381 3239 4217

7 אוֹתוֹ מִמִּזְרַח יָנוֹחָה׃ וְיָרַד מִיָּנוֹחָה עֲטָרוֹת וְנַעֲרָתָה וּפָגַע

it and touched to and ,Naarath to ,Ataroth from Janohah and went to ;Janohah eastward it

7071 5158 3220 1366 5927 8599 3383 3318 3405

8 בִּירִיחוֹ וְיָצָא הַיַּרְדֵּן׃ מִתַּפּוּחַ יֵלֵךְ הַגְּבוּל יָמָּה נַחַל קָנָה

,Kanah the torrent to west- ward the border went From Tappuah the at ,Jordan went and out on ,Jericho

669 1121 4294 5159 2088 3220 8444 1961

וְהָיוּ תֹצְאֹתָיו הַיָּמָּה זֹאת נַחֲלַת מַטֵּה בְנֵי־אֶפְרָיִם

of sons the ,Ephraim tribe the of inher- the of itance This (is) the at .sea its boundary and was

8432 669 1121 3995 5892 4940

9 לְמִשְׁפְּחֹתָם׃ וְהֶעָרִים הַמִּבְדָּלוֹת לִבְנֵי אֶפְרַיִם בְּתוֹךְ

the in of midst Ephraim (were) the of of sons separate the And cities their by .families

3423 3808 2691 5892 3605 4519/1121 5159

10 נַחֲלַת בְּנֵי־מְנַשֶּׁה כָּל־הֶעָרִים וְחַצְרֵיהֶן׃ וְלֹא הוֹרִישׁוּ אֶת־

did they expel And not their and .villages the cities all of sons the ,Manasseh inher- the of itance who lived in Gezer. And the Canaanite lives in the midst of Ephraim to this day, and is serving under tribute.

CHAPTER 17

1 And the lot came for the tribe of Manasseh, for he *was* the firstborn of Joseph, to Machir the firstborn of Manasseh, father of Gilead, for he had been a man of battle, and he had Gilead and Bashan. 2 And there was *a lot* remaining for the sons of Manasseh, for their families—for the sons of Abiezer, and for the sons of Helek, and for the sons of Asriel, and for the sons of Shechem, and for the sons of Hepher, and for the sons of Shemida; these *being* the sons of Manasseh the son of Joseph, by their families. 3 But Zelophehad the son of Hepher, the son of Gilead, the son of Machir, the son of Manasseh, had no sons, but daughters. And these *were* the names of his daughters: Mahlah, and Noah, Hoglah, Milcah, and Tirzah. 4 And they drew near before Eleazar the priest, and before Joshua the son of Nun, and before the rulers, saying, Jehovah commanded Moses to give to us an inheritance among our brothers; and at the mouth of Jehovah he gave to them an inheritance among their father's brothers. 5 And ten portions fell *to* Manasseh, besides that from the land of Gilead and Bashan beyond the Jordan; 6 because the daughters of Manasseh had inherited an inheritance among his sons; and the land of Gilead belonged to *the sons of* Manasseh who remained.

5704 669 7130 3669 3427 1507 3427 3669
הכנעני היושב בגזר וישב הכנעני בקרב אפרים עד
to Ephraim the in the and in who the
of midst Canaanite lives ;Gezer lived Canaanite
5647 4522 1961 3117
היום הזה ויהי למס-עבד׃
labor-forced A and this day
.slave is

CAP. XVII יז

CHAPTER 17

4353 3127 1060 4519 4294 1486 1961
1 ויהי הגורל למטה מנשה כי-הוא בכור יוסף למכיר
for ,Joseph first- the he for ,Manasseh the for lot the And
Machir of born (was) of tribe came
44:21 376 1961 1568 4519 1060
בכור מנשה אבי הגלעד כי הוא היה איש מלחמה
,battle a had he for ,Gilead father ,Manasseh the
of man been of of firstborn
3498 4519 1121 1961 1316 1568 1961
2 ויהי-לו הגלעד והבשן׃ ויהי לבני מנשה הנותרים
remaining ,Manasseh the for there And and Gilead he and
of sons was .Bashan had
844 1121 25-07/1121 44 1121 4940
למשפחתם לבני אביעזר ולבני-חלק ולבני אשריאל
,Asriel for and ,Helek for and ,Abiezer the for their for
of sons the of sons the of sons :families
4519 1121 8061 1121 2660/1121 7928 1121
ולבני-שכם ולבני-חפר ולבני שמידע אלה בני מנשה
Manasseh the these ;Shemidah for and ,Hepher for and ,Shechem and
of sons (were) of sons the of sons the of sons the for
1121 2660/1121 6765 4940 2145 3127/1121
3 בן-יוסף הזכרים למשפחתם׃ ולצלפחד בן-חפר בן
the ,Hepher the Zelophe- But their by male ,Joseph the
of son of son had .families of son
1323 1121 3808 4519/1121 4353/1121 1568
גלעד בן-מכיר בן-מנשה לא-היו לו בנים כי אם-בנות
.daughters but ,sons no had ,Manasseh the Machir the ,Gilead
of son of son
8656 4435 2295 5270 4244 1323 8034 428
ואלה שמות בנתיו מחלה ונעה חגלה מלכה ותרצה׃
and ,Milcah ,Hoglah and ,Mahlah his names the And
.Tirzah ,Noah :daughters of (were) these
6440 5126/1121/3091 6440 3548 499 6440 7126
4 ותקרבנה לפני אלעזר הכהן ולפני יהושע בן-נון ולפני
and ,Nun the Joshua and the Eleazar before they And
before of son before ,priest came
5159 5414 4872 6680 3068 559 5387
הנשיאים לאמר יהוה צוה את-משה לתת-לנו נחלה
an us give to Moses com- Jehovah ,saying ,rulers the
inheritance manded
251 8432 5159 3068 6310 5414 251 8432
בתוך אחינו ויתן להם אל-פי יהוה נחלה בתוך אחי
brothers among an ,Jehovah the by to he and our among
inheritance of mouth ,them gave ;brothers
1568 776 6235 4519 2256 5307 1
5 אביהן׃ ויפלו חבלי-מנשה עשרה לבד מארץ הגלעד
Gilead the from besides ,ten (to) portions And their
of land that Manasseh fell .father's
5159 5157 4519 1323 3588 3383 5676 834 1316
6 והבשן אשר מעבר לירדן׃ כי בנות מנשה נחלו נחלה
inher- an had Manasseh the because the beyond which and
itance inherited of daughters ;Jordan (were) ,Bashan
3498 4519 1121 5414 1568 776 1121 8432
בתוך בניו וארץ הגלעד היתה לבני-מנשה הנותרים׃
who Manasseh the to belonged Gilead the and his among
.remained of sons of land ;sons

[7]And the border of Manasseh *was* from Asher to Michmethah, which fronts on Shechem. And the border went up to the right to the inhabitants of En-tappuah—[8]the land of Tappuah belonged to Manasseh, but Tappuah on the border of Manasseh belonged to the sons of Ephraim—[9]and the border went down to the river Kanah, south of the river; these cities of Ephraim *were* in the midst of the cities of Manasseh, and the border of Manasseh *was* on the north of the river, and its boundary line was at the sea. [10]Southward, it was Ephraim's. And northward, it was Manasseh's, and the sea was its border. And they met in Asher on the north, and in Issachar on the east. [11]And Manasseh had in Issachar and in Asher, Beth-shean and its towns, and Ibleam and its towns, and the inhabitants of Dor and its towns, and the inhabitants of Endor and its towns, and the inhabitants of Taanach and its towns, and the inhabitants of Megiddo and its towns—three regions. [12]But the sons of Manasseh had not been able to occupy these cities, for the Canaanite determined to live in this land. [13]And it happened, when the sons of Israel became strong, they put the Canaanites to tribute, but did not completely expel him.

[14]And the sons of Joseph spoke with Joshua, saying, Why have you given to me one lot and one portion as an inheritance, since I *am* a numerous people? For Jehovah has blessed me until now. [15]And Joshua said to them, If you are a numerous people, go up to the forest for yourself, and you shall cut down for yourself there in the land of the Perizzite, and of the giants, if Mount Ephraim is

7 וַיְהִי גְבוּל־מְנַשֶּׁה מֵאָשֵׁר הַמִּכְמְתָת אֲשֶׁר עַל־פְּנֵי שְׁכֶם
;Shechem on fronts which Mich- to from Manasseh the And
,methah Asher of border
8 וְהָלַךְ הַגְּבוּל אֶל־הַיָּמִין אֶל־יֹשְׁבֵי עֵין תַּפּוּחַ׃ לִמְנַשֶּׁה
to tappuah En- the to the to the and
,Manasseh of inhabitants right border went
הָיְתָה אֶרֶץ תַּפּוּחַ וְתַפּוּחַ אֶל־גְּבוּל מְנַשֶּׁה לִבְנֵי אֶפְרָיִם׃
—Ephraim to was Manasseh the on but ,Tappuah the belonged
of sons the of border Tappuah of land
9 וְיָרַד הַגְּבוּל נַחַל קָנָה נֶגְבָּה לַנַּחַל עָרִים הָאֵלֶּה לְאֶפְרַיִם
Ephraim of these cities the of south ,Kanah the to the went and
(were) ;torrent river border down
בְּתוֹךְ עָרֵי מְנַשֶּׁה וּגְבוּל מְנַשֶּׁה מִצְּפוֹן לַנַּחַל וַיְהִי תֹצְאֹתָיו
boun- its and the of the on Manasseh the and ,Manasseh the the in
line dary was ,brook north of border of cities of midst
10 הַיָּמָּה׃ נֶגְבָּה לְאֶפְרַיִם וְצָפוֹנָה לִמְנַשֶּׁה וַיְהִי הַיָּם גְּבוּלוֹ
its the and was it north- and was it South- the at
;border sea was ,Manasseh's ward ,Ephraim's ward .sea
11 וּבְאָשֵׁר יִפְגְּעוּן מִצָּפוֹן וּבְיִשָּׂשכָר מִמִּזְרָח׃ וַיְהִי לִמְנַשֶּׁה
Manasseh And the on in and the on they in and
had .east Issachar ,north met Asher
בְּיִשָּׂשכָר וּבְאָשֵׁר בֵּית־שְׁאָן וּבְנוֹתֶיהָ וְיִבְלְעָם וּבְנוֹתֶיהָ
its and and its and shean Beth- in and Issachar in
towns Ibleam ,towns ,Asher
וְאֶת־יֹשְׁבֵי דֹאר וּבְנוֹתֶיהָ וְיֹשְׁבֵי עֵין־דֹּר וּבְנֹתֶיהָ וְיֹשְׁבֵי
the and its and dor En- the and its and Dor the and
in dwellers ,towns in dwellers ,towns in dwellers
תַעְנַךְ וּבְנֹתֶיהָ וְיֹשְׁבֵי מְגִדּוֹ וּבְנוֹתֶיהָ שְׁלֹשֶׁת הַנָּפֶת׃
.regions three its and Megiddo the and its and Taanach
,towns in dwellers ,towns
12 וְלֹא יָכְלוּ בְּנֵי מְנַשֶּׁה לְהוֹרִישׁ אֶת־הֶעָרִים הָאֵלֶּה וַיּוֹאֶל
for ,these cities occupy to Manasseh the had But
determined of sons able been not
13 הַכְּנַעֲנִי לָשֶׁבֶת בָּאָרֶץ הַזֹּאת׃ וַיְהִי כִּי חָזְקוּ בְּנֵי יִשְׂרָאֵל
,Israel the became when and ;this land in live to the
of sons strong ,was it Canaanite
14 וַיִּתְּנוּ אֶת־הַכְּנַעֲנִי לָמַס וְהוֹרֵשׁ לֹא הוֹרִישׁוֹ׃ וַיְדַבְּרוּ
spoke And drive did not but to Canaanites the that
.out him completely ,tribute put they
בְּנֵי יוֹסֵף אֶת־יְהוֹשֻׁעַ לֵאמֹר מַדּוּעַ נָתַתָּה לִּי נַחֲלָה גּוֹרָל
lot an as to you have Why ,saying Joshua with Joseph the
inheritance me given of sons
אֶחָד וְחֶבֶל אֶחָד וַאֲנִי עַם־רָב עַד אֲשֶׁר־עַד־כֹּה בֵּרְכַנִי
has now until for great a since ,one and one
me blessed ,people (am) I portion
15 יְהוָה׃ וַיֹּאמֶר אֲלֵיהֶם יְהוֹשֻׁעַ אִם־עַם־רַב אַתָּה עֲלֵה
up go you great a If ,Joshua them to said And Jehovah
,are people
לְךָ הַיַּעְרָה וּבֵרֵאתָ לְךָ שָׁם בְּאֶרֶץ הַפְּרִזִּי וְהָרְפָאִים
the of and the the in there for cut and the to for
,giants ,Perizzite of land yourself down forest yourself

4672 3808 3127 1121 559 669 2022 213
16 כי־אץ לך הר־אפרים: ויאמרו בני יוסף לא־ימצא לנו
for | be will | not | ,Joseph | the | said And | .Ephraim Mount | for | too is if
us | found | of sons | ,you | narrow

6010 776 3427 3669 1270 7393 2022
ההר ורכב ברזל בכל־הכנעני הישב בארץ־העמק
the | the in | who | Canaanite every | iron | a and | hill- The
,valley | of land | lives | (has) | of chariot | ;country

3157 6010 1323 1052
לאשר בבית־שאן ובנותיה ולאשר בעמק יזרעאל:
.Jezreel | the in | him of and | its and | shean | of | those
of valley | (is) who | ,towns | Beth- | are that

559 4519 669 3127 1004 3091 559
17 ויאמר יהושע אל־בית יוסף לאפרים ולמנשה לאמר
,saying | to and | to | ,Joseph | the to | Joshua | And
,Manasseh | Ephraim | of house | spoke

259 1486 1961 3808 1419 3581 7227
עם־רב אתה וכח גדול לך לא־יהיה לך גורל אחד:
,one | lot | you | shall not | ;have | great | and | You | numer- a
have | power (are) | ,ous people

8444 1961 1254 3293 2022/3588
18 כי הר יהיה־לך כי־יער הוא ובראתו והיה לך תצאתיו
outer its | ,yours | it and | cut shall you | is it | a for | ;yours is | the | for
;limits | be shall | ,down it | forest | hill

2388 1270 7393 3669 3423
כי־תוריש את־הכנעני כי רכב ברזל לו כי חזק הוא:
.(is) it | strong though it | iron | chariots though | the | shall you | for
,has | of | ,Canaanite | expel

too narrow for you. 16 And
the sons of Joseph said,
The hills will not come to
us. And every Canaanite
who lives in the land of the
valley *has* a chariot of iron,
those that are of Beth-
shean and its towns, and of
him who *is* in the valley of
Jezreel. 17 And Joshua
spoke to the house of
Joseph, to Ephraim and to
Manasseh, saying, You *are*
a numerous people, and
have great power; you shall
not have one lot, 18 be-
cause the hill is yours;
because it *is* a forest, you
shall cut it down, and its
outer limits shall be yours;
for you shall expel the
Canaanite, even though it
has chariots of iron; even
though it *is* strong.

CAP. XVIII יח

CHAPTER 18

8033 7931 7887 3478 1121 5712 6950
1 ויקהלו כל־עדת בני־ישראל שלה וישכינו שם את־
there | they and | at | Israel | the | the all | were And
established | ;Shiloh | of sons of | company | gathered

1121 3498 6440 3533 776 4150 168
2 אהל מועד והארץ נכבשה לפניהם: ויותרו בבני
among | were And | before | been had | the and | ;meeting | the
of sons the | left | .them | subdued | land | of tent

7626 7651 5159 2505 3808 834 3478
ישראל אשר לא־חלקו את־נחלתם שבעה שבטים:
.tribes | seven | their | had | not | who | ,Israel
inheritance | shared

7503 3478 1121 3091 559
3 ויאמר יהושע אל־בני ישראל עד־אנה אתם מתרפים
fail will | you | long How | ,Israel | the to | Joshua | said And
of sons

430 3068 5414 834 776 3423 935
לבוא לרשת את־הארץ אשר נתן לכם יהוה אלהי
the | Jehovah | to | has | which | land the | to | go to
of God | you | given | possess | in

7971 7626 582 7969 3053 1
4 אבותיכם: הבו לכם שלשה אנשים לשבט ואשלחם
shall I and | a of | men | three | from Give | your
;them send | ,tribe | you among | ?fathers

925 5159 3789 776 3212 6965
ויקמו ויתהלכו בארץ ויכתבו אותה לפי נחלתם ויבאו
and | their according | it | and | through | up go and | they and
come | ,inheritance to | map | ,land the down and | ;arise shall

5975 3063 2506 7651 2505
5 אלי: והתחלקו אתה לשבעה חלקים יהודה יעמד
shall | Judah | .portions | into | it | they And | to
stay | seven | divide shall | .me

6828 1366 5975 3127 1004 5045 1366
על־גבולו מנגב ובית יוסף יעמדו על־גבולם מצפון:
the on | their | within | shall | Joseph | the and | the on | his within
.north | border | stay | of house | ,south | border

CHAPTER 18
1 And all the company of
the sons of Israel were
gathered at Shiloh. And
they established the tabernacle of the congregation
there. And the land had
been subdued before them.
2 And seven tribes were left
among the sons of Israel
who had not shared their
inheritance. 3 And Joshua
said to the sons of Israel,
How long will you fail to go
in to possess the land
which He, Jehovah the God
of your fathers, has given to
you? 4 Give from among you
three men of a tribe, and I
shall send them. And they
shall go up and down
through the land, and map it
according to their inheritance; and then come to
me. 5 And they shall divide
it into seven parts. Judah
shall stay within their
border on the south, and
the house of Joseph shall
stay within their border on
the north. 6 And you shall

map the land *in* seven parts, and shall bring *it* to me here. And I shall cast a lot for you here before Jehovah our God. [7]For there shall be no portion to the Levites among you, for the priesthood of Jehovah *is* their inheritance. And Gad, and Reuben, and the half tribe of Manasseh have received their inheritance beyond the Jordan eastward, which Moses the servant of Jehovah gave to them.

[8]And the men rose up and went. And Joshua commanded those who were going to map out the land, saying, Go, and walk up and down through the land, and map it, and return to me. And I will cast a lot for you here before Jehovah at Shiloh. [9]And the men passed through the land, and mapped it by cities, in seven parts, in a book. And they came to Joshua, to the camp *at* Shiloh. [10]And Joshua cast lots for them in Shiloh before Jehovah. And Joshua apportioned the land to the sons of Israel there, according to their divisions.

[11]And the lot of the tribe of the sons of Benjamin came up, according to their families, and the border of their lot went out between the sons of Judah and the sons of Joseph. [12]And their border was at the north side from the Jordan, and the border went up to the side of Jericho on the north, and went up through the hills westward; and its boundary line was at the wilderness of Beth-aven; [13]and the border went up from there to Luz, to the side of Luz—it *is* Bethel—southward, and the border went down *to* Ataroth-adar, near the hill that is on the

6 ואתם תכתבו את־הארץ שבעה חלקים והבאתם אלי
7 הנה וירתי לכם גורל פה לפני יהוה אלהינו׃ כי אין
חלק ללוים בקרבכם כי־כהנת יהוה נחלתו וגד וראובן
וחצי שבט המנשה לקחו נחלתם מעבר לירדן מזרחה
8 אשר נתן להם משה עבד יהוה׃ ויקמו האנשים וילכו
ויצו יהושע את־ההלכים לכתב את־הארץ לאמר לכו
והתהלכו בארץ וכתבו אותה ושובו אלי ופה אשליך
9 לכם גורל לפני יהוה בשלה׃ וילכו האנשים ויעברו
בארץ ויכתבוה לערים לשבעה חלקים על־ספר ויבאו
10 אל־יהושע אל־המחנה שלה׃ וישלך להם יהושע גורל
בשלה לפני יהוה ויחלק־שם יהושע את־הארץ לבני
11 ישראל כמחלקתם׃ ויעל גורל מטה בני־בנימן
למשפחתם ויצא גבול גורלם בין בני יהודה ובין בני
12 יוסף׃ ויהי להם הגבול לפאת צפונה מן־הירדן ועלה
הגבול אל־כתף יריחו מצפון ועלה בהר ימה והיה
13 תצאתיו מדברה בית און׃ ועבר משם הגבול לוזה
אל־כתף לוזה נגבה היא בית־אל וירד הגבול עטרות

south of the lower Beth-
horon; [14]and the border
was drawn and went
around to the sea coast
southward, from the hill
which fronts on Beth-horon
southward; and its boun-
dary line was at the city of
Baal—it is Kirjath-jearim, a
city of the sons of Judah—
this is the west side. [15]And
the south side *was* from the
end of Kirjath-jearim; and
the border went out west-
ward, and went out to the
spring of the waters of
Nephtoah; [16]and the border
went down to the end of the
mountain that is before the
valley of the son of Hinnom,
which *is* in the Valley of the
Giants northward, and went
down the valley of Hinnom
to the side of the Jebusite
on the south, and went
down to En-rogel. [17]And it
was drawn from the north
and went out to En-
shemesh, and went out
toward Geliloth, which is
across from the ascent of
Adummim, and went down
to the stone of Bohan the
son of Reuben, [18]and
passed on to the side op-
posite to Arabah north-
ward, and went down to
Arabah. [19]And the border
passed on to the side of
Beth-hoglah northward,
and the boundary line was
at the north tongue of the
Salt Sea, to the extreme
south of the Jordan; this
was the southern border.
[20]And the Jordan borders it
on the east side. This was
the inheritance of the sons
of Benjamin, according to
its borders all around,
according to their families.

[21]And the cities for the
tribe of the sons of Ben-
jamin, by their families,
were Jericho, Beth-hoglah,
and the valley of Keziz,

[22]and Beth-arabah, and
Zemaraim, and Bethel,
[23]and Avvim, and Parah, and

8388 8481 1032 5045 834 2022 5853
14 אַדָּר עַל־הָהָר אֲשֶׁר מִנֶּגֶב לְבֵית־חֹרוֹן תַּחְתּוֹן׃ וְתָאַר
was And | the | horon | of | the on | that | the near | ,adar
drawn | lower | Beth- | south | is | hill

6440 5921 834 2022 5045 3220 6285 5437 1366
הַגְּבוּל וְנָסַב לִפְאַת־יָם נֶגְבָּה מִן־הָהָר אֲשֶׁר עַל־פְּנֵי
fronts | which | the | from | south- | sea the to | went and | the
on | hill | ward | coast | around | border

1168 7151 8444 1961 5045 1032
בֵית־חֹרוֹן נֶגְבָּה וְהָיָה תֹצְאֹתָיו אֶל־קִרְיַת־בַּעַל הִיא
is it | —Baal | the at | its | was and | south- | horon Beth-
of city | boundary | ward

5045 6285 3220 6285 2088 3063 1121 5892 7152
15 קִרְיַת יְעָרִים עִיר בְּנֵי יְהוּדָה זֹאת פְּאַת־יָם׃ וּפְאַת־נֶגְבָּה
south the And | west the | this | ;Judah sons the | a | jearim | Kirjath-
(was) side | side | is | of | of city

4325 4599 3318 3220 1366 3318 7152 7097
מִקְצֵה קִרְיַת יְעָרִים וְיָצָא הַגְּבוּל יָמָּה וְיָצָא אֶל־מַעְיַן מֵי
the spring the to | and | west- | the | went and | ;jearim Kirjath- | the from
of waters of | out went | ,ward | border | out | of end

1516 6440 834 2022 7097 1366 3381 4325
16 נֶפְתּוֹחַ׃ וְיָרַד הַגְּבוּל אֶל־קְצֵה הָהָר אֲשֶׁר עַל־פְּנֵי גֵּי
the | before | that | the | end the | to | the | came and | ;Nephtoah
of valley | is | mountain | of | border | down

2011 1516 3381 6828 7497 6010 834 1121
בֶן־הִנֹּם אֲשֶׁר בְּעֵמֶק רְפָאִים צָפוֹנָה וְיָרַד גֵּי הִנֹּם
Hinnom the went and | north- | the | the in | which ,Hinnom | the
of valley down | ,ward | giants | of valley | (is) | of son

6828 8388 5883 3381 5045 2983 3802
17 אֶל־כֶּתֶף הַיְבוּסִי נֶגְבָּה וְיָרַד עֵין רֹגֵל׃ וְתָאַר מִצָּפוֹן
the from | it and | ;rogel | to | went and | the on | the | the | to
north | drawn was | En- | down | ,south | Jebusite | of side

4608 5227 834 1553 3318 5885 3318
וְיָצָא עֵין שֶׁמֶשׁ וְיָצָא אֶל־גְּלִילוֹת אֲשֶׁר־נֹכַח מַעֲלֵה
the | opposite | which | toward | went and | ,shemesh En- | to | and
of ascent | is | ,Geliloth | out | out went

3801 5674 7205 1121 932 68 3381 131
18 אֲדֻמִּים וְיָרַד אֶבֶן בֹּהַן בֶּן־רְאוּבֵן׃ וְעָבַר אֶל־כֶּתֶף מוּל־
opposite | the | to | and | ,Reuben the | Bohan | the to | and ,Adummim
to | side | on passed | of son | of stone down went

1366 5674 6160 3381 6828 6160
19 הָעֲרָבָה צָפוֹנָה וְיָרַד הָעֲרָבָתָה׃ וְעָבַר הַגְּבוּל אֶל־
to | the | and | to | went and | north- | Arabah
border | on passed | ;Arabah | down | ,ward

1366 8444 1961 6828 1031 3801
כֶּתֶף בֵּית־חָגְלָה צָפוֹנָה וְהָיָה | תּוֹצְאוֹתָיו הַגְּבוּל אֶל־
at | the of | the | was and | ;northward | hoglah Beth- | the
border | boundary | of side

1366 2088 5045 3383 7097 6828 4417 3220 3956
לְשׁוֹן יָם־הַמֶּלַח צָפוֹנָה אֶל־קְצֵה הַיַּרְדֵּן נֶגְבָּה זֶה גְּבוּל
the | this | ;south | the of | the | to | ,north | Salt the | the
border | (was) | Jordan | extreme | Sea | of tongue

1121 5159 2088 6924 6285 1379 3383 5045
20 נֶגֶב׃ וְהַיַּרְדֵּן יִגְבֹּל־אֹתוֹ לִפְאַת־קֵדְמָה זֹאת נַחֲלַת בְּנֵי
the inher- | the This | .east | the on | it | borders | the And | .southern
of sons of | itance (was) | side | Jordan

4294 5892 1961 4940 5439 1367 1144
21 בִנְיָמִן לִגְבוּלֹתֶיהָ סָבִיב לְמִשְׁפְּחֹתָם׃ וְהָיוּ הֶעָרִים לְמַטֵּה
the for | the | And | to according | all | to according | ,Benjamin
of tribe | cities | were | .families their | ,around | borders its

6010 1031 3405 4940 1144 1121
בְּנֵי בִנְיָמִן לְמִשְׁפְּחוֹתֵיהֶם יְרִיחוֹ וּבֵית־חָגְלָה וְעֵמֶק
the and | hoglah | and | ,Jericho | their for | ,Benjamin | the
of valley | Beth- | :families | of sons

5757 1008 6787 1026 5010
22 23 קְצִיץ׃ וּבֵית הָעֲרָבָה וּצְמָרַיִם וּבֵית־אֵל׃ וְהָעַוִּים
and | and | and | arabah | and | ,Keziz
Avvim | ,Bethel | ,Zemaraim | Beth-

Ophrah, [24]and Chephar-haam-monai, and Ophni, and Gaba — twelve cities and their villages— [25]Gibeon, and Ramah, and Beeroth, [26]and Mizpeh, and Chephirah, and Mozah, [27]and Rekem, and Irpeel, and Taralah, [28]and Zelah, Eleph, and Jebusi, which *is* Jerusalem, Gibeath, *and* Kirjath—fourteen cities and their villages. This is the inheritance of the sons of Benjamin, by their families.

24 וְהַפָּרָה וְעָפְרָה׃ וּכְפַר הָעַמֹּנִי וְהָעָפְנִי וָגָבַע עָרִים

5892 1387 6078 3726 3723 6084 6511

cities and ,Gaba and ,Ophni ,haim-monai and -Chephar and ,Ophrah and ,Parah

25
26 שְׁתֵּים־עֶשְׂרֵה וְחַצְרֵיהֶן׃ גִּבְעוֹן וְהָרָמָה וּבְאֵרוֹת׃ וְהַמִּצְפֶּה

4708 881 7414 1391 2691 6240 8147

and ,Mizpeh and ,Beeroth and ,Ramah ,Gibeon their with ,villages twelve

27
28 וְהַכְּפִירָה וְהַמֹּצָה׃ וְרֶקֶם וְיִרְפְּאֵל וְתַרְאֲלָה׃ וְצֵלַע הָאֶלֶף

507 6762 8634 3416 7552 4681 3716

,Eleph and ,Zelah and ,Taralah and Irpeel and ,Rekem and ,Mozah and ,Chephirah

וְהַיְבוּסִי הִיא יְרוּשָׁלִַם גִּבְעַת קִרְיַת עָרִים אַרְבַּע־עֶשְׂרֵה

6240 702 7157 1388 3389 2983

fourteen cities (and) —Kirjath Gibeath ,Jerusalem which (is) and Jebusi

וְחַצְרֵיהֶן זֹאת נַחֲלַת בְּנֵי־בִנְיָמִן לְמִשְׁפְּחֹתָם׃

4940 1144 1121 5159 2088 2691

their by .families of sons the ,Benjamin of heritance This is their and .villages

CAP. XIX יט

CHAPTER 19

CHAPTER 19

[1]And the second lot came forth to Simeon, for the tribe of the sons of Simeon according to their families. And their inheritance was inside the inheritance of the sons of Judah. [2]And they *had* for their inheritance, Beer-sheba, and Sheba, and Moladah, [3]and Hazorshual, and Balah, and Azem, [4]and Eltolad, and Bethul, and Hormah, [5]and Ziklag, and Beth-marcaboth, and Hazar-susah, [6]and Beth-lebaoth, and Sharuhen—thirteen cities and their villages—[7]Ain, Remmon, and Ether, and Ashan—four cities and their villages—[8]and all the villages that were all around these cities to Baalath-beer, Ramah of the south. This is the inheritance of the tribe of the sons of Simeon according to their families. [9]The inheritance of the sons of Simeon *was* out of the portion of the sons of Judah. For the part of the sons of Judah *was* too much for them. Therefore, the sons of Simeon had their inheritance within their inheritance.

[10]And the third lot came up for the sons of Zebulun

1 וַיֵּצֵא הַגּוֹרָל הַשֵּׁנִי לְשִׁמְעוֹן לְמַטֵּה בְנֵי־שִׁמְעוֹן לְמִשְׁפְּחוֹתָם

4940 8095 1121 4294 8095 8145 1486 3318

to according .families their of sons the ,Simeon the for of tribe to ,Simeon second the lot came And forth

2 וַיְהִי נַחֲלָתָם בְּתוֹךְ נַחֲלַת בְּנֵי־יְהוּדָה׃ וַיְהִי לָהֶם

1961 3063 1121 5159 8432 5159 1961

they And of sons the .Judah inher- the of itance inside inher- their itance And was

3 בְּנַחֲלָתָם בְּאֵר־שֶׁבַע וְשֶׁבַע וּמוֹלָדָה׃ וַחֲצַר שׁוּעָל

2705 4137 7652 884 5159

shual and Hazor- and ;Moladah and ,Sheba sheba Beer- their for :inheritance

4 וּבָלָה וָעָצֶם׃ וְאֶלְתּוֹלַד וּבְתוּל וְחָרְמָה׃ וְצִקְלַג וּבֵית־

1024 6860 2767 1329 513 6107 1088

5 and Beth- and ,Ziklag and ,Hormah and ,Bethul and ,Eltolad and ,Azem and ,Balah

6 הַמַּרְכָּבוֹת וַחֲצַר סוּסָה׃ וּבֵית לְבָאוֹת וְשָׁרוּחֶן עָרִים

5892 8287 1034 2701 1024

cities and —Sharuhen lebaoth and Beth- ;susah Hazar- ,Marcaboth

7 שְׁלֹשׁ־עֶשְׂרֵה וְחַצְרֵיהֶן׃ עַיִן רִמּוֹן וָעֶתֶר וְעָשָׁן עָרִים

5892 6228 6281 7417 5871 2691 6240 7969

cities and —Ashan and ,Ether ,Remmon ,Ain their and —villages thirteen

8 אַרְבַּע וְחַצְרֵיהֶן׃ וְכָל־הַחֲצֵרִים אֲשֶׁר סְבִיבוֹת הֶעָרִים

5892 5439 834 2691 3605 2691 702

cities all around that (were) the villages and all their and —villages four

הָאֵלֶּה עַד־בַּעֲלַת בְּאֵר רָאמַת נֶגֶב זֹאת נַחֲלַת מַטֵּה בְנֵי־

1121 4294 5159 2088 5045 7414 1192 428

sons the of the of tribe the inheri- of tance the This (is) the .south Ramah of ,beer to Baalath- these

9 שִׁמְעוֹן לְמִשְׁפְּחֹתָם׃ מֵחֶבֶל בְּנֵי יְהוּדָה נַחֲלַת בְּנֵי שִׁמְעוֹן

8095 1121 5159 3063 1121 2256 4940 8095

. Simeon the of sons the inher- of itance The Judah (was) the of sons the of out of portion their by .families Simeon

כִּי־הָיָה חֵלֶק בְּנֵי־יְהוּדָה רַב מֵהֶם וַיִּנְחֲלוּ בְנֵי־שִׁמְעוֹן

8095 1121 5159 7227 3063 1121 2256 1961

Simeon the of sons has and inheritance their them for much too Judah the of sons the of part was For

10 בְּתוֹךְ נַחֲלָתָם׃ וַיַּעַל הַגּוֹרָל הַשְּׁלִישִׁי לִבְנֵי זְבוּלֻן

2074 1121 7992 1486 5927 2506 8432

Zebulun the for of sons third lot the came And up their .inheritance within

according to their families
And the border of their
inheritance was to Sarid.
11 And their border went up
toward the sea, and Mara-
lah, and reached to Dab-
basheth, and reached to the
torrent which *is* in front of
Jokneam, 12 and turned
east from Sarid toward the
rising of the sun, to the
border of The Flames of
Tabor, and goes out to
Daberath, and goes up the
Japhia. 13 And from there it
passes on along on the east
to Gittah-hepher, to Ittah-
kazin, and goes out to
Rimmon-methoar to Neah.
14 And the border goes
around it on the north side
to Hannathon, and its outer
limits are *in the* valley of
Jiphtahel, 15 and Kattath,
and Nahallal, and Shimron,
and Idalah, and Bethlehem
—twelve cities and their
villages. 16 This is the
inheritance of the sons of
Zebulun according to their
families, these cities and
their villages.
17 The fourth lot came out
to Issachar, for the sons of
Issachar according to their
families. 18 And their border
was toward Jezreel, and
Chesulloth, and Shunem,
19 and Hapharaim, and Shi-
hon, and Anaharath, 20 and
Rabbith, and Kishion, and
Abez, 21 and Remeth, and
En-gannim, and En-haddah,
and Beth-pazzez. 22 And
the border reaches to
Tabor, and Shahazimah,
and Beth-shemesh. And
the outer limits of their
border were at Jordan—
sixteen cities and their
villages. 23 This is the
inheritance of the tribe of
the sons of Issachar according to their families, the
cities and their villages.
24 And the fifth lot came
out for the tribe of the sons
of Asher, according to their
families. 25 And their border
was Helkath, and Hali, and
Beten, and Achshaph,
26 and Allammelech, and
Amad, and Misheal, and

1366 6927 8301 5704 5159 1366 1961 4940
11 למשפחתם ויהי גבול נחלתם עד־שריד׃ ועלה גבולם
their border | And up went | .Sarid | to | their inheritance | the of border | And was | their by .families

834 5158 6293 1708 6293 4831 3220
לימה ומרעלה ופגע בדבשת ופגע אל־הנחל אשר על־
in | which | the (is) torrent | to | and reached | Dab- ,basheth | to | and reached | and ,Maralah | toward ,sea the

1366 8121 4217 6924 8301 7725 3362 6440
12 פני יקנעם׃ ושב משריד קדמה מזרח השמש על־גבול
the of border | to | the of ,sun | toward rising the | east | from Sarid | and turned | ,Jokneam | front of

5694 8033 3309 5927 1705 3318 8396 3689
13 כסלת תבר ויצא אל־הדברת ועלה יפיע׃ ומשם עבר
it passes | from there | And | to .Japhia | and up goes | ,Daberath | to | and out goes | tabor | Chisloth-

8388 7417 6278 2660 4217 6924
קדמה מזרחה גתה חפר עתה קצין ויצא רמון המתאר
methoar | to | goes and out | Rimmon | ,kazin | to Ittah | ,hepher | to | Gittah- | east the | along on

1516 8444 1961 2615 6828 1366 5437
14 הנעה׃ ונסב אתו הגבול מצפון חנתן והיו תצאתיו גי
val-ley | its edges | and are | Hanna-thon | the on (to) north | the border | it goes And around | to .Neah

1035 3030 8110 5096 7005 3317
15 יפתח־אל׃ וקטת ונהלל ושמרון וידאלה ובית לחם
and —Bethlehem | and ,Idlah | and ,Shimron | and ,Nahallal | and ,Kattath | ,Jiphtahel

2074 1121 5159 2088 2691 6240 8147 5892
16 ערים שתים־עשרה וחצריהן׃ זאת נחלת בני־זבולן
Zebulun | the of sons | inher-itance | the of | This (is) | their and .villages | ten (and) | two | cities

3318 3485 2691 428 5892 4940
17 למשפחתם הערים האלה וחצריהן׃ ליששכר יצא
came out | to as Issachar | their with .villages | these | cities | their by ,families

1366 1961 4940 3485 1121 7243 1486
18 הגורל הרביעי לבני יששכר למשפחתם׃ ויהי גבולם
their border | And was | their by .families | Issachar | the for of sons | fourth | lot The

588 7866 2663 7766 3694 3157
19 יזרעאלה והכסולת ושונם׃ וחפרים ושיאן ואנחרת׃
and ,Anaharath | and ,Shihon | and ,Hapharaim | and ,Shunem | and ,Chesulloth | toward ,Jezreel

1048 5876 5873 7432 77 7191 7245
20 21 והרבית וקשיון ואבץ׃ ורמת ועין־גנים ועין חדה ובית
and Beth- | haddah En- | and gannim En- | and ,Remeth | and ,Abez | and ,Kishion | and ,Rabbith

1961 1053 7831 8396 1366 6293 1048
22 פצץ׃ ופגע הגבול בתבור ושחצומה ובית שמש והיו
And were | .shemesh Beth- | and | and ,Shahazimah | ,Tabor to | the border | And reaches | .pazzez

2088 2691 6240 8337 5892 3383 1366 8444
23 תצאות גבולם הירדן ערים שש־עשרה וחצריהן׃ זאת
This (is) | their with .villages | sixteen | cities | at —Jordan | their border | edges the of

2691 5892 4940 3485 1121 4294 5159
נחלת מטה בני־יששכר למשפחתם הערים וחצריהן׃
their and .villages | the cities | their by ,families | of sons the Issachar | the of tribe | inher-itance the

4940 836 1121 4294 2549 1486 3318
24 ויצא הגורל החמישי למטה בני־אשר למשפחותם׃
their by .families | of sons the Asher | the for of tribe | fifth | the lot | came And out

6008 487 407 991 2482 2520 1366 1961
25 26 ויהי גבולם חלקת וחלי ובטן ואכשף׃ ואלמלך ועמעד
and ,Amad | and ,Allammelech | and ,Achsaph | and ,Beten | and ,Hali | ,Helkath | their border | And was

reaches to Carmel westward, and to Shihor-libnath.
27And it turns toward the east to Beth-dagon, and *it* reaches to Zebulun, and to the valley of Jiphthahel toward the north side of Beth-emek, and Neiel, and goes out to Cabul on the left hand,
28and Hebron, and Rehob, and Hammon, and Kanah to great Sidon.
29And the border turns to Ramah, and to the strong city Tyre. And the border turns to Hosah, and the outer limits of it are at the sea from the line to Achzib,
30and Ummah, and Aphek, and Rehob —twenty-two cities and their villages.
31This is the inheritance of the tribe of the sons of Asher according to their families, these cities and their villages.
32The sixth lot came out to the sons of Naphtali, for the sons of Naphtali by their families.
33And their border was from Heleph, from Allon to Zaanannim, and Adami, Nekeb, and Jabneel, to Lakum. And its boundaries were at Jordan.
34And the border turns west toward Aznoth-tabor, and goes out from there to Hukkok, and reached to Zebulun on the south side, and reaches to Asher on the west side, and to Judah on Jordan toward the rising of the sun —
35and the fortified cities are Ziddim, Zer, and Hammath, Rakkath, and Chinnereth,
36and Adamah, and Ramah, and Hazor,
372and Kedesh, and Edrei, and En-hazor,
38and Iron, and Migdalel, Horem, and Beth-anath, and Beth-shemesh — nineteen cities and their villages.
39This is the inheritance of the tribe of the sons of Naphtali by their families, the cities and their villages.

40The seventh lot came out for the tribe of the sons of Dan by their families.

4217 2884 3220 3760 6293 4861
27 ומשאל ופגע בכרמל הימה ובשיחור לבנת: ושב מזרח
the toward And .libnath to and westward to and and
of rising turns it Shihor Carmel reaches ,Misheal

6828 3317 1516 2074 6293 1016 8121
השמש בית דגן ופגע בזבלון ובגי יפתח־אל צפונה
the to Jephthahel the to and to and dagon to sun the
side north of valley Zebulun reaches Beth-

7340 5683 8040 3521 3318 5272 1025
28 בית העמק ונעיאל ויצא אל־כבול משמאל: ועברן ורחב
and and the on Cabul to goes and and ,emek of
,Rehob ,Hebron hand left out ,Neiel Beth-

5704 7414 1366 7725 7227 6721 5704 7071 2540
29 וחמון וקנה עד צידון רבה: ושב הגבול הרמה ועד־
and to the And .great Sidon to and and
to ,Ramah border turns Kanah ,Hammon

3220 8444 1961 2621 1366 7725 6805 4013 5892
עיר מבצר־צר ושב הגבול חסה ויהיו תצאתיו הימה
the at its and to the And .Tyre strong the
sea boundaries are ,Hosah border turns city

8147 6242 5892 7340 663 5981 392 2256
30 מחבל אכזיבה: ועמה ואפק ורחב ערים עשרים ושתים
two twenty- cities and and also to the from
—Rehob ,Aphek ,Ummah ,Achzib line

4940 836 1121 4294 5159 2088 2691
31 וחצריהן: זאת נחלת מטה בני־אשר למשפחתם
their by of sons the tribe the inher- the This their with
,families Asher of of itance is ,villages

1486 3318 5320 6440 2691 428 5892
32 הערים האלה וחצריהן: לבני נפתלי יצא הגורל
lot The came ,Naphtali to as their with these cities
out of sons the ,villages

2501 1366 1961 4940 5320 1121 8345
33 הששי לבני נפתלי למשפחתם: ויהי גבולם מחלף
from their And their by Naphtali the for sixth
,Heleph border was ,families of sons

1961 3946 2995 5346 129 6815 438
מאלון בצעננים ואדמי הנקב ויבנאל עד־לקום ויהי
And .Lakum to and ,Nekeb and to from
were ,Jabneel ,Adami ,Zaanannim Allon

3318 243 3320 1366 7725 3383 8444
34 תצאתיו הירדן: ושב הגבול ימה אזנות תבור ויצא
and ,tabor toward west the And at its
out goes Aznoth border turns .Jordan boundaries

3063 3220 6293 834 5045 2074 6293 2712 8033
משם חקקה ופגע בזבלון מנגב ובאשר פגע מים וביהודה
to and the on reaches to and the on to and to from
Judah ,side west Asher ,side south Zebulun reaches ,Hukkok there

2575 6863 6661 4013 5892 8121 4217 3383
35 הירדן מזרח השמש: וערי מבצר הצדים צר וחמת
and ,Zer ,Ziddim fortified the And ..sun the rising the on
,Hammath :(were) cities of Jordan

154 6943 2674 7414 128 3672 7557
36
37 רקת וכנרת: ואדמה והרמה וחצור: וקדש ואדרעי
and and and and and and ,Rakkath
,Edrei ,Kedesh Hazor ,Ramah ,Adamah .Chinnereth

1053 1043 2765 4026 3375 5877
38 ועין חצור: ויראון ומגדל־אל חרם ובית־ענת ובית שמש
shemesh and ,anath and ,Horem and and ,hazor and
Beth- Beth- ,Migdalel ,Iron En-

5320 1121 4294 5159 2088 2691 6240 8672 5892
39 ערים תשע־עשרה וחצריהן: זאת נחלת מטה בני־נפתלי
Naphtali the the inher- the This their and ten (and) nine cities
of sons of tribe of tance (is) .villages

1835 1121 4294 2691 5892 4940
40 למשפחתם הערים וחצריהן: למטה בני־דן
Dan the the For their and the their by
of sons of tribe .villages cities ,families

[41]And the border of their inheritance was Zorah, and Eshtaol, and Ir-shemesh, [42]and Shaalabbin, and Ajalon, and Jethlah, [43]and Elon, and Timnathah, and Ekron,, [44]and Eltekeh, and Gibbethon, and Baalath, [45]and Jehud, and Bene-berak, and Gath-rimmon, [46]and Mejarkon, and Rakkon, with the border before Japho. [47]And the border of the sons of Dan came out *too little* for them. And the sons of Dan went up to fight against Leshem, and took it, and struck it with the mouth of the sword, and possessed it, and lived in it. And *they* called Leshem Dan, after the name of their father Dan. [48]This is the inheritance of the tribe of the sons of Dan by their families, these cities and their villages.

[49]When they had made an end of dividing the land for inheritance by their borders, the sons of Israel gave an inheritance to Joshua the son of Nun among them. [50]According to the mouth of Jehovah, they gave him the city which he asked, Timnath-serah in Mount Ephraim. And he built the city and lived in it.

[51]These are the inheritances which Eleazar the priest, and Joshua the son of Nun, and the heads of the fathers of the tribes of the sons of Israel divided for an inheritance by lot in Shiloh before Jehovah, at the door of the tabernacle of the congregation. So they finished dividing the country.

5159 1366 1961 7637 1486 3318 4940
41 למשפחתם יצא הגורל השביעי: ויהי גבול נחלתם
inher- their the And .seventh lot The came their by
itance of border was .out .families

3494 1357 8168 5905 5905 847 6881
42 צרעה ואשתאול ועיר שמש: ושעלבין ואילון ויתלה:
and and and ,shemesh Ir- and and ,Zorah
Jethlah ,Ajalon ,Shaalabbin ,Eshtaol

1191 1405 514 6138 8553 1356
43 ואילון ותמנתה ועקרון: ואלתקה וגבתון ובעלת:
44
and and and and Tim- and and
,Baalath ,Gibbethon ,Eltekeh ,Ekron ,nathah ,Elon

1366 7542 4313 1667 1139 3055
45 ויהד ובני־ברק וגת־רמון: ומי הירקון והרקון עם־הגבול
46
the with and and ,rimmon and ,berek and and
border ,Rakkon ,Mejarkon Gath- Bene- ,Jehud

3898 1835/1121 5927 1835/1121 1366 3318 3305
47 מול יפו: ויצא גבול בני־דן מהם ויעלו בני־דן וילחמו
fight to Dan the went And (too) Dan the border the And .Japho before
of sons up .them for (little) of sons of out came

3423 2719/6310 5221 3920 3954
עם־לשם וילכדו אותה ויכו אותה לפי־חרב וירשו
and the by it and it took and against
seized ,sword's edge struck ,Leshem

1 8034 1835 3959 7121 3427
אותה וישבו בה ויקראו ללשם דן כשם דן אביהם:
their Dan after ,Dan Leshem they And .it in and ,it
.father of name the called lived

428 5892 4940 1835/1121 4294 5159 2088
48 זאת נחלת מטה בני־דן למשפחתם הערים האלה
these cities their by Dan the the inher- the This
,families of sons of tribe of itance is

5414 1367 776 5157 3615 2691
49 וחצריהן: ויכלו לנחל את־הארץ לגבולתיה ויתנו
and their by land the dividing they And their with
gave ;borders inheritance for ended .villages

3068 6310 8437 5626/1121 3091 5159 3478 1121
50 בני־ישראל נחלה ליהושע בן־נון בתוכם: על־פי יהוה
Jehovah According among Nun the Joshua to in- an Israel the
of word the to .them of son heritance of sons

2022 = 8556 = 7592 834 5892 5414
נתנו לו את־העיר אשר שאל את־תמנת־סרח בהר
on serah Timnath- ,asked he which city the to they
Mount him gave

834 5159 428 3427 5892 1129 669
51 אפרים ויבנה את־העיר וישב בה: אלה הנחלת אשר
which inher- the These .it in and city the he And .Ephraim
itances are lived built

4294 1 7218 5126/1121 3091 3548 499 5157
נחלו אלעזר הכהן ויהושע בן־נון וראשי האבות למטות
the of the the and Nun the and the Eleazar alloted
of tribes fathers of heads of son Joshua ,priest

4150 168 6607 3068 6440 7887 1486 3478 1121
בני־ישראל בגורל בשלה לפני יהוה פתח אהל מועד
.meeting the the at ,Jehovah before in lot by of sons the
of tent of door Shiloh Israel

776 2505 3615
ויכלו מחלק את־הארץ:
.land the dividing they And
finished

CAP. XX כ

CHAPTER 20

CHAPTER 20

[1]And Jehovah spoke to Joshua, saying, [2]Speak to the sons of Israel, saying,

3478 1121 1696 559 3091 3068 1696
1 וידבר יהוה אל־יהושע לאמר: דבר אל־בני ישראל
2
,Israel the to Speak ,saying ,Joshua to Jehovah And
of sons spoke

Appoint cities of refuge for you, as I have spoken to you by the hand of Moses,
[3]that the manslayer who in innocence strikes anyone mortally, without knowing, may flee there. And they shall be your refuge from the avenger of blood. [4]And he shall flee to one of those cities, and shall stand at the entrance of the gate of the city, and shall declare his matter in the ears of the elders of that city. And they shall take him into the city to themselves, and shall give him a place, and he shall live with them. [5]And if the avenger of blood pursues him, then they shall not deliver the manslayer into his hand, for he has struck his neighbor without knowing, and did not hate him yesterday and the day before. [6]And he shall live in that city until he stands before the congregation for judgment, until the death of the high priest who is in those days. Then the manslayer shall return and come to his city, and to his house, to the city from where he fled.

[7]And they set apart Kadesh in Galilee, in the hills of Naphtali; and Shechem in the hills of Ephraim; and Kirjath-arba — it *is* Hebron — in the hills of Judah. [8]And beyond the Jordan, *at* Jericho eastward, they gave Bezer in the wilderness, on the tableland out of the tribe of Reuben; and Ramoth in Gilead out of the tribe of Gad; and Golan in Bashan out of the tribe of Manasseh. [9]These were the appointed cities for all the sons of Israel, and for the alien who was living in their

לאמר תנו לכם את־ערי המקלט אשר־דברתי אליכם
3 ביד־משה: לנוס שמה רוצח מכה־נפש בשגגה בבלי־
4 דעת והיו לכם למקלט מגאל הדם: ונס אל־אחת
מהערים האלה ועמד פתח שער העיר ודבר באזני
זקני העיר־ההיא את־דבריו ואספו אתו העירה אליהם
5 ונתנו־לו מקום וישב עמם: וכי ירדף גאל הדם אחריו
ולא־יסגרו את־הרצח בידו כי בבלי־דעת הכה את־רעהו
6 ולא־שנא הוא לו מתמול שלשום: וישב ׀ בעיר ההיא
עד־עמדו לפני העדה למשפט עד־מות הכהן הגדול
אשר יהיה בימים ההם אז ׀ ישוב הרוצח ובא אל־עירו
7 ואל־ביתו אל־העיר אשר־נס משם: ויקדשו את־קדש
בגליל בהר נפתלי ואת־שכם בהר אפרים ואת־קרית
8 ארבע היא חברון בהר יהודה: ומעבר לירדן יריחו
מזרחה נתנו את־בצר במדבר במישר ממטה ראובן
ואת־ראמת בגלעד ממטה־גד ואת־גולן בבשן ממטה
9 מנשה: אלה היו ערי המועדה לכל ׀ בני ישראל ולגר

midst, that he who had struck anyone mortally without knowing might flee there, and not die by the hand of the avenger of blood, until he stood before the congregation.

CHAPTER 21

[1]And the heads of the fathers of the Levites came near to Eleazar the priest, and to Joshua the son of Nun, and to the heads of the fathers of the tribes of the sons of Israel. [2]And they spoke to them in Shiloh, in the land of Canaan, saying, Jehovah commanded by the hand of Moses to give cities to us to live in, and their open land for our livestock. [3]And the sons of Israel gave to the Levites out of their inheritance these cities and their open land, at the command of Jehovah:

[4]And the lot came out for the families of the Kohathites. And the sons of Aaron the priest, of the Levites, had by lot out of the tribe of Judah, and out of the tribe of Simeon, and out of the tribe of Benjamin, thirteen cities.

[5]And the rest of the sons of Kohath had by lot out of the families of the tribe of Ephraim, and out of the tribe of Dan, and out of the half tribe of Manasseh, ten cities.

[6]And the sons of Gershon had by lot out of the families of the tribe of Issachar, and out of the tribe of Asher, and out of the tribe of Naphtali, and out of the half tribe of Manasseh in Bashan, thirteen cities.

[7]The sons of Merari by their families had out of the tribe of Reuben, and out of the tribe of Gad, and out of the tribe of Zebulun, twelve cities.

[8]And the sons of Israel gave by lot to the Levites

4191 3808 1847 5315 5221 3605 5127 8432 1481
הַגָּר בְּתוֹכָם לָנוּס שָׁמָּה כָּל־מַכֵּה־נֶפֶשׁ בִּשְׁגָגָה וְלֹא יָמוּת
should and without killed had who he ,there might that their in who
die not ,knowing anyone flee ,midst living was

5712 6440 5975 5704 1818 1350 3027
בְּיַד גֹּאֵל הַדָּם עַד־עָמְדוֹ לִפְנֵי הָעֵדָה׃
the before he until ,blood the the by
.congregation stood of avenger of hand

CAP. XXI כא

CHAPTER 21

1 3091 3548 499 3881 1 7218 5066
וַיִּגְּשׁוּ רָאשֵׁי אֲבוֹת הַלְוִיִּם אֶל־אֶלְעָזָר הַכֹּהֵן וְאֶל־יְהוֹשֻׁעַ
Joshua and the Eleazar to the fathers the the came And
to priest Levites of of heads near

2 1696 3478 1121 4294 1 7218 5126 1121
בִּן־נוּן וְאֶל־רָאשֵׁי אֲבוֹת הַמַּטּוֹת לִבְנֵי יִשְׂרָאֵל׃ וַיְדַבְּרוּ
they and ;Israel the of the father's the the and Nun the
spoke of sons of tribes of of heads to of son

4872 3027 6680 3068 559 3667 776 7887
אֲלֵיהֶם בְּשִׁלֹה בְּאֶרֶץ כְּנַעַן לֵאמֹר יְהוָה צִוָּה בְיַד־מֹשֶׁה
Moses the by com- Jehovah ,saying ,Canaan the in ,Shiloh in them to
of hand manded of land

3 1121 5414 929 4054 3427 5892 5414
לָתֶת־לָנוּ עָרִים לָשָׁבֶת וּמִגְרְשֵׁיהֶן לִבְהֶמְתֵּנוּ׃ וַיִּתְּנוּ בְנֵי־
the And our for open with live to cities us to to
of sons gave .cattle land their in give

428 5892 3068 6310 5159 3881 3478
יִשְׂרָאֵל לַלְוִיִּם מִנַּחֲלָתָם אֶל־פִּי יְהוָה אֶת־הֶעָרִים הָאֵלֶּה
these cities ,Jehovah the at their of out the to Israel
of mouth ,inheritance ,Levites

4 1961 6956 4940 1486 3318 4054
וְאֶת־מִגְרְשֵׁיהֶן׃ וַיֵּצֵא הַגּוֹרָל לְמִשְׁפְּחֹת הַקְּהָתִי וַיְהִי
And the the for the came And open their and
had .Kohathites of families lot out .land

8099 3063 4294 3881 3548 175 1121
לִבְנֵי אַהֲרֹן הַכֹּהֵן מִן־הַלְוִיִּם מִמַּטֵּה יְהוּדָה וּמִמַּטֵּה
from and ,Judah the from the of the Aaron the
of tribe the of tribe ,Levites ,priest of sons

6240 7969 5892 1486 1144 4294 8059
הַשִּׁמְעֹנִי וּמִמַּטֵּה בִנְיָמִן בַּגּוֹרָל עָרִים שְׁלֹשׁ עֶשְׂרֵה׃
.thirteen cities lot by ,Benjamin from and ,Simeon
of tribe the

5 4294 669 4294 4940 3498 6955 1121
וְלִבְנֵי קְהָת הַנּוֹתָרִים מִמִּשְׁפְּחֹת מַטֵּה־אֶפְרַיִם וּמִמַּטֵּה־
from and ,Ephraim the the from rest the Kohath And
of tribe the of tribe of families of sons the

6 1121 6235 5892 1486 4519 4294 2677 1835
דָן וּמֵחֲצִי מַטֵּה מְנַשֶּׁה בַּגּוֹרָל עָרִים עָשֶׂר׃ וְלִבְנֵי
had And .ten cities lot by ,Manasseh tribe from and ,Dan
of sons the of half the

4294 836 4294 3485 4294 4940 1648
גֵרְשׁוֹן מִמִּשְׁפְּחוֹת מַטֵּה־יִשָּׂשכָר וּמִמַּטֵּה־אָשֵׁר וּמִמַּטֵּה
from and ,Asher from and ,Issachar the the from Gershon
of tribe the of tribe the of tribe of families

7969 5892 1486 1316 4519 4294 2677 5320
נַפְתָּלִי וּמֵחֲצִי מַטֵּה מְנַשֶּׁה בַבָּשָׁן בַּגּוֹרָל עָרִים שְׁלֹשׁ
three cities lot by ,Bashan in ,Manasseh tribe from and ,Naphtali
of half the

7 7205 4294 4940 4847 1121 6240
עֶשְׂרֵה׃ לִבְנֵי מְרָרִי לְמִשְׁפְּחֹתָם מִמַּטֵּה רְאוּבֵן
,Reuben the from families their by Merari of sons The ten (and)
of tribe

8 5414 6240 8147 5892 2074 4294 1410 4294
וּמִמַּטֵּה־גָד וּמִמַּטֵּה זְבוּלֻן עָרִים שְׁתֵּים עֶשְׂרֵה׃ וַיִּתְּנוּ
gave And ten (and) two cities ,Zebulun from and Gad from and
of tribe the of tribe the

these cities with their open land, as Jehovah commanded by the hand of Moses.

[9]And they gave out of the tribe of the sons of Judah, and out of the tribe of the sons of Simeon, these cities which are called by name, [10]which the sons of Aaron had, being of the families of the Kohathites, who were of the sons of Levi. For theirs was the first lot. [11]And they gave them the city of Arba, the father of Anak—which *is* Hebron—in the hills of Judah, with its open lands around it. [12]But the fields of the city, and its villages, they gave to Caleb the son of Jephunneh for his own.

[13]So they gave Hebron and its open lands to the sons of Aaron the priest *as* a city of refuge for the slayer, and Libnah and its open lands, [14]and Jattir and its open lands, and Eshtemoa and its open lands, [15]and Holon and its open lands, and Debir and its open lands, [16]and Ain and its open lands, and Juttah and its open lands, and Beth-shemesh and its open lands—nine cities out of those two tribes. [17]And out of the tribe of Benjamin, Gibeon and its open lands, Geba and its open lands, [18]Anathoth and its open lands, and Almon and its open lands—four cities. [19]And all the cities of the sons of Aaron the priest *were* thirteen cities and their open land.

4054 428 5892 3881 3478 1121
בני־ישראל ללוים את־הערים האלה ואת־מגרשיהן
open their land and these cities the to Levites Israel the of sons

9 4294 5414 1486 4872 3027 3068 6680
כאשר צוה יהוה ביד־משה בגורל׃ ויתנו ממטה
the from of tribe they And gave .lot by Moses the by of hand Jehovah com- manded as

834 428 5892 8095 1121 4294 3063 1121
בני יהודה וממטה בני שמעון את הערים האלה אשר
which these cities ,Simeon the of sons from and of tribe the ,Judah the of sons

10 6956 4940 175 1121 1961 8034 7121
יקרא אתהן בשם׃ ויהי לבני אהרן ממשפחות הקהתי
the ,Kohathites the of families (being) ,Aaron the of sons which had by ,name are called

11 5414 7223 1486 1961 3881 1121
מבני לוי כי להם היה הגורל ראישנה׃ ויתנו להם את־
them And gave they .first lot the was to them for ,Levi from of sons the

3063 2022 2275 6061 1 7153
קרית ארבע אבי הענוק היא חברון בהר יהודה ואת־
with ,Judah the in of hill-country ,Hebron which (is) ,Anak the of father arba Kirjath-

12 5414 2691 5892 7704 5439 4054
מגרשה סביבתיה׃ ואת־שדה העיר ואת־חצריה נתנו
they gave its ,villages and ,city the the of fields But .it around open its lands

13 5414 3548 175 1121 272 3312 3612
לכלב בן־יפנה באחזתו׃ ולבני אהרן הכהן נתנו
they gave the ,priest Aaron the to And of sons his for .property of son the Jephunneh to Caleb

4054 2275 7523 4733 5892
את־עיר מקלט הרצח את־חברון ואת־מגרשיה ואת־
and, ,lands open its and Hebron the for ,slayer refuge a (as) of city

14 4054 8492 4054 3841
לבנה ואת־מגרשה ואת־יתר ואת־מגרשה ואת־
and ,lands open its and Jattir and ,lands open its and Libnah

15 4054 2473 4054 851
אשתמע ואת־מגרשה׃ ואת־חלן ואת־מגרשה ואת־
and ,lands open its and Holon and ,lands open its and Eshtemoa

16 3194 4054 5871 4054 1688
דבר ואת־מגרשה׃ ואת־עין ואת־מגרשה ואת־יטה
Juttah and ,lands open its and Ain and ,lands open its and Debir

8672 5892 4054 1053 4054
ואת־מגרשה את־בית שמש ואת־מגרשה ערים תשע
nine cities —lands open its and shemmesh Beth- ,lands open its and

17 1144 4294 428 7626 8147
מאת שני השבטים האלה׃ וממטה בנימן את־
Benjamin from And of tribe the .these tribes the two from

18 6068 4054 1387 4054 1391
גבעון ואת־מגרשה את־גבע ואת־מגרשה׃ את־ענתות
Anathoth ,lands open its and Geba ,lands open its and Gibeon

702 5892 4054 5960 4054
ואת־מגרשה ואת־עלמון ואת־מגרשה ערים ארבע׃
.four cities —lands open its and Almon and ,lands open its and

19 4054 5892 6240 7969 3548 175 1121 5892 3605
כל־ערי בני־אהרן הכהנים שלש־עשרה ערים ומגרשיהן׃
their and .land open cities (were) thirteen ,priests the Aaron the of sons the of cities All

[20]And the families of the
sons of Kohath, the Levites
who were left of the sons of
Kohath, even they had the
cities of their lot out of the
tribe of Ephraim. [21]And they
gave them Shechem and its
open land in Mount Ephraim
as a city of refuge *for* the
manslayer, and Gezer and
its open lands, [22]and Kibzaim and its open lands, and
Beth-horon and its open
lands—four cities. [23]And
out of the tribe of Dan,
Eltekeh and its open lands,
Gibbethon and its open
lands, [24]Aijalon and its
open lands, Gath-rimmon
and its open lands—four
cities. [25]And out of the half
tribe of Manasseh, Tanach
and its open lands, and
Gath-rimmon and its open
lands—two cities. [26]All the
cities *were* ten, and their
open land, for the families of
the sons of Kohath that
were left.

[27]And to the sons of
Gershon, of the families of
the Levites, from the half
tribe of Manasseh *they gave*
Golan in Bashan and its
open lands as a city of
refuge for the manslayer,
and Beesh-terah and its
open lands—two cities.
[28]And from the tribe of
Issachar *they gave* Kishon
and its open lands, and
Dabareh and its open lands,
[29]Jarmuth and its open
lands, En-gannim and its
open lands—four cities.

[30]And out of the tribe of
Asher, Mishal and its open
lands, Abdon and its open
lands, [31]Helkath and its
open lands, Rehob and its
open lands—four cities.

20 ולמשפחות בני־קהת הלוים הנותרים מבני קהת
,Kohath the of sons were who left the Levites Kohath the of sons the And of families

21 ויהי ערי גורלם ממטה אפרים: ויתנו להם את־עיר
the of city them they For gave .Ephraim the from of tribe their lot cities of even had they

מקלט הרצח את־שכם ואת־מגרשה בהר אפרים ואת־
and ,Ephraim in Mount lands open its and Shechem the (for) manslayer refuge

22 גזר ואת־מגרשה: ואת־קבצים ואת־מגרשה ואת־בית
Beth- and ,lands open its and Kibzaim and ,lands open its and Gezer

23 חרון ואת־מגרשה ערים ארבע: וממטה־דן את־
Dan from and of tribe the .four cities —lands open its and horon

24 אלתקא ואת־מגרשה את־גבתון ואת־מגרשה: את־אילון
Aijalon ,lands open its and Gibbethon ,lands open its and Elteke

ואת־מגרשה את־גת־רמון ואת־מגרשה ערים ארבע:
.four cities —lands open its and Gathrimmon ,lands open its and

25 וממחצית מטה מנשה את־תענך ואת־מגרשה ואת־גת
Gath- and ,lands open its and Tanach ,Manasseh tribe of from And half the

26 רמון ואת־מגרשה ערים שתים: כל־ערים עשר
.ten (were) cities the All .two cities —lands open its and rimmon

27 ומגרשיהן למשפחות בני־קהת הנותרים: ולבני גרשון
,Gershon to And of sons the were that .left Kohath the of sons the for of families their and lands open

ממשפחת הלוים מחצי מטה מנשה את־עיר מקלט
refuge city the of Manasseh tribe of the from half ,Levites the the of of families

הרצח את־גולן בבשן ואת־מגרשה ואת־בעשתרה ואת־
and terah Beesh- and ,lands open its and in Bashan Golan the for man-slayer

28 מגרשה ערים שתים: וממטה יששכר את־קשיון
Kishon Issachar (gave they) the from And of tribe .two cities open its —lands

29 ואת־מגרשה את־דברת ואת־מגרשה: את־ירמות ואת־
and Jarmuth ,lands open its and Dabarah ,lands open its and

מגרשה את־עין גנים ואת־מגרשה ערים ארבע:
.four cities —lands open its and gannin En- ,lands open its

30 וממטה אשר את־משאל ואת־מגרשה את־עבדון ואת־
and Abdon ,lands open its and Mishal ,Asher from And of tribe the

31 מגרשה: את־חלקת ואת־מגרשה ואת־רחב ואת־מגרשה
,lands open its and Rehob and ,lands open its and Helkath open its ,lands

[32]And out of the tribe of
Naphtali, Kedesh in Galilee
and its open lands as a city
of refuge for the manslayer,
and Hammoth-dor and its
open lands, and Kartan and
its open lands—three cities.
[33]All the cities of the
Gershonites according to
their families *were* thirteen
cities and their open land.

[34]And to the families of
the sons of Merari, the rest
of the Levites, out of the
tribe of Zebulun, *they gave*
Jokneam and its open
lands, and Kartah and its
open lands, [35]Dimnah and
its open lands, Nahalal and
its open lands—four cities.
[36]And out of the tribe of
Reuben, Bezer and its open
lands, and Jahazah and its
open lands, [37]Kedemoth
and its open lands, and
Mephaath and its open
lands—four cities. [38]And
out of the tribe of Gad,
Ramoth in Gilead and its
open lands as a city of
refuge for the manslayer,
and Mahanaim and its open
lands, [39]Heshbon and its
open land, Jazer and its
open lands—four cities in
all. [40]So all the cities for the
sons of Merari by their
families, *those* left of the
families of the Levites, *were*
by their lot twelve cities.
[41]All the cities of the
Levites within the possession of the sons of Israel
were forty-eight cities and
their open land. [42]These
cities were every one with
their open land around
them. So *it was* to all these
cities.

[43]And Jehovah gave to
Israel all the land which He
swore to give to their
fathers. And they possessed
it, and lived in it. [44]And
Jehovah gave them rest
round about, according to
all that He swore to their
fathers. And not a man of all

7523 4733 5892 5320 4294 702 5892
32 עָרִים אַרְבַּע׃ וּמִמַּטֵּה נַפְתָּלִי אֶת־עִיר ׀ מִקְלַט הָרֹצֵחַ
the (for) refuge ,slayer — city the of — ,Naphtali from And of tribe the — .four — cities

2576 4054 1551 6943
אֶת־קֶדֶשׁ בַּגָּלִיל וְאֶת־מִגְרָשֶׁהָ וְאֶת־חַמֹּת דֹּאר וְאֶת־
and dor Hammoth-and ,lands open its and Galilee in Kedesh

5892 7969 5892 4054 7178 4054
33 מִגְרָשֶׁהָ וְאֶת־קַרְתָּן וְאֶת־מִגְרָשֶׁהָ עָרִים שָׁלֹשׁ׃ כָּל־עָרֵי
the All of cities — three — cities —lands open its and Kartom and — open its .lands

4054 5892 7969 4940 1649
הַגֵּרְשֻׁנִּי לְמִשְׁפְּחֹתָם שְׁלֹשׁ־עֶשְׂרֵה עִיר וּמִגְרְשֵׁיהֶן׃
their and .land open — cities — (were) thirteen — to according families their — the Gershonites

2074 4294 3498 3881 4847 1121 4940
34 וּלְמִשְׁפְּחוֹת בְּנֵי־מְרָרִי הַלְוִיִּם הַנּוֹתָרִים מֵאֵת מַטֵּה זְבוּלֻן
:Zebulun — the from of tribe — ,of rest the — the Levites — ,Merari — the of sons — the to And of families

4054 7177 4054 3362
35 אֶת־יָקְנְעָם וְאֶת־מִגְרָשֶׁהָ אֶת־קַרְתָּה וְאֶת־מִגְרָשֶׁהָ׃ אֶת־
,lands open its and Kartah ,lands open its and Jokneam

702 5892 4054 5096 4054 1829
דִּמְנָה וְאֶת־מִגְרָשֶׁהָ אֶת־נַהֲלָל וְאֶת־מִגְרָשֶׁהָ עָרִים אַרְבַּע׃
.four cities —lands open its and Nahalal ,lands open its and Dimnah

7418 7523 4733 5892 1410 4294
36 וּמִמַּטֵּה־גָד אֶת־עִיר מִקְלַט הָרֹצֵחַ אֶת־רָמֹת
Ramoth — the (for) ,manslayer — refuge — city the of — ,Gad from And of tribe the

4054 4266 4054 1568
37 בַּגִּלְעָד וְאֶת־מִגְרָשֶׁהָ וְאֶת־מַחֲנַיִם וְאֶת־מִגְרָשֶׁהָ׃ אֶת־
,lands open its and Mahanaim and ,lands open its and Gilead in

5892 4054 3270 4054 2809
חֶשְׁבּוֹן וְאֶת־מִגְרָשֶׁהָ אֶת־יַעְזֵר וְאֶת־מִגְרָשֶׁהָ כָּל־עָרִים
cities all in —lands open its and Jazer ,lands open its and Heshbon

3498 4940 4847 1121 5892 3605 702
38 אַרְבַּע׃ כָּל־הֶעָרִים לִבְנֵי מְרָרִי לְמִשְׁפְּחֹתָם הַנּוֹתָרִים
who (those) left were — their by ,families — Merari — the for of sons — the cities — (So) all — .four

3605 6240 8147 5892 1486 1961 3881 4940
39 מִמִּשְׁפְּחוֹת הַלְוִיִּם וַיְהִי גּוֹרָלָם עָרִים שְׁתֵּים עֶשְׂרֵה׃ כֹּל
All — .twelve — cities — by lot their — were — the ,Levites — the of families

8083 703 5892 3478 1121 272 8432 3881 5892
עָרֵי הַלְוִיִּם בְּתוֹךְ אֲחֻזַּת בְּנֵי־יִשְׂרָאֵל עָרִים אַרְבָּעִים וּשְׁמֹנֶה
and eight — forty — cities — Israel (were) — the of sons — pos- the session — within — the Levities — the of cities

4054 428 5892 1961 4054
40 וּמִגְרְשֵׁיהֶן׃ תִּהְיֶינָה הֶעָרִים הָאֵלֶּה עִיר עִיר וּמִגְרָשֶׁיהָ
their and lands open — each one — These — cities — were — their and .lands open

3478 3068 5414 428 5892 3605 5439
41 סְבִיבֹתֶיהָ כֵּן לְכָל־הֶעָרִים הָאֵלֶּה׃ וַיִּתֵּן יְהוָה לְיִשְׂרָאֵל
Israel to Jehovah And gave — .these — cities — all to — So (was it) — around .them

3427 3423 7650 834 776 3605
אֶת־כָּל־הָאָרֶץ אֲשֶׁר נִשְׁבַּע לָתֵת לַאֲבוֹתָם וַיִּרָשׁוּהָ וַיֵּשְׁבוּ
and they lived — And it possessed — their .fathers — to give to — He swore — which — land the — all

7650 3605 5439 3068 5117
42 בָהּ׃ וַיָּנַח יְהוָה לָהֶם מִסָּבִיב כְּכֹל אֲשֶׁר־נִשְׁבַּע לַאֲבוֹתָם
their to .fathers — swore he — that — according all to — round ,about — them — Jehovah — And rest gave — .it in

*SEE NOTE ON PAGE 629, REGARDING VERSES 36 AND 37.

their enemies stood before them. Jehovah delivered all their enemies into their hand. [45]Not any good thing which Jehovah had spoken to the house of Israel failed. All came to pass.

341 3605 341 3605 6440 376 5975 3808
וְלֹא־עָמַד אִישׁ בִּפְנֵיהֶם מִכָּל־אֹיְבֵיהֶם אֵת כָּל־אֹיְבֵיהֶם
their all — their all of before a stood And
enemies ;enemies them man not

43 834 2896 1697 3605 1697 5307 3808 3027 3068 5414
נָתַן יְהוָה בְּיָדָם׃ לֹא־נָפַל דָּבָר מִכֹּל הַדָּבָר הַטּוֹב אֲשֶׁר־
which good word from word a did Not into Jehovah gave
any fall ,hand their

935 3605 3478 1004 3068 1696
דִּבֶּר יְהוָה אֶל־בֵּית יִשְׂרָאֵל הַכֹּל בָּא׃
came All .Israel the to Jehovah had
.pass to of house spoken

CAP. XXII כב

CHAPTER 22

CHAPTER 22

[1]Then Joshua called for the Reubenites, and the Gadites, and the half tribe of Manasseh, [2]and said to them, You have done all that which Moses the servant of Jehovah commanded you. And you have listened to my voice, to all that I have commanded you. [3]You have not left your brothers these many days until today, and have kept the observance of the command of Jehovah your God. [4]And now Jehovah your God has given rest to your brothers, as He spoke to them. And now you turn and go to your tents, to the land of your possession, which Moses the servant of Jehovah has given to you beyond the Jordan. [5]Only, diligently take heed to do the commands and the law which Moses the servant of Jehovah commanded you, to love Jehovah your God, and to walk in all His ways, and to keep His commandments, and to cleave to Him, and to serve Him with all your heart and with all your soul. [6]And Joshua blessed them and sent them away. And they went to their tents.

[7]And to the half tribe of Manasseh, Moses had given *possession* in Bashan. And to its *other* half Joshua

4519 4294 2677 1425 7206 3091 7121
1 אָז יִקְרָא יְהוֹשֻׁעַ לָרְאוּבֵנִי וְלַגָּדִי וְלַחֲצִי מַטֵּה מְנַשֶּׁה׃
,Manasseh tribe the and the and the for Joshua called Then
of half ,Gadites Reubenites

6680 834 3605 8104 559
2 וַיֹּאמֶר אֲלֵיהֶם אַתֶּם שְׁמַרְתֶּם אֵת כָּל־אֲשֶׁר צִוָּה אֶתְכֶם
you com- that all have You ,them to said and
manded observed

6680 834 3605 6963 8085 3068 5650 4872
מֹשֶׁה עֶבֶד יְהוָה וַתִּשְׁמְעוּ בְקוֹלִי לְכֹל אֲשֶׁר־צִוִּיתִי אֶתְכֶם׃
.you have I that all to my to you and ;Jehovah the Moses
commanded voice listened have of servant

2088 3117 5704 7227 3117 2088 251 5800 3808
3 לֹא־עֲזַבְתֶּם אֶת־אֲחֵיכֶם זֶה יָמִים רַבִּים עַד הַיּוֹם הַזֶּה
;this day to many days these your You not
brothers left have

5117 430 3068 4687 4931 8104
4 וּשְׁמַרְתֶּם אֶת־מִשְׁמֶרֶת מִצְוַת יְהוָה אֱלֹהֵיכֶם׃ וְעַתָּה הֵנִיחַ
given has And .God your Jehovah the observance the have and
rest now of command of kept

3212 6437 6258 1696 251 430 3068
יְהוָה אֱלֹהֵיכֶם לַאֲחֵיכֶם כַּאֲשֶׁר דִּבֶּר לָהֶם וְעַתָּה פְּנוּ וּלְכוּ
and you and to He as your to God your Jehovah
go turn ,now ;them spoke brothers

4872 5414 834 272 776 168
לָכֶם לְאָהֳלֵיכֶם אֶל־אֶרֶץ אֲחֻזַּתְכֶם אֲשֶׁר נָתַן לָכֶם מֹשֶׁה
Moses to has which your the to your to
you given possession of land ,tents

6213 3966 8104 7535 3383 5676 3068 5650
5 עֶבֶד יְהוָה בְּעֵבֶר הַיַּרְדֵּן׃ רַק שִׁמְרוּ מְאֹד לַעֲשׂוֹת אֶת־
do to very be ,Only the beyond Jehovah the
watchful .Jordan of servant

3068 5650 4872 6680 834 8451 4687
הַמִּצְוָה וְאֶת־הַתּוֹרָה אֲשֶׁר צִוָּה אֶתְכֶם מֹשֶׁה עֶבֶד־יְהוָה
,Jehovah the ,Moses you com- which law the and the
of servant manded commands

8104 1870 3605 3212 430 3068 157
לְאַהֲבָה אֶת־יְהוָה אֱלֹהֵיכֶם וְלָלֶכֶת בְּכָל־דְּרָכָיו וְלִשְׁמֹר
to and His all in to and ,God your Jehovah love to
keep ,ways walk

5315 3605 3824 3605 5647 1692 4687
מִצְוֹתָיו וּלְדָבְקָה־בוֹ וּלְעָבְדוֹ בְּכָל־לְבַבְכֶם וּבְכָל־נַפְשְׁכֶם׃
.soul your with and your with to and to to and His
all heart all Him serve ,Him cleave commands

6
7 2677 168 3212 7971 3091 1288
וַיְבָרְכֵם יְהוֹשֻׁעַ וַיְשַׁלְּחֵם וַיֵּלְכוּ אֶל־אָהֳלֵיהֶם׃ וְלַחֲצִי
to And their to they and sent and Joshua And
half the .tents went ;away them them blessed

5973 3091 5414 2677 1317 4872 5414 4519 7626
שֵׁבֶט הַמְנַשֶּׁה נָתַן מֹשֶׁה בַּבָּשָׁן וּלְחֶצְיוֹ נָתַן יְהוֹשֻׁעַ עִם־
with Joshua had its to and in Moses had ,Manasseh tribe
(land) given half (other) ,Bashan given of

had given *possession* with
their brothers beyond the
Jordan westward. And also
when Joshua had sent them
away to their tents, then he
blessed them. [8]And *he*
spoke to them, saying, You
are returning to your tents
with great treasures, and
with very much livestock,
with silver, and with gold,
and with bronze, and with
iron, and with much
clothing. Divide the spoil of
your enemies with your
brothers. [9]And the sons of
Reuben, and the sons of
Gad, and the half tribe of
Manasseh turned and left
the sons of Israel from
Shiloh in the land of
Canaan, to go to the land of
Gilead, to the land of their
possession in which they
have possession, according
to the command of Jehovah
by the hand of Moses.
[10]And when they came to
the regions of the Jordan in
the land of Canaan, then the
sons of Reuben, and the
sons of Gad, and the half
tribe of Manasseh built an
altar there by the Jordan, an
altar of grand appearance.
[11]And the sons of Israel
heard *it* said, Behold, the
sons of Reuben, and the
sons of Gad, and the half
tribe of Manasseh have built
an altar across from the land
of Canaan, in the regions of
the Jordan, at the border of
the sons of Israel. [12]And
the sons of Israel heard, and
all the company of the sons
of Israel were assembled *at*
Shiloh, to go up against
them to war.

[13]And the sons of Israel
sent to the sons of Reuben,
and to the sons of Gad, and
to the half tribe of
Manasseh, to the land of
Gilead, Phinehas the son of
Eleazar the priest, [14]and
ten rulers with him, one ruler

3091 7971 1571 3220 3383 5676 251
אחיהם מעבר הירדן ימה וגם כי שלחם יהושע אל־
to | Joshua | sent had away them | when | and also | west- :ward | the Jordan | beyond | their brothers

7227 5233 559 559 1288 168
8 אהליהם ויברכם׃ ויאמר אליהם לאמר בנכסים רבים
,great | with treasures | ,saying | ,them to | spoke and | he and ,them blessed | their .tents

2091 3701 3966 7227 4735 168 7725
שובו אל־אהליכם ובמקנה רב־מאד בכסף ובזהב
with and ,gold | with ,silver | ,very | much | with and livestock | your tents | to | Return

7998 2505 3966 7235 8008 1270 5178
ובנחשת ובברזל ובשלמות הרבה מאד חלקו שלל
the of spoil | divide | ;very | much | with and clothing | with and ,iron | with and ,copper

1121 7205 1121 3212 7725 251 341
9 איביכם עם־אחיכם׃ וישבו וילכו בני־ראובן ובני־
the and of sons | ,Reuben | the of sons | and left | And turned | your .brothers | with | your enemies

834 7887 3478 1121 4519 7626 2677 1410
גד וחצי שבט המנשה מאת בני ישראל משלה אשר־
which (is) | from ,Shiloh | ,Israel | the of sons | from | ,Manasseh | tribe of | the and half | ,Gad

272 776 1568 776 3212 3667 776
בארץ כנען ללכת אל־ארץ הגלעד אל־ארץ אחזתם
their ,possession | the of land | to | ,Gilead | the of land | to | go to | ,Canaan | the in of land

935 4872 3027 3068 6310 270 834
10 אשר נאחזו־בה על־פי יהוה ביד־משה׃ ויבאו אל־
to | when And came they | hand the by .Moses of | ,Jehovah | the by of mouth | ,it in | have they possession | which

1121 7205 1121 1129 3667 776 834 3383 1552
גלילות הירדן אשר בארץ כנען ויבנו בני־ראובן ובני־
the and of sons | ,Reuben | the of sons | Then built | .Canaan | the in of land | which (are) | the ,Jordan | regions the of

1419 4196 3383 4196 8033 4519 7626 2677 1410
גד וחצי שבט המנשה שם מזבח על־הירדן מזבח גדול
great | a altar | the ,Jordan | by | an altar | there | ,Manasseh | tribe of | the and half | ,Gad

7205 1121 1129 2009 559 3478 1121 8085 4758
11 למראה׃ וישמעו בני־ישראל לאמר הנה־בנו בני־ראובן
,Reuben | the of sons | have built | ,Behold | ,saying | Israel | the of sons | heard And (it) | .form in

776 4136 4196 4519 7626 2677 1410 1121
ובני־גד וחצי שבט המנשה את־המזבח אל־מול ארץ
the of land | opposite | altar an | ,Manasseh | tribe of | the and half | ,Gad | and of sons the

8085 3478 1121 5676 3383 1552 3667
12 כנען אל־גלילות הירדן אל־עבר בני ישראל׃ וישמעו
And heard | .Israel | the of sons | the of border | at | the ,Jordan | the of regions | in ,Canaan

5927 7887 3478 1121 5712 3605 6950 3478 1121
בני ישראל ויקהלו כל־עדת בני־ישראל שלה לעלות
up go to | (at) ,Shiloh | Israel | the of sons | the of company | all | were and assembled | ,Israel | the of sons

7205 1121 3478 1121 7971 6635
13 עליהם לצבא׃ וישלחו בני־ישראל אל־בני־ראובן
,Reuben | the of sons | to | Israel | the of sons | sent And | .war to | against them

1568 776 4519 7626 2677 1410 1121
ואל־בני־גד ואל־חצי שבט־מנשה אל־ארץ הגלעד את־
,Gilead | the of land | to | ,Manasseh | tribe of | the half | and to | ,Gad | the of sons | and to

259 5387 5387 6235 3548 499 1121 6372
14 פינחס בן־אלעזר הכהן׃ ועשרה נשאים עמו נשיא אחד
one | ruler | with ,him | rulers | ten and | ,priest the | Eleazar | the of son | Phinehas

each for the house of a
father, for all the tribes of
Israel, and each of them a
head of the house of their
fathers, for the thousands of
Israel. [15]And they came to
the sons of Reuben, and to
the sons of Gad, and to the
half tribe of Manasseh, to
the land of Gilead, and
spoke with them, saying,
[16]So says all the company of
Jehovah, What *is* this
treachery *with* which the
God of Israel *was* betrayed,
to turn back today from after
Jehovah, in *that* you built for
yourself an altar so that you
might rebel today against
Jehovah?

[17]Is the iniquity of Peor
too little for us, from which
we have not been cleansed
until this day? Yea, a plague
came on the company of
Jehovah; [18]that you turn
away today from following
after Jehovah? And it shall
be that today you rebel
against Jehovah, and
tomorrow He shall be angry
with all the company of
Israel. [19]And surely, if the
land of your possession *is*
unclean, you may cross over
to the land of the
possession of Jehovah,
there where the tabernacle
of Jehovah dwells, and have
possession among us. But
do not rebel against
Jehovah, and do not rebel
against us, by building for
yourselves an altar besides
the altar of Jehovah our
God. [20]Did not Achan the
son of Zerah commit a sin in
the cursed thing, and was
there not wrath on all the
company of Israel? And he
was not the only one to die
in his iniquity.

[21]And the sons of
Reuben, and the sons of
Gad, and the half tribe of
Manasseh answered and
spoke with the heads of the
thousands of Israel,
[22]Jehovah *is* the God of
gods; Jehovah *is* the God of

נָשִׂיא אֶחָד לְבֵית אָב לְכֹל מַטּוֹת יִשְׂרָאֵל וְאִישׁ רֹאשׁ
15 בֵּית־אֲבוֹתָם הֵמָּה לְאַלְפֵי יִשְׂרָאֵל: וַיָּבֹאוּ אֶל־בְּנֵי־רְאוּבֵן
וְאֶל־בְּנֵי־גָד וְאֶל־חֲצִי שֵׁבֶט־מְנַשֶּׁה אֶל־אֶרֶץ הַגִּלְעָד וַיְדַבְּרוּ
16 אִתָּם לֵאמֹר: כֹּה אָמְרוּ כֹּל ׀ עֲדַת יְהוָה מָה־הַמַּעַל
הַזֶּה אֲשֶׁר מְעַלְתֶּם בֵּאלֹהֵי יִשְׂרָאֵל לָשׁוּב הַיּוֹם מֵאַחֲרֵי
יְהוָה בִּבְנוֹתְכֶם לָכֶם מִזְבֵּחַ לִמְרָדְכֶם הַיּוֹם בַּיהוָה:
17 הַמְעַט־לָנוּ אֶת־עֲוֹן פְּעוֹר אֲשֶׁר לֹא־הִטַּהַרְנוּ מִמֶּנּוּ עַד
18 הַיּוֹם הַזֶּה וַיְהִי הַנֶּגֶף בַּעֲדַת יְהוָה: וְאַתֶּם תָּשֻׁבוּ הַיּוֹם
מֵאַחֲרֵי יְהוָה וְהָיָה אַתֶּם תִּמְרְדוּ הַיּוֹם בַּיהוָה וּמָחָר אֶל־
19 כָּל־עֲדַת יִשְׂרָאֵל יִקְצֹף: וְאַךְ אִם־טְמֵאָה אֶרֶץ אֲחֻזַּתְכֶם
עִבְרוּ לָכֶם אֶל־אֶרֶץ אֲחֻזַּת יְהוָה אֲשֶׁר שָׁכַן־שָׁם מִשְׁכַּן
יְהוָה וְהֵאָחֲזוּ בְּתוֹכֵנוּ וּבַיהוָה אַל־תִּמְרֹדוּ וְאֹתָנוּ אַל־
תִּמְרֹדוּ בִּבְנֹתְכֶם לָכֶם מִזְבֵּחַ מִבַּלְעֲדֵי מִזְבַּח יְהוָה
20 אֱלֹהֵינוּ: הֲלוֹא ׀ עָכָן בֶּן־זֶרַח מָעַל מַעַל בַּחֵרֶם וְעַל־
כָּל־עֲדַת יִשְׂרָאֵל הָיָה קָצֶף וְהוּא אִישׁ אֶחָד לֹא גָוַע
21 בַּעֲוֹנוֹ: וַיַּעֲנוּ בְנֵי־רְאוּבֵן וּבְנֵי־גָד וַחֲצִי שֵׁבֶט הַמְנַשֶּׁה
22 וַיְדַבְּרוּ אֶת־רָאשֵׁי אַלְפֵי יִשְׂרָאֵל: אֵל ׀ אֱלֹהִים ׀ יְהוָה

gods! He knows, and Israel shall know if *it is* in rebellion, and if *it is* in treachery against Jehovah, you shall not save us alive today. [23]*If we* built an altar for ourselves to turn away from following after Jehovah, or to sacrifice on it burnt offering and food offering, or to offer on it peace offerings, may Jehovah Himself require it. [24]But surely from anxiety, for a reason, we have done this, saying, In the future your sons shall speak to our sons, saying, What *is* to you and to Jehovah the God of Israel? [25]For Jehovah has put a border between you and us, O sons of Reuben, and sons of Gad: the Jordan. You have no portion in Jehovah! And your sons will cause our sons to fail, not fearing Jehovah. [26]And we said, Let us now prepare for ourselves, to build an altar, not for burnt offering and not for sacrifice, [27]but it *shall be* a witness between us and you, and between our generations after us, to do the service of Jehovah before Him with our burnt offerings, and with our sacrifices, and with our peace offerings; that your sons may not say to our sons in the future, You have no portion in Jehovah. [28]And we said, And it shall be, when they say to us, and to our generations hereafter, that we shall say, See the pattern of the altar of Jehovah, which our fathers made, not for burnt offering or for sacrifice, but it *is* a witness between us and you. [29]Far be it from us to rebel against Jehovah, and to turn away today from following after Jehovah, to build an altar for burnt

אֵל ׀ אֱלֹהִים ׀ יְהוָה הוּא יֹדֵעַ וְיִשְׂרָאֵל הוּא יֵדָע אִם־

if (is it) may know he Israel for as and knows He (is) Jehovah! gods the of God

23 בְּמֶרֶד וְאִם־בְּמַעַל בַּיהוָה אַל־תּוֹשִׁיעֵנוּ הַיּוֹם הַזֶּה׃ לִבְנוֹת

(we If) built this day shall you not alive us save against Jehovah in (is it) and treachery in rebellion

לָנוּ מִזְבֵּחַ לָשׁוּב מֵאַחֲרֵי יְהוָה וְאִם־לְהַעֲלוֹת עָלָיו עוֹלָה

burnt offering it on offer to or Jehovah from after following turn to away an altar for us

וּמִנְחָה וְאִם־לַעֲשׂוֹת עָלָיו זִבְחֵי שְׁלָמִים יְהוָה הוּא יְבַקֵּשׁ׃

may it require Him-self Jehovah peace offerings sacrifice it on perform to or food and offering

24 וְאִם־לֹא מִדְּאָגָה מִדָּבָר עָשִׂינוּ אֶת־זֹאת לֵאמֹר מָחָר

the In future saying this have we done a for reason from anxiety But surely

יֹאמְרוּ בְנֵיכֶם לְבָנֵינוּ לֵאמֹר מַה־לָּכֶם וְלַיהוָה אֱלֹהֵי

the of God to and Jehovah you to What (common is) saying our to sons your sons shall speak

25 יִשְׂרָאֵל׃ וּגְבוּל נָתַן־יְהוָה בֵּינֵנוּ וּבֵינֵיכֶם בְּנֵי־רְאוּבֵן וּבְנֵי־

and of sons Reuben O of sons you and between us Jehovah has put a For border ?Israel

גָד אֶת־הַיַּרְדֵּן אֵין־לָכֶם חֵלֶק בַּיהוָה וְהִשְׁבִּיתוּ בְנֵיכֶם

your sons cause will And fail to in !Jehovah (any) portion have you no the ;Jordan ,Gad

26 אֶת־בָּנֵינוּ לְבִלְתִּי יְרֹא אֶת־יְהוָה׃ וַנֹּאמֶר נַעֲשֶׂה־נָּא לָנוּ

for ,us now us Let prepare we And ,said Jehovah fear to not sons our

27 לִבְנוֹת אֶת־הַמִּזְבֵּחַ לֹא לְעוֹלָה וְלֹא לְזָבַח׃ כִּי עֵד הוּא

(shall) (be) it a witness but for sacrifice and not burnt for offering not ,altar an build to

בֵּינֵינוּ וּבֵינֵיכֶם וּבֵין דֹּרוֹתֵינוּ אַחֲרֵינוּ לַעֲבֹד אֶת־עֲבֹדַת

of service the to perform after ,us our generations and between ,you and between us

יְהוָה לְפָנָיו בְּעֹלוֹתֵינוּ וּבִזְבָחֵינוּ וּבִשְׁלָמֵינוּ וְלֹא־יֹאמְרוּ

shall say and not our with and ;offerings peace our with and ,sacrifices burnt our with ,offerings before Him Jehovah

28 בְנֵיכֶם מָחָר לְבָנֵינוּ אֵין־לָכֶם חֵלֶק בַּיהוָה׃ וַנֹּאמֶר וְהָיָה

it And be shall we And ,said in Jehovah (any) portion You not (have) our to sons the in ,future your sons

כִּי־יֹאמְרוּ אֵלֵינוּ וְאֶל־דֹּרֹתֵינוּ מָחָר וְאָמַרְנוּ רְאוּ אֶת־

See we that say shall here- ;after genera- tions our and to ,us to they say when

תַּבְנִית מִזְבַּח יְהוָה אֲשֶׁר־עָשׂוּ אֲבוֹתֵינוּ לֹא לְעוֹלָה וְלֹא

and not burnt for offering not ,fathers our made which Jehovah the of altar the of pattern

29 לְזֶבַח כִּי־עֵד הוּא בֵּינֵינוּ וּבֵינֵיכֶם׃ חָלִילָה לָּנוּ מִמֶּנּוּ

from it us to it be Far .you and between us (is) it a but witness for ,sacrifice

לִמְרֹד בַּיהוָה וְלָשׁוּב הַיּוֹם מֵאַחֲרֵי יְהוָה לִבְנוֹת מִזְבֵּחַ

altar an build to Jehovah from after today turn to and away against ,Jehovah rebel to

offering, for food offering, and for sacrifice, apart from the altar of Jehovah your God, which *is* before His tabernacle!

30And Phinehas the priest, and the rulers of the congregation, and the heads of the thousands of Israel with him heard the words which the sons of Reuben, and the sons of Gad, and the sons of Manasseh had spoken. And it was good in their eyes. 31And Phinehas the son of Eleazar the priest said to the sons of Reuben, and to the sons of Gad, and to the sons of Manasseh, Today we have known that Jehovah *is* among us, because you have not committed this treachery against Jehovah. Now you have delivered the sons of Israel out of the hand of Jehovah.

32And Phinehas the son of Eleazar the priest, and the rulers, returned from the sons of Reuben, and from the sons of Gad out of the land of Gilead to the land of Canaan, to the sons of Israel, and brought word back to them. 33And the thing was good in the eyes of the sons of Israel, and the sons of Israel blessed God and no more said to go up against them to war, to destroy the land which the sons of Reuben and the sons of Gad *were* living in. 34And the sons of Reuben, and the sons of Gad proclaimed regarding the altar, that it *was* a witness between us that Jehovah *is* God.

834 430 3068 4196 905 2077 4503 5930
לְעֹלָה לְמִנְחָה וּלְזָבַח מִלְּבַד מִזְבַּח יְהוָה אֱלֹהֵינוּ אֲשֶׁר
which (is) ,God our Jehovah the of altar apart from for and sacrifice food for ,offering burnt for ,offering

5712 5387 3548 6372 8085 4908 6440
30 לִפְנֵי מִשְׁכָּנוֹ׃ וַיִּשְׁמַע פִּינְחָס הַכֹּהֵן וּנְשִׂיאֵי הָעֵדָה
con- the ,gregation the and of rulers the ,priest Phinehas And heard His !tabernacle before

834 1697 834 3478 505 7218
וְרָאשֵׁי אַלְפֵי יִשְׂרָאֵל אֲשֶׁר אִתּוֹ אֶת־הַדְּבָרִים אֲשֶׁר
which words the with ,him who (were) Israel thou- of sands the the and of heads

5869 3190 4519 1121 1410/1121 7205/1121 1696
דִּבְּרוּ בְּנֵי־רְאוּבֵן וּבְנֵי־גָד וּבְנֵי מְנַשֶּׁה וַיִּיטַב בְּעֵינֵיהֶם׃
their in .eyes it And good was .Manasseh the and of sons Gad and of sons the ,Reuben the of sons had spoken

7205 1121 3548 499 1121 6372 559
31 וַיֹּאמֶר פִּינְחָס בֶּן־אֶלְעָזָר הַכֹּהֵן אֶל־בְּנֵי רְאוּבֵן וְאֶל־
to and ,Reuben the of sons to priest the Eleazar the of son Phinehas said And

3068 8432 3045 3117 4519 1121 1410/1121
בְּנֵי־גָד וְאֶל־בְּנֵי מְנַשֶּׁה הַיּוֹם יָדַעְנוּ כִּי־בְתוֹכֵנוּ יְהוָה
Jehovah (is) among ,us that have we known Today ,Manasseh the of sons and to Gad the of sons

5337 227 2088 4604 3068 4603 3808
אֲשֶׁר לֹא־מְעַלְתֶּם בַּיהוָה הַמַּעַל הַזֶּה אָז הִצַּלְתֶּם אֶת־
have you delivered now ;this treachery (with) Jehovah have you betrayed not because

3548 499 1121 6372 7725 3068 3027 3478 1121
32 בְּנֵי יִשְׂרָאֵל מִיַּד יְהוָה׃ וַיָּשָׁב פִּינְחָס בֶּן־אֶלְעָזָר הַכֹּהֵן
,priest the Eleazar the of son Phinehas And returned .Jehovah from of hand the Israel the of sons

1568 776 1410/1121 7205/1121 5387
וְהַנְּשִׂיאִים מֵאֵת בְּנֵי־רְאוּבֵן וּמֵאֵת בְּנֵי־גָד מֵאֶרֶץ הַגִּלְעָד
,Gilead the of out of land Gad the of sons and from Reuben the of sons from the and ,rulers

3190 1697 7725 3427 1121 3667 776
33 אֶל־אֶרֶץ כְּנַעַן אֶל־בְּנֵי יִשְׂרָאֵל וַיָּשִׁבוּ אוֹתָם דָּבָר׃ וַיִּיטַב
was and good word to ;them brought and back ,Israel the of sons to ,Canaan the of land to

3808 3478 1121 430 1288 3478 1121 5869 1697
הַדָּבָר בְּעֵינֵי בְּנֵי יִשְׂרָאֵל וַיְבָרְכוּ אֱלֹהִים בְּנֵי יִשְׂרָאֵל וְלֹא
no and more Israel the of sons God and blessed ,Israel the of sons the in of eyes the thing

1121 834 776 7843 6635 5927 559
אָמְרוּ לַעֲלוֹת עֲלֵיהֶם לַצָּבָא לְשַׁחֵת אֶת־הָאָרֶץ אֲשֶׁר בְּנֵי־
the of sons which the land destroy to ,war to against them up go to said

1410/1121 7205/1121 7121 3427 1410/1121 7205
34 רְאוּבֵן וּבְנֵי־גָד יֹשְׁבִים בָּהּ׃ וַיִּקְרְאוּ בְּנֵי־רְאוּבֵן וּבְנֵי־גָד
Gad and of sons the Reuben the of sons And proclaimed .in (were) living Gad and of sons the Reuben

430 3068 996 5707 4196
לַמִּזְבֵּחַ כִּי עֵד הוּא בֵּינֹתֵינוּ כִּי יְהוָה הָאֱלֹהִים׃
.God Jehovah (is) that between us it (was) a that witness the to as ,altar

CAP. XXIII כג

CHAPTER 23

1And it happened many days after Jehovah had given rest to Israel from all their enemies round about, that Joshua *was* old, going on in days. 2And Joshua

3605 3478 3068 5117 310 7227 3117 1961
1 וַיְהִי מִיָּמִים רַבִּים אַחֲרֵי אֲשֶׁר־הֵנִיחַ יְהוָה לְיִשְׂרָאֵל מִכָּל־
from all Israel to Jehovah given rest had after many days it And ,was

3091 7121 3117 935 2205 3091 5439 341
2 אֹיְבֵיהֶם מִסָּבִיב וִיהוֹשֻׁעַ זָקֵן בָּא בַּיָּמִים׃ וַיִּקְרָא יְהוֹשֻׁעַ
Joshua And called .days in on going old that Joshua round ,about their enemies

called for all Israel, for its
elders, and for its heads,
and for its judges, and for
its officers, and said to
them, I have become old;
I have gone on in days;
3and you have seen all
that Jehovah your God
has done to all these
nations because of you,
for Jehovah your God
was He who was fighting
for you. 4Behold, I have
caused to fall to you
these nations that are left
to be an inheritance for
your tribes, from Jordan,
with all the nations that I
have cut off, as far as the
Great Sea, toward the
going in of the sun. 5And
Jehovah your God will
thrust them out from be-
fore you, and will expel
them from before you,
and you shall possess
their land, as Jehovah
your God has spoken to
you.

6And you shall be very
strong to keep and to do all
that is written in the book of
the law of Moses, so as not
to turn aside from it to the
right or to the left; 7so as
not to go in among these
nations, these who are left
with you; and that you do
not make mention of the
name of their gods, nor
shall you swear, nor shall
you serve them, nor shall
you bow yourselves to
them. 8But you shall cling
to Jehovah your God, as
you have done until today.
9And Jehovah has expelled
from before you great and
mighty nations. And for you
no one has stood before
you until today. 10One man
of you shall pursue a
thousand; for Jehovah your
God *is* He who is fighting
for you, as He has spoken to
you. 11And you shall be
very watchful for yourselves

559 7860 8199 7218 2205 3478 3605
לְכָל־יִשְׂרָאֵל לִזְקֵנָיו וּלְרָאשָׁיו וּלְשֹׁפְטָיו וּלְשֹׁטְרָיו וַיֹּאמֶר
said and | its for and ,officers | its for and ,judges | its for and ,heads | its for ,elders | ,Israel | all for

3605 7200 3117 935 2204
3 אֲלֵהֶם אֲנִי זָקַנְתִּי בָּאתִי בַּיָּמִים׃ וְאַתֶּם רְאִיתֶם אֵת כָּל־
all | — | seen have | you and | ;days in | have I be- advanced | have I ;old come | ,them to

428 1471 3605 430 3068 6213
אֲשֶׁר עָשָׂה יְהוָה אֱלֹהֵיכֶם לְכָל־הַגּוֹיִם הָאֵלֶּה מִפְּנֵיכֶם
because ,you of | these | nations | all to | God your | Jehovah | has done | that

5307 2009 3898 430 3068 3588
4 כִּי יְהוָה אֱלֹהֵיכֶם הוּא הַנִּלְחָם לָכֶם׃ רְאוּ הִפַּלְתִּי לָכֶם
to you | have I fall made | ,Behold | .you for | was fighting | (was) who He | God your | Jehovah | For

3383 7626 5159 428 7604 1471
אֶת־הַגּוֹיִם הַנִּשְׁאָרִים הָאֵלֶּה בְּנַחֲלָה לְשִׁבְטֵיכֶם מִן־הַיַּרְדֵּן
from ,Jordan | your for ,tribes | an be to inheritance | these | are that left | nations

8121 3996 1419 3220 3772 834 1471/3605
וְכָל־הַגּוֹיִם אֲשֶׁר הִכְרַתִּי וְהַיָּם הַגָּדוֹל מְבוֹא הַשָּׁמֶשׁ׃
.sun the | the toward of in going | the Great | far as Sea as | have I ,off cut | that | the nations | with all

3423 6440 1920 430 3068
5 וַיהוָה אֱלֹהֵיכֶם הוּא יֶהְדֳּפֵם מִפְּנֵיכֶם וְהוֹרִישׁ אֹתָם
them | will and expel | from ,you before | thrust will out them | God your | And Jehovah

430 3068 1696 776 3423 6440
מִלִּפְנֵיכֶם וִירִשְׁתֶּם אֶת־אַרְצָם כַּאֲשֶׁר דִּבֶּר יְהוָה אֱלֹהֵיכֶם
God your | Jehovah | has spoken | as | their ,land | shall you and possess | from ;you before

3789 3605 6213 8104 3966 2388
6 לָכֶם׃ וַחֲזַקְתֶּם מְאֹד לִשְׁמֹר וְלַעֲשׂוֹת אֵת כָּל־הַכָּתוּב
is that written | all | do to and | keep to | very | shall you And strong be | to .you

8040 3225 5493 4872 8451 5612
בְּסֵפֶר תּוֹרַת מֹשֶׁה לְבִלְתִּי סוּר־מִמֶּנּוּ יָמִין וּשְׂמֹאול׃
the to or ;left | the to right | from ,it | turn to aside | as so not | ,Moses | the of Law | the in of Book

428 7604 428 1471 935 3808
7 לְבִלְתִּי־בוֹא בַּגּוֹיִם הָאֵלֶּה הַנִּשְׁאָרִים הָאֵלֶּה אִתְּכֶם
;you with | these | are who left | ,these | among nations | go to | as so not

5647 3808 7650 3808 2142 430 8034
וּבְשֵׁם אֱלֹהֵיהֶם לֹא־תַזְכִּירוּ וְלֹא תַשְׁבִּיעוּ וְלֹא תַעַבְדוּם
you shall ,them serve | nor | you shall ,swear | nor | not shall you mention | their gods | the and of name

1692 430 3068 7812 3808
8 וְלֹא תִשְׁתַּחֲווּ לָהֶם׃ כִּי אִם־בַּיהוָה אֱלֹהֵיכֶם תִּדְבָּקוּ
shall you cling | God your | Jehovah | to | but | ;them to | bow you shall yourselves | nor

6440 3068 3423 2088 3117 5704 6213
9 כַּאֲשֶׁר עֲשִׂיתֶם עַד הַיּוֹם הַזֶּה׃ וַיּוֹרֶשׁ יְהוָה מִפְּנֵיכֶם
before from you | Jehovah | has And expelled | this | day | until | have you done | as

5704 6440 376 5975 6099 1419 1471
גּוֹיִם גְּדֹלִים וַעֲצוּמִים וְאַתֶּם לֹא־עָמַד אִישׁ בִּפְנֵיכֶם עַד
up to | before you | one | has stood | no | for as ,you | ;mighty and | great | nations

3068 505 7291 259 376 2088 3117
10 הַיּוֹם הַזֶּה׃ אִישׁ־אֶחָד מִכֶּם יִרְדָּף־אָלֶף כִּי ׀ יְהוָה
Jehovah | for | a ;thousand | shall pursue | you of | One | man | .this | day

8104 1696 3898 430
11 אֱלֹהֵיכֶם הוּא הַנִּלְחָם לָכֶם כַּאֲשֶׁר דִּבֶּר לָכֶם׃ וְנִשְׁמַרְתֶּם
shall you and watchful be | ;you to | has He spoken | as | for ,you | is fighting | He who | your (is) God

to love Jehovah your God. [12]But if you at all turn away and cleave to the remnant of the nations, of those who are left to you, and intermarry with them, and go in to them, and they to you, [13]know certainly that Jehovah your God shall not continue to expel these nations from before you, and they shall be snares and traps to you, and scourges in your sides, and thorns in your eyes, until you perish from this good land which Jehovah your God has given you.

[14]And, behold, today I *am* going in the way of all the earth, and you know with all your heart and with all your soul that there has not failed one thing of all the good things which Jehovah your God has spoken concerning you; all of it has come to you; there has not one thing failed of it. [15]And it shall be, as every good thing which Jehovah your God has spoken to you comes to you, so shall Jehovah bring on you every evil thing, until He destroys you from off this good land which Jehovah your God has given to you. [16]When you transgress the covenant of Jehovah your God which He commanded you, and when you have gone and served other gods, and have bowed yourselves to

518 430 3068 157 3808 5315 3966
12 מְאֹד לְנַפְשֹׁתֵיכֶם לְאַהֲבָה אֶת־יְהוָה אֱלֹהֵיכֶם׃ כִּי ׀ אִם־
if But .God your Jehovah love to yourselves for very

7604 428 1471 3498 1692 7725 7725
שׁוֹב תָּשׁוּבוּ וּדְבַקְתֶּם בְּיֶתֶר הַגּוֹיִם הָאֵלֶּה הַנִּשְׁאָרִים
left are who these .nations the to of remnant and cling turn you away all at

854 854 935 2859
הָאֵלֶּה אִתְּכֶם וְהִתְחַתַּנְתֶּם בָּהֶם וּבָאתֶם בָּהֶם וְהֵם בָּכֶם׃
among ,you and they among ,them go and with ,them and intermarry with ,you of these

3423 430 3068 3054 3808 3045 3045
13 יָדוֹעַ תֵּדְעוּ כִּי לֹא יוֹסִיף יְהוָה אֱלֹהֵיכֶם לְהוֹרִישׁ אֶת־
— expel to God your Jehovah shall continue not that know surely

7850 4170 6341 1961 6440 428 1471
הַגּוֹיִם הָאֵלֶּה מִלִּפְנֵיכֶם וְהָיוּ לָכֶם לְפַח וּלְמוֹקֵשׁ וּלְשֹׁטֵט
and scourges and ,traps ,snares you to they and be shall from ,you before these nations

127 6 5704 5869 6796 6654
בְּצִדֵּיכֶם וְלִצְנִנִים בְּעֵינֵיכֶם עַד אֲבָדְכֶם מֵעַל הָאֲדָמָה
land from off you perish until your in eyes and thorns your in sides

2009 430 3068 5414 834 2896
14 הַטּוֹבָה הַזֹּאת אֲשֶׁר נָתַן לָכֶם יְהוָה אֱלֹהֵיכֶם׃ וְהִנֵּה
,And behold .God your Jehovah to you has given which this good

3824 3605 3045 776 3605 1870 3117 3212
אָנֹכִי הוֹלֵךְ הַיּוֹם בְּדֶרֶךְ כָּל־הָאָרֶץ וִידַעְתֶּם בְּכָל־לְבַבְכֶם
heart your all with you and know the earth all the in way of today (am) going I

1697 3605 259 1697 5307 5315 3605
וּבְכָל נַפְשְׁכֶם כִּי לֹא־נָפַל דָּבָר אֶחָד מִכֹּל ׀ הַדְּבָרִים
things the all of one thing has not fallen that soul your and all with

935 3605 430 3068 1696 834 2896
הַטּוֹבִים אֲשֶׁר דִּבֶּר יְהוָה אֱלֹהֵיכֶם עֲלֵיכֶם הַכֹּל בָּאוּ לָכֶם
to ;you has come all it of about ,you God your Jehovah has spoken which good

3605 935 1961 259 1697 5307
15 לֹא־נָפַל מִמֶּנּוּ דָּבָר אֶחָד׃ וְהָיָה כַּאֲשֶׁר־בָּא עֲלֵיכֶם כָּל־
every you to comes as it And be shall .one thing it of has not fallen

935 430 3068 3068 1696 834 2896 1697
הַדָּבָר הַטּוֹב אֲשֶׁר דִּבֶּר יְהוָה אֱלֹהֵיכֶם אֲלֵיכֶם כֵּן יָבִיא
shall bring so ,you to God your Jehovah has spoken which good thing

8045 5704 7451 1697 3605 3068
יְהוָה עֲלֵיכֶם אֵת כָּל־הַדָּבָר הָרָע עַד־הַשְׁמִידוֹ אוֹתְכֶם
you He destroys until ,evil thing every you on Jehovah

3068 5414 834 2088 2896 127
מֵעַל הָאֲדָמָה הַטּוֹבָה הַזֹּאת אֲשֶׁר נָתַן לָכֶם יְהוָה
Jehovah you to has given which this good land from off

6680 834 430 3068 1285 5674 430
16 אֱלֹהֵיכֶם׃ בְּעָבְרְכֶם אֶת־בְּרִית יְהוָה אֱלֹהֵיכֶם אֲשֶׁר צִוָּה
He commanded which God your Jehovah the of covenant you when transgress ;God your

7812 312 430 5647 3212
אֶתְכֶם וַהֲלַכְתֶּם וַעֲבַדְתֶּם אֱלֹהִים אֲחֵרִים וְהִשְׁתַּחֲוִיתֶם
bowed have and down other ,gods served and you when and gone have ,you

them, then the anger of Jehovah shall burn against you; and you shall perish quickly from off the good land which He has given to you.

CHAPTER 24

[1]And Joshua gathered all the tribes of Israel to Shechem, and called for the elders of Israel, and for its heads, and for its judges, and for its officers. And they presented themselves before God. [2]And Joshua said to all the people, So says Jehovah the God of Israel, Your fathers have in the past lived Beyond the River —Terah the father of Abraham and father of Nahor — and they served other gods. [3]And I took your father Abraham from Beyond the River, and caused him to go through all the land Canaan, and multiplied his seed, and gave Isaac to him. [4]And I gave Jacob and Esau to Isaac. And I gave Mount Seir to Esau, to possess it. And Jacob and his sons went down to Egypt. [5]And I sent Moses and Aaron and plagued Egypt, as I did in its midst. And afterward I brought you out. [6]And I brought your fathers out from Egypt, and you went into the sea, and the Egyptians pursued after your fathers with chariots and with horsemen, into the Red Sea. [7]And they cried to Jehovah, and He set thick darkness between you and the Egyptians, and brought the sea on them,

776 4120 6 3068 639 2734

לָהֶם וְחָרָה אַף־יְהוָה בָּכֶם וַאֲבַדְתֶּם מְהֵרָה מֵעַל הָאָרֶץ

the land | from off | quickly | you and perish shall | against ;you | anger the Jehovah of | shall then glow | to ,them

5414 834 2896

הַטּוֹבָה אֲשֶׁר נָתַן לָכֶם׃

to .you | has He given | which | good

CAP. XXIV כד

CHAPTER 24

7121 7927 3478 7626/3605 3091 622

1 וַיֶּאֱסֹף יְהוֹשֻׁעַ אֶת־כָּל־שִׁבְטֵי יִשְׂרָאֵל שְׁכֶמָה וַיִּקְרָא

and called | to ,Shechem | Israel | the of tribes | all | Joshua | And gathered

6440 3320 7860 8199 7218 3478 2205

לְזִקְנֵי יִשְׂרָאֵל וּלְרָאשָׁיו וּלְשֹׁפְטָיו וּלְשֹׁטְרָיו וַיִּתְיַצְּבוּ לִפְנֵי

before | they and themselves placed | its for and ;officers | its for and ,judges | for and heads its | ,Israel | the for of elders

3068 559 5971 3605 3091 559 430

2 הָאֱלֹהִים׃ וַיֹּאמֶר יְהוֹשֻׁעַ אֶל־כָּל־הָעָם כֹּה־אָמַר יְהוָה

,Jehovah | says | Thus | the ,people | all | to | Joshua | said And | .God

8646 5769 1 3427 5104 5674 3478 430

אֱלֹהֵי יִשְׂרָאֵל בְּעֵבֶר הַנָּהָר יָשְׁבוּ אֲבוֹתֵיכֶם מֵעוֹלָם תֶּרַח

Terah | the in :past | your fathers | lived | the —River | Beyond | ,Israel | the of God

3947 312 430 5647 5152 85 1

3 אֲבִי אַבְרָהָם וַאֲבִי נָחוֹר וַיַּעַבְדוּ אֱלֹהִים אֲחֵרִים׃ וָאֶקַּח

I And took | .other | gods | they and served | —Nahor and of father | Abraham | the of father

3605 3212 5104 5676 85 1

אֶת־אֲבִיכֶם אֶת־אַבְרָהָם מֵעֵבֶר הַנָּהָר וָאוֹלֵךְ אוֹתוֹ בְּכָל־

through all | him caused and go to | the ,River | from Beyond | Abraham | father your

3327 5414 2233 7235 3667 776

4 אֶרֶץ כְּנָעַן וָאַרְבֶּה אֶת־זַרְעוֹ וָאֶתֶּן־לוֹ אֶת־יִצְחָק׃ וָאֶתֵּן

I And gave | .Isaac | to him | and gave | ,seed his | and multiplied | Canaan | the of land

8165 2022 6215 5414 6215 3290 3327

לְיִצְחָק אֶת־יַעֲקֹב וְאֶת־עֵשָׂו וָאֶתֵּן לְעֵשָׂו אֶת־הַר שֵׂעִיר

Seir | Mount | to ,Esau | I and gave | ;Esau and | Jacob | to Isaac

7971 4714 3381 1121 3290 3423

5 לָרֶשֶׁת אוֹתוֹ וְיַעֲקֹב וּבָנָיו יָרְדוּ מִצְרָיִם׃ וָאֶשְׁלַח אֶת־

I And sent | .Egypt to | went down | his and sons | and Jacob | ;it | to possess

7130 6213 4714 5061 175 4872

מֹשֶׁה וְאֶת־אַהֲרֹן וָאֶגֹּף אֶת־מִצְרַיִם כַּאֲשֶׁר עָשִׂיתִי בְּקִרְבּוֹ

its in ;midst | did I | as | ,Egypt | and plagued | Aaron | and | Moses

4714 1 3318 3318 310

6 וְאַחַר הוֹצֵאתִי אֶתְכֶם׃ וָאוֹצִיא אֶת־אֲבוֹתֵיכֶם מִמִּצְרַיִם

from Egypt | fathers your | I And out brought | .you | brought I out | and later

7393 1 310 4713 7291 3220 935

וַתָּבֹאוּ הַיָּמָּה וַיִּרְדְּפוּ מִצְרַיִם אַחֲרֵי אֲבוֹתֵיכֶם בְּרֶכֶב

with chariots | fathers your | after | the Egyptians | and chased | the into ,sea | you and went

3990 7760 3068 6817 5488 3220 6571

7 וּבְפָרָשִׁים יַם־סוּף׃ וַיִּצְעֲקוּ אֶל־יְהוָה וַיָּשֶׂם מַאֲפֵל

thick darkness | and set He | Jehovah to | they and cried | .Reeds of Sea the | into | with and horsemen

3680 3220 5921 935 4713 996 996

בֵּינֵיכֶם ׀ וּבֵין הַמִּצְרִים וַיָּבֵא עָלָיו אֶת־הַיָּם וַיְכַסֵּהוּ

and him covered; | sea the | upon him | and brought | the Egyptians | and | between you

and covered them. And
your eyes saw that which I
have done in Egypt. And
you lived in the wilderness
many days. 8And I brought
you into the land of the
Amorite who lived beyond
the Jordan. And they fought
with you, and I gave them
into your hand, and you
possessed their land. And I
destroyed them before you.
9And Balak the son of
Zippor, the king of Moab,
rose up and fought against
Israel, and sent and called
for Balaam the son of Beor
to curse you. 10And I was
not willing to listen to
Balaam, and he greatly
blessed you. And I de-
livered you out of his hand.
11And you crossed over the
Jordan and came to
Jericho. And the masters of
Jericho fought against you,
the Amorite and the Perizzite, and the Caananite, and
the Hittite, and the Gir-
gashite, the Hivite, and the
Jebusite; and I gave them
into your hand. 12And I sent
the hornet before you, and it
cast them out before you,
two kings of the Amorite,
not by the sword nor by
your bow. 13And I have
given you a land for which
you have not labored, and
cities which you have not
built, and you live in them.
You are eating of vineyards
and oliveyards which you
did not plant.

14And now fear Jeho-
vah and serve Him in
sincerity and truth, and
turn away from the gods
that your fathers served
Beyond the River, and in
Egypt; and you serve
Jehovah. 15And if it
seems evil in your eyes to
serve Jehovah, choose
for you today whom you

3427 4714 6213 834 5869 7200
וַתִּרְאֶינָה עֵינֵיכֶם אֵת אֲשֶׁר־עָשִׂיתִי בְּמִצְרָיִם וַתֵּשְׁבוּ
you and lived | ;Egypt in | have I done | that which | eyes your | saw and

567 776 935 7227 3117 4057
8 בַּמִּדְבָּר יָמִים רַבִּים׃ וָאָבִאָה אֶתְכֶם אֶל־אֶרֶץ הָאֱמֹרִי
the Amorite | the of land | into | you | I And brought | .many | days | the in wilderness

3027 5414 3898 3383 5676 3427
הַיּוֹשֵׁב בְּעֵבֶר הַיַּרְדֵּן וַיִּלָּחֲמוּ אִתְּכֶם וָאֶתֵּן אוֹתָם בְּיֶדְכֶם
into ,hand your | them | I and gave | with ,you | they and fought | the ;Jordan | beyond | who lived

1111 6965 6440 8045 776 2423
9 וַתִּירְשׁוּ אֶת־אַרְצָם וָאַשְׁמִידֵם מִפְּנֵיכֶם׃ וַיָּקָם בָּלָק בֶּן
the of son | Balak | And rose | before .you | I and them destroyed | their ;land | and seized

1109 7121 7971 3478 3898 4124 4428 6834
צִפּוֹר מֶלֶךְ מוֹאָב וַיִּלָּחֶם בְּיִשְׂרָאֵל וַיִּשְׁלַח וַיִּקְרָא לְבִלְעָם
for Balaam | and called | and sent | against ,Israel | and fought | ,Moab | the of king | ,Zippor

1288 1109 8085 14 3808 7043/1160/1121
10 בֶּן־בְּעוֹר לְקַלֵּל אֶתְכֶם׃ וְלֹא אָבִיתִי לִשְׁמֹעַ לְבִלְעָם וַיְבָרֶךְ
he and blessed | to ,Balaam | to listen | was I willing | But not | .you | curse to | Beor | the of son

3383 5674 3027 5337 1288
11 בָּרוֹךְ אֶתְכֶם וָאַצִּל אֶתְכֶם מִיָּדוֹ׃ וַתַּעַבְרוּ אֶת־הַיַּרְדֵּן
Jordan the | you And crossed | of out .hand his | you | I and delivered | ;you | greatly

567 3405 1167 3898 3405 935
וַתָּבֹאוּ אֶל־יְרִיחוֹ וַיִּלָּחֲמוּ בָכֶם בַּעֲלֵי־יְרִיחוֹ הָאֱמֹרִי
the ,Amorite | masters the Jericho of | against ,you | and fought | ;Jericho | to | and came

5414 2983 2340 1622 2850 3669 6522
וְהַפְּרִזִּי וְהַכְּנַעֲנִי וְהַחִתִּי וְהַגִּרְגָּשִׁי הַחִוִּי וְהַיְבוּסִי וָאֶתֵּן
I and gave | the and ;Jebusite | the ,Hivite | the and ,Girgashite | the and ,Hittite | the and ,Canaanite | the and ,Perizzite

1644 6880 6440 7971 3027
12 אוֹתָם בְּיֶדְכֶם׃ וָאֶשְׁלַח לִפְנֵיכֶם אֶת־הַצִּרְעָה וַתְּגָרֶשׁ
it and out cast | ,hornet the | before you | I And sent | your into .hand | them

3808 2719 3808 567 4428 8147 6440
אוֹתָם מִפְּנֵיכֶם שְׁנֵי מַלְכֵי הָאֱמֹרִי לֹא בְחַרְבְּךָ וְלֹא
nor | your by sword | not | the ,Amorite | kings of | two | ,you before | them

5892 3021 834 776 5414 7198
13 בְּקַשְׁתֶּךָ׃ וָאֶתֵּן לָכֶם אֶרֶץ אֲשֶׁר לֹא־יָגַעְתָּ בָּהּ וְעָרִים
and cities | ,for | not have you labored | which | a land | to you | have I And given | your by .bow

3808 834 2132 3754 3427 1129 834
אֲשֶׁר לֹא־בְנִיתֶם וַתֵּשְׁבוּ בָּהֶם כְּרָמִים וְזֵיתִים אֲשֶׁר לֹא־
not | which | and oliveyards | of vineyards | in ;them | you and live | ,not have you built | which

5647 3068 3372 6258 398 5193
14 נְטַעְתֶּם אַתֶּם אֹכְלִים׃ וְעַתָּה יְראוּ אֶת־יְהוָה וְעִבְדוּ אֹתוֹ
Him | and serve | ,Jehovah | fear | ,Now ,then | are .eating | you | did you plant

1 5647 834 430 5493 571 8549
בְּתָמִים וּבֶאֱמֶת וְהָסִירוּ אֶת־אֱלֹהִים אֲשֶׁר עָבְדוּ אֲבוֹתֵיכֶם
your fathers | served | which | the from gods | turn and away | and ,truth | in sincerity

7451 3068 5647 4714 5104 5676
15 בְּעֵבֶר הַנָּהָר וּבְמִצְרַיִם וְעִבְדוּ אֶת־יְהוָה׃ וְאִם רַע
(is it) evil | And if | Jehovah | and serve | in and ;Egypt | the ,River | beyond

4310 3117 977 3068 5647 5869
בְּעֵינֵיכֶם לַעֲבֹד אֶת־יְהוָה בַּחֲרוּ לָכֶם הַיּוֹם אֶת־מִי
whom | today | for yourselves | choose | ,Jehovah | to serve | your in eyes

will serve — whether the
gods whom your fathers
served Beyond the River, or
the gods of the Amorites in
whose land you are living
—but as for me and my
house, we will serve
Jehovah.
[16]And the people replied
and said, Far be it from us to
forsake Jehovah, to serve
other gods. [17]For Jehovah
our God *is* He who has
brought us and our fathers
out of the land of Egypt, out
of the house of slaves,
and who has done these
great signs before our eyes,
and has preserved us in all
the way in which we have
gone, and among all the
people through whom we
have passed. [18]And
Jehovah has cast out all the
peoples, even the Amorite
inhabiting the land before
us. We also will serve
Jehovah, for He *is* our God.

[19]And Joshua said to the
people, You cannot serve
Jehovah, for He *is* a holy
God; He *is* a jealous God.
He will not lift up *from you*
your transgressions or your
sins. [20]When you forsake
Jehovah, and shall serve
strange gods, then He will
turn away and do evil to
you, and consume you, after
He has done good to you.
[21]And the people said to
Joshua, No, but we will
serve Jehovah. [22]And
Joshua said to the people,
You are witnesses against
yourselves, that you have
chosen Jehovah for your-
selves, to serve Him—for
they said, *We are* witnesses
—and now turn away from
the strange gods which *are*

834 1 5647 430 5647
תַּעֲבֹדוּן אִם אֶת־אֱלֹהִים אֲשֶׁר־עָבְדוּ אֲבוֹתֵיכֶם אֲשֶׁר
which your served whom gods the whether will you
(were) ,fathers —serve

3427 567 430 5104 5676
בְּעֵבֶר הַנָּהָר וְאִם אֶת־אֱלֹהֵי הָאֱמֹרִי אֲשֶׁר אַתֶּם יֹשְׁבִים
are you whose the of gods the or the beyond
dwelling Amorite ,River

16 559 5971 6030 3068 5647 1004 776
בְּאַרְצָם וְאָנֹכִי וּבֵיתִי נַעֲבֹד אֶת־יְהוָה׃ וַיַּעַן הָעָם וַיֹּאמֶר
,said and the And .Jehovah will we my and as but in
people spoke serve ,house me for —land

17 3588 312 430 5647 3068 5800 2486
חָלִילָה לָּנוּ מֵעֲזֹב אֶת־יְהוָה לַעֲבֹד אֱלֹהִים אֲחֵרִים׃ כִּי
for ;other gods serve to ,Jehovah to from it be Far
forsake us

776 1 5927 430 3068
יְהוָה אֱלֹהֵינוּ הוּא הַמַּעֲלֶה אֹתָנוּ וְאֶת־אֲבוֹתֵינוּ מֵאֶרֶץ
the of out fathers our and us has He our Jehovah
of land brought who ,(is) God

226 5869 6213 834 5650 1004 4714
מִצְרַיִם מִבֵּית עֲבָדִים וַאֲשֶׁר עָשָׂה לְעֵינֵינוּ אֶת־הָאֹתוֹת
signs before has and ,slaves a of out ,Egypt
eyes our done who of house

3212 1870 3605 8104 428 1419
הַגְּדֹלוֹת הָאֵלֶּה וַיִּשְׁמְרֵנוּ בְּכָל־הַדֶּרֶךְ אֲשֶׁר הָלַכְנוּ בָהּ
in have we way the all in has and ,these great
which gone us preserved

18 3068 1644 7130 5674 5971 3605
וּבְכָל הָעַמִּים אֲשֶׁר עָבַרְנוּ בְּקִרְבָּם׃ וַיְגָרֶשׁ יְהוָה אֶת־
Jehovah has And .through have we whom the and
out cast passed peoples all among

1871 6440 776 3427 567 5971 3605
כָּל־הָעַמִּים וְאֶת־הָאֱמֹרִי יֹשֵׁב הָאָרֶץ מִפָּנֵינוּ גַּם־אֲנַחְנוּ
we also ;us before ,land the in living Amorite the even the all
,peoples

19 5971 3091 559 430 3068 5647
נַעֲבֹד אֶת־יְהוָה כִּי־הוּא אֱלֹהֵינוּ׃ וַיֹּאמֶר יְהוֹשֻׁעַ אֶל־הָעָם
the to Joshua said And .God our (is) He for ,Jehovah shall
,people serve

410 6918 430 3068 5647 3201
לֹא תוּכְלוּ לַעֲבֹד אֶת־יְהוָה כִּי־אֱלֹהִים קְדֹשִׁים הוּא אֵל־
God a ;(is) He holy God a for ,Jehovah serve cannot You

20 5800 2403 6588 5375 7072
קַנּוֹא הוּא לֹא־יִשָּׂא לְפִשְׁעֲכֶם וּלְחַטֹּאותֵיכֶם׃ כִּי תַעַזְבוּ
you When ,sins your or your will He not He jealous
forsake transgressions up lift ;(is)

3615 7489 7725 5236 430 5647 3068
אֶת־יְהוָה וַעֲבַדְתֶּם אֱלֹהֵי נֵכָר וְשָׁב וְהֵרַע לָכֶם וְכִלָּה
and ,you to do and He then ,strange gods shall and ,Jehovah
consume evil turn will serve

21 3091 5971 559 3190 310
אֶתְכֶם אַחֲרֵי אֲשֶׁר־הֵיטִיב לָכֶם׃ וַיֹּאמֶר הָעָם אֶל־יְהוֹשֻׁעַ
,Joshua to the said And .you to good done has He after ,you
people

22 5707 5971 3091 559 5647 3068 3808
לֹא כִּי אֶת־יְהוָה נַעֲבֹד׃ וַיֹּאמֶר יְהוֹשֻׁעַ אֶל־הָעָם עֵדִים
witnesses the to Joshua said And will we Jehovah but ,No
people ,serve

5647 3068 977
אַתֶּם בָּכֶם כִּי־אַתֶּם בְּחַרְתֶּם לָכֶם אֶת־יְהוָה לַעֲבֹד אוֹתוֹ
.Him to ,Jehovah for have you that against You
serve yourselves chosen yourselves are

23 834 5236 430 5493 6258 5707 559
וַיֹּאמְרוּ עֵדִים׃ וְעַתָּה הָסִירוּ אֶת־אֱלֹהֵי הַנֵּכָר אֲשֶׁר
which the gods from turn And (are We) they And
(are) strange away ,now .witnesses ,said

among you, and incline
your heart to Jehovah the
God of Israel. 24And the
people said to Joshua, We
will serve Jehovah our God,
and we will listen to His
voice. 25And Joshua made
a covenant with the people
on that day, and laid on
them a statute and an
ordinance in Shechem.
26And Joshua wrote these
words in the book of the law
of God, and took a great
stone and raised it up there
under the oak by the
sanctuary of Jehovah.
27And Joshua said to all the
people, Behold, this stone
shall be a witness against
us, for it has heard all the
sayings of Jehovah which
He has spoken with us. And
it shall be against you for a
witness, that you not lie
against your God. 28And
Joshua sent the people
away, each to his inheritance.

29And it happened after
these things, the servant of
Jehovah, Joshua the son of
Nun died, being a son of a
hundred and ten. 30And
they buried him in the
border of his inheritance, in
Timnath-serah, which *is* in
the hills of Ephraim, on the
north of the Hill of Gaash.
31And Israel served
Jehovah all the days of
Joshua, and all the days of
the elders whose days were
prolonged after Joshua,
and who knew all the work
of Jehovah which he did to
Israel.

32And the bones of
Joseph which the sons of
Israel brought up out of
Egypt, they buried in
Shechem, in the portion of
the field which Jacob

בקרבכם והטו את־לבבכם אל־יהוה אלהי ישראל׃
24 ויאמרו העם אל־יהושע את־יהוה אלהינו נעבד ובקולו
25 נשמע׃ ויכרת יהושע ברית לעם ביום ההוא וישם לו
26 חק ומשפט בשכם׃ ויכתב יהושע את־הדברים האלה
בספר תורת אלהים ויקח אבן גדולה ויקימה שם תחת
27 האלה אשר במקדש יהוה׃ ויאמר יהושע אל־
כל־העם הנה האבן הזאת תהיה־בנו לעדה כי־היא
שמעה את כל־אמרי יהוה אשר דבר עמנו והיתה
28 בכם לעדה פן־תכחשון באלהיכם׃ וישלח יהושע
29 את־העם איש לנחלתו׃ ויהי אחרי הדברים האלה
וימת יהושע בן־נון עבד יהוה בן־מאה ועשר שנים׃
30 ויקברו אותו בגבול נחלתו בתמנת־סרח אשר בהר־
31 אפרים מצפון להר־געש׃ ויעבד ישראל את־יהוה כל
ימי יהושע וכל ימי הזקנים אשר האריכו ימים
אחרי יהושע ואשר ידעו את כל־מעשה יהוה אשר
32 עשה לישראל׃ ואת־עצמות יוסף אשר־העלו בני־
ישראל ממצרים קברו בשכם בחלקת השדה אשר

7192 3967 7927 1 2544/1121 3290 7069
קָנָה יַעֲקֹב מֵאֵת בְּנֵי־חֲמוֹר אֲבִי־שְׁכֶם בְּמֵאָה קְשִׂיטָה
silver a for Shechem the ,Hamor the from Jacob bought
pieces hundred of father of son

6912 4191 175/1121 499 5159 3127 1121
33 וַיִּהְיוּ לִבְנֵי־יוֹסֵף לְנַחֲלָה׃ וְאֶלְעָזָר בֶּן־אַהֲרֹן מֵת וַיִּקְבְּרוּ
they and ,died of son the And an for Joseph the to and
buried Aaron Eleazar .inheritance of sons were they

669 2022 5414 834 11:21 6372 1389
אֹתוֹ בְּגִבְעַת פִּינְחָס בְּנוֹ אֲשֶׁר נִתַּן־לוֹ בְּהַר אֶפְרָיִם׃
.Ephraim, the in to was which his Phinehas the in him
of hills him given ,son of hill

bought from the sons of Hamor the father of Shechem, for a hundred silver pieces. And they were for an inheritance to the sons of Joseph.

[33]And Eleazar the son of Aaron died, and they buried him in the hill of Phinehas his son, which was given to him in the hills of Ephraim.

NOTE ON CHAPTER 21, VERSES 36 AND 37

Both of these verses are supported by the majority of coddices, and they are not lacking in the early translations. Verses 7, 40, and 41 give internal evidence to their validity and to their importance to a full revelation of the divine words. The verses were left out of the Hebrew *Rabbinic Bible* by Rabbi Jacob ben Chasim in 1525. This was without right or reason. For full discussions, see Knobel, p.474; Keil, *Commentary on Joshua*, p. 457, note.

שופטים

LIBER JUDICUM

(THE) BOOK OF JUDGES

CAPUT. I א

CHAPTER 1

A LITERAL TRANSLATION
OF THE BIBLE
THE BOOK OF JUDGES

CHAPTER 1

[1]And it happened after the death of Joshua, the sons of of Israel inquired of Jehovah, saying, Who shall first go up for us against the Canaanites, to fight against them. [2]And Jehovah said, Judah shall go up. Behold, I have given the land into his hand. [3]And Judah said to his brother Simeon, Go up with me into my lot, and we shall fight against the Canaanites. And I also will go with you into your lot. And Simeon went with him. [4]And Judah went up, and Jehovah delivered the Canaanites and the Perizzites into their hand. And they struck them in Bezek, ten thousand men. [5]And they found Adoni-bezek in Bezek, and fought against him, and struck the Canaanites and the Perizzites. [6]And Adoni-bezek fled, and they pursued him and caught him, and cut off his thumbs and his big toes. [7]And Adoni-bezek said, Seventy kings *with* their thumbs and their big toes cut off used to *be* gathering *scraps* under my table. As I have done, so God has repaid me. And they brought him to Jerusalem, and he died there.

[8]And the sons of Judah fought against Jerusalem, and captured it, and struck it with the edge of the sword, and set the city on fire. [9]And afterward the sons of Judah went down to fight against the

559 3068 3478 1121 7592 3091 4194 310 1961
1 ויהי אחרי מות יהושע וישאלו בני ישראל ביהוה לאמר
,saying of Israel the that ,Joshua the after it And
Jehovah of sons inquired of death ,was

559 3898 8462 3669 5927
2 מי־יעלה־לנו אל־הכנעני בתחלה להלחם בו: ויאמר
said And against fight to ,first the against us for shall Who
?them Canaanites up go

559 3027 776 5414 2009 5927 3063 3068
3 יהוה יהודה יעלה הנה נתתי את־הארץ בידו: ויאמר
said And into the have I ,behold shall Judah ,Jehovah
hand his land given up go

3669 3898 1486 5927 251 8095 3063
יהודה לשמעון אחיו עלה אתי בגורלי ונלחמה בכנעני
the against us let and my to with Go his Simeon to Judah
;Canaanites fight ,allotment me up ,brother

5927 8095 3212 1486 1571 3212
4 והלכתי גם־אני אתך בגורלך וילך אתו שמעון: ויעל
And .Simeon with And your into with I also will and
went him went ,allotment you go

966 5221 3027 6522 3669 3068 5414 3063
יהודה ויתן יהוה את־הכנעני והפרזי בידם ויכום בבזק
in they and their into the and Canaanites the Jehovah and ,Judah
,Bezek them struck ;hand Perizzites gave

3898 966 966 113 4672 376 505 6235
5 עשרת אלפים איש: וימצאו את־אדני בזק בבזק וילחמו
fought and in bezek Adoni- they and ;men thousand ten
,Bezek found

7291 966 113 5127 6522 3669 5221
6 בו ויכו את־הכנעני ואת־הפרזי: וינס אדני בזק וירדפו
they and bezek Adoni- And the and the and against
chased fled .Perizzites Canaanites struck ,him

559 7272 3027 931 7112 270 310
7 אחריו ויאחזו אותו ויקצצו את־בהנות ידיו ורגליו: ויאמר
said And his and his large the cut and ,him and after
feet hands of digits off caught him

7272 3027 931 4428 7657 966/113
אדני־בזק שבעים | מלכים בהנות ידיהם ורגליהם
their and hands their the (with) kings Seventy ,bezek Adoni-
feet of digits large

6213 7979 8478 3950 7112
מקצצים היו מלקטים תחת שלחני כאשר עשיתי כן
so have I as ;table my under gathering (be) used off cut
done (scraps)

3898 8033 4191 3389 935 430 7999
8 שלם־לי אלהים ויביאהו ירושלם וימת שם: וילחמו
And .there he and to they and God me has
fought died ,Jerusalem him brought repaid

2719 6310 5221 3920 3389 3063/1121
בני־יהודה בירושלם וילכדו אותה ויכוה לפי־חרב ואת־
and the with and ,it and against Judah the
,sword's edge it struck captured ,Jerusalem of sons

3898 3063 1121 3381 310 784 7971 5892
9 העיר שלחו באש: ואחר ירדו בני יהודה להלחם
fight to Judah the went And .fire on set the
of sons down afterward city

Canaanites who inhabited Hebron — and the name of Hebron before *was* Kirjah-arba — and they struck Sheshai, and Ahiman, and Talmai. 11 And from there he went against the inhabitants of Debir — and the name of Debir before *was* Kirjath-sepher. 12 And Caleb said, *He* who strikes Kirjath-sepher and captures it, I will give to him my daughter Achsah for a wife. 13 And Othniel the son of Kenaz, Caleb's brother, the younger one, captured it. And he gave his daughter Achsah to him for a wife.

14 And it happened as she came, she persuaded him to ask a field from her father. And she alighted from the ass. And Caleb said to her, What for you? 15 And she said to him, Give a blessing to me, the land of the Negeb; also you shall give springs of water to me. And Caleb gave the upper springs and the lower springs to her.

16 And the sons of the Kenite, the father-in-law of Moses, had gone up out of the city of palms with the sons of Judah, to the wilderness of Judah, which is in the south of Arad. And they went and lived with the people.

17 And Judah went with his brother Simeon, and they struck the Canaanites inhabiting Zephath, and destroyed it. And the name of the city *was called* Hormah. 18 And Judah captured Gaza and its border, and Askelon and its border, and Ekron and its border. 19 And Jehovah was with Judah, and he occupied the hills, but did not

כְּנַעֲנִי יוֹשֵׁב הָהָר וְהַנֶּגֶב וְהַשְּׁפֵלָה׃ וַיֵּלֶךְ יְהוּדָה אֶל־ 10
against Judah went And the lowlands. and the Negeb and the hills living in the Canaanites against the

הַכְּנַעֲנִי הַיּוֹשֵׁב בְּחֶבְרוֹן וְשֵׁם־חֶבְרוֹן לְפָנִים קִרְיַת אַרְבַּע
-arba- Kirjath- formerly (was) Hebron the name of and Hebron in living the Canaanites

וַיַּכּוּ אֶת־שֵׁשַׁי וְאֶת־אֲחִימַן וְאֶת־תַּלְמָי׃ וַיֵּלֶךְ מִשָּׁם אֶל־ 11
against from there he went And .Talmai and ,Ahiman and ,Sheshai they struck and

יוֹשְׁבֵי דְבִיר וְשֵׁם־דְּבִיר לְפָנִים קִרְיַת־סֵפֶר׃ וַיֹּאמֶר כָּלֵב 12
,Caleb said and —Sepher Kirjath- formerly (was) Debir the name of and —Debir the dwellers of

אֲשֶׁר־יַכֶּה אֶת־קִרְיַת־סֵפֶר וּלְכָדָהּ וְנָתַתִּי לוֹ אֶת־עַכְסָה
Achsah to him will I give and it captures Sepher Kirjath- strikes (He) who

בִתִּי לְאִשָּׁה׃ וַיִּלְכְּדָהּ עָתְנִיאֵל בֶּן־קְנַז אֲחִי כָלֵב הַקָּטֹן 13
one the younger ,Caleb brother of ,Kenaz the son of Othniel captured it And .wife a for daughter my

מִמֶּנּוּ וַיִּתֶּן־לוֹ אֶת־עַכְסָה בִתּוֹ לְאִשָּׁה׃ וַיְהִי בְּבוֹאָהּ 14
she came as it happened And .wife a for daughter his Achsah him to he gave and ;him than

וַתְּסִיתֵהוּ לִשְׁאוֹל מֵאֵת־אָבִיהָ הַשָּׂדֶה וַתִּצְנַח מֵעַל הַחֲמוֹר
,ass the upon from she alighted and ;field a father her from ask to him persuaded she that

וַיֹּאמֶר־לָהּ כָּלֵב מַה־לָּךְ׃ וַתֹּאמֶר לוֹ הָבָה־לִּי בְרָכָה 15
;blessing a me to Give ,him to said she And ?you for What ,Caleb her to said and

כִּי אֶרֶץ הַנֶּגֶב נְתַתָּנִי וְנָתַתָּה לִי גֻּלֹּת מָיִם וַיִּתֶּן־לָהּ כָּלֵב
Caleb her to gave and ;water of springs me to you shall give that ,me given have you Negeb the of land the since

אֵת גֻּלֹּת עִלִּית וְאֵת גֻּלֹּת תַּחְתִּית׃ וּבְנֵי קֵינִי חֹתֵן 16
father-in-law ,Kenite the of sons the And .lower the springs and upper the springs the

מֹשֶׁה עָלוּ מֵעִיר הַתְּמָרִים אֶת־בְּנֵי יְהוּדָה מִדְבַּר יְהוּדָה
,Judah of wilderness the to Judah of sons the with palms of city the out of gone had ,Moses'

אֲשֶׁר בְּנֶגֶב עֲרָד וַיֵּלֶךְ וַיֵּשֶׁב אֶת־הָעָם׃ וַיֵּלֶךְ יְהוּדָה אֶת־ 17
with Judah went And .people the with lived and went they and ;Arad of south the in is which

שִׁמְעוֹן אָחִיו וַיַּכּוּ אֶת־הַכְּנַעֲנִי יוֹשֵׁב צְפַת וַיַּחֲרִימוּ אוֹתָהּ
;it annihilated and Zephath in living the Canaanites struck they and brother his Simeon

וַיִּקְרָא אֶת־שֵׁם־הָעִיר חָרְמָה׃ וַיִּלְכֹּד יְהוּדָה אֶת־עַזָּה 18
Gaza Judah captured And .Hormah city the of name the called was and

וְאֶת־גְּבוּלָהּ וְאֶת־אַשְׁקְלוֹן וְאֶת־גְּבוּלָהּ וְאֶת־עֶקְרוֹן וְאֶת־
and Ekron and ,border its and Askelon and ,border its and

גְּבוּלָהּ׃ וַיְהִי יְהוָה אֶת־יְהוּדָה וַיֹּרֶשׁ אֶת־הָהָר כִּי 19
but ,hills the occupied he and ,Judah with Jehovah was and ;border its

expel the inhabitants of the valley; for they had chariots of iron.
20And they gave Hebron to Caleb, As Moses had said. And he expelled the three sons of Anak from there.
21And the sons of Benjamin did ot expel the Jebusites living in Jerusalem. And the Jebusites live with the sons of Benjamin in Jerusalem until this day.

22And the house of Joseph went up; they also against Bethel. And Jehovah *was* with them. 23And the house of Joseph sent to spy around Bethel—and the name of the city formerly *was* Luz. 24And the guards saw a man coming out from the city, and said to him, Please show us the entrance of the city, and we will deal with you with mercy. 25And he showed them the entrance of the city. And they struck the city with the mouth of the sword; and they sent away the man and all his family. 26And the man went to the land of the Hittites and built a city, and called its name Luz; it *is* its name to this day.
27And Manasseh had not occupied Beth-shean and its daughter *villages*; or Taanach and its daughter *villages*; *nor struck* the inhabitants of Dor and its daughter *villages*; or the inhabitants of Ibleam and its daughter *villages*; or the inhabitants of Megiddo and its daughter *villages*. For the Canaanites desired to live in that land. 28But when Israel became strong, it happened that they put the Canaanites to tribute, but did not completely expel it.

29And Ephraim did not expel the Canaanites who lived in Gezer, and the Canaanites lived among them in Gezer.

5414 1270 7393 6010 3427 3423 3808
לֹא לְהוֹרִישׁ אֶת־יֹשְׁבֵי הָעֵמֶק כִּי־רֶכֶב בַּרְזֶל לָהֶם׃ וַיִּתְּנוּ 20
they And they iron chariots for the in- the expel did not
gave .had of valley of habitants

3423 4872 1696 2275 3612
לְכָלֵב אֶת־חֶבְרוֹן כַּאֲשֶׁר דִּבֶּר מֹשֶׁה וַיּוֹרֶשׁ מִשָּׁם אֶת־
from he and ;Moses had as ,Hebron to
there expelled said Caleb

3423 3389 3427 2983 6061 1121 7969
21 שְׁלֹשָׁה בְּנֵי הָעֲנָק׃ וְאֶת־הַיְבוּסִי יֹשֵׁב יְרוּשָׁלִַם לֹא הוֹרִישׁוּ
did not Jerusalem living Jebusites the And .Anak sons the
expel in of three

3117 5704 3389 1144 1121 2983 3427 1144 1121
בְּנֵי בִנְיָמִן וַיֵּשֶׁב הַיְבוּסִי אֶת־בְּנֵי בִנְיָמִן בִּירוּשָׁלִַם עַד הַיּוֹם
day until ,Jerusalem in Benjamin the with the and ;Benjamin the
of sons Jebusite live of sons

3068 1008/1004 1571 3127/1004 5927 2088
הַזֶּה׃ 22 וַיַּעֲלוּ בֵית־יוֹסֵף גַּם־הֵם בֵּית־אֵל וַיהוָה עִמָּם׃
with (was) and against ,they also Joseph the And .this
;them Jehovah ;Bethel of house up went

7200 3870 6440 5892 8034 1008/1004 3127/1004 8446
וַיָּתִירוּ בֵית־יוֹסֵף בְּבֵית־אֵל וְשֵׁם־הָעִיר לְפָנִים לוּז׃ וַיִּרְאוּ 23 24
and —Luz formerly the the and around Joseph the and
saw (was) city of name —Bethel of house scouted

4994 7200 559 5892 3318 376 8104
הַשֹּׁמְרִים אִישׁ יוֹצֵא מִן־הָעִיר וַיֹּאמְרוּ לוֹ הַרְאֵנוּ נָא אֶת־
Please show to said and the out coming a guards the
us ,him ,city from man

5892 3996 7200 2617 6213 5892 3996
מְבוֹא הָעִיר וְעָשִׂינוּ עִמְּךָ חָסֶד׃ 25 וַיַּרְאֵם אֶת־מְבוֹא הָעִיר
the entrance the he And with with we and the entrance
;city of them showed .mercy you deal will city's

4940 3605 376 2719/6310 5892 5221
וַיַּכּוּ אֶת־הָעִיר לְפִי־חָרֶב וְאֶת־הָאִישׁ וְאֶת־כָּל־מִשְׁפַּחְתּוֹ
family his all and the and the with the they and
man ;sword's edge city struck

8034 7121 5892 1129 2850 776 376 3212 7971
שִׁלֵּחוּ׃ 26 וַיֵּלֶךְ הָאִישׁ אֶרֶץ הַחִתִּים וַיִּבֶן עִיר וַיִּקְרָא שְׁמָהּ
its and a and the the to the and sent they
name called ,city built Hittites of land man went ;away

4519 3423 3808 2088 3117 5704 8034 3870
לוּז הוּא שְׁמָהּ עַד הַיּוֹם הַזֶּה׃ 27 וְלֹא־הוֹרִישׁ מְנַשֶּׁה
Manasseh taken had And .this day to its that ;Luz
of possession not name (is)

1323 8590 1323 = 1852 =
אֶת־בֵּית־שְׁאָן וְאֶת־בְּנוֹתֶיהָ וְאֶת־תַּעְנַךְ וְאֶת־בְּנֹתֶיהָ וְאֶת־
and daughter its and Taanach and daughter its and shean Beth-
(villages) .(villages)

1323 2991 3427 1323 1756 3427
יֹשֵׁב דּוֹר וְאֶת־בְּנוֹתֶיהָ וְאֶת־יוֹשְׁבֵי יִבְלְעָם וְאֶת־בְּנֹתֶיהָ
daughter its and Ibleam the and daughter its and Dor the
(villages) of dwellers .(villages) of dwellers

3027 3669 2974 1323 4023 3427
וְאֶת־יוֹשְׁבֵי מְגִדּוֹ וְאֶת־בְּנוֹתֶיהָ וַיּוֹאֶל הַכְּנַעֲנִי לָשֶׁבֶת
live to the were for daughter its and Megiddo the and
Canaanites on set .(villages) of dwellers

3669 7760 3478 2258 5414 776
בָּאָרֶץ הַזֹּאת׃ 28 וַיְהִי כִּי־חָזַק יִשְׂרָאֵל וַיָּשֶׂם אֶת־הַכְּנַעֲנִי
the they that ,Israel had when it but ;that in
Canaanites put strong become was land

3423 3808 669 3423 3808 3423 4522
לָמַס וְהוֹרֵישׁ לֹא הוֹרִישׁוֹ׃ 29 וְאֶפְרַיִם לֹא הוֹרִישׁ
did not And did not but for
dispossess Ephraim .them expel completely ,tribute

1507 7130 3669 3427 1507 3027 3669
אֶת־הַכְּנַעֲנִי הַיּוֹשֵׁב בְּגָזֶר וַיֵּשֶׁב הַכְּנַעֲנִי בְּקִרְבּוֹ בְּגָזֶר׃
in their in the and in living the
.Gezer midst Canaanites lived ,Gezer Canaanites

[30]Zebulun did not expel the inhabitants of Kitron, and the inhabitants of Nahalol; but the Canaanites lived among them, and they became burden-bearers.
[31]And Asher did not expel the inhabitants of Accho, and the inhabitants of Sidon, and Ahlab, and Achzib, and Helbah, and Aphik, and Rehob. [32]And the Asherites lived among the Canaanites, the inhabitants of the land, for they did not expel them.
[33]Naphtali did not expel the inhabitants of Beth-shemesh, and the inhabitants of Beth-anath, and they lived among the Canaanites, the inhabitants of the land. But the inhabitants of Beth-shemesh and Beth-anath became burden-bearers to them.
[34]And the Amorites pressed the sons of Dan into the hills; for they would not allow them to come down to the valley. [35]But the Amorites were determined to live in Mount Heres, in Aijalon, and in Shaalbim. Yet the hand of the house of Joseph prevailed, so that they became burden-bearers. [36]And the border of the Amorites *was* from the ascent of Akrabbim, from the rock and upward.

30 זבולן לא הוריש את־יושבי קטרון ואת־יושבי
the and ,Kitron dwellers the did not Zebulun
of dwellers of dispossess
31 נהלל וישב הכנעני בקרבו ויהיו למס: אשר לא
not Asher tribu- they and among the but ;Nahalol
.tary became ,them Canaanites lived
הוריש את־ישבי עכו ואת־יושבי צידון ואת־אחלב ואת־
and ,Ahlab and ,Zidon the and Accho the did
of dwellers of dwellers ,expel
32 אכזיב ואת־חלבה ואת־אפיק ואת־רחב: וישב האשרי
the and ;Rehob and ,Aphik and ,Helbah and ,Achzib
Asherites lived
33 בקרב הכנעני ישבי הארץ כי לא הורישו: נפתלי
Naphtali did they not for ,land the the Can- the the in
.him dispossess of dwellers ,naanites of midst
לא־הוריש את־ישבי בית־שמש ואת־ישבי בית־ענת
,anath Beth- the and ,shemesh Beth- the did not
of dwellers of dwellers expel
וישב בקרב הכנעני ישבי הארץ וישבי בית־שמש
shemesh Beth the and ,land the the Ca- the among they and
of dwellers of dwellers ,naanites lived
34 ובית ענת היו להם למס: וילחצו האמרי את־בני־דן
Dan the the And tribu- for became anath and
of sons Amorites pressed .tary them Beth-
35 ההרה כי־לא נתנו לרדת לעמק: ויואל האמרי לשבת
live to the were But the to come to did they not for the into
Amorite determined .valley down him grant ;country hill
בהר־חרס באילון ובשעלבים ותכבד יד בית־יוסף
Joseph the the was yet in and in ,Heres in
of house of hand heavy ;Shaalbim ,Aijalon Mount
36 ויהיו למס: וגבול האמרי ממעלה עקרבים מהסלע
the from ,Akrabbim the from (was) the the And tribu- they and
rock of ascent Amorites of border .taries became
ומעלה:
and
.upward

CAP. II ב

CHAPTER 2

CHAPTER 2

[1]And the Angel of Jehovah came up from Gilgal to The Place of Weeping, and said, I caused you to come up out of Egypt, and brought you into the land which I had sworn to your fathers, and said, I shall not break My covenant with you forever. [2]And you, you shall cut no covenant with the inhabitants of this land. You shall

1 ויעל מלאך־יהוה מן־הגלגל אל־הבכים ׃ ויאמר
,said and .Place the to Gilgal from Jehovah the And
Weeping of of Angel up came
אעלה אתכם ממצרים ואביא אתכם אל־הארץ אשר
which the into you and of out you caused I
land brought ,Egypt up go to
נשבעתי לאבתיכם ואמר לא־אפר בריתי אתכם
with My shall I not ,said and your to swore I
you covenant break ,fathers
2 לעולם: ואתם לא־תכרתו ברית ליושבי הארץ הזאת
,this land the with a shall you not ,you and ;forever
of dwellers covenant cut

break down their altars. Yet you have not listened to My voice. What *is* this you have done? [3]And I also have said, I shall not drive them out before you, and they shall become adversaries to you; and their gods shall become a snare to you. [4]And it happened when the Angel of Jehovah spoke these words to all the sons of Israel, the people lifted up their voice and wept.

[5]And they called the name of that place The Place of Weeping, and *they* sacrificed to Jehovah there.

[6]And Joshua sent the people away, and the sons of Israel each went to his inheritance, to possess the land. [7]And the people served Jehovah all the days of Joshua and all the days of the elders who prolonged *their* days after Joshua, who saw all the great work of Jehovah which He had done for Israel. [8]And Joshua the son of Nun, the servant of Jehovah, died, being a son of a hundred and ten years. [9]And they buried him in the border of his inheritance, in Timnath-heres, in the hills of Ephraim, on the north of Mount Gaash. [10]And also all that generation was gathered to their fathers, and another generation rose up after them, who had not known Jehovah, nor yet the works which He had done for Israel.

[11]And the sons of Israel did evil in the sight of Jehovah, and served the Baals. [12]And they forsook Jehovah, the God of their fathers, who brought them out from the land of Egypt. And they went after other gods, of the gods of the

מִזְבְּחוֹתֵיהֶם תִּתֹּצוּן וְלֹא־שְׁמַעְתֶּם בְּקֹלִי מַה־זֹּאת
this (is) what My to voice; have you listened Yet not shall you down break altars their

3 עֲשִׂיתֶם׃ וְגַם אָמַרְתִּי לֹא־אֲגָרֵשׁ אוֹתָם מִפְּנֵיכֶם וְהָיוּ
they and become shall before you them shall I out drive not have I said, And also have you done?

4 לָכֶם לְצִדִּים וֵאלֹהֵיהֶם יִהְיוּ לָכֶם לְמוֹקֵשׁ׃ וַיְהִי כְּדַבֵּר
when spoke it And was, snare a. you to shall become their and gods sides, to you

מַלְאַךְ יְהוָה אֶת־הַדְּבָרִים הָאֵלֶּה אֶל־כָּל־בְּנֵי יִשְׂרָאֵל
Israel, the of sons all to these words Jehovah the of Angel

5 וַיִּשְׂאוּ הָעָם אֶת־קוֹלָם וַיִּבְכּוּ׃ וַיִּקְרְאוּ שֵׁם־הַמָּקוֹם הַהוּא
that place name the of they And called and wept. voice their the lifted that people up

6 בֹּכִים וַיִּזְבְּחוּ־שָׁם לַיהוָה׃ וַיְשַׁלַּח יְהוֹשֻׁעַ אֶת־הָעָם
the people, Joshua sent And away to Jehovah sacrificed and there Place the Weeping of,

וַיֵּלְכוּ בְנֵי־יִשְׂרָאֵל אִישׁ לְנַחֲלָתוֹ לָרֶשֶׁת אֶת־הָאָרֶץ׃
land the. to possess his to inheritance each Israel the of sons and went

7 וַיַּעַבְדוּ הָעָם אֶת־יְהוָה כֹּל יְמֵי יְהוֹשֻׁעַ וְכֹל יְמֵי הַזְּקֵנִים
the elders days the of and all Joshua, the of days all Jehovah the people And served

אֲשֶׁר הֶאֱרִיכוּ יָמִים אַחֲרֵי יְהוֹשׁוּעַ אֲשֶׁר רָאוּ אֵת כָּל־
all saw who Joshua, after days prolonged who

8 מַעֲשֵׂה יְהוָה הַגָּדוֹל אֲשֶׁר עָשָׂה לְיִשְׂרָאֵל׃ וַיָּמָת יְהוֹשֻׁעַ
Joshua, And died Israel for. He done had which the great Jehovah of work

9 בִּן־נוּן עֶבֶד יְהוָה בֶּן־מֵאָה וָעֶשֶׂר שָׁנִים׃ וַיִּקְבְּרוּ אוֹתוֹ
him they And buried years. ten and a hundred son of a Jehovah's ser-vant, Nun the of son

בִּגְבוּל נַחֲלָתוֹ בְּתִמְנַת־חֶרֶס בְּהַר אֶפְרָיִם מִצְּפוֹן לְהַר־
of Mount north Ephraim, the in of hills heres, in Timnath inher-itance his the in of border

10 גָּעַשׁ׃ וְגַם כָּל־הַדּוֹר הַהוּא נֶאֶסְפוּ אֶל־אֲבוֹתָיו וַיָּקָם דּוֹר
gener-ation and rose fathers, his to was gathered that genera-tion all And also Gaash.

אַחֵר אַחֲרֵיהֶם אֲשֶׁר לֹא־יָדְעוּ אֶת־יְהוָה וְגַם אֶת־הַמַּעֲשֶׂה
the works nor yet Jehovah, did not know who after them another

11 אֲשֶׁר עָשָׂה לְיִשְׂרָאֵל׃ וַיַּעֲשׂוּ בְנֵי־יִשְׂרָאֵל אֶת־הָרַע
evil Israel sons the of And did for Israel. had He done which

12 בְּעֵינֵי יְהוָה וַיַּעַבְדוּ אֶת־הַבְּעָלִים׃ וַיַּעַזְבוּ אֶת־יְהוָה אֱלֹהֵי
the of God Jehovah they and forsook Baals, the and served Jehovah, the in of eyes

אֲבוֹתָם הַמּוֹצִיא אוֹתָם מֵאֶרֶץ מִצְרָיִם וַיֵּלְכוּ אַחֲרֵי אֱלֹהִים
gods after and went they ;Egypt the from of land them who out brought their fathers

peoples who *were* around
them, and bowed them-
selves to them, and
angered Jehovah. 13 Yea,
they forsook Jehovah, and
served Baal and the
Ashtoroths.
14 And the anger of
Jehovah burned against
Israel, and He gave them
into the hand of plunderers;
and they plundered them.
And He sold them into the
hand of their enemies all
around, and they were not
able to stand before
their enemies any longer.
15 Wherever they went, the
hand of Jehovah was
against them for evil, as
Jehovah had spoken, and
as Jehovah had sworn to
them. And *it* distressed
them very much. 16 And
Jehovah raised up judges,
and they saved them from
the hand of their plunderers.
17 But they also did not listen
to their judges, but went
whoring after other gods,
and bowed themselves to
them. They quickly turned
aside out of the way *in*
which their fathers walked
to obey the commands of
Jehovah. They did not do
so. 18 And when Jehovah
raised up judges to them,
then Jehovah was with the
judge, and rescued them
out of the hand of their
enemies all the days of the
judge. For Jehovah took
pity because of their groaning before their oppressors,
and those that crushed
them. 19 And at the death of
the judge, it happened that
they would turn and act
more corruptly than their
fathers, to go after other
gods, to serve them, and to
bow themselves to them.
And they did not fall away
from their own doings, and
from their stubborn way.
20 And the anger of Jehovah
glowed against Israel. And
He said, Because this
nation has transgressed My
covenant which I com-
manded their fathers, and
has not listened to My
voice, 21 I also from now on

אחרים מאלהי העמים אשר סביבותיהם וישתחוו להם
13 ויכעסו את־יהוה׃ ויעזבו את־יהוה ויעבדו לבעל
14 ולעשתרות׃ ויחר־אף יהוה בישראל ויתנם ביד שסים
וישסו אותם וימכרם ביד אויביהם מסביב ולא־יכלו עוד
15 לעמד לפני אויביהם׃ בכל ׀ אשר יצאו יד־יהוה היתה־
בם לרעה כאשר דבר יהוה וכאשר נשבע יהוה להם
16 ויצר להם מאד׃ ויקם יהוה שפטים ויושיעום מיד
17 שסיהם׃ וגם אל־שפטיהם לא שמעו כי זנו אחרי אלהים
אחרים וישתחוו להם סרו מהר מן־הדרך אשר הלכו
18 אבותם לשמע מצות־יהוה לא־עשו כן׃ וכי־הקים יהוה ׀
להם שפטים והיה יהוה עם־השפט והושיעם מיד איביהם
כל ימי השופט כי־ינחם יהוה מנאקתם מפני לחציהם
19 ודחקיהם׃ והיה ׀ במות השופט ישבו והשחיתו מאבותם
ללכת אחרי אלהים אחרים לעבדם ולהשתחות להם
20 לא הפילו ממעלליהם ומדרכם הקשה׃ ויחר־אף יהוה
בישראל ויאמר יען אשר עברו הגוי הזה את־בריתי
21 אשר צויתי את־אבותם ולא שמעו לקולי׃ גם־אני לא

will not drive out any from before them, of the nations that Joshua left when he died; [22]so that by them I may test Israel, whether they are keeping the way of Jehovah, to go in it, as their fathers kept *it*, or not. [23]And Jehovah left those nations, without driving them out quickly. And He did not deliver them into the hand of Joshua.

אוֹסִיף לְהוֹרִישׁ אִישׁ מִפְּנֵיהֶם מִן־הַגּוֹיִם אֲשֶׁר־עָזַב יְהוֹשֻׁעַ
22 וַיָּמֹת׃ לְמַעַן נַסּוֹת בָּם אֶת־יִשְׂרָאֵל הֲשֹׁמְרִים הֵם אֶת־
דֶּרֶךְ יְהוָה לָלֶכֶת בָּם כַּאֲשֶׁר שָׁמְרוּ אֲבוֹתָם אִם־לֹא׃
23 וַיַּנַּח יְהוָה אֶת־הַגּוֹיִם הָאֵלֶּה לְבִלְתִּי הוֹרִישָׁם מַהֵר וְלֹא
נְתָנָם בְּיַד־יְהוֹשֻׁעַ׃

CAP. III ג

CHAPTER 3

CHAPTER 3

[1]And these *are* the nations which Jehovah left in order to test Israel by them, all who did not know all the wars of Canaan; [2]only that the generations of the sons of Israel might know, to teach them war, only those who did not before know them: [3]five lords of the Philistines, and all the Canaanites, and the Sidonians, and the Hivites that lived in Mount Lebanon from Mount Baal-hermon to the entering of Hamath. [4]And they existed to test Israel by them, to know whether they would listen to the commands of Jehovah, which He had commanded their fathers by the hand of Moses.

[5]And the sons of Israel lived among the Canaanites, the Hittites, and the Amorites, and the Perizzites, and the Hivites, and the Jebusites. [6]And they took their daughters to them for wives, and gave their daughters to their sons; and they served their gods. [7]And the sons of Israel did that which was evil in the sight of Jehovah, and forgot Jehovah their God, and

1 וְאֵלֶּה הַגּוֹיִם אֲשֶׁר הִנִּיחַ יְהוָה לְנַסּוֹת בָּם אֶת־יִשְׂרָאֵל
2 אֵת כָּל־אֲשֶׁר לֹא־יָדְעוּ אֵת כָּל־מִלְחֲמוֹת כְּנָעַן׃ רַק לְמַעַן
דַּעַת דֹּרוֹת בְּנֵי־יִשְׂרָאֵל לְלַמְּדָם מִלְחָמָה רַק אֲשֶׁר־
3 לְפָנִים לֹא יְדָעוּם׃ חֲמֵשֶׁת ׀ סַרְנֵי פְלִשְׁתִּים וְכָל־הַכְּנַעֲנִי
וְהַצִּידֹנִי וְהַחִוִּי יֹשֵׁב הַר הַלְּבָנוֹן מֵהַר בַּעַל חֶרְמוֹן עַד
4 לְבוֹא חֲמָת׃ וַיִּהְיוּ לְנַסּוֹת בָּם אֶת־יִשְׂרָאֵל לָדַעַת הֲיִשְׁמְעוּ
5 אֶת־מִצְוֹת יְהוָה אֲשֶׁר־צִוָּה אֶת־אֲבוֹתָם בְּיַד־מֹשֶׁה׃ וּבְנֵי
יִשְׂרָאֵל יָשְׁבוּ בְּקֶרֶב הַכְּנַעֲנִי הַחִתִּי וְהָאֱמֹרִי וְהַפְּרִזִּי
6 וְהַחִוִּי וְהַיְבוּסִי׃ וַיִּקְחוּ אֶת־בְּנוֹתֵיהֶם לָהֶם לְנָשִׁים וְאֶת־
7 בְּנוֹתֵיהֶם נָתְנוּ לִבְנֵיהֶם וַיַּעַבְדוּ אֶת־אֱלֹהֵיהֶם׃ וַיַּעֲשׂוּ
בְנֵי־יִשְׂרָאֵל אֶת־הָרַע בְּעֵינֵי יְהוָה וַיִּשְׁכְּחוּ אֶת־יְהוָה

served the Baals and the
pillars. 8 And the anger of
Jehovah glowed against
Israel, and He sold them
into the hand of Chushan-
rishathaim, king of Meso-
potamia. And the sons of
Israel served Chushan-
rishathaim eight years.
9 And when the sons of
Israel cried to Jehovah,
Jehovah raised up a
deliverer to the sons of
Israel, Othniel the son of
Kenaz, the younger brother
of Caleb; and he saved
them. 10 And the Spirit of
Jehovah was on him; and
he judged Israel. And he
went out to war, and
Jehovah gave Chushan-
rishathaim king of Syria into
his hand, and his hand
prevailed over Chushan-
rishathaim. 11 And the land
had rest forty years. And
Othniel the son of Kenaz
died.

12 And the sons of Israel
again did evil in the eyes
of Jehovah. And Jehovah
made strong Eglon the king
of Moab against Israel,
because they had done evil
in the eyes of Jehovah.
13 And he gathered to him
the sons of Ammon and
Amalek. And *they* went and
struck Israel. And they
possessed the city of palm
trees. 14 And the sons of
Israel served Eglon king of
Moab eighteen years.

15 And the sons of Israel
cried to Jehovah. And
Jehovah raised up a
deliverer to them, Ehud the
son of Gera, son of a
Benjamite, a man impeded
in his right hand. And
the sons of Israel sent a
present by his hand to Eglon
king of Moab. 16 And Ehud
made for himself a
sword and it *had* two

639/2734 842 1168 5647 430
8 אֱלֹהֵיהֶם וַיַּעַבְדוּ אֶת־הַבְּעָלִים וְאֶת־הָאֲשֵׁרוֹת׃ וַיִּחַר־אַף
anger So .Ashtoreths the and Baals the and ,God their
glowed served

763 44,28 =3573= 3027 4376 3478 3068
יְהוָה בְּיִשְׂרָאֵל וַיִּמְכְּרֵם בְּיַד כּוּשַׁן רִשְׁעָתַיִם מֶלֶךְ אֲרַם
Meso- of king ,rishathaim Chushan- into sold He and against Jehovah's
of hand the them ,Israel

8083 =3573= 3478 1121 5647 763
נַהֲרַיִם וַיַּעַבְדוּ בְנֵי־יִשְׂרָאֵל אֶת־כּוּשַׁן רִשְׁעָתַיִם שְׁמֹנֶה
eight rishathaim Chushan- Israel the and ;potamia
of sons served

3462 3068 6965 3068 3478 1121 2199 8141
9 שָׁנִים׃ וַיִּזְעֲקוּ בְנֵי־יִשְׂרָאֵל אֶל־יְהוָה וַיָּקֶם יְהוָה מוֹשִׁיעַ
a Jehovah raised ,Jehovah to Israel the when And .years
deliverer up of sons cried

3672 251 7023/1121 6774 3462 3478 1121
לִבְנֵי יִשְׂרָאֵל וַיּוֹשִׁיעֵם אֵת עָתְנִיאֵל בֶּן־קְנַז אֲחִי כָלֵב
Caleb's brother ,Kenaz the Othniel (even) he and ,Israel the for
of of son them saved of sons

3478 8199 3068/7307 5921 1961 6996
10 הַקָּטֹן מִמֶּנּוּ׃ וַתְּהִי עָלָיו רוּחַ־יְהוָה וַיִּשְׁפֹּט אֶת־יִשְׂרָאֵל
;Israel he and ,Jehovah the upon And than younger
judged of Spirit ,him was .him

4428 =3573= 30:27 3068 5414 442 3318
וַיֵּצֵא לַמִּלְחָמָה וַיִּתֵּן יְהוָה בְּיָדוֹ אֶת־כּוּשַׁן רִשְׁעָתַיִם מֶלֶךְ
king rishathaim Chushan- into Jehovah and ,war to he and
of hand his gave out went

776 8252 =3573= 3027 5810 758
11 אֲרָם וַתָּעָז יָדוֹ עַל כּוּשַׁן רִשְׁעָתָיִם׃ וַתִּשְׁקֹט הָאָרֶץ
the had And .rishathaim Chushan- over his had and Aram
land rest hand power

1121 3254 7023/1121 6274 4191 8141 703
12 אַרְבָּעִים שָׁנָה וַיָּמָת עָתְנִיאֵל בֶּן־קְנַז׃ וַיֹּסִפוּ בְּנֵי
the And .Kenaz the Othniel And .years forty
of sons again of son died

5700 3068 2388 3068 5869 7451 6213 3478
יִשְׂרָאֵל לַעֲשׂוֹת הָרַע בְּעֵינֵי יְהוָה וַיְחַזֵּק יְהוָה אֶת־עֶגְלוֹן
Eglon Jehovah and ;Jehovah the in evil did Israel
strengthened of eyes

3068 5869 7451 6213 3478/5921 4124 4428
מֶלֶךְ־מוֹאָב עַל־יִשְׂרָאֵל עַל כִּי־עָשׂוּ אֶת־הָרַע בְּעֵינֵי יְהוָה׃
.Jehovah the in evil they because ,Israel against Moab the
of eyes done had of king

3478 5221 3318 6002 5983 1121 622
13 וַיֶּאֱסֹף אֵלָיו אֶת־בְּנֵי עַמּוֹן וַעֲמָלֵק וַיֵּלֶךְ וַיַּךְ אֶת־יִשְׂרָאֵל
;Israel and and and Ammon the to he And
struck went ,Amalek of sons him gathered

5700 3478 1121 5647 8558 5889 3423
14 וַיִּירְשׁוּ אֶת־עִיר הַתְּמָרִים׃ וַיַּעַבְדוּ בְנֵי־יִשְׂרָאֵל אֶת־עֶגְלוֹן
Eglon Israel the and palm the they and
of sons served ;trees of city possessed

3478 1121 2199 8141 6240 8083 41:24 44,28
15 מֶלֶךְ־מוֹאָב שְׁמוֹנֶה עֶשְׂרֵה שָׁנָה׃ וַיִּזְעֲקוּ בְנֵי־יִשְׂרָאֵל
Israel the And .years eighteen Moab the
of sons cried of king

1121 1612/1121 164 3462 3068 6965 3068
אֶל־יְהוָה וַיָּקֶם יְהוָה לָהֶם מוֹשִׁיעַ אֶת־אֵהוּד בֶּן־גֵּרָא בֶּן
a ,Gera the Ehud a for Jehovah and ,Jehovah to
of son of son deliverer them up raised

3027 3478 1121 7971 3225 334 376 3228
הַיְמִינִי אִישׁ אִטֵּר יַד־יְמִינוֹ וַיִּשְׁלְחוּ בְנֵי־יִשְׂרָאֵל בְּיָדוֹ
his by Israel the sent And his hand impeded a the
hand of sons right (in) man ,Benjamite

2719 164 6213 4124 44,28 5700 450:3
16 מִנְחָה לְעֶגְלוֹן מֶלֶךְ מוֹאָב׃ וַיַּעַשׂ לוֹ אֵהוּד חֶרֶב וְלָהּ
it and a Ehud for And .Moab king the Eglon to a
(had) sword himself made of present

edges, a cubit in length.
And he girded it under his
long robe, on his right
thigh. 17And he brought
the present to Eglon the
king of Moab; and Eglon
was a very fat man. 18And
it happened, when he had
finished offering the
present, he sent away the
people, the bearers of the
present. 19And he himself
turned back from the carved
images at Gilgal, and said, I
have a secret word for you,
O king. And he said, Be
silent! And all those standing beside him went out
from hin.. 20And Ehud
came to him. And he *was*
sitting by himself *in* the cool
roof room which he *had*.
And Ehud said, I have a
message from God to you.
And he rose out of his seat.
21And Ehud put out his left
hand and took the sword
from his right thigh, and
thrust it into *Eglon's* belly.
22And the haft also went in
after the blade; and the fat
closed on the blade; for he
did not draw the sword out
of his belly. And it came out
behind. 23Then Ehud went
out to the porch, and shut
the doors of the roof room
on him, and locked them.
24And when he had gone
out, his servants came. And
they looked, and, behold,
the doors of the roof room
were locked. And they said,
Surely he *is* covering his
feet in the cool roof room.

25And they waited until they
were ashamed. And, be-
hold, he did not open the
doors of the room. So they
took the key and opened
them. And, behold, their
master *had* fallen down to
the earth dead.
26And Ehud escaped
while they waited. And *he*
had passed by the images,
and had slipped away to

3409 5921/4055 8378 2296 753 1574 6366 8147
שְׁנֵי פֵיוֹת גֹּמֶד אָרְכָּהּ וַיַּחְגֹּר אוֹתָהּ מִתַּחַת לְמַדָּיו עַל יֶרֶךְ
thigh on his under it he and its a ,edges two
robe girded ;length cubit

5700 4124 4428 5700 4503 7126 3225
יְמִינוֹ׃ וַיַּקְרֵב אֶת־הַמִּנְחָה לְעֶגְלוֹן מֶלֶךְ מוֹאָב וְעֶגְלוֹן 17
and ;Moab the Eglon to present the he and his
(was) Eglon of king brought ;right

4503 7126 3615 1961 3966 1277 376
אִישׁ בָּרִיא מְאֹד׃ וַיְהִי כַּאֲשֶׁר כִּלָּה לְהַקְרִיב אֶת־הַמִּנְחָה 18
the offering had he when it And .very fat a
,present finished ,happened man

6456 7725 4503 5375 5971 7971
וַיְשַׁלַּח אֶת־הָעָם נֹשְׂאֵי הַמִּנְחָה׃ וְהוּא שָׁב מִן־הַפְּסִילִים 19
carved the from turned he and the bearers the sent he
images back himself ;present of people away

559 4428 5643 559 1537 834
אֲשֶׁר אֶת־הַגִּלְגָּל וַיֹּאמֶר דְּבַר־סֵתֶר לִי אֵלֶיךָ הַמֶּלֶךְ וַיֹּאמֶר
And .king O to I secret a ,said and ,Gilgal at which
,said he ,you have word (were)

935 164 5975 3605 3318 2013
הָס וַיֵּצְאוּ מֵעָלָיו כָּל־הָעֹמְדִים עָלָיו׃ וְאֵהוּד ׀ בָּא אֵלָיו 20
to came And beside those all from went And Be
him Ehud .him standing him out !silent

164 559 834 4747 5944 3427 1931
וְהוּא יֹשֵׁב בַּעֲלִיַּת הַמְּקֵרָה אֲשֶׁר־לוֹ לְבַדּוֹ וַיֹּאמֶר אֵהוּד
,Ehud said And by to which coolness roof the in (was) and
.himself him (was) of chamber sitting he

164 7971 3678 6965 430 1697
דְּבַר־אֱלֹהִים לִי אֵלֶיךָ וַיָּקָם מֵעַל הַכִּסֵּא׃ וַיִּשְׁלַח אֵהוּד 21
Ehud put And .seat his from he And to I God word a
out on rose .you have from

8628 3225 3409 5921 2719 3947 8040 3027
אֶת־יַד שְׂמֹאלוֹ וַיִּקַּח אֶת־הַחֶרֶב מֵעַל יֶרֶךְ יְמִינוֹ וַיִּתְקָעֶהָ
thrust and his thigh from the and left his hand
it ,right on sword took

1157 2459 5462 3851 310 5325 935 990
בְּבִטְנוֹ׃ וַיָּבֹא גַם־הַנִּצָּב אַחַר הַלַּהַב וַיִּסְגֹּר הַחֵלֶב בְּעַד 22
on fat the and the after the also And his into
closed ;blade haft in went .belly

6574 3318 990 2719 8025 3808 3851
הַלַּהַב כִּי לֹא שָׁלַף הַחֶרֶב מִבִּטְנוֹ וַיֵּצֵא הַפַּרְשְׁדֹנָה׃
.hole the it and of out sword the did he not for the
out went belly his draw ,blade

5774 5944 1817 5462 4528 164 3318
וַיֵּצֵא אֵהוּד הַמִּסְדְּרוֹנָה וַיִּסְגֹּר דַּלְתוֹת הָעֲלִיָּה בַּעֲדוֹ וְנָעָל׃ 23
and behind roof the doors the and ,porch the to Ehud Then
.them bolted him chamber of shut out went

5274 5944 1817 2009 7200 935 5650 3318
וְהוּא יָצָא וַעֲבָדָיו בָּאוּ וַיִּרְאוּ וְהִנֵּה דַּלְתוֹת הָעֲלִיָּה נְעֻלוֹת 24
were roof the doors the ,and they and ;came his had When
;bolted chamber of ,behold ,looked servants ,left he

2342 4947 2315 7272 5526 559
וַיֹּאמְרוּ אַךְ מֵסִיךְ הוּא אֶת־רַגְלָיו בַּחֲדַר הַמְּקֵרָה׃ וַיָּחִילוּ 25
they And .coolness room the in his he (is) Surely they and
waited of feet covering said

3947 5944 1817 6605 2009 954
עַד־בּוֹשׁ וְהִנֵּה אֵינֶנּוּ פֹתֵחַ דַּלְתוֹת הָעֲלִיָּה וַיִּקְחוּ אֶת־
they so roof the doors the (was) he be- ,and they until
took ;chamber of opening not ,hold ;ashamed were

164 4191 776 5307 113 2009 6605 4668
הַמַּפְתֵּחַ וַיִּפְתָּחוּ וְהִנֵּה אֲדֹנֵיהֶם נֹפֵל אַרְצָה מֵת׃ וְאֵהוּד 26
And .dead the to (was) their ,and and key the
Ehud earth fallen master ,behold ;opened

4422 6456 5674 4102 5704 2422
נִמְלַט עַד הִתְמַהְמְהָם וְהוּא עָבַר אֶת־הַפְּסִילִים וַיִּמָּלֵט
and carved the passed and their during escaped
away slipped ,images by he ,waiting

Seirath. [27]And it happened,
when he had come, he blew
a horn in the hills of
Ephraim. And the sons of
Israel came down with him
from the hills, and he before
them. [28]And he said to
them, Follow me, for
Jehovah has delivered your
enemies the Moabites into
your hand. And they went
down after him and took the
fords of the Jordan against
the Moabites. And *they* did
not allow a man to pass
over. [29]And they struck
about ten thousand men of
Moab at that time, every
lusty man, all mighty men.
And not a man escaped.
[30]So Moab was subdued
that day under the hand of
Israel. And the land had rest
eighty years.

[31]And after him was
Shamgar the son of Anath,
who struck six hundred
men of the Philistines with
an ox goad. And he also
delivered Israel.

669 2022 7782 8628 935 1961 8167
27 השעירתה: ויהי בבואו ויתקע בשופר בהר אפרים
;Ephraim the in the on he that he when it And .Seirath to
of hills horn blew ,come had was

559 6440 2022 3478/1121 3381
28 וירדו עמו בני־ישראל מן־ההר והוא לפניהם: ויאמר
he And before and the from Israel the with went and
said .them he ;hills of sons him down

4125 341 3068 5414 310 7291
אלהם רדפו אחרי כי־נתן יהוה את־איביכם את־מואב
the your Jehovah has for after chase ,them to
Moabites enemies given ,me (them)

4125 3383 4569 3920 310 3381 3027
בידכם וירדו אחריו וילכדו את־מעברות הירדן למואב
the against the the and after they And your into
,Moabites Jordan of fords captured ,him down went .hand

6235 6256 4124 5221 5674 376 5414 3808
29 ולא־נתנו איש לעבר: ויכו את־מואב בעת ההיא כעשרת
about ,that at Moab they And pass to a did and
ten time struck .over man grant not

376 2422 3808 2428 376/3605 8082/3605 376 505
אלפים איש כל־שמן וכל־איש חיל ולא נמלט איש:
a escaped and might men all robust every men thousand
.man not of .(men) of

776 8252 3478 3027/8478 3117 4124 3665
30 ויכנע מואב ביום ההוא תחת יד ישראל ותשקט הארץ
the had And .Israel the under that day Moab was So
land rest of hand subdued

5221 6067/1121 8044 1961 310 8141 8084
31 שמונים שנה: ואחריו היה שמגר בן־ענת ויך את־
he and Anath the Shamgar was And .years eighty
struck of son him after

1571 3462 1241 4451 376 3967 8337 6430
פלשתים שש־מאות איש במלמד הבקר ויושע גם־הוא
he also and the a with men hundred six the
delivered ox for goad Philistines

3478
את־ישראל:
.Israel

CAP. IV ד

CHAPTER 4

CHAPTER 4
[1]And the sons of Israel
did evil again in the sight of
Jehovah when Ehud was
dead. [2]And Jehovah sold
them into the hand of Jabin
the king of Canaan, who
ruled in Hazor. And his army
commander *was* Sisera;
and he lived in Harosheth of
the nations. [3]And the sons
of Israel cried to Jehovah,
for he had nine hundred
chariots of iron. And he
mightily oppressed the
sons of Israel twenty years.
[4]And Deborah the wife of
Lapidoth, a woman prophetess, *was* judging Israel at

4191 164 3068 5869 7451 6213 3478 1121 3254
1 ויספו בני ישראל לעשות הרע בעיני יהוה ואהוד מת:
was when Jehovah the in evil did Israel the And
.dead Ehud of eyes of sons again

2674 4427 834 3667 4428 2985 3027 3068 4376
2 וימכרם יהוה ביד יבין מלך־כנען אשר מלך בחצור
.Hazor in ruled who ,Canaan the Jabin the into Jehovah sold And
of king of hand them

6817 1471 2800 3427 5516 6635 8269
3 ושר־צבאו סיסרא והוא יושב בחרשת הגוים: ויצעקו
cried And the in (was) and (was) army's his And
.nations of Harosheth living he Sisera commander

1270 7393 3967 8672 3068 3478 1121
בני־ישראל אל־יהוה כי תשע מאות רכב־ברזל לו
he iron chariots hundred nine for ,Jehovah to Israel the
;had of of sons

8141 6242 2394 3478 1121 3905
והוא לחץ את־בני ישראל בחזקה עשרים שנה:
.years twenty forcibly Israel the oppressed and
of sons he

8199 3941 802 5031 802 1683
4 דבורה אשה נביאה אשת לפידות היא שפטה את־
(was) she ,Lapidoth's wife a a And
judging prophetess ,woman Deborah

that time. 5And she lived under the palm tree of Deborah, between Ramah and Bethel, in the hills of Ephraim. And the sons of Israel went up to her for judgment. 6And she sent and called for Barak, the son of Abinoam, out of Kedesh *in* Naphtali, and said to him, Has not Jehovah the God of Israel commanded? Go and draw toward Mount Tabor, and take ten thousand men of the sons of Naphtali, and of the sons of Zebulun with you. 7And I will draw to you *at* the Kishon River Sisera the army commander of Jabin, and his chariots, and his multitude, and shall give him into your hands. 8And Barak said to her, If you go with me, then I will go. And if you will not go with me, I will not go.

9And she said, I will certainly go with you; only, your glory shall surely not be on the way which you are going, for Jehovah shall sell Sisera into the hand of a woman. And Deborah rose up and went with Barak to Kedesh.

10And Barak called Zebulun and Naphtali together to Kedesh. And he went up *with* ten thousand men at his feet. And Deborah went up with him. 11And Heber the Kenite had broken away from the Kenites, *he being* of the children of Hobab, the father-in-law of Moses, And he pitched his tent by the oak in Zaanaim, near Kedesh. 12And they told Sisera that Barak the son of Abinoam had gone up to Mount Tabor. 13And Sisera mustered all his chariots, nine hundred chariots of iron, and all the people who

5 ישראל בעת ההיא׃ והיא יושבת תחת־תמר דבורה
,Deborah palm the under (was) and ;that at Israel
of tree living she time

בין הרמה ובין בית־אל בהר אפרים ויעלו אליה בני
the to went and ;Ephraim the in between and Ramah be-
of sons her up of hills ,Bethel tween

6 ישראל למשפט׃ ותשלח ותקרא לברק בן־אבינעם
,Abinoam the for and she And for Israel
of son ,Barak called sent .judgment

מקדש נפתלי ותאמר אליו הלא־צוה ׀ יהוה אלהי־
the Jehovah com- Had ,him to said and ,Naphtali from
of God manded not Kedesh-

ישראל לך ומשכת בהר תבור ולקחת עמך עשרת
ten with and ,Tabor toward draw and Go ?Israel
you take Mount

7 אלפים איש מבני נפתלי ומבני זבלון׃ ומשכתי אליך
to I and ;Zebulun of and Naphtali the of men thousand
you draw will of sons the of sons

אל־נחל קישון את־סיסרא שר־צבא יבין ואת־רכבו
his and ,Jabin the the Sisera ,Kishon the to
chariots of army of commander River

8 ואת־המונו ונתתיהו בידך׃ ויאמר אליה ברק אם־תלכי
go you If ,Barak her to said And your into shall and his and
hands him give multitude

9 עמי והלכתי ואם־לא תלכי עמי לא אלך׃ ותאמר הלך
Surely she And will I not with you not and I then with
,said .go ,me go will if ;go will ,me

אלך עמך אפס כי לא תהיה תפארתך על־הדרך אשר־
which the on your shall not ,only with will I
way glory be ;you go

אתה הולך כי ביד־אשה ימכר יהוה את־סיסרא ותקם
And .Sisera Jehovah shall a the into for (are) you
arose sell woman of hand ,going

10 דבורה ותלך עם־ברק קדשה׃ ויזעק ברק את־זבולן
Zebulun Barak called And to Barak with and Deborah
together .Kadesh went

ואת־נפתלי קדשה ויעל ברגליו עשרת אלפי איש ותעל
and ;men thousand ten his at and to Naphtali and
up went feet up went ;Kadesh

11 עמו דבורה׃ וחבר הקיני נפרד מקין מבני חבב חתן
father- ,Hobab the of from had the Now .Deborah with
in-law of sons Kenites the broken Kenite Heber him

12 משה ויט אהלו עד־אלון בצענים אשר את־קדש׃ ויגדו
they And .Kedesh near which in the by his he and ;Moses'
told (is) ,Zaanaim oak tent pitched

13 לסיסרא כי עלה ברק בן־אבינעם הר־תבור׃ ויזעק
And .Tabor to Abinoam the Barak had that Sisera
mustered Mount of son up gone

סיסרא את־כל־רכבו תשע מאות רכב ברזל ואת־כל־
all and ,iron chariots hundred nine his all Sisera
of ,chariots

were with him, from Harosheth of the nations, to the Kishon River.

[14]And Deborah said to Barak, Rise up, for this *is* the day in which Jehovah has given Sisera into your hand. Has not Jehovah gone out before you? And Barak went down from Mount Tabor, and ten thousand men after him. [15]And Jehovah routed Sisera, and all the chariots, and all the army, by the mouth of the sword, before Barak. And Sisera came down from the chariot and fled on his feet. [16]And Barak pursued the chariots and went after the army, to Harosheth of the nations. And all the army of Sisera fell by the mouth of the sword—there was not even one left. [17]And Sisera fled on his feet to the tent of Jael, the wife of Heber the Kenite. For *there was* peace between Jabin the king of Hazor and the house of Heber the Kenite. [18]And Jael went out to meet Sisera, and said to him, Turn in, my lord; turn in to me; do not fear. And he turned in to her into the tent; and she covered him with a rug. [19]And he said to her, Please give me a little water to drink, for I am thirsty. And she opened a skin of milk, and gave him drink, and covered him.

[20]And he said to her, Stand *at* the door of the tent, and it shall be if anyone comes in and asks you, and says, Is there a man here? Then you shall say, There is not. [21]And Jael the wife of Heber took a tent-peg, and took a hammer in her hand, and went to him quietly. And *she* drove the peg into his temple, and she beat *it* into

14 הָעָם אֲשֶׁר אִתּוֹ מֵחֲרֹשֶׁת הַגּוֹיִם אֶל־נַחַל קִישׁוֹן׃ וַתֹּאמֶר
said And .Kishon the to the from with who the
torrent nations of Harosheth him (were) people
דְּבֹרָה אֶל־בָּרָק קוּם כִּי זֶה הַיּוֹם אֲשֶׁר נָתַן יְהוָה אֶת־
Jehovah has in the this for Rise ,Barak to Deborah
given which day (is) ,up
סִיסְרָא בְּיָדֶךָ הֲלֹא יְהוָה יָצָא לְפָנֶיךָ וַיֵּרֶד בָּרָק מֵהַר
from Barak went And before gone Jehovah has your into Sisera
Mount down ?you out not ;hand
15 תָּבוֹר וַעֲשֶׂרֶת אֲלָפִים אִישׁ אַחֲרָיו׃ וַיָּהָם יְהוָה אֶת־
Jehovah And after men thousand ten and ,Tabor
routed .him
סִיסְרָא וְאֶת־כָּל־הָרֶכֶב וְאֶת־כָּל־הַמַּחֲנֶה לְפִי־חֶרֶב לִפְנֵי
before the by the all and the all and ,Sisera
sword's edge army ,chariots
16 בָרָק וַיֵּרֶד סִיסְרָא מֵעַל הַמֶּרְכָּבָה וַיָּנָס בְּרַגְלָיו׃ וּבָרָק
And his on and the from Sisera came and ;Barak
Barak .feet fled chariot on down
רָדַף אַחֲרֵי הָרֶכֶב וְאַחֲרֵי הַמַּחֲנֶה עַד חֲרֹשֶׁת הַגּוֹיִם וַיִּפֹּל
and the Harosheth to the and the after chased
fell ,nations of army after chariots
17 כָּל־מַחֲנֵה סִיסְרָא לְפִי־חֶרֶב לֹא נִשְׁאַר עַד־אֶחָד׃ וְסִיסְרָא
And .one even was not the by Sisera the all
Sisera left ;sword's edge of army
נָס בְּרַגְלָיו אֶל־אֹהֶל יָעֵל אֵשֶׁת חֶבֶר הַקֵּינִי כִּי שָׁלוֹם בֵּין
be- peace for the Heber the ,Jael the to his on fled
tween (existed) ;Kenite of wife of tent feet
18 יָבִין מֶלֶךְ־חָצוֹר וּבֵין בֵּית חֶבֶר הַקֵּינִי׃ וַתֵּצֵא יָעֵל לִקְרַאת
to Jael went And the Heber the and Hazor the Jabin
meet out .Kenite of house between of king
סִיסְרָא וַתֹּאמֶר אֵלָיו סוּרָה אֲדֹנִי סוּרָה אֵלַי אַל־תִּירָא
do not to turn my Turn ,him to said and ,Sisera
;fear ;me aside ,lord aside
19 וַיָּסַר אֵלֶיהָ הָאֹהֱלָה וַתְּכַסֵּהוּ בַּשְּׂמִיכָה׃ וַיֹּאמֶר אֵלֶיהָ
,her to He And a with she and the into her to he and
said .rug him covered tent aside turned
הַשְׁקִינִי־נָא מְעַט־מַיִם כִּי צָמֵאתִי וַתִּפְתַּח אֶת־נֹאוד הֶחָלָב
milk a she and am I for ,water a Please me give
of skin opened ;thirsty little drink to
20 וַתַּשְׁקֵהוּ וַתְּכַסֵּהוּ׃ וַיֹּאמֶר אֵלֶיהָ עֲמֹד פֶּתַח הָאֹהֶל וְהָיָה
it and the the (at) Stand ,her to he And covered and gave and
be shall ,tent of door said .him drink to him
אִם־אִישׁ יָבֹא וּשְׁאֵלֵךְ וְאָמַר הֲיֵשׁ־פֹּה אִישׁ וְאָמַרְתְּ אָיִן׃
There you then a here Is and asks and comes anyone if
.not is ,say shall ?man there ,says ,you
21 וַתִּקַּח יָעֵל אֵשֶׁת־חֶבֶר אֶת־יְתַד הָאֹהֶל וַתָּשֶׂם אֶת־הַמַּקֶּבֶת
a and ,tent the a Heber the Jael And
hammer placed of peg of wife took
בְּיָדָהּ וַתָּבוֹא אֵלָיו בַּלָּאט וַתִּתְקַע אֶת־הַיָּתֵד בְּרַקָּתוֹ
his into the and in him to and her in
;temple peg drove secrecy went ,hand

the ground. And he had
been fast asleep, and faint;
and he died. [22]And, behold,
as Barak followed Sisera,
Jael came out to meet him,
and said to him, Come, and
I will show you the man
whom you are seeking. And
he came in to her, and,
behold, Sisera had fallen
dead *with* the peg in his
temple. [23]And on that day
God humbled Jabin the
king of Canaan before the
sons of Israel. [24]And the
hand of the sons of Israel
went on, going on and
pressing hard on Jabin the
king of Canaan, until they
had cut off Jabin the king of
Canaan.

וַתִּצְנַח בָּאָרֶץ וְהוּא־נִרְדָּם וַיָּעַף וַיָּמֹת׃ 22 וְהִנֵּה בָרָק רֹדֵף
אֶת־סִיסְרָא וַתֵּצֵא יָעֵל לִקְרָאתוֹ וַתֹּאמֶר לוֹ לֵךְ וְאַרְאֶךָּ
אֶת־הָאִישׁ אֲשֶׁר־אַתָּה מְבַקֵּשׁ וַיָּבֹא אֵלֶיהָ וְהִנֵּה סִיסְרָא
נֹפֵל מֵת וְהַיָּתֵד בְּרַקָּתוֹ׃ 23 וַיַּכְנַע אֱלֹהִים בַּיּוֹם הַהוּא אֵת
יָבִין מֶלֶךְ־כְּנָעַן לִפְנֵי בְּנֵי יִשְׂרָאֵל׃ 24 וַתֵּלֶךְ יַד בְּנֵי־יִשְׂרָאֵל
הָלוֹךְ וְקָשָׁה עַל יָבִין מֶלֶךְ־כְּנָעַן עַד אֲשֶׁר הִכְרִיתוּ אֵת
יָבִין מֶלֶךְ־כְּנָעַן׃

CAP. V ה

CHAPTER 5

CHAPTER 5

[1]And Deborah and Barak
the son of Abinoam sang on
that day, saying:
[2]For the loosing of locks
of hair in Israel; for the
willing offering of the
people, bless Jehovah!
[3]Listen, O kings; give ear, O
princes. I, *even* I, will sing to
Jehovah; I will sing praise
to Jehovah the God of
Israel. [4]O Jehovah, when
You went forth out of Seir,
when You marched out of
the fields of Edom, the earth
trembled, and the heavens
dropped. Yea, the clouds
dropped water. [5]The
mountains quaked before
the face of Jehovah, this
Sinai *quaked* from before
Jehovah the God of Israel.
[6]In the days of Shamgar the
son of Anath, in the days of

1 וַתָּשַׁר דְּבוֹרָה וּבָרָק בֶּן־אֲבִינֹעַם בַּיּוֹם הַהוּא
לֵאמֹר׃ 2 בִּפְרֹעַ פְּרָעוֹת בְּיִשְׂרָאֵל בְּהִתְנַדֵּב
עָם בָּרְכוּ יְהוָה׃ 3 שִׁמְעוּ מְלָכִים הַאֲזִינוּ
רֹזְנִים אָנֹכִי לַיהוָה אָנֹכִי אָשִׁירָה אֲזַמֵּר
לַיהוָה אֱלֹהֵי יִשְׂרָאֵל׃ 4 יְהוָה בְּצֵאתְךָ
מִשֵּׂעִיר בְּצַעְדְּךָ מִשְּׂדֵה אֱדוֹם אֶרֶץ
רָעָשָׁה גַּם־שָׁמַיִם נָטָפוּ גַּם־עָבִים נָטְפוּ
מָיִם׃ 5 הָרִים נָזְלוּ מִפְּנֵי יְהוָה זֶה
סִינַי מִפְּנֵי יְהוָה אֱלֹהֵי יִשְׂרָאֵל׃ 6 בִּימֵי שַׁמְגַּר בֶּן־

Jael, the highways ceased,
and those going in the
paths traveled *in* byways.
[7]The leaders ceased in
Israel; they ceased until I,
Deborah, arose; I arose *as* a
mother in Israel. [8]They
chose new gods; then war
was at the gates! Neither a
shield nor a spear was seen
among forty thousand in
Israel. [9]My heart *was*
toward the lawgivers of
Israel, *who* freely offered
themselves among the
people; bless Jehovah!

[10]You that ride on white
asses, you that sit on rich
carpets, and you travelers
on the way, sing out!
[11]*Louder* than the voice of
the dividers between the
watering places, there they
shall tell of the righteous
acts of Jehovah, the
righteous acts of His
leaders in Israel. Then the
people of Jehovah went
down to the gates.

[12]Awake, Awake, Debor-
ah! Awake, awake, utter a
song! Rise, Barak, and lead
your captives captive, son
of Abinoam. [13]Then *He
caused me* to tread on the
remnant of the noble ones
of the people; Jehovah trod
for me among the warriors.
[14]Out of Ephraim *they
came, those* whose root
was against Amalek. After
you, Benjamin, among your
peoples; and out of Machir
came down commanders;
and out of Zebulun the ones

3212 734 2308 3278 3117 6067
עֲנָת בִּימֵי יָעֵל חָדְלוּ אֳרָחוֹת וְהֹלְכֵי
those and on going | the highways | ceased | Jael | the in of days | ,Anath

7 3478 6520 2308 6128 734 3212 5410
נְתִיבוֹת יֵלְכוּ אֳרָחוֹת עֲקַלְקַלּוֹת׃ חָדְלוּ פְרָזוֹן בְּיִשְׂרָאֵל
,Israel in | The leaders | ceased | crooked .ways | the | went on | the paths

6965 1683 6965 5704 2308
חָדֵלּוּ עַד שַׁקַּמְתִּי דְּבוֹרָה שַׁקַּמְתִּי
I arose | ,Deborah | I ,arose | until | they ceased

8 430 977 3478 517
אֵם בְּיִשְׂרָאֵל׃ יִבְחַר אֱלֹהִים
gods | they chose | .Israel | in | a mother

4043 8179 3901 2319
חֲדָשִׁים אָז לָחֶם שְׁעָרִים מָגֵן
a —shield | the at !gates | war (was) | then | ;new

505 703 7420 7200 518
אִם־יֵרָאֶה וָרֹמַח בְּאַרְבָּעִים אֶלֶף
thousand | among forty | a or —spear | was one if —seen

9 5069 3478 2710 3820 3478
בְּיִשְׂרָאֵל׃ לִבִּי לְחוֹקְקֵי יִשְׂרָאֵל הַמִּתְנַדְּבִים
(who) volunteered | ,Israel | the to of lawgivers | My (out went) heart | .Israel in

10 860 7392 3068 1288 5971
בָּעָם בָּרְכוּ יְהוָה׃ רֹכְבֵי אֲתֹנוֹת
asses | You of riders | !Jehovah | bless | among ;people the

1980 4055 5921 3427 6715
צְחֹרוֹת יֹשְׁבֵי עַל־מִדִּין וְהֹלְכֵי
you and travelers | rich ,carpets | on | you sitters | ,white

11 996 2686 6963 7891 1870 5921
עַל־דֶּרֶךְ שִׂיחוּ׃ מִקּוֹל מְחַצְצִים בֵּין
be- tween | the waterers | than (Louder) of voice the | !sing | the ,way | on

6666 3068 6662 8567 8033 4857
מַשְׁאַבִּים שָׁם יְתַנּוּ צִדְקוֹת יְהוָה צִדְקֹת
right- for acts eous | the | ,Jehovah | right- of acts eous | the | shall they recount | there | watering the ,places

5971 8179 3381 3478 6520
פִּרְזוֹנוֹ בְּיִשְׂרָאֵל אָז יָרְדוּ לַשְּׁעָרִים עַם־
the of people | the to gates | went down | Then | .Israel in | His leaders

12 5782 1683 5782 5782 3068
יְהוָה׃ עוּרִי עוּרִי דְּבוֹרָה עוּרִי
,Awake | !Deborah | ,awake | ,Awake | .Jehovah

1121 7617 7628 1301 6965 7892 1696 5782
עוּרִי דַּבְּרִי־שִׁיר קוּם בָּרָק וּשֲׁבֵה שֶׁבְיְךָ בֶּן
O of son | your ,captives | lead and captive | ,Barak | ,Rise | !song a | utter | ,awake

13 3068 5971 117 8300 7287 42
אֲבִינֹעַם׃ אָז יְרַד שָׂרִיד לְאַדִּירִים עָם יְהוָה
Jehovah | the ;people | noble the of ones | rem- of nant | the | tread Then upon | !Abinoam

14 8328 669 1368 7287
יְרַד־לִי בַּגִּבּוֹרִים׃ מִנִּי אֶפְרַיִם שָׁרְשָׁם
whose root | Ephraim (came they) | Out of | the among .warriors | me for trod

7971 1144 310 6002
בַּעֲמָלֵק אַחֲרֶיךָ בִנְיָמִין בַּעֲמָמֶיךָ מִנִּי
out of | your with ;peoples | ,Benjamin | after ,you | in (was) ;Amalek

that hold the staff of the
scribe. 15 And my com-
manders in Issachar *were*
with Deborah; as was
Issachar, so *was* Barak.
They were sent into the
valley at his feet. Among
the divisions of Reuben
resolves of heart *were*
great! 16 Why did you sit
between the sheepfolds, to
hear the bleatings of flocks?
At the divisions of Reuben
searchings of heart *were*
great! 17 Gilead remained
beyond the Jordan; and
why did Dan stay in ships?
Asher sat at the shore *by*
the water, and remained by
his havens. 18 Zebulun, a
people who despised his
life, *even* to death; also
Naphtali on the high places
of the field. 19 Kings came;
they fought; then the kings
of Canaan fought in
Taanach by the waters of
Megiddo; they took no gain
of silver. 20 The stars fought
from the heavens; from
their courses they fought
with Sisera. 21 The Kishon
River swept them away, the
ancient river, the Kishon
river. My soul, You trampled
in strength. 22 Then did the
hooves of horses beat, from

מָכִיר יָרְדוּ מְחֹקְקִים וּמִזְּבוּלֻן מֹשְׁכִים בְּשֵׁבֶט
the staff | that they hold | of out and Zebulun | ,commanders | came down | Machir

סֹפֵר׃ 15 וְשָׂרַי בְּיִשָּׂשכָר עִם־דְּבֹרָה וְיִשָּׂשכָר
was as Issachar | ;Deborah (were) with | in Issachar | My And commanders | the of scribe

כֵּן בָּרָק בָּעֵמֶק שֻׁלַּח
they sent were | the into valley | (was) So ;Barak

בְּרַגְלָיו בִּפְלַגּוֹת רְאוּבֵן גְּדֹלִים
great (were) | ,Reuben | the Among of divisions | his at .feet

חִקְקֵי־לֵב׃ 16 לָמָּה יָשַׁבְתָּ בֵּין
be- tween | did sit you | Why | .heart resolves of

הַמִּשְׁפְּתַיִם לִשְׁמֹעַ שְׁרִקוֹת עֲדָרִים לִפְלַגּוֹת
the Among divisions | of ?flocks | the bleatings | hear to | the sheepfolds

רְאוּבֵן גְּדוֹלִים חִקְרֵי־לֵב׃ 17 גִּלְעָד בְּעֵבֶר הַיַּרְדֵּן
the Jordan | beyond | Gilead | !heart search- of ings | (were there) great | of Reuben

שָׁכֵן וְדָן לָמָּה יָגוּר אֳנִיּוֹת אָשֵׁר
Asher | in ?ships | he did stay | why | and Dan | ;abode

יָשַׁב לְחוֹף יַמִּים וְעַל מִפְרָצָיו
his havens | by and | the water | the at of shore | sat

יִשְׁכּוֹן׃ 18 זְבֻלוּן עַם חֵרֵף נַפְשׁוֹ לָמוּת וְנַפְתָּלִי
and ,Naphtali | to ;death | life his | who despised | a people | Zebulun (is) | .abode

עַל מְרוֹמֵי שָׂדֶה׃ 19 בָּאוּ מְלָכִים
.Kings | came | the .field | high the of places | on

נִלְחָמוּ אָז נִלְחֲמוּ מַלְכֵי כְנַעַן בְּתַעְנַךְ
in Taanach | Canaan | the of kings | fought | then | they ;fought

עַל־מֵי מְגִדּוֹ בֶּצַע כֶּסֶף לֹא
not | silver | gain of | ;Megiddo | the by of waters

לָקָחוּ׃ 20 מִן־שָׁמַיִם נִלְחָמוּ הַכּוֹכָבִים
;stars the | fought | the heavens | From | they !(any) took

מִמְּסִלּוֹתָם נִלְחֲמוּ עִם סִיסְרָא׃ 21 נַחַל קִישׁוֹן
Kishon | the torrent | .Sisera | with | they fought | their from courses

גְּרָפָם נַחַל קְדוּמִים נַחַל קִישׁוֹן תִּדְרְכִי
You trod | .Kishon | the torrent | ,ancient | the river | them swept ,away

נַפְשִׁי עֹז׃ 22 אָז הָלְמוּ עִקְּבֵי־
the of hoofs | did beat | Then | in strength | My ,soul

the galloping, galloping of
his mighty stallions.
[23]Curse Meroz, said the
Angel of Jehovah; curse its
inhabitants bitterly, be-
cause they did not come to
the help of Jehovah, to the
help of Jehovah against the
warriors.
[24]Most blessed among
women is Jael, the wife of
Heber the Kenite; she is
blessed among women in
the tent. [25]He asked for
water; she gave *him* milk; in
a lordly bowl she brought
curd. [26]She put her hand
to the tent peg, and her
right hand to the work-
men's hammer; and she
hammered Sisera; she
smashed his head; she
struck through and pierced
his temple. [27]Between her
feet he bowed; he fell; he
lay down. Between her feet
he bowed; he fell! Where
he bowed, there he fell
down ruined. [28]Through the
window she looked out;
yea, she cried out, the
mother of Sisera, through
the lattice; Why does his
chariot delay to come? Why
have the steps of his chariot
tarried? [29]The wise ones of
her princesses answered
her; yea, she returned her
words to herself: [30]Do they
not find and divide the
plunder? A womb, two
wombs to *each* man's head;
a plunder of dyed *garments*

5483 סוס ,horses | 1726 מדהרות the from ,galloping | 1726 דהרות galloping of | 47 אביריו: mighty his stallions | 23 779 ארו Curse

47,89 מרוז Meroz | 559 אמר ,said | 4397 מלאך the of Angel | 3068 יהוה Jehovah | 779 779 ארו ארור bitterly curse

3427 ישביה its ,inhabitants | 935 כי לא־באו for not they did come | 5833 לעזרת the to of help | 3068 יהוה ,Jehovah | 5833 לעזרת the to of help

3068 יהוה Jehovah | 1368 בגבורים: the among !warriors | 24 1288 תברך Most is blessed | 802 מנשים among women

3278 יעל ,Jael | 802 אשת the of wife | 2268 חבר Heber | 7017 הקיני the ;Kenite | 802 מנשים among women

168 באהל the in tent | 1288 תברך: is she .blessed | 25 4325 מים water | 7592 שאל He asked for; | 2461 חלב milk

5414 נתנה she (him) gave | 5602 בספל a in bowl | 117 אדירים lordly | 7126 הקריבה she brought | 2529 חמאה: .curd | 26 3027 ידה Her hand

3489 ליתד the to tent-peg | 5414 תשלחנה put she. | 3225 וימינה her and hand right | 1989 להלמות the to hammer

6001 עמלים ;workmen's | 1986 והלמה she and hammered | 5516 סיסרא ,Sisera | 4277 מחקה she smashed | 7218 ראשו his ;head | 4272 ומחצה struck she through

2498 וחלפה and pierced | 7541 רקתו: his .temple | 27 996 בין Between | 7272 רגליה her feet | 3766 כרע he ,bowed | 5307 נפל he ,fell

7901 שכב lay he ;down | 996 בין between | 7272 רגליה her feet | 3766 כרע he ,bowed | 5307 נפל he ;fell | באשר where

3766 כרע he bowed, | שם there | 5307 נפל down fell | 7703 שדוד: .ruined (life of) | 28 בעד Through | 2474 החלון the window | 8259 נשקפה she out looked

2980 ותיבב she ,yea out cried | 517 אם the of mother | 5516 סיסרא Sisera | בעד through | 822 האשנב the lattice | 4100 מדוע Why

954 בשש delays | 7393 רכבו his chariot | 935 לבוא to ?come | 4100 מדוע Why | 309 אחרו have tarried | 6471 פעמי the of steps

4818 מרכבותיו: his ?chariot | 2450 חכמות The wise of ones | 8282 שרותיה her princesses | 6030 תעננה answered her | 29 637 אף ,yea

7725 היא תשיב she returned | 561 אמריה her words | לה: to herself | 30 3808 הלא Do not | 4672 ימצאו they find | 2505 יחלקו and divide

7998 שלל the ?spoil | 7356 רחם A ,womb | 7361 רחמתים two wombs | 7218 לראש a to head | 1397 גבר ;man's | 7998 שלל a of spoil

to Sisera, a plunder of embroidered dyed *garments;* two embroidered dyed *garments* for the necks of the plunder? [31]So all Your enemies shall perish, O Jehovah, and those who love Him *shall be* as the sun when it goes forth in its might.

And the land had rest forty years.

6648 7998 5516 6648
צְבָעִים לְסִיסְרָא שְׁלַל צְבָעִים
dyed a to dyed
(clothes) of spoil Sisera (cloths)

7998 6677 7553 6648 7553
31 רִקְמָה צֶבַע רִקְמָתַיִם לְצַוְּארֵי שָׁלָל׃ כֵּן
So the the for two dyed ,embroidered
?spoil of necks embroidered (cloths)

8121 3318 157 3068 341 3605 6
יֹאבְדוּ כָל־אוֹיְבֶיךָ יְהוָה וְאֹהֲבָיו כְּצֵאת הַשֶּׁמֶשׁ
sun the the as those but O Your all may
of forth going (be) Him loving ,Jehovah ,enemies perish

8141 703 776 8252 1369
בִּגְבֻרָתוֹ וַתִּשְׁקֹט הָאָרֶץ אַרְבָּעִים שָׁנָה׃
.years forty the had And its in
land rest !might

CAP. VI ו

CHAPTER 6

CHAPTER 6

1 [1]And the sons of Israel
did evil again in the sight of
Jehovah, and Jehovah gave
them into the hand of
Midian seven years. [2]And 2
the hand of Midian was
strong against Israel. And
the sons of Israel made
dens for themselves before
the faces of Midian, in the
mountains, and the caves,
and the strongholds. [3]And
3 it happened *after* Israel had
sown *crops*, Midian, and
Amalek, and the sons of the
east came; and they came
4 against them, [4]and
camped against them, and
destroyed the produce of
the land until you enter
Gaza. And they left no food
in Israel, either sheep, or ox,
or ass. [5]For they came up
5 with their livestock, and
with their tents. They came
in like locusts for number,
and there was no number to
them, to their camels. And
they came into the land to
destroy it. [6]And Israel was
brought very low before
6 Midian. And the sons of
Israel cried to Jehovah.
[7]And it happened when
the sons of Israel had cried
7 to Jehovah about Midian,
[8]Jehovah sent a man, a
prophet, to the sons of
Israel. And he said to them,
8 So says Jehovah the God of

3027 3068 5414 3068 5869 7451 3478 1121 6213
1 וַיַּעֲשׂוּ בְנֵי־יִשְׂרָאֵל הָרַע בְּעֵינֵי יְהוָה וַיִּתְּנֵם יְהוָה בְּיַד־
the into Jehovah and ;Jehovah the in evil Israel the And
of hand them gave of eyes of sons did

4080 6440 3478 4080 5810 3117 7651 4080
2 מִדְיָן שֶׁבַע שָׁנִים׃ וַתָּעָז יַד־מִדְיָן עַל־יִשְׂרָאֵל מִפְּנֵי מִדְיָן
Midian before ;Israel against Midian the was And .years seven Midian
of faces the of hand strong

2022 834 4492 3478 1121 6213
עָשׂוּ לָהֶם ׀ בְּנֵי יִשְׂרָאֵל אֶת־הַמִּנְהָרוֹת אֲשֶׁר בֶּהָרִים
the in which dens the Israel the for made
,mountains (are) of sons themselves

3478 2232 518 1961 4679 4631
3 וְאֶת־הַמְּעָרוֹת וְאֶת־הַמְּצָדוֹת׃ וְהָיָה אִם־זָרַע יִשְׂרָאֵל
,Israel had if it And .strongholds the and ,caves the and
sown ,happened

2583 5927 6924 1121 6002 4080 5927
4 וְעָלָה מִדְיָן וַעֲמָלֵק וּבְנֵי־קֶדֶם וְעָלוּ עָלָיו׃ וַיַּחֲנוּ עֲלֵיהֶם
against and against they and the and and Midian that
,them camped ,him came east of sons the Amalek came

7604 3808 5804 935 776 2981 7843
וַיַּשְׁחִיתוּ אֶת־יְבוּל הָאָרֶץ עַד־בּוֹאֲךָ עַזָּה וְלֹא־יַשְׁאִירוּ
they and ;Gaza your until the the
left not to coming land of produce destroyed

4735 2543 7794 7716 3478 4241
5 מִחְיָה בְּיִשְׂרָאֵל וְשֶׂה וָשׁוֹר וַחֲמוֹר׃ כִּי הֵם וּמִקְנֵיהֶם
their and they for ;ass or ,ox or either ,Israel in sus-
livestock ,sheep tenance

1581 428 7230 697 1767 935 168 5927
יַעֲלוּ וְאָהֳלֵיהֶם יָבֹאוּ כְדֵי־אַרְבֶּה לָרֹב וְלָהֶם וְלִגְמַלֵּיהֶם
their to and to and for like they their and came
camels ,them ;number locusts in came ;tents up

3966 3478 1809 7843 776 935 4557 369
6 אֵין מִסְפָּר וַיָּבֹאוּ בָאָרֶץ לְשַׁחֲתָהּ׃ וַיִּדַּל יִשְׂרָאֵל מְאֹד
very Israel was And destroy to the into and ;number there
low brought .it land came they no was

1961 3068 3478 1121 2199 4080 6440
7 מִפְּנֵי מִדְיָן וַיִּזְעֲקוּ בְנֵי־יִשְׂרָאֵל אֶל־יְהוָה׃ וַיְהִי כִּי־
when it And .Jehovah to Israel the and ,Midian before
happened of sons cried

3068 7971 4080 182 3068 3478 1121 2199
8 זָעֲקוּ בְנֵי־יִשְׂרָאֵל אֶל־יְהוָה עַל אֹדוֹת מִדְיָן׃ וַיִּשְׁלַח יְהוָה
Jehovah that ,Midian of because Jehovah to Israel the had
sent of sons cried

3068 559 559 3478 1121 5030 376
אִישׁ נָבִיא אֶל־בְּנֵי יִשְׂרָאֵל וַיֹּאמֶר לָהֶם כֹּה־אָמַר יְהוָה ׀
,Jehovah says Thus to he and ,Israel the to a a
,them said of sons ,prophet ,man

Israel, I have brought you up out of Egypt; and I have brought you out from a house of slavery. [9]And I have delivered you out of the hand of the Egyptians, and out of the hand of all your oppressors; and I have driven them out before you; and I have given you their land. [10]And I said to you, I *am* Jehovah your God. You shall not fear the gods of the Amorite *among* whom you *are* dwelling, in their land. But you have not listened to My voice.

[11]And the Angel of Jehovah came and sat under the oak which *is* in Ophrah, which *belonged* to Joash the Abiezrite. And his son Gideon was beating out wheat in the winepress, to hide it from the eyes of Midian. [12]And the Angel of Jehovah appeared to him, and said to him, Jehovah *is* with you, mighty warrior. [13]And Gideon said to him, O my Lord, if Jehovah is with us, then why has all this happened to us? And where *are* all His wonders which our fathers recounted to us, saying, Did not Jehovah bring us up out of Egypt? And now Jehovah has left us, and has given us into the hands of Midian. [14]And Jehovah turned to him and said, Go in this strength of yours, and you shall deliver Israel out of the hand of Midian. Have I not sent you? [15]And he said to Him, O my Lord, with what shall I deliver Israel? Behold, my family *is* the weakest in Manasseh, and I the least in my father's house. [16]And Jehovah said to him, Because I am with you, you shall strike Midian as one man. [17]And he said to Him, Please, if I have found grace

in Your eyes, then You shall give me a sign that You are speaking with me. [18]Please do not move from here until I come to You and bring my food offering and lay it before You. And He said, I will stay until you come back. [19]And Gideon went in and prepared a kid of the goats, and unleavened *bread* of an ephah of flour. He put the flesh in a basket, and he put the broth in a pot. And he brought it out to Him, under the oak, and offered *it*. [20]And the Angel of Jehovah said to him, Take the flesh and the unleavened *bread* and place *them* on this rock, and pour out the broth. And he did so. [21]And the Angel of Jehovah put forth the end of the staff in His hand and touched the flesh and the unleavened *bread*. And the fire rose up out of the rock and burned up the flesh and the unleavened *bread*. And the Angel of Jehovah departed out of his sight. [22]And Gideon saw that He *was* the Angel of Jehovah. And Gideon said, Alas, Lord Jehovah! Because I have seen the Angel of Jehovah face to face! [23]And Jehovah said to him, Peace to you, fear not. You shall not die. [24]And Gideon built an altar to Jehovah there, and called it Peace of Jehovah. It *is* still in Ophrah of the Abiezrites until today.

מְצָאתִי חֵן בְּעֵינֶיךָ וְעָשִׂיתָ לִּי אוֹת שָׁאַתָּה מְדַבֵּר עִמִּי׃

with One the You that a for then Your in favor have I
.me speaking (are) sign me perform ,eyes found

18 אַל־נָא תָמֻשׁ מִזֶּה עַד־בֹּאִי אֵלֶיךָ וְהֹצֵאתִי אֶת־מִנְחָתִי

food my will I and to my until from do Please not
offering out bring You coming here depart

19 וְהִנַּחְתִּי לְפָנֶיךָ וַיֹּאמַר אָנֹכִי אֵשֵׁב עַד שׁוּבֶךָ׃ וְגִדְעוֹן בָּא

went And you until will I He And before and
in Gideon .back come stay ,said .You it lay

וַיַּעַשׂ גְּדִי־עִזִּים וְאֵיפַת־קֶמַח מַצּוֹת הַבָּשָׂר שָׂם בַּסַּל

a in put he the unleavened flour an and the kid a and
,basket flesh ;bread of ephah goats of dressed

וְהַמָּרַק שָׂם בַּפָּרוּר וַיּוֹצֵא אֵלָיו אֶל־תַּחַת הָאֵלָה וַיַּגַּשׁ׃

and ,oak the under to he and a in put he the and
.(it) offered Him it brought ;pot broth

20 וַיֹּאמֶר אֵלָיו מַלְאַךְ הָאֱלֹהִים קַח אֶת־הַבָּשָׂר וְאֶת־הַמַּצּוֹת

unlea- the and the Take ,God the to said And
bread vened flesh of Angel him

21 וְהַנַּח אֶל־הַסֶּלַע הַלָּז וְאֶת־הַמָּרַק שְׁפוֹךְ וַיַּעַשׂ כֵּן׃ וַיִּשְׁלַח

put And .so And pour broth the and ,this rock on place and
forth did he .out (them)

מַלְאַךְ יְהוָה אֶת־קְצֵה הַמִּשְׁעֶנֶת אֲשֶׁר בְּיָדוֹ וַיִּגַּע בַּבָּשָׂר

the and His in which staff the the Jehovah the
flesh touched hand (was) of end of Angel

וּבַמַּצּוֹת וַתַּעַל הָאֵשׁ מִן־הַצּוּר וַתֹּאכַל אֶת־הַבָּשָׂר וְאֶת־

and the and the from fire went and un- the and
flesh consumed rock up ,bread leavened

22 הַמַּצּוֹת וּמַלְאַךְ יְהוָה הָלַךְ מֵעֵינָיו׃ וַיַּרְא גִּדְעוֹן כִּי־מַלְאַךְ

the that Gideon And of out went Jehovah the And unlea- the
of Angel saw .eyes his of Angel .bread vened

יְהוָה הוּא וַיֹּאמֶר גִּדְעוֹן אֲהָהּ אֲדֹנָי יְהוִה כִּי־עַל־כֵּן

because For !Jehovah Lord O ,Alas ,Gideon said and He Jehovah
;(was)

23 רָאִיתִי מַלְאַךְ יְהוָה פָּנִים אֶל־פָּנִים׃ וַיֹּאמֶר לוֹ יְהוָה

,Jehovah to said And !face to face Jehovah the have I
him of Angel seen

24 שָׁלוֹם לְךָ אַל־תִּירָא לֹא תָּמוּת׃ וַיִּבֶן שָׁם גִּדְעוֹן מִזְבֵּחַ

an Gideon there And shall you not ,fear not to Peace
altar built .die you

לַיהוָה וַיִּקְרָא־לוֹ יְהוָה שָׁלוֹם עַד הַיּוֹם הַזֶּה עוֹדֶנּוּ

(is) it this day until ;Peace Jehovah it and to
still of called Jehovah

[25]And it happened on that night, Jehovah said to him, Take your father's bullock, and the second bullock of seven years; and you shall throw down the altar of Baal which *belongs* to your father, and you shall

25 בְּעָפְרָת אֲבִי הָעֶזְרִי׃ וַיְהִי בַּלַּיְלָה הַהוּא וַיֹּאמֶר

that that night on And the in
said happened it ezrites Abi- of Ophrah

לוֹ יְהוָה קַח אֶת־פַּר־הַשּׁוֹר אֲשֶׁר לְאָבִיךָ וּפַר הַשֵּׁנִי

the and your to which bullock a the Take ,Jehovah to
second bullock ,father (is) of bull young him

שֶׁבַע שָׁנִים וְהָרַסְתָּ אֶת־מִזְבַּח הַבַּעַל אֲשֶׁר לְאָבִיךָ וְאֶת־

and your to which Baal the you and years seven
;father (belongs) of altar dash shall old

cut down the pillar beside it. 26 And you shall build an altar to Jehovah your God on the top of this stronghold, in an orderly way, and shall take the second bullock and offer a burnt offering with the wood of the pillar which you have cut down. 27 And Gideon took ten men from his servants and did as Jehovah had spoken to him. And it happened, since he feared his father's house and the men of the city, to do it by day, that he did it by night. 28 And the men of the city rose early in the morning. And, behold, the altar of Baal had been smashed, and the pillar beside it had been cut down. And the second bullock had been offered on the altar which was built. 29 And they each said to his neighbor, Who has done this thing? And they asked and sought. And they said, Gideon the son of Joash has done this thing. 30 And the men of the city said to Joash, Bring out your son, and he shall die, because he has broken down the altar of Baal, and because he has cut down the pillar beside it. 31 And Joash said to all that stood against him, You, will you contend for Baal? Or you, will you save him? *He* who contends for him shall be killed by the morning. If he *is* a god, let him contend for himself, because one has smashed his altar. 32 And on that day he called him Jerubbaal, saying, Let Baal contend against him, because he has smashed his altar.

33 And all Midian and Amalek, and the sons of the east, were gathered together, and crossed over, and camped in the valley of Jezreel. 34 And the Spirit of

26 האשרה אשר־עליו תכרת: ובנית מזבח ליהוה אלהיך
על ראש המעוז הזה במערכה ולקחת את־הפר השני
27 והעלית עולה בעצי האשרה אשר תכרת: ויקח גדעון
עשרה אנשים מעבדיו ויעש כאשר דבר אליו יהוה
ויהי כאשר ירא את־בית אביו ואת־אנשי העיר מעשות
28 יומם ויעש לילה: וישכימו אנשי העיר בבקר והנה
נתץ מזבח הבעל והאשרה אשר־עליו כרתה ואת הפר
29 השני העלה על־המזבח הבנוי: ויאמרו איש אל־רעהו
מי עשה הדבר הזה וידרשו ויבקשו ויאמרו גדעון בן
30 יואש עשה הדבר הזה: ויאמרו אנשי העיר אל־יואש
הוצא את־בנך וימת כי נתץ את־מזבח הבעל וכי כרת
31 האשרה אשר־עליו: ויאמר יואש לכל אשר־עמדו עליו
האתם תריבון לבעל אם־אתם תושיעון אותו אשר יריב
לו יומת עד־הבקר אם־אלהים הוא ירב לו כי נתץ את־
32 מזבחו: ויקרא־לו ביום־ההוא ירבעל לאמר ירב בו
33 הבעל כי נתץ את־מזבחו: וכל־מדין ועמלק ובני־
34 קדם נאספו יחדו ויעברו ויחנו בעמק יזרעאל: ורוח

Jehovah clothed Gideon *with Himself,* and he blew with a ram's horn. And the Abiezrites were called after
him. [35]And he sent messengers to all Manasseh, and it also was called after him. And he sent messengers to Asher and Zebulun, and to Naphtali. And they came up to meet them
[36]And Gideon said to God, If You are *to* deliver Israel by my hand, as You
have spoken, [37]behold, I *am* placing the fleece of wool on the grain-floor; if the dew is on the fleece only, and dryness on all the ground, then I will know that You will deliver Israel by my hand, as You have spoken. [38]And it was so. And he rose early on the next day and wrung the fleece, and drained dew out of the fleece, a bowl full of
water. [39]And Gideon said to God, Let not Your anger glow against me, and I shall speak only this time. Please let me try only this time with the fleece; please let there be dryness on the fleece alone; and let there be dew on all the ground. [40]And God did so on that night, and there was dryness only on the fleece, and there was dew on all the ground.

44 2199 7782 8628 1439 3847 3068
יְהוָה לָבְשָׁה אֶת־גִּדְעוֹן וַיִּתְקַע בַּשּׁוֹפָר וַיִּזָּעֵק אֲבִיעֶזֶר
the Abiezrites called after was and a with horn ram's he and blew ,Gideon clothed Jehovah (with Himself)

1571 2199 4519 3605 7971 4397 310
35 אַחֲרָיו׃ וּמַלְאָכִים שָׁלַח בְּכָל־מְנַשֶּׁה וַיִּזָּעֵק גַּם־הוּא
it also was and after called Manasseh all to sent he And messengers after .him

5927 5320 2074 836 7971 4397 310
אַחֲרָיו וּמַלְאָכִים שָׁלַח בְּאָשֵׁר וּבִזְבֻלוּן וּבְנַפְתָּלִי וַיַּעֲלוּ
they and up came to and ;Naphtali to and ,Zebulun to ,Asher sent he and messengers after ;him

3462 518 430 1439 559 7125
36 לִקְרָאתָם׃ וַיֹּאמֶר גִּדְעוֹן אֶל־הָאֱלֹהִים אִם־יֶשְׁךָ מוֹשִׁיעַ
(to going) deliver You are If ,God to Gideon said And meet to .them

1492 3322 2009 1696 3478 3027
37 בְּיָדִי אֶת־יִשְׂרָאֵל כַּאֲשֶׁר דִּבַּרְתָּ׃ הִנֵּה אָנֹכִי מַצִּיג אֶת־גִּזַּת
the fleece (am) placing I ,behold have You spoken as ,Israel my by hand

776 3605 1492 1961 2919 1637 6785
הַצֶּמֶר בַּגֹּרֶן אִם טַל יִהְיֶה עַל־הַגִּזָּה לְבַדָּהּ וְעַל־כָּל־הָאָרֶץ
the (is) ground all and on ,only the fleece on is the dew if the on ;grain-floor of wool

1696 3478 3027 3462 3045 2721
חֹרֶב וְיָדַעְתִּי כִּי־תוֹשִׁיעַ בְּיָדִי אֶת־יִשְׂרָאֵל כַּאֲשֶׁר דִּבַּרְתָּ׃
have You .spoken as ,Israel my by hand will You deliver that I then know shall dry- ,ness

1492 2919 4680 1492 2115 4283 7925 1961
38 וַיְהִי־כֵן וַיַּשְׁכֵּם מִמָּחֳרָת וַיָּזַר אֶת־הַגִּזָּה וַיִּמֶץ טַל מִן־הַגִּזָּה
the fleece out of dew and drained the ,fleece and wrung the on ,morrow he and early rose ,so it And was

2734 430 1439 559 4325 5602 4393
39 מְלוֹא הַסֵּפֶל מָיִם׃ וַיֹּאמֶר גִּדְעוֹן אֶל־הָאֱלֹהִים אַל־יִחַר
Let glow not ,God to Gideon said And .water bowl a fulness of

1492 6471 7535 4994/5254 6471 1696 639
אַפְּךָ בִּי וַאֲדַבְּרָה אַךְ הַפַּעַם אֲנַסֶּה־נָּא רַק־הַפַּעַם בַּגִּזָּה
the with ;fleece this time only please test me let ;time this only will I and speak against ,me Your anger

2919 / 1961 776 3605 5921 905 1492 2721 1961
יְהִי־נָא חֹרֶב אֶל־הַגִּזָּה לְבַדָּהּ וְעַל־כָּל־הָאָרֶץ יִהְיֶה־טָּל׃
.dew be let the ground all and on ,alone the fleece upon dry- ness Please let be

905 1492 2721 3915 430 6213
40 וַיַּעַשׂ אֱלֹהִים כֵּן בַּלַּיְלָה הַהוּא וַיְהִי־חֹרֶב אֶל־הַגִּזָּה לְבַדָּהּ
,alone the fleece on dryness and was ;that on night so God And did

2919 1961 776 3605 5921
וְעַל־כָּל־הָאָרֶץ הָיָה טָל׃
.dew there was the ground all and on

CAP. VII ז

CHAPTER 7

CHAPTER 7

[1]And Jerubbaal — he *is* Gideon—rose early, and all the people with him. And they camped by the spring of Harod, and the army of Midian was north of him on Mount Moreh, in the valley.
[2]And Jehovah said to Gideon, The people with

2583 834 5971 3605 1439 3378 7925
1 וַיַּשְׁכֵּם יְרֻבַּעַל הוּא גִדְעוֹן וְכָל־הָעָם אֲשֶׁר אִתּוֹ וַיַּחֲנוּ
they And camped with .him who (were) the people and all —Gideon he (is) —Jerubbaal rose And early

4176 1389 6828 1961 4080 4264 5878 5878
עַל־עֵין חֲרֹד וּמַחֲנֵה מִדְיָן הָיָה־לוֹ מִצָּפוֹן מִגִּבְעַת הַמּוֹרֶה
Moreh Mount on north of him was Midian the and army of ,Harod the by spring of

834 7971 7227 1439 3068 559 6010
2 בָּעֵמֶק׃ וַיֹּאמֶר יְהוָה אֶל־גִּדְעוֹן רַב הָעָם אֲשֶׁר אִתָּךְ
with you who the (are) people (are) (too) many ,Gideon to Jehovah said And the in .valley

you *are* too many for Me to give Midian into their hands, that Israel not glorify itself against Me, saying, My hand has delivered me. [3]And now then cry in the ears of the people, saying, Whoever is fearful and trembling, let him return and leave Mount Gilead. And twenty-two thousand of the people returned. And ten thousand were left. [4]And Jehovah said to Gideon, The people *are* still *too* many. Bring them down to the water, and I will refine them for you there. And it shall be, *he of* whom I say to you, this one shall go with you, he shall go with you. And any of whom I shall say to you, This one shall not go with you, he shall not go. [5]And he brought the people down to the water. And Jehovah said to Gideon, Everyone who laps of the water with his tongue, as a dog laps, you shall set him apart. And everyone who bows on his knees to drink, *set apart*.

[6]And the number of those lapping with their hand to their mouth *were* three hundred men. And all the rest of the people bowed down on their knees to drink water. [7]And Jehovah said to Gideon, I will deliver you by the three hundred men who lapped, and shall give Midian into your hand. And all the people shall go, each to his place. [8]And the people took the food in their hand, and their trumpets, and he sent away every man of Israel, each to his tent. But he kept hold on the three hundred men. And the camp of Midian was below him in the valley.

מִתִּתִּי אֶת־מִדְיָן בְּיָדָם פֶּן־יִתְפָּאֵר עָלַי יִשְׂרָאֵל לֵאמֹר יָדִי
3 הוֹשִׁיעָה לִּי׃ וְעַתָּה קְרָא נָא בְּאָזְנֵי הָעָם לֵאמֹר מִי־יָרֵא
וְחָרֵד יָשֹׁב וְיִצְפֹּר מֵהַר הַגִּלְעָד וַיָּשָׁב מִן־הָעָם עֶשְׂרִים
4 וּשְׁנַיִם אֶלֶף וַעֲשֶׂרֶת אֲלָפִים נִשְׁאָרוּ׃ וַיֹּאמֶר יְהוָה
אֶל־גִּדְעוֹן עוֹד הָעָם רָב הוֹרֵד אוֹתָם אֶל־הַמַּיִם וְאֶצְרְפֶנּוּ
לְךָ שָׁם וְהָיָה אֲשֶׁר אֹמַר אֵלֶיךָ זֶה ׀ יֵלֵךְ אִתָּךְ הוּא יֵלֵךְ
אִתָּךְ וְכֹל אֲשֶׁר־אֹמַר אֵלֶיךָ זֶה לֹא־יֵלֵךְ עִמָּךְ הוּא לֹא
5 יֵלֵךְ׃ וַיּוֹרֶד אֶת־הָעָם אֶל־הַמָּיִם וַיֹּאמֶר יְהוָה אֶל־
גִּדְעוֹן כֹּל אֲשֶׁר־יָלֹק בִּלְשׁוֹנוֹ מִן־הַמַּיִם כַּאֲשֶׁר יָלֹק הַכֶּלֶב
תַּצִּיג אוֹתוֹ לְבָד וְכֹל אֲשֶׁר־יִכְרַע עַל־בִּרְכָּיו לִשְׁתּוֹת׃
6 וַיְהִי מִסְפַּר הַמְלַקְקִים בְּיָדָם אֶל־פִּיהֶם שְׁלֹשׁ מֵאוֹת
אִישׁ וְכֹל יֶתֶר הָעָם כָּרְעוּ עַל־בִּרְכֵיהֶם לִשְׁתּוֹת מָיִם׃
7 וַיֹּאמֶר יְהוָה אֶל־גִּדְעוֹן בִּשְׁלֹשׁ מֵאוֹת הָאִישׁ הַמְלַקְקִים
אוֹשִׁיעַ אֶתְכֶם וְנָתַתִּי אֶת־מִדְיָן בְּיָדֶךָ וְכָל־הָעָם יֵלְכוּ
8 אִישׁ לִמְקֹמוֹ׃ וַיִּקְחוּ אֶת־צֵדָה הָעָם בְּיָדָם וְאֵת שׁוֹפְרֹתֵיהֶם
וְאֵת כָּל־אִישׁ יִשְׂרָאֵל שִׁלַּח אִישׁ לְאֹהָלָיו וּבִשְׁלֹשׁ־מֵאוֹת
הָאִישׁ הֶחֱזִיק וּמַחֲנֵה מִדְיָן הָיָה לוֹ מִתַּחַת בָּעֵמֶק׃

[9]And it happened on that night, Jehovah said to him, Rise up, go down to the camp, for I have given it into your hand. [10]And if you are afraid to go down, you and your young man Purah go down to the camp. [11]And you shall hear what they say. And afterward your hand shall be made stronger, and you shall go down against the army. And he went down, he and his young man Purah, to the edge of the battle alignment in the camp. [12]And Midian and Amalek, and all the sons of the east, *were* lying in the valley, as the locusts for multitude. And there was no number of their camels, *being* as the sand on the bank of the sea for multitude.

[13]And Gideon came; and, behold, a man *was* telling a dream to his companion. And he said, Behold, I have dreamed a dream. And, behold, a cake of barley bread *was* tumbling into the camp of Midian. And it came to the tent and struck it, and it fell, and turned it upside *down;* and the tent fell down. [14]And his companion answered and said, This is nothing but the sword of Gideon the son of Joash, a man of Israel. God has given Midian and all the army into his hand.

[15]And it happened when Gideon heard the telling of the dream, and its interpretation, he worshiped. And *he* returned to the army of Israel and said, Rise up, for Jehovah has given the army of Midian into your hand. [16]And he divided the three hundred men into three companies. And he put a trumpet in the hand of all of them, and empty jars, and torches inside the jars.

[17]And he said to them, Look at me, and do this; even behold, I am coming to the

4264 3381/6965 3068 559 3915 1961
9 וַיְהִי בַּלַּיְלָה הַהוּא וַיֹּאמֶר אֵלָיו יְהוָה קוּם רֵד בַּמַּחֲנֶה
the to go Rise ,Jehovah him to that ,that on it And
camp down ,up said night ,was

6313 3381 3381 3373 3027 5414
10 כִּי נְתַתִּיו בְּיָדֶךָ׃ וְאִם־יָרֵא אַתָּה לָרֶדֶת רֵד אַתָּה וּפֻרָה
and you go go to you are and your into have I for
,Purah down ,down afraid if ;hand it given

2388 310 1696 8085 4264 5288
11 נַעַרְךָ אֶל־הַמַּחֲנֶה׃ וְשָׁמַעְתָּ מַה־יְדַבֵּרוּ וְאַחַר תֶּחֱזַקְנָה
be shall and ,say they what you and the to your
strengthened afterward hear shall ;camp man young

7097 5288 6513 3381 4264 3381 3027
יָדֶיךָ וְיָרַדְתָּ בַּמַּחֲנֶה וַיֵּרֶד הוּא וּפֻרָה נַעֲרוֹ אֶל־קְצֵה
the to young his and he And the against you and your
of edge man ,Purah down went .camp down go shall hand

6924 1121 3605 6002 4080 4264 834 2571
12 הַחֲמֻשִׁים אֲשֶׁר בַּמַּחֲנֶה׃ וּמִדְיָן וַעֲמָלֵק וְכָל־בְּנֵי־קֶדֶם
the the and and and the in who by ranks
east of sons all ,Amalek Midian ;camp (were) five

2344 4557 369 1581 7230 697 6010 5307
נֹפְלִים בָּעֵמֶק כָּאַרְבֶּה לָרֹב וְלִגְמַלֵּיהֶם אֵין מִסְפָּר כַּחוֹל
(being) ,number there their of and for the as the in (were)
sand the as no was camels ;multitude locusts ,valley lying

5608 376 2009 1439 935 7230 3220 8193
13 שֶׁעַל־שְׂפַת הַיָּם לָרֹב׃ וַיָּבֹא גִדְעוֹן וְהִנֵּה־אִישׁ מְסַפֵּר
(was) man a ,and ;Gideon And for the lip the which
telling ,behold came .multitude sea of on (is)

3899 6742 2009 2492 2472 2009 559 2472 7453
לְרֵעֵהוּ חֲלוֹם וַיֹּאמֶר הִנֵּה חֲלוֹם חָלַמְתִּי וְהִנֵּה צְלוּל לֶחֶם
bread cake a ,and have I a ,Behold he And a his to
of ,behold dreamed dream ,said dream companion

5307 5221 168 935 4080 4264 2015 8184
שְׂעֹרִים מִתְהַפֵּךְ בְּמַחֲנֵה מִדְיָן וַיָּבֹא עַד־הָאֹהֶל וַיַּכֵּהוּ וַיִּפֹּל
it and and tent the to it and ,Midian the into (was) barley
,fell it struck came of camp tumbling

369 559 7453 6030 168 5307 4605 2015
14 וַיַּהַפְכֵהוּ לְמַעְלָה וְנָפַל הָאֹהֶל׃ וַיַּעַן רֵעֵהוּ וַיֹּאמֶר אֵין
is ,said and his And .tent the and upside- turned and
nothing companion replied down fell ;(down) it

5414 3478 376 3101 1121 1439 2719 2088
זֹאת בִּלְתִּי אִם־חֶרֶב גִּדְעוֹן בֶּן־יוֹאָשׁ אִישׁ יִשְׂרָאֵל נָתַן
has ;Israel a ,Joash the Gideon the except This
given of man of son of sword

8085 1961 4264 3605 4080 3027 430
15 הָאֱלֹהִים בְּיָדוֹ אֶת־מִדְיָן וְאֶת־כָּל־הַמַּחֲנֶה׃ וַיְהִי כִשְׁמֹעַ
when it And .army the all and Midian into God
heard was hand his

7725 7812 7667 2472 4557 1439
גִּדְעוֹן אֶת־מִסְפַּר הַחֲלוֹם וְאֶת־שִׁבְרוֹ וַיִּשְׁתָּחוּ וַיָּשָׁב אֶל־
to and he that its and dream the the Gideon
returned worshiped breaking of recounting

4264 3027 3068 5414 6965 559 3478 4264
מַחֲנֵה יִשְׂרָאֵל וַיֹּאמֶר קוּמוּ כִּי־נָתַן יְהוָה בְּיֶדְכֶם אֶת־מַחֲנֵה
army the into Jehovah has for Rise and ,Israel the
of hand your given ,up said of army

5414 7218 7969 376 3967 7969 2673 4080
16 מִדְיָן׃ וַיַּחַץ אֶת־שְׁלֹשׁ־מֵאוֹת הָאִישׁ שְׁלֹשָׁה רָאשִׁים וַיִּתֵּן
and ,heads into the hundred three he And .Midian
put he three men divided

3537 8432 3940 7386 3537 3605/3027 7782
שׁוֹפָרוֹת בְּיַד־כֻּלָּם וְכַדִּים רֵיקִים וְלַפִּדִים בְּתוֹךְ הַכַּדִּים׃
the inside and ,empty and of all the in a
,pitchers torches pitchers ,them of hand horn ram's

935 2009 6213 7200 559
17 וַיֹּאמֶר אֲלֵיהֶם מִמֶּנִּי תִרְאוּ וְכֵן תַּעֲשׂוּ וְהִנֵּה אָנֹכִי בָא
am I ,and ;do and ,Look me at ,them to he And
coming ,behold thus said

edge of the camp. And it
shall be, as I do, so you
shall do. 18And I shall
blow with a ram's horn, I
and all who *are* with me.
And you shall blow with
the ram's horns, you also
all around the camp. And
you shall shout. For
Jehovah and for Gideon!

19And Gideon came, and
the hundred men with him,
to the edge of the camp *at*
the beginning of the middle
watch—and they had but
newly set the watch. And
they blew with the
trumpets, and shattered the
jars in their hand. 20And
the three companies blew
with their trumpets, and
broke the jars, and held the
torches in their left hand;
and in their right hand the
trumpets to blow. And they
cried out, A sword for
Jehovah and for Gideon!
21And they each one stood
in his place, all around the
army. And all the army ran,
and they shouted, and they
fled. 22And the three
hundred blew the trumpets,
and Jehovah set a man's
sword against his com-
panion even in all the army.
And the army fled to Beth-
shittah, at Zererath, to the
border of Abel-meholah, by
Tabbath.

23And the men of Israel
were called from Naphtali,
and from Asher, and from all
Manasseh, and chased
Midian.
24And Gideon had sent
messengers to all the hills
of Ephraim, saying, Come
down to meet Midian, and
capture the waters before
them as far as Beth-barah

8628 6213 3651 6213 1961 4264 7097
18 בִּקְצֵה הַמַּחֲנֶה וְהָיָה כַאֲשֶׁר־אֶעֱשֶׂה כֵּן תַּעֲשׂוּן׃ וְתָקַעְתִּי
shall I And blow | you do shall | so | ,do I | as | it and be shall | the ,camp | the to of edge

1571 7782 8628 834 3605 7782
בַּשּׁוֹפָר אָנֹכִי וְכָל־אֲשֶׁר אִתִּי וּתְקַעְתֶּם בַּשּׁוֹפָרוֹת גַּם־
even | the with ,horns ram's | you and blow shall | with ,me | who (are) | and all | I | a with ,horn ram's

1439 3068 559 4264 3605 5439
אַתֶּם סְבִיבוֹת כָּל־הַמַּחֲנֶה וַאֲמַרְתֶּם לַיהוָה וּלְגִדְעוֹן׃
for and !Gideon | For Jehovah | shall and ,say | the camp | all | around | you

4264 7097 376 3967 1439 935
19 וַיָּבֹא גִדְעוֹן וּמֵאָה־אִישׁ אֲשֶׁר־אִתּוֹ בִּקְצֵה הַמַּחֲנֶה
,camp the | the to of edge | with him | who (were) | men (the) and hundred | Gideon | And came

8104 6965 6965 389 8484 821 7218
רֹאשׁ הָאַשְׁמֹרֶת הַתִּיכוֹנָה אַךְ הָקֵם הֵקִימוּ אֶת־הַשֹּׁמְרִים
;watch | the | they set had | newly | only | —middle | watch the | the (at) of head

8628 3027 834 3537 5310 7782 8628
20 וַיִּתְקְעוּ בַּשּׁוֹפָרוֹת וְנָפוֹץ הַכַּדִּים אֲשֶׁר בְּיָדָם׃ וַיִּתְקְעוּ
And blew | their ,hand | in which (were) | the pitchers | and shattered | the with ,horns ram's | they and blew

3027 2388 3537 7665 7782 7218 7969
שְׁלֹשֶׁת הָרָאשִׁים בַּשּׁוֹפָרוֹת וַיִּשְׁבְּרוּ הַכַּדִּים וַיַּחֲזִיקוּ בְיַד־
in hand | and held | the ,pitchers | broke and | their with ,horns ram's | heads the | three

7121 8628 7782 3225 3027 3940 8040
שְׂמֹאולָם בַּלַּפִּדִים וּבְיַד־יְמִינָם הַשּׁוֹפָרוֹת לִתְקוֹעַ וַיִּקְרְאוּ
they and ,cried | ;blow to | the horns ram's | their right | in and hand | the ,torches | left their

4264 5439 8478 376 5975 1439 3068 2719
21 חֶרֶב לַיהוָה וּלְגִדְעוֹן׃ וַיַּעַמְדוּ אִישׁ תַּחְתָּיו סָבִיב לַמַּחֲנֶה
;army the | all around | his in place | each one | they And stood | for and !Gideon | for Jehovah | A sword

3967 7969 8628 727 7321 4264 1323
22 וַיָּרָץ כָּל־הַמַּחֲנֶה וַיָּרִיעוּ וַיָּנִיסוּ׃ וַיִּתְקְעוּ שְׁלֹשׁ־מֵאוֹת
hundred | three | when And blew | and ,fled they | they and shouted | ,army the | all | and ran

3605 7453 376 2719 3068 7760 7782
הַשּׁוֹפָרוֹת וַיָּשֶׂם יְהוָה אֶת־חֶרֶב אִישׁ בְּרֵעֵהוּ וּבְכָל־
in even all | against companion his | man's a | sword of | Jehovah | and set | the horns, ram's

8193 5704 6888 = 1029 = 4264 5127 4264
הַמַּחֲנֶה וַיָּנָס הַמַּחֲנֶה עַד־בֵּית הַשִּׁטָּה צְרֵרָתָה עַד שְׂפַת־
the of lip | to | toward Zererath | ,shittah | Beth- as far | army the | and fled | the ;army

5320 3478 376 6817 2888 65 65
23 אָבֵל מְחוֹלָה עַל־טַבָּת׃ וַיִּצָּעֵק אִישׁ־יִשְׂרָאֵל מִנַּפְתָּלִי
from ,Naphtali | Israel | the of men | were And mustered | .Tabbath by | ,meholah | Abel-

4397 4080 310 7291 4519 3605 836
24 וּמִן־אָשֵׁר וּמִן־כָּל־מְנַשֶּׁה וַיִּרְדְּפוּ אַחֲרֵי מִדְיָן׃ וּמַלְאָכִים
And messengers | .Midian | after | and chased | ,Manasseh | all and from | ,Asher and from

4080 7125 3381 559 669 2022 3605 1439 7971
שָׁלַח גִּדְעוֹן בְּכָל־הַר אֶפְרַיִם לֵאמֹר רְדוּ לִקְרַאת מִדְיָן
,Midian | meet to | Come down | ,saying | ,Ephraim | the hills | all to | Gideon | sent

6817 3383 = 1012 = 5704/4325 3947
וְלִכְדוּ לָהֶם אֶת־הַמַּיִם עַד בֵּית בָּרָה וְאֶת־הַיַּרְדֵּן וַיִּצָּעֵק
was and mustered | .Jordan the and | barah | Beth- | as far | waters the | before them | and capture

= 1012 = 5704 4325 3920 669 376 3605
כָּל־אִישׁ אֶפְרַיִם וַיִּלְכְּדוּ אֶת־הַמַּיִם עַד בֵּית בָּרָה וְאֶת־
and | ,barah | Beth- | as far | the waters | they and captured | ,Ephraim | man | every of

and the Jordan. And every man of Ephraim was called up, and they captured the waters as far as Beth-barah and the Jordan. 25 And they captured the two rulers of Midian, Oreb and Zeeb. And Oreb was slain at the rock of Oreb; and they killed Zeeb at the winevat of Zeeb. And they pursued to Midian. And they brought the heads of Oreb and Zeeb to Gideon beyond the Jordan.

CHAPTER 8

1 And the men of Ephraim said to him, What *is* this thing you have done to us, not to call us when you went out to fight against Midian? And they contended with him sharply. 2 And he said to them, What have I done now in comparison to you? Are not the gleanings of Ephraim better than the vintage of Abiezer? 3 God has given the rulers of Midian, Oreb and Zeeb, into your hand. And what was I able to do like you? Then their spirit was abated toward him, when he said this word.

4 And Gideon came to the Jordan, he crossing over, and three hundred who *were* with him, *being* weary, yet pursuing. 5 And he said to the men of Succoth, Please give loaves of bread to the people at my feet, for they *are* weary; and I *am* chasing Zebah and Zalmunna, the kings of Midian. 6 And the rulers of Succoth said, *Is* the palm of Zebah and Zalmunna now in your hand, that we should give bread to your army? 7 And Gideon said, Because of this, when Jehovah has given Zebah and Zalmunna into my hand, I shall thresh your

2062 6159 4080 8269 8147 3920 3383
25 הירדן: וילכדו שני שרי מדין את־ערב ואת־זאב
;Zeeb and Oreb ,Midian rulers the they And the
of two captured .Jordan
2062/ 3342 2026 2062 6159 6697 6159 2026
ויהרגו את־עורב בצור־עורב ואת־זאב הרגו ביקב־זאב
Zeeb's at they Zeeb and ,Oreb the at Oreb they and
wine-vat killed of rock killed
1439 935 2062 6159 7218 4080 7291
וירדפו אל־מדין וראש־ערב וזאב הביאו אל־גדעון
Gideon to they and Oreb the And .Midian to they and
brought Zeeb of heads pursued
3383 5676
מעבר לירדן:
.Jordan the beyond

CAP. VIII ח

CHAPTER 8

6213 2088 669 376 559
1 ויאמרו אליו איש אפרים מה־הדבר הזה עשית לנו
to have you this thing What Ephraim the ,him to And
.us done (which) (is) of men said
7378 4080 3898 3212 7121
לבלתי קראות לנו כי הלכת להלחם במדין ויריבון
they And against fight to you when to call to not
contended ?Midian went us
3808 6258 6213 4100 559 2394
2 אתו בחזקה: ויאמר אליהם מה־עשיתי עתה ככם הלא
Are like now have What ,them to he And .sharply with
not ?you done I said him
430 5414 3027 44 1208 669 5955 2896
3 טוב עללות אפרים מבציר אביעזר: בידכם נתן אלהים
God has your into ?Abiezer the than Ephraim the better
given hand of vintage of gleanings
6213 3201 2062 6159 4080 8269
את־שרי מדין את־ערב ואת־זאב ומה־יכלתי עשות ככם
like do to I was and ,Zeeb and ,Oreb ,Midian the
?you able what of rulers
1439 935 2088 1696 7307 7503
4 אז רפתה רוחם מעליו בדברו הדבר הזה: ויבא גדעון
Gideon And .this word he when toward their abated Then
came said ,him spirit
5889 376 3967 7969 5674 3383
הירדנה עבר הוא ושלש־מאות האיש אשר אתו עיפים
weary with who the hundred and he crossing the to
him (were) men three ,over ,Jordan
5971 3899 3603 4994/5414/ 5523 582 559 7291
5 ורדפים: ויאמר לאנשי סכות תנו־נא ככרות לחם לעם
the to bread of loaves Please give ,Succoth the to he And yet
people of men said .pursuing
2078 310 7291 5889 7272 834
אשר ברגלי כי־עיפים הם ואנכי רדף אחרי זבח
Zebah after (am) I and they weary for my at who
chasing (are) feet (are)
2078 3709 5523 8269 559 4080 4428 6759
6 וצלמנע מלכי מדין: ויאמר שרי סכות הכף זבח
Zebah the (is) Succoth the ,said And .Midian the and
of palm of rulers of kings Zalmunna
1439 559 3899 6635 5414 3027 6258 6759
7 וצלמנע עתה בידך כי־נתן לצבאך לחם: ויאמר גדעון
Gideon And ?bread your to we that your in now and
said army give should ,hand Zalmunna
1758 3027 6759 2078 3068 5414
לכן בתת יהוה את־זבח ואת־צלמנע בידי ודשתי את־
shall I into Zalmunna and Zebah Jehovah when there-
thresh ,hand my given has fore

8 בְּשַׂרְכֶם אֶת־קוֹצֵי הַמִּדְבָּר וְאֶת־הַבַּרְקֳנִים׃ וַיַּעַל מִשָּׁם
פְּנוּאֵל וַיְדַבֵּר אֲלֵיהֶם כָּזֹאת וַיַּעֲנוּ אוֹתוֹ אַנְשֵׁי פְנוּאֵל
9 כַּאֲשֶׁר עָנוּ אַנְשֵׁי סֻכּוֹת׃ וַיֹּאמֶר גַּם־לְאַנְשֵׁי פְנוּאֵל לֵאמֹר
10 בְּשׁוּבִי בְשָׁלוֹם אֶתֹּץ אֶת־הַמִּגְדָּל הַזֶּה׃ וְזֶבַח וְצַלְמֻנָּע
בַּקַּרְקֹר וּמַחֲנֵיהֶם עִמָּם כַּחֲמֵשֶׁת עָשָׂר אֶלֶף כֹּל הַנּוֹתָרִים
מִכֹּל מַחֲנֵה בְנֵי־קֶדֶם וְהַנֹּפְלִים מֵאָה וְעֶשְׂרִים אֶלֶף אִישׁ
11 שֹׁלֵף חָרֶב׃ וַיַּעַל גִּדְעוֹן דֶּרֶךְ הַשְּׁכוּנֵי בָאֳהָלִים מִקֶּדֶם
לְנֹבַח וְיָגְבֳּהָה וַיַּךְ אֶת־הַמַּחֲנֶה וְהַמַּחֲנֶה הָיָה בֶטַח׃
12 וַיָּנוּסוּ זֶבַח וְצַלְמֻנָּע וַיִּרְדֹּף אַחֲרֵיהֶם וַיִּלְכֹּד אֶת־שְׁנֵי מַלְכֵי
13 מִדְיָן אֶת־זֶבַח וְאֶת־צַלְמֻנָּע וְכָל־הַמַּחֲנֶה הֶחֱרִיד׃ וַיָּשָׁב
14 גִּדְעוֹן בֶּן־יוֹאָשׁ מִן־הַמִּלְחָמָה מִלְמַעֲלֵה הֶחָרֶס׃ וַיִּלְכָּד־
נַעַר מֵאַנְשֵׁי סֻכּוֹת וַיִּשְׁאָלֵהוּ וַיִּכְתֹּב אֵלָיו אֶת־שָׂרֵי סֻכּוֹת
15 וְאֶת־זְקֵנֶיהָ שִׁבְעִים וְשִׁבְעָה אִישׁ׃ וַיָּבֹא אֶל־אַנְשֵׁי סֻכּוֹת
וַיֹּאמֶר הִנֵּה זֶבַח וְצַלְמֻנָּע אֲשֶׁר חֵרַפְתֶּם אוֹתִי לֵאמֹר הֲכַף
זֶבַח וְצַלְמֻנָּע עַתָּה בְּיָדֶךָ כִּי נִתֵּן לַאֲנָשֶׁיךָ הַיְּעֵפִים לָחֶם׃
16 וַיִּקַּח אֶת־זִקְנֵי הָעִיר וְאֶת־קוֹצֵי הַמִּדְבָּר וְאֶת־הַבַּרְקֳנִים
17 וַיֹּדַע בָּהֶם אֵת אַנְשֵׁי סֻכּוֹת׃ וְאֶת־מִגְדַּל פְּנוּאֵל נָתַץ

flesh with thorns of the
wilderness and with briers.
8 And he went up from there
to Penuel, and spoke to
them in this same way. And
the men of Penuel
answered him as the men of
Succoth had answered.
9 And he also spoke to the
men of Penuel, saying,
When I come back in
peace, I will break down
this tower.
10 And Zebah and Zal-
munna *were* in Karkor, and
their armies with them,
about fifteen thousand, all
who were left of all the army
of the sons of the east. And
those who fell *were* a
hundred and twenty thou-
sand men drawing sword.
11 And Gideon went up the
way of those who live in
tents, on the east of Nobah
and Jogbehah, and struck
the army; for the army was
at ease. 12 And Zebah and
Zalmunna fled; and he
chased them and captured
the two kings of Midian,
Zebah and Zalmunna. And
he caused all the army to
tremble.

13 And Gideon the son of
Joash returned from the
battle, at the ascent of
Mount Heres. 14 And he
captured a young man of
the men of Succoth, and
questioned him; and he
wrote out to him the rulers
of Succoth, and its elders,
seventy-seven men. 15 And
he came in to the men of
Succoth, and said, Behold,
Zebah and Zalmunna,
about whom you taunted
me, saying, *Is* the palm of
Zebah and Zalmunna now
in your hand that we should
give bread to your weary
men? 16 And he took the
elders of the city, and the
thorns of the wilderness,
and the briers, and taught
the men of Succoth with
them. 17 And he broke
down the tower of Penuel,

and killed the men of the
city.
[18]And he said to Zebah
and to Zalmunna, How
were the men whom you
killed in Tabor? And they
said, As you *are*, so they;
each one as a king's son in
appearance. [19]And he said,
They *were* my brothers,
sons of my mother. *As*
Jehovah lives, if you had
kept them alive, I would not
have killed you. [20]And he
said to his firstborn, Jether,
Rise up, kill them. But the
young man did not draw his
sword, for he was afraid, for
he *was* still a youth. [21]And
Zebah and Zalmunna said,
You rise up and fall on us,
for as the man, so *is* his
might. And Gideon rose up
and killed Zebah and Zal-
munna, and took the moon
crescents which *were* on
the necks of their camels.
[22]And the men of Israel
said to Gideon, rule over us,
both you and your son, and
your son's son, for you have
delivered us from the hand
of Midian. [23]And Gideon
said to them, I shall not rule
over you, nor shall my son
rule over you; Jehovah shall
rule over you.
[24]And Gideon said to
them, Let me ask of you a
request, that each man give
to me a ring from his
plunder; for they had gold
rings, because they *were*
Ishmaelites. [25]And they
said, We will certainly give.
And they spread out a
garment and each threw a
ring from their plunder
there. [26]And the weight of
the rings of gold which he
asked *was* a thousand and
seven hundred *shekels* of
gold, apart from the ornaments, and the pendants,
and the purple clothing that
was on the kings of Midian;
also apart from the neck-
laces that *were* on the

18 וַיַּהֲרֹג אֶת־אַנְשֵׁי הָעִיר׃ וַיֹּאמֶר אֶל־זֶבַח וְאֶל־צַלְמֻנָּע
אֵיפֹה הָאֲנָשִׁים אֲשֶׁר הֲרַגְתֶּם בְּתָבוֹר וַיֹּאמְרוּ כָּמוֹךָ
19 כְמוֹהֶם אֶחָד כְּתֹאַר בְּנֵי הַמֶּלֶךְ׃ וַיֹּאמַר אַחַי בְּנֵי־אִמִּי
20 הֵם חַי־יְהוָה לוּ הַחֲיִתֶם אוֹתָם לֹא הָרַגְתִּי אֶתְכֶם׃ וַיֹּאמֶר
לְיֶתֶר בְּכוֹרוֹ קוּם הֲרֹג אוֹתָם וְלֹא־שָׁלַף הַנַּעַר חַרְבּוֹ כִּי
21 יָרֵא כִּי עוֹדֶנּוּ נָעַר׃ וַיֹּאמֶר זֶבַח וְצַלְמֻנָּע קוּם אַתָּה וּפְגַע־
בָּנוּ כִּי כָאִישׁ גְּבוּרָתוֹ וַיָּקָם גִּדְעוֹן וַיַּהֲרֹג אֶת־זֶבַח וְאֶת־
צַלְמֻנָּע וַיִּקַּח אֶת־הַשַּׂהֲרֹנִים אֲשֶׁר בְּצַוְּארֵי גְמַלֵּיהֶם׃
22 וַיֹּאמְרוּ אִישׁ־יִשְׂרָאֵל אֶל־גִּדְעוֹן מְשָׁל־בָּנוּ גַּם־אַתָּה גַּם־
23 בִּנְךָ גַּם בֶּן־בִּנְךָ כִּי הוֹשַׁעְתָּנוּ מִיַּד מִדְיָן׃ וַיֹּאמֶר אֲלֵהֶם
גִּדְעוֹן לֹא־אֶמְשֹׁל אֲנִי בָּכֶם וְלֹא־יִמְשֹׁל בְּנִי בָּכֶם יְהוָה יִמְשֹׁל
24 בָּכֶם׃ וַיֹּאמֶר אֲלֵהֶם גִּדְעוֹן אֶשְׁאֲלָה מִכֶּם שְׁאֵלָה וּתְנוּ־לִי אִישׁ
25 נֶזֶם שְׁלָלוֹ כִּי־נִזְמֵי זָהָב לָהֶם כִּי יִשְׁמְעֵאלִים הֵם׃ וַיֹּאמְרוּ
נָתוֹן נִתֵּן וַיִּפְרְשׂוּ אֶת־הַשִּׂמְלָה וַיַּשְׁלִיכוּ שָׁמָּה אִישׁ נֶזֶם
26 שְׁלָלוֹ׃ וַיְהִי מִשְׁקַל נִזְמֵי הַזָּהָב אֲשֶׁר שָׁאָל אֶלֶף וּשְׁבַע־
מֵאוֹת זָהָב לְבַד מִן־הַשַּׂהֲרֹנִים וְהַנְּטִפוֹת וּבִגְדֵי הָאַרְגָּמָן
שֶׁעַל מַלְכֵי מִדְיָן וּלְבַד מִן־הָעֲנָקוֹת אֲשֶׁר בְּצַוְּארֵי

necks of their camels. [27]And Gideon made an ephod of it, and put it in his city, even in Ophrah. And all Israel went whoring after it there, and it became a snare to Gideon and to his house. [28]And Midian was subdued before the sons of Israel, and they did not lift up their heads any more.

And the land had rest forty years in the days of Gideon.

[29]And Jerubbaal the son of Joash departed and lived in his own house. [30]And seventy sons were *born* to Gideon, coming out of his loins; for he had many wives. [31]And his concubine in Shechem bore a son to him, she also; and he called his name Abimelech. [32]And Gideon the son of Joash died in a good old age, and was buried in the burial place of his father Joash, in Ophrah *of* the Abiezrites.

[33]And it happened, when Gideon *was* dead, the sons of Israel rebelled and went whoring after the Baals, and appointed Baal-berith for a god for themselves. [34]And the sons of Israel did not remember Jehovah their God who had delivered them out of the hand of all their enemies all around; [35]nor did they act with kindness on the house of Jerubbaal, Gideon, according to all the good which he did with Israel.

5892 3322 646 1439 6213 1581
27 גְמַלֵּיהֶם׃ וַיַּעַשׂ אוֹתוֹ גִדְעוֹן לְאֵפוֹד וַיַּצֵּג אוֹתוֹ בְעִירוֹ
his in it and an Gideon it of And their
city put ephod made .camels
1004 1439 1961 8033 310 3478 3605 2181 : 6084
בְּעָפְרָה וַיִּזְנוּ כָל־יִשְׂרָאֵל אַחֲרָיו שָׁם וַיְהִי לְגִדְעוֹן וּלְבֵיתוֹ
his to and to it and ;there after Israel all and in even
house Gideon became it whored ;Ophrah
5375 3254 3808 :3478 1121 6440 4080 3665 4170
28 לְמוֹקֵשׁ׃ וַיִּכָּנַע מִדְיָן לִפְנֵי בְּנֵי יִשְׂרָאֵל וְלֹא יָסְפוּ לָשֵׂאת
lifted again and ,Israel the before Midian was And .snare a
up they not of sons subdued
1439 3117 8141 703 776 8252 7218
רֹאשָׁם וַתִּשְׁקֹט הָאָרֶץ אַרְבָּעִים שָׁנָה בִּימֵי גִדְעוֹן׃
.Gideon the in years forty land the had And their
of days rest .heads
7657 1961/1439 1004 2416 3101/1121 3427 3212
29 30 וַיֵּלֶךְ יְרֻבַּעַל בֶּן־יוֹאָשׁ וַיֵּשֶׁב בְּבֵיתוֹ׃ וּלְגִדְעוֹן הָיוּ שִׁבְעִים
seventy were to And his in and Joash the Jerub- And
(born) ,Gideon .house own lived ,of son baal went
834 6370 7227 802 3409 5927 1121
31 בָּנִים יֹצְאֵי יְרֵכוֹ כִּי־נָשִׁים רַבּוֹת הָיוּ לוֹ׃ וּפִילַגְשׁוֹ אֲשֶׁר
who his and to were many wives for his coming sons
(was) ,concubine ;him ,loins of out
40 8034 7760 1121 3205 7927
בִּשְׁכֶם יָלְדָה־לּוֹ גַם־הִיא בֵּן וַיָּשֶׂם אֶת־שְׁמוֹ אֲבִימֶלֶךְ׃
.Abimelech his he and a she even to bore in
name gave ,son ,him ,Shechem
3101 6913 6912 2896 7872 3101 1121 1439 4191
32 וַיָּמָת גִּדְעוֹן בֶּן־יוֹאָשׁ בְּשֵׂיבָה טוֹבָה וַיִּקָּבֵר בְּקֶבֶר יוֹאָשׁ
,Joash the in was and ,good a in Joash the ,Gideon And
of place burial buried age old of son died
1439 4191 1961 = 33 = 6084 1
33 אָבִיו בְּעָפְרָה אֲבִי הָעֶזְרִי׃ וַיְהִי כַּאֲשֶׁר מֵת גִּדְעוֹן
,Gideon (was) when it And .ezrites the in his
dead ,was Abi- (of) Ophrah ,father
7760 1168 310 2181 3478 1121 7725
וַיָּשׁוּבוּ בְּנֵי יִשְׂרָאֵל וַיִּזְנוּ אַחֲרֵי הַבְּעָלִים וַיָּשִׂימוּ לָהֶם
for ap- and ,Baals the after whored Israel the that
themselves pointed of sons again
3068 : 3478 1121 2142 3808 430 =1170=
34 בַּעַל בְּרִית לֵאלֹהִים׃ וְלֹא זָכְרוּ בְּנֵי יִשְׂרָאֵל אֶת־יְהוָה
Jehovah Israel the re- did and a for berith Baal-
of sons member not ;god
3808 5439 341 3605 3027 5337 430
35 אֱלֹהֵיהֶם הַמַּצִּיל אוֹתָם מִיַּד כָּל־אֹיְבֵיהֶם מִסָּבִיב׃ וְלֹא־
and all their all from them had who ,God their
not ;around enemies of hand the delivered
6213 834 : 2896 3605 1439 3378 1004 2617 : 6213
עָשׂוּ חֶסֶד עִם־בֵּית יְרֻבַּעַל גִּדְעוֹן כְּכָל־הַטּוֹבָה אֲשֶׁר עָשָׂה
he which the according ,Gideon Jerub- the with with did
did good all to —baal of house kindness deal
3478
עִם־יִשְׂרָאֵל׃
.Israel with

CAP. IX ט

CHAPTER 9

[1]And Abimelech the son of Jerubbaal went to Shechem, to his mother's brothers, and spoke with them, and to all the family of the house of his mother's father, saying, [2]Please speak in the ears of all the

1696 517 251 7927 3378/1121 40 3212
1 וַיֵּלֶךְ אֲבִימֶלֶךְ בֶּן־יְרֻבַּעַל שְׁכֶמָה אֶל־אֲחֵי אִמּוֹ וַיְדַבֵּר
and his to to Jerubbaal the Abimelech And
spoke ,mother's brothers ,Shechem of son went
1696 559 517 1 1004 4940 3605
2 אֲלֵיהֶם וְאֶל־כָּל־מִשְׁפַּחַת בֵּית־אֲבִי אִמּוֹ לֵאמֹר׃ דַּבְּרוּ־
Speak ,saying his father the the all and ,them to
mother's of house of family to

leaders of Shechem, Which *is* best for you, seventy men ruling over you, all the sons of Jerubbaal, or one man ruling over you? And you should remember that I *am* your bone and your flesh. [3]And his mother's brothers spoke all these words about him in the ears of all the leaders of Shechem, and their heart inclined after Abimelech. For they said, He *is* our brother. [4]And they gave to him seventy silverlings out of the house of Baal-berith. And Abimelech hired worthless and reckless men with them; and they went after him. [5]And he went into his father's house at Ophrah, and killed his brothers, the sons of Jerubbaal, seventy men on one stone. But Jotham, the youngest son of Jerubbaal, was left; for he had hidden.

[6]And all the leaders of Shechem were gathered together, and all the house of Millo. And *they* came and caused Abimelech to reign as king at the oak of the outpost which *is* in Shechem. [7]And they told Jotham, and he went and stood on the top of Mount Gerizim. And *he* lifted up his voice and cried, and said to them, Listen to me, O leaders of Shechem, and God shall listen to you. [8]The trees went forth to anoint a king over them. And they said to the olive, Reign over us. [9]And the olive said to them, Should I cease from my fatness, by which they honor God and man, and go to hold sway over the trees? [10]And the trees said to the fig, You come, reign over us. [11]And

4910 2896 7927 1167 3605 241 4994
נָא בְּאָזְנֵי כָל־בַּעֲלֵי שְׁכֶם מַה־טּוֹב לָכֶם הַמְשֹׁל בָּכֶם
over ruling for better What ,Shechem the all the in please
,you ,you (is) of leaders of ears

259 376 4910 3378 1121 3605 376 7657
שִׁבְעִים אִישׁ כֹּל בְּנֵי יְרֻבַּעַל אִם־מְשֹׁל בָּכֶם אִישׁ אֶחָד
?one man over ruling or Jerub- the all ,men seventy
you ,baal of sons

517 251 1696 1320 6106 2142
3 וּזְכַרְתֶּם כִּי־עַצְמְכֶם וּבְשַׂרְכֶם אָנִי׃ וַיְדַבְּרוּ אֲחֵי־אִמּוֹ
his brothers And .(am) I your and your that And
mother's spoke flesh bone remember

5186 428 1697 3605 7927 1167/3605 241 5921
עָלָיו בְּאָזְנֵי כָּל־בַּעֲלֵי שְׁכֶם אֵת כָּל־הַדְּבָרִים הָאֵלֶּה וַיֵּט
and ,these words all ,Shechem the all the in about
inclined of leaders of ears him

5414 251 559 40 310 3820
4 לִבָּם אַחֲרֵי אֲבִימֶלֶךְ כִּי אָמְרוּ אָחִינוּ הוּא׃ וַיִּתְּנוּ־לוֹ
to And .(is) He our they for ,Abimelech after their
him gave they brother ,said heart

40 7936 1170 1004 3701 7657
שִׁבְעִים כֶּסֶף מִבֵּית בַּעַל בְּרִית וַיִּשְׂכֹּר בָּהֶם אֲבִימֶלֶךְ
Abimelech with hired and berith- Baal of out silver seventy
them of house the (pieces)

1 1004 935 310 6348 7386 582
5 אֲנָשִׁים רֵיקִים וּפֹחֲזִים וַיֵּלְכוּ אַחֲרָיו׃ וַיָּבֹא בֵּית־אָבִיו
his house he And after they and and worthless men
father's into went .him went ,reckless

376 7657 3378 1121 251 2026 6084
עָפְרָתָה וַיַּהֲרֹג אֶת־אֶחָיו בְּנֵי־יְרֻבַּעַל שִׁבְעִים אִישׁ עַל־
on ,men seventy Jerubbaal the his and at
of sons ,brothers killed ,Ophrah

2244 6996 3378 3147 3498 251 68
אֶבֶן אֶחָת וַיִּוָּתֵר יוֹתָם בֶּן־יְרֻבַּעַל הַקָּטֹן כִּי נֶחְבָּא׃
was he for the Jerubbaal son Jotham was but ;one stone
.hidden ;youngest of left

4427 3212 4407 1004 3605 7927 1167 3605 622
6 וַיֵּאָסְפוּ כָּל־בַּעֲלֵי שְׁכֶם וְכָל־בֵּית מִלּוֹא וַיֵּלְכוּ וַיַּמְלִיכוּ
caused and and ,Millo the and Shechem the all were And
reign to came of house all of leaders assembled

5046 7927 834 5324 437 4428 40
7 אֶת־אֲבִימֶלֶךְ לְמֶלֶךְ עִם־אֵלוֹן מֻצָּב אֲשֶׁר בִּשְׁכֶם׃ וַיַּגִּדוּ
they And in which the the at king as Abimelech
told .Shechem (is) outpost of oak

7121 6963 5375 1630 2022 7218 5975 3212 3147
לְיוֹתָם וַיֵּלֶךְ וַיַּעֲמֹד בְּרֹאשׁ הַר־גְּרִזִים וַיִּשָּׂא קוֹלוֹ וַיִּקְרָא
and his and Mount the on and and ,Jotham
,cried voice up lifted Gerizim of top stood went he

8085 7927 1167 8085 559
וַיֹּאמֶר לָהֶם שִׁמְעוּ אֵלַי בַּעֲלֵי שְׁכֶם וְיִשְׁמַע אֲלֵיכֶם
you to shall and ,Shechem O ,me to Listen ,them to and
listen of leaders said

559 4428 4886 6086 3212 3212 430
8 אֱלֹהִים׃ הָלוֹךְ הָלְכוּ הָעֵצִים לִמְשֹׁחַ עֲלֵיהֶם מֶלֶךְ וַיֹּאמְרוּ
they and a over to trees the went (Once) .God
said ;king them anoint forth

2308 2132 559 4427 2132
9 לַזַּיִת מְלוֹכָה עָלֵינוּ׃ וַיֹּאמֶר לָהֶם הַזַּיִת הֶחֳדַלְתִּי אֶת־
I should the them to said And .us over Reign the to
from cease ,olive ,olive

5921 5128 3212 582 430 3513 834 1880
דִּשְׁנִי אֲשֶׁר־בִּי יְכַבְּדוּ אֱלֹהִים וַאֲנָשִׁים וְהָלַכְתִּי לָנוּעַ עַל־
over to go and ,man and God they by which my
sway hold honor me ,fatness

5921 4427 3212 8384 6086 559 6086
10 הָעֵצִים׃ וַיֹּאמְרוּ הָעֵצִים לַתְּאֵנָה לְכִי־אַתְּ מָלְכִי עָלֵינוּ׃
over (and) You come the to trees the said And the
.us reign ,fig ?trees

the fig said to them, Should
I cease from my sweetness
and my good fruit, and go to
hold sway over the trees?
12 And the trees said to the
vine, You come, reign over
us. 13 And the vine said to
them, Should I cease from
my new wine, which
rejoices god and men, and
go to hold sway over the
trees?
14 And all the trees said to
the bramblebush, You
come, reign over us. 15 And
the bramblebush said to the
trees, If you truly anoint me
king over you, come seek
refuge in my shade. And if
not, let fire come out of the
bramblebush and burn up
the cedars of Lebanon.
16 And now if you have acted
in truth and integrity when
you made Abimelech king;
and if you have done well
with Jerubbaal and his
house; and you have done
to him as his hands did,
17 *in* which my father fought
for you, and cast aside his
life, and delivered you from
the hand of Midian. 18 And
you have risen against the
house of my father today
and have killed his sons,
seventy men on one stone,
and have made the son of
his slaaegirl king over the
leaders of Shechem — for
he *is* your brother;
19 yea, if in truth and in
sincerity you have acted
toward Jerubbaal and his
house this day, rejoice in
Abimelech, and he will
rejoice, even he in you.
20 And if not, may fire come
out from Abimelech and
consume the leaders of
Shechem and the house of
Millo; and may fire come

8570 4987 2308 8384 559
11 וַתֹּאמֶר לָהֶם הַתְּאֵנָה הֶחֳדַלְתִּי אֶת־מָתְקִי וְאֶת־תְּנוּבָתִי
my fruit | and | my sweetness | I Should cease from | ,fig the | them to | said And

1612 6086 559 6086 5128 3212 2896
12 הַטּוֹבָה וְהָלַכְתִּי לָנוּעַ עַל־הָעֵצִים׃ וַיֹּאמְרוּ הָעֵצִים לַגֶּפֶן
the to vine | trees the | said And | the ?trees | over | hold to sway | go and | ,good

2308 1612 559 4427 3212
13 לְכִי־אַתְּ מָלְכִי עָלֵינוּ׃ וַתֹּאמֶר לָהֶם הַגֶּפֶן הֶחֳדַלְתִּי אֶת־
I Should cease from | the vine | them to | said And | over .us | (and) reign | You come

5921 5128 3212 582 430 8056 8492
תִּירוֹשִׁי הַמְשַׂמֵּחַ אֱלֹהִים וַאֲנָשִׁים וְהָלַכְתִּי לָנוּעַ עַל־
over | hold to sway | go and | ,men and | god | which rejoices | new my ,wine

4427 3212 329 6086 3605 559 6086
14 הָעֵצִים׃ וַיֹּאמְרוּ כָל־הָעֵצִים אֶל־הָאָטָד לֵךְ אַתָּה מְלָךְ־
(and) reign | You | come | the ,bramble | to | trees the | all | said And | ?trees the

4886 571 6086 329 559 5921
15 עָלֵינוּ׃ וַיֹּאמֶר הָאָטָד אֶל־הָעֵצִים אִם בֶּאֱמֶת אַתֶּם מֹשְׁחִים
anoint | you | truly | If | ,trees the | to | the bramble | said And | over .us

784 3318 369 518 6738 2620 935 5921 4428
אֹתִי לְמֶלֶךְ עֲלֵיכֶם בֹּאוּ חֲסוּ בְצִלִּי וְאִם־אַיִן תֵּצֵא אֵשׁ
fire | let out come | not | and if | my in ;shade | seek refuge | come | ,you over | as king | me

571 518 6258 3844 730 398 329
16 מִן־הָאָטָד וְתֹאכַל אֶת־אַרְזֵי הַלְּבָנוֹן׃ וְעַתָּה אִם־בֶּאֱמֶת
truth in | if | And ,now | .Lebanon | the of cedars | and consume | the bramble | from

6213 2896 518 40 4427 6213 8549
וּבְתָמִים עֲשִׂיתֶם וַתַּמְלִיכוּ אֶת־אֲבִימֶלֶךְ וְאִם־טוֹבָה עֲשִׂיתֶם
have you acted | well | and if | ,Abimelech | you when king made | have you acted | in and integrity

834 6213 3027 1576 1004 3378
17 עִם־יְרֻבַּעַל וְעִם־בֵּיתוֹ וְאִם־כִּגְמוּל יָדָיו עֲשִׂיתֶם לוֹ׃ אֲשֶׁר־
(in) which | to —him | have you done | his hands | the as of doing | and if | his ;house | and with | Jerub- baal | with

5337 5048 5315 7993 1 3898
נִלְחַם אָבִי עֲלֵיכֶם וַיַּשְׁלֵךְ אֶת־נַפְשׁוֹ מִנֶּגֶד וַיַּצֵּל אֶתְכֶם
you | and delivered | ,aside | life his | and cast | ,you for | my father | fought

2026 3117 1 1004 6965 4080 3027
18 מִיַּד מִדְיָן׃ וְאַתֶּם קַמְתֶּם עַל־בֵּית אָבִי הַיּוֹם וַתַּהַרְגוּ אֶת־
have and killed | ,today | my father | the against of house | have risen | you and | ;Midian's | from hand

40 4427 259 68 376 7657 1121
בָּנָיו שִׁבְעִים אִישׁ עַל־אֶבֶן אֶחָת וַתַּמְלִיכוּ אֶת־אֲבִימֶלֶךְ
,Abimelech | have and king made | ,one | stone on | men | seventy | his ,sons

571 518 251 7927 1167 5921 519 1121
19 בֶּן־אֲמָתוֹ עַל־בַּעֲלֵי שְׁכֶם כִּי אֲחִיכֶם הוּא׃ וְאִם־בֶּאֱמֶת
truth in | and if | —(is) he | your brother | for —Shechem | the of leaders | over | his slavegirl's | son

8056 2088 3117 1004 3378 6213 8549
וּבְתָמִים עֲשִׂיתֶם עִם־יְרֻבַּעַל וְעִם־בֵּיתוֹ הַיּוֹם הַזֶּה שִׂמְחוּ
rejoice | ,this | day | his house with | and Jerubbaal with | have you acted | in and integrity

784 3318 369 518 8056 40
20 בַּאֲבִימֶלֶךְ וְיִשְׂמַח גַּם־הוּא בָּכֶם׃ וְאִם־אַיִן תֵּצֵא אֵשׁ
fire | may out come | not if But | .you in | he even | may and rejoice | in ,Abimelech

3318 4407 1004 7927 1167 398 40
מֵאֲבִימֶלֶךְ וְתֹאכַל אֶת־בַּעֲלֵי שְׁכֶם וְאֶת־בֵּית מִלּוֹא וְתֵצֵא
may and out come | ;Millo | the of house | and Shechem | the of leaders | and consume | from Abimelech

out from the leaders of Shechem and from the house of Millo and consume Abimelech.

[21]And Jotham hurried and fled, and went to Beer and lived there, away from the face of his brother Abimelech.

[22]And Abimelech ruled over Israel three years. [23]And God sent an evil spirit between Abimelech and the leaders of Shechem. And the leaders of Shechem dealt treacherously with Abimelech; [24]that the violence *against* Jerubbaal's seventy sons, even their blood, might be put on their brother Abimelech who killed them, and on the leaders of Shechem, who made his hands strong to kill his brothers. [25]And the leaders of Shechem set men in ambush at the tops of the mountains; and they robbed all who passed by them on the highway. And it was told to Abimelech.

[26]And Gaal, the son of Ebed, and his brothers came. And they passed on into Shechem; and the leaders of Shechem trusted in him. [27]And *they* went out into the fields and gathered their vineyards, and trod out, and made a festival, and went into the house of their god and ate and drank. And *they* cursed Abimelech.

[28]And Gaal the son of Ebed said, Who *is* Abimelech, and who *is* Shechem, that we should serve him? Is *he* not the son of Jerubbaal, and Zebul his commander? Serve the men of Hamor the father of Shechem! And, Why should we serve him? [29]And who will give this people in my hand? Then I would remove Abimelech. And he said to Abimelech, Multiply your army and come out.

[30]And Zebul, the leader of the city, heard the words

אש מבעלי שכם ומבית מלוא ותאכל את־אבימלך׃
21 וינס יותם ויברח וילך בארה וישב שם מפני אבימלך
22 אחיו׃ וישר אבימלך על־ישראל שלש שנים׃
23 וישלח אלהים רוח רעה בין אבימלך ובין בעלי שכם
24 ויבגדו בעלי־שכם באבימלך׃ לבוא חמס שבעים בני־
ירבעל ודמם לשום על־אבימלך אחיהם אשר הרג אותם
ועל בעלי שכם אשר־חזקו את־ידיו להרג את־אחיו׃
25 וישימו לו בעלי שכם מארבים על ראשי ההרים ויגזלו
את כל־אשר־יעבר עליהם בדרך ויגד לאבימלך׃
26 ויבא געל בן־עבד ואחיו ויעברו בשכם ויבטחו־בו בעלי
27 שכם׃ ויצאו השדה ויבצרו את־כרמיהם וידרכו ויעשו
הלולים ויבאו בית אלהיהם ויאכלו וישתו ויקללו את־
28 אבימלך׃ ויאמר ׀ געל בן־עבד מי־אבימלך ומי־שכם
כי נעבדנו הלא בן־ירבעל וזבל פקידו עבדו את־אנשי
29 חמור אבי שכם ומדוע נעבדנו אנחנו׃ ומי יתן את־
העם הזה בידי ואסירה את־אבימלך ויאמר לאבימלך
30 רבה צבאך וצאה׃ וישמע זבל שר העיר את־דברי

Gaal, the son of Ebed; and his anger glowed. [31]And he sent craftily sent messengers to Abimelech, saying, Behold, Gaal, the son of Ebed, and his brothers have come to Shechem. And, behold, they are fortifying the city against you. [32]And now rise up by night, you and the people with you, and lie in wait in the field. [33]And it shall be, in the morning, about the sun rise, you shall rise early and charge against the city. And, behold, he and the people with him *will* come out to you; and you shall do to him as you find your hand *able to do.*

[34]And Abimelech rose up by night, and all the people with him; and they lay in wait against Shechem *in* four companies. [35]And Gaal, the son of Ebed, went out and stood at the opening of the gate of the city. And Abimelech and the people with him rose up from the ambush. [36]And Gaal saw the people, and he said to Zebul, Behold, people *are* coming down from the top of the mountains! And Zebul said to him, You *are* seeing the shadow of the mountains like men. [37]And yet again Gaal spoke and said, Behold, people *are* coming from the high part of the land, and one head is coming by the way of the Sorcerers' Oak. [38]And Zebul said to him, Now where *is* your mouth *with* which you said, Who *is* Abimelech that we should serve him? Is this not the people you despised? Now please go out now and fight against it. [39]And Gaal went out before the face of the leaders of Shechem and fought against Abimelech; [40]and Abimelech chased him, and he fled before his face; and

40 4397 7971 639 2734 5651/1121 1603
31 געל בן־עבד ויחר אפו׃ וישלח מלאכים אל־אבימלך
Abimelech to messengers he And his and Ebed the Gaal
sent anger glowed of son

7927 935 251 5651/1121 1603 559 8699
בתרמה לאמר הנה געל בן־עבד ואחיו באים שכמה
;Shechem to have his and Ebed the Gaal ,Behold ,saying ,craftily
come brothers of son

39 151 6965 6258 5892 6696 2009
32 והנם צרים את־העיר עליך׃ ועתה קום לילה אתה
you ,night by up rise And against the (are) they ,and
,now you city besieging ,behold

2224 1242 1961 7704 693 7971
33 והעם אשר־אתך וארב בשדה׃ והיה בבקר כזרח
the about the in it and the in lie and with who the and
of rising ,morning be shall ;field wait in ,you (are) people

834 7971 2009 4892 6584 7925 8121
השמש תשכים ופשטת על־העיר והנה־הוא והעם אשר־
who the and he ,and the against and shall you sun the
(are) people ,behold ;city charge early rise

3027/ 4672 6213 3318
אתו יצאים אליך ועשית לו כאשר תמצא ידך׃
your shall as to will then ,you to (are) with
.hand find him do you out coming him

691 3915 5971 3605 40 6965
34 ויקם אבימלך וכל־העם אשר־עמו לילה ויארבו על־
against set and by with who the and Abimelech And
ambush an ,night ,him (were) people all arose

6607 5975 5651/1121 1603 3318 7218 702 7927
35 שכם ארבעה ראשים׃ ויצא געל בן־עבד ויעמד פתח
the at and Ebed the Gaal And .heads four (in) Shechem
of door stood of son out went

3993 834 5971 40 6965 5892 8179
שער העיר ויקם אבימלך והעם אשר־אתו מן־המארב׃
the from with who the and Abimelech rose and the the
;ambush him (were) people up ;city of gate

3381 5971 2009 2083 559 5971 1603 7200
36 וירא־געל את־העם ויאמר אל־זבל הנה־עם יורד
(are) people ,Behold ,Zebul to said and the Gaal And
coming ,people saw

2022 6738 2083 559 2022 7200
מראשי ההרים ויאמר אליו זבל את צל ההרים אתה
you moun- the the Zebul ,him to said And the the from
tains of shadow !mountains of top

7971/2009 559 1696 1603 5750 3254 582 7200
37 ראה כאנשים׃ ויסף עוד געל לדבר ויאמר הנה־עם
people Be- ,said and spoke Gaal yet And .men like (are)
,hold again seeing

437 1870 935 259 7218 776 2872 3381
ירדים מעם טבור הארץ וראש־אחד בא מדרך אלון
Oak the by is one and the high the from (are)
of way coming head ,land of part coming

559 834 6310 645 346 2083 559 6049
38 מעוננים׃ ויאמר אליו זבל איה אפוא פיך אשר תאמר
,said you (with) your where Now ,Zebul to said And .Sorcerers'
which mouth (is) ,him

3973 5647 3808 2088 5971 834 40
מי אבימלך כי נעבדנו הלא זה העם אשר־מאסתה בו
?whom you the this Is should we that Abimelech Who
despised people not ?him serve

7927 1167 6440 1603 3318 3898 6258 4994
39 צא־נא עתה והלחם בו׃ ויצא געל לפני בעלי שכם
Shechem the before Gaal And against and now Please
of leaders out went ,it fight (is) out go

5307 6440 5127 40 7291 40 3898
40 וילחם באבימלך׃ וירדפהו אבימלך וינס מפניו ויפלו
fell and before and Abimelech chased And against and
;him fled he him .Abimelech fought

many fell down wounded, to the door of the gate. [41]And Abimelech remained in Arumah. And Zebul threw out Gaal and his brothers from living in Shechem. [42]And it happened on the next day, people went out to the field, and *they* told Abimelech. [43]And he took the people and divided them into three heads and set an ambush in the field, and *they* watched. And, behold! The people *were* coming out from the city. And he rose against them and struck them. [44]And Abimelech and the heads who *were* with him charged forward and stood *at* the door of the gate of the city. And the two heads charged against all who *were* in the field and struck them. [45]And Abimelech fought against the city all that day, and captured the city. And he killed the people who *were* in it. And he broke down the city and sowed it *with* salt.

[46]And all the leaders of the tower of Shechem heard and went into the stronghold of the house of the god Berith. [47]And it was told to Abimelech that all the leaders had gathered in the tower of Shechem. [48]And Abimelech went up to Mount Zalmon, he and all the people who *were* with him. And Abimelech took the axes in his hand and cut off a bough of the trees. And *he* lifted it up and set *it* on his shoulder, and said to the people who *were* with him, You have seen what I have done, you hsurry and do likewise. [49]And all the people also, each man, cut down his bough and went after Abimelech, and set *them* at the stronghold and set afire the stronghold over them; and

חללים רבים עד־פתח השער׃ וישב אבימלך בארומה 41
;Arumah in Abimelech And .gate the the to many fatally remained of door wounded

42 ויגרש זבל את־געל ואת־אחיו משבת בשכם׃ ויהי
it And in from his and Gaal Zebul and ,was Shechem living brothers expelled

43 ממחרת ויצא העם השדה ויגדו לאבימלך׃ ויקח את־
he And .Abimelech (they) and the to the went that the on took told ;field people out ,day next

העם ויחצם לשלשה ראשים ויארב בשדה וירא והנה
,and and the in set and ,heads three into and the ,behold ;watched field ambush an them divided people

44 העם יצא מן־העיר ויקם עליהם ויכם׃ ואבימלך
And struck and against he and the from (were) the Abimelech .them them up rose ,city out coming people

והראשים אשר עמו פשטו ויעמדו פתח שער העיר
the gate the the (at) and charged with which the and ;city of of door stood forward him (were) heads

ושני הראשים פשטו על־כל־אשר בשדה ויכום׃
struck and the in who all against charged the and them ,field (were) heads two

45 ואבימלך נלחם בעיר כל היום ההוא וילכד את־העיר
the and ,that day all against fought And ;city captured city the Abimelech

ואת־העם אשר־בה הרג ויתץ את־העיר ויזרעה מלח׃
(with) sowed and the he and he it in who the and salt it city down broke ;killed (were) people

46 וישמעו כל־בעלי מגדל־שכם ויבאו אל־צריח
strong- the into and ,Shechem the the all heard And of hold went of tower of leaders

47 בית אל ברית׃ ויגד לאבימלך כי התקבצו כל־בעלי
the all had that Abimelech to it And .Berith the the of leaders assembled told was god of house

48 מגדל־שכם׃ ויעל אבימלך הר־צלמון הוא וכל־העם
the and he ,Zalmon to Abimelech And .Shechem the people all Mount up went of tower

אשר־אתו ויקח אבימלך את־הקרדמות בידו ויכרת
cut and his in the Abimelech and with who off hand axes took ;him (were)

שוכת עצים וישאה וישם על־שכמו ויאמר אל־העם
the to said and his on set and lifted and the bough a people ;shoulder (it) up it ,trees of

49 אשר־עמו מה ראיתם עשיתי מהרו עשו כמוני׃ ויכרתו
cut And .likewise and you have I you What with who down do hasten ,done seen have ,him (were)

גם־כל־העם איש שוכה וילכו אחרי אבימלך וישימו
set and ,Abimelech after and his each the all also (them) went bough man people

על־הצריח ויציתו עליהם את־הצריח באש וימתו גם
even and with the over and the at died ;fire stronghold them kindled stronghold

about a thousand men and women, all the men of the tower of Shechem, died also.

[50]And Abimelech went to Thebez and camped against Thebez and seized it. [51]And a strong tower was in the middle of the city. And all the men and women and all the leaders of the city fled there. And they shut *it* behind them and went up on the roof of the tower. [52]And Abimelech came to the tower and fought against it. And *he* drew near to the door of the tower to burn it with fire.

[53]And a certain woman threw a piece of a riding millstone on the head of Abimelech and crushed his skull. [54]And he quickly called to the young man bearing his weapons. And *he* said to him, Draw your sword and put me to death, lest they say of me, A woman killed him. And his young man ran him through and he died.

[55]And when the men of Israel saw that Abimelech *was* dead, then each one went to his place.

[56]And God turned back the evil of Abimelech which he did to his father, to kill his seventy brothers, [57]also all the wickedness of the men of Shechem, on their own heads. And the curse of Jothan the son of Jerubbaal came upon them.

כָּל־אַנְשֵׁי מִגְדַּל־שְׁכֶם כְּאֶלֶף אִישׁ וְאִשָּׁה׃ 50 וַיֵּלֶךְ

אֲבִימֶלֶךְ אֶל־תֵּבֵץ וַיִּחַן בְּתֵבֵץ וַיִּלְכְּדָהּ׃ וּמִגְדַּל־עֹז הָיָה 51

בְתוֹךְ־הָעִיר וַיָּנֻסוּ שָׁמָּה כָּל־הָאֲנָשִׁים וְהַנָּשִׁים וְכֹל בַּעֲלֵי

הָעִיר וַיִּסְגְּרוּ בַּעֲדָם וַיַּעֲלוּ עַל־גַּג הַמִּגְדָּל׃ וַיָּבֹא אֲבִימֶלֶךְ 52

עַד־הַמִּגְדָּל וַיִּלָּחֶם בּוֹ וַיִּגַּשׁ עַד־פֶּתַח הַמִּגְדָּל לְשָׂרְפוֹ

בָאֵשׁ׃ וַתַּשְׁלֵךְ אִשָּׁה אַחַת פֶּלַח רֶכֶב עַל־רֹאשׁ אֲבִימֶלֶךְ 53

וַתָּרִץ אֶת־גֻּלְגָּלְתּוֹ׃ וַיִּקְרָא מְהֵרָה אֶל־הַנַּעַר ׀ נֹשֵׂא כֵלָיו 54

וַיֹּאמֶר לוֹ שְׁלֹף חַרְבְּךָ וּמוֹתְתֵנִי פֶּן־יֹאמְרוּ לִי אִשָּׁה הֲרָגָתְהוּ

וַיִּדְקְרֵהוּ נַעֲרוֹ וַיָּמֹת׃ וַיִּרְאוּ אִישׁ־יִשְׂרָאֵל כִּי־מֵת אֲבִימֶלֶךְ 55

וַיֵּלְכוּ אִישׁ לִמְקֹמוֹ׃ וַיָּשֶׁב אֱלֹהִים אֵת רָעַת אֲבִימֶלֶךְ 56

אֲשֶׁר עָשָׂה לְאָבִיו לַהֲרֹג אֶת־שִׁבְעִים אֶחָיו׃ וְאֵת כָּל־רָעַת 57

אַנְשֵׁי שְׁכֶם הֵשִׁיב אֱלֹהִים בְּרֹאשָׁם וַתָּבֹא אֲלֵיהֶם קִלְלַת

יוֹתָם בֶּן־יְרֻבָּעַל׃

CAP. X י

CHAPTER 10

CHAPTER 10

[1]And after Abimelech, Tola the son of Puah, the son of Dodo, a man of Issachar, rose up to save Israel. And he lived in Shamir, in the hills of Ephraim. [2]And he judged Israel twenty-three years. And he died and was buried in Shamir.

וַיָּקָם אַחֲרֵי אֲבִימֶלֶךְ לְהוֹשִׁיעַ אֶת־יִשְׂרָאֵל תּוֹלָע בֶּן־פּוּאָה 1

בֶּן־דּוֹדוֹ אִישׁ יִשָּׂשכָר וְהוּא־יֹשֵׁב בְּשָׁמִיר בְּהַר אֶפְרָיִם׃

וַיִּשְׁפֹּט אֶת־יִשְׂרָאֵל עֶשְׂרִים וְשָׁלֹשׁ שָׁנָה וַיָּמָת וַיִּקָּבֵר 2

[3]And after him Jair, a Gileadite, rose up. And he judged Israel twenty-two years. [4]And he had thirty sons who rode on thirty ass colts. And they had thirty cities, which are called the Towns of Jair to this day, which *are* in the land of Gilead. [5]And Jair died and was buried in Kamon.

[6]And the sons of Israel did evil in the sight of Jehovah again, and served the Baals, and the Ashtoreths, and the gods of Syria, and the gods of Sidon, and the gods of Moab, and the gods of the sons of Ammon, and the gods of the Philistines. And they forsook Jehovah and did not serve Him. [7]And the anger of Jehovah glowed against Israel. And He sold them into the hands of the Philistines, and into the hand of the sons of Ammon. [8]And they crushed and oppressed the sons of Israel in that year, *for* eighteen years, all the sons of Israel that *were* beyond the Jordan in the land of the Amorites, which *is* in Gilead. [9]And the sons of Ammon crossed over the Jordan to fight against Judah also, and against Benjamin, and against the house of Ephraim. And Israel was greatly distressed.

[10]And the sons of Israel cried to Jehovah, saying, We have sinned against You, even because we have forsaken our God, and have served the Baals. [11]And Jehovah said to the sons of Israel, Did I not *save you* from the Egyptians, and from the Amorites, and from the sons of Ammon, and from the Philistines? [12]And the Sidonians, and Amalek,

3 בשמיר׃ ויקם אחריו יאיר הגלעדי וישפט את־ישראל
4 עשרים ושתים שנה׃ ויהי־לו שלשים בנים רכבים על־
שלשים עירים ושלשים עירים להם להם יקראו חות
5 יאיר עד היום הזה אשר בארץ הגלעד׃ וימת יאיר
6 ויקבר בקמון׃ ויספו בני ישראל לעשות הרע
בעיני יהוה ויעבדו את־הבעלים ואת־העשתרות ואת־
אלהי ארם ואת־אלהי צידון ואת אלהי מואב ואת אלהי
בני־עמון ואת אלהי פלשתים ויעזבו את־יהוה ולא
7 עבדוהו׃ ויחר־אף יהוה בישראל וימכרם ביד פלשתים
8 וביד בני עמון׃ וירעצו וירצצו את־בני ישראל בשנה
ההיא שמנה עשרה שנה את־כל־בני ישראל אשר בעבר
9 הירדן בארץ האמרי אשר בגלעד׃ ויעברו בני־עמון
את־הירדן להלחם גם־ביהודה ובבנימין ובבית אפרים
10 ותצר לישראל מאד׃ ויזעקו בני ישראל אל־יהוה לאמר
חטאנו לך וכי עזבנו את־אלהינו ונעבד את־הבעלים׃
11 ויאמר יהוה אל־בני ישראל הלא ממצרים ומן־
12 האמרי מן־בני עמון ומן־פלשתים׃ וצידונים ועמלק

and Maon have oppressed
you, and you cried to Me,
and I saved you out of their
hand. 13 Yet you have
forsaken Me, and served
other gods; therefore, I did
not save you again. 14 Go
and cry to the gods which
you have chosen; let them
save you in the time of your
distress. 15 And the sons
of Israel said to Jehovah,
We have sinned. Do to us
whatever *may be* good in
Your eyes; only please
deliver us this day. 16 And
they removed the gods of
the alien from among them,
and served Jehovah. And
His soul was grieved with
the misery of Israel. 17 And
the sons of Ammon were
called together, and
camped in Gilead. And the
sons of Israel were
gathered, and camped in
Mizpeh 18 And the people
said, The chief men of
Gilead, each man to his
neighbor, Who *will be* the
man who will begin to fight
against the sons of
Ammon? He shall be head
over all the people of
Gilead.

CAP. XI יא

CHAPTER 11

CHAPTER 11

1 And Jephthah the Gil-
eadite was a mighty warrior.
And he *was* the son of a
harlot woman; and Gilead
fathered Jephthah. 2 And
the wife of Gilead bore sons
to him. And the sons of the
wife grew up, and *they*
threw Jephthah out, and
said to him, You shall not
inherit in the house of your
father, for you *are* the son of
another woman. 3 And
Jephthah fled from the face
of his brothers, and lived in
the land of Tob. And
worthless men were

gathered to Jephthah, and went out with him.
4And it happened after some time, the sons of Ammon fought with Israel.
5And it happened when the sons of Ammon fought with Israel, the elders of Gilead went to bring Jephthah from the land of Tob.
6And they said to Jephthah, Come, and you shall be our commander, that we may fight against the sons of Ammon.
7And Jephthah said to the elders of Gilead, Have you not hated me? Yea, you threw me out from my father's house. Why have you come to me when you *are* in distress?
8And the elders of Gilead said to Jephthah, For this reason we have come back to you now; and you shall go with us and fight against the sons of Ammon. And you shall be our head, to all the people of Gilead.
9And Jephthah said to the elders of Gilead, If you take me back to fight against the sons of Ammon, and Jehovah gives them up before me, shall I be your head?
10And the elders of Gilead said to Jephthah, Jehovah shall be witness between us; surely we will do according to your word.
11And Jephthah went with the elders of Gilead, and the people appointed him head over them, and as commander. And Jephthah spoke all his words before Jehovah in Mizpeh.

12And Jephthah sent messengers to the king of the sons of Ammon, saying, What have you to do with me, that you have come in to me to fight in my land?
13And the king of the sons of Ammon said to the messengers of Jephthah, Because Israel took my land when he came up out of

3478 5983/1121 3898 3117 1961 5927
4 וַיֵּצְאוּ עִמּוֹ׃ וַיְהִי מִיָּמִים וַיִּלָּחֲמוּ בְנֵי־עַמּוֹן עִם־יִשְׂרָאֵל׃
.Israel with Ammon the that some after it And with they and
of sons fought time was .him out went

1568 2205 3212 3478 5983/1121 3898
5 וַיְהִי כַּאֲשֶׁר־נִלְחֲמוּ בְנֵי־עַמּוֹן עִם־יִשְׂרָאֵל וַיֵּלְכוּ זִקְנֵי גִלְעָד
Gilead the went ,Israel with Ammon the fought when And
of elders of sons

3212 3316 559 2897 776 3316 3947
6 לָקַחַת אֶת־יִפְתָּח מֵאֶרֶץ טוֹב׃ וַיֹּאמְרוּ לְיִפְתָּח לְכָה
,Come to they And .Tob the from Jephthah bring to
Jephthah said of land

3316 559 5983 1121 3898 7101 1961
7 וְהָיִיתָה לָּנוּ לְקָצִין וְנִלָּחֲמָה בִּבְנֵי עַמּוֹן׃ וַיֹּאמֶר יִפְתָּח
Jephthah said And .Ammon against we that com- a for us to you and
of sons the fight may ,mander be shall

1004 1644 8130 3808 1568 2205
לְזִקְנֵי גִלְעָד הֲלֹא אַתֶּם שְׂנֵאתֶם אוֹתִי וַתְּגָרְשׁוּנִי מִבֵּית
the from threw you ,Yea ?me hated you Have ,Gilead the to
of house out me not of elders

559 6887 6258 935 4100
8 אָבִי וּמַדּוּעַ בָּאתֶם אֵלַי עַתָּה כַּאֲשֶׁר צַר לָכֶם׃ וַיֹּאמְרוּ
said And to distress when ,now me to you have why my
?you (is) come ;father

3212 7725 6258 3316 1568 2205
זִקְנֵי גִלְעָד אֶל־יִפְתָּח לָכֵן עַתָּה שַׁבְנוּ אֵלֶיךָ וְהָלַכְתָּ עִמָּנוּ
with you and to have we now this For ,Jephthah to Gilead the
us go shall ;you back come reason of elders

1568 3427 3605 7218 1961 5983 1121 3898
וְנִלְחַמְתָּ בִּבְנֵי עַמּוֹן וְהָיִיתָ לָּנוּ לְרֹאשׁ לְכֹל יֹשְׁבֵי גִלְעָד׃
.Gilead the all to a for us to you and ;Ammon against fight and
of people ,head be shall of sons the

7725 1568 2205 3316 559
9 וַיֹּאמֶר יִפְתָּח אֶל־זִקְנֵי גִלְעָד אִם־מְשִׁיבִים אַתֶּם אוֹתִי
me you taking are If ,Gilead the to Jephthah said And
back of elders

1961 6440 3068 5414 5983 1121 3898
לְהִלָּחֵם בִּבְנֵי עַמּוֹן וְנָתַן יְהוָה אוֹתָם לְפָנָי אָנֹכִי אֶהְיֶה
shall ,I before them Jehovah and ,Ammon against fight to
be I ,me up gives of sons the

3068 1568/2205 559 7218
10 לָכֶם לְרֹאשׁ׃ וַיֹּאמְרוּ זִקְנֵי־גִלְעָד אֶל־יִפְתָּח יְהוָה יִהְיֶה
is Jehovah ,Jephthah to Gilead the said And ?head your
of elders

3316 3212 6213 1697 3808 996 8085
11 שֹׁמֵעַ בֵּינוֹתֵינוּ אִם־לֹא כִדְבָרְךָ כֵּן נַעֲשֶׂה׃ וַיֵּלֶךְ יִפְתָּח
Jephthah And will we according surely ;us between witness
went .do word your to

7101 7218 5971 7760 1568 2205
עִם־זִקְנֵי גִלְעָד וַיָּשִׂימוּ הָעָם אוֹתוֹ עֲלֵיהֶם לְרֹאשׁ וּלְקָצִין
for and for over him the and ,Gilead the with
.commander head ,them people appointed of elders

4709 3068 6440 1697 3605 3316 1696
וַיְדַבֵּר יִפְתָּח אֶת־כָּל־דְּבָרָיו לִפְנֵי יְהוָה בַּמִּצְפָּה׃
in Jehovah before words his all Jephthah And
.Mizpeh spoke

559 5983 1121 4428 4397 3316 7971
12 וַיִּשְׁלַח יִפְתָּח מַלְאָכִים אֶל־מֶלֶךְ בְּנֵי־עַמּוֹן לֵאמֹר מַה־לִּי
to What ,saying ,Ammon the the to messengers Jephthan And
me (is) of sons of king sent

1121 4428 559 776 3898 935
13 וָלָךְ כִּי־בָאתָ אֵלַי לְהִלָּחֵם בְּאַרְצִי׃ וַיֹּאמֶר מֶלֶךְ בְּנֵי־
the king the said And my in fight to ,me to have you that and
of sons of ?land come ,you to

5927 776 3478 3947 3316 4397 5983
עַמּוֹן אֶל־מַלְאֲכֵי יִפְתָּח כִּי־לָקַח יִשְׂרָאֵל אֶת־אַרְצִי בַּעֲלוֹתוֹ
he when my Israel took Be- ,Jephthah the to Ammon
up came land cause of messengers

Egypt, from Arnon even to
the Jabbok, and to the
Jordan. And now, restore
them in peace. 14 And
Jephthah again sent mes-
sengers to the king of the
sons of Ammon, 15 and said
to him, So says Jephthah,
Israel did not take the land
of Moab, and the land of the
sons of Ammon. 16 For when
they came up out of Egypt,
Israel went in the wilderness to the Red Sea, and
came in at Kadesh. 17 And
Israel sent messengers to
the king of Edom, saying,
Please let me pass on
through your land, and the
king of Edom did not listen.
And *Israel* sent also to the
king of Moab, and he was
not willing. And Israel
remained in Kadesh. 18 And
he went through the
wilderness, and went
around the land of Edom,
and the land of Moab, and
came in at the rising of the
sun to the land of Moab.
And they camped beyond
Arnon, and did not come
into the border of Moab, for
Arnon *was* the border of
Moab. 19 And Israel sent
messengers to Sihon, the
king of the Amorites, the
king of Heshbon, and Israel
said to him, Please let us
pass on through your land,
to my place. 20 And Sihon
did not trust Israel to pass
on through his border. And
Sihon gathered all his
people and they camped in
Jahaz, and fought with
Israel. 21 And Jehovah the
God of Israel gave Sihon
and all his people into the
hand of Israel, and they
struck them. And Israel took
possession of all the land of
the Amorites, the inhabi-
tants of that land. 22 And
they took possession of all

7725 6258 3383 2999 5704 769 4714
מִמִּצְרַיִם מֵאַרְנוֹן וְעַד־הַיַּבֹּק וְעַד־הַיַּרְדֵּן וְעַתָּה הָשִׁיבָה
restore and the to and the even from of out
.now ;Jordan .Jabbok to Arnon ,Egypt

4397 7971 3316 5750 3254 7965
אֶתְהֶן בְּשָׁלוֹם׃ וַיּוֹסֶף עוֹד יִפְתָּח וַיִּשְׁלַח מַלְאָכִים אֶל־ 14
to messengers sent Jephthah yet And .peace in them
again

3947 3316 559 559 5983 1121 4428
מֶלֶךְ בְּנֵי עַמּוֹן׃ וַיֹּאמֶר לוֹ כֹּה אָמַר יִפְתָּח לֹא־לָקַח 15
did not Jephthah says Thus ,him to said and ,Ammon the the
take of sons of king

3212 5983 1121 776 4124 776 3478
יִשְׂרָאֵל אֶת־אֶרֶץ מוֹאָב וְאֶת־אֶרֶץ בְּנֵי עַמּוֹן׃ כִּי בַּעֲלוֹתָם 16
they when for ,Ammon the the and ,Moab the Israel
up came of sons of land of land

6946 935 5488/3220 4057 3478 3212 4714
מִמִּצְרַיִם וַיֵּלֶךְ יִשְׂרָאֵל בַּמִּדְבָּר עַד־יַם־סוּף וַיָּבֹא קָדֵשָׁה׃
at and ,Reeds the to the in Israel went of out
.Kadesh in came of Sea wilderness ,Egypt

5674 559 123 4428 4397 3478 7971
וַיִּשְׁלַח יִשְׂרָאֵל מַלְאָכִים אֶל־מֶלֶךְ אֱדוֹם לֵאמֹר אֶעְבְּרָה־ 17
me Let ,saying ,Edom the to messengers Israel And
,on pass of king sent

4124 4428 7971 123 4428 8085 3808 776 4994
נָּא בְאַרְצֶךָ וְלֹא שָׁמַע מֶלֶךְ אֱדוֹם וְגַם אֶל־מֶלֶךְ מוֹאָב
,Moab the to and ;Edom the did but through please
of king also of king listen not ,land your

4057 3212 6946 3478 7725 14 3808 7971
שָׁלַח וְלֹא אָבָה וַיֵּשֶׁב יִשְׂרָאֵל בְּקָדֵשׁ׃ וַיֵּלֶךְ בַּמִּדְבָּר 18
the through he and in Israel and was he and (Israel)
,wilderness went ;Kadesh remained ;willing not ,sent

8121 4217 935 4124 776 123 776 5437
וַיָּסָב אֶת־אֶרֶץ אֱדוֹם וְאֶת־אֶרֶץ מוֹאָב וַיָּבֹא מִמִּזְרַח־שֶׁמֶשׁ
the the at and ,Moab the and Edom land the went and
sun of rising came of land of around

4124 1366 935 769 5676 2583 4124 776
לְאֶרֶץ מוֹאָב וַיַּחֲנוּן בְּעֵבֶר אַרְנוֹן וְלֹא־בָאוּ בִּגְבוּל מוֹאָב
,Moab the into did and ,Arnon beyond they and ;Moab the to
of border come not camped of land

4397 3478 7971 4124 1366 769
כִּי אַרְנוֹן גְּבוּל מוֹאָב׃ וַיִּשְׁלַח יִשְׂרָאֵל מַלְאָכִים אֶל־ 19
to messengers Israel sent And .Moab the Arnon for
of border (was)

3478 559 2809 4428 567 4428 5511
סִיחוֹן מֶלֶךְ־הָאֱמֹרִי מֶלֶךְ חֶשְׁבּוֹן וַיֹּאמֶר לוֹ יִשְׂרָאֵל
,Israel to said and ,Heshbon the the the ,Sihon
him of king ,Amorites of king

5511 539 3808 4725 5704 776 4994 5674
נַעְבְּרָה־נָּא בְאַרְצְךָ עַד־מְקוֹמִי׃ וְלֹא־הֶאֱמִין סִיחוֹן אֶת־ 20
Sihon did And .place my to through ,please us Let
trust not land your ,on pass

2583 5971 3605 5511 622 1366 5674 3478
יִשְׂרָאֵל עֲבֹר בִּגְבֻלוֹ וַיֶּאֱסֹף סִיחוֹן אֶת־כָּל־עַמּוֹ וַיַּחֲנוּ
he and his all Sihon and through pass to Israel
camped people gathered ,border his on

3478/430 3068 5414 3478 3898 3096
בְּיָהְצָה וַיִּלָּחֶם עִם־יִשְׂרָאֵל׃ וַיִּתֵּן יְהוָה אֱלֹהֵי־יִשְׂרָאֵל 21
,Israel the Jehovah And .Israel with and in
of God gave fought Jahaz

3478 3423 5221 3478 3027 5971 3605 5511
אֶת־סִיחוֹן וְאֶת־כָּל־עַמּוֹ בְּיַד יִשְׂרָאֵל וַיַּכּוּם וַיִּירַשׁ יִשְׂרָאֵל
Israel and they and ,Israel the into his all and Sihon
seized ,them struck of hand people

3423 776 3427 567 776 3605
אֵת כָּל־אֶרֶץ הָאֱמֹרִי יוֹשֵׁב הָאָרֶץ הַהִיא׃ וַיִּירְשׁוּ אֵת 22
they And .that land the the the all
seized of dwellers ,Amorites of land

the border of the Amorites
from Arnon, and to the
Jabbok, and from the
wilderness, and to the
Jordan. [23]And now,
Jehovah the God of Israel
has expelled the Amorite
from before His people
Israel. And would you
possess it? [24]Whatever
Chemosh your god causes
you to possess, do you not
possess it? And all that
which Jehovah our God has
expelled from before us, we
will possess! [25]And now,
are you at all any better than
Balak the son of Zippor, the
king of Moab? Did he
indeed ever strive with
Israel? Did he ever fight
against them? [26]When
Israel lived in Heshbon and
its towns, and in Aroer and
in its towns, in all the cities
which *were* by the sides of
Arnon three hundred years,
then why have you not
delivered them in that time?
[27]So I have not sinned
against you, and you are
doing me wrong to fight
against me. Jehovah the
Judge shall judge today
between the sons of Israel
and the sons of Ammon.

[28]And the king of the
sons of Ammon did not
listen to the words of
Jephthah which he sent to
him. [29]And the Spirit of
Jehovah was on Jephthah.
And he passed through
Gilead and Manasseh, and
passed through Mizpeh of
Gilead, and from Mizpeh of
Gilead he passed on to the
sons of Ammon. [30]And
Jephthah vowed a vow to
Jehovah, and said, If You
will indeed give the sons of
Ammon into my hand,
[31]then *it* shall be that
anything which comes out
from the doors of my house
to meet me when I return in
peace from the sons of
Ammon, it shall belong to

5704 4057 2999 769 567 1366 3605
כָּל־גְּבוּל הָאֱמֹרִי מֵאַרְנוֹן וְעַד־הַיַּבֹּק וּמִן־הַמִּדְבָּר וְעַד־
even to | the wilderness | and from | the Jabbok | even to | from Arnon | the Amorites | the of border | all

5984 3423 3478 430 3068 3383
23 הַיַּרְדֵּן׃ וְעַתָּה יְהוָה ׀ אֱלֹהֵי יִשְׂרָאֵל הוֹרִישׁ אֶת־הָאֱמֹרִי
the Amorite | has expelled | ,Israel | the of God | ,Jehovah | And ,now | the ,Jordan

3423 3423 3478 5971 6440
24 מִפְּנֵי עַמּוֹ יִשְׂרָאֵל וְאַתָּה תִּירָשֶׁנּוּ׃ הֲלֹא אֵת אֲשֶׁר יוֹרִישְׁךָ
you causes possess to | what- ever | Do not | would ?it possess | and you | ;Israel | His people | from before

3068 3423 834 3605 3423 430 3645
כְּמוֹשׁ אֱלֹהֶיךָ אוֹתוֹ תִירָשׁ וְאֵת כָּל־אֲשֶׁר הוֹרִישׁ יְהוָה
Jehovah | has expelled | that which | all | And | you ?possess | — | your god | Chemosh

2895 6258 3423 6440 430
25 אֱלֹהֵינוּ מִפָּנֵינוּ אוֹתוֹ נִירָשׁ׃ וְעַתָּה הֲטוֹב טוֹב אַתָּה
you | all at | (are) better | And ,now | will we .possess | from ,us before | God our

3478 7378 7378 4124 4428 6834 1111
מִבָּלָק בֶּן־צִפּוֹר מֶלֶךְ מוֹאָב הֲרוֹב רָב עִם־יִשְׂרָאֵל אִם־
Did | ?Israel with | he strive indeed | Did | Moab | the of king | ,Zippor | the of son | than Balak

1323 2809 3478 3427 3898 3898
26 נִלְחֹם נִלְחַם בָּם׃ בְּשֶׁבֶת יִשְׂרָאֵל בְּחֶשְׁבּוֹן וּבִבְנוֹתֶיהָ
its in and ,daughter-towns | in Heshbon | Israel | When lived | against ?them | fight | he indeed

769 3027 834 5892 3605 1323 6177
וּבְעַרְעוֹר וּבִבְנוֹתֶיהָ וּבְכָל־הֶעָרִים אֲשֶׁר עַל־יְדֵי אַרְנוֹן
Arnon | the of hands by | which (were) | the cities | in and all | its in and ,daughter-towns | in and Aroer

6256 5337 4100 8141 3967 7969
27 שְׁלֹשׁ מֵאוֹת שָׁנָה וּמַדּוּעַ לֹא־הִצַּלְתֶּם בָּעֵת הַהִיא׃ וְאָנֹכִי
I So | ?that | in time | you have not them delivered | Why | ,years | hundred | three

8199 3898 7451 853 6213 2398 3808
לֹא־חָטָאתִי לָךְ וְאַתָּה עֹשֶׂה אִתִּי רָעָה לְהִלָּחֶם בִּי יִשְׁפֹּט
May judge | against .me | fight to | ,wrong | me | are doing | but you | against ,you | have sinned | not

3808 5983 1121 996 3478 1121 996 3117 8199 3068
28 יְהוָה הַשֹּׁפֵט הַיּוֹם בֵּין בְּנֵי יִשְׂרָאֵל וּבֵין בְּנֵי עַמּוֹן׃ וְלֹא
And not | .Ammon | the of sons | and between | Israel | the of sons | between | today | the Judge | Jehovah

7971 834 3316 1696 5983 1121 4428 8085
שָׁמַע מֶלֶךְ בְּנֵי עַמּוֹן אֶל־דִּבְרֵי יִפְתָּח אֲשֶׁר שָׁלַח אֵלָיו׃
.him to | he sent | which | Jephthah | the of words | to | Ammon | the of sons | of king | the | did listen

1568 5674 3068 7307 3316 5921 1961
29 וַתְּהִי עַל־יִפְתָּח רוּחַ יְהוָה וַיַּעֲבֹר אֶת־הַגִּלְעָד וְאֶת־
and | Gilead | he and passed through | ;Jehovah | the of Spirit | Jephthah | on | And was

1121 5674 1568 4708 1568 4708 5674 4519
מְנַשֶּׁה וַיַּעֲבֹר אֶת־מִצְפֵּה גִלְעָד וּמִמִּצְפֵּה גִלְעָד עָבַר בְּנֵי
the (to) of sons | he passed on | Gilead | from And of Mizpeh | .Gilead | of Mizpeh | passed and through | Manas- seh

5414 5414 559 3068 5088 3316 5087 5983
30 עַמּוֹן׃ וַיִּדַּר יִפְתָּח נֶדֶר לַיהוָה וַיֹּאמַר אִם־נָתוֹן תִּתֵּן אֶת־
You give will | indeed | If | ,said and | to Jehovah | vow a | Jephthah | And vowed | .Ammon

1004 1817 3318 834 3318 1961 3027 5983 1121
31 בְּנֵי עַמּוֹן בְּיָדִי׃ וְהָיָה הַיּוֹצֵא אֲשֶׁר יֵצֵא מִדַּלְתֵי בֵיתִי
my house | the from of doors | comes out | which | thing the outcoming | it then be shall | my into hand | Ammon | the of sons

3068 1961 5983 1121 7965 7725 7125
לִקְרָאתִי בְּשׁוּבִי בְשָׁלוֹם מִבְּנֵי עַמּוֹן וְהָיָה לַיהוָה
to Jehovah | shall belong | Ammon | the from of sons | peace in | I when return | meet to me

וְהַעֲלִיתִהוּ עוֹלָה׃ וַיַּעֲבֹר יִפְתָּח אֶל־בְּנֵי עַמּוֹן לְהִלָּחֶם 32

בָּם וַיִּתְּנֵם יְהוָה בְּיָדוֹ׃ וַיַּכֵּם מֵעֲרוֹעֵר וְעַד־בּוֹאֲךָ מִנִּית 33

עֶשְׂרִים עִיר וְעַד אָבֵל כְּרָמִים מַכָּה גְּדוֹלָה מְאֹד וַיִּכָּנְעוּ

בְּנֵי עַמּוֹן מִפְּנֵי בְּנֵי יִשְׂרָאֵל׃ וַיָּבֹא יִפְתָּח הַמִּצְפָּה 34

אֶל־בֵּיתוֹ וְהִנֵּה בִתּוֹ יֹצֵאת לִקְרָאתוֹ בְּתֻפִּים וּבִמְחֹלוֹת

וְרַק הִיא יְחִידָה אֵין־לוֹ מִמֶּנּוּ בֵּן אוֹ־בַת׃ וַיְהִי כִרְאוֹתוֹ 35

אוֹתָהּ וַיִּקְרַע אֶת־בְּגָדָיו וַיֹּאמֶר אֲהָהּ בִּתִּי הַכְרֵעַ הִכְרַעְתִּנִי

וְאַתְּ הָיִית בְּעֹכְרָי וְאָנֹכִי פָּצִיתִי פִי אֶל־יְהוָה וְלֹא אוּכַל

לָשׁוּב׃ וַתֹּאמֶר אֵלָיו אָבִי פָּצִיתָה אֶת־פִּיךָ אֶל־יְהוָה 36

עֲשֵׂה לִי כַּאֲשֶׁר יָצָא מִפִּיךָ אַחֲרֵי אֲשֶׁר עָשָׂה לְךָ יְהוָה

נְקָמוֹת מֵאֹיְבֶיךָ מִבְּנֵי עַמּוֹן׃ וַתֹּאמֶר אֶל־אָבִיהָ יֵעָשֶׂה 37

לִּי הַדָּבָר הַזֶּה הַרְפֵּה מִמֶּנִּי שְׁנַיִם חֳדָשִׁים וְאֵלְכָה וְיָרַדְתִּי

עַל־הֶהָרִים וְאֶבְכֶּה עַל־בְּתוּלַי אָנֹכִי וְרֵעוֹתָי׃ וַיֹּאמֶר לֵכִי 38

וַיִּשְׁלַח אוֹתָהּ שְׁנֵי חֳדָשִׁים וַתֵּלֶךְ הִיא וְרֵעוֹתֶיהָ וַתֵּבְךְּ

עַל־בְּתוּלֶיהָ עַל־הֶהָרִים׃ וַיְהִי מִקֵּץ ׀ שְׁנַיִם חֳדָשִׁים 39

וַתָּשָׁב אֶל־אָבִיהָ וַיַּעַשׂ לָהּ אֶת־נִדְרוֹ אֲשֶׁר נָדָר וְהִיא

לֹא־יָדְעָה אִישׁ וַתְּהִי־חֹק בְּיִשְׂרָאֵל׃ מִיָּמִים ׀ יָמִימָה 40

Jehovah; and I will offer it *instead of* a burnt offering.
[32]And Jephthah passed over to the sons of Ammon to fight against them. And Jehovah delivered them into his hand. [33]And he struck them from Aroer until you come to Minnith, even twenty cities, and to the meadow of the vineyards, a very great destruction. And the sons of Ammon were humbled before the sons of Israel.

[34]And Jephthah came to Mizpeh to his house. And, behold, his daughter came out to meet him with timbrels, and with choruses. And she only, she alone; there was no *other* son or daughter to him. [35]And it happened when he saw her, he tore his garments, and said, Alas, my daughter! You have brought me very low, and you are among those making me bow. And surely I have opened my mouth to Jehovah, and I am not able to take it back. [36]And she said to him, My father, you have opened your mouth to Jehovah. Do to me whatever has gone out of your mouth, since Jehovah has taken vengeance for you on your enemies, on the sons of Ammon. [37]And she said to her father, Let this thing be done to me. Leave me alone two months, and let me go and go down on the mountains. And I will weep for my virginity, my friends and I. [38]And he said, Go. And he sent her away two months. And she went, she and her friends. And she wept for her virginity on the mountains. [39]And it happened at the end of two months, she returned to her father. And he did to her his vow which he had vowed. And she never knew a man. And it is a fixed custom in Israel, [40]from days to days,

the daughters of Israel go to tell again of the daughter of Jephthah the Gileadite, four days in a year.

702 1569 3316 8567 3478 1323 3212
תלכנה בנות ישראל לתנות לבת־יפתח הגלעדי ארבעת
four | the ,Gileadite | Jephthah | the of daughter of | tell to again | Israel | the of daughters | up go

8141 3117
ימים בשנה׃
the in .year | days

CAP. XII יב

CHAPTER 12

[1]And the men of Ephraim were called together, and went northward, and said to Jephthah, Why have you passed over to fight against the sons of Ammon, and you have not called on us to go with you? We will burn your house over you with fire. [2]And Jephthah said to them, I have been a man of war, my people and I, *having* great strife *with* the sons of Ammon. And I called you, and you did not save me out of their hands. [3]And seeing that you did not save *us*, I put my life in my hand and passed over against the Ammonites, and Jehovah delivered them into my hand. And why have you come up to me today to fight with me? [4]And Jephthah gathered all the men of Gilead, and fought with Ephraim. And the men of Gilead struck Ephraim, because they said, You Gileadites *are* fugitives from Ephraim, in the midst of Ephraim, in the midst of Manasseh. [5]And Gilead captured the fords of the Jordan before Ephraim. And it happened when the fugitives from Ephraim said, Let me pass over, then the men of Gilead said to him, You are an Ephraimite. And he said, No. [6]And they said to him, Please say Shibboleth. And he said, Sibboleth, and not could frame to speak so. And they would seize him and kill him at the fords of the Jordan. And at that time forty-two thousand of Ephraim fell.

4100 3316 559 6828 5674 669 376 6817
1 ויצעק איש אפרים ויעבר צפונה ויאמרו ליפתח מדוע
Why | to Jephthah | said and | ,northward | and crossed | Ephraim | the of men | were And called

3212 7121 3808 5983/1121 3898 5674
עברת ׀ להלחם בבני־עמון ולנו לא קראת ללכת עמך
with ?you | go to | have you called | not | for and us | Ammon | with of sons the | fight to | you have over crossed

7379 376 3316 559 784 8313 1004
2 ביתך נשרף עליך באש׃ ויאמר יפתח אליהם איש ריב
a feud | man A of | ,them to | Jephthah | And said | with .fire | over you | will We burn | your house

3462 3808 2199 3966 5983 1121 5971 1961
היתי אני ועמי ובני־עמון מאד ואזעק אתכם ולא־הושעתם
did you deliver | and not | ,you | I and called | great ;strife | the (with) ,Ammon | and of sons | my and people | I | have I ,been

5315 7760 3467 3588 7200 3027
3 אותי מידם׃ ואראה כי־אינך מושיע ואשימה נפשי
my life | put I | deliver (me) | did you not | that | when And saw I | their from hand | me

4100 3027 3068 5414 5983 1121 5674 3709
בכפי ואעברה אל־בני עמון ויתנם יהוה בידי ולמה
why and | into ;hand my | Jehovah | gave and them | ;Ammon | the of sons | to | passed and over | my in palm

3316 6908 3898 2088 3117 3212
4 עליתם אלי היום הזה להלחם בי׃ ויקבץ יפתח את־
Jephthah | And called up | with ?me | fight to | this | day | me to | you have up come

1568 582 5221 669 3898 1568 582
כל־אנשי גלעד וילחם את־אפרים ויכו אנשי גלעד את־
Gilead | the of men | and struck | ;Ephraim | with | and fought | ,Gilead | the of men | all

669 8432 1568 669 6412 559 669
אפרים כי אמרו פליטי אפרים אתם גלעד בתוך אפרים
,Ephraim | the in of midst | O ,Gileadites | ,You (are) | Ephraim | fugitives of | ,said they | for ;Ephraim

669 3383 4569 1568 3920 4519 8432
5 בתוך מנשה׃ וילכד גלעד את־מעברות הירדן לאפרים
before ;Ephraim | the Jordan | fords the of | Gilead | And captured | .Manasseh | the in of midst

582 559 5674 669 6412 559 1961
והיה כי יאמרו פליטי אפרים אעברה ויאמרו לו אנשי־
the of men | to him | said then | me Let ,over pass | ,Ephraim | fugi- from | the tives | said when | it and ,was

559 559 3808 559 673 1568
6 גלעד האפרתי אתה ויאמר לא׃ ויאמרו לו אמר־נא
Please say | to ,him | they Then said | !No | he And ,said | you !are | An Ephraimite | ,Gilead

270 1696 3559 3808 5451 559 7641
שבלת ויאמר סבלת ולא יכין לדבר כן ויאחזו אותו
him | they And seized | .so | speak to | could frame | and not | ,Sibboleth | he And ,said | Shib- .boleth

669 6256 5307 3383 4569 7819
וישחטוהו אל־מעברות הירדן ויפל בעת ההיא מאפרים
of Ephraim | that | at time | and fell | the ;Jordan | of fords the | at | killed and him

[7]And Jephthah judged Israel six years. And Jephthah the Gileadite died, and was buried in the cities of Gilead.
[8]And after him Ibzan of Bethlehem judged Israel. [9]And he had thirty sons. And he sent thirty daughters abroad, and he brought thirty daughters in from abroad for his sons. And he judged Israel seven years. [10]And Ibzan died, and was buried at Bethlehem.
[11]And after him Elon the Zebulunite judged Israel. And he judged Israel ten years. [12]And Elon the Zebulunite died, and was buried in Aijalon, in the land of Zebulun.

8337 3478 3316 8199 505 8147 703
7 ארבעים ושנים אלף: וישפט יפתח את־ישראל שש
six Israel Jephthah And judged .thousand two forty-

1568 5892 6912 1569 3316 4191 8141
שנים וימת יפתח הגלעדי ויקבר בערי גלעד:
.Gilead the in of cities was and buried the ,Gileadite Jephthah and died ;years

1961 =1035= 78 3478 310 8199
8
9 וישפט אחריו את־ישראל אבצן מבית לחם: ויהי־לו
to him And was .lehem of Beth- Ibzan Israel after him And judged

7970 2351 7971 1323 7970 1121 7970
שלשים בנים ושלשים בנות שלח החוצה ושלשים
and thirty ,abroad sent he daughters thirty and ;sons thirty

7651 3478 8199 2351 1121 935 1323
בנות הביא לבניו מן־החוץ וישפט את־ישראל שבע
seven Israel he And judged from .abroad his for sons he brought daughters

310 8199 =1035= 6912 78 4191 8141
10
11 שנים: וימת אבצן ויקבר בבית לחם: וישפט אחריו
after him And judged at .Bethlehem was and buried Ibzan And died .yaars

6235 3478 8199 2075 356 3478
את־ישראל אילון הזבולני וישפט את־ישראל עשר
ten Israel he and judged the ;Zebulunite ,Elon Israel

2074 776 357 6912 2075 356 4191 8141
12 שנים: וימת אילון הזבולני ויקבר באילון בארץ זבולן:
.Zebulun the in of land in ,Aijalon was and buried the ,Zebulunite ,Elon And died .years

[13]And after him Abdon the son of Hillel, the Pirathonite, judged Israel. [14]And he had forty sons, and thirty grandsons, who rode on seventy colts; and he judged Israel eight years. [15]And Abdon the son of Hillel, the Pirathonite, died, and was buried in Pirathon, in the land of Ephraim, in the hills of the Amalekites.

6553 1985/1121/5658 3478 310 8199
13 וישפט אחריו את־ישראל עבדון בן־הלל הפרעתוני:
Pira- .thonite the Hillel of son Abdon Israel after him And judged

5921 7392 1121 1121 797,0 1121 703 1961
14 ויהי־לו ארבעים בנים ושלשים בני בנים רכבים על־
on who rode sons sons of thirty and ,sons forty to him And was

4191 8141 8083 3478 8199 5895 7657
15 שבעים עירם וישפט את־ישראל שמנה שנים: וימת
And died .years eight Israel he and judged he-;asses seventy

669 776 6552 6912 6553 1985/1121/5650
עבדון בן־הלל הפרעתוני ויקבר בפרעתון בארץ אפרים
,Ephraim the in of land Pira- in ,thon was and buried Pira- the ,thonite ,Hillel the of son ,Abdon

6003 2022
בהר העמלקי:
the .Amalekites the in of hills

CAP. XIII יג

CHAPTER 13

[1]And the sons of Israel did evil again in the sight of Jehovah, and Jehovah gave them into the hands of the Philistines forty years.
[2]And there was a certain man of Zorah, of the family of the Danites, and his name was Manoah. And his wife was barren, and had not borne. [3]And the Angel

3068 5414 3068 5869 7457 6213 3478 1121 3254
1 ויספו בני ישראל לעשות הרע בעיני יהוה ויתנם יהוה
Jehovah and them gave ,Jehovah the in of eyes evil did Israel the of sons And again

6881 259 376 1961 8141 703 6430 3027
2 ביד־פלשתים ארבעים שנה: ויהי איש אחד מצרעה
of ,Zorah one man And was there .years forty Phil- istines the into of hand

3205 3808 6135 802 4495 8034 1839 4940
ממשפחת הדני ושמו מנוח ואשתו עקרה ולא ילדה:
had .borne and not (was) ,barren his And wife (was) .Manoah his and name the ,Danites the of family

of Jehovah appeared to the woman, and said to her, Behold now, you *are* barren and have not borne. But you shall conceive and bear a son. [4]And now take heed, and please do not drink wine or fermented drink; and do not eat any unclean *thing*. [5]For, behold, you *are* pregnant and bearing a son. And a razor shall not go on his head, for the boy shall be a Nazirite to God from the womb. And he shall begin to save Israel out of the hand of the Philistines.

[6]And the woman came and spoke to her husband, saying, A Man of God has come to me, and His appearance *was* like the appearance of the Angel of God, very terrifying. And I did not ask Him where He *was* from, and He did not tell me His name. [7]And He said to me, Behold, you *are* pregnant and will bear a son. And now do not drink wine or fermented drink, and do not eat any unclean *thing*, for the boy shall be a Nazirite to God from the womb, until the day of his death.

[8]Then Manoah prayed to Jehovah, and said, O my Lord, the Man of God whom You sent, please let Him come again to us and direct us what we shall do to the boy being born. [9]And God listened to the voice of Manoah, and the Angel of God came again to the woman. And she *was* sitting in a field; and her husband Manoah was not with her. [10]And the woman hurried and ran, and told her husband, and said to him, Behold, He has appeared to me, the Man who came to me *that* day.

[11]And Manoah rose up and went after his wife, and

3 וַיֵּרָא מַלְאַךְ־יְהוָה אֶל־הָאִשָּׁה וַיֹּאמֶר אֵלֶיהָ הִנֵּה־נָא אַתְּ־
you ,now Behold (are) ,her to said and the woman to Jehovah Angel the of And appeared
4 עֲקָרָה וְלֹא יָלַדְתְּ וְהָרִית וְיָלַדְתְּ בֵּן׃ וְעַתָּה הִשָּׁמְרִי נָא
please take heed And ,now a .son bear and you but conceive shall have ;borne and not barren
5 וְאַל־תִּשְׁתִּי יַיִן וְשֵׁכָר וְאַל־תֹּאכְלִי כָּל־טָמֵא׃ כִּי הִנָּךְ
,behold you ,For unclean any .(thing) do eat and not strong or ,drink (any) wine do drink and not
הָרָה וְיֹלַדְתְּ בֵּן וּמוֹרָה לֹא־יַעֲלֶה עַל־רֹאשׁוֹ כִּי־נְזִיר
a For to Nazirite his ,head upon shall up go not a and razor a ,son and bearing (are) pregnant
אֱלֹהִים יִהְיֶה הַנַּעַר מִן־הַבֶּטֶן וְהוּא יָחֵל לְהוֹשִׁיעַ אֶת־
deliver to shall begin and he the from ;womb the boy shall be God
6 יִשְׂרָאֵל מִיַּד פְּלִשְׁתִּים׃ וַתָּבֹא הָאִשָּׁה וַתֹּאמֶר לְאִישָׁהּ
her to ,husband spoke and the woman And came .Philistines the from of hand the Israel
לֵאמֹר אִישׁ הָאֱלֹהִים בָּא אֵלַי וּמַרְאֵהוּ כְּמַרְאֵה מַלְאַךְ
angel the of the like (was) of appearance His and appearance to me came God A of man ,saying
הָאֱלֹהִים נוֹרָא מְאֹד וְלֹא שְׁאִלְתִּיהוּ אֵי־מִזֶּה הוּא וְאֶת־שְׁמוֹ
His name and He (was) from where ask did I Him And not .very awesome ,God
7 לֹא־הִגִּיד לִי׃ וַיֹּאמֶר לִי הִנָּךְ הָרָה וְיֹלַדְתְּ בֵּן וְעַתָּה אַל־
not and now a ;son and bearing (are) pregnant ,Behold you to ,me He And said .me He tell did not
תִּשְׁתִּי ׀ יַיִן וְשֵׁכָר וְאַל־תֹּאכְלִי כָּל־טֻמְאָה כִּי־נְזִיר אֱלֹהִים
God a to Nazirite for unclean any ,(thing) do eat and not or intoxicant wine do drink
8 יִהְיֶה הַנַּעַר מִן־הַבֶּטֶן עַד־יוֹם מוֹתוֹ׃ וַיֶּעְתַּר מָנוֹחַ אֶל־
to Manoah Then prayed his .death the until of day the from womb the boy shall be
יְהוָה וַיֹּאמַר בִּי אֲדוֹנָי אִישׁ הָאֱלֹהִים אֲשֶׁר שָׁלַחְתָּ יָבוֹא־
Him let ,come ,sent You whom God the of Man my O ,Lord and ,said ,Jehovah
9 נָא עוֹד אֵלֵינוּ וְיוֹרֵנוּ מַה־נַּעֲשֶׂה לַנַּעַר הַיּוּלָּד׃ וַיִּשְׁמַע
And listened being .borne the to boy shall we do what and us teach us to again ,pray
הָאֱלֹהִים בְּקוֹל מָנוֹחַ וַיָּבֹא מַלְאַךְ הָאֱלֹהִים עוֹד אֶל־
to again God the of Angel and came ,Manoah the to of voice God
הָאִשָּׁה וְהִיא יוֹשֶׁבֶת בַּשָּׂדֶה וּמָנוֹחַ אִישָׁהּ אֵין עִמָּהּ׃
with .her was not her husband and Manoah the in ;field sitting she and (was) the ;woman
10 וַתְּמַהֵר הָאִשָּׁה וַתָּרָץ וַתַּגֵּד לְאִישָׁהּ וַתֹּאמֶר אֵלָיו הִנֵּה
Behold to ,him said and her ,husband and told and ran the woman And hurried
11 נִרְאָה אֵלַי הָאִישׁ אֲשֶׁר־בָּא בַיּוֹם אֵלָי׃ וַיָּקָם וַיֵּלֶךְ מָנוֹחַ
Manoah and went And arose .me to the on day (other) came who the Man ,me to has He appeared

אַחֲרֵי אִשְׁתּוֹ וַיָּבֹא אֶל־הָאִישׁ וַיֹּאמֶר לוֹ הַאַתָּה הָאִישׁ
12 אֲשֶׁר־דִּבַּרְתָּ אֶל־הָאִשָּׁה וַיֹּאמֶר אָנִי׃ וַיֹּאמֶר מָנוֹחַ עַתָּה
13 יָבֹא דְבָרֶיךָ מַה־יִּהְיֶה מִשְׁפַּט הַנַּעַר וּמַעֲשֵׂהוּ׃ וַיֹּאמֶר
מַלְאַךְ יְהוָה אֶל־מָנוֹחַ מִכֹּל אֲשֶׁר־אָמַרְתִּי אֶל־הָאִשָּׁה
14 תִּשָּׁמֵר׃ מִכֹּל אֲשֶׁר־יֵצֵא מִגֶּפֶן הַיַּיִן לֹא תֹאכַל וְיַיִן וְשֵׁכָר
אַל־תֵּשְׁתְּ וְכָל־טֻמְאָה אַל־תֹּאכַל כֹּל אֲשֶׁר־צִוִּיתִיהָ
15 תִּשְׁמֹר׃ וַיֹּאמֶר מָנוֹחַ אֶל־מַלְאַךְ יְהוָה נַעְצְרָה־נָּא אוֹתָךְ
16 וְנַעֲשֶׂה לְפָנֶיךָ גְּדִי עִזִּים׃ וַיֹּאמֶר מַלְאַךְ יְהוָה אֶל־מָנוֹחַ
אִם־תַּעְצְרֵנִי לֹא־אֹכַל בְּלַחְמֶךָ וְאִם־תַּעֲשֶׂה עֹלָה לַיהוָה
17 תַּעֲלֶנָּה כִּי לֹא־יָדַע מָנוֹחַ כִּי־מַלְאַךְ יְהוָה הוּא׃ וַיֹּאמֶר
מָנוֹחַ אֶל־מַלְאַךְ יְהוָה מִי שְׁמֶךָ כִּי־יָבֹא דְבָרְיךָ וְכִבַּדְנוּךָ׃
18 וַיֹּאמֶר לוֹ מַלְאַךְ יְהוָה לָמָּה זֶּה תִּשְׁאַל לִשְׁמִי וְהוּא־פֶלִאי׃
19 וַיִּקַּח מָנוֹחַ אֶת־גְּדִי הָעִזִּים וְאֶת־הַמִּנְחָה וַיַּעַל עַל־הַצּוּר
20 לַיהוָה וּמַפְלִא לַעֲשׂוֹת וּמָנוֹחַ וְאִשְׁתּוֹ רֹאִים׃ וַיְהִי בַעֲלוֹת
הַלַּהַב מֵעַל הַמִּזְבֵּחַ הַשָּׁמַיְמָה וַיַּעַל מַלְאַךְ־יְהוָה בְּלַהַב
הַמִּזְבֵּחַ וּמָנוֹחַ וְאִשְׁתּוֹ רֹאִים וַיִּפְּלוּ עַל־פְּנֵיהֶם אָרְצָה׃
21 וְלֹא־יָסַף עוֹד מַלְאַךְ יְהוָה לְהֵרָאֹה אֶל־מָנוֹחַ וְאֶל־אִשְׁתּוֹ

came to the Man. And *he* said to Him, *Are* You the Man who spoke to the woman? And He said, I *am*. 12 And Manoah said, Then let Your words come about. What shall be the way of the youth, and his undertaking? 13 And the Angel of Jehovah said to Manoah, Let her take heed of all that I said to the woman; 14 she shall not eat of anything that comes from the grapevine; and she shall not drink wine or fermented drink; and she shall not eat any unclean *thing*. She shall be careful of all that I commanded her.

15 And Manoah said to the Angel of Jehovah, Please let us keep You, and prepare before You a kid of the goats. 16 And the Angel of Jehovah said to Manoah, If you keep Me, I will not eat of your bread. And if you prepare a burnt offering, you shall offer it to Jehovah. For Manoah did not know that He *was* the Angel of Jehovah. 17 And Manoah said to the Angel of Jehovah, What is Your name? When Your words come about, then we shall honor You. 18 And the Angel of Jehovah said to him, Why do you ask this about My name? Yea, it *is* Wonderful.

19 And Manoah took the kid of the goats, and the food offering, and offered on the rock to Jehovah. And He did wonderfully, and Manoah and his wife *were* looking on. 20 And it happened as the flame from off the altar was going up to the heavens, that the Angel of Jehovah went up in the flame of the altar. And Manoah and his wife *were* watching. And they fell on their faces to the ground.

21 And the Angel of Jehovah did not appear any more to Manoah, or to his wife. Then Manoah knew

that He *was* the Angel of
Jehovah. [22]And Manoah
said to his wife, We shall
surely die, because we have
seen God. [23]And his wife
said to him, If Jehovah
desired to put us to death,
He would not have received
a burnt offering and a food
offering from our hands, nor
declared to us all these
things; nor would He *at this*
time have caused us to hear
such things as these.
[24]And the woman bore a
son, and called his name
Samson. And the youth
grew, and Jehovah blessed
him. [25]And the Spirit of
Jehovah began to move
him in the camp of Dan,
between Zorah and Eshtaol.

22 אָז יָדַע מָנוֹחַ כִּי־מַלְאַךְ יְהוָה הוּא׃ וַיֹּאמֶר מָנוֹחַ אֶל־
to Manoah said And He Jehovah the that Manoah knew then
(was) of Angel

23 אִשְׁתּוֹ מוֹת נָמוּת כִּי אֱלֹהִים רָאִינוּ׃ וַתֹּאמֶר לוֹ אִשְׁתּוֹ
his to said And have we God be- we surely his
wife him .seen cause ,die shall ,wife

לוּ חָפֵץ יְהוָה לַהֲמִיתֵנוּ לֹא־לָקַח מִיָּדֵנוּ עֹלָה וּמִנְחָה
food and burnt a our from would He not us put to Jehovah were If
offering offering hands received have .death to pleased

24 וְלֹא הֶרְאָנוּ אֶת־כָּל־אֵלֶּה וְכָעֵת לֹא הִשְׁמִיעָנוּ כָּזֹאת׃ וַתֵּלֶד
And (things) have would not and these all shown and
bore .these like hear us made now ,(things) us to not

הָאִשָּׁה בֵּן וַתִּקְרָא אֶת־שְׁמוֹ שִׁמְשׁוֹן וַיִּגְדַּל הַנַּעַר וַיְבָרְכֵהוּ
blessed and the and ;Samson his and a the
him ,boy up grew name called ,son woman

25 יְהוָה׃ וַתָּחֶל רוּחַ יְהוָה לְפַעֲמוֹ בְּמַחֲנֵה־דָן בֵּין צָרְעָה
Zorah be- Dan the in move to Jehovah the And .Jehovah
tween of camp him of Spirit began

וּבֵין אֶשְׁתָּאֹל׃
.Eshtaol and

CAP. XIV יד

CHAPTER 14

CHAPTER 14

[1]And Samson went down
to Timnath and saw a
woman in Timnath, of the
daughters of the Philistines.
[2]And *he* came up and told
his father and mother, and
said, I have seen a woman
in Timnath, of the daugh-
ters of the Philistines. And
now get her for me for a
wife. [3]And his father and his
mother said to him, Is there
not a woman among the
daughters of your brothers,
and among all my people,
that you must go to take a
woman from the uncir-
cumcised Philistines? And
Samson said to his father,
Get her for me, for she
pleases me very much.
[4]And his father and his
mother did not know that it
was from Jehovah, that He
was seeking an occasion
against the Philistines. For
at that time the Philistines
were ruling over Israel.
[5]And Samson and his
father and his mother went
down to Timnath. And they
came to the vineyards of
Timnath. And, behold, a

1 וַיֵּרֶד שִׁמְשׁוֹן תִּמְנָתָה וַיַּרְא אִשָּׁה בְּתִמְנָתָה מִבְּנוֹת
the of Timnath in a saw and to Samson And
of daughters woman Timnath down went

2 פְּלִשְׁתִּים׃ וַיַּעַל וַיַּגֵּד לְאָבִיו וּלְאִמּוֹ וַיֹּאמֶר אִשָּׁה רָאִיתִי
have I a ,said and his and his and came and the
seen woman ,mother father told up ,Philistines

בְתִמְנָתָה מִבְּנוֹת פְּלִשְׁתִּים וְעַתָּה קְחוּ־אוֹתָהּ לִי לְאִשָּׁה׃
a for for her get and Phil- the the of ,Timnath in
.wife me now ;istines of daughters

3 וַיֹּאמֶר לוֹ אָבִיו וְאִמּוֹ הַאֵין בִּבְנוֹת אַחֶיךָ וּבְכָל־עַמִּי אִשָּׁה
a my among and your among there Is his and his to said And
woman ,people all ,brothers' daughters not ,mother father him

כִּי־אַתָּה הוֹלֵךְ לָקַחַת אִשָּׁה מִפְּלִשְׁתִּים הָעֲרֵלִים וַיֹּאמֶר
said And uncir- the from wife a take to (are) you that
?cumcised Philistines . going

שִׁמְשׁוֹן אֶל־אָבִיו אוֹתָהּ קַח־לִי כִּי־הִיא יָשְׁרָה בְעֵינָי׃
my in is she for for Get her his to Samson
.eyes pleasing ,me father

4 וְאָבִיו וְאִמּוֹ לֹא יָדְעוּ כִּי מֵיְהוָה הִיא כִּי־תֹאֲנָה הוּא־מְבַקֵּשׁ
(was) He an that it from that did not his and his And
seeking occasion ,(was) Jehovah know mother father

מִפְּלִשְׁתִּים וּבָעֵת הַהִיא פְּלִשְׁתִּים מֹשְׁלִים בְּיִשְׂרָאֵל׃
over (were) the that at for the against
.Israel ruling Philistines time ;Philistines

5 וַיֵּרֶד שִׁמְשׁוֹן וְאָבִיו וְאִמּוֹ תִּמְנָתָה וַיָּבֹאוּ עַד־כַּרְמֵי תִמְנָתָה
.Timnath vine- the to they and to his and his and Samson And
of yards came ,Timnath mother father down went

young lion roaring to meet
him. [6]And the Spirit of
Jehovah came mightily on
him. And he tore it as the
cleaving of a kid. And there
was nothing in his hand;
and he did not tell his father
and his mother what he had
done. [7]And he went down
and talked with the woman.
And she was pleasing in the
eyes of Samson. [8]And
some days *later* he returned
to take her, and turned
aside to see the remains of
the lion. And, behold, a
bee-swarm in the carcase
of the lion, and honey.
[9]And he took it out on his
hands, and went on, eating
and walking. And he went
to his father and to his
mother, and gave *some* to
them. And they ate, but he
did not tell them that he
took the honey out of the
body of the lion.

[10]And his father went
down to the woman, and
Samson made a feast there,
for so the young men
usually did. [11]And it
happened when they saw
him, they took thirty com-
panions, and they were
with him. [12]And Samson
said to them, Please let me
riddle a riddle to you. If you
certainly declare it to me *in*
the seven days of the feast,
and find *it* out, then I shall
give you thirty linen garments and thirty changes of
clothing. [13]And if you are
not able to tell me, then you
shall give me thirty linen
garments and thirty
changes of clothing. And
they said to him, Riddle
your riddle, and we shall
hear it. [14]And he said to
them, Out of the eater came
forth food, and out of the
strong came forth sweet-
ness. And they were not
able to declare the riddle *in*
three days. [15]And it happened on the seventh day,

7307 5921 6743 7125 7580 738 3715 2009
6 וְהִנֵּה כְּפִיר אֲרָיוֹת שֹׁאֵג לִקְרָאתוֹ׃ וַתִּצְלַח עָלָיו רוּחַ
the upon came and meet to roaring the young a ,And
of Spirit him mightily him lions of lion ,behold

5046 3027 3972 1423 8156 8156 3068
יְהוָה וַיְשַׁסְּעֵהוּ כְּשַׁסַּע הַגְּדִי וּמְאוּמָה אֵין בְּיָדוֹ וְלֹא הִגִּיד
did he and his in there any- and ;kid a the as he and ,Jehovah
tell not ,hand not was thing of cleaving apart it tore

802 1696 3381 6213 517 1
7 לְאָבִיו וּלְאִמּוֹ אֵת אֲשֶׁר עָשָׂה׃ וַיֵּרֶד וַיְדַבֵּר לָאִשָּׁה
the with and he And had he what his and his
;woman talked down went .done mother father

7200 5493 3947 3117 7725 8123 5869 3474
8 וַתִּישַׁר בְּעֵינֵי שִׁמְשׁוֹן׃ וַיָּשָׁב מִיָּמִים לְקַחְתָּהּ וַיָּסַר לִרְאוֹת
see to turned and take to days some he And .Samson the in was she and
aside ,her (later) returned of eyes pleasing

738 1472 1682 5712 2009 738 4658
אֵת מַפֶּלֶת הָאַרְיֵה וְהִנֵּה עֲדַת דְּבוֹרִים בִּגְוִיַּת הָאַרְיֵה
,lion the the in bees swarm a ,and ;lion the the
of carcase (was) of ,behold of remains

3212 398 3212 3212 3709 7287 1706
9 וּדְבָשׁ׃ וַיִּרְדֵּהוּ אֶל־כַּפָּיו וַיֵּלֶךְ הָלוֹךְ וְאָכֹל וַיֵּלֶךְ אֶל־
to he and and walking and his to he And and
went ;eating ,on went ,palm out it scraped .honey

5046 3808 398 5414 517 1
אָבִיו וְאֶל־אִמּוֹ וַיִּתֵּן לָהֶם וַיֹּאכֵלוּ וְלֹא־הִגִּיד לָהֶם כִּי
that them did he but they and to gave and his and his
tell not ,ate ;them (some) mother to father

802 1 3381 1706 7287 738 1472
10 מִגְּוִיַּת הָאַרְיֵה רָדָה הַדְּבָשׁ׃ וַיֵּרֶד אָבִיהוּ אֶל־הָאִשָּׁה
the to his And the had he the the of out
,woman father down went .honey scraped lion of carcase

1961 970 6213 3651 4960 8123 8033 6213
11 וַיַּעַשׂ שָׁם שִׁמְשׁוֹן מִשְׁתֶּה כִּי כֵּן יַעֲשׂוּ הַבַּחוּרִים׃ וַיְהִי
it And young the (usually) so for ,feast a Samson there and
,was .men did made

559 1961 4828 7970 3947 7200
12 כִּרְאוֹתָם אוֹתוֹ וַיִּקְחוּ שְׁלֹשִׁים מֵרֵעִים וַיִּהְיוּ אִתּוֹ׃ וַיֹּאמֶר
said And with and ,companions thirty they that ,him they when
.him were they took saw

5046 5046 518 2420 4994 2330 8123
לָהֶם שִׁמְשׁוֹן אָחוּדָה־נָּא לָכֶם חִידָה אִם־הַגֵּד תַּגִּידוּ
you clearly if a you to Please me let ,Samson to
declare ;riddle riddle them

5414 4672 4960 3117 7651
אוֹתָהּ לִי שִׁבְעַת יְמֵי הַמִּשְׁתֶּה וּמְצָאתֶם וְנָתַתִּי לָכֶם
to I then find and ,feast the days the (in) me to it
you give shall ,out (it) of seven

3201 3808 899 2487 7970 899 7970
13 שְׁלֹשִׁים סְדִינִים וּשְׁלֹשִׁים חֲלִפֹת בְּגָדִים׃ וְאִם־לֹא תוּכְלוּ
are you not And .clothing changes and linen thirty
able if of thirty garments

7970 899 7970 5414 5046
לְהַגִּיד לִי וּנְתַתֶּם אַתֶּם לִי שְׁלֹשִׁים סְדִינִים וּשְׁלֹשִׁים
and linen thirty me to you then ,me to to
thirty garments give shall declare

8085 2420 2330 559 899 2487
חֲלִיפוֹת בְּגָדִים וַיֹּאמְרוּ לוֹ חוּדָה חִידָתְךָ וְנִשְׁמָעֶנָּה׃
shall we and your Riddle to they And .clothing changes
.it hear ,riddle ,him said of

3808 4966 3318 5794 3978 3318 398 559
14 וַיֹּאמֶר לָהֶם מֵהָאֹכֵל יָצָא מַאֲכָל וּמֵעַז יָצָא מָתוֹק וְלֹא
And sweet- came of out and food came the of Out to And
not .ness forth strong the forth eater ,them said he

7637 3117 1961 3117 7969 2420 5046 3201
15 יָכְלוּ לְהַגִּיד הַחִידָה שְׁלֹשֶׁת יָמִים׃ וַיְהִי ׀ בַּיּוֹם הַשְּׁבִיעִי
,seventh the on it And .days (in) the declare to they
day ,was three riddle able were

15 וַיֹּאמְרוּ לְאֵשֶׁת־שִׁמְשׁוֹן פַּתִּי אֶת־אִישֵׁךְ וְיַגֶּד־לָנוּ אֶת־
to he that your Entice ,Samson the to they that
us declare may ,husband of wife said
הַחִידָה פֶּן־נִשְׂרֹף אוֹתָךְ וְאֶת־בֵּית אָבִיךְ בָּאֵשׁ הַלְיָרְשֵׁנוּ
make to with your house and you we lest the
poor us ;fire father's burn ,riddle
16 קְרָאתֶם לָנוּ הֲלֹא׃ וַתֵּבְךְּ אֵשֶׁת שִׁמְשׁוֹן עָלָיו וַתֹּאמֶר
,said and before Samson's wife wept And not it Is for you have
,him ?(so) ?us called
רַק־שְׂנֵאתַנִי וְלֹא אֲהַבְתָּנִי הַחִידָה חַדְתָּ לִבְנֵי עַמִּי וְלִי
and my the to have you the riddle love do and you Only
me to ,people of sons riddled ;me not me hate
לֹא הִגַּדְתָּה וַיֹּאמֶר לָהּ הִנֵּה לְאָבִי וּלְאִמִּי לֹא הִגַּדְתִּי וְלָךְ
and de- I not my to and my to ,Behold to he And have you not
you to ,clared ,mother father ,her said .it declared
17 אַגִּיד׃ וַתֵּבְךְּ עָלָיו שִׁבְעַת הַיָּמִים אֲשֶׁר־הָיָה לָהֶם הַמִּשְׁתֶּה
the for were (on) days the before she And I shall
,feast them which seven him wept ?declare
וַיְהִי בַּיּוֹם הַשְּׁבִיעִי וַיַּגֶּד־לָהּ כִּי הֱצִיקַתְהוּ וַתַּגֵּד הַחִידָה
the she and she for ,her to he that the on it And
riddle declared ;him vexed (it) declared ,seventh day ,was
18 לִבְנֵי עַמָּהּ׃ וַיֹּאמְרוּ לוֹ אַנְשֵׁי הָעִיר בַּיּוֹם הַשְּׁבִיעִי בְּטֶרֶם
before the on the the to said And her the to
seventh day city of men him .people of sons
יָבֹא הַחַרְסָה מַה־מָּתוֹק מִדְּבַשׁ וּמֶה עַז מֵאֲרִי וַיֹּאמֶר לָהֶם
to he And a stronger And ?honey sweeter What the went
,them said ?lion than (is) what than (is) ,sun (down)
19 לוּלֵא חֲרַשְׁתֶּם בְּעֶגְלָתִי לֹא מְצָאתֶם חִידָתִי׃ וַתִּצְלַח עָלָיו
upon came And my would you not my with had you Unless
him mightily .riddle (out) found have ,heifer plowed
רוּחַ יְהוָה וַיֵּרֶד אַשְׁקְלוֹן וַיַּךְ מֵהֶם ׀ שְׁלֹשִׁים אִישׁ וַיִּקַּח
and ,men thirty of and to he and Jehovah the
took them struck Ashkelon down went of Spirit
אֶת־חֲלִיצוֹתָם וַיִּתֵּן הַחֲלִיפוֹת לְמַגִּידֵי הַחִידָה וַיִּחַר אַפּוֹ וַיַּעַל
he and his and the those to changes the and their
to went,anger glowed ;riddle declaring gave ,plunder
20 בֵּית אָבִיהוּ׃ וַתְּהִי אֵשֶׁת שִׁמְשׁוֹן לְמֵרֵעֵהוּ אֲשֶׁר רֵעָה לוֹ׃
for was who his Samson the And his the
.him feeder ,companion's of wife became .father of house

15 they said to Samson's wife, Entice your husband, that he may declare to us the riddle, lest we burn you and your father's house with fire. Have you called for us to make us poor? Is it not *so*? 16 And Samson's wife wept before him, and said, You only hate me, and do not love *me*. You have riddled the riddle to the sons of my people, and you have not declared it to me. And he said to her, Behold, I have not declared *it* to my father and to my mother, and shall I declare *it* to you? 17 And she wept before him the seven days *on* which they feasted. And it was on the seventh day, he told her, for she distressed him. And she told the riddle to the sons of her people. 18 And the men of the city said to him on the seventh day, before the sun went in, What *is* sweeter than honey? And what is stronger than a lion? And he said to them, Unless you had plowed with my heifer, you would not have found *out* my riddle.

19 And the Spirit of Jehovah came upon him. And he went down to Ashkelon and struck thirty men of them, and took their plunder. And *he* gave the changes to those who told the riddle; and his anger burned. And he went up to his father's house. 20 And Samson's wife became his companion's, who had been his feeder.

CAP. XV טו

CHAPTER 15

1 וַיְהִי מִיָּמִים בִּימֵי קְצִיר־חִטִּים וַיִּפְקֹד שִׁמְשׁוֹן אֶת־אִשְׁתּוֹ
his Samson that ,wheat the the in after- it And
,wife visited of harvest of days ,ward ,was
בִּגְדִי עִזִּים וַיֹּאמֶר אָבֹאָה אֶל־אִשְׁתִּי הֶחָדְרָה וְלֹא־נְתָנוֹ
would but inner the to my into will I and the a with
him grant not ;room ,wife go ,said ,goats of kid
2 אָבִיהָ לָבוֹא׃ וַיֹּאמֶר אָבִיהָ אָמֹר אָמַרְתִּי כִּי־שָׂנֹא שְׂנֵאתָהּ
,her you surely that said I Indeed her said And go to her
hated ,father .in father

CHAPTER 15

1 And it happened afterward, in the days of wheat harvest, that Samson visited his wife with a kid of the goats. And *he* said, I will go in to my wife, to the inner room. And her father would not allow him to go in. 2 And her father said, I certainly said that you would surely hate her, and I

gave her to your companion. Is not her sister, the young one, better than she? Please let her belong to you, instead of her. [3]And Samson said to them, This time I will be blameless regarding the Philistines, though I *am* doing evil with them. [4]And Samson went and caught three hundred foxes, and took torches, and turned tail to tail, and put a torch between the two tails, in the middle. [5]And *he* kindled fire on the torches, and sent *them* out into the grainstalks of the Philistines, and burned from the stacks and the grainstalks, and to the vineyard *and* the oliveyard.

[6]And the Philistines said, Who has done this? And they said, Samson, the son-in-law of the Timnite, because he took away his wife and gave her to his companion. And the Philistines went and burned her and her father with fire. [7]And Samson said to them, Though you do this, yet I shall be avenged on you; and afterwards I will stop. [8]And he struck them hip on thigh, a great slaughter, and went down and lived in the cleft of the rock Etam.

[9]And the Philistines went up and pitched in Judah, and were spread out in Lehi. [10]And the men of Judah said, Why have you come up against us? And they said, We have come up to bind Samson, to do to him as he has done to us. [11]And three thousand men of Judah went down to the cleft of the rock Etam, and said to Samson, Do you not know that the Philistines *are* rulers over us? And what *is* this that you have done to us? And he said to them, As they did to me, so I did to

1961 2896 6996 269 3808 4828 5414
וָאֶתְּנֶהָ לְמֵרֵעֶךָ הֲלֹא אֲחוֹתָהּ הַקְּטַנָּה טוֹבָה מִמֶּנָּה תְּהִי־
her let than better younger her is your to I and
be ?she sister not ;companion her gave

6458 5352 81:23 559 8478
3 נָא לְךָ תַּחְתֶּיהָ׃ וַיֹּאמֶר לָהֶם שִׁמְשׁוֹן נִקֵּיתִי הַפַּעַם
This be will I ,Samson to said And instead for Please
time blameless them .her of you

3920 8123 3212 7451 6213 6430
4 מִפְּלִשְׁתִּים כִּי־עֹשֶׂה אֲנִי עִמָּם רָעָה׃ וַיֵּלֶךְ שִׁמְשׁוֹן וַיִּלְכֹּד
and Samson And .evil with I (am) though regarding
caught went them doing ,Philistines the

7760 2180 2180/6437 3940 3947 7776 3967 7969
שְׁלֹשׁ־מֵאוֹת שׁוּעָלִים וַיִּקַּח לַפִּדִים וַיֶּפֶן זָנָב אֶל־זָנָב וַיָּשֶׂם
and ,tail to tail and ,torcnes and ,foxes hundred three
put turned took

3940 784 1197 8432 2180 8147/996 259 3940
5 לַפִּיד אֶחָד בֵּין־שְׁנֵי הַזְּנָבוֹת בַּתָּוֶךְ׃ וַיַּבְעֶר־אֵשׁ בַּלַּפִּידִים
the on fire and the in tails the between one torch
,torches kindled ,middle two

7054 1430 1197 6430 7054 7971
וַיְשַׁלַּח בְּקָמוֹת פְּלִשְׁתִּים וַיַּבְעֵר מִגָּדִישׁ וְעַד־קָמָה וְעַד
and the and the from and Phil- the the into sent and
to grainstalks stacks burned istines of grainstalks out them

8123 559 2088 6213 6430 559 2132 3754
6 כֶּרֶם זָיִת׃ וַיֹּאמְרוּ פְלִשְׁתִּים מִי עָשָׂה זֹאת וַיֹּאמְרוּ שִׁמְשׁוֹן
,Samson they And ?this has Who the said And the vine- the
said done ,Philistines oliveyard ,yard

5927 4828 5414 802 39 47 8554 2860
חֲתַן הַתִּמְנִי כִּי לָקַח אֶת־אִשְׁתּוֹ וַיִּתְּנָהּ לְמֵרֵעֵהוּ וַיַּעֲלוּ
And his to gave and his he because the son-
up went .companion her wife took ,Timnite's in-law

559 784 1 8313 6430
7 פְלִשְׁתִּים וַיִּשְׂרְפוּ אוֹתָהּ וְאֶת־אָבִיהָ בָּאֵשׁ׃ וַיֹּאמֶר לָהֶם
to said And with her and her and the
them .fire father burned Philistines

310 5358 518 2063 6213 518 81:23
שִׁמְשׁוֹן אִם־תַּעֲשׂוּן כָּזֹאת כִּי אִם־נִקַּמְתִּי בָכֶם וְאַחַר
and upon shall I surely like you If ,Samson
afterwards ,you avenged be this do

3427 3381 1419 4347 3409 5921 2785 5221 2308
8 אֶחְדָּל׃ וַיַּךְ אוֹתָם שׁוֹק עַל־יָרֵךְ מַכָּה גְדוֹלָה וַיֵּרֶד וַיֵּשֶׁב
and and ,great a thigh on hip them he And will I
lived down went slaughter struck .cease

3063 2583 6430 5927 5862 5553 5585
9 בִּסְעִיף סֶלַע עֵיטָם׃ וַיַּעֲלוּ פְלִשְׁתִּים וַיַּחֲנוּ בִּיהוּדָה
,Judah in and the went And .Etam the the in
camped Philistines up of rock of cleft

5927 4100 3063 376 559 3896 5203
10 וַיִּנָּטְשׁוּ בַּלֶּחִי׃ וַיֹּאמְרוּ אִישׁ יְהוּדָה לָמָה עֲלִיתֶם עָלֵינוּ
against you have Why ,Judah the said And in spread and
?us up come of men .Lehi out

6213 5927 8123 631 559
וַיֹּאמְרוּ לֶאֱסוֹר אֶת־שִׁמְשׁוֹן עָלִינוּ לַעֲשׂוֹת לוֹ כַּאֲשֶׁר
as to do to have we Samson bind To they And
him up come said

5585 3063 376 505 7969 3381 6213
11 עָשָׂה לָנוּ׃ וַיֵּרְדוּ שְׁלֹשֶׁת אֲלָפִים אִישׁ מִיהוּדָה אֶל־סְעִיף
the to Judah of men thousand three And .us to he
of cleft down went done has

4910 3045 3808 8123 559 5862 5553
סֶלַע עֵיטָם וַיֹּאמְרוּ לְשִׁמְשׁוֹן הֲלֹא יָדַעְתָּ כִּי־מֹשְׁלִים בָּנוּ
over (are) that you Do ,Samson to said and ,Etam the
us ruling know not of rock

6213 559 6213 2088 6430
פְלִשְׁתִּים וּמַה־זֹּאת עָשִׂיתָ לָּנוּ וַיֹּאמֶר לָהֶם כַּאֲשֶׁר עָשׂוּ
they As to he And to have you (is) And the
did ,them said ?us done this what ?Philistines

them. [12]And they said to
him, We have come down
to bind you, to give you into
the hands of the Philistines.
And Samson said to them,
Swear to me that you will
not fall on me yourselves.
[13]And they spoke to him,
saying, No, but we will
certainly bind you, and will
give you into their hand. But
we certainly will not kill
you. And they bound him
with two thick cords, new
ones, and brought him up
from the rock. [14]He came
to Lehi, and the Philistines
shouted to meet him. And
the Spirit of Jehovah came
upon him, and the thick
cords which *were* on his
arms were as flax which
they burn with fire. And his
bonds melted from his
hands. [15]And he found a
fresh jawbone of an ass,
and put out his hand and
took it. And *he* struck a
thousand men with it.
[16]And Samson said, With
the jawbone of an ass, a
heap, two heaps, with the
jawbone of an ass I have
killed a thousand men.
[17]And it happened when he
finished speaking, he threw
the jawbone out of his
hand. And *he* called that
place the Hill of the
Jawbone. [18]And he was
exceedingly thirsty, and
called to Jehovah and said,
Surely You have given this
great deliverance by the
hand of Your servant. And
now I am dying with thirst,
and will fall into the hand of
the uncircumcised. [19]And
God broke open the hollow
place which *is* in Lehi, and
water came out of it. And he
drank, and his spirit
returned, and he revived.
Therefore its name *is* called
the Fountain of the Praying
One, which *is* in Lehi to this
day.

5414 3381 631 559 6213 3651
12 לי כן עשיתי להם׃ ויאמרו לו לאסרך ירדנו לתתך
give to you | have We come down | bind to you | to him | they And said | to them | did I | so to me

6293 7650 8123 559 6430 3027
ביד־פלשתים ויאמר להם שמשון השבעו לי פן־תפגעון
will you fall | that not | to me Swear | ,Samson | to them | said And | the Philistines | the into hands of

5414 631 631 3808 559 559
13 בי אתם׃ ויאמרו לו לאמר לא כי־אסר נאסרך ונתנוך
give and you | will we bind ,you | cer-tainly | but | ,No | ,saying | to ,him | they And said | your-.selves | upon me

2319 5688 8147 631 4191 3808 4191 3027
בידם והמת לא נמיתך ויאסרהו בשנים עבתים חדשים
new | ropes | with two | they And him bound | will we not | .you kill | but surely | their into ,hand

7321 6430 3896 935 5553 5927
14 ויעלוהו מן־הסלע׃ הוא־בא עד־לחי ופלשתים הריעו
shouted | the and Philistines | ,Lehi | to | came He | the rock | from | brought and up him

834 5688 1961 3068 7307 5921 6743 7125
לקראתו ותצלח עליו רוח יהוה ותהיינה העבתים אשר
which (were) | ropes the | and became | ,Jehovah | the Spirit of | upon him | came and mightily | meet to ;him

612 4549 784 1197 834 6593 2220
על־זרועותיו כפשתים אשר בערו באש וימסו אסוריו
his bonds | and melted | with ;fire | (they) burn | which | flax | like | arms his on

3947 3027 7971 2961 2543 3895 4672 3027
15 מעל ידיו׃ וימצא לחי־חמור טריה וישלח ידו ויקחה
took and ,it | his hand | put and out | ,fresh | an of ass | jaw-a bone | he and found | his ,hands | from on

2565 2543 3895 8123 559 376 505 5221
16 ויך־בה אלף איש׃ ויאמר שמשון בלחי החמור חמור
,heap | ,ass an | the With of jawbone | ,Samson | said And | .men | a thousand | with and it struck

3615 1961 376 505 5221 2543 3895 2565
17 חמרתים בלחי החמור הכיתי אלף איש׃ ויהי ככלתו
he when finished | it And ,was | .men | a thousand | have I struck | ass an | the with of jawbone | two ,heaps

7413 4725 7121 3027 3895 7993 1696
לדבר וישלך הלחי מידו ויקרא למקום ההוא רמת
the of Height | that | place | and called | of out ,hand his | jaw-the bone | he that threw | ,speaking

5414 559 3068 7121 3966 6770 3895
18 לחי׃ ויצמא מאד ויקרא אל־יהוה ויאמר אתה נתת
have You given | ,said and | Jehovah to | and called | ,very | was he And thirsty | Jaw-.bone

4191 6258 2088 1419 8668 5650 3027
ביד־עבדך את־התשועה הגדלה הזאת ועתה אמות
am I dying | and now | ,this | great | deliverance | Your servant | the by of hand

430 1234 6189 3027 5307 6772
19 בצמא ונפלתי ביד הערלים׃ ויבקע אלהים את־
God | And open broke | uncir-.cumcised | the | the into of hand | will and fall | with ,thirst

7725 8354 4325 3318 3896 834 4388
המכתש אשר־בלחי ויצאו ממנו מים וישת ותשב
and returned | he and ;drank | ,water | it of | came and out | in ,Lehi | which (is) | hollow the place

3896 834 7121 5869 7121 3621 5921 2421 7307
רוחו ויחי על־כן קרא שמה עין הקורא אשר בלחי
in Lehi | which (is) | The ,Caller's | Spring | its name | (is) called | therefore | he and ;revived | his spirit

[20]And he judged Israel twenty years in the days of the Philistines.

CHAPTER 16

[1]And Samson went to Gaza, and saw a harlot, a woman, there, and went in to her. [2]The Gazites *were told*, saying, Samson has come here. And they encircled and set a trap for him all the night at the gate of the city, and kept quiet all night, saying, Until the light of the morning, then we will kill him. [3]And Samson lay down until the middle of the night, and rose up in the middle of the night. And *he* took hold on the leaves of the gate of the city, and on the two sideposts, and plucked them up with the bar, and put *them* on his shoulders. And *he* took them up to the top of the mountain that *is* before Hebron.

[4]And it happened afterward that he loved a woman in the valley of Sorek, and her name *was* Delilah. [5]And the Philistine rulers came to her and said to her, Entice him, and see in what *lies* his great strength, and by what we may prevail against him, so that we may bind him, to afflict him. And we will surely each give to you eleven hundred *of* silver. [6]And Delilah said to Samson, Now tell me in what your great strength *lies*, and with what you may be bound in order to afflict you. [7]And Samson said to her, If they bind me with seven green bow-strings which have not been dried, then I shall be weak, and shall be as any man. [8]And

6430 3117 3478 8199 . 2088 3117/5704
20 עַד הַיּוֹם הַזֶּה׃ וַיִּשְׁפֹּט אֶת־יִשְׂרָאֵל בִּימֵי פְלִשְׁתִּים
the Philistines | the in of days | Israel | he And judged | this | .day | to
8141 6242
עֶשְׂרִים שָׁנָה׃
.years twenty

CAP. XVI טז

CHAPTER 16

935 2181 802 8033 7200 5804 8123 3212
1 וַיֵּלֶךְ שִׁמְשׁוֹן עַזָּתָה וַיַּרְא־שָׁם אִשָּׁה זוֹנָה וַיָּבֹא אֵלֶיהָ׃
.her to | went and in | a ,harlot | a ,woman | there | and saw | to ,Gaza | Samson | And went
3605/ 691 5437 8123 935 559 5841
2 לַעַזָּתִים ׀ לֵאמֹר בָּא שִׁמְשׁוֹן הֵנָּה וַיָּסֹבּוּ וַיֶּאֶרְבוּ־לוֹ כָל־
all | for a set him trap | and they encircled And | .here | Samson | has come | ,(told was) ,saying | the to Gazites
216 5704/559 3915 3605/ 2790 5892 8179 3915
הַלַּיְלָה בְּשַׁעַר הָעִיר וַיִּתְחָרְשׁוּ כָל־הַלַּיְלָה לֵאמֹר עַד־אוֹר
the Until of light | ,saying | ,night | all | kept and quiet | the ,city | the at of gate | the night
6965 3915 2677 8123 7901 2026 1242
3 הַבֹּקֶר וַהֲרַגְנֻהוּ׃ וַיִּשְׁכַּב שִׁמְשׁוֹן עַד־חֲצִי הַלַּיְלָה וַיָּקָם ׀
and up rose | ,night the | the until of half | Samson | lay And down | will we then .him kill | the ,morning
4201 8147 5892 8179 1817 270 3915 2677
בַּחֲצִי הַלַּיְלָה וַיֶּאֱחֹז בְּדַלְתוֹת שַׁעַר־הָעִיר וּבִשְׁתֵּי הַמְּזוּזוֹת
,sideposts | on and two the | the ,city | the of gate | the on of doors | took and hold | the ,night | the in of half
7218 5927 3801 5921 7760 1280 5265
וַיִּסָּעֵם עִם־הַבְּרִיחַ וַיָּשֶׂם עַל־כְּתֵפָיו וַיַּעֲלֵם אֶל־רֹאשׁ
the of top | to | took and up them | his shoulders | on | put and (them) | the bar | with | pulled and up them
157 310 1961 2275 6440 834 2022
4 הָהָר אֲשֶׁר עַל־פְּנֵי חֶבְרוֹן׃ וַיְהִי אַחֲרֵי־כֵן וַיֶּאֱהַב
he that loved | ,afterward | it And was | .Hebron | before | which (is) | the mountain
5633 5927 1807 8034 7795 5158 802
5 אִשָּׁה בְּנַחַל שֹׂרֵק וּשְׁמָהּ דְּלִילָה׃ וַיַּעֲלוּ אֵלֶיהָ סַרְנֵי
the of lords | ,her to | came And | (was) .Delilah | her and name | ,Sorek | the in of torrent-bed | a woman
1419 3581 7200 6601 559 6430
פְלִשְׁתִּים וַיֹּאמְרוּ לָהּ פַּתִּי אוֹתוֹ וּרְאִי בַּמֶּה כֹּחוֹ גָדוֹל
,great | his strength | what in (lies) | and see | ,him | Entice | ,her to | said and | the Philistines
376 5414 5414 6031 631 3201
וּבַמֶּה נוּכַל לוֹ וַאֲסַרְנֻהוּ לְעַנֹּתוֹ וַאֲנַחְנוּ נִתֶּן־לָךְ אִישׁ
each | to you | will we give | and surely | afflict to ;him | we that ,him bind | against him | may we prevail | and what by
5046 8123 1807 559 3701 3967 505
6 אֶלֶף וּמֵאָה כָּסֶף׃ וַתֹּאמֶר דְּלִילָה אֶל־שִׁמְשׁוֹן הַגִּידָה־
tell | ,Samson | to | Delilah | said And | (of pieces) .silver | eleven hundred
559 6031 631 1419 3581 4994
7 נָּא לִי בַּמֶּה כֹּחֲךָ גָדוֹל וּבַמֶּה תֵאָסֵר לְעַנּוֹתֶךָ׃ וַיֹּאמֶר
said And | afflict to .you | may you bound be | with and what | ,great | your strength | in what | to Please me
834 3892 3499 7651 631 518 8123
אֵלֶיהָ שִׁמְשׁוֹן אִם־יַאַסְרֻנִי בְּשִׁבְעָה יְתָרִים לַחִים אֲשֶׁר
which | fresh | bowstrings | with seven | they me bind | If | ,Samson | her to
5633 5707 120 259 1961 2470 2717
8 לֹא־חֹרָבוּ וְחָלִיתִי וְהָיִיתִי כְּאַחַד הָאָדָם׃ וַיַּעֲלוּ־לָהּ סַרְנֵי
the of lords | her to brought And | .man | any as | will and be | will I then weak be | have ,dried been | not

Philistine rulers brought to
her seven fresh bowstrings
which had not been dried,
and she bound him with
them. 9And the ambush
was sitting for her in an
inner room. And she said to
him, The Philistines *are*
upon you, Samson! And he
broke the bowstrings like a
thread of tow when it
smells fire. And his strength
was not known.
10And Delilah said to
Samson, Behold, you have
trifled with me, and have
told me lies. Now, please
tell me with what you may
be bound. 11And he said
to her, If they really bind me
with new ropes, by which
no work has been done,
then I shall be weak and
shall be as any human
being. 12And Delilah took
new ropes and bound him
with them, and said to him,
Samson, the Philistines *are*
upon you! And the ambush
was sitting in the inner
room. And he tore them off
his arms like thread.

13And Delilah said to
Samson, Until now you
have trifled with me, and
have told me lies. Tell me
with what you may be
bound. And he said to her, If
you weave the seven locks
of my head with a web.
14And she fastened *it* with a
pin, and said to him,
Samson, the Philistines are
upon you! And he awoke
out of his sleep, and pulled
out the pin, the handloom,
and the web.
15And she said to him,
How can you say, I love you,
and your heart is not with
me. These three times you
have trifled with me, and
have not told me where
your great strength *lies*.
16And it happened, because
she distressed him with her
words all the days, and

פְּלִשְׁתִּים שִׁבְעָה יְתָרִים לַחִים אֲשֶׁר לֹא־חֹרָבוּ וַתַּאַסְרֵהוּ
9 בָּהֶם׃ וְהָאֹרֵב יֹשֵׁב לָהּ בַּחֶדֶר וַתֹּאמֶר אֵלָיו פְּלִשְׁתִּים
עָלֶיךָ שִׁמְשׁוֹן וַיְנַתֵּק אֶת־הַיְתָרִים כַּאֲשֶׁר יִנָּתֵק פְּתִיל־
10 הַנְּעֹרֶת בַּהֲרִיחוֹ אֵשׁ וְלֹא נוֹדַע כֹּחוֹ׃ וַתֹּאמֶר דְּלִילָה
אֶל־שִׁמְשׁוֹן הִנֵּה הֵתַלְתָּ בִּי וַתְּדַבֵּר אֵלַי כְּזָבִים עַתָּה
11 הַגִּידָה־נָּא לִי בַּמֶּה תֵּאָסֵר׃ וַיֹּאמֶר אֵלֶיהָ אִם־אָסוֹר
יַאַסְרוּנִי בַּעֲבֹתִים חֲדָשִׁים אֲשֶׁר לֹא־נַעֲשָׂה בָהֶם מְלָאכָה
12 וְחָלִיתִי וְהָיִיתִי כְּאַחַד הָאָדָם׃ וַתִּקַּח דְּלִילָה עֲבֹתִים
חֲדָשִׁים וַתַּאַסְרֵהוּ בָהֶם וַתֹּאמֶר אֵלָיו פְּלִשְׁתִּים עָלֶיךָ
שִׁמְשׁוֹן וְהָאֹרֵב יֹשֵׁב בֶּחָדֶר וַיְנַתְּקֵם מֵעַל זְרֹעֹתָיו כַּחוּט׃
13 וַתֹּאמֶר דְּלִילָה אֶל־שִׁמְשׁוֹן עַד־הֵנָּה הֵתַלְתָּ בִּי וַתְּדַבֵּר
אֵלַי כְּזָבִים הַגִּידָה לִּי בַּמֶּה תֵּאָסֵר וַיֹּאמֶר אֵלֶיהָ אִם־
14 תַּאַרְגִי אֶת־שֶׁבַע מַחְלְפוֹת רֹאשִׁי עִם־הַמַּסָּכֶת׃ וַתִּתְקַע
בַּיָּתֵד וַתֹּאמֶר אֵלָיו פְּלִשְׁתִּים עָלֶיךָ שִׁמְשׁוֹן וַיִּיקַץ מִשְּׁנָתוֹ
15 וַיִּסַּע אֶת־הַיְתַד הָאֶרֶג וְאֶת־הַמַּסָּכֶת׃ וַתֹּאמֶר אֵלָיו אֵיךְ
תֹּאמַר אֲהַבְתִּיךְ וְלִבְּךָ אֵין אִתִּי זֶה שָׁלֹשׁ פְּעָמִים הֵתַלְתָּ
16 בִּי וְלֹא־הִגַּדְתָּ לִּי בַּמֶּה כֹּחֲךָ גָדוֹל׃ וַיְהִי כִּי־הֵצִיקָה לּוֹ

urged him; and his soul was grieved to death,
[17]that he told her all his heart, and said to her, No razor has come on my head, for I *am* a Nazirite to God from my mother's womb. If I were shaved, my strength would go away from me, and I would be weak, and be like any *one of* men.
[18]And Delilah saw that he had told her all his heart. And she sent and called for the Philistine rulers, saying, Come, for this time he has told me all his heart. And the Philistine rulers came up to her, and brought the silver in their hand.
[19]And she made him sleep on her knees, and called for a man, and had *him* shave seven braids of his head, and began to afflict him. And his strength departed from him.

[20]And she said, Samson, the Philistines are upon you! And He awakened from his sleep, and said, I will go out and shake myself *free*, as time *after* time. But he did not know that Jehovah had departed from him.
[21]And the Philistines seized him, and bored out his eyes, and brought him down to Gaza. And they bound him with bands of bronze. And he *was* grinding in the house of prisoners.
[22]But the hair of his head began to grow, *for* he had been shaved.
[23]Then the Philistine rulers gathered to offer a great sacrifice to their god Dagon, and to exult. And they said, Our god has given our enemy Samson into our hand.
[24]And the people saw him, and praised their god. For they said, Our god has delivered our enemy into our hand, even the devastator of our land, who multiplied our

בִּדְבָרֶיהָ כָּל־הַיָּמִים וַתְּאַלְצֵהוּ וַתִּקְצַר נַפְשׁוֹ לָמוּת׃
17 וַיַּגֶּד־לָהּ אֶת־כָּל־לִבּוֹ וַיֹּאמֶר לָהּ מוֹרָה לֹא־עָלָה עַל־
רֹאשִׁי כִּי־נְזִיר אֱלֹהִים אֲנִי מִבֶּטֶן אִמִּי אִם־גֻּלַּחְתִּי וְסָר
18 מִמֶּנִּי כֹחִי וְחָלִיתִי וְהָיִיתִי כְּכָל־הָאָדָם׃ וַתֵּרֶא דְלִילָה
כִּי־הִגִּיד לָהּ אֶת־כָּל־לִבּוֹ וַתִּשְׁלַח וַתִּקְרָא לְסַרְנֵי פְלִשְׁתִּים
לֵאמֹר עֲלוּ הַפַּעַם כִּי־הִגִּיד לָהּ אֶת־כָּל־לִבּוֹ וְעָלוּ אֵלֶיהָ
19 סַרְנֵי פְלִשְׁתִּים וַיַּעֲלוּ הַכֶּסֶף בְּיָדָם׃ וַתְּיַשְּׁנֵהוּ עַל־בִּרְכֶּיהָ
וַתִּקְרָא לָאִישׁ וַתְּגַלַּח אֶת־שֶׁבַע מַחְלְפוֹת רֹאשׁוֹ וַתָּחֶל
20 לְעַנּוֹתוֹ וַיָּסַר כֹּחוֹ מֵעָלָיו׃ וַתֹּאמֶר פְּלִשְׁתִּים עָלֶיךָ שִׁמְשׁוֹן
וַיִּקַץ מִשְּׁנָתוֹ וַיֹּאמֶר אֵצֵא כְּפַעַם בְּפַעַם וְאִנָּעֵר וְהוּא לֹא
21 יָדַע כִּי יְהוָה סָר מֵעָלָיו׃ וַיֹּאחֲזוּהוּ פְלִשְׁתִּים וַיְנַקְּרוּ אֶת־
עֵינָיו וַיּוֹרִידוּ אוֹתוֹ עַזָּתָה וַיַּאַסְרוּהוּ בַּנְחֻשְׁתַּיִם וַיְהִי טוֹחֵן
22 בְּבֵית הָאֲסִירִים׃ וַיָּחֶל שְׂעַר־רֹאשׁוֹ לְצַמֵּחַ כַּאֲשֶׁר גֻּלָּח׃
23 וְסַרְנֵי פְלִשְׁתִּים נֶאֶסְפוּ לִזְבֹּחַ זֶבַח־גָּדוֹל לְדָגוֹן
אֱלֹהֵיהֶם וּלְשִׂמְחָה וַיֹּאמְרוּ נָתַן אֱלֹהֵינוּ בְּיָדֵנוּ אֵת שִׁמְשׁוֹן
24 אוֹיְבֵנוּ׃ וַיִּרְאוּ אֹתוֹ הָעָם וַיְהַלְלוּ אֶת־אֱלֹהֵיהֶם כִּי אָמְרוּ
נָתַן אֱלֹהֵינוּ בְיָדֵנוּ אֶת־אוֹיְבֵנוּ וְאֵת מַחֲרִיב אַרְצֵנוּ וַאֲשֶׁר

wounded. [25]And it happened when their heart *felt* good, they said, Call for Samson, and he shall entertain us. And they called for Samson from the prison-house. And he entertained them. And they made him stand between the pillars. [26]And Samson said to the young man grasping his hand, Let me alone, and let me feel the pillars on which the house rests, that I may lean on them. [27]And the house was full of men and women, and all the Philistine rulers *were* there. And about three thousand men and women *were* on the roof watching Samson entertaining. [28]And Samson called to Jehovah, and said, O Lord Jehovah, remember me, I pray, and please make me strong only this time, O God. And I shall be avenged *with* one vengeance on the Philistines, because of my two eyes. [29]And Samson grasped the two middle pillars on which the house rested, and on which it was supported; one with his right hand, and one with his left. [30]And Samson said, Let my soul die with the Philistines! And he bowed mightily, and the house fell on the rulers, and on all the people who *were* in it. And the dead that he killed in his death were more than those he killed in his life.

[31]And his brothers came down, and all his father's house, and lifted him up, and brought him up. And *they* buried him between Zorah and Eshtaol, in the burying-place of his father Manoah.

And he judged Israel twenty years.

7121 559 3820 2896 1961 2491 7235
25 הרבה את־חללינו: ויהי כי־טוב לבם ויאמרו קראו
Call they that their (felt) when And fatally our multi-
,said heart good was it .wounded plied

631 1004 8123 7121 7832 8123
לשמשון וישחק־לנו ויקראו לשמשון מבית האסירים
,prisoners the from for they and for shall he and for
of house Samson called :us sport ,Samson

559 5982 996 5975 6440 6711
26 ויצחק לפניהם ויעמידו אותו בין העמודים: ויאמר
said And .pillars the between him they and before he and
stand to caused them sported

4184 3240 3027 2388 5288 8123
שמשון אל־הנער המחזיק בידו הניחה אותי והימשני
let and ,me Let his grasping young the to Samson
feel me alone ,hand man

5921 8172 5921 3559 1004 834 5982
את־העמדים אשר הבית נכון עליהם ואשען עליהם:
upon may I that ,on is house the which the
.them lean established pillars

6430 5633 3605 8033 802 376 4376 1004
27 והבית מלא האנשים והנשים ושמה כל סרני פלשתים
the the all (were) and and men was the And
;Philistines of lords ,there woman of full house

7832 7200 802 582 505 7969 1406
ועל־הגג כשלשת אלפים איש ואשה הראים בשחוק
the during watching and men thousand about (were) the and
of sporting women three roof on

2142 3068/136 559 3068 8123 7121 8123
28 שמשון: ויקרא שמשון אל־יהוה ויאמר אדני יהוה זכרני
remem- ,Jehovah O ,said and ,Jehovah to Samson And .Samson
me ber Lord called

5359 5358 430 2088 6471 389 4994 2388 4994
נא וחזקני נא אך הפעם הזה האלהים ואנקמה נקם־
(with) me let and ;God O ,this time only ,pray I and ,pray I
vengeance avenged be me strengthen

8147 8123 3943 6430 5869 259
29 אחת משתי עיני מפלשתים: וילפת שמשון את־שני
two Samson And the of my because ,one
grasped .Philistines eyes two of

259 5921 5564 5921 3559 1004 834 8432 5982
עמודי התוך אשר הבית נכון עליהם ויסמך עליהם אחד
one ,on and on is the which the pillars the
supported established house middle of

5315 4191 8123 559 8040 259 3225
30 בימינו ואחד בשמאלו: ויאמר שמשון תמות נפשי עם־
with my Let ,Samson said and his with and his with
soul die left one ,hand right

5971 3605 5633 5921 1004 5307 3581 5186 6430
פלשתים ויט בכח ויפל הבית על־הסרנים ועל־כל־העם
the all and the on the and mightily And Phil- the
people on ,lords house fell bent he listines

7227 4194 4191 834 4191 1961
אשר־בו ויהיו המתים אשר־המית במותו רבים מאשר
those than more his in killed he whom the and ;it in who
that death dead were (were)

5375 1 1004 251 3381 2416 4191
31 המית בחייו: וירדו אחיו וכל־בית אביהו וישאו אתו
,him and his the and his came And his in he
up lifted ,father of house all brothers down .life killed

4495 6913 847 996 6881 996 6912 5927
ויעלו ויקברו אותו בין צרעה ובין אשתאול בקבר מנוח
Manoah the in ,Eshtaol and Zorah between him and bore and
of place burial buried (him)

8141 6242 3478 8199 1
אביו והוא שפט את־ישראל עשרים שנה:
.years twenty Israel had And his
judged he .father

CAP. XVII ין

CHAPTER 17

[1]And there was a man of the hills of Ephraim, and his name *was* Micah. [2]And he said to his mother, The eleven hundred pieces of silver which were taken from you, and you uttered a curse, even also speaking in my ear; behold, the silver *is* with me. I have taken it. And his mother said, Blessed *be* my son by Jehovah. [3]And he gave back the eleven hundred silver pieces to his mother. And his mother said, I have wholly consecrated the silver to Jehovah from my hand for my son, to make a graven image, and a molten image. And now, I am giving it back to you. [4]And he gave the silver back to his mother. And his mother took two hundred silver pieces and gave them to a refiner. And he made it a graven image, and a molten image. And it was in Micah's house. [5]And the man Micah had a house of gods. And he made an ephod, and household idols, and consecrated one of his sons. And he was a priest for him.

[6]And in those days there was no king in Israel; each man did the right in his *own* eyes.

[7]And there was a young man of Bethlehem in Judah, of the family of Judah; and he *was* a Levite. And he resided there. [8]And the man went out of the city, out of Bethlehem-judah, to live where he might find *a place*. And *he* came to the hills of Ephraim, to the house of Micah, to work his way. [9]And Micah said to him, From where do you come? And he said to him, I *am* a Levite of Bethlehem-judah, and I am going to live where I may find *a place*. [10]And Micah said to him, Live with

CHAPTER 17

517 559 4321 8034 669 2022 376 1961
1 וַיְהִי־אִישׁ מֵהַר־אֶפְרָיִם וּשְׁמוֹ מִיכָיְהוּ׃ וַיֹּאמֶר לְאִמּוֹ
2 his to he And (was) his and ,Ephraim hill- the of man a And
.mother said .Micah name of country was there

559 1422 3947 3701 3967 505
אֶלֶף וּמֵאָה הַכֶּסֶף אֲשֶׁר לֻקַּח־לָךְ וְאַתִּי אָלִית וְגַם אָמַרְתְּ
you even uttered and from were which silver eleven the
spoke also ,curse a you ,you taken pieces hundred

1288 517 559 3947 3701 241
בְּאָזְנַי הִנֵּה־הַכֶּסֶף אִתִּי אֲנִי לְקַחְתִּיו וַתֹּאמֶר אִמּוֹ בָּרוּךְ
Blessed his said And have I with the ,behold my in
(be) ,mother !it taken ;me (is) silver ;ears

559 517 3701 3967 505 7725 3068 1121
3 בְּנִי לַיהוָה׃ וַיָּשֶׁב אֶת־אֶלֶף־וּמֵאָה הַכֶּסֶף לְאִמּוֹ וַתֹּאמֶר
said and his to silver eleven the he And by my
;mother pieces hundred back gave .Jehovah son

1121 3027 3068 3701 6942 6942 517
אִמּוֹ הַקְדֵּשׁ הִקְדַּשְׁתִּי אֶת־הַכֶּסֶף לַיהוָה מִיָּדִי לִבְנִי
my for my from to the I wholly his
son hand Jehovah silver consecrated ,mother

7725 7725 6258 4541 6459 6213
4 לַעֲשׂוֹת פֶּסֶל וּמַסֵּכָה וְעַתָּה אֲשִׁיבֶנּוּ לָךְ׃ וַיָּשֶׁב אֶת־
he And to giving am I and mol- a and graven a make to
back gave .you back it ,now ;image ten ,image

6884 5414 3701 3967 517 3947 517 3701
הַכֶּסֶף לְאִמּוֹ וַתִּקַּח אִמּוֹ מָאתַיִם כֶּסֶף וַתִּתְּנֵהוּ לַצּוֹרֵף
a to gave and silver two his and his to the
;refiner them pieces hundred mother took ,mother silver

4321 376 4321 1004 1961 4541 6459 6213
5 וַיַּעֲשֵׂהוּ פֶּסֶל וּמַסֵּכָה וַיְהִי בְּבֵית מִיכָיְהוּ׃ וְהָאִישׁ מִיכָה
,Micah the And .Micah the in it and mol- a and graven a he and
man of house ,was ;image ten image it made

259 3027 4390 8655 646 6213 430 1004
לוֹ בֵּית אֱלֹהִים וַיַּעַשׂ אֵפוֹד וּתְרָפִים וַיְמַלֵּא אֶת־יַד אַחַד
one hand the he and house- and an he and ;gods a he
of filled idols hold ,ephod made of house had

3478 4428/369 3117 3548 1961 1121
6 מִבָּנָיו וַיְהִי־לוֹ לְכֹהֵן׃ בַּיָּמִים הָהֵם אֵין מֶלֶךְ בְּיִשְׂרָאֵל
,Israel in king there those in And a for to he and his of
no was days .priest him was ;sons

1035 1035 5288 1961 6213 5869 3477 376
7 אִישׁ הַיָּשָׁר בְּעֵינָיו יַעֲשֶׂה׃ וַיְהִי־נַעַר מִבֵּית לֶחֶם
of young a And .did his in the each
Bethlehem man was there eyes (own) right man

3212 1481 3881 3063 4940 3063
8 יְהוּדָה מִמִּשְׁפַּחַת יְהוּדָה וְהוּא לֵוִי וְהוּא גָר־שָׁם׃ וַיֵּלֶךְ
And .there so- he and a he and ,Judah the of in
out went journed ,Levite (was) of family ,Judah

4672 1481 3063 = 1035 = 5892 376
הָאִישׁ מֵהָעִיר מִבֵּית לֶחֶם יְהוּדָה לָגוּר בַּאֲשֶׁר יִמְצָא
might he where to ,Judah of out the of the
,find sojourn of Bethlehem- ,city man

559 1870 6213 4321 1004 669 935
9 וַיָּבֹא הַר־אֶפְרַיִם עַד־בֵּית מִיכָה לַעֲשׂוֹת דַּרְכּוֹ׃ וַיֹּאמֶר־
said And .way his work to ,Micah the to ,Ephraim the to he and
of house of hill-country came

= 1035 = 3881 559 935 370 4321
לוֹ מִיכָה מֵאַיִן תָּבוֹא וַיֹּאמֶר אֵלָיו לֵוִי אָנֹכִי מִבֵּית לֶחֶם
from (am) I a ,him to he And you do From ,Micah to
of Bethlehem Levite said ?come where him

4321 559 4672 1481 3212 3063
10 יְהוּדָה וְאָנֹכִי הֹלֵךְ לָגוּר בַּאֲשֶׁר אֶמְצָא׃ וַיֹּאמֶר לוֹ מִיכָה
Micah to said And find may I where to am and ,Judah
him .(place a) sojourn going I

me, and be a father and a
priest to me. I will give you
ten silver pieces for the
days, and a suit of garments, and your upkeep.
And the Levite went in.
[11]And the Levite was willing
to live with the man, and
the young man was to him
as one of his sons. [12]And
Micah consecrated the
hand of the Levite, and the
young man was a priest to
him; and he was in Micah's
house. [13]And Micah said,
Now I know that Jehovah
will do me good, for the
Levite is a priest to me.

6235 5414 3548 1 1961 3427
שבה עמדי והיה־לי לאב ולכהן ואנכי אתן־לך עשרת
ten you will give I and a priest and a father me to and be with me Live
2974 3881 3212 4241 899 6187 3117 3701
11 כסף לימים וערך בגדים ומחיתך וילך הלוי׃ ויואל
was willing And the Levite went And in your sustenance and garments order and the days for silver pieces
1121 259 5288 1961 376 3427 3881
הלוי לשבת את־האיש ויהי הנער לו כאחד מבניו׃
his sons of one as to him young man the and was the man with live to the Levite
1004 1961 3548 5288 1961 3881 3027 4318 4390
12 וימלא מיכה את־יד הלוי ויהי־לו הנער לכהן ויהי בבית
the house of in he was and a priest for young man the to him and was the Levite of hand the Micah And filled
3068 3190 3045 6258 4321 559 4321
13 מיכה׃ ויאמר מיכה עתה ידעתי כי־ייטיב יהוה לי כי
for me Jehovah will do good that know I Now Micah said And Micah.
3548 3881 1961
היה־לי הלוי לכהן׃
a priest for the Levite me to is

CAP. XVIII יח

CHAPTER 18

CHAPTER 18

[1]In those days there was
no king in Israel. And in
those days the tribe of the
Danites was seeking an
inheritance for itself to
inhabit. For to that day it
had not fallen to them by
inheritance among the
tribes of Israel. [2]And the
sons of Dan sent out of their
family five men from their
whole *number*, men, sons
of valor, from Zorah and
from Eshtaol, to spy out the
land, and to search it. And
they said to them, Go,
search the land. And they
came to the hills of
Ephraim, to Micah's house,
and lodged there. [3]They
were near the household of
Micah, and they recognized
the young man's voice, the
Levite. And *they* turned in
there, and said to him, Who
has brought you here? And
what are you doing in this
place? And what have you
here? [4]And he said to
them, This and this Micah
has done to me. And he
hired me, and I am a priest

1839 7626 3117 3478 4428 369 3117
1 בימים ההם אין מלך בישראל ובימים ההם שבט הדני
the Danites tribe the of those in and days Israel in king there was no those days In
3117 5307 3427 5159 1245
מבקש־לו נחלה לשבת כי לא־נפלה לו עד־היום ההוא
that day to them to had it fallen not for to inhabit inheritance an for itself was seeking
1835/1121 7971 5159 3478 7626 8432
2 בתוך שבטי־ישראל בנחלה׃ וישלחו בני־דן
Dan the sons of sent And out by inheritance Israel the tribes of the in midst of
2428 582 7098 582 2568 4940
ממשפחתם חמשה אנשים מקצותם אנשים בני־חיל
valor sons of men their from (number) whole men five their of family
559 2713 776 7270 847 6881
מצרעה ומאשתאל לרגל את־הארץ ולחקרה ויאמרו
they And said to and it search the land spy to out from and Eshtaol from Zorah
1004 669 2022 935 776 2713 3212
אלהם לכו חקרו את־הארץ ויבאו הר־אפרים עד־בית
the house of to hill-country of Ephraim the to they And came the land search Go them to
5234 4321 1004 8033 3885 4321
3 מיכה וילינו שם׃ המה עם־בית מיכה והמה הכירו
recognized and they Micah the household of near They (were) there and lodged Micah
935 559 8033 5493 3881 5288 6963
את־קול הנער הלוי ויסורו שם ויאמרו לו מי־הביאך
has brought you Who to him said and there turned and aside the Levite the man young voice the of
559 2088 6213 1988
4 הלם ומה־אתה עשה בזה ומה־לך פה׃ ויאמר אלהם
them to he And said here to And what (place) this in doing are you And what here
3548 7936 4321 6213 2088
כזה וכזה עשה לי מיכה וישכרני ואהי־לו לכהן׃
a priest for to him I and am he and hired me Micah for me has done as and this As this

to him. And they said to him, Please ask of God and we shall know whether our way *in* which we are going will be prosperous. 6And the priest said to them, Go in peace. Your way in which you go *is* before Jehovah. 7And the five men went out and came to Laish and saw the people living securely in its midst, according to the custom of the Sidonians, quiet and secure. And there (were) none to put to shame in a thing, *nor* possessing authority. And they *were* far away from the Sidonians, and not a word was to them with *any* one of men.

8And they came to their brothers at Zorah and Eshtaol. And their brothers said to them, What did you do? 9And they said, Rise up, and we shall go against them, for we have seen the land, and, behold, *it is* very good. And would you be silent? Do not hesitate to go to enter in to possess the land. 10When you go, you shall come to a secure people, and the land *is* large on both hands; for God has given it into your hand, a place in which there *is* no lack of anything which *is* in the land.

11And six hundred men of the family of the Danites from Zorah and from Eshtaol girded *themselves* with weapons of war, traveling from there. 12And they went up and camped in Kirjath-jearim, in Judah. Therefore they called that place a camp of Dan until this day—behold, *it is* behind Kirjath-jearim. 13And they passed on from there to the hills of Ephraim, and came into the house of

5 וַיֹּאמְרוּ לוֹ שְׁאַל־נָא בֵאלֹהִים וְנֵדְעָה הֲתַצְלִיחַ דַּרְכֵּנוּ
6 אֲשֶׁר אֲנַחְנוּ הֹלְכִים עָלֶיהָ׃ וַיֹּאמֶר לָהֶם הַכֹּהֵן לְכוּ
7 לְשָׁלוֹם נֹכַח יְהוָה דַּרְכְּכֶם אֲשֶׁר תֵּלְכוּ־בָהּ׃ וַיֵּלְכוּ
חֲמֵשֶׁת הָאֲנָשִׁים וַיָּבֹאוּ לָיְשָׁה וַיִּרְאוּ אֶת־הָעָם אֲשֶׁר־
בְּקִרְבָּהּ יוֹשֶׁבֶת לָבֶטַח כְּמִשְׁפַּט צִדֹנִים שֹׁקֵט ׀ וּבֹטֵחַ
וְאֵין־מַכְלִים דָּבָר בָּאָרֶץ יוֹרֵשׁ עֶצֶר וּרְחֹקִים הֵמָּה
8 מִצִּידֹנִים וְדָבָר אֵין־לָהֶם עִם־אָדָם׃ וַיָּבֹאוּ אֶל־אֲחֵיהֶם
צָרְעָה וְאֶשְׁתָּאֹל וַיֹּאמְרוּ לָהֶם אֲחֵיהֶם מָה אַתֶּם׃
9 וַיֹּאמְרוּ קוּמָה וְנַעֲלֶה עֲלֵיהֶם כִּי רָאִינוּ אֶת־הָאָרֶץ
וְהִנֵּה טוֹבָה מְאֹד וְאַתֶּם מַחְשִׁים אַל־תֵּעָצְלוּ לָלֶכֶת
10 לָבֹא לָרֶשֶׁת אֶת־הָאָרֶץ׃ כְּבֹאֲכֶם תָּבֹאוּ ׀ אֶל־עַם בֹּטֵחַ
וְהָאָרֶץ רַחֲבַת יָדַיִם כִּי־נְתָנָהּ אֱלֹהִים בְּיֶדְכֶם מְקוֹם אֲשֶׁר
11 אֵין־שָׁם מַחְסוֹר כָּל־דָּבָר אֲשֶׁר בָּאָרֶץ׃ וַיִּסְעוּ מִשָּׁם
מִמִּשְׁפַּחַת הַדָּנִי מִצָּרְעָה וּמֵאֶשְׁתָּאֹל שֵׁשׁ־מֵאוֹת אִישׁ חָגוּר
12 כְּלֵי מִלְחָמָה׃ וַיַּעֲלוּ וַיַּחֲנוּ בְּקִרְיַת יְעָרִים בִּיהוּדָה עַל־כֵּן
קָרְאוּ לַמָּקוֹם הַהוּא מַחֲנֵה־דָן עַד הַיּוֹם הַזֶּה הִנֵּה אַחֲרֵי
13 קִרְיַת יְעָרִים׃ וַיַּעַבְרוּ מִשָּׁם הַר־אֶפְרָיִם וַיָּבֹאוּ עַד־בֵּית

Micah. [14]And the five men who had gone to spy out the land of Laish answered and said to their brothers, Do you not know that there are in these houses an ephod, and household idols, and a graven image, and a molten image? And now, you know what you are to do. [15]And they turned in there, and came into the house of the young man, the Levite *in* Micah's house. And *they* asked him for the peace. [16]And the six hundred men of the sons of Dan girded with their weapons of war were standing *at* the opening of the gate. [17]And the five men, those who went to spy out the land, They came in there, *and* they took the graven image, and the ephod, and the household idols, and the molten image. And the priest was standing *at* the opening of the gate, and the six hundred men who were girded with weapons of war. [18]And these went into the house of Micah and took *the* graven image, the ephod, and the household idols, and the molten image, and the priest said to them, What are you doing? [19]And they said to him, Be quiet! Lay your hand on your mouth, and go with us, and be a father and a priest to us. Is it better for you to be a priest for one man's house, or for you to be a priest to a tribe and a family in Israel? [20]And the heart of the priest was glad. And he took the ephod, and the household idols, and the graven image, and went among the people.

[21]And they turned and departed, and put the little ones, and the livestock, and the valuables before them. [22]They had gone far away from Micah's house, and

14 מִיכָה׃ וַיַּעֲנוּ חֲמֵשֶׁת הָאֲנָשִׁים הַהֹלְכִים לְרַגֵּל אֶת־הָאָרֶץ
לַיִשׁ וַיֹּאמְרוּ אֶל־אֲחֵיהֶם הַיְדַעְתֶּם כִּי יֵשׁ בַּבָּתִּים הָאֵלֶּה
אֵפוֹד וּתְרָפִים וּפֶסֶל וּמַסֵּכָה וְעַתָּה דְּעוּ מַה־תַּעֲשׂוּ׃
15 וַיָּסוּרוּ שָׁמָּה וַיָּבֹאוּ אֶל־בֵּית־הַנַּעַר הַלֵּוִי בֵּית מִיכָה
16 וַיִּשְׁאֲלוּ־לוֹ לְשָׁלוֹם׃ וְשֵׁשׁ־מֵאוֹת אִישׁ חֲגוּרִים כְּלֵי
17 מִלְחַמְתָּם נִצָּבִים פֶּתַח הַשָּׁעַר אֲשֶׁר מִבְּנֵי דָן׃ וַיַּעֲלוּ
חֲמֵשֶׁת הָאֲנָשִׁים הַהֹלְכִים לְרַגֵּל אֶת־הָאָרֶץ בָּאוּ שָׁמָּה
לָקְחוּ אֶת־הַפֶּסֶל וְאֶת־הָאֵפוֹד וְאֶת־הַתְּרָפִים וְאֶת־הַמַּסֵּכָה
וְהַכֹּהֵן נִצָּב פֶּתַח הַשַּׁעַר וְשֵׁשׁ־מֵאוֹת הָאִישׁ הֶחָגוּר כְּלֵי
18 הַמִּלְחָמָה׃ וְאֵלֶּה בָּאוּ בֵּית מִיכָה וַיִּקְחוּ אֶת־פֶּסֶל הָאֵפוֹד
וְאֶת־הַתְּרָפִים וְאֶת־הַמַּסֵּכָה וַיֹּאמֶר אֲלֵיהֶם הַכֹּהֵן מָה אַתֶּם
19 עֹשִׂים׃ וַיֹּאמְרוּ לוֹ הַחֲרֵשׁ שִׂים־יָדְךָ עַל־פִּיךָ וְלֵךְ עִמָּנוּ
וֶהְיֵה־לָנוּ לְאָב וּלְכֹהֵן הֲטוֹב ׀ הֱיוֹתְךָ כֹהֵן לְבֵית אִישׁ
20 אֶחָד אוֹ הֱיוֹתְךָ כֹהֵן לְשֵׁבֶט וּלְמִשְׁפָּחָה בְּיִשְׂרָאֵל׃ וַיִּיטַב
לֵב הַכֹּהֵן וַיִּקַּח אֶת־הָאֵפוֹד וְאֶת־הַתְּרָפִים וְאֶת־הַפָּסֶל
21 וַיָּבֹא בְּקֶרֶב הָעָם׃ וַיִּפְנוּ וַיֵּלֵכוּ וַיָּשִׂימוּ אֶת־הַטַּף וְאֶת־
22 הַמִּקְנֶה וְאֶת־הַכְּבוּדָּה לִפְנֵיהֶם׃ הֵמָּה הִרְחִיקוּ מִבֵּית

the men who *were* in the
houses near Micah's house
had been called together,
and had overtaken the sons
of Dan. 23And *they* called to
the sons of Dan, and they
turned their faces and said
to Micah, What *ails* you,
that you have been called
together? 24And he said,
You have taken my gods
which I made, and the
priest, and you are leaving,
and what more do I have?
What *is* this you say to me,
What *ails* you? 25And the
sons of Dan said to him, Do
not let your voice be heard
among us, that men bitter in
soul not fall on you, and you
lose your life, and the lives
of your household.

26And the sons of Dan
went on their way. And
Micah saw that they were
stronger than he, and
turned and went back to his
house. 27And they took that
which Micah had made,
and the priest he had, and
came against Laish, against
a people quiet and secure.
And *they* struck them with
the edge of the sword, and
burned the city with fire.
28And there was no
deliverer, because it *was* far
from Sidon, and they had
no business with *any* men.
And it *was* in the valley
which *is* beside Beth-rehob.
And they built the city, and
lived in it. 29And they called
the name of the city, Dan,
by the name of their father
Dan, who was born to
Israel. And yet Laish *was*
the name of the city at first.
30And the sons of Dan
raised up for themselves
the graven image. And
Jonathan the son of
Gershom, the son of
Manasseh, he and his sons
were priests to the tribe of
the Danites until the day of

2199 4321 1004 834 1004 834 582 4321
מיכה והאנשים אשר בבתים אשר עם־בית מיכה נזעקו
been had Micah the near which the in who the and ,Micah
together called of house (were) houses (were) men

6440 5437 18:35/1121 2199 1835/1121 1692
23 וידביקו את־בני־דן׃ ויקראו אל־בני־דן ויסבו פניהם
their they and !Dan the to they And .Dan the had and
faces turned of sons called of sons overtaken

430 559 2199 43:21 559
24 ויאמרו למיכה מה־לך כי נזעקת׃ ויאמר את־אלהי
My he And been have you that ,you What ,Micah to said and
gods ,said ?together called (ails)

5750 3212 3548 3947 6213 834
אשר־עשיתי לקחתם ואת־הכהן ותלכו ומה־לי עוד ומה־
What more I do and you and ,priest the and have you made I which
(is) ?have what ,leaving are ,taken

8085 1835/1121 559 559
25 זה תאמרו אלי מה־לך׃ ויאמרו אליו בני־דן אל־תשמע
let do Not ,Dan the him to said And ?you What to you this
heard be of sons (ails) ,me say

622 5315 4751 582 6293 6963
קולך עמנו פן־יפגעו בכם אנשים מרי נפש ואספתה
take you and soul bitter men upon we lest among your
away of ,you fall ,us voice

43:21 7200 1835/1121 3212 1004 5315 5315
26 נפשך ונפש ביתך׃ וילכו בני־דן לדרכם וירא מיכה
Micah saw and their on Dan the And your the and your
,way of sons went ,household of lives ,life

3947 1004 7725 6437 2388
27 כי־חזקים המה ממנו ויפן וישב אל־ביתו׃ והמה לקחו
took And his to and and than they stronger that
they house back went turned ,he (were)

935 1961 834 3548 43:21 6213 834
את אשר־עשה מיכה ואת־הכהן אשר היה־לו ויבאו על־
against and to was who the and ,Micah had that
came him priest made which

5892 2719 6310 5221 982 8252 5971 3919
ליש על־עם שקט ובטח ויכו אותם לפי־חרב ואת־העיר
the and the the with them and and quiet against ,Laish
city sword of edge struck ,secure people a

1697 6721 7350 5337 784 8313
28 שרפו באש׃ ואין מציל כי רחוקה־היא מצידון ודבר
and from it far be- ,deliverer And .fire with burned
business ,Sidon (was) cause no was there

1129 1650 834 6010 120 369
אין־להם עם־אדם והיא בעמק אשר לבית־רחוב ויבנו
they and beside which the in it and (any) with to there
built ;Beth-rehob (is) valley (was) ;man them not was

1835 8034 18:35 5892 8034 7121 3427 5892
29 את־העיר וישבו בה׃ ויקראו שם־העיר דן בשם דן
Dan the by ,Dan the the called and ,it in and the
of name city of name lived ,city

5892 8034 3919 199 3478 3205 834 1
אביהם אשר יולד לישראל ואולם ליש שם־העיר
the the Laish however ;Israel to was who their
city of name (was) born father

1121 3093 6459 1835/1121 6965 7223
30 לראשנה׃ ויקימו להם בני־דן את־הפסל ויהונתן בן־
the and graven the Dan the for raised And the at
of son Jonathan ;image of sons themselves .first

5704 1839 7626 3548 1961 1121 4519/1121 1647
גרשם בן־מנשה הוא ובניו היו כהנים לשבט הדני עד
until the the for priests were his and he Manasseh the ,Gershom
Danites of tribe sons of son

the captivity of the land. [31]And they set up for themselves Micah's graven image, which he had made, all the days that the house of God *was* in Shiloh.

31 יוֹם גְּלוֹת הָאָרֶץ׃ וַיָּשִׂימוּ לָהֶם אֶת־פֶּסֶל מִיכָה אֲשֶׁר
עָשָׂה כָּל־יְמֵי הֱיוֹת בֵּית־הָאֱלֹהִים בְּשִׁלֹה׃

CAP. XIX ט׳

CHAPTER 19

CHAPTER 19

[1]And it happened in those days when there was no king in Israel, there was a man, a Levite, living on the further side of the hills of Ephraim. And he took a wife to himself, a concubine out of Bethlehem-judah. [2]And his concubine committed adultery against him. And she went away from him to her father's house, to Bethlehem-judah, and was there *many* days—four months. [3]And her husband rose up and went after her, to speak to her heart, to bring her back. And his young man *was* with him, and a team of asses. And she brought him into her father's house. And the young woman's father saw him, and rejoiced to meet him. [4]And his father-in-law, the young woman's father, detained him. And he stayed with him three days. And they ate and drank, and stayed there. [5]And it happened on the fourth day, they rose up early in the morning, and he rose up to go. And the young woman's father said to his son-in-law, Sustain your heart *with* a bit of food, and afterward you shall go on. [6]And they sat and ate, both of them together, and drank. And the young woman's father said to the man, Please be content and stay all night, and let your heart be good. [7]And the man rose up to go; and his father-in-law pressed him, and he turned back and stayed there. [8]And he rose up early in the morning to go on the fifth day. And the young woman's father said, Please refresh your heart. And they stayed until the

1 וַיְהִי בַּיָּמִים הָהֵם וּמֶלֶךְ אֵין בְּיִשְׂרָאֵל וַיְהִי ׀ אִישׁ לֵוִי
גָּר בְּיַרְכְּתֵי הַר־אֶפְרַיִם וַיִּקַּח־לוֹ אִשָּׁה פִילֶגֶשׁ מִבֵּית
2 לֶחֶם יְהוּדָה׃ וַתִּזְנֶה עָלָיו פִּילַגְשׁוֹ וַתֵּלֶךְ מֵאִתּוֹ אֶל־בֵּית
אָבִיהָ אֶל־בֵּית לֶחֶם יְהוּדָה וַתְּהִי־שָׁם יָמִים אַרְבָּעָה
3 חֳדָשִׁים׃ וַיָּקָם אִישָׁהּ וַיֵּלֶךְ אַחֲרֶיהָ לְדַבֵּר עַל־לִבָּהּ
לַהֲשִׁיבוֹ וְנַעֲרוֹ עִמּוֹ וְצֶמֶד חֲמֹרִים וַתְּבִיאֵהוּ בֵּית אָבִיהָ
4 וַיִּרְאֵהוּ אֲבִי הַנַּעֲרָה וַיִּשְׂמַח לִקְרָאתוֹ׃ וַיֶּחֱזַק־בּוֹ חֹתְנוֹ
אֲבִי הַנַּעֲרָה וַיֵּשֶׁב אִתּוֹ שְׁלֹשֶׁת יָמִים וַיֹּאכְלוּ וַיִּשְׁתּוּ וַיָּלִינוּ
5 שָׁם׃ וַיְהִי בַּיּוֹם הָרְבִיעִי וַיַּשְׁכִּימוּ בַבֹּקֶר וַיָּקָם לָלֶכֶת
וַיֹּאמֶר אֲבִי הַנַּעֲרָה אֶל־חֲתָנוֹ סְעַד לִבְּךָ פַּת־לֶחֶם וְאַחַר
6 תֵּלֵכוּ׃ וַיֵּשְׁבוּ וַיֹּאכְלוּ שְׁנֵיהֶם יַחְדָּו וַיִּשְׁתּוּ וַיֹּאמֶר אֲבִי
7 הַנַּעֲרָה אֶל־הָאִישׁ הוֹאֶל־נָא וְלִין וְיִטַב לִבֶּךָ׃ וַיָּקָם הָאִישׁ
8 לָלֶכֶת וַיִּפְצַר־בּוֹ חֹתְנוֹ וַיָּשָׁב וַיָּלֶן שָׁם׃ וַיַּשְׁכֵּם בַּבֹּקֶר
בַּיּוֹם הַחֲמִישִׁי לָלֶכֶת וַיֹּאמֶר ׀ אֲבִי הַנַּעֲרָה סְעָד־נָא לְבָבְךָ

turning of the day. And they ate, both of them. 9 And the man rose to go, he and his concubine, and his young man. And his father-in-law, the young woman's father, said to him, Please notice that the day has faded toward evening. Please stay the night. Behold, the day is declining. Stay here and let your heart be glad, and you shall rise early tomorrow for your journey. And you shall go to your tent. 10 But the man was not willing to stay the night. And he rose up and departed, and went until *he was* opposite Jebus—it is Jerusalem—and with him a team of saddle asses. And his concubine *was* with him.

11 They *were* near Jebus, and the day was spent. And the young man said to his master, Please come and we shall turn to this city of the Jebusites, and stay in it. 12 And his master said to him, Let us not turn to the city of an alien that *is* not of the sons of Israel, but we shall pass over to Gibeah. 13 And he said to his young man, Come and we shall draw near to one of these places, and shall stay in Gibeah, or in Ramah. 14 And they passed on and traveled on. And the sun went *down* on them near Gibeah, which belongs to Benjamin. 15 And they turned aside there, to go in to stay the night in Gibeah. And he went in and sat in a broad place of the city. Yet there was no man that took them into his house to spend the night.

16 And, behold, a man, an aged one, came from his work from the field in the evening. And the man *was* from the hills of Ephraim; and he *was* a sojourner in Gibeah. But the men of the place *were* sons of Benjamin. 17 And he lifted up his eyes and saw the man, the traveler, in a broad place of the city. And the aged man said, Where are

376 6965 8147 398 3117 5186 5704 4102
9 וְהִתְמַהְמְהוּ עַד־נְטוֹת הַיּוֹם וַיֹּאכְלוּ שְׁנֵיהֶם׃ וַיָּקָם הָאִישׁ
the And both they and the the. until they and
man rose ,them of ,ate ;day of turning lingered

5291 1 2859 559 5288 6370 3212
לָלֶכֶת הוּא וּפִילַגְשׁוֹ וְנַעֲרוֹ וַיֹּאמֶר לוֹ חֹתְנוֹ אֲבִי הַנַּעֲרָה
young the the father- his to said and his and his and he ,go to
,woman's father ,in-law him ;man young ,concubine

3885 3117 2583 2009 3885 6150 3117 7503 4994/2009
הִנֵּה־נָא רָפָה הַיּוֹם לַעֲרֹב לִינוּ־נָא הִנֵּה חֲנוֹת הַיּוֹם לִין
lodge the has ,behold ,Please lodge toward the has Please no-
;day fallen ;evening day faded tice

3212 1879 4279 7925 38:24 3190
פֹּה וְיִיטַב לְבָבֶךָ וְהִשְׁכַּמְתֶּם מָחָר לְדַרְכְּכֶם וְהָלַכְתָּ
you and your for tomorrow shall you and your and ,here
go shall ,journey early rise ,heart cheer

5704 935 3212 6965 3885 376 14 3808 168
10 לְאָהֳלֶךָ׃ וְלֹא־אָבָה הָאִישׁ לָלוּן וַיָּקָם וַיֵּלֶךְ וַיָּבֹא עַד
until and and he and to man the was But your to
went left rose lodge willing not .tent

2280 2543 6776 3389 2982 5227
נֹכַח יְבוּס הִיא יְרוּשָׁלָ͏ִם וְעִמּוֹ צֶמֶד חֲמוֹרִים חֲבוּשִׁים
,saddled asses a with and —Jerusalem (is) it —Jebus op-
of team him posite

5288 559 3966 3381 3117 29:82 6370
11 וּפִילַגְשׁוֹ עִמּוֹ׃ הֵם עִם־יְבוּס וְהַיּוֹם רַד מְאֹד וַיֹּאמֶר הַנַּעַר
young the and ,far gone the and Jebus near They with his and
man said day (were) ,him concubine

3885 2088 2983 5892 5493 4994/3212 113
אֶל־אֲדֹנָיו לְכָה־נָּא וְנָסוּרָה אֶל־עִיר־הַיְבוּסִי הַזֹּאת וְנָלִין
and this the city to us let and Please come his to
stay Jebusites of aside turn ,master

52:37 5892 5493 3808 113 559
12 בָּהּ׃ וַיֹּאמֶר אֵלָיו אֲדֹנָיו לֹא נָסוּר אֶל־עִיר נָכְרִי אֲשֶׁר
that an the to us Let not his him to said And .it in
alien of city aside turn ,master

5288 559 1390 5674 3478 1121 38.08
13 לֹא־מִבְּנֵי יִשְׂרָאֵל הֵנָּה וְעָבַרְנוּ עַד־גִּבְעָה׃ וַיֹּאמֶר לְנַעֲרוֹ
his to he And .Gibeah to we but ,here Israel the of (is)
,man young said cross will of sons not

7414 176 1390 3885 4725 259 7126 3212
לְךָ וְנִקְרְבָה בְּאַחַד הַמְּקֹמוֹת וְלַנּוּ בַגִּבְעָה אוֹ בָרָמָה׃
in or in shall and the one to will we and Come
,Ramah ,Gibeah lodge ,places of near draw

834 1390 681 8121 935 3212 5674
14 וַיַּעַבְרוּ וַיֵּלֵכוּ וַתָּבֹא לָהֶם הַשֶּׁמֶשׁ אֵצֶל הַגִּבְעָה אֲשֶׁר
which ,Gibeah near sun the on went and and they And
them (down) ;on went by passed

7339 3427 935 1390 3885 3212 5493 1144
15 לְבִנְיָמִן׃ וַיָּסֻרוּ שָׁם לָבוֹא לָלוּן בַּגִּבְעָה וַיָּבֹא וַיֵּשֶׁב בִּרְחוֹב
the in sat and he and in to go to there they And to belongs
of square in went ;Gibeah lodge in aside turned .Benjamin

376 2009 3885 1004 622 376 369 5892
16 הָעִיר וְאֵין אִישׁ מְאַסֵּף־אוֹתָם הַבַּיְתָה לָלוּן׃ וְהִנֵּה ׀ אִישׁ
an ,And to his into them that man there yet the
man ,behold .lodge house took no was ;city

669 2022 376 6153 7704 4639 935 2205
זָקֵן בָּא מִן־מַעֲשֵׂהוּ מִן־הַשָּׂדֶה בָּעֶרֶב וְהָאִישׁ מֵהַר אֶפְרַיִם
,Ephraim from the and the in the from his from came old
of hills the (was) man ,evening field work

5375 3228 1121 4725 582 1390 1481
17 וְהוּא־גָר בַּגִּבְעָה וְאַנְשֵׁי הַמָּקוֹם בְּנֵי יְמִינִי׃ וַיִּשָּׂא עֵינָיו
his he And Jamin of sons place the the but in a he and
eyes up lifted of men ,Gibeah visitor

2205 376 559 5892 7339 732 376 7200
וַיַּרְא אֶת־הָאִישׁ הָאֹרֵחַ בִּרְחוֹב הָעִיר וַיֹּאמֶר הָאִישׁ הַזָּקֵן
,old man the said and the the in the the and
;city of square ,traveler ,man saw

you going, and where do you come from? [18]And he said to him, We *are* passing from Bethlehem-judah to the other side of the hills of Ephraim. I *am* from there, and I am going to Bethlehem-judah. And I am going to the house of Jehovah. Yet there is no man to take me into the house. [19]But there is straw and food for our asses, and also there is bread and wine for me, and for your slave-girl, and for the young man with your servants; there is no lack of anything. [20]And the old man said, Peace to you. Only, all that you lack *shall be* on me. Only, do not spend the night in the open. [21]And he brought him to his house, and mixed *fodder* for the asses. And they washed their feet and ate and drank.

[22]They were making their hearts merry. And, behold, men of the city, sons of worthless men, went around the house, beating on the door. And they spoke to the old man, the housemaster, saying, Bring out the man who has come into your house, and we shall know him. [23]And the man, the housemaster, went out to them and said to them, No, my brothers, please do not do evil, since this man has come into my house; do not do this grave sin. [24]Behold, my daughter, a virgin, and his concubine. Please let me bring them out, and you humble them. And do to them that which is good in your eyes, but do not do this wicked thing to this man. [25]And the men were not willing to listen to him, and the man took hold on his concubine and brought *her* out to them outside. And they knew her,

18 אָנָה תֵלֵךְ וּמֵאַיִן תָּבוֹא׃ וַיֹּאמֶר אֵלָיו עֹבְרִים אֲנַחְנוּ מִבֵּית־
from We passing to he And you do and you do Where
Beth- (are) through ,him said ?come where from go

לֶחֶם יְהוּדָה עַד־יַרְכְּתֵי הַר־אֶפְרַיִם מִשָּׁם אָנֹכִי וָאֵלֵךְ עַד־
to am I and I (for) from hill-country the other the to Judah lehem
going ,(am) there ,Ephraim of of side of

בֵּית־לֶחֶם יְהוּדָה וְאֶת־בֵּית יְהוָה אֲנִי הֹלֵךְ וְאֵין אִישׁ מְאַסֵּף
taking man and am I Jehovah the and ;Judah lehem Beth-
no is ,to going of house of

19 אוֹתִי הַבָּיְתָה׃ וְגַם־תֶּבֶן גַּם־מִסְפּוֹא יֵשׁ לַחֲמוֹרֵינוּ וְגַם
and our for there fodder and straw But the into me
also ,asses is both .house

לֶחֶם וָיַיִן יֶשׁ־לִי וְלַאֲמָתֶךָ וְלַנַּעַר עִם־עֲבָדֶיךָ אֵין מַחְסוֹר
lack there your with the for and your for and for there and bread
of no is ;servants man young ,slave-girl ,me is wine

20 כָּל־דָּבָר׃ וַיֹּאמֶר הָאִישׁ הַזָּקֵן שָׁלוֹם לָךְ רַק כָּל־מַחְסוֹרְךָ
you that all ,only to Peace ,old man the said And .thing any
(be) lack ;you (be)

21 עָלָי רַק בָּרְחוֹב אַל־תָּלַן׃ וַיְבִיאֵהוּ לְבֵיתוֹ וַיָּבוֹל לַחֲמוֹרִים
the for mixed and his to he And do not the in only on
;asses ,house him brought lodge square ,me

22 וַיִּרְחֲצוּ רַגְלֵיהֶם וַיֹּאכְלוּ וַיִּשְׁתּוּ׃ הֵמָּה מֵיטִיבִים אֶת־לִבָּם
their making were They and ,ate and ,feet their they and
;hearts merry .drank washed

וְהִנֵּה אַנְשֵׁי הָעִיר אַנְשֵׁי בְנֵי־בְלִיַּעַל נָסַבּוּ אֶת־הַבַּיִת
the encircled worth- sons men the men the ,and
,house lessness of of ,city of ,behold

מִתְדַּפְּקִים עַל־הַדָּלֶת וַיֹּאמְרוּ אֶל־הָאִישׁ בַּעַל הַבַּיִת הַזָּקֵן
,old the the the to they and ;door the on pounding
house of master man spoke

23 לֵאמֹר הוֹצֵא אֶת־הָאִישׁ אֲשֶׁר־בָּא אֶל־בֵּיתְךָ וְנֵדָעֶנּוּ׃ וַיֵּצֵא
And may we that your into has who the Bring ,saying
went .him know house come man out

אֲלֵיהֶם הָאִישׁ בַּעַל הַבַּיִת וַיֹּאמֶר אֲלֵהֶם אַל־אַחַי אַל־
not my ,No ,them to said and the the the ,them to
,brothers ,house of master ,man

תָּרֵעוּ נָא אַחֲרֵי אֲשֶׁר־בָּא הָאִישׁ הַזֶּה אֶל־בֵּיתִי אַל־תַּעֲשׂוּ
do not my into this man has who since ,please do
;house come ,evil

24 אֶת־הַנְּבָלָה הַזֹּאת׃ הִנֵּה בִתִּי הַבְּתוּלָה וּפִילַגְשֵׁהוּ אוֹצִיאָה־
bring me let his and ,virgin a my ,behold ;this sin foolish
out !concubine ,daughter

נָּא אוֹתָם וְעַנּוּ אוֹתָם וַעֲשׂוּ לָהֶם הַטּוֹב בְּעֵינֵיכֶם וְלָאִישׁ
to but your in the to and ;them you and ,Please
man ,eyes good them do humble

25 הַזֶּה לֹא תַעֲשׂוּ דְּבַר הַנְּבָלָה הַזֹּאת׃ וְלֹא־אָבוּ הָאֲנָשִׁים
men the were And .this foolish thing do not ,this
willing not

לִשְׁמֹעַ לוֹ וַיַּחֲזֵק הָאִישׁ בְּפִילַגְשׁוֹ וַיֹּצֵא אֲלֵיהֶם הַחוּץ
;outside to brought and his on the took and to to
them (her) concubine man hold ,him listen

and rolled themselves on
her all night, until the
morning. And *they* sent her
away at the dawning of the
day. 26 And the woman
came in at the dawning of
the morning, and fell *at* the
door of the man's house,
where her master *was*, till it
was light. 27 And her master
rose up in the morning, and
opened the door of the
house, and went out to go
his way. And, behold, the
woman, his concubine, had
fallen *at* the door of the
house, and her hands were
on the threshold. 28 And he
said to her, Rise up, and we
will go. But there was no
answer. And he took her on
the ass, and the man rose
up and went to his place.
29 And *he* came to his house,
and took the knife and lay
hold on his concubine. And
he cut her in pieces to her
bones, into twelve pieces,
and sent her into all the
borders of Israel. 30 And it
was so: all who saw *it* said,
There has never been, and
never was seen, *a thing* like
this from the day the sons of
Israel came up out of the
land of Egypt until this day.
Set yourselves on it, take
counsel. Then speak.

וַיֵּדְעוּ אוֹתָהּ וַיִּתְעַלְּלוּ־בָהּ כָּל־הַלַּיְלָה עַד־הַבֹּקֶר וַיְשַׁלְּחוּהָ
26 בַּעֲלוֹת הַשָּׁחַר׃ וַתָּבֹא הָאִשָּׁה לִפְנוֹת הַבֹּקֶר וַתִּפֹּל
27 פֶּתַח בֵּית־הָאִישׁ אֲשֶׁר־אֲדוֹנֶיהָ שָּׁם עַד־הָאוֹר׃ וַיָּקָם
אֲדֹנֶיהָ בַּבֹּקֶר וַיִּפְתַּח דַּלְתוֹת הַבַּיִת וַיֵּצֵא לָלֶכֶת לְדַרְכּוֹ
וְהִנֵּה הָאִשָּׁה פִילַגְשׁוֹ נֹפֶלֶת פֶּתַח הַבַּיִת וְיָדֶיהָ עַל־הַסַּף׃
28 וַיֹּאמֶר אֵלֶיהָ קוּמִי וְנֵלֵכָה וְאֵין עֹנֶה וַיִּקָּחֶהָ עַל־הַחֲמוֹר
29 וַיָּקָם הָאִישׁ וַיֵּלֶךְ לִמְקֹמוֹ׃ וַיָּבֹא אֶל־בֵּיתוֹ וַיִּקַּח אֶת־
הַמַּאֲכֶלֶת וַיַּחֲזֵק בְּפִילַגְשׁוֹ וַיְנַתְּחֶהָ לַעֲצָמֶיהָ לִשְׁנֵים עָשָׂר
30 נְתָחִים וַיְשַׁלְּחֶהָ בְּכֹל גְּבוּל יִשְׂרָאֵל׃ וְהָיָה כָל־הָרֹאֶה
וְאָמַר לֹא־נִהְיְתָה וְלֹא־נִרְאֲתָה כָּזֹאת לְמִיּוֹם עֲלוֹת בְּנֵי־
יִשְׂרָאֵל מֵאֶרֶץ מִצְרַיִם עַד הַיּוֹם הַזֶּה שִׂימוּ־לָכֶם עָלֶיהָ
עֻצוּ וְדַבֵּרוּ׃

CAP. XX כ

CHAPTER 20

CHAPTER 20

1 And all the sons of Israel
went out, and the congre-
gation was assembled as
one man, from Dan even to
Beer-sheba, and the land of
Gilead, to Jehovah at
Mizpeh. 2 And the leaders
of all the people, of all the
tribes of Israel, presented
themselves in the assembly
of all the people of God, four
hundred thousand footmen
drawing swords. 3 And the

1 וַיֵּצְאוּ כָּל־בְּנֵי יִשְׂרָאֵל וַתִּקָּהֵל הָעֵדָה כְּאִישׁ אֶחָד לְמִדָּן
2 וְעַד־בְּאֵר שֶׁבַע וְאֶרֶץ הַגִּלְעָד אֶל־יְהוָה הַמִּצְפָּה׃ וַיִּתְיַצְּבוּ
פִּנּוֹת כָּל־הָעָם כֹּל שִׁבְטֵי יִשְׂרָאֵל בִּקְהַל עַם הָאֱלֹהִים
3 אַרְבַּע מֵאוֹת אֶלֶף אִישׁ רַגְלִי שֹׁלֵף חָרֶב׃ וַיִּשְׁמְעוּ

sons of Benjamin heard that the sons of Israel had gone up to Mizpeh. And the sons of Israel said, Speak up. How did this evil happen? [4]And the man, the Levite, husband of the woman who had been murdered, answered and said, I came into Gibeah which *is* to Benjamin, I and my concubine, to spend the night. [5]And the men of Gibeah rose up against me. And they went around the house against me at night; they had in mind to kill me, and they raped my concubine, and she died. [6]And I took hold on my concubine, and cut her in pieces, and sent her into all the land of the inheritance of Israel. For they have done evil and folly in Israel. [7]Behold, you *are* the sons of Israel. Give here your advice and counsel.

[8]And all the people rose up as one man, saying, Not one of us shall go to his tent, and not one of us shall return to his house. [9]And now, this *is* the thing which we shall do to Gibeah, *going* against it by lot. [10]And we shall take ten men of a hundred of all the tribes of Israel, and a hundred of a thousand, and a thousand of ten thousand, to take food for the people, that they may act when they come to Gibeah of Benjamin, according to all the folly which it has done in Israel. [11]And every man of Israel was gathered to the city, knit together as one man.

[12]And the tribes of Israel sent men to all the tribes of Benjamin, saying, What *is* this evil which has happened among you? [13]And now, give up the men, the worthless sons which *are* in Gibeah, and we shall put them to death.

בְּנֵי בִנְיָמִן כִּי־עָלוּ בְנֵי־יִשְׂרָאֵל הַמִּצְפָּה וַיֹּאמְרוּ בְּנֵי
4 יִשְׂרָאֵל דַּבְּרוּ אֵיכָה נִהְיְתָה הָרָעָה הַזֹּאת׃ וַיַּעַן הָאִישׁ
הַלֵּוִי אִישׁ הָאִשָּׁה הַנִּרְצָחָה וַיֹּאמַר הַגִּבְעָתָה אֲשֶׁר לְבִנְיָמִן
5 בָּאתִי אֲנִי וּפִילַגְשִׁי לָלוּן׃ וַיָּקֻמוּ עָלַי בַּעֲלֵי הַגִּבְעָה
וַיָּסֹבּוּ עָלַי אֶת־הַבַּיִת לָיְלָה אוֹתִי דִּמּוּ לַהֲרֹג וְאֶת־פִּילַגְשִׁי
6 עִנּוּ וַתָּמֹת׃ וָאֹחֵז בְּפִילַגְשִׁי וָאֲנַתְּחֶהָ וָאֲשַׁלְּחֶהָ בְּכָל־
7 שְׂדֵה נַחֲלַת יִשְׂרָאֵל כִּי עָשׂוּ זִמָּה וּנְבָלָה בְּיִשְׂרָאֵל׃ הִנֵּה
8 כֻלְּכֶם בְּנֵי יִשְׂרָאֵל הָבוּ לָכֶם דָּבָר וְעֵצָה הֲלֹם׃ וַיָּקָם
כָּל־הָעָם כְּאִישׁ אֶחָד לֵאמֹר לֹא נֵלֵךְ אִישׁ לְאָהֳלוֹ וְלֹא
9 נָסוּר אִישׁ לְבֵיתוֹ׃ וְעַתָּה זֶה הַדָּבָר אֲשֶׁר נַעֲשֶׂה לַגִּבְעָה
10 עָלֶיהָ בְּגוֹרָל׃ וְלָקַחְנוּ עֲשָׂרָה אֲנָשִׁים לַמֵּאָה לְכֹל ׀ שִׁבְטֵי
יִשְׂרָאֵל וּמֵאָה לָאֶלֶף וְאֶלֶף לָרְבָבָה לָקַחַת צֵדָה לָעָם
לַעֲשׂוֹת לְבוֹאָם לְגֶבַע בִּנְיָמִן כְּכָל־הַנְּבָלָה אֲשֶׁר עָשָׂה
11 בְּיִשְׂרָאֵל׃ וַיֵּאָסֵף כָּל־אִישׁ יִשְׂרָאֵל אֶל־הָעִיר כְּאִישׁ אֶחָד
12 חֲבֵרִים׃ וַיִּשְׁלְחוּ שִׁבְטֵי יִשְׂרָאֵל אֲנָשִׁים בְּכָל־שִׁבְטֵי
13 בִנְיָמִן לֵאמֹר מָה הָרָעָה הַזֹּאת אֲשֶׁר נִהְיְתָה בָּכֶם׃ וְעַתָּה
תְּנוּ אֶת־הָאֲנָשִׁים בְּנֵי־בְלִיַּעַל אֲשֶׁר בַּגִּבְעָה וּנְמִיתֵם

And we shall comsume evil
from Israel. But Benjamin
was not willing to listen to
the voice of their brothers,
the sons of Israel. [14]And
the sons of Benjamin were
gathered out of the cities to
Gibeah, to go out to battle
with the sons of Israel.
[15]And the sons of Benjamin counted themselves on
that day. Out of the cities
were twenty-six thousand
men drawing sword, be-
sides the inhabitants of
Gibeah *who* counted themselves seven hundred
chosen men. [16]Among all
this people *were* seven
hundred chosen men *who*
bound the right hand, each
of these able to sling a
stone at a hair. And he did
not miss! [17]And the men
of Israel numbered them-
selves, besides Benjamin,
four hundred thousand men
drawing sword, each of
these a man of war.

[18]And they rose up and
went up to Bethel and
asked of God. And the sons
of Israel said, Who shall go
up for us at the beginning of
the battle with the sons of
Benjamin? And Jehovah
said, Judah, at the beginning. [19]And the sons of
Israel rose up in the
morning and camped
against Gibeah. [20]And the
men of Israel went to battle
with Benjamin; and the
men of Israel set them-
selves in order against
them, *to* battle against
Gibeah. [21]And the sons of
Benjamin came out from
Gibeah. And on that day
they destroyed twenty-two
thousand to the earth in
Israel. [22]And the people,
the men of Israel, made
themselves strong, and
again set the battle in order
in the place where they set
themselves on the first day.
[23]And the sons of Israel
went up and wept before

6963 8085 1144 14 3808 3478 7451 1197
וּנְבַעֲרָה רָעָה מִיִּשְׂרָאֵל וְלֹא אָבוּ בִּנְיָמִן לִשְׁמֹעַ בְּקוֹל
the to of voice | to listen | Benjamin | was willing | But not | from .Israel | evil | we And consume shall

5892 1144 1121 622 3478 1121 251
14 אֲחֵיהֶם בְּנֵי־יִשְׂרָאֵל׃ וַיֵּאָסְפוּ בְנֵי־בִנְיָמִן מֵהֶעָרִים
the cities | out of | Benjamin | the of sons | were And gathered | .Israel | the of sons | their ,brothers

6485 3478 1121 4421 3318 1390
15 הַגִּבְעָתָה לָצֵאת לַמִּלְחָמָה עִם־בְּנֵי יִשְׂרָאֵל׃ וַיִּתְפָּקְדוּ
And mustered | .Israel | the with of sons | battle to | go to out | ,Gibeah to

376 505 8337 6242 5892 3117 1144 1121
בְנֵי בִנְיָמִן בַּיּוֹם הַהוּא מֵהֶעָרִים עֶשְׂרִים וְשִׁשָּׁה אֶלֶף אִישׁ
men thousand | twenty-six | of out cities the | that | on day | Benjamin | the of sons

3967 7651 6485 1390 3427 2719 8025
שֹׁלֵף חֶרֶב לְבַד מִיֹּשְׁבֵי הַגִּבְעָה הִתְפָּקְדוּ שְׁבַע מֵאוֹת
hundred | seven | mustering themselves | ,Gibeah | inhab- of itants | the besides | ,sword | draw- ing

977 376 3967 7651 2088 5971 3605 977 376
16 אִישׁ בָּחוּר׃ מִכֹּל ׀ הָעָם הַזֶּה שְׁבַע מֵאוֹת אִישׁ בָּחוּר
chosen | ,men | hundred | seven | this | people (were) | Among all | .chosen | men

2398 3808 8185 68 7049 3225/3027 334
אִטֵּר יַד־יְמִינוֹ כָּל־זֶה קֹלֵעַ בָּאֶבֶן אֶל־הַשַּׂעֲרָה וְלֹא יַחֲטִא׃
did he .miss | and not | ;hair the | at | the stone | could sling | these each of | ,right hand (the in) | bound

3967 702 1144 6485 3478 376
17 וְאִישׁ יִשְׂרָאֵל הִתְפָּקְדוּ לְבַד מִבִּנְיָמִן אַרְבַּע מֵאוֹת
hundred | four | ,Benjamin | besides | mustered .themselves | Israel | the And of men

5927 6965 4421 376 2719 8025 376 505
18 אֶלֶף אִישׁ שֹׁלֵף חֶרֶב כָּל־זֶה אִישׁ מִלְחָמָה׃ וַיָּקֻמוּ וַיַּעֲלוּ
and went | they And rose | .war | a of man | these each of | ,sword | drawing | men | thou- sand

5927 4310 3478 1121 559 430 7592 1008
בֵית־אֵל וַיִּשְׁאֲלוּ בֵאלֹהִים וַיֹּאמְרוּ בְּנֵי יִשְׂרָאֵל מִי יַעֲלֶה־
shall up go | Who | ,Israel | the of sons | said and | ;God | of | and asked | Bethel to

3063 3068 559 1144 1121 4421 8462
לָּנוּ בַתְּחִלָּה לַמִּלְחָמָה עִם־בְּנֵי בִנְיָמִן וַיֹּאמֶר יְהוָה יְהוּדָה
Judah | ,Jehovah | And said | ?Benjamin | the with of sons | the battle | of | the at beginning | for us

1390 2583 1242 3478 1121 6965 8462
19 בַּתְּחִלָּה׃ וַיָּקוּמוּ בְנֵי־יִשְׂרָאֵל בַּבֹּקֶר וַיַּחֲנוּ עַל־הַגִּבְעָה׃
;Gibeah | against | and camped | the in morning | Israel | the of sons | rose And up | the at .beginning

376 6186 1144 4421 3478 376 3318
20 וַיֵּצֵא אִישׁ יִשְׂרָאֵל לַמִּלְחָמָה עִם־בִּנְיָמִן וַיַּעַרְכוּ אִתָּם אִישׁ־
the of men | them | arrayed and against | Ben- jamin | with | battle | to | Israel | the of men | and went

1390 1144 1121 3318 1390 4421 3478
21 יִשְׂרָאֵל מִלְחָמָה אֶל־הַגִּבְעָה׃ וַיֵּצְאוּ בְנֵי־בִנְיָמִן מִן־הַגִּבְעָה
,Gibeah from | Benjamin | the of sons | came And out | against Gibeah | (to) ,battle | Israel

376 505 6242 8147 1931 3117 3478 7843
וַיַּשְׁחִיתוּ בְיִשְׂרָאֵל בַּיּוֹם הַהוּא שְׁנַיִם וְעֶשְׂרִים אֶלֶף אִישׁ
men | thousand | twenty- | two | that | day on | Israel in | and destroyed

4421 6186 3254 3478 376 5971 2388 776
22 אַרְצָה׃ וַיִּתְחַזֵּק הָעָם אִישׁ יִשְׂרָאֵל וַיֹּסִפוּ לַעֲרֹךְ מִלְחָמָה
the battle | arrayed for | and again | ,Israel | men the of | the ,people | took And courage | the to .earth

3478 1121 5927 7223 3117 8033 6186 4725
23 בַּמָּקוֹם אֲשֶׁר־עָרְכוּ שָׁם בַּיּוֹם הָרִאשׁוֹן׃ וַיַּעֲלוּ בְנֵי־יִשְׂרָאֵל
Israel | the of sons | And went | .first the | on day | there | they arrayed | where | the in place

Jehovah until the evening, and asked of Jehovah, saying, Shall I again draw near to battle with the sons of my brother Benjamin? And Jehovah said, Go up against him.

[24]And the sons of Israel drew near to the sons of Benjamin on the second day. [25]And Benjamin came out to meet them from Gibeah on the second day, and again destroyed to the earth eighteen thousand men of the sons of Israel; all these were swordsmen. [26]And all the sons of Israel went up, even all the people, and came to Bethel, and wept. And *they* sat there before Jehovah, and fasted on that day until the evening, and caused burnt offerings and peace offerings to ascend before Jehovah. [27]And the sons of Israel asked of Jehovah—and the ark of the covenant of God *was* there in those days, [28]and Phinehas the son of Eleazar, the son of Aaron was standing before it in those days—saying, Shall I again go out to battle with the sons of my brother Benjamin, or shall I cease? And Jehovah said, Go up, for tomorrow I will give him into your hand.

[29]And Israel set ambushers against Gibeah all around. [30]And the sons of Israel went up against the sons of Benjamin on the third day, and set themselves in order against Gibeah, as at other times. [31]And the sons of Benjamin came out to meet the people. They were drawn away out of the city, and began to strike the people *down* wounded as at other times, in the highways, of which one goes up to Bethel, and one to Gibeah in the field, about thirty men

ויבכו לפני־יהוה עד־הערב וישאלו ביהוה לאמר האוסף
לגשת למלחמה עם־בני בנימן אחי ויאמר יהוה עלו
24 אליו: ויקרבו בני־ישראל אל־בני בנימן ביום השני:
25 ויצא בנימן לקראתם מן־הגבעה ביום השני וישחיתו
בבני ישראל עוד שמנת עשר אלף איש ארצה כל־
26 אלה שלפי חרב: ויעלו כל־בני ישראל וכל־העם ויבאו
בית־אל ויבכו וישבו שם לפני יהוה ויצומו ביום־ההוא
27 עד־הערב ויעלו עלות ושלמים לפני יהוה: וישאלו
בני־ישראל ביהוה ושם ארון ברית האלהים בימים
28 ההם: ופינחס בן־אלעזר בן־אהרן עמד לפניו בימים
ההם לאמר האוסף עוד לצאת למלחמה עם־בני־בנימן
אחי אם־אחדל ויאמר יהוה עלו כי מחר אתננו בידך:
29 וישם ישראל ארבים אל־הגבעה סביב:
30 ויעלו בני
ישראל אל־בני בנימן ביום השלישי ויערכו אל־הגבעה
31 כפעם בפעם: ויצאו בני־בנימן לקראת העם הנתקו
מן־העיר ויחלו להכות מהעם חללים כפעם בפעם
במסלות אשר אחת עלה בית־אל ואחת גבעתה בשדה

כִּשְׁלֹשִׁים אִישׁ בְּיִשְׂרָאֵל׃ וַיֹּאמְרוּ בְּנֵי בִנְיָמִן נִגָּפִים הֵם 32
לְפָנֵינוּ כְּבָרִאשֹׁנָה וּבְנֵי יִשְׂרָאֵל אָמְרוּ נָנוּסָה וּנְתַקְּנֻהוּ
מִן־הָעִיר אֶל־הַמְסִלּוֹת׃ וְכֹל ׀ אִישׁ יִשְׂרָאֵל קָמוּ מִמְּקוֹמוֹ 33
וַיַּעַרְכוּ בְּבַעַל תָּמָר וְאֹרֵב יִשְׂרָאֵל מֵגִיחַ מִמְּקֹמוֹ מִמַּעֲרֵה־
גָבַע׃ וַיָּבֹאוּ מִנֶּגֶד לַגִּבְעָה עֲשֶׂרֶת אֲלָפִים אִישׁ בָּחוּר 34
מִכָּל־יִשְׂרָאֵל וְהַמִּלְחָמָה כָּבֵדָה וְהֵם לֹא יָדְעוּ כִּי־נֹגַעַת
עֲלֵיהֶם הָרָעָה׃ וַיִּגֹּף יְהוָה ׀ אֶת־בִּנְיָמִן לִפְנֵי יִשְׂרָאֵל 35
וַיַּשְׁחִיתוּ בְנֵי יִשְׂרָאֵל בְּבִנְיָמִן בַּיּוֹם הַהוּא עֶשְׂרִים וַחֲמִשָּׁה
אֶלֶף וּמֵאָה אִישׁ כָּל־אֵלֶּה שֹׁלֵף חָרֶב׃ וַיִּרְאוּ בְנֵי־בִנְיָמִן 36
כִּי נִגָּפוּ וַיִּתְּנוּ אִישׁ־יִשְׂרָאֵל מָקוֹם לְבִנְיָמִן כִּי בָטְחוּ אֶל־
הָאֹרֵב אֲשֶׁר שָׂמוּ אֶל־הַגִּבְעָה׃ וְהָאֹרֵב הֵחִישׁוּ וַיִּפְשְׁטוּ 37
אֶל־הַגִּבְעָה וַיִּמְשֹׁךְ הָאֹרֵב וַיַּךְ אֶת־כָּל־הָעִיר לְפִי־חָרֶב׃
וְהַמּוֹעֵד הָיָה לְאִישׁ יִשְׂרָאֵל עִם־הָאֹרֵב הֶרֶב לְהַעֲלוֹתָם 38
מַשְׂאַת הֶעָשָׁן מִן־הָעִיר׃ וַיַּהֲפֹךְ אִישׁ־יִשְׂרָאֵל בַּמִּלְחָמָה 39
וּבִנְיָמִן הֵחֵל לְהַכּוֹת חֲלָלִים בְּאִישׁ־יִשְׂרָאֵל כִּשְׁלֹשִׁים
אִישׁ כִּי אָמְרוּ אַךְ נִגּוֹף נִגָּף הוּא לְפָנֵינוּ כַּמִּלְחָמָה
הָרִאשֹׁנָה׃ וְהַמַּשְׂאֵת הֵחֵלָּה לַעֲלוֹת מִן־הָעִיר עַמּוּד עָשָׁן 40

of Israel. [32]And the sons of Benjamin said, They are destroyed before us, as at the beginning. But the sons of Israel said, Let us flee and draw them away out of the city, into the highways. [33]And all the men of Israel rose from their place and set themselves in order at Baal-tamar. And Israel's ambush came out of its place, out of the meadow of Gibeah. [34]And they came in across from Gibeah, ten thousand chosen men out of all Israel. And the battle *was* heavy. And they did not know that evil was striking against them. [35]And Jehovah struck Benjamin before Israel. And the sons of Israel destroyed twenty-five thousand, one hundred men on that day in Benjamin; all these *were* swordsmen. [36]And the sons of Benjamin saw that they were beaten. And the men of Israel had given place to Benjamin, for they trusted to the ambush which they had set against Gibeah. [37]And the ambush hurried and came against Gibeah, and the ambush drew itself out and struck all of the city by the mouth of the sword. [38]And there was a sign set to the men of Israel with the ambush, their causing a rising of smoke to go up from the city. [39]And the men of Israel turned in battle, and Benjamin had begun to strike, *causing some to be* slain of the men of Israel, about thirty men. For they said, Surely they are beaten down before us, as *at* the first battle. [40]And the rising *of smoke* began to go up from the city, a pillar. And

Benjamin turned around, and, behold, the whole city had gone up toward the heavens. [41]And the men of Israel turned, and the men of Benjamin were troubled. For they had seen that evil had struck them. [42]And they turned before the men of Israel, toward the way of the wilderness. And the battle followed them. And those who *were* from the city were destroying them in their midst. [43]They surrounded Benjamin, and they pursued them *without* rest. And *they* trod them down until *they were* opposite Gibeah, at the rising of the sun [44]And eighteen thousand men of Benjamin fell, all of these mighty men. [45]And they turned and fled toward the wilderness, to the rock of Rimmon. And they gleaned five thousand men of them in the highways, and caught them, to Gidom. And *they* struck two thousand men of them. [46]And all the ones of Benjamin who fell were twenty-five thousand men drawing the sword on that day; all of these mighty men. [47]And six hundred men turned and fled into the wilderness, to the rock of Rimmon. And they lived in the rock of Rimmon four months. [48]And the men of Israel turned back to the sons of Benjamin, and struck them by the mouth of the sword, from the entire city to livestock, to all that was found. Also they set fire to all the cities which were found.

ויפן בנימן אחריו והנה עלה כליל־העיר השמימה׃
41 ואיש ישראל הפך ויבהל איש בנימן כי ראה כי־נגעה
42 עליו הרעה׃ ויפנו לפני איש ישראל אל־דרך המדבר
והמלחמה הדביקתהו ואשר מהערים משחיתים אותו
43 בתוכו׃ כתרו את־בנימן הרדיפהו מנוחה הדריכהו
44 עד נכח הגבעה ממזרח־שמש׃ ויפלו מבנימן שמנה־
45 עשר אלף איש את־כל־אלה אנשי חיל׃ ויפנו וינסו
המדברה אל־סלע הרמון ויעללהו במסלות חמשת
אלפים איש וידביקו אחריו עד־גדעם ויכו ממנו אלפים
46 איש׃ ויהי כל־הנפלים מבנימן עשרים וחמשה אלף
איש שלף חרב ביום ההוא את־כל־אלה אנשי־חיל׃
47 ויפנו וינסו המדברה אל־סלע הרמון שש מאות איש
48 וישבו בסלע רמון ארבעה חדשים׃ ואיש ישראל
שבו אל־בני בנימן ויכום לפי־חרב מעיר מתם עד־
בהמה עד כל־הנמצא גם כל־הערים הנמצאות
שלחו באש׃

CAP. XXI כא

CHAPTER 21

1 וְאִישׁ יִשְׂרָאֵל נִשְׁבַּע בַּמִּצְפָּה לֵאמֹר אִישׁ מִמֶּנּוּ לֹא־יִתֵּן
2 בִּתּוֹ לְבִנְיָמִן לְאִשָּׁה׃ וַיָּבֹא הָעָם בֵּית־אֵל וַיֵּשְׁבוּ שָׁם עַד־
הָעֶרֶב לִפְנֵי הָאֱלֹהִים וַיִּשְׂאוּ קוֹלָם וַיִּבְכּוּ בְּכִי גָדוֹל׃
3 וַיֹּאמְרוּ לָמָה יְהוָה אֱלֹהֵי יִשְׂרָאֵל הָיְתָה זֹּאת בְּיִשְׂרָאֵל
4 לְהִפָּקֵד הַיּוֹם מִיִּשְׂרָאֵל שֵׁבֶט אֶחָד׃ וַיְהִי מִמָּחֳרָת
וַיַּשְׁכִּימוּ הָעָם וַיִּבְנוּ־שָׁם מִזְבֵּחַ וַיַּעֲלוּ עֹלוֹת וּשְׁלָמִים׃
5 וַיֹּאמְרוּ בְּנֵי יִשְׂרָאֵל מִי אֲשֶׁר לֹא־עָלָה בַקָּהָל מִכָּל־
שִׁבְטֵי יִשְׂרָאֵל אֶל־יְהוָה כִּי הַשְּׁבוּעָה הַגְּדוֹלָה הָיְתָה
לַאֲשֶׁר לֹא־עָלָה אֶל־יְהוָה הַמִּצְפָּה לֵאמֹר מוֹת יוּמָת׃
6 וַיִּנָּחֲמוּ בְּנֵי יִשְׂרָאֵל אֶל־בִּנְיָמִן אָחִיו וַיֹּאמְרוּ נִגְדַּע הַיּוֹם
7 שֵׁבֶט אֶחָד מִיִּשְׂרָאֵל׃ מַה־נַּעֲשֶׂה לָהֶם לַנּוֹתָרִים לְנָשִׁים
וַאֲנַחְנוּ נִשְׁבַּעְנוּ בַיהוָה לְבִלְתִּי תֵת־לָהֶם מִבְּנוֹתֵינוּ
8 לְנָשִׁים׃ וַיֹּאמְרוּ מִי אֶחָד מִשִּׁבְטֵי יִשְׂרָאֵל אֲשֶׁר לֹא־
עָלָה אֶל־יְהוָה הַמִּצְפָּה וְהִנֵּה לֹא בָא־אִישׁ אֶל־הַמַּחֲנֶה
9 מִיָּבֵישׁ גִּלְעָד אֶל־הַקָּהָל׃ וַיִּתְפָּקֵד הָעָם וְהִנֵּה אֵין־שָׁם
10 אִישׁ מִיּוֹשְׁבֵי יָבֵשׁ גִּלְעָד׃ וַיִּשְׁלְחוּ־שָׁם הָעֵדָה שְׁנֵים־

CHAPTER 21

1 And the men of Israel had sworn in Mizpeh, saying, Not one of us shall give his daughter to Benjamin for a wife. 2 And the people came to Bethel, and sat there before God until the evening. And *they* lifted up their voices and wept a great weeping. 3 And *they* said, O Jehovah, God of Israel, Why has this happened in Israel, to be lacking one tribe today from Israel? 4 And it happened on the next day, the people rose early and built an altar there, and offered burnt offerings and peace offerings. 5 And the sons of Israel said, Who *is* he that did not come up in the assembly out of all the tribes of Israel to Jehovah? For a great oath had been undertaken concerning him that did not come up to Jehovah to Mizpeh, saying, He shall surely be put to death.

6 And the sons of Israel repented concerning their brother Benjamin. And *they* said, One tribe from Israel has been cut off today. 7 What shall we do for them, for those who are left, for wives? For we surely have sworn by Jehovah not to give them of our daughters for wives. 8 And they said, What one out of the tribes of Israel did not come up to Jehovah to Mizpeh? And, behold, no one had come into the camp from Jabesh-gilead to the assembly. 9 And the people numbered themselves. And, behold, there was not a man of the inhabitants of Jabesh-gilead. 10 And the assembly sent twelve thousand men

there of the mighty sons, and commanded them, saying, Go, and you shall strike the inhabitants of Jabesh-gilead with the mouth of the sword, even the women and the little ones. [11]And this *is* the thing which you shall do. Every male, and every woman who has been known by lying with a male, you shall destroy. [12]And out of all the inhabitants of Jabesh-gilead they found four hundred young women, virgins, who had not known a man by lying with a male. And they brought them into the camp at Shiloh, which is in the land of Canaan. [13]And all the assembly sent and spoke to the sons of Benjamin who were in the rock of Rimmon, and called out peace to them. [14]And Benjamin came again at that time. And they gave the women whom they had kept alive, of the women of Jabesh-gilead. But they did not find *enough* for them.

[15]And the people repented as to Benjamin, for Jehovah had made a breach among the tribes of Israel. [16]And the elders of the assembly said, What shall we do to the remnant for wives, for the women have been destroyed out of Benjamin? [17]And they said, The one who escaped *shall be* a legacy of Benjamin, that a tribe may not be blotted out from Israel. [18]And we surely are not able to give wives to them from our daughters, for the sons of Israel have sworn, saying, Cursed *is* he who gives a wife to Benjamin. [19]And they said, Behold, there is a feast of Jehovah from year to year in Shiloh, which is on the north side of Bethel, toward the rising of the sun, by the highway which goes up from Bethel to Shechem, and on the south of Lebonah. [20]And they

3212 559 6680 2428 1121 376 505 6240
עֶשֶׂר אֶלֶף אִישׁ מִבְּנֵי הֶחָיִל וַיְצַוּוּ אוֹתָם לֵאמֹר לְכוּ
.Go ,saying ,them and ,mighty the of men thousand
commanded sons

2945 802 2719 : 6310 1568/3003 3427 5221
וְהִכִּיתֶם אֶת־יוֹשְׁבֵי יָבֵשׁ גִּלְעָד לְפִי־חֶרֶב וְהַנָּשִׁים וְהַטָּף׃
the and the even sword's with gilead Jabesh- inhab- the you and
.ones little women edge the of itants strike shall

4904 3045 802 3605 2145 6213 834 1697 2088
11 וְזֶה הַדָּבָר אֲשֶׁר תַּעֲשׂוּ כָּל־זָכָר וְכָל־אִשָּׁה יֹדַעַת מִשְׁכַּב־
by known woman and ,male every you which the this And
with lying every :do shall thing (is)

3967 702 1568 3003 3427 4672 2763 2145
12 זָכָר תַּחֲרִימוּ׃ וַיִּמְצְאוּ מִיּוֹשְׁבֵי יָבֵישׁ גִּלְעָד אַרְבַּע מֵאוֹת
hundred four gilead Jabesh- the among they And shall you a
of dwellers found .destroy male

935 2145 4904 376 3045 834 1330 5291
נַעֲרָה בְתוּלָה אֲשֶׁר לֹא־יָדְעָה אִישׁ לְמִשְׁכַּב זָכָר וַיָּבִאוּ
they and a lying by a had not who ,virgins young
brought ;male with ,man known ,women

7971 3667 776 834 7887 4264
13 אוֹתָם אֶל־הַמַּחֲנֶה שִׁלֹה אֲשֶׁר בְּאֶרֶץ כְּנָעַן׃ וַיִּשְׁלְחוּ
sent And .Canaan the in which at the into them
of land (is) ,Shiloh camp

7121 7417 5553 834 1144 1121 1696 5712 3605
כָּל־הָעֵדָה וַיְדַבְּרוּ אֶל־בְּנֵי בִנְיָמִן אֲשֶׁר בְּסֶלַע רִמּוֹן וַיִּקְרְאוּ
and ,Rimmon the in who Benjamin the to and the all
proclaimed of rock (were) of sons spoke assembly

802 5414 6256 1144 7725 7965
14 לָהֶם שָׁלוֹם׃ וַיָּשָׁב בִּנְיָמִן בָּעֵת הַהִיא וַיִּתְּנוּ לָהֶם הַנָּשִׁים
the to they and ;that at Benjamin And .peace to
women them gave time returned .them

5971 3651 4672 3808 1568 3003 802 2421
15 אֲשֶׁר חִיּוּ מִנְּשֵׁי יָבֵשׁ גִּלְעָד וְלֹא־מָצְאוּ לָהֶם כֵּן׃ וְהָעָם
the And .so for had they but ;gilead Jabesh- the of they whom
people them found not of women alive kept had

3478 7626 6556 3068 6213 1144 5162
נִחָם לְבִנְיָמִן כִּי־עָשָׂה יְהוָה פֶּרֶץ בְּשִׁבְטֵי יִשְׂרָאֵל׃
.Israel the among a Jehovah had for for re-
of tribes breach made ,Benjamin pented

802 3498 6213 57:12 2205 559
16 וַיֹּאמְרוּ זִקְנֵי הָעֵדָה מַה־נַּעֲשֶׂה לַנּוֹתָרִים לְנָשִׁים כִּי־
for ,wives for the to shall What the the said And
remnant do we ,assembly of elders

1144 6413 3425 559 802 1144 8045
17 נִשְׁמְדָה מִבִּנְיָמִן אִשָּׁה׃ וַיֹּאמְרוּ יְרֻשַּׁת פְּלֵיטָה לְבִנְיָמִן
of sur- the A they And the of out been have
,Benjamin vivor legacy ,said ?women Benjamin destroyed

5414 3201 3808 3478 7626 4229
18 וְלֹא־יִמָּחֶה שֵׁבֶט מִיִּשְׂרָאֵל׃ וַאֲנַחְנוּ לֹא־נוּכַל לָתֶת־
give to are not we But from tribe a be may that
able .Israel out blotted not

559 3478 1121 7650 1323 802
לָהֶם נָשִׁים מִבְּנוֹתֵינוּ כִּי־נִשְׁבְּעוּ בְנֵי־יִשְׂרָאֵל לֵאמֹר
,saying ,Israel the have for our from wives to
of sons sworn ,daughters them

7887 3068/2282 2009 559 1144 802 5414 779
19 אָרוּר נֹתֵן אִשָּׁה לְבִנְיָמִן׃ וַיֹּאמְרוּ הִנֵּה חַג־יְהוָה בְּשִׁלוֹ
in Jehovah a ,Behold they And to a who he Cursed
Shiloh of feast ,said .Benjamin wife gives (is)

8121 4217 1008 6828 834 3117 3117
מִיָּמִים יָמִימָה אֲשֶׁר מִצְּפוֹנָה לְבֵית־אֵל מִזְרְחָה הַשֶּׁמֶשׁ
the toward ,Bethel of the on which days to from
sunrising north (is) days

6680 3829 5045 7927 1008 5927 4546
20 לִמְסִלָּה הָעֹלָה מִבֵּית־אֵל שְׁכֶמָה וּמִנֶּגֶב לִלְבוֹנָה׃ וַיְצַוּ
And .Lebonah of on and to from which the by
told they south the ,Shechem Bethel up goes highway

commanded the sons of Benjamin, saying, Go, and you shall lie in wait in the vineyards. 21 And *you* shall watch. And, behold, if the daughters of Shiloh come out to dance in dances, then you shall go out from the vineyards and each of you catch his wife from the daughters of Shiloh, and go to the land of Benjamin. 22 And it shall be, when their fathers or their brothers come to plead to us, we shall say to them, Favor us *with* them, for we did not take for each man of them a wife in battle, for if you did not give to them as *at this* time, you would be guilty. 23 And the sons of Benjamin did so, and took women according to their number from the dancers whom they had seized. And they went and returned to their inheritance, and built the cities, and lived in them.

24 And the sons of Israel went up and down from there at that time, each to his tribe, and to his family. And they departed from there, every man to his inheritance.

25 In those days there was no king in Israel. Each man did that which was right in his *own* eyes.

7200 3754 693 3212 559 1144 1121
21 אֶת־בְּנֵי בִנְיָמִן לֵאמֹר לְכוּ וַאֲרַבְתֶּם בַּכְּרָמִים׃ וּרְאִיתֶם
shall and the in shall you and ,Go ,saying ,Benjamin the
,watch vineyards wait in lie of sons
3318 4246 2342 7887 1323 3318 2009
וְהִנֵּה אִם־יֵצְאוּ בְנוֹת־שִׁילוֹ לָחוּל בַּמְּחֹלוֹת וִיצָאתֶם מִן
from you then ,dances in to Shiloh the come if ,and
out go shall dance of daughters out ,behold
3212 7887 1323 802 376 2414 3754
הַכְּרָמִים וַחֲטַפְתֶּם לָכֶם אִישׁ אִשְׁתּוֹ מִבְּנוֹת שִׁילוֹ וַהֲלַכְתֶּם
go and ,Shiloh the from his each of and the
to of daughters wife man you catch vineyards
7378 251 1 935 1961 1144 776
22 אֶרֶץ בִּנְיָמִן׃ וְהָיָה כִּי־יָבֹאוּ אֲבוֹתָם אוֹ אֲחֵיהֶם לָרוֹב אֵלֵינוּ
,us to to their or their come when it And Ben- the
contend brothers fathers ,be shall jamin of land
802 376 3947 3808 2603 559
וְאָמַרְנוּ אֲלֵיהֶם חָנּוּנוּ אוֹתָם כִּי לֹא לָקַחְנוּ אִישׁ אִשְׁתּוֹ
his each did we not for (with) Favor ,them to we that
wife man take ,them us say shall
6213 816 6256 5414 3808 4421
23 בַּמִּלְחָמָה כִּי לֹא אַתֶּם נְתַתֶּם לָהֶם כָּעֵת תֶּאְשָׁמוּ׃ וַיַּעֲשׂוּ
did And would you as to did you not for ,battle in
,guilty be ,time (this) them give if
834 2342 4557 802 5375 1144 1121 3651
כֵן בְּנֵי בִנְיָמִן וַיִּשְׂאוּ נָשִׁים לְמִסְפָּרָם מִן־הַמְּחֹלְלוֹת אֲשֶׁר
whom the of out to according women and ,Benjamin the ,so
dancers number their took of sons
3427 5892 1129 5159 7725 3212 1497
גָּזָלוּ וַיֵּלְכוּ וַיָּשׁוּבוּ אֶל־נַחֲלָתָם וַיִּבְנוּ אֶת־הֶעָרִים וַיֵּשְׁבוּ
and ,cities the and their to and they and they
lived built inheritance returned went ;seized had
7626 376 6256 3478 1121 8033 3212
24 בָּהֶם׃ וַיִּתְהַלְּכוּ מִשָּׁם בְּנֵי־יִשְׂרָאֵל בָּעֵת הַהִיא אִישׁ לְשִׁבְטוֹ
his to each ,that at Israel the from up went And in
tribe time of sons there down and .them
369 3117 5159 376 8033 3318 4940
25 וּלְמִשְׁפַּחְתּוֹ וַיֵּצְאוּ מִשָּׁם אִישׁ לְנַחֲלָתוֹ׃ בַּיָּמִים הָהֵם אֵין
there those In in- his to every from they and his to and
no was days ,heritance man ,there departed ;family
6213 5869 3477 376 3478 4428
מֶלֶךְ בְּיִשְׂרָאֵל אִישׁ הַיָּשָׁר בְּעֵינָיו יַעֲשֶׂה׃
.did his in the each in king
eyes (own) right man ;Israel

רות

LIBER RUTH

(THE) BOOK OF RUTH

CAPUT. I א

A LITERAL TRANSLATION
OF THE BIBLE
THE BOOK OF RUTH

CHAPTER 1

[1]And it happened in the days that the judges judged, there was a famine in the land. And a man from Bethlehem-judah went to live in the fields of Moab, he and his wife, and his two sons. [2]And the name of the man *was* Elimelech; and the name of his wife Naomi. And the name of his two sons *were* Mahlon and Chilion, Ephrathites from Bethlehem-judah. And they came into the fields of Moab, and remained there. [3]And Naomi's husband Elimelech died; And she was left, and her two sons. [4]And they took wives to themselves, women of Moab. The name of the one *was* Orpah, and the name of the second, Ruth. And they lived there about ten years. [5]And they also died, both of them, Mahlon and Chilion. And the woman was bereaved of her two children and of her husband. [6]And she rose up, she and her daughters-in-law, and turned back from the fields of Moab. For she had heard in the fields of Moab that Jehovah had visited His people, to give food to them. [7]And she went out from the place where she had been, and her two daughters-in-law with her. And they went in the way to return to the land of Judah. [8]And Naomi said to her two daughters-in-law, Go, each return to the house of her mother. May Jehovah deal kindly with you, as you have done with the dead, and with me. [9]May Jehovah grant to you that you find

376 3212 776 7458 1961 8199 8199 3117 1961
1 וַיְהִי בִּימֵי שְׁפֹט הַשֹּׁפְטִים וַיְהִי רָעָב בָּאָרֶץ וַיֵּלֶךְ אִישׁ
man a and the in a that judges the the the in And
went ;land famine was of judging of days ,was it
8147 802 4124 7704 1481 3063 1035
מִבֵּית לֶחֶם יְהוּדָה לָגוּר בִּשְׂדֵי מוֹאָב הוּא וְאִשְׁתּוֹ וּשְׁנֵי
and his and he ,Moab the in to (in) lehem from
two ,wife of fields live Judah Beth-
8147 8034 5281 802 8034 458 376 8034 1121
2 בָנָיו׃ וְשֵׁם הָאִישׁ אֱלִימֶלֶךְ וְשֵׁם אִשְׁתּוֹ נָעֳמִי וְשֵׁם שְׁנֵי
two the and ,Naomi his the and (was) man the the And his
of name wife of name ,Elimelech of name sons
935 3063 1035 673 3630 4248 1121
בָנָיו מַחְלוֹן וְכִלְיוֹן אֶפְרָתִים מִבֵּית לֶחֶם יְהוּדָה וַיָּבֹאוּ
they And (in) lehem from Ephrathites and Mahlon his
came ,Judah Beth- ,Chilion ,sons
7604 5281 376 458 4191 7604 4124 7704
3 שְׂדֵי־מוֹאָב וַיִּהְיוּ־שָׁם׃ וַיָּמָת אֱלִימֶלֶךְ אִישׁ נָעֳמִי וַתִּשָּׁאֵר
she and ;Naomi's hus- ,Elimelech And .there and Moab the to
left was ,band died stayed of fields
259 8034 425 802 5375 1121 8147
4 הִיא וּשְׁנֵי בָנֶיהָ׃ וַיִּשְׂאוּ לָהֶם נָשִׁים מֹאֲבִיּוֹת שֵׁם הָאַחַת
the the women (as) them-to they And her and she
one of name ;Moab of wives ,selves took .sons two
4191 8141 6235 8033 3427 7327 8145 8034 6204
5 עָרְפָּה וְשֵׁם הַשֵּׁנִית רוּת וַיֵּשְׁבוּ שָׁם כְּעֶשֶׂר שָׁנִים׃ וַיָּמוּתוּ
they And .years ten about there they and ;Ruth the the and (was)
,died lived ,second of name ,Orpah
3206 8147 802 7604 3630 4248 8147 1571
גַם־שְׁנֵיהֶם מַחְלוֹן וְכִלְיוֹן וַתִּשָּׁאֵר הָאִשָּׁה מִשְּׁנֵי יְלָדֶיהָ
her two of woman the was and and Mahlon of both ,also
children bereaved ,Chilion ,them
4124 7704 7725 3668 6965 376
6 וּמֵאִישָׁהּ׃ וַתָּקָם הִיא וְכַלֹּתֶיהָ וַתָּשָׁב מִשְּׂדֵי מוֹאָב כִּי
for ,Moab the from and her and she she And her of and
of fields returned ,daughters-in-law ,arose .husband
3899 5414 5971 3068 6485 4124 7704 8085
שָׁמְעָה בִּשְׂדֵה מוֹאָב כִּי־פָקַד יְהוָה אֶת־עַמּוֹ לָתֵת לָהֶם
food give to ,people his Jehovah had that Moab the in had she
visited of fields heard
3618 8147 8033 1961 4725 3318
7 לָחֶם׃ וַתֵּצֵא מִן־הַמָּקוֹם אֲשֶׁר הָיְתָה־שָׁמָּה וּשְׁתֵּי כַלֹּתֶיהָ
daugh- her and there had she where the from she And to
ters-in-law two been place out went .them
5281 559 3063 776 7725 1870 3212
8 עִמָּהּ וַתֵּלַכְנָה בַדֶּרֶךְ לָשׁוּב אֶל־אֶרֶץ יְהוּדָה׃ וַתֹּאמֶר נָעֳמִי
Naomi said And .Judah the to to the in they and with
of land return way went ,her
3068 6213 517 1004 802 7725 3212 3618 8147
לִשְׁתֵּי כַלֹּתֶיהָ לֵכְנָה שֹּׁבְנָה אִשָּׁה לְבֵית אִמָּהּ יַעֲשֶׂה יְהוָה
Jehovah may her the to each return ,Go daugh- her to
deal ;mother of house ,ters-in-law two
3068 5414 4191 6213 2617
9 עִמָּכֶם חֶסֶד כַּאֲשֶׁר עֲשִׂיתֶם עִם־הַמֵּתִים וְעִמָּדִי׃ יִתֵּן יְהוָה
Jehovah may and the with have you as ,kindly with
grant ;me with dead done you

rest, each in the house of her husband. And she kissed them, and they lifted up their voice and wept. 10And they said to her, Surely we will go back with you to your people. 11And Naomi said, Turn back, my daughters. Why should you go with me? Are there yet sons to me in my belly that they should be husbands for you? 12Turn back, my daughters, go. For I am too old to belong to a husband. Though I should say, There is hope for me, and I should be tonight with a husband, and also I should bear sons; 13will you wait for them, that they might grow up? Will you shut yourselves up for them, not to belong to a husband? No, my daughters, for *it is* much more bitter for me than for you, for the hand of Jehovah has gone out against me. 14And they lifted up their voice and wept again. And Orpah kissed her mother-in-law, but Ruth clung to her. 15And she said, See, your sister-in-law has turned back to her people, and to her gods. You turn back after your sister-in-law. 16And Ruth said, Do not beg me to leave you, to turn back from following you. For where you go, I will go. And where you stay, I will stay. Your people *shall be* my people, and your God my God. 17Where you die, I will die, and there I will be buried. May Jehovah do to me, and more so, if *anything but* death part you and me.

18And she saw that she had made herself strong to go with her; and she ceased to speak to her. 19And they went, both of them, until they came into Bethlehem. And it happened as they came into Bethlehem, all the city was moved at them. And they said, Is this

5375 5401 375 1004 802 4496 4672
לָכֶם וּמְצֶאןָ מְנוּחָה אִשָּׁה בֵּית אִישָׁהּ וַתִּשַּׁק לָהֶן וַתִּשֶּׂאנָה
they and ,them she and her the in each ,rest you that to
up lifted kissed ;husband of house find you

5971 7725 559 1058 6963
10 קוֹלָן וַתִּבְכֶּינָה׃ וַתֹּאמַרְנָה לָּהּ כִּי־אִתָּךְ נָשׁוּב לְעַמֵּךְ׃
your to will we with ,No to they And .wept and their
.people return you her said voice

3212 4100 1323 7725 5281 559
11 וַתֹּאמֶר נָעֳמִי שֹׁבְנָה בְנֹתַי לָמָּה תֵלַכְנָה עִמִּי הַעוֹד־לִי
to Are with should why my Turn ,Naomi said And
me yet ?me go you ;daughters ,back

3212 7725 582 1961 4578 1121
12 בָנִים בְּמֵעַי וְהָיוּ לָכֶם לַאֲנָשִׁים׃ שֹׁבְנָה בְנֹתַי לֵכְןָ כִּי
for ;go my ,Return ?husbands for they that my in sons
,daughters you be should belly

1961 1571 8615 3426 559 376 1961 2204
זָקַנְתִּי מִהְיוֹת לְאִישׁ כִּי אָמַרְתִּי יֶשׁ־לִי תִקְוָה גַּם הָיִיתִי
should I even ,hope for There should I If a to be to am I
be (if) me is say ,husband (married) old too

5704 3427 3860 1121 1961 1571 376 3915
13 הַלַּיְלָה לְאִישׁ וְגַם יָלַדְתִּי בָנִים׃ הֲלָהֵן תְּשַׂבֵּרְנָה עַד
un- you would for ;sons should I and a to (married)
wait them bear (if) even ,husband tonight

1323 376 1961 5702 3860 1115 834
אֲשֶׁר יִגְדָּלוּ הֲלָהֵן תֵּעָגֵנָה לְבִלְתִּי הֱיוֹת לְאִישׁ אַל בְּנֹתַי
my ,No a to be to not you Would for they til
,daughters ?husband (married) endure ?them up grow

6963 5375 3068 3027 3318 3966 4843
14 כִּי־מַר־לִי מְאֹד מִכֶּם כִּי־יָצְאָה בִי יַד־יְהוָה׃ וַתִּשֶּׂנָה קוֹלָן
their they And Jeho- hand against has for than much for more for
voice up lifted .vah's me out gone ,you (for) (is it) me bitter

1692 7327 2545 6204 5401 5750 1058
וַתִּבְכֶּינָה עוֹד וַתִּשַּׁק עָרְפָּה לַחֲמוֹתָהּ וְרוּת דָּבְקָה־בָּהּ׃
.her to clung but mother- her Orpah and ;again wept and
Ruth ,in-law kissed

7725 430 5971 2994 7725 2009 559
15 וַתֹּאמֶר הִנֵּה שָׁבָה יְבִמְתֵּךְ אֶל־עַמָּהּ וְאֶל־אֱלֹהֶיהָ שׁוּבִי
return her and her to sister- your has ,Behold she And
;gods to ,people in-law returned said

7725 5800 6293 7327 559 2994 310
16 אַחֲרֵי יְבִמְתֵּךְ׃ וַתֹּאמֶר רוּת אַל־תִּפְגְּעִי־בִי לְעָזְבֵךְ לָשׁוּב
to leave to me Do not ,Ruth said And sister- your after
return ,you beg .in-law

5971 3885 3885 3212 3212 834 310
מֵאַחֲרָיִךְ כִּי אֶל־אֲשֶׁר תֵּלְכִי אֵלֵךְ וּבַאֲשֶׁר תָּלִינִי אָלִין עַמֵּךְ
your will I you and will I ,go you where to for after from
people ;stay stay where ,go :you

6912 8033 4191 4191 834 430 430 5971
17 עַמִּי וֵאלֹהַיִךְ אֱלֹהָי׃ בַּאֲשֶׁר תָּמוּתִי אָמוּת וְשָׁם אֶקָּבֵר
I will and will I you Where my your and my
;buried be there ,die ,die .God God ,people

6504 4194 3254 3068 6213
כֹּה יַעֲשֶׂה יְהוָה לִי וְכֹה יֹסִיף כִּי הַמָּוֶת יַפְרִיד בֵּינִי וּבֵינֵךְ׃
and me will death if ,more and to Jehovah may thus
.you part (alone) so ,me do

1696 2308 3212 553 7200
18 וַתֵּרֶא כִּי־מִתְאַמֶּצֶת הִיא לָלֶכֶת אִתָּהּ וַתֶּחְדַּל לְדַבֵּר אֵלֶיהָ׃
.her to to she and with go to she made that she And
speak ceased ,her strong herself saw

1035 935 1961 1035 935 5704 8147 3212
19 וַתֵּלַכְנָה שְׁתֵּיהֶם עַד־בֹּאָנָה בֵּית לָחֶם וַיְהִי כְּבֹאָנָה בֵּית
to they when it And .lehem to they until of both they And
Beth- came ,was Beth- came them went

5281 2088 589 5892 3605 1949 1035
לָחֶם וַתֵּהֹם כָּל־הָעִיר עֲלֵיהֶן וַתֹּאמַרְנָה הֲזֹאת נָעֳמִי׃
?Naomi Is they and of because the all that ,lehem
this ,said ;them city moved was

Naomi? [20]And she said to
them, Do not call me
Naomi. Call me Mara, for
the Almighty has dealt bitterly with me. [21]I went out
full, and Jehovah has
brought me back empty.
Why do you call me Naomi,
since Jehovah has set *His*
eye against me, and the
Almighty has done evil to
me?
[22]And Naomi returned,
and Ruth the Moabitess,
her daughter-in-law with
her, who returned from the
fields of Moab. And they
came to Bethlehem at the
beginning of barley harvest.

20 וַתֹּאמֶר אֲלֵיהֶן אַל־תִּקְרֶאנָה לִי נָעֳמִי קְרֶאןָ לִי מָרָא כִּי־
for ,Mara me call ;Naomi me call Do not to she And
,them said
21 הֵמַר שַׁדַּי לִי מְאֹד׃ אֲנִי מְלֵאָה הָלַכְתִּי וְרֵיקָם הֱשִׁיבַנִי
brought has and went full I .very me the made has
back me empty ,out Almighty bitter
יְהוָה לָמָּה תִקְרֶאנָה לִי נָעֳמִי וַיהוָה עָנָה בִי וְשַׁדַּי הֵרַע
done has the and ,me has since ,Naomi me you do why ;Jehovah
evil Almighty eyed Jehovah call
22 לִי׃ וַתָּשָׁב נָעֳמִי וְרוּת הַמּוֹאֲבִיָּה כַלָּתָהּ עִמָּהּ הַשָּׁבָה
one the with daugh- her the and Naomi and to
returning ,her ter-in-law ,Moabitess Ruth returned ?me
מִשְּׂדֵי מוֹאָב וְהֵמָּה בָּאוּ בֵּית לֶחֶם בִּתְחִלַּת קְצִיר שְׂעֹרִים׃
.barley harvest the at lehem to came and ;Moab the from
of beginning Beth- they of fields

CAP. II ב

CHAPTER 2

[1]And Naomi *had* a kinsman of her husband, a
mighty man of the family of
Elimelech. And his name
was Boaz. [2]And Ruth of
Moab said to Naomi, Let me
now go to the field and
glean among the ears of
grain after him in whose
sight I shall find favor. And
she said to her, Go, my
daughter. [3]And she went.
And *she* came and gleaned
in the field after the reapers.
And her chance happened
to be on the portion of the
field *belonging to* Boaz,
who *was* of Elimelech's
family. [4]And, behold, Boaz
came from Bethlehem, and
said to the reapers,
Jehovah be with you. And
hey answered him,
Jehovah bless you. [5]And
Boaz said to his young man
who had been set over the
reapers, Whose *is* this
young woman? [6]And the
young man who had been
set over the reapers
answered and said, She is a
young woman of Moab who
came with Naomi from the
fields of Moab. [7]And she
said, Please let me glean,
and I shall gather among
the *sheaves* after the
reapers. And she came and
has remained since morn-
ing, even until now. She sat

1 וּלְנָעֳמִי מְיֻדָּע לְאִישָׁהּ אִישׁ גִּבּוֹר חַיִל מִמִּשְׁפַּחַת אֱלִימֶלֶךְ
;Elimelech the of man mighty a her of kins- a to And
of family ,husband man (was) Naomi
2 וּשְׁמוֹ בֹּעַז׃ וַתֹּאמֶר רוּת הַמּוֹאֲבִיָּה אֶל־נָעֳמִי אֵלְכָה־נָּא
now go Let ,Naomi to Moabitess the Ruth said And (was) and
(me) .Boaz name his
הַשָּׂדֶה וַאֲלַקֳטָה בַשִּׁבֳּלִים אַחַר אֲשֶׁר אֶמְצָא־חֵן בְּעֵינָיו
whose in favor shall I him after the among glean and the to
eyes find grain of ears ,field
3 וַתֹּאמֶר לָהּ לְכִי בִתִּי׃ וַתֵּלֶךְ וַתָּבוֹא וַתְּלַקֵּט בַּשָּׂדֶה אַחֲרֵי
after the in and and she And my ,Go to she And
field gleaned ,came ,went .daughter ,her said
הַקֹּצְרִים וַיִּקֶר מִקְרֶהָ חֶלְקַת הַשָּׂדֶה לְבֹעַז אֲשֶׁר מִמִּשְׁפַּחַת
the of who (belonging) the por- the her hap- and har- the
of family (was) Boaz (to) field of tion chance upon pened ;vesters
4 אֱלִימֶלֶךְ׃ וְהִנֵּה־בֹעַז בָּא מִבֵּית לֶחֶם וַיֹּאמֶר לַקּוֹצְרִים
the to and lehem from came Boaz ,And .Elimelech
,harvesters said Beth- ,behold
5 יְהוָה עִמָּכֶם וַיֹּאמְרוּ לוֹ יְבָרֶכְךָ יְהוָה׃ וַיֹּאמֶר בֹּעַז לְנַעֲרוֹ
his to Boaz said And .Jehovah bless to they And with Jehovah
man young you ,him said .you be
6 הַנִּצָּב עַל־הַקּוֹצְרִים לְמִי הַנַּעֲרָה הַזֹּאת׃ וַיַּעַן הַנַּעַר הַנִּצָּב
set young the And ?this young Whose the over set
man replied woman (is) harvesters
עַל־הַקּוֹצְרִים וַיֹּאמַר נַעֲרָה מוֹאֲבִיָּה הִיא הַשָּׁבָה עִם־נָעֳמִי
Naomi with came who (is) she Moabitess young A ,said and har- the over
,woman vesters
7 מִשְּׂדֵה מוֹאָב׃ וַתֹּאמֶר אֲלַקֳטָה־נָּא וְאָסַפְתִּי בָעֳמָרִים אַחֲרֵי
after the among I and please me Let said And .Moab the from
sheaves gather will ,glean ,said of fields
הַקּוֹצְרִים וַתָּבוֹא וַתַּעֲמוֹד מֵאָז הַבֹּקֶר וְעַד־עַתָּה זֶה שִׁבְתָּהּ
sat she this ;now even the since has and she and the
until ,morning remained came ;harvesters

8And Boaz said to Ruth,
do you not hear, my
daughter? Do not go to
glean another field, and
also do not pass through
this. And you shall stay
close to my young women.
9Your eyes *shall be* on the
field which they shall reap,
and you shall go after them.
Have I not commanded the
young men not to touch
you? When you are thirsty,
then you shall go to the
vessels and shall drink from
that which the young men
draw. 10And she fell on
her face and bowed to the
earth, and said to him, Why
have I found grace in your
eyes, that you should notice
me, and I a foreigner?
11And Boaz answered and
said to her, It has been fully
revealed to me all that you
have done with your
mother-in-law after the
death of your husband. And
you left your father and your
mother, and the land of your
birth, and came to a people
which you had not known
before. 12Jehovah shall repay your work, and your
reward shall be complete
from Jehovah the God of
Israel, under whose wings
you have come to take
refuge. 13And she said, let
me find grace in your eyes,
my lord, because you have
comforted me, and be-
cause you have spoken to
the heart of your handmaid.
And I surely am not as one
of your handmaids. 14And
Boaz said to her, At meal-
time come here, and you
shall eat of the bread and
dip your morsel in the
vinegar. And she sat at the
side of the reapers, and he
reached out roasted grain
to her. And she ate and was
satisfied, and had *some* left
over. 15And she rose up to
glean. And Boaz com-
manded his young men,
saying, She shall glean
even between the sheaves,

1323 8085 3808 7327 1162 559 4592 1004
הַבַּיִת מְעָט׃ וַיֹּאמֶר בֹּעַז אֶל־רוּת הֲלוֹא שָׁמַעַתְּ בִּתִּי 8
my ,hear you Do ,Ruth to Boaz said And little a the in
?daughter not .while house

2088 5674 3808 1571 312 7704 3950 3212 408
אַל־תֵּלְכִי לִלְקֹט בְּשָׂדֶה אַחֵר וְגַם לֹא תַעֲבוּרִי מִזֶּה וְכֹה
and ;this do not and ,another field in to Do not
so on pass also glean go

3212 7114 834 7704 5869 5291 1692
תִדְבָּקִין עִם־נַעֲרֹתָי׃ עֵינַיִךְ בַּשָּׂדֶה אֲשֶׁר־יִקְצֹרוּן וְהָלַכְתְּ 9
you and shall they which the on eyes Your young my with shall you
go shall ,harvest field (be shall) .women stay

6770 5060 5288 6680 3808 310
אַחֲרֵיהֶן הֲלוֹא צִוִּיתִי אֶת־הַנְּעָרִים לְבִלְתִּי נָגְעֵךְ וְצָמִת
you When touch to not young the I have after
,thirst .you men ordered not ;them

5307 5288 7579 834 8354 3627 3212
וְהָלַכְתְּ אֶל־הַכֵּלִים וְשָׁתִית מֵאֲשֶׁר יִשְׁאֲבוּן הַנְּעָרִים׃ וַתִּפֹּל 10
she And young the draw that from shall and the to you then
fell .men which drink vessels go shall

2580 4672 4100 559 776 7812 6440
עַל־פָּנֶיהָ וַתִּשְׁתַּחוּ אָרְצָה וַתֹּאמֶר אֵלָיו מַדּוּעַ מָצָאתִי חֵן
favor I have Why ,him to said and the to bowed and her on
found ,earth herself ,face

5046 559 1162 6030 5237 5234 5869
בְּעֵינֶיךָ לְהַכִּירֵנִי וְאָנֹכִי נָכְרִיָּה׃ וַיַּעַן בֹּעַז וַיֹּאמֶר לָהּ הֻגֵּד 11
fully to said and Boaz And a and should you that your in
,her replied ?foreigner I ,me notice ,eyes

376 4194 310 2545 6213 834 3605 5046
הֻגַּד לִי כֹּל אֲשֶׁר־עָשִׂית אֶת־חֲמוֹתֵךְ אַחֲרֵי מוֹת אִישֵׁךְ
your the after your with have you that All to been has
;husband of death ,mother-in-law done me told

834 5971 3212 4138 776 517 5800
וַתַּעַזְבִי אָבִיךְ וְאִמֵּךְ וְאֶרֶץ מוֹלַדְתֵּךְ וַתֵּלְכִי אֶל־עַם אֲשֶׁר
which a to and your the and your and your you and
people came ,birth of land ,mother ,father left

1961 6466 3068 7999 8032 8543 3045 3808
לֹא־יָדַעַתְּ תְּמוֹל שִׁלְשׁוֹם׃ יְשַׁלֵּם יְהוָה פָּעֳלֵךְ וּתְהִי 12
may and your Jehovah May day the (and) yesterday had you not
be ,work repay .before known

935 834 3478 430 3068 8003 4909
מַשְׂכֻּרְתֵּךְ שְׁלֵמָה מֵעִם יְהוָה אֱלֹהֵי יִשְׂרָאֵל אֲשֶׁר־בָּאת
you ,Israel the Jehovah from complete wages your
come have of God

113 5869 2580 4672 559 3671 8478 2620
לַחֲסוֹת תַּחַת־כְּנָפָיו׃ וַתֹּאמֶר אֶמְצָא־חֵן בְּעֵינֶיךָ אֲדֹנִי כִּי 13
be- my your in favor me Let she And whose under take to
cause ,lord ,eyes find ,said ,wings refuge

259 1961 3808 8198 3820 5921 1696 5162
נִחַמְתָּנִי וְכִי דִבַּרְתָּ עַל־לֵב שִׁפְחָתֶךָ וְאָנֹכִי לֹא אֶהְיֶה כְּאַחַת
one as am not And hand- your heart have,you be-and have you
of I maid's to spoken cause ,me solaced

398 1988 5066 400 6256 1162 559 8198
שִׁפְחֹתֶיךָ׃ וַיֹּאמֶר לָהּ בֹעַז לְעֵת הָאֹכֶל גֹּשִׁי הֲלֹם וְאָכַלְתְּ 14
you and ,here Come ,meal the the at Boaz to said And hand-your
eat shall of time her maid's

7114 6654 3427 2558 6595 2881 3899
מִן־הַלֶּחֶם וְטָבַלְתְּ פִּתֵּךְ בַּחֹמֶץ וַתֵּשֶׁב מִצַּד הַקֹּצְרִים
the the at she And the in your dip and the of
,harvesters of side sat .vinegar morsel bread

6680 3950 6965 3498 7646 398 7039 6642
וַיִּצְבָּט־לָהּ קָלִי וַתֹּאכַל וַתִּשְׂבַּע וַתֹּתַר׃ וַתָּקָם לְלַקֵּט וַיְצַו 15
and glean to she And had and was and she and roasted to he and
told arose .over left ,satisfied ate grain her reached

3808 3950 6076 996 1571 559 5288 1162
בֹּעַז אֶת־נְעָרָיו לֵאמֹר גַּם בֵּין הָעֳמָרִים תְּלַקֵּט וְלֹא
and may she ,sheaves the be- Even ,saying his Boaz
not ,glean tween ,men young

and you shall not cause her
to be ashamed. 16And you
also shall surely pull out for
her of the bundles, and shall
leave; and she shall glean,
and you shall not restrain
her.

17And she gleaned in the
field until the evening, and
beat out that which she had
gleaned. And it was about
an ephah of barley. 18And
she took it up and went to
the city. And her mother-in-
law saw that which she had
gleaned. And she brought
out and gave to her that
which she had reserved
after she was satisfied.
19And her mother-in-law
said to her, Where have you
gleaned today? And where
have you worked? May he
who noticed you be
blessed. And she told her
mother-in-law with whom
she had worked, and said,
The name of the man with
whom I have worked today
is Boaz. 20And Naomi said
to her daughter-in-law,
Blessed *is* he of Jehovah
who has not forsaken his
kindness with the living and
with the dead. And Naomi
said to her, The man *is* near
of kin to us; he *is* of our
redeemers. 21And Ruth of
Moab said, And he surely
said to me, You shall stay
close, near to the young
men whom I have, until
they have completed the
whole harvest which I have.
22And Naomi said to her
daughter-in-law Ruth,
Good, my daughter, that
you go out with his young
women, and that *men* may
not attack you in another
field. 23And she stayed
close to the young women
of Boaz to glean, until the
end of the barley harvest,
and of the wheat harvest.
And she lived with her
mother-in-law.

5800 6653 7997 7997 1571 3637
16 תַכְלִימוּהָ׃ וְגַם שֹׁל־תָּשֹׁלּוּ לָהּ מִן־הַצְּבָתִים וַעֲזַבְתֶּם
shall and bundles the from for shall you surely and shall you
;leave her out pull her shame

2251 6153 5704 7704 3950 1605 3808 3950
17 וְלִקְּטָה וְלֹא תִגְעֲרוּ־בָהּ׃ וַתְּלַקֵּט בַּשָּׂדֶה עַד־הָעָרֶב וַתַּחְבֹּט
beat and the until the in she And .her shall you and she and
out evening field gleaned rebuke not ,glean shall

935 5375 8184 374 1961 3950 834
18 אֵת אֲשֶׁר־לִקֵּטָה וַיְהִי כְּאֵיפָה שְׂעֹרִים׃ וַתִּשָּׂא וַתָּבוֹא
and she And .barley an about it and had she what
went up it took of ephah was ,gleaned

5414 3318 3950 834 2545 7200 5892
הָעִיר וַתֵּרֶא חֲמוֹתָהּ אֵת אֲשֶׁר־לִקֵּטָה וַתּוֹצֵא וַתִּתֶּן־לָהּ
to and she and had she what mother- her And the to
her gave out brought ;gleaned in-law saw .city

375 2545 559 7648 3498 834
19 אֵת אֲשֶׁר־הוֹתִרָה מִשָּׂבְעָהּ׃ וַתֹּאמֶר לָהּ חֲמוֹתָהּ אֵיפֹה
Where mother- her to said And her beyond had she what
,in-law her .satiety over left

2545 5046 1288 5234 1961 6213 3117 3950
לִקַּטְתְּ הַיּוֹם וְאָנָה עָשִׂית יְהִי מַכִּירֵךְ בָּרוּךְ וַתַּגֵּד לַחֲמוֹתָהּ
mother- her she And .blessed who he may you did And ?today you did
in-law told you noticed be work where glean

6213 834 376 8034 559 6213 834
אֵת אֲשֶׁר־עָשְׂתָה עִמּוֹ וַתֹּאמֶר שֵׁם הָאִישׁ אֲשֶׁר עָשִׂיתִי
I whom the the ,said and ,with had she whom
worked man of name worked

3068 1288 3618 5281 559 1162 3117
20 עִמּוֹ הַיּוֹם בֹּעַז׃ וַתֹּאמֶר נָעֳמִי לְכַלָּתָהּ בָּרוּךְ הוּא לַיהוָה
of (be) Blessed her to Naomi said And (is) today with
Jehovah he ,daughter-in-law .Boaz

559 4191 2416 2617 5800 3808 834
אֲשֶׁר לֹא־עָזַב חַסְדּוֹ אֶת־הַחַיִּים וְאֶת־הַמֵּתִים וַתֹּאמֶר לָהּ
to said and the and the with his has not who
her ;dead with living kindness forsaken

4125 7327 559 1350 376 7138 5281
21 נָעֳמִי קָרוֹב לָנוּ הָאִישׁ מִגֹּאֲלֵנוּ הוּא׃ וַתֹּאמֶר רוּת הַמּוֹאֲבִיָּה
the Ruth ,said And he our of The to near Naomi
,Moabitess .(is) redeemers ;(is) man us (kin of)

5704 1692 834 5288 559 1571
גַּם ׀ כִּי־אָמַר אֵלַי עִם־הַנְּעָרִים אֲשֶׁר־לִי תִּדְבָּקִין עַד אִם
until shall You I whom the Near ,me to he surely And
close stay ,have men young said

7327 5281 559 834 7102 3605 3615
22 כִּלּוּ אֵת כָּל־הַקָּצִיר אֲשֶׁר־לִי׃ וַתֹּאמֶר נָעֳמִי אֶל־רוּת
Ruth to Naomi said And I which harvest the have they
.have whole completed

6293 3808 5291 3318 1323 2896 3618
כַּלָּתָהּ טוֹב בִּתִּי כִּי תֵצְאִי עִם־נַעֲרוֹתָיו וְלֹא יִפְגְּעוּ־בָךְ
you will (men) so young his with you that my ,Good daugh- her
attack not that ,women out go ,daughter (is it) .ter-in-law

3615 5704 3950 1162 5291 1692 312 7704
23 בְּשָׂדֶה אַחֵר׃ וַתִּדְבַּק בְּנַעֲרוֹת בֹּעַז לְלַקֵּט עַד־כְּלוֹת
the until ,glean to Boaz young the to she And .another in
of end of women close stayed field

2545 2406 7102 8184 7105
קְצִיר־הַשְּׂעֹרִים וּקְצִיר הַחִטִּים וַתֵּשֶׁב אֶת־חֲמוֹתָהּ׃
mother- her with she and ;wheat the and ,barley the
.in-law lived of harvest of harvest

CAP. III ג

CHAPTER 3

CHAPTER 3

1And her mother-in-law
Naomi said to her, My
daughter, do I not seek rest

4494 1245 3808 1323 2545 5281 559
1 וַתֹּאמֶר לָהּ נָעֳמִי חֲמוֹתָהּ בִּתִּי הֲלֹא אֲבַקֶּשׁ־לָךְ מָנוֹחַ
,rest for seek I do My mother- her Naomi, her to said And
you not ,daughter ,in-law

with you? 2 And now, is not Boaz of our kindred, with whose young women you have been? Behold, he *is* winnowing the threshing floor of barley tonight. 3 And you shall bathe, and anoint yourself, and put your garments on you, and go down to the threshing floor. Do not let yourself be known to the man until he has finished eating and drinking. 4 And it shall be, when he lies down, you shall note the place where he lies down, and shall go in and uncover his feet, and lie down. And he will tell you that which you are to do. 5 And she said to her, All that you say, I will do. 6 And she went down to the threshing floor and did according to all that her mother-in-law commanded her.

7 And Boaz ate and drank, and his heart *felt* good. And he went to lie down at the end of the heap. And she came secretly and uncovered his feet, and lay down. 8 And it happened in the middle of the night, that the man trembled and turned himself. And, behold, a woman *was* lying at his feet! 9 And he said, Who are you? And she said, I *am* your handmaid Ruth, and you shall spread your skirt over your handmaid, for you *are* a kinsman-redeemer. 10 And he said, Blessed *be* you of Jehovah, my daughter. You have dealt more kindly at the latter end than at the beginning, not to go after the young men, either poor or rich. 11 And now, my daughter, do not fear. All that you say I will do to you, for all the gate of my people know that you *are* an able woman. 12 And now, surely *it is* true that I *am* a kinsman-redeemer. But there also is a redeemer nearer than I. 13 Stay tonight, and it shall be in the

2 אֲשֶׁר יִיטַב־לָךְ׃ וְעַתָּה הֲלֹא בֹעַז מֹדַעְתָּנוּ אֲשֶׁר הָיִית אֶת־
with have you been | our of kindred | Boaz | is not | And now | ?you with | may it well be | that

נַעֲרוֹתָיו הִנֵּה־הוּא זֹרֶה אֶת־גֹּרֶן הַשְּׂעֹרִים הַלָּיְלָה׃
.tonight | barley | grain (at) floor the | win-nowing (is) | he ,Behold | whose ?women young

3 וְרָחַצְתְּ וָסַכְתְּ וְשַׂמְתְּ שִׂמְלֹתַיִךְ עָלַיִךְ וְיָרַדְתִּי הַגֹּרֶן אַל־
not | the to ;floor grain | o and down | upon ,you | your garments | and put | anoint and ,yourself | you And wash shall

4 תִּוָּדְעִי לָאִישׁ עַד כַּלֹּתוֹ לֶאֱכֹל וְלִשְׁתּוֹת׃ וִיהִי בְשָׁכְבוֹ
he when ,down lies | it And ,be shall | and .drinking | eating | has he finished | until | the to man | your-self let known be

וְיָדַעַתְּ אֶת־הַמָּקוֹם אֲשֶׁר יִשְׁכַּב־שָׁם וּבָאת וְגִלִּית מַרְגְּלֹתָיו
,feet his | and uncover | shall and in go | lies he ,down | where | the place | you that know shall

5 וְשָׁכָבְתְּ וְהוּא יַגִּיד לָךְ אֵת אֲשֶׁר תַּעֲשִׂין׃ וַתֹּאמֶר אֵלֶיהָ
to ,her | she And said | are you .do to | what | you | will tell | And he | lie and .down

6 כֹּל אֲשֶׁר־תֹּאמְרִי אֶעֱשֶׂה׃ וַתֵּרֶד הַגֹּרֶן וַתַּעַשׂ כְּכֹל
by all | and acted | the to floor grain | she And down went | will I .do | ,say you | that | All

7 אֲשֶׁר־צִוַּתָּה חֲמוֹתָהּ׃ וַיֹּאכַל בֹּעַז וַיֵּשְׁתְּ וַיִּיטַב לִבּוֹ וַיָּבֹא
he and went | his ;heart | and good | and ,drank | Boaz | And ate | mother-in-law | her commanded | that her

לִשְׁכַּב בִּקְצֵה הָעֲרֵמָה וַתָּבֹא בַלָּט וַתְּגַל מַרְגְּלֹתָיו וַתִּשְׁכָּב׃
lay and .down | feet his | and uncovered | secretly | And came she | .heap the | the at of end | lie to down

8 וַיְהִי בַּחֲצִי הַלַּיְלָה וַיֶּחֱרַד הָאִישׁ וַיִּלָּפֵת וְהִנֵּה אִשָּׁה
a woman | ,and ,behold | turned and ;himself | the man | that trembled | ,night the | the in of middle | it And ,was

9 שֹׁכֶבֶת מַרְגְּלֹתָיו׃ וַיֹּאמֶר מִי־אָתְּ וַתֹּאמֶר אָנֹכִי רוּת אֲמָתֶךָ
your ;handmaid | ,Ruth (am) I | she And said | are Who ?you | he And ,said | his at !feet | (was) lying

10 וּפָרַשְׂתָּ כְנָפֶךָ עַל־אֲמָתְךָ כִּי גֹאֵל אָתָּה׃ וַיֹּאמֶר בְּרוּכָה
Blessed | he And ,said | you .(are) | re-deemer a | for | your ,handmaid | over | your skirt | you and spread shall

אַתְּ לַיהוָה בִּתִּי הֵיטַבְתְּ חַסְדֵּךְ הָאַחֲרוֹן מִן־הָרִאשׁוֹן
the at ,beginning | more than | the end | in | your kindness | have you well done | my ;daughter | of ,Jehovah | (be) you

11 לְבִלְתִּי־לֶכֶת אַחֲרֵי הַבַּחוּרִים אִם־דַּל וְאִם־עָשִׁיר׃ וְעַתָּה
And ,now | .rich | or | poor either | young the ,men | after | go | to not

בִּתִּי אַל־תִּירְאִי כֹּל אֲשֶׁר־תֹּאמְרִי אֶעֱשֶׂה־לָּךְ כִּי יוֹדֵעַ כָּל־
of all knowing | (are) for | ,you for do | will I | say you | that | all | ;fear do not | my daughter

12 שַׁעַר עַמִּי כִּי אֵשֶׁת חַיִל אָתְּ׃ וְעַתָּה כִּי אָמְנָם כִּי אִם גֹּאֵל
re-deemer a | that | (is it) true | surely | And ,now | you .(are) | able | a woman | that | my people | the of gate

13 אָנֹכִי וְגַם יֵשׁ גֹּאֵל קָרוֹב מִמֶּנִּי׃ לִינִי הַלַּיְלָה וְהָיָה
it and be shall | ,tonight | Stay | .I than | nearer | re-a deemer | there is | but also | ,(am) I

morning, if he will redeem you, well; he will redeem. And if he does not delight to redeem you, *as* Jehovah lives, then I will redeem you. Lie down until the morning.

14 And she lay at his feet until the morning, and rose up before one could discern another. And he said, Let it not be known that a woman has come to the grain floor. 15 And he said, Give me the covering which is on you, and hold on to it. And she kept hold on it, and he measured six *measures* of barley, and lay *it* on her. And she went in to the city. 16 And she came in to her mother-in-law. And she said, Who *are* you, my daughter? And she told her all that the man had done to her. 17 And she said, He gave me these six *measures* of barley, for he said, You shall not go empty to your mother-in-law. 18 And she said, Sit, my daughter, until you shall know how the matter falls, for the man shall not rest until he has finished the matter today.

1350 2654 3808 518 1350 2896 1350 518 1242
בַּבֹּקֶר אִם־יִגְאָלֵךְ טוֹב יִגְאָל וְאִם־לֹא יַחְפֹּץ לְגָאֳלֵךְ
redeem to ,you | is he pleased | not | and if | will he ,redeem | ;good | will he ,you redeem | if | the in morning

7901 1242 5704 7901 3068 2416 1350
14 וּגְאַלְתִּיךְ אָנֹכִי חַי־יְהוָה שִׁכְבִי עַד־הַבֹּקֶר׃ וַתִּשְׁכַּב מַרְגְּלוֹתָו
his feet | at | she And lay | the .morning | until | Lie down | Jehovah (as) lives | ,I | will then you redeem

559 7453 376 5234 2958 6965 1242 5704
עַד־הַבֹּקֶר וַתָּקָם בִּטְרוֹם יַכִּיר אִישׁ אֶת־רֵעֵהוּ וַיֹּאמֶר אַל־
not | he And ,said | his .neighbor | a man | could discern | before | and arose | the morning | until

834 4304 3053 559 1637 802 935 3045
15 יִוָּדַע כִּי־בָאָה הָאִשָּׁה הַגֹּרֶן׃ וַיֹּאמֶר הָבִי הַמִּטְפַּחַת אֲשֶׁר־
which | the cloak | Give me | he And ,said | the to floor grain | the woman | came that | it Let known be

5921 7896 8184 8337 4058 270 270
עָלַיִךְ וְאֶחֳזִי־בָהּ וַתֹּאחֶז בָּהּ וַיָּמָד שֵׁשׁ־שְׂעֹרִים וַיָּשֶׁת עָלֶיהָ
on ;her | and (it) lay | (measures) ,barley of | six | he and measured | on ,it | she And hold kept | .it to | and on hold | on is ,you

1323 559 2545 935 5892 935
16 וַיָּבֹא הָעִיר׃ וַתָּבוֹא אֶל־חֲמוֹתָהּ וַתֹּאמֶר מִי־אַתְּ בִּתִּי
my ?daughter | ,you Who (are) | she and ,said | mother- .in-law | her to | she And came | the to .city | she and in went

8337 559 376 6213 834 3605 5046
17 וַתַּגֶּד־לָהּ אֵת כָּל־אֲשֶׁר עָשָׂה־לָהּ הָאִישׁ׃ וַתֹּאמֶר שֵׁשׁ־
of six | she And ,said | .man the | to her | had done | that | all | her | And told she

7387 935 408 559 5414 428 8184
הַשְּׂעֹרִים הָאֵלֶּה נָתַן לִי כִּי אָמַר אַל־תָּבוֹאִי רֵיקָם אֶל־
to | empty | shall You not go | he said | for | ,me | He gave | these | barley

5307 349 3045 834 5704 1323 3427 559 2545
18 חֲמוֹתֵךְ׃ וַתֹּאמֶר שְׁבִי בִתִּי עַד אֲשֶׁר תֵּדְעִין אֵיךְ יִפֹּל
falls | how | shall you know | until | my daughter | Sit | she And said | mother- your .in-law

3808 3117 1697 3615 518 376 8252 1697
דָּבָר כִּי לֹא יִשְׁקֹט הָאִישׁ כִּי־אִם־כִּלָּה הַדָּבָר הַיּוֹם׃
.today | the matter | has he completed | until | the man | shall rest | not | for | the ,matter

CAP. IV ד

CHAPTER 4

1 And Boaz went up to the gate and sat there. And, behold, the near kinsman of whom Boaz had spoken *was* passing by. And he said, Such a one, turn aside, sit down here. And he turned aside and sat down. 2 And he took ten men of the elders of the city, and said, Sit down here. And they sat down. 3 And he said to the near kinsman, Naomi, who has returned from the fields of Moab, will sell a portion of the field which *belonged* to our brother, to Elimelech. 4 And I said I would uncover your ear, saying, Buy *it* before those sitting, and before the elders of my people. If you will redeem,

1696 834 5674 1350 2009 8033 3427 8179 5927 1162
1 וּבֹעַז עָלָה הַשַּׁעַר וַיֵּשֶׁב שָׁם וְהִנֵּה הַגֹּאֵל עֹבֵר אֲשֶׁר דִּבֶּר־
had spoken | of whom | passing ,by | the kinsman | ,and ,behold | ;there | and sat | the to gate | went up | And Boaz

3427 5493 492 6423 3427 5493 559 1162
בֹּעַז וַיֹּאמֶר סוּרָה שְׁבָה־פֹּה פְּלֹנִי אַלְמֹנִי וַיָּסַר וַיֵּשֵׁב׃
sat and .down | he And turned | .one a | such | ,here | sit down | Turn ,aside | he And ,said | .Boaz

3427 3427 559 5892 2205 582 6235 3947
2 וַיִּקַּח עֲשָׂרָה אֲנָשִׁים מִזִּקְנֵי הָעִיר וַיֹּאמֶר שְׁבוּ־פֹה וַיֵּשֵׁבוּ׃
they And .down sat | .here | sit down | ,said and | the ,city | the of elders | men | ten | he And took

458 251 834 7704 2513 1350 559
3 וַיֹּאמֶר לַגֹּאֵל חֶלְקַת הַשָּׂדֶה אֲשֶׁר לְאָחִינוּ לֶאֱלִימֶלֶךְ
to Elimelech | our to ,brother | which (belonged) | the field | por- the of tion | the to ,kinsman | he And said

1540 559 4124 7704 7725 5281 4376
4 מָכְרָה נָעֳמִי הַשָּׁבָה מִשְּׂדֵה מוֹאָב׃ וַאֲנִי אָמַרְתִּי אֶגְלֶה
will I open | ,said | And | .Moab | the from of fields | has who returned | ,Naomi | will sell

1350 518 5971 2205 5048 3427 5048 7069 559 241
אָזְנְךָ לֵאמֹר קְנֵה נֶגֶד הַיֹּשְׁבִים וְנֶגֶד זִקְנֵי עַמִּי אִם־תִּגְאַל
will you ,redeem | If | my .people | the elders of | and before | sitting those | before (here) | Buy (it) | ,saying | your ,ear

redeem. But if you will not redeem, tell me so that I may know. For there is no one besides you to redeem, and I after you. And he said, I will redeem *it*. [5]And Boaz said, In the day you buy the field from Naomi's hand, then you have bought from Ruth of Moab, the wife of the dead, to raise up the name of the dead over his inheritance. [6]And the near kinsman said, I am not able to redeem for myself, that I not mar my own inheritance. You redeem for yourself my right of redemption, for I am not able to redeem.

[7]And this formerly *was done* in Israel for redemption, and for changing, to confirm every thing: A man would draw off his sandal and give to his neighbor. And this *was* the attestation in Israel. [8]And the near kinsman said to Boaz, Buy for yourself, and drew off his sandal. [9]And Boaz said to the elders, and all the people, You *are* witnesses today that I have bought all that *belonged* to Elimelech, and all that *was* to Chilion and Mahlon, from the hand of Naomi. [10]And also Ruth of Moab, the wife of Mahlon, I have bought for myself for a wife, to raise up the name of the dead over his inheritance. And the name of the dead shall not be cut off from among his brothers, and from the gate of his place. You *are* witnesses today. [11]And all the people who *were* in the gate, and the elders, said, *We are* witnesses. May Jehovah make the woman who is coming into your house as Rachel and as Leah, both of whom built the house of Israel. And may you do worthily in Ephratah, and proclaim the name in Bethlehem. [12]And let your house be as the house of Pharez, whom

גאל ואם־לא יגאל הגידה לי ואדע כי אין זולתך לגאול
5 ואנכי אחריך ויאמר אנכי אגאל׃ ויאמר בעז ביום־
קנותך השדה מיד נעמי ומאת רות המואביה אשת־המת
6 קניתי להקים שם־המת על־נחלתו׃ ויאמר הגאל לא
אוכל לגאול־לי פן־אשחית את־נחלתי גאל־לך אתה את־
7 גאלתי כי לא־אוכל לגאול׃ וזאת לפנים בישראל על־
הגאולה ועל־התמורה לקים כל־דבר שלף איש נעלו
8 ונתן לרעהו וזאת התעודה בישראל׃ ויאמר הגאל
9 לבעז קנה־לך וישלף נעלו׃ ויאמר בעז לזקנים וכל־
העם עדים אתם היום כי קניתי את־כל־אשר לאלימלך
10 ואת כל־אשר לכליון ומחלון מיד נעמי׃ וגם את־רות
המאביה אשת מחלון קניתי לי לאשה להקים שם־המת
על־נחלתו ולא־יכרת שם־המת מעם אחיו ומשער מקומו
11 עדים אתם היום׃ ויאמרו כל־העם אשר־בשער והזקנים
עדים יתן יהוה את־האשה הבאה אל־ביתך כרחל ׀
וכלאה אשר בנו שתיהם את־בית ישראל ועשה־חיל
12 באפרתה וקרא־שם בבית לחם׃ ויהי ביתך כבית פרץ

13068 5414 834 2233 3063 8559 3205 834
אֲשֶׁר־יָלְדָה תָמָר לִיהוּדָה מִן־הַזֶּרַע אֲשֶׁר יִתֵּן יְהוָה לְךָ
to Jehovah shall which seed the of ,Judah to Tamar bore whom
you give

802 1961 7327 1162 3947 2088 5291
13 מִן־הַנַּעֲרָה הַזֹּאת׃ וַיִּקַּח בֹּעַז אֶת־רוּת וַתְּהִי־לוֹ לְאִשָּׁה
,wife a to she and Ruth Boaz And .this young of
him became took woman

559 1121 3205 2032 3068 5414 935
14 וַיָּבֹא אֵלֶיהָ וַיִּתֵּן יְהוָה לָהּ הֵרָיוֹן וַתֵּלֶד בֵּן׃ וַתֹּאמַרְנָה
said And .son a she and con- her Jehovah and to he and
bore ,ception gave ;her in went

1350 7673 3808 834 3068 1288 5281 802
הַנָּשִׁים אֶל־נָעֳמִי בָּרוּךְ יְהוָה אֲשֶׁר לֹא הִשְׁבִּית לָךְ גֹּאֵל
re- a to caused has not who, ,Jehovah Blessed ,Naomi to the
deemer you fail to (be) women

5315 7725 1961 3478 8034 7121 3117
15 הַיּוֹם וְיִקָּרֵא שְׁמוֹ בְּיִשְׂרָאֵל׃ וְהָיָה לָךְ לְמֵשִׁיב נֶפֶשׁ
,life a for may And .Israel in his may and this
of restorer you become he name called be ;day

3205 159 834 3618 7872 3557
וּלְכַלְכֵּל אֶת־שֵׂיבָתֵךְ כִּי כַלָּתֵךְ אֲשֶׁר־אֲהֵבַתֶךְ יְלָדַתּוּ
borne has ;you loves who your for age old your a and
him daughter-in-law of nourisher

5281 3947 1121 7651 2896 834
16 אֲשֶׁר־הִיא טוֹבָה לָךְ מִשִּׁבְעָה בָּנִים׃ וַתִּקַּח נָעֳמִי אֶת־
Naomi took And .sons seven than to is she who
you better

7121 539 1961 2436 7896 3206
17 הַיֶּלֶד וַתְּשִׁתֵהוּ בְחֵיקָהּ וַתְּהִי־לוֹ לְאֹמֶנֶת׃ וַתִּקְרֶאנָה לוֹ
him called And .nurse to and her in laid and the
him became ,bosom him child

5744 8034 7121 5281 1121 3205 559 7934
הַשְּׁכֵנוֹת שֵׁם לֵאמֹר יֻלַּד־בֵּן לְנָעֳמִי וַתִּקְרֶאנָה שְׁמוֹ עוֹבֵד
;Obed his they and to son A has ,saying a neigh- the
name called ;Naomi borne been ,name women bor

3205 6557 6557 8435 428 1734 1 5448 1
18 הוּא אֲבִי־יִשַׁי אֲבִי דָוִד׃ וְאֵלֶּה תּוֹלְדוֹת פָּרֶץ פֶּרֶץ הוֹלִיד
fathered Pharez :Pharez gen- the And .David the Jesse the (is)he
of erations (are) these of father of father

3205 7410 7410 3205 2696 2696
19 אֶת־חֶצְרוֹן׃ וְחֶצְרוֹן הוֹלִיד אֶת־רָם וְרָם הוֹלִיד אֶת־
fathered and ,Ram fathered Hezron and ,Hezron
Ram

3205 5177 5177 3205 5992 5992
20 עַמִּינָדָב׃ וְעַמִּינָדָב הוֹלִיד אֶת־נַחְשׁוֹן וְנַחְשׁוֹן הוֹלִיד אֶת־
fathered and ,Nahshon fathered and ,Amminadab
Nahshon Amminadab

5744 3205 1162 1162 3205 8012 8012
21 שַׂלְמָה׃ וְשַׂלְמוֹן הוֹלִיד אֶת־בֹּעַז וּבֹעַז הוֹלִיד אֶת־עוֹבֵד׃
,Obed fathered and ,Boaz fathered and ,Salmon
Boaz Salmon

1732 3205 3448 3448 3205 5744
22 וְעֹבֵד הוֹלִיד אֶת־יִשָׁי וְיִשַׁי הוֹלִיד אֶת־דָּוִד׃
.David fathered and ,Jesse fathered and
Jesse Obed

Tamar bore to Judah, of the seed which Jehovah shall give to you of this young woman.

13 And Boaz took Ruth, and she became his wife. And he went in to her, and Jehovah gave her conception, and she bore a son. 14 And the women said to Naomi, Blessed *be* Jehovah, who has not left you this day without a redeemer; and may his name be called in Israel. 15 And may he be to you a restorer of life, and a nourisher of your old age, for your daughter-in-law who loves you has borne him, who is better to you than seven sons. 16 And Naomi took the child, and laid him in her bosom, and became nurse to him. 17 And the neighboring women gave him a name, saying, This is a son born to Naomi; and they called his name Obed. He is the father of Jesse, the father of David.

18 And these *are* the generations of Pharez: Pharez fathered Hezron; 19 and Hezron fathered Ram; and Ram fathered Amminadab; 20 and Amminadab fathered Nahshon; and Nahshon fathered Salmon; 21 and Salmon fathered Boaz; and Boaz fathered Obed; 22 and Obed fathered Jesse; and Jesse fathered David.

Made in the USA
Charleston, SC
15 December 2009